MACMILLAN Essential DICTIONARY

FOR LEARNERS OF AMERICAN ENGLISH

Macmillan Education
Between Towns Road, Oxford OX4 3PP
A division of Macmillan Publishers Limited
Companies and representatives throughout the world

ISBN
0 333 99211 3 paperback edition
0 333 99212 1 paperback edition + CD-ROM

First published 2003

The Macmillan Essential Dictionary was conceived, compiled and edited by the Reference and Electronic Media Division of Bloomsbury Publishing Plc.

This Dictionary includes words on the basis of their use in the English language today. Some words are identified as being trademarks or service marks. Neither the presence nor absence of such identification in this Dictionary is to be regarded as affecting in any way, or expressing a judgement on, the validity or legal status of any trademark, service mark, or other proprietary rights anywhere in the world.

World English Corpus
The definitions in the Macmillan Essential Dictionary have been based on information derived from 200,000,000 words of English which make up the World English Corpus. This consists of the Bloomsbury Corpus of World English® with additional material exclusively developed for this Dictionary, including ELT materials and a corpus of common errors made by learners of English.

Designed by Peter Burgess
Cover design by Boag Associates, London
Typeset by Selwood Systems, Midsomer Norton, Radstock, United Kingdom

Printed and bound in China

2007 2006 2005 2004 2003
10 9 8 7 6 5 4 3 2

CONTENTS

Editor-in-Chief
Michael Rundell

Associate Editor
Gwyneth Fox

EDITORIAL TEAM

Managing Editor
Michael Mayor

Editors
Robert Clevenger
Rosalind Combley
Korey Egge
Gloria George
Stephen Handorf
Dan Malt
Stella O'Shea
Elizabeth Potter
Glennis Pye
Howard Sargeant
Karen Stern
Penny Stock
Donald Watt

Phonetician
Dinah Jackson

Proofreaders
Sandra Anderson
Ruth Hillmore
Irene Lakhani

PROJECT TEAM

Project Manager
Katy McAdam

Database Manager
Edmund Wright

Production Editor
Nicky Thompson

Production Manager
Rowena Drewett

Production Director
Penny Edwards

Design
Peter Burgess
Helen Taylor

Dictionaries' Publisher
Faye Carney

Publishing Directors
Kathy Rooney
Sue Bale

Project Coordinators
Joel Adams
Katalin Süle

Database Administrator
James Orpin

Corpus Development
Gloria George

OTHER CONTRIBUTORS

Editorial and Keyboarding Assistance
Simon Arnold
Rebecca McKee
Lisa Milford
Ian M. Spackman

Illustrations
Ian Foulis and Associates
Peter Harper
Illustrated Arts
Stuart Lafford
Alan Male
Oxford Illustrators
Peter Richardson
Martin Shovel

ADVISORY PANEL

Chief Adviser

Professor Michael Hoey

Baines Professor of English Language and Director of the Applied English Language Studies Unit, University of Liverpool, U.K.

Professor Chen Lin
Professor of English, Foreign Languages University, Beijing, China

Simon Greenall
ELT author and trainer

Vaughan Jones
ELT author and teacher

Sue Kay
ELT author and teacher

Cindy Leaney
ELT author and trainer

Jane Magee
Course Director, English Language Teaching, University of St Andrews, U.K.

Amy Chi Man-lai
Instructor, Language Centre, Hong Kong University of Science and Technology, Hong Kong

Professor Kevin Mark
Professor, School of Politics and Economics, Meiji University, Japan

Ron Martinez
ELT author and trainer

Dr. Don R. McCreary
Associate Professor, Department of English, University of Georgia, Athens, Georgia, U.S.A.

Professor Rukmini Nair
Professor of Linguistics and English, Department of Humanities and Social Sciences, Indian Institute of Technology, Delhi, India

Dr. Hilary Nesi
Senior Lecturer, Centre for English Language Teacher Education, University of Warwick, U.K.

Philip Prowse
ELT author and trainer

Susan Stempleski
Coordinator of Faculty Development, Hunter College International English Language Institute, City University of New York, U.S.A.

Adrian Underhill
ELT consultant, trainer, and author

Sara Walker
Coordinator of the English Program, Brazilian Diplomatic Academy, Ministry of Foreign Relations, Brasilia DF, Brazil

ACKNOWLEDGMENTS

The publishers would like to thank the many people who have given valuable advice and support and who have helped to pilot the dictionary, in particular:

Maria Birkenmajer
Jan Borsbey
Claudia Finkbeiner
Christopher Gallagher
Galia Komarova
Anne McCabe
Vera Muller
Roy Norris
Vincent Ooi
Anne Pakir
Péter Rádai
Kim Jeong Ryeol
Piotr Steinbrich
Jerome Su
H. A. Swan
Ruth Swan
Michael Vaughan-Rees
Michael Vince

Introduction

Michael Rundell
Editor-in-Chief

The *Macmillan Essential Dictionary* has been specially designed to meet the needs of intermediate students of English. The word "essential" has two meanings, and both meanings are relevant to this dictionary. First, it provides the information that is *completely necessary* for your success as a learner of English. And second, it focuses on the most *basic and important* features of the English language—the things that you need to know most thoroughly in order to make effective progress.

Dictionaries exist in order to answer questions. To help us to give the right answers to the right questions, we—as dictionary makers—need to know who will be using the dictionary and what kinds of information they really need. All of this means making a careful *selection* from the enormous amount of data available to us. So how do we decide what is really "essential," and how can we be sure that we have made the *right* selection?

In creating the *Macmillan Essential Dictionary*, we have benefited from two valuable resources:

- high-quality linguistic data: our large language corpora and advanced software give us the tools to identify the essential facts about English
- expert advice: at every stage, experienced teachers, coursebook writers, and language students have contributed their suggestions and comments, telling us what learners really need to know

The *Macmillan Essential Dictionary* builds on the success of its sister dictionary, the *Macmillan English Dictionary*, adapting its unique features to the different needs of intermediate learners. These include:

- the "red words": the most frequent and useful words in English are shown in red, so that you can easily recognize the vocabulary that—as an intermediate learner—you need to know especially well. For this dictionary, we have identified 3,500 red words. More information about these words is given on the inside front cover.
- maximum coverage: our goal is to include as many vocabulary items as possible, and this dictionary has more entries than any other intermediate learners' dictionary
- special attention to "collocation" (the way words regularly combine with each other): over 130 new collocation boxes provide a unique bank of data on natural-sounding word combinations
- dozens of special notes: information on common errors and boxes that will help you to increase your vocabulary
- Study Pages: a 24-page central section, packed with ideas that will help you to become a better learner, including information on collocation, word formation, vocabulary development, and much more

We hope you will enjoy using the *Macmillan Essential Dictionary*, and we are confident that you will soon find that it is an essential part of your language-learning experience.

USING YOUR DICTIONARY

Finding a Word

Words with More Than One Entry

Sometimes the same word belongs to more than one word class: for example, the word **jet** can be a noun and a verb. Each word class is shown as a separate entry. The small number at the end of the headword tells you that a word has more than one entry.

jet¹ /dʒet/ noun ★
1 [C] an airplane that can fly very fast: *a jet fighter*
2 [C] a stream of liquid that comes out of something very quickly and with a lot of force: *The firefighter sprayed **a jet of water** on the flames.*
3 [U] a hard black shiny stone that is used for making jewelry

jet² /dʒet/ verb [I] to fly somewhere in an airplane: *They will be jetting off to Spain this weekend.*

Compound Words

These are shown as separate entries in the alphabetical list.

ˌjet-ˈblack adj very dark black in color

ˌjet ˈengine noun [C] a type of engine that combines air and burning fuel to create power for an airplane

ˈjet ˌlag noun [U] the feeling of being very tired because you have traveled on an airplane across parts of the world where the time is different —**jet-lag•ged** /ˈdʒetˌlægd/ adj

Derived Words

Some words are shown at the end of the entry for the word that they are derived from. These words can be understood by reading the definition for the main entry.

Word Classes (Noun, Verb, etc.)

There is a list of word classes on the inside front cover.

bite¹ /baɪt/ (past tense **bit** /bɪt/; past participle **bit•ten** /ˈbɪt(ə)n/) verb ★★
1 [I/T] to use your teeth to cut or break something, usually in order to eat it: *Stop biting your nails.* ♦ *I've just been bitten by a snake.* ♦ *Tom **bit into** his sandwich.*
2 [I] to have an unpleasant effect: *The economic slowdown is beginning to bite.*

PHRASES **bite the bullet** *informal* to force yourself to do something difficult or unpleasant

bite sb's head off *informal* to react angrily or rudely to someone, when this reaction seems too strong

bite your tongue to stop yourself from saying something that might upset or annoy someone

PHRASAL VERB **ˈbite sth ˌoff** to separate something from the main part by biting: *I bit off a chunk of chocolate.*

Idioms and Other Fixed Expressions

Some words are often used in idioms or other fixed expressions. These are shown at the end of the main entry, following the small box that says PHRASES. Look for fixed expressions at the entry for the first main word in the expression.

Phrasal verbs are shown after the entry for the main verb, following the small box that says PHRASAL VERB.

Finding the Meaning of a Word

Words with More Than One Meaning

Many words have more than one meaning, and each different meaning is shown by a number.

bi•lin•gual /baɪˈlɪŋgwəl/ adj **1** able to speak two languages **2** written in two languages: *a bilingual dictionary*

Some words have many different meanings, and so the entries can be long. Entries with five or more meanings have a "menu" at the top to make it easier to find the specific meaning you are looking for.

bill¹ /bɪl/ noun [C] ★★★

1 amount that you owe	4 in a restaurant
2 paper money	5 bird's beak
3 proposal for law	

1 a written statement that shows how much money you owe for goods or services that you have received: *a telephone bill* ♦ *I always **pay my bills** on time.* ♦ *I wonder what the bill for the repairs will be?*

Definitions

All the definitions are written using a carefully selected "defining vocabulary" of under 2,300 words so that it is easier to understand the definitions.

Any word in a definition that is not part of the defining vocabulary, and that is not the entry immediately before or after the one you are looking at, is shown in CAPITAL letters. You can find its meaning by looking it up in the dictionary.

ˈsalad ˌdressing noun [C/U] a sauce that adds flavor to salads, usually made by mixing oil, VINEGAR, and HERBS or SPICES

sa·la·mi /səˈlɑmi/ noun [C/U] a type of SAUSAGE containing strong SPICES, cut into thin pieces and served cold

Finding Out More About a Word

Red Words

Some words are printed in red with a "star rating" to show their frequency. This helps you to identify the words that you are most likely to need to use. For more information about red words, see the inside front cover.

dis·cov·er /dɪˈskʌvər/ verb [T] ★★★

friend·ly /ˈfren(d)li/ adj ★★

lo·cal[1] /ˈloʊk(ə)l/ adj ★

Pronunciation

The International Phonetic Alphabet shows you how a word is pronounced. A list of the symbols used is given on the inside back cover.

When British and American pronunciations are very different, both are given.

You can find the pronunciations for compound entries at the main entry for each of the words in the compound.

Stress marks tell you which part of a compound to stress when you are saying it.

a·ro·ma /əˈroʊmə/ noun [C] a smell that is strong but nice —**ar·o·mat·ic** /ˌærəˈmætɪk/ adj

lab·o·ra·to·ry /ˈlæbrəˌtɔri, *British* ləˈbɒrət(ə)ri/ noun [C] ★ a building or large room where people do scientific research: *our new research laboratory* ♦ *laboratory tests/experiments/studies* → LANGUAGE LABORATORY

ˈbaseball ˌcap noun [C] a hat that fits close to your head, with a flat curved part that sticks out above your eyes —*picture* → HAT

Inflections

Irregular inflections are shown.

do[1] /du/ (3rd person singular **does** /*weak* dəz, *strong* dʌz/; past tense **did** /dɪd/; past participle **done** /dʌn/) verb ★★★

Labels

Labels (in *italics*) show whether a word is used in only British or American English, or tell you whether it is used in informal contexts, specialized contexts etc. Lists of these labels are given on page 829.

pave·ment /ˈpeɪvmənt/ noun **1** [U] *American* the surface of a road **2** [C] *British* a SIDEWALK

prog·no·sis /prɑgˈnoʊsɪs/ (plural **prog·no·ses** /prɑgˈnoʊˌsiz/) noun [C] **1** *medical* a doctor's opinion about how a disease is likely to develop **2** *formal* a statement about what is likely to happen in a particular situation → DIAGNOSIS

Examples

Example sentences in *italics* show you how a word is used in context.

Information about collocation and syntax—how words combine and which structures they can be used with—is shown in **bold type**.

When a word has many collocations, these are shown in a box at the end of the entry.

pro•mote /prə'moʊt/ verb [T] ★★
1 to support something, or to help something to develop: *a campaign to promote recycling* ♦ *Young plants are exposed to bright light to* ***promote growth.***
2 to attract people's attention to a product or event, for example by advertising: *They are going on tour to promote their new album.*
3 to move someone to a job at a higher level: **promote sb to sth** *Steve Burrows was recently promoted to senior manager.*

Words often used with **promote**

Adverbs often used with ***promote*** *(sense 1)*
- **actively, heavily, strongly, vigorously** + PROMOTE: promote something in a determined way

Nouns often used with ***promote*** *(sense 1)*
- PROMOTE + **awareness, competition, development, efficiency, growth, interest, understanding, use**: increase the level of something

Grammar Boxes

Grammar boxes give extra information to help you to learn more about how a word is used.

The is not usually used before the names of streets, towns, countries, counties, states, or continents: *My parents live in Surrey.*

Notes are also given to help you to avoid common errors.

News looks like a plural, but it is never used with a plural verb and cannot be used with **a**: *I've got a wonderful* ***piece of news*** (NOT a wonderful news) for you. ♦ *Do you have* ***any news*** *about Laura's baby?* ♦ *Here's* ***some news*** *about the World Cup.*

Expanding Your Vocabulary

There are many ways that you can use this dictionary to expand your vocabulary.

Sometimes the opposite of a word is shown.

'left-,hand adj on the left side ≠ RIGHT-HAND: *The plates are on the left-hand side of the cabinet.*

Some definitions give you synonyms.

last•ly /'læstli/ adv used when you want to say one more thing before you finish speaking = FINALLY: *And lastly, remember that your reports are due tomorrow.*

Sometimes you are told to look at another word or page in the dictionary where you will find additional information, a related entry, or a picture.

hard•back /'hɑrd,bæk/ noun [C] a book that has a hard cover → PAPERBACK

"Word family" boxes bring together groups of words that are formed from the same "root word."

Word family: **compete**

Words in the same family as ***compete***
- **competition** *n*
- **competitor** *n*
- **competitive** *adj*
- **uncompetitive** *adj*

Vocabulary building boxes bring together words that are related to a particular subject, or suggest more specific alternatives for very common words.

Other ways of saying **famous**
- **eminent** famous and respected for doing important work
- **legendary** very famous and admired by many people
- **notorious/infamous** famous for something bad
- **well-known** fairly famous

NUMBERS THAT ARE ENTRIES

000 /ˌtrɪp(ə)lˈoʊ/ in Australia, the telephone number that you use in an emergency to call the police, the fire department, or an AMBULANCE

0800 num•ber /oʊ eɪt ˈhʌndrəd ˌnʌmbər/ noun [C] in the U.K., a telephone number beginning with 0800 that is free to use and is usually for calling business services

1 /wʌn/ abbrev used in e-mails and TEXT MESSAGES to replace "-one": *NE1* (=anyone)

1040 form /ˌten ˈfɔrti ˌfɔrm/ noun [C] a form used by people in the U.S. when they are calculating how much tax they have to pay on the money that they have earned

1099 /ˌten naɪnti ˈnaɪn/ noun [C] in the U.S., a document you send to the IRS (=the U.S. tax department) that gives details of money that you have earned in addition to your salary

12 /twelv/ in the U.K., a number given to a video that should only be watched by children who are at least 12 years old

12A /ˌtwelv ˈeɪ/ in the U.K., a number given to a movie that should only be watched by children under the age of 12 if they are with an adult

1471 /ˌwʌn fɔr sev(ə)n ˈwʌn/ in the U.K., a telephone number that you can call to find out which was the last telephone number to call you

15 /ˌfɪfˈtin/ in the U.K., a number given to a movie or video that should only be watched by children who are at least 15 years old

18 /ˌeɪˈtin/ in the U.K., a number given to a movie or video that should only be watched by people who are at least 18 years old

1800 num•ber /ˌwʌn eɪt ˈhʌndrəd ˌnʌmbər/ in Australia, a telephone number beginning with 1800 that is free to use and is usually for calling business services

18-wheel•er /ˌeɪtin ˈwilər/ noun [C] *American* a large truck that has 18 wheels

2 /tu/ abbrev **1** to or too: used in e-mails and TEXT MESSAGES: *it's up 2 U* (=it's up to you) ♦ *me 2* (=me too) **2** used for replacing "to-" in other words: *2day* (=today)

20/20 vi•sion /ˌtwenti ˌtwenti ˈvɪʒ(ə)n/ noun [U] the ability to see normally without wearing glasses

2.1 /ˌtuˈwʌn/ noun [C] in the U.K. and Australia, the second-highest grade for an UNDERGRADUATE degree from a university, lower than a **first** but higher than a **2.2**

2.2 /ˌtuˈtu/ noun [C] in the U.K. and Australia, the third-highest grade for an UNDERGRADUATE degree from a university, lower than a **2.1** but higher than a **third**

.22 /ˌtwentiˈtu/ noun [C] a type of gun that shoots small bullets

24/7 /ˌtwenti fɔr ˈsev(ə)n/ adv *informal* all the time: *He thinks about her 24/7.*

3-D /ˌθriˈdi/ adj a 3-D movie, picture, etc. looks as if it has length, depth, and width

4 /fɔr/ abbrev **1** for: used in e-mails and TEXT MESSAGES: *4 U* (=for you) **2** used for replacing "-fore" in other words: *B4* (=before)

401(k) /ˌfɔr oʊ wʌn ˈkeɪ/ noun [C] in the U.S., a special account in which people can save some of the money they earn for their RETIREMENT without paying taxes on it

4×4 /ˌfɔr baɪ ˈfɔr/ noun [C] a FOUR-WHEEL DRIVE vehicle

.45 /ˌfɔrtiˈfaɪv/ noun [C] a PISTOL (=small gun)

4-F /ˌfɔr ˈef/ adj if someone is **listed 4-F**, they are not allowed to serve in the U.S. military

4WD abbrev a FOUR-WHEEL DRIVE vehicle

$64,000 ques•tion, the /ˌsɪkstifɔrθaʊz(ə)nd dɑlər ˈkwestʃ(ə)n/ noun [singular] a question that is the most important and most difficult to answer concerning a particular problem or situation

8 /eɪt/ abbrev used in e-mails and TEXT MESSAGES to replace "-ate" or "-eat": *C U L8R* (=see you later) ♦ *GR8* (=great)

800 num•ber /ˌeɪt ˈhʌndrəd ˌnʌmbər/ noun [C] in the U.S., a telephone number that is free to use and is usually for calling business services

911 /ˌnaɪn wʌn ˈwʌn/ in the U.S., the telephone number that you use in an emergency to call the police, the fire department, or an AMBULANCE

9/11 /ˌnaɪn ɪˈlev(ə)n/ September 11, the date in 2001 when TERRORISTS attacked the U.S., flying planes into the World Trade Center and killing thousands of people

999 /ˌnaɪn naɪn ˈnaɪn/ in the U.K., the telephone number that you use in an emergency to call the police, the fire department, or an AMBULANCE

Roman Numerals

Roman numerals were used in ancient Rome to represent numbers. They are still sometimes used today, for example on clocks and watches and in official documents.

I	one	XVII	seventeen
II	two	XVIII	eighteen
III	three	XIX	nineteen
IV	four	XX	twenty
V	five	XXI	twenty-one
VI	six	XXX	thirty
VII	seven	XL	forty
VIII	eight	L	fifty
IX	nine	LX	sixty
X	ten	LXX	seventy
XI	eleven	LXXX	eighty
XII	twelve	XC	ninety
XIII	thirteen	C	one hundred
XIV	fourteen	CC	two hundred
XV	fifteen	D	five hundred
XVI	sixteen	M	one thousand

A a

a¹ or **A** /eɪ/ noun **1** [C/U] the first letter of the English alphabet **2 A** [C/U] a mark that a teacher gives to a student's work to show that it is excellent **3 A** [U] a common BLOOD TYPE

PHRASE **from A to B** from one place to another

a² /*weak* ə, *strong* eɪ/ or **an** /*weak* ən, *strong* æn/ determiner ★★★

> **A** and **an** are **indefinite articles.**
> - **A** is used when the next word begins with a consonant.
> - **An** is used when the next word begins with a vowel sound.

1 used when you are mentioning a person or a thing for the first time: *I have an idea.* ♦ *There's a concert on Sunday night.*
2 one: *I have a sister and two brothers.* ♦ *a hundred/thousand/million*
3 used when you mean any person or thing of a particular type, but not a specific one: *Do you have a car?* ♦ *Children must be accompanied by an adult.*
4 used when you say what job someone does: *Ruth was a lawyer.* ♦ *I want to be an actor.*
5 used when you say what type someone or something belongs to: *Maria is a Catholic.* ♦ *Greece has been a republic since 1973.*
6 used before a singular noun that represents every person or thing of a particular type: *A dog needs regular exercise.* ♦ *A molecule consists of two or more atoms.*
7 used in phrases showing prices, rates, or speeds to mean "each" or "every": *Meetings are held four times a year* (=four times every year). ♦ *Peaches are 99 cents a pound* (=each pound costs 99 cents). ♦ *90 miles an hour*
8 used in expressions of quantity such as "a lot," "a few," or "a great deal": *a lot of money* ♦ *a few friends* ♦ *We all appreciate a little encouragement.*
9 used before a noun that is formed from a verb and means a single action of that verb: *Can I have a try?* ♦ *Let's take a walk around the garden.*

A.A. /ˌeɪ ˈeɪ/ noun [C] Associate of Arts: a degree given by a U.S. COMMUNITY COLLEGE to students who have finished a two-year course of study

a•back /əˈbæk/ adv **be taken aback** to be very shocked or surprised

ab•a•cus /ˈæbəkəs/ noun [C] an object used for counting or doing simple calculations. An abacus consists of a frame with small balls in rows.

a•ban•don /əˈbændən/ verb [T] ★
1 to leave someone or something and never come back: *His mother abandoned him when he was five days old.* ♦ *The stolen car was abandoned only five miles away.*
2 to stop doing something before it is finished, or before you have achieved your goals: *The climbers finally abandoned their attempt on the mountain.*
—**a•ban•don•ment** noun [U]

a•ban•doned /əˈbændənd/ adj **1** left empty or no longer used: *an abandoned farm* **2** left alone by someone who should stay with you and take care of you: *a home for abandoned children*

a•bashed /əˈbæʃt/ adj embarrassed or ashamed about something that you have done

a•bate /əˈbeɪt/ verb [I] *formal* to gradually become less serious or extreme

ab•bey /ˈæbi/ noun [C] a large church with buildings attached for MONKS or NUNS to live in

ab•bre•vi•at•ed /əˈbriviˌeɪtɪd/ adj shorter because some parts have been removed

ab•bre•vi•a•tion /əˌbriviˈeɪʃ(ə)n/ noun [C] a short form of a word or phrase: *MIA is an abbreviation for "Missing in Action."*

ABC /ˌeɪ bi ˈsi/ Australian Broadcasting Corporation: one of the major television companies in Australia

ab•di•cate /ˈæbdɪˌkeɪt/ verb **1** [I/T] if a king or queen abdicates, he or she formally gives up being king or queen **2** [T] *formal* to stop accepting responsibility for something
—**ab•di•ca•tion** /ˌæbdɪˈkeɪʃ(ə)n/ noun [C/U]

ab•do•men /ˈæbdəmən, æbˈdoʊmən/ noun [C] *formal* the front part of your body below your waist

ab•dom•i•nal /æbˈdɑmɪn(ə)l/ adj in the abdomen

ab•duct /æbˈdʌkt/ verb [T] to take someone away using force = KIDNAP —**ab•duc•tion** /æbˈdʌkʃ(ə)n/ noun [C/U]

ab•er•ra•tion /ˌæbəˈreɪʃ(ə)n/ noun [C] *formal* something that is not normal, or not what you would usually expect

ab•hor•rent /əbˈhɔrənt/ adj *formal* if something is abhorrent, you hate it because it is immoral

a•bide /əˈbaɪd/ verb **can't abide sth** to hate something

PHRASAL VERB **aˈbide by sth** to follow a rule, decision, or instruction

a•bid•ing /əˈbaɪdɪŋ/ adj *formal* an abiding feeling or belief is one that you have had for a long time

a•bil•i•ty /əˈbɪləti/ noun [C/U] ★★★ the skill that you need in order to do something ≠ INABILITY: *She has good organizational abilities.* ♦ **ability to do sth** *Tiredness can affect your ability to drive.*

PHRASE **to the best of your ability** as well as you can: *Just try to do the job to the best of your ability.*

ab•ject /ˈæbˌdʒekt/ adj *formal* **1** used for emphasizing how bad something is: *abject poverty* **2** showing that you feel ashamed: *a look of abject embarrassment*

a•blaze /əˈbleɪz/ adj burning with a lot of flames

a•ble /ˈeɪb(ə)l/ adj ★★★ intelligent, or good at doing something

PHRASE **be able to do sth** used for saying that it is possible for someone to do

A

something: *I don't know if I'll be able to come.* ♦ *I'd love to be able to sing like you.*

> Word family: **able**
> *Words in the same family as* **able**
> - **ability** *n*
> - **unable** *adj*
> - **inability** *n*
> - **disability** *n*
> - **disabled** *adj*
> - **enable** *v*

able-bod·ied /ˌeɪb(ə)l ˈbɑdid/ adj not suffering from any disability

a·bly /ˈeɪbli/ adv very well, or very skillfully

ab·nor·mal /æbˈnɔrm(ə)l/ adj not normal, and therefore a sign that there is a problem: *abnormal behavior* ♦ *abnormal eating habits* —**ab·nor·ma·li·ty** /ˌæbnɔrˈmæləti/ noun [C/U], **ab·nor·mal·ly** adv: *Her blood pressure was abnormally high.*

a·board /əˈbɔrd/ adv, preposition in or on a ship, train, or airplane

a·bode /əˈboʊd/ noun [C] *literary* the place where you live=RESIDENCE

a·bol·ish /əˈbɑlɪʃ/ verb [T] to officially get rid of a law or system: *The U.S. abolished slavery in 1865.*

ab·o·li·tion /ˌæbəˈlɪʃ(ə)n/ noun [U] the official end to a law or system

a·bom·i·na·ble /əˈbɑmɪnəb(ə)l/ adj *formal* extremely bad —**a·bom·i·na·bly** adv

Ab·o·rig·i·ne /ˌæbəˈrɪdʒəni/ or **Ab·o·rig·i·nal** /ˌæbəˈrɪdʒən(ə)l/ noun [C] an Australian who belongs to the race of people who were living in Australia before Europeans arrived

a·bort /əˈbɔrt/ verb [T] **1** to stop something before it is finished: *The mission had to be aborted because of a technical problem.* **2** to remove a developing baby from a woman's body, so that it is not born alive

a·bor·tion /əˈbɔrʃ(ə)n/ noun [C/U] a medical operation in which a developing baby is removed from a woman's body, so that it is not born alive

a·bor·tive /əˈbɔrtɪv/ adj not finished, and therefore not successful: *abortive peace negotiations*

a·bound /əˈbaʊnd/ verb [I] to be present in large numbers or amounts

a·bout /əˈbaʊt/ grammar word ★★★

> **About** can be:
> - a **preposition**: *He told me about your problem.*
> - an **adverb** in British English: *Stop rushing about.*
> - followed by an infinitive with "to": *I was just about to explain.*

1 used for giving an amount, number, or time that is not exact=APPROXIMATELY: *About 250 people were killed in the explosion.* ♦ *I woke up at about 3 a.m.*
2 almost: *Pam's about the only person that I can trust.* ♦ *I'm **just about** ready to go.*
3 *British* in or to many different parts or areas=AROUND: *The children were running about the room.* ♦ *Dirty clothes were scattered about.*
4 used for stating who or what is being considered or discussed: *a book about American history* ♦ *They were talking about their vacation.* ♦ *There's nothing to get excited about.*

PHRASE **be about to do sth** to be going to happen very soon, or to be going to do something very soon: *I was about to get undressed when someone knocked.* ♦ *The show was about to begin.*

→ HOW, WHAT

aˌbout-ˈface noun [C] *American* **1** a complete change in the way you behave or think about something **2** the action of turning your whole body quickly so that you are facing in the opposite direction

a·bove /əˈbʌv/ grammar word ★★★

> **Above** can be:
> - a **preposition**: *The birds were flying high above the trees.*
> - an **adverb**: *She stared up at the stars above.*
> - an **adjective**: *Please reply to the above address.*

1 in a higher position at a higher level than something, or directly over it: *We lived in the room above the store.* ♦ *Her leg was broken above the knee.*
2 higher in amount or standard more than a particular number, amount, or level: *The company's profits were 23% above the previous year's.* ♦ *In most subjects the students scored well above average.*
3 louder or higher than another sound louder or higher than the other sounds that you can hear: *I couldn't hear his voice above all the noise.*
4 in an earlier part of writing in an earlier part of a piece of writing, or higher up on the same page: *Many of the documents mentioned above are now available on the Internet.*
5 with a higher rank higher in rank, or more important than someone else: *As a major, Stuart was a rank above me.*

PHRASE **above all** used for saying what is most important: *We hope you will learn new skills, meet new people, and above all enjoy yourself.*

> - Use **above** when something is not directly over something else, but at a higher level: *on the hillside above the river.*
> - Use **over** when something moves or stretches across the space above something else: *flying over Miami* ♦ *the bridge over the river.*
> - Use **over** when something covers something else: *She put a scarf over her hair.*

a·bove·board /əˈbʌvˌbɔrd/ adj completely honest and legal

ab·ra·sive /əˈbreɪsɪv/ adj **1** someone who is abrasive behaves in a way that seems rude **2** an abrasive substance has a rough surface that is used for rubbing other surfaces

a·breast /əˈbrest/ adv next to each other, facing or moving in the same direction

PHRASE **keep abreast of sth** to make sure that you know the most recent information about something

a·bridged /əˈbrɪdʒd/ adj an abridged book or play is shorter than the original

a·broad /əˈbrɔd/ adv ★★ in or to a foreign country: *We try to go abroad at least once a year.* ♦ *special arrangements for voters living abroad*

a·brupt /əˈbrʌpt/ adj **1** sudden and unexpected, often in an unpleasant way

2 someone who is abrupt speaks in an unfriendly way using very few words —**a•brupt•ly** adv

ab•scess /ˈæbˌses/ noun [C] a painful swollen area on your skin or inside your body

ab•scond /əbˈskɑnd/ verb [I] *formal* **1** to suddenly leave a place and take something with you that does not belong to you **2** to escape from a place where you are being kept as a punishment

ab•sence /ˈæbsəns/ noun ★
1 [C/U] a time when someone is not where they should be or where they usually are: *We are concerned about your child's frequent absences from school.* ♦ *Mark will be in charge* ***in my absence*** (=while I am away).
2 [U] the fact that something does not exist or is not present: *a complete absence of humor*

ab•sent /ˈæbsənt/ adj **1** not in the place where you should be ≠ PRESENT: *He's been absent from school for three days.* **2** *formal* missing from a place or situation: *The story has been absent from the news for weeks.*

ab•sen•tee /ˌæbsənˈti/ adj not able to do a job well because you are not in the place where you should be: *an absentee father*

ab•sen•tee•ism /ˌæbsənˈtiˌɪzəm/ noun [U] the habit of not being at school or work when you should be

ˌabsent-ˈminded adj likely to forget or not notice things because you are not paying attention —**ˌabsent-ˈmindedly** adv

ab•so•lute /ˈæbsəˌlut, ˌæbsəˈlut/ adj **1** used for emphasizing an opinion, feeling, or statement = TOTAL: *The way they've been treated is an absolute disgrace.* ♦ *You're talking absolute nonsense.* ♦ *I have absolute confidence in her.* **2** used for emphasizing that something is the most or least possible in a particular situation: *$4,000 is the absolute maximum we can spend.*

ab•so•lute•ly /ˈæbsəlutli, ˌæbsəˈlutli/ adv ★
1 completely: *Are you absolutely certain you saw him?* ♦ *The food was absolutely fantastic.* ♦ *They have absolutely no idea how this happened.*
2 *spoken* used for emphasizing that you agree or mean "yes": *"Are you sure it's OK?" "Absolutely!"*
PHRASE **absolutely not** used for showing that you disagree strongly, or used as a strong way of saying "no": *"Do you think I should forgive him?" "Absolutely not!"*

ab•solve /əbˈzɑlv/ verb [T] *formal* **1** to state officially that someone is not responsible for something bad **2** to forgive someone

ab•sorb /əbˈsɔrb, əbˈzɔrb/ verb [T] **1** to take in heat, light, liquid, or some other substance: *When wood gets wet, it absorbs water and expands.* ♦ *a device that produces energy by absorbing sunlight* ♦ **be absorbed into sth** *Caffeine is rapidly absorbed into the bloodstream.* **2** to make something become a part of something larger: *His music has absorbed influences from all over the world.* ♦ **be absorbed into sth** *After the war, the whole region was absorbed into the Roman Empire.* **3** to learn and understand new facts: *We had to absorb a lot of information.* **4** *business* to accept an increase in your costs, instead of increasing the prices that you charge: *Oil companies say they will absorb these tax increases.*

ab•sorbed /əbˈsɔrbd, əbˈzɔrbd/ adj completely interested or involved in something: *Richard was totally absorbed in his book.*

ab•sorb•ent /əbˈsɔrbənt, əbˈzɔrbənt/ adj an absorbent material can take in and hold liquids

ab•sorb•ing /əbˈsɔrbɪŋ, əbˈzɔrbɪŋ/ adj taking all your attention: *an absorbing book*

ab•sorp•tion /əbˈsɔrpʃ(ə)n, əbˈzɔrpʃ(ə)n/ noun [U] **1** the process by which something takes in heat, light, liquid, or some other substance **2** the process of becoming part of something larger

ab•stain /əbˈsteɪn/ verb [I] **1** to deliberately avoid doing something enjoyable **2** to decide not to vote

ab•sten•tion /əbˈstenʃ(ə)n/ noun [C] a decision not to vote

ab•sti•nence /ˈæbstɪnəns/ noun [U] the practice of avoiding something such as alcohol or sex

ab•stract /ˈæbˌstrækt, æbˈstrækt/ adj
1 abstract ideas are not related to physical objects or real events **2** abstract art expresses ideas or feelings, instead of showing the exact appearance of people or things —**ab•strac•tion** /æbˈstrækʃ(ə)n/ noun [C/U]

ˌabstract ˈnoun noun [C] a word that names a quality, idea, or feeling, such as "happiness" or "beauty"

ab•surd /əbˈsɜrd, əbˈzɜrd/ adj silly, unreasonable, or impossible to believe = RIDICULOUS —**ab•surd•i•ty** noun [C/U], **ab•surd•ly** adv

a•bun•dance /əˈbʌndəns/ noun [U] *formal* a very large quantity of something ≠ SCARCITY

a•bun•dant /əˈbʌndənt/ adj *formal* existing or available in large quantities ≠ SCARCE

a•bun•dant•ly /əˈbʌndəntli/ adv *formal* in large quantities
PHRASE **abundantly clear** very obvious

a•buse¹ /əˈbjus/ noun ★
1 [C/U] cruel, violent, or unfair treatment: *human rights abuses* ♦ *Many of the children were victims of* ***sexual abuse.***
2 [C/U] the use of something in a bad, dishonest, or harmful way: *alcohol/drug/substance abuse* ♦ *This is clearly* ***an abuse of executive power.***
3 [U] angry offensive comments: *racist abuse*

a•buse² /əˈbjuz/ verb [T] **1** to have sex with someone who is unable to refuse, especially a child: *She was abused as a child.* **2** to treat someone in a cruel or violent way **3** to use something in a bad, dishonest, or harmful way **4** to speak to someone in an angry, offensive way —**a•bus•er** noun [C]

a•bu•sive /əˈbjusɪv/ adj **1** offensive or insulting = RUDE: *abusive language* ♦ *When we asked him to leave, he became abusive.*
2 treating someone in a cruel way, either by being violent or by forcing them to have sex: *an abusive parent* —**a•bu•sive•ly** adv

a•bys•mal /əˈbɪzm(ə)l/ adj extremely bad = APPALLING

a•byss /əˈbɪs/ noun [C] **1** a very frightening or

A

dangerous situation **2** *literary* a large deep hole

a/c abbrev air conditioning

ac·a·dem·ic¹ /ˌækəˈdemɪk/ adj ★
1 relating to education, especially in colleges and universities: *We expect our students to meet high academic standards.* ♦ *We are approaching the end of* ***the academic year*** (=time during the year when there is teaching).
2 based on learning from study instead of practical skills and experience: *The college offers both academic and vocational qualifications.*
3 not relating to a real situation, and therefore not relevant: *Given the lack of funding, any discussion of future plans was somewhat academic.*
—**ac·a·dem·i·cal·ly** /ˌækəˈdemɪkli/ adv

ac·a·dem·ic² /ˌækəˈdemɪk/ noun [C] a teacher at a college or university

a·cad·e·my /əˈkædəmi/ noun [C] **1** a school or college that teaches a particular subject or skill **2** an organization that was created to encourage interest and development in a particular subject

ac·cel·er·ate /əkˈseləˌreɪt/ verb **1** [I] if a vehicle accelerates, it moves faster **2** [I/T] to happen at a faster rate, or to make something do this: *We want to accelerate the development process.* —**ac·cel·er·a·tion** /əkˌseləˈreɪʃ(ə)n/ noun [U]

ac·cel·er·a·tor /əkˈseləˌreɪtər/ noun [C] the PEDAL that you press with your foot to make a vehicle go faster —*picture* → C6

ac·cent¹ /ˈækˌsent/ noun ★
1 [C] a way of pronouncing words that shows what country, region, or social class you come from: *a Brooklyn accent* ♦ *Tom hasn't lost his strong Irish accent.*
2 [singular] the emphasis on a particular part of a word or phrase when you say it: *The accent is on the first syllable.*
3 [C] a mark above a letter that shows how you pronounce it
PHRASE **the accent is on sth** used for saying that a particular thing is given importance: *At the hotel, the accent is on luxury.*

> Words often used with **accent**
> *Adjectives often used with* ***accent*** *(noun, sense 1)*
> ■ **heavy, strong, thick** + ACCENT: used about accents that are easy to notice

ac·cent² /ækˈsent/ verb [T] to emphasize a word, sound, or feature

ac·cen·tu·ate /ækˈsentʃuˌeɪt/ verb [T] to make something more noticeable

ac·cept /əkˈsept/ verb ★★★

1 take sth offered	4 know sth bad is true
2 say yes to invitation	5 let sb be part of sth
3 recognize as true	

1 [T] to take something that someone gives you: *It gives me great pleasure to accept this award.* ♦ *Two police officers were accused of accepting bribes.*
2 [I/T] to say yes to an invitation, offer, or suggestion ≠ REJECT: *Our clients will never accept this proposal.* ♦ *They offered her a job, and she accepted without hesitation.*
3 [T] to recognize that something is true, fair, or right: *This argument is unlikely to be accepted by the court.* ♦ *We cannot* ***accept responsibility*** *for any damage.* ♦ **+that** *Most scientists accept that climate change is linked to pollution.*
4 [T] to recognize that a bad situation exists and cannot be changed: *I know it's not fair, but you'll just have to accept it.* ♦ *They found it hard to accept defeat.* ♦ **+that** *For a long time, he simply could not accept that she was dead.*
5 [T] to allow someone to become part of an organization or group: *Under the new law, gay people will be accepted in the armed forces.* ♦ **accept sb into sth** *The children soon accepted her into the family.*

> ■ Use **accept** to mean that you take something that someone gives you, or you recognize that something is true, fair, or right: *We accepted her gifts.* ♦ *They accepted the court's decision.*
> ■ Use **agree** to mean that you are willing to do something: *She agreed to work over the weekend.*
> ■ You **accept** something, but you **agree to do** something.

ac·cept·a·ble /əkˈseptəb(ə)l/ adj ★
1 if something is acceptable, most people approve of it or accept it ≠ UNACCEPTABLE: *That kind of behavior is not acceptable.* ♦ *an agreement that is* ***acceptable to*** *both sides*
2 good enough = REASONABLE ≠ UNACCEPTABLE: *A success rate of 65% is acceptable.*
—**ac·cept·a·bil·i·ty** /əkˌseptəˈbɪləti/ noun [U]

ac·cep·tance /əkˈseptəns/ noun [U]
1 agreement that something is true, reasonable, or cannot be changed ≠ REJECTION: *There is widespread acceptance of these principles.* **2** agreement to a plan, offer, or suggestion ≠ REJECTION: *The union has recommended acceptance of the pay offer.* **3** an attitude of accepting a bad situation because it cannot be changed: *a religion that teaches acceptance of suffering* **4** the fact of being accepted into an organization or group: *my acceptance into Stanford University*

ac·cept·ed /əkˈseptəd/ adj thought by most people to be reasonable, right, or normal

ac·cess¹ /ˈækˌses/ noun [U] ★★
1 the right or opportunity to have or to use something: *Only a small number of our students have* ***access to*** *the Internet.* ♦ *Some groups still have difficulty* ***gaining access*** *to health care.*
2 the means by which you get to a place: *An elevator provides* ***access to*** *the upper floors.*
3 official permission to see someone: *All prisoners have* ***access to*** *a lawyer.*

ac·cess² /ˈækˌses/ verb [T] to get information, especially from a computer

ˈaccess ˌcourse noun [C] *British* a course of study in which you learn enough about a subject to allow you to go to a college or university to continue studying the subject

ac·ces·si·ble /əkˈsesəb(ə)l/ adj **1** easy to obtain, use, or understand ≠ INACCESSIBLE: *information that should be accessible to the*

A

public **2** easy to find or get to ≠ INACCESSIBLE: *The city is easily accessible by road, train, or air.* —**ac·ces·si·bil·i·ty** /əkˌsesəˈbɪləti/ noun [U]

ac·ces·so·ry /əkˈsesəri/ noun [C] **1** an additional object or piece of equipment that makes something more attractive or useful **2** a small thing that you wear such as a piece of jewelry or a belt **3** *legal* someone who helps a criminal

ac·ci·dent /ˈæksɪdənt/ noun [C] ★★★
1 a crash involving a car, train, or other vehicle: *The accident was caused by ice on the road.*
2 an unexpected event that causes injury or damage: *He was killed in a climbing accident.* ♦ *I didn't mean to break the vase, it was an accident.*
3 something that happens without being planned: *To be honest, my second pregnancy was an accident.*
PHRASE **by accident** by chance, without being planned or intended: *I discovered the answer by accident.*

Words often used with accident

Adjectives often used with ***accident*** *(sense 1)*
- **bad, horrific, nasty, serious, fatal, tragic** + ACCIDENT: used about accidents that cause serious injuries or death
- **minor, slight** + ACCIDENT: used about accidents that are not serious

Verbs often used with ***accident*** *(sense 1)*
- **be involved in, have** + ACCIDENT: have an accident

ac·ci·den·tal /ˌæksɪˈdent(ə)l/ adj not intended ≠ DELIBERATE: *accidental death* ♦ *an accidental release of dangerous chemicals* —**ac·ci·den·tal·ly** adv

ac·claim /əˈkleɪm/ noun [U] public praise

ac·claimed /əˈkleɪmd/ adj publicly praised

ac·cli·mate /əˈklaɪmət, ˈæklɪˌmeɪt/ verb [I/T] *American* to gradually become more comfortable in a new place

ac·cli·ma·tize /əˈklaɪməˌtaɪz/ verb [I/T] to acclimate

ac·co·lade /ˈækəˌleɪd/ noun [C] an honor or praise that someone is given for their work

ac·com·mo·date /əˈkɑməˌdeɪt/ verb [T] **1** to provide a room or a place for someone to stay: *The hotel can accommodate 600 guests.* ♦ *The teams will be accommodated in luxury hotels.* **2** to provide enough space for something or someone: *The new office will easily accommodate 50 desks.* **3** *formal* to do what someone asks you to do: *We will do our best to accommodate your request.*

ac·com·mo·dat·ing /əˈkɑməˌdeɪtɪŋ/ adj helpful and easy to work with = OBLIGING: *The staff was very accommodating.*

ac·com·mo·da·tions /əˌkɑməˈdeɪʃ(ə)nz/ noun [plural] *American* ★★
1 a place to live, especially a temporary place such as a hotel room: *accommodations for guests/students/workers*
2 special arrangements for someone's particular need

ac·com·pa·ni·ment /əˈkʌmpənɪmənt/ noun **1** [C/U] music that supports someone who is singing or playing the main tune **2** [C] something that you provide as an addition, especially to a meal

ac·com·pa·ny /əˈkʌmpəni/ verb [T] **1** *formal* to go with someone to a place or event: *Children must be accompanied by an adult.* **2** to happen or exist with something else: *A sore throat sometimes accompanies a fever.* ♦ *The book is accompanied by a CD-ROM.* **3** to play music while someone sings or plays the main tune

ac·com·plice /əˈkʌmplɪs/ noun [C] someone who helps another person to do something illegal

ac·com·plish /əˈkʌmplɪʃ/ verb [T] to succeed in doing something difficult → MISSION

ac·com·plished /əˈkʌmplɪʃt/ adj good at doing something that needs a lot of skill

ac·com·plish·ment /əˈkʌmplɪʃmənt/ noun [C/U] something difficult that you succeed in doing

ac·cord¹ /əˈkɔrd/ noun [C] a formal agreement between countries or groups
PHRASE **do sth of your own accord** to do something without being asked, forced, or helped to do it

ac·cord² /əˈkɔrd/ verb [T] *formal* to give someone something such as power, respect, or status

ac·cor·dance /əˈkɔrd(ə)ns/ noun **in accordance with** in a way that follows a rule, system, or someone's wishes

ac·cord·ing·ly /əˈkɔrdɪŋli/ adv **1** as a result of something = CONSEQUENTLY: *No formal complaint was made; accordingly, the police took no action.* **2** in a way that is appropriate: *They have broken the rules and will be punished accordingly.*

ac·cord·ing to /əˈkɔrdɪŋ ˌtu/ preposition ★★★
1 used for stating where information or ideas have come from: *According to newspaper reports, fighting has broken out in the northern provinces.*
2 in a way that agrees with or obeys a particular plan, system, or set of rules: *The game was played according to the rules.* ♦ *If everything* ***goes according to plan****, they should finish by Thursday.*
3 used for saying that something changes or is different depending on the situation: *The amount of tax people pay varies according to where they live.*

ac·cor·di·on /əˈkɔrdiən/ noun [C] a musical instrument that is played by moving the ends of a box in and out while pressing buttons

ac·cost /əˈkɔst/ verb [T] *formal* to stop someone and speak to them, especially when this annoys them

ac·count¹ /əˈkaʊnt/ noun ★★

1 agreement with bank	5 regular customer
2 report/description	6 for e-mail
3 financial records	+ PHRASES
4 agreement with store	

1 [C] an arrangement in which a bank takes care of your money: *There was only $50 in his bank account.* ♦ *How do I* ***open an account*** (=start having an account)? → CHECKING ACCOUNT
2 [C] a written or spoken report about something that has happened: *a brief*

A

account of the meeting ♦ *He was too shocked to give a clear* ***account*** *of events.*
3 accounts [plural] a detailed record that a business keeps of the money it receives and spends: *The accounts showed a loss of $498 million.*
4 [C] an arrangement that you have with a store or other business that allows you to pay for goods or services later: *I have an account with Macy's.*
5 [C] *business* a company that regularly buys goods or services from another company
6 [C] an arrangement with a company or Internet PROVIDER to use a service they provide: *an e-mail account*
PHRASES **by/from all accounts** according to what people say
on sb's account if you do something on someone's account, you do it because you think they want you to: *Please don't stay home on my account.*
on account of because of someone or something: *She can't work too many hours on account of the children.*
on no account used for emphasizing that something must not happen
take account of sth or **take sth into account** to consider something when you are trying to make a decision: *A good transportation strategy must take account of the environmental issues.* ♦ *If you take inflation into account, the cost of computers has fallen in the last ten years.*

ac·count² /əˈkaʊnt/ verb ★★★ PHRASAL VERB
acˈcount for sth 1 to form a particular amount or part of something: *Electronic goods account for over 30% of our exports.* **2** to be the reason for something: *The increase in carbon dioxide emissions may account for changes in the climate.* **3** to give an explanation for something: *How do you account for this sudden improvement in his test scores?*

ac·count·a·ble /əˈkaʊntəb(ə)l/ adj in a position where people can criticize you or ask you why something happened ≠ UNACCOUNTABLE —**ac·count·a·bil·i·ty** /əˌkaʊntəˈbɪləti/ noun [U]

ac·count·an·cy /əˈkaʊntənsi/ noun [U] the work or profession of an accountant

ac·count·ant /əˈkaʊntənt/ noun [C] someone whose job is to prepare or check financial records

ac·count·ing /əˈkaʊntɪŋ/ noun [U] the work of accountants, or the methods they use

ac·cred·it·ed /əˈkredɪtəd/ adj having official approval

ac·cu·mu·late /əˈkjumjəˌleɪt/ verb **1** [T] to get more and more of something over a period of time: *Over the years, I had accumulated hundreds of books.* **2** [I] to increase in quantity over a period of time: *The snow accumulated in the streets overnight.*
—**ac·cu·mu·la·tion** /əˌkjumjəˈleɪʃ(ə)n/ noun [U]

ac·cu·ra·cy /ˈækjərəsi/ noun [U] the ability to do something in an accurate way, or the quality of being accurate ≠ INACCURACY: *The accuracy of the report is being checked.*

ac·cu·rate /ˈækjərət/ adj ★ correct in every detail, and without any mistakes = PRECISE ≠ INACCURATE: *We need to get an accurate estimate of what the new building will cost.* ♦ *accurate measurements* ♦ *an accurate description of the events* —**ac·cu·rate·ly** adv

ac·cu·sa·tion /ˌækjəˈzeɪʃ(ə)n/ noun [C] a claim that someone has done something illegal or wrong: *The police officer denied the accusation that she had lied.*

ac·cuse /əˈkjuz/ verb [T] ★★ to say that someone has done something wrong or illegal: **accuse sb of doing sth** *Are you accusing me of lying?* ♦ **accuse sb of sth** *Her boss accused her of theft.* —**ac·cus·er** noun [C]

ac·cused, the /əˈkjuzd/ (plural **the ac·cused**) noun [C] someone who is accused of a crime in a court of law

ac·cus·ing /əˈkjuzɪŋ/ adj showing that you think someone has done something wrong: *an accusing stare* —**ac·cus·ing·ly** adv

ac·cus·tomed /əˈkʌstəmd/ adj **be/get accustomed to sth** to think that something is normal or natural because you have experienced it regularly over a period of time: *He had become accustomed to living without electricity.*

ace¹ /eɪs/ noun [C] in card games, a card with only one symbol and either the highest or lowest value —*picture* → C16

ace² /eɪs/ verb [T] *American informal* to get the best grade possible on a test, a piece of written work, etc.

ace³ /eɪs/ adj *informal* very good or skillful

ache¹ /eɪk/ noun [C] a pain that is continuous but usually not very strong

ache² /eɪk/ verb [I] to feel a continuous but not very strong pain in part of your body

a·chieve /əˈtʃiv/ verb ★★★
1 [T] to succeed in doing or having something: *We have achieved what we set out to do.* ♦ *Most of the students achieved high test scores.*
2 [I] to be successful and do things that people admire: *Many athletes are driven by a desire to achieve.*
—**a·chiev·a·ble** adj

a·chieve·ment /əˈtʃivmənt/ noun ★★
1 [C] a particular thing that someone has achieved: *Winning the gold medal was a remarkable achievement.*
2 [U] the fact of achieving something: *It was hard work, but the sense of achievement is huge.*

ac·id /ˈæsɪd/ noun [C/U] a strong chemical that can damage other substances

a·cid·ic /əˈsɪdɪk/ adj **1** containing acid **2** very sour

ˌacid ˈrain noun [U] rain that contains a high level of acid that can damage the environment

ˌacid ˈtest noun [singular] a fact, event, or situation that proves whether something is true or effective

ac·knowl·edge /əkˈnɑlɪdʒ/ verb [T] **1** to accept that something exists, is true, or has a particular quality: *She won't acknowledge that there's a problem.* ♦ *He is acknowledged as one of our greatest medical experts.* **2** to thank someone for something that they have given you, or for helping you: *We gratefully acknowledge the efforts of everyone who helped us.*

A

ac•knowl•edg•ment or **ac•knowl•edge•ment** /ək'nɑlɪdʒmənt/ noun **1** [singular/U] something that shows that you accept that something exists or is true **2** [C/U] something that you say or write to thank someone, or to tell them that you have received something that they sent you

ACLU, the /ˌeɪ si el 'ju/ the American Civil Liberties Union: an organization that protects and defends people in situations where their CIVIL RIGHTS (=freedom, fair treatment, etc.) are not being respected

ac•ne /'ækni/ noun [U] a medical condition in which your face is covered in PIMPLES

a•corn /'eɪˌkɔrn/ noun [C] the nut of an OAK tree

a•cous•tic /ə'kustɪk/ adj **1** relating to sound **2** an acoustic musical instrument does not use electricity to make sounds louder —**a•cous•ti•cal•ly** /ə'kustɪkli/ adv

a•cous•tics /ə'kustɪks/ noun [plural] the way that sound is heard in a room

ac•quain•tance /ə'kweɪntəns/ noun [C] someone who you know but who is not a close friend

ac•quaint•ed /ə'kweɪntəd/ adj *formal* **1** if two people are acquainted, they know each other, but usually not very well **2** if you are acquainted with something, you know about it

ac•quire /ə'kwaɪr/ verb [T] **1** to get something: *She has acquired an impressive reputation as a negotiator.* **2** *business* to buy something, especially a company or a share in a company

ac•qui•si•tion /ˌækwɪ'zɪʃ(ə)n/ noun **1** [U] the process of getting something: *the acquisition of knowledge* **2** [C] *business* something that someone has bought

ac•quit /ə'kwɪt/ verb [T] to state officially that someone is not guilty of a crime: *He was eventually acquitted of the charges.*

ac•quit•tal /ə'kwɪt(ə)l/ noun [C/U] an official judgment that someone is not guilty of a crime

a•cre /'eɪkər/ noun [C] a unit for measuring large areas of land, equal to 4,840 square yards or 4,047 square meters

ac•rid /'ækrɪd/ adj very strong, bitter, and unpleasant: *an acrid smell*

ac•ri•mo•ni•ous /ˌækrɪ'moʊniəs/ adj unpleasant because people feel angry toward each other: *an acrimonious meeting*

ac•ro•bat /'ækrəˌbæt/ noun [C] a performer who balances, jumps, and turns their body in skillful ways

ac•ro•bat•ics /ˌækrə'bætɪks/ noun [plural] the skills or movements of an acrobat —**ac•ro•bat•ic** adj

ac•ro•nym /'ækrəˌnɪm/ noun [C] a word made from the first letters of a series of words: *NATO is an acronym for the North Atlantic Treaty Organization.*

a•cross /ə'krɔs/ grammar word ★★★

> **Across can be:**
> - a **preposition**: *I walked across the road.*
> - an **adverb**: *Our host hurried across to meet us.*

1 moving, looking, or reaching from one side of something to the other: *Over 70 airlines fly across the Atlantic between Europe and North America.* ♦ *Barbara looked across the room at her husband.* ♦ *There are four bridges across the Cedar River.*
2 on the opposite side of a road, river, or line: *There's a bus stop just across the road.* ♦ *They had opened a new factory across the border in Mexico.* ♦ *I'm staying at a little hotel just **across from** the Libyan Embassy.*
3 in many parts of something, or covering all of an area or surface: *an insurance company with 120 offices across America* ♦ *There has been growth across all areas of the economy.*

aˌcross-the-'board adj involving everyone or everything in a place or situation: *across-the-board budget cuts* —**aˌcross the 'board** adv

a•cryl•ic /ə'krɪlɪk/ adj made from a chemical substance that is used for making cloth and paint

act¹ /ækt/ noun ★★★

1 single thing sb does	5 performer/performers
2 law	6 behavior hiding truth
3 part of play	+ PHRASES
4 performance	

1 [C] a single thing that someone does: *an **act of violence against innocent people** ♦ a simple **act of kindness** ♦ groups committing **criminal acts***
2 [C] a law: *an act of Congress*
3 [C] one of the major divisions of a play, opera, or BALLET
4 [C] a short performance: *Her act includes singing and dancing.*
5 [C] a person or group who performs on stage: *They're one of rock music's most exciting live acts.*
6 [singular] a way of behaving that is not sincere: *She isn't really upset: it's all an act.*

PHRASES **act of God** something bad such as a flood that people cannot control because it is produced by natural forces
be a hard/tough act to follow *informal* to do something so well that it is hard for other people to be as good as you
get your act together *informal* to organize your life or work in a better way
get in on the act *informal* to take part in an activity in order to gain the same advantages as other people

act² /ækt/ verb ★★★

1 behave	4 have an effect
2 do sth	5 do a particular job
3 perform in plays	+ PHRASAL VERBS

1 [I] to behave in a particular way: *He's been acting strangely all day.* ♦ *Despite her problems, she **acted as if** nothing was wrong.*
2 [I] to do something: *Now is the time to act.* ♦ *I'm **acting on the advice of** my doctor.* ♦ *She claims that she **acted out of necessity*** (=because she had to).
3 [I/T] to perform in plays or movies: *I've always wanted to act.* ♦ *Burt Lancaster **acted the part of** Joseph.*
4 [I] to have a particular effect: *Don't expect the medicine to act immediately.* ♦ *The measures are intended to **act as** a deterrent to criminals.*

A

5 [I] to do the job of a particular kind of person: *You speak Greek – will you **act as** our interpreter?*

PHRASAL VERBS ˌ**act sth ˈout** to copy events that happened by pretending to be the people involved

ˌ**act ˈup** *informal* **1** if children act up, they behave badly **2** if a part of your body or a piece of equipment acts up, it develops problems

act·ing[1] /ˈæktɪŋ/ adj doing someone else's job for a short time: *the acting manager*

act·ing[2] /ˈæktɪŋ/ noun [U] the job or skill of being an actor

ac·tion /ˈækʃ(ə)n/ noun ★★★

1 process of doing sth	4 events in play/movie
2 sth sb does	5 movement of object
3 fighting in war	+ PHRASE

1 [U] the process of doing something: *Police say they will **take** tough **action** against drug dealers.* ♦ *If a student complains of harassment, what is the most appropriate **course of action*** (=way of dealing with the problem)*?* ♦ *We aren't quite ready to **put** our plans **into action*** (=start doing something). ♦ *It's interesting to watch a good salesman **in action*** (=doing his job).

2 [C] something that you do: *How can you justify your actions?*

3 [U] fighting in a war: *a list of soldiers **missing in action***

4 [singular] the events that form part of a play or movie: *In Scene 1, the action takes place in an expensive restaurant.*

5 [singular/U] the movement of an object or machine: *This switch slows down **the action** of the pump.*

PHRASE **out of action 1** unable to do your usual activities because you are injured or sick **2** equipment that is out of action is unable to be used because it is broken or being repaired

ˈ**action-packed** adj full of exciting events

ac·ti·vate /ˈæktɪveɪt/ verb [T] to make a piece of equipment or a process start working

ac·tive /ˈæktɪv/ adj ★★★

1 always doing things, especially with energy and enthusiasm: *Rose is still active at the age of 87.* ♦ *She continues to be **active in** politics.* ♦ *He is **an active member of** the American Cancer Society.*

2 an active VOLCANO is likely to ERUPT (=explode and pour out fire) at any time → EXTINCT

3 *linguistics* an active verb or sentence has the person or thing doing the action as the SUBJECT → PASSIVE

—**ac·tive·ly** adv

Word family: active

*Words in the same family as **active***

- **activate** *v*
- **actively** *adv*
- **activity** *n*
- **inactive** *adj*
- **interactive** *adj*
- **proactive** *adj*

ac·tive, the /ˈæktɪv/ noun [singular] *linguistics* the active form of a verb → PASSIVE

ac·tiv·ist /ˈæktɪvɪst/ noun [C] someone who is an active member of an organization that aims to achieve political or social change: *environmental activists*

ac·tiv·i·ty /ækˈtɪvəti/ noun ★★★

1 [C/U] things that people do in order to achieve a goal: *an increase in criminal activity in the area* ♦ *We plan to expand our business activities in East Africa.*

2 [U] a situation in which a lot of things are happening: *On Saturdays, there's always lots of activity in the streets.* ♦ *a high level of electrical activity in the atmosphere*

3 [C] something enjoyable or interesting that people do: *Guests can enjoy activities like swimming and surfing.* ♦ *We have several activities in which students work in groups.*

ac·tor /ˈæktər/ noun [C] ★★★ someone who performs in plays and movies

ac·tress /ˈæktrəs/ noun [C] a woman who performs in plays and movies. Many women performers prefer to be called actors instead of actresses.

ac·tu·al /ˈæktʃuəl/ adj ★★ real, true, or exact: *The actual number of people killed is not yet known.* ♦ *The actual situation was very different from the way she described it.* ♦ *The play is based on actual events.*

ac·tu·al·ly /ˈæktʃuəli/ adv ★★★

1 used for emphasizing what is really true or what really happened: *We've spoken on the phone but we've never actually met.*

2 used for emphasizing that something is surprising: *I think she actually agreed to go out with him.*

3 *spoken* used when correcting a statement: *It was yesterday, no actually it was Monday morning.*

4 *spoken* used for admitting something: *"Did you spend much money?" "Well, yes. Quite a lot, actually."*

ac·u·punc·ture /ˈækjuˌpʌŋktʃər/ noun [U] a medical treatment that involves putting needles into particular parts of someone's body —**ac·u·punc·tur·ist** /ˈækjuˌpʌŋktʃərɪst/ noun [C]

a·cute /əˈkjut/ adj **1** very serious or severe: *an acute pain in his chest* ♦ *acute food shortages* **2** able to notice things very quickly and easily: *an acute sense of smell* **3** an acute angle is less than 90 degrees —*picture* → C8 **4** an acute ACCENT is the mark ´ above a letter in some languages that shows it is pronounced in a particular way → GRAVE[3]

a·cute·ly /əˈkjutli/ adv used for emphasizing that a feeling is very strong: *He was acutely aware of his public image.*

ad /æd/ noun [C] *informal* ★ an ADVERTISEMENT → AD HOC

A.D. /ˌeɪ ˈdi/ abbrev used after a date to show that it is later than the birth of Jesus Christ → B.C.

ad·age /ˈædɪdʒ/ noun [C] a well-known phrase about life and human experience

ad·a·mant /ˈædəmənt/ adj determined not to change a belief or decision: *He was adamant that he was right.* —**ad·a·mant·ly** adv

Adam's ˈapple noun [C] the lump at the front of a man's throat

a·dapt /əˈdæpt/ verb **1** [I] to change your ideas or behavior in order to deal with a new situation: *The children adapted quickly to the new school.* **2** [T] to make something

A

more appropriate for a new use or situation

a·dapt·a·ble /ə'dæptəb(ə)l/ adj able to change or be changed easily to deal with new situations

a·dap·ta·tion /ˌædæp'teɪʃ(ə)n/ noun **1** [C] a movie or TV program made from a book or play **2** [U] the process of changing something so that it can be used for a different purpose

a·dapt·er or **a·dapt·or** /ə'dæptər/ noun [C] an object for connecting two pieces of equipment of different types

add /æd/ verb ★★★
1 [T] to put something with another thing: *When the sauce has thickened, add the cheese.* ♦ **add sth to sth** *They've added two major companies to their list of clients.*
2 [I/T] to calculate the total of two or more numbers: *What do you get if you add 75 and 63?*
3 [T] to say something more: *"Don't worry," Jenny added hastily.* ♦ **+(that)** *I should add that I am not happy about this decision.*
4 [T] to give something an extra quality: **add sth to sth** *The Italian chairs add a touch of elegance to the room.*
PHRASAL VERBS ˌ**add sth 'on** to include something extra: *If you add on legal fees, the total cost is over $1000.*
'**add to sth** to make a quality more extreme: *The arrival of five more guests only added to the confusion.*
ˌ**add (sth) 'up 1** to calculate the total of several numbers or amounts **2 not add up** if information does not add up, it does not seem true because it does not match other information that you have

add·ed /'ædəd/ adj extra or additional: *Baby food should contain no added sugar or salt.*

ad·dict /'ædɪkt/ noun [C] **1** someone who cannot stop taking illegal or harmful drugs: *a heroin addict* **2** someone who likes doing a particular activity very much: *a TV addict*

ad·dict·ed /ə'dɪktəd/ adj **1** unable to stop taking an illegal or harmful drug: *He was addicted to cocaine.* **2** doing a particular activity as much as you can: *I admit I'm addicted to that show.*

ad·dic·tion /ə'dɪkʃ(ə)n/ noun [C/U] a strong need to keep taking an illegal or harmful drug

ad·dic·tive /ə'dɪktɪv/ adj **1** an addictive drug is difficult to stop taking **2** an addictive activity is difficult to stop doing

ad·di·tion /ə'dɪʃ(ə)n/ noun ★★
1 [C] something that is added to something else: *The latest **addition to** her business empire is a chain of clothing stores.*
2 [U] the process of adding two or more numbers or amounts together to make a total
3 [C] *American* a room or area added to a building
PHRASE **in addition** as well as something else: *About 30 people were killed in the explosion. In addition, 120 people were injured.* ♦ *In addition to the twins, Jason has another child by his first wife.*

ad·di·tion·al /ə'dɪʃ(ə)nəl/ adj extra: *The new factory will create an additional 400 jobs.* —**ad·di·tion·al·ly** adv: *150 trucks were sent with supplies, and additionally, two cargo ships brought food and medicine.*

ad·di·tive /'ædətɪv/ noun [C] a chemical substance that is added to food to make it last longer or look or taste better

ad·dress¹ /ə'dres, 'ædres/ noun [C] ★★★
1 the exact name of the place where you live or work: *I'll need your name and address.* ♦ *My address is 125 Carter Street.*
2 a series of letters, numbers, and symbols that you use to find a particular WEBSITE on the Internet, or to send someone an e-mail
3 /ə'dres/ a formal speech

ad·dress² /ə'dres/ verb [T] **1** to write a name and address on an envelope or package: *This letter is addressed to Alice McQueen.* **2** to speak to a person or group: *He stood up to address the meeting.* **3** to call someone a particular name or title when you are speaking to them: *The neighbor's children address him as "Mr. H."* **4** to try to deal with a problem or question: *Governments have been slow to address the problem of global warming.*

'address ˌ**book** noun [C] a book or a piece of software in which you write people's names, addresses, telephone numbers, and e-mail addresses in alphabetical order

a·dept /ə'dept/ adj skillful at doing something: *He had quickly become adept at handling difficult customers.*

ad·e·quate /'ædəkwət/ adj ★
1 good enough or large enough = SUFFICIENT ≠ INADEQUATE: *The state has an adequate supply of trained teachers.* ♦ *It's a small office but it's **adequate for** our needs.*
2 satisfactory, but not extremely good ≠ INADEQUATE: *an adequate knowledge of the subject*
—**ad·e·quate·ly** adv

ad·here /əd'hɪr/ verb [I] *formal* to stick to something
PHRASAL VERB **ad'here to sth** to do the things that are stated in a rule, law, or agreement

ad·he·sive /əd'hisɪv/ noun [C] a substance that you use for making things stick together —**ad·he·sive** adj

ad hoc /ˌæd 'hɑk/ adj done only when it is needed for a specific purpose: *Members of the committee are elected on an ad hoc basis.*

adj. abbrev adjective

ad·ja·cent /ə'dʒeɪs(ə)nt/ adj next to or near something else: *The fire spread to an adjacent office block.*

ad·jec·ti·val /ˌædʒək'taɪv(ə)l/ adj relating to or used as an adjective

ad·jec·tive /'ædʒəktɪv/ noun [C] ★ a word used for describing a noun or pronoun

ad·join·ing /ə'dʒɔɪnɪŋ/ adj next to and connected to another building, room, or area

ad·journ /ə'dʒɜrn/ verb [I/T] to stop something such as a meeting or a trial for a short time and continue it later —**ad·journ·ment** noun [C/U]

ad·ju·di·cate /ə'dʒudɪˌkeɪt/ verb [I/T] to make an official decision about a problem or legal disagreement —**ad·ju·di·ca·tion** /əˌdʒudɪ'keɪʃ(ə)n/ noun [U], **ad·ju·di·ca·tor** noun [C]

A

ad•junct /ˈædʒʌŋkt/ adj *American* not a permanent member of the staff where you work

ad•just /əˈdʒʌst/ verb **1** [T] to change or move something slightly so that it works or fits better: *She stopped to adjust the strap on her sandal.* ♦ *Use the thermostat to adjust the temperature.* **2** [I] to get used to a new situation by changing your ideas or the way you do things: *It took her two years to adjust to life in England.*

ad•just•a•ble /əˈdʒʌstəb(ə)l/ adj something that is adjustable can be changed in order to make it work or fit better: *an adjustable strap/seat*

ad•just•ment /əˈdʒʌstmənt/ noun [C/U] a small change that you make to improve something: *I made a few adjustments – I think it's working better now.*

ad-lib /ˌæd ˈlɪb/ verb [I/T] to say something in a speech or play without preparing or writing it: *I lost the notes for my talk and had to ad-lib.*

ad•min•is•ter /ədˈmɪnɪstər/ verb [T] **1** to be responsible for managing or organizing something **2** *formal* to give someone a drug or medical treatment

ad•min•is•tra•tion /ədˌmɪnɪˈstreɪʃ(ə)n/ noun ★★
1 [U] the activities, processes, or people involved in managing a business, organization, or institution: *Too much money is spent on administration.*
2 the administration [C] the government of a country at a particular time, especially in the U.S.: *the Reagan administration*
—**ad•min•is•tra•tive** /ədˈmɪnɪˌstreɪtɪv/ adj

ad•min•is•tra•tor /ədˈmɪnɪˌstreɪtər/ noun [C] someone whose job is to manage a business, organization, or institution

ad•mi•ra•ble /ˈædmərəb(ə)l/ adj an admirable quality, action, or person deserves to be admired and respected —**ad•mi•ra•bly** adv

ad•mi•ral /ˈædmərəl/ noun [C] an officer of high rank in the navy

ad•mi•ra•tion /ˌædməˈreɪʃ(ə)n/ noun [U] a feeling of respect and approval: *We're full of admiration for all your hard work.*

ad•mire /ədˈmaɪr/ verb [T] ★
1 to greatly respect and approve of someone or something: *I've always admired her dedication and commitment.* ♦ *Ferguson is widely **admired for** his team management skills.*
2 to look at someone or something that you think is attractive: *We stopped to admire the view.*
—**ad•mir•er** noun [C]

> **Word family: admire**
> *Words in the same family as admire*
> ■ **admirable** *adj* ■ **admirer** *n*
> ■ **admiration** *n*

ad•mir•ing /ədˈmaɪrɪŋ/ adj full of admiration for someone or something —**ad•mir•ing•ly** adv

ad•mis•si•ble /ədˈmɪsəb(ə)l/ adj admissible evidence can be legally used in a trial

ad•mis•sion /ədˈmɪʃ(ə)n/ noun **1** [C] a statement accepting that something bad is true, or that you have done something wrong: *an admission of guilt* **2** [U] the act of accepting someone into a place, organization, or institution: *Several people were refused admission* (=not allowed in).
3 [U] the amount that you pay to enter a place or event: *Admission to the game is free.*

ad•mit /ədˈmɪt/ verb ★★★
1 [I/T] to agree that something bad is true, or to agree that you have done something wrong: **admit (to) doing sth** *Davis admitted driving the car into his neighbor's tree.* ♦ *In court, he admitted to lying about the accident.* ♦ **+(that)** *She freely admits that she made mistakes.*
2 [T] to allow someone to enter a place, join an organization, or be treated in a hospital: *Children under five will not be admitted.* ♦ **admit sb to sth** *The Baltic States were admitted to the United Nations in 1991.*
PHRASE **admit defeat** to accept that you cannot succeed at something, and stop trying to do it

ad•mit•tance /ədˈmɪt(ə)ns/ noun [U] *formal* permission to enter a place or to join an organization

ad•mit•ted•ly /ədˈmɪtədli/ adv used for saying that you accept that something is true even though it does not support the main point of what you are saying: *Admittedly, she's not very experienced, but she can do the job.*

ad•o•les•cence /ˌædəˈles(ə)ns/ noun [U] the period of your life when you are changing from being a child to being an adult, especially when you are a young teenager: *He spent his adolescence in a children's home.*

ad•o•les•cent /ˌædəˈles(ə)nt/ noun [C] a young teenager who is changing from being a child into being an adult —**ad•o•les•cent** adj

a•dopt /əˈdɑpt/ verb ★
1 [I/T] to legally become the parent of another person's child: *The couple are hoping to adopt a baby girl.*
2 [T] to start using a new or different way of doing something: *He decided to adopt a more radical approach to the problem.*
3 [T] to formally accept a proposal, usually by voting

a•dopt•ed /əˈdɑptəd/ adj an adopted child has been legally made the son or daughter of someone who is not their natural parent

a•dop•tion /əˈdɑpʃ(ə)n/ noun **1** [C/U] the process of making a child legally part of your family: *For many childless couples, adoption is the best solution.* **2** [U] the decision to start using a new or different way of doing something

a•dop•tive /əˈdɑptɪv/ adj adoptive parents have ADOPTED a child

a•dor•a•ble /əˈdɔrəb(ə)l/ adj extremely attractive

ad•o•ra•tion /ˌædəˈreɪʃ(ə)n/ noun [U] a feeling of great love and respect for someone

a•dore /əˈdɔr/ verb [T] **1** to love someone very much **2** *informal* to like something very much

a•dor•ing /əˈdɔrɪŋ/ adj an adoring person or group of people has a great feeling of love and admiration for someone: *Adoring crowds lined the streets to wait for her.*
—**a•dor•ing•ly** adv

a•dorn /əˈdɔrn/ verb [T] to decorate something —**a•dorn•ment** noun [C/U]

a•dren•a•lin or **a•dren•a•line** /əˈdren(ə)lɪn/ noun [U] a chemical that your body produces when you are frightened, excited, or angry

a•drift /əˈdrɪft/ adj floating on the water without being tied to anything or controlled by anyone

a•droit /əˈdrɔɪt/ adj *formal* clever or skillful

ADSL /ˌeɪ di es ˈel/ noun [U] *computing* asymmetric digital subscriber line: a method of connecting a computer to the Internet that allows very fast exchange of information, and allows you to be connected at all times without having to pay any extra money

ad•u•la•tion /ˌædʒəˈleɪʃ(ə)n/ noun [U] great praise or admiration, especially for someone who is famous

a•dult[1] /əˈdʌlt, ˈædʌlt/ noun [C] ★★★
1 someone who is not a child anymore and is legally responsible for their actions: *Tickets are $2.50 for adults and $1.50 for children.*
2 a fully grown animal or bird

a•dult[2] /əˈdʌlt, ˈædʌlt/ adj **1** relating to or typical of adults: *About 59% of the adult population said they were suffering from stress.* **2** adult magazines, movies, and books are about sex **3** an adult animal, bird, etc. is fully grown

a•dul•ter•y /əˈdʌltəri/ noun [U] sex between a married person and someone who is not their husband or wife

a•dult•hood /əˈdʌltˌhʊd, ˈædʌltˌhʊd/ noun [U] the period of your life when you are an adult

adv. abbrev adverb

ad•vance[1] /ədˈvæns/ noun **1** [C] an instance of progress in science, technology, human knowledge, etc.: *major advances in computer technology* **2** [C] a forward movement toward someone or something, especially by an army **3** [C] a payment for work that is given before the work is complete **4 advances** [plural] an attempt to have a sexual relationship with someone, especially when the other person does not want this
PHRASE **in advance** done in preparation for a particular time or event in the future: *You have to make reservations six months in advance.*

ad•vance[2] /ədˈvæns/ verb **1** [I/T] to progress and become better or more developed, or to help something to do this: *Technology has advanced dramatically since the 1960s.* ♦ *He will do anything to advance his career.* **2** [I] if an army advances, it moves forward and toward something —**ad•vance•ment** noun [C/U]

ad•vance[3] /ədˈvæns/ adj **1** done before a particular time or event: *advance notice/warning* **2** sent to a place before a larger group that will arrive later: *an advance party/team/unit*

ad•vanced /ədˈvænst/ adj ★
1 based on the most recent methods or ideas: *advanced technology*
2 having achieved a high standard or level: *She is very advanced for her age.*
3 at a high academic level: *a dictionary for advanced students*

ad•van•tage /ədˈvæntɪdʒ/ noun ★★
1 [C/U] something that makes one person or thing more likely to succeed than others =BENEFIT: *the advantages of a good education* ♦ *The home team usually **has an advantage over** its opponent.* ♦ *Her teaching experience **gives her an advantage** when working with children.* ♦ *It would be **to your advantage** (=make you more likely to succeed) to prepare questions in advance.*
2 [C] a good feature or quality that something has ≠ DISADVANTAGE: *Having children when you're older has both advantages and disadvantages.* ♦ *The equipment **has the additional advantage of** being easy to carry.*
PHRASES **take advantage of sb** to unfairly use the fact that someone is nice or trusts you in order to get what you want from them: *salesmen who take advantage of elderly customers*
take advantage of sth to use a situation or opportunity in a way that will help you or be good for you: *Many schools don't **take full advantage of** the Internet.*

ad•van•ta•geous /ˌædvənˈteɪdʒəs/ adj likely to make someone or something more successful

ad•vent /ˈædˌvent/ noun **the advent of sth** the introduction of a new product, idea, custom, etc.: *the advent of the personal computer*

ad•ven•ture /ədˈventʃər/ noun [C/U] ★ an exciting, unusual, and sometimes dangerous experience: *The trip was quite an adventure.* ♦ *The children were looking for adventure.*

ad•ven•tur•ous /ədˈventʃərəs/ adj **1** eager to try new or exciting things ≠ UNADVENTUROUS **2** new, exciting, and possibly dangerous ≠ UNADVENTUROUS: *an adventurous skiing trip*

ad•verb /ˈædˌvɜrb/ noun [C] ★ a word used for describing a verb, an adjective, another adverb, or a whole sentence. Adverbs in English often consist of an adjective with "-ly" added, for example "quickly." —**ad•ver•bi•al** /ədˈvɜrbiəl/ adj

ad•ver•sar•y /ˈædvərˌseri/ noun [C] *formal* an enemy or opponent

ad•verse /ædˈvɜrs/ adj not good, or likely to cause problems: *adverse weather conditions* ♦ *an adverse reaction from the public* —**ad•verse•ly** adv

ad•ver•si•ty /ædˈvɜrsəti/ noun [C/U] a time in your life during which you have a lot of bad things happening to you

ad•ver•tise /ˈædvərˌtaɪz/ verb [I/T] ★
1 to announce a product, service, or event on television, on the Internet, in newspapers, etc. so that people will buy it, use it, or go to it: *The perfume has been advertised in all the major women's magazines.*
2 to invite people to apply for a job by announcing it in a newspaper, on the Internet, etc.: *We need to **advertise for** a new chef.*
—**ad•ver•tis•er** noun [C]

ad•ver•tise•ment /ædˈvɜrtɪsmənt,

A

ˌædvərˈtaɪzmənt/ noun [C] an announcement in a newspaper, on television, on the Internet, etc. that is designed to persuade people to buy a product or service, go to an event, or apply for a job

ad·ver·tis·ing /ˈædvərˌtaɪzɪŋ/ noun [U] ★ the business of making advertisements, or advertisements in general: *We spend $5 million a year on advertising.* ♦ *an advertising agency*

Talking or writing about advertising

- **ad** (*informal*) an advertisement
- **advertisement** an announcement in a newspaper, or on the television or radio, that encourages people to buy something
- **billboard** a large outdoor sign used for advertising
- **campaign** a series of advertisements and events used for advertising something
- **the classified ads** small advertisements printed together in newspapers and magazines
- **commercial** an advertisement on the television or radio
- **flyer** a small piece of paper with a printed advertisement on it. Flyers are given to people on the street, or delivered to their homes
- **the personals** a section in a newspaper or magazine where people advertise when they want to meet someone to have a relationship with
- **poster** a large piece of paper with a printed advertisement on it
- **slogan** a short sentence used for advertising something

ad·vice /ədˈvaɪs/ noun [U] ★★★ an opinion that someone gives you about the best thing to do in a particular situation: *Ask your father for advice.* ♦ *We are here to* ***give*** *people* ***advice about*** *health issues.* ♦ *I* ***took his advice*** (=did what he advised) *and left.* ♦ *She's* ***acting on*** *her lawyer's* ***advice****.*

Words often used with advice

Verbs often used with ***advice***

- **give, offer, provide** + ADVICE: give someone advice
- **ask for, seek** + ADVICE: ask for advice
- **accept, act on, follow, take** + ADVICE: do what someone advises
- **disregard, ignore, reject** + ADVICE: not do what someone advises

Advice is never used in the plural and cannot be used with **an**: *She gave me* ***a useful piece of advice*** (NOT a useful advice). ♦ *Do you have* ***any advice*** *about the best places to eat?* ♦ *His son asked him for* ***some advice****.*

ad·vis·a·ble /ədˈvaɪzəb(ə)l/ adj if something is advisable, it is a good idea to do it, especially in order to avoid problems ≠ INADVISABLE: *It is advisable to keep your belongings with you at all times.*

ad·vise /ədˈvaɪz/ verb [I/T] ★★
1 to give your opinion to someone about the best thing to do in a particular situation: **advise sb to do sth** *Her doctor advised her to rest.* ♦ *I* ***strongly advise*** *you to reject the offer.* ♦ **advise sb against sth** *Police are advising the public against traveling in the fog.* ♦ **+that** *Experts advise that suntan lotion should be reapplied on an hourly basis.*
2 *formal* to tell someone facts or information that they need to know: **advise sb of sth** *The committee will advise all applicants of its decision by June 30th.*

Word family: advise

Words in the same family as ***advise***

- **advice** *n*
- **advisable** *adj*
- **adviser** *n*
- **advisory** *adj*
- **inadvisable** *adj*

ad·vis·er or **ad·vis·or** /ədˈvaɪzər/ noun [C] ★ someone whose job is to give advice on subjects that they know a lot about: *the president's closest advisers* ♦ *a financial adviser*

ad·vi·so·ry /ədˈvaɪz(ə)ri/ adj existing in order to give advice about a particular subject: *an advisory board/committee/panel*

ad·vo·ca·cy /ˈædvəkəsi/ noun [U] strong public support for something

ad·vo·cate¹ /ˈædvəˌkeɪt/ verb [T] to publicly support a particular policy or way of doing something

ad·vo·cate² /ˈædvəkət/ noun [C] **1** someone who strongly and publicly supports someone or something: *an advocate of political reform* **2** a LAWYER → DEVIL'S ADVOCATE

aer·i·al /ˈeriəl/ adj **1** from an airplane: *an aerial view* **2** taking place in the air

aer·o·bic /eˈroʊbɪk/ adj aerobic exercise is a very active type of exercise that makes your heart and lungs stronger

aer·o·bics /eˈroʊbɪks/ noun [U] very active physical exercises done to music, often in a class

aer·o·dy·nam·ic /ˌeroʊdaɪˈnæmɪk/ adj shaped in a way that makes it easier for something to move forward or through the air smoothly and quickly

aer·o·dy·nam·ics /ˌeroʊdaɪˈnæmɪks/ noun [U] the science of how objects move through the air

aer·o·plane /ˈerəˌpleɪn/ noun [C] *British* an AIRPLANE

aer·o·sol /ˈerəˌsɑl/ noun [C] a container in which a liquid such as paint or PERFUME is kept under high pressure so that it can be SPRAYED (=forced out in very small drops): *an aerosol can/spray*

aer·o·space /ˈeroʊˌspeɪs/ adj relating to the science or business of building and flying airplanes and space vehicles

aes·thet·ic /esˈθetɪk/ adj relating to beauty —**aes·thet·i·cal·ly** /esˈθetɪkli/ adv

aes·thet·ics /esˈθetɪks/ noun [U] the study of beauty, especially in art

a·far /əˈfɑr/ adv **from afar** *literary* from a distance

af·fa·ble /ˈæfəb(ə)l/ adj friendly, relaxed, and easy to talk to —**af·fa·bly** adv

af·fair /əˈfer/ noun ★★★
1 affairs [plural] events and activities relating to the government, politics, economy, etc. of a country or region: *The Senator is an expert on foreign affairs.* ♦ *a government spokesperson on consumer affairs* → CURRENT AFFAIRS

2 [C] a sexual relationship between two people, especially when one of them is married to someone else: *Her husband denied that he was **having an affair**.*
3 affairs [plural] things relating to your personal life, for example what is happening in your family or with your financial situation: *We are friends, but I don't know much about their private affairs.*
4 [C] something that happens, especially something shocking, in public or political life: *The president's popularity was unaffected by the whole affair.*

af•fect /əˈfekt/ verb [T] ★★★
1 to change or influence something, often in a negative way: *Did the newspapers really affect the outcome of the election?* ♦ *The disease affects many different organs of the body.*
2 to have a strong effect on someone's emotions: *She had been deeply affected by her parents' divorce.*

af•fec•ta•tion /ˌæfekˈteɪʃ(ə)n/ noun [C/U] something that is not part of your natural personality but that you do or say to impress people

af•fect•ed /əˈfektəd/ adj not natural, but done to impress other people

af•fec•tion /əˈfekʃ(ə)n/ noun [U] a feeling of liking and caring about someone or something: *He has great affection for the country.*

af•fec•tion•ate /əˈfekʃənət/ adj showing that you love or care about someone or something —**af•fec•tion•ate•ly** adv

af•fi•da•vit /ˌæfɪˈdeɪvɪt/ noun [C] a legal document containing a written promise that something is true

af•fil•i•ate /əˈfɪliˌeɪt/ verb **be affiliated with sth** to be officially connected with a larger organization or group—**af•fil•i•at•ed** adj, **af•fil•i•a•tion** /əˌfɪliˈeɪʃ(ə)n/ noun [C/U]

af•fin•i•ty /əˈfɪnəti/ noun [singular] a feeling that you understand and like someone or something because they are like you

af•firm /əˈfɜrm/ verb [T] *formal* to state that something is true or that you agree with it —**af•fir•ma•tion** /æfɜrˈmeɪʃ(ə)n/ noun [C]

af•fir•ma•tive /əˈfɜrmətɪv/ adj an affirmative statement or answer means "yes"

afˌfirmative ˈaction noun [U] the practice of choosing someone for a job or course of education who belongs to a group that is often treated in an unfair way because of their race, sex, health, etc.

af•fix /ˈæˌfɪks/ noun [C] *linguistics* a part added to the beginning or end of a word that changes its meaning → PREFIX, SUFFIX

af•flict /əˈflɪkt/ verb [T] *formal* if you are afflicted by an illness or serious problem, you suffer from it

af•flic•tion /əˈflɪkʃ(ə)n/ noun [C/U] *formal* an illness or serious problem

af•flu•ent /ˈæfluənt/ adj rich —**af•flu•ence** /ˈæfluəns/ noun [U]

af•ford /əˈfɔrd/ verb [T] ★★★
1 can afford or **be able to afford** to have enough money to pay for something: *I'm not sure how they are able to afford such expensive vacations.* ♦ **can afford to do sth** *The company simply cannot afford to keep all its staff.*
2 can afford or **be able to afford** to be able to do something without having to worry about the problems that it might cause you: *We can't afford any more delays.* ♦ **can afford to do sth** *No politician can afford to ignore the power of television.*

af•ford•a•ble /əˈfɔrdəb(ə)l/ adj inexpensive enough for ordinary people to afford: *a shortage of affordable housing*

af•front /əˈfrʌnt/ noun [C] something insulting that makes you shocked and angry

a•field /əˈfild/ adv **far afield** far away

a•float /əˈfloʊt/ adj **1** floating on water **2** able to pay the money that you owe

a•fraid /əˈfreɪd/ adj ★★★
1 frightened: *Don't be afraid – I won't hurt you.* ♦ *Everyone seems to be **afraid of** her.*
2 worried that something bad might happen: **+(that)** *I was afraid that you'd miss the flight.* ♦ **afraid to do sth** *The boy was afraid to say that he didn't know the answer.* ♦ **afraid of doing sth** *A lot of people are afraid of losing their jobs.*
PHRASE **I'm afraid** *spoken* used for politely telling someone something that might make them sad, disappointed, or angry: *I can't help you, I'm afraid.* ♦ **+(that)** *I'm afraid I really don't agree.*

Af•ri•can A•mer•i•can /ˌæfrɪkən əˈmerɪkən/ adj **1** someone who is African American is from the U.S., but their family originally came from Africa **2** relating to the language or culture of African Americans —**African Aˈmerican** noun [C]

af•ter /ˈæftər/ grammar word ★★★

> **After** can be:
> - a **preposition**: *I went for a swim after breakfast.*
> - an **adverb**: *He died on June 3rd and was buried the day after.*
> - a **conjunction**: *After you'd left, I got a phone call from Stuart.*

1 at a later time when a particular time has passed, or when an event or action has ended: *You can call us any time after 6:00 this evening.* ♦ *After the war, my parents moved to the U.S.* ♦ *This message arrived after everyone had gone home.* ♦ *It seems noisy at first, but **after a while** you get used to it.* ♦ **after doing sth** *Wash your hands after touching raw meat.*
2 saying how much later used for saying how much later something is: *His birthday is two days after mine.* ♦ *I can start work tomorrow or **the day after**.* ♦ *You shouldn't go swimming **right after** a big meal.*
3 at a later position in a list following someone or something else in order in a list or in a piece of writing: *N comes after M in the alphabet.* ♦ *Germany is our largest export market after Japan.*
4 past a place farther along a road, railroad, etc.: *You turn right just after the bank.* ♦ *We get off at the station after Providence.*
5 trying to get sb/sth trying to catch, find, or get someone or something: *I ran after her to apologize.* ♦ *Watch out, he's only after*

A

your money. ♦ *The police are after him for burglary.*
6 time past the hour *American* used in telling the time, for giving the number of minutes past the hour: *It's ten after nine* (=9:10).
7 because of sth used for saying how someone is influenced by something that happened in the past: *After what happened last time, I was careful not to make the same mistakes.*
8 despite sth despite everything that was done in the past: *After everything that I'd done for her, she didn't even say thank you.*
PHRASES **after all 1** despite what was said or planned before: *I'm sorry, but we've decided not to come after all.* ♦ *Maybe she was right after all.* **2** used when giving a reason to explain what you have just said: *She shouldn't be working so hard – she is 70, after all.*
after you *spoken* used for politely telling someone that they can do something before you or walk somewhere in front of you
day after day/year after year etc. happening again and again every day/year etc. for a long time: *Many families come back to our hotel year after year.*
one after another or **one after the other** used for saying that each person or thing is immediately followed by the next: *One day I had three different exams one after the other.*

af·ter·ef·fect /ˈɑftərɪˌfekt/ noun [C] an unpleasant effect that lasts for a long time after an event or situation: *the aftereffects of the storm*

af·ter·life /ˈæftərˌlaɪf/ noun [singular] another life that some people believe begins after you die

af·ter·math, the /ˈæftərˌmæθ/ noun [singular] the effects and results of something bad or important: *In the aftermath of the shootings, there were calls for new gun laws.*

af·ter·noon /ˌæftərˈnun/ noun [C/U] ★★★ the period of time between the middle of the day and the beginning of the evening: *What are you doing tomorrow afternoon?* ♦ *an afternoon nap/class* ♦ *I might go shopping **this afternoon**.*

af·ter·shave /ˈæftərˌʃeɪv/ noun [C/U] a liquid with a nice smell that a man puts on his face after SHAVING

af·ter·shock /ˈæftərˌʃɑk/ noun [C] a small EARTHQUAKE that happens after a bigger one

af·ter·taste /ˈæftərˌteɪst/ noun [C] a taste that remains in your mouth after you eat or drink something

af·ter·thought /ˈæftərˌθɔt/ noun [C] something that you say or do after something else because you did not think of it at first

af·ter·ward /ˈæftərwərd/ or **af·ter·wards** /ˈæftərwərdz/ adv ★★ after something else that you have already mentioned: *Let's go see a movie, and afterward we could get something to eat.*

a·gain /əˈgen/ adv ★★★
1 one more time: *If you fail the exam you will have to take it again.* ♦ *Oh no, now I'll have to start **all over again*** (=a second time from the beginning). ♦ *I read through her letter **again and again*** (=many times). ♦ ***Once again*** (=it has already happened more than once) *the troops moved forward, and once again they were driven back.* → ONCE
2 returning to the same condition as before: *I turned over and went back to sleep again.* ♦ *The streets of the city are quiet again.*
3 *spoken* used for asking someone to repeat something that they have already told you: *That friend of yours – what's her name again?*
PHRASE **then again** used for introducing a statement that makes what you have just said seem less true: *The hotel was awful. But then again, you can't expect much for $30 a night.*

a·gainst /əˈgenst/ preposition ★★★
1 in opposition to sth used for stating which plan, idea, or action someone opposes and thinks is wrong: *I'm against all forms of censorship.* ♦ *She argued against changing the design.* ♦ *the fight against drugs in our city's schools*
2 competing with sb/sth used for stating who or what you are trying to defeat in a game, race, or fight: *The Dodgers have won their last three games against the Cardinals.*
3 directed toward sb/sth in a negative way used for stating who or what a negative feeling or action is directed toward: *illegal discrimination against minority employees* ♦ *There was growing resentment against the military government.* ♦ *Police are expected to bring criminal charges against Warren.*
4 touching or hitting sb/sth touching, hitting, or being supported by the surface of something: *I fell heavily against the bookshelves.* ♦ *Ron's bike was leaning against a tree.*
5 providing protection from sth used for stating what someone or something is being protected from: *All the children have been vaccinated against diseases such as polio.*
6 not allowing sth if there is a law against doing something, it is illegal: *The state has a law against cruelty to animals.*
7 in the opposite direction in the opposite direction of the wind, the current, etc.: *We were sailing against a strong easterly wind.*
PHRASES **against the law/rules** not allowed by the law/rules: *It is against the law to park here overnight.*
against your will if someone makes you do something against your will, you do not want to do it: *No one will be forced to leave home against their will.*
against sb's wishes/advice even though someone does not want you to do something/advises you not to do it: *She took the two children away against her husband's wishes.*
have something against sb/sth to dislike or not approve of someone or something for a particular reason: *I think he has something against artists.*

age[1] /eɪdʒ/ noun ★★★

1 how old sb is	5 being/becoming old
2 how old sth is	6 long time
3 time of life for sth	+ PHRASE
4 period of history	

A

1 [C/U] the number of years that someone has lived: *The average age of the delegates was over 60.* ♦ *At the age of 10, I went to live with my aunt.* ♦ *The movie is designed to appeal to people of all ages.* ♦ *Darren's very tall for his age.*
2 [C/U] the number of years that something has existed: *The value of the furniture depends on its age and condition.* ♦ *It's hard to guess the age of the object.*
3 [C/U] the time of life when it is possible, legal, or typical for people to do something: *young people who have reached voting age*
4 [C] a period of history: *We live in a materialistic age.* ♦ *It was an age of great scientific progress.*
5 [U] the state of being old or of becoming old: *His face is starting to show signs of age.* ♦ *Good wines improve with age.*
6 ages [plural] *informal* a long time: *She's lived here for ages.* ♦ *For the first time in ages, we sat down and talked.*
PHRASE **come of age** to reach the age when you are legally an adult

Talking or writing about someone's age

asking about age
- **how old** used for asking someone their age
- **what age** used for talking about someone's age at a time in the past or future. Say "How old are you?", not "What age are you?", when you are asking someone their age

saying how old someone is
- **be 2/10/40 etc. (years old)** the most usual way of saying how old someone is
- **be 2/9/18 months old** used for saying how old a baby or young child is
- **aged 2/10/40 etc.** used in writing, for example in newspapers, for saying how old someone is
- **a 2-/10-/40-year-old** someone who is 2/10/40 years old
- **a 2-year-old child/a 10-year-old girl/a 40-year-old man** used for saying that someone is 2/10/40 years old

when you are not saying exactly how old someone is
- **in your teens/twenties/thirties etc.** used for saying that someone is aged between 13–19, 20–29, 30–39, etc.
- **twenty-something/thirty-something etc.** used as an adjective or noun for talking about someone aged between 20–29, 30–39, etc.
- **teenage** aged between 13 and 19
- **teenager** someone aged between 13 and 19
- **middle-aged** no longer young, but not yet old, usually used for someone aged between 40 and 60

age² /eɪdʒ/ verb [I/T] to become older or look older, or to make someone do this: *Her father had aged a lot since she had last seen him.*

aged¹ /eɪdʒd/ adj ★★ someone who is aged 18, 35, 70, etc. is 18, 35, 70, etc. years old

ag·ed² /ˈedʒəd/ adj very old

ˈage ˌgroup noun [C] all the people between two particular ages, considered as a group: *a game for children in the 7–10 age group*

ˈage ˌlimit noun [C] the oldest or the youngest age at which you are allowed to do something

a·gen·cy /ˈeɪdʒənsi/ noun [C] ★★
1 a government department or organization that deals with a particular subject: *the official Chinese news agency* ♦ *law enforcement agencies*
2 a business that provides a service: *an employment/advertising agency*

a·gen·da /əˈdʒendə/ noun [C] **1** all the things that need to be done or thought about: *Cutting the number of workers is not on the agenda.* **2** someone's plans or intentions for what they want to achieve: *Beth wanted to get married, but her boyfriend had his own agenda.* ♦ *Getting in shape is at the top of my agenda.* **3** a list of things that people will discuss at a meeting

a·gent /ˈeɪdʒənt/ noun [C] ★
1 someone whose job is to help a person by finding work for them, or to help a person or company by dealing with their business for them: *a literary/shipping/travel agent*
2 someone who works for a government or police department and collects secret information = SPY

ˌage-ˈold adj having existed for a long time: *the age-old problem of poverty*

ag·gra·vate /ˈæɡrəˌveɪt/ verb [T] **1** to make something bad become worse: *His headache was aggravated by all the noise.* **2** *spoken* to annoy someone —**ag·gra·va·tion** /ˌæɡrəˈveɪʃ(ə)n/ noun [C/U], **ag·gra·vat·ing** /ˈæɡrəˌveɪtɪŋ/ adj

ag·gres·sion /əˈɡreʃ(ə)n/ noun [U] **1** a situation in which a person or country attacks another person or country: *an act of aggression against a neighboring country* **2** an angry feeling that makes you want to behave violently or attack someone else

ag·gres·sive /əˈɡresɪv/ adj **1** behaving in an angry or rude way that shows you want to fight, attack, or argue with someone: *The taxis have features that protect drivers from aggressive passengers.* ♦ *aggressive behavior* **2** very determined to win or be successful: *an aggressive election strategy* —**ag·gres·sive·ly** adv

ag·gres·sor /əˈɡresər/ noun [C] a country that starts a war, or someone who starts a fight

ag·grieved /əˈɡrivd/ adj feeling angry and unhappy because you think that you have been treated unfairly

a·ghast /əˈɡæst/ adj shocked and upset

ag·ile /ˈæˌdʒəl/ adj able to move your body quickly and easily —**a·gil·i·ty** /əˈdʒɪləti/ noun [U]

ag·ing¹ /ˈeɪdʒɪŋ/ adj becoming old: *a town with an aging population*

ag·ing² /ˈeɪdʒɪŋ/ noun [U] the process of becoming old: *the aging process*

ag·i·tate /ˈædʒɪˌteɪt/ verb [I] to try to cause social or political changes by arguing or protesting, or through other political activity: *students agitating for more freedom* —**ag·i·ta·tor** noun [C]

ag·i·tat·ed /ˈædʒɪˌteɪtəd/ adj worried or upset ≠ CALM: *She became increasingly agitated as the interview proceeded.* —**ag·i·ta·tion** /ˌædʒɪˈteɪʃ(ə)n/ noun [U]

ag·nos·tic /æɡˈnɑstɪk/ noun [C] someone who believes that it is not possible to know whether God exists or not —**ag·nos·tic** adj,

A

ag•nos•ti•cism /æg'nɑstɪˌsɪzəm/ noun [U]

a•go /ə'goʊ/ adv ★★★

> Ago follows a word or expression that refers to a period of time. It is usually used with a past tense, not with a perfect tense.

used for saying how much time has passed since something happened: *Your wife called a few minutes ago.* ♦ ***How long ago** did this happen?* ♦ ***Long ago** in a far-off land, there was a king called Midas.*

> - Use **ago** to say how long before the present time something happened: *He died two years ago.*
> - Use **before** to say how long before a time in the past something had happened: *I remembered that I had met her ten years before.*
> - Use **for** to say how long something in the past continued: *Their marriage lasted for fifteen years.*

ag•o•nize /'ægəˌnaɪz/ verb [I] to spend a long time worrying about something, especially when you have to make a decision: *For days I agonized over whether to accept his offer.*

ag•o•niz•ing /'ægəˌnaɪzɪŋ/ adj **1** making you feel very worried and upset for a long time **2** very painful

ag•o•ny /'ægəni/ noun [C/U] **1** great pain **2** extreme worry or sadness: *She had to go through the agony of leaving her children.*

a•gree /ə'gri/ verb ★★★

1 [I/T] to have the same opinion as someone else: *Doreen thought that the house was too small, and Jim agreed.* ♦ *I **agree with** my mother about most things.* ♦ *The committee members **agreed on** the need for more information.* ♦ **+(that)** *We all agree that we should celebrate this event.*

2 [I] to say that you will do something that someone else wants or suggests: *I asked her to marry me, and she agreed.* ♦ *We have **agreed to** their request for a full investigation.* ♦ **agree to do sth** *The school agreed to send the students on the field trip.*

3 [I/T] to decide together what will be done and how it will be done: *We need to **agree on** a date for our next meeting.* ♦ *Management and unions have **agreed to** a pay deal.*

4 [I] if two pieces of information agree, they are the same or they suggest the same thing: *The observations **agree with** the predictions we made earlier.*

→ ACCEPT

PHRASAL VERBS **a'gree with sb** if food or drink does not agree with you, it makes you feel sick

a'gree with sth to think that something is the right thing to do: *I don't agree with corporal punishment in schools.*

> **Word family: agree**
>
> *Words in the same family as **agree***
> - **agreeable** *adj*
> - **agreement** *n*
> - **disagree** *v*
> - **disagreeable** *adj*
> - **disagreement** *n*

a•gree•a•ble /ə'griəb(ə)l/ adj **1** acceptable: *a compromise that is agreeable to both sides* **2** *formal* friendly or nice ≠ DISAGREEABLE **3** *formal* willing to do or accept something —**a•gree•ab•ly** adv

a•greed /ə'grid/ adj **1** an agreed price, limit, date, etc. is one that people have talked about and accepted **2** if people are agreed, they all agree about what to do

a•gree•ment /ə'grimənt/ noun ★★★

1 [C] an arrangement or decision about what to do, made by two or more people, groups, or organizations: *Our agreement was that you would pay by the first of the month.* ♦ *NAFTA is the trade **agreement between** Canada, the United States, and Mexico.* ♦ *a license **agreement with** the software company* ♦ *an **agreement on** military cooperation* ♦ *Management announced that it had **reached an agreement** with the unions.*

2 [U] a situation when people have the same opinion or make the same decision: *After a long discussion, there was still no **agreement about** what to do next.* ♦ *We are all **in agreement** that Mr. Ross should resign.*

ag•ri•cul•ture /'ægrɪˌkʌltʃər/ noun [U] the work or business of farming —**ag•ri•cul•tur•al** /ˌægrɪ'kʌltʃ(ə)rəl/ adj

a•ground /ə'graʊnd/ adv **run aground** if a ship runs aground, it becomes stuck on a piece of ground under the water

ah /ɑ/ interjection **1** used for showing that you see or understand something **2** used for showing that you are interested, surprised, pleased, or annoyed

a•ha /ɑ'hɑ/ interjection used for showing that you have suddenly realized or understood something

a•head /ə'hed/ adv ★★★

1 in front of sb in the direction in front of you: *There's a motel just a few miles ahead.* ♦ *She walked **ahead of** him along the corridor.* ♦ *We're almost there! That's the place **up ahead**.* ♦ *Instead of turning left, he drove **straight ahead** toward the river.*

2 in the future used for saying what will happen in the future: *Where will the money come from in the years ahead?* ♦ *Looking ahead to next summer, where would you like to go?* ♦ *We have a busy day **ahead of** us.*

→ LIE[1]

3 before sb leaving or arriving before someone else: *You go on ahead and tell them we're coming.* ♦ *David finished **ahead of** me in last year's race.*

4 achieving more success or making more progress than someone else: *The Russians were now **ahead of** the U.S. in space research.* ♦ *If you want to **get ahead** in politics* (=become more successful), *you have to look confident.*

5 referring to the time in different places if one place is ahead of another, the clocks there show a later time: *New York is three hours ahead of Los Angeles.*

PHRASES **ahead of your/its time** very advanced or modern: *As a writer, Sterne was ahead of his time.*

ahead of time/schedule at an earlier time than was planned

→ GO AHEAD

a·hold /ə'hoʊld/ adv
PHRASES **get ahold of sb** to manage to talk to someone especially by telephone
get ahold of sth *spoken* to obtain or buy something after trying to get it for a long time
get/grab/take ahold of sth to take something firmly in your hand and hold it tightly there

aid¹ /eɪd/ noun ★★
1 [U] money, food, or other help that a government or organization gives to people who need it: *financial aid* ♦ *foreign aid*
2 [U] help with doing something: *Chromosomes can be seen **with the aid of** a microscope.* ♦ *Several people heard her screams, but no one **went to her aid**.*
3 [C] something that makes it easier to do something: *Hypnosis can be **an aid to** giving up smoking.*
4 *American* another spelling of **aide**

aid² /eɪd/ verb [T] *formal* to help someone to do something, or to help to make something happen more easily: *Gentle exercise aids the circulation of blood around the body.*
PHRASE **aid and abet** *legal* to help someone to commit a crime

aide /eɪd/ noun [C] someone whose job is to help another person in their work

AIDS /eɪdz/ noun [U] acquired immune deficiency syndrome: a serious disease that destroys the body's ability to defend itself against infection

ail·ing /'eɪlɪŋ/ adj not strong, healthy, or successful: *an ailing business*

ail·ment /'eɪlmənt/ noun [C] a minor illness

aim¹ /eɪm/ verb ★★★
1 [I/T] to point something such as a gun at a person or thing that you want to hit: *He was **aiming at** the tree but he missed.* ♦ **aim sth at sb/sth** *I looked up to see Betty aiming a gun at me.*
2 [I] to intend or hope to achieve something: *Most of the students were **aiming for** jobs in television.* ♦ **aim to do sth** *The project aims to provide support for young musicians.*
3 [T] **be aimed at sb** to be intended to be read, watched, or used by people of a particular type: *The book is aimed at people with no specialized knowledge.*
4 [T] **be aimed at doing sth** to have the goal of achieving a particular thing: *an energy program that is aimed at reducing our dependence on fossil fuels*

aim² /eɪm/ noun ★★★
1 [C] the thing that you hope to achieve by doing something = GOAL: *My main aim in therapy is to gain confidence.* ♦ *We visit schools with **the aim of** getting young people interested in the theater.* ♦ ***The aim of** this project is to help patients to be more independent.*
2 [singular] your ability to hit something when you throw, kick, or shoot something at it: *My aim isn't very good.*
PHRASE **take aim (at)** to point a gun at something before you shoot

aim·less /'eɪmləs/ adj without any particular purpose or plan —**aim·less·ly** adv

ain't /eɪnt/ *spoken* a way of saying "am not," "is not," "are not," "has not," or "have not." Many people think that "ain't" is not correct.

air¹ /er/ noun ★★★
1 [U] the mixture of gases that we breathe: *She breathed in the cold air.* ♦ *I'd like to open the window – I need some air.*
2 **the air** [singular] the space around things and above the ground: *They threw their hats up into the air.* ♦ *birds flying through the air*
3 [singular] a feeling or attitude: *She spoke with her usual air of authority.*
PHRASES **by air** traveling in an airplane
sth is in the air used for saying that people all have a similar feeling, especially a feeling that something exciting or new is happening: *Spring is in the air.*
off the air or **off air** not broadcasting on radio or television anymore
on the air or **on air** on radio or television
up in the air if a plan is up in the air, you have not yet decided what will happen
→ CLEAR², FRESH AIR, OPEN AIR

air² /er/ verb **1** [T] to broadcast something on radio or television: *The show was first aired in 1978.* **2** [T] to publicly make a complaint or state your opinion: *In an interview, the singer aired his views on family life.* **3** [I/T] if you air a place or piece of clothing, or if they air, you let fresh air pass through them until they smell clean and fresh
PHRASAL VERB ˌ**air (sth) 'out** *American* same as air² 3

ˈ**air ˌbag** noun [C] a piece of equipment in a car that protects people in a crash by immediately filling with air

air·borne /'erˌbɔrn/ adj moving or carried in the air

air con·di·tion·ing /ˌer kən'dɪʃ(ə)nɪŋ/ noun [U] a system that makes the air inside a building, room, or vehicle colder —ˈ**air-conˌditioned** adj: *air-conditioned rooms*

air·craft /'erˌkræft/ (plural **air·craft**) noun [C] ★★★ an airplane, HELICOPTER, or other vehicle that flies

ˈ**aircraft ˌcarrier** noun [C] a ship that carries military airplanes

air·fare /'erˌfer/ noun [C] the money that you pay to go somewhere by airplane

air·field /'erˌfild/ noun [C] a small airport for military or private aircraft

ˈ**air ˌforce** noun [C] the part of a country's military forces that fights using airplanes

air·lift /'erˌlɪft/ noun [C] an action by which people or things are taken into or away from a dangerous place by aircraft —**air·lift** verb [T]

air·line /'erˌlaɪn/ noun [C] ★ a company that owns aircraft and takes people or goods by airplane from one place to another

air·lin·er /'erˌlaɪnər/ noun [C] a large airplane for passengers

air·mail /'erˌmeɪl/ noun [U] the system for sending mail by airplane

air·plane /'erˌpleɪn/ noun [C] *American* ★ an aircraft with wings and at least one engine = PLANE —*picture* → C7

air·port /'erˌpɔrt/ noun [C] ★★★ a place where airplanes arrive and leave

air·space /'erˌspeɪs/ noun [U] the sky above a particular country

A

air·tight /ˈerˌtaɪt/ adj not allowing air to enter or leave: *an airtight container*

ˈair ˌtime noun [U] the amount of time that is given to someone or something in a radio or television broadcast

ˌair traffic conˈtroller noun [C] someone whose job is to organize the movement of airplanes in a particular area by giving instructions to pilots by radio

air·waves /ˈerˌweɪvz/ noun [plural] radio waves that are used for sending signals for radio, television, and CELLPHONES

air·y /ˈeri/ adj with a lot of fresh air and space

aisle /aɪl/ noun [C] a passage between rows of seats, for example in a theater, church, or airplane, or between the shelves of a supermarket

a·jar /əˈdʒɑr/ adj a door that is ajar is slightly open —*picture* → OPEN[1]

AK abbrev Alaska

aka /ˌeɪ keɪ ˈeɪ/ also known as: used when giving someone's real name followed by a different name that they also use

AL abbrev Alabama

à la carte /ˌɑ lɑ ˈkɑrt/ adj, adv priced separately on a menu instead of as part of a meal

à la mode /ˌɑ lɑ ˈmoʊd/ adj, adv *American* served with ICE CREAM

a·larm[1] /əˈlɑrm/ noun ★★

1 [C] a piece of electrical equipment that warns you of danger by making a loud noise: *a burglar/fire/smoke alarm*

2 [C] an ALARM CLOCK: *I'll set the alarm for eight.*

3 [U] the worried feeling that something unpleasant or dangerous might happen: *There was a note of alarm in her voice.*

PHRASE **sound/raise the alarm** to tell people about something dangerous that is happening

→ FALSE ALARM

a·larm[2] /əˈlɑrm/ verb [T] to make someone worried that something unpleasant or dangerous might happen: *School officials were alarmed by the number of children with the disease.*

aˈlarm ˌbells noun [plural] if something rings alarm bells, or sets off alarm bells, it makes you very careful because you think something bad is going to happen

aˈlarm ˌclock noun [C] a clock that wakes you up at a particular time by making a noise

a·larmed /əˈlɑrmd/ adj **1** worried that something unpleasant or dangerous might happen **2** protected by an ALARM

a·larm·ing /əˈlɑrmɪŋ/ adj frightening or worrying —**a·larm·ing·ly** adv

a·larm·ist /əˈlɑrmɪst/ adj causing unnecessary fear or worry

a·las /əˈlæs/ interjection *often humorous* an old word used for saying that you are sad about something

al·be·it /ɔlˈbiɪt/ conjunction *formal* although: *The United States finally agreed, albeit unwillingly, to support the U.N. action.*

al·bum /ˈælbəm/ noun [C] **1** a CD, record, or CASSETTE with several songs or pieces of music on it **2** a book in which you can collect things such as photographs or stamps

al·co·hol /ˈælkəˌhɔl/ noun [U] ★

1 drinks such as wine and beer that can make people drunk: *a ban on the advertising of alcohol*

2 the substance in drinks such as wine and beer that makes you drunk

al·co·hol·ic[1] /ˌælkəˈhɔlɪk/ adj **1** containing alcohol ≠ NONALCOHOLIC: *alcoholic drinks* **2** affected by ALCOHOLISM: *alcoholic patients*

al·co·hol·ic[2] /ˌælkəˈhɔlɪk/ noun [C] someone who finds it difficult to control the amount of alcohol that they drink

al·co·hol·ism /ˈælkəhɔˌlɪzəm/ noun [U] a medical condition that makes it difficult to control the amount of alcohol that you drink

al·cove /ˈælˌkoʊv/ noun [C] a small area in a room that has been created by building part of a wall farther back than the rest of the wall

ale /eɪl/ noun [C/U] a type of dark-colored beer

a·lert[1] /əˈlɜrt/ adj **1** able to think clearly: *He's remarkably alert for his age.* **2** paying attention to what is happening and ready to react to it: *Parents must be alert to the symptoms of the disease.* —**a·lert·ly** adv

a·lert[2] /əˈlɜrt/ verb [T] to tell someone about a danger or problem

a·lert[3] /əˈlɜrt/ noun [C] a warning about something dangerous

PHRASE **on the alert** or **on full alert** ready to deal with a dangerous situation

al·gae /ˈældʒi/ noun [plural] plants with no leaves that grow in water

al·ge·bra /ˈældʒəbrə/ noun [U] a type of mathematics that uses letters and symbols to represent numbers —**al·ge·bra·ic** /ˌældʒəˈbreɪɪk/ adj

a·li·as[1] /ˈeɪliəs/ noun [C] a different name that someone uses instead of their real name

a·li·as[2] /ˈeɪliəs/ preposition used before a different name that someone uses instead of their real name: *Zeljko Raznatovic, alias Arkan*

al·i·bi /ˈæləˌbaɪ/ noun [C] evidence that someone was not in a particular place when a crime was committed there

a·li·en[1] /ˈeɪliən/ noun [C] **1** someone who is not a citizen of the country they are living in **2** a creature from another planet

a·li·en[2] /ˈeɪliən/ adj **1** not familiar = STRANGE **2** from another planet

al·ien·ate /ˈeɪliəˌneɪt/ verb [T] **1** to make someone dislike you or not want to help you: *Their campaign has alienated the public.* **2** to make someone feel that they do not belong in a place or group —**al·ien·a·tion** /ˌeɪliəˈneɪʃ(ə)n/ noun [U]

al·ien·at·ed /ˈeɪliəˌneɪtəd/ adj feeling that you do not belong in a place or group: *angry and alienated teenagers*

a·light[1] /əˈlaɪt/ adj burning

a·light[2] /əˈlaɪt/ verb [I] *formal* to get off a train, bus, or other vehicle

a·lign /əˈlaɪn/ verb [T] **1** to give your support to a group or country: *Many women do not want to align themselves with the movement.* **2** to organize things so that they are in the correct position in relation to other things —**a·lign·ment** noun [C/U]

a•like¹ /əˈlaɪk/ adj similar: *The sisters don't really look alike.*

a•like² /əˈlaɪk/ adv **1** in the same way or in a similar way: *Students of both sexes dressed alike.* **2** used for referring to two people or things equally: *It's a show that appeals to young and old alike.*

al•i•mo•ny /ˈælɪˌmoʊni/ noun [U] *American* money that someone pays to support a husband or wife who they are no longer married to

a•live /əˈlaɪv/ adj ★★★
1 living and not dead: *My father died last year but my mother is still alive.* ♦ *He is lucky to be alive after his fall.* ♦ *The family was stealing food just to **stay alive**.*
2 still existing and not gone or forgotten: *Memories of the war are still very much alive.* ♦ *They struggled to **keep** their language and traditions **alive**.*
3 full of excitement or activity: *The waterfront really **comes alive** at Christmas.* ♦ *The street was **alive with** the sound of children playing.*
PHRASE **alive and well/kicking 1** still living **2** still existing and not gone or forgotten

al•ka•line /ˈælkəˌlaɪn/ adj not ACID

all /ɔl/ grammar word ★★★

> **All** can be:
> - a **determiner**: *All children deserve encouragement.*
> - a **pronoun**: *I want to invite all of you.* ♦ *We can all relax.*
> - an **adverb**: *Bernard was all alone in a strange city.*

1 the whole of an amount, thing, situation, or period of time: *Have you spent all your money?* ♦ *There's no cake left. They've eaten it all.* ♦ *I've been awake all night worrying.* ♦ *You can't blame it all on David.* ♦ *Oh, look, you spilled it all over the carpet.* ♦ *Make sure that **all of** the equipment has been checked.*
2 every person or thing: *We all enjoyed the party.* ♦ *No one can solve all these problems.* ♦ *All seven astronauts were killed in the explosion.* ♦ *I want **all of** you to listen carefully.* ♦ ***Not all** lawyers have large incomes.* ♦ *We play **all kinds of** music – rock, reggae, jazz, even classical.*
3 used for emphasizing something: *I'm all in favor of giving children more freedom.* ♦ *Now we're going to be late, and it's **all because** of you.* ♦ *The exam season is so stressful – I'll be glad when it's **all over*** (=completely finished).
4 used for saying that there is nothing more than what you are mentioning: *All I have left is four dollars.* ♦ *All we can do is sit and wait.* ♦ *I wasn't interfering. I was just trying to help, **that's all**.*
PHRASES **all along** during the whole time that something is happening: *Mary knew all along what I was planning to do.*
all but almost: *The job is all but finished.*
all in all used for showing that you are considering every aspect of something: *All in all, I think it has been a very successful conference.*
all of a sudden or **all at once** very suddenly: *All of a sudden there was a knock at the door.*
first/best/most etc. of all before anything else/better than anything else/more than anything else etc.: *First of all, I want to welcome our guest speaker.* ♦ *His music was the thing he loved most of all.*
for all sth despite something: *For all its faults, she loved the city.*
for all I know/care *spoken* used for saying that even if something was true, you would not know/care about it: *He might be a murderer, for all we know.*
go all out to use all your energy, strength, and determination in order to achieve something
in all or **all told** when the whole amount or number is included: *In all, there are over 120 languages spoken in the city's schools.*
not all that good/bad/big etc. used for saying that something is not very good/bad/big etc.: *I didn't finish the book – it wasn't all that interesting.*
→ AT

Al•lah /ˈɑlə, ˈælə/ the name of God in Islam

ˌall-aˈround adj good at doing a lot of different things, especially in sports: *a superb all-around athlete*

al•lay /əˈleɪ/ verb [T] *formal* if you allay feelings such as fears or worries, you make someone feel less afraid or worried

ˌall-ˈclear, the noun [singular] **1** a statement from a doctor that someone is well again **2** a signal or statement that a period of danger has ended

ˌall-ˈday adj continuing or available for the whole day: *an all-day meeting* ♦ *an all-day breakfast*

al•le•ga•tion /ˌæləˈgeɪʃ(ə)n/ noun [C] a statement claiming that someone has done something wrong or illegal

al•lege /əˈledʒ/ verb [T] to say that someone has done something wrong or illegal, even though this has not been proved

al•leged /əˈledʒd/ adj claimed to be true but not proved: *his alleged part in a terrorist plot* —**al•leg•ed•ly** /əˈledʒədli/ adv

al•le•giance /əˈlidʒəns/ noun [C/U] loyalty to a person, group, idea, or country

al•le•go•ry /ˈæləgɔri/ noun [C/U] a story, poem, or picture in which events and characters are used as symbols to express a moral or political idea —**al•le•gor•i•cal** /ˌæləˈgɔrɪk(ə)l/ adj

al•ler•gic /əˈlɜrdʒɪk/ adj **1** affected by an allergy: *I'm allergic to nuts.* **2** caused by an allergy: *an allergic reaction*

al•ler•gy /ˈælərdʒi/ noun [C/U] a medical condition in which you become sick as a reaction to something that you eat, breathe, or touch

al•le•vi•ate /əˈliviˌeɪt/ verb [T] to make something less painful, severe, or serious

al•ley /ˈæli/ or **al•ley•way** /ˈæliˌweɪ/ noun [C] a narrow street or passage between buildings

al•li•ance /əˈlaɪəns/ noun [C] **1** an arrangement in which people, groups, or countries agree to work together: *The two companies have formed a strategic alliance.* ♦ *an alliance between the two parties* **2** an arrangement in which two or more countries join together

A

to defend themselves against an enemy

al·lied /ˈæˌlaɪd, əˈlaɪd/ adj **1** joined together in a military alliance: *the allied army* **2** if something is allied to or with something else, it is connected with it

al·li·ga·tor /ˈælɪˌɡeɪtər/ noun [C] a large REPTILE with a long pointed mouth and sharp teeth. Alligators look like CROCODILES.

ˌall-imˈportant adj very important, or the most important of all

ˌall-ˈnight adj continuing or available for the whole night: *an all-night party* ♦ *an all-night restaurant*

al·lo·cate /ˈæləˌkeɪt/ verb [T] **1** to provide something for someone: *We allocate a personal tutor to each student.* **2** to decide to use something for a particular purpose: *Extra money has been allocated for equipment.* —**al·lo·ca·tion** /ˌæləˈkeɪʃ(ə)n/ noun [C/U]

al·lot /əˈlɑt/ verb [T] to give someone a share of something, such as time, money, or work

ˌall-ˈout adj using everything available in order to succeed in something

al·low /əˈlaʊ/ verb [T] ★★★

1 to give someone permission to do something or have something: *I'm sorry, sir, but smoking is not allowed.* ♦ **allow sb to do sth** *She only allows the children to watch television on the weekends.* ♦ **allow sb sth** *Some prisoners are allowed visitors.*

2 to give someone or something the time or opportunity to do something: **allow sth to do sth** *Allow the cake to cool for five minutes before taking it out of the pan.* ♦ **allow sb to do sth** *a program that allows you to create web pages*

3 to make certain that you have enough of something such as time, food, or money for a particular purpose: *How much rice do you allow for each person?*

PHRASAL VERB **alˈlow ˌfor sth** to consider something when you are making a plan or calculation: *The cost will be about $17 million, allowing for inflation.*

al·low·a·ble /əˈlaʊəb(ə)l/ adj allowed by a set of rules or by the law

al·low·ance /əˈlaʊəns/ noun [C] **1** an amount of money that someone receives regularly to pay for things that they need: *a housing/clothing allowance* **2** an amount of something that you are officially allowed: *Your baggage allowance is 75 pounds.*

PHRASE **make allowances (for)** to accept behavior that you would not normally accept because you know why someone has behaved that way: *We have to make allowances for his lack of experience.*

al·loy /ˈæˌlɔɪ/ noun [C/U] a metal made by combining two or more other metals

ˈall-ˌpurpose adj able to be used in a lot of different ways

all ˈright¹ adj, adv *spoken* ★★

1 fairly good	4 not hurt/sick
2 going well	5 for making sb calm
3 for permission	+ PHRASE

1 satisfactory or fairly nice, but not excellent: *Chicago's all right, but I'd rather live in New York.*

2 going well or happening successfully: *Did the party go all right?* ♦ *My brother was unemployed for years but he's* ***doing all right*** *now* (=he's fairly successful).

3 used for asking for or giving permission to do something: **be all right if sb does sth** *Is it all right if I open the window?* ♦ **be all right to do sth** *It's all right to use that computer.*

4 not hurt or sick: *You look terrible, are you all right?*

5 used for making someone feel less worried or upset: *It's all right, I'm here.*

PHRASE **that's all right** used when someone has thanked you or said sorry to you: *"Thanks for the ride." "That's all right."*

ˌall ˈright² interjection **1** used for agreeing to something: *"Can't we stay a little longer?" "Oh, all right, but just five minutes."* **2** used for checking that someone understands or agrees: *I'm playing football after school today, all right?* **3** used for showing that you have heard or understood what someone has said: *"We need to leave in ten minutes." "All right, I'll be ready."*

ˈall-ˌtime adj used for comparing all the people or things of a particular type that have ever existed: *Interest rates are at an all-time high.* ♦ *the all-time worst player*

al·lude /əˈlud/ PHRASAL VERB **alˈlude ˌto sth** *formal* to mention someone or something in an indirect way

al·lure /əˈlʊr/ noun [U] an exciting and attractive quality

al·lur·ing /əˈlʊrɪŋ/ adj attractive in an exciting way

al·lu·sion /əˈluʒ(ə)n/ noun [C/U] a statement that refers to something in an indirect way

al·ly¹ /ˈæˌlaɪ, əˈlaɪ/ noun [C] **1** a country that makes an agreement to help another country, especially in a war: *the United States and its European allies* **2** someone who helps you, especially against people who are causing problems for you: *If you're going to succeed in this job you will need allies.*

al·ly² /əˈlaɪ, ˈæˌlaɪ/ verb **ally yourself with** to support another country, group, or person

ˌall-you-can-ˈeat adj *American* serving you as much food as you want for one price: *all-you-can-eat breakfast*

al·ma ma·ter /ˌɑlmə ˈmɑtər/ noun [singular] the high school, college, or university where you were a student

al·might·y /ɔlˈmaɪti/ adj **1 Almighty** with power over everyone and everything: *Almighty God* **2** *informal* used for emphasizing how great, loud, or serious something is

al·mond /ˈɑmənd, ˈælmənd/ noun [C] a flat white nut that has a brown skin and can be eaten

al·most /ˈɔlmoust/ adv ★★★ nearly but not completely: *"Are you ready?" "Almost! I'm just putting my shoes on."* ♦ *It's been almost a year since she died.* ♦ *Almost all of the students here are from South America.* ♦ **almost as...as** *Sam's almost as tall as his mother.*

a•lone /əˈloʊn/ adj, adv ★★

> **Alone** can be:
> - an **adjective**: *I was alone in the house.*
> - an **adverb**: *Kim prefers to travel alone.*

1 if you are alone, no one else is with you: *Shelley is divorced and lives alone.* ♦ *She was **all alone** in a dark forest.* ♦ *It was the first time he had been **alone with** Maria* (=just the two of them and nobody else).
2 without any help from other people: *Was the killer acting alone?*
3 without including numbers or amounts from anywhere else: *Last year, she earned over a million dollars from television advertisements alone.*
4 used for emphasizing that a particular person or thing is the only one that has something or can do something: *Time alone will show whether the voters made the right choice.* ♦ **alone in (doing) sth** *Am I alone in thinking that Biggs could be wrong?*
PHRASE **go it alone** to live, work, or make decisions on your own, without any help from other people

a•long /əˈlɔŋ/ grammar word ★★★

> **Along** can be:
> - a **preposition**: *Go along South Street and turn left.*
> - an **adverb**: *Can I bring the children along?*

1 moving forward on a line, path, or near the edge of something: *Mrs. Klein was hurrying along the path toward us.* ♦ *We walked along in silence.* ♦ *They were sailing along the southern coast of Australia.*
2 placed in a line beside a road, river, wall, etc.: *a line of trees along the river bank*
3 used for saying that you go somewhere with someone, or you take someone or something with you: *Do you mind if I come along too?* ♦ *Be sure to take your notes along with you.*
4 coming to the place where someone is: *Finally a taxi came along, and we jumped in.*
PHRASES **along with** in addition to: *Ramos was arrested along with 11 other men.*
be getting/coming along used for saying how well someone is progressing or succeeding: *How is your garden coming along?* ♦ *How are you **getting along with** your Russian?*

a•long•side /əˈlɔŋˌsaɪd/ grammar word

> **Alongside** can be:
> - a **preposition**: *A police car drove up alongside us.*
> - an **adverb**: *Peter was riding on a donkey with his father walking alongside.*

1 along the side of someone or something, or close to their side: *The railroad track runs alongside the road.* **2** working together with someone in the same place: *We worked alongside people from 71 other countries.* **3** existing at the same time as another system, process, or idea: *In Hong Kong, a communist government and a capitalist economy operate alongside each other.* **4** in comparison with another person or thing: *Our profits seem small alongside the amounts that the big companies make.*

a•loof /əˈluf/ adj **1** not friendly **2** not willing to be involved in something

a•loud /əˈlaʊd/ adv loud enough for other people to hear

al•pha•bet /ˈælfəˌbet/ noun [C] ★ a set of letters in a particular order that are used for writing a language

al•pha•bet•i•cal /ˌælfəˈbetɪk(ə)l/ adj arranged according to the order of letters in the alphabet: *Here is a list of words in alphabetical order.* —**al•pha•bet•i•cal•ly** /ˌælfəˈbetɪkli/ adv

al•read•y /ɔlˈredi/ adv ★★★
1 before now, or before another point in time: *He's only 24, but he's already achieved worldwide fame.* ♦ *The gang leader had already left the country.*
2 used for saying that a situation has started to exist and still continues: *By the time the doctor arrived, I was already feeling better.*
3 sooner than you expected: *Are you tired already? I don't believe it!* ♦ *Is it 12 o'clock already?*
→ YET

al•right /ɔlˈraɪt/ adj, adv ALL RIGHT. Many people think that this is incorrect.

al•so /ˈɔlsoʊ/ adv ★★★
1 used for adding another fact or idea to what you have already said: *Ken is a good photographer who also loves to paint.* ♦ *The electric drill can also be used as a screwdriver.* ♦ ***Not only** is it more expensive, it's **also** a horrible color.*
2 used for showing that what you have just said about someone or something is true about another person or thing: *Jeremy is now at Cornell College, where his father also studied.* ♦ *The movie was popular **not only** with children, **but also** with their parents.*

> **Also**, **as well**, and **too** all have a similar meaning.
> - **As well** and **too** come at the end of a clause: *My wife speaks French as well/too.* But **also** usually comes before the verb, or after an auxiliary or modal verb or the verb **to be**: *She also speaks French.* ♦ *She can also speak French.* ♦ *He was also a fine musician.*
> - **Also** is not normally used with negatives. **Not...either** is used instead: *I don't speak French, and I don't speak German either.*

al•tar /ˈɔltər/ noun [C] a table where religious ceremonies are performed

al•ter /ˈɔltər/ verb [I/T] to change, or to make changes to something = MODIFY: *He had altered all the information on the forms.* ♦ *After all these years, the town has hardly altered.*

al•ter•a•tion /ˌɔltəˈreɪʃ(ə)n/ noun [C] a change in something or someone = MODIFICATION

al•ter•nate¹ /ˈɔltərˌneɪt/ verb [I/T] to change from one thing, idea, or feeling to another, and keep repeating that pattern: *The government alternates between tough talk and silence.* ♦ *The class allows students to alternate work with education.*

al•ter•nate² /ˈɔltərnət, ɔlˈtɜrnət/ adj
1 happening or coming one after another, in a regular pattern: *alternate periods of good and bad weather* **2** *American* ALTERNATIVE: *You'll have to find an alternate route.* **3** happening on one day,

A

week, etc., but not on the day, week, etc. that immediately follows: *I go and visit him on alternate weekends.* —**al•ter•nate•ly** adv

al•ter•na•tive¹ /ɔlˈtɜrnətɪv/ noun [C] ★★ something that you can choose to do instead of something else: *There was **no alternative** – we had to close the bridge.*

al•ter•na•tive² /ɔlˈtɜrnətɪv/ adj ★★
1 able to be used or done instead of something else: *We are now looking for an alternative method.*
2 not traditional, or not done in the usual way: *an alternative lifestyle*

al•ter•na•tive•ly /ɔlˈtɜrnətɪvli/ adv used for making another suggestion: *We could drive all the way. Alternatively, we could fly.*

alˌternative ˈmedicine noun [U] medical treatments that are based on traditional ideas, not on modern methods

al•though /ɔlˈðoʊ/ conjunction ★★★
1 used for introducing a statement that makes your main statement seem surprising = THOUGH: *She used to call me "Tiny" although I was at least as tall as she was.*
2 used for introducing a statement that makes what you have just said seem less true or less likely: *The Lamberts liked their new home, although they missed their friends.*

al•ti•tude /ˈæltɪˌtud/ noun [C] the height of a place or object above SEA LEVEL

al•to•geth•er /ˌɔltəˈgeðər/ adv ★★
1 including everyone or everything: *How many guests will there be altogether?*
2 completely: *These rare animals may soon disappear altogether.*

> Do not confuse **altogether** with **all together**, which means "everyone or everything together": *Write down the numbers and add them all together.*

al•tru•is•tic /ˌæltruˈɪstɪk/ adj doing something for the benefit of other people ≠ SELFISH —**al•tru•ism** /ˈæltruˌɪzəm/ noun [U]

al•u•min•i•um /ˌæləˈmɪniəm/ the British spelling of **aluminum**

a•lu•mi•num /əˈlumɪnəm/ noun [U] a light silver-colored metal

aˌluminum ˈfoil noun [U] a very thin light sheet of shiny metal that you can wrap food in to keep it fresh

a•lum•ni /əˈlʌmˌnaɪ, əˈlʌmni/ noun [plural] the people who were students at a particular school, college, or university

al•ways /ˈɔlˌweɪz/ adv ★★★
1 on every occasion: *I always get the eight o'clock bus.* ♦ *Starting a new job is always a little bit of a shock.*
2 all the time: *Is he always this silly?*
3 for all time in the past or future: *I'll always remember how kind she was.* ♦ *Jimmy was always a difficult boy.*
4 used for saying that something happens often, especially when this annoys you: *He's always forgetting my name.*

PHRASES **as always** as on every other occasion: *As always, her father was there to meet her.*
I/you/they etc. could always... *spoken* used for making a suggestion: *You could always call him yourself.*
there's always... used for making a suggestion: *There's always Sue if Jane isn't available.*

Alz•heim•er's dis•ease /ˈɑltshaɪmərz dɪˌziz/ noun [U] a serious illness that affects someone's brain and memory

am /*weak* əm, *strong* æm/ *see* **be**

a.m. /ˌeɪ ˈem/ abbrev used after a time for showing that it is between midnight and noon → P.M.

a•mal•ga•mate /əˈmælgəˌmeɪt/ verb [I/T] to join two or more organizations, companies, etc. to make a single large one, or to be joined in this way —**a•mal•ga•ma•tion** /əˌmælgəˈmeɪʃ(ə)n/ noun [C/U]

a•mass /əˈmæs/ verb [T] to collect a lot of money or information

am•a•teur¹ /ˈæmətər, ˈæməˌtʃʊr/ adj **1** done for pleasure instead of as a job ≠ PROFESSIONAL: *amateur photography* **2** done or made badly: *a very amateur performance*

am•a•teur² /ˈæmətər, ˈæməˌtʃʊr/ noun [C]
1 someone who does something because they enjoy it, instead of as a job ≠ PROFESSIONAL **2** someone who does not do something very well

am•a•teur•ish /ˈæmətərɪʃ, ˈæməˌtʃʊrɪʃ/ adj done or made without much skill

a•maze /əˈmeɪz/ verb [T] to surprise someone very much by being very impressive or unusual: *What amazes me is that they never get tired.*

a•mazed /əˈmeɪzd/ adj very surprised: *Frankly, I was amazed that he was interested.*

a•maze•ment /əˈmeɪzmənt/ noun [U] a feeling of being very surprised: *They were shaking their heads in amazement.*

a•maz•ing /əˈmeɪzɪŋ/ adj ★ very good, surprising, or impressive: *Her story was quite amazing.* ♦ *Their last CD sold an amazing 2 million copies.* —**a•maz•ing•ly** adv

am•bas•sa•dor /æmˈbæsədər/ noun [C] a senior official who lives in a foreign country and represents his or her own country there

am•ber /ˈæmbər/ noun [U] a hard yellow-brown substance used for making jewelry

am•bi•dex•trous /ˌæmbɪˈdekstrəs/ adj able to use both hands with equal skill

am•bi•ence or **am•bi•ance** /ˈæmbiəns/ noun [C/U] the character of a place, or the general feeling that you have in a place = ATMOSPHERE

am•bi•gu•i•ty /ˌæmbɪˈgjuəti/ noun [C/U] something that is not clear because it has more than one possible meaning

am•big•u•ous /æmˈbɪgjuəs/ adj something that is ambiguous is not clear because it has more than one possible meaning or intention ≠ UNAMBIGUOUS: *The wording of his statement was highly ambiguous.* —**am•big•u•ous•ly** adv

am•bi•tion /æmˈbɪʃ(ə)n/ noun ★
1 [C] something that you very much want to achieve: *His ambition was to become a successful writer.* ♦ *I had no idea about Jesse's political ambitions.*

A

2 [U] determination to become successful, rich, or famous

am•bi•tious /æmˈbɪʃəs/ adj **1** determined to become successful, rich, or famous: *an ambitious young lawyer* **2** an ambitious plan or attempt will need a lot of hard work and skill in order for it to be successful

am•biv•a•lent /æmˈbɪvələnt/ adj having two different opinions about something at the same time —**am•biv•a•lence** /æmˈbɪvələns/ noun [U]

am•ble /ˈæmb(ə)l/ verb [I] to walk in a slow relaxed way

am•bu•lance /ˈæmbjələns/ noun [C] ★ a vehicle for taking people to the hospital

am•bush /ˈæmˌbʊʃ/ verb [T] to attack someone suddenly from a hidden position —**am•bush** noun [C/U]

a•men /ɑˈmen, eɪˈmen/ interjection said at the end of a Christian or Jewish prayer

a•me•na•ble /əˈminəb(ə)l/ adj willing to do something, or willing to agree with someone

a•mend /əˈmend/ verb [T] to make changes that improve a document, law, or agreement

a•mend•ment /əˈmendmənt/ noun [C] a change to a document, law, or agreement

a•mends /əˈmendz/ noun **make amends** to try to make a situation better after you have done something wrong

a•men•i•ties /əˈmenətiz/ noun [plural] things that make it comfortable or enjoyable to live or work somewhere: *Amenities include a gym and a pool.*

A•mer•i•can Dream, the /əˌmerɪkən ˈdrim/ noun [singular] the idea that anyone can be successful in the U.S. if they work hard enough

A•mer•i•can foot•ball /əˌmerɪkən ˈfʊtbɔl/ noun [U] *British* the game of FOOTBALL

A•mer•i•can In•di•an /əˌmerɪkən ˈɪndiən/ noun [C] a NATIVE AMERICAN —**Aˌmerican ˈIndian** adj

A•mer•i•can•ize /əˈmerɪkəˌnaɪz/ verb [T] to make a language or culture more American —**A•mer•i•can•i•za•tion** /əˌmerɪkənɪˈzeɪʃ(ə)n/ noun [U]

am•e•thyst /ˈæməθɪst/ noun [C/U] a purple stone that is used in jewelry

a•mi•a•ble /ˈeɪmiəb(ə)l/ adj friendly and easy to like

am•i•ca•ble /ˈæmɪkəb(ə)l/ adj friendly and without arguments: *an amicable divorce* —**am•i•ca•bly** adv

a•mid /əˈmɪd/ or **a•midst** /əˈmɪdst/ preposition **1** while something is happening or changing: *Banks and stores closed yesterday amid growing fears of violence.* **2** surrounded by things or people

a•mi•no ac•id /əˌminoʊ ˈæsɪd/ noun [C] one of the substances in the body that combine to make proteins

a•miss /əˈmɪs/ adj if something is amiss, it is not as it should be

am•mo•nia /əˈmoʊniə/ noun [U] a poisonous gas or liquid with a strong unpleasant smell, used in cleaning products

am•mu•ni•tion /ˌæmjəˈnɪʃ(ə)n/ noun [U] **1** bullets and bombs that can be fired from a weapon **2** facts that can be used against someone in an argument

am•ne•sia /æmˈniʒə/ noun [U] a medical condition that makes you unable to remember things

am•nes•ty /ˈæmnəsti/ noun [C] an official order not to punish people who have committed a particular crime

a•moe•ba /əˈmibə/ noun [C] a very small ORGANISM (=living thing) that consists of a single cell —**a•moe•bic** /əˈmibɪk/ adj

a•mok /əˈmɑk/ adv **run amok** to behave in an uncontrolled and often violent way

a•mong /əˈmʌŋ/ or **a•mongst** /əˈmʌŋst/ preposition ★★★

1 included in a particular group of people or things: *Robert was the only one among them who had ever ridden a horse.* ♦ *They discussed,* ***among other things,*** *the future of the oil industry.* ♦ *The winner was selected* ***from among*** *500 candidates.*

2 used for saying what happens within a particular group of people: *The suicide rate among young male prisoners is high.* ♦ *The team were fighting* ***among themselves.***

3 used for saying that different people receive parts of something when it is divided up: *The money has to be divided among several projects.*

4 with other people or things all around: *It was pleasant strolling among the olive trees.*

> **Between** and **among** are used in similar ways.
> - Use **between**, not **among**, when just two people are mentioned: *It was an agreement between Carl and me.*
> - When three or more people are mentioned, you can use either, but **among** is more formal: *The money was divided up among/between the four children.*
> - Use **between** for saying that there are people or things on two sides of someone or something: *I sat between my parents.*
> - Use **among** for saying that someone or something is in the middle of a group of people or things: *We strolled among the trees.*

a•mor•al /ˌeɪˈmɔrəl/ adj someone who is amoral does not care if their behavior is right or wrong

am•o•rous /ˈæmərəs/ adj involving sexual love

a•mount[1] /əˈmaʊnt/ noun [C] ★★★ a quantity of something: *This amount* (=quantity of money) *should be paid within two weeks.* ♦ *A computer can store vast* ***amounts of*** *information.*

PHRASE **no amount of sth** used for saying that something will never be enough to have an effect: *No amount of training could have prepared him for this.*

> **Amount** and **number** are both used for talking about quantities, but they are used in different ways.
> - **Number** is used with plural nouns: *a small number of cars* ♦ *a certain number of people.*
> - **Amount** is used with uncountable nouns: *a small amount of milk* ♦ *a certain amount of confidence.*
> - Say a **large** or **small** number/amount and NOT a **big** or **little** number/amount.

a•mount[2] /əˈmaʊnt/ PHRASAL VERB **aˈmount to sth 1** to be the same as something else,

A

or to have the same effect as something else: *Most people believe his statements amount to a declaration of war.* **2** to add up to a particular total: *His monthly earnings amount to about $3,500.*

amp /æmp/ or **am·pere** /ˈæmpɪr/ noun [C] *science* a unit for measuring an electric current

am·phet·a·mine /æmˈfetəˌmin/ noun [C/U] a drug that increases energy and excitement

am·phib·i·an /æmˈfɪbiən/ noun [C] an animal that can live both in water and on land

am·phib·i·ous /æmˈfɪbiəs/ adj living, being used, or happening both in water and on land

am·phi·the·a·ter /ˈæmfɪˌθiətər/ noun [C] a large circular building with no roof that is used for sports competitions or plays

am·ple /ˈæmp(ə)l/ adj **1** enough, and often more than you need **2** used for referring to a part of someone's body that is large: *an ample bosom* —**am·ply** adv

am·pli·fi·er /ˈæmplɪˌfaɪr/ noun [C] a piece of electronic equipment that makes sounds louder

am·pli·fy /ˈæmplɪˌfaɪ/ verb [T] to make sounds louder —**am·pli·fi·ca·tion** /ˌæmplɪfɪˈkeɪʃ(ə)n/ noun [C/U]

am·pu·tate /ˈæmpjəˌteɪt/ verb [I/T] to cut off a part of someone's body in a medical operation —**am·pu·ta·tion** /ˌæmpjəˈteɪʃ(ə)n/ noun [C/U]

a·muse /əˈmjuz/ verb [T] **1** to do or say something that other people think is funny or entertaining **2** to keep someone interested or entertained, so that they do not get bored: *We need something that will amuse a 10-year-old for an afternoon.*

a·mused /əˈmjuzd/ adj showing that you think that something is funny or entertaining: *an amused expression*

a·muse·ment /əˈmjuzmənt/ noun **1** [U] a feeling of being amused **2** [C] an enjoyable activity

aˈmusement ˌpark noun [C] a place where people pay money to go on RIDES (=large machines that you ride on for pleasure)

a·mus·ing /əˈmjuzɪŋ/ adj funny or entertaining: *an amusing birthday card*

an /*weak* ən, *strong* æn/ determiner ★★★ used instead of "a" when the next word begins with a vowel sound: *an accident* ♦ *an hour* ♦ *an X-ray*

a·nach·ro·nism /əˈnækrəˌnɪzəm/ noun [C] something that is no longer appropriate for modern times —**a·nach·ro·nis·tic** /əˌnækrəˈnɪstɪk/ adj

a·naes·the·tize /əˈnesθəˌtaɪz/ another spelling of **anesthetize**

an·a·gram /ˈænəˌɡræm/ noun [C] a word or phrase that you can form from another word or phrase by putting the letters in a different order

a·nal /ˈeɪn(ə)l/ adj relating to the ANUS

a·nal·o·gous /əˈnæləɡəs/ adj *formal* similar to another situation, process, etc.

a·nal·o·gy /əˈnælədʒi/ noun [C/U] a comparison between two things that shows how they are similar: *He uses the analogy of the family to explain the role of the state.*

an·a·lyse /ˈæn(ə)lˌaɪz/ the British spelling of analyze

a·nal·y·sis /əˈnæləsɪs/ (plural **a·nal·y·ses** /əˈnæləˌsiz/) noun ★

1 [C/U] the process of examining something in order to understand it, or to find out what it contains: *The blood samples have been sent away for analysis.* ♦ *The study included an analysis of accident statistics.*

2 [U] PSYCHOANALYSIS

PHRASE **in the final analysis** used for giving the facts that are most relevant in a situation: *In the final analysis, it is up to the students to decide.*

an·a·lyst /ˈæn(ə)lɪst/ noun [C] **1** someone whose job is to carefully examine a situation, event, etc. in order to provide other people with information about it: *a stock market analyst* **2** a PSYCHOANALYST

an·a·lyt·i·cal /ˌænəˈlɪtɪk(ə)l/ or **an·a·lyt·ic** /ˌænəˈlɪtɪk/ adj examining a problem or issue by separating it into its different parts or aspects: *analytical skills* —**an·a·lyt·i·cal·ly** /ˌænəˈlɪtɪkli/ adv

an·a·lyze /ˈæn(ə)lˌaɪz/ verb [T] to examine something in detail in order to understand or explain it: *Scientists analyzed samples of leaves taken from the area.*

an·ar·chist /ˈænərkɪst/ noun [C] someone who believes that there should be no government or laws

an·ar·chy /ˈænərki/ noun [U] a situation in which people ignore normal rules and laws, and are unable to be controlled

a·nath·e·ma /əˈnæθəmə/ noun [singular/U] *formal* something that you strongly dislike or strongly disagree with

a·nat·o·my /əˈnætəmi/ noun **1** [C] the body of a human or animal, or the structure of a plant **2** [U] the scientific study of the physical structure of an animal or plant —**an·a·tom·i·cal** /ˌænəˈtɑmɪk(ə)l/ adj

an·ces·tor /ˈænˌsestər/ noun [C] someone who lived a long time ago and is related to you —**an·ces·tral** /ænˈsestrəl/ adj → DESCENDANT

an·ces·try /ˈænˌsestri/ noun [singular/U] your ancestors and family history: *His family was of Danish ancestry.*

an·chor¹ /ˈæŋkər/ noun [C] **1** a heavy object that is dropped into the water to prevent a boat from moving **2** *American* the main person who presents the news on a television or radio news program

an·chor² /ˈæŋkər/ verb **1** [I/T] to prevent a boat from moving by dropping its anchor into the water **2** [T] to present the news on television or radio **3** [T] to attach something firmly somewhere

an·cho·vy /ˈænˌtʃoʊvi, ænˈtʃoʊvi/ noun [C/U] a type of small fish that tastes of salt and is often preserved in oil

an·cient /ˈeɪnʃənt/ adj ★★

1 very old: *an ancient city/book/tradition*

2 relating to a period of history a very long time ago: *the ancient Greeks/Britons/Egyptians*

and /*weak* ən, *weak* ənd, *strong* ænd/ grammar word ★★★

And can be:
- a **conjunction**: *Rachel plays the piano and sings.*

■ a way of starting a new sentence and relating it to the previous sentence: *The telephone isn't working. And that's not the only problem.*

1 used for connecting words or phrases together: *the lakes and mountains of Scotland* ♦ *Everyone was singing and dancing.* ♦ *You make lunch, and I'll take care of the children.*

When more than two words or phrases are joined in a list, **and** is used only between the last two: *She speaks German, French, Spanish, and English.*

2 used for showing that one thing happens after another: *He turned off the television and went to bed.*
3 used after verbs such as "go," "come," "try," or "wait," for showing what your purpose is: *I'll try and find out where we can buy tickets.* ♦ *Come and see our new kitchen.*
4 used for showing that one thing causes another: *He lied to us before, and now no one believes him.*
5 used for connecting words that are repeated for emphasis: *The situation is getting more and more complicated.* ♦ *I've tried and tried, but I can't understand it.*
6 *spoken* used in calculations for showing that numbers are added together: *Two and two is four.*
7 *spoken* used in numbers after the word "hundred" or "thousand," or between whole numbers and fractions: *a hundred and ten feet* ♦ *two and three quarters* (=2¾)

an·ec·dot·al /ˌænəkˈdoʊt(ə)l/ adj based on someone's personal experience or on what they say rather than on facts that can be checked

an·ec·dote /ˈænəkˌdoʊt/ noun [C] a story that you tell people about something interesting or funny that has happened to you

a·ne·mi·a /əˈnimiə/ noun [U] a medical condition in which your blood contains too few red blood cells —**a·ne·mic** /əˈnimɪk/ adj

an·es·the·si·ol·o·gist /ˌænəsˌθiziˈɑlədʒɪst/ noun [C] *American* a doctor who is trained to give people anesthetics

an·es·thet·ic /ˌænəsˈθetɪk/ noun [C/U] a drug or gas given to someone before a medical operation to stop them from feeling pain

a·nes·the·tist /əˈnesθətɪst/ noun [C] an ANESTHESIOLOGIST

a·nes·the·tize /əˈnesθəˌtaɪz/ verb [T] to give someone an ANESTHETIC so that they do not feel pain during a medical operation

an·gel /ˈeɪndʒəl/ noun [C] **1** a spirit that in some religions is believed to live in heaven with God. In pictures, angels are shown as beautiful people with wings. **2** *spoken* a very kind person —**an·gel·ic** /ænˈdʒelɪk/ adj

an·ger¹ /ˈæŋgər/ noun [U] ★★ the strong feeling you get that makes you want to hurt someone or shout at them: *Some people express their anger through violence.*

an·ger² /ˈæŋgər/ verb [T] to make someone feel angry: *The school board's decision angered many students and parents alike.*

an·gle¹ /ˈæŋg(ə)l/ noun [C] ★★
1 the shape that is made where two lines or surfaces join each other: *An angle that measures 90 degrees is a right angle.*
2 the direction from which something comes, or the direction from which you look at something, especially when it is not directly in front of you: *Guns were firing at them from several different angles.*
3 a particular way of thinking about something: *We have considered the whole subject from many different angles.*
PHRASE **at an angle** not straight, but leaning to one side: *Hold the knife at a slight angle.*

an·gle² /ˈæŋg(ə)l/ verb [T] to make something move or point in a direction that is not directly in front of you
PHRASAL VERB **ˈangle for sth** *informal* to try to make someone give you something without asking for it directly: *She didn't want Ron to think that she was angling for sympathy.*

An·gli·can /ˈæŋglɪkən/ noun [C] a Christian who is a member of the Church of England —**An·gli·can** adj

an·gli·cize /ˈæŋglɪˌsaɪz/ verb [T] to make someone or something more English

Anglo- /æŋgloʊ/ prefix involving or related to England or the U.K.: *an Anglo-Russian trading agreement*

an·gry /ˈæŋgri/ adj ★★★ very annoyed: *There's no point in **getting angry**.* ♦ *His attitude **makes** me really **angry**.* ♦ *He is very **angry about** the way he's been treated.* ♦ *Are you **angry with** me?* ♦ **+(that)** *Anne was a little angry that no one told her about the party.* —**an·gri·ly** adv

angst /æŋst/ noun [U] a strong feeling of worry

an·guish /ˈæŋgwɪʃ/ noun [U] *formal* a feeling of great physical or emotional pain: *The rejection filled him with anguish.* —**an·guished** /ˈæŋgwɪʃt/ adj: *an anguished cry*

an·i·mal¹ /ˈænɪm(ə)l/ noun [C] ★★★
1 a living creature that is not a human, bird, fish, or insect: *lions, tigers, and other wild animals*
2 any living creature, including humans
3 *informal* someone who behaves in a very violent, cruel, or rude way

an·i·mal² /ˈænɪm(ə)l/ adj **1** relating to animals: *animal behavior* **2** relating to people's basic physical needs such as food and sex: *animal instincts/urges/desires*

an·i·mat·ed /ˈænɪˌmeɪtəd/ adj **1** lively or active: *an animated conversation* **2** an animated movie consists of a series of drawings that look as if they are moving

an·i·ma·tion /ˌænɪˈmeɪʃ(ə)n/ noun [U]
1 ANIMATED movies, or the process of making them **2** energy and excitement

an·i·mos·i·ty /ˌænɪˈmɑsəti/ noun [U] a strong feeling of disliking someone or something =HOSTILITY

an·kle /ˈæŋk(ə)l/ noun [C] the part at the bottom of your leg where your foot joins your leg —*picture* → C14

an·nex¹ /əˈneks, ˈæˌneks/ verb [T] to take control of a country or region by force —**an·nex·a·tion** /ˌænekˈseɪʃ(ə)n/ noun [C/U]

an·nex² /ˈæˌneks/ noun [C] a building added

A

to a larger building or built next to it

an•ni•hi•late /əˈnaɪəˌleɪt/ verb [T] to completely destroy or defeat a group of people or things —**an•ni•hi•la•tion** /əˌnaɪəˈleɪʃ(ə)n/ noun [U]

an•ni•ver•sa•ry /ˌænɪˈvɜrs(ə)ri/ noun [C] a date when you celebrate something that happened in a previous year that is important to you: *a wedding anniversary* ♦ *the 10th anniversary of the end of the war*

an•nounce /əˈnaʊns/ verb [T] ★
1 to make a public statement about a plan or decision: *There was a press release announcing the Senator's resignation.* ♦ **+(that)** *I am pleased to announce that the Board has agreed to our proposal.*
2 to tell people something clearly or loudly: **+(that)** *Bill suddenly announced he was taking the day off.*
3 to give information over a LOUDSPEAKER in a public place such as an airport: *When your flight is announced, make your way to the departure lounge.*

an•nounce•ment /əˈnaʊnsmənt/ noun ★
1 [C] a public statement that gives people information about something: *Observers expect the president to* ***make an announcement*** *about his plans tonight.* ♦ **+(that)** *Ms. Baker stunned her fans with an announcement that she was quitting the music business.*
2 [U] the act of publicly stating something: ***The announcement of*** *his visit caused widespread media interest.*
3 [C] a short statement in a newspaper or a card you send out, telling people about something such as a birth or marriage

an•nounc•er /əˈnaʊnsər/ noun [C] someone whose job is to give information or describe a sports event on TV or radio

an•noy /əˈnɔɪ/ verb [T] to make someone feel slightly angry or impatient =IRRITATE: *I don't dislike her – she just annoys me sometimes.*

an•noy•ance /əˈnɔɪəns/ noun **1** [U] a slightly angry or impatient feeling **2** [C] something that makes you feel slightly angry

an•noyed /əˈnɔɪd/ adj ★★ feeling slightly angry or impatient: *We were all* ***annoyed with*** *him* ***for*** *forgetting.* ♦ **+(that)** *I was really annoyed that I hadn't been invited.*

an•noy•ing /əˈnɔɪɪŋ/ adj ★ making you feel slightly angry or impatient: *an annoying habit/problem* ♦ *What's really annoying is that we made the same mistake last time.*

an•nu•al /ˈænjuəl/ adj ★★
1 happening once a year =YEARLY: *an annual festival/vacation/report*
2 calculated over a period of one year =YEARLY: *an annual salary*
—**an•nu•al•ly** /ˈænjuəli/ adv

an•nul /əˈnʌl/ verb [T] to state officially that something such as a marriage or an agreement has no legal authority —**an•nul•ment** noun [C/U]

a•nom•a•ly /əˈnɑməli/ noun [C] *formal* something unusual or unexpected

an•o•nym•i•ty /ˌænəˈnɪməti/ noun [U] a situation in which the name of a person is not known or is kept secret

a•non•y•mous /əˈnɑnɪməs/ adj **1** if someone is anonymous, no one knows their name: *an anonymous caller* **2** done or written by someone whose name is not known: *an anonymous phone call/letter*
—**a•non•y•mous•ly** adv

an•o•rex•i•a /ˌænəˈreksiə/ noun [U] a serious illness that makes you want to stop eating. It mainly affects young women. → BULIMIA

an•o•rex•ic /ˌænəˈreksɪk/ adj extremely thin and suffering from anorexia —**an•o•rex•ic** noun [C]

an•oth•er /əˈnʌðər/ grammar word ★★★

> **Another** can be:
> - a **determiner:** *Can I have another glass of water, please?*
> - a **pronoun:** *We're changing from one system to another.*

1 one more person or thing of the same type as before: *Peter's mom is expecting another baby in June.* ♦ *"These sandwiches are delicious." "Would you like another?"* ♦ *Another 200 nurses are needed in local hospitals.* ♦ *We're doing a big concert tomorrow night and* ***another one*** *on Saturday.* ♦ *They are having* ***another of*** *their parties.*
2 a different person or thing of the same type: *Isn't there another word that has the same meaning?* ♦ *Fatima's husband was working in another part of the country.*
→ ONE ANOTHER

an•swer[1] /ˈænsər/ verb [I/T] ★★★
1 to give a spoken or written reply to a question, letter, etc.: *Mark answered my letter right away.* ♦ *I'm still waiting for you to answer.* ♦ *What's the matter? Answer me!* ♦ *"I don't have it," he answered truthfully.* ♦ **+that** *We asked him if he agreed with us, and he answered that he did.*
2 to come to the door when someone arrives at your house, or to pick up the phone when it rings: *I knocked and a young man answered the door.*
3 to try to give the correct reply to a question in a test or competition: *Not everyone answered correctly.*

PHRASAL VERBS ˈ**answer for sth** to be responsible for explaining something that you have done: *You have to answer for any problems that happen during the show.*
ˈ**answer to sb** to have to explain to someone why you did something

an•swer[2] /ˈænsər/ noun [C] ★★★
1 a spoken or written reply to something such as a question, a letter, or a telephone call: *I wrote to her in May but I never got an answer.* ♦ *I'll* ***give you a definite answer*** *tomorrow.* ♦ *The* ***answer to*** *your question is yes.*
2 a spoken or written reply to a question in a test or competition: *I'm sorry, but "Paris" is the wrong answer.* ♦ *Do you know the* ***answer to*** *question 10?*
3 a way of dealing with a problem =SOLUTION: *There are no easy* ***answers to*** *this crisis.*

an•swer•ing ma•chine /ˈæns(ə)rɪŋ məʃin/ noun [C] a machine that answers your telephone and records messages that people leave for you

ant /ænt/ noun [C] a small insect that lives under the ground in large organized groups —*picture* → C13

an·tag·o·nism /æn'tægə,nɪzəm/ noun [U] a strong feeling of disliking someone or of opposing something: *the growing antagonism between the two groups* —**an·tag·o·nis·tic** /æn,tægə'nɪstɪk/ adj

an·tag·o·nize /æn'tægə,naɪz/ verb [T] to make someone feel angry with you and dislike you

Ant·arc·tic, the /æn'tɑrktɪk/ the extremely cold region that is the most southern part of the world → ARCTIC

an·te /'ænti/ noun **up/raise the ante** to try to get a greater advantage from a situation by taking a bigger risk

an·te·lope /'æntɪ,loʊp/ noun [C] a brown animal with horns and long thin legs. It can run very fast.

an·ten·na /æn'tenə/ noun [C] **1** (plural **an·ten·nas** or **an·ten·nae**) a wire or metal pole used for receiving radio and television signals —*picture* → C1 **2** (plural **an·ten·nae**) one of the two long thin parts on an insect's head that it uses to feel things with

an·them /'ænθəm/ noun [C] the official song of a particular country

an·thol·o·gy /æn'θɑlədʒi/ noun [C] a book containing poems, stories, or songs that were written by different people

an·thrax /'æn,θræks/ noun [U] a very serious illness that affects cows and sheep and sometimes people

an·thro·pol·o·gy /,ænθrə'pɑlədʒi/ noun [U] the study of human societies, customs, and beliefs —**an·thro·po·log·i·cal** /,ænθrəpə'lɑdʒɪk(ə)l/ adj, **an·thro·pol·o·gist** /,ænθrə'pɑlədʒɪst/ noun [C]

anti- /ænti/ prefix **1** opposing: *antiwar protesters* **2** with the opposite qualities: *an antihero* **3** preventing or curing: *antibacterial*

an·ti·bi·ot·ic /,æntibaɪ'ɑtɪk, ,æntaɪbaɪ'ɑtɪk/ noun [C] a drug that cures illnesses and infections caused by bacteria

an·ti·bod·y /'æntɪ,bɑdi/ noun [C] a substance in your blood that helps your body to fight illnesses and infections

an·tic·i·pate /æn'tɪsɪ,peɪt/ verb [T] **1** to think that something will probably happen: *Organizers say they do not anticipate any difficulties.* ♦ *We anticipate that the river level will rise very slowly.* **2** to guess that something will happen, and be ready to deal with it: *The businesses that survive are those that anticipate changes in technology.*

an·tic·i·pa·tion /æn,tɪsɪ'peɪʃ(ə)n/ noun [U] a feeling of excitement about something enjoyable that is going to happen soon
PHRASE **in anticipation of sth** if you do something in anticipation of an event, you do something to prepare for it

an·ti·cli·max /,ænti'klaɪ,mæks/ noun [C] something that is not as exciting as you expected it to be

an·tics /'æntɪks/ noun [plural] behavior that is funny or silly

an·ti·de·pres·sant /,æntidɪ'pres(ə)nt/ noun [C] a drug that is used for treating someone who is DEPRESSED

an·ti·dote /'æntɪ,doʊt/ noun [C] **1** a substance that prevents a poison from having bad effects **2** something that helps to improve the effects of something bad: *The game was a welcome antidote to the day's worries.*

an·ti·freeze /'æntɪ,friz/ noun [U] a chemical that you add to the water in a car engine to prevent it from freezing

an·tip·a·thy /æn'tɪpəθi/ noun [U] *formal* a strong feeling of not liking someone or something

an·ti·quat·ed /'æntɪ,kweɪtəd/ adj too old or old-fashioned to be useful

an·tique /æn'tik/ noun [C] an old valuable object such as a piece of furniture or jewelry

an·tiq·ui·ty /æn'tɪkwəti/ noun **1** [U] ancient times **2 antiquities** [plural] objects or buildings that existed in ancient times and still exist

an·ti-Se·mit·ic /,ænti sə'mɪtɪk, ,æntaɪ sə'mɪtɪk/ adj showing a feeling of hate toward Jewish people —**an·ti-Sem·i·tism** /,ænti 'semɪ,tɪzəm, ,æntaɪ 'semɪ,tɪzəm/ noun [U]

an·ti·sep·tic /,æntɪ'septɪk/ noun [C/U] a substance that you use for cleaning injured skin and preventing infections —**an·ti·sep·tic** adj

an·ti·so·cial /,ænti'soʊʃ(ə)l, ,æntaɪ'soʊʃ(ə)l/ adj **1** not interested in meeting other people or not enjoying friendly relationships with them **2** showing a lack of care for other people: *antisocial activities*

an·tith·e·sis /æn'tɪθəsɪs/ noun [singular] *formal* the exact opposite of something

an·ti·trust /,æntɪ'trʌst, ,æntaɪ'trʌst/ adj *American legal* intended to prevent companies from controlling prices and reducing competition: *antitrust laws*

ant·lers /'æntlərz/ noun [plural] the horns on the head of a male DEER

an·to·nym /'æntənɪm/ noun [C] a word that means the opposite of another word → SYNONYM

a·nus /'eɪnəs/ noun [C] the hole in your bottom through which you get rid of solid waste

anx·i·e·ty /æŋ'zaɪəti/ noun **1** [U] a worried feeling that you have because you think that something bad might happen: *There was a lot of anxiety about the results of the talks.* **2** [C] something that you are worried about

anx·ious /'æŋkʃəs/ adj ★
1 worried because you think that something bad might happen: *His silence made me anxious.* ♦ *People are naturally* ***anxious about*** *these tests.*
2 wanting something very much and feeling nervous, excited, or impatient: *We were all* ***anxious for*** *peace.* ♦ **anxious to do sth** *We're anxious to hear from anyone who can help.* ♦ **+(that)** *They were anxious that everyone should enjoy themselves.*
—**anx·ious·ly** adv

an·y /'eni/ grammar word ★★★

> **Any** can be:
> ■ a **determiner**: *Any intelligent child can use this software.*

A

- a **pronoun**: *I needed milk, but there wasn't any.* ♦ *Have you read any of his books?*
- an **adverb**: *Are you feeling any better?*

1 used instead of "some" in negatives, questions, and conditional sentences: *Did you bring any warm clothes?* ♦ *He didn't do any work at all.* ♦ *I tried to get a ticket but there weren't any left.* ♦ *If you need any help, just let me know.* ♦ *Did* ***any of*** *her friends come?*
2 used when something is true for every person or thing in a group: *Pick any design you want – they're all the same price.* ♦ *It was the first time that* ***any of*** *us had been in a plane.*
3 in any way, or by any amount: *If your headache gets any worse, you should see a doctor.* ♦ *I was too tired to walk any further.*
4 *spoken* used for emphasis after a verb to mean "at all": *Have things improved any?*
PHRASES **any day now** or **any time now** or **any minute now** very soon: *He should be home any minute now.*
be any use/good used for saying or asking whether something is at all good or effective: *It isn't any use complaining – they never listen.*
→ ANYMORE

an·y·bod·y /ˈeniˌbɑdi/ pronoun ★★★ anyone: *Would anybody like a cup of coffee?* ♦ *Is there anybody who doesn't understand?*

an·y·how /ˈeniˌhaʊ/ adv ANYWAY

an·y·more /ˌeniˈmɔr/ adv ★ used when talking or asking about a situation that has ended: *Don't you love me anymore?* ♦ *They don't live here anymore.*

an·y·one /ˈeniˌwʌn/ pronoun ★★★
1 used instead of "someone" in negatives, questions, and conditional sentences: *I don't know anyone here.* ♦ *Was there anyone at home?* ♦ *If anyone wants coffee, here it is.* ♦ *Is* ***anyone else*** *coming with us?*
2 used for referring to any person, when it does not matter which person, or when you do not know which person: *Anyone can make a mistake.* ♦ *You can invite anyone you want.* ♦ *Jackie knows more than* ***anyone else*** *about this.*

an·y·place /ˈeniˌpleɪs/ grammar word *American* ANYWHERE: *With this ticket you get to go anyplace you want to.*

an·y·thing /ˈeniˌθɪŋ/ pronoun ★★★
1 used instead of "something" in negatives, questions, and conditional sentences: *Don't do anything stupid.* ♦ *He never does anything to help.* ♦ *Do you know anything about baseball?* ♦ *If anything happens, call me.* ♦ *Do you want* ***anything else*** *to eat?*
2 used when something is true for every thing in a group, or for every possible thing: *You can buy anything you want on the Internet.* ♦ *She would do anything for her children.* ♦ *Pigs will eat* ***just about anything.*** ♦ *Get me a sandwich –* ***anything but*** *cheese* (=anything except cheese).
PHRASES **anything like** used in questions or negatives to mean "at all similar to": *Is Tom anything like his brother?*
...or anything *spoken* used for referring to a group of similar things without being specific: *I wasn't in any pain or anything.*

an·y·time /ˈeniˌtaɪm/ adv at any time: *You can come and see me anytime you like.*

an·y·way /ˈeniˌweɪ/ adv *spoken* ★★★
1 used when you want to change the subject of a conversation, or end the conversation: *What are you doing here, anyway?* ♦ *Anyway, I have to go now.*
2 used for showing why something is not important, or is not a problem: *I don't understand politics, and anyway I'm not really interested.* ♦ *I'll get some bread – I was going to the store anyway.*
3 despite something that you have previously mentioned: *It's illegal to park here, but people do it anyway.*
4 used for adding a statement that limits what you have just said: *It's something I can't tell you – not just now, anyway.*

an·y·where /ˈeniˌwer/ grammar word ★★

Anywhere can be:
- an **adverb**: *I'm not going anywhere today.*
- a **pronoun**: *a village a long way from anywhere.*

1 used instead of "somewhere" in negatives, questions, and conditional sentences: *He never travels anywhere without his camera.* ♦ *Have you seen Mike anywhere?* ♦ *If we go* ***anywhere else,*** *we'll let you know.*
2 used when something is true for every place, and it is not important which: *You can sit anywhere you like.* ♦ *A trained teacher can find work anywhere.*
3 used for saying that a number or amount is within a particular range: *The trip can take* ***anywhere from*** *20 minutes* ***to*** *an hour.*
PHRASE **not be getting/going anywhere** to not be making any progress or achieving anything
→ NEAR[1]

a·part /əˈpɑrt/ grammar word ★★★

Apart can be:
- an **adverb**: *We had to take the engine apart.*
- used after the verb "to be": *I'm never happy when we're apart.*
- used in the preposition phrase **apart from**: *Everyone was there apart from Ann.*

1 at a distance away from each other, or away from someone or something else: *Stand with your feet apart.* ♦ *Their two farms are about a mile apart.* ♦ *Aitken and his wife are living apart.* ♦ *He doesn't like being apart from his family.*
2 broken or separated into different pieces: *The book* ***came apart*** *in my hands.* ♦ *I had to* ***take*** *the printer* ***apart*** *to fix it.*
3 used for saying how much time there is between events: *The two brothers were born six years apart.*
4 different from each other or from other people or things: *Our political views are very far apart.* ♦ *His style* ***sets him apart*** *from other writers.* → TELL SB/STH APART
PHRASE **apart from** not including someone or something: *Do you speak any languages apart from English?*

a·part·heid /əˈpɑrtˌheɪt, əˈpɑrtˌhaɪt/ noun [U] the political system that existed in the past in South Africa, in which only white people had political rights and power

a·part·ment /əˈpɑrtmənt/ noun [C] *American* ★★★ a set of rooms for living in, usually on one floor of a large building

aˈpartment ˌbuilding or **aˈpartment ˌhouse** noun [C] *American* a building containing many apartments —*picture* → C1

aˈpartment ˌcomplex noun [C] *American* a large group of apartment buildings

ap·a·thet·ic /ˌæpəˈθetɪk/ adj not interested in anything, or not enthusiastic about anything —**ap·a·thet·i·cal·ly** /ˌæpəˈθetɪkli/ adv

ap·a·thy /ˈæpəθi/ noun [U] a feeling of not being interested in anything or not enthusiastic about anything

ape /eɪp/ noun [C] a large monkey without a tail

a·pe·ri·tif /əˌperəˈtif/ noun [C] an alcoholic drink that you have before a meal

ap·er·ture /ˈæpərtʃər/ noun [C] *formal* a small hole or space

a·pex /ˈeɪˌpeks/ noun [C] the pointed top part of something

aph·ro·dis·i·ac /ˌæfrəˈdɪziˌæk/ noun [C] a food, drink, or drug that makes people want to have sex

a·piece /əˈpis/ adv for each one: *Tickets were being sold for $20 apiece.*

a·poc·a·lypse /əˈpɑkəlɪps/ noun [singular] **1** a time when the whole world will be destroyed **2** a situation in which many people die and many things are destroyed

a·poc·a·lyp·tic /əˌpɑkəˈlɪptɪk/ adj describing a time when very bad things will happen

a·pol·o·get·ic /əˌpɑləˈdʒetɪk/ adj showing that you are sorry for doing something wrong —**a·pol·o·get·i·cal·ly** /əˌpɑləˈdʒetɪkli/ adv

a·pol·o·gize /əˈpɑləˌdʒaɪz/ verb [I] ★★ to tell someone that you are sorry for doing something wrong: *I **apologize for** taking so long to reply.* ♦ *You should **apologize to** your brother.*

a·pol·o·gy /əˈpɑlədʒi/ noun [C] a statement that tells someone that you are sorry for doing something wrong: *They were kind enough to accept my apology.* ♦ *I think I owe you an apology.*

a·pos·tro·phe /əˈpɑstrəfi/ noun [C] the symbol ' used in English to show the POSSESSIVE form of a noun, for example "Bob's car," or to mark the place where a letter has been removed to make a word shorter, for example "isn't"

ap·palled /əˈpɔld/ adj offended or shocked: *I'm appalled that a doctor would behave like that.* —**ap·pall** verb [T]

ap·pall·ing /əˈpɔlɪŋ/ adj extremely bad or shocking: *The conditions they live in are appalling.* ♦ *appalling weather*

ap·pa·ra·tus /ˌæpəˈrætəs, ˌæpəˈreɪtəs/ noun [U] equipment: *divers wearing underwater breathing apparatus*

ap·par·el /əˈperəl/ noun [U] *American* clothes

ap·par·ent /əˈperənt/ adj ★

1 easy to see or understand = OBVIOUS: **+(that)** *It was apparent that the two women knew each other.* ♦ *It should be **apparent to** anyone that the letter was written by a child.*

2 an apparent quality, feeling, or situation seems to exist although it may not be real: *His apparent lack of interest in her work always annoyed her.*

ap·par·ent·ly /əˈperəntli/ adv ★

1 based only on what you have heard, not on what you are certain is true: *Apparently, she resigned because she had an argument with her boss.*

2 used for saying what seems to be true when people do not yet know all the facts of a situation: *Seven people were shot yesterday in two apparently unrelated incidents.*

ap·pa·ri·tion /ˌæpəˈrɪʃ(ə)n/ noun [C] *formal* a strange image or creature that someone sees

ap·peal[1] /əˈpil/ verb ★

1 [I] to make an urgent request for people to do something or give something: **appeal to sb to do sth** *She appealed to her former husband to return their baby son.* ♦ **appeal to sb for sth** *They're appealing to local businesses for money.*

2 [I] if something appeals to you, you like it or want it: *The show's mixture of comedy and songs will **appeal to** children.*

3 [I/T] to formally ask a court of law to change its decision: *Green's family say they will appeal the verdict.*

ap·peal[2] /əˈpil/ noun ★

1 [C] an urgent request for people to do something or give something: *There have been several **appeals for** an end to the fighting.* ♦ *The organization has **launched an appeal** to send food to the flood victims.*

2 [U] a quality that something has that makes people like it or want it: *How do you explain **the appeal of** horror movies?* → SEX APPEAL

3 [C] a formal request for a court of law to change its decision

ap·peal·ing /əˈpilɪŋ/ adj attractive and interesting: *The building has an appealing old-fashioned charm.* ♦ *We've tried to make the design more appealing to young people.*

ap·pear /əˈpɪr/ verb ★★★

1 seem	4 be written/printed
2 begin to be seen	5 be on TV etc.
3 start to exist	

1 [linking verb] to make other people think that you are something, or that you feel something: *Matt appears unaffected by all the media attention.* ♦ ***There appears to be** very little we can do about the problem.* ♦ ***It appears that** she's changed her mind.* ♦ **appear to do sth** *No one appeared to notice me.*

2 [I] if someone or something appears somewhere, you see them suddenly or for the first time: *Cracks began to appear in the ceiling.*

3 [I] to start to exist, or to start to be available for the first time: *the latest Internet guide to appear on the market*

4 [I] to be written or printed somewhere: *Jane's name did not appear on the list.*

5 [I] to be on television or in a play, movie, or concert: *She is currently appearing in a Broadway musical.*

ap·pear·ance /əˈpɪrəns/ noun ★★★

1 [U] the way that someone or something

A

A

looks: *The twins are almost identical in* ***appearance.*** ♦ *He always* ***gives the appearance of*** *being very busy.*

2 [U] the time when something starts to exist, or starts to be seen: ***the appearance*** *of shopping malls in every large town*

3 [U] the fact that someone arrives somewhere: *She was startled by Julie's sudden appearance in the doorway.*

4 [C] an occasion when you are on television or in a play, movie, or concert: *a public appearance* ♦ *She has* ***made*** *numerous* ***appearances*** *on TV game shows.*

PHRASE **put in/make an appearance** to go somewhere because you think that you should go there: *I think I ought to put in an appearance at the office before lunch.*

ap•pease /əˈpiz/ verb [T] to give someone what they want because you want to avoid arguing or fighting —**ap•pease•ment** noun [U]

ap•pen•di•ci•tis /əˌpendɪˈsaɪtɪs/ noun [U] an illness in which your appendix becomes infected and has to be removed

ap•pen•dix /əˈpendɪks/ noun [C] **1** (plural **ap•pen•dix•es**) a small tube in your body near your stomach **2** (plural **ap•pen•di•ces** /əˈpendɪˌsiz/) an extra section at the end of a book

ap•pe•tite /ˈæpəˌtaɪt/ noun [C] ★

1 the natural feeling of wanting to eat: *a child with a healthy appetite* ♦ *Don't have any more chocolate – you'll* ***spoil your appetite*** (=make you want to eat less at the next meal).

2 a feeling of wanting something: *Young children have a natural* ***appetite for*** *stories.*

ap•pe•tiz•er /ˈæpəˌtaɪzər/ noun [C] a food that you eat before the main part of a meal

ap•pe•tiz•ing /ˈæpəˌtaɪzɪŋ/ adj appetizing food smells or looks very good ≠ UNAPPETIZING

ap•plaud /əˈplɔd/ verb **1** [I/T] to show that you enjoyed someone's performance by hitting the palms of your hands together = CLAP **2** [T] to praise a decision or action

ap•plause /əˈplɔz/ noun [U] the sound made by people applauding: *Let's have a round of applause for all the organizers.*

ap•ple /ˈæp(ə)l/ noun [C/U] ★★★ a hard round green or red fruit that is white inside and grows on trees —*picture* → C10

ap•pli•ance /əˈplaɪəns/ noun [C] a piece of electrical equipment that you have in your home: *appliances such as washing machines and refrigerators*

ap•pli•ca•ble /ˈæplɪkəb(ə)l, əˈplɪkəb(ə)l/ adj relevant to a particular situation or group of people: *This section of the law is applicable only to corporations.*

ap•pli•cant /ˈæplɪkənt/ noun [C] someone who applies for a job

ap•pli•ca•tion /ˌæplɪˈkeɪʃ(ə)n/ noun [C] ★★

1 a formal request to do something or have something, for example a job: *His* ***application for*** *membership was rejected.* ♦ **application to do sth** *her application to study at Columbia University*

2 a particular use that something has: *the practical applications of this technology*

3 *computing* a piece of computer software

appliˈcation ˌform noun [C] a printed list of questions that you answer as part of a formal request for something

ap•ply /əˈplaɪ/ verb ★★★

1 [I] to make a formal request to do something or have something: *Students can* ***apply for*** *money to help with their living costs.* ♦ *You have to* ***apply to*** *the U.S. embassy for a visa.* ♦ **apply to do sth** *Bill is applying to join the fire department.*

2 [I] to be relevant to a particular person or thing: *The rule no longer* ***applies to*** *him, because he's over 18.*

3 [T] to use something: **apply sth to sth** *A similar technique can be applied to the treatment of cancer.*

4 [T] to put a layer of something such as paint onto a surface

ap•point /əˈpɔɪnt/ verb [T] ★★ to choose someone to do a particular job: *We need to appoint a new treasurer.*

ap•point•ment /əˈpɔɪntmənt/ noun ★★★

1 [C/U] an arrangement to see someone, for example a doctor, at a particular time: *Why don't you* ***make an appointment with*** *one of our doctors?* ♦ **appointment to do sth** *I have an appointment to see my lawyer next Saturday.*

2 [C] a job: *academic appointments*

3 [U] the decision to give someone a job: *his* ***appointment as*** *governor of California*

apˈpointment ˌbook noun [C] *American* a book that has spaces or pages for each day of the year, where you can write down things you plan to do = CALENDAR, DATEBOOK, PLANNER

ap•pre•cia•ble /əˈpriʃəb(ə)l/ adj enough to be noticed: *an appreciable improvement in the student's test scores* —**ap•pre•cia•bly** adv

ap•pre•ci•ate /əˈpriʃiˌeɪt/ verb ★★

1 [T] to understand a situation and know why it is important or serious = REALIZE: **+how/why/what** *Doctors are beginning to appreciate how dangerous this drug can be.* ♦ **+(that)** *We appreciate that you cannot make a decision immediately.*

2 [T] to be grateful for something: *I really appreciate all your help.*

3 [T] to realize that someone or something has good qualities: *She feels that her family doesn't really appreciate her.*

4 [I] to increase in value ≠ DEPRECIATE

PHRASE **I/we etc. would appreciate it if...** *spoken* used for politely asking someone to do something: *We'd appreciate it if you didn't smoke in here.*

ap•pre•ci•a•tion /əˌpriʃiˈeɪʃ(ə)n/ noun **1** [U] the feeling of being grateful: *The award is given in appreciation of her huge contribution to the movie industry.* **2** [singular/U] pleasure that comes from understanding something good or beautiful: *We share an appreciation of music.* **3** [U] the ability to understand a situation and know why it is important or serious: *Most people have no appreciation of the dangers involved in the process.*

ap•pre•cia•tive /əˈpriʃətɪv/ adj showing that you are grateful, or that you enjoyed something: *an appreciative audience* —**ap•pre•cia•tive•ly** adv

ap•pre•hen•sion /ˌæprɪˈhenʃ(ə)n/ noun [C/U] a feeling of worry that something bad might happen = ANXIETY

ap·pre·hen·sive /ˌæprɪˈhensɪv/ adj slightly worried or nervous —**ap·pre·hen·sive·ly** adv

ap·pren·tice /əˈprentɪs/ noun [C] someone who is learning how to do a particular job

ap·pren·tice·ship /əˈprentɪsʃɪp/ noun [C/U] the time when someone works as an apprentice

ap·proach¹ /əˈproʊtʃ/ verb ★★

1 [I/T] to move closer in distance or time: *She heard footsteps approaching from behind.* ♦ *A strange boat was approaching the shore.* ♦ *The day of the election approached.*

2 [T] to formally ask someone for something, or formally offer something: **approach sb about sth** *I have already approached my boss about a raise.*

3 [T] to almost reach a particular level or condition: *They played in temperatures approaching 100 degrees.*

4 [T] to deal with a situation in a particular way: *There are several ways of approaching this problem.*

ap·proach² /əˈproʊtʃ/ noun ★★

1 [C] a way of dealing with something: *He has a relaxed* ***approach to*** *life.*

2 [singular] the fact that something is coming closer in time or in distance: *the approach of war*

3 [C] the action of asking for something, or of offering something formally: *The company has* ***made some approaches to*** *the Department of Commerce.*

4 [C] a path or road: *All approaches to the palace have been closed by the police.*

ap·proach·a·ble /əˈproʊtʃəb(ə)l/ adj friendly and easy to talk to ≠ UNAPPROACHABLE

ap·pro·pri·ate /əˈproʊpriət/ adj ★★★ right or correct for a particular situation ≠ INAPPROPRIATE: *This isn't the appropriate time to discuss the problem.* —**ap·pro·pri·ate·ly** adv

ap·prov·al /əˈpruv(ə)l/ noun [U] ★

1 a positive opinion about someone or something ≠ DISAPPROVAL: *Children are constantly looking for signs of approval from their parents.*

2 official permission: *The mayor has not yet* ***given the plan her approval.***

ap·prove /əˈpruv/ verb ★

1 [I] to think that someone or something is good ≠ DISAPPROVE: *You're leaving college! Do your parents approve?* ♦ *He seemed to* ***approve of*** *my choice.* ♦ **approve of sb doing sth** *I don't really approve of children wearing makeup.*

2 [T] to give official permission for something: *The new stamps were approved by a special panel of artists.*

> **Word family: approve**
>
> *Words in the same family as* ***approve***
> - **approval** *n*
> - **disapproval** *n*
> - **approving** *adj*
> - **disapproving** *adj*
> - **disapprove** *v*

ap·prov·ing /əˈpruvɪŋ/ adj showing that you like someone or something ≠ DISAPPROVING: *an approving smile* —**ap·prov·ing·ly** adv

ap·prox·i·mate /əˈprɑksɪmət/ adj not exact, but close to an exact amount or number: *the approximate cost of the repairs*

ap·prox·i·mate·ly /əˈprɑksɪmətli/ adv ★ used for showing that an amount or number is not exact = ROUGHLY: *Approximately 60,000 people filled the stadium.* ♦ *We have approximately 300 copies left.*

a·pri·cot /ˈæprɪˌkɑt/ noun [C] a fruit with an orange-yellow skin and a large hard seed inside —*picture* → C10

A·pril /ˈeɪprəl/ noun [C/U] ★★★ the fourth month of the year, between March and May: *Her birthday is in April.* ♦ *My appointment is on April 8th.*

a·pron /ˈeɪprən/ noun [C] something that you wear to protect the front of your clothes when you are cooking

apt /æpt/ adj very appropriate: *It seemed apt that the winning goal was scored by the captain.*

PHRASE **be apt to do sth** to have a tendency to do something

—**apt·ly** adv

ap·ti·tude /ˈæptɪˌtud/ noun [C/U] natural ability that makes it easy for you to do something well: *an aptitude for math*

a·quar·i·um /əˈkweriəm/ noun [C] **1** a glass container for fish and other water animals **2** a building with aquariums in it

A·quar·i·us /əˈkweriəs/ noun [U] one of the 12 signs of the ZODIAC. An **Aquarius** or **Aquarian** is someone who is born between January 20 and February 19.

a·quat·ic /əˈkwætɪk/ adj living in or near water: *aquatic birds*

AR abbrev Arkansas

Ar·ab /ˈerəb/ noun [C] someone from the Middle East or North Africa who speaks Arabic —**Ar·ab** adj

Ar·a·bic /ˈerəbɪk/ noun [U] the language that most people speak in the Middle East and North Africa —**Ar·a·bic** adj

ar·bi·ter /ˈɑrbɪtər/ noun [C] **1** someone who has the official power to settle disagreements **2** someone whose opinions about art, fashion, food, etc. have a lot of influence

ar·bi·trar·y /ˈɑrbɪˌtreri/ adj not done for any particular reason and therefore often unfair: *an arbitrary decision* —**ar·bi·trar·i·ly** /ˈɑrbɪˌtrerəli, ˌɑrbɪˈtrerəli/ adv

ar·bi·tra·tion /ˌɑrbɪˈtreɪʃ(ə)n/ noun [U] the official process of trying to settle a disagreement —**ar·bi·trate** /ˈɑrbɪˌtreɪt/ verb [I], **ar·bi·tra·tor** /ˈɑrbɪˌtreɪtər/ noun [C]

arc /ɑrk/ noun [C] a curved shape, or a curved line

ar·cade /ɑrˈkeɪd/ noun [C] **1** a VIDEO ARCADE **2** a covered area with stores on both sides

arch¹ /ɑrtʃ/ noun [C] **1** a shape or structure with straight sides and a curved top. The curved top part is also called an arch. **2** the curved bottom part of your foot

arch² /ɑrtʃ/ verb [T] to make something curve: *The cat arched its back.*

ar·chae·ol·o·gist /ˌɑrkiˈɑlədʒɪst/ noun [C] someone who studies archaeology

ar·chae·ol·o·gy /ˌɑrkiˈɑlədʒi/ noun [U] the study of ancient societies, done by looking at old bones, buildings, and other objects —**ar·chae·o·log·i·cal** /ˌɑrkiəˈlɑdʒɪk(ə)l/ adj

ar·cha·ic /ɑrˈkeɪɪk/ adj old and no longer used or useful

A

arch•bish•op /ˈɑrtʃbɪʃəp/ noun [C] a priest of the highest rank in some Christian churches

ar•che•ol•o•gist /ˌɑrkiˈɑlədʒɪst/ another spelling of **archaeologist**

ar•che•ol•o•gy /ˌɑrkiˈɑlədʒi/ another spelling of **archaeology**

arch•er•y /ˈɑrtʃəri/ noun [U] the sport of shooting ARROWS from a BOW —**arch•er** noun [C]

ar•che•typ•al /ˌɑrkəˈtaɪp(ə)l, ˈɑrkəˌtaɪp(ə)l/ adj very typical of a particular type of person or thing

ar•chi•tect /ˈɑrkɪˌtekt/ noun [C] someone whose job is to design buildings

ar•chi•tec•ture /ˈɑrkɪˌtektʃər/ noun [U] **1** a particular style of building: *The church is a typical example of Gothic architecture.* **2** the study or practice of designing buildings —**ar•chi•tec•tu•ral** /ˌɑrkɪˈtektʃərəl/ adj

ar•chive /ˈɑrˌkaɪv/ noun [C] **1** a collection of historical documents, or the place where it is kept **2** *computing* a collection of computer files that have been saved together in COMPRESSED form

arch•way /ˈɑrtʃˌweɪ/ noun [C] a curved roof over an entrance or passage

Arc•tic, the /ˈɑrktɪk/ the cold region that is the most northern part of the world —**Arc•tic** adj → ANTARCTIC

ar•dent /ˈɑrd(ə)nt/ adj feeling a particular emotion very strongly: *ardent supporters of the president* —**ar•dent•ly** adv

ar•du•ous /ˈɑrdjuəs/ adj extremely difficult and involving a lot of effort

are /*weak* ər, *strong* ɑr/ *see* **be**

ar•e•a /ˈeriə/ noun ★★★

1 [C] a part of a place or building: *Bus service in rural areas is not very good.* ♦ *The hotel has a spacious and comfortable reception area.* ♦ *My family has lived in this* ***area of*** *New England for years.*

2 [C] a particular subject or type of activity: *His* ***area of*** *expertise is engineering.* ♦ *What is your main* ***area of*** *concern?*

3 [C] a place on the surface of something, for example on a part of your body: *sensitive areas of your skin*

4 [U] the amount of space that the surface of a place or shape covers: *The screen has a large surface area.*

ˈarea ˌcode noun [C] a series of numbers that you have to DIAL when you are making a telephone call to someone in a different area

a•re•na /əˈrinə/ noun [C] **1** a large area surrounded by seats, used for sports or entertainment **2** the people and activities that are involved with a particular subject: *Today, businesses must be able to compete in the international arena.*

aren't /ɑrnt/ short form **1** the usual way of saying "are not": *We aren't going to Florida this year.* **2** the usual way of saying "am not" in questions: *I'm looking thinner, aren't I?*

ar•gu•a•ble /ˈɑrgjuəb(ə)l/ adj **1** *formal* if a fact or statement is arguable, there is evidence that it may be true: *It is arguable that we should have sold the company at that point.* **2** not clearly true or correct: *Whether good students make good teachers is arguable.*

ar•gu•a•bly /ˈɑrgjuəbli/ adv used for stating your opinion or belief, especially when you think that other people may disagree: *Ali was arguably the best boxer of all time.*

argue

ar•gue /ˈɑrˌgju/ verb ★★★

1 [I] to discuss something that you disagree about, usually in an angry way: *Those girls are always arguing!* ♦ *Don't* ***argue with*** *me – you know I'm right.* ♦ *We used to* ***argue about*** *who should drive.*

2 [I/T] to give reasons why you believe that something is right or true: *Woolf's report* ***argued for*** (=supported) *an improvement in prison conditions.* ♦ **+that** *Reuben opposed the new road, arguing that it wasn't worth $25 million.*

> **Words often used with argue**
>
> *Adverbs often used with* ***argue*** *(sense 2)*
>
> ■ ARGUE + **convincingly, forcefully, persuasively, plausibly**: used for saying that someone's arguments convince people
>
> ■ ARGUE + **passionately, strongly**: used for saying that someone's beliefs are strong

ar•gu•ment /ˈɑrgjəmənt/ noun ★★★

1 [C] an angry disagreement between people: *The decision led to a heated argument* (=extremely angry disagreement). ♦ *My girlfriend and I* ***had an argument.*** ♦ *Every time we visit my family, he* ***gets into an argument with*** *my sister.* ♦ *I try to avoid* ***arguments about*** *money.*

2 [C/U] a set of reasons that you use for persuading people to support your opinion: *There are powerful* ***arguments against*** *releasing them from prison.* ♦ *You could* ***make an argument for*** *working shorter hours.*

ar•gu•men•ta•tive /ˌɑrgjəˈmentətɪv/ adj often arguing or disagreeing with people

ar•id /ˈerɪd/ adj very dry with few plants

Ar•ies /ˈeriz/ noun [C/U] one of the 12 signs of the ZODIAC. An **Aries** is someone who is born between March 21 and April 20.

a•rise /əˈraɪz/ (past tense **a•rose** /əˈroʊz/; past participle **a•ris•en** /əˈrɪz(ə)n/) verb [I] to begin to exist or develop: *Problems arose over plans to build a new supermarket here.* ♦ *We can have another meeting if the need arises.*

ar•is•toc•ra•cy /ˌerəˈstɑkrəsi/ noun [C] the people in the highest class of society, who usually have money, land, and power and who often have special titles

a•ris•to•crat /əˈrɪstəˌkræt/ noun [C] a member

A

of the aristocracy —**a•ris•to•crat•ic** /əˌrɪstəˈkrætɪk/ adj

ar•ith•met•ic /əˈrɪθmətɪk/ noun [U] the part of mathematics that involves basic calculations such as adding or multiplying numbers

arm¹ /ɑrm/ noun [C] ★★★
1 one of the two long parts of your body with your hands at the end: *I put my arm around his shoulders.* ♦ *She was holding the baby **in her arms**.* ♦ *Jim was carrying a package **under his arm**.* ♦ *She **folded her arms** across her chest.* ♦ *Lovers were strolling by **arm in arm**.* —*picture* → C14
2 the part of a chair that you rest your arm on when you are sitting in it
3 a part of an organization that deals with a particular subject or activity: *the insurance arm of a major bank*
PHRASES **at arm's length 1** held away from your body with your arm stretched out straight: *He held the baby out at arm's length.* **2** in a situation where you avoid becoming involved with someone else: *She never gives interviews, and tends to keep the media at arm's length.*
up in arms angry and complaining about something: *Residents are up in arms about the closure of the local library.*
→ ARMS, OPEN¹

arm² /ɑrm/ verb [T] to provide someone with weapons

ar•ma•ments /ˈɑrməmənts/ noun [plural] weapons and military equipment used by the military

arm•band /ˈɑrmˌbænd/ noun [C] a small piece of cloth that you wear around one arm

arm•chair /ˈɑrmˌtʃer/ noun [C] a large comfortable chair with parts for you to rest your arms on —*picture* → CHAIR¹

armed /ɑrmd/ adj ★★
1 carrying a weapon, or involving the use of weapons: *armed robbery* ♦ *a bank robber armed with a shotgun*
2 **armed with sth** having useful or impressive equipment, information, etc.: *a group of reporters armed with telephoto cameras*

ˌarmed ˈforces, the noun [plural] a country's army, navy, and air force

arm•ful /ˈɑrmˌfʊl/ noun [C] the amount of something that you can carry in your arms

ar•mi•stice /ˈɑrmɪstɪs/ noun [C] a formal agreement to stop fighting a war
→ CEASEFIRE

ar•mor /ˈɑrmər/ noun [U] metal clothing that soldiers wore in the past to protect their bodies

ar•mored /ˈɑrmərd/ adj an armored vehicle is covered with layers of hard metal to protect it from attack

arm•pit /ˈɑrmpɪt/ noun [C] the part of your body that is under your arm, where your arm joins your shoulder

arms /ɑrmz/ noun [plural] weapons such as guns or bombs: *the international arms trade*

ˈarms conˌtrol noun [U] agreements between countries to reduce or limit the number of weapons in the world

ˈarms ˌrace noun [C] competition between countries to increase the number or power of their weapons

ar•my /ˈɑrmi/ noun [C] ★★★
1 a large organization of soldiers who are trained to fight wars on land: *an army officer/colonel* ♦ *Both of her sons are **in the army**.*
2 a large group of people who are doing the same thing or are in the same situation: ***Armies** of rescue workers are sorting through the rubble.*

a•ro•ma /əˈroʊmə/ noun [C] a smell that is strong but nice —**ar•o•mat•ic** /ˌærəˈmætɪk/ adj

a•ro•ma•ther•a•py /əˌroʊməˈθerəpi/ noun [U] a health treatment in which oils with a nice smell are used to make you feel relaxed —**a•ro•ma•ther•a•pist** noun [C]

arose the past tense of **arise**

a•round /əˈraʊnd/ grammar word ★★★

> **Around** can be:
> - a **preposition**: *We walked around the old town.*
> - an **adverb**: *She turned around and smiled at me.*
> - used after the verb "to be": *Don't discuss this when the children are around.*

1 **in or to many places** in or to many different parts or areas: *We drove around looking for a hotel.* ♦ *I glanced around the room, but I couldn't see him.* ♦ *The Games were watched by millions of people around the world.*
2 **in the opposite direction** moving so that you face in the opposite direction: *I turned around to see what the noise was.*
3 **to the other side** moving to the other side of something: *At that moment a truck came around the corner.*
4 **in a place** in or close to a place: *the quiet country roads around my hometown* ♦ *There's a phone around here somewhere.* ♦ *Is your wife around? I'd like to talk to her.*
5 **moving in circles** moving in a circular way: *The Earth goes around the Sun.* ♦ *The wheels spun around.*
6 **surrounding sth** surrounding or enclosing something: *Arrange the chairs around the table.* ♦ *a cabin with woods all around* ♦ *Sam had his arm around Mandy's waist.*
7 **not exact** used for giving a number, amount, or time that is not exact =APPROXIMATELY: *There must have been around 500 people there.* ♦ *We got back at around 11.*
8 **doing nothing useful** spending time not doing anything important or useful: *We got tired of waiting around.*
9 **existing now** available or existing at this time: *There are some really good new video games around.* ♦ *It's one of the biggest shopping malls around.*

aˌround-the-ˈclock adj *American* ROUND-THE-CLOCK

a•rouse /əˈraʊz/ verb [T] **1** to cause an emotion or attitude: *These rumors have aroused interest among investors.* **2** to make someone feel sexually excited

ar•range /əˈreɪndʒ/ verb [T] ★★★
1 to make plans for something to happen, and to manage the details of it: *I'm trying to arrange a meeting with the sales director.*

A

♦ *Who's arranging the wedding?* ♦ **arrange to do sth** *They arranged to go swimming the following day.* ♦ **arrange for sb/sth to do sth** *Please arrange for a taxi to pick me up at six.*
2 to put things in a neat, attractive, or useful order: *Here is the list arranged chronologically.* ♦ *We'll need to arrange the chairs around the table.*

ar·range·ment /əˈreɪndʒmənt/ noun ★★★
1 **arrangements** [plural] practical plans for organizing and managing the details of something: *sleeping/seating arrangements* ♦ *Her husband is away, so she'll have to* ***make*** *other childcare* ***arrangements.***
2 [C] an agreement or plan that you make with someone else: *They have an* ***arrangement with*** *Pepsi-Cola to share distribution facilities.*
3 [C/U] a set of things that have been arranged to look attractive, or the way that they have been arranged: *a floral arrangement*

ar·ray /əˈreɪ/ noun [C] a large group of people or things that are related in some way: *a dazzling array of products*

ar·rears /əˈrɪrz/ noun **in arrears** late in making a regular payment: *We are writing to inform you that your mortgage payment is a month in arrears.*

ar·rest¹ /əˈrest/ verb [T] ★★
1 if the police arrest someone, they take that person to a police station because they think that he or she has committed a crime: *Police raided the building and arrested six men.* ♦ **arrest sb for sth** *He was arrested for possession of illegal drugs.*
2 *formal* to stop a process or bad situation from continuing or developing: *A cut in interest rates failed to arrest the decline in prices.*

ar·rest² /əˈrest/ noun [C/U] a situation in which the police arrest someone: *The information led to the arrest of three suspects.* ♦ *Six men are under arrest in connection with the drug smuggling operation.* ♦ *We hope to make an arrest in the near future.*
→ CARDIAC ARREST, HOUSE ARREST

ar·ri·val /əˈraɪv(ə)l/ noun ★★
1 [singular/U] the time when someone or something arrives at a place from somewhere else: *Her arrival livened up the party.* ♦ ***The arrival of*** *Flight 106 from Boston has been delayed.*
2 [U] the time when something begins: ***the arrival of*** *spring*
3 [C] someone who has arrived or who has joined a group

ar·rive /əˈraɪv/ verb [I] ★★★
1 to reach a place: *What time does your plane arrive?* ♦ *A letter arrived for you this morning.* ♦ *Four police officers suddenly* ***arrived at*** *their house.*
2 to happen, or to begin to exist: *Society changed forever when television arrived.* ♦ *The baby arrived* (=was born) *earlier than we expected.*
PHRASAL VERB **arˈrive at sth** to reach a result, decision, or solution to a problem: *The two studies arrive at very different conclusions.*

- You **arrive in** a town or country, and you **arrive at** a building or place: *What time will she arrive in New York?* ♦ *He arrived at the airport early.*
- You can also say that you **reach** or **get to** a town, country, or building. **Reach** is more formal than **get to**: *The ambulance took 30 minutes to reach the hospital.* ♦ *I'll call you when I get to my hotel.*

ar·ro·gant /ˈærəgənt/ adj someone who is arrogant thinks that they are better or more important than other people —**ar·ro·gance** /ˈærəgəns/ noun [U], **ar·ro·gant·ly** adv

ar·row /ˈæroʊ/ noun [C] **1** a weapon in the form of a thin straight stick with a sharp point at one end and feathers at the other. It is fired using a **bow**. **2** a sign that looks like an arrow →, used for showing people where to go or look

ar·se·nal /ˈɑrs(ə)nəl/ noun [C] a large collection of weapons

ar·se·nic /ˈɑrs(ə)nɪk/ noun [U] a strong poison

ar·son /ˈɑrs(ə)n/ noun [U] the crime of deliberately burning a building —**ar·son·ist** noun [C]

art /ɑrt/ noun ★★★

1 painting, drawing, etc.	4 film, theater, etc.
2 beautiful objects	5 special skills
3 non-scientific subjects	

1 [U] the activity or study of creating paintings, drawings, and other objects that are beautiful or interesting → WORK²
2 [U] paintings, drawings, and other objects that are created in order to be beautiful or interesting: *the art of ancient Mexico* ♦ *Do you like* ***modern art?***
3 **arts** [plural] subjects of study that are not scientific, such as history, literature, and languages: *the College of Arts and Sciences*
4 **the arts** [plural] activities such as art, music, film, theater, and dance
5 [C] an activity that needs special skill: ***the art of*** *letter-writing*

ar·te·fact /ˈɑrtɪˌfækt/ another spelling of **artifact**

ar·ter·y /ˈɑrtəri/ noun [C] **1** one of the tubes in your body that carries blood from your heart to the rest of your body → VEIN **2** an important road, railroad, or river —**ar·te·ri·al** /ɑrˈtɪriəl/ adj

ar·thri·tis /ɑrˈθraɪtɪs/ noun [U] a serious medical condition that makes your JOINTS swollen and painful —**ar·thrit·ic** /ɑrˈθrɪtɪk/ adj

ar·ti·choke /ˈɑrtɪtʃoʊk/ noun [C/U] a round green vegetable with layers of thick pointed leaves

ar·ti·cle /ˈɑrtɪk(ə)l/ noun [C] ★★★
1 a piece of writing in a newspaper or magazine: *He has written several articles for* The New York Times. ♦ *an* ***article on/about*** *women in politics*
2 an object: *an article of clothing* ♦ *The store sells small household articles.*
3 *linguistics* a type of word that is used before a noun. The **indefinite article** in English is "a" or "an" and the **definite article** is "the."

A

ar·tic·u·late¹ /ɑrˈtɪkjulət/ adj someone who is articulate speaks very well because they use words effectively ≠ INARTICULATE —**ar·tic·u·late·ly** adv

ar·tic·u·late² /ɑrˈtɪkjuleɪt/ verb **1** [T] to use words effectively to express your ideas **2** [I/T] to say words clearly —**ar·tic·u·la·tion** /ɑrˌtɪkjuˈleɪʃ(ə)n/ noun [U]

ar·ti·fact /ˈɑrtɪˌfækt/ noun [C] an interesting object from the past

ar·ti·fi·cial /ˌɑrtɪˈfɪʃ(ə)l/ adj ★
1 not natural or real, but made by people: *The growers use both natural and artificial light.* ♦ *artificial flowers/fur/snow* ♦ *The product contains no artificial colors or flavors.*
2 not sincere = FALSE: *an artificial laugh* —**ar·ti·fi·cial·ly** /ˌɑrtɪˈfɪʃəli/ adv

ˌartificial inˈtelligence noun [U] the use of computer technology to make computers and machines think like people

ar·til·ler·y /ɑrˈtɪl(ə)ri/ noun [U] large powerful guns that soldiers use

ar·ti·san /ˈɑrtɪzən/ noun [C] someone who uses traditional skills and tools to make things

art·ist /ˈɑrtɪst/ noun [C] ★★
1 someone who creates paintings or other objects that are beautiful or interesting
2 a professional performer in music, dance, or the theater

ar·tiste /ɑrˈtist/ noun [C] a singer, dancer, or other professional entertainer

ar·tis·tic /ɑrˈtɪstɪk/ adj **1** good at drawing and painting: *You don't need to be very artistic to produce great designs.* **2** relating to painting, music, or other forms of art: *high artistic standards* —**ar·tis·ti·cal·ly** /ɑrˈtɪstɪkli/ adv

art·ist·ry /ˈɑrtɪstri/ noun [U] great skill

art·sy /ˈɑrtsi/ adj *American* showing a great interest in art, but in a way that may not be sincere: *artsy intellectual types*

art·work /ˈɑrtˌwɜrk/ noun [U] **1** paintings, drawings, and other objects that artists create **2** the pictures or photographs in a book or magazine

as /*weak* əz, *strong* æz/ grammar word ★★★

As can be:
- a **conjunction**: *As I was leaving, the phone rang.*
- a **preposition**: *He works as a waiter.*
- an **adverb**: *I'm as fast as you.*

1 used in comparisons used for comparing one person, thing, or situation with another: *Simon isn't* ***as*** *tall* ***as*** *his brother.* ♦ *I don't play football* ***as much as*** *I used to.* ♦ *There were twice* ***as many*** *visitors* ***as*** *last weekend.* ♦ *We need to collect* ***as much*** *information* ***as possible.*** ♦ *Barbara's hair looks exactly* ***the same as*** *mine.* ♦ *We all need exercise, but a healthy diet is* ***just as*** (=equally) *important.* → LESS
2 used for referring to what is known used for referring to something that has already been talked about: *As you know, Jack is leaving next month.*
3 in a particular way happening or done in a particular way: *Leave everything just as you found it.* ♦ *I invested the money as you suggested.* ♦ *Judith was late,* ***as usual.***
4 saying what sb/sth is used when you are saying what someone or something is or does: *As a parent, you naturally want the best for your children.* ♦ *a portrait of the actor as a child* ♦ *An electric drill can also be used as a screwdriver.*
5 saying how sb/sth is considered considered or described in a particular way: *Van Dyck was regarded as the greatest painter of his time.* ♦ *Madeira is described as having the best climate in the world.*
6 when or while happening at the same time as something else: *As we were sitting down to dinner, the phone rang.* ♦ *We got to the check-in desk* ***just as*** *they were about to close.* ♦ *I'm ready to go out* ***as soon as*** *it stops raining.*
7 because used for giving a reason for something: *As it was getting late, we decided to go home.*

PHRASES **as for** used for introducing a subject that is related to what you have just been talking about: *As for me, I went home and left them to deal with it.*
as if or **as though 1** in such a way that something seems to be true: *It looks as if it's going to rain.* ♦ *Jack smiled as though he knew the answer.* **2** used when you imagine an explanation for something that you know is not the real one: *My car looked as if an elephant had sat on it.*
as is in the original condition, including any faults or problems: *We've agreed to take the house as is.*
as it is already: *I've got enough problems as it is.*
as to *formal* concerning: *There is some doubt as to his true identity.*
→ YET

asap /ˌeɪ es eɪ ˈpi/ as soon as possible: *I want those files on my desk asap.*

as·bes·tos /æsˈbestəs, æzˈbestəs/ noun [U] a substance that was used in buildings in the past. You get very sick if you breathe the dust from it.

as·cend /əˈsend/ verb [I/T] *formal* to go upward, or to climb something ≠ DESCEND

as·cen·dan·cy /əˈsendənsi/ noun [U] the advantage, power, or influence that one person or group has over another: *the party's political ascendancy*

as·cent /əˈsent/ noun **1** [C/U] the process of climbing or of going upward ≠ DESCENT: *the airplane's ascent to 35,000 feet* **2** [C] a path that goes up a hill **3** [C/U] the process of becoming more important or famous

as·cer·tain /ˌæsərˈteɪn/ verb [T] *formal* to find out something: *Police are trying to ascertain the facts of the case.*

as·cribe /əˈskraɪb/ PHRASAL VERB **aˈscribe sth to sth** *formal* to believe that something is the cause of something else: *Their defeat was ascribed to a poor defense.*

a·sex·u·al /eɪˈsekʃuəl/ adj **1** an asexual animal has no sex organs **2** not interested in sex

ash /æʃ/ noun **1** [U] the gray powder that remains after something has burned **2** [C] a tree with a smooth gray BARK **3 ashes** [plural] the substance that remains after a person's body has been CREMATED (=burned after death)

A

a•shamed /əˈʃeɪmd/ adj feeling guilty or embarrassed about something that you have done: *He's extremely ashamed of his behavior last night.*
PHRASE **ashamed of sb** disappointed and upset by someone else's behavior: *I'm ashamed of you – lying to your teacher!*

a•shore /əˈʃɔr/ adv onto land from the ocean: *He quickly rowed ashore.*

ash•tray /ˈæʃtreɪ/ noun [C] a small container for ASH and cigarettes that have been smoked

A•sian /ˈeɪʒ(ə)n, ˈeɪʃ(ə)n/ adj **1** of or from the countries in East and Southeast Asia, such as China, Japan, Thailand, or Korea **2** *British* of or from the countries of South Asia (India, Pakistan, Bangladesh, and Sri Lanka) —**A•sian** noun [C]

ˌAsian Aˈmerican noun [C] someone who lives in the U.S. but whose family is from Asia —**ˌAsian Aˈmerican** adj

a•side¹ /əˈsaɪd/ adv ★
PHRASES **aside from** except for: *Aside from hanging around in the street, there's nothing for kids to do here.*
leave sth aside to deliberately not consider something: *Let's leave aside the issue of money.*
move/step aside to move away from someone or something: *Helen stepped aside to let him pass.*
set/put sth aside to keep something such as time or money for a particular purpose: *Try to set aside half an hour every day for something you really enjoy doing.*

a•side² /əˈsaɪd/ noun [C] a remark about something that is not the main subject of your discussion

ask /æsk/ verb ★★★
1 [I/T] to speak to someone in order to get information from them: *I wondered who had given her the ring but was afraid to ask.* ♦ *The police wanted to **ask** us **a few questions**.* ♦ **ask (sb) why/how/whether etc.** *She asked me how I knew about it.* ♦ **ask (sb) about sth** *Did you ask about the money?*
2 [I/T] to speak to someone because you want them to give you something, or do something for you: *If you need any help, just ask.* ♦ *Can I ask you a favor?* ♦ **ask (sb) for sth** *The children were asking for drinks.* ♦ **ask sb to do sth** *He asked us to move over a little.* ♦ **ask to do sth** *I asked to see the manager.* ♦ **ask (sb) if/whether** *Ask if we can go backstage.*
3 [T] to invite someone to do something, or to go somewhere with you: *We waited for half an hour before he asked us in* (=invited us to come inside). ♦ **ask sb to do sth** *They asked me to stay the night.*
4 [T] to expect someone to do something, or to give you something: *It's a nice house, but they're asking over half a million dollars.*
PHRASES **be asking for it/trouble** to behave in a way that makes something bad likely to happen: *She's asking for trouble if she speaks to the boss like that.*
don't ask me *spoken* used for telling someone that you do not know the answer to their question, when you are annoyed or surprised that they have asked you
if you ask me *spoken* used before you give someone your opinion about something: *If you ask me, she doesn't really want the job.*
PHRASAL VERB **ˌask sb ˈout** to invite someone to go somewhere with you because you want to start a romantic relationship with them

a•skew /əˈskju/ adj not as straight as it should be

a•sleep /əˈslip/ adj ★★ not awake: *The children are **fast asleep*** (=sleeping deeply). ♦ *She was so tired she **fell asleep*** (=began sleeping) *in her chair.*

as•par•a•gus /əˈsperəgəs/ noun [U] a long thin green vegetable with pointed ends —*picture* → C11

as•pect /ˈæspekt/ noun [C] ★★ a particular part, feature, or quality of something: *The Internet affects every aspect of our business.* ♦ *This chapter covers several important aspects of the teaching process.*

as•per•sions /əˈspɜrʒ(ə)nz/ noun **cast aspersions (on)** to criticize someone or something

as•phalt /ˈæsˌfɔlt/ noun [U] a black sticky substance that is used for making the surface of a road

as•phyx•i•ate /æsˈfɪksiˌeɪt/ verb [I/T] to kill someone by preventing them from breathing, or to die in this way =SUFFOCATE —**as•phyx•i•a•tion** /æsˌfɪksiˈeɪʃ(ə)n/ noun [U]

as•pi•ra•tion /ˌæspɪˈreɪʃ(ə)n/ noun [C] a strong wish to achieve something =AMBITION: *He has no political aspirations.*

as•pire /əˈspaɪr/ PHRASAL VERB **aˈspire to sth** to want to achieve something: *students who aspire to be professional actors*

as•pirin /ˈæsprɪn/ noun [C/U] a drug that cures minor pain, or a pill that contains the drug

as•pir•ing /əˈspaɪrɪŋ/ adj trying to be successful at something: *an aspiring actor*

ass /æs/ noun [C] an old word for a DONKEY

as•sail•ant /əˈseɪlənt/ noun [C] *formal* someone who violently attacks another person

as•sas•sin /əˈsæsɪn/ noun [C] someone who deliberately kills an important person

as•sas•si•nate /əˈsæsɪˌneɪt/ verb [T] to kill an important person deliberately —**as•sas•si•na•tion** /əˌsæsɪˈneɪʃ(ə)n/ noun [C/U]

as•sault¹ /əˈsɔlt/ noun [C/U] a violent attack, or the crime of physically attacking someone: *an assault on a young student*

as•sault² /əˈsɔlt/ verb [T] to attack someone violently: *An elderly woman was assaulted and robbed.*

as•sem•ble /əˈsemb(ə)l/ verb **1** [I/T] to bring a group together, or to come together and form a group: *The children assembled outside the building.* **2** [T] to build something by putting all its parts together: *You have to assemble the shelves yourself.* ♦ *They are assembling a peace-keeping force to send to the region.*

as•sem•bly /əˈsembli/ noun **1** [C] a group of people who have been chosen to make laws or deal with particular issues: *the French National Assembly* **2** [C/U] a regular meeting of students and teachers in a school **3** [U] the process of building something by putting all its parts together

as'sembly ˌline noun [C] a system for making products in a factory. Each worker or machine does a single job as the product moves past them = PRODUCTION LINE

as•sent /ə'sent/ noun [U] formal agreement or approval

as•sert /ə'sɜrt/ verb [T] **1** to state firmly that something is true **2** to behave in a determined or confident way: *He quickly asserted his authority as a leader.* ♦ *It's hard for shy people to assert themselves in a group.*

as•ser•tion /ə'sɜrʃ(ə)n/ noun [C] a statement in which you say that something is definitely true

as•ser•tive /ə'sɜrtɪv/ adj expressing your opinions firmly and confidently = FORCEFUL —**as•ser•tive•ness** noun [U]

as•sess /ə'ses/ verb [T] to think about something carefully and make a judgment about it: *We tried to assess his suitability for the job.* ♦ *Our agent will assess the value of your property.* —**as•sess•ment** noun [C/U]: *a clear assessment of the investment's risks*

as•set /'æset/ noun [C] **1** something such as money or property that a company owns **2** something that gives you benefits: *He is a definite asset to the team.* ♦ *Youth is a tremendous asset in this job.*

as•sid•u•ous /ə'sɪdʒuəs/ adj formal someone who is assiduous works very hard and does things carefully

as•sign /ə'saɪn/ verb [T] **1** to give someone a particular job: *We assigned her the job of maintaining our website.* **2** to put someone in a particular group, or send them to a particular place: *Tina has been assigned to the intermediate learners' group.* **3** to give someone money or equipment so that they can use it for a particular purpose

as•sign•ment /ə'saɪnmənt/ noun [C] a piece of work that you must do: *a homework assignment* ♦ *His first assignment as a reporter was to cover the local election.*

as•sim•i•late /ə'sɪmɪˌleɪt/ verb **1** [I/T] to feel that you belong to the new community that you have started to live in, or to make someone feel like this **2** [T] to learn new ideas or information: *Picasso assimilated an amazing variety of techniques in his art.* —**as•sim•i•la•tion** /əˌsɪmɪ'leɪʃ(ə)n/ noun [U]

as•sist /ə'sɪst/ verb [I/T] ★ to help someone or something: *Her job is to assist the head chef.* ♦ *Several designers* ***assisted in the creation*** *of the garden.*

as•sis•tance /ə'sɪstəns/ noun [U] ★ help: *financial/military assistance* ♦ *He's been running the company* ***with the assistance of*** *his son.*

as•sis•tant¹ /ə'sɪstənt/ noun [C] ★★ someone whose job is to help another person in their work, for example by doing the easier parts of it: *a personal assistant*

as•sis•tant² /ə'sɪstənt/ adj an assistant manager, teacher, etc. is someone whose job is to help the main manager or teacher

as•so•ci•ate¹ /ə'soʊʃiˌeɪt/ verb [T] **1** to connect people or things in your mind: *Most people associate food with pleasure.* **2** if one thing is associated with another, they are connected: *The problem is often associated with heavy drinking.*

PHRASAL VERB **as'sociate with sb** formal to spend time with someone

as•so•ci•ate² /ə'soʊʃiət/ noun [C] someone that you work with

as•so•ci•ate³ /ə'soʊʃiət/ adj an associate position or job is not at the highest level: *an associate professor/director* ♦ *an associate producer/editor*

asˌsociate de'gree noun [C] the qualification you get when you have completed a two-year course of study at a COMMUNITY COLLEGE in the U.S.

as•so•ci•a•tion /əˌsoʊʃi'eɪʃ(ə)n/ noun ★

1 [C] an organization for people who have similar interests or goals: *the Parent Teacher Association*

2 [C] a connection between people or things: *Smoking has a close* ***association with*** *lung cancer.*

3 associations [plural] memories or feelings that are connected with a particular place or event: *The town has many happy childhood associations for me.*

PHRASE **in association with** with the help of a person or organization

as•sort•ed /ə'sɔrtəd/ adj including various types

as•sort•ment /ə'sɔrtmənt/ noun [C] a group of things of various types

as•sume /ə'sum/ verb [T] ★

1 to believe that something is true, even though you cannot be certain: **+(that)** *I'm assuming everyone here has an e-mail address.*

2 formal to start to control something or take an important position: *His first priority was assuming control of the army.*

3 formal to pretend to have a particular feeling or attitude: *Fay assumed an air of innocence.*

as•sumed name /əˌsumd 'neɪm/ noun [C] a name that someone uses so that no one will know their real name

as•sum•ing /ə'sumɪŋ/ conjunction if: sometimes used for emphasizing that something may not be true

as•sump•tion /ə'sʌmpʃ(ə)n/ noun **1** [C] something that you think is likely to be true, although you cannot be certain **2** [U] the process of starting to have power or responsibility

as•sur•ance /ə'ʃʊrəns/ noun **1** [C] a statement in which you tell someone that something is definitely true or will definitely happen **2** [U] the feeling of being certain or confident about something

as•sure /ə'ʃʊr/ verb [T] **1** formal to tell someone that something is definitely true or will definitely happen: *There's no mistake, I can assure you.* **2** to make certain that something happens

as•sured /ə'ʃʊrd/ adj confident and certain → SELF-ASSURED —**as•sur•ed•ly** /ə'ʃʊrədli/ adv

as•ter•isk /'æstərɪsk/ noun [C] the symbol *, used for showing that more information is given in a FOOTNOTE

as•ter•oid /'æstəˌrɔɪd/ noun [C] a mass of rock that moves around in space

asth•ma /'æzmə/ noun [U] a medical condition that makes it difficult to breathe

asth•mat•ic /æz'mætɪk/ noun [C] someone

who suffers from asthma —**asth•mat•ic** adj

a•ston•ish /əˈstɑnɪʃ/ verb [T] to surprise someone very much

a•ston•ished /əˈstɑnɪʃt/ adj very surprised: *We were astonished to hear that she'd lost her job.*

a•ston•ish•ing /əˈstɑnɪʃɪŋ/ adj very surprising: *It's astonishing that so many people watch that program.* —**a•ston•ish•ing•ly** adv

a•ston•ish•ment /əˈstɑnɪʃmənt/ noun [U] very great surprise

a•stound /əˈstaʊnd/ verb [T] to surprise or shock someone very much

a•stound•ed /əˈstaʊndəd/ adj very surprised or shocked

a•stound•ing /əˈstaʊndɪŋ/ adj very surprising or shocking

a•stray /əˈstreɪ/ adv
PHRASES **go astray** to become lost: *The check I sent them seems to have gone astray.*
lead sb astray to make someone behave badly

a•stride /əˈstraɪd/ preposition with one leg on each side of something: *sitting astride a bicycle*

as•trol•o•gy /əˈstrɑlədʒi/ noun [U] the study of how the stars and planets influence people's lives —**as•trol•o•ger** noun [C], **as•tro•log•i•cal** /ˌæstrəˈlɑdʒɪk(ə)l/ adj

as•tro•naut /ˈæstrəˌnɔt/ noun [C] someone who travels in space

as•tro•nom•i•cal /ˌæstrəˈnɑmɪk(ə)l/ adj
1 *informal* an astronomical amount is extremely large: *astronomical prices*
2 relating to the scientific study of the stars and planets

as•tron•o•my /əˈstrɑnəmi/ noun [U] the scientific study of stars and planets —**as•tron•o•mer** noun [C]

as•tute /əˈstut/ adj good at making decisions that benefit you: *an astute judge of the stock market* —**as•tute•ly** adv

a•sy•lum /əˈsaɪləm/ noun **1** [U] the right to stay in a country that you have come to because you were in a dangerous situation in your own country **2** [C] *old-fashioned* a hospital for people with mental illnesses

a•sy•lum seek•er /əˈsaɪləm ˌsikər/ noun [C] someone who wants permission to stay in another country because their own country is dangerous

a•sym•met•ri•cal /ˌeɪsɪˈmetrɪk(ə)l/ or **a•sym•met•ric** /ˌeɪsɪˈmetrɪk/ adj something that is asymmetrical does not have the same shape and size on both sides

at /*weak* ət, *strong* æt/ preposition ★★★
1 **in a place** in a particular place: *I'll meet you at the main entrance.* ♦ *Does this train stop at Newport?* ♦ *We live at 23 Brookfield Avenue.* ♦ *Andy's at the doctor's – he'll be back soon.* ♦ *I'm babysitting at Sally's* (=at Sally's house) *tomorrow night.* ♦ *He wants to spend more time* ***at home*** *with his family.* ♦ *Dad should be* ***at work*** *by now.*
2 **near sth** sitting or standing close to something: *She was standing at the window, staring out.* ♦ *Why isn't he at his desk?*
3 **used for saying when sth happens** used for saying what time something happens, or someone's age when something happens: *The game starts at three o'clock.* ♦ ***At night*** *temperatures sometimes fall to 30 degrees below zero.* ♦ *Mozart was already composing music* ***at the age of*** *five.*
4 **during a process** in a particular part of a process or series of events: *He dies right* ***at the start of*** *the movie.* ♦ ***At some point*** *things started to go wrong.*
5 **doing sth** taking part in an activity, or involved in a situation: *We were at a party last night when you called.*
6 **used for talking about reactions** used for stating what causes a particular reaction: *Audiences still laugh at his jokes.* ♦ *She was annoyed at being interrupted.*
7 **used with levels and amounts** used for showing the level of prices, temperatures, speeds, etc.: *His Ferrari crashed at 120 miles an hour.* ♦ *The plastic pipes will melt at high temperatures.*
8 **in a particular direction** used for saying where an action such as looking, pointing, or hitting is directed: *Why are you staring at me like that?* ♦ *She swung her bat at the ball, but missed.*
9 **used for talking about abilities** used for saying which skills or abilities someone has or does not have: *I've never been very good at sports.* ♦ *He is an expert at getting what he wants.*
10 **used for giving phone numbers** *American* used for stating the phone number where someone can be reached: *You can reach us at 555-3964.*
PHRASES **at all** used for emphasis when you are saying or asking whether something is even slightly true: *Has the situation improved at all?* ♦ *Don't you have* ***any money at all?*** ♦ *He knows* ***nothing at all*** *about computers.*
at sth's best/worst/strongest etc. showing the best/worst etc. qualities of something: *This is British cooking at its best.*

ate the past tense of **eat**

a•the•ist /ˈeɪθiɪst/ noun [C] someone who believes that God does not exist → AGNOSTIC —**a•the•ism** /ˈeɪθiˌɪzəm/ noun [U]

ath•lete /ˈæθˌlit/ noun [C] someone who is good at sports and takes part in sports competitions

ath•let•ic /æθˈletɪk/ adj **1** physically strong and good at sports **2** relating to athletes or ATHLETICS

ath•let•ics /æθˈletɪks/ noun [U] *American* sports and other physical activities

at•las /ˈætləs/ noun [C] a book of maps

ATM /ˌeɪ ti ˈem/ noun [C] automated teller machine: a machine that you use to take money out of your bank account

at•mos•phere /ˈætməˌsfɪr/ noun [singular] ★★
1 the mood that exists in a place and affects the people there: *There is an* ***atmosphere of*** *tension in the city today.*
2 the air around the Earth or around another planet: *The Earth's atmosphere is getting warmer.*
3 the air inside a room or other place

at•mos•pher•ic /ˌætməˈsferɪk/ adj **1** existing in the atmosphere **2** creating a special mood or feeling

at•om /ˈætəm/ noun [C] the smallest unit of a chemical element

ˈatom ˌbomb or **aˌtomic ˈbomb** noun [C] a bomb that causes a very large nuclear explosion

a·tom·ic /əˈtɑmɪk/ adj *science* **1** using the energy that is produced by SPLITTING atoms (=breaking them apart) **2** relating to the atoms in a substance

a·tone /əˈtoʊn/ verb [I] *formal* to do something that shows that you are sorry —**a·tone·ment** noun [U]

a·tro·cious /əˈtroʊʃəs/ adj extremely bad: *atrocious weather conditions* —**a·tro·cious·ly** adv

a·troc·i·ty /əˈtrɑsəti/ noun [C/U] something very cruel and violent that someone does

at·tach /əˈtætʃ/ verb [T] ★

1 attach sth to sth to fasten one thing to another: *Attach the rope to the branch of a tree.*

2 to send another document with a letter or an e-mail: *I attach a copy of his reply.*

3 be attached to if one thing is attached to another, it is part of it: *There is a riding school attached to the farm.*

4 be attached to to be sent to work temporarily in a different place: *She is now attached to the American Embassy in Beijing.*

PHRASE **attach importance/significance/value/weight to sth** to think that something is important or true and that it should be considered seriously

at·tached /əˈtætʃt/ adj **1** joined or fixed to something **2 attached to sth/sb** if you are attached to something or someone, you like them very much: *Danny is very attached to his teddy bear.*

at·tach·ment /əˈtætʃmənt/ noun **1** [C/U] a feeling of liking a person or place very much **2** [C] a computer file that you send with an e-mail **3** [C] a special tool that you attach to something in order to do a particular job

at·tack¹ /əˈtæk/ noun ★★★

1 [C/U] a violent attempt to harm someone or something: *a vicious **attack on** an unarmed man* ♦ *The city was **under attack** throughout the night.*

2 [C] strong criticism: *The book is seen as **an attack on** the education system.*

3 [C] an occasion when you are affected by an illness, or when you have a particular strong feeling: *an asthma attack* ♦ ***an attack of nerves*** → HEART ATTACK

4 [C] an attempt to score points in a game

> **Words often used with attack**
>
> *Adjectives often used with **attack** (noun, sense 2)*
> ■ **bitter, fierce, scathing, stinging** + ATTACK: used about attacks that show strong criticism
>
> *Verbs often used with **attack** (noun, sense 2)*
> ■ **launch, mount** + ATTACK: make an attack

at·tack² /əˈtæk/ verb ★★★

1 [I/T] to use violence against a person or place: *It was shortly before midnight when the terrorists attacked.* ♦ **attack sb with sth** *Two prison officers were brutally attacked with a knife.*

2 [T] to strongly criticize someone or something: **attack sb/sth for (doing) sth** *Congress is being attacked for failing to take action.*

3 [I/T] to cause damage or disease in something: *The virus attacks the body's red blood cells.*

4 [I/T] to try to score points in a game: *They attack well, but their defense is weak.*

> **Words often used with attack**
>
> *Adverbs often used with **attack** (verb, sense 2)*
> ■ ATTACK + **bitterly, fiercely, openly, strongly, vigorously**: used for saying that someone expresses strong criticism

at·tack·er /əˈtækər/ noun [C] someone who physically attacks someone else

at·tain /əˈteɪn/ verb [T] *formal* to succeed in achieving something that involves a lot of effort = ACHIEVE —**at·tain·a·ble** adj, **at·tain·ment** noun [C/U]

at·tempt¹ /əˈtempt/ noun [C] ★★

1 an effort to do something: **an attempt to do sth** *the president's final attempt to reach a settlement with the rebel forces* ♦ *an **attempt on** the world record* ♦ *It's his fourth **attempt at** flying a balloon around the world.*

2 an attack on someone that is intended to kill them but fails: *an assassination attempt*

at·tempt² /əˈtempt/ verb [T] ★★ to try to do something: *Few people knew that she had once attempted suicide.* ♦ **attempt to do sth** *The book attempts to explain the origins of the war.*

at·tempt·ed /əˈtemptəd/ adj used about crimes that someone tries to commit without success: *attempted murder*

at·tend /əˈtend/ verb [I/T] ★★

1 to be present at an event or activity: *Most of his colleagues attended the wedding.*

2 to go regularly to a place such as a school or a church: *Born in India, he attended high school in Madras.*

PHRASAL VERB **atˈtend to sth** to deal with something: *We still have a number of other matters to attend to.*

at·ten·dance /əˈtendəns/ noun **1** [C/U] the number of people who are present at an event or in a place such as a school or church: *Church attendance dropped sharply in the 1970s.* ♦ *Attendance at the first meeting was high* (=there were a lot of people). **2** [U] the fact that someone is present in a place, or goes there regularly

PHRASE **in attendance** *formal* present at an important event

at·ten·dant /əˈtendənt/ noun [C] someone whose job is to help customers or people who visit a public place: *a museum attendant*

at·ten·tion /əˈtenʃ(ə)n/ noun [U] ★★★

1 the fact that you are listening to someone or something, or you are looking at them: *May I please **have your attention** – I have an important announcement.* ♦ *The man **paid** no **attention to** them.*

2 the fact that you know about something or notice something: *I have been asked to **draw your attention to** the following matters.* ♦ *We should **bring the problem to their attention**.*

3 special care, help, or treatment: *She needs urgent medical attention.*

atˈtention ˌspan noun [singular] the length of time that you can pay attention to one thing

A

without becoming bored or thinking about something else

at•ten•tive /əˈtentɪv/ adj **1** listening to or watching something carefully **2** behaving in a way that shows that you care about someone —**at•ten•tive•ly** adv, **at•ten•tive•ness** noun [U]

at•tic /ˈætɪk/ noun [C] the top floor of a house, directly under the roof —*picture* → C1

at•ti•tude /ˈætɪˌtud/ noun ★★★
1 [C/U] opinions or feelings that you show by your behavior: *We can win if we keep a positive attitude.* ♦ ***Attitudes toward** the older members of the group will have to change.*
2 [U] *informal* a proud confident way of behaving that some people think is rude: *There's no denying the guy has attitude.*

at•tor•ney /əˈtɜrni/ noun [C] *American* a lawyer

atˌtorney ˈgeneral noun [C] the most senior lawyer in some countries or U.S. states

at•tract /əˈtrækt/ verb [T] ★★
1 to make someone like something, or be interested in something: *The show attracts viewers from every sector of society.* ♦ **attract sb to sth** *What first attracted you to Buddhism?*
2 to cause people to behave in a particular way toward something: *His paintings have attracted considerable criticism.* ♦ *The trial attracted a lot of media interest.*
3 if you are attracted to someone, you are interested in them in a romantic or sexual way: *She's old enough now to be attracted to boys.*
4 to make something move near someone or something: *Insects are often attracted by smells that aren't obvious to us.*
PHRASE **attract (sb's) attention** to make someone notice someone or something

at•trac•tion /əˈtrækʃ(ə)n/ noun **1** [C] an interesting place or object that people come to see **2** [singular/U] the feeling of liking someone in a romantic or sexual way **3** [C/U] a reason for liking something or being interested in it

at•trac•tive /əˈtræktɪv/ adj ★★
1 nice to look at ≠ UNATTRACTIVE: *a stunningly attractive movie star*
2 worth having, thinking about, or doing: *a company that will be increasingly **attractive to** investors*

at•trib•ut•a•ble /əˈtrɪbjətəb(ə)l/ adj caused by a particular event, situation, or activity: *illnesses attributable to cigarette smoking*

at•trib•ute¹ /əˈtrɪˌbjut/ PHRASAL VERB
atˈtribute sth to sb/sth to believe that something was caused by something else, or done by someone else: *a painting attributed to Picasso*

at•trib•ute² /ˈætrɪˌbjut/ noun [C] *formal* a quality or feature

au•ber•gine /ˈoʊbərʒin/ noun [C/U] *British* an EGGPLANT

au•burn /ˈɔbərn/ adj auburn hair is red-brown in color

auc•tion¹ /ˈɔkʃ(ə)n/ noun [C] a public occasion when things are sold to the people who offer the most money for them

auc•tion² /ˈɔkʃ(ə)n/ verb [T] to sell something at an auction

auc•tion•eer /ˌɔkʃəˈnɪr/ noun [C] someone whose job is to sell things at an auction

au•da•cious /ɔˈdeɪʃəs/ adj done with extreme confidence, or behaving with extreme confidence

au•dac•i•ty /ɔˈdæsəti/ noun [U] the confidence to say or do what you want, despite difficulties, risks, or the negative attitudes of other people

au•di•ble /ˈɔdɪb(ə)l/ adj loud enough for people to hear —**au•di•bly** adv

au•di•ence /ˈɔdiəns/ noun [C] ★★★
1 the people who watch or listen to a performance: *Chaplin's movies were loved by audiences throughout the world.* ♦ *His jokes offended many people in the audience.*
2 all the people who watch a particular television program, read a particular book, etc.: *The series has attracted an audience of more than 10 million.*
3 a formal meeting with a very important person: ***an audience with** the Pope*

au•di•o /ˈɔdiˌoʊ/ adj relating to sound that is recorded or broadcast

au•di•o•vis•u•al /ˌɔdioʊˈvɪʒuəl/ adj using both recorded sounds and images

au•dit¹ /ˈɔdɪt/ noun [C] an official examination of a company's financial or tax records

au•dit² /ˈɔdɪt/ verb [T] **1** to officially examine the financial or tax records of a company **2** *American* to go regularly to a college class without asking for or receiving CREDIT for it

au•di•tion¹ /ɔˈdɪʃ(ə)n/ noun [C] an occasion when you sing, dance, or act so that someone can decide if you are good enough to perform

au•di•tion² /ɔˈdɪʃ(ə)n/ verb [I] to perform at an audition: *She auditioned for a part in Tarantino's next movie.*

au•di•tor /ˈɔdɪtər/ noun [C] someone whose job is to examine the financial or tax records of a company

au•di•to•ri•um /ˌɔdɪˈtɔriəm/ noun [C] a large room or building used for meetings, lectures, or public performances

aug•ment /ɔgˈment/ verb [T] *formal* to increase the size, amount, or value of something

au•gur /ˈɔgər/ verb [I/T] *formal* to be a sign of what may happen in the future: *The look on her face did not augur well.*

Au•gust /ˈɔgəst/ noun [C/U] ★★★ the eighth month of the year, between July and September: *We'll be on vacation in August.* ♦ *It's my birthday on August 6th.*

aunt /ænt/ noun [C] ★★ the sister of your mother or father, or the wife of your UNCLE: *I loved visiting my aunt and uncle.* ♦ *Hello, Aunt Betty.* —*picture* → FAMILY TREE

au pair /oʊ ˈper/ noun [C] a young woman who lives with a family in a foreign country and helps to take care of their children

au•ra /ˈɔrə/ noun [C] a quality that seems to come from a person or place: *an aura of innocence*

aus•pi•ces /ˈɔspɪsəz/ noun **under the auspices of** *formal* with the help and support of a particular person or organization

aus•pi•cious /ɔˈspɪʃəs/ adj *formal* showing

signs that suggest that something will be successful

Aus•sie /ˈɔzi/ noun [C] *informal* someone from Australia

aus•tere /ɔˈstɪr/ adj **1** plain or simple in style **2** severe or strict in manner

aus•ter•i•ty /ɔˈsterəti/ noun [U] **1** a bad economic situation in which people do not have much money **2** the quality of being austere

Aus•tral•a•sia /ˌɔstrəˈleɪʒə/ a region that includes Australia, New Zealand, New Guinea, and some South Pacific islands

au•then•tic /ɔˈθentɪk/ adj **1** real, not false or copied = GENUINE: *The letter is certainly authentic.* **2** based on facts: *an authentic account of life in rural China* —**au•then•tic•i•ty** /ˌɔθenˈtɪsəti/ noun [U]

au•thor[1] /ˈɔθər/ noun [C] ★★
1 someone who writes books or articles as their job
2 the person who wrote a particular document or other piece of writing: *the author of the report*

au•thor[2] /ˈɔθər/ verb [T] to write a book or article

au•thor•i•tar•i•an /ɔˌθɔrɪˈteriən/ adj controlling everything and forcing people to obey strict rules

au•thor•i•ta•tive /ɔˈθɔrɪˌteɪtɪv/ adj based on careful research and the most reliable information: *an authoritative report on climate change*

au•thor•i•ty /ɔˈθɔrəti/ noun ★★

1 power	4 expert in subject
2 people with power	5 official permission
3 organization	

1 [U] the power to make decisions and make people do what you want: *The president's authority is being questioned in the press.* ♦ *Parents **have legal authority over** their children.* ♦ *I don't **have the authority to** hire staff.*
2 the authorities [plural] the police or other organizations with legal power to make people obey laws: *The French authorities have refused to issue him a visa.*
3 [C] an organization or institution that controls a public service: *the Port Authority of New York and New Jersey*
4 [C] an expert on a particular subject: *Charles was an **authority on** antique musical instruments.*
5 [U] *formal* official permission to do something: *We do not release the names of our customers without their authority.*

au•thor•ize /ˈɔθəˌraɪz/ verb [T] to give official permission for something: *The guard is authorized to carry a gun.* —**au•thor•i•za•tion** /ˌɔθərɪˈzeɪʃ(ə)n/ noun [U]

au•tism /ˈɔˌtɪzəm/ noun [U] a serious mental condition that makes it difficult to communicate with other people —**au•tis•tic** /ɔˈtɪstɪk/ adj

au•to /ˈɔtoʊ/ adj *American* relating to cars: *auto parts*

au•to•bi•og•ra•phy /ˌɔtoʊbaɪˈɑgrəfi/ noun [C] a book about your life that you write yourself —**au•to•bi•o•graph•i•cal** /ˌɔtoʊbaɪəˈgræfɪk(ə)l/ adj

au•to•crat•ic /ˌɔtəˈkrætɪk/ adj ruling in a strict or cruel way —**au•to•crat** noun [C]

au•to•graph /ˈɔtəˌgræf/ noun [C] a famous person's name that they sign on something —**au•to•graph** verb [T]

au•to•mak•er /ˈɔtoʊˌmeɪkər/ noun [C] *American* a company that produces cars

au•to•mat•ed /ˈɔtəˌmeɪtəd/ adj using machines instead of people

au•to•mat•ic[1] /ˌɔtəˈmætɪk/ adj ★
1 an automatic machine can work by itself without being operated by people: *an automatic garage door* → MANUAL[2], SEMIAUTOMATIC
2 happening as part of an established process, without a special decision being made: *Taxpayers who do not send in their forms face an automatic penalty.*
3 an automatic action is something that you do without thinking, or without intending to do it: *an automatic response* —**au•to•mat•i•cal•ly** /ˌɔtəˈmætɪkli/ adv: *He automatically assumed that the engineer would be a man.*

au•to•mat•ic[2] /ˌɔtəˈmætɪk/ noun [C] **1** a car in which the GEARS change by themselves **2** a weapon that shoots bullets until you take your finger off the TRIGGER

au•to•ma•tion /ˌɔtəˈmeɪʃ(ə)n/ noun [U] a system that uses machines to do work instead of people, or the process of changing to such a system

au•to•mo•bile[1] /ˈɔtəməˌbil/ adj relating to cars

au•to•mo•bile[2] /ˈɔtəməˌbil/ noun [C] *old-fashioned* a car

au•to•mo•tive /ˌɔtəˈmoʊtɪv/ adj relating to cars: *the automotive industry*

au•ton•o•my /ɔˈtɑnəmi/ noun [U] **1** the right of a state, region, or organization to govern itself = INDEPENDENCE **2** the power to make your own decisions = INDEPENDENCE —**au•ton•o•mous** /ɔˈtɑnəməs/ adj

au•top•sy /ˈɔˌtɑpsi/ noun [C] a medical examination of a dead person's body that is done in order to find out why they died

au•tumn /ˈɔtəm/ noun [C/U] the season of the year that comes between summer and winter —**au•tum•nal** /ɔˈtʌmnəl/ adj

aux•il•ia•ry /ɔgˈzɪljəri/ adj **1** additional and available for use: *an auxiliary engine* **2** helping more senior or permanent workers: *auxiliary nurses*

auxˌiliary ˈverb noun [C] *linguistics* a verb that is used with another verb to form questions, tenses, and negative or passive phrases. The main auxiliary verbs in English are "be," "have," and "do."

a•vail[1] /əˈveɪl/ noun **to no avail** *formal* without getting the effect that you wanted

a•vail[2] /əˈveɪl/ verb **avail yourself of sth** *formal* to use something

a•vail•a•ble /əˈveɪləb(ə)l/ adj ★★
1 able to be obtained, taken, or used ≠ UNAVAILABLE: *We'll notify you as soon as tickets become available.* ♦ *Not all the facts are made **available to** us.* ♦ *There is no money **available for** this project.*
2 not too busy to do something ≠ UNAVAILABLE: *I'm available next Tuesday if you want to meet then.* ♦ **available to do sth**

A

A

My professor is always available to talk to her students.
—**a•vail•a•bil•i•ty** /əˌveɪləˈbɪləti/ noun [U]: *Parents are concerned about the availability of drugs in the school.*

av•a•lanche /ˈævəˌlæntʃ/ noun [C] **1** a large amount of snow that suddenly falls down a mountain **2** a large quantity of things that arrive suddenly: *an avalanche of letters*

a•vant-garde /ˌɑvɑŋˈgɑrd/ adj very modern in style

Ave. abbrev Avenue: used in addresses

a•venge /əˈvendʒ/ verb [T] *formal* to react to something wrong by punishing the person who did it

av•e•nue /ˈævəˌnu/ noun [C] **1** a wide straight road in a town or city **2** a method of achieving something: *We tried every avenue, but couldn't borrow the money we needed.*

av•er•age¹ /ˈæv(ə)rɪdʒ/ noun ★
1 [C/U] the typical amount or level: *Unemployment here is twice the national average.* ♦ *Her performance in the test was* ***below average****.*
2 [C] an amount that is calculated by adding several numbers together and dividing the total by the number of things that you added together = MEAN
PHRASE **on average** used for talking about what is usually true, although it may not be true in every situation: *On average, women live longer than men.*

av•er•age² /ˈæv(ə)rɪdʒ/ adj ★★
1 usual or ordinary: *He's about average height.*
2 not very good = MEDIOCRE: *a very average performance*
3 calculated by adding several numbers together and dividing the total by the number of things that you added together: *winds with an average speed of 15 miles per hour*

av•er•age³ /ˈæv(ə)rɪdʒ/ verb [T] to usually do, have, or involve a particular level or amount: *The cost of developing a new drug now averages around $500 million.*

a•verse /əˈvɜrs/ adj **not averse to sth** if you are not averse to something, you like it or feel positive about it

a•ver•sion /əˈvɜrʒ(ə)n/ noun [C/U] *formal* a strong feeling that you dislike someone or something

a•vert /əˈvɜrt/ verb [T] to prevent something bad from happening: *We managed to avert disaster this time.*
PHRASE **avert your eyes** to look away from something that you do not want to see

a•vi•a•tion /ˌeɪviˈeɪʃ(ə)n/ noun [U] the activity of flying or making airplanes

av•id /ˈævɪd/ adj very enthusiastic —**av•id•ly** adv

av•o•ca•do /ˌævəˈkɑdoʊ/ noun [C/U] a fruit with green or black skin, a very large seed in the middle, and pale green flesh —*picture* → C10

a•void /əˈvɔɪd/ verb [T] ★★★
1 to stay away from someone or something: *We went early to avoid the crowds.*
2 to try to prevent something from happening: *Try to avoid confrontation.* ♦ **avoid doing sth** *I want to avoid being drawn into the argument.*
3 to choose not to do something: *He will avoid work whenever he can.* ♦ **avoid doing sth** *Where possible, we have avoided using technical terms.*
—**a•void•ance** /əˈvɔɪdəns/ noun [U]: *the avoidance of confrontation*

a•void•a•ble /əˈvɔɪdəb(ə)l/ adj capable of being prevented ≠ UNAVOIDABLE: *avoidable costs/mistakes/errors*

a•wait /əˈweɪt/ verb [T] *formal* **1** to wait for something: *They were awaiting the birth of their first child.* **2** if something awaits you, it will happen to you: *Well, I wonder what surprises await us today.*

a•wake¹ /əˈweɪk/ adj ★ not sleeping: *I've been awake for hours.* ♦ *Do you* ***lie awake*** *at night, worrying about things?* ♦ *I managed to* ***stay awake*** *long enough to watch the movie.* ♦ *We've been* ***kept awake*** *all night by the noise.* ♦ *When the alarm went off, I was already* ***wide awake*** (=completely awake).

a•wake² /əˈweɪk/ (past tense **a•woke** /əˈwoʊk/; past participle **a•wok•en** /əˈwoʊkən/) verb [I/T] to wake up, or to wake someone up: *They awoke to find that several inches of snow had fallen.*

a•wak•en /əˈweɪkən/ verb *formal* **1** [T] to make someone have a particular feeling **2** [I/T] to wake up, or to wake someone up

a•wak•en•ing /əˈweɪkənɪŋ/ noun [singular] the moment when you first realize or experience something

a•ward¹ /əˈwɔrd/ noun [C] ★★
1 a prize that is given to someone who has achieved something: *She won the Player of the Year award.* ♦ *an* ***award for*** *outstanding services to the industry*
2 an amount of money that is given by a court of law or other authority: *an award for compensation*

a•ward² /əˈwɔrd/ verb [T] ★
1 to give someone a prize: *Students who complete the training successfully will be awarded a diploma.*
2 to officially give someone something such as a contract or an amount of money: *He has been awarded a scholarship to do research.*

a•ware /əˈwer/ adj ★★★
1 knowing about a situation or fact ≠ UNAWARE: ***As far as I'm aware****, he didn't tell her anything.* ♦ **+that** *I was not aware that she had already talked to you.* ♦ *They're* ***aware of*** *the dangers.* ♦ *I was* ***well aware*** *of this fact.*
2 interested and involved in something: *The organization aims to create a new generation of* ***environmentally aware*** *consumers.*
3 if you become aware of someone or something, you notice them: *I became aware of someone following me.* ♦ **+that** *He suddenly became aware that the music had stopped.*
—**a•ware•ness** noun [U]: *The aim of our campaign is to* ***raise awareness about*** (=make people learn about) *heart disease.*

a•wash /əˈwɑʃ/ adj **1** thoroughly covered with a liquid **2** full of something or having a lot of something: *The town is awash with tourists this time of year.*

a·way¹ /əˈweɪ/ adv ★★★

1 in a different direction in a direction that takes you farther from a person, place, or thing: *When Sykes saw the police, he ran away.* ♦ *Bruce was staring at her, but she looked away.* ♦ *Please move **away from** the doors.*

2 not in your usual place not at home, or not at the place where you work or study: *My brother takes care of the farm while I'm away.* ♦ *Amy has spent a lot of time **away from** school.*

3 not near at a distance from someone or something: *The nearest hospital is 30 miles away.* ♦ *Keep **away from** the stove – it's very hot.*

4 removing sth used for showing that something is removed: *We need to have this garbage taken away.* ♦ *She wiped away her tears.*

5 after a period of time used for saying how much time will pass before something happens: *Final exams are less than three weeks away.*

6 gradually disappearing used for saying that something gradually disappears: *The sound of their voices faded away into the distance.*

7 doing sth continuously doing something continuously or for a long time: *Molly was at her desk working away as usual.*

8 in a safe or usual place in a safe place, or in the place where something is usually kept: *Put your toys away before you go to bed.*

a·way² /əˈweɪ/ adj an away game is one in which a team goes to their opponents' place to play

awe /ɔ/ noun [U] a feeling of great respect and admiration: *He is totally in awe of his father.*

ˈawe-inˌspiring adj making you feel great respect and admiration

awe·some /ˈɔsəm/ adj **1** very impressive and sometimes a little frightening **2** *informal* extremely good

aw·ful /ˈɔf(ə)l/ adj ★★ extremely bad =TERRIBLE: *This wine tastes awful.* ♦ *That's an awful thing to say.* ♦ *He had the awful feeling that everyone was laughing at him.*

PHRASES **an awful lot** *spoken* a very large amount: *There were an awful lot of people just standing around.*

look/feel awful to look or feel sick or sad

aw·ful·ly /ˈɔf(ə)li/ adv *spoken* extremely: *It's awfully cold in here.*

a·while /əˈwaɪl, əˈhwaɪl/ adv for a short time

awk·ward /ˈɔkwərd/ adj **1** difficult and embarrassing: *Luckily, nobody asked any awkward questions.* **2** not comfortable, relaxed, or confident: *He stood there looking stiff and awkward in his uniform.* **3** an object that is awkward is difficult to use or carry because of its shape or position

awk·ward·ly /ˈɔkwərdli/ adv **1** in a way that shows you are not comfortable, relaxed, or confident: *They smiled awkwardly at the camera.* **2** in a way that is not graceful: *He scrambled awkwardly to his feet.*

awn·ing /ˈɔnɪŋ/ noun [C] a sheet of cloth above a window or door, used as protection against the rain or sun

awoke the past tense of **awake²**

awoken the past participle of **awake²**

a·wry /əˈraɪ/ adj **go awry** to not happen in the way that was planned

ax¹ or **axe** /æks/ noun [C] a tool used for cutting wood, consisting of a long wooden handle and a heavy metal blade

ax² /æks/ verb [T] to end or reduce something: *The program was almost axed by the network.*

ax·is /ˈæksɪs/ (plural **ax·es** /ˈækˌsiz/) noun [C] **1** an imaginary line through the middle of an object, around which the object spins **2** one of the two fixed lines that are used for showing measurements on a GRAPH

ax·le /ˈæks(ə)l/ noun [C] a metal bar that connects a pair of wheels on a car or other vehicle

aye /aɪ/ noun [C] *formal* a vote in support of something, or someone who votes this way

AZ abbrev Arizona

Bb

b or **B** /bi/ noun **1** [C] the second letter of the English alphabet **2 B** [C] a grade that is given in a school, college, or university for work that is better than average **3 B** [U] a common BLOOD TYPE

B abbrev be: used in e-mails and TEXT MESSAGES

b. abbrev born: used before the date of someone's birth

B & B /ˌbi ən ˈbi/ noun [C] a BED AND BREAKFAST

B.A. /ˌbi ˈeɪ/ noun [C] Bachelor of Arts: a first degree from a college or university in a subject such as languages or history: *Jen has a B.A. in literature.*

baa /bɑ/ verb [I] to make the sound that a sheep makes —**baa** noun [C]

bab·ble¹ /ˈbæb(ə)l/ verb [I/T] to speak quickly in a way that is boring or difficult to understand

bab·ble² /ˈbæb(ə)l/ noun [singular] the noise of a lot of voices all talking at the same time

babe /beɪb/ noun [C] **1** *literary* a baby **2** *informal* an attractive young woman or man. Many women think that this word is offensive.

ba·boon /bəˈbun/ noun [C] a type of large monkey from Africa or South Asia

ba·by /ˈbeɪbi/ noun [C] ★★★

1 young child	4 sb you love
2 sb being weak or silly	5 project you care about
3 young animal	

1 a very young child who cannot yet talk or walk: *their new baby daughter* ♦ *Sally's*

B

*going to **have a baby** (=give birth) in May.* —*picture* → CHILD
2 someone who is behaving in a way that is weak, silly, or not brave: *Don't be such a big baby!*
3 a very young animal: *a baby elephant*
4 *spoken* used for talking to someone you love: *What's the matter, baby?*
5 *informal* a project or piece of work that you care about a lot, especially because it was your idea: *Steve has always seen the book as his baby.*

ˈbaby ˌboomer noun [C] someone who was born during the period after World War Two when many babies were born

ˈbaby ˌcarriage noun [C] *American* a type of bed for a baby to sit or lie in, that has four wheels and a handle to push it with

ba•by•ish /ˈbeɪbiɪʃ/ adj *showing disapproval* appropriate only for a baby or young child

ˈbaby ˌoil noun [C/U] a type of oil that you put on your skin to make it softer

ba•by•sit /ˈbeɪbiˌsɪt/ (past tense and past participle **ba•by•sat** /ˈbeɪbiˌsæt/) verb [I/T] to take care of children while their parents are not at home —**ba•by•sit•ter** noun [U], **ba•by•sit•ting** noun [U]

bach•e•lor /ˈbætʃələr/ noun [C] a man who has never been married

ˈbachelor ˌparty noun [C] *American* a party for men only, to celebrate the fact that one of them will be getting married soon

ˈbachelor's deˌgree noun [C] a first university degree

back¹ /bæk/ adv ★★★

1 returning to place	5 away from sb/sth
2 as reply or reaction	6 in/into the past
3 to earlier state	7 in a different place
4 away from the front	+ PHRASE

1 returning to a place or position: *Put those CDs back where you found them.* ♦ *Can we go back to what we were talking about earlier?*
2 as a reply or reaction to what someone else has said or done: *Jane called, and I said you'd call her back later.* ♦ *Just because he hit you doesn't mean you have to hit him back.*
3 returning to an earlier state or condition: *We're hoping things will be back to normal again soon.* ♦ *I couldn't get back to sleep.*
4 in the direction that is behind you: *Don't look back, but there's a man following us.*
5 away from a person, thing, or position: *Get back – he has a gun!* ♦ *The band started playing as the curtain slowly went back.*
6 in or to a time in the past: *Back in the '70s, disco music was very popular.* ♦ *Think back; don't you remember anything?*
7 used for talking about a place that you mentioned or were in before: *I have no idea what's going on back home.* ♦ *Back at the hospital, the baby had just been born.*
PHRASE **back and forth** moving first in one direction and then in the opposite direction many times
→ BACK-TO-BACK

back² /bæk/ adj ★★
1 farthest from the front ≠ FRONT: *There's a map on the back page.*
2 used for describing money that is owed from an earlier date and has not been paid yet: *back pay/taxes/rent*
PHRASE **back street/road** a street/road that is away from any main streets/roads

back³ /bæk/ noun [C] ★★★
1 the part of your body between your neck and your bottom, on the opposite side to your chest and stomach: *I have a pain in my back.* ♦ *She was lying **flat on her back** on the bed.* —*picture* → C14
2 the part or side of something that is farthest from the front ≠ FRONT: *Get in **the back of** the car.* ♦ *The sun burned **the back** of my neck.* ♦ *a cotton dress with a bow **in back*** ♦ *I'll put my name **on the back of** the envelope.* —*picture* → C14
3 an outside area behind a building: *The kids are playing **out back**.* ♦ *We caught them hiding **in back of** (=behind) the house.*
4 the part of a chair that you lean on when you are sitting on it: *What's that mark on the back of the sofa?*
PHRASES **behind sb's back** if you do something bad or unkind behind someone's back, you do it without them knowing
get off my back *spoken* used for telling someone to stop criticizing you or to stop telling you what to do
have your back to the wall to be in a difficult situation with few choices, so that you have to work or fight very hard
in the back of your mind if something is in the back of your mind, you are slightly conscious of it all the time
on sb's back *informal* criticizing someone, or telling them to do things
on the back of sth because of something, or helped by something: *Share prices rose sharply on the back of a rise in profits.*
when sb's back is turned when someone is not there, or is not paying attention: *As soon as her back is turned, he's flirting with other women!*
→ TURN¹

back⁴ /bæk/ verb ★
1 [T] to support a person, organization, or plan, so that they are more likely to succeed: *Both main parties are backing these proposals.*
2 [I/T] to move backward, or to make a person or a vehicle move backward: *She **backed out of** the room carrying a tray.* ♦ **back sb into sth** *Steve backed me into a corner at the party.*
3 [T] to risk an amount of money by saying that a particular person or animal will win a race or competition
PHRASAL VERBS **ˌback ˈdown** to stop asking for something, or to stop saying that you will do something, because a lot of people oppose you: *Neither side is willing to back down.*
ˌback ˈoff 1 to move backward in order to get farther away from something **2** to stop criticizing someone or telling them what to do: *Back off, OK? I'll tell you when I'm ready!*
ˌback ˈout to refuse to do something that you agreed to do: *We're hoping that no one will **back out of** the deal.*

ˌback ˈup to move backward a short distance
ˌback (sth) ˈup **1** to make a copy of information on your computer **2** to make a car go backward
ˌback sb ˈup to give support to someone by telling other people that you agree with them: *If I file a complaint, will you back me up?*
ˌback sth ˈup to show that an explanation or belief is probably true: *All the evidence backs up her story.*

back•ache /ˈbækˌeɪk/ noun [C/U] pain in your back

back•board /ˈbækˌbɔrd/ noun [C] in basketball, the board behind the BASKET (=net) —*picture* → C15

back•bone /ˈbækˌboʊn/ noun **1** [C] the row of small bones that goes down the middle of your back=SPINE **2** [U] the determination and strong personality that you need in order to deal with a difficult situation

PHRASE **the backbone of sth** the part of something that makes it successful or strong: *Our volunteers are the backbone of our organization.*

back•date /ˌbækˈdeɪt/ verb [T] **1** to make a rule or law start to be effective from a date in the past **2** to write a date on a document or check that is earlier than the real date

back•drop /ˈbækˌdrɑp/ noun [C] the situation or place in which something happens: *Negotiations were carried out against a backdrop of continued fighting.*

back•er /ˈbækər/ noun [C] someone who gives help or money to a plan or organization

back•fire /ˈbækˌfaɪr/ verb [I] **1** if a plan or idea backfires, it has the opposite effect of the one that you wanted **2** if a car backfires, its engine makes a loud noise like an explosion

back•gam•mon /ˈbækˌgæmən/ noun [U] a game for two people that you play on a board using DICE and two sets of round pieces —*picture* → C16

back•ground /ˈbækˌgraʊnd/ noun ★★

1 sb's experiences	4 extra sounds
2 information	5 general situation
3 position behind sb/sth	+ PHRASE

1 [C] the general experiences and influences that have formed someone's character, or the type of education and training they have had: *students from very different backgrounds* ♦ *We are looking for writers with* ***a background in*** *law.*
2 [singular/U] information and details that help you to understand a situation: *We need to know* ***the background to*** *the case.* ♦ *You'll need some* ***background information*** *on the local economy.*
3 [C] the part of a picture or pattern that is behind the main people or things in it ≠ FOREGROUND, THE: *a picture of palm trees with mountains* ***in the background***
4 [singular] the sounds that you can hear in addition to the main thing that you are listening to: *background noise/music* ♦ *I could hear a TV* ***in the background.***
5 [singular/U] the general situation in which something happens: *The statement was made* ***against a background of*** *intense pressure from the government.*

PHRASE **in the background** in a place or situation in which people do not notice you: *Jo does the publicity work, while Ed stays pretty much in the background.*

> **Words often used with background**
> *Adjectives often used with* ***background*** *(sense 1)*
> ■ **cultural, educational, ethnic, religious, social** + BACKGROUND: used about a particular type of background

back•hand /ˈbækˌhænd/ noun [C] in tennis and similar sports, a movement made to hit the ball in which the back of your hand moves toward the ball

back•ing /ˈbækɪŋ/ noun [U] support, help, or strong approval: *The new policy has the backing of several leading Democrats.*

back•lash /ˈbækˌlæʃ/ noun [C] a strong, negative, and often angry reaction to something that has happened

back•log /ˈbækˌlɑg/ noun [singular] an amount of work that you should already have finished

back•pack /ˈbækˌpæk/ noun [C] a large bag that you carry on your back —*picture* → BAG

back•pack•er /ˈbækˌpækər/ noun [C] someone, especially a young person without much money, who travels around an area on foot or public transportation —**back•pack•ing** noun [U]

back•ped•al /bækˈped(ə)l, ˈbækˌped(ə)l/ verb [I] to show that you are no longer certain about a previous opinion, intention, or promise: *Congress is backpedaling on the proposed legislation.*

ˌback ˈseat noun [C] a seat behind the driver of a car

PHRASE **take a back seat** to become less important: *Other issues must take a back seat to this crisis.*

ˌback seat ˈdriver noun [C] someone in a car who keeps telling the driver how to drive

back•side /ˈbækˌsaɪd/ noun [C] *informal* the part of your body that you sit on

back•slash /ˈbækˌslæʃ/ noun [C] the symbol \ used for separating words or numbers, especially in the names of computer files

back•stage /bækˈsteɪdʒ/ adv in the area behind the stage in a theater, which includes the rooms where the actors get dressed

back•swing /ˈbækˌswɪŋ/ noun [C] the first part of the movement you make when hitting a ball in golf, starting with the CLUB on the ground and moving it into the air above your head

ˌback-to-ˈback adj, adv **1** happening one after the other: *back-to-back games* **2** with the back of someone or something against the back of someone or something else: *chairs placed back-to-back*

back•track /ˈbækˌtræk/ verb [I] **1** to go back in the direction from which you have come **2** to show that you have become less likely to do something that you said you would do: *The government is backtracking on its commitment to increase spending.*

back•up /ˈbækˌʌp/ noun **1** [C] *computing* a copy of information on your computer that you make in case you lose the original information **2** [C/U] people or equipment that can be used when extra help is needed: *The gang was armed, so the police called for backup.* ♦ *a backup generator/crew*

B

back·ward¹ /ˈbækwərd/ or **back·wards** /ˈbækwərdz/ adv ★★★

1 in the direction that is behind you: *The car rolled backward down the hill.*

2 in the opposite way or order from usual: *Count backward from ten to one.* ♦ *Your shirt is on backward.*

3 toward a time in the past: *We should plan for the future, not look backward.*

PHRASE **backward and forward** moving first in one direction and then in the opposite direction

→ BEND¹

back·ward² /ˈbækwərd/ adj **1** moving or looking in the direction that is behind you: *a backward glance* **2** not developing quickly, normally, or successfully: *a remote and backward region*

back·wa·ter /ˈbækˌwɔtər/ noun [singular] a place far from main cities where nothing exciting or important happens

back·yard /ˌbækˈjɑrd/ noun [C] *American* an area behind a house, usually with grass and plants

PHRASE **in your (own) backyard** *informal* close to where you live, or in a situation that you are directly involved in

ba·con /ˈbeɪkən/ noun [U] meat from a pig that is treated with smoke or salt, and is often cooked in RASHERS (=thin pieces)

bac·te·ri·a /bækˈtɪriə/ noun [plural] very small living things that consist of a single cell. Some types of bacteria cause diseases. —**bac·te·ri·al** adj

bad¹ /bæd/ (comparative **worse** /wɜrs/; superlative **worst** /wɜrst/) adj ★★★

1 not nice or enjoyable	5 painful/injured
2 causing problems	6 evil/behaving badly
3 of low quality/skill	7 not fresh anymore
4 not appropriate	+ PHRASES

1 not nice or enjoyable: *The weather was really bad – it rained all week.* ♦ *I'm afraid I have some bad news for you.*

2 causing major problems, harm, or damage: *a bad accident/mistake/case of the flu* ♦ *I tried to help, but I just made things worse.* ♦ *Too much salt can be* **bad for** *your heart.*

3 showing a lack of quality or skill: *one of this year's worst movies* ♦ *a bad driver/teacher* ♦ *I'm really* **bad at** *remembering people's names.*

4 not appropriate or convenient: *I can come back later if this is a bad time for you.*

5 painful or injured: *a bad back/leg/stomach*

6 cruel, evil, or morally wrong

7 no longer fresh or good to eat or drink: *It will* **go bad** *if you don't put it in the refrigerator.*

PHRASES **feel bad (about)** to feel guilty or unhappy about something: *Tim felt bad about leaving without saying goodbye.*

not bad *informal* fairly good, or better than you expected: *Those pictures aren't bad for a beginner.*

too bad *spoken* **1** used for showing that you are sorry or sympathetic about something: *That's too bad about your sister losing her job.* **2** used for showing that you are not sympathetic at all, or that you do not really care what someone else thinks: *If you don't like the truth, that's just too bad.*

→ BADLY

Words that you can use instead of bad

Bad is a very general word. Here are some words with more specific meanings that sound more natural and appropriate in particular situations.

meal/film/TV show/weather/behavior/book/party	appalling, awful, terrible (*informal*)
person	horrible, mean, nasty, unpleasant, wicked
illness/injury/problem	major, serious, severe
performance/piece of work/teacher/singer	not much good (*informal*), poor, terrible (*informal*), useless (*informal*)
something that causes harm or bad effects	damaging, dangerous, harmful, poisonous, toxic, unhealthy

bad² /bæd/ adv *spoken* badly. Many people think that this use is incorrect.

ˌbad ˈblood noun [U] angry feelings that people still have toward each other because of something that happened in the past

ˌbad ˈdebt noun [C] money that someone owes but will never pay

badge /bædʒ/ noun [C] a special piece of metal, cloth, or plastic with words or symbols on it. You wear it or carry it to show your official position: *a police badge*

badg·er¹ /ˈbædʒər/ verb [T] to try to make someone do something by asking them many times: *They keep badgering me to take them to the show.*

badg·er² /ˈbædʒər/ noun [C] a wild animal with dark fur and a white area on its head. It lives in a hole in the ground. —*picture* → C13

bad ˈlanguage noun [U] rude words

bad·ly /ˈbædli/ (comparative **worse** /wɜrs/; superlative **worst** /wɜrst/) adv ★★

1 in a way that is not skillful, effective, or successful: *She spoke French so badly I couldn't understand her.* ♦ *a badly organized meeting*

2 in a serious or severe way: *One of the prisoners had been badly beaten by guards.*

3 in an unkind, unfair, or unreasonable way: *She feels she has been badly treated.*

4 if you need or want something badly, you need or want it very much

ˌbadly ˈoff adj BAD OFF

bad·min·ton /ˈbædmɪntən/ noun [U] a game in which two or four players use RACKETS to hit a SHUTTLECOCK (=a small light object with feathers on it) to each other across a net

bad·mouth /ˈbædˌmaʊθ/ verb [T] *informal* to criticize someone or something

ˌbad ˈoff (comparative **ˌworse ˈoff**; superlative **ˌworst ˈoff**) adj *American spoken* someone who is bad off does not have much money

bad-tem•pered /ˌbæd ˈtempərd/ adj made annoyed or angry very easily

baf•fle /ˈbæf(ə)l/ verb [T] to be confusing or difficult for someone to understand or solve: *Detectives remain baffled by these murders.* —**baf•fling** adj

bag /bæg/ noun [C] ★★★
1 a container made of paper, plastic, or cloth, used for carrying or storing things: *Put your dirty clothes in the plastic bag.* ♦ *He was weighed down by shopping bags.*
2 a container that someone, especially a woman, uses for carrying small personal things=PURSE
3 a suitcase or similar container in which you carry clothes and other things that you need when you are traveling: *The customs officials may want to search your bags.*
4 the things in a bag, or the amount that it contains: *I've already used about half **a bag of** flour.*
PHRASE **bags under your eyes** loose dark areas of skin below your eyes

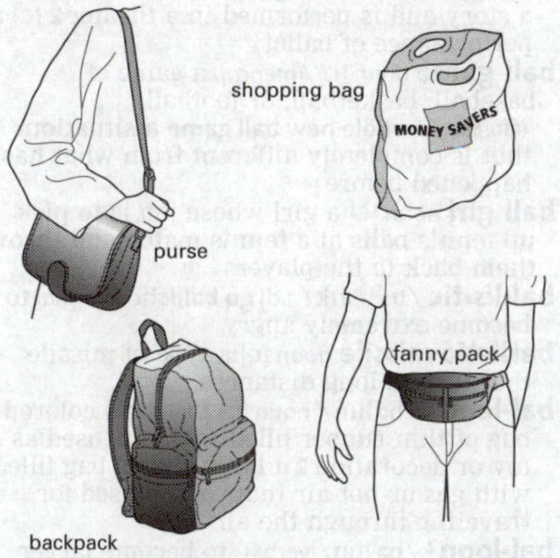

bags

ba•gel /ˈbeɪg(ə)l/ noun [C] a type of bread that is small and round with a hole in the middle

bag•gage /ˈbægɪdʒ/ noun [U] **1** the suitcases and bags that you take with you when you travel=LUGGAGE **2** *informal* problems that someone's past experiences sometimes cause in new situations: *emotional baggage*

> **Baggage** is never used in the plural and cannot be used with **a**: *You may take **a piece of baggage*** (NOT a baggage) *onto the plane.* ♦ *Do you have **any baggage**?* ♦ *There was **some baggage** lying around in the hallway.*

bag•gy /ˈbægi/ adj baggy clothes are very loose and comfortable

bag•pipes /ˈbægˌpaɪps/ noun [plural] a Scottish musical instrument consisting of a bag with several pipes sticking out of it. You play bagpipes by blowing air through one of the pipes.

ba•guette /bæˈget/ noun [C] a long thin LOAF of bread that is soft inside and hard outside

bail¹ /beɪl/ noun [U] money that is given to a court so that someone is allowed to stay out of prison until their trial=BOND: *She was released on bail later that day.* ♦ *The judge set bail at $50,000.*

bail² /beɪl/ verb [I] *American spoken* to BAIL OUT of a project, situation, or relationship
PHRASAL VERBS ˌ**bail ˈout** *American spoken* to leave a project, situation, or relationship, especially when it becomes difficult
ˌ**bail sb ˈout** to give money to a court so that someone is allowed to stay out of prison while they wait for their trial
ˌ**bail sb/sth ˈout** to help a person or organization that is having financial problems

bail•iff /ˈbeɪlɪf/ noun [C] *American* someone whose job is to guard prisoners in a court

bail•out /ˈbeɪlˌaʊt/ noun [C] money that someone gives or lends to a person or organization with financial problems

bait¹ /beɪt/ noun [C/U] **1** food that is used for attracting and catching fish, birds, or animals **2** something that is offered in order to persuade someone to do something

bait² /beɪt/ verb [T] **1** to deliberately try to make someone angry **2** to put food on a hook or in a TRAP in order to catch fish, birds, or animals

bake /beɪk/ verb [I/T] ★ to cook food such as bread and cakes in an oven: *She baked me a cake for my birthday.* ♦ *a baked potato*

baked beans /ˌbeɪkt ˈbinz/ noun [plural] beans in a sweet SPICY brown sauce

baked po•ta•to /ˌbeɪkt pəˈteɪtoʊ/ noun [C] a potato that is baked and served with its skin on

bak•er /ˈbeɪkər/ noun [C] someone whose job is to make bread, cakes, etc.

bak•er•y /ˈbeɪk(ə)ri/ noun [C] a building where bread, cakes, etc. are made or sold

bal•ance¹ /ˈbæləns/ noun ★★

1 ability to stay upright	4 emotional calm
2 correct relationship	5 majority of sth
3 amount of money	+ PHRASES

1 [U] the ability to remain steady in an upright position: *He **lost his balance** and tipped backward in the chair.* ♦ *Ted kept pulling my arm, throwing me **off balance**.*
2 [C/U] a situation in which different aspects or features are treated equally or exist in the correct relationship to each other: *A healthy diet is about getting the correct **balance of** a variety of foods.* ♦ *We're trying to **strike a balance between** fun and learning.*
3 [C] the amount of money in a bank account or remaining to be paid for something
4 [U] mental or emotional calm: *She quickly recovered her balance after the outburst.*
5 [singular] the majority of information, opinions, or facts: *The balance of public opinion was against the proposal.* → TIP²
PHRASES **balance of payments** the difference between the amount of money that a country pays to foreign countries and the amount it receives from them
balance of power the way in which military or political power is divided between countries or groups
be/hang in the balance if something is in the balance, you do not know whether it will succeed or fail

on balance after thinking about all the relevant facts: *On balance, I think we made the right decision.*

bal•ance² /ˈbæləns/ verb ★
1 [I] to keep your body steady without falling over, or to put something in a steady position so that it does not fall: *We had to balance our plates on our knees.*
2 [T] to create or preserve a good or correct balance between different features or aspects: *We have to balance the needs and tastes of all our customers.* ♦ **balance sth with sth** *There is a need to balance the demands of the workplace with those of family life.*
PHRASE **balance the budget/books** to make sure that you do not spend more money than you receive

bal•anced /ˈbælənst/ adj **1** thinking about all arguments, opinions, or aspects fairly and equally = UNBIASED: *We aim to provide balanced reporting of this difficult issue.* **2** with a sensible and reasonable attitude toward life **3** with all parts combining well together or existing in the correct amounts: *a balanced diet*

ˈbalance ˌsheet noun [C] a written statement showing the value of a company at a particular time

bal•anc•ing act /ˈbælənsɪŋ ˌækt/ noun [C] a difficult process in which you try to keep different groups satisfied, or try to do many different things at the same time

bal•co•ny /ˈbælkəni/ noun [C] **1** a place sticking out from the outside of a building where you can sit or stand **2** an upper floor in a theater that sticks out over the main floor

bald /bɔld/ adj **1** with little or no hair on your head **2** a bald tire is no longer safe because its surface is worn smooth —**bald•ness** noun [U]

ˌbald ˈeagle noun [C] a large bird with a white head and neck that lives in North America and is the national bird of the U.S.

bald•ing /ˈbɔldɪŋ/ adj beginning to lose your hair

bald•ly /ˈbɔldli/ adv speaking in a direct way, without trying to be sensitive or polite

bale /beɪl/ noun [C] a large quantity of something such as paper, cotton, or HAY that is tied tightly together

balk /bɔk/ verb [I] to refuse to do something or let something happen: *They really wanted the apartment, but they balked at paying such high rent.*

ball /bɔl/ noun ★★★

1 round object	4 part of foot/hand
2 game	5 social event
3 fun	+ PHRASES

1 [C] a round object that you use in games and sports, or an object that is shaped like this: *a tennis/golf ball* ♦ *a ball of dough*
2 [U] a game that you play with a ball, especially baseball
3 [singular] *American informal* a lot of fun: *Why don't you come – we'll **have a ball!***
4 [C] the part of your foot, hand, or thumb that is slightly round and sticks out
5 [C] a formal social event at which there is dancing
PHRASES **get/set/start the ball rolling** to make something start happening
on the ball *informal* quick to understand what is happening and what must be done

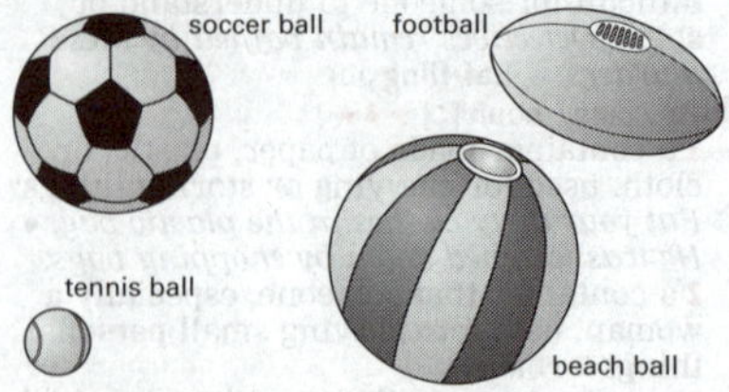

balls

bal•lad /ˈbæləd/ noun [C] a popular love song

ˈball ˌboy noun [C] a boy whose job is to pick up tennis balls at a tennis match and throw them back to the players

bal•le•ri•na /ˌbæləˈrinə/ noun [C] a woman who performs in ballets

bal•let /ˈbæˌleɪ, bæˈleɪ/ noun **1** [U] a type of complicated dancing that is used for telling a story and is performed in a theater **2** [C] a performance of ballet

ˈball ˌgame noun [C] *American* a game of baseball, basketball, or football
PHRASE **a whole new ball game** a situation that is completely different from what has happened before

ˈball ˌgirl noun [C] a girl whose job is to pick up tennis balls at a tennis match and throw them back to the players

bal•lis•tic /bəˈlɪstɪk/ adj **go ballistic** *informal* to become extremely angry

balˌlistic ˈmissile noun [C] a type of missile that travels long distances

bal•loon¹ /bəˈlun/ noun [C] **1** a small colored bag of thin rubber filled with air, used as a toy or decoration **2** a large strong bag filled with gas or hot air that can be used for traveling through the air

bal•loon² /bəˈlun/ verb [I] to become larger and rounder in shape

bal•lot¹ /ˈbælət/ noun **1** [C/U] a secret vote to decide about an issue or to decide who wins an election **2** [C] a piece of paper that you write your vote on

bal•lot² /ˈbælət/ verb [T] to ask people to vote in a ballot

ˈballot ˌbox noun **1** [C] a box in which you put a piece of paper with your vote on **2** [singular] the democratic system of voting

ball•park¹ /ˈbɔlˌpɑrk/ noun [C] a place where baseball games are played

ball•park² /ˈbɔlˌpɑrk/ adj not calculated exactly: *a ballpark figure*

ball•point /ˈbɔlˌpɔɪnt/ or **ˌballpoint ˈpen** noun [C] a pen with a very small ball at the end from which ink flows —*picture* → PEN

ball•room /ˈbɔlˌrum/ noun [C] a very large room used for formal dances

ˌballroom ˈdancing noun [U] a type of formal dancing done by two people together, using a fixed series of movements

balm /bɑm/ noun [C/U] an oil with a nice smell for rubbing on sore skin

balm•y /ˈbɑmi/ adj balmy weather is warm and pleasant

ba•lo•ney /bəˈlouni/ noun [U] *informal* **1** *spoken* nonsense or lies **2** BOLOGNA

Bal•tic /ˈbɔltɪk/ adj relating to the Baltic Sea in northern Europe and to the countries in this region

bam•boo /bæmˈbu/ noun [C/U] a tall tropical plant with thick light-brown stems, used for making things such as furniture

ban¹ /bæn/ verb [T] ★

1 to say officially that something is illegal or not allowed: *a new law that bans tobacco advertising* ♦ **ban sth from sth** *The book was banned from school libraries.*

2 to say officially that someone is not allowed to do something: **ban sb from (doing) sth** *She was banned from competing for two years after failing a drug test.*

ban² /bæn/ noun [C] an official statement ordering people not to do something: *There is a total ban on smoking anywhere in the college.*

ba•nal /bəˈnɑl/ adj boring, with no new, interesting, or unusual qualities —**ba•nal•i•ty** /bəˈnæləti/ noun [C/U]

ba•nan•a /bəˈnɑnə/ noun [C/U] a long curved fruit with a yellow skin —*picture* → C10

band¹ /bænd/ noun [C] ★★★

1 group of musicians	4 narrow circular object
2 group of same type	5 line of color/light
3 range of values/levels	

1 a group of musicians who play popular music: *He used to play in a band.*

2 a group of people who do something together or who share a particular feature: *a band of warriors*

3 a range of values, prices, etc. in a system for measuring or organizing something: *students in the age band 11 to 14*

4 a flat narrow piece of something in the shape of a ring: *She wore a band around her hair.* ♦ *a rubber band*

5 a line of something such as color or light: *The male bird has a brown band across its chest.*

band² /bænd/ PHRASAL VERB ˌ**band toˈgether** to form a group in order to achieve a goal

band•age¹ /ˈbændɪdʒ/ noun [C/U] a long thin piece of cloth that you wrap around an injured part of your body

band•age² /ˈbændɪdʒ/ verb [T] to wrap a bandage around part of your body

ˈ**Band-ˌAid** *American trademark* a piece of TAPE that you stick over a cut on your skin

ban•dit /ˈbændɪt/ noun [C] a member of a group of thieves who attack people while they are traveling

band•stand /ˈbændˌstænd/ noun [C] a building without walls in a park, used for musical performances

band•wag•on /ˈbændˌwægən/ noun [C] an idea or activity that suddenly becomes very popular: *Every business was trying to jump on the "dot-com" bandwagon.*

band•width /ˈbændˌwɪdθ/ noun [C/U] *computing* the amount of information that can be sent each second through an Internet connection

bang¹ /bæŋ/ verb **1** [T] to hit or move something with a lot of force, making a loud noise: *We could hear them banging their drums.* ♦ *She banged her fist on the table.* **2** [I] to move with a lot of force, making a loud noise: *We heard a door bang.* ♦ *Who's banging around upstairs?* **3** [I/T] to knock against something when you are moving: *Be careful not to bang your head.* ♦ *She banged into me.*

bang² /bæŋ/ noun [C] a short loud noise, for example the sound of a door closing with a lot of force

PHRASE **with a bang** in a very exciting or successful way

→ BANGS

bang³ /bæŋ/ interjection **1** used by children for representing the sound made by a gun **2** used for showing that something happens very suddenly

ban•gle /ˈbæŋg(ə)l/ noun [C] a stiff circular BRACELET (=jewelry worn around the wrist)

bangs /bæŋz/ noun [plural] *American* short hair that hangs over your forehead —*picture* → HAIRSTYLE

ban•ish /ˈbænɪʃ/ verb [T] **1** to officially order someone to leave a place as a punishment **2** to get rid of something such as a problem or worry

ban•is•ter /ˈbænɪstər/ noun [C] a structure like a fence along the edge of stairs —*picture* → C1

ban•jo /ˈbændʒoʊ/ noun [C] a musical instrument like a small round guitar

bank¹ /bæŋk/ noun [C] ★★★

1 a financial institution where people can keep their money, or can borrow money: *I need to go to the bank this morning.*

2 a raised sloping area of land, for example along the side of a river: *We climbed a steep bank.*

3 a large collection or store of something: *a blood bank*

4 a large mass of cloud or FOG

bank² /bæŋk/ verb [I] **1** to have a bank account with a particular bank: *Who do you bank with?* **2** if an airplane banks, it turns quickly in the air, with one wing higher than the other

PHRASAL VERB **bank on sb/sth** to depend on someone doing something or on something happening

ˈ**bank acˌcount** noun [C] an arrangement with a bank that allows you to keep your money there: *We'll pay the money into your bank account.*

ˈ**bank ˌcard** noun [C] a small plastic card for making payments or for getting money from the bank

bank•er /ˈbæŋkər/ noun [C] someone who has an important position in a bank

bank•ing /ˈbæŋkɪŋ/ noun [U] the work done by banks

bank•roll¹ /ˈbæŋkˌroul/ noun [singular] a supply of money for a particular purpose

bank•roll² /ˈbæŋkˌroul/ verb [T] to provide the money for something

bank•rupt¹ /ˈbæŋkˌrʌpt/ adj a person or business that is bankrupt has officially admitted that they have no money and cannot pay what they owe = INSOLVENT

bank•rupt² /ˈbæŋkˌrʌpt/ verb [T] to make a person, business, or country BANKRUPT or very poor

B

bank•rupt³ /ˈbæŋk,rʌpt/ noun [C] someone who is officially bankrupt

bank•rupt•cy /ˈbæŋk,rʌptsi/ noun [C/U] a situation in which a person or business becomes BANKRUPT

ˈbank ˌstatement noun [C] a document showing the money that went into or out of a bank account during a particular period

ban•ner¹ /ˈbænər/ noun [C] **1** a wide piece of cloth with a message on it **2** *computing* an advertisement across a WEBSITE
PHRASE **under the banner of sth 1** because of a particular principle or belief **2** controlled or supported by a particular organization

ban•ner² /ˈbænər/ adj *American* extremely successful: *a banner year for the company*

ban•quet /ˈbæŋkwɪt/ noun [C] a formal meal for a large number of people

ban•ter /ˈbæntər/ noun [U] friendly conversation in which people make jokes about each other

bap•tism /ˈbæp,tɪzəm/ noun [C/U] a ceremony in which someone is covered or touched with water in order to welcome them into the Christian religion

Bap•tist /ˈbæptɪst/ noun [C] a member of a Protestant religious group that believes that only adults should be baptized
—**Bap•tist** adj

bap•tize /bæpˈtaɪz/ verb [T] **1** to welcome someone into the Christian religion by touching or covering them with water **2** to name a child when it is baptized

bar¹ /bɑr/ noun ★★★

1 place serving alcohol	5 profession of a lawyer
2 flat surface for drinks	6 sth that prevents sth
3 long piece of metal	7 on computer screen
4 block of sth solid	+ PHRASE

1 [C] a place where you go to buy and drink alcoholic drinks
2 [C] the COUNTER where alcoholic drinks are served
3 [C] a long narrow piece of metal: *an old house with iron bars on the windows*
4 [C] a solid block of a substance: *a bar of soap ♦ a candy bar*
5 the bar [singular] the profession of being a lawyer
6 [C] something that prevents another thing from happening: *The fact that you are a woman should not be* ***a bar to success.***
7 [C] a long narrow shape along one of the sides of a WINDOW on a computer screen: *a scroll/tool bar*
PHRASE **behind bars** in prison

bar² /bɑr/ verb [T] **1** to officially say that something is not allowed: *The new rule bars the export of live animals.* **2** to put something across a door or window so that no one can get through it **3** to prevent someone from going somewhere by standing in their way: *Three vicious-looking dogs barred our way.*

bar•bar•i•an /bɑrˈberiən/ noun [C] someone who does not respect culture or who is extremely violent and cruel

bar•bar•ic /bɑrˈberɪk/ adj extremely violent and cruel

bar•ba•rous /ˈbɑrbərəs/ adj extremely violent and cruel

bar•be•cue¹ /ˈbɑrbə,kju/ noun [C] **1** a meal at which food is cooked and eaten outside **2** a piece of equipment used for cooking food outside

bar•be•cue² /ˈbɑrbə,kju/ verb [T] to cook food outside on a barbecue

barbed /bɑrbd/ adj barbed comments contain cruel but clever criticisms

ˌbarbed ˈwire noun [U] thick wire with a lot of sharp points sticking out of it

bar•bell /ˈbɑr,bel/ noun [C] a long metal bar with weights at each end. You lift it in order to make your muscles bigger.
—*picture* → C16

bar•ber /ˈbɑrbər/ noun [C] someone whose job is to cut men's hair

bar•bi•tu•rate /bɑrˈbɪtʃərət/ noun [C] a strong drug that can make people calm or help them to sleep

ˈbar ˌcode noun [C] a set of printed lines on a product that contains information such as its price

bare¹ /ber/ adj **1** not covered by any clothes **2** a bare surface has nothing on it **3** basic, with nothing extra: *the bare essentials like food and clothing*
PHRASE **with your bare hands** without using any equipment or weapons

bare² /ber/ verb [T] to show something that was covered, for example a part of your body

bare•foot /ˈber,fʊt/ adj, adv without any shoes or socks on

bare•ly /ˈberli/ adv ★
1 used for saying that something only just happens or exists, or is only just possible =HARDLY, SCARCELY: *He could barely stand. ♦ The roads were barely wide enough for two cars to pass.*
2 used for emphasizing that something happened a very short time before something else: *Roy had barely left the room before they started to laugh.*
3 used for emphasizing how small an amount is: *He's barely 12 years old.*

barf /bɑrf/ verb [I] *very informal* to VOMIT

bar•gain¹ /ˈbɑrgən/ noun [C] **1** something you buy that costs much less than normal: *Her dress was a real bargain.* **2** an agreement in which each person or group promises something

bar•gain² /ˈbɑrgən/ verb [I] to try to persuade someone to agree to a price or deal that is better for you
PHRASE **more than you bargained for** something that is worse or more difficult than you expected

barge¹ /bɑrdʒ/ noun [C] a long flat boat that is used on rivers and CANALS

barge² /bɑrdʒ/ verb [I] to move in a fast careless way, often hitting people or things: *He barged past me without looking.*
PHRASAL VERB **ˌbarge ˈin** to enter a room suddenly in a rude way

ˈbar ˌgraph noun [C] a GRAPH that represents amounts as thick lines of different lengths

bar•i•tone /ˈberɪ,toʊn/ noun [C] a man with a fairly deep singing voice, between a TENOR and a BASS

bark¹ /bɑrk/ verb [I] to make the short loud sound that a dog makes

PHRASE **barking up the wrong tree** *informal* doing something that will not get the result that you want

bark² /bɑrk/ noun **1** [U] the hard substance that covers a tree —*picture* → TREE **2** [C] the short loud sound that a dog makes

bar•ley /ˈbɑrli/ noun [U] a type of grain that is used for making food, beer, and WHISKEY

bar mitz•vah /bɑr ˈmɪtsvə/ noun [C] a Jewish ceremony held when a boy is 13, after which he is considered to be an adult in his religious life

barn /bɑrn/ noun [C] a large building on a farm where animals, crops, or machines are kept

ba•rom•e•ter /bəˈrɑmətər/ noun [C] **1** a piece of equipment that measures pressure in the air and tells you what kind of weather to expect **2** something that shows how a situation is changing or how people feel about something: *Investment levels are seen as a good barometer of business confidence.*

bar•on /ˈberən/ noun [C] **1** a male member of the NOBILITY with low rank **2** a powerful person in a particular type of business: *the steel barons*

ba•roque /bəˈroʊk, bəˈrɑk/ adj relating to the very detailed style of art, building, or music that was popular in Europe in the 17th and early 18th centuries

bar•racks /ˈberəks/ noun [plural] a group of buildings where members of the military live and work

bar•rage /bəˈrɑʒ/ noun **1** [singular] a lot of criticisms, complaints, or questions that are directed at someone **2** [C] a long continuous attack of guns or bombs

bar•rel /ˈberəl/ noun [C] **1** a large round container with a flat top and bottom, used for storing liquids **2** the part of a gun that a bullet is fired through

PHRASE **have sb over a barrel** *informal* to have someone in a difficult situation in which they will have to do what you want

bar•ren /ˈberən/ adj **1** barren land is dry and plants cannot grow there **2** *old-fashioned* a woman who is barren cannot have babies

bar•rette /bəˈret/ noun [C] *American* a small plastic or metal object used for keeping a woman's hair in place

bar•ri•cade¹ /ˌberɪˈkeɪd/ noun [C] a temporary structure that is built across a road, gate, or door to prevent people from getting through

bar•ri•cade² /ˌberɪˈkeɪd/ verb [T] to block something with a barricade

bar•ri•er /ˈberiər/ noun [C] ★

1 a structure that stops people or vehicles from entering a place: *Fans broke through the barriers and rushed onto the field.*

2 something that prevents progress or makes it difficult for people to communicate or achieve a goal = OBSTACLE: *High levels of debt are **a major barrier to** economic development.*

3 something that separates one thing from another: *The river is the last barrier between the rebel army and the city.*

bar•ring /ˈbɑrɪŋ/ preposition unless the thing mentioned happens or exists: *Barring any further delays, we should be able to start tomorrow.*

bar•tend•er /ˈbɑrˌtendər/ noun [C] *American* someone whose job is to serve drinks in a bar

bar•ter /ˈbɑrtər/ verb [I/T] to exchange goods or services for other goods or services instead of using money —**bar•ter** noun [U]

base¹ /beɪs/ noun [C] ★★★

1 lowest part of sth	5 ideas etc. to start from
2 place for military	6 in baseball
3 place for doing sth	+ PHRASE
4 supporters/customers	

1 the bottom part, edge, or surface of something: *The statue stands on a large round base. ♦ The pituitary gland is at **the base of the brain.***

2 a place where members of the military live and work: *a U.S. naval base*

3 a place from which an activity can be planned, started, or carried out: *Hikers find this **a** convenient **base for** their mountain expeditions.*

4 a group of people or organizations that support someone or something: *They have built a loyal customer base.*

5 a set of ideas, facts, achievements, etc. from which something can develop: *The company lacks a strong financial base. ♦ **a** broad **base of** experience/knowledge/ expertise*

6 one of the four places on a baseball field that a player must touch in order to score points → FIRST BASE —*picture* → C15

PHRASE **off base** *American informal* not right or accurate: *A Ford spokesman says that the company's critics are way off base.*

base² /beɪs/ verb ★★★

PHRASE **be based in** to have somewhere as your main office or place of work, or the place where you live: *Our parent company is based in Osaka. ♦ Where are you based now?*

PHRASAL VERB ˈ**base sth on sth 1** to use particular ideas or facts to make a decision, do a calculation, or develop a theory: *Her theories are based largely on personal experience.* **2** to use something as a model for a movie, piece of writing, or work of art: *The movie is based on a true story.*

base³ /beɪs/ adj *literary* not moral at all

base•ball /ˈbeɪsˌbɔl/ noun ★

1 [U] a game played by two teams of nine players who score points by hitting a ball with a BAT and then running around four bases —*picture* → C15

2 [C] the small hard ball used in the game of baseball

ˈ**baseball ˌcap** noun [C] a hat that fits close to your head, with a flat curved part that sticks out above your eyes —*picture* → HAT

base•less /ˈbeɪsləs/ adj *formal* not based on facts or evidence

base•line /ˈbeɪsˌlaɪn/ noun [C] the line that marks the back of the playing area in games such as tennis

base•ment /ˈbeɪsmənt/ noun [C] the part of a building below the level of the ground —*picture* → C1

ba•ses /ˈbeɪˌsiz/ the plural of **basis**

B

B

bash¹ /bæʃ/ verb [I/T] *informal* to hit someone or something very hard, often causing injury or serious damage

bash² /bæʃ/ noun [C] *informal* a party or celebration

bash•ful /ˈbæʃfəl/ adj easily embarrassed when you are with other people = SHY —**bash•ful•ly** adv

ba•sic /ˈbeɪsɪk/ adj ★★★
1 forming the main or most important part or aspect of something: *Rice is the basic ingredient of the dish.* ♦ *First you need to understand the basic principles of computers.*
2 simple, with nothing special or extra: *The state provides only basic health care.* ♦ *Sales reps receive a basic salary plus commission.* ♦ *It's an inexpensive hotel, and the accommodations are quite basic.*

ba•si•cally /ˈbeɪsɪkli/ adv ★
1 in the most important aspects, without thinking about the specific details: *The book is basically a love story.*
2 *spoken* used for emphasizing the most important point or idea in what you are saying: *Basically, you should have asked me first.*

ba•sics, the /ˈbeɪsɪks/ noun [plural] the most important aspects or principles of something: *The basics of the game can be learned very quickly.*

bas•il /ˈbeɪz(ə)l, ˈbæz(ə)l/ noun [U] a plant with sweet leaves that are used in salads and cooking

ba•sil•i•ca /bəˈzɪlɪkə, bəˈsɪlɪkə/ noun [C] a large important Roman Catholic church

ba•sin /ˈbeɪs(ə)n/ noun [C] **1** a large area of land from which water flows into a particular river or lake: *the Colorado River Basin* **2** a large round open container that is used for holding water or washing things in **3** a sink in a bathroom

ba•sis /ˈbeɪsɪs/ (plural **bas•es** /ˈbeɪˌsiz/) noun [C] ★
1 a particular method or system that is used for doing or organizing something: *Salaries are paid **on a weekly basis**.* ♦ *Tickets will be sold **on a first-come, first-served basis**.*
2 the reason why something is done: *Don't make your decision **on the basis of** cost alone.*
3 the important ideas, facts, or actions from which something can develop = FOUNDATION: *Bernard's work forms the **basis of** all modern physiology.* ♦ *The agreement provides the **basis for** future negotiations.*

bask /bæsk/ verb [I] **1** to relax and enjoy yourself by lying in the sun **2** to enjoy people's attention and approval: *For now, she is content to bask in her newfound fame.*

bas•ket /ˈbæskət/ noun [C] ★★
1 a container for carrying or keeping things in, made from thin pieces of plastic, wire, or wood woven together: *a laundry basket* ♦ *a basket of food*
2 the net that you throw the ball through in basketball, or a point scored by throwing the ball through it —*picture* → C15

bas•ket•ball /ˈbæskətˌbɔl/ noun ★
1 [U] a game played by two teams of five players who score points by throwing a ball through a net —*picture* → C15
2 [C] the ball used in the game of basketball

bass¹ /beɪs/ noun **1** [C/U] the lowest male singing voice, or a man who sings with this type of voice **2** [U] the lower half of the full range of musical notes → TREBLE **3 bass** or **bass guitar** [C] an electric guitar that produces very low notes **4** [C] a DOUBLE BASS —**bass** adj: *a bass drum/voice*

bass² /bæs/ (plural **bass**) noun [C/U] a fish that lives in rivers and the ocean

bas•si•net /ˌbæsiˈnet/ noun [C] a bed like a basket for a baby

bas•soon /bəˈsun/ noun [C] a musical instrument consisting of a long wooden tube that you hold upright and play by blowing into a thin metal pipe —*picture* → WOODWIND

bas•tard /ˈbæstərd/ noun [C] *offensive* **1** an insulting word for an unpleasant or annoying man **2** *old-fashioned* someone whose parents are not married to each other

baste /beɪst/ verb [I/T] to cover meat with hot fat or its own juices while it is cooking

bas•tion /ˈbæstʃ(ə)n/ noun [C] an organization, community, or system that supports and defends a particular way of life, tradition, or belief: *an all-male bastion of conservatism*

bat¹ /bæt/ noun [C] **1** a long wooden object used for hitting the ball in games such as baseball and CRICKET **2** a small animal that flies at night and looks like a mouse with large wings
PHRASE **right off the bat** *American informal* immediately or right from the start

bat² /bæt/ verb [I] to try to hit the ball with a bat in a game such as baseball or CRICKET

batch /bætʃ/ noun [C] a quantity of people or things that arrive, are made, or are dealt with at the same time: *a batch of cookies*

bat•ed /ˈbeɪtəd/ adj **with bated breath** worried or excited about what will happen

bath /bæθ/ noun [C] ★★★
1 the process of washing yourself or someone else in a BATHTUB: *Do I have time to take a bath?*
2 the water in a BATHTUB: *Can you run a bath* (=fill a bathtub with water) *for me?*

bathe /beɪð/ verb **1** [I/T] *American* to wash yourself or someone else in a BATHTUB **2** [T] to cover a part of your body with a liquid, especially in order to clean or treat a cut **3** [T] to fill an area with light: *The valley was bathed in warm light.*

ˈbathing ˌsuit noun [C] a piece of clothing worn for swimming = SWIMSUIT —*picture* → C5

bath•robe /ˈbæθˌroʊb/ noun [C] a loose piece of clothing like a soft coat that you wear before or after taking a bath or shower —*picture* → C5

bath•room /ˈbæθˌrum/ noun [C] ★★ a room containing a toilet and often a bathtub or shower
PHRASE **go to the bathroom** *American* to use the toilet

bath•tub /ˈbæθˌtʌb/ noun [C] a long deep container that you fill with water and wash yourself in

ba•ton /bəˈtɑn, ˈbæt(ə)n/ noun [C] **1** a stick that

the CONDUCTOR of an orchestra uses **2** a stick that you spin and throw in the air

bat·tal·ion /bəˈtæljən/ noun [C] a large group of soldiers

bat·ter¹ /ˈbætər/ verb [I/T] to hit someone or something many times: *Huge waves battered the little ship.*

bat·ter² /ˈbætər/ noun **1** [C/U] a liquid mixture of milk, flour, and eggs, that is used in cooking and baking **2** [C] a player who tries to hit the ball in baseball *—picture* → C15

bat·tered /ˈbætərd/ adj **1** old and slightly damaged: *a battered old car* **2** having experienced a lot of problems: *his battered reputation* **3** *old-fashioned* treated violently by a member of your family

bat·ter·y /ˈbæt(ə)ri/ noun ★
1 [C] an object that fits into something such as a radio, clock, or car and supplies it with electricity
2 [U] *legal* the crime of hitting someone
→ RECHARGE

bat·tle¹ /ˈbæt(ə)l/ noun ★★
1 [C/U] a fight between two armies in a war: *one of the bloodiest battles of World War Two* ♦ *soldiers wounded **in battle*** ♦ *the Battle of Waterloo*
2 [C] a situation in which people or groups compete with each other: *The couple are locked in a bitter legal battle over custody of their children.* ♦ ***the battle for** the leadership of the Democratic Party*
3 [C] a situation in which someone is trying very hard to deal with a difficult situation: *She has lost her **battle against** breast cancer.* ♦ **a battle to do sth** *It was a daily battle to get my son to go to school.*

bat·tle² /ˈbæt(ə)l/ verb **1** [I/T] to try very hard to deal with a difficult situation: *Surgeons battled to save the man's life.* **2** [I] to compete with someone: *the three men battling for the world title*

bat·tle·field /ˈbæt(ə)lˌfild/ or **bat·tle·ground** /ˈbæt(ə)lˌgraʊnd/ noun [C] a place where a battle takes place or where one took place in the past

bat·tle·ments /ˈbæt(ə)lmənts/ noun [plural] a wall around the top of a castle, with spaces through which weapons could be fired

bat·tle·ship /ˈbæt(ə)lˌʃɪp/ noun [C] the largest type of WARSHIP

bau·ble /ˈbɔb(ə)l/ noun [C] an inexpensive decoration or piece of jewelry

baulk /bɔk/ another spelling of **balk**

bawl /bɔl/ verb **1** [I] to cry loudly **2** [I/T] to shout in a loud angry way
PHRASAL VERB ˌ**bawl sb ˈout** *informal* to speak angrily to someone because of something they have done wrong

bay /beɪ/ noun [C] **1** an area of the coast where the land curves inward **2** an area in a building or vehicle that is used for a particular purpose: *a loading/cargo bay*
PHRASE **keep/hold sth at bay** to prevent something serious, dangerous, or unpleasant from affecting you

ˈ**bay ˌleaf** noun [C] a leaf used in cooking for adding flavor

bay·o·net /ˈbeɪənɪt/ noun [C] a long sharp blade that is attached onto the end of a RIFLE

bay·ou /ˈbaɪˌu/ noun [C] a large area of water that flows very slowly and has a lot of water plants and animals living in it

ˌ**bay ˈwindow** noun [C] a large window that sticks out from the main wall of a house *—picture* → C1

ba·zaar /bəˈzɑr/ noun [C] **1** a market, especially in the Middle East and South Asia **2** a sale to raise money for a particular project or organization

BBC, the /ˌbi bi ˈsi/ the British Broadcasting Corporation: an organization that broadcasts television and radio programs and is owned by the British government

BB gun /ˈbi bi ˌgʌn/ noun [C] *American* a gun that shoots small round bullets called **BBs**

BBQ abbrev barbecue

B.C. abbrev before Christ: used after a date to show that it refers to a time before the birth of Jesus Christ

be /bi/ verb ★★★

> Be can have many different forms depending on its subject and on its tense:
>
> | | |
> |---|---|
> | *present tense* | I **am** |
> | | he/she/it **is** |
> | | we/you/they **are** |
> | *past tense* | I/he/she/it **was** |
> | | we/you/they **were** |
> | *past participle* | **been** |
> | *present participle* | **being** |

1 [auxiliary verb] used with a present participle for forming a PROGRESSIVE tense of a verb: *I am studying English Literature.* ♦ *We were having breakfast when Terry phoned.*
2 [auxiliary verb] used with a past participle for forming the passive form of a verb: *Her husband was killed in a car accident.* ♦ *The orchestra will be conducted by David Norton.*
3 [linking verb] used for giving information about someone or something, for example their name, job, or position: *Our teacher is Miss Tiwana.* ♦ *He wants to be an actor.* ♦ *It was a cold frosty morning.* ♦ *Baltimore is not far from Washington.* ♦ *Nancy is tall and very thin.*
4 [linking verb] used for saying how someone behaves, or for telling them how to behave: *They are being very silly.* ♦ *Be quiet!*
PHRASES **have been to...** used for saying that someone has gone to a place and returned: *Have you ever been to Venice?*
there is/are used for saying that someone or something exists, happens, or can be found: *There is a problem with the car.* ♦ *How many people were there at the party?* ♦ *There have been six serious accidents on this road.*

> Questions and negatives with "be" are formed without "do": *Are you busy?* ♦ *The book was not expensive.*

beach /bitʃ/ noun [C] ★★ an area of sand or small stones beside the ocean or a lake
→ SHORE

beach·front /ˈbitʃˌfrʌnt/ adj facing a beach or very close to a beach: *a large beachfront hotel*

bea·con /ˈbikən/ noun [C] a bright light that is used as a signal to warn people or to show them the way somewhere

bead /bid/ noun [C] **1** a small round piece of plastic, glass, metal, etc. that is used for making jewelry: *a string of beads* **2** a small drop of a liquid such as blood or SWEAT

B

bead•y /ˈbidi/ adj beady eyes are small, round, and bright

bea•gle /ˈbig(ə)l/ noun [C] a dog with short hair and long ears

beak /bik/ noun [C] the hard curved or pointed part of a bird's mouth

beak•er /ˈbikər/ noun [C] a glass or plastic container with straight sides, used in a laboratory

beam¹ /bim/ verb **1** [I] to have a big smile on your face because you are very happy **2** [I/T] to send out light, heat, or radio or television signals: *Pictures of the famine were beamed to television audiences all over the world.*

beam² /bim/ noun [C] **1** a long thick piece of wood, metal, or CONCRETE that supports a roof **2** a line of light or energy: *a laser beam*

bean /bin/ noun [C] **1** a seed of various plants that is cooked and eaten, or a plant that produces these seeds **2** a dried bean that you GRIND and use to make drinks such as coffee and COCOA → SPILL¹

bear¹ /ber/ (past tense **bore** /bɔr/; past participle **borne** /bɔrn/) verb [T] ★

1 (not) like sb/sth	6 have bad feeling
2 accept bad situation	7 give birth to
3 have particular quality	+ PHRASES
4 have writing/design	+ PHRASAL VERBS
5 support weight	

1 if you cannot bear someone or something, you do not like them at all or cannot accept them: *She **couldn't bear the thought of** moving again.* ♦ **can't bear doing sth/to do sth** *Sue can't bear to be separated from her baby daughter.*

2 to accept a difficult or unpleasant situation, especially without complaining: *She bore all her suffering with incredible patience.* ♦ *The pain was **more than I could bear**.*

3 to seem to be a particular kind of thing or to have particular qualities: *His description **bore no relation to reality**.*

4 *formal* if something bears writing or a design, it has writing or a design on it: *a blue banner bearing the words "Civil Rights March"*

5 to support the weight of something: *The old floorboards could not bear the weight of the grand piano.*

6 to have a bad feeling toward someone: *I hope you don't still **bear a grudge against** me* (=continue to be angry about something I did in the past).

7 *formal* to give birth to a child

PHRASES **bear fruit** if a plan or effort bears fruit, it is eventually successful

bear sth in mind to remember to think about something when you are involved in doing something else: **+(that)** *When you speak to Lee, bear in mind he's still upset about what happened.*

bear left/right to turn left/right

bear the responsibility/blame to be responsible for something: *The company **bears the responsibility for** the actions of its employees.*

bear witness *formal* to show signs that prove that something happened or was true

PHRASAL VERBS ˌ**bear ˈdown on sb/sth** to move quickly toward someone in a determined and threatening way: *I could see a police car bearing down on us.*

ˌ**bear sb/sth ˈout** to show that someone is telling the truth or that something is true: *Scientific evidence bears out the claim that stress and disease are linked.*

ˌ**bear ˈup** to behave in a brave way in a very sad or difficult situation: *Let's see how he **bears up under** the pressure.*

ˈ**bear ˌwith sb** *spoken* used as a polite way of asking someone to be patient while you do something: *Bear with me – I won't be long.*

bear² /ber/ noun [C] **1** a large wild animal with thick fur **2** *business* someone who expects the price of company STOCK to fall, so they sell them → BULL 3

bear•a•ble /ˈberəb(ə)l/ adj something that is bearable is difficult or unpleasant, but you are able to accept or deal with it ≠ UNBEARABLE

beard /bɪrd/ noun [C] hair that grows on a man's chin and cheeks —**beard•ed** adj

bear•er /ˈberər/ noun [C] someone who brings you a particular type of news or information: *I hate to be the bearer of bad news.*

bear•ing /ˈberɪŋ/ noun [singular] the particular way in which someone stands, moves, or behaves

PHRASES **get/find your bearings** to find out where you are and where other things are

have some/no bearing on sth to be relevant/not relevant to something: *His private life has no bearing on his competence as a manager.*

lose your bearings to become confused about where you are and where other things are

ˈ**bear ˌmarket** noun [C] *business* a situation in which the prices of STOCKS are falling

beast /bist/ noun [C] **1** an animal, especially a dangerous or strange one **2** *old-fashioned* a cruel or immoral person

beat¹ /bit/ (past tense **beat**; past participle **beat•en**) verb ★★★

1 hit sb several times	6 of heart
2 defeat sb	7 mix foods well
3 arrive before sb	+ PHRASES
4 be better than sth	+ PHRASAL VERBS
5 hit sth several times	

1 [T] to hit someone violently several times: *They were arrested for beating their children.* ♦ *The two men had been **beaten to death**.*

2 [T] to defeat someone in a game, competition, election, or BATTLE: *Hingis needed to beat Davenport to get to the final.*

3 [T] to arrive before someone else: *See if you can beat me back to the house!*

4 [T] *informal* to be better than something else: *For me, surfing the Net beats watching TV any time.*

5 [I/T] to hit something many times or for a long period of time: *The rain **was beating against** the windows.*

6 [I] if someone's heart beats, it makes regular sounds and movements: *The shock had made my heart beat faster.*

7 [T] to mix foods together using a fork or a special tool or machine

PHRASES **beats me** *spoken* used for saying that you do not know or understand something: *"Why did he do such a stupid thing?" "Beats me."*

beat sb to it to do something before someone else: *When I went to take the keys I found that someone had beaten me to it.*

you can't beat sth used for saying that something is very good: *You can't beat a good book.*

PHRASAL VERBS **ˌbeat ˈdown 1** if the rain beats down, it rains very hard **2** if the sun beats down, it shines very brightly

ˌbeat sb ˈoff to prevent someone from attacking you by hitting them: *He had to beat the dogs off with a stick.*

ˌbeat sb ˈout *American informal* to succeed in winning or gaining something that someone else wants: *Atlanta beat out Athens for the privilege of hosting the 1996 Olympics.*

ˌbeat sb ˈup *informal* to hurt someone by hitting or kicking them many times: *They threatened to beat me up if I didn't give them my wallet.*

beat² /bit/ noun **1** [C] the regular sound or movement of your heart: *I could feel the beat of his heart.* **2** [singular] the main pattern of regular strong sounds in a piece of music: *music with a slow bluesy beat* **3** [singular] a single regular sound, or a series of regular sounds, especially of two things hitting together: *the beat of the bird's wings* **4** [C] an area that a police officer has responsibility for and must walk around regularly

beat³ /bit/ adj *spoken* very tired: *You look beat.*

beat·en /ˈbit(ə)n/ adj **off the beaten path/track** far away from the places that people usually visit, and hard to get to

beat·ing /ˈbitɪŋ/ noun [C] an act of hitting someone hard a number of times in a fight or as a punishment

PHRASE **take a beating** to be badly damaged or criticized

ˈbeat-ˌup adj *informal* old and in bad condition: *a beat-up old bicycle*

beau·ti·cian /bjəˈtɪʃ(ə)n/ noun [C] someone whose job is to give people beauty treatments or cut and style women's hair

beau·ti·ful /ˈbjutɪf(ə)l/ adj ★★★

1 a beautiful woman or child is extremely attractive ≠ UGLY: *What a beautiful baby!*

2 very nice to look at, hear, or experience = LOVELY: *The weather has been beautiful this week.* ♦ *a beautiful song/dress*

—**beau·ti·ful·ly** adv: *They were all beautifully dressed.*

> Other ways of saying **beautiful**
>
> - **attractive** used for describing men and women whose looks make other people sexually interested in them
> - **cute** used for describing children who are nice to look at and who behave in a nice way. It is also used for describing a man or woman who is sexually attractive
> - **good-looking** used for describing adults and older children who are nice to look at.
> - **gorgeous** very beautiful or handsome
> - **handsome** used for describing men who are nice to look at
> - **pretty** used for describing young women and girls who have nice faces

beau·ti·fy /ˈbjutɪˌfaɪ/ verb [T] to make something look more beautiful

beau·ty¹ /ˈbjuti/ noun ★★

1 [U] the quality of being beautiful: *He was impressed by her beauty and charm.* ♦ *the beauty of the landscape*

2 [C] *informal* something that you think is very good, or is a good example of its type: *I love old cars, and that one's a beauty.*

PHRASE **the beauty of sth** the advantage or good quality that something has: *The beauty of working at home is that you don't have to travel to work.*

beau·ty² /ˈbjuti/ adj designed to make people look more beautiful: *beauty products/treatments*

ˈbeauty ˌparlor noun [C] a store where you can get beauty treatments for your skin or hair

bea·ver /ˈbivər/ noun [C] a small North American animal that has a wide flat tail and thick fur

became the past tense of **become**

be·cause /bɪˈkɔz, bɪkəz/ grammar word ★★★

> Because can be:
>
> - a **conjunction**: *We went by bus because it was cheaper.*
> - used in the preposition phrase **because of**: *The game was canceled because of the snow.*

used for giving the reason for something: *I couldn't call you because I didn't have your number.* ♦ *It's a really useful book, because it explains everything very clearly.* ♦ *Our profits fell* ***because of*** *the recession.* → JUST¹

beck /bek/ noun **at sb's beck and call** available to do things for another person whenever they want

beck·on /ˈbekən/ verb [I/T] **1** to signal to someone to come toward you **2** to seem to be an attractive possibility to someone: *A bright future beckoned.*

be·come /bɪˈkʌm/ (past tense **be·came** /bɪˈkeɪm/; past participle **be·come**) linking verb ★★★ to change and start to be something different: *The sky became dark.* ♦ *People were becoming increasingly angry about the delay.* ♦ *Christine decided to become a writer.* ♦ *São Paulo has become the largest city in South America.*

PHRASE **what has/will become of** used for asking what has happened to someone or something, or what will happen to them: *If she is sent to prison, what will become of her children?*

bed /bed/ noun ★★★

1 [C/U] a piece of furniture that you sleep on: *The room had two beds in it.* ♦ *It's midnight – why aren't you* ***in bed?*** ♦ *I never* ***get out of bed*** *before 10 a.m.* ♦ *I got home at 11 p.m. and* ***went straight to bed.***

2 [C] the ground at the bottom of an ocean or river: *a dried-up river bed*

3 [C] an area of ground that has been

prepared for growing plants in → FLOWERBED

PHRASES **bed and breakfast** a small hotel or private house that provides a room for the night and a meal the next morning

go to bed with sb *informal* to have sex with someone

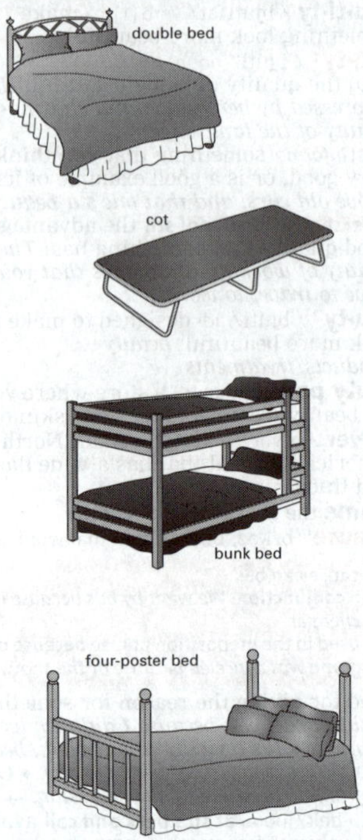

beds

bed•clothes /ˈbedˌkloʊðz, ˈbedˌkloʊz/ noun [plural] sheets and covers that are used on beds

bed•ding /ˈbedɪŋ/ noun [U] sheets and covers that are used on beds

be•drag•gled /bɪˈdræg(ə)ld/ adj wet, dirty, and messy

bed•rid•den /ˈbedˌrɪd(ə)n/ adj unable to get out of bed because you are too sick

bed•rock /ˈbedˌrɑk/ noun [singular] **1** the principles on which a system is based **2** the solid rock under the ground that supports the soil above it

bed•room /ˈbedˌrum/ noun [C] ★★ a room that you sleep in: *Your mom can stay in the spare bedroom.* ♦ *a two-bedroom apartment* ♦ *the bedroom door*

bed•side /ˈbedˌsaɪd/ noun [singular] the area near your bed: *a bedside lamp*

bed•spread /ˈbedˌspred/ noun [C] a top cover for a bed

bed•time /ˈbedˌtaɪm/ noun [U] the time when you usually go to bed: *Come on, kids – it's bedtime!* ♦ *a bedtime story*

bee /bi/ noun [C] a flying insect that has a black and yellow body, makes HONEY, and can sting you —*picture* → C13

beech /bitʃ/ noun [C/U] a large tree with smooth gray BARK and small nuts, or the wood of this tree

beef¹ /bif/ noun [U] ★ the meat from a cow: *a slice of roast beef*

beef² /bif/ PHRASAL VERB ˌ**beef sth ˈup** *informal* to increase or improve something

beef•y /ˈbifi/ adj *informal* a beefy person has a large heavy body

bee•hive /ˈbiˌhaɪv/ noun [C] a large box that people keep BEES in when they want to get the HONEY that the bees produce

been the past participle of **be**

beep¹ /bip/ verb **1** [I] if a piece of electronic equipment beeps, it makes a short high sound **2** [I/T] if you beep the horn in your car, it makes a short loud noise

beep² /bip/ noun [C] **1** a short high sound made by a piece of electronic equipment **2** the short loud noise that a car horn makes

beep•er /ˈbipər/ noun [C] a small piece of electronic equipment that you carry that makes a sound when someone sends you a message = PAGER

beer /bɪr/ noun ★

1 [U] a yellow or brown alcoholic drink made from grain: *a barrel of beer*

2 [C] a glass or bottle of this drink: *Would you like another beer?*

beet /bit/ noun [C/U] *American* a round purple vegetable that is cooked and eaten —*picture* → C11

bee•tle /ˈbit(ə)l/ noun [C] an insect with a smooth hard back —*picture* → C13

beet•root /ˈbitˌrut/ noun [C/U] *British* a BEET

be•fall /bɪˈfɔl/ (past tense **be•fell** /bɪˈfel/; past participle **be•fall•en** /bɪˈfɔlən/) verb [I/T] *literary* if something unpleasant befalls you, it happens to you

be•fit /bɪˈfɪt/ verb [T] *formal* to be appropriate for someone or something: *She dressed as befitted the daughter of a millionaire.* —**be•fit•ting** adj

be•fore /bɪˈfɔr/ grammar word ★★★

> **Before** can be:
> - a **conjunction**: *Think carefully before you choose.*
> - a **preposition**: *We'll finish the project before Christmas.*
> - an **adverb**: *I'd met him once before.*

1 earlier than something earlier than a particular time, event, or action: *I went for a run before breakfast.* ♦ *The others had gotten there before us.* ♦ *Have another drink before you go!* ♦ *I joined the police in 1999. Before that I was in the army.* ♦ *Haven't we met somewhere before?* ♦ *Don was here the* ***day before yesterday.*** ♦ **before doing sth** *You should seek legal advice before signing anything.*

2 earlier in series placed earlier than something else in a list or series: *"Barnes" comes before "Brown" on the list.*

3 passed first in a place that you reach as you go toward another place: *Our house is just before the end of the road.*

4 used in warnings or threats *spoken* used for warning or threatening that something

bad could happen: *Get out, before I lose my temper.*
5 in front of sb/sth *formal* in front of someone or something: *Lawrence knelt before the king.*
→ AGO

be•fore•hand /bɪˈfɔrˌhænd/ adv before a particular event: *If you do most of the cooking beforehand, you'll enjoy the evening more.*

be•friend /bɪˈfrend/ verb [T] to become someone's friend and treat them in a kind way

beg /beg/ verb [I/T] **1** to ask for something in a way that shows you want it very much: *She had written a letter begging him to come back.* ♦ *We begged her for another chance.* ♦ *"Don't go!" he begged.* **2** to ask people for money or food: *homeless people begging on the streets*
PHRASE **I beg your pardon** *spoken formal* **1** used for asking someone to repeat something **2** used for saying that you are sorry when you make a small mistake: *Oh, I beg your pardon, I didn't realize this was your chair.*

began the past tense of **begin**

beg•gar /ˈbegər/ noun [C] someone who lives by asking people for money or food

be•gin /bɪˈgɪn/ (past tense **be•gan** /bɪˈgæn/; past participle **be•gun** /bɪˈgʌn/; present participle **be•gin•ning**) verb ★★★
1 [I] to start happening, or to be the first thing to happen: *The ceremony will begin at noon.* ♦ *We usually use "an" before a word that **begins with** a vowel.*
2 [I/T] to start doing something: **begin doing sth** *He began yelling at them.* ♦ **begin to do sth** *Now we were beginning to feel excited.* ♦ **begin (sth) as sth** *He began his working life as a waiter.* ♦ **begin (sth) with sth** *We began the meeting with a discussion about the budget.*
PHRASE **to begin with 1** before or during the first part of an activity: *How did you get involved to begin with?* **2** *spoken* used for introducing the first thing in a list of things: *"Why were you annoyed?" "Well, to begin with, I missed my bus."*

be•gin•ner /bɪˈgɪnər/ noun [C] someone who has just started to learn or do something =NOVICE

be•gin•ning /bɪˈgɪnɪŋ/ noun ★★★
1 [singular] the first part of something =START ≠ END: *I loved **the beginning of** the book but hated the rest.* ♦ *It was **the beginning of** a friendship that would last his whole life.* ♦ ***In the beginning** I found it hard to concentrate.*
2 beginnings [plural] the origin of something, for example where or how it started: *It was a decade that saw **the beginnings of** the space program.*

be•grudge /bɪˈgrʌdʒ/ verb [T] **1** to feel annoyed because someone has something that you think they do not deserve **2** to feel annoyed because you have to do something =RESENT

begun the past participle of **begin**

be•half /bɪˈhæf/ noun ★
PHRASE **on sb's behalf** or **on behalf of sb**
1 instead of someone, or as a representative of someone: *A lawyer read out a statement on behalf of the victim's family.* **2** in order to help someone: *I offered to speak to the manager on his behalf.*

be•have /bɪˈheɪv/ verb ★★
1 [I] to do things in a particular way: *The children behaved very badly.* ♦ *a badly behaved dog* ♦ *You **behaved like** a complete idiot!* ♦ *He **behaved as though** he hadn't seen Ellie.*
2 [I/T] to be polite and not cause trouble: *Mom's always telling me to behave when we go out.* ♦ *I hope the children **behave themselves**.*

be•hav•ior /bɪˈheɪvjər/ noun [U] ★★★
1 the way that someone behaves: *Anna was sick of her brother's annoying behavior.*
2 *science* the way that a substance reacts in particular conditions: *Scientists are studying the behavior of the new gas.*

be•hav•iour /bɪˈheɪvjər/ the British spelling of **behavior**

be•head /bɪˈhed/ verb [T] to cut off someone's head as a punishment

be•hind¹ /bɪˈhaɪnd/ grammar word ★★★

> **Behind** can be:
> - a **preposition**: *The car behind us was flashing its lights.*
> - an **adverb**: *I stayed behind to take care of the children.*

1 at the back of sb/sth at the back of someone or something, or following them: *The teacher was standing behind me.* ♦ *Some papers had fallen behind the bookcase.* ♦ *Shut the door behind you.* ♦ *You walk ahead and we'll follow along behind.* ♦ *Someone grabbed me **from behind**.*
2 late in doing sth late or too slow in doing things that you have to do: *The project is already a month behind schedule.* ♦ *I've been sick, and now I'm **behind with** my work.*
3 remaining after people leave remaining in a place after people have left: *A few people stayed behind to clean up.* ♦ *Some of the equipment got left behind.*
4 achieving less progress or success with less success or progress than others: *Technology in Eastern Europe was at least 20 years behind the West.* ♦ *At half time, our team was behind by 12 points.*
5 used for stating the real cause of sth used for stating what the true cause of something is, or what the true facts are in a situation: *Police believe that a racist group is behind the attacks.* ♦ *People want to know the truth behind these rumors.*
6 supporting sb/sth supporting a person, action, or idea: *I want you to know we're behind you all the way.*
7 in the past in the past, and no longer affecting you: *All those bad times are behind me now.*
PHRASE **behind the times** old-fashioned: *A business without its own website is definitely way behind the times.*

be•hind² /bɪˈhaɪnd/ noun [C] *informal* the part of your body that you sit on

beige /beɪʒ/ adj very pale brown in color —**beige** noun [U]

B

be·ing /ˈbiːŋ/ noun [C] a person: *We are social beings as well as individuals.*
PHRASE **come into being** to start to exist

be·lat·ed /bɪˈleɪtəd/ adj happening or arriving late: *a belated apology* —**be·lat·ed·ly** adv

belch¹ /beltʃ/ verb **1** [I] to let air from your stomach come out through your mouth in a noisy way=BURP **2** [T] to produce a lot of smoke or steam

belch² /beltʃ/ noun [C] the action or sound of someone belching

be·lea·guered /bɪˈligərd/ adj having a lot of problems or criticism to deal with

be·lie /bɪˈlaɪ/ verb [T] *formal* **1** to make something appear different from how it really is **2** to seem to show that something is not true

be·lief /bɪˈlif/ noun ★★★
1 [C] a strong feeling that something is true, real, or good: *a **belief in** the possibility of a perfect society* ♦ *It is my **firm belief** that the government should act now.* ♦ **+that** *the mistaken belief that cocaine is not an addictive drug*
2 beliefs [plural] a set of ideas that you are certain are true: *Christian/Buddhist beliefs* ♦ *Everyone is entitled to **express** their own personal **beliefs**.* ♦ *our traditional **beliefs about** the origins of life*
PHRASE **beyond belief** used for emphasizing how bad or surprising something is: *The conditions they are living in are beyond belief.*

be·liev·a·ble /bɪˈlivəb(ə)l/ adj something that is believable seems possible or likely to be true=PLAUSIBLE

be·lieve /bɪˈliv/ verb ★★★
1 [T] to think that something is true: *Astronomers knew the Earth was round, but few people believed it.* ♦ *The police didn't believe her.* ♦ **+(that)** *I don't believe she's his sister at all.* ♦ *It is **widely believed*** (=believed by a lot of people) *that the disease originally came from monkeys.* ♦ *She **found it hard to believe** that he was a real businessman.*
2 [T] to have an opinion about what is true or what might happen, although there is no proof=THINK: **+(that)** *Scientists believe a cure for the disease will be discovered soon.* ♦ *We were **led to believe*** (=people told us) *we could make a large profit.*
3 [I] to have a religious belief
PHRASES **I can't/don't believe it** *spoken* **1** used for emphasizing that you are extremely surprised or shocked: *"He graduated from Harvard." "I don't believe it!"* **2** used when something annoys you: *I just don't believe it! I left my keys in the car again.*
would you believe it? *spoken* used for showing that you think something is surprising or funny: *And they want me to sing – would you believe it?*
PHRASAL VERB **beˈlieve ˌin sb/sth** **1** to think that someone or something exists: *I don't believe in miracles.* **2** to think that someone or something is good: *She used to say she didn't believe in marriage.*

> **Word family: believe**
> *Words in the same family as **believe***
> - **belief** *n*
> - **disbelief** *n*
> - **believable** *adj*
> - **unbelievable** *v*
> - **disbelieve** *adj*

be·liev·er /bɪˈlivər/ noun [C] someone who believes in God, a religion, or a set of principles
PHRASE **be a great/firm believer in sth** to believe that a particular idea or activity is good: *I'm a great believer in healthy eating and exercise.*

be·lit·tle /bɪˈlɪt(ə)l/ verb [T] to say that someone or something is not very good or important

bell /bel/ noun [C] ★★
1 a metal object that makes a noise when its sides are hit by a metal piece inside it: *the sound of church bells ringing*
2 a piece of equipment that makes a ringing sound, used for getting someone's attention: *There was no one at the counter, so I rang the bell.*
→ RING¹

bel·lig·er·ent /bəˈlɪdʒ(ə)rənt/ adj very unfriendly and angry=AGGRESSIVE —**bel·lig·er·ence** noun [U]

bel·low /ˈbeloʊ/ verb [I/T] to shout very loudly

ˈbell ˌpepper noun [C] *American* a HOLLOW green, red, or yellow vegetable with small white seeds inside. It can be eaten raw or cooked. *—picture* → C11

bel·ly /ˈbeli/ noun [C] *informal* your stomach, or the front part of your body between your chest and your legs

ˈbelly ˌbutton noun [C] *informal* a person's NAVEL

be·long /bɪˈlɔŋ/ verb [I] ★★★
1 to be in the right place: *That lamp belongs on the desk.* ♦ *When you're done put the books back where they belong.*
2 to feel happy and comfortable in a particular place or group: *I just don't feel that I belong here.*
PHRASAL VERBS **beˈlong ˌto sb** to be owned by someone: *The car belongs to the woman next door.* ♦ *Who does this coat belong to?*
beˈlong ˌto sth to be a member of a group or organization: *She belongs to the school computer club.*

be·long·ings /bɪˈlɔŋɪŋz/ noun [plural] the things that you own

be·lov·ed /bɪˈlʌvɪd/ adj *literary* a beloved person, place, or thing is one that you love very much

be·low /bɪˈloʊ/ grammar word ★★★

> **Below** can be:
> - a **preposition**: *The lake is almost 900 feet below sea level.*
> - an **adverb**: *I heard someone calling from the street below.*

1 in a lower place or position: *There was a party in the apartment below.* ♦ *a gunshot wound below the left shoulder*
2 less than a particular number, amount, or level: *The temperature fell below zero.* ♦ *His score on the test was below average.*
3 lower in rank or less important than

someone else: *officers below the rank of captain*
4 in a later part of a piece of writing: *For further information, see below.*

belt[1] /belt/ noun [C] ★
1 a narrow piece of leather or cloth that you wear around your waist
2 a circular band that turns or moves something in a machine
3 an area of land where there is a particular industry or activity: *the corn belt*
PHRASE **get/have sth under your belt** *informal* to achieve something that is important and useful: *You need to get a few more computer programming courses under your belt.*
→ TIGHTEN

belt[2] /belt/ verb [T] *informal* to hit someone or something very hard
PHRASAL VERB **,belt sth 'out** *informal* to sing something loudly

belt·way /ˈbeltˌweɪ/ noun [C] *American* a road that goes around the edge of a city to keep traffic away from the center

be·mused /bɪˈmjuzd/ adj confused

bench[1] /bentʃ/ noun **1** [C] a hard seat for two or more people to sit on outside: *a park bench* —*picture* → CHAIR **2 the bench** [singular] a place where people in a sports team sit when they are not playing **3 the bench** [singular] the position of being a judge in a court of law, or the place where a judge sits **4** [C] a long table that you use when you are working with tools

bench[2] /bentʃ/ verb [T] *American* to make a sports player stop playing a game for a short time

bench·mark /ˈbentʃˌmɑrk/ noun [C] a level or standard that you can use for judging how good other things are

bend[1] /bend/ (past tense and past participle **bent** /bent/) verb [I/T] ★★
1 to lean forward and downward: ***Bend over** and touch your toes.* ♦ *Helen **bent down** to pick up her pen.*
2 to curve or fold something, or to be curved or folded: *Use thin wire than can be easily bent.* ♦ *His arm was so stiff he couldn't bend it at all.* ♦ *The slim branches were bending under the weight of their fruit.*
PHRASES **bend over backward (to do sth)** *informal* to do everything that you can do in order to help
bend the rules (for sb) to allow something that is not usually allowed

bend[2] /bend/ noun [C] a curve in something such as a road or river: *We came to a sharp bend in the road.*

bend·y /ˈbendi/ adj *informal* easy to bend

be·neath /bɪˈniθ/ grammar word ★★
1 directly under something, or at a lower level: *We sheltered beneath a tree.* ♦ *You can see through the clear water to the coral reefs beneath.*
2 if something is beneath you, you think that you are too good or important to have to do it

ben·e·fac·tor /ˈbenəˌfæktər/ noun [C] someone who helps a person or organization by giving them money

ben·e·fi·cial /ˌbenəˈfɪʃ(ə)l/ adj something that is beneficial has a good effect or influence ≠ DETRIMENTAL, HARMFUL

ben·e·fi·ci·ar·y /ˌbenəˈfɪʃiˌeri, ˌbenəˈfɪʃəri/ noun [C] **1** someone who gets money or property from someone who has died **2** *formal* someone who gets an advantage from a situation

ben·e·fit[1] /ˈbenəfɪt/ noun ★★
1 [C] something good that you get from your employer as part of your job: *The benefits include medical insurance and a company car.*
2 [C/U] an advantage that you get from a situation: *He has **had the benefit of** the best education money can buy.* ♦ *Consider the potential **benefits of** the deal for the company.* ♦ *We are working **for the benefit** of the whole community.*
3 [C] an event that is organized in order to make money for a CHARITY: *a benefit concert/performance*
4 [C/U] *British* payment for people who are sick or unemployed: *housing/sickness/disability benefit*
PHRASE **give sb the benefit of the doubt** to accept what someone says, although you know that they might be lying

ben·e·fit[2] /ˈbenəfɪt/ (present participle **ben·e·fit·ing** or **ben·e·fit·ting**; past tense and past participle **ben·e·fit·ed** or **ben·e·fit·ted**) verb [I/T] ★★ to get an advantage, or to give someone an advantage: *Thousands of households could benefit under the plan.* ♦ *The system mainly benefited people in the cities.* ♦ *Some patients have **benefited** greatly **from** this treatment.*

be·nev·o·lent /bəˈnevələnt/ adj kind and helpful —**be·nev·o·lence** noun [U]

be·nign /bəˈnaɪn/ adj **1** a benign TUMOR (=lump in your body) is not cancer and will not kill you ≠ MALIGNANT **2** *formal* kind and nice

bent[1] /bent/ adj a bent object has a curved or twisted shape

bent[2] the past tense and past participle of **bend**[1]

be·queath /bɪˈkwið, bɪˈkwiθ/ verb [T] *formal* to give someone money or property after you die by making a legal document called a WILL

be·quest /bɪˈkwest/ noun [C] *formal* money or property that you give to someone after you die by making a legal document called a WILL

be·reaved /bɪˈrivd/ adj a bereaved person is someone whose close friend or family member has recently died

be·reave·ment /bɪˈrivmənt/ noun [C/U] an occasion when a close friend or family member dies

be·reft /bɪˈreft/ adj *literary* **bereft of sth** lacking something that you need

be·ret /ˈbeˌreɪ/ noun [C] a round flat soft hat that fits tightly on the top of your head

ber·ry /ˈberi/ noun [C] a small fruit that does not have a PIT inside it

ber·serk /bəˈzɜrk/ adj **go berserk 1** *informal* to become very excited **2** to become violent because you are very angry

berth /bɜrθ/ noun [C] **1** a place at a port where a ship stays for a period of time **2** a bed on a train or ship

B

be·side /bɪˈsaɪd/ preposition ★★ at the side of someone or something: *Who's that standing beside Jeff?* ♦ *We found a picnic area down beside the river.*

PHRASES **beside the point** not relevant to the subject that you are discussing

beside yourself unable to think clearly because you are very upset or excited

be·sides /bɪˈsaɪdz/ grammar word ★

> **Besides** can be:
> - a **preposition**: *Did you talk to anyone besides Joan?*
> - an **adverb**: *I've read all the books on the list, and a few others besides.*

1 in addition to someone or something else: *A lot of them are studying other things besides Italian.* ♦ *Besides being a teammate, he's my friend.* ♦ *There are cakes and sandwiches, and lots more besides.*

2 used when you are adding another reason to support what you are saying: *It's too late to invite any more people. Besides, Tim hates parties.*

be·siege /bɪˈsidʒ/ verb [T] **1** to make more requests or complaints than someone can deal with: *The department has been besieged with letters from angry students.* **2** if soldiers besiege a place, they surround it and prevent the people there from getting food and supplies

best /best/ grammar word ★★★

> **Best** can be:
> - an **adjective**: *Which apples are best for cooking?* ♦ *It was the best party I've ever been to.*
> - an **adverb**: *We'll choose the system that works best.*
> - a **noun**: *I'll do my best.*

1 the superlative form of "good" and "well," used for describing the person, thing, or way that is the most satisfactory, appropriate, skillful, etc. ≠ WORST: *the best hotel in town* ♦ *You need to find out which program works best on your computer.* ♦ *In the world of ballet she was simply the best.* ♦ *The new drug is safe and effective, and **best of all**, inexpensive.* ♦ *What kind of soil is **best for** growing roses?* ♦ *I'll try to deal with all these problems **as best I can**.*

2 liked or known more than anyone or anything else ≠ WORST: *What kind of music do you **like best**?* ♦ *The Mona Lisa is probably the world's **best known** painting.*

PHRASES **at best** used for stating what is the best or biggest possible thing, when this is not very good: *You can hope for a 5% profit at best.*

at sb's/sth's best feeling or showing the most impressive or attractive qualities possible: *I'm not at my best early in the morning.*

be for the best used for saying that something that seems bad will in fact make the situation better

sb's best friend the friend that someone likes best

the best of both worlds a situation where you have two different advantages at the same time

best wishes used as a polite and friendly greeting before you sign your name on a letter or card

do/try your best to try as hard as you can

make the best of it to try to deal with a bad or difficult situation as well as you can

→ PART[1]

ˌbest ˈman noun [singular] the friend who helps a BRIDEGROOM at his wedding

be·stow /bɪˈstoʊ/ verb [T] *formal* to give someone something good or valuable

best·sell·er /ˌbestˈselər/ noun [C] a book that many people buy

bet[1] /bet/ (past tense and past participle **bet**) verb [I/T] ★ to risk an amount of money by saying what you think will happen in a race or game: *Thousands of people **bet on** the result of the game.* ♦ **bet sth on sth** *I bet $10 on each of the horses.* ♦ **bet (sb) that** *He bet me $20 that I couldn't keep quiet for ten minutes.*

PHRASE **you bet** *spoken* used for saying "yes" in an enthusiastic way

bet[2] /bet/ noun [C] an agreement in which you bet money on what will happen, or the amount of money that you bet: *He likes to have a bet on his home team, even though they always lose.*

PHRASE **a safe bet** something that is likely to happen, or someone or something that is likely to be successful: *It's a safe bet that the others won't make the same mistake.*

→ BETTING

be·tray /bɪˈtreɪ/ verb [T] **1** if you betray your country, your family, or your friends, you deliberately do something that harms them **2** if you betray a feeling that you want to hide, your words or face make the feeling clear to people: *The woman's face betrayed no emotion.* **3** if you betray your beliefs or principles, you do something that does not agree with them

be·tray·al /bɪˈtreɪəl/ noun [C/U] an act of betraying someone or something

bet·ter /ˈbetər/ grammar word ★★★

> **Better** can be:
> - an **adjective**: *a better method of teaching languages*
> - an **adverb**: *Our opponents played better than we did.*
> - a **noun**: *There has been a change for the better.*

1 the comparative form of "good" and "well," used for describing a person, thing, or way that is more satisfactory, appropriate, skillful, etc. than another ≠ WORSE: *She's trying to find a better job.* ♦ *The machine works better if you change the oil regularly.* ♦ *The situation started to **get better**.* ♦ *It's a good book, but her first one was **far better**.* ♦ *The results were **better than** we had expected.* ♦ *Maggie's a **better** cook **than** me.* ♦ *It's not much, but it's **better than nothing**.*

2 healthy again, or no longer painful ≠ WORSE: *You shouldn't go back to school until you're better.* ♦ *Is your headache better?* ♦ *If you want to **get better**, you have to take your medicine.*

3 liked or known more than someone or something else: *I've always **liked** Susan **better** than her sister.* ♦ *He is **better known** by the name "Pele."*

PHRASES **better yet/still** used when you are adding a new idea that you think is better: *Come for a weekend or, better yet, come for a whole week.*

for the better if something changes for the better, it improves ≠ FOR THE WORSE

get the better of sb 1 if a feeling gets the better of you, it is too strong for you to control **2** to defeat someone in a game or argument

(had) better do sth *spoken* used for saying that someone should do something: *You'd better take an umbrella – it's going to rain.* ♦ *Do you think we'd better go now?*

the sooner/bigger/quicker etc. the better used for saying that you want something to be as soon/big/quick etc. as possible: *I want you to get rid of those people, and the sooner the better.*

ˌbetter ˈoff adj someone who is better off is in a better situation, or has more money: *You'd be better off living on your own.*

bet·ting /ˈbetɪŋ/ noun [U] the activity of trying to win money by placing a BET (=guessing the result of a race or game)

be·tween /bɪˈtwin/ grammar word ★★★

> **Between** can be:
> - a **preposition**: *the distance between two places*
> - an **adverb**: *two classes with a short break between*

1 with sb/sth on each side or end in a position with people or things on each side or end: *Hold the needle between your finger and thumb.* ♦ *Trains running between Boston and New York were delayed.* ♦ *A sandwich is two slices of bread with something* ***in between***. ♦ *Charlotte sat* ***in between*** *her two sons.*

2 with times or events before and after in the period after one time or event and before the next: *The office will be closed between Christmas and New Year.* ♦ *I have two classes this morning, with a short break* ***in between***.

3 within a range within a range of numbers or amounts: *children between the ages of 4 and 13*

4 involving two people or things used for showing which people or things are involved in something: *a conversation between the Prime Minister and the President* ♦ *Scientists believe there is a link between diet and cancer.* ♦ *tonight's game between Dallas and San Francisco* → AMONG

5 talking about differences used for showing which people or things are similar or different: *Does a five-year-old know the difference between right and wrong?* ♦ *There are parallels between computer systems and the human brain.*

6 shared or divided used for showing how something is shared or divided: *We agreed to split the profits equally between us.*

7 talking about choices used for showing that you can choose one of two or more things: *You can choose between pasta, pizza, or burgers.*

PHRASE **between you and me** used when you are telling someone something that you do not want anyone else to know

bev·er·age /ˈbev(ə)rɪdʒ/ noun [C] *formal* a drink

be·ware /bɪˈwer/ verb [I/T] if someone tells you to beware of something, they are warning you that it might be dangerous: *Beware of the dog!*

be·wil·dered /bɪˈwɪldərd/ adj confused and not certain what to do

be·wil·der·ing /bɪˈwɪldərɪŋ/ adj making you feel confused and not certain what to do

be·wil·der·ment /bɪˈwɪldərmənt/ noun [U] a feeling of being confused

be·yond /bɪˈjɑnd/ grammar word ★★★

> **Beyond** can be:
> - a **preposition**: *the world beyond the prison wall*
> - an **adverb**: *The empire extended to the Danube River and beyond.*

1 past a place farther away than something else or outside a particular area: *I could see the ocean beyond the fields.* ♦ *Dr. Barnard's fame had spread far beyond South Africa.*

2 not within the limits of sth outside the range or limits of a subject, quality, or activity: *Their behavior went far beyond what is acceptable.*

3 except used in negative sentences to mean "except": *We know nothing about him beyond these few facts.*

4 not able to be done used for saying that something cannot be done: *The situation is already* ***beyond our control***. ♦ *I'm afraid the watch is damaged* ***beyond repair***. ♦ *The center of the city has changed* ***beyond recognition***.

5 after a time or age, or above an amount continuing after a particular time or age, or moving past a particular level: *She never went beyond tenth grade in school.* ♦ *Inflation has risen beyond ten percent.*

PHRASE **be beyond sb** to be too difficult for someone to understand or deal with: *It's beyond me why anyone would want to marry him.*

bi·as /ˈbaɪəs/ noun [singular/U] **1** an attitude that makes you treat someone in a way that is unfair or different from the way you treat other people: *Ideally we'd choose judges who are without political bias.* **2** emphasis on one thing more than others: *a French course with a bias toward the spoken language*

bi·ased /ˈbaɪəst/ adj preferring one person, thing, or idea to another in a way that is unfair ≠ UNBIASED

bib /bɪb/ noun [C] a piece of cloth that is tied around a baby's neck to protect its clothes while it is eating

bi·ble /ˈbaɪb(ə)l/ noun **1 the Bible** [singular] the holy book of the Christian and Jewish religions **2** [C] a copy of the Bible **3** [C] the most important book for a particular subject

bib·li·cal /ˈbɪblɪk(ə)l/ adj from the Bible, or described in the Bible

bib·li·og·ra·phy /ˌbɪbliˈɑgrəfi/ noun [C] a list of books and articles on a particular subject

bi·ceps /ˈbaɪˌseps/ (plural **bi·ceps**) noun [C] the muscle between your shoulder and elbow on the front of your arm

B

bick•er /ˈbɪkər/ verb [I] to argue about things that are not important —**bick•er•ing** /ˈbɪkərɪŋ/ noun [U]

bi•cy•cle /ˈbaɪsɪk(ə)l/ noun [C] a vehicle with two wheels that you ride by pushing PEDALS with your feet —*picture* → C7

bid[1] /bɪd/ (past tense and past participle **bid**; present participle **bid•ding**) verb **1** [I/T] to offer a particular amount of money for something: *They bid $300 for the painting.* **2** [I] to offer to do work or provide a service for a particular amount of money: *Several firms are bidding for the job.* —**bid•der** noun [C]: *The house will be sold to the highest bidder.*

bid[2] /bɪd/ noun [C] **1** an offer to pay a particular amount of money for something: *We received a bid of $12,000 for the table.* **2** an offer to do work or provide a service for a particular amount of money: *They've put in a bid for the construction project.* **3** an attempt to do something: *a bid to win the championship*

bid•ding /ˈbɪdɪŋ/ noun [U] the process of making bids for things
PHRASE **do sb's bidding** to do what someone asks or tells you to do

bide /baɪd/ verb **bide your time** to wait in a patient way for an opportunity to do something

bi•det /biˈdeɪ/ noun [C] a large bowl in a bathroom that you sit on to wash your bottom

bi•en•ni•al /baɪˈeniəl/ adj happening once every two years

big /bɪg/ adj ★★★

1 large	4 older
2 important	5 enthusiastic
3 successful	

1 large in size: *big brown eyes* ♦ *A big man stood in the doorway.* ♦ *At the end of the road was a great big house.*
2 important or serious: *We have another big game next week.*
3 powerful or successful: *The place was full of big businessmen.* ♦ *It was her dream to make it big as a singer.* ♦ *Her mother is big in local television.*
4 *informal* your big sister or big brother is older than you ≠ LITTLE: *This is my big brother, Jake.*
5 enthusiastic: *They were big fans of the Beatles.*

Words that you can use instead of big

Big is a very general word. Here are some words with more specific meanings that sound more natural and appropriate in particular situations.

people	large, tall
animals/plants	enormous, gigantic, great big, huge, large, massive
objects	bulky, colossal, enormous, gigantic, immense, large, massive
buildings	high, huge, large, rambling, tall
places/areas/cities	huge, large, massive, vast
rooms	airy, spacious
groups/organizations/ systems	enormous, huge, large, massive
numbers/amounts	colossal, considerable, high, huge, immense, massive, significant, sizeable, substantial, tremendous
changes	drastic, major, radical, significant, sweeping
problems	considerable, important, major, serious

big•a•my /ˈbɪgəmi/ noun [U] the crime of being married to more than one person at the same time —**big•a•mist** noun [C]

ˌBig ˈApple, the an informal name for New York City

ˌBig ˈBang, the an explosion that some scientists believe was the origin of the universe

ˌBig ˈBrother noun [singular] a person or organization that watches people all the time and tries to control everything that they say or do

ˌbig ˈbusiness noun [U] important business activity that makes a lot of money

Big Dip•per, the /ˌbɪg ˈdɪpər/ *American* a CONSTELLATION (=group of stars) made up of seven stars that can be seen in the northern half of the world

ˌbig ˈgovernment noun [U] government that seems to have too much control over people's lives

ˌbig ˈmoney noun [U] *informal* a lot of money

ˌbig ˈname noun [C] *informal* a famous person

big•ot /ˈbɪgət/ noun [C] someone who has very strong and unreasonable opinions about politics, race, or religion —**big•ot•ed** adj

big•ot•ry /ˈbɪgətri/ noun [U] very strong and unreasonable opinions about politics, race, or religion

ˌbig ˈscreen, the noun [singular] the movies

ˌbig ˌshot noun [C] *informal* an important person in an organization

ˈbig-ˌticket adj *informal* expensive: *big-ticket items like stereos and DVD players*

ˈbig ˌtime adv *spoken* used for emphasizing what you are saying: *"Did you have problems with it?" "Yeah, big time."*

ˈbig ˌtime, the noun [singular] the highest and most successful level in a profession

big•wig /ˈbɪgˌwɪg/ noun [C] *informal* an important and powerful person in an organization

bike[1] /baɪk/ noun [C] *informal* ★★★ a BICYCLE or a MOTORCYCLE

bike[2] /baɪk/ verb [I] *informal* to ride somewhere on a bicycle

bik•er /ˈbaɪkər/ noun [C] someone who rides a MOTORCYCLE

bi•ki•ni /bɪˈkini/ noun [C] a swimming suit for women, with two separate parts that cover the breasts and the lower part of the body —*picture* → C5

bi•lat•er•al /ˌbaɪˈlæt(ə)rəl/ adj involving two groups or countries: *bilateral negotiations/talks* —**bi•lat•er•al•ly** adv

bile /baɪl/ noun [U] **1** a bitter liquid that your liver produces to help your body to DIGEST food **2** *literary* angry words or feelings

bi·lin·gual /baɪˈlɪŋgwəl/ adj **1** able to speak two languages **2** written in two languages: *a bilingual dictionary*

bill[1] /bɪl/ noun [C] ★★★

1 amount that you owe	4 in a restaurant
2 paper money	5 bird's beak
3 proposal for law	

1 a written statement that shows how much money you owe for goods or services that you have received: *a telephone bill* ♦ *I always **pay my bills** on time.* ♦ *I wonder what **the bill for** the repairs will be?*

2 *American* a piece of paper money: *a $100 bill*

3 a written document that contains a proposal for a new law

4 a CHECK in a restaurant = CHECK

5 a bird's beak

→ FOOT[2]

bill[2] /bɪl/ verb [T] to send or give someone a written statement that shows how much money they owe: *We were billed for three nights when we were only there for two.*

PHRASE **be billed as** to be advertised or described in a particular way: *It was billed as the wedding of the year.*

bill·board /ˈbɪlˌbɔrd/ noun [C] a large board for advertisements

bill·fold /ˈbɪlˌfoʊld/ noun [C] *American* a WALLET

bil·liards /ˈbɪljərdz/ noun [U] a game in which two people use long sticks called CUES to hit balls into POCKETS at the edges and corners of a table → POOL[1] 3

bill·ing /ˈbɪlɪŋ/ noun [U] **1** the process of sending bills for payment **2** the importance that is given to a performer or an event in advertising material: *I got top billing.*

bil·lion /ˈbɪljən/ number the number 1,000,000,000

ˌBill of ˈRights, the the part of the U.S. CONSTITUTION that describes the rights of citizens

bil·low /ˈbɪloʊ/ verb [I] **1** to rise or move in clouds: *Black smoke billowed over the city.* **2** to be filled with air and swell out like a sail: *Their robes billowed in the wind.*

bim·bo /ˈbɪmboʊ/ noun [C] *informal* an insulting word for a young woman who is attractive but not very intelligent

bin /bɪn/ noun [C] **1** a container for storing something: *a recycling bin* **2** *British* a container for putting garbage in: *He tore up the letter and put it in the bin.*

bi·na·ry /ˈbaɪnəri/ adj **1** *computing* based on a system in which information is represented using combinations of the numbers 0 and 1 **2** *technical* consisting of two parts

bind /baɪnd/ (past tense and past participle **bound** /baʊnd/) verb [T] **1** to tie things together with rope or string: *Their hands were bound behind their backs.* **2** to make two people or groups feel closely connected to each other: *The troubles they had shared bound them much closer together.* **3** to limit what someone is allowed to do by making them obey a rule or agreement: *He is bound by a contract that prevents him from working for competitors.*

bind·er /ˈbaɪndər/ noun [C] a hard cover that holds loose papers together

bind·ing[1] /ˈbaɪndɪŋ/ adj a binding agreement, contract, or decision must be obeyed

bind·ing[2] /ˈbaɪndɪŋ/ noun [C] the cover of a book

binge /bɪndʒ/ noun [C] an occasion when someone does too much of something that they enjoy, such as eating —**binge** verb [I]

bin·go /ˈbɪŋgoʊ/ noun [U] a game in which players try to match numbers on their cards with numbers that are called out

bin·oc·u·lars /bɪˈnɑkjələrz/ noun [plural] a piece of equipment that you look through to see distant objects. It has a separate part for each eye.

bi·o·chem·i·cal /ˌbaɪoʊˈkemɪk(ə)l/ adj involving chemical substances and processes in living things

bi·o·chem·is·try /ˌbaɪoʊˈkemɪstri/ noun [U] the study of chemical processes in living things —**bi·o·chem·ist** noun [C]

bi·o·de·grad·a·ble /ˌbaɪoʊdɪˈgreɪdəb(ə)l/ adj decaying naturally in a way that is not harmful to the environment

bi·o·di·ver·si·ty /ˌbaɪoʊdaɪˈvɜrsəti/ noun [U] the variety of different types of plant and animal life in a particular region

bi·o·graph·er /baɪˈɑgrəfər/ noun [C] someone who writes a book about someone else's life

bi·o·graph·i·cal /ˌbaɪəˈgræfɪk(ə)l/ adj relating to the facts of someone's life

bi·og·ra·phy /baɪˈɑgrəfi/ noun [C] a book that someone writes about someone else's life

bi·o·log·i·cal /ˌbaɪəˈlɑdʒɪk(ə)l/ adj **1** relating to living things **2** using dangerous bacteria to harm people: *biological weapons/warfare* —**bi·o·log·i·cal·ly** /ˌbaɪəˈlɑdʒɪkli/ adv

bi·ol·o·gist /baɪˈɑlədʒɪst/ noun [C] a scientist who studies living things

bi·ol·o·gy /baɪˈɑlədʒi/ noun [U] the scientific study of living things

bi·op·sy /ˈbaɪˌɑpsi/ noun [C] a medical test in which cells are taken from your body and are examined to find out if they are healthy

bi·o·tech·nol·o·gy /ˌbaɪoʊtekˈnɑlədʒi/ noun [U] *science* the use of bacteria and cells from plants and animals for industrial or scientific purposes

bi·par·ti·san /baɪˈpɑrtɪzən/ adj involving two political parties

birch /bɜrtʃ/ noun [C/U] a tree with thin branches and an outer layer that comes off in thin strips

bird /bɜrd/ noun [C] ★★★ an animal with feathers, two wings, and a BEAK (=a hard pointed mouth)

PHRASE **bird of prey** a bird that hunts and eats other animals

→ EARLY BIRD

ˌbird's-eye ˈview noun [singular] a good view of something from a high position

birth /bɜrθ/ noun ★★

1 [C/U] the occasion when a baby is born: *We are happy to announce **the birth of** our son Andrew.* ♦ *James has been blind **since birth**.* ♦ *children who have medical problems*

B

at birth ♦ *Her place of birth was listed as Reno.* → DATE[1]
2 [singular] the beginning of something: ***the birth of** a new era in Latin American politics*
3 [U] your position in society according to your family, or according to the place where you were born: *She's French **by birth**.*
PHRASE **give birth (to sb)** to produce a baby from inside your body: *She gave birth to a baby boy.*

'birth cer,tificate noun [C] an official document that shows your name, details of when and where you were born, and who your parents are

'birth con,trol noun [U] the practice of avoiding becoming pregnant, or the methods that people use for this = CONTRACEPTION

birth·day /ˈbɜrθˌdeɪ/ noun [C] ★★ the day each year with the same date as the day when you were born: *It's her seventeenth birthday tomorrow.* ♦ *Her birthday is on June 7th.* ♦ *a birthday party/card/present* ♦ *Happy birthday, Tessa!*

birth·mark /ˈbɜrθˌmɑrk/ noun [C] a red or brown mark on the skin that some people are born with

'birth ,parent noun [C] one of the parents that someone had when they were born, rather than one of the parents who ADOPTED them

birth·place /ˈbɜrθˌpleɪs/ noun [C] **1** the place where someone was born **2** the place where something first started

'birth ,rate noun [C] the official number of births in a particular year or place

bis·cuit /ˈbɪskɪt/ noun [C] **1** *American* a small round soft type of bread **2** *British* a COOKIE

bi·sex·u·al /baɪˈsekʃuəl/ adj sexually attracted to both men and women → HETEROSEXUAL, HOMOSEXUAL
—**bi·sex·u·al·i·ty** /ˌbaɪsekʃuˈæləti/ noun [U]

bish·op /ˈbɪʃəp/ noun [C] **1** a senior Christian priest who is responsible for all the churches in a particular area **2** a piece in the game of CHESS, shaped like a bishop's hat —*picture* → C16

bi·son /ˈbaɪs(ə)n/ (plural **bi·son**) noun [C] a large wild animal like a cow with long hair and a big head

bis·tro /ˈbistroʊ/ noun [C] a small restaurant or bar

bit¹ /bɪt/ grammar word ★★

> **A bit can be:**
> - an **adverb**: *We waited a bit, and then decided to go.* ♦ *It's a bit cold in here, isn't it?*
> - a **pronoun**: *She only ate a little bit.* ♦ *I could use a bit of help.*

PHRASES **a (little) bit** *informal* **1** slightly, or a little: *I'm feeling a little bit tired.* **2** a small amount of something: *"Would you like some more sauce?" "Just a little bit."* ♦ *I know **a bit of** German.* **3** to a limited degree: *I used to surf a little bit when I was younger.* **4** a short time
a bit of a... *informal* used for saying that someone or something has a particular quality or effect: *My letter has caused a bit of a problem.*
every bit as just as: *Her new book is every bit as good as the first one.*
a good/fair bit *British* a fairly large amount of something: *We've still got a fair bit to do.*
quite a bit *informal* a lot: *You can fly there, but it costs quite a bit.*

bit² /bɪt/ noun [C] ★★
1 a small piece or part of something: *There were **bits of** broken glass everywhere.*
2 *computing* the basic unit of computer information → BYTE
3 the part of a horse's BRIDLE that fits inside the horse's mouth
PHRASES **bit by bit** gradually, or in small stages: *I'll move my things into the apartment bit by bit.*
to bits *informal* **1** into small pieces **2** very much: *He's thrilled to bits.*

bit³ the past tense of **bite¹**

bitch¹ /bɪtʃ/ noun [C] **1** *offensive* an insulting word for a woman **2** a female dog

bitch² /bɪtʃ/ verb [I] *informal* to complain or say unkind things about someone or something

bitch·y /ˈbɪtʃi/ adj *informal* rude or cruel toward someone

bite¹ /baɪt/ (past tense **bit** /bɪt/; past participle **bit·ten** /ˈbɪt(ə)n/) verb ★★
1 [I/T] to use your teeth to cut or break something, usually in order to eat it: *Stop biting your nails.* ♦ *I've just been bitten by a snake.* ♦ *Tom **bit into** his sandwich.*
2 [I] to have an unpleasant effect: *The economic slowdown is beginning to bite.*
PHRASES **bite the bullet** *informal* to force yourself to do something difficult or unpleasant
bite sb's head off *informal* to react angrily or rudely to someone, when this reaction seems too strong
bite your tongue to stop yourself from saying something that might upset or annoy someone
PHRASAL VERB **'bite sth ,off** to separate something from the main part by biting: *I bit off a chunk of chocolate.*

bite

bite² /baɪt/ noun **1** [C] an act of cutting or breaking something with your teeth, usually in order to eat it: *Anthony ate half his burger in one bite.* **2** [C] a mark where an animal or insect has bitten you **3 bite** or **bite to eat** [singular] a small meal, especially one that you eat in a hurry = SNACK

bite-sized /ˈbaɪtˌsaɪzd/ or **bite-size** /ˈbaɪtˌsaɪz/ adj small enough to be put into your mouth whole

bit·ing /ˈbaɪtɪŋ/ adj **1** a biting wind is extremely cold and unpleasant **2** a biting remark is cruel

bitten the past participle of **bite¹**

bit·ter /ˈbɪtər/ adj ★

1 feeling angry	4 with a sharp taste
2 showing anger	5 extremely cold
3 making sb unhappy	+ PHRASE

1 angry or upset because you think that you have been treated unfairly: *I'm still **bitter about** the whole affair.*
2 involving very angry feelings: *a bitter dispute*
3 making you feel very unhappy or disappointed: *It was **a bitter blow** when he lost his job.*
4 something that is bitter has a strong sharp taste that is not sweet
5 extremely cold in an unpleasant way: *a bitter north wind*
PHRASE **to the bitter end** continuing until the end of a difficult or unpleasant situation or period
—**bit·ter·ness** noun [U]

bit·ter·ly /ˈbɪtərli/ adv **1** in an extremely angry, upset, or disappointed way: *He complained bitterly that no one had bothered to ask his opinion.* **2** in a determined and angry way: *Many people are bitterly opposed to the idea.*
PHRASE **bitterly cold** extremely cold

bit·ter·sweet /ˈbɪtərˌswit/ adj **1** involving feelings of happiness and sadness at the same time: *a bittersweet love story* **2** tasting bitter and sweet at the same time

bi·zarre /bɪˈzɑr/ adj strange and difficult to explain: *a bizarre situation* —**bi·zarre·ly** adv

blab /blæb/ verb [I/T] *informal* to tell people about something that should be kept secret

black¹ /blæk/ adj ★★★

1 of darkest color	5 angry or sad
2 of a race with dark skin	6 sad or unpleasant
3 with no milk in it	+ PHRASE
4 involving sth bad/sad	

1 of the darkest color, like the sky at night: *clouds of thick black smoke*
2 black or **Black** belonging to a race of people with dark skin, especially people whose families were originally from Africa: *a famous black actor*
3 coffee or tea that is black has no milk in it
4 making people lose hope or feel sad: *It's a black day for the automobile industry.*
5 showing angry or unhappy feelings: *a black mood/look*
6 involving sad or unpleasant things: *black humor*
PHRASE **black and blue** covered in BRUISES (=dark marks on your skin where you have been hit)
—**black·ness** noun [U]

Words that avoid giving offense: black

Use the adjective **black** (sometimes spelled **Black**) to refer to people with dark skin whose families originally came from Africa. Do not use **black** as a noun because it is offensive. Black Americans usually prefer to be called **African American.** In Australian English, **black** refers to people whose families were living in Australia before Europeans arrived.

black² /blæk/ noun ★
1 [U] the darkest color, like the color of the sky at night: *You look good in black* (=wearing black clothes).
2 black or **Black** [C] *offensive* a black person
PHRASE **in the black** with money in your bank account ≠ IN THE RED: *We've managed to stay in the black for over a year now.*

black³ /blæk/ PHRASAL VERB **ˌblack ˈout** to suddenly become unconscious = FAINT

ˌblack-and-ˈwhite adj **1** using only black, white, and gray ≠ COLOR: *a black-and-white photograph* **2** a black-and-white situation, description, or issue makes the difference between right and wrong seem very clear: *His version of the story sounds a little too black-and-white for me.*
PHRASE **in black and white** in a written or printed form: *We've got her confession right here in black and white.*

ˈblack ˌbelt noun [C] the highest level of skill in JUDO or KARATE, or someone who has achieved this level of skill

black·ber·ry /ˈblækˌberi/ noun [C] a small soft dark fruit that grows on a bush

black·bird /ˈblækˌbɜrd/ noun [C] a bird that is common in Europe and North America. The male is black with an orange BEAK.

black·board /ˈblækˌbɔrd/ noun [C] a large dark board that a teacher writes on with CHALK = CHALKBOARD

ˌblack ˈbox noun [C] a piece of equipment in an airplane that records details about the cause of a crash

black·en /ˈblækən/ verb [I/T] to become black, or to make something black
PHRASE **blacken sb's reputation/name/character** to say things in order to harm someone's reputation

ˌblack ˈeye noun [C] a dark mark on the skin around your eye that is caused by someone hitting you

black·head /ˈblækˌhed/ noun [C] a small black spot on your skin, caused by dirt or oil blocking a PORE

ˌblack ˈhole noun [C] *science* an area in outer space that pulls everything around it into it

black·jack /ˈblækˌdʒæk/ noun [U] a card game in which players try to collect cards that add up to no more than 21

black·list¹ /ˈblækˌlɪst/ verb **be blacklisted** to be included on a list of people or things that are not approved of

black·list² /ˈblækˌlɪst/ noun [C] a list of people or things that you do not approve of and want to prevent from being successful

ˌblack ˈmagic noun [U] magic that is used for evil purposes

black·mail /ˈblækˌmeɪl/ noun [U] the crime of forcing someone to do something for you by threatening to tell people embarrassing information about them —**black·mail** verb [T], **black·mail·er** noun [C]

ˌblack ˈmarket noun [singular] the illegal trade in goods that are difficult or expensive to obtain legally: *Rhino horns can fetch up to $5,000 on the black market.* —**black mar·ket·eer** /ˌblæk mɑrkəˈtɪr/ noun [C]

black·out /ˈblækˌaʊt/ noun [C] **1** a short period when the electricity supply is stopped at night=POWER FAILURE **2** a period during a war when the lights are turned off so that an enemy cannot see them at night **3** a period when you suddenly become unconscious for a short time **4** a situation in which reporters are officially prevented from reporting news about something

ˌblack ˈpepper noun [U] pepper that is produced from dried crushed pepper seeds and their hard black cover

ˌblack ˈsheep noun [C] someone who is not approved of by the other members of their family or group

black•smith /ˈblækˌsmɪθ/ noun [C] someone whose job is to make HORSESHOES and other objects out of metal

ˌblack ˈtie noun [U] very formal men's clothes worn for a social event, usually including a black BOW TIE —**ˌblack-ˈtie** adj

black•top /ˈblækˌtɑp/ noun [C/U] *American* a thick black substance used for covering a road, or a road covered with this substance

ˌblack ˈwidow noun [C] a very poisonous SPIDER that lives in parts of North America and Asia

blad•der /ˈblædər/ noun [C] the part inside your body where URINE collects

blade /bleɪd/ noun [C] **1** the thin sharp part of a knife, tool, or weapon **2** a long thin leaf of grass **3** a flat wide part of a machine or piece of equipment → SHOULDER BLADE

blah¹ /blɑ/ noun **blah, blah, blah** *spoken* used for completing a sentence when you do not have to be definite, or when the subject is boring: *They say they want to cut taxes, improve education, blah, blah, blah.*

blah² /blɑ/ adj *spoken* **1** not very interesting or exciting **2** feeling slightly tired or sick

blame¹ /bleɪm/ verb [T] ★★ to say or think that someone or something is responsible for an accident, problem, or bad situation: *If it doesn't work, don't blame me.* ♦ *The hospital has launched an investigation to find out who was* **to blame for** *the mistake.* ♦ **blame sth on sb/sth** *You can't blame all your problems on your family.* ♦ **blame sb/sth for sth** *Organizers blame the weather for the low turnout.*

PHRASE **I don't blame you/him/her/them** *spoken* used for saying that you understand why someone did something, or why they feel the way they do: *"Then I told him to leave." "I don't blame you!"*

blame² /bleɪm/ noun [U] responsibility for an accident, problem, or bad situation: *Why do I always get the blame for everything?* ♦ *The management has to take the blame* (=accept they are responsible) *for recent failures.*

blame•less /ˈbleɪmləs/ adj not responsible for anything bad

bland /blænd/ adj **1** not interesting or exciting: *The movie is a bland adaptation of the novel.* **2** not having a strong taste and not very interesting to eat —**bland•ly** adv

blank¹ /blæŋk/ adj **1** showing no emotion, or no sign of understanding something or recognizing someone: *a blank look/expression* **2** containing no writing, pictures, or sound: *a blank sheet of paper* ♦ *a blank tape/disk* ♦ *rows of blank screens* ♦ *The last three boxes should be left blank.*

PHRASE **go blank** if your mind goes blank, you are unable to remember something

blank² /blæŋk/ noun [C] an empty space on a piece of paper where you can write something: *Please put either a check or an X in the blanks.*

ˌblank ˈcheck noun [C] **1** a check that has been signed but does not have an amount of money written on it **2** freedom and authority to do whatever is necessary to deal with a problem

blan•ket¹ /ˈblæŋkɪt/ noun **1** [C] a thick cover made of wool or another material that you use to keep warm in bed **2** [singular] a thick layer of something that completely covers an area: *a blanket of snow*

blan•ket² /ˈblæŋkɪt/ adj affecting everyone or everything equally, even when this is not sensible or fair: *a blanket ban on tobacco advertising*

blan•ket³ /ˈblæŋkɪt/ verb [T] to cover something with a layer of something, for example snow

blank•ly /ˈblæŋkli/ adv without showing any emotion, reaction, or understanding: *She gazed at him blankly.*

ˌblank ˈverse noun [U] poetry that does not have lines that RHYME

blare /bler/ verb [I/T] to make a loud unpleasant noise —**blare** noun [singular]

blas•phe•my /ˈblæsfəmi/ noun [C/U] something that is considered to be offensive to God or to someone's religious beliefs —**blas•phe•mous** /ˈblæsfəməs/ adj

blast¹ /blæst/ noun **1** [C] an explosion: *Ten people were injured in the blast.* **2** [C] a strong current of air, wind, or heat: *a blast of cold air* **3** [C] a sudden short loud sound: *a sudden blast of music* **4** [singular] *spoken* a very enjoyable experience: *We had a real blast!*

PHRASE **(at) full blast** as loudly or with as much power as possible: *The radio was on full blast.*

blast² /blæst/ verb **1** [T] to damage or destroy something with a bomb or gun: *A massive car bomb blasted the police headquarters.* **2** [I] to make a loud sound: *Music blasted from the open window.* **3** [T] to criticize someone very strongly: *Government officials have blasted the United Nations for its failure to take action.*

PHRASAL VERB **ˌblast ˈoff** if a SPACECRAFT blasts off, it leaves the ground

ˈblast-ˌoff noun [U] *informal* the moment when a SPACECRAFT leaves the ground=LIFT-OFF

bla•tant /ˈbleɪt(ə)nt/ adj done in an obvious way that shows you are not embarrassed or ashamed to be doing something bad or illegal: *a blatant lie* —**bla•tant•ly** adv

blaze¹ /bleɪz/ verb [I] **1** to burn strongly and brightly: *A fire blazed in the fireplace.* **2** to shine very brightly: *A car roared toward them with its headlights blazing.*

blaze² /bleɪz/ noun **1** [C] a large fire that causes a lot of damage: *Firefighters were called to a blaze at a warehouse yesterday.* **2** [singular] a strong bright light or area of color

PHRASE **a blaze of publicity/glory** a lot of

public excitement and attention from newspapers, radio, and television

blaz•er /ˈbleɪzər/ noun [C] a light jacket for a man that is a different color from his pants

blaz•ing /ˈbleɪzɪŋ/ adj **1** burning very strongly: *a blazing building* **2** very hot: *the blazing sun* **3** showing a lot of anger or emotion: *the blazing fury in his eyes*

bleach[1] /blitʃ/ noun [U] a strong chemical that is used for killing bacteria or for making colored things white

bleach[2] /blitʃ/ verb [T] to remove the color from something

bleach•ers /ˈblitʃərz/ noun [plural] *American* a structure with several rows of seats where people can watch sports games

bleak /blik/ adj **1** with no reason to feel happy or hopeful: *Textile workers face a bleak future.* **2** cold and unpleasant: *bleak winter days* —**bleak•ly** adv

blear•y /ˈblɪri/ adj not able to see clearly because you are tired —**blear•i•ly** adv

bleat /blit/ verb [I] **1** to make the sound that a sheep or goat makes **2** to complain in a weak voice, or in an annoying way

bleed /blid/ (past tense and past participle **bled** /bled/) verb [I] to have blood flowing from your body, for example from a cut: *He was bleeding from a wound in his shoulder.* —**bleed•ing** noun [U]: *They had to act quickly to stop the bleeding.*

bleep /blip/ noun [C] a short high sound made by a piece of electronic equipment —**bleep** verb [I]

blem•ish /ˈblemɪʃ/ noun [C] **1** a mark or spot that spoils the appearance of something **2** a mistake or dishonest action that spoils someone's reputation

blend[1] /blend/ verb **1** [T] to mix things together: *Blend the flour with a little milk to make a smooth paste.* **2** [I] to combine with other things: *The pale blue of the curtains blends perfectly with the color scheme.*

PHRASAL VERB **ˌblend ˈin** to be similar to the other people or things in the same place or situation: *Security men were trying to blend in with the crowd.*

blend[2] /blend/ noun [C] **1** a combination of different tastes, styles, or qualities that produces an attractive or effective result: *a blend of modern and traditional Portuguese songs* **2** a mixture of different types of tea, coffee, alcoholic drinks, or tobacco

blend•er /ˈblendər/ noun [C] a piece of electrical equipment that mixes foods, or turns soft food into a liquid —*picture* → C2

bless /bles/ verb [T] **1** to say a prayer asking God to help and protect someone or something **2** to make something holy, so that it can be used in a religious ceremony

PHRASES **be blessed with sth** to have something very good or special

bless you *spoken* used when someone has SNEEZED

bless•ed /ˈblesəd/ adj **1** holy, or loved by God **2** *literary* making you feel happy or grateful: *We found a patch of blessed shade under the trees.*

bless•ing /ˈblesɪŋ/ noun **1** [C] something good that you feel grateful or lucky to have: *It's a blessing that your children live so near.* → MIXED BLESSING **2** [singular] permission or support for something: *Mike finally gave up his stressful job with his wife's blessing.* **3** [U] protection and help from God

PHRASE **a blessing in disguise** something that seems to cause problems, but that you later realize is a good thing

blew the past tense of **blow**[1]

blight /blaɪt/ noun [singular] something that damages or spoils something else —**blight** verb [T]

blind[1] /blaɪnd/ adj ★

1 unable to see. Some people think that this word is offensive and prefer to use the expression **visually impaired** ≠ SIGHTED: *Blind and sighted children attend the same school.* ♦ *The disease made her go blind.*

2 a blind emotion or belief is so strong that you do not question it, even if it is unreasonable: *blind faith* ♦ *In a **blind panic**, I dropped the bag and ran.*

3 unable to realize or admit the truth about something: *He was **blind to** the importance of the occasion.*

4 a blind corner is one where you cannot see what is coming toward you

PHRASE **turn a blind eye (to sth)** to pretend that you do not notice something bad or illegal

—**blind•ness** noun [U]

blind[2] /blaɪnd/ verb [T] **1** to damage someone's eyes so that they are unable to see: *Jimmy was temporarily blinded by the bright light.* **2** to prevent someone from realizing or admitting the truth about something: *Her hatred blinded her to the fact that Joe could have helped her.*

blind[3] /blaɪnd/ noun [C] a window cover that you pull down from the top to the bottom

ˌblind ˈdate noun [C] an arrangement in which two people who have never met before spend some time together, in order to find out whether they would like to start a relationship

blind•ers /ˈblaɪndərz/ noun [plural] *American* **1** something that stops you from seeing the truth or from understanding all parts of a situation **2** things that partly cover a horse's eyes so that it can only look straight forward

blind•fold[1] /ˈblaɪndˌfoʊld/ noun [C] something that is tied over someone's eyes so that they cannot see

blind•fold[2] /ˈblaɪndˌfoʊld/ verb [T] to tie a cover over someone's eyes so that they cannot see

blind•ing /ˈblaɪndɪŋ/ adj **1** extremely bright: *a blinding light* **2** very great, or severe: *a blinding headache/rage/pain*

blind•ly /ˈblaɪndli/ adv **1** without thinking or knowing enough about what you are doing: *This group is blindly loyal to the president.* **2** without being able to see: *She felt her way blindly toward the door.*

blind•side /ˈblaɪnˌsaɪd/ verb [T] *American informal* **1** to hit the side of a moving vehicle in an accident **2** to give someone an unpleasant surprise by doing something that they were not expecting

ˈblind ˌspot noun [C] **1** an area that you cannot see when you are driving **2** a subject that you do not understand well, often because you do not want to know or admit the truth about it

B

blink¹ /blɪŋk/ verb **1** [I/T] to close your eyes and quickly open them again **2** [I] if a light blinks, it goes on and off continuously

blink² /blɪŋk/ noun [C] the act of closing and opening your eyes quickly

blink·ered /ˈblɪŋkərd/ adj blinkered opinions or attitudes are very limited and conservative = NARROW-MINDED

blink·ers /ˈblɪŋkərz/ noun [plural] *American* the small lights on a vehicle that flash to show that it is turning

blip /blɪp/ noun [C] **1** a small flashing light on the screen of a piece of equipment **2** *informal* a minor problem

bliss /blɪs/ noun [U] complete happiness

bliss·ful /ˈblɪsfəl/ adj giving you great pleasure —**bliss·ful·ly** adv

blis·ter /ˈblɪstər/ noun [C] a swollen area on your skin that contains liquid and is caused by being burned or rubbed —**blis·ter** verb [I/T]

blis·ter·ing /ˈblɪstərɪŋ/ adj **1** very fast: *a blistering shot to the baseline* **2** blistering criticism is very severe **3** blistering heat or temperatures are extremely hot

blithe·ly /ˈblaɪðli/ adv without worrying about possible problems, or without realizing that anything is wrong: *He blithely ignores all our warnings.* —**blithe** adj

blitz /blɪts/ noun **1** [C] a situation in football when a lot of players attack the QUARTERBACK **2** [singular] a special effort to deal with something quickly and thoroughly: *It's time we had a blitz on the paperwork.* **3** [C] a sudden military attack —**blitz** verb [T]

bliz·zard /ˈblɪzərd/ noun [C] a storm with a lot of snow and strong winds

bloat·ed /ˈbloʊtəd/ adj **1** having an uncomfortable feeling in your stomach after eating or drinking too much **2** a bloated organization or system is not effective because it is too large or has too many workers

blob /blɑb/ noun [C] **1** a small amount of a thick liquid **2** something that seems to have no definite shape

bloc /blɑk/ noun [C] a group of countries or people with the same political goals

block¹ /blɑk/ noun [C] ★★

1 solid piece of sth	5 large building
2 distance along street	6 sth stopping progress
3 area in a town	7 when you cannot think
4 amount of sth	

1 a solid piece of wood, stone, ice, etc. with straight sides: ***a block of marble***

2 *American* the distance along a street, from the place where one street crosses it to the place where the next street crosses it: *The school was only a few blocks from where she lived.*

3 an area of buildings in a town or city with streets on all four sides: *I was early, so I walked around the block a couple of times.*

4 an amount of something that you think of as a unit: *We need to find a two-hour block when we are all free for this seminar.* ♦ *You can move **blocks of** text using the mouse.*

5 a large building with a lot of different levels: *an apartment block*

6 something that stops you from doing something or making progress: *The issue of vacation pay was the major block in reaching an agreement.*

7 a short time when you are unable to think clearly or remember something: *a mental block*

→ STUMBLING BLOCK

block² /blɑk/ verb [T] ★

1 to stop something from moving along or passing through something: *A car was blocking the road.* ♦ *Something is blocking the flow of water through the pipe.*

2 to stop someone from going past you by standing in front of them: *A crowd of people **blocked his way** to the gate.*

3 to stop something from happening or succeeding: *She accused him of blocking her promotion.* ♦ *The plan to build a new school was blocked by local residents.*

4 to be in front of someone so that they cannot see something, or so that light cannot reach them: *Don't stand in the doorway, you're blocking the light.*

PHRASAL VERBS ˌ**block sth ˈoff** to cover or close something completely so that nothing can move through it: *Snow had blocked off several streets.*

ˌ**block sth ˈout 1** to stop light or sound from reaching something: *That tree in the neighbor's yard blocks out a lot of light.* **2** to stop yourself from thinking about or remembering something: *He had always managed to block out the incident.*

ˌ**block sth ˈup** *same as* **block²** 1: *Falling leaves had blocked up the drains.*

block·ade /blɑˈkeɪd/ noun [C] an official action that is intended to prevent people or goods from moving from one place to another —**block·ade** verb [T]

block·age /ˈblɑkɪdʒ/ noun [C] something that blocks a tube or pipe

block·bust·er /ˈblɑkˌbʌstər/ noun [C] a very successful movie, show, or novel

ˈ**block ˌparty** noun [C] *American* a party that takes place outside for all the people who live in a particular area

blond¹ or **blonde** /blɑnd/ adj **1** blond hair is pale yellow in color **2** with pale yellow hair

blond² or **blonde** /blɑnd/ noun [C] a person with pale yellow hair

blood /blʌd/ noun [U] ★★★

1 the red liquid that flows around inside your body: *Oxygen is carried in the blood.* ♦ *His face was covered in blood.* ♦ *a blood test*

2 the family, nation, or group that you belong to through your parents and grandparents: *Like many Canadians, she had some Scottish blood.*

3 violence and death: *The conflict continued for years, with a lot of **blood spilled*** (=deaths caused) *on both sides.*

PHRASES **sth is in your blood** used for saying that it is natural for you to do something because your family has done it in the past

new/fresh blood people who join an organization with new ideas or new ways of doing things

→ BAD BLOOD, DRAW[1], FLESH[1]

ˈblood ˌbank noun [C] a place where blood is stored so that it can be given to people during operations

blood•bath /ˈblʌdˌbæθ/ noun [singular] a period of fighting in which a lot of people are killed or injured

blood•cur•dling /ˈblʌdˌkɜrdlɪŋ/ adj very frightening

ˈblood ˌdonor noun [C] someone who gives some of their blood so that hospitals can use it to treat other people

blood•hound /ˈblʌdˌhaʊnd/ noun [C] a large dog that can smell very well

blood•less /ˈblʌdləs/ adj involving no violence or killing: *a bloodless revolution*

ˈblood ˌpressure noun [U] the pressure at which blood flows from your heart around your body. Blood pressure that is either very high or very low can be dangerous to your health.

blood•shed /ˈblʌdʃed/ noun [U] a situation in which people are killed or injured in fighting

blood•shot /ˈblʌdʃɑt/ adj bloodshot eyes are red in the part where they should be white

ˈblood ˌsports noun [plural] activities such as hunting that involve killing animals or birds

blood•stained /ˈblʌdˌsteɪnd/ adj marked with blood —**blood•stain** noun [C]

blood•stream /ˈblʌdˌstrim/ noun [singular] the blood that moves around your body

blood•thirst•y /ˈblʌdˌθɜrsti/ adj someone who is bloodthirsty enjoys being violent, or enjoys watching violence

ˈblood transˌfusion noun [C] a medical treatment in which blood from another person is put into someone's body

ˈblood ˌtype noun [C] one of the groups that human blood can be divided into

ˈblood ˌvessel noun [C] a tube that carries blood around your body

blood•y /ˈblʌdi/ adj **1** covered in blood **2** a bloody fight or war is one in which a lot of people are killed or injured

bloom[1] /blum/ verb [I] **1** if a tree or plant blooms, flowers appear and open **2** to develop in a successful or healthy way

bloom[2] /blum/ noun [C] *literary* a flower: *beautiful red blooms*

PHRASE **in (full) bloom** if a tree or plant is in bloom, it is covered with flowers

bloop•er /ˈblupər/ noun [C] *American informal* a silly or embarrassing mistake

blos•som[1] /ˈblɑsəm/ noun [C/U] a flower on a tree, or all the flowers on a tree —*picture* → TREE

blos•som[2] /ˈblɑsəm/ verb [I] **1** if a plant or tree blossoms, flowers appear and open **2** to develop and become more successful: *Their romance blossomed on a trip to Key West.*

blot[1] /blɑt/ verb [T] to remove liquid from the surface of something using a piece of paper or cloth

PHRASAL VERB **ˌblot sth ˈout 1** to cover something so that you can no longer see it: *Dark clouds overhead had blotted out the sun.* **2** to forget something unpleasant: *She tried hard to blot out the bitter memories of the divorce.*

blot[2] /blɑt/ noun [C] a drop of ink or another liquid on the surface of something

blotch /blɑtʃ/ noun [C] a colored mark on something

blotch•y /ˈblɑtʃi/ adj covered with blotches

blouse /blaʊs/ noun [C] a shirt for women —*picture* → C5

blow[1] /bloʊ/ (past tense **blew** /blu/; past participle **blown** /bloʊn/) verb ★★

1 when wind/air moves	6 waste an opportunity
2 move with the wind	7 waste money
3 push air from mouth	8 when sth electric stops
4 move/form sth	+ PHRASES
5 play an instrument	+ PHRASAL VERBS

1 [I] if wind or air blows, the air moves: *The wind was blowing across the desert.*

2 [I/T] if something blows somewhere, or if it is blown somewhere, the wind moves it there: *The wind was blowing snow along the street.* ♦ *Newspapers and plastic bags were blowing around in the wind.*

3 [I] to push out air from your mouth: *He bent toward the candle and blew gently.*

4 [T] to move something or form something by pushing out air from your mouth: *We were sitting on the steps, blowing bubbles.* ♦ **blow sth off/away** *She picked up a book and blew the dust off it.*

5 [I/T] to make a musical sound by pushing air through something: *The conductor blew his whistle and the train started.* ♦ *Behind them they heard horns blowing.*

6 [T] *informal* to destroy your own chance of succeeding, or to waste a good opportunity: *I've completely blown my diet.* ♦ *We've been working very hard, and we don't intend to* ***blow it*** *now.*

7 [T] *informal* to spend a lot of money quickly on things that you do not need

8 [I/T] if something electrical blows, it stops working because of a fault

PHRASES **blow (sb) a kiss** to kiss your hand and pretend to blow the kiss to someone

blow sb's mind *informal* to impress someone very much or make them feel very excited: *To see him perform on stage just blew my mind.*

blow your nose to clean your nose by forcing air through it

blow the whistle to tell the public or someone in authority that someone is doing something wrong or illegal: *People should be able to* ***blow the whistle on*** *corruption without losing their jobs.*

PHRASAL VERBS **ˌblow sb aˈway** *informal* to impress someone very much, or make someone very excited: *When I heard that song for the first time it just blew me away.*

ˌblow (sth) ˈout if you blow out a flame, or if it blows out, it stops burning because you blow on it, or because of the wind: *He blew out all 60 candles on his birthday cake.*

ˌblow ˈover if a dangerous or embarrassing situation blows over, people stop worrying about it and soon forget about it: *The scandal soon blew over.*

ˌblow (sth) ˈup if something blows up, or if someone blows something up, it explodes and is destroyed: *Terrorists had threatened to blow up the embassy.*

B

blow sth ˈup to fill something with air or gas: *We blew up lots of balloons and hung them around the room.*

blow up

blow² /bloʊ/ noun [C] **1** an event that makes you feel very sad, disappointed, or shocked: *Her mother's death was a real blow to her.* **2** a hard hit from someone's hand or an object: *The victim was killed by a blow to the head.* **3** an act of blowing air from your mouth or nose
PHRASES **come to blows** if two people come to blows, they start hitting each other
soften the blow to make something that is unpleasant easier to deal with or accept

ˌblow-by-ˈblow adj including a lot of details: *a blow-by-blow account of her trip*

ˈblow-ˌdry verb [T] to dry your hair with a blow dryer

ˈblow ˌdryer noun [C] a small machine that blows air, and that you use to dry your hair

blown the past participle of **blow**[1]

blow•out /ˈbloʊˌaʊt/ noun [C] **1** an occasion when a tire on a moving vehicle suddenly bursts **2** *American informal* an easy victory in a game or competition **3** *informal* a celebration during which people eat and drink a lot

blub•ber¹ /ˈblʌbər/ verb [I] *informal* to cry in a noisy and uncontrolled way

blub•ber² /ˈblʌbər/ noun [U] a layer of fat around the body of an ocean animal such as a WHALE

bludg•eon /ˈblʌdʒən/ verb [T] to hit someone hard with a heavy object

blue¹ /blu/ adj ★★★
1 something that is blue is the same color as the sky on a clear sunny day: *He looked at her with his pale blue eyes.*
2 *informal* feeling slightly sad: *She usually calls her mother when she's feeling blue.*
3 *old-fashioned* dealing with sex in a way that some people find offensive: *a blue movie*
PHRASES **once in a blue moon** *informal* not very often at all
till you are blue in the face *informal* doing something continually and for a long time, but without success: *You can say "don't do it" till you're blue in the face, but if kids want to do it, they will.*

blue² /blu/ noun [C/U] ★ the color of the sky on a clear sunny day: *The boy was dressed all in blue.* ♦ *bright blues and yellows*
PHRASE **out of the blue** happening in a way that is sudden and unexpected: *Out of the blue she said, "Your name's John, isn't it?"*
→ BLUES

blue•bell /ˈbluˌbel/ noun [C] a wild plant with small blue flowers that are shaped like bells

blue•ber•ry /ˈbluˌberi/ noun [C/U] a small dark blue fruit that grows on a bush —*picture* → C10

blue•bird /ˈbluˌbɜrd/ noun [C] a small blue bird found in North America

blue-blood•ed /ˌbluˈblʌdəd/ adj from a royal family, or from a family of a very high social class

ˈblue ˌbook noun [C] *American* a book with no words written in it, used for writing the answers to an examination in

ˌblue ˈcheese noun [C/U] a strong-tasting cheese that is white or pale yellow and has blue lines in it

ˈblue ˌchip noun [C] a company or INVESTMENT that is considered safe to invest in —**ˈblue-chip** adj

ˌblue-ˈcollar adj blue-collar workers do physical work in places such as factories and mines → WHITE-COLLAR

blue•grass /ˈbluˌgræs/ noun [U] a type of music from the southern U.S. that is played on instruments such as VIOLINS and BANJOS

blue•jay /ˈbluˌdʒeɪ/ noun [C] a common blue North American bird

blue•print /ˈbluˌprɪnt/ noun [C] **1** a drawing that shows how to build something such as a building or a machine **2** a detailed plan for doing something

ˌblue ˈribbon noun [C] *American* a small piece of blue material that you give to the winner of a competition

blues /bluz/ noun **1** [U] a type of slow sad music that developed from the songs of black SLAVES in the southern U.S. **2 the blues** [plural] *informal* a feeling of sadness and loss

bluff¹ /blʌf/ verb [I/T] to try to trick someone by pretending that you know something or that you will do something: *They said they'd had another offer, but we knew they were just bluffing.*

bluff² /blʌf/ noun [C/U] an attempt to bluff someone
PHRASE **call sb's bluff** to ask someone to do what they are threatening to do, because you believe that they do not really intend to do it

blu•ish /ˈbluɪʃ/ adj similar to blue

blun•der¹ /ˈblʌndər/ noun [C] a careless or embarrassing mistake

blun•der² /ˈblʌndər/ verb [I] **1** to make a careless or embarrassing mistake **2** to move around in a careless way

blunt /blʌnt/ adj **1** not pointed or sharp: *a blunt pencil/razor* **2** saying what is true or what you really think, even if this offends or upsets people —**blunt•ness** noun [U]

blunt•ly /ˈblʌntli/ adv speaking in a direct and honest way, even if this offends or upsets people

blur¹ /blɜr/ verb [I/T] **1** to become less clear, or to make something less clear: *The letters blurred together on the page.* **2** if the difference between two things blurs, or if something blurs it, they become more similar: *The law seems to blur the line between hard drugs and soft drugs.*

blur² /blɜr/ noun [C] **1** a shape that is difficult to see clearly, for example because it is moving very fast: *a blur of activity/*

B

movement **2** a thought or memory that is not very clear in your mind: *I remember a big house, but the rest of it is a blur.*

blurb /blɜrb/ noun [singular] information about a book that is printed on its back cover

blurred /blɜrd/ or **blur·ry** /ˈblɜri/ adj **1** difficult to see clearly, or causing difficulty in seeing something clearly: *blurred photographs* ♦ *blurry vision* **2** difficult to remember clearly: *blurred memories*

blurt /blɜrt/ or **ˌblurt sth ˈout** verb [T] to say something suddenly and without thinking about the effect that it will have

blush¹ /blʌʃ/ verb [I] if you blush, your cheeks become red because you feel embarrassed or ashamed

blush² /blʌʃ/ noun [U] *American* a red powder or cream that women put on their cheeks —*picture* → MAKEUP

blus·ter /ˈblʌstər/ noun [U] angry or threatening things that someone says because they are frightened or nervous —**blus·ter** verb [I/T]

blus·ter·y /ˈblʌst(ə)ri/ adj with strong winds: *blustery weather*

Blvd. abbrev Boulevard

B.O. /ˌbi ˈoʊ/ noun [U] body odor: an unpleasant smell that comes from someone who has not washed or has been exercising

bo·a con·stric·tor /ˈboʊə kənˌstrɪktər/ noun [C] a large snake that kills animals by squeezing them

boar /bɔr/ noun [C] **1** a wild pig **2** a male pig

board¹ /bɔrd/ noun ★★★

1 long piece of wood	4 group of managers
2 thin flat surface	5 meals
3 for information	+ PHRASE

1 [C] a long thin flat piece of wood that is used for building: *There's a loose board in the bedroom floor.*

2 [C] a thin flat piece of wood or other material that is used for a particular purpose: *a cutting/ironing board* ♦ *We wanted to play chess, but I couldn't find the board.*

3 [C] a flat wide surface such as a BULLETIN BOARD or BLACKBOARD that is used for showing information: *The final grades were posted on the board.*

4 [C] a group of people who control an organization or company: *an advisory/ editorial board* ♦ *The company's board of directors voted against the proposal.*

5 [U] meals provided for you when you stay at a hotel, live at another person's house, etc. → ROOM¹

PHRASE **on board 1** on a ship or an airplane: *The airplane had 125 passengers and crew on board.* **2** involved in a project or organization, or working for a company: *Welcome to the team. It's great to have you on board.*

→ ACROSS-THE-BOARD

board² /bɔrd/ verb **1** [I/T] to get onto a ship, aircraft, train, or bus **2** [I] if a plane or ship is boarding, passengers are being allowed to get on it **3** [I] to live at another person's house in a room that you pay for

PHRASAL VERB **ˌboard sth ˈup** to cover a window or door with wooden boards: *a row of boarded up stores*

board·er /ˈbɔrdər/ noun [C] someone who pays to live in someone else's house

ˈboard ˌgame noun [C] any game in which you move objects round on a special board

ˈboarding ˌhouse noun [C] *old-fashioned* a house in which people pay to live as guests with the family who owns it

ˈboarding ˌpass noun [C] a card that each passenger has to show before they are allowed to get on an airplane

ˈboarding ˌschool noun [C] a school in which the students live during the part of the year that they have classes

board·room /ˈbɔrdˌrum/ noun [C] a room where the directors of a company have meetings

board·walk /ˈbɔrdˌwɔk/ noun [C] a path made of boards on sand at the edge of the ocean or across wet ground

boast¹ /boʊst/ verb **1** [I/T] to talk about your abilities, achievements, or possessions in a way that sounds too proud = BRAG: *The men sat at the bar boasting about their win.* ♦ *Mrs. White liked to boast that she knew every person in the village.* **2** [T] *formal* to have something good that other people admire: *The island boasts the highest number of tourists in the area.*

boast² /boʊst/ noun [C] a statement in which you talk about your abilities, achievements, or possessions in a way that sounds too proud

boast·ful /ˈboʊstf(ə)l/ adj too eager to tell other people about your abilities, achievements, or possessions ≠ MODEST

boat /boʊt/ noun [C] ★★★

1 a small vehicle for traveling on water: *The only way to get there was **by boat**.*

→ ROWBOAT, SAILBOAT

2 a ship that carries passengers

PHRASE **in the same boat** in the same difficult or unpleasant situation

→ BURN¹, ROCK²

boat·ing /ˈboʊtɪŋ/ noun [U] the activity of sailing in a boat for enjoyment

bob¹ /bɑb/ verb [I] to move up and down with short regular movements, especially in the water

bob² /bɑb/ noun [C] a woman's hairstyle in which her hair is cut to an even length at the level of her chin —*picture* → HAIRSTYLE

bob·by pin /ˈbɑbi ˌpɪn/ noun [C] *American* a small piece of wire that women use to hold their hair in place

bob·cat /ˈbɑbˌkæt/ noun [C] a large North American wild cat

bode /boʊd/ verb **bode well/ill** *formal* to be a sign that something good/bad will happen

bod·i·ly /ˈbɑdɪli/ adj relating to your body, or affecting your body: *bodily injury* ♦ *bodily fluids*

bod·y /ˈbɑdi/ noun ★★★

1 of human/animal	5 of car/plane
2 not arms/legs	6 main part of sth
3 of a dead person	7 collection of work, etc.
4 group of people	8 appearance of hair

B

1 [C] the whole physical structure of a person or animal, including the head, arms, and legs: *My whole body ached.*
2 [C] the main part of a person's or animal's body, not including the head, arms, or legs
3 [C] the body of a dead person = CORPSE
4 [C] a group of people who have official responsibility for something: *the legislative body* (=group that makes laws) *of the government* ♦ *the school's governing body*
5 [C] the main outer part of a car or airplane, not including the engine, wheels, or wings
6 [singular] the main part of something that has many parts: *You can find more details in the body of the report.*
7 [C] a large amount of knowledge, information, or work: *There is a growing body of evidence to support this theory.*
8 [U] the thick healthy appearance of your hair
→ FOREIGN BODY

ˈbody ˌblow noun [C] a serious problem, or a great disappointment

bod•y•build•ing /ˈbɑdiˌbɪldɪŋ/ noun [U] regular physical exercises with weights that make your muscles bigger —**bod•y•build•er** noun [C]

bod•y•guard /ˈbɑdiˌgɑrd/ noun [C] a person whose job is to protect an important person from being attacked

ˈbody ˌlanguage noun [U] the movements or positions of your body that show other people what you are thinking or feeling

bod•y•work /ˈbɑdiˌwɜrk/ noun [U] the painted metal outer part of a car or other vehicle

bog¹ /bɔg/ noun [C/U] an area of ground that is always very wet and soft

bog² /bɑg/ verb **be/get bogged down (in sth)** to be or become so involved with one particular thing that you cannot make any progress: *The trial got bogged down in legal complications.*

bog•gle /ˈbɑg(ə)l/ verb [I/T] if your mind boggles, or if something boggles your mind, you cannot imagine or understand it

bog•gy /ˈbɔgi/ adj boggy ground is always very wet and soft

bo•gus /ˈboʊgəs/ adj not real, but pretending to be real: *bogus insurance claims*

bo•he•mi•an /boʊˈhimiən/ adj living or behaving in an informal way that is thought to be typical of artists and writers = UNCONVENTIONAL

boil¹ /bɔɪl/ verb ★
1 [I/T] if a liquid boils, or if you boil it, it becomes so hot that BUBBLES rise to the surface: *When the water boils, add the rice.*
2 [I/T] to cook something in boiling water, or to be cooked in this way: *How long does it take to boil an egg?*
3 [I] to feel something such as anger very strongly
PHRASAL VERBS **ˌboil ˈdown to sth** to be the main reason for something, or the most basic part of something: *They're both good jobs – I guess it just boils down to who will pay better.*
ˌboil ˈover 1 to flow over the top of a container while boiling **2** if a situation or feeling boils over, people cannot control their anger and start to fight or argue: *Racial tensions in the area were boiling over.*

boil² /bɔɪl/ noun [C] a painful lump on your skin that has become infected
PHRASES **bring sth to a boil** to heat something until it boils
come to a boil if a liquid comes to a boil, it starts to boil

boil•er /ˈbɔɪlər/ noun [C] a machine that heats water and provides hot water for a heating system

boil•ing /ˈbɔɪlɪŋ/ or **ˈboiling ˌhot** adj extremely hot: *It was a boiling hot day.*

ˈboiling ˌpoint noun [C/U] the temperature at which a liquid boils

bois•ter•ous /ˈbɔɪst(ə)rəs/ adj lively and noisy

bold¹ /boʊld/ adj **1** confident and not afraid of risks: *a bold plan to reduce crime* **2** clear, bright, and strong in color: *a shirt with bold blue and yellow stripes* —**bold•ly** adv, **bold•ness** noun [U]

bold² /boʊld/ noun [U] a way of printing letters that makes them thicker and darker than usual: *Try putting the title in bold.*

bo•lo•gna /bəˈloʊni/ noun [U] *American* a type of SAUSAGE made from different meats, often eaten in sandwiches

bol•ster /ˈboʊlstər/ verb [T] to make something stronger or more effective: *The central bank cut interest rates in an attempt to bolster the economy.*

bolt¹ /boʊlt/ noun [C] **1** a type of screw without a point that is used for fastening things together **2** a metal bar that you slide across a door or window in order to lock it

bolt² /boʊlt/ verb **1** [I] to run away suddenly, especially because you are frightened: *There was a gunshot and the horse bolted.*
2 [T] to lock a door or window using a bolt
3 [T] to fasten two things together using a bolt: *The chairs were all bolted to the floor.*
4 bolt or **bolt sth down** [T] to eat food very quickly: *She bolted down her lunch and rushed back to work.*

bolt³ /boʊlt/ adv **bolt upright** with your back very straight

bomb¹ /bɑm/ noun [C] ★ a weapon that is made to explode at a particular time or when it hits something: *The bomb had been planted in a busy street.* ♦ *Bombs fell on the city every night for two weeks.*

bomb² /bɑm/ verb **1** [T] to attack a place with bombs: *NATO aircraft bombed the town again last night.* **2** [I] *informal* to be very unsuccessful: *The movie bombed at the box office* (=not many people went to see it).
3 [I/T] *informal* to fail a test very badly: *I bombed my geography quiz.*

bom•bard /bɑmˈbɑrd/ verb [T] to attack a place by dropping a lot of bombs on it, or by firing guns at it for a long time
PHRASE **bombard sb with questions/messages/advice etc.** to ask someone so many questions or give them so much information that it is difficult for them to deal with it all
—**bom•bard•ment** noun [C/U]

bombed /bɑmd/ adj *informal* extremely drunk

bomb•er /ˈbɑmər/ noun [C] **1** a large military airplane that drops bombs **2** someone who puts a bomb in a public place

bomb•shell /ˈbɑmʃel/ noun [C] *informal* an

event or piece of news that is unexpected and shocking

bo•na fi•de /ˌbounə ˈfaɪd/ adj a bona fide person or thing is really what they seem or claim to be

bo•nan•za /bəˈnænzə/ noun [C] a situation in which people quickly become very rich or successful

bond¹ /bɑnd/ noun **1** [C] a close special feeling of connection with other people or groups: *The experience formed a close bond between us.* **2** [C] a document that a government or a company gives to someone who invests money in it. The government or company promises to pay back the money with interest. **3** [U] *American* an amount of money paid so that someone can leave prison before their trial = BAIL **4** [C] the way that two surfaces stick together

bond² /bɑnd/ verb **1** [I] to develop a close special feeling toward other people: *He never felt like he bonded with any of the other students.* **2** [I/T] to attach two things firmly together, or to become attached in this way —**bond•ing** noun [U]

bond•age /ˈbɑndɪdʒ/ noun [U] **1** the activity of tying someone up for sexual pleasure **2** *formal* a situation in which someone is a SLAVE or has no freedom

bone¹ /boun/ noun ★★

1 [C] one of the hard parts that form the frame inside your body: *She fell and broke a bone in her foot.*

2 [U] the substance that bones are made of

PHRASES **a bone of contention** a subject that people disagree about: *The main bone of contention between us is money.*

chilled/frozen to the bone feeling very cold

have a bone to pick with sb *informal* to be annoyed with someone and want to talk to them about it

make no bones about sth to talk about something without feeling ashamed or embarrassed: *He makes no bones about the fact that he wants my job.*

bone² /boun/ verb [T] to remove the bones from meat or fish before cooking it

ˈbone ˌmarrow noun [U] the soft substance inside bones

bon•fire /ˈbɑnˌfaɪr/ noun [C] a large fire built outside for burning garbage or for a celebration

bon•net /ˈbɑnət/ noun [C] **1** a hat that ties under the chin **2** *British* the HOOD of a car

bo•nus /ˈbounəs/ noun [C] **1** something good that you get in addition to what you expect: *Customers will receive a free CD as a bonus.* **2** extra money that you are paid in addition to your usual salary: *a Christmas bonus*

bon•y /ˈbouni/ adj a bony part of the body is so thin that the shape of the bones can be seen: *bony fingers*

boo¹ /bu/ (3rd person singular **boos**; present participle **boo•ing**; past tense and past participle **booed**) verb [I/T] to shout at a performer or sports team in order to show that you think they are not very good

boo² /bu/ interjection **1** you shout "boo" suddenly to frighten someone as a joke **2** you shout "boo" at a performer or sports team in order to show that you think they are not very good

boobs /bubz/ noun [plural] *informal* a woman's breasts

boob tube, the /ˈbub ˌtub/ noun [singular] *American informal* the television

boob•y prize /ˈbubi ˌpraɪz/ noun [C] a prize that is given as a joke to someone who comes last in a competition

boob•y trap /ˈbubi ˌtræp/ noun [C] a hidden bomb that explodes when someone touches something connected to it

boog•er /ˈbʊgər/ noun [C] *American informal* **1** a piece of the soft substance from inside your nose **2** an annoying person

boog•ey•man /ˈbʊgiˌmæn/ noun [C] *American* in children's stories, a man who frightens people

boog•ie /ˈbʊgi/ verb [I] *informal* to dance to fast popular music —**boog•ie** noun [C]

book¹ /bʊk/ noun ★★★

1 [C] a written work that is printed on pages fastened together inside a cover: *Please **open your books to page 25.** ♦ Have you **read** any **books** by John Grisham? ♦ **a book about** American history ♦ She has **written** over 20 **books** on the subject.*

2 [C] something that you write in, consisting of pages fastened together inside a cover: *an exercise book ♦ an address book*

3 [C] a set of small objects, such as stamps, tickets, or matches, fastened together inside a paper cover

4 the books [plural] the financial records of an organization or business

PHRASES **by the book** correctly, following all the rules or systems for doing something

in sb's bad/good books *informal* used for saying that someone is annoyed with you/pleased with you

> **Talking or writing about books**
> - **autobiography** a book about your own life
> - **biography** a book about someone's life
> - **cookbook** a book of instructions for cooking
> - **guidebook** a book for tourists
> - **hardcover/hardback** a book with a hard cover
> - **manual** a book of instructions
> - **notebook** a book with empty pages for writing in
> - **novel** a book that tells a story
> - **paperback** a book with a thick paper cover
> - **textbook** a book that you use for studying at school or college

book² /bʊk/ verb ★

1 [I/T] to buy tickets for an event or trip before you go, or to arrange to stay in a hotel at a particular time in the future: *Do you want me to book a room for you?* ♦ **book sb on sth** *Could you book me on the 8:30 flight* (=get a ticket for me)*?*

2 [T] to arrange for someone to perform or speak at a public event: **book sb to do sth** *Several leading businessmen were booked to speak at the conference.*

3 [T] if the police book someone, they take them to the police station and make a record of their crime

book•case /ˈbʊkˌkeɪs/ noun [C] a piece of furniture with shelves in it for books

ˈbook ˌclub noun [C] **1** a group of people who

meet regularly to discuss books that they have read **2** an organization that sells books at low prices to its members, usually by MAIL ORDER

B

book·ie /ˈbʊki/ noun [C] *informal* a BOOKMAKER

book·ing /ˈbʊkɪŋ/ noun [C] an arrangement to do something such as buy a travel ticket or stay in a hotel room in the future =RESERVATION

book·keep·ing /ˈbʊkˌkipɪŋ/ noun [U] the job of recording a business's financial accounts —**book·keep·er** noun [C]

book·let /ˈbʊklət/ noun [C] a small thin book that contains information: *a 12-page booklet called "You and Your Child's Health"*

book·mak·er /ˈbʊkˌmeɪkər/ noun [C] someone whose job is to take BETS from people and to pay them money if they win

book·mark /ˈbʊkˌmɑrk/ noun [C] **1** something that you put inside a book so that you can find the page you want again **2** a way of marking an Internet WEBSITE so that you can easily find it again —**book·mark** verb [T]

book·shelf /ˈbʊkʃelf/ (plural **book·shelves** /ˈbʊkʃelvz/) noun [C] a shelf that you put books on

book·store /ˈbʊkˌstɔr/ noun [C] a store that sells books

book·worm /ˈbʊkˌwɜrm/ noun [C] *informal* someone who spends a lot of time reading books

boom¹ /bum/ noun [C] **1** a sudden increase in economic activity or success: *the economic boom of the 1980s* ♦ *The island is experiencing a boom in tourism.* **2** a deep loud sound that continues for some time **3** a pole with a camera or MICROPHONE attached to it, used in making movies

PHRASE **boom and bust** a situation in which a country's economy regularly goes through periods of success followed by periods of failure

boom² /bum/ verb [I] **1** to make a deep loud sound that continues for some time **2** if a place or an industry is booming, it is experiencing a period of economic success: *The housing market is booming.* **3** if an activity is booming, it is becoming very popular

boo·mer·ang /ˈbuməˌræŋ/ noun [C] a curved stick that comes back to you when you throw it

boon /bun/ noun [singular] something that brings you benefits or makes your life easier: *Falling PC prices are a boon for consumers.*

boon·docks, the /ˈbunˌdɑks/ noun [plural] *American informal* a place that is a long way from a town or city

boor·ish /ˈbʊrɪʃ/ adj rude and not caring about other people's feelings

boost¹ /bust/ verb [T] **1** to help something to increase or improve: *The cold weather boosted demand for electricity.* ♦ *The new coach has boosted the team's confidence.* **2** to lift someone up to a higher position

boost² /bust/ noun [singular] something that helps something to increase or improve: *The festival has been a major boost for the local economy.*

PHRASE **give sb a boost (up)** to lift someone up to a higher position

boost·er /ˈbustər/ noun [C] **1** an extra amount of a medical drug that you are given so that a drug you had before will continue to be effective **2** an extra engine on a SPACECRAFT that gives it enough power to leave the Earth's atmosphere **3** *American* someone who publicly supports a person, plan, or organization

boot¹ /but/ noun [C] ★

1 a type of shoe that covers all of your foot and part of your leg: *walking/riding/hiking boots* ♦ *a pair of black boots* —*picture* → SHOE

2 *British* the TRUNK of a car

PHRASES **get the boot** to be forced to leave your job

to boot used for adding an extra thing to a list of comments: *The trains are slow, dirty, and very unreliable to boot.*

boot² /but/ verb [T] *informal* to kick something or someone hard: *He booted the ball over the line.*

PHRASAL VERBS ˌ**boot sb ˈout** *informal* to make someone leave a place or an organization: *They were booted out of the club for fighting.*

ˌ**boot ˈup** *computing* if a computer boots up, or if you boot it up, it starts working and becomes ready to use

ˈ**boot ˌcamp** noun [C] a camp for training people who have just joined the U.S. military

booth /buð, buθ/ noun [C] **1** a small enclosed space where you do something private, especially vote or make a phone call **2** a small enclosed space where you can buy things or use a service: *a ticket booth* **3** a private, enclosed table in a restaurant

boot·leg /ˈbutˌleg/ adj bootleg goods are products that are made and sold illegally —**boot·leg·ger** noun [C]

boo·ty /ˈbuti/ noun [U] *literary* valuable goods that someone takes illegally or by force, especially in a war

booze /buz/ noun [U] *informal* alcoholic drinks

bor·der¹ /ˈbɔrdər/ noun [C] ★★

1 the official line that separates two countries or states: *border guards* ♦ *the **border between** Texas and Mexico* ♦ *Argentina's northern **border with** Bolivia* ♦ *Thousands of refugees were fleeing **across the border**.* ♦ *a town **on the** Canadian **border*** (=near it)

2 a narrow decorated area around the edge of something: *cotton sheets with a lace border*

bor·der² /ˈbɔrdər/ verb [T] **1** to be next to another country or region: *Georgia borders Florida to the north.* **2** to form a line along the edge of something: *The canal is bordered by poplar trees.*

PHRASAL VERB ˌ**border ˈon sth** to be nearly the same as a particular quality, feeling, or state: *a feeling of mistrust bordering on hatred*

bor·der·line¹ /ˈbɔrdərˌlaɪn/ adj in a position between two standards or types, and therefore difficult to judge: *students with borderline test scores*

bor·der·line² /ˈbɔrdərˌlaɪn/ noun [singular] an imaginary point that divides one feeling or condition from another: *the borderline between friendship and love*

bore¹ /bɔr/ verb [T] **1** to make someone feel bored: *I hope I'm not boring you.* **2** to make a deep hole in something hard

bore² /bɔr/ noun **1** [C] someone who talks too much about things that are not interesting **2** [singular] a boring or annoying activity or situation

bore³ the past tense of **bear¹**

bored /bɔrd/ adj ★★ feeling impatient and annoyed because nothing is interesting: *The waiter looked very bored.* ♦ *Steve was getting **bored with** the game.*

- **Bored** describes how you feel: *I hated school, and I was always bored.*
- **Boring** describes things or situations that make you feel bored: *I always found school very boring.*

bore·dom /ˈbɔrdəm/ noun [U] the feeling of being bored

bor·ing /ˈbɔrɪŋ/ adj ★★ not at all interesting: *a boring badly-paid job* ♦ *Our math teacher is so boring!* → BORED

born /bɔrn/ adj ★★★

1 when a baby is born, it comes out of its mother's body and starts its life: *Her grandfather died before she was born.* ♦ *The twins were born on August 29, 1962.* ♦ *a German-born tennis player* (=who was born in Germany) ♦ *He was born blind* (=he was blind when he was born).

2 used for saying that someone has a natural ability to do something well: *a born salesman/leader/optimist*

3 if something such as a new organization or idea is born, it begins to exist

ˌborn-again ˈChristian noun [C] a Christian who wants to tell other people about their strong religious beliefs

bor·ough /ˈbɜroʊ/ noun [C] a town, or a district in a big city

bor·row /ˈbɔroʊ/ verb ★★

1 [T] to receive and use something that belongs to someone else, and promise to give it back: *Can I borrow your calculator?* ♦ **borrow sth from sb/sth** *I borrowed a camera from Alex.*

2 [I/T] to borrow money from a bank and pay it back gradually: *We borrowed $20,000 to start up the business.*

3 [I/T] to use something such as an idea or word that was first used by another person or used in another place: *A lot of English words were borrowed from other languages.*

- If you **borrow** something from someone, they give it to you and you agree to give it back: *Can I borrow your umbrella?*
- If you **lend** something to someone, you give it to them and they agree to give it back to you: *Could you lend me your umbrella?*

bor·row·er /ˈbɔroʊər/ noun [C] someone who borrows money from a bank

bor·row·ings /ˈbɔroʊɪŋz/ noun [plural] money that a business, country, or organization has borrowed

bos·om /ˈbʊzəm, ˈbuzəm/ noun [singular] a woman's breasts

PHRASE **bosom friend/buddy/pal** a very close friend

boss¹ /bɔs, bɑs/ noun [C] ★★

1 the person who is in charge of you at work: *I'll ask my boss for a day off next week.*

2 someone who has a powerful position in an organization

PHRASE **be your own boss** to work for yourself and not be employed by someone else

boss² /bɔs, bɑs/ PHRASAL VERB **ˌboss sb aˈround** *informal* to keep telling other people what to do: *He's always bossing his little brother around.*

boss·y /ˈbɔsi, ˈbɑsi/ adj someone who is bossy is annoying because they keep telling other people what to do

bot·a·nist /ˈbɑt(ə)nɪst/ noun [C] someone who studies plants

bot·a·ny /ˈbɑt(ə)ni/ noun [U] the scientific study of plants —**bo·tan·i·cal** /bəˈtænɪk(ə)l/ adj

botch /bɑtʃ/ verb [T] *informal* to do something very badly or carelessly: *The police botched the entire investigation.* —**botched** /bɑtʃt/ adj

both /boʊθ/ grammar word ★★★

Both can be:
- a **determiner**: *Both children are at school.*
- a **pronoun**: *They are both good singers.* ♦ *Both of them are learning English.*

1 used for showing that you are referring to two people or things, and that you are saying the same thing about the two of them: *You can write on both sides of the paper.* ♦ *Both my parents are doctors.* ♦ *I like them both.* ♦ ***Both of** my brothers play on the football team.*

Do not use **both** in negative sentences. Use **neither**: *Neither of my parents wanted me to leave school* (=my mother did not and my father did not).

PHRASE **both...and...** used for emphasizing that each of two things is true: *a plant that grows in both Chile and Argentina* ♦ *The results of the research are both impressive and alarming.*

both·er /ˈbɑðər/ verb ★★

1 [I] if you do not bother to do something, you do not do it because it is not sensible or because you feel lazy: **bother to do sth** *It was such a stupid question, I didn't even bother to reply.* ♦ **bother doing sth** *Don't bother inviting Janet.*

2 [T] to annoy someone by interrupting them: *I hope the children aren't bothering you.*

3 [T] to make someone feel worried, frightened, or upset: *There was something about him that really bothered her.* ♦ *If he keeps bothering you, you should call the police.* ♦ **it bothers sb that/when** *Does it bother you that people think you're older than him?*

4 [T] to cause someone pain: *His knee was bothering him.*

PHRASES **I can't be bothered** *British informal* used for saying that you will not do something because you feel lazy

sorry to bother you *spoken* used for politely

asking someone to do something for you: *Sorry to bother you, but would you move your bag?*

B

bot·ox /ˈboʊtɑks/ noun [U] botulinum toxin: a substance that can be INJECTED into someone's face to make the muscles relax and the skin look smoother and younger

bot·tle¹ /ˈbɑt(ə)l/ noun [C] ★★★

1 a glass or plastic container for liquids: *an empty beer bottle* ♦ ***a bottle of** cooking oil*

2 the amount of liquid that a bottle contains: *They drank the whole bottle.*

bot·tle² /ˈbɑt(ə)l/ verb [T] to put a liquid into bottles in order to sell it —**bot·tled** /ˈbɑt(ə)ld/ adj: *bottled beer/water*

PHRASAL VERB ˌ**bottle sth ˈup** to stop yourself from showing negative emotions: *You've been bottling up your anger for years.*

bot·tle·neck /ˈbɑt(ə)lˌnek/ noun [C] **1** a place where traffic moves slowly because the road is narrow or blocked **2** a problem that causes delays

bot·tom¹ /ˈbɑtəm/ noun ★★★

1 lowest part of sth	4 part of body you sit on
2 ground under ocean	5 pants
3 lowest level in status	+ PHRASE

1 [singular] the lowest part of sth: *The page had a line missing from the bottom.* ♦ *She ran down to **the bottom of** the hill.* ♦ *The date and time are shown **at the bottom of** your screen.* ♦ *Read what is says **on the bottom of** the box* (=on the surface at the bottom).

2 [singular] the ground under the ocean or under a lake or river

3 [singular] the lowest level or position: *She started at the bottom and ended up running the company.* ♦ *The company finally **hit bottom*** (=reached its lowest level of success) *when it lost a major contract.*

4 [C] the part of your body that you sit on

5 **bottoms** [plural] the pants that are part of a set of loose clothes or sports clothes: *pajama bottoms*

PHRASE **get to the bottom of sth** to find out the true cause or explanation of a bad situation

bot·tom² /ˈbɑtəm/ adj in the lowest part or position: *She sat on the bottom step.* ♦ *the bottom half of the page* ♦ *students in the bottom 25% of their class*

bot·tom³ /ˈbɑtəm/ PHRASAL VERB ˌ**bottom ˈout** if something such as an economy or price bottoms out, it reaches its lowest level before starting to improve again

bot·tom·less /ˈbɑtəmləs/ adj **1** having no limits: *There isn't a bottomless pit* (=an unlimited supply) *of public money.*
2 extremely deep: *a bottomless lake*

ˌ**bottom ˈline, the** noun [singular] **1** *business* the amount of money that a business makes or loses **2** the most important fact in a situation: *The bottom line is that he lied to Congress.*

bough /baʊ/ noun [C] *literary* a branch of a tree

bought the past tense and past participle of buy¹

boul·der /ˈboʊldər/ noun [C] a large rock

boul·e·vard /ˈbʊləˌvɑrd/ noun [C] a wide road in a city

bounce¹ /baʊns/ verb

1 hit sth & move off	5 of e-mail
2 move up and down	+ PHRASE
3 of check	+ PHRASAL VERB
4 move in lively way	

1 [I/T] if a ball or other object bounces, or if you bounce it, it hits a surface then immediately moves away: *The ball bounced twice before hitting the net.* ♦ *Hailstones were bouncing off the roof.* ♦ *Josh bounced the ball down the street.* **2** [I/T] to move up and down, or to move something up and down: *She was bouncing the baby on her knee.* ♦ *The kids love bouncing on the bed.* **3** [I] if a check bounces, the bank refuses to pay it because there is not enough money in the account of the person who wrote it **4** [I] to move quickly and with a lot of energy: *The band came bouncing onto the stage.* **5** [I] if an e-mail message bounces, it is sent back to you without reaching the person you sent it to

PHRASE **bounce ideas off sb** to discuss ideas with someone in order to get their opinion

PHRASAL VERB ˌ**bounce ˈback** to become healthy, happy, or successful again after something bad has happened to you

bounce² /baʊns/ noun [C] the movement of a ball when it hits a surface and moves away again

bounc·er /ˈbaʊnsər/ noun [C] someone whose job is to stop violent behavior in a bar or club

bounc·y /ˈbaʊnsi/ adj **1** a bouncy ball BOUNCES well when it hits a surface **2** a bouncy surface moves up and down when you walk or jump on it **3** a bouncy person is happy, lively, and enthusiastic

bound¹ /baʊnd/ adj ★

1 **bound to do sth** something that is bound to happen will almost certainly happen: *If you have problems at home, it's bound to affect your work.*

2 **bound to do sth** used for saying that you must do something or you should do something: *We **felt bound to** tell her that her son had been taking drugs.*

PHRASE **bound for sth** traveling toward a place: *The plane was bound for Los Angeles.*

bound² /baʊnd/ verb [I] to run or jump with large steps

PHRASE **be bounded by sth** *formal* if an area is bounded by something such as a fence, the fence goes around the edge of the area

bound³ /baʊnd/ noun **1 bounds** [plural] limits that affect and control what can happen or what people are able to do **2** [C] *literary* a long or high jump

PHRASE **out of bounds 1** if a place is out of bounds, you are not allowed to go there **2** if a subject is out of bounds, you are not allowed to talk about it or know about it **3** outside the playing area in some sports such as football or basketball
→ LEAP²

bound⁴ the past tense and past participle of **bind**

bound·a·ry /ˈbaʊnd(ə)ri/ noun ★

1 [C] the edge of an area of land, or a line that marks the edge: *The road once formed*

the boundary between the two villages. ♦ *a boundary fence/wall*
2 boundaries [plural] the limits of an activity or experience: *new research that pushes back the boundaries of genetic science*

bound·less /ˈbaʊndləs/ adj very great

boun·ti·ful /ˈbaʊntɪf(ə)l/ adj *literary* available in large quantities = ABUNDANT

boun·ty /ˈbaʊnti/ noun **1** [C] money that is offered as a reward for catching or killing a criminal **2** [singular] *literary* the good things that something provides

bou·quet /boʊˈkeɪ, buˈkeɪ/ noun [C] flowers that are tied together in an attractive way and given to someone as a present

bour·bon /ˈbɜrbən/ noun [C/U] American WHISKEY, or a glass of this drink

bour·geois /bʊrˈʒwɑ, ˈbʊrˌʒwɑ/ adj *showing disapproval* typical of middle-class people and their attitudes

bour·geoi·sie, the /ˌbʊrʒwɑˈzi/ noun [singular] the middle class

bout /baʊt/ noun [C] **1** a short period when you have a particular illness or you do a particular activity: *a bout of flu* **2** a BOXING match or WRESTLING match

bou·tique /buˈtik/ noun [C] a small fashionable store, especially one that sells clothes

bo·vine /ˈboʊˌvaɪn/ adj *technical* relating to cows

bow¹ /baʊ/ verb **1** [I] to bend your body forward from the waist in order to show respect for someone **2** [I/T] to bend your head forward so that you are looking down
PHRASAL VERBS **ˌbow ˈout** to give up a job or position
ˈbow to sth/sb to agree to do something in an unwilling way: *They finally bowed to political pressure and signed the agreement.*

bow² /baʊ/ noun [C] **1** a forward movement of the top part of your body that you make in order to show respect for someone **2** the front part of a ship

bow³ /boʊ/ noun [C] **1** a weapon made from a curved piece of wood. It is used for shooting ARROWS. **2** a knot that has two circular parts and two loose ends: *The ribbon was tied in a bow.* **3** an object that you use for playing instruments such as the VIOLIN and the CELLO

bowels /ˈbaʊəlz/ noun [plural] the organ near your stomach where solid waste is formed and pushed out of your body
PHRASE **the bowels of sth** the inner parts of something

bowl¹ /boʊl/ noun [C] ★★
1 a round container that you use for eating, serving, or preparing food: *In a large bowl, mix together the eggs, sugar, and butter.* ♦ *a bowl of fruit/soup*
2 the food in a bowl, or the amount that a bowl contains: *I always eat **a bowl of** cereal for breakfast.*
3 a large container without a lid, used for holding liquids

bowl² /boʊl/ verb [I/T] to play the sport of BOWLING
PHRASAL VERB **ˌbowl sb ˈover** to surprise someone by being very impressive or unexpected: *We were bowled over by the beauty of the landscape.*

bow·leg·ged /ˌboʊ ˈlegəd/ adj with legs that curve out sideways at the knees

bowl·er /ˈboʊlər/ noun [C] someone who plays the sport of BOWLING

bowl·ing /ˈboʊlɪŋ/ noun [U] an indoor game in which players roll heavy balls along a track and try to knock down a group of PINS (=objects that look like bottles)

bow tie /ˈboʊ ˌtaɪ/ noun [C] a man's formal NECKTIE in the shape of a BOW —*picture* → C4

box¹ /bɑks/ noun [C] ★★★
1 a container with straight sides and a flat base: *a cardboard box*
2 the things in a box, or the amount that a box contains: *We ate the whole **box of chocolates.***
3 a space for writing information on a printed form, or a space on a computer screen with information in it: *a dialog box*
4 a small private space with seats in a theater or sports ground

box² /bɑks/ verb **1** [I] to fight in the sport of BOXING **2** [T] to put something into a box
PHRASAL VERB **ˌbox sb ˈin** to surround someone so that they cannot move

box·car /ˈbɑksˌkɑr/ noun [C] *American* a railroad car for carrying goods

box·er /ˈbɑksər/ noun [C] **1** someone who takes part in the sport of BOXING **2** a large dog with smooth hair and a flat face

box·ers /ˈbɑksərz/ or **ˈboxer ˌshorts** noun [plural] loose underwear for men

box·ing /ˈbɑksɪŋ/ noun [U] a sport in which two people fight each other wearing large leather GLOVES

ˈbox ˌoffice noun [C] **1** the place in a theater where you buy tickets **2** the number of people who buy tickets for a movie or play: *a box-office success/failure* ♦ *The play was a huge success at the box office* (=a lot of people went to see it).

boy¹ /bɔɪ/ noun ★★★
1 [C] a male child, or a young man: *a 10-year-old boy* ♦ *Mr. and Mrs. Wylie have three boys.* ♦ *How old is your little boy* (=your son)*?*
2 [C] a man of any age, especially used for talking about where he comes from: *The Minnesota farm boy became a national hero.*
3 the boys [plural] *informal* a group of men who are friends

boy² /bɔɪ/ interjection used for expressing a strong reaction: *Boy, was she mad!*

ˈboy ˌband noun [C] a POP group consisting of attractive young men who sing and dance

boy·cott /ˈbɔɪˌkɑt/ verb [T] to protest about something by not taking part in an event or not buying certain products: *Turkey threatened to boycott the conference.*
—**boy·cott** noun [C]

boy·friend /ˈbɔɪˌfrend/ noun [C] ★ a man or boy that you are having a sexual or romantic relationship with: *She has a new boyfriend.* → GIRLFRIEND 1

boy·hood /ˈbɔɪˌhʊd/ noun [U] *literary* the time when someone is a boy

boy·ish /ˈbɔɪɪʃ/ adj *showing approval* like a boy, or typical of a boy: *boyish good looks*

ˌBoy ˈScout noun [C] a boy who is a member of

the **Boy Scouts**, an organization that encourages boys to learn practical skills and help other people → GIRL SCOUT

B

bra /brɑ/ noun [C] a piece of underwear that supports a woman's breasts

brace¹ /breɪs/ verb [I/T] to get ready for something unpleasant: *Smith braced himself to give her the bad news.* ♦ *The stock market is braced for another week of falling prices.*

brace² /breɪs/ noun **1 braces** [plural] *American* a set of wires that you wear on your teeth to push them into the correct position **2** [C] an object that is designed to support something or to hold it in the correct position: *a back/neck brace*

brace•let /ˈbreɪslət/ noun [C] a piece of jewelry that you wear around your wrist → BANGLE —*picture* → JEWELRY

brac•ing /ˈbreɪsɪŋ/ adj cold in a way that makes you feel full of energy

brack•et /ˈbrækət/ noun **1** [C] one of the groups that people or things are divided into, according to a feature that they all share: *people in the $75,000–$100,000 income bracket* **2** [C] a piece of wood, metal, or plastic that is attached to a wall to support something like a shelf **3 brackets** or **square brackets** [plural] *American* a pair of symbols [ ], used for showing that the words or numbers between them can be considered separately **4 brackets** [plural] *British* PARENTHESES

brag /bræg/ verb [I] to talk about your achievements or possessions in a proud way that annoys other people = BOAST: *She's always bragging about her famous father.*

braid¹ /breɪd/ noun **1** [C] a piece of long hair divided into three sections that are twisted around each other —*picture* → HAIRSTYLE **2** [U] twisted colored rope that is used for decorating clothes, curtains, or furniture

braid² /breɪd/ verb [T] to put someone's hair into braids —**braid•ed** adj

braille /breɪl/ noun [U] a reading system for blind people that uses small raised marks that they feel with their fingers

brain /breɪn/ noun [C] ★★
1 the organ inside your head that allows you to think and feel, and controls your body: *a brain tumor/scan/operation*
2 mental ability or intelligence: *He's good-looking, and he **has brains**.*
3 an intelligent person: *The best brains in the company can't solve the problem.*
PHRASES **the brains behind sth** the person who is responsible for inventing, developing, or organizing something
pick sb's brains *informal* to talk to someone who knows more about something than you do, in order to learn more about it
rack your brain(s) to try very hard to remember something or to solve a problem

brain•child /ˈbreɪnˌtʃaɪld/ noun [singular] a clever system, organization, or plan that someone thinks of and develops

brain•less /ˈbreɪnləs/ adj *informal* extremely stupid

brain•storm¹ /ˈbreɪnˌstɔrm/ noun [C] *American* a sudden very good idea that someone has

brain•storm² /ˈbreɪnˌstɔrm/ verb [I/T] to discuss ideas in a brainstorming discussion

brain•storm•ing /ˈbreɪnˌstɔrmɪŋ/ noun [U] a way of developing new ideas, in which people suggest lots of ideas and the best ones are chosen

brain•wash /ˈbreɪnˌwɑʃ/ verb [T] to force someone to accept an idea by repeating it many times —**brain•wash•ing** noun [U]

brain•wave /ˈbreɪnˌweɪv/ noun [C] an electrical signal sent by your brain that can be recorded and measured

brain•y /ˈbreɪni/ adj *informal* very intelligent

brake¹ /breɪk/ noun [C] ★
1 the equipment in a vehicle or bicycle that you use for slowing down or stopping: *I saw the child run out, so I **slammed on the brakes*** (=stopped suddenly). —*picture* → C6
2 an action or a situation that prevents something from developing: *The high level of debt **put a brake on** economic recovery.*

brake² /breɪk/ verb [I] to use the brakes to stop or slow down a vehicle or bicycle

ˈbrake ˌlight noun [C] a light on the back of a vehicle that comes on when you use the brakes —*picture* → C6

bran /bræn/ noun [U] the outside parts of the grains of plants such as wheat or OATS

branch¹ /bræntʃ/ noun [C] ★★

1 part of tree	4 part of area of study
2 store/office	5 part of family
3 part of organization	6 part of river

1 one of the parts of a tree that grows out of its TRUNK (=main stem) —*picture* → TREE
2 a store or office representing a large company or organization in a particular area: *The store has branches in over 50 cities.*
3 one part of a government or large organization that has particular responsibilities: *the local branch of the teachers' union* ♦ *the legislative branch of the U.S. government*
4 a part of a particular area of study or knowledge: *Mechanics is a branch of physics.*
5 a section of a family who are all related to one person who lived in the past
6 a part of a river that leads away from the main part

branch² /bræntʃ/ verb [I] to divide into two or more parts: *The road branched into four paths.*
PHRASAL VERB ˌ**branch ˈout** to start doing something new or different

brand¹ /brænd/ noun [C] ★
1 a product or group of products that has its own name and is made by one particular company: *I tried using a new **brand of** soap.*
2 a particular type of something: *He has his own special **brand of** humor.*

brand² /brænd/ verb [T] **1** to describe someone or something as a bad person or thing = LABEL: *The men were branded liars by the judge.* **2** to burn a mark into a farm animal, in order to show who owns it

bran•dish /ˈbrændɪʃ/ verb [T] to wave a weapon or other object around in your hand so that other people can see it

ˈbrand ˌname noun [C] the name that a company chooses for its particular BRAND of product=TRADE NAME → TRADEMARK

ˈbrand-ˌname adj brand-name goods are made by well-known companies and have the company name on them

ˌbrand-ˈnew adj extremely new

bran•dy /ˈbrændi/ noun [U] a strong alcoholic drink made from wine

brash /bræʃ/ adj *showing disapproval* **1** a brash person talks and behaves in a loud confident way **2** big, bright, or colorful

brass /bræs/ noun [U] **1** a shiny yellow metal that is a mixture of COPPER and ZINC **2** musical instruments made of brass such as TRUMPETS

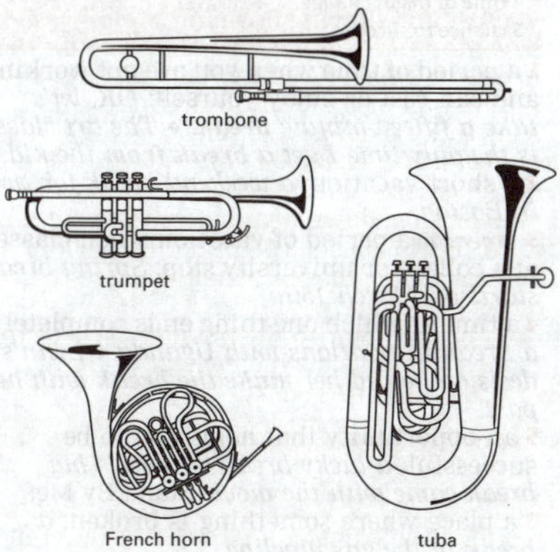

brass instruments

ˌbrass ˈband noun [C] a group of musicians who play brass instruments

brat /bræt/ noun [C] *informal* an annoying child who behaves badly

bra•va•do /brəˈvɑdoʊ/ noun [U] a brave, confident way of behaving, especially when you are in fact frightened

brave¹ /breɪv/ adj ★★ able to deal with danger, pain, or trouble without being frightened or worried=COURAGEOUS ≠COWARDLY: *the brave soldiers who fought and died for their country* ♦ *his brave fight against corruption in the police force* —**brave•ly** adv

brave² /breɪv/ verb [T] to deal with a difficult situation in order to achieve something

brav•er•y /ˈbreɪvəri/ noun [U] brave behavior =COURAGE ≠COWARDICE

bra•vo /brɑˈvoʊ/ interjection used for showing that you admire what someone has done, or that you have enjoyed their performance

brawl /brɔl/ noun [C] a noisy fight in a public place —**brawl** verb [I]

bray /breɪ/ verb [I] **1** to make the sound that a DONKEY makes **2** *showing disapproval* to talk or laugh very loudly

bra•zen /ˈbreɪz(ə)n/ adj *showing disapproval* behaving badly, and not caring if other people are shocked —**bra•zen•ly** adv

breach¹ /britʃ/ noun [C] **1** an action or situation in which a law, rule, or agreement is broken: *a clear breach of copyright* ♦ *The company was in breach of environmental regulations.* **2** *formal* a serious disagreement: *a breach in our relationship with China*

breach² /britʃ/ verb [T] *formal* to break a law, rule, or agreement

bread /bred/ noun [U] ★★★ a common food made from flour, water, and usually YEAST: *a slice/loaf of bread* ♦ *white/brown bread*

PHRASE **bread and butter** *informal* something that provides your main income: *Tourism is the island's bread and butter.*

bread•box /ˈbredˌbɑks/ noun [C] a container used for storing bread —*picture* → C2

bread•crumbs /ˈbredˌkrʌmz/ noun [plural] very small pieces of bread, used in cooking

breadth /bredθ/ noun **1** [C/U] the distance from one side of an object to the other =WIDTH: *5 feet in breadth* **2** [U] the wide range of different things or ideas that something includes: *The book demonstrates a remarkable breadth of knowledge.*
→ LENGTH

bread•win•ner /ˈbredˌwɪnər/ noun [C] the person who earns the money to support a family

break¹ /breɪk/ (past tense **broke** /broʊk/; past participle **brok•en** /ˈbroʊkən/) verb ★★★

1 separate into pieces	10 when waves fall
2 stop working	11 when the day starts
3 not obey rule/law	12 when a storm starts
4 not keep agreement	13 weather: change
5 make a hole/cut	14 when sb is upset
6 make sth end	15 of a boy's voice
7 when news is told	+ PHRASES
8 tell sb bad news	+ PHRASAL VERBS
9 destroy confidence	

1 [I/T] if something breaks, or if you break it, it separates into two or more pieces when it is hit, dropped etc.: *I broke two dishes this morning.* ♦ *Joey broke three bones in his foot.* ♦ ***Break** the spaghetti **in half*** (=in the middle). ♦ *The glass **broke into tiny pieces**.*
2 [I/T] if a piece of equipment breaks, or if you break it, it stops working correctly: *Don't play with the camera – you'll break it.*
3 [T] to fail to obey a rule or law: *Students who break these rules will be punished.*
4 [T] to not do something that you promised or agreed to do: *Elliot claims that his business partner broke her contract.*
5 [T] to make a hole or cut in the surface of something: *The dog bit his leg, but didn't break the skin.*
6 [T] to make something end: *A bird's call broke the silence.* ♦ *I found it hard to **break the habit** of eating in the afternoons.*
7 [I/T] if important news breaks, or if a newspaper or television station breaks it, it becomes publicly known: *He was back in France when the news broke.*
8 [T] to tell someone bad news in a kind way: *I didn't know how to break it to her.*
9 [T] to destroy someone's confidence, determination, or happiness: *Twenty years in prison had not broken his spirit.*
10 [I] if waves break, they reach their highest point and start to fall
11 [I] when day breaks, it starts to get light in the morning=DAWN
12 [I] if a storm breaks, it starts
13 [I] if the weather breaks, it changes unexpectedly

14 [I] if someone's voice breaks, they cannot speak clearly, usually because they are upset
15 [I] when a boy's voice breaks, it starts to become deeper and sound like a man's

B

PHRASES **break even** if a person or business breaks even, they neither make a profit nor lose money
break sb's fall to stop someone who is falling from hitting the ground directly
break free 1 to escape from someone who is trying to hold you **2** to escape from an unpleasant situation that controls your life
break sb's heart to make someone feel extremely sad
break the ice to do or say something that makes people feel less shy or nervous when they first meet
break a record to do something better than anyone else has done before in a particular activity, especially a sport

PHRASAL VERBS **ˌbreak aˈway** to escape from a person, place, or situation: *Anna tried to break away, but he held her tight.*
ˌbreak ˈdown 1 if a machine or vehicle breaks down, it stops working **2** if a relationship or discussion breaks down, it stops being successful: *At one point, the talks broke down completely.* **3** to start crying, especially in public: *People broke down and wept when they heard the news.*
ˌbreak sth ˈdown to hit something such as a door or wall very hard so that it falls down: *Firefighters had to break down the door.*
ˌbreak (sth) ˈdown if a substance breaks down, or if it is broken down, it separates into the parts that it is made up of: *The substance is easily broken down by bacteria.*
ˌbreak ˈin 1 to enter a building by force, especially in order to steal things: *Someone had broken in through the bedroom window.* **2** to interrupt when someone is talking: *"Hilary," he broke in gently, "I'm just trying to help."*
ˌbreak ˈinto sth 1 to enter a building by force, especially in order to steal things: *A house in our neighborhood was broken into last night.* **2** to start doing something: *The kids saw the beach and broke into a run.*
ˌbreak ˈoff to stop speaking: *Linda broke off, realizing that she was wrong.*
ˌbreak (sth) ˈoff if a part of something breaks off, or if you break it off, it becomes separated from the main part: *Part of the chimney broke off and fell to the ground.*
ˌbreak ˈsth off to end a relationship or a discussion: *The two countries have broken off diplomatic relations.*
ˌbreak ˈout 1 if something bad such as a war, fire, or disease breaks out, it starts **2** to start to appear on the skin: *An ugly rash broke out on my arm.* **3** to escape from a prison
ˌbreak ˈthrough (sth) if something that was hidden breaks through, it appears: *The sun broke through the clouds.*
ˌbreak ˈup 1 if two people break up, or if a relationship breaks up, the relationship ends: *He's just broken up with his girlfriend.* **2** if a meeting or event breaks up, it ends: *The talks didn't break up until after midnight.* **3** if the sound on a radio or cell phone breaks up, you cannot hear it clearly
ˌbreak (sth) ˈup to break into smaller pieces, or to make something do this: *Break the chocolate up into squares.*
ˌbreak sth ˈup to stop a fight
ˌbreak with sth 1 to leave a group that you have worked with, because of a disagreement **2** if someone breaks with the past or with tradition, they start doing things in a new way

break² /breɪk/ noun [C] ★★

1 time for rest	6 where sth is broken
2 a short vacation	7 pause in program
3 vacation	8 a space in sth
4 time of major change	+ PHRASE
5 chance to succeed	

1 a period of time when you are not working and can rest or enjoy yourself: *OK, let's take a fifteen-minute* ***break.*** ♦ *The art class is the only time I get* ***a break from*** *the kids.*
2 a short vacation: *a weekend break for two in Boston*
3 *American* a period of vacation when classes at a college or university stop: *Spring break starts on March 15th.*
4 a time at which one thing ends completely: *a break in relations with Uganda* ♦ *Lynn's decision helped her* ***make the break*** *with her past.*
5 an opportunity that helps you to be successful: *a lucky break* ♦ *Kiefer's big break came with the movie* Stand By Me.
6 a place where something is broken: *a break in the gas pipeline*
7 a pause between television or radio programs, especially when advertisements are broadcast: *We'll be back after the break.*
8 a space in something: *a break in the traffic/clouds*

PHRASE **give sb a break** to stop being unkind or making things difficult for someone: *Give the boy a break – he's just learning.* ♦ *Oh,* ***give me a break*** (=stop annoying me). *I was just kidding.*

break·a·ble /ˈbreɪkəb(ə)l/ adj a breakable object can break easily
break·a·way /ˈbreɪkəˌweɪ/ adj consisting of people who have decided to separate from a larger group: *a breakaway republic*
break·down /ˈbreɪkˌdaʊn/ noun [C] **1** a situation in which something has failed or is beginning to fail: *a breakdown in communication* **2** information that has been separated into different groups: *We'll need to see a breakdown of these figures.* **3** NERVOUS BREAKDOWN **4** a situation in which a machine or vehicle stops working
break·er /ˈbreɪkər/ noun [C] a large wave that comes onto a beach
break·fast /ˈbrekfəst/ noun [C/U] ★★ the first meal that you have in the morning: *What did you* ***have for breakfast*** *this morning?*
ˈbreak-in noun [C] an occasion when someone enters a building illegally using force
break·ing point /ˈbreɪkɪŋ ˌpɔɪnt/ noun [singular] a situation in which there are so many problems that it is impossible to deal with them
break·neck /ˈbreɪkˌnek/ adj **at breakneck speed** very fast, in a way that is dangerous

break·out¹ /ˈbreɪkˌaʊt/ noun [C] **1** an occasion when prisoners escape from a prison **2** *American* an appearance of PIMPLES on your skin

break·out² /ˈbreɪkˌaʊt/ adj *American* involving great success that makes someone or something very popular

break·through /ˈbreɪkˌθru/ noun [C] **1** a discovery or achievement that comes after a lot of hard work: *Scientists predict a major breakthrough within six months.* **2** a time when you begin to be successful: *The breakthrough came when they discovered how to slow the virus down.*

break·up /ˈbreɪkˌʌp/ noun [C] **1** the end of a marriage or serious relationship **2** the division of something such as an organization or country into smaller parts

breast /brest/ noun ★
1 [C] one of the two round soft parts on the front of a woman's body —*picture* → C14
2 [C] *literary* your chest and heart, thought of as the part of your body where you feel emotions
3 [C] the front part of a bird's body
4 [C/U] meat from the front part of a bird or some animals: *chicken breasts*

breast·feed /ˈbrestˌfid/ (past tense and past participle **breast·fed** /ˈbrestˌfed/) verb [I/T] to feed a baby with milk from your breasts —**breast·feed·ing** noun [U]

breast·stroke /ˈbres(t)ˌstroʊk/ noun [U] a style of swimming in which you lie on your front and pull both arms back from your chest at the same time

breath /breθ/ noun [C/U] ★★ the air that goes in and out of your body when you breathe, or the action of getting air into your lungs: *His breath smelled of alcohol.* ♦ *She **took a deep breath*** (=filled her lungs with air). ♦ *Simon **held his breath*** (=breathed in and held the air inside) *and dived under the water.* ♦ *I was **out of breath*** (=breathing fast and with difficulty) *from running.*

PHRASES **a breath of fresh air 1** a short time outside a building when you have been inside **2** *informal* someone or something that is new, interesting, and exciting: *Young's singing style is a breath of fresh air for pop music.*

catch your breath to have a short rest after doing something tiring, so that you can start breathing normally again

don't hold your breath *spoken* used for telling someone not to expect something to happen because it probably will not: *Dan said he was coming, but don't hold your breath.*

in the same breath used for saying that someone has said two things that cannot both be true

take your breath away to be extremely impressive, beautiful, or shocking

under your breath said in a very quiet way, so that it is difficult for people to hear → CATCH¹

Breath·a·lyz·er /ˈbreθəˌlaɪzər/ *trademark* a piece of equipment used by the police for checking how much alcohol a driver has drunk

breathe /brið/ verb ★★
1 [I/T] to take air into your lungs through your nose or mouth and let it out again: *Doctors said he was having difficulty breathing.* ♦ *We begin the exercise by **breathing deeply*** (=breathing large amounts of air). ♦ *She leaned against the door, **breathing heavily*** (=with difficulty).
2 [T] to bring other substances than air into your body as you breathe: *I don't want to breathe other people's smoke.*

PHRASES **breathe down sb's neck** to watch closely what someone is doing, in a way that annoys them

not breathe a word to keep something a secret

PHRASAL VERBS ˌ**breathe (sth) ˈin** to take air or other substances into your lungs through your nose or mouth

ˌ**breathe (sth) ˈout** to send air or other substances out of your lungs through your nose or mouth

breath·er /ˈbriðər/ noun [singular] *informal* a short rest from work or activity

breath·ing /ˈbriðɪŋ/ noun [U] the process of taking air into your lungs and letting it out again

ˈ**breathing ˌroom** noun [singular/U] a period of rest from a difficult situation that allows you to get your energy back

breath·less /ˈbreθləs/ adj **1** breathing very fast and hard, for example after running **2** experiencing a very strong emotion, especially excitement —**breath·less·ly** adv, **breath·less·ness** noun [U]

breath·tak·ing /ˈbreθˌteɪkɪŋ/ adj extremely impressive or beautiful —**breath·tak·ing·ly** adv

ˈ**breath ˌtest** noun [C] a test in which police officers check how much alcohol a driver has drunk

breed¹ /brid/ (past tense and past participle **bred** /bred/) verb **1** [I] if animals breed, they become the parents of young animals **2** [T] to produce new plants or animals from existing ones **3** [T] to make bad feelings or situations develop: *Secrecy breeds distrust.*

breed² /brid/ noun [C] **1** a particular type of animal that is different from others, but not so different that it is another SPECIES: *different breeds of dog* **2** a particular type of person or thing: *the new breed of Internet millionaires*

breed·er /ˈbridər/ noun [C] someone who breeds animals or plants

breed·ing /ˈbridɪŋ/ noun [U] **1** the process of MATING and producing young animals **2** the activity of keeping animals or plants in order to produce new animals or plants **3** *old-fashioned* polite behavior that is thought to be connected with the type of family that you come from

breeze¹ /briz/ noun [C] a light wind: *a gentle/light/slight breeze*

breeze² /briz/ verb [I] to go somewhere in a very confident way: *He breezed into the meeting and took charge.*

PHRASAL VERB ˈ**breeze through sth** to do something very easily or confidently

breez·y /ˈbrizi/ adj **1** with a lot of light wind **2** lively, confident, and informal —**breez·i·ly** adv

brev·i·ty /ˈbrevəti/ noun [U] *formal* **1** the use of

only a few words **2** the fact that something only lasts for a short time

brew /bru/ verb **1** [I/T] to make beer **2** [I/T] if tea or coffee is brewing, or if you are brewing it, you have made it and left it to develop more flavor **3** [I] to begin to happen: *A storm was brewing.*

brew·er /ˈbruər/ noun [C] a company or person that makes beer

brew·er·y /ˈbruəri/ noun [C] **1** a place where beer is made **2** a company that makes beer

bribe¹ /braɪb/ verb [T] to give money or presents to someone so that they will help you by doing something wrong or illegal: *They tried to bribe the judge to find their brother not guilty.*

bribe² /braɪb/ noun [C] money or a present that you give to someone so that they will help you by doing something wrong or illegal: *Some officials had accepted bribes from a major oil company.*

brib·er·y /ˈbraɪbəri/ noun [U] the act of giving money or presents to someone so that they will help you by doing something wrong or illegal

bric-a-brac /ˈbrɪkəˌbræk/ noun [U] small objects for your home that are not very expensive

brick /brɪk/ noun [C/U] ★★ a small block used as a building material to make walls, houses, etc.: *The church was built entirely of brick.* → WALL¹

brick·lay·er /ˈbrɪkˌleɪər/ noun [C] someone whose job is to build walls, houses, etc. using bricks —**brick·lay·ing** noun [U]

bri·dal /ˈbraɪd(ə)l/ adj relating to a bride

bride /braɪd/ noun [C] a woman who is getting married, or one who has recently gotten married

bride·groom /ˈbraɪdˌgrum/ noun [C] a man who is getting married, or one who has recently gotten married

brides·maid /ˈbraɪdzˌmeɪd/ noun [C] a girl or young woman who helps a BRIDE at her wedding

bridge¹ /brɪdʒ/ noun ★★

1 for crossing river/road	4 card game
2 connection	5 upper part of nose
3 part of ship	

1 [C] a structure that supports a road, railroad, or path going over a river, over another road, etc.: *Go over the bridge and then turn right.* ♦ *a railroad bridge*

2 [C] something that forms a connection between two groups or situations: *Preschool acts as **a bridge between** home and school.*

3 [C] the part of a ship from which it is controlled

4 [U] a card game for four players who make two teams

5 [C] the thin part of your nose between your eyes

bridge² /brɪdʒ/ verb [T] to reduce the differences that separate two things or groups: *ways to bridge the gap between income and spending*

bri·dle¹ /ˈbraɪd(ə)l/ noun [C] a set of leather bands that go over a horse's head

bri·dle² /ˈbraɪd(ə)l/ verb [I] to show that you are angry or offended

brief¹ /brif/ adj ★★

1 lasting for only a short time: *a brief visit*

2 using only a few words: *I'll make my comments brief.*

PHRASE **in brief** using as few words as possible, and without many details

→ BRIEFLY

brief² /brif/ noun [C] **1** *American* a short written summary or report **2** a document giving the facts of a legal case → BRIEFS

brief³ /brif/ verb [T] to give someone official information about a situation: *The President's military advisors are briefing him on the situation.*

brief·case /ˈbrifˌkeɪs/ noun [C] a case for carrying documents —*picture* → C3

brief·ing /ˈbrifɪŋ/ noun [C] a meeting or document in which people receive official information

brief·ly /ˈbrifli/ adv **1** in a way that does not take much time or give many details: *Tell me briefly what your story is about.* **2** for a short time: *I saw her briefly yesterday before she left for the airport.*

briefs /brifs/ noun [plural] short tight UNDERPANTS for men

bri·gade /brɪˈgeɪd/ noun [C] **1** a large group of soldiers **2** *showing disapproval* a group of people who have the same opinions: *the anti-hunting brigade*

brig·a·dier·gen·er·al /ˌbrɪgədɪr ˈdʒen(ə)rəl/ noun [C] an officer of high rank in the U.S. Army, MARINES, or Air Force

bright /braɪt/ adj ★★★

1 bright colors are strong but not dark: *She was wearing a bright red scarf.* ♦ *They have used warm bright colors all through the house.*

2 full of strong shining light: *It was a bright sunny day.* ♦ *I could see a bright light in the sky.*

3 intelligent: *one of the brightest students in the class*

4 happy and lively = CHEERFUL: *She gave him a bright smile.*

PHRASE **look on the bright side** to think about the good parts of a situation that is mainly bad

—**bright·ly** adv, **bright·ness** noun [U]

bright·en /ˈbraɪt(ə)n/ verb **1** [I/T] to start to have more color or light, or to give something more color or light **2** [I] to start looking or feeling happier

PHRASAL VERBS ˌ**brighten ˈup** *same as* **brighten** 2: *Viola brightened up when she saw him.*

ˌ**brighten (sth) ˈup** to start to have more color or light, or to give something more color or light: *It was beginning to brighten up* (=the weather was beginning to improve).

brights /braɪts/ noun [plural] *American* car HEADLIGHTS (=lights on the front of a car) when they are shining as brightly as possible

bril·liance /ˈbrɪljəns/ noun [U] **1** great skill or intelligence **2** great brightness

bril·liant /ˈbrɪljənt/ adj **1** very intelligent: *a brilliant scientist* **2** very skillful, impressive, or successful: *The goalkeeper* *made a brilliant save.* **3** extremely bright: *a brilliant light* —**bril•liant•ly** adv: *Their plan worked brilliantly.* ♦ *brilliantly colored birds*

brim[1] /brɪm/ noun [C] **1** the part of a hat that sticks out from the base **2** the top edge of a cup or bowl

brim[2] /brɪm/ PHRASAL VERB ˈ**brim with sth 1** to be extremely full of something liquid: *Her eyes were brimming with tears.* **2** to be feeling a strong emotion

bring /brɪŋ/ (past tense and past participle **brought** /brɔt/) verb [T] ★★★

1 take sb/sth with you	6 start a legal case
2 move sth somewhere	7 used to change subject
3 attract to a place	+ PHRASES
4 cause sth	+ PHRASAL VERBS
5 make sth reach a total	

1 to take someone or something with you from one place to another: *Bring a coat in case it gets cold.* ♦ **bring sth for sb** *I brought that book for you.* ♦ **bring sb sth** *Could you bring me a plate from the kitchen?* ♦ **bring sth to sb** *Don't get up – I'll bring your tea to you.*

2 to move something somewhere: **bring sth down/up** *She reached up to the shelf and brought down a box.*

3 to make someone or something come to a place: **bring sb/sth to sth** *Government investment has brought thousands of new jobs to the area.* ♦ *What brought you to Chicago in the first place?*

4 to be the cause of a state, situation, or feeling: *efforts to bring peace to the region* ♦ *My work* ***brings*** *me* ***into contact with*** *all kinds of people.* ♦ **bring sb sth** *The baby has brought them great joy.*

5 to make a number reach a particular total: *He scored 10 points, bringing the team's total to 85.*

6 to start a legal case against someone: *The authorities are expected to* ***bring charges.***

7 to come to a particular point as you are talking or writing: *This brings us to the end of this part of the discussion.*

PHRASES **bring sth to an end/a close** to make something stop

can't bring yourself to do sth to be unable to do something because it is too unpleasant, embarrassing, or sad: *He can't even bring himself to talk to me.*

PHRASAL VERBS ˌ**bring sth aˈbout** to cause changes in a situation

ˌ**bring sb/sth aˈlong** to take someone or something with you when you go somewhere

ˌ**bring sth ˈback 1** to cause ideas, feelings, or memories to be in your mind again: *Do these stories bring back any memories?* **2** to start using or doing things that were used or done in the past: *He wants to bring back the glamour of the old Hollywood movies.* **3** to bring something with you when you come back from a place

ˌ**bring sth ˈdown 1** to reduce the rate, level, or amount of something: *policies designed to bring down inflation* **2** to cause a government or politician to lose power **3** to make someone or something move or fall to the ground

ˌ**bring sth ˈin 1** to use the skills of a particular group or person: *This is an opportunity to bring in new talent.* **2** to cause someone or something to get money or customers: *Renting out a spare room can bring in $350 a month.*

ˌ**bring sth ˈon** to be the cause of something bad: *Stress can bring on headaches.*

ˌ**bring sth ˈout 1** to produce a new product and start to sell it = RELEASE: *They have recently brought out a new CD.* **2** to make a particular quality appear in someone or something: *Tragedies like this sometimes* ***bring out the best*** *in people* (=make them show their best qualities).

ˌ**bring sb ˈup** to take care of a child until he or she becomes an adult = RAISE: *She brought up three sons on her own.* ♦ **bring sb up to be/do sth** *Our parents brought us up to believe in our own abilities.*

ˌ**bring sth ˈup** to start discussing a subject: *I hate to bring this up, but you still owe me $50.*

If you **bring** or **take** something, you hold it and go with it to another place. But which word you choose depends on the situation.

- **Bring** describes movement to another place when the speaker or listener is already there: *Bring the photos when you come to visit me.* ♦ *I'll bring the photos to your house tonight.*
- **Take** describes movement to another place when the speaker or listener is NOT already there: *Take the photos when you go to visit her.* ♦ *I'll take the photos to her house.*

brink /brɪŋk/ noun **the brink of sth** the point in time when something very bad or very good is about to happen: *The crisis brought the two nations to the brink of war.*

brisk /brɪsk/ adj **1** moving or acting quickly **2** if business is brisk, a lot of things are being sold quickly —**brisk•ly** adv

bris•tle[1] /ˈbrɪs(ə)l/ noun [C] **1** a short stiff fiber in a brush **2** a short stiff hair

bris•tle[2] /ˈbrɪs(ə)l/ verb [I] to be angry or offended

Brit /brɪt/ noun [C] *informal* someone who comes from the U.K.

Brit•ish /ˈbrɪtɪʃ/ adj **1** of the U.K., or from the U.K. **2 the British** the people of the U.K.

Brit•on /ˈbrɪt(ə)n/ noun [C] *mainly journalism* someone from the U.K.

brit•tle /ˈbrɪt(ə)l/ adj hard and easily broken

broach /broʊtʃ/ verb [T] to begin discussing a subject that may make someone upset or embarrassed: *He decided it was time to broach the subject of a pay raise.*

broad /brɔd/ adj ★★★

1 wide ≠ NARROW: *He had very broad shoulders.* ♦ *a broad shady path*

2 including many different things or people ≠ NARROW: *I meet* ***a broad range of*** *people in my job.*

3 expressed in a general way, without many details: *We need a broad strategy for the company's future development.* ♦ *This chapter can only give* ***a broad outline*** *of the subject.*

4 a broad ACCENT (=way of speaking) is very noticeable and typical of the area you come from: *a broad southern accent*

B

PHRASE **in broad daylight** during the day, when people can easily see what is happening: *They robbed the bank in broad daylight.*
→ BROADLY

broad•band /ˈbrɔdˌbænd/ noun [U] a type of connection between a computer and the Internet that allows you to send or receive a large amount of information in a short time

broad•cast¹ /ˈbrɔdˌkæst/ (past tense and past participle **broad•cast** or **broad•cast•ed**) verb [I/T] to send out messages or programs to be received by radios or televisions: *NBC will be broadcasting the game live from Chicago.* —**broad•cast•ing** noun [U]

broad•cast² /ˈbrɔdˌkæst/ noun [C] a program that is broadcast: *Channel 5's main news broadcast*

broad•cast•er /ˈbrɔdˌkæstər/ noun [C] someone whose job is to speak on radio or television programs

broad•en /ˈbrɔd(ə)n/ verb [I/T] **1** to start to include more things or people, or to make something include more things or people: *We have broadened the scope of the investigation.* **2** to become wider, or to make something wider: *There are plans to broaden the road.*

broad•ly /ˈbrɔdli/ adv **1** in a general way, although not in every detail: *The proposal was broadly welcomed by teachers.* **2** in a way that includes a large number of people or things: *a broadly-based committee*

broad-mind•ed /ˌbrɔdˈmaɪndəd/ adj willing to accept different types of behavior and not easily shocked ≠ NARROW-MINDED

broad•side¹ /ˈbrɔdˌsaɪd/ verb [T] *American* to crash into the side of another vehicle

broad•side² /ˈbrɔdˌsaɪd/ adv with the side facing toward something: *His van hit the car broadside.*

broad•side³ /ˈbrɔdˌsaɪd/ noun [C] a strong written or spoken attack

Broad•way /ˈbrɔdˌweɪ/ a street in New York City that is famous for having many theaters

bro•cade /brəˈkeɪd/ noun [U] expensive thick cloth with a pattern woven into it

broc•co•li /ˈbrɑkəli/ noun [U] a vegetable consisting of green stems with many small green or purple parts on the ends —*picture* → C11

bro•chure /broʊˈʃʊr/ noun [C] a small magazine containing details of goods or services that you can buy

broil /brɔɪl/ verb [I/T] *American* to cook something by putting it close to strong heat above or below it

broil•er /ˈbrɔɪlər/ noun [C] *American* a piece of equipment that cooks food using strong heat from above

broil•ing /ˈbrɔɪlɪŋ/ adj very hot

broke¹ /broʊk/ adj *informal* without any money: *Can you lend me $5? I'm completely broke.*

broke² the past tense of **break¹**

bro•ken¹ /ˈbroʊkən/ adj ★★★

1 damaged and in pieces	4 extremely sad
2 not working	5 not as promised
3 injured and cracked	+ PHRASES

1 a broken object has been damaged with the result that it is in two or more pieces: *Nearly all the houses had broken windows.* ♦ *Be careful not to step on the broken glass.*
2 if a piece of equipment is broken, it is not working correctly: *You can't use the microwave – it's broken.*
3 a broken bone has a crack in it: *He had several broken ribs.* ♦ *a broken arm*
4 *literary* if your heart is broken, you feel extremely sad
5 a broken promise is one that someone has not kept

PHRASES **broken English** English with a lot of mistakes, spoken by someone who does not know it very well
a broken home a family in which the parents no longer live together

Words that you can use instead of broken

Broken is a very general word. Here are some words with more specific meanings that sound more natural and appropriate in particular situations.

cars/machines/equipment	faulty, not working
houses/buildings	falling down, in disrepair
systems/computers	down, not working
objects	chipped, cracked, dented, smashed
containers	burst, leaky, split
fabric	frayed, ripped, split, torn
paper	in shreds, ripped, torn

bro•ken² the past participle of **break¹**

ˌbroken-ˈdown adj not working anymore, or in very bad condition

bro•ken-heart•ed /ˌbroʊkən ˈhɑrtəd/ adj extremely sad

bro•ker¹ /ˈbroʊkər/ noun [C] **1** someone who buys and sells things like property or insurance for other people **2** someone who arranges an agreement

bro•ker² /ˈbroʊkər/ verb [T] to arrange the details of a deal so that everyone can agree to it

bro•ker•age /ˈbroʊkərɪdʒ/ noun [C] a company where brokers work

bron•chi•tis /brɑŋˈkaɪtɪs/ noun [U] an illness that affects your breathing and makes you cough

bronze /brɑnz/ noun **1** [U] a hard brown metal made from COPPER and TIN **2** [U] a red-brown color **3** [C] a BRONZE MEDAL

bronzed /brɑnzd/ adj with attractive brown skin because of spending time in the sun

ˌbronze ˈmedal noun [C] a round flat piece of metal that you get as a prize for coming third in a competition

brooch /broʊtʃ/ noun [C] a piece of jewelry that you fasten to your clothes —*picture* → JEWELRY

brood¹ /brud/ verb [I] to think and worry about something a lot

brood² /brud/ noun [C] a group of young birds that are born at the same time to the same mother

brook /brʊk/ noun [C] a small river

broom /brum/ noun [C] a brush with a long handle, used for cleaning floors

broth /brɔθ/ noun [U] a thin soup with a meat or vegetable flavor

broth•el /ˈbrɑθ(ə)l/ noun [C] a place where men pay to have sex

broth•er[1] /ˈbrʌðər/ noun [C] ★★★
1 a boy or man who has the same parents as you: *his younger/older/little/big brother —picture* → FAMILY TREE
2 *American* a black man. This word is mainly used by black people.
3 used by men for referring to a man that they feel loyalty and friendship toward
4 a man who is a member of a religious group, especially a MONK

broth•er[2] /ˈbrʌðər/ interjection used for showing that you are surprised or annoyed: *Oh brother, what a mess.*

broth•er•hood /ˈbrʌðərˌhʊd/ noun **1** [U] the friendship and support that a group of people get from one another **2** [C] a group of people who have similar interests

ˈbrother-in-ˌlaw (plural **ˈbrothers-in-ˌlaw**) noun [C] **1** your sister's husband **2** the brother of your husband or wife —*picture* → FAMILY TREE

broth•er•ly /ˈbrʌðərli/ adj typical of the feelings that a brother shows

brought the past tense and past participle of bring

brow /braʊ/ noun [C] **1** *literary* the part of your face above your eyes **2** an EYEBROW **3** the highest part of a hill

brown[1] /braʊn/ adj ★★★ having the same color as wood or coffee: *brown eyes* —**brown** noun [C/U]: *The skirt is also available in brown.*

brown[2] /braʊn/ verb [I/T] to cook something until it turns brown, or to become brown in this way

brown•field /ˈbraʊnˌfild/ adj relating to land in a town that was previously used for industry and where new buildings can now be built: *brownfield sites*

brown•ie /ˈbraʊni/ noun [C/U] a type of flat chocolate cake that is served in squares

browse /braʊz/ verb **1** [I] to look at information or pictures in a book or magazine, without looking for anything in particular: *I sat in the waiting room and browsed through the magazines.* **2** [I/T] *computing* to look for information on a computer, especially on the Internet **3** [I] to look at things in a store without being sure whether you want to buy anything

brows•er /ˈbraʊzər/ noun [C] *computing* a computer program that allows you to use the Internet

bruise[1] /bruz/ verb [T] to cause a bruise on someone's skin or on a piece of fruit: *She bruised her leg when she fell.* —**bruis•ing** noun [U]

bruise[2] /bruz/ noun [C] a dark mark on your body or on a piece of fruit where it has been hit: *He had a large bruise over his eye.*

brunch /brʌntʃ/ noun [C/U] a meal that combines breakfast and lunch

bru•nette /bruˈnet/ noun [C] a woman with dark brown hair → BLOND[2]

brunt, the /brʌnt/ noun **bear/take the brunt of sth** to suffer the worst effects of something

brush[1] /brʌʃ/ noun ★★
1 [C] an object that you use for painting, cleaning things, or making your hair neat, consisting of a handle with fibers attached to it: *Remove any loose dirt using a soft brush.*
2 [C] a short experience of a dangerous or unpleasant situation: *He'd had a few* ***brushes with the law, but nothing serious.***
3 [singular] a very gentle movement against something

brush[2] /brʌʃ/ verb ★
1 [T] to make something clean or neat using a brush: *She hadn't bothered to* ***brush her hair****.* ♦ *How often do you* ***brush your teeth****?*
2 [T] to remove something by moving your hands or a brush quickly over a surface: *Maggie* ***brushed away*** *her tears as she listened.* ♦ **brush sth from/off sth** *We had to brush the snow off the windshield.*
3 [I/T] to touch someone or something for a very short time as you go past: *She* ***brushed past*** *him.*

PHRASAL VERBS **ˌbrush sth aˈside** to refuse to accept that something is important or true: *The defendant brushed aside accusations that he had lied.*
ˌbrush ˈup on sth to improve your skills or knowledge of something: *I took a class to brush up on my German.*

brusque /brʊsk/ adj speaking quickly in an unfriendly way using very few words = CURT —**brusque•ly** adv

Brus•sels /ˈbrʌs(ə)lz/ the capital city of Belgium, where the HEADQUARTERS of the European Union is. People often use "Brussels" for referring to the government of the European Union.

ˌBrussels ˈsprout noun [C] a small round vegetable consisting of many green leaves —*picture* → C11

bru•tal /ˈbrut(ə)l/ adj **1** extremely violent: *brutal attacks/atrocities* **2** extremely honest, in a way that seems unkind: *Let's be brutal here – he's not good enough.* —**bru•tal•i•ty** /bruˈtæləti/ noun [C/U], **bru•tal•ly** adv

brute[1] /brut/ noun [C] a strong man who acts in a cruel or violent way

brute[2] /brut/ adj **brute force/strength** great physical force/strength

brut•ish /ˈbrutɪʃ/ adj *literary* cruel and lacking intelligence

B.S. /ˌbi ˈes/ noun [C] *American* Bachelor of Science: a first degree from a college or university in a scientific subject

BSc /ˌbi es ˈsi/ noun [C] *British* a B.S.

BTW abbrev by the way: used in e-mails and TEXT MESSAGES for introducing additional information

bub•ble[1] /ˈbʌb(ə)l/ noun [C] a ball of air or gas in a liquid or other substance: *Heat the milk until bubbles form around the edge of the pan.*

bub•ble[2] /ˈbʌb(ə)l/ verb [I] if liquid bubbles, bubbles form and move in it: *When the sauce starts to bubble, remove it from the heat.*

PHRASAL VERB **ˈbubble ˌwith sth** or **ˌbubble ˈover with sth** to be full of a happy or excited feeling

B

ˈbubble ˌgum noun [C/U] a type of brightly colored candy that you blow into to form bubbles, but do not swallow

bub•bly /ˈbʌbli/ adj **1** lively, happy, and friendly **2** full of BUBBLES

buck /bʌk/ noun [C] **1** *American informal* a dollar: *You can get batteries for a few bucks at any drugstore.* **2** a male deer → DOE

PHRASE **pass the buck** to make someone else deal with something that you should take responsibility for

buck•et /ˈbʌkət/ noun [C] **1** a round open container with a handle, used for carrying liquid and other substances **2** the amount that a bucket contains: *a bucket of soapy water*

buck•le¹ /ˈbʌk(ə)l/ noun [C] a metal object used for fastening a belt, shoe, or bag

buck•le² /ˈbʌk(ə)l/ verb [I/T] **1** to fasten a buckle, or to be fastened with a buckle: *The bag buckles at the side.* **2** to bend, or to make something bend under pressure: *The pillars began to buckle under the strain.*

bud /bʌd/ noun [C] **1** a part of a plant that opens to form a leaf or flower: *yellow rose buds* **2** *American spoken* used for talking to a male friend → NIP, TASTE BUDS

Bud•dha /ˈbudə/ the title used for referring to the religious leader Siddhartha Gautama, the founder of Buddhism

Bud•dhism /ˈbuˌdɪzəm/ noun [U] the set of religious beliefs based on the teaching of Siddhartha Gautama, the Buddha —**Bud•dhist** adj, noun [C]

bud•ding /ˈbʌdɪŋ/ adj just beginning or developing: *a budding musician*

bud•dy /ˈbʌdi/ noun [C] *American* **1** *spoken* used for talking to a man whose name you do not know: *Hey buddy, what are you doing?* **2** *informal* a friend

budge /bʌdʒ/ verb [I/T] to move, or to make something move, especially something that is difficult to move: *I pulled again, but the wheel wouldn't budge.*

PHRASE **not budge** to refuse to change your opinion or decision → INCH¹

budg•et¹ /ˈbʌdʒət/ noun [C] ★ the amount of money a person, organization, or government has to spend, or their plan to spend it: *Two-thirds of their budget goes on labor costs.* ♦ *Make a monthly budget and stick to it.* ♦ *The movie is already **over budget*** (=it has cost more than was expected).

budg•et² /ˈbʌdʒət/ verb [I] to carefully plan the way you will spend your money: *As a student, you have to learn how to budget.*

budg•et³ /ˈbʌdʒət/ adj very inexpensive: *a budget hotel*

buff /bʌf/ noun [C] someone who is very interested in and knows a lot about a particular subject: *a movie/computer/wine buff*

buf•fa•lo /ˈbʌfəloʊ/ noun [C] **1** a large animal similar to a cow with curved horns **2** a BISON

buff•er /ˈbʌfər/ noun [C] something that protects someone or something from harm: *The air bag acts as a buffer between the driver and the steering wheel.*

buf•fet¹ /bʌˈfeɪ/ noun [C] a meal at which all the food is put on a table and people go and choose what they want

buf•fet² /ˈbʌfət/ verb [T] to keep hitting against something with force

bug¹ /bʌg/ noun [C] **1** *informal* an insect **2** *informal* a minor infectious illness: *a flu bug* **3** a minor fault in a computer system or in a computer program **4** a small piece of electronic equipment that is used for secretly listening to people

bug² /bʌg/ verb [T] **1** *informal* to annoy someone: *It really bugs me when people smoke in restaurants.* **2** to hide a piece of electronic equipment somewhere so that you can secretly listen to people

bu•gle /ˈbjug(ə)l/ noun [C] a musical instrument, consisting of a curved metal tube that is wide at one end

build¹ /bɪld/ (past tense and past participle **built** /bɪlt/) verb ★★★

1 [I/T] to make a building or other large structure by putting its parts together: *Do you know when this house was built?* ♦ *They're building a new bridge over the river.* ♦ *The cabin was **built of** logs.*

2 [T] to develop something: *He set out to build a business empire and succeeded.*

3 [I/T] to increase, or to make something increase: *The company has worked hard to build sales.*

PHRASAL VERBS **ˌbuild sth ˈin/ˈinto sth** to make something part of a plan, system, or calculation: *The cost of renting equipment is built into the price.*

ˈbuild ˌon/uˌpon sth to do something in addition to what you have already achieved: *We need to build on the ideas we have had so far.*

ˌbuild (sth) ˈup *same as* **build¹** 3: *These exercises are good for building up leg strength.* → BUILDUP

ˌbuild sth ˈup *same as* **build¹** 2: *Stevens played a key role in building up the company.*

ˌbuild ˈup to sth to prepare for something: *She'd been building up to telling them she was leaving.*

build² /bɪld/ noun [singular] the size and shape of someone's body: *He was of medium build and about my height.*

> **Words often used with build**
>
> *Adjectives often used with **build** (noun)*
>
> - **muscular, solid, stocky, sturdy** + BUILD: used about someone with a big body
> - **slender, slim, wiry** + BUILD: used about someone with a thin body

build•er /ˈbɪldər/ noun [C] someone whose job is to build and repair houses

build•ing /ˈbɪldɪŋ/ noun ★★★

1 [C] a structure such as a house that has a roof and walls: *The city hall was a large impressive building.*

2 [U] the process of building houses, factories, office buildings, etc.: *the building of a new hospital* ♦ *building materials/regulations*

ˈbuilding ˌblock noun [C] one of the basic parts from which something is made: *Proteins are the essential building blocks of the body's cells.*

build•up /ˈbɪldˌʌp/ noun [C] **1** a gradual

increase in the amount or level of something: *a buildup of carbon dioxide in the atmosphere* **2** the time before an event when people are preparing for it

built the past tense and past participle of **build**[1]

ˌ**built-ˈin** adj forming part of something, and not separate from it

ˌ**built-ˈup** adj a built-up area has many buildings in it

bulb /bʌlb/ noun [C] **1** a glass object with a very thin wire inside, that produces light when it is connected to an electricity supply **2** the part of a plant from which it grows. Bulbs are shaped like onions.

bul•bous /ˈbʌlbəs/ adj big and round

bulge[1] /bʌldʒ/ noun [C] a shape that curves outward on the surface of something

bulge[2] /bʌldʒ/ verb [I] to stick out in a curved shape

bulg•ing /ˈbʌldʒɪŋ/ adj **1** completely full: *a bulging suitcase/briefcase* **2** sticking out

bu•lim•i•a /bʊˈlɪmiə/ noun [U] a serious illness in which you try to control your weight by VOMITING (=bringing food up from your stomach and out of your mouth) → ANOREXIA

bulk /bʌlk/ noun [U] the fact of being large

PHRASES **the bulk of sth** the majority or largest part of something: *Women still do the bulk of domestic work in the home.*

in bulk in large quantities: *large companies that buy and sell in bulk*

bulk•y /ˈbʌlki/ adj too big to be carried or stored easily

bull /bʊl/ noun **1** [C] a male cow —*picture* → C12 **2** [U] *informal* something someone says that is stupid or not true = NONSENSE **3** [C] *business* someone who expects the price of company STOCK to rise → BEAR[2] 2

PHRASE **take the bull by the horns** to deal with a problem in a direct confident way

bull•dog /ˈbʊlˌdɔg/ noun [C] a dog with short hair, a short neck and large head, and short thick legs

bull•doze /ˈbʊlˌdoʊz/ verb [I/T] to clear an area with a bulldozer

bull•doz•er /ˈbʊlˌdoʊzər/ noun [C] a heavy vehicle with a large curved open container at the front, used for moving earth and stones and destroying buildings

bul•let /ˈbʊlɪt/ noun [C] ★ a small piece of metal that is shot from a gun: *a bullet wound/hole* → BITE[1]

bul•le•tin /ˈbʊlətɪn/ noun [C] **1** a newspaper that a club or organization produces regularly for its members **2** a short news broadcast

ˈ**bulletin ˌboard** noun [C] **1** *American* a board on a wall where you can put information or pictures for other people to see **2** *computing* a place on a computer system or on the Internet where you can leave and read messages

ˈ**bullet ˌpoint** noun [C] a printed circle, square, etc. before each item on a list in order to emphasize it

bul•let•proof /ˈbʊlɪtˌpruf/ adj made from a material that stops bullets from passing through

bull•fight /ˈbʊlˌfaɪt/ noun [C] a traditional entertainment in Spain, Mexico, and Portugal in which someone fights a BULL (=male cow) —**bull•fight•er** noun [C], **bull•fight•ing** noun [U]

bull•horn /ˈbʊlˌhɔrn/ noun [C] *American* a MEGAPHONE

bul•lion /ˈbʊljən/ noun [U] gold or silver in the form of solid blocks

bull•ish /ˈbʊlɪʃ/ adj expecting a successful future = OPTIMISTIC

ˈ**bull ˌmarket** noun [C] *business* a situation in which prices of STOCKS are rising → BEAR MARKET

ˈ**bull's-ˌeye** noun [C] the circle in the center of a TARGET that you try to hit

bul•ly[1] /ˈbʊli/ noun [C] someone who uses their strength or status to threaten or frighten people

bul•ly[2] /ˈbʊli/ verb [T] to frighten or hurt someone who is smaller or weaker than you —**bul•ly•ing** noun [U]

bul•wark /ˈbʊlwərk/ noun [C] *formal* someone or something that protects or defends something

bum[1] /bʌm/ noun [C] *informal* **1** *American* a lazy person **2** *American* someone without a job or place to live. This word is now considered offensive by some people. **3** *British* the part of your body that you sit on = BOTTOM

bum[2] /bʌm/ verb [T] *informal* to ask someone to give you something without making you pay: *Can I bum a cigarette?*

PHRASAL VERB ˌ**bum aˈround sth** *informal* to spend time traveling around a place

bum[3] /bʌm/ adj *informal* **1** bad or unfair: *I think we got a bum deal.* **2** *American* injured or not working correctly: *a bum knee/leg/wrist*

bum•ble•bee /ˈbʌmb(ə)lˌbi/ noun [C] a large BEE (=flying insect)

bum•bling /ˈbʌmblɪŋ/ adj confused or badly organized

bummed out /ˌbʌmd ˈaʊt/ adj *American spoken* disappointed or annoyed: *I was so bummed out when they told me I couldn't go.*

bum•mer /ˈbʌmər/ noun [singular] *informal* something that is annoying or disappointing

bump[1] /bʌmp/ verb **1** [I/T] to hit against something solid, or to accidentally make something do this: *I bumped my knee on the corner of the desk.* **2** [I] to move over a surface that is not even: *The truck bumped across a field.*

PHRASAL VERBS ˌ**bump ˈinto sb** to meet someone unexpectedly: *I bumped into your mother at the supermarket.*

ˌ**bump sth ˈup** *informal* to increase something

bump[2] /bʌmp/ noun [C] **1** a raised part on your skin where you have been injured: *Her body was covered in bumps and bruises.* **2** a raised part on a surface: *a bump in the road* **3** a hit or knock against something solid: *We felt a bump as the boat hit something.*

bump•er[1] /ˈbʌmpər/ noun [C] a long thin bar on the front or back of a vehicle that protects the vehicle if it hits anything —*picture* → C6

bump•er[2] /ˈbʌmpər/ adj bigger or more successful than usual: *a bumper crop*

ˈ**bumper ˌsticker** noun [C] a small sign that you stick on your car

bump·y /ˈbʌmpi/ adj **1** a bumpy surface is rough **2** a bumpy trip is uncomfortable because of bad weather or a bad road

bun /bʌn/ noun [C] **1** a small round piece of bread: *a burger in a bun* **2** a hairstyle in which a woman's hair is tied in a tight round ball at the back of her head **3** *British* a small round cake

bunch¹ /bʌntʃ/ noun **1** [C] a group or set of similar things that are fastened together: *a bunch of grapes/flowers/keys* **2** [singular] *informal* a group of people: *They're a great bunch who have made me feel welcome.*

PHRASE **a bunch** *American informal* a large number or amount: *I have a bunch of stuff I have to do before lunch.*

bunch² /bʌntʃ/ or ˌ**bunch (sth) ˈup** verb [I/T] to form a group or a tight round shape, or to make something do this

bun·dle¹ /ˈbʌnd(ə)l/ noun [C] **1** a group of things that have been tied together: *bundles of firewood* **2** a group of things that are sold or offered as a set

PHRASES **a bundle** *informal* a lot of money

be a bundle of sth *informal* used for emphasizing that someone has a lot of a particular quality: *Susan is a bundle of energy.*

bun·dle² /ˈbʌnd(ə)l/ verb [T] **1** to wrap or tie things together **2** to make someone go to a particular place by pushing them in a rough way: *He was quickly bundled into a police car.* **3** to put things together so that they can be sold or offered as a single product

PHRASAL VERB ˌ**bundle sth ˈup** to put warm clothes on yourself or someone else, or wrap someone in something warm

bun·ga·low /ˈbʌŋgəloʊ/ noun [C] a small house that is often all on one level

bun·gee jump·ing /ˈbʌndʒi ˌdʒʌmpɪŋ/ noun [U] the sport of jumping from a very high place while attached to a long piece of rubber

bun·gle /ˈbʌŋg(ə)l/ verb [I/T] to spoil something by doing it very badly

bunk /bʌŋk/ noun [C] a narrow bed attached to a wall

ˈ**bunk ˌbeds** noun [plural] two small beds that are joined together with one above the other —*picture* → BED

bun·ker /ˈbʌŋkər/ noun [C] a room with very strong walls that is built underground as a shelter against bombs

bun·ny /ˈbʌni/ noun [C] a RABBIT. This word is used by or to children.

buoy¹ /bɔɪ, ˈbui/ noun [C] an object that floats on water to show ships where there is danger

buoy² /bɔɪ, ˈbui/ or ˌ**buoy sb ˈup** verb [T] to encourage someone and make them feel confident

buoy·ant /ˈbɔɪənt, ˈbujənt/ adj **1** capable of floating **2** happy and confident **3** successful and likely to remain successful: *The housing market remains buoyant.* —**buoy·an·cy** /ˈbɔɪənsi, ˈbujənsi/ noun [U]

bur·den¹ /ˈbɜrd(ə)n/ noun [C] **1** a serious or difficult responsibility that you have to deal with **2** *literary* something heavy that you have to carry

PHRASE **the burden of proof** *legal* the responsibility of proving that something is true in a court of law

bur·den² /ˈbɜrd(ə)n/ verb [T] to create a problem or serious responsibility for someone

bu·reau /ˈbjʊroʊ/ (plural **bu·reaus**) noun [C] **1** a government department, or part of a government department: *the Federal Bureau of Investigation* **2** an organization that collects or provides information: *an advice bureau* **3** *American* a piece of furniture with drawers for holding clothes **4** *British* a piece of furniture a top part that opens to make a writing table

bu·reauc·ra·cy /bjəˈrɑkrəsi/ noun **1** [U] a complicated and annoying system of rules and processes **2** [C/U] the people employed to run government organizations —**bu·reau·crat·ic** /ˌbjʊrəˈkrætɪk/ adj

bu·reau·crat /ˈbjʊrəˌkræt/ noun [C] *showing disapproval* someone who is employed to help to run an office or government department

bur·geon·ing /ˈbɜrdʒənɪŋ/ adj growing or developing quickly

burg·er /ˈbɜrgər/ noun [C] *informal* a HAMBURGER

bur·glar /ˈbɜrglər/ noun [C] someone who enters a building illegally in order to steal things

ˈ**burglar aˌlarm** noun [C] a piece of equipment that makes a loud noise if someone enters a building

bur·glar·ize /ˈbɜrgləˌraɪz/ verb [T] *American* to enter a building and steal things

bur·gla·ry /ˈbɜrgləri/ noun [C/U] the crime of entering a building illegally in order to steal things

bur·gle /ˈbɜrg(ə)l/ verb [T] *British* to BURGLARIZE a building

bur·gun·dy /ˈbɜrgəndi/ noun [U] a dark red color —**bur·gun·dy** adj

bur·i·al /ˈberiəl/ noun [C/U] the process of burying a dead body

bur·ly /ˈbɜrli/ adj a burly man is fat and strong

burn¹ /bɜrn/ (past tense and past participle **burned** or **burnt** /bɜrnt/) verb ★★★

1 damage with fire	**7** when cheeks are pink
2 be on fire	**8** feel strong emotion
3 produce light/heat	**9** put information on CD
4 spoil food	+ PHRASES
5 cause injury	+ PHRASAL VERBS
6 of chemicals	

1 [T] to damage or destroy something with fire: *Demonstrators burned flags outside the embassy.* ♦ *The old part of the city was **burned to the ground*** (=completely destroyed by fire).

2 [I] if something is burning, it is being damaged or destroyed by fire: *Homes were burning all over the village.*

3 [I] if a fire or flame burns, it produces light and heat

4 [I/T] if food burns, or if you burn it, it gets spoiled by being cooked for too long or at too high a temperature: *Have you burned the toast?*

5 [T] to injure someone or a part of your body with something hot: *The sand was so hot it burnt my feet.*

6 [I/T] if a chemical burns something, it causes damage or pain: *The acid had burned a hole in my shirt.*
7 [I] if your cheeks are burning, they are red because you are embarrassed
8 [I] to feel a very strong emotion or a great need for someone or something: *I was **burning with** curiosity.*
9 [T] to put information onto a CD-ROM
PHRASES **burn your bridges** to do something that makes it impossible for you to return to the situation you were in before: *She had burned her bridges in Hollywood, and returned to Denver.*
get burned to suffer by being treated badly or by losing money
PHRASAL VERBS **ˌburn (sth) ˈdown** to destroy something large with fire, or to be destroyed in this way: *The entire house burned down in 20 minutes.*
ˌburn sth ˈoff to use up energy or get rid of fat from your body by doing physical activity: *Swimming can help you burn off calories.*
ˌburn sth ˈup *same as* **burn sth off**: *Dancers burn up a lot of calories.*

burn² /bɜrn/ noun [C] an injury or mark caused by heat or fire

burned-out /ˌbɜrnd ˈaʊt/ adj **1** a burned-out building or vehicle has had everything inside it destroyed by fire **2** *informal* very tired or ill, usually because of too much work or worry

burn•ing /ˈbɜrnɪŋ/ adj **1** being destroyed by fire **2** very hot **3** painful, and feeling as if a part of your body is touching something hot: *She felt a burning sensation in her mouth.* **4** felt extremely strongly: *burning ambition*
PHRASE **burning issue/question** something that people have strong opinions about and think is very important

burnt a past tense and past participle of **burn**¹

ˌburnt-ˈout adj BURNED-OUT

burp /bɜrp/ verb [I] to make a noise when air from your stomach passes out through your mouth —**burp** noun [C]

bur•ri•to /bəˈritoʊ/ noun [C] a type of food made with a TORTILLA (=a piece of flat thin bread) that is folded over and filled with meat or beans and cheese

bur•row¹ /ˈbʌroʊ/ verb [I] **1** to make a hole or tunnel in the ground **2** to search for something, especially using your hands: *She burrowed in her purse, and came up with a bunch of keys.*

bur•row² /ˈbʌroʊ/ noun [C] a hole or tunnel in the ground made by an animal

bur•sar /ˈbɜrsər/ noun [C] someone who is in charge of financial business in a school, college, or university

burst¹ /bɜrst/ (past tense and past participle **burst**) verb ★★
1 [I] to move quickly or suddenly: *A man burst into the room.* ♦ *The door burst open and in came Sam.*
2 [I/T] if an object bursts, or if you burst it, it breaks suddenly: *She burst the little boy's balloon.*
PHRASAL VERBS **ˌburst ˈin on sb/sth** to suddenly enter a room where someone is doing something
ˈburst ˌinto sth 1 to suddenly start doing something: *Terri keeps bursting into tears* (=starting to cry) *for no reason.* **2 burst into flames** to suddenly start burning
ˌburst ˈout 1 to suddenly say or shout something: *"I hate you!" Julia suddenly burst out.* **2 burst out laughing/crying** to suddenly start laughing or crying

burst² /bɜrst/ noun [C] a sudden short noise, activity, or feeling: *a burst of anger* ♦ *After an initial burst of enthusiasm, she lost interest in her job.*

burst•ing /ˈbɜrstɪŋ/ adj **1** if you are bursting with something such as love or energy, you feel a lot of it **2** very eager to do something: *She was bursting to tell us what had happened.* **3** if a place is bursting, it is very full

bur•y /ˈberi/ verb [T] ★

1 put body in ground	4 push sth into sth else
2 put sth under ground	5 avoid feeling/memory
3 cover sth	+ PHRASE

1 to put someone's dead body in the ground during a funeral ceremony: *All his family are buried in the same cemetery.*
2 to put something in the ground and cover it with earth: *There's supposed to be treasure buried around here.*
3 to cover something with a layer or pile of things: *My homework is buried somewhere under this pile of books.*
4 to push one thing into another very hard =SINK: *Diane screamed as the dog **buried** its teeth **in** her arm.*
5 to try to stop yourself from having a feeling or memory, by not allowing yourself to think about it: *feelings of anger that had been buried for years*
PHRASE **bury your face/head in sth** to hide your face or head with something: *She buried her face in her hands.*
→ HATCHET

bus¹ /bʌs/ noun [C] ★★★ a large road vehicle that people pay to travel on: *The children go to school **by bus**.* ♦ *If you hurry, you can catch the next bus.* —picture → C7

bus² /bʌs/ (present participle **bus•ing** or **bus•sing**; past tense and past participle **bused** or **bussed**) verb [T] **1** to take someone somewhere by bus **2** *American* to remove dirty dishes from the tables in a restaurant

bus•boy /ˈbʌsˌbɔɪ/ noun [C] *American* a boy or man who removes dirty dishes from the tables in a restaurant

bush /bʊʃ/ noun ★★
1 [C] a plant that is smaller than a tree and has a lot of thin branches: *a holly/rose/blackberry bush*
2 **the bush** [singular] wild areas in hot places like Australia and Africa that are not used for growing crops

bushed /bʊʃt/ adj *informal* extremely tired

bush•el /ˈbʊʃ(ə)l/ noun [C] a unit for measuring grain, vegetables, etc. equal to 35.24 liters in the U.S. or 36.4 liters in the U.K.

bush•y /ˈbʊʃi/ adj bushy hair or fur is very thick

bus•i•ly /ˈbɪzɪli/ adv in a busy way

busi•ness /ˈbɪznəs/ noun ★★★

1 buying and selling	5 sth to deal with
2 people who buy/sell	6 sth that is private
3 the work that you do	7 event
4 organization	+ PHRASES

B

1 [U] the work of buying or selling products or services: *the music/fashion business* ♦ *They're trying to **attract** new **business*** (=get more customers) *by cutting prices.* ♦ *We have been **in business** since 1983* (=buying or selling products or services). ♦ *It was a mistake to **go into business** with my brother.* ♦ *I found them very easy to **do business** with.*
2 [U] people who work in business: *The conference brought together representatives from business, the media, and politics.* ♦ *the business community*
3 [U] the work that you do as your job: *a business trip* ♦ *Jon was away **on business**.*
4 [C] an organization that buys or sells products or services: *a small family business* ♦ *Sheryl's parents **run a** small clothing **business**.* ♦ *After leaving school, Bob **started his own** computer **business**.*
5 [singular/U] something that you have to deal with: *Disposing of industrial waste can be a dangerous business.* ♦ *We've still got some **unfinished business** to settle* (=things that need to be dealt with).
6 [U] something that affects or involves a particular person and no one else: *It's my business who I go out with.*
7 [singular] something that has happened, especially something that has caused problems: *Ever since that business with her boyfriend, Becky's been really depressed.*
PHRASES **get down to business** to start doing something that you need to do
go out of business if a company goes out of business, it stops doing business permanently, usually because it has failed
have no business doing sth to do something you should not do, because it does not affect or involve you at all: *You had no business interfering in a family argument.*
mean business to be very serious about something you have to do: *This is not a game. We mean business.*
mind your own business *spoken* used for telling someone rudely that you are not going to tell them about something because it does not affect or involve them: *"Who were you with last night?" "Mind your own business."*
→ MONKEY BUSINESS

ˈbusiness ˌclass noun [U] part of an airplane that is more comfortable and has better service than the part where most people sit

busi•ness•like /ˈbɪznəsˌlaɪk/ adj serious and effective in the way that you deal with things = EFFICIENT

busi•ness•man /ˈbɪznəsˌmæn/ (plural **busi•ness•men** /ˈbɪznəsˌmen/) noun [C] a man who works at a fairly high level in business

busi•ness•per•son /ˈbɪznəsˌpɜrs(ə)n/ (plural **busi•ness•peo•ple** /ˈbɪznəsˌpip(ə)l/) noun [C] someone who works at a fairly high level in business

ˈbusiness ˌplan noun [C] a document giving details of a company's plans for the future

busi•ness•wom•an /ˈbɪznəsˌwʊmən/ (plural **busi•ness•wom•en** /ˈbɪznəsˌwɪmɪn/) noun [C] a woman who works at a fairly high level in business

ˈbus ˌshelter noun [C] a structure that protects you from the weather while you are waiting for a bus

ˈbus ˌstation noun [C] a building where buses start and finish their trips

ˈbus ˌstop noun [C] a place marked by a sign at the side of a road where buses stop to let passengers get on and off

bust[1] /bʌst/ noun **1** [C] a model of the head and shoulders of a person **2** [C] a woman's breasts **3** [singular] *informal* a complete failure = FLOP: *The movie was a total bust.*

bust[2] /bʌst/ verb [T] *informal* **1** to break or damage something **2** to arrest someone, especially for offenses relating to drugs
PHRASE **bust your butt** *American spoken* to put a lot of effort into doing something

bust[3] /bʌst/ adj *informal* a company or organization that has gone bust has lost all its money and can no longer continue to operate = BANKRUPT

bus•tle[1] /ˈbʌs(ə)l/ noun [U] a lot of noisy activity in a crowded place

bus•tle[2] /ˈbʌs(ə)l/ verb [I] **bustle around** to do something or go somewhere quickly because you are very busy

bus•tling /ˈbʌs(ə)lɪŋ/ adj full of noise and activity: *a bustling city/market/street*

bus•y[1] /ˈbɪzi/ adj ★★★
1 having many things to do: *He is an extremely busy man.* ♦ *It's been a very busy day.* ♦ *We have enough work here to **keep** us **busy** for weeks.* ♦ *Irina and Marcus were **busy with** preparations for their wedding.* ♦ **busy doing sth** *We're all busy preparing for Christmas.*
2 full of people or vehicles: *a busy highway* ♦ *Stores are always busier on weekends.*
3 if someone's telephone is busy, it is being used when you try to call

bus•y[2] /ˈbɪzi/ verb **busy yourself** to make yourself busy by doing a particular job or activity

bus•y•bod•y /ˈbɪziˌbɑdi/ noun [C] *informal* someone who is too interested in other people's private lives

ˈbusy ˌsignal noun [C] *American* the sound you hear when you call someone and they are already talking on the phone

but /*weak* bət, *strong* bʌt/ grammar word ★★★

> **But** can be:
> - a **conjunction**: *She's 83 but she still goes swimming every day.*
> - a **preposition**: *There's been nothing but trouble since he came.*

1 used for introducing a different idea used for joining two ideas or statements when the second one is different from the first, or surprising after the first: *Anna's an intelligent girl, but she's lazy.* ♦ *a simple but effective way of filtering water* ♦ *I thought I had solved the problem. But I'd forgotten one thing.*
2 used for changing the subject *spoken* used when you are saying that you should not say any more about a particular subject: *It*

was really awful. But you don't want to hear about that.

3 used in polite questions and statements *spoken* used after expressions such as "I'm sorry" and "excuse me" to introduce a polite question, request, or statement: *Excuse me, but is there a post office anywhere around here?* ♦ *I'm sorry, but all our operators are busy at the moment.*

4 except used especially after words such as "nothing," "everyone," or "anything" to mean "except": *She does nothing but complain all day long.*

5 used for expressing surprise *spoken* used for showing that you are surprised or annoyed, or that you disagree: *"I've decided to resign." "But why?"* ♦ *But you promised not to do anything without asking me first.*

butch•er¹ /ˈbʊtʃər/ noun [C] someone whose job is to sell meat. The store they work in is called a **butcher's shop**.

butch•er² /ˈbʊtʃər/ verb [T] **1** to kill an animal and cut it up so that it can be eaten **2** to kill someone, often many people, in a cruel way

but•ler /ˈbʌtlər/ noun [C] the most important male servant in a rich person's house

butt¹ /bʌt/ noun [C] **1** *American informal* the part of your body that you sit on = BOTTOM **2** the part of a cigarette or CIGAR that is left after you have finished smoking it **3** the end of the handle of a gun

PHRASE **be the butt of sth** if you are the butt of jokes or criticism, people often make jokes about you or criticize you

butt² /bʌt/ verb [T] to hit someone or something with your head

PHRASAL VERBS ˌ**butt ˈin** *informal* to join a conversation or activity without being asked to

ˌ**butt ˈout** *spoken* used for telling someone rudely to go away or not get involved in something

but•ter¹ /ˈbʌtər/ noun [U] ★★ a solid yellow food made from cream that you spread on bread or use in cooking —**but•ter•y** adj → BREAD

but•ter² /ˈbʌtər/ verb [T] to spread butter on something

PHRASAL VERB ˌ**butter sb ˈup** *informal* to be nice to someone so that they will help or support you

but•ter•cup /ˈbʌtərˌkʌp/ noun [C] a plant with small bright yellow flowers —*picture* → C9

but•ter•fly /ˈbʌtərˌflaɪ/ noun **1** [C] an insect with large colorful wings —*picture* → C13

2 the butterfly or **the butterfly stroke** [singular] a way of swimming in which you lie on your front and move both your arms together above your head

PHRASE **have butterflies (in your stomach)** to feel very nervous or excited about something important that you have to do

but•ter•milk /ˈbʌtərˌmɪlk/ noun [U] the liquid that remains when fat is removed from cream in order to make butter, used in cooking or as a drink

but•tocks /ˈbʌtəks/ noun [plural] the two round parts of your body that you sit on —*picture* → C14

but•ton¹ /ˈbʌt(ə)n/ noun [C] ★★

1 a small object that you press to make a machine do something: *Push this button to start the computer.* ♦ *a push-button phone*

2 a small round object that is used for fastening clothes by pushing it through a hole: *He had undone the top button of his shirt.*

3 *American* a small round object that fastens onto your clothes with a pin and usually has a picture or writing on it

but•ton² /ˈbʌt(ə)n/ or ˌ**button sth ˈup** verb [I/T] to fasten something with buttons, or to be fastened with buttons ≠ UNBUTTON

but•ton•hole /ˈbʌt(ə)nˌhoʊl/ noun [C] a small hole in a piece of clothing through which you push a button to fasten it

bux•om /ˈbʌksəm/ adj a buxom woman is slightly fat in an attractive way, with large breasts

buy¹ /baɪ/ (past tense and past participle **bought** /bɔt/) verb ★★★

1 [I/T] to get something by paying money for it: *I need to buy some clothes.* ♦ **buy sb sth** *He's always buying me presents.* ♦ **buy sth for sb** *When I go away on business, I usually buy something for my daughter.* ♦ **buy sth for $50/$60 etc.** *They offered to buy the car for $4,000.* ♦ **buy sth from sb** *Do you like my new carpet? I bought it from that Swedish store.*

2 [T] *spoken* to believe or accept something that is unlikely to be true: *"I told her I had to work late." "She'll never buy that!"*

3 [T] if you buy time, you delay something in order to get more time to do or finish something else: *That should buy us another week.*

PHRASE **buy sb (off)** *informal* to give someone something so that they will do something dishonest for you

PHRASAL VERBS ˈ**buy into sth 1** to buy part of a business, especially in order to get control of it: *Moves to buy into other companies have failed.* **2** *informal* to start to believe something that a lot of other people believe: *You don't buy into all this garbage, do you?*

ˌ**buy sb ˈout** to pay money to your business partner so that you can control all of a business you previously owned together: *The board members have offered to buy me out.*

ˌ**buy sth ˈup** to buy large amounts of something or all of it that is available: *Developers bought up old factories and converted them into luxury apartments.*

buy² /baɪ/ noun [C] something that you buy

buy•er /ˈbaɪər/ noun [C] **1** someone who buys something **2** someone whose job is to choose and buy products for a large store to sell

buy•out /ˈbaɪˌaʊt/ noun [C] *business* a situation in which a group of people buy the company that they work for

buzz¹ /bʌz/ verb [I] **1** to make a rough continuous sound like a fly or an electric tool **2** if a place is buzzing, there is a lot of noise or activity

PHRASAL VERB ˌ**buzz ˈoff** *informal* used for telling someone in a rude way to go away

buzz² /bʌz/ noun [singular] **1** a continuous noise like the sound of a fly **2** *American informal* a pleasant feeling of being slightly drunk **3** *informal* a strong feeling of pleasure or excitement

B

buz•zard /ˈbʌzərd/ noun [C] *American* a VULTURE

buzz•er /ˈbʌzər/ noun [C] a small piece of equipment that makes a sound when you press it

buzz•word /ˈbʌzˌwɜrd/ noun [C] a word relating to a particular activity or subject that has become very popular: *The buzzword of the moment is "accountability."*

by /baɪ/ grammar word ★★★

> **By** can be:
> - a **preposition**: *The building was destroyed by fire.*
> - an **adverb**: *As time went by, things improved.*

1 stating who or what does sth used for stating who does or makes something, or what causes something: *She was helped by her friends.* ♦ *Children are fascinated by magic.* ♦ *The fabric had been faded by the sun.* ♦ *a painting by Goya*
2 stating how sth is done using a particular method or in a particular way: *Reading is taught by traditional methods here.* ♦ *We decided to go by car.* ♦ *We'll send you the tickets by mail.* ♦ *Every bit of lace is made* ***by hand*** (=not using a machine). ♦ *We met completely* ***by chance.*** ♦ **by doing sth** *By using the Internet you can do your shopping from home.*
3 before not later than a particular time or date: *The meeting should have finished by 4:30.* ♦ *Application forms must be received by March 31st.* ♦ ***By the time*** *I arrived, everyone had left.*
4 past moving past someone or something: *She walked right by me without saying a word.* ♦ *A police car drove by.*
5 saying that time passes used for saying that time passes, or how it passes: *As time went by, people's attitudes changed.* ♦ *The days seem to fly by.*
6 stating changes or differences used for stating how large a change or difference is: *House prices rose by 23% last year.* ♦ *Owen broke the world record by 2.4 seconds.*
7 beside beside or close to someone or something: *She was sitting over there by the window.*
8 according to rules according to rules, laws, or standards: *By law, the hospital must treat patients whether or not they can pay.* ♦ *You can't judge children and adults by the same standard.*
9 visiting a place used for saying that someone stops somewhere for a short time: *Why don't you stop by on your way home from work?* ♦ *Peggy dropped by the office this afternoon.*
10 used for stating how you hold sb/sth used for saying which part you take in your hand when you hold someone or something: *She took me by the hand.* ♦ *Always pick up a CD by the outer edge.*
11 in calculations and measurements used for stating what numbers or units are involved in calculations and measurements: *I am paid by the hour.* ♦ *To convert gallons to liters multiply by 3.785.* ♦ *a 4 by 6 inch photograph*
12 gradually used when saying that something happens gradually in small units: *Little by little Philip got more confident.* ♦ *His condition is improving* ***day by day.*** ♦ ***One by one*** *the men were given their medals.*

PHRASES **(all) by yourself/itself/himself etc.** **1** alone: *I want to be by myself for a while.* **2** without being helped by anyone else: *You can't carry that big table all by yourself.*
by and large used for saying that something is generally true: *By and large I think you're right.*
by night/day during the night/day: *We traveled by night to avoid the heat.*
by the way *spoken* used for adding a remark that is not relevant to the main subject of your conversation: *By the way, Jeff called this afternoon.*

bye /baɪ/ or **bye-bye** interjection ★ goodbye: *Bye for now – see you later.*

by•gone /ˈbaɪˌgɔn/ adj happening or existing during a period of time in the past

by•gones /ˈbaɪˌgɔnz/ noun **let bygones be bygones** to decide to forget about a disagreement or something unpleasant that has happened in the past

by•line /ˈbaɪˌlaɪn/ noun [C] a line at the top of an article in a magazine or newspaper giving the writer's name

by•pass¹ /ˈbaɪˌpæs/ noun [C] **1** a road that goes around a town or city so that you can avoid going through its center **2** a medical operation to make someone's blood flow past a blocked or damaged part of their heart

by•pass² /ˈbaɪˌpæs/ verb [T] **1** to avoid dealing with someone or something because you think you can do something more quickly without using them **2** to avoid the center of a town or city by using a road that goes around it

by•prod•uct /ˈbaɪˌprɑdʌkt/ noun [C] **1** a product that is made as a result of making something else **2** something that happens unexpectedly as a result of something else

by•stand•er /ˈbaɪˌstændər/ noun [C] someone who sees an event happen, but who is not directly involved in it

byte /baɪt/ noun [C] *computing* a basic unit for storing computer information, used for measuring the size of a document

by•way /ˈbaɪˌweɪ/ noun [C] a quiet minor road

by•word /ˈbaɪˌwɜrd/ noun **a byword for sth** someone or something that has a strong reputation for a particular quality: *The company's name had become a byword for bad service and overpriced goods.*

Cc

c or **C** /si/ noun [C/U] **1** the third letter of the English alphabet **2 C** a grade that a teacher gives to a student's work to show that it is average → C-SECTION

C abbrev **1** Celsius **2** see: used in e-mails and TEXT MESSAGES
c. abbrev **1** cents **2** century **3** **c.** or **ca.** circa: used before a date that is not exact
© a symbol meaning "copyright"
CA abbrev California
cab /kæb/ noun [C] **1** a taxi **2** the front part of a bus, train, or truck where the driver sits
cab·a·ret /ˌkæbəˈreɪ/ noun [C/U] entertainment in a restaurant or club that is performed while you eat or drink
cab·bage /ˈkæbɪdʒ/ noun [C/U] a hard round vegetable with green or purple leaves *—picture* → C11
cab·bie or **cab·by** /ˈkæbi/ noun [C] *informal* a taxi driver
cab·in /ˈkæbɪn/ noun [C] **1** a small simple wooden house in the mountains or in a forest **2** the part of an airplane where the passengers sit **3** a bedroom on a ship
ˈcabin ˌcrew noun [C] the people on an airplane whose job is to take care of the passengers
cab·i·net /ˈkæbɪnət/ noun [C] ★
1 a cupboard that you use for storing or showing things: *a medicine cabinet —picture* → C2
2 a group of advisers who are chosen by the leader of a government
ca·ble /ˈkeɪb(ə)l/ noun **1** [U] CABLE TELEVISION **2** [C/U] thick wire used for carrying electricity or electronic signals **3** [C/U] strong thick metal rope
ˈcable ˌcar noun [C] a small vehicle that hangs from a cable. It is used for taking people up and down mountains.
ˌcable ˈtelevision or **ˌcable TV** noun [U] a system for broadcasting television programs in which signals are sent through underground wires
ca·boose /kəˈbus/ noun [C] *American* the back part of a train where the train workers sit
cache /kæʃ/ noun [C] **1** a quantity of things that have been hidden, or the place where they have been hidden **2** *computing* an area of a computer's memory for storing information that is frequently needed
cack·le /ˈkæk(ə)l/ verb [I/T] to laugh in a loud unpleasant way —**cack·le** noun [C]
ca·coph·o·ny /kəˈkɑfəni/ noun [singular] an unpleasant mixture of loud sounds
cac·tus /ˈkæktəs/ (plural **cac·ti** /ˈkækˌtaɪ/) noun [C] a desert plant with thick stems and sharp points
CAD /kæd/ noun [U] computer-aided design: the use of computers to design things
ca·dav·er /kəˈdævər, kəˈdɑvər/ noun [C] *science* a dead human body = CORPSE
cad·dy /ˈkædi/ noun [C] someone who carries the GOLF CLUBS for a golf player
ca·det /kəˈdet/ noun [C] a young person who is training to be a police officer or military officer
ca·fé /ˈkæˌfeɪ, kəˈfeɪ/ noun [C] ★★ a small informal restaurant serving drinks and snacks
caf·e·te·ri·a /ˌkæfəˈtɪriə/ noun [C] a restaurant in which you take the food to the table yourself
ca·fe·tière /ˌkæfəˈtjer/ noun [C] *British* a glass container for making and serving coffee
caf·feine /ˈkæˌfin/ noun [U] a substance in coffee and tea that makes you feel awake
cage /keɪdʒ/ noun [C] a container that is made of wire or metal bars, used for keeping birds or animals in
caged /keɪdʒd/ adj kept in a cage
ca·gey /ˈkeɪdʒi/ adj *informal* not saying much about something, because you do not want people to know about it
ca·jole /kəˈdʒoʊl/ verb [I/T] to persuade someone to do something by being nice to them
cake /keɪk/ noun ★★
1 [C/U] a sweet food made by baking a mixture of sugar, eggs, flour, and butter or oil: *a chocolate cake* ♦ ***She was making a cake for Peter's birthday.***
2 [C] a small amount of food formed into a flat round shape and cooked: *rice/potato cakes*
3 [C] a small hard block of something: *a cake of soap*
PHRASES **have your cake and eat it too** to try to have all the benefits of a situation, when, in fact, you can only have some of them
a piece of cake *informal* something that is very easy: *The test was a piece of cake.*
→ ICING
caked /keɪkd/ adj covered with a thick layer of something
ca·lam·i·ty /kəˈlæməti/ noun [C/U] an event that causes serious damage or makes a lot of people suffer = DISASTER
cal·ci·um /ˈkælsiəm/ noun [U] a white chemical element that is an important part of bones and teeth
cal·cu·late /ˈkælkjəˌleɪt/ verb [T] ★★
1 to discover a number or amount by using mathematics: *Calculate the size of the angle.* ♦ **+(that)** *He calculates that the proposal would cost $4 million.*
2 to make a judgment about what is likely to happen or be true: *It's difficult to calculate the long-term effects of these changes.*
PHRASE **be calculated to do sth** to be deliberately intended to have a particular result
cal·cu·lat·ed /ˈkælkjəˌleɪtəd/ adj done deliberately in order to have a particular effect
cal·cu·lat·ing /ˈkælkjəˌleɪtɪŋ/ adj using careful planning to get what you want, even if it hurts other people
cal·cu·la·tion /ˌkælkjəˈleɪʃ(ə)n/ noun ★★
1 [C/U] numbers or symbols that you write when you are calculating something, or the process of calculating something: *a piece of paper covered with calculations*
2 [C] a judgment about what is likely to happen, based on available information
cal·cu·la·tor /ˈkælkjəˌleɪtər/ noun [C] a small piece of electronic equipment that is used for doing calculations *—picture* → C3
cal·cu·lus /ˈkælkjələs/ noun [U] a type of mathematics, used for calculating such things as the slopes of curves
cal·en·dar /ˈkæləndər/ noun [C] **1** a set of pages showing the days, weeks, and months of a particular year **2** a list of important events and the dates on which they take place: *the*

college football calendar **3** a system for measuring and dividing a year: *the Jewish/Roman calendar* **4** *American* an APPOINTMENT BOOK

calf /kæf/ (plural **calves** /kævz/) noun [C] **1** a young cow **2** the thick back part of your leg between your knee and your ANKLE

C

cal•i•ber /ˈkælıbər/ noun **1** [U] the high standard or quality of someone or something **2** [C] the width of a bullet, or of a gun BARREL (=the tube through which the bullet travels)

cal•i•brate /ˈkælıˌbreıt/ verb [T] to check or change a piece of equipment that is used for measuring things in order to make it accurate —**cal•i•bra•tion** /ˌkælıˈbreıʃ(ə)n/ noun [U]

call¹ /kɔl/ verb ★★★

1 telephone sb	5 speak loudly
2 describe sb/sth	6 organize sth
3 ask/tell sb to come	+ PHRASES
4 use a name for sb/sth	+ PHRASAL VERBS

1 [I/T] to telephone someone: *He called her from the hospital.* ♦ *Can you call a taxi for me?* ♦ *For more information call 1-800-555-3820.* → COLLECT²

2 [T] to describe or refer to someone or something in a particular way: **call sb/sth sth** *One candidate called it a scandal.* ♦ *The other kids* ***called her names*** (=said unkind things about her).

3 [T] to ask or tell someone by phone to come to a place: **call sb across/up/over/to etc.** *She called me up to her office.*

4 [T] to use a particular name or title for someone or something: *They called the area the Gold Coast.* ♦ **call sb/sth sth** *Her name's Elizabeth, but we call her Liz.*

5 [I/T] to say something loudly, or to shout to someone: *Did you call me?* ♦ *When I call your name, raise your hand.*

6 [T] to organize something: *Harris wants to call a meeting.*

PHRASES **call (sb's) attention to** to make someone notice and think about a person or thing

call it a day/night to decide that you have finished doing something

what do you call it/him/her/them? *spoken* used when you are trying to think of the correct name for someone or something: *Do you have a – what do you call it – lemon reamer?*

(now) that's what I call sth *spoken* used for emphasizing that something is a very good example of what you are talking about: *Now that's what I call a real cup of coffee!*

→ BLUFF²

PHRASAL VERBS **ˌcall (sb) ˈback** to telephone someone again, or to telephone someone who telephoned you earlier: *Can you call me back later?*

ˈcall for sth 1 to say publicly that something must happen: *Several of the newspapers were calling for his resignation.* **2** to make something necessary or appropriate: *I think that calls for a celebration!* → UNCALLED FOR

ˌcall ˈin to telephone the place where you work and tell them something: *Harry's* ***called in sick again*** (=telephoned to say he is sick).

ˌcall sb ˈin to ask someone to come and deal with something: *The company has called in the police to investigate.*

ˌcall sth ˈoff to decide that something will not happen = CANCEL: *She's called off the wedding.*

ˈcall on sb 1 to officially ask someone to do something: *He called on both sides to stop fighting.* **2** if a teacher calls on a student, the teacher asks them to answer a question

ˌcall (sth) ˈout to shout something when you are trying to get someone's attention: *"In here!" she called out.*

ˌcall (sb) ˈup to telephone someone: *I called him up and told him the news.*

ˌcall sth ˈup to make information in a computer appear on the screen: *Call up the menu and click on "Documents."*

ˈcall upon *formal same as* **call on sb** 1

call² /kɔl/ noun ★★★

1 act of telephoning	6 announcement
2 shout	7 guess
3 formal request	8 decision
4 animal sound	+ PHRASE
5 short visit	

1 [C] an act of telephoning someone = PHONE CALL: *Can you wait while I* ***make a call?*** ♦ *He* ***took the call*** *in his study.* ♦ *Why don't you* ***give me a call*** *in the morning?*

2 [C] a loud shout to someone who is not near you: *A hiker heard his* ***calls for*** *help.*

3 [C] a formal or public request that something should happen: *The government has rejected* ***calls for*** *tougher immigration laws.*

4 [C/U] the sound that a bird or animal usually makes

5 [C] *old-fashioned* a short visit to someone

6 [C] an announcement in an airport telling passengers to go to their airplane because it is leaving soon: *This is the last call for flight UA 554 to Denver.*

7 [C] a guess about what will happen: *The election looks so close that it's anybody's call.*

8 [C] a decision that is the responsibility of a particular person: *"Do we offer him the job?" "It's your call."*

PHRASE **on call** available in case you are needed at work: *Tim's on call this weekend.*

CALL /kɔl/ noun [U] computer-assisted language learning: the use of computers for learning languages

ˈcall ˌbox noun [C] **1** *American* a telephone at the side of a road that you use to call for help **2** *British* a PHONE BOOTH

ˈcall ˌcenter noun [C] a place where a large number of people are employed to deal with customers by telephone

call•er /ˈkɔlər/ noun [C] someone who makes a telephone call

cal•lig•ra•phy /kəˈlıgrəfi/ noun [U] beautiful writing that you do using special pens or brushes

ˈcall-ˌin noun [C] *American* a radio or television program that broadcasts the opinions or questions of people who telephone the program

call•ing /ˈkɔlıŋ/ noun [C] a strong feeling that you must do a particular type of job

cal·lous /ˈkæləs/ adj not caring about other people's trouble or pain =HEARTLESS

call wait·ing /ˈkɔl ˌweɪtɪŋ/ noun [U] a system that lets you answer a second telephone call without ending your first telephone call

calm¹ /kɑm/ adj ★★
1 not affected by strong emotions: *a calm voice* ♦ *Try to* ***stay calm****.*
2 peaceful: *The city appears calm after last night's missile attack.*
3 if the weather is calm, there is very little wind
4 calm water does not move very much
—**calm·ly** adv

calm² /kɑm/ verb [T] to make someone feel more relaxed and less emotional
PHRASAL VERB ˌ**calm (sb)** ˈ**down** to begin to feel more relaxed and less emotional, or to make someone do this: *Calm down and tell us what's going on.*

calm³ /kɑm/ noun [U] **1** a situation in which everything is peaceful: *the calm of the evening* **2** a state in which you are not affected by strong emotions
PHRASE **the calm before the storm** a quiet time just before problems or arguments start

cal·o·rie /ˈkæləri/ noun [C] a unit for measuring how much energy you get from food

cal·o·rif·ic /ˌkæləˈrɪfɪk/ adj containing a lot of calories and therefore likely to make you fat

calves the plural of **calf**

cam·cord·er /ˈkæmˌkɔrdər/ noun [C] a small camera used for recording pictures and sound onto VIDEOTAPE

came the past tense of **come**

cam·el /ˈkæm(ə)l/ noun [C] a large animal with one or two HUMPS (=large round raised parts) on its back

cam·e·o /ˈkæmiˌoʊ/ noun [C] **1** a small part that a well-known actor plays in a movie or play **2** a piece of jewelry with a design of a woman's head on it in a different color

cam·er·a /ˈkæm(ə)rə/ noun [C] ★★★
1 a piece of equipment for taking photographs
2 a piece of equipment for making television programs, movies, or videos

cam·er·a·man /ˈkæm(ə)rəˌmæn/ (plural **cam·er·a·men** /ˈkæm(ə)rəˌmen/) noun [C] someone who operates a camera for making movies or television programs

cam·ou·flage /ˈkæməˌflɑʒ/ noun [singular/U] colors or clothes that hide people, objects, or animals by making them look like the natural background —**cam·ou·flage** verb [T]

camp¹ /kæmp/ noun ★★
1 [C/U] a place where people, especially children, go for a vacation that often has tents or other temporary shelters: *music camp* ♦ *Boy/Girl scout camp*
2 [C] a place where soldiers or prisoners live during a war
3 [C] a group of people who support a particular person or idea: *People in the Brown camp* (=who support Brown) *deny this rumor.*
PHRASE **set up camp** to put tents somewhere and stay there for a while

camp² /kæmp/ verb [I] **1** to stay somewhere for a short time in a tent or another temporary shelter: *They camped for two nights in the forest.* **2** to stay outside a place until you get what you want: *Reporters had camped in front of the house.*
PHRASAL VERB ˌ**camp** ˈ**out 1** to sleep outside, with or without a tent or another temporary shelter **2** *same as* **camp²** 2

camp³ /kæmp/ adj a man who is camp behaves in a way that does not follow traditional ideas about male behavior

cam·paign¹ /kæmˈpeɪn/ noun [C] ★
1 a series of actions that are intended to achieve something such as a social or political change: *an election/advertising campaign* ♦ *Local people have launched a* ***campaign against*** *closing the hospital.* ♦ **campaign to do sth** *There's been a campaign by local fishermen to ban imported fish.*
2 a series of actions by an army trying to win a war: *a bombing campaign*

cam·paign² /kæmˈpeɪn/ verb [I] **1** to try to win an election: *The party has campaigned hard in the Midwest.* **2** to try to achieve a social or a political change by persuading other people or the government to do something

camp·er /ˈkæmpər/ noun [C] **1** someone who is staying in a campground **2** a vehicle used for living in on vacations

camp·ground /ˈkæmpˌgraʊnd/ noun [C] *American* a place where people on vacation can stay in tents or other temporary shelters

camp·ing /ˈkæmpɪŋ/ noun [U] the activity of living in a tent or other temporary shelter for fun: *We don't go camping as much as we used to.*

camp·site /ˈkæmpˌsaɪt/ noun [C] *American* a piece of land that one person or group camps on

cam·pus /ˈkæmpəs/ noun [C/U] an area of land containing all the main buildings of a university or college

can¹ /*weak* kən, *strong* kæn/ modal verb ★★★

- **Can** is usually followed by an infinitive without "to": *I can speak French.* Sometimes it is used without a following infinitive: *Come and help us, if you can.*
- **Can** has no participles and no infinitive form. It does not change its form, so the third person singular form does not end in "-s": *She can speak Japanese.*
- Questions and negatives are formed without "do": *Can you swim?*
- The negative form **cannot** is often shortened in conversation or informal writing to **can't**: *I can't find my brown jacket.*
- **Could** is used as the past tense of **can** when it means that someone had the ability to do something, or that something was possible: *New York was a place where anyone could start a business.* But **was/were able to** is used for saying that someone actually succeeded in doing something: *By climbing on the table he was able to reach the window.*

1 **able to do sth** to have the ability to do something: *"Can you swim?" "No I can't."* ♦ *The machine can translate messages into 24 different languages.* ♦ *I will help as much*

as I can. ♦ *I can hear someone crying.*
2 for saying what is possible used for saying that something is possible, or that it might happen: *Tickets can be bought from the Tourist Information Center.* ♦ *Even minor head injuries can be serious.*
3 be allowed to do sth to be allowed to do something, or to have the right or power to do it: *You can borrow my calculator if you want.* ♦ *Anyone aged 18 or over can vote.* ♦ *You can't sit there. Those seats are reserved.*
4 in requests, offers, etc. *spoken* used in requests, or when offering or suggesting something: *Can you tell me where Mr. Lawson's office is?* ♦ *Can I have another piece of cake?*
5 when you are fairly certain used for saying that you feel fairly sure about something: *The hotel can't be far from here.* ♦ *Can there be any doubt that he is lying?* ♦ *I can't tell you how pleased I am to see you.*
6 when sth should not happen used for emphasizing that something should not happen or should not continue: *We can't let them cheat and get away with it.*
7 for expressing surprise *spoken* used for showing how surprised or shocked you are: *He can't be here already!*
8 for emphasizing how you feel *spoken* used with verbs such as "say," "imagine," or "believe" for emphasizing how strongly you feel: *I can imagine how upset you must be.*

can² /kæn/ noun [C] ★★
1 a metal container with round sides, used for holding food, or drink or other liquids: *empty beer cans* ♦ *There's a little paint left in the can.* ♦ *a garbage can* ♦ ***a can of** beans*
2 the amount that a can holds: *Add two **cans of** tomatoes to the sauce and stir.*

can³ /kæn/ verb [T] to preserve food in metal containers by storing it without air

ca·nal /kəˈnæl/ noun [C] an artificial river

ca·nar·y /kəˈneri/ noun [C] a small yellow bird that is kept as a pet

can·cel /ˈkæns(ə)l/ (present participle **can·cel·ing** or **can·cel·ling**; past tense and past participle **can·celed** or **can·celled**) verb [T] **1** to say that something that has been arranged will not now happen = CALL STH OFF: *This afternoon's meeting has been canceled.* **2** to say officially that you do not want to receive something: *Did you remember to cancel the taxi?*

PHRASAL VERB ˌ**cancel sth ˈout** if two things cancel each other out, they stop each other from having any effect

can·cel·la·tion /ˌkæns(ə)lˈeɪʃ(ə)n/ noun **1** [C/U] a decision to stop something that has been arranged from taking place **2** [C] a ticket or place that becomes available because someone else has said they do not want it

can·cer /ˈkænsər/ noun [U] ★ a serious illness that is caused when cells in the body increase in an uncontrolled way: *He died of lung cancer.* —**can·cer·ous** adj

Can·cer /ˈkænsər/ noun [U] one of the 12 signs of the ZODIAC. A **Cancer** or a **Cancerian** is someone who was born between June 22 and July 22.

can·did /ˈkændɪd/ adj honest and direct, even when the truth is not pleasant —**can·did·ly** adv

can·di·da·cy /ˈkændɪdəsi/ noun [U] the fact that someone is a candidate in an election

can·di·date /ˈkændɪˌdeɪt, ˈkændɪdət/ noun [C] ★ one of the people who is competing in an election or competing for a job: *the Democratic/Republican candidate* ♦ *There were two **candidates for** the position.*

can·dle /ˈkænd(ə)l/ noun [C] a stick of WAX with a string in it that you burn to give light

can·dle·light /ˈkænd(ə)lˌlaɪt/ noun [U] the light from a burning candle

can·dle·lit /ˈkænd(ə)lˌlɪt/ adj lit only by CANDLES

can·dle·stick /ˈkænd(ə)lˌstɪk/ noun [C] an object for holding a CANDLE

ˌ**can-ˈdo** adj always eager to try hard in order to succeed: *a can-do attitude*

can·dor /ˈkændər/ noun [U] honesty, even when the truth is not pleasant

can·dy /ˈkændi/ noun [C/U] *American* ★ a sweet food made of cooked sugar or chocolate but not containing flour, or a piece of this

ˈ**candy ˌbar** noun [C] *American* a bar of candy, usually covered with chocolate

ˈ**candy ˌcane** noun [C] *American* a long thin piece of red and white candy that is shaped like a hook

cane /keɪn/ noun **1** [C] a long thin stick that a person uses to help them to walk **2** [C/U] the hard light stem of some plants, often used for making furniture: *cane chairs*

ca·nine /ˈkeɪˌnaɪn/ adj relating to dogs

can·is·ter /ˈkænɪstər/ noun [C] a metal container for storing a gas or dry foods such as sugar and flour

can·na·bis /ˈkænəbɪs/ noun [U] MARIJUANA

canned /kænd/ adj canned food has been preserved in a metal container without air

can·ni·bal /ˈkænɪb(ə)l/ noun [C] someone who eats human flesh —**can·ni·bal·ism** /ˈkænɪb(ə)lˌɪzəm/ noun [U]

can·non /ˈkænən/ noun [C] **1** a large gun used in the past to shoot heavy metal balls **2** a large gun on a ship or TANK

can·not /ˈkæˌnɑt, kəˈnɑt/ modal verb ★★★ the negative form of CAN: *You cannot escape the law.*

ca·noe¹ /kəˈnu/ noun [C] a light narrow boat that you push through the water using a PADDLE

ca·noe² /kəˈnu/ verb [I] to travel in a canoe —**ca·noe·ing** noun [U]

can·on /ˈkænən/ noun [C] a Christian priest who works in a CATHEDRAL

ˈ**can ˌopener** noun [C] a piece of equipment, used for opening cans —*picture* → C2

can·o·py /ˈkænəpi/ noun [C] a cloth cover above something such as a bed or chair

can't /kænt/ short form the usual way of saying or writing "cannot." This is not often used in formal writing: *I can't remember where my keys are.*

can·ta·loupe /ˈkænt(ə)lˌup/ noun [C] a gray-green MELON (=large round fruit) with sweet orange flesh

can·tan·ker·ous /kænˈtæŋkərəs/ adj always complaining or arguing and easily annoyed

can·teen /kænˈtin/ noun [C] a CAFETERIA

can·ter /ˈkæntər/ verb [I] if a horse canters, it

runs fairly fast but not as fast as it can

can•vas /ˈkænvəs/ noun **1** [U] strong heavy cotton cloth that is used for making tents, shoes, and sails **2** [C/U] cloth on which artists paint, or a painting done on this cloth

can•vass /ˈkænvəs/ verb **1** [I/T] to encourage people to vote for someone or support something: *We were canvassing for the Republican candidate.* **2** [T] to ask people for their opinions about something: *We will be canvassing the views of teachers all over the country.*

can•yon /ˈkænjən/ noun [C] a long valley with steep sides made of rock

cap¹ /kæp/ noun [C] ★★
1 a soft hat with a stiff part that comes out above your eyes: *a baseball cap*
2 a lid or part that fits over the top of something: *Meg screwed the cap back on the bottle.*

cap² /kæp/ verb [T] to set a limit on the amount of money that someone can spend or charge

ca•pa•bil•i•ty /ˌkeɪpəˈbɪləti/ noun [C/U] the ability to do something: *the company's manufacturing capability* ♦ *We have the capability to produce faster trains.*

ca•pa•ble /ˈkeɪpəb(ə)l/ adj ★★
1 **capable of (doing) sth** able to do something ≠ INCAPABLE: *The port is capable of handling 10 million tons of coal a year.* ♦ *I don't think I've achieved everything I'm capable of.*
2 very good at doing a job: *The staff all seem very capable.*

ca•pac•i•ty /kəˈpæsəti/ noun ★
1 [C/U] the amount of something that can be put in a container, or the number of people that a place has room for: *a concert hall with **a seating capacity of** 800* ♦ *All the country's prisons are **filled to capacity*** (=completely full). ♦ *The games attract **capacity crowds*** (=audiences that fill a place).
2 [C/U] the ability to do something: **capacity to do sth** *They are worried about their capacity to invest for the future.* ♦ *Harry had a tremendous **capacity for** work.*
3 [U] the amount of goods that a company can produce: *The factory is now operating **at full capacity*** (=doing as much work as possible).
4 [singular] the job or position you have when you do something: *Elizabeth Taylor was there **in her capacity as** patron of the charity.*

cape /keɪp/ noun [C] **1** a type of coat that has no sleeves and hangs from your shoulders **2** a large area of land that continues farther out into the ocean than the land that it is part of

cap•il•lar•y /ˈkæpɪˌleri/ noun [C] *science* a very small tube that carries blood around your body

cap•i•tal¹ /ˈkæpɪt(ə)l/ noun ★★★
1 **capital** or **capital city** [C] the city where a country or region has its government: *Madrid is **the capital of** Spain.*
2 **capital** or **capital letter** [C] the large form of a letter that you use at the beginning of a sentence or name, for example "A" or "B": *He wrote the title **in capitals**.*
3 [C] the most important place for an activity or industry: *Houston is **the capital of the** American oil industry.*
4 [U] money or property that you use to start a business or that you invest

cap•i•tal² /ˈkæpɪt(ə)l/ adj a capital letter is the large form of a letter that you use at the beginning of a sentence or name

ˌcapital-inˈtensive adj a capital-intensive business or activity needs to have a lot of money invested in it → LABOR-INTENSIVE

cap•i•tal•ism /ˈkæpɪt(ə)lˌɪzəm/ noun [U] an economic system in which property and businesses are owned by individual people, not by the government

cap•i•tal•ist /ˈkæpɪt(ə)lɪst/ noun [C] someone who supports the system of capitalism —**cap•i•tal•ist** adj

cap•i•tal•ize /ˈkæpɪt(ə)lˌaɪz/ verb [T] to write something using capital letters
PHRASAL VERB **ˈcapitalize ˌon sth** to use an event or situation to help you to get an advantage: *The team needed to capitalize on their early successes.*

ˌcapital ˈletter noun see **capital¹** 2

ˌcapital of ˈfense noun [C] a crime for which the punishment is death

ˌcapital ˈpunishment noun [U] the punishment of legally killing someone who has committed a serious crime

Cap•i•tol, the /ˈkæpɪt(ə)l/ the building in Washington, D.C. or in the main city of each U.S. state where government officials meet to make laws

ˌCapitol ˈHill the U.S. Congress, or the area in Washington D.C. where members of Congress work

ca•pit•u•late /kəˈpɪtʃəˌleɪt/ verb [I] *formal* to stop opposing or fighting someone, and agree to what they want —**ca•pit•u•la•tion** /kəˌpɪtʃəˈleɪʃ(ə)n/ noun [U]

cap•puc•ci•no /ˌkæpəˈtʃinoʊ/ noun [C/U] strong coffee made with hot FROTHY milk, or a cup of this coffee

ca•pri•cious /kəˈprɪʃəs/ adj suddenly and unexpectedly changing your opinion or behavior for no reason

Cap•ri•corn /ˈkæprɪˌkɔrn/ noun [C/U] one of the 12 signs of the ZODIAC. A **Capricorn** is someone who is born between 22 December and 19 January.

cap•size /ˈkæpˌsaɪz, kæpˈsaɪz/ verb [I] if a boat capsizes, it turns over in the water

cap•sule /ˈkæpsəl, ˈkæpˌsjul/ noun [C] **1** a small round container filled with medicine that you swallow **2** the part of a space vehicle in which people travel

cap•tain¹ /ˈkæptɪn/ noun [C] ★★
1 the person who is in charge of a ship or aircraft
2 an officer of middle rank in the military and the police
3 the person who is in charge of a team or organization: *She was **captain of the** Olympic swimming team.*

cap•tain² /ˈkæptɪn/ verb [T] to be the captain of a team, organization, ship, or aircraft

cap•tion /ˈkæpʃ(ə)n/ noun [C] words printed near a picture that explain what the picture is about

C

cap•ti•vate /ˈkæptɪˌveɪt/ verb [T] to attract or interest someone very much

cap•ti•vat•ing /ˈkæptɪˌveɪtɪŋ/ adj very interesting or attractive in a way that takes all your attention: *a captivating story*

cap•tive¹ /ˈkæptɪv/ adj **1** kept as a prisoner: *She was kidnapped and held captive for over a week.* **2** a captive wild animal is kept in a park or zoo

cap•tive² /ˈkæptɪv/ noun [C] someone who is being kept as a prisoner

ˌcaptive ˈaudience noun [C] a group of people who must listen to something because they cannot leave

cap•tiv•i•ty /kæpˈtɪvəti/ noun [U] **1** a situation in which wild animals are kept in a place such as a park or zoo: *crocodiles that were born in captivity* **2** a situation in which a person is being kept as a prisoner

cap•tor /ˈkæptər/ noun [C] someone who is keeping someone else as a prisoner

cap•ture¹ /ˈkæptʃər/ verb [T] ★★

1 to catch a person or animal and stop them from escaping: *Most of the men had been either killed or captured.*

2 to get control of something, for example in a war or in business: *Rebel forces have captured the village.*

3 to express what someone or something is really like in a way that people can clearly recognize: *The movie succeeds in capturing the mood of the 1960s.*

4 to record an event in a movie or photograph: *The whole incident was captured by a young American photographer.*

PHRASE **capture sb's interest/imagination/attention** to make someone interested in something, or excited about something: *Her story captured the interest of the world's media.*

cap•ture² /ˈkæptʃər/ noun [U] **1** the act of catching someone so that they become your prisoner: *He tried to avoid capture by leaving the country.* **2** the act of getting control of something, for example in a war or in business

car /kɑr/ noun [C] ★★★

1 a road vehicle for one driver and a few passengers: *a car accident/factory/manufacturer ♦ We usually go to work in my husband's car. ♦ She **got into a** black **car** and drove away. ♦ It's quicker to go **by car**. ♦ She's learning to **drive a car**.* —*picture* → C6, C7

2 *American* one of the separate sections of a train: *Our car was near the front of the train.*

ca•rafe /kəˈræf, kəˈrɑf/ noun [C] a glass container with a wide top, used for serving wine

car•a•mel /ˈkerəˌmel, ˈkɑrməl/ noun [C/U] soft or hard candy made from sugar, butter, and milk

car•at /ˈkerət/ noun [C] a unit for measuring the weight of DIAMONDS and other jewels

car•a•van /ˈkerəˌvæn/ noun [C] **1** a group of people and animals who are traveling together in a desert **2** *British* a TRAILER

car•bo•hy•drate /ˌkɑrboʊˈhaɪˌdreɪt/ noun [C/U] a substance in foods such as bread and potatoes that gives your body heat and energy

car•bon /ˈkɑrbən/ noun [U] a chemical element that exists in all living things and in coal and DIAMONDS

car•bon•at•ed /ˈkɑrbəˌneɪtəd/ adj a carbonated drink has small BUBBLES in it

ˌcarbon ˈcopy noun [C] someone or something that is almost exactly like another person or thing

car•bon di•ox•ide /ˌkɑrbən daɪˈɑkˌsaɪd/ noun [U] the gas that is produced when you breathe out

ˌcarbon eˈmissions noun [plural] carbon dioxide and carbon monoxide that vehicles and factories produce and send into the atmosphere

car•bon mon•ox•ide /ˌkɑrbən məˈnɑkˌsaɪd/ noun [U] the poisonous gas that is produced by the engines of vehicles

ˈcarbon ˌtax noun [C/U] a tax on vehicles or factories that produce a lot of CARBON EMISSIONS

car•bu•re•tor /ˈkɑrbəˌreɪtər/ noun [C] the part of a car engine that mixes air and gas

car•cass /ˈkɑrkəs/ noun [C] the body of a dead animal

car•cin•o•gen /kɑrˈsɪnədʒən, ˈkɑrs(ə)nəˌdʒen/ noun [C] *medical* a substance that can cause cancer

car•cin•o•gen•ic /ˌkɑrsɪnəˈdʒenɪk/ adj *medical* likely to cause cancer

card¹ /kɑrd/ noun ★★★

1 for money	5 for playing games
2 with information	6 games
3 for sending greetings	7 in a computer
4 postcard	+ PHRASES

1 [C] a small flat piece of plastic that you use for buying things, or for getting money from a bank: *I gave the waiter my card.*

2 [C] a small piece of thick stiff paper or plastic that shows who you are: *a library/membership card*

3 [C] a folded piece of thick stiff paper with a picture and a message on it: *a birthday/Christmas card*

4 [C] a POSTCARD

5 [C] one of a set of 52 small pieces of thick stiff paper, used for various games = PLAYING CARD: *I'll teach you some new card games.* —*picture* → C16

6 cards [plural] the activity of playing games with a set of 52 cards: *Let's **play cards** this evening. ♦ Do you have time for **a game of cards**?*

7 [C] *computing* a part inside a computer that holds a CHIP

PHRASES **have a card up your sleeve** to have a secret advantage that you can use later

in the cards very likely to happen

lay your cards on the table to tell people exactly what you are thinking or what you are intending to do

card² /kɑrd/ verb [T] *American* to ask someone to show a document that proves their age

card•board /ˈkɑrdˌbɔrd/ noun [U] very thick stiff paper that is used for making boxes

car•di•ac /ˈkɑrdiˌæk/ adj *medical* relating to your heart

ˌcardiac arˈrest noun [C] *medical* a HEART ATTACK

car·di·gan /ˈkɑrdɪɡən/ noun [C] a piece of wool clothing that fastens in the front, worn on the top part of your body *—picture* → C5

car·di·nal¹ /ˈkɑrdɪn(ə)l/ noun [C] **1** a bright red North American bird **2** a senior priest in the Roman Catholic Church

car·di·nal² /ˈkɑrdɪn(ə)l/ adj *formal* very important: *The cardinal rule in this job is never to take any risks.*

ˌcardinal ˈnumber noun [C] an ordinary number such as 1, 2, or 3

car·di·o·vas·cu·lar /ˌkɑrdioʊˈvæskjələr/ adj *medical* connected with the heart and the BLOOD VESSELS

care¹ /ker/ verb [I/T] ★★★ to be interested in someone or something and think that they are important: *Her son didn't care enough to come and visit her.* ♦ *I don't think she* ***cares about*** *him at all.* ♦ **+what/why etc.** *Of course I care what happens to the school!* ♦ *They* ***cared deeply*** *about the environment.*

PHRASES **sb couldn't care less** used for emphasizing that someone thinks that something is unimportant: *I couldn't care less how you do it – just do it.*

not care for to not like someone or something: *I don't really care for chocolate.*

who cares? *spoken* used for saying that you do not think that something is important and that you are not worried about it: *Who cares whether he lied or not?*

would you care for sth *spoken formal* used for asking someone politely whether they would like something: *Would you care for some coffee?*

PHRASAL VERBS **ˈcare for sb 1** to love someone: *He really cared for her.* **2** to do the necessary things for someone who needs help or protection = TAKE CARE OF: *Teach your children how to care for their pets.*

ˈcare for sth to treat something carefully so that it stays in good condition = TAKE CARE OF: *Your clothes won't last as long if you don't care for them properly.*

Word family: care

Words in the same family as ***care***

- **careful** *adj*
- **carefully** *adv*
- **caring** *adj*
- **uncaring** *adj*
- **careless** *adj*
- **caregiver** *n*

care² /ker/ noun ★★★

1 [U] the effort that you make when you avoid making mistakes or causing harm: *The label on the box said "Handle with care."* ♦ *He was choosing his words* ***with great care.***

2 [U] the activity of looking after someone who needs help or protection: *specialist medical care* ♦ *I left him* ***in your care*** *– you should have watched him!*

3 [U] the activity of keeping something in good condition: *skin care* ♦ *advice on* ***the proper care of*** *your new car*

4 [C] something that makes you feel worried: *She acted like she* ***didn't have a care in the world*** (=was not worried about anything).

PHRASES **take care 1** to be careful: **+(that)** *Take care that you don't fall.* ♦ **take care (not) to do sth** *Please take care not to step on the cables.* **2** *spoken* used for saying goodbye to someone in a friendly way: *Bye now! Take care!*

take care of 1 to do the necessary things for someone who needs help or protection: *Who will take care of the children?* **2** to treat something carefully so that it stays in good condition: *All the neighbors take very good care of their yards.* **3** to deal with a person or situation: *Can you take care of this customer, please?*

ca·reen /kəˈrin/ verb [I] **careen down/along/off/across sth** to move forward quickly and suddenly, going from side to side in an uncontrolled way: *The car hit a guardrail and careened across the freeway.*

ca·reer¹ /kəˈrɪr/ noun [C] ★★

1 a job or profession that you work at for some time: *the problems of combining a career and a family* ♦ *Rosen had decided on an academic career.* ♦ *He felt like having* ***a career change*** *and went into teaching.* ♦ *a* ***career in*** *computer science* ♦ *He has just started out on* ***a career as*** *a photographer.*

2 the period of someone's life that they spend doing their job: *the most important game of her career* ♦ *the injury that ended his playing career*

Words often used with career

Adjectives often used with ***career*** *(noun, sense 2)*

- **brilliant, distinguished, glittering, successful** + CAREER: used about a career that is successful

ca·reer² /kəˈrɪr/ adj a career politician, soldier, teacher, etc. wants to stay in their profession for a long time and be successful

ca·reer³ /kəˈrɪr/ verb [I] to move very quickly in an uncontrolled way

care·free /ˈkerˌfri/ adj happy and without any worries, problems, or responsibilities

care·ful /ˈkerf(ə)l/ adj ★★★ thinking about what you do, so that you avoid problems, damage, or danger: *She took a few careful steps into the water.* ♦ *After careful consideration, we are giving the prize to a children's book.* ♦ *Please* ***be very careful*** *with those plates!* ♦ **be careful to do sth** *Marta was careful to keep her records up to date.* **—care·ful·ly** adv: *He washed everything carefully.*

care·giv·er /ˈkerˌɡɪvər/ noun [C] someone who takes care of a child or an adult who is unable to care for themselves

care·less /ˈkerləs/ adj ★

1 not thinking about what you are doing, so that you cause problems or damage: *careless driving* ♦ *The letter was full of careless spelling mistakes.*

2 natural and relaxed: *a careless laugh* **—care·less·ly** adv, **care·less·ness** noun [U]

ˈcare ˌpackage noun [C] *American* a present of food, clothes, or other necessary things that you send to someone, especially a student

ca·ress /kəˈres/ verb [T] to move your hands gently over someone's face or body in a way that shows love **—ca·ress** noun [C]

care·tak·er /ˈkerˌteɪkər/ noun [C] someone whose job is to take care of a house or land while the owner is away

car·go /ˈkɑrɡoʊ/ (plural **car·goes**) noun [C/U] things that are being sent by ship, airplane, train, or truck: *The ship and all its cargo sank.* ♦ *a cargo ship*

C

ˈcargo ˌpants noun [plural] loose pants made of heavy cotton with pockets on the legs

car•i•ca•ture /ˈkerɪkəˌtʃʊr/ noun [C] a drawing or description of someone that emphasizes particular features in order to make them seem silly —**car•i•ca•ture** verb [T]

C

car•ing /ˈkerɪŋ/ adj kind, helpful, and sympathetic toward other people

car•jack•ing /ˈkɑrˌdʒækɪŋ/ noun [C/U] a crime in which someone attacks the driver of a car and steals the car —**car•jack•er** noun [C]

car•nage /ˈkɑrnɪdʒ/ noun [U] a situation in which there is a lot of death and destruction

car•nal /ˈkɑrn(ə)l/ adj *literary* involving sex

car•na•tion /kɑrˈneɪʃ(ə)n/ noun [C] a flower that is often worn as a decoration on formal occasions —*picture* → C9

car•ni•val /ˈkɑrnɪv(ə)l/ noun **1** [C/U] a festival in the streets in which people play music, dance, and wear colorful clothes **2** [C] *American* a FAIR where there are machines for riding on and games in which you can win prizes

car•ni•vore /ˈkɑrnɪˌvɔr/ noun [C] an animal that eats other animals

car•niv•o•rous /kɑrˈnɪvərəs/ adj a carnivorous animal eats other animals

car•ol /ˈkerəl/ noun [C] a traditional song that people sing at Christmas

car•ou•sel /ˌkerəˈsel/ noun [C] **1** a moving surface in an airport from which you collect your bags **2** *American* a MERRY-GO-ROUND

ˈcar ˌpark noun [C] *British* a PARKING LOT or PARKING GARAGE

car•pen•ter /ˈkɑrpəntər/ noun [C] someone whose job is to make or repair wooden things

car•pen•try /ˈkɑrpəntri/ noun [U] the activity of making and repairing wooden things

car•pet¹ /ˈkɑrpət/ noun ★★
1 [C/U] a thick soft cover for a floor
2 [C] *literary* a layer of something soft covering the ground: ***a carpet of** autumn leaves*

car•pet² /ˈkɑrpət/ verb [T] to cover a floor with a carpet

ˈcarpet-ˌbomb verb [T] to drop a lot of bombs from airplanes, so that everything on the ground is destroyed

car•pet•ed /ˈkɑrpətəd/ adj a carpeted room has carpet on the floor

ˈcar ˌpool noun [C] a group of people who travel together to work, school, etc., so that only one car is used

ˈcar-ˌpool verb [I] *American* to regularly travel in the same car as other people when you are going to work, school, etc., in order to save fuel

car•riage /ˈkerɪdʒ/ noun [C] a vehicle pulled by horses, used in the past for carrying passengers

car•ri•er /ˈkeriər/ noun [C] **1** a company that moves goods or people from one place to another **2** a vehicle or ship used for moving goods or people → AIRCRAFT CARRIER **3** someone who can infect another person with a disease without getting it themselves **4** *American* a company that provides telephone, television, or insurance service

car•rot /ˈkerət/ noun **1** [C/U] a long hard orange vegetable that grows under the ground —*picture* → C11 **2** [C] *informal* something that someone promises you to encourage you to do something

car•ry /ˈkeri/ verb ★★★

1 take in your hands	8 accept responsibility
2 in your pocket/bag	9 win election
3 transport sb/sth	10 lead to punishment
4 have goods for sale	11 have message
5 publish/broadcast sth	12 of smells/sounds
6 spread disease	+ PHRASES
7 develop	+ PHRASAL VERBS

1 [T] to hold someone or something using your hands, arms, or body and take them somewhere: *Do you mind carrying this box for me?* ♦ *Sarah carried her cup of coffee back to her desk.* ♦ *Luke was carrying the boy on his shoulders.*

2 [T] to have something with you, usually in your pocket or bag: *I never carry much cash with me.* ♦ *British police officers normally don't carry guns.*

3 [T] to transport someone or something from one place to another: *a plane carrying 225 passengers* ♦ *They carried the message back to their villages.* ♦ *a cable carrying electricity*

4 [T] if a store carries goods or products, it has them for sale: *We carry several models of microwaves.*

5 [T] to publish or broadcast a news story: *All the papers carried the story the next day.*

6 [T] to have a disease and be capable of infecting someone else with it

7 [T] to do or develop something to a particular level: *If this behavior is carried to extremes, it can be destructive.*

8 [T] if you carry responsibility or blame for something, you accept it

9 [T] *American* to win an election in a particular state or district

10 [T] if a crime carries a particular punishment, that is the punishment that people will receive for committing it

11 [T] if something carries a message, the message is written on it: *Packs of cigarettes must carry a government health warning.*

12 [I] if a sound carries, it can be heard far away: *The child's cries carried down the quiet street.*

PHRASES **carry a tune** to be able to sing musical notes correctly

carry weight to be respected and have influence: *Dr. Watson's opinions carry a lot of weight in court.*

get carried away to become so excited or involved in something that you lose control of your feelings or behavior

PHRASAL VERBS **ˌcarry sth ˈoff** to deal successfully with something difficult

ˌcarry (sth) ˈon 1 to continue doing something: *She moved to Atlanta to carry on her work.* **2** *informal* to behave in an angry, excited, or emotional way

ˌcarry sth ˈout 1 to do something that you have been told to do or that you have promised to do: *Maybe she ought to have carried out her threat to go to the police.* ♦ *Your orders have been carried out, sir.* **2** to do a particular piece of work: *The construction work was carried out by a local contractor.*

ˈcarry-ˌon adj carry-on bags or suitcases are ones that you can keep with you on an airplane

car•ry•o•ver /ˈkeriˌoʊvər/ noun [singular] **1** something that is the result of a situation that existed in the past **2** an amount of money that has not been used within a period of time and can be kept and used later

car•sick /ˈkɑrˌsɪk/ adj feeling sick from traveling in a car —**car•sick•ness** noun [U]

cart¹ /kɑrt/ noun [C] **1** an open vehicle with four wheels that is pulled by a horse **2** *American* a small table with wheels, for moving food or other objects around

cart² /kɑrt/ verb [T] *informal* to carry something large or heavy somewhere

carte blanche /ˌkɑrt ˈblɑntʃ/ noun [U] the freedom to do what you want in a particular situation

car•tel /kɑrˈtel/ noun [C] a group of companies who agree to sell something at the same price so that they do not have to compete with one another

car•ti•lage /ˈkɑrt(ə)lɪdʒ/ noun [U] a substance that surrounds the JOINTS in your body

car•ton /ˈkɑrt(ə)n/ noun [C] a container for liquids made of stiff thick paper, or the amount of liquid that can be put into this container

car•toon /kɑrˈtun/ noun [C] **1** a movie or TV show made by photographing a series of drawings so that things in them seem to move **2** a humorous drawing in a newspaper or magazine **3** a COMIC STRIP

car•tridge /ˈkɑrtrɪdʒ/ noun [C] **1** a small container with ink inside that you put into a printer or pen **2** a metal tube that you put into a gun, containing a bullet and a substance that will explode

cart•wheel /ˈkɑrtˌwil, ˈkɑrtˌhwil/ noun [C] a movement in which you throw yourself sideways onto your hands, swing your legs over your head, and land on your feet

carve /kɑrv/ verb [I/T] **1** to make an object by cutting it from stone or wood, or to make a pattern by cutting into stone or wood **2** to cut a large piece of meat into pieces before you serve it

PHRASAL VERBS **ˌcarve ˈout sth (for yourself)** to develop a career or position for yourself by working hard

ˌcarve sth ˈup to divide something such as land between different people or countries, usually unfairly

carv•ing /ˈkɑrvɪŋ/ noun [C] an object or pattern made by cutting stone or wood

ˈcar ˌwash noun [C] a place with special equipment for washing cars

cas•cade /kæˈskeɪd/ verb [I] to flow or hang down in large amounts —**cas•cade** noun [C]

case /keɪs/ noun [C] ★★★

1 situation affecting sth	5 instance of disease
2 legal matter for court	6 situation/person
3 set of reasons	7 container/cover
4 crime	+ PHRASES

1 a situation that involves a particular person or thing: *In the majority of cases, it's easy to keep costs down.* ♦ ***If that's the case****, I'm not surprised she was angry.* ♦ *It was* ***a case of*** *love at first sight.* ♦ *"I don't need it tonight." "****In that case****, I'll keep it until tomorrow."*

2 a legal matter that will be decided in a court: *He was confident that the case against him would be dropped.* ♦ *a murder/rape/libel case*

3 a set of facts used to support one side of an argument or legal matter: *The lawyers told me I had* ***a strong case*** (=had a good chance of winning in court).

4 a crime that the police are trying to solve: *a murder case*

5 an instance of a disease: *a bad case of food poisoning*

6 a situation or person that an official is dealing with: *Each social worker was assigned 30 cases.*

7 a container or cover for something: *Have you seen my glasses' case anywhere?* ♦ ***a case of wine***

PHRASES **a case in point** used for giving an example of the situation or behavior that you are talking about

in any case whatever the situation is, was, or will be: *Traffic may be bad, but in any case we'll be there in time for dinner.*

in case 1 if: *In case you can't come, give me a call.* **2** in order to be prepared for something that may happen: *Take an umbrella in case it rains.* ♦ *I'll make some sandwiches,* ***just in case*** *we get hungry later.* ♦ ***In case of*** (=if there is) *bad weather, the wedding will be held indoors.*

ˈcase ˌstudy noun [C] a piece of research that records details of how a situation develops over a period of time

cash¹ /kæʃ/ noun [U] ★★★ money in the form of bills and coins: *Do you want to pay in cash or by credit card?*

cash² /kæʃ/ verb [T] to exchange a check for its value in bills and coins

PHRASAL VERB **ˌcash ˈin** to use an opportunity to make a profit or gain an advantage

cash•ew /ˈkæʃu, kæˈʃu/ or **ˈcashew ˌnut** noun [C] a curved nut that you can eat

C

ˈcash ˌflow noun [U] *business* the process of money coming into and going out of a company

cash•ier /kæˈʃɪr/ noun [C] someone whose job is to receive or give money to customers in a store, bank, etc.

ˈcash ˌmachine noun [C] an ATM

cash•mere /ˈkæʃmɪr/ noun [U] very soft wool that comes from a type of goat

cash•point /ˈkæʃˌpɔɪnt/ noun [C] *British* an ATM

ˈcash ˌregister noun [C] a machine that holds bills and coins and shows customers in stores how much they have to pay

cas•ing /ˈkeɪsɪŋ/ noun [C] a layer of a substance covering the outside of something to protect it

ca•si•no /kəˈsinoʊ/ noun [C] a place where people GAMBLE (=risk money in the hope of winning more)

cas•ket /ˈkæskət/ noun [C] *American* the box that a dead person is buried in

cas•se•role /ˈkæsəˌroʊl/ noun [C/U] a deep dish with a lid, used for cooking in the oven, or the mixture of food that is cooked

cas•sette /kəˈset/ noun [C] a flat plastic case that contains TAPE for playing and recording sound or pictures

cast[1] /kæst/ (past tense and past participle **cast**) verb ★

1 [T] to choose an actor for a particular part, or to choose all the actors for a particular play, movie, etc.: **cast sb as sth** *She was always cast as a mother.*

2 [T] to make light or a shadow appear in a particular place

3 [I/T] to throw a FISHING LINE or net into the water

4 [T] to form an object by pouring liquid metal or liquid plastic into a MOLD

PHRASES **cast doubt on sth** to make something seem less certain, good, or real: *The latest information casts doubt on his story.*

cast your eyes over/cast a glance at to look at someone or something: *Harry cast his eyes around the room.*

cast (new/fresh) light on sth to provide information that helps people to understand something more clearly

cast a shadow over sth to make a situation seem less hopeful or more likely to end badly

cast a spell on/over sb to use magic to make something happen to someone, or to seem to do this

cast a vote/ballot to vote in an election

PHRASAL VERBS **ˌcast sb/sth aˈside** to get rid of someone or something because they are no longer interesting or valuable

ˌcast ˈoff to remove the rope that is fastening your boat to the land, so that you can sail away

ˌcast sb/sth ˈoff to get rid of someone or something: *It took many years for Chicago to cast off its violent reputation.*

cast[2] /kæst/ noun [C] **1** all the performers in a movie, play, etc. **2** *medical* a hard cover for protecting a broken part of your body while it is getting better **3** an object made by pouring a liquid into a MOLD that is removed when the liquid is hard

cast•a•way /ˈkæstəˌweɪ/ noun [C] someone whose ship has sunk and who is left alone on an island

caste /kæst/ noun [C] one of the social classes that people are born into in Hindu society

cas•ti•gate /ˈkæstɪˌgeɪt/ verb [T] *formal* to criticize someone or something severely

ˌcasting ˈvote noun [C] the vote that gives one group a majority when the other votes are equally divided

ˌcast ˈiron noun [U] very hard iron used for making objects such as cooking pans and fences

ˌcast-ˈiron adj **1** made of cast iron **2** very definite, and certain to be effective: *a cast-iron alibi*

cas•tle /ˈkæs(ə)l/ noun [C] ★★

1 a large strong building with thick walls that was built in the past to protect the people inside from being attacked

2 one of the pieces used in the game of CHESS —*picture* → C16

cas•trate /ˈkæˌstreɪt/ verb [T] to remove the TESTICLES (=pair of sexual organs) of a male animal or a man —**cas•tra•tion** /kæˈstreɪʃ(ə)n/ noun [U]

ca•su•al /ˈkæʒuəl/ adj

1 relaxed/informal	4 not planned
2 comfortable to wear	5 temporary
3 without strong feeling	

1 relaxed and informal: *The bar has a casual atmosphere.* **2** casual clothes are comfortable and appropriate for wearing in informal situations **3** not involving strong feelings or emotions: *casual relationships/friendships* **4** happening without being planned or thought about: *a casual meeting/remark* **5** used for describing temporary employment, and the people involved in it —**ca•su•al•ly** adv

ca•su•al•ty /ˈkæʒuəlti/ noun [C] **1** someone who is injured or killed in an accident or war: *There were reports of heavy casualties* (=many people injured or killed). **2** someone or something that is damaged or harmed as a result of something: *Education has again been a casualty of government spending cuts.*

cat /kæt/ noun [C] ★★★

1 an animal with soft fur, a long thin tail, and WHISKERS. It is kept as a pet or for catching mice.

2 a wild animal that looks like a big cat, for example a lion

PHRASES **cat and mouse** a situation in which two people use skill or tricks to try to defeat each other: *Hammond played cat and mouse with the police for weeks.*

let the cat out of the bag to tell someone something that was intended to be secret

→ FAT CAT

cat•a•clysm /ˈkætəˌklɪzəm/ noun [C] *literary* a sudden violent change or event

cat•a•clys•mic /ˌkætəˈklɪzmɪk/ adj changing a situation in a sudden, violent, and unpleasant way

cat•a•log[1] /ˈkæt(ə)lˌɔg/ noun [C] **1** a book that contains pictures of things that you can buy: *a mail order catalog* **2** a list of all the courses at a college or university, or of the things in a library, museum, art sale, etc.

3 a series of bad things that happen: *a catalog of disasters*

cat·a·log[2] /ˈkæt(ə)ˌlɔg/ verb [T] to make a list of all the things in a collection

cat·a·logue /ˈkæt(ə)ˌlɔg/ the British spelling of **catalog**

cat·a·lyst /ˈkæt(ə)lɪst/ noun [C] **1** someone or something that causes something to happen or change **2** *science* a substance that causes a chemical reaction to happen more quickly

cat·a·pult /ˈkætəˌpʌlt/ verb [T] **1** to suddenly put someone into an important position: *The song catapulted the band to fame in the 1960s.* **2** to fire something through the air very quickly

cat·a·ract /ˈkætəˌrækt/ noun [C] a white area that grows on your eye as a result of disease. It makes you gradually lose your sight.

ca·tas·tro·phe /kəˈtæstrəfi/ noun [C] an event that causes a lot of damage, or makes a lot of people suffer = DISASTER: *an economic/natural catastrophe*

cat·a·stroph·ic /ˌkætəˈstrɑfɪk/ adj causing a lot of damage, or making a lot of people suffer: *catastrophic floods*
—**cat·a·stroph·i·cal·ly** /ˌkætəˈstrɑfɪkli/ adv

catch[1] /kætʃ/ (past tense and past participle **caught** /kɔt/) verb ★★★

1 stop a falling object	9 talk to/telephone sb
2 stop an escape	10 get stuck on sth
3 find and arrest	11 discover a problem
4 get on public vehicle	12 hear sth that sb says
5 discover sb doing sth	13 get sb's attention etc.
6 get disease/illness	14 of light
7 find sb not prepared	+ PHRASES
8 get into bad situation	+ PHRASAL VERBS

1 [I/T] to stop something that is falling or moving through the air, and hold it: *Stewart caught the ball with one hand.* ♦ *A bucket stood under the hole to catch the rain.*

2 [T] to get hold of and stop a person or animal so that they cannot escape: *She raced to catch the child before he got to the edge.* ♦ *Wolves hunt and catch their prey in packs.* ♦ *Laura shouted, "Wait!" and* ***caught hold of*** *his arm.* ♦ *Did you* ***catch*** *any* ***fish*** (=using a fishing rod or net)?

3 [T] if the police catch someone, they find them and arrest them

4 [I/T] to get on a train, bus, airplane, or boat that is traveling somewhere: *I caught the next train to New York.* ♦ *I have a flight to catch at 4:40.*

5 [T] to find someone doing something that they do not expect or want you to see: **catch sb doing sth** *Several times she'd caught him staring at her.* ♦ *Diana was* ***caught red-handed*** (=caught while doing something wrong).

6 [T] to get a disease or illness: **catch sth from sb/sth** *Brian caught chickenpox from his nephew.*

7 [T] to surprise someone in an unpleasant way, by doing something that they are not prepared for: *The question* ***caught*** *their spokesperson* ***by surprise.*** ♦ *Harry looked up suddenly,* ***catching*** *Emily* ***off guard*** (=when she was not ready).

8 [T] to become unexpectedly involved in an unpleasant situation: *We were* ***caught in*** *a heavy storm.* ♦ *She* ***got caught up in*** *a clash between protesters and police.*

9 [T] *informal* to find someone available to talk by going to them or telephoning them: *Margaret caught me just as I was leaving.*

10 [I/T] to become stuck on something, or to make something get stuck: *I must have* ***caught*** *my shirt* ***on*** *a nail.*

11 [T] to discover a problem or medical condition and stop it from becoming worse: *Doctors assured her that they had caught the cancer in time.*

12 [T] to hear something that someone says: *I'm sorry, I didn't catch what you said.*

13 [T] to have a sudden effect on someone's attention or imagination: *It was Myra's red hair that first caught my attention.*

14 [T] if light catches something, or if something catches the light, the light makes it look bright and shiny

PHRASES **catch your breath 1** to take time to start to breathe normally again after physical exercise **2** to stop breathing suddenly for a short time because you are surprised or impressed

catch sb's eye 1 if something catches your eye, you suddenly notice it: *There was one painting that caught my eye.* **2** to get someone's attention by looking at them

catch sight of/a glimpse of to see someone or something for a very short time

PHRASAL VERBS **ˌcatch ˈon 1** to become popular or fashionable: *We were surprised at how quickly the idea caught on.* **2** to understand: *He didn't catch on at first.*

ˌcatch (sb/sth) ˈup 1 to go faster so that you reach the person or vehicle in front of you: *We left first, but they caught up with us.* **2** to improve in order to reach the same standard or rate as someone or something: *He's missed so much school that he's going to find it hard to catch up.* ♦ *Recently, salaries have* ***caught up with*** *inflation.*

ˌcatch ˈup on sth to do something that you have not done enough of before: *I just want to go home and catch up on some sleep.*

ˌcatch ˈup with sb to talk to someone who you have not seen for some time and find out what they have been doing: *Come over tomorrow and we can catch up.*

catch

catch[2] /kætʃ/ noun ★★

1 [C] an act of stopping and holding a ball that is moving through the air: *Good catch!*

2 [U] a game in which children throw a ball to each other

3 [C] a hidden problem or difficulty in something that seems extremely good: *It sounds so cheap – is there a catch?*

4 [C] an object used for fastening something

such as a window, door, or container

catch-22 /ˌkætʃ twentiˈtu/ noun [C] a difficult situation that is impossible to escape from because each part of the problem must be solved first

ˈcatch-ˌall noun [C] a word, phrase, or group that includes a lot of different things

catch·er /ˈkætʃər/ noun [C] in baseball, the person who catches any balls that are not hit —*picture* → C15

catch·phrase /ˈkætʃˌfreɪz/ noun [C] a short phrase that many people know from television, movies, etc.

catch·y /ˈkætʃi/ adj a tune or phrase that is catchy gets your attention and is easy to remember

cat·e·gor·i·cal·ly /ˌkætəˈgɔrɪkli/ adv in a very clear and definite way —**cat·e·gor·i·cal** adj

cat·e·go·rize /ˈkætəgəˌraɪz/ verb [T] to put people or things into groups according to their qualities =CLASSIFY —**cat·e·go·ri·za·tion** /ˌkætəgəriˈzeɪʃ(ə)n/ noun [U]

cat·e·go·ry /ˈkætəgəri/ noun [C] a group of people or things that have similar qualities: *There will be two winners in each category.* ♦ *The proposal would ban some categories of weapons.*

ca·ter /ˈkeɪtər/ verb [I/T] to provide food and drinks at an event such as a party or meeting —**ca·ter·er** noun [C]

PHRASAL VERB ˈ**cater to sb** to provide a particular group of people with something that they want or need: *TV shows catering to young male audiences*

ca·ter·ing /ˈkeɪtərɪŋ/ noun [U] the job of organizing the food and drinks for an event such as a party or meeting

cat·er·pil·lar /ˈkætərˌpɪlər/ noun [C] an insect with many legs that develops into a BUTTERFLY or MOTH —*picture* → C13

cat·fish /ˈkætˌfɪʃ/ noun [C] a fish with long hard hairs near its mouth. It lives in lakes and rivers.

ca·thar·sis /kəˈθɑrsɪs/ noun [U] the process of expressing strong feelings that have been affecting you so that they do not upset you anymore —**ca·thar·tic** adj

ca·the·dral /kəˈθidrəl/ noun [C] the most important church in the area that a BISHOP controls

Cath·o·lic /ˈkæθ(ə)lɪk/ noun [C] a member of the Roman Catholic Church —**Cath·o·lic** adj, **Ca·thol·i·cism** /kəˈθɑlɪˌsɪzəm/ noun [U]

cat·tle /ˈkæt(ə)l/ noun [plural] cows and BULLS that are kept by farmers for their milk or meat

cat·ty /ˈkæti/ adj saying cruel or unpleasant things about other people

cat·walk /ˈkætˌwɔk/ noun [C] **1** the raised area at a FASHION SHOW that the MODELS walk along **2** a structure for people to walk on, built high on a building or above a stage

Cau·ca·sian /kɔˈkeɪʒ(ə)n/ adj *formal* used for describing a white person, for example someone from North America, Europe, or Australia —**Cau·ca·sian** noun [C]

cau·cus /ˈkɔkəs/ noun [C] **1** a meeting of members of a political party at which they choose who will represent the party in the election for president **2** a group of politicians with special interests or responsibilities

caught the past tense and past participle of catch[1]

caul·dron /ˈkɔldrən/ noun [C] a large round metal container that you use for cooking over a fire

cau·li·flow·er /ˈkɑliˌflaʊr/ noun [C/U] a vegetable with a hard round white central part surrounded by green leaves —*picture* → C11

ˈcause conjunction *informal* because

cause[1] /kɔz/ noun ★★★

1 [C] an event, thing, or person that makes something happen: ***The cause of death was found to be a heart attack.*** ♦ ***an essay on the causes of World War I***

2 [C/U] a reason for behaving in a particular way, or for feeling a particular emotion: *He wouldn't have done it without **good cause*** (=a good reason). ♦ *His departure was **cause for celebration** in the village.* ♦ *The doctor's report states that there is **no cause for concern**.*

3 [C] a goal, idea, or organization that you support or work for: *Campaigners hope that people will be sympathetic to their cause.* ♦ *Please give as much as you can: it's **for a good cause**.*

→ LOST CAUSE

cause[2] /kɔz/ verb [T] ★★★ to make something happen, usually something bad: *Police confirmed that the explosion was **caused by** a bomb.* ♦ *Indigestion is **caused by** excess acid in the stomach.* ♦ *Bad weather continues to **cause problems** for travelers.* ♦ **cause sb/sth to do sth** *A small sound caused him to turn his head.* ♦ **cause sb sth** *He apologizes for causing you any embarrassment.*

> **Words often used with cause**
>
> *Nouns often used with **cause***
>
> ■ CAUSE + **alarm, concern, confusion, damage, distress, embarrassment, harm, problems, suffering, trouble**: cause a bad situation

cause·way /ˈkɔzˌweɪ/ noun [C] a raised road or path across ground that is wet or covered by water

caus·tic /ˈkɔstɪk/ adj expressing severe criticism, often in a funny or clever way

cau·tion[1] /ˈkɔʃ(ə)n/ noun [U] **1** careful thought and lack of hurry in order to try to avoid risks or danger: *He was instructed to act with extreme caution.* ♦ *Politicians should exercise greater caution with taxpayers' money.* **2** advice that you should be careful: *A word of caution: the roads are very icy.*

cau·tion[2] /ˈkɔʃ(ə)n/ verb [T] *formal* to warn someone about a possible danger or problem: *Researchers cautioned that the drug is only partly effective.*

cau·tion·ar·y /ˈkɔʃ(ə)nˌeri/ adj warning someone that they should be careful: *cautionary remarks*

cau·tious /ˈkɔʃəs/ adj careful to avoid problems or danger —**cau·tious·ly** adv

cav·a·lier /ˌkævəˈlɪr/ adj not caring enough about other people's feelings or about a serious situation: *a cavalier attitude*

cav·al·ry /ˈkævəlri/ noun [U] the part of an army that consists of soldiers who ride horses

cave¹ /keɪv/ noun [C] a large hole in the side of a hill or under the ground

cave² /keɪv/ PHRASAL VERB ˌ**cave ˈin 1** if a roof or wall caves in, it falls down or inward **2** to suddenly stop opposing something because someone has persuaded you

ca·ve·at /ˈkæviˌæt, ˈkeɪviˌæt/ noun [C] *formal* a warning of the limits of a particular agreement or statement

cave·man /ˈkeɪvˌmæn/ (plural **cave·men** /ˈkeɪvˌmen/) noun [C] someone who lived thousands of years ago when people lived in CAVES

cav·ern /ˈkævərn/ noun [C] a large CAVE

cav·ern·ous /ˈkævərnəs/ adj a cavernous room or building is very large and dark

cav·i·ar /ˈkæviˌɑr/ noun [U] fish eggs that are eaten as a special and expensive food

cav·i·ty /ˈkævəti/ noun [C] **1** a hole or space inside a solid object or your body **2** a hole in a tooth, caused by decay

cc /ˌsi ˈsi/ abbrev **1** used on a business letter or e-mail for saying that a copy is being sent to the person mentioned: *To Jack Brown, cc: Paul Davis.* **2** cubic centimeter: used for measuring the amount of a liquid or the size of an engine: *a 750cc motorcycle*

CCTV noun [U] closed-circuit television: a system of cameras and television screens that allows someone to see what is happening in different parts of a building or town

CD /ˌsi ˈdi/ noun [C] ★
1 compact disc: a small round piece of hard plastic with sound recorded on it or computer information stored on it
2 certificate of deposit: an arrangement in which you save a particular amount of money with a bank for a fixed amount of time for a fixed amount of interest

ˌ**CD ˌburner** noun [C] a CD WRITER

ˌ**CD ˌplayer** noun [C] a piece of equipment used for playing CDs with music on them

CD-ROM /ˌsi di ˈrɑm/ noun [C/U] compact disc read-only memory: a CD that stores large amounts of information for use by a computer

CD-RW /ˌsi di ɑr ˈdʌb(ə)lju/ abbrev compact disc rewritable: a CD that you can use for recording music or information from a computer

ˌ**CD ˌwriter** noun [C] a piece of equipment used for recording information onto CDs

cease /sis/ verb [I/T] *formal* to stop happening or continuing, or to stop something happening or continuing: *Conversation ceased when she entered the room.* ♦ *The government has ceased all contact with the rebels.* ♦ *He had ceased caring what she did.*

cease·fire /ˈsisˌfaɪr/ noun [C] an agreement to stop fighting for a period of time

cease·less /ˈsisləs/ adj *formal* continuing without stopping —**cease·less·ly** adv

ce·dar /ˈsidər/ noun [C/U] a tall EVERGREEN tree, or the wood from this tree

cede /sid/ verb [T] *formal* to allow someone to take something such as power or land away from you

ceil·ing /ˈsilɪŋ/ noun [C] ★
1 the surface that is above you in a room: *There were cracks in the walls and the ceiling.*
2 an upper limit set on the number or amount of something: *A ceiling of $100 was put on all donations.*
→ GLASS CEILING

ce·leb /səˈleb/ noun [C] *informal* a CELEBRITY

cel·e·brate /ˈseləˌbreɪt/ verb ★★
1 [I/T] to do something enjoyable in order to show that an occasion or event is special: *Let's have a party to celebrate.* ♦ *They're celebrating the end of their exams.*
2 [T] *formal* to show admiration for someone or something in a piece of writing, music, or art, or in a ceremony: *The songs celebrate the ancient culture.*

cel·e·brat·ed /ˈseləˌbreɪtəd/ adj famous and praised by many people: *a celebrated artist*

cel·e·bra·tion /ˌseləˈbreɪʃ(ə)n/ noun ★★★
1 [C] a party or special event at which you celebrate something: *The whole family showed up for our anniversary celebration.*
2 [U] the activity of celebrating something: *It was a night of dancing and celebration.* ♦ *He's having a party* ***in celebration of*** *his 84th birthday.*

ce·leb·ri·ty /səˈlebrəti/ noun [C] ★ a famous entertainer or sports personality: *TV/sports celebrities*

cel·er·y /ˈseləri/ noun [U] a pale green vegetable with long stems that are eaten raw or cooked —*picture* → C11

ceˌlestial ˈbody noun [C] *technical* a star or planet

cel·i·bate /ˈseləbət/ adj someone who is celibate does not have sex —**cel·i·ba·cy** /ˈseləbəsi/ noun [U]

cell /sel/ noun [C] ★★
1 the smallest part of a living human being, animal, or plant that can operate as an independent unit: *nerve/blood/brain/cancer cells*
2 a small room where a prisoner is kept: *a police/prison cell*

cel·lar /ˈselər/ noun [C] a room under a building, below the ground

cel·lo /ˈtʃeloʊ/ noun [C] a large musical instrument with strings. You hold it between your legs and play it with a BOW. —*picture* → STRINGED INSTRUMENT —**cel·list** /ˈtʃelɪst/ noun [C]

cel·lo·phane /ˈseləˌfeɪn/ noun [U] a very thin clear material that you use for wrapping things

cell·phone /ˈselˌfoʊn/ noun [C] *American* a telephone that you can carry around with you —*picture* → C3

cel·lu·lar /ˈseljələr/ adj **1** relating to human, animal, or plant cells **2** relating to cellphones

ˌ**cellular ˈphone** noun [C] *formal* a CELLPHONE

cel·lu·lite /ˈseljəˌlaɪt/ noun [U] small lumps of fat just below the skin

cel·lu·loid /ˈseljəˌlɔɪd/ noun [U] a thin clear plastic material that was used in the past for making FILM

Cel·si·us /ˈselsiəs/ noun [U] a system for measuring temperature in the METRIC SYSTEM → FAHRENHEIT

ce•ment¹ /səˈment/ noun [U] a gray powder used in building. It becomes very hard when it is mixed with sand and water.

ce•ment² /səˈment/ verb [T] **1** to make a relationship or idea stronger or more certain **2** to cover a surface with cement

cem•e•ter•y /ˈseməˌteri/ noun [C] an area of ground where dead people are buried → GRAVEYARD

cen•sor /ˈsensər/ verb [T] to remove parts of a book, movie, or letter for moral, religious, or political reasons —**cen•sor** noun [C]

cen•sor•ship /ˈsensərʃɪp/ noun [U] the process of removing parts of books, movies, or letters that are considered inappropriate for moral, religious, or political reasons

cen•sure /ˈsenʃər/ verb [T] *formal* to criticize someone severely —**cen•sure** noun [U]

cen•sus /ˈsensəs/ noun [C] an occasion when government officials count all the people in a country and record information about them

cent /sent/ noun [C] ★ a small unit of money used in many countries, for example the U.S., Canada, and Australia. There are 100 cents in a dollar.

cen•ten•a•ry /senˈtenəri, ˈsent(ə)nˌeri/ noun [C] a CENTENNIAL

cen•ten•ni•al /senˈteniəl/ noun [C] a day or year that people celebrate exactly 100 years after an important event

cen•ter¹ /ˈsentər/ noun ★★★

1 middle	5 not left- or right-wing
2 a building for sth	6 in basketball
3 important place for sth	7 in football
4 main subject/cause	+ PHRASE

1 [C] the middle of a space or area: *chocolates with soft centers* ♦ *in **the center of** the room*
2 [C] a building or group of buildings that is used for a particular activity, or for providing a particular service: *a conference center* ♦ *a shopping center*
3 [C] a place where a particular thing is important, or where a particular thing exists in large amounts or numbers: *one of the world's most important financial centers* ♦ *a **center of** industry*
4 [singular] **the center of sth** the main subject or cause of something: *He's very shy and hates being **the center of attention**.*
5 the center [singular] political views or parties that are between left-wing and the right-wing
6 [C] a player in basketball whose position is near the basket —*picture* → C15
7 [C] a player in football whose position is in the middle of the line of attacking players

PHRASE **center of gravity** the point in any object around which its weight balances

cen•ter² /ˈsentər/ verb [T] to put something in the center of an area

PHRASAL VERB **ˈcenter (sth) aˌround sb/sth** or **ˈcenter (sth) ˌon sb/sth** to make something the main subject of attention or interest: *The debate centered around the issue of finance.*

cen•ter•piece /ˈsentərˌpis/ noun [C] **1** the most important feature of something: *Health care is the centerpiece of our campaign.* **2** a decoration or arrangement of flowers that you put in the middle of a table

ˌcenter ˈstage noun [U] a situation in which someone or something is attracting a lot of attention

cen•ti•grade /ˈsentɪˌgreɪd/ noun [U] *old-fashioned* CELSIUS

cen•ti•li•ter /ˈsentɪˌlitər/ noun [C] a unit for measuring an amount of liquid or gas in the METRIC SYSTEM. There are 100 centiliters in one liter.

cen•ti•me•ter /ˈsentɪˌmitər/ noun [C] a unit for measuring length in the METRIC SYSTEM. There are 100 centimeters in one meter.

cen•ti•me•tre /ˈsentɪˌmitər/ the British spelling of **centimeter**

cen•ti•pede /ˈsentɪˌpid/ noun [C] a small insect with a narrow body and many pairs of legs

cen•tral /ˈsentrəl/ adj ★★★
1 in the middle of a space or area: *central Boston* ♦ *The hotel is built around a central courtyard.*
2 main or major: *He played a central role in the development of U.S. economic policy.* ♦ *skills that are **central to*** (=very important for) *a child's development*
3 belonging to the main organization that controls other smaller organizations: *the Communist Party's central committee*
—**cen•tral•ly** /ˈsentrəli/ adv

ˌcentral ˈheating noun [U] a system that heats a whole building by sending hot air or water through pipes to all the rooms

cen•tral•ize /ˈsentrəˌlaɪz/ verb [T] to give control of a country, organization, or industry to one central group of people

ˌcentral ˈnervous ˌsystem noun [C] the part of your NERVOUS SYSTEM that consists of your brain and your SPINAL CORD

cen•tre /ˈsentər/ the British spelling of **center**

cen•tu•ry /ˈsentʃəri/ noun [C] ★★★
1 a period of 100 years, usually counted from a year ending in –00: *16th century paintings* ♦ *His family has ruled Morocco since the 17th century.*
2 any period of 100 years: *the worst storm in nearly a century* ♦ *The tribe had died out centuries* (=hundreds of years) *before.*

CEO /ˌsi i ˈoʊ/ noun [C] Chief Executive Officer: the most senior manager in a corporation

ce•ram•ic /səˈræmɪk/ adj made from baked clay

ce•ram•ics /səˈræmɪks/ noun **1** [U] the art or process of making ceramic objects **2** [plural] ceramic objects

ce•re•al /ˈsɪriəl/ noun **1** [C/U] a food made from grain. You eat it with milk for breakfast. **2** [C] any grain that can be made into flour, or a plant that produces grain

cer•e•bral /ˈserəbrəl, səˈribrəl/ adj *medical* relating to your brain, or affecting your brain

cer•e•bral pal•sy /ˌserəbrəl ˈpɔlzi/ noun [U] a medical condition that affects someone's ability to control their movement and speech

cer•e•mo•ni•al /ˌserəˈmoʊniəl/ adj connected with a ceremony

cer•e•mo•ny /ˈserəˌmoʊni/ noun ★
1 [C] a formal public event with special traditions, actions, or words: *a ceremony to honor those who died in the war* ♦ *an award ceremony*

2 [U] the formal traditions, actions, and words used for celebrating a public or religious event: *They celebrated Easter with lavish ceremony.*

cer·tain¹ /ˈsɜrt(ə)n/ adj ★★★
1 having no doubts that something is true =SURE ≠ UNCERTAIN: *I'm not absolutely certain, but I think I'm right.* ♦ **+(that)** *You can be pretty certain she's not going to like it.* ♦ **+who/how/why etc.** *We still can't be certain who is going to win.* ♦ *I've never been more **certain of** anything in my entire life.*
2 definitely going to happen, or definitely known: *One thing was certain: someone had been in his room.* ♦ **be certain to do sth** *Interest rates seem certain to rise next month.* ♦ **+(that)** *It's not certain that this method would work.* ♦ *Mexico is now **certain of** a place in the finals.*
PHRASE **make certain** to take action in order to be sure that something happens or be sure that something is true =MAKE SURE: **+(that)** *Call the office to make certain everything is OK.*

cer·tain² /ˈsɜrt(ə)n/ determiner ★★ used for referring to someone or something without being specific about who or what they are: *There are certain things we need to discuss.*
PHRASE **a certain** some, but not very much: ***A certain amount of** fat in your diet is good for you.*

cer·tain·ly /ˈsɜrt(ə)nli/ adv ★★★
1 used for emphasizing that something is definitely true or will definitely happen: *There certainly wasn't any point in going now.*
2 *spoken* used for expressing agreement or for giving permission: *"We'd like you to explain your proposal to us in greater detail." "Certainly."* ♦ *"Can I borrow your car?" "Certainly not!"*

cer·tain·ty /ˈsɜrt(ə)nti/ noun **1** [C] something that will definitely happen, or that you feel very sure about: *Victory looked like a certainty.* **2** [U] the feeling of being completely sure about something =CONVICTION: *I can say with certainty that there will be no more information today.*

cer·tif·i·cate /sərˈtɪfɪkət/ noun [C] ★★
1 an official document that states that particular facts are true: *a birth/marriage certificate*
2 an official document that proves that you have passed an examination or have successfully completed a course

cer·ti·fied /ˈsɜrtɪfaɪd/ adj **1** a certified professional person has done all the training that they officially need to do **2** having an official document that shows official facts

ˌcertified ˈmail noun [U] *American* mail that is recorded when you send it and again when the post office delivers it

cer·ti·fy /ˈsɜrtɪˌfaɪ/ verb [T] **1** to state officially that something is true, accurate, or satisfactory **2** to give someone an official document that proves that they have passed an examination or have successfully completed a training course

cer·vi·cal /ˈsɜrvɪk(ə)l/ adj *medical* relating to a woman's CERVIX

cer·vix /ˈsɜrvɪks/ noun [C] the entrance to the UTERUS (=the part of a woman's body where a baby grows)

ce·sar·e·an /sɪˈzeriən/ or **ceˌsarean ˈsection** noun [C] a medical operation in which a baby is born by being removed from the woman's body through a cut made in her ABDOMEN

ces·sa·tion /seˈseɪʃ(ə)n/ noun [C/U] *formal* an end to something: *a cessation of hostilities*

CFC /ˌsi ef ˈsi/ noun [C] chlorofluorocarbon: a gas used in REFRIGERATORS and in some AEROSOLS

chafe /tʃeɪf/ verb [I/T] to rub the skin on a part of your body and make it sore

chain¹ /tʃeɪn/ noun ★★
1 [C/U] a series of metal rings that are connected to each other: *The crate was attached to the deck with a chain.* ♦ *a gold chain* ♦ *Women prisoners were kept **in chains**.*
2 [C] a series of people or things that are connected: *a chain of events that eventually led to murder* ♦ ***a chain of** small islands*
3 [C] a group of businesses that all belong to the same company: *Japan's leading hotel chain* ♦ ***a chain of** appliance stores*

chain

chain² /tʃeɪn/ verb [T] to use a chain to fasten something so that it cannot be stolen, or to fasten a prisoner with a chain so that they cannot escape

ˌchain reˈaction noun [C] a series of events or chemical reactions that happens very fast, with each one causing the next one

ˈchain ˌsaw noun [C] a tool with a motor, used for cutting down trees or cutting up wood

ˈchain ˌstore noun [C] one of a group of stores that all belong to the same company

chair¹ /tʃer/ noun [C] ★★★
1 a piece of furniture for one person to sit on, with a back, legs, and sometimes two arms —*picture* → NEXT PAGE
2 the person who is in charge of a meeting, committee, corporation, or organization: *All questions must be addressed to the chair.* ♦ *He is the former **chair of** the Atomic Energy Commission.* → CHAIRMAN, CHAIRPERSON, CHAIRWOMAN
3 *American* someone who is in charge of a department in a university

chair² /tʃer/ verb [T] to be the person in charge of a meeting, committee, corporation, or organization

chair·man /ˈtʃermən/ (plural **chair·men** /ˈtʃermən/) noun [C] ★ the person who is in charge of a meeting, committee, corporation, or organization

chair·man·ship /ˈtʃermənˌʃɪp/ noun [C/U] the position of being a chairman, or the time

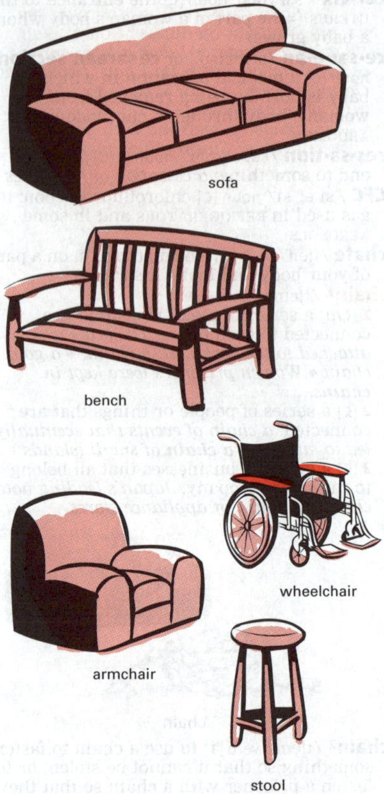

chairs

during which someone is a chairman

chair•per•son /ˈtʃerˌpɜrsən/ (plural **chair•per•sons** /ˈtʃerˌpɜrsəns/) noun [C] the person who is in charge of a meeting, committee, corporation, or organization

chair•wom•an /ˈtʃerˌwʊmən/ (plural **chair•wom•en** /ˈtʃerˌwɪmɪn/) noun [C] the woman who is in charge of a meeting, committee, corporation, or organization

cha•let /ʃæˈleɪ/ noun [C] a wooden house in a mountain area

chalk¹ /tʃɔk/ noun **1** [U] a type of soft white stone **2** [C/U] a stick of chalk used for writing or drawing

chalk² /tʃɔk/ PHRASAL VERB **ˌchalk sth ˈup** achieve or win something

chalk•board /ˈtʃɔkˌbɔrd/ noun [C] *American* a smooth hard surface that you write on with chalk = BLACKBOARD

chalk•y /ˈtʃɔki/ adj similar to CHALK, or containing CHALK

chal•lenge¹ /ˈtʃæləndʒ/ noun ★★

1 [C/U] something that needs a lot of skill, energy, and determination to deal with or achieve: *I felt I needed a new challenge at work.* ♦ *Are western nations ready to **meet** the environmental **challenges** that lie ahead?* ♦ *The company **faces the challenge** of completing the building on time.*

2 [C] an action or idea that questions whether something is true, fair, accurate, legal, etc.: *Recent discoveries **present a** serious **challenge to** accepted views on the age of the universe.* ♦ *The strike was **a** direct **challenge to** the authority of the government.*

3 [C] an occasion when someone tries to win a game or competition

> **Words often used with challenge**
>
> *Adjectives often used with **challenge** (noun, sense 1)*
>
> ■ **daunting, formidable, major, serious** + CHALLENGE: used about a challenge that worries or frightens you
>
> *Verbs often used with **challenge** (noun, sense 1)*
>
> ■ **accept, rise to** + CHALLENGE: deal with a challenge in a brave way
>
> ■ **pose, present** + CHALLENGE: create a challenge that you must deal with
>
> ■ **enjoy, relish** + CHALLENGE: enjoy being challenged

chal•lenge² /ˈtʃæləndʒ/ verb [T] **1** to question whether something is true, fair, accurate, legal, etc.: *This decision is likely to be challenged by the oil companies.* ♦ *The president has accused the governor of challenging his leadership.* **2** to invite someone to compete or fight: *The girls challenged the boys to a game of basketball.*

chal•lenged /ˈtʃælɪndʒd/ adj unable to do particular things without difficulty because of being disabled

chal•leng•ing /ˈtʃælɪndʒɪŋ/ adj difficult to deal with or achieve, but interesting and enjoyable ≠ UNCHALLENGING

cham•ber /ˈtʃeɪmbər/ noun **1** [C] a room used for a particular purpose: *a torture chamber* ♦ *the debating chamber* **2** [C] an enclosed space, especially one inside a machine or someone's body: *the chambers of the heart* **3** [C] one of the sections of a legislature: *the upper/lower chamber* **4 chambers** [plural] the offices used by judges

PHRASE **chamber of commerce** an organization of business owners whose aim is to improve conditions for business in their town

cham•ber•maid /ˈtʃeɪmbərˌmeɪd/ noun [C] a woman whose job is to clean the bedrooms in a hotel

ˈchamber ˌmusic noun [U] a type of classical music that is played by a small group of musicians

cham•o•mile /ˈkæməˌmaɪl/ noun [C/U] a plant with a pleasant smell often used for making tea

champ /tʃæmp/ noun [C] *informal* a CHAMPION

cham•pagne /ʃæmˈpeɪn/ noun [U] a type of French SPARKLING wine that people drink on special occasions

cham•pi•on¹ /ˈtʃæmpiən/ noun [C] ★

1 someone who has won an important competition, especially in a sport: *the world heavyweight boxing champion*

2 someone who publicly supports or defends something: *a champion of the rights of developing nations*

cham·pi·on² /ˈtʃæmpiən/ verb [T] to publicly support or defend something

cham·pi·on·ship /ˈtʃæmpiənʃɪp/ noun ★
1 [C] a competition to find the best player or team in a sport or game: *the World Chess Championships*
2 [singular] the position of being a champion: *Two more points and the championship will be his!*

chance¹ /tʃæns/ noun ★★★
1 [C] an opportunity to do something, especially something that you want to do =OPPORTUNITY: **the chance to do sth** *Students are given the chance to learn another language.* ♦ *We work together whenever we* ***get a chance.*** ♦ *I warned her that this was her* ***last chance.***
2 [C/U] the possibility that something will happen: **a chance of (doing) sth** *I think she has a good chance of getting the job.* ♦ **+(that)** *Is there any chance they will reverse their decision?* ♦ *He* ***doesn't stand a chance*** *of winning the tournament* (=it is not at all likely that he will win).
3 [U] the way that things happen without being planned or expected =LUCK: *The results may simply be due to chance.* ♦ *It was simply* ***by chance*** *that Nicholson was cast in the movie.*
PHRASES **by any chance** *spoken* used when you are asking questions to find out whether something is true: *Do you remember his name, by any chance?*
sb's chances how likely someone is to achieve something: **sb's chances of (doing) sth** *What are their chances of survival?*
(the) chances are *spoken* used for saying that something is likely to happen but is not certain
take a chance (on) or **take chances** to do something even though it involves risk

chance² /tʃæns/ verb [T] to do something even though you know it involves a risk: *It looked like rain so I decided not to chance it and brought my umbrella.*

chance³ /tʃæns/ adj not planned or expected: *a chance meeting/discovery*

chan·cel·lor /ˈtʃænsələr/ noun [C] **1** someone who is the official leader of a university **2** the leader of the government in some countries

chan·de·lier /ʃændəˈlɪr/ noun [C] a light that hangs from a ceiling and has a lot of branches for holding lights or CANDLES

change¹ /tʃeɪndʒ/ verb ★★★

1 become different	5 get on different vehicle
2 start sth new	6 exchange money
3 of clothes	+ PHRASES
4 replace sth	+ PHRASAL VERBS

1 [I/T] to become different, or to make someone or something different: *After a few days the weather changed.* ♦ *The law was changed in 1989.* ♦ *The leaves are already starting to* ***change color*** (=become a different color). ♦ **change (sth) from sth to sth** *The town has changed from a small fishing village to a modern tourist center.*
2 [I/T] to stop doing one thing and start doing something different: *Dave said he might change jobs.* ♦ **change (sth) to sth** *Consumers are increasingly changing to low-fat milk.*
3 [I/T] to take off the clothes that you are wearing and put on different ones: *Wait, I'll go and change.* ♦ *I took a bath and changed my clothes.* ♦ *Do I have time to* ***get changed*** *before we go?* ♦ *You should* ***change into*** *some dry socks.*
4 [T] to replace something with a new or different thing: *Can you help me change a tire?*
5 [I/T] to leave one airplane, train, bus, etc. to get on another: *We changed planes in Miami.*
6 [T] to exchange one type of money for another: *Can anyone change a twenty-dollar bill?* ♦ *I need to change some dollars into pesos.*
PHRASES **change hands** to be given or sold by one person to another
change your mind to change a decision you have made or an opinion you have about something: *I've* ***changed my mind about*** *Steve.*
change the subject to stop talking about one thing and start talking about another
PHRASAL VERBS ˈ**change (sth) ˌinto sth** to stop being in one condition or form and start being in another, or to make something do this: *At what point does boiling water change into steam?*
ˌ**change ˈover** to stop doing or using one thing and start doing or using something else: *When did the school change over to the phonics system?*

Other ways of saying change

- **adapt** to change something in order to make it suitable for a specific situation
- **adjust** to change something slightly so that it is exactly the way you want it
- **alter** a more formal word for "change"
- **convert** to change something so that it can be used for a different purpose
- **modify** to make small changes to a machine or system in order to make it suitable for a different situation
- **transform** to change something completely so that it looks or works much better than before

change² /tʃeɪndʒ/ noun ★★★
1 [C/U] a situation or process in which something becomes different or is replaced, or the result of this process: *A number of changes have taken place since the 1960s.* ♦ *Older people sometimes find it hard to accept change.* ♦ *We* ***made a few changes to*** *the schedule.* ♦ ***a change in*** *the law* ♦ ***a change from*** *military* ***to*** *civilian rule*
2 [U] the money that someone gives back to you when you give more money than it costs to buy something: *Here's your change.*
3 [U] coins instead of bills: *I'm sorry I don't have any change.* ♦ *Do you have change for a ten-dollar bill* (=bills or coins of lower value that you can exchange for it)?
PHRASES **a change of clothes/socks/underwear etc.** another set of clothes, socks, etc. that you take with you so that you can wear them later
a change of heart an occasion when you change your opinion or plan

for a change instead of what usually happens: *It's nice to hear some good news for a change.*
→ SEA CHANGE

Words often used with change
*Adjectives often used with **change** (noun, sense 1)*
■ **dramatic, fundamental, major, radical +** CHANGE: used about big changes

change·a·ble /ˈtʃeɪndʒəb(ə)l/ adj tending to change suddenly and often =UNPREDICTABLE

changed /tʃeɪndʒd/ adj different from before ≠ UNCHANGED

change·o·ver /ˈtʃeɪndʒˌoʊvər/ noun [C] a change from one method, system, or activity to another

ˈchange ˌpurse noun [C] *American* a small bag in which to keep coins

chan·nel¹ /ˈtʃæn(ə)l/ noun [C] ★★
1 a television station and the programs that it broadcasts: *What's on the other channel?*
2 a way of communicating or expressing something: *It is important to keep **channels of communication open**.* ♦ *a **channel for** her creative energies*
3 a narrow passage made in the ground so that water can go along it
4 a narrow area of water that joins two oceans

chan·nel² /ˈtʃæn(ə)l/ verb [T] **1** to use money or supplies for a particular purpose: *The company has channeled $1.2 million into developing new products.* **2** to use your energy, ability, feelings, or ideas for a particular purpose

chant /tʃænt/ verb [I/T] to shout or sing a word or phrase many times —**chant** noun [C]

Cha·nu·kah /ˈhɑnəkə/ another spelling of **Hanukkah**

cha·os /ˈkeɪˌɑs/ noun [U] a situation in which everything is confused and not organized

cha·ot·ic /keɪˈɑtɪk/ adj happening in a confused way and without any order or organization —**cha·ot·i·cal·ly** /keɪˈɑtɪkli/ adv

chap·el /ˈtʃæp(ə)l/ noun [C] a small church, or a special room used as a church

chap·lain /ˈtʃæplən/ noun [C] a priest who works in an institution such as a school or hospital, or in the army

chapped /tʃæpt/ adj chapped skin is dry and painful because of cold weather

chap·ter /ˈtʃæptər/ noun [C] ★★★
1 one of the sections of a book: *See Chapter Three for more details.*
2 a period of someone's life, or a period in history: *The war was now entering its final chapter.*
3 a local club or organization that is part of a much larger one

char·ac·ter /ˈkerəktər/ noun ★★★

1 personality	5 sb in book, movie, etc.
2 qualities of sth	6 letter/number/symbol
3 attractive qualities	7 determination
4 unusual person	

1 [C] the qualities that make up someone's personality: *This selfishness was one aspect of Steve's character that I didn't like.* ♦ *Why did Simon refuse? It seems so **out of character*** (=not typical of his usual behavior).
2 [C/U] the qualities that make something clearly different from anything else: *The two towns are similar in size but very different **in character**.*
3 [U] qualities that make someone or something good, interesting, or attractive: *a traditional inn with a lot of character and charm*
4 [C] a person of a particular type: *a shady/suspicious character*
5 [C] a person in a book, play, movie, etc.: *The movie's **main character** is played by George Clooney.*
6 [C] a letter, number, or symbol that is written or printed: *Your computer password may be up to 12 characters long.*
7 [U] the qualities of being brave and determined: *She showed real character in standing up to her parents.*

char·ac·ter·ise /ˈkerəktəˌraɪz/ a British spelling of **characterize**

char·ac·ter·is·tic¹ /ˌkerəktəˈrɪstɪk/ noun [C] a typical quality or feature: *the main characteristics of 20th-century culture*

char·ac·ter·is·tic² /ˌkerəktəˈrɪstɪk/ adj typical of someone or something ≠ UNCHARACTERISTIC: *Sue answered with her characteristic truthfulness.* —**char·ac·ter·is·ti·cal·ly** /ˌkerəktəˈrɪstɪkli/ adv

char·ac·ter·i·za·tion /ˌkerəktərɪˈzeɪʃ(ə)n/ noun [U] the way in which a writer creates CHARACTERS

char·ac·ter·ize /ˈkerəktəˌraɪz/ verb [T] **1 be characterized as** to be described as a particular type of person or thing: *The military is usually characterized as being conservative.* **2 be characterized by** to have something as a typical quality or feature: *The 1980s were characterized by high inflation and high unemployment.*

cha·rade /ʃəˈreɪd/ noun [C] an attempt to pretend that a situation is good when it is not

cha·rades /ʃəˈreɪdz/ noun [U] a game in which you can use only actions to help the other players to guess a word or phrase

char·coal /ˈtʃɑrˌkoʊl/ noun [U] a black substance made from burned wood. It is used as a fuel and for drawing.

charge¹ /tʃɑrdʒ/ noun ★★★

1 amount of money	4 amount of electricity
2 when sb is accused	5 an attack running fast
3 a claim sb/sth is bad	+ PHRASES

1 [C/U] an amount of money that you have to pay when you visit a place, or when someone does something for you: *There is no **charge for** using the library.* ♦ *The organization provides a range of services **free of charge*** (=with no charge). ♦ *There's a small **admission charge**.*
2 [C] an official statement that accuses someone of committing a crime: *murder/corruption/fraud charges* ♦ *In the end we decided not to **press charges*** (=officially accuse someone of a crime). ♦ *They faced **charges of** conspiracy and murder.* ♦ *The investigation resulted in criminal **charges against** three police officers.*

3 [C] a claim that someone or something is bad, or that they have done something bad: ***charges of racism*** ♦ **+that** *The leadership rejected charges that its policies were not effective.*
4 [singular/U] the amount of electricity that something holds or carries
5 [C] an attack by people or animals running very fast toward someone or something
PHRASES **in charge (of)** if you are in charge, you have control over someone or something and are responsible for them: *Who's in charge here?* ♦ *He was* ***put in charge of*** *the whole investigation.*
take charge (of) to take control and become responsible for someone or something: *Heather arrived and took charge of the project.*

charge² /tʃɑrdʒ/ verb ★★★

1 ask sb to pay money	4 run to attack
2 arrange for sb to pay	5 put electricity into
3 accuse sb of crime	

1 [I/T] to ask someone to pay an amount of money for something: *How much do you* ***charge for delivery?*** ♦ **charge sb sth (for sth)** *They charged us $24 for three drinks.* ♦ **be charged at sth** *Phone calls are charged at $1.00 per minute.*
2 [T] to arrange to pay for something later: **charge sth to sb/sth** *The flights were charged to his personal account.*
3 [T] to accuse someone of committing a crime: *Two men have been charged in connection with the fire.* ♦ **charge sb with sth** *The police have charged him with murder.*
4 [I/T] to attack someone or something by running very fast toward them
5 [I/T] to put electricity into a BATTERY: *The phone won't work if it isn't charged.*

ˈcharge ˌcard noun [C] a CREDIT CARD that you can use only in a particular store

cha•ris•ma /kəˈrɪzmə/ noun [U] a strong personal quality that makes other people like you and feel attracted to you = CHARM —**char•is•mat•ic** /ˌkerɪzˈmætɪk/ adj

char•i•ta•ble /ˈtʃerɪtəb(ə)l/ adj **1** intended to give money and help to people who need it **2** kind to other people and not judging them too severely ≠ UNCHARITABLE

char•i•ty /ˈtʃerəti/ noun ★★
1 [C/U] an organization that gives money and help to people who need it: *a registered charity*
2 [U] money or food that is given to people who need it: *The event* ***raised*** *$59,000* ***for charity.***
3 [U] kind behavior

charm¹ /tʃɑrm/ noun **1** [C/U] an attractive quality: *President Roosevelt's charm and humor* ♦ *The building has kept its traditional charm.* **2** [C] an object that brings luck or has magic powers

charm² /tʃɑrm/ verb [T] to make someone like you, or make them want to do something for you: *He charmed my mother into giving him money.*

charmed /tʃɑrmd/ adj extremely lucky: *a charmed life*

charm•ing /ˈtʃɑrmɪŋ/ adj attractive and pleasant: *a charming man/smile* ♦ *a charming little restaurant*

chart¹ /tʃɑrt/ noun **1** [C] a list, drawing, or GRAPH that shows information **2** [C] a map used for planning a trip by ship or aircraft **3 the charts** [plural] a list of the CDs that people have bought the most copies of in the previous week

chart² /tʃɑrt/ verb [T] **1** to record how something develops and changes: *A team visits every week to chart their progress.* **2** to make a map of an area

char•ter¹ /ˈtʃɑrtər/ noun **1** [C] a document that describes the goals of an organization or the rights of a group of people **2** [C/U] the process of renting a boat, airplane, or bus, or the vehicle that is rented

char•ter² /ˈtʃɑrtər/ verb [T] to rent a boat, airplane, or bus

ˈcharter ˌflight noun [C] an airplane trip that is arranged by a travel company

ˌcharter ˈmember noun [C] *American* one of the people who started a club or organization

chase¹ /tʃeɪs/ verb ★
1 [I/T] to follow someone or something quickly in order to catch them = PURSUE: *The band has often been chased down the street by enthusiastic fans.* ♦ *I* ***chased after*** *the robbers for several blocks.*
2 [T] to follow someone or something quickly in order to make them go away: *We chased the cat out of the house.* ♦ *Suddenly a man came out and* ***chased*** *the kids* ***away.***
3 [T] to try hard to get something such as a job, prize, or money: *Tiger Woods was chasing another European title.*

chase

chase² /tʃeɪs/ noun **1** [C] the action of following someone or something quickly because you want to catch them: *a high-speed car chase* **2** [singular] the act of trying to get something that you want

chasm /ˈkæzəm/ noun [C] **1** a very big difference that separates one person or group from another = GULF **2** a very deep crack in rock or ice

chas•sis /ˈʃæsi/ (plural **chas•sis** /ˈʃæsiz/) noun [C] the frame and wheels of a vehicle

chas•tise /tʃæˈstaɪz/ verb [T] *formal* to criticize or punish someone

chat¹ /tʃæt/ verb [I] ★
1 to talk in a friendly way: *They sat waiting,* ***chatting about*** *their families.*
2 *computing* to exchange messages with someone using computers, in a way that lets you see each other's messages immediately

chat² /tʃæt/ noun [C/U] a friendly conversation

ˈchat ˌroom noun [C] a WEBSITE that people can use for exchanging messages → NEWSGROUP

chat•ter /ˈtʃætər/ verb [I] **1** to talk in a fast informal way about unimportant subjects

C

2 if your teeth chatter, they knock together from fear or cold —**chat•ter** noun [U]

chat•ty /ˈtʃæti/ adj **1** someone who is chatty enjoys talking a lot **2** a chatty writing style is friendly and informal

chauf•feur /ˈʃoʊfər, ʃoʊˈfɜr/ noun [C] someone whose job is to drive a rich or important person around in their car —**chauf•feured** /ˈʃoʊfərd/ adj: *a chauffeured limousine*

chau•vin•ist /ˈʃoʊvɪnɪst/ noun [C] someone who believes that their own country, race, sex, or group is better than any other —**chau•vin•ism** noun [U], **chau•vin•ist•ic** adj

cheap¹ /tʃip/ adj ★★★

1 not expensive	4 unkind/unfair
2 not of good quality	5 without value
3 not spending money	

1 not expensive: *People should have access to cheap, fresh food.*

2 not expensive and not of good quality: *cheap wine*

3 not happy about spending money even on necessary things: *She's so cheap she wouldn't even buy her own mother a birthday card.*

4 a cheap action or remark is unfair or unkind

5 not considered important or valuable: *It happened during the war when life was cheap.*

—**cheap•ly** adv

cheap² /tʃip/ adv at a low price: *I can't believe I managed to get it so cheap.*

cheat¹ /tʃit/ verb ★

1 [I] to behave dishonestly, or to not obey rules: *Kids have always found ways of cheating on tests.*

2 [T] to treat someone dishonestly: *He trusted these people and they cheated him.* ♦ **cheat sb (out) of sth** *He was accused of cheating investors out of their life savings.*

3 [I] to do something that is not correct but makes it easier to succeed: *You can cheat by adding a little flour.*

PHRASAL VERB **ˈcheat ˌon sb 1** to secretly have sex with someone other than your husband, wife, or partner: *He discovered that she'd been cheating on him.* **2** to cheat by not obeying the rules on something: *They say she cheated on her taxes.*

cheat² /tʃit/ noun [C] someone who cheats

check¹ /tʃek/ verb ★★★

1 [I/T] to examine something in order to get information, or to find out whether it is good or correct: *Always check your spelling.* ♦ *You should have your eyes checked regularly.* ♦ *The doctor* ***checked for*** *a pulse.* ♦ **check sth for sth** *Check our website for details of our special offers.*

2 [I/T] to make certain of something, for example by looking at the information again or by asking someone: *I think he's gone home – but let me check.* ♦ *I'll check the dates.* ♦ **+that** *First, check that you have everything you need.* ♦ **+if/whether** *Could you please check whether a package has arrived for me?* ♦ *For further information,* ***check with*** *your local fire department.* ♦ *He* ***checked to see if*** *Gail was still there.*

3 [T] *American* to make a mark ✓ to show that something is correct, that you agree with it, etc: *Check the appropriate boxes on the form.*

4 [T] to give your bags and suitcases to an official at an airport so that they can be put on an airplane: *How many bags do you have to check?*

PHRASAL VERBS **ˈcheck sth aˌgainst sth** to find out whether information is accurate or useful by comparing it with other information

ˌcheck ˈin 1 to arrive at a hotel and give your personal information to the person at the RECEPTION desk: *Have you checked in yet?* **2** to arrive at an airport and show your ticket to an official

ˌcheck ˈinto sth 1 to arrive at a hotel and give your personal information to the person at the RECEPTION desk: *We won't be able to check into the hotel until 3 o'clock.* **2** to try to find out more information about a particular subject: *I'll check into the tours and see how much they cost.*

ˌcheck sth ˈoff to mark things on a list to show that you have dealt with them or that they are correct

ˈcheck ˌon sb/sth to look at someone or something so that you are certain they are safe, satisfactory, etc.: *I sent Michael to check on the kids.*

ˌcheck ˈout 1 to leave a hotel after you have paid the bill: *Joan had already* ***checked out of*** *the hotel.* **2** *American* to pay for your goods before leaving a supermarket or other large store **3** *American* to borrow a book from a library

ˌcheck sb/sth ˈout to examine someone or something in order to be certain that everything is correct, true, or satisfactory: *I've been taking lots of photographs, just to check out the camera.*

ˌcheck ˈover to look at something in order to make certain that it is good or correct: *Check over your writing for spelling mistakes.*

ˌcheck ˈup ˌon sb to find out information about someone, especially secretly: *Ken told me someone had been checking up on me.*

check² /tʃek/ noun ★★★

1 examination of sb/sth	5 sth controlling sth else
2 for paying from bank	6 pattern of squares
3 amount you owe	+ PHRASE
4 mark of agreement	

1 [C] an examination of something that is intended to find out whether it is good or correct: *a* ***check for*** *errors* ♦ *routine* ***checks on*** *the condition of the planes* ♦ *They'll be* ***running a*** *sound* ***check*** *before the concert.*

→ SPOT CHECK

2 [C] one of the pieces of printed paper that your bank gives you so that you can pay for things without using money: ***a check for*** *$50* ♦ *Can I* ***pay by check?***

3 [C] *American* a piece of paper that you are given in a restaurant showing you how much money you owe = BILL: *Could we get the check, please?*

4 [C] *American* a mark ✓ that you put next to something to show that it is correct or that you have dealt with it

5 [C] something that controls another thing and stops it from becoming worse or more extreme: *Economic forces act as* ***a check on*** *political power.*
6 [C/U] a pattern of squares: *a sheet with red and white checks*
PHRASE **keep sb/sth in check** to control someone or something that might cause damage or harm: *Attempts to keep global warming in check are being made by many countries.*

check•book /ˈtʃekˌbʊk/ noun [C] *American* a small book of printed pieces of paper that you can sign and use instead of money

checked /tʃekt/ adj printed or woven in a pattern of squares: *a red-and-blue checked shirt*

check•ered /ˈtʃekərd/ adj with a pattern of squares in two different colors, all of the same size: *a checkered tablecloth*

check•ers /ˈtʃekərz/ noun [U] *American* a game for two people, played on a board with 64 squares, using 24 round pieces *—picture* → C16

ˈcheck-in noun [singular/U] the place that you go to when you arrive at an airport or hotel, or the process that you go through before you go to your flight or room

ˈchecking acˌcount noun [C] *American* a bank account in which you keep money that you can take whenever you want

check•list /ˈtʃekˌlɪst/ noun [C] a list of all the things that you need to do or consider

check•out /ˈtʃekˌaʊt/ noun **1** [C] the place where you pay in a supermarket or other large store **2** [C/U] the time when you have to leave a hotel room

check•point /ˈtʃekˌpɔɪnt/ noun [C] a place where traffic can be stopped by soldiers or police

check•up /ˈtʃekˌʌp/ noun [C] an examination that a doctor or DENTIST does in order to make sure that you are healthy: *a regular dental/physical checkup*

ched•dar /ˈtʃedər/ noun [U] a type of hard yellow cheese

cheek /tʃik/ noun [C] ★ the soft part on each side of your face below your eyes: *Sarah kissed her on the cheek. —picture* → C14

cheek•bone /ˈtʃikˌboʊn/ noun [C] the bone in your cheek

cheer[1] /tʃɪr/ verb [I/T] to give a loud shout of happiness or approval: *The crowd cheered and threw flowers.*
PHRASAL VERBS **ˌcheer sb ˈon** to shout loudly in order to encourage someone
ˌcheer (sb) ˈup to become less sad, or to make someone feel less sad: *I tried to cheer him up, but he just kept staring out the window.*

cheer[2] /tʃɪr/ noun [C] a loud shout of happiness or approval → CHEERS

cheer•ful /ˈtʃɪrf(ə)l/ adj **1** behaving in a happy friendly way: *Stephen was a cheerful, affectionate child.* **2** pleasant or enjoyable, and making you feel happy: *bright cheerful colors* —**cheer•ful•ly** adv, **cheer•ful•ness** noun [U]

cheer•lead•er /ˈtʃɪrˌlidər/ noun [C] one of a group of young women who sing and dance together at a sports event

cheers /tʃɪrz/ interjection **1** used for expressing good wishes before you drink something **2** *British spoken* thank you

cheer•y /ˈtʃɪri/ adj feeling or showing happiness

cheese /tʃiz/ noun [C/U] ★★ a solid food made from milk: *a slice of cheese*

cheese•burg•er /ˈtʃizˌbɜrgər/ noun [C] a BURGER with a piece of cheese on top of the meat

cheese•cake /ˈtʃizˌkeɪk/ noun [C/U] a type of sweet cake made with soft cheese

chees•y /ˈtʃizi/ adj *informal* lacking style or good quality and slightly silly: *cheesy songs*

chee•tah /ˈtʃitə/ noun [C] a large African wild cat that can run extremely fast *—picture* → C12

chef /ʃef/ noun [C] someone whose job is to cook food in a restaurant

chem•i•cal[1] /ˈkemɪk(ə)l/ noun [C] ★★★ a substance used in chemistry, or one produced by a process that involves chemistry: *toxic chemicals* ♦ *the chemical industry*

chem•i•cal[2] /ˈkemɪk(ə)l/ adj involving chemistry, or produced by a method used in chemistry: *chemical processes*

chem•ist /ˈkemɪst/ noun [C] **1** a scientist who studies chemistry **2 chemist** or **chemist's** *British* a DRUGSTORE

chem•is•try /ˈkemɪstri/ noun [U] **1** the scientific study of the structure of substances and the way they react with other substances **2** the chemical structure of something and the reactions that take place in it **3** the emotional relationship between people

che•mo•ther•a•py /ˌkimoʊˈθerəpi/ noun [U] the treatment of cancer using drugs

cheque /tʃek/ the British spelling of **check[2]** 2

cher•ish /ˈtʃerɪʃ/ verb [T] **1** to think that something is very important and to want to keep it: *I cherished my independence.* **2** to take care of someone or something because you love them very much

cher•ry /ˈtʃeri/ noun [C] **1** a small round red or black fruit *—picture* → C10 **2** a tree that produces cherries, or the wood from this tree

chess /tʃes/ noun [U] a game that two people play on a board with black and white squares. The pieces that you use have different shapes and move in different ways. *—picture* → C16

chess•man /ˈtʃesˌmæn/ (plural **chess•men** /ˈtʃesˌmen/) or **chess piece** /ˈtʃes ˌpis/ noun [C] one of the pieces used for playing CHESS *—picture* → C16

chest /tʃest/ noun [C] ★★★
1 the upper front part of your body between your neck and your stomach: *a broad/hairy chest* ♦ *chest pains —picture* → C14
2 a large strong box, used for moving or storing things
PHRASES **chest of drawers** a piece of wooden furniture with several drawers for storing clothes
get something off your chest to talk to someone about something that has been worrying you, so that you feel better about it

chest•nut /ˈtʃesˌnʌt/ noun [C] **1** a large smooth

red-brown nut that you can eat **2 chestnut** or **chestnut tree** a tall tree that produces chestnuts —*picture* → C9

chew /tʃu/ verb [I/T] ★
1 to use your teeth to bite food in your mouth into small pieces: *She chewed her food slowly.*
2 to bite something continuously but not swallow it: *We're not allowed to chew gum in class.* ♦ *The dog was* ***chewing on*** *an old bone.*
PHRASAL VERB ˌ**chew sb ˈout** *American informal* to speak angrily to someone because they have done something wrong

chew·ing gum /ˈtʃuɪŋ ˌɡʌm/ noun [U] a type of candy that you chew for a long time but do not swallow

chew·y /ˈtʃui/ adj chewy food needs to be CHEWED a lot before you can swallow it

chic /ʃik/ adj fashionable and attractive in style

chick /tʃɪk/ noun [C] a baby bird

chick·a·dee /ˈtʃɪkəˌdi/ noun [C] a small black and white North American bird

chick·en¹ /ˈtʃɪkən/ noun ★★
1 [C] a bird that is kept for its eggs and meat —*picture* → C12
2 [U] the meat of a chicken: *fried/roast/grilled chicken*
→ COUNT¹

chick·en² /ˈtʃɪkən/ adj *informal* not brave enough to do something: *I didn't want the other kids to think I was chicken.*

chick·en³ /ˈtʃɪkən/ PHRASAL VERB ˌ**chicken ˈout** *informal* to not do something because you are too frightened

chick·en·pox /ˈtʃɪkənˌpɑks/ noun [U] an infectious disease that most children get once, in which the skin is covered with red spots

chick·pea /ˈtʃɪkˌpi/ noun [C/U] a round yellow-brown seed that can be cooked and eaten

chief¹ /tʃif/ adj ★★
1 main, or most important: *the company's chief competitor* ♦ *Unemployment was the chief cause of poverty during the 1930s.*
2 highest in authority, position, or rank: *the government's chief negotiator at the talks*

chief² /tʃif/ noun [C] **1** the person who is in charge of an organization or department, or who has the main responsibility for something: *the chief of the Red Cross mission in the war zone* **2** the leader of a TRIBE = CHIEFTAIN

ˌ**chief exˈecutive** noun [C] the most senior person in a company or organization who is responsible for running it = CEO

chief·ly /ˈtʃifli/ adv mainly or mostly, but not completely: *He will be remembered chiefly for his years of dedicated service to the school.*

chief·tain /ˈtʃiftən/ noun [C] the leader of a TRIBE

chif·fon /ʃɪˈfɑn, ˈʃɪˌfɑn/ noun [U] very thin transparent cloth made from silk or NYLON

chi·hua·hua /tʃɪˈwɑwə/ noun [C] a very small dog with pointed ears

child /tʃaɪld/ (plural **chil·dren** /ˈtʃɪldrən/) noun [C] ★★★
1 a young person from the time when they are born until they are about 14 years old: *The center has places for 30 children.* ♦ *He can't understand – he's just a child.*
2 someone's son or daughter of any age: *All of our children are grown and married.* ♦ *They're expecting their second child in May.* ♦ ***I was an only child*** (=with no brothers or sisters).

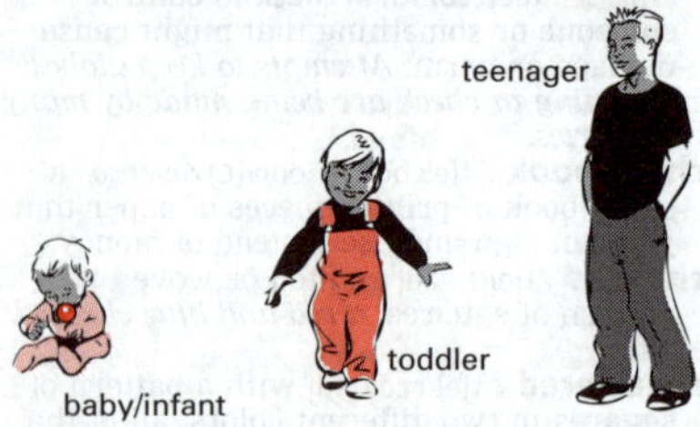

ˈ**child aˌbuse** noun [U] bad treatment of a child by an adult

child·birth /ˈtʃaɪldˌbɜrθ/ noun [U] the process of giving birth to a baby

child·care /ˈtʃaɪldˌker/ noun [U] the job of taking care of children, especially while their parents are working = DAY CARE: *the high cost of childcare*

child·hood /ˈtʃaɪldˌhʊd/ noun [C/U] the time of your life when you are a child: *We spent our childhood in a small town in the mountains.*

child·ish /ˈtʃaɪldɪʃ/ adj **1** behaving in a silly and annoying way, like a small child **2** typical of a child —**child·ish·ly** adv, **child·ish·ness** noun [U]

child·like /ˈtʃaɪldˌlaɪk/ adj similar to the way that a child looks, behaves, or thinks: *childlike excitement*

child·proof /ˈtʃaɪldˌpruf/ adj something that is childproof is designed so that children cannot use it, open it, or hurt themselves on it: *a bottle of pills with a childproof lid*

children the plural of **child**

ˈ**child supˌport** noun [U] money that a parent pays to support a child who does not live with him or her

chil·i /ˈtʃɪli/ (plural **chil·ies**) noun **1** [U] a Mexican meal made from meat, beans, and chilies cooked together **2 chili** or **chili pepper** [C/U] a red or green vegetable with a hot taste

chill¹ /tʃɪl/ verb **1** [I/T] if you chill food or drink, or if it chills, it becomes cold enough to eat or drink **2** [I] *informal* to relax and stop being angry or nervous, or to spend time relaxing: *I'm just going to chill this weekend.*
PHRASAL VERB ˌ**chill ˈout** *informal same as* **chill¹ 2**

chill² /tʃɪl/ noun **1** [singular] a feeling of being cold: *a chill in the air* **2** [C] a feeling of fear: *The cry sent a chill down her spine.* **3** [C] a minor illness like a COLD

chill·ing /ˈtʃɪlɪŋ/ adj making you feel suddenly very frightened or worried: *The chilling truth is that the killers are still out there.* —**chill·ing·ly** adv

chill·y /ˈtʃɪli/ adj **1** cold enough to be unpleasant: *The evenings are getting chilly.* **2** unfriendly

C

chime /tʃaɪm/ verb [I/T] to make a high ringing sound like a bell: *Somewhere a clock chimed midnight.* —**chime** noun [C]

PHRASAL VERB **ˌchime ˈin** to join a conversation by saying something

chim•ney /ˈtʃɪmni/ noun [C] a passage that takes smoke from a fire up through a building and out through the roof —*picture* → C1

chim•pan•zee /ˌtʃɪmpænˈzi/ noun [C] an African APE (=animal like a monkey)

chin /tʃɪn/ noun [C] ★★ the center of the bottom part of your face, below your mouth and above your neck —*picture* → C14

chi•na /ˈtʃaɪnə/ noun [U] plates and cups of good quality

chink /tʃɪŋk/ noun [C] a very small space in a wall or between two things

chi•nos /ˈtʃinoʊz/ noun [plural] pants made from thick strong cotton cloth

chip¹ /tʃɪp/ noun [C] ★★

1 piece of potato/tortilla	5 in games for money
2 in computers	6 potato cooked in oil
3 small piece	+ PHRASES
4 missing piece of sth	

1 *American* a very thin piece of fried potato or TORTILLA: *chips and salsa* ♦ *Would you like some chips with your sandwich?*
2 a very small piece of SILICON that is marked with electronic connections. It is used in computers and other machines =MICROCHIP, SILICON CHIP
3 a small piece of something such as wood or glass that has broken off something: *wood chips*
4 a place on a plate, cup, etc. where a small piece of it has broken off: *The cup had a tiny* ***chip in it.***
5 a small piece of plastic that people use instead of money when they are GAMBLING (=playing games for money)
6 *British* a FRENCH FRY

PHRASES **have a chip on your shoulder** to feel offended and angry whenever people mention a particular subject

when the chips are down *spoken* used for saying what happens when a situation becomes difficult

→ BLUE CHIP

chip² /tʃɪp/ verb [I/T] if something hard chips, or if you chip it, a small piece of it breaks off: *These cups chip easily.*

PHRASAL VERBS **ˌchip (sth) aˈway 1** to gradually make something weaker, smaller, or less effective: *Her comments were beginning to chip away at his self-confidence.*
2 to remove small pieces from something hard by hitting it with a tool: *She was chipping away at the ice with a shovel.*

ˌchip ˈin (sth) *informal* if people chip in, they each give some money to help to pay for something: *The three of us chipped in and bought the boat for Dad.*

chip•munk /ˈtʃɪpˌmʌŋk/ noun [C] a small furry Asian and North American animal with bands of darker color on its back

chi•ro•prac•tor /ˈkaɪrəˌpræktər/ noun [C] someone whose job is to treat illnesses by pressing on bones in the body, especially the SPINE

chirp /tʃɜrp/ verb [I] when a bird or an insect chirps, it makes a short high sound —**chirp** noun [C]

chis•el /ˈtʃɪz(ə)l/ noun [C] a tool with a flat metal blade used for cutting wood or stone

chit•chat /ˈtʃɪtˌtʃæt/ noun [U] *informal* friendly conversation about things that are not very important

chiv•al•ry /ˈʃɪvəlri/ noun [U] polite and kind behavior by men toward women —**chiv•al•rous** /ˈʃɪvəlrəs/ adj

chives /tʃaɪvz/ noun [plural] a plant with long thin leaves that taste like onion

chlo•ri•nat•ed /ˈklɔrɪˌneɪtəd/ adj chlorinated water has had chlorine added to it in order to kill bacteria

chlo•rine /ˈklɔrin/ noun [U] a gas that is used for killing bacteria in water

choc•o•late /ˈtʃɑklət/ noun ★★
1 [U] a sweet brown food that is used for making candy or flavoring other food: *a bar of chocolate* ♦ *chocolate cake*
2 [C] a small piece of candy made from chocolate: *a box of chocolates*
→ HOT CHOCOLATE

choice¹ /tʃɔɪs/ noun ★★★
1 [singular/U] the opportunity or right to choose between different things: *We try to provide greater choice for our customers.* ♦ *Students have* ***a choice between*** *studying French or German.* ♦ *These people* ***have the choice of*** *whether to buy a house or rent one.* ♦ *If you were* ***given the choice****, would you prefer a cat or a dog?* ♦ ***I had no choice*** *– I had to believe what he said.*
2 [C] a decision to choose someone or something: *He wants people to* ***make*** *their* ***own choices.*** ♦ *Our childhood experiences can influence our* ***choice of*** *career.* ♦ *He was facing a difficult* ***choice between*** *staying with his family or working abroad.*
3 [C] a range of things that you can choose from: *The restaurant offers a good* ***choice of*** *dishes.* ♦ *New York has* ***a wide choice*** *of plays and movies.*
4 [C] someone or something that you choose: *Disney World is a popular choice for a family vacation.* ♦ *I think Yale University would be my* ***first choice.***

PHRASE **by choice** if you do something by choice, you do it because you want to and not because you have to

choice² /tʃɔɪs/ adj *formal* of very high quality: *the choicest ingredients*

choir /kwaɪr/ noun [C] a group of singers who perform together, for example in a church or school: *the church/school choir*

choke¹ /tʃoʊk/ verb **1** [I/T] if you choke, or if something chokes you, you cannot breathe because there is not enough air, or because something is blocking your throat: *Joe took a bite of the steak and started to choke.* ♦ *Ruth almost choked on a mouthful of cake.*
2 [T] to squeeze someone's neck so that they cannot breathe **3** [I] *informal* to fail to achieve something because you lose confidence

PHRASAL VERBS **ˌchoke sth ˈback** to stop yourself from showing a feeling or emotion: *Ms. Ross choked back tears as she described what had happened.*

ˌchoke (sb) ˈup if someone chokes up, or if

something chokes them up, they cannot speak because they are starting to cry

choke² /tʃoʊk/ noun [C] the part of a vehicle that helps it to start by reducing the amount of air going into the engine —*picture* → C6

C

choked up /ˌtʃoʊkt ˈʌp/ adj *informal* feeling so much emotion that it is difficult to speak

chol•er•a /ˈkɑlərə/ noun [U] a serious disease that affects your stomach and INTESTINES

cho•les•ter•ol /kəˈlestərɑl/ noun [U] a substance in your blood that can cause heart disease if you have too much of it

chomp /tʃɑmp/ verb [I/T] *informal* to bite something several times in a noisy way

choose /tʃuz/ (past tense **chose** /tʃoʊz/; past participle **cho•sen** /ˈtʃoʊz(ə)n/) verb [I/T] ★★★
1 to decide which person or thing you want from a number of people or things: *Do you feel that you chose the wrong career?* ♦ *There is a huge range of vacations **to choose from**.* ♦ *She is forced to **choose between** her husband and her parents.* ♦ **+which/where/whether etc.** *How do you choose which car you are going to buy?* ♦ **choose sb/sth out of sb/sth** *The winner was chosen out of thousands who sent in photos.*
2 to decide to do something: **choose to do sth** *More and more people are choosing to live alone.*
PHRASE **choose your words (carefully)** to think carefully about what you are saying

choos•y /ˈtʃuzi/ adj someone who is choosy has definite ideas about what they like and is not willing to accept other things

chop¹ /tʃɑp/ verb [T] to cut something such as food or wood into pieces: *Chop the meat into small cubes.* —*picture* → C2
PHRASAL VERBS ˌ**chop sth** ˈ**down** to make a tree or tall plant fall down by cutting through it
ˌ**chop sth** ˈ**off** to remove something by cutting
ˌ**chop sth** ˈ**up** *same as* **chop¹**: *Sarah was busy chopping up onions.*

chop² /tʃɑp/ noun [C] **1** a small piece of meat with a bone in it: *lamb/pork chops* **2** an act of hitting someone or something hard with the side of your hand or a sharp tool

chop•per /ˈtʃɑpər/ noun [C] *informal* a helicopter

chop•py /ˈtʃɑpi/ adj choppy water has a lot of waves because the wind is blowing across it

chop•sticks /ˈtʃɑpˌstɪks/ noun [plural] a pair of thin sticks used in East Asian cultures for eating food

cho•ral /ˈkɔrəl/ adj sung by a CHOIR: *choral music/singing*

chord /kɔrd/ noun [C] two or more musical notes played together
PHRASE **strike/touch a chord (with sb)** to produce an emotion such as sympathy in someone

chore /tʃɔr/ noun [C] an ordinary, boring, or unpleasant job that must be done: *You can go play after you've done your chores.*

cho•re•og•raph•y /ˌkɔriˈɑgrəfi/ noun [U] the art of planning the movements of dancers, or the steps that the dancers perform —**cho•re•o•graph•er** noun [C], **cho•re•o•graph** /ˈkɔriəˌgræf/ verb [T]

cho•rus /ˈkɔrəs/ noun [C] **1** the part of a song that is repeated several times **2** a large group of people who sing together **3** a piece of music that is sung by a large group of people: *the Prisoners' Chorus from* Fidelio **4** an opinion that several people express at the same time: *a chorus of disapproval*

chose the past tense of **choose**

chosen the past participle of **choose**

Christ /kraɪst/ Jesus Christ, whose ideas the Christian religion is based on

chris•ten /ˈkrɪs(ə)n/ verb [T] **1** to BAPTIZE a baby and officially give it a name **2** to give a name to someone or something

chris•ten•ing /ˈkrɪs(ə)nɪŋ/ noun [C] a Christian religious ceremony during which a baby is BAPTIZED and is officially given a name = BAPTISM

Chris•tian /ˈkrɪstʃ(ə)n/ noun [C] someone whose religion is Christianity —**Chris•tian** adj

Chris•ti•an•i•ty /ˌkrɪstʃiˈænəti, ˌkrɪstiˈænəti/ noun [U] the religion that is based on the ideas of Jesus Christ

Christ•mas /ˈkrɪsməs/ noun [C/U] ★★★
1 December 25, celebrated by Christians as the day that Jesus Christ was born: *Did you get a lot of Christmas presents this year?*
2 the period before and after December 25: *We spent Christmas in the Bahamas last year.*

ˈ**Christmas** ˌ**card** noun [C] a card that you send to your friends and family at Christmas

ˌ**Christmas** ˈ**carol** noun [C] a song that people sing at Christmas

ˌ**Christmas** ˈ**Day** noun [C/U] December 25, celebrated by Christians as the day that Jesus Christ was born

ˌ**Christmas** ˈ**Eve** noun [C/U] the day or evening before Christmas Day

Christ•mas•time /ˈkrɪsməsˌtaɪm/ noun [U] the period of time around Christmas

ˈ**Christmas** ˌ**tree** noun [C] a tree that people cover with lights and other decorations at Christmas

chrome /kroʊm/ noun [U] a hard metal substance used for covering other metals to make them shiny

chro•mo•some /ˈkroʊməˌsoʊm/ noun [C] one of the parts of all living cells that contains genes

chron•ic /ˈkrɑnɪk/ adj **1** a chronic illness or pain is serious and lasts for a long time **2** a chronic problem is always happening and is very difficult to solve: *chronic energy shortages*

chron•i•cle /ˈkrɑnɪk(ə)l/ noun [C] a record of events that happened in the past, in the order in which they happened —**chron•i•cle** verb [T]

chron•o•log•i•cal /ˌkrɑnəˈlɑdʒɪk(ə)l/ adj arranged or described in the order in which events happened —**chron•o•log•i•cal•ly** /ˌkrɑnəˈlɑdʒɪkli/ adv

chry•san•the•mum /krɪˈsænθəməm, krɪˈzænθəməm/ noun [C] a plant with large round brightly colored flowers —*picture* → C9

chub•by /ˈtʃʌbi/ adj *informal* slightly fat

chuck /tʃʌk/ verb [T] *informal* **1** to throw

something **2** to get rid of something that you do not want

PHRASAL VERB ˌ**chuck sth ˈout** *informal same as* **chuck** 2

chuck•le /ˈtʃʌk(ə)l/ verb [I] to laugh quietly —**chuck•le** noun [C]

chug /tʃʌg/ verb [I] if a vehicle chugs, it moves slowly making a series of low sounds

chunk /tʃʌŋk/ noun [C] **1** a large thick piece of something: *chunks of meat* **2** a large amount or part of something

chunk•y /ˈtʃʌŋki/ adj thick and square in shape

church /tʃɜrtʃ/ noun ★★★

1 [C/U] a building that Christians go to in order to worship: *the church choir ♦ She doesn't go to church very often these days.*

2 [C] a group of Christian churches with its own particular beliefs and structures: *the Roman Catholic Church*

church•go•er /ˈtʃɜrtʃˌgoʊr/ noun [C] someone who goes to church regularly

churl•ish /ˈtʃɜrlɪʃ/ adj rude and unfriendly

churn[1] /tʃɜrn/ verb **1** [I/T] if a liquid churns, or if something churns it, it moves around violently **2** [I] if your stomach churns, you feel sick **3** [T] to mix milk or cream in a special container in order to make butter

PHRASAL VERBS ˌ**churn sth ˈout** to produce something in large quantities quickly and often carelessly

ˌ**churn sth ˈup** *same as* **churn**[1] 1

churn[2] /tʃɜrn/ noun [C] a container in which butter is made

chute /ʃut/ noun [C] a tube or narrow open structure that people or things slide down

CIA, the /ˌsi aɪ ˈeɪ/ the Central Intelligence Agency: a U.S. government organization that collects secret information about other countries and protects secret information about the U.S. → FBI

ci•der /ˈsaɪdər/ noun [U] **1** *American* a drink made from apples **2** alcoholic cider

ci•gar /sɪˈgɑr/ noun [C] a thick tube of dried tobacco leaves that people smoke

cig•a•rette /ˌsɪgəˈret, ˈsɪgəˌret/ noun [C] ★★ a narrow paper tube containing tobacco that people smoke: *a pack of cigarettes*

ci•lan•tro /sɪˈlæntroʊ/ noun [U] *American* the leaves of the CORIANDER plant

cin•der /ˈsɪndər/ noun [C] a small piece of something that has been burned almost completely

ˈ**cinder ˌblock** noun [C] *American* a large light brick made from CEMENT and cinders

Cin•der•el•la sto•ry /ˌsɪndəˈrelə ˌstɔri/ noun [C] a situation in which someone or something with good qualities is treated badly or ignored

cin•e•ma /ˈsɪnəmə/ noun [C] a MOVIE THEATER

cin•e•mat•ic /ˌsɪnəˈmætɪk/ adj relating to movies

cin•na•mon /ˈsɪnəmən/ noun [U] a brown powder or small stick used for giving a special taste to food

cir•ca /ˈsɜrkə/ preposition *formal* used before a date for showing that it is not exact

cir•cle[1] /ˈsɜrk(ə)l/ noun [C] ★★★

1 a curved line that creates a round enclosed space and is the same distance from the center at every point —*picture* → C8

2 a group of people or things arranged in a circle: *a circle of stones*

3 a group of people who know one another or are interested in the same things: *international financial circles ♦ They have a large circle of friends.*

PHRASES **come/go full circle** if a situation comes or goes full circle, it becomes the same again as it was at the beginning

go around in circles to do something for a long time without achieving any results because you always return to the same problem

cir•cle[2] /ˈsɜrk(ə)l/ verb **1** [I/T] to move in a circle, or to move something in a circle **2** [T] to draw a circle around something

cir•cuit /ˈsɜrkɪt/ noun [C] **1** the complete path around which an electric current flows → SHORT CIRCUIT **2** a series of places that someone regularly goes to: *He is a performer on the New York comedy-club circuit.* **3** a track around which cars, bicycles, etc. race

ˈ**circuit ˌboard** noun [C] a board with electrical connections or computer chips on it, fitted inside a piece of electronic equipment

ˈ**circuit ˌbreaker** noun [C] a piece of equipment that is designed to stop an electric current automatically if it becomes dangerous

ˈ**circuit ˌcourt** noun [C] a court of law that deals with local cases

ˈ**circuit ˌjudge** noun [C] a judge who visits courts of law in an area regularly in order to deal with local cases

cir•cu•lar[1] /ˈsɜrkjələr/ adj **1** in the shape of a circle, or moving in a circle **2** a circular argument or theory does not mean anything because it consists of a series of causes and effects that lead you back to the original cause

cir•cu•lar[2] /ˈsɜrkjələr/ noun [C] a document or advertisement that is sent to a lot of people at the same time

cir•cu•late /ˈsɜrkjəˌleɪt/ verb **1** [I/T] to move around continuously inside a system or area, or to make something do this: *a machine designed to circulate warm air* **2** [I] if information or ideas circulate, more and more people start to know about them **3** [T] to send something to all the people in a group **4** [I] to move around at a party, talking to different people

cir•cu•la•tion /ˌsɜrkjəˈleɪʃ(ə)n/ noun **1** [U] the movement of blood around your body **2** [U] the continuous movement of liquid, air, etc. inside a system or area **3** [singular] the number of copies of a newspaper or magazine that are sold each day, week, etc. **4** [U] the process by which something such as information passes from one person to another

cir•cum•cise /ˈsɜrkəmˌsaɪz/ verb [T] to remove the skin at the end of a boy's PENIS, or to remove part of a girl's sex organs —**cir•cum•ci•sion** /ˌsɜrkəmˈsɪʒ(ə)n/ noun [C/U]

cir•cum•fer•ence /sərˈkʌmf(ə)rəns/ noun [C/U] the distance measured around the edge of a circle or a round object —*picture* → C8

cir•cum•flex /ˈsɜrkəmˌfleks/ noun [C] the symbol ^ that is written above a vowel in some languages → ACUTE 4, GRAVE[3]

cir·cum·stance /ˈsɜrkəmstəns/ noun ★★

1 [C] the facts or conditions that affect a situation: *The circumstances of this case are unusual.* ♦ *It's amazing that they did so well* ***under the circumstances*** (=because the situation was difficult or unusual).

2 [plural] the conditions in which you live, especially how much money you have: *It is very important to make a will, whatever your circumstances.*

3 [U] *formal* events and situations that cannot be controlled

PHRASE **under no circumstances** used for emphasizing that you mean "never": *Under no circumstances will I give you any more money.*

cir·cum·stan·tial /ˌsɜrkəmˈstænʃ(ə)l/ adj *legal* circumstantial evidence makes it seem likely that something is true but does not prove it

cir·cum·vent /ˌsɜrkəmˈvent, ˈsɜrkəmˌvent/ verb [T] *formal* to find a clever way of avoiding a rule or law

cir·cus /ˈsɜrkəs/ noun **1** [C] a group of people who travel from place to place and entertain people by performing tricks

2 [singular] a situation in which there is too much excitement and uncontrolled activity

cis·tern /ˈsɪstərn/ noun [C] a large container for holding water

ci·ta·tion /saɪˈteɪʃ(ə)n/ noun [C] **1** *American* an official statement ordering someone to pay money or appear in a court of law because they did something illegal **2** an official statement praising someone for something that they have done

cite /saɪt/ verb [T] **1** to mention something as an example, explanation, or proof **2** *American* to officially order someone to pay money or appear in a court of law because they did something illegal **3** to officially mention someone in a legal case **4** to officially praise someone for something that they have done

cit·i·zen /ˈsɪtɪz(ə)n/ noun [C] ★★

1 someone who has the right to live permanently in a particular country: *She married an American and became a U.S. citizen.*

2 someone who lives in a particular town or city: *the citizens of San Diego*

cit·i·zen·ship /ˈsɪtɪz(ə)nʃɪp/ noun [U] the legal right to be a citizen of a particular country

cit·rus fruit /ˈsɪtrəs ˌfrut/ noun [C/U] a fruit such as a lemon or orange

cit·y /ˈsɪti/ noun [C] ★★★

1 a large important town: *an industrial city* ♦ *Tokyo is Japan's* ***capital city*** (=most important city).

2 the institutions of a city: *The city has agreed to pay for the rebuilding.* ♦ *the city hospital*

ˌcity ˈhall noun [C/U] the officials who manage a city, or the building where they work

cit·y·wide /ˈsɪtiˌwaɪd/ adj involving the whole of a city

civ·ic /ˈsɪvɪk/ adj relating to a town or city

civ·il /ˈsɪvɪl/ adj ★★★

1 polite	4 of state not religion
2 private not criminal	5 not military
3 involving citizens	

1 polite, but not friendly: *He could barely force himself to be civil to them.*

2 relating to private legal disagreements between people, rather than to criminal law: *civil court*

3 involving protests or fighting by the people of a country: *civil disturbances*

4 done by the state, rather than by religious authorities: *We were married in a civil ceremony.*

5 involving ordinary people, not the armed forces: *civil employees*

ˌcivil deˈfense noun **1** [U] the organization and training of ordinary people to help their country's military during a war **2 civil defenses** [plural] the preparations that a country makes to prepare for an attack by an enemy

ˌcivil engiˈneering noun [U] the job of designing and building roads, bridges, etc. —**civil engiˈneer** noun [C]

ci·vil·ian /sɪˈvɪljən/ noun [C] someone who does not belong to the military or the police —**ci·vil·ian** adj

civ·i·li·za·tion /ˌsɪvɪlɪˈzeɪʃ(ə)n/ noun **1** [C/U] a society that has developed its own culture and institutions **2** [U] *often humorous* a place such as a large city where modern things make life easy

civ·i·lize /ˈsɪvɪˌlaɪz/ verb [T] **1** to make someone behave in a more polite and reasonable way **2** *old-fashioned* to help a society to develop its culture and institutions

civ·i·lized /ˈsɪvɪˌlaɪzd/ adj **1** a civilized country or society has developed an advanced culture and advanced institutions **2** polite and reasonable: *Let's discuss this in a civilized way.* **3** pleasant and comfortable

ˌcivil ˈlaw noun [U] the part of law that deals with disagreements between people, rather than with crime

ˌcivil ˈliberties noun [plural] the basic freedom that all citizens have to do or say what they want

ˌcivil ˈrights noun [plural] the basic rights that all people in a society have, for example the right to be treated fairly by the law

ˌcivil ˈservant noun [C] someone who works for a government department

ˌcivil ˈservice, the noun [singular] a country's government departments and the people who work in them

ˌcivil ˈwar noun [C/U] a war that is fought between different groups of people within the same country

cl abbrev centiliter

clad /klæd/ adj wearing a particular type of clothing

claim[1] /kleɪm/ verb ★★★

1 [T] to say that something is true, even though there is no definite proof: **+(that)** *He claims he is innocent.* ♦ **claim to do sth** *The organization claims to represent more than 20,000 firms.*

2 [I/T] to ask for something that belongs to you, or to ask for something that you have a right to: *The back of the form tells you how to claim your refund.* ♦ *Has anyone claimed the wallet I turned in yesterday?* ♦ *She claimed political asylum in 1986.*

3 [T] if war, disease, or an accident claims

someone's life, they die as a result of it: *The flood has now claimed over 500 lives.*
4 [T] to need something such as your attention or time: *Several more urgent matters were claiming her attention.*
PHRASE **claim credit/responsibility/victory etc.** to say that you have achieved or done something: *I can't claim all the credit for our success.*

claim² /kleɪm/ noun [C] ★★★
1 a statement that something is true but with no definite proof: ***claims of bullying*** ♦ **+that** *I don't believe his claim that he fought in Vietnam.*
2 an official request for something that you believe you have a right to: *an insurance claim* ♦ ***a claim for asylum***
3 a legal or moral right to something: *She has no **claim on** her husband's estate.*
4 claim on sth a right to someone's attention, love, etc.: *There are so many competing claims on our attention these days.*
PHRASE **claim to fame** *often humorous* the thing that makes a person or place famous or interesting

claim·ant /ˈkleɪmənt/ noun [C] **1** someone who makes an official request for money **2** someone who says that they have a right to something

clair·voy·ant /klerˈvɔɪənt/ noun [C] someone who claims to know what will happen in the future —**clair·voy·ant** adj

clam /klæm/ noun [C] a small sea animal with a hard shell. It can be eaten.

clam·ber /ˈklæmbər/ verb [I] to climb something with difficulty, using your hands and feet = SCRAMBLE

clam·my /ˈklæmi/ adj cold and wet in an unpleasant way

clam·or¹ /ˈklæmər/ noun [singular/U] **1** a very loud noise made by a lot of people or things **2** urgent requests from a lot of people who want something

clam·or² /ˈklæmər/ verb [I] to say loudly that you must have something: *children clamoring for attention*

clamp¹ /klæmp/ verb [T] **1** to put or hold something firmly in position **2** to hold two things together using a clamp
PHRASAL VERB ˌ**clamp ˈdown** to make a determined attempt to stop people from doing something bad or illegal: *Police are clamping down on local drug dealers.*

clamp² /klæmp/ noun [C] a tool used for holding two things together firmly

clamp·down /ˈklæmpˌdaʊn/ noun [C] a determined attempt by someone in authority to stop people from doing something bad or illegal

clan /klæn/ noun [C] a large group of families that are related to each other

clan·des·tine /klænˈdestɪn, ˈklændəˌstin/ adj secret and often illegal

clang /klæŋ/ verb [I/T] if something made of metal clangs, it makes a loud sound —**clang** noun [C]

clank /klæŋk/ verb [I/T] if a heavy metal object clanks, it makes a short loud sound —**clank** noun [C]

clap¹ /klæp/ verb **1** [I/T] to hit your hands together many times as a way of showing that you liked something, or in order to get attention: *At the end of the speech everyone clapped.* **2** [T] to suddenly put something somewhere: *The boy clapped his hands over his ears.* —**clap·ping** noun [U]

clap² /klæp/ noun [C] a sudden loud sound: *a clap of thunder*

clar·i·fi·ca·tion /ˌklerɪfɪˈkeɪʃ(ə)n/ noun [U] *formal* an explanation that makes something easier to understand

clar·i·fy /ˈklerɪˌfaɪ/ verb [T] *formal* to explain something more clearly so that it is easier to understand

clar·i·net /ˌklerɪˈnet/ noun [C] a musical instrument consisting of a long black tube that you play by blowing into it —*picture* → WOODWIND —**clar·i·net·ist** noun [C]

clar·i·ty /ˈklerəti/ noun [U] **1** the ability to think clearly or understand things clearly **2** the quality of being easy to see, hear, or understand

clash¹ /klæʃ/ noun [C] **1** a very angry argument or fight between two people or groups: *violent clashes between police and protesters* **2** a situation in which two people or things are so different that they cannot exist or work together: *a personality clash between a student and a teacher* **3** a loud sound that is made when two metal objects hit each other **4** an annoying situation in which two events happen at the same time

clash² /klæʃ/ verb [I] **1** if two groups of people clash, they suddenly start fighting with each other **2** if colors or patterns clash, they do not look good together **3** if two events clash, they happen at the same time

clasp¹ /klæsp/ noun [C] a metal object used for fastening something such as a bag or a piece of jewelry

clasp² /klæsp/ verb [T] to hold someone or something tightly

class¹ /klæs/ noun ★★★

1 group of students	5 standard of service
2 teaching period	6 type of thing/person
3 series of classes	7 natural ability
4 group in society	

1 [C] a group of students who are taught together: *Do you like the other kids in your class?*
2 [C/U] a period of time during which a group of students is taught together: *We had to write an essay in class.* ♦ *I have classes all afternoon.*
3 [C] a series of classes in a particular subject: *I go to my **art class** on Mondays.*
4 [C/U] one of the groups into which people in a society are divided according to education, income, etc.: *tax cuts for the middle class* ♦ *the relationship between social class and your level of education*
5 [C] one of the standards of service that are available to someone traveling by train, airplane, etc.: *The man was sitting in first class.*
6 [C] a group of things, animals, or people with similar features or qualities: *The race has competitions for ten classes of boat.*
7 [U] *informal* impressive natural style, social ability, or skill: *Hilary has too much class to say something like that.*

class² /klæs/ verb [T] to include someone or something in a particular group: *She is now classed as a professional athlete.*

ˌclass ˈact noun [C] *informal* a person or group with great style and skill

C

clas•sic¹ /ˈklæsɪk/ adj **1** a classic song, book, play, etc. is very good and has been popular for a long time **2** a classic style of clothes, furniture, etc. is beautiful in a very simple way **3** completely typical: *a classic example of poor management*

clas•sic² /ˈklæsɪk/ noun [C] a song, book, play, etc. that is very good and has been popular for a long time → CLASSICS

clas•si•cal /ˈklæsɪk(ə)l/ adj **1** following the original or traditional standard for something: *classical economics* **2** relating to Ancient Greece and Rome: *classical mythology* **3** relating to CLASSICAL MUSIC: *classical composers* —**clas•sic•al•ly** /ˈklæsɪkli/ adv

ˌclassical ˈmusic noun [U] serious music that is played on instruments such as the piano and the VIOLIN

clas•sics /ˈklæsɪks/ noun [U] the study of the language, literature, and culture of Ancient Greece and Rome

clas•si•fi•ca•tion /ˌklæsɪfɪˈkeɪʃ(ə)n/ noun [C/U] the process of putting people or things into particular groups according to the features that they have, or one of these groups

clas•si•fied /ˈklæsɪˌfaɪd/ adj classified information is officially secret and can only be known by a few government officials or military officials

ˌclassified ˈad noun [C] a short advertisement that you put in a newspaper, for example so that you can sell something = WANT AD

clas•si•fy /ˈklæsɪˌfaɪ/ verb [T] to put people or things into groups according to the features that they have = CATEGORIZE: *Families were classified according to their incomes.*

class•less /ˈklæsləs/ adj not divided into social classes

class•mate /ˈklæsˌmeɪt/ noun [C] someone who is in your class at school

class•room /ˈklæsˌrum/ noun [C] ★★ a room where you have classes in a school

class•y /ˈklæsi/ adj *informal* expensive, fashionable, and very good: *a classy hotel*

clat•ter /ˈklætər/ verb [I] if a hard object clatters, it makes a lot of loud short noises as it hits something hard —**clat•ter** noun [singular]

clause /klɔz/ noun [C] ★

1 a part of a legal document or law

2 *linguistics* a group of words that includes a verb and a SUBJECT

claus•tro•pho•bi•a /ˌklɔstrəˈfoʊbiə/ noun [U] fear of being in a small space

claus•tro•pho•bic /ˌklɔstrəˈfoʊbɪk/ adj **1** feeling afraid because you are in a small space **2** a claustrophobic place makes you uncomfortable because it is small or crowded

claw¹ /klɔ/ noun [C] one of the sharp curved nails that some birds and animals have on their feet

claw² /klɔ/ verb [I/T] to attack someone or damage something using claws

clay /kleɪ/ noun [U] **1** a type of heavy wet dirt used for making cups, plates, and other objects **2** *American* a soft colored substance that children use for making shapes and models

clean¹ /klin/ adj ★★★

1 not dirty or polluted: *Go and put on a clean shirt.* ♦ *the clean country air* ♦ *Tom had scrubbed the floor clean.*

2 a clean piece of paper does not have anything written on it

3 not illegal or unfair, or not involved in anything illegal or unfair: *It was a good clean fight.*

4 clean language or humor does not offend people because it does not involve sex or swearing

PHRASES **a clean slate** a situation in which everything bad that you have done in the past has been forgiven or forgotten: *We have the chance to start over, with a clean slate.*

come clean to tell the truth about something that you have kept secret

→ SQUEAKY CLEAN

clean² /klin/ verb ★★★

1 [T] to remove the dirt from something: *Paul is cleaning his car.*

2 [I/T] to remove the dirt and dust in a house: *We've cleaned the house from top to bottom.* ♦ *I was cleaning all morning.*

PHRASAL VERBS **ˌclean sth ˈout 1** to make a place clean or neat by removing things that are not wanted and by getting rid of dirt: *They spent the day cleaning out the garage.* **2** *informal* to use all of your money: *This will clean me out. I'll have to sell the house.*

ˌclean (sth) ˈup 1 to make a place completely clean and neat: *Let's start getting this place cleaned up.* **2** to wash someone who is dirty: *I cleaned myself up and got ready for dinner.*

ˌclean sth ˈup to stop bad or criminal behavior in a place or activity: *Does the government have plans to clean up the banking system?*

ˌclean ˈup ˌafter sb to clean a place after someone has made it dirty or messy: *Residents have been told to clean up after their dogs.*

Other ways of saying clean

- **brush** to clean something by rubbing it with a brush
- **cleanse** (*formal*) to clean your skin thoroughly using a special liquid or cream
- **dust** to remove dust from furniture and other surfaces using a soft cloth
- **scrub** to clean something by rubbing it hard with a brush and soap and water
- **sweep** to clean a floor using a brush with a long handle
- **wash** to clean something using water and soap
- **wipe** to clean a surface such as a table using a cloth that is slightly wet

clean³ /klin/ adv *informal* used for emphasizing that something happens completely: *The blast blew the windows clean out of the building.*

ˌclean-ˈcut adj a clean-cut man looks clean and neat

clean•er /ˈklinər/ noun **1** [C] a chemical substance used for cleaning things **2** the cleaner's [singular] a place where you can get clothes DRY-CLEANED (=cleaned with chemicals)=DRY CLEANER'S

clean·ing /ˈklinɪŋ/ noun [U] the activity or job of making rooms in a building clean

clean·li·ness /ˈklenlinəs/ noun [U] the process of keeping yourself and your possessions clean

clean·ly /ˈklinli/ adv **1** with one smooth movement **2** without creating a lot of mess or pollution

cleanse /klenz/ verb [T] to clean your skin thoroughly → ETHNIC CLEANSING

cleans·er /ˈklenzər/ noun [C/U] a special substance that you use for cleaning your face

ˌclean-ˈshaven adj a clean-shaven man does not have a BEARD or MUSTACHE

clean·up /ˈklinʌp/ noun [C/U] the process of cleaning a place thoroughly

clear¹ /klɪr/ adj ★★★

1 easy to understand	5 easy to see/hear
2 obvious	6 not blocked
3 transparent	7 not confused
4 without clouds	8 without guilty feelings

1 easy to understand: *Clear instructions are provided.* ♦ *Let me **make this clear** – I will not help you again!*

2 obvious and certain to be true: *There was clear evidence that showed he was at the scene of the crime.* ♦ **+(that)** *It was very clear that something was worrying him.* ♦ **it is not clear whether** *It is not clear whether the firemen are still alive.*

3 transparent: *a clear glass bottle*

4 if the sky is clear, there are no clouds

5 easy to see or hear: *"I did it," she said in a clear voice.* ♦ *The picture was clear and sharp.*

6 if a surface, road, or passage is clear, there is nothing that blocks it: *a clear view of the mountains* ♦ *All the main roads are **clear of** snow.*

7 not confused: *Are you **clear about** the purpose of the meeting?*

8 not affected by guilty feelings: *She had done her duty, and her **conscience was clear**.*

→ COAST¹, CRYSTAL CLEAR

Word family: clear

*Words in the same family as **clear***

- **clarity** *n*
- **clearly** *adv*
- **unclear** *adj*

clear² /klɪr/ verb ★★★

1 empty a place	6 pass without touching
2 remove sth	7 accept check
3 prove sb not guilty	8 start to disappear
4 weather: improve	+ PHRASES
5 give/get permission	+ PHRASAL VERBS

1 [T] to remove people or things from a place, or to become empty when people leave or things are removed: *Millions of acres of tropical forest have been cleared.* ♦ *The room cleared quickly after the speech.*

2 [T] to remove something that is blocking a place: *The police cleared a path through to the front of the building.*

3 [T] to prove officially that someone did not do something wrong: *Yesterday the two men **were cleared of** murder.*

4 [I] if the sky or the weather clears, it becomes brighter with no clouds or rain

5 [T] to give or obtain permission for something to happen: *You'll have to **clear** this project **with** the head office.*

6 [T] to go over, under, or past an object without touching it: *The horse cleared the fence.*

7 [I/T] if a check clears, or if a bank clears it, the bank allows the money to be used

8 [I] if something such as smoke clears, it starts to disappear

PHRASES **clear the air** to discuss a problem or difficult situation with someone in order to make it better

clear your throat to make a noise in your throat before you speak, so that you can speak without any difficulty

PHRASAL VERBS **ˌclear ˈup** if the weather clears up, the clouds or rain go away

ˌclear sth ˈup to solve a problem or a mystery

clear³ /klɪr/ adv /klɪr/ completely away from something: *Stan grabbed her hands and pulled her clear.*

PHRASE **keep/stay/steer clear of** to avoid someone or something unpleasant or dangerous: *No one mentioned the divorce, so Lisa decided to steer clear of that subject.*

clear⁴ /klɪr/ noun **in the clear** no longer believed to be guilty of something bad or illegal

clear·ance /ˈklɪrəns/ noun [U] **1** official permission to do something: **clearance to do sth** *The pilot has just received clearance to land.* **2** an amount of space between two things that keeps them from touching each other

ˌclear-ˈcut adj definite and easy to understand or make a decision about

clear·ing /ˈklɪrɪŋ/ noun [C] an area in a forest where there are no trees or bushes

clear·ly /ˈklɪrli/ adv ★★★

1 in a way that people can easily see, hear, or understand: *His contract clearly states that he cannot leave before next year.* ♦ *The road signs were clearly visible.*

2 in a way that is sensible and not confused: *You can't think clearly on four hours' sleep.*

3 used for emphasizing that what you are saying is true=OBVIOUSLY: *Both companies clearly like to do things their own way.*

cleav·age /ˈklivɪdʒ/ noun [C] the space between a woman's breasts

clef /klef/ noun [C] a symbol written at the beginning of a line of music to show the PITCH of the notes

clem·en·cy /ˈklemənsi/ noun [U] *formal* a decision not to punish someone severely, made by someone in a position of authority

clench /klentʃ/ verb **clench your teeth/jaw/fist** to press your teeth or fingers together tightly because you are angry or upset

cler·gy /ˈklɜrdʒi/ noun [plural] priests and other people who lead religious services

cler·ic /ˈklerɪk/ noun [C] *formal* a member of the clergy

cler·i·cal /ˈklerɪk(ə)l/ adj **1** connected with the ordinary work that people do in offices **2** relating to priests

clerk /klɜrk/ noun [C] **1** *American* someone whose job is to serve people in a store **2** *American* someone whose job is to welcome guests to a hotel and provide them with information **3** someone whose job is to take care of the documents in an office

clev•er /ˈklevər/ adj **1** good at achieving what you want, especially by using unusual or slightly dishonest methods **2** a clever tool or idea is effective because it was designed in an intelligent way —**clev•er•ly** adv

cli•ché /kliˈʃeɪ, ˈkliʃeɪ/ noun [C] a phrase or idea that is boring because people use it a lot and it is no longer original —**cli•chéd** adj

click¹ /klɪk/ verb **1** [I/T] to make a short high sound like the sound of a switch, or to make an object make this sound: *The cameras continued clicking as they drove away.* ♦ *The young soldier clicked his heels and saluted.* **2** [I/T] *computing* to make a computer do something by pressing a button on the mouse: *To send the message, click on the "send" button.* **3** [I] *informal* if something clicks, you suddenly understand or realize it **4** [I] *informal* if two people click, they realize immediately that they like each other and understand each other

click² /klɪk/ noun [C] **1** a short sound like the sound of a switch **2** *computing* the action of making a computer do something by pressing a button on the mouse

cli•ent /ˈklaɪənt/ noun [C] someone who uses the services of a professional person such as a lawyer, or of a business or organization that provides help or advice: *Our clients are not all wealthy people.*

cli•en•tele /ˌklaɪənˈtel/ noun [singular] the customers of a store, hotel, or restaurant

cliff /klɪf/ noun [C] the steep side of an area of high land

cliff•hang•er /ˈklɪfˌhæŋər/ noun [C] *informal* an exciting end to a part of a book or television show

cli•mac•tic /klaɪˈmæktɪk/ adj a climactic event or moment is the most exciting or important one in a series

cli•mate /ˈklaɪmət/ noun ★★
1 [C/U] the climate of a country or region is the type of weather it has: *Mexico is renowned for its hot climate and spicy food.* **2** [C] the general situation or attitudes that people have at a particular time: *We are unable to increase wages in the current economic climate.* ♦ *a climate of fear and mistrust*

cli•mat•ic /klaɪˈmætɪk/ adj relating to the type of weather that a place has

cli•max¹ /ˈklaɪˌmæks/ noun [C] the most exciting or important moment in a story, event, or situation, usually near the end: *the climax to this season's playoffs*

cli•max² /ˈklaɪˌmæks/ verb [I/T] if a story, event, or situation climaxes, it reaches the most exciting or important moment

climb¹ /klaɪm/ verb ★★★
1 [I/T] to use your hands and feet to move up, over, down, or across something: *He climbed onto the roof.* ♦ *We escaped by climbing through a window.* ♦ *I didn't think he could climb the wall.*
2 [T] to walk up a slope or up some steps: *We left the road and climbed the hill.* ♦ *They had to climb ten flights of stairs.*
3 [I] to get into or out of something, especially by stepping to a higher or lower position: *Sara climbed wearily into bed.*
4 [I] if something such as a temperature, price, or level climbs, it becomes higher: *Their profits climbed from $20 million to $50 million last year.*

climb

climb² /klaɪm/ noun [singular] an occasion when you go up a slope or up some steps

climb•er /ˈklaɪmər/ noun [C] someone who takes part in the activity of climbing

climb•ing /ˈklaɪmɪŋ/ noun [U] the activity of climbing mountains and rocks for enjoyment and exercise

clinch /klɪntʃ/ verb [T] to manage to win or achieve something by doing one final thing that makes it certain

cling /klɪŋ/ (past tense and past participle **clung** /klʌŋ/) verb [I] **1** to hold onto something or someone tightly, for example because you are afraid: *Some children were crying and clinging to their mothers.* **2** to stick to something, or to fit very tightly on something: *Gareth's wet clothes clung to his body.*
PHRASAL VERB **cling to sth 1** to keep believing that something is right or real, even though other people do not: *Older people cling to the religion they had as children.* **2** to try very hard to keep something: *The Prime Minister is still clinging to power.*

cling•y /ˈklɪŋi/ adj *informal* a clingy child or person wants to be with another person all the time

clin•ic /ˈklɪnɪk/ noun [C] **1** a place where people go to receive a particular type of medical treatment or advice **2** *American* a group of doctors who work together in one building =PRACTICE **3** an occasion when an expert teaches a class on their subject

clin•i•cal /ˈklɪnɪk(ə)l/ adj **1** involving working with people who are sick, rather than in a laboratory: *a clinical study of the drug* **2** not showing any excitement or emotion: *a cold and clinical manner* **3** done perfectly, but not in a way that is original or interesting —**clin•i•cal•ly** /ˈklɪnɪkli/ adv

clink /klɪŋk/ verb [I/T] to make a short high sound like glass or metal objects hitting each other —**clink** noun [singular]

clip¹ /klɪp/ verb **1** [I/T] to fasten something somewhere using a small object, or to be fastened somewhere in this way: *Clip the* *microphone to your shirt.* **2** [T] to cut off small parts of something in order to make it neat: *I clipped my nails.* **3** [T] to hit something accidentally while passing it

clip² /klɪp/ noun [C] **1** a small object that holds something in position: *hair clips* **2** a short part of a movie or television program that is shown separately

clip•board /ˈklɪpˌbɔrd/ noun [C] **1** a small board that you carry and attach papers to so that you can write while you are moving around **2** *computing* the part of a computer program where you store information that you are going to copy to another document

clipped /klɪpt/ adj if someone speaks in a clipped voice, they speak clearly and quickly but they seem unfriendly

clip•pers /ˈklɪpərz/ noun [plural] an object used for cutting things to make them neat, consisting of two blades that you press or push together: *nail clippers*

clip•ping /ˈklɪpɪŋ/ noun [C] **1** an article that you have cut from a newspaper or magazine **2** a small piece that you remove when you cut something to make it neat

clique /klik/ noun [C] a small group of people who seem unfriendly to other people

clit•o•ris /ˈklɪtərɪs/ noun [C] a woman's sexual organ above her VAGINA

cloak¹ /kloʊk/ noun **1** [C] a long coat without sleeves that fastens around your neck **2** [singular] something that covers or hides something else: *a cloak of secrecy*

cloak² /kloʊk/ verb [T] to cover or hide something: *The whole investigation has been cloaked in secrecy.*

clob•ber /ˈklɑbər/ verb [T] *informal* **1** to hit someone very hard **2** to have a very bad effect on someone or something

clock¹ /klɑk/ noun [C] ★★★ an object that shows the time. The similar object that you wear on your wrist is called a **watch**: *The only sound was the clock ticking.* ♦ *I glanced at the kitchen clock.*

PHRASES **against the clock** as fast as possible in order to finish something before a particular time: *We are working against the clock to meet the deadline.*

around the clock all day and all night: *Rescuers worked around the clock to free people trapped in the wreckage.*

turn/set/put the clock back 1 to change the time on a clock to an earlier time **2** to return to a time in the past: *If we could turn the clock back, would you actually change anything?*

clock² /klɑk/ verb [T] to measure the speed that something is traveling at

clock•wise /ˈklɑkˌwaɪz/ adj, adv moving in a circle in the same direction as the HANDS on a clock ≠ COUNTERCLOCKWISE

clock•work /ˈklɑkˌwɜrk/ noun

PHRASES **like clockwork** happening or working correctly, with no problems

(as) regular as clockwork very regularly

clog /klɑg/ verb [I/T] to block something such as a pipe, or to become blocked

clogs /klɑgz/ noun [plural] shoes with wooden SOLES (=bottom part)

clois•tered /ˈklɔɪstərd/ adj kept away from the unpleasant responsibilities of ordinary life

clone¹ /kloʊn/ noun [C] **1** *science* an exact copy of an animal or plant that has been created in a laboratory **2** *informal* something that is exactly like something else

clone² /kloʊn/ verb [T] *science* to create an exact copy of an animal or plant in a laboratory

close¹ /kloʊz/ verb ★★★

1 shut	5 stop people entering
2 stop doing business	6 of computer program
3 stop operating	+ PHRASAL VERBS
4 end/finish	

1 [I/T] if you close something, or if it closes, it moves to cover an open area: *I was just closing my eyes to go to sleep when the phone rang.* ♦ *Did the fridge door close completely?*

2 [I/T] to stop doing business for a short time: *We close the office at noon Fridays.* ♦ *Snow forced both airports to close.*

3 [I/T] to stop existing as a business, or to stop something operating as a business: *The company plans to close 10 coal mines.* ♦ *Small stores are closing because of competition from the large chains.*

4 [I/T] if an activity or event closes, or if you close it, it ends: *Her latest show closed after only three performances.* ♦ **close sth by doing sth** *He closed the meeting by thanking everyone for coming.*

5 [T] to stop people from entering a place or using a road: *The bridge will have to be* ***closed for repairs.***

6 [I/T] *computing* if a computer program closes, or if you close it, it stops operating and disappears from your computer screen

PHRASAL VERBS **ˌclose (sth) ˈdown 1** *same as* **close¹** 3: *We had to close down the factory.* **2** *same as* **close¹** 6: *Close down all the programs that are running.*

ˌclose ˈin to move nearer to someone, especially in order to surround them: *Armed police began* ***closing in on*** *the house.*

ˌclose sth ˈoff to prevent people from entering a place or using a road

ˌclose (sth) ˈup to lock the doors of a building

close² /kloʊs/ adj ★★★

1 short distance away	7 related to you directly
2 short time away	8 involved with sb a lot
3 likely to happen soon	9 almost equal to sth
4 careful	10 won by small amount
5 similar but different	11 dangerous
6 connected by feelings	

1 only a short distance away: *We can walk to the mall – it's very close.* ♦ *The hotel is* ***close to*** *the historical district.*

2 only a short time away: *Sam's birthday is* ***close to*** *Christmas.*

3 likely to happen soon: *Everyone believes that a peace deal is close.* ♦ **close to doing sth** *We're closer to signing a contract after today's meeting.* ♦ *She was* ***close to tears*** (=almost crying) *as she said goodbye to her sister.*

4 giving careful attention to every detail: *I'll take a closer look at it tomorrow.* ♦ *The local police* ***kept a close eye on*** *his activities.*

5 similar to something but not exactly the

C

same: *That's not exactly the shade of blue, but it's close.* ♦ *The sensation is **close to** the feeling of floating.*
6 connected by shared feelings such as love and respect: *My brother and I are very close.* ♦ ***close friends*** ♦ *She's **close to** both her parents.*
7 related to you directly, for example by being your parent, child, brother, or sister: *my close relatives*
8 directly involved with someone and communicating with them a lot: *a close business associate* ♦ *We worked in close cooperation with local people.*
9 almost the same as a particular amount or number: *Unemployment on the island is **close to** 12 percent.*
10 if a game, competition, or election is close, the scores of the players, teams, etc. are nearly equal: *The game was close, but Denver finally won in overtime.*
11 *spoken* very dangerous or unpleasant: *That was close! He almost hit us.* ♦ *We had **a close call*** (=were in a dangerous situation) *on our bikes today.*
—**close•ness** noun [U]

close³ /kloʊs/ adv ★★★
1 only a short distance away: *She moved closer, trying to hear what Jack was saying.* ♦ *He clutched his bag **close to** his chest.*
2 only a short time away: *As the summer grew closer, we started to think about a vacation.*
3 **close to sth** almost a particular amount or number: *Close to 500 people attended the meeting.*
PHRASES **close up** or **up close** from only a short distance away: *I didn't see his face close up.*
come close to (doing) sth to nearly do something: *I came close to giving up several times.*

close⁴ /kloʊz/ noun [singular] the end of something such as a period of time or an event: *toward the close of the 18th century*

closed /kloʊzd/ adj ★★
1 if something such as a door or window is closed, it is not open: *All the doors are closed and locked.*
2 not operating or doing business ≠ OPEN: *All the stores were closed.* ♦ *This part of the museum is **closed to** the public.*
PHRASE **behind closed doors** in a place where other people cannot see or know what is happening

ˌclosed-ˌcircuit teleˈvision noun [U] CCTV

close-knit /ˌkloʊs ˈnɪt/ adj consisting of people who like and support each other: *a close-knit family*

close•ly /ˈkloʊsli/ adv ★★
1 in a way that is very similar to something, or that has a strong connection with it: *The Northern Ireland economy is closely linked to that of the rest of the United Kingdom.*
2 in a way that involves careful attention to every detail: *Our accountants will examine the accounts very closely.*
3 in a way that involves sharing ideas, thoughts, or feelings: *We are all working closely with each other.*
4 with very little time or distance between one thing and another

clos•et¹ /ˈklɑzət/ noun [C] *American* a small room or space built into a wall for storing things
PHRASE **come out of the closet** *informal* to say publicly that you are gay

clos•et² /ˈklɑzət/ adj keeping your beliefs or activities secret: *I've always been a closet fan of science-fiction books.*

close-up /ˈkloʊs ˌʌp/ noun [C] a photograph of someone or something that is taken from a position very near them

clos•ing /ˈkloʊzɪŋ/ adj happening at the end of something: *the closing moments of the game*

ˈclosing ˌdate noun [C] the date by which you must do something

clo•sure /ˈkloʊʒər/ noun [C/U] an occasion when a business or institution stops operating permanently, or the process of stopping it: *an increase in hospital closures*

clot¹ /klɑt/ verb [I] if blood or another liquid clots, it becomes thick and stops flowing

clot² /klɑt/ noun [C] a lump consisting of thick blood or another liquid

cloth /klɑθ/ noun ★★★
1 [C/U] material used for making things such as clothes and curtains: *linen/cotton cloth*
2 [C] a piece of cloth that is used for a particular purpose such as cleaning or covering a table

clothe /kloʊð/ verb [T] to provide someone with clothes

clothed /kloʊðd/ adj dressed in a particular way

clothes /kloʊðz/ noun [plural] ★★★ shirts, dresses, pants, and other things that you wear: *a pile of dirty clothes* ♦ *I'm going to* ***put on*** *some clean* ***clothes.*** ♦ *Why don't you* ***take*** *those wet* ***clothes off?***

- **Clothes** is a general word meaning "things that you wear." It is always plural: *His clothes were dirty.* ♦ *I bought some new clothes.* If you want to talk about "one thing that you wear" use **a piece/an item of clothing**.
- **Dress** is a less common word and refers to special clothes that are typical of a particular country or time: *men in national dress*
- A **dress** is a single piece of clothing worn by a woman.

clothes•line /ˈkloʊðzˌlaɪn/ noun [C] a rope for hanging wet clothes on, so that they dry

cloth•ing /ˈkloʊðɪŋ/ noun [U] ★ clothes: *a piece/item/article of clothing* ♦ *waterproof clothing* ♦ *the clothing industry*

cloud¹ /klaʊd/ noun [C] ★★★
1 a white or gray mass of drops of water in the sky: *a few white clouds in the sky*
2 a large amount of something such as smoke or dust in the air: *a huge* ***cloud of*** *black smoke*
3 something unpleasant that spoils a situation: *Violent protests* ***cast a cloud over*** *the president's visit.*
PHRASE **under a cloud** with your reputation damaged

cloud² /klaʊd/ verb **1** [T] to affect your ability to think in a sensible way: *Make sure that your feelings do not cloud your judgment.* **2** [T] to make something more complicated or confusing: *Unanswered questions have further clouded the issue.* **3** [T] to spoil an event **4** [I/T] if something such as glass clouds, or if something clouds it, it becomes difficult to see through
PHRASAL VERB ˌ**cloud ˈover** to become darker because gray clouds are forming in the sky

cloud•less /ˈklaʊdləs/ adj a cloudless sky has no clouds in it

cloud•y /ˈklaʊdi/ adj **1** full of clouds **2** a cloudy liquid is not clear

clout /klaʊt/ noun [U] *informal* the authority to make decisions, or the power to influence events: *political/financial/economic clout*

clove /kloʊv/ noun [C] **1** a brown dried flower BUD used for flavoring food **2** a section of a BULB of GARLIC

clo•ver /ˈkloʊvər/ noun [U] a small plant with leaves that have three round parts

clown¹ /klaʊn/ noun [C] **1** a performer in a CIRCUS who wears funny clothes and does silly things **2** someone who is stupid or annoying

clown² /klaʊn/ or ˌ**clown aˈround** verb [I] to do funny or annoying things

club¹ /klʌb/ noun ★★★

1 society for activity	4 for hitting ball in golf
2 sports team & staff	5 suit of playing cards
3 place for dancing	

1 [C] an organization for people who take part in a particular activity, or the building that they use: *a sailing club* ♦ *Why don't you* ***join*** *a chess* ***club?*** ♦ *Are you* ***a member of*** *the club?*
2 [C] a team of sports players and the staff who work with them: *the Waterville baseball club*
3 [C] a place where you go in the evening to dance and drink = NIGHTCLUB
4 [C] an object used for hitting the ball in golf = GOLF CLUB
5 **clubs** [plural] the suit (=group) of playing cards that has a pattern of three black balls on a black stem: *the king of clubs* —*picture* → C16

club² /klʌb/ verb [T] to hit someone with a heavy object

club•house /ˈklʌbˌhaʊs/ noun [C] the building used by members of a sports club

ˌ**club ˈsoda** noun [U] *American* a clear drink made by adding a gas to water

cluck /klʌk/ verb [I] if a chicken clucks, it makes its usual short low sound —**cluck** noun [C]

clue /klu/ noun [C] ★
1 an object or fact that helps someone to solve a crime or mystery: *Detectives were brought in to help* ***search for clues.*** ♦ *Police still have no* ***clues as to*** *the identity of the killer.*
2 a piece of information that helps you to understand something: *His face gave her no* ***clue to*** *what he was thinking.*
3 a word or phrase provided to help you to guess the answer in a CROSSWORD
PHRASE **not have a clue** *informal* to not know or understand something: *"What's wrong with him?" "I don't have a clue."*

clue•less /ˈkluləs/ adj *informal* someone who is clueless knows nothing or is stupid

clump /klʌmp/ noun [C] a group of trees or plants growing very close together

clum•sy /ˈklʌmzi/ adj **1** a clumsy person often has accidents because they are not careful **2** showing a lack of skill in judging people or situations **3** a clumsy object is too large and heavy to be useful —**clum•si•ly** adv, **clum•si•ness** noun [U]

clung the past tense and past participle of **cling**

clus•ter¹ /ˈklʌstər/ noun [C] a small group of things that are very close to one another

clus•ter² /ˈklʌstər/ verb [I] to form a small close group

clutch¹ /klʌtʃ/ verb [T] to hold someone or something firmly

clutch² /klʌtʃ/ noun **1** [C] a piece of equipment in a vehicle that you press with your foot when you change GEAR —*picture* → C6
2 **clutches** [plural] power or control over someone: *They left the country to escape the clutches of the secret police.*

clut·ter[1] /ˈklʌtər/ noun [U] the mess created when there are too many things in a place

clut·ter[2] /ˈklʌtər/ or ˌ**clutter sth ˈup** verb [T] to put too many things in a place so that it looks messy

C

cm. abbrev centimeter

CO abbrev Colorado

Co. /koʊ/ abbrev **1** Company **2** County

c/o abbrev care of: used in an address on a letter that you are sending to someone at another person's house

coach[1] /koʊtʃ/ noun ★★
1 [C] someone who trains a sports player or team: *a baseball coach*
2 [U] *American* a less expensive type of seat on an airplane or a train: *We flew coach to New Orleans.*
3 [C] a vehicle pulled by horses, used in the past
4 [C] *British* a comfortable bus for long trips

coach[2] /koʊtʃ/ verb [T] **1** to train a sports player or team **2** to teach someone a particular skill

coach·ing /ˈkoʊtʃɪŋ/ noun [U] the process of giving a student extra private teaching in a particular subject

co·ag·u·late /koʊˈægjəˌleɪt/ verb [I] if a liquid coagulates, it becomes thick and hard

coal /koʊl/ noun ★
1 [U] a hard black substance that is dug from the ground and burned as fuel: *a piece of coal* ♦ *the coal industry*
2 coals [plural] pieces of burning coal

co·a·li·tion /ˌkoʊəˈlɪʃ(ə)n/ noun [C] a government formed by different political parties that are working together for a short time

ˈ**coal ˌmine** noun [C] a place where coal is dug up from under the ground

coarse /kɔrs/ adj **1** not smooth or soft, or consisting of rough or thick pieces: *She had short, coarse hair.* **2** rude and offensive —**coarse·ly** adv

coast[1] /koʊst/ noun [C] ★★ an area of land along the edge of an ocean: *the east coast of the United States* ♦ *a little town on the coast* → SHORE
PHRASE **the coast is clear** used for saying that it is safe to do something because there is no one to catch you

coast[2] /koʊst/ verb [I] **1** to be successful without making much effort **2** to continue to move in a car or on a bicycle after you have turned off the engine or stopped PEDALING

coast·al /ˈkoʊst(ə)l/ adj relating to a coast, or existing on or near a coast: *coastal areas/roads*

coast·er /ˈkoʊstər/ noun [C] a small flat object that you put under a cup to protect the table

ˈ**Coast ˌGuard, the** a military organization in the U.S. that watches for ships in danger and works to prevent illegal activities in the ocean

coast·line /ˈkoʊstˌlaɪn/ noun [C] the land along a coast, or the shape that it makes

coat[1] /koʊt/ noun [C] ★★★
1 a piece of clothing with long sleeves that you wear over your other clothes when you go outside: *a fur coat* ♦ *Put your coat on – we're going out.*
2 a layer of something such as paint that you put onto a surface
3 the fur or hair on an animal's skin
PHRASE **coat of arms** a special design that is used as the symbol of a family, institution, city, etc.

coat[2] /koʊt/ verb [T] to cover something with a layer of a substance

ˈ**coat ˌhanger** noun [C] a frame used for hanging clothes on

coat·ing /ˈkoʊtɪŋ/ noun [C] a thin layer that covers a surface

coat·tails /ˈkoʊtˌteɪlz/ noun **on sb's coattails** using someone else's success to get an advantage for yourself

coax /koʊks/ verb [T] to gently persuade someone to do something

co·balt /ˈkoʊˌbɔlt/ noun [U] a blue-green color

cob·ble /ˈkɑbl/ PHRASAL VERB ˌ**cobble sth toˈgether** to make something quickly, using whatever is available

cob·bled /ˈkɑb(ə)ld/ adj a cobbled street or road surface is made from many small round stones fastened closely together

cob·bler /ˈkɑblər/ noun [C] *old-fashioned* someone who repairs shoes as a job

cob·ble·stones /ˈkɑb(ə)lˌstoʊnz/ noun [plural] small stones with round tops used in the past to make the surface of a road

co·bra /ˈkoʊbrə/ noun [C] a poisonous African or Asian snake

cob·web /ˈkɑbˌweb/ noun [C] a net that a SPIDER makes out of thin sticky strings to catch insects in

co·caine /koʊˈkeɪn, ˈkoʊˌkeɪn/ noun [U] a strong illegal drug, usually sold in the form of a white powder

cock[1] /kɑk/ noun [C] a male bird, especially a male chicken

cock[2] /kɑk/ verb [T] to raise a part of your body, or to move it to one side

cock·er·el /ˈkɑkrəl/ noun [C] a young male chicken

cock·ney or **Cock·ney** /ˈkɑkni/ noun **1** [U] a type of informal English spoken in London **2** [C] someone who speaks cockney —**cock·ney** adj

cock·pit /ˈkɑkˌpɪt/ noun [C] the place where the pilot sits in a plane or where the driver sits in a racing car

cock·roach /ˈkɑkˌroʊtʃ/ noun [C] an insect similar to a BEETLE that lives in places where food is kept —*picture* → C13

cock·tail /ˈkɑkˌteɪl/ noun [C] **1** an alcoholic drink made by mixing different drinks together **2** a combination of substances, for example drugs

ˈ**cocktail ˌlounge** noun [C] a bar, often in a hotel or club

ˈ**cocktail ˌparty** noun [C] a small formal party in the early evening

cock·y /ˈkɑki/ adj *informal* very confident in an annoying way

co·coa /ˈkoʊkoʊ/ noun **1** [U] a brown powder made from a type of bean. It is used for making chocolate and chocolate-flavored food and drinks. **2** [C/U] a hot drink made from this powder

co•co•nut /ˈkoʊkəˌnʌt/ noun **1** [C] a large nut that has a hard brown shell and white flesh —*picture* → C10 **2** [U] the white flesh of a coconut, that can be eaten

co•coon¹ /kəˈkun/ noun [C] a cover that some young insects make to protect themselves while they change into their adult form

co•coon² /kəˈkun/ verb [T] to keep someone safe and protected

cod /kɑd/ (plural **cod**) noun [C/U] a large sea fish that can be eaten

C.O.D. /ˌsi oʊ ˈdi/ abbrev cash on delivery: a system by which you pay for goods that you have ordered when they are delivered to you

code /koʊd/ noun ★★

1 [C/U] a system of words, numbers, or signs used for sending secret messages: *The message was written **in code**.* ♦ *They never **cracked** the enemy's **code*** (=discovered how it worked).

2 [C] a set of rules about how something should be done or how people should behave: *the company's code of conduct*

3 [C] a set of numbers, letters, or symbols used for a particular purpose, for example to give information about a product or as part of a phone number

cod•ed /ˈkoʊdəd/ adj written using a secret system of words or signs

ˈ**code** ˌ**name** noun [C] a name for someone or something that you use when you want to keep their real name secret

co•ed /ˈkoʊˌed/ adj including students of both sexes

co•erce /koʊˈɜrs/ verb [T] to make someone do something by using force or threats

co•er•cion /koʊˈɜrʃ(ə)n/ noun [U] the use of force or threats to make someone do something

co•ex•ist /ˌkoʊɪɡˈzɪst/ verb [I] *formal* to live or exist at the same time or in the same place —**co•ex•is•tence** /ˌkoʊɪɡˈzɪstəns/ noun [U]

cof•fee /ˈkɑfi/ noun ★★★

1 [U] a hot brown drink made by pouring hot water over crushed beans: *Would you like a cup of coffee?* ♦ *Do you take sugar in your coffee?*

2 [C] a cup of this drink: *Can we have three regular coffees please?*

3 [U] a light brown color

ˈ**coffee ma**ˌ**chine** noun [C] **1** a machine that you put money into in order to get a hot drink **2** a machine for making coffee

ˈ**coffee** ˌ**maker** noun [C] a machine for making coffee —*picture* → C2

ˈ**coffee** ˌ**shop** noun [C] **1** a small café where tea, coffee, sandwiches, cakes, etc. are served **2** *American* an informal restaurant that serves inexpensive meals

ˈ**coffee** ˌ**table** noun [C] a small low table in a LIVING ROOM

cof•fers /ˈkɑfərz/ noun [plural] the supply of money that an organization has available to spend

cof•fin /ˈkɑfɪn/ noun [C] a box in which a dead person is buried

cog /kɑɡ/ noun [C] a wheel in a machine that fits into the edge of another wheel and makes it turn

co•gnac /ˈkɑnˌjæk/ noun [U] a type of French BRANDY

cog•ni•tive /ˈkɑɡnətɪv/ adj *technical* connected with the way the brain recognizes or understands things: *cognitive changes/skills*

co•hab•it /ˌkoʊˈhæbɪt/ verb [I] *formal* to live with someone in a sexual relationship without being married —**co•hab•i•ta•tion** /koʊˌhæbɪˈteɪʃ(ə)n/ noun [U]

co•her•ent /koʊˈhɪrənt/ adj clear and sensible, or capable of being understood ≠ INCOHERENT —**co•her•ent•ly** adv

co•he•sion /koʊˈhiʒ(ə)n/ noun [U] a situation in which people or things combine well to form a unit

co•he•sive /koʊˈhisɪv/ adj combining to form a strong well-organized unit

coil¹ /kɔɪl/ noun [C] a long piece of rope, hair, or wire, that forms several circles, each on top of the other

coil² /kɔɪl/ verb [I/T] to make something into a coil —**coiled** /kɔɪld/ adj

coin¹ /kɔɪn/ noun [C] ★★★ a flat round piece of metal used as money: *Put a coin into the slot.*

PHRASES **flip/toss a coin** to throw a coin in the air to make a decision. Your decision depends on which side of the coin is on top when it lands.

the other side of the coin a different aspect of a situation

two sides of the same coin two different aspects of the same situation

coin² /kɔɪn/ verb [T] to use a word or phrase that no one has used before

co•in•cide /ˌkoʊɪnˈsaɪd/ verb [I] to happen at the same time as something else

co•in•ci•dence /koʊˈɪnsɪdəns/ noun [C/U] an unusual situation in which two things happen by chance at the same time or in the same way

co•in•ci•den•tal /koʊˌɪnsɪˈdent(ə)l/ adj happening or existing by chance and not because of being planned or intended —**co•in•ci•den•tal•ly** adv

Col. abbrev Colonel

co•la /ˈkoʊlə/ noun [U] a sweet brown drink with bubbles in it

col•an•der /ˈkʌləndər/ noun [C] a bowl with small holes in it. You put food into it to remove any liquid.

cold¹ /koʊld/ adj ★★★

1 with a low temperature, or a temperature that is lower than normal ≠ HOT: *The water was too cold for a shower.* ♦ *a cold winter morning* ♦ *I was cold and hungry.* ♦ *Their house is always **freezing cold**.*

2 not seeming friendly or sympathetic: *Her father was a cold and distant man.*

3 cold food has been cooked but is not eaten hot: *cold chicken*

PHRASES **get/be given the cold shoulder** *informal* to be treated in an unfriendly way by someone you know

get cold feet to suddenly feel nervous about something that you have planned or agreed to do: *Two days before the wedding he got cold feet.*

in cold blood in a cruel way without showing any sympathy

C

Other ways of saying that the weather is cold

- **chilly** cold enough to make you feel uncomfortable
- **cool** slightly cold in a nice, comfortable way
- **freezing cold/freezing** extremely cold

cold² /koʊld/ noun ★★
1 [C] a minor illness that blocks your nose and makes you cough: *I didn't go to the game because I **had a cold**. ♦ I must have **caught a cold** on my trip.*
2 [U] cold air or temperatures: *Plants need protection against extreme cold. ♦ Heavy curtains help to keep **the cold** out.*

cold³ /koʊld/ adv if you do something cold, you do it without preparing for it
PHRASE **out cold** completely unconscious

cold-blood·ed /ˌkoʊld ˈblʌdəd/ adj **1** deliberately cruel and showing no emotion **2** cold-blooded animals have a body temperature that changes to suit their environment

ˈcold ˌcuts noun [plural] thin pieces of cooked meat that you eat cold

cold-heart·ed /ˌkoʊld ˈhɑrtəd/ adj with no sympathy for other people ≠ WARM-HEARTED

cold·ly /ˈkoʊldli/ adv in a way that is unfriendly or not sympathetic

ˌcold-ˈshoulder verb [T] to be unfriendly toward someone you know

cole·slaw /ˈkoʊlˌslɔ/ noun [U] a type of salad made from raw CABBAGE and CARROTS mixed with MAYONNAISE

col·ic /ˈkɑlɪk/ noun [U] pain that a baby has in its stomach

col·lab·o·rate /kəˈlæbəˌreɪt/ verb [I] **1** to work with someone in order to produce something **2** to work secretly to help an enemy or opponent —**col·lab·o·ra·tor** noun [C]

col·lab·o·ra·tion /kəˌlæbəˈreɪʃ(ə)n/ noun [U] **1** the process of working with someone to produce something **2** help that someone secretly gives to an enemy or opponent

col·lab·o·ra·tive /kəˈlæbərətɪv/ adj involving people working together: *collaborative efforts*

col·lage /kɑˈlɑʒ/ noun [C] a picture made by sticking pieces of different materials together on a surface

col·lapse¹ /kəˈlæps/ verb [I] ★
1 if a building or other structure collapses, it suddenly falls down: *There were fears that the roof would collapse.*
2 to suddenly fail or stop existing: *The country's economy is collapsing.*
3 to suddenly fall down and become very sick or unconscious: *A man had collapsed on the hospital steps.*
4 an object that collapses can be folded or separated into parts, so that it takes up less space

col·lapse² /kəˈlæps/ noun **1** [U] a situation in which something fails or stops existing: *the collapse of the military government* **2** [U] an occasion when a building or other structure falls down **3** [C/U] an occasion when someone falls down and becomes very sick or unconscious

col·laps·i·ble /kəˈlæpsəb(ə)l/ adj able to be folded into a smaller size: *a collapsible bicycle*

col·lar /ˈkɑlər/ noun [C] ★ a thin piece of leather or plastic that a dog or cat wears around its neck

col·lar·bone /ˈkɑlərˌboʊn/ noun [C] the bone along the front of your shoulder

col·lat·er·al /kəˈlæt(ə)rəl/ noun [U] property that you agree to give to a bank if you fail to pay back money that you have borrowed

col·league /ˈkɑˌlig/ noun [C] ★★ someone who works in the same organization or department as you: *Friends and colleagues will remember him with affection.*

col·lect¹ /kəˈlekt/ verb ★★★
1 [T] to get things and keep them together for a particular reason: *A lot of families collect newspapers for recycling.*
2 [T] to get and keep objects because they are interesting or valuable: *I didn't know she collected modern art.*
3 [T] to get money from someone for a particular purpose: *She is collecting money for charity.*
4 [I] to gradually come together, or to become present = GATHER: *Rain often collects in the corners of flat roofs.*
PHRASE **collect your thoughts** to spend a short time thinking about a decision or forming an opinion

col·lect² /kəˈlekt/ adv **call sb collect** *American* to make a phone call that is paid for by the person who receives the call

colˈlect ˌcall noun [C] *American* a phone call that the person you are calling agrees to pay for

col·lect·ed /kəˈlektəd/ adj **sb's collected works/poems/letters etc.** all of someone's work, poetry, etc. published together

col·lect·i·ble /kəˈlektəb(ə)l/ adj valuable because of being something that people want to own —**col·lect·i·ble** noun [C]

col·lec·tion /kəˈlekʃ(ə)n/ noun ★★★
1 [C] a group of similar things that are kept together: *a book borrowed from John's huge collection ♦ a **collection of** baseball cards ♦ The gallery has one of the finest **collections** of Impressionist art.*
2 [C/U] the process of collecting things for a particular purpose, or an instance of this: *garbage collection ♦ **the collection and analysis of** information*
3 [C/U] the activity of collecting money for a particular purpose, or the money that is collected: *The door-to-door collection raised $255.41.*
4 [C] a group of people: *a motley **collection** of protesters and student groups*

col·lec·tive¹ /kəˈlektɪv/ adj involving all the members of a group ≠ INDIVIDUAL: *collective responsibility* —**col·lec·tive·ly** adv

col·lec·tive² /kəˈlektɪv/ noun [C] a business run by a group of workers

col·lec·tor /kəˈlektər/ noun [C] **1** someone who collects things for fun: *a stamp collector* **2** someone whose job is to collect something from people: *the ticket collector*

col·lege /ˈkɑlɪdʒ/ noun ★★★
1 [C] *American* in the U.S., a university, often a smaller one: *Boston College ♦ Colleges all*

over the country are receiving government money.
2 [U] *American* the situation or time when you are studying at a college or university: *his junior year of college* ♦ *Kaitlin's **going to college** next year.* ♦ *It happened while my sister was away **at college**.*
3 [C] one of the parts that some universities are divided into: *the University of Mexico's College of Arts and Sciences*

col•le•giate /kəˈlidʒət/ adj relating to colleges or intended for students at college

col•lide /kəˈlaɪd/ verb [I] if people or things collide, they crash into each other: *The truck collided with a row of parked cars.*

col•li•sion /kəˈlɪʒ(ə)n/ noun [C/U] an accident in which a person or vehicle that is moving crashes into something: *The stolen car was involved in a head-on collision with a truck* (=the front of the vehicles hit each other).

col•lo•qui•al /kəˈloʊkwiəl/ adj used in informal conversation rather than in writing or formal language —**col•lo•qui•al•ly** adv

col•lo•qui•al•ism /kəˈloʊkwiəˌlɪzəm/ noun [C] a colloquial word or expression

col•lu•sion /kəˈluʒ(ə)n/ noun [U] *formal* the secret activities of people who work together to do something dishonest

co•logne /kəˈloʊn/ noun [C/U] a liquid with a nice smell that you put on your skin

co•lon /ˈkoʊlən/ noun [C] **1** the symbol : used in writing, for example before an explanation or a list **2** *medical* the lower part of your BOWELS

colo•nel /ˈkɜrn(ə)l/ noun [C] an officer of high rank in the army, the MARINES, or the U.S. Air Force

co•lo•ni•al /kəˈloʊniəl/ adj **1** relating to a system or period in which one country rules another: *years of colonial rule* **2** made in a style that was common in North America in the 18th century —*picture* → C1

co•lo•ni•al•ism /kəˈloʊniəˌlɪzəm/ noun [U] a situation in which one country rules another —**co•lo•ni•al•ist** adj

col•o•nist /ˈkɑlənɪst/ noun [C] one of the people who establish a COLONY or go to live in it

col•o•nize /ˈkɑləˌnaɪz/ verb [T] to take control of another country by going to live there or by sending people to live there —**col•o•ni•za•tion** /ˌkɑlənɪˈzeɪʃ(ə)n/ noun [U]

col•o•ny /ˈkɑləni/ noun [C] **1** a country that is controlled by another country **2** a group of people or animals of a particular type who live together: *an ant colony*

col•or[1] /ˈkʌlər/ noun ★★★
1 [C/U] red, blue, green, yellow, etc.: *Pink is my favorite color.* ♦ *a light brown color* ♦ *The soil is reddish **in color**.* ♦ *Many fruits **change color** as they become ripe.*
2 [U] the quality of having color: *Plants add color to a room.* ♦ *Are the pictures in black and white or **in color**?*
3 [C/U] the color of someone's skin as a sign of their race: *people of all races and colors*
4 [C/U] the color of someone's face when it shows how they are feeling: *Suddenly, the color drained from his cheeks.*
→ FLYING[1], OFF-COLOR

> **Talking or writing about colors**
>
> *general*
> - **shade** one of the light or dark types of a particular color
> - **tone** one of the different types of a particular color
> - **-ish** used with colors to make adjectives that describe things that look a little like that color
>
> *dark colors*
> - **dark** used for describing colors that look more like black than like white
> - **deep** used for describing dark colors that look attractive
> - **rich** used for describing dark colors that look beautiful and expensive
> - **somber** dark in a way that seems appropriate for a serious occasion
>
> *bright colors*
> - **bright** strong and noticeable
> - **vibrant** bright in a way that looks exciting
> - **colorful** brightly colored, or having a lot of bright colors
> - **loud** bright in a way that you think looks silly or ugly
> - **gaudy** very brightly colored in a way that you think shows bad taste
> - **garish** very brightly colored in a way that looks ugly
>
> *pale colors*
> - **pale** like white with a small amount of a color mixed in
> - **light** pale
> - **faded** used for describing something that is pale because it has been washed a lot, or because the sun has shone on it

col•or[2] /ˈkʌlər/ verb [T] **1** to add color to something to make it a different color: *I think I'll color my hair.* **2** to affect someone's decision or opinion about something: *Don't allow her opinions to color your judgment.* **3** to use pens, pencils, or CRAYONS to add color to a picture

PHRASAL VERB ˌ**color sth** ˈ**in** *same as* **color[2]** 3

> **Word family: color**
>
> *Words in the same family as color*
> - **colored** *adj*
> - **discolored** *adj*
> - **colorful** *adj*
> - **colorless** *adj*
> - **coloring** *n*

col•or[3] /ˈkʌlər/ adj **1** consisting of different colors rather than just black and white: *color pictures* **2** a color television, MONITOR, etc. shows color pictures, not black and white ones

ˈ**color-**ˌ**blind** adj unable to recognize a difference between some colors, especially red and green —ˈ**color** ˌ**blindness** noun [U]

col•ored /ˈkʌlərd/ adj **1** red, green, blue, etc. rather than transparent or black or white: *pieces of colored paper* **2** *offensive* a colored person has dark skin

col•or•ful /ˈkʌlərf(ə)l/ adj **1** with bright colors, or a lot of different colors: *a colorful carpet* **2** interesting, exciting, and sometimes funny or shocking: *colorful characters* ♦ *a colorful past* —**col•or•ful•ly** adv

col•or•ing /ˈkʌlərɪŋ/ noun **1** [U] the color of something, especially someone's hair and skin **2** [C/U] a substance that you add to change the color of food

col•or•less /ˈkʌlərləs/ adj **1** without any color: *a colorless, odorless poison* **2** not interesting, exciting, or original

co•los•sal /kəˈlɑs(ə)l/ adj extremely great or large: *It was a colossal waste of money.*

C

col•our /ˈkʌlər/ the British spelling of **color**[1]

col•our•ful /ˈkʌlərf(ə)l/ the British spelling of **colorful**

colt /koʊlt/ noun [C] a young male horse

col•umn /ˈkɑləm/ noun [C] ★★

1 tall thick post	4 in newspaper
2 sth rising into the air	5 line of people/vehicles
3 of writing/numbers	

1 a tall thick post that is used for supporting a roof, decorating a building, or reminding people of an important event or person: *marble columns*
2 something that rises up into the air in a straight line: *a column of smoke and ash*
3 a series of short lines of writing or numbers arranged one below the other on a page
4 a regular newspaper or magazine article on a particular subject or by a particular reporter: *an advice column*
5 a long line of people or vehicles moving together: *a column of soldiers*

column

col•um•nist /ˈkɑləmnɪst/ noun [C] someone who writes a regular series of articles for a particular newspaper or magazine

com abbrev *computing* commercial organization: used in Internet addresses

co•ma /ˈkoʊmə/ noun [C] a state in which someone is unconscious for a long time: *She was in a coma for a week.*

comb[1] /koʊm/ noun [C] an object with one row of thin pointed parts that you use to make your hair neat

comb[2] /koʊm/ verb [T] **1** to make your hair neat with a comb **2** to search a place thoroughly: *Dozens of officers combed the area with search dogs.*

com•bat[1] /ˈkɑmˌbæt/ noun [U] fighting during a war: *soldiers killed in combat* ♦ *combat forces/troops/aircraft*

com•bat[2] /ˈkɑmˌbæt, kəmˈbæt/ verb [T] to try to stop something bad from happening or a bad situation from becoming worse: *the need for effective action to combat global warming* ♦ *measures to combat crime*

com•bat•ant /ˈkɑmbət(ə)nt, kəmˈbæt(ə)nt/ noun [C] *formal* a person, group, or country that takes part in a war

com•bat•ive /kəmˈbætɪv/ adj ready to fight, argue, or oppose someone: *He has a reputation as a combative player.*

com•bi•na•tion /ˌkɑmbɪˈneɪʃ(ə)n/ noun [C] ★
1 something that combines several things: *a striking color combination* ♦ *a* ***combination of*** *text, illustration, and graphics*
2 a series of numbers or letters used for opening a lock: *I've forgotten the combination.*

com•bine /kəmˈbaɪn/ verb [I/T] ★★ if you combine things, or if they combine, they are used, done, or put together: *an attempt to combine the advantages of two systems* ♦ **combine sth with sth** *Combine the excitement of a week in Florida with a few days at Disneyworld.* ♦ **combined with sth** *High tides combined with strong winds caused severe flooding.* ♦ **combine to do sth** *One oxygen and two hydrogen atoms combine to form a molecule of water.*

com•bined /kəmˈbaɪnd/ adj **1** done by people or groups working together = JOINT: *a combined effort* **2** formed by adding things together: *What is your combined family income?*

com•bo /ˈkɑmboʊ/ noun [C] *informal* a combination of people or things: *a chicken combo meal with fries and coleslaw*

com•bus•ti•ble /kəmˈbʌstəb(ə)l/ adj *formal* able to burn easily

com•bus•tion /kəmˈbʌstʃ(ə)n/ noun [U] *formal* the process of burning

come /kʌm/ (past tense **came** /keɪm/; past participle **come**) verb [I] ★★★

1 move/travel (to here)	6 happen
2 start doing sth	7 be produced/sold
3 reach particular state	8 be somewhere in order
4 reach particular point	+ PHRASES
5 be received	+ PHRASAL VERBS

1 to move to the place where the person who is speaking is, or to the place that they are going, or to the place that they are talking about: *Billy, I want you to come here right now!* ♦ *A tall woman in black was* ***coming across*** *the lawn.* ♦ *All the glasses* ***came crashing*** *onto the floor.* ♦ **come to do sth** *Someone is supposed to come this morning to fix the computer.* ♦ **come and do sth** *Come and tell me all about it.*
2 to start being a different state or condition: *The new changes will* ***come into effect*** *next month.* ♦ *As we turned the corner, the Eiffel Tower* ***came into view*** (=started to be seen).
3 to reach a particular state: *We* ***came to the conclusion that*** *she must be telling the truth.* ♦ *All good things must* ***come to an end.*** ♦ *When the Freedom Party* ***came to power*** *they continued these policies.*
4 to reach a particular point or level: *The road comes as far as the post office and then ends.* ♦ *The water* ***came up to*** *my shoulders.*
5 if something such as a letter or message comes, you receive it: *The news came at the perfect time.*
6 to happen: *Gorbachev's resignation came after seven tough years in office.* ♦ ***It came as no surprise that*** *she left the company.*
7 to be produced or sold: *The dress* ***comes in*** *yellow or blue.* ♦ *All new cars* ***come with*** *one year's free insurance.*

8 to be in a particular position in a series or list or at the end of a race: *July **comes before** August.* ♦ *She **came first** in a national poetry competition.*

PHRASES **come naturally/easily/easy (to sb)** to be easy for someone to do: *Fame and fortune have come easily to Carmen.*

come undone/untied/unstuck etc. to become UNDONE/UNTIED/UNSTUCK etc.: *Your buttons have come undone.*

here comes sb used for telling another person that someone is moving toward you: *Here comes Dad, and he doesn't look very happy.*

to come in the future: *We were to remain enemies for years to come.*

PHRASAL VERBS **ˌcome aˈbout** to happen, especially by chance: *The company's growth has come about through the use of advanced technology.*

ˌcome aˈcross to make someone have a particular opinion of you when they meet you: *She **comes across as** very self-confident.*

ˌcome aˈcross sb/sth to meet someone or find something by chance: *I came across a word I'd never seen before.*

ˌcome ˈafter sb to try to find or catch someone, in order to punish or harm them

ˌcome aˈlong 1 to arrive, or to become available: *He decided to give the money to the first stranger who came along.* **2** to go somewhere with someone: *I've never seen a baseball game – do you mind if I come along?* **3** to make progress, or to get better in quality, skill, or health: *The building work was coming along nicely.*

ˌcome aˈpart to separate easily into pieces

ˌcome aˈround 1 to change your opinion or decision because someone has persuaded you to agree with them: *He'll come around eventually.* **2** to become conscious again

ˈcome at sb to move toward someone in order to threaten them or attack them physically: *A stranger came at him with a knife.*

ˌcome ˈback 1 to return to a place: *We **come back to** Cape Cod every summer.* **2** to be remembered again: *I can't think of her name right now, but I'm sure it'll **come back to** me.* **3** to become fashionable again

ˌcome beˈtween sb to cause a disagreement or argument between people: *He didn't want this to come between them.*

ˌcome ˈby (sth) to go to the place where someone is for a short visit: *I'll come by this afternoon and we can talk.*

ˈcome ˌby sth to get something, especially something that is hard to get: *At that time, teaching jobs were **hard to come by**.*

ˌcome ˈdown to become less in amount, level, price, etc.: *Interest rates have come down a lot lately.*

ˌcome ˈdown on sb to criticize or punish someone severely: *She came down on us pretty hard for making a mess.*

ˌcome ˈdown to sth to be the most important aspect of a situation or problem: *In the end, it all comes down to who wants the job the most.*

ˌcome ˈdown with sth to become sick with a particular disease, usually one that is not serious

ˌcome ˈforward to offer help or information: *Police said that several people had **come forward** with information about the attack.*

ˈcome from sth 1 to have been born or lived in a particular place: *My parents came from Italy.* **2** to be produced by a particular place or thing, or to start from there: *The word comes from an African language.* ♦ *I can't tell where the noise is coming from, can you?*

ˌcome ˈin 1 to enter a room, building, or other place: *Come in and sit down.* **2** to arrive somewhere: *What time does his train come in?* **3** if something such as a message comes in, it is received by someone: *Reports are coming in of a major air accident.* **4** to finish a race in a particular position: *My horse came in third.* **5** when the TIDE comes in, the sea moves higher up the beach ≠ GO OUT **6 come in handy** to be useful for a particular situation: *A big sheet of plastic always comes in handy when you're camping.*

ˌcome ˈinto sth to get money when someone dies

ˈcome of sth to be the result of something: *I looked for work for months, but nothing came of my efforts.*

ˌcome ˈoff (sth) 1 be removed from something: *I pulled at the drawer, and the handle came off.* ♦ *The grease won't come off your skin with ordinary soap.* **2 come off it** *spoken* used for telling someone to stop saying something because you do not believe them, or they are annoying you

ˌcome ˈon 1 to start working by being switched on: *I saw a light come on in an upstairs window.* **2** *spoken* used for telling someone to hurry or for encouraging them to do something: *Come on! We're going to be late.* **3** *spoken* used for telling someone that you do not believe what they are saying

ˌcome ˈout 1 if something such as a book or a movie comes out, it becomes available to buy or see: *Our new album is coming out in the spring.* **2** to become known: ***It** eventually **came out that** she was already married.* **3** to be spoken, heard, or understood in a particular way: *She had tried to say "sorry," but it had **come out all wrong**.* **4** to be removed from something by washing or rubbing: *The stains still haven't come out.* **5** to tell people that you are gay **6** to state a decision or opinion officially or publicly: *The commission has come out against the takeover.* **7** if the sun, moon, or stars come out, they start to be able to be seen in the sky

ˌcome ˈout with sth to say something suddenly, usually something that surprises or shocks people: *You never know what the children are going to come out with.*

ˌcome ˈover to visit someone in the place where they are, especially their house: *Why don't you come over for dinner?*

ˌcome ˈover sb if a feeling comes over you, it suddenly affects you in a strong way

ˌcome ˈthrough 1 if something such as a signal or a message comes through, you receive it **2** if a document that you are expecting comes through, it is sent to you: *The job offer still hasn't come through.*

ˌcome ˈthrough sth 1 to be still alive, working, or making progress after a difficult or dangerous experience: *It's been a very upsetting time but we've come through it*

C

together. **2** to do something that you have agreed or promised to do: *The team came through when it mattered.*

ˈcome to *same as* **come around** 2

ˈcome to sb if something comes to you, you think of it or remember it: *The idea came to me while we were on vacation.*

ˈcome to sth to reach a particular total when everything is added together: *The total came to $752,000.*

ˈcome at sth to examine or deal with something such as a problem in a particular way: *Try coming at it from a different angle.*

ˈcome ˌunder sth to be forced to experience something unpleasant: *President Bush has* ***come under pressure*** *to step up the sanctions.*

ˌcome ˈup 1 if a problem comes up, it happens and needs to be dealt with immediately: *I'm going to have to cancel our lunch – something's come up.* **2** to be about to happen soon: *We've got a busy period coming up in a couple of weeks.* **3** to be mentioned and need to be considered: *A number of interesting points came up at today's meeting.* **4** to move toward someone, usually because you want to talk to them: *Strangers* ***come up to*** *him in the street and say how much they enjoy his books.* **5** if the sun or the moon comes up, it starts to appear in the sky

ˌcome ˈup aˌgainst sth to have to deal with something difficult or unpleasant: *In the first week, we came up against a problem.*

ˌcome ˈup to sth to be as good as you want, need, or expect something to be: *The food didn't come up to her standards.*

ˌcome ˈup with sth to think of something such as an idea or a plan: *Is that the best you can come up with?*

ˈcome upˌon sb/sth *literary* to meet someone or find something by chance

ˈcome with sth to exist or develop as a result of something: *He has the kind of skill that comes with years of practice.*

come·back /ˈkʌmˌbæk/ noun [C] **1** a period when someone or something becomes successful or popular again: *Seventies styles have been making a comeback.* **2** a quick clever reply to a comment or criticism

co·me·di·an /kəˈmidiən/ noun [C] someone whose job is to entertain people by making them laugh = COMIC

com·e·dy /ˈkɑmədi/ noun ★

1 [C] a funny movie, play, or television program

2 [U] entertainment intended to make people laugh

com·et /ˈkɑmət/ noun [C] a bright object in space that has a tail of gas and dust

com·fort[1] /ˈkʌmfərt/ noun ★

1 [U] a physically relaxed state, without pain or other unpleasant feelings: *The airline is attempting to improve passenger comfort.* ♦ *There is plenty of room to lie down and sleep* ***in comfort****.*

2 [U] a feeling of being less sad or worried about something than you were previously: *My mother was always there to offer comfort.* ♦ ***I take comfort from*** *the fact that his friends are there to help him.*

3 [C] someone or something that makes you feel better when you are sad or worried: *Her children have been* ***a great comfort to*** *her.*

4 [U] a pleasant way of life in which you have everything you need: *Now he can live* ***in comfort*** *for the rest of his life.*

5 comforts [plural] things that make your life easier and more pleasant: ***the comforts of*** *home*

> Word family: **comfort**
>
> *Words in the same family as* ***comfort***
> - **comfortable** *adj*
> - **uncomfortable** *adj*
> - **comforting** *adj*
> - **discomfort** *n*

com·fort[2] /ˈkʌmfərt/ verb [T] to make someone feel less sad, worried, or disappointed —**com·fort·ing** adj

com·fort·a·ble /ˈkʌmfərtəb(ə)l/ adj ★★

1 feeling physically relaxed, without pain or other unpleasant feelings ≠ UNCOMFORTABLE: *If you're not comfortable, try changing positions.* ♦ ***Make yourself comfortable*** *and I'll be back in a minute.*

2 making you have a pleasant satisfied feeling in your body: *loose comfortable clothes* ♦ *The bed looked warm and comfortable.*

3 not worried about something and willing to accept it: *Is everyone* ***comfortable with*** *the arrangement?*

4 rich enough to pay for everything that you need

—**com·fort·a·bly** /ˈkʌmfərtəbli/ adv

com·fort·er /ˈkʌmfərtər/ noun [C] *American* a bed cover that is filled with something such as feathers

com·fy /ˈkʌmfi/ adj *informal* comfortable

com·ic[1] /ˈkɑmɪk/ adj funny

com·ic[2] /ˈkɑmɪk/ noun **1** [C] someone whose job is to entertain people by telling jokes and stories to make them laugh = COMEDIAN **2 the comics** [plural] the COMIC STRIPS in a newspaper

com·i·cal /ˈkɑmɪk(ə)l/ adj funny in a strange or silly way —**com·i·cal·ly** /ˈkɑmɪkli/ adv

ˈcomic ˌbook noun [C] a magazine that contains stories told in a series of drawings

ˈcomic ˌstrip noun [C] a series of drawings that tell a story, especially a funny story

com·ing[1] /ˈkʌmɪŋ/ adj happening soon, or happening next: *the coming elections*

com·ing[2] /ˈkʌmɪŋ/ noun

PHRASES **the coming of** the time when someone or something arrives or happens: *the coming of spring*

comings and goings activity that consists of people arriving and leaving many times

com·ma /ˈkɑmə/ noun [C] the symbol , used in writing and printing between parts of a sentence or things in a list

com·mand[1] /kəˈmænd/ noun ★

1 [C] an official order to do something: *He refuses to obey my commands.*

2 [U] control of a group of people or of a situation: *Franco was* ***in command of*** *the military.* ♦ *The home team soon* ***took command of*** *the game.*

3 [C] an instruction that you give to a computer to make it do something: *the log-on command*

PHRASE **command of sth** knowledge of a particular subject, especially the ability to speak a foreign language

com•mand² /kə'mænd/ verb **1** [T] to be in charge of an activity that involves a group of people: *Lovell commanded the Apollo 13 mission to the moon.* **2** [I/T] to officially order someone to do something: *He commanded his men to retreat.* **3** [T] to have something such as people's respect or attention: *He commands the respect of everyone who works for him.*

com•man•dant /'kɑmən,dænt, ,kɑmən'dɑnt/ noun [C] a military officer of high rank who controls a particular institution or group of people

com•man•deer /,kɑmən'dɪr/ verb [T] to officially take someone's property for military use

com•man•der /kə'mændər/ noun [C] **1** an officer who is in charge of a military group or operation **2** an officer of middle rank in the U.S. Navy or the U.S. Coast Guard

com•mand•ing /kə'mændɪŋ/ adj powerful and impressive: *his commanding voice/presence*

com•mand•ment /kə'mæn(d)mənt/ noun [C] according to the Bible, one of the ten rules of behavior that God gave people to obey

com•man•do /kə'mændoʊ/ noun [C] a soldier who is trained to attack in areas controlled by an enemy

com•mem•o•rate /kə'memə,reɪt/ verb [T] to show that you remember an important person or event: *A huge bronze statue commemorating the Canadian poet stands in the main square.* —**com•mem•o•ra•tion** /kə,memə'reɪʃ(ə)n/ noun [C/U]

com•mem•o•ra•tive /kə'memərətɪv/ adj produced for an important event in order to help you to remember it: *a commemorative stamp*

com•mence /kə'mens/ verb [I/T] *formal* to begin, or to begin something: *The trial will commence in 30 days.*

com•mence•ment /kə'mensmənt/ noun **1** [C] *American* a GRADUATION ceremony **2** [singular/U] *formal* the beginning of something

com•mend /kə'mend/ verb [T] *formal* to praise someone or something formally or publicly: *They were commended for the way they handled the job.* —**com•men•da•tion** /,kɑmən'deɪʃ(ə)n/ noun [C/U]

com•mend•a•ble /kə'mendəb(ə)l/ adj *formal* deserving praise or admiration —**com•mend•a•bly** adv

com•men•su•rate /kə'menʃərət/ adj *formal* intended to be suitable for the quality, status, or value of something or someone: *a pay increase commensurate with job performance*

com•ment¹ /'kɑ,ment/ noun [C/U] ★★★ a written or spoken remark giving an opinion: *I've had enough of your sarcastic comments.* ♦ *Did she **make any comment** about Eddie?* ♦ *We would welcome your **comments on** our work.*

PHRASE **no comment** *spoken* used for saying that you are not willing to answer a question that a reporter asks

com•ment² /'kɑ,ment/ verb [I/T] ★★ to make a written or spoken remark about someone or something: *I'm afraid I can't **comment on** that.* ♦ **+that** *Researchers who read the report commented that it had many errors.*

com•men•tar•y /'kɑmən,teri/ noun **1** [C] a spoken description of an event that is given as the event is happening, especially on radio or television **2** [C/U] a discussion of something such as an event or theory: *a commentary on seventh-century English life*

com•men•ta•tor /'kɑmən,teɪtər/ noun [C] **1** someone whose job is to give a description of an event on television or radio as it happens **2** someone whose job is to write about or discuss a particular subject

com•merce /'kɑ,mɜrs/ noun [U] the activity of buying and selling goods and services

com•mer•cial¹ /kə'mɜrʃ(ə)l/ adj ★
1 relating to the business of buying and selling goods and services: *One of their first commercial products was an electronic typewriter.*
2 relating to making a profit: *The movie's commercial success made her a star.*
3 making money by broadcasting advertisements instead of being given money by the government: *commercial broadcast stations*
—**com•mer•cial•ly** adv

com•mer•cial² /kə'mɜrʃ(ə)l/ noun [C] an advertisement on television or radio

com•mer•cial•ism /kə'mɜrʃ(ə)l,ɪzəm/ noun [U] the activities or attitudes of people who think that making a profit is more important than anything else

com•mer•cial•ized /kə'mɜrʃ(ə)l,aɪzd/ adj done or changed in order to make a profit: *the increasingly commercialized world of soccer*

com•mis•er•ate /kə'mɪzə,reɪt/ verb [I] to express sympathy to someone who is unhappy about something = SYMPATHIZE —**com•mis•er•a•tion** /kə,mɪzə'reɪʃ(ə)n/ noun [U]

com•mis•sion¹ /kə'mɪʃ(ə)n/ noun ★
1 [C/U] an extra amount of money that someone earns when they sell a product or get a new customer: *All our salespeople **work on commission*** (=are paid according to how much they sell).
2 [C] a group of people that is officially put in charge of something or asked to find out about something: *the Interstate Commerce Commission*
3 [C] a request for an artist, writer, or musician to produce a piece of work for someone in exchange for payment

PHRASE **out of commission** not being used, or not able to be used: *Five of their rescue vehicles were out of commission.*

com•mis•sion² /kə'mɪʃ(ə)n/ verb [T] to officially ask someone to do some work or to produce something for you: *We have commissioned a full survey of the property.* ♦ *She's been commissioned to write a symphony.*

com•mis•sion•er /kə'mɪʃ(ə)nər/ noun [C] an official who is in charge of something: *New York's Police Commissioner*

C

com•mit /kə'mɪt/ verb ★★★

1 do sth illegal/wrong	4 in relationships
2 (make sb) agree to sth	5 send sb to prison
3 say sb/sth will be used	+ PHRASES

1 [T] to do something that is illegal or morally wrong: *The study aims to find out what makes people **commit crimes**.* ♦ *He had admitted to **committing adultery**.* ♦ *Reports suggest that the singer **committed suicide*** (=killed himself).
2 [I/T] to agree to do something, or to make someone agree to do something: **commit sb to (doing) sth** *The agreement commits them to a minimum of three years in the program.* ♦ **commit to (doing) sth** *I do not want to commit to any particular date.*
3 [T] to say that you will use available people or things for a particular purpose: **commit sth to sth** *They'll have to commit more money to the project if they want it to succeed.*
4 [I] to decide to have a permanent relationship with someone: *He's not ready to commit.*
5 [T] to say officially that someone must go to prison
PHRASES **commit sth to memory** to study something carefully so that you can remember it exactly
commit yourself 1 to agree to do something: *Take a little time to think before committing yourself.* **2** to give a definite opinion, or to make a definite decision: *She won't commit herself either way.*

com•mit•ment /kə'mɪtmənt/ noun ★★
1 [C/U] a promise to do something: *I want to honor my father's **commitment to** the people who farm here.* ♦ **make a commitment (to do sth)** *We've made a commitment to help, and we will.*
2 [U] enthusiasm for something and a determination to work hard at it: *There is a high **level of commitment** amongst employees.*
3 [C] a duty or responsibility that you have accepted: *I couldn't make it because of **work commitments**.* ♦ *He has huge **financial commitments**.*

com•mit•ted /kə'mɪtəd/ adj loyal to a belief, organization, or group, and willing to work hard for it

com•mit•tee /kə'mɪti/ noun [C] ★★★ a group of people who represent a larger group or organization and are chosen to do a particular job: *the Senate Foreign Relations committee* ♦ *committee meetings* ♦ *He's **on** the golf club **committee**.*

com•mod•i•ty /kə'mɑdəti/ noun [C] a product that can be bought and sold

com•mon¹ /'kɑmən/ adj ★★★
1 happening frequently, or existing in large amounts or numbers: *Today smog **is a common occurrence** in many major cities.* ♦ *It's **common practice** in most companies these days.* ♦ **it is common for sb/sth to do sth** *It was common for children to play in the street.*
2 used, done, or shared by two or more people: *Members also agreed to pursue a common trade policy.* ♦ *These issues are **common to** all our clients.*
3 ordinary, with no special status or rank: *a common soldier/criminal*
PHRASE **the common good** the benefit of everyone

com•mon² /'kɑmən/ noun [C] a large piece of open land in a town or city where anyone can walk or play games
PHRASES **have sth in common (with sb)** to have the same interests or opinions as someone else: *We have a lot in common.*
have sth in common (with sth) to have the same features as something else
→ HOUSE OF COMMONS

ˌcommon 'cold, the noun [singular] a minor illness that makes you SNEEZE and cough

ˌcommon 'ground noun [U] something that people can agree about when they disagree about other things

ˌcommon 'knowledge noun [U] something that everyone knows

ˌcommon 'law¹ noun [U] the system of law that has developed from customs and judges' decisions instead of from laws made by politicians

ˌcommon 'law² adj involved in a relationship that has continued long enough to be considered a marriage, even though it is not official: *a common law husband/wife*

com•mon•ly /'kɑmənli/ adv usually, or frequently

com•mon•place /'kɑmənˌpleɪs/ adj completely normal: *It is now commonplace for people to use the Internet at home.*

ˌcommon 'sense noun [U] the ability to use good judgment and make sensible decisions

com•mon•wealth /'kɑmənˌwelθ/ noun [C] **1** a group of countries that have the same political or economic interests **2** a part of the U.S. that is not a state and has its own government, for example Puerto Rico

com•mo•tion /kə'moʊʃ(ə)n/ noun [C/U] noise and confused activity

com•mu•nal /kə'mjun(ə)l/ adj owned or used by everyone in a group: *a communal kitchen/garden*

com•mune¹ /'kɑˌmjun/ noun [C] a group of people who live together and share work, food, income, and possessions

com•mune² /kə'mjun/ verb [I] *literary* to communicate with someone or something without using words

com•mu•ni•cate /kə'mjunɪˌkeɪt/ verb ★
1 [I/T] to express thoughts, feelings, or information to someone else: *How do whales communicate?* ♦ *We **communicate with** each other via e-mail.* ♦ **communicate sth to sb** *The information was communicated to officials in July 1981.*
2 [I/T] to make someone understand an emotion or idea without expressing it in words: *She has an amazing ability to communicate enthusiasm.*
3 [I] to let someone know what you are feeling or thinking, so that you have a good relationship: *She says that they no longer seem to communicate.*

com•mu•ni•ca•tion /kəˌmjunɪ'keɪʃ(ə)n/ noun ★★★
1 [U] the process of giving or exchanging information or of making emotions or ideas known to someone: *efforts to improve*

communication among the staff ♦ *There was a breakdown in communication.* ♦ *The two groups are **in regular communication**.* ♦ *She has no **communication with** her family.* ♦ *a workshop to improve teachers' **communication skills***
2 communications [plural] a system for sending information: *satellite communications*
3 [C] *formal* a message such as a letter, phone call, or e-mail

com·mu·ni·ca·tive /kəˈmjunɪˌkeɪtɪv, kəˈmjunɪkətɪv/ adj willing to tell things to other people

com·mun·ion /kəˈmjunjən/ noun [U] **1 Communion** or **Holy Communion** a Christian ceremony in which people eat bread and drink wine in order to remember Jesus Christ **2** *formal* communication with someone or something without using words

com·mu·ni·qué /kəˌmjunɪˈkeɪ, kəˈmjunɪˌkeɪ/ noun [C] an official statement

com·mu·nism /ˈkɑmjəˌnɪzəm/ noun [U] a political and economic system in which individual people do not own property or industries and in which people of all social classes are treated equally

com·mu·nist /ˈkɑmjənɪst/ noun [C] someone who believes in communism —**com·mu·nist** adj

com·mu·ni·ty /kəˈmjunəti/ noun ★★★
1 [C] the people who live in an area: *small rural communities* ♦ *I wanted to work somewhere where I could serve the community.*
2 [C] a group of people in a larger society who are the same in some way: *areas where there are large Jewish communities*
3 [U] the feeling that you belong to a group and that this is a good thing: *One of the major goals is to develop **a sense of community**.*

comˈmunity ˌcollege noun [C] a college that offers students a two-year course of study → JUNIOR COLLEGE

comˈmunity ˌservice noun [U] **1** work that someone does as a punishment, instead of going to prison **2** work without payment that someone does to help their local community

com·mute¹ /kəˈmjut/ verb **1** [I] to travel regularly to and from work **2** [T] *legal* to change a punishment to one that is less severe

com·mute² /kəˈmjut/ noun [singular] the trip to and from work every day

com·mut·er /kəˈmjutər/ noun [C] someone who travels regularly to and from work

com·pact¹ /kəmˈpækt, ˈkɑmˌpækt/ adj smaller than most things of the same kind: *a compact car/camera*

com·pact² /kəmˈpækt/ verb [T] to make something smaller or firmer by pressing it

com·pact³ /ˈkɑmˌpækt/ noun [C] **1** *American* a small car **2** a small flat container for FACE POWDER, with a mirror inside

ˌcompact ˈdisc noun [C] a CD

com·pan·ion /kəmˈpænjən/ noun [C] someone who is with you or who you spend a lot of time with

com·pan·ion·ship /kəmˈpænjənˌʃɪp/ noun [U] the relationship that you have with a good friend who spends a lot of time with you

com·pa·ny /ˈkʌmpəni/ noun ★★★
1 [C] an organization that sells services or goods: *Max works for a large oil company.*
2 [C] a group of actors, singers, or dancers who perform together: *a dance/theater company*
3 [U] the activity of being with other people: *I thought you might want some company tonight.* ♦ *We always enjoy his company.* ♦ *She's not coming – she has company* (=a guest or guests).
PHRASES **be good company** to be someone who people enjoy spending time with
keep sb company to spend time with someone so that they will not feel lonely

> **Talking or writing about companies**
> - **business** a company that makes or sells goods, or provides a service
> - **cooperative** a company that is owned and run by all the people who work in it
> - **corporation** a large company that employs a lot of people
> - **firm** a company, especially one that provides professional or financial services
> - **multinational** a large company that operates in many different countries
> - **subsidiary** a company that is owned by a larger company

com·pa·ra·ble /ˈkɑmp(ə)rəb(ə)l/ adj fairly similar to another thing, so that it is reasonable to compare them ≠ INCOMPARABLE: *The salary is comparable with that of a junior doctor.*

com·par·a·tive¹ /kəmˈperətɪv/ adj **1** judged in comparison with something such as a previous situation or state = RELATIVE: *We expected to win with comparative ease.* **2** involving the comparison of two or more things: *a comparative analysis* **3** *linguistics* the comparative form of an adjective or adverb is the form that shows that something has more of a quality than it previously had or more of a quality than something else has. For example, "newer" is the comparative form of "new." → SUPERLATIVE²

com·par·a·tive² /kəmˈperətɪv/ noun [C] *linguistics* a comparative form of an adjective or adverb: *The comparative of "good" is "better."*

com·par·a·tive·ly /kəmˈperətɪvli/ adv as compared with something else or with a previous situation or state = RELATIVELY: *The technology is still comparatively new.*

com·pare /kəmˈper/ verb ★★★
1 [T] to consider the ways in which people or things are similar or different: *The research **compares and contrasts** the two policies* (=shows how they are similar and how they are different). ♦ **compare sth with/to sth** *Compare the one that has been cleaned with the others.*
2 [I] to be as good or bad as someone or something else: ***How does** Mexico's performance **compare with** performance in other Latin countries?*
3 [T] to say that one person or thing is similar to another: **compare sth to sth** *The*

band has been compared to the Beatles.

PHRASE **compare notes** to discuss something with someone who has also experienced it or thought about it

C

Word family: compare

Words in the same family as ***compare***

- comparative *adj*
- comparatively *adv*
- comparable *adj*
- incomparable *adj*
- comparison *n*

com•pared /kəm'perd/ adj **compared with/to** used for talking about the ways in which two people or things are different, or about the ways in which someone or something has changed: *Profits were good compared with last year.*

com•par•i•son /kəm'perɪsən/ noun [C/U] ★★ the process of considering the ways in which people or things are similar or different: *It is very difficult to* ***make comparisons with*** *other schools.* ♦ *We cannot* ***make a comparison between*** *the two languages.* ♦ *There was some* ***comparison of*** *the techniques used by the different players.*

PHRASES **in/by comparison (with)** used for talking about the ways in which two people or things are different: *Our lives seem so dull in comparison with theirs.*

there's no comparison used for saying that one person or thing is much better than another

com•part•ment /kəm'pɑrtmənt/ noun [C] **1** one of the separate parts of a container or place where things are stored **2** one of the separate spaces into which a railroad passenger car or airplane is divided

com•pass /'kʌmpəs/ noun [C] **1** a piece of equipment used for finding your way, with a needle that always points to the north **2** a piece of equipment in the shape of the letter V, used for drawing circles

com•pas•sion /kəm'pæʃ(ə)n/ noun [U] sympathy for someone who is in a bad situation

com•pas•sion•ate /kəm'pæʃ(ə)nət/ adj caring about someone who is in a bad situation

com•pat•i•ble /kəm'pætəb(ə)l/ adj **1** able to exist together with another idea or system: *The proposed new regulation is not compatible with our existing policy.*
2 *computing* able to be used together with another piece of computer equipment or software **3** likely to have a good relationship because of being similar ≠ INCOMPATIBLE: *We're just not compatible.* —**com•pat•i•bil•i•ty** /kəm,pætə'bɪləti/ noun [U]

com•pa•tri•ot /kəm'peɪtriət/ noun [C] someone who is from the same country as you

com•pel /kəm'pel/ verb [T] to force someone to do something

com•pel•ling /kəm'pelɪŋ/ adj **1** interesting or exciting enough to keep your attention completely: *a compelling story* **2** able to persuade someone to do or believe something: *compelling evidence*

com•pen•sate /'kɑmpən,seɪt/ verb **1** [I] to change or remove the bad effect of something: *Their enthusiasm compensates for their lack of skill.* **2** [I/T] to pay someone money because they have suffered an injury or loss: *They were compensated for the damage to the house.*

com•pen•sa•tion /,kɑmpən'seɪʃ(ə)n/ noun
1 [C/U] something that changes or removes the bad effect of something: *He uses speed as compensation for his lack of strength.*
2 [U] money that someone receives because something bad has happened to them: *She was awarded $350,000 compensation for her injuries.*

com•pete /kəm'pit/ verb [I] ★★
1 to try to be more successful than other companies or people in business: *We're too small to* ***compete with*** *a company like that.*
2 to try to win a competition: *Her dream was to* ***compete in the Olympics.*** ♦ *You will be* ***competing against*** *the best athletes in the world.* ♦ *Ten teams will* ***compete for the*** *trophy.*

Word family: compete

Words in the same family as ***compete***

- competition *n*
- competitor *n*
- competitive *adj*
- uncompetitive *adj*

com•pe•tence /'kɑmpɪtəns/ noun [U] the ability to do something well: *I am not questioning your competence.*

com•pe•tent /'kɑmpɪtənt/ adj **1** capable of doing something well **2** good enough, but not extremely good ≠ INCOMPETENT —**com•pe•tent•ly** adv

com•pet•ing /kəm'pitɪŋ/ adj competing arguments, claims, or theories cannot all be true

com•pe•ti•tion /,kɑmpə'tɪʃ(ə)n/ noun ★★★
1 [U] the activities of companies that are trying to be more successful than others: *intense* ***competition between*** *the two computer giants*
2 [U] the activities of people who are trying to get something that other people also want: *There is a lot of* ***competition for*** *jobs.* ♦ *We must emphasize that we are not* ***in competition with*** (=competing with) *you.*
3 [C] an organized event in which people try to win prizes by being better than other people: *He* ***entered a competition*** *in the local newspaper.*
4 the competition [singular] the person, company, or thing that someone is competing with: *Let's look at what the competition is doing and do it better.*

com•pet•i•tive /kəm'petətɪv/ adj ★★
1 a competitive activity is one in which companies or teams are competing against each other: *the struggle to survive in a* ***highly competitive*** *marketplace*
2 less expensive than others: *a wide range of goods at very competitive prices*
3 always trying to be more successful than other people: *a* ***highly competitive*** *player* —**com•pet•i•tive•ly** adv, **com•pet•i•tive•ness** noun [U]

com•pet•i•tor /kəm'petɪtər/ noun [C] **1** a company that sells the same goods or services as another **2** someone who takes part in a sports competition

com•pi•la•tion /,kɑmpɪ'leɪʃ(ə)n/ noun [C] a set of things such as songs or stories that are brought together from different places

com•pile /kəm'paɪl/ verb [T] to make a list or

book using information from many different places

com•pla•cent /kəmˈpleɪs(ə)nt/ adj too confident and relaxed because you think you can deal with something easily, even though this may not be true —**com•pla•cen•cy** /kəmˈpleɪs(ə)nsi/ noun [U], **com•pla•cent•ly** adv

com•plain /kəmˈpleɪn/ verb [I/T] ★★★ to say that you are not satisfied with something: *What are you **complaining about**?* ♦ *He threatened to **complain to the boss**.* ♦ **+(that)** *She complained that it was too hot.*
PHRASAL VERB **comˈplain of sth** to say that you have a pain or an illness

com•plaint /kəmˈpleɪnt/ noun ★★
1 [C/U] a statement that you are not satisfied with something: *I intend to **make a complaint**.* ♦ *There's been a **complaint about** your work.* ♦ *Several **complaints** have been made **against** him.* ♦ **+that** *complaints that the building is not safe*
2 [C] something that someone complains about: *The main complaint was the noise.*
3 [C] an illness or other medical problem

com•ple•ment[1] /ˈkɑmpləˌment/ verb [T] to combine well with something: *a simple sweater that was complemented by elegant jewelry*

com•ple•ment[2] /ˈkɑmpləmənt/ noun [C]
1 something that combines well with something else: *Our sauces are the perfect complement to any meal.* 2 the number of people or things that something has: *We already have our full complement of workers.* 3 *linguistics* a word or phrase after a verb such as "be" that tells you about the SUBJECT. For example, in "He was a nice man," the complement is "a nice man."

com•ple•men•ta•ry /ˌkɑmpləˈment(ə)ri/ adj combining well together, or looking attractive together

com•plete[1] /kəmˈplit/ adj ★★★
1 including everything ≠ INCOMPLETE: *a complete set of her novels*
2 finished: *When the chart is complete, stick it on the wall.*
3 used for emphasizing that someone or something has a particular quality: *He's a complete idiot.*
PHRASE **complete with** including something: *All our machines come complete with a three-year service guarantee.*

com•plete[2] /kəmˈplit/ verb [T] ★★★
1 to finish something: *The work was completed in March.*
2 to add the missing parts of something in order to finish it: *Complete the following sentence by writing in the correct form of the present tense.* ♦ *Please complete this form* (=write in the blank spaces).

com•plete•ly /kəmˈplitli/ adv ★★★ used for emphasis: *Ellen's suggestion took us completely by surprise.*

com•ple•tion /kəmˈpliʃ(ə)n/ noun [U] ★ the process of finishing an activity or job: *Nothing must delay the **completion of** the project.* ♦ *You will get a certificate **on completion of** the course.*

com•plex[1] /kəmˈpleks, ˈkɑmˌpleks/ adj ★★ containing many details or small parts and therefore difficult to understand or deal with: *These rules are very complex.*

com•plex[2] /ˈkɑmˌpleks/ noun [C] 1 a group of buildings, or a building with several parts 2 an emotional problem caused by unreasonable fears or worries: *I used to have a complex about being so tall.*

com•plex•ion /kəmˈplekʃ(ə)n/ noun 1 [C] the appearance and color of the skin on your face 2 [singular] the typical features of something

com•plex•i•ty /kəmˈpleksəti/ noun 1 [U] the complicated nature of something
2 **complexities** [plural] the features of something that make it confusing or difficult to deal with

com•pli•ance /kəmˈplaɪəns/ noun [U] *formal* the practice of obeying a law, rule, or request: *All building work must be carried out in compliance with safety regulations.*

com•pli•ant /kəmˈplaɪənt/ adj extremely willing to do what people tell you to do

com•pli•cate /ˈkɑmplɪˌkeɪt/ verb [T] to make something more difficult to deal with or understand

com•pli•cat•ed /ˈkɑmplɪˌkeɪtəd/ adj ★★ difficult to do, deal with, or understand ≠ SIMPLE

com•pli•ca•tion /ˌkɑmplɪˈkeɪʃ(ə)n/ noun 1 [C] a new medical problem that makes a medical condition more serious 2 [C/U] something that makes a process or activity more difficult to deal with

com•plic•i•ty /kəmˈplɪsəti/ noun [U] the fact that someone is involved in or knows about something bad

com•pli•ment[1] /ˈkɑmplɪmənt/ noun [C] something nice that you say to praise someone ≠ INSULT: *He kept paying me compliments on my cooking.*
PHRASE **with the compliments of sb** used for saying that you do not have to pay for something

com•pli•ment[2] /ˈkɑmplɪˌment/ verb [T] to say something nice to or about someone: *Everybody complimented her on the way she handled the emergency.*

com•pli•men•ta•ry /ˌkɑmplɪˈment(ə)ri/ adj 1 free: *complimentary tickets* 2 saying nice things about someone or something: *She was very complimentary about your work.*

com•ply /kəmˈplaɪ/ verb [I] to obey a rule or law, or to do what someone asks you to do: *You are legally obliged to comply with any investigations.*

> **Words often used with comply**
>
> *Nouns often used with **comply***
> - COMPLY WITH + **demand, order, request, requirement**: do something that someone says
> - COMPLY WITH + **legislation, regulation, rule**: obey a law or rule

com•po•nent /kəmˈpoʊnənt/ noun [C] ★
1 a part of a machine or piece of equipment
2 an individual quality or feature of something

Words often used with component

Adjectives often used with **component** *(sense 2)*

- **essential, key, major, principal, vital** + COMPONENT: used about a feature that is important or necessary

C

com•pose /kəmˈpoʊz/ verb ★
1 [I/T] to write a piece of music: *The song was composed for their wedding.*
2 [T] *formal* to write something after thinking carefully about it: *He sat down and composed a letter of resignation.*
PHRASES **be composed of sth** to consist of something: *Muscle is composed of two different types of protein.*
compose yourself to make yourself calm after being very angry, upset, or nervous

com•posed /kəmˈpoʊzd/ adj calm and relaxed

com•pos•er /kəmˈpoʊzər/ noun [C] someone who writes music

com•pos•ite /kəmˈpɑzɪt/ adj made up of separate parts —**com•pos•ite** noun [C]

com•po•si•tion /ˌkɑmpəˈzɪʃ(ə)n/ noun ★
1 [U] the way in which something is formed from separate parts or people: *Households differ widely in their size and composition.*
2 [C] a piece of music, a piece of writing, or a painting
3 [U] the skill or process of producing music, writing, or paintings

com•post /ˈkɑmˌpoʊst/ noun [U] a mixture of decaying plants and vegetables that is added to soil to improve it

com•po•sure /kəmˈpoʊʒər/ noun [U] the feeling of being calm and relaxed

com•pound¹ /ˈkɑmˌpaʊnd/ noun [C] **1** *science* a chemical substance that consists of two or more elements **2** an enclosed area where a particular group of people live or exercise **3** *linguistics* a combination of two or more words used as a single word

com•pound² /kəmˈpaʊnd/ verb [T] to make a problem or difficult situation worse

com•pre•hend /ˌkɑmprəˈhend/ verb [I/T] *formal* to understand something

com•pre•hen•si•ble /ˌkɑmprəˈhensəb(ə)l/ adj able to be understood ≠ INCOMPREHENSIBLE

com•pre•hen•sion /ˌkɑmprəˈhenʃ(ə)n/ noun [U] the ability to understand something: *These acts of cruelty are beyond my comprehension* (=impossible for me to understand).

com•pre•hen•sive /ˌkɑmprəˈhensɪv/ adj including everything: *a comprehensive guide to university courses*

com•press /kəmˈpres/ verb [T] **1** to press something so that it fits into a smaller space **2** to make something last for less time than usual —**com•pres•sion** /kəmˈpreʃ(ə)n/ noun [U]

com•prise /kəmˈpraɪz/ verb [T] *formal* to form something: *People aged 65 and over comprise 20% of the population.*
PHRASE **be comprised of** to consist of two or more things: *The force is comprised of U.S. and British troops.*

com•pro•mise¹ /ˈkɑmprəˌmaɪz/ noun [C/U] a way of solving a disagreement in which both people accept that they cannot have everything that they want: *Neither of them is willing to make compromises.* ♦ *Both sides have agreed to try to reach a compromise.*

com•pro•mise² /ˈkɑmprəˌmaɪz/ verb **1** [I] to solve a disagreement by accepting that you cannot have everything that you want: *Can we compromise on the schedule if not on pay?* **2** [T] to risk harming or losing something important: *We will not compromise the safety of our workers.* **3** [T] to do things that do not agree with your beliefs or principles: *The party is obviously compromising its principles.*

com•pro•mis•ing /ˈkɑmprəˌmaɪzɪŋ/ adj likely to damage your reputation

com•pul•sion /kəmˈpʌlʃ(ə)n/ noun **1** [C] an extremely strong feeling of wanting to do something **2** [U] an obligation to do something

com•pul•sive /kəmˈpʌlsɪv/ adj **1** impossible to control: *a compulsive need to succeed* **2** unable to control a habit: *a compulsive liar* —**com•pul•sive•ly** adv

com•pul•so•ry /kəmˈpʌlsəri/ adj ★ something that is compulsory must be done or used because of a rule or law ≠ OPTIONAL: *compulsory exams*

com•put•er /kəmˈpjutər/ noun [C] ★★★ an electronic machine that has programs on it for storing, writing, and calculating information. It also allows you to communicate on the Internet: *a computer program/game* —*picture* → C3

com•put•er-aid•ed de•sign /kəmˌpjutərˌeɪdɪd dɪˈzaɪn/ noun [U] CAD

com•put•er•ize /kəmˈpjutəˌraɪz/ verb [T] to use computers to do a particular job —**com•put•er•iz•a•tion** /kəmˌpjutəraɪˈzeɪʃ(ə)n/ noun [U]

comˌputer-ˈliterate adj able to use a computer

com•put•ing /kəmˈpjutɪŋ/ noun [U] the activity or skill of using or PROGRAMMING computers

com•rade /ˈkɑmˌræd/ noun [C] *formal* a friend who you work with or who is in the same army as you —**com•rade•ship** noun [U]

con¹ /kɑn/ noun [C] *informal* a trick for making someone believe something that is not true in order to get money from them

con² /kɑn/ verb [T] *informal* to make someone believe something that is not true in order to get money from them

con•cave /kɑnˌkeɪv, kɑnˈkeɪv/ adj curved inward ≠ CONVEX

con•ceal /kənˈsil/ verb [T] *formal* to hide something, or to keep something secret: *She could not conceal her annoyance.*

con•cede /kənˈsid/ verb **1** [T] to admit that something is true: *Myers was forced to concede that competition had badly affected profits.* **2** [I/T] to stop trying to win something because you realize that you cannot: *He finally had to concede defeat.* **3** [T] to give something that you own or control to someone, although you do not want to: *Some territory has been conceded to the rebels.*

con•ceit /kənˈsit/ noun [U] a conceited attitude or way of behaving

con•ceit•ed /kənˈsitəd/ adj *showing disapproval* behaving in a way that shows that you think you are very intelligent, skillful, or attractive

con•ceiv•a•ble /kənˈsivəb(ə)l/ adj possible, or possible to imagine ≠ INCONCEIVABLE —**con•ceiv•a•bly** adv

con•ceive /kənˈsiv/ verb **1** [T] to think of a new idea, plan, or design: *The facilities had been conceived with families in mind.* **2** [I/T] to imagine something, or to think of doing something: *How can they even conceive of cutting back on welfare?* **3** [I/T] to become pregnant

con•cen•trate /ˈkɑnsənˌtreɪt/ verb ★★★
1 [I/T] to give all your attention to the thing that you are doing: *Shh! I'm trying to concentrate.* ♦ *Just* ***concentrate on*** *your work.*
2 [T] **be concentrated** to exist mainly in a particular area: *The violence was concentrated mostly in the north.*

con•cen•trat•ed /ˈkɑnsənˌtreɪtəd/ adj
1 concentrated liquids or substances have been made stronger by having water removed **2** directed completely at one thing, person, or place: *The presidential palace has been hit again by concentrated artillery fire.*

con•cen•tra•tion /ˌkɑnsənˈtreɪʃ(ə)n/ noun ★★★
1 [U] the process of giving all your attention to something: *It took all his concentration to stay awake.*
2 [C/U] a large number of people or things in one area: *The largest concentrations of ancient sites are around Cairo and Luxor.*

ˌconcenˈtration ˌcamp noun [C] a prison where ordinary people are kept during a war in very unpleasant conditions

con•cen•tric /kənˈsentrɪk/ adj concentric circles all have the same center

con•cept /ˈkɑnˌsept/ noun [C] ★★★ an idea: *It's important that children learn to understand* ***the concept of*** *sharing.* —**con•cep•tu•al** /kənˈseptʃuəl/ adj

con•cep•tion /kənˈsepʃ(ə)n/ noun **1** [C] a belief about what something is like: *His conception of the world is a very strange one.* **2** [U] the moment when a woman becomes pregnant

con•cern¹ /kənˈsɜrn/ noun ★★★
1 [C/U] a feeling of worry, or something that worries you: *There's a lot of* ***public concern about*** *modern farming methods.* ♦ *The trip was canceled because of* ***concerns over*** *safety.* ♦ *It's* ***a matter of major concern to*** *employers* (=it worries them). ♦ *Her doctor said her condition was* ***causing concern.***
2 [C/U] something that you think is important: *My only concern is to find my daughter.*
3 [singular] a responsibility: *If those children are skipping school, then that is the parents' concern.*
4 [C] a business: *a large concern employing 600 people*

> Words often used with **concern**
>
> *Adjectives often used with* ***concern*** *(noun, sense 2)*
> - **central, chief, main, major, overriding, primary, principal** + CONCERN: used about something that is very important
>
> *Verbs often used with* ***concern*** *(noun, sense 1)*
> - **express, raise, voice** + CONCERN: tell people that you are worried
> - **be a cause for, be a matter of, cause** + CONCERN: make someone worried

C

con•cern² /kənˈsɜrn/ verb [T] ★★★
1 to worry someone: ***It concerns me that*** *these people are not getting the support they need.*
2 to be about a particular subject: *The story concerns a friend of mine.*
3 to involve or affect someone: *My past doesn't concern you.*
PHRASE **concern yourself** to think about or worry about something: *I'm too busy to concern myself with the details.*

con•cerned /kənˈsɜrnd/ adj ★★★
1 *formal* worried about something ≠ UNCONCERNED: *The police said they were very* ***concerned about*** *the boy's safety.*
2 caring about what happens to someone: *I think she's genuinely* ***concerned about*** *you.*
3 involved in something, or affected by something: *I suggest you talk with the person concerned.*
4 giving your attention to something that you think is important: *Don't be so* ***concerned with*** *what other people think of you.*
PHRASES **as far as I'm concerned** used for giving your opinion about something: *As far as I'm concerned, the issue is over and done with.*
as far as sb/sth is concerned used for saying which person or thing you are talking about: *I make the decisions as far as finance is concerned.*

con•cern•ing /kənˈsɜrnɪŋ/ preposition *formal* ★★ about a particular subject: *a newspaper article concerning pollution*

con•cert /ˈkɑnsərt/ noun [C] ★★ an event at which an orchestra, band, or musician plays or sings in front of an audience

con•cert•ed /kənˈsɜrtəd/ adj involving a lot of people working together in a determined way: *a concerted effort*

con•cer•to /kənˈtʃertoʊ, kənˈtʃɜrtoʊ/ noun [C] a piece of music for a musical instrument and an orchestra: *Beethoven's Violin Concerto*

con•ces•sion /kənˈseʃ(ə)n/ noun [C]
1 something that you agree to in order to reach an agreement: *He said they would not make concessions to the union.* **2** a right that is given to a person or group to sell something or perform a particular activity: *timber concessions to Korean companies* **3** a reduction in the rate of something for a particular group of people: *tax concessions*

conˈcession ˌstand noun [C] *American* a STAND at a sports event, theater, etc. where people can buy food and drinks

con•cierge /kɑnˈsjerʒ/ noun [C] someone in a hotel whose job is to help people with problems and to give them information

con•cil•i•a•tion /kənˌsɪliˈeɪʃ(ə)n/ noun [U] the process of trying to end an argument between two people or groups

con•cil•i•a•to•ry /kənˈsɪliəˌtɔri/ adj trying to end an argument and make people feel less angry

C

con•cise /kən'saɪs/ adj expressed clearly using only a few words —**con•cise•ly** adv

con•clude /kən'klud/ verb ★★
1 [T] to decide that something is true after looking at all the evidence: **+that** *The report concluded that a recession was unlikely.*
2 [T] *formal* to officially arrange something: *We hope to conclude an agreement by the end of the day.*
3 [I/T] *formal* to end, or to end something: *The article concludes with the names and addresses of organizations that can help.* ♦ *The president will conclude his visit with a trip to Munich.*

con•clud•ing /kən'kludɪŋ/ adj happening or done at the end of something: *concluding remarks*

con•clu•sion /kən'kluʒ(ə)n/ noun ★★★
1 [C] something that you decide is true after looking at all the evidence: *I finally **came to the conclusion** that Lenny wasn't interested in me.* ♦ *Hubble **reached the conclusion** that the universe was expanding.*
2 [singular] *formal* the end of something: *a successful **conclusion to the season***
PHRASES **in conclusion** finally: *In conclusion, I would like to thank my wife and children.*
jump to conclusions to make a decision about something before you know all the facts

con•clu•sive /kən'klusɪv/ adj conclusive evidence, proof, or information proves that something is true ≠ INCONCLUSIVE —**con•clu•sive•ly** adv

con•coct /kən'kɑkt/ verb [T] **1** to invent a false explanation or false information **2** to produce something unusual by mixing things in a new way —**con•coc•tion** /kən'kɑkʃ(ə)n/ noun [C/U]

con•course /'kɑŋˌkɔrs/ noun [C] a large open area in an airport or train station, or in front of a public building

con•crete[1] /'kɑŋˌkrit/ adj ★
1 made of concrete
2 based on facts: *concrete evidence*

con•crete[2] /'kɑŋˌkrit, kɑŋ'krit/ noun [U] a hard substance used in building that is made by mixing CEMENT, sand, small stones, and water

con•crete[3] /kɑŋ'krit, 'kɑŋˌkrit/ or **'concrete ˌover sth** verb [T] to cover something with concrete

'concrete ˌnoun noun [C] *linguistics* a noun that refers to an object that you can see or touch rather than to an idea or feeling

con•cur /kən'kɜr/ verb [I] *formal* to agree

con•cus•sion /kən'kʌʃ(ə)n/ noun [C/U] a head injury that makes someone feel sick or become unconscious for a short time

con•demn /kən'dem/ verb [T] ★
1 to say publicly that you think someone or something is bad or wrong: *Politicians have condemned the attacks.* ♦ **condemn sb/sth as sth** *The mayor condemned the proposal as "very damaging."*
2 to give a punishment to someone who has committed a crime: *Fifty rebels were **condemned to death.***
3 to order something such as a building or machine to be destroyed because it is not safe

con•dem•na•tion /ˌkɑndem'neɪʃ(ə)n/ noun [C/U] a public statement in which you criticize someone or something severely

con•den•sa•tion /ˌkɑnden'seɪʃ(ə)n/ noun [U] water that forms when steam or warm air changes into liquid

con•dense /kən'dens/ verb **1** [T] to make something shorter or smaller **2** [I/T] if gas or steam condenses, or if something condenses it, it changes into a liquid

con•de•scend•ing /ˌkɑndə'sendɪŋ/ adj showing that you think you are more important or intelligent than someone else —**con•des•cend** /ˌkɑndə'send/ verb [I], **con•des•cen•sion** /ˌkɑndə'senʃ(ə)n/ noun [U]

con•di•ment /'kɑndɪmənt/ noun [C] *formal* something such as salt, pepper, or a sauce that you put on food to make it taste better

con•di•tion[1] /kən'dɪʃ(ə)n/ noun ★★★
1 [singular/U] the physical state of something or someone: *Engineers will examine the condition of the damaged buildings.* ♦ *The five people who were rescued were all **in good condition.***
2 conditions [plural] the situation or environment in which something happens or someone lives: *Their role is to create **the conditions for** peace in the region.* ♦ *The project aims to provide better **living conditions** for elderly people.*
3 [C] something that must be true or must be done before another thing can happen: *Read the **terms and conditions** of the contract carefully.* ♦ *You will have to **meet** strict financial **conditions** to get the loan.*
4 [C] an illness or health problem that lasts a long time and affects the way you live: *a heart condition* ♦ *Both children suffer from the same **medical condition.***
PHRASES **in no condition to do sth** too sick, upset, or drunk to do something
on condition (that) used for saying that one thing will happen only if another thing also happens: *They agreed to speak on condition that their names would not be used in the article.*

con•di•tion[2] /kən'dɪʃ(ə)n/ verb [T] **1** to make your hair feel softer by putting a special liquid on it after you have washed it **2** to influence someone over a long period so that they think or behave in a particular way —**con•di•tion•ing** /kən'dɪʃ(ə)nɪŋ/ noun [U]

con•di•tion•al /kən'dɪʃ(ə)nəl/ adj ★
1 something that is conditional will only happen if something else happens: *The job offer is **conditional on** passing a medical examination.*
2 *linguistics* a conditional CLAUSE usually begins with "if" or "unless" and says what must happen or exist in order for the information in the main part of the sentence to be true

con•di•tion•er /kən'dɪʃ(ə)nər/ noun [C/U] a liquid that you put on your hair after you have washed it in order to make it feel softer

con•do /'kɑndoʊ/ noun [C] *American informal* a CONDOMINIUM

con•do•len•ces /kən'doʊlənsɪz/ noun [plural] the things that you say in order to show sympathy when someone has just died

con•dom /ˈkɑndəm/ noun [C] a thin rubber tube that a man covers his PENIS with during sex in order to prevent a woman from becoming pregnant and to protect against diseases

con•do•min•i•um /ˌkɑndəˈmɪniəm/ noun [C] *American* a building containing apartments that are owned by the people who live there, or one of these apartments

con•done /kənˈdoʊn/ verb [T] to approve of behavior that most people think is wrong

con•du•cive /kənˈdusɪv/ adj **conducive to sth** creating a situation that helps something to happen

con•duct¹ /kənˈdʌkt/ verb ★★

1 [T] to do something in an organized way: *The interview was conducted by telephone.*

2 [I/T] to stand in front of an orchestra or group of singers and direct the way they play or sing

3 [T] if something conducts heat or electricity, heat or electricity can move through it

PHRASE **conduct yourself** *formal* to behave in a particular way

con•duct² /ˈkɑnˌdʌkt/ noun [U] *formal* ★

1 the way someone behaves: *The coach criticized his team for their conduct.*

2 the way in which a process or activity is managed

con•duc•tor /kənˈdʌktər/ noun [C] **1** someone who directs the musicians in an orchestra or a group of singers **2** someone on a bus who checks tickets and collects money **3** a substance that allows heat or electricity to move through it

cone /koʊn/ noun [C] **1** an object with a circular base that rises to a point *—picture* → C8 **2** an object shaped like a cone that you put ICE CREAM in. You can also eat the cone. **3** the fruit of a PINE tree

con•fed•er•a•tion /kənˌfedəˈreɪʃ(ə)n/ noun [C] a group of people or organizations that are united

con•fer /kənˈfɜr/ verb **1** [I] to take part in a discussion about a particular subject **2** [T] *formal* to give something such as a legal right or an honor to someone

con•fer•ence /ˈkɑnf(ə)rəns/ noun [C] ★★

1 a large meeting where people who are interested in a particular subject discuss ideas: *a conference hall/room/center* ♦ *an international* ***conference on*** *the control of illegal drugs*

2 a group of teams that play against each other

3 a meeting where a small number of people have formal discussions

ˈ**conference ˌcall** noun [C] a telephone call involving three or more people

con•fess /kənˈfes/ verb [I/T] **1** to admit that you have done something illegal or wrong: *Simpson has confessed to taking the money.* ♦ *He confessed that he had been seeing another woman.* **2** to admit something that you are embarrassed about: *He confessed he did not understand financial matters at all.* **3** to tell a priest about the bad things that you have done and ask to be forgiven

con•fes•sion /kənˈfeʃ(ə)n/ noun [C/U] **1** a statement in which you admit that you have done something illegal or wrong **2** a statement that you make to a priest about the bad things that you have done

con•fet•ti /kənˈfeti/ noun [U] small pieces of colored paper that people throw in the air to celebrate a wedding

con•fi•dant /ˈkɑnfɪˌdænt, ˈkɑnfɪˌdɑnt/ noun [C] someone who you trust and discuss your private feelings with

con•fi•dante /ˈkɑnfɪˌdænt, ˈkɑnfɪˌdɑnt/ noun [C] a woman who you trust and discuss your private feelings with

con•fide /kənˈfaɪd/ verb [I/T] to tell someone about something that is private or secret: *She confided to friends that she was scared of her mother.*

con•fi•dence /ˈkɑnfɪdəns/ noun [U] ★★★

1 the belief that you are able to do things well: *You should* ***have more confidence in*** *your yourself.* ♦ *I'm taking this course mainly to* ***gain*** *a little* ***confidence.*** ♦ *The more he fails, the more he* ***loses confidence.***

2 the belief that someone or something is good and that you can trust them: *Public* ***confidence in*** *the police is very low.* ♦ *I have complete* ***confidence in*** *our chairman.* ♦ *Many businesses have* ***lost confidence in*** *the government's economic policies.* ♦ *It took me a while to* ***gain*** *her* ***confidence*** (=make her feel that she could trust me).

3 the belief that something is true: *I can say* ***with confidence*** *that all our targets have now been met.* ♦ **+that** *He expressed his confidence that the project would be a success.*

PHRASE **in confidence** if you tell someone something in confidence, you trust them not to tell anyone else: *Any information you give us will be treated* ***in the strictest confidence.***

con•fi•dent /ˈkɑnfɪdənt/ adj ★★★

1 certain about your abilities and not nervous or frightened: *a confident mood/smile/manner* ♦ *I was starting to feel more* ***confident about*** *the exam.*

2 certain that something will happen or be successful: *We were* ***confident of*** *victory.* ♦ **+that** *They are confident that the show will open on Thursday.*

con•fi•den•tial /ˌkɑnfɪˈdenʃ(ə)l/ adj **1** secret: *confidential information* **2** keeping information secret: *a confidential service* **—con•fi•den•tial•ly** /ˌkɑnfɪˈdenʃ(ə)li/ adv

con•fig•u•ra•tion /kənˌfɪgjəˈreɪʃ(ə)n, kənˌfɪgəˈreɪʃ(ə)n/ noun [C/U] *technical* the way in which the different parts of something are arranged **—con•fig•ure** /kənˈfɪgjər, kənˈfɪgər/ verb [T]

con•fine /kənˈfaɪn/ verb [T] **1** to keep someone or something in a particular place: *Chris was sick, and confined to bed.* **2** *formal* to keep an activity within particular limits: *Try to confine the discussion to general principles.*

PHRASE **be confined to** to happen only in a particular area, or to affect a particular group of people: *The risk of infection is confined to a few small groups.*

con•fined /kənˈfaɪnd/ adj a confined space is small and difficult to move around in

con•fine•ment /kənˈfaɪnmənt/ noun [U] a situation in which someone is forced to stay in a place

con•fines /ˈkɑnˌfaɪnz/ noun [plural] the borders

of a place, or the limits of an activity

con•firm /kənˈfɜrm/ verb ★★★

1 [T] to show or say that something is true: *The study confirms the findings of earlier research.* ♦ **+(that)** *The doctor may run a test to confirm that you are pregnant.*

2 [I/T] to tell someone that something will definitely happen at the time or in the way that has been arranged: *You can make an appointment now, and then call nearer the time to confirm.*

—**con•fir•ma•tion** /ˌkɑnfərˈmeɪʃ(ə)n/ noun [U]: *The hotel will send you written confirmation of your booking.*

con•firmed /kənˈfɜrmd/ adj always living or behaving in a particular way, or having a particular belief

con•fis•cate /ˈkɑnfɪˌskeɪt/ verb [T] to officially remove someone's possessions —**con•fis•ca•tion** /ˌkɑnfɪˈskeɪʃ(ə)n/ noun [C/U]

con•flict[1] /ˈkɑnˌflɪkt/ noun [C/U] ★★

1 angry disagreement between people or groups: *a* ***conflict between*** *the press and the police* ♦ *The management team is eager to resolve the* ***conflict over*** *wages.*

2 fighting between countries or groups: *a bloody border conflict*

3 a situation in which two things cannot easily exist together, or cannot both be true: *The two recommendations seem to* ***be in conflict with*** *each other.*

PHRASE **conflict of interest** a situation in which someone cannot make fair decisions because they will be affected by the results

con•flict[2] /kənˈflɪkt/ verb [I] if different statements or suggestions conflict, they cannot all be right or they cannot all happen: *His story conflicted with reports from other journalists.*

con•form /kənˈfɔrm/ verb [I] **1** to behave in the way that people expect you to behave: *There is great pressure on women to conform.* **2** to obey a rule, or to follow an accepted pattern: *Products are tested to make sure that they conform to safety standards.*

—**con•form•i•ty** /kənˈfɔrməti/ noun [U]

con•form•ist /kənˈfɔrmɪst/ adj behaving in a way that most people think is correct or suitable —**con•form•ist** noun [C]

con•found /kənˈfaʊnd/ verb [T] to make someone feel surprised or confused by not behaving in the way they expect

con•front /kənˈfrʌnt/ verb [T] **1** to deal with a difficult situation: *It takes courage to confront your fears.* **2** to go close to someone in a threatening way: *The guard was confronted by an armed man.*

PHRASE **be confronted by/with sth** to be forced to deal with a difficult situation: *She was confronted with the biggest crisis of her political life.*

con•fron•ta•tion /ˌkɑnfrənˈteɪʃ(ə)n/ noun [C/U] a situation in which people are fighting or arguing angrily: *violent confrontations with the police*

con•fron•ta•tion•al /ˌkɑnfrənˈteɪʃ(ə)nəl/ adj behaving in a way that shows that you want to fight or have an argument

con•fuse /kənˈfjuz/ verb [T] ★

1 to make someone feel that they do not understand something: *Don't confuse the reader with too much extra detail.*

2 to make something more complicated: *This latest piece of information just confuses the issue.*

3 to make the mistake of thinking that one thing is another thing: *It's easy to confuse the two containers because they're so similar.*

con•fused /kənˈfjuzd/ adj ★

1 unable to understand something or think clearly about it: *She was completely confused.* ♦ *I'm still a little* ***confused about*** *what happened.*

2 complicated and not well organized or explained: *Their ideas were a little confused.* ♦ *The situation is still fairly confused.*

con•fus•ing /kənˈfjuzɪŋ/ adj ★ not easy to understand: *She left a very confusing message.*

con•fu•sion /kənˈfjuʒ(ə)n/ noun ★

1 [U] a feeling that you do not understand something or cannot decide what to do: *There seems to be some* ***confusion about*** *who actually won.* ♦ *These changes have just* ***caused*** *more* ***confusion.***

2 [U] a situation in which things are messy, badly organized, or not clear: *Inside the building was a scene of total confusion.* ♦ ***In the confusion****, I lost my bag.*

3 [singular/U] a situation in which you make the mistake of thinking that one person or thing is another: *I've put them in different colored folders to* ***avoid confusion.***

con•geal /kənˈdʒil/ verb [I] if a liquid congeals, it becomes thick and almost solid —**con•gealed** /kənˈdʒild/ adj

con•gen•ial /kənˈdʒiniəl/ adj *formal* making you feel welcome or comfortable

con•gen•i•tal /kənˈdʒenɪt(ə)l/ adj a congenital medical condition is one that someone has had since they were born

con•gest•ed /kənˈdʒestəd/ adj **1** so full of vehicles or people that it is difficult to move around: *Many of Europe's major airports are heavily congested.* **2** blocked with a liquid: *His nose was congested.*

con•ges•tion /kənˈdʒestʃ(ə)n/ noun [U] a situation or condition in which something is blocked

con•glom•er•ate /kənˈglɑmərət/ noun [C] a large business that was formed by joining together several businesses

con•glom•er•a•tion /kənˌglɑməˈreɪʃ(ə)n/ noun [C] a collection of many different types of things

con•grat•u•late /kənˈgrætʃəˌleɪt/ verb [T] ★ to tell someone that you are pleased about their success, good luck, or happiness on a special occasion: **congratulate sb on sth** *I congratulated him on his recent promotion.*

con•grat•u•la•tions /kənˌgrætʃəˈleɪʃ(ə)nz/ noun [plural] *spoken* used for telling someone that you are pleased about their success, good luck, or happiness on a special occasion: *Congratulations on your graduation!*

con•gre•gate /ˈkɑŋgrəˌgeɪt/ verb [I] to come together in a group

con•gre•ga•tion /ˌkɑŋgrəˈgeɪʃ(ə)n/ noun [C] a group of people who go to a religious service

con•gress /ˈkɑŋgrəs/ noun [C] **1** a large formal

meeting **2** a group of people who are elected to make laws in some countries

Con·gress /ˈkɑŋgrəs/ the group of people in the U.S. who are elected to make laws

con·gress·man /ˈkɑŋgrəsmən/ (plural **con·gress·men** /ˈkɑŋgrəsmən/) noun [C] a man who is a member of the U.S. Congress

con·gress·wom·an /ˈkɑŋgrəsˌwʊmən/ (plural **con·gress·wom·en** /ˈkɑŋgrəsˌwɪmɪn/) noun [C] a woman who is a member of the U.S. Congress

con·i·cal /ˈkɑnɪk(ə)l/ adj with a circular base that rises to a point

con·i·fer /ˈkɑnɪfər/ noun [C] a type of tree that produces CONES (=hard brown fruit) and stays green all year —**co·nif·er·ous** /koʊˈnɪfərəs/ adj

con·jec·ture /kənˈdʒektʃər/ noun [C/U] a theory based on information that is not complete

con·ju·gal /ˈkɑndʒəg(ə)l/ adj *formal* relating to marriage

con·ju·gate /ˈkɑndʒəˌgeɪt/ verb [T] *linguistics* to state the different forms that a verb can have —**con·ju·ga·tion** /ˌkɑndʒəˈgeɪʃ(ə)n/ noun [C/U]

con·junc·tion /kənˈdʒʌŋkʃ(ə)n/ noun [C] *linguistics* a word that is used to join words, phrases, and sentences, for example "and," "because," and "although"

PHRASE **in conjunction with** combined with

con·jure /ˈkʌndʒər/ verb [I/T] to perform magic tricks using quick hand movements

PHRASAL VERB **ˌconjure sth ˈup 1** to bring something such as a feeling or memory to your mind **2** to create or achieve something as if by magic

con·jur·er or **con·jur·or** /ˈkʌndʒərər/ noun [C] someone who performs magic tricks using quick hand movements

con·nect /kəˈnekt/ verb ★★★

1 join things	4 show a relationship
2 join to energy supply	5 in changing vehicles
3 with phone/computer	+ PHRASAL VERB

1 [I/T] to join two things together: *She carefully connected the two wires.* ♦ *This cable* ***connects to*** *the back of the TV.* ♦ **connect sth to/with sth** *one of the bridges connecting Manhattan to the rest of New York*

2 [T] to join something to a supply of electricity, water, or gas: *Check that your printer is connected and that the power is turned on.*

3 [I/T] to make it possible for someone to communicate using a telephone or computer system: *Please wait, we are trying to connect you.* ♦ *Your modem enables you to* ***connect to*** *the Internet.*

4 [T] to show a relationship between one person or thing and another: *There was no evidence then to connect smoking and lung cancer.* ♦ **connect sb to/with sth** *Police found nothing that connected him with the murder.*

5 [I] to arrive in time for you to continue your trip on another airplane, train, bus, etc.: *a connecting flight*

PHRASAL VERB **conˌnect sth ˈup** *same as* **connect** 2: *The plumber came and connected up the dishwasher.*

con·nect·ed /kəˈnektəd/ adj **1** related to each other ≠ UNCONNECTED: *Were the two deaths connected?* **2** joined to each other or to something else: *connected underground tunnels* **3** able to communicate using a telephone or computer system

con·nec·tion /kəˈnekʃ(ə)n/ noun ★★★

1 relationship	5 of energy supply
2 liking sb	6 for phone/computer
3 in transportation	7 people you know
4 where things join	+ PHRASE

1 [C] a relationship between things or people: *I don't see* ***a connection between*** *the two cases.* ♦ *She was alleged to have* ***connections with*** *the secret police.*

2 [singular] a feeling that you like, understand, and are similar to someone else: *I felt a connection with him, as soon as we met.*

3 [C] a train, bus, or airplane that allows you to continue a trip: *My train was late and I* ***missed my connection.***

4 [C] a place where two things join: *The light keeps flickering – there must be a loose connection.*

5 [U] the process of joining something to a supply of electricity, water, or gas: *a connection charge*

6 [C] a means of communicating using a telephone or computer system: ***high-speed*** *Internet connections*

7 connections [plural] people you know who are able to use their influence to help you: *He used his connections to get a government job.*

PHRASE **in connection with sth** *formal* relating to something: *Police want to talk to him in connection with the murder.*

con·nect·or /kəˈnektər/ noun [C] an object that is attached to the end of a wire, used for connecting two pieces of equipment

con·nois·seur /ˌkɑnəˈsɜr/ noun [C] someone who knows a lot about a particular thing and enjoys it very much

con·no·ta·tion /ˌkɑnəˈteɪʃ(ə)n/ noun [C] an additional idea that a word suggests to you, that is not part of its usual meaning

con·quer /ˈkɑŋkər/ verb **1** [I/T] to take control of land or people using force **2** [T] to gain control of a situation or emotion by making a great effort

con·quer·or /ˈkɑŋkərər/ noun [C] someone who has taken control of land or people by force

con·quest /ˈkɑŋˌkwest/ noun [C/U] the process of taking control of something, or the thing or place that you take control of

con·science /ˈkɑnʃəns/ noun [C/U] the ideas and feelings you have that tell you whether something that you are doing is right or wrong: *The decision must be a matter of individual conscience.* ♦ *Maybe he has a guilty conscience* (=a bad feeling because he knows he has done something wrong). ♦ *We want to leave with a clear conscience* (=the knowledge that we have done nothing wrong).

PHRASE **on your conscience** causing you to feel guilty

C

con•sci•en•tious /ˌkɑnʃiˈenʃəs/ adj working hard, and careful to do things well —**con•sci•en•tious•ly** adv

con•scious /ˈkɑnʃəs/ adj ★
1 noticing that something exists or is happening and realizing that it is important = AWARE: *He was **conscious of** the fact that everyone was waiting for him.* ♦ **+(that)** *We are conscious that some people may not wish to work at night.*
2 awake and able to see, hear, and think ≠ UNCONSCIOUS: *The patient was fully conscious throughout the operation.*
3 done deliberately by someone who knows what the effect will be: *a conscious effort*

con•scious•ly /ˈkɑnʃəsli/ adv in a deliberate way

con•scious•ness /ˈkɑnʃəsnəs/ noun **1** [U] the state of being awake and able to see, hear, and think: *The pain was so bad that I lost consciousness.* **2** [singular/U] the knowledge or understanding that something exists or is important: *We want to increase students' consciousness of health issues.*

con•script¹ /kənˈskrɪpt/ verb [T] to make someone join the military —**con•scrip•tion** /kənˈskrɪpʃ(ə)n/ noun [U]

con•script² /ˈkɑnˌskrɪpt/ noun [C] someone who has been forced to join the military

con•se•crate /ˈkɑnsəˌkreɪt/ verb [T] to perform a religious ceremony in order to make a place or a thing holy —**con•se•cra•tion** /ˌkɑnsəˈkreɪʃ(ə)n/ noun [C/U]

con•sec•u•tive /kənˈsekjətɪv/ adj following one after another: *her fifth consecutive defeat* —**con•sec•u•tive•ly** adv

con•sen•su•al /kənˈsenʃuəl/ adj *formal* agreed to by all the people involved

con•sen•sus /kənˈsensəs/ noun [singular/U] agreement among all the people involved: *We have finally reached a consensus on this issue.*

con•sent¹ /kənˈsent/ noun [U] permission to do something: *He entered the building without the owner's consent.*

con•sent² /kənˈsent/ verb [I] to give someone permission to do something, or to agree to do something: *The child's parents would not consent to the treatment.*

con•se•quence /ˈkɑnsəkwəns/ noun [C] ★★★ a result or effect of something: *Climate change could have **disastrous consequences**.* ♦ *the economic **consequences of** government policies* ♦ *Demand for oil increased and, **as a consequence**, the price went up.*
PHRASE **of no consequence** *formal* not important in any way

> Words often used with **consequence**
> *Adjectives often used with **consequence***
> ■ **dire, disastrous, fatal, serious, tragic, unfortunate** + CONSEQUENCES: used about consequences that are very bad
> *Verbs often used with **consequence***
> ■ **accept, face, suffer, take** + CONSEQUENCES: accept the bad results of something

con•se•quent /ˈkɑnsəkwənt/ adj *formal* happening as a result of something

con•se•quent•ly /ˈkɑnsəkwəntli/ adv ★ as a result: *They've employed more staff and consequently the service is better.*

con•ser•va•tion /ˌkɑnsərˈveɪʃ(ə)n/ noun [U] ★
1 the management of land and water in ways that prevent it from being damaged or destroyed: *a wildlife conservation project* ♦ *groups calling for **the conservation of** the northern forests*
2 the careful use of supplies of things such as electricity or water, so that they are not wasted: *energy conservation measures*

con•ser•va•tion•ist /ˌkɑnsərˈveɪʃ(ə)nɪst/ noun [C] someone who works to protect the environment from damage or destruction

con•ser•va•tism /kənˈsɜrvəˌtɪzəm/ noun [U] **1** a tendency to dislike change **2** a political belief that it is better for society to change only gradually

con•ser•va•tive¹ /kənˈsɜrvətɪv/ adj ★
1 not willing to accept much change: *The small farming communities tend to be very conservative.*
2 supporting or relating to right-wing ideas: *conservative voters/values*
3 conservative clothing or styles are traditional
4 a conservative guess about a price or a number is usually less than the actual amount
—**con•ser•va•tive•ly** adv: *She dresses very conservatively.*

con•ser•va•tive² /kənˈsɜrvətɪv/ noun [C] someone who is conservative

Conˈservative ˌParty, the one of the three main political parties in the U.K. It supports right-wing policies.

con•ser•va•to•ry /kənˈsɜrvəˌtɔri/ noun [C] a school where students study to become musicians or actors

con•serve /kənˈsɜrv/ verb [T] to use very little of something such as electricity or water so that it is not wasted

con•sid•er /kənˈsɪdər/ verb ★★★
1 [I/T] to think about something carefully before you make a decision: *The jury went out to consider its verdict.* ♦ *He is **considering whether** to accept another job offer.* ♦ **consider doing sth** *At one time I seriously considered leaving.*
2 [T] to have a particular opinion about someone or something: **consider sb/sth (to be) sth** *We all considered him a hero.*
3 [I/T] to think that something may exist or be true: *Have you **considered the possibility** that he just doesn't like you?*
4 [T] to think about someone's feelings or reactions: *I'm not the only one involved – there's my daughter to consider as well.*

con•sid•er•a•ble /kənˈsɪd(ə)rəb(ə)l/ adj ★ large in size, amount, or degree: *a considerable amount of money* ♦ *a matter of considerable importance*

con•sid•er•a•bly /kənˈsɪd(ə)rəbli/ adv a lot: *It was considerably colder in the mountains.*

con•sid•er•ate /kənˈsɪdərət/ adj thinking about the feelings and needs of other people ≠ INCONSIDERATE

con•sid•er•a•tion /kənˌsɪdəˈreɪʃ(ə)n/ noun ★
1 [U] careful thought before you make a decision about something: *We have **given** careful **consideration to** your request.* ♦ *Several possibilities are **under consideration*** (=being thought about). ♦ *We*

will take your good driving record into consideration (=think about it before deciding something).
2 [C] something that you must think about carefully before you make a decision: *practical/ethical/political considerations*
3 [U] a kind way of behaving that shows that you care about other people's feelings and needs: *She treats all her patients with consideration and respect.*

con·sid·er·ing /kən'sɪd(ə)rɪŋ/ grammar word ★ used for showing that your opinion about something is affected by a particular fact: *They've made remarkable progress, considering they only started last week.*

con·sign /kən'saɪn/ verb [T] *formal* to put someone or something somewhere because you do not want to deal with them

con·sign·ment /kən'saɪnmənt/ noun [C] goods that are being delivered somewhere

con·sist /kən'sɪst/ verb ★★★ PHRASAL VERB
con'sist of sth to be made of particular parts or things: *Breakfast consisted of dry bread and a cup of tea.* ♦ **consist of doing sth** *My job seemed to consist of standing and smiling at people.*

con·sis·ten·cy /kən'sɪstənsi/ noun 1 [U] the ability to remain the same in behavior, attitudes, or qualities 2 [C/U] the degree to which a substance is thick, smooth, or firm

con·sis·tent /kən'sɪstənt/ adj ★
1 not changing in behavior, attitudes, or qualities ≠ INCONSISTENT: *A good manager is flexible but consistent.*
2 continuing or developing steadily in the same way: *a consistent improvement*
3 containing statements or ideas that are similar or have the same goal: *the need for a unified and consistent policy* ♦ *These results are **consistent with** the findings of the previous study.*
—**con·sis·tent·ly** adv

con·so·la·tion /ˌkɑnsə'leɪʃ(ə)n/ noun [C/U] something that makes you feel less unhappy or disappointed

con·sole¹ /kən'soʊl/ verb [T] to try to make someone feel better when they are unhappy or disappointed

con·sole² /'kɑnˌsoʊl/ noun [C] 1 a board with switches that controls a machine or piece of equipment 2 a small piece of electronic equipment used for playing video games

con·sol·i·date /kən'sɑlɪˌdeɪt/ verb 1 [T] to make something stronger or more effective 2 [I/T] to combine several small things into one large unit, or to become one large unit —**con·sol·i·da·tion** /kənˌsɑlɪ'deɪʃ(ə)n/ noun [C/U]

con·so·nant /'kɑnsənənt/ noun [C] *linguistics* ★ any letter of the English alphabet except for "a," "e," "i," "o," and "u"

con·sor·tium /kən'sɔrʃəm/ (plural **con·sor·tiums** or **con·sor·tia** /kən'sɔrʃə/) noun [C] a group of companies or people who have agreed to work together

con·spic·u·ous /kən'spɪkjuəs/ adj very noticeable, or easy to see ≠ INCONSPICUOUS —**con·spic·u·ous·ly** adv

con·spir·a·cy /kən'spɪrəsi/ noun [C/U] a secret plan by a group of people to do something that is bad or illegal

con·spir·a·tor /kən'spɪrətər/ noun [C] someone who is involved in making a secret plan to do something that is bad or illegal

con·spir·a·to·ri·al /kənˌspɪrə'tɔriəl/ adj showing that you share knowledge of a secret with someone —**con·spir·a·to·ri·al·ly** adv

con·spire /kən'spaɪr/ verb [I] 1 to secretly plan with someone to do something that is bad or illegal 2 **conspire to do sth** to produce a bad situation

con·stant /'kɑnstənt/ adj ★★
1 continuous or regular over a long period of time: *the constant noise of traffic* ♦ *His health has been a constant source of concern.*
2 continuing at the same rate, level, or amount over a particular period of time: *Maintain a constant speed.*

con·stant·ly /'kɑnstəntli/ adv always or regularly

con·stel·la·tion /ˌkɑnstə'leɪʃ(ə)n/ noun [C] a group of stars that are named for the pattern they form

con·ster·na·tion /ˌkɑnstər'neɪʃ(ə)n/ noun [U] *formal* a shocked or worried feeling

con·sti·pa·tion /ˌkɑnstɪ'peɪʃ(ə)n/ noun [U] a condition in which you cannot easily move solid waste out of your body —**con·sti·pat·ed** /'kɑnstɪˌpeɪtəd/ adj

con·stit·u·en·cy /kən'stɪtʃuənsi/ noun [C] an area of a country that elects a representative to a legislature, or all the people who live in that area

con·stit·u·ent /kən'stɪtʃuənt/ noun [C]
1 someone who votes in a particular constituency 2 one of the parts of something

con·sti·tute /'kɑnstɪˌtut/ linking verb *formal* 1 to be a particular thing: *This letter does not constitute an offer of employment.* 2 to be one of the parts of something

con·sti·tu·tion /ˌkɑnstɪ'tuʃ(ə)n/ noun 1 [C] a set of basic laws or rules that control how a country is governed or how an organization operates 2 [singular] your general physical condition

con·sti·tu·tion·al /ˌkɑnstɪ'tuʃ(ə)nəl/ adj
1 allowed by the constitution of a country or organization ≠ UNCONSTITUTIONAL
2 relating to the constitution of a country or organization: *constitutional reform*

con·strain /kən'streɪn/ verb [T] *formal* to limit someone's freedom to do what they want

con·straint /kən'streɪnt/ noun [C] a limit on something = LIMITATION: *The time constraints on the project are quite strict.*

con·strict /kən'strɪkt/ verb *formal* 1 [T] to limit what someone is able or allowed to do 2 [I/T] to become smaller or narrower, or to make something do this —**con·stric·tion** /kən'strɪkʃ(ə)n/ noun [C/U]

con·struct /kən'strʌkt/ verb [T] ★★ to build or make something: *The tunnel was constructed in 1996.* ♦ *She is able to construct simple sentences in Spanish.*

con·struc·tion /kən'strʌkʃ(ə)n/ noun ★★★
1 [U] the process of building something: *The company will finance the construction of a new sports center.* ♦ *This website is **under construction*** (=being built).
2 [C/U] the way in which words are put

together to form a sentence or phrase: *difficult grammatical constructions*

con'struction ,paper noun [U] *American* thick paper that is produced in a variety of colors

con•struc•tive /kən'strʌktɪv/ adj intended to be useful or helpful —**con•struc•tive•ly** adv

con•strue /kən'stru/ verb [T] *formal* to understand the meaning of something in a particular way

con•sul /'kɑns(ə)l/ noun [C] a government official who lives in another country and whose job is to help the citizens of their own country who go there —**con•sul•ar** /'kɑnsələr/ adj

con•su•late /'kɑnsələt/ noun [C] the government building in which a consul works

con•sult /kən'sʌlt/ verb ★
1 [T] to ask for advice from someone who has professional knowledge: *Consult your doctor before going on a diet.* ♦ **consult sb about sth** *I consulted my attorney about the matter.*
2 [I/T] to discuss something with someone before you make a decision: **consult sb about sth** *Why wasn't I consulted about this?*
3 [T] to look in a book or at a document in order to find information = REFER TO STH

con•sul•tan•cy /kən'sʌlt(ə)nsi/ noun [C] a company that has expert knowledge about something and provides professional help and advice to other companies

con•sult•ant /kən'sʌlt(ə)nt/ noun [C] an expert whose job is to give help and advice on a particular subject

con•sul•ta•tion /,kɑns(ə)l'teɪʃ(ə)n/ noun [C/U] **1** a process in which people give their opinions before an important decision is made **2** a meeting with a professional person in order to get advice or discuss a problem

con•sume /kən'sum/ verb [T] **1** to use a supply of something such as time, energy, or fuel **2** to eat or drink something

con•sum•er /kən'sumər/ noun [C] ★★ someone who buys and uses goods and services: *The technology means better service for consumers.* ♦ *consumer protection groups*

con•sum•ing /kən'sumɪŋ/ adj extremely important or interesting to you

con•sump•tion /kən'sʌmpʃ(ə)n/ noun [U] *formal* the use of something such as energy or fuel, or the amount of something that people use or buy: *We've reduced our energy consumption by 10%.*

con•tact[1] /'kɑn,tækt/ noun ★★★
1 [C/U] communication between people, countries, or organizations: *Do you and Jo still* ***keep in contact****? ♦ I still haven't managed to* ***make contact with*** *Joe.* ♦ *There was no direct* ***contact between*** *the two sides in the dispute.* ♦ *I have* ***lost contact with*** *most of my college friends* (=no longer talk or write to them).
2 [U] a situation in which people or things touch each other: *The disease is spread through sexual contact.* ♦ *Are you likely to* ***come into contact with*** *any dangerous chemicals?*
3 [C] *informal* a CONTACT LENS
4 [C] someone you know who can help you, for example by giving you information

con•tact[2] /'kɑn,tækt/ verb [T] ★★★ to communicate with someone by phone, e-mail, letter, etc.: *Please contact us if you have any information.*

'contact ,lens noun [C] a small piece of plastic that you wear in your eye to help you to see more clearly

con•ta•gious /kən'teɪdʒəs/ adj **1** a contagious disease spreads easily from one person to another **2** a contagious feeling spreads quickly from one person to another

con•tain /kən'teɪn/ verb [T] ★★★
1 to have something inside: *boxes containing toys and books* ♦ *The envelope contained a few old photographs.*
2 to have or include something as a part: *Milk contains many important vitamins and minerals.* ♦ *I disagreed with some of the points* ***contained in*** *the report.*
3 to control something: *I couldn't contain my excitement any longer.* ♦ *Firefighters are still battling to contain the blaze.*

con•tain•er /kən'teɪnər/ noun [C] ★★
1 something used for storing or keeping things in, for example a box, bottle, or bowl
2 a very large metal or wooden box that has been designed to be loaded easily onto ships and trucks

con•tain•ment /kən'teɪnmənt/ noun [U] the process of controlling something that could become harmful or dangerous

con•tam•i•nate /kən'tæmɪ,neɪt/ verb [T] **1** to make something dirty, polluted, or poisonous by adding a harmful substance: *Industrial sewage continues to contaminate our beaches.* **2** to affect something or someone in a negative way —**con•tam•i•na•tion** /kən,tæmɪ'neɪʃ(ə)n/ noun [U]

con•tem•plate /'kɑntəm,pleɪt/ verb **1** [T] to think about something that might be possible: *Have you ever contemplated working abroad?* **2** [I/T] to think about or look at something very carefully for a long time —**con•tem•pla•tion** /,kɑntəm'pleɪʃ(ə)n/ noun [U]

con•tem•po•rar•y[1] /kən'tempə,reri/ adj ★
1 modern, or relating to the present time: *contemporary art/music/literature/dance*
2 alive, or existing at the same time as a particular event or person: *contemporary evidence/documents/sources*

con•tem•po•rar•y[2] /kən'tempə,reri/ noun [C] someone who is or was alive at the same time as someone else: *He was a contemporary of Charles Dickens.*

con•tempt /kən'tempt/ noun [U] a feeling that someone or something is stupid, unimportant, or deserves no respect: *I have nothing but contempt for their ridiculous opinions.*

con•temp•tu•ous /kən'temptʃuəs/ adj showing that you do not respect someone or something at all —**con•temp•tu•ous•ly** adv

con•tend /kən'tend/ verb [T] *formal* to claim that something is true
PHRASAL VERB **con'tend with sth** to have to deal with problems or difficulties: *They had to contend with winds of over 40 miles an hour.*

con·tend·er /kənˈtendər/ noun [C] someone who competes with other people for a prize or job

con·tent¹ /ˈkɑnˌtent/ noun ★★★
1 contents [plural] the things that are inside something such as a box, bottle, building, or room: *The entire contents of the house will be sold.* ♦ *He emptied out the contents of his pockets.*
2 contents [plural] the things that are contained in a book, letter, document, etc., or a list of these: *The contents of the report remain secret.*
3 [U] the subject, ideas, or story that a piece of writing, television program, etc. deals with: *the design and content of your website*
4 [singular] the amount of a substance that something contains: *a cereal with a high sugar content*

con·tent² /kənˈtent/ adj happy and satisfied with your life or with a particular situation: *When I last saw her, she seemed content.* ♦ *I'm content with the relationship the way it is.*

con·tent³ /kənˈtent/ verb **content yourself with sth** to accept what you have, although you would prefer to have something else

con·tent·ed /kənˈtentəd/ adj happy and satisfied —**con·tent·ed·ly** adv

con·ten·tion /kənˈtenʃ(ə)n/ noun *formal* **1** [U] disagreement: *The subject is a source of contention in the family.* **2** [C] an opinion or statement that something is true

con·ten·tious /kənˈtenʃəs/ adj likely to cause arguments = CONTROVERSIAL

con·tent·ment /kənˈtentmənt/ noun [U] a feeling of happiness and satisfaction

con·test¹ /ˈkɑnˌtest/ noun [C] **1** a competition: *a writing contest* **2** a situation in which two or more people or groups are competing to gain power or an advantage

con·test² /kənˈtest/ verb [T] **1** to state formally that you disagree with something = DISPUTE **2** to compete for a job or for success in a competition

con·tes·tant /kənˈtestənt/ noun [C] someone who takes part in a contest

con·text /ˈkɑnˌtekst/ noun [C/U] ★★
1 the general situation in which something happens, that helps to explain it: *the historical context of the events* ♦ *This fall in prices has to be seen **in context**.*
2 the words surrounding a particular word, that help to give it its meaning: *In this context, "development" means economic growth.*
PHRASE **take sth out of context** to use only part of something that someone said, so that the original meaning is changed

con·ti·nent /ˈkɑntɪnənt/ noun [C] ★★ one of the very large areas of land on the Earth, for example Asia or Africa

con·ti·nen·tal /ˌkɑntɪˈnent(ə)l/ adj relating to or belonging to a continent: *the wildlife of continental North America*

con·tin·gen·cy /kənˈtɪndʒənsi/ noun [C] something bad that might happen in the future

con·tin·gent /kənˈtɪndʒənt/ noun [C] **1** a group of people who represent a particular place or organization **2** a group of soldiers or police officers that forms part of a larger group

con·tin·u·al /kənˈtɪnjuəl/ adj **1** continuing without stopping **2** happening again and again, often in an annoying way —**con·tin·u·al·ly** adv

con·tin·u·a·tion /kənˌtɪnjuˈeɪʃ(ə)n/ noun **1** [C/U] a situation in which something continues without stopping **2** [C] a situation in which something begins again after a pause

con·tin·ue /kənˈtɪnju/ verb ★★★
1 [I/T] to keep doing something, or to keep happening without stopping: *Doctors advised him to continue the treatment for another six weeks.* ♦ *She decided to **continue with** her studies for another two years.* ♦ **continue doing sth** *He continued typing while he spoke.*
2 [T] to start doing something again after stopping: *She looked up briefly, and then continued reading.*
3 [I] to go farther in the same direction: *The path continued for another fifty yards.* ♦ *The woman pushed past me and **continued down** the road.*

> **Word family: continue**
> *Words in the same family as* ***continue***
> - **continual** *adj*
> - **continuous** *adj*
> - **continuation** *n*
> - **continuity** *n*
> - **discontinue** *v*
> - **discontinued** *adj*

con·tin·ued /kənˈtɪnjud/ adj provided, happening, or done regularly or for a long period: *We thank our customers for their continued support.*

conˌtinuing eduˈcation noun [U] **1** *American* classes in which professional people learn the latest information relating to their professions **2** classes for adults in a wide variety of subjects

con·ti·nu·i·ty /ˌkɑntɪˈnuəti/ noun [U] a situation in which something happens or exists for a long time without stopping or changing

con·tin·u·ous /kənˈtɪnjuəs/ adj ★★
1 continuing without stopping: *a continuous flow of water*
2 *linguistics* the continuous form of a verb includes "be" and the PRESENT PARTICIPLE of a verb to show that an activity is in progress. For example in "He is running to catch the bus," "is running" is the continuous form of "run." = PROGRESSIVE
—**con·tin·u·ous·ly** adv: *It rained continuously for five days.*

con·tort /kənˈtɔrt/ verb [I/T] if your face or body contorts, or if you contort it, it twists into an unusual shape —**con·tor·tion** /kənˈtɔrʃ(ə)n/ noun [C]

con·tort·ed /kənˈtɔrtəd/ adj twisted into an unusual shape or position

con·tour /ˈkɑnˌtʊr/ noun [C] **1** the shape of the outside edge of something **2 contour** or **contour line** a line on a map joining points that are the same height above or below sea level

con·tra·cep·tion /ˌkɑntrəˈsepʃ(ə)n/ noun [U] the methods that are used for preventing a woman from becoming pregnant, or the use of these methods

C

con·tra·cep·tive[1] /ˌkɑntrəˈseptɪv/ noun [C] a drug, method, or object that is used for preventing a woman from becoming pregnant

con·tra·cep·tive[2] /ˌkɑntrəˈseptɪv/ adj designed to prevent a woman from becoming pregnant

con·tract[1] /ˈkɑnˌtrækt/ noun [C] ★★★ a written legal agreement between two people or organizations: *After six months she was offered an employment contract.* ♦ *He has **signed a** six-year **contract with** the Denver Broncos.* —**con·trac·tu·al** /kənˈtræktʃuəl/ adj

> **Words often used with contract**
> *Verbs often used with **contract** (noun)*
> ■ **enter into, negotiate, renew, secure, sign, win** + CONTRACT: start or get a contract

con·tract[2] /kənˈtrækt, ˈkɑnˌtrækt/ verb **1** [I/T] to make a formal agreement that work will be done or that something will happen: *They had contracted to supply the machinery by June.* **2** [I] to get smaller: *The steel contracts as it cools.* **3** [T] *medical* to get a serious disease

con·trac·tion /kənˈtrækʃ(ə)n/ noun **1** [U] the process of becoming smaller **2** [C] *medical* a strong painful movement of a muscle that helps to push a baby out during birth **3** [C] *linguistics* a short form of a word that is made by leaving out a letter or letters. For example "can't" is a contraction of the word "cannot."

con·trac·tor /ˈkɑnˌtræktər, kənˈtræktər/ noun [C] a person or company that provides goods or does work, especially building, for someone else

con·tra·dict /ˌkɑntrəˈdɪkt/ verb [T] **1** to say the opposite of what someone else has said **2** if one statement, piece of evidence, story, etc. contradicts another, they are different and cannot both be true

con·tra·dic·tion /ˌkɑntrəˈdɪkʃ(ə)n/ noun [C/U] a difference between two statements, ideas, stories, etc. that makes it impossible for both of them to be true

con·tra·dic·to·ry /ˌkɑntrəˈdɪktəri/ adj contradictory statements, information, stories, etc. are different from each other and cannot both be true

con·trap·tion /kənˈtræpʃ(ə)n/ noun [C] a machine or piece of equipment that looks strange or complicated

con·trar·y /ˈkɑnˌtreri/ adj completely different, or opposed to something else: *a contrary view/opinion*

con·trar·y, the /ˈkɑnˌtreri/ noun
PHRASES **on the contrary** used for emphasizing that the opposite of what has been said is true: *The situation hasn't improved – on the contrary, it's getting worse.*
to the contrary making you think that the opposite may be true: *Despite all evidence to the contrary, he believed his plan would succeed.*

con·trast[1] /ˈkɑnˌtræst/ noun ★★
1 [C/U] a noticeable difference between people or things: *There is a striking **contrast between** these two attitudes.* ♦ ***In contrast to** deserts in the south, the northern part of the state is very green.*
2 [C] something that is different from something else in a very noticeable way: *The little village was a total **contrast to** Athens.*
3 [U] the differences in light or color that you can see in a painting or photograph, or in a television picture

con·trast[2] /kənˈtræst/ verb **1** [I] if one thing contrasts with another, the two things are very different from each other **2** [T] to compare two things in order to show the ways in which they are different

con·trast·ing /kənˈtræstɪŋ/ adj different from each other in a noticeable or interesting way: *contrasting styles/opinions/colors*

con·tra·vene /ˌkɑntrəˈvin/ verb [T] *formal* to do something that is not allowed by a rule, law, or agreement —**con·tra·ven·tion** /ˌkɑntrəˈvenʃ(ə)n/ noun [C/U]

con·trib·ute /kənˈtrɪbjut, ˈkɑntrɪˌbjut/ verb ★★★
1 [I/T] to give money, goods, or your time and effort in order to help someone to achieve something: *Many local businesses offered to **contribute to** the fund.* ♦ **contribute sth to/toward sth** *He promised to contribute $5,000 toward the cost of the lawsuit.*
2 [I/T] to be a part of a group or an activity and help it to be successful: **contribute sth to sth** *Davis didn't really contribute much to the game in the second half.*
3 [I] to be one of the causes of something: *The scandal **contributed to** the party's defeat in the last election.*
4 [I/T] to write stories or articles for a newspaper or magazine

con·tri·bu·tion /ˌkɑntrɪˈbjuʃ(ə)n/ noun [C] ★★★
1 something that you give or do that helps someone to achieve something or helps to make something successful: *We are asking all parents for a **contribution toward** the cost of the trip.*
2 a story or article that is written for a newspaper or magazine

> **Words often used with contribution**
> *Adjectives often used with **contribution** (sense 1)*
> ■ **great, huge, important, major, outstanding, significant, valuable** + CONTRIBUTION: used about contributions that are important and useful

con·trib·u·tor /kənˈtrɪbjətər/ noun [C]
1 someone who gives or does something in order to help someone to achieve something **2** someone who writes a story or article for a newspaper or magazine

con·trib·u·to·ry /kənˈtrɪbjəˌtɔri/ adj partly responsible for a situation or event

con·trite /kənˈtraɪt, ˈkɑnˌtraɪt/ adj very sorry or ashamed because you have done something bad —**con·tri·tion** /kənˈtrɪʃ(ə)n/ noun [U]

con·trive /kənˈtraɪv/ verb [T] *formal* **1** to succeed in doing something difficult by using clever or dishonest methods **2** to invent or make something in a clever or unusual way

con·trived /kənˈtraɪvd/ adj artificial, or not natural

con•trol¹ /kən'troʊl/ noun ★★★
1 [U] the power to make decisions about what happens in a situation: *The island is now **under** French **control**.* ♦ *When Marie's father died, **control of** the business passed to her.* ♦ *When we **took control of** the company, it was losing money.* ♦ *Democrats are hoping to **gain control of** the House of Representatives.* ♦ *I **lost control of** the car, and it skidded off the road.*
2 [C/U] a law, agreement, or method that limits something: *new **controls on** the importing of live animals* ♦ *an international agreement on **arms control***
3 [C] a part of a machine that you use to make it do something: *There was an experienced pilot **at the controls*** (=operating the controls of a plane).
4 [U] the process of checking something, or the place where it is checked: *She is responsible for quality control of all our products.*
PHRASES **in control** with the power to decide what happens or what someone or something does: *Dr. Marion is in control of all medical decisions in the hospital.*
out of control impossible to stop or deal with successfully: *Forest fires can easily get out of control.*
under control being managed or dealt with successfully: *He sometimes has difficulty keeping his temper under control.*

con•trol² /kən'troʊl/ verb [T] ★★★
1 to have the power to make decisions about what happens in a situation: *The rebel army now controls the northern half of the country.* ♦ *New teachers often find it difficult to control their classes.*
2 to make something operate in the way that you want: *I hit a patch of ice and couldn't control the car.* ♦ *The temperature in the museum is carefully controlled.*
3 to prevent something harmful from spreading or becoming more dangerous: *We must do more to control the spread of the virus.*
4 to remain calm and not show that you are angry or upset: *Carol struggled to control her anger.*

con'trol ˌfreak noun [C] *informal* someone who wants to control every aspect of a situation and will not allow other people to share in making decisions

con•trol•ler or **comp•trol•ler** /kən'troʊlər/ noun [C] someone whose job is to manage an organization's money

con'trol ˌtower noun [C] a tall building at an airport from which airplanes are given permission to take off and land

con•tro•ver•sial /ˌkɑntrə'vɜrʃ(ə)l/ adj ★ causing strong feelings of disagreement ≠ UNCONTROVERSIAL: *controversial plans to build a new freeway*

con•tro•ver•sy /'kɑntrəˌvɜrsi/ noun [C/U] a disagreement that a lot of people have strong feelings about: *the recent controversy over the school's new teaching methods* ♦ *The decision is sure to cause controversy in Europe.*

con•ur•ba•tion /ˌkɑnər'beɪʃ(ə)n/ noun [C] a large city area

con•va•lesce /ˌkɑnvə'les/ verb [I] to spend time resting after an illness in order to get better —**con•val•es•cent** /ˌkɑnvə'les(ə)nt/ adj

con•vene /kən'vin/ verb [I/T] to arrange a formal meeting, or to gather for a meeting

con•ven•ience /kən'viniəns/ noun **1** [U] a condition that helps you to avoid wasting time or effort: *Her hair was cut short for convenience rather than fashion.* **2** [C] a piece of equipment that makes things easier for you: *The kitchen was equipped with a range of modern conveniences.*

con'venience ˌfood noun [C/U] food that is quick and easy to prepare such as food that has already been cooked and only needs to be heated → FAST FOOD

con'venience ˌstore noun [C] *American* a store that is open for long hours and sells a variety of goods

con•ven•ient /kən'viniənt/ adj ★★
1 easy for you to do, or appropriate for your needs ≠ INCONVENIENT: *If it's convenient, call me tomorrow.* ♦ *Traveling on the subway is fast and convenient.*
2 near to the place where you want to go: *a house that is convenient for the expressway*
—**con•ven•i•ent•ly** adv

con•vent /'kɑnvənt, 'kɑnˌvent/ noun [C] a building where NUNS (=women members of a religious organization) live and work

con•ven•tion /kən'venʃ(ə)n/ noun ★★
1 [C] a large meeting of people from a particular profession or organization
2 [C/U] a way of behaving that is generally accepted as normal and right: *social conventions* ♦ *She rebelled against convention and refused to marry.*
3 [C] a formal agreement between governments: *the European Convention on Human Rights*

con•ven•tion•al /kən'venʃ(ə)nəl/ adj ★★
1 using ordinary or traditional methods, not new ideas or new technology: *a conventional oven* ♦ *conventional weapons* (=not nuclear or chemical weapons)
2 someone who is conventional follows traditional ways of thinking and behaving in their society ≠ UNCONVENTIONAL: *Her boyfriend is nice, but he's very conventional.*
3 conventional medical treatments are those that are based on drugs and operations → ALTERNATIVE
—**con•ven•tion•al•ly** adv: *a conventionally dressed young man*

con•verge /kən'vɜrdʒ/ verb [I] to come to the same place from different places or directions: *Top diplomats were converging on Washington from all over the world.*

con•ver•sant /kən'vɜrs(ə)nt/ adj *formal* if you are conversant with something, you know about it and understand it

con•ver•sa•tion /ˌkɑnvər'seɪʃ(ə)n/ noun [C/U] ★★★ an informal talk between two or more people: *He's so boring – his only **topic of conversation** is football.* ♦ ***conversations between friends*** ♦ ***a conversation with** my neighbor* ♦ *She **had a long conversation** with her mother.*
PHRASE **make conversation** *informal* to talk to someone that you do not know well in order to be polite

C

—**con•ver•sa•tion•al** adj: *conversational skills*

con•verse /kən'vɜrs/ verb [I] *formal* to have a conversation

con•verse, the /'kɑn‚vɜrs/ noun [singular] *formal* the opposite of a statement or situation

con•verse•ly /kən'vɜrsli, 'kɑn‚vɜrsli/ adv used for introducing one part of a sentence that says the opposite of an earlier part: *Some wrong answers were marked right and, conversely, some right answers had been rejected.*

con•ver•sion /kən'vɜrʒ(ə)n/ noun **1** [U] the process of changing from one system or use to another **2** [C] a change in someone's religious or political beliefs

con•vert¹ /kən'vɜrt/ verb [I/T] ★
1 to change from one system or use to another, or to make something change in this way: *Farmers are converting to new production methods.* ♦ **convert sth into sth** *They converted the old school into luxury apartments.*
2 to change your religious or political beliefs, or to persuade someone to change their beliefs

con•vert² /'kɑn‚vɜrt/ noun [C] someone who has changed their religious or political beliefs

con•vert•i•ble¹ /kən'vɜrtəb(ə)l/ noun [C] a car with a roof that can be folded back or removed

con•vert•i•ble² /kən'vɜrtəb(ə)l/ adj something that is convertible can be changed from one form or use to another

con•vex /kən'veks, 'kɑn‚veks/ adj a convex surface curves outward ≠ CONCAVE

con•vey /kən'veɪ/ verb [T] ★
1 to communicate ideas, feelings, or information: *A good photograph can convey far more than words.* ♦ *Please convey our thanks to the organizers.*
2 *formal* to move something from one place to another = TRANSPORT

con•vey•or belt /kən'veɪər ‚belt/ noun [C] a machine that has a flat surface that moves and carries objects from one part of a factory to another

con•vict¹ /kən'vɪkt/ verb [T] ★ to prove in a court of law that someone is guilty of a crime: *There wasn't enough evidence to convict her.* ♦ **convict sb of sth** *Robinson was convicted of the murder of his brother.*
—**con•vict•ed** adj: *a convicted thief*

con•vict² /'kɑn‚vɪkt/ noun [C] someone who is in prison because they have committed a crime

con•vic•tion /kən'vɪkʃ(ə)n/ noun ★★
1 [C] a strong belief or opinion: *deep religious convictions*
2 [C] a decision by a court of law that someone is guilty of a crime: *a murder/drug/felony conviction* ♦ *He had two earlier convictions for assault.*
3 [U] the feeling or appearance of being confident: *"Everything will be fine," she said with conviction.*

con•vince /kən'vɪns/ verb [T] ★★
1 to make someone believe that something is true = PERSUADE: **convince sb of sth** *He failed to convince the court of his innocence.* ♦ **convince sb (that)** *Maria had convinced herself that Juan didn't love her.*
2 to persuade someone to do something: **convince sb to do sth** *They tried to convince him to buy a cheaper car.*

con•vinced /kən'vɪnst/ adj certain that something is true

con•vinc•ing /kən'vɪnsɪŋ/ adj something that is convincing makes you believe that it is true or good ≠ UNCONVINCING
—**con•vinc•ing•ly** adv

con•voy /'kɑn‚vɔɪ/ noun [C] a group of vehicles or ships that are traveling together

con•vul•sions /kən'vʌlʃənz/ noun [plural] sudden violent movements of your body that you cannot control, caused by illness

cook¹ /kʊk/ verb ★★★
1 [I/T] to prepare and heat food so that it is ready to eat: *What's the best way to cook fish?* ♦ *When did you learn to cook?* ♦ **cook sth for sb** *Joe's cooking dinner for me tonight.* ♦ **cook sb sth** *He offered to cook me lunch.*
2 [I] when food cooks, it is heated until it is ready to eat: *The potatoes need to cook for about 20 minutes.*

Word family: cook

Words in the same family as cook

- **cooked** *adj*
- **cooking** *n*
- **overcooked** *adj*
- **undercooked** *adj*

Other ways of saying cook

- **bake** to cook food such as bread or cakes in an oven
- **boil** to cook food in very hot water
- **broil** *American* to cook food under or over a very strong heat. The British word is **grill**.
- **fry** to cook food in hot oil
- **grill** *American* to cook food on metal bars over a fire
- **roast** to cook meat or vegetables in an oven with fat or oil
- **simmer** to boil something very gently

cook² /kʊk/ noun [C] someone who cooks food, either as their job or for pleasure

cook•book /'kʊk‚bʊk/ noun [C] a book that contains RECIPES (=instructions for preparing and cooking food)

cook•er /'kʊkər/ noun [C] *British* a STOVE

cook•ie /'kʊki/ noun [C] **1** *American* a small sweet cake that is usually flat and in the shape of a circle **2** *computing* a file that is sent by an Internet WEBSITE to a computer that visits it. If the computer visits the same website again, the file collects information about the computer user.
PHRASE **tough/smart cookie** *informal* someone who has a strong character or is intelligent, and deals well with problems and disappointments

'cookie ‚sheet noun [C] *American* a metal sheet used for baking cookies or other food on

cook•ing /'kʊkɪŋ/ noun [U] the activity of preparing food, or a particular way of preparing it

cook•out /'kʊk‚aʊt/ noun [C] *American* an informal meal with food that is cooked and eaten outside on a GRILL

cook•ware /'kʊk‚wer/ noun [U] pans and other equipment used in cooking

cool[1] /kul/ adj ★★★

1 fairly cold	5 good
2 fashionable	6 likeable
3 calm and relaxed	+ PHRASE
4 not friendly	

1 fairly cold ≠ WARM: *The water was wonderfully cool and refreshing.* ♦ *the cool evening air*
2 fashionable and attractive ≠ UNCOOL: *one of America's coolest young designers*
3 calm and relaxed: *her cool way of handling the situation*
4 not friendly or enthusiastic: *Relations between the two countries were becoming increasingly cool.*
5 *spoken* good or enjoyable: *The scenery in the mountains was so cool.* ♦ *"We could go to see a movie." "Cool."*
6 *spoken* a cool person is one that you like or admire
PHRASE **play it cool** *informal* to behave calmly and not show your emotions
→ COOLLY

cool[2] /kul/ verb **1** [I/T] to become cooler, or to make something cooler: *Allow the cake to cool completely.* **2** [I] if an emotion such as love or anger cools, it becomes less strong
PHRASAL VERBS **ˌcool ˈdown** *informal* to become less angry
ˌcool (sth) ˈdown *same as* **cool**[2] 1
ˌcool ˈoff 1 to become cooler after being very hot **2** *informal* to become less angry or excited

cool[3] /kul/ noun
PHRASES **keep your cool** to remain calm in a difficult situation
lose your cool to become angry or excited in a difficult situation

cool·ly /ˈkulli/ adv **1** calmly, without getting excited or angry **2** in an unfriendly way

cooped up /ˌkupt ˈʌp/ adj in a place that you cannot leave or cannot move around in

co·op·er·ate /koʊˈɑpəˌreɪt/ verb [I] **1** to work with other people in order to achieve something: *Residents are refusing to cooperate with the authorities.* **2** to do what someone asks you to do: *They threatened to harm him if he didn't cooperate.*

co·op·er·a·tion /koʊˌɑpəˈreɪʃ(ə)n/ noun [U] a situation in which people help each other or work together to achieve something

co·op·er·a·tive[1] /koʊˈɑp(ə)rətɪv/ adj
1 someone who is cooperative is willing to do what you ask them ≠ UNCOOPERATIVE: *One of the prisoners was very cooperative.*
2 done by different groups working together: *a cooperative research project*

co·op·er·a·tive[2] /koʊˈɑp(ə)rətɪv/ noun [C] a business that is owned by all the people who work in it

co·or·di·nate /koʊˈɔrdɪˌneɪt/ verb [T] to organize an activity so that all the people who are involved in it work together effectively: *Jean is coordinating the project.*

co·or·di·nat·ed /ˈkoʊˈɔrdɪˌneɪtəd/ adj able to control the movements of your body well: *She's very coordinated for a two-year-old.*

co·or·di·nates /koʊˈɔrdɪnəts/ noun [plural] a set of two numbers that give the exact position of something on a map or GRAPH

co·or·di·na·tion /koʊˌɔrdɪˈneɪʃ(ə)n/ noun [U] **1** the ability to control the parts of your body so that they move well together **2** the process of organizing people or things so that they work together effectively: *He asked for better coordination between NATO and the United Nations.*

co·or·di·na·tor /koʊˈɔrdɪˌneɪtər/ noun [C] someone whose job is to organize an activity and to make sure that the people who are involved in it work well together

cop /kɑp/ noun [C] *informal* a police officer

cope /koʊp/ verb [I] ★★ to deal successfully with a difficult situation: *Considering how bad her injuries are, she's coping very well.* ♦ *The safety system is designed to* ***cope with*** *engine failure.*

cop·i·er /ˈkɑpiər/ noun [C] a machine that makes exact copies of documents and pictures = COPY MACHINE, PHOTOCOPIER —*picture* → C3

co·pi·lot /ˈkoʊˌpaɪlət/ noun [C] a pilot who helps the main pilot to fly an aircraft —**co·pi·lot** verb [T]

co·pi·ous /ˈkoʊpiəs/ adj *formal* in large amounts

ˈcop-ˌout noun [C] *showing disapproval* something that you say or do in order to avoid doing what you should do

cop·per /ˈkɑpər/ noun [U] a red-brown metal, that is used especially for making wire or pipes

cop·u·late /ˈkɑpjəˌleɪt/ verb [I] *technical* to have sex —**cop·u·la·tion** /ˌkɑpjəˈleɪʃ(ə)n/ noun [U]

cop·y[1] /ˈkɑpi/ noun [C] ★★★
1 something that is exactly like something else: *This is not the original painting – it's a copy.* ♦ *Please send* ***a copy of*** *your birth certificate.* ♦ ***I made copies of*** *the report.*
2 a single newspaper, book, CD, etc., that is one of many that are all exactly the same: *Her first album sold 100,000 copies.* ♦ *Do you have* ***a copy of*** *yesterday's newspaper?*
→ HARD COPY

cop·y[2] /ˈkɑpi/ verb ★★★
1 [T] to make a copy that is the same as the original thing: *They were illegally copying videotapes and selling them.* ♦ *You can use the mouse to copy text from one part of the document to another.* —*picture* → DRAW
2 [I/T] to do something in the same way as someone else = IMITATE: *Children learn by copying their parents.*
3 [T] to use someone else's ideas or methods: *Their style of music was copied by a lot of other bands.*
4 [I/T] to look at someone else's work and dishonestly write the same as they have written, especially in an examination
PHRASAL VERBS **ˌcopy sb ˈin** to send someone a copy of an e-mail or letter that you are sending to another person: *I'll e-mail her about it, and copy you in.*
ˈcopy sth ˌto sb to send a copy of a message or letter to someone: *I accidentally copied the e-mail to everyone in the company.*

Other ways of saying copy

- **make a copy** to copy something, especially using a machine

- **photocopy** to copy a document using a special machine
- **reproduce** to copy a picture, sound, or piece of writing, especially using modern technology
- **trace** to copy a picture by placing transparent paper on top of it and following the lines with a pencil
- **plagiarize** to copy someone else's words or ideas and pretend that they are your own
- **pirate** to make an illegal copy of something such as a book, software, or a video

cop·y·cat /ˈkɑpiˌkæt/ adj similar to something else: *a copycat murder/shooting*

ˈcopy maˌchine noun [C] *American* a COPIER

cop·y·right /ˈkɑpiˌraɪt/ noun [C/U] the legal right to decide who can make and sell copies of a book, show a movie, perform a piece of music, etc.

cor·al /ˈkɔrəl/ noun [U] a hard pink, white, or red substance that grows in the ocean: *a coral necklace* ♦ *a coral reef* (=large area of coral under the sea)

cord /kɔrd/ noun **1** [C] an electrical wire that connects a machine to the main supply of electricity **2** [C/U] strong thick string → CORDS

cor·dial /ˈkɔrdʒəl/ adj *formal* friendly —**cor·dial·ly** adv

cord·less /ˈkɔrdləs/ adj a cordless piece of equipment works without being connected to the electricity supply

cor·don¹ /ˈkɔrd(ə)n/ noun [C] a line of police officers or soldiers who stop other people from going somewhere

cor·don² /ˈkɔrd(ə)n/ PHRASAL VERB **ˌcordon sth ˈoff** to prevent people from entering a place, by putting a rope around it or by surrounding it with police officers or soldiers

cords /kɔrdz/ noun [plural] pants made of corduroy

cor·du·roy /ˈkɔrdəˌrɔɪ/ noun **1** [U] thick cotton cloth with a RIDGED surface (=covered with raised lines) **2 corduroys** [plural] pants made of corduroy

core¹ /kɔr/ noun [C] ★

1 the most important or most basic part of something: ***the core of the problem*** ♦ *The club has **a small core of** active members.*

2 the center of something: *the seeds in an apple core* ♦ *the Earth's core*

PHRASE **to the core** used for emphasizing that an aspect of someone's character is very strong and will not change: *She's a feminist to the core.*

core² /kɔr/ adj most important, or most basic: *Selling insurance is still our core business.*

co·ri·an·der /ˌkɔriˈændər/ noun [U] *British* CILANTRO

cork /kɔrk/ noun **1** [U] a soft light substance from the BARK (=outside part) of a special type of tree **2** [C] an object made from cork, used for closing the top of a bottle of wine

cork·screw /ˈkɔrkˌskru/ noun [C] a tool used for pulling the corks out of wine bottles

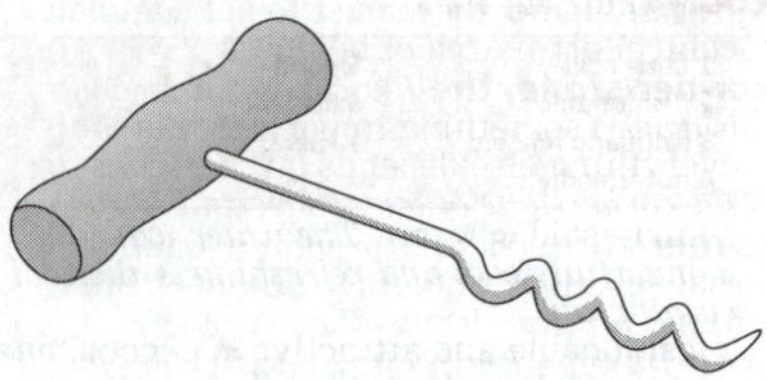

corkscrew

corn /kɔrn/ noun **1** [U] tall plants with large yellow seeds on a COB (=thick piece of stem), or the seeds when they are cooked and eaten → SWEET CORN **2** [C] a small piece of painful hard skin on your foot

PHRASE **corn on the cob** the top part of a CORN plant, cooked and eaten as a vegetable —*picture* → C11

ˈcorn ˌbread noun [U] bread made from CORN

ˈcorn ˌdog noun [C] *American* a HOT DOG covered with CORNMEAL (=flour made from maize), usually served on a stick

cor·ner¹ /ˈkɔrnər/ noun [C] ★★★

1 where two sides meet	4 small (quiet) area
2 where roads meet	5 difficult situation
3 end of mouth/eye	+ PHRASES

1 the part of an object, space, or room where two edges or sides meet: *The baby banged his head on **the corner of** the table.* ♦ *The "Start" button is in **the** left-hand **corner of** the screen.* ♦ *She sat **in the corner** reading.*

2 a place where two roads meet, or where there is a sharp bend in the road: *I get my newspaper from the shop **on the corner**.* ♦ *As she **turned the corner** (=went around it), she saw us.* ♦ *people begging on **street corners***

3 the end of your mouth or eye: *A tear fell from **the corner of** her eye.*

4 a particular area, especially one that is quiet, peaceful, or private: *Plant it in **a** sunny **corner of** your garden.*

5 a difficult situation that you cannot easily escape from = PREDICAMENT: *The administration has been **backed into a corner** by the unions.*

PHRASES **around the corner** not far away in distance or time: *The kids go to school just around the corner.* ♦ *Spring is just around the corner.*

out of the corner of your eye without looking at something directly

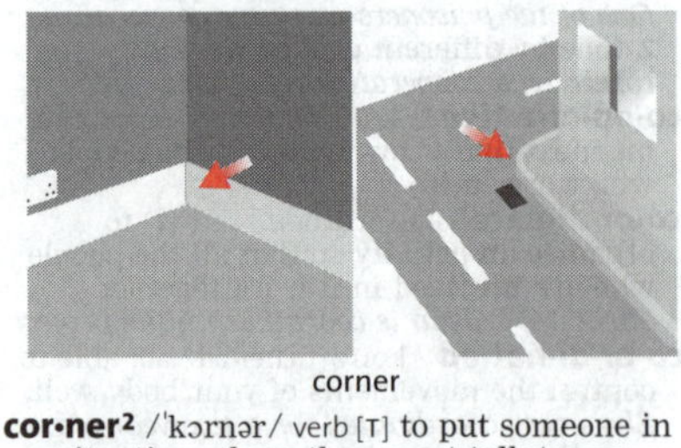

corner

cor·ner² /ˈkɔrnər/ verb [T] to put someone in a situation where they must talk to you, fight you, or do what you want: *Carl cornered me by the coffee machine.*

PHRASE **corner the market** to get complete control of an area of business

cor·ner·stone, the /ˈkɔrnərˌstoʊn/ noun [singular] something important that everything else depends on: *Elections are the cornerstone of our democratic system.*

ˌcorner ˈstore noun [C] *American* a small store that sells food and other products, often found on the corner of a street

corn·flakes /ˈkɔrnˌfleɪks/ noun [plural] a breakfast food made of small flat dried pieces of CORN. You eat them with milk.

corn·starch /ˈkɔrnˌstɑrtʃ/ noun [U] *American* white flour made from CORN that you use in cooking to make liquids thicker

corn·y /ˈkɔrni/ adj corny stories or jokes have been told so often that they seem silly

cor·o·nar·y /ˈkɔrəˌneri/ adj relating to your heart

cor·o·na·tion /ˌkɔrəˈneɪʃ(ə)n/ noun [C] a ceremony at which someone officially becomes a king or queen

cor·o·ner /ˈkɔrənər/ noun [C] a public official whose job is to decide how someone died

Corp. abbrev corporation

cor·po·ral /ˈkɔrp(ə)rəl/ noun [C] an OFFICER of low rank in the military

ˌcorporal ˈpunishment noun [U] punishment that consists of hitting someone

cor·po·rate /ˈkɔrp(ə)rət/ adj ★ relating to a corporation: *corporate culture*

cor·po·ra·tion /ˌkɔrpəˈreɪʃ(ə)n/ noun [C] ★ a large business company: *a big tobacco corporation* ♦ *the Microsoft Corporation*

corps /kɔr/ (plural **corps** /kɔrz/) noun [C] **1** a part of an army that has particular responsibilities **2** a group of people who all do the same type of job: *the press/diplomatic corps*

corpse /kɔrps/ noun [C] the body of a dead person

cor·pus /ˈkɔrpəs/ noun [C] *linguistics* a collection of written and spoken language that is stored on computer and used for language research and writing dictionaries

cor·rect¹ /kəˈrekt/ adj ★★★
1 right according to the facts or rules ≠ INCORRECT: *The first person to give the correct answer wins the contest.* ♦ *If my calculations are correct, we should arrive in exactly 17 minutes.* ♦ *a grammatically correct sentence*
2 behaving in a way that is considered socially acceptable or morally right: *My father was always very formal and correct.* —**cor·rect·ly** adv: *She guessed my age correctly.* ♦ *They refused, correctly, to give this information to the police.* —**cor·rect·ness** noun [U]

> **Word family: correct**
> *Words in the same family as **correct***
> - **correction** *n*
> - **correctly** *adv*
> - **corrective** *adj*
> - **incorrect** *adj*
> - **incorrectly** *adv*

cor·rect² /kəˈrekt/ verb [T] **1** to show that something is wrong, and make it right: *I want to correct this false impression that people have of me.* **2** to look at a piece of writing and make marks to show where the mistakes are: *She sat correcting the students' homework.* **3** to make something work in the way that it should: *She had surgery to correct a defect in her left eye.* **4** to tell someone that something they have said is not right: *I want to correct you on one point.*

PHRASE **correct me if I'm wrong** *spoken* used for politely disagreeing with someone

cor·rec·tion /kəˈrekʃ(ə)n/ noun ★
1 [C] a change that makes something correct or solves a problem: *I read the report and made a few small corrections.* ♦ ***minor corrections to the car's steering mechanism***
2 [U] the process of changing something in order to make it correct: *some factual errors that need correction* ♦ ***the correction of sight problems by surgery***
3 [C] *business* a fall in values on the STOCK MARKET after values have risen a lot

corˈrections ˌofficer noun [C] *American* someone whose job is to guard prisoners in a prison

cor·rec·tive /kəˈrektɪv/ adj *formal* designed to solve a problem or improve a bad situation

cor·re·late /ˈkɔrəˌleɪt/ verb [I/T] *formal* if two or more things correlate, or if one thing correlates with another, they are connected

cor·re·la·tion /ˌkɔrəˈleɪʃ(ə)n/ noun [C/U] *formal* a connection or relationship between things

cor·re·spond /ˌkɔrəˈspɑnd/ verb [I] **1** to be the same as something else, or very similar to something else: *Unfortunately, their statements did not correspond.* **2** *formal* if two people correspond with each other, they regularly write letters to each other

cor·re·spon·dence /ˌkɔrəˈspɑndəns/ noun [U] the process of sending and receiving letters, or the letters that someone sends and receives

ˌcorreˈspondence ˌcourse noun [C] an educational course that you take at home. You send and receive work by mail or by e-mail.

cor·re·spon·dent /ˌkɔrəˈspɑndənt/ noun [C] a reporter who deals with a particular subject: *an education/arts correspondent*

cor·re·spond·ing /ˌkɔrəˈspɑndɪŋ/ adj related to something or similar to something —**cor·re·spond·ing·ly** adv

cor·ri·dor /ˈkɔrɪˌdɔr/ noun [C] **1** a long passage inside a building with doors on each side **2** a long narrow area of land

PHRASE **the corridors of power** *mainly journalism* the places where major political decisions are made

cor·rob·o·rate /kəˈrɑbəˌreɪt/ verb [T] *formal* to support what someone says by giving information or evidence

cor·rode /kəˈroʊd/ verb [I/T] if metal or another substance corrodes, or if something corrodes it, it is gradually destroyed by a chemical reaction

cor·ro·sion /kəˈroʊʒ(ə)n/ noun [U] damage that is caused to metal or stone when it is corroded

cor·ro·sive /kəˈroʊsɪv/ adj a corrosive substance contains chemicals that gradually cause damage

cor·ru·gat·ed /ˈkɔrəˌgeɪtəd/ adj corrugated

metal, paper, or CARDBOARD has a surface of curved parallel folds

cor•rupt¹ /kəˈrʌpt/ adj **1** doing dishonest or illegal things in order to get money or power: *corrupt politicians/officials* **2** corrupt computer files are damaged and do not operate correctly —**cor•rupt•ly** adv

cor•rupt² /kəˈrʌpt/ verb [T] **1** to encourage someone to do dishonest, illegal, or immoral things **2** to damage a computer file

cor•rup•tion /kəˈrʌpʃ(ə)n/ noun [U] ★
1 dishonest or illegal behavior by powerful people: *The men were arrested on charges of corruption.*
2 the process of corrupting someone or something: ***corruption of the database***

cor•ti•sone /ˈkɔrtɪˌzoʊn/ noun [U] a drug that is used to improve medical conditions such as ARTHRITIS and ALLERGIES

cos•met•ic /kɑzˈmetɪk/ adj **1** *showing disapproval* cosmetic changes affect only the appearance of something = SUPERFICIAL **2** relating to the improvement of someone's appearance: *cosmetic products* —**cos•met•i•cal•ly** /kɑzˈmetɪkli/ adv

cos•met•ics /kɑzˈmetɪks/ noun [plural] substances that you use on your hair or skin to make yourself look more attractive

cosˌmetic ˈsurgery noun [U] medical operations that improve someone's appearance

cos•mic /ˈkɑzmɪk/ adj relating to the planets and space

cos•mo•pol•i•tan /ˌkɑzməˈpɑlɪt(ə)n/ adj showing the influence of many different countries and cultures

cos•mos, the /ˈkɑzməs, ˈkɑzˌmoʊs/ noun [singular] the universe

cost¹ /kɔst/ noun ★★★
1 [C/U] the amount of money that you need in order to buy something or to do something: *The **cost of** basic foods has risen dramatically.* ♦ *We need money to **cover the cost of** hiring a lawyer* (=to have enough to pay for it). ♦ *We're organizing a trip to New York, **at a cost of** $100 per person.*
2 [C/U] damage or loss: *A new road is needed, but the **costs to the environment** would be too high.* ♦ *the **social costs of** unemployment*
3 **costs** [plural] money that you have to spend regularly in order to live somewhere or to run a business: *New technology has helped us to **cut costs*** (=reduce them). ♦ *manufacturing/operating costs*
4 **costs** [plural] *legal* money that someone who is involved in a legal case must give to pay for the lawyers and the court
PHRASES **at all costs** or **at any cost** used for saying that something must be done, even if it causes damage or harm
the cost of living the amount of money that people need in order to pay for basic things such as food and a place to live

> **Words often used with cost**
> *Verbs often used with **cost** (noun, sense 1)*
> ■ **bear, cover, pay** + COST: pay the cost of something
> ■ **cut, reduce, slash** + COST: make the cost of something lower
> ■ **drive up, increase, push up** + COST: make the cost of something greater
> ■ **offset, recoup, recover** + COST: get back money that you paid

cost² /kɔst/ (past tense and past participle **cost**) verb [T] ★★★
1 if something costs an amount of money, you need that amount to pay for it or to do it: *A new computer costs between $500 and $3,000.* ♦ **cost sb sth** *Unemployment costs the taxpayer billions of dollars each year.* ♦ **cost sth to do sth** *How much does it cost to rent a bike?*
2 to cause someone to lose something good or valuable: *The merger of the two companies will cost jobs.* ♦ **cost sb sth** *His decision to take the car cost him his life.*
3 (past tense and past participle **cost•ed**) to calculate how much something will cost: *We have costed our proposals and sent them to the committee.*
PHRASE **cost a fortune** or **cost an arm and a leg** *informal* to cost a lot of money

co•star /ˈkoʊˌstɑr/ noun [C] an actor's costars are the other actors who have main parts in a movie or play —**coˌstar** verb [I/T]

ˈcostˌcutting noun [U] actions taken to reduce the costs of a business or organization

ˌcost-efˈfective adj a cost-effective way of doing something brings the most profit or advantage for the money that is spent —**ˌcost-efˈfectively** adv

cost•ly /ˈkɔs(t)li/ adj *formal* **1** causing problems and wasting money **2** expensive

cos•tume /ˈkɑsˌtum/ noun [C/U] **1** clothes that the actors wear in a play or movie **2** clothes that are typical of a particular place or period in history

ˈcostume ˌdrama noun [C] a play or movie about a particular historical period in which the actors wear clothes that are typical of that period

ˈcostume ˌjewelry noun [U] jewelry that is not valuable but looks expensive

cot /kɑt/ noun [C] **1** *American* a small narrow bed that can be folded up —*picture* → BED **2** *British* a CRIB for a baby to sleep in

cot•tage /ˈkɑtɪdʒ/ noun [C] a small house in the country

ˌcottage ˈcheese noun [U] a soft white cheese that does not contain much fat

ˌcottage ˈindustry noun [C] a small business that involves people producing things at home

cot•ton¹ /ˈkɑt(ə)n/ noun [U] ★★
1 cloth made from the white fibers of a plant called a **cotton plant**: *a cotton dress*
2 plants with white fibers used for making cotton cloth: *the southern states that grow cotton*

cot•ton² /ˈkɑt(ə)n/ PHRASAL VERB **ˌcotton ˈon** *informal* to begin to realize or understand something

ˈcotton ˌball noun [C] a small ball of cotton used for removing MAKEUP, cleaning a cut on your skin, or cleaning a baby

ˌcotton ˈcandy noun [U] *American* a sweet food that consists of many long thin strings of sugar

couch¹ /kaʊtʃ/ noun [C] a long seat that you can sit or lie on = SOFA

couch² /kaʊtʃ/ verb **be couched in sth** *formal* to be expressed in a particular way

ˌcouch poˈtato noun [C] *showing disapproval* someone who spends a lot of time watching television

cou•gar /ˈkugər/ noun [C] a large wild cat found in North and South America

cough¹ /kɑf/ verb ★

1 [I] to force air up through your throat with a sudden noise, especially when you have a cold or when you want to get someone's attention: *My chest felt painful, and I was coughing uncontrollably.*

2 [T] to force something such as blood out of your lungs by coughing

—**cough•ing** noun [U]

PHRASAL VERB **ˌcough sth ˈup** *same as* **cough¹ 2**

cough² /kɑf/ noun [C] **1** the action of coughing, or the sound that you make when you cough **2** an illness in which you cough a lot and your throat hurts

ˈcough ˌsyrup noun [C/U] *American* a liquid medicine that you take to help cure a cough

could /*weak* kəd, *strong* kʊd/ modal verb ★★★

- **Could** is used as the past tense of **can** when it means that someone had the ability to do something, or that something was possible: *The Roman army could march 30 miles in a day.*
- **Could** is usually followed by an infinitive without "to": *I'm glad you could come.* Sometimes it is used without a following infinitive: *I came as quickly as I could.*
- **Could** has no tenses, no participles, and no infinitive form. It does not change its form, so the third person singular form does not end in "-s": *She could play the violin when she was six.*
- Questions and negatives are formed without "do": *Could he help you?* ♦ *I could not breathe.*
- The negative form **could not** is often shortened in conversation or informal writing to **couldn't**: *I couldn't find her phone number.*

1 past tense of "can" used for saying that someone was able to do something: *Renee could read when she was four.* ♦ *In the distance I could see a cloud of smoke.*

2 for saying what is possible used for saying that something is possible or that it may happen: *We could still win.* ♦ *In a situation like this, anything could happen.*

3 in requests *spoken* used for asking something politely: *Could I have a glass of water?* ♦ *Could you mail this letter for me?* → CAN¹

4 for making a suggestion *spoken* used for suggesting to someone what they might do: *You could come and stay with us.* ♦ *You* ***could always*** *sell the car if you need extra money.*

5 for emphasis *spoken* used for emphasizing how strong your feelings are: *You could have said you were sorry!* ♦ *How could you be so stupid!*

PHRASES **could have** *spoken* **1** used for saying that something was possible in the past, even though it did not happen: *You could have been killed.* ♦ *She could have married Gerald if she'd wanted to.* **2** used for saying that perhaps something was true, although you are not sure: *The explosion could have been caused by a gas leak.*

couldn't be better/worse/nicer etc. *spoken* used for emphasizing that someone or something is extremely good/bad/nice etc.: *I was so nervous, but she couldn't have been nicer to me.*

could•n't /ˈkʊd(ə)nt/ short form the usual way of saying or writing "could not." This is not often used in formal writing: *I couldn't go to her party.*

coun•cil /ˈkaʊns(ə)l/ noun [C] ★★

1 the elected politicians who govern a city or local area, or the organization they work for: *The council has rejected their suggestion.* ♦ *Mount Vernon City Council*

2 a group of people who are chosen to make official decisions or give advice

coun•cil•man /ˈkaʊns(ə)lmən/ (plural **coun•cil•men** /ˈkaʊns(ə)lmən/) noun [C] *American* a man who is an elected member of the government of a city in the U.S.

coun•cil•or /ˈkaʊns(ə)lər/ noun [C] *American* a member of a council

coun•cil•wom•an /ˈkaʊns(ə)lˌwʊmən/ (plural **coun•cil•wom•en** /ˈkaʊns(ə)lˌwɪmɪn/) noun [C] *American* a woman who is an elected member of the government of a city in the U.S.

coun•sel¹ /ˈkaʊns(ə)l/ (present participle **coun•sel•ing** or **coun•sel•ling**; past tense and past participle **coun•seled** or **coun•selled**) verb [T] to give someone advice about their problems, especially as your job: *She spent five years counseling rape victims.*

coun•sel² /ˈkaʊns(ə)l/ noun **1** [C] a lawyer who represents someone in a court of law **2** [C/U] *formal* advice and help

coun•sel•ing or **coun•sel•ling** /ˈkaʊns(ə)lɪŋ/ noun [U] professional advice given to someone who has problems: *marriage counseling* (=for people with problems in their marriage)

coun•sel•or or **coun•sel•lor** /ˈkaʊns(ə)lər/ noun [C] **1** someone whose job is to give advice to people with problems **2** *American* someone who takes care of children at a SUMMER CAMP

count¹ /kaʊnt/ verb ★★★

1 say how many	5 consider as sth
2 say numbers	+ PHRASES
3 include in calculation	+ PHRASAL VERBS
4 be important	

1 [I/T] to calculate how many people or things there are in a group: *All the votes have been counted.* ♦ *At least 60 people were injured, but we're still counting.*

2 [I] to say numbers one after another in order: *I can count up to ten in German.*

3 [I/T] to include something or someone in a calculation, or to be included in a calculation: *Points scored after the bell do not count.* ♦ *The test scores for this project* ***count toward*** *your final grade.* ♦ **+as** *Do public holidays count as part of vacation time?*

4 [I] to be important: *You're late, but you're here; and* ***that's what counts.*** ♦ *They made me feel that my views* ***didn't count for anything.***

C

5 [I/T] to consider someone or something in a particular way, or to be considered in a particular way: *We can **count ourselves lucky** that none of us got hurt.* ♦ **count sth as sth** *Is geography counted as a science subject?*

PHRASES **count the days/hours/minutes etc.** to be impatient for something good to happen

don't count your chickens (before they're hatched) used for telling someone not to make plans that depend on the success of something that has not happened yet

PHRASAL VERBS **ˌcount aˈgainst sb** to be a disadvantage for someone

ˌcount sb ˈin to include someone

ˈcount on sb to be sure that someone will do what you want or expect them to do: **count on sb for sth** *You can always count on him for good advice.* ♦ **count on sb to do sth** *I knew I could count on you to be on time.*

ˈcount on sth to expect that something will happen: *Tournament directors are counting on good weather.*

ˌcount sb ˈout to not include someone

ˌcount sth ˈup to count all the things or people in a group

count² /kaʊnt/ noun [C] ★★

1 counting process	4 amount of sth in sth
2 saying numbers	5 person of high status
3 each crime	+ PHRASES

1 the process of counting the people or things in a group, or the number of people or things that are counted: *After the count, Ellison had 25% of the votes.* ♦ ***At last count**, 400 people had agreed to join.*

2 the process of saying numbers in order: *Hold your breath for a count of ten.*

3 *legal* each crime that someone is charged with: *Brown was put in jail on three counts of corruption.*

4 the amount of a substance that is present in another substance: *the pollen count* ♦ *a low sperm count*

5 **Count** a NOBLEMAN in some European countries

PHRASES **keep count (of sth)** to remember or record a number as it changes over a period of time: *It seemed like a long time, but I didn't keep count of the days.*

lose count (of sth) used for emphasizing that something has happened many times

on both/all/several counts in both/all/several ways

count·a·ble /ˈkaʊntəb(ə)l/ adj *linguistics* a countable noun is a noun that has a plural and can be used after "a" when it is singular. Countable nouns are marked "[C]" in this dictionary ≠ UNCOUNTABLE

count·down /ˈkaʊntˌdaʊn/ noun [C] **1** the action of counting numbers backward before something important happens **2** the period of time just before an important event

coun·ter¹ /ˈkaʊntər/ noun [C] **1** a long flat surface where customers are served, for example in a store or a bank **2** a long flat surface in a kitchen where you prepare food —*picture* → C2

PHRASES **over the counter** drugs and medicines that are available over the counter can be bought without a doctor's PRESCRIPTION

under the counter bought or sold secretly and illegally

coun·ter² /ˈkaʊntər/ verb **1** [I/T] to reply to a criticism or statement that you disagree with **2** [T] to oppose or stop something

coun·ter³ /ˈkaʊntər/ adj, adv opposite, or with an opposite purpose: *a counter argument*

counter- /kaʊntər/ prefix opposing something: *a counter-proposal*

coun·ter·act /ˌkaʊntərˈækt/ verb [T] to reduce the negative effect of something by doing something that has an opposite effect

coun·ter·at·tack /ˈkaʊntərəˌtæk/ noun [C] an attack that you make against someone who has just attacked you in a war, game, or argument —**coun·ter·at·tack** verb [I]

coun·ter·clock·wise /ˌkaʊntərˈklɑkˌwaɪz/ adv *American* moving in the opposite direction to the way clock HANDS move

coun·ter·feit /ˈkaʊntərˌfɪt/ adj counterfeit money, documents, or products are illegal copies

coun·ter·part /ˈkaʊntərˌpɑrt/ noun [C] a person or thing that is similar to another in a different country or organization

coun·ter·pro·duc·tive /ˌkaʊntərprəˈdʌktɪv/ adj having a result that is the opposite of the one that you intended

coun·ter·top /ˈkaʊntərˌtɑp/ noun [C] *American* the surface of a COUNTER in a kitchen

count·ess /ˈkaʊntəs/ noun [C] a woman who is the wife of an EARL or COUNT

count·less /ˈkaʊntləs/ adj very many: *The temple attracts countless visitors.*

ˈcount ˌnoun noun [C] a COUNTABLE noun

coun·try /ˈkʌntri/ noun ★★★

1 area of land	4 country music
2 people of a country	5 area of particular type
3 areas away from cities	+ PHRASE

1 [C] an area of land that has its own government and official borders: *We have offices in 15 countries.* ♦ *soldiers who fight for their country*

2 **the country** [singular] all the people who live in a country: *a crime that has shocked **the whole country***

3 **the country** [singular] areas away from towns and cities, consisting of fields, farms, villages, etc. = COUNTRYSIDE: *We went for a picnic in the country.*

4 [U] COUNTRY MUSIC

5 [U] an area that is known for a particular product, activity, person, etc.: *East of here is mostly farming country.*

PHRASE **country and western** COUNTRY MUSIC

ˈcountry ˌclub noun [C] an expensive private club where the members hold social events and play sports such as golf and tennis

coun·try·man /ˈkʌntrimən/ (plural **coun·try·men** /ˈkʌntrimən/) noun [C] someone who is from the same country as you

ˈcountry ˌmusic noun [U] a type of popular music from the southern U.S. = COUNTRY, COUNTRY AND WESTERN

coun·try·side /ˈkʌntriˌsaɪd/ noun [U] areas

away from towns and cities, with farms, fields, and trees

coun•ty /ˈkaʊnti/ noun [C] a region that has its own local government

coup /ku/ noun [C] **1 coup** or **coup d'état** an occasion when a group of people take control of a country using military force **2** an impressive and surprising success

cou•pe /kup/ noun [C] a car with two side doors and a back door that slopes downward

cou•ple[1] /ˈkʌp(ə)l/ noun ★★★
1 [singular] *informal* two things or people of the same type: *"Has he had any serious girlfriends?" "A couple."* ♦ *Take **a couple of** aspirin – you'll soon feel better.*
2 [singular] a small number of things or people: *There are **a couple of** things I want to discuss.* ♦ *I invited a couple of friends over.*
3 [C] two people who are married to each other, or who have a romantic relationship with each other
4 [C] two people who are doing something together: *The room was full of dancing couples.*

cou•ple[2] /ˈkʌp(ə)l/ verb [T] **1** if one thing is coupled with another, they are combined **2** to join vehicles or pieces of equipment so that they work together

cou•pon /ˈkuˌpɑn/ noun [C] a piece of paper that allows you to buy something at a reduced price

cour•age /ˈkʌrɪdʒ/ noun [U] ★ the ability to do things that are dangerous, frightening, or very difficult: *I didn't **have the courage** to admit that I was wrong.* ♦ *Eventually I **plucked up the courage*** (=tried to make myself feel brave enough) *to ask her to dance.*

cou•ra•geous /kəˈreɪdʒəs/ adj very brave and determined —**cou•ra•geous•ly** adv

cour•gette /kɔrˈʒet/ noun [C/U] *British* a ZUCCHINI

cou•ri•er /ˈkʊriər, ˈkɜriər/ noun [C] **1** someone whose job is to deliver documents or packages **2** *British* a TOUR GUIDE

course[1] /kɔrs/ noun [C] ★★★

1 series of classes	5 part of meal
2 action sb chooses	6 area for sports
3 way things develop	+ PHRASES
4 direction sth follows	

1 a series of classes in an academic subject or a practical skill: *a drama/secretarial/Spanish course* ♦ *You could **take a** language **course** abroad.* ♦ *The school **runs courses** for beginners.* ♦ *an introductory **course in** economics*
2 the things that you choose to do in a particular situation: *What **course of action** do you recommend?*
3 the way that things develop over a period of time: *In **the normal course of events**, he would have left on time.* ♦ *a speech that changed **the course of history***
4 the direction that a ship or airplane is traveling in: *The captain had to change course quickly.*
5 one of the parts of a meal: *We both chose fish as our **main course**.*
6 an area where a race or sport takes place: *a golf/race course*

PHRASES **in/over the course of sth** while something is happening or continuing: *In the course of the morning I learned a lot about the project.*
on course for sth or **on course to do sth** very likely to achieve something or to have a particular result
run/take its course to develop in the usual way and stop naturally: *We have to let the illness run its course.*
→ DUE[1], OF COURSE

course[2] /kɔrs/ adv *spoken* OF COURSE

course•book /ˈkɔrsˌbʊk/ noun [C] *British* a TEXTBOOK

course•work /ˈkɔrsˌwɜrk/ noun [U] school work that a student must do as part of a course of study

court[1] /kɔrt/ noun ★★★
1 [C/U] a place where trials take place and legal cases are decided: *a court case* ♦ *The man will **appear in court** on Monday.* ♦ *Lynn **took** her employers **to court*** (=began a court case against them).
2 the court [singular] the people in a court, especially the judge and JURY: *A police officer told the court that he had seen Brown leaving the house.*
3 [C] an area marked with lines where some sports are played, including tennis and basketball: *a tennis court*
4 [C/U] the place where a king or queen lives and works

PHRASE **court of law** a court where legal trials take place

court[2] /kɔrt/ verb [T] to try to impress someone because you want them to help you

PHRASES **court disaster/danger** to behave in a way that is likely to cause serious trouble
court popularity/publicity to try very hard to make yourself popular or well-known

cour•te•ous /ˈkɜrtiəs/ adj polite in a formal way ≠ DISCOURTEOUS —**cour•te•ous•ly** adv

cour•te•sy[1] /ˈkɜrtəsi/ noun [U] polite behavior: *You could have had the courtesy to return my calls.*

PHRASE **courtesy of 1** used for saying who has provided something, and for thanking them for it **2** as a result of

cour•te•sy[2] /ˈkɜrtəsi/ adj provided free

court•house /ˈkɔrtˌhaʊs/ noun [C] *American* a building that has one or more courts in it for legal trials

ˌcourt-ˈmartial noun [C] a trial of a member of the military who has broken military laws —**ˌcourt-ˈmartial** verb [T]

ˈcourt ˌorder noun [C] an order from a court of law that tells someone that they must do something

court•room /ˈkɔrtˌrum/ noun [C] a room where legal cases are judged

court•ship /ˈkɔrtʃɪp/ noun [C/U] *old-fashioned* the romantic relationship that a man and a woman have before they get married

court•yard /ˈkɔrtˌjɑrd/ noun [C] a square area outside that is surrounded by buildings or walls

cous•cous /ˈkusˌkus/ noun [U] crushed wheat that is used in North African cooking

cous•in /ˈkʌz(ə)n/ noun [C] ★★ a child of your UNCLE or AUNT —*picture* → FAMILY TREE

C

cove /koʊv/ noun [C] a small area of ocean that is partly surrounded by land

cov•e•nant /ˈkʌvənənt/ noun [C] a legal agreement, often an agreement to give money

cov•er¹ /ˈkʌvər/ verb [T] ★★★

1 put sth over sth else	6 pay for
2 be all over sth	7 travel a distance
3 include and deal with	+ PHRASES
4 report/describe	+ PHRASAL VERBS
5 provide insurance	

1 to put one thing over another in order to protect or hide it: *Cover the food until you are ready to eat it.* ♦ *The noise was so loud I had to cover my ears.* ♦ **cover sb/sth with sth** *They covered the baby with a blanket.*
2 to be all over a surface or object: *Bruises covered his entire body.* ♦ **be covered with sth** *His clothes were covered with mud.*
3 to deal with a particular situation or subject: *The program covers all aspects of health and safety at work.*
4 to give a report of an event on television or radio, or in a newspaper: *We will be covering the game on Saturday afternoon.*
5 if an insurance agreement covers a situation or person, it provides protection against loss or damage
6 to have enough money to pay for something: *We need $700 a month to cover the rent.*
7 to travel a particular distance: *We had to cover the last three miles on foot.*
PHRASES **cover your tracks** to try to hide evidence of something bad that you have done
cover yourself or **cover your back** to take action to protect yourself against criticism, blame, or legal problems
PHRASAL VERBS **ˈcover for sb 1** to do someone's work while they are sick or not there **2** to protect someone from punishment, for example by telling a lie for them
ˌcover ˈup to put more clothes on
ˌcover sth ˈup 1 *same as* **cover¹** 1 **2** to hide the truth about something: *The school tried to cover the whole thing up.*

cov•er² /ˈkʌvər/ noun ★★★

1 for putting over sth	5 piece of music
2 outside of book/CD	6 cover charge
3 place for shelter	7 sheets/blankets
4 false story	+ PHRASES

1 [C] something that you put over something else in order to hide it, protect it, or close it: *She put plastic covers on all the furniture.* ♦ *cushion covers*
2 [C] the outside page on the front or back of a book or magazine: *Her face was once **on the cover of*** Vogue *magazine.* ♦ *On the airplane I **read** the newspaper **from cover to cover*** (=read it all).
3 [U] places such as buildings or trees where people or animals can hide or shelter from the weather: *Everybody **ran for cover** as the rain started to fall.*
4 [singular] a false story that is used for hiding who someone really is
5 [C] a song that is recorded by someone who is not the original performer
6 [C/U] *American* a COVER CHARGE
7 **the covers** [plural] sheets and BLANKETS that you lie under in bed
PHRASES **under cover** pretending to be someone else in order to find out secret information
under cover of night/darkness hidden by darkness

cov•er•age /ˈkʌv(ə)rɪdʒ/ noun [U] **1** news about something on television or radio or in the newspapers: *live coverage of the main Olympic events* **2** the amount of attention that television, radio, and newspapers give to something, or the way in which something is reported **3** *American* the amount and type of protection that an insurance agreement gives you

ˈcover ˌgirl noun [C] an attractive young woman whose photograph is on the front of a magazine

cov•er•ing /ˈkʌv(ə)rɪŋ/ noun [singular] something that covers something else

ˈcover ˌletter noun [C] *American* a letter that you send with something, to explain what you are sending

co•vert /ˈkoʊˌvɜrt, koʊˈvɜrt/ adj secret ≠ OVERT —**co•vert•ly** adv

ˈcover-ˌup noun [C] an attempt to stop people from discovering the truth about something bad

ˈcover ˌversion noun [C] a COVER of a popular song

cov•et /ˈkʌvət/ verb [T] *formal* to want something that someone else has

cov•et•ed /ˈkʌvətid/ adj a coveted thing is something that a lot of people want to have

cow¹ /kaʊ/ noun [C] ★★
1 an animal that is kept by farmers for its milk or meat —*picture* → C12
2 the female of some types of animal such as an elephant or a WHALE

cow² /kaʊ/ verb [T] to make someone do what you want by frightening them = INTIMIDATE: *They refused to be cowed.*

cow•ard /ˈkaʊərd/ noun [C] someone who is not brave enough to do something that they should do

cow•ard•ice /ˈkaʊərdɪs/ noun [U] behavior that shows that you are not brave enough to do something that you should do

cow•ard•ly /ˈkaʊərdli/ adj **1** a cowardly person is not brave enough to do something that they should do **2** cruel toward someone who is weaker than you: *a cowardly attack*

cow•boy /ˈkaʊˌbɔɪ/ noun [C] a man whose job is to take care of cows on a RANCH in the U.S.

ˈcowboy ˌhat noun [C] a high hat with a wide BRIM (=the flat part that surrounds a hat) —*picture* → HAT

cow•er /ˈkaʊr/ verb [I] to move your body down and away from someone because you are frightened = CRINGE

ˈco-ˌworker noun [C] someone who works with you

coy /kɔɪ/ adj pretending to be shy in order to seem more attractive —**coy•ly** adv

coy•o•te /kaɪˈoʊti, ˈkaɪˌoʊt/ noun [C] a small wild North American dog

co•zy¹ /ˈkoʊzi/ adj warm and comfortable, relaxing, or friendly=SNUG: *a cozy chair* ♦ *a cozy evening by the fire*

co•zy² /ˈkoʊzi/ PHRASAL VERB **ˌcozy ˈup to sb** to try to become friendly with someone to get some benefit for yourself

CPA /ˌsi pi ˈeɪ/ noun [C] a certified public accountant: someone with all the qualifications needed to be an ACCOUNTANT in the U.S.

crab /kræb/ noun [C/U] a SHELLFISH with two large CLAWS that walks sideways, or the meat from this fish

crab•by /ˈkræbi/ adj easily annoyed =IRRITABLE

crab•meat /ˈkræbˌmit/ noun [U] the meat from a CRAB

crack¹ /kræk/ verb ★

1 break so line appears	5 lose control of yourself
2 break sth open	6 when voice shakes
3 make short loud noise	+ PHRASES
4 hit part of body hard	+ PHRASAL VERBS

1 [I/T] if something cracks, or if you crack it, a line or long narrow hole appears on its surface, but it does not break into pieces: *The ice was starting to crack at the edges.* ♦ *I dropped a plate and cracked it.*

2 [T] to break something open in order to get what is inside: *Crack the egg open with a knife.*

3 [I] to make a short loud noise like a small explosion: *Thunder cracked overhead.*

4 [T] to accidentally hit a part of your body against something with a lot of force: *Dad fell and cracked his head against the door.*

5 [I] to say or do things that you would not normally say or do, because you are very tired or because someone is threatening you: *She won because her opponent **cracked under the pressure**.*

6 [I] if your voice cracks, it goes higher and lower in a way that you cannot control

PHRASES **crack a joke** *informal* to tell a joke
sth is not all it's cracked up to be *informal* used for saying that something is not as good as people say it is

PHRASAL VERBS **ˌcrack ˈdown** to start dealing with someone or something much more strictly than before: *The school is **cracking down on** smoking.*
ˌcrack ˈup *informal* to become mentally ill
ˌcrack (sb) ˈup to suddenly laugh a lot at something, or to make someone laugh a lot: *Little kids crack me up with the things they say.*

crack² /kræk/ noun ★

1 line where sth breaks	5 attempt
2 narrow opening	6 rude/insulting joke
3 sign sth is weak	7 illegal drug
4 short loud noise	+ PHRASES

1 [C] a line on a surface where something is beginning to break apart: *cracks in the walls*

2 [C] a narrow opening between two things: *She looked through the crack in the curtains.*

3 [C] a sign that an organization, relationship, or plan is becoming weak: *Cracks had started to appear in their marriage.*

4 [C] a short loud noise

5 [C] *informal* an attempt to do something: *We thought we'd **take a crack at** running our own business.*

6 [C] *informal* a rude or insulting joke about someone or something

7 [U] a pure form of the illegal drug COCAINE

PHRASES **at the crack of dawn** extremely early in the morning
slip/fall through the cracks to not be helped by a system that is designed to help you

crack³ /kræk/ adj very skillful as a result of being trained well

crack•down /ˈkrækˌdaʊn/ noun [C] strong action that someone in authority takes to stop a particular activity=CLAMPDOWN: *a new crackdown on drug dealing*

crack•er /ˈkrækər/ noun [C] **1** a type of small thin dry bread that is often eaten with cheese **2** *American* an insulting word for a poor white person

crack•le /ˈkræk(ə)l/ verb [I] **1** to continually make short sounds like the sound of wood burning **2** to be full of something such as nervousness or excitement: *The atmosphere crackled with expectation.*

crack•ling /ˈkræk(ə)lɪŋ/ noun [singular/U] the sound that something makes when it crackles

crack•pot /ˈkrækˌpɑt/ noun [C] a crazy person —**crack•pot** adj

cra•dle¹ /ˈkreɪd(ə)l/ noun [C] **1** a small bed for a baby that can swing from side to side **2** the part of a telephone where you put the RECEIVER **3** the place where something began=BIRTHPLACE: *a region that is regarded as the cradle of African culture*

cra•dle² /ˈkreɪd(ə)l/ verb [T] to hold something gently in your hands or arms

craft¹ /kræft/ noun **1** [C] a traditional skill of making things by hand, or something such as furniture or jewelry that is made by hand: *traditional Egyptian arts and crafts* **2** [C/U] the skill needed for a particular profession **3** [C] a boat or ship

craft² /kræft/ verb [T] to make or produce something skillfully

crafts•man /ˈkræftsmən/ noun [C] a man who makes beautiful or practical objects

crafts•man•ship /ˈkræftsmənʃɪp/ noun [U] the skill involved in making something beautiful or practical, or the beauty of something that has been made with skill

crafts•per•son /ˈkræftsˌpɜrs(ə)n/ noun [C] someone who makes beautiful or practical objects

crafts•wom•an /ˈkræftsˌwʊmən/ noun [C] a woman who makes beautiful or practical objects

craft•y /ˈkræfti/ adj good at getting what you want, especially dishonestly —**craft•i•ly** adv

crag /kræg/ noun [C] a very steep rough part of a cliff or mountain

crag•gy /ˈkrægi/ adj **1** a craggy face looks strong and has deep lines in it=RUGGED **2** steep with a lot of rough rocks

cram /kræm/ verb **1** [T] to put people or things into a space that is too small: *The sacks of rice were crammed under a table.* ♦ *The hall was crammed with children.* **2** [I] *informal* to study hard in order to learn a lot in a short time

cramp /kræmp/ noun **1** [C] a sudden severe pain in a tired muscle that becomes very tight **2 cramps** [plural] *American* pains that a woman sometimes gets during her PERIOD

cramped /kræmpt/ adj small and crowded: *cramped offices*

cran·ber·ry /ˈkrænˌberi/ noun [C] a small sour red fruit: *a glass of cranberry juice*

crane[1] /kreɪn/ noun [C] **1** a very tall machine that is used for moving heavy objects and for building tall buildings **2** a large water bird with long legs and a long neck

crane[2] /kreɪn/ verb [I/T] to stretch your neck out to try to see something

cra·ni·um /ˈkreɪniəm/ noun [C] *medical* your SKULL

crank[1] /kræŋk/ noun [C] a piece of equipment that turns to make something move or start

crank[2] /kræŋk/

PHRASAL VERBS **ˌcrank ˈout** *informal* to produce things in large numbers without caring about quality: *He cranked out one hit song after another.*

ˌcrank sth ˈup *informal* to increase the level or amount of something

crank·y /ˈkræŋki/ adj *American informal* easily annoyed = IRRITABLE

craps /kræps/ noun [U] a game of DICE in which you risk money

crash[1] /kræʃ/ verb ★

1 hit sth noisily	4 make sudden noise
2 when vehicle hits sth	5 when computer fails
3 when plane falls	6 of stock market

1 [I/T] to hit something hard and make a loud noise: *A ball came crashing through the window.* ♦ *The waves crashed against the rocks.*

2 [I] if a vehicle crashes, it hits something: *Three people were killed when their car crashed into a tree.*

3 [I/T] if a plane crashes, or if someone crashes it, it falls from the sky

4 [I] to make a sudden loud noise, as if something is being hit

5 [I] if a computer or a computer program crashes, it suddenly stops working

6 [I] if the STOCK MARKET crashes, its value falls suddenly

crash[2] /kræʃ/ noun [C] ★

1 an accident that happens when a vehicle hits something = WRECK: *He was seriously injured in the crash.* ♦ *It was the worst train crash in thirty years.*

2 an occasion when a computer or a computer program suddenly stops working

3 a loud noise like the sound of things hitting each other and breaking

4 a sudden fall in prices or in the value of the STOCK MARKET

ˈcrash ˌcourse noun [C] a course of study in which you are taught a lot about a subject in a short time

ˈcrash ˌhelmet noun [C] a hard round hat that you wear to protect your head while driving a MOTORCYCLE or RACE CAR —*picture* → HAT

ˌcrash ˈlanding noun [C] an occasion when an aircraft has to land in a sudden and dangerous way

crass /kræs/ adj offensive and not sensitive to other people's feelings —**crass·ly** adv

crate /kreɪt/ noun [C] a container for storing or moving things

cra·ter /ˈkreɪtər/ noun [C] **1** the round hole at the top of a VOLCANO **2** a large round hole in the ground that is caused by an explosion

crave /kreɪv/ verb [I/T] to feel a very strong need that is hard to control: *As a child he craved attention.*

crav·ing /ˈkreɪvɪŋ/ noun [C] a very strong feeling of wanting something: *a craving for chocolate*

crawl[1] /krɔl/ verb [I] **1** to move along the ground on your hands and knees: *We crawled through the bushes.* **2** to move forward very slowly: *Traffic crawled along the main road.* **3** if an insect crawls, it moves forward using its legs **4** if time crawls by, it seems to pass very slowly

PHRASE **be crawling with 1** to be too full of people: *The town was crawling with police.* **2** to be full of unpleasant insects or animals

crawl

crawl[2] /krɔl/ noun [singular] **1** a very slow speed **2** a style of swimming in which you move one arm over your head and then the other while you are kicking your legs

cray·fish /ˈkreɪˌfɪʃ/ noun [C] a creature like a small LOBSTER

cray·on /ˈkreɪˌɑn/ noun [C] a stick of colored WAX that is used for drawing

craze /kreɪz/ noun [C] something that suddenly becomes very popular for a short time

crazed /kreɪzd/ adj completely crazy and uncontrolled

cra·zy /ˈkreɪzi/ adj *informal* ★★ not at all sensible or practical: *It's crazy. Who would do a thing like that?* ♦ **be crazy to do sth** *She knew she would be completely crazy to refuse.*

PHRASES **crazy about sb** very much in love with someone

crazy about sth very enthusiastic about something

drive/make sb crazy to make someone very annoyed

go crazy 1 to become very angry about something **2** to become very bored and upset **3** to become very excited

like crazy to a very great degree: *The games are selling like crazy.*

—**cra·zi·ly** adv

Words that may cause offense: crazy

Avoid using words like **crazy**, and **insane** about people who have mental illnesses or mental health problems. Instead, use an expression such as **mentally ill**.

creak /krik/ verb [I] if something creaks, it makes a high noise when it moves, or when you put weight on it —**creak** noun [C], **creak•y** adj

cream¹ /krim/ noun ★★
1 [C/U] a thick smooth substance that you put on your skin, for example when it is dry. Some medicines are in the form of a cream.
2 [U] a yellow-white color
3 [U] a thick yellow-white liquid that is taken from the top of milk
PHRASE **the cream of the crop** the best people or things of a particular type
—**cream•y** adj

cream² /krim/ adj yellow-white in color

ˌcream ˈcheese noun [U] a soft smooth white cheese that you spread on bread and similar foods

crease¹ /kris/ noun [C] **1** a line made on cloth or paper when it is folded or crushed **2** a line on someone's skin = WRINKLE

crease² /kris/ verb [I/T] to make lines on cloth or paper by folding or crushing it, or to become covered in these lines

creased /krist/ adj creased cloth or paper is marked with a crease

cre•ate /kriˈeɪt/ verb [T] ★★★ to make something new exist or happen: *His comments have created a lot of confusion.* ♦ *How do I create a new file?* ♦ *In the last week, 170 new jobs have been created.* ♦ *He was only 22 when he created this masterpiece.*

cre•a•tion /kriˈeɪʃ(ə)n/ noun ★★
1 [U] the act of creating something: *The government is to provide more money for job creation.* ♦ ***the creation of** new industries*
2 [C] something that has been created using skill or imagination: *Have you seen my latest creation?*

cre•a•tive /kriˈeɪtɪv/ adj ★
1 involving a lot of imagination and new ideas: *Painting is a creative process.* ♦ *the creative use of technology in everyday life*
2 having a lot of imagination and new ideas: *The program offers children the chance to be creative.*
—**cre•a•tive•ly** adv

creˌative ˈwriting noun [U] the activity of writing stories and poems

cre•a•tiv•i•ty /ˌkrieɪˈtɪvəti/ noun [U] the ability to create new ideas or things using your imagination: *We want to encourage creativity in our employees.*

cre•a•tor /kriˈeɪtər/ noun **1** [C] someone who has created something **2 the Creator** God

crea•ture /ˈkritʃər/ noun [C] ★★
1 anything that lives except plants: *a small furry creature*
2 an imaginary living thing that is strange or frightening: *The Gorgon was a mythical creature.*

cre•dence /ˈkrid(ə)ns/ noun **give/lend/add credence to sth** *formal* to make people think that something is likely to be true

cre•den•tials /krəˈdenʃ(ə)lz/ noun [plural]
1 personal qualities, achievements, or experiences that make someone appropriate for something: *His credentials as a football coach are impressive.*
2 documents that prove who you are, or that show your qualifications

cred•i•bil•i•ty /ˌkredɪˈbɪləti/ noun [U] qualities that someone or something has that make people believe them or trust them: *The government is losing credibility by its failure to act quickly.*

cred•i•ble /ˈkredɪb(ə)l/ adj **1** able to be believed or trusted: *credible evidence*
2 considered likely to happen or likely to be successful: *a credible opponent/candidate* —**cred•i•bly** adv

cred•it¹ /ˈkredɪt/ noun ★★

1 when you pay later	5 money you pay in
2 money you can use	6 who made movie etc.
3 praise for sth you did	+ PHRASES
4 at college/university	

1 [U] an arrangement to receive money from a bank, or receive goods from a store, and to pay for them later ≠ DEBIT: *I don't like buying things **on credit**.* ♦ *Some suppliers will not **offer credit** to their customers.*
2 [C] an amount of money that you have a right to use: *tax credits*
3 [U] praise for something that you have done: *He always **takes the credit** for my ideas.* ♦ *You deserve **credit for** all the help you gave us.*
4 [C] a part of a college or university program that you have completed successfully
5 [C] an amount of money that you add to an account
6 **the credits** [plural] a list at the beginning or end of a movie or television show that shows the people who were involved in making it
PHRASES **be a credit to sb** if you are a credit to someone, they should be proud of you
give sb credit for sth to believe that someone is good at something, or that they have a particular good quality
to sb's credit used for saying that someone deserves praise: *Jane, to her credit, helped the woman without knowing the situation.*

cred•it² /ˈkredɪt/ verb [T] to add an amount of money to an account ≠ DEBIT: *The money will be credited to your account.*
PHRASE **credit sb with sth** to believe that someone has achieved something, or that they have particular good qualities

cred•it•a•ble /ˈkredɪtəb(ə)l/ adj good enough to deserve some praise or admiration

ˈcredit ˌcard noun [C] a small plastic card that you use to buy things now and pay for them later

ˈcredit ˌlimit noun [C] the maximum amount of money that a customer can borrow using a particular credit card

cred•i•tor /ˈkredɪtər/ noun [C] a person or company that is owed money by another person or company ≠ DEBTOR

creed /krid/ noun [C] *formal* a set of beliefs

creek /krik, krɪk/ noun [C] **1** a narrow stream **2** a long narrow area of ocean that stretches into the land
PHRASE **be up the creek (without a paddle)** *informal* to be in a difficult situation

creep¹ /krip/ (past tense and past participle **crept** /krept/) verb [I] **1** to move slowly and quietly:

Sue crept up the stairs. ♦ *The fog was creeping across the bay.* **2** to gradually happen or start: *A smile crept over her face.*

PHRASAL VERB **ˌcreep ˈup on sb 1** if something creeps up on you, it happens so gradually that you do not notice it **2** to move toward someone quietly and slowly, so that they do not hear you

creep² /krip/ noun [C] *informal* an unpleasant person

PHRASE **give sb the creeps** to make someone feel nervous or frightened

creep•y /ˈkripi/ adj *informal* unpleasant in a way that makes you feel frightened

cre•mate /krəˈmeɪt, ˈkriˌmeɪt/ verb [T] to burn the body of a dead person —**cre•ma•tion** /krəˈmeɪʃ(ə)n/ noun [C/U]

cre•ma•to•ri•um /ˌkreməˈtɔriəm/ noun [C] a building where the bodies of dead people are cremated

crepe /kreɪp/ noun **1** [C] a light thin PANCAKE **2** [U] a light type of rubber **3** [U] a soft thin cloth with small folds in its surface

ˌcrepe ˈpaper noun [U] thin paper that stretches easily and is often used for making decorations

crept the past tense and past participle of **creep¹**

cres•cen•do /krəˈʃendoʊ/ noun [C] a gradual increase in sound in a piece of music

cres•cent /ˈkrez(ə)nt/ noun [C] a curved shape that is wide in the middle and pointed at the ends —*picture* → C8

crest /krest/ noun [C] **1** a set of feathers on the top of the heads of some birds **2** the top of a hill, mountain, or wave

crest•fall•en /ˈkrestˌfɔlən/ adj sad and disappointed

cre•vasse /krəˈvæs/ noun [C] a very deep crack in rock or ice

crev•ice /ˈkrevɪs/ noun [C] a narrow crack in rock or in a wall

crew /kru/ noun ★★

1 [C] the people who work on a ship, aircraft, etc.: *All the passengers and crew on board the jet were killed.*

2 [C] the people on a military ship or aircraft who are not officers

3 [C] a group of people with a particular skill who work together: *a movie crew* ♦ *an ambulance crew*

4 [C/U] the sport of ROWING boats in races, or a team of people who do this

crew•man /ˈkrumən/ (plural **crew•men** /ˈkrumən/) noun [C] a man who is a member of the CREW of a ship, aircraft, etc.

ˈcrew ˌneck noun [C] a SWEATER with a round neck —*picture* → NECKLINE

crib /krɪb/ noun [C] *American* a bed for a baby with tall bars at the sides

crick /krɪk/ noun [C] a sudden pain in your neck or back that you get when the muscles become stiff

crick•et /ˈkrɪkɪt/ noun **1** [C] a brown insect that makes a loud noise at night **2** [U] a game in which teams get points by hitting a ball with a **bat** and running between two sets of sticks

cried the past tense and past participle of **cry¹**

crime /kraɪm/ noun ★★★

1 [C] an illegal activity or action: *She was unaware that she had **committed a crime**.* ♦ *It took police eight years to **solve the crime*** (=find out who did it).

2 [U] illegal activities in general: *new laws to help **fight crime*** ♦ ***The crime rate*** (=the number of crimes) *in the city has risen sharply.* ♦ ***Rising crime*** (=crime that is increasing) *is a key election issue.*

3 [singular] something that is bad, wrong, or unfair: *It's not a crime to be curious.*

ˈcrime ˌwave noun [C] a sudden increase in the number of crimes in a particular area

crim•i•nal¹ /ˈkrɪmɪn(ə)l/ noun [C] ★★ someone who has committed a crime: *The program is designed to help former criminals find jobs.*

> **Words often used with criminal**
>
> *Adjectives often used with **criminal** (noun)*
>
> ■ **habitual, hardened, known, notorious** + CRIMINAL: used about someone who has committed many crimes

crim•i•nal² /ˈkrɪmɪn(ə)l/ adj ★★

1 relating to illegal acts, or to the parts of the legal system that deal with crime: *criminal behavior* ♦ *a criminal investigation* (=one that is dealing with a crime) ♦ *the criminal justice system* ♦ *a criminal offense*

2 bad, wrong, or unfair in a way that makes you angry: *That's a criminal waste of resources.*

crim•i•nal•ize /ˈkrɪmɪn(ə)lˌaɪz/ verb [T] to make an activity illegal by making a new law

ˌcriminal ˈlaw noun [U] the system of laws that deals with crimes and the punishment of criminals

crim•i•nal•ly /ˈkrɪmɪn(ə)li/ adv according to criminal law: *criminally insane*

ˌcriminal ˈrecord noun [C] an official list of crimes that someone has committed

crimp /krɪmp/ verb [T] **1** to make small folds or wave shapes in something **2** *American informal* to prevent something from increasing or developing

crim•son /ˈkrɪmz(ə)n/ adj dark purple-red in color

cringe /krɪndʒ/ verb [I] **1** to move back slightly from something that is unpleasant or frightening **2** to feel embarrassed or ashamed about something

crin•kle /ˈkrɪŋk(ə)l/ verb [I/T] if skin or cloth crinkles, or if you crinkle it, a lot of small folds appear in it —**crin•kled** /ˈkrɪŋk(ə)ld/ adj, **crin•kly** /ˈkrɪŋkli/ adj

crip•ple¹ /ˈkrɪp(ə)l/ verb [T] **1** to make someone physically disabled **2** to destroy something or damage it severely

crip•ple² /ˈkrɪp(ə)l/ noun [C] *offensive* an offensive word for someone who is physically disabled

crip•pling /ˈkrɪplɪŋ/ adj **1** causing severe damage or problems: *crippling taxes* **2** making someone physically disabled, or causing them to have severe health problems: *a crippling disease*

cri•sis /ˈkraɪsɪs/ (plural **cri•ses** /ˈkraɪˌsiz/) noun [C/U] ★★ an urgent and difficult or dangerous situation: ***political crisis*** ♦ *The nursing profession is **in crisis**.* ♦ *the current **crisis in** the farming industry*

crisp¹ /krɪsp/ adj **1** crisp food is firm in a pleasant way: *a crisp apple/carrot* **2** crisp weather is pleasant because it is cold and dry: *crisp night air* **3** crisp cloth or paper is smooth, clean, and fresh: *crisp sheets*

crisp² /krɪsp/ noun [C] *British* a POTATO CHIP

crisp·y /ˈkrɪspi/ adj food that is crispy is firm in a pleasant way

criss·cross /ˈkrɪsˌkrɔs/ verb **1** [I/T] to form a pattern of straight lines that cross each other **2** [T] to go across a place and back again many times, taking a different path each time

cri·te·ri·a /kraɪˈtɪriə/ (singular **cri·te·ri·on** /kraɪˈtɪriən/) noun [plural] ★ standards that are used for judging something or for making a decision about something: *Everyone whose qualifications **meet** our **criteria** will be considered.* ♦ *What **criteria** do you have **for** selecting patients for treatment?*

crit·ic /ˈkrɪtɪk/ noun [C] ★
1 someone whose job is to give their opinions about things such as books, movies, or plays
2 someone who does not like something and states their opinion about it: ***a critic of** the government's tax proposals*

crit·i·cal /ˈkrɪtɪk(ə)l/ adj ★★

1 saying sth is wrong	4 according to critics
2 very important	5 considering carefully
3 seriously sick/injured	

1 expressing your opinion when you think something is wrong or bad: *Her father was a very critical man.* ♦ *Warren was **critical of** the way she handled the affair.*
2 an event, time, or issue that is critical is very important, often because it affects the future: *a critical moment* ♦ *Winning the award is **critical to** our success.*
3 very seriously sick or injured: *Six of the patients were **in critical condition**.*
4 according to the book, movie, or theater CRITICS: *The show has won much **critical acclaim**.*
5 considering something carefully and deciding what is good or bad about it: *a critical look at modern life*

crit·i·cal·ly /ˈkrɪtɪkli/ adv **1** extremely and seriously: *critically ill* **2** carefully judging something: *We teach children to think critically.* **3** in a way that shows that you do not like something: *Nobody spoke critically of the government.* **4** if a book, movie, or play is critically acclaimed, it is said to be good by people whose job is to give their opinion

ˌcritical ˈmass noun [singular/U] the smallest number of people or things that are needed for something to happen

crit·i·cise /ˈkrɪtɪˌsaɪz/ a British spelling of **criticize**

crit·i·cism /ˈkrɪtɪˌsɪzəm/ noun ★★
1 [C/U] a comment or comments that show that you think something is wrong or bad: *a valid/fair criticism* ♦ ***criticism of** the team's performance* ♦ *The new plans drew **fierce criticism** from local people.*
2 [U] the activity of giving your professional opinion about things such as new books, movies, or plays

Words often used with criticism

*Adjectives often used with **criticism** (sense 1)*
- **fierce, outspoken, severe, strong** + CRITICISM: showing that you think that something is very bad

crit·i·cize /ˈkrɪtɪˌsaɪz/ verb [I/T] ★★ to say what you think is wrong or bad about something: *We were told not to criticize the policy publicly.* ♦ **criticize sb/sth for (doing) sth** *The new proposals have been criticized for not going far enough to change the system.*

Word family: criticize

*Words in the same family as **criticize***
- **critic** *n*
- **criticism** *n*
- **critical** *adj*
- **uncritical** *adj*
- **critically** *adv*

cri·tique /krɪˈtik/ noun [C] a careful written examination of a subject that includes the writer's opinions —**cri·tique** verb [T]

crit·ter /ˈkrɪtər/ noun [C] *American informal* a creature

croak /kroʊk/ verb **1** [I] when a FROG croaks, it makes a low loud rough sound **2** [I/T] to speak or say something in a low rough voice **3** [I] *very informal* to die —**croak** noun [C]

cro·chet /kroʊˈʃeɪ/ verb [I/T] to make something with YARN using a large needle with a hook on the end

croc·o·dile /ˈkrɑkəˌdaɪl/ noun [C] a large REPTILE with many sharp teeth that lives in water in hot countries —*picture* → C13

cro·cus /ˈkroʊkəs/ noun [C] a small yellow, white, or purple flower that appears early in spring

crois·sant /krwɑˈsɑnt, krwɑˈsɑ̃/ noun [C] a type of light bread with a curved shape

cro·ny /ˈkroʊni/ noun [C] *showing disapproval* a friend or supporter of someone who is powerful

cro·ny·ism /ˈkroʊniˌɪzəm/ noun [U] *showing disapproval* the practice of giving jobs and other advantages to friends

crook /krʊk/ noun [C] **1** *informal* someone who is dishonest or is a thief **2** the place where something bends inward: *the crook of your arm*

crook·ed /ˈkrʊkəd/ adj **1** not straight **2** *informal* dishonest = CORRUPT —**crook·ed·ly** adv

croon /krun/ verb [I/T] to sing slowly in a soft voice —**croon·er** noun [C]

crop¹ /krɑp/ noun ★
1 [C] a plant that is grown for food: *They're all out planting the crops today.* ♦ *Japan bought large amounts of rice overseas because of a **crop failure*** (=the crops did not grow).
2 [C] the amount of crops that are grown in a particular year: *a good crop of potatoes* ♦ *Last year we had **a bumper crop** of strawberries* (=a very large crop).
3 [singular] several things that happen or exist at the same time: *this summer's **crop** of Hollywood movies* ♦ *the current **crop of** young players*

crop² /krɑp/ verb [T] to make something shorter or smaller by cutting it

PHRASAL VERB **ˌcrop ˈup** *informal* to appear or happen suddenly or unexpectedly = COME UP

cro·quet /ˈkroʊki/ noun [U] a game in which players hit balls through curved pieces of metal using long wooden hammers

cross¹ /krɔs/ verb ★★★

1 [I/T] to go from one side of something to the other: *She watched the children cross the road.* ♦ *It was dark when we crossed the French border.*

2 [I] if things such as roads or lines cross, they go across each other = INTERSECT: *the point where the two paths cross*

3 [T] to combine one type of animal or plant with another to produce a genetic mix

4 [T] if an expression crosses someone's face or lips, it appears there for a short time

PHRASES **cross your arms** to put one arm over the other in front of your body, so that each hand is on the opposite elbow

cross your fingers to put your middle finger over your first finger as a wish for good luck

cross your legs to sit with one leg placed over the other at the knee

cross the line to go beyond accepted limits or standards of behavior

cross sb's mind if something crosses your mind, you think of it, but not for very long: *It suddenly crossed his mind that maybe Stephanie had been right.*

PHRASAL VERBS **ˌcross sth ˈoff** to draw a line through something on a list to show that you have dealt with it

ˌcross sth ˈout to draw an X or a line through writing because it is wrong, or because you want to write something else

cross

cross² /krɔs/ noun ★★

1 [C] a shape or an object with one long straight upright part and another shorter one across it, used as a symbol of Christianity → CRUCIFIXION

2 the Cross [singular] the structure on which Jesus Christ died according to the Bible

3 [C] a mixture of two different types of animals, plants, or things: *Most of their music is a* ***cross between jazz and rock****.*

4 [C] *British* the symbol X

cross³ /krɔs/ adj angry

cross·bar /ˈkrɔsˌbɑr/ noun [C] **1** the bar that joins the two upright posts of a goal **2** the metal bar between the seat and the front of a bicycle

cross·bow /ˈkrɔsˌboʊ/ noun [C] a weapon used for firing short heavy pointed sticks

ˌcross-ˈcountry adj **1** going across the countryside, not using tracks or roads **2** from one side of a country to the other —**ˌcross-ˈcountry** adv

ˌcross-examiˈnation noun [C] an occasion when someone is asked a lot of questions by a lawyer during a trial —**ˌcross-exˈamine** verb [T]

cross-eyed /ˌkrɔs ˈaɪd/ adj someone who is cross-eyed has eyes that look toward each other slightly

cross·fire /ˈkrɔsˌfaɪr/ noun [U] **1** bullets that come from two directions **2** arguments or violence that might affect people who are not directly involved

cross·ing /ˈkrɔsɪŋ/ noun [C] **1** a trip across a river or ocean: *a transatlantic crossing* **2** a place where you are allowed to cross something such as a road or border: *a pedestrian crossing*

cross-leg·ged /ˌkrɔs ˈlegəd/ adj, adv in a sitting position on the floor, with your knees bent and your lower legs crossing each other —*picture* → POSTURE

cross·o·ver /ˈkrɔsˌoʊvər/ noun [C] a change from one situation or style to another

ˌcross ˈreference noun [C] a note in a book that tells you to look at another page for more information

cross·roads /ˈkrɔsˌroʊdz/ (plural **cross·roads**) noun [C] **1** a place where one road crosses another **2** a point in time when you have to make an important decision about what to do next

ˈcross ˌsection noun **1** [C/U] the inside of an object that you can see by cutting through the middle of it, or a picture of this **2** [C] a group that contains an example of most types of people or things: *a cross section of the city's population*

ˌcross-trainer noun [C] a piece of exercise equipment that you stand on and move your legs and arms backward and forward —*picture* → C16

ˈcross-ˌtraining noun [U] the activity of training in more than one sport —**cross-ˈtrain** verb [I]

cross·walk /ˈkrɔsˌwɔk/ noun [C] *American* a painted path that people use for crossing a street

cross·word /ˈkrɔsˌwɜrd/ or **crossword ˌpuzzle** noun [C] a word game in which the answers to questions are written in rows of squares that cross each other

crotch /krɑtʃ/ noun [C] the area between your legs where they join your body, or the part of a piece of clothing that covers this area

crotch·et·y /ˈkrɑtʃəti/ adj *informal* easily annoyed

crouch /kraʊtʃ/ verb [I] **1** to move your body close to the ground by bending your knees and leaning forward slightly: *She crouched down and spoke to the little boy.* —*picture* → POSTURE **2** to lean forward with your head and shoulders bent: *Five or six men were crouched over the desk.*

crou·ton /ˈkruˌtɑn/ noun [C] a small piece of bread that is served on soup and in salads

crow¹ /kroʊ/ noun [C] a large black bird that makes a loud sound

crow² /kroʊ/ verb [I] **1** if a ROOSTER (=male chicken) crows, it makes a loud high noise **2** to talk very proudly about something that you have done = BOAST

crow·bar /ˈkroʊˌbɑr/ noun [C] a metal bar with a curved end, used for forcing things open

crowd[1] /kraʊd/ noun ★★★
1 [C] a large number of people in the same place: *The boys disappeared into the crowd.* ♦ *Crowds of people began making their way to the station.*
2 [C] the audience at an event: *He takes off his shirt and the crowd goes wild.*
3 [singular] *informal* a group of friends: *I spent an evening out with the usual crowd.*

crowd[2] /kraʊd/ verb **1** [I] to move to a place at the same time as a lot of other people: *We crowded into the kitchen.* **2** [T] to fill a place: *Hundreds of people crowded the streets.*
PHRASAL VERB ˌ**crowd sth ˈout** to become more successful than another group so that they can no longer compete

crowd·ed /ˈkraʊdəd/ adj ★ containing a lot of people or things: *a crowded street/train/restaurant* ♦ *Was the pool crowded?* ♦ *a crowded schedule*

crown[1] /kraʊn/ noun [C]

1 on king's/queen's head	4 cover for tooth
2 position of winner	5 unit of money
3 top part of head/hat	

1 a circular decoration that a king or queen wears on their head **2** the position of being the winner of an important sports competition: *France lost their World Cup crown.* **3** the top part of your head or of a hat **4** a cover that is used to repair a tooth **5** a unit of money used in some European countries

crown[2] /kraʊn/ verb [T] **1** to make someone a king or queen: *James III was crowned at Kelso Abbey.* **2** to give someone a title for winning an important sports competition: *Schumacher went on to be crowned world champion.* **3** to put a cover on a tooth in order to repair it

crown·ing /ˈkraʊnɪŋ/ adj better or greater than anything else: *The garden is the hotel's crowning glory.*

cru·cial /ˈkruʃ(ə)l/ adj ★ extremely important: *Your involvement is **crucial to** the success of the project.* ♦ *The talks are considered **crucial for** ending the violence.* ♦ **it is crucial that** *It is crucial that all students develop these basic skills.* —**cru·cial·ly** adv

cru·ci·fix /ˈkrusɪˌfɪks/ noun [C] a model of Jesus Christ dying on a CROSS

cru·ci·fix·ion /ˌkrusɪˈfɪkʃ(ə)n/ noun [C/U] a method of killing someone by crucifying them

cru·ci·fy /ˈkrusɪˌfaɪ/ verb [T] **1** to kill someone by fastening them to a CROSS with nails or rope **2** *informal* to criticize someone in a very cruel way

crude[1] /krud/ adj **1** done or made using very simple methods = BASIC: *a crude home-made bomb* **2** referring to sex in a way that offends people: *crude language*

crude[2] /krud/ or ˌ**crude ˈoil** noun [U] oil that is still in its natural state

cru·el /ˈkruəl/ adj ★★
1 causing pain to people or animals: *I can't stand to see people being **cruel to** animals.*
2 making someone unhappy or upset: *Closing the school would be **a cruel blow** to this community.*
—**cru·el·ly** adv

cru·el·ty /ˈkruəlti/ noun [C/U] cruel behavior: *cruelty to children/animals* ♦ *the cruelties he witnessed during the war*

cruise[1] /kruz/ noun [C] a trip on a ship for pleasure, often visiting a series of places

cruise[2] /kruz/ verb [I] **1** to travel at a steady speed in a car or airplane **2** to sail in a ship for pleasure **3** to achieve success easily in a race, game, or competition: *The Rams cruised to victory this afternoon.*

ˌ**cruise ˈmissile** noun [C] a missile that is controlled by a computer and can travel very long distances

cruis·er /ˈkruzər/ noun [C] **1** a fast military ship **2** a large boat with a motor that is used for sailing in for pleasure **3** *American informal* a police car

crumb /krʌm/ noun [C] **1** a very small piece that falls off a dry food such as bread or cake **2** a very small amount of something

crum·ble /ˈkrʌmb(ə)l/ verb **1** [I/T] to break into very small pieces, or to make something do this: *The soft earth crumbled under his feet.* **2** [I] to stop existing or being effective: *My determination crumbled as soon as I saw her.*

crum·ple /ˈkrʌmp(ə)l/ verb **1** [I/T] to crush something so that it forms messy folds, or to be crushed in this way: *I quickly crumpled up the letter and put it in my pocket.* **2** [I] to fall to the ground suddenly, with your body, legs, and arms bent, because you are injured, sick, or upset
PHRASAL VERB ˌ**crumple (sth) ˈup** *same as* **crumple** 1

crunch[1] /krʌntʃ/ verb **1** [I/T] to bite hard food, causing it to make a loud noise **2** [I] to make a noise like something being crushed

crunch[2] /krʌntʃ/ noun **1** [singular] the noise that something makes when you crunch it **2** [C] *informal* a situation that is very difficult because you do not have enough of something, especially time or money: *a credit/budget crunch*

crunch·y /ˈkrʌntʃi/ adj crunchy foods make a loud noise when you bite them

cru·sade /kruˈseɪd/ noun [C] an effort over a long time to achieve something that you strongly believe is right = CAMPAIGN
—**cru·sad·er** /kruˈseɪdər/ noun [C]

crush[1] /krʌʃ/ verb [T] **1** to press something so hard that you damage it or break it into small pieces —*picture* → C2 **2** to injure or kill someone by pressing on them very hard **3** to completely defeat an opponent

crush[2] /krʌʃ/ noun **1** [C] *informal* a strong feeling of love for someone **2** [singular] a crowd of people in an area that is too small for them

crush·ing /ˈkrʌʃɪŋ/ adj **1** complete and achieved very easily: *a crushing defeat/victory* **2** very severe: *It's a crushing blow for the president's foreign policy.*

crust /krʌst/ noun [C/U] **1** the hard brown edges of a piece of bread, or the outer part of a PIE **2** a hard layer on the surface of something

crust·y /ˈkrʌsti/ adj covered with a hard CRUST

crutch /krʌtʃ/ noun **1** [C] a stick that fits under your arm and that helps you to walk when your leg or foot is injured **2** [singular] *showing disapproval* something that you depend on for support or help

crux /krʌks/ noun **the crux (of sth)** the most important aspect of something

C

cry[1] /kraɪ/ (past tense and past participle **cried** /kraɪd/) verb [I/T] ★★★ **1** to have tears coming from your eyes because you are sad or hurt: *I'm sorry – please don't cry.* ♦ *She was crying for her mother.* ♦ *Don't waste time crying over him.* **2** to shout something: *"That's not what I meant," Polly cried.* ♦ *Ted could hear a woman crying for help.*

PHRASAL VERBS ˌ**cry ˈout** to make a loud noise because you are in pain or because you are afraid or shocked: *The girl cried out in alarm.*

ˌ**cry (sth) ˈout** *same as* cry[1] 2: *"Be careful!" Miss Lee cried out.*

ˌ**cry ˈout for sth** to need something a lot in a way that is obvious: *This room is crying out for some new furniture.*

cry[2] /kraɪ/ noun [C] **1** a loud expression of emotion: *a cry of pain* **2** something that someone shouts: *There was a cry of "Fire!"* **3** the noise that an animal or bird makes

PHRASE **be a far cry from** *informal* to be very different from someone or something

crypt /krɪpt/ noun [C] a room where dead people are buried, usually under a church

cryp•tic /ˈkrɪptɪk/ adj expressing something in a mysterious or indirect way

crys•tal /ˈkrɪst(ə)l/ noun **1** [U] very good quality glass **2** [C] a regular shape with many sides that is formed when a substance becomes solid: *ice/salt/sugar crystals* **3** [C/U] a clear rock that looks like glass

ˌ**crystal ˈball** noun [C] a glass ball that some people believe can show the future

ˌ**crystal ˈclear** adj **1** completely transparent and very bright **2** extremely obvious or easy to understand

crys•tal•lize /ˈkrɪst(ə)ˌlaɪz/ verb [I/T] **1** to change into CRYSTALS, or to make something change into CRYSTALS **2** to become definite or easily understood, or to make something definite or easily understood

C-sec•tion /ˈsi ˌsekʃ(ə)n/ noun [C/U] a CESAREAN

CT abbrev Connecticut

cub /kʌb/ noun [C] a young bear, lion, or other wild animal

cube[1] /kjub/ noun [C] **1** an object like a box with six square sides that are all the same size *—picture* → C8 **2 the cube of sth** *technical* the result of multiplying a number by itself twice: *The cube of 2 is 8.*

cube[2] /kjub/ verb [T] **1** *technical* to multiply a number by itself twice **2** to cut something into cubes = DICE

cu•bic /ˈkjubɪk/ adj cubic units are used for measuring VOLUME (=the amount of space in an object)

cu•bi•cle /ˈkjubɪk(ə)l/ noun [C] a small enclosed area in a room

ˈ**Cub** ˌ**Scouts, the** noun *American* the division of the BOY SCOUTS for the youngest boys

cuck•oo /ˈkʊˌku/ noun [C] a bird that leaves its eggs in other birds' NESTS and makes a call that sounds like its name

cu•cum•ber /ˈkjuˌkʌmbər/ noun [C/U] a long, dark green vegetable that is usually eaten raw in salads *—picture* → C11

cud•dle[1] /ˈkʌd(ə)l/ verb [I/T] to put your arms around someone and hold them close to show that you like or love them

PHRASAL VERB ˌ**cuddle ˈup** to sit or lie with your body against someone else's because you want to feel warm or loved

cud•dle[2] /ˈkʌd(ə)l/ noun [C] an act of cuddling someone

cud•dly /ˈkʌdli/ adj soft and pleasant to cuddle

cue /kju/ noun [C] **1** an event, action, or statement that shows someone what they should do: *Greg's arrival seemed to be the cue for everyone to get up and start dancing.* **2** something that an actor does or says as a signal to another actor to do or say something **3** a long thin stick that you use for hitting the ball in games such as POOL

PHRASES **(right) on cue** *often humorous* at exactly the right moment, or exactly when you expect

take your cue from sb to behave in the same way as someone else

cuff[1] /kʌf/ noun [C] the part of a sleeve that fits around your wrist → OFF-THE-CUFF

cuff[2] /kʌf/ verb [T] *informal* to HANDCUFF someone

cui•sine /kwɪˈzin/ noun [C/U] a particular style of cooking: *Thai/Italian cuisine*

cul-de-sac /ˌkʌl də ˈsæk, ˌkʊl də ˈsæk/ noun [C] a short street that is closed at one end

cu•li•nar•y /ˈkjulɪˌneri, ˈkʌlɪˌneri/ adj relating to food and how to cook it

cull[1] /kʌl/ verb [T] **1** to collect something such as information from different places **2** to kill animals in order to stop the population from becoming too large

cull[2] /kʌl/ noun [C] an act of culling animals

cul•mi•nate /ˈkʌlmɪˌneɪt/ PHRASAL VERB ˈ**culminate in sth** to have or lead to an important result: *A series of financial disasters culminated in the collapse of the country's largest bank.*

cul•mi•na•tion /ˌkʌlmɪˈneɪʃ(ə)n/ noun [singular] the final result of a process or situation

cul•pa•ble /ˈkʌlpəb(ə)l/ adj *formal* responsible for doing something bad or illegal

cul•prit /ˈkʌlprɪt/ noun [C] **1** someone who is responsible for doing something bad or illegal **2** the cause of something bad that happens

cult[1] /kʌlt/ noun [C] **1** a religious group with beliefs that most people consider strange or dangerous **2** extreme admiration for someone or something: *the cult of beauty*

cult[2] /kʌlt/ adj very popular with a particular group of people: *a cult figure/hero/movie*

cul•ti•vate /ˈkʌltɪˌveɪt/ verb [T] **1** to prepare land for growing crops or plants **2** to grow crops or plants: *Rice is cultivated throughout the coastal regions.* **3** to develop something: *He's trying to cultivate a more caring image.* —**cul•ti•va•tion** /ˌkʌltɪˈveɪʃ(ə)n/ noun [U]

cul•ti•vat•ed /ˈkʌltɪˌveɪtəd/ adj **1** a cultivated person is well educated and knows how to behave politely **2** cultivated land is used for growing crops or plants **3** cultivated plants are developed from wild plants and grown on farms or in gardens

cul·tur·al /ˈkʌltʃərəl/ adj ★★
1 relating to the culture of a particular group, country, or society: *cultural diversity ♦ the cultural traditions of our society*
2 relating to music, literature, and other arts: *During the summer New York offers a variety of cultural events. ♦ The country enjoys a rich cultural life.*
—**cul·tur·al·ly** adv

cul·ture /ˈkʌltʃər/ noun ★★★
1 [U] activities involving music, literature, and other arts: *If you're looking for culture, then Paris is the place for you. ♦ Mexico's literary culture*
2 [C/U] *science* a group of bacteria or cells that have been grown in a scientific experiment, or the process by which they are grown
3 [C/U] a set of ideas, beliefs, and ways of behaving: *societies that share the same language and culture ♦ The two firms have very different corporate cultures. ♦ Some organizations encourage **a culture of** secrecy.*
4 [C] a society that has its own set of ideas, beliefs, and ways of behaving: *people from different cultures ♦ ancient cultures*

cul·tured /ˈkʌltʃərd/ adj well educated and polite = REFINED

cum·ber·some /ˈkʌmbərsəm/ adj
1 complicated, slow, and difficult to use
2 large, heavy, and difficult to move or carry

cu·mu·la·tive /ˈkjumjəˌleɪtɪv, ˈkjumjələtɪv/ adj developing or increasing gradually as a result of more and more additions: *We studied the cumulative effect of long periods of stress on the body.*

cun·ning¹ /ˈkʌnɪŋ/ adj good at tricking or cheating people —**cun·ning·ly** adv

cun·ning² /ˈkʌnɪŋ/ noun [U] the use of clever methods for tricking or cheating people

cup¹ /kʌp/ noun [C] ★★★
1 a small round container for a drink, usually with a handle: *She filled my cup with hot tea.*
2 the drink contained in a cup: *I've already had two cups. ♦ Would you like **a cup of** coffee?*
3 the amount that a cup contains, used in the U.S. as a unit for measuring quantities of food when you are cooking: *Mix one **cup of** sugar with three cups of flour.*
4 a large round metal container with two handles given as a prize to the winner of a competition, or the competition for which this prize is given: *the winners of the World Cup*

cups

cup² /kʌp/ verb [T] to hold something in your hands, with your hands in a curved shape

cup·board /ˈkʌbərd/ noun [C] a piece of furniture that is used for storing things, with shelves inside and one or two doors at the front

cup·cake /ˈkʌpˌkeɪk/ noun [C] a small round cake

cup·ful /ˈkʌpˌfʊl/ noun [C] the amount of something that a cup contains

cur·a·ble /ˈkjʊrəb(ə)l/ adj possible to cure ≠ INCURABLE

cu·ra·tor /kjəˈreɪtər/ noun [C] someone whose job is to take care of the objects in a museum

curb¹ /kɜrb/ noun [C] **1** *American* the edge of a SIDEWALK (=path built beside a road) that is closest to the road **2** a rule or control that stops or limits something

curb² /kɜrb/ verb [T] to control or limit something that is harmful or may cause problems: *efforts to curb inflation*

curd /kɜrd/ noun [C/U] the solid substance that forms in milk when it becomes sour

cur·dle /ˈkɜrd(ə)l/ verb [I/T] if milk or another liquid curdles, or if something makes it curdle, lumps begin to form in it

cure¹ /kjʊr/ noun [C] ★
1 a medicine or treatment that makes a sick person healthy: *Doctors say there are several possible cures. ♦ There's no **cure for** the disease.*
2 a solution to a problem: *It's the only possible **cure for** high unemployment.*

cure² /kjʊr/ verb [T] **1** to stop someone from being affected by an illness: *Only an operation will cure her. ♦ The disease is easy to prevent but almost impossible to cure.* **2** to solve a problem **3** to preserve meat, fish, or other foods by drying them, or by using smoke or salt

cur·few /ˈkɜrˌfju/ noun [C] a period of time during which people must not go outside according to an order from the government

cu·ri·os·i·ty /ˌkjʊriˈɑsəti/ noun **1** [U] a strong feeling of wanting to find out about something **2** [C] something that is unusual and interesting

cu·ri·ous /ˈkjʊriəs/ adj ★
1 wanting to find out about something: *People were **curious to know** why the accident happened. ♦ Children are **curious about** animals and how they live.*
2 unusual and interesting: *He felt a curious mixture of happiness and fear. ♦ **It is curious that** you've never mentioned this before.*
—**cu·ri·ous·ly** /ˈkjʊriəsli/ adv

curl¹ /kɜrl/ verb **1** [I/T] to form a curved or round shape, or to give something this shape: *As she talked, she curled a strand of hair on one finger.* **2** [I] to move in a curving or twisting way: *Smoke curled from tall chimneys.* **3** [I] to curve up or down at the edges: *The pages had begun to yellow and curl.*
PHRASAL VERB ˌ**curl ˈup** to sit or lie in a comfortable position, with your legs bent and close to your body

curl² /kɜrl/ noun [C] **1** a section of hair that forms a curved shape **2** something long and thin that has a curved shape: *a curl of smoke*

C

curl•er /ˈkɜrlər/ noun [C] a plastic or metal tube that you wrap your hair around in order to curl it=ROLLER

curl•y /ˈkɜrli/ adj forming curves: *curly hair*

cur•rant /ˈkʌrənt/ noun [C] a small round fruit that may be red, black, or white

cur•ren•cy /ˈkʌrənsi/ noun ★★
1 [C/U] the money that is used in a particular country: *Russian currency*
2 [U] the state of being accepted or used by many people: *The idea of withdrawing from the war has **gained wide currency**.*

cur•rent¹ /ˈkʌrənt/ adj ★★★
1 happening or existing now: *Production is likely to remain at current levels.* ♦ *There are several reasons for the current political situation.*
2 believed or used by many people now: *current thinking on prison reform* ♦ *current methods of funding research*
3 correct or legal now: *Is this your current address?* ♦ *a current license*

cur•rent² /ˈkʌrənt/ noun **1** [C] a strong movement of water or air in one direction **2** [C/U] a flow of electricity

ˌcurrent afˈfairs noun [plural] political, social, and economic events that are happening now

cur•rent•ly /ˈkʌrənt(ə)li/ adv ★★★ at the present time: *Davis is currently appearing in a Broadway play.* ♦ *the largest memory chips currently available*

cur•ric•u•lum /kəˈrɪkjələm/ noun [C] ★★ the subjects that students study at a particular school or college: *the science curriculum* ♦ *curriculum planning/development*

cur•ry /ˈkʌri/ noun [C/U] an Indian food consisting of meat, fish, or vegetables cooked in a sauce with a hot flavor

curse¹ /kɜrs/ verb **1** [I] to use offensive or impolite language: *She looked at her watch, cursed, and ran for a taxi.* **2** [T] to say or think offensive or impolite words about someone or something: *She cursed herself for being such a fool.* **3** [T] to use magic powers to make bad things happen to someone

curse² /kɜrs/ noun [C] **1** an offensive or impolite word or phrase **2** the words that are used for causing bad luck **3** an unpleasant situation or influence

cur•sor /ˈkɜrsər/ noun [singular] a small flashing line on a computer screen that you move to mark the point where you are going to type or do something

cur•so•ry /ˈkɜrsəri/ adj *formal* quick and not thorough=SUPERFICIAL: *a cursory examination/search*

curt /kɜrt/ adj using few words in a way that shows that you are impatient or angry =BRUSQUE —**curt•ly** adv

cur•tail /kərˈteɪl/ verb [T] *formal* to reduce or limit something

cur•tain /ˈkɜrt(ə)n/ noun ★★★
1 [C] a long piece of cloth that hangs down to cover a window: *She **closed the curtains**.* ♦ ***Open the curtains** and let some light in.*
2 [C] a large piece of cloth that hangs in front of the stage in a theater, or that divides one part of a room from another: *The audience cheered wildly as the curtain rose.*
3 [singular/U] a large amount of a substance that is too thick to see through: *A dark curtain of cloud hung over the valley.*

curt•sy or **curt•sey** /ˈkɜrtsi/ noun [C] a formal greeting in which a woman bends her knees with one leg behind the other —**curt•sy** verb [I]

curve¹ /kɜrv/ noun [C] a shape or line with a gradual smooth bend

curve² /kɜrv/ verb [I/T] to form a curve, or to make something form a curve

curved /kɜrvd/ adj forming a curve

cush•ion¹ /ˈkʊʃ(ə)n/ noun [C] **1** a cloth bag filled with something soft, used for making a seat more comfortable **2** something that gives protection against the effects of something bad

cush•ion² /ˈkʊʃ(ə)n/ verb [T] to protect a person or thing from the harmful effects of something

cuss /kʌs/ verb [I/T] *informal* to swear

cus•tard /ˈkʌstərd/ noun [C/U] a soft firm sweet food made from milk, eggs, and sugar

cus•to•di•al sen•tence /kʌˌstoʊdiəl ˈsent(ə)ns/ noun [C] *legal* a punishment that involves sending someone to prison

cus•to•di•an /kʌˈstoʊdiən/ noun [C] **1** *American* someone whose job is to clean a building and to fix things that are broken **2** someone who is responsible for something valuable

cus•to•dy /ˈkʌstədi/ noun [U] **1** the protection or care of someone or something, especially given by a court: *The father was given custody of the children.* **2** a situation in which someone is kept in prison: *One of the men is still in custody.*

cus•tom /ˈkʌstəm/ noun [C/U] ★★ something that people do that is traditional or usual: *local customs and traditions* → HABIT → CUSTOMS

cus•tom•ar•y /ˈkʌstəˌmeri/ adj usual —**cus•tom•ar•i•ly** /kʌstəˈmerəli/ adv

ˌcustom-ˈbuilt adj designed and built for one particular person

cus•tom•er /ˈkʌstəmər/ noun [C] ★★★
1 a person or company that buys goods or services: *Supermarkets use a variety of tactics to attract customers.* ♦ *customer services/relations/support* ♦ *Discounts are available for our **regular customers**.*
2 *informal* a particular type of person: *a cool customer* ♦ *a tricky/awkward/tough customer*

cus•tom•ize /ˈkʌstəˌmaɪz/ verb [T] to change the way that something looks or works so that it is exactly what you want or need

ˌcustom-ˈmade adj designed and made for one particular person

cus•toms /ˈkʌstəmz/ noun [plural] **1** the place at a port, airport, or border where officials check that people are not bringing anything into a country illegally **2** a government department that collects taxes on goods that people bring into a country

cut¹ /kʌt/ (past tense and past participle **cut**) verb [T] ★★★

1 use knife/sharp tool	5 stop sth working
2 injure part of body	+ PHRASES
3 reduce sth	+ PHRASAL VERBS
4 remove parts of sth	

1 to use a knife or other sharp tool to divide something into pieces, or to remove a piece of something: *I need a sharp knife to cut the bread with.* ♦ *The telephone wires had been cut.* ♦ *I'm going to **have my hair cut** tomorrow.* ♦ **cut sth in half/two** *The apples had been cut in half.* ♦ **cut sth into pieces/quarters/three etc.** *Cut the cake into small pieces.* ♦ **cut sb sth** *Will you cut me a slice of pizza?* ♦ **cut sth in/through sth** *Firefighters had to cut a hole in the car roof to get him out.*
2 to injure a part of your body with something sharp that cuts the skin: *Be careful not to cut your finger.* ♦ *He cut himself shaving.*
3 to reduce an amount or level: *Supermarkets are drastically cutting prices.* ♦ *We have cut our spending by 33%.* ♦ *Manufacturing companies have already cut thousands of jobs.*
4 to remove parts of something such as a piece of writing or a computer document: ***Cut and paste** the file* (=cut and move a computer file) *into your "documents" folder.* ♦ **cut sth from sth** *They have cut some sex scenes from the movie.* ♦ **cut sth by sth** *You need to cut your speech by about ten minutes.*
5 to stop the supply of something or stop something working: *The injury had cut the oxygen to her brain.*

PHRASES **cut corners** to do something quickly and carelessly because you want to save time or money
cut-and-dried already clearly decided or settled: *It's a pretty cut-and-dried case.*
cut sb short to interrupt someone who is talking
cut sth short to make something last for less time than it was planned to last for: *I'm sorry we had to cut our visit short.*

PHRASAL VERBS **ˌcut aˈcross sth 1** to go across an area of land instead of going around it: *We cut across the field to save time.* **2** to affect two or more different groups: *These problems cut across class boundaries.*
ˌcut (sth) ˈback to reduce something, or do less of something: *plans to cut back investment in education* ♦ *If you **cut back on** fat and sugar, you'll lose weight.*
ˌcut (sth) ˈdown to reduce something or do less of something: *These improvements will cut traffic noise down.* ♦ *I'm trying to **cut down on** salt.*
ˌcut sth ˈdown to cut through a tree and make it fall to the ground
ˌcut sb ˈoff if you are cut off when you are talking on the telephone, something makes the telephone line stop working
ˌcut sth ˈoff 1 *same as* **cut**[1] 5: *They cut off the electricity last week.* **2** to make a place impossible to enter, leave, or communicate with: *The floods completely cut off the town.* ♦ **cut sth off from sth** *Our house was cut off from the rest of the village.* **3** to remove something by cutting it: *Cut the tops off the carrots.* ♦ *Why did you cut off all your hair?*
ˌcut ˈout if an engine or machine cuts out, it suddenly stops working
ˌcut sth ˈout 1 to remove something from a larger piece by cutting: **cut sth out of sth** *I cut this article out of a magazine for you.* **2** to stop eating something or doing something because it is bad for your health: *I'm trying to cut out chocolate completely.* **3 cut it/that out** *spoken* used for telling someone to stop doing something that you do not like **4 not be cut out for sth/to do sth** to lack the right qualities or character for doing something: *Bill was never cut out to be a parent.* → WORK[2]
ˌcut ˈthrough sth to go through an area instead of going around it: *He decided to cut through the woods.*
ˌcut sth ˈup to cut something into several pieces: *You have to cut food up for young children.*

cut[2] /kʌt/ noun [C] ★★★

1 injury from sth sharp	**5** part removed from sth
2 mark/hole	**6** sb's part of money
3 reduction in sth	+ PHRASE
4 piece of meat	

1 an injury on your skin where something sharp has cut it: *My son's face was covered with cuts and bruises.*
2 a mark or hole in a surface where something sharp has cut it: *Make a series of small cuts in the meat.*
3 a reduction in something: *job/tax/pay/defense cuts* ♦ ***a cut in** education spending*
4 a piece of meat: *a lean cut of beef* → COLD CUTS
5 a part that has been removed from something such as a speech or a piece of writing
6 *informal* someone's part of a total amount of money: *The agent will take a 10% cut.*

PHRASE **be a cut above** to be much better than someone or something else

cut·back /ˈkʌtˌbæk/ noun [C] a reduction in something such as the amount of money that is available to spend: *Many hospitals face cutbacks in services.*

cute /kjut/ adj **1** attractive: *a cute little house* **2** *informal* sexually attractive: *There are a couple of really cute guys at work.*

cut·ler·y /ˈkʌtləri/ noun [U] the knives, forks, and spoons that you use for eating food =SILVERWARE

cut·let /ˈkʌtlət/ noun [C] a flat piece of meat with a bone in it

cut·off /ˈkʌtˌɔf/ noun **1** [C] a level or limit at which something stops: *the cutoff date by which all applications must be received* **2 cutoffs** [plural] short pants that you make by cutting part of the legs off old pants

ˈcut-ˌrate adj *American* cheaper than the normal price

cut·ter /ˈkʌtər/ noun [C] a tool that is used for cutting something

cut·throat /ˈkʌtˌθroʊt/ adj a cutthroat activity or situation is one in which people behave in an unfair or immoral way in order to get an advantage

cut·ting /ˈkʌtɪŋ/ adj a cutting remark is cruel and intended to upset someone

ˌcutting ˈedge noun [singular] **1** the most modern and advanced point in the development of something: *These models are at the cutting edge of computer design.* **2** a feature that gives someone or something an advantage

ˌcutting-ˈedge adj extremely modern and advanced: *cutting-edge technology*

CV /ˌsi ˈvi/ noun [C] *British* a RÉSUMÉ

cy·a·nide /ˈsaɪəˌnaɪd/ noun [U] a very poisonous chemical

cy·ber·ca·fé /ˈsaɪbərkæˌfeɪ/ noun [C] a café with computers for using the Internet

cy·ber·space /ˈsaɪbərˌspeɪs/ noun [U] the imaginary place that e-mails pass through when they are going from one computer to another

cy·cle[1] /ˈsaɪk(ə)l/ noun [C] ★★ a series of events that happen again and again in the same order or at the same times: ***the cycle** of hate and violence in the world*

cy·cle[2] /ˈsaɪk(ə)l/ verb [I] to go somewhere on a bicycle

cy·cli·cal /ˈsɪklɪk(ə)l/ adj cyclical events happen again and again in the same order or at the same times

cy·clist /ˈsaɪklɪst/ noun [C] someone who rides a bicycle

cy·clone /ˈsaɪˌkloʊn/ noun [C] a severe storm in which the wind spins in a circle

cyg·net /ˈsɪgnət/ noun [C] a young SWAN

cyl·in·der /ˈsɪlɪndər/ noun [C] **1** an object shaped like a wide tube *—picture* → C8 **2** a metal container for gas or liquid **3** the tube in an engine that a PISTON moves up and down in

cy·lin·dri·cal /sɪˈlɪndrɪk(ə)l/ adj shaped like a cylinder

cym·bal /ˈsɪmb(ə)l/ noun [C] a musical instrument that is a thin circular piece of metal. You hit it with a stick or hit two of them together. *—picture* → PERCUSSION

cyn·ic /ˈsɪnɪk/ noun [C] someone who believes that people care only about themselves and are not sincere or honest

cyn·i·cal /ˈsɪnɪk(ə)l/ adj **1** someone who is cynical believes that people care only about themselves and are not sincere or honest **2** willing to harm other people in order to get an advantage: *a cynical attempt to damage the president's reputation* —**cyn·i·cal·ly** /ˈsɪnɪkli/ adv

cyn·i·cism /ˈsɪnɪˌsɪzəm/ noun [U] **1** the belief that people care only about themselves and are not sincere or honest **2** the attitude of someone who is willing to harm other people in order to get an advantage

cyst /sɪst/ noun [C] a lump containing liquid that grows under your skin or inside your body

czar /zɑr/ noun [C] **1** a senior official who is chosen by the government to make decisions about a particular subject: *the drugs czar* **2** a man who ruled Russia before 1917

cza·rina /zɑˈrinə/ noun [C] a woman who ruled Russia before 1917

Dd

d or **D** /di/ noun [C/U] **1** the fourth letter of the English alphabet **2 D** a grade that a teacher gives to a student's work to show that it is below average

-'d short form a way of writing "had" or "would." This is not often used in formal writing: *He realized she'd asked him something.* ♦ *I'd like a glass of milk, please.*

D.A. /ˌdi ˈeɪ/ abbrev district attorney

dab[1] /dæb/ noun [C] a small amount of a substance that is put on a surface

dab[2] /dæb/ verb [I/T] to touch a surface gently several times with something such as a cloth, for example in order to dry it: *Marge dabbed at her eyes with a handkerchief.*

dab·ble /ˈdæb(ə)l/ verb [I] to be involved in an activity for a short time in a way that is not very serious: *When he was younger he dabbled in astrology.*

dachs·hund /ˈdæksənd/ noun [C] a small dog with very short legs and a long body

dad /dæd/ noun [C] *informal* ★★ your father: *His dad works in my office.* ♦ *Can I borrow some money, Dad?*

dad·dy /ˈdædi/ noun [C] *informal* your father. This word is usually used by and to young children.

daf·fo·dil /ˈdæfədɪl/ noun [C] a tall yellow flower that grows in the spring *—picture* → C9

dag·ger /dægər/ noun [C] a weapon like a very small sword

dai·ly[1] /ˈdeɪli/ adj ★★
1 done or happening every day: *The information is updated **on a daily basis**.*
2 a daily newspaper is published every day
3 a daily amount is the amount for one day: *Workers stood waiting to receive their daily wages.*

dai·ly[2] /ˈdeɪli/ adv every day: *Fresh bread is delivered daily.*

dai·ly[3] /ˈdeɪli/ noun [C] a newspaper that is published every day

ˌdaily ˈlife noun [C/U] all the things that happen or that you do regularly

dain·ty /ˈdeɪnti/ adj small and attractive in a delicate way —**dain·ti·ly** adv

dair·y[1] /ˈderi/ noun [C] **1** a company that sells milk and makes foods such as butter and cheese **2** a building on a farm where milk is kept and where foods such as butter and cheese are made

dair·y[2] /ˈderi/ adj dairy products include milk and foods such as butter and cheese

dai·sy /ˈdeɪzi/ noun [C] a small white flower with a yellow center *—picture* → C9

Dal·ma·tian /dælˈmeɪʃ(ə)n/ noun [C] a large dog with smooth white hair and black spots

dam[1] /dæm/ noun [C] a wall built across a river to create a lake or to help to produce electricity

dam² /dæm/ verb [T] to stop a river or stream from flowing by building a dam across it

dam·age¹ /ˈdæmɪdʒ/ noun ★★★
1 [U] physical harm: *a new drug to treat nerve damage ♦ Luckily, no serious **damage** had been done. ♦ The house **suffered** only superficial **damage** in the fire. ♦ **Damage to** the building could take six months to repair.*
2 [U] negative effects on someone or something: *The **damage to** the bank's image is extremely serious.*
3 damages [plural] money that a court orders you to pay someone because you have harmed them or their property

dam·age² /ˈdæmɪdʒ/ verb [T] ★★★
1 to harm something physically: *Many buildings had been damaged in the blast. ♦ The house had been **severely damaged** by fire.*
2 to have a negative effect on someone or something: *His political reputation has been **seriously damaged** by the scandal.*

dam·ag·ing /ˈdæmɪdʒɪŋ/ adj causing physical harm, or having a bad or negative effect: *The chemicals have a damaging effect on the environment.*

damn¹ /dæm/ interjection *impolite* used when you are annoyed about something: *Damn! I've broken one of my nails.*

damn² /dæm/ or **damned** /dæmd/ adj, adv *impolite* used for emphasizing what you are saying: *I can't open the damn window. ♦ She works damn hard.*

damn³ /dæm/ verb [T] to criticize someone or something extremely severely
PHRASE **damn it/you/him etc.** *impolite* used when you are annoyed about something

damn⁴ /dæm/ noun **not give a damn (about)** *impolite* to not care at all about someone or something

damn·ing /ˈdæmɪŋ/ adj showing that something is wrong or bad: *a damning report into the way the case was handled*

damp¹ /dæmp/ adj ★ something that is damp is slightly wet, often in an unpleasant way or when it should be dry: *The wood won't burn if it's damp.* —**damp·ness** noun [U]

damp² /dæmp/ noun [U] slightly wet areas in the walls of a building

damp·en /ˈdæmpən/ verb [T] **1** to make something slightly wet **2** to make something such as a feeling or hope less strong: *Not even defeat could dampen the enthusiasm of his supporters.*

damp·er /ˈdæmpər/ noun **put a damper on sth** *informal* **1** to make something less successful: *The rise in unemployment put a damper on the economy.* **2** to make people feel less enthusiastic or hopeful about something

dance¹ /dæns/ verb [I/T] ★★★ to move your body in movements that follow the sound of music: *I was too shy to ask you to dance. ♦ They **danced to** the music of a Latin band. ♦ Who were you **dancing with**?* —**danc·er** noun [C], **danc·ing** noun [U]

dance² /dæns/ noun ★★★
1 [C] a social event with music for people to dance to: *a high school dance*
2 [C] a pattern of movements that you make with your feet and your body, following the sound of music: *They **did a** traditional Mexican **dance**.*
3 [C] a piece of music that is played for people to dance to: *dance tunes*
4 [U] the activity of dancing in order to entertain people: *She teaches drama and dance. ♦ a dance teacher/school/class*

ˈdance ˌmusic noun [U] a type of music with a strong beat for dancing to in clubs

dan·de·li·on /ˈdænd(ə)lˌaɪən/ noun [C] a wild plant with a yellow flower —*picture* → C9

dan·druff /ˈdændrəf/ noun [U] small white pieces of dry skin in your hair

dan·ger /ˈdeɪndʒər/ noun ★★★
1 [U] a situation in which serious harm, death, or damage is possible: *The sign said "Danger! Keep Out!" ♦ There is **danger from** exposure to radiation. ♦ His actions **put** the child's life **in danger**.*
2 [C/U] a situation in which something unpleasant might happen: **+(that)** *There is a danger that the money will simply be wasted.* ♦ **in danger of (doing) sth** *The peace talks are now in danger of collapse.*
3 [C] a person or thing that might cause serious harm or damage: *a campaign to warn children of **the dangers of** electricity ♦ The animal is **a danger to** the public.*

dan·ger·ous /ˈdeɪndʒərəs/ adj ★★★ likely to cause serious harm, or to have a bad effect: *a dangerous dog ♦ a dangerous stretch of road ♦ an exciting but **highly dangerous** sport ♦ We don't know whether these chemicals are **dangerous to** humans.* ♦ **it is dangerous (for sb) to do sth** *It's dangerous to walk around here at night.* —**dan·ger·ous·ly** adv: *Fuel levels were dangerously low.*

dan·gle /ˈdæŋg(ə)l/ verb [I/T] if you dangle something, or if it dangles, it hangs or swings without anything stopping it: *A single light bulb dangled from the ceiling.*

dank /dæŋk/ adj a dank place is unpleasant because it is cold and slightly wet

dap·pled /ˈdæp(ə)ld/ adj with areas of lighter and darker color or light and shadow

dare¹ /der/ verb ★★
1 [I] to not be afraid to do something, even though it may be dangerous or may cause trouble: *I drove as fast as I dared.* ♦ **dare to do sth** *Sakharov was one of the few people who dared to protest.* ♦ **dare do sth** *Nobody dared argue with him.*
2 [T] to try to persuade someone to prove that they are not afraid to do something =CHALLENGE: *Go on, pick it up, I dare you!* ♦ **dare sb to do sth** *The older boys dared Jimmy to go up on the roof.*
PHRASES **don't you dare** *spoken* used for telling someone not to do something, when you are warning them that you will be very angry if they do it: *Don't you dare come near me!*
how dare you *spoken* used for telling someone that you are shocked and angry about something that they have done or said

dare² /der/ noun [C] an attempt to persuade someone to do something dangerous in order to prove that they are brave =CHALLENGE

dare·dev·il /ˈderˌdev(ə)l/ noun [C] someone who does dangerous things without worrying about the risk —**dare•dev•il** adj

dar•ing¹ /ˈderɪŋ/ adj **1** involving brave behavior **2** new and different in a way that might offend or upset some people: *a daring and highly original movie* —**dar•ing•ly** adv

dar•ing² /ˈderɪŋ/ noun [U] the brave attitude of someone who does new or dangerous things

D

dark¹ /dɑrk/ adj ★★★
1 with very little or no light: *a dark and stormy night* ♦ *When Maggie woke up, it was still dark.* ♦ *It was very dark in the bedroom.* ♦ *When they left, it was already starting to* ***get dark*** (=become dark at the end of a day).
2 close to black in color: *He was dressed in a dark suit.* ♦ *She glanced up at the dark clouds above the cliffs.* ♦ *a dark blue shirt*
3 involving unpleasant or frightening things: *the darkest days of the war*

dark² /dɑrk/ noun [singular] ★★ **the dark** a situation or place in which there is very little or no light: *Tim is afraid of the dark.* ♦ *Why are you sitting here* ***in the dark****?*
PHRASES **after dark** after it has become night: *Do not go out on your own after dark.*
before dark before it becomes night: *We were hoping to get home before dark.*
in the dark (about sth) not knowing much about something because other people have not given you information: *We are still completely in the dark about how the money was lost.*

dark•en /ˈdɑrkən/ verb [I/T] to become darker, or to make something darker: *The sky darkened and heavy rain began to fall.*

ˌdark ˈhorse noun [singular] **1** someone with a secret ability or achievement that surprises you when you discover it **2** someone who wins a race or competition unexpectedly

dark•ly /ˈdɑrkli/ adv in an angry and threatening way

dark•ness /ˈdɑrknəs/ noun [U] the lack of light: *The front rooms were all in darkness.* ♦ *The search had to be abandoned when darkness fell* (=it got dark).

dar•ling¹ /ˈdɑrlɪŋ/ noun [C] **1** *spoken* used for talking to someone you love: *Are you sleepy, darling?* **2** someone who is very kind: *She's such a darling, isn't she?* **3** someone who is liked or admired very much by a particular group of people: *He quickly became the darling of the middle classes.*

dar•ling² /ˈdɑrlɪŋ/ adj loved very much by someone: *my darling wife*

darn¹ /dɑrn/ interjection *informal* used when you are annoyed about something

darn² /dɑrn/ or **darned** /dɑrnd/ adj, adv *informal* used for emphasizing what you are saying when you are annoyed about something: *I can't see a darn thing with these glasses!*

darn³ /dɑrn/ verb [I/T] to repair a piece of clothing by sewing stitches across the hole

dart¹ /dɑrt/ noun **1** [C] a small pointed object that you throw or fire from a gun **2** [singular] a sudden short movement

dart² /dɑrt/ verb [I] to make a sudden quick movement somewhere: *A child darted out in front of our car.*

darts /dɑrts/ noun [U] a game in which you throw darts at a round board

Dar•win•i•an /dɑrˈwɪniən/ adj relating to Darwinism

Dar•win•ism /ˈdɑrwɪˌnɪzəm/ noun [U] a theory of EVOLUTION

dash¹ /dæʃ/ verb **1** [I] to go somewhere in a hurry: *I dashed out into the street, still in my pajamas.* **2** [I/T] to hit something violently, or to throw something violently against a surface: *Huge waves dashed against the side of the boat.*
PHRASE **dash sb's hopes** to make it impossible for someone to do what they had hoped to do: *Saturday's defeat has dashed their hopes of success in the league this year.*

dash² /dæʃ/ noun

1 small amount of sth	4 where car controls are
2 act of hurrying	5 short very fast race
3 symbol in writing	

1 [C] a small amount of something: *a dash of soy sauce* **2** [singular] an act of going somewhere quickly: *She made a dash for the door.* **3** [C] the symbol – used in writing to separate different parts of a sentence **4** [C] *informal* the DASHBOARD of a car **5** [C] *American* a short race in which people run as fast as they can = SPRINT

dash•board /ˈdæʃˌbɔrd/ noun [C] the part inside a car where the SPEEDOMETER and other instruments are —*picture* → C6

DAT /dæt/ noun [C] digital audio tape: a type of TAPE that is used for recording sound or information

da•ta /ˈdætə, ˈdeɪtə/ noun [U] ★★★
1 information in a form that a computer can use: *data storage/processing*
2 information that is used for making calculations or decisions: *The document contained data from tests of biological weapons.*

da•ta•base /ˈdeɪtəˌbeɪs/ noun [C] *computing* a large amount of information that is stored in a computer in an organized way

da•ta pro•cess•ing /ˌdeɪtə ˈprɑsesɪŋ/ noun [U] *computing* the operations that are performed by a computer in order to store, organize, or find information

date¹ /deɪt/ noun [C] ★★★
1 a particular day, month, or year, or its name or number: *What was* ***the date of*** *the last meeting we had?* ♦ *"What's* ***today's date****?" "The 25th."* ♦ *Should we* ***set a date*** *for the next meeting* (=decide when it will happen)*?* ♦ *The exact details of the plan will be worked out* ***at a later date*** (=at some time in the future).
2 an arrangement to meet someone who you are having a romantic relationship with: *I* ***have a date*** *with one of the guys from my class tonight.*
3 a brown fruit that grows on PALM trees
PHRASES **date of birth** the day, month, and year when you were born
make a date (with sb) to arrange to meet someone on a particular day
to date *formal* until now: *There have been no reports of car theft to date.*
→ OUT-OF-DATE, UP-TO-DATE

date² /deɪt/ verb ★★

1 [I/T] *American* to have a sexual or romantic relationship with someone: *They've been dating for over six months now.* ♦ *At college he dated a medical student.*
2 [T] to write the date on something: *The letter was dated February 23.*
3 [T] to discover exactly how old something is or when it was made: *The paintings have not been accurately dated yet.*
4 [I] to seem to be no longer modern or fashionable: *This style has hardly dated at all.*
PHRASAL VERB **ˈdate from sth** or **ˌdate ˈback to sth** to have been made at a particular time in the past: *Some of the objects date from the middle of the 7th century.*

date·book /ˈdeɪtbʊk/ noun [C] *American* an APPOINTMENT BOOK

dat·ed /ˈdeɪtəd/ adj no longer modern or fashionable

ˈdate ˌrape noun [C/U] a crime in which one person RAPES another (=forces them to have sex) while on a DATE with them —**ˈdate-ˌrape** verb [T]

daub /dɔb/ verb [T] to spread a wet substance such as paint on a surface in a careless way

daugh·ter /ˈdɔtər/ noun [C] ★★★ your female child —*picture* → FAMILY TREE

ˈdaughter-in-ˌlaw noun [C] the wife of your son —*picture* → FAMILY TREE

daunt·ing /ˈdɔntɪŋ/ adj something that is daunting makes you worried because you think that it will be very difficult or dangerous to do

daw·dle /ˈdɔd(ə)l/ verb [I] to go somewhere or do something so slowly that people become annoyed with you

dawn¹ /dɔn/ noun [C/U] the beginning of the day, when it begins to get light = DAYBREAK: *We had to get up at the crack of dawn* (=very early in the morning).
PHRASE **the dawn of sth** *literary* the time when something such as a new period in history begins

dawn² /dɔn/ verb [I] if a day or period dawns, it begins
PHRASAL VERB **ˈdawn on sb** if something dawns on you, you realize it for the first time: *It suddenly dawned on me that she hadn't told me the truth.*

day /deɪ/ noun ★★★

1 24 hours	4 time in past/future
2 when it is light	5 period of time
3 when you are available	+ PHRASES

1 [C] one of the 7 periods of time that a week is divided into. It is equal to 24 hours: *We're going away for five days.* ♦ *The animals are kept inside for 14 hours a day.* ♦ *The store is open **24 hours a day*** (=during the whole of the day and night).
2 [C/U] the period of time when it is light outside ≠ NIGHT: *There was not enough of the day left to finish the game.* ♦ *The restaurant is only open **during the day**.* ♦ ***By day*** (=during the day) *he is a banker, but by night he sings in a club.*
3 [C] the period of time when you are awake and doing things: *She came home exhausted after **a hard day** at the office* (=a difficult or unpleasant day). ♦ *What do you do at home **all day**?* ♦ *Next week, I have **a day off*** (=a day when you do not work).
4 [singular] a time in the past or future: *We look forward to the day when nuclear weapons will no longer exist.* ♦ ***The day may come** when our air becomes too polluted to breathe.*
5 days [plural] a period of time when something is happening or is successful: *I think **my days as** a basketball player are coming to an end.* ♦ *That was **back in the days of** the horse and buggy.* ♦ *She became famous **in the early days of** television.*
PHRASES **sb's day** the period of time when someone was young: *The place has changed completely since my day.*
day after day every day for a long time, often in a way that is boring or unpleasant
the day after tomorrow two days from now: *We're going on vacation the day after tomorrow.*
the day before yesterday two days ago: *I got back home the day before yesterday.*
day by day in small slow stages as each day passes: *She's getting stronger day by day.*
day in, day out used for emphasizing that something is boring because it is the same every day
from day one ever since the very beginning of something
from day to day 1 in a way that changes quickly or often: *He seems to change his opinion from day to day.* **2** without thinking about what is going to happen in the future: *They lived from day to day.*
have had your/its day to have stopped being successful or fashionable: *I think the show has had its day. Our viewers want something more fun.*
make sb's day to make someone feel very happy
one day 1 at some time in the future: *She hopes to own her own business one day.* **2** on a day in the past: *One day he just walked out and never came back.*
one of these days *spoken* at some time in the future: *One of these days I'm finally going to read that book.*
the other day *informal* recently: *I saw Kim the other day.*
some day at some time in the future: *I'll go back there some day.*
these days *spoken* used for talking about things that are happening or are true now: *Children grow up much more quickly these days.*

day·break /ˈdeɪˌbreɪk/ noun [U] the time when light first appears in the morning = DAWN

ˈday ˌcare noun [U] *American* care given to young children while their parents are at work

day·dream /ˈdeɪˌdrim/ verb [I] to spend time thinking about something pleasant when you should be doing something more serious —**day·dream** noun [C], **day·dream·er** noun [C]

day·light /ˈdeɪˌlaɪt/ noun [U] the light outside that you see during the day

ˌdaylight ˈrobbery noun [U] *British spoken* HIGHWAY ROBBERY

day·time /ˈdeɪˌtaɪm/ noun [U] the period of time during the day when it is light

ˌday-to-ˈday adj happening every day as part of your normal life

daze /deɪz/ noun **in a daze** unable to think clearly or to understand what is happening

dazed /deɪzd/ adj unable to think clearly or to understand what is happening

D

daz·zle /ˈdæz(ə)l/ verb [T] **1** if a bright light dazzles you, you cannot see for a short time **2** to impress someone a lot

daz·zling /ˈdæzlɪŋ/ adj **1** a dazzling light is so bright that it makes you unable to see for a short time **2** extremely impressive: *a dazzling display of flowers*

de·ac·ti·vate /diˈæktɪˌveɪt/ verb [T] to prevent something such as a bomb or an ALARM from being able to work

dead¹ /ded/ adj ★★★

1 not alive	5 having no feeling
2 not working	6 complete
3 not interesting	+ PHRASE
4 no longer important	

1 no longer alive: *The shootings left 14 people dead.* ♦ *I raked up the dead leaves.* ♦ *The police don't know whether she's* ***alive or dead****.* ♦ *Rescue workers are still pulling* ***dead bodies*** *out of the rubble.* ♦ *Several children are among* ***the dead*** (=people who have died).

2 a piece of equipment that is dead is not working: *The battery was completely dead.* ♦ *The phone suddenly* ***went dead****.*

3 boring because there is no activity or noise: *The street seems dead without all the children.*

4 no longer important or likely to be successful: *It seems that the peace process is now dead.*

5 if a part of your body is dead, you cannot feel it: *My legs had* ***gone completely dead****.*

6 complete: *dead silence* ♦ *The bullet hit the target* ***dead center*** (=exactly in the center). ♦ *The truck suddenly came to* ***a dead stop****.*

PHRASE **sb wouldn't be seen dead** *spoken* used for saying that someone would never do something because they hate it or because it is not fashionable: *I wouldn't be seen dead in a jacket like that!*

dead² /ded/ adv *informal* **1** completely: *Rachel stopped dead in her tracks* (=completely and suddenly stopped moving) *when she saw me with Andy.* ♦ *The editor is dead set on finishing the book by Christmas* (=determined to finish it). **2** directly: *I can see the service station dead ahead.*

dead³ /ded/ noun **in the dead of night/winter** *literary* in the middle of the night or in the middle of the winter, when everything is quiet

dead·beat /ˈdedˌbit/ noun [C] *informal* **1** *American* someone who tries to avoid paying money that they owe **2** someone who is lazy

dead·en /ˈded(ə)n/ verb [T] **1** to make a feeling less strong **2** to make a sound less loud

ˌdead ˈend noun [C] **1** a road that has no way out at one end **2** a situation in which no more progress is possible

ˌdead-end ˈjob noun [C] a job that provides you with no chance of getting a better job

ˌdead ˈheat noun [C] a situation in which two people, horses, cars, etc. are very near each to other in a race or competition so that either might win

dead·line /ˈdedˌlaɪn/ noun [C] a time or date by which you have to do something: *The deadline for applications was last Friday.* ♦ *If we can't meet the deadline* (=finish something in time), *they won't give us another contract.*

dead·lock /ˈdedˌlɑk/ noun [singular/U] a disagreement between people who are not willing to change their opinions or decisions: *Hopes of breaking the deadlock* (=ending it) *are fading.* —**dead·locked** /ˈdedˌlɑkt/ adj

dead·ly¹ /ˈdedli/ adj **1** capable of killing people: *This is a potentially deadly disease.* ♦ *a deadly weapon* **2** complete: *Tom hit the target with deadly accuracy.*

dead·ly² /ˈdedli/ adv extremely: *Politics is a deadly serious business.*

dead·pan /ˈdedˌpæn/ adj pretending to be serious when you are really joking: *deadpan humor*

ˌdead ˈwood noun [U] useless people or things

deaf /def/ adj ★★ not able to hear anything, or not able to hear very well. Some people think that this word is offensive and prefer to use the expression **hearing impaired**: *I'm a little* ***deaf*** *in one ear.*

PHRASE **deaf to sth** not willing to listen to something

—**deaf·ness** noun [U]

deaf·en /ˈdef(ə)n/ verb [T] **1** if a noise deafens you, you cannot hear anything else because it is so loud **2** to make someone unable to hear, either for a short time or for ever

deaf·en·ing /ˈdef(ə)nɪŋ/ adj so loud that you can hear nothing else

deal¹ /dil/ noun ★★★

1 [C] a formal agreement: ***a deal with a*** *Japanese TV company* ♦ ***I got a really good deal*** *on my new computer* (=I got it for a low price). ♦ *We think there was a* ***deal*** *between the CIA and the FBI.* ♦ *We've* ***cut a deal*** *with Germany* (=made an agreement with them) *on wine imports.* → DEALING

2 [singular] the way in which you are treated by other people: *Unions are demanding* ***a fair deal*** *for nurses.*

3 [singular] the act of giving cards to the people who are playing a game of cards: *Whose deal is it next?*

4 the deal [singular] *spoken* what is happening or going to happen: *So, what's the deal? Is she coming or not?*

PHRASES **a big deal** *spoken* something that is very important: *Water is a big deal in the Southwest.* ♦ ***It's no big deal*** (=it's not important) *if you can't pay me back right now.*

big deal *spoken* used for showing that you do not think that something is very good or impressive: *So she has a part in the school play? Big deal!*

a good/great deal of sth a large amount of something: *A great deal of research has been done already.*

deal[2] /diːl/ (past tense and past participle **dealt** /delt/) verb [I/T] ★★★
1 to give cards to the people who are playing a game of cards: *Each player is dealt three cards.*
2 to buy and sell illegal drugs: *Many drug addicts often deal as well.*
PHRASE **deal a blow to** to harm or shock someone or something
PHRASAL VERBS ˈ**deal in sth** to buy and sell something: *a small company that deals in rare books*
ˌ**deal (sth) ˈout** same as **deal**[2] 1: *He dealt all the cards out.*
ˈ**deal with sth 1** to take action to solve a problem: *The administration must now deal with the problem of high unemployment.* **2** to be about a subject: *Chapter 5 deals with employment law.*
ˈ**deal with sb** to buy goods or services from someone, or to sell them to someone: *We have dealt with the company for years.*

deal•er /ˈdiːlər/ noun [C] **1** a person or company that buys and sells a particular product **2** someone who sells illegal drugs **3** the person who gives cards to the people who are playing a game of cards

deal•er•ship /ˈdiːlərʃɪp/ noun [C] a business that sells the products of a particular company: *a Chevrolet dealership*

deal•ing /ˈdiːlɪŋ/ noun **1** [U] the business of buying and selling: *property/drug dealing* **2 dealings** [plural] the business relationship that you have with another person or organization

dealt the past tense and past participle of **deal**[2]

dean /diːn/ noun [C] **1** a senior official at a college or university **2** a senior Christian priest

dear[1] /dɪr/ adj ★★★
1 **Dear** used in front of someone's name or title at the beginning of a letter to them: *Dear Diana, I hope you're feeling better now.* ♦ *Dear Sir or Madam*
2 loved, or liked very much: *a dear friend*

dear[2] /dɪr/ noun [C] *spoken old-fashioned* used for talking to someone that you love: *Did you have a nice day, dear?*

dear[3] /dɪr/ interjection used when you are upset, disappointed, annoyed, or worried about something: *Oh dear, I spilled the coffee.*

dear•est /ˈdɪrəst/ adj **1** used about something that you want or hope for more than anything else: *her dearest wish* **2 Dearest** *old-fashioned* used in front of the name of someone you love at the beginning of a letter to them

dear•ly /ˈdɪrli/ adv very much: *I love him dearly in spite of all his faults.*

dearth /dɜrθ/ noun [singular] *formal* a situation in which there is not enough of something =LACK: *a dearth of talented students*

death /deθ/ noun ★★★
1 [C/U] the end of someone's life: *Sandra was very close to death.* ♦ *the rising number of deaths on the roads every year* ♦ *These people will **starve to death** unless they receive help soon.* ♦ *The **cause of death** has not yet been discovered.*
2 [singular] the end of something: ***the death** of apartheid in South Africa*
PHRASE **to death** *informal* very, or very much: *bored/scared/worried to death*
→ MATTER[1]

death•bed /ˈdeθˌbed/ noun [singular] a bed in which someone has died or is about to die
PHRASE **on your deathbed** *often humorous* going to die very soon

ˈ**death cerˌtificate** noun [C] an official document signed by a doctor that provides details of how and when someone died

death•ly /ˈdeθli/ adj making you think of death or a dead person: *a deathly silence/hush* —**death•ly** adv: *deathly pale/white*

ˈ**death ˌpenalty, the** noun [singular] legal punishment by death, usually for a serious crime such as murder

ˈ**death ˌrate** noun [C] the number of deaths in a particular area in one year

death row /ˈdeθ ˌroʊ/ noun [U] *American* the part of a prison for criminals who are going to be EXECUTED (=legally killed)

ˈ**death ˌsentence** noun [C] a judge's official statement that orders someone to be punished by death

ˈ**death ˌsquad** noun [C] a group of people who illegally kill their political opponents

ˈ**death ˌtoll** noun [C] the number of people who are killed on a particular occasion

ˈ**death ˌtrap** noun [C] *informal* a building or vehicle that is in such bad condition that it could be dangerous to people

ˈ**death ˌwish** noun [C] a feeling that you want to die

de•ba•cle /deɪˈbɑk(ə)l/ noun [C] something that fails completely in an embarrassing way

de•bar /dɪˈbɑr/ verb [T] to officially prevent someone from doing something

de•base /dɪˈbeɪs/ verb [T] *formal* to reduce the value, quality, or status of something

de•bat•a•ble /dɪˈbeɪtəb(ə)l/ adj something that is debatable is not certain because it is possible for people to have different opinions about it

de•bate[1] /dɪˈbeɪt/ noun ★★★
1 [C/U] a discussion in which people or groups state different opinions about a subject: *The proposals provoked **a fierce debate**.* ♦ *There has been intense **debate over** the treatment of illegal immigrants.*
2 [C] a formal discussion that ends with a decision made by voting

de•bate[2] /dɪˈbeɪt/ verb [I/T] **1** to discuss a subject formally before making a decision, usually by voting: *Congress is still debating the bill.* **2** to consider an action or situation carefully before you decide what to do: *I debated whether or not to call her parents.*

de•bauch•er•y /dɪˈbɔtʃəri/ noun [U] immoral behavior that involves a lot of sex, alcohol, or illegal drugs —**de•bauched** /dɪˈbɔtʃt/ adj

de•bil•i•tat•ing /dɪˈbɪlɪˌteɪtɪŋ/ adj *formal* making someone physically or mentally weak: *a debilitating illness/condition*

deb•it[1] /ˈdebɪt/ noun [C] an amount of money that is taken from a bank account ≠ CREDIT

deb•it[2] /ˈdebɪt/ verb [T] if a bank debits your account, it takes money out of it ≠ CREDIT

ˈ**debit ˌcard** noun [C] a plastic card that you use to pay for things. It automatically takes the money you pay out of your bank account. → CREDIT CARD

de•brief /dɪ'brif/ verb [T] to get information from someone who has just finished an important job for the military or the government

de•brief•ing /dɪ'brifɪŋ/ noun [C/U] a meeting where someone gives a report about an important job that they have just finished for the military or the government

D

de•bris /də'bri/ noun [U] the broken pieces that are left when something large has been destroyed

debt /det/ noun ★★★

1 [C] an amount of money that you owe: *By this time we had debts of over $15,000.* ♦ *Many people experience difficulty in **paying off their debts**.*

2 [U] a situation in which you owe money to other people: *I don't like **being in debt**.* ♦ *She was terrified of **getting into debt**.*

3 [singular] an obligation to be grateful to someone because they have done something for you: *I'm forever **in your debt**.*

debt•or /'detər/ noun [C] a person, organization, or country that owes money ≠ CREDITOR

'debt re,lief noun [U] the practice of allowing poor countries not to pay back what they owe to rich countries

de•bug /di'bʌg/ verb [T] *computing* to look for and remove mistakes from a computer program

de•bunk /di'bʌŋk/ verb [T] to prove that something such as an idea or belief is false and silly

de•but¹ /deɪ'bju, 'deɪ,bju/ noun [C] the first time a performer or sports player appears in public: *Easton made his debut in 2002.*

de•but² /deɪ'bju, 'deɪ,bju/ adj a debut CD, performance, novel, etc. is the first that a performer, sports player, writer, etc. makes

de•but³ /'deɪ,bju/ verb [I] to perform, or to be performed, in public for the first time

dec•ade /'dekeɪd/ noun [C] ★★★ a period of ten years: *Prices have risen sharply in the last decade.*

dec•a•dent /'dekədənt/ adj involving a lot of immoral pleasure —**dec•a•dence** /'dekədəns/ noun [U]

de•caf /'dikæf/ noun [C/U] *informal* decaffeinated coffee, or a cup of this drink

de•caf•fein•at•ed /di'kæfɪ,neɪtəd/ adj decaffeinated coffee or tea has had the CAFFEINE (=a chemical substance that keeps you awake) removed

de•cal /'di,kæl, dɪ'kæl/ noun [C] *American* a piece of paper with a picture on it that you can put onto a surface

de•cap•i•tate /dɪ'kæpɪ,teɪt/ verb [T] *formal* to cut off someone's head

de•cath•lon /dɪ'kæθ,lɑn/ noun [C] a sports event that consists of ten different sports

de•cay /dɪ'keɪ/ verb **1** [I/T] to be gradually destroyed as a result of a natural process, or to destroy something in this way: *As dead trees decay, they feed the soil.* ♦ *Too much sugar will decay your teeth.* **2** [I] if a building or an area decays, its condition gradually gets worse because it has not been taken care of —**de•cay** noun [U]: *tooth decay* ♦ *urban decay*

de•ceased /dɪ'sist/ adj *formal* **1** dead **2 the deceased** a dead person or dead people

de•ceit /dɪ'sit/ noun [C/U] dishonest behavior that is intended to trick someone

de•ceit•ful /dɪ'sitfəl/ adj behaving dishonestly in order to trick people → DECEPTIVE 2

de•ceive /dɪ'siv/ verb [T] **1** to trick someone by behaving in a dishonest way: *He was deceived into giving them all his money.* **2** to make someone believe something that is not true

De•cem•ber /dɪ'sembər/ noun [C/U] ★★★ the twelfth month of the year, between November and January: *House prices fell slightly in December.* ♦ *I received a letter from them on December 15th.*

de•cen•cy /'dis(ə)nsi/ noun [U] behavior that is moral, good, or reasonable: *You didn't even have the decency to say you're sorry!*

de•cent /'dis(ə)nt/ adj **1** good, or good enough: *Are there any decent restaurants around here?* **2** if you behave in a decent way toward other people, you are honest, fair, and nice **3** *informal old-fashioned* wearing enough clothes to not be embarrassed to let other people see you —**de•cent•ly** adv

de•cen•tral•ize /di'sentrə,laɪz/ verb [T] to take power from a central government or organization and give it to several smaller and more local ones —**de•cen•tral•i•za•tion** /,disentrəlɪ'zeɪʃ(ə)n/ noun [U]

de•cep•tion /dɪ'sepʃ(ə)n/ noun [C/U] the act of tricking someone by telling them something that is not true

de•cep•tive /dɪ'septɪv/ adj **1** if something is deceptive, it seems very different from the way it really is: *a deceptive calmness in his voice* **2** if someone is being deceptive, they trick other people by telling them something that is not true: *deceptive advertising* —**de•cep•tive•ly** adv

de•ci•bel /'desɪb(ə)l, 'desɪ,bel/ noun [C] a unit for measuring how loud a sound is

de•cide /dɪ'saɪd/ verb ★★★

1 [I/T] to make a choice about what you are going to do: **decide to do sth** *He decided to stay and see what would happen.* ♦ **+(that)** *I decided that it would be best to tell George everything.* ♦ **+what/whether/how/when etc.** *I can't decide where to go.* ♦ *She needs to decide whether or not she wants to keep the car.*

2 [T] to produce a particular result: *Today's game will decide the championship.*

PHRASAL VERBS **de,cide a'gainst sb/sth** to not choose someone or something: *We decided against the house because it was too small.*

de'cide ,on sb/sth to choose someone or something from a number of possible choices: *We finally decided on the red curtains.*

Word family: decide

Words in the same family as ***decide***

- **decided** *adj*
- **decision** *n*
- **decisive** *adj*
- **undecided** *adj*
- **indecision** *n*
- **indecisive** *adj*

de•cid•ed /dɪ'saɪdəd/ adj impossible to doubt

and easy to see: *a decided improvement on last year* —**de•cid•ed•ly** adv

de•cid•u•ous /dɪˈsɪdʒuəs/ adj deciduous trees lose all their leaves each fall

dec•i•mal¹ /ˈdesɪm(ə)l/ noun [C] a number that consists of numbers on either side of a DECIMAL POINT. 0.5, 25.75, and 873.4 are all decimals

dec•i•mal² /ˈdesɪm(ə)l/ adj based on the number ten

ˌdecimal ˈpoint noun [C] the symbol . in a DECIMAL

dec•i•mate /ˈdesɪˌmeɪt/ verb [T] to damage or destroy a large number of people or things

de•ci•pher /dɪˈsaɪfər/ verb [T] to discover the meaning of something that is difficult to read or understand

de•ci•sion /dɪˈsɪʒ(ə)n/ noun ★★★
1 [C] a choice that you make after you have thought carefully about something: *The committee will **make a decision** by the end of the week.* ♦ *Have you **come to a decision** yet?* ♦ **a decision to do sth** *Mrs. Osman has announced her decision to retire.*
2 [U] the ability to make choices quickly, confidently, and effectively: *He acted with decision.*

deˈcision-ˌmaking noun [U] the process of deciding what to do about something

de•ci•sive /dɪˈsaɪsɪv/ adj **1** if something is decisive, it makes the final result of a situation certain: *The U.S. has played a decisive role in these negotiations.* **2** a decisive person can decide what to do quickly and confidently ≠ INDECISIVE **3** a decisive victory or defeat is one in which the winner does much better than the LOSER —**de•ci•sive•ly** adv

deck¹ /dek/ noun [C] **1** the outside top part of a ship that you can walk on **2** one of the levels on a ship, train, or STADIUM **3** *American* a wooden floor that is built onto the outside of the back of a house **4** a set of cards used for playing card games —*picture* → C16

deck² /dek/ verb [T] **1** *informal* to hit someone so hard that they fall to the ground **2** *same as* **deck sb/sth out**
PHRASAL VERB **ˌdeck sb/sth ˈout** to decorate a person or object with something, usually for a special occasion

dec•la•ra•tion /ˌdekləˈreɪʃ(ə)n/ noun [C/U] an important or official statement about something: *a declaration of war* ♦ *his declaration of love*

de•clare /dɪˈkler/ verb [T] ★★
1 to announce officially that something is true or is happening: *I was in Germany when war was declared.* ♦ **+that** *Mrs. Armitage declared that she would fight to clear her name.* ♦ **declare sb/sth (to be) sth** *Sarah was declared the winner.*
2 to state officially the value of the things that you have earned or bought, so that you can pay the correct amount of tax: *All income from investments must also be declared.*

de•clas•si•fied /diˈklæsɪˌfaɪd/ adj declassified information is officially not secret anymore —**de•clas•si•fy** verb [T]

de•cline¹ /dɪˈklaɪn/ verb ★★
1 [I] to become less or worse: *The number of people buying their own homes has declined.* ♦ *Stock prices declined sharply last week.*
2 [I/T] to say politely that you will not accept something or do something: *They offered to fly him to Brussels, but he declined.* ♦ *We asked her to the reception, but she declined the invitation.* ♦ **decline to do sth** *The mayor declined to comment on the rumors.*

de•cline² /dɪˈklaɪn/ noun [C/U] ★★ a reduction in the amount or quality of something: *a sharp/steep/dramatic decline* ♦ *There has been **a steady decline in** public services over recent years.*

D

de•code /diˈkoʊd/ verb [T] to succeed in understanding the meaning of a message that is written in CODE = DECIPHER ≠ DECODE

de•col•o•ni•za•tion /diˌkɑlənɪˈzeɪʃ(ə)n/ noun [U] the process by which a COLONY becomes independent from the country that used to control it —**de•col•on•ize** verb [T]

de•com•mis•sion /ˌdikəˈmɪʃ(ə)n/ verb [T] to stop using something such as a weapon, ship, or nuclear power station

de•com•pose /ˌdikəmˈpoʊz/ verb [I] to be destroyed by a slow natural process

de•com•press /ˌdikəmˈpres/ verb [T] to reduce the pressure on something —**de•com•pres•sion** /ˌdikəmˈpreʃ(ə)n/ noun [U]

de•cor or **dé•cor** /ˈdeɪˌkɔr, deɪˈkɔr/ noun [C/U] the style of decoration and furniture in a building

dec•o•rate /ˈdekəˌreɪt/ verb [T] ★
1 to make something more attractive by putting nice things on it or in it: *The room had been **decorated with** balloons.*
2 to give someone a MEDAL because they have done something brave

dec•o•ra•tion /ˌdekəˈreɪʃ(ə)n/ noun **1** [C/U] something nice that you use to make something else look more attractive **2** [C] a MEDAL given to someone who has done something brave

dec•o•ra•tive /ˈdek(ə)rətɪv, ˈdekəˌreɪtɪv/ adj attractive rather than useful: *decorative objects*

de•co•rum /dɪˈkɔrəm/ noun [U] *formal* polite behavior

de•coy /ˈdikɔɪ, dɪˈkɔɪ/ noun [C] a person or thing that you use to trick someone into going somewhere or doing something

de•crease¹ /dɪˈkris/ verb **1** [I] to become less ≠ INCREASE: *The number of visitors has decreased significantly.* **2** [T] to reduce something

Other ways of saying decrease

- **be/go/come down** to become less in number, value, or price
- **drop/fall** to decrease in number or quality by a large amount
- **dwindle** to decrease slowly and steadily until there is almost nothing left
- **plummet/plunge** to decrease suddenly and very quickly
- **slump** to decrease to a very low level or value, when this is seen as a bad thing

de•crease² /ˈdikris/ noun [C/U] the process of becoming less, or the amount by which something is less ≠ INCREASE

de•cree /dɪˈkri/ noun [C] **1** a judgment that is

made by a court of law **2** an official decision or order that is made by a leader or government —**de•cree** verb [T]

de•crep•it /dɪˈkrepɪt/ adj old and not in good condition anymore

de•crim•i•nal•ize /diˈkrɪmɪn(ə)lˌaɪz/ verb [T] to change the law so that something that was illegal becomes legal —**de•crim•i•nal•i•za•tion** /ˌdikrɪmɪn(ə)lɪˈzeɪʃ(ə)n/ noun [U]

D

ded•i•cate /ˈdedɪˌkeɪt/

PHRASAL VERBS **ˈdedicate sth to sth** to spend your time and effort doing something =DEVOTE: **dedicate sth to doing sth** *This woman has dedicated her life to helping others.*

ˈdedicate sth to sb to say that a book or song that you have written was written for a person that you love or admire

ded•i•cat•ed /ˈdedɪˌkeɪtəd/ adj believing something is important and spending a lot of time and effort on it: *a dedicated teacher*

ded•i•ca•tion /ˌdedɪˈkeɪʃ(ə)n/ noun **1** [U] the belief that something is good or right that makes you spend a lot of time and effort doing or supporting it: *his dedication to the fight against AIDS* **2** [C] a statement that dedicates a song or book to someone

de•duce /dɪˈdus/ verb [T] *formal* to decide that something is true by considering the information that you have

de•duct /dɪˈdʌkt/ verb [T] to take an amount or number from a total

de•duct•i•ble[1] /dɪˈdʌktəb(ə)l/ adj if money is deductible, it can be taken away from the total amount of money on which you pay tax

de•duct•i•ble[2] /dɪˈdʌktəb(ə)l/ noun [C] *American* an amount of money that someone has to pay toward the cost of something when an insurance company is going to pay the rest

de•duc•tion /dɪˈdʌkʃ(ə)n/ noun [C/U] **1** an amount or number taken from a total, or the process of taking an amount or number away from a total **2** something that you know from the information you have, or the process of finding something out from the information you have

deed /did/ noun [C] **1** an official document that gives the details about who owns a building or piece of land **2** *literary* something that someone does: *a good deed*

deem /dim/ verb [T] *formal* to decide that someone or something has a particular quality

deep[1] /dip/ adj ★★★

1 a long way down	6 color: dark and strong
2 measuring a distance	7 sleep: hard to wake up
3 going a long way in	8 breathing a lot of air
4 feeling: strong	9 serious
5 sound: low	+ PHRASES

1 going a long way down from the top or surface of something ≠ SHALLOW: *The river is pretty deep here.*

2 used for talking about the distance from the surface to the bottom of something: *The pond needs to be about four feet deep.* ♦ ***How deep is the snow?***

3 going a long way in from the front, edge, or surface: *a deep cut on my arm* ♦ *We were **deep inside** the national park.*

4 a deep feeling is very strong: *I told him my deepest fears.*

5 a deep sound is low: *a deep voice*

6 a deep color is dark and strong: *a beautiful deep red*

7 a deep sleep is one that you do not wake up easily from

8 a deep breath or deep breathing brings a lot of air into and out of your body

9 involving very serious thoughts, ideas, or feelings

PHRASES **deep in thought/conversation** so involved in thinking or talking to someone that you do not notice anything else

thrown in at the deep end having to deal with something difficult without being prepared for it

deep[2] /dip/ adv ★★★

1 a long way down from the top or the surface, or a long way into something: *men who work deep under the ground* ♦ *They continued deep into the forest.*

2 if people or things are two deep, three deep, etc., there are two, three, etc. rows of them

PHRASE **deep down** used for saying that you know something is true, although you do not like to admit it: *Deep down, I knew that Caroline was right.*

deep•en /ˈdipən/ verb [I/T] to become, or to make something become, worse, stronger, deeper, etc.: *a deepening crisis* ♦ *Both sides are deepening their commitment to peace.*

ˌdeep-ˈfried adj cooked in a lot of hot oil

deep•ly /ˈdipli/ adv ★★

1 very, or very much: *Your mother is deeply concerned.*

2 a long way into something: *The needle had penetrated deeply into his skin.*

3 if you breathe or SIGH deeply, you breathe a lot of air into or out of your body

deep-root•ed /dipˈrutəd/ adj DEEP-SEATED

ˌdeep-ˈsea adj in the deep areas of the ocean

deep-seat•ed /ˌdip ˈsitəd/ adj a deep-seated feeling or belief is strong and difficult to change

ˌdeep-ˈset adj deep-set eyes seem to be a long way back into your face

ˌDeep ˈSouth, the the states of Alabama, Georgia, Louisiana, Mississippi, and South Carolina in the southern part of the U.S.

deer /dɪr/ noun [C] a large brown animal with long thin legs —*picture* → C12

de•face /dɪˈfeɪs/ verb [T] to deliberately damage something, usually by writing on it

def•a•ma•tion /ˌdefəˈmeɪʃ(ə)n/ noun [U] *legal* the offense of writing or saying something bad about someone that is not true —**de•fam•a•to•ry** /dɪˈfæməˌtori/ adj

de•fault[1] /dɪˈfɔlt/ noun [C] the way that something will automatically appear or be done on a computer if you do not change it

PHRASES **by default 1** if something happens by default, it happens only because you do not do something else **2** if you win something by default, you win because the other person does not play or does not finish the game

in default *formal* not having done something that you were officially told to do

de•fault² /dɪˈfɔlt/ verb [I] to fail to pay money that you owe: *They defaulted on the loan.*

de•feat¹ /dɪˈfit/ noun [C/U] ★★ failure to win a competition or to succeed in doing something ≠ VICTORY: *Wisconsin suffered a 23–7 defeat.*

de•feat² /dɪˈfit/ verb [T] ★★
1 to win against someone = BEAT: *The Yankees defeated the Red Sox 2–1.*
2 to prevent something from happening or being successful: *The proposal was defeated by 16 votes to 5.*

de•fect¹ /ˈdiˌfekt/ noun [C] a fault in someone or something

de•fect² /dɪˈfekt/ verb [I] to leave one country or political party and go to another one —**de•fec•tion** /dɪˈfekʃ(ə)n/ noun [C/U], **de•fec•tor** noun [C]

de•fec•tive /dɪˈfektɪv/ adj not made correctly, or not working correctly = FAULTY

de•fence /dɪˈfens/ the British spelling of defense

de•fend /dɪˈfend/ verb ★★
1 [T] to protect someone or something from attack: *Can the military **defend** the city **against** attack?*
2 [T] to say things to support someone or something: *We will defend their right to free speech.*
3 [I/T] to be the lawyer in a court case who tries to prove that someone is not guilty
4 [T] to attempt to win a competition that you won last time: *Baxter will defend his heavyweight championship.*

Word family: defend
*Words in the same family as **defend***
- **defense** *n*
- **defenseless** *adj*
- **defendant** *n*
- **defender** *adj*
- **defensive** *adv*
- **indefensible** *adj*

de•fen•dant /dɪˈfendənt/ noun [C] *legal* someone who has been accused of a crime and is on trial

de•fend•er /dɪˈfendər/ noun [C] **1** someone who works to prevent something from being lost or taken away **2** a player who tries to stop the other team from scoring in a game
→ PUBLIC DEFENDER

de•fense /dɪˈfens/ noun ★★★

1 protecting a place	4 attempt to win again
2 protection for sb/sth	5 in sports
3 proof sb/sth is right	6 in court case

1 [C/U] the weapons, equipment, and people that are used to protect a country or place: *Huge amounts of government money are spent on defense.*
2 [C/U] protection for someone or something that is being attacked: *new drugs that work by strengthening the body's own defenses*
3 [C/U] something that you say to support someone or something that is being criticized: *Several people **spoke in my defense**.* ♦ *The president responded with a strong **defense of** his foreign policy.*
4 [singular] an attempt by someone to win a competition that they won last time
5 /ˈdifens/ [U] the players in a team game who try to prevent the other team from scoring
6 the defense [singular] the people in a court case who try to prove that someone is not guilty
→ SELF-DEFENSE

de•fense•less /dɪˈfensləs/ adj weak and unable to protect yourself

de•fen•sive¹ /dɪˈfensɪv/ adj **1** becoming angry or offended when you think that someone is criticizing you: *Don't get so defensive!* **2** intended or used for protecting a place during an attack **3** a defensive player tries to stop the other team from scoring points —**de•fen•sive•ly** adv

de•fen•sive² /dɪˈfensɪv/ noun **on the defensive** trying to defend something from attacks or criticism

de•fer /dɪˈfɜr/ verb [T] to arrange for something to happen later than you had planned = POSTPONE

def•er•ence /ˈdef(ə)rəns/ noun [U] behavior that shows that you respect someone —**def•er•en•tial** /ˌdefəˈrenʃ(ə)l/ adj

de•fi•ance /dɪˈfaɪəns/ noun [U] refusal to obey a person or rule: *Goods were exported in defiance of the treaty.*

de•fi•ant /dɪˈfaɪənt/ adj refusing to obey a person or rule —**de•fi•ant•ly** adv

de•fi•cien•cy /dɪˈfɪʃ(ə)nsi/ noun [C/U] a lack of something, or a fault in someone or something

de•fi•cient /dɪˈfɪʃ(ə)nt/ adj lacking something, or not good enough: *a diet deficient in vitamin C* ♦ *a deficient education system*

def•i•cit /ˈdefəsɪt/ noun [C] the amount by which something is less than you need or should have: *the budget deficit*

de•fine /dɪˈfaɪn/ verb [T] ★★
1 to describe clearly and exactly what something is, or what something means: *No one has defined the goals of the project.* ♦ *How would you define the word "love?"*
2 to show clearly the shape or edges of something
—**de•fined** /dɪˈfaɪnd/ adj: *a sharply defined image*

def•i•nite /ˈdefənɪt/ adj ★★
1 clearly decided and specific: *We haven't arranged a definite date for our visit yet.*
2 certain: *This book will be a definite bestseller.*

ˌdefinite ˈarticle noun [C] *linguistics* the word "the" in English, or a similar type of word in another language

def•i•nite•ly /ˈdefənətli/ adv ★★
1 without any doubt: *I'm definitely going to Ben's party.*
2 used for emphasizing that you mean "yes": *"So we'll see you on Sunday at 7:00?" "Definitely!"*

def•i•ni•tion /ˌdefəˈnɪʃ(ə)n/ noun ★★
1 [C] a statement of what a word or expression means: *The **definition of** "family" has changed over the years.*
2 [U] the quality of being clear: *Some of the photographs lack definition.*
PHRASE **by definition** as a part of the basic nature of something: *Being a soldier, by definition, involves risks.*

de•fin•i•tive /dɪˈfɪnətɪv/ adj **1** better than all others **2** certain and unlikely to change —**de•fin•i•tive•ly** adv

de•flate /dɪˈfleɪt/ verb **1** [I/T] if a tire or

D

BALLOON deflates, or if you deflate it, air comes out of it ≠ INFLATE **2** [T] to make someone feel less confident or important

de·flat·ed /dɪˈfleɪtəd/ adj feeling less confident and happy

de·flect /dɪˈflekt/ verb **1** [T] to direct criticism, attention, or blame away from yourself and toward someone else **2** [I/T] if something deflects, or if it is deflected, it hits something and starts to move in a different direction —**de·flec·tion** /dɪˈflekʃ(ə)n/ noun [C/U]

de·for·es·ta·tion /diˌfɔrəˈsteɪʃ(ə)n/ noun [U] the process of removing the trees from an area of land

de·formed /dɪˈfɔrmd/ adj something that is deformed is not attractive because it has a different shape from what is usual or natural

de·for·mi·ty /dɪˈfɔrməti/ noun [C/U] a part of someone's body that is not the normal shape

de·frag·ment /diˈfrægˌment/ verb [T] *computing* to make a computer do an operation that brings together all free space and all similar files, in order to increase the speed at which it operates

de·fraud /dɪˈfrɔd/ verb [I/T] to get money from a person or organization in a dishonest way

de·frost /diˈfrɔst/ verb **1** [I/T] if frozen food defrosts, or if you defrost it, it becomes warmer until it is no longer frozen **2** [I/T] if a FREEZER defrosts, or if you defrost it, you switch it off so that the ice inside it MELTS **3** [T] *American* to remove ice from the windows of a car using warm air

deft /deft/ adj done quickly and with skill —**deft·ly** adv

de·funct /dɪˈfʌŋkt/ adj not existing or working anymore

de·fuse /diˈfjuz/ verb [T] **1** to make a situation more relaxed by making people less angry or worried **2** to stop a bomb from exploding by removing its FUSE

de·fy /dɪˈfaɪ/ verb [T] to refuse to obey someone or something = DISOBEY

PHRASE **defy belief/explanation etc.** to be almost impossible to believe, explain, etc.

de·gen·er·ate¹ /dɪˈdʒenəˌreɪt/ verb [I] to become worse

de·gen·er·ate² /dɪˈdʒen(ə)rət/ adj immoral

de·grade /dɪˈgreɪd/ verb **1** [T] to treat someone very badly so that they lose the respect of other people **2** [I] *science* if a substance degrades, it separates into the different substances that it consists of —**deg·ra·da·tion** /ˌdegrəˈdeɪʃ(ə)n/ noun [U]

de·grad·ing /dɪˈgreɪdɪŋ/ adj something that is degrading causes you to have less respect for yourself or for someone else

de·gree /dɪˈgri/ noun ★★★

1 [C/U] an amount of something such as a feeling or a quality: *The job requires a* ***high degree of skill.*** ♦ *What you say is* ***true to some degree*** (=partly true).

2 [C] a qualification that you get after completing a course at a college or university: *a biology degree* ♦ *a master's degree in English literature*

3 [C] a unit for measuring temperature, that is often shown as a number followed by the symbol °: *It is 82 degrees and sunny outside.*

4 [C] a unit for measuring angles, that is often shown as a number followed by the symbol °: *The two lines meet at a 90 degree angle.*

de·hy·drate /diˈhaɪˌdreɪt/ verb **1** [I] to lose so much water from your body that you feel weak or sick **2** [T] *science* to remove the water from something —**de·hy·dra·tion** /ˌdihaɪˈdreɪʃ(ə)n/ noun [U]

de·hy·drat·ed /diˈhaɪˌdreɪtəd/ adj **1** feeling weak or sick because you have lost a lot of water from your body **2** dehydrated food has been preserved by having all of its water removed

de·i·ty /ˈdiəti/ noun [C] a god

dé·jà vu /ˌdeɪʒɑ ˈvu/ noun [U] the feeling that you are having exactly the same experience as one that you have had before

de·ject·ed /dɪˈdʒektəd/ adj someone who is dejected has lost all of their hope or enthusiasm —**de·jec·tion** /dɪˈdʒekʃ(ə)n/ noun [U]

de·lay¹ /dɪˈleɪ/ verb ★

1 [I/T] to do something later than is planned or expected: *They delayed the decision for as long as possible.*

2 [T] to make someone or something late, or to slow them down: *His plane was delayed for five hours.*

de·lay² /dɪˈleɪ/ noun [C/U] ★★ a situation in which something happens later or more slowly than you expected: *After a long delay, the plane finally took off.* ♦ **delay in doing sth** *Who is responsible for the delay in reaching an agreement?*

del·e·gate¹ /ˈdeləˌgeɪt/ verb **1** [I/T] to give part of your work or responsibilities to someone else **2** [T] to choose someone to do a job for you or to represent you

del·e·gate² /ˈdeləgət/ noun [C] someone who is chosen to represent a group of other people at a meeting

del·e·ga·tion /ˌdeləˈgeɪʃ(ə)n/ noun **1** [C] a group of people who represent a country, government, or organization **2** [U] the process of giving some of your work or responsibilities to someone else

de·lete /dɪˈlit/ verb [T] to remove something that has been written, recorded, or stored in a computer: *I deleted the file by mistake.*

de·le·tion /dɪˈliʃ(ə)n/ noun [C/U] the process of deleting something, or something that has been deleted

del·i /ˈdeli/ noun [C] *informal* a DELICATESSEN

de·lib·er·ate¹ /dɪˈlɪb(ə)rət/ adj ★

1 intended, and not done by chance or by accident = INTENTIONAL ≠ ACCIDENTAL: *This was a deliberate attack on unarmed civilians.*

2 slow and careful: *deliberate steps*

de·lib·er·ate² /dɪˈlɪbəˌreɪt/ verb [I/T] to think about or discuss something very carefully

de·lib·er·ate·ly /dɪˈlɪb(ə)rətli/ adv ★

1 with a definite intention, and not by chance or by accident: *The police believe the fire was started deliberately.*

2 in a slow careful way: *He spoke deliberately.*

de·lib·er·a·tion /dɪˌlɪbəˈreɪʃ(ə)n/ noun **1** [C/U]

long and careful thought or discussion **2** [U] a slow and careful way of speaking or moving

del·i·ca·cy /ˈdelɪkəsi/ noun **1** [C] a rare or expensive type of food **2** [U] a sensitive and careful way of doing something **3** [U] the quality of being delicate

del·i·cate /ˈdelɪkət/ adj **1** easily damaged, broken, or hurt: *Delicate skin must be protected from the sun.* ♦ *delicate fabrics* **2** needing care and skill: *The negotiations are at a very delicate stage.* **3** small and attractive: *delicate pink flowers* **4** a delicate taste, smell, or color is pleasant and not too strong —**del·i·cate·ly** adv

del·i·ca·tes·sen /ˌdelɪkəˈtes(ə)n/ noun [C] a store that sells food such as cooked meat and cheese

de·li·cious /dɪˈlɪʃəs/ adj ★ with a very pleasant taste or smell: *This sauce is delicious with fish or vegetables.* —**de·li·cious·ly** adv

de·light¹ /dɪˈlaɪt/ noun **1** [U] a feeling of great happiness: *The children slid down the hill, shrieking with delight.* **2** [C] something that gives you pleasure

de·light² /dɪˈlaɪt/ verb [T] to give someone a lot of enjoyment or pleasure

PHRASAL VERB **deˈlight ˌin doing sth** to get a lot of pleasure from something

de·light·ed /dɪˈlaɪtəd/ adj **1** very happy about something: *We're delighted with our new grandson.* ♦ *The company is delighted at the response to its advertisement.* **2** used for saying politely that you are pleased about something: *"Will you come?" "I'd be delighted."*

de·light·ful /dɪˈlaɪtfəl/ adj very nice —**de·light·ful·ly** adv

de·lin·quent¹ /dɪˈlɪŋkwənt/ adj **1** behaving in a criminal or immoral way **2** failing to pay money that you owe —**de·lin·quen·cy** noun [U]

de·lin·quent² /dɪˈlɪŋkwənt/ noun [C] a young person whose behavior is criminal or very bad

de·lir·i·ous /dɪˈlɪriəs/ adj **1** talking in a confused way because you are sick **2** extremely happy = ECSTATIC —**de·lir·i·ous·ly** adv

de·lir·i·um /dɪˈlɪriəm/ noun [U] a confused state caused by illness

de·liv·er /dɪˈlɪvər/ verb ★★★

1 take sth to a place	4 give a statement
2 do what you promised	5 help at a birth
3 give a formal talk	

1 [T] to take something such as goods or letters to a place and give them to someone: *I can deliver the letter this afternoon.* ♦ *You can have groceries* ***delivered to your door.***
2 [I/T] to do something that you have promised to do or are expected to do: *We're looking for a supplier who can deliver a reliable service.* ♦ *How will the governor* ***deliver on*** *his campaign promises?*
3 [T] *formal* to give a formal talk: *He delivered a speech lasting 40 minutes.*
4 [T] to officially give your decision or a message: *The jury has delivered its verdict.*
5 [T] to help a baby to be born: *Paramedics delivered the baby.*

de·liv·er·y /dɪˈlɪv(ə)ri/ noun ★★
1 [C/U] the process of bringing goods or letters to a place: *Please allow ten days for delivery.* ♦ *When do you* ***make deliveries?***
2 [U] the process of providing a service: *We need to improve* ***delivery of*** *health care.*
3 [C/U] the process of giving birth to a baby

del·ta /ˈdeltə/ noun [C] an area where a river divides into smaller rivers that flow into the ocean

de·lude /dɪˈlud/ verb [T] to make someone think something that is not true —**de·lud·ed** adj

del·uge¹ /ˈdeljudʒ/ noun [singular] **1** a lot of things all happening or arriving at the same time = FLOOD **2** a very heavy fall of rain = DOWNPOUR

del·uge² /ˈdeljudʒ/ verb **be deluged with sth** to have a lot of things to deal with

de·lu·sion /dɪˈluʒ(ə)n/ noun [C/U] a belief that is not true

de·luxe /dəˈlʌks/ adj better in quality and more expensive than other things of the same type = LUXURY: *the deluxe model/version*

delve /delv/ verb [I] **1** to try hard to find out information **2** to search for something in a bag or pocket

de·mand¹ /dɪˈmænd/ verb [T] ★★★
1 to say firmly that you want something: *The demonstrators demanded the release of all prisoners.* ♦ **demand to do sth** *She demanded to know what was happening.* ♦ **+(that)** *The panel demanded that the report be made public.*
2 to expect something, or to make something necessary: *I demand absolute loyalty from my staff.* ♦ *a situation that demands careful handling*

de·mand² /dɪˈmænd/ noun ★★★
1 [C] a firm statement that you want something: *They* ***made demands*** *that our government could never accept.* ♦ ***demands for*** *a pay increase*
2 demands [plural] the things or qualities that are needed in a particular situation: ***the demands of*** *his new job* ♦ *She has a lot of* ***demands on*** *her time.*
3 [U] the amount of a product or service that people want, or the fact that they want it: *18,400 new houses will be needed to cope with the demand.* ♦ ***Demand for*** *organic food is increasing.*

PHRASES **be in demand** to be wanted by a lot of people: *The software is in demand all over the world.*
by popular demand because a lot of people have asked for it
on demand whenever people want it

de·mand·ing /dɪˈmændɪŋ/ adj needing a lot of attention, time, or energy ≠ UNDEMANDING: *a demanding child/job*

de·mean·ing /dɪˈminɪŋ/ adj making people have less respect for someone = DEGRADING

de·mean·or /dɪˈminər/ noun [U] *formal* the way that you look and behave

de·ment·ed /dɪˈmentəd/ adj *informal* crazy

de·men·tia /dɪˈmenʃə/ noun [C/U] *medical* a

D

serious illness affecting your brain and memory

de•mise /dɪˈmaɪz/ noun [singular] *very formal* the time when something or someone stops existing

dem•o /ˈdemoʊ/ noun [C] *informal* something such as a piece of recorded music or software that is made to show what a product is like

D

de•moc•ra•cy /dɪˈmɑkrəsi/ noun ★★
1 [U] a system of government in which people choose their political representatives in elections
2 [C] a country that has democracy
3 [U] a way of running an organization in which everyone can share in making decisions

dem•o•crat /ˈdeməˌkræt/ noun [C] someone who supports democracy

Dem•o•crat /ˈdeməˌkræt/ noun [C] a member of the Democratic Party in the U.S.

dem•o•crat•ic /ˌdeməˈkrætɪk/ adj ★★
1 based on the principle that all people should share in making decisions ≠ UNDEMOCRATIC: *a democratic organization*
2 involving elections in which people vote for their political representatives: *the democratic system*
—**dem•o•crat•i•cal•ly** /ˌdeməˈkrætɪkli/ adv

Demoˈcratic ˌParty, the one of the two main political parties in the U.S.

dem•o•graph•ic /ˌdeməˈgræfɪk/ adj relating to populations

dem•o•graph•ics /ˌdeməˈgræfɪks/ noun [plural] the particular features of a population

de•mol•ish /dɪˈmɑlɪʃ/ verb [T] **1** to destroy a building **2** to completely defeat someone, or to destroy their hopes or their confidence

dem•o•li•tion /ˌdeməˈlɪʃ(ə)n/ noun [C/U] the deliberate destruction of a building

de•mon /ˈdimən/ noun [C] an evil spirit

de•mon•ic /dɪˈmɑnɪk/ adj like a demon

de•mon•stra•ble /dɪˈmɑnstrəb(ə)l, ˈdemənstrəb(ə)l/ adj *formal* clear or obvious —**de•mon•stra•bly** adv

dem•on•strate /ˈdemənˌstreɪt/ verb ★★
1 [T] to show someone how to do something or how something works: *We will demonstrate various techniques.* ♦ *Let me demonstrate how we achieve this effect.*
2 [T] to show that something is true or exists: *Her story demonstrates the importance of staying in shape.* ♦ **+that** *The study demonstrates that children are affected by advertising.*
3 [I] to protest about something in a public place: *the right to demonstrate peacefully* ♦ *Students were* ***demonstrating against*** *the war.*

dem•on•stra•tion /ˌdemənˈstreɪʃ(ə)n/ noun ★★
1 [C/U] an occasion when someone shows how something works or how to do something: *cooking demonstrations*
2 [C] an occasion when people protest about something in public: *Angry students held* ***demonstrations.*** ♦ ***demonstrations against*** *the new tax*
3 [C] an event or action that proves a fact: *This is* ***a demonstration of*** *the president's popularity.*

de•mon•stra•tive /dɪˈmɑnstrətɪv/ adj showing love in the way that you behave toward someone

dem•on•stra•tor /ˈdemənˌstreɪtər/ noun [C] **1** someone who takes part in a public protest **2** someone whose job is to show how something works or how to do something

de•mor•al•ized /dɪˈmɔrəˌlaɪzd/ adj feeling unhappy and without any confidence

de•mor•al•iz•ing /dɪˈmɔrəˌlaɪzɪŋ/ adj making you feel unhappy and without any confidence

de•mote /dɪˈmoʊt/ verb [T] to give someone or something lower status or a less important position —**de•mo•tion** /dɪˈmoʊʃ(ə)n/ noun [C/U]

de•mure /dɪˈmjʊr/ adj a demure woman is quiet, shy, and polite —**de•mure•ly** adv

den /den/ noun [C] **1** *American* a room in a house where someone can go to relax **2** a place where people take part in secret or illegal activities: *a gambling den* **3** a place where a wild animal such as a lion lives

de•ni•al /dɪˈnaɪəl/ noun **1** [C/U] a statement that something is not true: *the company's denial of the charges against it* **2** [U] *technical* the refusal to accept the unpleasant truth about something **3** [U] the refusal to let someone have or do something: *the denial of health care to poor patients*

den•i•grate /ˈdenɪˌgreɪt/ verb [T] to criticize something in a way that shows that you think it has no value at all

den•im /ˈdenɪm/ noun [U] thick cotton cloth that is usually blue and is used for making JEANS

de•nom•i•na•tion /dɪˌnɑmɪˈneɪʃ(ə)n/ noun [C] **1** a religious group within one of the main religions **2** the value of a particular coin or piece of paper money

de•nounce /dɪˈnaʊns/ verb [T] to criticize someone or something severely in public

dense /dens/ adj **1** consisting of a lot of things, people, trees, etc. that are all very close together: *a dense crowd/forest* **2** thick and difficult to see through: *dense smoke/cloud/fog* **3** *informal* someone who is dense is stupid **4** *science* a dense substance is very heavy in relation to its size —**dense•ly** adv

den•si•ty /ˈdensəti/ noun [U] **1** the number of people or things in a particular area **2** *science* the relationship between the weight and the size of an object

dent¹ /dent/ noun [C] a place where a surface has been pushed or knocked inward

dent² /dent/ verb [T] to make a dent in a surface

den•tal /ˈdent(ə)l/ adj relating to teeth: *dental hygiene*

ˈdental ˌfloss noun [U] a substance like very thin string that you use to clean between your teeth

den•tist /ˈdentɪst/ noun [C] someone whose job is to examine and treat people's teeth

den•tist•ry /ˈdentɪstri/ noun [U] **1** the job of examining and treating people's teeth **2** the medical study of the teeth and mouth

den•tures /ˈdentʃərz/ noun [plural] artificial teeth

de·nun·ci·a·tion /dɪˌnʌnsiˈeɪʃ(ə)n/ noun [C/U] strong public criticism of someone or something

de·ny /dɪˈnaɪ/ verb [T] ★★★
1 to say that something is not true: **+(that)** *A spokesman denied that the company had acted irresponsibly.* ♦ **deny doing sth** *He still denies murdering his wife.*
2 to refuse to admit that you have a particular feeling, illness, or problem: *I had been denying this anger for years.*
3 to not allow someone to do or have something: *Doctors were accused of denying treatment to older patients.*

de·o·dor·ant /diˈoʊdərənt/ noun [C/U] a substance that you put on your skin to prevent your body from having an unpleasant smell

de·part /dɪˈpɑrt/ verb [I] *formal* to leave a place and start a trip
PHRASAL VERB **deˈpart from sth** to not do something in the usual or traditional way

de·part·ment /dɪˈpɑrtmənt/ noun [C] ★★★
1 a section in a government, organization, or business that deals with a particular type of work: *the Department of Health* ♦ *the sales department*
2 an area in a large store that sells a particular type of goods: *the menswear department*

deˈpartment ˌstore noun [C] a large store that is divided into separate sections, with each section selling a different type of thing

de·par·ture /dɪˈpɑrtʃər/ noun [C/U] **1** an act of leaving a place, job, or organization **2** an airplane, train, ship, etc. that leaves to start a trip **3** a way of doing something that is different from the usual or traditional way

de·pend /dɪˈpend/ verb ★★★
PHRASE **it/that depends** *spoken* used for saying that you cannot give a definite answer until certain details of the situation are described: *"How much will I have to pay for a car?" "It **depends what** type of car you want."*
PHRASAL VERBS **deˈpend ˌon sth** if one thing depends on another, it is changed or affected by the other thing: *Their future depends on how well they do in school.*
deˈpend ˌon sb/sth to need someone or something in order to continue to exist or to be successful = RELY ON SB/STH: *The project's success depends on the support of everyone concerned.*
deˈpend ˌon sb if you can depend on someone to do something, you can trust them to do it: *I knew I could depend on you.*

de·pend·a·ble /dɪˈpendəb(ə)l/ adj always behaving or working in the way that you expect = RELIABLE: *a dependable friend/worker/machine*

de·pend·ence /dɪˈpendəns/ or **de·pend·en·cy** /dɪˈpendənsi/ noun [U] **1** a situation in which you need someone or something in order to live or succeed = RELIANCE: *the industry's dependence on coal* **2** the fact that someone is ADDICTED to a drug or to alcohol

de·pend·ent¹ /dɪˈpendənt/ adj ★★
1 if you are dependent on someone or something, you need them in order to live or succeed: *a married couple with dependent children* ♦ *They hate being **dependent on** their parents.*
2 if one thing is dependent on another, it is affected by the other thing and changes if the other thing changes: *Your pay is **dependent on** your work experience.*

de·pend·ent² /dɪˈpendənt/ noun [C] a child or other relative that you are legally responsible for supporting

de·pict /dɪˈpɪkt/ verb [T] to describe someone or something using words or pictures

de·plete /dɪˈplit/ verb [T] to reduce the amount of something or the number of things —**de·ple·tion** /dɪˈpliʃ(ə)n/ noun [U]

de·plet·ed /dɪˈplitəd/ adj with a smaller amount of something or a smaller number of things than you want or need

de·plor·a·ble /dɪˈplɔrəb(ə)l/ adj *formal* extremely bad and shocking —**de·plor·a·bly** adv

de·plore /dɪˈplɔr/ verb [T] *formal* to think that something is bad and immoral

de·ploy /dɪˈplɔɪ/ verb [T] if a government or army deploys soldiers or weapons, it uses them —**de·ploy·ment** noun [U]

de·port /dɪˈpɔrt/ verb [T] to send someone back to the country that they came from —**de·por·ta·tion** /ˌdipɔrˈteɪʃ(ə)n/ noun [C/U]

de·pose /dɪˈpoʊz/ verb [T] to force someone out of their position of power

de·pos·it¹ /dɪˈpɑzɪt/ noun [C] ★
1 an amount of money that you pay when you rent something. You get the money back if the thing is not damaged when you return it.
2 a payment that you make as the first part of a total amount that you will have to pay later: *I paid a $100 deposit.*
3 a payment that you make into a bank account
4 a layer of something that is formed by natural or chemical processes: *rich mineral deposits*

de·pos·it² /dɪˈpɑzɪt/ verb [T] **1** to pay money into a bank account **2** *formal* to put something somewhere

de·pot /ˈdepoʊ, ˈdipoʊ/ noun [C] **1** *American* a railroad station or a bus station **2** a large building where things are stored until they are needed

de·praved /dɪˈpreɪvd/ adj immoral or evil —**de·prav·i·ty** /dɪˈprævəti/ noun [U]

de·pre·ci·ate /dɪˈpriʃiˌeɪt/ verb [I] to become less valuable —**de·pre·ci·a·tion** /dɪˌpriʃiˈeɪʃ(ə)n/ noun [U]

de·press /dɪˈpres/ verb [T] **1** to make someone feel unhappy and without any enthusiasm or hope: *It depresses me to see all that money being wasted.* **2** *formal* to make something such as a price or value go down

de·pressed /dɪˈprest/ adj ★
1 very unhappy and without any feelings of hope or enthusiasm: *She got very depressed after her husband left her.*
2 a depressed area, industry, or economy is not successful

de·press·ing /dɪˈpresɪŋ/ adj making you feel very unhappy and without any feelings of hope or enthusiasm —**de·press·ing·ly** adv

D

de·pres·sion /dɪˈpreʃ(ə)n/ noun ★
1 [U] a feeling of great sadness that is sometimes so extreme that it is considered to be a mental illness: *Many children show signs of anxiety and depression after a divorce in the family.*
2 [C/U] a period of time when there is a lot of unemployment and POVERTY because there is very little economic activity: *the world depression of the 1930s*
3 [C] *formal* an area on a surface that is lower than the parts around it

dep·ri·va·tion /ˌdeprɪˈveɪʃ(ə)n/ noun [U] a situation in which people are very poor and do not have the basic things that they need

de·prive /dɪˈpraɪv/ verb [T] to prevent someone from having something that they need or want: *people who are deprived of their freedom*

de·prived /dɪˈpraɪvd/ adj not having enough of the basic things that you need, for example food or money: *deprived children in the inner cities*

depth /depθ/ noun ★★★
1 [C/U] a distance relating to how deep something is, for example the ocean, a river, or a hole: ***What's the depth of the water here?***
2 [U] the distance from the front to the back of something: *the depth of the shelf*
3 [C/U] interesting qualities or ideas that are not obvious at first: *His first album had more depth than this one.*
4 [U] a high level of something such as a feeling or the amount of information that is given: *The newspaper is proud of the **depth of** its coverage.*
PHRASES **the depths of sth 1** a place that is very far inside an area: *the depths of the forest* **2** the worst part of an unpleasant time, feeling, or situation: *She was **in the depths of** despair.*
in depth in a very detailed way and giving a lot of information: *This subject will be covered in depth next term.*

dep·u·ty /ˈdepjəti/ noun [C] ★★
1 someone whose job is the second most important in a department or organization. A deputy does the job of the most important person in some situations.
2 a police officer who works for the SHERIFF in some parts of the U.S.

de·rail /dɪˈreɪl/ verb [I] if a train derails, or if something derails it, it comes off its tracks —**de·rail·ment** noun [C/U]

de·ranged /dɪˈreɪndʒd/ adj behaving in an uncontrolled or dangerous way because of a mental illness

der·by /ˈdɜrbi/ noun [C] *informal* a race or competition

de·reg·u·la·tion /diˌregjəˈleɪʃ(ə)n/ noun [U] the process of removing the rules that control something such as an industry —**de·reg·u·late** /diˈregjəˌleɪt/ verb [T]

der·e·lict /ˈderəlɪkt/ adj a derelict building or area is empty, not used, and in bad condition

de·ride /dɪˈraɪd/ verb [T] *formal* to say that someone or something is stupid or useless

de·ri·sion /dɪˈrɪʒ(ə)n/ noun [U] the attitude that someone or something is stupid or useless

de·ri·sive /dɪˈraɪsɪv/ adj showing that you think that someone or something is stupid or useless —**de·ri·sive·ly** adv

de·ri·so·ry /dɪˈraɪsəri/ adj if money that you are offered or given is derisory, you feel insulted because it is not very much

der·i·va·tion /ˌderɪˈveɪʃ(ə)n/ noun [C/U] *linguistics* the original form from which something such as a word developed

de·rive /dɪˈraɪv/ verb [T] to get something from something else

der·ma·tol·o·gist /ˌdɜrməˈtɑlədʒɪst/ noun [C] a doctor who treats diseases of the skin —**der·ma·tol·o·gy** noun [U]

de·rog·a·to·ry /dɪˈrɑgəˌtɔri/ adj intended to criticize or insult

de·scend /dɪˈsend/ verb **1** [I/T] *formal* to go down something such as a mountain, a slope, or stairs ≠ ASCEND **2** [I] to move closer to the ground from the air or from a high point **3 be descended from** to be related to a person or animal that lived long ago
PHRASAL VERBS **desˈcend ˌinto sth** to develop into a very bad state: *Filming descended into chaos after further arguments.*
desˈcend on sb/sth if people descend on a person or a place, a lot of them arrive together

de·scen·dant /dɪˈsendənt/ noun [C] a relative of a person who lived in the past

de·scent /dɪˈsent/ noun **1** [C/U] the act of moving down to a lower place or position ≠ ASCENT: *The plane began its descent.* **2** [U] the origin of your parents or other older members of your family: *They're all of Irish descent.* **3** [singular] the process of gradually changing to a worse condition: *her gradual descent into alcoholism*

de·scribe /dɪˈskraɪb/ verb [T] ★★★ to give details about someone or something in order to explain to another person what they are like: *It's hard to describe my feelings.* ♦ **describe sb/sth as sth** *The attacker is described as tall, with dark hair.* ♦ **describe sb/sth to sb** *Could you describe her to me?*

> **Word family: describe**
> *Words in the same family as **describe***
> ■ **description** *n* ■ **indescribable** *adj*
> ■ **descriptive** *adj* ■ **nondescript** *adj*

de·scrip·tion /dɪˈskrɪpʃ(ə)n/ noun [C] ★★★ a statement about what someone or something is like: ***a brief description of the** area* ♦ *Barry was unable to **give the police a description of** his attacker.*

de·scrip·tive /dɪˈskrɪptɪv/ adj describing something: *descriptive writing*

des·e·crate /ˈdesəˌkreɪt/ verb [T] to deliberately spoil something that is special or holy —**des·e·cra·tion** /ˌdesəˈkreɪʃ(ə)n/ noun [U]

de·seg·re·ga·tion /ˌdisegrəˈgeɪʃ(ə)n/ noun [U] the process of ending a system in which people of different races are separated —**de·seg·re·gate** /diˈsegrəˌgeɪt/ verb [T]

de·sert¹ /ˈdezərt/ noun [C/U] ★★ a large area of land with few plants and dry weather

de·sert² /dɪˈzɜrt/ verb **1** [T] to leave a person or place and not come back **2** [I] if soldiers desert, they leave the army without permission —**de·ser·tion** /dɪˈzɜrʃ(ə)n/ noun [C/U]

de·sert·ed /dɪˈzɜrtəd/ adj a deserted place has no people in it

de·sert·er /dɪˈzɜrtər/ noun [C] someone who leaves the military without permission

des·ert is·land /ˌdezərt ˈaɪlənd/ noun [C] a small tropical island with no people living on it

de·serve /dɪˈzɜrv/ verb [T] ★★
1 if you deserve something, it is right that you get it, because of the way that you are or the way that you have behaved: *After five hours on your feet you deserve a break.* ♦ **deserve to do sth** *I think I deserve to be well paid.* ♦ *Chambers* ***got what he deserved*** (=was punished correctly for something he did).
2 to be worth spending time on or giving thought to: *an issue that deserves careful thought*

de·serv·ing /dɪˈzɜrvɪŋ/ adj worth supporting or helping

de·sign[1] /dɪˈzaɪn/ noun ★★★
1 [C/U] the way that something is made so that it works and looks a certain way, or a drawing that shows what it will look like: *The car has a new design.* ♦ ***designs for*** *the new bridge*
2 [U] the process of deciding how something will be made, how it will work, and what it will look like, or the study of this process: *software design* ♦ *the design and construction of new buildings* ♦ *I studied design at college.*
3 [C] a pattern that decorates something: *simple geometric designs*
PHRASE **by design** *formal* deliberately

de·sign[2] /dɪˈzaɪn/ verb [T] ★★★ to decide how something will be made, how it will work, or what it will look like, and often to make drawings of it: *The bride wore a dress that she designed herself.* ♦ *She has a job designing websites.*

des·ig·nate /ˈdezɪɡˌneɪt/ verb [T] **1** to formally choose someone or something for a particular purpose **2** *formal* to give someone or something a particular name —**des·ig·na·tion** /ˌdezɪɡˈneɪʃ(ə)n/ noun [C/U]

de·sign·er[1] /dɪˈzaɪnər/ noun [C] ★ someone whose job is to decide how to make things, how they will work, and what they will look like: *a fashion designer*

de·sign·er[2] /dɪˈzaɪnər/ adj designer clothes and products are expensive and fashionable

de·sir·a·ble /dɪˈzaɪrəb(ə)l/ adj **1** something that is desirable has qualities that make you want it **2** sexually attractive

de·sire[1] /dɪˈzaɪr/ noun ★★
1 [C/U] a strong feeling of wanting to have or do something: **a desire to do sth** *his desire to travel* ♦ ***a desire for*** *peace*
2 [U] *literary* a strong feeling that you want to have sex with someone

de·sire[2] /dɪˈzaɪr/ verb [T] **1** *formal* to want something **2** *literary* to want someone as a sexual partner
PHRASE **leave a lot to be desired** *spoken* used for saying that something is of a very low standard

de·sired /dɪˈzaɪrd/ adj making you want to have or achieve something

desk /desk/ noun ★★★
1 [C] a table that you sit at to write or work, often with drawers in it
2 [singular] a place that provides information or a service, for example in a hotel: *the information desk*
3 [singular] a particular department of an organization such as a television company or a newspaper: *the sports desk*

ˈdesk ˌorganizer noun [C] a container that you keep on top of a desk and use for holding pens and other small pieces of office equipment —*picture* → C3

desk·top /ˈdeskˌtɑp/ noun [C] the main screen on a computer that shows the programs that are available

ˌdesktop ˈpublishing noun [U] the use of small computers to produce newspapers, magazines, or professional documents

des·o·late /ˈdesələt/ adj **1** a desolate place is completely empty with no pleasant features **2** feeling very sad and alone —**des·o·la·tion** /ˌdesəˈleɪʃ(ə)n/ noun [U]

de·spair[1] /dɪˈsper/ noun [U] the feeling that a situation is so bad that nothing can change it —**de·spair·ing** adj

de·spair[2] /dɪˈsper/ verb [I] to feel that a situation is so bad that nothing can change it

des·per·ate /ˈdesp(ə)rət/ adj ★
1 very upset and willing to do anything because you are in a bad situation: *The missing man's family is getting increasingly desperate.* ♦ *In* ***a desperate attempt*** *to escape, he killed a guard.*
2 extremely severe or serious: *Parts of this school are* ***in desperate need of*** *repair.*
3 needing or wanting something very much: **be desperate to do sth** *She was desperate to see him again.*
—**des·per·ate·ly** adv, **des·per·a·tion** /ˌdespəˈreɪʃ(ə)n/ noun [U]

des·pi·ca·ble /dɪˈspɪkəb(ə)l/ adj extremely unpleasant: *despicable crimes*

de·spise /dɪˈspaɪz/ verb [T] to hate someone or something and have no respect for them

de·spite /dɪˈspaɪt/ preposition ★★★ used for saying that something happens or is true even though something else makes it seem unlikely =SPITE: *He still loves her,* ***despite the fact that*** *she left him.*
PHRASE **despite yourself** even though you did not intend or expect to do something: *I began to enjoy the party despite myself.*

de·spon·dent /dɪˈspɑndənt/ adj very unhappy because you do not believe that an unpleasant situation will improve —**de·spon·den·cy** noun [U]

des·sert /dɪˈzɜrt/ noun [C/U] ★ sweet food that you eat after the main part of a meal =PUDDING

de·sta·bi·lize /diˈsteɪb(ə)lˌaɪz/ verb [T] to cause problems for a country, government, or person in authority so that they become less effective —**de·sta·bi·li·za·tion** /ˌdisteɪb(ə)lɪˈzeɪʃ(ə)n/ noun [U]

des·ti·na·tion /ˌdestɪˈneɪʃ(ə)n/ noun [C] ★ the place where someone or something is going

des·tined /ˈdestɪnd/ adj **1** certain to do

something, or certain to happen: *We felt that we were destined to meet.* **2** traveling, or being sent, to a particular place

des·ti·ny /ˈdestəni/ noun **1** [C] the things that you will do or the type of person that you will become **2** [U] a power that some people believe controls everything that happens

des·ti·tute /ˈdestɪˌtut/ adj with no money or possessions

D

de·stroy /dɪˈstrɔɪ/ verb [T] ★★★ to damage or harm something so severely that it cannot exist as it was before: *An earthquake destroyed the town.* ♦ *This action destroyed any hope of reaching an agreement.*

Word family: **destroy**

Words in the same family as ***destroy***

- **destroyer** *n*
- **destruction** *n*
- **destructive** *adj*
- **indestructible** *adj*
- **self-destruct** *v*

de·stroy·er /dɪˈstrɔɪər/ noun [C] a small fast ship that is used for fighting enemy ships

de·struc·tion /dɪˈstrʌkʃ(ə)n/ noun [U] ★ damage that is so severe that something cannot exist as it was before: ***the destruction of the environment***

de·struc·tive /dɪˈstrʌktɪv/ adj causing severe damage or harm

de·tach /dɪˈtætʃ/ verb [I/T] to remove a part from something, or to become removed from something = SEPARATE

PHRASE **detach yourself (from)** to stop being involved in something in an emotional way

de·tach·a·ble /dɪˈtætʃəb(ə)l/ adj able to be removed and put back on again

de·tached /dɪˈtætʃt/ adj not feeling involved in something in an emotional way

de·tach·ment /dɪˈtætʃmənt/ noun **1** [U] a feeling of not being involved with someone or something in a close or emotional way **2** [C] a small group of soldiers who are sent to do a particular job

de·tail[1] /dɪˈteɪl, ˈdiˌteɪl/ noun ★★★
1 [C/U] one of many small facts or pieces of information relating to a situation: *No details of the offer were revealed.* ♦ *She talked* ***in detail*** (=including many smaller facts) *about her plans.* ♦ *Mr. Shaw refused to go* ***into detail*** (=talk about more than general facts) *about the discussions.*
2 [U] all the small aspects or features that something has, especially when they are difficult to notice: ***Attention to detail*** *is important in this job.*

de·tail[2] /dɪˈteɪl/ verb [T] to list all the facts or aspects of a situation

de·tailed /dɪˈteɪld, ˈdiˌteɪld/ adj ★★ including many small facts or aspects: *a detailed description/report*

de·tain /dɪˈteɪn/ verb [T] **1** to not allow someone to leave a POLICE STATION or prison **2** *formal* to delay someone who has to go somewhere

de·tect /dɪˈtekt/ verb [T] **1** to notice something when it is not obvious: *I thought I detected a hint of irony in her words.* **2** to prove that something is present by using scientific methods —**de·tec·tion** /dɪˈtekʃ(ə)n/ noun [U]

de·tec·tive /dɪˈtektɪv/ noun [C] ★
1 a police officer whose job is to try to discover information about a crime
2 someone who is paid by other people to find out information

de·tec·tor /dɪˈtektər/ noun [C] a piece of equipment that is used for checking whether something is present

de·ten·tion /dɪˈtenʃ(ə)n/ noun **1** [U] the state of being kept in a POLICE STATION or prison and not being allowed to leave **2** [C/U] a punishment in which a child has to stay at school after other children have left

de·ter /dɪˈtɜr/ verb [T] to make someone decide not to do something

de·ter·gent /dɪˈtɜrdʒənt/ noun [C/U] a liquid or powder that you use for washing clothes or dishes

de·te·ri·o·rate /dɪˈtɪriəˌreɪt/ verb [I] to become worse —**de·te·ri·o·ra·tion** /dɪˌtɪriəˈreɪʃ(ə)n/ noun [U]

de·ter·mi·na·tion /dɪˌtɜrmɪˈneɪʃ(ə)n/ noun [U] ★ the refusal to let anything stop you from doing what you want to do: **determination to do sth** *The president's determination to pursue the rebels was clear.*

Words often used with **determination**

Adjectives often used with ***determination***

- **dogged, fierce, grim, sheer, steely** + DETERMINATION: used for saying that someone is very determined

Verbs often used with ***determination***

- **demonstrate, show, signal, underline** + DETERMINATION: show people that you are determined

de·ter·mine /dɪˈtɜrmɪn/ verb **1** [I/T] to officially decide something: *The court must determine whether she is guilty.* **2** [T] to control what something will be: *Our prices are determined by the market.* **3** [I/T] to calculate something, or to discover it by examining evidence = FIND OUT: *Technicians were trying to determine why the missile didn't fire.*

de·ter·mined /dɪˈtɜrmɪnd/ adj ★ not willing to let anything stop you from doing what you want to do: *a strong, determined woman* ♦ **determined to do sth** *I was determined to be a jazz musician.*

de·ter·min·er /dɪˈtɜrmɪnər/ noun [C] *linguistics* a word such as "a," "the," "this," or "some" that is used before a noun for showing which thing or things you are talking about

de·ter·rent /dɪˈterənt/ noun [C] **1** something that stops people from doing something by making them afraid of what will happen if they do it **2** a weapon whose purpose is to make other countries afraid to attack the country that owns it

de·test /dɪˈtest/ verb [T] to hate someone or something

det·o·nate /ˈdet(ə)nˌeɪt/ verb [I/T] to explode, or to make something such as a bomb explode —**det·o·na·tion** /ˌdet(ə)nˈeɪʃ(ə)n/ noun [C/U]

det·o·na·tor /ˈdet(ə)nˌeɪtər/ noun [C] a piece of equipment on a bomb that makes it explode

de·tour /ˈdiˌtʊr/ noun [C] a way of going from one place to another that is not the shortest or usual way —**de·tour** verb [I]

de·tox /ˈdiˌtɑks/ noun [U] *informal* treatment to

help someone to stop taking drugs or drinking alcohol

de·tract /dɪˈtrækt/ PHRASAL VERB **deˈtract from sth** to make something seem less good, attractive, or important: *The ugly high-rise buildings detract from the view.*

det·ri·ment /ˈdetrɪmənt/ noun [U] *formal* harm that is caused to something as a result of something else

det·ri·men·tal /ˌdetrɪˈment(ə)l/ adj harmful or damaging ≠ BENEFICIAL

de·val·ue /diˈvælju/ verb **1** [T] to treat someone or something as if they are not important **2** [I/T] *business* to officially reduce the value of a country's money
—**de·val·u·a·tion** /ˌdivæljuˈeɪʃ(ə)n/ noun [C/U]

dev·as·tate /ˈdevəˌsteɪt/ verb [T] **1** to destroy or seriously damage something **2** to make someone feel very shocked and upset: *Mary's death devastated the family.*
—**dev·as·ta·tion** /ˌdevəˈsteɪʃ(ə)n/ noun [U]

dev·as·tat·ed /ˈdevəˌsteɪtəd/ adj feeling very shocked and upset

dev·as·tat·ing /ˈdevəˌsteɪtɪŋ/ adj **1** causing a lot of harm or damage: *a devastating fire/storm/flood* **2** very shocking or upsetting: *a devastating loss* **3** very impressive or attractive: *devastating good looks*

de·vel·op /dɪˈveləp/ verb ★★★

1 grow/change	5 create new product
2 start to exist	6 use land for sth
3 be affected by	7 become complete
4 change	8 prepare photograph

1 [I/T] to change, grow, or improve, or to make something grow, change, or improve: *All children develop at different rates.* ♦ *The area is working to develop its tourist industry.* ♦ *As the economy developed, social change took place.* ♦ *The cell **develops into** an embryo.*
2 [I] to start to exist, or to start to be noticeable: *Their friendship developed at college.* ♦ *A rash developed on my arm.*
3 [T] to start to have something or be affected by something: *Rob died two years after developing the illness.* ♦ *The engine developed a problem soon after takeoff.*
4 [I] if a situation develops, it changes as events happen or conditions change: *We're waiting to see how things develop before we make a decision.*
5 [T] to create a new product or method: *We've recently developed new communications software.*
6 [T] to use land for a particular purpose that increases its value
7 [I/T] if an idea or story develops, or if you develop it, it becomes clear and complete as you add details to it
8 [T] to treat film with chemicals in order to make photographs

de·vel·oped /dɪˈveləpt/ adj **1** a developed skill, idea, or quality has reached a high level: *a well-developed sense of smell* **2** a developed country, region, or economy has a lot of industries

de·vel·op·er /dɪˈveləpər/ noun [C] someone who buys land or buildings in order to put new or better buildings there

de·vel·op·ing /dɪˈveləpɪŋ/ adj a developing country is poor and does not have many industries

de·vel·op·ment /dɪˈveləpmənt/ noun ★★★
1 [U] change, growth, or improvement over a period of time: *a child's physical development* ♦ *the development of the region's economy*
2 [C] a new event that changes a situation: *Were there any further developments in the case?*
3 [U] the process of creating a new product or method, or the product or method that is created: *software development* ♦ ***developments in medical research***
4 [C/U] the process of putting new buildings on land, or a group of new buildings

de·vi·ant /ˈdiviənt/ adj deviant behavior is not considered normal or morally correct

de·vi·ate /ˈdiviˌeɪt/ verb [I] to start doing something different from what is expected

de·vi·a·tion /ˌdiviˈeɪʃ(ə)n/ noun [C/U] a difference in the usual or expected way of doing something

de·vice /dɪˈvaɪs/ noun [C] ★★
1 a machine or piece of equipment that does a particular job: *a listening device* ♦ ***a device for** measuring humidity in the air*
2 a bomb

dev·il /ˈdev(ə)l/ noun **1 the Devil** [singular] the most powerful evil spirit in many religions **2** [C] an evil spirit
PHRASE **talk/speak of the devil** *spoken* used when someone that you have just been talking about arrives unexpectedly

ˌdevil's ˈadvocate noun **play/be devil's advocate** to pretend to disagree with someone in order to start an argument or discussion

de·vi·ous /ˈdiviəs/ adj dishonest and clever = CUNNING

de·vise /dɪˈvaɪz/ verb [T] ★ to invent a method of doing something

de·void /dɪˈvɔɪd/ adj **devoid of sth** lacking something, especially a good quality

de·vote /dɪˈvoʊt/
PHRASAL VERBS **deˈvote sth to sth 1** to spend a lot of time or effort doing something = DEDICATE: *He devoted most of his time to his painting.* **2** to use a particular amount of time, space, or money for dealing with something
deˈvote yourself to sth to spend a lot of your time or effort doing something: *Few people are able to devote themselves fully to their career.*

de·vot·ed /dɪˈvoʊtəd/ adj **1** loving someone very much: *a devoted family man* **2 devoted to sth** containing or dealing with one particular thing = DEDICATED: *an exhibit devoted to Rembrandt's etchings* **3** very enthusiastic about something

de·vo·tion /dɪˈvoʊʃ(ə)n/ noun [U] **1** great love, admiration, or loyalty **2** the process of spending a lot of time or energy on an activity **3** strong religious feeling

de·vour /dɪˈvaʊr/ verb [T] **1** to eat something very fast because you are hungry **2** to read, watch, or listen to something with a lot of interest **3** if you are devoured by a feeling, you feel it very strongly and cannot get rid of it

D

de•vout /dɪˈvaʊt/ adj **1** very religious **2** very enthusiastic about something —**de•vout•ly** adv

dew /du/ noun [U] small drops of water that form on the ground at night

dex•ter•i•ty /dekˈsterəti/ noun [U] great skill in using your hands or your mind

dex•ter•ous /ˈdekst(ə)rəs/ adj able to use your hands skillfully

di•a•be•tes /ˌdaɪəˈbitiz/ noun [U] *medical* a serious medical condition in which your body cannot reduce the amount of sugar in your blood

di•a•bet•ic /ˌdaɪəˈbetɪk/ noun [C] *medical* someone who has diabetes —**di•a•bet•ic** adj

di•a•bol•i•cal /ˌdaɪəˈbɑlɪk(ə)l/ adj evil or cruel

di•ag•nose /ˈdaɪəgˌnoʊz/ verb [T] to find out what physical or mental problem someone has by examining them: *Eva's been diagnosed with cancer.*

di•ag•no•sis /ˌdaɪəgˈnoʊsɪs/ (plural **di•ag•nos•es** /ˌdaɪəgˈnoʊˌsiz/) noun [C/U] a statement about what disease someone has, based on examining them

di•ag•nos•tic /ˌdaɪəgˈnɑstɪk/ adj used for making a diagnosis

di•ag•o•nal /daɪˈægənəl/ adj a diagonal line is straight and sloping —*picture* → C8 —**di•ag•o•nal•ly** adv

di•a•gram /ˈdaɪəˌgræm/ noun [C] ★ a drawing that explains something: ***a diagram of the*** *manufacturing process*

di•al¹ /ˈdaɪəl/ (present participle **di•al•ing** or **di•al•ling**; past tense and past participle **di•aled** or **di•alled**) verb [I/T] to push the buttons or turn the dial on a telephone in order to call someone

di•al² /ˈdaɪəl/ noun [C] **1** a round control on a piece of equipment that you turn to change something **2** the round part of a clock, watch, or machine that has numbers on it

di•a•lect /ˈdaɪəˌlekt/ noun [C/U] a way of speaking a language that is used only in a particular area or by a particular group

di•a•log /ˈdaɪəˌlɔg/ another spelling of dialogue

ˈdialog ˌbox noun [C] *computing* a small area that appears on a computer screen for you to type messages, instructions, or choices

di•a•logue /ˈdaɪəˌlɔg/ noun ★★

1 [C/U] a process in which two people or groups have discussions in order to solve problems: *They are trying to start a* ***dialogue with*** *the opposing party.*

2 [U] all the words that characters speak in a book, play, or movie, or a particular conversation in a book, play, or movie

ˈdial ˌtone noun [C] *American* the sound that a telephone makes when you pick it up

ˈdial-ˌup adj *computing* a dial-up service or system is one that connects with your computer using a telephone line

di•am•e•ter /daɪˈæmətər/ noun [C/U] a straight line that crosses a circle through the center, or the length of this line —*picture* → C8

di•a•mond /ˈdaɪəmənd/ noun **1** [C/U] a very hard clear COLORLESS stone that is used in expensive jewelry: *a diamond ring/ necklace/bracelet* **2** [C] a shape with four straight equal sides that stands on one of its corners —*picture* → C8 **3** [C] a playing card with a red diamond shape on it —*picture* → C16 **4** [C] the diamond-shaped area of a baseball field —*picture* → C15

di•a•per /ˈdaɪ(ə)pər/ noun [C] *American* a piece of cloth or plastic that a baby wears before it has learned to use the toilet

di•a•phragm /ˈdaɪəˌfræm/ noun [C] **1** a large muscle that helps you to breathe **2** a round rubber object that a woman uses as a CONTRACEPTIVE (=to avoid having a baby)

di•ar•rhe•a /ˌdaɪəˈriə/ noun [U] an illness in which the solid waste from your body is like a liquid

di•a•ry /ˈdaɪəri/ noun [C] a book in which you write your experiences each day =JOURNAL: *She's kept a diary since she was twelve.*

dice¹ /daɪs/ (plural **dice**) noun [C] a small block with a number of spots on each side, that you use for playing games —*picture* → C16

dice² /daɪs/ verb [T] to cut food into small square pieces —*picture* → C2

dic•ey /ˈdaɪsi/ adj *informal* involving danger or risk

di•chot•o•my /daɪˈkɑtəmi/ noun [C] *formal* a difference between two opposite things or ideas

dic•tate /ˈdɪkˌteɪt/ verb **1** [I/T] to say something that someone else will write down for you **2** [I/T] to tell someone exactly what to do and how to behave **3** [T] to influence or control how something is done: *The situation dictates that we act cautiously.*

dic•ta•tion /dɪkˈteɪʃ(ə)n/ noun **1** [U] the act of saying something that someone else then writes down **2** [C/U] an activity in which a teacher reads sentences to students that they write down so that the teacher can see how well they understand and write a language

dic•ta•tor /ˈdɪkteɪtər/ noun [C] someone who uses force to take and keep power in a country —**dic•ta•to•ri•al** /ˌdɪktəˈtɔriəl/ adj

dic•ta•tor•ship /dɪkˈteɪtərʃɪp/ noun [C/U] government by someone who takes power by force and does not allow elections

dic•tion /ˈdɪkʃ(ə)n/ noun [U] the way that you pronounce words

dic•tion•ar•y /ˈdɪkʃəˌneri/ noun [C] a book that gives an alphabetical list of words with their meanings or their translations

did the past tense of do¹

did•n't /ˈdɪd(ə)nt/ short form the usual way of saying or writing "did not." This is not often used in formal writing: *I didn't hear the phone ringing.*

die /daɪ/ (past tense and past participle **died**; present participle **dy•ing**) verb ★★★

1 [I/T] to stop being alive: *My grandfather died at the age of 86.* ♦ *Several people in the village have died violent deaths.* ♦ *She is* ***dying of*** *cancer.* ♦ *Tragically, Keats* ***died young.***

2 [I] to disappear, or to stop existing: *Our memory of her will never die.*

PHRASES **be dying for sth/to do sth** *spoken* to want something very much, or to want to do something very much: *I'm dying for a cup of coffee.*

I could have died *spoken* used for saying that you were very embarrassed or shocked by something

PHRASAL VERBS ˌ**die ˈdown** if something dies down, it becomes much less noisy, powerful, or active: *I waited for the laughter to die down before I spoke.*

ˌ**die ˈoff** if a group dies off, the members die one by one until none exist

ˌ**die ˈout** to gradually disappear or stop existing: *The tribe's traditional way of life is dying out.*

Words that may cause offense: die

When someone has died, people usually avoid mentioning death directly when they speak to the family and friends of the person who has died. They often say **pass away** or **pass on** instead of **die**, or they use indirect expressions such as "I am sorry for your loss" or "I was sorry to hear about your father/mother."

die•hard /ˈdaɪˌhɑrd/ noun [C] someone who refuses to accept change or new ideas —**die•hard** adj

die•sel /ˈdiz(ə)l/ noun [U] heavy oil that is used as fuel instead of gas in some engines

di•et[1] /ˈdaɪət/ noun ★★

1 [C/U] the food that a person or animal usually eats: *Try to eat **a balanced diet**.* ♦ *The bird has a **diet of** nuts and berries.*

2 [C] a limited range or amount of food that someone chooses to eat in order to be healthy or to become thinner: *I can't button my jeans – I'll have to **go on a diet**.*

Words often used with diet

*Adjectives often used with **diet** (noun, sense 1)*

- **balanced, healthy, varied** + DIET: used about foods that are healthy

di•et[2] /ˈdaɪət/ verb [I] to control your eating in order to become thinner —**di•et•ing** noun [U]

di•et[3] /ˈdaɪət/ adj containing less sugar or fat than other similar foods: *diet cola*

di•e•tar•y /ˈdaɪəˌteri/ adj relating to the foods you eat

dif•fer /ˈdɪfər/ verb [I] **1** to be different from something else: *Our approach differs from theirs in several ways.* **2** to disagree with someone about a subject: *Experts differ on the causes of the disease.*

dif•fer•ence /ˈdɪf(ə)rəns/ noun ★★★

1 [C/U] something that makes one person or thing not the same as another person or thing ≠ SIMILARITY: *cultural/social/political differences* ♦ *What's **the difference between** these two computers?* ♦ *There's **a** big **difference in** the attitudes of town and country people.*

2 [C] the amount by which one thing is different from another thing: *The same car costs $500 less here which is quite a difference!* ♦ *Despite this **age difference**, they fell in love.*

3 **differences** [plural] disagreements about something: *Joe and I have **had our differences**, but we work well together.*

PHRASES **a difference of opinion** a disagreement about something

make a difference to have an important effect on something, especially a good effect: *The extra space **makes a big difference**.* ♦ *This program will certainly **make a difference in** the way I do my job.*

make no/little difference to not be important, or to not have any effect: *Anybody can enjoy yoga, and your age makes absolutely no difference.*

tell the difference to notice what is different between similar people or things: *How do you **tell the difference between** the kittens?*

Word family: difference

*Words in the same family as **difference***

- **differ** *v*
- **different** *adj*
- **differentiate** *v*
- **indifference** *n*
- **indifferent** *adj*

dif•fer•ent /ˈdɪf(ə)rənt/ adj ★★★

1 not the same as another person or thing, or not the same as before ≠ SIMILAR: *Her new glasses make her look **completely different**.* ♦ *This job is a lot **different from** what I'm used to.* ♦ *The two cars are **different in** shape.*

2 separate, but of the same type: *Six different boys asked me to dance.* ♦ *Her money is in different bank accounts.*

3 unusual and not like other things of the same kind: *I wanted something a little bit different, so I painted the room green.* —**dif•fer•ent•ly** adv: *My sister and I look at life very differently.* ♦ *six differently shaped chairs*

dif•fer•en•tial /ˌdɪfəˈrenʃ(ə)l/ noun [C] the difference between two amounts, values, or rates

dif•fer•en•ti•ate /ˌdɪfəˈrenʃiˌeɪt/ verb **1** [I/T] to see or show a difference between things = DISTINGUISH: *Neil is color-blind and cannot differentiate between red and green.* **2** [T] to be the quality or fact that makes one thing different from another: *The ability to speak differentiates humans from other animals.* —**dif•fer•en•ti•a•tion** /ˌdɪfərenʃiˈeɪʃ(ə)n/ noun [U]

dif•fi•cult /ˈdɪfɪkəlt/ adj ★★★

1 not easy to do, deal with, or understand = HARD ≠ EASY: *Choosing the winner was a difficult task.* ♦ *The exam questions were too difficult.* ♦ *Talking to teenagers can be **difficult for** parents.* ♦ **it is difficult to do sth** *It's difficult to say what time I will get home.*

2 causing a lot of problems and making it hard for you to succeed: *She had a difficult childhood.*

3 never seeming happy or satisfied: *Martin was a difficult baby.*

dif•fi•cul•ty /ˈdɪfɪkəlti/ noun ★★★

1 [C] a problem: *Many students have serious financial difficulties.*

2 [U] the state of not being able to do something easily ≠ EASE: *Grandpa was speaking **with difficulty**.* ♦ **have difficulty (in) doing sth** *She still has difficulty walking.* ♦ **have difficulty with sth** *She's having difficulty with her schoolwork this year.*

3 [U] the degree to which something is difficult: *The courses vary in content and difficulty.*

dif•fi•dent /ˈdɪfɪdənt/ adj not confident —**dif•fi•dence** noun [U]

dif•fuse¹ /dɪˈfjuz/ verb **1** [T] *formal* to spread something such as information, ideas, or power among a large group of people **2** [I/T] if light diffuses, or if something diffuses it, it shines over a large area but not very brightly —**dif•fu•sion** /dɪˈfjuʒ(ə)n/ noun [U]

dif•fuse² /dɪˈfjus/ adj *formal* existing over a large area or in many areas

D

dig¹ /dɪg/ (past tense and past participle **dug** /dʌg/; present participle **dig•ging**) verb [I/T] ★★ to make a hole in earth using your hands, a machine, or a tool: *The children like to dig in the sand.* ♦ *We dug a hole and planted the tree.* ♦ *The boys were* ***digging for*** *worms.*

PHRASE **dig your heels in** to refuse to do something even though other people are trying to persuade you

PHRASAL VERBS ˌ**dig ˈin** *informal* to start eating food with a lot of enthusiasm: *Come on, everybody – dig in!*

ˌ**dig ˈinto sth** to press hard into something: *The seat belt was digging into my shoulder.*

ˌ**dig sth ˈout** to find something that you have not used or seen for a long time: *I'll dig out my old college notes later.*

ˌ**dig sth ˈup 1** to find information by searching carefully: *When we investigated, we dug up some interesting facts.* **2** to remove something from under the ground by digging: *They dug up a body in his yard.*

dig² /dɪg/ noun [C] **1** *informal* a remark that criticizes someone or makes a joke about them **2** an attempt to find ancient objects by digging in the ground

di•gest /daɪˈdʒest/ verb [T] **1** to change food in your stomach into the substances that your body needs **2** to try to understand information when it is difficult or unexpected = ABSORB, TAKE STH IN —**di•gest•i•ble** adj

di•ges•tion /daɪˈdʒestʃ(ə)n/ noun [U] the process of digesting food

di•ges•tive /daɪˈdʒestɪv/ adj relating to digestion: *the digestive process*

dig•it /ˈdɪdʒɪt/ noun [C] **1** *formal* one of the written numbers from 0 to 9 **2** *technical* one of your fingers or toes

dig•i•tal /ˈdɪdʒɪt(ə)l/ adj ★
1 storing information such as sound or pictures as numbers or electronic signals: *a digital recording*
2 a digital clock or instrument shows information as a row of numbers

ˌ**digital ˈcamera** noun [C] a camera that takes and stores pictures in the form of electronic signals

dig•ni•fied /ˈdɪgnɪˌfaɪd/ adj behaving in a calm way that people respect ≠ UNDIGNIFIED: *a dignified manner*

dig•ni•tar•y /ˈdɪgnɪˌteri/ noun [C] someone who has an important official position

dig•ni•ty /ˈdɪgnəti/ noun [U] calm behavior that makes people respect you: *She faced her death with dignity.*

di•gress /daɪˈgres/ verb [I] to start to talk or write about something different from the subject that you were discussing —**di•gres•sion** /daɪˈgreʃ(ə)n/ noun [C/U]

dike /daɪk/ noun [C] a wall that prevents a lake or river from flooding the surrounding land

di•lap•i•dat•ed /dɪˈlæpɪˌdeɪtəd/ adj old and in bad condition: *a dilapidated farm* —**di•lap•i•da•tion** /dɪˌlæpɪˈdeɪʃ(ə)n/ noun [U]

di•late /daɪˈleɪt/ verb [I] if part of your body dilates, it becomes bigger and wider —**di•la•tion** /daɪˈleɪʃ(ə)n/ noun [U]

di•lem•ma /dɪˈlemə, daɪˈlemə/ noun [C] a situation in which you have to make a difficult decision = PREDICAMENT, QUANDARY

dil•i•gent /ˈdɪlɪdʒənt/ adj *formal* working very hard and very carefully = HARD-WORKING —**dil•i•gence** noun [U], **dil•i•gent•ly** adv

di•lute¹ /dɪˈlut, daɪˈlut/ verb [T] to make a liquid less strong by adding water or another liquid

di•lute² /dɪˈlut, daɪˈlut/ adj a dilute liquid has been mixed with another liquid to make it less strong

dim¹ /dɪm/ adj **1** not bright or clear: *a dim light/room* **2** a dim memory is something from long ago that you cannot remember very well ≠ CLEAR —**dim•ly** adv

dim² /dɪm/ verb [I/T] if a light dims, or if you dim it, it becomes less bright

dime /daɪm/ noun [C] a coin worth ten CENTS in the U.S. and Canada

di•men•sion /daɪˈmenʃ(ə)n/ noun **1** [C] length, height, or width **2** [C] an aspect of a situation that influences the way that you think about the situation: *Doing volunteer work has added a whole new dimension to my life.* **3 dimensions** [plural] the size of something: *Can you mark the dimensions of the room on the diagram?*

di•min•ish /dɪˈmɪnɪʃ/ verb [I/T] to become less, or to make something become less: *The intensity of the sound diminished gradually.*

di•min•u•tive /dɪˈmɪnjətɪv/ adj *formal* very small = TINY

dim•ple /ˈdɪmp(ə)l/ noun [C] a small area on your cheek, chin, etc. that goes inward

din /dɪn/ noun [singular] a very loud unpleasant noise that lasts for a long time

dine /daɪn/ verb [I] *formal* to eat DINNER (=your evening meal)

din•er /ˈdaɪnər/ noun [C] **1** *American* a small restaurant that sells simple inexpensive food **2** someone who is eating a meal at a restaurant

ding-dong /ˈdɪŋˌdɑŋ/ noun [U] the sound that a bell makes

din•ghy /ˈdɪŋi/ noun [C] a small boat

din•gy /ˈdɪndʒi/ adj dirty and dark: *a dingy room*

din•ing room /ˈdaɪnɪŋ ˌrum, ˈdaɪnɪŋ ˌrʊm/ noun [C] the room in a house or hotel where you eat meals

din•ner /ˈdɪnər/ noun [C/U] ★★★ the main meal of the day, usually eaten in the evening: *I haven't had dinner yet.* ♦ *Are we having chicken for dinner again?*

di•no•saur /ˈdaɪnəˌsɔr/ noun [C] a large animal that lived a very long time ago but is now EXTINCT (=all of them have died)

di•o•cese /ˈdaɪəsɪs/ noun [C] an area that a BISHOP (=a senior Christian priest) is in charge of

dip¹ /dɪp/ verb **1** [T] to lower something into a liquid for a moment and then take it out again **2** [I] to become less: *Our profits dipped 30%.*

PHRASAL VERB ˈ**dip into sth 1** to take some money from an amount that you have saved **2** to read different parts of a book, but not the whole book

dip[2] /dɪp/ noun **1** [C/U] a thick cold sauce for dipping pieces of food into before eating them **2** [C] a reduction in the amount or level of something: *a dip in the price of new homes* **3** [C] a place in a surface that is lower than the surrounding area: *a dip in the road* **4** [C] *informal* a quick swim: *Let's take a dip in the pool.*

diph•the•ri•a /dɪfˈθɪriə, dɪpˈθɪriə/ noun [U] a serious disease affecting your throat that makes it difficult for you to breathe

di•plo•ma /dɪˈploʊmə/ noun [C] an official document that proves you have successfully finished all the work in a course of study → CERTIFICATE, DEGREE

di•plo•ma•cy /dɪˈploʊməsi/ noun [U] **1** the profession or skill of creating friendly relationships between countries **2** the ability to deal with people well, so that they are not upset or offended

dip•lo•mat /ˈdɪpləˌmæt/ noun [C] an official whose job is to represent their government in a foreign country

dip•lo•mat•ic /ˌdɪpləˈmætɪk/ adj **1** relating to the profession or skill of DIPLOMACY: *a diplomatic mission* **2** able to deal with people well, so that they are not upset or offended ≠ UNDIPLOMATIC: *a diplomatic answer* —**dip•lo•mat•ic•al•ly** /ˌdɪpləˈmætɪkli/ adv

dire /daɪr/ adj very severe, serious, or bad: *dire warnings*

di•rect[1] /dɪˈrekt, daɪˈrekt/ adj ★★★

1 involving only the two people or things that are mentioned and with no one or nothing else between ≠ INDIRECT: *Employees have little direct contact with management.* ♦ *Their study found a direct link between poverty and crime.*

2 going straight to a place without stopping or changing direction: *direct flights from San Francisco to Tokyo*

3 saying what you really think in a very clear honest way: *I love New Yorkers – they're so funny and direct.*

4 exact: *That's a direct quote from the man himself.*

di•rect[2] /dɪˈrekt, daɪˈrekt/ verb [T] ★★

1 aim sth	4 tell/show way
2 tell actors what to do	5 order sb to do sth
3 control/organize sth	

1 to aim something at a particular person or thing: **direct sth to/at etc. sb/sth** *The incident directed public attention to pollution in the North Sea.* ♦ *At the time, all the criticism was directed at her instead of me.*

2 to be in charge of telling all the actors and technical staff who are involved in a movie, play, or program what to do → PRODUCE

3 to control or organize how a person or group of people does something: *The manager's job is mainly to direct the activities of others.*

4 to tell or show someone the way to go: **direct sb to sth** *Could you direct me to the bus station?*

5 *formal* to order someone to do something: *The jury was directed to disregard everything Robinson had said.*

di•rect[3] /dɪˈrekt, daɪˈrekt/ adv **1** going straight to a place and not stopping or changing direction: *All the major airlines fly direct to Los Angeles.* **2** in a way that involves only the two people or things that are mentioned, with no one or nothing else between: *You can buy direct from the manufacturer.*

di•rec•tion /dɪˈrekʃ(ə)n, daɪˈrekʃ(ə)n/ noun ★★★

1 of movement/look	4 purpose
2 instructions	5 control/management
3 way sb/sth changes	6 of movie/play

1 [C] the place that someone or something moves, faces, or points toward: *Are you sure we're **going in the right direction**?* ♦ *The wind has **changed direction**.* ♦ *We drove off **in the direction of** the mountains.* ♦ *I'd give you a ride, but I'm going **in the opposite direction**.* ♦ *Michelle's always getting lost because of her terrible **sense of direction**.*

2 directions [plural] instructions for doing something or for getting to a place: ***Follow the directions** on the label.* ♦ *She gave the driver **directions** to her house.*

3 [C/U] the general development or progress of someone or something: *He was determined to change **the direction of** the business.*

4 [U] the feeling of having a definite purpose: *Your life seems to **lack direction**.*

5 [U] LEADERSHIP or management: *The project was **under the direction of** Henry Richardson.*

6 [U] the work of directing a movie, program, or play

di•rec•tive /dɪˈrektɪv, daɪˈrektɪv/ noun [C] an official order

di•rect•ly /dɪˈrek(t)li, daɪˈrek(t)li/ adv ★★★

1 in a way that involves only the two people or things that are mentioned, with no one or nothing else between: *I prefer to deal directly with the manager.* ♦ *You are directly responsible for this.* ♦ *Price is directly related to size.*

2 going straight to a place without stopping or changing direction: *We landed at the airport and went directly to the hotel.*

3 exactly: *The post office is directly opposite the town hall.*

4 in a very clear and honest way: *Jackson avoided saying directly that he disapproved.*

ˌ**direct** ˈ**object** noun [C] *linguistics* the noun or pronoun in a sentence that is affected by the action of a TRANSITIVE verb. In the sentence "Harry was reading a book," "a book" is the direct object of the verb "was reading."

di•rec•tor /dɪˈrektər, daɪˈrektər/ noun [C] ★★★

1 someone whose job is to tell the actors and technical staff who are involved in a movie, play, or program what to do

2 someone whose job is to manage all or part of a company, organization, or institution: *the finance/marketing/personnel director*

di•rec•to•ry /dɪˈrektəri, daɪˈrektəri/ noun [C] **1** a book or list of people's names, addresses, telephone numbers, or other information **2** a computer file that contains other files, documents, or programs

D

di͵rectory as'sistance noun [U] *American* the service that you phone to find out someone's telephone number =INFORMATION

dirt /dɜrt/ noun [U] **1** soil or MUD: *children playing in the dirt ♦ a dirt road/path* **2** a substance that makes something dirty: *Angelo brushed the dirt off his coat.* **3** *informal* information about someone that could damage their reputation if people knew about it

͵dirt 'cheap adj, adv *informal* very inexpensive

͵dirt 'poor adj *American informal* extremely poor

dirt•y¹ /dɜrti/ adj ★★★

1 not clean: *piles of dirty laundry ♦ dirty fingernails*

2 dealing with sex in a way that offends some people: *dirty jokes/movies*

3 dishonest or unfair: *dirty tricks*

PHRASE **do sb's dirty work** to do an unpleasant job for someone so that they do not have to do it themselves

dirt•y² /dɜrti/ verb [T] to make something dirty

dis•a•bil•i•ty /͵dɪsəˈbɪləti/ noun [C/U] a condition in which someone is not able to use a part of their body or brain normally: *children with learning disabilities*

dis•a•bled /dɪˈseɪb(ə)ld/ adj ★

1 unable to use part of your body or brain normally

2 the disabled people who are disabled. Many people think this word is offensive and prefer to use the expression **people with disabilities.**

> **Words that avoid giving offense: disabled**
>
> You can use the adjective **disabled** to describe people who have a permanent physical condition that makes them unable to do something, but you should avoid referring to these people as **the disabled**. Similarly, you can use **blind** to refer to someone who cannot see, and **deaf** to refer to someone who cannot hear, but you should avoid referring to these people as **the blind** and **the deaf**. Many people now prefer the expressions **the visually impaired** and **the hearing impaired.**

dis•ad•van•tage /͵dɪsədˈvæntɪdʒ/ noun [C] ★ something that makes someone or something less effective, successful, or attractive: *One of the **disadvantages of** the job is the long hours I work. ♦ Anyone not familiar with the Internet is **at a** serious **disadvantage**.* —**dis•ad•van•ta•geous** /͵dɪsædvənˈteɪdʒəs/ adj

dis•ad•van•taged /͵dɪsədˈvæntɪdʒd/ adj not having the same advantages of money or education as other people

dis•af•fect•ed /͵dɪsəˈfektəd/ adj no longer feeling any loyalty toward a group or leader

dis•a•gree /͵dɪsəˈgri/ verb [I] ★

1 to have a different opinion from someone else: *Teenagers and their parents often disagree. ♦ I **disagree with** you – I think she's done a very good job. ♦ Dole and Evans **disagree about** many aspects of the new policy.*

2 to contain different information, or to produce different results: *Two pathologists examined the body, but their findings disagreed.*

PHRASAL VERB **disa'gree ͵with sb** if something that you eat or drink disagrees with you, it makes you feel sick

dis•a•gree•a•ble /͵dɪsəˈgriəb(ə)l/ adj *formal* **1** not nice or enjoyable **2** not friendly or polite —**dis•a•gree•a•bly** adv

dis•a•gree•ment /͵dɪsəˈgrimənt/ noun ★

1 [C/U] a situation in which people do not agree: *Bowen quit the team following **a disagreement with** the head coach. ♦ There has been considerable **disagreement about** how best to deal with the crisis.*

2 [U] a difference between things that should be the same: *There was some **disagreement between** the two statements he had given.*

dis•ap•pear /͵dɪsəˈpɪr/ verb [I] ★★★

1 to no longer happen or exist: *The symptoms should disappear within a few days.*

2 to become impossible to see or find: *The letter I had left on my desk had disappeared. ♦ The train **disappeared from view**. ♦ The couple **disappeared without trace** while on vacation in France.*

—**dis•ap•pear•ance** noun [C/U]

dis•ap•point /͵dɪsəˈpɔɪnt/ verb [I/T] to make someone feel unhappy or not satisfied: *I hate to disappoint you, but the cake's all gone.*

dis•ap•point•ed /͵dɪsəˈpɔɪntəd/ adj ★ unhappy because something did not happen or because someone or something was not as good as you expected: **+(that)** *She was disappointed that he never replied to her letter. ♦ I am very **disappointed at** not getting the job. ♦ I'm really **disappointed in** you, Ruth.*

dis•ap•point•ing /͵dɪsəˈpɔɪntɪŋ/ adj not as good as you had hoped or expected: *This year's sales figures were very disappointing.*

dis•ap•point•ment /͵dɪsəˈpɔɪntmənt/ noun ★

1 [U] the feeling of being unhappy because something did not happen or because someone or something was not as good as you expected: *Diplomats expressed **disappointment at** the lack of progress. ♦ Jackson canceled the concert, **to the disappointment of** his fans.*

2 [C] someone or something that is not as good as you thought they would be: *Newcombe has described the defeat as the biggest disappointment of his career. ♦ I'm such **a disappointment to** her.*

dis•ap•prov•al /͵dɪsəˈpruv(ə)l/ noun [U] a feeling of not approving of someone or something: *He made no secret of his disapproval of the way the affair was handled.*

dis•ap•prove /͵dɪsəˈpruv/ verb [I] ★ to not approve of someone or something: *Why do you always have to **disapprove of** everything I do?*

dis•ap•prov•ing /͵dɪsəˈpruvɪŋ/ adj a disapproving expression or reaction shows that someone does not approve of something —**dis•ap•prov•ing•ly** adv

dis•arm /dɪsˈɑrm/ verb **1** [I] if a country or organization disarms, it reduces or gets rid of its weapons or military **2** [T] to take someone's weapons so that they can no longer use them **3** [T] to make someone feel less angry or unfriendly: *Interviewers are disarmed by her straightforward approach.*

dis·ar·ma·ment /dɪsˈɑrməmənt/ noun [U] the process by which a country reduces or gets rid of its weapons or military

dis·arm·ing /dɪsˈɑrmɪŋ/ adj making someone feel less angry or unfriendly: *her disarming honesty*

dis·ar·ray /ˌdɪsəˈreɪ/ noun [U] a situation in which people are very confused or things are not organized: *The committee was in complete disarray.*

dis·as·ter /dɪˈzæstər/ noun ★
1 [C/U] something very bad that happens and causes a lot of damage or kills a lot of people: *A series of disasters forced the company to close down.* ♦ ***natural disasters*** (=floods, earthquakes, etc.)
2 [C] a very bad or annoying situation, or a complete failure: *Our party was a complete disaster.*

disˈaster ˌarea noun **1** [C] a place or region that has been badly affected by a disaster **2** [singular] *humorous* a person, place, or system that is very messy

dis·as·trous /dɪˈzæstrəs/ adj very bad, harmful, or unsuccessful: *The spending cuts would be disastrous for schools.* ♦ *a disastrous start to the meeting*

dis·band /dɪsˈbænd/ verb [I/T] if a group of people disbands, or if it is disbanded, its members stop working together

dis·be·lief /ˌdɪsbɪˈlif/ noun [U] the feeling of not believing someone or something: *Liz stared at us in disbelief as we told her what had happened.*

dis·be·lieve /ˌdɪsbɪˈliv/ verb [T] to not believe someone or something

disc another spelling of **disk**

dis·card /dɪsˈkɑrd/ verb [T] to get rid of something that you no longer want or need: *Discard the melon seeds.*

dis·cern /dɪˈsɜrn/ verb [T] *formal* to notice, see, or understand something: *It's hard to discern exactly what his motives are.* —**dis·cern·i·ble** adj

dis·cern·ing /dɪˈsɜrnɪŋ/ adj showing good judgment about things such as art, music, or fashion —**dis·cern·ment** noun [U]

dis·charge¹ /ˈdɪsˌtʃɑrdʒ, dɪsˈtʃɑrdʒ/ verb **1** [T] to allow or force someone to leave a hospital, a prison, or the army **2** [T] *formal* to perform a duty or responsibility **3** [I/T] to allow liquid or gas to leave a place **4** [T] *formal* to fire a weapon

dis·charge² /ˈdɪsˌtʃɑrdʒ, dɪsˈtʃɑrdʒ/ noun [C/U] **1** official permission to leave a hospital, a prison, or the army **2** a liquid, gas, or other substance that comes out of something else

dis·ci·ple /dɪˈsaɪp(ə)l/ noun [C] someone who admires and is influenced by a political or religious leader

dis·ci·pli·nar·i·an /ˌdɪsəplɪˈneriən/ noun [C] someone who forces people to obey rules

dis·ci·pli·nar·y /ˈdɪsəplɪˌneri, ˌdɪsəˈplɪnəri/ adj connected with the punishment of people who do not obey rules

dis·ci·pline¹ /ˈdɪsəplɪn/ noun ★★
1 [U] the practice of making people obey rules and punishing them if they do not: *He believes in strict discipline.*
2 [U] the ability to control your own behavior: *Many of the students lacked the discipline to learn.*
3 [C] a subject that people study, especially at a university: *academic disciplines*

dis·ci·pline² /ˈdɪsəplɪn/ verb [T] to punish someone for something wrong that they have done

dis·ci·plined /ˈdɪsəplɪnd/ adj well organized and following rules or standards ≠ UNDISCIPLINED: *the team's disciplined approach*

ˈdisc ˌjockey noun [C] a DJ

dis·claim·er /dɪsˈkleɪmər/ noun [C] a statement in which someone says that they do not take responsibility for something

dis·close /dɪsˈkloʊz/ verb [T] to give people information that was secret: *They failed to disclose that profits had fallen.*

dis·clo·sure /dɪsˈkloʊʒər/ noun [C/U] the act of telling people information that was secret, or the information that is told: *a series of disclosures that almost wrecked his career*

dis·co /ˈdɪskoʊ/ noun [U] a type of popular dance music from the 1970s

dis·col·ored /dɪsˈkʌlərd/ adj changed in color and no longer looking new, clean, or healthy: *discolored wallpaper* —**dis·col·or** verb [I/T], **dis·col·or·a·tion** /dɪsˌkʌləˈreɪʃ(ə)n/ noun [C/U]

dis·com·fort /dɪsˈkʌmfərt/ noun **1** [U] a feeling of slight pain: *discomfort in my lower back* **2** [C] something that makes you feel slightly sick or uncomfortable: *the discomforts of life in the desert*

dis·con·cert·ed /ˌdɪskənˈsɜrtəd/ adj feeling worried, confused, or surprised

dis·con·cert·ing /ˌdɪskənˈsɜrtɪŋ/ adj making you feel worried, confused, or surprised: *a disconcerting habit/tendency* —**dis·con·cert** verb [T]

dis·con·nect /ˌdɪskəˈnekt/ verb [T] **1** to separate two things that were connected to each other: *A bomb disposal expert was called in to disconnect the timer.* **2** to stop someone's telephone service or supply of gas, water, or electricity: *His telephone has been disconnected.*

dis·con·tent /ˌdɪskənˈtent/ or **dis·con·tent·ment** /ˌdɪskənˈtentmənt/ noun [U] the unhappy feeling that you have when you are not satisfied with something: *Public discontent with the government is growing.* —**dis·con·tent·ed** adj

dis·con·tin·ue /ˌdɪskənˈtɪnju/ verb [T] **1** to stop doing something that you were doing regularly **2** to stop providing a product or service

dis·cord /ˈdɪsˌkɔrd/ noun [U] *formal* disagreement between people —**dis·cor·dant** adj

dis·count¹ /ˈdɪsˌkaʊnt/ noun [C] a reduction in the price of something: *Air Canada is currently offering a 10% discount on selected airfares.*

dis·count² /dɪsˈkaʊnt/ verb [T] **1** to reduce the price of something **2** to decide that something is not important, possible, or likely: *Police have discounted the possibility that this was a terrorist attack.*

dis•cour•age /dɪsˈkʌrɪdʒ/ verb [T] **1** to make someone feel less confident or hopeful: *What she said didn't discourage me.* **2** to try to prevent something from happening ≠ ENCOURAGE: *We hope the bad weather won't discourage people from coming.* —**dis•cour•age•ment** noun [C/U]

D

dis•cour•aged /dɪsˈkʌrɪdʒd/ adj feeling less confident or hopeful: *Don't get discouraged – just keep trying.*

dis•cour•ag•ing /dɪsˈkʌrɪdʒɪŋ/ adj making you feel less confident or hopeful ≠ ENCOURAGING

dis•course /ˈdɪsˌkɔrs/ noun [C] *formal* a long serious speech or piece of writing on a particular subject

dis•cour•te•ous /dɪsˈkɜrtiəs/ adj *formal* rude and lacking respect

dis•cov•er /dɪˈskʌvər/ verb [T] ★★★
1 to find something that was hidden or that no one knew about before: *William Herschel discovered Uranus in 1781.* ♦ *New antimalarial drugs have been discovered.*
2 to find out something that you did not know before: **+(that)** *He became very friendly when he discovered that she was my sister.*
3 to recognize the ability of someone and help to make them famous

dis•cov•er•y /dɪˈskʌvəri/ noun ★★
1 [C/U] the act of finding or learning about someone or something that was hidden or not known: *Police announced the **discovery of** the body late last night.* ♦ *We **made** some interesting **discoveries about** our new neighbors.* ♦ **+that** *Mr. Andrews told of his family's joy following the discovery that his son was alive.*
2 [C] something that is found, or something new that is learned: *This is one of the most important archaeological discoveries of the century.*

dis•cred•it /dɪsˈkredɪt/ verb [T] to make people stop believing or respecting someone or something: *She claims there was a conspiracy to discredit her.* —**dis•cred•it** noun [U]

dis•creet /dɪˈskrit/ adj careful not to say anything that is secret or that could upset someone ≠ INDISCREET —**dis•creet•ly** adv

dis•crep•an•cy /dɪˈskrepənsi/ noun [C/U] a difference between things that should be the same: *a discrepancy between estimated and actual spending*

dis•cre•tion /dɪˈskreʃ(ə)n/ noun [U] **1** careful and sensitive behavior that does not upset or offend people ≠ INDISCRETION **2** the right or ability to make a judgment or decision: *The funds may be spent **at the manager's discretion*** (=according to decisions made by the manager).

dis•cre•tion•ar•y /dɪˈskreʃ(ə)nˌeri/ adj based on someone's judgment of a particular situation rather than on a set of rules: *a discretionary payment/budget*

dis•crim•i•nate /dɪˈskrɪmɪˌneɪt/ verb **1** [I] to treat someone unfairly because of their religion, race, or other personal features: *laws that discriminate against women* **2** [I/T] to recognize the difference between things

dis•crim•i•nat•ing /dɪˈskrɪmɪˌneɪtɪŋ/ adj able to judge whether or not something is good or suitable ≠ UNDISCRIMINATING

dis•crim•i•na•tion /dɪˌskrɪmɪˈneɪʃ(ə)n/ noun [U] ★
1 unfair treatment of someone because of their religion, race, or other personal features: *sex/racial/age discrimination* ♦ ***discrimination against women***
2 the ability to judge whether something is good or suitable

dis•crim•i•na•to•ry /dɪˈskrɪmɪnəˌtɔri/ adj *formal* treating a particular group of people unfairly because of their religion, race, or other personal features: *discriminatory policies/practices*

dis•cus, the /ˈdɪskəs/ noun [singular] a sports event in which a heavy circular flat object is thrown

dis•cuss /dɪˈskʌs/ verb [T] ★★★
1 to talk about something with someone: *We're meeting to discuss the matter next week.* ♦ **discuss sth with sb** *You should discuss this problem with your doctor.*
2 to write or talk about a subject in detail: *The causes of stress have already been discussed in Chapter 3.*

dis•cus•sion /dɪˈskʌʃ(ə)n/ noun [C/U] ★★★ a conversation about something important: *We need to **have a discussion about** your school work.* ♦ *an interesting **discussion on** Internet censorship* ♦ ***Discussions with** management have broken down.* ♦ *Proposals for changing the system are **under discussion*** (=being discussed).

dis•dain /dɪsˈdeɪn/ noun [U] the feeling that someone or something is not important and does not deserve any respect —**dis•dain•ful** adj

dis•ease /dɪˈziz/ noun [C/U] ★★★ an illness that affects people, animals, or plants: *liver/heart/lung disease* ♦ *Studies have revealed that vegetarians **suffer** less **from** heart **disease**.* ♦ *Smoking can **cause** fatal **diseases**.* —**dis•eased** /dɪˈzizd/ adj

dis•em•bark /ˌdɪsɪmˈbɑrk/ verb [I] *formal* to get off a ship or airplane

dis•em•bod•ied /ˌdɪsɪmˈbɑdid/ adj a disembodied voice comes from someone who you cannot see

dis•en•chant•ed /ˌdɪsɪnˈtʃæntəd/ adj disappointed and no longer enthusiastic about someone or something —**dis•en•chant•ment** noun [U]

dis•en•gage /ˌdɪsɪnˈgeɪdʒ/ verb [T] if you disengage part of a machine, it is no longer connected to the main part of the machine

dis•en•tan•gle /ˌdɪsɪnˈtæŋg(ə)l/ verb [T] to separate something from the thing that is holding it or that is twisted around it
PHRASE **disentangle yourself (from)** to get yourself out of a situation that you no longer want to be involved in

dis•fig•ure /dɪsˈfɪgjər/ verb [T] to spoil the appearance of someone or something

dis•grace[1] /dɪsˈgreɪs/ noun **1** [U] the loss of other people's respect because of something bad that you have done **2** [singular] someone or something that makes you angry because they are very bad: *The way he treats his dogs is a disgrace.*

dis·grace² /dɪsˈgreɪs/ verb [T] *formal* to harm the reputation of a person or group by doing something bad or immoral

dis·grace·ful /dɪsˈgreɪsfəl/ adj extremely bad or shocking —**dis·grace·ful·ly** adv

dis·grun·tled /dɪsˈgrʌnt(ə)ld/ adj disappointed and annoyed

dis·guise¹ /dɪsˈgaɪz/ verb [T] **1** to hide something such as your feelings or intentions: *He didn't try to disguise his bitterness.* **2** to change the way that someone looks so that other people will not recognize them **3** to make something look, sound, or seem like something else

dis·guise² /dɪsˈgaɪz/ noun [C/U] something that you wear in order to change the way that you look so that people will not recognize you: *He often went out in disguise to avoid being recognized.*

dis·gust¹ /dɪsˈgʌst/ noun [U] **1** a very strong feeling of not liking something **2** the feeling that you are going to be physically sick when you see, smell, or taste something very unpleasant **3** a strong feeling of anger about something bad or immoral

dis·gust² /dɪsˈgʌst/ verb [T] **1** to be so bad or immoral that you feel angry and upset: *You attitude disgusts me.* **2** to make you feel physically sick

dis·gust·ed /dɪsˈgʌstəd/ adj **1** feeling very angry and upset about something that you do not approve of: *I was disgusted by the way he treated those women.* **2** feeling physically sick because something is extremely unpleasant to see, smell, or taste

dis·gust·ing /dɪsˈgʌstɪŋ/ adj **1** extremely unpleasant = REVOLTING **2** very bad or shocking —**dis·gust·ing·ly** adv

dish¹ /dɪʃ/ noun ★★

1 [C] a container similar to a plate or bowl that is used for serving or cooking food: *Place the fruit in a large shallow dish.*

2 [C] food that has been prepared and cooked in a particular way: *Do you have any vegetarian dishes?*

3 dishes [plural] the plates, pans, etc. that have to be washed after a meal: *Who's going to do the dishes?*

4 [C] a round piece of equipment that sends or receives radio or television messages: *a satellite dish*

dish² /dɪʃ/ PHRASAL VERBS **ˌdish sth ˈout** *informal* to give things to a number of people **ˌdish (sth) ˈup** to put food into on plates so that people can eat it

dis·heart·ened /dɪsˈhɑrt(ə)nd/ adj no longer confident or enthusiastic about something

dis·heart·en·ing /dɪsˈhɑrt(ə)nɪŋ/ adj making you less confident or enthusiastic

di·shev·eled /dɪˈʃev(ə)ld/ adj with hair and clothes that do not look neat

dis·hon·est /dɪsˈɑnəst/ adj willing to do things that are not honest ≠ HONEST —**dis·hon·est·ly** adv

dis·hon·es·ty /dɪsˈɑnəsti/ noun [U] behavior that is not honest

dish·tow·el /ˈdɪʃˌtaʊəl/ noun [C] a large cloth that you use to dry dishes that have been washed —*picture* → C2

dish·wash·er /ˈdɪʃˌwɑʃər/ noun [C] a machine that washes dishes —*picture* → C2

dis·il·lu·sion /ˌdɪsɪˈluʒ(ə)n/ verb [T] to make someone disappointed by showing them that something is not as good as they thought it was —**dis·il·lu·sion·ment** noun [U]

dis·il·lu·sioned /ˌdɪsɪˈluʒ(ə)nd/ adj disappointed because you realize that some-thing is not as good as you thought it was

dis·in·fect /ˌdɪsɪnˈfekt/ verb [T] to clean something by putting a substance on it that kills bacteria

dis·in·fec·tant /ˌdɪsɪnˈfektənt/ noun [C/U] a chemical substance that kills bacteria. It is used for cleaning things.

dis·in·te·grate /dɪsˈɪntɪˌgreɪt/ verb [I] **1** to be completely destroyed by breaking into lots of very small pieces **2** to become less effective and stop working —**dis·in·te·gra·tion** /dɪsˌɪntɪˈgreɪʃ(ə)n/ noun [U]

dis·in·ter·est·ed /dɪsˈɪntrəstəd/ adj not involved in something and therefore able to judge it fairly → UNINTERESTED

dis·joint·ed /dɪsˈdʒɔɪntəd/ adj consisting of different parts that are not clearly connected: *a strange disjointed dream*

disk /dɪsk/ noun [C] **1** a small flat circular object that is used for storing information from a computer **2** a flat circular object or shape **3** a CD or DVD **4** a round flat piece of a substance called CARTILAGE between the bones in your back

ˈdisk ˌdrive noun [C] the part of a computer that reads information from a disk or records information onto a disk

disk·ette /dɪˈsket/ noun [C] a FLOPPY DISK for storing computer information

dis·like¹ /dɪsˈlaɪk/ verb [T] ★ to not like someone or something ≠ LIKE: *She knew Philip disliked her.* ♦ **dislike doing sth** *Cats dislike getting their fur wet.*

> **Other ways of saying dislike**
>
> - **not like** to have negative feelings about someone or something
> - **not be crazy about** (*informal*) used for saying that you do not like something, in situations where you do not want to sound rude
> - **hate** to dislike someone or something very much
> - **can't stand** to dislike someone or something so strongly that it makes you feel angry or upset
> - **detest/loathe** used for emphasizing that you strongly dislike someone or something

dis·like² /dɪsˈlaɪk/ noun **1** [singular/U] a feeling of not liking someone or something: *her dislike of small children* **2** [C] something that you do not like: *We were asked to list our likes and dislikes.*

dis·lo·cate /ˈdɪsləˌkeɪt/ verb [T] to do something that forces a bone out of its normal position —**dis·lo·ca·tion** /ˌdɪsləˈkeɪʃ(ə)n/ noun [C/U]

dis·lodge /dɪsˈlɑdʒ/ verb [T] to force something out of a position where it is attached

dis·loy·al /dɪsˈlɔɪəl/ adj not loyal to someone who you have a close relationship with or to an organization that you belong to ≠ LOYAL —**dis·loy·al·ty** noun [U]

D

dis•mal /ˈdɪzməl/ adj **1** making you feel unhappy and without hope or enthusiasm: *dismal living conditions* **2** very bad —**dis•mal•ly** adv

dis•man•tle /dɪsˈmænt(ə)l/ verb [T] **1** to separate the parts of something so that they no longer form a single unit **2** to end a political or economic system, or to get rid of an institution

dis•may /dɪsˈmeɪ/ noun [U] the feeling of being very worried, disappointed, or sad about something that is surprising or shocking —**dis•mayed** /dɪsˈmeɪd/ adj

dis•mem•ber /dɪsˈmembər/ verb [T] to cut someone's body into pieces

dis•miss /dɪsˈmɪs/ verb [T] ★★
1 to refuse to accept that something could be true or important: *The senator dismissed the allegations.* ♦ **dismiss sth as sth** *Their evidence was dismissed as completely worthless.*
2 to force someone to leave their job = FIRE, SACK: **dismiss sb from sth** *Jackson was dismissed from her post.*
3 to give someone permission to leave a place: *The class is dismissed.*
4 to officially decide that a court case should not continue

dis•miss•al /dɪsˈmɪs(ə)l/ noun **1** [C/U] an act of making someone leave their job: *The investigation led to five dismissals.* **2** [U] a refusal to accept that something could be true or important: *the committee's dismissal of their complaints* **3** [C/U] a decision to allow someone to leave a place **4** [C/U] a decision that a court case should not continue

dis•mis•sive /dɪsˈmɪsɪv/ adj showing that you do not think that something is worth paying attention to —**dis•mis•sive•ly** adv

dis•mount /dɪsˈmaʊnt/ verb [I] *formal* to get off a horse or bicycle

dis•o•be•di•ence /ˌdɪsəˈbidiəns/ noun [U] behavior in which you refuse to obey orders or rules

dis•o•be•di•ent /ˌdɪsəˈbidiənt/ adj refusing to do what someone in authority has told you to do or to obey orders or rules ≠ OBEDIENT

dis•o•bey /ˌdɪsəˈbeɪ/ verb [I/T] to deliberately not pay attention to a rule or an order from someone in authority = DEFY ≠ OBEY

dis•or•der /dɪsˈɔrdər/ noun **1** [U] a situation in which things are not neat **2** [C/U] *medical* an illness, or a medical condition **3** [U] a situation in which people behave in a noisy or violent way

dis•or•dered /dɪsˈɔrdərd/ adj not neat, or not well organized

dis•or•der•ly /dɪsˈɔrdərli/ adj **1** behaving in a noisy or violent way **2** not neat

dis•or•gan•ized /dɪsˈɔrgəˌnaɪzd/ adj **1** not arranged according to a clear plan or system **2** not good at dealing with things in a clear or sensible way

dis•o•ri•ent /dɪsˈɔriənt/ verb [T] to make someone confused about where they are or what direction they are moving in —**dis•o•ri•en•ta•tion** /dɪsˌɔriənˈteɪʃ(ə)n/ noun [U]

dis•own /dɪsˈoʊn/ verb [T] to say that you no longer want to be connected with someone or something: *I think my parents would disown me if I ever got a tattoo.*

dis•par•ag•ing /dɪˈsperɪdʒɪŋ/ adj showing that you have no respect for someone or something: *disparaging comments*

dis•pa•rate /ˈdɪspərət, dɪˈsperət/ adj *formal* belonging to very different groups or classes

dis•par•i•ty /dɪˈsperəti/ noun [singular/U] *formal* a difference between things

dis•patch[1] /dɪˈspætʃ/ verb [T] *formal* to send someone or something somewhere

dis•patch[2] /dɪˈspætʃ/ noun [C] a report that someone sends from a foreign country

dis•pel /dɪˈspel/ verb [T] to get rid of unpleasant feelings or false beliefs

dis•pen•sa•tion /ˌdɪspənˈseɪʃ(ə)n/ noun [C/U] *formal* official permission to do something that people are not normally allowed to do

dis•pense /dɪˈspens/ verb [T] to provide people with something
PHRASAL VERB **diˈspense with sb/sth** *formal* to stop using someone or something because you no longer want or need them

dis•pens•er /dɪˈspensər/ noun [C] a machine or container from which you can get something such as drinks or money

dis•per•sal /dɪˈspɜrs(ə)l/ noun [U] the process of spreading people or things in different directions over a wide area

dis•perse /dɪˈspɜrs/ verb [I/T] **1** if a crowd of people disperses, or if someone disperses it, the people separate and go in different directions: *Soldiers fired tear gas to disperse the crowds.* **2** to spread in different directions over a wide area, or to make things do this

dis•pir•it•ed /dɪˈspɪrɪtəd/ adj no longer feeling any hope, enthusiasm, or interest

dis•place /dɪsˈpleɪs/ verb [T] **1** to force someone to leave their own country and live somewhere else **2** to take the place of someone or something —**dis•place•ment** /dɪsˈpleɪsmənt/ noun [U]

dis•play[1] /dɪˈspleɪ/ noun [C] ★★
1 an arrangement of things for people to look at: *a window display* ♦ ***a display of*** *exotic plants*
2 a performance for people to look at: *a fireworks display* ♦ ***a display of*** *circus skills*
3 an occasion when someone shows a particular feeling, quality, or attitude: ***Displays of*** *emotion disgusted her.* ♦ *a very public* ***display of*** *Anglo-American unity*
4 a computer screen, or a similar piece of equipment that shows information
PHRASE **on display** if something is on display, it is in a place where it can be seen by many people: *Her work is on display at the gallery.*

dis•play[2] /dɪˈspleɪ/ verb [T] ★★
1 to put something in a particular place so that people can see it easily: *She displayed some of her paintings at the local art exhibit.*
2 to show a feeling, quality, or attitude by the way that you behave: *From an early age he displayed a talent for singing.*
3 to show information on a computer screen

dis•pleased /dɪsˈplizd/ adj *formal* annoyed or angry

dis•pleas•ure /dɪsˈpleʒər/ noun [U] *formal* the feeling of being annoyed or angry

dis•pos•a•ble /dɪˈspoʊzəb(ə)l/ adj designed to be thrown away after being used once or a few times

disˌposable ˈincome noun [U] money that you have left to spend after you have paid your bills

dis•pos•al /dɪˈspoʊz(ə)l/ noun **1** [U] the process of getting rid of something: *the disposal of nuclear waste* **2** [C] *American* a GARBAGE DISPOSAL

PHRASE **at sb's disposal** available for someone to use at any time

dis•pose /dɪˈspoʊz/ PHRASAL VERB **disˈpose of sth** to get rid of something that you no longer need or want: *Please dispose of litter in the containers provided.*

dis•posed /dɪˈspoʊzd/ adj *formal* **1 be disposed to sth** likely to behave or think in a particular way **2 be disposed to do sth** to be willing to do something

dis•po•si•tion /ˌdɪspəˈzɪʃ(ə)n/ noun [singular] the way that someone normally thinks and behaves: *a warm and friendly disposition*

dis•pro•por•tion•ate /ˌdɪsprəˈpɔrʃ(ə)nət/ adj too big or too small in comparison with something else —**dis•pro•por•tion•ate•ly** adv

dis•prove /dɪsˈpruv/ verb [T] to prove that something is not correct or true

dis•pute¹ /dɪˈspjut/ noun [C/U] ★★ a serious disagreement, especially one that involves groups of people and lasts for a long time: *The two companies are still **in dispute**. ♦ a territorial **dispute between** rival gangs ♦ a **dispute over** pay ♦ We got involved in a dispute with the neighbors.*

dis•pute² /dɪˈspjut/ verb **1** [T] to say that something is not true or correct **2** [I/T] to argue about something

dis•qual•i•fi•ca•tion /dɪsˌkwɑlɪfɪˈkeɪʃ(ə)n/ noun [C/U] a situation in which someone is not allowed to take part in something, usually because they have done something wrong

dis•qual•i•fy /dɪsˈkwɑlɪˌfaɪ/ verb [T] to not allow someone to take part in something, usually because they have done something wrong

dis•qui•et /dɪsˈkwaɪət/ noun [U] *formal* a feeling of being very worried or nervous

dis•re•gard¹ /ˌdɪsrɪˈgɑrd/ verb [T] to not think that something is important, or to not pay any attention to it

dis•re•gard² /ˌdɪsrɪˈgɑrd/ noun [singular/U] the attitude of someone who does not respect something or does not think that it is important

dis•re•pair /ˌdɪsrɪˈper/ noun [U] *formal* a broken or damaged state

dis•rep•u•ta•ble /dɪsˈrepjətəb(ə)l/ adj not respected, and thought to be dishonest or illegal

dis•re•pute /ˌdɪsrɪˈpjut/ noun **bring sb/sth into disrepute** *formal* to cause people to stop respecting someone or something

dis•re•spect /ˌdɪsrɪˈspekt/ noun [U] a lack of respect for someone or something —**dis•re•spect•ful** adj

dis•rupt /dɪsˈrʌpt/ verb [T] to interrupt something and prevent it from continuing: *Protesters tried to disrupt the meeting.* —**dis•rup•tion** /dɪsˈrʌpʃ(ə)n/ noun [C/U]

dis•rup•tive /dɪsˈrʌptɪv/ adj causing difficulties that interrupt something and prevent it from continuing —**dis•rup•tive•ly** adv

dis•sat•is•fac•tion /dɪsˌsætɪsˈfækʃ(ə)n/ noun [U] the annoyed feeling that you get when something is not as good as you expected it to be

dis•sat•is•fied /dɪsˈsætɪsˌfaɪd/ adj annoyed because something is not as good as you expected it to be: *a dissatisfied customer*

dis•sect /dɪˈsekt, daɪˈsekt/ verb [T] *technical* to cut the body of a dead person or animal into pieces in order to examine it —**dis•sec•tion** /dɪˈsekʃ(ə)n/ noun [C/U]

dis•sem•i•nate /dɪˈsemɪˌneɪt/ verb [T] *formal* to make something such as information available to a lot of people —**dis•sem•i•na•tion** /dɪˌsemɪˈneɪʃ(ə)n/ noun [U]

dis•sent /dɪˈsent/ noun [U] strong disagreement, especially with what people in authority think or with what the majority of people think —**dis•sent** verb [I]

dis•sent•ing /dɪˈsentɪŋ/ adj expressing strong disagreement, especially with what people in authority think or with what the majority of people think

dis•ser•ta•tion /ˌdɪsərˈteɪʃ(ə)n/ noun [C] a long piece of writing on a particular subject that you do as part of a university degree

dis•serv•ice /dɪˈsɜrvɪs/ noun **do a disservice to sb/sth** *formal* to have a bad effect on someone or something

dis•si•dent /ˈdɪsɪdənt/ noun [C] someone who disagrees publicly with a government —**dis•si•dent** adj

dis•sim•i•lar /dɪˈsɪmɪlər/ adj different from someone or something else

dis•si•pate /ˈdɪsɪˌpeɪt/ verb [I/T] *formal* to gradually disappear by becoming less strong, or to make something do this

dis•so•ci•ate /dɪˈsoʊʃiˌeɪt/ or **dis•as•so•ci•ate** /ˌdɪsəˈsoʊʃiˌeɪt/ verb **dissociate yourself from** to show clearly that you are not connected with someone or something —**dis•so•ci•a•tion** /dɪˌsoʊʃiˈeɪʃ(ə)n/ noun [U]

dis•so•lu•tion /ˌdɪsəˈluʃ(ə)n/ noun [U] the process of officially ending the existence of an organization, institution, or agreement

dis•solve /dɪˈzɑlv/ verb **1** [I/T] if a solid substance dissolves in a liquid, or if you dissolve it, it mixes into the liquid and becomes included in it **2** [T] to officially end the existence of an organization, institution, or agreement

dis•suade /dɪˈsweɪd/ verb [T] *formal* to persuade someone not to do something

dis•tance¹ /ˈdɪstəns/ noun [C/U] ★★★ the amount of space between two people or things: ***the distance from** the Earth **to** the sun ♦ The house is **within walking distance** of the university. ♦ They started to walk the **short distance** to the camp. ♦ We watched the fighting **from a safe distance**.*

PHRASES **at/from a distance** at/from a place that is not close: *I've only ever seen him from a distance.*

in/into the distance at/to a place that is very far from where you are, although you can still see or hear things that are there: *The peaks of the Rockies could be seen in the*

distance. ♦ *He stared into the distance.*
keep your distance to avoid going near someone or something
→ STRIKE[1]

dis•tance[2] /ˈdɪstəns/ verb **distance yourself from** to act in a way that shows that you are not connected with someone or something

D

ˈdistance ˌlearning noun [U] a system in which students work at home and send work to their teachers by mail or e-mail

dis•tant /ˈdɪstənt/ adj ★
1 far away from the place where you are: *the distant sound of traffic* ♦ *stories from distant countries*
2 far away in time: *our ancestors from the **distant past***
3 related, but not in a close way: *a distant relative/cousin*
4 unfriendly or not showing strong feelings: *Laura was cold and distant.*
—**dis•tant•ly** /ˈdɪstəntli/ adv: *distantly related cousins* ♦ *Ivan smiled distantly.*

dis•taste /dɪsˈteɪst/ noun [U] a feeling of dislike for someone or something that you do not approve of

dis•taste•ful /dɪsˈteɪstfəl/ adj unpleasant in a way that upsets or offends you

dis•till /dɪˈstɪl/ verb [I/T] to make a liquid stronger or purer by heating it until it becomes a gas and then making it a liquid again —**dis•til•la•tion** /ˌdɪstɪˈleɪʃ(ə)n/ noun [C/U]

dis•till•er•y /dɪˈstɪləri/ noun [C] a place where strong alcoholic drinks such as WHISKEY are made

dis•tinct /dɪˈstɪŋkt/ adj **1** separate and different in a way that is clear: *The animals were put into two distinct groups.* **2** able to be clearly seen, heard, smelled, or tasted ≠ INDISTINCT: *a distinct smell of burning*
3 definite and obvious: *a distinct disadvantage*

dis•tinc•tion /dɪˈstɪŋkʃ(ə)n/ noun ★
1 [C] a difference between two things: *the clear **distinction between** rich and poor* ♦ *The school does not **make a distinction between** education for girls and boys.*
2 [U] *formal* the excellent skills or features that someone or something has, or the high status that comes from these skills or features: *a writer **of great distinction*** ♦ *She **held the distinction of** being the first woman to edit a national newspaper.*

dis•tinc•tive /dɪˈstɪŋktɪv/ adj easy to recognize because of being different from other people or things of the same type
—**dis•tinc•tive•ly** adv

dis•tinct•ly /dɪˈstɪŋk(t)li/ adv **1** clearly: *I distinctly remember seeing him.* **2** extremely: *Lucy felt distinctly uncomfortable.*

dis•tin•guish /dɪˈstɪŋgwɪʃ/ verb ★
1 [I/T] to recognize the differences between things = DIFFERENTIATE: *He learned to distinguish the songs of different birds.* ♦ *information on how to **distinguish between** the different diseases* ♦ **distinguish sth from sth** *the ability to distinguish right from wrong*
2 [T] to be a feature that makes someone or something clearly different from other similar people or things = DIFFERENTIATE: **distinguish sb/sth from sb/sth** *What distinguished Alex from the rest of us was his exceptional ability as a writer.*
3 [T] *formal* to be able to hear, see, smell, or taste something clearly
PHRASE **distinguish yourself** to do something very well so that people notice and respect you

dis•tin•guish•a•ble /dɪˈstɪŋgwɪʃəb(ə)l/ adj
1 clearly different from other people or things of the same type ≠ INDISTINGUISHABLE
2 easy to see, hear, smell, or taste

dis•tin•guished /dɪˈstɪŋgwɪʃt/ adj successful and respected by many people

dis•tort /dɪˈstɔrt/ verb [T] **1** to change something so that it is no longer true or accurate **2** to change the way that something looks, sounds, or behaves so that it becomes strange or difficult to recognize
—**dis•tor•tion** /dɪˈstɔrʃ(ə)n/ noun [C/U]

dis•tract /dɪˈstrækt/ verb [T] to get someone's attention and prevent them from concentrating on something: *The noise was distracting me.*

dis•tract•ed /dɪˈstræktəd/ adj not able to concentrate on something —**dis•tract•edly** adv

dis•trac•tion /dɪˈstrækʃ(ə)n/ noun [C/U] something that gets your attention and prevents you from concentrating on something else
PHRASE **drive sb to distraction** to annoy someone so much that they become angry or upset

dis•traught /dɪˈstrɔt/ adj extremely worried, upset, or confused

dis•tress[1] /dɪˈstres/ noun [U] **1** a feeling that you have when you are very unhappy, worried, or upset **2** a situation in which a ship or aircraft is in great danger and likely to sink or crash: *a message from a ship in distress* —**dis•tressed** /dɪˈstrest/ adj

dis•tress[2] /dɪˈstres/ verb [T] to make someone feel very unhappy, worried, or upset

dis•tress•ing /dɪˈstresɪŋ/ adj making you feel extremely unhappy, worried, or upset: *distressing news*

dis•trib•ute /dɪˈstrɪˌbjut/ verb [T] ★
1 to give something such as food, clothes, or money to a group of people, especially so that each person gets an equal share: *The two men were distributing antigovernment leaflets.* ♦ **distribute sth to sb** *We distributed beans and corn to the refugees.*
2 to supply goods from one central place: *Hollywood movies are distributed worldwide.*
3 to spread something over an area: *Water beds distribute body pressure much more evenly than conventional beds.*

dis•tri•bu•tion /ˌdɪstrɪˈbjuʃ(ə)n/ noun ★
1 [U] the process of giving something such as food, clothes, or money to a group of people: ***the distribution of** food and clothing in the disaster area*
2 [C/U] the way in which something is shared among people or spread over an area: *Brazil has a very unequal **distribution of** income and wealth.*

3 [U] the process of supplying goods from one central place: *the marketing and distribution of the software*

dis•trib•u•tor /dɪˈstrɪbjətər/ noun [C] a company that supplies goods to stores and businesses

dis•trict /ˈdɪstrɪkt/ noun [C] ★★★
1 an area of a town or country: *They live in one of the most exclusive districts of Paris.* ♦ *the new financial district*
2 one of the areas into which a town or country is divided for official purposes: *Schools in the district continue to perform badly.* ♦ *a district judge*

ˌdistrict atˈtorney noun [C] a lawyer who works for a state or COUNTY government in the U.S. and whose job is to bring people accused of crimes to trial

dis•trust /dɪsˈtrʌst/ noun [U] a feeling that you cannot trust someone or something → MISTRUST —**dis•trust** verb [T]

dis•turb /dɪˈstɜrb/ verb [T] ★★
1 to interrupt someone and stop them from continuing what they were doing: *Sorry to disturb you, but do you know where Miss Springer is?*
2 to upset and worry someone a lot: *We were disturbed by her resignation.*
3 to make something move: *A soft breeze gently disturbed the surface of the pool.*

dis•tur•bance /dɪˈstɜrbəns/ noun [C] **1** an occasion on which people behave in a noisy or violent way in a public place **2** something that interrupts you and stops you from continuing what you were doing

dis•turbed /dɪˈstɜrbd/ adj **1** extremely worried or upset **2** affected by mental or emotional problems

dis•turb•ing /dɪˈstɜrbɪŋ/ adj making you feel extremely worried or upset

ditch¹ /dɪtʃ/ noun [C] a long narrow hole that is dug along the side of a road or field

ditch² /dɪtʃ/ verb [T] *informal* to get rid of someone or something because you no longer like or need them

dith•er /ˈdɪðər/ verb [I] *showing disapproval* to be unable to make a decision about something

dit•zy /ˈdɪtsi/ adj *informal* silly and not reliable

di•va /ˈdivə/ noun [C] a famous female singer, especially of opera

dive¹ /daɪv/ (past tense **dived** or **dove** /doʊv/) verb [I] **1** to jump into water with your head first and with your arms stretched out in front of you **2** to swim UNDERWATER using special equipment so that you can breathe **3** to move quickly and suddenly toward the ground, or in a particular direction: *The plane dove suddenly.* ♦ *She dove for the gun.*

dive² /daɪv/ noun [C] **1** a jump into water with your head first and your arms stretched out in front of you **2** a quick sudden movement toward the ground, or in a particular direction: *The plane lost control and went into a dive.* **3** *informal* a bar or club that is dirty, inexpensive, and unpleasant **4** a sudden fall in the value of something: *The stock market took a dive yesterday.*

div•er /ˈdaɪvər/ noun [C] someone who swims deep under water

di•verge /daɪˈvɜrdʒ/ verb [I] **1** to go in separate directions **2** to develop and become different after being the same

di•ver•gence /daɪˈvɜrdʒəns/ noun [C/U] a difference in the way that two or more things develop from the same thing

di•verse /dɪˈvɜrs, daɪˈvɜrs/ adj very different from each other: *a diverse range of issues*

di•ver•si•fy /dɪˈvɜrsɪfaɪ, daɪˈvɜrsɪfaɪ/ verb [I/T] *business* to develop additional products or activities —**di•ver•si•fi•ca•tion** /dɪˌvɜrsɪfɪˈkeɪʃ(ə)n, daɪˌvɜrsɪfɪˈkeɪʃ(ə)n/ noun [U]

di•ver•sion /dɪˈvɜrʒ(ə)n, daɪˈvɜrʒ(ə)n/ noun **1** [C] something that is intended to take your attention away from something else: *One man created a diversion while the other ran for the door.* **2** [C/U] a change in the use or purpose of something: *a diversion of funds* **3** [C] *formal* an activity that you do for fun

di•ver•si•ty /dɪˈvɜrsəti, daɪˈvɜrsəti/ noun [singular/U] the fact that very different people or things exist within a group or place: *ethnic and cultural diversity*

di•vert /dɪˈvɜrt, daɪˈvɜrt/ verb [T] **1** to take someone's attention away from something: *The state claimed that Cooper was trying to divert attention from his financial problems.* **2** to make something move or travel in a different direction **3** to use something for a purpose that is different from its original or main purpose

di•vest /dɪˈvest, daɪˈvest/ PHRASAL VERB **diˈvest sb of sth** *formal* to take something from someone

di•vide¹ /dɪˈvaɪd/ verb ★★★

1 separate/be separated	4 cause disagreement
2 separate and share	5 in mathematics
3 be in between	+ PHRASAL VERB

1 [I/T] to separate into groups or parts, or to make people or things separate into groups or parts: **divide sth into sth** *Divide the class into three groups.* ♦ *The problem **is divided into** four parts.*
2 [T] to separate something into smaller parts and share the parts between people or things: *Decide how you would like to divide the money.* ♦ **divide sth between/among sb** *After his death his property was divided among his children.* ♦ **divide sth between sth and sth** *She divides her time between teaching and research.*
3 [T] to keep two or more areas or parts separate: **divide sth from sth** *A busy road divides the hotel from the beach.*
4 [T] to be the cause of disagreement between people: *This is a subject that divides the nation.*
5 [I/T] to do a calculation to find out how many times a number contains a smaller number. This is usually shown by the symbol ÷: **divide sth by sth** *Divide 9 by 3.* ♦ *10 divided by 2 is 5.*

PHRASAL VERB **diˌvide sth ˈup 1** *same as* **divide¹** 1: *Divide the children **up into** groups of four.* **2** *same as* **divide¹** 2: *The money will be **divided up between** five different charities.*

di•vide² /dɪˈvaɪd/ noun [C] an important difference or disagreement between people: *a cultural/political divide*

D

D

di,vided 'highway noun [C] *American* a road with two or more LANES (=lines) of traffic going in each direction

div•i•dend /ˈdɪvɪˌdend/ noun [C] a part of the profits of a company that is paid to the people who own the company's STOCK

di•vid•ing line /dɪˈvaɪdɪŋ ˌlaɪn/ noun [singular] something that clearly shows the difference between one thing and another

di•vine /dɪˈvaɪn/ adj relating to a god, or sent by a god

div•ing /ˈdaɪvɪŋ/ noun [U] **1** the activity or sport of swimming deep under water **2** the activity or sport of jumping into water with your head first and your arms stretched out in front of you

di•vin•i•ty /dɪˈvɪnəti/ noun [U] the study of religions and religious belief

di•vi•sion /dɪˈvɪʒ(ə)n/ noun ★★★

1 separation into groups	4 a difference
2 separation & sharing	5 part of organization
3 a disagreement	6 in mathematics

1 [C/U] the process of separating people or things into groups or parts: *The civil war led to a permanent **division of** the country.* ♦ **division of sth into sth** *the division of the land into small fields*

2 [C/U] the process of separating something into parts and sharing it between people: **division of sth between/among sb** *the division of responsibilities among members of the committee*

3 [C/U] a disagreement between people: *deep divisions within the Republican Party*

4 [C] a difference between people: ***the** growing **division between** rich and poor*

5 [C] one of the parts into which a large organization is divided: *the company's electronics division*

6 [C/U] a calculation in mathematics of how many times a number is contained in a larger number

di•vi•sion•al /dɪˈvɪʒ(ə)nəl/ adj relating to a division of an organization

di•vi•sive /dɪˈvaɪsɪv/ adj likely to cause arguments between people

di•vorce¹ /dɪˈvɔrs/ noun [C/U] ★ a legal way of ending a marriage: *I want a divorce.* ♦ *Is it true Tom's **getting a divorce**?* ♦ *Both of her marriages **ended in divorce**.*

di•vorce² /dɪˈvɔrs/ verb **1** [I/T] to take legal action to end your marriage to someone **2** [T] to completely separate one thing from another: *Politics should not be divorced from the lives of ordinary people.*

di•vorced /dɪˈvɔrst/ adj ★ no longer married because your marriage has been legally ended: *a divorced mother of three* ♦ *After they **got divorced**, she never remarried.*

di•vor•cée /dɪˌvɔrˈseɪ/ noun [C] a woman who is divorced

di•vulge /dɪˈvʌldʒ/ verb [T] *formal* to give information about something that should be kept secret

diz•zy /ˈdɪzi/ adj **1** feeling that the things around you are spinning and that you are going to fall **2** feeling excited or confused, or making you feel like this: *We were dizzy with excitement.* —**diz•zi•ness** noun [U]

DJ /ˈdiˌdʒeɪ/ noun [C] disc jockey: someone who plays CDs and records in a club or on the radio

DNA /ˌdi en ˈeɪ/ noun [U] a chemical substance in cells that contains genetic information

do¹ /du/ (3rd person singular **does** /*weak* dəz, *strong* dʌz/; past tense **did** /dɪd/; past participle **done** /dʌn/) verb ★★★

1 for forming questions and negatives [auxiliary verb] used before another verb for forming a question or a negative: *Do you like cheese?* ♦ *What did the doctor say?* ♦ *Didn't they tell you I was coming?* ♦ *I did not know the answer.* ♦ *Max doesn't live here any more.*

In conversation and informal written English the negative forms of the auxiliary verb "do," **does not, do not, did not** are shortened to **doesn't, don't**, and **didn't**.

2 for referring back to a previous verb [I] used instead of repeating the same verb that was used earlier: *"You promised to come with me." "No I didn't."* ♦ *She doesn't travel around as much as I do.* ♦ *I like Chinese food, but George doesn't.* ♦ *"I enjoyed our trip to New Orleans." "So did I."*

3 for emphasis [auxiliary verb] used for emphasizing the meaning of a positive statement: *I've forgotten her name, but I do remember her face.* ♦ *I did lock the door. I'm absolutely sure.*

4 perform an action, activity, or job [T] to perform an action or job, take part in an activity, or complete a piece of work: *I've done something awful.* ♦ *Have you done your math assignment yet?* ♦ *I just need to do my hair* (=brush and arrange it). ♦ ***I do the cooking**, and Peggy washes the dishes.* ♦ *There's **nothing to do** around here.* ♦ *I'm not sure **what she does for a living*** (=what her job is).

5 for talking about health or success [I] used for talking about someone's health, progress, or their general situation: *Hi Sam! How are you doing?* ♦ *He **did well** on the test.*

6 have an effect [T] to have a particular effect on someone or something: *The doctor gave him some special medicine, but it didn't do a lot of good.* ♦ *Frost can **do a lot of damage**.* ♦ **do sth to sth** *What have you done to your hair?* ♦ **do sth to sb** *I'll never forgive him for what he did to me.*

PHRASES **what is sb/sth doing...?** *spoken* used for asking why someone or something is in a particular place: *What's my diary doing on your desk?*

will do used for saying that something is enough or is appropriate for a particular purpose: *If you don't have a bandage, a piece of clean cloth will do.*

PHRASAL VERBS **,do a'way with sth** to get rid of something: *They discussed whether to do away with the agency completely.*

,do sth 'over *American informal* to do something again from the beginning

'do with sth 1 could do with sth *spoken* used for saying that you want or need something: *I could do with a cup of coffee right now.* **2 have something/anything to do with sth** to be connected with something: *The problem* *had something to do with his mother.* **3 have nothing to do with sth** to not be connected with sth: *Her resignation had nothing to do with her health.* **4 what is sb doing with sth?** *spoken* used for asking why someone has something: *What are you doing with my CD player?*

ˌdo withˈout (sb/sth) to succeed in living or working without someone or something: *I couldn't do without my washing machine.*

do² /du/ noun [C] *informal* a social event such as a party

PHRASE **do's and don'ts** instructions and warnings about what you should and should not do in a particular situation

doc·ile /ˈdɑs(ə)l, ˈdɑˌsaɪl/ adj well-behaved and easy to control

dock¹ /dɑk/ noun [C] an area in a port where ships stay while goods are taken on or off or while repairs are done

dock² /dɑk/ verb **1** [I/T] if a ship docks, it arrives at a dock **2** [I/T] if a SPACECRAFT docks, it joins to another spacecraft while they are still in space **3** [T] to take money out of someone's salary as a punishment

dock·ing sta·tion /ˈdɑkɪŋ ˌsteɪʃ(ə)n/ noun [C] *computing* a piece of equipment to which you can connect a PORTABLE computer for a short time, so that you can use it like a PC

dock·yard /ˈdɑkˌjɑrd/ noun [C] a place where ships are built or repaired.

doc·tor¹ /ˈdɑktər/ noun [C] ★★★
1 someone whose job is to treat people who are sick or injured: *Have you seen a doctor yet?* ♦ *Consult your doctor before trying these exercises.* ♦ *Doctor Jones specializes in heart problems.*
2 someone who has the highest degree that a college or university gives: *a doctor of theology* ♦ *The research team is led by Doctor Beth Levinson.*

doc·tor² /ˈdɑktər/ verb [T] to change something in order to get an unfair advantage: *The evidence had been doctored.*

doc·tor·ate /ˈdɑktərət/ noun [C] the highest degree that a college or university gives —**doc·tor·al** adj

doc·trine /ˈdɑktrɪn/ noun [C/U] a set of religious or political beliefs

doc·u·ment¹ /ˈdɑkjəmənt/ noun [C] ★★★
1 a piece of paper or a set of papers containing official information: *He refused to sign the documents.* ♦ *A secret policy document was leaked to the newspapers.*
2 *computing* a computer file that you can write in: *The program will automatically save any documents you have open.*

doc·u·ment² /ˈdɑkjəˌment/ verb [T] **1** to record something in writing or on film: *Her report documents the effects of climate change.* **2** to support something with evidence: *Their allegations are fully documented.*

doc·u·men·ta·ry¹ /ˌdɑkjəˈment(ə)ri/ noun [C] a movie or television program that deals with real people and events

doc·u·men·ta·ry² /ˌdɑkjəˈment(ə)ri/ adj **1** dealing with real people and events: *a documentary film* **2** in the form of documents: *documentary evidence*

doc·u·men·ta·tion /ˌdɑkjumənˈteɪʃ(ə)n/ noun [U] **1** documents that can be used for proving that something is true **2** written instructions about how to use a computer or computer program

dodge /dɑdʒ/ verb **1** [I/T] to avoid someone or something by moving quickly —*picture* → C15 **2** [T] to avoid doing something in a clever or dishonest way: *He tried to dodge the question.* —**dodge** noun [C]

doe /doʊ/ noun [C] a female DEER or RABBIT

does 3rd person singular of the present tense of **do¹**

does·n't /ˈdʌz(ə)nt/ short form the usual way of saying or writing "does not." This is not often used in formal writing: *Sara doesn't live here anymore.*

dog¹ /dɔg/ noun [C] ★★★ an animal kept as a pet, for guarding buildings, or for hunting

dog² /dɔg/ verb [T] **1** to cause trouble for someone over a long period of time: *These rumors had dogged the president for years.* **2** to follow someone closely in a way that annoys them

ˈdog ˌcollar noun [C] **1** a collar around a dog's neck that you can fasten to a LEASH (=a long piece of rope, leather, etc.) **2** a white round collar that is worn by priests in the Christian church

dog-eared /ˈdɑg ˌɪrd/ adj a dog-eared page or book has been used so much that the corners or edges have become damaged or torn

dog·ged /ˈdɔgəd/ adj determined to achieve something despite difficulties =TENACIOUS —**dog·ged·ly** adv

dog·house /ˈdɔghaʊs/ noun [C] *American* a small building for a dog to sleep in

PHRASE **in the doghouse** *informal* if you are in the doghouse, someone is angry with you because you have done something wrong

dog·ma /ˈdɔgmə/ noun [C/U] a belief or set of beliefs that people are expected to accept without asking questions about them

dog·mat·ic /dɔgˈmætɪk/ adj so sure that your beliefs and ideas are right that you expect other people to accept them

do-good·er /ˌdu ˈgʊdər/ noun [C] someone who always tries to help people in a way that is unnecessary or inappropriate

do·ing¹ the present participle of **do**

do·ing² /ˈduɪŋ/ noun **take some doing** to be very difficult to do

ˌdo-it-yourˈself noun [U] the activity of making or repairing things yourself instead of paying someone to do it for you

dol·drums, the /ˈdoʊldrəmz, ˈdɑldrəmz/ noun [plural] a situation in which there is a lack of success, activity, or improvement

dole /doʊl/ PHRASAL VERB **ˌdole sth ˈout** *informal* to give something such as food or money to a group of people

dole·ful /ˈdoʊlfəl/ adj looking sad —**dole·ful·ly** adv

doll /dɑl/ noun [C] a children's toy in the shape of a small person

dol·lar /ˈdɑlər/ noun ★★★
1 [C] the unit of money used in the U.S. and in several other countries such as Canada, Australia, and Singapore. Its symbol is $: *a coat costing one hundred dollars* ♦ *Payment must be in U.S. dollars.*

2 [C] a BILL or coin that is worth a dollar: *a dollar bill*
3 **the dollar** [singular] used for talking about the value of U.S. money, especially in comparison with that of other countries

dol·lop /ˈdɑləp/ noun [C] *informal* a large lump of a soft substance, especially food

dol·phin /ˈdɑlfɪn/ noun [C] a large sea animal, similar to a fish, with a long nose

D

do·main /doʊˈmeɪn/ noun [C] **1** a particular area of activity or life **2** *computing* a DOMAIN NAME

doˈmain ˌname noun [C] an address on the Internet

dome /doʊm/ noun [C] a roof shaped like the top half of a ball —**domed** /doʊmd/ adj: *a domed roof/building*

do·mes·tic /dəˈmestɪk/ adj ★★
1 relating to a particular country: *domestic politics* ♦ *domestic and international flights*
2 relating to people's homes and family life: *domestic chores* ♦ *domestic appliances*
3 enjoying activities relating to your home, such as cooking and taking care of children
4 kept as a pet or on a farm ≠ WILD: *the domestic cat*

do·mes·ti·cat·ed /dəˈmestɪˌkeɪtəd/ adj a domesticated animal has been trained to live with or work for humans

do·mes·tic·i·ty /ˌdoʊmeˈstɪsəti/ noun [U] the activities relating to your home and family life

dom·i·nance /ˈdɑmɪnəns/ noun [U] a situation in which one person or thing has more influence or power than any other: *the growing dominance of the Green Party in the north of the country* ♦ *Japanese dominance of the electronics market*

dom·i·nant /ˈdɑmɪnənt/ adj more important, powerful, or successful than the other people or things of the same type: *The company cannot preserve its dominant position in the market.*

dom·i·nate /ˈdɑmɪˌneɪt/ verb ★★
1 [I/T] to control someone or something by having more power or influence: *She tends to dominate the conversation.*
2 [T] if an object dominates a place, it is so big or high that it is easy to notice: *a little room dominated by a huge fireplace*
3 [I/T] to be the most important aspect or feature of a particular situation: *The earthquake once again dominated the news.*

dom·i·na·tion /ˌdɑmɪˈneɪʃ(ə)n/ noun [U] control or power over other people or things: *the team's domination of football in the 1990s*

dom·i·neer·ing /ˌdɑmɪˈnɪrɪŋ/ adj trying to control other people and make them obey you

do·min·ion /dəˈmɪnjən/ noun *formal* **1** [U] control, or the right to rule over something **2** [C] an area that is ruled by one person or government

dom·i·no /ˈdɑmɪnoʊ/ noun **1 dominoes** [plural] a game in which players take turns to try to place each domino next to another one with the same number of spots on it **2** [C] a small flat piece of wood with spots on it, used in the game of dominoes

don /dɑn/ verb [T] *literary* to put on a piece of clothing

do·nate /ˈdoʊˌneɪt/ verb **1** [I/T] to give something such as money or goods to an organization: *Many big corporations donate to political parties.* **2** [T] to give something such as blood, SPERM, or a part of your body to help someone else

do·na·tion /doʊˈneɪʃ(ə)n/ noun **1** [C] money or goods that you give to an organization: *a generous donation* **2** [C/U] the process of giving something such as blood, SPERM, or a part of your body to help someone else

done[1] /dʌn/ adj **1** finished doing something or using something: *I'm almost done.* **2** if a job is done, it has been finished: *Is the painting done?* **3** cooked long enough to be eaten: *That chicken must be done by now.*
PHRASE **all done** *spoken* used for saying that you have finished doing something

done[2] the past participle of **do**

don·key /ˈdɑŋki/ noun [C] a gray or brown animal like a small horse with long ears —*picture* → C12

do·nor /ˈdoʊnər/ noun [C] **1** someone who gives something such as blood, SPERM, or a part of their body to help someone else **2** someone who gives something such as money or goods to an organization

don't /doʊnt/ short form the usual way of saying or writing "do not." This is not often used in formal writing: *I don't believe you!*

do·nut /ˈdoʊˌnʌt/ an American spelling of **doughnut**

doo·dle /ˈdud(ə)l/ verb [I] to draw patterns or pictures because you are bored or thinking about other things —**doo·dle** noun [C]

doom /dum/ noun [U] a bad event that cannot be avoided such as death, destruction, or complete failure
PHRASE **doom and gloom** a feeling that a situation is very bad and without hope

doomed /dumd/ adj certain to end in death, destruction, or complete failure

door /dɔr/ noun [C] ★★★
1 a large flat object that you open when you want to enter or leave a building, room, or vehicle: *open/close/shut the door* ♦ *the bedroom/car door* ♦ *the back/front/side door* ♦ ***I knocked on the door** and a voice said "Come in."* ♦ *Go and **answer the door*** (=go to see who is there)! ♦ *There's someone **at the door*** (=outside the door to your house). ♦ *We'll **deliver the goods to your door*** (=directly to your house) *within 24 hours.* —*picture* → C1, C6
2 the space created when you open a door = DOORWAY
PHRASE **(from) door to door 1** used for talking about the total length of a trip from the place where you start to the place where you arrive: *It takes two hours door to door.* **2** going to all the houses in an area, trying to sell things or asking for information or votes
→ CLOSED

door·bell /ˈdɔrˌbel/ noun [C] a button near the front door of a house that you press to make a sound to tell the person in the house that you are there —*picture* → C1

door·knob /ˈdɔrˌnɑb/ noun [C] a round handle

on a door that you turn in order to open it

door•man /ˈdɔrmən/ noun [C] someone whose job is to be in charge of the main entrance of a building and help people when they go in or come out

door•mat /ˈdɔrˌmæt/ noun [C] a piece of material on which you clean the SOLES (=bottoms) of your shoes before you go into a building

door•step /ˈdɔrˌstep/ noun [C] a small step outside the main door to a building —*picture* → C1

PHRASE **on your doorstep** very close to where you live

ˌdoor-to-ˈdoor adj **1** going to all the houses in a particular area in order to sell something or ask for information or votes **2** taking someone or something directly from one place to the place they need to go to

door•way /ˈdɔrˌweɪ/ noun [C] the space that is created when you open a door

dope¹ /doʊp/ noun *informal* **1** [C] a stupid person **2** [U] an illegal drug

dope² /doʊp/ verb [T] *informal* **1** to give someone a drug in order to take away their pain or make them sleep **2** to give a person or an animal a drug so that they run faster in a race

dork /dɔrk/ noun [C] *informal* an insulting word for someone that you think is stupid and not fashionable

dorm /dɔrm/ noun [C] *informal* a DORMITORY

dor•mant /ˈdɔrmənt/ adj not active or developing now, but possibly becoming active in the future

dor•mi•to•ry /ˈdɔrmɪˌtɔri/ noun [C] *American* a large building in a college or university, where students live

dos•age /ˈdoʊsɪdʒ/ noun [C/U] the amount of a medicine or drug that you take at one time

dose¹ /doʊs/ noun [C] **1** a particular amount of a drug or medicine that has been measured so that you can take it: *a low dose of painkiller* **2** an amount of something, especially something bad: *I can only put up with Dave in small doses* (=for short periods of time).

dose² /doʊs/ or **ˌdose sb ˈup** verb [T] to give someone an amount of a drug or medicine that has been measured for them to take

dos•si•er /ˈdɑsiˌeɪ/ noun [C] a set of documents about a person or situation

dot¹ /dɑt/ noun [C] **1** a very small spot of ink or color **2** the way you say the symbol . in an Internet or e-mail address **3** something that looks very small because it is far away: *The house was a tiny dot in the valley below.*

PHRASE **on the dot** at exactly the time that you mention: *He arrived at 8 o'clock on the dot.*

dot² /dɑt/ verb [T] **1** to put people or things in many parts of a place: *The company has more than thirty branches dotted around Spain.* **2** to put a dot over a letter of the alphabet **3** to put something, such as paint, on a surface in small amounts with spaces between

dot-com /ˌdɑtˈkɑm/ noun [C] a company that began by selling its products and services only on the Internet —**ˌdot-ˈcom** adj

dote /doʊt/ PHRASAL VERB **ˈdote on sb** to love someone so much that you do not notice their faults

dot•ing /ˈdoʊtɪŋ/ adj a doting relative or friend loves you so much that they do not notice your faults

dot•ted line /ˌdɑtəd ˈlaɪn/ noun [C] a line of small spots of ink that are very close together

PHRASE **sign on the dotted line** to sign a contract or other legal agreement

dou•ble¹ /ˈdʌb(ə)l/ adj ★★

1 consisting of two things or parts: *He went through the double doors.* ♦ *a double murder* ♦ *She suspected his words might have* ***a double meaning*** (=two different meanings).

2 containing or consisting of twice as much as normal: *Sometimes I would work a double shift.* ♦ ***a double helping*** *of mashed potatoes*

3 large enough for two people or things: *a double room/bed/garage*

dou•ble² /ˈdʌb(ə)l/ verb ★

1 [I/T] to become twice as big, twice as much, or twice as many, or to make something do this: *The number of people out of work has doubled in the last five years.* ♦ *The state doubled the tax on liquor.* ♦ *Their house has* ***doubled in value*** *since they bought it.*

2 [T] to fold something so that it has two layers of equal size

PHRASAL VERBS **ˈdouble as sth** to have another use or job as something: *an old couch that doubled as Simon's bed*

ˌdouble ˈback to turn and go back in the direction that you have come from

ˌdouble sth ˈover *same as* **double**² 2: *The map on his desk was doubled over so I couldn't see it.*

ˌdouble (sb) ˈover to bend forward because you are in pain or because you are laughing a lot: **be doubled over with sth** *She was doubled over with pain.*

ˌdouble (sb) ˈup *same as* **double (sb) over**

ˌdouble ˈup as sth *same as* **double as sth**

dou•ble³ /ˈdʌb(ə)l/ noun

1 a drink twice usual size	4 another actor
2 room for two people	5 twice as much money
3 sb looking like sb else	6 game played in pairs

1 [C] an amount of a strong alcoholic drink that is twice the usual amount **2** [C] a room or bed for two people to sleep in **3** [C] someone who looks very similar to another person: *He's his father's double.* **4** [C] an actor who takes the place of another actor when making difficult or dangerous parts of a movie **5** [U] twice as much money: *I get double for working evenings.* **6 doubles** [U] a game such as tennis that is played by pairs of players

dou•ble⁴ /ˈdʌb(ə)l/ determiner twice as much, or twice as many: *He now earns double the amount he used to.*

ˌdouble ˈbass noun [C] a large musical instrument shaped like a VIOLIN that you rest on the floor and play standing up —*picture* → STRINGED INSTRUMENT

ˌdouble ˈbed noun [C] a bed for two people —*picture* → BED

dou•ble-breast•ed /ˌdʌb(ə)l ˈbrestəd/ adj a

D

double-breasted jacket or coat has two parallel lines of buttons down the front when it is fastened

ˌdouble-ˈcheck verb [I/T] to check something for a second time

ˈdouble-ˌclick verb [I/T] *computing* to give an instruction to a computer by quickly pressing the MOUSE twice with your finger —**ˈdouble ˌclick** noun [C]

ˌdouble-ˈcross verb [T] to cheat someone who is helping you to do something dishonest or illegal

dou·ble-deck·er /ˌdʌb(ə)l ˈdekər/ or **ˌdouble-decker ˈbus** noun [C] a bus that has both an upper and a lower level where people can sit

ˌdouble-ˈdigit adj *American* a double-digit number is between 10 and 99

ˌdouble ˈdigits noun [plural] *American* the numbers 10 to 99

ˌdouble ˈlife noun [C] a completely separate way of life that you have some of the time and keep secret from other people

dou·ble-sid·ed /ˌdʌb(ə)l ˈsaɪdəd/ adj able to be used on both sides: *double-sided disks*

ˌdouble ˈstandard noun [C] a rule or principle that is applied to some people but not to others, in a way that is unfair

ˌdouble ˈtake noun **do a double take** to react after a slight pause, because you are surprised by what you have just seen or heard

dou·bly /ˈdʌbli/ adv **1** by a much greater amount, or to a much greater degree than usual **2** for two reasons or in two ways

doubt¹ /daʊt/ noun [C] ★★★ a feeling of not being certain about something: *I have serious **doubts about** whether this system will work.* ♦ ***I have no doubt that** he will succeed.* ♦ ***There's no doubt about it** – we are in trouble.* ♦ *The accident **raises doubts about** (=makes people have doubts about) the safety of the aircraft.* ♦ *She is **without a doubt** one of our most talented students.*

PHRASES **be in doubt 1** if something is in doubt, it is not certain whether it will succeed or continue: *The future of the company is still in doubt.* **2** if you are in doubt about something, you do not know what to do about it

beyond (any) doubt if something is beyond doubt, it is completely certain

if in doubt if you are not certain: used when giving advice: *If in doubt, get someone to help you.*

→ BENEFIT¹

doubt² /daʊt/ verb [T] ★★

1 to think that something is probably not true, probably does not exist, or probably will not happen: *"Do you think they'll win?" "I doubt it."* ♦ *I know a few people doubted my story.* ♦ **+(that)** *I doubt it will work, but we can try.*

2 to feel that you cannot trust or believe someone

doubt·ful /ˈdaʊtfəl/ adj **1** not certain or likely to happen or to be true: *It is doubtful whether he will survive.* **2** not feeling certain about something: *Eddie looked doubtful, but agreed.* —**doubt·ful·ly** adv

dough /doʊ/ noun [C/U] a mixture of flour, water, SHORTENING, etc. that is baked to make bread or PASTRY

dough·nut /ˈdoʊˌnʌt/ noun [C] a sweet food, often in the shape of a ring, that is made by cooking DOUGH in oil

dour /daʊr, dʊr/ adj very serious, and not smiling or friendly

douse /daʊs/ verb [T] **1** to cover someone or something with a liquid **2** to make a fire stop burning by pouring water over it

dove¹ /dʌv/ noun [C] **1** a white bird. Doves are often used as a sign of peace. **2** a politician who wants to use only peaceful methods to solve problems

dove² /doʊv/ *American* the past tense of **dive¹**

dow·dy /ˈdaʊdi/ adj not attractive or fashionable

Dow Jones Av·er·age, the /ˌdaʊ ˈdʒoʊnz ævərɪdʒ/ *trademark* a number that represents an average of the SHARE value of important companies in the U.S.

down¹ /daʊn/ grammar word ★★★

> **Down** can be:
> - a **preposition**: *She was walking down the street.*
> - an **adverb**: *She lay down and fell asleep.*
> - used after the verb "to be": *Oil prices are down.*
> - an **adjective**: *I've been feeling rather down lately.*

1 to or toward a lower place to or toward a lower place, position, or surface: *He slipped on the ice and fell down.* ♦ *Tears were rolling down his cheeks.* ♦ *Get down off that roof!* ♦ *Put the box down on the table.* ♦ *the down escalator*

2 in a lower place in a lower place, or at a lower level: *It was dark and cold down in the cellar.* ♦ *Your name's farther down the list.* ♦ *We could hear noises coming from **down below**.*

3 in or into a sitting or lying position with your body in or moving into a sitting, bending, or lying position: *Why don't you lie down and rest?* ♦ *exercises you can do while you are sitting down*

4 in a direction away from you in or toward a place that is in a direction away from you: *I was walking down the street with a couple of friends.*

5 when sth is reduced at or to a smaller amount or a lower or weaker level than before: *Turn down the radio.* ♦ *Crime is **down 15% from last year**.*

6 when you write sth used for saying that you write something on a piece of paper: *Let me write that down before I forget it.*

7 south in or toward the south: *My mom and dad go down to Florida every winter.*

8 when you eat or drink sth if food or drink goes down, it goes from your mouth to your stomach

9 sad *informal* unhappy: *He's been feeling very down.*

10 losing a game with a lower score than your opponent: *At the end of the first half we were down three points.*

11 not working if a computer system is down, it is not working

12 already done used for saying how many things you have dealt with and how many

more still need to be dealt with: *That's two classes down and four to go.*
PHRASE **down to** used for emphasizing that everyone or everything is included: *Everything had been carefully planned, right down to the last detail.*

down[2] /daʊn/ noun [U] the small soft feathers of a bird

down[3] /daʊn/ verb [T] to drink all of something quickly

ˌdown-and-ˈout adj very poor, with nowhere to live and no job

down•cast /ˈdaʊnˌkæst/ adj **1** sad or upset **2** downcast eyes are looking downward

down•er /ˈdaʊnər/ noun [singular] *informal* something that makes you feel sad or disappointed

down•fall /ˈdaʊnˌfɔl/ noun [singular] a sudden loss of power, status, or success, or something that causes this loss: *bad investments that led to the company's downfall* ♦ *His greed was his downfall.*

down•grade /ˈdaʊnˌgreɪd/ verb [T] **1** to treat something in a way that makes it seem less important than before **2** to move someone to a job that is less important

down•heart•ed /ˌdaʊnˈhɑrtəd/ adj sad and feeling that things will not get better

down•hill /ˌdaʊnˈhɪl/ adv toward the bottom of a hill or slope
PHRASE **go downhill** to get worse
—**down•hill** adj

Down•ing Street /ˈdaʊnɪŋ ˌstrit/ noun [U] the prime minister or the government of the U.K.

down•load[1] /ˈdaʊnˌloʊd/ verb [I/T] *computing* to move information to your computer from a computer system or from the Internet

down•load[2] /ˈdaʊnˌloʊd/ noun [C/U] *computing* the process of downloading information to your computer, or a file that you have downloaded

ˌdown ˈpayment noun [C] a first payment that you make when you buy something and will pay the rest later

down•play /ˈdaʊnˌpleɪ/ verb [T] to deliberately make a situation seem less serious or important than it is = PLAY STH DOWN

down•pour /ˈdaʊnˌpɔr/ noun [C] a large amount of rain that falls quickly = DELUGE

down•right /ˈdaʊnˌraɪt/ adv *informal* completely or extremely: *She was downright mean!* —**down•right** adj

down•side /ˈdaʊnˌsaɪd/ noun [singular] the disadvantage or negative aspect of something ≠ UPSIDE

down•size /ˈdaʊnˌsaɪz/ verb [I/T] *business* to reduce the number of workers in a company or organization

down•stairs[1] /ˌdaʊnˈsterz/ adv ★ to or on a lower floor of a building, especially the floor at ground level ≠ UPSTAIRS: *I ran downstairs.* —**down•stairs** /ˈdaʊnsterz/ adj: *a downstairs window*

down•stairs[2] /ˌdaʊnˈsterz/ noun [singular] the floor of a building that is at ground level ≠ UPSTAIRS

down•stream /ˌdaʊnˈstrim/ adv in the direction that a river or stream is flowing ≠ UPSTREAM

ˈDown ˌsyndrome noun [U] a medical condition that makes someone develop mentally and physically in a different way from most people

ˈdown ˌtime noun [U] **1** time when a computer or other machine is not working **2** time when you can relax and not work

ˌdown-to-ˈearth adj practical and sensible

down•town[1] /ˈdaʊnˌtaʊn/ adj, adv ★ *American* in or near the business or shopping center of a city ≠ UPTOWN: *the streets of downtown Las Vegas* ♦ *Let's go downtown.*

down•town[2] /ˈdaʊnˌtaʊn/ noun [C/U] the business or shopping center of a city

down•trod•den /ˈdaʊnˌtrɑd(ə)n/ adj treated in a cruel or unfair way by someone with power

down•turn /ˈdaʊnˌtɜrn/ noun [C] a reduction in economic or business activity

down•ward[1] /ˈdaʊnwərd/ adv toward a lower place or level ≠ UPWARD
PHRASE **face downward 1** lying on the front of your body **2** lying on the side that normally faces up

down•ward[2] /ˈdaʊnwərd/ adj going toward a lower place or level ≠ UPWARD: *a downward slope/movement*

down•wards /ˈdaʊnwərdz/ adv DOWNWARD

down•wind /ˌdaʊnˈwɪnd/ adj, adv in the same direction that the wind is moving

down•y /ˈdaʊni/ adj covered in very soft small hairs or feathers

dow•ry /ˈdaʊri/ noun [C] money and property that, in some cultures, a woman's family gives to her husband when they get married

doz. abbrev dozen

doze /doʊz/ verb [I] to sleep for a short time, especially during the day
PHRASAL VERB **ˌdoze ˈoff** to start to sleep without intending to

doz•en /ˈdʌz(ə)n/ (plural **doz•en**) determiner **1** a set of 12 things or people: *a dozen red roses* ♦ *We need half a dozen (=six) eggs for the cake.* **2 dozens** [plural] lots of things or people: *Dozens of people were injured.*

Dr. abbrev **1** doctor **2** drive

drab /dræb/ adj not colorful or interesting

draft[1] /dræft/ noun [C] **1** cold air that blows into a room and makes you feel uncomfortable **2** a piece of writing or a drawing that may have changes made to it before it is finished: *a first draft of the letter* **3 the draft** *American* a system in which people are ordered to join the military
PHRASE **on draft** beer that is on draft is served directly from a BARREL

draft[2] /dræft/ verb [T] **1** to write a document, speech, or letter that may have changes made to it before it is finished **2** *American* to order someone to join the military

draft[3] /dræft/ adj draft beer is served directly from a BARREL

draft•y /ˈdræfti/ adj a drafty room or building is uncomfortable because it has cold air blowing through it

drag[1] /dræg/ verb ★

1 pull sth	5 when time seems slow
2 pull sb	6 in computing
3 make sb leave	+ PHRASE
4 touch ground	+ PHRASAL VERBS

D

1 [T] to pull something along with difficulty, especially something heavy: **drag sth down/along/through sth** *She dragged her suitcase to the car.*
2 [T] to pull someone strongly or violently when they do not want to go with you: *I grabbed his arm and dragged him over to the window.*
3 [T] to make someone leave or go to a place when they do not want to: *You dragged me away from my meeting just to tell me this!*
4 [I] if something drags on or along the ground, it touches the ground as you move along, because it is too long or too heavy: *I heard a chain **dragging along the ground**.*
5 [I] if time drags, it seems to pass very slowly
6 [T] *computing* to move something across a computer screen using the MOUSE
PHRASE **drag your feet** to do something very slowly because you do not really want to do it
PHRASAL VERBS **ˌdrag sb ˈinto sth** to make someone become involved in a situation when they do not want to: *The U.S. was afraid of being dragged into the war.*
ˌdrag ˈon to continue for longer than you want or think is necessary: *Some cases drag on for years.*
ˌdrag sth ˈout to make something continue for longer than necessary: *Let's not drag this meeting out any more than we have already.*

drag² /dræg/ noun **1** [singular] *informal* something that is boring or annoying **2** [U] women's clothes worn by a man, or men's clothes worn by a woman **3** [C] an act of breathing in smoke from a cigarette → MAIN DRAG

drag•on /ˈdrægən/ noun [C] in stories, an imaginary large animal that breathes out fire

drag•on•fly /ˈdrægənˌflaɪ/ noun [C] an insect with a long narrow brightly colored body and transparent wings

drain¹ /dreɪn/ verb **1** [I/T] if liquid drains, or if you drain it, it flows away from something: *Put the meat aside to let the fat drain off.* ♦ **drain sth from sth** *Drain the water from the tank.* —*picture* → C2 **2** [T] to get rid of the water in an area of land so that it can be used for other purposes **3** [T] to use so much of someone's energy or strength that they feel very tired

drain² /dreɪn/ noun **1** [C] a pipe or passage through which water or waste liquid flows away **2** [singular] something that uses a lot of something such as money or supplies
PHRASE **down the drain** *informal* completely lost or wasted: *That's three years' work down the drain!*

drain•age /ˈdreɪnɪdʒ/ noun [U] a system of pipes and passages that take away water or waste liquid from an area, or the process of taking this waste away

drain•board /ˈdreɪnˌbɔrd/ noun [C] *American* the place next to the SINK in a kitchen where you leave wet dishes to dry —*picture* → C2

drained /dreɪnd/ adj feeling as though you have no mental or physical energy left

dra•ma /ˈdrɑmə/ noun ★
1 [C] a play for the theater, television, or radio
2 [U] plays in general or as a subject that you study: *He teaches drama.* ♦ *a drama class*
3 [C/U] something unusual or exciting that happens: *a game full of drama*

dra•mat•ic /drəˈmætɪk/ adj ★
1 sudden and surprising, or easy to notice: *a dramatic increase in sales*
2 exciting and impressive: *a dramatic game*
3 dramatic behavior is done to impress other people
4 relating to the theater or plays
—**dra•mat•i•cal•ly** /drəˈmætɪkli/ adv

dra•mat•ics /drəˈmætɪks/ noun [U] the activity of performing plays

dram•a•tize /ˈdræməˌtaɪz/ verb **1** [T] to make a book or story into a play **2** [I/T] to treat a situation as more serious or exciting than it really is —**dram•a•ti•za•tion** /ˌdræmətɪˈzeɪʃ(ə)n/ noun [C/U]

drank the past tense of **drink**

drape /dreɪp/ verb [T] to put something made of cloth over or around something

drapes /dreɪps/ noun [plural] *American* curtains made of heavy cloth

dras•tic /ˈdræstɪk/ adj a drastic action or change has a very big effect —**dras•ti•cal•ly** /ˈdræstɪkli/ adv

draught /dræft/ the British spelling of **draft¹**

draw¹ /drɔ/ (past tense **drew** /dru/; past participle **drawn** /drɔn/) verb ★★★

1 create picture	7 compare two things
2 take money	8 make sb notice sth
3 choose sb/sth	9 get particular reaction
4 move slowly/smoothly	+ PHRASES
5 pull sth	+ PHRASAL VERBS
6 get information from	

1 [I/T] to create a picture by making lines with a pen or pencil: *I can't draw faces very well.* ♦ *The kids **drew on the sidewalk with** chalk.*
2 [T] to take money from a bank account: *Customers can **draw** up to $250 a day **from** most accounts.*
3 [T] to choose someone or something from a group of similar things: *Elliot's name was drawn from over 200 entries.* ♦ *I **drew** two cards **from** the pack.*
4 [I] to move somewhere slowly or smoothly: *As we **drew nearer**, I noticed that the front door was open.*
5 [T] to pull something somewhere: *He drew a handkerchief out of his pocket.* ♦ *The curtains were still drawn at noon.*
6 [T] to get ideas, information, or knowledge from somewhere: **draw sth from sth** *She drew inspiration for her stories from her childhood.*
7 [T] to consider the ways in which two things are different or similar: *The writer drew comparisons between the two societies.*
8 [T] to make someone notice something: *My eyes were drawn to a painting over the fireplace.* ♦ *We tried to get in without **drawing attention to ourselves**.*
9 [T] to get a particular reaction from people: *The new exhibit has been drawing a lot of criticism.*

PHRASES **draw a blank** to fail to find something, or to be unable to remember something
draw blood to make someone BLEED
draw a conclusion to decide what you believe about something after you have thought about all the facts
draw the line *informal* to say that you will definitely not allow or accept something: *I draw the line at breaking the law.*
draw to a close/an end to end

PHRASAL VERBS **ˈdraw on sth** to use something that you have gained or saved: *As an actor, you often draw on your own life experiences.*
ˌdraw sth ˈout to make something continue for longer than usual
ˌdraw sth ˈup to prepare and write something such as a document or plan: *Guidelines have been drawn up for dealing with emergencies.*
ˈdraw uˌpon sth *same as* **draw on sth**

draw² /drɔ/ noun [C] a way of choosing something such as a name or number by chance

draw·back /ˈdrɔˌbæk/ noun [C] a feature of something that makes it less useful than it could be: *The main drawback of the plan is its expense.*

draw·er /drɔr/ noun [C] ★ a part of a piece of furniture that slides in and out and is used for keeping things in —*picture* → C2

draw·ing /ˈdrɔɪŋ/ noun ★★
1 [C] a picture that someone has drawn: *The children did **drawings of** themselves.*
2 [U] the activity or skill of making pictures with a pen or pencil: *I'm not very good at drawing.*

ˈdrawing ˌboard noun **go back to the drawing board** to try to think of a completely new idea because the one that you tried before was not successful

drawl /drɔl/ noun [singular] a slow way of speaking, with long vowel sounds —**drawl** verb [I/T]

drawn¹ /drɔn/ adj looking very tired, sick, or worried

drawn² /drɔn/ the past participle of **draw**

ˌdrawn-ˈout adj continuing for a long time so that you become bored: *a long-drawn out explanation*

dread¹ /dred/ verb [T] to feel very worried about something that will or could happen: *She started to dread seeing him.*
PHRASE **I dread to think** *spoken* used for saying that you are worried about a situation: *I dread to think what the operation will cost.*

dread² /dred/ noun [singular/U] fear of something bad that will or could happen: *The thought of making a speech fills me with dread.*

dread·ed /ˈdredəd/ adj *often humorous* a dreaded event, person, or thing is one that you do not want to happen or to see

dread·ful /ˈdredfəl/ adj very unpleasant —**dread·ful·ly** adv

dread·locks /ˈdredˌlɑks/ noun [plural] twisted pieces of long hair, worn especially by RASTAFARIANS

dream¹ /drim/ noun [C] ★★★
1 something that you experience in your mind while you are sleeping: *I **had a** strange **dream** last night.* ♦ *The idea came to him **in a dream**.*
2 something good that you hope that you will have or will achieve in the future: *a dream job/vacation/home* ♦ *She watched her **dreams of** success fade away.* ♦ *Finding my father again was **a dream come true*** (=something that you really wanted to happen).
PHRASES **beyond your (wildest) dreams** much better than you imagined or hoped
go/work like a dream to happen in the best way possible

dream² /drim/ (past tense and past participle **dreamed**) verb [I/T] ★★
1 to experience things in your mind while you are sleeping: *I was **dreaming about** a black cat.* ♦ **+(that)** *He dreamed that he saw Rosa.*
2 to think about something that you hope to do: **dream of doing sth** *She had always dreamed of going to Africa.*
PHRASE **would not dream of doing sth** used for emphasizing that you would definitely

not do something: *I wouldn't dream of asking him for money.*
PHRASAL VERB ˌ**dream sth ˈup** to think of a new idea

dream·er /ˈdrimər/ noun [C] someone who has a lot of ideas, but not very sensible ones

dreamt a past tense and past participle of **dream**

D

dream·y /ˈdrimi/ adj showing that you are thinking about something pleasant rather than paying attention: *a dreamy look*

drea·ry /ˈdrɪri/ adj making you feel bored or unhappy: *dreary weather*

dredge /dredʒ/ verb [T] to remove dirt from the bottom of a river or lake, often in order to look for something
PHRASAL VERB ˌ**dredge sth ˈup** to tell people a secret from someone's past that they do not want other people to know about

dregs /dregz/ noun [plural] *informal* the least important or valuable part of something: *the dregs of society*

drench /drentʃ/ verb [T] to make someone or something very wet —**drenched** /drentʃt/ adj

dress¹ /dres/ verb ★★★
1 [I] to wear clothes of a particular type: *He tends to* ***dress in*** *dark colors.* ♦ *The nurses* ***dressed as*** *clowns for Halloween.*
2 [I] to put clothes on yourself or on someone else: *It only took her ten minutes to shower and dress.*
3 [T] to clean an injury and cover it with a piece of soft cloth
PHRASAL VERB ˌ**dress ˈup 1** to put on clothes that make you look like someone else, for fun: *They had* ***dressed up as*** *princes and princesses.* **2** to put on clothes that are more formal than the clothes that you usually wear: *Do I have to dress up for dinner?*

dress² /dres/ noun ★★
1 [C] a piece of clothing that covers a woman's body and part of her legs: *a blue cotton dress* —*picture* → C4
2 [U] the type of clothes that are typical of a particular place, time in history, or occasion: *traditional Norwegian dress*
→ CLOTHES

dressed /drest/ adj **1** wearing clothes of a particular type: *She was dressed in a black suit.* ♦ *a well-dressed man* **2** someone who is dressed is wearing clothes ≠ UNDRESSED: *Just a minute, I'm not dressed yet.*
PHRASE **get dressed** to put your clothes on: *I got dressed and went downstairs.*

dress·er /ˈdresər/ noun [C] *American* a piece of bedroom furniture with a lot of drawers

dress·ing /ˈdresɪŋ/ noun **1** [C/U] a mixture of liquids that you pour over salad **2** [C/U] *American* STUFFING that you put inside meat **3** [C] a piece of material that is used for protecting a skin injury

ˈ**dressing ˌroom** noun [C] **1** a small room in a clothing store for trying on clothes **2** a room that is used by a performer or sports players for preparing for a performance or game

ˈ**dress reˌhearsal** noun [C] the last occasion when performers practice before a concert, play, etc.

dress·y /ˈdresi/ adj dressy clothes are worn on formal occasions

drew the past tense of **draw¹**

drib·ble /ˈdrɪb(ə)l/ verb [I/T] **1** if a liquid dribbles, or if you dribble it, it flows slowly in small drops **2** to move forward with a ball by BOUNCING or kicking it —*picture* → C15 —**drib·ble** noun [C/U]

dried /draɪd/ adj dried food, milk, or flowers have had the water removed from them

drift¹ /drɪft/ verb [I] **1** to be pushed along slowly by the movement of air or water: *The boat started to drift out to sea.* **2** to do something or happen in a way that is not planned: *I just drifted into nursing really.* **3** to move somewhere slowly as though you do not know where you are going: *For three months, Paul drifted from town to town.* **4** if snow or sand drifts, the wind blows it into a large pile
PHRASAL VERBS ˌ**drift aˈpart** if two or more people drift apart, their relationship gradually ends
ˌ**drift ˈoff** to start to sleep

drift² /drɪft/ noun **1** [C] a large pile of snow or sand that has been formed by the wind **2** [singular] *informal* the meaning that someone is trying to express: *Do you get my drift?* **3** [singular] a slow gradual change or movement

drill¹ /drɪl/ noun **1** [C] a tool that is used for making a hole in something —*picture* → TOOL **2** [C/U] a way of teaching people something by making them repeat it several times

drill² /drɪl/ verb **1** [I/T] to make a hole using a drill: *Drill two holes in the wall.* **2** [T] to teach someone by making them repeat something many times

dri·ly /ˈdraɪli/ adv in a way that expresses humor while appearing to be serious

drink¹ /drɪŋk/ (past tense **drank** /dræŋk/; past participle **drunk** /drʌŋk/) verb ★★★
1 [I/T] to take liquid into your body through your mouth: *Drink your orange juice, Thomas.* ♦ *Rosie* ***drank*** *thirstily* ***from*** *the mug.* → TAKE
2 [I] to drink alcohol, especially regularly or too often: *Dan had been out drinking with his friends.* ♦ *My parents don't drink.*
PHRASAL VERBS ˈ**drink to sb/sth** to express a

wish for health, happiness, or success, then lift your glass and drink from it: *We will now **drink a toast to** the bride and groom.*

ˌdrink (sth) ˈup to drink all of your drink

drink² /drɪŋk/ noun [C/U] ★★★

1 an amount of liquid that someone drinks, or drinks in general: *They had had no food or drink all day.* ♦ *I need **a drink of** water.*

2 an alcoholic drink, or alcohol in general: *We **went for a drink** after work.*

drink·er /ˈdrɪŋkər/ noun [C] **1** someone who often drinks alcohol: *a heavy drinker* (=someone who drinks a lot of alcohol) **2** someone who often drinks a particular drink: *tea/beer/wine drinker*

drink·ing /ˈdrɪŋkɪŋ/ noun [U] the activity of drinking alcohol

ˈdrinking ˌwater noun [U] water that is safe to drink

drip¹ /drɪp/ verb **1** [I/T] if a liquid drips, or if you drip it somewhere, it falls in very small drops: *Red paint had dripped on the floor.* **2** [I] to produce small drops of liquid: *The faucet was dripping.*

drip gush

drip² /drɪp/ noun [C] a small drop of liquid that falls from something, or the sound or action of it falling

drip·ping /ˈdrɪpɪŋ/ adj very wet

drive¹ /draɪv/ (past tense **drove** /droʊv/; past participle **driv·en** /ˈdrɪv(ə)n/) verb ★★★

1 control vehicle	6 force into bad state
2 take sb in vehicle	7 make sb determined
3 provide power to move	+ PHRASE
4 push sth strongly	+ PHRASAL VERBS
5 force sb to leave	

1 [I/T] to control a vehicle so that it moves somewhere, or to go somewhere by doing this: *Usually, my sister drives and I read the map.* ♦ *Please **drive carefully**.* ♦ *He **drove along** for several miles before he saw anyone.* ♦ *We're **driving to** Florida this year.*

2 [T] to take someone somewhere in a vehicle that you drive: **drive sb to/from sth** *Lee drove me to the airport.*

3 [T] to provide the power that makes something move: *The pump is driven by an electric motor.*

4 [T] to push, hit or kick something using a lot of force: *He drove the nail into the wall.*

5 [T] to force someone to leave the place where they live: **drive sb from/out of sth** *Thousands of people have been driven from their homes by the fighting.*

6 [T] to force someone or something into a bad situation or state: *Supermarkets are driving small stores out of business.* ♦ *Would you be quiet – you're **driving me crazy**!*

7 [T] to make someone determined to do something: *What drives her to succeed?*

PHRASE **drive a hard bargain** to be very firm when you are making an agreement or a deal

PHRASAL VERBS **ˌdrive sb aˈway** to make someone stop wanting something: *Increasing your prices will only drive customers away.*

ˌdrive ˈoff 1 if a vehicle or driver drives off, the vehicle starts moving and leaves **2** to force someone to go away, especially when they are attacking or threatening you

- **Drive** means to move and control a vehicle such as a car or truck: *Do you walk or drive to work?* ♦ *He drives a bus.*
- **Ride** means to move and control a bicycle or horse. You can also **ride** in a vehicle that is controlled by someone else: *She rides her bike to school.* ♦ *We rode all over town on the bus.*

drive² /draɪv/ noun ★★

1 trip in car	6 power from engine
2 part of computer	7 gear position
3 feeling causing action	8 hard hit/kick of ball
4 determination	9 wide path for car
5 effort to achieve sth	

1 [C] a trip in a car: *The hotel is only 10 minutes' drive from the airport.* ♦ *We **went for a drive** in Jack's new car.*

2 [C] *computing* a part of a computer that reads and stores information: *a disk/hard/CD-ROM drive*

3 [C] a feeling that makes you act in a particular way: *the human sex drive*

4 [U] the energy and determination that makes you try hard to achieve something: *I admire her drive and ambition.*

5 [C] a big effort to achieve something, especially by a company or government: *The company is launching a major recruitment drive.*

6 [U] the power from an engine that turns the wheels of a vehicle: *front-wheel drive*

7 [U] the position of the gears in an AUTOMATIC car, that lets the car move forward

8 [C] a hard hit or kick of a ball

9 [C] *British* a DRIVEWAY

ˈdrive-ˌby noun [C] an act of shooting someone from a moving car —**ˈdrive-ˌby** adj

ˈdrive-ˌin noun [C] *American* a movie theater or restaurant where you sit in your car to watch a movie or eat a meal —**ˈdrive-ˌin** adj

driv·el /ˈdrɪv(ə)l/ noun [U] stupid and unimportant things that someone says or writes

driv·en the past participle of **drive¹**

driv·er /ˈdraɪvər/ noun [C] ★★★ someone who drives a vehicle, especially as their job: *a taxi driver*

ˈdriver's ˌlicense noun [C] *American* an official card that you need in order to drive

ˈdrive-ˌthrough noun [C] a restaurant, bank, etc. that serves you through a special window, so that you do not have to leave your car —**ˈdrive-ˌthrough** adj

drive·way /ˈdraɪvˌweɪ/ noun [C] a wide path for a car that joins someone's house to a street —*picture* → C1

D

driv·ing /ˈdraɪvɪŋ/ adj **1** driving snow or rain falls very fast **2** having a strong influence, or making something happen: *Williams was the driving force behind the business.*

driz·zle /ˈdrɪz(ə)l/ noun [singular/U] very light rain —**driz·zle** verb [I]

drone¹ /droʊn/ verb [I] to make a low continuous noise
PHRASAL VERB ˌ**drone ˈon** to talk about something for a long time in a very boring way

drone² /droʊn/ noun [singular] a low continuous sound

drool /drul/ verb [I] **1** to let SALIVA (=the liquid in your mouth) come out of your mouth **2** to look at someone or something with great pleasure

droop /drup/ verb [I] to hang downward: *The leaves were drooping in the heat.*

drop¹ /drɑp/ verb ★★★

1 let sth fall	5 not include sth/sb
2 fall	6 speak less loudly
3 reduce/get less	+ PHRASES
4 not continue with sth	+ PHRASAL VERBS

1 [T] to let something fall: *The box was so heavy I almost dropped it.* ♦ **drop sth off sth** *The children were dropping stones off the bridge.* ♦ **drop sth into sth** *He dropped a few coins into my hand.*
2 [I] to fall: *She took off her jacket and let it drop to the floor.* ♦ *Everyone cheered as the ball* ***dropped into*** *the hole.* ♦ *Teresa* ***dropped into*** *the chair, exhausted.*
3 [I/T] to reduce the amount or rate of something, or to fall to a lower amount or rate: *We had to drop the price of our house to sell it.* ♦ *In the winter the temperature often* ***drops below*** *freezing.*
4 [T] to stop doing something: *I decided to drop chemistry and take biology instead.* ♦ *He told me to* ***drop everything*** *and come over right away.* ♦ *To her relief, Julius* ***dropped the subject*** (=stopped talking about it).
5 [T] to not include something or someone: *Rogers has been* ***dropped from*** *the team because of a knee injury.*
6 [I/T] if you drop your voice, or if your voice drops, you speak less loudly
PHRASES **drop the ball** *American* to fail to do something that other people expected you to do
drop dead *informal* to die suddenly and unexpectedly: *He dropped dead of a heart attack.*
drop a hint/hints to say something in an indirect way
drop sb a line/note to write a short letter to someone
→ FLY²
PHRASAL VERBS ˌ**drop ˈback** or ˌ**drop ˈbehind** to start walking, running, driving, etc. behind other people in a group or race
ˌ**drop ˈby** or ˌ**drop ˈin** *informal* to make a short visit somewhere: *Why don't you drop by for coffee some time?*
ˌ**drop sb ˈoff** to take someone to a place in a car: *Can you drop the kids off at school this morning?*
ˌ**drop ˈoff** to become weaker or smaller in amount: *Her popularity has dropped off recently.*
ˌ**drop sth ˈoff** to take something to a place and not stay there very long: *Can I drop the documents off later?*
ˌ**drop ˈout** to leave something before you have finished what you intended to do: *Too many students* ***drop out of*** *college after only one year.*

drop² /drɑp/ noun [C] ★
1 a very small amount of liquid with a round shape: *a tear drop* ♦ *There were* ***drops of*** *blood on his arm.*
2 a fall in the amount or value of something: *The company announced a 15% drop in profits.* ♦ *There was* ***a sharp drop*** *in temperature overnight.*
3 a distance down to the ground from a high place: *At the edge of the cliff is a 100-foot drop.*
PHRASES **at the drop of a hat** immediately
a drop in the bucket a very small amount that will not have much effect

ˈ**drop-down** ˌ**menu** noun [C] *computing* a list of choices on your computer screen that goes away when you choose one

drop·let /ˈdrɑplət/ noun [C] a very small drop of liquid

drop·out /ˈdrɑpˌaʊt/ noun [C] someone who leaves school or college without finishing their course of study

drop·pings /ˈdrɑpɪŋz/ noun [plural] the FECES (=solid waste) of animals or birds

drought /draʊt/ noun [C/U] a long period of time when there is little or no rain

drove the past tense of **drive¹**

drown /draʊn/ verb ★
1 [I] to sink under water and die: *Thirty people drowned when the boat sank in a storm.*
2 [T] to kill someone by pushing them under water
3 [T] to cover something completely with a liquid: *shellfish drowned in a spicy sauce*
4 [T] *same as* **drown sth out**
PHRASAL VERB ˌ**drown sth ˈout** to prevent a sound from being heard by making a louder noise: *The music almost drowned out the sound of his voice.*

drows·y /ˈdraʊzi/ adj feeling that you want to sleep —**drows·i·ly** adv

drudg·er·y /ˈdrʌdʒəri/ noun [U] boring and unpleasant work

drug¹ /drʌg/ noun [C] ★★★
1 an illegal substance that affects someone physically or mentally when they put it into their body: *drug smuggling* ♦ *a drug addict* (=someone who cannot stop using illegal drugs) ♦ *She had never* ***taken drugs*** *in her life.* ♦ *He acted like he was* ***on drugs*** (=had taken drugs).
2 a substance that a doctor gives you in order to treat a disease or medical problem: *Your doctor may prescribe drugs for this condition.* ♦ *a new anti-cancer drug*

drug² /drʌg/ verb [T] to give a drug to someone so that they will go to sleep or become unconscious

ˈ**drug** ˌ**lord** noun [C] *American* a powerful person that buys and sells illegal drugs

drug·store /ˈdrʌgˌstɔr/ noun [C] *American* a store that sells medicines, beauty products, and other goods = PHARMACY

D

drum¹ /drʌm/ noun [C] ★
1 a musical instrument that consists of a tight skin stretched over a round frame. You hit it with your hands or a stick. —*picture* → PERCUSSION
2 a large round container for liquids: *an oil drum*

drum² /drʌm/ verb **1** [I] to play a drum **2** [I/T] to make a continuous sound by hitting a surface —**drum•ming** noun [U]
PHRASAL VERBS ˌ**drum sth ˈinto sb** to make someone learn or understand something by repeating it many times
ˌ**drum sth ˈup** to try to make people support you or buy something from you: *They've been in London trying to drum up business.*

drum•mer /ˈdrʌmər/ noun [C] someone who plays drums

drunk¹ /drʌŋk/ adj ★ unable to control your actions or behavior because you have drunk too much alcohol ≠ SOBER: *Everyone else was **getting drunk** and enjoying themselves.*

drunk² /drʌŋk/ noun [C] *showing disapproval* someone who has drunk too much alcohol or who regularly drinks too much alcohol

drunk³ the past participle of **drink¹**

drunk•ard /ˈdrʌŋkərd/ noun [C] *showing disapproval* a DRUNK

ˌ**drunk ˈdriving** or ˌ**drunken ˈdriving** noun [U] *American* driving when you have drunk too much alcohol

drunk•en /ˈdrʌŋkən/ adj *showing disapproval* **1** a drunken person is drunk **2** involving or affecting someone who is drunk —**drunk•en•ly** adv, **drunk•en•ness** noun [U]

dry¹ /draɪ/ adj ★★★

1 with no water in/on it	5 food: with little liquid
2 without rain	6 joking in serious way
3 no longer liquid	7 boring/serious
4 hair/skin: rough	8 without alcohol

1 something that is dry has little or no water or other liquid inside or on it ≠ WET: *Are your hands dry?* ♦ *Vegetables should be stored in a cool dry place.*
2 with no rain ≠ WET: *warm dry places like southern Spain* ♦ *The weather is usually **dry and sunny** at this time of year.*
3 when a liquid such as paint is dry, it has become hard or solid ≠ WET: *Someone walked on the concrete before it was dry.*
4 dry hair or skin feels rough ≠ GREASY
5 dry food contains little or no liquid: *The chicken was overcooked and dry.* ♦ *dry bread*
6 dry humor involves saying funny things in a serious way
7 very serious and boring: *The style was a little too dry for a children's book.*
8 a dry place does not allow alcohol to be sold there
—**dry•ness** noun [U]

dry² /draɪ/ verb ★★
1 [T] to remove the water from something by wiping it, heating it, or blowing air onto it: *We washed and dried all the sheets.* ♦ *Dry your hands on this towel.*
2 [I] to become dry: *I usually let my hair dry naturally.*
3 [I] when a liquid such as paint dries, it becomes hard or solid: *Leave the varnish to dry overnight.*
4 [T] to remove the water from food or plants as a way of preserving them: *dried fruit/herbs/flowers*
→ CUT¹
PHRASAL VERBS ˌ**dry (yourself/sth) ˈoff** if something dries off, or if you dry it off, all the water comes out of it or is wiped from its surface: *My boots dried off in the sun.* ♦ *He got out of the shower and dried himself off.*
ˌ**dry (sth) ˈout** if something dries out, or if it is dried out, some or all the water comes out of it: *Water the plant regularly to stop the soil from drying out.*
ˌ**dry ˈup** to stop being available: *What will happen when the money dries up?*
ˌ**dry (sth) ˈup** if something dries up, or if it is dried up, all the water comes out of it: *The land had dried up and no crops would grow.*

ˌ**dry-ˈclean** verb [T] to clean clothes using chemicals rather than water

ˌ**dry ˈcleaner's** noun [singular] a store where you take your clothes to be dry-cleaned

dry•er /ˈdraɪr/ noun [C] a machine that dries things such as clothes

ˌ**dry ˈland** noun [U] land, rather than the ocean

dry•ly /ˈdraɪli/ another spelling of **drily**

DSL noun [U] *computing* digital subscriber line: a way of connecting to the Internet that allows a very fast exchange of information using ordinary phone connections

du•al /ˈduəl/ adj with two aspects, parts, or uses: *a dual role*

dub /dʌb/ verb [T] **1** *mainly journalism* to give someone or something a particular name: *The press have dubbed her "the Silent Star."* **2** to change the sound in a movie by replacing the original speech with words spoken in a different language

du•bi•ous /ˈdubiəs/ adj **1** not sure about something: *I'm dubious about his ability to do the job.* **2** not completely good, safe, or honest: *a dubious reputation* **3** used for saying that something is the opposite of the good thing that you are describing it as: *a dubious honor/pleasure/distinction* —**du•bi•ous•ly** adv

duch•ess /ˈdʌtʃəs/ noun [C] a woman who has the same position as a DUKE, or the wife of a duke

duck¹ /dʌk/ noun **1** [C] a water bird with short legs and a large flat beak —*picture* → C12 **2** [U] the meat of a duck

duck² /dʌk/ verb **1** [I/T] to lower your head and body quickly, in order to move under something or to avoid being hit: *He ducked to avoid the blow.* **2** [T] to avoid something that is difficult: *Stop trying to duck the issue – who paid you for this?* **3** [I] to move quickly into or behind something to avoid being seen: *She ducked behind the wall.*

duck•ling /ˈdʌklɪŋ/ noun [C] a young duck

duct /dʌkt/ noun [C] **1** a narrow tube inside your body that carries liquid: *tear ducts* **2** a tube in a building that carries air or protects wires: *air-conditioning ducts*

dud /dʌd/ noun [C] **1** a bomb or other EXPLOSIVE object that fails to explode **2** *informal* something that does not work correctly or is disappointing

dude /dud/ noun [C] *American informal* a man

due¹ /du/ adj ★★★
1 expected to happen or to be somewhere: *Her baby is due in May* (=expected to be born). ♦ *I'm due at a meeting in ten minutes.* ♦ **due to do sth** *The case is due to go to court next month.* ♦ *The prisoners are not* ***due for*** *release until next year.*
2 if money is due, it is time for it to be paid: *The rent is due on the first day of each month.*
3 according to the usual standards or rules: *A driver has to have* ***due regard for*** *the safety of other road users.*
4 if something is due to someone, they should receive it: *Some* ***credit is due to*** *the government for this improvement.*
PHRASES **in due course** *formal* later, when it is the right time, and not before
with (all) due respect used when you are going to disagree with someone or criticize someone, in order to sound more polite
→ DUE TO

due² /du/ noun **to give sb their due** used when you are going to say something good about someone, after you have been criticizing them → DUES

due³ /du/ adv **due north/south/east/west** directly toward the north, south, east, or west

du•el /ˈduəl/ noun [C] **1** *mainly journalism* a competition or fight between two people or teams **2** a fight between two men with guns or swords —**duel** verb [I]

ˌdue ˈprocess noun [U] *American legal* the correct way of dealing with legal matters

dues /duz/ noun [plural] money that someone pays regularly to be a member of a club or union

du•et /duˈet/ noun [C] a piece of music that is sung or played by two people

due to /ˈdu tu/ preposition ★★★ because of something: *We had problems due to poor management.* ♦ *These fears are usually due to ignorance.*

dug the past tense and past participle of **dig¹**

dug•out /ˈdʌɡˌaʊt/ noun [C] **1** a hole or tunnel in the ground, used as a shelter by soldiers during a battle **2** a small shelter by the side of a sports field

duh /dɜr/ interjection *informal* used for saying that you think something that someone has said or done is stupid

DUI /ˌdi ju ˈaɪ/ abbrev *American* Driving Under the Influence: the crime of driving after you have drunk too much alcohol

duke /duk/ noun [C] a man with a very high social position, just below that of a PRINCE

dull¹ /dʌl/ adj

1 boring	4 low and not clear
2 not bright/shiny	5 not sharp
3 weak and continuous	

1 boring, or not interesting **2** not bright or shiny **3** a dull pain is not very strong but continues for a long time **4** a dull sound is low and not very clear **5** a dull blade is not sharp

dull² /dʌl/ verb [T] to make something slower or weaker: *The drug is used to dull the pain.*

du•ly /ˈduli/ adv *formal* in a way that is correct or appropriate

dumb¹ /dʌm/ adj *informal* stupid

dumb² /dʌm/ PHRASAL VERB **ˌdumb (sth) ˈdown** to spoil something by trying to make it easier to understand or more popular

dumb•found•ed /dʌmˈfaʊndəd/ adj so surprised that you do not know what to do or say

dum•my¹ /ˈdʌmi/ noun [C] **1** something that is made to look like a real object **2** a model of a person's body **3** *informal* someone who is not very intelligent

dum•my² /ˈdʌmi/ adj designed to look real but in fact not real: *a dummy corporation*

dump¹ /dʌmp/ verb [T] **1** *informal* to put something somewhere in a careless way: *She dumped her bags on the floor.* **2** to get rid of something that you no longer want or need: *Waste chemicals were being dumped into the ocean.* **3** *informal* to end a sexual or romantic relationship with someone in an unkind way

dump² /dʌmp/ noun [C] **1** a place where large amounts of garbage are taken **2** *informal* a place that is dirty or unpleasant
PHRASE **(down) in the dumps** *informal* feeling unhappy

dump•ling /ˈdʌmplɪŋ/ noun [C] a small solid lump of cooked food made from flour and water

Dump•ster /ˈdʌmpstər/ *American trademark* a very large metal container used for garbage

dune /dun/ noun [C] a hill of sand that has been formed by the wind or sea = SAND DUNE

dung /dʌŋ/ noun [U] waste from the body of a large animal

dun•geon /ˈdʌndʒən/ noun [C] a dark underground room in a castle that was used as a prison in the past

dunk /dʌŋk/ verb [T] **1** to put something into liquid for a short time before taking it out again **2** to throw the ball downward into the basket during a game of basketball —*picture* → C15

du•o /ˈduˌoʊ/ noun [C] two people who perform together or do something else together

dupe /dup/ verb [T] to trick someone into believing or doing something stupid or illegal

du•plex /ˈduˌpleks/ noun [C] *American* a house that is joined to another house on one side

du•pli•cate¹ /ˈduplɪˌkeɪt/ verb [T] **1** to make an exact copy of something such as a document **2** to create a situation that is exactly like another one

du•pli•cate² /ˈduplɪkət/ adj made as an exact copy of something else —**du•pli•cate** noun [C]

du•pli•ca•tion /ˌduplɪˈkeɪʃ(ə)n/ noun [U] **1** a situation in which one thing has the same purpose or effect as another **2** the process of making an exact copy of something

du•ra•ble /ˈdʊrəb(ə)l/ adj **1** able to stay in good condition for a long time, even after being used a lot **2** continuing to exist or be effective for a long time —**du•ra•bil•i•ty** /ˌdʊrəˈbɪləti/ noun [U]

du•ra•tion /dʊˈreɪʃ(ə)n/ noun [C/U] the period of time during which something continues to happen or exist

du•ress /dʊˈres/ noun **under duress** *formal* if you

do something under duress, you do it because someone has forced or threatened you

dur•ing /ˈdʊrɪŋ/ preposition ★★★ **1** at one point within a period of time: *During his visit to South Africa, the president met Archbishop Tutu.* **2** through all of a period of time: *Many creatures stay underground during daylight hours.*

dusk /dʌsk/ noun [U] the period of time at the end of the day just before it gets dark

dust¹ /dʌst/ noun [U] ★ very small pieces of dirt or another substance that form a layer on a surface or a cloud in the air: *The books were old and covered in dust.* ♦ *He drove off, leaving us in **a cloud of dust**.*
PHRASE **let the dust settle** to wait for a situation to become calm or normal again after something exciting or unusual has happened

dust² /dʌst/ verb **1** [I/T] to wipe the dust off the surface of something such as furniture **2** [T] to put a thin layer of powder on something
PHRASAL VERB ˌ**dust sth ˈoff** to wipe dust or dirt off the surface of something

dust•pan /ˈdʌstˌpæn/ noun [C] a small flat container that you put on the floor and brush dirt into

dust•y /ˈdʌsti/ adj **1** covered with dust **2** covered with dry earth or sand

du•ti•ful /ˈdutɪfəl/ adj *formal* careful to do things that other people ask or expect you to do —**du•ti•ful•ly** adv

du•ty /ˈduti/ noun [C/U] ★★★ **1** something that you should do as a legal or moral obligation: **sb's duty to do sth** *It is your duty as a parent to protect your children.* ♦ *The company **has a duty to** its stockholders.* ♦ *I was just **doing my duty** as a good citizen.* **2** a tax that you must pay on something, especially something that you bring into one country from another
PHRASES **off duty** not working at that moment: *I was off duty when they called me in.*
on duty working at that moment: *The nurse on duty called for a doctor.*

ˌ**duty-ˈfree¹** adj duty-free goods cost less than the usual price because you do not pay any tax on them —ˌ**duty-ˈfree** adv

ˌ**duty-ˈfree²** noun [U] goods such as cigarettes and alcohol that you buy without paying tax on them

DVD /ˌdi vi ˈdi/ noun [C] an object like a CD that has a movie or television program recorded on it

dwarf¹ /dwɔrf/ (plural **dwarves** /dwɔrvz/ or **dwarfs**) noun [C] an imaginary creature in children's stories that looks like a very small old man

dwarf² /dwɔrf/ verb [T] to make someone or something seem small or unimportant

dwell /dwel/ (past tense and past participle **dwelled** or **dwelt** /dwelt/) verb [I] *literary* to live somewhere
PHRASAL VERB ˈ**dwell on sth** to spend a lot of time thinking or talking about something unpleasant

dwell•er /ˈdwelər/ noun [C] someone who lives in a particular type of place: *a city/country/cave dweller*

dwell•ing /ˈdwelɪŋ/ noun [C] *formal* a building that someone lives in

dwin•dle /ˈdwɪnd(ə)l/ verb [I] to get gradually less or smaller over a period of time until almost nothing remains

dye¹ /daɪ/ noun [C/U] a substance that is used for changing the color of something such as cloth or hair

dye² /daɪ/ (present participle **dye•ing**; past tense and past participle **dyed**) verb [T] to change the color of something such as cloth or hair using dye

dy•ing¹ /ˈdaɪɪŋ/ adj not likely to live or exist for much longer: *a dying man*

dy•ing² the present participle of **die**

dyke /daɪk/ another spelling of **dike**

dy•nam•ic /daɪˈnæmɪk/ adj **1** very lively and enthusiastic, with a lot of energy and determination: *dynamic leadership* **2** continuously changing, growing, or developing: *a dynamic process/situation/business* —**dy•nam•i•cal•ly** /daɪˈnæmɪkli/ adv

dy•na•mite /ˈdaɪnəˌmaɪt/ noun [U] **1** a substance that is used for causing explosions **2** *informal* someone or something that is very impressive or exciting

dy•na•mo /ˈdaɪnəˌmoʊ/ noun [C] **1** a piece of equipment that changes the movement of a machine into electricity **2** *informal* someone with a lot of energy and determination

dy•nas•ty /ˈdaɪnəsti/ noun [C] **1** a family whose members rule a country or region for a long time **2** a family whose members are very successful in business or politics for a long time —**dy•nas•tic** /daɪˈæstɪk/ adj

dys•en•ter•y /ˈdɪs(ə)nˌteri/ noun [U] a serious disease that causes severe diarrhea

dys•func•tion•al /dɪsˈfʌŋkʃən(ə)l/ adj dysfunctional relationships do not work well and are not happy or successful

dys•lex•i•a /dɪsˈleksiə/ noun [U] a medical condition that makes it difficult for someone to read, write, and spell words correctly —**dys•lex•ic** /dɪsˈleksɪk/ adj

Ee

e or **E** /i/ noun [C/U] **1** the fifth letter of the English alphabet **2 E** *informal* the illegal drug ECSTASY

E. abbrev **1** East **2** Eastern

e- /i/ prefix on or using the Internet: *e-learning* ♦ *e-business*

each /itʃ/ grammar word ★★★

> **Each can be:**
> - a **determiner**: *in each corner of the room*
> - a **pronoun**: *three windows, with a different view from each* ♦ *I want each of you to fill out an application.*

used for referring to all the people or things in a group, when you are thinking about every one separately: *Each child will read a poem to the group.* ♦ *The United States, Russia, and Germany each won two gold medals.* ♦ *New batteries cost $1.99 each.* ♦ *I locked all the doors and then checked* ***each one*** *again.* ♦ ***Each of us*** *has a job to do.*

ˌeach ˈother pronoun ★★★
1 used for saying that each person or thing does something to the other or others: *The women looked at each other.*
2 used for saying that each person or thing is related in the same way to the other or others: *Suitcases were piled on top of each other.*

E

ea•ger /ˈigər/ adj very enthusiastic about doing something, or excited about something that is going to happen: *The girls were eager for new experiences.* ♦ **eager to do sth** *He's so eager to learn that he stays late every evening.* —**ea•ger•ly** adv: *the most eagerly awaited film of the year* —**ea•ger•ness** noun [U]

ea•gle /ˈig(ə)l/ noun [C] a large bird that eats other animals

ea•gle-eyed /ˌig(ə)l ˈaɪd/ adj able to see things that are very difficult to see

ear /ɪr/ noun ★★★
1 [C] one of the two parts on the sides of your head that you hear with —*picture* → C14
2 [singular] the ability to hear and judge sounds: *She has* ***a very good ear for*** *music.*
3 [C] the part at the top of a plant such as wheat that contains the grain: *ears of corn*
PHRASES **be all ears** *informal* to be ready to pay attention to what someone has to say
play it by ear to deal with a situation without having a plan, by reacting to things as they happen

ear•ache /ˈɪrˌeɪk/ noun [C] pain in your ear

ear•drum /ˈɪrˌdrʌm/ noun [C] the part inside your ear that VIBRATES when sound reaches it

earl /ɜrl/ noun [C] a man with a very high social position in the U.K.

ear•li•er /ˈɜrliər/ adv used for referring to a time before the present or before the time that you are talking about: *A few days earlier, he had been in London.* —**ear•li•er** adj: *an earlier period in history*

ear•li•est, the /ˈɜrliəst/ noun [singular] the earliest time that something can happen or be done: *The earliest we could be there is 7:30.*

ear•lobe /ˈɪrˌloʊb/ noun [C] the soft part at the bottom of your ear

ear•ly¹ /ˈɜrli/ adv ★★★
1 before the usual or expected time ≠ LATE: *I don't get up very early.* ♦ *The flight arrived ten minutes early.*
2 near the beginning of a period of time ≠ LATE: *Let's meet again early next week.* ♦ *He showed great musical talent very* ***early in life.***
3 near the beginning of a piece of writing ≠ LATE: *This point was discussed earlier in the chapter.*
4 soon enough to avoid problems: *If we begin treatment early, we have a better chance of success.*

ear•ly² /ˈɜrli/ adj ★★★
1 before the time that something usually happens or is expected to happen ≠ LATE: *Spring was early that year.* ♦ *My train was ten minutes early.* ♦ *I think I'll have* ***an early night*** (=go to bed earlier than usual).
2 near the beginning of a period of time ≠ LATE: *the early 19th century* ♦ *Julia is in her early thirties.* ♦ *It's too early to say what will happen.*
3 used about the first people or things of a particular type: *The early settlers used to heat their cabins with wood.*
→ EARLIEST

ˈearly ˌbird noun [C] *informal* someone who gets up early in the morning, or who does something before other people do

ear•mark /ˈɪrˌmɑrk/ verb [T] to decide to use an amount of money for a particular purpose: *Part of the housing budget is earmarked for regenerating urban areas.*

earn /ɜrn/ verb ★★
1 [I/T] to receive money for work that you do: *Most people here earn about $60,000 a year.* ♦ *She* ***earns a good living*** *as a financial adviser* (=she gets a good salary).
2 [T] to make a profit from business or from money that you have in the bank: *The company earned profits of $22 million last year.*
3 [T] to get something as a result of your efforts or your behavior: *Have a good rest now – you've earned it.* ♦ *You have to earn your employees' respect.*

earn•er /ˈɜrnər/ noun [C] **1** someone who earns money by working: *a wage earner* **2** something that earns money: *Tourism is a major earner of foreign currency.*

ear•nest /ˈɜrnɪst/ adj serious, determined, and sincere
PHRASE **in earnest 1** with more energy or determination than before: *After the rainy season, building work can begin in earnest.* **2** serious, and meaning what you say
—**ear•nest•ly** adv

earn•ings /ˈɜrnɪŋz/ noun [plural] **1** the amount of money that you earn **2** the profit made by a company

ear•phones /ˈɪrˌfoʊns/ noun [plural] a piece of equipment that you wear over your ears to listen to recorded sound = HEADPHONES

ear•plug /ˈɪrˌplʌg/ noun [C] a small object that you put in your ear to keep noise or water out

ear•ring /ˈɪrɪŋ/ noun [C] a piece of jewelry you wear on your ear —*picture* → JEWELRY

ear•shot /ˈɪrʃɑt/ noun
PHRASES **out of earshot** too far away for you to hear
within/in earshot close enough for you to hear

ˈear-ˌsplitting adj extremely loud

earth /ɜrθ/ noun ★★★
1 **Earth** or **earth** [singular/U] the planet on which we live: *the planet Earth* ♦ *the Earth's surface* ♦ *the origins of life* ***on Earth***
2 **the earth** [singular] the land on which we live: *They felt the earth shake.*
3 [U] the substance in which plants grow, that covers most of the land: *Cover the seeds with earth, then water them.*

PHRASES **on earth** used for emphasizing that someone or something is the best, worst, biggest, etc. in the world: *the largest man-made structure on earth*
on/from the face of the earth on/from the whole of the earth
what/why/how/where on earth *spoken* used for adding emphasis to questions: *Why on earth would I want to work for you?*

earth·en /ˈɜrθən/ adj made of dirt or clay

earth·en·ware /ˈɜrθənˌwer/ noun [U] bowls, cups, etc. that are made of baked clay

earth·ly /ˈɜrθli/ adj used for giving emphasis to negative statements or to questions: *There's no earthly reason why we should pay.*

earth·quake /ˈɜrθˌkweɪk/ noun [C] a sudden shaking movement of the ground

ˌearth ˈscience noun [C/U] a science that involves studying the Earth

earth·worm /ˈɜrθˌwɜrm/ noun [C] a type of WORM that lives in soil

earth·y /ˈɜrθi/ adj **1** looking or smelling like earth **2** showing an attitude to sex and the human body that is honest and direct

ease[1] /iz/ verb **1** [I/T] to make something that is bad become less severe, or to become less severe: *Sometimes a mild painkiller is enough to ease the pain.* ♦ *The city's traffic problems are beginning to ease a little.* **2** [I/T] to move somewhere slowly and carefully, or to make something move in this way: *Joseph eased himself off the bed.* **3** [T] to make a rule or punishment less severe: *Sanctions against the country should be eased.*

PHRASAL VERB **ˌease ˈoff** or **ˌease ˈup** if something unpleasant eases off, it becomes weaker: *The pain should ease off after a couple of hours.* ♦ *They waited for the storm to ease up.*

ease[2] /iz/ noun [U] the ability to do something easily, or the fact that something is easy ≠ DIFFICULTY: *Children usually master computer games with ease.*

PHRASES **at ease** confident and relaxed
ill at ease not confident or relaxed

ea·sel /ˈiz(ə)l/ noun [C] a frame that you rest a painting on while you are painting it

eas·i·ly /ˈizəli/ adv ★★★
1 without difficulty or effort: *You could easily get there in a day.*
2 used for saying that something is likely to happen or be true: *The situation could easily get worse.*
3 definitely: *This is easily his best album in years.*
4 more quickly or more often than is usual or normal: *Some babies cry more easily than others.*

east[1] /ist/ noun ★★★
1 [U] the direction that is in front of you when you are facing the rising sun: *driving from east to west*
2 the east [singular] the part of a place that is in the east: *They live in **the east of** the city.* ♦ *Most of the region's forests are **in the east**.*
3 the East [singular] the eastern part of the world, especially China and Japan
4 the East [singular] *American* the eastern part of the U.S.

east[2] /ist/ adv toward the east: *Drive east until you come to the river.* ♦ *She lives 40 miles east of Chicago.*

east[3] /ist/ adj **1** in the east, or facing toward the east **2** an east wind blows from the east

east·bound /ˈis(t)ˌbaʊnd/ adj going toward the east

ˌEast ˈCoast, the the eastern part of the U.S., along the Atlantic Ocean

East·er /ˈistər/ noun [C/U] a day when Christians celebrate the time when Jesus Christ died and then returned to life

ˈEaster ˌegg noun [C] a chocolate egg that you eat in celebration of Easter

east·er·ly /ˈistərli/ adj **1** an easterly wind blows from the east **2** toward or in the east

east·ern /ˈistərn/ adj ★★ in the east of a place: *eastern Arizona* ♦ *the eastern shore of Lake Michigan*

east·ern·er /ˈistərnər/ noun [C] someone who lives in or was born in the eastern part of a country

east·ern·most /ˈistərnˌmoʊst/ adj farthest toward the east

east·ward[1] /ˈistwərd/ adv toward the east

east·ward[2] /ˈistwərd/ adj toward or in the east

eas·y[1] /ˈizi/ adj ★★★
1 not difficult, or not needing much work: *The test was easy.* ♦ *The easiest way to get to Hartford is on the train.* ♦ *It is easy to see why she likes him.* ♦ **easy to do** *This cake is very easy to make.*
2 happy, confident, and not worried about anything: *Doug had an easy charm.*

PHRASES **the easy way out** an easy way of doing something, but not the right or best way
I'm easy *spoken* used for saying that you will accept any choice or decision that someone else makes

eas·y[2] /ˈizi/ adv ★★

PHRASES **easier said than done** *informal* used for saying that something is a good idea but will be difficult to achieve
go easy on sb *spoken* to not be very angry or severe with someone
go easy on/with sth *spoken* to not use, eat, or drink too much of something
take it easy 1 *informal* to rest and not do things that will make you tired **2** *spoken* used for telling someone to be calm **3** *spoken* used for saying goodbye to someone

ˈeasy ˌchair noun [C] a large comfortable chair

eas·y·go·ing /ˌiziˈgoʊɪŋ/ adj relaxed, calm, and not easy to upset

eas·y lis·ten·ing /ˌizi ˈlɪs(ə)nɪŋ/ noun [U] music that is relaxing and does not have complicated tunes or beats

eat /it/ (past tense **ate** /eɪt/; past participle **eat·en** /ˈit(ə)n/) verb ★★★
1 [I/T] to put food into your mouth and swallow it: *Did you eat your sandwich?* ♦ *My sister doesn't eat meat, but she eats fish.* ♦ *Don't talk while you're eating.* ♦ *Where can we get **something to eat** (=food)?* → TAKE
2 [I] to have a meal: *Are you ready to eat?* ♦ *We **ate at** a small Chinese restaurant.*

PHRASE **eat sb out of house and home** to eat too much of someone's food when you are a guest in their house

PHRASAL VERBS ˈ**eat ˌinto sth** to use up more of your time and money than you intended: *The cost of new computer systems is eating into our profits.*
ˌ**eat ˈout** to have a meal in a restaurant instead of at home
ˌ**eat sth ˈup** to use large amounts of your available time or money: *Having children eats up a lot of a family's income.*

Other ways of saying eat

- **chew** to use your teeth to break up the food in your mouth
- **eat up** to finish all the food that you have been given
- **have breakfast/lunch/dinner** to eat a particular meal
- **have something to eat** to eat something, or to have a meal
- **munch** to eat something noisily
- **nibble** to take very small bites from your food
- **have a snack** to eat something small between your main meals

eat•er /ˈitər/ noun [C] **1** someone who eats in a particular way: *a messy/noisy eater* **2** a person or animal that eats a particular type of food: *a meat eater*
eat•ing dis•or•der /ˈitɪŋ dɪsˌɔrdər/ noun [C] a medical condition in which someone does not eat normally, and wrongly believes that they are too fat
eaves /ivz/ noun [plural] the bottom edge of a roof that continues out over the walls
eaves•drop /ˈivzˌdrɑp/ verb [I] to listen to other people's conversation when they do not know that you are listening

eavesdrop

ebb¹ /eb/ noun [singular]
PHRASES **be at/reach (a) low ebb** to be in a very weak state
the ebb and flow a situation in which something keeps getting larger or stronger, then smaller or weaker
ebb² /eb/ verb [I] *literary* to gradually become smaller or less: *He felt his confidence ebbing away.*
eb•on•y /ˈebəni/ noun [C/U] a tree with hard black wood, or the wood of this tree
ˈ**e-ˌbusiness** noun [C/U] *business* business done on the Internet, or an Internet company
ec•cen•tric /ɪkˈsentrɪk/ adj **1** an eccentric person often behaves in slightly strange or unusual ways **2** an eccentric action or decision is strange or unusual —**ec•cen•tric** noun [C]
ec•cen•tric•i•ty /ˌeksenˈtrɪsəti/ noun [C/U] strange or unusual behavior

ec•cle•si•as•ti•cal /ɪˌkliziˈæstɪk(ə)l/ adj relating to the Christian Church
ech•e•lon /ˈeʃəˌlɑn/ noun [C] one of the levels of status in an organization, or the people in that level: *the upper/lower echelons of society*
ech•o¹ /ˈekoʊ/ verb **1** [I] if a sound echoes, it is repeated because the sound hits a surface and returns: *Gunfire echoed across the streets.* **2** [I] if a place echoes, noises echo easily there **3** [T] to express the same words, ideas, or feelings that someone else has expressed: *Blake echoed the views of many players.*
ech•o² /ˈekoʊ/ (plural **ech•oes**) noun [C] **1** a sound that is repeated because the sound hits a surface and returns: *the echo of footsteps in the alley* **2** an idea or phrase that is like one that has been expressed before: *echoes of the past*
e•clec•tic /ɪˈklektɪk/ adj *formal* consisting of many different types
e•clipse¹ /ɪˈklɪps/ noun [C] a short period when all or part of the Sun or Moon becomes dark: *a total eclipse of the Sun* (=when all of the Sun is dark)
e•clipse² /ɪˈklɪps/ verb [T] to make someone or something seem less successful or important, by becoming more important than they are: *His performance was eclipsed by Francisco's winning home run.*
ˈ**eco-ˌfriendly** adj designed to cause as little harm as possible to the environment
ec•o•log•i•cal /ˌekəˈlɑdʒɪk(ə)l/ adj relating to the environment and the way living things affect each other: *an ecological disaster* —**ec•o•log•i•cal•ly** /ˌekəˈlɑdʒɪkli/ adv
e•col•o•gy /ɪˈkɑlədʒi/ noun [U] the study of the environment and the way living things affect each other —**e•col•o•gist** noun [C]
e-ˈcommerce noun [U] buying and selling goods on the Internet
ec•o•nom•ic /ˌikəˈnɑmɪk, ˌekəˈnɑmɪk/ adj ★★★
1 relating to the economy, business, and trade: *economic development/growth* ♦ *the government's economic policies* ♦ *The project will bring great social and economic benefits to the region.*
2 providing a satisfactory profit from business activities: *It is no longer economic to mine coal here.*
ec•o•nom•i•cal /ˌikəˈnɑmɪk(ə)l, ˌekəˈnɑmɪk(ə)l/ adj not spending or costing much money: *The material is an economical substitute for plastic or steel.* ♦ *It's more economical to run the machines at night.*
ec•o•nom•i•cal•ly /ˌikəˈnɑmɪkli, ˌekəˈnɑmɪkli/ adv **1** done so that not much is wasted or little money is spent: *We aim to do the job as economically as possible.* **2** relating to the economy or to money: *Politically and economically, the country is going through some enormous changes.*
ˌ**economic ˈmigrant** noun [C] someone who goes to live in a new country because living conditions or opportunities for jobs are not good in their own country
ec•o•nom•ics /ˌikəˈnɑmɪks, ˌekəˈnɑmɪks/ noun [U] the study of the way that goods and services are produced and sold and the way

that money is managed: *an economics professor*

e·con·o·mist /ɪˈkɑnəmɪst/ noun [C] an expert in ECONOMICS

e·con·o·mize /ɪˈkɑnəˌmaɪz/ verb [I] to try to waste as little as possible of something such as money or fuel

e·con·o·my[1] /ɪˈkɑnəmi/ noun ★★★
1 [C] the system by which a country's trade, industry, and money are organized, and all the business, industry, and trade in that system: *a modern industrial economy* ♦ *The economy grew at an average of about 3 percent per year.* ♦ *The tax cuts are designed to* ***boost the economy*** (=make it stronger).
2 [C/U] the careful use of something so that very little is wasted, or an example of using something carefully: *In those days, fuel economy was a central factor in car design.* ♦ *If we* ***make a few economies*** (=spend money more carefully), *we can afford it.*
3 [U] the cheapest seats on a plane

e·con·o·my[2] /ɪˈkɑnəmi/ adj **1** economy goods are sold in large quantities so that they are less expensive **2** economy travel is the least expensive type of air travel available

eˈconomy ˌclass noun [U] the cheapest seats on a plane —**eˈconomy ˌclass** adj, adv

ec·o·sys·tem /ˈekoʊˌsɪstəm/ noun [C] *science* all the plants and animals in an area, considered as a system with parts that depend on each other

ec·o·tour·ism /ˈekoʊˌtʊrɪzəm/ noun [U] the business of creating and selling vacations that cause as little damage to the environment as possible —**ec·o·tour·ist** noun [C]

ec·sta·sy /ˈekstəsi/ noun **1** [C/U] a feeling of great happiness and pleasure **2** [U] an illegal drug that young people take, especially in NIGHTCLUBS

ec·stat·ic /ɪkˈstætɪk/ adj extremely happy or pleased —**ec·stat·i·cal·ly** /ɪkˈstætɪkli/ adv

ec·ze·ma /ˈeksəmə, ɪɡˈzimə/ noun [U] a medical condition that makes your skin dry, sore, and ITCHY

ed. abbrev **1** edition **2** editor **3** education

ed·dy /ˈedi/ noun [C] a current of water or air that moves in a circular pattern

edge[1] /edʒ/ noun ★★★
1 [C] the part of something that is farthest from its center: *Victoria was sitting on* ***the edge of*** *the bed.* ♦ *A new mall is to be built* ***on the edge of*** *town.*
2 [C] the sharp side of a blade or tool that is used for cutting things
3 [singular] an advantage over other people or things: *Training can* ***give you the edge over*** *your competitors.*
4 [singular] an unusual quality that makes something interesting or exciting
PHRASES **on edge** nervous and unable to relax because you are worried
on the edge of your seat very excited and interested, because you want to know what happens next

edge[2] /edʒ/ verb **1** [I/T] to move slowly and carefully, or to make something do this: *Michael was edging toward the door.* **2** [I] to gradually increase or become less: *Food prices edged up by 0.2 percent in November.* **3** [T] to put something around the edge of another thing: *white plates edged with gold*
PHRASAL VERB **ˌedge sb ˈout** to beat someone in a competition by a small amount

edge·ways /ˈedʒˌweɪz/ or **edge·wise** /ˈedʒˌwaɪz/ adv sideways

edg·y /ˈedʒi/ adj **1** in a bad mood because you are worried or nervous = IRRITABLE **2** edgy music, movies, books, etc. have an unusual quality that is interesting or exciting

ed·i·ble /ˈedəb(ə)l/ adj safe to eat, or good enough to eat ≠ INEDIBLE: *edible mushrooms* ♦ *The food in the cafeteria is barely edible* (=it tastes very bad).

e·dict /ˈidɪkt/ noun [C] *formal* an official order that is given by a government or someone in authority

ed·i·fice /ˈedəfɪs/ noun [C] *formal* a large impressive building

ed·it[1] /ˈedɪt/ verb [T] **1** to make changes to a book or document so that it is ready to be published **2** to be the EDITOR in charge of a book, newspaper, or magazine **3** to make changes to a movie or to a television or radio program before it is shown or broadcast

ed·it[2] /ˈedɪt/ noun [U] a menu in some computer programs that allows you to cut, copy, or move parts of a document, or look for particular words in it

e·di·tion /ɪˈdɪʃ(ə)n/ noun [C] a set of copies of a book, newspaper, or magazine that are published at the same time: *the Sunday edition of the local newspaper* ♦ *the 1993 edition of the* Guinness Book of Records

ed·i·tor /ˈedɪtər/ noun [C] ★
1 someone who is in charge of a newspaper or magazine, or in charge of one of its sections
2 someone whose job is to EDIT books, documents, or movies
3 a computer program that is used for writing or EDITING documents, files, or programs

ed·i·to·ri·al[1] /ˌedəˈtɔriəl/ noun [C] a newspaper article in which the editor gives their opinion on an issue in the news

ed·i·to·ri·al[2] /ˌedəˈtɔriəl/ adj relating to the EDITING of books, magazines, newspapers, etc.

edu abbrev educational institution: used in Internet addresses

ed·u·cate /ˈedʒəˌkeɪt/ verb ★
1 [T] to teach someone, especially at a school, college, or university: *More and more parents are choosing to educate their children at home.* ♦ **educate sb at sth** *She was educated at Smith College and Yale Law School.*
2 [I/T] to give someone necessary or useful knowledge: **educate sb about sth** *The mining museum was built to educate people about their local history.*

ed·u·cat·ed /ˈedʒəˌkeɪtəd/ adj an educated person has received a good education and has a lot of knowledge ≠ UNEDUCATED: *The people who work here are well educated and open-minded.*
PHRASE **an educated guess** a guess that is based on knowledge of the situation

ed·u·ca·tion /ˌedʒəˈkeɪʃ(ə)n/ noun ★★★
1 [U] the activity of educating people in schools, colleges, and universities, and all the policies and arrangements concerning this: *Education is a major concern for voters.* ♦ *the Secretary of Education*
2 [singular] someone's experience of learning or being taught: *Did you have a college education?* ♦ *He wants his children to* ***get an education****.*
3 [U] the process of providing people with information about an important issue: *a health education campaign*

Word family: **education**	
Words in the same family as ***education***	
■ **educate** *v*	■ **educational** *adj*
■ **educated** *adj*	■ **uneducated** *adj*

ed·u·ca·tion·al /ˌedʒəˈkeɪʃ(ə)nəl/ adj ★★
1 relating to education: *educational opportunities for women*
2 giving people useful knowledge: *The program was educational and entertaining too.*

ed·u·ca·tor /ˈedʒəˌkeɪtər/ noun [C] someone who teaches, or someone who is an expert on education

ed·u·tain·ment /ˌedʒəˈteɪnmənt/ noun [U] television programs, videos, software, etc. that entertain you while teaching you something

eel /il/ noun [C] a long thin fish that looks like a snake

ee·rie /ˈɪri/ adj strange and mysterious, and sometimes frightening —**ee·ri·ly** adv

ef·fect[1] /ɪˈfekt/ noun ★★★
1 [C/U] a change that is produced in one person or thing by another: *Scientists are studying the chemical's* ***effect on*** *the environment.* ♦ *Any change in lifestyle will* ***have an effect on*** *your health.* ♦ *The new tax rates will* ***have little effect on*** *most ordinary people.*
2 [C] an appearance or reaction that is deliberately produced, for example by a writer or artist: *Students should learn how they can* ***achieve*** *different* ***effects*** *in their writing.*
3 effects [plural] special artificial images and sounds that are created for a movie =SPECIAL EFFECTS
4 effects or **personal effects** [plural] *formal* the things that belong to you

PHRASES **come into effect** if a rule or law comes into effect, it starts to be used
for effect if you do something for effect, you do it in order to impress people
in effect 1 used for giving a summary of what you think the situation really is: *In effect, this means we'll have to work more hours for the same pay.* **2** if a law or rule is in effect, it is operating
put sth into effect to start to use a plan or idea
take effect 1 to start to produce the results that were intended: *The tax cuts are beginning to take effect.* **2** if a rule or law takes effect, it starts to be used
to the effect that used for showing that you are giving a general idea of what someone said, but not their actual words: *Harry said something to the effect that they would all meet Margaret very soon.*
→ SIDE EFFECT

Words often used with **effect**
Adjectives often used with ***effect*** *(noun, sense 1)*
■ **adverse, damaging, detrimental, harmful, negative** + EFFECT: used about bad effects
■ **beneficial, positive** + EFFECT: used about good effects
■ **dramatic, major, profound, significant, substantial** + EFFECT: used about big effects

ef·fect[2] /ɪˈfekt/ verb [T] *formal* to make something happen =BRING STH ABOUT: *Swift action was necessary if real change was to be effected.*

Word family: **effect**	
Words in the same family as ***effect***	
■ **effective** *adj*	■ **ineffectual** *adj*
■ **effectively** *adv*	

ef·fec·tive /ɪˈfektɪv/ adj ★★★
1 working well and producing the result that was intended ≠ INEFFECTIVE: *You need more effective communication within the organization.* ♦ *This is a very effective way of controlling pests and weeds.* ♦ *The new vaccine is highly* ***effective against*** *all strains of the disease.*
2 *formal* when a law or agreement becomes effective, it officially starts to be used: *Government ministers reached a 30-month agreement,* ***effective from*** *July 1.*
—**ef·fec·tive·ness** noun [U]

ef·fec·tive·ly /ɪˈfektɪvli/ adv ★★
1 in a way that works well and produces the result that you intended: *The system could deliver services to local communities more effectively.*
2 used for saying what the situation really is, although it might seem to be different: *With Australia 24 points ahead at halftime, the game was effectively over.*

ef·fem·i·nate /ɪˈfemɪnət/ adj *showing disapproval* an effeminate man looks, behaves, or speaks like a woman

ef·fer·ves·cent /ˌefərˈves(ə)nt/ adj
1 producing a lot of small BUBBLES **2** lively and enthusiastic

ef·fi·cien·cy /ɪˈfɪʃ(ə)nsi/ noun [U] ★ the ability to work well and produce good results, using the available time, money, supplies, etc. in the most effective way: *new technology aimed at improving efficiency and customer service*

ef·fi·cient /ɪˈfɪʃ(ə)nt/ adj ★★ working well and producing good results by using the available time, money, supplies, etc. in the most effective way ≠ INEFFICIENT: *The new machine is far more efficient than the old one.* ♦ *The most efficient way to plan your work is to put your tasks in order of importance.* ♦ *The hotel staff is friendly and efficient.* —**ef·fi·cient·ly** adv

ef·fi·gy /ˈefɪdʒi/ noun [C] a model of someone, especially one that is destroyed in a protest against them

ef·flu·ent /ˈefluənt/ noun [C/U] liquid waste

ef·fort /ˈefərt/ noun ★★★
1 [C/U] an attempt to do something that is

difficult or involves hard work: *Detectives are talking to other witnesses **in an effort to** find out more about the girl.* ♦ *I've **made an effort** to drink less tea and coffee.* ♦ **an effort to do sth** *The changes were part of an effort to push profits up.*
2 [singular/U] physical or mental energy needed to do something: *Writing a book **takes** a lot of time and **effort**.* ♦ *Mary **put** a lot **of effort into** this project.*
3 [C] the activities of people who are working together to achieve a particular goal: *international relief efforts*

Words often used with effort

*Adjectives often used with **effort** (sense 1)*

- **big, determined, great, massive, valiant** + EFFORT: used when someone tries very hard to do something
- **combined, concerted, joint, team** + EFFORT: used about an effort that is made by a lot of people together

ef•fort•less /ˈefərtləs/ adj done well or successfully and without any effort —**ef•fort•less•ly** adv
ef•fu•sive /ɪˈfjusɪv/ adj expressing happiness, praise, etc. in an extremely enthusiastic way
EFL /ˌi ef ˈel/ noun [U] English as a Foreign Language: English taught to people who do not live in an English-speaking country
e.g. or **eg** /ˌi ˈdʒi/ abbrev for example: used for giving an example of what you mean
e•gal•i•tar•i•an /ɪˌɡælɪˈteriən/ adj supporting a social system in which everyone has the same status, money, and opportunities
egg¹ /eɡ/ noun ★★★
1 [C] the round object with a shell that a baby bird develops in: *The chicken had **laid an egg**.*
2 [C/U] a HEN's egg used as food: *We had boiled eggs for breakfast.* ♦ *an egg salad sandwich*
3 [C] a small object produced by a female insect, FROG, snake, etc., that a young animal comes out of
4 [C] a cell produced inside a woman or female animal that can develop into a baby
PHRASE **have/get egg on your face** *informal* to be embarrassed or appear stupid because something you tried to do has gone wrong

eggs

egg² /eɡ/ PHRASAL VERB ˌ**egg sb ˈon** to encourage someone to do something that they should not do
egg•plant /ˈeɡˌplænt/ noun [C/U] *American* a vegetable with a smooth, dark purple skin —*picture* → C11
egg•shell /ˈeɡʃel/ noun [C] the hard outside layer of an egg
ˈ**egg ˌwhite** noun [C/U] the clear part of an egg that becomes white when you cook it
e•go /ˈiɡoʊ/ noun [C] the opinion that you have of yourself and your own importance: *a guy with a huge ego* ♦ *Being asked to speak was a real boost to her ego.*
e•go•tis•ti•cal /ˌiɡoʊˈtɪstɪk(ə)l/ adj thinking that you are more important than other people and need not care about them —**e•go•tist** /ˈiɡoʊtɪst/ noun [C]
eh /eɪ/ interjection used for asking someone to agree with you: *Pretty good, eh?*
eight /eɪt/ number the number 8
eight•een /eɪˈtin/ number the number 18 —**eight•eenth** /eɪˈtinθ/ number
eighth /eɪtθ/ number **1** in the place or position counted as number 8 **2** one of 8 equal parts of something
eight•y /ˈeɪti/ number the number 80 —**eight•i•eth** /ˈeɪtiəθ/ number
ei•ther /ˈiðər/ grammar word ★★★

Either can be:

- a **conjunction**: *Students could choose either French or Spanish.* ♦ *You can either come by bus or take a taxi.*
- a **pronoun**: *You could have fish or chicken, but I don't like either.* ♦ *Does either of you speak Chinese?*
- an **adverb**: *Jerry wasn't there either.*
- a **determiner**: *a long room with a door at either end*

1 one or the other of two people or things, especially when it does not matter which: *Check or credit card – you can use either.* ♦ *Applications are welcomed from people of either sex and any age.* ♦ *It was a long time before **either of** them spoke.*
2 used instead of "also" in negative statements: *I can't come tonight, and nobody else can either.* ♦ *We tried another method, but that didn't work either.* ♦ *"I don't like horror movies." "Me either* (=I also do not like them)."
3 used instead of "both" in negative statements: *Jackie could play the piano and sing, but I couldn't do either.* ♦ *I didn't like **either of** the candidates.* → ALSO
PHRASES **either...or** used for showing two or more possibilities or choices: *You must answer either yes or no.* ♦ *You can contact us either by phone, by e-mail, or by letter.*
either side/end/hand etc. each of two sides/ends/hands, etc.: *Her parents were sitting on either side of her.*

When **either** is the subject of a sentence, it is usually used with a singular verb: *Is either of them at home?* But in spoken English a plural verb is sometimes used: *Are either of them at home?*

e•jac•u•late /ɪˈdʒækjəˌleɪt/ verb [I/T] if a man ejaculates, SEMEN comes out of his PENIS —**e•jac•u•la•tion** /ɪˌdʒækjəˈleɪʃ(ə)n/ noun [C/U]
e•ject /ɪˈdʒekt/ verb **1** [T] to make something such as a TAPE or CD come out from a machine **2** [T] to make someone leave a place, especially using physical force: *A group of noisy protesters were ejected from the meeting.* **3** [I] to jump out of a plane before it crashes —**e•jec•tion** /ɪˈdʒekʃ(ə)n/ noun [U]

eke /ik/ verb **eke out a living** to get just enough money to be able to live

e•lab•o•rate¹ /ɪˈlæb(ə)rət/ adj very detailed and complicated: *elaborate geometrical patterns* ♦ *an elaborate system of inspections and reports*

e•lab•o•rate² /ɪˈlæbəˌreɪt/ verb [I] to give more details or information about something: *The police refused to elaborate on the circumstances of the arrest.* —**e•lab•o•ra•tion** /ɪˌlæbəˈreɪʃ(ə)n/ noun [U]

E

e•lapse /ɪˈlæps/ verb [I] *formal* if time elapses, it passes

e•las•tic¹ /ɪˈlæstɪk/ noun [U] a material that stretches or bends easily and can return to its original shape

e•las•tic² /ɪˈlæstɪk/ adj **1** made of elastic **2** able to stretch or bend and then return to its original shape

e•lat•ed /ɪˈleɪtəd/ adj extremely happy and excited —**e•la•tion** /ɪˈleɪʃ(ə)n/ noun [U]

el•bow¹ /ˈelboʊ/ noun [C] ★★ the part in the middle of your arm, where it bends: *She sat with her elbows on the table.* —*picture* → C14

el•bow² /ˈelboʊ/ verb [T] to push or hit someone with your elbow

eld•er¹ /ˈeldər/ noun [C] **1** someone in your family or community who is older than you **2** an older member of an organization or community who is given respect and authority

eld•er² /ˈeldər/ adj older than someone, especially someone in your family: *advice from my elder brother*

eld•er•ly /ˈeldərli/ adj ★★
1 old: *Not all elderly people can live with their relatives.*
2 the elderly old people

eld•est /ˈeldəst/ adj oldest of the people in a group, especially the children in a family: *He was the eldest of three sons.*

e•lect¹ /ɪˈlekt/ verb [T] ★★ to choose someone to represent you or to hold an official position, by voting for them: *Every nation should have a right to elect its own government.* ♦ **elect sb to sth** *Carol Moseley became the first black woman to be elected to the Senate.* ♦ **elect sb as sth** *Lee Yuan-tzu was elected the next day as Vice President.* ♦ **elect sb sth** *She was elected president of the association.*

PHRASE **elect to do sth** *formal* to choose to do something: *They had elected to remain at home.*

e•lect² /ɪˈlekt/ adj elected to an important position, but not yet officially holding it: *the president-elect*

e•lec•tion /ɪˈlekʃ(ə)n/ noun ★★★
1 [C] an occasion when people vote for someone to represent them, especially in government: *an election victory/defeat* ♦ *He won the first national election for president.* ♦ *The new regime is promising to **hold** free **elections** as soon as possible.*
2 [U] the process of electing a person or group of people: ***the election of** a new leader* ♦ *a candidate for **election to the** Council* ♦ *His **election as** President will mean changes in foreign policy.*

e•lec•tive¹ /ɪˈlektɪv/ adj **1** an elective position is one that you hold because people have voted for you **2** done because someone chooses it, not because they have to do it: *elective surgery*

e•lec•tive² /ɪˈlektɪv/ noun [C] *American* a course or class that you choose to do, rather than one that you must do

e•lec•tor /ɪˈlektər/ noun [C] someone who has the right to vote in an election

e•lec•tor•al /ɪˈlekt(ə)rəl/ adj relating to elections: *a new electoral system*

e•lec•tor•ate /ɪˈlekt(ə)rət/ noun [C] all the people who are allowed to vote in an election

e•lec•tric /ɪˈlektrɪk/ adj ★
1 using or relating to electricity: *an electric motor/drill/toothbrush* ♦ *an electric outlet/plug/cord* ♦ *an electric current*
2 extremely exciting: *The atmosphere was electric.*

- **Electric** describes things that use electricity to make them work: *an electric iron/shaver/guitar*
- **Electrical** is used in more technical contexts, when you are talking about how electricity is made or used: *an electrical engineer*

e•lec•tri•cal /ɪˈlektrɪk(ə)l/ adj ★ working by or relating to electricity: *electrical equipment/appliances* ♦ *an electrical fault*

eˌlectric ˈchair, the noun [singular] a chair used for legally killing someone as a punishment, using a strong electrical current

e•lec•tri•cian /ɪˌlekˈtrɪʃ(ə)n, ˌilekˈtrɪʃ(ə)n/ noun [C] someone whose job is to repair or fit electrical equipment

e•lec•tric•i•ty /ɪˌlekˈtrɪsəti, ˌilekˈtrɪsəti/ noun [U] ★★ a form of energy that can produce light, heat, and power for computers, televisions, etc.: *The machines run on electricity.* ♦ *a supply of electricity*

eˌlectric ˈshock noun [C] a sudden strong pain that is caused by electricity passing through your body

e•lec•tri•fy /ɪˈlektrəˌfaɪ/ verb [T] **1** to make someone feel extremely excited **2** to provide something with a supply of electricity —**e•lec•tri•fi•ca•tion** /ɪˌlektrəfɪˈkeɪʃ(ə)n/ noun [U]

e•lec•tro•cute /ɪˈlektrəˌkjut/ verb [T] to kill or injure someone with electricity —**e•lec•tro•cu•tion** /ɪˌlektrəˈkjuʃ(ə)n/ noun [U]

e•lec•trode /ɪˈlekˌtroʊd/ noun [C] a small metal object that allows electricity to flow through it

e•lec•tron /ɪˈlekˌtrɑn/ noun [C] a part of an atom that has a negative electrical CHARGE → NEUTRON

e•lec•tron•ic /ɪˌlekˈtrɑnɪk, ˌilekˈtrɑnɪk/ adj ★★
1 using electricity and extremely small electrical parts such as MICROCHIPS: *an electronic calculator* ♦ *The information is held **in electronic form** (=on computer disks).*
2 involving the use of electronic equipment, especially computers: *an electronic voting system* —**e•lec•tron•i•cal•ly** /ɪˌlekˈtrɑnɪkli/ adv

e•lec•tron•ics /ɪˌlekˈtrɑnɪks, ˌilekˈtrɑnɪks/ noun [U] the science and technology of electronic equipment

el•e•gant /ˈeləgənt/ adj beautiful in a graceful simple way: *She always looks so elegant.* ♦ *an elegant room/restaurant* —**el•e•gance** noun [U], **el•e•gant•ly** adv

el•e•gy /ˈelədʒi/ noun [C] a poem or other piece of writing that expresses sadness

el•e•ment /ˈelɪmənt/ noun ★★★

1 basic part of sth	4 for heating
2 in science	5 weather
3 small amount	+ PHRASES

1 [C] an important basic part of something, for example a system or plan: *Fieldwork is a key **element of** this course.* ♦ *Advertising is not the only **element in** the marketing process.*
2 [C] *science* a substance that consists of only one type of atom: *hydrogen, oxygen, and other elements*
3 [singular] a small but important amount of a quality or feeling: *There is **an element of** truth in what she said.*
4 [C] the part of a piece of electrical equipment that produces heat
5 the elements [plural] the weather, especially wind and rain
PHRASES **be in your element** to feel very happy and comfortable in a situation
be out of your element to feel unhappy and uncomfortable in a situation

el•e•men•ta•ry /ˌeləˈment(ə)ri/ adj **1** relating to the most basic and important part of something=BASIC: *He made a few elementary errors.* **2** easy: *elementary tasks* **3** relating to the first years of school: *elementary education*

eleˈmentary ˌschool noun [C] in the U.S., a school for children between the ages of five and about eleven=GRADE SCHOOL

el•e•phant /ˈeləfənt/ noun [C] a very large wild animal that lives in Africa and Asia. It has thick gray skin and a very long nose called a **trunk**. —*picture* → C12

el•e•vate /ˈeləˌveɪt/ verb [T] *formal* **1** to improve someone or something, or to make them more important: *We need to work together to elevate the position of women in society.* **2** to raise something to a higher physical position=RAISE —**el•e•vat•ed** /ˈeləˌveɪtəd/ adj, **el•e•va•tion** /ˌeləˈveɪʃ(ə)n/ noun [C/U]

el•e•va•tor /ˈeləˌveɪtər/ noun [C] *American* a machine that carries people up and down between the levels of a tall building

e•lev•en /ɪˈlev(ə)n/ number the number 11

e•lev•enth /ɪˈlev(ə)nθ/ number **1** in the place or position counted as number 11 **2** one of 11 equal parts of something

elf /elf/ (plural **elves** /elvz/) noun [C] a small imaginary person with magic powers

e•lic•it /ɪˈlɪsɪt/ verb [T] *formal* to get something such as a reaction or information from someone: *The question elicited a positive response.*

el•i•gi•ble /ˈelɪdʒəb(ə)l/ adj **1** allowed by rules or laws to do something ≠ INELIGIBLE: *She will be eligible to compete in the next Winter Games.* **2** considered to be a good marriage partner —**el•i•gi•bil•i•ty** /ˌelɪdʒəˈbɪləti/ noun [U]

e•lim•i•nate /ɪˈlɪmɪˌneɪt/ verb [T] **1** to get rid of something that is not wanted or needed: *Many infectious diseases have been virtually eliminated.* ♦ **eliminate sth from sth** *He had to eliminate dairy products from his diet.* **2** to remove someone from a competition: *Five candidates were eliminated after the first interview.* **3** to decide that someone or something is not responsible for something: *We've eliminated the possibility that the fire was started deliberately.*

e•lim•i•na•tion /ɪˌlɪmɪˈneɪʃ(ə)n/ noun **1** [U] the process of getting rid of something that is not wanted **2** [C] defeat in a competition
PHRASE **a process of elimination** a way of solving a problem by getting rid of wrong solutions first

e•li•sion /ɪˈlɪʒ(ə)n/ noun [U] *linguistics* the practice of leaving a sound out when you say a word or group of words quickly in ordinary conversation

e•lite /ɪˈlit/ noun [C] **1** a small group of people who have a lot of power or advantages: *the political elite* **2** the best or most skillful people in a group: *This book puts him among the elite of British novelists.* ♦ *an elite group of athletes*

e•lit•ism /ɪˈlitˌɪzəm/ noun [U] the belief that a small group of people should keep the most power and influence —**e•lit•ist** adj

el•lip•ti•cal /ɪˈlɪptɪk(ə)l/ adj in the shape of a circle that is longer than it is wide

elm /elm/ noun [C] a large tree with round leaves that fall off in winter

e•lon•gat•ed /ɪˈlɔŋˌgeɪtəd/ adj longer and narrower than is normal

e•lope /ɪˈloʊp/ verb [I] to go away secretly in order to get married

el•o•quent /ˈeləkwənt/ adj expressing something clearly and effectively: *an eloquent speech/speaker* —**el•o•quence** noun [U], **el•o•quent•ly** adv

else /els/ adv ★★★ used after question words, or words such as "anyone," "something," "everywhere," and "nobody," to mean "in addition" or "other": *No one else was willing to help.* ♦ *Would you like to go somewhere else?* ♦ *What else have you been doing wrong, Kelly?* ♦ *The police had already interviewed everyone else.*
PHRASE **or else 1** used for stating the second of two possibilities: *You could drive to Chicago, or else fly there and rent a car.* **2** used for saying that there will be a bad result if something does not happen: *We'd better leave now or else we'll miss our train.* → NOTHING

else•where /ˈelsˌwer/ adv ★★ in or to another place or other places: *Gas prices are higher in San Francisco than elsewhere in California.*

ELT /ˌi el ˈti/ noun [U] English Language Teaching: the teaching of English to students whose first language is not English

e•lu•ci•date /ɪˈlusɪˌdeɪt/ verb [I/T] *formal* to make something easier to understand by giving more information

e•lude /ɪˈlud/ verb [T] *formal* **1** if something eludes you, you cannot achieve it, understand it, or remember it: *Financial success eluded him.* **2** to manage to escape or hide from someone or something=EVADE

E

e•lu•sive /ɪˈlusɪv/ adj **1** difficult or impossible to find or catch **2** difficult or impossible to achieve or understand
elves the plural of **elf**
'em /əm/ short form a way of writing "them" that shows how it sounds in informal conversation
e•ma•ci•at•ed /ɪˈmeɪʃiˌeɪtəd/ adj extremely thin
e-mail or **e•mail** /ˈiˌmeɪl/ noun ★★★
1 [U] a system for sending messages from one computer to another: *We communicate by e-mail.* ♦ *Do you know her* ***e-mail address****?*
2 [C] a written message sent by e-mail: *Send me an e-mail with the details.*
—**ˈe-ˌmail** verb [T]
em•a•nate /ˈeməˌneɪt/ PHRASAL VERB
ˈemanate from sth *formal* to come from a particular place: *Wonderful smells emanated from the kitchen.*
e•man•ci•pa•tion /ɪˌmænsɪˈpeɪʃ(ə)n/ noun [U] *formal* the process of giving freedom and rights to someone —**e•man•ci•pate** /ɪˈmænsɪˌpeɪt/ verb [T], **e•man•ci•pat•ed** /ɪˈmænsɪˌpeɪtəd/ adj
em•balm /ɪmˈbɑm/ verb [T] to preserve a dead body using chemicals
em•bank•ment /ɪmˈbæŋkmənt/ noun [C] a sloping wall of earth or stone beside a road, railroad, or river
em•bar•go /ɪmˈbɑrgoʊ/ (plural **em•bar•goes**) noun [C] a government order preventing trade with another country: *an arms/oil/trade embargo*
em•bark /ɪmˈbɑrk/ verb [I] to get on a ship ≠ DISEMBARK —**em•bar•ka•tion** /ˌembɑrˈkeɪʃ(ə)n/ noun [C/U]
PHRASAL VERB **emˈbark ˌon sth** or **emˈbark uˌpon sth** to start a new project or activity
em•bar•rass /ɪmˈberəs/ verb [T] to make someone feel nervous, ashamed, or stupid: *It embarrassed me to have to give my opinion in public.*
em•bar•rassed /ɪmˈberəst/ adj ★ feeling slightly ashamed, and worried about what other people will think of you: *She looked embarrassed when we asked her about her boyfriend.* ♦ **embarrassed to do sth** *I was too embarrassed to tell anyone about my illness.*
em•bar•rass•ing /ɪmˈberəsɪŋ/ adj ★ making you feel nervous, ashamed, or stupid: *an embarrassing situation* —**em•bar•rass•ing•ly** adv
em•bar•rass•ment /ɪmˈberəsmənt/ noun **1** [U] a feeling of being embarrassed: *I felt my face burning with embarrassment.* **2** [C] someone or something that makes you feel embarrassed: *He is such an embarrassment to his family.*
em•bas•sy /ˈembəsi/ noun [C] a group of officials who represent their government in a foreign country, or the building where they work: *the Canadian Embassy in Paris*
em•bat•tled /ɪmˈbæt(ə)ld/ adj *mainly journalism* experiencing a lot of problems and likely to be defeated or destroyed
em•bed•ded /ɪmˈbedəd/ adj fixed firmly in something: *A piece of metal had become embedded in her leg.*
em•bel•lish /ɪmˈbelɪʃ/ verb [I/T] to make something more interesting or beautiful by adding things to it
em•bers /ˈembərz/ noun [plural] pieces of wood or coal that are still hot and red after a fire has stopped burning
em•bez•zle /ɪmˈbez(ə)l/ verb [I/T] to steal money that you are trusted to take care of as part of your work —**em•bez•zle•ment** noun [U]
em•bit•ter•ed /ɪmˈbɪtərd/ adj angry and unhappy about things that have happened to you in the past
em•bla•zoned /ɪmˈbleɪz(ə)nd/ adj printed, drawn, or decorated in a way that is very easy to notice
em•blem /ˈembləm/ noun [C] a design or object that is a symbol of something such as a country, organization, or idea
em•bod•i•ment /ɪmˈbɑdɪmənt/ noun **the embodiment of sth** the best possible example of a particular idea, quality, or principle
em•bod•y /ɪmˈbɑdi/ verb [T] to be the best possible example of a particular idea, quality, or principle
em•brace /ɪmˈbreɪs/ verb **1** [T] *formal* to accept something new with enthusiasm: *Many older people have embraced new technology.*
2 [I/T] to put your arms around someone in order to show love or friendship —**em•brace** noun [C]
em•broi•der /ɪmˈbrɔɪdər/ verb [I/T] **1** to decorate cloth with a design of colored stitches **2** to make a story more interesting by adding details that you have invented
em•broi•der•y /ɪmˈbrɔɪdəri/ noun [C/U] a design of colored stitches on cloth, or the activity of decorating cloth in this way
em•broiled /ɪmˈbrɔɪld/ adj involved in a difficult situation: *The mayor is embroiled in another scandal.*
em•bry•o /ˈembriˌoʊ/ noun [C] an animal or human before it is born, when it is beginning to develop and grow
em•bry•on•ic /ˌembriˈɑnɪk/ adj **1** just beginning to develop and grow: *an embryonic industry* **2** relating to an animal or human embryo
em•er•ald /ˈem(ə)rəld/ noun [C] a bright green stone used in expensive jewelry
e•merge /ɪˈmɜrdʒ/ verb [I] ★★
1 to come out of something, or out from behind something: *After a few weeks, the caterpillar* ***emerges from*** *its cocoon.* ♦ *The doors opened and people began to emerge into the street.*
2 to stop being involved in a difficult situation or period of time: *The country is slowly* ***emerging from*** *a recession.*
3 to become known or recognized: *Cities like Atlanta are* ***emerging as*** *important new financial centers.* ♦ **+that** *It has emerged that Americans were among those injured.*
e•mer•gence /ɪˈmɜrdʒəns/ noun [U] the process of appearing or becoming recognized: *the emergence of the modern French state*
e•mer•gen•cy /ɪˈmɜrdʒənsi/ noun [C] ★★ an unexpected situation in which immediate action is necessary, often because there is danger: *The club is now facing a financial emergency.* ♦ *We always carry a medical kit*

for emergencies. ♦ *emergency surgery* ♦ ***In an emergency**, call this number.*

e'mergency ˌbrake noun [C] *American* the BRAKE in a car that prevents it from moving when it is parked —*picture* → C6

e'mergency ˌroom noun [C] *American* the part of a hospital where you take someone who needs immediate care

e'mergency ˌservices noun [plural] the organizations that deal with fire, crime, accidents, and injuries

e•merg•ing /ɪ'mɜrdʒɪŋ/ adj just beginning to exist or be noticed: *emerging businesses/ technologies*

em•i•grant /'emɪgrənt/ noun [C] someone who leaves their country in order to live in another country

em•i•grate /'emɪˌgreɪt/ verb [I] to leave your country in order to live in another country —**em•i•gra•tion** /ˌemɪ'greɪʃ(ə)n/ noun [U]

em•i•nent /'emɪnənt/ adj important, respected, and admired

em•i•nent•ly /'emɪnəntli/ adv *formal* very: *eminently qualified*

e•mis•sion /ɪ'mɪʃ(ə)n/ noun **1** [C] a substance, especially a gas, that goes into the air: *a proposal to reduce carbon dioxide emissions* **2** [U] the process of sending gas, light, or heat into the air

e•mit /ɪ'mɪt/ verb [T] to send out gas, light, heat, or sound

e•mo•ti•con /ɪ'moʊtɪˌkɑn/ noun [C] a symbol that you type in an e-mail or TEXT MESSAGE to show how you feel

e•mo•tion /ɪ'moʊʃ(ə)n/ noun [C/U] ★★ a feeling that you experience, for example love, fear, or anger: *Jealousy is an uncomfortable emotion.*

e•mo•tion•al /ɪ'moʊʃ(ə)nəl/ adj ★★
1 relating to feelings and the way in which they affect your life: *He is in need of emotional support.*
2 affected by and expressing strong emotion: *It was an emotional reunion.*
3 causing strong emotions: *This is such an emotional issue.*
—**e•mo•tion•al•ly** adv

e•mo•tive /ɪ'moʊtɪv/ adj causing strong feelings

em•pa•thize /'empəˌθaɪz/ verb [I] to understand how someone else feels

em•pa•thy /'empəθi/ noun [U] the ability to understand how someone else feels

em•per•or /'empərər/ noun [C] a man who rules an EMPIRE

em•pha•sis /'emfəsɪs/ (plural **em•pha•ses** /'emfəˌsiz/) noun [C/U] ★★
1 special importance or attention that is given to one thing in particular: *We **place great emphasis on** employee development.*
2 the extra loudness with which you say a particular phrase, word, or part of a word = STRESS: ***The emphasis is on** the first syllable.*

em•pha•size /'emfəˌsaɪz/ verb [T] ★
1 to give particular importance or attention to something: *The report emphasizes the need for better health education.* ♦ **+that** *He emphasized that no one should be above the law.*
2 to say a phrase, word, or part of a word more loudly
3 to make something more noticeable: *Naomi's white dress emphasized her suntan.*

em•phat•ic /em'fætɪk/ adj **1** said or shown in a very strong clear way: *an emphatic shake of the head* **2** with a very clear result: *an emphatic victory/defeat* —**em•phat•i•cal•ly** /em'fætɪkli/ adv

em•phy•se•ma /ˌemfə'simə/ noun [U] a very serious illness that affects your lungs

em•pire /'empaɪr/ noun [C] ★
1 a number of countries that are ruled by one person or government: *the Roman empire*
2 a large powerful group of companies that are controlled by one person or company: *an international media empire*

em•pir•i•cal /em'pɪrɪk(ə)l/ adj based on real experience or scientific experiments rather than on theory —**em•pir•i•cal•ly** adv

em•ploy /ɪm'plɔɪ/ verb [T] ★★
1 to pay someone regularly to work for you: *a large automobile factory that employs over 8,000 people* ♦ **employ sb as sth** *Jean was employed as a computer programmer.*
2 *formal* to use something for a particular purpose: *They employed an imaginative marketing strategy.*

> **Word family: employ**
> *Words in the same family as **employ***
> - **employed** *adj*
> - **unemployed** *adj*
> - **employment** *n*
> - **unemployment** *n*
> - **employer** *n*
> - **employee** *n*

em•ploy•ee /ɪm'plɔɪi, ˌɪmplɔɪ'i/ noun [C] ★★ someone who is paid regularly to work for a person or organization: *part-time employees*

em•ploy•er /ɪm'plɔɪər/ noun [C] ★★ a person or organization that pays workers to work for them: *The factory is the largest single employer in the area.*

em•ploy•ment /ɪm'plɔɪmənt/ noun [U] ★★★
1 work that you are paid regularly to do: *Many qualified nurses are unable to **find employment**.*
2 a situation in which people have regular paid work ≠ UNEMPLOYMENT: *Employment has risen among people over 55.*

em•pow•er /em'paʊr/ verb [T] **1** *formal* to give a person or organization the legal authority to do something **2** to make someone feel that they have control over their life and their work: *Our goal is to empower everyone on our staff.* —**em•pow•er•ment** noun [U]

em•press /'emprɪs/ noun [C] a woman who rules an EMPIRE or who is married to an EMPEROR

emp•ty¹ /'empti/ adj ★★★
1 containing no things or people ≠ FULL: *an empty jar* ♦ *The room was empty.* ♦ *empty streets*
2 lacking emotion, interest, or purpose: *Her life felt empty and meaningless.*
3 not true or serious: *an empty promise/ threat/gesture*
—**emp•ti•ness** noun [U]

emp•ty² /'empti/ verb **1** [T] to make something empty ≠ FILL **2** [I] if a place empties, all the people in it leave

E

PHRASAL VERB ˌempty sth ˈout *same as* empty² 1

emp·ty-hand·ed /ˌempti ˈhændəd/ adj without getting anything for your effort: *They returned empty-handed from the peace negotiations.*

em·u·late /ˈemjəˌleɪt/ verb [T] *formal* to try to be like someone or something else

en·a·ble /ɪnˈeɪb(ə)l/ verb [T] ★★★ to give someone the ability or opportunity to do something: **enable sb to do sth** *This will enable users to conduct live video conversations.*

en·act /ɪnˈækt/ verb [T] to make a proposal into a law —**en·act·ment** noun [C/U]

e·nam·el /ɪˈnæm(ə)l/ noun [C/U] **1** a hard shiny substance that is used for protecting or decorating glass, metal, or clay **2** the hard white outer layer of teeth

en·camp·ment /ɪnˈkæmpmənt/ noun [C] a large group of tents or temporary shelters

en·cap·su·late /ɪnˈkæpsjəˌleɪt/ verb [T] to express something in a short clear form that gives the most important facts or ideas about it

en·case /ɪnˈkeɪs/ verb [T] to completely cover or enclose something

en·chant·ed /ɪnˈtʃæntəd/ adj **1** very attracted by something, or getting great pleasure from it: *She performed a Beethoven sonata, and we were all enchanted by her playing.* **2** affected by magic

en·chant·ing /ɪnˈtʃæntɪŋ/ adj very attractive, or giving great pleasure

en·chi·la·da /ˌentʃɪˈlɑdə/ noun [C] a Mexican food consisting of a piece of flat bread rolled up and filled with meat and cheese, served with a hot sauce

en·cir·cle /ɪnˈsɜrk(ə)l/ verb [T] to completely surround something

en·clave /ˈenˌkleɪv, ˈɑŋˌkleɪv/ noun [C] an area of a country or city where a particular group of people lives

en·close /ɪnˈkloʊz/ verb [T] **1** to surround someone or something: *The swimming pool was enclosed by a high fence.* **2** to send something such as a document with a letter: *Please enclose a copy of your birth certificate with your application.* —**en·closed** /ɪnˈkloʊzd/ adj

en·clo·sure /ɪnˈkloʊʒər/ noun [C] an area that is surrounded by a fence or wall

en·com·pass /ɪnˈkʌmpəs/ verb [T] *formal* to include a lot of people or things: *The term "world music" encompasses a wide range of musical styles.*

en·core /ˈɑŋˌkɔr/ noun [C] a short performance given after the main performance, because the audience asks for more

en·coun·ter¹ /ɪnˈkaʊntər/ verb [T] **1** to experience or deal with something, especially a problem: *We encountered one small problem during the first test.* **2** *formal* to meet someone or see something for the first time

en·coun·ter² /ɪnˈkaʊntər/ noun [C] **1** a meeting, especially one that was not planned **2** an experience or DISCOVERY of a particular kind: *my earliest encounter with ballet*

en·cour·age /ɪnˈkʌrɪdʒ/ verb [T] ★★★
1 to try to persuade someone to do something that you believe would be good ≠ DISCOURAGE: *We encourage student participation in our classes.* ♦ **encourage sb to do sth** *Mom always encouraged us to discuss our problems.*
2 to provide conditions that make it easier for something to happen ≠ DISCOURAGE: *Bad hygiene encourages the spread of disease.*
3 to give someone confidence or hope ≠ DISCOURAGE: *His optimism encouraged me.*
—**en·cour·age·ment** noun [C/U]

> **Word family: encourage**
> *Words in the same family as encourage*
> - **encouraging** *adj*
> - **encouragement** *n*
> - **discourage** *v*
> - **discouraging** *adj*
> - **discouragement** *n*
> - **discouraged** *adj*

en·cour·ag·ing /ɪnˈkʌrɪdʒɪŋ/ adj giving you confidence or hope ≠ DISCOURAGING: *They are testing a new Aids drug, and the first results are encouraging.* —**en·cour·ag·ing·ly** adv

en·croach /ɪnˈkroʊtʃ/ PHRASAL VERB **enˈcroach on sth** or **enˈcroach uˌpon sth 1** to gradually take something such as power or authority from someone else: *The federal government is encroaching on states' rights.* **2** to gradually cover more land

en·crust·ed /ɪnˈkrʌstəd/ adj covered with a hard layer of something

en·cy·clo·pe·di·a /ɪnˌsaɪkləˈpidiə/ noun [C] a book or set of books that gives information about a lot of different subjects or one particular subject

end¹ /end/ noun [C] ★★★

1 final part	4 part in activity
2 when sth stops	5 purpose
3 part farthest out	+ PHRASES

1 the final part of a period of time: *We're going on vacation* ***at the end of*** *this month.* ♦ *They'll make their decision* ***at the very end of*** *the week.* ♦ *The work should be completed* ***by the end of*** *the year.*
2 the time when a situation or an event stops: *Are you going to stay until* ***the end of*** *the game?* ♦ *After* ***the end of*** *the war many promises were made.* ♦ *We both knew that the partnership had* ***come to an end.*** ♦ *We want to* ***put an end to*** (=stop) *discrimination.* ♦ *the final battle that* ***brought*** *the war* ***to an end*** (=made it end)
3 the part of something that is furthest away from the center: *Hold both ends of the rope.* ♦ *The only door was* ***at the far end of*** *the corridor.*
4 *spoken* the part that you have in an activity or situation: *Kate is more involved in the research end of things.* ♦ *I've* ***kept my end of the bargain*** (=done what I promised), *but he hasn't kept his.*
5 *formal* something that you want to achieve: *She used people* ***for her own ends.***

PHRASES **at the end of the day** *spoken* used for saying that something is the most important aspect of a situation: *There were problems, but at the end of the day, everyone got what they wanted.*

hours/days/weeks etc. on end used for emphasizing how long something continues:

He talks for hours on end about absolutely nothing.

in the end *spoken* finally: *In the end, I decided not to buy the shoes.*

make ends meet to have just enough money to buy the things that you need
→ DEEP[1], HAIR, MEANS

end² /end/ verb ★★★
1 [T] to be in a particular place or state at the end of a period: *We ended the day in a more hopeful mood.* ♦ *The team looks likely to end the season as champions.*
2 [I/T] to stop existing, or to make something stop existing: *The marriage ended after only 11 months.* ♦ *The injury ended his career.*
3 [I/T] if you end by doing or saying something, it is the last thing that you do or say: *Let's **end** the meeting **with** a short prayer.*
PHRASAL VERBS **ˈend in sth** to have something as a final result: *All of our attempts ended in failure.*
ˌend ˈup *spoken* to be in a place or state after doing something, or because of doing something: *Keep on doing that and you'll end up in serious trouble.* ♦ *Somehow they all ended up at my house.* ♦ **end up doing sth** *I ended up spending the night in the airport.*

en·dan·ger /ɪnˈdeɪndʒər/ verb [T] to put someone or something into a situation where they might be harmed

en·dan·gered spe·cies /ɪnˌdeɪndʒərd ˈspiʃiz/ noun [C] a type of animal or plant that may soon stop existing because not many of them are left in the world

en·dear /ɪnˈdɪr/ PHRASAL VERB **enˈdear yourself to sb** to make someone like you

en·dear·ing /ɪnˈdɪrɪŋ/ adj making people like you

en·deav·or /ɪnˈdevər/ verb [I] *formal* to try very hard to do something

en·dem·ic /enˈdemɪk/ adj very common in a place or situation

end·ing /ˈendɪŋ/ noun ★
1 [C] the way in which a story, movie, or play ends: *Children usually prefer books with a happy ending.*
2 [singular] a time when something stops permanently: *Officials have announced **the ending of** price controls.*
3 [C] the last group of letters in a word: *a plural ending*

en·dive /ˈenˌdaɪv/ noun [C/U] *American* a vegetable with a bitter taste used in salads

end·less /ˈendləs/ adj lasting or continuing for a very long time: *There seemed to be an endless supply of food at the meeting.* ♦ *endless questions* —**end·less·ly** adv

en·dorse /ɪnˈdɔrs/ verb [T] to say publicly that you support someone or something —**en·dorse·ment** noun [C/U]

en·dow /ɪnˈdaʊ/ verb **be endowed with sth** to have a good ability or quality

ˌend ˈproduct noun [C] the thing that is produced at the end of a process

en·dur·ance /ɪnˈdʊrəns/ noun [U] the ability to continue doing something that is difficult or tiring

en·dure /ɪnˈdʊr/ verb **1** [T] to suffer something unpleasant without becoming upset **2** [I] to last for a long time

en·dur·ing /ɪnˈdʊrɪŋ/ adj lasting for a long time

ˈend ˌzone noun [C] the area at the end of a football field where you have to take the ball in order to score points —*picture* → C15

en·e·my /ˈenəmi/ noun [C] ★★
1 someone who is opposed to someone else and tries to harm them ≠ FRIEND: *They searched for information on political enemies.* ♦ *Terrorists are described as **enemies of the state**.* ♦ *It's easy to **make enemies** in a job like this.*
2 a country that is fighting another country in a war ≠ ALLY: *enemy aircraft/soldiers/tanks* ♦ *They had to prevent **the enemy** from attacking.*

en·er·get·ic /ˌenərˈdʒetɪk/ adj an energetic person has a lot of energy and is very active —**en·er·get·ic·al·ly** /ˌenərˈdʒetɪkli/ adv

en·er·gy /ˈenərdʒi/ noun [U] ★★★
1 the power that your body needs in order to do physical things: *She didn't even **have the energy** to get out of bed.*
2 electricity and other forms of power used for making things work: *energy sources/supplies* ♦ *Turning off lights is a good way to **save energy**.*

en·force /ɪnˈfɔrs/ verb [T] to make people obey a law, rule, etc.: *Troops were sent in to enforce the treaty.* ♦ *The regulation was never enforced.* —**en·force·ment** noun [U]

Eng. abbrev England or English

en·gage /ɪnˈgeɪdʒ/ verb **1** [I/T] if a part of a machine engages, or if you engage it, it fits into another part and they start to move together ≠ DISENGAGE **2** [T] *formal* to attract someone's interest or attention and keep it **3** [T] *formal* to employ someone
PHRASE **engage sb in conversation** to start having a conversation with someone

en·gaged /ɪnˈgeɪdʒd/ adj ★ if two people are engaged, they have formally agreed to get married: *She's **engaged to** someone she met at work.* ♦ *We **got engaged** about this time last year.*

en·gage·ment /ɪnˈgeɪdʒmənt/ noun [C] **1** a formal agreement to get married: *an engagement ring* **2** an arrangement to meet someone or do something

en·gag·ing /ɪnˈgeɪdʒɪŋ/ adj attractive and pleasant

en·gen·der /ɪnˈdʒendər/ verb [T] *formal* to make people have a particular feeling

en·gine /ˈendʒɪn/ noun [C] ★★★
1 the part of a vehicle that makes it move: *the ship's engine* ♦ *a jet/gasoline/diesel/steam engine*
2 a vehicle that pulls a train = LOCOMOTIVE

en·gi·neer¹ /ˌendʒɪˈnɪr/ noun [C] ★
1 someone who designs things such as roads, railroads, or machines
2 *American* someone whose job is to drive a train

en·gi·neer² /ˌendʒɪˈnɪr/ verb [T] to arrange something in a clever or secret way

en·gi·neer·ing /ˌendʒɪˈnɪrɪŋ/ noun [U] ★ the activity of designing things such as roads, railroads, or machines

en·grave /ɪnˈgreɪv/ verb [T] to cut words or pictures into a hard surface such as stone, metal, or glass —**en·grav·er** noun [C]

E

en·grav·ing /ɪnˈgreɪvɪŋ/ noun [C] a picture that is printed using a piece of metal that has the picture cut into its surface

en·grossed /ɪnˈgroʊst/ adj so interested or involved in something that you do not think about anything else

en·gulf /ɪnˈgʌlf/ verb [T] **1** to cover something in a way that destroys it: *Within minutes, the car was engulfed in flames.* **2** to have a very strong effect on someone or something: *Feelings of panic engulfed them.*

E

en·hance /ɪnˈhæns/ verb [T] to improve something, or to make something more attractive: *We've enhanced the quality of the picture.* —**en·hance·ment** noun [U]

e·nig·ma /ɪˈnɪgmə/ noun [C] someone or something that is mysterious and difficult to understand

en·ig·mat·ic /ˌenɪgˈmætɪk/ adj mysterious and difficult to understand

en·joy /ɪnˈdʒɔɪ/ verb [T] ★★★
1 to get pleasure from something: *Did you enjoy your dinner?* ♦ **enjoy doing sth** *I don't enjoy going to the movies as much as I used to.*
2 *formal* to have a particular good feature: *The hotel enjoys a magnificent view of the harbor.*
PHRASE **enjoy yourself** to get pleasure from something that you do: *I haven't enjoyed myself so much for a long time.*

en·joy·a·ble /ɪnˈdʒɔɪəb(ə)l/ adj something that is enjoyable gives you pleasure: *an enjoyable evening* ♦ *Most students find the course very enjoyable.*

en·joy·ment /ɪnˈdʒɔɪmənt/ noun [U] pleasure that you get from an activity or experience: *their enjoyment of life*

en·large /ɪnˈlɑrdʒ/ verb [T] to make something bigger: *I sent the pictures back to be enlarged.*

en·large·ment /ɪnˈlɑrdʒmənt/ noun [C/U] the process of making something bigger, or something that has been made bigger

en·light·en /ɪnˈlaɪt(ə)n/ verb [T] to give someone information about something so that they understand more about it —**en·light·en·ing** adj

en·light·ened /ɪnˈlaɪt(ə)nd/ adj with sensible modern attitudes

en·light·en·ment /ɪnˈlaɪt(ə)nmənt/ noun [U] the process of understanding something clearly: *spiritual enlightenment*

en·list /ɪnˈlɪst/ verb **1** [I] to join the military **2** [T] if you enlist someone or enlist their help, you ask them to help or support you

en·liv·en /ɪnˈlaɪv(ə)n/ verb [T] *formal* to make something more interesting or lively

en masse /ɑn ˈmæs/ adv all together as a group

en·mi·ty /ˈenməti/ noun [C/U] *formal* a feeling of hate

e·nor·mi·ty /ɪˈnɔrməti/ noun [U] the fact that something is very big, important, or wrong: *the enormity of the problem*

e·nor·mous /ɪˈnɔrməs/ adj ★★ very large in size or quantity: *an enormous birthday cake* ♦ *The stress they're under is enormous.* ♦ *an enormous amount of money*

e·nor·mous·ly /ɪˈnɔrməsli/ adv extremely, or very much: *an enormously valuable experience*

e·nough /ɪˈnʌf/ grammar word ★★★

> **Enough** can be:
> - a **determiner**: *There isn't enough time.* ♦ *Have I made enough sandwiches?*
> - a **pronoun**: *I've only got $12 – will that be enough?*
> - an **adverb**: *The rope isn't long enough.* ♦ *She didn't move quickly enough.*

1 as much or as many as is necessary: *He doesn't have enough experience as a teacher.* ♦ *"Would you like something more to eat?" "No thanks, I've had enough."* ♦ *There aren't **enough of** us to make up a team.* ♦ *Do we have **enough** knives and forks **for** everyone?* ♦ *You've had **more than enough** time to finish the job.* ♦ **enough to do sth** *Some of the workers don't earn enough to live on.*
2 with as much of a particular quality as is necessary: *Ken wants to join the army when he's old enough.* ♦ *He told me I wasn't working hard enough.* ♦ **be good/stupid/lucky etc. enough to do sth** *I was lucky enough to meet her once.* ♦ *She's intelligent enough to understand that!*
3 *spoken* used for saying that you do not want to experience any more of something because it is annoying or boring: *I've only been to one of her lectures, and that was enough!* ♦ *I'm leaving. I've **had enough of** work for today.* ♦ ***That's enough!** Stop that noise!*
4 used after an adjective or adverb for emphasis: *It's natural enough to be upset, after what happened.*
PHRASES **it's bad/difficult/hard enough** used for saying that a situation is already bad and something else would make it even worse: *It's bad enough that you were late, without lying about the reason.*
strangely/oddly/funnily enough used for showing that you think a particular fact is strange or surprising: *Funnily enough, Robert was saying exactly the same thing yesterday.*

en·quire /ɪnˈkwaɪr/ another spelling of **inquire**

en·quir·y /ɪnˈkwaɪri/ another spelling of **inquiry**

en·rage /ɪnˈreɪdʒ/ verb [T] to make someone extremely angry —**en·raged** /ɪnˈreɪdʒd/ adj

en·rich /ɪnˈrɪtʃ/ verb [T] to make something better or more enjoyable: *Doing volunteer work has enriched my life.* —**en·rich·ment** noun [U]

en·roll /ɪnˈroʊl/ verb [I/T] to put your name on the official list of students who go to a particular school, university, course, etc., or to put another person's name on the list for them —**en·roll·ment** noun [C/U]

en route /ɑn ˈrut/ adv on the way: *We went through Little Rock en route to Memphis.*

en·sconce /ɪnˈskɑns/ verb **be ensconced** *formal* to be in a comfortable or safe place

en·sem·ble /ɑnˈsɑmb(ə)l/ noun [C] **1** a group of musicians, dancers, or actors who perform together **2** a group of things that look good together

en·shrine /ɪnˈʃraɪn/ verb **be enshrined in** *formal* to be officially accepted by being included in a document

en•slave /ɪnˈsleɪv/ verb [T] **1** to keep someone in a bad situation from which they cannot escape **2** to make someone a SLAVE —**en•slave•ment** noun [U]

en•sue /ɪnˈsu/ verb [I] to happen after something else, often as a result of it: *A fight quickly ensued.* —**en•su•ing** adj

en suite /ɑ̃ ˈswit/ adj *British* an en suite bathroom is one that is joined to a bedroom

en•sure /ɪnˈʃʊr/ verb [T] ★★ to make certain that something happens or is done: **+(that)** *Our new system ensures that everyone gets paid on time.*

en•tail /ɪnˈteɪl/ verb [T] *formal* to involve something, or to make something necessary: *These cuts will entail some job losses.*

en•tan•gled /ɪnˈtæŋg(ə)ld/ adj **1** so involved in a complicated situation that it is difficult to get out **2** stuck in something such as ropes or wires —**en•tan•gle•ment** noun [U]

en•ter /ˈentər/ verb ★★★

1 go or come in	4 take part in sth
2 start to do sth	5 start a period of time
3 write sth	+ PHRASAL VERB

1 [I/T] to go or come into a place: *The man had entered through the back door.* ♦ *They were imprisoned for illegally entering the country.*

2 [T] to start to do something: *There are dozens of new companies entering the software market.* ♦ *She had hoped to enter the legal profession.*

3 [T] to write something somewhere, for example in a book, on a form, or on a computer: *Enter your user name and password.*

4 [I/T] to arrange to be in a race or competition, or to arrange for someone else to do this: *The competition is free, and anyone over the age of 18 can enter.*

5 [T] to start or reach a period of time: *The war had already entered its third week.*

PHRASAL VERB **ˌenter ˈinto sth 1** to start to take part in something: *Adams agreed to enter into talks with the British government.* **2** to be an important aspect of a situation: *When companies are trying to save money, loyalty to workers doesn't enter into it.*

en•ter•prise /ˈentərˌpraɪz/ noun **1** [C] a business: *Euro Disney is a much smaller enterprise than the American Disney parks.*
2 [C] a large or important project, especially a new one: *an exciting scientific enterprise*
3 [U] the ability to create new businesses or projects: *The success of the band is mainly due to Jim's initiative and enterprise.*

en•ter•pris•ing /ˈentərˌpraɪzɪŋ/ adj willing to try or think of new ideas or methods

en•ter•tain /ˌentərˈteɪn/ verb ★

1 [T] to give a performance that people enjoy: *The children sang and danced to entertain the crowd.*

2 [I/T] to receive someone as a guest and give them food and drink: *The front room is used for entertaining visitors.*

3 [T] *formal* to consider an idea or feeling and allow it to develop in your mind: *Edberg entertained hopes of winning the championship.*

en•ter•tain•er /ˌentərˈteɪnər/ noun [C] someone whose job is to entertain people

en•ter•tain•ing /ˌentərˈteɪnɪŋ/ adj enjoyable or interesting: *an entertaining talk/evening/program*

en•ter•tain•ment /ˌentərˈteɪnmənt/ noun [U] ★★ performances that people enjoy: *A jazz band provided entertainment for the evening.*

en•thrall /ɪnˈθrɔl/ verb [I/T] to make you so interested in something that you give it all your attention: *This is a story that enthralls listeners.* —**en•thrall•ing** adj

en•thu•si•asm /ɪnˈθuziˌæzəm/ noun [U] ★ the feeling of being very interested in something or excited by it: *His **enthusiasm for** music has stayed strong.*

en•thu•si•ast /ɪnˈθuziæst/ noun [C] someone who is very interested in something and spends time doing it or learning about it

en•thu•si•as•tic /ɪnˌθuziˈæstɪk/ adj ★ very interested in something, or excited by it ≠ UNENTHUSIASTIC: *Business leaders gave an enthusiastic welcome to the proposal.* ♦ *For a while, we were **enthusiastic about** the idea.* —**en•thu•si•as•ti•cal•ly** /ɪnˌθuziˈæstɪkli/ adv

en•tice /ɪnˈtaɪs/ verb [T] to persuade someone to do something by offering them an advantage or reward —**en•tic•ing** adj: *an enticing offer*

en•tire /ɪnˈtaɪr/ adj ★★ whole or complete: *She has spent her entire life in London.*

en•tire•ly /ɪnˈtaɪrli/ adv ★★★ completely, or in every way: *We have entirely different tastes in music.* ♦ *I'm not entirely sure I believe him.*

en•tire•ty /ɪnˈtaɪrəti/ noun **in its/their entirety** with all or everything included: *The movie was shown in its entirety.*

en•ti•tle /ɪnˈtaɪt(ə)l/ verb [T] **1** to give someone the right to do something: **entitle sb to sth** *Membership entitles you to cheaper tickets.* ♦ **entitle sb to do sth** *Some children are entitled to claim free school meals.* **2** to give a title to a book, poem, or piece of music: *Her first novel was entitled* More Innocent Times.

en•ti•tle•ment /ɪnˈtaɪt(ə)lmənt/ noun [C/U] the right to receive something or to do something

enˈtitlement ˌprogram noun [C] *American* a government program that provides money or care for people who are old, sick, or unemployed

en•ti•ty /ˈentəti/ noun [C] *formal* something that exists separately from other things and has its own character

en•tou•rage /ˈɑntʊˌrɑʒ/ noun [C] a group of people who go somewhere with an important person

en•trance /ˈentrəns/ noun ★★★

1 [C] the place where you can enter a room, building, or area ≠ EXIT: *I'll meet you at the **main entrance** at six o'clock.* ♦ *The statue stands at **the entrance to** the harbor.*

2 [U] The right or ability to enter a place, or to join an organization: *Entrance to the museum is free.* ♦ *There is a $10 **entrance fee**.*

3 [C] the act of going into a place: *Crowds cheered as she **made her entrance**.*

en•tranced /ɪnˈtrænst/ adj so impressed by

someone or something that you cannot look at or think about anything else

en·trant /ˈentrənt/ noun [C] someone who enters a competition or examination

en·trée /ˈɑnˌtreɪ/ noun [C] the main part of a meal, especially at a restaurant

en·trenched /ɪnˈtrentʃt/ adj entrenched attitudes have existed for a long time and are difficult to change

en·tre·pre·neur /ˌɑntrəprəˈnʊr/ noun [C] someone who uses money to start businesses and make business deals —**en·tre·pre·neur·i·al** adj

E

en·trust /ɪnˈtrʌst/ verb [T] to give someone responsibility for an important job or activity

en·try /ˈentri/ noun ★★★

1 into a place	4 for a competition
2 right to be a member	5 entrance
3 information	

1 [U] the right or ability to go into a place: *Entry to the exhibition costs $5.50.* ♦ *They were charged with illegal **entry into** the U.S.* ♦ *We had to remove the lock on the door to **gain entry*** (=get in).
2 [U] the right to become a member of an organization, profession, or other group: *Older students are being denied **entry into** full-time education.*
3 [C] a set of information that is written in a book, on a list, or on a computer: *the dictionary entry for the word "play"*
4 [C] a piece of work that you do to try to win a competition: *The contest attracted entries from all over the country.*
5 [C] an entrance to a building

en·twine /ɪnˈtwaɪn/ verb [T] to curl or twist one thing around another
PHRASE **be entwined** to be closely connected

en·vel·op /ɪnˈveləp, enˈveləp/ verb [T] to surround someone or something completely

en·ve·lope /ˈenvəˌloʊp, ˈɑnvəˌloʊp/ noun [C] ★★★ a flat paper case that you put a letter in before you send it

en·vi·a·ble /ˈenviəb(ə)l/ adj an enviable quality or situation is one that someone has and that other people would like to have ≠ UNENVIABLE

en·vi·ous /ˈenviəs/ adj unhappy because you want something that someone else has → JEALOUS

en·vi·ron·ment /ɪnˈvaɪrənmənt, ɪnˈvaɪərnmənt/ noun ★★★
1 [C] the place in which people live and work, including all the physical conditions that affect them: *Parents are responsible for providing the right environment for their children to learn in.* ♦ *He grew up in a harsh urban environment.*
2 **the environment** [singular] the natural world, including the land, water, air, plants, and animals: *Industrial development is causing damage to the environment.*

> Words often used with **environment**
>
> *Adjectives often used with **environment** (sense 1)*
> ■ **safe, stable** + ENVIRONMENT: used about environments that people like
> ■ **classroom, rural, school, urban** + ENVIRONMENT: used about particular types of environment
>
> *Verbs often used with **environment** (sense 2)*
> ■ **damage, destroy, pollute** + THE ENVIRONMENT: have a bad effect on the environment
> ■ **preserve, protect** + THE ENVIRONMENT: not allow the environment to be damaged

en·vi·ron·men·tal /ɪnˌvaɪrənˈment(ə)l, ɪnˌvaɪərnˈment(ə)l/ adj ★★★
1 relating to the natural world and the effect that human activity has on it: *Both candidates discussed environmental issues.*
2 intended to help or protect the environment: *Some environmental groups are opposed to tourism on the island.*
—**en·vi·ron·men·tal·ly** adv

en·vi·ron·men·tal·ist /ɪnˌvaɪrənˈment(ə)lɪst, ɪnˌvaɪərnˈment(ə)lɪst/ noun [C] someone who wants to protect the environment

en͵vironmentally ˈfriendly adj not harming the natural environment

en·vi·sion /ɪnˈvɪʒ(ə)n/ or **en·vis·age** /ɪnˈvɪzɪdʒ/ verb [T] to imagine that something will happen in the future

en·voy /ˈenvɔɪ/ noun [C] an official who represents their government in another country

en·vy¹ /ˈenvi/ noun [U] the unhappy feeling that you have when you want something that someone else has
PHRASE **be the envy of** to have good qualities that people admire and would like to have themselves

en·vy² /ˈenvi/ verb [T] to have the unhappy feeling of wanting what someone else has
PHRASE **I don't envy you/him etc.** *spoken* used for saying that you would not like to do what someone else has to do

en·zyme /ˈenˌzaɪm/ noun [C] a natural substance that is produced by animal and plant cells and that causes chemical reactions

e·phem·er·al /ɪˈfem(ə)rəl/ adj lasting for only a short time

ep·ic¹ /ˈepɪk/ noun [C] a long book, poem, or movie that contains a lot of exciting events

ep·ic² /ˈepɪk/ adj very long and exciting: *an epic journey*

ep·i·dem·ic¹ /ˌepɪˈdemɪk/ noun [C] **1** a situation in which a disease spreads very quickly and infects many people **2** a sudden increase in something bad or unpleasant that affects many people

ep·i·dem·ic² /ˌepɪˈdemɪk/ adj happening a lot and affecting many people: *In some cities, drug use has reached epidemic proportions.*

ep·i·lep·sy /ˈepɪˌlepsi/ noun [U] a brain disease that makes you suddenly shake in an uncontrolled way or become unconscious

ep·i·lep·tic /ˌepɪˈleptɪk/ noun [C] someone who has epilepsy —**ep·i·lep·tic** adj

ep·i·logue /ˈepɪˌlɑg/ noun [C] an extra comment or piece of information at the end of a book or play

E·pis·co·pal Church, the /ɪˌpɪskəp(ə)l ˈtʃɜrtʃ/ noun a Protestant Church that developed from the Anglican Church

ep·i·sode /ˈepɪˌsoʊd/ noun [C] **1** one part of a

series in a television or radio story **2** an important event in a story, in someone's life, or during a particular period of time

ep·i·taph /ˈepɪˌtæf/ noun [C] a piece of writing that honors a dead person, especially one written on their GRAVE (=place where they are buried)

e·pit·o·me /ɪˈpɪtəmi/ noun **the epitome of** the best possible example of a particular type of person or thing

e·pit·o·mize /ɪˈpɪtəˌmaɪz/ verb [T] to be the best possible example of a particular type of person or thing

ep·och /ˈepək, ˈɪˌpɑk/ noun [C] a long period of time in history

e·qual[1] /ˈikwəl/ adj ★★★

1 the same in value, amount, or size: *All the workers have an equal share in the profits.* ♦ *One unit of alcohol* ***is equal to*** *one small glass of wine.* ♦ *The two companies are* ***equal in size.*** ♦ *Every game is* ***of equal importance*** *to us.*

2 having or deserving the same rights, status, and opportunities as other people: *He believed that men and women were equal.* ♦ *They are equal partners in every aspect of their lives.*

PHRASE **on an equal footing** or **on equal terms** with the same rights and conditions as someone else: *In the early part of the century women got the vote, on equal terms with men.*

e·qual[2] /ˈikwəl/ (present participle **e·qual·ing** or **e·qual·ling**; past tense and past participle **e·qualed** or **e·qualled**) verb [T] **1** to be the same in value or amount as something else: *Five plus three equals eight.* **2** to be as good as someone or something else: *She equaled the record with a time of 27.69 seconds.*

e·qual[3] /ˈikwəl/ noun [C] someone or something that has the same value, rights, or importance as another person or thing

e·qual·i·ty /ɪˈkwɑləti/ noun [U] ★ the state of being equal, especially in having the same rights, status, and opportunities as other people ≠ INEQUALITY

e·qual·ize /ˈikwəˌlaɪz/ verb [T] to make something the same in size, amount, or importance

e·qual·ly /ˈikwəli/ adv ★★

1 in equal amounts or quantities: *The money raised will be divided equally among the charities.*

2 to the same degree: *This recipe works equally well with whole wheat flour.*

3 in a way that is fair and the same for everyone: *We will treat all the cases equally.*

ˌequal opporˈtunity noun [C/U] a situation in which people have the same opportunities in life as other people, without being treated in an unfair way because of their race, sex, religion, or age

ˈequal ˌsign or **ˈequals ˌsign** noun [C] the sign = used in mathematics to show that two sets of numbers are the same in quantity or amount

e·quate /ɪˈkˌweɪt/ verb [T] to consider something to be the same as something else: *These people seem to equate honesty with weakness.*

e·qua·tion /ɪˈkweɪʒ(ə)n/ noun [C] a statement in mathematics that two sets of numbers or expressions are equal: *Solve the equation* $5x - 3 = 27$.

e·qua·tor, the /ɪˈkweɪtər/ noun [singular] an imaginary line that goes around the center of the Earth and divides it into northern and southern parts —**e·qua·to·ri·al** /ˌekwəˈtɔriəl/ adj

e·ques·tri·an /ɪˈkwestriən/ adj connected with riding horses

e·qui·lib·ri·um /ˌikwɪˈlɪbriəm, ˌekwɪˈlɪbriəm/ noun [C/U] a situation in which there is a balance between different forces or aspects

e·quip /ɪˈkwɪp/ verb [T] **1** to provide a person or place with the things that they need for a particular purpose: *They received a grant to build and equip a new clinic.* **2** to provide someone with the skills or qualities that they need in order to deal with a situation successfully: *The training had equipped her to deal with emergency situations.*

e·quip·ment /ɪˈkwɪpmənt/ noun [U] ★★★ the tools, machines, or other things that you need for a particular job or activity: *camping equipment* ♦ *A computer is the most important* ***piece of equipment*** *you will buy.*

eq·ui·ta·ble /ˈekwɪtəb(ə)l/ adj *formal* fair and reasonable because everyone is treated in the same way: *an equitable distribution of funds*

eq·ui·ty /ˈekwəti/ noun [U] *formal* a fair and reasonable way of behaving toward people, so that everyone is treated equally

e·quiv·a·lent[1] /ɪˈkwɪvələnt/ adj ★ of the same size, value, importance, or meaning as something else: *The price is $30,000, or the equivalent amount in Euros.* ♦ *a distance* ***equivalent to*** *a return flight from Moscow to Beijing*

e·quiv·a·lent[2] /ɪˈkwɪvələnt/ noun [C] someone or something that has the same size, value, importance, or meaning as someone or something else

ER /ˌi ˈɑr/ noun [C] *American* an EMERGENCY ROOM in a hospital

e·ra /ˈerə, ˈɪrə/ noun [C] a historical period of time that has a particular quality or character: *The president promised to bring about a new era of peace.*

e·rad·i·cate /ɪˈrædɪˌkeɪt/ verb [T] to get rid of something bad completely —**e·rad·i·ca·tion** /ɪˌrædɪˈkeɪʃ(ə)n/ noun [U]

e·rase /ɪˈreɪs/ verb [T] to remove all the writing, sound, or pictures from something: *The virus erases all the files on your hard drive.*

e·ras·er /ɪˈreɪsər/ noun [C] **1** a piece of rubber for removing marks on paper made by a pencil —*picture* → C3 **2** an object that you use for removing marks from a BLACKBOARD or WHITEBOARD

e·rect[1] /ɪˈrekt/ verb [T] *formal* to build something, or to put something in an upright position: *Police erected barriers to control the crowds.*

e·rect[2] /ɪˈrekt/ adj in a straight upright position: *the erect posture of a professional soldier*

e·rec·tion /ɪˈrekʃ(ə)n/ noun **1** [C] a stiff PENIS **2** [U] *formal* the process of erecting something such as a building or fence

er•go•nom•ics /ɜrgəˈnɑmɪks/ noun [U] the study of the way in which furniture and equipment can be designed so that the user is comfortable and can work effectively —**er•go•nom•ic** /ɜrgəˈnɑmɪk/ adj

e•rode /ɪˈroʊd/ verb [I/T] **1** to gradually damage the surface of rock or land so that it begins to disappear, or to be gradually damaged in this way **2** to gradually reduce the strength, importance, or value of something, or to be gradually reduced in this way —**e•ro•sion** /ɪˈroʊʒ(ə)n/ noun [U]

E

e•rot•ic /ɪˈrɑtɪk/ adj containing scenes or descriptions that make you sexually excited: *erotic movies*

err /ɜr/ verb [I] *formal* to make a mistake
PHRASE **err on the side of sth** to do more than is really necessary in order to avoid a particular situation: *We are erring on the side of caution and have closed the school.*

er•rand /ˈerənd/ noun [C] a small job that involves going to get or deliver something

er•rant /ˈerənt/ adj *formal* behaving in a way that is bad or wrong

er•rat•ic /ɪˈrætɪk/ adj changing often, or not following a regular pattern =UNPREDICTABLE: *erratic behavior* —**er•rat•ic•al•ly** /ɪˈrætɪkli/ adv

er•ro•ne•ous /ɪˈroʊniəs/ adj *formal* not correct: *reports based on erroneous information* —**er•ro•ne•ous•ly** adv

er•ror /ˈerər/ noun ★★★
1 [C/U] a mistake, for example in a calculation or a decision: *an* ***error in*** *our calculations* ♦ *He admitted that he'd* ***made an error*** *in rejecting their offer.* ♦ *I was guilty of* ***an error of judgment*** *in allowing myself to be placed in this situation.* ♦ *The computer had been turned off* ***in error****.*
2 [C] a failure in a computer process: *an error message* (=telling you that something is wrong)
→ TRIAL

e•rupt /ɪˈrʌpt/ verb [I] **1** if a VOLCANO erupts, it explodes inside and flames, rocks, and LAVA come out of the top **2** to start suddenly with a lot of violence or noise: *Heavy fighting erupted in the city on Sunday.* **3** to suddenly become very angry, excited, or noisy: *The crowd erupted into wild cheers.* —**e•rup•tion** /ɪˈrʌpʃ(ə)n/ noun [C/U]

es•ca•late /ˈeskəˌleɪt/ verb **1** [I/T] to become much worse or more serious, or to make something much worse or more serious **2** [I] to increase at an uncontrolled rate: *escalating costs* —**es•ca•la•tion** /ˌeskəˈleɪʃ(ə)n/ noun [C/U]

es•ca•la•tor /ˈeskəˌleɪtər/ noun [C] a set of moving stairs that take people from one level of a building to another

es•ca•pade /ˈeskəˌpeɪd/ noun [C] something exciting or dangerous that someone is involved in

es•cape¹ /ɪˈskeɪp/ verb ★★
1 [I] to get away from a dangerous or unpleasant place: *Three people died in the fire, but John escaped through the bedroom window.* ♦ *She was shot while trying to* ***escape from*** *prison.*
2 [I/T] to avoid a dangerous or unpleasant experience: *Two security guards escaped injury in the attack.* ♦ *San Diego narrowly escaped defeat in their first game of the season.*
3 [I] to come out of a container by accident: *How will we know if there's any gas escaping?*
4 [T] if something escapes you, you cannot remember it or you do not notice it: *His name escapes me right now.*
—**es•caped** /ɪˈskeɪpt/ adj: *an escaped prisoner*

es•cape² /ɪˈskeɪp/ noun ★
1 [C/U] an act of avoiding or getting away from a person, place, or bad situation: *She was relieved to* ***make her escape from*** *the meeting.* ♦ *A couple* ***had a narrow escape*** (=were almost killed) *when a tree fell just in front of their car.*
2 [C/U] a way of helping yourself to stop thinking about an unpleasant situation you are in: *He used alcohol as a means of escape.*
3 [U] *computing* the ESCAPE KEY on a computer

esˈcape ˌkey noun [C] *computing* a key on a computer keyboard that allows you to stop an action or leave a program

es•cap•ism /ɪˈskeɪˌpɪzəm/ noun [U] a pleasant or exciting activity or entertainment that helps you to forget about real life —**es•cap•ist** adj

es•cort¹ /ɪˈskɔrt/ verb [T] **1** to go somewhere with a person or vehicle, to protect them or prevent them from escaping **2** to go with another person to a social event as their partner

es•cort² /ˈesˌkɔrt/ noun [C] **1** a person or a group of people or vehicles that go somewhere with someone in order to protect them or prevent them from escaping: *He arrived in court under police escort.* **2** someone, especially a man, who goes with another person to a social event as their partner

Es•ki•mo /ˈeskɪmoʊ/ noun [C] *old-fashioned* a member of the Inuit people. Some people think that this word is offensive and prefer to use the word **Inuit**.

ESL /ˌi es ˈel/ noun [U] English as a Second Language: the activity of teaching English to people whose first language is not English, but who live in an English-speaking country

ESOL /ˈiˌsɑl/ noun [U] English for Speakers of Other Languages: the activity of teaching English to people whose first language is not English

es•o•ter•ic /ˌesəˈterɪk/ adj known about or understood by very few people

ESP /ˌi es ˈpi/ noun [U] English for Specific or Special Purposes: the activity of teaching English to people whose first language is not English, but who need to speak English for their job or for another purpose

esp. abbrev especially

es•pe•cial•ly /ɪˈspeʃ(ə)li/ adv ★★★
1 used when mentioning conditions that make something more relevant, important, or true =PARTICULARLY: *It was a very cold house, especially in the winter.*
2 used for showing that what you are saying affects one person or thing more than others =PARTICULARLY: *Don't talk to anyone about this – especially not my mother.*
3 very, or very much =PARTICULARLY: *I'm*

not especially interested in sports. 4 for a particular purpose, or for a particular person: *a service **especially for** local people*

es•pi•o•nage /ˈespiəˌnɑʒ/ noun [U] attempts to discover the secrets of a country that is your enemy

es•pouse /ɪˈspaʊz/ verb [T] *formal* to support an idea, principle, or belief

es•pres•so /eˈspresoʊ/ noun [C/U] a small cup of very strong coffee, or this type of coffee

es•say /ˈeˌseɪ/ noun [C] ★ a short piece of writing on a particular subject, especially by a student: *We have to write **an essay about** Romantic poetry.*

es•sence /ˈesəns/ noun **1** [singular/U] the most important and typical part of something: *images that captured the essence of life in our country before the war* **2** [C/U] a liquid that contains the strong taste or smell of the plant that it is taken from

PHRASE **in essence** *formal* used for emphasizing what is the most important feature of something

es•sen•tial /ɪˈsenʃ(ə)l/ adj ★★★
1 completely necessary: *It is absolutely essential that all these issues are discussed.* ♦ *A good dictionary is **essential for** learning English.* ♦ ***It is essential to** involve your staff in the decision.*
2 basic and important: *food, fuel, and other essential supplies*

es•sen•tial•ly /ɪˈsenʃ(ə)li/ adv ★★
1 used for emphasizing the most important aspect of something: *That, essentially, is the difference between them.*
2 used for saying that something is mostly true, but not completely true: *The list is essentially complete.*

es•sen•tials /ɪˈsenʃ(ə)lz/ noun [plural] things that are completely necessary or basic

es•tab•lish /ɪˈstæblɪʃ/ verb [T] ★★
1 to make something start to exist or start to happen: *Mandela was eager to establish good relations with the business community.* ♦ *A proper procedure for complaints should be established.*
2 to start an organization or company: *The company was established in 1860.*
3 to achieve success, so that people recognize your skill, qualities, or power: **establish yourself/sb (as sth)** *Reagan quickly established himself as a promising movie actor.*
4 to discover, prove, or decide that something is true: *The cause of death has not yet been established.* ♦ **+(that)** *We have established that you were present that afternoon.*

es•tab•lished /ɪˈstæblɪʃt/ adj having existed or done something for a long time, and therefore recognized as good or successful: *an old established family firm*

es•tab•lish•ment /ɪˈstæblɪʃmənt/ noun ★★
1 [C] *formal* an institution, organization, or business: *a research/training establishment*
2 **the establishment** [singular] the most important and powerful people in a country or section of society
3 [U] the process of starting or creating something: *Davis proposed the establishment of the committee.*

es•tate /ɪˈsteɪt/ noun [C] ★
1 a large piece of land that belongs to one person with a big house on it
2 *British* a DEVELOPMENT of houses
3 *British* a STATION WAGON

es•teem /ɪˈstim/ noun [U] *formal* a feeling of admiration and respect for someone =REGARD

es•teemed /ɪˈstimd/ adj *very formal* admired and respected

es•thet•ic /esˈθetɪk/ an American spelling of aesthetic

es•thet•ics /esˈθetɪks/ an American spelling of aesthetics

es•ti•mate¹ /ˈestɪˌmeɪt/ verb [T] ★★ to guess or calculate an amount or value by using available information: *It is impossible to **estimate how many** of the residents were affected.* ♦ **estimate sth at sth** *The total cost was estimated at $600,000.* ♦ **+(that)** *We estimate that 20 percent of the harvest has been lost.*

es•ti•mate² /ˈestɪmət/ noun [C] ★
1 an amount that you guess or calculate by using the information that is available: *The figure mentioned is just **a rough estimate**.*
2 a statement that tells a customer how much money you will charge if they employ you to do a particular piece of work: *Can you give us an estimate for the repairs to the roof?*

> **Words often used with estimate**
>
> *Adjectives often used with **estimate** (noun, sense 1)*
>
> ■ **accurate, realistic, reliable** + ESTIMATE: used about an estimate that is likely to be correct
>
> ■ **approximate, rough, unofficial** + ESTIMATE: used about an estimate that might not be correct

es•ti•ma•tion /ˌestɪˈmeɪʃ(ə)n/ noun [singular] *formal* someone's opinion

es•tranged /ɪˈstreɪndʒd/ adj *mainly journalism* **1** no longer living with your husband or wife **2** no longer seeing friends or relatives because of a disagreement

es•tro•gen /ˈestrədʒən/ noun [U] a HORMONE (=chemical substance) produced in a woman's body

es•tu•ar•y /ˈestʃuˌeri/ noun [C] the part of a large river where it becomes wide and flows into the ocean

etc. /et ˈset(ə)rə/ abbrev et cetera: used after a list of things to mean "and others of the same type," when you do not want to mention everything

etch /etʃ/ verb [I/T] to make marks on a hard surface by cutting into it

e•ter•nal /ɪˈtɜrn(ə)l/ adj continuing and never ending —**e•ter•nal•ly** /ɪˈtɜrn(ə)li/ adv

e•ter•ni•ty /ɪˈtɜrnəti/ noun **1** [U] all time, with no beginning and no end **2** [singular] an extremely long time: *After what seemed like an eternity, he gave his answer.*

E•ther•net /ˈiθərˌnet/ *trademark* a system in which several computers in an area are directly connected to each other by wires

eth•ic /ˈeθɪk/ noun **1** [singular] a general principle or belief that affects the way that people behave: *a strong team ethic* **2 ethics**

[plural] a set of principles that people use to decide what is right and what is wrong: *business/medical/professional ethics*

eth·i·cal /ˈeθɪk(ə)l/ adj **1** involving the principles that people use for deciding what is right and what is wrong: *ethical issues/standards/objections* **2** morally right ≠ UNETHICAL: *Is it really ethical to keep animals in zoos?* —**eth·i·cal·ly** /ˈeθɪkli/ adv

eth·nic /ˈeθnɪk/ adj ★
1 relating to a group of people who have the same culture and traditions: *The country's population consists of three main ethnic groups.*
2 belonging a particular ethnic group that lives in a place where most people are from a different ethnic group: *ethnic Albanians living in Kosovo*
3 involving people from different ethnic groups: *ethnic conflict/violence*
4 ethnic clothing, food, or music comes from countries outside Western Europe and North America
—**eth·ni·cal·ly** /ˈeθnɪkli/ adv

eth·nic cleans·ing /ˌeθnɪk ˈklenzɪŋ/ noun [U] the use of violence to force people who belong to a particular ethnic group to leave an area

eth·nic·i·ty /eθˈnɪsəti/ noun [C/U] the fact that someone belongs to a particular ETHNIC group

ˌethnic miˈnority noun [C] a group of people with the same culture and traditions who live in a place where most people have a different culture and different traditions

e·thos /ˈiˌθɑs/ noun [singular] *formal* the set of attitudes and beliefs that are typical of an organization or a group of people

et·i·quette /ˈetɪˌket/ noun [U] a set of rules for behaving correctly in social situations

et·y·mol·o·gy /ˌetɪˈmɑlədʒi/ noun **1** [U] the study of the origins and development of words **2** [C] the origin and development of a particular word —**et·y·mo·log·i·cal** /ˌetɪməˈlɑdʒɪk(ə)l/ adj

EU, the /ˌi ˈju/ the European Union

eu·lo·gy /ˈjulədʒi/ noun [C] a speech at a funeral about the person who has died

eu·phe·mism /ˈjufəˌmɪzəm/ noun [C] a word or expression that people use when they want to talk about something unpleasant or embarrassing without mentioning the thing itself: *"Social exclusion" seems to be the latest euphemism for poverty.*

eu·pho·ri·a /juˈfɔriə/ noun [U] a feeling of great happiness that lasts for a short time only —**eu·phor·ic** /juˈfɔrɪk/ adj

eu·ro /ˈjʊroʊ/ noun [C] ★ the unit of money that is used in most countries in the European Union. Its symbol is €.

Eu·rope /ˈjʊrəp/ noun **1** the large area of land between Asia and the Atlantic Ocean **2** the European Union

Eu·ro·pe·an[1] /ˌjʊrəˈpiən/ adj **1** of Europe, or from Europe **2** relating to the European Union

Eu·ro·pe·an[2] /ˌjʊrəˈpiən/ noun [C] someone from Europe

ˌEuropean ˈUnion, the noun an organization of European countries whose aim is to improve trade among its members and encourage closer political connections

eu·tha·na·sia /ˌjuθəˈneɪʒə/ noun [U] the practice of killing a very old or very sick person in order to stop them from suffering

e·vac·u·ate /ɪˈvækjuˌeɪt/ verb [I/T] to leave a place because it is not safe, or to make people leave a place because it is not safe: *The building was immediately evacuated.*
—**e·vac·u·a·tion** /ɪˌvækjuˈeɪʃ(ə)n/ noun [U]

e·vac·u·ee /ɪˌvækjuˈi/ noun [C] someone who is evacuated from their home because of a dangerous situation such as a war

e·vade /ɪˈveɪd/ verb [T] **1** to avoid dealing with someone or something that you should deal with: *He had become an expert at evading responsibility.* **2** to avoid being caught: *The armed robbers managed to evade the police.*

e·val·u·ate /ɪˈvæljuˌeɪt/ verb [T] to think carefully about something before you make a judgment about its value, importance, or quality —**e·val·u·a·tion** /ɪˌvæljuˈeɪʃ(ə)n/ noun [C/U]

e·van·gel·i·cal /ˌivænˈdʒelɪk(ə)l/ adj relating to a form of Christianity in which people express their religious beliefs in an enthusiastic way

e·van·gel·ism /ɪˈvændʒəˌlɪzəm/ noun [U] the practice of teaching people about Christianity

e·van·gel·ist /ɪˈvændʒəlɪst/ noun [C] someone who travels around trying to persuade people to become Christians

e·vap·o·rate /ɪˈvæpəˌreɪt/ verb [I] **1** if liquid evaporates, it changes into gas or steam **2** if something such as a feeling or quality evaporates, it suddenly disappears
—**e·vap·o·ra·tion** /ɪˌvæpəˈreɪʃ(ə)n/ noun [U]

e·va·sion /ɪˈveɪʒ(ə)n/ noun **1** [U] the practice of avoiding doing something that you should do **2** [C/U] something that you say in order to avoid telling the truth about something

e·va·sive /ɪˈveɪsɪv/ adj not talking or answering questions in an honest way
PHRASE **take evasive action** to do something to avoid a dangerous situation
—**e·va·sive·ly** adv

eve /iv/ noun **on the eve of sth** on the day before an important event, or during the period of time just before it
→ CHRISTMAS EVE, NEW YEAR'S EVE

e·ven[1] /ˈiv(ə)n/ adv ★★★
1 used when you are saying something that is surprising: *It always feels cold in this room, even in summer.* ♦ *Even the dog refused to eat it.* ♦ *They didn't even offer me a glass of water.* ♦ ***Even now**, after all these years, he still misses her.*

> When emphasizing verbs, **even** comes before an ordinary verb: *They even served champagne at breakfast.* But **even** comes after an auxiliary verb, a modal verb, or the verb "to be": *She doesn't even know his name.* ♦ *Some computers can even talk to you.*

2 used for emphasizing that something is bigger, better, etc. than something else that is also big, good, etc.: *Things are bad, but they were even worse before you came.* ♦ *She works **even more** quickly than I do.*
PHRASES **even if** used for emphasizing that

although something may happen, another situation remains the same: *She won't apologize, even if she's proved wrong.*

even so used for introducing a statement that seems surprising after what you said before: *Crashes are rare, but, even so, there should be stricter safety regulations.*

even though used for introducing a fact that makes the main statement in your sentence very surprising: *Most of us ignore this good advice, even though we know it to be true.* ♦ *Even though I have a master's degree in business administration, I can't fill out my tax form.*

e·ven² /ˈiv(ə)n/ adj **1** flat and level ≠ UNEVEN: *The table kept wobbling because the floor wasn't quite even.* **2** not changing much in rate, level, or amount ≠ UNEVEN: *an even temperature* **3** an even number can be divided exactly by two ≠ ODD **4** with both teams or people having an equal chance of winning: *an even match*

PHRASES **be even** *informal* if two people are even, neither of them owes the other anything

get even (with sb) *informal* to punish someone by causing them as much trouble or harm as they have caused you

→ BREAK[1], KEEL

e·ven³ /ˈiv(ə)n/ PHRASAL VERB **ˌeven (sth) ˈout** if things even out, or if you even them out, they show fewer changes or differences

eve·ning¹ /ˈivnɪŋ/ noun [C/U] ★★★ the part of the day between the end of the afternoon and night: *We spend most evenings reading or listening to music.* ♦ *I'll see you on Monday evening, OK?* ♦ *We usually go to the movies on Thursday evenings* (=every Thursday evening). ♦ *an evening meal/ performance/newspaper* ♦ *I'm so tired* ***in the evenings****, all I want to do is sit and watch television.* ♦ *The incident took place at around 9 o'clock* ***yesterday evening****.*

eve·ning² /ˈivnɪŋ/ interjection used for greeting someone in the evening

e·ven·ly /ˈiv(ə)nli/ adv **1** in an equal or regular way: *Sprinkle the sugar evenly over the cake.* **2** with each person having an equal chance to win: *The two teams are fairly evenly matched.*

e·vent /ɪˈvent/ noun [C] ★★★

1 something that happens: *the most important event of my life* ♦ *a series of events*

2 an organized occasion such as a party or sports competition: *The concert is an annual event.* ♦ *Staff at the hospital helped to organize the event.*

3 one of the planned activities that take place during an occasion such as a sports competition: *the winner of the first event*

PHRASES **in any event** whatever happens or has happened: *In any event, the project would never have succeeded.*

in the event of sth used for saying what will happen in a particular situation: *the procedures to be followed* ***in the event of fire***

e·vent·ful /ɪˈventf(ə)l/ adj with a lot of exciting or unusual things happening ≠ UNEVENTFUL

e·ven·tu·al /ɪˈventʃuəl/ adj happening or existing at the end of a long process or period of time = ULTIMATE: *This mistake led to his eventual capture and imprisonment.*

e·ven·tu·al·ly /ɪˈventʃuəli/ adv ★★★ at the end of a long process or period of time: *Eventually, we became good friends.* ♦ *the scientific research that we hope will eventually produce a cure*

ev·er /ˈevər/ adv ★★★ used for meaning "at any time in the past, present, or future," especially in questions, negatives, and CONDITIONAL sentences: *Have you ever been to Las Vegas?* ♦ *Don't ever do that again.* ♦ *If you ever need any help, just let me know.* ♦ *It* ***hardly ever*** (=almost never) *rains here in the summer.* ♦ *Isabel's looking prettier* ***than ever****.* ♦ *It was her* ***first time ever*** *on an airplane.*

E

PHRASES **all sb ever does/wants/gets etc.** *spoken* used for emphasizing that the same thing happens all the time: *All he ever does is complain.*

ever since during the whole period of time since something happened: *I met Harry in high school and we've been friends ever since.* ♦ *Ever since his wife left him, he's been depressed.*

→ FOREVER

ev·er·green /ˈevərˌgrin/ noun [C] a tree or plant that does not lose its leaves in winter —**ev·er·green** adj

ev·er·last·ing /ˌevərˈlæstɪŋ/ adj continuing forever

eve·ry /ˈevri/ determiner ★★★

1 used for referring to all the people or things of a particular type: *Every bedroom has its own private bathroom.* ♦ *She wrote to every member of the committee.* ♦ *This is a decision that affects* ***every single*** *one of us.*

2 used for showing how often something happens or how far apart things are: *Take one pill every four hours.* ♦ *There are army checkpoints every few miles along the road.* ♦ *I have to work* ***every other*** *weekend* (=on the first, third, fifth, etc.). ♦ ***Every once in a while*** (=not too frequently) *an event occurs that changes public attitudes.*

3 used for showing how common something is by giving a number as a part of a larger number: *Almost one in every five computers was found to be faulty.*

4 used before some words for emphasis: *You have every reason to feel proud of your performance.*

PHRASE **every time** whenever something happens: *We can't keep calling the doctor every time you get a headache.*

→ BIT[1]

- A noun subject that follows **every** is used with a singular verb.
- In formal writing, pronouns or possessive adjectives that refer back to a subject with **every** are usually singular: *Every employee has his or her own key to the building.* But in speech and informal writing, plural pronouns and possessive adjectives are more usual, although some people consider this incorrect: *Every employee has their own key to the building.*

eve·ry·bod·y /ˈevriˌbɑdi/ pronoun ★★★ everyone: *Has everybody remembered to bring a pen?* ♦ *Bill had the courage to say* *what everybody else was thinking.*

ev·ery·day /ˈevriˌdeɪ/ adj very common or completely normal: *everyday life*

ev·ery·one /ˈevriˌwʌn/ pronoun ★★★
1 every person in a group: *Happy New Year, everyone!* ♦ *Everyone is thrilled about Jean's baby.* ♦ *James made a point of shaking everyone's hand.* ♦ ***Everyone else** had finished eating.*
2 used for talking about people in general: *Everyone needs a friend.* ♦ ***Not everyone** can afford to take a big trip every year.*

E

- When **everyone** is a subject, it is used with a singular verb.
- In formal writing, pronouns or possessive adjectives that refer back to **everyone** are usually singular: *Everyone should bring his or her own lunch.* But in speech and informal writing, plural pronouns and possessive adjectives are more usual, although some people consider this incorrect: *Everyone should bring their own lunch.*

ev·ery·place /ˈevriˌpleɪs/ grammar word *American informal* everywhere

ev·ery·thing /ˈevriˌθɪŋ/ pronoun ★★★
1 all the things, activities, etc. that are involved in a situation: *The earthquake destroyed everything within 25 miles.* ♦ *Everything's done by computer nowadays.* ♦ *If you put the books back on the shelves, I'll put **everything else** away.*
2 life in general, or a particular situation: *You look upset – is everything all right?*
PHRASES **and everything** *spoken* used for referring to other similar things without saying exactly which: *Did you say goodbye and everything?*
be/mean everything to be more valuable or important than anyone or anything else: *Beauty isn't everything, you know!*

ev·ery·where /ˈevriˌwer/ adv in or to every place: *Everywhere in the world people know his name.* ♦ *Rosie travels everywhere with me.* ♦ *My keys must be in the desk, I've searched everywhere else.*

e·vict /ɪˈvɪkt/ verb [T] to legally force someone to leave the house that they are living in —**e·vic·tion** /ɪˈvɪkʃ(ə)n/ noun [C/U]

ev·i·dence /ˈevɪdəns/ noun [U] ★★★
1 facts or physical signs that help to prove something: **+that** *The study found no evidence that fish feel pain.* ♦ *the historical **evidence for** his theories* ♦ *We are seeing more **evidence of** economic growth.*
2 facts, statements, or objects that help to prove whether someone has committed a crime: *The police didn't have enough evidence to convict him.* ♦ *The **evidence against** them is overwhelming.*

ev·i·dent /ˈevɪdənt/ adj *formal* easy to see, notice, or understand

ev·i·dent·ly /ˈevɪdəntli/ adv **1** used for showing that a statement is based on known facts: *Evidently, these plants don't do well in a cold climate.* **2** used for saying that something is obvious: *Evidently annoyed, he left the room.*

e·vil[1] /ˈiv(ə)l/ adj **1** very bad or cruel: *a dangerous and evil dictator* **2** very unpleasant: *an evil-smelling chemical*

e·vil[2] /ˈiv(ə)l/ noun [U] a power that makes people do very bad and cruel things ≠ GOOD
PHRASE **the evils of sth** the bad effects that something can have
→ LESSER[1], NECESSARY

e·voc·a·tive /ɪˈvɑkətɪv/ adj *formal* bringing a particular emotion, idea, or memory into your mind

e·voke /ɪˈvoʊk/ verb [T] *formal* to bring a particular emotion, idea, or memory into your mind

ev·o·lu·tion /ˌevəˈluʃ(ə)n/ noun [U] **1** the theory that plants and animals change over long periods of time to become more appropriate for their environment **2** the way in which something gradually changes and develops —**ev·o·lu·tion·ar·y** /ˌevəˈluʃ(ə)nˌeri/ adj

e·volve /ɪˈvɑlv/ verb **1** [I] to gradually change and develop over a period of time: *Computer software will continue to evolve in response to users' needs.* ♦ *a debate as to whether birds evolved from dinosaurs* **2** [T] to develop something gradually: *Teachers are evolving new ways of working.*

ewe /ju/ noun [C] a female sheep

ex /eks/ noun [C] *informal* the person that someone used to be married to or used to have a romantic relationship with

ex- /eks/ prefix used with nouns that describe someone's job, rank, or relationship to someone, showing that they do not have that job, rank, or relationship any more: *an ex-boyfriend*

ex·ac·er·bate /ɪɡˈzæsərˌbeɪt/ verb [T] *formal* to make a problem worse

ex·act[1] /ɪɡˈzækt/ adj ★ done, made, or described in a very thorough way, with all the details correct: *the exact sequence of events leading up to the accident* ♦ *The exact number of wounded people is unknown.*
PHRASE **the exact opposite** used for emphasizing that two things or people are completely different: *She's very friendly, the exact opposite of her sister.*

ex·act[2] /ɪɡˈzækt/ verb [T] *formal* to get something from someone by threatening or forcing them

ex·act·ing /ɪɡˈzæktɪŋ/ adj needing a lot of skill and effort

ex·act·ly /ɪɡˈzæk(t)li/ adv ★★★
1 no more and no less than a particular amount or time = PRECISELY: *It's exactly three o'clock.* ♦ *The wood should measure five centimeters exactly.*
2 in every way, or in every detail = JUST: *She sounds exactly like her mother.* ♦ *The house is **exactly the same** as it was 20 years ago.*
3 used for emphasizing that you are referring to one particular thing and no other = JUST: *She was standing exactly where you are now.*
4 *spoken* used as a reply for saying that you completely agree with someone: *"If he does that again, he could lose his job." "Exactly!"*
PHRASES **not exactly** *spoken* **1** *often humorous* used for emphasizing that someone or something does not have a particular quality: *She's not exactly the world's greatest singer.* **2** used for saying that

something that someone says is not completely right: *"You're leaving, aren't you?" "Not exactly, I'm just going on vacation."*
what/where/when etc. exactly used for asking someone for more details about something: *What exactly did he say?*

ex·ag·ger·ate /ɪɡˈzædʒəˌreɪt/ verb [I/T] ★ to describe something in a way that makes it seem better, worse, larger, more important, etc. than it really is: *Don't exaggerate! It wasn't that bad!* ♦ *We should not exaggerate the importance of this agreement.*

ex·ag·ger·at·ed /ɪɡˈzædʒəˌreɪtəd/ adj **1** describing something in a way that makes it seem better, worse, larger, more important, etc. than it really is: *exaggerated claims* **2** done in a way that does not seem sincere or natural: *a tone of exaggerated politeness*

ex·ag·ger·a·tion /ɪɡˌzædʒəˈreɪʃ(ə)n/ noun **1** [C] a comment or description that makes something seem better, worse, larger, more important, etc. than it really is **2** [U] the act of making a comment or description of this type

ex·alt·ed /ɪɡˈzɔltəd/ adj *formal* very important

ex·am /ɪɡˈzæm/ noun [C] ★★
1 an important test of your knowledge, especially one that you take at school: *I'm **taking the exam** in June.* ♦ *She really needs to **pass this exam**.*
2 *American* a medical examination: *an eye exam*

ex·am·i·na·tion /ɪɡˌzæmɪˈneɪʃ(ə)n/ noun ★★★
1 [C/U] a careful look at something or someone: *The doctor will give you a full examination.* ♦ *Engineers made **a thorough examination of** the wreckage.*
2 [C] *formal* an exam: *Students will take an examination at the end of the year.*
3 [C/U] a careful study of something: ***a close examination** of the language of a text*
4 [C/U] an occasion when a lawyer asks someone questions in court

ex·am·ine /ɪɡˈzæmɪn/ verb [T] ★★★
1 to look at something or someone carefully: *She opened the suitcase and examined the contents.* ♦ *Dr. Greene has come to examine the patient.*
2 to study or consider something carefully: *The committee will examine four proposals.*
3 to ask someone questions in a legal trial
4 *formal* to give students an examination to test their knowledge

ex·am·in·er /ɪɡˈzæmɪnər/ noun [C] someone whose job is to test people's knowledge or ability

ex·am·ple /ɪɡˈzæmp(ə)l/ noun [C] ★★★
1 something that you mention in order to show the type of thing that you are talking about and to help to explain what you mean: *Many sports are still dominated by men – football is an obvious example.* ♦ *He gave several **examples of** how we could change things.* ♦ *The Mustang is **a classic example*** (=a typical example) *of a great American car.*
2 a person or way of behaving that is considered as a model for other people to copy: *You should be **setting an example** for your little brother.*

PHRASE **for example** used when mentioning something that shows the type of thing that you are talking about and helps to explain what you mean: *There are good deals available – people under 25, for example, can get discounts of up to 50%.*

ex·as·per·at·ed /ɪɡˈzæspəˌreɪtəd/ adj extremely annoyed —**ex·as·per·ate** verb [T]

ex·as·per·at·ing /ɪɡˈzæspəˌreɪtɪŋ/ adj making you feel extremely annoyed

ex·as·per·a·tion /ɪɡˌzæspəˈreɪʃ(ə)n/ noun [U] the feeling of being extremely annoyed

ex·ca·vate /ˈekskəˌveɪt/ verb [I/T] to dig in the ground in order to find things from the past —**ex·ca·va·tion** /ˌekskəˈveɪʃ(ə)n/ noun [C/U]

ex·ceed /ɪkˈsid/ verb [T] *formal* **1** to be greater than a number or amount: *a claim exceeding $500* **2** to go above an official limit: *drivers who exceed the speed limit*

ex·ceed·ing·ly /ɪkˈsidɪŋli/ adv *formal* extremely

ex·cel /ɪkˈsel/ verb [I] to do something extremely well

ex·cel·lence /ˈeksələns/ noun [U] the quality of being extremely good: *academic excellence*

ex·cel·lent /ˈeksələnt/ adj ★★★ extremely good: *The food was absolutely excellent.* ♦ *It's an old bike, but it's **in excellent condition**.* —**ex·cel·lent·ly** adv

ex·cept /ɪkˈsept/ grammar word ★★★

> **Except** can be:
> - a **preposition**: *We haven't told anyone except Leslie's dad.*
> - a **conjunction**: *I'd go and see him myself, except I don't know where he lives.*
> - used before a **conjunction**: *I don't know much about the man, except that he's an idiot.*
> - used in the prepositional phrase **except for**: *Everything was perfect except for the weather.*

1 used for introducing the only thing, person, or fact that is not included in your main statement: *The whole team was there, except Pete.* ♦ *The store is open every day, except on Sundays.* ♦ *I never get a chance to study, except when the children have gone to bed.* ♦ *She was dressed all in black **except for** a white scarf.* ♦ **+(that)** *I don't know anything except that the flight is delayed.* ♦ **except do sth** *He did nothing all day except watch television.*
2 *spoken* used for introducing a statement that makes what you have just said seem less true or less possible: **+(that)** *I'd be glad to help, except that I'm going away this weekend.*

ex·cep·tion /ɪkˈsepʃ(ə)n/ noun [C/U] ★★ someone or something that is different and cannot be included in a general statement: *There are some **exceptions to** every grammatical rule.* ♦ *The boat race always attracts a large crowd and this year **is no exception**.* ♦ ***With the exception of** the Metropole, all the hotels have their own restaurants.*

PHRASE **make an exception** to deal with something differently on one particular occasion only: *I don't usually lend people money, but in your case I'll make an exception.*

ex•cep•tion•al /ɪk'sepʃən(ə)l/ adj **1** extremely good or impressive in a way that is unusual ≠ UNEXCEPTIONAL: *Her scores were exceptional.* **2** unusual and not likely to happen or exist very often = EXTREME: *exceptional circumstances* **3** much more or greater than usual: *the exceptional difficulty of this task* —**ex•cep•tion•al•ly** adv

ex•cerpt /'ekˌsɜrpt/ noun [C] a short piece of writing or music that is taken from a longer piece = PASSAGE

E

ex•cess¹ /ɪk'ses, 'ekˌses/ noun **1** [singular/U] a larger amount of something than is usual or necessary **2 excesses** [plural] behavior that is thought to be wrong because it is too extreme: *the worst excesses of the regime*

PHRASES **in excess of sth** more than a particular amount

to excess if you do something to excess, you do it so much that it harms you or causes problems

ex•cess² /'ekˌses/ adj more than is usual or necessary: *Drain off any excess liquid.*

ex•ces•sive /ɪk'sesɪv/ adj much more than is reasonable or necessary

ex•change¹ /ɪks'tʃeɪndʒ/ noun ★★

1 [C/U] a situation in which one person gives, does, or says something and another person gives, does, or says something in return: *a frank exchange of views* ♦ ***an exchange of prisoners of war*** ♦ *Russia supplied crude oil to Cuba* ***in exchange for*** *raw sugar.*

2 [U] the process of changing the money of one country for the money of another country: *a foreign exchange dealer* ♦ ***What is the rate of exchange for U.S. dollars?***

3 [C] an arrangement in which people or groups from different countries visit each other: *a cultural/educational exchange* ♦ *an exchange student from Spain*

→ STOCK EXCHANGE

ex•change² /ɪks'tʃeɪndʒ/ verb [T] ★★

1 to give someone something in return for something that they give you: *We exchanged addresses and promised to write to each other.* ♦ **exchange sth for sth** *The certificates can be exchanged for goods in any of our stores.*

2 to say or do something to someone who says or does something to you: *We exchanged greetings.*

3 to change the money of one country for the money of another country

ex'change ˌrate noun [C] the value of the money of one country when you change it for the money of another country

ex•cise /'ekˌsaɪz/ noun [U] *technical* a government tax on services used and goods sold within a country

ex•cit•a•ble /ɪk'saɪtəb(ə)l/ adj easily excited or upset

ex•cite /ɪk'saɪt/ verb [T] **1** to make someone feel very happy and enthusiastic about something good that is going to happen: *The idea of working in Australia really excites me.* **2** to make someone feel lively, nervous, or upset: *We were warned by the doctors not to excite him.* **3** to make someone feel that they want to have sex

ex•cit•ed /ɪk'saɪtəd/ adj ★★

1 very happy and enthusiastic because something good is going to happen: *I was so excited I couldn't sleep.* ♦ *I'm so* ***excited about the trip!***

2 upset, worried, or angry about something: *Look, Dad, stop getting so excited – I'm sure she'll be home soon.*

3 feeling that you want to have sex —**ex•cit•ed•ly** adv: *He talked excitedly about his plans.*

- **Excited** describes how you feel: *I'm excited about my vacation.* ♦ *She didn't seem very excited.*
- **Exciting** describes things or situations that make you feel excited: *I think basketball games are very exciting.* ♦ *It was such an exciting adventure.*

ex•cite•ment /ɪk'saɪtmənt/ noun [U] ★★ the feeling of being excited: *The long wait only added to our excitement.* ♦ ***the excitement of winning a major championship***

ex•cit•ing /ɪk'saɪtɪŋ/ adj ★★

1 making you feel excited and enthusiastic ≠ UNEXCITING: *an exciting opportunity*

2 interesting and full of action ≠ BORING: *an exciting story of adventure*

ex•claim /ɪk'skleɪm/ verb [I/T] to say something suddenly and loudly because you are surprised or angry

ex•cla•ma•tion /ˌekskləˈmeɪʃ(ə)n/ noun [C] something that you say because you are surprised or angry

excla'mation ˌpoint noun [C] the symbol ! used in writing to show that someone says something suddenly and loudly because they are surprised or angry

ex•clude /ɪk'sklud/ verb [T] ★★

1 to deliberately not include something ≠ INCLUDE: *These figures exclude administration costs.*

2 to deliberately prevent someone or something from being part of something or from entering a place ≠ INCLUDE: *I felt as though the other women were excluding me.* ♦ **exclude sb from sth** *The committee has decided to exclude him from the competition.*

3 to decide that something is not possible or not worth considering: *We cannot* ***exclude the possibility*** *that the patient has cancer.*

ex•clud•ing /ɪk'skludɪŋ/ preposition not including: *The cost of hiring equipment, excluding insurance, is around $600 a year.*

ex•clu•sion /ɪk'skluʒ(ə)n/ noun [U] a situation in which someone or something is deliberately prevented from being part of something or from entering a place ≠ INCLUSION: *the team's exclusion from the competition*

PHRASE **to the exclusion of sth** when you do something to the exclusion of other things, you only do that one thing and not the other things

ex•clu•sive¹ /ɪk'sklusɪv/ adj **1** very expensive and available only to people who have a lot of money: *an exclusive store/restaurant/neighborhood* **2** limited to a particular person or group and not shared with others: *The road is for the exclusive use of residents.* **3** published or reported by only one newspaper, magazine, or television station: *an exclusive interview*

PHRASE **exclusive of sth** not including something: *The cost is $20 exclusive of delivery charges.*

ex•clu•sive² /ɪk'sklusɪv/ noun [C] a piece of news that is published or reported by only one newspaper, magazine, or television station

ex•clu•sive•ly /ɪk'sklusɪvli/ adv only: *a club exclusively for women*

ex•cre•ment /'ekskrəmənt/ noun [U] *formal* the solid waste that your body gets rid of

ex•crete /ɪk'skrit/ verb [I/T] *formal* to get rid of waste from your body

ex•cru•ci•at•ing /ɪk'skruʃiˌeɪtɪŋ/ adj causing extreme physical pain —**ex•cru•ci•at•ing•ly** adv

ex•cur•sion /ɪk'skɜrʒ(ə)n/ noun [C] a short trip that you take for pleasure

ex•cuse¹ /ɪk'skjuz/ verb [T] ★★

1 to forgive someone for something: *Please excuse my messy handwriting.* ♦ **excuse sb for (doing) sth** *I hope you'll excuse us for leaving so early.*

2 to provide a reason or explanation for something bad that someone has done, in order to make it seem less bad: *I know he's over 70, but that doesn't excuse his sexist attitudes.*

3 to give someone permission not to do something that they usually have to do: **excuse sb from (doing) sth** *You're excused from doing the dishes tonight.*

4 to give someone permission to leave: *Now if you'll excuse us, we have to get going.*

PHRASES **excuse me** *spoken* **1** used for politely getting someone's attention, or for showing that you are sorry for interrupting or touching them: *Excuse me, do you know what time it is?* **2** *American* used for asking someone to repeat something: *"How old are you?" "Excuse me?"* **3** used for politely asking someone to move so that you can get past them **4** used for politely telling someone that you are leaving: *Excuse me for a moment – I have to make a phone call.*

excuse yourself to politely say that you are going to leave a place

ex•cuse² /ɪk'skjus/ noun [C] ★★

1 a reason that you give to explain why you have done something bad, or why you have not done something that you should have done: *a reasonable/valid/legitimate excuse* ♦ *He **made** some **excuse** about having a lot of work to do.* ♦ *What **excuse** did they **give** for the delay?*

2 a reason for doing something that you want to do: *Birthdays are always **a good excuse for** a party.* ♦ **an excuse to do sth** *Emily was glad to have an excuse to change the subject.*

3 *American* a note written by your parent or your doctor that explains why you have missed work or school

PHRASE **there is no excuse for sth 1** used for emphasizing that you think that someone's behavior is very bad: *There's no excuse for treating a child that way.* **2** used for saying that someone should definitely do something: *She only lives five minutes away, so there's really no excuse for not visiting her.*

ex•e•cute /'eksəˌkjut/ verb [T] **1** to kill someone as a punishment for a crime: *The prisoner is due to be executed next week.* **2** *formal* to complete something that you have agreed or planned to do: *They were able to execute their task successfully.*

ex•e•cu•tion /ˌeksə'kjuʃ(ə)n/ noun **1** [C/U] the act of killing someone as a punishment for a crime **2** [U] *formal* the act of completing something that you have agreed or planned to do

ex•e•cu•tion•er /ˌeksə'kjuʃ(ə)nər/ noun [C] someone whose job is to EXECUTE criminals

ex•ec•u•tive¹ /ɪg'zekjətɪv/ noun [C] ★

1 a senior manager in a business or other organization: *a meeting with some of the company's top executives*

2 a group of people who are responsible for making important decisions in an organization: *This matter will be decided by the party's national executive.*

ex•ec•u•tive² /ɪg'zekjətɪv/ adj **1** involved in making important decisions in an organization or government: *the executive director of the museum* ♦ *executive powers* **2** designed for rich or important people: *an executive jet*

ex'ecutive ˌbranch, the noun [singular] the part of government that makes certain that laws are being applied as planned. The other two parts of government are the **legislative branch** and the **judicial branch**.

ex•em•pla•ry /ɪg'zempləri/ adj *formal* excellent, or done in a way that other people should try to copy

ex•em•pli•fy /ɪg'zemplɪˌfaɪ/ verb [T] to be a typical example of something

ex•empt¹ /ɪg'zempt/ adj allowed to ignore something such as a rule, obligation, or payment

ex•empt² /ɪg'zempt/ verb [T] to allow someone to ignore something such as a rule, obligation, or payment —**ex•emp•tion** /ɪg'zempʃ(ə)n/ noun [C/U]

ex•er•cise¹ /'eksərˌsaɪz/ noun ★★★

1 physical activity	4 written questions
2 physical action	5 for particular purpose
3 learning activity	6 use of power etc.

1 [U] physical activity that you do in order to stay healthy and make your body stronger: *Try to do 20 minutes of exercise every day.* ♦ *I **get plenty of exercise** being an aerobics instructor.*

2 [C] a physical action that you repeat several times in order to make a part of your body stronger or more healthy: *Roll over and repeat the exercise on the other leg.* ♦ *breathing exercises*

3 [C] an activity or set of activities that you do in order to learn or practice a skill: *military training exercises* ♦ *When did you **do** your piano **exercises**?*

4 [C] a set of written questions that you answer in order to help you to learn something: *Next I'd like you to **do the exercises** on page 10.*

5 [singular] *formal* an action that has a particular plan, purpose, or result: *a cost-cutting exercise* ♦ *Good management is often **an exercise in** compromise.*

E

6 [U] *formal* the use of your power, rights, or skills: *General de Gaulle's military training influenced his exercise of power.*

ex·er·cise² /ˈeksərˌsaɪz/ verb ★★★
1 [I/T] to do a physical activity in order to stay healthy and to make your body stronger: *Do you eat right and exercise regularly?* ♦ *The doctor said I should exercise my knee every morning.*
2 [T] *formal* to use power, skill, or a personal quality: *For centuries, the Church exercised authority over people's lives.*

E

ˈexercise ˌbike noun [C] a bicycle that stays in one place, used for physical exercise —*picture* → C16

ex·ert /ɪgˈzɜrt/ verb [T] *formal* to use influence, authority, or strength in order to affect or achieve something
PHRASE **exert yourself** to use a lot of physical or mental effort

ex·er·tion /ɪgˈzɜrʃ(ə)n/ noun [C/U] great physical or mental effort

ex·hale /eksˈheɪl/ verb [I/T] to breathe air out through your mouth or nose ≠ INHALE

ex·haust¹ /ɪgˈzɔst/ verb [T] **1** to make someone feel extremely tired and without energy: *Caring for young children can exhaust you physically and mentally.* **2** to use all that you have of something: *The expedition was forced to turn back when it exhausted its food supply.*

ex·haust² /ɪgˈzɔst/ noun **1** [C] an EXHAUST PIPE **2** [U] gases or steam that are produced by an engine as it works

ex·haust·ed /ɪgˈzɔstəd/ adj extremely tired and without enough energy to do anything else: *After two days of travel the children were completely exhausted.*

ex·haust·ing /ɪgˈzɔstɪŋ/ adj extremely tiring

ex·haus·tion /ɪgˈzɔstʃ(ə)n/ noun [U] a feeling of being extremely tired and without energy

ex·haus·tive /ɪgˈzɔstɪv/ adj thorough, or complete: *The list is by no means exhaustive.*

exˈhaust ˌpipe noun [C] a pipe that carries the gases or steam out of an engine —*picture* → C6

ex·hib·it¹ /ɪgˈzɪbɪt/ verb **1** [I/T] to put something interesting in a public place so that people can go look at it: *His work will be exhibited in Moscow later this year.* **2** [T] *formal* to show a particular feeling, quality, ability, or form of behavior: *She was exhibiting symptoms of stress.*

ex·hib·it² /ɪgˈzɪbɪt/ noun [C] **1** an object that is part of an exhibition **2** *American* an exhibition of art or other interesting things **3** an object or document that is used as evidence in a court of law

ex·hi·bi·tion /ˌeksɪˈbɪʃ(ə)n/ noun [C] ★★
1 a public show where art or other interesting things are put so that people can go and look at them: *an exhibition hall/center/space* ♦ *an* ***exhibition of*** *paintings by Henri Matisse*
2 a particular way of behaving or performing = DISPLAY: *a fine* ***exhibition of*** *skillful and exciting basketball*

ex·hib·i·tor /ɪgˈzɪbɪtər/ noun [C] a person, company, or organization that shows their work or products in a public place

ex·hil·a·rat·ed /ɪgˈzɪləˌreɪtəd/ adj extremely happy, excited, and full of energy —**ex·hil·a·ra·tion** /ɪgˌzɪləˈreɪʃ(ə)n/ noun [U]

ex·hil·a·rat·ing /ɪgˈzɪləˌreɪtɪŋ/ adj making you feel extremely happy, excited, and full of energy

ex·ile¹ /ˈegˌzaɪl, ˈekˌsaɪl/ noun **1** [U] a situation in which someone is forced to live in a foreign country, usually for political reasons: *He died in exile in 1986.* **2** [C] someone who has been forced to live in a foreign country

ex·ile² /ˈegˌzaɪl, ˈekˌsaɪl/ verb [T] to force someone to live in a foreign country, usually for political reasons

ex·ist /ɪgˈzɪst/ verb [I] ★★★
1 to be present in a particular place, time, or situation: *Several exciting career opportunities exist in our company.* ♦ *The company officially* ***ceased to exist*** *at midnight on March 31st.*
2 to be real, not imaginary: *Dragons don't exist.*
3 to manage to live, especially when conditions are difficult = SURVIVE: *You can't exist for long without water.*

ex·is·tence /ɪgˈzɪstəns/ noun ★★★
1 [U] the state of being a real or living thing, or of being present in a particular place, time, or situation: *The tests confirm* ***the existence of*** *a brain tumor.* ♦ *The company* ***came into existence*** *at the end of the 1980s.* ♦ *the only copy of the book that is* ***still in existence***
2 [C] the way that someone lives their life: *Jones led a miserable existence in an isolated village.*

ex·ist·ing /ɪgˈzɪstɪŋ/ adj ★★★ used for describing something that exists now, especially when it might soon be changed or replaced: *The existing system needs to be changed.*

ex·it¹ /ˈeksɪt/ noun [C] ★
1 a door that leads out of a public place such as a room or building ≠ ENTRANCE: *Passengers should leave the airplane by the nearest* ***emergency exit.***
2 a minor road that you use to drive off a highway: *Take the next exit going north.*
3 the act of leaving a place: *They* ***made a*** *hasty* ***exit*** *through the back door.*

ex·it² /ˈeksɪt/ verb [I/T] **1** *formal* to leave a place **2** to make a computer program stop running

ex·o·dus /ˈeksədəs/ noun [singular] a situation in which a lot of people leave a place at the same time

ex·on·er·ate /ɪgˈzɑnəˌreɪt/ verb [T] *formal* to officially say that someone is not to blame for something

ex·or·bi·tant /ɪgˈzɔrbɪtənt/ adj an exorbitant price or amount of money is much more than is reasonable

ex·or·cise /ˈeksɔrˌsaɪz/ verb [T] to get rid of an evil spirit using a ceremony or prayer —**ex·or·cism** noun [C/U], **ex·or·cist** noun [C]

ex·ot·ic /ɪgˈzɑtɪk/ adj interesting or exciting because of being unusual or not familiar

ex·pand /ɪkˈspænd/ verb [I/T] ★★
1 to become larger, or to make something larger: *The population is expanding*

rapidly. ♦ *There are plans to expand the national park.*
2 if a business or service expands, or if you expand it, it grows by including more people and moving into new areas: *We are expanding the program to provide more student places.*
PHRASAL VERB **ex'pand on sth** to talk or write more about something, adding more details or information

ex·panse /ɪk'spæns/ noun [C] a large area of land, water, or sky

ex·pan·sion /ɪk'spænʃ(ə)n/ noun [U] **1** an increase in size **2** the process of developing to include more people, places, or things

ex·pan·sion·ist /ɪk'spænʃ(ə)nˌɪst/ adj an expansionist government or nation tries to get control over other regions and countries

ex·pan·sive /ɪk'spænsɪv/ adj friendly, generous, or willing to talk

ex·pa·tri·ate /ek'speɪtriət/ noun [C] someone who lives in a foreign country —**ex·pa·tri·ate** adj

ex·pect /ɪk'spekt/ verb [T] ★★★
1 to think that something will happen: *We're expecting good weather this weekend.* ♦ *As* ***expected****, the party was a great success.* ♦ **expect sb/sth to do sth** *I didn't really expect you to understand.* ♦ **+(that)** *Investors expect that interest rates will rise.* → WAIT
2 to think that it is right or reasonable that something should happen: *Our customers expect good service.* ♦ **expect to do sth** *I expect to get paid on time.* ♦ **expect sb/sth to do sth** *It's not fair to expect me to do all the housework.*
3 to be waiting for someone or something to arrive: *Are you expecting a package?* ♦ *What time do you expect Sara home?*
PHRASES **be expecting (a baby)** to be pregnant
I expect *spoken* used for saying that you think that something is probably true: **+(that)** *I expect you're hungry.*

Word family: expect
Words in the same family as ***expect***
- **expected** *adj*
- **unexpected** *adj*
- **expectation** *n*
- **expectancy** *n*
- **expectant** *adj*

ex·pec·tant /ɪk'spektənt/ adj **1** feeling excited about something that you think is going to happen **2** an expectant mother or father will soon be a parent of a new baby —**ex·pec·tan·cy** noun [U], **ex·pec·tant·ly** adv

ex·pec·ta·tion /ˌekspek'teɪʃ(ə)n/ noun ★★
1 [C] a belief or hope that something will be good, or that someone will do well: *We have* ***high expectations*** *of our students* (=expect them to succeed). ♦ *We had heard so much about the restaurant, but it did not* ***live up to our expectations*** (=was not as good as we expected).
2 [C/U] the belief that something will happen: *The team set off without any* ***expectation*** *of success.*

ex·pect·ed /ɪk'spektəd/ adj likely to happen or be true: *Events did not follow their expected course.*

ex·pe·di·en·cy /ɪk'spidiənsi/ noun [C/U] *formal* a way of dealing with something that produces the result that you want in a particular situation, especially when this is not the best or most honest thing to do

ex·pe·di·ent /ɪk'spidiənt/ adj an expedient action produces the result that you want in a particular situation, especially when this is not the best or most honest thing to do

ex·pe·di·tion /ˌekspə'dɪʃ(ə)n/ noun [C] **1** a long trip to a dangerous or distant place **2** a short trip for pleasure

ex·pel /ɪk'spel/ verb [T] **1** to officially force someone to leave a place, organization, or school, for example because of their bad behavior **2** *technical* to force something out of a container or out of someone's body

ex·pend /ɪk'spend/ verb [T] *formal* to spend time, energy, or money on something

ex·pend·a·ble /ɪk'spendəb(ə)l/ adj someone or something that is expendable is no longer useful or necessary to you

ex·pen·di·ture /ɪk'spendɪtʃər/ noun **1** [C/U] the amount of money that is spent by a government, organization, or person =SPENDING **2** [U] *formal* the use of time, money, or energy to do something

ex·pense /ɪk'spens/ noun ★★
1 [C] an amount of money that you spend in order to buy or do something: *traveling/medical/legal expenses* ♦ *Rent is our biggest expense.*
2 [U] the high cost of something: *A powerful computer is worth the expense if you use it regularly.* ♦ *Previously, the chemical had to be imported* ***at great expense****.*
3 **expenses** [plural] money that you spend as part of your job that your employer gives back to you later: *Your salary will be $70,000 a year, plus expenses.*
PHRASES **at sb's expense 1** used for saying who pays for something: *He did a six-month training course at his own expense.* **2** if someone has a joke at your expense, you are the person that the joke is about
at the expense of sth if one thing exists or happens at the expense of another, the second thing suffers because of the first

ex·pen·sive /ɪk'spensɪv/ adj ★★★ something that is expensive costs a lot of money ≠INEXPENSIVE: *He always wears expensive clothes.* ♦ *It can be very expensive to train new personnel.* —**ex·pen·sive·ly** adv

ex·pe·ri·ence[1] /ɪk'spɪriəns/ noun ★★★
1 [U] knowledge and skill that you get by doing a particular job or activity: *You don't need any experience to work here.* ♦ *business/teaching experience* ♦ *Do you have any previous* ***experience with*** *children?* ♦ *She* ***has*** *years* ***of experience*** *in the computer industry.*
2 [U] the knowledge that you get from life and from being in different situations: *I can say* ***from personal experience*** *that it's hard not having a job.* ♦ *Helen knew* ***from past experience*** *that there was no point in arguing with him.*
3 [C] something that happens to you, or a situation that you are involved in: *our childhood experiences* ♦ *I had* ***a bad experience*** *in the last place I worked.*

ex·pe·ri·ence[2] /ɪk'spɪriəns/ verb [T] ★★★
1 if you experience a problem or situation,

you have that problem or are in that situation: *Almost every country of the industrial world is experiencing economic problems.* ♦ *How can we end the discrimination experienced by older people?*
2 to feel an emotion or a physical feeling: *Are you experiencing any pain?*

ex•pe•ri•enced /ɪk'spɪriənst/ adj ★ someone who is experienced has skill at something because they have done it a lot ≠ INEXPERIENCED: *I'm a lot more experienced than him.* ♦ *an experienced sailor* ♦ *She's* ***experienced in*** *dealing with difficult customers.*

E

ex•per•i•ment[1] /ɪk'sperɪmənt, ɪk'sperɪment/ noun [C] ★★
1 a scientific test to find out what happens to someone or something in particular conditions: *laboratory experiments* ♦ *a series of* ***experiments on*** *animals* ♦ *Researchers now need to* ***conduct*** *further* ***experiments.***
2 an occasion when you test a new idea, method, or activity in order to find out what the result will be: ***an experiment in*** *tax reform*

ex•per•i•ment[2] /ɪk'sperɪˌment/ verb [I] **1** to try new ideas, methods, or activities in order to find out what results they will have: *a designer who is not afraid to experiment* **2** to perform scientific tests in order to find out what happens to someone or something in particular conditions: *This lab does not experiment on animals.*

ex•per•i•men•tal /ɪkˌsperɪ'ment(ə)l/ adj **1** using new ideas or methods that you have not tried before **2** relating to scientific experiments —**ex•per•i•men•tal•ly** adv

ex•per•i•men•ta•tion /ɪkˌsperɪmen'teɪʃ(ə)n/ noun [U] the process of testing ideas, methods, or activities to see what effect they have

ex•pert[1] /'ekˌspɜrt/ noun [C] ★★ someone who has a particular skill or knows a lot about a particular subject: *a safety/health/computer expert* ♦ ***an expert in*** *radio communications*

ex•pert[2] /'ekˌspɜrt/ adj having special skills in or knowledge about something —**ex•pert•ly** adv

ex•per•tise /ˌekspər'tiz/ noun [U] special skill or knowledge that you get from experience, training, or study

ex•pi•ra•tion /ˌekspɪ'reɪʃ(ə)n/ noun [U] *American* the end of a period of time during which an agreement, offer, or official document can be used

expi'ration ˌdate noun [C] *American* the date after which something can no longer be used or is no longer safe to eat

ex•pire /ɪk'spaɪr/ verb [I] if an agreement, offer, or official document expires, the period of time during which it can be used comes to an end = RUN OUT

ex•plain /ɪk'spleɪn/ verb ★★★
1 [T] to tell someone something in a way that helps them to understand it better: **explain sth to sb** *The doctor explained the risks to me before the operation.* ♦ **+how/when/what etc.** *I will try to explain how a car engine works.* ♦ **+(that)** *He explained that he would be moving to another city.*
2 [I/T] to give a reason for something that happens: *Science cannot explain everything.* ♦ *"Tom is in the hospital." "That explains why he wasn't in school today."* ♦ *Wait! Let me explain!*
PHRASAL VERB **exˌplain sth a'way** to tell someone about something in a way that makes it seem unimportant, so that they do not ask questions about it: *She made up stories to explain away the missing money.*

Word family: explain
Words in the same family as ***explain***
- **explanation** *n*
- **explanatory** *adj*
- **inexplicable** *adj*
- **unexplained** *adj*

ex•pla•na•tion /ˌeksplə'neɪʃ(ə)n/ noun [C/U] ★★★
1 a reason that you give for something that has happened or something that you have done: *I expected an explanation and an apology.* ♦ ***The explanation for*** *this is simple.* ♦ *He gave* ***a detailed explanation of*** *the events leading up to the accident.*
2 a description of how something works or of how to do something: *This book provides a clear* ***explanation of*** *how to use the Internet.*

ex•plan•a•to•ry /ɪk'splænəˌtɔri/ adj intended to help you to understand something

ex•ple•tive /'eksplətɪv/ noun [C] *formal* a swear word

ex•plic•it /ɪk'splɪsɪt/ adj **1** showing or describing sex or violence in a lot of detail **2** extremely clear —**ex•plic•it•ly** adv

ex•plode /ɪk'sploʊd/ verb ★
1 [I/T] to burst with a lot of force and a loud noise, or to make something do this, usually in a way that causes a lot of damage: *Bombs were exploding all over the city.* ♦ *France first exploded a nuclear device in 1960.*
2 [I] to suddenly express a strong emotion, especially anger: *She suddenly* ***exploded with*** *rage, and stormed off.*
3 [I] to increase a lot over a very short period of time: *The increased availability of food has caused the deer population to explode.*

ex•ploit[1] /ɪk'splɔɪt/ verb [T] ★
1 to treat someone unfairly in order to get some benefit for yourself: *Children are being exploited in many of these factories.*
2 to use a situation so that you get an advantage from it, even if it is wrong or unfair to do this: *A lot of ads just exploit our insecurities.*
3 to make the best use of something so that you get from it as much as possible: *They're just beginning to exploit the country's natural resources.*
—**ex•ploi•ta•tion** /ˌeksplɔɪ'teɪʃ(ə)n/ noun [U]

ex•ploit[2] /'ekˌsplɔɪt/ noun [C] something unusual that someone does that you think is brave, exciting, or entertaining

ex•plo•ra•tion /ˌeksplə'reɪʃ(ə)n/ noun [C/U] **1** a trip around an area in order to learn about it or in order to search for something valuable such as oil **2** a thorough examination or discussion of something

ex•plor•a•to•ry /ɪk'splɔrəˌtɔri/ adj done in order to learn more about something

ex•plore /ɪk'splɔr/ verb ★★
1 [I/T] to travel around an area in order to learn about it, or in order to search for something valuable such as oil: *The town is a good base from which to explore this part of New England.*
2 [T] to examine or discuss something in order to see if it is possible or is worth doing: *We are **exploring the possibility** of taking legal action against the company.*

ex•plor•er /ɪk'splɔrər/ noun [C] someone who travels around a place that other people do not know much about in order to find out what is there

ex•plo•sion /ɪk'sploʊʒ(ə)n/ noun [C] ★
1 an occasion when something such as a bomb explodes: *a gas/nuclear explosion* ♦ *The explosion could be heard for miles around.*
2 a very large increase in something over a very short period of time: *a **population explosion***
3 a sudden expression of a strong emotion, especially anger

ex•plo•sive¹ /ɪk'sploʊsɪv/ adj **1** something that is explosive is used for causing an explosion, or is capable of exploding: *This gas is highly explosive.* **2** likely to become violent or very difficult: *an explosive situation/issue* **3** increasing quickly: *the explosive growth in street crime*

ex•plo•sive² /ɪk'sploʊsɪv/ noun [C/U] a substance or object that can cause an explosion

ex•po•nent /ɪk'spoʊnənt/ noun [C] *formal* someone who tries to persuade other people to support an idea, theory, policy, etc.: *a leading exponent of free trade*

ex•port¹ /'ekˌspɔrt/ noun ★★
1 [U] the business or process of selling goods to other countries ≠ IMPORT: *They are now manufacturing more goods for export.*
2 [C] a product that is sold to another country ≠ IMPORT: *There has been a rapid increase in oil **exports to** the West.* ♦ *Agricultural produce is the country's largest export.*

ex•port² /ɪk'spɔrt/ verb ★
1 [I/T] to send a product to another country so that it can be sold there ≠ IMPORT: *Their flowers are exported around the world.* ♦ *Weapons are being illegally **exported to** other countries.*
2 [T] to introduce an idea, tradition, or activity into another country ≠ IMPORT: *Blues music was exported throughout the Western world.*
3 [T] *computing* to copy information from one part of a computer to another part, or to copy it to a place where it can be stored ≠ IMPORT

ex•port•er /ɪk'spɔrtər/ noun [C] a person, business, or country that sells goods to another country: *Saudi Arabia is the world's largest oil exporter.*

ex•pose /ɪk'spoʊz/ verb [T]

1 put in danger	4 give sb experience
2 let sth be seen	5 let light reach film
3 make sth known	

1 to put someone or something into a situation that involves danger or risk: *Many of the soldiers had been exposed to radiation.* **2** to remove something that is covering something else so that it is no longer hidden or protected: *The snow had melted and exposed the rock underneath.* **3** to tell the public about something shocking or illegal that was previously not known **4** to give someone a particular experience: *These children are exposed to art at a very early age.* **5** to allow light to reach the FILM in a camera so that you can take a photograph

ex•po•sé /ˌekspoʊ'zeɪ/ noun [C] a story in a newspaper or on television that tells the truth about something shocking

ex•posed /ɪk'spoʊzd/ adj **1** not covered or hidden **2** not protected from attack or from the bad effects of something

ex•po•sure /ɪk'spoʊʒər/ noun

1 being in danger	4 experience of sth
2 telling public sth	5 being out in cold
3 public attention	6 single photograph

1 [C/U] the state of not being protected from something harmful: *exposure to the sun*
2 [C/U] the act of making something publicly known because you believe that it is wrong or illegal: *the exposure of corruption within the government* **3** [U] the fact that something is mentioned in newspapers and on television and is well known **4** [C/U] the act of giving someone a particular experience: *Children who have exposure to books in their early years are likely to read earlier.*
5 [U] the harmful effect of very cold weather on your body: *Two of the climbers died of exposure.* **6** [C] *technical* the amount of FILM that is used for taking one photograph

ex•pound /ɪk'spaʊnd/ verb [I/T] *formal* to explain something, or to express your opinion about it in detail

ex•press¹ /ɪk'spres/ verb [T] ★★★
1 to say or write about what your opinion is or what your feelings are about something: *His teachers expressed concern about his progress at school.* ♦ *The government has expressed an interest in the plan.*
2 to show your feelings in the way that you look or behave: *Her eyes expressed total shock.*
3 *American* to send something using a service that will deliver it very quickly: *I'll express those documents to you.*
PHRASE **express yourself 1** to talk in a way that other people can understand: *She finds it difficult to express herself in English.* **2** to show your feelings in a particular way

ex•press² /ɪk'spres/ adj much faster than the usual service: *an express train* ♦ *express delivery*

ex•press³ /ɪk'spres/ noun [C] a fast train or bus

ex•pres•sion /ɪk'spreʃ(ə)n/ noun ★★★
1 [C] a look on someone's face that shows what their thoughts or feelings are: *She had a puzzled expression on her face.* ♦ *I noticed his **expression of** disgust.*
2 [C/U] the act of showing what your thoughts or feelings are
3 [C] a word or phrase: *He uses childish expressions like "choo-choo."*

E

ex•pres•sion•less /ɪk'spreʃ(ə)nləs/ adj not showing your feelings in your face or voice

ex•pres•sive /ɪk'spresɪv/ adj clearly showing your thoughts or feelings: *She has wonderfully expressive features.*

ex•press•ly /ɪk'spresli/ adv *formal* in a way that is clear and definite: *Smoking is expressly forbidden.*

ex•pres•so /ek'spresoʊ/ noun [C] an ESPRESSO

ex•press•way /ɪk'spres,weɪ/ noun [C] *American* a highway with several LANES (=lines of traffic) going each direction

E

ex•pul•sion /ɪk'spʌlʃ(ə)n/ noun [C/U] an occasion when someone is officially forced to leave an organization, institution, or country

ex•qui•site /ɪk'skwɪzɪt, 'ekskwɪzɪt/ adj extremely beautiful and delicate: *an exquisite hand-painted vase*

ex•tend /ɪk'stend/ verb ★★★

1 increase size/length	4 stretch arm/leg out
2 of distance/time	5 offer greeting
3 include sb/sth	

1 [T] to increase the size, time, or range of something: *The course has been extended to include the history of art.* ♦ *I asked if I could extend my vacation.*

2 [I] to continue for a particular distance or time: *an area **extending from** the Baltic coast **to** the Alps*

3 [I] to include someone or something: *This law **extends to** children under the age of 14 only.*

4 [T] to stretch out an arm or a leg

5 [T] *formal* to offer something such as thanks or a welcome: *We extend our sympathy to all the families of the victims.*

ex,tended 'family noun [C] the family that you belong to, including people such as your grandparents, COUSINS, etc. → NUCLEAR FAMILY

ex•ten•sion /ɪk'stenʃ(ə)n/ noun ★★

1 extra time allowed	4 sth that develops
2 telephone line	5 special classes
3 extra part added	6 computer file name

1 [C] an extra period of time that is added to the original period: *Brady wants a two-year **extension to** his contract.* ♦ *Will the bank give you an **extension on** the loan?*

2 [C] a telephone line that is one of two or more lines in the same building: *I'm at extension 334.*

3 [C] an extra part that is added to a building: *The company is building an extension onto the side of the factory.*

4 [C] something that develops from something else: *He sees local history as an extension of family history.*

5 [U] extra courses for people who cannot go to ordinary college classes

6 [C] *computing* the last part of the name of a computer file. For example "exe" and "doc" are extensions.

ex•ten•sive /ɪk'stensɪv/ adj ★

1 very large in amount or degree: *The accident caused extensive damage to both cars.*

2 involving a lot of details and information: *extensive knowledge/research*

3 spreading over a large area: *The hotel has extensive grounds, including a private lake.*
—**ex•ten•sive•ly** adv: *The building was extensively damaged by fire.*

ex•tent /ɪk'stent/ noun ★★★

1 [singular/U] the degree to which something happens, or the degree to which something is affected: *They were shocked at **the extent of** the damage.* ♦ *Languages vary in **the extent to which** they rely on word order.*

2 [U] the size or area of something: *Open the table to its fullest extent.*

PHRASES **to a large/great extent** mainly: *The complaints were to a large extent valid.*
to some/a certain/a limited extent partly, but not completely: *To a certain extent, I was relieved.*

ex•te•ri•or¹ /ɪk'stɪriər/ noun [C] **1** the outside part of a building ≠ INTERIOR **2** the way that someone seems to be: *Beneath that gruff exterior is a very kind person.*

ex•te•ri•or² /ɪk'stɪriər/ adj on the outside of something ≠ INTERIOR: *exterior walls*

ex•ter•mi•nate /ɪk'stɜrmɪ,neɪt/ verb [T] to kill all the insects, animals, or people in a particular area —**ex•ter•mi•na•tion** /ɪk,stɜrmɪ'neɪʃ(ə)n/ noun [C/U]

ex•ter•nal /ɪk'stɜrn(ə)l/ adj ★★

1 on, or relating to, the outside of something ≠ INTERNAL: *external doors/walls* ♦ *Her external appearance was calm and cool.*

2 from outside an organization or country ≠ INTERNAL: *We will need to find external sources of finance.*
—**ex•ter•nal•ly** adv

ex•tinct /ɪk'stɪŋkt/ adj **1** if something such as a type of animal or plant is extinct, it no longer exists **2** an extinct VOLCANO no longer ERUPTS

ex•tinc•tion /ɪk'stɪŋkʃ(ə)n/ noun [U] a situation in which something such as a type of animal or plant stops existing: *Several species of monkey are in danger of extinction.*

ex•tin•guish /ɪk'stɪŋgwɪʃ/ verb [T] *formal* to make a fire or cigarette stop burning

ex•tin•guish•er /ɪk'stɪŋgwɪʃər/ noun [C] a FIRE EXTINGUISHER

ex•tol /ɪk'stoʊl/ verb [T] *formal* to praise something in a very enthusiastic way

ex•toll /ɪk'stoʊl/ an American spelling of **extol**

ex•tort /ɪk'stɔrt/ verb [T] to illegally get money or information from someone by using force or threats

ex•tor•tion /ɪk'stɔrʃ(ə)n/ noun [U] a crime of getting money or information from someone by using force or threats —**ex•tor•tion•ist** noun [C]

ex•tor•tion•ate /ɪk'stɔrʃ(ə)nət/ adj an extortionate price is much higher than it should be

ex•tra¹ /'ekstrə/ adj ★★★ in addition to the usual amount: *There's no extra money for emergencies.* ♦ *We need extra space for guests.*

PHRASE **be extra** to cost an additional amount of money: *It's $19.95 for dinner, and drinks are extra.*

ex•tra² /'ekstrə/ noun [C] **1** something that is added to a basic service, product, etc.: *A virus checker is available as an optional* *extra for your computer.* **2** someone who has a very small part in a movie

ex·tra³ /ˈekstrə/ adv **1** more than a particular amount of money: *You have to pay extra for insurance.* **2** very: *Be extra careful when you go out alone at night.*

ex·tract¹ /ɪkˈstrækt/ verb [T] **1** to remove something from something else = OBTAIN: *a method of extracting sulfur from copper ore* **2** to get information from someone using force

ex·tract² /ˈekˌstrækt/ noun **1** [C/U] a substance that has been taken from a plant or from another substance **2** [C] a short piece of writing that is taken from something such as a book or letter = EXCERPT

ex·trac·tion /ɪkˈstrækʃ(ə)n/ noun [C/U] the process of taking something from somewhere

PHRASE **of Chinese/German/British etc. extraction** belonging to a family that was originally from China, Germany, Britain, etc.

ex·tra·cur·ric·u·lar /ˌekstrəkəˈrɪkjələr/ adj extracurricular activities are things that you do at school or college that are not part of your usual classes

ex·tra·dite /ˈekstrəˌdaɪt/ verb [T] to send someone who is wanted for a crime back to the country or state where the crime was committed, so that they can be judged in a law court there —**ex·tra·di·tion** /ˌekstrəˈdɪʃ(ə)n/ noun [C/U]

ex·traor·di·nar·y /ɪkˈstrɔrd(ə)nˌeri/ adj ★
1 very unusual and surprising: *It's an extraordinary story.* ♦ *It's extraordinary that no one disagreed with him.*
2 much better or worse than is usual: *The picture does not capture her extraordinary beauty.*
—**ex·traor·di·nar·i·ly** /ɪkˌstrɔrd(ə)nˈerəli/ adv

ex·trap·o·late /ɪkˈstræpəˌleɪt/ verb [I/T] *formal* to say what is likely to happen or be true by using information that you already have —**ex·trap·o·la·tion** /ɪkˌstræpəˈleɪʃ(ə)n/ noun [C/U]

ex·tra·ter·res·tri·al /ˌekstrətəˈrestriəl/ adj existing on planets other than Earth

ex·trav·a·gance /ɪkˈstrævəgəns/ noun **1** [U] the act of spending a lot of money, especially spending it on something that is not really necessary **2** [C] something that you spend a lot of money on

ex·trav·a·gant /ɪkˈstrævəgənt/ adj **1** spending or costing a lot of money: *an extravagant present/lifestyle* **2** extreme or unreasonable: *an extravagant claim* —**ex·trav·a·gant·ly** adv

ex·trav·a·gan·za /ɪkˌstrævəˈgænzə/ noun [C] a large and impressive event

ex·treme¹ /ɪkˈstrim/ adj ★★
1 very great in degree: *extreme poverty/hardship/cold*
2 extreme actions or opinions are considered unreasonable by most people: *It seemed a little extreme to call the police.* ♦ *extreme right-wing views*
3 very unusual = EXCEPTIONAL: *In extreme cases, your membership may be canceled.*
4 farthest away from the center of something: *My friend is on the extreme left of the picture.*

ex·treme² /ɪkˈstrim/ noun [C] a very large or very small degree of something: *extremes of temperature*

PHRASE **go to extremes** or **take/carry sth to extremes** to do something much more than is usual or reasonable: *This is political correctness taken to extremes.*

ex·treme·ly /ɪkˈstrimli/ adv ★★★ very: *He knows the area extremely well.* ♦ *It is extremely important to record everything that happens.*

exˈtreme ˌsport noun [C] a sport or activity that is exciting and dangerous

ex·trem·ist /ɪkˈstrimɪst/ noun [C] someone who has beliefs that most people think are extremely unreasonable —**ex·trem·ism** noun [U], **ex·trem·ist** adj

ex·trem·i·ty /ɪkˈstreməti/ noun *formal* **1** [C] a part of something that is farthest from the main part: *the southern extremity of the island* **2 extremities** [plural] your fingers or toes

ex·tri·cate /ˈekstrɪˌkeɪt/ verb [T] *formal* to get someone or yourself out of a difficult situation or a dangerous place

ex·tro·vert /ˈekstrəˌvɜrt/ noun [C] someone who is very confident, lively, and likes social situations ≠ INTROVERT —**ex·tro·vert·ed** adj

ex·u·ber·ant /ɪgˈzubərənt/ adj happy, excited, and full of energy —**ex·u·ber·ance** noun [U]

ex·ude /ɪgˈzud/ verb [T] *formal* if you exude a particular quality, you obviously have a lot of it

eye¹ /aɪ/ noun [C] ★★★
1 one of the two parts of your face that you use for seeing: *Close your eyes and go to sleep.* ♦ *He gazed into her eyes as she spoke.* ♦ *He has blond hair and blue eyes.* —*picture* → C14
2 used for talking about the expression on someone's face: *He spoke to her with slight amusement in his eyes.*
3 used for saying what someone is looking at: *I fixed my eye on the clock.*
4 the hole at the top of a needle

PHRASES **can't take your eyes off** to be unable to stop looking at someone or something that is attractive, surprising, or interesting

an eye for an eye the idea that someone who has harmed another person should be punished by having the same thing done to them

have an eye for to have a natural ability for seeing or noticing something: *Proofreaders need to have a good eye for detail.*

have your eye on sth to want to have or buy something: *I've got my eye on a new DVD player.*

have/keep your eye on sb to watch someone carefully because you think they are going to do something wrong

have/keep your eye on sth to keep looking at something, especially to avoid making a mistake: *It's important to keep your eye on the ball at all times.*

have one eye on sth to be giving some attention to something at the same time that you are doing something else: *I had one eye on the clock the whole time.*

E

in sb's eyes according to what someone thinks or feels: *In his mother's eyes, the boy can do no wrong.*
keep an eye on to take care of someone or something: *Will you keep an eye on things here until I get back?*
keep an eye out for to try to notice someone or something: *He asked me to keep an eye out for any houses to rent.*
keep your eyes open/peeled to keep looking for something that you hope to find: *Keep your eyes open for a gas station.*
look sb in the eye to look directly at someone, especially as a way to show that you are being honest: *Look me in the eye and tell me you didn't do it.*
see eye to eye (with sb) to have the same opinion as someone: *I don't see eye to eye with my father on many things.*
set/lay eyes on to see someone or something, especially for the first time
with your eyes (wide) open if you do something with your eyes wide open, you know all about any problems that there are likely to be
→ BLIND[1]

eye[2] /aɪ/ verb [T] **1** to look at someone or something carefully **2** *American* to look at someone in a way that shows that you are sexually attracted to them

eye·ball /ˈaɪˌbɔl/ noun [C] the round ball that forms your eye

eye·brow /ˈaɪˌbraʊ/ noun [C] the line of hair above an eye

ˈ**eye-ˌcatching** adj something that is eye-catching is attractive, impressive, or unusual, so that you notice it very easily

ˈ**eye ˌcontact** noun [U] a situation in which two people look at each other's eyes

eye·lash·es /ˈaɪlæʃɪz/ noun [plural] the hairs along the edges of your eyelids

eye·lid /ˈaɪˌlɪd/ noun [C] one of the two pieces of skin that cover your eye when it is closed

eye·lin·er /ˈaɪˌlaɪnər/ noun [U] a type of MAKEUP used for drawing a line around the edges of your eyes —*picture* → MAKEUP

ˈ**eye ˌopener** noun [C] a situation that shows you things you did not know before: *Visiting people in prison was a real eye opener for me.*

ˈ**eye ˌshadow** noun [U] a type of colored MAKEUP that you put on your EYELIDS —*picture* → MAKEUP

eye·sight /ˈaɪˌsaɪt/ noun [U] the ability to see =SIGHT: *Reading in poor light can damage your eyesight.*

eye·sore /ˈaɪˌsɔr/ noun [C] something that is ugly or unpleasant to look at, especially a building

eye·wit·ness /ˈaɪˌwɪtnəs/ noun [C] someone who has seen a crime or an accident happen: *Eyewitnesses describe the man as tall with brown hair.*

e-zine /ˈiˌzin/ noun [C] a magazine that you can read on the Internet

Ff

f or **F** /ef/ noun [C/U] **1** the sixth letter of the English alphabet **2 F** a grade that a teacher gives to a student's work to show that they have failed

F abbrev **1** Fahrenheit **2** false **3** female

fa·ble /ˈfeɪb(ə)l/ noun [C] a traditional story about animals that teaches a moral lesson

fa·bled /ˈfeɪb(ə)ld/ adj very famous =LEGENDARY

fab·ric /ˈfæbrɪk/ noun ★
1 [C/U] cloth that is used for making things such as clothes or curtains =MATERIAL: *plain/patterned/floral fabric* ♦ *a wide range of fabrics*
2 [singular] the basic structure of something: *Drug abuse poses a major threat to the **fabric of society**.*

fab·ri·cate /ˈfæbrɪˌkeɪt/ verb [T] to make up a story or piece of information in order to trick someone —**fab·ri·ca·tion** /ˌfæbrɪˈkeɪʃ(ə)n/ noun [C/U]

fab·u·lous /ˈfæbjələs/ adj **1** *informal* extremely good =WONDERFUL: *You look fabulous.* ♦ *a fabulous opportunity* **2** very large or great: *fabulous wealth* —**fab·u·lous·ly** /ˈfæbjələsli/ adv

fa·cade or **fa·çade** /fəˈsɑd/ noun **1** [C] the front of a large building **2** [singular] a way of behaving that hides your real feelings or character

face[1] /feɪs/ noun [C] ★★★
1 the front part of your head, where your eyes, nose, and mouth are: *She wiped her face.* ♦ *He had a big smile on his face.* ♦ *The ball hit me in the face.*
2 a side of something: *the mountain's north face* ♦ *the faces of a coin/cube*
3 a person: *There were a lot of famous faces at the party.* ♦ *Look out for a couple of new faces in the team.*
4 the way that something appears to people: *players who **changed the face of** tennis* ♦ *This is **the new face of** banking in America.*

PHRASES **face down** with the front or face toward the ground
face to face 1 in a situation where you are talking to another person directly: *It would be better if we talked face to face.* ♦ *I **came face to face with** his mother.* **2** in a situation where you are forced to deal directly with a problem: *Her work brings her face to face with human suffering.*
face up with the front or face upward
in the face of in an unpleasant or difficult situation: *They won in the face of stiff competition from all over the country.*
lose face to lose people's respect
make a face to put a silly or rude expression on your face, or an expression that shows that you dislike someone or something
on the face of it used for saying that something appears to be true, although it

may not be true: *He didn't have to pay any rent, so on the face of it he didn't need much money.*

save face to avoid being embarrassed or losing people's respect

to sb's face if you say something to someone's face, you say it to them directly

→ BLUE[1], EGG[1], FACE-TO-FACE, FLY[1], IN-YOUR-FACE, PRETTY[2], STRAIGHT[1]

face[2] /feɪs/ verb ★★★

1 be turned to	5 compete against sb
2 deal with problem	+ PHRASES
3 accept	+ PHRASAL VERB
4 talk to sb	

1 [I/T] to have your face or front toward someone or something: *The two men faced each other across the table.* ♦ *I turned to face the sun.* ♦ *My room faces north.*

2 [T] if you face a problem, or if it faces you, you have to deal with it: **be faced with/by sth** *The country is now faced with the prospect of war.* ♦ **face doing sth** *Many of the shipyard workers face losing their jobs.*

3 [T] to accept that a bad situation exists and try to deal with it: *She had to **face the fact that** she still missed him.*

4 [T] to talk to someone when this is difficult or embarrassing: *I'll never be able to face her again after what happened.*

5 [T] to compete against someone: *Williams will face Capriati for the title.*

PHRASES **can't face sth** *spoken* to not want to do something because it is too difficult or unpleasant: *He couldn't face the housework, so he left it until the morning.* ♦ **can't face doing sth** *I just can't face attending another conference.*

let's face it *spoken* used before saying something that people might not want to accept, although it is true: *Let's face it, we played badly today.*

PHRASAL VERB **ˌface ˈup to sth** *same as* face[2] 3: *He was the only one who faced up to the situation.*

face·less /ˈfeɪsləs/ adj a faceless person does not seem to be an individual because they represent a large organization

face·lift /ˈfeɪsˌlɪft/ noun [C] **1** a medical operation to make someone's face look younger **2** work that is done to make something look more attractive

ˈface-ˌsaving adj done in order to stop people from losing respect for you

fac·et /ˈfæsɪt/ noun [C] an aspect of something

fa·ce·tious /fəˈsiʃəs/ adj trying to be funny in a way that is not appropriate
—**fa·ce·tious·ly** adv

ˌface-to-ˈface adj involving two people who are together in the same place: *a face-to-face meeting*

ˌface ˈvalue noun **take sb/sth at face value** to accept someone or something without thinking about whether they really are what they claim to be: *These threats should not be taken at face value.*

fa·cial[1] /ˈfeɪʃ(ə)l/ adj on your face: *facial expressions/features/injuries*

fa·cial[2] /ˈfeɪʃ(ə)l/ noun [C] a beauty treatment in which someone rubs your face and puts creams on it

fac·ile /ˈfæˌsaɪl/ adj too simple to deal with the difficulties of a real situation: *facile conclusions*

fa·cil·i·tate /fəˈsɪləˌteɪt/ verb [T] *formal* to make it possible or easier for something to happen

fa·cil·i·ty /fəˈsɪləti/ noun ★★★

1 [C] *American* an area or building used for a particular purpose: *He works at the company's manufacturing facility in Texas.* ♦ *Haynes was taken to a psychiatric facility for evaluation.*

2 facilities [plural] places, services, or pieces of equipment that are provided for people: *There are plans to improve the restroom facilities at the bus station.* ♦ *Does the company offer any facilities for staff with young children?*

3 [C] a feature of a machine or system that allows you to do something: *the text messaging facility on your phone*

fac·sim·i·le /fækˈsɪməli/ noun [C] **1** an exact copy of a book or document **2** *formal* a FAX

fact /fækt/ noun ★★★

1 [C] a piece of true information: *The classes are designed to help children discover basic scientific facts.* ♦ ***The fact is,*** *he lost because he didn't try very hard.* ♦ *He has never hidden **the fact that** he doesn't like me.* ♦ ***The fact remains that*** (=it is still true that) *women are paid less than men.* ♦ ***I know for a fact that*** *he was lying.*

2 [U] things that are true or that really happened, rather than things that are imaginary or not true: *The story is based on historical fact.* ♦ *Children soon learn the difference between **fact and fiction**.*

PHRASES **the facts of life** the facts about sex and how babies are made

in (actual) fact 1 used for saying what is really true, when this is surprising or different from what people think: *He was paid money for a job that did not in fact exist.* ♦ *In actual fact, she was quite right.* **2** used when you are adding something to what you have just said, especially something surprising: *She's a friend of mine, a very close friend in fact.*

→ MATTER[1]

fac·tion /ˈfækʃ(ə)n/ noun [C] a small group within a larger group, consisting of people with different opinions from the rest

fac·tor /ˈfæktər/ noun [C] ★★★

1 one of the things that influence whether an event happens or the way that it happens: *Several factors have contributed to the increase in the number of road accidents.* ♦ *Public pressure was a **factor in** the administration's decision.*

2 *technical* a number that you can divide a larger number by exactly: *2 and 3 are factors of 6.*

Words often used with factor

*Adjectives often used with **factor***

- **crucial, deciding, decisive, determining, important, key** + FACTOR: used about factors that are very important

fac·to·ry /ˈfækt(ə)ri/ noun [C] ★★★ a building where large quantities of goods are produced using machines: *She works in a factory.* ♦ *a car factory* ♦ *factory workers/bosses*

fac·tu·al /ˈfæktʃuəl/ adj based on facts, rather than on theories or opinions: *factual information* —**fac·tu·al·ly** adv: *factually correct*

fac·ul·ty /ˈfæk(ə)lti/ noun **1** [C] a department or group of departments in a university: *the Faculty of Medicine* **2** [U] *American* all the teachers in a university, college, or school **3** [C] a natural ability that most people have: *the faculty of speech*

fad /fæd/ noun [C] something that is popular or fashionable for a short time only

F

fade /feɪd/ verb [I] **1** to gradually become less clear, bright, loud, or strong: *It was late afternoon and the light was fading.* ♦ *Hopes that he will be found alive are fading.* ♦ *They heard footsteps go past the room, then fade into the distance.* **2** to become less famous or less important: *After one hit record he faded into obscurity.* —**fad·ed** /ˈfeɪdɪd/ adj

PHRASAL VERB ˌ**fade aˈway** *same as* **fade** 2: *Most of these fashions just fade away and are forgotten.*

Fah·ren·heit /ˈferənˌhaɪt/ noun [U] a system for measuring temperature in which water freezes at 32° and boils at 212°

fail[1] /feɪl/ verb ★★★

1 be unsuccessful	4 stop working
2 not do sth expected	5 lose quality/ability
3 not do well enough	+ PHRASE

1 [I] to be unsuccessful ≠ SUCCEED: *It looks as if the negotiations are going to fail.* ♦ *He **failed in** his attempt to get compensation.* ♦ **fail to do sth** *They have failed to think of any practical solutions.*

2 [I] to not do something that people expect you to do: **fail to do sth** *He failed to come home at the usual time.*

3 [I/T] to not achieve a satisfactory standard in a test, or to decide that someone or something has not achieved a satisfactory standard ≠ PASS: *The new airplane failed a safety test.* ♦ *Teachers failed nearly 30% of the students.*

4 [I] to stop working, developing, or existing: *The brakes failed and the van crashed into a tree.* ♦ *He is old now and his health is starting to fail.* ♦ *If interest rates go up, more small businesses will fail.*

5 [T] if a quality or ability fails you, you suddenly lose it when you need it: *At the last minute, her courage failed her.*

PHRASE **if all else fails** used for saying that, if other methods do not succeed, there is one last thing that you can try to do

fail[2] /feɪl/ noun **without fail** used for emphasizing that something always happens in the same way or at the same time

failed /feɪld/ adj unsuccessful: *a failed attempt*

fail·ing[1] /ˈfeɪlɪŋ/ noun [C] a fault that makes someone or something less effective: *the failings of the educational system*

fail·ing[2] /ˈfeɪlɪŋ/ preposition used for saying that there is something else you can try: *We could try the bank, or, failing that, ask my parents for the money.*

fail·ure /ˈfeɪljər/ noun ★★★

1 [U] a lack of success ≠ SUCCESS: *Their first attempt to climb Everest **ended in failure**.* ♦ ***The failure of** the talks has made the situation worse.* ♦ **failure to do sth** *She is depressed by her continued failure to find a job.*

2 [U] a situation in which you do not do something that someone expects you to do: ***the failure of** teachers to inform parents about the problem* ♦ **failure to do sth** *Failure to follow safety procedures could put people in danger.*

3 [U] a situation in which a machine or a part of your body stops working correctly: *The crash seems to have been caused by engine failure.* ♦ *He died from liver failure.*

4 [C] someone or something that has not been successful ≠ SUCCESS: *I feel like such a failure.* ♦ *The party was **a total failure**.*

faint[1] /feɪnt/ adj **1** not strong or clear: *the faint glow of a light through the fog* ♦ *a faint memory* ♦ *a faint hope/possibility* **2** feeling that you are going to become unconscious —**faint·ly** /ˈfeɪntli/ adv

faint[2] /feɪnt/ verb [I] to suddenly become unconscious for a short time

faint·est /ˈfeɪntəst/ adj **not have the faintest idea** used for emphasizing that you do not know or understand something

fair[1] /fer/ adj ★★★

1 if a situation is fair, everyone is treated equally and in a reasonable way ≠ UNFAIR: *free and fair elections* ♦ **it is not fair to sb** *It wouldn't be fair to the others if she is paid more.*

2 reasonable and morally right: *a fair deal/price/share* ♦ **it is (not) fair to do sth** *It is not fair to blame him for our mistakes.*

3 not bad, but not very good = AVERAGE

4 fair hair is BLOND (=light yellow) or very light brown in color ≠ DARK

PHRASES **have your fair share of sth** to have a lot of something, especially something bad

to be fair used for making your criticism of someone or something seem less strong: *I don't like their music but, to be fair, millions of people disagree with me.*

fair[2] /fer/ noun [C] **1** an event where people ride on special machines and play games to win prizes **2** an event where companies bring their products for you to look at or buy

fair[3] /fer/ adv

PHRASES **fair and square** in a way that is clear and fair, so that no one can complain or disagree

play fair to behave in a fair and honest way

ˌ**fair ˈgame** noun [U] someone or something that it is fair to criticize: *The media see politicians as fair game.*

fair·ground /ˈferˌgraʊnd/ noun [C] an area of land that is used for FAIRS

fair·ly /ˈferli/ adv ★★

1 to some degree, but not completely or extremely = RATHER, REASONABLY: *We went to the theater fairly often.* ♦ *He enjoys fairly good health.*

2 in a fair way: *I do my best to treat all my children fairly.*

fair·ness /ˈfernəs/ noun [U] behavior that is fair and reasonable

PHRASE **in (all) fairness** used for making your criticism of someone or something seem less strong = TO BE FAIR

fair•way /ˈferˌweɪ/ noun [C] the long part of a GOLF COURSE that you hit the ball along to get to the hole

fair•y /ˈferi/ noun [C] an imaginary creature with magic powers that looks like a small person with wings

ˈfairy ˌtale noun [C] a traditional children's story in which magic things happen

fair•y•tale /ˈferiˌteɪl/ adj extremely good, beautiful, or happy: *a fairytale romance*

faith /feɪθ/ noun ★★

1 [U] a strong belief that someone or something is good: *I'm delighted to know you **have such faith in** me.* ♦ *The public have **lost faith in** what the government is doing.* ♦ *Maybe we **put** too much **faith in** doctors and medicine.*

2 [C/U] a religion, or religious belief: *people of many different faiths* ♦ ***Faith in** God helped him through his illness.*

PHRASE **in good faith** if you do something in good faith, you honestly believe that it is right or fair

faith•ful /ˈfeɪθfəl/ adj **1** continuing to support someone or something, even in difficult situations = LOYAL: *a faithful friend/servant/follower* ♦ *He remained faithful to his beliefs.* **2** showing or describing something in a way that is exactly correct: *a faithful reproduction of the original painting* **3** not having sex with anyone other than your partner ≠ UNFAITHFUL: *Ken has always been faithful to his wife.*
—**faith•ful•ness** noun [U]

faith•ful•ly /ˈfeɪθfəli/ adv **1** in a loyal and honest way **2** accurately

fake[1] /feɪk/ adj **1** made to look like something real in order to trick people: *a fake passport/visa/document* **2** made to look like something expensive: *fake fur/pearls/leather*

fake[2] /feɪk/ noun [C] **1** a copy of something such as a painting that is intended to trick people **2** someone who pretends to have skills that they do not really have

fake[3] /feɪk/ verb [T] **1** to pretend to do or feel something: *He left the country after faking his own death.* **2** to make an exact copy of something in order to trick people

fal•con /ˈfælkən/ noun [C] a bird that is often trained to hunt small animals

fall[1] /fɔl/ (past tense **fell** /fel/; past participle **fall•en** /ˈfɔlən/) verb [I] ★★★

1 move quickly down	7 hang down
2 hit ground by accident	8 belong to group
3 come from sky	9 happen
4 get lower in amount	+ PHRASES
5 start to be/do sth	+ PHRASAL VERBS
6 lose power	

1 to move quickly downward from a higher position by accident: *I keep **falling off** my bike.* ♦ *It's not unusual for small children to **fall out of** bed.*

2 to go quickly down onto the ground from an upright position by accident: *I slipped and almost fell.* ♦ *We heard the crash of falling trees.* ♦ *He collapsed and **fell to the ground**.*

3 to come down to the ground from the sky: *Snow began to fall.* ♦ *Bombs fell on the city throughout the night.*

4 to become lower in level or amount ≠ RISE: *The temperature has been falling all day.* ♦ *Inflation has **fallen to** 3%.*

5 to change into another state or condition: *I climbed into bed and **fell into** a deep sleep.* ♦ *Shortly before Christmas she **fell sick**.*

6 to lose a position of power

7 *literary* to hang down

8 to belong to a particular group or area of activity: *Those items **fall into** the category of luxury goods.*

9 to happen on a particular day or date: *Christmas falls on a Saturday this year.*

PHRASES **fall in love** to start to love someone

fall into place 1 if something falls into place, you suddenly understand how the different pieces of it are connected **2** if things fall into place, events happen in a way that is satisfactory for you

fall short to not reach a particular level

fall to pieces to be in a very bad condition because of being old or badly made
→ FOOT[1]

PHRASAL VERBS **ˌfall aˈpart 1** to break because of being old or badly made **2** if something such as an organization or system falls apart, it stops existing, or stops being effective

ˌfall ˈback to move so that you are behind someone or something

ˌfall ˈback on sth to do something else after other things have failed: *She always has her teaching experience to fall back on.*

ˌfall beˈhind sb 1 to make less progress than other people **2** to be behind other people because you have moved more slowly

ˌfall ˈdown 1 *same as* **fall[1]** 2: *I fell down and hurt my knee.* **2** if a building is falling down, it is in very bad condition

ˈfall for sb to fall in love with someone

ˈfall for sth to believe that a trick or a joke is true

ˌfall ˈoff if the amount, level, or value of something falls off, it gets smaller: *Sales always fall off in the winter months.*

ˌfall ˈover 1 if something falls over, it falls so that its side is on the ground **2** if you fall over, you fall to the ground

ˌfall ˈthrough if something such as a plan or arrangement falls through, it fails to happen

Words often used with fall

*Adverbs often used with **fall** (verb, sense 3)*

- FALL + **dramatically, rapidly, sharply, steeply**: used when a level becomes much lower very quickly

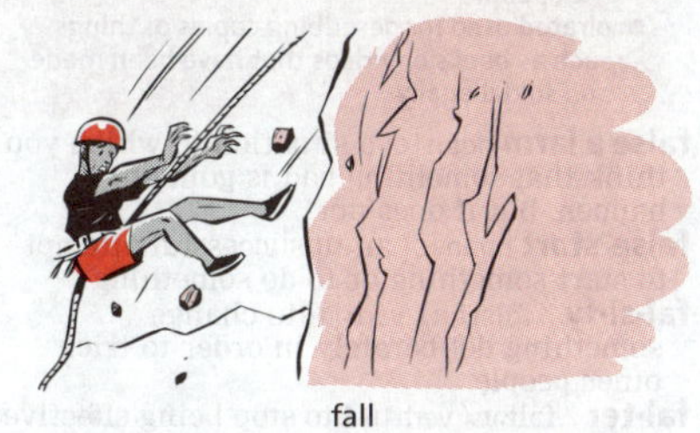

fall

fall² /fɔl/ noun ★★★

1 season	4 when amount etc. falls
2 when sb/sth falls	5 defeat or loss of power
3 amount that falls	6 waterfall

1 [singular] *American* the season between summer and winter: *He will go away to college in the fall.*
2 [C] an occasion when someone or something falls to the ground: *Her brother was killed in **a fall from** a horse.*
3 [C] an amount of something that falls to the ground: *a heavy **fall of snow***
4 [C] an occasion when an amount or level falls ≠ RISE: *There has been **a sharp fall in** unemployment.*
5 [singular] someone's defeat or loss of power
6 falls [plural] a WATERFALL: *We went to swim under the falls.*

fal•la•cy /ˈfæləsi/ noun [C] an idea or belief that is false but that many people think is true

fallen the past participle of **fall¹**

fal•li•ble /ˈfæləb(ə)l/ adj not perfect, and likely to be wrong or to make mistakes

fall•out /ˈfɔlˌaʊt/ noun **1** [singular/U] the unpleasant effects of something **2** [U] the dangerous dust produced by a nuclear explosion

false /fɔls/ adj ★★

1 not true	4 tricking people
2 not accurate	5 not sincere
3 like sth real	+ PHRASE

1 not true ≠ TRUE: *The report was dismissed as totally false.* ♦ *a false statement/claim/accusation*
2 based on a mistake or on wrong information: *a false impression/belief/hope*
3 made to look like something real =ARTIFICIAL: *false eyelashes*
4 not real and intended to trick people: *a false passport*
5 not showing what you really feel or intend =INSINCERE: *a false smile*

PHRASE **under false pretenses** by tricking people
—**false•ly** adv

Other ways of saying false

- **artificial** made to have the same qualities as something else that exists naturally
- **counterfeit** made to look exactly like real money and used illegally to trick people
- **fake** made to look like something valuable or important, often in order to trick people
- **forged** made to look exactly like something valuable or important and used illegally to trick people
- **pirated** used for describing copies of things such as books or videos that have been made and sold illegally

ˌfalse aˈlarm noun [C] a situation in which you think that something bad is going to happen, but it does not

ˌfalse ˈstart noun [C] an unsuccessful attempt to start something or to do something

fal•si•fy /ˈfɔlsɪˌfaɪ/ verb [T] to change something deliberately in order to trick other people

fal•ter /ˈfɔltər/ verb [I] **1** to stop being effective **2** to do something in a way that shows that you are weak or are not confident

fame /feɪm/ noun [U] the state of being famous: *Tarantino's rise to fame began with his movie* Reservoir Dogs. → CLAIM²

famed /feɪmd/ adj famous: *a restaurant famed for its seafood*

fa•mil•iar /fəˈmɪljər/ adj ★★
1 well known to you, or easily recognized by you ≠ UNFAMILIAR: *People are more relaxed in familiar surroundings.* ♦ *His face looked **vaguely familiar** but I couldn't remember where we'd met.* ♦ *I'm pleased to see so many **familiar faces** here tonight.* ♦ *The name Harry Potter will be **familiar to** many readers.*
2 something that is familiar happens a lot or exists in most places: *Horses used to be **a familiar sight** on our streets.* ♦ *an **all-too familiar** problem*
3 behaving in an informal way that shows a lack of respect for someone: *Don't be too **familiar with** the customers.*

PHRASE **familiar with sth** if you are familiar with something, you know about it: *Are you familiar with Windows software?*

fa•mil•iar•i•ty /fəˌmɪlɪˈerəti/ noun **1** [U] knowledge that you have of something because you have dealt with it before: *a familiarity with international law* **2** [C/U] informal behavior that shows a lack of respect for someone

fa•mil•iar•ize /fəˈmɪljəˌraɪz/ verb [T] to show or teach someone something: *It's my job to familiarize new employees with office procedures.*

fam•i•ly¹ /ˈfæm(ə)li/ noun ★★★
1 [C] a group consisting of parents and children: *Is the Watson family going to be there?* ♦ *The tent is big enough for a family of six.*
2 [C/U] all the people who are related to you, including people who are now dead: *Does your family have any history of heart disease?* ♦ *She did not want the property to go to anyone outside the family.* ♦ *The business had been **in his family** (=belonged to his family) for four generations.*
3 [C] children: *They want to get married and **start a family** (=have children).* ♦ *It's difficult to **bring up a family** on one salary.*
4 [C] a group of things such as animals or plants that are related: *Kidney beans belong to the bean family.*

fam•i•ly² /ˈfæm(ə)li/ adj **1** relating to families, or typical of families: *Quarrels are a normal part of family life.* **2** appropriate for a family with children: *family entertainment*

ˈfamily ˌname noun [C] the part of your name that all the people in your family have =LAST NAME, SURNAME

ˌfamily ˈplanning noun [U] the practice of controlling the number of children that you have by using CONTRACEPTIVES (=drugs or objects that stop a woman from becoming pregnant)

ˌfamily ˈtree noun [C] a drawing that shows the names of everyone in a family and shows the relationships among them

fam•ine /ˈfæmɪn/ noun [C/U] a serious lack of

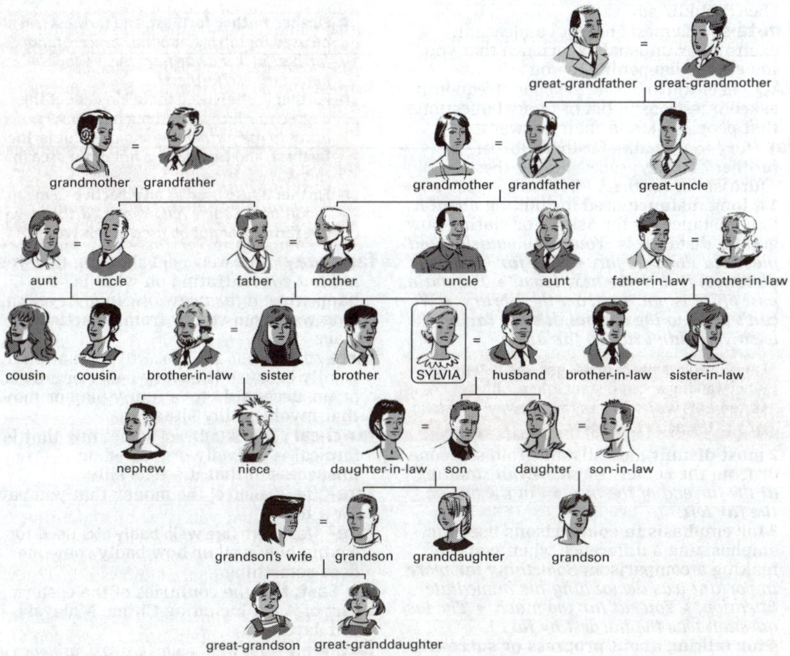

family tree

food that causes many people to become sick or to die

fam•ished /fæmɪʃt/ adj *informal* very hungry

fa•mous /ˈfeɪməs/ adj ★★★ if someone or something is famous, a lot of people know their name or have heard about them: *He dreamed of becoming a famous actor.* ♦ *The town of Gouda is **famous for** its cheese.* ♦ *She became **famous as** a teacher and a writer.* → INFAMOUS
—**fa•mous•ly** /ˈfeɪməsli/ adv

> Other ways of saying **famous**
> - **eminent** famous and respected for doing important work
> - **legendary** very famous and admired by many people
> - **notorious/infamous** famous for something bad
> - **well-known** fairly famous

fan¹ /fæn/ noun [C] ★★
1 someone who likes someone or something very much: *a crowd of football fans* ♦ *I'm a big fan of Madonna.*
2 a machine that makes the air in a room move so that it feels less hot
3 a flat object that you wave in front of your face in order to make yourself feel less hot

fan² /fæn/ verb [T] **1** to wave a flat object in front of someone's face in order to make them feel less hot **2** to make a fire burn more strongly by moving air onto it
PHRASAL VERB ˌ**fan ˈout** if a group of people fan out, they spread out while moving forward

fa•nat•ic /fəˈnætɪk/ noun [C] **1** someone who has strong beliefs that make them behave in an unreasonable way **2** someone who likes a sport or activity very much
—**fa•nat•i•cal** /fəˈnætɪk(ə)l/ adj

fan•ci•ful /ˈfænsɪf(ə)l/ adj not serious or sensible: *a fanciful suggestion*

ˈ**fan ˌclub** noun [C] an organization for people who like a particular famous player, performer, or team

fan•cy¹ /ˈfænsi/ adj **1** with a lot of features or decorations: *fancy computer graphics*
2 expensive and fashionable: *a fancy hotel*

fan•cy² /ˈfænsi/ noun [singular] *literary* a feeling of wanting or liking someone or something: *One of the boys has taken a fancy to my daughter.*

fan•fare /ˈfænˌfer/ noun [C] a short loud piece of music that is played to announce a special person or event

fang /fæŋ/ noun [C] one of the long pointed teeth that some animals have

ˈ**fanny ˌpack** noun [C] *American* a small bag with a belt that you wear around your waist —*picture* → BAG

fan•ta•size /ˈfæntəˌsaɪz/ verb [I/T] to imagine that something pleasant, exciting, or unusual is happening to you

fan•tas•tic /fænˈtæstɪk/ adj **1** *informal* extremely good or pleasant: *You've done a fantastic job.* ♦ *He looked absolutely fantastic.* **2** *informal* extremely large: *You've all put in a fantastic amount of work.*
3 strange, or imaginary: *fantastic*

F

creatures/stories —**fan•tas•ti•cal•ly** /fænˈtæstɪkli/ adv

fan•ta•sy /ˈfæntəsi/ noun [C] a pleasant, exciting, or unusual experience that you imagine is happening to you

FAQ /ˌef eɪ ˈkju/ noun [C] *computing* frequently asked questions: a list of typical questions that people ask and their answers

far /fɑr/ (comparative **far•ther** /ˈfɑrðər/ or **fur•ther** /ˈfɜrðər/; superlative **far•thest** /ˈfɑrðəst/ or **fur•thest** /ˈfɜrðəst/) adj, adv ★★★

1 a long distance used for talking about a long distance, or for asking or stating how great a distance is: *You can go outside and play, but don't go far.* ♦ ***How far*** (=what distance) *is it to the next town?* ♦ *The main post office is not **far from** the library.* ♦ *We can't walk to the cinema, it's **too far**.* ♦ *I wish you didn't live so **far away**.*

> **Far** is used mainly in questions and negatives when talking about distance. In positive statements we usually say **a long way**: *It's a long way to the nearest hospital.*

2 most distant most distant from someone or from the center: *He saw Lynn standing at the far end of the bar.* ♦ *I'm the one on **the far left**.*

3 for emphasis in comparisons used for emphasizing a difference when you are making a comparison: *Something far more important was demanding his immediate attention.* ♦ *You eat **far too** much.* ♦ *The last question was the hardest **by far**.*

4 for talking about progress or success used for saying or asking how much progress someone or something makes: *We're not going to get very far if we don't trust each other.* ♦ *With her talent and enthusiasm Linda should **go far*** (=be very successful).

5 to a particular degree used for talking about the degree to which something happens or how extreme an action is: *The opinion polls show how far his popularity has fallen.* ♦ *Do you think feminism has **gone too far*** (=become too extreme)? ♦ *He even **went as far as** to accuse me of betraying him.*

6 for talking about time a long time before or after: *A castle has stood on this site since **as far back as** 1230.* ♦ *She will be remembered **far into** the future.* ♦ *The date of an election is not normally announced so **far in advance**.*

PHRASES **as far as I know/can remember/can see/can tell** *spoken* used for stating what you think is true: *No one has complained, as far as I know.*

far from used for saying that the real situation is the opposite of what you mention: *The battle is far from over.*

the far right/left people whose political views are extremely right-wing/extremely left-wing

so far 1 until now: *So far we have considered only the local area.* **2** up to a particular point or degree: *You can only get so far on good looks alone.*

so far, so good used for saying that something has been successful up to this point

→ CONCERNED, CRY², FARTHER, FARTHEST

> - **Further, farther, furthest**, and **farthest** can all be used for talking about distance: *Stand further/farther away from me.* ♦ *Who can jump furthest/farthest?*
> - **Further** is often used for talking about the degree to which something happens: *I expect prices to rise further (=rise more).* But **farther, farthest**, and **furthest** are not often used in this way.
> - **Further** is also used as an **adjective** to mean "additional": *There has been no further news.* But **farther** cannot be used in this way.

far•a•way /ˌfɑrəˈweɪ/ adj **1** showing that you are not concentrating on what is happening: *a faraway look in her eyes* **2** a long way from you or from a particular place

farce /fɑrs/ noun **1** [singular/U] a situation that is silly because it is very badly organized or unsuccessful **2** [C] a funny play or movie that involves silly situations

far•ci•cal /ˈfɑrsɪk(ə)l/ adj something that is farcical is so badly organized or unsuccessful that it seems silly

fare¹ /fer/ noun [C] the money that you pay for a trip

fare² /fer/ verb **fare well/badly etc.** used for saying how well or how badly someone does something

ˌFar ˈEast, the the countries of the eastern part of Asia, including China, Malaysia, and Japan

fare•well¹ /ferˈwel/ noun [C/U] *old-fashioned* an occasion when you say goodbye to someone

fare•well² /ferˈwel/ adj done in order to celebrate the fact that someone is leaving a place or job: *a farewell dinner/party/speech*

far-fetched /ˌfɑr ˈfetʃt/ adj very unlikely to be true and therefore difficult to believe

farm¹ /fɑrm/ noun [C] an area of land that is used for growing crops or keeping animals

farm² /fɑrm/ verb [I/T] to use land for growing crops or keeping animals

farm•er /ˈfɑrmər/ noun [C] someone who owns or manages a farm

farm•house /ˈfɑrmˌhaʊs/ (plural **farm•hous•es** /ˈfɑrmˌhaʊzəz/) noun [C] the main house on a farm

farm•ing /ˈfɑrmɪŋ/ noun [U] the business of being a farmer

farm•land /ˈfɑrmˌlænd/ noun [U] land that is used for farming

farm•yard /ˈfɑrmˌjɑrd/ noun [C] an area that is surrounded by the buildings on a farm

ˌfar-ˈoff adj far away in distance or in time

far-reach•ing /ˌfɑr ˈritʃɪŋ/ adj affecting a lot of people or things in an important way

far•sight•ed /ˌfɑrˈsaɪtəd/ adj *American* **1** good at judging what will happen in the future **2** not able to see things clearly if they are close to you

fart /fɑrt/ verb [I] *impolite* to allow gases from your stomach to come out through your ANUS —**fart** noun [C]

far•ther /ˈfɑrðər/ adj, adv ★ in or to a place that is more distant: *I live farther up the road.* ♦ *The children were too tired to walk any farther.*

far·thest /ˈfɑrðəst/ adj, adv in or to a place that is most distant: *Sam had chosen to sit farthest away from the door.*

fas·ci·nate /ˈfæsɪˌneɪt/ verb [T] to attract and interest you very much

fas·ci·nat·ed /ˈfæsɪˌneɪtəd/ adj very interested in, or attracted by, someone or something

fas·ci·nat·ing /ˈfæsɪˌneɪtɪŋ/ adj ★ extremely interesting: *a fascinating story/person/place* ♦ **it is fascinating to do sth** *It will be fascinating to see who they appoint.* ♦ **find sb/sth fascinating** *I find him absolutely fascinating.*

fas·ci·na·tion /ˌfæsɪˈneɪʃ(ə)n/ noun [singular/U] **1** the state of being very interested in something or very attracted by something **2** the power to interest or attract people very strongly

fas·cism /ˈfæʃɪzəm/ noun [U] a very right-wing political system in which the government completely controls society and the economy

fas·cist /ˈfæʃɪst/ noun [C] **1** someone who supports or believes in fascism **2** an insulting word for someone who has very right-wing opinions —**fas·cist** adj

fash·ion¹ /ˈfæʃ(ə)n/ noun ★★

1 [U] the state of being popular at a particular time: *His ideas have **gone right out of fashion**.* ♦ *High heels are **back in fashion**.*

2 [C] a style of dress or an activity that is popular at a particular time: *She was always dressed in **the latest fashions**.* ♦ ***the fashion for** naming children for pop stars*

3 [U] the activity or business that involves styles of clothes and people's appearance: *the world of fashion* ♦ *an Italian fashion designer*

4 [singular] a particular way of doing something: *The elections took place **in a** peaceful and orderly **fashion**.*

fash·ion² /ˈfæʃ(ə)n/ verb [T] *formal* to make something using a lot of skill or care

fash·ion·a·ble /ˈfæʃ(ə)nəb(ə)l/ adj ★★

1 popular at a particular time ≠ UNFASHIONABLE: *fashionable clothes* ♦ **it is fashionable to do sth** *It is now fashionable to buy organic food.*

2 popular with rich and successful people, and often expensive: *London's most fashionable shopping district*

—**fash·ion·a·bly** adv: *a fashionably dressed young woman*

fast¹ /fæst/ adj ★★★

1 moving, happening, or doing something quickly: *Simon loves fast cars.* ♦ *The government has promised a fast response to the crisis.* ♦ *We were expected to work **at a fast pace**.*

2 if a clock is fast, it shows a time that is later than the correct time: *My watch is a few minutes fast.*

fast² /fæst/ adv ★★★

1 quickly: *I can't run very fast.* ♦ *You need to get help fast!*

2 firmly and strongly or tightly: *She held fast to the chair and refused to move.* ♦ *The van was stuck fast in the mud.*

PHRASE **fast asleep** sleeping in a way that makes it difficult to wake you

fast³ /fæst/ verb [I] to eat no food or very little food for a period of time, usually for religious reasons —**fast** noun [C]

fas·ten /ˈfæs(ə)n/ verb ★★★

1 [I/T] to close something such as a piece of clothing or a bag by fixing together the two parts of it, or to be closed in this way ≠ UNFASTEN: *Please keep your seat belts fastened.* —*picture* → CLOSE

2 [T] to attach one thing to another using something such as string or nails so that it is held firmly in position: **fasten sth to sth** *We fastened our boat to a post in the river.*

3 [T] to use something such as a lock in order to close a door, gate, or window: *I checked that all the windows were properly fastened.* —*picture* → CLOSE

fas·ten·er /ˈfæs(ə)nər/ or **fas·ten·ing** /ˈfæs(ə)nɪŋ/ noun [C] **1** something such as a lock that you use to keep a door, gate, or window closed **2** something that you use to attach the two parts of something such as a piece of clothing or a bag to each other

ˌfast ˈfood noun [U] food that is made and served very quickly, and that you can take away with you

ˌfast-ˈforward verb [I/T] if you fast-forward a TAPE, or if it fast-forwards, it goes forward quickly —**ˌfast ˈforward** noun [U]

fas·tid·i·ous /fəˈstɪdiəs/ adj caring a lot about small details and wanting everything to be correct and neat

ˈfast ˌtrack noun [singular] a way of achieving something more quickly than usual: *on the fast track to success*

fat¹ /fæt/ adj ★★

1 a person or animal that is fat has too much flesh on their body and weighs too much: *She can eat whatever she likes and she never **gets fat**.*

2 a fat object is thicker than other objects of the same type: *a big fat cigar*

3 *informal* used about an amount of money that is very large: *I bet he gets a nice fat salary!*

PHRASE **fat chance** *spoken* used for emphasizing that you think that something is extremely unlikely

> **Other ways of saying fat**
> - **big/large** tall and fairly fat
> - **chubby** used especially for describing babies and children who look fat in a healthy attractive way
> - **obese** very fat in a way that is dangerous to your health
> - **overweight** heavier than you should be
> - **plump** slightly fat in a way that looks nice

fat² /fæt/ noun ★

1 [U] a soft white substance that you store in a layer under your skin

2 [C/U] a food substance like oil that is used by your body to create energy: *Reduce the amount of fat in your diet.*

3 [C/U] oil in a solid or liquid form that is obtained from plants or animals and is used in cooking: *Fry the meat in a small amount of fat.*

fa·tal /ˈfeɪt(ə)l/ adj ★

1 causing someone to die: *a fatal accident/*

injury/disease ♦ *The condition can* ***prove fatal*** (=cause death).
2 with very bad effects: *I* ***made the fatal mistake*** *of falling in love with him.*
—**fa•tal•ly** /ˈfeɪt(ə)li/ adv

fa•tal•ism /ˈfeɪt(ə)lˌɪzəm/ noun [U] the belief that you cannot prevent bad things from happening —**fa•tal•is•tic** /ˌfeɪt(ə)lˈɪstɪk/ adj

fa•tal•i•ty /fəˈtæləti/ noun [C] *formal* a death that is caused by an accident, war, violence, or disease

ˈfat ˌcat noun [C] *informal showing disapproval* a very rich and powerful person, usually in business or politics

F

fate /feɪt/ noun ★
1 [C] the things that happen to someone: *a meeting that would decide* ***the fate of*** *thousands of employees*
2 [U] a power that some people believe controls everything that happens in their lives: *Fate has dealt these people a cruel blow.*

fate•ful /ˈfeɪtfəl/ adj affecting what happens in the future in an important and usually bad way

fa•ther¹ /ˈfɑðər/ noun ★★★
1 [C] your male parent: *My father taught me to drive.* —*picture* → FAMILY TREE
2 **Father** used for talking to or about a Roman Catholic priest

fa•ther² /ˈfɑðər/ verb [T] to make a woman pregnant and become the father of a child

ˈfather ˌfigure noun [C] an older man who you go to for help and advice

fa•ther•hood /ˈfɑðərˌhʊd/ noun [U] the state of being a father

ˈfather-in-ˌlaw noun [C] the father of your husband or wife —*picture* → FAMILY TREE

fa•ther•ly /ˈfɑðərli/ adj typical of a good, kind father

fath•om /ˈfæðəm/ verb [T] to understand something that is complicated or mysterious: *For some reason she couldn't fathom, he seemed angry.*

fa•tigue /fəˈtig/ noun [U] **1** a feeling of being extremely tired: *He was suffering from fatigue and acute headaches.* **2** a tendency for metal or wood to break as a result of too much pressure —**fa•tigued** /fəˈtigd/ adj

fa•tigues /fəˈtigz/ noun [plural] simple loose clothes worn by soldiers

fat•ten /ˈfæt(ə)n/ verb [T] to make an animal fat so that it will be more appropriate for eating
PHRASAL VERB **ˌfatten sb/sth ˈup** to make a person or animal fatter

fat•ten•ing /ˈfæt(ə)nɪŋ/ adj likely to make you fat: *Avoid fattening foods and take more exercise.*

fat•ty /ˈfæti/ adj containing a lot of fat: *fatty foods*

fat•u•ous /ˈfætʃuəs/ adj *formal* stupid

fau•cet /ˈfɔsɪt/ noun [C] *American* a piece of equipment that you turn to control the flow of water from a pipe —*picture* → C2

fault¹ /fɔlt/ noun ★★
1 [C/U] the fact of being responsible for a bad or unpleasant situation: *The teacher was* ***at fault*** *for not telling the child's parents.* ♦ **be sb's fault** *It's my fault – I forgot to give him the message.* ♦ **be sb's own fault** *If you didn't get enough sleep, it's your own fault.*
2 [C] a feature that makes someone or something less good: *She has her faults, but on the whole she's very nice.* ♦ *The book's main fault is that it is too long.*
3 [C] a problem with a machine or piece of equipment that stops it from working correctly: *The fire was caused by* ***an electrical fault.***
4 [C] a crack on or below the Earth's surface: *the San Andreas Fault*
PHRASE **find fault with** to criticize someone or something after deliberately looking for mistakes

fault² /fɔlt/ verb [T] to find something bad or wrong in a person or thing

fault•less /ˈfɔltləs/ adj containing no mistakes at all

fault•y /ˈfɔlti/ adj not working correctly, or not made correctly: *faulty brakes*

fau•na /ˈfɔnə/ noun [U] *formal* all the animals that live in a particular area

faux pas /ˌfoʊ ˈpɑ/ noun [C] *formal* an embarrassing mistake in a social situation

fa•vor¹ /ˈfeɪvər/ noun ★★
1 [C] something that you do for someone in order to help them: **do sb a favor** *Could you do me a favor?* ♦ *He wouldn't take any money for the job because he said he was doing it* ***as a favor.***
2 [U] support or admiration from people: *This approach has* ***found more favor*** *in the U.S. than in Britain.*
3 [C] *American* a small present given to a guest at a party
PHRASES **be in favor/out of favor** to be popular/no longer popular at a particular time: *The microskirt is currently* ***out of favor with*** *American women.*
in sb's favor helping you, or giving you an advantage: *The delay might actually work in our favor.*
in favor of 1 supporting a person, idea, or proposal: *All those in favor of the motion, please raise your hands.* **2** preferring someone or something that you believe is better than another choice: *The downtown area was rejected in favor of the harbor as the site for the festival.*

fa•vor² /ˈfeɪvər/ verb [T] ★
1 to prefer someone or something that you believe is better than another choice: *The report strongly favors reform of the electoral system.*
2 to give someone an unfair advantage: *more tax cuts that favor the rich*

fa•vor•a•ble /ˈfeɪv(ə)rəb(ə)l/ adj **1** showing that you like or approve of someone or something ≠ UNFAVORABLE: *Reaction to the plan has been generally favorable.*
2 showing that something good is likely to happen: *a favorable weather forecast*
—**fa•vor•a•bly** /ˈfeɪv(ə)rəbli/ adv

fa•vor•ite¹ /ˈfeɪv(ə)rɪt/ adj ★★ your favorite person or thing of a particular type is the one that you like the best: *What's your favorite food?*

fa•vor•ite² /ˈfeɪv(ə)rɪt/ noun [C] ★
1 the person or thing that you like the best:

The hot dog is still a national favorite.
2 someone who is treated better than others because someone such as a teacher or parent prefers them: *Eric's always been mom's favorite.*
3 the person, team, or animal that is expected to win a race or competition: *The Yankees are favorite to win the series.*

fa•vor•it•ism /ˈfeɪv(ə)rɪˌtɪzəm/ noun [U] the unfair practice of giving someone help or advantages that you do not give to others

fa•vour /ˈfeɪvər/ the British spelling of **favor**

fa•vour•a•ble /ˈfeɪv(ə)rəb(ə)l/ the British spelling of **favorable**

fa•vour•ite /ˈfeɪv(ə)rɪt/ the British spelling of **favorite**

fa•vour•it•ism /ˈfeɪv(ə)rɪˌtɪzəm/ the British spelling of **favoritism**

fawn¹ /fɔn/ noun [C] a young DEER

fawn² /fɔn/ PHRASAL VERB **ˈfawn over sb** or **ˈfawn on sb** to be extremely nice to someone because you want them to like you or to give you something

fawn³ /fɔn/ adj light brown in color

fax¹ /fæks/ noun **1 fax** or **fax machine** [C] a piece of equipment that is used for sending and receiving copies of documents in electronic form: *What's your fax number?* *—picture* → C3 **2** [C] a document that has been sent by a fax machine **3** [U] the system of sending documents using a fax machine: *Send me the details by fax.*

fax² /fæks/ verb [T] to send a message to someone using a fax machine: *Could you fax me the application form?*

faze /feɪz/ verb [T] *informal* to make someone feel confused, shocked, or upset

FBI, the /ˌef bi ˈaɪ/ the Federal Bureau of Investigation: a U.S. government department that deals with serious crimes that affect more than one state

FDA, the /ˌef di ˈeɪ/ the Food and Drug Administration: a U.S. government department that controls the food and drugs that are allowed to be sold

fear¹ /fɪr/ noun ★★★
1 [U] the feeling that you have when you are frightened: *She eventually managed to overcome her **fear of** the dark.* ♦ *Martin screamed **in fear**.* ♦ *She was **shaking with fear**.* ♦ *Many of these people **live in fear*** (=are afraid all the time).
2 [C] something bad or unpleasant that you are afraid might happen: *He expressed **fears for** his missing wife's safety.* ♦ *This latest case has raised **fears of** an epidemic.* ♦ *There are **fears about** the safety of the nuclear plant.* ♦ **+that** *There are fears that the building might collapse.*
PHRASE **for fear of (doing) sth** or **for fear (that)** in case you make something bad happen: *I didn't tell Susan about our meeting for fear of upsetting her.*

fear² /fɪr/ verb [T] ★★
1 to feel worried and afraid that something bad will happen: *The refugees fear persecution if they return to their own country.* ♦ *One person is still **missing, feared dead**.* ♦ **+(that)** *Health experts fear that there may be a flu epidemic this winter.*
2 to feel afraid of someone or something because they might harm you: *He was hated and feared by his colleagues.*
PHRASAL VERB **ˈfear for sb/sth** to feel worried about someone or something because you think that something bad may happen: *I fear greatly for their safety.*

fear•ful /ˈfɪrf(ə)l/ adj frightened —**fear•ful•ly** /ˈfɪrf(ə)li/ adv

fear•less /ˈfɪrləs/ adj *showing approval* not afraid of anyone or anything —**fear•less•ly** adv

fear•some /ˈfɪrsəm/ adj very frightening

fea•si•ble /ˈfizəb(ə)l/ adj possible, or likely to succeed: *There seems to be only one feasible solution.* —**fea•si•bil•i•ty** /ˌfizəˈbɪləti/ noun [U]

feast¹ /fist/ noun [C] a large meal, usually for a special occasion

feast² /fist/ PHRASAL VERB **ˈfeast on sth** to eat a lot of a particular food with enjoyment: *We feasted on strawberries and ice cream.*

feat /fit/ noun [C] something that is impressive that someone does

feath•er /ˈfeðər/ noun [C] one of the narrow tubes with thin soft hairs on each side that cover a bird's body

feath•er•y /ˈfeðəri/ adj like a feather

fea•ture¹ /ˈfitʃər/ noun [C] ★★★
1 an important part or aspect of something: *The latest model has a lot of new safety features.* ♦ *the natural **features of** the landscape*
2 a part of your face such as your eyes, nose, or mouth: *Her large blue eyes were her best feature.*
3 a newspaper or magazine article, or a part of a television or radio program that concentrates on a particular subject: ***a special feature on** new children's books*

> **Words often used with feature**
>
> *Adjectives often used with **feature** (noun, sense 1)*
> - **important, key, main** + FEATURE: used about aspects of something that are important
> - **distinctive, striking, unusual** + FEATURE: used about impressive or unusual features

fea•ture² /ˈfitʃər/ verb ★★
1 [T] if something features a particular person or thing, they are an important part of it: *a concert featuring music by Haydn and Mozart* ♦ **feature sb/sth as** *The movie features Minnie Driver as a young French student.*
2 [I] to be an important part or aspect of something: *She has already **featured in** two award-winning movies this year.*

ˈfeature ˌfilm noun [C] a long movie that is made to be shown in a movie theater

Feb. abbrev February

Feb•ru•ar•y /ˈfebruˌeri/ noun [C/U] ★★★ the second month of the year, between January and March: *I'm starting my new job in February.* ♦ *The first examination is on February 3rd.*

fe•ces /ˈfisiz/ noun [plural] solid waste from your body

feck•less /ˈfekləs/ adj a feckless person is not reliable and does not care about achieving anything

fed the past tense and past participle of **feed**¹

F

fed•er•al /ˈfed(ə)rəl/ adj ★★★
1 a federal country or system is one in which individual states make their own laws, but with a national government that is responsible for areas such as defense and foreign policy
2 connected with the national government of a country rather than with the government of one of its member states

fed•er•al•ism /ˈfed(ə)rəˌlɪzəm/ noun [U] a FEDERAL political system —**fed•er•al•ist** noun [C], adj

ˌFederal Reˈserve, the the organization that controls the U.S. national bank

fed•er•a•tion /ˌfedəˈreɪʃ(ə)n/ noun [C] **1** a country that is made up of individual states with the power to make their own decisions, but with a national government that is responsible for areas such as defense and foreign policy **2** a large organization that is made up of several smaller organizations that share similar goals

ˌfed ˈup adj *informal* annoyed or bored with something that you feel you have accepted for too long: *I'm fed up with this job.*

fee /fi/ noun [C] ★★
1 money that you pay to a professional person or institution for their work: *tuition fees* ♦ *He will have to pay legal fees of $2,000.*
2 an amount of money that you pay to be allowed to do something such as join an organization: *The gallery charges a small entrance fee.*

fee•ble /ˈfib(ə)l/ adj **1** physically weak **2** not good enough to achieve the intended result: *a feeble attempt* ♦ *a feeble excuse* **3** not strong enough to be seen or heard clearly: *a feeble light/voice* —**fee•bly** adv

feed[1] /fid/ (past tense and past participle **fed** /fed/) verb ★★★
1 [T] to give food to a person or an animal: *We've been feeding the ducks on the river.* ♦ *All the children will be properly fed and cared for.* ♦ **feed sth to sb/sth** *The leftover food is fed to the pigs.*
2 [I] if an animal or baby feeds, it eats: *Young babies need to feed every three to four hours.*
3 [T] to provide a supply of something for a person or a machine: **feed sth into sth** *Information is fed into the computer and stored in a database.* ♦ **feed sb with sth** *He's been feeding the police with information about terrorist activities.*
4 [T] to push something into a machine: **feed sth into sth** *She saw him feeding documents into the shredder.*
PHRASAL VERB ˈ**feed on sth** if an animal feeds on something, it eats it as its usual food

feed[2] /fid/ noun [C/U] food that is given to animals: *Hay is used as winter feed for the cows.*

feed•back /ˈfidˌbæk/ noun [U] comments about how well or how badly someone is doing something, which are intended to help them to do it better: *Initial feedback from parents has been very positive.*

feed•ing /ˈfidɪŋ/ noun [C] *American* an occasion on which you give milk to a baby

feel[1] /fil/ (past tense and past participle **felt** /felt/) verb ★★★

1 be in state mentioned	7 be affected by sth
2 have emotion/feeling	8 give sb a feeling
3 think particular way	9 try to find with hands
4 touch to discover sth	+ PHRASES
5 seem when touched	+ PHRASAL VERBS
6 notice sth	

1 [linking verb] to be in a particular state as a result of an emotion or a physical feeling: *I was feeling very happy when we began our trip.* ♦ *Are you feeling sick?* ♦ *How do you feel now?* ♦ ***I felt as though** someone had just punched me in the stomach.* ♦ *When I came back to England, **I felt like** a stranger.*
2 [T] to experience a particular emotion or physical feeling: *He felt a sudden pain in his chest.* ♦ *Richard felt no guilt at all for what he had done.* ♦ *Cara **felt the need to** talk to someone.* ♦ *Children don't seem to **feel the cold** as much as adults do.*
3 [I/T] to have a particular way of thinking about something: **+(that)** *I feel that more should be done to help young people.* ♦ *I know that Sally **feels strongly about** this issue.*
4 [T] to touch something with your hand so that you can discover what it is like: *She felt the child's forehead to see if he was hot.*
5 [linking verb] if something feels soft, hard, etc., that is what it is like when you touch it: *Your hair feels so soft.*
6 [T] to notice something that is touching you or something that is happening to you or near you: *Can you feel the draft coming from under the door?* ♦ **+(that)** *I felt I was being watched.*
7 [T] to be affected by something: *People should **feel the benefits of** the tax cuts by next year.*
8 [linking verb] if something feels nice, good, strange, etc., it gives you this feeling: *It certainly felt good to be back home.* ♦ *The clock said it was only eight o'clock but it **felt like** midnight.*
9 [I] to try to find something with your hands: *I felt around on the ground but couldn't find the flashlight.*
PHRASES **feel your age** to realize that you are becoming older and less able or willing to do things that younger people do
feel free *spoken* used for telling someone that they can do something if they want to: *Feel free to contact us at any time.*
feel like *spoken* to want something: *I feel like a cup of coffee.* ♦ **feel like doing sth** *Do you feel like going out tonight?*
feel your way 1 to move slowly and carefully, touching things with your hands because you cannot see **2** to make decisions and changes slowly, because you are not certain about what you are doing
→ HOME[1]
PHRASAL VERBS ˈ**feel for sb** to feel sympathy for someone
ˌ**feel ˈup to sth** to feel that you are strong or healthy enough to do something: *I don't feel up to eating anything.*

feel[2] /fil/ noun [singular] **1** the way that something seems when you touch it or when it touches you: *Ben was enjoying the*

feel of the breeze in his hair. **2** the way that something such as a place generally seems to you: *The town has a nice friendly feel.* **3** an act of touching someone or something
PHRASES **get a feel for sth** or **get the feel of sth** *informal* to develop a good knowledge or understanding of something
have a feel for sth *informal* to have a natural ability to do or understand something

feel•ers /ˈfilərz/ noun [plural] the two long thin parts on an insect's head that it uses for feeling things

ˈfeel-ˌgood adj intended to make you happy and satisfied: *a feel-good movie*

feel•ing /ˈfilɪŋ/ noun ★★★
1 [C] an emotional state, for example anger or happiness: *He found it difficult to express his feelings.* ♦ *I didn't want to* ***hurt his feelings*** (=upset him). ♦ *Stephen had a sudden* ***feeling of*** *panic.*
2 [C] an opinion that you have about something, which is based on general thoughts: *My feeling is that we should wait a week or two.* ♦ *Sarah has very strong* ***feelings about*** *environmental issues.*
3 [C] something that you feel physically in your body: ***a feeling of*** *nausea*
4 [U] the ability to feel something such as pain or heat in your body: *She had lost all the feeling in her right arm.*
PHRASES **bad/ill feeling** angry feelings that remain between people after a disagreement
have/get the feeling (that) or **have/get a feeling (that)** to be conscious of something but not certain about it: *I have a feeling we've met before.*
I know the feeling *spoken* used for showing sympathy
→ HARD[1]

feet the plural of **foot**[1]

feign /feɪn/ verb [T] *formal* to pretend to have a particular feeling

feist•y /ˈfaɪsti/ adj full of energy and determination

fe•line /ˈfiˌlaɪn/ adj connected with cats —**fe•line** noun [C]

fell[1] /fel/ verb [T] to cut down a tree

fell[2] the past tense of **fall**[1]

fel•low[1] /ˈfeloʊ/ adj used for talking about people who are similar to you or are in the same situation as you: *his fellow students/workers/citizens*

fel•low[2] /ˈfeloʊ/ noun [C] **1** *old-fashioned* a man **2** a member of a professional society or educational institution

fel•low•ship /ˈfeloʊʃɪp/ noun **1** [U] a feeling of friendship and support between people who do the same work or have the same interests **2** [C] an amount of money that is given to an advanced student for teaching and doing research

fel•on /ˈfelən/ noun [C] *American legal* someone who has committed a serious crime

fel•o•ny /ˈfeləni/ noun [C/U] *American legal* a serious crime → MISDEMEANOR

felt[1] /felt/ noun [U] a thick soft cloth made from wool, hair, or fur fibers that have been rolled and pressed flat

felt[2] the past tense and past participle of **feel**[1]

ˌfelt-ˈtip or **ˌfelt-tip ˈpen** noun [C] a pen that has a piece of felt as its writing point

fe•male[1] /ˈfiˌmeɪl/ adj ★★★
1 a female person or animal belongs to the sex that can produce babies or eggs ≠ MALE
2 a female plant is one that produces fruit

fe•male[2] /ˈfiˌmeɪl/ noun [C] a female person or animal ≠ MALE

fem•i•nine /ˈfemənɪn/ adj **1** having qualities that are traditionally considered to be typical of women ≠ MASCULINE: *The look this year is soft and feminine.* ♦ *conventional notions of feminine beauty* **2** *linguistics* in some languages, feminine nouns, pronouns, and adjectives have different forms from MASCULINE or NEUTER words

fem•i•nin•i•ty /ˌfeməˈnɪnəti/ noun [U] qualities that are considered to be typical of women ≠ MASCULINITY

fem•i•nism /ˈfemɪˌnɪzəm/ noun [U] the belief that women should have the same rights and opportunities as men —**fem•i•nist** /ˈfemɪnɪst/ adj, noun [C]

fence[1] /fens/ noun [C] ★
1 a flat upright structure made of wood or wire that surrounds an area of land —*picture* → C1
2 a structure that horses jump over in a competition or race

fence[2] /fens/ verb **1** [I] to fight with a light thin sword as a sport **2** [T] to put a fence around something
PHRASAL VERBS **ˌfence sth ˈin** *same as* fence[2] 2
ˌfence sth ˈoff to separate an area by surrounding it with a fence

fenc•ing /ˈfensɪŋ/ noun [U] **1** the sport of fighting with a light thin sword **2** fences, or the materials that are used for making them

fend /fend/ PHRASAL VERBS **ˌfend for yourˈself** to take care of yourself without help from anyone else: *The kittens have been fending for themselves since they were six weeks old.*
ˌfend sb/sth ˈoff to defend yourself against criticism or an attack: *He tried to fend off accusations of corruption.*

fend•er /ˈfendər/ noun [C] *American* a part of a vehicle that covers or protects the area around a wheel —*picture* → C6

feng shui /ˌfʌŋ ˈʃweɪ/ noun [U] a Chinese system of designing buildings according to special rules about the flow of energy that is thought to influence people's lives

fen•nel /ˈfen(ə)l/ noun [U] a pale green vegetable with seeds and leaves that are used for adding flavor to food —*picture* → C11

fer•ment[1] /fərˈment/ verb [I/T] if a food or drink ferments, or if it is fermented, a chemical change happens to it and the sugar in it produces alcohol —**fer•men•ta•tion** /ˌfɜrmenˈteɪʃ(ə)n/ noun [U]

fer•ment[2] /ˈfɜrˌment/ noun [U] a time of great excitement or activity that usually leads to change or violence: *a period of intense political ferment*

fern /fɜrn/ noun [C] a plant with no flowers and leaves that are shaped like feathers

fe•ro•cious /fəˈroʊʃəs/ adj violent and able to cause serious damage or injury: *a ferocious attack* —**fe•ro•cious•ly** adv

fe•roc•i•ty /fəˈrɑsəti/ noun [U] violence, or extreme force

fer•ret¹ /ˈferət/ noun [C] a small thin furry animal with a long tail that people sometimes use for hunting

fer•ret² /ˈferət/ PHRASAL VERB **ˌferret sth ˈout** to find something by searching in a determined way

fer•ris wheel /ˈferɪs ˌwil/ noun [C] a large upright structure shaped like a wheel in an AMUSEMENT PARK with seats hanging from it that people sit in as it goes around

F

fer•rous /ˈferəs/ adj *science* containing or connected with iron

fer•ry¹ /ˈferi/ or **fer•ry•boat** /ˈferiˌboʊt/ noun [C] a boat that makes short regular trips between two or more places: *They took the ferry to Staten Island.* —*picture* → C7

fer•ry² /ˈferi/ verb [T] to carry people or goods between two or more places: *Passengers were ferried to the island in a small airplane.*

fer•tile /ˈfɜrt(ə)l/ adj **1** fertile land is able to produce good crops or plants **2** a fertile person, animal, or plant is able to produce babies, young animals, or new plants ≠ INFERTILE **3** a fertile mind or situation is able to produce good ideas or results: *a child's fertile imagination*

fer•til•i•ty /fɜrˈtɪləti/ noun [U] **1** the ability of the soil to produce a lot of good crops or plants **2** a woman's ability to have babies: *fertility treatment*

fer•til•ize /ˈfɜrtəˌlaɪz/ verb [T] **1** to make an egg, a woman, or an animal start to produce a baby **2** to add a substance to soil in order to help plants to grow —**fer•til•i•za•tion** /ˌfɜrt(ə)lɪˈzeɪʃ(ə)n/ noun [U]

fer•til•iz•er /ˈfɜrt(ə)lˌaɪzər/ noun [C/U] a substance that is added to soil in order to help plants to grow

fer•vent /ˈfɜrv(ə)nt/ adj very enthusiastic and sincere about something that you believe in or support —**fer•vent•ly** adv

fer•vor /ˈfɜrvər/ noun [U] excitement caused by strong feelings or beliefs

fer•vour /ˈfɜrvər/ the British spelling of fervor

fes•ter /ˈfestər/ verb [I] **1** if an injury festers, it becomes infected **2** if a problem or unpleasant feeling festers, it becomes worse because no one has dealt with it: *This festering hatred could tear the community apart.*

fes•ti•val /ˈfestɪv(ə)l/ noun [C] **1** a series of performances of movies, plays, music, or dancing that is usually organized in the same place at the same time each year **2** a day or period when there is a public holiday, often to celebrate a religious event: *the Hindu festival of Holi*

fes•tive /ˈfestɪv/ adj connected with a festival or celebration: *the festive season* (=Christmas)

fes•tiv•i•ties /feˈstɪvətiz/ noun [plural] lively and enjoyable activities in which people celebrate something

fes•toon /feˈstun/ verb [T] to decorate something with bright colorful objects

fe•tal /ˈfit(ə)l/ adj *medical* relating to a FETUS (=baby that is still developing)

fetch /fetʃ/ verb [T] **1** to be sold for a particular amount of money: *The painting is expected to fetch up to $220,000.* **2** *old-fashioned* to go and get someone or something: *He went to fetch his coat.*

fête or **fete** /feɪt/ verb [T] to honor or entertain someone at a public celebration

fet•ish /ˈfetɪʃ/ noun [C] **1** an unusual sexual interest in a particular object or material **2** something that someone enjoys a lot, in a way that is unusual or unreasonable: *an exercise fetish*

fe•tus /ˈfitəs/ noun [C] a developing baby human or animal, before it is born

feud /fjud/ noun [C] an angry disagreement between two people or groups that continues for a long time: *a bitter feud between rival gangs* —**feud** verb [I]

feu•dal /ˈfjud(ə)l/ adj relating to the social system that existed in Europe in the Middle Ages, in which most people worked and fought for the more powerful people who owned their land —**feu•dal•ism** noun [U]

fe•ver /ˈfivər/ noun **1** [C/U] a medical condition in which the temperature of your body is very high = TEMPERATURE **2** [U] strong excitement and enthusiasm: *The whole country was in the grip of election fever.* —**fe•vered** /ˈfivərd/ adj

fe•ver•ish /ˈfiv(ə)rɪʃ/ adj **1** affected by fever **2** extremely excited: *There was a lot of feverish activity backstage.* —**fe•ver•ish•ly** adv

few /fju/ (comparative **fewer**; superlative **fewest**) grammar word ★★★

> **Few** or **a few** can be:
> - a **determiner**: *Few people live there now.* ♦ *There were a few animals in the barn.*
> - a **pronoun**: *Many have tried, but few have succeeded.* ♦ *A few of the visitors left early.*
>
> **Few** can be:
> - an **adjective**: *Her few decent clothes were now dirty.*

1 some, but not many: *I spoke with **a few** friends about it.* ♦ *I'm not sure how many I'll need, so give me **a few more**.* ♦ *Everything is expected to change in the **next few** years.* ♦ *Clean the cage **every few** days.* ♦ ***A few of** the plates were chipped.*
2 very small in number: *Few managers attend the meetings.* ♦ *Why are there **so few** women in the Senate?* ♦ *We get **very few** complaints about racial discrimination.* ♦ ***Few of** the companies offer a home delivery service.* ♦ *Poe is among **the few** to have tackled this question.*

> - **A few** usually has a positive meaning and refers to a number of people or things that is not very large: *I've got a few questions for you.*
> - **Few** usually has a negative meaning and refers to a number that is smaller than you would like or expect: *Very few people came to her party.* **Few** is rather formal when used in this negative way and in spoken English it is more usual to say **not many**.

PHRASES **few and far between** not happening very often, or not existing in many places: *Opportunities for promotion are few and far between.*
quite a few a fairly large number of people

or things: *The letter arrived quite a few days ago.*
→ LESS

Both **fewer** and **less** can be used to refer to an amount that is smaller than another amount.
- Use **fewer** before plural nouns: *Fewer people came than we expected.* ♦ *There are fewer restaurants in the area these days.*
- Use **less** before uncountable nouns: *It took less time than I thought.*

fi•an•cé /ˌfiɑnˈseɪ/ noun [C] the man that a woman is going to marry

fi•an•cée /ˌfiɑnˈseɪ/ noun [C] the woman that a man is going to marry

fi•as•co /fiˈæskoʊ/ noun [C] a complete and embarrassing failure

fib /fɪb/ verb [I] *informal* to tell a lie about something that is not important —**fib** noun [C]

fi•ber /ˈfaɪbər/ noun **1** [U] the parts of fruit, vegetables, and grains that help food to pass through your body but that your body does not use: *foods that are high in fiber* **2** [C] a type of cloth, or one of the very thin natural or artificial pieces that cloth is made from: *natural fibers such as linen and cotton* **3** [C/U] one of the thin pieces that form the nerves and muscles in your body

fi•ber•glass /ˈfaɪbərˌglæs/ noun [U] a light hard substance made from very thin pieces of glass

fi•bre /ˈfaɪbər/ the British spelling of **fiber**

fick•le /ˈfɪk(ə)l/ adj **1** always changing your mind about who or what you like **2** weather that is fickle changes often and unexpectedly

fic•tion /ˈfɪkʃ(ə)n/ noun ★★
1 [U] books and stories about imaginary events and people ≠ NONFICTION: *Hardy wrote poetry as well as fiction.*
2 [C/U] a report, story, or explanation that is not true: *His account of what happened was pure fiction.*
→ SCIENCE FICTION

fic•tion•al /ˈfɪkʃən(ə)l/ adj invented for a book, play, or movie: *a fictional character/place*

fic•ti•tious /fɪkˈtɪʃəs/ adj invented and not real or true

fid•dle¹ /ˈfɪd(ə)l/ verb [I] to keep touching or moving something: *Mary fiddled with her keys.*
PHRASAL VERB ˌ**fiddle aˈround 1** *same as* **fiddle¹ 2** to waste time doing things that are not important or useful

fid•dle² /ˈfɪd(ə)l/ noun [C] *informal* a VIOLIN

fi•del•i•ty /fɪˈdeləti/ noun [U] **1** the attitude or behavior of someone who is willing to have sex only with their partner ≠ INFIDELITY **2** *formal* loyalty to someone or something

fidg•et /ˈfɪdʒɪt/ verb [I] to keep making small quick movements because you are bored, nervous, or impatient —**fidg•et•y** adj

field¹ /fild/ noun [C] ★★★

1 area for farming	5 where force has effect
2 area for sports	6 area with gas, coal, etc.
3 subject or type of work	7 area that can be seen
4 space for information	+ PHRASE

1 an area of land that is used for keeping animals or growing food: *a **field** of wheat*
2 an area of land that is covered in grass and used for sports: *a football field*
3 a subject that you study, or a type of work that you do: *Professor Edwards is one of the main experts in his field.* ♦ *the **field of** organic chemistry*
4 a space where you can type information in a computer program: *Type your name in the User field.*
5 an area where a particular force has an effect: *a magnetic field*
6 an area where gas, coal, oil, or other useful substances are found
7 an area that a person or piece of equipment can see at one time: *A man walked into my **field of vision**.* ♦ *a telescope's **field of view***
PHRASE **in the field** in conditions that you find in the real world, not in a laboratory or classroom: *The new drugs have not yet been tested in the field.*

field² /fild/ verb [T] **1** to catch or pick up the ball in a sport such as baseball when a player from the other team hits it **2** to use a person or group of people as your team or representative: *The party will be fielding a very strong candidate in the election.* **3** to deal with something such as a difficult question or a telephone call

ˈ**field** ˌ**day** noun **have a field day** to have the chance to do something that you really enjoy

field•er /ˈfildər/ noun [C] a player in a sport such as baseball whose job is to catch or pick up the ball when a player from the other team hits it

ˈ**field e**ˌ**vent** noun [C] a sports event that is not a race, for example throwing something or jumping

ˈ**field** ˌ**goal** noun [C] in football, a kick worth three points scored by kicking the ball over the BAR of the goal

ˈ**field** ˌ**hockey** noun [U] *American* an outdoor game played by two teams who use curved sticks to try to hit a ball into the other team's goal

ˈ**field** ˌ**test** noun [C] a test of something that involves using it in real conditions, rather than in a laboratory —ˈ**field-**ˌ**test** verb [T]

ˈ**field** ˌ**trip** noun [C] a visit to a place that gives students the chance to study something in a real environment, rather than in a classroom or laboratory

field•work /ˈfildˌwɜrk/ noun [U] work that involves going outside your classroom or laboratory to study something in a real environment

fiend /find/ noun [C] **1** a very evil person = MONSTER **2** *informal* someone who is extremely enthusiastic about something: *a soccer fiend*

fiend•ish /ˈfindɪʃ/ adj **1** a fiendish plan or idea is very clever but cruel **2** a fiendish problem or question is very difficult to solve or deal with —**fiend•ish•ly** adv

fierce /fɪrs/ adj ★
1 very angry, or ready to attack: *a fierce dog*
2 involving very strong feelings such as determination, anger, or hate: *a fierce debate*
3 very strong, or severe: *a fierce storm* ♦ *fierce competition*
—**fierce•ly** adv

F

fier•y /ˈfaɪri/ adj **1** expressing strong feelings, especially anger: *a fiery speech* **2** very bright in color

fi•es•ta /fiˈestə/ noun [C] a public celebration or religious festival, especially in countries where people speak Spanish

FIFA /ˈfifə/ the international organization that makes rules and decisions relating to the sport of soccer

fif•teen /fɪfˈtin/ number the number 15

fif•teenth /fɪfˈtinθ/ number **1** in the place or position counted as number 15 **2** one of 15 equal parts of something

fifth[1] /fɪfθ/ number **1** in the place or position counted as number five **2** one of five equal parts of something

fifth[2] /fɪfθ/ noun [C] *American* a bottle of an alcoholic drink containing one fifth of a GALLON

ˌFifth Aˈmendment, the the part of the U.S. Constitution that says that anyone accused of a crime does not have to give information in court if it proves that they are guilty

PHRASE **take/plead the Fifth (Amendment)** *often humorous* to say that you do not want to answer a question

fif•ties /ˈfɪftiz/ noun [plural] **1** the years from 1950 to 1959 **2** a temperature in the fifties is between 50 and 59 degrees Fahrenheit

PHRASE **in your fifties** aged between 50 and 59

fif•ti•eth /ˈfɪftiəθ/ number **1** in the place or position counted as number 50 **2** one of 50 equal parts of something

fif•ty /ˈfɪfti/ number the number 50

ˌfifty-ˈfifty adj, adv equal, or into two equal parts: *a fifty-fifty chance of winning* ♦ *The bills were split fifty-fifty.*

fig /fɪg/ noun [C] a fruit with purple or green skin and many small seeds *—picture* → C10

fig. abbrev figure: a picture in a book

fight[1] /faɪt/ (past tense and past participle **fought** /fɔt/) verb ★★★

1 use weapons	5 try not to show/do sth
2 hit/kick/bite	+ PHRASES
3 disagree/argue	+ PHRASAL VERBS
4 try hard to do sth	

1 [I/T] if people fight, they use guns or other weapons against each other: *Dan fought in the Gulf War.* ♦ *We were **fighting for** freedom.*

2 [I/T] if people or animals fight, they hit, kick, or bite each other: *Protesters **fought with** the police outside.* ♦ *Children **fought over** scraps of food.*

3 [I] to disagree or argue about something: *What are you two **fighting about** now?* ♦ *I don't want to **fight over** this.*

4 [I/T] to try very hard to achieve something, or to stop something bad from happening: *She spent her life fighting racism.* ♦ *We **fought** hard **for** our rights.* ♦ **fight to do sth** *Local campaigners are fighting to save the building.*

5 [T] to try very hard not to show a feeling, or not to do something that you want to do: *She **fought the urge to** run after him.*

PHRASES **fight a fire/blaze** to try to stop a large fire from burning

fight it out to fight or argue until something is decided

have a fighting chance to have a good chance of being successful

PHRASAL VERBS **ˌfight ˈback** to hit or kick someone who is attacking you, or to argue when someone criticizes you

ˌfight sth ˈback to try very hard not to show an emotion = HOLD BACK: *Mary fought back her tears.*

ˌfight sb ˈoff to stop someone who is trying to attack you

ˌfight sth ˈoff if your body fights off an illness, it prevents the illness from making you sick

Words often used with fight

*Nouns often used with **fight** (verb, sense 4)*

- FIGHT + **corruption, crime, discrimination, prejudice, racism, terrorism:** stop something bad

fight[2] /faɪt/ noun [C] ★★★

1 a situation in which people hit each other: *He **had a fight with** a man in the bar.* ♦ ***fights between** rival gangs*

2 a situation in which people disagree or argue with each other = DISAGREEMENT: *All teenagers **have fights with** their parents.*

3 a determined attempt to achieve something, or to stop something bad from happening = STRUGGLE: ***the fight against** terrorism* ♦ **a fight to do sth** *the fight to protect our children.*

4 an occasion when people fight in a BOXING match

PHRASE **put up a good fight** to try hard to achieve something even though you do not succeed

fight•er /ˈfaɪtər/ noun [C] **1** a military aircraft that is designed for battles with other aircraft **2** someone who refuses to be defeated even in the most difficult situations **3** someone who takes part in the sport of BOXING

fig•ment /ˈfɪgmənt/ noun **a figment of your imagination** something that you have imagined, which therefore does not really exist

fig•u•ra•tive /ˈfɪgjərətɪv/ adj a figurative meaning is not the usual LITERAL meaning of a word or phrase, but makes a description more interesting: *"My love is like a red, red rose" is an example of the figurative use of language.* —**fig•u•ra•tive•ly** adv

fig•ure[1] /ˈfɪgjər/ noun [C] ★★

1 number	5 drawing in a book
2 amount of money	6 mathematical shape
3 person	+ PHRASE
4 woman's shape	

1 a number that has been counted or calculated: *This year's sales figures were excellent.*

2 a price, cost, or other amount of money: *It's difficult to **put an exact figure on** the rebuilding work.*

3 a person: *A small figure appeared in the doorway.* ♦ *She was the dominant figure in British politics in the 1980s.*

4 the shape of a woman's body: *She has a beautiful figure.*

5 a drawing in a book that gives information =DIAGRAM, ILLUSTRATION
6 *technical* a shape in mathematics: *a five-sided figure*
PHRASE **figure of speech** an expression in which the words are used in a figurative way

fig·ure² /ˈfɪgjər/ verb ★★
1 [I/T] *informal* to think that something is true, although you do not know for certain: **+(that)** *I figured that Joe would have my letter by now.*
2 [I] to be an important part of something: *Marriage doesn't figure in their plans.*
PHRASE **it/that figures** *spoken* used for saying that you are not surprised about something that happens
PHRASAL VERBS **ˌfigure sb ˈout** to understand what someone is like and why they behave in the way that they do
ˌfigure sth ˈout to be able to understand something, or to solve a problem

ˌfigure ˈeight noun [C] *American* the shape of the number 8

fig·ure·head /ˈfɪgjərˌhed/ noun [C] a leader who has no power or influence

file¹ /faɪl/ noun [C] ★★★
1 a set of documents or records that you keep because they contain information: *medical files* ♦ *We have all your information **on file*** (=kept in a file). ♦ *The police **file on** the case has now been closed.*
2 a set of information that is stored on a computer and that is given a particular name
3 a metal tool that is used for making wood or metal smooth

file² /faɪl/ verb ★★
1 [T] to put a document into a container with other documents: *File the forms in alphabetical order.*
2 [T] to make an official statement or complaint by giving it to people in authority: *The family has filed a lawsuit against the company.* ♦ *The couple **filed for a divorce*** (=told the court that they wanted to be divorced) *last month.*
3 [I] if people file somewhere, they walk there in a line: *Students filed into the lecture hall.*
4 [T] to rub something with a metal tool in order to make it smooth, or in order to cut it
PHRASE **file a report** to send an official news report to a newspaper or television station

ˈfile exˌtension noun [C] *computing* the second part of the name of a computer file, that tells you what kind of file it is

fi·let /fɪˈleɪ/ another spelling of **fillet¹**

ˈfiling ˌcabinet noun [C] a tall piece of furniture with drawers in which you keep documents *—picture* → C3

fil·ings /ˈfaɪlɪŋz/ noun [plural] very small pieces of metal that have been FILED off a larger piece

fill¹ /fɪl/ verb ★★★

1 make sth full	6 feel emotion strongly
2 become full of sth	7 spend time doing sth
3 put sth in hole/gap	+ PHRASE
4 of sound/smell/light	+ PHRASAL VERBS
5 be given job/position	

1 [T] to make something full: *Let me fill your glass.* ♦ *The room was **filled with** thick smoke.* ♦ **fill sth with sth** *She filled the bowl with warm water.*
2 [I] to become full of something: *The bar was slowly **filling with** people.*
3 [T] to put something into a hole or GAP so that the hole or GAP no longer exists: *We used cement to fill the cracks.*
4 [T] if sound, smell, or light fills a place, it is very strong or noticeable: *Bright sunlight filled the whole room.*
5 [T] if someone fills a job or position, they are given that job or position: *All the vacancies have now been filled.*
6 [T] if something fills you with a particular emotion, you feel that emotion very strongly: **fill sb with sth** *The sound of his voice filled me with dread.*
7 [T] if you fill a period of time, you spend it doing something
PHRASE **fill a need/gap/void/vacuum** to provide something that is missing or needed
PHRASAL VERBS **ˌfill ˈin** to do someone's job for them while they are away =STAND IN: *I'm **filling in for** the receptionist today.*
ˌfill sb ˈin *informal* to give someone details about something: *Carol will **fill you in on** what happened in the meeting.*
ˌfill sth ˈin to add information in the empty spaces on an official document =FILL STH OUT: *Please fill in the application form.*
ˌfill ˈout *informal* if someone fills out, their body becomes less thin
ˌfill sth ˈout to add information in the empty spaces on an official document =FILL STH IN: *Have you filled out the form?*
ˌfill ˈup *same as* **fill¹** 2: *The room was beginning to fill up.*
ˌfill sth ˈup *same as* **fill¹** 1: *Would you fill up that pitcher for me?*

fill² /fɪl/ noun **have your fill of sth** to experience so much of something that you do not want any more

fil·let¹ /fɪˈleɪ/ noun [C/U] a piece of meat or fish with no bones in it

fil·let² /fɪˈleɪ/ verb [T] to prepare fish or meat for cooking by removing the bones

fill·ing¹ /ˈfɪlɪŋ/ noun **1** [C/U] the cream, fruit, etc. that forms the inside part of a cake or PIE **2** [C] a small amount of metal or plastic that is used for filling a hole in a tooth

fill·ing² /ˈfɪlɪŋ/ adj food that is filling makes you feel full

film¹ /fɪlm/ noun ★★
1 [C/U] the material that is used for taking photographs or for recording moving pictures: *I need some new film for my camera.*
2 [U] the job or business of making movies: *the film industry*
3 [C] moving pictures that tell a story =MOVIE: *We watched a **film about** prison life.*
4 [C] a very thin layer of something that forms on a surface: ***a film of** oil on the water*

film² /fɪlm/ verb [I/T] to use a camera to record moving pictures: *The program was filmed in South Africa.*

film·ing /ˈfɪlmɪŋ/ noun [U] the activity of making a movie

film·mak·er /ˈfɪlmˌmeɪkər/ noun [C] a movie director

fil·ter¹ /ˈfɪltər/ noun [C] a piece of equipment that removes substances that are not wanted from a liquid or gas: *a water filter*

fil·ter² /ˈfɪltər/ verb **1** [T] to pass something through a filter in order to remove particular things that are contained in it **2** [I] if light or sound filters into a place, only a little of it enters that place: *The August sunlight filtered in through the blinds.* **3** [I] if information filters out or through to people, they receive it after a period of time: *News of the decision filtered out to reporters.*

PHRASAL VERB ˌ**filter sth ˈout** to use a filter to remove something that is not wanted

F

filth /fɪlθ/ noun [U] **1** *informal* words or pictures that are very offensive, usually dealing with sex **2** dirt that is especially unpleasant

filth·y /ˈfɪlθi/ adj **1** very dirty **2** *informal* very offensive and usually dealing with sex

fin /fɪn/ noun [C] a thin flat part that sticks out of the body of a fish

fi·nal¹ /ˈfaɪn(ə)l/ adj ★★★

1 existing at the end of a process: *These issues will be discussed in the final report.* ♦ *The **final score** was 21–14.*

2 last in a series: *The final payment is due next month.*

3 if something is final, it cannot be changed: *The editor's decision is final.*

4 showing that something has finished: *the final buzzer of the game*

fi·nal² /ˈfaɪn(ə)l/ noun **1** [C] the last game, race, etc. in a competition, that decides who wins the whole competition **2** [C] *American* the last examination that students take before they finish a class at a school or university **3 finals** [plural] the last set of examinations that students take before they finish at a college or university

fi·nal·e /fɪˈnæli, fɪˈnɑli/ noun [C] the last part of a performance with the most exciting music and dancing

fi·nal·ist /ˈfaɪnəlɪst/ noun [C] a player or team that takes part in the final game in a competition

fi·nal·ize /ˈfaɪn(ə)lˌaɪz/ verb [T] to make the final decisions or arrangements for something

fi·nal·ly /ˈfaɪn(ə)li/ adv ★★★

1 after a long time, process, or series of events: *We finally arrived home at midnight.*

2 *spoken* as the last thing that you want to say: *Finally, I'd like to say thank you.*

3 *formal* decided or agreed in a way that cannot be changed: *The exact amount has not been finally decided.*

fi·nance¹ /ˈfaɪˌnæns, fɪˈnæns/ noun ★

1 [U] decisions on how money is spent or invested: *the company's finance committee*

2 finances [plural] money that is used to pay for something such as a large project: *Where will we get the finances for the project?*

3 finances [plural] the money that you have, and how well you spend it or save it: *My finances are a mess at the moment.*

fi·nance² /ˈfaɪˌnæns, fɪˈnæns/ verb [T] to pay for something such as a large project: *The program is being financed by private individuals.*

fi·nan·cial /fɪˈnænʃ(ə)l, faɪˈnænʃ(ə)l/ adj ★★★ involving money: *banks and other financial institutions* ♦ *We offer a range of **financial services**.* —**fi·nan·cial·ly** adv: *The decision does not affect us financially.*

fin·an·cier /ˌfɪnənˈsɪr/ noun [C] a person or organization that manages or lends large amounts of money

fi·nanc·ing /ˈfaɪnænsɪŋ/ noun [U] money that you borrow to buy or do something expensive

finch /fɪntʃ/ noun [C] a small bird with a short thick beak

find¹ /faɪnd/ (past tense and past participle **found** /faʊnd/) verb [T] ★★★

1 discover (by searching)	5 make formal decision
2 get sth	6 have enough of sth
3 experience sth	+ PHRASES
4 have as opinion	+ PHRASAL VERB

1 to discover or to notice something, often after searching: *Did you find your shoes?* ♦ *We hope to find the answers to these questions.* ♦ **find sb doing sth** *I found her wandering in the streets.*

2 to get something: *Have you found a place to live yet?* ♦ *It is very difficult for young people in this area to **find work**.*

3 to experience something in a particular way: *William now finds walking very difficult.*

4 to have something as an opinion because of things that you have experienced: **+(that)** *I find that children need a lot of encouragement.*

5 to make a formal decision about something after listening to all the facts: *He was **found guilty** and sentenced to three years in prison.* ♦ **+(that)** *The court found that the company had broken the law.*

6 if you find the time or money to do something, you have enough time or money to do it

PHRASES **be found** if something is found in a particular place, it lives, grows, or exists there: *The flower is found only in the French Alps.*

find your way to manage to arrive in a place that you were not sure how to get to

find yourself doing sth to realize that you are doing something that you had not intended to do: *I found myself agreeing with everything she said.*

PHRASAL VERB ˌ**find ˈout** to discover a fact or piece of information: *I don't want Jerry to **find out about** this.* ♦ **+who/what/why etc.** *I want to find out what happened.* ♦ **+(that)** *Her parents found out that she had a boyfriend.*

find² /faɪnd/ noun [C] something good that you find by chance

find·ings /ˈfaɪndɪŋz/ noun [plural] information or opinions that come from doing research

fine¹ /faɪn/ adj ★★★

1 good enough	4 difficult to notice
2 healthy	5 thin and narrow
3 of high quality	+ PHRASE

1 good enough, or acceptable: *"Is your room*

all right?" "Yes, it's fine, thanks." ♦ *Your blood pressure is absolutely fine.*
2 healthy and happy: *"How are you?" "Fine, thanks."*
3 of very good quality: *fine clothes/food/wine*
4 fine details are small and difficult to notice: *He spent hours explaining the finer points of the plan.*
5 very thin and narrow, not thick or heavy: *fine hair* ♦ *a fine layer of dust*
PHRASE **a fine line between** if there is a fine line between two things, they are almost the same as each other

fine² /faɪn/ adv *informal* in a way that is acceptable and good enough: *My car's running fine now.*

fine³ /faɪn/ noun [C] an amount of money that you must pay because you have broken the law: *I had to pay a $40 fine for parking on the street overnight.* ♦ *The court has the right to impose heavy fines* (=large fines).

> Words often used with **fine**
> *Adjectives often used with **fine** (noun)*
> ■ **heavy, hefty, large, stiff, substantial** + FINE: used when you have to pay a lot of money

fine⁴ /faɪn/ verb [T] to make someone pay an amount of money as a punishment for breaking the law: *She was fined for speeding.*

ˌfine ˈart noun [U] objects such as paintings that are created to be beautiful or interesting

fine•ly /ˈfaɪnli/ adv **1** into very small pieces: *Add one onion, finely chopped.* **2** exactly, or with great care: *a finely crafted machine*

ˌfine ˈprint noun [U] the details of an agreement, that are usually printed in very small letters

fi•nesse /fɪˈnes/ noun [U] a skillful quality in the way that you move or deal with difficult situations

ˌfine-ˈtune verb [T] to make small changes to something in order to make it as good as possible

fin•ger¹ /ˈfɪŋgər/ noun [C] ★★★
1 the long thin parts on the end of your hands
2 a long thin piece of something
PHRASE **(keep your) fingers crossed** used for saying that you hope things will happen in the way that you want them to
→ LAY¹, POINT², PULSE¹, SLIP¹

fin•ger² /ˈfɪŋgər/ verb [T] **1** to touch something with your fingers **2** *informal* to tell someone in authority that someone has done something wrong

fin•ger•nail /ˈfɪŋgərˌneɪl/ noun [C] any of the hard smooth parts at the ends of your fingers

fin•ger•print /ˈfɪŋgərˌprɪnt/ noun [C] a mark on something that you have touched that shows the pattern of lines on your fingers

fin•ger•tip /ˈfɪŋgərˌtɪp/ noun [C] the end of your finger
PHRASE **at your fingertips** available for you to use immediately: *He has all the information at his fingertips.*

fin•ick•y /ˈfɪnɪki/ adj someone who is finicky wants things to be correct in every detail

fin•ish¹ /ˈfɪnɪʃ/ verb ★★★
1 [I/T] to do the last part of something so that it is complete: *I've almost finished my work.* ♦ **finish doing sth** *I haven't finished eating yet.*
2 [I] to stop happening: *The game finished with the score tied.*
3 [T] to eat, drink, or use all of something so that there is none left: *We finished the bottle of wine.*
4 [I/T] to be in a particular position at the end of a race or competition: *She finished fifth.*
PHRASE **the finishing touch/touches** the last small details that make something complete
PHRASAL VERBS **ˌfinish sth ˈoff 1** *same as* **finish¹** 1: *They hired a smaller company to finish off the job.* **2** *same as* **finish¹** 3: *Do you want to finish off these sandwiches?*
ˌfinish sth ˈup *same as* **finish¹** 3: *Finish up your drinks, please.*
ˈfinish with sth if you are finished with something, you have stopped using it and no longer need it: *Are you finished with the scissors yet?*

fin•ish² /ˈfɪnɪʃ/ noun [C] **1** the end of something **2** the appearance of a surface, for example whether it is smooth or rough

fin•ished /ˈfɪnɪʃt/ adj **1** something that is finished has been completed: *We can move in as soon as construction is finished.* **2** if you are finished, you have completed the job that you were doing

fi•nite /ˈfaɪˌnaɪt/ adj *formal* existing only in limited numbers or amounts, or continuing only for a limited time or distance
≠ INFINITE

fir /fɜr/ noun [C] a tree with thin sharp leaves that do not fall off in winter —*picture* → C9

fire¹ /faɪr/ noun ★★★
1 [C/U] flames and heat from something that is burning in an uncontrolled way: *Lightning may have **started the fire**.* ♦ *A tree in the middle of the field was **on fire*** (=burning). ♦ *Suddenly the curtains **caught fire*** (=began to burn). ♦ *That night a **fire broke out** in the nightclub.* ♦ *The boys **set fire to*** (=started a fire on) *an old couch.*
2 [C] a small pile of burning wood, coal, etc. that you make in order to produce heat: *Bill started to **build a fire**.*
3 [U] shots from a gun: *machine-gun fire* ♦ *One of the men **opened fire on*** (=started shooting at) *the police.*
→ PLAY¹

fire² /faɪr/ verb ★★
1 [I/T] if a weapon fires, or if someone fires it, someone uses it to shoot something: *The rebels fired their machine guns into the air.* ♦ *Jed lifted his rifle and **fired at** the target.*
2 [T] to make someone leave their job as a punishment: *She was fired for refusing to include the information in her report.*

ˈfire aˌlarm noun [C] a piece of equipment that makes a loud noise to warn people that there is a fire

fire•arm /ˈfaɪrˌɑrm/ noun [C] *formal* a gun

fire•crack•er /ˈfaɪrˌkrækər/ noun [C] a FIREWORK that makes a loud noise when it explodes

ˈfire deˌpartment noun [C] *American* an organization of people whose job is dealing with fires in a particular area

ˈfire ˌdrill noun [C] an occasion when all the people in a building pretend that there is a fire inside and practice getting out safely

fired up /ˌfaɪrd ˈʌp/ adj *informal* very excited and enthusiastic about something

ˈfire ˌengine noun [C] a large vehicle that takes FIREFIGHTERS and their equipment to a fire

ˈfire eˌscape noun [C] a metal STAIRCASE on the outside of a building that people use in order to escape when there is a fire

ˈfire exˌtinguisher noun [C] a metal container that is filled with water or with a chemical that stops fires

F

fire•fight•er /ˈfaɪrˌfaɪtər/ noun [C] someone whose job is to put out fires and help people to escape from other dangerous situations

fire•fly /ˈfaɪrˌflaɪ/ noun [C] an insect that produces a flashing light when it flies

fire•house /ˈfaɪrˌhaʊs/ noun [C] *American* a FIRE STATION

ˈfire ˌhydrant noun [C] a water pipe in a street from which water is taken to stop a fire

fire•light /ˈfaɪrˌlaɪt/ noun [U] the light that a fire in a FIREPLACE produces

fire•man /ˈfaɪrmən/ (plural **fire•men** /ˈfaɪrmən/) noun [C] a male FIREFIGHTER

fire•place /ˈfaɪrˌpleɪs/ noun [C] a place in a room where a fire burns

fire•proof /ˈfaɪrˌpruf/ adj a fireproof object cannot be damaged by fire

fire•side /ˈfaɪrˌsaɪd/ noun [C] the part of a room that is near a fire

ˈfire ˌstation noun [C] the building where FIREFIGHTERS have their office and keep their equipment

ˈfire ˌtruck noun [C] *American* a FIRE ENGINE

fire•wall /ˈfaɪrˌwɔl/ noun [C] *computing* a computer program that prevents people from entering a computer system illegally

fire•wood /ˈfaɪrˌwʊd/ noun [U] wood that is used as fuel for a fire

fire•works /ˈfaɪrˌwɜrks/ noun [plural] objects that make loud noises and colored lights in the sky when they explode

ˈfiring ˌsquad noun [C] a group of soldiers who shoot and kill someone as a punishment

firm¹ /fɜrm/ adj ★★

1 solid but not hard ≠ SOFT: *a firm mattress*

2 definite and not changing: *Have you set a firm date for the meeting?* ♦ *The institution has the firm support of the local people.* ♦ *Mark's* ***a firm believer in*** *discipline for children.*

3 showing that you are in control of a situation: *What the party needs now is firm leadership.* ♦ *You sometimes have to* ***be firm with*** *young children.*

4 physically or mentally strong: *She took a firm hold of the stick and pulled.*

—**firm•ly** adv: *I firmly believe that we must act at once.* —**firm•ness** noun [U]

firm² /fɜrm/ noun [C] ★★ a business, or a company: *a building/engineering/law firm* ♦ *a firm of accountants/architects/lawyers*

firm³ /fɜrm/ PHRASAL VERB **ˌfirm sth ˈup** to make something more definite

first /fɜrst/ grammar word ★★★

> **First** can be:
> - a **number**: *This is the first car I've ever owned.*
> - a **pronoun**: *Her second husband was much older than her first.*
> - an **adverb**: *First, I want to explain the purpose of this meeting.*
> - a **noun**: *That visit was a first for me.*

1 before any others coming, happening, or starting before any others: *What was your first job?* ♦ *This will be Kenny's first trip overseas.* ♦ *Julia got there first.* ♦ *He's had a lot of girlfriends, but Lucy was* ***the first.*** ♦ *Take the first road on the right.* ♦ *He cooked me a meal, which was* ***a first*** (=he had never done it before).

2 before doing other things before you do something else: *First, let's go around the room and introduce ourselves.* ♦ *Can't I just finish reading this article first?*

3 at the beginning at the beginning of a period of time, a situation, an activity, etc.: *When I first started running, I could do a mile in nine minutes.* ♦ *The first few days of our vacation were wonderful.*

4 most important used for referring to the main or most important thing: *His first love was music.* ♦ *Our first consideration must be the safety of the passengers.* ♦ *My children will always* ***come first.***

5 best in a competition better than anyone or anything else in a game, competition, etc.: *Karen has always been first in her class.* ♦ *His painting won* ***first prize*** *in a competition.*

PHRASES **at first** in the beginning, before something changes: *At first he wouldn't even talk about it.*

at first sight/glance when you first see something or find out about something, before you know more details: *At first glance, the theory seems to make a lot of sense.*

sb's first choice the thing or person that someone likes more than all the others

first come, first served used for saying that if you arrive before other people you will be served or dealt with before them

first of all *spoken* **1** used for introducing the first of several things that you are going to say: *First of all, I'd like to give you a little background information.* **2** before doing anything else: *First of all, clean the surface that you are going to paint.*

first thing (in the morning) at the very beginning of the day

first things first used for saying that the most important things should be dealt with before anything else

in the first place 1 used for stating the most basic reason for something: *I'm not going because, in the first place, I can't afford it.* **2** at the beginning of a situation: *If you don't like her, why invite her in the first place?*

make the first move to take action before anyone else

ˌfirst ˈaid noun [U] basic medical treatment that is given as soon as someone is injured or sick

ˌfirst ˈaid ˌkit noun [C] a small box or bag with

the equipment that you need to give first aid

ˌFirst Aˈmendment, the the part of the U.S. Constitution that says that people have the right to express their opinions, to practice their own religion, and to meet together in groups

ˌfirst ˈbase noun [singular] the first successful step in an attempt to achieve something: *Our project never got to first base.*

ˌfirst ˈclass¹ noun [U] **1** the most expensive and most comfortable way to travel on an airplane, train, or ship **2** the class of mail that is used for sending letters

ˌfirst ˈclass² adj **1** providing the most expensive and most comfortable way to travel on an airplane, train, or ship: *a first class ticket* **2** of the best quality, or of the highest standard: *first class service* **3** used for first class mail

ˌfirst ˈclass³ adv using the most expensive form of transportation or mail: *She always travels first class.*

ˌfirst ˈcousin noun [C] a child of your AUNT or UNCLE

ˌfirst-deˈgree adj **1** *American* a first-degree murder is the most serious type, in which someone deliberately plans to kill someone **2** a first-degree burn is the least serious type

ˌfirst eˈdition noun [C] one of the first printed copies of a book, newspaper, or magazine

ˌfirst ˈfloor, the noun [singular] **1** *American* the floor of a building that is at the same level as the ground = GROUND FLOOR **2** *British* the second floor of a building

ˌfirst ˈgear noun [U] the lowest GEAR in a vehicle, used for starting or moving slowly

ˌfirst geneˈration noun [singular] **1** the GENERATION of people in a family who were the first from their country to go and live in another country **2** the first type of a particular machine or piece of equipment to be produced —**ˌfirst-geneˈration** adj

ˌfirst ˈhalf noun [C] the first part of a sports game

ˌfirst-ˈhand adj obtained by experiencing something yourself, not by learning about it from other people: *first-hand knowledge/information/experience* ♦ *a first-hand account of the situation* —**ˌfirst-ˈhand** adv

ˌFirst ˈLady, the the wife of the president of the U.S. or of a GOVERNOR of a U.S. state

ˌfirst ˈlanguage noun [C] **1** the first language that you learn to speak **2** the main language that people speak in a region or country

first·ly /ˈfɜrs(t)li/ adv used for beginning a list of things that are in a particular order

ˈfirst ˌname noun [C] the name that comes before your family name

ˌfirst ˈperson, the noun [singular] **1** *linguistics* the pronouns "I" and "we" and the verbs and object pronouns that are used with them **2** a way of writing a story as if it had happened to you

ˌfirst-ˈrate adj of the highest quality

ˌfirst-ˈstring adj the first-string players on a sports team are the best players

ˌFirst World ˈWar, the WORLD WAR I

fis·cal /ˈfɪsk(ə)l/ adj relating to money and financial matters —**fis·cal·ly** adv

ˌfiscal ˈyear noun [C] *American* a period of 12 months that a business uses to calculate how much profit it has made and how much it owes

fish¹ /fɪʃ/ (plural **fish** or **fish·es**) noun [C/U] ★★★ an animal that lives in water and swims, or the meat of this animal

PHRASE **fish and chips** a meal of fish and long thin pieces of potato, cooked in hot oil

fish² /fɪʃ/ verb [I] **1** to try to catch fish **2** to try to find something by feeling inside a bag, a box, etc.: *She fished around in her bag for the keys.* **3** to try to make someone tell you something without asking directly: *"Having trouble?" he asked casually, fishing for information.*

PHRASAL VERB **ˌfish sth ˈout** to pull something out from inside something else: *She reached into her bag and fished out a pen.*

fish·er·man /ˈfɪʃərmən/ (plural **fish·er·men** /ˈfɪʃərmən/) noun [C] a man who catches fish for fun, or as his job

fish·ing /ˈfɪʃɪŋ/ noun [U] the activity, sport, or business of catching fish: *We're going fishing tomorrow.*

ˈfishing ˌrod or **ˈfishing ˌpole** noun [C] a long thin pole that you use for catching fish

ˈfish ˌstick noun [C] *American* a long thin piece of fish that is covered in BREADCRUMBS and cooked

fish·y /ˈfɪʃi/ adj **1** not completely right, honest, or legal **2** tasting or smelling like fish

fis·sure /ˈfɪʃər/ noun [C] a long deep crack in something

fist /fɪst/ noun [C] your hand when your fingers are closed tightly: *She was holding something tightly in her fist.*

fist·ful /ˈfɪstʃʊl/ noun [C] the amount of something that you can hold in your fist

fit¹ /fɪt/ (past tense and past participle **fit** or **fit·ted**) verb [I/T] ★★★

1 to be small enough or the right size and shape to go somewhere, or to manage to put someone or something in a space: *I don't think that box will fit.* ♦ *The book is small enough to fit in your pocket.* ♦ *The cover fits neatly over the chair.* ♦ **fit sth into/onto/over sth** *She can fit two more people into her car.*

2 if clothes fit, they are the right size for you: *It is important that children's shoes fit correctly.* ♦ *I like the suit, but the jacket doesn't fit me.* ♦ *The dress fit her **like a glove*** (=fit extremely well).

3 to be appropriate or right for something: *We need a name that fits our image.* ♦ *A dark wooden table wouldn't **fit with** the decor in here.*

4 to be the truth, or to be the same as something that someone describes or asks for: *He fits the description of a man seen running away from the scene.* ♦ *Something in her story did not fit.*

PHRASAL VERBS **ˌfit ˈin 1** to be accepted by a group of people because you are similar to them: *I tried to fit in, but they were all much younger than I was.* **2** to be a part of a group, plan, or situation: *He explained the*

project to me and how my job fits in.
ˌ**fit sb ˈin** to have enough time to deal with someone or something: *Dr. Halden can fit you in this morning at 10.*
ˌ**fit ˈin with sth** to be correct, appropriate, or sensible in relation to something else: *His explanation didn't fit in with what I saw.*
ˌ**fit ˈtogether** if things such as ideas or facts fit together, they make a sensible story or explanation when you put them together: *We have all the evidence, but we don't know yet how it fits together.*

fit² /fɪt/ adj ★
1 healthy, strong, and able to do physical exercise ≠ UNFIT: *Running around after the kids keeps me fit.*
2 of a good enough standard for something ≠ UNFIT: *The house was not fit for human habitation.* ♦ **fit to do sth** *I don't think he's fit to be a teacher.*
PHRASE **see/think fit** to decide that something is the best thing to do: *The court will deal with the matter as it thinks fit.*

fit³ /fɪt/ noun **1** [C] a strong sudden physical reaction or emotion that you cannot control: *a coughing/sneezing fit* ♦ *a fit of rage* **2** [C] *informal* an occasion when someone becomes unconscious for a short time and their body shakes **3** [singular] used for saying whether something is the right size and shape for someone or something: *When buying shoes, it is important to get a good fit.* **4** [C/U] used for saying whether people or things are appropriate for each other: *There was a good fit between the managers' goals and the staff.*
PHRASE **have/throw a fit** *informal* to get very angry and shout or become violent

fit•ful /ˈfɪtfəl/ adj starting and stopping often: *fitful sleep* —**fit•ful•ly** adv

fit•ness /ˈfɪtnəs/ noun [U] **1** the state of being physically healthy and strong: *a high level of physical fitness* **2** how appropriate someone or something is: *There are questions as to his fitness for office.*

fit•ted /ˈfɪtəd/ adj made to fit the shape of something closely: *a fitted shirt*

fit•ting /ˈfɪtɪŋ/ adj appropriate for a particular situation: *The dinner was a fitting end to Carter's 25 years with the company.*

ˈ**fitting ˌroom** noun [C] a room in a clothing store where you can put on clothes before you buy them

fit•tings /ˈfɪtɪŋz/ noun [plural] small parts that you connect to something: *pipe fittings*

five /faɪv/ number [C] the number 5

ˈ**five-ˌstar** adj a five-star hotel or restaurant is of excellent quality

fix¹ /fɪks/ verb [T] ★★

1 make sth work again	5 set price/amount/date
2 prepare food/drink	6 cheat
3 arrange hair/clothing	+ PHRASAL VERBS
4 fasten so cannot move	

1 to repair something: *Jessica fixed my watch.* ♦ *I have to get my car fixed.*
2 *American* to prepare food or drink: *I'll fix dinner.* ♦ **fix sb sth** *Jackie fixed me a drink.*
3 *American* to arrange your hair or clothing so that you look nicer: *How should I fix my hair?*
4 to fasten something somewhere so that it cannot move: **fix sth to/onto/on sth** *Smoke detectors should be fixed to the ceiling.*
5 to decide what a price, amount, or date will be: *Interest rates have been fixed at 5%.* ♦ *A delivery date has not yet been fixed.*
6 to dishonestly arrange the result of something such as a game or election
PHRASAL VERBS ˈ**fix sth on sb/sth** if you fix your eyes or your attention on someone or something, you look straight at them and at nothing else
ˌ**fix sb ˈup** *informal* to arrange for two people to meet so that they might begin a romantic relationship: **fix sb up with sb** *Jimmy wants to fix Joe up with his sister.*
ˌ**fix sth ˈup** to clean, repair, or decorate something: *I'm going to fix up the house before my mother-in-law arrives.*

fix² /fɪks/ noun **1** [C] something that solves a problem or corrects a mistake: *We need a long-term solution, not just a quick fix* (=a fast solution, but one that is usually only temporary). **2** [singular] an amount of a drug that someone feels that they need to take regularly

fix•a•tion /fɪkˈseɪʃ(ə)n/ noun [C] a very strong interest in something that prevents you from paying attention to anything else: *Doug has a fixation with sports cars.* —**fix•at•ed** /fɪkˈseɪtəd/ adj

fixed /fɪkst/ adj ★
1 not changing, or not able to be changed: *a fixed price* ♦ *a fixed smile* ♦ *My mother has fixed ideas about how to bring up children.*
2 fastened in one position and not able to be moved: *Make sure bookcases are securely fixed to the wall.*

ˌ**fixed ˈincome** noun [C] an income that does not change or get bigger over time

fix•ture /ˈfɪkstʃər/ noun [C] a piece of furniture or equipment that is built into a building so that you do not take it with you when you move: *light fixtures*

fizz /fɪz/ noun [U] the small gas BUBBLES that are in some drinks —**fizz** verb [I], **fizz•y** adj

fiz•zle /ˈfɪz(ə)l/ or ˌ**fizzle ˈout** verb [I] to gradually fail, become less enthusiastic, or disappear: *The group's efforts at reform fizzled out after their leader left.*

fjord /fiˈɔrd, fjɔrd/ noun [C] a narrow section of ocean that is between high rocks

FL abbrev Florida

flab /flæb/ noun [U] *informal* loose fat flesh

flab•ber•gast•ed /ˈflæbərˌgæstəd/ adj very surprised or shocked

flab•by /ˈflæbi/ adj with a lot of loose fat: *a flabby stomach*

flack /flæk/ another spelling of **flak**

flag¹ /flæg/ noun [C] a piece of cloth with colors or a pattern on it, used as a signal or for representing a country or organization

flag² /flæg/ verb **1** [I] to become tired or weak, or to begin to lack enthusiasm: *After a long day, his energy flagged.* **2** [T] to mark something so that you will be able to find it again
PHRASAL VERB ˌ**flag sb/sth ˈdown** to wave at

the driver of a car so that they stop: *tourists trying to flag down a cab*

flag·pole /ˈflægˌpoʊl/ noun [C] a tall thin pole, used for hanging a flag on

fla·grant /ˈfleɪgrənt/ adj done in an obvious way that shows that you do not care what people think: *a flagrant disregard for the law* —**fla·grant·ly** adv

flag·ship /ˈflægʃɪp/ noun [C] the biggest, most important, or best thing in a group

flail /fleɪl/ verb [I/T] to move your arms and legs around in an uncontrolled way

flair /fler/ noun [U] an attractive, skillful, or interesting way of doing something: *She always dresses with flair.*
PHRASE **have a flair for sth** to be very skillful at something

flak /flæk/ noun [U] *informal* criticism and argument: *The policy is getting a lot of flak.*

flake¹ /fleɪk/ noun [C] **1** a small flat piece of something **2** *American informal* someone who acts in a strange way or who often does not do what they say they will do

flake² /fleɪk/ verb [I] **1** to come off a surface in small flat pieces: *Her skin was itchy and beginning to flake.* **2** *American informal* to behave in a strange way, or to fail to do what you have said you would do: *Craig was supposed to meet us at 3, but he flaked again.*
PHRASAL VERBS ˌ**flake ˈoff** *same as* **flake**² 1
ˌ**flake ˈout** *informal same as* **flake**² 2

flak·y /ˈfleɪki/ adj **1** *American informal* crazy **2** breaking off easily into small flat pieces: *flaky chocolate*

flam·boy·ant /flæmˈbɔɪənt/ adj behaving or dressing in a way that deliberately attracts attention —**flam·boy·ant·ly** adv

flame¹ /fleɪm/ noun [C] ★ the brightly burning gas that you see coming from a fire: *He sat by the fire staring at the flames.* ♦ *The whole building was soon* ***in flames.*** ♦ *A car had overturned and* ***burst into flames.*** → OLD FLAME

flame² /fleɪm/ verb [I/T] *computing* to send an angry or insulting message over the Internet

fla·men·co /fləˈmeŋkoʊ/ noun [C/U] a traditional lively dance from Spain, or the music for this dance

flam·ing /ˈfleɪmɪŋ/ adj **1** burning brightly: *flaming torches* **2** brightly colored red, orange, or yellow: *a flaming orange sunset*

fla·min·go /fləˈmɪŋgoʊ/ noun [C] a large pink tropical water bird with a long neck and long legs

flam·ma·ble /ˈflæməb(ə)l/ adj likely to burn very quickly and easily = INFLAMMABLE ≠ NONFLAMMABLE

> **Flammable** and **inflammable** both describe something that burns easily and quickly, but most people use **flammable** because **inflammable** looks as if it means **not flammable**.

flank¹ /flæŋk/ verb [T] to be at the side of something or someone: *The president entered the room, flanked by his advisors.*

flank² /flæŋk/ noun [C] **1** the side of an animal's body **2** a position on the right or left side of a team or army, or the people in that position

flan·nel /ˈflæn(ə)l/ noun [U] soft cloth that is used for making clothes and sheets

flap¹ /flæp/ noun [C] a thin flat piece of something that is attached to something else along one edge

flap² /flæp/ verb **1** [I/T] if a bird's wings flap, or if the bird flaps them, they move quickly up and down **2** [I] to be blown noisily by the wind: *I was running fast, my coat flapping in the wind.*

flare¹ /fler/ noun [C] **1** a bright light or flame that is used as a signal in the dark **2** a bright flame that burns for a short time

flare² /fler/ verb [I] **1** to suddenly burn or shine brightly **2** to suddenly become worse or more violent **3** to become wider at one end: *The horse's nostrils flared.*
PHRASAL VERB ˌ**flare ˈup 1** *same as* **flare**² 1: *The fire could flare up again at any time.* **2** *same as* **flare**² 2: *It looked as if the fighting might flare up again.*

flared /flerd/ adj much wider at the bottom than at the top: *flared pants/skirts*

ˈ**flare-ˌup** noun [C] **1** an occasion when people suddenly start behaving in an angry or violent way **2** an occasion when a disease suddenly returns

flash¹ /flæʃ/ verb ★
1 [I/T] to shine on and off very quickly, or to make a light do this: *A truck behind me was flashing its headlights.* ♦ *His watch flashed in the sunlight.*
2 [I/T] to appear, or to make something appear, for a very short time before disappearing: *Tom flashed me a smile from across the room.* ♦ *The headlines flashed across the screen.*
3 [I] to pass very quickly: *The thought that I might die flashed through my mind.*
—**flash·ing** adj

flash² /flæʃ/ noun [C] **1** a bright light that appears for a very short time: *a flash of lightning* **2** a bright light on a camera that flashes as you take a photograph **3** a moment when you suddenly understand or feel something: *a flash of anger/genius*
PHRASES **a flash in the pan** *spoken* someone or something that is popular or successful for only a very short time
in/like a flash very quickly

flash·back /ˈflæʃˌbæk/ noun **1** [C] a sudden clear memory of something that happened in the past **2** [C/U] a part of a book, movie, or play that tells you what happened earlier

flash·card /ˈflæʃˌkɑrd/ noun [C] a small card printed with words, pictures, or numbers that helps someone to learn something

ˌ**flash ˈflood** noun [C] a sudden unexpected flood

flash·light /ˈflæʃˌlaɪt/ noun [C] *American* an electric light that you hold in your hand

flash·point /ˈflæʃˌpɔɪnt/ noun [C] a situation or place in which serious problems or violence will probably develop: *The site has become a flashpoint of religious tensions.*

flash·y /ˈflæʃi/ adj very bright, fashionable, or expensive in a way that is intended to impress people: *a flashy car*

flask /flæsk/ noun [C] a small flat bottle that

F

fits in your pocket, used especially for carrying alcohol

flat[1] /flæt/ adj ★★★

1 level/smooth	6 spoken directly
2 object: not thick	7 tire: no air
3 lying on surface	8 drink: no bubbles
4 rate/amount: fixed	9 musical note: lower
5 lacking emotion	

1 smooth and level on the surface, with no lumps or slopes: *The farmland is very flat.* ♦ *a firm flat stomach* ♦ *You need a flat surface to work on.*
2 not curving inwards or outwards, and not very thick: *a monitor with a flat screen*
3 stretched out, or lying on a surface: *She was flat on her back asleep.*
4 a flat rate or amount is the same in all situations: *The bank charges* ***a flat fee*** *of $15 for money transfers.*
5 lacking emotion, interest, or excitement: *The celebrations seemed a little flat.*
6 said directly and definitely: *a flat refusal*
7 a flat tire does not have enough air in it
8 a drink that is flat has lost its gas BUBBLES
9 slightly lower than the musical note that should be played or sung

flat[2] /flæt/ adv **1** stretched out, or lying on a surface: *He laid the map out flat on the table.* ♦ *Carole was lying flat on her back.* **2** *informal* in exactly the very short period of time that you mention: *I fell asleep in five seconds flat!*
PHRASE **fall flat** to not succeed in entertaining someone or making them laugh

flat[3] /flæt/ noun **1** [C] *informal* a flat tire **2 flats** [plural] shoes with no heels, or with very low heels **3** [C] *British* an APARTMENT
PHRASE **the flat of sth** a flat surface or part of something: *She hit the table with the flat of her hand.*

flat·ly /ˈflætli/ adv **1** in a firm, definite way: *He flatly denied being near the scene of the crime.* **2** without showing any emotion or interest: *"How can I help you?" the clerk asked flatly.*

flat·ten /ˈflæt(ə)n/ verb [I/T] to become flat, or to make something flat: *This exercise helps to flatten a flabby stomach.*
PHRASAL VERB ˌ**flatten (sth) ˈout 1** *same as* **flatten**: *The mountainous region flattens out to a vast plateau.* **2** *business* to become lower in price or amount, or to make a price or amount lower: *The price of crude oil is expected to flatten out this summer.*

flat·ter /ˈflætər/ verb [T] **1** to praise someone in order to make them feel special, often in a way that is not sincere: *She flattered him and told him what he wanted to hear.* **2** if something flatters you, it makes you look good when you use it or wear it
PHRASE **flatter yourself** to persuade yourself that you are better, more attractive, more important, etc. than you are
—**flat·ter·er** noun [C], **flat·ter·ing** adj

flat·tered /ˈflætərd/ adj feeling pleased that someone notices and admires you: *I'm flattered that you would ask me to speak at the convention.*

flat·ter·y /ˈflætəri/ noun [U] praise that is not sincere: *She decided that a little flattery might get results.*

flat·ware /ˈflætˌwer/ noun [U] *American* knives, forks, and spoons that you use for eating rather than serving or cooking

flaunt /flɔnt/ verb [T] to deliberately try to make people notice something that you have so that they admire you: *Lawrence didn't flaunt his wealth.*

fla·vor[1] /ˈfleɪvər/ noun ★
1 [C] the particular taste that a food or drink has: *The drink has a strong citrus flavor.* ♦ *What flavor is the ice cream?*
2 [U] the quality of having a pleasant or strong taste: *This beer has no flavor.* ♦ *Add flavor to your meal by using more herbs and garlic.*
3 [singular/U] a particular quality that is typical of something: *She catches the flavor of small town life in the story.*

fla·vor[2] /ˈfleɪvər/ verb [T] to add something to food or drink that changes its taste or gives it a particular taste

fla·vored /ˈfleɪvərd/ adj with a particular taste: *grape-flavored candy*

fla·vor·ing /ˈfleɪvərɪŋ/ noun [C/U] a substance that is added to food or drink to give it a particular flavor

fla·vour /ˈfleɪvər/ the British spelling of **flavor**

flaw /flɔ/ noun [C] a mark, mistake, or fault that makes someone or something less than perfect: *There was a tiny flaw in the diamond.* ♦ *My father definitely had his flaws and failings.*

flawed /flɔd/ adj spoiled by something such as a mark, fault, or mistake: *The current healthcare system is seriously flawed.*

flaw·less /ˈflɔləs/ adj with no mistakes, marks, or bad features = PERFECT: *a flawless performance* —**flaw·less·ly** adv

flea /fli/ noun [C] a small jumping insect that lives on animals and bites them

ˈ**flea ˌmarket** noun [C] a market where old things are sold at low prices

fleck /flek/ noun [C] a small mark, piece, or amount of something: *flecks of gray in his hair*

flecked /flekt/ adj with small spots of color: *green eyes flecked with brown*

fled the past tense and past participle of **flee**

fledg·ling /ˈfledʒlɪŋ/ adj recently formed and still developing, without very much experience: *fledgling democracies*

flee /fli/ (past tense and past participle **fled** /fled/) verb [I/T] to escape from a dangerous situation or place

fleece /flis/ noun **1** [C/U] the wool on a sheep **2** [U] a type of soft artificial cloth that is used for making clothes

fleet /flit/ noun [C] **1** a group of vehicles that are owned by one organization or person **2** a group of ships, or all the ships in a nation's navy: *the French/U.S./Greek fleet* ♦ *Europe's largest fishing fleet*

fleet·ing /ˈflitɪŋ/ adj continuing for only a very short time —**fleet·ing·ly** adv

flesh[1] /fleʃ/ noun [U] ★
1 the soft substance under your skin that consists mostly of muscle and fat: *The dog's teeth sank into my flesh.*

2 the soft part of a fruit or vegetable that is under the skin: *Cut the avocado in half and scoop out the flesh.*
PHRASES **in the flesh** present here and now, instead of on a screen or in a picture =PERSON: *He was finally going to see her in the flesh.*
sb's (own) flesh and blood someone's relative
→ THORN

flesh² /fleʃ/ PHRASAL VERB ˌ**flesh sth ˈout** to add more details to something

flesh·y /ˈfleʃi/ adj with a lot of flesh

flew the past tense of **fly**¹

flex /fleks/ verb [T] to bend a part of your body in order to stretch it or exercise it
PHRASE **flex your muscles** to show how powerful or strong you are as a warning to someone: *The country's military is just flexing its muscles.*

flex·i·bil·i·ty /ˌfleksəˈbɪləti/ noun [U] **1** the ability to make changes or to deal with a situation that is changing **2** the ability to bend or move easily

flex·i·ble /ˈfleksəb(ə)l/ adj ★
1 able to make changes or deal with a situation that is changing: *A more flexible approach is needed.* ♦ *The job offers flexible working hours.*
2 able to bend or move easily ≠ RIGID: *a flexible rubber strip*

flick¹ /flɪk/ verb **1** [I/T] to move quickly and suddenly, or to make something move quickly and suddenly: *She flicked back her long dark hair.* **2** [T] to move a switch in order to turn something on or off: *He flicked on the light.*

flick² /flɪk/ noun [C] **1** a sudden quick movement **2** *informal* a movie

flick·er¹ /ˈflɪkər/ verb [I] **1** if a flame or light flickers, it does not burn evenly, or it goes on and off **2** to last for only a moment and then disappear

flick·er² /ˈflɪkər/ noun [C] **1** a light that goes quickly on and off **2** a feeling that lasts for a very short time

fli·er /ˈflaɪər/ noun [C] **1** an announcement or advertisement that is printed on paper and given to people = LEAFLET **2** an aircraft pilot or passenger

flight /flaɪt/ noun ★★★
1 [C] a trip in an airplane: *My flight has been delayed.* ♦ *The flight from New York to London took about 5 hours.*
2 [U] the process of moving through the air, or the ability to move through the air: *a flock of geese **in flight***
3 [C/U] the act of running away, or of trying to escape from someone or something: *the refugees' desperate flight from their city*
4 [C] a set of stairs that go from one level to another: *The restrooms are two flights up.* ♦ ***A flight of stairs** leads down to the courtyard.*

ˈflight atˌtendant noun [C] someone whose job is to take care of passengers on an airplane

flim·sy /ˈflɪmzi/ adj **1** made of a thin or light substance: *a flimsy cotton blouse* **2** badly made and likely to break easily: *a flimsy wooden fence* **3** not very reliable, or not easy to believe: *a flimsy excuse*

flinch /flɪntʃ/ verb [I] to make a sudden small movement because you are afraid, surprised, or in pain

fling¹ /flɪŋ/ (past tense and past participle **flung** /flʌŋ/) verb [T] **1** to throw something carelessly or with a lot of force: *She pulled off her coat and flung it on the chair.* **2** to move something quickly and with a lot of force: *He flung open the window.*

fling² /flɪŋ/ noun [C] **1** a sexual relationship that does not last long and is not serious **2** a short time during which you have a lot of fun

flint /flɪnt/ noun [U] a hard gray stone that was used in the past for making tools

flip¹ /flɪp/ verb **1** [I/T] to turn over quickly, or to make something turn over: *His car flipped over and crashed.* ♦ *Flip a coin to decide who goes first.* **2** [T] to change the position of something, or exchange the positions of two or more things: *Flip the last two numbers around and there's your answer.* ♦ *All you have to do is flip a switch to start the machine running.* **3** [I] *informal* to become very angry or excited
PHRASAL VERBS ˌ**flip ˈout** *informal same as* **flip**¹ 3
ˌ**flip ˈthrough sth** to quickly look at the pages of a magazine or book

flip² /flɪp/ noun [C] an action of jumping up and completely turning over in the air

ˈflip ˌchart noun [C] large sheets of paper that are connected at the top. You use them to show pictures or to write things on when you are talking to a group of people.

ˈflip-ˌflop noun [C] a rubber shoe without a top or back, held to your foot by a STRAP in the shape of a "V" that goes between your toes —*picture* → SHOE

flip·pant /ˈflɪpənt/ adj treating a serious subject or situation in a way that is not serious enough

flip·per /ˈflɪpər/ noun [C] **1** a wide flat part like an arm on the bodies of some sea animals **2** a wide flat rubber shoe that you wear when you swim under water

ˈflip ˌside, the noun [singular] the negative aspects of something

flirt¹ /flɜrt/ verb [I] to behave toward someone in a way that shows that you are sexually attracted to them
PHRASAL VERB ˈ**flirt with sth** to consider an idea or plan, but not very seriously

flirt² /flɜrt/ noun [C] someone who flirts a lot

flir·ta·tion /flɜrˈteɪʃ(ə)n/ noun **1** [U] behavior that shows someone that you are sexually attracted to them **2** [C] a short period of time when someone is interested in a new idea or activity

flit /flɪt/ verb [I] to move quickly from one place to another without stopping long

float¹ /floʊt/ verb ★
1 [I] to rest or move slowly on the surface of a liquid and not sink ≠ SINK: *Leaves and twigs **floated on the water**.*
2 [I] to move slowly through the air: *A cloud floated across the moon.*
3 [T] to suggest an idea for people to consider: *Various explanations for his resignation are being floated.*
4 [T] *business* to start to sell a company's SHARES

float² /floʊt/ noun [C] **1** a large vehicle that is decorated and driven through the streets as part of a PARADE **2** *American* a SOFT DRINK with ice cream floating in it

float·ing /ˈfloʊtɪŋ/ adj not fixed or permanent, and therefore likely to change: *a floating exchange rate*

flock¹ /flɑk/ noun [C] **1** a group of birds, sheep, or goats **2** a large group of people

flock² /flɑk/ verb [I] to gather together in a large group

flog /flɑg/ verb [T] to hit someone very hard with a stick or WHIP as a punishment —**flog·ging** noun [C/U]

F

flood¹ /flʌd/ verb ★

1 [I/T] to cover a place with water, or to become covered with water: *Water burst through the dam and flooded local villages.* ♦ *The ground floor of the house was flooded.*

2 [I] if a river floods, water rises up over its BANKS and covers the land around it

3 [I/T] if people or things flood somewhere, they go there or arrive there in large numbers: *Two million visitors **flood into** our city each year.* ♦ **be flooded with sth** *The TV station was flooded with complaints.*

4 [I/T] to fill a place with light, or to become filled with light: *I opened the curtains and light **flooded into** the room.*

PHRASE **flood the market** to make such a large number of goods available for sale that they cannot all be sold and the price falls

PHRASAL VERB ˌ**flood ˈback** if memories or feelings flood back, you suddenly remember them very clearly: *When he told me his name, it all came flooding back.*

flood² /flʌd/ noun ★

1 [C/U] a large amount of water that covers an area that was dry before: *Florida has been badly hit by floods.* ♦ *After three weeks the flood waters finally receded.*

2 [C] a large number of people or things that move somewhere or arrive somewhere at the same time: *We received **a flood of** letters protesting the change.*

flood·gates /ˈflʌdˌgeɪts/ noun **open the floodgates** to suddenly make it possible for a lot of things to happen

flood·ing /ˈflʌdɪŋ/ noun [U] a situation in which water from a river or from heavy rain covers large areas of land

flood·light /ˈflʌdˌlaɪt/ noun [C] a very strong light that is used for lighting a public building or sports event at night

flood·lit /ˈflʌdˌlɪt/ adj lit at night using floodlights

floor¹ /flɔr/ noun ★★★

1 flat area you walk on	4 audience at debate
2 level in building	5 lowest level allowed
3 of ocean/valley etc.	

1 [C] the flat area that you walk on inside a building or room: *The house has polished wooden floors.* ♦ *We were sitting **on the floor** watching TV.*

2 [C] one of the levels in a building: *a first-floor apartment* ♦ *The toy department is **on the second floor**.*

3 [C] the ground at the bottom of something: *a map of the ocean floor*

4 [singular] the audience at a public discussion or debate: *The speaker will now take questions from the floor.*

5 [singular] *business* the lowest level that an amount is allowed to reach

→ SHOP FLOOR

floor² /flɔr/ verb [T] **1** to make someone feel so surprised and confused that they cannot react **2** *American informal* to press the ACCELERATOR of a vehicle down to the floor in order to increase its speed

floor·board /ˈflɔrˌbɔrd/ noun [C] a long wooden board that is part of a floor

floor·ing /ˈflɔrɪŋ/ noun [U] materials that are used for making or covering a floor

flop¹ /flɑp/ verb [I] **1** to sit or lie down in a heavy way by letting your body fall: *He came home and flopped into a chair.* **2** to move or hang in a loose way: *Her long hair flopped down over her eyes.* **3** *informal* if a play, movie, or new product flops, it is completely unsuccessful

flop² /flɑp/ noun [C] *informal* a complete failure

flop·py /ˈflɑpi/ adj soft and hanging down in a loose or heavy way

ˌ**floppy ˈdisk** or **floppy** /ˈflɑpi/ noun [C] *computing* a small square plastic object that you use for storing information from a computer

flo·ral /ˈflɔrəl/ adj made of flowers, or decorated with pictures of flowers

flo·rist /ˈflɔrɪst/ noun [C] someone whose job is to arrange and sell flowers

floss /flɑs/ verb [I/T] to clean between your teeth with DENTAL FLOSS

flo·ta·tion /floʊˈteɪʃ(ə)n/ noun [C/U] *business* the sale of STOCK in a company for the first time

flounce /flaʊns/ verb [I] to walk in an impatient angry way

floun·der /ˈflaʊndər/ verb [I] **1** to experience difficulties and be likely to fail **2** to feel confused and not know what to say or do next **3** to move with great difficulty and in an uncontrolled way

flour /flaʊr/ noun [U] a white or brown powder made from grain. It is used for making bread, cakes, and pasta.

flour·ish¹ /ˈflɜrɪʃ/ verb **1** [I] to grow well and be healthy: *Most plants flourish in this rich soil.* **2** [I] to be very successful **=** THRIVE: *His new business is flourishing.* **3** [T] to wave something in the air so that people notice it: *She came in flourishing a photograph.*

flour·ish² /ˈflɜrɪʃ/ noun [C] a confident movement that you make so that other people notice it

flout /flaʊt/ verb [T] to deliberately refuse to obey a rule or custom

flow¹ /floʊ/ noun [C/U] ★★

1 the continuous movement of something: *the flow of blood to the heart*

2 a supply of something that continues without stopping: *the agency's work flow* ♦ *The television provided **a steady flow of** information about the war.*

3 a way of talking or thinking in an easy natural way, without any pauses or difficulties: *The phone rang, interrupting **the flow of** his thoughts.*

PHRASE **go with the flow** *spoken* to do what seems to be the easiest thing in a particular situation

flow² /floʊ/ verb [I] ★★
1 to move continuously: *Hot water flows through the pipes.* ♦ *A constant stream of people flowed past.* ♦ *Blood flowed from the wound on her face.*
2 if a supply of something flows, it continues without stopping: *Millions of dollars of new investment are flowing into the region.*
3 if words or ideas flow, they follow each other in an easy, natural, continuous way: *The conversation did not flow smoothly.*
4 if hair or clothing flows, it falls or moves in a smooth graceful way around someone's body

'flow ,chart noun [C] a drawing that uses different shapes connected with lines to show the steps in a complicated process

flow•er¹ /'flaʊr/ noun [C] ★★★
1 the colored part of a plant from which the plant's seeds develop: *The plant has small white flowers.* —*picture* → C9
2 a plant that is grown because its flowers are attractive: *I'm going to plant more flowers in the front yard this year.*

flow•er² /'flaʊr/ verb [I] to produce flowers

flow•er•bed /'flaʊr,bed/ noun [C] an area of ground where flowers are grown —*picture* → C1

flow•er•y /'flaʊri/ adj **1** decorated with a pattern of flowers **2** flowery language uses many complicated words that are intended to make it more attractive

flown the past participle of **fly**¹

fl. oz. abbrev FLUID OUNCE

flu /flu/ noun [U] a very common infectious disease that lasts for a short time and makes you feel weak and tired

fluc•tu•ate /'flʌktʃu,eɪt/ verb [I] to change frequently —**fluc•tu•a•tion** /,flʌktʃu'eɪʃ(ə)n/ noun [C/U]

flu•ent /'fluənt/ adj able to speak a foreign language very well: *I'm fluent in three languages.* ♦ *Steve speaks fluent Japanese.* —**flu•en•cy** noun [U], **flu•ent•ly** adv

fluff¹ /flʌf/ noun [U] very small pieces of hair, dust, or cloth that stick together

fluff² /flʌf/ verb [T] **1** to shake something so that more air goes into it and it becomes larger and softer: *Fluff the pillows after you use them.* **2** *informal* to do something badly
PHRASAL VERB **,fluff sth 'out** or **,fluff sth 'up** *same as* **fluff**² 1

fluff•y /'flʌfi/ adj **1** covered with very soft hair or feathers **2** made of something that is very soft

flu•id¹ /'fluɪd/ noun [C/U] *formal* a liquid: *Drink lots of fluids during exercise.* ♦ *cleaning fluid*

flu•id² /'fluɪd/ adj **1** graceful and continuous: *a fluid movement* **2** likely to change: *The situation remains fluid.*

,fluid 'ounce noun [C] a unit for measuring an amount of a liquid, equal to .02957 liters

fluke /fluk/ noun [C] *informal* something good that happens unexpectedly because of good luck

flung the past tense and past participle of **fling**¹

flunk /flʌŋk/ verb [I/T] *informal* to fail a test or a course in school, or to give a student a failing grade
PHRASAL VERB **,flunk 'out** *informal* to have to leave a school because your work is not satisfactory

fluo•res•cent /flɔr'res(ə)nt/ adj **1** a fluorescent color is very bright and seems to reflect light **2** a fluorescent substance produces light when you pass electricity through it

fluo'rescent ,light noun [C] a very bright light that consists of a long glass tube containing fluorescent gas

fluor•ide /'flɔ,raɪd/ noun [U] a chemical that protects your teeth

flur•ry /'flɜri/ noun [C] **1** a small amount of snow **2** a short period of activity or emotion

flush¹ /flʌʃ/ verb **1** [I/T] if you flush a toilet, or if it flushes, water passes through it **2** [I] if someone flushes, their face becomes red because they feel hot, angry, embarrassed, or excited: *Mark flushed with annoyance, but said nothing.* **3** [T] to get rid of something by putting it into a toilet and flushing it
PHRASAL VERB **,flush sb/sth 'out** to force a person or animal to leave a place where they have been hiding

flush² /flʌʃ/ noun [singular] a red color that appears on someone's face because they feel hot, angry, embarrassed, or excited

flush³ /flʌʃ/ adj, adv fitted so that two surfaces or edges are exactly level

flushed /flʌʃt/ adj with a red face

flus•tered /'flʌstərd/ adj feeling confused, embarrassed, or nervous

flute /flut/ noun [C] a musical instrument that you hold sideways to your mouth and play by blowing over a hole at one end —*picture* → WOODWIND

flut•ter /'flʌtər/ verb **1** [I/T] to move with quick light movements, or to make something move in this way: *The bird fluttered from branch to branch.* **2** [I] if your heart or stomach flutters, you feel excited or nervous —**flut•ter** noun [singular]

flux /flʌks/ noun [U] a condition of continuous change: *The climate appears to be in a state of flux.*

fly¹ /flaɪ/ (past tense **flew** /flu/; past participle **flown** /floʊn/) verb ★★★

1 move with wings	6 move quickly
2 travel on airplane	7 about time
3 take sb/sth on airplane	8 when flag is on pole
4 control airplane	+ PHRASES
5 move fast through air	

1 [I] to use wings to move through the air: *Not all insects can fly.*
2 [I] to travel on an airplane: *Sometimes it's cheaper to fly.* ♦ *I flew from Miami to New York.* ♦ *We flew into O'Hare on Monday evening.*
3 [T] to take people or goods somewhere on an airplane: *They flew her home for urgent medical treatment.* ♦ **fly sb/sth in/out** *Helicopters are being used to fly in supplies.*
4 [I/T] to control an airplane when it is in the air: *He had always wanted to learn to fly.* ♦ *The pilots refused to fly the airplanes in icy conditions.*
5 [I] to move very fast through the air: *A bullet flew past his head.*

6 [I] to move suddenly or quickly: *The door **flew open** and the principal marched in.*
7 [I] if time flies, it seems to pass very quickly
8 [I/T] if you fly a flag, or if it is flying, it is on the top of a pole or building
PHRASES **fly in the face of sth** to be completely opposite to something that most people believe or accept: *This behavior flies in the face of all the ideals we've worked toward.*
fly into a rage *literary* to suddenly become extremely angry
fly off the handle *informal* to suddenly become extremely angry without a good reason: *He flies off the handle every time the mail is late.*
go flying *informal* to move quickly through the air and fall to the ground: *I tripped over a tree root and went flying.*

fly² /flaɪ/ (plural **flies**) noun [C] **1** a common small insect with wings —*picture* → C13
2 *American* the opening at the front of a pair of pants
PHRASES **dropping like flies** *informal* getting sick or dying in large numbers very quickly
on the fly in a very quick and informal way
sb wouldn't hurt a fly *spoken* used for saying that someone is very gentle and kind

fly·er /ˈflaɪər/ another spelling of **flier**

fly·ing¹ /ˈflaɪɪŋ/ adj **1** able to fly: *a flying insect* **2** moving fast through the air: *About 20 people were injured by flying glass.*
PHRASE **with flying colors** very successfully

fly·ing² /ˈflaɪɪŋ/ noun [U] **1** the activity of traveling in an aircraft: *I'm afraid of flying.*
2 the activity of operating or controlling an aircraft: *flying lessons*

ˌflying ˈsaucer noun [C] a round flat vehicle from another planet

ˌflying ˈstart noun [C] a very good beginning

fly·swat·ter /ˈflaɪˌswɑtər/ noun [C] an object used for killing flies that consists of a flat piece of plastic on a long handle

FM /ˌef ˈem/ noun [U] frequency modulation: a system that is used for broadcasting radio signals of high quality

foal /foʊl/ noun [C] a young horse

foam /foʊm/ noun [U] **1** a lot of BUBBLES that stick together on the surface of a liquid **2** a soft thick substance that contains a lot of BUBBLES. It is used for cleaning, washing, or stopping fires. **3** a soft light rubber or plastic substance that contains a lot of small holes: *foam mattresses/pillows/cushions*

fo·cal point /ˈfoʊk(ə)l ˌpɔɪnt/ noun [C] the most important, interesting, or attractive part of something

fo·cus¹ /ˈfoʊkəs/ (present participle **fo·cus·ing** or **fo·cus·sing**; past tense and past participle **fo·cused** or **fo·cussed**) verb [I/T] ★ if your eyes focus, or if you focus your eyes, you look at something carefully until you start to see it clearly: *It took a while for my eyes to focus in the dim light of the cave.*
PHRASAL VERBS **ˈfocus on sth** to concentrate on something and pay particular attention to it: *The course focuses on three main topics.*
ˈfocus sth on sth to turn a camera toward something: *The cameras seemed to be focused on the crowd.*

fo·cus² /ˈfoʊkəs/ noun ★
1 [singular] the thing that people are concentrating on or paying particular attention to: *The oil crisis became **the focus of** Western concern in the early 1970s.* ♦ *We have chosen six communities as **the focus for** our study.*
2 [singular/U] particular attention that people pay to something: *The report calls for greater **focus on** the needs of the poor.*
3 [singular/U] the act of concentrating on a particular goal: *Each course unit has a very clear focus.* ♦ *I think this campaign has lost its focus.*
PHRASES **in focus** able to be seen clearly
out of focus unable to be seen clearly: *Some of these photographs are out of focus.*

fo·cused /ˈfoʊkəst/ adj *showing approval* concentrating on a particular goal and not wasting time or energy on other things

ˈfocus ˌgroup noun [C] a group of people who are asked to give their opinions about particular subjects

fod·der /ˈfɑdər/ noun [U] food for animals such as cows and horses

foe /foʊ/ noun [C] *literary* an enemy

foe·tal /ˈfit(ə)l/ the British spelling of **fetal**

fog¹ /fɔg/ noun [U] thick clouds that form close to the ground and are difficult to see through

fog² /fɔg/ PHRASAL VERB ˌ**fog ˈup** to become covered with steam and difficult to see through: *All the windows had fogged up.*

fog·gy /ˈfɔgi/ adj full of fog, or covered with fog
PHRASE **not have the foggiest (idea)** *spoken* used for emphasizing that you do not know anything at all about something

ˈfog ˌlight noun [C] a bright light on a car that helps drivers to see in the FOG —*picture* → C6

foi·ble /ˈfɔɪb(ə)l/ noun [C] a way of thinking or behaving that is strange or annoying

foil¹ /fɔɪl/ noun **1** [U] very light thin sheets of metal that are used for wrapping food **2** [C] something that makes another thing seem better because it is different from it: *The plain stone floor is a perfect foil to the highly decorated walls.*

foil² /fɔɪl/ verb [T] to prevent someone from doing something that they want to do

foist /fɔɪst/ PHRASAL VERB **ˈfoist sth ˌon sb** or **ˈfoist sth uˌpon sb** to force someone to accept or deal with something that they do not want

fold¹ /foʊld/ verb ★★★
1 [T] to bend a piece of paper or cloth and press one part of it over another part: *Carrie folded the note and slid it into her purse.* ♦ *Fold the paper in half.*
2 [I/T] if something folds, or if you fold it, you bend part of it so that it becomes smaller and easier to carry or store: *Jed folded the pocket knife and put it into his front pocket.* ♦ *The bed **folds away** conveniently for storage.*
3 [I] if a business folds, it closes because it is not able to make enough money
PHRASE **fold your arms** to cross one arm over the other
PHRASAL VERB ˌ**fold sth ˈup** to make something smaller by bending it over on

itself more than once: *His clothes were neatly folded up on a chair.*

fold² /fould/ noun **1** [C] a line that you make on a piece of paper or cloth when you press one part of it over another **2** [C] a curved piece of cloth that hangs in a loose way **3 the fold** [singular] a group of people who share the same ideas or goals or who live or work together

-fold /fould/ suffix used with numbers to make adjectives and adverbs describing how much something increases

fold·er /ˈfouldər/ noun [C] **1** a thin flat container for sheets of paper **2** a group of programs or documents that are stored in a computer

fo·li·age /ˈfouliidʒ/ noun [U] the leaves of a plant or tree

folk¹ /fouk/ noun **1 folk** or **folks** [plural] *informal* people: *A lot of folks are upset at the changes.* ♦ *city folk* **2 folks** [plural] *spoken* used for talking to a group of people: *What do you folks think?* **3 folks** [plural] someone's parents **4** [U] FOLK MUSIC

folk² /fouk/ adj **1** traditional in a particular region: *folk art* **2** based on the beliefs and methods of ordinary people: *folk medicine/wisdom*

folk·lore /ˈfoukˌlɔr/ noun [U] traditional stories, sayings, and beliefs from a particular region or community

ˈfolk ˌmusic noun [U] traditional music from a particular country, region, or community, or music played in a traditional style

folk·sy /ˈfouksi/ adj *American* informal in a friendly way that makes you feel relaxed

fol·low /ˈfɑlou/ verb ★★★

1 walk/drive behind sb	7 understand sth
2 happen after sth else	8 do same as sb else
3 watch/listen carefully	9 happen in a pattern
4 obey order/advice	10 to have to be true
5 go along road/river	+ PHRASE
6 watch progress	+ PHRASAL VERBS

1 [I/T] to walk, drive, etc. behind someone who is going in the same direction as you: *Ralph set off down the hill, and I followed.* ♦ *I was convinced there was someone following me.* ♦ *Jim opened the door and followed me down the hall.*
2 [I/T] to happen or come after something else: *The weather report follows our show.* ♦ *In the weeks that followed the situation was very tense.*
3 [T] to pay close attention to what someone or something is doing or saying: *He followed every word of the trial.*
4 [T] to obey an order, or to do what someone has advised you to do: *She refused to **follow** our **advice**.* ♦ *The soldiers claimed they were only **following orders**.* ♦ ***Follow the instructions** carefully.*
5 [T] to go along a road, river, etc. in the same direction as it does: *Follow the road down the hill into an intersection.*
6 [T] to be interested in the progress of someone or something: *My father followed the Yankees for 40 years.*
7 [T] to understand something that is long or complicated: *I couldn't follow what Professor Hope was saying.*
8 [I/T] to do the same thing that someone else has done: *The U.S. may **follow** Canada's **example** by banning these products.* ♦ *Other students **followed** her **lead** and boycotted classes.* ♦ *They began to offer takeout food, and other restaurants **followed suit*** (=did the same).
9 [T] to happen according to a particular pattern or order: *All the murders have followed the same horrible pattern.*
10 [I] if something follows, it must be true because of something else that is true: **+that** *If the two groups have the same goal, then it should follow that they work together.*

PHRASE **as follows** used when you are going to give more details about something: *The first line of the poem goes as follows:* I wandered lonely as a cloud...

→ FOOTSTEP

PHRASAL VERBS **ˌfollow sb aˈround** to follow someone wherever they go: *Henry's been following me around like a puppy!*

ˌfollow (sth) ˈthrough to continue doing something until it is finished: *Jack hasn't followed through on one project this year.*

ˌfollow sth ˈup to do something in addition to what you have already done: *Follow up the phone call with a written confirmation.*

fol·low·er /ˈfɑlouər/ noun [C] **1** someone who believes in a religion or system of ideas, or who supports the person who established it **2** someone who is interested in the progress of something = SUPPORTER

fol·low·ing¹ /ˈfɑlouɪŋ/ grammar word ★★★

> **Following** can be:
> - a **preposition**: *Following the lecture, there will be the opportunity to ask questions.*
> - an **adjective**: *She arrived the following day.*
> - a **pronoun**: *Please read the following carefully.*

1 after something happens, or as a result of something that happens: *Following his military service, Wilkins returned to his hometown.*
2 the following day, month, page, etc. is the next one: *The problem will be discussed in the following chapter.*
3 used for referring to something that you are going to say or mention next: *Combine the following ingredients: brown sugar, flour, and butter.* ♦ *Make sure you bring the following: sunglasses, suntan lotion, and a swimsuit.*

fol·low·ing² /ˈfɑlouɪŋ/ noun [C] a group of people who support or admire another person or group

ˈfollow-ˌup noun **1** [C/U] something that is done in order to complete something or to check that an earlier action was effective **2** [C] a book, movie, or article that is based on or develops from an earlier one = SEQUEL
—**ˈfollow-ˌup** adj

fond /fɑnd/ adj ★
1 fond of sb/sth liking and caring about someone or something very much: *I was very fond of my Uncle Jim.* ♦ *I'm not fond of children.*
2 fond of (doing) sth getting enjoyment and satisfaction from something that you do

PHRASE **fond memory** something that you remember with pleasure: *Jane has fond*

memories of a happy childhood.
—**fond•ness** noun [U]

fon•dle /ˈfɑnd(ə)l/ verb [T] to squeeze or touch someone or something gently, often for sexual pleasure

fond•ly /ˈfɑndli/ adv in a way that shows that you like and care about someone or something: *She smiled fondly at her brother.*

font /fɑnt/ noun [C] a set of letters and numbers in a particular size and style

food /fud/ noun ★★★
1 [U] the things that people or animals eat: *The prices of food and clothing have risen recently.* ♦ *All the food is cooked and served by volunteers.* ♦ *good fresh food*
2 [C/U] a particular type of food: *I can't eat spicy food.* ♦ *Italian/Chinese/French food*
PHRASE **food for thought** something that makes you think a lot about a particular subject

F

ˈfood ˌchain noun [singular] the natural process in which one living thing is eaten by another, which is then eaten by another, etc.

ˈfood ˌpoisoning noun [U] an illness caused by eating food that contains harmful bacteria

ˈfood ˌprocessor noun [C] a piece of electrical equipment, used for cutting food into very small pieces or for mixing foods together —*picture* → C2

fool¹ /ful/ noun [C] someone who does not behave in an intelligent or sensible way
PHRASES **make a fool of yourself** to make yourself seem stupid by behaving in a silly or embarrassing way
make a fool (out) of sb to deliberately make someone seem stupid

fool² /ful/ verb [T] to trick someone by making them believe something that is not true
PHRASE **you could have fooled me** *spoken* used for saying that you do not believe something that someone is telling you
PHRASAL VERBS **ˌfool ˈaround 1** to behave in a silly way for fun **2** to have a sexual relationship with someone who is not your usual partner
ˌfool aˈround with sth or **ˈfool ˌwith sth** to handle or use something in a stupid or careless way: *The kids were fooling around with the rake, and one of them got hurt.*

fool•har•dy /ˈfulˌhɑrdi/ adj *formal* ignoring obvious dangers in a stupid way = RECKLESS

fool•ish /ˈfulɪʃ/ adj **1** behaving in a way that is stupid and likely to have bad results **2** embarrassed because of something stupid that you have done —**fool•ish•ly** adv, **fool•ish•ness** noun [U]

fool•proof /ˈfulˌpruf/ adj a foolproof method, plan, or system is so well designed that it cannot go wrong or fail

foot¹ /fʊt/ (plural **feet** /fit/) noun ★★★
1 [C] the part of your body at the end of your leg, on which you stand: *He wiped his feet on the mat.* ♦ *She injured her right foot playing basketball.* → SHOOT¹, STAND¹ —*picture* → C14
2 (plural **feet** or **foot**) [C] a unit used for measuring length that is equal to 12 INCHES or about 30 CENTIMETERS: *He's over six foot tall.* ♦ *We had over two feet of snow last night.*
3 [singular] **the foot of sth** the bottom or far end of something: *She paused **at the foot of** the stairs.* ♦ *We camped at the foot of the mountain.*
PHRASES **back on your feet** well or successful again after being sick or having problems: *Jim's hoping he'll be back on his feet by next week.*
get/leap/rise etc. to your feet to stand up in a particular way: *Steve jumped to his feet.*
get off/start off on the wrong foot to immediately have a bad relationship with someone when you first meet them: *I got off on the wrong foot with Patrick.*
have/keep your feet on the ground to have a sensible practical attitude to life
land on your feet to be lucky and get into a good situation after being in a difficult one: *Tim always manages to land on his feet.*
on your feet standing: *I'm exhausted – I've been on my feet all afternoon.*
on foot walking: *We started toward town on foot.*
put your feet up to sit down and relax with your feet raised off the ground
put your foot down to refuse very firmly to do or accept something: *Things can't carry on like this; you'll have to put your foot down.*
put your foot in your mouth to accidentally say something that is embarrassing or that upsets or annoys someone
set foot to go to a place: *It was the first time I had set foot on French soil.*
under sb's feet if someone is under your feet, they are annoying you by stopping you from doing what you need to do

foot² /fʊt/ verb **foot the bill (for sth)** *informal* to pay for something: *Are we expected to foot the bill for this?*

foot•age /ˈfʊtɪdʒ/ noun [U] a movie of a particular event

foot•ball /ˈfʊtˌbɔl/ noun ★★
1 [U] *American* a game in which two teams of eleven players run with, throw, or kick a ball to the end of a field to score
2 [C] a ball used for playing football —*picture* → BALL
3 [U] *British* soccer

foot•bridge /ˈfʊtˌbrɪdʒ/ noun [C] a narrow bridge for people to walk across

foot•hills /ˈfʊtˌhɪlz/ noun [plural] the low hills next to high mountains

foot•hold /ˈfʊtˌhoʊld/ noun [C] **1** a position from which you can improve your status or become more successful **2** a place on a surface where you can put your foot to support yourself when climbing

foot•ing /ˈfʊtɪŋ/ noun [singular] **1** a firm position for your feet on a surface **2** the basic conditions in which something operates or develops: *a firm financial footing*

foot•lights /ˈfʊtˌlaɪts/ noun [plural] a row of very bright lights at the front edge of a theater stage

foot•note /ˈfʊtˌnoʊt/ noun [C] a note at the bottom of a page that gives more detailed information about something on the page

foot•print /ˈfʊtˌprɪnt/ noun [C] a mark made by a human or animal foot in a soft surface such as earth, snow, or sand

foot·step /ˈfʊtˌstep/ noun [C] the sound of a foot touching the ground as someone walks
PHRASE **follow in sb's footsteps** to do the same work, or to achieve the same success, as someone else has done before you: *She followed in her mother's footsteps and became a doctor.*

foot·stool /ˈfʊtˌstul/ noun [C] a small low piece of furniture for resting your feet on

foot·wear /ˈfʊtˌwer/ noun [U] things that you wear on your feet, such as shoes or boots

foot·work /ˈfʊtˌwɜrk/ noun [U] the way that you move your feet when you are dancing or playing sports

for /*weak* fər, *strong* fɔr/ preposition ★★★
1 intended to benefit sb/sth used for saying who or what is intended to receive something or get the benefit of it: *Claudia, this present is for you.* ♦ *The academy provides training for young musicians.* ♦ *They'll have to buy furniture for the new house.* ♦ *Betty will take care of things for us while we're away.*
2 stating a purpose used for stating the purpose of an object or action: *We use the basement for storage.* ♦ *The red button is for turning the machine off.*
3 stating a length of time used for saying how long something continues: *I've been waiting for 20 minutes.* ♦ *We haven't seen Kim for a while.* → SINCE
4 stating a distance used for saying how far something reaches, or how far someone goes: *They must have walked for at least three miles.* ♦ *The desert stretched for as far as we could see.*
5 employed by sb/sth used for stating the person or organization that employs someone: *She works for an accounting firm downtown.*
6 stating the cost of sth used for stating the cost of a product or a service: *I sold my car for $1500.*
7 saying who experiences sth used for saying who is affected by a situation or feeling: *For me, it was a complete disaster.* ♦ *Living conditions for most people have improved.*
8 saying who or what your feelings are related to used for showing that your feelings are directed toward a particular person or thing: *I'm so happy for you!* ♦ *She felt sorry for his wife.*
9 saying who or what does sth used after some adjectives, nouns, and verbs for saying who or what does an action: *It's time for us to go.* ♦ *All I want is for you to be happy.*
10 enough to make sth possible used for saying what is possible with a particular amount of time, money, space, etc.: *We don't have the money for a new car.* ♦ *Is there enough time for a drink?*
11 saying who or what you support used for saying which person or thing you support or agree with: *There is a lot of support for the reforms.* ♦ *Of course, I'm* ***all for*** (=I completely support) *freedom of speech.*
12 representing sb used for saying who you represent when you say or do something: *I'm speaking for all of us when I say how sorry we are.*
13 going to a place used for saying where you are going when you leave a place: *What time are you leaving for home?* ♦ *He got on the next airplane for San Francisco.*
14 intended to happen at a particular time used for saying the time or date when something is planned to happen: *The meeting was planned for 10 o'clock.*
15 in order to celebrate in order to celebrate a holiday or special occasion: *We haven't decided what to do for her birthday.*
16 considering what sb/sth is used for saying that something is surprising when you consider who or what someone is: *She sings amazingly well for a child.*
17 showing what sth means used for saying what something means or represents: *What's the Italian word for "Goodbye?"*
PHRASES **for all 1** despite: *For all his complaining, I think he actually enjoyed the day.* **2** considering how large or small an amount is: *I might as well have said nothing, for all the difference it made.*
for the first/last etc. time used for saying how often something has happened: *He was late this morning for the third time this week.*
for now or **for the moment** or **for the time being** for a short time, until a situation changes: *You'll have to stay here for now.*
it is for sb to do sth it is someone's right, responsibility, or duty to do something: *It's not for me to decide whether you should quit your job.*

for·age /ˈfɔrɪdʒ/ verb [I] to search in a wide area for food

for·ay /ˈfɔˌreɪ/ noun [C] **1** an attempt at doing something new or something that you do not usually do **2** a sudden quick attack on an enemy

forbade the past tense of **forbid**

for·bid /fərˈbɪd/ (past tense **for·bade**; past participle **for·bid·den** /fərˈbɪd(ə)n/) verb [T] to say that something is not allowed =PROHIBIT: *The army forbids soldiers from talking to reporters.* ♦ *She was forbidden to see him again.*

for·bid·den /fərˈbɪd(ə)n/ adj ★ not allowed according to a rule or law: *Smoking is forbidden in all parts of the building.* ♦ *The use of cellphones in the library is* ***strictly forbidden.***

for·bid·ding /fərˈbɪdɪŋ/ adj someone who is forbidding seems unfriendly or threatening

force[1] /fɔrs/ noun ★★★
1 [U] physical strength, violence, or energy: ***The force of*** *the bomb blast shattered windows in 15 buildings.* ♦ *They accused the police of* ***using excessive force*** *during the arrest.* ♦ *The army took control of the region* ***by force.*** ♦ *You can achieve more by talking than by* ***brute force*** (=physical force alone).
2 [C] a group of people doing military or police work: *Both countries have now withdrawn their forces from the area.* ♦ *a U.N. peacekeeping force*
3 [U] the power that something or someone has to influence people or events: *We have convinced people by* ***the force of*** *our argument.*

F

4 [C] someone or something that has a lot of influence on what happens: *the political forces that shape people's lives* ♦ *The U.N. should be a major **force for** stability in the area.*

PHRASES **in force** if a law or rule is in force, it is being applied and people must obey it: *The ban on arms exports remains in force.*

join/combine forces to work with someone else in order to achieve something together: *Aid workers have joined forces with police to get supplies to the town.*

out of force of habit without thinking, because you always do a particular thing: *I locked the door out of force of habit.*

F

force² /fɔrs/ verb [T] ★★★

1 to make someone do something that they do not want to do=COMPEL: **force sb to do sth** *The judge was forced to resign.* ♦ **force yourself to do sth** *Despite the pain, she forced herself to get out of bed.*

2 to use physical force to move something or to move somewhere: *She forced the package through the slot.* ♦ *We had to **force** the windows **open**.*

3 to make something happen: *Opposition to the plans forced a rapid change of policy.*

PHRASE **force a smile/laugh** to smile or laugh when you do not really want to

PHRASAL VERBS ˌ**force sth ˈback** if you force back tears, you try very hard not to cry

ˌ**force sth ˈdown** to eat or drink something even though you do not want to

ˈ**force sth on sb** or ˈ**force sth uˌpon sb** to make someone accept something that they do not want: *She took over the meeting and forced her views on everyone.*

forced /fɔrst/ adj **1** not sincere or natural: *a forced smile* **2** done or happening because the situation makes it necessary or because someone makes you do it

force•ful /ˈfɔrsfəl/ adj **1** confident and good at influencing people=ASSERTIVE **2** likely to persuade people: *a forceful argument* —**force•ful•ly** adv

for•ceps /ˈfɔrˌseps/ noun [plural] a medical tool that is used for holding or pulling things

forc•i•ble /ˈfɔrsəb(ə)l/ adj involving the use of force —**forc•i•bly** adv

fore•arm /ˈfɔrˌɑrm/ noun [C] the lower part of your arm, between your elbow and your wrist

fore•bears /ˈfɔrˌberz/ noun [plural] the people in your family who lived before you

fore•bod•ing /fɔrˈboʊdɪŋ/ noun [U] a strong feeling that something very bad is going to happen

fore•cast¹ /ˈfɔrˌkæst/ noun [C] a statement about what is likely to happen, usually relating to the weather, business, or the economy

fore•cast² /ˈfɔrˌkæst/ (past tense and past participle **fore•cast** or **fore•cast•ed**) verb [T] to make a statement about what is likely to happen, usually relating to the weather, business, or the economy

fore•cast•er /ˈfɔrˌkæstər/ noun [C] someone whose job is to say what is likely to happen, for example what the weather will be like or what will happen in the economy

fore•close /fɔrˈkloʊz/ verb [I] *legal* to take someone's property because they failed to pay back the money that they borrowed to buy it —**fore•clo•sure** /fɔrˈkloʊʒər/ noun [C/U]

fore•fa•thers /ˈfɔrˌfɑðərz/ noun [plural] *formal* people belonging to your family or nation who lived a long time ago=ANCESTOR

fore•fin•ger /ˈfɔrˌfɪŋgər/ noun [C] the finger that is next to your thumb=INDEX FINGER

fore•foot /ˈfɔrˌfʊt/ noun [C] one of the two front feet of an animal that has four feet

fore•front, the /ˈfɔrˌfrʌnt/ noun [singular] a leading or important position

fore•gone con•clusion /ˌfɔrgɔn kənˈkluʒ(ə)n/ noun [singular] a result that you can be certain about before it happens

fore•ground, the /ˈfɔrˌgraʊnd/ noun [singular] the front part of a scene or picture ≠BACKGROUND

fore•hand /ˈfɔrˌhænd/ noun [C] a way of hitting the ball in tennis with the palm of your hand toward your opponent

fore•head /ˈfɔrəd, ˈfɔrˌhed/ noun [C] the upper part of your face, between your eyes and your hair —*picture* → C14

for•eign /ˈfɔrən/ adj ★★★

1 from another country, or in another country: *Working in **a foreign country** takes some getting used to.* ♦ *Do you speak any **foreign languages**?*

2 dealing with, or relating to, other countries: *foreign policy*

3 not typical of something or someone and therefore not expected or familiar=ALIEN: *emotions that were totally **foreign to** her nature*

ˌ**foreign ˈbody** noun [C] *formal* something that has entered a place where it should not be: *a foreign body in her eye*

for•eign•er /ˈfɔrənər/ noun [C] someone who comes from another country

ˌ**foreign exˈchange** noun [C/U] a system for changing the money of one country for the money of another, or the money used in this system

fore•leg /ˈfɔrˌleg/ noun [C] one of the two front legs of an animal that has four legs

fore•man /ˈfɔrmən/ (plural **fore•men** /ˈfɔrmən/) noun [C] **1** a man who is in charge of a team of workers **2** the person who is chosen to be the leader of a JURY

fore•most /ˈfɔrˌmoʊst/ adj most important, or most well known

fo•ren•sic /fəˈrenzɪk/ adj relating to the use of scientific methods to solve crimes

fo•ren•sics /fəˈrenzɪks/ noun [U] scientific methods that are used to solve crimes

fore•run•ner /ˈfɔrˌrʌnər/ noun [C] an institution, custom, or thing that existed before a newer but similar thing =PRECURSOR

fore•see /fɔrˈsi/ (past tense **fore•saw** /fɔrˈsɔ/; past participle **fore•seen** /fɔrˈsin/) verb [T] to see or know something that will happen in the future=PREDICT

fore•see•a•ble /fɔrˈsiəb(ə)l/ adj a foreseeable event or time is one that can easily be imagined or known about before it happens =PREDICTABLE ≠UNFORESEEABLE

PHRASE **the foreseeable future** the time in the near future in which you can guess what might happen

fore·shad·ow /fɔrˈʃædoʊ/ verb [T] if something foreshadows a future event, it shows or gives a warning that it will happen

fore·sight /ˈfɔrˌsaɪt/ noun [U] the ability to think about and plan for what might happen

fore·skin /ˈfɔrˌskɪn/ noun [C] the loose skin that covers the front part of a man's PENIS

for·est /ˈfɔrəst/ noun [C/U] ★★★ a large area of land that is covered by trees and other plants growing close together

fore·stall /fɔrˈstɔl/ verb [T] to do something to prevent something from happening

for·est·ed /ˈfɔrəstəd/ adj covered with trees

ˈforest ˌranger noun [C] someone whose job is to protect and manage a forest on public land

for·est·ry /ˈfɔrəstri/ noun [U] the science or activity of caring for forests

fore·tell /fɔrˈtel/ (past tense and past participle **fore·told** /fɔrˈtoʊld/) verb [T] *literary* to say what will happen in the future = PREDICT

fore·thought /ˈfɔrθɔt/ noun [U] careful thought and planning that prepares you well for a future event

foretold the past tense and past participle of **foretell**

for·ev·er /fərˈevər/ adv ★
1 for all time in the future, or for as long as you can imagine: *They promised to love each other forever.*
2 *informal* for a long time, usually longer than you would like: *The movie seemed to go on forever.*

fore·warn /fɔrˈwɔrn/ verb [T] to warn someone about a problem or dangerous situation that is likely to happen

fore·word /ˈfɔrˌwɜrd/ noun [C] a short introduction to a book

for·feit¹ /ˈfɔrfɪt/ verb [T] to be forced to give up something, usually because you have broken a rule or law

for·feit² /ˈfɔrfɪt/ noun [C] something that you must give, pay, or do because you have done something wrong = PENALTY

forgave the past tense of **forgive**

forge¹ /fɔrdʒ/ verb [T] **1** to develop or achieve something: *During the 1970s, the U.S. forged trade links with China.* **2** to make an illegal copy of something in order to cheat people: *Someone forged my signature.*
PHRASAL VERB **ˌforge aˈhead** to make strong steady progress

forge² /fɔrdʒ/ noun [C] a place where metal objects are made

forg·er /ˈfɔrdʒər/ noun [C] a criminal who makes illegal copies of documents or works of art

for·ger·y /ˈfɔrdʒəri/ noun **1** [U] the crime of making illegal copies of documents or works of art **2** [C] an illegal copy of a document or a work of art

for·get /fərˈget/ (present participle **for·get·ting**; past tense **for·got** /fərˈgɑt/; past participle **for·got·ten** /fərˈgɑt(ə)n/) verb [I/T] ★★★
1 to be unable to remember something: *I've forgotten her phone number.* ♦ *Did you **forget about** our agreement?* ♦ **+where/how etc.** *She always forgets where her car is parked.* ♦ **+(that)** *I'd forgotten that you'd already given me the money.*
2 to not remember to do something that you intended to do: *She had **forgotten all about** mailing the letter.* ♦ **forget to do sth** *Don't forget to lock the door when you leave.*
3 to not take something with you when you should have taken it: *She forgot her sunglasses.* ♦ *I remembered everything else but I **forgot about** the beach towels.* → LEAVE
4 to stop thinking or worrying about something: *Try to **forget about** him.* ♦ **+that** *People forget that women didn't always have the right to vote.*
PHRASES **forget it** *spoken* used for telling someone not to worry about something because it is not important
forget yourself to behave in a way that is silly or embarrassing

Word family: forget
*Words in the same family as **forget***
- **forgetful** *adj*
- **unforgettable** *adj*
- **forgetfulness** *n*

for·get·ful /fərˈgetfəl/ adj often unable to remember things —**for·get·ful·ness** noun [U]

for·give /fərˈgɪv/ (past tense **for·gave** /fərˈgeɪv/; past participle **for·giv·en** /fərˈgɪv(ə)n/) verb [T] ★ to decide to stop being angry with someone who has done something that is bad: *John has never **forgiven himself** for the accident.* ♦ **forgive sb for doing sth** *She eventually forgave him for forgetting her birthday.*

for·give·ness /fərˈgɪvnəs/ noun [U] the action of forgiving someone

for·giv·ing /fərˈgɪvɪŋ/ adj willing to forget your anger toward someone

for·go /fɔrˈgoʊ/ (past tense **for·went** /fɔrˈwent/; past participle **for·gone** /fɔrˈgɔn/) verb [T] *formal* to decide not to do or have something

for·got the past tense of **forget**

for·got·ten¹ /fərˈgɑt(ə)n/ adj a forgotten thing is something that most people do not remember anymore

for·got·ten² the past participle of **forget**

fork¹ /fɔrk/ noun [C] ★
1 an object that you use for eating, with a handle and three or four points on the end —*picture* → C2
2 a place where a road divides into two parts to form a shape like a "Y"

fork² /fɔrk/ verb [I] if a road forks, it divides into two separate parts
PHRASAL VERB **ˌfork (sth) ˈout** or **ˌfork (sth) ˌover** *informal* to spend money on something: *I'm not forking out $400 on ski clothes!*

forked /fɔrkt/ adj divided into two separate parts in a "Y" shape

for·lorn /fərˈlɔrn/ adj someone who is forlorn looks lonely and sad

form¹ /fɔrm/ noun ★★★

1 type of sth	4 official document
2 way sth appears/exists	5 shape of sb/sth
3 level of ability	

1 [C] a type of something: *He developed a rare **form of** cancer.* ♦ *Everyone agrees that the kids must receive **some form of** punishment.*
2 [C/U] the particular way in which

something appears or exists: *The information is also available in electronic form.* ♦ *Help arrived* ***in the form of*** *six heavily armed police officers.* ♦ *The aid might* ***take the form of*** *food or medical supplies.*
3 [C] the level of someone's ability at a particular time, especially in a sport: *Williams blames a foot injury for her recent loss of form.* ♦ *The band's new CD marks a welcome return to form* (=to a previous high standard). ♦ *She is hoping to* ***be in top form*** *in time for the Olympics.*
4 [C] an official document with spaces where you write information: *Use the order form to get new office supplies.* ♦ *Make sure you* ***fill in the application form.***
5 [C] the body of a person, or the shape of an object: *Three forms gradually emerged out of the darkness.*

form² /fɔrm/ verb ★★★
1 [I/T] to start to exist, or to make something develop: *The club was formed in 1972.* ♦ *A change in temperature causes moisture to form on the windows.* ♦ *A plan began to form in her mind.* ♦ *The interview will give you a chance to* ***form an impression of*** *the company.*
2 [linking verb] to be something, or to be the parts that something consists of: *Research forms an important part of the course.* ♦ *Mountains form a natural barrier that keeps invaders out.*
3 [T] to make or shape something: *Use your hands to form the damp clay into a small ball.* ♦ *The children formed a line behind their teacher.*
4 [T] to influence the development of something: *His political views were formed by years of service in the army.*

for·mal /ˈfɔrm(ə)l/ adj ★★★
1 following the correct official methods ≠ INFORMAL: *The government is promising a formal investigation.* ♦ *We intend to make* ***a formal*** *written* ***complaint.***
2 appropriate for serious situations or occasions ≠ INFORMAL: *"Ameliorate" is a more formal way of saying "improve."*
3 you get a formal education or formal training from studying rather than from working at a job
—**for·mal·ly** adv

for·mal·i·ty /fɔrˈmæləti/ noun **1** [C] something that you must do as part of an official process, even though it may not seem necessary or sensible: *We went through the usual formalities at customs and passport control.* **2** [U] a formal style of writing, speaking, behaving, or dressing

for·mal·ize /ˈfɔrm(ə)l͵aɪz/ verb [T] to make something such as a plan or agreement official

for·mat¹ /ˈfɔr͵mæt/ noun [C/U] ★
1 the arrangement, size, or shape of something: *Changes have been proposed to* ***the format of*** *the competition.*
2 *computing* the way that information is arranged and organized on a computer DISK

for·mat² /ˈfɔr͵mæt/ verb [T] *computing* **1** to prepare a computer DISK so that information can be stored on it **2** to change the size, shape, or arrangement of the words in a computer file

for·ma·tion /fɔrˈmeɪʃ(ə)n/ noun ★
1 [U] the process of starting or developing something: *factors that affect* ***the formation of*** *children's personalities*
2 [C/U] a pattern that people or things are arranged into: *airplanes flying* ***in formation***

form·a·tive /ˈfɔrmətɪv/ adj strongly influencing the development of someone's character and beliefs

for·mer /ˈfɔrmər/ grammar word ★★★

> **Former** can be:
> - an **adjective**: *She still visits her former husband.*
> - a **pronoun**: *He could resign or be dismissed, and he chose the former.*

1 used for stating the job, title, status, etc. that someone or something had in the past: *former president Bill Clinton* ♦ *the former Soviet Union*
2 *formal* used for referring to times in the past: *memories of former times*
3 the former *formal* used for referring to the first of two people or things that you have mentioned: *He attended with his wife and daughter, the former wearing a black dress.*
→ LATTER

for·mer·ly /ˈfɔrmərli/ adv in the past

for·mi·da·ble /ˈfɔrmɪdəb(ə)l, fərˈmɪdəb(ə)l/ adj very impressive in size, power, or skill and therefore deserving respect

for·mu·la /ˈfɔrmjələ/ (plural **for·mu·las** or **for·mu·lae** /ˈfɔrmjəli/) noun **1** [C] a way of achieving something, or of dealing with a problem: *There is no magic formula for economic success.* **2** [C] a group of letters or numbers that represents a rule in science **3** [C] a list of the substances that you mix in order to make something **4** [U] *American* a liquid food for babies that is similar to milk

for·mu·la·ic /͵fɔrmjəˈleɪɪk/ adj using a standard method that is effective but boring

for·mu·late /ˈfɔrmjə͵leɪt/ verb [T] **1** to develop something by thinking carefully about its details: *He formulated a plan to improve the team's performance.* **2** to express an idea in words that you choose carefully
—**for·mu·la·tion** /͵fɔrmjəˈleɪʃ(ə)n/ noun [C/U]

for·sake /fərˈseɪk/ (past tense **for·sook** /fərˈsʊk/; past participle **for·sak·en** /fərˈseɪkən/) verb [T] **1** *literary* to leave someone when they still need you = ABANDON **2** *formal* to stop doing something

fort /fɔrt/ noun [C] **1** a strong building that is used by soldiers for defending a place **2** *American* a place where an army lives or trains

for·te /ˈfɔr͵teɪ, fɔrt/ noun [singular] something that someone is very good at

forth /fɔrθ/ adv *literary* **1** away from a place **2** forward, or out → SO

forth·com·ing /fɔrθˈkʌmɪŋ/ adj **1** happening or coming soon: *the forthcoming Presidential election* **2** helpful and willing to tell you things ≠ UNFORTHCOMING: *James was more forthcoming than I expected.* **3** *formal* provided when someone asks for it

forth·right /ˈfɔrθ͵raɪt/ adj saying exactly what you think without being afraid of other people's reactions

forth•with /fɔrθˈwɪθ, fɔrθˈwɪð/ adv *formal* immediately

for•ti•eth /ˈfɔrtiəθ/ number **1** in the place or position counted as number 40 **2** one of 40 equal parts of something

for•ti•fi•ca•tions /ˌfɔrtɪfɪˈkeɪʃ(ə)nz/ noun [plural] strong buildings and walls that have been built to defend a place

for•ti•fy /ˈfɔrtɪˌfaɪ/ verb [T] **1** to protect a place against attack by building strong walls, towers, or other structures around it **2** to add a substance to food in order to make it healthier **3** to give someone energy or confidence

for•ti•tude /ˈfɔrtɪˌtud/ noun [U] *formal* a brave and determined attitude

for•tress /ˈfɔrtrəs/ noun [C] a strong building that is used by soldiers for defending a place

for•tu•i•tous /fɔrˈtuɪtəs/ adj *formal* happening by chance in a way that is good for you —**for•tu•i•tous•ly** adv

for•tu•nate /ˈfɔrtʃənət/ adj lucky ≠ UNFORTUNATE: *Not everyone is as fortunate as we are.* ♦ **fortunate to do sth** *She was extremely fortunate to escape without injury.* ♦ **fortunate enough to do sth** *I was fortunate enough to have a very supportive family.* ♦ **it is fortunate that** *It is very fortunate that the doctor was here today.*

for•tu•nate•ly /ˈfɔrtʃənətli/ adv ★ used for emphasizing that something good has happened by chance = LUCKILY ≠ UNFORTUNATELY: *I arrived at the station late, but fortunately the train was delayed.*

for•tune /ˈfɔrtʃ(ə)n/ noun ★

1 [C] a large amount of money: *They must have **spent a fortune** on flowers.* ♦ *He had **made a fortune** from mining.*

2 [U] good luck: ***I had the good fortune to** know the manager of the company.*

3 fortunes [plural] the good or bad things that happen to someone: *a career that illustrates **the changing fortunes of** the Democratic Party*

PHRASE **tell sb's fortune** to use magic powers to find out what will happen to someone in the future

ˈfortune-ˌteller noun [C] someone who tells you what will happen to you in the future, for example by looking at the lines on your hand

for•ty /ˈfɔrti/ number the number 40

fo•rum /ˈfɔrəm/ noun [C] **1** a large meeting where people discuss something **2** a WEBSITE, newspaper, television program, etc. where people can express their ideas and opinions

for•ward[1] /ˈfɔrwərd/ grammar word ★★★

> **Forward** can be:
> - an **adverb**: *I stepped forward to greet him.*
> - an **adjective**: *the forward section of the aircraft*

1 in the direction in front moving or looking in the direction in front of you: *The car started to roll forward.* ♦ *She made a sudden forward movement.* ♦ *I reached forward to touch her hand.*

2 nearer the front in a position that is toward the front of a room or vehicle: *Let's sit farther forward so that we can see the stage better.* ♦ *the forward part of the train*

3 toward the future or a better state thinking about the future or moving toward a better state in the future: *We are looking forward to new possibilities.* ♦ *a giant leap forward in computer technology*

4 confident saying what you think in a confident and direct way that is not socially appropriate

5 to a later time on a clock if you set a clock or watch forward, you change the time it shows to a later time

> **Forward** and **forwards** have similar meanings and uses, but speakers of American English usually use the form **forward**. Speakers of British English often use the form **forwards** for senses 1, 2, and 5.

for•ward[2] /ˈfɔrwərd/ verb [T] to send a letter, package, e-mail, etc. that has been sent to your address to someone else at another address

for•ward[3] /ˈfɔrwərd/ noun [C] a player in a game such as basketball, soccer, or HOCKEY whose job is to attack the other team and score —*picture* → C15

for•ward•ing ad•dress /ˈfɔrwərdɪŋ ˌædres/ noun [C] an address that someone can send your letters to after you leave a place

for•ward-look•ing /ˈfɔrwərd ˌlʊkɪŋ/ adj planning for the future in a positive way by considering new ideas = PROGRESSIVE

for•wards /ˈfɔrwərdz/ adv FORWARD

ˈforward ˌslash noun [C] the symbol / used in Internet addresses and computer instructions

forwent the past tense of **forgo**

fos•sil /ˈfɑs(ə)l/ noun [C] an animal or plant from the past that has been preserved in rock

ˈfossil ˌfuel noun [C/U] coal or oil used as fuel

fos•sil•ized /ˈfɑsəˌlaɪzd/ adj preserved in rock

fos•ter[1] /ˈfɑstər/ verb **1** [T] to help something to develop over a period of time = PROMOTE **2** [I/T] to take care of someone else's child as part of your family for a period of time → ADOPT

fos•ter[2] /ˈfɑstər/ adj a foster child is a child who is being temporarily taken care of in someone else's family

fought the past tense and past participle of fight[1]

foul[1] /faʊl/ adj **1** very dirty, or very unpleasant: *a foul smell* **2** a foul move or throw in a game is one that is not allowed by the rules **3** if someone has a foul TEMPER or is in a foul mood, they are very angry

foul[2] /faʊl/ verb **1** [I/T] to break the rules of a game **2** [T] to make something very dirty

PHRASAL VERB **ˌfoul (sth) ˈup** to do something wrong, or to spoil something

foul[3] /faʊl/ noun [C] **1** something that you do in a game that is not allowed by the rules **2 foul** or **foul ball** a ball that has been hit outside the playing area in a game of baseball

ˌfoul ˈplay noun [U] dishonest or illegal behavior

ˈfoul-ˌup noun [C] *informal* a mistake that causes problems in a process or system

found[1] /faʊnd/ verb [T] ★ to start an organization or institution: *The newspaper was founded in 1909.*
PHRASE **be founded on sth** to be based on a particular idea or principle: *a society founded on the belief that all people are equal*

found[2] the past tense and past participle of **find**[1]

foun·da·tion /faʊnˈdeɪʃ(ə)n/ noun ★★

1 basic part of sth	4 creating an organization
2 base of building	5 face cream/powder
3 an organization	+ PHRASE

F

1 [C] the most basic part of something from which the rest of it develops=BASIS: *The first two years of study provide **a** solid **foundation in** computing.* ♦ *a business partnership that **lays the foundation for** future success* ♦ *He believes that religion is **the foundation of** a civilized society.*
2 [C] the part of a building that is below the ground and that supports the rest of the building
3 [C] an organization that provides money for things such as medical research or for a CHARITY: *the Ford Foundation*
4 [U] the process of starting an organization or institution: ***the foundation of** the state of Israel*
5 [C/U] a cream the same color as your skin that you put on your face before the rest of your MAKEUP —*picture* → MAKEUP
PHRASE **be without foundation** or **have no foundation** to not be based on fact and therefore not possible to prove

foun·der /ˈfaʊndər/ noun [C] someone who starts an organization or institution

found·ry /ˈfaʊndri/ noun [C] a factory where metal is MELTED and made into different objects

foun·tain /ˈfaʊnt(ə)n/ noun [C] a decoration for gardens and streets in which a stream of water is sent up into the air

ˈfountain ˌpen noun [C] a type of pen that you fill with ink —*picture* → PEN

four[1] /fɔr/ number the number 4

four[2] /fɔr/ noun **on all fours** with your hands, knees, and feet on the ground —*picture* → POSTURE

ˌfour-by-ˈfour noun [C] a FOUR-WHEEL DRIVE

ˌfour-ˈposter noun [C] an old-fashioned bed with four tall posts at the corners —*picture* → BED

four·some /ˈfɔrsəm/ noun [C] a group of four people

four·teen /fɔrˈtin/ number the number 14

four·teenth /fɔrˈtinθ/ number **1** in the place or position counted as number 14 **2** one of 14 equal parts of something

fourth /fɔrθ/ number **1** in the place or position counted as number four **2** *American* one of four equal parts of something=QUARTER

ˌFourth of Juˈly a U.S. public holiday that celebrates the time when the United States became an independent country

ˌfour-wheel ˈdrive noun [C] a car with big wheels that is designed for driving on rough ground

fowl /faʊl/ (plural **fowl** or **fowls**) noun [C] a chicken or other bird that is kept on a farm for its eggs and meat

fox /fɑks/ noun [C] a wild animal similar to a small dog, with red-brown fur and a thick tail —*picture* → C13

foy·er /ˈfɔɪər, ˈfwɑˌjeɪ/ noun [C] **1** *American* a small space just inside the front door of a house **2** a large open space just inside the entrance to a hotel or theater=LOBBY

fra·cas /ˈfreɪkəs, ˈfrækəs/ noun [singular] a noisy fight or argument

frac·tion /ˈfrækʃ(ə)n/ noun [C] **1** a part of a whole number, for example $\frac{1}{2}$ or $\frac{3}{4}$ **2** a small part or amount of something: *His investment is now worth only a fraction of its original value.* —**frac·tion·al** adj

frac·tion·al·ly /ˈfrækʃ(ə)n(ə)li/ adv by a very small amount

frac·ture[1] /ˈfræktʃər/ noun [C] a break or crack in a bone or piece of rock

frac·ture[2] /ˈfræktʃər/ verb [I/T] if something hard such as a bone fractures, or if it is fractured, it breaks or cracks —**frac·tured** /ˈfræktʃərd/ adj

frag·ile /ˈfrædʒəl/ adj **1** easy to break or damage **2** not very strong or healthy: *His health has always been fragile.* —**fra·gil·i·ty** /frəˈdʒɪləti/ noun [U]

frag·ment[1] /ˈfrægmənt/ noun [C] **1** a small piece of a larger object that has broken into a lot of pieces: *Police found fragments of glass on his clothing.* **2** a small part of something: *fragments of conversation*

frag·ment[2] /ˈfrægˌment/ verb [I/T] if something fragments, or if it is fragmented, it breaks into a lot of separate pieces or parts —**frag·ment·ed** adj

fra·grance /ˈfreɪgrəns/ noun [C/U] **1** a nice smell **2** PERFUME

fra·grant /ˈfreɪgrənt/ adj with a nice smell

frail /freɪl/ adj **1** physically weak and not very healthy **2** not strong and therefore likely to be damaged or destroyed

frail·ty /ˈfreɪlti/ noun [C/U] the condition of being physically or morally weak

frame[1] /freɪm/ noun ★★

1 border of picture, etc.	5 box on Internet page
2 basic structure	6 of pair of glasses
3 one photograph	+ PHRASE
4 shape of sb's body	

1 [C] a structure that forms the border of something: *a silver picture frame* ♦ *The window frames need painting.*
2 [C] the part of an object that forms its basic structure: *the frame of a bed/bike*
3 [C] one of the single photographs that form a movie
4 [C] the particular shape or size of someone's body: *A shiver shook her small frame.*
5 [C] *computing* a box on an Internet page that contains information that you can SCROLL through (=go up and down by using the mouse)
6 **frames** [plural] the part of a pair of GLASSES that holds the LENSES (=parts that you see through) and that has pieces that go over your ears
PHRASE **frame of mind** the mood that someone is in

HOUSE

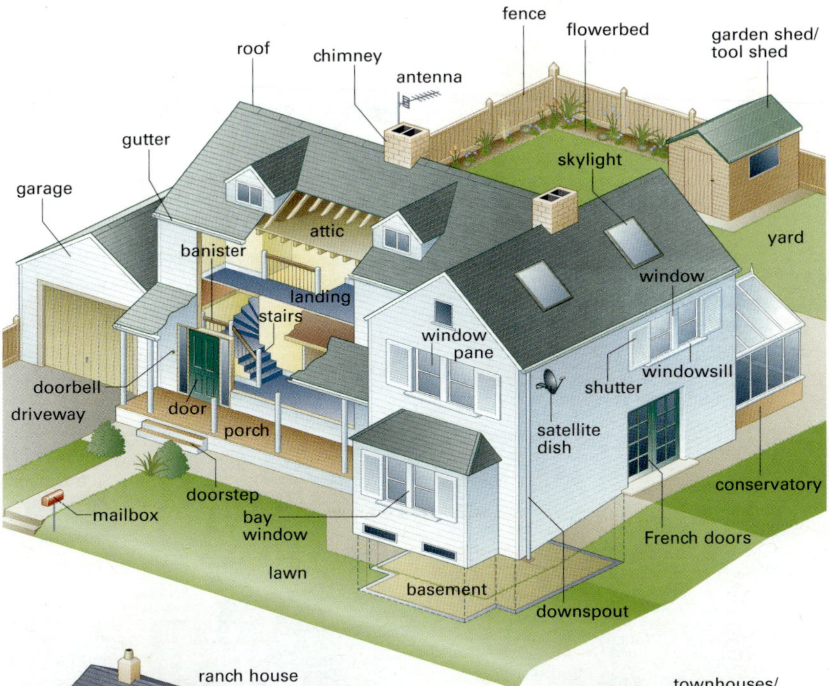

ranch house

townhouses/
row houses

apartment
building

colonial house

KITCHEN

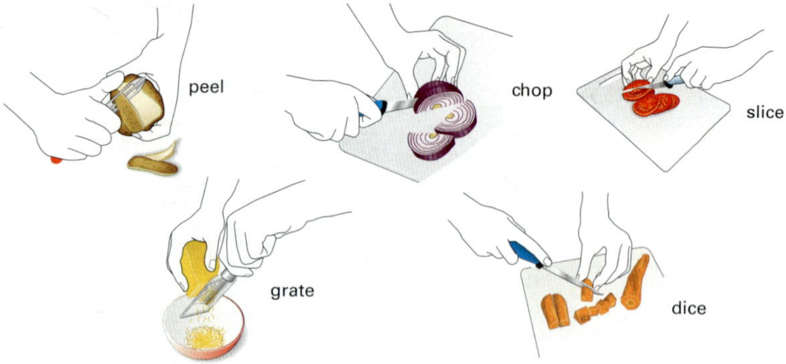
peel
chop
slice
grate
dice

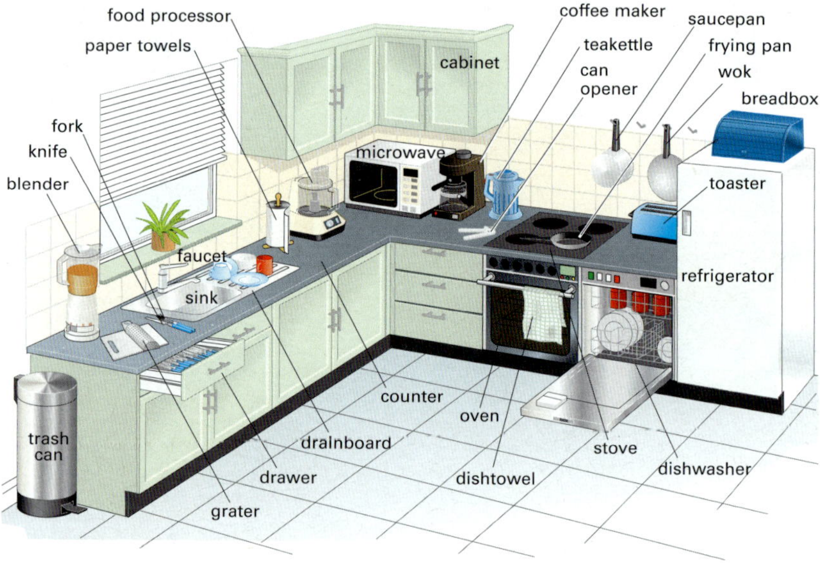
food processor
paper towels
coffee maker
saucepan
teakettle
frying pan
cabinet
can opener
wok
breadbox
fork
knife
microwave
blender
toaster
faucet
sink
refrigerator
counter
oven
trash can
drainboard
stove
dishwasher
drawer
dishtowel
grater

crush
drain
mix
whisk

OFFICE

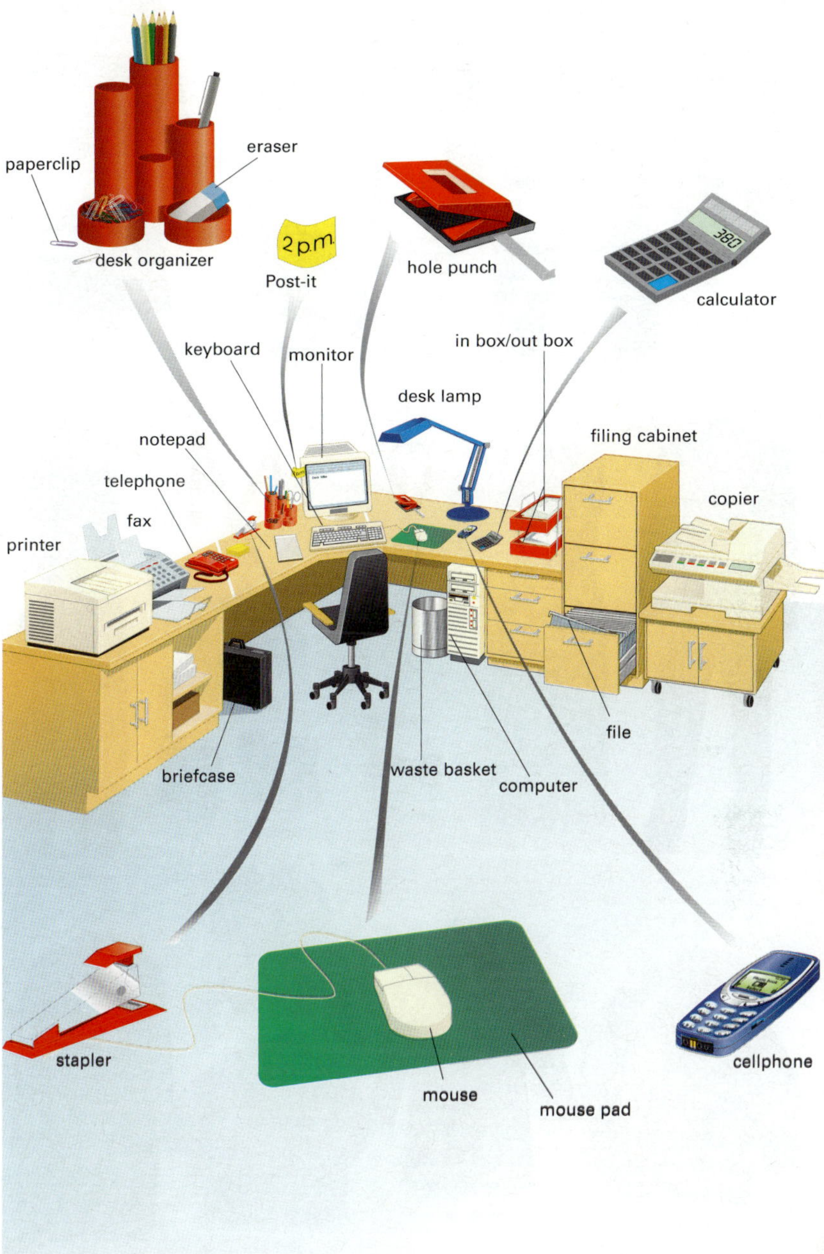
paperclip
eraser
desk organizer
2 p.m.
Post-it
hole punch
calculator
380
keyboard
monitor
in box/out box
desk lamp
notepad
filing cabinet
telephone
fax
copier
printer
file
briefcase
waste basket
computer
stapler
cellphone
mouse
mouse pad

CLOTHES

jeans
overalls
leggings
sweatpants
kilt
shorts
suit
jacket
pants
dress
tie
bow tie
suspenders
scarf
gloves
mittens
vest
pants
parka
raincoat
fleece
jacket
overcoat

CLOTHES

T-shirt

blouse

shirt

undershirt

sweatshirt

cardigan

sweater

pantyhose

stockings

socks

trunks

bikini

bathing suit

nightdress

pajamas

bathrobe

CAR

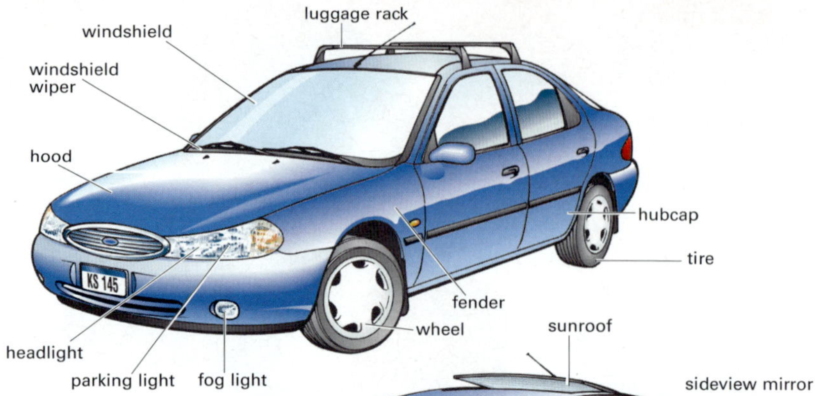
luggage rack
windshield
windshield wiper
hood
hubcap
tire
fender
wheel
headlight
parking light
fog light

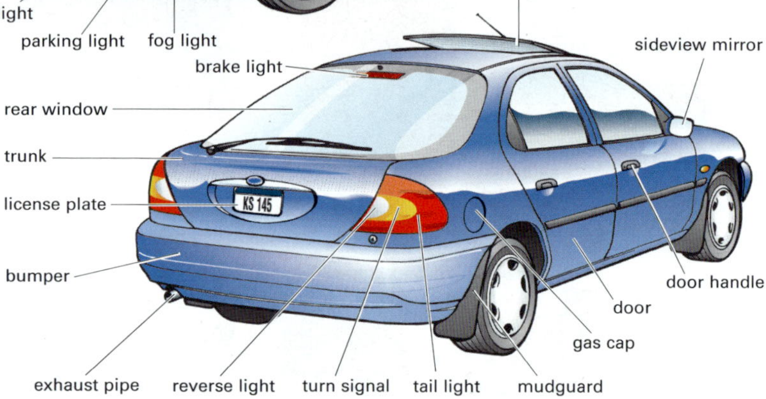
sunroof
sideview mirror
brake light
rear window
trunk
license plate
bumper
door handle
door
gas cap
exhaust pipe
reverse light
turn signal
tail light
mudguard

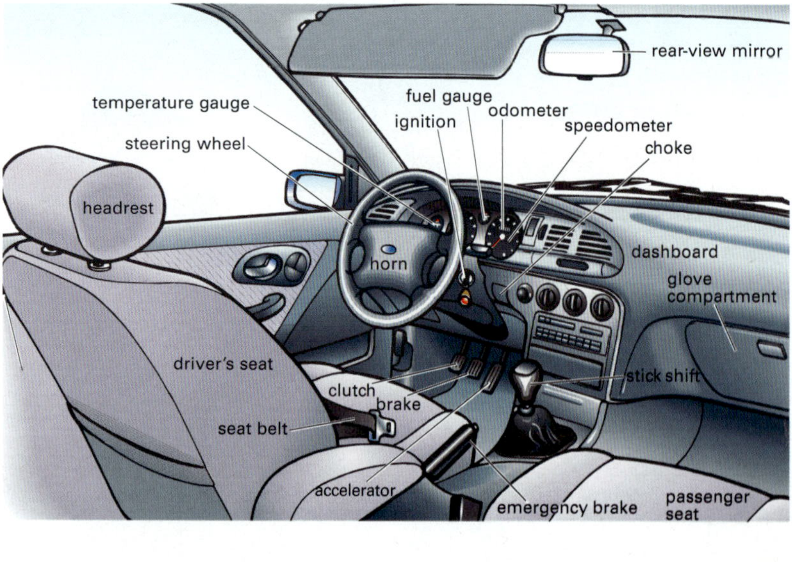
rear-view mirror
temperature gauge
fuel gauge
odometer
ignition
speedometer
steering wheel
choke
headrest
horn
dashboard
glove compartment
driver's seat
stick shift
clutch
brake
seat belt
accelerator
emergency brake
passenger seat

TRANSPORTATION

SHAPES

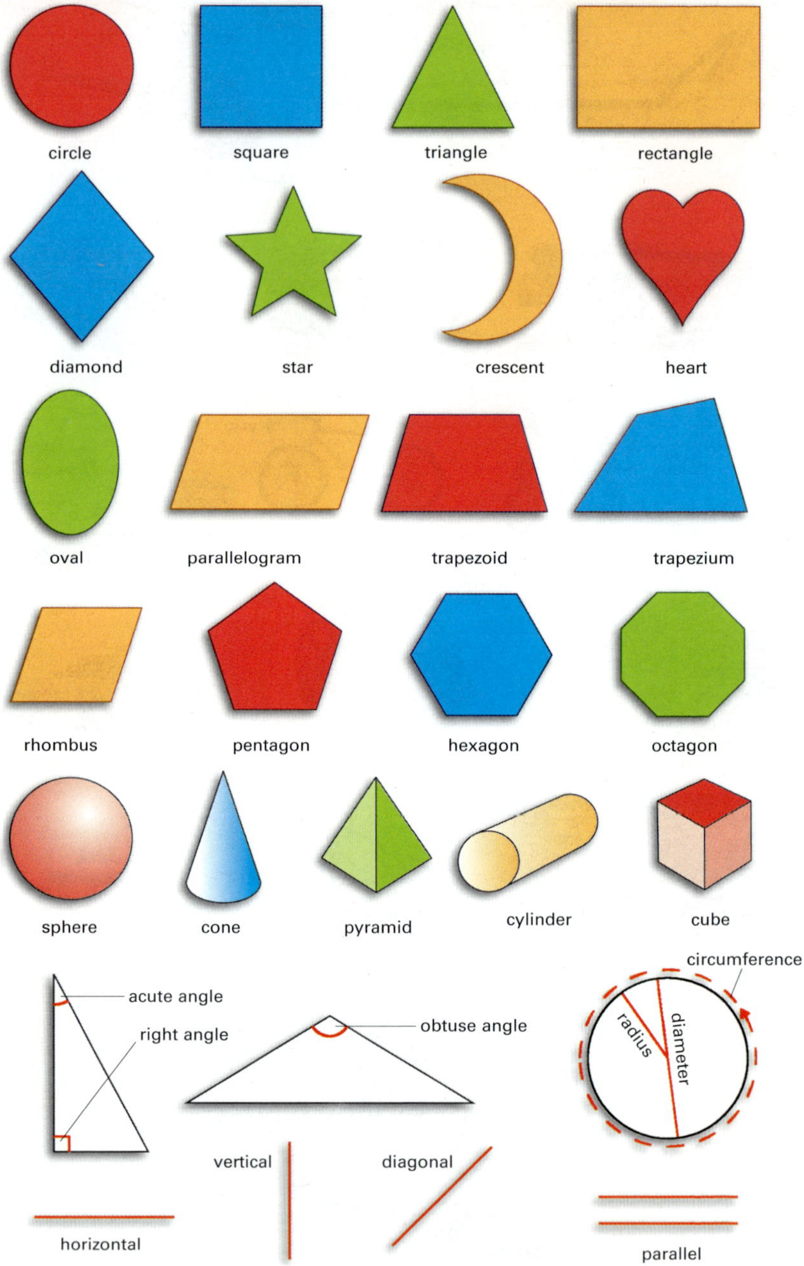
circle
square
triangle
rectangle
diamond
star
crescent
heart
oval
parallelogram
trapezoid
trapezium
rhombus
pentagon
hexagon
octagon
sphere
cone
pyramid
cylinder
cube
acute angle
right angle
obtuse angle
circumference
radius
diameter
vertical
diagonal
horizontal
parallel

frame² /freɪm/ verb [T] **1** to put a picture or photograph in a frame **2** *informal* to make someone seem to be guilty of a crime when they are not, for example by lying to the police **3** to express something in a particular way: *He was thinking about how to frame the question.*

frame·work /ˈfreɪmˌwɜrk/ noun [C] ★
1 a set of principles or rules: ***a framework for the study of television's effect on society***
2 a structure that supports something and makes it a particular shape: ***the wooden framework of the roof***

fran·chise /ˈfrænˌtʃaɪz/ noun **1** [C] an arrangement in which someone operates a business using the name and the products of a big company **2** [C] a business that operates under a franchise system
3 [singular/U] the right to vote in elections

frank /fræŋk/ adj honest about a situation or your opinions, even if this offends people
PHRASE **to be frank** *spoken* used when you are going to say something that other people might not like to hear
—**frank·ness** noun [U]

frank·furt·er /ˈfræŋkˌfɜrtər/ noun [C] a long thin SAUSAGE (=meat that is cut into very small pieces and put inside a thin skin). It is often eaten inside a long bread roll. =HOT DOG

frank·ly /ˈfræŋkli/ adv **1** used for emphasizing that you are speaking honestly: *Frankly, I don't care what you think.* **2** in an honest and direct manner

fran·tic /ˈfræntɪk/ adj **1** done in a very urgent way: *frantic attempts to rescue people from the fire* **2** very worried —**fran·ti·cal·ly** /ˈfræntɪkli/ adv

frat /fræt/ noun [C] *American informal* a student FRATERNITY

fra·ter·nal /frəˈtɜrn(ə)l/ adj of a brother, or like a brother

fra·ter·ni·ty /frəˈtɜrnəti/ noun **1** [C] *American* a private club for male students at a university or college in the U.S. **2** [C/U] people who have similar jobs or interests: *members of the legal fraternity* **3** [U] feelings of friendship, trust, and support between people

frat·er·nize /ˈfrætərˌnaɪz/ verb [I] *formal* to spend time with someone as a friend

fraud /frɔd/ noun **1** [C/U] the crime of obtaining money from someone by tricking them **2** [C] someone who pretends to be an official or professional person in order to trick people

fraud·u·lent /ˈfrɔdʒələnt/ adj done dishonestly or illegally with the intention of tricking someone —**fraud·u·lent·ly** adv

fraught /frɔt/ adj **fraught with sth** full of problems or dangers

fray /freɪ/ verb **1** [I/T] if cloth frays, or if something frays it, its fibers come apart at the edge **2** [I] if someone's nerves fray, they get nervous, and if someone's TEMPER frays, they get angry —**frayed** /freɪd/ adj

fray, the /freɪ/ noun [singular] **1** an exciting situation in which people compete with each other **2** a fight, or an argument

frayed /freɪd/ adj **1** with fibers that are coming apart at the edge **2** if your nerves are frayed, you are nervous, and if your TEMPER is frayed, you are angry

freak¹ /frik/ noun [C] **1** a very strange person or thing **2** *informal* someone who is extremely interested in a particular subject: *a fitness/health freak*

freak² /frik/ adj extremely unusual and unexpected: *He was killed in a freak accident.*

freak³ /frik/ or ˌ**freak (sb) ˈout** verb [I/T] *informal* to suddenly become very angry, excited, or frightened, or to make someone very angry, excited, or frightened

freck·les /ˈfrek(ə)lz/ noun [plural] small brown spots that are on someone's skin

free¹ /fri/ adj ★★★

1 not costing anything	5 not busy
2 not prisoner	6 not being used
3 not tied/attached	+ PHRASES
4 not limited by rules	

1 something that is free does not cost anything: *There is plenty of free parking.* ♦ *The swimming pool is **free for** hotel guests.*
2 not a prisoner or a SLAVE: *He'll soon be **a free man**.*
3 not held, tied, or attached to something: *Hand me the free end of the rope.* ♦ *Sally struggled to **get free** from the branches.*
4 not limited or controlled by rules: *We like to believe we live in a free society.* ♦ **free to do sth** *You are free to choose your own lawyer.*
5 available to see someone or do something: *I'm busy at the moment, but I'll be free this afternoon.* ♦ *Are you **free for** lunch?*
6 available for someone to use: *Is this seat free?* ♦ *I don't have much **free time** in this job.*
PHRASES **be free from/of sth** to be not containing or involving something that is unpleasant: *a world free from violence* ♦ *Doctors try to keep their patients free of pain.*
feel free *spoken* used for giving someone permission in a friendly way: *"Can I use the phone?" "Feel free."* ♦ *Feel free to help yourself to coffee.*
a free hand the right to make your own decisions without asking someone's permission: *The board gave me a free hand to reorganize the company.*

free² /fri/ verb [T] ★
1 to let someone leave a prison or similar place =RELEASE: *The organization works to free political prisoners.*
2 to help someone to get out of a place: **free sb/sth from sth** *They helped to free the injured driver from the wreckage.*
3 to remove something unpleasant that affects someone: **free sb/sth from sth** *Morphine was given to free her from pain.* ♦ **free sb/sth of sth** *He has been freed of direct responsibility for his staff.*
4 to make someone or something available to be used: **free sb/sth for sth** *We need to free more police officers for street duties.* ♦ **free sb/sth to do sth** *A classroom assistant frees teachers to concentrate on teaching.*
PHRASAL VERB ˌ**free sb/sth ˈup** *same as* **free²** 4: *We can probably free up $20,000 for new computer equipment.*

free³ /fri/ adv **1** without paying any money: *We got in free.* ♦ *Children can stay free of charge.* **2** out of a place where you are being kept: *The prisoner suddenly broke free and ran toward the car.* **3** without being controlled or stopped: *dogs running free*

ˌfree ˈagent noun [C] someone who is free to do what they want

free•bie /ˈfribi/ noun [C] *informal* something that someone gives you that you do not have to pay for

free•dom /ˈfridəm/ noun ★★★

1 [U] the right or opportunity to do what you want: *a law that restricts religious freedom* ♦ *The school gives students **freedom of choice** about what to wear.* ♦ **freedom to do sth** *My parents gave me total freedom to do whatever I liked.*

2 freedoms [plural] different types of freedom: *basic/fundamental/political freedoms*

PHRASES **freedom from sth** a situation in which you are not affected by something that is unpleasant: *freedom from hunger/disease/poverty*

freedom of speech the legal right to express your opinions without being prevented or punished

ˈfreedom ˌfighter noun [C] someone who fights against a cruel or unfair government

ˌfree ˈenterprise noun [U] an economic system in which businesses can compete with each other without being controlled by government

ˈfree-for-ˌall noun [C] *informal* **1** a situation in which people compete with each other using unfair or cruel methods **2** a noisy fight or argument that involves a lot of people

free•lance /ˈfriˌlæns/ adj working for different companies rather than being permanently employed by a particular company —**free•lance** verb [I]

free•lanc•er /ˈfriˌlænsər/ or **free•lance** /ˈfriˌlæns/ noun [C] a SELF-EMPLOYED person who works for different companies

free•ly /ˈfrili/ adv

1 without limits	4 in an honest way
2 without pauses	5 in many places
3 generously	

1 without being controlled by rules: *The shares could be traded freely on the open market.* **2** without being stopped or interrupted: *The traffic is moving quite freely this morning.* **3** generously, or in a willing way: *They give their time freely to support our cause.* **4** without trying to hide anything = OPENLY: *I freely admit I've made mistakes.* **5** something that is freely available is easy to obtain or buy

ˌfree ˈmarket noun [C] an economic system in which the government does not control trade and prices

ˌfree-ˈrange adj free-range farm animals live outside in a lot of space

ˌfree ˈspeech noun [U] the legal or natural right to say what you believe is true, without being prevented or punished

ˌfree ˈtrade noun [U] a system in which companies do not pay high taxes on goods that are bought from other countries or are sold in other countries

free•ware /ˈfriˌwer/ noun [U] *computing* computer software that is available free on CD-ROM or from the Internet

free•way /ˈfriˌweɪ/ noun [C] *American* a large divided highway that does not cost anything to use

ˌfree ˈwill noun [U] people's ability to control their own lives, based on their own decisions

PHRASE **of your own free will** if you do something of your own free will, you do it because you want to do it, not because you are forced to

freeze¹ /friz/ (past tense **froze** /froʊz/; past participle **fro•zen** /ˈfroʊz(ə)n/) verb ★

1 become hard with cold	4 feel extremely cold
2 preserve food	5 stop moving
3 not increase a level	

1 [I/T] to become solid or hard because of extreme cold, or to make something solid or hard: *The lake freezes in the winter.* ♦ *The water had **frozen solid**.*

2 [T] to preserve food or drink by making it extremely cold in a freezer: *You should freeze meat on the day that you buy it.*

3 [T] to decide officially that the level of something will not increase: *Wages were frozen until the end of December.*

4 [I] to feel extremely cold: *You'll freeze if you go out in that thin coat.* ♦ *The lambs looked as if they had **frozen to death** in the snow.*

5 [I] to stop moving and keep completely still: *Kate froze in horror when she saw all the blood.*

freeze² /friz/ noun [C] **1** an official decision to prevent any increase in something: *a pay/wage/price freeze* **2** a period of extremely cold weather

freez•er /ˈfrizər/ noun [C] a large piece of electrical equipment that is used for freezing food

freez•ing¹ /ˈfrizɪŋ/ adj *informal* very cold: *It's absolutely freezing in here.*

freez•ing² /ˈfrizɪŋ/ noun [U] the temperature at which water freezes and becomes ice: *five degrees below freezing*

ˈfreezing ˌpoint noun [C] the temperature at which a particular liquid freezes

freight /freɪt/ noun [U] goods that are carried by vehicles

freight•er /ˈfreɪtər/ noun [C] a large ship or airplane that carries goods

ˌFrench ˈdoors noun [plural] a pair of doors made mostly of glass that both open from the middle —*picture* → C1

ˌFrench ˈfries noun [plural] long thin pieces of potato that have been cooked in boiling oil

ˌFrench ˈhorn noun [C] a musical instrument consisting of a long curved metal tube that is very wide at one end —*picture* → BRASS

fre•net•ic /frəˈnetɪk/ adj done very fast and with a lot of energy, often by someone who is in a hurry —**fre•net•i•cal•ly** /frəˈnetɪkli/ adv

fren•zied /ˈfrenzid/ adj done in an extremely uncontrolled way, often by someone who is crazy

fren•zy /ˈfrenzi/ noun [singular] **1** the feeling of being unable to control your feelings or behavior: *She was in a frenzy of rage.* **2** a period when there is a lot of activity

fre·quen·cy /ˈfrikwənsi/ noun **1** [U] the number of times that something happens during a period of time: *We hope this treatment will reduce the frequency of heart disease.* **2** [C] the WAVELENGTH on which a radio program is broadcast

fre·quent¹ /ˈfrikwənt/ adj ★ happening often ≠ INFREQUENT: *Their arguments were becoming more and more frequent.* ♦ *He was a frequent visitor to our house.* ♦ *Inspections must be carried out **at frequent intervals*** (=regularly).

fre·quent² /friˈkwent/ verb [T] *formal* if you frequent a place, you go there regularly

fre·quent·ly /ˈfrikwəntli/ adv ★★ often ≠ RARELY, SELDOM: *He has frequently been compared to Michael Jackson.* ♦ *The ten most frequently asked questions are listed below.*

fresh /freʃ/ adj ★★★

1 new	6 with feeling of energy
2 food: not preserved	7 of flowers
3 food: still good to eat	8 water: with no salt
4 replacing sth	+ PHRASE
5 recently done/made	

1 clearly new and different: *We need a completely fresh approach to the problem.* ♦ *The program **takes a fresh look at** this difficult issue.* ♦ *She regarded the birth of her children as **a fresh start*** (=a chance to start living in a better way).

2 fresh food has not been preserved in any way: *You can use fresh or canned tomatoes for this recipe.*

3 food that is fresh is still good to eat because it was prepared or produced recently ≠ STALE: *Cooked meat will **stay fresh** for several days in the refrigerator.*

4 replacing or adding to a previous thing: *The police made a fresh appeal for witnesses.* ♦ *I've put fresh towels in your room.*

5 recently made or experienced: *fresh footprints in the snow* ♦ *The details are still fresh in my mind.*

6 if you feel fresh, you have a lot of energy

7 fresh flowers have been recently PICKED (=taken from the place that they were growing in)

8 fresh water is water in lakes and rivers that does not contain any salt

PHRASE **fresh from/out of sth** if someone is fresh from a particular place or situation, they have recently come from there: *He was just a kid, fresh out of law school.*

—**fresh·ness** noun [U]

ˌfresh ˈair noun [U] the air outside that is nice to breathe → BREATH

fresh·en /ˈfreʃ(ə)n/ verb [T] to make something fresher, cleaner, or more attractive

PHRASAL VERBS **ˌfreshen ˈup** to wash your hands and face and make yourself cleaner and neater

ˌfreshen sth ˈup *same as* **freshen**: *Freshen up your walls and ceilings with a coat of paint.*

fresh·ly /ˈfreʃli/ adv recently

fresh·man /ˈfreʃmən/ (plural **fresh·men** /ˈfreʃmən/) noun [C] *American* a student who is in their first year at a HIGH SCHOOL or university

fresh·wa·ter /ˈfreʃˌwɔtər/ adj living in water that does not contain salt

fret /fret/ verb [I] to worry about something continuously

fret·ful /ˈfretf(ə)l/ adj someone who is fretful is worried and unhappy

Fri. abbrev Friday

fri·ar /ˈfraɪər/ noun [C] a man who is a type of MONK (=a member of a Christian religious community)

fric·tion /ˈfrɪkʃ(ə)n/ noun [U] **1** disagreement: *There is some friction between the various departments.* **2** the fact that one surface rubs against another

Fri·day /ˈfraɪdeɪ/ noun [C/U] ★★★ the day after Thursday and before Saturday: *My birthday is on a Friday this year.* ♦ *The museum closes Fridays* (=every Friday). ♦ *She leaves next Friday.* ♦ *Let's go swimming **on Friday**.*

fridge /frɪdʒ/ noun [C] *informal* ★ a REFRIGERATOR

fried /fraɪd/ adj cooked in hot oil

friend /frend/ noun [C] ★★★ someone who you know well and like who is not a member of your family: *She's visiting friends in Illinois.* ♦ *Helga is **a close friend** of mine.* ♦ *May I introduce Peter Flint, a very old **friend of the family**.* ♦ *I'm having lunch **with an old friend*** (=someone who has been a friend for a long time). ♦ *She has a wide **circle of friends*** (=group of friends). ♦ *They used to **be friends*** (=with each other). ♦ *They **made friends with** the children next door* (=started to be their friends).

Words often used with friend

*Adjectives often used with **friend***

- **best, close, dear, good, great, lifelong, old, trusted** + FRIEND: someone who you know very well

friend·ly /ˈfren(d)li/ adj ★★

1 someone who is friendly is always pleasant and helpful toward other people ≠ UNFRIENDLY: *He will be remembered as a kind, friendly person.* ♦ *The local people were very **friendly toward** us.*
→ SYMPATHETIC

2 if you are friendly with someone, you are their friend: *Janet and I used to **be** very **friendly**.* ♦ *Doctors shouldn't get too **friendly with** their patients.*

-friendly /fren(d)li/ suffix **1** used for showing that something does not harm something else: *wildlife-friendly farming methods* ♦ *environmentally-friendly cleaning materials* **2** appropriate for a particular type of person: *child-friendly restaurants*

friend·ship /ˈfren(d)ʃɪp/ noun [C/U] ★ a relationship between people who are friends: *Whatever happened, I did not want to lose Sarah's friendship.* ♦ *his **friendship with** a local businessman* ♦ *She formed **a close friendship** with Vera Brittain.*

fries /fraɪz/ noun [plural] FRENCH FRIES

frig·ate /ˈfrɪgət/ noun [C] a small fast ship that is used by a navy

fright /fraɪt/ noun [singular/U] a sudden strong feeling of being afraid: *He was shaking with fright.* ♦ *Kelly cried out in fright.*

F

fright·en /ˈfraɪt(ə)n/ verb [T] ★ to make someone feel afraid = SCARE: *The thought of war frightens me.* ♦ *It frightens me how quickly children grow up these days.* ♦ **frighten sb into doing sth** *ads that frighten people into buying expensive security equipment*

PHRASAL VERB ˌ**frighten sb/sth aˈway** or ˌ**frighten sb/sth ˈoff 1** to make a person or animal so afraid that they run away **2** to make someone so worried or nervous that they decide not to become involved with something: *The fall in share prices has frightened off possible investors.*

F

fright·ened /ˈfraɪt(ə)nd/ adj ★ feeling or showing fear = SCARED: *The puppy looked cold and frightened.* ♦ *Bruckner was watching him with wide, frightened eyes.* ♦ *There's nothing to be* ***frightened about.*** ♦ *I've always been* ***frightened of*** *snakes.* ♦ **+(that)** *I was frightened that he might see us.* ♦ **frightened to do sth** *Now he is frightened to go out at night.*

- **Frightened** describes how you feel: *I am frightened of spiders.* ♦ *She looked very frightened.*
- **Frightening** describes things or situations that make you feel frightened: *The look on his face was frightening.* ♦ *It was a very frightening experience.*

fright·en·ing /ˈfraɪt(ə)nɪŋ/ adj ★ making you feel afraid, nervous, or worried: *a frightening noise/thought/experience* ♦ *It was supposed to be a horror film but it wasn't very frightening.* ♦ *It's frightening that people like him get elected.* —**fright·en·ing·ly** adv

frig·id /ˈfrɪdʒɪd/ adj **1** *formal* extremely cold **2** extremely formal and unfriendly = ICY **3** a frigid woman does not enjoy having sex

frill /frɪl/ noun [C] a decoration that consists of a long narrow piece of cloth with many small folds in it

PHRASE **no frills** used for referring to something that is good enough but that has no unnecessary extra features

frill·y /ˈfrɪli/ adj decorated with a lot of frills

fringe¹ /frɪndʒ/ noun [C] **1** the outer edge of something: *factories on the northern fringe of the city* **2** people or activities that are considered strange **3** a decoration that consists of a row of fibers or thin pieces of cloth that hang down

fringe² /frɪndʒ/ verb [T] to form a line around the edge of something = BORDER

fringe³ /frɪndʒ/ adj involving people who do not form the main part of a group and are sometimes thought to be strange: *fringe meetings/issues/politics*

ˈ**fringe ˌbenefit** noun [C] something that you get from your employer in addition to your salary, for example a car

frisk /frɪsk/ or ˌ**frisk sb ˈdown** verb [T] to search someone with your hands in order to see if they are carrying anything illegal such as a gun or drugs

frisk·y /ˈfrɪski/ adj feeling lively and full of fun

frit·ter /ˈfrɪtər/ PHRASAL VERB ˌ**fritter sth aˈway** to waste time or money on things that are not important: *He frittered away all his winnings.*

fri·vol·i·ty /frɪˈvɑləti/ noun [U] silly behavior or attitudes

friv·o·lous /ˈfrɪvələs/ adj **1** behaving in a silly way in situations in which you should be serious or sensible **2** lacking any real purpose or importance: *frivolous complaints*

friz·zy /ˈfrɪzi/ adj frizzy hair has small tight stiff curls

fro /froʊ/ *see* **to**

frog /frɔg/ noun [C] a small animal with smooth skin and long back legs that lives near water → TOAD

frog·man /ˈfrɔgmən/ (plural **frog·men** /ˈfrɔgmən/) noun [C] someone who does police or military work under water. Frogmen wear special clothes and use special equipment.

frol·ic /ˈfrɑlɪk/ verb [I] to play in a happy way with a lot of energy

from /*weak* frəm, *strong* frɑm/ preposition ★★★

1 given, sent, or provided by sb used for saying who gives, sends, or provides something: *The watch was a present from his daughter.* ♦ *She got a letter from Tom.* ♦ *I borrowed the money from my parents.*

2 stating sb's origin used for saying where someone was born, where they live or work, or the type of family they were born with: *I'm originally from North Carolina.* ♦ *Rosie Miller from Eugene, Oregon, received the award.* ♦ *a team of experts from the bank* ♦ *Those from poor families should not have to pay.*

3 giving distances used for saying how far away something is in relation to something else: *We live a few miles from the city.*

4 giving a range used for giving a range of things, times, prices, etc.: *music ranging from classical to punk*

5 giving a reason used for saying what has caused something or why you have a particular opinion: *Her hair was wet from the rain.* ♦ *She's been suffering from stress.* ♦ *I could see from his expression that he was upset.*

6 saying where sb does sth used for saying where someone is when they see, hear, or do something: *He works from home.* ♦ *Let's watch the fireworks from the roof.*

7 made of sth used for saying what substance has been used for making something: *The toys are made from a very durable plastic.*

8 describing a change used for saying what someone or something was before changing to something else: *Colesville changed* ***from*** *a sleepy little town* ***to*** *a busy city.*

9 saying what is prevented used for saying what has been prevented or protected against: *Protect delicate plants from frost.* ♦ *His restlessness kept him from sleeping.*

10 showing differences used for talking about differences between two or more people or things: *This recipe is different from the one I usually use.* ♦ *He should know right from wrong by now.*

11 starting at a particular time starting at a point in time and continuing: *She will be* *working here full-time from tomorrow.* ♦ *He wanted to be an actor from the age of 10.* ♦ ***From now on**, things are going to be different.*

12 saying where sb/sth started used for saying where someone or something started a trip, or where they were before moving: *the 3 o'clock flight from Chicago* ♦ *imports from Japan* ♦ *He took a hammer from his tool box.* ♦ *What time does he come home from school?* ♦ *We drove **from** Los Angeles **to** Denver.*

frond /frɑnd/ noun [C] a large long leaf that is divided into many narrow sections

front¹ /frʌnt/ noun ★★★

1 part facing forward	5 not sincere behavior
2 part farthest forward	6 in war
3 aspect of situation	7 in weather
4 activity to hide secret	+ PHRASES

1 the front [singular] the surface of something that faces forward ≠ BACK: *Go around to the front* (=of the building) *and I'll let you in.* ♦ *Attach a recent photograph to **the front of** your application.* ♦ *a book with a picture of a tiger **on the front***

2 the front [singular] the part of something that is nearest the direction it faces ≠ BACK: *If you can't see the blackboard, come and sit **at the front**.* ♦ *Tom was sitting **at the front of** the bus.* ♦ *He had signed his name **in the front of** the book.*

3 [C] a particular aspect of a situation: *There's bad news on the job front – two factories are going to close.* ♦ *His main problems were in math and science, but he has made progress on both fronts.*

4 [C] an organization or activity that exists in order to hide something that is secret or illegal: *They used the store as **a front for** dealing in stolen goods.*

5 [singular] behavior that is not sincere because you want to hide your real feelings: *He always pretended he didn't care but we knew it was just a front.* ♦ *She's putting on a brave front, but she's really very worried.*

6 [C] a FRONT LINE in a war

7 [C] *technical* a line where a large area of cold air meets a large area of warm air

PHRASES **in front 1** a little farther forward than someone or something else: *I passed the car in front.* **2** winning a competition, game, or election that is not yet finished: *Owen scored to put his team in front.*

in front of sb 1 if something is in front of you, it is in a position where you can see it if you look forward: *In front of her, the highway stretched for miles.* **2** in a situation where someone is there with you: *I would never say this in front of my mother.* **3** in a situation where someone is watching you do something: *The game took place in front of a crowd of 60,000 people.*

in front of sth 1 in a position where you can see a particular thing when you look forward: *She just sits in front of the television all day long.* **2** into a place where a moving vehicle might hit you: *He stepped onto the road in front of a bus.*

up front if you pay money up front, you pay it before you have received the goods that you are buying, or before someone starts to do work for you: *I'll need $500 up front for the cost of materials.*

front² /frʌnt/ adj ★★★ at, in, or on the front of something: *You can go and play in the front yard.* ♦ *the front seat of the car* ♦ *front legs/paws*

fron•tal /ˈfrʌnt(ə)l/ adj *formal* at, in, or on the front part of something

ˌfront ˈdoor noun [C] the main door at the front of a house

fron•tier /frʌnˈtɪr/ noun **1** [C] a border between two countries **2 the frontiers** [plural] the most advanced or recent ideas about something: *Their work was on the frontiers of science.*

ˌfront ˈline noun [C] the area where two armies face each other and fight during a war — **ˌfront-ˈline** adj

ˌfront-ˈpage adj important enough to be printed on the first page of a newspaper: *front-page news/stories/headlines*

ˌfront-ˈrunner noun [C] the person or thing that is thought to be the most likely to win a competition, game, or election

frost¹ /frɔst/ noun **1** [U] a thin white layer of ice that looks like powder and that forms on things outside when the weather is very cold: *bushes covered with frost* **2** [C/U] a period of weather that is cold enough to form frost

frost² /frɔst/ verb [T] *American* to put FROSTING on a cake

PHRASAL VERB **ˌfrost (sth) ˈover** or **ˌfrost (sth) ˈup** to cover something completely with frost, or to become completely covered with frost: *The windows were all frosted over.*

frost•bite /ˈfrɔs(t)ˌbaɪt/ noun [U] a medical condition in which cold weather seriously damages your fingers, toes, ears, or nose

frost•bit•ten /ˈfrɔs(t)ˌbɪt(ə)n/ adj affected by frostbite

ˌfrosted ˈglass noun [U] glass that has a rough surface so that you cannot see clearly through it

frost•ing /ˈfrɔstɪŋ/ noun [U] *American* a smooth sweet substance that is usually made from sugar, butter, and liquid, used for covering cakes = ICING

frost•y /ˈfrɔsti/ adj **1** cold enough to produce FROST, or covered with FROST: *a frosty morning* **2** unfriendly: *a frosty look*

froth¹ /frɔθ/ noun [singular/U] a mass of small air BUBBLES that form on the surface of a liquid

froth² /frɔθ/ verb [I] to produce froth

froth•y /ˈfrɔθi/ adj covered with or consisting of froth

frown¹ /fraʊn/ verb [I] to move your EYEBROWS down and closer together because you are annoyed, worried, or thinking hard

PHRASAL VERB **ˈfrown ˌon sb/sth** to not approve of something: *Personal phone calls are frowned on at work.*

frown² /fraʊn/ noun [C] an expression on your face that is made by moving your EYEBROWS down and closer together. It shows that you are annoyed, worried, or thinking hard.

froze the past tense of **freeze¹**

fro·zen[1] /ˈfroʊz(ə)n/ adj ★
1 preserved by being made extremely cold and stored at a very low temperature: *frozen food/meals* ♦ *frozen vegetables/fish/yogurt*
2 covered with a layer of ice, or made very hard because the weather is very cold: *a frozen pond* ♦ *the frozen ground*
3 *spoken* feeling very cold: *I'm frozen – can't we go inside?* ♦ *We were* ***frozen stiff*** (=extremely cold) *waiting for the bus.*

fro·zen[2] the past participle of **freeze**[1]

fru·gal /ˈfrug(ə)l/ adj **1** spending very little money and only on things that are really necessary **2** a frugal meal is simple, inexpensive, and not very big —**fru·gal·ly** adv

F

fruit /frut/ noun [C/U] ★★★ (plural **fruit** or **fruits**) a type of food that grows on trees or plants, for example apples and oranges: *Eat plenty of fresh fruit and vegetables.* ♦ *She always has* ***a piece of fruit*** *for dessert.*
PHRASES **bear fruit** to have a successful result: *Our policies must be given time to bear fruit.*
the fruit/fruits of sth the good results that you get from something such as hard work: *The book is the fruit of a collaboration between several groups.*

fruit·ful /ˈfrutfəl/ adj producing good results ≠ FRUITLESS: *a fruitful meeting/discussion*

fru·i·tion /fruˈɪʃ(ə)n/ noun [U] *formal* the result that you wanted to achieve from a plan or idea: *Nobody was sure whether the deal would ever come to fruition.*

fruit·less /ˈfrutləs/ adj producing no good results ≠ FRUITFUL: *a fruitless search*

ˌfruit ˈsalad noun [C/U] a food consisting of small pieces of different types of fresh fruit, usually eaten as a DESSERT

fruit·y /ˈfruti/ adj tasting or smelling like fruit

frus·trate /ˈfrʌˌstreɪt/ verb [T] **1** to make someone feel annoyed and impatient by preventing them from doing or getting something **2** to prevent someone or something from succeeding: *The bad weather frustrated their plans for a picnic.*

frus·trat·ed /ˈfrʌˌstreɪtəd/ adj feeling annoyed and impatient because you are prevented from achieving something: *Parents are increasingly frustrated with the local school system.*

frus·trat·ing /ˈfrʌˌstreɪtɪŋ/ adj making you feel annoyed and impatient because you are prevented from achieving something: *It's frustrating to wait all day for a repairman who doesn't show up.*

frus·tra·tion /frʌˈstreɪʃ(ə)n/ noun [C/U] an annoyed or impatient feeling that you get when you are prevented from doing what you want: *There is a growing sense of frustration among hospital staff.*

fry /fraɪ/ verb [I/T] ★ to cook food in hot oil or fat, or to be cooked in this way: *the smell of chicken frying in the kitchen* → STIR-FRY

fry·ing pan /ˈfraɪɪŋ ˌpæn/ noun [C] a flat metal pan with a long handle that is used for cooking food in hot oil or fat = SKILLET —*picture* → C2

ft. abbrev foot or feet: *a 3 ft. deep pond*

fuch·sia /ˈfjuʃə/ noun [C/U] a small bush with pink, red, or white flowers that hang down —*picture* → C9

fudge[1] /fʌdʒ/ noun [U] a soft brown sweet food made from sugar, butter, milk or cream, and usually chocolate

fudge[2] /fʌdʒ/ verb **1** [T] to change the details of something: *Journalists have always tended to fudge the facts.* **2** [I/T] to avoid giving a clear decision or answer about something: *People have accused us of fudging the issue.*

fu·el[1] /ˈfjuəl/ noun ★★
1 [C/U] a substance such as oil, gas, coal, or wood that produces heat or power when it is burned: *a shortage of food and fuel*
2 [U] gas or DIESEL used in vehicles: *The stolen car was abandoned when it ran out of fuel.*

fu·el[2] /ˈfjuəl/ (present participle **fu·el·ing** or **fu·el·ling**; past tense and past participle **fu·eled** or **fu·elled**) verb [T] to make something increase or become worse: *People's fear of crime is fueled by sensationalist reports.*

ˈfuel ˌcell noun [C] *technical* the piece of equipment that produces the power in an electric vehicle

fu·gi·tive /ˈfjudʒətɪv/ noun [C] someone who has done something that is illegal and is trying to avoid being caught by the police

ful·fil /fʊlˈfɪl/ the British spelling of **fulfill**

ful·fill /fʊlˈfɪl/ verb [T]

1 have purpose	4 do sth promised
2 reach standard	5 satisfy sb
3 achieve sth wanted	

1 to do a particular job or have a particular purpose: *The bus really fulfills a need for this community.* ♦ *The sports center fulfills a necessary role in this town.* **2** to reach a particular standard or have the qualities that are necessary for something: *Several of the applicants do not fulfill the entry requirements for the course.* **3** to achieve something that you wanted to do, or to get something that you hoped for: *The trip fulfilled a lifelong dream.* ♦ *He never really* ***fulfilled his potential*** (=achieved as much as he could) *as a player.* **4** to do what you must do or what you said that you will do: *Landlords who refuse to fulfill their obligations may be fined.* ♦ *The government has failed to fulfill its election promises.* **5** to make you happy and satisfied because you are using your skills and abilities: *This job doesn't really fulfill me.*

ful·filled /fʊlˈfɪld/ adj happy and satisfied because you are doing something important or are using your skills and abilities ≠ UNFULFILLED

ful·fill·ing /fʊlˈfɪlɪŋ/ adj making you feel fulfilled: *a fulfilling career*

ful·fill·ment /fʊlˈfɪlmənt/ noun **1** [U] a feeling of happiness and satisfaction because you are doing something important or using your abilities: *Being a doctor gives me a real sense of fulfillment.* **2** [U] the act of doing or achieving something that is promised or expected: *Is there anything that might interfere with the fulfillment of your duties?* **3** [C/U] the act of something happening or being made to happen: *the fulfillment of a prediction*

ful·fil·ment /fʊlˈfɪlmənt/ the British spelling of **fulfillment**

full /fʊl/ adj ★★★

1 containing all that fits	5 busy
2 complete	6 body: large
3 unable to eat more	+ PHRASES
4 as much as possible	

1 containing the largest amount that will fit in a particular place ≠ EMPTY: *The gas tank is almost full.* ♦ *a full parking lot* ♦ *This potato chip bag is only **half full**.* ♦ *cans full of garbage*
2 complete: *full details/instructions* ♦ *She is expected to make a full recovery.* ♦ *Please give your **full name and address**.*
3 not wanting to eat any more because you have eaten a lot
4 used for emphasizing that something is as loud, powerful, fast, etc. as possible: *He turned the radio on full volume.* ♦ *He drove **at full speed** along the road.*
5 busy: *a full day at the office* ♦ *She leads a very full life* (=she takes part in many different activities).
6 if part of someone's body is full, it is large, wide, or has a round shape: *full lips*
PHRASES **be full of sth** to have or contain a lot of something: *Your pants are full of holes!*
be full of yourself *informal* to be always talking about yourself or your achievements in a way that annoys other people
in full completely, including the whole of something: *Fines must be paid in full within 30 days.*
to the fullest as much as possible: *My goal is to enjoy life to the fullest.*

ˌfull-ˈblown adj in the most complete and developed form

ˌfull-ˈfledged adj *American* completely developed or trained

ˌfull-ˈgrown adj FULLY-GROWN

ˌfull ˈhouse noun [singular] a situation in which every seat in a theater or sports STADIUM has someone sitting in it

ˌfull-ˈlength adj **1** a full-length coat, dress, or skirt goes down to your feet **2** a full-length mirror or picture shows someone's whole body including their feet **3** a full-length book, movie, etc. is the normal length

ˌfull ˈmoon noun [C] the moon when it looks like a complete circle

ˌfull-ˈpage adj printed on a whole page of a newspaper or magazine

ˈfull-ˌscale adj **1** complete, or not limited in any way: *a full-scale investigation into the murder* **2** a full-scale model or drawing of something is as big as the real thing

ˌfull ˈstop noun [C] *British* a PERIOD used in writing

ˈfull-ˌtime adj done or doing something for the number of hours that people normally work or study in a complete week: *a full-time job* —**full-ˌtime** adv

ful·ly /ˈfʊli/ adv ★★★ completely: *He was lying on the bed, fully dressed.* ♦ *I did not fully appreciate the seriousness of the situation.* ♦ *She still hasn't fully recovered from her shoulder injury.*

ˌfully-ˈfledged adj FULL-FLEDGED

ˌfully-ˈgrown adj a fully-grown person or animal has reached its biggest size and will not grow any more

fum·ble /ˈfʌmb(ə)l/ verb **1** [I] to try to hold, move, or find something using your hands in a way that is not skillful or graceful **2** [I/T] to drop the ball in a game of football —*picture* → C15 —**fum·ble** noun [C]

fume /fjum/ verb [I] **1** to be very angry **2** to send out smoke or gas

fumes /fjumz/ noun [plural] smoke or gas that has an unpleasant smell and that may be harmful

fu·mi·gate /ˈfjumɪˌgeɪt/ verb [T] to treat a place with smoke or with gas in order to kill bacteria or insects —**fu·mi·ga·tion** /ˌfjumɪˈgeɪʃ(ə)n/ noun [U]

fun¹ /fʌn/ noun [U] ★★ enjoyment from an activity that is not important or serious: *I hate to spoil your fun but it's time to go home now.* ♦ *We haven't **had such fun** for years.* ♦ *The kids **had a lot of fun** with that old tent.*
PHRASES **be no fun** or **not be any fun** to not be enjoyable: *It's no fun living by yourself.*
for fun or **for the fun of it** because something is enjoyable or funny, not for any important or serious reason: *I swim every day for fun.*
in fun said or done as a joke, and not intended to annoy anyone: *The teasing was all in fun.*
make fun of to make jokes about someone or something in an unkind way: *The other children made fun of her because she was always so serious.*

fun² /fʌn/ adj enjoyable: *a fun day at the zoo*

- **Funny** is used for talking about something or someone that makes you laugh: *He told a funny joke.* ♦ *She's one of the funniest people I know.* ♦ *Don't laugh; it isn't funny.*
- **Fun** is used for talking about something that is enjoyable or someone that you enjoy being with: *Barcelona is a fun city.* ♦ *Our day at the beach was really fun.* ♦ *My sister is a fun person.*

func·tion¹ /ˈfʌŋkʃ(ə)n/ noun ★★★
1 [C/U] a job that something is designed to do, or the duties or responsibilities that someone has in their job: *The function of advertising is to create a unique image for your company.*
2 [C] a social event such as a party: *an official function*

func·tion² /ˈfʌŋkʃ(ə)n/ verb [I] to work or operate in a particular way: *We need to get this department functioning efficiently.*
PHRASAL VERB **ˈfunction as sth** to be used or work as something: *a phrase that functions as an adverb*

func·tion·al /ˈfʌŋkʃən(ə)l/ adj **1** designed to be effective, practical, and simple, with no unnecessary features or decorations
2 operating in the correct way

ˈfunction ˌkey noun [C] *computing* a special button on a computer keyboard that is used for a particular operation in a program

fund¹ /fʌnd/ noun ★★
1 [C] an amount of money that you collect, save, or invest: *an investment/retirement fund* → TRUST FUND

F

2 funds [plural] money: *I'm a little low on funds right now.*
→ FUNDING

fund² /fʌnd/ verb [T] to provide the money for something: *publicly funded legal services*

fun·da·men·tal /ˌfʌndəˈment(ə)l/ adj ★★ relating to the basic nature or character of something: *There is **a fundamental flaw** in his argument.* ♦ *We'll have to make some **fundamental changes** in the way we do business.*

fun·da·men·tal·ism /ˌfʌndəˈment(ə)lˌɪzəm/ noun [U] the belief that religious or political laws should be followed very strictly and should not be changed

fun·da·men·tal·ist /ˌfʌndəˈment(ə)lɪst/ noun [C] someone who believes that religious or political laws should be followed very strictly and should not be changed —**fun·da·men·tal·ist** adj

fun·da·men·tal·ly /ˌfʌndəˈment(ə)li/ adv **1** in a very important or basic way: *His entire approach to the problem is fundamentally flawed.* **2** used for emphasizing the basic nature or character of something: *Fundamentally, she is a children's writer.*

fun·da·men·tals, the /ˌfʌndəˈment(ə)lz/ noun [plural] the most basic and important aspects of something: *the fundamentals of classic French cooking*

fund·ing /ˈfʌndɪŋ/ noun [U] money that a government or organization provides for a specific purpose

fund·rais·er /ˈfʌndˌreɪzər/ noun [C] a social event that is organized to make money for a CHARITY or political party

fund·rais·ing /ˈfʌndˌreɪzɪŋ/ noun [U] the activity of trying to persuade people or organizations to give money to a CHARITY or political party

fu·ner·al /ˈfjun(ə)rəl/ noun [C] ★ a ceremony that takes place after someone dies, and the formal process of taking the body to the place where it is buried or CREMATED: *He flew home to arrange his father's funeral.* ♦ *a funeral service/procession*

ˈfuneral diˌrector noun [C] someone whose job is to organize funerals = UNDERTAKER

ˈfuneral ˌhome or **ˈfuneral ˌparlor** noun [C] a place where the body of a dead person is prepared and kept before a funeral

fun·gus /ˈfʌŋgəs/ (plural **fun·gi** /ˈfʌŋˌdʒaɪ, ˈfʌŋˌgaɪ/; plural **fun·gus·es**) noun [C/U] a type of plant without leaves, flowers, or green color that grows in wet conditions or on decaying substances

funk /fʌŋk/ noun [U] a type of lively music with a strong beat that developed from SOUL and ROCK

funk·y /ˈfʌŋki/ adj **1** fashionable in a way that is unusual and that shows a lot of imagination **2** funky music has a strong simple beat that is good for dancing

fun·nel /ˈfʌn(ə)l/ noun [C] **1** a tube that is wide at the top and narrow at the bottom. It is used for pouring a liquid or powder into a container. **2** a tube that lets out smoke and steam from the engine of a boat or an old-fashioned train

fun·nies, the /ˈfʌniz/ noun [plural] *American* the section of a newspaper that contains COMIC STRIPS (=series of drawings that tell a story)

fun·ni·ly /ˈfʌnɪli/ adv in a strange or unusual way

PHRASE **funnily enough** *spoken* used for saying that you think that something is surprising or unusual: *Funnily enough, I heard someone say the exact same thing this morning.*

fun·ny /ˈfʌni/ adj ★★★
1 someone or something that is funny makes you laugh: *a funny story* ♦ *one of America's funniest comedians* ♦ *I don't think that's at all funny.* ♦ *Wouldn't it be funny if we played a trick on him?* → FUN
2 strange or unusual: *This milk tastes funny.* ♦ *You're in a funny mood today.* ♦ ***That's funny** – she was here a minute ago.*

PHRASE **feel funny** *informal* to feel slightly sick

> Other ways of saying **funny**
>
> - **amusing** funny in a way that makes you smile
> - **comical/comic** funny and silly or strange
> - **hilarious/hysterical** very funny
> - **humorous** used for describing stories or remarks that are meant to be funny
> - **lighthearted** dealing with a serious subject in a funny way that is meant to entertain people
> - **witty** used for describing remarks that are funny and intelligent, or for describing people who often make remarks like this

fur /fɜr/ noun **1** [U] the soft hair that covers the body of some animals **2** [C/U] an animal skin that is covered with soft hair, used for making clothes: *a fur coat*

fu·ri·ous /ˈfjʊriəs/ adj **1** extremely angry **2** done with a lot of speed, energy, or determination: *The game was played at a furious pace.* —**fu·ri·ous·ly** adv

furl /fɜrl/ verb [T] to fold or roll a piece of cloth or paper

fur·long /ˈfɜrˌlɔŋ/ noun [C] a unit for measuring distance in horse races

fur·lough /ˈfɜrloʊ/ noun [C/U] a period of time during which someone is allowed to be away from a job or the military

fur·nace /ˈfɜrnɪs/ noun [C] a large enclosed container in which you burn fuel. It is used for heating a building or for an industrial process.

fur·nish /ˈfɜrnɪʃ/ verb [T] **1** to provide someone with something that they need, especially information: *Lyall's evidence may have furnished the police with a vital clue.* **2** to provide furniture for a room or house

fur·nished /ˈfɜrnɪʃt/ adj a furnished house, apartment, or room is one that you rent with furniture already in it ≠ UNFURNISHED

fur·nish·ings /ˈfɜrnɪʃɪŋz/ noun [plural] the things in a room such as furniture, carpets, and curtains

fur·ni·ture /ˈfɜrnɪtʃər/ noun [U] ★★ the chairs, tables, beds, etc. that you put in a room or house so that you can live in it

> **Furniture** is never used in the plural and cannot be used with **a**: *That's **a** lovely **piece of furniture*** (NOT a lovely furniture). ♦ *We don't need **any** more **furniture** for this room.* ♦ *I helped her to move **some furniture**.*

fu·ror /ˈfjʊˌrɔr/ noun [singular] a lot of anger, excitement, or activity

fur·row[1] /ˈfɜroʊ/ noun [C] **1** a line that a farmer digs in the dirt with a PLOW in order to grow plants **2** a deep line in the skin of someone's face

fur·row[2] /ˈfɜroʊ/ verb [I/T] if your BROW furrows, or if you furrow it, deep lines appear on your forehead

fur·ry /ˈfɜri/ adj covered with fur or with something like fur

fur·ther[1] /ˈfɜrðər/ grammar word ★★★

> Further can be:
> - an **adverb**: *She walked further up the hill.*
> - used after the verb "to be": *By road it's only six miles, but it's further if you follow the river.*
> - an **adjective**: *Further details are available from the office.*

1 to or at a greater distance from a place: *A little **further ahead**, you'll come to a crossroads.* ♦ *I would like to live **further** from the interstate.* ♦ *Paul threw the ball **further than** Steve.*
2 additional: *I have nothing further to say on the subject.* ♦ *We need a further $10,000 to complete the work.*
3 more, or to a greater degree: *The situation was further complicated by Stuart's arrival.*
4 some time before or after a particular point: *His problems started a lot **further back** than his divorce.* ♦ *Six years **further on** and still there's been no decision.*
PHRASE **go further 1** to say or do something more extreme: *By sending Lister to prison, the judge went further than the law normally allows.* **2** to continue talking about something: *Before we go any further, shall we break for lunch?*
→ FAR, NOTICE[2]

fur·ther[2] /ˈfɜrðər/ verb [T] to help something to progress or to succeed: *efforts to further the peace process*

fur·ther·more /ˈfɜrðərˌmɔr/ adv *formal* used before adding another statement to what you have just said: *What you did was extremely irresponsible. Furthermore, it achieved nothing.*

fur·thest /ˈfɜrðəst/ adj, adv **1** at the greatest distance from something: *My car is parked in the space furthest away from the building.* **2** most distant: *Merlin's fame had spread to the furthest corners of the land.* → FAR

fur·tive /ˈfɜrtɪv/ adj done quickly and secretly in order to avoid being noticed: *a furtive glance* —**fur·tive·ly** adv

fu·ry /ˈfjʊri/ noun [singular/U] **1** a feeling of very strong anger: *She was speechless with fury.* **2** the noise and force of a strong wind, storm, or flood

fuse[1] /fjuz/ noun [C] **1** an object in electrical equipment that makes it stop working when there is too much electricity flowing through it **2** an object like string, or a piece of electrical equipment, that is used for making a bomb explode

fuse[2] /fjuz/ verb [I/T] to join two substances together to form one thing, or to become joined together in this way

fu·se·lage /ˈfjuzəˌlɑʒ/ noun [C] the main part of an aircraft that the wings are attached to

fu·sion /ˈfjuʒ(ə)n/ noun [C/U] a process in which different things combine to form something new

fuss[1] /fʌs/ noun [singular/U] unnecessary worry or excitement about something: *What is all the fuss about?*
PHRASE **make a fuss over** to give a person or animal a lot of attention in order to show that you love them

fuss[2] /fʌs/ verb [I] to behave in a way that shows that you are nervous or worried, especially about unimportant things
PHRASAL VERB ˈ**fuss ˌover sb/sth** to give a person or animal a lot of attention in order to show that you love them

fuss·y /ˈfʌsi/ adj **1** only satisfied if things are exactly as you want them to be **2** *American* a fussy baby cries easily **3** containing too many small parts or details

fu·tile /ˈfjut(ə)l/ adj certain to fail or be unsuccessful: *a futile attempt* —**fu·til·i·ty** /fjuˈtɪləti/ noun [U]

fu·ton /ˈfuˌtɑn/ noun [C] a type of firm MATTRESS, used as a bed or SOFA

fu·ture[1] /ˈfjutʃər/ noun ★★★
1 the future [singular] the time that follows the present time: *It's important to plan for the future.* ♦ *Check if the computer can be upgraded **in the future**.* ♦ *I have no plans to travel **in the near future**.*
2 [C] the things that will happen to someone or something after the present time: *Jack went on vacation to think about his future.* ♦ *The people of this village face an uncertain future.*
3 [C] the chance that something will continue to exist or be successful: *We see no future in continuing the negotiations.*
4 the future [singular] *linguistics* the FUTURE TENSE of a verb
PHRASE **in the future** from the present time continuing forward in time: *In the future, please ask before you borrow my clothes.*
→ FORESEEABLE

fu·ture[2] /ˈfjutʃər/ adj ★★★
1 expected to exist or happen during the time following the present time: *at some future date* ♦ *future developments* ♦ *We need to protect the rain forest for future generations.* ♦ *his future wife* (=the woman he is going to marry)
2 *linguistics* relating to the FUTURE TENSE of a verb
PHRASE **for future reference 1** so that you can find some information in the future: *Keep this document for future reference.* **2** used for telling someone something that you feel they should know, often when you are slightly annoyed with them: *For future reference, I expect all employees to be on time.*

ˌfuture ˈperfect, the noun [singular] *linguistics* the verb tense that is used for showing that an action will be finished at a particular time in the future, as in "He will have finished the work by Friday."

ˌfuture ˈtense, the noun [singular] *linguistics* the verb tense that is used for talking about future time

fu·tur·is·tic /ˌfjutʃəˈrɪstɪk/ adj very modern in a way that seems to belong to the future

fuzz /fʌz/ noun [U] **1** a lot of short soft hairs

F

or fibers like hairs **2** *American* a small mass of fibers that usually come from clothes =FLUFF

fuzz•y /ˈfʌzi/ adj **1** a fuzzy picture or image is not clear so that you cannot see all its details **2** covered with short soft hairs or fibers like hair

fwy abbrev *American* freeway

FYI abbrev for your information: used in e-mails and TEXT MESSAGES as a way of introducing a useful piece of information

G g

g¹ or **G** /dʒi/ noun [C/U] the seventh letter of the English alphabet

g² abbrev gram

G¹ /dʒi/ noun [C] *science* gravity: a measurement of the force of GRAVITY

G² /dʒi/ abbrev *American* General Audiences: used for saying that a movie is appropriate for anyone to watch

GA abbrev Georgia

gab•ble /ˈgæb(ə)l/ verb [I/T] *informal* to talk very quickly in a way that is difficult for people to understand

ga•ble /ˈgeɪb(ə)l/ noun [C] the top part of a wall of a building just below the roof. A gable is shaped like a TRIANGLE.

gadg•et /ˈgædʒət/ noun [C] a small tool or piece of equipment that does something that is useful or impressive

gag¹ /gæg/ verb **1** [I] *informal* to be unable to swallow because you feel as if you are going to VOMIT (=bring food back up from your stomach) **2** [T] to tie a piece of cloth over someone's mouth so that they cannot speak or make a noise **3** [T] to officially prevent someone from talking about or publishing something

gag² /gæg/ noun [C] **1** a piece of cloth that you tie over someone's mouth in order to stop them from speaking or making a noise **2** *informal* a joke, trick, or story that makes people laugh

gag•gle /ˈgæg(ə)l/ noun [C] **1** a group of GEESE **2** *informal* a noisy and uncontrolled group of people

gai•ly /ˈgeɪli/ adv in a happy and lively way

gain¹ /geɪn/ verb ★★★

1 [T] to get or achieve something, usually as a result of a lot of effort: *Bolivia gained independence from Spain in 1825.* ♦ *Her theories have only recently gained acceptance.* ♦ *He* ***gained entry*** *to the building by showing a fake pass.*

2 [T] to get more of something, usually as a result of a gradual process: *I've* ***gained a lot of weight*** *this winter.* ♦ *The property has* ***gained steadily in value*** *since they bought it.* ♦ **gain sth from/by (doing) sth** *She hopes to gain experience by working abroad for a year.*

3 [I/T] to get a benefit or advantage for yourself: *Even if you fail, you will* ***gain from the experience.*** ♦ *When the business is sold, all the brothers* ***stand to gain*** (=are likely to benefit).

PHRASE **gain ground** to become more successful, popular, or accepted

PHRASAL VERB ˌ**gain on sb/sth** to gradually get closer to someone or something that you are trying to catch

gain² /geɪn/ noun **1** [C/U] an improvement or increase in something: *We have seen impressive gains in productivity over the last 12 months.* **2** [C] a benefit or advantage: *It is a policy that will bring significant gains to all sections of the community.* **3** [U] the money or other benefits that you can get from something: *He entered politics only for personal gain.* → ILL-GOTTEN GAINS

gait /geɪt/ noun [singular] the way that someone walks

gal /gæl/ noun [C] *American informal* a girl or woman

ga•la /ˈgeɪlə, ˈgɑlə/ noun [C] a special performance or event that celebrates something

gal•ax•y /ˈgæləksi/ noun [C] an extremely large group of stars and planets —**ga•lac•tic** /gəˈlæktɪk/ adj

gale /geɪl/ noun [C] a very strong wind

gall /gɔl/ noun [U] an attitude toward other people that shows a lack of respect: *He had the gall to call me a bad parent!*

gal•lant /ˈgælənt/ adj **1** *literary* brave **2** /ˈgælənt, gəˈlænt/ *old-fashioned* a man who is gallant treats women in an extremely polite and helpful way **3** a gallant effort, attempt, or fight is one in which you try very hard, but do not succeed —**gal•lant•ly** adv

ˈ**gall ˌbladder** noun [C] the organ in your body that stores BILE

gal•ler•y /ˈgæl(ə)ri/ noun [C] **1** a public building where you can look at paintings and other works of art **2** an upper level in a building such as a church or court

gal•ley /ˈgæli/ noun [C] **1** the kitchen on a boat or an airplane **2** a long ancient Greek or Roman ship that used sails and SLAVES with OARS to move it

gal•lon /ˈgælən/ noun [C] ★ a unit for measuring an amount of liquid, equal to 3.79 liters: *a gallon of gas*

gal•lop /ˈgæləp/ verb [I] if a horse gallops, it runs at its fastest speed —**gal•lop** noun [singular]

gal•lows /ˈgæloʊz/ (plural **gal•lows**) noun [C] a wooden frame that is used for hanging criminals as a way of killing them

ga•lore /gəˈlɔr/ adj used for emphasizing how large an amount or quantity is: *There will be competitions galore, with terrific vacations to be won.*

gal•va•nize /ˈgælvəˌnaɪz/ verb [T] to shock or affect someone enough to produce a strong and immediate reaction

gam•bit /ˈgæmbɪt/ noun [C] something that you say or do in an attempt to gain an advantage

gam•ble¹ /ˈgæmb(ə)l/ verb [I/T] **1** to risk money in the hope of winning more if you are lucky: *We used to gamble at the casinos in*

Atlantic City. **2** to do something that involves risks but may result in benefits if things happen as you hope they will: *Some foreign investors are gambling on an economic recovery.* —**gam•bler** noun [C], **gam•bling** noun [U]

gam•ble² /ˈgæmb(ə)l/ noun [singular] an action or plan that involves risks but will bring benefits if it is successful

game¹ /geɪm/ noun ★★★

1 activity you do for fun	5 sth not important
2 type of sport	6 hunted animals, etc.
3 particular competition	+ PHRASES
4 major sports event	

1 [C] an activity that you take part in for fun, usually one that has rules: *Monopoly is a game for all the family.* ♦ *The children were **playing** noisy **games** in the yard.* ♦ *computer/video games*
2 [C] a type of sport: *They take **the game of** football very seriously here.*
3 [C] a particular event in which people take part in a competition: *He won the money in a poker game.* ♦ *We **played a game of** volleyball.*
4 games [plural] an event where people from different countries compete in sports such as running, jumping, and swimming: *the Olympic Games*
5 [C] an activity or situation that someone seems to be treating less seriously than it should be treated: *Marriage is just a game to them.* ♦ *They are **playing political games** with people's safety.*
6 [U] wild animals, birds, and fish that people hunt, usually for food
PHRASES **ahead of the game** in a situation that is likely to lead to success as the result of good planning, advice, or luck: *In terms of technology, this company is way ahead of the game.*
give the game away to let people know a secret when you did not intend to let them know: *The expression on her face gave the game away.*
→ BALL GAME, BOARD GAME, FAIR GAME, NAME¹

game² /geɪm/ adj prepared to try a new, difficult, or dangerous activity: *"Do you want to try it?" "Sure, I'm game."*

game•keep•er /ˈgeɪmˌkipər/ noun [C] someone whose job is to take care of the wild animals, birds, and fish on a piece of private land

ˈgame ˌshow noun [C] a television program in which people play games or answer questions in order to win prizes

gam•ut /ˈgæmət/ noun [singular] the complete range of things of a particular type

gan•der /ˈgændər/ noun [C] a male GOOSE

gang¹ /gæŋ/ noun [C] **1** a group of young people who spend time together and often cause trouble: *a study of Chicago street gangs* **2** a group of criminals working together: *a gang of thieves* **3** *informal* a group of friends

gang² /gæŋ/ PHRASAL VERB **ˌgang ˈup on sb** to join together in a group in order to hurt, frighten, or fight someone

gang•land /ˈgæŋˌlænd/ adj relating to organized criminal activities, or to the people who are involved in them

gan•gling /ˈgæŋglɪŋ/ or **gan•gly** /ˈgæŋgli/ adj very tall and thin, and not graceful

gang•ster /ˈgæŋstər/ noun [C] a member of an organized group of criminals

gaol /dʒeɪl/ a British spelling of **jail¹**

gap /gæp/ noun [C] ★★
1 a space or opening in the middle of something or between things: *He has **a gap between** his teeth.* ♦ *We waited for **a gap in** the busy traffic and crossed the street.*
2 something missing from a situation or a system that prevents it from being complete or perfect: *There are still some **gaps in** our knowledge.*
3 a large difference between things or groups: ***the gap between** rich and poor*
4 a period of time in which something does not happen: *The second book in the series came out after **a gap of** seven years.*
PHRASE **a gap in the market** an opportunity to produce something that is not yet available but that people would like to have

gape /geɪp/ verb [I] **1** to look at someone or something with your mouth open because you are very surprised **2** to open wide, or to be wide open: *The mouth of the bag gaped open.*

gap•ing /ˈgeɪpɪŋ/ adj a gaping hole is very large

ga•rage /gəˈrɑʒ, gəˈrɑdʒ/ noun ★
1 [C] a building for keeping a car in —*picture* → C1
2 [C] a place that repairs cars
3 [C] a place where you go to buy gas = GAS STATION
4 [U] a type of U.S. dance music that developed in the 1980s

gaˈrage ˌsale noun [C] *American* an occasion when someone puts things that they do not want anymore in their garage and sells them

garb /gɑrb/ noun [U] *formal* clothes: *military/formal/work garb*

gar•bage /ˈgɑrbɪdʒ/ noun [U] ★
1 waste material that you are throwing away, for example food that you do not want or empty containers
2 *informal* something that someone says or writes that is completely false, silly, or wrong

ˈgarbage ˌcan noun [C] *American* a large deep container with a lid that you keep outside for holding garbage

ˈgarbage colˌlector noun [C] *American* someone whose job is to collect garbage

ˈgarbage disˌposal noun [C] *American* a piece of electrical equipment under the kitchen SINK that cuts food waste into very small pieces

gar•bage•man /ˈgɑrbɪdʒˌmæn/ (plural **gar•bage•men** /ˈgɑrbɪdʒˌmen/) noun [C] *American* a man whose job is to collect garbage

ˈgarbage ˌtruck noun [C] *American* a large truck used for collecting garbage

gar•ban•zo /gɑrˈbɑnzoʊ/ or **garˈbanzo ˌbean** noun [C] *American* a CHICKPEA

gar•bled /ˈgɑrb(ə)ld/ adj not correctly organized or explained, and difficult to understand: *a garbled explanation/message*

G

gar·den[1] /ˈgɑrd(ə)n/ noun ★★★
1 [C] an area of land next to or near a house that is used for growing flowers or vegetables
2 **gardens** [plural] a large area of grass, flowers, and trees that is open to the public for their enjoyment: *They spent the afternoon wandering around the Botanical Gardens.*
3 [C] *British* a YARD

gar·den[2] /ˈgɑrd(ə)n/ verb [I] to take care of a garden and its plants —**gar·den·er** noun [C]

ˈ**garden ˌcenter** noun [C] a large store that sells plants and the tools and equipment that you need for taking care of a garden

gar·den·ing /ˈgɑrd(ə)nɪŋ/ noun [U] the activity of taking care of a garden

ˈ**garden ˌparty** noun [C] a formal party in a large yard

ˌ**garden ˈshed** noun [C] a small building for storing garden tools, bicycles, and other equipment —*picture* → C1

ˈ**garden-vaˌriety** adj *American* ordinary and not very interesting

gar·gle /ˈgɑrg(ə)l/ verb [I] to move liquid around in the back of your mouth, in order to clean your mouth and throat

gar·ish /ˈgerɪʃ/ adj very bright and colorful in an ugly way

gar·land /ˈgɑrlənd/ noun [C] a ring of flowers or leaves that you decorate something with

gar·lic /ˈgɑrlɪk/ noun [U] a round white vegetable that is made up of sections. You use the sections in cooking in order to give it a strong flavor. —*picture* → C11

gar·ment /ˈgɑrmənt/ noun [C] *formal* a piece of clothing

gar·nish /ˈgɑrnɪʃ/ noun [C] something that you add to a dish of food to make it look more attractive —**gar·nish** verb [T]

gar·ri·son /ˈgerɪs(ə)n/ noun [C] a group of soldiers who live in a particular place and defend it

gas[1] /gæs/ noun ★★★
1 [U] *American* a liquid fuel that is used for producing power in the engines of cars =GASOLINE
2 [C/U] a substance such as air that is neither a solid nor a liquid: *gases such as carbon dioxide*
3 [U] a gas that is burned as fuel, for example to heat your house or cook food: *Can you smell gas?* ♦ *a gas stove/heater/boiler* ♦ *She couldn't pay her gas bill.*
4 [U] *American* a gas that is produced inside your body by your stomach
PHRASE **run out of gas** *American* to no longer have the energy to continue or finish something

gas[2] /gæs/ verb [T] to attack or kill someone by making them breathe a poisonous gas

ˈ**gas ˌcap** noun [C] *American* the cover that fits on the hole where you put the gas in your car —*picture* → C6

ˈ**gas ˌchamber** noun [C] a room that is used for killing prisoners by filling the air with a poisonous gas

gash /gæʃ/ noun [C] a long deep cut in your skin or in the surface of something —**gash** verb [T]

ˈ**gas ˌmask** noun [C] a special covering for your face that protects you from a poisonous gas

gas·o·line /ˈgæsəˌlin, ˌgæsəˈlin/ noun [C/U] *American* GAS that you put in your car

gasp /gæsp/ verb [I] **1** to breathe in suddenly because you are surprised, shocked, or in pain: *He gasped as the freezing water hit his body.* **2** to make a violent effort to breathe because you need more air: *Laura coughed and spluttered as she gasped for air.* —**gasp** noun [C]: *a gasp of pain/surprise/relief*

ˈ**gas ˌpedal** noun [C] *American informal* the flat object you press with your foot to make a vehicle go faster

ˈ**gas ˌpump** noun [C] *American* the machine at a gas station that the gas you put in your car comes out of

ˈ**gas ˌstation** noun [C] *American* a place that sells gas, oil, and other things that you need for your car

ˈ**gas ˌtank** noun [C] *American* the container inside a vehicle that holds the gas that it uses in order to run

gas·tric /ˈgæstrɪk/ adj *medical* relating to your stomach

gas·tro·nom·ic /ˌgæstrəˈnɑmɪk/ adj *formal* relating to skillful methods of cooking food, or to the enjoyment of good food

gate /geɪt/ noun [C] ★★
1 a door in a fence or wall that you go through in order to enter or leave a place: *Be sure to close the gate when you leave.*
2 the place at an airport where people get on an airplane: *Delta Airlines Flight 17 to New York is now boarding at Gate 21.*

gate·crash·er /ˈgeɪtˌkræʃər/ noun [C] someone who comes to a party or social event without being invited

gate·way /ˈgeɪtˌweɪ/ noun [C] **1** an entrance that is opened and closed with a gate **2 a gateway to sth** a way of going somewhere or doing something: *Bombay was considered the gateway to India.* **3** *computing* a way of connecting two computer NETWORKS so that information can pass between them

gath·er /ˈgæðər/ verb ★★

1 come together	4 increase
2 find information	5 bring things together
3 find things you need	6 believe sth

1 [I/T] if people gather, or if someone gathers them, they come together in one place in order to do something: *She gathered her children and ran for shelter.* ♦ ***A crowd gathered** outside the hotel.*
2 [T] to look for and find information or documents in different places: *The information has been gathered from all parts of the country.* ♦ *The police have been gathering evidence against him.*
3 [T] to search for and find similar things that you need or want: *Bees were gathering pollen.*
4 [T] if something gathers force, speed, or strength, its force, speed, or strength increases: *The train pulled away slowly, then **gathered speed**.*
5 [T] to bring things closer together, for example in order to protect something or make it neat: *She gathered her hair into a knot at the back of her head.*
6 [I/T] to believe that something is true,

although no one has directly told you about it: ***From what I can gather** she's madly in love with him.* ♦ *I **gather that** the storm caused a power failure.*

gath•er•ing /ˈgæð(ə)rɪŋ/ noun [C] a group of people meeting together: *a large social/family gathering*

gaud•y /ˈgɔdi/ adj brightly colored and ugly or of bad quality

gauge¹ /geɪdʒ/ noun [C] **1** a piece of equipment that measures the amount of something: *the fuel/gas/pressure gauge* **2** a fact or event that can be used for judging someone or something: *New orders are a gauge of how well manufacturers are doing.* **3** a measurement of how thick or wide something is, or of how far apart two things are: *heavy-gauge plastic*

gauge² /geɪdʒ/ verb [T] **1** to make a judgment or guess about something using the information that you have: *He looked at her, trying to gauge her response.* **2** to measure the amount, strength, or speed of something

gaunt /gɔnt/ adj looking very thin, tired, and not healthy

gaunt•let /ˈgɔntlət/ noun [C] a thick heavy GLOVE that you wear to protect your hand and lower arm

PHRASES **run the gauntlet** to experience a difficult situation, for example a lot of questions, criticism, or attacks

throw down the gauntlet to make it clear that you want to argue or fight with someone about something

gauze /gɔz/ noun [U] white cotton cloth that is very thin and has been woven in a loose way. It is often used for covering a cut or an injury.

gave the past tense of **give**

gawk /gɔk/ verb [I] *informal* to look at someone or something for a long time in a rude or stupid way

gay¹ /geɪ/ adj **1** sexually attracted to people of the same sex **2** *old-fashioned* brightly-colored, or attractive **3** *old-fashioned* happy and excited

Words that avoid giving offense: gay

Use **gay** to describe men who are sexually attracted to other men. Avoid using **gay** as a noun, especially in the singular. **Gay** can also be used about women who are sexually attracted to other women, but the more usual word is **lesbian**.

gay² /geɪ/ noun [C] someone who is sexually attracted to people of the same sex

gaze¹ /geɪz/ verb [I] to look at someone or something for a long time: *They gazed into each other's eyes.*

gaze² /geɪz/ noun [singular] a look at someone or something that lasts for a long time: *His gaze remained fixed on her face.*

GDP /ˌdʒi di ˈpi/ noun [C] gross domestic product: the total value of the goods and services that a country produces in a year. It does not include income that is received from money that is invested in other countries. → GNP

gear¹ /gɪr/ noun ★

1 [C/U] the part of an engine that changes engine power into movement: ***in first/second/third gear*** ♦ *Helen **changed gears** as she approached the intersection.*

2 [U] the special clothes and equipment that you use for a particular activity: *We took down the tent and packed all the gear away.* ♦ *The police were dressed in riot gear.* ♦ *Don't forget to bring hiking gear.*

3 [U] a machine, or a part of a machine, that does a particular job: *heavy lifting gear*

gear² /gɪr/ verb [I/T] **be geared to/toward/for** to be organized in a way that is appropriate for a particular person or thing: *The museum is geared toward children.*

PHRASAL VERB ˌ**gear (yourself)** ˈ**up** to prepare for an activity or event: *The town is gearing up for the carnival this weekend.*

GED /ˌdʒi i ˈdi/ noun [C] *American* general equivalency diploma: a document given to students who have not completed HIGH SCHOOL but have passed an examination in several subjects at that level

gee /dʒi/ interjection *American* used to express a reaction such as surprise or admiration

geek /gik/ noun [C] *informal* someone who is boring, strange, or seems to be interested only in computers —**geek•y** adj

geese the plural of **goose**

geez /dʒiz/ another spelling of **jeez**

gel¹ /dʒel/ noun [C/U] a sticky substance that is used in products for your hair and skin

gel² /dʒel/ verb [I] **1** if a group gels, the people in it form a successful or friendly relationship **2** if a thought or idea gels, it becomes clearer **3** if a substance gels it becomes thicker

gel•a•tin /ˈdʒelət(ə)n/ noun [U] a clear substance used in cooking to make liquids become thick and firm

gem /dʒem/ noun [C] **1** a valuable stone that is used to make jewelry **2** someone or something that is special in some way: *She's a real gem.*

Gem•i•ni /ˈdʒemɪˌnaɪ/ noun [C/U] one of the 12 signs of the ZODIAC. A **Gemini** is someone who was born between May 22 and June 21.

gen•der /ˈdʒendər/ noun **1** [C/U] *formal* the fact of being either male or female = SEX: *The job is open to all applicants regardless of age, race, or gender.* **2** [C] all male people, or all female people = SEX: *the entire male gender* **3** [C/U] *linguistics* the gender of a word is whether it is MASCULINE, FEMININE, or NEUTER

gene /dʒin/ noun [C] *science* a pattern of chemicals within a cell. The chemicals carry information about the qualities that are passed from parent animals, plants, or organisms to their children.

ge•ne•al•o•gy /ˌdʒiniˈælədʒi/ noun **1** [C/U] the study of the history of families, or the history of one family **2** [C] the history of a particular family, including how all the people are related to each other —**ge•ne•a•log•i•cal** /ˌdʒiniəˈlɑdʒɪk(ə)l/ adj, **ge•ne•al•o•gist** /ˌdʒiniˈælədʒɪst/ noun [C]

gen•er•al¹ /ˈdʒen(ə)rəl/ adj ★★★

1 not specific, exact, or detailed: *Could you just give us a general description of the work you do?* ♦ *I'm probably not making myself very clear, but you get **the general idea**.*

G

2 involving or true for most people, things, or situations: *There was general agreement at the meeting that the plan was too expensive.* ♦ *The fighting could escalate into a more general war.* ♦ ***As a general rule,*** *shorter sentences are easier to understand.*
3 used for describing the whole of something, without considering the details: *Your general health seems very good.*
4 dealing with all areas of a subject or activity, rather than concentrating on a particular area: *a good general introduction to the subject* ♦ *general knowledge*
PHRASE **in general 1** in most situations or for most people: *I don't think people in general give much thought to the environment.* **2** as a whole, without giving details: *In general, the standard of your work is very high.*

G

gen·er·al² /ˈdʒen(ə)rəl/ noun [C] an officer of high rank in the army, air force, or MARINES

ˌgeneral anesˈthetic noun [C/U] a substance that a doctor puts into your body so that you will sleep and not feel any pain during an operation → LOCAL ANESTHETIC

ˌgeneral eˈlection noun [C] an election in which every adult in the country can vote for the people who will represent them

gen·er·al·i·za·tion /ˌdʒen(ə)rəlɪˈzeɪʃ(ə)n/ noun [C/U] a statement that seems to be true in most situations but that may not be true in all situations

gen·er·al·ize /ˈdʒen(ə)rəˌlaɪz/ verb [I] **1** to make a statement or remark about a group of people or things without giving details: *We can generalize and say that most of our students are middle-class.* **2** to give an opinion about a group of people or things that is often unfair, because it makes them all seem the same when they are not

gen·er·al·ly /ˈdʒen(ə)rəli/ adv ★★★
1 used for saying what is usually true or typical: *The food is generally pretty good in this restaurant.*
2 used for describing or considering something as a whole, without details: *His attitude to me was generally unfriendly.*
3 by most people, or in most instances: *Scientists generally agree that the new disease is caused by a virus.* ♦ *The church is generally accepted as one of the world's greatest buildings.*
→ SPEAK

ˌgeneral ˈpublic, the noun [singular] ★ ordinary people in society, rather than a particular group

ˈgeneral ˌstore noun [C] *American* a store that sells a wide range of products, often found in small communities

ˌgeneral ˈstrike noun [C] a situation in which most or all workers stop working in order to try to get better working conditions or higher pay

gen·er·ate /ˈdʒenəˌreɪt/ verb [T] ★★
1 to produce something, or to cause something to exist: *The food processing industry generates billions of dollars a year.* ♦ *These new policies will generate jobs.*
2 to make people express feelings or opinions about something: *The advertising campaign generated a lot of interest in our work.*
3 to produce power or heat: *75% of France's electricity is generated by nuclear reactors.*

gen·er·a·tion /ˌdʒenəˈreɪʃ(ə)n/ noun ★★★
1 [C] all the people, a group of people, or the members of a family who are born and live around the same time: *The site was preserved as a monument for future generations.* ♦ *Many people from her generation still remember the war.* ♦ *a candidate that appeals mainly to the* ***older/younger generation*** (=the people in society at a particular time who are old or young) ♦ ***Generations of*** *schoolchildren have sat at these desks.*
2 [C] the number of years that usually pass between someone's birth and the birth of their children: *Within a generation, the family had lost all its wealth.*
3 [C] a group of products that were made at about the same time: *a new generation of cellphones*
4 [U] the process of producing something: *cheap electricity generation*

geneˈration ˌgap, the noun [singular] the difference in opinions or behavior between older and younger people

ˌGeneration ˈX noun *American* the people born in the 1960s and 1970s, who are sometimes seen as having no strong moral values

ˌGeneration ˈY noun *American* the people born in the 1980s and 1990s

gen·er·a·tor /ˈdʒenəˌreɪtər/ noun [C] a machine that produces electricity

ge·ner·ic /dʒəˈnerɪk/ adj **1** *formal* relating to, or appropriate for, a particular group of similar things **2** a generic drug or other product does not have a TRADEMARK and is sold without a company's name on it —**ge·ner·i·cal·ly** /dʒəˈnerɪkli/ adv

gen·er·os·i·ty /ˌdʒenəˈrɑsəti/ noun [U] kindness in giving things to people

gen·er·ous /ˈdʒen(ə)rəs/ adj ★
1 giving people more of your time or money than is usual or expected: *She is a warm and generous human being.* ♦ **generous of sb (to do sth)** *That's very generous of you.*
2 larger than is usual or necessary: *a generous helping of salad*
—**gen·er·ous·ly** adv

ge·net·ic /dʒəˈnetɪk/ adj ★ relating to genes or to the study of them: *a genetic disease* ♦ *We inherit* ***genetic characteristics*** *from our parents.* —**ge·net·i·cal·ly** /dʒəˈnetɪkli/ adv

ge·net·i·cal·ly mod·i·fied /dʒəˌnetɪkli ˈmɑdɪˌfaɪd/ adj a genetically modified substance or crop has had its genetic structure changed in order to make it more suited to a particular purpose

geˌnetic engiˈneering noun [U] the practice or science of changing the genes of a living thing

ge·net·i·cist /dʒəˈnetəsɪst/ noun [C] a scientist who studies or works in genetics

ge·net·ics /dʒəˈnetɪks/ noun [U] the study of how features of living things are passed through their genes to their children

gen·ial /ˈdʒiniəl/ adj friendly and kind

gen·i·tals /ˈdʒenɪt(ə)lz/ noun [plural] the outer sex organs of a person or animal —**gen·i·tal** adj

gen·ius /ˈdʒiniəs/ noun **1** [C] someone who is

much more intelligent or skillful than other people **2** [U] a very high level of intelligence or skill: *At the time, his appointment seemed like a stroke of genius* (=a very intelligent act or idea).

gen•o•cide /ˈdʒenəˌsaɪd/ noun [U] the murder of large numbers of people belonging to a particular race

ge•nome /ˈdʒiˌnoʊm/ noun [C] *science* the complete set of genes in a living thing

gen•re /ˈʒɑnrə/ noun [C] a particular type of movie, writing, or art, that can be recognized by specific features

gen•teel /dʒenˈtil/ adj polite and typical of people belonging to a high social class

gen•tle /ˈdʒent(ə)l/ adj ★
1 kind and calm: *Joe is such a gentle, loving boy.*
2 not using or needing a lot of force or effort: *gentle exercise*
3 a gentle slope or curve is gradual, with no sudden changes
4 not strong or unpleasant: *a gentle breeze* ♦ *a gentle voice*
—**gen•tly** adj

gen•tle•man /ˈdʒent(ə)lmən/ (plural **gen•tle•men** /ˈdʒent(ə)lmən/) noun [C] **1** a polite honest man who thinks about what other people want or need **2** used for referring politely to a man whose name you do not know: *This gentleman has a question.*

gen•tri•fi•ca•tion /ˌdʒentrɪfɪˈkeɪʃ(ə)n/ noun [U] the process by which an area where poor people lived becomes an area where middle-class people live, as they buy the houses and repair them —**gen•tri•fy** /ˈdʒentrɪˌfaɪ/ verb [T]

gen•try, the /ˈdʒentri/ noun [plural] people from a high social class

gen•u•ine /ˈdʒenjuɪn/ adj ★
1 real, and not pretended or false ≠ FAKE: *Morley looked at her with genuine concern.* ♦ *a genuine 18th century desk*
2 honest, friendly, and sincere: *Greg was a humble, genuine person.*
—**gen•u•ine•ly** adv

ge•nus /ˈdʒinəs/ noun [C] *science* a group that includes all living things that have similar features → SPECIES

ge•o•graph•i•cal /ˌdʒiəˈɡræfɪk(ə)l/ or **ge•o•graph•ic** /ˌdʒiəˈɡræfɪk/ adj relating to an area or place, or to geography —**ge•o•graph•i•cal•ly** /ˌdʒiəˈɡræfɪkli/ adv

ge•og•ra•phy /dʒiˈɑɡrəfi/ noun [U] the study of the Earth's physical features and the people, plants, and animals that live in different regions of the world
—**ge•og•ra•pher** noun [C]

ge•ol•o•gy /dʒiˈɑlədʒi/ noun [U] the scientific study of the structure of the Earth
—**ge•o•log•i•cal** /ˌdʒiəˈlɑdʒɪk(ə)l/ adj, **ge•ol•o•gist** noun [C]

ge•o•met•ric /ˌdʒiəˈmetrɪk/ or **ge•o•met•ri•cal** /ˌdʒiəˈmetrɪk(ə)l/ adj **1** relating to geometry **2** relating to simple or regular shapes

ge•om•e•try /dʒiˈɑmətri/ noun [U] the part of mathematics that deals with the relationships between lines, angles, and surfaces

ge•ra•ni•um /dʒəˈreɪniəm/ noun [C] a plant with soft round leaves and bright pink, red, or white flowers —*picture* → C9

ger•i•at•ric /ˌdʒeriˈætrɪk/ adj *medical* relating to old age, or to the process of getting older

ger•i•at•rics /ˌdʒeriˈætrɪks/ noun [U] the medical study, treatment, and care of old people and their diseases

germ /dʒɜrm/ noun **1** [C] a form of bacteria that spreads disease **2** [singular] something that could develop into a greater idea or plan: *the germ of an idea*

ˌGerman ˈmeasles noun [U] an infectious disease that causes red spots on the skin = RUBELLA

ˌGerman ˈshepherd noun [C] a large dog with thick brown and black fur and pointed ears

ger•mi•nate /ˈdʒɜrmɪˌneɪt/ verb [I/T] to develop from a seed and begin to grow into a plant, or to make a seed begin to grow —**ger•mi•na•tion** /ˌdʒɜrmɪˈneɪʃ(ə)n/ noun [U]

ger•und /ˈdʒerənd/ noun [C] *linguistics* a noun that is formed from a verb by adding "-ing." A gerund describes an action, for example "running" or "believing."

ges•ta•tion /dʒəˈsteɪʃ(ə)n/ noun [U] the time and process during which a baby develops inside its mother

ges•tic•u•late /dʒəˈstɪkjəˌleɪt/ verb [I] to make movements with your hands and arms when you are talking

ges•ture¹ /ˈdʒestʃər/ noun [C] ★
1 a movement that communicates a feeling or instruction: *an impatient gesture* ♦ *Joan raised her arms in a gesture of triumph.*
2 something that you do to communicate your intentions: *Offering to drive us there was a very nice gesture.* ♦ ***a gesture of support***

ges•ture² /ˈdʒestʃər/ verb [I] to make a movement in order to communicate something to someone

get /ɡet/ (past tense **got** /ɡɑt/; past participle **gotten** /ˈɡɑt(ə)n/) verb ★★★

1 obtain/receive	**13** send sth
2 buy sth	**14** make progress
3 bring sth	**15** fit/put sth in a place
4 think/feel sth	**16** understand
5 start to be sick	**17** be able to do sth
6 start to be	**18** catch/punish sb
7 be/become	**19** answer door/phone
8 cause to be	**20** use particular vehicle
9 do sth/have sth done	**21** prepare meal
10 make sb do sth	**22** talk to sb by phone
11 move to/from	+ PHRASAL VERBS
12 arrive	

1 [T] to obtain, receive, or be given something: *Ross's father got a new job.* ♦ *Did you get tickets for the game?* ♦ *You get ten points for each correct answer.* ♦ *Young players will* ***get the chance*** *to meet one of their heroes.* ♦ **get sth from sb** *She got a ring from her grandmother.* ♦ **get sb sth** *The agency got the family a new apartment.*
2 [T] to buy something: *They had to stop and get some gas.* ♦ **get sb sth/get sth for sb** *I got my dad a sweater for his birthday.*
3 [T] to go and bring something back from somewhere else: *She went and got a photograph from the desk.* ♦ **get sb sth/get sth for sb** *Will you get me a glass of water?*

G

4 [T] to start to have an idea or feeling: *I got a strange feeling as we walked toward the house.* ♦ *I **got the impression** they were finding the work difficult.*
5 [T] to start to have an illness or a medical condition: *I hope I don't get the flu this winter.*
6 [linking verb] to start to be in a particular state, or to start to have a particular quality =BECOME: *It's getting late – I have to go.* ♦ *It was raining and we all got wet.* ♦ *Things are starting to get difficult at home.*
7 [linking verb] to be or become: used with past participles to form PASSIVES: *I'm sick of getting yelled at for things that aren't my fault.* ♦ *Somehow the paper got ripped.* ♦ *You should wash that cut – it might get infected.*

G

8 [T] to cause someone or something to be in a particular state: *I'll get the children dressed.* ♦ *It took them three hours to get the fire under control.* ♦ *He got his suit all dirty.*
9 [T] to do something, or to have it done for you: **get sth done** *You need to get your hair cut.* ♦ *I should be able to get the first chapter finished by tonight.* ♦ **get sth doing sth** *Hal managed to get my e-mail working again.*
10 [T] to make someone do something, or to persuade them to do it: **get sb to do sth** *I'll get Andrew to give you a call.* ♦ *She couldn't get them to understand what she was saying.*
11 [I/T] to move to or from a position or place, or to make someone or something do this: *Dad stopped the car and told me to **get in**.* ♦ *A car stopped and two men **got out**.* ♦ *Half the audience **got up** and walked out.* ♦ **get sb/sth in/into sth** *Let's get you into the house where it's warm.* ♦ **get sb/sth out (of sth)** *Get that dog out of my kitchen.*
12 [I] to arrive at a place: *What time did you **get home** last night?* ♦ *When will we **get there**?* ♦ *How long does it take to **get from** St. Louis **to** Chicago?* ♦ *I usually **get to** work at about 8:30.* → ARRIVE
13 [T] to send something to a person or place: **get sth to sb/sth** *We'll get the schedule to you as soon as we have it.*
14 [I] to make progress: *How far did you get with your homework?* ♦ *I'm **not getting anywhere** with this paper* (=not making any progress). ♦ *At last she is starting to **get somewhere** in her career* (=make some progress). ♦ *Everyone finds driving difficult at first, but you're **getting there*** (=making progress).
15 [T] **get sth into/in/onto sth** to fit or put something in a place: *You can get a lot of things into this bag.*
16 [T] *informal* to understand someone or something: *Everyone laughed, but Harold didn't seem to **get the joke**.* ♦ ***I don't get it** – what's happening?*
17 [I/T] to have the opportunity or be able to do something: **get to do sth** *Did you get to visit the Vietnam Memorial when you were in Washington?*
18 [T] to catch or punish someone: *The police need to get the person who did this.*
19 [T] *spoken* to answer the door or phone: *It's OK, I'll get it.*
20 [T] to use a particular vehicle to travel somewhere: *It's easiest if you get a taxi from the station.*
21 [T] to prepare a meal: *It's time to start getting dinner.*
22 [T] to succeed in talking to someone by phone: *Could you get me the New York office right away, please.*
→ HOLD², KNOW¹

PHRASAL VERBS ˌ**get sth aˈcross** to make people understand something: **get sth across to sb** *What message are you trying to get across to the consumer?*
ˌ**get aˈhead** to become more successful or progress more quickly than other people: *The best way to get ahead is through hard work.* ♦ *Sometimes you have to be ruthless to get ahead in business.*
ˌ**get aˈlong 1** if people get along, they like each other and are friendly to each other: *Richard and his sister don't get along.* ♦ *I **get along well with** most of my colleagues.* **2** to manage to continue doing something, or to manage to make progress in a situation: *I got along much better in my new job.* ♦ *How are you **getting along with** your schoolwork?*
ˌ**get aˈround** if news gets around, a lot of people hear it
ˌ**get aˈround sth** to solve a problem, or to avoid a difficulty that something is causing: *There are ways of getting around the tax rules.* ♦ *You can't get around the fact she lied.*
ˌ**get aˈround to sth** to do something after you have intended to do it for some time: *I meant to call you, but somehow I never got around to it.* ♦ **get around to doing sth** *We have to get around to cleaning those windows.*
ˈ**get at sth 1** to manage to reach or touch something: *I keep the cookies up here where the children can't get at them.* **2** to try to suggest something without saying it directly: *What are you getting at?*
ˌ**get aˈway 1** to escape from a person or place: *A police officer grabbed him, but he got away.* ♦ *The dog **got away from** me in the park.* **2** to manage to leave a place: *He said he'd meet me for lunch if he could get away.* **3** to go somewhere different from where you live in order to have a rest or a vacation: *On days like today, I just want to **get away from it all**.*
ˌ**get aˈway with sth** to manage to do something bad without being punished or criticized for it: *They have repeatedly broken the law and gotten away with it.* ♦ **get away with doing sth** *How can he get away with speaking to her like that?*
ˌ**get ˈback 1** to return to a place: *It's late, I ought to get back.* ♦ *What time does Sara **get back from work**?* **2** to begin doing something again after not doing it for a period of time: *She was eager to **get back to work** after she had her baby.* **3** to return to the state or condition that you were in before: *I woke early and couldn't **get back to sleep**.*
ˌ**get sb ˈback** to hurt or upset someone because they have hurt or upset you
ˌ**get sth ˈback** to receive or have something again after a time when it was taken away from you or lost: *She left her briefcase on the train and she doesn't know how to get it back.*

ˌget ˈback at sb to hurt or upset someone because they have hurt or upset you: *She was trying to get back at him for embarrassing her.*

ˌget ˈback to sb *spoken* to call, write, or speak to someone at a later time because you were busy or could not answer their question earlier: *Can you **get back to** me on those figures by the end of the day?*

ˌget beˈhind if you get behind with work or payments, you have not done as much work or made as many payments as you should have done

ˌget ˈby to have just enough of something such as money or knowledge so that you can do what you need to do: *My math isn't very good, but I get by.* ♦ *I can **get by on** $1,500 a month if I'm careful.* ♦ *You could probably **get by with** that computer, but a more powerful one would be better.*

ˌget sb ˈdown *informal* to make someone feel sad or lose hope: *Doing the same thing every day can get you down.*

ˌget ˈdown to sth to start doing something seriously or with a lot of effort: *After lunch we got down to discussing the issue of pay.*

ˌget ˈin 1 if a train, airplane, etc. gets in, it arrives: *Our flight got in on time.* **2** to be accepted to study at a school, or to be chosen to play for a team

ˌget ˈin on sth *informal* to become involved in something

ˌget ˈinto sth 1 *informal* to start enjoying something, or to become enthusiastic about it: *You feel shy when you start your speech, but then you get into it.* **2** to become involved in a bad situation: *Those kids are always **getting into trouble**.* **3** to be accepted to study at a school, or to be chosen to play for a team

ˌget ˈoff to not be punished severely, or to not be punished at all, for something that you have been accused of in court: *He was charged with manslaughter, but got off.* ♦ *At best you can hope to **get off with** a $100 fine.*

ˌget ˈoff (sth) to leave the place you work at the end of the day: *What time do you **get off work**?*

ˌget ˈoff (sb/sth) 1 used for telling someone to stop touching someone or something: *Get off – you're hurting my back.* ♦ *Get off the grass right now!* **2 where does sb get off doing sth?** *American spoken* used for saying that you think someone is wrong to behave in a particular way

ˌget sth ˈoff to have a particular period of time as a vacation: *Do you **get much time off** at Christmas?*

ˌget ˈoff on sth *informal* to enjoy something and become very excited about it

ˌget ˈon sb *American* to remind someone to do something: *Get on Bill to see if he can come up with those numbers for you.*

ˌget ˈon sth to be chosen to be part of a group or team: *Claire got on the school board.*

ˌget ˈonto sth 1 to start talking about a subject: *How did we get onto this subject?* **2** *same as* **get on sth**: *Things changed when he got onto the selection committee.*

ˌget ˈon with sth to give your time to something and make progress with it: *Let's finish the speeches, so we can get on with the celebration.* ♦ **get on with doing sth** *I want to get on with fixing lunch.*

ˌget ˈout 1 used for telling someone to leave: *The teacher screamed at him to get out.* ♦ ***Get out of** my house!* **2** if something secret gets out, a lot of people find out about it: *There was a huge public outcry when the news got out.* ♦ **+that** *It quickly got out that Mariel was leaving Danny.*

ˌget sth ˈout to manage to say something: *He tried to protest, but couldn't get the words out.*

ˌget ˈout of sth 1 to avoid doing something that you should do, or that you said that you would do: *I said I'd meet him, but now I want to get out of it.* ♦ **get out of doing sth** *Ruth always tries to get out of doing the dishes.* **2 get out of here** *American spoken* used for saying that you do not believe what someone is telling you

ˌget sth ˈout of sb to persuade someone to give you information or money

ˌget sth ˈout of sth to get pleasure or a benefit from something: *He gets a lot of satisfaction out of being a teacher.*

ˌget ˈover sth 1 to start to feel happy or well again after something bad has happened to you: *It can take weeks to get over an illness like that.* ♦ *Don's pretty upset, but he'll get over it.* **2 can't get over sth** used for saying that you are very surprised by something, or that you think it is funny: *I just can't get over how well we played!*

ˌget sth ˈover with to do something, or to allow something to happen, because you want it to be finished: *I wanted to get the interview over with as quickly as possible.*

ˌget ˈthrough to succeed in talking to someone by phone: *I couldn't get through – the line was busy.* ♦ *I finally **got through to** Warren on his cellphone.*

ˌget ˈthrough sth to manage to deal with a difficult situation, or to stay alive until it is over: *The refugees will need help to get through the winter.*

ˌget ˈthrough to sb to make someone understand what you are trying to say: *I feel I'm not getting through to some of the kids in my class.*

ˈget to sb *informal* to annoy or upset someone: *After a while his teasing started to get to me.*

ˌget toˈgether 1 if people get together, they meet in order to do something or in order to spend time together: *The whole family usually gets together at least once a year.* ♦ *He **got together with** some friends to plan a party for her.* **2 get it together** to be in control of your life, so that you are successful and are doing what you want to do

ˌget ˈup to get out of bed after sleeping: *He never gets up before nine.*

ˌget sb ˈup to wake someone and tell them to get out of bed: *Will you get me up at six tomorrow?*

ˌget ˈup to sth *spoken* to do something, especially something that you should not do: *The children get up to all sorts of mischief when I'm not here.*

ˈget with *spoken* **get with the program** to pay attention to what is happening and start doing what you should be doing

G

get·a·way /ˈgetəˌweɪ/ noun **make a getaway** **1** to escape after committing a crime **2** to get away from a boring social situation

ˈget-toˌgether noun [C] an informal social occasion

gey·ser /ˈgaɪzər/ noun [C] a place where hot water and steam move very quickly and suddenly up out of the earth

ghast·ly /ˈgæs(t)li/ adj very bad or unpleasant

ghet·to /ˈgetoʊ/ noun [C] an area in a city where people live in poor conditions

ghost /goʊst/ noun [C] the spirit of a dead person that someone believes that they can see or hear

ghost·ly /ˈgoʊs(t)li/ adj reminding you of a ghost

ˈghost ˌtown noun [C] a town that most people have left

ghoul /gul/ noun [C] an imaginary creature that eats dead people

GI /ˌdʒi ˈaɪ/ noun [C] a soldier

gi·ant[1] /ˈdʒaɪənt/ noun [C] **1** a person in stories who is much bigger than a normal human **2** a very large successful company, or a successful important person: *the Dutch electronics giant Phillips*

gi·ant[2] /ˈdʒaɪənt/ adj extremely large: *a giant bronze statue*

gib·ber·ish /ˈdʒɪbərɪʃ/ noun [U] *informal* nonsense

gibe /dʒaɪb/ noun [C] a remark that is intended to hurt someone or to make them feel stupid

gid·dy /ˈgɪdi/ adj very excited and happy

gift /gɪft/ noun [C] ★★

1 something that you give to someone as a present: *a gift from a friend* ♦ *He* ***bought gifts for everyone.***

2 a natural ability to do something well: *She* ***has a gift for*** *languages.*

3 something good that you are grateful that you have: ***the gift of sight***

ˈgift cerˌtificate noun [C] *American* a document that you buy in a store as a present for someone, so that they can exchange it for something they want to buy

gift·ed /ˈgɪftəd/ adj a gifted person has an impressive natural ability

ˈgift ˌwrap noun [U] attractive colored paper that you use for wrapping presents

gift-wrapped /ˈgɪftˌræpt/ adj an object that is gift-wrapped is covered in attractive paper so that it can be given as a present —**gift-ˌwrap** verb [T]

gig /gɪg/ noun [C] a public performance of popular music or jazz

gi·ga·byte /ˈgɪgəˌbaɪt/ noun [C] *computing* a unit for measuring computer information, equal to 1,024 MEGABYTES

gi·gan·tic /dʒaɪˈgæntɪk/ adj extremely large

gig·gle /ˈgɪg(ə)l/ verb [I] to laugh in a nervous, excited, or silly way —**gig·gle** noun [C]

gild /gɪld/ verb [T] to cover a surface with a very thin layer of gold

gill /gɪl/ noun [C] one of the organs behind the head of a fish that allows it to breathe

gilt /gɪlt/ noun [U] a thin layer of gold or gold paint —**gilt** adj

gim·me /ˈgɪmi/ short form *informal* a way of writing "give me" that shows how it sounds in informal conversation

gim·mick /ˈgɪmɪk/ noun [C] something that is intended to impress you or get your attention but is not necessary or useful: *a sales gimmick* ♦ *a gimmick to win votes* —**gim·mick·y** adj

gin /dʒɪn/ noun [C/U] a strong clear alcoholic drink, or a glass of this drink

gin·ger /ˈdʒɪndʒər/ noun [U] a light brown root with a strong flavor that is used in cooking —*picture* → C11

gin·ger·ly /ˈdʒɪndʒərli/ adv in a very slow and careful way

gip·sy /ˈdʒɪpsi/ a British spelling of **gypsy**

gi·raffe /dʒəˈræf/ noun [C] a tall African animal that has a very long neck and very long legs —*picture* → C12

gird·er /ˈgɜrdər/ noun [C] a large metal bar that is used for making the frame of a building or a bridge

gir·dle /ˈgɜrd(ə)l/ noun [C] a piece of tight underwear that some women wear to make them look thinner

girl /gɜrl/ noun ★★★

1 [C] a female child: *There are 15 girls in my son's class.* ♦ *What a pretty* ***little girl!***

2 [C] a daughter: *Mary's two girls still live at home.*

3 [C] a young adult woman. Many people think that this use is offensive: *Who was that beautiful girl I saw you with last night?*

4 **the girls** [plural] a woman's female friends. Some people think that this use is offensive when it is used by men.

girl·friend /ˈgɜrlˌfrend/ noun [C] ★

1 a woman that you are having a romantic or sexual relationship with: *Do you have a girlfriend?*

2 a woman's female friend

girl·ish /ˈgɜrlɪʃ/ adj looking or behaving like a young girl

ˌGirl ˈScout noun [C] *American* a girl who is a member of the Scout Association, an organization for young people

girth /gɜrθ/ noun [C/U] the distance around something, for example a tree

gist, the /dʒɪst/ noun [singular] the main idea, or the general meaning of something

give[1] /gɪv/ (past tense **gave** /geɪv/; past participle **giv·en** /ˈgɪv(ə)n/) verb ★★★

1 provide sb with sth	8 help sb
2 make sb owner of sth	9 allow sb to do sth
3 put medicine in sb	10 pass illness to sb else
4 have an effect	11 pay money
5 make sb believe sth	12 stretch/bend/break
6 communicate	+ PHRASE
7 perform action	+ PHRASAL VERBS

1 [T] to provide someone with something: **give sb sth** *Could you give me that pen?* ♦ *We don't know what to give Dad for Christmas.* ♦ **give sth to sb** *I gave the keys to John yesterday.*

2 [T] to make someone the owner of something that you owned: **give sb sth** *Ken gave me his old tennis racket.* ♦ **give sth to sb** *He gave the house to his children.*

3 [T] to put medicine into someone's body using a particular method: *The drug is normally given by injection.*
4 [T] to cause a general result or effect: **give sb/sth sth** *The results gave us a distinct shock.* ♦ *Some laundry detergents give cotton a softer feel.*
5 [T] to make someone think or believe something: *We don't want to* ***give the impression*** *that every child is at risk.* ♦ *The hotel isn't as comfortable as we were* ***given to understand*** (=as we were told).
6 [T] to show or communicate information: *The answers are given on page 78.* ♦ *Someone from the university will* ***give a talk*** *on the future of education.* ♦ **give sb sth/ give sth to sb** *If you see him, will you give him a message from me?*
7 [T] to perform an action: *I'd never ridden a horse before, but I was prepared to* ***give it a try*** (=try to do it). ♦ **give sb/sth sth** *I gave him a hug before he left.* ♦ *I'll* ***give you a call*** (=phone you) *on Sunday.*
8 [I/T] to do something good or helpful for someone: *a relationship where one partner gives more than the other* ♦ **give sth to sb/sth** *Aid will be given to areas where the flooding is worst.*
9 [T] to allow someone to do something: *We asked to go out, and the teacher* ***gave her permission.*** ♦ **give sb sth** *They should have given us more time to finish the test.*
10 [T] to pass an illness or disease to another person: **give sb sth** *She gave the whole office the flu.* ♦ **give sth to sb** *You could easily give the disease to your partner.*
11 [T] *spoken* to pay money for something: **give sb sth** *Martin gave me $500 for my computer.*
12 [I] to stretch, bend, or break: *The bridge has to be able to give a little in the wind.*
PHRASE **give or take** used for saying that a number or quantity may be a little more or less than the number or quantity mentioned: *Each talk lasts half an hour, give or take five minutes.*
→ WAY[1]
PHRASAL VERBS ˌ**give sth aˈway 1** to let someone know a secret, often by accident: *If captured, they might give away vital military secrets.* ♦ *Her expression gave nothing away.* **2** to provide someone with something that you no longer want or need: *I gave my plants* ***away to*** *the neighbors.*
ˌ**give sth ˈback** to give someone something that they had or owned before: *The company had to give back all the money.* ♦ **give sb back sth** *We just want them to give us back our home.*
ˌ**give ˈin** to stop competing or arguing and accept that you cannot win: *The government has said that it will never* ***give in to*** *terrorist threats.*
ˌ**give ˈoff sth** to produce something such as heat or a smell: *When they die, plants give off gases.*
ˌ**give ˈout** to stop working correctly: *His heart finally gave out under the strain.*
ˌ**give sth ˈout** to give something to several people: *The office gives out financial advice to students.*
ˌ**give ˈup (sth)** to stop trying to do something because it is too difficult: *I give up. Tell me the answer.* ♦ **give up doing sth** *We've given up trying to persuade them to change.*
ˌ**give sth ˈup 1** to stop doing something that you do regularly: *I'm trying to give up smoking.* **2** to allow someone to have something that was yours: *The new arrangement would mean giving up some of their political independence.*
ˌ**give ˈup on sb** to stop hoping that someone will improve, and stop trying to help them or to change them: *Most of the teachers gave up on her years ago.*

give² /gɪv/ noun [U] the tendency to bend or stretch
PHRASE **give and take** *informal* if there is give and take between people, each person allows the other to get something that they want

give·a·way /ˈgɪvəˌweɪ/ noun [singular] a movement, action, or expression on someone's face that shows the truth about something: *I knew she'd passed. Her face was a dead giveaway* (=an obvious giveaway).

giv·en¹ /ˈgɪv(ə)n/ adj **1** used for referring to a particular thing = PARTICULAR: *In a given situation, more than one method may be used.* **2** a given period has previously been decided on: *Many people pay off the money owed within a given time.*

giv·en² /ˈgɪv(ə)n/ preposition because of a particular fact = CONSIDERING: *Given that conflict happens, we need to learn how to manage it.*

giv·en³ the past participle of **give¹**

ˈ**given ˌname** noun [C] the name that your parents give you when you are born = FIRST NAME → NAME

gla·cial /ˈgleɪʃ(ə)l/ adj relating to, or created by, glaciers

gla·cier /ˈgleɪʃər/ noun [C] a very large mass of ice that moves very slowly

glad /glæd/ adj ★★ happy and pleased about something: *"We're having a great time." "I'm so glad."* ♦ **+(that)** *I'm glad he finally called you.* ♦ **glad to do sth** *Maggie was glad to be home.* → GLADLY
PHRASE **glad to do sth** willing or ready to do something: *I'd be glad to watch the kids for you this afternoon.*

glade /gleɪd/ noun [C] *literary* an area in a forest where there are no trees or bushes = CLEARING

glad·i·a·tor /ˈglædiˌeɪtər/ noun [C] in ancient Rome, someone who fought people or wild animals as a form of public entertainment

glad·ly /ˈglædli/ adv in a willing or happy way

glam·or /ˈglæmər/ an American spelling of **glamour**

glam·or·ize /ˈglæməˌraɪz/ verb [T] to make someone or something seem to be more attractive or exciting than they really are

glam·or·ous /ˈglæm(ə)rəs/ adj **1** attractive or exciting in an unusual way: *a glamorous lifestyle* **2** a glamorous person is attractive, rich, and famous

glam·our /ˈglæmər/ noun [U] a special quality that makes someone or something seem to be very attractive or exciting

G

glance[1] /glæns/ verb [I] ★ to look somewhere quickly and then look away: *"I have to go," Jen said, **glancing at** her watch.* ♦ *Robin **glanced around** the room.*
PHRASAL VERB ˈ**glance off sth** to hit something at an angle and then move away in a different direction

glance[2] /glæns/ noun [C] a quick look at someone or something: *After a quick glance around the room, she turned and left.*
PHRASE **at a glance** if you know something at a glance, you know it as soon as you see someone or something
→ FIRST

G

gland /glænd/ noun [C] a part of your body that produces a substance that your body needs —**glan•du•lar** /ˈglændʒələr/ adj

glare[1] /gler/ verb [I] **1** to look at someone or something in a very angry way: *Dan glared at me and immediately left the room.* **2** to shine with a very bright light that makes you feel uncomfortable

glare[2] /gler/ noun **1** [singular/U] a very bright light that makes you feel uncomfortable **2** [C] an angry look

glar•ing /ˈglerɪŋ/ adj **1** a glaring mistake is very obvious **2** a glaring light shines very brightly in a way that makes you feel uncomfortable —**glar•ing•ly** adv: *glaringly obvious*

glass /glæs/ noun ★★★
1 [U] a hard clear substance that is used for making objects such as windows or bottles: *the sound of breaking glass* ♦ *a glass bowl*
2 [C] a small container made of glass that you use for drinking from, or the drink in it: *a wine/brandy/beer glass* ♦ *She drank three **glasses of** milk.*
3 [U] attractive objects made of glass: *a beautiful collection of Italian glass*

glass ˈceiling noun [C] an unfair system that prevents some people from reaching the most senior positions in a company or organization

glass•es /ˈglɑsəz/ noun [plural] an object that you wear in front of your eyes in order to help you to see better

glass•ware /ˈglæsˌwer/ noun [U] objects made of glass

glass•y /ˈglæsi/ adj **1** smooth and shiny like glass **2** glassy eyes show no interest or emotion, for example because of illness or drugs

glaze /gleɪz/ noun [C/U] **1** a thin layer of milk, sugar, or egg that you put on foods to make them look shiny **2** a clear liquid that you put on paintings or clay objects to protect them and make them shiny —**glaze** verb [T]

glazed /gleɪzd/ adj **1** a glazed look or expression shows that you are not at all interested in something **2** decorated or protected by a smooth shiny surface: *glazed pastries* **3** made of glass, or decorated with glass: *glazed doors*

gleam[1] /glim/ verb [I] **1** to shine brightly **2** if your eyes gleam, you look excited or happy =SHINE

gleam[2] /glim/ noun [C] **1** a bright light that is reflected from something **2** a look of emotion or excitement in someone's eyes

glean /glin/ verb [T] to gradually get small pieces of information about something

glee /gli/ noun [U] a feeling of excitement and happiness, usually because of your own good luck or someone else's bad luck —**glee•ful** adj, **glee•ful•ly** adv

glib /glɪb/ adj **1** a glib person speaks easily and confidently, but is not sincere **2** a glib remark is made without careful thought —**glib•ly** adv

glide /glaɪd/ verb [I] **1** to move in a smooth easy way with no noise **2** to fly without using power, carried by the wind

glid•er /ˈglaɪdər/ noun [C] a light airplane with no engine

glid•ing /ˈglaɪdɪŋ/ noun [U] the activity of flying in a glider

glim•mer[1] /ˈglɪmər/ noun [C] a soft weak light that is not steady
PHRASE **a glimmer of hope** a very small sign that something might improve or succeed

glim•mer[2] /ˈglɪmər/ verb [I] to shine with a soft weak light that is not steady

glimpse[1] /glɪmps/ noun [C] **1** an occasion when you see someone or something for a very short time: *I only caught a glimpse of it, but I think it was a fox.* **2** an experience that gives you an idea of what something is like: *a glimpse of what the future might be like*

glimpse[2] /glɪmps/ verb [T] to see someone or something for a moment or not completely =CATCH SIGHT OF

glint /glɪnt/ verb [I] **1** to shine with quick flashes of light **2** if your eyes glint, they show a strong emotion such as anger —**glint** noun [C]

glis•ten /ˈglɪs(ə)n/ verb [I] if something glistens, it shines because it is wet or covered with oil

glitch /glɪtʃ/ noun [C] *informal* a small problem that prevents something from operating correctly =HITCH

glit•ter[1] /ˈglɪtər/ verb [I] **1** to shine with a lot of small flashes of light =SPARKLE **2** if your eyes glitter, they show a strong emotion such as anger

glit•ter[2] /ˈglɪtər/ noun [U] **1** an attractive exciting quality: *the glitter and glare of Las Vegas* **2** small shiny pieces of metal or plastic that you stick on things to make them shine and look attractive **3** a lot of small flashes of light

glit•ter•ing /ˈglɪtərɪŋ/ adj **1** bright and shining with a lot of flashes of light **2** exciting and successful

glitz /glɪts/ noun [U] *informal* a special quality that makes something seem very exciting and attractive although it has no real value —**glitz•y** adj

gloat /gloʊt/ verb [I] *showing disapproval* to show that you are happy about your own success or someone else's failure =CROW

glob /glɑb/ noun [C] *very informal* a small amount of a soft thick substance

glob•al /ˈgloʊb(ə)l/ adj ★★
1 including or affecting the whole world: *The **global economy** has become increasingly unstable.*

2 *formal* complete, including all parts of something: *global changes* —**glob•al•ly** adv

glob•al•i•za•tion /ˌgloʊbəlɪˈzeɪʃ(ə)n/ noun [U] the idea that the world is developing a single economy and culture as a result of improved communications and the influence of very large corporations

glob•al•ize /ˈgloʊbəˌlaɪz/ verb [T] **1** to make something become generally accepted all over the world **2** to make a business begin operating all over the world

ˌglobal ˈwarming noun [U] the increase in the temperature of the Earth that is caused partly by increasing amounts of CARBON DIOXIDE in the atmosphere

globe /gloʊb/ noun **1** [C] a round object that has a map of the world on it **2** [C] a round object **3** [singular] the world

glob•ule /ˈglɑbjul/ noun [C] a small round drop of a thick liquid —**glob•u•lar** adj

gloom /glum/ noun [U] **1** darkness in which it is difficult to see clearly **2** a feeling of sadness and a lack of hope → DOOM

gloom•y /ˈglumi/ adj **1** feeling sad and without hope **2** showing that things are not going well and will probably not get better quickly: *The economic news is gloomy.* **3** dark in a way that makes you feel sad or a little afraid: *gloomy weather* —**gloom•i•ly** adv

glo•ri•fied /ˈglɔrəˌfaɪd/ adj used for saying what something is really like when other people have described it as more impressive than it really is: *The "yacht" we rented was just a glorified sailboat.*

glo•ri•fy /ˈglɔrəˌfaɪ/ verb [T] **1** to make someone or something seem to be more impressive than they really are **2** *literary* to praise someone —**glo•ri•fi•ca•tion** /ˌglɔrəfɪˈkeɪʃ(ə)n/ noun [U]

glo•ri•ous /ˈglɔriəs/ adj **1** very beautiful in a way that makes you feel happy: *What glorious weather!* **2** extremely successful and likely to be remembered for a long time: *reminders of the country's glorious past* —**glo•ri•ous•ly** adv

glo•ry¹ /ˈglɔri/ noun [U] **1** admiration and praise that you get because you have done something impressive: *I did the hard work and someone else got all the glory.* **2** great beauty: *It will cost millions of dollars to restore the mansion to its former glory.*

glo•ry² /ˈglɔri/ PHRASAL VERB **ˈglory in sth** to get a lot of pleasure from something = REVEL

gloss¹ /glɔs/ noun **1** [singular/U] the shiny surface of something **2** [C] a short explanation of what something means **3** [U] GLOSS PAINT

gloss² /glɔs/ verb [T] to give an explanation of a word or a piece of writing
PHRASAL VERB **ˌgloss ˈover sth** to ignore or avoid unpleasant facts

glos•sa•ry /ˈglɔsəri/ noun [C] a list of difficult words with explanations of their meaning

ˈgloss ˌpaint noun [U] paint that is shiny when it is dry

gloss•y /ˈglɔsi/ adj **1** shiny in an attractive way **2** printed on shiny paper with a lot of bright pictures: *a glossy magazine*

glove /glʌv/ noun [C] a piece of clothing that covers your fingers and hand: *a pair of gloves* —*picture* → C4

ˈglove comˌpartment noun [C] the small cupboard or shelf in front of the passenger seat of a car —*picture* → C6

glow¹ /gloʊ/ verb [I] **1** to shine with a soft warm light: *The tip of a cigarette glowed in the darkness.* **2** to show that you are happy: *She glowed with satisfaction.* **3** if your face or body is glowing, it looks pink or red, for example because you are healthy or embarrassed

glow² /gloʊ/ noun [singular] **1** a soft warm light **2** the pink or red color that your skin has when you are healthy, hot, embarrassed, or emotional **3** a pleasant feeling: *Anne felt a glow of pride at Sarah's words.*

glow•er /ˈglaʊr/ verb [I] to look angrily at someone = GLARE

glow•ing /ˈgloʊɪŋ/ adj full of praise: *a glowing reference from her former employer*

glu•cose /ˈgluˌkoʊz/ noun [U] a natural sugar that exists in some foods

glue¹ /glu/ noun [C/U] a sticky substance that you use for attaching things to each other

glue² /glu/ verb [T] to stick things to each other with glue
PHRASE **be glued to sth** to be looking at something and not paying attention to anything else

glum /glʌm/ adj unhappy —**glum•ly** adv

glut /glʌt/ noun [singular] an amount of something that is more than people want or need

glu•ti•nous /ˈglut(ə)nəs/ adj thick and sticky, often in an unpleasant way

glut•ton /ˈglʌt(ə)n/ noun [C] someone who eats too much
PHRASE **a glutton for punishment** someone who seems to enjoy doing something that is difficult or unpleasant

glut•ton•y /ˈglʌt(ə)ni/ noun [U] *literary* the bad habit of eating or drinking too much

GMO /ˌdʒi em ˈoʊ/ noun [C] genetically modified organism: a plant or animal whose genes have been changed

GMT /ˌdʒi em ˈti/ noun [U] Greenwich Mean Time: the time at Greenwich in England, used as an international standard

gnarled /nɑrld/ adj old and twisted and covered in lines: *gnarled hands*

gnat /næt/ noun [C] a very small flying insect that bites but is not dangerous

gnaw /nɔ/ verb [I/T] to keep biting something
PHRASAL VERB **ˈgnaw ˌat sb** or **ˌgnaw aˈway at sb** if something gnaws at you, you keep worrying about it or feeling upset about it

gnaw•ing /ˈnɔɪŋ/ adj continuously causing you pain or worrying you: *a gnawing fear that something had happened to her father*

gnome /noʊm/ noun [C] an imaginary little man in children's stories who wears a pointed hat

GNP /ˌdʒi en ˈpi/ noun [U] Gross National Product: the total value of all the goods and services that a country produces in a year

go[1] /goʊ/ (past tense **went** /went/; past participle **gone** /gɔn/) verb ★★★

1 move to place	14 when time passes
2 leave a place	15 to be spent/used
3 move to do sth	16 disappear
4 travel to activity	17 leave a job
5 continue to place	18 move/make a sound
6 happen	19 about story/music
7 change condition	20 begin doing sth
8 be in state	21 spend time doing sth
9 stop working	22 operate correctly
10 be kept somewhere	23 say
11 fit somewhere	+ PHRASES
12 be right/attractive	+ PHRASAL VERBS
13 be sent	

G

1 [I] to move or travel to a place that is away from where you are now: *Where did Sue go?* ♦ *We're planning to* ***go to*** *Arizona this winter.* ♦ *She* ***went into*** *the bathroom and rinsed her face in cold water.* ♦ *Are you* ***going by train*** *or are you flying?*
2 [I] to leave a place: *What time are you going tomorrow?* ♦ *I'm tired; let's go.*
3 [I] to move or travel to a place, or to leave a place, in order to do a particular thing: *They've* ***gone to*** *a concert in town tonight.* ♦ *He* ***went into the hospital*** *for an operation last Tuesday.* ♦ *They* ***went for a walk.*** ♦ *On hot days the kids would* ***go swimming*** *in the river.* ♦ **go to do sth** *Jim went to buy some ice cream about ten minutes ago.* ♦ **go and do sth** *I have to go and pick up my friends at the airport.*
4 [I] to travel to a particular place regularly in order to take part in an activity: *None of her brothers* ***went to college.*** ♦ *When I was young, we* ***went to church*** *every Sunday.*
5 [I] to continue from one place or time to another: *The highway* ***going from*** *Georgetown* ***to*** *Brazil was built with World Bank funds.*
6 [I] to happen in a particular way: *How are things going at work?* ♦ *I think the interview went very well.* ♦ ***The way things are going*** (=because things are not happening in the best way), *we won't finish until next year!*
7 [linking verb] to change to another condition, usually a worse one: *Louise had* ***gone*** *completely* ***blind*** *before she died.* ♦ *The milk smells like it's* ***going bad.***
8 [linking verb] to be in a particular state or situation, especially one in which you do not have something or in which something is not done: *We* ***went barefoot*** *all summer.* ♦ *Her comment* ***went unnoticed.*** ♦ *Thousands of people are being allowed to* ***go hungry.***
9 [I] to start being in a worse state, or to stop working correctly, as a result of becoming old or damaged: *Her hearing is really starting to go.* ♦ *The battery in this watch is going.*
10 [I] to be usually kept or put in a particular place: *The spoons* ***go in*** *the other drawer.*
11 [I] if something goes in a particular place, it fits there because it is the right size or shape: *There's no way all this stuff will go in the box.*
12 [I] to be appropriate, right, or attractive in a particular place or in a particular combination: *It's the kind of furniture that would go well in any room.*
13 [I] to be sent: *The memo should* ***go to*** *all employees.* ♦ *I'd like this letter to* ***go airmail.***
14 [I] if time goes in a particular way, it passes in that way: *This week's gone so fast – I can't believe it's Friday already.*
15 [I] to be spent or used: *We were worried because the food was going fast.* ♦ *Half of the money* ***went on*** *new shoes for the kids.*
16 [I] to disappear: *I put my book on the table, and now it's gone.*
17 [I] to leave a job or organization, usually because you are forced to: *They can fire me, but I won't go quietly.*
18 [T] to make a particular sound or movement: *Cows go "moo."* ♦ *He kept going like this with his head.*
19 [I/T] to consist of a particular series of words, facts, or musical notes: *That's not the way the song goes.*
20 [I] to begin doing something: *Nobody starts until I say "Go."* ♦ *We've planned every detail and are* ***ready to go.*** ♦ *It won't take me long once I* ***get going.***
21 [I/T] to continue or last for a particular amount of time while doing something: *He went several days without eating a single thing.*
22 [I] if a machine or piece of equipment goes, it operates correctly = WORK: *My old watch is still going.*
23 [T] *spoken* used when you are telling a story for saying what someone has said: *So he goes, "I know what I'm doing," and she goes, "I don't think so."*

PHRASES **be going to do sth 1** to intend to do something: *I'm going to watch TV tonight.* **2** to be about to do something: *You're going to fall if you're not careful.*
don't go there *spoken* used for saying that you do not want to hear about, discuss, or consider a particular subject
go all out (to do sth/for sth) to try as hard as you can to achieve something: *We're going all out for a big win in Saturday's game.*
go and do sth *spoken* to do something that is silly or annoying: *She'll probably go and tell everyone our secret.*
go do sth *spoken* used for telling someone to do something, especially when you are annoyed: *If you hate this job so much, go get another one!*
to go 1 remaining: *There are just three weeks to go before the end of the semester.* **2** if you order food to go from a restaurant, you take it and eat it somewhere else: *Do you want this pizza to go?*

PHRASAL VERBS **ˌgo aˈbout sth 1** to do something that you normally do in your usual way: *I watched the inspectors as they* ***went about their business.*** **2** to start dealing with a problem, situation, or job in a particular way: *I think I'd go about it quite differently.* ♦ **go about doing sth** *How did you go about finding a job?*
ˌgo ˈafter sb to try to catch or stop someone: *You'd better go after her and tell her you're sorry.*
ˌgo ˈafter sth to try to get something that other people are also competing for: *Many recent college graduates are going after jobs that they would not have considered before.*
ˌgo aˈgainst sb if something such as a decision

or judgment goes against you, you do not get the decision or judgment that you wanted to get

ˌgo aˈgainst sb/sth to oppose someone or something: *Building a road here would go against the wishes of the local community.*

ˌgo aˈhead 1 to start, or continue to do something, especially after waiting for permission to do it: *"Go ahead," he insisted. "I won't interrupt again."* ♦ *The city will **go ahead with** its plans for a new stadium.* ♦ **go ahead and do sth** *Go ahead and eat before everything gets cold.* **2** to happen or take place: *The party went ahead as planned.* **3** to go to a place before someone else that you are with: *You go ahead and we'll wait here for Sally.* ♦ *Don **went ahead of** the others to try to find help.*

ˌgo aˈlong to continue doing something: *You'll learn a lot as you go along.*

ˌgo aˈlong with sb/sth to agree with someone or something: *I think Alice's point goes along with what Tim was saying.*

ˌgo aˈround 1 to behave or be dressed in a particular way: *Why do you always go around without any shoes on?* ♦ **go around doing sth** *You can't go around saying things like that!* **2** if something such as an illness or a piece of news is going around, people are giving it or telling it to each other: *He caught the flu virus that's going around.* **3** to be enough so that everyone can have one or some: *In some classes, there aren't even enough books to go around.*

ˈgo at sth to do something with a lot of enthusiasm or energy

ˌgo aˈway 1 to move away from, or to travel away from, a person or place: *If he's bothering you, tell him to go away.* **2** to leave your home for a period of time, especially for a vacation: *We've decided to go away for the weekend.* **3** to stop existing or being noticeable: *The pain should go away in a couple of hours.*

ˌgo ˈback 1 to return to a person, place, subject, or activity: *It started to rain, so we decided to go back.* ♦ *I left my keys in the office and had to **go back for** them.* ♦ *She should be well enough to **go back to** work on Wednesday.* ♦ **go back to doing sth** *The computer breaks down and you go back to writing things down on pieces of paper.* **2** to have existed since or for a particular time: *My interest in the subject goes back many years.*

ˌgo ˈback on sth to not do something that you have promised or agreed to do: *I don't think that the president would go back on his word.*

ˌgo ˈby if time goes by, it passes: *Last month went by so fast.*

ˌgo ˈby sth 1 to base an opinion on something: *It's never very wise to go by appearances.* **2** to move past a place: *I went by the post office on the way home.*

ˌgo ˈdown 1 to become less: *No one expects house prices to go down in the near future.* ♦ *How long will it take for the swelling to go down?* ♦ *The crime rate shows no signs of going down.* **2** when the sun goes down, it moves below the HORIZON so that you cannot see it anymore = SET **3** if something such as a computer or an electrical system goes down, it stops working for a period of time **4** to sink below the surface of the water: *The ship went down off the coast of Africa.* **5** to fall to the ground: *The plane went down during a thunderstorm.* **6** to be remembered or recorded in a particular place or way: *Hansen will **go down as** one of the best teachers this school has ever had.* ♦ *The efforts they made will **go down in history**.* **7** to produce a particular reaction: *The plan to raise rents has not **gone down well with** tenants.*

ˈgo for sb *informal* to attack someone physically

ˈgo for sth 1 *informal* to try to get something that you have to compete for: *There were 200 people going for just three jobs.* **2** *informal* to choose a particular thing: *I think I'll go for the steak. What are you having?* **3** to be sold for a particular amount of money: *We expect the house to go for about $200,000.* **4 go for it** *spoken* used for encouraging someone to do something or to try very hard

ˈgo for sb/sth 1 to be true or relevant for someone or something: *We expect you boys to behave yourselves, and the same goes for the girls.* **2** *informal* to like a particular type of person or thing: *So what type of men do you go for?*

ˌgo ˈinto sth 1 to start working in a particular type of job or business: *Alex has decided to go into nursing.* **2** to deal with something in detail: *That's a good question, but I don't want to go into it now.* ♦ *The company is refusing to **go into detail** about its offer.* **3** to be used or spent in order to do something: *Over 50% of the budget went into the design of the equipment.* ♦ **go into doing sth** *Months of hard work have gone into making tonight's ceremony a success.*

ˌgo ˈoff 1 to explode or be fired: *The gun went off while he was cleaning it.* **2** to start making a noise as a signal or warning: *I was lying in bed waiting for the alarm to go off.* **3** if something such as a light or an electricity supply goes off, it stops working or being available **4** to leave a place, especially for a particular purpose: *Dave's **gone off to** the mountains for the summer.* ♦ **go off to do sth** *He went off to have lunch in the cafeteria.* **5** to happen in a particular way: *The whole conference **went off without a hitch*** (=without any problems).

ˌgo ˈon 1 to continue happening or doing something in the same way as before: *The meeting went on a lot longer than I expected.* ♦ *Burton smiled and **went on with** his work.* ♦ **go on doing sth** *She can't go on pretending that everything is fine when it clearly isn't.* **2** to happen: *I wonder what's going on next door – they're making a lot of noise.* **3** to talk so much that people become bored or annoyed: *He **went on and on about*** (=talked for a long time about) *me being late for work again.* **4** to start talking again after a pause or interruption: *Please go on – I didn't mean to interrupt you.* **5** if time goes on, it passes **6** *spoken* used for encouraging someone to do something: *Go on, try it – it's really good.* **7** if something such as a light or an electricity supply goes on, it starts working

G

or becomes available: *I heard the TV go on in the next room.*

ˌgo on sth to base an opinion or decision on something: *Since there were no witnesses, the police had little to go on.*

ˌgo ˈout 1 to leave your house and go somewhere, especially to do something enjoyable: *I wanted the evenings free for **going out with friends**.* ♦ **go out doing sth** ♦ *We haven't gone out dancing in a long time.* ♦ **go out to do sth** *Let's go out to eat tonight.* **2** to have a romantic or sexual relationship with someone and spend a lot of time with them: *How long have Rob and Ally been going out?* ♦ *Greg used to **go out with** Karla.* ♦ *We've been **going out together** for three months now.* **3** to stop burning or shining: *The fire must have gone out during the night.* **4** to stop being fashionable: *That hairstyle went out about ten years ago.* ♦ *Classic jewelry like this will never **go out of fashion**.* **5** when the TIDE goes out, the water in the ocean flows away from the land

ˌgo ˈover sth 1 to check something carefully: *Could you go over this report and correct any mistakes?* **2** to repeat a series of things or think about them again in order to remember or understand them completely

ˌgo ˈthrough if a request or proposal goes through, it is officially accepted or approved

ˌgo ˈthrough sth 1 to examine or search something very carefully: *Someone had broken into the office and gone through all the drawers.* **2** to experience something difficult or unpleasant: *We can't really imagine what they're going through.* **3** to use, spend, or eat all of something: *He'd gone through all his money by the end of the first week of his vacation.*

ˌgo ˈthrough with sth to do something that you have planned or agreed to do: *I can't believe he went through with the divorce.*

ˌgo toˈgether 1 if two things go together, they seem good, natural, or attractive in combination with each other: *I don't think the colors go together very well.* **2** if two or more things go together, they frequently exist together: *Too often greed and politics seem to go together.* **3** *informal* if two people are going together, they have a romantic or sexual relationship with each other

ˌgo toˈward sth to be used to help to pay for something: *The proceeds from the sale of the land will go toward a new stadium.* ♦ **go toward doing sth** *The money raised will go toward rebuilding the children's hospital.*

ˌgo ˈunder 1 if a business goes under, it fails completely and stops operating **2** to sink below the surface of the water: *The crowd watched as the ship went slowly under.*

ˌgo ˈup 1 to increase: *The price of oil has gone up by over 50 percent in less than a year.* **2** to be built: *A new office building is going up on State Street.* **3** if something such as a notice or sign goes up somewhere, it is put in a place where people can see it: *Posters for the show are going up all over town.* **4** to explode, or to start burning quickly: *The whole building went up in just a few minutes.* ♦ *From the air, it looked as if the entire city was **going up in flames**.*

ˈgo with sb *informal* to have a romantic or sexual relationship with someone: *I heard that Carol is going with the guy who works downstairs.*

ˈgo with sth 1 to be provided or offered together with something: *the book that goes with the CD-ROM* ♦ *Does a car go with the job?* **2** to seem good, natural, or attractive in combination with something: *Which shoes go best with this dress?* **3** to choose or accept something: *I think we should go with yellow for the walls.*

ˌgo withˈout sth to live without something that you need or would like to have: *Three areas have gone without water for days.* ♦ **go without doing sth** *He went without sleeping for two days.*

go² /goʊ/ (plural **goes** /goʊz/) noun [C] an attempt to do something

PHRASE **be on the go** *informal* to be very busy or active

goad /goʊd/ verb [T] to deliberately make someone feel very angry or upset so that they react in a particular way

ˈgo-aˌhead noun **give/get the go-ahead** to give/get permission to do something

goal /goʊl/ noun [C] ★★★

1 an area or structure that a ball must go into or through to score points in some sports

2 the action of putting a ball into a goal: *Nielsen **scored two goals** in the last ten minutes.*

3 something that you hope to achieve: *His goal is to win a medal at the Olympics.*

goal·ie /ˈgoʊli/ noun [C] *informal* a GOALKEEPER

goal·keep·er /ˈgoʊlˌkipər/ noun [C] the player whose job is to stop the ball from going into the goal in games such as soccer

goal·post /ˈgoʊlˌpoʊst/ noun [C] one of the two posts that the ball must go between to score a goal in games such as soccer —*picture* → C15

goal·tend·er /ˈgoʊlˌtendər/ noun [C] *American* a GOALKEEPER

goat /goʊt/ noun [C] an animal similar to a sheep but with longer legs and a thinner coat —*picture* → C12

goat·ee /goʊˈti/ noun [C] a small pointed BEARD

gob·ble /ˈgɑb(ə)l/ verb [T] to eat something quickly

gob·ble·de·gook or **gob·ble·dy·gook** /ˈgɑb(ə)ldiˌguk/ noun [U] *informal* **1** very complicated or technical language **2** nonsense

ˈgo-beˌtween noun [C] someone who takes messages between people who cannot meet or do not want to meet

gob·let /ˈgɑblət/ noun [C] a metal or glass cup with no handles that was used in the past

gob·lin /ˈgɑblɪn/ noun [C] a small ugly creature in children's stories that enjoys causing trouble

ˈgo-ˌcart noun [C] a small low vehicle with no roof, used for racing or for fun

god /gɑd/ noun [C] ★

1 one of the male spirits with special powers that some people believe in and worship: *Poseidon was the Greek god of the sea.*

2 a man who many people admire or find attractive

God¹ /gɑd/ the spirit or force that some people believe created and controls the universe

PHRASE **God (only) knows** *spoken* used for emphasizing that you do not know something

God² /gɑd/ interjection used for expressing strong feelings such as anger, surprise, or worry. Some people think that this expression is offensive.

god•child /ˈgɑdˌtʃaɪld/ (plural **god•chil•dren** /ˈgɑdˌtʃɪldrən/) noun [C] a child that a GODPARENT promises to take care of, especially by making certain that he or she gets a religious education

god•dess /ˈgɑdəs/ noun [C] **1** one of the female spirits with special powers that some people believe in and worship **2** a woman who many people admire or find attractive

god•fa•ther /ˈgɑdˌfɑðər/ noun [C] **1** a male GODPARENT **2** *informal* a man who controls a large criminal organization

god•for•sak•en /ˈgɑdfərˌseɪkən/ adj a godforsaken place is not at all interesting or attractive

god•less /ˈgɑdləs/ adj *showing disapproval* not believing in God, or not living according to religious rules

god•like /ˈgɑdˌlaɪk/ adj better or more impressive than an ordinary human

god•ly /ˈgɑdli/ adj showing respect for God and living according to religious rules

god•moth•er /ˈgɑdˌmʌðər/ noun [C] a female godparent

god•par•ent /ˈgɑdˌperənt/ noun [C] an adult who promises during the Christian ceremony of BAPTISM to take care of a child, especially by making certain that he or she gets a religious education

god•send /ˈgɑdˌsend/ noun [singular] something that you are very grateful for because it helps you in a difficult situation

go-get•ter /goʊˈgetər/ noun [C] *informal* someone who is determined to succeed and works hard to achieve this —**go-ˈgetting** adj

gog•gle-eyed /ˌgɑg(ə)l ˈaɪd/ adj *informal* looking at someone or something in a way that shows that you are very surprised or impressed by them

gog•gles /ˈgɑg(ə)lz/ noun [plural] special GLASSES that protect your eyes

go•ing¹ /ˈgoʊɪŋ/ noun [U] **1** used for talking about how fast or easily you make progress: *We'd reached the summit by six o'clock, which was good going.* ♦ *The first half of the movie is pretty slow going* (=is rather boring). **2** an occasion when someone leaves a place or job permanently: *None of us knew the reasons for his going.* → COMING² **3** the condition of the ground for a horse race

PHRASE **do sth while the going is good** *informal* to do something before any problems happen that will prevent you from doing it

go•ing² /ˈgoʊɪŋ/ adj available: *It's one of the best jobs going in television.* → RATE¹

ˌgoing conˈcern noun [C] a business that seems likely to continue to make a profit

ˌgoings-ˈon noun [plural] *informal* events or activities that are strange, dishonest, or illegal

gold¹ /goʊld/ noun ★★

1 [U] a valuable yellow metal that is used for making jewelry: *The picture frames were made of solid gold.*

2 [C/U] a MEDAL made of gold that is given to the winner of a race: *We always thought Sally was going to win gold.* ♦ *So Australia gets the gold and Britain the silver.*

3 [C/U] the color of gold: *The boat was painted in black and gold.*

gold² /goʊld/ adj **1** something that is gold is the color of gold: *blue fabric decorated with gold stars* **2** made of gold: *a gold ring/chain/watch*

gold•en /ˈgoʊld(ə)n/ adj ★

1 bright yellow in color: *golden hair* ♦ *Fry the chicken in the oil until* ***golden brown.***

2 very happy or successful: *The seventies were the* ***golden years*** *of Australian tennis.*

3 *literary* made of gold: *The queen wore a golden crown.*

ˌgolden ˌage noun [singular] a period of time in the past when something was the most successful that it has ever been: *the golden age of radio*

ˌgolden opporˈtunity noun [C] a very good chance to do something

ˌgolden ˈrule noun [C] an important basic principle that you should always obey when doing a particular activity

gold•fish /ˈgoʊldˌfɪʃ/ (plural **gold•fish**) noun [C] a small orange fish that is often kept as a pet

ˌgold ˈmedal noun [C] a MEDAL that is given to the winner of a race or competition

ˌgold ˈmedalist noun [C] someone who wins a gold medal

gold•mine /ˈgoʊldˌmaɪn/ noun [C] **1** *informal* a business or an activity that makes large amounts of money very easily **2** a place under the ground where there are rocks containing gold

golf /gɔlf/ noun [U] ★ a game in which you use GOLF CLUBS to hit a small white ball into a hole in the ground: *I usually play a* ***round of golf*** (=a game of golf) *on Saturday.* —**golf•er** noun [C]

ˈgolf ˌball noun [C] a small white ball that you use for playing golf

ˈgolf ˌclub noun [C] **1** a long stick that you use for hitting the ball in golf **2** a place with a golf course and CLUBHOUSE where people go to play golf and meet their friends

ˈgolf ˌcourse noun [C] a large area of land that is designed for playing golf

gone¹ /gɔn/ adj **1** someone who is gone is no longer present in a place **2** something that is gone no longer exists or has all been used

gone² the past participle of **go¹**

gon•na /ˈgɔnə/ short form a way of writing "going to" that shows how it sounds in informal conversation

goo /gu/ noun [U] *informal* a thick sticky unpleasant substance

G

good[1] /gʊd/ (comparative **bet•ter** /ˈbetər/; superlative **best** /best/) adj ★★★

1 of high quality	8 kind/helpful
2 able to do sth well	9 giving benefits
3 appropriate	10 fairly large
4 giving pleasant feeling	11 able to be used
5 showing pleasure	12 thorough and complete
6 morally correct	13 more than amount, etc.
7 behaving well	+ PHRASES

1 of a high quality or standard: *We saw a really good movie last night.* ♦ *They were all dressed in their best clothes.* ♦ *How good is his English?*
2 able to do something well: *Francine was a very good cook.* ♦ *Bob is pretty **good at** fixing things.* ♦ *Gina has always been **good with** animals.*
3 appropriate and likely to produce the results or conditions that you want: *What's the best way to get to the freeway from here?* ♦ *Now would be **a good time** to ask for a raise.* ♦ *Thursday is **good for** me – can you make it then?*
4 giving you a happy or pleasant feeling: *We had such **a good time** in Las Vegas.* ♦ *One more piece of **good news**: Beth had a baby girl!* ♦ **it is/feels good to do sth** *It's good to finally meet you.*
5 *spoken* used for saying that you are pleased with someone or pleased about something: *"They should be here in half an hour." "Good."* ♦ *Oh, good, you remembered to buy the milk.*
6 honest and morally correct: *George had always tried to lead **a good life**.*
7 willing to obey and behave in a socially correct way: *Ruth's children are always so good.* ♦ ***Be a good boy** and play quietly.*
8 kind, generous, and willing to help: *Helen's parents were always **good to us**.* ♦ *Sheryl's brother has been **good about** helping out with the new baby.*
9 producing benefits for someone or something: *Exercise is **good for** you.* ♦ *The recent tax cuts will be **good for** business.* ♦ **it is good (for sb) to do sth** *It's not good to eat so much junk food.*
10 fairly large in amount, size, range, etc.: *He earns a good salary as a consultant.* ♦ *They've known each other for **a good many** years.*
11 still able to be used: *Do you think the eggs are still good?* ♦ *Make sure your passport is good before your trip.* ♦ *I think these pants are **good for** another few months.*
12 thorough and complete: *The witness said she got a good look at his face.*
13 *informal* more than a particular distance, amount, age, etc.: *We've been waiting for a good half hour.*

PHRASES **as good as** almost: *They've as good as admitted it was their fault.*
as good as new something that is as good as new is in almost the same good condition as it was before it was damaged or injured: *After the surgery your back should be as good as new.*
good for sb used for saying that you are happy about something good that someone has done
a good friend someone that you know very well and like a lot
good Heavens/Lord/God/grief used for showing that you are very surprised, angry, or upset
it's a good thing that used for saying that you are pleased that something has happened because it prevents something bad from happening: *It's a good thing you called – Mom was starting to get worried.*
too good to be true/to last so good that you cannot believe that such a situation is possible or can continue: *If you think the deal they are offering is too good to be true, it probably is.*

Words that you can use instead of good

Good is a very general word. Here are some words with more specific meanings that sound more natural and appropriate in particular situations.

movies/books/events	excellent, fabulous, fantastic, great, terrific
food/meals	delicious, tasty, wonderful
performance/piece of work	excellent, outstanding, terrific
people	decent, kind, moral, nice, respectable
ideas/suggestions	appealing, brilliant, excellent, great, interesting

good[2] /gʊd/ noun [U] ★★★
1 advantage, or benefit: *I think a trip to the beach would **do us all a lot of good**.* ♦ *I'm doing this **for your own good**.* ♦ *Hartman should resign **for the good of** the party.*
2 morally correct behavior ≠ EVIL: *the battle between **good and evil***

PHRASES **do no good** or **not do any good** to not have any effect or success: *I'll talk to her, but it won't do any good.*
for good permanently, without the possibility of change in the future: *It looks like Jamie has left for good this time.*
no good or **not any good** or **not much good 1** of a low quality or standard: *Most of the pictures I took weren't any good.* **2** not able to do something well: *I'm **no good at** chemistry.* ♦ *Ken's **not much good with** kids.* **3** not useful or effective: *My shoes are **no good for** hiking.* ♦ **it's no good doing sth** *It's no good trying to persuade her to come with us.* **4** not appropriate or convenient: *Tomorrow's no good – I'm busy.*
up to no good *informal* doing or planning something bad, illegal, or immoral
→ GOODS

good[3] /gʊd/ adv *spoken* a way of saying "well" that many people think is not correct: *He's doing pretty good at his new job.*

ˌgood afterˈnoon interjection *formal* used for saying hello or goodbye to someone in the afternoon

good•bye[1] /gʊdˈbaɪ/ interjection ★★★ used when you are leaving someone or when someone is leaving you, or when you are finishing a telephone call: *"Goodbye, Mr. Taylor." "Goodbye, John."*

good•bye[2] /gʊdˈbaɪ/ noun [C] a word or phrase that you say when you leave someone or when someone leaves you: *I said goodbye to everyone and left.* ♦ *It was heartbreaking saying our goodbyes at the airport.*

ˌgood ˈevening interjection *formal* used for saying hello to someone in the evening

ˈgood-for-ˌnothing noun [C] someone who is lazy and never does anything useful

ˌGood ˈFriday noun [C/U] the Friday before Easter, when Christians believe that Jesus Christ died

ˈgood ˌguy noun [C] someone who does what is morally right, especially a character in a movie

good-hu·mored /gʊdˈ hjumərd/ adj friendly, happy, and not easily annoyed or upset

good·ies /ˈgʊdiz/ noun [plural] *informal* things that are nice to eat

good-look·ing /gʊdˈlʊkɪŋ/ adj physically attractive

ˌgood ˈlooks noun [plural] the physically attractive appearance of someone

ˌgood ˈmorning interjection *formal* used for saying hello or goodbye to someone in the morning

good-na·tured /gʊdˈneɪtʃərd/ adj kind and friendly, and not easily annoyed —**ˌgood-ˈnaturedly** adv

good·ness¹ /ˈgʊdnəs/ interjection used for showing that you are surprised: *My goodness, you're so tall!*

PHRASE **for goodness sake** used for showing that you are annoyed, impatient, worried, or surprised

→ THANK

good·ness² /ˈgʊdnəs/ noun [U] **1** the quality of being morally good **2** substances such as VITAMINS and proteins that are contained in some foods and help you to stay healthy

ˌgood ˈnight interjection used for saying goodbye to someone in the evening or at night, or before they go to bed at night

goods /gʊdz/ noun [plural] ★★★ objects that are produced for sale: *leather/electrical goods* ♦ *Wilkins was found in possession of $8,000 worth of **stolen goods**.* ♦ *The cost of household **goods and services** fell.*

PHRASE **come up with/deliver the goods** *informal* to do what you have said you will do or what people expect

good·will /gʊdˈwɪl/ noun [U] a feeling of wanting to be friendly and helpful to someone ≠ ILL WILL: *As a gesture of goodwill, we agreed to do the work free of charge.*

good·y /ˈgʊdi/ interjection *informal* used by children for saying that they are happy or excited about something

ˈgoody-ˌgoody or **ˌgoody-ˈtwo-ˌshoes** *informal* noun [C] *showing disapproval* someone who always tries to please people in authority

goo·ey /ˈgui/ adj *informal* sticky and soft

goof /guf/ verb [I] to make a stupid mistake —**goof** noun [C]

PHRASAL VERBS **ˌgoof aˈround** *American informal* to behave in a silly way

ˌgoof ˈoff *American informal* to waste time when you should be working

ˌgoof ˈup *informal same as* **goof**

goof·y /ˈgufi/ adj *informal* silly, but in a funny or pleasant way

goop /gup/ noun [U] *American informal* a thick sticky unpleasant substance

goose /gus/ (plural **geese** /gis/) noun **1** [C/U] a large white or gray bird with a long beak —*picture* → C12 **2** [U] the meat of a goose

ˈgoose ˌbumps noun [plural] very small lumps that appear on your skin because you are cold, frightened, or excited

GOP, the /ˌdʒi oʊ ˈpi/ *American* the Grand Old Party: the Republican Party in the U.S.

go·pher /ˈgoʊfər/ noun [C] a small furry animal with a short tail that lives in holes in the ground in North and Central America

gore¹ /gɔr/ noun [U] thick blood from an injured person

gore² /gɔr/ verb [T] if an animal such as a BULL gores someone, it injures them with its horns

gorge¹ /gɔrdʒ/ noun [C] a deep valley with high straight sides

gorge² /gɔrdʒ/ verb **gorge yourself (on sth)** to eat or drink so much of something that you cannot eat or drink any more

gor·geous /ˈgɔrdʒəs/ adj very beautiful or pleasant

go·ril·la /gəˈrɪlə/ noun [C] a large strong African wild animal that is similar to a monkey but much larger. Gorillas live in forests. —*picture* → C12

go·ry /ˈgɔri/ adj involving a lot of blood, killing, or injuries

gosh /gɑʃ/ interjection used for showing that you are surprised or a little annoyed

gos·ling /ˈgɑzlɪŋ/ noun [C] a young GOOSE

gos·pel /ˈgɑsp(ə)l/ noun **1 gospel** or **gospel music** [U] a type of Christian music that was developed by African Americans **2** [C] one of the four books in the Bible that tell about the life of Jesus Christ **3 the gospel** [singular] the things that Jesus Christ said and taught according to the Bible

PHRASE **the gospel truth** the complete truth

gos·sip¹ /ˈgɑsɪp/ noun **1** [C/U] talk or a conversation about things that are not important or about people's private lives: *an interesting piece of gossip* **2** [C] someone who enjoys talking about other people

gos·sip² /ˈgɑsɪp/ verb [I] to talk about other people or about things that are not important

got¹ /gɑt/ verb **have got** *spoken* used especially in speech to mean "have": *I've got an extra apple if you want one.*

got² the past tense of **get**

got·ta /ˈgɑtə/ short form a way of writing "got to" that shows how it sounds in informal conversation

got·ten the American past participle of **get**

gouge /gaʊdʒ/ verb [T] to cut long deep holes in something —**gouge** noun [C]

PHRASAL VERB **ˌgouge sth ˈout** to remove something from a surface by cutting or digging with a sharp object

gourd /gɔrd/ noun [C] a type of fruit with a hard thick skin

gour·met¹ /gʊrˈmeɪ/ adj **1** gourmet food and wine is of a very high quality **2** a gourmet cook is someone who can make very good food

gour·met² /gʊrˈmeɪ/ noun [C] someone who

knows a lot about good food and wine

gov•ern /ˈgʌvərn/ verb ★
1 [I/T] to officially control and manage a country or area and its people=RULE: *The region is now governed by Morocco.* ♦ *The party will not be able to govern alone.*
2 [T] to control or influence the way that things happen or develop: *the laws that govern the movements of the stars* ♦ *Fear governed their lives.*

gov•ern•ess /ˈgʌvərnəs/ noun [C] a woman whose job is to take care of and teach her employer's children in their home

gov•ern•ment /ˈgʌvərnmənt/ noun ★★★
1 [C/U] the people who control a country or area and make decisions about its laws and taxes: *The Mexican government has announced its plans to raise the minimum wage next year.* ♦ *a democratically elected government* ♦ *government policy*
2 [U] the process, method, or effects of governing a country or area: *I'm not sure these reforms will necessarily lead to more effective government.*
—**gov•ern•ment•al** /ˌgʌvərnˈment(ə)l/ adj

gov•er•nor /ˈgʌvərnər/ noun [C] someone who is in charge of an area such as a U.S. state: *the governor of California* —**gov•er•nor•ship** noun [C/U]

gown /gaʊn/ noun [C] **1** a long dress that a woman wears for a special occasion **2** a long loose piece of clothing that a doctor or patient wears during an operation in a hospital

GPA /ˌdʒi pi ˈeɪ/ noun [C] *American* grade point average: a number between 0 and 4 that is an average of a student's grades. The number 4 is the same as an A, 3 is a B, 2 is a C, 1 is a D, and 0 is an F.

grab¹ /græb/ verb [T] ★
1 to take hold of something in a rough or rude way: *He grabbed the knife before I could get to it.* ♦ *I **grabbed hold of** his hair.* ♦ **grab sb by sth** *Ben grabbed Marco by the arm.*
2 to succeed in getting something, especially by being quick or by being the best at something: *We got there early and grabbed seats at the front.* ♦ *It's often the bad characters in a story who **grab our attention**.* ♦ *I grabbed the chance to escape for a few minutes.*
3 *informal* if you grab food or sleep, you eat quickly or sleep for a short time: *I'll grab a sandwich back at the hotel.*
PHRASAL VERB ˈ**grab at sth** to try to take hold of something in a rough or rude way: *Suddenly he was on his feet, grabbing at her sleeve.*

grab² /græb/ noun [singular] an attempt to take hold of something: *Rose rushed at David and made a grab at his wrist.*
PHRASE **up for grabs** *informal* if something is up for grabs, it is available and many people are trying to get it or win it

grace¹ /greɪs/ noun **1** [U] a smooth and beautiful way of moving: *She moved with natural grace.* **2** [U] kind, polite, and fair behavior: *He should have the grace to admit he was wrong.* ♦ *Davis accepted the defeat with good grace* (=in a pleasant way). **3** [U] extra time that you are given to do something such as pay money that you owe: *Could you give me a couple of days' grace to pay the rent?* **4** [singular/U] a short prayer that some people say before they eat in order to thank God for the food

grace² /greɪs/ verb [T] to make something more attractive, pleasing, or interesting: *Her photograph graced many a magazine cover.*

grace•ful /ˈgreɪsfəl/ adj **1** a graceful movement is smooth and beautiful **2** a graceful shape or object is attractive
3 showing good manners and respect for other people: *She was extremely graceful in defeat.* —**grace•ful•ly** adv

gra•cious¹ /ˈgreɪʃəs/ adj **1** showing kindness and good manners ≠ UNGRACIOUS **2** relating to a style of life that is enjoyed by people who have enough money to buy beautiful things —**gra•cious•ly** adv

gra•cious² /ˈgreɪʃəs/ interjection *old-fashioned* used for expressing surprise

grad /græd/ noun [C] *informal* a GRADUATE —**grad** adj: *a grad student*

gra•da•tion /grəˈdeɪʃ(ə)n/ noun [C] one of the steps in a series that shows how one thing slowly becomes something else

grade¹ /greɪd/ noun [C] ★
1 one of the levels of school in the U.S. that lasts for one year: *The topic is covered in the seventh grade.* ♦ *eighth grade students*
2 a letter or number that shows the quality of a student's work: *You need to improve your grades.*
3 a level of quality or importance: *Their wool is suitable for finer grades of cloth.* ♦ *He demanded to be put on a higher salary grade.*
PHRASE **make the grade** to succeed in doing something because you are good enough

grade² /greɪd/ verb [T] **1** to judge the quality of a student's work by giving it a letter or number **2** to separate things into different groups according to quality, size, importance, etc.

ˈ**grade point** ˌ**average** noun [C] *American* a GPA

ˈ**grade** ˌ**school** noun [C/U] *American* an ELEMENTARY SCHOOL

gra•di•ent /ˈgreɪdiənt/ noun [C] a measure of how steep a slope is

grad•u•al /ˈgrædʒuəl/ adj happening slowly and by small amounts: *a gradual change in the climate*

grad•u•al•ly /ˈgrædʒuəli/ adv ★★ slowly and in small stages or amounts: *She gradually built up a reputation as a successful lawyer.* ♦ *Gradually add the flour.*

grad•u•ate¹ /ˈgrædʒuət/ noun [C] ★
1 *American* someone who has finished their studies at a HIGH SCHOOL, college, or university: *Is Jane a high school graduate?* ♦ *All three were **graduates of** the same university.*
2 someone who has a degree from a university or college: *careers for history graduates* ♦ *a Yale graduate* ♦ *Candidates should be **graduates in** science or engineering.*

grad•u•ate² /ˈgrædʒuˌeɪt/ verb [I] ★
1 to complete your studies at a school such

as a HIGH SCHOOL, college, or university and get a DIPLOMA or a degree: *He **graduated from** Yale University in 1936.* ♦ *one of the first women to **graduate in** history and languages at the Sorbonne*
2 graduate (from sth) to sth to make progress, or to reach a higher position: *He eventually graduated from clerical work to his present role.* ♦ *Some children had graduated to reading books without pictures.*

grad·u·ate[3] /ˈgrædʒuət/ adj relating to or studying for a second degree such as a MASTER'S DEGREE or a DOCTORATE

grad·u·at·ed /ˈgrædʒuˌeɪtəd/ adj **1** organized according to a series of levels **2** increasing by regular amounts

grad·u·a·tion /ˌgrædʒuˈeɪʃ(ə)n/ noun **1** [U] the act of receiving a DIPLOMA or degree after finishing a course of study at a school such as a HIGH SCHOOL, college, or university
2 [C/U] a ceremony at which you are given a DIPLOMA or degree

graf·fi·ti /grəˈfiti/ noun [U] words or pictures that are drawn on walls in public places

graft[1] /græft/ noun **1** [U] *American informal* dishonest or illegal activities in politics or business that involve giving people money or advantages in exchange for their help or support **2** [C] a piece of skin or bone from one part of your body that is used to replace or repair a damaged part of your body **3** [C] a piece that is taken from a plant and joined to a cut that has been made in another plant, so that it can grow there

graft[2] /græft/ verb [T] **1** to take a piece of skin or bone from one part of someone's body and use it to replace or repair a damaged part of their body **2** to take a piece from a plant and join it to a cut that has been made in another plant, so that it can grow there

gra·ham crack·er /ˈgreɪəm ˌkrækər/ noun [C] *American* a type of COOKIE made from flour, sugar, and water

grain /greɪn/ noun

1 seed	4 small amount of quality
2 plants used for food	5 pattern of fibers
3 very small piece of sth	+ PHRASE

1 [C/U] a seed, or the seeds from plants such as wheat, rice, or CORN that are used for food **2** [U] plants that are used for food such as wheat, rice, or CORN **3** [C] a very small individual piece of a substance such as sand, salt, or sugar **4** [singular] a very small amount of a quality or feeling: *There was more than a grain of truth in what he'd said.* **5** [U] the pattern or direction of the fibers in substances such as wood, stone, cloth, or paper
PHRASE **go against the grain** to be completely different from what you feel is right, natural, or normal for you
→ SALT[1]

gram /græm/ noun [C] a unit for measuring weight in the METRIC SYSTEM

gram·mar /ˈgræmər/ noun ★★
1 [U] the set of rules that describe the structure of a language and control the way that sentences are formed: *errors in spelling and grammar* ♦ *The book covers all the essential points of English grammar.*
2 [C] a book explaining the rules of a language

ˈgrammar ˌschool noun [C] **1** *American* an ELEMENTARY SCHOOL **2** a school in the U.K. for children between the ages of 11 and 18 who have passed a special examination in order to be allowed to go there

gram·mat·i·cal /grəˈmætɪk(ə)l/ adj **1** relating to grammar: *grammatical errors* **2** a grammatical sentence correctly follows the rules of grammar ≠ UNGRAMMATICAL
—**gram·mat·i·cal·ly** adv

gramme /græm/ another spelling of **gram**

gran·a·ry /ˈgræn(ə)ri, ˈgreɪn(ə)ri/ noun [C] a building where grain is kept

grand[1] /grænd/ adj ★
1 very impressive: *The house was spacious and grand.* ♦ *The ball was **a very grand affair**.*
2 most important: *the grand prize*

grand[2] /grænd/ noun [C] **1** (plural **grand**) *informal* a thousand dollars **2** a GRAND PIANO

grand·child /ˈgræn(d)ˌtʃaɪld/ (plural **grand·chil·dren** /ˈgræn(d)ˌtʃɪldrən/) noun [C] the son or daughter of one of your children

grand·dad /ˈgræn(d)ˌdæd/ noun [C] *informal* a GRANDFATHER

grand·daugh·ter /ˈgræn(d)ˌdɔtər/ noun [C] the daughter of one of your children —*picture* → FAMILY TREE

gran·deur /ˈgrændʒər, ˈgrænˌdʒʊr/ noun [U] an impressive quality

grand·fa·ther /ˈgræn(d)ˌfɑðər/ noun [C] ★ the father of one of your parents —*picture* → FAMILY TREE

ˌgrandfather ˈclock noun [C] an old-fashioned clock in a tall wooden box that stands on the floor

gran·di·ose /ˈgrændiˌoʊs/ adj intended to achieve something that is important or difficult, but unlikely to be successful because of not being sensible

ˌgrand ˈjury noun [C] a group of people in the U.S. legal system who decide if someone accused of a crime should go to trial in a court of law

grand·ly /ˈgrændli/ adv in a way that tries to impress you but often does not

grand·ma /ˈgræn(d)ˌmɑ/ noun [C] *informal* a GRANDMOTHER

grand·moth·er /ˈgræn(d)ˌmʌðər/ noun [C] ★ the mother of one of your parents —*picture* → FAMILY TREE

grand·pa /ˈgræn(d)ˌpɑ/ noun [C] *informal* a GRANDFATHER

grand·par·ent /ˈgræn(d)ˌperənt/ noun [C] ★ the mother or father of your mother or father

ˌgrand piˈano noun [C] a type of large piano

Grand Prix /ˌgrɑn ˈpri/ noun [C] an international competition for RACE CARS or MOTORCYCLES

ˌgrand ˈslam noun [C] **1** a HOME RUN in baseball in which you score four RUNS (=points) because there is a player on each of the four BASES **2** a situation in which you win all of a set of important competitions in a particular sport in the same year

grand·son /ˈgræn(d)ˌsʌn/ noun [C] the son of one of your children —*picture* → FAMILY TREE

grand•stand /ˈɡræn(d)ˌstænd/ noun [C] a large structure with rows of seats from which people watch sports events

ˌgrand ˈtotal noun [C] a final total of all the amounts or totals that must be added together

gran•ite /ˈɡrænɪt/ noun [U] a type of very hard stone

gran•ny /ˈɡræni/ noun [C] *informal* a GRANDMOTHER

gra•no•la /ɡrəˈnoʊlə/ noun [U] *American* a mixture of grains and dried fruit that is eaten as a breakfast food

grant¹ /ɡrænt/ verb [T] *formal* ★★ to allow someone to have or to do what they want: *The Board has refused to **grant your request**.* ♦ *His **wish** was finally **granted**.*

PHRASES **I grant you** used for admitting that something is true: *You're thorough, I grant you that, but we don't need all this detail.*

take sb for granted to expect someone to always do things for you even when you do not show that you are grateful

take sth for granted to expect something always to happen or exist in a particular way and not think about any possible problems or difficulties: *Losing my job taught me never to take anything for granted.*

grant² /ɡrænt/ noun [C] ★★ an amount of money that the government or an organization gives you for a specific purpose and does not ask you to pay back: *a research grant*

gran•ule /ˈɡrænˌjul/ noun [C] a small hard round piece of something: *coffee granules*

grape /ɡreɪp/ noun [C] a small green or purple fruit that grows in BUNCHES on a VINE and that is often used for making wine —*picture* → C10

grape•fruit /ˈɡreɪpˌfrut/ noun [C/U] a fruit like a large orange that is yellow on the outside, yellow or red inside, and has sour juice —*picture* → C10

grape•vine /ˈɡreɪpˌvaɪn/ noun [singular] *informal* the way in which information spreads quickly from one person to another through conversation: *I heard through the grapevine that you had a baby.*

graph /ɡræf/ noun [C] a picture that uses lines or curves to show the relationship between numbers or measurements that change

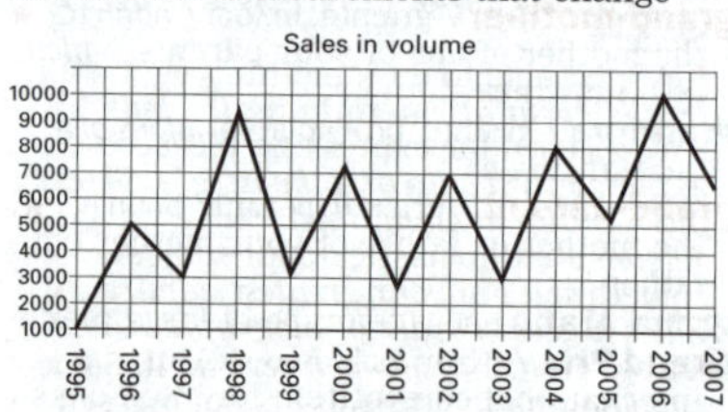

graph

graph•ic /ˈɡræfɪk/ adj **1** containing a lot of detail so that you have a clear idea of something: *a graphic description* **2** relating to drawing —**graph•i•cal•ly** /ˈɡræfɪkli/ adv

ˌgraphic deˈsign noun [U] the art of designing pictures and TEXT for magazines, advertisements, etc. —**graphic deˈsigner** noun [C]

graph•ics /ˈɡræfɪks/ noun [plural] pictures that are produced by a computer, or that are included in a document, magazine, etc.

graph•ite /ˈɡræˌfaɪt/ noun [U] a soft black substance that is used in pencils

grap•ple /ˈɡræp(ə)l/ PHRASAL VERB ˈ**grapple ˌwith sth** to try hard to understand a difficult idea or solve a difficult problem

grasp¹ /ɡræsp/ verb [T] **1** to take and hold someone or something very tightly: *He grasped her firmly by the shoulders.* **2** to understand something: *Charlie grasped the point at once.* → NETTLE

PHRASAL VERB ˈ**grasp at sth** to try to take hold of something

grasp² /ɡræsp/ noun [singular] **1** the ability to understand something: *a good grasp of English* **2** the ability to achieve something: *Victory was now within their grasp.* **3** a very tight hold of someone or something: *Suddenly he broke free from her grasp.*

grass /ɡræs/ noun ★★★
1 [U] a very common plant with thin green leaves that covers the ground: *We should cut the grass before it starts raining.* ♦ *Stephen was lying on the grass.*
2 [C] a particular type of grass: *tall flowering grasses*
3 [U] *informal* MARIJUANA

grass•hop•per /ˈɡræsˌhɑpər/ noun [C] a large insect with long back legs that moves by jumping and that makes short high sounds —*picture* → C13

grass•land /ˈɡræsˌlænd/ noun [U] a large area of land where wild grass grows

grass•roots, the /ˈɡræsˌruts/ noun [plural] the ordinary people in a community, country, or organization instead of its leaders

grass•y /ˈɡræsi/ adj covered in grass

grate¹ /ɡreɪt/ verb **1** [T] to rub food against a GRATER in order to cut it into small pieces —*picture* → C2 **2** [I] to rub against something and make an unpleasant annoying sound: *Her nails grated against the wall.* **3** [I] to have an annoying effect on someone: *His constant talking began to grate on her nerves.*

grate² /ɡreɪt/ noun [C] a frame of metal bars used for holding coal or wood in a FIREPLACE (=the opening in a wall where you can light a fire)

grate•ful /ˈɡreɪtfəl/ adj ★ feeling that you want to thank someone because they have given you something or done something for you ≠ UNGRATEFUL: *Thanks for coming with me. I'm really grateful.* ♦ *I'm very **grateful for** all your help with the party.* ♦ **grateful to sb for sth** *She was grateful to them for letting her stay at their house.* ♦ **+(that)** *You should be grateful that I didn't tell your parents.* —**grate•ful•ly** adv

grat•er /ˈɡreɪtər/ noun [C] a tool with a rough sharp surface that you rub foods such as cheese and vegetables against in order to cut them into very small pieces —*picture* → C2

grat•i•fy /ˈɡrætɪˌfaɪ/ verb [T] *formal* to make someone feel pleased or satisfied —**grat•i•fi•ca•tion** /ˌɡrætɪfɪˈkeɪʃ(ə)n/ noun [U]

grat·ing[1] /ˈgreɪtɪŋ/ noun [C] a metal frame with bars across it that is used for covering a hole or window

grat·ing[2] /ˈgreɪtɪŋ/ adj a grating voice, laugh, or sound is unpleasant and annoying

grat·i·tude /ˈgrætɪˌtud/ noun [U] the feeling of being grateful ≠ INGRATITUDE

gra·tu·i·tous /grəˈtuɪtəs/ adj done or shown without any good reason: *There's too much gratuitous violence in the movie.*

grave[1] /greɪv/ noun ★

1 [C] the place where a dead body is buried in a deep hole in the ground: *He's never even visited his mother's grave.*

2 the grave [singular] *literary* death: *His secret will go with me to the grave* (=I will die without telling anyone).

grave[2] /greɪv/ adj **1** so serious that you feel worried: *You're in grave danger.* **2** looking serious and worried: *a grave expression/face* —**grave·ly** adv

grave[3] /grɑv/ or **ˌgrave ˈaccent** noun [C] the mark ` above a letter in French and some other languages that is used in order to show how it is pronounced → ACUTE 4, CIRCUMFLEX

grav·el /ˈgræv(ə)l/ noun [U] small pieces of stone that are used for making paths and roads

grav·el·ly /ˈgræv(ə)li/ adj a gravelly voice sounds low and rough

grave·stone /ˈgreɪvˌstoʊn/ noun [C] a stone by a GRAVE that shows the name of the person who is buried there and the dates when he or she was born and died

grave·yard /ˈgreɪvˌjɑrd/ noun [C] an area of land where dead people are buried, usually around a church

grav·i·tate /ˈgrævɪˌteɪt/ verb [I] *formal* to be attracted to someone or something and tend to move toward them

grav·i·ta·tion·al /ˌgrævɪˈteɪʃən(ə)l/ adj *science* relating to the force of gravity

grav·i·ty /ˈgrævəti/ noun [U] **1** the force that makes something fall to the ground: *the laws of gravity* **2** the serious or important quality of something: *I'm sure you can appreciate the gravity of the situation.* → CENTER[1]

gra·vy /ˈgreɪvi/ noun [U] a sauce made from the juices of cooked meat mixed with flour

gray[1] /greɪ/ adj ★

1 shade of black	4 with a lot of clouds
2 when hair goes whiter	5 boring
3 when face looks pale	

1 between black and white in color: *He wore a dark gray suit.*

2 if someone goes or turns gray, their hair starts to become white: *She seems to have gone gray very quickly.*

3 if someone's face is gray, they look pale because they are sick or shocked: *His face was gray with pain.*

4 used for describing the weather or the light when it is not very bright because there are a lot of clouds: *a gray day in February* ♦ *The rain stopped and the gray skies began to clear.*

5 boring: *the drab gray tedium of his life*

gray[2] /greɪ/ noun [C/U] a color that is between black and white

gray[3] /greɪ/ verb [I] **1** to become gray in color **2** if a person or their hair is graying, their hair is becoming white

ˌgray ˈarea noun [C] a situation in which the rules are not clear, or in which you are not sure what is right or wrong

graze[1] /greɪz/ verb **1** [I] to eat grass that is growing somewhere: *Goats grazed on the hillside.* **2** [I/T] to touch something slightly when you pass it: *She let her fingers graze lightly against his skin.* **3** [T] to break the surface of your skin: *He fell off the swing and grazed his knee.*

graze[2] /greɪz/ noun [C] a break in the surface of your skin: *a graze on my elbow*

GRE, the /ˌdʒi ɑr ˈi/ Graduate Record Exam: a test that someone must take in order to be accepted at a U.S. university as a GRADUATE STUDENT (=a student who already has at least one degree)

grease[1] /gris/ noun [U] **1** a thick substance similar to oil that is used on machine parts for making them work smoothly **2** fat that comes out of meat when you cook it

grease[2] /gris/ verb [T] to put grease, fat, or oil on something

greas·y /ˈgrisi/ adj **1** prepared with a lot of oil or fat: *greasy french fries* **2** covered in GREASE or oil: *greasy hands/jeans* **3** producing a lot of natural oil ≠ DRY: *greasy hair/skin*

great[1] /greɪt/ adj ★★★

1 good/enjoyable	5 able to do sth well
2 more than usual	6 for showing pleasure
3 for emphasis	7 enthusiastic
4 important/powerful	

1 *informal* very good, enjoyable, or nice: *You looked great in that outfit.* ♦ *We had a great day.* ♦ *He's a great guy.*

2 bigger or more than is usual: *They could be in great danger.* ♦ *He was in a great hurry.* ♦ *It gives me great pleasure to welcome our next guest.* → DEAL[1]

3 *spoken* used for emphasizing the large size or amount of something: *a **great big** piece of chocolate*

4 important or powerful: *a great military power* ♦ *the greatest environmental disaster in decades* ♦ *one of the greatest writers of the modern age*

5 *informal* able to do something very well: *Paul's **great at** entertaining the kids.*

6 *spoken* used for expressing pleasure or agreement: *It's great to be here.* ♦ *Great! I'll pick you up at eight, then.*

7 *informal* enthusiastic about someone or something: *I'm your greatest admirer.* ♦ *She's a great reader of biographies.*

great[2] /greɪt/ adv *informal* very well. Some people think that this use is not correct: *You're doing great.*

great[3] /greɪt/ noun [C] someone or something that is well known and admired by a lot of people: *Pete Sampras is one of the all-time greats of tennis.*

ˌGreat ˈBritain the island that consists of England, Scotland, and Wales

ˌgreat-ˈgrandchild noun [C] the GRANDCHILD of your son or daughter

G

G

great·ly /ˈgreɪtli/ adv very much: *Your support is greatly appreciated.* ♦ *greatly reduced costs*

great·ness /ˈgreɪtnəs/ noun [U] a position of power, success, or respect: *a woman destined for greatness*

greed /grid/ noun [U] a strong wish to have more money, possessions, or power than you need

greed·y /ˈgridi/ adj wanting more money, possessions, or power than you need —**greed·i·ly** adv

green¹ /grin/ adj ★★★

1 like grass in color	5 not experienced
2 made of green leaves	6 with lots of plants
3 not ready to be eaten	7 of Green Party
4 caring for nature	

1 something that is green is the same color as grass: *green eyes* ♦ *The first **bright green** leaves were showing.*
2 made from the green leaves of vegetables: *a green salad*
3 not yet ready to be eaten: *green tomatoes*
4 concerned with protecting the environment: *wind farms and other green energy projects* ♦ *green campaigners*
5 someone who is green is young and has no experience of life
6 a green area has a lot of grass, plants, or trees: *a campaign to protect the city's green spaces*
7 Green relating to the GREEN PARTY

green² /grin/ noun ★★

1 color of grass	4 green vegetables
2 area of grass	5 Green Party member
3 area in golf	

1 [C/U] the color of grass: *She was dressed in green.*
2 [C] a large area of grass where people can walk, sit, or play games: *They moved to a house overlooking the green.*
3 [C] in golf, the area of short grass around a hole
4 greens [plural] *spoken* vegetables that have green leaves
5 Green [C] a member of the GREEN PARTY

green·back /ˈgrinˌbæk/ noun [C] *American informal* a U.S. dollar

ˌgreen ˈbean noun [C] a long thin green vegetable that grows on a tall climbing plant —*picture* → C11

ˈgreen ˌcard noun [C] *American* an official document that allows someone who is not a U.S. citizen to live and work in the U.S.

green·er·y /ˈgrinəri/ noun [U] plants or leaves

green·house /ˈgrinˌhaʊs/ noun [C] a building made of glass that is used for growing plants that need protection from the weather

ˈgreenhouse efˌfect, the noun [singular] the situation in which heat is unable to escape from the atmosphere, which causes the temperature of the Earth to rise

ˈgreenhouse ˌgas noun [C] a gas that stops heat from escaping from the atmosphere and causes the greenhouse effect

green·ish /ˈgriniʃ/ adj similar to green

ˌgreen ˈlight noun [singular] official approval for something to be done

ˌgreen ˈonion noun [C] *American* a type of onion with a small white round part and a long thin green stem = SCALLION

ˈGreen ˌParty, the a political organization whose main goal is to protect the environment

Green·peace /ˈgrinˌpis/ an international organization whose goal is to protect the environment

greet /grit/ verb [T] **1** to behave in a polite or friendly way toward someone when you meet them: *Natalie rushed to open the door and greet the guests.* **2** to react to an action or news in a particular way: *The decision was greeted by violent demonstrations.* **3** if you are greeted by a sight, sound, or smell, it is the first thing that you notice

greet·ing /ˈgritɪŋ/ noun **1** [C/U] something polite or friendly that you say or do when you meet someone: *They exchanged greetings and sat down.* **2** [C] a friendly message that you send to someone on a special occasion such as their birthday

gre·gar·i·ous /grəˈgeriəs/ adj a gregarious person enjoys being with other people

gre·nade /grəˈneɪd/ noun [C] a small bomb that someone throws or fires from a gun

grew the past tense of **grow**

grey /greɪ/ another spelling of **gray**

grey·hound /ˈgreɪˌhaʊnd/ noun [C] a tall thin dog that can run very fast. It is used in races.

grid /grɪd/ noun [C] **1** a pattern of straight lines that cross each other to form squares: *streets laid out in a grid* **2** a pattern of straight lines that form squares on a map, that you use to find a particular place: *a grid reference* **3** a set of metal bars that are arranged in a pattern of straight lines

grid·dle /ˈgrɪd(ə)l/ noun [C] a round flat iron pan that is used on top of a hot surface for cooking

grid·i·ron /ˈgrɪdˌaɪrn/ noun [C] *American* a field on which football is played

grid·lock /ˈgrɪdˌlɑk/ noun [U] **1** a situation in which it is impossible to make progress **2** a situation in which there are so many cars on the roads that traffic cannot move

grief /grif/ noun [U] a strong feeling of sadness, usually because someone has died → GOOD¹

griev·ance /ˈgrivəns/ noun [C] a feeling or complaint that you have been treated unfairly

grieve /griv/ verb [I/T] to feel extremely sad because someone has died

griev·ous /ˈgrivəs/ adj *formal* extremely serious or severe: *He has made a grievous error.*

grift·er /ˈgrɪftər/ noun [C] *American informal* someone who tricks people into giving them their money or possessions

grill¹ /grɪl/ noun [C] **1** a flat frame of metal bars on which food can be placed and cooked over a fire **2** *British* a BROILER

grill² /grɪl/ verb **1** [I/T] to cook something over a fire on a frame of metal bars **2** [T] to ask someone a lot of difficult questions for a long period of time **3** [I/T] *British* to BROIL something

grille or **grill** /grɪl/ noun [C] a metal frame with bars or wire across it that is used for protecting a door, a window, or the front of a car

grim /grɪm/ adj **1** grim news, situations, and events are unpleasant and make you feel upset and worried: *the grim reality of unemployment* **2** very serious and unfriendly: *a grim expression* **3** a grim place is ugly and unpleasant —**grim•ly** adv

grim•ace /ˈgrɪməs/ verb [I] to make an ugly expression by twisting your face, for example because you are in pain or because you do not like something —**grim•ace** noun [C]

grime /graɪm/ noun [U] thick dirt on a surface

grim•y /ˈgraɪmi/ adj very dirty

grin /grɪn/ verb [I] to smile showing your teeth —**grin** noun [C]

grind[1] /graɪnd/ (past tense and past participle **ground** /graʊnd/) verb [T] **1** to break something into very small pieces or powder, either by using a machine or by crushing it between two hard surfaces: *The mill was used for grinding corn.* **2** to use a machine in order to cut food, especially raw meat, into very small pieces **3** to press something down onto a surface using a lot of force: *She ground a half-smoked cigarette into the ashtray.*

PHRASES **grind your teeth** to rub your top and bottom teeth together in a way that makes a noise

grind to a halt 1 if a vehicle grinds to a halt, it moves more and more slowly until it finally stops **2** if a process or a country grinds to a halt, things gradually get worse until they finally stop

grind[2] /graɪnd/ noun [singular] *informal* something that is hard work, boring, and tiring

grind•ing /ˈgraɪndɪŋ/ adj **a grinding halt** a situation in which something stops operating completely

grip[1] /grɪp/ noun **1** [singular] a firm strong hold: *Pete tightened his grip on her arm.* **2** [singular] power and control over someone or something: *The President struggled to regain his grip on power.* **3** [singular/U] if shoes or tires have grip, they hold a surface firmly and do not slip

PHRASES **be in the grip of sth** to be in a difficult or unpleasant situation

come to grips with sth to start to deal with a problem, situation, or job that you have to do

get a grip (on yourself) *spoken* to make an effort to control your emotions or your behavior

grip[2] /grɪp/ verb **1** [T] to hold something tightly: *She gripped Frank's hand firmly.* **2** [T] to have a strong effect on someone: *A feeling of fear gripped the crowd.* **3** [T] to keep someone very interested in something: *The case has gripped the public because of the celebrities involved.* **4** [I/T] if shoes or tires grip, they hold a surface firmly and therefore do not slip

gripe /graɪp/ noun [C] *informal* a complaint about something that is annoying but not very important —**gripe** verb [I]

grip•ping /ˈgrɪpɪŋ/ adj very exciting and interesting

gris•ly /ˈgrɪzli/ adj involving death or violence in a shocking way = GRUESOME

grit[1] /grɪt/ noun [U] very small pieces of stone or sand

grit[2] /grɪt/ verb **grit your teeth 1** to press your teeth together tightly, for example because you are angry or in pain **2** to show determination in a difficult situation

grit•ty /ˈgrɪti/ adj **1** firm in your intentions: *a gritty determination to succeed* **2** showing life as it really is, even when it is not nice or attractive: *a gritty television drama* **3** containing grit, or covered with grit

griz•zled /ˈgrɪz(ə)ld/ adj with gray hair

griz•zly bear /ˈgrɪzli ˌber/ or **griz•zly** /ˈgrɪzli/ noun [C] a very large bear with brown fur that lives in the mountains of the north western U.S.

G

groan /groʊn/ verb **1** [I] to make a long low sound because you are unhappy or in pain **2** [I/T] to speak about something in a way that shows that you are unhappy —**groan** noun [C]

gro•cer /ˈgroʊsər/ noun [C] someone who owns or works in a GROCERY

gro•cer•ies /ˈgroʊs(ə)riz/ noun [plural] food and other goods for the home that you buy regularly

gro•cer•y[1] /ˈgroʊs(ə)ri/ noun [C] *American* a small store that sells food and other goods

gro•cer•y[2] /ˈgroʊs(ə)ri/ adj relating to groceries or stores that sell groceries

grog•gy /ˈgrɑgi/ adj feeling tired, weak, or confused because you are sick or because you have not had enough sleep

groin /grɔɪn/ noun [C] the area where your legs join the front of your body

groom[1] /grum/ noun [C] **1** a BRIDEGROOM **2** someone who takes care of horses

groom[2] /grum/ verb [T] **1** to clean and brush an animal **2** to prepare someone for a particular job or activity

groove /gruv/ noun [C] a line that has been cut into a surface

grope /groʊp/ verb **1** [I] to try to find something by feeling with your hands: *She was groping around in her purse for her keys.* ♦ *I groped my way to the door.* **2** [I] to search for an idea or a way to say something without being certain of what you are doing: *She hesitated, seeming to grope for words.* **3** [T] to touch someone sexually, especially someone who does not want to be touched

gross[1] /groʊs/ adj **1** a gross amount of money is the total amount before taxes or costs have been taken out **2** extreme and unreasonable: *a gross distortion of the truth* **3** *legal* gross actions are extremely bad and are considered immoral by most people: *gross misconduct* **4** *informal* extremely unpleasant

gross[2] /groʊs/ verb [T] to earn a particular amount of money before taxes or other costs have been taken out

ˌgross doˌmestic ˈproduct noun [U] GDP

gross•ly /ˈgroʊsli/ adv extremely: *grossly unfair*

ˌgross ˌnational ˈproduct noun [U] GNP

gross 'profit noun [C] *business* the difference between the price that someone sells goods for and what it costs to produce them

gro·tesque /groʊ'tesk/ adj **1** extremely ugly and strange **2** unreasonable or offensive —**gro·tesque·ly** adv

grouch[1] /graʊtʃ/ noun [C] *informal* someone who complains a lot or is often in a bad mood

grouch[2] /graʊtʃ/ verb [I] *informal* to complain a lot, often without good reason =GRUMBLE

grouch·y /'graʊtʃi/ adj *informal* often in a bad mood or complaining a lot =GRUMPY

ground[1] /graʊnd/ noun ★★★

1 surface of Earth	6 reason for sth
2 layer of soil/rock	7 subject/idea
3 area of land	8 level of progress
4 area used for sth	9 wire
5 land around house	+ PHRASES

1 [singular/U] the top part of the Earth's surface that people walk on: *People were sitting **on the ground** in small groups.* ♦ *They were working 250 feet **below ground**.*
2 [singular] the layer of soil and rock that forms the Earth's surface: *the destruction caused by getting coal out of the ground* ♦ *Prepare the ground for planting.*
3 [U] an area of land: *an acre of ground*
4 [C] an area of land or ocean that is used for a particular purpose: *soldiers on the parade ground* ♦ *a regular fishing ground*
5 grounds [plural] the land and gardens that surround a large house or public building: *She found him wandering around the grounds.*
6 grounds [plural] a reason for what you say or do: *The army turned him down **on medical grounds**.* ♦ *The Act prohibits discrimination **on the grounds of** sex or marital status.* ♦ *There do seem to be some **grounds for** their complaints.*
7 [singular/U] the subject, idea, or information that people are talking about or writing about: *We'll be **covering** a lot of new **ground** in today's lecture.* ♦ *Henry seems anxious to return to more **familiar ground**.*
8 [U] the level of success or progress that someone or something has achieved: *Most stock markets **lost ground** after their recent gains.*
9 [C] *American* a wire that makes electrical equipment safe by allowing the current to flow into the ground

PHRASES **get (sth) off the ground** to start successfully, or to get something started successfully
on the ground 1 on the surface of the earth, rather than in the air **2** *mainly journalism* in the place or situation that is being discussed
stand your ground 1 to not move when someone attacks you or is going to attack you **2** to refuse to change your opinions, beliefs, or decisions despite pressure to change them

ground[2] /graʊnd/ verb [T] **1** to stop an airplane from leaving the ground: *All of their planes have been grounded.* **2** *American* to make a piece of electrical equipment safe by putting in a wire that takes the current to the ground **3** to base an idea or decision on a particular thing: *Kim's theory is grounded in practical experience.* **4** to punish a child or young person by stopping them from going to places that they enjoy: *His parents grounded him for two weeks.*

ground[3] the past tense and past participle of grind[1]

ˌground 'beef noun [U] *American* meat from a cow that has been cut into very small pieces =HAMBURGER

ground·break·ing /'graʊn(d)ˌbreɪkɪŋ/ adj using new methods or achieving new results

ˌground 'floor noun [singular] *British* the floor of a building that is at or near the level of the ground

ground·hog /'graʊndˌhɔg/ noun [C] a small furry animal with short legs that is found in North America and that lives in holes in the ground

ground·ing /'graʊndɪŋ/ noun [singular] a basic knowledge of a subject

ground·less /'graʊn(d)ləs/ adj not based on evidence or good reasons

'ground ˌrules noun [plural] the basic rules or principles that govern the way that something is done

ground·swell /'graʊn(d)ˌswel/ noun [singular] a sudden increase in people's feelings about something

ground·work /'graʊn(d)ˌwɜrk/ noun [U] work that you do in order to prepare for something: *The agreement will lay the groundwork* (=do the work that is necessary) *for peaceful relations between the two countries.*

ˌground 'zero noun [U] **1** a place where a lot of people have been killed, or a lot of damage has been done, especially because of a nuclear explosion **2** a place where changes are happening quickly or violently

group[1] /grup/ noun [C] ★★★
1 several people or things that are together or that are related to each other in some way: *Why don't you join the local drama group?* ♦ *Companies should employ more people in the over-55 age group.* ♦ *a group decision/activity* (=involving all the people in a group) ♦ *There was a **group of** girls following him.*
2 a small set of musicians who play POP MUSIC =BAND: *members of a pop group*

group[2] /grup/ verb [T] to put people or things into groups: *The students are grouped according to ability.* ♦ *The new offices will be grouped around a central courtyard.*

group·ie /'grupi/ noun [C] *informal* someone who admires a particular famous person and tries to meet them or make friends with them

group·ing /'grupɪŋ/ noun [C] a set of people or things that are considered as a group

grouse[1] /graʊs/ noun [C] a large brown bird that lives on the ground and is hunted for its meat

grouse[2] /graʊs/ verb [I] *informal* to complain about something that is unimportant

grove /groʊv/ noun [C] a group of trees that are arranged in lines

grov·el /'grɑv(ə)l/ verb [I] to show too much

respect for someone, or to be too willing to obey someone

grow /groʊ/ (past tense **grew** /gru/; past participle **grown** /groʊn/) verb ★★★

1 become taller	4 start to have quality
2 about hair/nails	5 take care of plants
3 get bigger/stronger	+ PHRASAL VERBS

1 [I] if children, animals, or plants grow, they become taller: *She must have grown at least four inches since the last time I saw her.* ♦ *a fully grown lion* ♦ *Some of these creatures* ***grew to a length of*** *over 12 feet.*
2 [I/T] if your hair or nails grow, or if you grow them, they become longer: *My nails grow really quickly.* ♦ *Her husband is growing a beard.*
3 [I] to increase in size, strength, or importance: *The world's population is growing faster than anyone thought it would.* ♦ *The problem continues to grow.* ♦ *She could feel the anger growing inside her.* ♦ *The sound* ***grew to*** *a deafening roar.* ♦ *The economy has* ***grown by*** *7% over the past year.* ♦ *She was* ***growing in*** *confidence every day.*
4 [linking verb] *literary* used for saying that a feeling or quality gradually starts to exist: *The nights were growing darker.* ♦ *Nina was growing bored.* ♦ *She had* ***grown used to*** *the old man's habits.* ♦ **grow to do/be sth** *They had grown to love the place and the people.*
5 [T] if you grow plants, you take care of them and help them to develop =CULTIVATE, PRODUCE: *They grew all their own vegetables.* ♦ *Various crops are grown here.* ♦ *the country's largest rice-growing area*

PHRASAL VERBS ˌ**grow aˈpart** if people grow apart, their relationship gradually changes and they become less close
ˈ**grow into sth 1** to develop and become a particular thing or person: *She had grown into a beautiful woman.* **2** if children grow into clothes, they become the right size to wear clothes that were too big
ˈ**grow on sb** if something or someone grows on you, you start to like them more: *The new house slowly began to grow on her.*
ˌ**grow ˈout of sth 1** if children grow out of clothes, they grow bigger and the clothes become too small for them **2** if someone grows out of a habit, they stop doing it because they have become older or wiser **3** to develop from something: *The idea grew out of a wish to improve the lives of the children in the region.*
ˌ**grow ˈup 1** to change from being a child to being an adult: *She's really starting to grow up now.* ♦ *He rarely saw his father while he was growing up.* **2** to stop behaving like a child and become more sensible: *It wasn't until my marriage ended that I really started to grow up.*

Word family: grow

Words in the same family as ***grow***

- **grown** *adj*
- **growing** *adj*
- **growth** *n*
- **outgrow** *v*
- **overgrown** *adj*
- **undergrowth** *n*

grow·ing /ˈgroʊɪŋ/ adj ★★
1 becoming more severe or extreme: *There is* ***growing public concern*** *over the effects of this policy.*
2 becoming greater in size or amount: *the growing popularity of the Internet* ♦ *A* ***growing number of*** *people are choosing to eat less red meat.* ♦ *the country's* ***fastest growing*** *international airport*

growl /graʊl/ verb **1** [I] if an animal growls, it makes a frightening low noise **2** [I/T] to say something in an unfriendly and angry way —**growl** noun [C]

grown[1] /groʊn/ adj adult: *a grown man/woman*

grown[2] the past participle of **grow**

ˈ**grown-ˌup**[1] noun [C] an ADULT: used when talking to children

ˈ**grown-ˌup**[2] adj adult, or intended for adults: *She has two grown-up sons.* ♦ *grown-up entertainment*

growth /groʊθ/ noun ★★★
1 [singular/U] an increase in the number, size, or importance of something: *We are entering a* ***period of*** *rapid population* ***growth.*** ♦ *The annual* ***rate of growth*** *was 12 percent.* ♦ *a substantial* ***growth in*** *the number of available jobs* ♦ *the international* ***growth of*** *capitalism*
2 [singular/U] an increase in the size or development of a living thing: *There is no evidence that the drug increases hair growth.*
3 [C] a lump on someone's body that is caused by a disease: *a cancerous growth*

Words often used with growth

Verbs often used with ***growth*** *(sense 1)*

- **encourage, foster, increase, promote, stimulate** + GROWTH: make something increase
- **inhibit, stunt** + GROWTH: prevent something from increasing

ˈ**growth ˌindustry** noun [C] an industry that is growing quickly

grub·by /ˈgrʌbi/ adj dirty

grudge /grʌdʒ/ noun [C] a feeling of anger toward someone because they have done something unfair to you: *There's a whole list of people who might bear a grudge against him.*

grudg·ing /ˈgrʌdʒɪŋ/ adj done in an unwilling way —**grudg·ing·ly** adv

gru·el·ing /ˈgru(ə)lɪŋ/ adj involving a lot of continuous effort =DEMANDING

grue·some /ˈgrusəm/ adj something that is gruesome is very unpleasant because it involves violent injury or death

gruff /grʌf/ adj **1** rude and unfriendly **2** a gruff voice has a rough low sound —**gruff·ly** adv

grum·ble /ˈgrʌmb(ə)l/ verb [I] to complain about something that is unimportant —**grum·ble** noun [C]

grump·y /ˈgrʌmpi/ adj someone who is grumpy complains a lot or is often unhappy —**grump·i·ly** adv

grun·gy /ˈgrʌndʒi/ adj *very informal* dirty and messy

grunt /grʌnt/ verb [I] **1** to make a short low sound in your throat and nose **2** if a pig grunts, it makes its usual low sound —**grunt** noun [C]

G

guar·an·tee[1] /ˌgerənˈti/ noun [C] ★ **1** something that makes something else certain to happen: *Massive investment is no **guarantee of** success.* ♦ **+(that)** *There's no guarantee you will get in without a ticket.* **2** a written promise that a company will repair something that you buy from them if it stops working = WARRANTY: *Many companies offer a 30-day **money-back guarantee**.* ♦ *My watch is still **under guarantee*** (=protected by a company's guarantee). **3** a promise that something will definitely happen: **give (sb) a guarantee** *I can't give you any guarantees at the moment.* ♦ **+(that)** *The company has given a guarantee that there will be no layoffs.*

G

guar·an·tee[2] /ˌgerənˈti/ verb [T] ★ **1** to make it certain that something will happen or will exist = ASSURE: *Our agency provides help for small businesses, but it cannot **guarantee** their **success**.* ♦ **+(that)** *We can't guarantee that you will get the cheapest tickets possible.* ♦ **guarantee sb sth** *This win guarantees them a place in the finals.* **2** if a company guarantees something that you buy, they promise to repair it if it stops working: *All our products are guaranteed for three years.* **3** to promise that something will happen: **+(that)** *He guaranteed they would be paid on time.*

guar·an·teed /ˌgerənˈtid/ adj if something is guaranteed, you will definitely get it

guard[1] /gɑrd/ noun [C] ★★ **1** someone whose job is to protect a place or person: *a prison guard* ♦ *There was an **armed guard** on duty outside his door.* **2** an object that covers something and protects it: *All boxers wear a mouth guard.* **3** in basketball, one of two players who are responsible for moving the ball round the court in order to create opportunities for their team to score —*picture* → C15

PHRASES **let your guard down** or **drop your guard 1** to relax and trust people, even though this might be dangerous **2** to stop being careful while you are being attacked

off (your) guard not concentrating on something and therefore likely to do something that you did not intend to do

on your guard being careful not to do something that you did not intend to do

under guard protected by a guard, or prevented from escaping by a guard: *He was taken to prison under police guard.*

guard[2] /gɑrd/ verb [T] **1** to protect someone or something from danger or harm: **guard sth/sb from sth** *the trees that guarded the farm from the wind* **2** to prevent someone from escaping from a place: *There were two soldiers guarding the main gate.* **3** to try very hard to keep something that is important to you: *The company is fiercely guarding its technology.*

PHRASAL VERB ˈ**guard aˌgainst sth** to try to prevent something from happening: *We need to guard against the possibility of failure.*

guard·ed /ˈgɑrdəd/ adj careful not to give much information or show your real feelings

guard·i·an /ˈgɑrdiən/ noun [C] **1** someone who is legally responsible for someone else's child **2** a person or organization that protects something

ˌ**guardian ˈangel** noun [C] **1** a helpful spirit who some people believe takes care of a particular person **2** someone who continuously supports someone else

gu·ber·na·to·ri·al /ˌgubərnəˈtoriəl/ adj *very formal* relating to the position of GOVERNOR

guer·ril·la /gəˈrɪlə/ noun [C] a member of a military group that fights to change a political situation: *guerrilla groups/fighters/leaders*

guess[1] /ges/ verb [I/T] ★★ **1** to say or decide what you think is true, without being certain about it: *a contest to guess the weight of the pig* ♦ *Whoever **guesses correctly** will win two tickets to the show.* ♦ *I could only **guess at** her age.* ♦ **+what/how etc.** *Would anyone like to guess what this object is?* ♦ **+(that)** *She guessed that it was about noon from the position of the sun.* **2** to be correct about something that you guess: *He had already **guessed the answer**.* ♦ *Surely she would **guess the truth**.* ♦ **+(that)** *Tim guessed she was awake.*

PHRASES **guess what** *spoken* used before you tell someone something that you are pleased or excited about: *Guess what! I won a trip to the Caribbean!*

I guess *informal* used when you are saying something that you think is probably true or correct: *"So you won't be going there again?" "**I guess not*** (=no)*."* ♦ *"Were you happy with the result?" "Well, **I guess so*** (=yes, but not very happy)*."* ♦ **+(that)** *I guess I'll never be able to explain.*

guess[2] /ges/ noun [C] ★ an occasion when you say what you think is true without being certain: *We can only **hazard a guess** at what happened* (=make a guess that will probably not be accurate). ♦ ***Make a guess** and then check it on your calculator.* ♦ *I could probably make **an educated guess*** (=one that is based on some knowledge).

PHRASE **sth is anyone's guess** used for saying that no one knows a particular thing: *What this all means is anybody's guess.* ♦ *It's anyone's guess who'll win the election.*

Words often used with guess

*Adjectives often used with **guess** (noun)*

- **educated, good, informed** + GUESS: used about a guess that is likely to be accurate
- **rough, wild** + GUESS: used about a guess that is not likely to be accurate

guess·ing game /ˈgesɪŋ ˌgeɪm/ noun [C] a situation in which people have to guess what is going to happen

guess·ti·mate /ˈgestɪmət/ noun [C] *informal* a calculation that you make when you do not have all the facts about something

guess·work /ˈgesˌwɜrk/ noun [U] the guesses that you make when you try to find the answer to something

guest[1] /gest/ noun [C] ★★ **1** someone that you have invited to your home or your party: *We have guests staying with us this weekend.* ♦ *advice about getting rid of unwanted guests* ♦ *He was a **guest at** our wedding.*

2 someone who is paying to stay at a hotel or eat in a restaurant: *There is live music to entertain guests.* ♦ *The pool is free for hotel guests.*
3 someone who appears on a television or radio show that they do not regularly appear on: *My first guest tonight is famous for both her singing and acting talent.*
PHRASES **be my guest** *spoken* used for saying yes as a polite reply to a request: *"Do you mind if I sit down?" "Be my guest."*
guest of honor an important guest at a meeting, party, or other event

guest² /gest/ adj **1** provided for guests to use: *a set of guest towels* **2** appearing by invitation to perform at an event: *Tonight's guest speaker is Peter Bell.*

ˈguest ˌhouse noun [C] a small hotel or private home where people can pay to stay the night

guid·ance /ˈgaɪd(ə)ns/ noun [U] advice: *I need some guidance on which university I should choose.*

guide¹ /gaɪd/ noun [C] ★★
1 a book that gives information: *It is worth buying a good travel guide.* ♦ *I bought a copy of* A Beginner's Guide to Building Your Own Home.
2 something or someone that helps you to make a judgment about something: *The doctor will give you **a guide as to** how much you should weigh.* ♦ *The color of a plant's leaves is **a good guide to** its health.* ♦ *Opinion polls only serve as **a rough guide** to how people really vote.*
3 someone whose job is to give information to people who are visiting a place: *a tour guide*

guide² /gaɪd/ verb [T] ★
1 to show someone where to go by going with them: **guide sb through/to/along etc. sth** *He guided them through the forest.*
2 to help someone to do something or make a decision: *There was no research to guide them.* ♦ *His entire life was guided by his religious beliefs.*
3 to try to make a situation develop in a particular way: **guide sth toward sth** *Harry tried to guide the conversation toward the subject of money.*

guide·book /ˈgaɪdˌbʊk/ noun [C] a book for tourists that provides information about a place

guide·lines /ˈgaɪdˌlaɪnz/ noun [plural] official instructions or advice about how to do something: *strict guidelines on the training of police officers*

guild /gɪld/ noun [C] an organization of people who all have the same job or interests

guile /gaɪl/ noun [U] *formal* clever ways of tricking people = CUNNING

guil·lo·tine /ˈgɪləˌtin/ noun [C] a machine that was used in the past for cutting off someone's head —**guil·lo·tine** verb [T]

guilt /gɪlt/ noun [U] **1** a feeling of being ashamed and sorry because you have done something wrong: *The failure of the company left her with an overwhelming sense of guilt.* **2** the fact that someone has committed a crime: *The court will decide on his guilt or innocence.*

guilt·y /ˈgɪlti/ adj ★★
1 ashamed and sorry because you have done something wrong: *a guilty look/expression* ♦ *It was a clear sign that he had **a guilty conscience*** (=a feeling that he had done something wrong). ♦ *You shouldn't **feel guilty** all the time – you've done nothing to be ashamed of.* ♦ *I still feel **guilty about** things I said to my mother when I was a teenager.*
2 someone who is guilty has committed a crime or has done something wrong: *Patrick knew that he was **guilty of** lying.* ♦ **find sb guilty/not guilty of sth** (=officially decide that they are guilty/not guilty) *He was found guilty of murder.*
—**guilt·i·ly** adv

guin·ea pig /ˈgɪni ˌpɪg/ noun [C] **1** a small furry animal with short ears and no tail. It is often kept as a pet. **2** someone who is used in an experiment

guise /gaɪz/ noun [C] *formal* the way that someone or something appears to people: *Revolutions come in many guises.* ♦ *Arms dealers have been operating under the guise of* (=pretending to be) *import agents.*

gui·tar /gɪˈtɑr/ noun [C] ★★ a musical instrument with six strings that can be ACOUSTIC or electric: *Her son **plays the guitar** in a rock band.* —*picture* → STRINGED INSTRUMENT —**gui·tar·ist** noun [C]

gulf /gʌlf/ noun [C] **1** a large area of ocean that is almost surrounded by land: *the Persian Gulf* **2** a large and important difference between people or groups = CHASM: *trying to close the widening gulf between the rich and the poor*

gull /gʌl/ noun [C] a large white bird that lives near the ocean = SEAGULL

gul·li·bil·i·ty /ˌgʌləˈbɪləti/ noun [U] the tendency to be gullible

gul·li·ble /ˈgʌləb(ə)l/ adj a gullible person is easy to trick because they always trust people ≠ CYNICAL

gul·ly /ˈgʌli/ noun [C] a long narrow valley with steep sides

gulp /gʌlp/ verb **1** [T] to swallow food or drink quickly **2** [I] to make the movement of swallowing because you are surprised, excited, or afraid —**gulp** noun [C]
PHRASAL VERB ˌ**gulp sth ˈdown** *same as* **gulp** 1

gum /gʌm/ noun **1** [C] the firm pink flesh in your mouth that your teeth are attached to **2** [U] CHEWING GUM **3** [U] a sticky substance that comes from some trees

gump·tion /ˈgʌmpʃ(ə)n/ noun [U] the ability to be sensible and brave enough to do the right thing in a difficult situation

gun¹ /gʌn/ noun [C] ★★★
1 a weapon that shoots bullets or large SHELLS: *Enemy guns fired a shell every two or three minutes.* ♦ *a gang **armed with** machine **guns*** ♦ *He **pointed the gun** directly **at** me.* ♦ *She was learning how to **fire a gun**.* ♦ *Their police officers all carry guns.* ♦ *A police **gun went off*** (=was fired) *accidentally.* ♦ *Suddenly the officer **pulled a gun on** them* (=took it out and pointed it at them).
2 a tool that forces something out of its container using pressure: *a paint/glue/staple gun*
→ JUMP¹, STICK TO STH 3

gun² /gʌn/ verb [T] to make a car go fast, or to make a car's engine go fast when the car is not moving
PHRASAL VERB ˌ**gun sb** ˈ**down** *mainly journalism* to shoot someone and kill them

gun•boat /ˈgʌnˌboʊt/ noun [C] a small navy ship with large guns

ˈ**gun conˌtrol** noun [U] laws that prevent people from keeping and using guns

gun•fire /ˈgʌnˌfaɪr/ noun [U] shots from guns, or the sound of shots

gunk /gʌŋk/ noun [U] *informal* any soft, sticky, or dirty substance —**gunk•y** adj

gun•man /ˈgʌnmən/ (plural **gun•men** /ˈgʌnmən/) noun [C] *mainly journalism* someone who uses a gun when they are fighting or committing a crime

gun•point /ˈgʌnˌpɔɪnt/ noun **at gunpoint** in the position of threatening someone with a gun, or being threatened with a gun

gun•shot /ˈgʌnˌʃɑt/ noun **1** [C] the sound that is made when someone fires a gun **2** [U] the bullets that are shot from a gun: *a gunshot wound*

gur•gle /ˈgɜrg(ə)l/ verb [I] **1** to make the low sound that water makes when it is poured quickly from a bottle **2** if a person gurgles, they make a low sound in their throat —**gur•gle** noun [C]

gur•ney /ˈgɜrni/ noun [C] *American* a bed on wheels that is used in hospitals for moving people around

gu•ru /ˈguˌru/ noun [C] **1** a spiritual leader in some religions **2** someone who other people respect and ask for advice about a particular subject: *a style/fitness guru*

gush¹ /gʌʃ/ verb [I] **1** if a liquid gushes, it flows quickly and in large quantities —*picture* → DRIP **2** to express a lot of admiration or pleasure in a way that does not seem to be sincere

gush² /gʌʃ/ noun [C] **1** a large quantity of liquid or gas that quickly flows out of something **2** a strong sudden feeling

gush•ing /ˈgʌʃɪŋ/ adj *informal* expressing admiration or pleasure in a way that does not seem to be sincere

gust¹ /gʌst/ noun [C] a sudden strong wind —**gust•y** adj

gust² /gʌst/ verb [I] if a wind gusts, it blows very strongly for short periods of time

gus•to /ˈgʌstoʊ/ noun **with gusto** with a lot of enthusiasm

gut¹ /gʌt/ noun [C] the tube in your body that carries food away from your stomach
PHRASE **gut feeling/instinct** a feeling that you are certain is right, although you can give no good reason why
→ GUTS

gut² /gʌt/ verb [T] **1** to destroy the inside of a building or vehicle: *The entire building was gutted by the fire.* **2** to remove the organs from inside a fish or animal before you cook it

ˌ**gut reˈaction** noun [C] something that you feel or believe strongly without stopping to think about it

guts /gʌts/ noun [plural] *informal* **1** the quality of being brave and determined: *She had the guts to go for what she wanted.* ♦ *It takes a lot of guts and hard work to get where he is.* **2** your stomach and the organs near it

guts•y /ˈgʌtsi/ adj *informal* brave and determined

gut•ted /ˈgʌtəd/ adj if a building is gutted, it is completely destroyed

gut•ter /ˈgʌtər/ noun **1** [C] an open piece of pipe that is attached to the edge of a roof in order to carry rain water away —*picture* → C1 **2** [C] the edge of a road, where water flows away **3 the gutter** [singular] the bad social conditions of the poorest people in society

gut•tur•al /ˈgʌt(ə)rəl/ adj a guttural sound is deep and made at the back of your throat

guy /gaɪ/ noun ★★
1 [C] *informal* a man: *Bob's a really nice guy.* ♦ *She's going out with some French guy she met on vacation.* ♦ *He looks like the kind of guy you would trust with your life savings.*
2 guys [plural] *spoken* used for talking to a group of people: *Okay, guys. What should we do now?*

guz•zle /ˈgʌz(ə)l/ verb [T] *informal* to drink a lot quickly

gym /dʒɪm/ noun **1** [C] a room or club with equipment for doing physical exercises **2** [U] the activity of doing indoor physical exercises at a school

gym•na•si•um /dʒɪmˈneɪziəm/ noun [C] *formal* a GYM

gym•nast /ˈdʒɪmˌnæst, ˈdʒɪmnəst/ noun [C] someone who does gymnastics

gym•nas•tics /dʒɪmˈnæstɪks/ noun [U] a sport in which you perform physical exercises that involve bending and balancing —**gym•nas•tic** adj

gy•nae•col•o•gy /ˌgaɪnəˈkɑlədʒi/ the British spelling of **gynecology**

gy•ne•col•o•gy /ˌgaɪnəˈkɑlədʒi/ noun [U] the treatment of medical conditions that affect women's REPRODUCTIVE organs —**gy•ne•co•log•i•cal** /ˌgaɪnəkəˈlɑdʒɪk(ə)l/ adj, **gy•ne•col•o•gist** /ˌgaɪnəˈkɑlədʒɪst/ noun [C]

gyp•sy /ˈdʒɪpsi/ noun [C] **1** someone who does not live in one place but travels around **2** *offensive* a ROMANY

gy•rate /ˈdʒaɪˌreɪt/ verb [I] **1** to move around quickly in circles **2** *humorous* to dance in a sexual way

Hh

h or **H** /eɪtʃ/ noun [C/U] the eighth letter of the English alphabet

ha /hɑ/ interjection used for showing that you are pleased because you have discovered or achieved something

hab•it /ˈhæbɪt/ noun ★★
1 [C/U] something that you do often: *healthy eating habits* ♦ **be in the habit of doing sth**

They were in the habit of taking long walks. ♦ **get in/into the habit of doing sth** *George has gotten in the habit of calling me regularly.*
2 [C] something that is bad that you often do without realizing it, or without being able to stop: *Over 10 million smokers have succeeded in* ***kicking the habit*** (=stopping it). ♦ **have the habit of doing sth** *He had the annoying habit of tapping the table when he was nervous.*
3 [C] a simple dress that is worn by NUNS and other members of religious communities

Words often used with habit

Adjectives often used with ***habit*** *(sense 2)*
- **annoying, dirty, disgusting, filthy** + HABIT: used about a habit that is very unpleasant

- A **habit** is something that someone does often or regularly, as a normal part of their life: *Eating candy is a bad habit.* ♦ *I soon got into the habit of getting up early.*
- A **custom** is something that a particular group of people do because it is traditional and usual: *the custom of shaking hands*

hab•it•a•ble /ˈhæbɪtəb(ə)l/ adj a building that is habitable is good enough to live in ≠ UNINHABITABLE

hab•i•tat /ˈhæbɪˌtæt/ noun [C] the type of place that an animal normally lives in or that a plant normally grows in

hab•i•ta•tion /ˌhæbɪˈteɪʃ(ə)n/ noun [U] *formal* the fact that people are living in a place

ha•bit•u•al /həˈbɪtʃuəl/ adj **1** used for describing a person who has a particular bad habit: *a habitual smoker/drinker/liar/criminal* **2** usual, or typical: *He spoke to the workers with his habitual honesty.* — **ha•bit•u•al•ly** adv

hack¹ /hæk/ verb [I/T] to cut something in a rough way or with a lot of energy: *The boys were hacking at the bushes with heavy sticks.*
PHRASE **can't hack it** to be unable to deal with something because it is too difficult or boring
PHRASAL VERB ˈ**hack into sth** to use a computer in order to connect secretly and illegally to someone else's computer: *They hack into banks and transfer huge amounts of cash.*

hack² /hæk/ noun [C] *informal* a reporter, artist, or writer who does boring work or work that is not very good

hack•er /ˈhækər/ noun [C] someone who uses a computer in order to connect secretly and illegally to other people's computers

hack•les /ˈhæk(ə)lz/ noun [plural] if your hackles rise, you begin to feel very angry

hack•neyed /ˈhæknid/ adj hackneyed words or ideas have been used so often that they do not seem interesting or original any more

had the past tense and past participle of **have**

had•dock /ˈhædək/ (plural **had•dock**) noun [C/U] a large fish that lives in the North Atlantic Ocean and that is eaten as food

had•n't /ˈhæd(ə)nt/ short form the usual way of saying or writing "had not." This is not often used in formal writing: *I wish I hadn't sent that e-mail.*

hae•mo•phil•i•a /ˌhiməˈfɪliə/ the British spelling of **hemophilia**

hae•mo•phil•i•ac /ˌhiməˈfɪliæk/ the British spelling of **hemophiliac**

haem•or•rhage /ˈhemərɪdʒ/ the British spelling of **hemorrhage**

haem•or•rhoids /ˈheməˌrɔɪdz/ the British spelling of **hemorrhoids**

hag•gard /ˈhægərd/ adj looking very tired, worried, or sick

hag•gle /ˈhæg(ə)l/ verb [I] to argue in order to agree on the price of something

hah /hɑ/ another spelling of **ha**

ˌ**ha** ˈ**ha** interjection used for representing the sound of laughter, or for showing that you think something is not funny

hail¹ /heɪl/ verb **1** [I] if it hails, small balls of ice fall from the sky **2** [T] *formal* to shout to someone as a way of attracting their attention: *I stepped out into the street and hailed a taxi.*
PHRASE **be hailed as sth** to be publicly praised for being very good: *The ruling was hailed as one of the most important legal decisions of the last 20 years.*

hail² /heɪl/ noun [U] rain that falls as small balls of ice
PHRASE **a hail of bullets/arrows/bottles** a lot of things such as bullets that come at you very quickly

hail•stones /ˈheɪlˌstoʊnz/ noun [plural] small balls of ice that form hail

hair /her/ noun ★★★
1 [U] the thing that grows on your head in a mass of thin fibers: *long black hair* ♦ *brush/comb your hair* —picture → C14
2 [C] a single fiber of hair: *a few gray hairs* ♦ *dog hairs on the furniture*
PHRASES **let your hair down** *informal* to relax and enjoy yourself
make sb's hair stand on end *humorous* to make someone feel very frightened
→ SPLIT¹

Words often used with hair

Adjectives often used with ***hair*** *(sense 1)*
- **curly, fine, long, short, straight, thick, wavy** + HAIR: used about a particular type of hair

When **hair** is used to refer to the thing that grows on your head as a mass, it has no plural and cannot be used with **a**: *She has beautiful hair* (NOT *a beautiful hair*). ♦ *All the children have curly hair.* ♦ *I found* ***some hair*** *in the bath.*

hair•cut /ˈherˌkʌt/ noun [C] **1** an act of cutting someone's hair: *He was badly dressed and needed a haircut.* **2** the style that your hair has been cut in: *a short stylish haircut*

hair•do /ˈherˌdu/ noun [C] *informal* a woman's hairstyle

hair•dress•er /ˈherˌdresər/ noun [C] someone whose job is to cut people's hair

hair•dry•er or **hair•dri•er** /ˈherˌdraɪr/ noun [C] a piece of electrical equipment that you use for drying your hair after you have washed it

hair•line¹ /ˈherˌlaɪn/ noun [C] the line at the top of your forehead where your hair begins

hair•line² /ˈherˌlaɪn/ adj a hairline crack is very narrow

H

hair·pin /ˈherˌpɪn/ noun [C] a metal object that is used for holding a woman's hair in position

ˌhairpin ˈcurve noun [C] *American* a very sharp curve in a road, where the road forms a "U" shape

hair-rais·ing /ˈherˌreɪzɪŋ/ adj very frightening but exciting at the same time

hairs·breadth /ˈherzˌbredθ/ noun [singular] the smallest possible distance, amount, or degree

hair·style /ˈherˌstaɪl/ noun [C] the shape that your hair has been cut or arranged in

hairstyles

hair·y /ˈheri/ adj **1** with a lot of hair: *a hairy chest* **2** *informal* frightening, or dangerous

hajj or **haj** /hædʒ/ noun [C] a trip to the holy city of Mecca that Muslims make as a religious duty

haj·ji /ˈhædʒi/ noun [C] a Muslim who has made a hajj

ha·lal /həˈlɑl, ˈhælæl/ adj halal meat has been prepared according to the religious laws of Islam

half /hæf/ (plural **halves** /hævz/) grammar word ★★★

Half can be:
- a **determiner**: *We live half a mile up the road.*
- a **pronoun**: *Let's share the prize money. You can have half.* ♦ *Half of us are still unemployed.*
- an **adjective**: *We ordered a half bottle of red wine.*
- an **adverb**: *I was only half awake.* ♦ *A nurse only earns half as much as a doctor.*
- a **noun**: *The group was divided into two halves.*
- a **number**: *Emma could talk well by the age of two and a half.*

1 one of two equal parts of a number, amount, group, or object: *Only half the population voted in the election.* ♦ *The students spend half their time on practical work.* ♦ *The fabric is half nylon, half cotton.* ♦ *Jasmine started school when she was four **and a half**.* ♦ *We had to wait **half an hour** for a bus.* ♦ *Peel the potatoes and **cut them in half**.* ♦ *The risk of developing lung cancer has been **reduced by half**.* ♦ ***half a dozen*** (=6) *eggs* ♦ *Prices rose by over 15% during the second **half of 1988**.*
2 partly but not completely: *The door was half open.* ♦ *I only half understood the instructions.* ♦ *a half-empty milk bottle*
3 one of the two equal periods of time into which a game of football, basketball, etc. is divided

PHRASES **half the battle** the most important part of what you have to do in order to achieve something: *Winning people's trust is half the battle.*
half the fun/problem/trouble etc. a large part of the fun/problem/trouble etc. that is involved in something: *Putting up the decorations is half the fun of Christmas.*
half one/two/three etc. *British spoken* thirty minutes after one o'clock/two o'clock etc.
half past one/two etc. thirty minutes after one o'clock/two o'clock etc.: *The stores close at half past five.*
not half as good/bad/much etc. as used for emphasizing that one person or thing is not nearly as good/bad etc. as another: *It wasn't half as difficult as I expected.*

half-baked /ˌhæf ˈbeɪkt/ adj *informal* a half-baked idea is not practical because it has not been thought about carefully

ˈhalf ˌbrother noun [C] a brother who has either the same mother or the same father as you have

half-heart·ed /ˌhæf ˈhɑrtəd/ adj done with no real interest or enthusiasm —**ˌhalf-ˈheartedly** adv

ˌhalf-ˈhour¹ adj lasting for 30 minutes: *a half-hour meeting*

ˌhalf-ˈhour² or **half an ˈhour** noun [C] a period of 30 minutes: *Shannon waited another half-hour and then left.*

ˌhalf-ˈhourly adj happening every 30 minutes: *half-hourly news programs*

ˌhalf-ˈmast noun **at half-mast** a flag that is at half-mast has been lowered to the middle of a pole in order to show respect for someone who has died

ˌhalf ˈmeasures noun [plural] methods that are not effective enough

ˈhalf ˌsister noun [C] a sister who has either the same mother or the same father as you have

ˈhalf ˌstep noun [C] *American technical* an amount by which one sound is higher or lower than another, equal to $\frac{1}{12}$ of an OCTAVE. This difference occurs between any two notes that are next to each other on a piano.

ˌ**half ˈterm** noun [C/U] *British* a vacation from school or college at MIDTERM

half•time /ˈhæfˌtaɪm/ noun [U] in football, basketball, and some other team sports, a period of rest between the two halves of a game

half•way /hæfˈweɪ/ adj, adv in the middle of a space or period of time: *at the halfway stage of the competition* ♦ *Their house is about halfway up the street.*

hal•i•but /ˈhælɪbət/ (plural **hal•i•but**) noun [C/U] a large flat ocean fish, or this fish eaten as food

hall /hɔl/ noun [C] ★★★

1 a building or large room that is used for public events: *Hundreds of students had packed into the dining hall.* ♦ *a concert at Carnegie Hall*

2 an area or passage inside the front door of a building that leads to other rooms: *Leave your shoes in the hall.* ♦ *The house has a large* ***entrance hall.***

3 hall or **hall of residence** *British* a DORMITORY

→ TOWN HALL

hall•mark /ˈhɔlˌmɑrk/ noun [C] **1** a typical feature **2** an official mark on an object made of gold or silver that shows its quality

Hal•low•een /ˌhæloʊˈin/ noun [C/U] the night of October 31, when children wear COSTUMES and go TRICK-OR-TREATING (=go from house to house in order to ask neighbors for candy)

hal•lu•ci•nate /həˈlus(ə)nˌeɪt/ verb [I] to see or hear something that is not really there because you are sick or because you have taken drugs —**hal•lu•ci•na•tion** /həˌlusnˈeɪʃ(ə)n/ noun [C/U]

hall•way /ˈhɔlˌweɪ/ noun [C] an area or passage inside the front door of a building that leads to other rooms = HALL

ha•lo /ˈheɪloʊ/ noun [C] a circle of light that is shown around the head of a holy person in religious paintings

halt¹ /hɔlt/ noun [singular] the fact that something stops moving or stops happening: *The taxi came to a halt outside his front door.* ♦ *Traffic was brought to a halt* (=stopped) *by the demonstration.* ♦ *He has appealed for a halt to the fighting.*

PHRASE **call a halt to sth** to end something formally

→ GRIND¹

halt² /hɔlt/ verb [I/T] if you halt something, or if it halts, it stops moving or happening: *Building work had been halted by the bad weather.* ♦ *She halted at the door and turned towards him.*

halt•ing /ˈhɔltɪŋ/ adj with a lot of pauses between words or movements because you are nervous or not confident —**halt•ing•ly** adv

halve /hæv/ verb **1** [I/T] to reduce something to half its original size or amount, or to become half the original size or amount: *Many stores have halved their prices.* ♦ *The number of hospitals in the country has halved over the last five years.* **2** [T] to cut something into two pieces of equal size

halves the plural of **half**

ham /hæm/ noun [U] the meat from a pig's leg: *a slice of ham* ♦ *a ham sandwich*

ham•burg•er /ˈhæmˌbɜrgər/ noun **1** [C] a food made by pressing small pieces of BEEF (=meat from a cow) into a flat round shape and cooking it. Hamburgers are usually eaten in a **bun**. **2** [U] *American* meat from a cow that is cut up into very small pieces = GROUND BEEF

ham•let /ˈhæmlət/ noun [C] a small village

ham•mer¹ /ˈhæmər/ noun [C] a tool used for hitting nails into wood. It consists of a handle and a heavy metal top. —*picture* → TOOL

ham•mer² /ˈhæmər/ verb [I/T] **1** to hit something with a hammer **2** to hit something hard, or to hit it many times

PHRASAL VERB ˌ**hammer sth ˈout** to reach an agreement after a long discussion

ham•mock /ˈhæmək/ noun [C] a bed consisting of a long piece of cloth or net that is tied at each end to a post or tree

ham•per¹ /ˈhæmpər/ verb [T] to prevent something from happening normally, or to prevent someone from moving normally

ham•per² /ˈhæmpər/ noun [C] **1** *American* a large basket in which you keep dirty clothes until you wash them **2** a large basket with a lid, especially one that contains food

ham•ster /ˈhæmstər/ noun [C] a very small furry animal with a short tail. It is often kept as a pet.

ham•string /ˈhæmˌstrɪŋ/ noun [C] a TENDON that is behind your knee

ham•strung /ˈhæmˌstrʌŋ/ adj prevented from doing what you want to do

hand¹ /hænd/ noun ★★★

1 body part	5 set of cards
2 help	6 clapping
3 advantages	+ PHRASES
4 part of clock	

1 [C] the part of your body at the end of each arm that you use for holding things: *Mrs. Bennet put her hands over her ears to shut out the noise.* ♦ *The park was full of young couples* ***holding hands*** (=holding each other's hands). ♦ *The two men introduced themselves and* ***shook hands.*** ♦ *He was* ***holding*** *a cup of coffee* ***in his left hand.*** —*picture* → C14

2 [singular] help: *Do you need* ***a hand with*** *the dusting?* ♦ *Lydia said she would* ***lend a hand*** (=help) *with the costumes.* ♦ *Can you* ***give me a hand*** (=help me) *with these boxes?*

3 [singular] *informal* the advantages that you have in a situation: *Everything depends on how the company* ***plays its hand*** (=uses its advantages).* ♦ *The trick is not to* ***show your hand*** *too early* (=let an opponent know what your advantages are).

4 [C] the hands on a clock are the long parts that move around and show the time

5 [C] the cards that have been given to you in a game of cards —*picture* → C16

6 [singular] if people give someone a hand, they CLAP their hands to show that they have enjoyed a performance

PHRASES **at hand** very close to you and easy to reach: *Help is always at hand if you need it.* ♦ *I always keep my calculator* ***close at hand.***

by hand 1 using your hands rather than a machine **2** if a letter is delivered by hand, it is not delivered by the mail service
first/second/third hand if you experience something first hand, you experience it yourself. If you experience something second hand or third hand, someone else tells you about it.
get/lay your hands on sth to manage to obtain something: *I couldn't lay my hands on a copy of the book.*
go hand in hand to happen or exist together
hands off *spoken* used for telling someone not to touch or take something
hands up *spoken* **1** used for asking people to tell you if they know the answer to a question **2** used for asking people to tell you if they want something
have a hand in sth to help to make something happen
have your hands full to be extremely busy
in hand if something is in hand, you are dealing with it
in sb's hands if something is in someone's hands, they are responsible for it: *I knew that the dog was* ***in safe hands*** *with my parents.*
keep your hands off *informal* to not touch someone or something
on hand 1 if someone is on hand, they are available to help you if you need them **2** if something is on hand, it is available to be used
on the one hand ... on the other hand used for giving two different opinions about something
out of hand not well controlled: *We decided to leave before things* ***got out of hand.***
out of your hands if something is out of your hands, someone else is now responsible for it
take/get your hands off *informal* to stop touching someone or something

hand² /hænd/ verb [T] ★★ to give something to someone by holding it in your hand and offering it to them: **hand sth to sb** *Talbot handed the paper to the man.* ♦ **hand sb sth** *Sarah handed me an envelope.*

PHRASAL VERBS ˌ**hand sth ˈback** to give something back to someone: **hand sth back to sb** *Jean handed the letter back to Doug.* ♦ **hand sb sth back** *The officer handed me my passport back.*
ˌ**hand sth ˈdown** to give something to a younger person who will use it after you have died: *These skills have been handed down from generation to generation.*
ˌ**hand sth ˈin** to give something to a person in authority: *Please hand in your keys when you leave the hotel.*
ˌ**hand sth ˈout** to give things to different people in a group: *Would you hand these papers out for me?*
ˌ**hand sb ˈover** to give someone to the police or another authority: **hand sb over to sb** *The suspects have now been handed over to the French authorities.*
ˌ**hand sth ˈover 1** to give something to someone by holding it in your hand and offering it to them: *Albert bowed and handed over the letter.* ♦ **hand sth over to sb** *He handed the car keys over to Stella.* **2** to give power or control to someone else: **hand sth over to sb** *They formally hand power over to the new government next week.*

hand·bag /ˈhæn(d)ˌbæg/ noun [C] a woman's PURSE

hand·book /ˈhæn(d)ˌbʊk/ noun [C] a small book that gives information or instructions

hand·cuff /ˈhæn(d)ˌkʌf/ verb [T] to put handcuffs on someone

hand·cuffs /ˈhæn(d)ˌkʌfs/ noun [plural] metal rings that a police officer puts around a prisoner's wrists to stop them from using their hands

hand·ful /ˈhæn(d)ˌfʊl/ noun **1** [C] the quantity of something that you can hold in your hand: *a handful of coins* **2** [singular] a very small number of people or things: *Only a handful of people attended the meeting.* **3** [singular] *informal* someone who is difficult to control: *Their children are a real handful at school.*

ˈ**hand greˌnade** noun [C] a small bomb that explodes after a soldier throws it

hand·gun /ˈhæn(d)ˌgʌn/ noun [C] any small gun that is used with one hand

hand·held /ˈhændˌheld/ adj small enough to hold in your hands: *a handheld computer*

hand·i·cap /ˈhændiˌkæp/ noun [C] a disadvantage that prevents you from doing something well

hand·i·capped /ˈhændiˌkæpt/ adj *old-fashioned* someone who is handicapped has a permanent injury, illness, or other problem that makes them unable to use their body or mind normally. People now think that this word is offensive and prefer to say that someone is **disabled**.

hand·i·ly /ˈhændɪli/ adv *American* easily, without much effort

hand·i·work /ˈhændiˌwɜrk/ noun [U] something that someone has done or created

hand·ker·chief /ˈhæŋkərtʃɪf/ noun [C] a small piece of cloth or paper that you use for wiping your nose or eyes

han·dle¹ /ˈhænd(ə)l/ verb [T] ★★★ **1** to deal with someone or something: *The government was criticized for the way it handled the crisis.* ♦ *The newer computers can handle massive amounts of data.* ♦ *Flight attendants are trained to handle difficult passengers.* ♦ *I left the job because I couldn't handle the pressure.* **2** to touch or hold something: *All chemicals must be* ***handled with care.*** **3** to buy and sell goods, especially illegally: *He denied burglary but admitted* ***handling stolen goods.*** **4** to control an animal or a vehicle using your hands: *She handled the horse very confidently.*

han·dle² /ˈhænd(ə)l/ noun [C] ★ the part of something that you use for holding it: *knives with plastic handles* ♦ *a door handle*

han·dle·bars /ˈhænd(ə)lˌbɑrz/ noun [plural] the part of a bicycle that you hold with your hands and use for controlling it

han·dling /ˈhændlɪŋ/ noun [U] the way that someone deals with a particular situation

ˈ**hand ˌluggage** noun [U] CARRY-ON luggage

hand•made /ˌhæn(d)ˈmeɪd/ adj made by a person, not by a machine

hand•out /ˈhændˌaʊt/ noun [C] **1** *showing disapproval* money or goods that are given to people who need them **2** a piece of paper with information on it that a teacher gives to everyone in a class

hand•o•ver /ˈhændˌoʊvər/ noun [C] the process of formally giving something to someone else

hand•picked /ˌhæn(d)ˈpɪkt/ adj chosen very carefully for a particular purpose

hand•set /ˈhæn(d)ˌset/ noun [C] **1** the part of a telephone that you hold next to your ear **2** a small piece of electronic equipment that you hold and use for controlling another piece of equipment from a distance

ˈhands-ˌfree adj hands-free equipment can be operated without using your hands, for example by using a HEADSET or a REMOTE CONTROL

hand•shake /ˈhæn(d)ʃeɪk/ noun [C] the act of shaking someone's hand, for example as a greeting

hand•some /ˈhænsəm/ adj ★★
1 a handsome man or boy has a very attractive face = GOOD-LOOKING
2 a handsome amount of money is large: *a handsome profit/donation*

ˌhands-ˈon adj **1** hands-on experience involves you doing something, not just reading about it **2** someone who is hands-on is involved in something and does not make other people do the work

ˌhand-to-ˈmouth adj, adv with just enough money or food to live on

hand•writ•ing /ˈhændˌraɪtɪŋ/ noun [U] the particular way that someone writes when they use a pen or pencil

hand•writ•ten /ˈhændˌrɪt(ə)n/ adj written using a pen or pencil, not printed or TYPED

hand•y /ˈhændi/ adj **1** useful: *a handy tool* **2** close to you and therefore easy to reach or easy to get to: *Keep your pills handy just in case you feel seasick.* **3** good at doing things with your hands: *He's very handy with a paintbrush* (=good at painting).
PHRASE **come in handy** to be useful: *A spare set of keys might come in handy.*

hand•y•man /ˈhændiˌmæn/ (plural **hand•y•men** /ˈhændiˌmen/) noun [C] someone who is good at making and repairing things

hang¹ /hæŋ/ (past tense and past participle **hung** /hʌŋ/) verb ★★★
1 [I/T] to attach the top part of something to a place and leave its bottom part free to move, or to be in this position: *Hang your jacket there.* ♦ **hang sth on/over sth** *Phillip hung his hat on a hook behind the door.* ♦ *The children's coats were **hanging on** pegs behind the door.* ♦ *Her dark hair **hung down** over her shoulders.*
2 (past tense and past participle **hanged**) [T] to kill someone by putting a rope around their neck and making them fall: *He was **hanged** for murder in 1942.* ♦ *After his wife left, he tried to **hang himself**.*
3 [I] if something such as smoke or a smell hangs in the air, it remains there: *A thick mist **hung over** the fields.*
PHRASAL VERBS **ˌhang aˈround** *informal* to spend time in a place waiting or doing nothing: *I hung around outside, waiting for the others.* ♦
ˌhang aˈround with sb *informal* to spend time with someone
ˌhang ˈback to not do something immediately because you are not confident or certain about it = HESITATE
ˌhang ˈon 1 to hold tightly to something **2** *spoken* to wait, or to be patient: *I think we should hang on and see the end of the game.*
ˌhang ˈonto sth *informal* to keep something: *She still hung onto her wedding ring, even after the divorce.*
ˌhang ˈout *informal* to spend time in a particular place or with particular people: *She knew all the clubs where he usually hung out.*
ˌhang ˈup to put the telephone down at the end of a conversation: *Greg hung up and sat back in his chair.* ♦ *"Get lost!" she shouted, and **hung up on** me.*
ˌhang sth ˈup to hang a piece of clothing on something: *The women hung up their coats and sat down.*

hang² /hæŋ/ noun **get the hang of sth** *informal* to learn to do something

han•gar /ˈhæŋər/ noun [C] a very large building where airplanes are kept

hang•er /ˈhæŋər/ noun [C] a small frame for hanging clothes such as jackets or shirts on = COAT HANGER

ˌhangers-ˈon noun [plural] *showing disapproval* people who spend time with a rich or important person so that they can get an advantage for themselves

ˈhang ˌglider noun [C] a simple aircraft with no engine that you hang under and control by moving your body —**hang ˌgliding** noun [U]

hang•ing /ˈhæŋɪŋ/ noun [C/U] a punishment in which someone is killed by hanging their body from a rope around their neck

hang•out /ˈhæŋˌaʊt/ noun [C] *informal* a place where a particular person likes to spend time

hang•o•ver /ˈhæŋˌoʊvər/ noun [C] the feeling of being tired and sick because you have drunk too much alcohol

ˈhang-ˌup noun [C] *informal* **1** something that you are worried or embarrassed about **2** *American* a problem that causes a delay or difficulty

han•ker /ˈhæŋkər/ verb [I] *informal* to have a strong feeling of wanting something —**han•ker•ing** noun [singular]

han•kie or **han•ky** /ˈhæŋki/ noun [C] *informal* a HANDKERCHIEF

han•ky-pan•ky /ˌhæŋki ˈpæŋki/ noun [U] *informal* sexual activity

Ha•nuk•kah /ˈhɑnəkə/ noun [C/U] an important Jewish religious festival that takes place in November or December

hap•haz•ard /hæpˈhæzərd/ adj done in a way that is not carefully planned or organized —**hap•haz•ard•ly** adv

hap•less /ˈhæpləs/ adj a hapless person is someone that you feel sorry for because bad things have happened to them

hap•pen /ˈhæpən/ verb [I] ★★★ to take place, usually without being planned = OCCUR: *The accident happened at about 4:30 p.m.*

H

yesterday. ♦ *He seemed to be unaware of what was happening around him.* ♦ *What happens if I press this button?* ♦ *Let's just wait and see* ***what happens.***
PHRASES **happen to do sth** to do something by chance: *I happened to meet an old friend in town.*
it just so happens that *spoken* used for saying that something is true, although it is surprising: *It just so happens that I have a bike I can lend you.*
whatever happens used for saying that nothing will change a situation: *Whatever happens tomorrow, this experience has been very valuable.*
PHRASAL VERB **ˈhappen to sb/sth** to be affected by something: *This is the best thing that's ever happened to me.* ♦ *We don't understand what is happening to the economy.*

hap·pen·ing /ˈhæpənɪŋ/ noun [C] an unusual or important event

hap·pi·ly /ˈhæpɪli/ adv **1** in a happy way: *He and his wife are happily settled in their new home.* **2** used when you are pleased about something: *Happily, nobody was injured.* **3** in a willing way: *I'll happily make dinner if you want me to.*

hap·pi·ness /ˈhæpinəs/ noun [U] the feeling of being happy

hap·py /ˈhæpi/ adj ★★★
1 feeling pleased and relaxed, with no worries ≠ UNHAPPY: *The children seem very happy at school.* ♦ *Sarah* ***felt happy*** *for the first time in her life.* ♦ *Money alone will never* ***make you happy.*** ♦ *You deserve all this success. We're very* ***happy for you.*** ♦ *Anna was excited and* ***happy about*** *the baby.* ♦ **happy doing sth** *So you're happy living in Baltimore?*
2 satisfied that something is good or right: *Rising profits* ***keep*** *the bosses* ***happy.*** ♦ *Are you* ***happy with*** *this arrangement?* ♦ *I'm not very* ***happy about*** *the children being out so late.* ♦ **+that** *We were happy that a decision has finally been made.* ♦ **happy to do sth** *Her parents were happy to know she'd gotten a good job.*
3 making you feel happy, or showing that you feel happy: *a happy marriage/childhood/life* ♦ *a happy smile/expression*
PHRASES **be happy to do sth** if you are happy to do something, you are very willing to do it
Happy Birthday/Easter/Anniversary used as a greeting on a particular occasion

ˌhappy-go-ˈlucky adj a happy-go-lucky person does not usually worry about the future

ˈhappy ˌhour noun [C/U] a short period of time when drinks in a bar cost less than usual, usually in the early evening

ˌhappy ˈmedium noun [singular] a way of doing something that is between two extreme positions or that is satisfactory to everyone

ha·rangue /həˈræŋ/ verb [T] to criticize someone angrily —**ha·rangue** noun [C]

ha·rass /ˈherəs, həˈræs/ verb [T] to annoy or upset someone, for example by regularly criticizing them or treating them in a way that is offensive

ha·rass·ment /ˈherəsmənt, həˈræsmənt/ noun [U] annoying or unpleasant behavior toward someone that takes place regularly: *the victims of racial/sexual harassment*

har·bor[1] /ˈhɑrbər/ noun [C/U] an area of water next to the land where boats can stop

har·bor[2] /ˈhɑbər/ verb [T] **1** to hide someone who has done something wrong so that the police will not find them **2** to keep a particular thought or feeling in your mind for a long time

har·bour /ˈhɑrbər/ the British spelling of **harbor**[1]

hard[1] /hɑrd/ adj ★★★

1 not easy to break	5 not frightened
2 difficult to do	6 unkind/angry
3 involving effort	+ PHRASES
4 full of problems	

1 stiff, firm, and not easy to bend or break: *hard wooden benches* ♦ *The ice on the lake was so hard we could walk on it.*
2 difficult to do: *Some of the questions were very hard.* ♦ **find sth hard** *I found the English test extremely hard.* ♦ **hard for sb to do sth** *It is hard for young people to get jobs in this area.* ♦ **hard to do sth** *It's hard to explain why I love this place so much.*
3 involving a lot of effort: *Lifting stones this size is pretty* ***hard work.*** ♦ *I need to relax at the end of* ***a hard day.***
4 unpleasant and full of problems: *My grandmother had a very* ***hard life.*** ♦ *The family has* ***had a hard time*** *recently.* ♦ *It's very* ***hard on*** *parents when their children are rebellious.*
5 strong and not easily frightened: *He likes to pretend he's hard, but he's really soft underneath.*
6 unkind, or angry: *Don't be too* ***hard on*** *her, she was only trying to help.*
PHRASES **be hard on sth** *informal* to cause damage to something: *These exercises are hard on the knees.*
give sb a hard time *informal* to be unpleasant to someone, or to criticize them a lot
hard of hearing unable to hear well
hard to come by *informal* difficult to find or get: *Good teachers are hard to come by.*
learn the hard way to learn how to do something by trying to do it and making a lot of mistakes
no hard feelings *spoken* used for telling someone that you are not angry with them after an argument or disagreement, and that you hope that they are not angry with you

hard[2] /hɑrd/ adv ★★★
1 using a lot of effort or force: *The whole team has worked very hard.* ♦ *I was trying very hard to remember her name.* ♦ *I didn't mean to hit him so hard.*
2 if it is raining or snowing hard, a lot of rain or snow is falling
PHRASE **take sth hard** to be very upset by something

ˌhard-and-ˈfast adj not able to be changed

hard·back /ˈhɑrdˌbæk/ noun [C] a book that has a hard cover → PAPERBACK

hard·ball /ˈhɑrdˌbɔl/ noun **play hardball** to use unfair or dishonest methods in order to defeat someone

hard·board /ˈhɑrdˌbɔrd/ noun [U] a type of thin wooden board

hard-boiled /ˌhɑrd ˈbɔɪld/ adj a hard-boiled egg has been cooked in boiling water until it is solid inside

ˈ**hard ˌcopy** noun [U] *computing* a printed copy of information that is held on a computer → SOFT COPY

ˈ**hard ˌcore** noun [singular] the most determined or enthusiastic people in a group

ˈ**hard-ˌcore** adj very determined and completely unwilling to change your opinions or behavior: *hard-core opposition* ♦ *hard-core criminals*

hard·cov·er /ˈhɑrdˌkʌvər/ noun [C] a HARDBACK

ˌ**hard ˈcurrency** noun [U] money from a country with a strong economy

ˌ**hard ˈdisk** or ˈ**hard ˌdrive** noun [C] the part inside a computer that stores information → FLOPPY DISK

ˌ**hard ˈdrugs** noun [plural] illegal drugs that are ADDICTIVE, for example HEROIN

hard·en /ˈhɑrd(ə)n/ verb [I/T] **1** to become hard or firm, or to make something hard or firm ≠ SOFTEN: *The bread will harden if you don't cover it.* **2** to become less sympathetic or emotional, or to make someone less sympathetic or emotional ≠ SOFTEN: *His eyes hardened when he saw her.* **3** to become strong, or to make someone or something strong ≠ SOFTEN: *The soldiers have been hardened by months in the field.*

hard·ened /ˈhɑrd(ə)nd/ adj someone who is hardened has had a lot of unpleasant experiences and is no longer upset by unpleasant things: *hardened criminals/convicts* ♦ *The children became hardened to the violence.*

hard·hat /ˈhɑrdˌhæt/ noun [C] a hat made of metal or hard plastic worn by workers to protect their heads —*picture* → HAT

ˌ**hard-ˈheaded** adj able to make decisions without being influenced by your emotions

hard-heart·ed /ˌhɑrd ˈhɑrtəd/ adj someone who is hard-hearted has no sympathy for other people

hard-hit·ting /ˌhɑrd ˈhɪtɪŋ/ adj making criticisms in a very honest and direct way

hard·line /ˈhɑrdˌlaɪn/ adj strict or extreme in your beliefs or opinions, and not willing to change them —**hard·lin·er** noun [C]: *He's a right-wing hardliner.*

hard·ly /ˈhɑrdli/ adv ★★
1 used for saying that something is almost not true, or almost does not happen at all: *He hardly spoke except to say hello.* ♦ *Alice was so busy she hardly noticed the days pass by.* ♦ *He had **hardly changed at all**.* ♦ ***Hardly anyone** believed the man's story.* ♦ *It **hardly ever** rains here in the summer.* ♦ *We could **hardly** afford to pay the rent.*
2 used for saying that something had only just happened when something else happened: *She had hardly arrived when she started talking about leaving again.*
3 used when you think it is obvious that something is not true, not possible, not surprising, etc.: *This is hardly the time to start discussing finances.* ♦ ***It's hardly surprising** that people complained.*

> **Hardly** is a negative word and is often used with words like "any" and "ever," but it should not be used with other negative words such as "not" or "never."

hard-nosed /ˌhɑrd ˈnoʊzd/ adj determined to succeed and not influenced by your emotions

ˌ**hard-ˈpressed** adj not having enough money for the things that you need
PHRASE **be hard-pressed to do sth** to find it very difficult to do something

ˌ**hard ˈsell** noun [singular] **1** any method of selling in which someone tries very hard to persuade customers to buy something **2** *American* a situation in which you have difficulty persuading someone to do something

hard·ship /ˈhɑrdʃɪp/ noun [C/U] the state of having a difficult life, or something that makes life very difficult: *financial hardship*

ˌ**hard ˈup** adj *informal* not having much money

hard·ware /ˈhɑrdˌwer/ noun [U] **1** computer equipment **2** the equipment and vehicles that are used in an activity, especially in the military

ˈ**hardware ˌstore** noun [C] a store that sells things for your home or garden such as pans, knives, tools, and chemicals

ˌ**hard-ˈwired** adj a machine that is hard-wired works in a particular way because of the way it was built, and it cannot be changed by the person using it

ˈ**hard-ˈwon** adj achieved only after a lot of effort: *hard-won success*

hard·wood /ˈhɑrdˌwʊd/ noun [C/U] hard strong wood from trees such as OAK or MAHOGANY

ˌ**hard-ˈworking** adj putting a lot of effort into your work

har·dy /ˈhɑrdi/ adj strong and able to deal with unpleasant or extreme conditions

hare /her/ noun [C] an animal that is similar to a RABBIT but bigger

hare-brained /ˈherˌbreɪnd/ adj silly, or very unlikely to succeed

har·em /ˈherəm/ noun [C] **1** the wives of a rich man in some Muslim societies in the past **2** a part of a Muslim home in which only women live

hark /hɑrk/ PHRASAL VERB ˌ**hark ˈback to sth** to remember something from the past, or to be similar to something from the past

har·lot /ˈhɑrlət/ noun [C] an old word meaning PROSTITUTE

harm[1] /hɑrm/ noun [U] ★ injury, damage, or problems caused by something that you do: *Eating candy occasionally won't **do you any harm**.* ♦ *Changes to the law may **do more harm than good*** (=make things worse not better).
PHRASES **not mean any harm** to not intend to hurt, damage, or upset someone or something
out of harm's way in a safe place
there's no harm in (doing) sth used for saying that something may be helpful: *There's no harm in trying.*

harm[2] /hɑrm/ verb [T] to injure, damage, or have a bad effect on someone or something: *chemicals that harm the environment* ♦ *Does* *watching violence on TV really harm children?*

harm•ful /ˈhɑrmfəl/ adj causing harm: *the harmful effects of cigarette smoke* ♦ *The fungus is not harmful to humans.*

harm•less /ˈhɑrmləs/ adj not causing any harm —**harm•less•ly** adv

har•mon•i•ca /hɑrˈmɑnɪkə/ noun [C] a musical instrument that you play by blowing and sucking as you move it from side to side between your lips

har•mo•ni•ous /hɑrˈmoʊniəs/ adj **1** friendly and peaceful: *a harmonious environment/relationship/society* **2** looking, sounding, or combining well with each other —**har•mo•ni•ous•ly** adv

har•mo•nize /ˈhɑrməˌnaɪz/ verb **1** [I/T] to combine with other things in a pleasant way, or to make things combine in this way **2** [T] to make laws or policies that work with those of a different country, organization, etc. **3** [I] to sing or play different notes at the same time, producing a pleasant sound

har•mo•ny /ˈhɑrməni/ noun **1** [U] a situation in which people live and work in a happy, peaceful way with others: *racial/social/domestic harmony* **2** [C/U] musical notes that are sung or played at the same time, making a pleasant sound

har•ness¹ /ˈhɑrnəs/ noun [C] **1** strong leather bands that are used for fastening an animal to a vehicle that it pulls **2** strong bands of leather, cloth, or rope that are used for fastening someone in a particular place, or for fastening something to their body

har•ness² /ˈhɑrnəs/ verb [T] **1** to get control of something in order to use it for a particular purpose: *Humans first harnessed the power of electricity over 200 years ago.* **2** to put a harness on a person or animal

harp /hɑrp/ noun [C] a musical instrument that consists of a row of strings stretched over a large upright frame —*picture* → STRINGED INSTRUMENT

har•poon /hɑrˈpun/ noun [C] a pole with a blade that is attached to a rope, used for hunting WHALES —**har•poon** verb [T]

har•ried /ˈhærɪd/ adj tired and annoyed

har•row•ing /ˈheroʊɪŋ/ adj extremely upsetting or frightening

harsh /hɑrʃ/ adj **1** harsh conditions, places, or weather are unpleasant and difficult to live in **2** strict, unkind, and often unfair =SEVERE: *harsh words/punishment* **3** unpleasantly loud or bright: *the harsh glare of the sun* —**harsh•ly** adv

har•vest¹ /ˈhɑrvəst/ noun [C] **1** the activity of collecting a crop, or the time when crops are collected: *the corn/potato/grape harvest* **2** the amount of a crop that is collected

har•vest² /ˈhɑrvəst/ verb [I/T] to collect a crop from the fields

has 3rd person singular of the present tense of have

has-been /ˈhæz ˌbɪn/ noun [C] an insulting word for someone who was important in the past but that is not important now

hash¹ /hæʃ/ noun **1** [C/U] a meal made from small pieces of meat and potato that are cooked together **2** [U] *informal* a form of the drug MARIJUANA

hash² /hæʃ/ PHRASAL VERB ˌ**hash sth ˈout** *informal* to discuss a plan or agreement in order to agree about the details

ˌ**hash ˈbrowns** noun [plural] potatoes that have been cut up into very small pieces, pressed together, and cooked in oil

has•n't /ˈhæz(ə)nt/ short form the usual way of saying or writing "has not" when "has" is an AUXILIARY VERB. This is not often used in formal writing: *He hasn't arrived yet.*

has•sle¹ /ˈhæs(ə)l/ noun [C/U] *informal* a situation that causes annoying problems for you: *If it's too much hassle, we can do it another time.*

has•sle² /ˈhæs(ə)l/ verb [T] to annoy someone, or to cause problems for them

haste /heɪst/ noun [U] *formal* great speed in doing something because you do not have much time

PHRASE **in haste** too quickly, without careful planning or thought

has•ten /ˈheɪs(ə)n/ verb [T] to make something happen sooner or more quickly

PHRASES **hasten to add** used when you add something to what you have just said, in order to make your meaning clear: *I hasten to add that I am not accusing you of lying.*

hasten to do sth to do or say something very quickly without waiting

hast•y /ˈheɪsti/ adj done in a hurry, without thinking carefully, or doing something too quickly: *a hasty marriage* ♦ *Don't be hasty about making this decision.* —**hast•i•ly** adv

hat /hæt/ noun [C] ★★ a piece of clothing that you wear on your head: *a brown fur hat* → DROP²

hatch¹ /hætʃ/ verb [I/T] if a baby bird, fish, or insect hatches, or if it is hatched, it comes out of its egg and is born

hatch² /hætʃ/ noun [C] a small door in a floor or ceiling, or above the ground in a wall

hatch•back /ˈhætʃˌbæk/ noun [C] a type of car that has a door on the back that opens from the bottom

hatch•et /ˈhætʃət/ noun [C] a tool like a small AX

PHRASE **bury the hatchet** to become friendly with someone again after a disagreement

hate¹ /heɪt/ verb [T] ★★★

1 to dislike someone or something very much ≠ LOVE: *I hate the smell of cigarettes.* ♦ *I really* ***hate his guts*** (=hate him very much).

2 if you hate a particular situation or activity, you think that it is unpleasant or upsetting: *I* ***hate it when*** *my parents argue.* ♦ **hate to do sth** *Glen hates to lose.*

PHRASES **I hate to bother/interrupt you** *spoken* a polite way of saying that you are sorry for bothering or interrupting someone

I hate to say/admit used for showing that it is unpleasant for you to say something: *I hate to say this, but I think you've probably lost your money.*

I hate to think *spoken* used for emphasizing that what you are going to talk about is upsetting: *I hate to think how much money I have spent.*

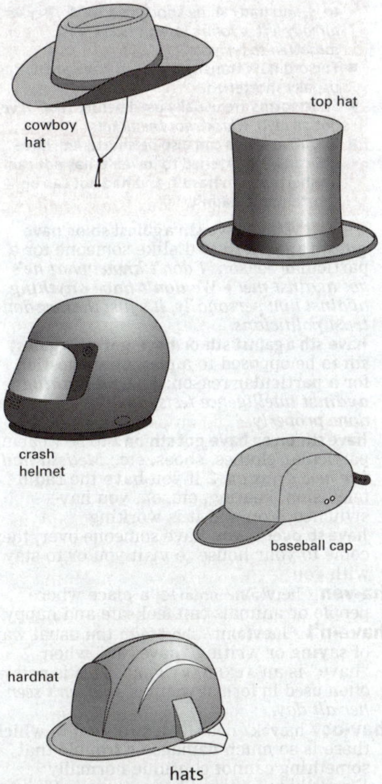

hats

hate² /heɪt/ noun [U] the feeling of hating someone or something ≠ LOVE

hate·ful /ˈheɪtfəl/ adj extremely bad, unpleasant, or cruel

ˈhate ˌmail noun [U] letters that contain threats or offensive remarks

ha·tred /ˈheɪtrəd/ noun [U] *formal* a feeling of hate

haugh·ty /ˈhɔti/ adj proud and unfriendly

haul¹ /hɔl/ verb [T] **1** to pull or carry something that is heavy from one place to another with a lot of effort = DRAG: *I hauled my luggage to the nearest hotel.* **2** to move someone by pulling them = DRAG: *He grasped Judy's arm and hauled her to her feet.*

PHRASAL VERB **ˌhaul sb ˈoff** to take someone away to a place that they do not want to go to

haul² /hɔl/ noun [C] **1** a large amount of something illegal such as drugs that is found by the police **2** the amount of fish that is caught in a net → LONG-HAUL

haunches /ˈhɔnʃɪz/ noun [plural] the top parts of your legs and your BUTTOCKS

haunt¹ /hɔnt/ verb [T] **1** if a place is haunted by the spirit of a dead person, people believe that it appears there **2** to make someone feel worried and upset for a long time: *Images from the war still haunt him.* ♦ *Our past mistakes are returning to haunt us.*

haunt² /hɔnt/ noun [C] a place that someone visits often because they enjoy going there

haunt·ed /ˈhɔntəd/ adj **1** lived in or visited by the spirit of a dead person **2** looking frightened or worried

haunt·ing /ˈhɔntɪŋ/ adj beautiful and sad in a way that stays in your memory: *haunting melodies*

have /*weak* əv, həv, *strong* hæv/ (3rd person singular **has** /*weak* əz, həz, *strong* hæz/; past tense and past participle **had** /*weak* əd, həd, *strong* hæd/) verb ★★★

1 used for forming perfect tenses [auxiliary verb] used for forming the PERFECT TENSES of verbs. The perfect tenses are used for talking about what happened or began before now, or before another point in time: *Has anybody seen Dave this afternoon?* ♦ *I've been looking for you everywhere.* ♦ *"Have you washed your hands?" "Of course I have."* ♦ *We didn't get a chance to talk to her, but I wish we had.*

2 have or **have got: used for describing sb/sth** [T] used for saying what the features or qualities of someone or something are: *Dr. Morel had dark piercing eyes.* ♦ *The house didn't have electricity.* ♦ *She's got a lot of talent.* ♦ *The museum has a large section devoted to modern art.*

3 have or **have got: own or hold sth** [T] to own something, or to be carrying something: *They have a house in the suburbs.* ♦ *If you had a computer, I could e-mail you.* ♦ *What's that you've got in your hand?* ♦ *Do you have a pen I could borrow?* ♦ **have sth on you** *I don't have any money on me.*

4 do sth [T] to do or experience something: *Can I have a look at your photos?* ♦ *You should have a nap.* ♦ *We almost had an accident on the freeway.* ♦ *I had a feeling I was being watched.* ♦ *Have a nice weekend!*

5 have or **have got: stating a relationship** [T] used for stating someone's relationship with another person or other people: *Stephen has a sister in Minneapolis.* ♦ *I've got a friend who works at NBC.* ♦ *Gary knew he had some dangerous enemies.*

6 eat or drink sth [T] to eat or drink something: *Can I have another piece of cake?* ♦ *Why don't you stay and have lunch with us?* ♦ *I'll have the roast beef, please.*

7 have or **have got: saying what is available** [T] used for saying what is available: *Do you have a double room available?* ♦ *She didn't have space for me in her car.* ♦ *I didn't **have time to** cook anything.* ♦ *We've got time for a quick swim before breakfast.*

8 arrange for sth to be done [T] to arrange for someone to do something: **have sth done** *They've had the house redecorated.* ♦ *I'm having my hair cut today.* ♦ **have sb do sth** *I'll have someone bring your luggage up.*

9 have or **have got: place or arrange sth** [T] used for saying that you have put something in a particular position, or you have arranged it in a particular way: *Ralph had his back to the door, so he didn't see me come in.* ♦ *She had the book open in front of her.*

10 have or **have got: suffer from sth** [T] to

suffer from an illness, disease, injury, or pain: *I've got a terrible headache.* ♦ *James had malaria while he was working in West Africa.* ♦ *The X-rays show that he has a broken ankle.*
11 have or **have got: receive sth** [T] to receive a message, advice, criticism, etc.: *We haven't had any news from home.* ♦ *I've had a lot of phone calls today.* ♦ *Did you have any help from your friends?* ♦ *The airline has had thousands of complaints.*
12 have or **have got: be employed** [T] to be employed to do a particular job: *He can't pay the rent because he doesn't have a job.*
13 have or **have got: referring to arrangements** [T] used for saying that you have arranged or planned to do something: *I have an appointment tomorrow afternoon.* ♦ *We have friends coming to dinner.* ♦ **have sth to do** *She has a lot of work to do today.*
14 have or **have got: hold sb** [T] to be holding someone by a particular part of their body so that they cannot get away: **have sb by sth** *The guard had her by the arm.*
15 give birth [T] to give birth to a baby: *Linda's having a baby in June.*

PHRASES **sb had better do sth** used for saying what someone should do: *You'd better be careful.*
have (got) it in for sb *informal* to want to cause trouble for someone because you dislike them
have (got) it made *informal* to be in a very good situation: *Jerry's got it made – he only has to work half the year.*
have had it *spoken* **1** to be so annoyed with someone or something that you do not want to be involved with them any longer: *He says he's **had it with** politics.* ♦ *I've **had it up to here** with Kevin – he never stops complaining.* **2** if something has had it, it cannot be used any longer because it is in such bad condition
have it out to talk to someone honestly about a disagreement between you: *He decided to **have it out with** Rose there and then.*
have to do sth or **have got to do sth** if you have to do something, you must do it because it is necessary: *I have to get up early tomorrow.* ♦ *You have to ask Jane if you want any drinks.* ♦ *You **don't have to come*** (=it is not necessary to come) *if you don't want to.*

- Questions and negatives using the auxiliary verb **have** are formed without **do**: *Has the meeting finished?* ♦ *You haven't eaten anything.*
- For many transitive senses of **have**, **have got** can also be used in the present tense. Questions and negatives with these senses can be formed using **do** or sometimes **have got**: *Does the car have four doors?* ♦ *Has he got red hair?* ♦ *Lou doesn't have a cellphone.* ♦ *I haven't got the courage to tell her.*
- Questions and negatives with other transitive senses of **have** are formed with **do**: *Did you have a nice walk?* ♦ *I didn't have breakfast this morning.*
- In conversation or informal writing the auxiliary use of **have** is often shortened. **Have** can be shortened to **'ve**, **has** can be shortened to **'s**, and **had** can be shortened to **'d**: *They've already left.* ♦ *John's lost his ticket.* ♦ *I'd forgotten to tell you.*
- The ordinary transitive uses of **have** are not usually shortened.
- Short forms are usually used before "got": *I've got an idea.* ♦ *Jack's got the tickets.*
- Negative forms can also be shortened: **have not** can be shortened to **haven't**, **has not** can be shortened to **hasn't**, and **had not** can be shortened to **hadn't**.

PHRASAL VERBS **ˈhave sth aˌgainst sb** or **have ˈgot sth aˌgainst sb** to dislike someone for a particular reason: *I don't know what he's got against me.* ♦ *We **don't have anything against** him personally, it's just that we don't trust politicians.*
ˈhave sth aˌgainst sth or **have ˈgot sth aˌgainst sth** to be opposed to a plan or suggestion for a particular reason: *I've **got nothing against** intelligence tests, as long as they're done properly.*
ˌhave sth ˈon or **have ˌgot sth ˈon 1** to be wearing particular clothes, shoes, etc.: *Melissa had her new dress on.* **2** if you have the radio, television, heating, etc. on, you have switched it on and it is working
ˌhave sb ˈover if you have someone over, they come to your house to visit you or to stay with you

ha·ven /ˈheɪv(ə)n/ noun [C] a place where people or animals can feel safe and happy

have·n't /ˈhæv(ə)nt/ short form the usual way of saying or writing "have not" when "have" is an AUXILIARY VERB. This is not often used in formal writing: *I haven't seen her all day.*

hav·oc /ˈhævək/ noun [U] a situation in which there is so much damage or trouble that something cannot continue normally: *Floods have wreaked havoc* (=caused havoc) *on the town.*

hawk /hɔk/ noun [C] **1** a large bird that kills other birds and animals for food **2** a politician who prefers using military force to more peaceful methods ≠ DOVE

hay /heɪ/ noun [U] long grass that has been cut and dried so that it can be used for feeding animals

ˈhay ˌfever noun [U] a medical condition that affects your nose and eyes. It is caused by POLLEN (=powder produced by flowers).

hay·wire /ˈheɪˌwaɪr/ adj **go haywire** *informal* to stop working or behaving correctly

haz·ard¹ /ˈhæzərd/ noun [C] something that could be dangerous or could cause damage: *a fire/radiation/traffic hazard* ♦ *Pollution is a major health hazard* (=something that is dangerous to your health).

haz·ard² /ˈhæzərd/ verb [T] to make a guess or suggestion when you are not sure if it is true

ˈhazard ˌlights noun [plural] the lights on a car that flash on and off to warn other drivers of danger

haz·ard·ous /ˈhæzərdəs/ adj dangerous to people's health or safety: *hazardous driving conditions*

haze /heɪz/ noun [C/U] smoke, dust, or water in the air that makes it difficult to see clearly

ha•zel /ˈheɪz(ə)l/ adj light brown and slightly green in color

haz•y /ˈheɪzi/ adj **1** not clear because there is smoke, dust, or water in the air **2** not exact or sure: *hazy memories from childhood*

he /*weak* i, *strong* hi/ pronoun ★★★
1 used for referring to a man, boy, or male animal, when they have already been mentioned, or when it is obvious which one you are referring to: *I told William, but he didn't believe me.* ♦ *Like all dogs, he'll chase a rabbit if he sees one.*
2 *old-fashioned* used in a general way for referring to any person whether they are male or female: *Everyone has a right to say what he thinks.*

Words that may cause offense

He, him, his, and **himself** are sometimes used for referring to a person of either sex, but many people avoid this use because it suggests that women are not included, or that men are more important than women. To avoid causing offense, you can use expressions such as **he or she, he/she, s/he, him/her,** or **him/herself** in writing. In conversation, many people say **they, them, their,** and **themselves** to avoid mentioning whether the person is male or female.

head¹ /hed/ noun [C] ★★★

1 top part of body	4 top/front part of sth
2 your mind & thoughts	5 main teacher
3 leader of group	+ PHRASES

1 the top part of your body that has your brain, eyes, mouth, etc. in it: *Lynn had a bruise on the side of her head.* ♦ *She **shook her head*** (=moved it from side to side). ♦ *Ron **nodded his head*** (=moved it up and down) *but said nothing.* —*picture* → C14
2 your mind and thoughts: *A thought suddenly came into my head.* ♦ *He added the numbers quickly **in his head**.* ♦ *I can't get that song **out of my head*** (=cannot stop thinking about it).
3 the leader or most important person in a group: *the head waiter* ♦ *I'm meeting **the head of** the department tomorrow.*
4 the top or front part of something: *We walked straight to **the head of** the line.*
5 *British* the PRINCIPAL of a school

PHRASES **a/per head** for each person: *The meal cost $20 per head.*
come to a head *informal* if a situation comes to a head, it suddenly becomes worse
go over sb's head 1 if an idea, joke, or remark goes over someone's head, they cannot understand it **2** if you go over someone else's head, you speak directly to a person who is more important than the person who you should speak to
go to your head *informal* if success goes to your head, it makes you think that you are better or more important than you really are
head over heels completely in love with someone or something
(in) over your head involved in a situation in which you do not have the skills, knowledge, or money to succeed
keep your head above water *informal* to manage to live or keep a business working even though you are not earning much money
laugh/scream your head off *informal* to laugh or scream very loudly
→ BITE¹, BURY, TOP¹

head² /hed/ verb ★★★
1 [I] to go in a particular direction: *They headed north, across the desert.* ♦ *We decided to **head for** home.*
2 [T] to be in control of a group or an organization: *Detective Tim Reynolds will head the investigation.*
3 [T] to be first on a list, or first in a line of people: *Williams heads the police's list of suspects.*
4 [T] to hit the ball with your head in soccer

PHRASES **be heading/headed for sth** if you are heading or headed for a situation, you are likely to be in that situation soon: *It appears that the current champions are heading for victory again.*
head of state the leader of a country, for example a king, queen, or president

PHRASAL VERBS **ˌhead ˈoff** *informal* to leave: *We should be heading off soon.*
ˌhead sth ˈoff to prevent something from taking place: *The report claims that the security officials could have headed off the terrorist attack.*
ˌhead sth ˈup *same as* **head² 2**: *Judy Leighton was chosen to head up the department.*

head•ache /ˈhedˌeɪk/ noun [C] ★
1 a pain in your head: *I had a bad headache yesterday.*
2 *informal* something that causes you a lot of problems

ˈhead ˌcount noun [C] an occasion when you count all the people in a place or organization, or the number of people that are counted

head•ed /ˈhedəd/ adj with a particular title: *a document headed "The Future of Farming"*

head•er /ˈhedər/ noun [C] something that is printed at the top of a page or a computer document

ˌhead ˈfirst or **head•first** /ˌhedˈfɜrst/ adv with your head in such a position that it hits something before the rest of your body

head•gear /ˈhedˌgɪr/ noun [U] hats and other things that you wear on your head

head•hunt /ˈhedˌhʌnt/ verb [T] to try to persuade someone to leave their job in order to work for another company

head•hunt•er /ˈhedˌhʌntər/ noun [C] a person or company who searches for good staff and tries to persuade them to leave their jobs in order to work for another company

head•ing /ˈhedɪŋ/ noun [C] the title at the top of a page or piece of writing

head•light /ˈhedˌlaɪt/ noun [C] one of the two lights on the front of a vehicle —*picture* → C6

head•line¹ /ˈhedˌlaɪn/ noun **1** [C] the title of a newspaper story, printed in large letters **2 the headlines** [plural] the most important stories in the news: *The fuel crisis continues to dominate the headlines.* ♦ *Did the story **make the headlines*** (=appear as one of the main reports)?

head•line² /ˈhedˌlaɪn/ verb **1** [T] to give a headline to a story in a newspaper **2** [I/T] to be the most famous performer at a concert

H

or show where many other people are also performing

head•long /ˈhedˌlɔŋ/ adj, adv **1** moving with your head going first **2** very quickly and without thinking about what you are doing

ˌ**head ˈoffice** noun [C] the main office of an organization or company

ˌ**head-ˈon** adv **1** if two vehicles crash head-on, the front of one hits the front of the other **2** if you deal with a problem head-on, you deal with it in a very direct way —**head-ˌon** adj: *a head-on crash*

head•phones /ˈhedˌfoʊnz/ noun [plural] a piece of equipment that you wear over your ears in order to listen to the radio or recorded sound

head•quar•tered /ˈhedˌkwɔrtərd/ adj a company or organization that is headquartered in a place has its main offices in that place

head•quar•ters /ˈhedˌkwɔrtərz/ noun [plural] the place where a company, organization, or military unit has its main offices or its main center of control

head•rest /ˈhedˌrest/ noun [C] the part of a chair or car seat that you lean your head against —*picture* → C6

head•room /ˈhedˌrum/ noun [U] **1** the amount of space between your head and a ceiling, especially in a car **2** the amount of space between the top of a vehicle and a bridge

head•set /ˈhedˌset/ noun [C] a piece of radio or telephone equipment that you wear over your ears with a part that you can speak into

ˌ**head ˈstart** noun [C] **1** an advantage over other people who are in the same situation as you: *The reading program gives young children a head start.* **2** a situation in which you start a race before or in front of your opponent

head•stone /ˈhedˌstoʊn/ noun [C] a piece of stone that marks a GRAVE (=place where a dead person is buried)

head•strong /ˈhedˌstrɔŋ/ adj determined to do what you want even if other people warn you not to do it

ˌ**heads-ˈup**[1] adj *American informal* lively and intelligent

ˌ**heads-ˈup**[2] noun [singular] *American informal* a warning: *They gave us a heads-up that the deal might not happen.*

head•teach•er /ˌhedˈtitʃər/ noun [C] *British* the PRINCIPAL of a school

ˌ**head-to-ˈhead** adj, adv competing or meeting directly with someone or something else: *The two teams go head-to-head* (=compete) *on Sunday.*

head•way /ˈhedˌweɪ/ noun **make headway** to make progress with something that you are trying to achieve

head•wind /ˈhedˌwɪnd/ noun [C] a wind that blows in the opposite direction to the one in which you are moving

head•y /ˈhedi/ adj giving you a strong feeling of pleasure or excitement

heal /hil/ verb **1** [I/T] if an injury heals, or if someone heals it, the skin or bone grows back together and becomes healthy again: *The wound took a long time to heal.* **2** [T] to make people stop fighting and become friendly again

PHRASAL VERB ˌ**heal ˈup** if an injury heals up, the skin or bone grows back together and becomes healthy again

heal•ing[1] /ˈhilɪŋ/ adj making someone feel better after they have been sick or unhappy: *a plant with healing properties*

heal•ing[2] /ˈhilɪŋ/ noun [U] the process of becoming healthy again

health /helθ/ noun [U] ★★★

1 the condition of your body, especially whether or not you are sick: *His health improved once he stopped working.* ♦ *She's had serious* ***health problems.*** ♦ *Lola is 85 and still* ***in very good health.*** ♦ *My father has been* ***in poor health*** *for some time.*

2 how successful something is: *Officials are worried about* ***the health of*** *the local technology industry.*

ˈ**health ˌcare** noun [U] the services that take care of people's health: *Homeless people need better access to health care.* —**health•care** /ˈhelθˌker/ adj

ˈ**health ˌcenter** noun [C] *American* a building where several doctors can provide medical care to the people in a particular area

ˈ**health ˌclub** noun [C] a club where members can go to do physical exercises

ˈ**health ˌfood** noun [C/U] food that is good for you because it does not contain artificial substances

ˈ**health inˌsurance** noun [U] a type of insurance that pays for your medical treatment when you are sick or injured

ˈ**health ˌservice** noun [C] a public service that is responsible for providing medical care

health•y /ˈhelθi/ adj ★★

1 physically strong and not sick ≠ UNHEALTHY: *a healthy baby* ♦ *I feel very healthy at the moment.*

2 making you strong and not sick ≠ UNHEALTHY: *healthy food* ♦ *a healthy diet/lifestyle*

3 working well and likely to continue to be successful ≠ UNHEALTHY: *The country still has a healthy economy.*

4 a healthy attitude is good and sensible ≠ UNHEALTHY

—**health•i•ly** adv

heap[1] /hip/ noun [C] a large messy pile of something: *a heap of old car parts* ♦ *Dirty rags lay in a heap on the floor.*

heap[2] /hip/ verb [T] **1** to make a big messy pile of things: *Clothing was heaped on the floor.* **2** if you heap praise or blame on someone, you praise or blame them a lot

heap•ing /ˈhipɪŋ/ adj *American* **1** a heaping spoon is completely full **2** filled or covered with a lot of something in a high pile: *a heaping plate of stew*

hear /hɪr/ (past tense and past participle **heard** /hɜrd/) verb ★★★

1 [I/T] to realize that someone or something is making a sound: *Mary heard the sound of voices.* ♦ *Shh, I can't hear.* ♦ *No one could* ***hear what*** *she said.* ♦ **hear sb/sth do sth** *He heard the door slam.* ♦ **hear sb/sth doing sth** *She heard the dog barking outside.*

2 [I/T] to receive information about something: *Did you* ***hear about*** *Jim's party?* ♦ *I came home as soon as I* ***heard what*** *happened.* ♦ **+(that)** *I heard he has a new job.*

3 [T] to listen to something such as a speech, performance, or program: *I want to hear the news on the radio before I go.* ♦ **hear sb do sth** *He's got a great voice – you should hear him sing.*

4 [T] to listen to and judge a legal case in a court of law

PHRASES **have heard it (all) before** *spoken* to not believe what someone is saying, or to not be impressed by it

not want to hear sth to not be willing to discuss or consider something: *I don't want to hear another word on the subject.*

PHRASAL VERBS **ˈhear from sb 1** if you hear from someone, they write to you or call you on the telephone: *It's years since I heard from Jill.* **2** to listen to someone who is speaking about a particular thing: *The Commission heard from over thirty witnesses.*

ˈhear of sb/sth if you have heard of someone or something, you know about their existence: *Have you heard of the author James Bomford?*

ˌhear sb ˈout to let someone finish what they are saying without interrupting them: *I'm serious about this; hear me out, please.*

- When you **hear** a sound, you become conscious of it: *Did you hear the thunder last night?* ♦ *I didn't hear the door open.*
- When you **listen**, you deliberately pay attention to a sound in order to hear it: *I listened carefully but I couldn't hear what she was saying.* ♦ *I always listen to the radio in my car.*
- You **hear** something, but you **listen to** something.

hear•ing /ˈhɪrɪŋ/ noun **1** [U] your ability to hear sounds: *My hearing is getting worse as I get older.* **2** [C] a meeting of a court of law or official organization in order to find out the facts about something

ˈhearing ˌaid noun [C] a small piece of equipment that someone wears in their ear in order to help them to hear

ˈhearing-imˌpaired adj unable to hear as well as most people can

hear•say /ˈhɪrˌseɪ/ noun [U] information that you have heard without having any proof that it is true

hearse /hɜrs/ noun [C] a large car that is used for carrying a dead person in a COFFIN

heart /hɑrt/ noun ★★★

1 organ in your chest	4 shape
2 your feelings	5 suit of playing cards
3 inner central part	+ PHRASES

1 [C] the organ in your chest that pumps blood around your body: *I could hear his heart beating.* ♦ *Did you know he had a weak heart?*

2 [C] your feelings when they are considered as part of your character: *You have to do what your heart tells you is right.*

3 [C] the central part of something: *a beautiful house deep **in the heart of** the Blue Ridge Mountains*

4 [C] a shape that represents love —*picture* → C8

5 hearts [plural] the SUIT of playing cards that have red heart shapes on them —*picture* → C16

PHRASES **at heart** used for saying what someone's basic character is: *I'm really a country person at heart.*

break sb's heart to upset someone very much, especially by showing them that you do not love them

by heart if you know something by heart, you can remember all the words or music in it

have your heart set on (doing) sth to decide that you want something very much

sb's heart goes out to sb used for saying that someone feels sorry for someone else

sb's heart is in the right place used for saying that someone tries to do good things even though it does not always seem like this

sb's heart is not in sth used for saying that someone does not really care about something that they are doing

lose heart to feel disappointed and try less hard because of this

not have the heart to do sth to not want to do something because it seems cruel

(straight) from the heart being completely honest about your feelings

take sth to heart to think about something seriously, often so that it upsets you

to your heart's content as much or as often as you like

heart•ache /ˈhɑrtˌeɪk/ noun [U] great sadness or worry

ˈheart atˌtack noun [C] an occasion when someone suddenly has a lot of pain because their heart stops working normally

heart•beat /ˈhɑrtˌbit/ noun [C] the movement or sound of your heart as it pumps blood around your body

PHRASE **in a heartbeat** used for saying that you are willing and eager to do something

heart•break /ˈhɑrtˌbreɪk/ noun [U] a feeling of great sadness

heart•break•ing /ˈhɑrtˌbreɪkɪŋ/ adj making you feel very sad or upset

heart•bro•ken /ˈhɑrtˌbroʊkən/ adj extremely sad and upset

heart•burn /ˈhɑrtˌbɜrn/ noun [U] a pain that feels like burning in your chest and is a type of INDIGESTION

ˈheart disˌease noun [U] a serious medical condition that affects your heart

heart•ened /ˈhɑrt(ə)nd/ adj feeling happier and more hopeful than before

ˈheart ˌfailure noun [U] a serious medical condition in which your heart stops working normally

heart•felt /ˈhɑrtˌfelt/ adj *formal* a heartfelt emotion, remark, or action is very sincere

hearth /hɑrθ/ noun [C] the floor around a FIREPLACE

heart•i•ly /ˈhɑrtɪli/ adv **1** in a loud or enthusiastic way: *Jones laughed heartily at his little joke.* **2** if you eat heartily, you eat everything on your plate with enthusiasm **3** completely, or extremely: *They are heartily sorry for the trouble they've caused.*

heart•land /ˈhɑrtˌlænd/ noun [C] *mainly journalism* a part of a country where a particular activity or belief is especially common

heart•less /ˈhɑrtləs/ adj feeling or showing no sympathy or kindness = CALLOUS

heart-stop·ping /ˈhɑrtˌstɑpɪŋ/ adj extremely frightening or exciting: *For one heart-stopping moment, I thought she was going to kiss me.*

heart·strings /ˈhɑrtˌstrɪŋz/ noun **tug/pull at sb's heartstrings** to make someone feel a lot of love or sympathy

ˌheart-to-ˈheart noun [C] a private conversation between two people about their personal feelings

heart·warm·ing /ˈhɑrtˌwɔrmɪŋ/ adj making you feel happy because people are being kind

heart·y /ˈhɑrti/ adj **1** friendly and enthusiastic **2** a hearty meal is large

heat¹ /hit/ noun ★★★

1 hot quality	4 for cooking
2 very hot weather	5 part of competition
3 system in building	+ PHRASES

1 [singular/U] the quality of being hot, or how hot something is: *We felt the intense heat from the fire.* ♦ *He could feel **the heat of** the sun on his back.*

2 the heat [singular] very hot weather: *The local people get out of the city to escape the heat.*

3 [U] *American* the system in a building that keeps it warm

4 the heat [singular] the flame or hot area on a STOVE that you cook on: *I turned the heat down a little.*

5 [C] a game or race at the start of a competition

PHRASES **in heat** a female animal that is in heat is ready to MATE with a male

in the heat of the moment at a time when you are too angry or excited to think carefully

heat² /hit/ verb [I/T] ★ to make something hot, or to become hot: *Heat the oil gently in a large frying pan.*

PHRASAL VERBS **ˌheat ˈup** if a situation heats up, it becomes more exciting, dangerous, or serious: *The dispute was already heating up.*

ˌheat sth ˈup *same as* **heat²**: *I was just heating up some soup.*

heat·ed /ˈhitəd/ adj **1** angry and excited: *a heated discussion/argument/debate* **2** made warm enough for people to use: *a heated swimming pool* —**heat·ed·ly** adv

heat·er /ˈhitər/ noun [C] a piece of equipment that is used for making a place warm, or for heating water → SPACE HEATER

heath·er /ˈheðər/ noun [C/U] a plant with small purple or white flowers that grows on hills

ˈheat ˌwave noun [C] a continuous period of very hot weather

heave¹ /hiv/ verb **1** [I/T] to push, pull, throw, or lift an object using a lot of effort: *Paul heaved the last box into the truck.* **2** [I] to move up and down with large regular movements: *Her chest heaved as she struggled to control her breathing.*

PHRASE **heave a sigh** to let out a deep breath, for example because you are pleased about something

heave² /hiv/ noun [C] a strong pulling, pushing, throwing, or lifting movement

heav·en /ˈhev(ə)n/ noun **1 heaven** or **Heaven** [U] the place where God is believed to live **2 the heavens** [plural] *literary* the sky

PHRASE **for heaven's sake/sakes** *spoken* used for emphasizing that you are annoyed or impatient with someone

heav·en·ly /ˈhev(ə)nli/ adj **1** in or from heaven **2** *informal* extremely nice, enjoyable, or beautiful = DIVINE

heav·i·ly /ˈhevɪli/ adv **1** in large amounts: *She had been smoking heavily since her teens.* ♦ *They had borrowed heavily to buy the boat.* **2** very, or to a large degree: *heavily populated areas* ♦ *Her work was heavily influenced by her father's.* ♦ *The men were heavily armed* (=carrying a lot of weapons). **3** with a lot of force or effort: *She leaned heavily on the table.* ♦ *The older man was now breathing heavily.* **4** slowly, in a way that shows that you feel sad or tired: *She grabbed the chair and pulled herself up heavily.*

heav·y /ˈhevi/ adj ★★★

1 with a lot of weight	4 serious/difficult
2 many things	5 of food
3 with physical effort	6 big or powerful

1 a heavy object weighs a lot ≠ LIGHT: *She was struggling with a heavy suitcase.* ♦ *He was too heavy for the nurses to lift.*

2 used for saying that there is a lot of something, or that something is done a lot: *Traffic is very heavy on the interstate tonight.* ♦ *The school places **a heavy emphasis** on music.* ♦ ***heavy rain** and strong winds* ♦ *There was **heavy fighting** in the capital yesterday.* ♦ *Sandra is **a heavy smoker*** (=she smokes a lot).

3 involving a lot of physical effort or force ≠ LIGHT: *a heavy blow to the head* ♦ *They did most of **the heavy work** in the morning.*

4 too serious, difficult, or frightening to be good or enjoyable: *She felt their relationship was getting too heavy.* ♦ *His new book is pretty heavy.* ♦ *a heavy responsibility*

5 food that is heavy is too solid and not enjoyable ≠ LIGHT

6 large, thick, or powerful: *The men wore heavy coats and gloves.* ♦ *a small fishing boat struggling in heavy seas* ♦ *Do not operate any **heavy machinery** while taking this medication.*

ˌheavy-ˈduty adj strong and not easily damaged: *heavy-duty plastic*

heav·y-hand·ed /ˌhevi ˈhændəd/ adj using too much force, or not considering people's feelings enough when you are dealing with a situation

ˌheavy ˈhitter noun [C] *informal* a person or organization with a lot of influence and power

ˌheavy ˈindustry noun [U] industry that produces materials such as coal or steel or large objects such as cars or ships

ˌheavy ˈmetal noun [U] a type of loud ROCK music that developed in the 1970s = METAL

heav·y·weight /ˈheviˌweɪt/ noun [C] **1** a BOXER or WRESTLER in the heaviest weight group **2** someone or something that has a lot of influence, status, or knowledge: *political heavyweights*

He·brew¹ /ˈhiˌbru/ noun **1** [U] one of the official languages of Israel **2** [C] a Jewish person in ancient times

He•brew² /ˈhiˌbru/ adj **1** relating to the Hebrew language **2** of Jewish people

heck•le /ˈhek(ə)l/ verb [I/T] to interrupt a speaker or performer by shouting at them —**heck•ler** noun [C], **heck•ling** noun [U]

hec•tare /ˈhektər, ˈhekˌtɑr/ noun [C] a unit for measuring an area of land, equal to 10,000 square meters

hec•tic /ˈhektɪk/ adj full of busy activity

he'd /*weak* id, *strong* hid/ short form **1** the usual way of saying or writing "he had" when "had" is an AUXILIARY VERB. This is not often used in formal writing: *He knew he'd seen her before.* **2** the usual way of saying or writing "he would." This is not often used in formal writing: *He'd come if you asked him.*

hedge¹ /hedʒ/ noun [C] a line of bushes or small trees that are growing close together around a yard or a field

PHRASE **a hedge against sth** a way of trying to protect yourself against a problem or risk: *a hedge against inflation*

hedge² /hedʒ/ verb [I] to avoid answering a question directly, or to avoid making a definite decision

PHRASE **hedge your bets** to organize a situation so that you have several choices available to you, in order to increase your chances of success

hedge•hog /ˈhedʒˌhɔg/ noun [C] a small wild animal with a round body that is covered with sharp SPINES

he•don•ist /ˈhid(ə)nɪst/ noun [C] someone who believes that pleasure is the most important thing in life —**he•don•ism** noun [U], **he•don•is•tic** /ˌhid(ə)nˈɪstɪk/ adj

heed¹ /hid/ verb [T] *formal* to listen carefully to someone's advice or warning, and do what they suggest

heed² /hid/ noun **pay heed to** or **take heed of** *formal* to give careful attention to someone's advice or warning

heel /hil/ noun [C] **1** the back part of your foot, below your ANKLE —*picture* → C14 **2** the part underneath the back of a shoe

PHRASE **(hard/hot/close) on the heels of** **1** following close behind someone or something **2** happening soon after another event

→ DIG¹, HEAD¹

heft•y /ˈhefti/ adj **1** large and heavy **2** a hefty amount of money is very large

heif•er /ˈhefər/ noun [C] a young cow

height /haɪt/ noun ★★★

1 [C/U] how high something is, or how tall someone is: *He was about the same height as his wife.* ♦ *What height do you want the picture at?*

2 [singular] the time or level of greatest activity: *The excitement was **at its height**.* ♦ *Jeans were once again **the height of** fashion.*

3 heights [plural] a high place or position: *Dave was trying to overcome his **fear of heights**.*

4 heights [plural] a high level of activity or success: *His popularity has **reached new heights**.*

height•en /ˈhaɪt(ə)n/ verb [I/T] if something heightens a feeling or emotion, or if a feeling or emotion heightens, it becomes stronger

hei•nous /ˈheɪnəs/ adj *very formal* a heinous act or crime is extremely evil

heir /er/ noun [C] someone who will receive money, property, or a title when another person dies

heir•ess /ˈerəs/ noun [C] a woman or girl who will receive money or property when another person dies

heir•loom /ˈerˌlum/ noun [C] a valuable or special possession that has belonged to one family for many years

held the past tense and past participle of **hold**¹

hel•i•cop•ter /ˈhelɪˌkɑptər/ noun [C] an aircraft with large metal blades on top that spin round and lift it into the air —*picture* → C7

he•li•um /ˈhiliəm/ noun [U] a gas that is lighter than air

he'll /*weak* il, *strong* hil/ short form the usual way of saying or writing "he will." This is not often used in formal writing: *He'll be here around noon.*

hell /hel/ noun [U] **1 hell** or **Hell** in some religions, the place where bad people are sent to suffer when they die **2** a situation that is extremely unpleasant

PHRASES **all hell breaks loose** *informal* used for saying that people start fighting or arguing because they are angry or upset

for the hell of it *informal* just for fun, and not for any serious reason

the sth from hell *informal* an especially unpleasant example of a person or thing: *the boss from hell*

like hell *spoken* with a lot of speed or effort: *I got out of the truck and ran like hell.*

a/one hell of a *spoken* **1** used for emphasizing what you are saying: *It must be a hell of a job trying to organize all this information.* **2** used for emphasizing how good something is

what the hell *spoken* used for showing that something does not matter

ˌhell-ˈbent adj determined to do or achieve something

hel•lo /həˈloʊ/ interjection ★★★

1 used as a greeting when you meet someone or begin to talk to someone on the telephone: *Hello, my name is Anna.*

2 used for calling to someone to get their attention: *Hello! We're over here!*

3 *very informal* used for saying that you think someone is being stupid: *Hello! There's no way anyone will give you a job with that haircut.*

helm /helm/ noun [C] a wheel or handle used for making a boat go in the direction that you want it to go in

PHRASE **at the helm** in charge, or in the position of a leader

hel•met /ˈhelmət/ noun [C] a hard hat that you wear to protect your head

help¹ /help/ verb [I/T] ★★★

1 to give someone support or information so that they can do something more easily: **help sb (to) do sth** *Can you help me find my glasses?* ♦ **help sb with sth** *Her brother offered to help her with her homework.* ♦ *Her work involves helping people to find jobs.*

2 to make something better or easier:

Organic farming methods help the environment. ♦ **help (to) do sth** *We hope this helps to clarify the situation.*

PHRASES **cannot/can't help sth** used for saying that someone cannot stop themselves from doing something: *She couldn't help laughing when she saw it.*

sb cannot/can't help it if used for saying that someone cannot be blamed for a situation: *I can't help it if you're upset.*

help yourself *spoken* used for giving someone permission to do or use something: *"Do you mind if I use the phone?" "Help yourself."*

help yourself to sth to take food or drink that someone has offered: *Help yourselves to more wine.*

PHRASAL VERB **ˌhelp (sb) ˈout** to help someone by doing a particular job, or by giving them money: *My family has always helped me out.* ♦ *He always **helped out with** the housework.*

H

Word family: help

Words in the same family as **help**
- **helpful** *adj*
- **helping** *n*
- **unhelpful** *adj*
- **helpless** *adj*

help² /help/ noun ★★★
1 [U] the process of helping someone, or something that you do to help someone: *Do you want some **help with** that?*
2 [singular/U] a person or thing that helps: *You've been a real help to me, Carrie.*
3 [U] the part of a computer program that gives you information: *Try the help menu.*

help³ /help/ interjection used for asking for urgent help: *Help! I'm going to fall.*

ˈhelp ˌdesk noun [C] a service that is provided by a company to give information and support to its customers

help·er /ˈhelpər/ noun [C] someone who helps a person or organization

help·ful /ˈhelpfəl/ adj ★
1 a helpful person helps you by doing something, or by giving you useful advice or information ≠ UNHELPFUL: *a traditional hotel with very helpful staff*
2 useful, or providing help: **it's helpful to do sth** *It's helpful to have a calculator for this exam.* ♦ **helpful for/in doing sth** *Exercise is helpful for controlling high blood pressure.*
—**help·ful·ly** adv

help·ing /ˈhelpɪŋ/ noun [C] an amount of food that is served to one person at a meal =SERVING

help·less /ˈhelpləs/ adj not able to do anything without help —**help·less·ly** adv

hem¹ /hem/ noun [C] the bottom edge of something made of cloth that is folded and sewn in place

hem² /hem/ PHRASAL VERB **ˌhem sb ˈin** if someone is hemmed in, they are prevented from leaving or doing what they want

hem·i·sphere /ˈhemɪˌsfɪr/ noun [C] **1** one half of the Earth **2** one half of the brain

he·mo·phil·i·a /ˌhiməˈfɪliə/ noun [U] a serious illness that prevents your blood from CLOTTING (=becoming thick) when it should

he·mo·phil·i·ac /ˌhiməˈfɪliæk/ noun [C] someone who has hemophilia

hem·or·rhage¹ /ˈhemərɪdʒ/ noun [C/U] an instance of blood flowing out of an injured organ inside someone's body

hem·or·rhage² /ˈhemərɪdʒ/ verb [I] to lose a lot of blood

hem·or·rhoids /ˈheməˌrɔɪdz/ noun [plural] painful swollen areas around your ANUS (=the hole where solid waste comes out of your body)

hemp /hemp/ noun [U] a plant that is used for making rope. It is also used for making the drug MARIJUANA.

hen /hen/ noun [C] a female chicken

hence /hens/ adv *formal* therefore: *Alcohol can cause liver failure and hence death.*

hench·man /ˈhentʃmən/ (plural **hench·men** /ˈhentʃmən/) noun [C] someone who helps a powerful person by doing immoral or violent things

hep·a·ti·tis /ˌhepəˈtaɪtɪs/ noun [U] an infectious disease of the liver

her /*weak* ər, hər, *strong* hɜr/ grammar word ★★★

Her can be:
- a **pronoun**: *If you see Mary, give her my love.*
- a **determiner**: *She was holding her baby.*

1 the object form of "she," used for referring to a woman, girl, or female animal when they have already been mentioned or when it is obvious which one you are referring to: *Where's Susan? Has anyone seen her?* ♦ *Mary asked me to write to her.*
2 belonging to a woman, girl, or female animal that has already been mentioned: *Emma's invited us to her party.* ♦ *She parked her car across the road.* ♦ *She makes **her own** clothes.*

her·ald /ˈherəld/ verb [T] **1** to announce something, or to be a sign that something is going to happen soon **2** to praise something loudly or in a public way

herb /ɜrb/ noun [C] a plant that you use for adding flavor to food or as a medicine

herb·al /ˈɜrb(ə)l/ adj containing herbs, or made from herbs

her·bi·cide /ˈɜrbɪˌsaɪd/ noun [C/U] a chemical that you use for killing WEEDS (=plants that you do not want in your garden)

her·bi·vore /ˈɜrbɪˌvɔr/ noun [C] an animal that eats only plants

herd¹ /hɜrd/ noun [C] a large group of animals of the same type that live and move around together

herd² /hɜrd/ verb [T] to make a group of animals or people move somewhere together

here /hɪr/ grammar word ★★★

Here can be:
- an **adverb**: *Wait here. I'll be back in a minute.*
- an **interjection**: *Here, have a drink of water.*

1 in or to this place in or to the place where you are, or where you are pointing: *We've lived here for over 20 years.* ♦ *Come here.* ♦ *Just sign your name here, at the bottom of the page.* ♦ *You can see the lighthouse **from here**.* ♦ *There aren't many good restaurants **around here**.* ♦ *It's freezing cold **out here**.* ♦ *She wrote her novels **right here** in this room.*
2 when offering or giving sth *spoken* used when you are offering or giving something to someone: *Here, use my handkerchief.* ♦ *Here's $20 – go and buy yourself something*

nice. ♦ ***Here you go, two cups of coffee.***

3 at this point at this point in a process, discussion, or series of events: *Let's stop here and consider what we've said so far.* ♦ *The question is, where does the peace process go **from here**?*

4 when sb/sth arrives or is found *spoken* used for saying that someone or something has just arrived, or has just been found: *I'm waiting for Linda. Oh, here she is.* ♦ *Here are my glasses. I thought I'd lost them.* ♦ ***Here comes** the bus.*

5 happening now happening at the present time, or in the present situation: *Summer is here at last.*

6 for stating a purpose used for saying what purpose someone is working for: *I'm **here** for an interview.* ♦ **here to do sth** *Our staff is here to help.*

PHRASES **here and there** in or to several different places: *Papers were scattered here and there.*

here goes or **here we go** *spoken* used when you are going to try to do something and you are not sure whether you will be successful: *I'm not much good at making speeches, but anyway here goes.*

here to stay if something is here to stay, it will continue to exist for a long time

here•by /hɪrˈbaɪ/ adv *legal* used for stating that something that has been said or written is now official

he•red•i•tar•y /həˈredɪˌteri/ adj a hereditary disease or quality is passed from a parent to a child in their genes

he•red•i•ty /həˈredəti/ noun [U] the genetic process by which a parent's qualities or diseases are passed to their child

her•e•sy /ˈherəsi/ noun [C/U] a belief that is considered wrong because it is very different from what most people believe, or because it opposes the official principles of a religion

her•e•tic /ˈherətɪk/ noun [C] someone who believes things that are considered wrong because they are very different from what most people believe or because they oppose the official principles of a religion
—**he•ret•i•cal** /həˈretɪk(ə)l/ adj

her•i•tage /ˈherɪtɪdʒ/ noun [C/U] the art, buildings, traditions, and beliefs that a society considers to be important parts of its history and culture

her•mit /ˈhɜrmɪt/ noun [C] someone who chooses to live alone, or someone who spends most of their time alone

her•ni•a /ˈhɜrniə/ noun [C] a medical condition in which an organ pushes itself through the muscles around it

he•ro /ˈhɪroʊ/ (plural **he•roes**) noun [C]
1 someone who has done something very brave **2** someone who you admire a lot **3** the main male character of a book, movie, or play ≠ VILLAIN **4 hero** or **hero sandwich** *American* a type of sandwich that consists of meat, cheese, and vegetables on a long narrow piece of bread

he•ro•ic /hɪˈroʊɪk/ adj **1** very brave =COURAGEOUS **2** showing great determination to achieve something: *their heroic effort to protect the future of the local hospital* —**he•ro•i•cal•ly** /hɪˈroʊɪkli/ adv

he•ro•ics /hɪˈroʊɪks/ noun [plural] actions that are very brave but that are also dangerous and unnecessary

her•o•in /ˈheroʊɪn/ noun [U] a powerful illegal drug

her•o•ine /ˈheroʊɪn/ noun [C] **1** the main female character of a book, movie, or play **2** a woman who you admire a lot =HERO

her•o•ism /ˈheroʊˌɪzəm/ noun [U] actions that prove that someone is very brave

her•on /ˈherən/ noun [C] a large bird with a long neck that lives near water

her•pes /ˈhɜrpiz/ noun [U] an infectious disease that can make sore red spots appear on someone's sex organs or near their mouth

her•ring /ˈherɪŋ/ noun [C/U] a long thin silver ocean fish, or this fish eaten as food → RED HERRING

hers /hɜrz/ pronoun ★★ a POSSESSIVE form of "she," used for referring to something that belongs to a woman, girl, or female animal that has already been mentioned: *Mrs. Lansbury claims the money is all hers.* ♦ *His hand reached out and touched hers.* ♦ *My Japanese isn't as good as hers.* ♦ *She introduced us to some friends **of hers**.*

her•self /*weak* ərˈself, *strong* hərˈself/ pronoun ★★★
1 the REFLEXIVE form of "she," used for showing that the woman, girl, or female animal that does something is also affected by what she does: *Lizzie had locked herself in the bathroom.* ♦ *She's going to buy herself a new jacket.* ♦ *Pam was looking at herself in the mirror.*
2 used for emphasizing that you are referring to a particular woman, girl, or female animal and not to anyone else: *It was Christina herself who told me that she was unhappy.* ♦ *The queen herself will attend the meeting.* ♦ *She has enough money to pay for it herself.*

PHRASES **(all) by herself 1** alone: *Annie's too young to travel by herself.* **2** without help from anyone else: *Sally had organized the whole party by herself.*

(all) to herself not sharing something with anyone else: *Everyone had gone away, and she had the apartment to herself.*

be/feel/seem herself to be in a normal mental or physical state: *Beth wasn't quite herself that evening.*

hertz /hɜrts/ (plural **hertz**) noun [C] a unit for measuring sound and radio waves

he's /*weak* iz, *strong* hiz/ short form **1** the usual way of saying or writing "he is." This is not often used in formal writing: *He's in Seattle this weekend.* **2** the usual way of saying or writing "he has" when "has" is an AUXILIARY VERB. This is not often used in formal writing: *He's decided to move.*

hes•i•tant /ˈhezɪtənt/ adj doing something slowly because you are nervous or not certain about it —**hes•i•tant•ly** adv

hes•i•tate /ˈhezɪˌteɪt/ verb [I] ★ to pause before doing something because you are nervous or not certain about it: *He hesitated a moment, and then knocked on the door.*

PHRASE **don't hesitate to do sth** *spoken* used

for encouraging someone to do something: *Don't hesitate to call me if you need any help.*

hes•i•ta•tion /ˌhezɪˈteɪʃ(ə)n/ noun [C/U] a pause before doing something, or a feeling that you should not do it, because you are nervous or not certain about it

het•er•o•sex•u•al /ˌhetəroʊˈsekʃuəl/ adj sexually attracted to people of the opposite sex —**het•er•o•sex•u•al** noun [C]

hex•a•gon /ˈheksəˌgɑn/ noun [C] a GEOMETRIC shape that has six straight sides —*picture* → C8 —**hex•a•gon•al** /heksˈægən(ə)l/ adj

hey /heɪ/ interjection ★
1 used for getting someone's attention, or for showing that you are surprised or annoyed: *Hey! Watch where you're going!*
2 *American* hello: *Hey, Dan. How are you?*

hey•day /ˈheɪˌdeɪ/ noun [C] the time when a person, idea, or object was most successful

hi /haɪ/ interjection *informal* ★ hello: *Hi, I'm Tom.*

HI abbrev Hawaii

hi•a•tus /haɪˈeɪtəs/ noun [C] *formal* a period of time when something does not happen

hi•ber•nate /ˈhaɪbərˌneɪt/ verb [I] if an animal hibernates, it sleeps through the winter —**hi•ber•na•tion** /ˌhaɪbərˈneɪʃ(ə)n/ noun [U]

hic•cup[1] /ˈhɪˌkʌp/ noun [C] **1** a short repeated sound that you make in your throat because you have been eating or drinking too quickly **2** *informal* a small problem, or a problem that causes a short delay

hic•cup[2] /ˈhɪˌkʌp/ (present participle **hic•cup•ping**; past tense and past participle **hic•cupped**) verb [I] to make a hiccup sound

hick•o•ry /ˈhɪkəri/ noun [C/U] a tree that produces nuts and that grows mainly in North America, or the hard wood of a hickory tree

hid the past tense of **hide**[1]

hid•den[1] /ˈhɪd(ə)n/ adj ★
1 if something is hidden, most people do not know about it or understand it: *the* ***hidden costs*** *of being in the hospital*
2 a hidden object or place is not easy to find: *a hidden camera* ♦ *hidden valleys*

hid•den[2] the past participle of **hide**[1]

ˌhidden aˈgenda noun [C] a secret plan to do something because you will get an advantage from it

hide[1] /haɪd/ (past tense **hid** /hɪd/; past participle **hidden** /ˈhɪd(ə)n/) verb ★★★

1 put in secret place	5 try to avoid sth
2 go to secret place	+ PHRASE
3 not allow to be seen	+ PHRASAL VERB
4 not show feelings	

1 [T] to put something in a place so that no one can find it or see it: **hide sth in/at/under etc. sth** *She hid the key in the drawer.* ♦ **hide sth from sb** *I wanted to hide his present from him until his birthday.*
2 [I] to go somewhere or be somewhere where no one can find you or see you: *He ran and* ***hid behind*** *a bush.* ♦ *Robert is* ***hiding from*** *us.*
3 [T] to make something difficult or impossible to see clearly: *Dark clouds hid the sun.*
4 [T] to prevent people from knowing your thoughts or feelings, or the truth: *He could not hide his disappointment.*
5 [I] to try not to accept something, or to try not to be affected by something: *You can't* ***hide from*** *your feelings forever.*

PHRASE **have nothing to hide** to not be afraid of what people may discover, because you have done nothing wrong

PHRASAL VERB **ˌhide ˈout** to go somewhere where no one can find you: *We used to hide out from our parents here.*

hide[2] /haɪd/ noun [C/U] the skin of an animal such as a cow that is used for making leather

ˌhide-and-ˈseek or **ˌhide-and-go-ˈseek** noun [U] a children's game in which one player lets the other players hide, and then tries to find them

hide•a•way /ˈhaɪdəˌweɪ/ noun [C] a private place where someone goes to relax or to be alone

hid•e•ous /ˈhɪdiəs/ adj very ugly, frightening, or unpleasant —**hid•e•ous•ly** adv

hide•out /ˈhaɪdˌaʊt/ noun [C] a place where someone can hide

hid•ing /ˈhaɪdɪŋ/ noun [U] a situation in which someone hides: *Davis, fearing arrest, went into hiding.*

hi•er•ar•chi•cal /ˌhaɪəˈrɑrkɪk(ə)l/ adj a hierarchical society or organization is one in which differences in status are considered to be very important

hi•er•ar•chy /ˈhaɪəˌrɑrki/ noun **1** [C/U] a system for organizing people according to their status **2** [C] the group of people who control an organization

high[1] /haɪ/ adj ★★★

1 large in size	7 affected by drugs
2 a long way up	8 happy/excited
3 measuring things	9 about sounds
4 large in amount	10 winds: very strong
5 very good	11 best/most extreme
6 important	+ PHRASE

1 large in size from the top to the ground ≠ LOW: *Kilimanjaro is the highest mountain in Africa.* ♦ *The fence is too high to climb over.*
2 in a position that is a long way above the ground ≠ LOW: *high clouds* ♦ *the highest shelf*
3 used in measurements of how big or how far above the ground an object is: *Some of the waves are fifteen feet high.* ♦ ***How high*** *is that ceiling?*
4 large in amount ≠ LOW: *high prices/temperatures/wages* ♦ *This is an area of* ***high unemployment.*** ♦ *Ice cream is very* ***high in*** *calories* (=contains a lot of calories).
5 very good or excellent ≠ LOW: *high quality products* ♦ *She has* ***a very high opinion of*** *herself.*
6 important compared to other people or things ≠ LOW: *What is the highest rank in the army?* ♦ *Both parties are giving* ***high priority*** *to education.*
7 *informal* affected by an illegal drug: *He was* ***high on*** *cocaine.*
8 *informal* very happy or excited: *The children have been* ***in high spirits*** *all day.*
9 a high sound is near the upper end of a

range of sounds ≠ LOW: *Women's voices are usually higher than men's.* → HIGH-PITCHED
10 high winds are very strong
11 used in some expressions for referring to the greatest or most extreme example or part of something: *Their soldiers were **on high alert** all along the border.* ♦ *In the 1980s this was **high fashion**.*

PHRASE **high hopes/expectations** if you have high hopes or EXPECTATIONS, you hope or expect that something very good will happen

- **High** is used for talking about things that are a long way from the ground. It is also used to talk about mountains: *a high shelf* ♦ *a high window* ♦ *the world's highest mountain*
- **Tall** is used about people or things that measure more than is usual from their bottom to their top: *a tall thin bottle* ♦ *a tall tree* ♦ *the tallest boy in the class*

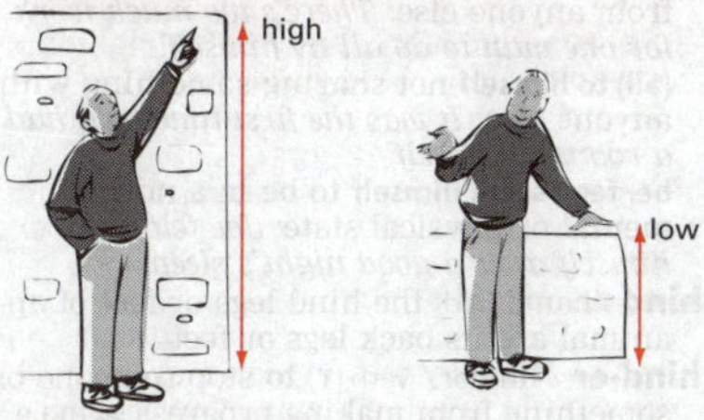

high² /haɪ/ adv ★★★
1 a long distance above the ground, or above a particular position ≠ LOW: *a first-class hotel built high on the hillside* ♦ *the sound of war planes flying **high above** the city*
2 reaching up a long way: *She stretched her arms up high.*
3 to or at an important position ≠ LOW: *She rose high in the company.* ♦ *A colonel ranks higher than a major.*
4 near the upper end of a range of sounds ≠ LOW: *I can't sing that high.*

high³ /haɪ/ noun [C] **1** a period or situation in which something reaches its highest level ≠ LOW: *Temperatures today are expected to reach a high of 105 degrees.* **2** a feeling of great happiness or excitement ≠ LOW

high•brow /ˈhaɪˌbraʊ/ adj likely to interest people who are interested in learning, culture, and art

ˈ**high ˌchair** noun [C] a tall chair that very young children sit in to have their meals

ˌ**high-ˈclass** adj very good in quality or ability

ˈ**high-ˌend** adj high-end goods and services are more expensive and more advanced than other similar goods and services

high•er¹ /ˈhaɪər/ adj at a more advanced level, or involving a greater degree of knowledge: *higher mathematics*

high•er² /ˈhaɪər/ the COMPARATIVE of **high**

ˌ**higher ˌeduˈcation** noun [U] education at a university, or at a college

ˌ**high ˈfive** noun [C] the action of holding your hand up and hitting your palm flat against that of another person

ˌ**high ˈflier** noun [C] someone who has achieved a lot and is determined to continue being successful —ˌ**high-ˈflying** adj

ˌ**high-ˈgrade** adj very good in quality

ˌ**high ˈground, the** noun [singular] an advantage that you have in a situation or competition, especially because you have behaved more fairly or more honestly than your opponent

high-hand•ed /ˌhaɪ ˈhændəd/ adj speaking or acting without considering other people's opinions = ARROGANT

ˌ**high ˈheels** or **high-heeled shoes** /ˌhaɪ hild ʃuz/ noun [plural] women's shoes that have high heels —*picture* → SHOE

ˈ**high ˌjump, the** noun [singular] a sports event in which people try to jump over a bar that can be raised higher after each jump

high•lands /ˈhaɪləndz/ noun [plural] an area of land that consists of hills and mountains ≠ LOWLANDS —**high•land** adj

ˌ**high-ˈlevel** adj **1** involving people in important or powerful positions: *a high-level meeting* **2** at a more extreme or advanced level than usual: *high-level radiation*

high•light¹ /ˈhaɪˌlaɪt/ verb [T] ★
1 to report or describe something in a way that makes people notice it and think about it: *The case highlights the need for adequate controls on such experiments.*
2 to make something easier to see or notice: *Using contrasting colors will highlight the shape and dimensions of your room.*
3 to mark a word, picture, computer file, etc. so that you can see it more easily

high•light² /ˈhaɪˌlaɪt/ noun [C] the most exciting, impressive, or interesting part of something: *The highlight of the trip was visiting the Great Wall of China.*

high•light•er /ˈhaɪˌlaɪtər/ noun [C] a brightly colored pen that you use for marking particular words on a document

high•lights /ˈhaɪˌlaɪts/ noun [plural] parts of your hair that have been made a lighter color using chemicals

high•ly /ˈhaɪli/ adv ★★★
1 used before some adjectives to mean "very," or "very well": *It now seems **highly unlikely** that the project will be finished on time.* ♦ *She's a **highly educated** young woman.*
2 used for saying that someone or something is very good or very important: *a **highly valued** member of the staff* ♦ *Everyone we talked to **spoke very highly of** him.*

High•ness /ˈhaɪnəs/ noun **Your/His/Her Highness** used for talking to or about a king, queen, PRINCE, or PRINCESS

ˌ**high-ˈpitched** adj a high-pitched voice or sound is very high

ˈ**high ˌpoint** noun [C] the best part of something = HIGHLIGHT

high-pow•ered /ˌhaɪˈpaʊərd/ adj **1** important and powerful: *a high-powered job* **2** very powerful and effective: *a high-powered rifle*

ˌ**high-ˈprofile** adj often seen or mentioned in newspapers or on television: *a high-profile campaign/company/politician*

ˈ**high-ˌrise** adj very tall with many floors: *high-rise apartment buildings* —ˈ**high-ˌrise** noun [C]

ˈ**high ˌschool** noun [C/U] ★★
1 in the U.S., a school for children between the ages of 14 and 18

2 in the U.K., a school for children between the ages of 11 and 18 = SECONDARY SCHOOL

ˌhigh ˈseas, the noun [plural] the parts of the oceans that are far away from land and that are not owned by any country

ˌhigh ˈseason noun [singular/U] the part of the year when many tourists visit a place

ˌhigh-ˈstrung adj *American* a high-strung person becomes angry or emotional very quickly

high-tech /ˌhaɪ ˈtek/ adj using the most advanced technology

ˌhigh techˈnology noun [U] technology that involves the most advanced methods

ˌhigh ˈtide noun [C/U] the time when the ocean reaches the highest level ≠ LOW TIDE

high•way /ˈhaɪˌweɪ/ noun [C] *American* ★ a wide road that has been built for fast travel between towns and cities

H

ˈhighway paˌtrol noun [U] the U.S. police officers who make certain that people obey the law while driving

hi•jack /ˈhaɪˌdʒæk/ verb [T] **1** to illegally take control of an airplane by using violence or threats **2** *showing disapproval* to take control of an organization or activity for your own purposes —**hi•jack•er** /ˈhaɪˌdʒækər/ noun [C], **hi•jack•ing** noun [C/U]

hike[1] /haɪk/ noun [C] **1** a long walk in the countryside **2** *informal* a sudden large increase, for example in prices or taxes

hike[2] /haɪk/ verb **1** [I/T] to go for a long walk in the countryside **2** [T] to suddenly increase the amount or level of something, for example a price or tax

PHRASAL VERB **ˌhike sth ˈup** *informal same as* **hike**[2] 2

hik•ing /ˈhaɪkɪŋ/ noun [U] the activity of walking for long distances in the countryside —**hik•er** noun [C]

hi•lar•i•ous /hɪˈleriəs/ adj extremely funny —**hi•lar•i•ous•ly** adv

hill /hɪl/ noun [C] ★★★ an area of land that is higher than the land surrounding it but that is smaller and lower than a mountain: *They climbed slowly to the top of the hill.* ♦ *The village is built on a steep hill.*

PHRASE **over the hill** *informal* no longer young and therefore unable to do things that you could do in the past

hill•side /ˈhɪlˌsaɪd/ noun [C] the land on a hill below the top

hill•top /ˈhɪlˌtɑp/ noun [C] the top of a hill

hill•y /ˈhɪli/ adj with a lot of hills: *a hilly landscape*

hilt /hɪlt/ noun **to the hilt** *informal* as much as possible, or to the highest level possible: *Mike's friends were prepared to defend him to the hilt.*

him /*weak* ɪm, *strong* hɪm/ pronoun ★★★

1 the object form of "he," used for referring to a man, boy, or male animal when they have already been mentioned or when it is obvious which one you are referring to: *Luke wants me to marry him.* ♦ *I'm expecting a call from Jake. That must be him now.*

2 *old-fashioned* used in a general way for referring to any person: *Each patient should receive the treatment that the doctor thinks is best for him.* → HE

him•self /*weak* ɪmˈself, *strong* hɪmˈself/ pronoun ★★★

1 the REFLEXIVE form of "he," used for showing that the man, boy, or male animal that does something is also affected by what he does: *Will slipped once, but he didn't hurt himself.* ♦ *That man ought to be ashamed of himself.*

2 used for emphasizing that you are referring to a particular man, boy, or male animal and not to anyone else: *It is said that Shakespeare himself once acted in this play.* ♦ *You mean to tell me Jack built the whole cabin himself?*

3 *old-fashioned* used in a general way for referring back to the subject of a sentence when they may be either male or female: *Everyone has to look after himself.* → HE

PHRASES **(all) by himself 1** alone: *I noticed Ben sitting all by himself.* **2** without help from anyone else: *There's too much work for one man to do all by himself.*

(all) to himself not sharing something with anyone else: *It was the first time he'd had a room to himself.*

be/feel/seem himself to be in a normal mental or physical state: *Joe felt more himself after a good night's sleep.*

hind /haɪnd/ adj the hind legs or feet of an animal are its back legs or feet

hind•er /ˈhɪndər/ verb [T] to stop someone or something from making progress ≠ HELP

hin•drance /ˈhɪndrəns/ noun [C] something that delays or prevents progress

hind•sight /ˈhaɪn(d)ˌsaɪt/ noun [U] the opportunity to judge or understand past events using knowledge that you have gained since then

Hin•du /ˈhɪnˌdu/ noun [C] someone whose religion is Hinduism —**Hin•du** adj

Hin•du•ism /ˈhɪnduˌɪzəm/ noun [U] the main religion of India

hinge[1] /hɪndʒ/ noun [C] an object that fastens a door to a wall, or a lid to a container, and allows it to open and shut

hinge[2] /hɪndʒ/ PHRASAL VERB **ˈhinge on sth** to depend on something: *The result of the trial hinges on her evidence.*

hint[1] /hɪnt/ noun ★

1 [C] something that you say in order to show what you are thinking or feeling, without saying it directly: *She hoped he would* ***take the hint*** *and leave her alone.* ♦ *Sam keeps* ***dropping hints*** *about what he wants for his birthday.*

2 [C] a small piece of information that helps someone guess something: *"You'll never guess who I saw today." "****Give me a hint.****"*

3 [singular] a small amount of something: *There was* ***a hint of*** *impatience in his voice.*

4 [C] a useful suggestion or piece of advice = TIP: *hints on how to improve your computer skills*

> **Words often used with hint**
>
> *Adjectives often used with* ***hint*** *(noun, sense 1)*
>
> ■ **gentle, slight, subtle, vague, veiled** + HINT: used when you say what you mean indirectly

hint[2] /hɪnt/ verb [I/T] to say what you are thinking or feeling in an indirect way:

Officials are hinting at the possibility of signing an agreement this week.

hin·ter·land /ˈhɪntərˌlænd/ noun [C] an area that is far away from towns and cities and is not on the coast

hip[1] /hɪp/ noun [C] one of the two parts at either side of your body between your waist and the top of your legs: *She stood with her hands on her hips, waiting.* ♦ *He fell downstairs and broke his hip.* —*picture* → C14

hip[2] /hɪp/ adj *informal* modern and fashionable

ˈhip ˌhop noun [U] a type of music that uses RAP and SAMPLES (=short pieces of recorded music or sound)

hip·pie /ˈhɪpi/ noun [C] someone in the 1960s who was opposed to war and traditional attitudes, and who showed this by their long hair and informal clothes

hip·po /ˈhɪpoʊ/ noun [C] *informal* a hippopotamus

hip·po·pot·a·mus /ˌhɪpəˈpɑtəməs/ noun [C] a large African animal with a wide head and mouth and thick gray skin —*picture* → C12

hip·py /ˈhɪpi/ another spelling of **hippie**

hire /haɪr/ verb ★

1 [I/T] to pay someone to work for you =EMPLOY: *I hired someone to paint the house.*

2 [T] *British* to RENT something such as a car or room

his /*weak* ɪz, *strong* hɪz/ grammar word ★★★

> His is the possessive form of "he," which can be:
> - a **determiner**: *He gave me his address.*
> - a **pronoun**: *My computer didn't cost as much as his.*

1 used for showing that something belongs to or is connected with a man, boy, or male animal that has already been mentioned: *She was attracted by his smile.* ♦ *Brad lost both his legs in a flying accident.* ♦ *The house isn't his, it's mine.* ♦ *I saw her parents at the wedding, but I didn't see his.* ♦ *He saved enough money to start **his own** business.*

2 *old-fashioned* used in a general way for showing that something belongs to or is connected with any person, whether they are male or female: *Each child can choose his favorite story.* → HE

His·pan·ic /hɪˈspænɪk/ adj ★

1 used for describing someone whose family originally came from a country where Spanish is spoken

2 relating to countries where Spanish is spoken, or to the culture of these countries —**His·pan·ic** noun [C]

hiss /hɪs/ verb **1** [I] to make a long "s" sound like the sound that a snake makes **2** [I/T] to say something in a quiet but angry way —**hiss** noun [C]

his·to·ri·an /hɪˈstɔriən/ noun [C] someone who studies history

his·tor·ic /hɪˈstɔrɪk/ adj important enough to be remembered as a part of history: *historic events* ♦ *Charleston's historic buildings*

his·tor·i·cal /hɪˈstɔrɪk(ə)l/ adj ★★

1 connected with history or with the past: *The painting depicts an actual historical event.* ♦ *historical research/evidence*

2 based on people or events that existed in the past: *a historical novel* —**his·tor·i·cal·ly** /hɪˈstɔrɪkli/ adv

his·to·ry /ˈhɪst(ə)ri/ noun ★★★

1 [singular/U] all time before now or since something began to exist, and everything that happened in that time: *Attitudes toward gender roles have changed throughout history.* ♦ *The university has a distinguished history.* ♦ ***the history of Spain***

2 [U] the study of the events of the past: *He teaches history at the high school.* ♦ *history books*

3 [C] an account of the events that happened during a particular period of the past: *He's writing **a history of** the Romans.*

PHRASES **have a history of sth 1** to be well known for doing something because you have often done it in the past: *The country has a long history of political kidnappings.* **2** if you have a history of a medical condition or other problem, you have had it before: *He has a history of heart disease.*

make history to do something that many people will remember because it is very important

hit[1] /hɪt/ (past tense and past participle **hit**) verb ★★★

1 touch sth with force	5 press switch, etc.
2 hurt sb	+ PHRASES
3 have bad effect on	+ PHRASAL VERBS
4 realize sth	

1 [I/T] to move quickly against something, or to move an object quickly against something, touching it with force: *The glass smashed as it hit the ground.* ♦ **hit sth with sth** *The child was hitting the table with a toy hammer.*

2 [I/T] to move your hand or an object hard against someone's body, so that you hurt them: *Stop hitting your brother!* ♦ **hit sb on sth** *He hit me on the shoulder.* ♦ **hit sb in sth** *They hit me in the stomach.*

3 [I/T] to have a sudden or bad effect on someone or something: *They were halfway down the mountain when the storm hit.* ♦ *The recession has **hit** small businesses **hard**.*

4 [T] if an idea hits you, you suddenly realize it =STRIKE: *It suddenly hit her that she would never see him again.*

5 [T] *spoken* to press something such as a switch on a machine, vehicle, or computer: *Just hit the Save button every few minutes.*

PHRASES **hit it off** *spoken* if two people hit it off, they like each other when they first meet =GET ALONG

hit the nail on the head to say something that is exactly right

hit the road *informal* to leave, or to start a trip

hit the roof *spoken* to become very angry

PHRASAL VERBS **ˌhit ˈback** to criticize someone who has criticized you

ˈhit on sb *informal* to try to start a conversation with someone because you are sexually attracted to them

ˈhit on sth or **ˈhit uˌpon sth** to suddenly have an idea =COME UP WITH STH: *They hit on an excellent solution.*

hit[2] /hɪt/ noun [C] ★

1 successful record	4 when player hits ball
2 sth successful/popular	5 use of Internet
3 when sb/sth is hit	6 computer result

1 a song that sells a very large number of

copies: *They played a lot of old hits from the 70s and 80s.* ♦ *an album of Madonna's **greatest hits***

2 something or someone that is very successful and popular: *The movie was a massive hit at the box office.* ♦ *His magic act was **a hit with** the children.*

3 an occasion when someone or something touches another person or thing with a lot of force

4 an occasion when a player hits the ball in a game

5 *computing* an occasion when someone looks at a particular document on the Internet: *Their website gets a couple of hundred hits a day.*

6 *computing* a piece of information that a computer program finds for you

ˌhit-and-ˈrun adj a hit-and-run accident is one in which a driver does not stop after their vehicle has hit a person or another car

hitch¹ /hɪtʃ/ verb **1** [I/T] *informal* to hitchhike **2** [T] to fasten something to something else: *We hitched a trailer to the back of our car.*

PHRASAL VERB **ˌhitch sth ˈup** to pull up something that you are wearing: *She hitched up her skirt and ran.*

hitch² /hɪtʃ/ noun [C] a problem that is not very serious: *The airplane was delayed due to a last-minute hitch.*

hitch•hike /ˈhɪtʃˌhaɪk/ verb [I] to travel by asking other people to take you in their car. You do this by standing on the side of a road and holding out your thumb or a sign. —**hitch•hik•er** noun [C]

hith•er•to /ˌhɪðərˈtu, ˈhɪðərˌtu/ adv *very formal* until the present time = PREVIOUSLY

HIV /ˌeɪtʃ aɪ ˈvi/ noun [U] human immunodeficiency virus: a VIRUS that can cause AIDS

hive /haɪv/ noun [C] a place in which BEES live and make HONEY

ˌHIV ˈpositive adj infected with HIV

hm or **hmm** /m, hm/ interjection **1** used for representing a sound that you make when you pause to think before saying something else **2** used for representing a sound that you make to show you do not believe something

HMO /ˌeɪtʃ em ˈoʊ/ noun [C] health maintenance organization: an organization in the U.S. that provides medical care

hoard¹ /hɔrd/ verb [I/T] to get and keep a large amount of something because it might be valuable later

hoard² /hɔrd/ noun [C] a large amount of something that someone has hidden somewhere

hoarse /hɔrs/ adj speaking in a low rough voice —**hoarse•ly** adv

hoax /hoʊks/ noun [C] a trick in which someone tells people that something bad is going to happen or that something is true when it is not

hob•ble /ˈhɑb(ə)l/ verb [I] to walk slowly and with difficulty because your feet are sore or injured

hob•by /ˈhɑbi/ noun [C] something that you enjoy doing when you are not working: *Mike's hobbies include reading and chess.*

ho•bo /ˈhoʊˌboʊ/ noun [C] *old-fashioned* someone who travels from place to place because they do not have a home or a job

hock•ey /ˈhɑki/ noun [U] **1** *American* a game that is played on ice by two teams of six players who try to score goals by hitting a small object with a long stick **2** *British* FIELD HOCKEY

hoe /hoʊ/ noun [C] a tool with a long handle that you use for turning over the soil in a garden —**hoe** verb [I/T]

hog¹ /hɔg/ noun [C] *American* a PIG

PHRASE **go whole hog** *informal* to do something in a very thorough or enthusiastic way

hog² /hɔg/ verb [T] *informal* to take or use a lot of something in a way that prevents other people from having it

hoist¹ /hɔɪst/ verb [T] to lift something or someone, often using special equipment

hoist² /hɔɪst/ noun [C] a piece of equipment that is used for lifting heavy objects

hok•ey /ˈhoʊki/ adj *American informal* describing or showing emotions in a way that seems silly or not sincere

hold¹ /hoʊld/ (past tense and past participle **held** /held/) verb ★★★

1 carry	**10** organize event
2 stop sb/sth moving	**11** wait on telephone
3 put arms around sb	**12** support weight
4 be able to contain	**13** have quality/feeling
5 have a job/position	**14** keep having feeling
6 keep prisoner	**15** own sth
7 store information	**16** not lose to opponent
8 continue in same state	+ PHRASES
9 believe	+ PHRASAL VERBS

1 [T] to carry something or someone using your hands or arms: *Can you hold my bag for a moment?* ♦ **hold sth in/under/between sth** *Barry was holding a coin between his finger and thumb.* ♦ *She was holding a baby in her arms.*

2 [T] to keep someone or something in a particular position so that they do not move: *Can you hold the wrapping paper for me so I can tape it up?* ♦ *His silk tie was **held in place** with a small diamond pin.* ♦ **hold sb down** *Four people held him down* (=held him on the floor so that he could not move).

3 [T] to put your arms around someone for a long time because you love them or because they are unhappy: *He sat beside her and held her.* ♦ *She kissed him and held him tight.*

4 [T] to be able to fit an amount of something inside: *The stadium holds 80,000 people.* ♦ *How much does this pitcher hold?*

5 [T] to have a job or position: *She is the first woman to hold this post.* ♦ *President Mitterrand **held office** for 14 years.*

6 [T] to keep someone as a prisoner: *The four men had been **held captive** for over two years.*

7 [T] to keep information, for example on a computer: *His data was held on a disk.*

8 [I] to stay in the same state or at the same level: *The fine weather should hold until Tuesday.* ♦ *The coffee market has **held steady** for a few months.*

9 [T] to have a particular belief or opinion:

She holds some pretty unpleasant views. ♦ *Most people **hold** the president **responsible** for the riots.* ♦ **+(that)** *Baxter holds that significant changes in the population can occur within a decade.*
10 [T] to organize something such as a meeting or event: *The government agreed to hold a referendum.*
11 [I/T] to wait to speak to someone on the telephone: *"Do you want to call back later?" "No, I'll hold."*
12 [T] to support the weight of someone or something: *Do you think this branch will hold us?*
13 [T] *formal* to have a particular quality: *The project holds a great deal of promise.* ♦ *He holds no authority over us.*
14 [T] to continue to have a particular feeling: *I no longer hold any resentment toward him.*
15 [T] *formal* to own something or have the right to use something: *Three percent of our shares are now held by U.S. investors.* ♦ *He holds a U.S. passport.*
16 [T] to keep control of something: *Rebel fighters have held the territory for five years.*
PHRASES **hold it** *spoken* **1** used for telling someone not to move: *Just hold it right there! Where do you think you're going with that?* **2** used for telling someone to wait: *Hold it, you two, wait for us!*
hold true to be true, or to remain true
hold your own to be as good as other more experienced or stronger people
PHRASAL VERBS **ˌhold sth aˈgainst sb** to feel angry with someone because of something that they have done in the past: *He knows it was an accident, I don't think he'll hold it against her.*
ˌhold ˈback to decide not to do or say something: *He held back, remembering the mistake he had made before.*
ˌhold sb/sth ˈback 1 to stop someone or something from moving forward: *Ollie had to hold Tom back to prevent him from fighting.* ♦ *Her hair was held back by two clips.* **2** to stop someone or something from being as successful as they should be: *Her parents worried that her classmates were holding her back.*
ˌhold sth ˈdown 1 to stop prices or numbers from rising: *a deal to hold down wages and prices* **2 hold down a job** to succeed in keeping a job: *Half of them have never held down a regular job.*
ˌhold ˈoff to delay doing something: *He may decide to hold off for a few days.* ♦ **hold off doing sth** *She held off calling him until the last possible moment.*
ˌhold sb ˈoff to stop someone who is trying to attack you from coming close
ˌhold ˈon 1 to hold something tightly or carefully so that you do not drop it or do not fall: *Hold on tight everyone, the boat's getting ready to go.* **2** to wait: *Hold on! You forgot your card!*
ˌhold ˈon to sth or **ˌhold ˈonto sth 1** to hold something tightly or carefully so that you do not drop it or do not fall: *Hold on to the seat in front when we go around the corner.* **2** to not lose something or not let someone else have it **=** KEEP: *Hold on to the instructions in case you have any problems.* **3** to continue feeling or believing something
ˌhold ˈout 1 to continue to be enough, or to continue to exist: *How long will your money hold out?* **2** to continue to defend a place that is being attacked
ˌhold sth ˈout 1 to hold something where other people can reach it: *She held out her hand to him.* **2 hold out hope** to think that something is likely to happen or succeed
ˌhold ˈout for sth to not accept an offer because you hope to get a better one
ˈhold sb to sth to make someone do what they have promised or decided
ˌhold sb/sth ˈup 1 to cause a delay, or to make someone late: *Sorry I'm late, but my flight was held up.* ♦ *She got held up at work.* **2** to steal from a business, from a vehicle, or from people by threatening violence: *An armed robber held up the bank last week.*

hold[2] /hoʊld/ noun ★
1 [singular] the fact that you are holding something: *His hold on her arm tightened.* ♦ *Bobby **grabbed hold of** the railing* (=suddenly started holding it). ♦ *She **took hold of** his hand* (=started holding it).
2 [singular] power or control over someone or something: *The rebels have a firm **hold over** the northern area.* ♦ *Does he have some sort of **hold on** you?*
3 [C] the area in an airplane or ship that is used for goods, vehicles, or suitcases
PHRASES **get hold of sb** to manage to talk to someone: *Can you get hold of Mike and tell him the meeting's postponed?*
get hold of sth 1 to get something that you need or want: *I've managed to get hold of some very good wine.* **2** to start holding something with your hands: *Just get hold of the antenna and move it around to see if you can get a better picture.*
keep hold of sth 1 to not take your hands away from something that you are holding: *She kept hold of his arm.* **2** to not lose something or not let someone else get it: *They managed to keep hold of the lead in the second half.*
on hold 1 if something is on hold, you have stopped it from happening now, but it may happen later: *After the accident her career had to be put on hold.* **2** waiting to speak to someone on the telephone, after your call has been answered: *They've put me on hold.*
take hold to become stronger and difficult to stop: *They were fortunate to escape before the fire took hold.* ♦ *A sense of dread **took hold of** him.*

hold·er /ˈhoʊldər/ noun [C] **1** someone who owns something or who has been given something **2** something that is designed to hold or support another object

hold·ing /ˈhoʊldɪŋ/ noun [C] a part of a company that someone owns

ˈholding ˌcompany noun [C] a company that owns the majority of the SHARES in another company

hold·o·ver /ˈhoʊldˌoʊvər/ noun [C] *American* **1** an idea or attitude from the past that is not appropriate anymore **2** someone who worked for an organization that existed in the past and who now works for the organization that has replaced it

ˈhold-up noun [C] **1** a delay **2** a situation in which someone with a weapon steals money from a bank or store

hole¹ /hoʊl/ noun [C] ★★★

1 a space that has been dug in the surface of the ground: *Workers dug a 30-foot hole in the ground.* ♦ *rabbit holes*

2 a space in the surface of something that goes partly or completely through it: *All my socks have **holes in** them.* ♦ *Rain poured through a **gaping hole** in the roof* (=a very large hole).

3 a part of something such as an idea or explanation where important details are missing: *His argument was full of holes.*

4 in golf, a small space in the ground that you have to hit the ball into

hole² /hoʊl/ PHRASAL VERB **ˌhole (sb) ˈup** if you hole up somewhere, or if you are holed up somewhere, you stay there, especially because you are hiding

ˈhole ˌpunch noun [C] a piece of equipment used for putting small holes in paper —*picture* → C3

hol•i•day¹ /ˈhɑlɪˌdeɪ/ noun ★★★

1 [C] a day that is a celebration of something special, on which you do not have to work or go to school: *May 1st is a holiday in many European countries.*

2 [C/U] *British* a VACATION

hol•i•day² /ˈhɑlɪˌdeɪ/ verb [I] *British* to VACATION

ho•lis•tic /hoʊˈlɪstɪk/ adj **1** treating the whole body, and not just the part of it that is sick: *holistic medicine/healthcare* **2** thinking about all of something, and not just dealing with particular aspects: *a holistic approach to the region's development*

hol•low¹ /ˈhɑloʊ/ adj **1** empty inside: *hollow chocolate eggs* **2** not sincere or with any real meaning: *a hollow display of friendship* ♦ *a hollow victory* **3** a hollow sound is a low sound like something empty being hit **4** hollow eyes or cheeks seem to have sunk into your head

hol•low² /ˈhɑloʊ/ PHRASAL VERB **ˌhollow sth ˈout** to make a hole in something by removing what is inside it

hol•low³ /ˈhɑloʊ/ noun [C] a small area in the ground that is lower than the ground around it

hol•ly /ˈhɑli/ noun [C/U] a tree with dark green leaves with sharp points and small bright red BERRIES —*picture* → C9

Hol•ly•wood /ˈhɑliˌwʊd/ noun [U] the part of the U.S. movie industry that has a reputation for making very successful movies that cost a lot of money to produce

hol•o•caust /ˈhɑləˌkɔst/ noun [C] a war in which very many people are killed

hol•o•gram /ˈhɑləˌgræm/ noun [C] a special kind of picture that is THREE-DIMENSIONAL (=does not look flat)

hol•ster /ˈhoʊlstər/ noun [C] a leather container for a small gun, that is attached to a belt

ho•ly /ˈhoʊli/ adj ★★

1 important in a religion, or used in worship =SACRED: *the holy book of the Sikhs* ♦ *the holy city of Jerusalem*

2 respected for living a very religious life: *a holy man and his followers*

—**ho•li•ness** noun [U]

hom•age /ˈhɑmɪdʒ/ noun [singular/U] something that someone does or says in order to show respect or admiration

home¹ /hoʊm/ noun ★★★

1 place where you live	5 where people get care
2 where parents live	6 where sth started
3 your country/city, etc.	7 base for sports team
4 place to buy/rent	+ PHRASES

1 [C/U] the place where you live: *We go to a school close to our home.* ♦ *a child in need of a loving home* ♦ *Peter isn't **at home** today.* ♦ *I hate being **away from home**.* → HOUSE

2 [U] the place where your parents live and where you grew up: *He is 43 and still living **at home**.* ♦ *I **left home** when I was 18* (=stopped living there).

3 [U] the country, state, or city where you live: *a great opportunity in markets both **at home** and abroad* ♦ ***Back home**, the weather is much better.*

4 [C] a building for people to buy or rent: *One thousand new homes are being built in the area.* ♦ *There is a shortage of homes for rent.*

5 [C] a building where people who need special care can live and be cared for: *They didn't want to put their mother in a home.* ♦ *a **home for** orphans*

6 [singular] the place where something first started or was first made: *New Jersey is **the home of** professional basketball.*

7 [U] the place where a sports team is based and plays most of its games: *The Diamondbacks are playing **at home** tonight.*

PHRASES **be/feel at home** to be/feel relaxed and comfortable in a particular place or situation: *They did everything they could to make me feel at home.*

make yourself at home to feel relaxed and behave in the same way as you do in your own home: *Make yourself at home while I go and find those photographs.*

home² /hoʊm/ adv ★★★

1 to the place where you live: *I decided to walk home.* ♦ *What time are you **coming home**?* ♦ *I went home to France.* ♦ ***On the way home** from school, I met my friend Sue.*

2 at the place where you live: *Is Kathryn home?* ♦ *I'll be home all day Tuesday.*

home³ /hoʊm/ adj **1** relating to your home rather than your work: *Write your home address at the top of the page.* **2** done, made, or experienced at home: *home cooking/shopping/banking* **3** relating to things that happen within a country, rather than between different countries: *These cameras sell well in the home market.* **4** relating to the place where a sports team is based: *a home win* ♦ *the team's home ground* (=where they usually play)

home⁴ /hoʊm/ PHRASAL VERB **ˌhome ˈin on sth** to aim at something and move quickly and directly to it: *a missile homing in on its target*

home•bod•y /ˈhoʊmˌbɑdi/ noun [C] *American* someone who likes to spend most of their time at home

home•com•ing /ˈhoʊmˌkʌmɪŋ/ noun [C]

1 *American* a celebration that happens once a year at schools and universities when ALUMNI (=students who went to the school before) return for parties **2** an occasion when someone returns to a place where they used to live

ˈhome ˌfries noun [plural] *American* potatoes that have been cooked, cut up, and then cooked in oil

ˌhome-ˈgrown adj **1** grown in someone's garden, not on a large farm **2** from a particular local area or small place: *home-grown companies*

ˌhome ˈimprovement noun [C/U] work that you do to your house to make it better

home•land /ˈhoʊmˌlænd/ noun [C] the country where someone comes from

ˈhome ˌlanguage noun [C] *American* someone's native language

home•less /ˈhoʊmləs/ adj **1** without a place to live **2 the homeless** people who are homeless

home•ly /ˈhoʊmli/ adj **1** *American* ugly **2** *British* HOMEY

ˌhome-ˈmade adj made in someone's home rather than in a factory

home•mak•er /ˈhoʊmˌmeɪkər/ noun [C] *American* someone who cooks, cleans, and washes clothes for their family as their main job

ˈhome ˌoffice noun [C] **1** a room with a telephone, computer, etc. where someone works inside their own home **2** *American* the place where a company has its main office

ho•me•o•path•ic /ˌhoʊmiəˈpæθɪk/ adj homeopathic medicines or doctors use a way of treating an illness in which people are given very small amounts of natural substances that, in large amounts, would cause the illness —**ho•me•op•a•thy** /ˌhoʊmiˈɑpəθi/ noun [U]

ˈhome ˌpage noun [C] *computing* **1** a place on the Internet where a person or an organization gives information about themselves or their business **2** a place on the Internet that you choose to appear first on your computer screen each time you look at the Internet

ˈhome ˌplate noun [U] in baseball and similar sports, the place you stand when you hit the ball —*picture* → C15

hom•er /ˈhoʊmər/ noun [C] *American informal* a HOME RUN

ˈhome ˌroom noun [U] *American* a place where students go for a period of time at the beginning of each school day when the teacher makes announcements to the class and takes ATTENDANCE (=checks which students are not in school)

ˌhome ˈrule noun [U] a form of government in which people have control in their own country, rather than being controlled by another country

ˌhome ˈrun noun [C] a point in baseball that is scored when a player hits the ball and then runs around all four BASES

home•sick /ˈhoʊmˌsɪk/ adj feeling sad and alone because you are far from home

home•stead /ˈhoʊmˌsted/ noun [C] *American* **1** a farm, including any buildings that are on the land **2** an area of land that was given to people in the past by the U.S. government to live on and farm

ˌhome ˈtown noun [C] the city or town where you lived as a child

home•work /ˈhoʊmˌwɜrk/ noun [U] ★ work that a teacher gives a student to do at home: *Have the kids **done their homework**?*

PHRASE **do your homework** to prepare for something by learning as much as you can about it: *You could tell that the interviewer hadn't really done his homework.*

hom•ey /ˈhoʊmi/ adj *American* pleasant in a way that reminds you of home

hom•i•cid•al /ˌhɑmɪˈsaɪd(ə)l/ adj likely to kill someone, or wanting to kill someone

hom•i•cide /ˈhɑmɪˌsaɪd/ noun [C/U] *American legal* the crime of killing someone

ho•mo•ge•ne•ous /ˌhoʊməˈdʒiniəs, ˌhɑməˈdʒiniəs/ adj consisting of things that are similar or all of the same type

hom•o•nym /ˈhɑmənɪm/ noun [C] *linguistics* a word that is spelled the same as another word but that has a different meaning

ho•mo•pho•bi•a /ˌhoʊməˈfoʊbiə/ noun [U] hate of gay people —**ho•mo•pho•bic** adj

hom•o•phone /ˈhɑməˌfoʊn, ˈhoʊməˌfoʊn/ noun [C] *linguistics* a word that sounds the same as another word but that has a different spelling and meaning

ho•mo•sex•u•al¹ /ˌhoʊmoʊˈsekʃuəl/ noun [C] a person who is attracted sexually to people of the same sex

ho•mo•sex•u•al² /ˌhoʊmoʊˈsekʃuəl/ adj attracted sexually to people of the same sex —**ho•mo•sex•u•al•i•ty** /ˌhoʊmoʊsekʃuˈæləti/ noun [U]

hone /hoʊn/ verb [T] to improve a skill or TALENT that is already well developed

hon•est /ˈɑnəst/ adj ★

1 a person who is honest does not tell lies or cheat people, and obeys the law ≠ DISHONEST: *an honest man*

2 telling the truth, or not cheating people: *I want you to give me **an honest answer**.* ♦ *I gave her the wrong amount of money, but it was **an honest mistake*** (=not intended).

3 honest work is a job that you work fairly hard at: *When is the last time Charlie did any honest work?* ♦ *I'm just trying to earn **an honest living*** (=earn money by working hard).

PHRASE **to be honest** *spoken* used when telling someone what you really think: *To be honest, the meal was terrible.*

Word family: honest

Words in the same family as ***honest***

- **honesty** *n*
- **honestly** *adv*
- **dishonest** *adj*
- **dishonesty** *n*

hon•est•ly /ˈɑnəs(t)li/ adv **1** *spoken* used for emphasizing that what you are saying is true: *I honestly can't remember.* **2** in a way that is honest: *She was trying to do her job honestly and fairly.* **3** *spoken* used for expressing slight anger at someone: *Oh honestly, now look what he's done!*

hon•es•ty /ˈɑnəsti/ noun [U] an honest way of behaving, speaking, or thinking: *She is a woman of honesty and integrity.*

PHRASE **in all honesty** *spoken* used when

telling someone what you really think: *I can't, in all honesty, say that I enjoyed it.*

hon•ey /ˈhʌni/ noun **1** [U] a sweet sticky yellow or brown food made by BEES **2** [C] *spoken* used for talking to someone who you like very much: *Hi, honey, I'm home!*

hon•ey•moon /ˈhʌniˌmun/ noun [C] a vacation that two people take after they get married

honk /hɑŋk/ verb [I/T] to make a loud noise using the horn of a car —**honk** noun [C]

hon•or¹ /ˈɑnər/ noun

1 respect	4 prize for achievement
2 moral belief/practice	5 high achievement
3 sth you are proud to do	+ PHRASE

1 [U] the respect that people have for someone who achieves something great, is very powerful, or behaves in a way that is morally right: *They were prepared to die for the honor of their country.* **2** [U] the behavior of someone who has high moral standards =INTEGRITY: *a man of honor* (=someone who always behaves in a morally correct way) ♦ *It's not just a legal matter, it's a matter of honor.* **3** [C] something that you do that you are proud of: *Performing at Carnegie Hall is an honor for any singer.* ♦ **be an honor to do sth** *It's a great honor to be invited here tonight.* **4** [C] a prize that someone is given because they have done something important: *Bob Dylan was among the recipients of the annual Kennedy Center honors.* ♦ *The romantic comedy received top honors at the Golden Globe Awards.* **5 honors** [plural] if you graduate with honors, you have reached the highest level of achievement at college or HIGH SCHOOL

PHRASE **in honor of** in order to show respect and admiration for someone or something: *St. Petersburg was renamed Leningrad in honor of Lenin.*

hon•or² /ˈɑnər/ verb [T] **1** to show your respect or admiration for someone by giving them a prize or a title, or by praising them publicly: *We are here today to honor the men and women who gave their lives for their country.* **2** to do what you promised to do or what it is your duty to do: *Once a contract has been signed, it has to be honored.*

hon•or•a•ble /ˈɑn(ə)rəb(ə)l/ adj morally good and deserving respect: *Your father was an honorable man.* ♦ *the honorable thing to do* —**hon•or•a•bly** adv

hon•or•ar•y /ˈɑnəˌreri/ adj **1** an honorary university degree or title is given to honor someone, although they have not earned it in the usual way **2** an honorary member of a group is someone who is allowed to join without applying or without having the usual qualifications

hon•ored /ˈɑnərd/ adj **1** proud that you have been given special respect or a special opportunity: *I feel deeply honored to have been invited here today.* **2** deserving special respect: *an honored guest*

ˈhonor ˌguard noun [C] a group of soldiers who stand or march together at an important official occasion

ˈhonor ˌroll noun [C] *American* a list of the students with the best grades

ˈhonor ˌsystem noun [C] *American* a system in which people are expected to be honest in situations in which they have the opportunity to cheat

hon•our /ˈɑnər/ the British spelling of **honor¹**

hon•our•a•ble /ˈɑn(ə)rəb(ə)l/ the British spelling of **honorable**

hon•oured /ˈɑnərd/ the British spelling of **honored**

hood /hʊd/ noun [C] **1** the part of a coat or jacket that covers your head **2** *American* the part of a car that covers the engine and that can be raised —*picture* → C6

hood•ed /ˈhʊdəd/ adj with a hood

hoof /huf/ (plural **hoofs or hooves** /huvz/) noun [C] the hard part of a horse's foot

hook¹ /hʊk/ noun [C] **1** a curved piece of metal or plastic, used for hanging things on or for catching fish: *He hung his coat on a hook on the back of the door.* **2** a way of hitting someone with your arm bent: *a left hook to the jaw*

PHRASE **off the hook 1** if a telephone is off the hook, the part that you speak into has not been put into its place, so that you cannot receive any calls **2** *informal* having avoided a duty, an unpleasant situation, or a punishment: *I can't believe his boss has let him off the hook again.*

hook² /hʊk/ verb **1** [I/T] to hang something on something else, or to be fastened to something else with a hook: *He hooked the umbrella over his arm and went outside.* **2** [T] to put your arm, finger, leg, etc. around something to hold it or bring it closer to you: *Kathy hooked her arm through Peter's.* **3** [T] to catch a fish with a hook

PHRASAL VERB **ˌhook sth ˈup** to connect two pieces of electronic equipment, or to connect a piece of equipment to a computer or power supply

hooked /hʊkt/ adj **1** attracted by or interested in something so much that you want to do it as much as possible **2** if you are hooked on drugs, you cannot stop taking them **3** shaped like a hook

hook•er /ˈhʊkər/ noun [C] *informal* a PROSTITUTE

hook•y /ˈhʊki/ noun *American* **play hooky** to stay away from school without permission

hoo•li•gan /ˈhulɪgən/ noun [C] someone who is noisy or violent in public places

hoop /hup/ noun **1** [C] an object in the shape of a circle, usually made of metal, plastic, or wood **2 hoops** [plural] *American* the game of basketball: *in the gym shooting hoops* (=playing basketball)

hoo•ray /huˈreɪ/ interjection *old-fashioned* a word that you shout to show that you are excited and happy about something

hoot¹ /hut/ noun [C] **1** a short loud sound made by people who are laughing or criticizing something **2** the deep sound that an OWL makes

hoot² /hut/ verb [I/T] **1** to make a short loud sound when you laugh or criticize something **2** to make the deep sound that an OWL makes

hooves a plural of **hoof**

hop¹ /hɑp/ verb [I] **1** to move forward by jumping on one foot **2** if a bird or animal hops, it uses both or all four feet to jump forward **3** *informal* to get into, onto, or out of a vehicle quickly: *Hop in. I'll give you a lift into town.*

hop[2] /hɑp/ noun [C] **1** a quick jump on one foot **2** a short quick jump by a small animal or a bird

PHRASE **a short hop** a short trip

hope[1] /hoʊp/ verb [I/T] ★★★ to want and expect something to happen or be true: *It wouldn't be sensible to **hope for** immediate success.* ♦ **+(that)** *I hope that you'll enjoy your stay with us.* ♦ **hope to do sth** *The university is hoping to raise $3,000,000.*

PHRASES **I hope not** *spoken* used in replies to questions for saying that you do not want something to happen or to be true: *"Do you have to work late tonight?" "I hope not."*

I hope so *spoken* used in replies to questions for saying that you would like something to happen: *"Do you think the Mets have a chance to win this game?" "I hope so."*

I hope (that) used for showing that you do not like what someone is doing or is thinking of doing: *I hope you're not going to use all the milk.*

hope[2] /hoʊp/ noun [C/U] ★★★ **1** the feeling or belief that something that you want to happen is likely to happen: *She arrived in New York, young and **full of hope**.* ♦ *These young people have no **hope for the future**.* ♦ *The team's **hopes of** a championship are fading fast.* ♦ *The research **raises hopes** of a significant improvement in the treatment of cancer.* ♦ **hope of doing sth** *Rescuers refused to give up hope of finding more survivors.* ♦ *He had **lost hope** of seeing his children again.*

2 someone or something that offers a chance of improvement: *Our **only hope** was to get her to a hospital fast.* ♦ *Many people saw the new president as their **last hope** for political change.*

PHRASES **have high hopes for sb** to hope and expect that someone will be very successful

in the hope that/of wanting something to happen: *The police are carrying out a search in the hope of finding the missing girl.*

hope·ful[1] /ˈhoʊpfəl/ adj **1** believing that something will happen in the way that you want it to: *In spite of our differences, we remain hopeful that a solution can be found.* ♦ *a hopeful look* **2** making you believe that something will happen in the way that you want it to: *a hopeful sign*

hope·ful[2] /ˈhoʊpfəl/ noun [C] someone who wants to succeed or who seems likely to win

hope·ful·ly /ˈhoʊpfəli/ adv **1** used for saying that you hope that something will happen: *Hopefully, we'll get more news next week.* **2** feeling or showing hope: *He looked at her hopefully.*

hope·less /ˈhoʊpləs/ adj **1** if a situation is hopeless, it seems very unlikely to succeed or improve **2** *informal* not skillful at all: *I am hopeless at tennis.* —**hope·less·ly** adv, **hope·less·ness** noun [U]

horde /hɔrd/ noun [C] a large number of people

ho·ri·zon, the /həˈraɪz(ə)n/ noun [singular] the line in the distance where the sky seems to meet the Earth

PHRASE **on the horizon** likely to happen soon

ho·ri·zons /həˈraɪz(ə)nz/ noun [plural] the limits of your experience

hor·i·zon·tal /ˌhɔrɪˈzɑnt(ə)l/ adj straight and parallel to the ground ≠ VERTICAL —*picture* → C8

hor·mone /ˈhɔrˌmoʊn/ noun [C] a substance that is produced by your body that helps it to develop and grow —**hor·mon·al** /hɔrˈmoʊn(ə)l/ adj

horn /hɔrn/ noun [C] **1** the object in a vehicle that makes a loud warning noise when you press it —*picture* → C6 **2** one of the two hard pointed parts that grow on the heads of some animals, for example cows or goats **3** a metal musical instrument that is wide at one end, and that you play by blowing → BULL

hor·o·scope /ˈhɔrəˌskoʊp/ noun [C] a description of someone's character and the likely events in their life that is based on ASTROLOGY (=the position of the stars and the date they were born)

hor·ren·dous /həˈrendəs/ adj extremely bad or shocking —**hor·ren·dous·ly** adv

hor·ri·ble /ˈhɔrəb(ə)l/ adj ★ very unpleasant or unkind: *I've had a horrible day at work.* ♦ *The medicine tasted horrible.* ♦ *Stop being so **horrible to** me.* —**hor·rib·ly** /ˈhɔrəbli/ adv

hor·rid /ˈhɔrɪd/ adj very unpleasant, or very unkind

hor·rif·ic /həˈrɪfɪk/ adj shocking and upsetting —**hor·rif·i·cal·ly** /həˈrɪfɪkli/ adv

hor·ri·fy /ˈhɔrɪˌfaɪ/ verb [T] to shock someone very much —**hor·ri·fy·ing** adj

hor·ror /ˈhɔrər/ noun **1** [C/U] a strong feeling of shock or fear, or the thing that makes you feel shocked or afraid: *Millions watched in horror as the disaster unfolded on TV.* **2** [U] a type of book or movie that is intended to frighten people: *a horror story/movie*

hors d'oeuvre /ˌɔr ˈdɜrv/ noun [C] a small amount of food that is served before the main part of a meal

horse[1] /hɔrs/ noun [C] ★★★ a large animal that people ride

horse[2] /hɔrs/ PHRASAL VERB **ˌhorse aˈround** to play in a very lively or rough way

horse·back /ˈhɔrsˌbæk/ noun **on horseback** riding on a horse

ˈhorseback ˌriding noun [U] the activity of riding a horse

ˈhorse-ˌdrawn adj pulled by one horse or by several horses

horse·pow·er /ˈhɔrsˌpaʊr/ (plural **horse·power**) noun [C] *technical* a unit for measuring the power of a vehicle's engine

horse·shoe /ˈhɔrsʃu/ noun [C] a curved piece of iron that is fastened to the bottom of a horse's HOOF (=foot)

hor·ti·cul·ture /ˈhɔrtɪˌkʌltʃər/ noun [U] the activity of growing and studying plants —**hor·ti·cul·tur·al** /ˌhɔrtɪˈkʌltʃ(ə)rəl/ adj

hose /hoʊz/ noun **1** [C] a very long tube that water can flow through **2** [plural] socks, STOCKINGS, PANTYHOSE, and TIGHTS

ho·sier·y /ˈhoʊziəri/ noun [U] socks, STOCKINGS, PANTYHOSE, and TIGHTS

hos·pice /ˈhɑspɪs/ noun [C] **1** a hospital that

H

cares for people who are dying **2** a program of care for a dying person in his or her home, provided by a hospice organization

hos·pi·ta·ble /hɑˈspɪtəb(ə)l, ˈhɑspɪtəb(ə)l/ adj friendly and generous toward visitors

hos·pi·tal /ˈhɑspɪt(ə)l/ noun [C] ★★★ a place where sick or injured people receive medical treatment: *He spent a week **in the hospital** with food poisoning.* ♦ *He **went into the hospital** last week for a heart operation.*

hos·pi·tal·i·ty /ˌhɑspɪˈtæləti/ noun [U] friendly and generous behavior toward visitors

hos·pi·tal·ize /ˈhɑspɪt(ə)lˌaɪz/ verb **be hospitalized** to be kept in hospital for medical treatment
—**hos·pi·tal·i·za·tion** /ˌhɑspɪt(ə)lɪˈzeɪʃ(ə)n/ noun [C/U]

H

host[1] /hoʊst/ noun [C] ★

1 sb who invites	4 a lot of people/things
2 on television/radio	5 main computer
3 sth arranging event	

1 someone who invites people to a meal or a party, or to stay for a short time in their home: *They had brought a present for their hosts.*
2 someone who introduces and talks to the people taking part in a television or radio program: *a game show/talk show host*
3 a place or organization that arranges a special event and provides the area, equipment, or services needed for it: *Korea and Japan **played host to** the 2002 World Cup.*
4 a lot of people or things: ***a host of** possibilities*
5 *computing* the main computer in a system, which controls particular processes or files

host[2] /hoʊst/ verb [T] **1** to arrange a special event and provide the area, equipment, or services needed for it **2** to introduce and talk to the people taking part in a television or radio program **3** *computing* to organize WEBSITES by providing the equipment and software that is needed

hos·tage /ˈhɑstɪdʒ/ noun [C] a person who is the prisoner of someone who threatens to kill them if they do not get what they want: *Six visiting businessmen were taken hostage by rebel groups.*

hos·tel /ˈhɑst(ə)l/ noun [C] a YOUTH HOSTEL

host·ess /ˈhoʊstəs/ noun [C] **1** a woman who invites someone to a meal or a party, or to stay for a short time in her home **2** a woman who introduces and talks to the people taking part in a television or radio program **3** *American* a woman whose job is to welcome customers in a restaurant and to take them to their table

hos·tile /ˈhɑst(ə)l/ adj **1** behaving in a very unfriendly or threatening way **2** opposing something: *The local community was hostile to plans for a new highway.* **3** a hostile place or situation is difficult or dangerous to be in

hos·til·i·ty /hɑˈstɪləti/ noun **1** [U] unfriendly or threatening behavior: *She said she had experienced hostility from her male colleagues.* **2** [U] opposition to something: *There is always some hostility to new technology.* **3 hostilities** [plural] *formal* fighting between enemies in a war

hot /hɑt/ adj ★★★

1 high in temperature	5 clever/skillful
2 food: with spices	6 difficult/dangerous
3 exciting	7 involving sex
4 with strong feelings	

1 very high in temperature ≠ COLD: *Cook the fish on a hot grill for 5 minutes.* ♦ *Take your jacket off if you're hot.* ♦ *It's going to be hot again today.* ♦ *hot countries such as India*
2 hot food contains a lot of SPICES that create a burning feeling in your mouth = SPICY
3 *informal* exciting and interesting: *the hot new look in women's fashions* ♦ *one of Hollywood's hottest young directors*
4 involving strong feelings: *Health care became **a hot topic** during the presidential campaign.* ♦ *Our coach has **a really hot temper*** (=gets angry easily).
5 *informal* clever or skillful: *a hot tip* (=a useful piece of advice) ♦ *Kyle's pretty **hot at** tennis.*
6 difficult or dangerous: *When things got too **hot for** her at home, she'd stay with a friend.*
7 *informal* involving sexual feelings or images: *love scenes that are too hot for TV*

Other ways of saying hot

- **boiling (hot)** very hot in a way that is unpleasant or uncomfortable. Also used for referring to the temperature of a liquid when it starts to bubble
- **lukewarm** used for describing water that is only slightly hot
- **scalding (hot)** used for describing a liquid that is hot enough to burn your skin
- **sweltering** used for describing weather that is so hot that you feel uncomfortable
- **tepid** used for describing drinks that are not hot enough
- **warm** hot in a pleasant way

ˌhot-ˈair balˌloon noun [C] an extremely large bag full of hot air, with a basket attached that people can ride through the air in

hot·bed /ˈhɑtˌbed/ noun [C] a place where there are a lot of people involved in a particular activity: *a hotbed of invention/crime*

ˌhot ˈchocolate noun [C/U] a drink made with chocolate powder and hot milk or water

ˈhot ˌdog noun [C] a hot SAUSAGE inside a long piece of bread

ho·tel /hoʊˈtel/ noun [C] ★★★ a building where you pay to stay in a room: *He always **stays in** the best **hotels**.* ♦ *We **checked into** a luxury **hotel**.*

ho·te·lier /ˌoʊtelˈjeɪ, hoʊˈteljər/ noun [C] the owner or manager of a hotel

ˈhot ˌkey noun [C] *computing* a key on a computer keyboard that provides a quick way of performing a set of actions

hot·line /ˈhɑtˌlaɪn/ noun [C] a telephone number that people can call for information

hot·ly /ˈhɑtli/ adv **1** in a way that shows that you have very strong feelings about something: *Rumors of a split have been hotly denied by the band's manager.* **2** involving people who are competing very hard with one another: *a hotly contested election*

hot·plate /ˈhɑtˌpleɪt/ noun [C] a piece of electrical equipment with one or two flat surfaces that you cook food on

ˌhot poˈtato noun [C] *informal* a difficult issue that people try to avoid dealing with

ˈhot ˌrod noun [C] *informal* a car whose engine has been changed so that it can go much faster

hot·shot /ˈhɑtʃɑt/ noun [C] *informal* someone who is very successful and confident

ˈhot ˌspot noun [C] *informal* **1** a place where there is often a lot of violence or fighting **2** a place that is fashionable, popular, and lively **3** *computing* a small area on a computer screen that you CLICK on in order to make the computer do something

ˌhot ˈtub noun [C] a deep round container that is filled with hot water for people to relax in

ˌhot-ˈwater ˌbottle noun [C] a rubber container that you fill with hot water, used for keeping a bed or a part of your body warm

hound¹ /haʊnd/ noun [C] a dog that is used for hunting or racing

hound² /haʊnd/ verb [T] **1** to follow someone in a determined way in order to get something from them: *She was sick of being hounded by the press.* **2** to force someone to leave a place or job by always being unpleasant to them: *His political opponents hounded him out of office.*

hour /aʊr/ noun ★★★

1 60 minutes of time	4 particular time of day
2 a long time	5 point in history/life
3 time when you do sth	+ PHRASE

1 [C] a period of time that consists of 60 minutes: *He left about **an hour ago**.* ♦ *Annapolis is only **an hour away*** (=it takes an hour to get there). ♦ *I earn $15 **an hour*** (=for each hour spent working).

2 hours [plural] a long time: *I'm hungry and it's hours until dinner.*

3 hours [plural] the time during which you do something such as work or study: *My job is very flexible – I can fit my hours around my children.* ♦ *Jo has to work very **long hours**.*

4 [C] a particular time in the day or night: *You can call me at any hour of the day or night.* ♦ *You get cars coming down here **at all hours*** (=at any time, even at night).

5 [singular] a particular point in history or in someone's life or career: *His **finest hour** came in 1982 when his movie* Gandhi *won eight Oscars.*

PHRASE **after hours** after the time when a place such as an office or bar usually closes

hour·ly /ˈaʊrli/ adj **1** happening once every hour: *hourly news bulletins* **2** relating to one hour of work: *His hourly fee is $75.* —**hour·ly** adv: *Buses run hourly.*

house¹ /haʊs/ (plural **hous·es** /ˈhaʊzəz/) noun ★★★

1 building for living in	4 restaurant/hotel, etc.
2 people in a house	5 area for audience
3 company	6 type of music

1 [C] a building for living in, usually where only one family lives: *a three-bedroom house*

2 [singular] the people who are in a house or who live there: *The noise woke the entire house.*

3 [C] a company or organization that is involved in a particular activity: *a publishing house*

4 the house [singular] a restaurant, hotel, bar, or club: *Seafood is the specialty of the house.* ♦ *Your first drink is **on the house*** (=free).

5 [C] the part of a theater, CONCERT HALL, etc. that contains the audience: *Her new show has been playing to **packed houses**.*

6 [U] a type of modern dance music

- A **house** is a building for living in: *She lives in that big house.* ♦ *They're building some new houses on our street.*
- Someone's **home** is the place where they live: *This little cabin is the home of a family of eight.*
- Do not use **to** before **home**: *They all went to Dan's house, but I went home.*

house² /haʊz/ verb [T] ★

1 to give someone a place to live: *A large number of families are still waiting to be housed.*

2 to contain or provide a place for something: *These buildings house hazardous materials.*

House, the /haʊs/ the House of Representatives in the U.S., or the House of Commons or the House of Lords in the U.K.

ˈhouse arˌrest noun **be under house arrest** to be officially prevented from leaving your home because you have been accused of a political crime

house·boat /ˈhaʊsˌboʊt/ noun [C] a boat that someone lives in

house·bound /ˈhaʊsˌbaʊnd/ adj unable to leave your house because you are sick or disabled

house·bro·ken /ˈhaʊsˌbroʊkn/ adj *American* a pet that is housebroken knows that it must go outside or use a special container inside when it needs to go to the toilet

house·hold¹ /ˈhaʊsˌhoʊld/ noun [C] the people who live in a house or an apartment

house·hold² /ˈhaʊsˌhoʊld/ adj used in homes, or relating to homes: *household goods/appliances*

PHRASE **be a household name** to be very well known

house·hold·er /ˈhaʊsˌhoʊldər/ noun [C] a person who owns or rents a house or an apartment

ˈhouse ˌhusband noun [C] a man who does not work outside the home and whose main job is taking care of his children, cooking, cleaning, etc.

house·keep·er /ˈhaʊsˌkipər/ noun [C] someone whose job is to clean or cook in a large house or a hotel

house·keep·ing /ˈhaʊsˌkipɪŋ/ noun [U] the jobs that need to be done in a house, for example cleaning and cooking

ˌHouse of ˈCommons, the the part of the PARLIAMENT (=legislature) in the U.K. or Canada that consists of politicians who have been elected by the people

ˌHouse of ˈLords, the the part of the PARLIAMENT (=legislature) in the U.K. that

H

consists of politicians who are not elected by the people

ˌHouse of Repreˈsentatives, the the larger and less powerful part of the U.S. CONGRESS (=the national legislature in the U.S.)

house•plant /ˈhaʊsˌplænt/ noun [C] a plant that you keep inside your house for decoration

ˌhouse-to-ˈhouse adj, adv involving visits to every house in an area

house•wares /ˈhaʊsˌwerz/ noun [plural] *American* things that people buy to use at home, for example plates, kitchen tools, and small electrical APPLIANCES

house•warm•ing /ˈhaʊsˌwɔrmɪŋ/ noun [C] a party that you give in a house that you have just moved into

H

house•wife /ˈhaʊsˌwaɪf/ (plural **house•wives** /ˈhaʊsˌwaɪvz/) noun [C] a woman who does not work outside the home and whose main job is taking care of her children, cooking, cleaning, etc.

house•work /ˈhaʊsˌwɜrk/ noun [U] the work that you do in order to keep your house clean and neat

hous•ing /ˈhaʊzɪŋ/ noun [U] ★ buildings for people to live in: *Land had to be found for new housing.* ♦ *a housing shortage*

ˈhousing deˌvelopment noun [C] *American* a large group of houses that were built at the same time and in the same style

ˈhousing ˌproject noun [C] *American* a large apartment building or group of buildings or houses that are owned by the government and rented to people with low incomes =PROJECT

hov•er /ˈhʌvər/ verb [I] **1** if a bird, insect, or aircraft hovers, it keeps itself in the same position in the air **2** to stay somewhere because you are waiting to do something or because you cannot decide what to do: *The waiter was hovering by their table.*

hov•er•craft /ˈhʌvərˌkræft/ noun [C] a vehicle that can move over both land and water, raising itself above the surface by blowing air downward *—picture* → C7

how /haʊ/ adv, conjunction ★★★
1 used for asking or talking about the way that something happens or is done: *How can I get from here to the Empire State Building?* ♦ *Louis is the only person who understands how the camera works.* ♦ *How did she react when you mentioned my name?* ♦ *Cut her hair short if that's how she wants it.* ♦ **how to do sth** *Would you show me how to send an e-mail?*
2 used for asking or talking about the quantity or degree of something: *How difficult will it be to change the system?* ♦ *I've forgotten* ***how old*** *she is.* ♦ *I wonder* ***how far*** *we've walked today.* ♦ ***How many*** *grandchildren do you have now?*
3 used for asking what someone thinks about an experience: *How's life in the army?* ♦ *How was school today?* ♦ ***How did*** *your driving test go?*
4 used for emphasizing a particular fact or quality: *How wonderful! This means we can all travel together.* ♦ *I was amazed at just* ***how easy*** *it is to shop on the Internet.* ♦ *You know* ***how much*** *I love you.*

PHRASES **how about...?** *spoken* **1** used for suggesting a possible choice: *How about dinner tonight?* ♦ *How about Friday evening? Would that be convenient?* ♦ **how about doing sth?** *How about joining us for a game of cards?* **2** used for asking about another person or thing: *How about Philip? Is he coming too?* ♦ *I'm having coffee. How about you?*
how are things? or **how's it going?** or **how are you doing?** *spoken* used for asking someone about their progress or their general situation
how are you? *spoken* used for asking in a polite way about someone's health
how come? *spoken* why: *How come you're not at work today?*
how do you do? *spoken formal* used as a polite greeting when you are introduced to someone for the first time
how much is/are...? used for asking the price of something: *How much was that CD player of yours?*

how•dy /ˈhaʊdi/ interjection *American informal* a word that some people use as a way of saying "hello"

how•ev•er /haʊˈevər/ adv, conjunction ★★★
1 used for adding a statement that seems surprising or that makes a previous statement seem less true: *He seemed to be studying hard. His grades, however, did not improve.*
2 used when you are changing the subject: *I'm delighted I could be here today. However, I didn't come here to talk about myself.*
3 used for saying that it makes no difference how good, bad, difficult, etc. something is or how much there is of something: *She would still love him however badly he behaved.* ♦ *We're determined to have a wonderful vacation,* ***however much*** *it costs.* ♦ *I'm going to solve this problem,* ***however long*** *it takes.*
4 in whatever way someone chooses: *We let the kids decorate their rooms however they want to.*

howl /haʊl/ verb [I] **1** if a dog or other animal howls, it makes a long loud sound **2** to cry very loudly in pain, anger, or sadness **3** if the wind howls, it blows with a long loud sound **4** to laugh very loudly **—howl** noun [C]

HQ /ˌeɪtʃ ˈkju/ noun [plural] headquarters

hr. abbrev hour

HTML /ˌeɪtʃ ti em ˈel/ noun [U] *computing* hypertext markup language: the computer language that is used for writing pages on the Internet

http /ˌeɪtʃ ti ti ˈpi/ noun [U] *computing* hypertext transfer (or transport) protocol: the system that is used on the Internet to exchange documents in HTML

hub /hʌb/ noun [C] **1** the most important place where a particular activity takes place: *Bombay is the financial hub of India.* **2** the part at the center of a wheel **3** a central airport that passengers can fly to from smaller local airports

hub•bub /ˈhʌˌbʌb/ noun [singular/U] the noise of a lot of people talking at the same time

hub•cap /ˈhʌbˌkæp/ noun [C] a metal cover for the central part of a wheel on a car *—picture* → C6

hud·dle¹ /ˈhʌd(ə)l/ verb [I] to move close together in order to stay warm, feel safe, or talk

PHRASAL VERBS ˌ**huddle toˈgether** *same as* **huddle**

ˌ**huddle ˈup** *same as* **huddle**

hud·dle² /ˈhʌd(ə)l/ noun [C] a group of people who are close together

hue /hju/ noun [C] *literary* a color

huff¹ /hʌf/ noun **in a huff** feeling annoyed and upset because someone has offended you

huff² /hʌf/ verb **huff and puff** to breathe loudly and with difficulty

hug¹ /hʌg/ verb **1** [I/T] to put your arms around someone in order to show your love or friendship: *Mike picked up his daughter and hugged her tight.* **2** [T] to stay close to something: *They kept to the back of the crowd, hugging the wall.* **3** [T] to hold something close to your chest: *Emma was sitting on the floor hugging her knees.*

hug² /hʌg/ noun [C] the action of putting your arms around someone in order to show your love or friendship

huge /hjudʒ/ adj ★★★

1 extremely large ═ENORMOUS: *She arrived carrying two huge suitcases.* ♦ *Many top players earn huge amounts of money.* ♦ *The concert turned out to be **a huge success**.*

2 extremely successful and well known: *The band is huge in both Britain and the U.S.*

—**huge·ly** adv: *a hugely popular TV show*

huh /hʌ/ interjection *informal* **1** used for asking someone to repeat something because you did not hear what they said: *"Did you enjoy it?" "Huh?" "Did you enjoy the movie?"* **2** used after you have said something in order to show that you are asking for agreement: *Great shot, huh?* **3** used as a way of showing that you do not like, believe, or agree with something: *What's wrong with you, huh?*

hulk /hʌlk/ noun [C] **1** the shape of something such as a large ship or building after the inside of it has been destroyed **2** someone who is very tall and heavy

hull /hʌl/ noun [C] the main part of a ship

hum¹ /hʌm/ verb **1** [I/T] to make musical sounds with your lips closed: *If you don't know the words, just hum the tune.* **2** [I] to make a low continuous sound: *The refrigerator hummed in the kitchen.* **3** [I] if a place hums, it is full of noise and activity: *The whole stadium was humming with excitement.*

hum² /hʌm/ noun [singular] a low continuous noise made by a machine or by a lot of people talking

hu·man¹ /ˈhjumən/ adj ★★★

1 relating to people: *the human brain* ♦ *the study of **human behavior*** ♦ *Tests show that the meat is **unfit for human consumption*** (=not safe for people to eat).

2 showing normal human feelings: ***It is only human** to want revenge when someone hurts you.*

PHRASE **sb is only human** used for saying that someone has been weak in the ways that most people are weak and should not be blamed for their behavior

hu·man² /ˈhjumən/ or ˌ**human ˈbeing** noun [C] ★★ a person: *The disease can be fatal in humans.*

hu·mane /hjuˈmeɪn/ adj caring about the quality of people's or animals' lives and trying to be kind to them ≠ CRUEL, INHUMANE —**hu·mane·ly** adv

ˌ**human ˈerror** noun [U] a mistake made by a person who is controlling a machine or process, rather than something wrong with the machine or process itself

ˌ**human ˈinterest** noun [U] the part of a true story that interests people because it is about someone's life or experiences

hu·man·i·tar·i·an /hjuˌmænɪˈteriən/ adj relating to people who live in very bad conditions and to other people's efforts to help them

hu·man·i·ties, the /hjuˈmænətiz/ noun [plural] subjects that you study such as history and literature, rather than science or mathematics

hu·man·i·ty /hjuˈmænəti/ noun [U] **1** all people, thought of as a group: *Weapons of this type are a threat to the survival of humanity.* **2** a kind and sympathetic attitude toward other people ≠ INHUMANITY: *He was a man of great humanity who was deeply affected by the suffering of others.* **3** the state of being human

hu·man·kind /ˈhjumənˌkaɪnd, ˌhjumənˈkaɪnd/ noun [U] all people, thought of as a group

hu·man·ly /ˈhjumənli/ adv **humanly possible** possible for a person to do: *We will deal with the matter as soon as is humanly possible.*

ˌ**human ˈnature** noun [U] the attitudes, feelings, and reactions that are typical of most people

ˌ**human ˈrace, the** noun [singular] all people, thought of as a group

ˌ**human reˈsources** noun [U] the department within a company that is responsible for employing and training people, and for taking care of workers who have problems ═PERSONNEL

ˌ**human ˈrights** noun [plural] the rights that everyone should have in a society, including the right to express opinions or to have protection from harm

hum·ble¹ /ˈhʌmb(ə)l/ adj **1** not proud, and not thinking that you are better than other people **2** from a low social class, or with low social status —**hum·bly** adv

hum·ble² /ˈhʌmb(ə)l/ verb [T] to make someone realize that they are not as important, good, or intelligent as they thought they were

hum·drum /ˈhʌmˌdrʌm/ adj boring because nothing new or interesting ever happens

hu·mid /ˈhjumɪd/ adj hot and wet in a way that makes you feel uncomfortable: *a humid climate*

hu·mid·i·fi·er /hjuˈmɪdɪˌfaɪr/ noun [C] a machine that makes the air in a room less dry

hu·mid·i·ty /hjuˈmɪdəti/ noun [U] the amount of water that is in the air

hu·mil·i·ate /hjuˈmɪliˌeɪt/ verb [T] to make someone feel very embarrassed and ashamed —**hu·mil·i·a·tion** /hjuˌmɪliˈeɪʃ(ə)n/ noun [C/U]

H

hu•mil•i•at•ing /hjuˈmɪliˌeɪtɪŋ/ adj making you feel very embarrassed and ashamed

hu•mil•i•ty /hjuˈmɪləti/ noun [U] a way of behaving that shows that you do not think that you are better or more important than other people

hu•mor[1] /ˈhjumər/ noun ★
1 [U] the quality that makes something funny: *a novel that is full of humor*
2 [U] the ability to know when something is funny and to laugh at funny situations: *Lynne is a friendly person with a great sense of humor.*
3 [singular] *formal* someone's mood: *He laughed again, obviously* ***in a good humor****.*

hu•mor[2] /ˈhjumər/ verb [T] to do what someone wants, or to pretend to agree with them, so that they do not become angry or upset

H

hu•mor•less /ˈhjumərləs/ adj unable to see when something is funny, or showing that you do not think that something is funny

hu•mor•ous /ˈhjumərəs/ adj funny: *a humorous story* —**hu•mor•ous•ly** adv

hu•mour /ˈhjumər/ the British spelling of **humor[1]**

hump /hʌmp/ noun [C] **1** a large round shape that rises above a surface or above the ground **2** a large round part on the back of an animal or person

hunch[1] /hʌntʃ/ noun [C] a feeling that something is true or will happen, although you do not know any definite facts about it

hunch[2] /hʌntʃ/ verb [I/T] to sit or stand with your back and shoulders curved forward

hunch•back /ˈhʌntʃˌbæk/ noun [C] *offensive* an offensive word for someone who has a large round part on their back

hun•dred[1] /ˈhʌndrəd/ number ★★
1 the number 100
2 hundreds a very large number or amount of people or things: *We received* ***hundreds of*** *applications for the job.*

hun•dred[2] /ˈhʌndrəd/ noun [C] a piece of paper money that is worth 100 dollars

hun•dredth /ˈhʌndrədθ/ number **1** in the place or position that is counted as number 100 **2** one of 100 equal parts of something

hung the past tense and past participle of **hang**

hun•ger /ˈhʌŋgər/ noun **1** [U] the feeling that you have when you need to eat: *a nutritious snack that will satisfy your hunger* **2** [U] a lack of food that can cause illness or death =STARVATION: *a new chance to fight world hunger and poverty* **3** [C/U] the feeling that you have when you want something very much: *his hunger for success/power*

ˈhunger ˌstrike noun [C] a refusal to eat for a long time by someone who is protesting against something

hung•o•ver /ˈhʌŋˌoʊvər/ adj tired and sick in the morning because you drank too much alcohol the night before

hun•gry /ˈhʌŋgri/ adj ★
1 feeling that you want to eat: *We were cold, tired, and hungry.* ♦ *She was beginning to* ***feel hungry*** *again.*
2 wanting something very much: *a hungry young actor* ♦ *People are* ***hungry for*** *news.*
PHRASE **go hungry** to not have enough food
—**hun•gri•ly** adv

hunk /hʌŋk/ noun [C] **1** a large piece of a solid substance: *a hunk of meat/bread* **2** *informal* a strong and sexually attractive man

hunt[1] /hʌnt/ verb [I/T] **1** to catch and kill animals: *Crocodiles were hunted and killed for their teeth.* ♦ *Wild dogs usually hunt in packs.* ♦ *We hunted for rabbits in the hills.* **2** to try to find someone or something =LOOK FOR SB/STH: *Police are still hunting the killer.* ♦ *Detectives have been hunting for clues to the murderer's identity.*
PHRASAL VERB ˌ**hunt sb/sth ˈdown** to try very hard to find someone or something: *They'll actually hunt down old books for you.*

hunt[2] /hʌnt/ noun [C] **1** a search for someone or something: *the hunt for the missing child* **2** an attempt to catch and kill animals

hunt•er /ˈhʌntər/ noun [C] a person or animal that catches and kills wild animals

hunt•ing /ˈhʌntɪŋ/ noun [U] **1** the activity of catching and killing wild animals **2** the activity of looking for a particular thing that you want or need: *bargain hunting* ♦ *apartment hunting*

hur•dle /ˈhɜrd(ə)l/ noun **1** [C] one of several problems that you must solve before you can do something successfully: *Finding investors is the biggest hurdle we face.* **2** [C] an upright frame that a person or horse jumps over during a race **3 hurdles** [plural] a race in which people or horses jump over a series of upright frames

hurl /hɜrl/ verb [T] **1** to throw something using a lot of force **2** to direct angry remarks or criticism at someone: *The rival gangs began hurling abuse at each other.*

hur•ray /hʊˈreɪ/ or **hur•rah** /hʊˈrɑ/ interjection a word that you shout to show that you are excited and happy about something

hur•ri•cane /ˈhʌrɪˌkeɪn/ noun [C] a violent storm with extremely strong winds and heavy rain

hur•ried /ˈhʌrid/ adj done quickly, because you do not have enough time =RUSHED ≠ UNHURRIED —**hur•ried•ly** adv

hur•ry[1] /ˈhʌri/ verb [I/T] ★ to do something or to move somewhere very quickly, or to make someone do this: *We'd better hurry or we'll be late.* ♦ *Alex had to hurry home, but I decided to stay.* ♦ *She* ***hurried along*** *the corridor toward his office.* ♦ **hurry sb away/in/out etc.** *Liz took Anna's arm and hurried her away.* ♦ **hurry sb into doing sth** *Don't let them hurry you into signing anything.*
PHRASAL VERB ˌ**hurry ˈup 1** *spoken* used for telling someone to do something more quickly: *Hurry up and finish your soup.* **2** to do something or to move somewhere more quickly, or to make someone do this: *She wished George would hurry up with her cup of tea.*

hur•ry[2] /ˈhʌri/ noun ★
PHRASES **in a hurry** doing something or going somewhere quickly, because you do not have much time: *Donna's letter looked as though she had written it in a great hurry.*
in no hurry or **not in any hurry 1** able to wait to do something, because you have plenty of time: *I'm not in any hurry to get there.*

2 unwilling to do something, or not wanting to do it until a future time: *Lou's in no hurry to get married.*
(there's) no hurry *spoken* used for telling someone that they do not need to do something soon or quickly: *I'm ready whenever you are – there's no hurry.*

hurt¹ /hɜrt/ (past tense and past participle **hurt**) verb ★★★
1 [I/T] to cause someone physical pain or injury: *You're hurting my arm!* ♦ *These new boots hurt.* ♦ **hurt yourself doing sth** *Don't hurt yourself exercising.*
2 [I/T] to cause someone emotional pain: *His comments hurt her deeply.* ♦ *I never meant to **hurt your feelings**.*
3 [I] to feel pain somewhere in your body: *Fred's knees hurt after skiing all day.*
4 [T] to cause damage or problems, or to harm someone's chance to succeed at something: *The weakness of the dollar has hurt auto sales.*
PHRASE **sth won't/doesn't/can't hurt** *spoken* used for saying that something helps or cannot harm a situation: *One more drink won't hurt.*

hurt² /hɜrt/ adj **1** injured, or feeling physical pain ≠ UNHURT: *Two young men were badly hurt in the accident.* **2** feeling emotional pain, usually because of someone's behavior: *She left feeling angry and deeply hurt.*

Words often used with hurt

*Adverbs often used with **hurt** (adjective, sense 1)*
- **badly, seriously** + HURT: used when someone is injured severely

*Adverbs often used with **hurt** (adjective, sense 2)*
- **deeply, extremely, terribly** + HURT: used when someone is very upset

hurt³ /hɜrt/ noun [C/U] a feeling of emotional pain that is caused by someone's behavior

hurt·ful /ˈhɜrtfəl/ adj causing emotional pain

hur·tle /ˈhɜrt(ə)l/ verb [I] to move very quickly in an uncontrolled way

hus·band /ˈhʌzbənd/ noun [C] ★★★ the man that a woman is married to —*picture* → FAMILY TREE

hush¹ /hʌʃ/ verb **1** [I] *spoken* used for telling someone to be quiet: *Hush! You'll wake the baby!* **2** [I] *spoken* used for trying to calm someone who is upset: *Hush, sweetheart, it's OK now.* **3** [I/T] to stop talking, crying, or making noise, or to make someone do this
PHRASAL VERB ˌ**hush sth** ˈ**up** if someone in authority hushes something up, they try to keep it secret

hush² /hʌʃ/ noun [singular/U] a silence

hushed /hʌʃt/ adj very quiet: *People were talking in hushed voices.*

ˌ**hush-**ˈ**hush** adj used for talking about official activities that very few people should know about

hus·ky¹ /ˈhʌski/ noun [C] a large dog that is used for pulling SLEDS over snow

hus·ky² /ˈhʌski/ adj **1** a husky voice is deep and sounds HOARSE (=as if you have a sore throat), often in an attractive way **2** *American* a husky boy or man is big and strong

hus·tle¹ /ˈhʌs(ə)l/ verb **1** [T] to make someone go quickly to the place where you want them to go: *As soon as he arrived in the country, he was hustled off to prison.* **2** [I/T] *American* to get or sell things in a dishonest way **3** [I/T] *American* to move or to do something in a quick effective way

hus·tle² /ˈhʌs(ə)l/ noun **1** [U] a lot of noisy activity: *the hustle and bustle of the city* **2** [C] *American* a dishonest way of making money

hus·tler /ˈhʌslər/ noun [C] *American* someone who obtains money dishonestly or by having sex

hut /hʌt/ noun [C] a small simple shelter

hutch /hʌtʃ/ noun [C] **1** *American* a large piece of wooden furniture with shelves and drawers for storing dishes and kitchen tools **2** a box for keeping RABBITS in

hy·a·cinth /ˈhaɪəˌsɪnθ/ noun [C] a plant with small blue, pink, or white sweet-smelling flowers that grow close together on the stem —*picture* → C9

hy·brid /ˈhaɪbrɪd/ noun [C] **1** an animal or plant that has been produced from two different types of animal or plant **2** a mixture of different things or styles —**hy·brid** adj

hy·drant /ˈhaɪdrənt/ noun [C] an upright water pipe in the street that the FIRE DEPARTMENT gets water from

hy·drau·lic /haɪˈdrɔlɪk/ adj using the pressure of water or oil to make a machine work

hy·dro·e·lec·tric /ˌhaɪdroʊɪˈlektrɪk/ adj using water power to produce electricity

hy·dro·foil /ˈhaɪdrəˌfɔɪl/ noun [C] a boat with wing-shaped pieces attached to the bottom that lift the boat onto the surface of the water as it starts to travel quickly —*picture* → C7

hy·dro·gen /ˈhaɪdrədʒən/ noun [U] a gas that has no color or smell and that is lighter than air

hy·dro·plane /ˈhaɪdrəˌpleɪn/ verb [I] *American* if a car hydroplanes, it slides on a wet road

hy·giene /ˈhaɪdʒin/ noun [U] the practice of keeping yourself and the things around you clean in order to prevent illness and disease

hy·gien·ic /haɪˈdʒinɪk, haɪˈdʒenɪk/ adj clean and not likely to cause illness or disease

hymn /hɪm/ noun [C] a religious song that Christians sing in churches

hype¹ /haɪp/ noun [U] *informal* the use of a lot of advertisements and information to interest people

hype² /haɪp/ verb [T] *informal* to publish and broadcast a lot of advertisements and information in order to interest people
PHRASAL VERB ˌ**hype sth** ˈ**up** *informal* to make something sound more interesting or impressive than it really is

hy·per /ˈhaɪpər/ adj *informal* behaving in an excited and nervous way

hy·per·ac·tive /ˌhaɪpərˈæktɪv/ adj very lively and finding it difficult to concentrate or relax —**hy·per·ac·tiv·i·ty** /ˌhaɪpərækˈtɪvəti/ noun [U]

hy·per·bo·le /haɪˈpɜrbəli/ noun [C/U] *formal* a way of emphasizing something by describing it as far more extreme than it really is

hy·per·link /ˈhaɪpərˌlɪŋk/ noun [C] *computing* a

word or image in a computer document that you can CLICK on in order to move to a related document, word, or image —**hy•per•link** verb [T]

hy•per•sen•si•tive /ˌhaɪpərˈsensɪtɪv/ adj **1** very easily upset or offended **2** *medical* extremely sensitive to certain substances

hy•per•ten•sion /ˌhaɪpərˈtenʃ(ə)n/ noun [U] *medical* a condition in which your blood pressure is extremely high

hy•per•text /ˈhaɪpərˌtekst/ noun [U] *computing* a computer system in which you can CLICK on a word or image in order to move to a related document, word, or image

hy•per•ven•ti•late /ˌhaɪpərˈvent(ə)lˌeɪt/ verb [I] to breathe very fast because you are frightened or nervous

hy•phen /ˈhaɪfən/ noun [C] the short line - used for joining two words or parts of words, or for dividing a word at the end of a line of writing

hy•phen•at•ed /ˈhaɪfəˌneɪtəd/ adj written with a hyphen

hyp•no•sis /hɪpˈnoʊsɪs/ noun [U] a very relaxed state in which you seem to be sleeping but can still react to someone else's suggestions, or the practice of putting people into this state

hyp•not•ic /hɪpˈnɑtɪk/ adj **1** something that is hypnotic makes you feel like sleeping, because it is repeated in a regular way: *the hypnotic rhythm of the drums* **2** relating to hypnosis, or caused by hypnosis: *a hypnotic trance*

hyp•no•tist /ˈhɪpnətɪst/ noun [C] someone who hypnotizes people for medical reasons or for entertainment —**hyp•no•tism** /ˈhɪpnəˌtɪzəm/ noun [U]

hyp•no•tize /ˈhɪpnəˌtaɪz/ verb [T] to put someone into a state that is similar to sleep, but in which they can still hear and react to suggestions

hy•po•al•ler•gen•ic /ˌhaɪpoʊælərˈdʒenɪk/ adj unlikely to cause an ALLERGIC reaction (=an illness or skin reaction produced in some people by certain substances)

hy•po•chon•dri•ac /ˌhaɪpoʊˈkɑndriˌæk/ noun [C] someone who worries a lot about their health and thinks that they are sick when they are not

hy•poc•ri•sy /hɪˈpɑkrəsi/ noun [C/U] behavior in which someone pretends to be morally good or to believe something but does things that show that they are not sincere

hyp•o•crite /ˈhɪpəkrɪt/ noun [C] someone who pretends to be morally good or to believe something but who behaves in a way that shows that they are not sincere

hy•po•crit•i•cal /ˌhɪpəˈkrɪtɪk(ə)l/ adj someone who is hypocritical pretends to be morally good or to believe something but behaves in a way that shows that they are not sincere —**hyp•o•crit•i•cal•ly** /ˌhɪpəˈkrɪtɪkli/ adv

hy•po•ther•mi•a /ˌhaɪpoʊˈθɜrmiə/ noun [U] a serious medical condition in which your body temperature is very low

hy•poth•e•sis /haɪˈpɑθəsɪs/ (plural **hy•poth•e•ses** /haɪˈpɑθəˌsiz/) noun [C] an idea that attempts to explain something, but that has not yet been tested or been proved to be correct=THEORY

hy•po•thet•i•cal /ˌhaɪpəˈθetɪk(ə)l/ adj based on situations or events that seem possible rather than on actual ones=THEORETICAL —**hy•po•thet•i•cal•ly** /ˌhaɪpəˈθetɪkli/ adv

hys•ter•ec•to•my /ˌhɪstəˈrektəmi/ noun [C] a medical operation to remove a woman's UTERUS (=the part of her body where a baby can grow)

hys•ter•i•a /hɪˈstɪriə/ noun [U] a state of uncontrolled excitement or extreme fear

hys•ter•i•cal /hɪˈsterɪk(ə)l/ adj **1** behaving in an uncontrolled way because you are extremely excited, afraid, or upset **2** *spoken* extremely funny —**hys•ter•i•cal•ly** /hɪˈsterɪkli/ adv

hys•ter•ics /hɪˈsterɪks/ noun [plural] an uncontrolled emotional state in which you are extremely excited, afraid, or upset
PHRASE **in hysterics** *informal* laughing in an excited and uncontrolled way

Hz abbrev hertz

Ii

i or **I** /aɪ/ noun [C/U] the ninth letter of the English alphabet

I¹ /aɪ/ abbrev *American* interstate: an important road between states in the U.S.

I² /aɪ/ pronoun ★★★ used as the subject of a verb for referring to yourself, when you are the person speaking or writing: *I don't like cats.* ♦ *I didn't hurt you, did I?* ♦ *Peter and I will do the cooking.*

IA abbrev Iowa

I•be•ri•a /aɪˈbɪriə/ the part of Europe that includes Spain and Portugal —**I•be•ri•an** /aɪˈbɪriən/ adj

ice¹ /aɪs/ noun [U] ★★ water that has frozen and become solid: *a block of ice* ♦ *Ice was forming on the windshield.* ♦ *a drink with plenty of ice*
PHRASES **break the ice** to make people feel more relaxed and ready to talk, for example at the beginning of a party: *Roni told a few jokes, which helped to break the ice.*
keep/put sth on ice *informal* to delay doing anything about something such as a plan or idea: *The whole deal was put on ice when the stock market fell sharply.*

ice² /aɪs/ verb [T] *British* to cover a cake with FROSTING
PHRASAL VERB ˌ**ice ˈover** or ˌ**ice ˈup** to become covered with ice

ice•berg /ˈaɪsˌbɜrg/ noun [C] a very large piece of ice floating in the ocean with only a small amount of it above the surface of the water

ice•box /ˈaɪsˌbɑks/ noun [C] *American old-fashioned* a REFRIGERATOR

ˈ**ice ˌcap** noun [C] a large area of ice that covers the land and ocean around the North or South Pole

ˌice-ˈcold adj very cold

ˌice ˈcream noun [U] a frozen sweet food made from cream or milk and sugar, often with fruit or chocolate added to flavor it

ˈice ˌcube noun [C] a small piece of ice that you put in a drink to make it cold

iced /aɪst/ adj an iced drink is very cold and contains pieces of ice

ˈice ˌhockey noun [U] a game that is played on ice by two teams of six players. The players use long sticks to try to hit a small round flat object called a **puck** into the other team's goal = HOCKEY

ˈice ˌpack noun [C] **1** a bag full of ice that you hold against an injured or painful part of your body to stop it from swelling or to make it less painful **2** an area of small pieces of ice floating in the ocean

ˈice ˌrink noun [C] a large flat area of ice inside a building, where people can go to ICE-SKATE and where ICE HOCKEY games are played

ˈice ˌskate noun [C] a special boot with a metal blade on the bottom that you wear to move smoothly across ice

ˈice-ˌskate verb [I] to move around on ice wearing ice skates —**ice ˌskater** noun [C]

ˈice-ˌskating noun [U] the activity or sport of moving around on ice wearing ICE SKATES

i•ci•cle /ˈaɪsɪk(ə)l/ noun [C] a long thin piece of ice that hangs down from somewhere such as a roof

ic•ing /ˈaɪsɪŋ/ noun [U] a mixture of sugar and water or butter that is used for covering cakes = FROSTING

PHRASE **the icing on the cake** something that makes a good situation even better

i•con /ˈaɪˌkɑn/ noun [C] **1** a small picture on a computer screen that you choose by pressing a button with your MOUSE in order to open a particular program **2** someone who is very famous and who people think represents a particular idea **3** a picture or model of a holy person that is used in religious worship in the Russian or Greek Orthodox Church

ic•y /ˈaɪsi/ adj **1** very cold, in an unpleasant way **2** covered with ice **3** showing that you do not like someone and do not want to be friendly with them: *an icy stare*

I'd /aɪd/ short form **1** the usual way of saying or writing "I had." This is not often used in formal writing: *I'd never seen so much money in my life.* **2** the usual way of saying or writing "I would." This is not often used in formal writing: *I'd love to go to Brazil.*

ID[1] /ˌaɪˈdi/ noun [C/U] a document that gives the details of your name, address, and date of birth, sometimes with a photograph

ID[2] abbrev Idaho

i•de•a /aɪˈdiə/ noun ★★★

1 [C] a thought that you have about how to do something or how to deal with something: *What a great idea!* ♦ *Then I **had an idea**: We could stay with Mark.* ♦ *Then she **got the idea of** sending the poems to a publisher.* ♦ *an **idea for** a new TV show*

2 [C] an opinion, or a belief: *I don't agree with his **ideas on** education.* ♦ *She **has** some pretty strange **ideas about** how to raise children.* ♦ *We didn't have a clear **idea of** what to expect from the training course.*

3 [singular/U] information or knowledge that you have about something: *They **had no idea** what time they were supposed to arrive.* ♦ *I had only a basic **idea of** how the machine worked.*

4 [C/U] a purpose. or an intention: *My parents wanted me to be a doctor, but I had other ideas.*

PHRASES **get the idea** *informal* to understand something, often something that is not expressed directly: *Okay, I get the idea. You two want to be alone.* ♦ **+(that)** *I got the idea that he didn't want to answer the question.*

get the wrong idea *informal* to believe something that is not true: *I'll explain everything to George. I wouldn't want him to get the wrong idea.*

it's a good idea to do sth used for giving someone advice about what they should do: *It's a good idea to get someone else's opinion about it first.*

put ideas into sb's head *informal* to make someone think that they can or should do something: *Don't talk to Ralph about joining the army. I don't want you putting ideas into his head.*

i•de•al[1] /aɪˈdiəl/ adj ★

1 of the best or most appropriate type: *Upgrading your computer seems **the ideal solution**.* ♦ *Conditions were **ideal for** racing.*

2 as good as you can imagine, and probably too good to be real = PERFECT: ***In an ideal world** there would be no poverty.*

i•de•al[2] /aɪˈdiəl/ noun [C] ★

1 an idea that you try to follow about what is good and right = PRINCIPLE: *the socialist ideal of equality for all members of society*

2 the best example of something that you can think of: *Sophie represented his **ideal** of beauty.*

i•de•al•ism /aɪˈdiəˌlɪzəm/ noun [U] a very strong belief in something that is good but probably impossible to achieve

i•de•al•ist /aɪˈdiəlɪst/ noun [C] someone who is idealistic

i•de•al•is•tic /aɪˌdiəˈlɪstɪk/ adj an idealistic person believes very firmly in something that is good but probably impossible to achieve

i•de•al•ize /aɪˈdiəˌlaɪz/ verb [T] to believe or suggest that someone or something is perfect or better than they really are —**i•de•al•i•za•tion** /aɪˌdiəlɪˈzeɪʃ(ə)n/ noun [C/U]

i•de•al•ly /aɪˈdiəli/ adv **1** used for saying what you would like to happen or how things should be: *Ideally, we should finish everything by this afternoon.* **2** in the best possible way: *The lake is ideally suited for sailing.*

i•den•ti•cal /aɪˈdentɪk(ə)l/ adj ★ exactly the same: *This house is almost **identical to** the one where I lived as a child.* —**i•den•ti•cal•ly** /aɪˈdentɪkli/ adv

iˌdentical ˈtwin noun [C] identical twins are TWINS of the same sex who look exactly like each other

i•den•ti•fi•a•ble /aɪˈdentɪˌfaɪəb(ə)l/ adj able to be recognized, or easy to recognize

i•den•ti•fi•ca•tion /aɪˌdentɪfɪˈkeɪʃ(ə)n/ noun [U] **1** something that proves who you are, especially a document with your name and a photograph = ID: *Can you show me some identification?* **2** the action of recognizing someone or something: *the identification and arrest of two suspects* **3** a feeling that you understand someone else and know how they feel

i•den•ti•fy /aɪˈdentɪˌfaɪ/ verb [T] ★★★
1 to recognize someone and be able to say who they are: *One of the thieves has been identified by witnesses.*
2 to recognize something and to understand exactly what it is: *Several key problems have already been identified.*
PHRASAL VERBS **iˈdentify with sb/sth** to feel that you can understand and share someone else's feelings: *He didn't seem to be able to identify with ordinary people and their hopes.*
iˈdentify sb/sth with sth to think that someone or something is connected with a particular group or opinion
iˈdentify sth with sth *formal* to think that something is the same as something else or is closely related to it

i•den•ti•ty /aɪˈdentəti/ noun [C/U] ★★
1 the fact of who you are or what your name is: *Do you have any **proof of identity**?* ♦ *It was just a case of **mistaken identity*** (=when you wrongly think that someone is someone else).
2 the qualities that make someone or something what they are and different from other people: *The countries have kept their own political and cultural identities.* ♦ *Lorna went through a bit of **an identity crisis*** (=was not certain about her identity) *after her divorce.*

i•de•o•log•i•cal /ˌaɪdiəˈlɑdʒɪk(ə)l, ˌɪdiəˈlɑdʒɪk(ə)l/ adj based on or relating to an IDEOLOGY —**id•e•o•log•i•cal•ly** /ˌaɪdiəˈlɑdʒɪkli/ adv

i•de•ol•o•gy /ˌaɪdiˈɑlədʒi, ˌɪdiˈɑlədʒi/ noun [C/U] a system of ideas and principles on which a political or economic theory is based: *Marxist/socialist/revolutionary ideology*

id•i•o•cy /ˈɪdiəsi/ noun **1** [U] very stupid ideas or behavior **2** [C] a very stupid thing to say or do

id•i•om /ˈɪdiəm/ noun [C] an expression whose meaning is different from the meaning of the individual words. For example, "to have your feet on the ground" is an idiom meaning "to be sensible."

id•i•o•mat•ic /ˌɪdiəˈmætɪk/ adj **1** expressing things in a way that sounds natural: *an idiomatic translation* **2** containing idioms, or consisting of an idiom: *idiomatic expressions* —**id•i•o•mat•i•cal•ly** /ˌɪdiəˈmætɪkli/ adv

id•i•o•syn•cra•sy /ˌɪdiəˈsɪŋkrəsi/ noun [C/U] an idiosyncratic feature or way of behaving

id•i•o•syn•crat•ic /ˌɪdiəsɪŋˈkrætɪk/ adj unusual or strange, and not typical of anyone or anything else: *her own idiosyncratic style of painting*

id•i•ot /ˈɪdiət/ noun [C] *informal* someone who behaves in an extremely stupid way

id•i•ot•ic /ˌɪdiˈɑtɪk/ adj done or behaving in an extremely stupid way —**id•i•ot•i•cal•ly** /ˌɪdiˈɑtɪkli/ adv

i•dle[1] /ˈaɪd(ə)l/ adj **1** not working or being used: *Valuable machinery is left to lie idle for long periods.* **2** lazy **3** lacking a good reason or real purpose: *idle talk/gossip* —**i•dle•ness** noun [U], **i•dly** /ˈaɪd(ə)li/ adv

i•dle[2] /ˈaɪd(ə)l/ verb [I/T] if an engine idles, it runs slowly and does not produce any movement

i•dol /ˈaɪd(ə)l/ noun [C] **1** someone that you admire very much **2** a picture or STATUE that is worshiped as a god

i•dol•ize /ˈaɪd(ə)ˌlaɪz/ verb [T] to think that someone is perfect

i•dyl•lic /aɪˈdɪlɪk/ adj extremely beautiful and peaceful: *an idyllic scene* —**i•dyl•li•cal•ly** /aɪˈdɪlɪkli/ adv

i.e. abbrev used when you are explaining the exact meaning of something that you have mentioned: *Senior officers – i.e. anyone with the rank of colonel or above – get their own administrative staff.*

if /ɪf/ conjunction ★★★
1 in a possible or imagined situation used for introducing a situation when you are talking about its likely or imaginary results: *If we miss the last bus, we'll have to walk home.* ♦ *If Luke paid more attention in class, he would get better results.* ♦ *If I had known who he was, I wouldn't have spoken to him like that.* ♦ *I'd like to be back here by 10:30 **if possible**.* ♦ ***What if** the boss walked in here now and saw us?*
2 when sth is always true used for introducing a situation that always has the same effect or meaning: *I get a headache if I watch too much television.* ♦ *If you drive without insurance, you're breaking the law.*
3 whether used when you are asking or talking about something that is not certain: *She asked me if I was fond of music.* ♦ *Can you tell me if they're planning to come?* ♦ *I haven't decided if I want to play.*
4 saying why sb may need information used for introducing the reason that you think someone may want to know something: *There are plenty of taxis if you're in a hurry.* ♦ *If anyone asks you where I am, I'll be in the library.*
5 saying how you feel about a possibility used for saying how you feel about the possibility that something may be true: *I'm sorry if I've upset you.* ♦ *I don't care if I never see her again.*
6 in requests *spoken* used when you are politely asking someone to do something, or when you are asking for permission: *I would be grateful if you would send me further details.* ♦ ***If you don't mind**, I'd like to sit in the back.*
PHRASES **if I were you** *spoken* used when you are giving someone advice: *If I were you, I'd stay away from that man.*
if only *spoken* used for saying that you would like a situation to be different: *If only we could afford to buy a place of our own.*
→ AS

if•fy /ˈɪfi/ adj *spoken* **1** not certain = DOUBTFUL: *It's still iffy whether she'll be able to come to the party.* **2** not very good: *That engine sounds a little iffy to me.*

ig•loo /ˈɪglu/ noun [C] a building made from snow or ice

ig·nite /ɪgˈnaɪt/ verb **1** [I/T] *formal* to start to burn, or to make something start to burn **2** [T] to start a war or argument = SPARK

ig·ni·tion /ɪgˈnɪʃ(ə)n/ noun **1** [singular] the place where you put in the key to make a car's engine start —*picture* → C6 **2** [U] *formal* the process of making something start to burn

ig·no·min·i·ous /ˌɪgnəˈmɪniəs/ adj *formal* very embarrassing = HUMILIATING: *an ignominious defeat* —**ig·no·min·i·ous·ly** adv

ig·no·rance /ˈɪgnərəns/ noun [U] lack of knowledge about something

ig·no·rant /ˈɪgnərənt/ adj not knowing something that you should know or that you need to know —**ig·no·rant·ly** adv

ig·nore /ɪgˈnɔr/ verb [T] ★★
1 to not consider something, or to not let it influence you: *We had ignored the fact that it was getting darker.* ♦ *My son gets good advice but he just ignores it.*
2 to pretend that you have not noticed someone or something: *He completely ignored her and kept on walking.*

i·gua·na /ɪˈgwɑnə/ noun [C] a large LIZARD with sharp points on its back that lives in tropical parts of North and South America —*picture* → C13

i·kon /ˈaɪˌkɑn/ see **icon** 3

IL abbrev Illinois

ill[1] /ɪl/ adj ★
1 not healthy because of a medical condition or an injury: *She was too ill to travel.* ♦ *Her husband is **seriously ill** in the hospital.* → SICK
2 *formal* bad or harmful: *The fish didn't taste fresh, but we suffered no **ill effects**.*

> **Words often used with ill**
> *Adverbs often used with ill (adj, sense 1)*
> ■ **critically, gravely, seriously** + ILL: used for saying that someone is very ill

ill[2] /ɪl/ adv *formal* badly: *He was ill prepared for the demands of being a father.*
PHRASE **can ill afford (to do) sth** used for saying that someone should definitely not do something because it will cause problems: *These are issues that we can ill afford to ignore.* → BODE

ill[3] /ɪl/ noun [C] *formal* a problem, or a difficulty: *a cure for all the nation's ills*

I'll /aɪl/ short form the usual way of saying or writing "I will." This is not often used in formal writing: *I'll see you later.*

ill-ad·vised /ˌɪl ədˈvaɪzd/ adj likely to have a bad effect

ill-con·ceived /ˌɪl kənˈsivd/ adj an ill-conceived idea or plan is not sensible

il·le·gal /ɪˈlig(ə)l/ adj ★★ not allowed by the law: *illegal drugs* ♦ **it is illegal (for sb) to do sth** *It is illegal for employers to discriminate on the grounds of race.* —**il·le·gal·i·ty** /ˌɪliˈgæləti/ noun [U], **il·le·gal·ly** adv

il͵legal ˈalien noun [C] *American* an ILLEGAL IMMIGRANT

il͵legal ˈimmigrant noun [C] someone who enters a country illegally, or who stays for a longer time than they are legally allowed

il·leg·i·ble /ɪˈledʒəb(ə)l/ adj difficult or impossible to read —**il·leg·i·ble** /ɪˈledʒəbli/ adv

il·le·git·i·mate /ˌɪləˈdʒɪtɪmət/ adj an illegitimate child is born to parents who are not legally married

ill-e·quip·ped /ˌɪlɪ ˈkwɪpt/ adj *formal* lacking the necessary equipment, skills, or abilities to do something

ill-fat·ed /ɪlˈfeɪtəd/ adj likely to end in failure or death

͵ill-ˈfitting adj *formal* ill-fitting clothes are the wrong size for the person wearing them

ill-got·ten gains /ˌɪl gɑt(ə)n ˈgeɪnz/ noun [plural] *often humorous* money or property that someone has obtained in an illegal or dishonest way

il·lic·it /ɪˈlɪsɪt/ adj **1** an illicit relationship, activity, or situation is one that people do not approve of **2** not allowed by the law = ILLEGAL: *illicit drugs* —**il·lic·it·ly** adv

͵ill-inˈformed adj lacking knowledge of a particular subject

il·lit·er·ate /ɪˈlɪt(ə)rət/ adj **1** not able to read or write **2** containing a lot of mistakes in grammar and spelling **3** lacking knowledge in a particular subject: *politically illiterate* —**il·lit·er·a·cy** /ɪˈlɪt(ə)rəsi/ noun [U]

͵ill-ˈmannered adj *formal* not polite = RUDE ≠ WELL-MANNERED

ill·ness /ˈɪlnəs/ noun ★★★
1 [U] the state of feeling sick or having a disease: *He missed five days of school because of illness.*
2 [C] a particular disease, or a period of being sick: *She has had no serious illnesses before this.*

> **Other ways of saying illness**
> ■ **bug** (*informal*) a minor illness that is caused by a virus or bacteria and lasts only a short time
> ■ **condition** a medical problem that affects someone for a long time
> ■ **disease** a serious illness that usually lasts a long time
> ■ **infection** an illness that is caused by bacteria and that usually lasts a short time only
> ■ **virus** an illness that is caused by a very small germ

il·log·i·cal /ɪˈlɑdʒɪk(ə)l/ adj not sensible, or not based on clear facts or reasons: *an illogical argument* —**il·log·i·cal·ly** /ɪˈlɑdʒɪkli/ adv

͵ill-ˈtreat verb [T] *formal* to treat someone in a cruel or unkind way = MALTREAT: *None of the prisoners were ill-treated.* —**͵ill-ˈtreatment** noun [U]

il·lu·mi·nate /ɪˈlumɪˌneɪt/ verb [T] *formal* **1** to make something bright with light or lights, or to shine a light on something = LIGHT **2** to make something clear and easier to understand —**il·lu·mi·na·tion** /ɪˌlumɪˈneɪʃ(ə)n/ noun [C/U]

il·lu·mi·nat·ing /ɪˈlumɪˌneɪtɪŋ/ adj *formal* making something clearer and easier to understand

il·lu·sion /ɪˈluʒ(ə)n/ noun [C] **1** a false or wrong belief or idea **2** an appearance or effect that is different from the way that things really are

il·lu·so·ry /ɪˈlus(ə)ri/ or **il·lu·sive** /ɪˈlusɪv/ adj *formal* not real, but seeming real: *the illusory benefits of the program*

il•lus•trate /ˈɪləˌstreɪt/ verb [T] ★★
1 to show or explain something by using examples, pictures, lists of numbers, etc.: *The process is illustrated in Figure 4.* ♦ *Miriam quoted three case studies to* ***illustrate her point.***
2 to draw the pictures in a book, or to put pictures in a book: *The cookbook is* ***beautifully illustrated*** *with color photographs.*

il•lus•tra•tion /ˌɪləˈstreɪʃ(ə)n/ noun ★
1 [C] a picture, drawing, or photograph that is used for decorating a book or for explaining something: *a children's book with beautiful illustrations*
2 [U] the art of illustrating books
3 [C/U] an example, event, or fact that explains something or shows that something is true: *The project* ***provides a good illustration of*** *how people can work together.*

il•lus•tra•tor /ˈɪləˌstreɪtər/ noun [C] someone whose job is to draw pictures for books or magazines

il•lus•tri•ous /ɪˈlʌstriəs/ adj *formal* famous and respected because of what you have achieved = DISTINGUISHED

ˌill ˈwill noun [U] a strong feeling of disliking someone and wanting something bad to happen to them = ANIMOSITY ≠ GOODWILL

I'm /aɪm/ short form the usual way of saying or writing "I am." This is not often used in formal writing.

im•age /ˈɪmɪdʒ/ noun ★★★
1 [C/U] an opinion that people have about someone or something: *The company needs to shake off its outdated image.* ♦ *We have* ***an image of*** *the U.S. as a very rich country.*
2 [C] a picture, especially one in a mirror, on a computer or television screen, or in a movie theater: *She stared at her image in the bathroom mirror.* ♦ *Images of Germany appeared across the screen.*
3 [C] a picture or idea of someone or something in your mind: *I had a sudden* ***mental image*** *of Robert waiting for me with flowers.*
4 [C] a description of something that uses language or combines ideas in an interesting way

im•age•ry /ˈɪmɪdʒ(ə)ri/ noun [U] **1** pictures, photographs, or objects that represent an idea **2** the use of words and phrases in literature to create an image of something

i•mag•i•na•ble /ɪˈmædʒɪnəb(ə)l/ adj possible to imagine: *a situation that was hardly imaginable ten years ago*

i•mag•i•nar•y /ɪˈmædʒɪˌneri/ adj not real, but only created in your mind: *A lonely child sometimes creates an imaginary friend to play with.*

i•mag•i•na•tion /ɪˌmædʒɪˈneɪʃ(ə)n/ noun [C/U] ★ the ability to form pictures or original ideas in your mind: *Was he scared, or was it just my imagination?* ♦ *a child with* ***a vivid imagination*** ♦ ***Try to use your imagination*** *when planning main meals.* ♦ *Her essay showed a remarkable* ***lack of imagination.*** ♦ *They didn't* ***have the imagination to*** *deal with such complex problems.* → FIGMENT, STRETCH²

> **Word family: imagination**
> *Words in the same family as* ***imagination***
> ■ **imagine** *v* ■ **imaginary** *adj*
> ■ **imaginable** *adj* ■ **unimaginable** *adj*
> ■ **imaginative** *adj* ■ **unimaginative** *adj*

i•mag•i•na•tive /ɪˈmædʒɪnətɪv/ adj
1 involving new, different, or exciting ideas = CREATIVE ≠ UNIMAGINATIVE: *the imaginative use of computers in the classroom* **2** able to produce new, different, or exciting ideas ≠ UNIMAGINATIVE —**i•mag•i•na•tive•ly** adv

i•mag•ine /ɪˈmædʒɪn/ verb [T] ★★★
1 to form a picture of someone or something in your mind: *She tried to imagine the scene.* ♦ *Imagine my surprise when they announced I had won!* ♦ **+(that)** *He had never imagined that digging would be such hard work.* ♦ **+what/how etc.** *You can imagine what the newspapers would do if they ever found out about this.*
2 to have an idea that something exists or is happening, when in fact it does not exist or is not happening: *There's nothing there – you're just* ***imagining things!***
3 to think that something is probably true = SUPPOSE: *It's difficult,* ***I imagine,*** *to keep your interest alive after doing the job for 30 years.* ♦ **+(that)** *I imagine they've left already.*

im•ag•ing /ˈɪmədʒɪŋ/ noun [U] the process of producing an image by using a machine that passes an electronic BEAM over something

im•bal•ance /ɪmˈbæləns/ noun [C/U] a situation in which the balance between two things is not equal or fair

im•be•cile /ˈɪmbəs(ə)l, ˈɪmbəˌsaɪl/ noun [C] an insulting word for someone who behaves in a very stupid way = IDIOT

im•bue /ɪmˈbju/ PHRASAL VERB **imˈbue sb/sth with sth** *formal* to fill someone or something with a particular quality or emotion

IMF, the /ˌaɪ em ˈef/ the International Monetary Fund: an international organization that works to manage the world's economy

im•i•tate /ˈɪmɪˌteɪt/ verb [T] **1** to copy what someone does or says, often in order to make people laugh = MIMIC **2** to copy something: *Italian ice cream is imitated all over the world.* —**im•i•ta•tor** noun [C]

im•i•ta•tion¹ /ˌɪmɪˈteɪʃ(ə)n/ noun **1** [C/U] the act of copying someone's actions, words, or behavior, often in order to make people laugh **2** [C/U] the act of copying something **3** [C] something that is a copy of something else, and not as good as the original thing: *Her ring is just a cheap imitation.*

im•i•ta•tion² /ˌɪmɪˈteɪʃ(ə)n/ adj made to look like something that is more valuable or expensive: *imitation fur/leather/marble*

im•mac•u•late /ɪˈmækjələt/ adj **1** completely clean and neat = SPOTLESS **2** correct or perfect in every way —**im•mac•u•late•ly** adv

im•ma•te•ri•al /ˌɪməˈtɪriəl/ adj not important or relevant

im•ma•ture /ˌɪməˈtʃʊr/ adj **1** behaving in a silly way, as though you are much younger than you really are ≠ MATURE **2** not fully grown or developed ≠ MATURE

—**im•ma•tur•i•ty** /ˌɪməˈtʃʊrəti/ noun [U]

im•meas•ur•a•ble /ɪˈmeʒərəb(ə)l/ adj *formal* impossible to measure because of being so large or extreme —**im•meas•ur•a•bly** /ɪˈmeʒərəbli/ adv

im•me•di•ate /ɪˈmidiət/ adj ★★★

1 without delay	4 next to sb/sth
2 urgent	5 closely connected
3 directly before/after	

1 happening or done now, without delay: *Our government must take immediate action.* ♦ *The rebels demanded the immediate release of the prisoners.* ♦ *My immediate response was to say yes.*
2 existing now and needing urgent action: *There doesn't seem to be any immediate danger.*
3 existing in the period of time directly before or after an event: *plans for the **immediate future***
4 next to a person or place: *There are several nice hikes **in the immediate vicinity*** (=very near).
5 closely connected to you: *She is **my immediate superior*** (=the person directly in charge of me). ♦ *Only **immediate family*** (=parents, children, brothers, and sisters) *will be allowed to attend the ceremony.*

im•me•di•ate•ly /ɪˈmidiətli/ adv ★★★
1 very quickly and without delay = AT ONCE: *When she saw him come in, she decided to leave immediately.* ♦ *I immediately saw how serious the situation was.*
2 with no one or nothing between: *We could hear noises coming from the room immediately below us.*
3 just before or just after an event: *She was with Roosevelt immediately before his death.*

im•mense /ɪˈmens/ adj extremely large = HUGE: *an immense amount of money*

im•mense•ly /ɪˈmensli/ adv very, or very much: *an immensely talented singer*

im•men•si•ty /ɪˈmensəti/ noun [U] the very large size of something

im•merse /ɪˈmɜrs/ verb [T] *formal* to put someone or something in a liquid so that they are covered completely
PHRASE **immerse yourself in sth** to spend most of your time doing something or thinking about it: *Sandra immersed herself in work to try and forget her problems at home.*
—**im•mer•sion** /ɪˈmɜrʃ(ə)n, ɪˈmɜrʒ(ə)n/ noun [U]

im•mi•grant /ˈɪmɪɡrənt/ noun [C] someone who comes to live in a country from another country → EMIGRANT

im•mi•grate /ˈɪmɪˌɡreɪt/ verb [I] to come into a country because you want to live there

im•mi•gra•tion /ˌɪmɪˈɡreɪʃ(ə)n/ noun [U] **1** the process in which people enter a country in order to live there permanently **2** the place where you show your passport and are officially allowed into a country

im•mi•nent /ˈɪmɪnənt/ adj likely to happen very soon, or certain to do so —**im•mi•nence** noun [U], **im•mi•nent•ly** adv

im•mo•bile /ɪˈmoʊb(ə)l/ adj **1** not moving = MOTIONLESS **2** not able to move —**im•mo•bil•i•ty** /ˌɪmoʊˈbɪləti/ noun [U]

im•mo•bi•lize /ɪˈmoʊb(ə)ˌlaɪz/ verb [T] **1** to make someone unable to move **2** to stop something from working: *a device that immobilizes the car if anyone tries to steal it* —**im•mo•bi•li•za•tion** /ɪˌmoʊb(ə)lɪˈzeɪʃ(ə)n/ noun [U]

im•mor•al /ɪˈmɔrəl/ adj morally wrong: *immoral behavior* —**im•mor•al•i•ty** /ˌɪməˈræləti/ noun [U], **im•mor•al•ly** adv

im•mor•tal /ɪˈmɔrt(ə)l/ adj **1** very well known and likely to be remembered for a long time **2** living or existing for all time —**im•mor•tal•i•ty** /ˌɪmɔrˈtæləti/ noun [U]

im•mor•tal•ize /ɪˈmɔrt(ə)ˌlaɪz/ verb [T] to make someone or something famous for a very long time

im•mov•a•ble /ɪˈmuvəb(ə)l/ adj **1** impossible to move **2** with opinions or feelings that you refuse to change —**im•mov•a•bly** adv

im•mune /ɪˈmjun/ adj **1** safe from a disease, because you cannot be infected by it **2** relating to the body's IMMUNE SYSTEM **3** not influenced or affected by something: *Greg seemed totally immune to criticism.* **4** not affected by something such as a law, because of a special arrangement: *Diplomats are immune from prosecution.* —**im•mu•ni•ty** /ɪˈmjunəti/ noun [C/U]

imˈmune ˌsystem noun [C] the system in your body that protects you against diseases

im•mu•ni•ty /ɪˈmjunəti/ noun [C/U] a situation in which someone is not affected by something such as a law because they have a special job or position

im•mu•nize /ˈɪmjəˌnaɪz/ verb [T] to prevent someone from getting a particular illness by putting a substance into their body —**im•mu•ni•za•tion** /ˌɪmjənɪˈzeɪʃ(ə)n/ noun [C/U]

imp /ɪmp/ noun [C] an imaginary creature that looks like a small child and likes to have fun by behaving badly

im•pact¹ /ˈɪmˌpækt/ noun ★★★
1 [C] an effect or influence: *Her paper discusses **the likely impact of** global warming.* ♦ *Internet shopping has begun to have a serious **impact on** the traditional bookstores.*
2 [C/U] the force or act of one object hitting another: *the point of impact* ♦ *I was thrown to the ground by **the impact of** the blast.* ♦ *The missile exploded **on impact**.*

Words often used with impact

*Adjectives often used with **impact** (noun, sense 1)*
- **adverse, devastating, negative, serious** + IMPACT: used about a bad effect
- **dramatic, major, profound, significant** + IMPACT: used about a big effect

*Verbs often used with **impact** (noun, sense 1)*
- **absorb, cushion, lessen, minimize, soften** + IMPACT: reduce the effect of something

im•pact² /ɪmˈpækt/ verb [I/T] to have an effect or influence on someone or something

im•pair /ɪmˈper/ verb [T] *formal* to make something less good or effective by damaging it

im•paired /ɪmˈperd/ adj not fully able to do something: *methods of correcting impaired vision*

im•pair•ment /ɪmˈpermənt/ noun [C/U] the

fact that a part of your body is unable to do something fully

im•pale /ɪmˈpeɪl/ verb [T] to push a pointed object through someone or something

im•part /ɪmˈpɑrt/ verb [T] *formal* **1** to give something such as information, knowledge, or beliefs to someone **2** to give something a particular quality

im•par•tial /ɪmˈpɑrʃ(ə)l/ adj not influenced by, or not preferring, one particular person or group —**im•par•ti•al•i•ty** /ˌɪmpɑrʃiˈæləti/ noun [U], **im•par•tial•ly** adv

im•pass•a•ble /ɪmˈpæsəb(ə)l/ adj an impassable road or path is impossible to travel along

im•passe /ˈɪmˌpæs/ noun [singular] a situation in which progress is not possible because none of the people involved is willing to change their opinion or decision =DEADLOCK

im•pas•sioned /ɪmˈpæʃ(ə)nd/ adj expressing a lot of emotion

im•pas•sive /ɪmˈpæsɪv/ adj not showing any emotion —**im•pas•sive•ly** adv

im•pa•tient /ɪmˈpeɪʃ(ə)nt/ adj ★
1 annoyed because something is not happening as quickly as you want or in the way that you want: *"Come on!" said Maggie, becoming impatient.* ♦ *He gets* ***impatient with*** *people who don't agree with him.*
2 wanting something to happen as soon as possible: *They were* ***impatient for*** *news of their father.* ♦ **impatient to do sth** *After a couple of days, she was impatient to get back to work.*
—**im•pa•tience** /ɪmˈpeɪʃ(ə)ns/ noun [U], **im•pa•tient•ly** adv

im•peach /ɪmˈpitʃ/ verb [T] to formally accuse a public official of a serious crime relating to their job —**im•peach•ment** noun [C/U]

im•pec•ca•ble /ɪmˈpekəb(ə)l/ adj perfect in every way =FAULTLESS —**im•pec•ca•bly** adv

im•pede /ɪmˈpid/ verb [T] *formal* to make it more difficult for someone to do something or for something to happen

im•ped•i•ment /ɪmˈpedɪmənt/ noun [C] **1** *formal* something that makes it more difficult for someone to do something or for something to happen **2** a physical or PSYCHOLOGICAL problem that affects how well someone can do something

im•pel /ɪmˈpel/ verb [T] *formal* if a feeling or idea impels you to do something, it forces you to do it

im•pend•ing /ɪmˈpendɪŋ/ adj going to happen very soon: *He was unaware of the impending disaster.*

im•pen•e•tra•ble /ɪmˈpenətrəb(ə)l/ adj **1** impossible to get into, get through, or see through **2** impossible to understand: *impenetrable writing*

im•per•a•tive[1] /ɪmˈperətɪv/ adj **1** *formal* extremely important and urgent **2** *linguistics* the imperative form of a verb expresses an order to do something, for example "Go!"

im•per•a•tive[2] /ɪmˈperətɪv/ noun **1 the imperative** [singular] *linguistics* the form of a verb that expresses an order **2** [C] *formal* something that is very important and urgent

im•per•cep•ti•ble /ˌɪmpərˈseptəb(ə)l/ adj something that is imperceptible is so slight or small that it is very difficult to notice —**im•per•cep•ti•bly** adv

im•per•fect /ɪmˈpɜrfɪkt/ adj **1** something that is imperfect has some faults or other bad qualities **2** *linguistics* an imperfect form of a verb describes an action in the past that is continuous, repeated, or not finished —**im•per•fec•tion** /ˌɪmpərˈfekʃ(ə)n/ noun [C/U], **im•per•fect•ly** adv

im•per•fect, the /ɪmˈpɜrfɪkt/ noun [singular] *linguistics* the form of a verb that describes an action in the past that is continuous, repeated, or not finished

im•pe•ri•al /ɪmˈpɪriəl/ adj **1** relating to an EMPIRE (=a group of several countries that are ruled by one country) or the person who rules it **2** belonging to a system of measurement in which weight is measured in pounds, length is measured in FEET, and VOLUME is measured in PINTS → METRIC

im•pe•ri•al•ism /ɪmˈpɪriəˌlɪzəm/ noun [U] the actions of a powerful country that tries to gain control of other countries —**im•pe•ri•al•ist** adj, noun

im•per•il /ɪmˈperəl/ verb [T] *formal* to put someone or something in danger =ENDANGER

im•per•son•al /ɪmˈpɜrs(ə)nəl/ adj not showing your personal feelings or ideas: *His manner was cold and impersonal.* —**im•per•son•al•ly** adv

im•per•son•ate /ɪmˈpɜrs(ə)nˌeɪt/ verb [T] **1** to pretend to be someone else by copying the way that they look, speak, or behave in order to trick people **2** to copy the way that someone speaks and behaves in order to pretend to be that person or to make people laugh =IMITATE —**im•per•son•a•tion** /ɪmˌpɜrs(ə)nˈeɪʃ(ə)n/ noun [C/U], **im•per•son•a•tor** noun [C]

im•per•ti•nent /ɪmˈpɜrt(ə)nənt/ adj *formal* rude and not showing respect for someone —**im•per•ti•nence** noun [U], **im•per•ti•nent•ly** adv

im•per•vi•ous /ɪmˈpɜrviəs/ adj **1 impervious to sth** not affected by something: *He continued talking, impervious to the effect his words were having.* **2** something that is impervious to a substance does not let the substance pass through it

im•pet•u•ous /ɪmˈpetʃuəs/ adj doing things quickly, without thinking about the results =RASH —**im•pet•u•ous•ly** adv

im•pe•tus /ˈɪmpətəs/ noun [singular/U] something that makes a process happen or develop more quickly

im•pinge /ɪmˈpɪndʒ/ PHRASAL VERB **imˈpinge on sth** or **imˈpinge uˌpon sth** *formal* to have an effect on something

imp•ish /ˈɪmpɪʃ/ adj behaving in a way that is slightly bad but that makes people smile =MISCHIEVOUS —**imp•ish•ly** adv

im•plac•a•ble /ɪmˈplækəb(ə)l/ adj having or expressing very angry or determined feelings that will not change —**im•plac•a•bly** adv

im•plant[1] /ɪmˈplænt/ verb [T] **1** to put something into someone's body in a medical operation **2** to put an idea or attitude into someone's mind

im•plant[2] /ˈɪmˌplænt/ noun [C] an object that

is put into someone's body in a medical operation

im•plau•si•ble /ɪmˈplɔzəb(ə)l/ adj difficult to accept as true=UNCONVINCING —**im•plau•si•bly** adv

im•ple•ment[1] /ˈɪmpləˌment/ verb [T] to make something such as an idea, plan, system, or law start to work and be used=CARRY STH OUT —**im•ple•men•ta•tion** /ˌɪmpləmənˈteɪʃ(ə)n/ noun [U]

im•ple•ment[2] /ˈɪmpləmənt/ noun [C] a tool, or a simple piece of equipment

im•pli•cate /ˈɪmplɪˌkeɪt/ verb [T] to show or claim that someone or something is involved in an activity that is illegal or morally wrong

im•pli•ca•tion /ˌɪmplɪˈkeɪʃ(ə)n/ noun ★

1 [C] a possible future effect or result: *What are the **implications of** this new technology?* ♦ *Improving your diet **has** important **implications for** your future health.*

2 [C/U] something that you suggest is true, although you do not say it directly: **+that** *I resent the implication that my work is not thorough.*

3 [U] the fact of suggesting or showing that someone is involved in something illegal or morally wrong

im•plic•it /ɪmˈplɪsɪt/ adj **1** not stated directly, but expressed or suggested indirectly ≠EXPLICIT: *an implicit criticism* **2** without any doubts or questions: *an implicit belief in the goodness of people* **3 implicit in sth** forming a necessary part of something —**im•plic•it•ly** adv

im•plode /ɪmˈploʊd/ verb [I] to break up violently and fall inward

im•plore /ɪmˈplɔr/ verb [T] *formal* to ask someone in an emotional way to do something, because you want it very much=BEG

im•ply /ɪmˈplaɪ/ verb [T] ★ to show or suggest that something exists or is true: **+(that)** *I didn't mean to imply that you were interfering.*

im•po•lite /ˌɪmpəˈlaɪt/ adj not polite=RUDE —**im•po•lite•ly** adv

im•port[1] /ˈɪmˌpɔrt/ noun [C/U] ★ a product that is imported, or the process of importing products ≠EXPORT: *oil/food/coal imports* ♦ *cheap imports from South American countries* ♦ *We need controls on **the import of** meat.*

im•port[2] /ɪmˈpɔrt/ verb [T] ★

1 to buy a product from another country and bring it to your country ≠EXPORT: *We import most of our coal from other countries.* ♦ *imported luxury goods*

2 *computing* to move information into a file or program ≠EXPORT —**im•por•ta•tion** /ˌɪmpɔrˈteɪʃ(ə)n/ noun [U], **im•port•er** noun [C]

im•por•tance /ɪmˈpɔrt(ə)ns/ noun [U] ★★★ the fact of being important, or the degree to which something or someone is important: *The company recognizes **the importance of** training its employees.* ♦ *The issue has special **importance for** people in rural areas.* ♦ *I pretended the incident **was of no importance**.*

im•por•tant /ɪmˈpɔrt(ə)nt/ adj ★★★

1 something that is important has a major effect on someone or something: *Music was **an important part of** the life of the community.* ♦ *Winning the game yesterday was **important for** us.* ♦ *Your interest and support are **important to** your child.* ♦ **it is important to do sth** *It is important to stress that the study only involved a small number of people.*

2 important people have a lot of influence or power: *We can't afford to lose such an important customer.*

Words often used with important

*Adverbs often used with **important** (sense 1)*

■ **crucially, extremely, most, particularly, terribly, vitally** + IMPORTANT: used for saying that something is very important

Words you can use instead of important

Important is a very general word. Here are some words with more specific meanings that sound more natural and appropriate in particular situations.

people	influential, leading, prominent, senior, top
events	key, historic, landmark, major, main, momentous
issues/problems	critical, major, significant
achievements/ discoveries	groundbreaking, historic, landmark, significant
effects	far-reaching, lasting, main, major, significant
facts	notable, noteworthy, significant
things that are important because you must have or do them	critical, crucial, essential, necessary, urgent, vital

im•por•tant•ly /ɪmˈpɔrt(ə)ntli/ adv **1** used for emphasizing that something is important: *How did Jamie know? And, more importantly, what did he know?* **2** in a way that shows that you think you are important

im•pose /ɪmˈpoʊz/ verb ★

1 [T] to force people to accept something: *If she lied under oath, the court will impose a severe penalty.* ♦ **impose sth on sb** *I wouldn't want to impose my views on anyone.*

2 [I] to cause extra work for someone: *They invited me to dinner, but I didn't want to impose.* ♦ *Please come and stay. You wouldn't be **imposing on** us at all.*

People often use this word when they are politely refusing an invitation, or when they are politely persuading someone to accept an invitation.

im•pos•ing /ɪmˈpoʊzɪŋ/ adj large and impressive

im•po•si•tion /ˌɪmpəˈzɪʃ(ə)n/ noun **1** [C] an unfair or unreasonable situation that you are expected to accept **2** [U] the introduction of something that people are forced to accept

im•pos•si•ble /ɪmˈpɑsəb(ə)l/ adj ★★★

1 if something is impossible, no one can do

it or it cannot happen: *We were faced with an impossible task.* ♦ **it is impossible to do sth** *It would be impossible to gather this information without using computers.*
2 extremely difficult to do or to deal with: *Dealing with her illness makes life pretty impossible for the rest of the family.* ♦ *Young children are impossible at times.*
—**im•pos•si•bil•i•ty** /ɪmˌpɑsəˈbɪləti/ noun [C/U]

im•pos•si•bly /ɪmˈpɑsəbli/ adv extremely: *impossibly high heels*

im•pos•tor or **im•pos•ter** /ɪmˈpɑstər/ noun [C] someone who pretends to be someone else

im•po•tent /ˈɪmpət(ə)nt/ adj **1** a man who is impotent cannot have sex because his PENIS does not stay hard **2** unable to do anything that is effective because of a lack of power —**im•po•tence** noun [U]

im•pound /ɪmˈpaʊnd/ verb [T] if the police or other officials impound something, they take it away from someone who has done something that is illegal = CONFISCATE

im•pov•er•ished /ɪmˈpɑv(ə)rɪʃt/ adj very poor

im•prac•ti•cal /ɪmˈpræktɪk(ə)l/ adj **1** not sensible, or not likely to be effective or successful **2** not good at doing practical things —**im•prac•ti•cal•i•ty** /ɪmˌpræktɪˈkæləti/ noun [C/U]

im•pre•cise /ˌɪmprəˈsaɪs/ adj not exact, accurate, or clear —**im•pre•cise•ly** adv

im•preg•na•ble /ɪmˈpregnəb(ə)l/ adj a place that is impregnable is very well protected and difficult to attack

im•preg•nate /ɪmˈpregˌneɪt/ verb [T] **1** to make a substance such as a liquid spread all the way through something **2** *formal* to make a woman or female animal pregnant
—**im•preg•na•tion** /ˌɪmpregˈneɪʃ(ə)n/ noun [U]

im•press /ɪmˈpres/ verb [T] ★★ if someone or something impresses you, you admire them: *Her ability to deal with problems impresses me.* ♦ *I was extremely impressed by the novel.*
PHRASAL VERB **imˈpress sth on sb** to try to make someone understand how important something is: *They impressed on us the need to keep the project completely secret.*

im•pres•sion /ɪmˈpreʃ(ə)n/ noun [C] ★★
1 an opinion, feeling, or idea about someone or something that is not based on much information, or that is only based on the way that they look, sound, or behave: *It is important to* ***make a good impression*** *at the interview.* ♦ *He* ***gave me the impression that*** *he really didn't care.* ♦ ***I have the impression that*** *she's very good at her job.* ♦ *Her* ***first impression*** *was that he was dead.* ♦ ***I was under the impression*** (=thought) *that we had met before.*
2 a performance in which someone copies the way another person speaks or behaves in order to make people laugh = IMITATION: *Jill* ***does impressions of*** *famous singers.*
3 *formal* a mark that is made when an object is pressed onto a surface

im•pres•sion•a•ble /ɪmˈpreʃ(ə)nəb(ə)l/ adj easily impressed and influenced by other people

im•pres•sion•is•tic /ɪmˌpreʃ(ə)nˈɪstɪk/ adj based on reactions or opinions, rather than on specific facts or details

im•pres•sive /ɪmˈpresɪv/ adj ★ if someone or something is impressive, you admire them ≠ UNIMPRESSIVE: *an impressive performance* ♦ *The list of their achievements is pretty impressive.* —**im•pres•sive•ly** adv

im•print¹ /ˈɪmˌprɪnt/ noun [C] **1** a mark that an object leaves on a surface when it is pressed into it **2** a strong permanent influence on someone or something

im•print² /ɪmˈprɪnt/ verb [T] **1** to leave a mark on a surface by pressing an object into it **2** to make something have a strong permanent influence on someone or something

im•pris•on /ɪmˈprɪz(ə)n/ verb [T] to put someone in a prison, or to keep them in a place that they cannot escape from
—**im•pris•on•ment** noun [U]

im•prob•a•ble /ɪmˈprɑbəb(ə)l/ adj **1** not likely to happen or be true = UNLIKELY **2** strange and unexpected —**im•prob•a•bly** adv

im•promp•tu /ɪmˈprɑmpˌtu/ adj not planned or prepared —**im•promp•tu** adv

im•prop•er /ɪmˈprɑpər/ adj **1** not appropriate or right according to accepted standards of behavior = INAPPROPRIATE **2** not legal or honest = UNLAWFUL —**im•prop•er•ly** adv

im•pro•pri•e•ty /ˌɪmprəˈpraɪəti/ noun [C/U] *formal* behavior that is not honest, professional, or socially acceptable

im•prove /ɪmˈpruv/ verb [I/T] ★★★ to become better, or to make something better: *Your English will improve with practice.* ♦ *More money is needed to improve airline security.*
PHRASAL VERB **imˈprove on sth** or **imˈprove uˌpon sth** to make something better than it was before, or to do something better than you did before: *We hope to improve upon last year's performance.*

> **Words often used with improve**
>
> *Adverbs often used with* ***improve***
>
> ■ IMPROVE + **considerably, dramatically, greatly, markedly, significantly, vastly**: used for saying that something improves a lot

im•prove•ment /ɪmˈpruvmənt/ noun ★★★
1 [C/U] the state of being better than before, or the process of making something better than it was before: *The school is performing well, but we recognize the need for further improvement.* ♦ *There has been* ***an improvement in relations between*** *the two countries.*
2 [C] a change that you make to something in order to make it better: *home improvements*

im•pro•vise /ˈɪmprəˌvaɪz/ verb **1** [I/T] to do something or to make something without any previous preparation or using only what is available at the time: *I don't have a recipe, but we can improvise.* **2** [I] to perform something that has not been written down or practiced earlier = AD-LIB —**im•prov•i•sa•tion** /ˌɪmprɑvɪˈzeɪʃ(ə)n/ noun [C/U]

im•pu•dent /ˈɪmpjəd(ə)nt/ adj behaving in a rude way that shows no respect
—**im•pu•dence** noun [U], **im•pu•dent•ly** adv

im•pulse /ˈɪmˌpʌls/ noun **1** [C/U] a sudden strong feeling that you must do something **2** [C] *science* an electrical signal

im•pul•sive /ɪmˈpʌlsɪv/ adj tending to do things without thinking about what will happen as a result —**im•pul•sive•ly** adv

im•pu•ni•ty /ɪmˈpjunəti/ noun [U] *formal* freedom from any risk of being punished

im•pure /ɪmˈpjʊr/ adj containing another substance that should not be there

im•pu•ri•ty /ɪmˈpjʊrəti/ noun **1** [C] a substance that is wrongly present in another substance **2** [U] the quality of not being pure

in[1] /ɪn/ grammar word ★★★

> In can be:
> - a **preposition**: *The children are in the back yard.*
> - an **adverb**: *Come in and sit down.*
> - used after the verb "to be": *Is Philip in?*

1 contained within sth inside or within a container, place, or substance: *His passport was in his coat pocket.* ♦ *Have you seen a bag with some tools in it?* ♦ *The books are printed in Hong Kong.* ♦ *a picnic in the park* ♦ *There wasn't a cloud in the sky.*

2 into sth moving, falling, or looking into a place or substance: *The door was open so I just walked in.* ♦ *The guards fired a few shots in the air.* ♦ *I invited her in for a drink.* ♦ *The roof of the cave fell in.* ♦ *Look in the top drawer of my desk.*

3 inside a building at home or at work: *Most evenings we stay in and watch television.* ♦ *I asked to speak to the manager but she wasn't in.*

4 arriving somewhere arriving somewhere, especially your home or place of work: *The ferry won't be in for another hour.* ♦ *What time did you get in last night?*

5 during a particular time during a particular period, month, season, or year, or during a part of the day: *Mel Gibson was born in 1956.* ♦ *In the winter the lake freezes over.* ♦ *Let's meet again in the morning, at around 9:30.* ♦ *Our anniversary is in April.* ♦ *Unemployment has risen by over 15% in the past year.*

6 at the end of a period of time at the end of a period of time in the future: *The exams are in six weeks.* ♦ *I'll be ready in a few minutes.*

7 involved with an activity involved with or relating to a particular type of activity: *Bailey was in the long-distance bicycle race.* ♦ *Her husband works in publishing.* ♦ *There have been amazing advances in medical science.* ♦ *a university degree in economics*

8 for describing a situation or relationship used for describing the state, situation, or relationship that exists for someone or something: *She's 85 and still in good health.* ♦ *Their lives were in danger.* ♦ *Are we all in agreement?*

9 wearing sth used for stating what someone is wearing: *She looked so beautiful in her wedding dress.* ♦ *a man in a tall hat* ♦ *a woman in black* (=wearing black clothes)

10 for saying what changes used for saying what changes, increases, improves, etc.: *There's going to be a change in the weather.* ♦ *the recent rise in oil prices*

11 for talking about the way sth is done using a particular method, style, or language: *We are trying to teach mathematics in a more interesting way.* ♦ *The houses are all built in the traditional style.* ♦ *You have to pay in cash.* ♦ *Go on, say something in French.* ♦ *a drawing done in ink*

12 included as part of sth used for saying which group, book, movie, etc. someone or something is part of: *Kenny's been in the Boy Scouts since he was eight.* ♦ *Who's in the new movie with Brad Pitt?*

13 written or drawn to complete sth written or drawn where something is needed: *Fill in your name and address at the top of the form.* ♦ *I typed in my password and my e-mail address.*

14 referring to an aspect of sth used for saying what aspect of something you are referring to: *The words are similar but there is a difference in meaning.* ♦ *She's so selfish in her attitude toward other people.*

15 for describing how things are arranged arranged in a particular order, shape, or pattern: *We all sat around in a circle.* ♦ *The trees are planted in rows.* ♦ *The names are listed in alphabetical order.*

16 available to buy used for saying that something is available to buy: *They have fresh fish in on Fridays.*

17 affected by weather affected by a particular type of weather: *Have you been waiting outside in the rain?* ♦ *Flags were fluttering in the breeze.*

18 given or received given or sent to someone, or received by someone: *Homework must be handed in tomorrow morning.* ♦ *Have you sent in your application form?* ♦ *Changes to the proposal must be in by April 15th.*

19 fashionable fashionable: *Pale colors are definitely in this summer.*

20 when the ocean is high if the TIDE is in, the ocean has reached its highest level on the land

PHRASES **be in for sth** *informal* to be going to experience something: *It looks as if we're in for some stormy weather.*

be in on sth to be involved in something that is being planned: *I don't know what they agreed to because I wasn't in on the deal.*

in[2] noun **the ins and outs (of sth)** all the details or facts that you need to know in order to deal with a complicated situation or process

IN abbrev Indiana

in•a•bil•i•ty /ˌɪnəˈbɪləti/ noun [U] **inability to do sth** the fact of not being able to do something

in•ac•ces•si•ble /ˌɪnəkˈsesəb(ə)l/ adj difficult or impossible to reach = REMOTE —**in•ac•ces•si•bil•i•ty** /ˌɪnəksesəˈbɪləti/ noun [U]

in•ac•cu•ra•cy /ɪnˈækjərəsi/ noun [C/U] something that is not accurate, or the failure to be accurate

in•ac•cu•rate /ɪnˈækjərət/ adj not accurate or correct —**in•ac•cu•rate•ly** adv

in•ac•tion /ɪnˈækʃ(ə)n/ noun [U] lack of action

in•ac•tive /ɪnˈæktɪv/ adj **1** not taking part in physical activity or exercise **2** not working or operating —**in•ac•tiv•i•ty** /ˌɪnækˈtɪvəti/ noun [U]

in•ad•e•qua•cy /ɪnˈædəkwəsi/ noun **1** [C/U] the failure to be good enough **2** [U] a lack of confidence that makes someone feel that they are not good enough

in•ad•e•quate /ɪnˈædəkwət/ adj ★ not enough, or not good enough: *Some people feel inadequate when they are faced with new responsibilities.* ♦ *The heating system is totally inadequate.* ♦ *The machinery is inadequate for the job.* ♦ **inadequate to do sth** *The roads are inadequate to deal with this amount of traffic.* —**in•ad•e•quate•ly** adv

in•ad•mis•si•ble /ˌɪnədˈmɪsəb(ə)l/ adj *legal* inadmissible evidence cannot be used in a court of law

in•ad•ver•tent•ly /ˌɪnədˈvɜrt(ə)ntli/ adv *formal* without intending to do something —**in•ad•ver•tent** adj

in•ad•vis•a•ble /ˌɪnədˈvaɪzəb(ə)l/ adj not sensible and likely to have bad results

in•al•ien•a•ble /ɪnˈeɪliənəb(ə)l/ adj *formal* an inalienable right cannot be taken away from you

in•ane /ɪˈneɪn/ adj completely stupid =IDIOTIC —**in•ane•ly** adv

in•an•i•mate /ɪnˈænɪmət/ adj not alive

in•ap•pro•pri•ate /ˌɪnəˈproʊpriət/ adj not appropriate in a particular situation: *inappropriate behavior* ♦ *The material is inappropriate for our students.* ♦ **it is inappropriate to do sth** *It would be inappropriate to publish the story.* —**in•ap•pro•pri•ate•ly** adv

in•ar•tic•u•late /ˌɪnɑrˈtɪkjələt/ adj not able to express clearly what you want to say —**in•ar•tic•u•late•ly** adv

in•as•much as /ˌɪnəzˈmʌtʃ æz/ conjunction *formal* used for adding a comment that explains or makes clearer what you have just said

in•au•di•ble /ɪnˈɔdəb(ə)l/ adj difficult or impossible to hear **in•au•di•bly** adv

in•au•gu•ral /ɪˈnɔgjərəl/ adj made or happening at the beginning of something new: *the president's inaugural address*

in•au•gu•rate /ɪˈnɔgjəˌreɪt/ verb [T] **1** to have an official ceremony to celebrate the beginning of something =OPEN **2** *formal* to start or introduce something that is new and important —**in•au•gu•ra•tion** /ɪˌnɔgjəˈreɪʃ(ə)n/ noun [C/U]

in•born /ɪnˈbɔrn/ adj something that is inborn has existed in you since you were born =INNATE

ˈin ˌbox noun [C] *American* a flat open container on your desk where you put documents that you still have to deal with —*picture* → C3

in•box /ˈɪnˌbɑks/ noun [C] *computing* the place on a computer program where e-mails arrive for you

Inc. abbrev Incorporated: used in the U.S. after the name of a large company

in•can•des•cent /ˌɪnkænˈdes(ə)nt/ adj producing light as a result of being made very hot —**in•can•des•cence** noun [U]

in•ca•pa•ble /ɪnˈkeɪpəb(ə)l/ adj **incapable of sth** unable to do something

in•ca•pac•i•tate /ˌɪnkəˈpæsɪˌteɪt/ verb [T] *formal* to make someone or something unable to live or work normally

in•ca•pac•i•ty /ˌɪnkəˈpæsəti/ noun [U] **1** the condition of being unable to live normally because you are sick or weak **2** *formal* a lack of ability

in•car•cer•ate /ɪnˈkɑrsəˌreɪt/ verb [T] *formal* to put someone in prison =IMPRISON —**in•car•cer•a•tion** /ɪnˌkɑrsəˈreɪʃ(ə)n/ noun [U]

in•car•na•tion /ˌɪnkɑrˈneɪʃ(ə)n/ noun **1** [singular] a person or thing that is an extremely strong example of a particular quality **2** [C] according to some religions, one in a series of lives that a person may have

in•cen•di•ar•y /ɪnˈsendiˌeri/ adj **1** designed to cause a fire **2** likely to cause anger or violence =INFLAMMATORY

in•cense /ˈɪnˌsens/ noun [U] a substance that creates a strong but pleasant smell when it is burned

in•censed /ɪnˈsenst/ adj extremely angry

in•cen•tive /ɪnˈsentɪv/ noun [C/U] ★ something that makes you want to do something or to work harder, because you know that you will benefit by doing this: *The high rate of pay is a great incentive.* ♦ **incentive to do sth** *Many farmers have little incentive to work for the environment.*

in•cep•tion /ɪnˈsepʃ(ə)n/ noun [U] *formal* the beginning of something

in•ces•sant /ɪnˈses(ə)nt/ adj continuing for a long time without stopping =CONSTANT —**in•ces•sant•ly** adv

in•cest /ˈɪnˌsest/ noun [U] sexual activity between people who are closely related —**in•ces•tu•ous** /ɪnˈsestʃuəs/ adj

inch¹ /ɪntʃ/ noun [C] ★★ a unit for measuring length that is equal to 2.54 CENTIMETERS: *The insect was about an inch long.*

PHRASES **every inch (of sth)** the whole of an area or place

not give/budge an inch to completely refuse to change your opinion or decision

inch² /ɪntʃ/ verb [I/T] to move somewhere very slowly and gradually, or to make something do this

in•ci•dence /ˈɪnsɪd(ə)ns/ noun [singular] the number of times that something happens

in•ci•dent /ˈɪnsɪdənt/ noun [C] ★★ something that happens that is unusual, violent, or dangerous: *an embarrassing incident* ♦ *The police are appealing for witnesses to the incident.*

in•ci•den•tal /ˌɪnsɪˈdent(ə)l/ adj related to something, but thought to be less important than it

in•ci•den•tal•ly /ˌɪnsɪˈdent(ə)li/ adv used for adding related but less important information to what has just been said, or for suddenly introducing a new subject

in•cin•er•ate /ɪnˈsɪnəˌreɪt/ verb [T] to burn something completely —**in•cin•er•a•tion** /ɪnˌsɪnəˈreɪʃ(ə)n/ noun [U]

in•cin•er•a•tor /ɪnˈsɪnəˌreɪtər/ noun [C] a machine that destroys garbage or other material by burning it

in•cip•i•ent /ɪnˈsɪpiənt/ adj *formal* just beginning to appear or develop

in•ci•sion /ɪnˈsɪʒ(ə)n/ noun [C/U] a cut made into your body during a medical operation

in•ci•sive /ɪnˈsaɪsɪv/ adj expressed in a clear and direct manner —**in•ci•sive•ly** adv

in•cite /ɪnˈsaɪt/ verb [T] to encourage people to be violent or to commit crimes by making them angry or excited

in·cli·na·tion /ˌɪnklɪˈneɪʃ(ə)n/ noun [C/U] **1** a feeling that you want to do something **2** a tendency to behave in a particular way or to have a particular interest

in·cline¹ /ɪnˈklaɪn/ verb [I/T] *formal* to slope in a particular direction, or to make something do this

in·cline² /ˈɪnˌklaɪn/ noun [C] a slope

in·clined /ɪnˈklaɪnd/ adj **1** feeling that you want to do something: *Karen didn't feel inclined to help.* **2** tending to behave in a particular way, or to be interested in a particular thing: *Joe is inclined to be moody.* PHRASE **inclined to think/believe/agree etc.** having an opinion, but not completely sure about it: *I'm inclined to agree with you.*

in·clude /ɪnˈklud/ verb [T] ★★★ **1** to contain, or to have someone or something as a part: *The book includes activities, stories, and practical advice.* **2** to make someone or something be part of a group, set, or collection of things ≠ EXCLUDE: *Please include a photograph of yourself with your application.* ♦ **include sth in sth** *His work was recently included in an exhibition of young painters.*

in·clud·ed /ɪnˈkludəd/ adj **1** contained in something as part of the whole **2** forming part of a group, set, or collection of things

in·clud·ing /ɪnˈkludɪŋ/ preposition ★★★ used for mentioning that someone or something is part of a particular group or amount: *He will make stops in five Midwestern cities, including Chicago and Detroit.* ♦ *The news delighted everyone, including me.*

in·clu·sion /ɪnˈkluʒ(ə)n/ noun **1** [U] the action of including someone or something ≠ EXCLUSION **2** [C] someone or something that is added or included

in·clu·sive /ɪnˈklusɪv/ adj **1** including all costs **2** deliberately aiming to involve all types of people

in·co·her·ent /ˌɪnkoʊˈhɪrənt/ adj **1** badly organized or expressed and therefore difficult to understand **2** unable to express yourself clearly —**in·co·her·ence** noun [U], **in·co·her·ent·ly** adv

in·come /ˈɪnˌkʌm/ noun [C/U] ★★★ money that someone gets from working or from investing money: *What is your approximate annual income?* ♦ *an average household income of $27,000*

ˈincome ˌtax noun [C/U] a tax that is based on your income

in·com·ing /ˈɪnˌkʌmɪŋ/ adj **1** recently elected, or recently chosen for a job or position ≠ OUTGOING **2** coming in, or arriving ≠ OUTGOING

in·com·pa·ra·ble /ɪnˈkɑmpərəb(ə)l/ adj so good that nothing else can be as good —**in·com·pa·ra·bly** adv

in·com·pat·i·ble /ˌɪnkəmˈpætəb(ə)l/ adj not able to work or exist together —**in·com·pat·i·bil·i·ty** /ˌɪnkəmˌpætəˈbɪləti/ noun [U]

in·com·pe·tent /ɪnˈkɑmpət(ə)nt/ adj lacking the ability or skills to do something —**in·com·pe·tence** noun [U], **in·com·pe·tent·ly** adv

in·com·plete /ˌɪnkəmˈplit/ adj not finished, not completely developed, or lacking one or more parts

in·com·pre·hen·si·ble /ɪnˌkɑmprəˈhensəb(ə)l/ adj impossible to understand —**in·com·pre·hen·si·bly** adv

in·con·ceiv·a·ble /ˌɪnkənˈsivəb(ə)l/ adj impossible to believe or imagine: *It is inconceivable that he would lose his job.* —**in·con·ceiv·a·bly** adv

in·con·clu·sive /ˌɪnkənˈklusɪv/ adj not producing a definite result or complete proof of something: *inconclusive evidence* —**in·con·clu·sive·ly** adv

in·con·gru·ous /ɪnˈkɑŋgruəs/ adj strange because of being very different from other things that happen or exist in the same situation —**in·con·gru·i·ty** /ˌɪnkənˈgruəti/ noun [U], **in·con·gru·ous·ly** adv

in·con·se·quen·tial /ɪnˌkɑnsɪˈkwenʃəl/ adj not important = UNIMPORTANT

in·con·sid·er·ate /ˌɪnkənˈsɪdərət/ adj not thinking about other people and their feelings = THOUGHTLESS —**in·con·sid·er·ate·ly** adv

in·con·sis·tent /ˌɪnkənˈsɪstənt/ adj **1** containing parts that do not match each other: *an inconsistent account of what happened* **2** not always behaving in the same way or producing the same results —**in·con·sis·ten·cy** /ˌɪnkənˈsɪstənsi/ noun [C/U]

in·con·spic·u·ous /ˌɪnkənˈspɪkjuəs/ adj not easily seen or noticed ≠ NOTICEABLE —**in·con·spic·u·ous·ly** adv

in·con·ti·nent /ɪnˈkɑntɪnənt/ adj unable to control your BLADDER or BOWELS —**in·con·ti·nence** noun [U]

in·con·ven·ience¹ /ˌɪnkənˈviniəns/ noun [C/U] a problem or situation that causes difficulties or needs extra effort

in·con·ven·ience² /ˌɪnkənˈviniəns/ verb [T] to cause difficulties for someone

in·con·ven·ient /ˌɪnkənˈviniənt/ adj causing difficulties or extra effort —**in·con·ven·ient·ly** adv

in·cor·po·rate /ɪnˈkɔrpəˌreɪt/ verb **1** [T] to add or include something as a part of something else = INCLUDE: *We'll incorporate some of these ideas in the final report.* **2** [I/T] *business* to form a corporation —**in·cor·po·ra·tion** /ɪnˌkɔrpəˈreɪʃ(ə)n/ noun [U]

in·cor·po·rat·ed /ɪnˈkɔrpəˌreɪtɪd/ adj *business* an incorporated company has the legal status of a corporation

in·cor·rect /ˌɪnkəˈrekt/ adj wrong, or not accurate or true ≠ RIGHT —**in·cor·rect·ly** adv

in·cor·ri·gi·ble /ɪnˈkɔrɪdʒəb(ə)l/ adj *often humorous* someone who is incorrigible does bad things or has bad habits and will not change

in·crease¹ /ɪnˈkris/ verb [I/T] ★★★ to become larger in number or amount, or to make something do this: *We have managed to increase the number of patients treated.* ♦ *The population has* ***increased by*** *15 percent.* ♦ *The club has been* ***increasing in*** *popularity.* ♦ *The chances of having twins increase with a mother's age.*

I

Other ways of saying **increase**

- **be on the increase** to be increasing steadily
- **go up** to increase in price or level
- **double** to increase to twice the original amount or level
- **push sth up** to increase the price or level of something
- **mount** to increase steadily
- **rise** to increase
- **rocket** (*informal*) to increase quickly and suddenly
- **soar** to increase quickly to a very high level
- **triple** to increase to three times the original amount or level

in·crease[2] /ˈɪnˌkris/ noun [C/U] ★★★ a rise in the number, amount, or degree of something: *price increases* ♦ *There has been a significant* ***increase in*** *the number of young people who smoke.* ♦ *Workplace stress* ***is on the increase*** (=increasing).

Words often used with **increase**

Adjectives often used with ***increase*** *(noun)*

- **dramatic, huge, large, marked, massive, sharp, significant, substantial** + INCREASE: used about increases that are big

in·creased /ɪnˈkrist/ adj ★★ greater in size, amount, or degree: *an increased demand for qualified doctors* ♦ *The factory was unable to cope with the increased demand for new models.* ♦ *These conditions can lead to* ***an increased risk of*** *lung cancer.*

in·creas·ing·ly /ɪnˈkrisɪŋli/ adv ★★ more and more over a period of time: *Her job has become increasingly difficult.*

in·cred·i·ble /ɪnˈkredəb(ə)l/ adj **1** surprising or difficult to believe: *They all have incredible stories to tell.* **2** great, extreme, or extremely good: *an incredible amount of money*

in·cred·i·bly /ɪnˈkredəbli/ adv **1** extremely: *That's an incredibly important issue.* **2** used for saying that something is difficult to believe: *Incredibly, his wife did not know the truth.*

in·cred·u·lous /ɪnˈkredʒələs/ adj not believing something, or showing that you do not believe something —**in·cre·du·li·ty** /ˌɪnkrəˈduləti/ noun [U], **in·cred·u·lous·ly** adv

in·cre·ment /ˈɪŋkrəmənt/ noun [C] **1** one in a series of increases in amount or value, for example a regular increase in pay **2** the amount by which something increases

in·cre·men·tal /ˌɪŋkrəˈment(ə)l/ adj increasing gradually

in·crim·i·nate /ɪnˈkrɪmɪˌneɪt/ verb [T] to show that someone is guilty of a crime, or to make someone seem guilty of it —**in·crim·i·na·tion** /ɪnˌkrɪmɪˈneɪʃ(ə)n/ noun [U], **in·crim·i·na·to·ry** /ɪnˈkrɪmɪnəˌtɔri/ adj

in·cum·bent[1] /ɪnˈkʌmbənt/ noun [C] *formal* someone who has an elected job at the present time

in·cum·bent[2] /ɪnˈkʌmbənt/ adj *formal* holding an elected job at the present time

PHRASE **it is incumbent on sb to do sth** *formal* it is someone's duty or responsibility to do something

in·cur /ɪnˈkɜr/ verb [T] to experience something that is unpleasant as a result of something that you have done

in·cur·a·ble /ɪnˈkjʊrəb(ə)l/ adj **1** not able to be cured **2** not able to be changed: *an incurable romantic* —**in·cur·a·bly** adv

in·cur·sion /ɪnˈkɜrʒ(ə)n/ noun [C] a sudden attack on, or move into, an area that is controlled by other people

in·debt·ed /ɪnˈdetəd/ adj **1** grateful to someone for their help **2** owing money

in·de·cent /ɪnˈdis(ə)nt/ adj offensive or shocking —**in·de·cen·cy** /ɪnˈdis(ə)nsi/ noun [U], **in·de·cent·ly** adv

in·de·ci·sion /ˌɪndɪˈsɪʒ(ə)n/ noun [U] the feeling that you are unable to make a decision

in·de·ci·sive /ˌɪndɪˈsaɪsɪv/ adj **1** unable to make decisions **2** not producing a clear result or winner: *an indecisive election* —**in·de·ci·sive·ly** adv

in·deed /ɪnˈdid/ adv *formal* ★

1 used for adding a statement that supports and increases the effect of what you have just said: *The service will benefit young people, and, indeed, all Americans.*

2 used for emphasizing that something is true when there is some doubt about it: *Three of the pictures were indeed genuine Rembrandts.*

3 used for emphasis in statements, questions, and short answers: *It is indeed a great tragedy that he died so young.*

in·de·fen·si·ble /ˌɪndɪˈfensəb(ə)l/ adj impossible to defend from criticism —**in·de·fen·si·bly** adv

in·de·fin·a·ble /ˌɪndɪˈfaɪnəb(ə)l/ adj impossible to describe or explain clearly —**in·de·fin·a·bly** adv

in·def·i·nite /ɪnˈdef(ə)nɪt/ adj **1** continuing into the future with no fixed end **2** not clear —**in·def·i·nite·ly** adv

inˌdefinite ˈarticle noun [C] *linguistics* the word "a" or "an" in the English language, or a word in another language that is used in a similar way → DEFINITE ARTICLE

in·del·i·ble /ɪnˈdelɪb(ə)l/ adj impossible to remove or forget —**in·del·i·bly** adv

in·del·i·cate /ɪnˈdelɪkət/ adj rude and likely to offend people —**in·del·i·cate·ly** adv

in·dem·ni·ty /ɪnˈdemnəti/ noun *legal* **1** [U] insurance or protection against an injury or loss **2** [C] a payment that is made to someone who has suffered an injury or loss

in·dent /ɪnˈdent/ verb [T] to start a line of writing or printing farther from the edge of the page than the other lines —**in·dent·ed** /ɪnˈdentəd/ adj

in·den·ta·tion /ˌɪndenˈteɪʃ(ə)n/ noun **1** [C] a mark or hole in the surface of something **2** [C/U] the action of indenting lines of writing, or the space that is made by indenting a line

in·de·pend·ence /ˌɪndɪˈpendəns/ noun [U] ★★

1 freedom from control by another country or organization: *Lithuania was the first of the Soviet republics to* ***declare its independence.***

2 the ability to make decisions and live your life free from the control or influence of other people: *Employment gave young women a measure of independence.*

in•de•pend•ent[1] /ˌɪndɪˈpendənt/ adj ★★★
1 not influenced by anyone else, and therefore fair: *an independent investigation* ♦ *Seek **independent legal advice** before entering into an agreement.*
2 not controlled by another country or organization: *an independent nation*
3 not depending on other people ≠ DEPENDENT: *Michelle is young, independent, and confident.*
4 not connected with or joined to anything else: *The equipment has its own independent power supply.*
—**in•de•pend•ent•ly** adv

> **Words often used with independent**
> *Adverbs often used with **independent** (adj, sense 2)*
> ■ **completely, entirely, genuinely, totally, truly** + INDEPENDENT: used for saying that someone or something is very independent

in•de•pend•ent[2] /ˌɪndɪˈpendənt/ noun [C] a politician who does not belong to any political party
ˈin-ˌdepth adj thorough and detailed: *an in-depth study*
in•de•scrib•a•ble /ˌɪndɪˈskraɪbəb(ə)l/ adj something that is indescribable is impossible to describe because it is so extreme —**in•de•scrib•a•bly** adv
in•de•struc•ti•ble /ˌɪndɪˈstrʌktəb(ə)l/ adj impossible, or very difficult, to destroy
in•de•ter•mi•nate /ˌɪndɪˈtɜrmɪnət/ adj not known, or not clearly established
in•dex[1] /ˈɪnˌdeks/ (plural **in•dex•es** or **in•di•ces** /ˈɪndɪˌsiz/) noun [C] ★★
1 an alphabetical list of subjects or names at the back of a book that shows on which page they are mentioned: *Look up the term you want in the index.*
2 *business* a number that shows the price, value, or level of something that is compared with something else: *the Dow Jones index* ♦ *a wage/price index*
3 **index of sth** a measure of how something is changing: *The test provides parents with a reliable index of their child's progress.*
in•dex[2] /ˈɪnˌdeks/ verb [T] to arrange information in an alphabetical list
ˈindex ˌcard noun [C] one of a set of small cards on which you write information
ˈindex ˌfinger noun [C] the finger next to your thumb —*picture* → C14
In•di•an /ˈɪndiən/ adj relating to NATIVE AMERICANS or their culture. Some people think that this word is offensive and prefer to use the word Native American. —**In•di•an** noun [C]
in•di•cate /ˈɪndɪˌkeɪt/ verb [T] ★★★
1 to be a sign or symbol of something: *Each pin on the map indicates a district office.*
2 to show that something will happen, is true, or exists: *Test results will **indicate whether** the treatment was successful.* ♦ **+(that)** *A survey indicated that 89 percent of people recycle paper.*
3 to express an intention, opinion, or wish in an indirect way: *Both sides indicated a willingness to solve the problem.* ♦ **+(that)** *She indicated that she would like the job.*
4 to point toward someone or something: *"Here it is," she said, indicating the house.*
in•di•ca•tion /ˌɪndɪˈkeɪʃ(ə)n/ noun [C/U] a sign that something will happen, is true, or exists
in•dic•a•tive /ɪnˈdɪkətɪv/ adj *formal* showing that something will happen, is true, or exists: *These latest figures are indicative of a slowing economy.*
in•dic•a•tive, the /ɪnˈdɪkətɪv/ noun [singular] *linguistics* a form of a verb that is used for making statements or asking questions
in•di•ca•tor /ˈɪndɪˌkeɪtər/ noun [C] something that shows you what condition something is in: *economic indicators*
indices a plural of **index**[1]
in•dict /ɪnˈdaɪt/ verb [T] *legal* to officially accuse someone of committing a serious crime =CHARGE
in•dict•ment /ɪnˈdaɪtmənt/ noun **1** [C] **indictment of sth** something that shows how bad or wrong something is **2** [C/U] *legal* an official statement accusing someone of committing a serious crime =CHARGE
in•dif•fer•ent /ɪnˈdɪfrənt/ adj lacking interest or sympathy —**in•dif•fer•ence** /ɪnˈdɪfrəns/ noun [U], **in•dif•fer•ent•ly** adv
in•dig•e•nous /ɪnˈdɪdʒənəs/ adj **1** indigenous people lived in a place for a very long time before other people came to live there **2** indigenous plants and animals belong to a region because they developed there
in•di•ges•tion /ˌɪndɪˈdʒestʃ(ə)n/ noun [U] pain that you get in your stomach when your body has difficulty in DIGESTING the food that you have eaten
in•dig•nant /ɪnˈdɪgnənt/ adj angry, because a situation is unfair —**in•dig•nant•ly** adv
in•dig•na•tion /ˌɪndɪgˈneɪʃ(ə)n/ noun [U] anger about an unfair situation
in•dig•ni•ty /ɪnˈdɪgnəti/ noun [C/U] a situation that makes you feel embarrassed or ashamed
in•di•rect /ˌɪndɪˈrekt, ˌɪndaɪˈrekt/ adj ★
1 not using the shortest or simplest way: *We took an indirect route through the mountains.* ♦ ***an indirect approach** to the problem*
2 not directly connected with something but done or obtained in some other way: *an indirect criticism of the president* ♦ *indirect evidence of ancient building methods*
3 not communicated in a direct way: *He made only indirect references to his opponent.*
—**in•di•rect•ly** adv
ˌindirect ˈdiscourse noun [U] *linguistics* the words that you use for reporting what someone else has said, for example "She said that we must leave" =REPORTED SPEECH
ˌindirect ˈobject noun [C] *linguistics* in a sentence with two objects, the person or thing that receives something through the action of the verb. For example "me" is the indirect object in "He gave me the book."
ˌindirect ˈquestion noun [C] *linguistics* the words that you use to report a question that someone else has asked, for example "She asked me where I was going"
ˌindirect ˈspeech noun [U] *linguistics* INDIRECT DISCOURSE
in•dis•creet /ˌɪndɪˈskrit/ adj telling or showing

something that should be private —**in•dis•creet•ly** adv

in•dis•cre•tion /ˌɪndɪˈskreʃ(ə)n/ noun [U] the behavior of someone who fails to keep something private

in•dis•crim•i•nate /ˌɪndɪˈskrɪmɪnət/ adj done in a careless way that causes extra harm or damage —**in•dis•crim•i•nate•ly** adv

in•dis•pen•sa•ble /ˌɪndɪˈspensəb(ə)l/ adj something that is indispensable is so useful or important that you must have it =ESSENTIAL

in•dis•put•a•ble /ˌɪndɪˈspjutəb(ə)l/ adj a fact that is indisputable is so certain that nobody can say that it is not true =UNDENIABLE —**in•dis•put•a•bly** adv

in•dis•tinct /ˌɪndɪˈstɪŋkt/ adj difficult to see or hear clearly =UNCLEAR ≠ CLEAR —**in•dis•tinct•ly** adv

in•dis•tin•guish•a•ble /ˌɪndɪˈstɪŋgwɪʃəb(ə)l/ adj people or things that are indistinguishable are so similar that you cannot see any difference between them

in•di•vid•u•al[1] /ˌɪndɪˈvɪdʒuəl/ adj ★★★
1 considered separately from other people or things: *individual pieces of furniture*
2 intended for one person only or for a particular person ≠ COLLECTIVE: *individual rights/freedom/liberty* ♦ *Choose a vacation to match your individual needs.*
3 unusual or different in an interesting way: *a very individual style*

in•di•vid•u•al[2] /ˌɪndɪˈvɪdʒuəl/ noun [C] ★★★ a person: *We believe in **the freedom of the individual**.* ♦ *The colleges were usually built with money from **private individuals*** (=people who represent only themselves, not organizations).

in•di•vid•u•al•ism /ˌɪndɪˈvɪdʒuəˌlɪzəm/ noun [U] the behavior of someone who does things in their own way and is not afraid to be different from others —**in•di•vid•u•al•ist** noun [C], **in•di•vid•u•al•ist•ic** /ˌɪndɪˌvɪdʒuəˈlɪstɪk/ adj

in•di•vid•u•al•i•ty /ˌɪndɪvɪdʒuˈæləti/ noun [U] the qualities that make someone or something different from all others

in•di•vid•u•al•ly /ˌɪndɪˈvɪdʒuəli/ adv as a separate person or thing, not as part of a group

in•doc•tri•nate /ɪnˈdɑktrɪˌneɪt/ verb [T] to teach someone a set of beliefs so thoroughly that they do not accept any other ideas =BRAINWASH —**in•doc•tri•na•tion** /ɪnˌdɑktrɪˈneɪʃ(ə)n/ noun [U]

in•door /ˈɪndɔr/ adj done or used inside a building ≠ OUTDOOR: *an indoor swimming pool* ♦ *indoor plants*

in•doors /ɪnˈdɔrz/ adv in or into a building ≠ OUTDOORS: *I stayed indoors all day.*

in•duce /ɪnˈdus/ verb [T] to cause a mental or physical condition

in•duce•ment /ɪnˈdusmənt/ noun [C/U] something that someone offers you in order to persuade you to do something

in•duct /ɪnˈdʌkt/ verb [T] *American formal* to officially accept someone into a group or organization

in•duc•tion /ɪnˈdʌkʃ(ə)n/ noun [C/U] the process of formally making someone part of a group or organization

in•dulge /ɪnˈdʌldʒ/ verb **1** [I/T] to allow yourself to have something enjoyable: *The new job gave him the chance to indulge his passion for music.* **2** [I] **indulge in sth** to do something that people do not approve of: *He had indulged in affairs with several women.* **3** [T] to allow someone to do what they want when you should be more strict

in•dul•gence /ɪnˈdʌldʒəns/ noun **1** [U] the act of doing something that is not good for you: *indulgence in alcohol* **2** [C] something enjoyable that you do for pleasure **3** [U] kind behavior in a situation where strict behavior is needed

in•dul•gent /ɪnˈdʌldʒənt/ adj allowing someone to have what they want when you should be more strict: *indulgent parents* —**in•dul•gent•ly** adv

in•dus•tri•al /ɪnˈdʌstriəl/ adj ★★★
1 relating to industries or to the people who work in industries: *industrial development/production*
2 an industrial region or country has a lot of industries in it
—**in•dus•tri•al•ly** adv

in•dus•tri•al•ist /ɪnˈdʌstriəlɪst/ noun [C] someone who owns a large industrial company

in•dus•tri•al•ized /ɪnˈdʌstriəˌlaɪzd/ adj an industrialized country or society has a lot of industries

inˌdustrial ˈpark noun [C] an area where there are many factories

inˌdustrial reˈlations noun [plural] the relationship between the workers and managers in an industry or company

in•dus•tri•ous /ɪnˈdʌstriəs/ adj *formal* someone who is industrious works very hard

in•dus•try /ˈɪndəstri/ noun ★★★
1 [U] the production of goods in factories: *The town was severely hit by the decline in industry.* ♦ *industry experts/leaders/officials*
2 [C] all the businesses involved in producing a particular type of goods or services: *the oil/fishing/electronics industry*
3 [C] an activity that has become very popular or successful and earns money for businesses: *the fitness industry*
→ COTTAGE INDUSTRY, GROWTH INDUSTRY

in•e•bri•at•ed /ɪˈnibriˌeɪtəd/ adj *formal* drunk

in•ed•i•ble /ɪnˈedəb(ə)l/ adj too unpleasant or poisonous to eat

in•ef•fec•tive /ˌɪnɪˈfektɪv/ adj something that is ineffective does not work correctly or does not do what you want it to do

in•ef•fec•tu•al /ˌɪnɪˈfektʃuəl/ adj someone who is ineffectual does not have the ability or confidence to do something well

in•ef•fi•cient /ˌɪnɪˈfɪʃ(ə)nt/ adj people or methods that are inefficient do not work well because they waste time, energy, materials, or money —**in•ef•fi•cien•cy** /ˌɪnɪˈfɪʃ(ə)nsi/ noun [C/U], **in•ef•fi•cient•ly** adv

in•el•i•gi•ble /ɪnˈelɪdʒəb(ə)l/ adj not officially allowed to do something

in•ept /ɪˈnept/ adj someone who is inept does something badly ≠ CAPABLE —**in•ep•ti•tude** /ɪˈneptɪˌtud/ noun [U], **in•ept•ly** adv

in•e•qual•i•ty /ˌɪnɪˈkwɑləti/ noun [C/U] an

unfair situation in which some people have more opportunities, power, or money than other people ≠ EQUALITY

in·ert /ɪˈnɜrt/ adj **1** not moving **2** *science* an inert substance does not produce a chemical reaction when it is mixed with other substances

in·er·tia /ɪˈnɜrʃə/ noun [U] **1** a feeling of not wanting to do anything **2** a situation in which no progress is made **3** *science* the force that makes an object stay in the same position

in·es·cap·a·ble /ˌɪnɪˈskeɪpəb(ə)l/ adj impossible to avoid or ignore

in·ev·i·ta·ble /ɪnˈevɪtəb(ə)l/ adj ★
1 impossible to avoid or prevent: *War now seems almost inevitable.* ♦ **it is inevitable that** *It is perhaps inevitable that new technology will create unemployment.*
2 the inevitable something that is certain to happen: *You must face the inevitable and try to deal with it.*
—**in·ev·i·ta·bil·i·ty** /ɪnˌevɪtəˈbɪləti/ noun [U], **in·ev·i·ta·bly** adv

in·ex·cus·a·ble /ˌɪnɪkˈskjuzəb(ə)l/ adj inexcusable behavior is so bad that you cannot forgive the person who behaved like that = UNFORGIVABLE

in·ex·haust·i·ble /ˌɪnɪgˈzɔstəb(ə)l/ adj never completely used up, and therefore always available

in·ex·pen·sive /ˌɪnɪkˈspensɪv/ adj something that is inexpensive does not cost much money = CHEAP —**in·ex·pen·sive·ly** adv

in·ex·pe·ri·enced /ˌɪnɪkˈspɪriənst/ adj lacking experience —**in·ex·pe·ri·ence** noun [U]

in·ex·pli·ca·ble /ˌɪnɪkˈsplɪkəb(ə)l/ adj impossible to explain —**in·ex·pli·ca·bly** adv

in·ex·tri·ca·bly /ˌɪnɪkˈstrɪkəbli/ adv *formal* used for emphasizing that you cannot separate two things

in·fa·mous /ˈɪnfəməs/ adj well known for something bad = NOTORIOUS: *an infamous criminal*

in·fan·cy /ˈɪnfənsi/ noun [U] the time when you are a very young child
PHRASE **in its infancy** something that is in its infancy has only just started to exist

in·fant /ˈɪnfənt/ noun [C] a very young child —*picture* → CHILD

in·fan·tile /ˈɪnfənˌtaɪl/ adj infantile behavior annoys you because it is very silly

in·fan·try /ˈɪnfəntri/ noun [U] soldiers who fight on foot, not on horses or in TANKS or other vehicles

in·fat·u·at·ed /ɪnˈfætʃuˌeɪtəd/ adj in love with someone in a way that seems silly

in·fat·u·a·tion /ɪnˌfætʃuˈeɪʃ(ə)n/ noun [C/U] a strong feeling of love that seems silly

in·fect /ɪnˈfekt/ verb [T] **1** to make someone get a disease: *Thousands of people have been infected with the disease.* **2** if a computer VIRUS infects a computer, it enters the computer and causes problems

in·fect·ed /ɪnˈfektəd/ adj **1** someone who is infected has a disease **2** containing bacteria or other substances that cause disease

in·fec·tion /ɪnˈfekʃ(ə)n/ noun ★★
1 [U] the process of becoming infected with a disease: *There are ways to reduce your risk of infection.*
2 [C] a disease that is caused by bacteria or by a VIRUS: *a throat infection*

in·fec·tious /ɪnˈfekʃəs/ adj **1** an infectious disease can spread from one person to another **2** behavior that is infectious makes other people behave in the same way: *an infectious laugh*

in·fer /ɪnˈfɜr/ verb [T] *formal* to form an opinion about something that is based on information that you already have → IMPLY

in·fer·ence /ˈɪnfərəns/ noun [C] an opinion about something that is based on information that you already have: *It's impossible to make inferences from such a small sample.*

in·fe·ri·or[1] /ɪnˈfɪriər/ adj not good, or not as good as someone or something else ≠ SUPERIOR: *This design is inferior to the one the German company proposed.*
—**in·fe·ri·or·i·ty** /ɪnˌfɪriˈɔrəti/ noun [U]

in·fe·ri·or[2] /ɪnˈfɪriər/ noun [C] someone who has a lower status than someone else

inferiˈority ˌcomplex noun [C] a strong feeling that you are not as good or important as other people

in·fer·no /ɪnˈfɜrnoʊ/ noun [C] a large and dangerous fire

in·fer·tile /ɪnˈfɜrt(ə)l/ adj not physically able to have children —**in·fer·til·i·ty** /ˌɪnfərˈtɪləti/ noun [U]

in·fest /ɪnˈfest/ verb [T] if a place is infested with animals or insects, there are so many of them that they might cause damage or disease

in·fi·del·i·ty /ˌɪnfɪˈdeləti/ noun [C/U] a situation in which someone has sex with someone other than their husband, wife, or partner

in·field /ˈɪnˌfild/ noun [C] in baseball, the central part of the field —*picture* → C15

in·fight·ing /ˈɪnˌfaɪtɪŋ/ noun [U] disagreements about power among the members of a group

in·fil·trate /ˈɪnfɪlˌtreɪt, ɪnˈfɪlˌtreɪt/ verb [I/T] to join an organization in order to secretly get information for its enemies —**in·fil·tra·tion** /ˌɪnfɪlˈtreɪʃ(ə)n/ noun [U]

in·fi·nite /ˈɪnfɪnɪt/ adj **1** very great, and seeming to have no limit: *a teacher with infinite patience* ♦ *The possibilities are infinite.* **2** with no physical end or limit: *Space is infinite.*

in·fi·nite·ly /ˈɪnfɪnɪtli/ adv very, or very much: *I'm infinitely grateful for your help.*

in·fin·i·tive /ɪnˈfɪnɪtɪv/ noun [C] *linguistics* the basic form of a verb. In English, it often has the word "to" in front of it.

in·fin·i·ty /ɪnˈfɪnəti/ noun [U] **1** a space, time, or distance that has no limit **2** *technical* a number that is larger than any that exists

in·flame /ɪnˈfleɪm/ verb [T] to make a situation worse by making people more angry or excited

in·flamed /ɪnˈfleɪmd/ adj swollen and painful because of an infection or injury

in·flam·ma·ble /ɪnˈflæməb(ə)l/ adj something that is inflammable burns easily ≠ NONFLAMMABLE → FLAMMABLE

in·flam·ma·tion /ˌɪnfləˈmeɪʃ(ə)n/ noun [C/U] an area on your body that is swollen and painful because of an infection or injury

in•flam•ma•to•ry /ɪnˈflæməˌtɔri/ adj likely to make people feel angry: *inflammatory remarks*

in•flat•a•ble /ɪnˈfleɪtəb(ə)l/ adj an inflatable object must be filled with air or gas before you can use it

in•flate /ɪnˈfleɪt/ verb **1** [I/T] to fill something with air or gas, or to become full of air or gas = BLOW STH UP ≠ DEFLATE **2** [T] to make a number or price higher than it should be —**in•flat•ed** adj

in•fla•tion /ɪnˈfleɪʃ(ə)n/ noun [U] ★★
1 an economic process in which prices increase so that money becomes less valuable: ***Inflation has risen** again this month.* ♦ *countries with **high inflation*** ♦ ***The rate of inflation** is 3.2%.*
2 the process of filling something with air or gas

in•fla•tion•ar•y /ɪnˈfleɪʃ(ə)nˌeri/ adj likely to cause an increase in prices

in•flec•tion /ɪnˈflekʃ(ə)n/ noun **1** [U] the way in which the sound of your voice becomes higher and lower when you speak **2** [C/U] *linguistics* a change in the basic form of a word that gives information about the tense, number, etc.

in•flex•i•ble /ɪnˈfleksəb(ə)l/ adj **1** stiff and not able to bend ≠ FLEXIBLE **2** not willing to change your ideas or decisions: *an inflexible attitude/system*

in•flict /ɪnˈflɪkt/ verb [T] to cause something unpleasant to happen: *the environmental damage we are inflicting on the Earth*

in•flu•ence¹ /ˈɪnfluəns/ noun ★★★
1 [C/U] the effect that a person or thing has on someone or something: *He couldn't hope to **exert** any real **influence** in the new department.* ♦ *Teachers have considerable **influence over** what is taught in the classroom.*
2 [C] a person or thing that has an effect on someone or something

PHRASE **under the influence** drunk

in•flu•ence² /ˈɪnfluəns/ verb [T] ★★★ to affect someone or something: *What factors **influenced** your **decision** to take the job?* ♦ *Research has shown that the weather can **influence** people's **behavior**.*

> **Words often used with influence**
> *Adverbs often used with **influence** (verb)*
> ■ INFLUENCE + **greatly, heavily, profoundly, significantly, strongly**: used when the influence is great
> *Nouns often used with **influence** (verb)*
> ■ INFLUENCE + **behavior, choice, decision, outcome, policy**: influence something that someone does

in•flu•en•tial /ˌɪnfluˈenʃəl/ adj able to influence the way that other people think or behave

in•flux /ˈɪnˌflʌks/ noun [C] a large number of people or things coming to a place

in•fo /ˈɪnfoʊ/ noun [U] *informal* INFORMATION

in•form /ɪnˈfɔrm/ verb [T] ★★★ to officially tell someone about something: *The President has been **fully informed** of the recent developments.* ♦ **inform sb of/about sth** *Please inform us of any changes in your circumstances.* ♦ **inform sb (that)** *Parents were informed that the school was closing early.*

in•for•mal /ɪnˈfɔrm(ə)l/ adj ★
1 relaxed, friendly, and not official: *The hotel has an informal atmosphere.* ♦ *They cooperate with other groups **on an informal basis**.*
2 suitable for relaxed friendly situations: *informal clothes/language*
—**in•for•mal•i•ty** /ˌɪnfɔrˈmæləti/ noun [U], **in•for•mal•ly** adv

in•form•ant /ɪnˈfɔrmənt/ noun [C] someone who secretly gives information about someone to the police

in•for•ma•tion /ˌɪnfərˈmeɪʃ(ə)n/ noun [U] ★★★
1 knowledge or facts about someone or something: *We're not allowed to give you any **information about** our client's medical records.* ♦ *We were able to **get the information** we needed from the Internet.* ♦ *If you require any **further information**, please call back at any time.* ♦ *He gave us a very interesting **piece of information**.*
2 *American* DIRECTORY ASSISTANCE

> **Information** is never used in the plural and cannot be used with **an**: *I've just discovered **an** interesting **piece of information*** (NOT an interesting information) about the company. ♦ *Do you have **any information** about local attractions?* ♦ *I found **some information** on the Net about cheap flights to Egypt.*

inforˌmation techˈnology noun [U] the use of computers and electronic systems for storing information

in•form•a•tive /ɪnˈfɔrmətɪv/ adj giving a lot of useful information ≠ UNINFORMATIVE

in•formed /ɪnˈfɔrmd/ adj **1** based on good knowledge ≠ UNINFORMED: *an informed choice/decision* **2** someone who is informed has a lot of knowledge about something ≠ UNINFORMED

in•form•er /ɪnˈfɔrmər/ noun [C] an INFORMANT

in•frac•tion /ɪnˈfrækʃ(ə)n/ noun [C/U] *formal* a situation in which someone breaks a law or a rule

in•fra•red /ˌɪnfrəˈred/ adj using a type of light that cannot be seen: *infrared sensors*

in•fra•struc•ture /ˈɪnfrəˌstrʌktʃər/ noun [C] the set of systems in a country or organization that affect how well it operates, for example telephone and transportation systems

in•fre•quent /ɪnˈfrikwənt/ adj something that is infrequent does not happen very often = RARE —**in•fre•quent•ly** adv

in•fringe /ɪnˈfrɪndʒ/ verb **1** [T] to break a law or a rule **2** [I/T] to limit someone's legal rights or freedom —**in•fringe•ment** noun [C]

in•fu•ri•ate /ɪnˈfjʊriˌeɪt/ verb [T] to make someone extremely angry

in•fu•ri•at•ing /ɪnˈfjʊriˌeɪtɪŋ/ adj extremely annoying

in•fuse /ɪnˈfjuz/ verb [T] to give someone or something a particular quality: *Her paintings are infused with a natural strength.*

in•fu•sion /ɪnˈfjuʒ(ə)n/ noun [C/U] **1** a drink, medicine, or beauty treatment made by putting something such as leaves in hot water **2** the addition of something such as money or a particular quality

in•gen•ious /ɪnˈdʒiniəs/ adj **1** using new and clever ideas **2** good at inventing things or solving problems —**in•gen•ious•ly** adv

in•ge•nu•i•ty /ˌɪndʒəˈnuəti/ noun [U] the ability to solve problems in new and clever ways

in•gest /ɪnˈdʒest/ verb [T] *technical* to eat or drink something

in•grained /ɪnˈgreɪnd/ adj an ingrained attitude or habit has existed for a long time and cannot easily be changed

in•gra•ti•ate /ɪnˈgreɪʃiˌeɪt/ verb **ingratiate yourself with sb** *showing disapproval* to try to get someone's approval by doing things that will please them

in•gra•ti•at•ing /ɪnˈgreɪʃiˌeɪtɪŋ/ adj *showing disapproval* done in an attempt to get someone's approval

in•grat•i•tude /ɪnˈgrætəˌtud/ noun [U] the fact that someone is not grateful for something when you think they should be grateful

in•gre•di•ent /ɪnˈgridiənt/ noun [C] **1** one of the foods or liquids that you use in making a particular meal: *Mix all the ingredients together carefully.* **2** one of the things that give something its character or make it effective: *Good communication is an essential ingredient of good management.*

in•hab•it /ɪnˈhæbɪt/ verb [T] to live in a particular place

in•hab•i•tant /ɪnˈhæbɪt(ə)nt/ noun [C] a person or animal that lives in a particular place

in•hab•it•ed /ɪnˈhæbɪtəd/ adj a place that is inhabited has people living in it ≠ UNINHABITED

in•hale /ɪnˈheɪl/ verb [I/T] to breathe air, smoke, or other substances into your lungs =BREATHE (STH) IN ≠ EXHALE —**in•ha•la•tion** /ˌɪnhəˈleɪʃ(ə)n/ noun [C/U]

in•her•ent /ɪnˈhɪrənt, ɪnˈherənt/ adj an inherent quality is a basic feature that gives something its character —**in•her•ent•ly** adv

in•her•it /ɪnˈherɪt/ verb [T] **1** to receive property or money from someone when they die **2** to be born with the same appearance or character as one of your parents: *The boys inherited Derek's good looks.* **3** to have something because it was left by someone who was in your situation before you: *These are problems we inherited from the previous government.*

in•her•i•tance /ɪnˈherɪt(ə)ns/ noun [C] property or money that you receive from someone when they die

in•hib•it /ɪnˈhɪbɪt/ verb [T] **1** to prevent something from developing in a normal way **2** to make someone feel too embarrassed to behave in a normal way

in•hib•it•ed /ɪnˈhɪbɪtəd/ adj too embarrassed to do something ≠ UNINHIBITED

in•hi•bi•tion /ˌɪnhɪˈbɪʃ(ə)n/ noun [C/U] a feeling of being too embarrassed to do what you want to do

in•hos•pi•ta•ble /ˌɪnhɑˈspɪtəb(ə)l, ɪnˈhɑspɪtəb(ə)l/ adj **1** an inhospitable place is unpleasant to live in **2** unfriendly to guests

in•hu•man /ɪnˈhjumən/ adj someone who is inhuman does not care when other people are suffering

in•hu•mane /ˌɪnhjuˈmeɪn/ adj inhumane treatment is very cruel ≠ HUMANE —**in•hu•mane•ly** adv

in•hu•man•i•ty /ˌɪnhjuˈmænəti/ noun [C/U] extremely cruel behavior

in•i•tial[1] /ɪˈnɪʃ(ə)l/ adj ★★ happening at the beginning of a process, or when you first see or hear about something: ***the initial** stages of the project* ♦ *My **initial reaction** was to panic.*

in•i•tial[2] /ɪˈnɪʃ(ə)l/ noun [C] the first letter of a name

in•i•tial[3] /ɪˈnɪʃ(ə)l/ (present participle **in•i•tial•ing** or **in•i•tial•ling**; past tense and past participle **in•i•tialed** or **in•i•tialled**) verb [T] to write your initials on something

in•i•tial•ly /ɪˈnɪʃ(ə)li/ adv ★★ at the beginning =ORIGINALLY: *Initially she worked for us as an intern.* ♦ *I had initially thought I wanted to write novels.*

in•i•ti•ate /ɪˈnɪʃiˌeɪt/ verb [T] **1** *formal* to make something start **2** to make someone a member of a group, often with a special ceremony **3** to teach someone about an activity that they have never done before —**in•i•ti•a•tion** /ɪˌnɪʃiˈeɪʃ(ə)n/ noun [singular/U]

in•i•tia•tive /ɪˈnɪʃətɪv/ noun ★★
1 [U] the ability to take action in an independent way: *Employees are encouraged to **use their initiative** if faced with a problem.* ♦ *He developed the plan **on his own initiative**.*
2 [C] *American legal* a process by which people can suggest a new law by signing a PETITION
3 the initiative [singular] the opportunity to take action before other people do: *She would have to **take the initiative** in order to improve their relationship.*
4 [C] an important action that is intended to solve a problem: *a number of initiatives designed to address the problem of child poverty*

in•ject /ɪnˈdʒekt/ verb [T] **1** to put a drug into your body through your skin using a SYRINGE **2** to add something new to a situation: *Young designers are injecting new life into the fashion industry.*

inject

in•jec•tion /ɪnˈdʒekʃ(ə)n/ noun [C/U] ★
1 a drug that is injected into your body, or the process of injecting it into your body: *vaccines that are given by injection* ♦ **give sb an injection** *Did the doctor give you a measles injection?*
2 the act of providing more money for something: ***an injection of cash***

in•junc•tion /ɪnˈdʒʌŋkʃ(ə)n/ noun [C] *legal* an official order from a court that prevents someone from doing something

in•jure /ˈɪndʒər/ verb [T] ★ to hurt someone: *Nine people died and 54 were injured in the accident.* ♦ *No one was **seriously injured**.*

in•jured /ˈɪndʒərd/ adj hurt in an accident or attack: *The injured man was taken to a hospital.*

in•ju•ry /ˈɪndʒəri/ noun [C/U] ★★★ physical harm: *an eye/leg injury* ♦ *All the passengers in the vehicle **escaped injury**.* ♦ *Both drivers sustained* (=received) ***multiple injuries**.*

> Words often used with **injury**
>
> *Adjectives often used with **injury***
> - **serious, severe** + INJURY: used when someone is injured a lot
> - **minor, slight** + INJURY: used when the injury is not very bad

I

in•jus•tice /ɪnˈdʒʌstɪs/ noun [C/U] an unfair way of treating someone
PHRASE **do sb an injustice** to treat someone in an unfair way, for example by saying something bad about them that is not true

ink /ɪŋk/ noun [U] a black or colored liquid that is used for writing, drawing, or printing

ˈink-jet ˌprinter noun [C] a type of printer for computers that prints using very small drops of ink

in•kling /ˈɪŋklɪŋ/ noun **have an inkling** to think that something might be happening because of a small piece of information that you have

in•land¹ /ˈɪnˌlænd, ˈɪnlənd/ adj not near a coast

in•land² /ˈɪnˌlænd/ adv in a direction away from the coast

ˈin-ˌlaws noun [plural] the parents or other relatives of your husband or wife

in•let /ˈɪnlət/ noun [C] a long narrow area of water that continues into the land from a lake or ocean

ˌin-line ˈskating noun [U] the activity of moving on boots called **in-line skates** that each have a single row of narrow wheels on them

in-line skates

in•mate /ˈɪnˌmeɪt/ noun [C] someone who is kept in a prison or similar institution

inn /ɪn/ noun [C] a small hotel or bar

in•nate /ɪˈneɪt/ adj an innate quality or ability is one that you have always had =INHERENT —**in•nate•ly** adv

in•ner /ˈɪnər/ adj ★
1 inside or farther toward the center of something ≠ OUTER: *your inner ear*
2 close to the center of a city: *inner London*
3 private, or personal: *inner feelings*

ˌinner ˈcircle noun [C] a small group of people who have a lot of power within a larger group

ˌinner ˈcity noun [C] an area near the center of a large city where a lot of social problems exist —**ˈinner-ˌcity** adj

in•ner•most /ˈɪnərˌmoʊst/ adj **1** your innermost thoughts and feelings are very personal and private **2** closest to the center of something ≠ OUTERMOST

in•no•cence /ˈɪnəs(ə)ns/ noun [U] **1** the state of not being guilty of a crime or anything bad: *This new evidence would hopefully prove his innocence.* **2** lack of experience in life that makes you trust people too much

in•no•cent /ˈɪnəs(ə)nt/ adj ★
1 not guilty of a crime or anything bad ≠ GUILTY: *Under the law, everyone is considered innocent until proven guilty.* ♦ *the **innocent victims** of terrorism* ♦ *She was completely **innocent of** any crime.*
2 not intended to harm or upset anyone: *an innocent remark/mistake*
3 someone who is innocent does not have much experience of life and tends to trust people too much
—**in•no•cent•ly** adv

in•noc•u•ous /ɪˈnɑkjuəs/ adj not likely to offend or upset anyone

in•no•va•tion /ˌɪnəˈveɪʃ(ə)n/ noun [C/U] a new idea or piece of equipment, or the use of new ideas or equipment

in•no•va•tive /ˈɪnəˌveɪtɪv/ adj new and advanced

in•nu•en•do /ˌɪnjuˈendoʊ/ (plural **innuendoes** or **innuendos**) noun [C/U] a remark that deliberately suggests something about sex but does not say it directly, or the use of remarks like this

in•nu•mer•a•ble /ɪˈnumərəb(ə)l/ adj *formal* too many to be counted: *There are innumerable examples of his generous nature.*

in•of•fen•sive /ˌɪnəˈfensɪv/ adj unlikely to offend anyone

in•or•di•nate /ɪnˈɔrdɪnət/ adj *formal* much more than you expect or want —**in•or•di•nate•ly** adv

in•pa•tient /ˈɪnˌpeɪʃ(ə)nt/ noun [C] someone who stays and sleeps in a hospital while they are getting treatment → OUTPATIENT

in•put¹ /ˈɪnˌpʊt/ noun [U] **1** comments and suggestions that you make as part of a discussion **2** information that you put into a computer ≠ OUTPUT **3** electrical power that is put into a machine

in•put² /ˈɪnˌpʊt/ (present participle **in•put•ting**; past tense and past participle **in•put**) verb [T] to put information into a computer

in•quest /ˈɪŋˌkwest/ noun [C] an official attempt by a court to find the cause of someone's death

in•quire /ɪnˈkwaɪr/ verb [I/T] to ask someone for information about something: *I am writing to inquire whether you have any jobs available.* —**in•quir•er** noun [C]
PHRASAL VERB **inˈquire ˌinto sth** to try to find out the truth about something: *The committee inquired into complaints made by several prisoners.*

in•quir•ing /ɪnˈkwaɪrɪŋ/ adj **1** eager to learn

about new things: *an inquiring mind* **2** showing that you want more information about something: *an inquiring look/expression*

in·quir·y /ɪnˈkwaɪri, ˈɪŋkwəri/ noun ★★
1 [C] a question that is intended to get information about someone or something: *There have already been over 300 inquiries from people interested.*
2 [C/U] a process of trying to find out more information about something: *The public is demanding **an official inquiry into** the incident.*

in·quis·i·tive /ɪnˈkwɪzətɪv/ adj eager to learn about a lot of different things, and asking a lot of questions = CURIOUS: *an inquisitive reporter* —**in·quis·i·tive·ly** adv

in·roads /ˈɪnˌroʊdz/ noun **make inroads into/in/on sth** to take or use a large part of something: *European cars have started to make inroads into the Japanese market.*

in·sane /ɪnˈseɪn/ adj **1** *informal* very stupid or crazy: *You'd be totally insane to see him again.* **2** suffering from very severe mental illness —**in·sane·ly** adv

in·san·i·ty /ɪnˈsænəti/ noun [U] **1** very severe mental illness **2** *informal* very stupid or crazy behavior

in·sa·tia·ble /ɪnˈseɪʃəb(ə)l/ adj always wanting more and never feeling satisfied —**in·sa·tia·bly** adv

in·scribe /ɪnˈskraɪb/ verb [T] to write or cut words on or in something: *a gold watch inscribed with her initials*

in·scrip·tion /ɪnˈskrɪpʃ(ə)n/ noun [C] a piece of writing that is written on or cut into something

in·scru·ta·ble /ɪnˈskrutəb(ə)l/ adj making it impossible for other people to understand what you are thinking or feeling: *Anna's face remained inscrutable and unsmiling.*

in·seam /ˈɪnˌsim/ noun [C] *American* the length of your leg measured on the inside from the top to the foot

in·sect /ˈɪnˌsekt/ noun [C] ★ a small animal that has six legs and often has wings

in·sec·ti·cide /ɪnˈsektɪˌsaɪd/ noun [C] a chemical for killing insects

in·se·cure /ˌɪnsəˈkjʊr/ adj **1** not confident about yourself: *She's always been very insecure about the way she looks.* **2** not safe or protected: *In this economy, all our jobs are insecure.* —**in·se·cu·ri·ty** /ˌɪnsəˈkjʊrəti/ noun [C/U]

in·sem·i·na·tion /ɪnˌsemɪˈneɪʃ(ə)n/ noun [U] the process of putting SPERM into a woman or female animal to make her pregnant

in·sen·si·tive /ɪnˈsensətɪv/ adj not noticing or caring about other people's feelings and not worrying that the things you say or do may upset them —**in·sen·si·tive·ly** adv, **in·sen·si·tiv·i·ty** /ɪnˌsensəˈtɪvəti/ noun [U]

in·sep·a·ra·ble /ɪnˈsepər(ə)b(ə)l/ adj **1** people who are inseparable spend all their time together **2** things that are inseparable cannot exist or be considered separately: *His personal morality was inseparable from his religious beliefs.* —**in·sep·a·ra·bly** adv

in·sert[1] /ɪnˈsɜrt/ verb [T] to put something into something else: **insert sth into/in sth** *Insert the plug into the earphone socket.* —**in·ser·tion** /ɪnˈsɜrʃ(ə)n/ noun [C/U]

insert

in·sert[2] /ˈɪnˌsɜrt/ noun [C] something that is put into something else: *advertising inserts in the Sunday newspaper*

in·set /ˈɪnˌset/ noun [C] **1** a small picture or map inside a larger one **2** something that is put in something else: *a gold ring with diamond insets*

in·side[1] /ɪnˈsaɪd/ grammar word ★★★

> **Inside** can be:
> - a **preposition**: *What's inside the envelope?* **Inside of** is sometimes used instead of **inside**: *The beetles live inside of the tree.*
> - an **adverb**: *I opened the box and looked inside.*
> - an **adjective**: *the inside pages of a newspaper*

1 within a container or place, or in the inner part of something ≠ OUTSIDE: *I always keep important papers locked inside my desk.* ♦ *There were lights on inside and I could hear voices.* ♦ *houses without running water or an inside toilet* ♦ *She was standing just inside the door.* ♦ *The melon was still green inside.* ♦ *What's **inside of** the box?*
2 into a place or container ≠ OUTSIDE: *As I walked past the door, I glanced inside.* ♦ *You're not allowed to go inside the museum without paying.* ♦ *What did he put inside of the trunk?* ♦ *She reached inside her handbag and pulled out an envelope.*
3 within an organization or group ≠ OUTSIDE: *There is a battle being fought inside the Reform Party.* ♦ *The rumors are coming from inside the company.*
4 only known by people who belong to a particular organization or group: *The thieves clearly had inside information.*

in·side[2] /ɪnˈsaɪd/ noun [C] the inner part of something: *I had never seen the inside of a prison before.*

ˌinside ˈout adv with the inside part facing out: *Your sweater is on inside out.*
PHRASE **know sb/sth inside out** to know someone or something very well

in·sid·er /ɪnˈsaɪdər/ noun [C] someone within an organization or group who knows about all the things happening in it

inˌsider ˈtrading noun [U] the crime of buying or selling STOCK in a company using information that is available only to people working for that company

in·sid·i·ous /ɪnˈsɪdiəs/ adj something that is insidious is dangerous because it seems to be harmless or not important but in fact causes harm or damage: *the insidious effects of gossip* —**in·sid·i·ous·ly** adv

in·sight /ˈɪnˌsaɪt/ noun [C/U] the ability to notice and understand a lot about people or situations, or a chance to do this:

Children can sometimes show remarkable insight.

in·sig·ni·a /ɪnˈsɪgniə/ (plural **in·sig·ni·a**) noun [C] a mark or sign that shows someone's rank or status, or shows what organization they belong to

in·sig·nif·i·cant /ˌɪnsɪgˈnɪfɪkənt/ adj not large or important enough to be worth considering: *insignificant details* —**in·sig·nif·i·cance** /ˌɪnsɪgˈnɪfɪkəns/ noun [U], **in·sig·nif·i·cant·ly** adv

in·sin·cere /ˌɪnsɪnˈsɪr/ adj not expressing your feelings or opinions honestly: *an insincere smile* —**in·sin·cere·ly** adv, **in·sin·cer·i·ty** /ˌɪnsɪnˈserəti/ noun [U]

in·sin·u·ate /ɪnˈsɪnjuˌeɪt/ verb [T] to say something unpleasant in an indirect way: *He even went as far as insinuating that Roger was a liar.* —**in·sin·u·a·tion** /ɪnˌsɪnjuˈeɪʃ(ə)n/ noun [C/U]

I

in·sip·id /ɪnˈsɪpɪd/ adj *formal* boring, dull, or pale, with no interesting features

in·sist /ɪnˈsɪst/ verb [I/T] ★★
1 to say very firmly that something must happen or be done: *You must see a doctor immediately – I insist.* ♦ *Some companies* ***insist on*** *staff undergoing regular medical checks.* ♦ **+(that)** *She insisted that we stay at her house instead of a hotel.*
2 to keep saying very firmly that something is true: *He has* ***insisted on*** *his innocence from the beginning.* ♦ **+(that)** *The school insists that it is doing everything it can to cooperate.*
PHRASAL VERB **inˈsist ˌon sth** or **inˈsist uˌpon sth 1** to say that you must have something: *She insists upon fresh fruit every morning.* **2 insist on/upon doing sth** to keep doing something that annoys people: *Why do you insist on leaving your dirty clothes all over the floor?*

in·sis·tence /ɪnˈsɪstəns/ noun [U] a very firm statement that something must happen or that something is true: *Despite his insistence that he wasn't involved, most people think he's dishonest.*

in·sis·tent /ɪnˈsɪstənt/ adj saying very firmly that something must happen or that something is true: *John was insistent that we shouldn't tell anyone else about our plans.* —**in·sis·tent·ly** adv

in·so·far as /ˌɪnsoʊˈfɑr æz/ conjunction *formal* to the degree that something happens or is true: *She cites other scholars' work only insofar as it supports her own theories.*

in·so·lent /ˈɪnsələnt/ adj rude, especially when you should be showing respect ≠ POLITE —**in·so·lence** /ˈɪnsələns/ noun [U], **in·so·lent·ly** adv

in·sol·u·ble /ɪnˈsɑljəb(ə)l/ adj **1** an insoluble substance does not DISSOLVE in liquid **2** impossible to solve

in·sol·vent /ɪnˈsɑlvənt/ adj *formal* not having enough money to pay what you owe = BANKRUPT —**in·sol·ven·cy** /ɪnˈsɑlvənsi/ noun [U]

in·som·ni·a /ɪnˈsɑmniə/ noun [U] a medical condition in which you have difficulty sleeping —**in·som·ni·ac** /ɪnˈsɑmniˌæk/ noun [C]

in·spect /ɪnˈspekt/ verb [T] **1** to check something by looking at it carefully = EXAMINE: *Engineers will inspect the site later today.* ♦ *Make sure you inspect the goods carefully as soon as you receive them.* ♦ **inspect sth for sth** *The young plants are regularly inspected for disease and insects.* **2** to officially visit a place and check to see that everything is as it should be: *Restaurants are inspected regularly by the health department.*

in·spec·tion /ɪnˈspekʃ(ə)n/ noun [C/U] ★
1 an official process of checking that things are as they should be: *All countries must allow international* ***inspection of*** *their nuclear weapons sites.*
2 an action of looking at something carefully to check it: *The documents are* ***available for public inspection.***

in·spec·tor /ɪnˈspektər/ noun [C] **1** an official whose job is to check that things are in the correct condition, or that people are doing what they should: *health inspectors* **2** a senior police officer

in·spi·ra·tion /ˌɪnspɪˈreɪʃ(ə)n/ noun [C/U] someone or something that gives you the enthusiasm and new ideas to create something, or a feeling of enthusiasm like this: *Her short story was the original inspiration for the movie.*
PHRASE **be an inspiration to sb** to be so successful, or to deal with a difficult situation so well, that other people admire you and want to be like you: *She has been an inspiration to other young athletes from a similar background.*
—**in·spi·ra·tion·al** adj

in·spire /ɪnˈspaɪr/ verb [T] **1** to give someone the enthusiasm or idea to do or create something: *The sea inspired many of the artist's later paintings.* **2** to give people a particular feeling: *His athletic ability inspires awe in everyone who sees him in action.* ♦ *Her resignation will do little to inspire confidence in a company that is already struggling.* —**in·spir·ing** adj

in·spired /ɪnˈspaɪrd/ adj very special, or very impressive ≠ UNINSPIRED: *an inspired performance*

in·sta·bil·i·ty /ˌɪnstəˈbɪləti/ noun [U] a situation or someone's mental state that keeps changing, so that you do not know what might happen: *This policy would lead to greater instability in the region.*

in·stall /ɪnˈstɔl/ verb [T] ★ to put a piece of equipment somewhere or a piece of software into a computer and make it ready for use: *Have you installed a smoke alarm in your office?* ♦ *It's important to install a virus checker.* —**in·stal·la·tion** /ˌɪnstəˈleɪʃ(ə)n/ noun [C/U]

in·stall·ment /ɪnˈstɔlmənt/ noun [C] **1** one of several payments that an amount of money you owe is divided into: *We paid for the television in twelve monthly installments.* **2** one of several parts of a story or article that are published at different times in a magazine or newspaper

in·stance /ˈɪnstəns/ noun [C] ★★★ an example of something happening: *I have not found* ***a single instance*** *where someone was actually denied their right to vote.* ♦ *The* *study discusses **instances of** water pollution in this neighborhood.*

PHRASE **for instance** for example: *They intend to provide information, via the Internet for instance.*

in·stant¹ /ˈɪnstənt/ adj **1** immediate: *We can't promise instant solutions, but we can promise to listen.* ♦ *They took an instant liking to each other.* **2** instant food or drink can be prepared very quickly, usually by adding hot water: *instant coffee/soup/pudding* —**in·stant·ly** adv

in·stant² /ˈɪnstənt/ noun [C] a moment: *It took only an instant for him to react.*

PHRASE **this instant** *spoken* immediately: *Pick up that garbage this instant!*

in·stan·ta·ne·ous /ˌɪnstənˈteɪniəs/ adj immediate —**in·stan·ta·ne·ous·ly** adv

ˌ**instant ˈmessaging** noun [U] *computing* the activity of communicating with someone directly over the Internet and replying to their messages as soon as they arrive

ˌ**instant ˈreplay** noun [C] *American* an action in a sports event on television that is immediately shown again

in·stead /ɪnˈsted/ adv ★★★ used for saying that one person, thing, or action replaces another: *If you don't have olive oil, you can use sunflower oil instead.* ♦ *Tickets will cost only $5, **instead of** the usual $8.* ♦ **instead of doing sth** *Can't we deal with this now instead of waiting until tomorrow?*

in·step /ˈɪnˌstep/ noun [C] the raised part in the middle of your foot —*picture* → C14

in·sti·gate /ˈɪnstɪˌgeɪt/ verb [T] *formal* to make something start —**in·sti·ga·tion** /ˌɪnstɪˈgeɪʃ(ə)n/ noun [U], **in·sti·ga·tor** noun [C]

in·still /ɪnˈstɪl/ verb [T] to make someone have a particular feeling or belief: *His parents had instilled a lasting love of music in him.*

in·stinct /ˈɪnstɪŋkt/ noun [C/U] ★

1 a natural tendency to behave in a particular way: *the instinct of ducklings to follow their mother* ♦ *the **basic instinct for** survival*

2 a natural ability to know what to do in a particular situation: *Instinct told me that it would be unwise to return home.* ♦ ***My first instinct** was to turn and run.* ♦ *It's always best to **trust your instincts**.*

in·stinc·tive /ɪnˈstɪŋktɪv/ adj done without thinking, because of a natural tendency or ability: *His reaction was purely instinctive.* —**in·stinc·tive·ly** adv

in·sti·tute¹ /ˈɪnstɪˌtut/ noun [C] an organization that does a particular type of research or educational work

in·sti·tute² /ˈɪnstɪˌtut/ verb [T] *formal* to start something such as a system or an official process: *The company has instituted new security measures for its staff.*

in·sti·tu·tion /ˌɪnstɪˈtuʃ(ə)n/ noun [C] ★★★

1 a large organization such as a bank, hospital, university, or prison: *a financial/educational/charitable institution* ♦ *an **institution of** higher education*

2 a hospital or other building where people are taken care of for a long time, for example if they are disabled or mentally ill

3 an important tradition on which society is based: *the **institution of** marriage* —**in·sti·tu·tion·al** adj

in·struct /ɪnˈstrʌkt/ verb [T] *formal* **1** to tell someone to do something, especially officially: *He instructed his men to collect information about troop movements.* **2** to teach someone a particular subject or skill: *All children are instructed in the use of the library.*

in·struc·tion /ɪnˈstrʌkʃ(ə)n/ noun ★★★

1 [C] a statement of something that must be done, or an explanation of how to do or use something: ***Step-by-step instructions for** assembling the workbench are included.* ♦ *I tried to **follow** her **instructions**, but I got confused.* ♦ **instructions to do sth** *The players were given strict instructions not to leave the hotel.*

2 [U] the teaching of a particular subject or skill: *golf/ski/math instruction*

> **Words often used with instruction**
>
> *Verbs often used with **instruction** (sense 1)*
>
> - **disobey, disregard, ignore** + INSTRUCTION: not do what someone tells you to do
> - **carry out, follow, obey** + INSTRUCTION: do what someone tells you to do
> - **give, issue, provide** + INSTRUCTION: tell someone what to do

in·struc·tive /ɪnˈstrʌktɪv/ adj giving useful information

in·struc·tor /ɪnˈstrʌktər/ noun [C] someone whose job is to teach a particular subject, skill, or sport

in·stru·ment /ˈɪnstrəmənt/ noun [C] ★★★

1 a tool that is used in science, medicine, or technology: ***scientific instruments** such as microscopes*

2 a MUSICAL INSTRUMENT, for example a piano or a guitar: *Do you **play an instrument**?*

3 a piece of equipment that measures something such as position, speed, or temperature: *Your compass and clock are the most essential instruments in sailing.*

in·stru·men·tal /ˌɪnstrəˈment(ə)l/ adj **1** involved in an important way in making something happen: *The general was instrumental in helping both sides to reach a compromise.* **2** instrumental music is played by instruments only instead of being sung

in·sub·or·di·nate /ˌɪnsəˈbɔrd(ə)nət/ adj *formal* not obeying or not showing respect to someone who has authority over you —**in·sub·or·di·na·tion** /ˌɪnsəbɔrd(ə)nˈeɪʃ(ə)n/ noun [U]

in·sub·stan·tial /ˌɪnsəbˈstænʃəl/ adj *formal* not very large or strong: *insubstantial evidence*

in·suf·fi·cient /ˌɪnsəˈfɪʃ(ə)nt/ adj not enough: *There are insufficient funds in your account.* —**in·suf·fi·cient·ly** adv

in·su·lar /ˈɪnsələr, ˈɪnsjələr/ adj not interested in meeting new people or learning new things —**in·su·lar·i·ty** /ˌɪnsəˈlerəti, ˌɪnsjəˈlerəti/ noun [U]

in·su·late /ˈɪnsəˌleɪt, ˈɪnsjəˌleɪt/ verb [T] **1** to cover something in order to prevent heat, cold, noise, or electricity from passing through it **2** to protect someone from unpleasant knowledge or harmful experiences

in•su•la•tion /ˌɪnsəˈleɪʃ(ə)n, ˌɪnsjəˈleɪʃ(ə)n/ noun [U] material that is used for preventing heat, cold, noise, or electricity from passing through something

in•su•lin /ˈɪnsəlɪn/ noun [U] a substance that is produced in your body that controls the level of sugar in your blood

in•sult¹ /ˈɪnˌsʌlt/ noun [C] **1** an offensive remark **2** something that seems to show a lack of respect for someone or something: *This exam is an insult to my students' intelligence.*

PHRASE **add insult to injury** to do something that makes a bad situation even worse

in•sult² /ɪnˈsʌlt/ verb [T] ★ to say or do something that is offensive: *She has no right to insult us like that.* ♦ *You'll insult the cook if you don't at least taste the meal.* —**in•sult•ing** adj

in•sur•ance /ɪnˈʃʊrəns/ noun ★★★

1 [U] an arrangement in which you regularly pay a company an amount of money so that they will give you money if something that you own is damaged, lost, or stolen, or if you die or are sick or injured: *health/life/car insurance* ♦ *an insurance company/policy/agent* ♦ *Do you* ***have insurance for*** *the house yet?*

2 [singular/U] a situation or action that is intended to prevent something bad from happening or affecting you: *The hostages were being held as* ***insurance against*** *further bombing raids.*

in•sure /ɪnˈʃʊr/ verb **1** [T] to buy or provide insurance for someone or something: *They've insured the painting for over half a million dollars.* **2** another spelling of **ensure**

in•sur•mount•a•ble /ˌɪnsərˈmaʊntəb(ə)l/ adj *formal* impossible to deal with successfully

in•sur•rec•tion /ˌɪnsəˈrekʃ(ə)n/ noun [C/U] an attempt by a large group of people to take control of their country by force

in•tact /ɪnˈtækt/ adj not harmed, damaged, or lacking any parts

in•take /ˈɪnˌteɪk/ noun **1** [singular] the amount of something that you eat or drink: *You should reduce your intake of salt.*

2 [singular/U] the number of people who are accepted by an institution such as a school, university, or company at one time

in•tan•gi•ble /ɪnˈtændʒəb(ə)l/ adj not able to be touched or measured, and difficult to describe or explain: *She has that intangible quality that a player must possess to be a champion.*

in•te•gral /ˈɪntəgrəl, ɪnˈtegrəl/ adj forming an essential part of something and needed to make it complete: *Home visits by our trained technicians are an integral part of the service.* —**in•te•gral•ly** adv

in•te•grate /ˈɪntəˌgreɪt/ verb **1** [T] to change the rules of a place, institution, or organization so that people of all races can enter it: *Laws were finally passed integrating all the restaurants.* **2** [I/T] to become a full member of a society or group and be involved completely in its activities, or to help someone to do this **3** [T] to connect or combine two or more things so that together they form an effective unit or system: *We provide resources that can be integrated into the national teaching program.*

in•te•grat•ed /ˈɪntəˌgreɪtəd/ adj **1** combining things, people, or ideas of different types in one effective unit, group, or system: *a modern integrated approach to learning* **2** able to be used or shared by people of all races: *integrated schools*

in•te•gra•tion /ˌɪntəˈgreɪʃ(ə)n/ noun [U] **1** the process of allowing people of all races to use a place, institution, or organization =DESEGREGATION: *the integration of schools* **2** the process of combining with other things in a single larger unit or system **3** the process of becoming a full member of a society or group, and becoming involved completely in its activities: *a strategy to ease their integration into the community*

in•teg•ri•ty /ɪnˈtegrəti/ noun [U] the quality of always behaving honestly and according to moral principles

in•tel•lect /ˈɪnt(ə)lˌekt/ noun [U] the ability to think in an intelligent way and to understand difficult or complicated ideas and subjects: *a lawyer of great intellect*

in•tel•lec•tu•al¹ /ˌɪnt(ə)lˈektʃuəl/ adj **1** well educated and interested in serious subjects at an advanced level **2** relating to the ability to think in an intelligent way and to understand things —**in•tel•lec•tu•al•ly** adv

in•tel•lec•tu•al² /ˌɪnt(ə)lˈektʃuəl/ noun [C] someone who is well educated and interested in serious subjects at an advanced level

ˌintellectual ˈproperty noun [U] *legal* something that someone has created or invented and that no one else is legally allowed to make, copy, or sell

in•tel•li•gence /ɪnˈtelɪdʒəns/ noun [U] ★★

1 the ability to understand and think about things, and to gain and use knowledge: *Maria had spirit and intelligence as well as beauty.* ♦ *a person of* ***average intelligence***

2 information that is collected about the secret plans and activities of a foreign government, enemy, etc.: *military intelligence*

in•tel•li•gent /ɪnˈtelɪdʒənt/ adj ★★ good at thinking, understanding, and learning =SMART ≠ UNINTELLIGENT: *He was* ***highly intelligent****, but disliked studying.* —**in•tel•li•gent•ly** adv

Other ways of saying intelligent

- **bright** intelligent and quick to understand things
- **brilliant** extremely intelligent
- **quick** able to understand things quickly and react to them quickly
- **sharp** quick to notice and understand things
- **smart** able to understand and learn things quickly
- **wise** able to use your knowledge and experience to judge what is right or true

in•tel•li•gi•ble /ɪnˈtelɪdʒəb(ə)l/ adj clear or simple enough to understand ≠ UNINTELLIGIBLE

in•tend /ɪnˈtend/ verb [T] ★★★

1 to have a plan in your mind to do something: **intend to do sth** *What do you*

intend to do about this? ♦ **intend for sb/sth to do sth** *I never intended for it to turn out like that.* ♦ **intend sb sth** *She felt certain that he intended her no harm.*
2 to want something to have a particular meaning: **intend sth as sth** *Perhaps it was intended as a joke.* ♦ **intend sth by sth** *She wondered what he intended by that statement.*
PHRASE **be intended for** to be made, done, or said for a particular purpose or person: *The book is intended for use in the classroom.* ♦ *The meat was never intended for human consumption.*

Word family: **intend**	
Words in the same family as **intend**	
■ **intended** *adj*	■ **unintended** *adj*
■ **intentional** *adj*	■ **unintentional** *adj*
■ **intention** *n*	■ **intent** *n*

in•tense /ɪnˈtens/ adj ★
1 very great, or extreme: *The pain was intense.* ♦ *the intense heat of the midday sun* ♦ *He's been under* ***intense pressure.***
2 involving or done with a lot of effort, energy, attention, etc.: *This type of work requires intense concentration.*
3 feeling and showing emotions in a very strong way: *an intense person/personality/nature*
—**in•tense•ly** adv, **in•ten•si•ty** noun [U]

in•ten•si•fy /ɪnˈtensɪˌfaɪ/ verb [I/T] if something intensifies, or if you intensify it, it becomes greater, stronger, or more extreme —**in•ten•si•fi•ca•tion** /ɪnˌtensɪfɪˈkeɪʃ(ə)n/ noun [U]

in•ten•sive /ɪnˈtensɪv/ adj involving a lot of effort, energy, learning, or attention in a short period of time: *three weeks of intensive negotiations* —**in•ten•sive•ly** adv

inˌtensive ˈcare noun [U] the department of a hospital for people who are very sick or badly injured and must be watched closely by doctors and nurses

in•tent¹ /ɪnˈtent/ noun [singular/U] *formal* the intention to do something: *Congress has declared its intent to reform the welfare system.*

in•tent² /ɪnˈtent/ adj **1** concentrating hard on something **2** determined to do something: *The people of the area are intent on keeping their club open.* —**in•tent•ly** adv

in•ten•tion /ɪnˈtenʃ(ə)n/ noun [C/U] ★★★ a plan in your mind to do something: *We* ***have no intention of*** *giving up.* ♦ ***I had every intention of*** *calling* (=I really intended to call) *her this morning, but I didn't get a chance.* ♦ *No one goes to college* ***with the intention of*** *failing.* ♦ **intention to do sth** *It wasn't my intention to upset you.*

in•ten•tion•al /ɪnˈtenʃən(ə)l/ adj deliberate ≠ UNINTENTIONAL: *I'm sorry I hurt you, but it wasn't intentional.* —**in•ten•tion•al•ly** adv

in•ter•act /ˌɪntərˈækt/ verb [I] **1** if people interact, they communicate with and react to each other: *In large classes, children feel that they cannot interact with the teacher.* **2** if things interact, they affect or change each other in some way —**in•ter•ac•tion** /ˌɪntərˈækʃ(ə)n/ noun [C/U]

in•ter•ac•tive /ˌɪntərˈæktɪv/ adj **1** an interactive computer program, video, etc. reacts to the information and instructions that you give it **2** involving people communicating with each other and reacting to each other —**in•ter•ac•tive•ly** adv

in•ter•cept /ˌɪntərˈsept/ verb [T] to stop, catch, or take control of someone or something before they can get to the place they are going to: *Townsend intercepted a pass and ran half the length of the field to score.* —**in•ter•cep•tion** /ˌɪntərˈsepʃ(ə)n/ noun [U]

in•ter•change•a•ble /ˌɪntərˈtʃeɪndʒəb(ə)l/ adj things that are interchangeable can be put or used in place of each other with the same effect —**in•ter•change•a•bly** adv

in•ter•com /ˈɪntərˌkɑm/ noun [C] a system that allows people in different parts of a building, aircraft, or ship to speak to each other

in•ter•con•ti•nen•tal /ˌɪntərkɑntɪˈnent(ə)l/ adj between CONTINENTS: *intercontinental flights*

in•ter•course /ˈɪntərˌkɔrs/ noun [U] SEXUAL INTERCOURSE

in•ter•de•pend•ent /ˌɪntərdɪˈpendənt/ adj things that are interdependent are related to each other in such a close way that each one needs the others in order to exist —**in•ter•de•pend•ence** noun [U]

in•ter•est¹ /ˈɪntrəst/ noun ★★★

1 a need to know	5 advantage/benefit
2 activity you enjoy	6 right to own part of sth
3 money paid/received	+ PHRASE
4 quality attracting you	

1 [singular/U] a feeling of wanting to know about or take part in something: ***an interest in*** *politics* ♦ *Apparently several buyers have* ***expressed an interest in*** *the deal.* ♦ *People are* ***losing interest*** *in the election.*
2 [C] an activity that you enjoy doing when you are not working: *Tell us about your interests and hobbies.*
3 [U] the money that a bank charges or pays you when you borrow or save money: *an increase in the interest charged on personal loans* ♦ *low* ***interest rates*** ♦ *We were required to repay the loan* ***with interest.***
4 [U] the quality that something has that makes you notice it and want to know about it or take part in it: *The city has lots of museums and* ***places of interest.*** ♦ *publications that may* ***be of interest to*** *the self-employed* → HUMAN INTEREST
5 [C/U] an advantage or benefit to someone or something: *Publication of the documents is not* ***in the public interest.*** ♦ ***It's in their own interest*** *to cooperate.* ♦ *The president doesn't believe the plan is* ***in the best interest*** *of the company.*
6 [C] *business* a legal right to own part of a business or property
PHRASE **in the interest(s) of sth** in order to preserve, develop, or achieve something: *It is vital that we reform the system in the interest of fairness to everyone.*

in•ter•est² /ˈɪntrəst/ verb [T] to make someone want to know about or take part in something: *Oceanography has always interested me.*

in•ter•est•ed /ˈɪntrəstəd/ adj ★★★
1 wanting to know about or take part in

something ≠ UNINTERESTED: *Joe's always been **interested in** sports.*
2 willing or eager to do something: *We're going to the movies. Are you interested* (=would you like to come too)? ♦ *Is anyone **interested in** a quick walk before lunch?*

Words often used with interested

*Adverbs often used with **interested** (sense 1)*

- **deeply, extremely, genuinely, seriously** + INTERESTED: used for saying that someone is very interested

- **Interested** describes how you feel: *I am interested in art.* ♦ *She didn't look very interested.*
- **Interesting** describes things or situations that make you feel interested: *I find history very interesting.* ♦ *It was a really interesting lecture.*

in·ter·est·ing /ˈɪntrəstɪŋ/ adj ★★★ making you want to pay attention or know more: *an interesting topic* ♦ *She's a very interesting speaker.* ♦ *It would be interesting to hear their views on this problem.* ♦ **it is interesting that/how** *It's interesting that she suddenly changed her attitude.* —**in·ter·est·ing·ly** adv

ˈinterest ˌrate noun [C] the percentage that a bank charges or pays you in interest when you borrow money from it or keep money in an account

in·ter·face /ˈɪntərˌfeɪs/ noun [C] *computing* a point in a computer system where information passes from one part of the system to another, or from the computer to the person using it

in·ter·fere /ˌɪntərˈfɪr/ verb [I] to deliberately become involved in a situation, although you have no right to do this: *I don't want to interfere, but maybe you'd better listen to me.* ♦ *I don't want your mother interfering in our affairs.*
PHRASAL VERB **interˈfere with sth** to prevent something from happening or developing in the correct way: *Mom says I can get a job if it doesn't interfere with my homework.*

in·ter·fer·ence /ˌɪntərˈfɪrəns/ noun [U] **1** the process of deliberately becoming involved in a situation, although you have no right to do this: *They expressed resentment at outside interference in their domestic affairs.* **2** radio signals that make the sound or picture of a radio or television program difficult to hear or see clearly, or the noise caused by this **3** in sports such as football, the act of touching or standing in front of an opponent in order to prevent them from moving

in·ter·im[1] /ˈɪntərɪm/ adj intended to last or to perform an activity only until someone or something permanent or final is available: *an interim government/president/report*

in·ter·im[2] /ˈɪntərɪm/ noun **in the interim** during the time between one thing happening and another

in·te·ri·or /ɪnˈtɪriər/ noun **1** [C] the inside part of something ≠ EXTERIOR: *The car has a surprisingly spacious interior.* **2 the interior** [singular] the inner part of a country or region

inˌterior deˈsigner or **inˌterior ˈdecorator** noun [C] someone whose job is to choose the colors of the walls and carpets and the style of the furniture for the inside of a room or building —**inˌterior deˈsign** noun [U]

in·ter·ject /ˌɪntərˈdʒekt/ verb [I/T] *formal* to say something suddenly that interrupts the person who is speaking

in·ter·jec·tion /ˌɪntərˈdʒekʃ(ə)n/ noun [C] *linguistics* a word or phrase that you use in speech for expressing a strong emotion such as surprise or anger. "Oh" and "ouch" are interjections. = EXCLAMATION

in·ter·lude /ˈɪntərˌlud/ noun [C] a short period of time between two longer periods

in·ter·me·di·ar·y /ˌɪntərˈmidiˌeri/ noun [C] someone who talks to each of the people or groups that are involved in something in order to help them to agree about it

in·ter·me·di·ate /ˌɪntərˈmidiət/ adj **1** at an academic level below advanced: *an intermediate English course* **2** in between two stages, places, levels, times, etc.: *The cells have a series of intermediate stages before they develop fully.* —**in·ter·me·di·ate·ly** adv

in·ter·mi·na·ble /ɪnˈtɜrmɪnəb(ə)l/ adj continuing for a long time in a boring or annoying way: *an interminable speech/wait/meeting* —**in·ter·mi·na·bly** adv

in·ter·mis·sion /ˌɪntərˈmɪʃ(ə)n/ noun [C] a short break in the middle of a play, movie, concert, etc.

in·ter·mit·tent /ˌɪntərˈmɪt(ə)nt/ adj happening sometimes but not regularly or often: *a dull day with intermittent rain* —**in·ter·mit·tent·ly** adv

in·tern[1] /ˈɪnˌtɜrn/ noun [C] *American* **1** someone who has recently obtained a qualification as a doctor and is continuing their training by working in a hospital **2** a student who works in a job in order to get experience —**in·tern·ship** /ɪnˈtɜrnʃɪp/ noun [C/U]

in·tern[2] /ɪnˈtɜrn/ verb [T] to put someone in a prison without officially accusing them of a crime, especially for political reasons —**in·tern·ment** noun [U]

in·ter·nal /ɪnˈtɜrn(ə)l/ adj ★★
1 existing or happening within a country, organization, or system ≠ EXTERNAL: *an internal memo* ♦ *They were opposed to foreign involvement in their **internal affairs**.*
2 existing or happening inside your body or your mind: *internal bleeding/injuries/organs* ♦ *an internal struggle*
3 existing or happening inside an object or building ≠ EXTERNAL: *internal walls* —**in·ter·nal·ly** adv

in·ter·na·tion·al /ˌɪntərˈnæʃən(ə)l/ adj ★★★ involving several countries, or existing between countries: *international trade/relations/diplomacy* ♦ *an international flight* ♦ ***International aid organizations** are appealing for donations from western governments.* —**in·ter·na·tion·al·ly** adv

ˌinternational comˈmunity, the noun [singular] political leaders and important organizations from all parts of the world

In·ter·net, the /ˈɪntərˌnet/ noun [singular] ★★★ a computer system that allows people in different parts of the world to exchange information: *Do you have access to the Internet?* ♦ *The group posted the names of the men* ***on the Internet.*** → WORLD WIDE WEB

in•ter•nist /ɪnˈtɜrnɪst/ noun [C] *American* a doctor who treats illnesses without SURGERY

in•ter•per•son•al /ˌɪntərˈpɜrsən(ə)l/ adj involving relationships between people

in•ter•play /ˈɪntərˌpleɪ/ noun [U] the way that people or things affect each other or react when they are put together: *the interplay of emotions*

in•ter•pret /ɪnˈtɜrprət/ verb ★★
1 [I/T] to translate what someone is saying into another language: *I speak Spanish. Would you like me to interpret for you?*
2 [T] to understand an action, situation, etc. in a particular way: *This move can be interpreted in two ways.* ♦ *Low voter turnout can be* ***interpreted as*** *a sign of satisfaction with the current government.*
3 [T] to explain the meaning of something: *We'll need some help to* ***interpret*** *all this* ***data.***

in•ter•pre•ta•tion /ɪnˌtɜrprəˈteɪʃ(ə)n/ noun [C/U] ★★
1 an explanation of the meaning or importance of something: *The Catholic* ***interpretation of*** *the Bible is slightly different.*
2 a way of performing a piece of music, a part in a play, etc. that shows how you understand it and feel about it: *He was best known for his* ***interpretation of*** *English folk music.*

in•ter•pret•er /ɪnˈtɜrprətər/ noun [C] someone whose job is to translate what someone is saying into another language → TRANSLATOR

in•ter•pre•tive /ɪnˈtɜrprətɪv/ adj relating to how you explain or understand something or perform a piece of music, a part in a play, etc.

in•ter•ra•cial /ˌɪntərˈreɪʃ(ə)l/ adj involving or consisting of people who belong to different races —**in•ter•ra•cial•ly** adv

in•ter•re•lat•ed /ˌɪntərɪˈleɪtəd/ adj things that are interrelated affect each other because they are connected in some way

in•ter•ro•gate /ɪnˈterəɡeɪt/ verb [T] to ask someone a lot of questions in order to get information: *The suspects were interrogated by the police.* —**in•ter•ro•ga•tion** /ɪnˌterəˈɡeɪʃ(ə)n/ noun [C/U], **in•ter•ro•gat•or** noun [C]

in•ter•rog•a•tive /ˌɪntəˈrɑɡətɪv/ noun [C] *linguistics* a word or phrase that you use for asking a question, for example "what?" or "how?" —**in•ter•rog•a•tive** adj

in•ter•rupt /ˌɪntəˈrʌpt/ verb ★
1 [I/T] to say or do something that stops someone when they are speaking or concentrating on something: *Please don't interrupt her while she's working.* ♦ *She tried to explain, but he interrupted her as soon as she started talking.*
2 [T] to make something stop for a period of time: *Rain interrupted the tournament for an hour this afternoon.*
—**in•ter•rup•tion** /ˌɪntəˈrʌpʃ(ə)n/ noun [C/U]

in•ter•sect /ˌɪntərˈsekt/ verb [I/T] if roads or lines intersect, they cross each other, or they join

in•ter•sec•tion /ˈɪntərˌsekʃ(ə)n/ noun [C] a place where roads, lines, etc. join or cross each other: *The school is at the intersection of two main roads.*

in•ter•sperse /ˌɪntərˈspɜrs/ verb [T] to put something in various places in or among something else: *The text can be interspersed with full-page illustrations.*

in•ter•state¹ /ˈɪntərˌsteɪt/ adj existing or taking place between states, especially between the states in the U.S. or Australia: *interstate commerce*

in•ter•state² /ˈɪntərˌsteɪt/ noun [C] in the U.S., a wide road with several lines of traffic going in each direction

in•ter•val /ˈɪntərv(ə)l/ noun [C] ★
1 a period of time between two events: *Planes pass overhead* ***at regular intervals.*** ♦ *Progress is reviewed* ***at monthly intervals.***
2 a space or distance between two things

in•ter•vene /ˌɪntərˈvin/ verb [I] **1** to become involved in a situation in order to try to stop or change it: *The police had to intervene when the protesters blocked traffic.* **2** to happen between two events, often in a way that delays the second event: *Several months intervened before we met again.*

in•ter•ven•ing /ˌɪntərˈvinɪŋ/ adj happening between two events or times: *Not much has changed during the intervening six years.*

in•ter•ven•tion /ˌɪntərˈvenʃ(ə)n/ noun [C/U] a situation in which someone becomes involved in a particular issue, problem, etc. in order to influence what happens

in•ter•view¹ /ˈɪntərˌvju/ noun ★★
1 [C] a meeting in which someone asks another person, especially a famous person, questions about themselves, their work, or their ideas: *This is her first interview since she won an Olympic medal.* ♦ *He doesn't give interviews to the press.* ♦ *The magazine has an exclusive* ***interview with*** *the couple.*
2 [C/U] a formal meeting in which someone asks you questions in order to find out if you are the right person for a job, course of study, etc.: *I have an interview tomorrow for a job as an interpreter.*

in•ter•view² /ˈɪntərˌvju/ verb ★
1 [T] to ask someone, especially someone famous, questions about themselves, their work, or their ideas: *He was interviewed on the radio this morning.*
2 [I/T] to meet with someone and ask them questions in order to find out if they are the right person for a job, course of study, etc.: ***Applicants will be interviewed*** *early next month.*
—**in•ter•view•er** noun [C]

in•tes•tine /ɪnˈtestɪn/ noun [C] the long tube in your body that processes food and carries waste out of your body —**in•tes•ti•nal** /ɪnˈtestɪn(ə)l/ adj

in•ti•ma•cy /ˈɪntɪməsi/ noun [singular/U] a close personal relationship

in•ti•mate¹ /ˈɪntɪmət/ adj **1** an intimate friend is someone who you know very well and like very much = CLOSE **2** relating to very private or personal things: *The magazine published intimate details of their affair.*

3 private and friendly and making you feel relaxed and comfortable: *It's a small hotel with an intimate atmosphere.* **4** an intimate relationship is a very close personal relationship, especially a sexual one PHRASE **intimate knowledge of sth** detailed knowledge of something
—**in•ti•mate•ly** adv

in•ti•mate² /ˈɪntɪˌmeɪt/ verb [T] *formal* to tell people something in an indirect way
—**in•ti•ma•tion** /ˌɪntɪˈmeɪʃ(ə)n/ noun [C/U]

in•tim•i•date /ɪnˈtɪmɪˌdeɪt/ verb [T] to make someone feel frightened so that they will do what you want —**in•tim•i•da•tion** /ɪnˌtɪmɪˈdeɪʃ(ə)n/ noun [U]

in•tim•i•dat•ed /ɪnˈtɪmɪˌdeɪtəd/ adj feeling nervous or frightened of someone or something: *Children cannot learn if they feel intimidated.*

in•tim•i•dat•ing /ɪnˈtɪmɪˌdeɪtɪŋ/ adj making you feel nervous, frightened, or less confident: *Working with such talented people can be intimidating.*

in•to /*weak* ˈɪntə, ˈɪntʊ, *strong* ˈɪntu/ preposition ★★★
1 moving to the inside moving from the outside to the inside of a place or container: *She got into her car and drove away.* ♦ *Hundreds of athletes marched into the stadium for the opening ceremony.* ♦ *He put his hands into his pockets.*
2 toward sth used for stating the direction in which someone or something looks, faces, or points: *She was gazing into the mirror.* ♦ *Please speak into the microphone.*
3 hitting sth moving toward something and hitting it: *Their car had crashed into a tree.* ♦ *He was so angry he slammed his fist into the wall.*
4 changing to sth used for stating the result of a change from one thing to another: *Julie had grown into a beautiful woman.* ♦ *The dispute turned into a major battle.* ♦ *Roll the dough into a ball.* ♦ *She fell into a deep sleep.* ♦ *Her stories have been translated into more than 30 languages.*
5 starting to be involved in sth used for saying that someone becomes involved in an activity or situation, or becomes part of a group: *Ted is trying to get into the financial industry* (=get a job in it). ♦ *She always manages to get into trouble.* ♦ *He went into the army when he left school.*
6 finding out about sth used for saying what you are trying to find out about: *I promise to look into the matter.*
7 interested in sth *informal* used for saying what activity or subject someone is interested in and enjoys: *I'm into yoga and things like that.*

in•tol•er•a•ble /ɪnˈtɑlərəb(ə)l/ adj impossible to bear or deal with —**in•tol•er•a•bly** adv

in•tol•er•ance /ɪnˈtɑlərəns/ noun [U] someone's refusal to accept behavior, beliefs, or opinions that are different from their own: *political/racial/religious intolerance*

in•tol•er•ant /ɪnˈtɑlərənt/ adj not willing to accept behavior, beliefs, or opinions that are different from your own

in•to•na•tion /ˌɪntəˈneɪʃ(ə)n/ noun [C/U] the way in which your voice rises and falls when you speak

in•tox•i•cat•ed /ɪnˈtɑksɪˌkeɪtəd/ adj **1** *formal* drunk **2** *literary* extremely excited or happy —**in•tox•i•ca•tion** /ɪnˌtɑksɪˈkeɪʃ(ə)n/ noun [U]

in•trac•ta•ble /ɪnˈtræktəb(ə)l/ adj *formal* very difficult or impossible to deal with

in•tra•mu•ral /ˌɪntrəˈmjʊrəl/ adj *American* existing or happening among the students of a particular school or college: *intramural sports*

in•tra•net /ˈɪntrəˌnet/ noun [C] *computing* a NETWORK (=system connecting computers) that only members of a particular organization can use → INTERNET

in•tran•si•gent /ɪnˈtrænsɪdʒənt/ adj *formal* refusing to change your ideas or behavior with no good reason = STUBBORN
—**in•tran•si•gence** noun [U]

in•tran•si•tive /ɪnˈtrænzətɪv/ adj *linguistics* an intransitive verb has no direct object. In the sentence "The children played" the verb "play" is intransitive. Intransitive verbs are marked "[I]" in this dictionary.

in•tra•ve•nous /ˌɪntrəˈvinəs/ adj put directly into a VEIN —**in•tra•ve•nous•ly** adv

in•trep•id /ɪnˈtrepɪd/ adj not afraid to do dangerous things = DARING

in•tri•ca•cy /ˈɪntrɪkəsi/ noun **1 intricacies** [plural] the complicated parts or details of something such as a system or problem: *the intricacies of international law* **2** [U] the quality of being intricate

in•tri•cate /ˈɪntrɪkət/ adj very detailed in design or structure: *an intricate tunnel system* —**in•tri•cate•ly** adv

in•trigue¹ /ɪnˈtrig/ verb [T] to make someone very interested in knowing more about something: *That old house has always intrigued me.*

in•trigue² /ˈɪnˌtrig, ɪnˈtrig/ noun [C/U] a secret plan to harm or cheat someone, or the process of making such a plan

in•trigu•ing /ɪnˈtrigɪŋ/ adj very interesting and making you want to know more: *an intriguing subject for researchers*
—**in•trigu•ing•ly** /ɪnˈtrigɪŋli/ adv

in•trin•sic /ɪnˈtrɪnsɪk/ adj *formal* relating to the essential qualities or features of something or someone: *Providing good service is intrinsic to a successful business.*
—**in•trin•si•cal•ly** /ɪnˈtrɪnsɪkli/ adv

in•tro /ˈɪntroʊ/ noun [C] *informal* the introduction to something

in•tro•duce /ˌɪntrəˈdus/ verb [T] ★★★
1 to tell someone another person's name when they meet for the first time: *He introduced himself as* (=said his name was) *Michael Sullivan.* ♦ **introduce sb to sb** *I would like to introduce you to my friend Martin.*
2 to bring something into existence or use for the first time: *City schools have introduced stricter rules for dealing with drug users.*
3 to provide someone with a new experience: **introduce sb to sth** *My father first introduced me to jazz when I was about five.*
4 to tell an audience about a program, performer, performance, etc. that they are going to see or hear: *It is my pleasure to introduce tonight's speaker.*

in•tro•duc•tion /ˌɪntrəˈdʌkʃ(ə)n/ noun ★★
1 [U] the process of bringing something into existence or use for the first time: *Opposition to the tax has decreased since its introduction last year.* ♦ ***the introduction of** new cancer-fighting drugs*
2 [C] the part at the beginning of a book, report, etc. that gives a general idea of what it is about
3 [C] something that provides an opportunity to learn or experience something for the first time: *My **introduction to** sailing happened on a weekend trip to Lake George.*
4 [C] the process of telling someone another person's name when they meet for the first time

in•tro•duc•to•ry /ˌɪntrəˈdʌkt(ə)ri/ adj
1 providing basic information about a subject, especially for people who know nothing about it: *introductory classes* **2** an introductory offer or price is a low price that is intended to encourage people to buy a new product

in•tro•spec•tive /ˌɪntrəˈspektɪv/ adj tending to examine your own thoughts, feelings, or ideas instead of communicating with other people

in•tro•vert /ˈɪntrəˌvɜrt/ noun [C] someone who tends to concentrate on their own thoughts and feelings instead of communicating with other people ≠ EXTROVERT —**in•tro•vert•ed** adj

in•trude /ɪnˈtrud/ verb [I] to become involved in a situation in which you are not wanted, or to enter a place where you are not allowed to go: *I was very concerned about her, but I didn't want to intrude.*

in•trud•er /ɪnˈtrudər/ noun [C] someone who enters a place where they are not allowed to go

in•tru•sion /ɪnˈtruʒ(ə)n/ noun [C/U] something that interrupts a peaceful situation or a private event

in•tru•sive /ɪnˈtrusɪv/ adj becoming involved in something in a way that is not welcome

in•tu•i•tion /ˌɪntuˈɪʃ(ə)n/ noun [C/U] an ability to know or understand something through your feelings, instead of by considering facts or evidence

in•tu•i•tive /ɪnˈtuɪtɪv/ adj based on your feelings instead of on facts or evidence: *an intuitive judgment* —**in•tu•i•tive•ly** adv

In•u•it /ˈɪnuɪt, ˈɪnjuɪt/ (plural **In•u•it**) noun [C/U] a member of a group of people who live in northern Siberia, Canada, Alaska, and Greenland, or the language that they speak —**In•u•it** adj

in•un•date /ˈɪnənˌdeɪt/ verb [T] to send or provide much more of something than someone can easily deal with: *We've been inundated with calls.*

in•vade /ɪnˈveɪd/ verb **1** [I/T] to take or send an army into another country in order to get control of it: *The island was invaded during the war.* **2** [T] to enter a place, especially in large numbers or in a way that causes problems: *The town is invaded by tourists every summer.* —**in•vad•er** noun [C]

in•va•lid[1] /ɪnˈvælɪd/ adj not legally effective ≠ VALID: *Your ticket is invalid.*

in•va•lid[2] /ˈɪnvəlɪd/ noun [C] someone who is sick or injured and cannot take care of themselves

in•val•u•a•ble /ɪnˈvæljuəb(ə)l/ adj extremely useful

in•var•i•a•bly /ɪnˈveriəbli/ adv always, or almost always

in•va•sion /ɪnˈveɪʒ(ə)n/ noun [C/U] **1** an occasion when one country's army goes into another country in order to take control of it **2** a situation in which a very large number of people come to a place
PHRASE **invasion of privacy** an occasion when someone finds out or uses information about your private life, especially illegally

in•vent /ɪnˈvent/ verb [T] ★★
1 to design or create something that did not exist before: *Alfred Nobel invented dynamite.* ♦ *The mountain bike was invented in California.*
2 to make up a story, excuse, etc. that is not true

in•ven•tion /ɪnˈvenʃ(ə)n/ noun [C/U] ★
1 something that someone has made, designed, or thought of for the first time, or the act of inventing something: *Inventions like the electric light bulb changed the way people lived.* ♦ ***the invention of** the Internet*
2 a story, excuse, etc. that is not true

in•ven•tive /ɪnˈventɪv/ adj **1** good at thinking of new ideas or methods **2** used about new and original ideas, methods, etc.: *an inventive strategy*

in•ven•tor /ɪnˈventər/ noun [C] someone who has invented something, or whose job is to invent things

in•ven•to•ry /ˈɪnvənˌtɔri/ noun **1** [U] *American* all the goods that are available for sale in a store at a particular time **2** [C] a list that gives the details of all the things in a place

in•vert /ɪnˈvɜrt/ verb [T] *formal* to turn something upside down, or to put it in the opposite position —**in•ver•sion** /ɪnˈvɜrʒ(ə)n/ noun [C/U]

in•vest /ɪnˈvest/ verb [I/T] ★ to use your money with the goal of making a profit from it, for example by buying STOCK in a company: *Banks **invested** $20 million **in** the deal.* ♦ *We've **invested heavily*** (=invested a lot of money) *in foreign markets.* —**in•ves•tor** noun [C]
PHRASAL VERB **inˈvest in sth 1** to spend money on something in order to improve it or to make it more successful: *This government believes in investing in education.* **2** to buy something that you will use a lot: *I finally invested in a new computer.*

in•ves•ti•gate /ɪnˈvestɪˌgeɪt/ verb [I/T] ★★ to try to find out all the facts about something in order to learn the truth about it: *We sent a reporter to investigate the rumor.* ♦ *Customer "complaints" are **investigated** quickly and efficiently.* ♦ **+what/why/whether etc.** *The research aims to investigate why schools are not doing better.* —**in•ves•ti•ga•tor** noun [C]

in•ves•ti•ga•tion /ɪnˌvestɪˈgeɪʃ(ə)n/ noun [C/U] ★★★ the process of trying to find out all the facts about something in order to learn who or what caused it or how it happened: *The **murder investigation** is continuing.* ♦ *She is still **under investigation*** (=being investigated) *by the Spanish police.* ♦ *the **investigation into** the crash of Flight 803*

in·ves·ti·ga·tive /ɪnˈvestɪˌgeɪtɪv/ adj intended to discover new details and facts about something: *investigative journalism/techniques*

in·vest·ment /ɪnˈvestmənt/ noun ★★★
1 [C/U] money that is used in a way that may earn you more money, for example money used for buying STOCK in a company: *Her **investments** were mainly **in** technology stocks.* ♦ *The new laws will attract foreign **investment**.*
2 [U] the process of spending money in order to improve something or make it more successful: ***Investment in** new technology is critical to our success.*
3 [C] something that you are willing to spend money on because it will give you benefits in the future: *Computer courses are a **good investment** for your career.*

in·vet·er·ate /ɪnˈvetərət/ adj always doing a particular thing and unlikely to change: *an inveterate liar/gambler/critic*

in·vig·or·ate /ɪnˈvɪgəˌreɪt/ verb [T] to give someone more energy = REFRESH

in·vin·ci·ble /ɪnˈvɪnsəb(ə)l/ adj too strong to be defeated

in·vis·i·ble /ɪnˈvɪzəb(ə)l/ adj something that is invisible cannot be seen —**in·vis·i·bil·ity** /ɪnˈvɪzəbɪləti/ noun [U], **in·vis·i·bly** adv

in·vi·ta·tion /ˌɪnvɪˈteɪʃ(ə)n/ noun [C] ★★ a request for someone to come to an event or to do something: *a wedding invitation* ♦ *The senator **refused** our **invitation to speak**.* ♦ *an **invitation to** the party*

in·vite[1] /ɪnˈvaɪt/ verb [T] ★★★
1 to ask someone to come to see you or to spend time with you socially: *How many people did you invite?* ♦ *We've **invited** all the neighbors **to** the party.* ♦ *Why don't you **invite** them **for** a drink?* ♦ **invite sb to do sth** *They've invited me to eat at their house tonight.*
2 to formally ask someone to do something or go somewhere: *Leaders of the two countries were invited to attend peace talks in Geneva.*
3 to do something that makes something bad or unpleasant more likely to happen: *His policies invited widespread criticism.*
PHRASAL VERBS **inˌvite sb ˈin** to ask someone to come into your house: *Did she invite you in for a cup of coffee?*
inˌvite sb ˈover to invite someone to your house: *They had invited some friends over for dinner.*

in·vite[2] /ˈɪnˌvaɪt/ noun [C] *informal* an invitation to a social event

in·vit·ing /ɪnˈvaɪtɪŋ/ adj attractive in a way that makes you want to do something ≠ UNINVITING: *an inviting outdoor pool* —**in·vit·ing·ly** adv

in·voice[1] /ˈɪnˌvɔɪs/ noun [C] a document giving details of goods or services that someone has bought and must pay for

in·voice[2] /ˈɪnˌvɔɪs/ verb [T] to send someone an invoice for goods or services

in·voke /ɪnˈvoʊk/ verb [T] *formal* to use a law or rule in order to achieve something

in·vol·un·tar·y /ɪnˈvɑlənˌteri/ adj an involuntary movement, sound, or reaction is a sudden one that you cannot control —**in·vol·un·tar·i·ly** adv

in·volve /ɪnˈvɑlv/ verb [T] ★★★
1 to include something as a necessary part of an activity, event, or situation: *The course involves a lot of hard work.* ♦ **involve doing sth** *The job involved working with a software development team.*
2 to include or affect someone or something in an important way: *Forty-six vehicles were involved in the accident.*
3 to encourage or allow someone to take part in something: **involve sb in sth** *The goal is to involve workers in the decision-making process.*

in·volved /ɪnˈvɑlvd/ adj **1** affected by or included in an activity, event, or situation: *They became involved in a lengthy dispute.* **2** someone who is involved in something takes part in it: *We want all departments to be involved.* ♦ *We were involved in the talks until today.* ♦ *He denied that he was involved with organized crime.* **3** complicated and difficult to understand: *a long involved explanation* **4** if you are involved with someone, you have a sexual or emotional relationship with them

in·volve·ment /ɪnˈvɑlvmənt/ noun [C/U] ★★ the act of taking part in an activity, event, or situation: *Our **involvement with** this project started in 1989.* ♦ *There is no evidence of his direct **involvement in** the bombing.* ♦ *the **involvement of** the local government*

in·ward[1] /ˈɪnwərd/ adj **1** felt in your own mind but not obvious to other people **2** going toward the inside or center of something ≠ OUTWARD

in·ward[2] /ˈɪnwərd/ adv toward the inside of something

in·ward·ly /ˈɪnwərdli/ adv in a hidden way that is not obvious to other people ≠ OUTWARDLY

in·wards /ˈɪnwərdz/ adv INWARD

ˌin-your-ˈface adj *informal* extremely direct, in a way that is deliberately intended to shock or annoy people

IOU /ˌaɪ oʊ ˈju/ noun [C] *informal* a piece of paper that you sign to say that you owe someone an amount of money

IPA /ˌaɪ pi ˈeɪ/ noun [U] International Phonetic Alphabet: a system of symbols that are used to represent speech sounds

IPO /ˌaɪ pi ˈoʊ/ noun [C] *business* initial public offering: an occasion when STOCK in a company is first sold to the public

IQ /ˌaɪ ˈkju/ noun [C] intelligence quotient: a number that represents someone's intelligence

i·rate /aɪˈreɪt/ adj very angry

i·ris /ˈaɪrɪs/ noun [C] **1** a tall, usually purple, flower —*picture* → C9 **2** the colored part of your eye

i·ron[1] /ˈaɪrn/ noun ★★
1 [U] a hard heavy metal that is used for making steel
2 [C] a heated object that you push across clothes in order to make them smooth

i•ron² /ˈaɪrn/ verb [I/T] to push an iron across clothes in order to make them smooth: *She ironed her skirt.*

PHRASAL VERB ˌ**iron sth ˈout** to remove the last difficulties in order to solve a problem: *We have to iron out the final details of the contract.*

iron

i•ron³ /ˈaɪrn/ adj **1** made of iron **2** very strong, strict, or severe: *an iron will*

i•ron•ic /aɪˈrɑnɪk/ adj **1** expressing the opposite of what you really think, especially in order to be humorous: *an ironic comment* **2** an ironic event or situation is interesting, because it is the opposite of what you expect

i•ron•i•cal•ly /aɪˈrɑnɪkli/ adv **1** used for saying that a situation has developed in an unexpected or humorous way **2** in an ironic way

i•ron•ing /ˈaɪrnɪŋ/ noun [U] the job of making clothes smooth with an iron, or the clothes that must be made smooth with an iron: *I'll do the ironing.*

ˈ**ironing** ˌ**board** noun [C] a tall narrow table that you use to do the ironing

i•ro•ny /ˈaɪrəni/ noun **1** [U] a form of humor in which you use words to express the opposite of what the words really mean **2** [C/U] a strange, funny, or sad situation in which things happen in the opposite way to what you expect

ir•ra•tion•al /ɪˈræʃən(ə)l/ adj without clear or sensible reasons, or not thinking in a sensible way: *irrational violence/fear/panic* —**ir•ra•tion•al•ly** adv

ir•rec•on•cil•a•ble /ɪˌrekənˈsaɪləb(ə)l/ adj irreconcilable opinions, aims, or disagreements are so opposed to each other that it is impossible to reach an agreement

ir•reg•u•lar /ɪˈregjələr/ adj **1** not happening regularly: *His breathing had become irregular.* **2** not even, smooth, or straight in shape or appearance: *an irregular surface* **3** not following the rules, laws, or usual ways of doing things **4** *linguistics* not following the usual rules of grammar. For example, "eat" is an irregular verb because its past tense is "ate" and its past participle is "eaten." —**ir•reg•u•lar•ly** adv

ir•reg•u•lar•i•ty /ɪˌregjəˈlerəti/ noun **1** [C] a situation in which the rules, laws, or usual ways of doing things have not been followed: *irregularities in the election process* **2** [C] a shape or appearance that is not even, smooth, or straight: *irregularities in the surface* **3** [C/U] a situation in which events do not happen at regular times

ir•rel•e•vant /ɪˈreləvənt/ adj not important, or not relevant to what you are doing: *an irrelevant remark* —**ir•rel•e•vance** /ɪˈreləvəns/ noun [C/U]

ir•rep•a•ra•ble /ɪˈrep(ə)rəb(ə)l/ adj *formal* irreparable harm or damage is extremely bad and cannot be repaired

ir•re•place•a•ble /ˌɪrɪˈpleɪsəb(ə)l/ adj valuable and impossible to replace if used, lost, or destroyed

ir•re•press•i•ble /ˌɪrɪˈpresəb(ə)l/ adj lively, confident, and impossible to control

ir•re•sis•ti•ble /ˌɪrɪˈzɪstəb(ə)l/ adj **1** strong or powerful and impossible to control: *an irresistible urge to laugh* **2** impossible to refuse, not want, or not like: *an irresistible smile* —**ir•re•sis•ti•bly** adv

ir•re•spec•tive /ˌɪrɪˈspektɪv/ adv **irrespective of sth** despite a particular fact, situation, or quality

ir•re•spon•si•ble /ˌɪrɪˈspɑnsəb(ə)l/ adj **1** done or said without thinking about the possible results: *It was irresponsible of you to leave her alone.* **2** not sensible, or not able to be trusted to be reasonable: *an irresponsible driver* —**ir•re•spon•si•bly** adv

ir•rev•er•ent /ɪˈrevrənt/ adj showing no respect for traditions, rules, or religious beliefs

ir•re•vers•i•ble /ˌɪrɪˈvɜrsəb(ə)l/ adj impossible to change or bring back to a previous condition or situation: *irreversible damage to the environment*

ir•rev•o•ca•ble /ɪˈrevəkəb(ə)l/ adj *formal* impossible to change or stop —**ir•rev•o•ca•bly** adv

ir•ri•gate /ˈɪrɪˌgeɪt/ verb [T] to bring water to land through a system of pipes, DITCHES, etc. in order to make plants grow —**ir•ri•ga•tion** /ˌɪrɪˈgeɪʃ(ə)n/ noun [U]

ir•ri•ta•ble /ˈɪrɪtəb(ə)l/ adj likely to become easily annoyed or made angry —**ir•ri•ta•bil•i•ty** /ˌɪrɪtəˈbɪləti/ noun [U], **ir•ri•ta•bly** adv

ir•ri•tant /ˈɪrɪtənt/ noun [C] **1** something that annoys you **2** *medical* something that makes part of your body become painful or swollen

ir•ri•tate /ˈɪrɪˌteɪt/ verb [T] **1** to make you feel annoyed or angry: *That little noise he makes really irritates me.* **2** to make part of your body painful or swollen —**ir•ri•ta•tion** /ˌɪrɪˈteɪʃ(ə)n/ noun [U]

ir•ri•tat•ed /ˈɪrɪˌteɪtəd/ adj **1** annoyed or angry about something: *I was beginning to get irritated.* **2** painful or swollen

ir•ri•tat•ing /ˈɪrɪˌteɪtɪŋ/ adj making you feel annoyed or angry: *He had an irritating habit of cracking his knuckles.* —**ir•ri•tat•ing•ly** adv

IRS, the /ˌaɪ ɑr ˈes/ the Internal Revenue Service: the U.S. government department that collects taxes

is 3rd person singular of the present tense of **be**

-ish /ɪʃ/ suffix "slightly" or "fairly": *a bluish tint*

Is•lam /ɪsˈlɑm, ɪzˈlɑm, ˈɪzˌlɑm/ noun [U] the religion that is based on the ideas of Muhammad, or the people and countries who follow this religion —**Is•lam•ic** /ɪsˈlɑmɪk, ɪzˈlɑmɪk/ adj

is•land /ˈaɪlənd/ noun [C] ★★★ a piece of land that is completely surrounded by water: *the best hotel on the island* ♦ *islands off the west coast of Canada*

is•land•er /ˈaɪləndər/ noun [C] someone who lives on a small island

isle /aɪl/ noun [C] *literary* an island

is•n't /ˈɪz(ə)nt/ short form the usual way of saying or writing "is not." This is not often used in formal writing: *Isn't she here yet?*

i•so•late /ˈaɪsəˌleɪt/ verb [T] **1** to keep someone in a place that is away from other people **2** to prevent a country or group from communicating with, doing business with, or getting support from other countries or groups **3** to separate something from other similar things so that you can consider it by itself

i•so•lat•ed /ˈaɪsəˌleɪtəd/ adj **1** an isolated place is a long way from other places and is often difficult to get to = REMOTE: *isolated mountain villages* **2** happening only once, or existing only in one place: *an isolated incident* **3** feeling alone and unhappy, with no friends: *Many victims feel isolated and unable to talk about their experiences.* **4** an isolated country or organization is one that others refuse to deal with

i•so•la•tion /ˌaɪsəˈleɪʃ(ə)n/ noun [U] **1** the state of being separated from other people, or a situation in which you do not have support from other people: *Isolation from family and friends can lead to feelings of anxiety.* **2** a situation in which a country or group is alone and without support because other countries or groups stop dealing with it

PHRASE **in isolation 1** if something is considered in isolation, it is considered separately from other similar things **2** in a place that is away from other people, animals, or things: *The prisoners were kept in isolation.*

i•so•la•tion•ism /ˌaɪsəˈleɪʃ(ə)nˌɪzəm/ noun [U] a country's policy of not having political or economic relationships with other countries —**i•so•la•tion•ist** adj

ISP /ˌaɪ es ˈpi/ noun [C] Internet service provider: a company that provides a connection to the Internet

is•sue[1] /ˈɪʃu/ noun [C] ★★★

1 a subject or problem that people discuss or argue about: *environmental issues* ♦ *Education was one of the biggest issues in the campaign.* ♦ *The chairman* ***raised the issue*** (=started discussing the issue) *of funding.*

2 a magazine that is published at a particular time: *The article appeared in the November issue.*

PHRASES **make an issue out of sth** to treat something as an important problem when it is not

take issue with sb/sth to disagree with someone, or to disagree about something

> **Words often used with issue**
>
> *Verbs often used with* ***issue*** *(noun, sense 1)*
>
> - **address, confront, tackle, take up** + ISSUE: deal with an issue
> - **dodge, duck, evade** + ISSUE: avoid dealing with an issue
> - **cloud, complicate, confuse** + ISSUE: make an issue more difficult to understand, or more difficult to deal with
> - **consider, examine, explore** + ISSUE: think about an issue

is•sue[2] /ˈɪʃu/ verb [T] ★★

1 to announce something officially: *The banks issued a warning that charges will rise.*

2 if you issue someone something, you officially give it to them: *All visitors to the factory must be* ***issued with*** *protective goggles.*

3 to officially make things available for people to buy or use: *The post office is issuing a new range of stamps.*

it /ɪt/ pronoun ★★★

1 referring to sth that has been mentioned used for referring to something that has already been mentioned, or when it is obvious which thing you mean: *I can't find my ticket. I think I must have lost it.* ♦ *You should come to Rome – it's a wonderful city.* ♦ *The dog was howling, so she fed it.* ♦ *I can't move the baby without waking it.*

2 used as the subject/object of a sentence used instead of the subject or object of a sentence, when the real subject or object is a phrase or CLAUSE at the end of the sentence: *It's nice to be home again.* ♦ *It's strange that she never mentioned the wedding.* ♦ *The new law made it easier to get a divorce.* ♦ *I hate it when people talk about me behind my back.*

3 referring to sb's life or situation used for referring to someone's life, work, or general situation: *What's it like in the army these days?*

4 talking about weather conditions used for talking about the weather, the temperature, or the light: *It rained last night.* ♦ *It's a beautiful day.* ♦ *It's cooler inside the house.* ♦ *It gets dark at around five.*

5 talking about times and dates used for saying or asking what the time, day, or date is: *"What time is it?" "It's four o'clock."* ♦ *Thank goodness it's Saturday tomorrow.*

6 talking about distance used for saying how large a distance is: *It's about ten miles from here to Billings.*

7 emphasizing who or what you mean used with the verb "to be" for emphasizing that you are referring to a particular person or thing: *It's your brother I want to speak to.*

8 saying or asking who sb is *spoken* used for telling someone who you are, or asking who someone else is, especially on the telephone: *"Ted, you've got a phone call." "Find out who it is."* ♦ *Hello, it's me, Jeff.*

PHRASE **it seems/looks/appears** used for saying what seems to be true: *It seems that no one is willing to accept responsibility for what happened.* ♦ *It looks as if we're going to lose our jobs.*

IT /ˌaɪ ˈti/ noun [U] information technology: the use of computers and other electronic equipment to store, process, and send information

i•tal•ics /ɪˈtælɪks/ noun [plural] italics are

letters that slope to the right, like the letters in examples in this dictionary

itch[1] /ɪtʃ/ verb [I] if your skin itches, you want to SCRATCH it (=rub it with your nails)
PHRASE **be itching to do sth** *informal* to feel very impatient because you want to do something immediately

itch[2] /ɪtʃ/ noun [singular] a feeling on your skin that makes you want to SCRATCH it (=rub it with your nails)

itch·y /ˈɪtʃi/ adj if you feel itchy, you want to SCRATCH your skin (=rub it with your nails)

it'd /ˈɪtəd/ short form **1** a way of saying or writing "it would." This is not often used in formal writing: *It'd be better to wait until later.* **2** a way of saying or writing "it had" when "had" is an AUXILIARY VERB. This is not often used in formal writing: *It'd been a difficult night.*

i·tem /ˈaɪtəm/ noun [C] ★★★
1 one of several things in a group or on a list: *The first item to be discussed was the new computer system.* ♦ *Several items of equipment needed to be repaired.*
2 an article in a newspaper or magazine, or one part of a news program on the television or radio

i·tem·ize /ˈaɪtəˌmaɪz/ verb [T] to make a detailed list of a number of things —**i·tem·ized** /ˈaɪtəˌmaɪzd/ adj

i·tin·er·ant /aɪˈtɪnərənt/ adj traveling around frequently: *itinerant workers*

i·tin·er·ar·y /aɪˈtɪnəˌreri/ noun [C] a written plan that shows the details of a trip

it'll /ˈɪt(ə)l/ short form the usual way of saying or writing "it will." This is not often used in formal writing: *It'll be fun!*

it's /ɪts/ short form **1** the usual way of saying or writing "it is." This is not often used in formal writing: *It's cold outside.* **2** the usual way of saying or writing "it has" when "has" is an AUXILIARY VERB. This is not often used in formal writing: *It's been raining for hours.*

its /ɪts/ determiner ★★★

Its is the possessive form of **it**.

belonging or relating to something, when it has already been mentioned or when it is obvious which thing you are referring to: *The chair lay on its side.* ♦ *Europe and its many great cities* ♦ *The bull had a ring through its nose.*

Its should not be confused with **it's**, which is the short form of "it is" or "it has."

it·self /ɪtˈself/ pronoun ★★★
1 the REFLEXIVE form of "it," used for showing that an action affects the thing that does the action: *The young bird cannot feed itself.* ♦ *The government needs to defend itself against these attacks.*
2 used for emphasizing that you are referring to a particular thing and not to anything else: *The problem is not with the software, but with the computer itself.*
PHRASES **(all) by itself 1** not near or with any other thing: *His house stood by itself on the edge of the town.* **2** without help: *The door opened by itself.* ♦ *Can the baby stand up all by itself?*
in itself used for stating what is true about one particular thing, without considering anything else: *The fact that he lied to the police does not in itself prove that he is guilty.*

IV /ˌaɪ ˈvi/ noun [C] *American* a tube used in hospitals for putting liquid into your body

I've /aɪv/ short form the usual way of saying or writing "I have." This is not often used in formal writing: *I've been meaning to call you.*

IVF /ˌaɪ vi ˈef/ noun [U] in vitro fertilization: the medical process in which a woman's egg is FERTILIZED outside her body and then put back inside so that it can grow into a baby

i·vo·ry[1] /ˈaɪvəri/ noun [U] the bone that an elephant's TUSKS are made of

i·vo·ry[2] /ˈaɪvəri/ adj pale yellow-white in color

i·vy /ˈaɪvi/ noun [U] a dark green plant that spreads and grows up walls —*picture* → C9

ˌIvy ˈLeague adj belonging to a group of eight important universities in the northeastern part of the U.S.

J

J j

j or **J** /dʒeɪ/ noun [C/U] the tenth letter of the English alphabet

jab[1] /dʒæb/ verb [I/T] to push something narrow or pointed into or toward something else with a sudden movement

jab[2] /dʒæb/ noun [C] a hard straight push with something narrow or pointed

jack[1] /dʒæk/ noun [C] **1** a piece of equipment for lifting and supporting a heavy object, for example a car **2** a PLAYING CARD that has a picture of a young man on it —*picture* → C16

jack[2] /dʒæk/ PHRASAL VERB **ˌjack sth ˈup** *informal* to increase the price, rate, or number of something by a large amount

jack·al /ˈdʒæk(ə)l/ noun [C] a wild African or Asian animal like a dog

jack·et /ˈdʒækət/ noun [C] ★★
1 a short coat: *a linen/denim/leather jacket* ♦ *a suit jacket* —*picture* → C4
2 a cover for a book

ˈjack-in-the-ˌbox noun [C] a toy that consists of a box with a model of a man inside that jumps up when the box opens

jack·knife /ˈdʒækˌnaɪf/ verb [I] if a truck or train jackknifes in an accident, it bends in the middle and its parts fold toward each other

jack-o'-lan·tern /ˌdʒækəˈlæntərn/ noun [C] an empty PUMPKIN with a face cut into it and a light inside that can be seen through the holes

jack·pot /ˈdʒækˌpɑt/ noun [C] the largest

amount of money that someone can win in a game

PHRASE **hit the jackpot** to be very successful at something

Ja•cuz•zi /dʒəˈkuzi/ *trademark* a type of hot bath with BUBBLY water in which people sit to relax

jade /dʒeɪd/ noun [U] a hard green stone that is used for making jewelry

jad•ed /ˈdʒeɪdəd/ adj bored and no longer enthusiastic about something

jag•ged /ˈdʒægəd/ adj a jagged surface or edge has a lot of rough pointed parts

jag•uar /ˈdʒægˌwɑr/ noun [C] a large wild cat with black spots from Central and South America

jail[1] /dʒeɪl/ noun [C/U] ★ a place where people are put as punishment for a crime = PRISON: *Adam spent 3 years **in jail** for drug possession.* ♦ *They **put** her **in jail** for murder.*

jail[2] /dʒeɪl/ verb [T] to put someone in jail: *He was jailed for drunk driving.*

J

Jain /dʒaɪn/ noun [C] a member of a religious group in India that believes that people should not be violent toward any living creature —**Jain** adj, **Jain•ism** noun [U]

jal•a•pe•ño /ˌhɑləˈpeɪnjoʊ/ or ˌ**jalapeño ˈpepper** noun [C] a small green or red PEPPER often used in Mexican cooking

jam[1] /dʒæm/ noun **1** [C/U] a sweet sticky food made from boiled fruit and sugar, that is usually spread onto bread: *strawberry jam* **2** [C] an occasion when a machine does not work because something prevents its parts from moving: *a paper jam in the printer*

PHRASE **be in a jam** *informal* to be in a difficult situation

→ TRAFFIC JAM

jam[2] /dʒæm/ verb **1** [T] to use force to put something into a small space: *I tried to jam some paper into the cracks.* **2** [T] if people or things jam a place, there are so many of them that it is difficult to move: *The streets were jammed with cars.* **3** [I/T] if a machine, lock, window, etc. jams, or if something jams it, it does not work because something stops it from moving: *He fired one shot before his gun jammed.* **4** [T] to block a radio, television, or other electronic signal

jam•bo•ree /ˌdʒæmbəˈri/ noun [C] a large celebration with a lot of music and entertainment

ˌ**jam-ˈpacked** adj completely full

Jan. abbrev January

Jane Doe /ˌdʒeɪn ˈdoʊ/ noun [C] *American* a woman whose name is not known

jan•gle /ˈdʒæŋg(ə)l/ verb [I/T] if small metal objects jangle, they make a noise when they hit against each other

jan•i•tor /ˈdʒænɪtər/ noun [C] someone whose job is to clean and take care of a public building

Jan•u•ar•y /ˈdʒænjuˌeri/ noun [C] ★★★ the first month of the year: *My class begins in January.* ♦ *The new year begins on January 1st.*

jar[1] /dʒɑr/ noun [C] a glass container for food, with a lid and a wide opening: *a jar of pickles*

jar[2] /dʒɑr/ verb **1** [I/T] to accidentally push something hard against something else, in a way that causes pain or damage: *The shock of the fall jarred every bone in his body.* **2** [I] to be unpleasant or not appropriate in a particular situation

jar•gon /ˈdʒɑrgən/ noun [U] *showing disapproval* special words and phrases that are only understood by people who do the same kind of work: *medical/computer jargon*

jar•ring /ˈdʒɑrɪŋ/ adj surprising, unpleasant, or slightly shocking

jaun•dice /ˈdʒɔndɪs/ noun [U] an illness that makes your skin and the white part of your eyes become yellow

jaun•diced /ˈdʒɔndɪst/ adj showing dislike of something, or criticizing it

jaunt /dʒɔnt/ noun [C] a short trip that you take for fun

jaun•ty /ˈdʒɔnti/ adj lively and confident

jave•lin /ˈdʒævəlɪn/ noun [C/U] a long pointed stick that is thrown in a sports competition, or the sport of throwing this stick

jaw /dʒɔ/ noun [C] **1** the part of your mouth where your teeth grow **2** the lower part of your face that includes your chin and stretches back almost to your ear *—picture* → C14

PHRASE **sb's jaw dropped** used for saying that someone was very surprised or shocked

jazz[1] /dʒæz/ noun [U] a type of music with a strong lively beat which players often IMPROVISE (=make up the music as they play)

jazz[2] /dʒæz/ PHRASAL VERB ˌ**jazz sth ˈup** *informal* to make something more lively or interesting

jeal•ous /ˈdʒeləs/ adj ★
1 upset because someone has something that you would like to have, or can do something that you would like to do: *I expect some of your colleagues will be jealous.*
2 angry and upset because someone who you love is giving attention to another person: *He would dance with other women to **make** her **jealous**.*
—**jeal•ous•ly** adv

jeal•ous•y /ˈdʒeləsi/ noun [U] **1** a feeling of anger and sadness because someone has something that you would like to have: *Professional jealousy can cause problems at work.* **2** a strong feeling of anger and sadness because someone who you love is giving their attention to someone else: *sexual jealousy*

jeans /dʒinz/ noun [plural] ★★ informal pants made of DENIM (=heavy cotton cloth): *a pair of faded blue jeans —picture* → C4

Jeep /dʒip/ *trademark* a car with no roof that can drive over all types of land

jeer /dʒɪr/ verb [I/T] to shout or laugh at someone in an unkind way —**jeer** noun [C]

jeez /dʒiz/ interjection *spoken* used when you are very surprised or angry about something

Jell-O /ˈdʒeloʊ/ *American trademark* a soft food made from fruit juice, sugar, and GELATIN that shakes when you touch it

jel•ly /ˈdʒeli/ noun [C/U] a sweet sticky food made from boiled fruit juice and sugar, often spread on bread

jel•ly•fish /ˈdʒeliˌfɪʃ/ noun [C] a soft transparent sea animal that can sting you

jeop•ard•ize /ˈdʒepərˌdaɪz/ verb [T] to risk damaging or destroying something important: *Cuts in funding could jeopardize our research.*

jeop•ard•y /ˈdʒepərdi/ noun **in jeopardy** likely to be damaged or destroyed

jerk¹ /dʒɜrk/ verb [I/T] to move suddenly, or to make something move suddenly: *The train jerked forward.*

PHRASAL VERB ˌ**jerk sb aˈround** *informal* to treat someone in an unfair or dishonest way

jerk² /dʒɜrk/ noun [C] **1** a quick sudden movement **2** *impolite* someone who does stupid, annoying, or unkind things

jerk•y¹ /ˈdʒɜrki/ adj a jerky movement consists of several separate short movements —**jerk•i•ly** adv

jerk•y² /ˈdʒɜrki/ noun [U] meat cut in thin STRIPS and dried

jer•sey /ˈdʒɜrzi/ noun [U] a soft cloth made from wool or cotton

Je•sus Christ /ˌdʒizəs ˈkraɪst/ or **Jesus** the man on whose ideas Christianity is based

jet¹ /dʒet/ noun ★

1 [C] an airplane that can fly very fast: *a jet fighter*

2 [C] a stream of liquid that comes out of something very quickly and with a lot of force: *The firefighter sprayed **a jet of water** on the flames.*

3 [U] a hard black shiny stone that is used for making jewelry

jet² /dʒet/ verb [I] to fly somewhere in an airplane: *They will be jetting off to Spain this weekend.*

ˌ**jet-ˈblack** adj very dark black in color

ˌ**jet ˈengine** noun [C] a type of engine that combines air and burning fuel to create power for an airplane

ˈ**jet ˌlag** noun [U] the feeling of being very tired because you have traveled on an airplane across parts of the world where the time is different —**jet-lag•ged** /ˈdʒetˌlægd/ adj

ˈ**Jet ˌSki** *trademark* a very small fast boat for one or two people that you drive standing up

jet•ti•son /ˈdʒetɪs(ə)n/ verb [T] **1** to get rid of something that is not useful or successful: *We may have to jettison some parts of the business.* **2** to throw goods, equipment, or fuel from a ship or airplane in order to make it less likely to sink or crash

jet•ty /ˈdʒeti/ noun [C] a long narrow structure that goes from the land out into a lake, ocean, or river to provide a place for boats to stop

Jew /dʒu/ noun [C] someone who believes in Judaism or who belongs to a family that believed in Judaism in the past

jew•el /ˈdʒuəl/ noun [C] a hard valuable stone that has been cut and made shiny

jew•eled /ˈdʒuəld/ adj a jeweled object has been decorated with jewels

jew•el•er /ˈdʒuələr/ noun [C] someone who makes, repairs, or sells jewelry

jew•el•lery /ˈdʒuəlri/ the British spelling of jewelry

jew•el•ry /ˈdʒuəlri/ noun [U] ★★ objects such as rings that you wear as decoration: *My mother doesn't wear **much jewelry**.*

→ COSTUME JEWELRY

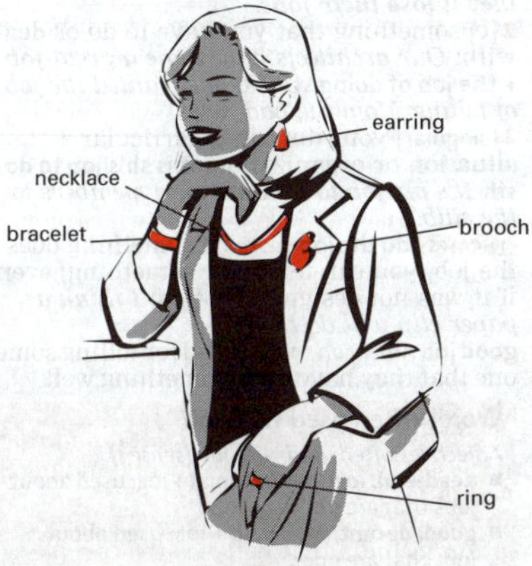

jewelry

Jew•ish /ˈdʒuɪʃ/ adj **1** someone who is Jewish was born in the Jewish culture, and may practice Judaism **2** relating to Jews, their culture, or their religion

jibe¹ /dʒaɪb/ noun [C] a comment that is intended to annoy or offend someone

jibe² /dʒaɪb/ verb [I] *American* if one piece of information jibes with another, it shows that it is true

jig /dʒɪg/ noun [C] a fast traditional dance, or the music for this dance

jig•ger /ˈdʒɪgər/ noun [C] a very small glass for measuring alcohol

jig•gle /ˈdʒɪg(ə)l/ verb [I/T] to move quickly up and down or from side to side, or to make something move in this way: *If the toilet won't flush, just jiggle the handle a little.*

jig•saw /ˈdʒɪgˌsɔ/ or ˈ**jigsaw ˌpuzzle** noun [C] a picture made of a lot of small pieces that you have to fit together

jim•my /ˈdʒɪmi/ verb [T] *American* to break open a lock, door, or window, usually with a long piece of metal

jin•gle¹ /ˈdʒɪŋg(ə)l/ noun [C] **1** a short phrase, usually with music, that is easy to remember. Jingles are used in advertising. **2** the sound that small metal objects make when they hit each other

jin•gle² /ˈdʒɪŋg(ə)l/ verb [I/T] if small metal objects jingle, or if you jingle them, they hit each other to make a noise

jinx /dʒɪŋks/ noun [C] *informal* someone or something that causes bad luck: *There seems to be a jinx on that family.* —**jinx** verb [T], **jinxed** /dʒɪŋkst/ adj

jit•ters /ˈdʒɪtərz/ noun [plural] *informal* a nervous feeling that you get when you do not know what will happen

jit•ter•y /ˈdʒɪtəri/ adj feeling nervous, often so that you cannot keep still

job /dʒɑb/ noun ★★★

1 [C] work that you do regularly to earn money: *a part-time/full-time job* ♦ *Andy **got a job** at Krispy Kreme.* ♦ *Emma **finally found a job** (=got a job after looking).* ♦ *My son* has been ***offered a job*** in Tokyo. ♦ *Dan **quit** his **job*** (=stopped working at a particular job). ♦ *Many steelworkers are worried that they'll **lose their jobs**.*

2 [C] something that you have to do or deal with: *Our architects have **done a** great **job**.* ♦ **the job of doing sth** *No one wanted the job of telling Mom the bad news.*

3 [singular] your duty in a particular situation or organization: **it is sb's job to do sth** *It's my job to welcome new members to the club.*

PHRASES **do the job** *spoken* if something does the job, you can use it for something, even if it was not designed for this: *I think a paper clip will do the job.*

good job *American spoken* used for telling someone that they have done something well

Words often used with job

*Adjectives often used with **job** (sense 1)*

- **dead-end, low-paid, menial** + JOB: used about jobs that are not very good
- **good, decent, well-paid** + JOB: used about jobs that are good
- **full-time, part-time, permanent, temporary** + JOB: used about a job that you do for a particular period of time

Talking or writing about jobs

general

- **job** what you do regularly to earn money
- **work** something that you do to earn money, or the place where you go to do it
- **career** the jobs that someone does over a period of time that involve a particular type of work
- **profession** a type of job that you need a lot of education or special training to do
- **post** a particular job within a company or organization, especially a job with some responsibility
- **position** a particular job: used especially in advertisements for jobs

getting a job

- **apply** to officially say, usually in a letter or on a special form, that you would like to be considered for a particular job
- **résumé** a list of your qualifications and work experience
- **applicant** someone who applies for a particular job
- **candidate** someone who is competing with other people for a particular job
- **interview** a meeting with the people you are hoping to work for where they ask you questions and find out more about you
- **interviewee** an applicant who is asked to come for an interview

not having a job

- **unemployed** *or* **jobless** *or* **out of work** used for describing someone who does not have a job
- **retired** used for describing someone who is not working because they have reached a certain age

ˈjob deˌscription noun [C] a list of all the things that someone must do in their job

job·less /ˈdʒɑbləs/ adj *mainly journalism* without a job, or relating to people without a job =UNEMPLOYED: *a jobless steelworker* ♦ *Canada's jobless rate was 10.3 percent.*

J

ˈjob seˌcurity noun [U] the knowledge that you will not be forced to leave your job

job-shar·ing /ˈdʒɑb ʃerɪŋ/ noun [U] a system in which two people share the work from a single job, so that each one works fewer hours

jock /dʒɑk/ noun [C] *American informal* a student who plays a lot of sports

jock·ey¹ /ˈdʒɑki/ noun [C] someone whose job is to ride horses in races → DISC JOCKEY

jock·ey² /ˈdʒɑki/ verb **jockey for position** to try to get into the best situation possible when you are competing for something

joc·u·lar /ˈdʒɑkjələr/ adj *formal* humorous

jog¹ /dʒɑg/ verb **1** [I] to run at a slow steady speed, usually for exercise: *Let's jog around the lake.* **2** [T] to knock something so that it moves a little

PHRASE **jog sb's memory** to make someone remember something

jog² /dʒɑg/ noun [C] a run for exercise at a slow steady speed: *We went for a jog around the park.* —**jog·ger** noun [C]

jog·ging /ˈdʒɑgɪŋ/ noun [U] the activity of running at a slow steady speed: *I go jogging every morning.*

John Doe /ˌdʒɑn ˈdoʊ/ noun [C] *American* a man whose name is not known

join /dʒɔɪn/ verb ★★★

1 [I/T] to connect two things, or to become connected at a particular point ≠ DISCONNECT, SEPARATE: *The two roads join about five miles south of the city.* ♦ **join sth together** *First, join the two pipes together.*

2 [T] to become a member of an organization, club, or group, or to start working for an organization ≠ LEAVE: *I'm thinking of joining a choir.* ♦ *Martin joined the firm in 1999.* ♦ *He wants to **join the army**.*

3 [T] to come together with other people or things: *Wendy went off to join her friends in the bar.* ♦ *The police car was soon joined by two ambulances.* ♦ **join sb for sth** *Why don't you join us for dinner tonight?*

PHRASE **join forces (with sb)** to work together with someone else in order to achieve something

PHRASAL VERBS **ˌjoin ˈin (sth)** to do an activity with people who are already doing it: *She laughed and Tom joined in.* ♦ *Pat didn't feel like joining in the celebrations.*

ˌjoin ˈup to become a member of the armed forces

ˌjoin (sth) ˈup *same as* **join** 1: *You need to join up these two lines.*

joint¹ /dʒɔɪnt/ adj ★★ involving two or more people, or done by two or more people together: *a joint decision* ♦ *The two presidents issued a joint statement.* —**joint·ly** adv: *a jointly owned property*

joint² /dʒɔɪnt/ noun [C]

1 part of your body	4 restaurant, bar, etc.
2 connection	5 piece of meat
3 marijuana cigarette	

1 a part of your body that can bend where two bones meet: *a knee joint* **2** a place where two parts of something are connected: *Make sure you seal the joints of the pipes with tape.* **3** *informal* a MARIJUANA cigarette

4 *informal* a restaurant, bar, or club **5** a large piece of meat that is cooked in an oven: *a joint of beef*

ˌjoint ˈventure noun [C] *business* an agreement between two companies to work together on a particular job

joke¹ /dʒoʊk/ noun [C] ★ something that you say or do that is intended to make people laugh: *Do you want to hear a good joke?* ♦ *Greg sprayed her with water* ***as a joke***. ♦ *The kids were* ***telling jokes*** (=short stories with funny endings). ♦ *Stephen decided to* ***play a joke on*** (=trick) *his teacher*.

PHRASES **be a joke** *informal* to be bad or silly in a way that is annoying: *That price is just a joke!*

sb can take a joke if you can take a joke, you are able to laugh when someone makes a joke about you or does something to trick you

joke² /dʒoʊk/ verb [I] to say things that are intended to make people laugh: *You shouldn't joke about such serious things.*

PHRASE **be joking** to say something but not mean it to be true: *I thought he was joking when he said he'd resigned.*
—**jok•ing•ly** adv

jok•er /ˈdʒoʊkər/ noun [C] **1** someone who likes to make people laugh **2** a type of PLAYING CARD that is used only in some card games —*picture* → C16

jol•ly /ˈdʒɑli/ adj friendly and happy

jolt¹ /dʒoʊlt/ verb **1** [I/T] to move with a sudden violent movement, or to make something move like this **2** [T] to give someone a sudden shock

jolt² /dʒoʊlt/ noun [C] **1** a sudden violent movement: *The bus stopped with a jolt and we were all flung forward.* **2** a sudden strong feeling of surprise or shock: *I realized with a jolt that everyone was staring at me.*

Jone•ses /ˈdʒoʊnzəz/ noun **keep up with the Joneses** *informal* to try to be as rich, successful, etc. as your neighbors

jos•tle /ˈdʒɑs(ə)l/ verb **1** [I/T] to push against someone in order to move past them in a crowd: *We managed to jostle our way to the front.* **2** [I] to compete for something: *The two parties are jostling for control of the parliament.*

jot /dʒɑt/ PHRASAL VERB **ˌjot sth ˈdown** to write something in a quick informal way on a piece of paper so that you remember it

jour•nal /ˈdʒɜrn(ə)l/ noun [C] **1** a newspaper or magazine that contains articles relating to a particular profession or subject: *a scientific journal* ♦ *the Wall Street Journal* **2** a book in which you write about what happens to you every day = DIARY

jour•nal•ism /ˈdʒɜrn(ə)lˌɪzəm/ noun [U] the activity of reporting the news for a newspaper, magazine, radio program, or television program

jour•nal•ist /ˈdʒɜrn(ə)lɪst/ noun [C] ★ someone whose job is to report the news for a newspaper, magazine, radio program, or television program = REPORTER

jour•ney /ˈdʒɜrni/ noun [C] ★ an occasion when you travel from one place to another, especially over a long distance: *We had* ***a long journey*** *ahead of us.* ♦ *It's a seven-hour journey to Boston from here.* ♦ *He* ***makes the journey*** *to Moscow three times a year.*

jo•vi•al /ˈdʒoʊviəl/ adj happy and friendly

joy /dʒɔɪ/ noun **1** [U] a feeling of great happiness: *Penny could have shouted with joy.* **2** [C] something that makes you feel very happy or pleased: *the joys of skiing* → PRIDE¹

joy•ful /ˈdʒɔɪf(ə)l/ adj very happy, or causing happiness —**joy•ful•ly** adv

joy•ous /ˈdʒɔɪəs/ adj *literary* causing happy feelings —**joy•ous•ly** adv

joy•pad /ˈdʒɔɪˌpæd/ noun [C] a small piece of equipment with buttons that you press in order to control the movement of the images in a computer game

joy•rid•ing /ˈdʒɔɪˌraɪdɪŋ/ noun [U] *informal* the crime of stealing a car and driving it for pleasure —**joy•rid•er** noun [C]

joy•stick /ˈdʒɔɪˌstɪk/ noun [C] an upright handle that you use to control an aircraft or the movement of the images in a computer game

Jr. abbrev junior

ju•bi•lant /ˈdʒubɪlənt/ adj extremely happy because something good has happened —**ju•bi•lant•ly** adv, **ju•bi•la•tion** /ˌdʒubɪˈleɪʃ(ə)n/ noun [U]

ju•bi•lee /ˈdʒubɪli, ˌdʒubɪˈli/ noun [C] a celebration on a date on which something important happened in an earlier year

Ju•da•ism /ˈdʒudəˌɪzəm/ noun [U] the religion of Jewish people, based on the writings of the Torah and the Talmud

judge¹ /dʒʌdʒ/ noun [C] ★★
1 someone whose job is to make decisions in a court of law: *The judge sentenced her to ninety days in prison.* → MAGISTRATE
2 someone who decides who the winner of a competition will be: *All entries will be examined by* ***a panel of judges***.

PHRASE **be a good/bad/shrewd etc. judge of sth** to be someone whose opinions about something are usually right, wrong, intelligent, etc.

judge² /dʒʌdʒ/ verb ★★
1 [I/T] to form an opinion about something after considering all the details or facts: **+that** *He left the room when he judged that she was asleep.* ♦ **judge sb/sth on sth** *Universities are judged on their graduation rates.* ♦ **judge sth (to be) sth** *The water was judged to be of good quality.*
2 [I/T] to decide who or what is the winner of a competition: **judge sb/sth on sth** *The paintings will be judged on imagination and technique.* ♦ **judge sth (to be) sth** *In the end, Debbie's cake was judged the winner.*
3 [I/T] to criticize someone because you think their moral behavior is not very good: *It's difficult not to* ***judge people*** *sometimes.*
4 [T] to decide in a court of law whether or not someone is guilty

PHRASE **judging by/from sth** used for giving the reason why you think something is true: *Judging by his face, he was angry.*

judg•ment or **judge•ment** /ˈdʒʌdʒmənt/ noun ★★
1 [C/U] an opinion that you have after thinking carefully about something: *It is still too soon to* ***form a judgment about*** *this.* ♦ *He's too quick to* ***make judgments about***

J

other people. ♦ *She is not someone who* ***passes judgment*** *without knowing all the facts.* ♦ ***In my judgment****, he was not very good at his job.*
2 [U] your ability to understand a situation and make good decisions: *I trust your judgment.* ♦ *Her decision shows good judgment.*
3 [C/U] a decision that is made by a judge in a court of law = VERDICT

> **Words often used with judgment**
> *Verbs often used with* ***judgment*** *(sense 2)*
> - **affect, cloud** + JUDGMENT: cause someone to make an unreasonable judgment
> - **exercise, use** + JUDGMENT: be sensible when you are making a judgment

judg·men·tal or **judge·men·tal** /dʒʌdʒˈment(ə)l/ adj too willing to criticize other people

ju·di·cial /dʒuˈdɪʃ(ə)l/ adj relating to judges or to courts of law

juˈdicial ˌbranch, the noun [singular] the part of government that consists of all the judges and courts in a country. It makes decisions about which laws people must obey and whether people have not obeyed them. The other two parts of government are the **executive branch** and the **legislative branch**.

ju·di·ci·ar·y, the /dʒuˈdɪʃiˌeri/ noun [singular] all the judges and courts in a country

ju·di·cious /dʒuˈdɪʃəs/ adj *formal* showing intelligence and good judgment

ju·do /ˈdʒudoʊ/ noun [U] a sport in which you fight using balance and the weight of your body to throw your opponent to the ground

jug /dʒʌg/ noun [C] **1** *American* a large container for liquids, with a very narrow top that can be closed by a CORK **2** a PITCHER

jug·gle /ˈdʒʌg(ə)l/ verb **1** [I/T] to keep objects moving through the air by catching them and throwing them back into the air **2** [T] to try to do several important things at the same time: *the pressures of juggling a career and children*

juggle

jug·gler /ˈdʒʌg(ə)lər/ noun [C] someone who juggles objects in order to entertain people

juice /dʒus/ noun ★★
1 [C/U] the liquid that comes out of fruit or vegetables, often used as a drink: *orange/apple/carrot juice* ♦ *a selection of fruit juices*
2 [C/U] the liquid that comes out of meat when you cook it
3 [U] *informal* fuel or electricity

juic·y /ˈdʒusi/ adj **1** containing a lot of juice: *a sweet juicy apple* **2** *informal* slightly shocking but interesting or fun to listen to: *a juicy piece of gossip*

juke·box /ˈdʒukˌbɑks/ noun [C] a machine that plays music when you put money in it

Jul. abbrev July

Ju·ly /dʒuˈlaɪ/ noun [C/U] ★★★ the seventh month of the year, between June and August: *We're moving into our new house in July.* ♦ *The wedding is on July 19th.*

jum·ble[1] /ˈdʒʌmb(ə)l/ noun [singular] a collection of different things that are mixed together: *a jumble of buildings, neon signs, and billboards*

jum·ble[2] /ˈdʒʌmb(ə)l/ or **ˌjumble sth ˈup** verb [T] to mix things in a confusing or messy way

jum·bo /ˈdʒʌmboʊ/ adj larger than other things of the same type: *jumbo shrimp/sausages*

ˈjumbo ˌjet noun [C] a large airplane for a lot of passengers

jump[1] /dʒʌmp/ verb ★★★

1 move off the ground	5 increase very quickly
2 move over sth	6 move between ideas
3 move because of shock	+ PHRASES
4 move suddenly	+ PHRASAL VERB

1 [I] to push your body off the ground using your legs: *The cat* ***jumped up*** *onto my lap.* ♦ *The children were all* ***jumping up and down*** *and cheering.*
2 [T] to move over something by pushing yourself off the ground using your legs: *Terry jumped the fence and walked across the field.*
3 [I] to get a shock and suddenly move your body slightly because of this: *The noise* ***made her jump****.*
4 [I] to move somewhere quickly and suddenly: *He jumped in the car and drove off.* ♦ *Maggie jumped out of bed.*
5 [I] to increase or improve very quickly = SHOOT UP: *Profits jumped by 15% last year.* ♦ *Williams jumped from 39th to 5th in the world rankings.*
6 [I] to move quickly from one idea to another: *The conversation suddenly jumped back to what had happened yesterday.*
PHRASES **jump down sb's throat** to criticize someone immediately, in an unfair way
jump the gun to do or say something too soon
PHRASAL VERB **ˈjump at sth** to take an opportunity that is offered to you in a very enthusiastic way: ***I jumped at the chance*** *to go with him.*

jump[2] /dʒʌmp/ noun [C] **1** a movement in which you jump off the ground **2** a movement in which you jump from a high place: *a parachute/bungee jump* **3** a sudden increase = LEAP: *There has been another sharp jump in property prices.* **4** a structure that a horse or runner jumps over

ˈjump ˌball noun [C] in basketball, an occasion when the ball is thrown straight up so that one player from each team can jump for it —*picture* → C15

jump·er /ˈdʒʌmpər/ noun [C] *American* a dress without sleeves that is usually worn over a shirt

ˈjumper ˌcables noun [plural] *American* a pair of wires that you use to start a car by connecting it to the engine of another car

ˌjumping ˈjack noun [C] a type of exercise in which you spread your legs and point your hands straight up, then bring your legs together and let your hands fall

ˈjump ˌrope noun [C] *American* a rope that you pass over your head and under your feet as you jump

ˈjump ˌshot noun [C] the movement that a basketball player makes by jumping into the air and throwing the ball toward the basket —*picture* → C15

jump•suit /ˈdʒʌmpˌsut/ noun [C] a tight piece of clothing that covers the body and legs, and sometimes the arms

jump•y /ˈdʒʌmpi/ adj *informal* nervous

Jun. abbrev June

junc•tion /ˈdʒʌŋkʃ(ə)n/ noun [C] a place where two or more highways, railroad lines, or rivers join together

junc•ture /ˈdʒʌŋktʃər/ noun [C] *formal* a point in a process or period of time

June /dʒun/ noun [C/U] ★★★ the sixth month of the year, between May and July: *I'll finish school in June.* ♦ *Our last class is on June 5th.*

jun•gle /ˈdʒʌŋg(ə)l/ noun [C/U] a thick tropical forest

jun•ior[1] /ˈdʒuniər/ adj ★★

1 a junior person does not have a lot of responsibility or power in their job ≠ SENIOR: *a junior partner at the law firm*

2 intended for young people, or involving them: *the world junior swimming championship*

jun•ior[2] /ˈdʒuniər/ noun [C] a student in the U.S. who is in the year before their last year at a university or HIGH SCHOOL

PHRASE **be two years/ten years etc. sb's junior** to be younger than someone else by a particular amount

jun•ior[3] /ˈdʒuniər/ used after the name of a man who has the same name as his father

ˌjunior ˈcollege noun [C/U] a college in the U.S. where students can study practical subjects or follow a two year course of study that prepares them to enter a university = COMMUNITY COLLEGE

ˌjunior ˈhigh school or **ˌjunior ˈhigh** noun [C/U] a school in the U.S. for children between the ages of 12 and 15

ˌjunior ˈvarsity noun [singular] *American* a sports team for the players in a school who are either not old enough or not good enough to play on the best team

junk /dʒʌŋk/ noun [U] old things that are not valuable or not wanted = GARBAGE

ˈjunk ˌfood noun [C/U] food that is not healthy because it contains a lot of fat, salt, or sugar

junk•ie /ˈdʒʌŋki/ noun [C] *informal* **1** someone who is unable to stop taking illegal drugs **2** *often humorous* a person who likes doing something very much and does it a lot: *a computer games junkie*

ˈjunk ˌmail noun [U] advertising and other information that is sent to you, but that you did not ask for

junk•yard /ˈdʒʌŋkˌjɑrd/ noun [C] a place that buys machines and other things that are old, not useful, or broken, and sells them or their parts to other people

jun•ta /ˈhʊntə/ noun [C] a group of military officers that governs a country

ju•ris•dic•tion /ˌdʒʊrɪsˈdɪkʃ(ə)n/ noun [U] the right or power to make legal decisions

ju•ror /ˈdʒʊrər/ noun [C] a member of a jury

ju•ry /ˈdʒʊri/ noun [C] ★★

1 a group of members of the public who decide whether someone is guilty in a court case: *The jury found him guilty.*

2 a group of people who judge a competition

PHRASE **the jury is still out (on sth)** used for saying that people have not yet decided what they think about something

just[1] /dʒʌst/ adv ★★★

1 a moment ago a short time ago, or a short time before something that happened in the past: *Mom just left to go to the grocery store.* ♦ *Agassi had just arrived in Australia the day before.* ♦ *Just last week it was freezing, and now it's too hot.* ♦ *What were you saying to Lisa **just now** (=a moment ago)?*

2 at this time at the same time as something else: ***Just then** a knock at the door interrupted our conversation.* ♦ *Mark was **just about to** leave when someone called him.* ♦ *I was **just going to** ask you the same question.*

3 only not more, bigger, more important, etc. than what you are mentioning: *The medicine costs just a few cents to produce.* ♦ *It was just a stupid mistake.* ♦ *We just wanted to make sure everyone was safe.* ♦ *No, I don't want to buy anything. I'm just looking.* ♦ *It's **not just** me. Other people are complaining too.*

4 exactly exactly: *He's just like his father.* ♦ *Thank you so much, it was just what I wanted.* ♦ *Cameron's plan failed, **just as** I expected it would.*

5 slightly slightly before, after, nearer, or farther: *I spoke with him just after he won the award.* ♦ *Her parents were seated just behind her.*

6 used for emphasis *spoken* used for emphasizing what you are saying: *It was just awful seeing her so miserable.* ♦ *Just be quiet, will you?*

7 when sth almost does not happen used for saying that although something happens, it almost does not happen: *We should just get there on time if we hurry.*

8 used in requests *spoken* used for making a request more polite: *Could I just borrow your pen for a second?*

PHRASES **just about** very nearly: *I think we've just about finished.* ♦ *Another scandal would be just about the worst thing that could happen.*

just a minute/moment/second *spoken* **1** used for asking someone to wait for a short time: *Just a moment. We're not ready for you yet.* **2** used when interrupting someone, especially when you disagree with what they are saying: *Just a minute. You can't make accusations like that.*

just as...(as) used for emphasizing that something is equally large, good, bad, etc.: *Less expensive machines are just as good or*

even better. ♦ *Animals feel pain just as much as we do.*
just because... *spoken* used for saying that even if one thing is true, this is not a reason for thinking that something else is true: *Just because he's rich doesn't mean he's better than us.*
it/that is just as well *spoken* used for saying that a situation is good, even though it is not what you planned: *We canceled the trip, which was just as well, because it rained.*
→ LIKE

just² /dʒʌst/ adj *formal* fair and morally right =FAIR ≠ UNJUST: *a just society*

jus•tice /ˈdʒʌstɪs/ noun [U] ★★
1 treatment of people that is fair and morally right ≠ INJUSTICE: *The people want peace and justice.* ♦ *Victims are calling for justice.*
2 the legal process of judging and punishing people: *the criminal justice system* ♦ *Whoever committed these crimes must be* ***brought to justice*** (=judged in a court of law).
PHRASE **do sb/sth justice** to show or emphasize all the good qualities of someone or something

ˌJustice of the ˈPeace noun [C] a government official similar to a judge who works in the lower courts and can perform marriage ceremonies =MAGISTRATE

jus•ti•fi•a•ble /ˈdʒʌstɪˌfaɪəb(ə)l/ adj if something is justifiable, there is a good reason for it —**jus•ti•fi•a•bly** adv

jus•ti•fi•ca•tion /ˌdʒʌstɪfɪˈkeɪʃ(ə)n/ noun [C/U] a reason why something is correct and morally right: *There can be no justification for such rude behavior.*

jus•ti•fied /ˈdʒʌstɪˌfaɪd/ adj if something is justified, there is a good reason for it

jus•ti•fy /ˈdʒʌstɪˌfaɪ/ verb [T] ★★
1 to show that there is a good reason for something: *The results justify all our hard work.* ♦ **justify doing sth** *How can you justify spending all that money?*
2 *technical* to make the left or right edges of writing form a straight line when typing or printing

jut /dʒʌt/ PHRASAL VERB **ˌjut ˈout** to be farther forward than other things, or farther forward than normal

ju•ve•nile¹ /ˈdʒuvən(ə)l/ adj **1** relating to young people **2** silly and not appropriate for an adult

ju•ve•nile² /ˈdʒuvən(ə)l/ noun [C] a young person

ˌjuvenile deˈlinquent noun [C] a young person who has committed a crime

jux•ta•pose /ˈdʒʌkstəˌpoʊz/ verb [T] *formal* to put different things together so that people can see how they are different —**jux•ta•po•si•tion** /ˌdʒʌkstəpəˈzɪʃ(ə)n/ noun [C/U]

JV /ˌdʒeɪ ˈvi/ abbrev *American* junior varsity

K k

k or **K** /keɪ/ noun [C/U] the eleventh letter of the English alphabet

K¹ /keɪ/ abbrev **1** kilobyte **2** kilometer **3** kindergarten

K² /keɪ/ (plural **K**) noun [C] *informal* one thousand dollars, or one thousand pounds

K-12 /ˌkeɪ ˈtwelv/ abbrev *American* kindergarten through twelfth: used for talking about the 13 years of school before your college education

ka•lei•do•scope /kəˈlaɪdəˌskoʊp/ noun [C] **1** a scene, situation, or experience that keeps changing and has many different aspects **2** a toy that shows changing patterns. It consists of a tube with colored pieces inside.

kan•ga•roo /ˌkæŋgəˈru/ noun [C] a large Australian animal that moves by jumping and carries its baby in a POUCH (=pocket on the front of its body) —*picture* → C13

kar•a•o•ke /ˌkeriˈoʊki/ noun [U] a type of entertainment in which people sing popular songs while recorded music is played

kar•at /ˈkerət/ noun [C] *American* a unit for measuring how pure gold is

ka•ra•te /kəˈrɑti/ noun [U] a way of fighting from Japan, in which people hit each other using their hands, feet, arms, and legs

kar•ma /ˈkɑrmə/ noun [U] in Hinduism and Buddhism, a belief that the way you behaved in past lives affects your present life, and the way you behave in this life will affect your future lives

kay•ak /ˈkaɪˌæk/ noun [C] a small covered CANOE (=narrow boat with a point at each end)

keel /kil/ noun [C] a long thin piece of wood or metal along the bottom of a boat that helps it to balance in the water
PHRASE **on an even keel** operating or happening without problems

keen /kin/ adj **1** keen sight, hearing, etc. makes you very good at seeing, hearing, etc. **2** very strong: *a manager who takes a keen interest in his employees* **3** wanting to do something or wanting other people to do something: *I was quite keen on the idea of going to live in a bigger city.* —**keen•ly** /ˈkinli/ adv, **keen•ness** noun [U]

keep¹ /kip/ (past tense and past participle **kept** /kept/) verb ★★★

1 stay in state/position	8 do what you said
2 continue/repeat	9 take care of animals
3 make sb/sth continue	10 of food etc.
4 continue to have	11 delay sb
5 stay within limit	12 provide money for
6 store sth somewhere	+ PHRASES
7 store information	+ PHRASAL VERBS

1 [I/T] to stay in a state, position, or place without changing or moving, or to make someone or something do this: ***Keep still***

while I brush your hair. ♦ *People* ***kept quiet*** *because they were afraid.* ♦ ***Keep*** *her* ***warm*** *and give her plenty to drink.*
2 [T] to do something many times, or to continue doing something: *Keep taking the tablets.* ♦ *I keep forgetting to turn the burglar alarm on.* ♦ *Keep going straight until you reach the river.*
3 [T] to make someone or something continue doing something: *Sorry to* ***keep you waiting.***
4 [T] to continue to have or own something: *We should keep this car and sell the other one.* ♦ *I've got two copies, you can keep that one.*
5 [T] to control something so that it stays within a limit: *Expenses must be kept to a minimum.*
6 [T] to store something in a particular place so that you know where it is: *Where do you keep the soap?* ♦ *Read this letter carefully, and* ***keep it in a safe place.***
7 [T] to store information by writing it or putting it into a computer: *Some companies do not* ***keep*** *detailed* ***records.*** ♦ *Every member of the group has to* ***keep a diary.***
8 [T] to do what you said you would do: *If you cannot* ***keep*** *your* ***appointment,*** *please let us know.* ♦ *I have tried to* ***keep*** *my* ***promise.***
9 [T] to own animals and take care of them: *A few cows are kept to provide milk, cheese, and cream.*
10 [I] if food or other substances keep for a particular period of time, they stay in good condition for that period of time: *The cranberry sauce will* ***keep for*** *two weeks in the refrigerator.*
11 [T] *spoken* to delay someone: *What kept you?* ♦ *I won't keep you long.*
12 [T] to provide money for yourself or someone else, in order to pay for the food, clothes, and other things that you or they need

PHRASES **keep going 1** to continue to do something although it is difficult: *They forced themselves to keep going even though they felt exhausted.* **2** to continue to move without stopping: *The truck kept going and disappeared from view.*
keep to yourself to stay alone or with your family rather than spending time with other people: *They were a quiet couple who kept to themselves.*
keep sth to yourself to not tell anyone else about something
→ EYE[1]

PHRASAL VERBS **ˌkeep ˈat sth** to continue doing something even if you want to stop: *The secret of dieting is to keep at it.*
ˌkeep aˈway to avoid someone or something, or to not go near someone or something: *I've told him to keep away, but he won't listen.* ♦ *You should* ***keep away from*** *fried foods.*
ˌkeep sth ˈdown to control something and prevent it from increasing in size or number: *We have to try and keep our costs down.*
ˈkeep sb from sth to prevent someone from doing something, or to prevent something from happening: *These worries kept her from sleeping properly.*
ˈkeep sth from sb to not tell someone something: *I kept the news from him for a while.*
ˌkeep sth ˈoff (sth) to not touch something, or to prevent something from touching something: *Keep the flies off the food.* ♦ *Keep your hands off, it's mine.*
ˈkeep (sb/sth) off sth to not go onto a particular area of land: *Dogs must be kept off the beach.* ♦ *Keep off the grass.*
ˌkeep sb ˈon to continue to employ someone: *Only highly skilled people were kept on after the merger.*
ˌkeep ˈon doing sth to continue to do something: *My sister kept on asking me question after question.*
ˌkeep sb/sth ˈout 1 to prevent someone or something from entering a place: *Cars should be kept out of the national park.* **2 keep out** used on signs to tell people not to go into a place
ˌkeep ˈout of sth to not become involved with something: *You keep out of this. It's none of your business.*
ˈkeep to sth to follow an agreement or a rule, by doing what you should do or what you said you would do: *Try to keep to a regular schedule when you travel overseas.*
ˈkeep sth to sth to prevent an amount or number from passing a limit: *You should keep your intake of alcohol to two drinks per day.*
ˌkeep ˈup to move or develop at the same speed as someone or something: *By studying hard, she managed to keep up.* ♦ *He had to hurry to* ***keep up with*** *her.*
ˌkeep sb ˈup to prevent someone from going to bed: *It's late, I'd better not keep you up any longer.*
ˌkeep sth ˈup to continue to do something: *Keep up the good work.* ♦ *The unions continued to keep up pressure for higher wages.*

keep[2] /kip/ noun [U] the cost of the food and the other things such as clothes that you need to live

keep•er /ˈkipər/ noun [C] someone who is responsible for taking care of a place, a group of animals, or a collection of objects

keep•ing /ˈkipɪŋ/ noun **in/out of keeping with sth** in or not in the same manner or style as something else

keg /keg/ noun [C] a small BARREL (=round container with a flat top and bottom) that is used for storing beer or other drinks

ken•nel /ˈken(ə)l/ noun [C] **1** a small building where a dog sleeps and is protected from bad weather **2** a place where dogs stay while their owners are away

kept the past tense and past participle of **keep**[1]

kerb /kɜrb/ the British spelling of **curb**

ker•nel /ˈkɜrn(ə)l/ noun [C] **1** the soft part inside a nut or a seed **2** the central or most important part of something

ker•o•sene /ˈkerəˌsin/ noun [U] *American* a clear oil with a strong smell that is used for fuel

ketch•up /ˈketʃəp/ noun [U] a thick red sauce made from tomatoes

ket•tle /ˈket(ə)l/ noun [C] a TEAKETTLE

K

key¹ /ki/ noun [C] ★★★

1 for opening/locking	5 in music
2 for achieving sth	6 list of symbols
3 on keyboard	7 list of answers
4 on instrument	

1 a small piece of metal that is used for opening or locking a door or a container, or for starting the motor of a vehicle: *a bunch of keys ♦ house/car keys ♦ I could hear someone* ***turning the key in the lock.*** *♦ Where's the* ***key to*** *the back door?*
2 the thing that will do most to help you to achieve something: *Proper planning is the* ***key to*** *success. ♦ Tourism* ***holds the key*** *to the region's economic recovery.*
3 one of the parts that you press on a keyboard to make it produce letters, numbers, and symbols: *Highlight the file you want to open and* ***press the*** *RETURN* ***key.***
4 one of the parts that you press on a musical instrument to make it produce sounds: *piano keys*
5 a set of musical notes that are based on one particular note: *a major/minor key ♦ a piece written* ***in the key of*** *C*
6 a list of the symbols that are used on a map or a drawing
7 a list of answers to the questions in a test or in a book
→ LOCK²

key² /ki/ adj ★★★ very important: *The Steelers have lost two key players because of injuries. ♦ Foreign policy had been* ***a key issue*** *in the campaign.*

key³ /ki/ or ˌ**key sth ˈin** verb [T] to put information into a computer or other electronic machine using a keyboard

key·board /ˈkiˌbɔrd/ noun [C] **1** a piece of computer equipment with keys on it, used for putting information into a computer —*picture* → C3 **2** the part of a musical instrument such as a piano that has the keys that you touch to make sounds **3** a musical instrument that has a keyboard, especially an electric piano

key·hole /ˈkiˌhoul/ noun [C] the hole in a lock where you put the key

key·note /ˈkiˌnout/ adj a keynote speech is the most important speech at a formal meeting or event

key·pad /ˈkiˌpæd/ noun [C] a part of a piece of equipment that has keys that you press

ˈ**key ˌring** noun [C] a metal ring that you use for keeping your keys together

key·word /ˈkiˌwɜrd/ noun [C] **1** a word that you type into a computer in order to find information about a particular subject **2** a word that represents the main feature or idea of something

kg abbrev kilogram

khak·i /ˈkæki/ adj green-brown or brown-yellow in color —**khak·i** noun [U]

kick¹ /kɪk/ verb ★★★
1 [I/T] to hit someone or something with your foot: *Mom! Jimmy kicked me! ♦* **kick sth open/closed/shut** *Jerry kicked the door open. ♦* **kick sb in the stomach/face/head etc.** *She felt as if she had been kicked in the stomach. ♦* **kick sth around** *A couple of children were kicking a ball around.*
2 [I/T] to move your legs as if you were kicking something: *A beetle lay on its back kicking its legs in the air.*
3 [T] *informal* to stop doing something that is bad for you: *Do you smoke and want to* ***kick the habit?***
PHRASE **kick yourself** to be annoyed with yourself because you have made a mistake, or have missed an opportunity to do something
→ ALIVE
PHRASAL VERBS ˌ**kick ˈback** *informal* to relax: *At 5:00 we can kick back and forget about work.*
ˌ**kick ˈin** *informal* to start to have an effect: *The medicine took some time to kick in.*
ˌ**kick (sth) ˈoff** *informal* to begin, or to begin something: *The game kicks off at noon. ♦ I'd like to* ***kick off with*** *a quick look at last month's sales figures.*
ˌ**kick sb ˈout** *informal* to force someone to leave a place or organization: **kick sb out of sth** *Sonia was kicked out of her house.*

kick

kick² /kɪk/ noun **1** [C] a hit with your foot: *Bobby gave the door a good kick.* **2** [singular] *informal* a feeling of excitement or pleasure: *I get a real kick out of seeing my children do well in school. ♦ I just play the banjo for kicks – I'm not very good at it.*

kick·back /ˈkɪkˌbæk/ noun [C/U] *American informal* money paid illegally to another person in exchange for something they have done for you

kick·er /ˈkɪkər/ noun [C] *American informal* something that is very surprising

kick·off /ˈkɪkˌɔf/ noun [C] the beginning of a game of soccer or football, when one player kicks the ball down the field

ˈ**kick-ˌstart** verb [T] to make something start again after it has stopped or slowed down —ˈ**kick-ˌstart** noun [C]

kid¹ /kɪd/ noun ★★
1 [C] *informal* a child or young adult: *There was a group of kids playing in the street. ♦ a bunch of middle-class college kids ♦ When I was a kid, I was very shy.*
2 [C] a young goat
3 [U] leather made from a young goat's skin

kid² /kɪd/ verb [I/T] to say something that is not true, especially as a joke: *He said that? You're kidding me.* ♦ *Just kidding. Don't worry.*
PHRASE **are you kidding?** *spoken* used for saying that you do not believe or agree with what someone is saying

kid³ /kɪd/ adj *informal* your kid brother or sister is your younger brother or sister

kid·die or **kid·dy** /ˈkɪdi/ noun [C] *informal* a young child

kid·nap¹ /ˈkɪdˌnæp/ verb [T] to illegally take someone away and make them a prisoner, especially in order to make their family or a government give you money —**kid·nap·per** noun [C]

kid·nap² /ˈkɪdˌnæp/ or **kid·nap·ping** /ˈkɪdˌnæpɪŋ/ noun [C/U] the act of kidnapping someone

kid·ney /ˈkɪdni/ noun [C] one of the two organs in your body that clean your blood by removing waste liquids

ˈkidney ˌbean noun [C] a red bean eaten as a vegetable —*picture* → C11

kill¹ /kɪl/ verb ★★★
1 [I/T] to make a person or other living thing die: *Each year thousands of people are killed and injured on the roads.* ♦ *Many people believe that killing animals for sport is morally wrong.*
2 [T] to stop something from continuing: *The nurse will give you something to kill the pain.*
3 [T] *informal* if part of your body is killing you, it is causing you a lot of pain: *My back's killing me.*
4 [T] to spend time doing a particular activity while you are waiting for something: *We killed a few hours watching reruns.* ♦ *Shopping can be a good way to **kill time** at the airport.*
PHRASE **sb will kill sb** *spoken* used for saying that someone will be very angry with another person
PHRASAL VERB **ˌkill sb/sth ˈoff** **1** to destroy living things so that most or all of them are dead: *Antibiotics may kill off beneficial bacteria.* **2** to make something stop or fail completely: *Opponents hope to kill off the plan to extend the airport.*

Other ways of saying kill

- **assassinate** to kill an important or famous person for political reasons or for money
- **commit suicide** to deliberately kill yourself
- **execute** to kill someone legally as a punishment for a serious crime
- **massacre** to kill a very large number of people in a violent or cruel way
- **murder** to deliberately kill someone
- **put sth down** or **put sth to sleep** to kill an animal because it is sick or in pain

kill² /kɪl/ noun [singular] an act in which a hunted animal is killed

kill·er /ˈkɪlər/ noun [C] **1** someone who kills another person: *The young woman's killer has not yet been found.* **2** something that kills people: *Cancer is the second largest killer in the U.S.* **3** something that kills or destroys something else: *weed killer*

kill·ing /ˈkɪlɪŋ/ noun [C] an act in which someone is deliberately killed

kiln /kɪln/ noun [C] a type of oven that is used for baking clay and bricks to make them hard

ki·lo /ˈkiloʊ/ noun [C] a KILOGRAM

kil·o·byte /ˈkɪləˌbaɪt/ noun [C] *computing* a unit for measuring computer information, containing 1024 BYTES

kil·o·gram /ˈkɪləˌgræm/ noun [C] a unit for measuring weight in the METRIC system, containing 1000 grams

ki·lom·e·ter /kɪˈlɑmətər/ noun [C] a unit for measuring distance in the METRIC system, containing 1000 meters

ki·lom·e·tre /kɪˈlɑmətər/ the British spelling of **kilometer**

kil·o·watt /ˈkɪləˌwɑt/ noun [C] a unit for measuring electrical power, containing 1000 WATTS

kilt /kɪlt/ noun [C] a type of traditional Scottish clothing, similar to a skirt, worn by men —*picture* → C4

kin /kɪn/ noun [U] *formal* all the people in your family → NEXT

kind¹ /kaɪnd/ noun [C] ★★★ a type of person or thing = SORT: *I guess I'm not the marrying kind.* ♦ *The bridge is the largest **of its kind** in the world.* ♦ *We've all had disappointments **of some kind**.* ♦ *There was no financial link between us **of any kind**.* ♦ *What **kind of** person is she?* ♦ *Francis taught me **all kinds of** stuff.* ♦ *Many people like to try lots of **different kinds of** food.*
PHRASES **in kind** payments or benefits in kind are in the form of goods or services rather than money
kind of *spoken* used when you are talking about someone or something in a general way without being very exact or definite: *He was kind of strange, but I liked him.*

kind² /kaɪnd/ adj ★ behaving in a way that shows you care about other people and want to help them ≠ UNKIND: *Thank you, Mark, you've been very kind.* ♦ *We are grateful for your **kind offer**.* ♦ *She was very **kind to** me when the children were sick.* ♦ **it is kind of sb to do sth** *It was kind of you to help them.*

kin·da /ˈkaɪndə/ adv a way of writing "kind of" that shows how it sounds in informal conversation

kin·der·gar·ten /ˈkɪndərˌgɑrt(ə)n, ˈkɪndərˌgɑrd(ə)n/ noun [C/U] **1** *American* the first year of formal education in the U.S., for children aged 5 or 6 **2** *British* a NURSERY SCHOOL

kin·dle /ˈkɪnd(ə)l/ verb [T] **1** to start a strong interest or emotion in someone: *His interest in history was kindled by visits to the museum.* **2** to start a fire by lighting small pieces of wood or paper that will burn easily

kin·dling /ˈkɪndlɪŋ/ noun [U] small pieces of wood that you use for starting a fire

kind·ly¹ /ˈkaɪndli/ adj *old-fashioned* a kindly person behaves in a kind way toward other people

kind·ly² /ˈkaɪndli/ adv **1** in a kind way: *"Don't worry about it," she said kindly.* **2** *spoken formal* used for making a polite request: *Would you kindly stop making that noise?* ♦

Kindly return one copy of the letter to me.

kind•ness /ˈkaɪndnəs/ noun [U] kind behavior, or kind feelings

king /kɪŋ/ noun [C] ★★★
1 a man who rules a country and is the senior male member of the royal family: *Oswald became king in 634.* ♦ *King George VI*
2 a man who is the best at doing a particular thing: *Elvis, **the king of** rock and roll*
3 a PLAYING CARD with the picture of a king on it: ***the king of spades*** —*picture* → C16
4 one of the two most important pieces in the game of CHESS —*picture* → C16

king•dom /ˈkɪŋdəm/ noun [C] a country or area that is ruled by a king or queen
PHRASE **the animal/plant kingdom** all the animals or plants that exist in the world

king•pin /ˈkɪŋˌpɪn/ noun [C] the most important person in a group or organization, usually connected with crime

king-size /ˈkɪŋ ˌsaɪz/ or **king-sized** /ˈkɪŋ ˌsaɪzd/ adj bigger than usual

kink /kɪŋk/ noun [C] **1** a bend or twist in something that is usually straight
2 something that is a problem or that seems strange: *We need time to iron out any kinks in the new system.*

kin•ship /ˈkɪnʃɪp/ noun [singular/U] *formal* the fact of being related to someone

ki•osk /ˈkiˌɑsk, kiˈɑsk/ noun [C] a very small store that sells newspapers, drinks, etc.

kiss¹ /kɪs/ verb [I/T] ★ to touch someone with your lips to show love or as a greeting: *They kissed again, and then he was gone.* ♦ *We all **hugged and kissed** each other.* ♦ *He went upstairs to **kiss** his son **good night**.*
PHRASAL VERB **ˌkiss ˈup to sb** *American informal* to try to please a powerful person, because you want them to do something for you

kiss² /kɪs/ noun [C] an act of kissing someone: *Julius gave her another kiss.*

kit /kɪt/ noun [C] **1** a set of tools or equipment for a particular activity: *Cyclists should carry a repair kit.* ♦ *a sewing/shaving kit*
2 all the pieces that you need to build something such as a vehicle or a computer

kitch•en /ˈkɪtʃ(ə)n/ noun [C] ★★★ a room where you prepare and cook food, and wash dishes: *We sometimes eat in the kitchen.* ♦ *kitchen utensils/appliances* —*picture* → C2

kite /kaɪt/ noun [C] a toy that flies in the air while you hold it by a long string

kit•ten /ˈkɪt(ə)n/ noun [C] a young cat

kit•ty /ˈkɪti/ noun [C] **1** an amount of money collected by a group, to be spent by the group **2** an amount of money collected by the people playing a game, to be paid to the winner

ki•wi fruit /ˈkiwi ˌfrut/ noun [C/U] a fruit with green flesh, small black seeds, and a brown skin —*picture* → C10

Kleen•ex /ˈkliˌneks/ *trademark* a small paper HANDKERCHIEF

km abbrev kilometer

knack /næk/ noun [singular] *informal* a particular skill or way of doing something: *She had a knack of making people feel really special.*

knead /nid/ verb [T] to prepare DOUGH (=a mixture for making bread) or clay by pressing it continuously

knee /ni/ noun [C] ★★★
1 the part in the middle of your leg, where it bends: *a serious knee injury* ♦ ***Bend your knees** when you pick up heavy objects.* ♦ *We were **up to our knees** in mud.* ♦ *He **got down on his knees** for a closer look.* —*picture* → C14
2 the upper part of your legs when you are sitting down, where you can hold a child or object = LAP: *He was sitting in the armchair with the cat curled up **on his knees**.*
PHRASE **bring sb/sth to their knees** to almost defeat someone or something

knee•cap /ˈniˌkæp/ noun [C] the bone at the front of your knee

ˈknee-ˌjerk adj a knee-jerk reaction is immediate and not carefully considered

kneel /nil/ (past tense and past participle **knelt** /nelt/ or **kneeled**) or **ˌkneel ˈdown** verb [I] to put or have your knee or both knees on the ground: *She knelt in front of the fire to warm herself.* ♦ *He was kneeling at her feet.* —*picture* → POSTURE

knew the past tense of **know**

knick•ers /ˈnɪkərz/ noun [plural] *British* PANTIES

knife¹ /naɪf/ (plural **knives** /naɪvz/) noun [C] ★★★ an object with a blade, used for cutting food or as a weapon: *knives and forks* ♦ *a kitchen/bread/carving knife* ♦ *The girls were threatened with a knife.* —*picture* → C2

knife² /naɪf/ verb [T] to injure or kill someone with a knife

knight /naɪt/ noun [C] **1** in the past, a European soldier from a high social class who wore a suit of ARMOR (=a metal suit) and rode a horse **2** a piece in the game of CHESS that is shaped like a horse's head —*picture* → C16

knight•hood /ˈnaɪtˌhʊd/ noun [C] an honor given by a British king or queen that allows a man to use the title "Sir" before his name

knit /nɪt/ (past tense and past participle **knit•ted** or **knit**) verb [I/T] to make something such as a piece of clothing using wool and KNITTING NEEDLES → CLOSE-KNIT

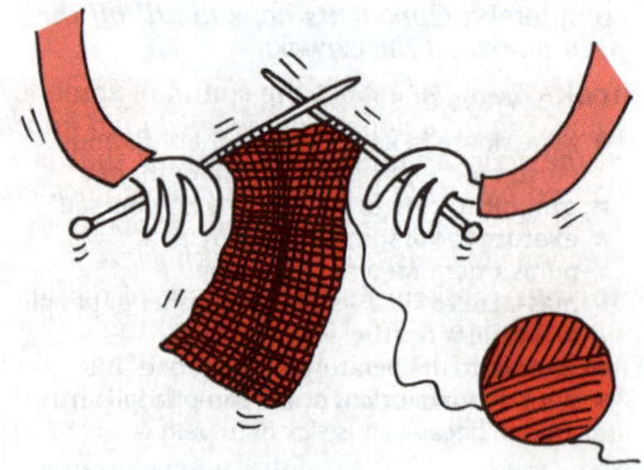

knit

knit•ting /ˈnɪtɪŋ/ noun [U] **1** the activity or process of knitting things **2** something that is being knitted

knit•wear /ˈnɪtˌwer/ noun [U] clothes that have been KNITTED

knives the plural of **knife¹**

knob /nɑb/ noun [C] **1** a round handle on a door or drawer **2** a round switch on a piece of equipment

knock¹ /nɑk/ verb ★★★

1 hit a door	4 hit sth hard
2 move sth by hitting	5 criticize sb/sth
3 hit sb hard	+ PHRASAL VERBS

1 [I] to hit a door with your hand or with a knocker: *They walked up to the door and knocked loudly.* ♦ *I* ***knocked on*** *his door but got no answer.*
2 [T] to hit something so that it moves somewhere: **knock sth off sth** *I knocked a picture off the wall.* ♦ **knock sth into sth** *He knocked a couple of nails into the door.*
3 [T] to hit someone very hard, so that they fall or become unconscious: *They knocked him to the ground.* ♦ *The driver had been* ***knocked unconscious*** *by the impact.*
4 [T] to hit something hard against an object: *Mike had knocked his leg against a table.*
5 [T] *informal* to criticize someone or something

PHRASAL VERBS ˌ**knock sth ˈdown** to destroy a building or wall: *The far wall could be knocked down to make the room bigger.*
ˌ**knock ˈoff** to stop working
ˌ**knock sth ˈoff (sth)** *informal* to reduce a price or an amount: *Kelly knocked two seconds off her previous time.*
ˌ**knock sb ˈout 1** to make someone unconscious **2** to make someone leave a competition by defeating them: *The home team was knocked out of the tournament in the first round.* **3** *informal* to impress or surprise someone very much

knock

knock² /nɑk/ noun [C] **1** the sound of someone knocking on a door: *There was a loud knock at the door.* **2** damage or an injury that is caused by being knocked: *a nasty knock on the head* **3** something bad that happens to someone: *Life is full of hard knocks.*

knock•er /ˈnɑkər/ noun [C] a piece of metal on a door that you use for knocking

knock•out /ˈnɑkˌaʊt/ noun [C] a hit that knocks a BOXER down, so that they cannot get up

knot /nɑt/ noun [C] **1** a point where string, rope, or cloth is tied or twisted together and pulled tight: *Can you tie a knot in the end of this thread?* **2** a unit for measuring the speed of ships, aircraft, and wind, equal to one NAUTICAL MILE per hour

knot•ted /ˈnɑtəd/ adj with knots: *a scarf with knotted corners*

know¹ /noʊ/ (past tense **knew** /nu/; past participle **known** /noʊn/) verb ★★★

1 have information	6 experience
2 be familiar with	7 speak a language
3 feel certain about	8 have learned sth
4 use particular name	+ PHRASES
5 remember sb for sth	+ PHRASAL VERB

1 [I/T] to have information about something, or to understand something: *How do you know my name?* ♦ *"Have they arrived yet?" "I don't know."* ♦ *If you don't* ***know the answer****, just guess.* ♦ **+(that)** *I knew she wasn't really happy.* ♦ **+what/why/who etc.** *None of us really knew what had gone wrong.* ♦ *I don't* ***know if*** *she's made a decision yet.* ♦ **know sth about sth** *Do you know anything about computers?* ♦ **be known to be/do sth** *Some drugs are known to cause damage to unborn children.*
2 [T] to be familiar with someone or something, for example because you have met someone before or been to a place before: *Do you know Terry Davis?* ♦ *Jane and I have* ***known each other*** *for years.* ♦ *Do you* ***know*** *Rome* ***well****?*
3 [I/T] to feel certain about something: **+(that)** *She knew it was Steven before she picked up the phone.*
4 [T] to use a particular name for someone or something: *They know all their professors by their first names.* ♦ **be known as sth** *The place was known as Boot Hill.*
5 [T] to remember someone because of a particular skill or quality: *We know her mostly for her poetry.* ♦ *He was* ***best known as*** *a painter.*
6 [T] to experience something: *It was the only comfort and warmth she had ever known.* ♦ **have never known sb (to) do sth** *I've never known her to tell a joke.*
7 [T] to be able to speak a language: *Do you know any Spanish?*
8 [T] to have learned a poem, story, or song, so that you can say it or sing it

PHRASES **for all I know** used for emphasizing that you do not know something: *He could be a murderer for all I know.*
get to know to start to be familiar with someone or something: *It took a while to get to know the city properly.*
how should I know? *spoken* used for saying in an annoyed way that you do not know something
I don't know 1 used for politely disagreeing or giving your opinion: *"It'll be boring." "Oh I don't know, it might be fun."* ♦ **+that** *I don't know that we need to discuss this.* **2** used for criticizing someone: **+what/how/why etc.** *I don't know how he could do that.*
I know 1 used for agreeing with what someone says: *"He's a complete idiot." "Yeah, I know."* **2** used for showing that you understand someone and feel sympathy for them: *I know how hard this is for you.* **3** used for showing that you understand that there is a problem, but you do not think it is important: *I know, I should have told you I'd be late.* ♦ *I know the plan is pretty rough, but you get the idea.* **4** used when you have a sudden idea: *I know, let's go to the movies instead.*

K

know best to be in the best position to decide something

know better 1 to understand that you should not do something, because you are sensible or experienced: *She should know better than to try to fool him.* **2** to know that what someone else says or thinks is wrong: *Everyone thought it was an innocent mistake, but I knew better.*

let sb know to tell someone something: *Let me know when he arrives.*

you know *spoken* **1** *informal* used while you think about what to say next: *My whole leg was, you know, soaked in blood.* **2** used when you are giving extra information about something: *Have you seen that bowl, you know, the blue one?* **3** used for emphasis: *Things are different now, you know.* **4** used before you start to talk about a particular person or thing: *You know the woman next door, well, she's expecting a baby.*

you never know *spoken* used for saying that something good might happen

PHRASAL VERB ˈ**know of sb/sth 1** to know about someone or something: *I only know of one case in which this has happened.* ♦ *Do you know of anyone who's looking for a new car?* **2 not that I know of** *spoken* used for answering that you think that something is not true, although you are not completely certain

L

Word family: know

Words in the same family as ***know***

- **knowing** *adj*
- **knowingly** *adv*
- **knowledge** *n*
- **knowledgeable** *adj*
- **known** *adj*
- **unknowingly** *adv*
- **unknown** *adj*

know² /noʊ/ noun **in the know** having more information about something than other people

ˈ**know-ˌhow** noun [U] *informal* the knowledge that is needed to do something

know•ing /ˈnoʊɪŋ/ adj showing that you know about something: *Tom gave me a knowing look.*

know•ing•ly /ˈnoʊɪŋli/ adv **1** in a way that shows that you know something: *She smiled knowingly.* **2** deliberately, knowing that something is wrong or illegal: *Had her grandmother knowingly taken the money?*

ˈ**know-it-ˌall** noun [C] *informal* someone who is annoying because they always think that they know everything

knowl•edge /ˈnɑlɪdʒ/ noun [U] ★★★

1 what you know, or what is known about a particular subject: *She had a lot of knowledge and experience.* ♦ *the pursuit of knowledge* ♦ *Candidates should have a good* ***knowledge of*** *Russian.*

2 the fact that you know that something is happening: *This was done without my knowledge.* ♦ *Daniels has denied all* ***knowledge of*** *the events.* ♦ **+that** *The staff had no knowledge that the company was in trouble.*

PHRASE **to (the best of) my knowledge** used for saying that you think that something is true, but you are not completely certain

→ COMMON KNOWLEDGE

Knowledge is never used in the plural and cannot be used with **a**: ***a very important piece of knowledge*** (NOT a very important knowledge) ♦ *They claim not to have* ***any knowledge*** *about what happened.* ♦ *Most of the students have* ***some knowledge*** *of computers.*

knowl•edge•a•ble /ˈnɑlɪdʒəb(ə)l/ adj knowing a lot about one subject or many subjects

known¹ /noʊn/ adj **1** discovered or known about by people: *a disease with no known cure* **2** famous: *internationally known TV personalities*

known² the past participle of **know¹**

knuck•le /ˈnʌk(ə)l/ noun [C] one of the parts where your fingers can bend, or where they join your hand

ko•a•la /koʊˈɑlə/ or **koˈala ˌbear** noun [C] an Australian animal with gray fur, large ears, and no tail. It lives in trees. *—picture* → C12

Ko•ran, the /kəˈræn/ the holy book of Islam

ko•sher /ˈkoʊʃər/ adj approved or allowed by Jewish laws concerning food

Krem•lin, the /ˈkremlɪn/ the government of Russia or, in the past, of the Soviet Union

KS abbrev Kansas

ku•dos /ˈkuˌdoʊs/ noun [U] praise and respect because of something that you have achieved

kung fu /ˌkʌŋ ˈfu, ˌkʊŋ ˈfu/ noun [U] a Chinese sport in which people fight using their hands and feet

kW abbrev kilowatts

KY abbrev Kentucky

Ll

l¹ or **L** /el/ noun [C/U] the 12th letter of the English alphabet

l² abbrev liter

L abbrev large: used on clothes labels

LA abbrev Louisiana

L.A. /el ˈeɪ/ Los Angeles, California

lab /læb/ noun [C] *informal* a LABORATORY

la•bel¹ /ˈleɪb(ə)l/ noun [C] ★★

1 a piece of paper or material fastened to an object that gives information about the object: *Always read the label on medical products.*

2 a word or phrase that is used for describing someone or something: *a group of writers who were given the label "Angry Young Men"*

3 a company that designs and makes expensive clothes: *After working with Armani, he launched his own label.*

4 a company that produces records: *Their album was released on the Digital label.*

la•bel² /ˈleɪb(ə)l/ (present participle **la•bel•ing** or **la•bel•ling**; past tense and past participle **la•beled** or **la•belled**) verb [T] **1** to use a word or phrase in order to describe someone or something, especially in a way that is not fair or true=BRAND: *We shouldn't label these boys as criminals so early in their lives.* **2** to put a label on an object —**la•bel•ing** noun [U]

la•bor¹ /ˈleɪbər/ noun ★★
1 [U] all the workers in a country, industry, or company when they are thought of as a group: *labor costs ♦ a plentiful supply of **cheap labor** ♦ the demand for **skilled labor***
2 [U] workers' organizations and their leaders when they are thought of as a group: *a meeting between management and labor ♦ a labor dispute*
3 [C/U] work, especially physical work: *The price includes the cost of labor.*
4 [singular/U] the process by which a baby is pushed from its mother's body when it is being born: *labor pains ♦ She was **in labor** for six hours. ♦ She **went into labor** early this morning.*

la•bor² /ˈleɪbər/ verb [I] to work hard, or to put a lot of effort into something

lab•o•ra•to•ry /ˈlæbrəˌtɔri, *British* ləˈbɒrət(ə)ri/ noun [C] ★ a building or large room where people do scientific research: *our new research laboratory ♦ laboratory tests/experiments/studies* → LANGUAGE LABORATORY

ˈLabor ˌDay noun [C/U] in the U.S., the first Monday in September, when there is a public holiday in honor of working people

la•bored /ˈleɪbərd/ adj **1** if someone's breathing is labored, they are breathing with difficulty **2** not natural because of being done with too much effort: *a labored performance*

la•bor•er /ˈleɪbərər/ noun [C] someone whose job involves hard physical work

ˈlabor ˌforce noun [C] all the people who work in an industry or country

ˌlabor-inˈtensive adj needing a lot of workers rather than machines

la•bo•ri•ous /ləˈbɔriəs/ adj long, difficult, and boring: *a laborious task* —**la•bo•ri•ous•ly** adv

ˈlabor ˌmarket noun [C] the number of people who are available to work

ˈlabor ˌmovement, the noun [singular] political parties and other organizations whose goal is to improve conditions for workers

ˈlabor ˌunion noun [C] *American* an organization of workers in a particular industry that tries to improve workers' pay and conditions

la•bour /ˈleɪbər/ the British spelling of **labor**

La•bour /ˈleɪbər/ the British LABOUR PARTY

ˈLabour ˌParty, the one of the three main political parties in the U.K.

Lab•ra•dor /ˈlæbrəˌdɔr/ noun [C] a large dog with short fur

lab•y•rinth /ˈlæbəˌrɪnθ/ noun [C] a place with a lot of paths or streets where you can easily become lost=MAZE

lace¹ /leɪs/ noun **1** [U] light delicate cloth with patterns of small holes in it **2** [C] a thick piece of string that is used for tying shoes or clothing

lace² /leɪs/ verb **1** [I/T] to fasten something with a lace, or to be fastened with a lace **2** [T] to put strong alcohol, a drug, or poison into a drink or food
PHRASAL VERB **ˌlace (sth) ˈup** *same as* lace² 1

lac•er•a•tion /ˌlæsəˈreɪʃ(ə)n/ noun [C/U] a deep cut in your skin

lack¹ /læk/ noun [singular/U] ★★ a situation in which you do not have something, or do not have enough of something: *The game was canceled because of **lack of interest**. ♦ **a lack of confidence** ♦ The court case was dismissed **for lack of evidence**.*

lack² /læk/ verb [T] ★ to not have something, or to not have enough of something: *He lacked the skills required for the job. ♦ Many people lack confidence in their own abilities.*

lack•ing /ˈlækɪŋ/ adj if something is lacking, there is none of it, or not enough of it: *She seems to be lacking in common sense.*

lack•lus•ter /ˈlækˌlʌstər/ adj not lively, exciting, or impressive

lac•quer /ˈlækər/ noun [C/U] a liquid that you put on wood or metal in order to make it shiny —**lac•quer** verb [T]

lac•tose /ˈlækˌtoʊs/ noun [U] a type of sugar that is in milk

lac•y /ˈleɪsi/ adj made of LACE, or looking like LACE

lad•der /ˈlædər/ noun [C] ★
1 a piece of equipment for reaching high places that consists of two long pieces of wood or metal joined by smaller pieces called **rungs**: *A fireman **climbed the ladder**.*
2 a system that has different levels through which you can progress: *She rose to a high position on the **corporate ladder**.*

ladder

lad•en /ˈleɪd(ə)n/ adj carrying or supporting something heavy: *Passengers got off the train laden with boxes and suitcases.*

la•dle /ˈleɪd(ə)l/ noun [C] a large deep spoon with a long handle that is used for serving liquid food such as soup —**la•dle** verb [T]

la•dy /ˈleɪdi/ noun [C] ★★★
1 a woman. Some people think that this use is polite, but other people think that it is old-fashioned and prefer to use "woman": *Go and ask that lady over there.*
2 a woman who behaves politely and in a way that was traditionally considered appropriate for a woman: *She doesn't talk like a lady.*
PHRASE **ladies and gentlemen** *formal* used for addressing an audience of men and women
→ FIRST LADY

La•dy /ˈleɪdi/ in the U.K., used as a title for some women in high social positions

la•dy•bug /ˈleɪdiˌbʌg/ noun [C] *American* an insect with a round red or yellow body with black spots —*picture* → C13

la•dy•like /ˈleɪdiˌlaɪk/ adj behaving in a quiet

polite way that was traditionally thought to be appropriate for a woman

lag[1] /læg/ verb [I] **1** to not be as successful or advanced as other people or organizations =TRAIL: *Their software tends to lag behind other producers.* **2** to walk more slowly than the people you are with

lag[2] /læg/ noun [singular] a period of time or delay between one event and another → JET LAG

la•ger /ˈlɑgər/ noun [C/U] a type of light-colored beer, or a glass of this beer

la•goon /ləˈgun/ noun [C] *American* an area of water, especially a small one beside a larger one

laid the past tense and past participle of **lay**[1]

ˌlaid-ˈback adj *informal* calm and relaxed

lain the past participle of **lie**[1]

lair /ler/ noun [C] a place where a wild animal lives

lais•sez-faire /ˌleseɪ ˈfer/ adj allowing someone to do what they want to do, and to do it in any way that they want to

lake /leɪk/ noun [C] ★★ a large area of water surrounded by land: *There were some boys swimming in the lake.*

L

lamb /læm/ noun [C/U] a young sheep, or its meat

lam•bast /læmˈbæst/ verb [T] *mainly journalism* to criticize someone angrily, especially in public

lame /leɪm/ adj **1** not at all impressive or likely to persuade someone: *a lame excuse* **2** a lame animal cannot walk very well because its leg or foot is damaged —**lame•ly** adv

ˌlame-ˈduck adj *American* a lame-duck leader or government is one that is not powerful

la•ment /ləˈment/ verb [I/T] to show publicly that you feel sad or disappointed about something: *Some older people lament the loss of close local communities.* —**la•ment** noun [C]

lam•i•nate /ˈlæmɪˌneɪt/ verb [T] to cover something with a thin layer of plastic that protects it

lamp /læmp/ noun [C] ★★
1 an electric light that stands on a floor or table —*picture* → C3
2 an oil or gas light
3 a piece of equipment that produces light and heat: *an ultra-violet lamp*

lam•poon /læmˈpun/ verb [T] to publicly criticize someone or something by making jokes about them —**lam•poon** noun [C]

lamp•post /ˈlæmpˌpoʊst/ noun [C] a tall post at the side of a street with a light on top

lamp•shade /ˈlæmpˌʃeɪd/ noun [C] a cover for a light that makes it less bright

LAN /læn/ noun [C] *computing* local area network: a system that allows computers in the same building or area to exchange information

lance /læns/ noun [C] a very long pointed weapon that was used in the past by soldiers on horses

land[1] /lænd/ noun ★★★
1 [U] an area of ground, especially one used for a particular purpose such as farming or building: *Some of his land had been flooded.* ♦ *The land around here is very fertile.* ♦ *acres of* ***agricultural land***
2 [U] the part of the Earth's surface that is not water: *The vehicle can travel* ***on land*** *or in water.*
3 [C] *literary* a real or imaginary country: ***a land of abundant wildlife and great beauty***
→ COUNTRY, NO-MAN'S-LAND

land[2] /lænd/ verb ★★

1 of airplane	4 be in bad situation
2 arrive by boat	5 get sth you wanted
3 fall or fly to the ground	

1 [I/T] if an aircraft lands, or if you land it, it comes down to the ground ≠ TAKE OFF: *The* ***plane landed*** *a couple of hours before dawn.* ♦ *The pilot was able to* ***land*** *the aircraft safely.*
2 [I] to arrive at a place by boat: *The refugees landed on the east side of the island.*
3 [I] to come down to a surface after falling or flying: *She fell from the window, and landed in the bushes.*
4 [I/T] to put someone in an unexpected or unpleasant situation, or to be in this kind of situation: **land sb in sth** *His attitude could land him in trouble.*
5 [T] to get something that you wanted: *At age 19 she* ***landed a part*** *in a Broadway play.*
→ FOOT[1]

land•fill /ˈlændˌfɪl/ or **ˈlandfill ˌsite** noun [C] a large hole in the ground where garbage from people's homes or from industry is buried

land•ing /ˈlændɪŋ/ noun **1** [C/U] the process of moving an airplane down from the air onto the ground: *The pilot was forced to make an emergency landing.* **2** [C] the area at the top of a set of stairs —*picture* → C1

land•la•dy /ˈlændˌleɪdi/ noun [C] a woman who owns a house, apartment, or room that people can rent → LANDLORD

land•line /ˈlændˌlaɪn/ noun [C] a telephone that is not a cellphone

land•locked /ˈlændˌlɑkt/ adj a landlocked country is surrounded by land

land•lord /ˈlændˌlɔrd/ noun [C] a man who owns a house, apartment, or room that people can rent → LANDLADY

land•mark /ˈlændˌmɑrk/ noun [C] **1** a famous building or object that you can easily recognize **2** something that marks an important stage in a process, and influences how it will develop: *This book has become a landmark in art criticism.*

ˈland ˌmass noun [C] a CONTINENT or a large area of land that is surrounded by ocean

land•mine /ˈlændˌmaɪn/ noun [C] a bomb hidden under the ground that explodes when someone moves over it

land•own•er /ˈlændˌoʊnər/ noun [C] someone who owns a large amount of land

land•scape[1] /ˈlændˌskeɪp/ noun **1** [C] an area of land that has particular features: *a green, rural landscape* **2** [C] a painting of an area of land **3** [U] a way of arranging a page so that its long sides are at the top and bottom → PORTRAIT

land•scape[2] /ˈlændˌskeɪp/ verb [T] to add features such as plants and paths to a piece of land —**land•scap•ing** noun [U]

land·slide /ˈlænd,slaɪd/ noun [C] **1** a heavy fall of earth and rocks down the side of a mountain **2** a victory by a very big majority in an election: *Cardenas was elected in a landslide last May.*

lane /leɪn/ noun [C] ★★
1 one of the parts that a wide road or highway is divided into. A lane is intended for one line of traffic: *the fast/slow lane* ♦ *The truck suddenly crossed into my lane.*
2 the part of a RACING TRACK or SWIMMING POOL that is used by one person in a competition
3 a course that a ship or aircraft follows
4 *British* a narrow road, especially in the countryside

lan·guage /ˈlæŋgwɪdʒ/ noun ★★★
1 [U] the method of human communication using spoken or written words: *language skills* ♦ *a new study of how a child **learns language*** ♦ *a comparison between **spoken and written language***
2 [C] the particular form of words and speech that is used by the people of a country, area, or social group: *African languages* ♦ *English and French are the official languages of Canada.* ♦ *Do you **speak** any other **languages**?*
3 [C/U] signs, symbols, sounds, and other methods of communicating information or ideas: *computer languages* ♦ ***the language of dance***
PHRASE **speak/talk the same language** to have the same ideas and attitudes as someone else
→ BODY LANGUAGE, FIRST LANGUAGE, SECOND LANGUAGE

ˈlanguage ˌlaboratory noun [C] a room with special equipment such as computers, TAPE RECORDERS and VCRS for students who are learning a foreign language

lan·guid /ˈlæŋgwɪd/ adj very slow and relaxed

lan·guish /ˈlæŋgwɪʃ/ verb [I] to remain in a difficult or unpleasant situation

lank·y /ˈlæŋki/ adj tall, thin, and not very graceful: *a lanky teenager*

lan·tern /ˈlæntərn/ noun [C] a light inside a transparent container that has a handle for carrying it

lap[1] /læp/ noun [C] **1** the top half of your legs above your knees when you sit down: *The cat settled on Christine's lap.* **2** one complete trip around a course in a race

lap[2] /læp/ verb **1** [T] if an animal laps water, it drinks it with its tongue **2** [I/T] if water laps against something, it moves against it gently with a soft sound **3** [T] to pass someone else in a race when you are ahead of them by a whole lap
PHRASAL VERB ˌ**lap sth ˈup** to enjoy something very much: *There are photographers following her wherever she goes, but she's lapping it up.*

la·pel /ləˈpel/ noun [C] one of the two parts on each side of the front of a coat or jacket that are folded back

lapse[1] /læps/ noun [C] **1** a short period when you fail to do something, or fail to show a quality: *He suffers from memory lapses.* ♦ *lapses in concentration* **2** a period of time between two events: *There was a lapse of ten years between his visits.*

lapse[2] /læps/ verb [I] **1** to stop gradually or for a short time: *At this point conversation lapsed.* **2** if an official document, decision, or right lapses, it is no longer effective
PHRASAL VERB ˈ**lapse into sth** to change to a different way of speaking or behaving: *She often lapses into French* (=starts speaking French).

lap·top /ˈlæp,tɑp/ noun [C] a small computer that you can carry with you = NOTEBOOK

lard /lɑrd/ noun [U] white fat that is used in cooking

large /lɑrdʒ/ adj ★★★ bigger than usual in size, number, or amount: *a house with a very large yard* ♦ *a large software company* ♦ *large sums of money* ♦ *A large crowd had gathered outside the American Embassy.* ♦ *She's a rather large woman with red hair.*
PHRASES **at large** not yet caught and put into prison or into a cage: *The murderer is still at large.*
the public/population/community etc. at large most people in a particular group: *the opinions of American society at large*
larger than life with a very strong, impressive personality
→ BY

large·ly /ˈlɑrdʒli/ adv ★ mainly: *Our success is largely due to your efforts.* ♦ *Her poetry has largely been forgotten.*

ˈlarge-ˌscale adj **1** involving a large number of people or things, or happening over a large area **2** a large-scale map is one that shows a lot of details

lark /lɑrk/ noun [C] a small brown bird that is known for its singing

lar·va /ˈlɑrvə/ (plural **lar·vae** /ˈlɑr,vi/) noun [C] an insect that looks like a small WORM, before it changes into an insect with wings

la·sa·gna or **la·sa·gne** /ləˈzænjə/ noun [C/U] an Italian meal made with layers of flat pasta with a sauce, cheese, and meat or vegetables

la·ser /ˈleɪzər/ noun [C] a piece of equipment that produces a powerful line of light that can be used as a tool, or the line of light that is produced: *laser surgery*

ˈlaser ˌprinter noun [C] a type of computer printer that uses a laser to produce clear letters and images

lash[1] /læʃ/ noun [C] **1** an EYELASH **2** a hit with a WHIP or a thin stick

lash[2] /læʃ/ verb **1** [T] to tie something firmly to something else **2** [I/T] to hit against something with a very strong force: *Waves lashed the shore.* **3** [T] to hit someone or something with a WHIP or a thin stick
PHRASAL VERB ˌ**lash ˈout 1** to speak angrily to or about someone **2** to try to hit or attack someone suddenly and violently

las·so /ˈlæsoʊ, ləˈsu/ noun [C] a long rope with one end tied in a circle that is used for controlling horses, cows, etc., especially in North America —**las·so** verb [T]

last[1] /læst/ grammar word ★★★

> **Last** can be:
> ■ a **determiner**: *I wasn't here last time.*

L

- an **adjective**: *I ate the last piece of cake.* ♦ *I was last in the race.*
- a **pronoun**: *Their new CD is even better than the last.*
- an **adverb**: *I put my shoes on last.*
- a **noun**: *I drank up the last of the wine.*

1 happening, coming, or ending most recently: *I don't agree with that last comment.* ♦ *During the last hour the storms have been getting worse.* ♦ *I last saw her three years ago.* ♦ ***The last time** we met, you were moving to Greenwich.* ♦ *How did you boys sleep **last night**?* ♦ *We went to the play **the night before last*** (=two nights ago).
2 happening or coming at the end, after all the others: *Fry the onions until crisp, and add them last.* ♦ *That's **the last time** I'm ever going out with him.* ♦ ***The last of** the guests had arrived.* ♦ *Baker finished **next to last*** (=one before the last) *in the 1500 meters race.* ♦ *Janice was **the last to** leave.*
3 remaining after all the rest have gone: *the last book left on the shelf* ♦ *Who wants **the last of** the ice cream?* ♦ *He is **the last** great writer **of** his generation.*
4 used for emphasizing that someone or something is not at all likely, appropriate, or wanted: *Hurting you is **the last thing** I'd want to do.* ♦ *I'm **the last person** you should be asking for advice.*
PHRASES **at the last minute/moment** when it is almost too late: *At the last minute she decided not to come after all.*
at (long) last used for saying that something that you have been waiting for finally happens: *I'm so glad to meet you at last.*
have the last word 1 to win an argument by making the last statement **2** to make the final decision about something: *The president has the last word.*
→ LAST-MINUTE, RESORT[1]

last[2] /læst/ verb ★★★
1 [I] to continue happening for a particular period, or until a particular time: *The game lasted four hours.* ♦ *The conference will **last for** two weeks.* ♦ *The party **lasted until** the early morning.*
2 [I] to continue in a good state without changing or failing: *I hope the good weather will last.* ♦ *These cars are built **to last**.*
3 [I/T] to continue to be available, or to be enough for what people need: *The water won't last long.* ♦ *Ninety dollars usually lasted him about a week.*

ˈlast-ˌditch adj a last-ditch attempt, effort, etc. is a final try at achieving something difficult, when other attempts have already failed

last•ing /ˈlæstɪŋ/ adj continuing to exist or to have an effect for a long time: *We have an opportunity here for a lasting peace.*

last•ly /ˈlæstli/ adv used when you want to say one more thing before you finish speaking = FINALLY: *And lastly, remember that your reports are due tomorrow.*

ˌlast-ˈminute adj happening or done at the latest possible time: *You can do any last-minute shopping at the airport.*

ˈlast ˌname noun [C] the name that you share with the other members of your family. In English, it comes at the end of your full name = FAMILY NAME, SURNAME

ˌlast ˈword, the noun [singular] the newest and best type of something: *a five-star hotel that is the last word in luxury*

latch[1] /lætʃ/ noun [C] an object for keeping a door, gate, etc. shut

latch[2] /lætʃ/
PHRASAL VERBS **ˌlatch ˈonto sb** *informal* to go with someone who does not want to be with you
ˌlatch ˈonto sth *informal* to immediately become very interested in something that you discover

late /leɪt/ adj, adv ★★★
1 arriving somewhere or doing something after the expected or usual time ≠ EARLY: *The buses are all running about 15 minutes late.* ♦ *She called to say she'd **be late**.* ♦ *Sheila was **late for** work again this morning.*
2 near the end of an evening or night: *Late one night I heard a knock on the door.* ♦ *It was **getting late** and all the kids were sleepy.* ♦ *We had **a late night** last night* (=went to bed when it was late).
3 near the end of a period of time ≠ EARLY: *the late 18th century* ♦ *These bulbs bloom in late spring.* ♦ *a girl in her late teens*
4 used for talking about someone who has died, especially recently: *my late aunt*
PHRASES **better late than never** used for saying that it is good that something has happened, but that it would have been better if it had been earlier
too late if you are too late, you have missed the best or only time for doing something: *The ambulance arrived, but it was too late.*

late•com•er /ˈleɪtˌkʌmər/ noun [C] someone who arrives late

late•ly /ˈleɪtli/ adv recently: *Have you seen either of them lately?*

ˈlate-ˌnight adj happening late at night: *a late-night movie*

la•tent /ˈleɪt(ə)nt/ adj something that is latent exists, but it is not obvious and has not developed yet: *latent aggression*

lat•er[1] /ˈleɪtər/ adv ★★★ at some time in the future, or after the time that you have been talking about: *She'll be home later.* ♦ *We can schedule an appointment for later in the week.*
PHRASES **later on** at a time in the future, or after the time that you have been talking about: *I'll come and see you later on.*
see you later *informal* used for saying goodbye: *Okay, I'm leaving now. See you later.*

lat•er[2] /ˈleɪtər/ adj **1** happening at some time in the future, or after the time that you have been talking about: *We can settle on the price at a later date.* **2** near the end of a period of time, or near the end of someone's life or career: *Her views changed in her later years.*

lat•er•al /ˈlætərəl/ adj *technical* on the side of something, or moving sideways

lat•est /ˈleɪtəst/ adj ★★★ most recent or newest: *The latest figures show steady growth.*

lat•est, the /ˈleɪtəst/ noun [singular] the most recent event, thing, piece of news, etc.: *Have you heard the latest? He's getting a divorce.*
PHRASE **at the latest** no later than a particular time

la•tex /ˈleɪˌteks/ noun [U] a substance that is used for making rubber, paint, and glue

lath•er /ˈlæðər/ noun [singular] the white mass of BUBBLES that is produced when you mix soap and water

Lat•in¹ /ˈlæt(ə)n/ noun [U] the language that people spoke in ancient Rome. Modern European languages such as Italian, Spanish, and French developed from it.

Lat•in² /ˈlæt(ə)n/ adj **1** written in Latin **2** relating to people who speak languages that developed from Latin, or to their culture

La•ti•na /læˈtinə/ noun [C] a woman or girl whose family is from Latin America —**La•ti•na** adj

ˌLatin Aˈmerican adj from or relating to Mexico, Central America, or South America —**ˌLatin Aˈmerican** noun [C]

La•ti•no /ləˈtinoʊ/ noun [C] ★ someone whose family is Latin American —**La•ti•no** adj

lat•i•tude /ˈlætəˌtud/ noun [C/U] *technical* the distance of a point on the Earth from the EQUATOR (=the imaginary line around the center of the Earth), measured in degrees north or south → LONGITUDE

lat•te /ˈlɑteɪ/ noun [C/U] a drink made by mixing ESPRESSO (=strong coffee) with hot milk

lat•ter /ˈlætər/ grammar word

> Latter can be:
> - an **adjective**: *He considered his students either geniuses or idiots, and I fell into the latter category.*
> - a **pronoun**: *Given a choice between Tahiti and Hawaii, I prefer the latter.*

1 *formal* used for referring to the second of two people, things, or groups that have just been mentioned: *He did well in both schoolwork and sports and won a number of medals in the latter* (=in sports). → FORMER **2** used for describing the later part of a period of time: *the latter half of 1998*

laugh¹ /læf/ verb [I] ★★★
1 to make the noise with your voice that shows that you think that something is funny: *We talked and laughed late into the night.* ♦ *The audience didn't **laugh at** his jokes.* ♦ *They were still **laughing about** the experience years later.* ♦ *She **burst out laughing** when she saw what he was wearing.*
2 to show that you think that someone or something is stupid or deserves no respect: *When I told them my idea, they just laughed.* ♦ *Are you **laughing at** me?*
PHRASAL VERB **ˌlaugh sth ˈoff** to joke about something in order to show that you think that it is not important or serious

> Other ways of saying **laugh**
> - **chuckle** to laugh quietly in a private or secret way
> - **giggle** to laugh in a nervous or excited way at something silly
> - **snicker** to laugh secretly and quietly in an unkind way, or to laugh at something that is rude
> - **be in hysterics/stitches** to laugh in an excited and uncontrolled way

laugh² /læf/ noun [C] ★ the sound that you make when you laugh: *a hearty laugh*
PHRASE **have the last laugh** to finally be more successful than someone who was unpleasant to you

laugh•a•ble /ˈlæfəb(ə)l/ adj stupid, or unreasonable —**laugh•a•bly** adv

laugh•ing stock /ˈlæfɪŋ ˌstɑk/ noun [C] someone or something that everyone thinks is stupid or silly

laugh•ter /ˈlæftər/ noun [U] ★ the sound or action of someone laughing: *The children's laughter drifted down the street.*

launch¹ /lɔntʃ/ verb [T] ★★
1 to send a space vehicle, missile, or other object into space or into the air: *The agency will launch a new weather satellite next month.*
2 to start a major activity such as a military attack, a public project, or a new career: *The armies launched their attack at dawn.*
3 to make a new product available for the public to buy for the first time: *The company will launch a new version of the software in July.*
4 to put a boat or ship into water, especially for the first time
PHRASAL VERB **ˈlaunch into sth** to enthusiastically start something such as an explanation, criticism, or description: *He launched into a detailed account of his trip.*

launch² /lɔntʃ/ noun [C] **1** the act of sending a space vehicle, missile, or other object into the air or into space: *the launch of the space shuttle* **2** the start of a major activity such as a military attack, a public project, or a new career **3** an occasion on which a company makes a new product available for the public to buy

Laun•dro•mat /ˈlɔndrəˌmæt/ *American trademark* a place where people go to wash clothes in machines that they pay to use

laun•dry /ˈlɔndri/ noun [U] dirty clothes, sheets, etc. that you are washing, or clean clothes, sheets, etc. that have just been washed: *My husband does* (=washes) *the laundry.* ♦ *a laundry basket*

ˈlaundry deˌtergent noun [C/U] *American* soap used for cleaning clothes

ˈlaundry ˌlist noun [C] *American* a long list of things that someone needs, wants, or has to do: *a laundry list of complaints*

ˈlaundry ˌroom noun [C] a separate room in a house or apartment building where machines for washing clothes are

lau•rel /ˈlɔrəl/ noun [C/U] a small tree with shiny dark green leaves
PHRASE **rest on your laurels** to be satisfied with your achievements so that you do nothing to achieve more

la•va /ˈlɑvə/ noun [U] rock in the form of extremely hot liquid that flows from a VOLCANO

lav•a•to•ry /ˈlævəˌtɔri/ noun [C] a small room with a toilet and a sink on an airplane

lav•en•der¹ /ˈlævəndər/ noun [C] a plant with small light purple flowers that have a pleasant smell

lav•en•der² /ˈlævəndər/ adj light purple in color

lav•ish¹ /ˈlævɪʃ/ adj given very generously, or very expensive —**lav•ish•ly** adv

lav•ish² /ˈlævɪʃ/ PHRASAL VERB **ˈlavish sth on sb** or **ˈlavish sth uˌpon sb** to give someone a lot of something such as praise, attention, or presents

law /lɔ/ noun ★★★

1 the law [singular] the system of rules that must be obeyed in society: *Failing to declare any extra income is **against the law**.* ♦ *How can I bring my boyfriend into the country without **breaking the law*** (=doing something that is not allowed by the law)*?*

2 [C/U] an official rule that people must obey, or a set of these rules: *The new law will be passed by the Senate in the spring.* ♦ *Several traffic **laws** had been **broken**.* ♦ *a **law against** shoplifting*

3 [U] the academic study of laws, or the profession of working as a judge, lawyer, etc.: *a degree in law* ♦ *My son is at law school.* ♦ *Anne's been **practicing law*** (=working as a lawyer) *for 20 years.*

4 [C] an explanation of a natural or scientific process: ***the laws of physics/gravity***

PHRASES **law and order** safe and peaceful conditions in society that result when people obey the law

take the law into your own hands to punish someone in your own way without involving the police or the courts, often by doing something illegal → LAY STH DOWN

L

ˈlaw-aˌbiding adj obeying the law

ˈlaw enˌforcement noun [U] the job of making sure that people obey the law

ˈlaw enˌforcement officer noun [C] *American formal* a member of the police or other organization that makes sure that people obey the law

ˈlaw ˌfirm noun [C] a company consisting of a group of lawyers who provide legal advice and services

law•ful /ˈlɔf(ə)l/ adj allowed by law ≠ UNLAWFUL —**law•ful•ly** adv

law•less /ˈlɔləs/ adj ignoring the laws of society —**law•less•ness** noun [U]

law•mak•er /ˈlɔˌmeɪkər/ noun [C] *American mainly journalism* a politician whose job is to help to make the laws of a country or state

lawn /lɔn/ noun [C/U] an area of grass that is cut short, especially in a yard —*picture* → C1

ˈlawn ˌchair noun [C] *American* a light chair that folds up, used outside in warm weather

lawn mow•er /ˈlɔn ˌmoʊr/ noun [C] a machine for cutting grass = MOWER

law•suit /ˈlɔˌsut/ noun [C] a situation in which a disagreement between people or groups is formally judged in a law court: *The singer has filed a $100 million lawsuit against his record company.*

law•yer /ˈlɔjər/ noun [C] ★★ someone whose profession is to provide people with legal advice and services: *Mayer's lawyer spoke to the press today.*

lax /læks/ adj not paying enough attention to rules, or not caring enough about quality or safety

lax•a•tive /ˈlæksətɪv/ noun [C] a medicine, food, or drink that helps solid waste to leave the body —**lax•a•tive** adj

lay¹ /leɪ/ (past tense and past participle **laid** /leɪd/) verb [T] ★★★

1 to put someone or something down in a careful way, especially so that they are lying flat: **lay sb/sth on sth** *Lay the baby on her back.* ♦ **lay sb/sth across sth** *He laid his coat across the arm of the chair.*

2 if a female animal such as a bird or fish lays an egg, it produces the egg by pushing it from its body

3 to carefully plan and prepare something: *an agreement that laid the foundations for a lasting peace* ♦ *The gunman realized the police had **laid a trap** and surrendered.*

PHRASES **be laid up (in bed) with sth** to have to stay in bed as a result of being sick or injured: *He's still laid up with a bad back.*

lay the blame/responsibility (for sth) on to say that someone or something is responsible for something that has happened: *Don't try to lay the blame on me.*

not lay a finger on sb to not hit or harm someone in any way

PHRASAL VERBS **ˌlay sth ˈdown 1** to state officially what someone must do, or how they must do it: *The Department has laid down tough standards for water quality.* **2 lay down the law** to tell someone what to do and expect them to obey you completely: *With kids like that you have to lay down the law.*

ˌlay ˈinto sb *informal* to attack someone physically, or to criticize them angrily: *My parents really laid into me for being so late.*

ˌlay sb ˈoff to stop employing someone because there is not enough work for them: *They had to lay off 2000 workers.*

ˌlay ˈoff (sb/sth) *informal* to stop doing something that is annoying someone: *Lay off! I'm trying to study.*

ˌlay sth ˈout 1 to spread something out or arrange things so that you can see them easily: *I had my dress all ready and laid out on the bed.* **2** to arrange something according to a plan: *The city was laid out with the capitol on a hill in its center.* **3** to explain something carefully and clearly: *The documents lay out the principles clearly enough.*

- **Lay** means to put something in a particular place or position: *I always lay my clothes carefully on the chair when I undress.* ♦ *He laid the book on the desk.*
- **Lie** means to be in a particular place or position: *I found the cat lying in front of the fire.* ♦ *He loves to lie on the beach all day.* ♦ *Papers were lying all over the desk.*
- **Lay** is also the past form of the verb **lie**: *The book lay on the floor where I'd left it.*

lay² /leɪ/ adj lacking professional or advanced knowledge of a particular subject: *a book intended for a lay audience*

lay³ the past tense of **lie**¹

lay•er /ˈleɪr/ noun [C] ★★

1 an amount or sheet of a substance that covers a surface or lies between two things: *Glue the layers together and let them dry.* ♦ *Put **a layer of** grated cheese on top.*

2 a level or rank within an organization or system: *another **layer of** bureaucracy*

lay·man /ˈleɪmən/ noun [C] someone who does not have professional or advanced knowledge of a particular subject

lay·off /ˈleɪˌɔf/ noun [C] a situation in which an employer ends a worker's employment

lay·out /ˈleɪˌaʊt/ noun [C] the way in which the different parts of something are arranged: *the layout of the keyboard*

lay·o·ver /ˈleɪˌoʊvər/ noun [C] *American* a short stop in a long airplane trip

laze /leɪz/ or **ˌlaze aˈround** verb [I] to relax and enjoy yourself, doing no work: *We found some time to swim and laze in the sun.*

la·zy /ˈleɪzi/ adj ★

1 not willing to work or do anything that involves effort: *Get out of bed, you lazy slob!*

2 a lazy period of time is spent resting and relaxing: *a lazy afternoon in the sun*

—**la·zi·ly** adv, **la·zi·ness** noun [U]

lb. (plural **lbs.** or **lb.**) abbrev pound

lead¹ /lid/ (past tense and past participle **led** /led/) verb ★★★

1 take sb somewhere	6 make sb do sth
2 go somewhere	7 live life particular way
3 be winning	+ PHRASE
4 be best	+ PHRASAL VERBS
5 be in charge of sb/sth	

1 [T] to take someone to a place by going there with them, usually in front of them: **lead sb into/across/to etc.** *The real estate agent led us into the kitchen.* ♦ *She took the boy by the hand and led him from the room.*

2 [I/T] if something such as a road, river, or door leads somewhere, or if it leads you there, it goes there: *The road leads west for three miles, then turns south.* ♦ *This door leads you to a large entrance hall.*

3 [I/T] to be winning at a particular time during a race or competition: *The polls show the Republicans leading with only 10 days left until the election.* ♦ **lead sb by sth** *The Giants led the Lions at halftime by a score of 10 to 7.*

4 [I/T] to be the most successful, popular, or advanced of all the people or groups that are involved in a particular activity: *They **lead the world in** oil production.*

5 [T] to be in charge of an organization, group of people, or an activity: *She led the team for over twelve years.*

6 [T] to influence someone to do or think something: *I had been **led to believe** that the job was mine if I wanted it.*

7 [T] to live your life in a particular way: *He had always **led a quiet life** until he met Emma.*

PHRASE **lead the way 1** to show other people the way to a place: *Sheila turned and led the way downstairs.* **2** to be the first person to do something and to show other people how to do it: *It is a country that has always led the way with its conservation policies.*

PHRASAL VERBS **ˌlead sb ˈon** to encourage someone to believe that you are attracted to them when you are not

ˈlead to sth to begin a process that causes something to happen: *There is no doubt that stress can lead to physical illness.*

ˌlead ˈup to sth to happen in the period of time before something else happens: *the events that led up to the war*

lead² /lid/ noun ★★★

1 first position	5 sth that others copy
2 winning amount	6 first piece of news
3 main part or actor	+ PHRASE
4 useful information	

1 [singular] the first position at any particular time during a race or competition: *He regained his lead in the final lap.* ♦ *The latest polls show the Democratic candidate **in the lead*** (=winning).

2 [singular] the distance, amount of time, number of points, etc. by which someone is winning a race or competition: *They increased their lead by three points on the next play.*

3 [C] the main person or part in a play, film, or television show: *She's **playing the lead** in her school play.*

4 [C] a piece of information that may help to solve a crime or help to find out the truth about something

5 [C] an action that is an example for someone to copy: *North Korea is to **follow** China's **lead** in attracting foreign investment.*

6 [C] the most important story on the front page of a newspaper, or the first piece of news on a news broadcast

PHRASE **take the lead 1** to start winning a race or competition: *She took the lead ten miles into the marathon.* **2** to do something first, especially as an example for other people to follow: *British farmers took the lead by sending tons of grain to the disaster area.*

Words often used with lead

*Verbs often used with **lead** (noun, sense 1)*

■ **establish, have, hold, keep, maintain** + LEAD: be or stay in the first position

lead³ /led/ noun **1** [U] a soft heavy gray metal **2** [C/U] the part of a pencil that you make marks with

lead·er /ˈlidər/ noun [C] ★★★

1 someone who is in charge of a group, organization, or country: *a political/military/religious leader* ♦ ***the leader of** the French delegation*

2 someone or something that is winning at a particular time during a race or competition: *She remains the leader after the 17th hole.*

3 someone or something that is the most successful, most popular, most advanced, etc.: *He is **a world leader in** his field.*

lead·er·ship /ˈlidərʃɪp/ noun ★★

1 [U] the qualities and skills of a good leader

2 [C] the people who are in charge of an organization or country

3 [U] the position of being a leader: *The war was fought **under** the emperor's **leadership**.*

lead·ing /ˈlidɪŋ/ adj ★★ main, most important, or most successful: *He very soon became **a leading figure** in the London art world.* ♦ ***a leading brand** of toothpaste* ♦ *She **played a leading role in** the country's independence movement.*

ˌleading-ˈedge adj of the most modern or advanced type: *leading-edge technology*

L

ˌleading ˈquestion noun [C] a question that you ask in a way that tricks someone, or that forces them to give the answer that you want

leaf[1] /lif/ (plural **leaves** /livz/) noun [C] ★★★
1 a flat, thin, usually green part of a tree or plant that grows on a branch or stem: *The **autumn leaves** were beginning to fall.* —*picture* → TREE
2 a page of a book
PHRASE **turn over a new leaf** to change your life by starting to be a better person or by stopping a bad habit

leaf[2] /lif/ PHRASAL VERB **ˌleaf ˈthrough sth** to turn pages quickly and without looking at them carefully

leaf•let /ˈliflət/ noun [C] a printed sheet of paper that is provided free and gives information about something = FLIER

leaf•y /ˈlifi/ adj covered with a lot of leaves: *leafy green vegetables*

league /lig/ noun [C] ★★★
1 an organized group of teams or players who regularly compete against each other: *the National Football League* ♦ *They were the **league champions** twice during the 1990s.*
2 a group of people, organizations, or countries that have joined together because they have the same interests or aims: *the League of Nations*
PHRASES **be in league with sb** to be secretly working together with someone in order to do something bad
in a different league or **not in the same league** not nearly as good as someone or something else

leak[1] /lik/ verb **1** [I/T] if a pipe, container, roof, etc. leaks, or if it leaks something, liquid or gas comes out of it through a hole: *The roof is still leaking.* **2** [I] if a liquid or gas leaks, it comes out of a pipe, container, roof, etc. through a hole: *Oil was leaking from the pipeline.* **3** [T] to give secret information about the organization you work for to a reporters or to the public: *The story was leaked to the press.*
PHRASAL VERB **ˌleak ˈout** to become known by the public

leak[2] /lik/ noun [C] **1** a hole or crack in something that a liquid or gas comes out of, or the liquid or gas that comes out **2** an occasion when secret information about an organization is told to a reporter or to the public

leak•age /ˈlikɪdʒ/ noun [C/U] an amount of gas or liquid that leaks out of something

leak•y /ˈliki/ adj a leaky object or container has a hole or crack in it so that liquid or gas comes out of it

lean[1] /lin/ verb ★★
1 [I] to move your body by bending at the waist, bringing yourself closer to or farther from someone or something: *The other girl **leaned forward** to hear what was going on.* ♦ *I **leaned over** her shoulder to study the maps.*
2 [I] to stand or be placed at an angle against something for support, instead of being upright: *There was a small ladder **leaning against** the wall.* ♦ *He walked in, **leaning heavily on** a cane.* —*picture* → POSTURE
3 [T] to put something at an angle against an object for support: **lean sth against sth** *John leaned his rake against the side of the barn.*
PHRASAL VERB **ˈlean on sb** to depend on someone: *Everybody needs someone to lean on in times of trouble.*

lean[2] /lin/ adj **1** someone who is lean does not have any fat on their body and looks physically fit and healthy **2** lean meat contains very little fat

lean•ing /ˈlinɪŋ/ noun [C] a tendency to prefer, support, or be interested in a particular idea or activity

leap[1] /lip/ (past tense and past participle **leaped** /lipt/ or **leapt** /lept/) verb [I] **1** to move somewhere suddenly and quickly: *He leaped out of bed.* ♦ *She leaped to her feet* (=suddenly stood up) *when she saw me.* **2** to jump into the air or over a long distance: *People leaped from the burning building.*
PHRASE **leap at the chance/opportunity/offer** to accept something quickly and enthusiastically: *Klein leapt at the chance to appear in the show.*

leap[2] /lip/ noun [C] **1** a jump, especially one that is long or high **2** a sudden increase or improvement = JUMP: *a huge leap in the price of gasoline*
PHRASE **by/in leaps and bounds** used for saying that something improves quickly or increases a lot: *Building work on the library is moving ahead in leaps and bounds.*

leap•frog /ˈlipˌfrɔg/ noun [U] a children's game in which one child bends down so that another child can jump over them

leapt a past tense and past participle of **leap**[1]

ˈleap ˌyear noun [C] a year that has 366 days instead of 365. This happens once every four years.

learn /lɜrn/ (past tense and past participle **learned** /lɜrnt/) verb ★★★
1 [I/T] to gain knowledge or experience of something, for example by being taught: *What did you **learn at school** today?* ♦ **learn to do sth** *The children are learning to swim this summer.* ♦ **learn how to do sth** *I want to learn how to ride a motorcycle.*
2 [T] to study something so that you remember it exactly = MEMORIZE: *I have a list of German verbs to learn tonight.*
3 [I/T] to gain new information about a situation, event, or person = FIND OUT: *We didn't **learn about** the situation until it was too late.* ♦ **+(that)** *We were distressed to learn that American troops were the targets of the attack.*
4 [I] to improve your behavior as a result of gaining greater experience or knowledge of something: *His girlfriend's left him again. Some people never learn, do they?*
PHRASE **learn your lesson** to be unlikely to do something stupid or wrong again, because last time you did it something unpleasant happened

- When you **learn**, you gain knowledge or skills through experience or as a result of practicing, reading, or being taught: *I am learning to play the guitar.* ♦ *He wanted to learn about life in ancient Rome.*

- When you **study**, you make an effort to learn a particular subject, usually by going to classes or reading and doing research: *He studied geography at college.* ♦ *If you want to learn English you must study hard.*

learn•ed /ˈlɜrnəd/ adj having or showing a lot of knowledge about academic subjects: *a learned man*

learn•er /ˈlɜrnər/ noun [C] someone who is learning something: *a learner driver*

learn•ing /ˈlɜrnɪŋ/ noun [U] **1** the process of gaining knowledge and experience, for example by studying **2** knowledge that someone has gained, especially by studying

ˈlearning ˌcurve noun [C] the rate at which you learn something: *I've never done this kind of work before, so I'm on a steep learning curve* (=I have to learn a lot in a short time).

lease¹ /lis/ noun [C] a legal contract in which you agree to pay to use someone else's building, land, or equipment for a particular period of time

PHRASE **a new lease on life 1** new energy and enthusiasm, or better health **2** a change to something that makes it more modern or useful

lease² /lis/ verb [T] to have a legal agreement in which someone pays you to use your building, land, or equipment

leash /liʃ/ noun [C] a long thin piece of material attached to a dog's collar so that it can be controlled in a public place: *All dogs must be kept on a leash while on the beaches.*

least /list/ grammar word ★★★

Least can be:
- a **determiner**: *This method takes the least time.*
- a **pronoun**: *Of all the girls, she seemed to know the least.*
- an **adverb**: *Doug is probably the least appropriate person for the job.*
- an **adjective**: *At the least sign of trouble, he quits.*

1 a smaller amount than any other ≠ MOST: *I earn the least out of all of us.* ♦ *His most popular songs are always the ones he spends the least time on.* ♦ *Let me pay for the dinner – it's **the least I can do*** (=I should probably do more).
2 to a smaller degree or less often than any other, or than at any other time: *This is one of the least polluted industrial cities.* ♦ *Troubles come when you least expect them.* ♦ *The new taxes hurt those who are least able to pay.*

PHRASES **at least 1** not less than a particular amount or number: *The disease killed at least 120 people in New England last year.* ♦ *The trip will take a year, **at the very least*** (=a year is the shortest time possible). **2** even if nothing else happens or is true: *At least no one can accuse me of hiding the truth.* ♦ *You could at least have waited for me.* **3** used for talking about an advantage that exists despite something else: *The work is difficult, but at least the pay is good.* **4** used when you are saying something that changes or limits what you have just said: *No one saw anything, or at least they say they didn't.*
in the least or **the least bit** used for emphasizing a negative statement or question: *I'm not interested in him in the least.* ♦ *Aren't you the least bit worried?*
least of all used after a negative statement for saying that something applies to a particular person, thing, or group more than any other: *There is not much there to attract tourists, least of all the weather.*
to say the least used for suggesting that something is worse or more extreme than you are saying: *He was a difficult person to deal with, to say the least.*

leath•er /ˈleðər/ noun [C] ★ a strong material made from animal skin that is used for making shoes, clothes, bags, etc.: *leather pants*

leave¹ /liv/ (past tense and past participle **left** /left/) verb ★★★

1 go away from place	8 cause a feeling
2 go away permanently	9 not do sth
3 stop doing sth	10 let sb decide
4 cause sth that remains	11 not use sth
5 forget to take sth	12 give sth when you die
6 end relationship	+ PHRASES
7 put sth somewhere	+ PHRASAL VERBS

1 [I/T] to go away from a place: *We left Boston at three in the afternoon.* ♦ *Your plane leaves in ten minutes.* ♦ *She **leaves for** work at 7:30 every morning.*
2 [I/T] to go away from a place permanently: *He didn't **leave home** until he was 24.*
3 [I/T] to stop working for an organization, or to stop going to school or college: *He decided to leave the company after 15 years.*
4 [T] to produce something that remains after you have gone: *The government left the economy in ruins.* ♦ *The ants **leave a trail** of chemicals for others to follow.*
5 [T] to put something somewhere and forget to take it away with you: *I left my homework on the bus.*
6 [I/T] to end a relationship with someone and stop living with them: *His wife has threatened to leave him.*
7 [T] to put something somewhere, especially in a place where it will stay: *Leave your stuff by the door.* ♦ *I'll leave a note for Leigh.*
8 [T] to produce a feeling or opinion: **leave sb with sth** *I was left with the feeling that she wasn't being quite honest.* ♦ **leave sb doing sth** *Kate's sudden departure left us all wondering what was going to happen.*
9 [T] to not do something that can be done later, or that can be done by someone else: *Leave the dishes and do them in the morning.* ♦ **leave sth to sb** *Don't worry – just leave everything to me.*
10 [T] to not make a decision and let someone else make it: *Leave questions of guilt or innocence for the jury to decide.*
11 [T] to not use something: *You've left half your dinner.* ♦ *There **was** some material **left over** when I'd finished making the dress.* ♦ **have sth left** *We don't have much money left.*
12 [T] to say that you want someone to have your money, property, etc. after you die: **leave sth to sb** *She left her jewels to her*

favorite niece. ♦ **leave sb sth** *He left her all his money.*

PHRASES **leave it at that** to not do anything more about something

leave a lot to be desired to be of a very low quality or standard: *The food left a lot to be desired.*

PHRASAL VERBS **ˌleave sb/sth beˈhind** **1** to forget to take someone or something with you: *When she was halfway home, she realized that she'd left her purse behind.* **2** to improve or progress much faster than someone or something else

ˌleave sb/sth ˈout to not include someone or something: *We decided to leave the chapter out of the book altogether.* ♦ *She **feels left out** because the other children don't play with her.*

Other ways of saying leave

- **depart** (*formal*) to leave a place: used mainly about airplanes, trains, and other types of transportation
- **go** a general word used for talking about leaving a place or situation
- **go away** to leave a place: often used for ordering someone to leave
- **set off** to leave a place at the beginning of a trip
- **storm out** to leave a place in an angry way
- **walk out** to leave a job or relationship suddenly

- Both **forget** and **leave** can be used to talk about not taking something that you need with you.
- Use **leave**, not **forget**, when you mention the place where the thing is: *Oh no, I've forgotten my keys.* ♦ *Don't forget your wallet.* ♦ *I can't find my keys – I must have left them somewhere.* ♦ *Don't leave your bag in your hotel room.*

leave[2] /liv/ noun [U] a period of time when you are officially away from your job, school, or the military: *You are entitled to six weeks annual leave.*

leaves the plural of **leaf**[1]

lech•er•ous /ˈletʃərəs/ adj behaving in an unpleasant way that shows you are sexually interested in someone

lec•ture[1] /ˈlektʃər/ noun [C] ★

1 a talk to a group of people about a particular subject, especially at a college or university: ***a lecture on** Dickens* ♦ *Tomorrow she will be **giving a lecture** at London University.*

2 *showing disapproval* a long serious talk that criticizes or warns someone: *I don't need any lectures from you about being late!*

lec•ture[2] /ˈlektʃər/ verb **1** [I] to give a lecture or a series of lectures **2** [T] *showing disapproval* to talk to someone seriously in order to criticize or warn them about something

lec•tur•er /ˈlektʃərər/ noun [C] **1** someone who gives a lecture **2** *British* a teacher at a university or college

led the past tense and past participle of **lead**[1]

ledge /ledʒ/ noun [C] **1** a narrow surface that sticks out from the side of a cliff or wall **2** a narrow shelf at the bottom of a window = SILL

ledg•er /ˈledʒər/ noun [C] a book that contains the financial records of a business

leech /litʃ/ noun [C] a small soft creature that sticks to the skin of other animals in order to feed on their blood

leek /lik/ noun [C] a long thin vegetable that tastes similar to an onion and is white at one end with green leaves at the other

leer /lɪr/ verb [I] to look at someone in an unpleasant way that shows you are sexually interested in them —**leer** noun [C]

lee•way /ˈliˌweɪ/ noun [U] the amount of freedom that someone has to make their own decisions or to take action

left[1] /left/ adj ★★★

1 on the side of your body that is opposite to the right ≠ RIGHT: *He wore a wedding ring on his left hand.*

2 on the left side of something: *the bottom left corner of the screen* ♦ *We took a left turn when we should have gone right.*

left[2] /left/ noun [singular] ★★

1 the left side or direction: *My office is the third door **on your left**.* ♦ ***On the left of** the picture you can see his grandmother.* ♦ *The car swerved **to the left**.*

2 the left or **the Left** people or groups with left-wing political opinions: *He received strong criticism from **the left of** the party.*

left[3] /left/ adv **1** toward the left side: *Turn left at the end of the street.* **2** toward the left in politics

left[4] the past tense and past participle of **leave**[1]

ˈleft-ˌclick verb [I] *computing* to press the button on the left side of a computer MOUSE with your finger

ˈleft ˌfield noun **come out of left field** *American informal* to be unexpected and surprising

ˈleft-ˌhand adj on the left side ≠ RIGHT-HAND: *The plates are on the left-hand side of the cabinet.*

left-hand•ed /left ˈhændəd/ adj **1** born with a natural tendency to use the left hand to do things ≠ RIGHT-HANDED **2** designed for or done with the left hand ≠ RIGHT-HANDED —**left-hand•ed•ness** noun [U]

left•o•ver /ˈleftˌoʊvər/ adj remaining after you have finished using the amount that you want or need

left•o•vers /ˈleftˌoʊvərz/ noun [plural] the food that remains at the end of a meal after you have finished eating

ˌleft ˈwing, the noun [singular] the members of a political organization whose aims and ideas are more SOCIALIST than the other members, because they believe that property, money, and power should be shared more equally

ˌleft-ˈwing adj someone who is left-wing believes that property, money, and power should be shared more equally ≠ RIGHT-WING —**ˌleft-ˈwinger** noun [C]

leg /leg/ noun [C] ★★★

1 part of body	4 part of furniture
2 clothing covering leg	5 part of trip/race
3 meat from animal leg	+ PHRASE

1 one of the parts of a person's or animal's body to which the feet are attached: *an exercise to strengthen the leg muscles* ♦ *She*

sat down and crossed her legs. —picture → C14
2 the part of a piece of clothing that covers one of your legs: *There was dirt on his **pants leg**.*
3 a piece of meat that comes from an animal's leg: *roast leg of lamb*
4 the part of a piece of furniture that supports it and raises it off the floor: *a stool with three legs ♦ a table leg*
5 a part of a trip or race
PHRASE **not have a leg to stand on** *informal* to not have any way of proving that you are right about something
→ PULL[1], STRETCH[1]

leg·a·cy¹ /ˈlegəsi/ noun [C] **1** money or property that you arrange for someone to have after you die **2** something such as a tradition or problem that exists as a result of something that happened in the past

leg·a·cy² /ˈlegəsi/ adj *computing* legacy software or equipment is still in use, but is not the most recent or advanced type that is available

le·gal /ˈlig(ə)l/ adj ★★★
1 relating to the law or lawyers: *You may wish to seek **legal advice** before signing the contract. ♦ China's **legal system** ♦ Parents are **taking legal action** to challenge the school's closure.*
2 allowed by the law or done according to the law ≠ ILLEGAL: *It is perfectly legal to import these goods under European law. ♦ They are the child's legal guardians.*
—**le·gal·ly** /ˈlig(ə)li/ adv

ˌlegal ˈaid noun [U] a system in which the government pays for people to get legal help when they do not have much money

le·gal·i·ty /liˈgæləti/ noun [U] the fact that something is legal

le·gal·ize /ˈligəlˌaɪz/ verb [T] to make something legal by creating a new law —**le·gal·i·za·tion** /ˌligələˈzeɪʃ(ə)n/ noun [U]

leg·end /ˈledʒənd/ noun [C] **1** an old story about imaginary people and events in the past: *Greek myths and legends* **2** someone who a great many people know about and admire: *the Hollywood legend, Elizabeth Taylor*

leg·en·dar·y /ˈledʒənˌderi/ adj **1** mentioned or described in a legend **2** very famous or well known for a long time

leg·gings /ˈlegɪŋz/ noun [plural] pants worn by women and girls that stretch and fit very closely to their legs *—picture* → C4

leg·i·ble /ˈledʒəb(ə)l/ adj legible writing is clear and neat enough to be read ≠ ILLEGIBLE —**leg·i·bly** adv

le·gion /ˈlidʒən/ noun [C] a large group of soldiers forming part of an army

leg·is·late /ˈledʒɪˌsleɪt/ verb [I/T] to create a law: *The state has legislated new safety measures.* —**leg·is·la·tor** /ˈledʒɪˌsleɪtər/ noun [C]

leg·is·la·tion /ˌledʒɪˈsleɪʃ(ə)n/ noun [U] a law, or a set of laws: *a complex piece of legislation ♦ Congress should pass legislation to limit the powers of the police.*

leg·is·la·tive /ˈledʒɪˌsleɪtɪv/ adj **1** relating to laws or to the process of creating new laws: *the legislative power of Congress* **2** used for talking about groups of people who have the power to create new laws: *a legislative body*

ˈlegislative ˌbranch, the noun [singular] the part of government that makes and changes laws

leg·is·la·tor /ˈledʒɪˌsleɪtər/ noun [C] someone who is elected to take part in the process of making laws

leg·is·la·ture /ˈledʒɪˌsleɪtʃər/ noun [C] ★ the part of a government that has the power to create laws: *Georgia's state legislature*

le·git·i·mate /ləˈdʒɪtəmət/ adj **1** allowed by the law, or correct according to the law: *Are the premises being used for legitimate business purposes?* **2** fair and reasonable: *Did he have a legitimate excuse for being late?* **3** a legitimate child is born to parents who are legally married —**le·git·i·ma·cy** /ləˈdʒɪtəməsi/ noun [U], **le·git·i·mate·ly** adv

lei·sure /ˈliʒər, ˈleʒər/ noun [U] **1** activities that are relaxing or fun: *leisure pursuits/activities* **2** the time when you are not working or are not busy: *I'm looking forward to more leisure time in my retirement.*
PHRASE **at your leisure** *formal* when you have free time and it is convenient for you: *Read it at your leisure.*

lei·sure·ly /ˈliʒərli, ˈleʒərli/ adj slow and relaxed

lem·on /ˈlemən/ noun [C/U] a fruit with a hard yellow skin and sour juice: *Add the juice of half a lemon. —picture* → C10

lem·on·ade /ˌleməˈneɪd/ noun [C/U] a drink that has a lemon flavor, or a glass of this drink

lend /lend/ (past tense and past participle **lent** /lent/) verb ★★★
1 [T] to give someone something for a short time, expecting that they will give it back to you later: *The local library will lend books for a month without charge.* ♦ **lend sb sth** *She lent me her very expensive coat.* ♦ **lend sth to sb** *Joe lent this car to us for the weekend.* → BORROW
2 [I/T] to give someone money that you expect them to pay back later: **lend sth to sb** *Banks will lend large amounts of money to new businesses.*
3 [T] to give something a particular quality: **lend sth sth** *The smile lent his face a certain boyish charm.*
4 [T] to give someone support or help: *Patricia is always ready to **lend a hand**.*
PHRASE **lend itself to sth** to be suitable for a particular purpose: *The story lends itself to being adapted for film.*

lend·er /ˈlendər/ noun [C] a person or financial institution that lends money

length /leŋθ/ noun ★★★

1 how long in size	4 how long book is
2 distance end to end	5 long thin piece
3 how long in time	+ PHRASES

1 [C/U] a measurement of how long something is in size: *The boat was 16 feet **in length**.*
2 [C] the distance from one end of something to the other: *Carter ran half **the length of** the field to score.*

3 [C/U] a measurement of how long something takes to do or of how long it lasts: ***The length of** your talk must be at least 10 minutes.*
4 [C/U] a measurement of how big a book or piece of writing is: *His latest novel is twice **the length of** his previous one.*
5 [C] a piece of something that is long and thin: ***a length of** pipe/rope/string*
PHRASES **at (great) length** for a long time and with a lot of detail: *Austin was questioned at length by detectives.*
at length *literary* after a long time
go to great/extreme/any etc. lengths to try in a very determined way to achieve something: *They have gone to great lengths to make us feel welcome.*
the length and breadth of sth every part of a large area

length•en /ˈleŋθən/ verb [I/T] to become longer, or to make something longer

length•ways /ˈleŋθˌweɪz/ or **length•wise** /ˈleŋθˌwaɪz/ adv in the direction of the longest side of something

length•y /ˈleŋθi/ adj continuing for a long time, especially for too long: *a lengthy period of negotiation*

le•ni•ent /ˈliniənt/ adj punishing someone less severely than they deserve —**le•ni•en•cy** /ˈliniənsi/ noun [U], **le•ni•ent•ly** adv

lens /lenz/ noun [C] **1** a thin piece of curved glass or plastic that makes things seem smaller, bigger, or clearer **2** the part of the eye that bends light to produce an image on the RETINA **3** a CONTACT LENS

lent the past tense and past participle of **lend**

Lent /lent/ the period of 40 days before Easter, when for religious reasons some Christians stop doing or eating something that they enjoy

len•til /ˈlent(ə)l/ noun [C/U] a small round flat dried seed that you boil before you eat it

Le•o /ˈliˌoʊ/ noun [C/U] one of the 12 signs of the ZODIAC. A **Leo** is someone who was born between July 23 and August 22.

leop•ard /ˈlepərd/ noun [C] a large wild animal from Africa and Southern Asia that has yellow fur with black spots —*picture* → C12

le•o•tard /ˈliəˌtɑrd/ noun [C] a piece of clothing that covers the body tightly from the neck to the top of the legs and is used for dancing or exercising

lep•er /ˈlepər/ noun [C] someone who has leprosy

lep•ro•sy /ˈleprəsi/ noun [U] a serious disease that affects the skin, nerves, and bones and can cause people's fingers and toes to fall off

les•bi•an /ˈlezbiən/ noun [C] a woman who is sexually attracted to women —**les•bi•an** adj

le•sion /ˈliʒ(ə)n/ noun [C] *medical* an area of damaged skin = WOUND

less /les/ grammar word ★★★

> **Less** can be:
> - a **determiner**: *Schools put less emphasis on being creative.*
> - a **pronoun**: *Connie did less than anyone else.* ♦ *He seemed to spend less of his time with her.*
> - an **adverb**: *The red jacket is less expensive.*

1 a smaller amount ≠ MORE: *You should eat less and exercise more.* ♦ *The industry operates with less government control these days.* ♦ *The new Ford is designed to use **less** fuel **than** earlier models.* ♦ *I aim to spend **less of** my time traveling.* ♦ *I wish you'd do **a little less** talking and a little more work.*
2 to a smaller degree, or not as often ≠ MORE: *We've been trying to use the telephone less this month.* ♦ *The homework was less difficult than I expected.* ♦ *My husband worries about things less than I do.* ♦ *We talk a lot **less than** we used to.*
PHRASES **less and less** gradually getting smaller in amount or degree: *Fishing was growing less and less profitable.*
the less...the less/more used for saying that when a particular activity, feeling, etc. is reduced, it causes something else to change at the same time: *Sometimes it seems like the less I do, the more tired I feel.*
no less than used before a number or amount for showing that it is large and surprising: *Exports have risen by no less than 80% in the last ten years.*

> Both **fewer** and **less** can be used to refer to an amount that is smaller than another amount.
> - Use **fewer** before plural nouns: *Fewer people turned up than expected.*
> - Use **less** before uncountable nouns: *You'll get a smoother finish if you use less paint.*
> - In informal English, some people now use **less** instead of **fewer** before plural nouns, although many people think that this is not correct.

less•en /ˈles(ə)n/ verb [I/T] to become smaller in amount, level, or importance, or to make something do this

less•er[1] /ˈlesər/ adj *formal* smaller, less important, or less serious than something else: *She was encouraged by her mother and, to a lesser extent, her father.*
PHRASE **the lesser of two evils** the less unpleasant or harmful of two possible choices

less•er[2] /ˈlesər/ adv less: *one of the lesser known English poets*

les•son /ˈles(ə)n/ noun [C] ★★
1 a period of time in which someone is taught a skill: *a driving/dancing/swimming lesson*
2 something that you learn from life, an event, or an experience: *I hope you've **learned a lesson** from this!* ♦ ***the lessons of** war/history/experience*
3 *British* a class in school on a particular subject

let /let/ (past tense and past participle **let**) verb ★★★
1 [T] to allow something to happen, or to allow someone to do something: **let sb/sth do sth** *Alice's mom won't let her come with us.* ♦ *I stepped back and let him pass.* ♦ **let sth in/out/through etc.** *The large windows let in a lot of light.*
2 [T] used for offering to do something: *Here, let me help you.*
3 [I/T] *British* to rent a room, apartment, house, etc. to someone
PHRASES **let alone** used for saying that something is even less likely to happen than another unlikely thing: *I hardly have time*

to think these days, let alone relax.
let sb go 1 to allow a person or animal to go free＝RELEASE: *The police had to let her go because of insufficient evidence.* **2** *informal* to officially tell someone that they can no longer work at a job: *We had to let several people go.*
let sth go/pass to not react to something annoying that someone says: *The remark made me furious, but I let it pass.*
let sb have it *informal* to attack or criticize someone severely
let sb know to tell someone something: *Let us know what time your plane arrives.*
let's 1 used for suggesting that you and one or more other people do something: *Let's eat now.* **2 let's face it** used for saying that someone must admit that a situation exists: *Let's face it – he just can't do this job.* **3 let's hope** used for saying that you hope something is true or will happen: *Let's hope she never finds out the truth.* **4 let's say (that)** used for suggesting that a possible situation needs to be considered: *Let's say you lose. What will you do then?*
let's see 1 used for suggesting that you and one or more other people should find the answer to something: ***Let's see if it works.*** **2 let's see** or **let me see** *spoken* used for saying that you need a moment to think about something: *Let's see – where was I?*
let yourself go *informal* **1** to relax and stop trying to control your emotions or behavior **2** to stop caring about your health or appearance: *He's really let himself go in the past few years.*

PHRASAL VERBS ˌ**let sb ˈdown** to make someone feel disappointed by not doing something that they are expecting you to do: *The families of the victims feel that the justice system has let them down.*
ˌ**let sb ˈin 1** to allow someone to enter a house, room, etc. **2 let yourself in for sth** *informal* to put yourself in a difficult situation: *She didn't know what she was letting herself in for when she married John.*
ˌ**let sb ˈin on sth** to tell someone a secret: *They were planning something, but they wouldn't let me in on it.*
ˌ**let sb ˈoff** to give someone little or no punishment for something that they did wrong: *I was pulled over for speeding, but I was let off with a warning.*
ˌ**let sb/sth ˈout** to allow a person or animal to leave a place
ˈ**let sth ˌout** to make a noise: *As he walked away, he let out a sigh of relief.*
ˌ**let ˈup** if something bad or unpleasant lets up, it slows down or stops: *The icy wind never let up for a moment.*

let•down /ˈletˌdaʊn/ noun [singular] something that makes you feel disappointed because it is not as good as you expected

le•thal /ˈliθl/ adj very dangerous and capable of killing you

le•thar•gic /ləˈθɑrdʒɪk/ adj lacking energy and not wanting to do anything

leth•ar•gy /ˈleθərdʒi/ noun [U] the feeling of being lethargic

let•ter /ˈletər/ noun [C] ★★★
1 a piece of paper that you write a message on and send to someone: *Most of the soldiers **wrote** long **letters** home.* ♦ *I **sent** them **a letter** complaining about it.* ♦ ***I get letters from** them every week.* ♦ ***a letter to** a friend*
2 a symbol used for writing words: *a word starting with the letter J*

PHRASE **follow/obey sth to the letter** to do exactly what you are told to do

let•tuce /ˈletəs/ noun [C/U] a vegetable with large thin green leaves that you eat raw in a salad —*picture* → C11

let•up /ˈletˌʌp/ noun [singular] a pause or reduction in something unpleasant

leu•ke•mi•a /luˈkimiə/ noun [U] a type of cancer that people get in their blood

lev•el[1] /ˈlev(ə)l/ noun ★★★

1 amount	5 floor in building
2 height of sth	6 way of understanding
3 standard	7 for checking if flat
4 part/stage of system	

1 [C] the amount of something that exists at a particular time: *Unemployment is now at its lowest level for 15 years.* ♦ *Many people have to cope with high **levels of** stress at work.*
2 [C] the height of something in a container or on a surface: *The river is at its highest level for several years.* ♦ *Check **the level of** the fluid in the tank.*
3 [C/U] a standard of academic ability: *This is an excellent book for **advanced level** students.*
4 [C/U] a part or stage in a system that has several parts or stages: *Decisions should be made at local, not national, level.* ♦ *These social changes will affect everyone, at all **levels of** society.*
5 [C/U] one of the floors in a building: *a garage at basement level*
6 [C] a particular way of relating to someone or something: *I get along with Frank very well **on a personal level**, but we just can't work together!*
7 [C] *American* a tool for measuring how flat something is

lev•el[2] /ˈlev(ə)l/ adj ★★
1 flat, smooth, and not sloping up or down: *We found a nice level spot for a picnic.*
2 at the same height: *They stood so that their shoulders were level.* ♦ *My head was **level with** George's chin.*

lev•el[3] /ˈlev(ə)l/ verb [T] **1** to make something flat: *Level the ground carefully before you pour the cement.* **2** to destroy a building or group of buildings

PHRASAL VERBS ˈ**level sth aˌgainst sb** *same as* **level sth at sb** 2
ˈ**level sth at sb 1** to point a weapon at someone **2** to criticize or accuse someone: *Several criticisms have been leveled at the company's board of directors.*
ˌ**level ˈoff** or ˌ**level ˈout 1** to stop sloping or moving up or down **2** to stop becoming more or less, and remain the same: *Oil prices should level out now that the war is over.*
ˌ**level sth ˈoff** or ˌ**level sth ˈout** to make something flat
ˈ**level with sb** *informal* to be honest with someone

ˌ**level-ˈheaded** adj behaving in a calm sensible way, even in a difficult situation

L

ˌlevel ˈplaying-ˌfield noun [singular] a situation that is fair for all the people involved

lev•er[1] /ˈlevər/ noun [C] **1** a long handle that you pull or push to operate a machine **2** a long metal bar that you put under a heavy object to move it

lev•er[2] /ˈlevər/ verb [T] to move something using a lever

lev•er•age /ˈlev(ə)rɪdʒ/ noun [U] **1** the power to make someone do what you want **2** the power that a lever gives you to move things

lev•i•tate /ˈlevɪˌteɪt/ verb [I/T] to rise and float in the air as if by magic, or to make something do this —**lev•i•ta•tion** /ˌlevɪˈteɪʃ(ə)n/ noun [U]

lev•y[1] /ˈlevi/ noun [C] an amount of money that you have to pay, for example as a tax

lev•y[2] /ˈlevi/ verb [T] to officially request payment of something such as a tax

lewd /lud/ adj referring to sex in a rude or unpleasant way

li•a•bil•i•ty /ˌlaɪəˈbɪləti/ noun **1** [U] legal responsibility for causing damage or injury, or for paying something **2** [C] someone or something that causes problems for someone

li•a•ble /ˈlaɪəb(ə)l/ adj legally responsible for causing damage or injury, so that you have to pay something or be punished: *The hospital was held liable for negligence.*
PHRASE **liable to do sth** likely to do something bad or unpleasant: *Be careful, the door handle is liable to break.*

li•ai•son /liˈeɪz(ə)n/ noun **1** [singular/U] an exchange of information between people or organizations, so that they understand each other and work well together **2** [C] a secret sexual or romantic relationship between two people

li•ar /ˈlaɪr/ noun [C] someone who tells lies

li•bel[1] /ˈlaɪb(ə)l/ noun [C/U] the illegal act of writing bad things that are not true about someone → SLANDER —**li•bel•ous** /ˈlaɪbələs/ adj

li•bel[2] /ˈlaɪb(ə)l/ verb [T] to write bad things that are not true about someone → SLANDER

lib•er•al[1] /ˈlɪb(ə)rəl/ adj **1** willing to accept ideas and ways of behaving that are different from your own: *Their views on marriage and divorce are very liberal.*
2 believing that people should have social and political freedom, and that they should be allowed to make their own decisions about moral issues: *liberal politicians*
3 giving or consisting of a larger amount than is usual: *There was a liberal supply of food and wine.* —**lib•er•al•ism** /ˈlɪb(ə)rəˌlɪzəm/ noun [U], **lib•er•al•ly** adv

lib•er•al[2] /ˈlɪb(ə)rəl/ noun [C] someone who has liberal social or political beliefs

ˌliberal ˈarts noun [plural] academic subjects, such as history, literature and science, as opposed to subjects that develop practical skills

lib•er•al•ize /ˈlɪb(ə)rəˌlaɪz/ verb [T] to make laws or rules less strict —**lib•er•al•i•za•tion** /ˌlɪb(ə)rəlɪˈzeɪʃ(ə)n/ noun [U]

lib•er•ate /ˈlɪbəˌreɪt/ verb [T] **1** to make a place or the people in it free from soldiers who have been controlling it **2** to give someone the freedom to do what they want —**lib•er•a•tion** /ˌlɪbəˈreɪʃ(ə)n/ noun [U], **lib•er•a•tor** noun [C]

lib•er•at•ed /ˈlɪbəˌreɪtəd/ adj not accepting traditional ideas or rules about the way you should behave

lib•er•at•ing /ˈlɪbəˌreɪtɪŋ/ adj making you feel that you have more freedom to do what you want to do

lib•er•ty /ˈlɪbərti/ noun [U] **1** the freedom to think or behave in the way that you want and not be controlled by anyone else
2 freedom from being kept in prison
PHRASE **be at liberty to do sth** *formal* to be allowed to do something

li•bi•do /lɪˈbidoʊ/ noun [C/U] *formal* someone's level of sexual energy and enthusiasm

Li•bra /ˈlibrə/ noun [C/U] one of the 12 signs of the ZODIAC. A **Libra** or **Libran** is someone who was born between September 23 and October 22.

li•brar•i•an /laɪˈbreriən/ noun [C] someone who works in a library, or who is in charge of a library

li•brar•y /ˈlaɪˌbreri/ noun [C] ★★★
1 a place where books, documents, CDs, etc. are available for you to look at or borrow: *the university/school library*
2 a private collection of books, or the room that it is kept in

lice /laɪs/ noun [plural] small insects that live on people's skin and in their hair. Lice is the plural of LOUSE.

li•cence /ˈlaɪs(ə)ns/ the British spelling of **license**[1]

li•cense[1] /ˈlaɪs(ə)ns/ noun ★★
1 [C] an official document that gives someone permission to do or use something: *a liquor license* (=giving permission to sell alcohol) ♦ *She was arrested for practicing medicine without a license.* ♦ *a driver's license*
2 [C/U] *formal* freedom to say or do what you want

li•cense[2] /ˈlaɪs(ə)ns/ verb [T] **1** if someone is licensed to do something, they have official permission to do it **2** if something is licensed, people have official permission to use it

li•censed /ˈlaɪs(ə)nst/ adj **1** someone who is licensed has official permission to do something, for example to drive or to do a particular job **2** licensed products are products that someone has official permission to use or to own

li•cens•ee /ˌlaɪs(ə)nˈsi/ noun [C] someone who has a license to do something

ˈlicense ˌplate noun [C] *American* the group of letters and numbers on the back and sometimes the front of a car that shows its official number and the state where it was licensed —*picture* → C6

li•chen /ˈlaɪken/ noun [C/U] a small soft plant that grows on surfaces such as trees and walls

lick[1] /lɪk/ verb [I/T] to move your tongue across something: *The boy licked his ice cream.*

lick[2] /lɪk/ noun [C] the action of licking something
PHRASE **a lick of paint** a layer of paint that you put on something to make it look better

lic•o•rice /ˈlɪkərɪs, ˈlɪkərɪʃ/ noun [U] a black

substance with a strong flavor, used for making candy

lid /lɪd/ noun [C] ★
1 a cover for a container: *a lid for the casserole dish*
2 the piece of skin that covers your eye when it is closed = EYELID

lie[1] /laɪ/ (present participle **lying** /ˈlaɪɪŋ/; past tense **lay** /leɪ/; past participle **lain** /leɪn/) verb [I] ★★★

1 be/put yourself flat	5 be in particular state
2 be on surface	6 say sth that is not true
3 be in position/place	+ PHRASES
4 consist of	+ PHRASAL VERBS

1 to be or put yourself in a position in which your body is flat on a surface such as the floor or a bed: *She was **lying on the beach** reading a book.* ♦ *Emma was **lying on her stomach** on the couch.* → LAY —*picture* → POSTURE
2 to be on a particular surface: *The gun was lying on the ground next to him.*
3 to be in a particular position or place: *The farm lay a few miles to the north.*
4 used for talking about things such as plans, ideas, and qualities and what they consist of: *The difficulty **lies in** knowing what to do next.*
5 if something lies in a particular state, it is in that state: *The castle **lay in ruins**.*
6 (past tense and past participle **lied** /laɪd/) to deliberately say something that is not true: *It was obvious that she was lying.* ♦ *He had to **lie about** his age to get into the army.* ♦ *She admitted **lying to** the police.*

PHRASES **lie ahead** to be going to happen in the future: *A grand future lies ahead of him.*
lie in wait (for sb) to hide so that you can attack someone when they pass you
lie low to hide, or to try to avoid attracting attention to yourself

PHRASAL VERBS **ˌlie aˈround 1** to have been left somewhere instead of being put in the correct place: *Never leave cash lying around.* **2** to spend a lot of time relaxing and not doing anything: *We lay around the house all day just talking.*
ˌlie ˈback to move from a sitting position into a position in which you are lying on a surface
ˌlie ˈdown 1 to put yourself in a position in which your body is flat on a surface, especially in order to rest or to sleep: *I'm going to **go and lie down** for a while.* **2 not take sth lying down** to not accept unfair treatment, by complaining about it or trying to change it
ˈlie with sb to be someone's responsibility

lie[2] /laɪ/ noun [C] ★★ something that you say or write that is not true and that you know is not true: *He told them he could drive, but it was a lie.* ♦ *All children **tell** their parents little **lies** sometimes.*

ˈlie deˌtector noun [C] a piece of equipment that is used for checking whether someone is telling the truth

lieu /lu/ noun **in lieu (of)** instead, or instead of

lieu·ten·ant /luˈtenənt/ noun [C] **1** an officer of low rank in the military **2** a police officer of middle rank

life /laɪf/ (plural **lives** /laɪvz/) noun ★★★

1 time sb is alive	5 time sth exists/lasts
2 way of living	6 activity/excitement
3 state of being alive	7 punishment
4 living things	+ PHRASES

1 [C/U] the period of time from someone's birth until their death: *He had a long and happy life.* ♦ *Don't **spend your whole life** worrying about money.* ♦ *She's lived in California **all her life**.*
2 [C/U] your particular way of living and the experiences that you have: *His life revolves around his children.* ♦ *I never liked city life* (=the experiences people have in a city). ♦ ***The life of** a movie star is not always a glamorous one.* ♦ *I just want to be able to **lead a normal life**.*
3 [C/U] the state of being alive: *He believed his life was in danger.* ♦ *They **risk their lives** to protect the people they love.* ♦ *Thousands of people **lost their lives*** (=died) *in the earthquake.* ♦ *It was a police officer who **saved her life**.*
4 [U] living things such as plants and animals: *Is there life on other planets?* ♦ *the great variety of **bird life** in the area*
5 [C] the period of time during which something exists or continues: ***The average life of** a television is about ten years.*
6 [U] the quality of being lively or exciting: *There's not much life in this little town.*
7 [U] *informal* a punishment in which someone is sent to prison for the rest of their life

PHRASES **bring sth to life** to make something exciting or interesting: *a book that brings the subject to life*
come to life to start to be exciting or interesting: *a new TV series in which history really comes to life*
get a life *spoken* used for telling someone that they are boring
that's life used for encouraging someone to accept that bad things happen to everyone, not just them
the time of your life a very enjoyable experience: *The children were having the time of their lives.*
→ MATTER[1]

life·boat /ˈlaɪfˌboʊt/ noun [C] a small boat that is kept on a ship for emergencies

life·buoy /ˈlaɪfˌbui, ˈlaɪfˌbɔɪ/ noun [C] something that you throw to someone to save them when they have fallen into water

ˈlife ˌcycle noun [C] the series of changes that happen to an animal or plant during its life

ˌlife exˈpectancy noun [C/U] the length of time that someone is likely to live

life·guard /ˈlaɪfˌgɑrd/ noun [C] someone whose job is to save swimmers who are in danger

ˈlife inˌsurance noun [U] a type of insurance that pays money to your family when you die

ˈlife ˌjacket noun [C] something you wear on a boat to make you float if you fall into the water

life·less /ˈlaɪfləs/ adj **1** not interesting or exciting **2** dead, or seeming to be dead **3** without any living or growing things

life·like /ˈlaɪfˌlaɪk/ adj a lifelike picture, model, etc. looks real

life•line /ˈlaɪfˌlaɪn/ noun [C] someone or something that you depend on to help you when you are in a difficult situation

life•long /ˈlaɪfˌlɔŋ/ adj continuing all through your life: *a lifelong friendship*

life pre•serv•er /ˈlaɪf prɪˌzɜrvər/ noun [C] *American* something you wear or put around you that keeps you from sinking in the water

life•sav•ing /ˈlaɪfˌseɪvɪŋ/ or **ˈlife-ˌsaving** adj done in order to prevent someone from dying

ˌlife ˈsentence noun [C] a punishment in which someone is sent to prison for the rest of their life, or for a very long time

ˈlife-ˌsize adj a life-size picture, model, etc. of something is the same size as the real thing

life•span /ˈlaɪfˌspæn/ noun [C] the length of time that someone lives for, or the length of time that something exists

ˈlife ˌstory noun [C] a description of all the things that have happened to someone during their life

life•style /ˈlaɪfˌstaɪl/ noun [C/U] the type of life that someone has, for example the type of things that they own and the type of activities that they do: *a healthy, outdoor lifestyle*

ˈlife-ˌthreatening adj a life-threatening disease or situation is one that could kill you

life•time /ˈlaɪfˌtaɪm/ noun [C] **1** the period of time when someone is alive **2** the length of time that something exists or works

ˈlife ˌvest noun [C] a LIFE JACKET

lift¹ /lɪft/ verb ★★★

1 [T] to move something to a higher position: *Lie on the floor and lift your legs slowly.* ♦ *The phone rang and he lifted the receiver immediately.* ♦ *Always bend your knees when lifting heavy loads.* —*picture* → CARRY

2 [T] to improve the situation that someone or something is in, or to make someone feel happier: **lift sb out of sth** *economic measures designed to lift the country out of recession* ♦ *Being outdoors can really* ***lift your spirits.***

3 [T] to officially end a rule or law that stopped someone from doing something: *They're hoping to get the* ***ban lifted*** *soon.*

4 [I] if something such as cloud or FOG lifts, it disappears

PHRASE **not lift a finger** *informal* to not help at all in a situation in which someone else is working

PHRASAL VERB **ˌlift ˈoff** if a space vehicle lifts off, it goes up from the ground into the air

lift² /lɪft/ noun [C] **1** a movement in which something is lifted **2** a RIDE in someone's car **3** *British* an ELEVATOR

ˈlift-ˌoff noun [C/U] the time when a space vehicle goes up from the ground into the air

lig•a•ment /ˈlɪgəmənt/ noun [C] a part inside your body that holds bones together or keeps organs in place

light¹ /laɪt/ noun ★★★

1 [U] brightness from the sun or from a light, which allows you to see things: *a beam/flash/ray of light* ♦ *The house could be clearly seen* ***by the light of*** *the moon.*

2 [C] a piece of electrical equipment that produces brightness: *Could somebody* ***put the light on?*** ♦ *I* ***turned the lights off*** *and shut the door.* ♦ *All the* ***lights went out.***

3 [C] a TRAFFIC LIGHT: *Turn left at the lights.*

4 [singular] something that is used for lighting a cigarette: *Do you have a light?*

PHRASES **bring sth to light** or **come to light** if facts are brought to light or come to light, people discover them

in a bad/new/different etc. light used for talking about someone's opinion of a particular person or thing: *This incident made me see him in a completely different light.*

in light of sth because of a particular fact: *In light of your good driving record, we've decided to overlook this offense.*

light at the end of the tunnel something that makes you think that a difficult situation will improve

see the light to suddenly realize or understand something

see the light (of day) 1 if an object sees the light of day, it is brought out of a place where it has been for a long time **2** if something such as an idea, plan, or rule sees the light of day, it starts to exist

set light to sth to make something start burning

throw/shed/cast light on sth to provide new information that helps you to understand something

light² /laɪt/ adj ★★★

1 bright/well lit	7 gentle
2 not dark	8 not serious
3 pale in color	9 about food/drink
4 not weighing much	10 about sleep
5 small/not much	+ PHRASE
6 not severe	

1 very bright because of light from the sun ≠ DARK: *The room is light and airy.*

2 if it is light, you can see because it is day and not night ≠ DARK: *It gets light around 5 a.m.*

3 pale in color, not dark ≠ DARK: *a light blue shirt*

4 not weighing much, or weighing less than you expect ≠ HEAVY: *The table is a lot lighter than it looks.*

5 not much in quantity: *Traffic was fairly light as we left the city.* ♦ *a light frost* ♦ *light refreshments*

6 a light punishment is not very severe ≠ HARSH: *a light prison sentence*

7 not strong, hard, or loud: *a light breeze* ♦ *a light kiss on the cheek* ♦ *She heard a light knock at the window.*

8 enjoyable and not very serious or difficult: *a little light reading*

9 food or drink that is light has less fat or alcohol than other similar food or drink: *light beer/cream cheese*

10 a light sleep is one in which you wake up often ≠ DEEP

PHRASE **make light of sth** to treat something as not being very serious

light³ /laɪt/ (past tense and past participle **lit** /lɪt/) verb ★★

1 [I/T] to start to burn, or to make something

start to burn: *The fire won't light if the wood is wet.* ♦ *Amy **lit a cigarette**.*
2 [T] to make a place brighter by giving it more light: *a dimly lit hallway* ♦ *The room was lit by candlelight.*
3 [T] if you light someone's way, you use a light to lead them through a dark place
PHRASAL VERBS ˌ**light ˈup** to start to shine: *A warning signal lit up on the dashboard.*
ˌ**light (sth) ˈup 1** *informal* to light a cigarette **2** if someone's face or eyes light up, they express a strong emotion, usually happiness or excitement: *a smile that lit up her whole face* ♦ *Antony's eyes lit up when Keiko walked into the room.*

light[4] /laɪt/ adv if you travel light, you do not take many things with you

ˌ**light ˈaircraft** noun [C] a very small airplane

ˈ**light ˌbulb** noun [C] a glass object that you put in an electric light to produce light

light•en /ˈlaɪt(ə)n/ verb **1** [I/T] if a situation or someone's mood lightens, or if something lightens the mood, it becomes more relaxed **2** [T] to reduce an amount of work **3** [I/T] to become brighter or lighter in color, or to make something brighter or lighter in color **4** [I/T] to become less heavy, or to make something less heavy
PHRASAL VERB ˌ**lighten ˈup 1** *same as* **lighten** 1 **2** *informal* used for telling someone to be less serious

ˌ**light enterˈtainment** noun [U] entertainment that involves things such as singing, dancing, and telling jokes

light•er /ˈlaɪtər/ noun [C] a small object that produces a flame, used for lighting cigarettes

light•head•ed /ˌlaɪtˈhedəd/ adj feeling as though you might fall down or become unconscious, for example because you are drunk

light•heart•ed /ˌlaɪtˈhɑrtəd/ adj **1** happy and not worried about anything **2** funny and not intended to be serious

light•house /ˈlaɪtˌhaʊs/ noun [C] a tower that is built next to the ocean with a powerful light that warns ships of danger

ˌ**light ˈindustry** noun [U] industry in which small goods are produced, for example electronic equipment → HEAVY INDUSTRY

light•ing /ˈlaɪtɪŋ/ noun [U] light of a particular type or quality, or the equipment that produces it

light•ly /ˈlaɪtli/ adv

1 without much force	4 cooked for a short time
2 without thought	5 waking up very easily
3 in small amounts	+ PHRASE

1 without using much force or pressure **2** without considering something carefully and seriously: *The decision was not made lightly.* **3** in small amounts, or using only a small amount of something **4** cooked for a short time: *a lightly boiled egg* **5** if you sleep lightly, you wake up very easily
PHRASE **get off/be let off lightly** to not be harmed or punished as severely as you might have been

light•ning /ˈlaɪtnɪŋ/ noun [U] the bright flashes of light that you see in the sky during a storm: *The ship was struck by lightning soon after it left the port.* ♦ *She lay awake, listening to the thunder and lightning.*

lightning

light•weight[1] /ˈlaɪtˌweɪt/ adj weighing less than other similar things

light•weight[2] /ˈlaɪtˌweɪt/ noun [C] **1** someone who is not important or does not have much influence **2** a BOXER or WRESTLER who belongs to one of the lower weight groups

ˈ**light ˌyear** noun **1** [C] the distance that light travels in a year, used as a unit for measuring distances in space **2 light years** [plural] *informal* a very long way in time, distance, or quality

lik•a•ble /ˈlaɪkəb(ə)l/ adj pleasant, friendly, and easy to like

like[1] /laɪk/ grammar word ★★★

> **Like can be:**
> - a **preposition**: *He looks like his father.*
> - a **conjunction**: *She looked like she was about to cry.*
> - an **adverb**: *I said, like, you can't do this to me.*

1 similar similar to someone or something else: *No one could play the trumpet like he did.* ♦ *I went and bought myself a new pen **just like** yours.* ♦ *Doesn't he **look like** Mark?* ♦ *The cloth **felt like** silk against her skin.* ♦ *Once it's washed and ironed it'll be **like new**.* ♦ *an animal **something like** a shark*
2 such as used for introducing an example of someone or something that you have just mentioned: *It eats small animals like birds and mice.*
3 typical typical of a particular person: *It's not **like** him to lie.*
4 as if *spoken* used for saying that something seems to be true but may not be: *He sounded like he'd just woken up.*
5 when you pause *spoken* used when you pause while you are speaking: *He hasn't called me in, like, three weeks.*
6 used when reporting speech *very informal* used when you are reporting what someone has said: *And I'm like, give me a chance, Simon.*
PHRASES **like crazy/mad** in a very extreme, noticeable, or fast way: *His new book is selling like crazy.*
like I say/said *spoken* used when you are saying something again that you have already said: *It's unfortunate but, like I said, it's a decision we have to make.*
like this used when showing someone exactly how to do something: *Click on the "Mail" icon, like this.*
more like used for giving a number or amount that you think is more accurate

L

than another one: *I'd guess it's more like 40 percent than 60 percent .*

what is sb/sth like? used for asking or talking about the qualities or features that someone or something has: *I haven't met Alan – what's he like?* ♦ *She took Andrew with her to show him what the club was like.*

→ ANYTHING

like[2] /laɪk/ verb [T] ★★★

1 to enjoy something, or to think that someone or something is pleasant or attractive: *Do you like my new hairstyle?* ♦ *You never did like John, did you?* ♦ *Which of her novels did you* ***like best?*** ♦ *Jamie doesn't* ***like it when*** *you correct him.* ♦ **like doing sth** *I like going to parties.* ♦ **like to do sth** *He always liked to sleep late on Sundays.* ♦ *"****How did you like*** *Paris?""I loved it!"*

2 to prefer to do something in a particular way, or to prefer to have something done in a particular way: *How do you like your eggs?* ♦ **like sb to do sth** *She likes us to hand our work in on time.* ♦ **like to do sth** *I don't like to interrupt her when she's in a meeting.*

PHRASES **(whether you) like it or not** used for saying that you cannot change a situation even if it is unpleasant: *Whether we like it or not, we are part of a global economy.*

would like used for stating politely what someone wants: *I'd like a large whiskey, please.* ♦ **would like to do sth** *I'd like to thank everyone who made this evening a success.*

would you like...? used for offering something to someone or for inviting them to do something: *Would you like some cake?* ♦ **would you like to do sth?** *Would you like to go for a drink?* ♦ **would you like sb/sth to do sth** *Would you like me to help you with your homework?*

> Other ways of saying **like**
>
> - **adore** (*informal*) to like someone or something very much
> - **be crazy about** (*informal*) to like someone or something very much
> - **be fond of** to like someone or something very much
> - **enjoy** to like doing a particular activity
> - **love** to like something very much. **Love** is also used for saying that you care about someone very much
> - **prefer** to like one thing more than another

like[3] /laɪk/ noun

PHRASES **sb's likes and dislikes** the things that someone likes or does not like

the likes of *informal* people or things of a particular type

-like /laɪk/ suffix similar to something: *a childlike face* ♦ *The illness causes flu-like symptoms.*

like·li·hood /ˈlaɪkliˌhʊd/ noun [singular/U] the chance that something might happen: *The likelihood of developing cancer is increased in people who smoke.* ♦ *a strong likelihood that he will run for president*

like·ly[1] /ˈlaɪkli/ adj ★★★

1 probably going to happen, or probably true ≠ UNLIKELY: **likely to do sth** *Is anyone likely to see Fran?* ♦ **+(that)** *It seems likely that interest rates will rise.*

2 suitable, or almost certain to be successful ≠ UNLIKELY: *a likely candidate for the job*

like·ly[2] /ˈlaɪkli/ adv probably: *They'll quite likely ask you to pay.*

like-ˈminded adj like-minded people have similar interests and opinions

lik·en /ˈlaɪkən/ PHRASAL VERB **ˈliken sb/sth to sb/sth** *formal* to say that someone or something is similar to someone or something else

like·ness /ˈlaɪknəs/ noun [C] a picture, model, etc. of someone that looks just like them

like·wise /ˈlaɪkˌwaɪz/ adv *formal* in a similar way: *Most fathers said that they had too little time with their children. Likewise, kids wanted more time with their dads.*

lik·ing /ˈlaɪkɪŋ/ noun [singular] a feeling of enjoying something: *a liking for science*

PHRASES **take a liking to** to begin to like someone or something

to sb's liking if something is to someone's liking, they like it

li·lac /ˈlaɪlək/ noun [C/U] a small tree with pale purple or white flowers

lilt /lɪlt/ noun [singular] a pleasant rising and falling pattern of sounds in the way that someone talks or in a piece of music —**lilt·ing** adj

lil·y /ˈlɪli/ noun [C] a large flower in the shape of a bell —*picture* → C9

li·ma bean /ˈlaɪmə ˌbin/ noun [C] a flat pale green bean

limb /lɪm/ noun [C] an arm, or a leg

PHRASE **out on a limb** in a situation where you have no support from other people

lim·ber /ˈlɪmbər/ adj able to bend and move easily

lim·bo /ˈlɪmboʊ/ noun **in limbo** in a situation where you have to wait to find out what will happen next

lime /laɪm/ noun **1** [C/U] a fruit with a hard green skin and sour juice —*picture* → C10 **2** [U] a white substance used for making CEMENT

lime·light, the /ˈlaɪmˌlaɪt/ noun [singular] a situation in which you are getting a lot of public attention: *DiCaprio has been in the limelight since the age of 12.*

lim·er·ick /ˈlɪmərɪk/ noun [C] a humorous poem with five lines

lim·it[1] /ˈlɪmɪt/ noun [C] ★★★

1 the greatest amount or level of something that is possible or allowed: ***The speed limit*** *here is forty miles an hour.* ♦ *There is* ***a limit to*** *what we can do in two weeks.*

2 the outer edge of an area: *No bombs landed within the city limits.*

PHRASE **off limits 1** if a place is off limits, you are not allowed to go there **2** not allowed or approved of: *Discussion of these subjects is off limits.*

> Words often used with **limit**
>
> *Nouns often used with* ***limit*** *(noun, sense 1)*
> - **age, speed, time, weight** + LIMIT: nouns that can come immediately before limit
>
> *Verbs often used with* ***limit*** *(noun, sense 1)*
> - **impose, place, put** + LIMIT + ON: limit something
> - **define, set, specify** + LIMIT: say what the limits are

- **extend, raise** + LIMIT: increase the limit
- **lower, reduce** + LIMIT: make the limit lower

lim·it² /ˈlɪmɪt/ verb [T] ★★★
1 to prevent a number, amount, or effect from increasing past a particular point: *The new laws should limit environmental damage.* ♦ **limit sth to sth** *We want to limit classes to a maximum of twenty-five students.*
2 to reduce or control someone's freedom or ability to be effective = RESTRICT: **be limited by sth** *They were limited by the amount of money they could spend on the production.* ♦ **limit sb to sth** *Try to limit yourself to two or three glasses of wine a week.*
3 be limited to if something is limited to a particular place or group, it happens only in that place or within that group: *The right to vote was limited to men.*

lim·i·ta·tion /ˌlɪmɪˈteɪʃ(ə)n/ noun **1 limitations** [plural] weak points that make someone or something less effective: *There are several limitations to this method.* **2** [C/U] a rule or situation that puts a limit on something, or the process of limiting something: *a limitation on the use of cars in the city*

lim·it·ed /ˈlɪmɪtəd/ adj ★★
1 not allowed to go above a particular number, amount, or level ≠ UNLIMITED: *The promotional pack will be on sale for a limited period only.*
2 not very good, or not very great in amount: *a limited grasp of economics*
3 *British* used after the name of a company to show that it is a limited company

ˌlimited ˈcompany noun [C] a company, especially in the U.K., whose owners are legally responsible for only a limited amount of its DEBTS

lim·it·ing /ˈlɪmɪtɪŋ/ adj preventing someone or something from developing or improving

lim·it·less /ˈlɪmɪtləs/ adj very great, or without any limits

lim·ou·sine /ˈlɪməˌzin/ noun [C] **1** a large expensive comfortable car in which a rich or important person travels **2** *American* a small bus that takes people to and from airports

limp¹ /lɪmp/ verb [I] to walk with difficulty because of an injured leg or foot —**limp** noun [singular]

limp² /lɪmp/ adj not firm, stiff, or strong

line¹ /laɪn/ noun ★★★

1 long thin mark	8 telephone connection
2 on someone's skin	9 series of events etc.
3 row of people/things	10 way of thinking etc.
4 people waiting	11 series of words
5 string/rope/wire	12 part of railroad system
6 border	13 direction/path
7 imaginary limit	+ PHRASES

1 [C] a long thin mark on the surface of something: *Draw a straight line.* ♦ *It was hard to tell whether the ball had crossed the line.*
2 [C] a thin mark on someone's skin that appears especially as they get older = WRINKLE
3 [C] a row of people or things: ***a line of*** *palm trees*
4 [C/U] a row of people who are waiting for something: *The line went out the door and into the street.* ♦ *We **stood in line** for an hour.*
5 [C] a piece of string, rope, or wire used for a particular purpose: *a washing line*
6 [C] a border between two regions: *the Arizona – California state line*
7 [C] an imaginary limit or border between two situations or conditions: *There is **a fine line between** helping and interfering.*
8 [C] a telephone connection or service: *an advice line* ♦ *It's **a very bad line** – I'll call you back.*
9 [C] a series of people or events that are connected: *the latest in **a long line of** scandals*
10 [C] a way of thinking, talking, or finding out about something: *a persuasive line of argument* ♦ *The government is **taking a hard line** on street crime* (=dealing with it firmly).
11 [C] a series of words in a book, song, play, etc.: *The actors kept forgetting their lines.* ♦ ***a line of** poetry*
12 [C] a part of a railroad system
13 [C] the direction or path along which someone or something moves or looks: *He was so drunk he couldn't walk in **a straight line**.*

PHRASES **along the lines of** similar to, or based on: *an ad campaign along the lines of the one we did last year*
along similar/different/the same lines in a way that is similar/different/the same
be in line for to be likely to receive something
down the line at a later stage in a process: *The situation will be very different two months down the line.*
in/out of line with 1 similar to/different from someone or something: *The costs were very much in line with what we expected.* **2** changing/not changing in the same way as another thing: *The increase in pay is in line with the cost of living.*
on line connected to a computer system or to the Internet → ONLINE
on the line 1 at risk: *His job could be on the line if results do not improve.* **2** on the telephone: *We have a caller on the line from California.*
out of line behaving in a way that other people do not approve of: *That comment was way out of line.*

line² /laɪn/ verb [T] **1** to cover the inside of something with a layer of something else: *He wore a black coat lined with dark gray silk.* ♦ **line sth with sth** *Line the cake pan with aluminum foil.* **2** to form rows along the sides of something: *Crowds lined the streets to watch the parade.*

PHRASE **line your pockets** to obtain money, especially by acting dishonestly

PHRASAL VERBS **ˌline (sb/sth) ˈup** to form a row, or to put people or things in a row: *The books are lined up on a shelf above the desk.* ♦ *All children must line up when the whistle goes.*
ˌline sth ˈup to organize or prepare things for an event: *We have a series of activities lined up to keep you entertained.*

lin·e·ar /ˈlɪniər/ adj *formal* consisting of lines, or of a straight line

lined /laɪnd/ adj **1** lined paper has lines printed on it **2** clothing that is lined has another layer of cloth on the inside **3** lined skin has a lot of lines on it

lin·en /ˈlɪnən/ noun [C/U] **1** a cloth like thick cotton that CREASES easily **2** things made of cloth that are used in the house, such as sheets and TABLECLOTHS

lin·er /ˈlaɪnər/ noun [C] **1** something that you use inside another thing to keep it clean or protect it: *a garbage can liner* **2** a large passenger ship that people travel on for pleasure

line·up /ˈlaɪnˌʌp/ noun [C] **1** the players from a team who will play in a particular game **2** a line of people the police use to find out if someone who saw a crime recognizes any of them **3** a group of television or radio programs that play one after another

lin·ger /ˈlɪŋgər/ verb [I] **1** to stay somewhere for a long time, or to do something for a long time: *I like to linger over breakfast and read the newspapers.* **2** to continue for a long time: *Doubts still linger about his honesty.*

PHRASAL VERB ˌ**linger ˈon** *same as* **linger** 2

L

lin·ge·rie /ˌlɑnʒəˈreɪ, ˈlɑnʒəri/ noun [U] women's underwear

lin·ger·ing /ˈlɪŋgərɪŋ/ adj lasting for a long time: *lingering doubts/fears*

lin·guist /ˈlɪŋgwɪst/ noun [C] **1** someone who studies and speaks a lot of languages **2** someone who teaches or studies LINGUISTICS

lin·guis·tic /lɪŋˈgwɪstɪk/ adj relating to languages, words, or linguistics

lin·guis·tics /lɪŋˈgwɪstɪks/ noun [U] the study of language and how it works

lin·ing /ˈlaɪnɪŋ/ noun [C/U] **1** a piece of cloth that is attached to the inside of something such as clothes or curtains to make them thicker **2** something that you put on the inside of another thing to keep it clean or protect it

link[1] /lɪŋk/ verb [T] ★★★

1 if people, things, or events are linked, they are related to each other in some way: *Police suspect that the two murder cases are linked.* ♦ **be linked to/with sth** *Rock music has often been linked with the drug culture.*

2 to say or show that two things are related, or that one of the things causes the other: **link sb/sth to sth** *Scientists have linked certain types of cancer to people's diets.*

3 to connect two or more places or things: *Several new roads will link the southern and northern regions of the country.* ♦ **link sth to/with sth** *Link the supply cable to the fitting at the rear of the machine.*

PHRASAL VERB ˌ**link ˈup** to make a connection between two or more things: *The space shuttle will **link up with** the space station this afternoon.*

link[2] /lɪŋk/ noun [C] ★★★

1 a connection	4 on the Internet
2 a relationship	5 ring in a chain
3 way to travel etc.	

1 a connection between two or more people, places, facts, or events: *They are studying **the links between** carbon emissions and climate change.*

2 a relationship between two or more people, organizations, or countries: *Back in the 1980s, the bank was criticized for its **links with** South Africa.*

3 a means of travel or communication that connects two or more places: *a satellite link between Hong Kong and New York*

4 *computing* a connection between one Internet file or section and another, for example a connection on a WEBSITE =HYPERLINK: *Click on this link to find out more.*

5 one of the rings that are connected to each other to form a chain

ˈ**linking ˌverb** noun [C] *linguistics* a verb such as "be" or "seem" that connects the subject of a sentence with its COMPLEMENT (=the part of the sentence that describes the subject)

link·up /ˈlɪŋkˌʌp/ noun [C] a connection between machines or electronic equipment

li·no·le·um /lɪˈnoʊliəm/ noun [U] a hard flat substance with a shiny surface, used for covering floors

lint /lɪnt/ noun [U] *American* small pieces of thread or wool that come off cloth or clothes

li·on /ˈlaɪən/ noun [C] a large African wild cat with yellow fur —*picture* → C12

li·on·ess /ˈlaɪənəs/ noun [C] a female lion

lip /lɪp/ noun [C] ★★★

1 one of the two edges that form the top and bottom parts of your mouth —*picture* → C14

2 the place on the edge of a glass or container where you pour out liquid

PHRASES **on everyone's lips** if something is on everyone's lips, a lot of people are talking about it

pay lip service to sth to say publicly that you agree with an idea, but not do anything to support it

lip-read /ˈlɪp ˌrid/ verb [I] to look at someone's lips in order to understand what they are saying because you cannot hear them

lip·stick /ˈlɪpˌstɪk/ noun [C/U] a colored substance in the form of a small stick that women put on their lips, or a stick of this —*picture* → MAKEUP

liq·ue·fy /ˈlɪkwəˌfaɪ/ verb [I/T] to become a liquid, or to make something become a liquid

li·queur /lɪˈkɜr, lɪˈkjʊr/ noun [C/U] a sweet strong alcoholic drink that you have at the end of a meal

liq·uid[1] /ˈlɪkwɪd/ noun [C/U] ★★ a substance such as water that can flow and is not a solid or gas: *a glass of colorless liquid*

liq·uid[2] /ˈlɪkwɪd/ adj ★ in the form of a liquid: *liquid detergent*

ˌ**liquid ˈassets** noun [plural] *business* the money that a company or person has, and anything else that can easily be exchanged for money

liq·ui·date /ˈlɪkwɪˌdeɪt/ verb [I/T] to close a business and sell everything that it owns in order to pay money that it owes —**liq·ui·da·tion** /ˌlɪkwɪˈdeɪʃ(ə)n/ noun [U]

liq·uor /ˈlɪkər/ noun [U] alcoholic drinks, especially strong alcoholic drinks

ˈ**liquor ˌstore** noun [C] *American* a store that sells alcoholic drinks

lisp /lɪsp/ noun [singular] if someone has a lisp, they pronounce "s" sounds as "th" —**lisp** verb [I/T]

list¹ /lɪst/ noun [C] ★★★
1 a set of names, numbers, etc. that are written or printed one below another: *a shopping list* ♦ *I'd better **make a list**, or I'll forget who I've invited.* ♦ *I couldn't see my name **on the list**.* ♦ ***a list of** the world's richest people*
2 a set of things that you put in a particular order in your mind, according to how important they are: *Painting the house is **high on our list** of things to do.*

list² /lɪst/ verb ★★
1 [T] to mention or write things one after another: *The ingredients in food must be listed on the package.* ♦ *Chris lists his hobbies as cycling, gardening, and chess.*
2 [T] if a telephone number is listed, it is published in a book
3 [I] if a ship lists, it leans to one side

lis·ten /ˈlɪs(ə)n/ verb [I] ★★★
1 to pay attention to a sound, or to try to hear a sound: *Do you like **listening to** music?* ♦ ***Listen carefully** to the instructions.* ♦ *She was **listening for** the sound of his key in the lock.* → HEAR
2 to pay attention to what someone tells you and do what they suggest: *I've tried to give Jerry advice, but he just won't listen.* ♦ *Don't **listen to** him – he doesn't know anything about it.*

PHRASAL VERBS ˌ**listen ˈin** to secretly listen to what someone says = EAVESDROP: *Rachel was **listening in on** our conversation.*
ˌ**listen ˈup** *spoken* used for getting the attention of a noisy group of people: *Hey, listen up everybody!*

> **Words often used with listen**
> *Adverbs often used with listen (sense 1)*
> ■ LISTEN + **attentively, carefully, closely, hard, intently**: used for saying that someone is giving all their attention

lis·ten·er /ˈlɪs(ə)nər/ noun [C] **1** someone who listens to the radio, or to a particular radio program or radio station **2** someone who listens to a person speaking

list·ing /ˈlɪstɪŋ/ noun **1** [C] a list, or a position on a list **2 listings** [plural] a list of things such as movies, plays, and exhibits printed in a newspaper

list·less /ˈlɪstləs/ adj feeling as if you have no energy and no interest in anything

list·serv /ˈlɪstˌsɜrv/ *trademark* a piece of software that automatically sends a copy of every e-mail received to all members of a group

lit the past tense and past participle of **light³**

lite /laɪt/ adj a spelling of "light" that is often used in the names of foods and drinks that contain less sugar, fat, or alcohol than usual

li·ter /ˈlitər/ noun [C] **1** a unit for measuring an amount of liquid or gas in the METRIC SYSTEM, containing 1000 milliliters **2** a unit for measuring the size of a vehicle's engine

lit·er·a·cy /ˈlɪt(ə)rəsi/ noun [U] the ability to read and write

lit·er·al /ˈlɪt(ə)rəl/ adj **1** the literal meaning of a word is its most basic meaning → FIGURATIVE **2** a literal translation is one in which each word is translated separately in a way that does not sound natural

lit·er·al·ly /ˈlɪt(ə)rəli/ adv **1** used for showing that what you are saying is really true: *Now there are literally thousands of companies using our software.* **2** used when you are describing something in an extreme way that cannot be true: *When I told him the news he literally exploded.* **3** in the most basic, obvious meanings of the words that are used: *There's an Italian dessert called tiramisu, which literally means "pull me up."* **4** if you translate something literally, you translate each word separately in a way that does not sound natural

lit·er·ar·y /ˈlɪtəˌreri/ adj **1** relating to literature **2** typical of words that are used only in stories or poems, and not in normal writing or speech

lit·er·ate /ˈlɪt(ə)rət/ adj able to read and write ≠ ILLITERATE

lit·er·a·ture /ˈlɪt(ə)rətʃər, ˈlɪt(ə)rəˌtʃʊr/ noun [U] ★★
1 stories, poems, and plays, especially those that are considered to have value as art: *She is studying German literature.*
2 books or other printed information about a subject: *Police discovered racist literature in his home.*

lithe /laɪð/ adj moving and bending in a graceful way

lit·i·gate /ˈlɪtɪˌgeɪt/ verb [I] *legal* to ask a court of law to make a decision about a disagreement

lit·i·ga·tion /ˌlɪtɪˈgeɪʃ(ə)n/ noun [U] use of the legal system to settle a disagreement

lit·mus test /ˈlɪtməs ˌtest/ noun [C] an event, decision, etc. that provides a clear sign of what someone is really like, or of what their intentions are

li·tre /ˈlitər/ the British spelling of **liter**

lit·ter¹ /ˈlɪtər/ noun **1** [U] things that people have dropped on the ground in a public place, making it messy **2** [C] a group of baby animals that are born at the same time

lit·ter² /ˈlɪtər/ verb **1** [T] **be littered with** if a place is littered with things, they are spread around there: *The room was littered with books and papers.* **2** [T] **be littered with** if something is littered with things, there are many of them in it: *The book is littered with references from the Bible.* **3** [I] to leave litter in a place

lit·tle¹ /ˈlɪt(ə)l/ (comparative **less** /les/; superlative **least** /list/) grammar word ★★★

> **Little** can be:
> ■ a **determiner**: *Little progress has been made.*
> ■ a **pronoun**: *They manage to survive on very little.* ♦ *Can I take a little of this sugar?*
> ■ an **adverb**: *I go there very little.*

1 an extremely small amount of something: *Little has been revealed about his background.* ♦ *He's an excellent manager, so there's **very little** tension in the office.* ♦ *There was too much rain and **too little** sun.* ♦ *The company **did little** to prevent the disaster.*
2 not very often, or only to a small degree: *In her last years I saw her **very little**.* ♦ *They*

spoke of him ***as little as possible.*** ♦ *a little* ***known*** *fact* (=not known by many people)

PHRASES **a little 1** a small amount: *We managed to save a little money.* ♦ *Mix in* ***a little*** *of the flour.* ♦ *Doesn't Helen speak* ***a little bit*** *of Chinese?* ♦ *I have a* ***little more*** *patience than you.* **2** to a small degree: *The whole situation makes me a little nervous.* ♦ *I held her a little closer.* ♦ *This may be* ***a little bit*** *painful.* **3** for a short time: *You should rest a little.* ♦ *Come talk with me for* ***a little bit.***

little by little very gradually: *Little by little his eyes adjusted to the light.*

> **Little** and **a little** are both used for talking about a small amount of something. But they have slightly different meanings.
> - **Little** means "not much" or "not enough," and is used when you would like there to be more of something: *There is little hope of finding survivors.* ♦ *There has been little change since this morning.*
> - **A little** means "some," and is used for emphasizing that an amount is small, but greater than you might expect: *There is still a little time to finish the game.* ♦ *I had a little money left so I took a taxi.*

L

lit·tle² /ˈlɪt(ə)l/ adj ★★★

1 small in size or number: *Use the little pan for making the sauce.* ♦ *There's a little group of us who meet once a week.* ♦ *a* ***tiny little*** *garden* → SMALL

2 short in time or distance: *Molly carried her a little way toward the house.* ♦ *I'll be with you in* ***a little while.***

3 young, and often small ≠ BIG: *a little boy/girl/child* ♦ *When I was little, we didn't have computers in school.* ♦ *Is this your* ***little brother*** (=younger brother)? ♦ ***My little girl*** (=my daughter) *is three years old.*

4 not important = MINOR: *There are just some little details to sort out.*

ˌlittle ˈfinger noun [C] the smallest finger on your hand —*picture* → C14

ˈLittle ˌLeague noun [singular] a group of baseball clubs for children

liv·a·ble /ˈlɪvəb(ə)l/ adj nice enough to live in

live¹ /lɪv/ verb ★★★

1 [I] to be alive, or to stay alive: *Aunt Joan* ***lived to be*** *86.* ♦ *Hippodamus* ***lived in*** *the early fifth century B.C.* ♦ **live to do sth** (=live long enough to do it) *He lived to see the first talking pictures.*

2 [I] to have your home in a particular place: *Paris is a nice place to live.* ♦ *They* ***lived in*** *a studio apartment in Manhattan.* ♦ *I think he* ***lives somewhere near*** *Kansas City.* ♦ *Do you still* ***live at home*** (=in your parents' home)?

3 [I/T] to have a particular kind of life: *Food is inexpensive here, so you can live quite cheaply.* ♦ *people* ***living in*** *poverty* ♦ *Millions of families are* ***living on*** *benefits.* ♦ *Now they have retired and want to* ***live a quiet life.***

4 [I] to have an interesting and exciting life: *Come on, you have to live a little!*

PHRASES **can live with sth** used for saying that you can accept something: *It's a little less than I asked for, but I can live with that.*

live it up to do enjoyable and exciting things that involve spending a lot of money

PHRASAL VERBS **ˈlive by sth** to behave according to a particular set of beliefs or principles: *Even criminals have standards that they live by.*

ˌlive sth ˈdown to make people forget about something embarrassing or silly that you have done: *I'm never going to live this down!*

ˈlive for sb/sth to think that someone or something is so important that they are your main reason for living: *She lives for her work.*

ˈlive off sb/sth to depend on someone or something for the money or food that you need: *He's 25 and still living off his parents.*

ˌlive ˈon to continue to be alive, or to continue to exist: *These traditions live on in the villages in the mountains.*

ˈlive on sth 1 to have a particular amount of money to buy the things that you need to live: *They have to live on a Social Security check of $500 a month.* **2** to eat a particular kind of food: *These fish live on small sea creatures such as shrimp.*

ˈlive through sth to experience a dangerous or unpleasant situation and still be alive after it

ˈlive toˌgether if two people live together, they are not married but live in the same house and have a sexual relationship

ˌlive ˈup to sth to be as good as what was expected or promised: *The beautiful scenery certainly lived up to expectations.*

ˈlive with sb to live in the same house and have a sexual relationship with someone that you are not married to

ˈlive with sth to accept something unpleasant that you cannot change: *How does she live with the guilt?*

live² /laɪv/ adj ★

1 living	4 with electricity
2 broadcast	5 bullets
3 performance	

1 living and not dead: *The law deals with the transportation of live animals.*

2 a live television or radio program shows something that is happening at the same time as you are watching it or listening to it

3 a live performance is given in front of an audience: *We found a bar that has* ***live music*** *on Friday nights.*

4 a live wire or piece of equipment is connected to the electricity supply and has electricity going through it

5 live bullets or AMMUNITION are real, rather than BLANKS or rubber or plastic bullets

live³ /laɪv/ adv **1** if something is broadcast live, it is happening at the same time as you are watching it or listening to it **2** if something is performed live, it is performed in front of an audience

live·li·hood /ˈlaɪvliˌhʊd/ noun [C/U] something such as your work that provides the money that you need to live

live·ly /ˈlaɪvli/ adj **1** full of energy and enthusiasm: *a lively group/debate/discussion* **2** full of people: *lively bars and restaurants*

li·ven /ˈlaɪv(ə)n/ **PHRASAL VERB** **ˌliven (sth) ˈup** to make something more interesting or exciting, or to become more interesting or exciting: *We need some music to liven things up.*

liv•er /ˈlɪvər/ noun **1** [C] the organ in your body that cleans your blood **2** [C/U] the liver of some animals eaten as food

lives the plural of **life**

live•stock /ˈlaɪvˌstɑk/ noun [plural] animals such as cows, sheep, and pigs that are kept on farms

liv•id /ˈlɪvɪd/ adj *informal* extremely angry

liv•ing¹ /ˈlɪvɪŋ/ adj [C] ★★
1 alive at the present time: *He has no living relatives.*
2 living things are animals or plants that are alive, rather than objects such as rocks
PHRASE **be living proof of sth** to show that something is true or exists by being a clear example of it: *She's living proof that anyone can succeed in this business.*

liv•ing² /ˈlɪvɪŋ/ noun **1** [C] money that you earn to live on: *Do you know what she does for a living* (=does as a job)? ♦ *She makes a living as a music teacher.* **2** [U] a particular type of life: *the stresses of modern living*

ˈliving ˌroom noun [C] the main room in a house where you usually relax in comfortable chairs =LOUNGE

ˈliving ˌstandards noun [plural] the way in which people live, for example how comfortable their houses are or how much money they have to spend

liz•ard /ˈlɪzərd/ noun [C] a small REPTILE with a long tail —*picture* → C13

load¹ /loʊd/ noun [C] ★★
1 something that a person, animal, or vehicle carries: *a truck carrying **a load of** wood*
2 a quantity of clothes that you put in a washing machine
3 an amount of work that a person, piece of equipment, or system has to do at one time =WORKLOAD: *Teaching loads have increased this year.*

load² /loʊd/ verb ★
1 [I/T] to put a load onto or into something such as a vehicle or container: *Down at the docks, ships were loading and unloading.*
2 [T] to put something into a piece of equipment so that it is ready to use: *Did you **load the dishwasher**?* ♦ **load sth with/into sth** *My camera is loaded with color film.*
3 [T] to put bullets into a gun
PHRASAL VERBS **ˌload sb ˈdown 1** if you are loaded down with a lot of heavy things, you are carrying them: *She was loaded down with luggage.* **2** if you are loaded down with responsibilities, problems or work, you have more than you can deal with
ˌload (sth) ˈup *same as* **load²** 1: *The trucks were being loaded up and driven away.*

load•ed /ˈloʊdəd/ adj

1 carrying a load	4 with second meaning
2 very full	5 very rich
3 containing bullets	

1 carrying a load: *a truck loaded with fruit* **2** having a large amount of a particular thing or quality: *mass-produced cakes that are loaded with fat and sugar* **3** a loaded gun has bullets in it **4** a loaded question, word, statement, etc. has a hidden or second meaning **5** *informal* very rich

loaf /loʊf/ (plural **loaves** /loʊvz/) noun [C] bread in a long, round, or square shape that you cut into SLICES (=thin flat pieces) for eating

loan¹ /loʊn/ noun ★
1 [C] an amount of money that a person, business, or country borrows, especially from a bank: *Jim **took out a loan** to pay for his car.* ♦ *How soon do you have to **pay off the loan**?*
2 [singular] a situation in which someone lends something to someone: *He had accepted Tom's offer of **the loan of** his cabin.*
PHRASE **on loan** if something is on loan, someone has borrowed it: *That book is already **out on loan**.* ♦ *These paintings are **on loan from** the Guggenheim in Bilbao.*

loan² /loʊn/ verb [T] to lend something to someone

loath /loʊθ/ adj *formal* very unwilling to do something =RELUCTANT

loathe /loʊð/ verb [T] to dislike someone or something very much =DETEST —**loath•ing** noun [U]

loaves the plural of **loaf**

lob /lɑb/ verb [T] **1** to throw, hit, or kick something so that it goes high into the air **2** to hit or kick a ball high into the air and usually over the head of another player

lob•by¹ /ˈlɑbi/ noun [C] **1** an organized group of people who try to influence politicians **2** the area just inside the entrance to a hotel, theater, or other large building

lob•by² /ˈlɑbi/ verb [I/T] to try to influence politicians

lob•by•ist /ˈlɑbiɪst/ noun [C] someone who lobbies politicians

lob•ster /ˈlɑbstər/ noun [C/U] a large SHELLFISH with a long body and eight legs, or the meat from this fish

lo•cal¹ /ˈloʊk(ə)l/ adj ★
1 in or related to a particular area, especially the place where you live: *Ask for the book in your local library.* ♦ *Local calls are free.*
2 affecting only a small area of the body: *a local infection*

lo•cal² /ˈloʊk(ə)l/ noun [C] someone who lives in a particular place

ˌlocal ˌanesˈthetic noun [C/U] a type of ANESTHETIC (=a drug or gas a doctor gives you to stop you from feeling pain) that affects only one part of your body
→ GENERAL ANESTHETIC

ˌlocal area ˈnetwork noun [C] *computing* a LAN

lo•cale /loʊˈkæl/ noun [C] *formal* the place where something happens

ˌlocal ˈgovernment noun [U] the organizations that provide public services in a particular area

lo•cal•i•ty /loʊˈkæləti/ noun [C] *formal* a particular area or district

lo•cal•ized /ˈloʊk(ə)lˌaɪzd/ adj *formal* existing only in a particular area

lo•cal•ly /ˈloʊk(ə)li/ adv in the area where you live or that you are talking about

ˈlocal ˌtime noun [U] the time in a particular part of the world

lo·cate /ˈloʊˌkeɪt/ verb [T] ★
1 to find out the exact place where someone or something is: *Engineers are still trying to locate the flaw.*
2 to establish something in a particular place: *The company wants to locate the factory near the railroad tracks.*
PHRASE **be located** to exist in a particular place: *The pituitary gland is located at the base of the brain.* ♦ *The center is* ***conveniently located*** *close to many historical sites.* ♦ *The hotel is* ***located in*** *downtown Hartford.*

lo·ca·tion /loʊˈkeɪʃ(ə)n/ noun ★★
1 [C] the place or position where someone or something is, or where something happens: *The talks are taking place at a secret location.*
2 [C/U] a place where a movie or TV program is made, away from a STUDIO: *a thriller filmed entirely* ***on location***

lock¹ /lɑk/ verb [I/T] ★★
1 to fasten something such as a door with a key, or to be fastened with a key ≠ UNLOCK: *Have you locked the car?* ♦ *This drawer won't lock.* ♦ **lock sth in sth** *She locked the documents in the safe.* —picture → CLOSE
2 to become fixed in one position, or to fix something in one position: *The brakes locked and the car spun off the road.* ♦ *He locked his arms around her waist.*
PHRASE **locked in a debate/dispute etc.** involved in a discussion or argument that lasts a long time: *The two sides were locked in fierce debate.*
PHRASAL VERBS **ˌlock sth aˈway** to put something in a place or container that you fasten with a lock: *Valuable items should be locked away.*
ˌlock sb ˈin to put someone in a room and lock the door so that they cannot leave: *She went to her room and locked herself in.*
ˌlock sb ˈout to prevent someone from coming into a room or building by locking the door: *I locked myself out again – could I use your phone?*
ˌlock sb ˈup to put someone in prison: *He was locked up for 12 years for armed robbery.*
ˌlock (sth) ˈup to lock all the doors and windows of a building so that no one can get in: *I locked up and went to bed.* ♦ *The last person to leave locks up the store.*

lock² /lɑk/ noun [C] ★
1 the thing that is used for fastening a door, drawer, etc. so that no one can open it: *All the windows were equipped with locks.*
2 a piece of equipment used for preventing someone from using a vehicle, machine, etc.: *a bicycle lock*
3 a small piece of hair on your head: *She cut off a lock of his hair.*
4 a place on a river or CANAL that allows boats to move to a higher or lower water level
PHRASE **under lock and key** in a room or container that is fastened with a lock

lock·er /ˈlɑkər/ noun [C] a cabinet that you store clothes, books, and other personal things in temporarily, for example while you are at school

ˈlocker ˌroom noun [C] a room with lockers in a large building such as a factory or school

lock·et /ˈlɑkət/ noun [C] a piece of jewelry that consists of a very small case that you wear around your neck on a chain

lo·co·mo·tive /ˌloʊkəˈmoʊtɪv/ noun [C] the vehicle that pulls a train = ENGINE

lodge¹ /lɑdʒ/ verb **1** [I/T] to become firmly stuck somewhere, usually accidentally: *A piece of meat lodged in his throat.* **2** [T] to formally make something such as a complaint or claim: *She lodged a complaint with the city council.*

lodge² /lɑdʒ/ noun [C] a house in the countryside that people stay in, for example when they go hunting or fishing

lodg·ing /ˈlɑdʒɪŋ/ noun [C/U] a place that you pay to live in for a short time

loft /lɔft/ noun [C] a room or space under the roof of a building

loft·y /ˈlɔfti/ adj **1** very tall or high **2** lofty goals or principles are based on high moral standards = NOBLE

log¹ /lɔg/ noun [C] **1** a thick piece of wood that has been cut from a tree **2** a written record of things that happen, especially on a ship or an airplane

log² /lɔg/ verb [T] to make an official record of things that happen
PHRASAL VERBS **ˌlog ˈoff** or **ˌlog ˈout** *computing* to finish using a computer system
ˌlog ˈon or **ˌlog ˈin** *computing* to start using a computer system, for example by typing a PASSWORD

ˌlog ˈcabin noun [C] a small simple house made of LOGS

log·ger·heads /ˈlɔgərˌhedz/ noun **at loggerheads (with sb)** disagreeing very strongly with someone

log·ging /ˈlɔgɪŋ/ noun [U] the work of cutting down trees for wood

log·ic /ˈlɑdʒɪk/ noun [U] **1** the way that someone connects ideas when they are explaining something or giving a reason **2** the study of the way that ideas can be connected and used to explain things

log·i·cal /ˈlɑdʒɪk(ə)l/ adj sensible and reasonable ≠ ILLOGICAL: *a logical argument* ♦ *It seems like the most logical solution to the problem.* —**log·i·cal·ly** /ˈlɑdʒɪkli/ adv: *She presented her ideas clearly and logically.*

log·in /ˈlɔgɪn/ noun [C/U] *computing* the process of starting to use a computer program or system

lo·gis·tics /ləˈdʒɪstɪks/ noun [plural] the practical arrangements that are necessary in order to organize something successfully —**lo·gis·ti·cal** adj

lo·go /ˈloʊgoʊ/ noun [C] a symbol that represents an organization or company

loins /lɔɪnz/ noun [plural] *literary* the part of your body below your waist, where your sex organs are

loi·ter /ˈlɔɪtər/ verb [I] to stand or wait in a public place for no particular reason = HANG AROUND —**loi·ter·ing** noun [U]

loll /lɑl/ verb [I] **1** to sit, stand, or lie in a relaxed position **2** if your tongue or your head lolls, it hangs down in an uncontrolled way

lol·li·pop or **lol·ly·pop** /ˈlɑlipɑp/ noun [C] a hard candy on the end of a stick

lone /loʊn/ adj single, or alone

lone·ly /ˈloʊnli/ adj ★

1 unhappy because you are alone or have no friends: *a lonely childhood* ♦ *She must feel really **lonely** with all her family in Scotland.*

2 a lonely place is far from where people live or go = REMOTE: *a lonely stretch of country road*

—**lone·li·ness** noun [U]

lon·er /ˈloʊnər/ noun [C] someone who likes to be alone

lone·some /ˈloʊnsəm/ adj LONELY

long[1] /lɔŋ/ adj ★★★

1 not short	5 of document
2 lasting a long time	6 of clothes
3 giving a measurement	+ PHRASES
4 seeming long	

1 measuring a large amount from one end to the other ≠ SHORT: *It's the longest tunnel in Europe.* ♦ *There was **a long line** outside the bank.* ♦ *a woman with **long blonde hair***

2 lasting for a large amount of time ≠ SHORT: *a long history of mental illness* ♦ *It's been **a long time** since I saw Rachel.*

3 used for saying how long something lasts, or how long something is from one end to the other: *The room was ten feet long.* ♦ ***How long** was the movie?*

4 seeming to last for a very long time because you are bored or tired: *It had been a long week.*

5 a long book, letter, report, etc. has a lot of pages ≠ SHORT

6 long dresses, pants, sleeves, etc. cover your arms or legs ≠ SHORT: *a shirt with **long sleeves***

PHRASES **go a long way toward doing sth** to help someone to achieve something: *The money will go a long way toward paying for her medical treatment.*

have a long way to go to need to do a lot more before you are successful: *We've raised $500 so far, but we still have a long way to go.*

have come a long way to have achieved a lot of things and made progress: *Technology has come a long way since the days of telegrams.*

in the long run/term not immediately, but at some time in the future: *In the long run, this will be a better solution for the company.*

long hours or **a long day** if you work long hours, or a long day, you work more than usual

a long shot *informal* an attempt or guess that is not likely to be successful but that is worth trying: *It's a long shot, but I'll ask her.*

not by a long shot *informal* used for saying that something is not true at all: *We haven't finished yet – not by a long shot.*

long[2] /lɔŋ/ adv ★★★

1 for a long period of time: *I hope you haven't been **waiting long**.* ♦ *People are **living longer** nowadays.*

2 much earlier or later than a particular event or period: ***long before/after** the war* ♦ *I should have ended the relationship **long ago**.*

PHRASES **all day/year/week etc. long** for the whole day/year/week etc.: *I don't think I could take care of children all day long.*

as/so long as used before explaining the conditions that will make something else happen or be true: *My parents don't care what job I get, as long as I'm happy.*

before long soon: *She joined the company in 1995, and before long she was promoted to sales manager.*

be/take long used for saying or asking whether you will have to wait a long time for someone or something: *Will you be long, or should I wait?* ♦ *It didn't take long to get there.*

for long for a long period of time: *I haven't known them for long.*

no longer or **not any longer** used when something happened or was true in the past but is not true now: *He no longer plays in an orchestra.*

long[3] /lɔŋ/ verb [I] to want something very much: *She longed to see him again.*

long-a·wait·ed /ˌlɔŋ əˈweɪtəd/ adj a long-awaited event has been expected for a long time

ˌlong-ˈdistance adj **1** traveling between two places that are far apart: *a long-distance runner* **2** a long-distance phone call is one that you make to someone far away —**ˌlong-ˈdistance** adv

ˌlong-drawn-ˈout adj continuing for too long = PROTRACTED

ˈlong-ˌhaul adj traveling a long distance, especially by air ≠ SHORT-HAUL

long·ing /ˈlɔŋɪŋ/ noun [C/U] a strong feeling of wanting someone or something —**long·ing·ly** adv

lon·gi·tude /ˈlɑndʒɪˌtud/ noun [C/U] the position of a place in the world when it is measured in relation to east or west, not to north or south → LATITUDE

ˈlong ˌjump, the noun [singular] a sports event in which each person tries to jump farther than the other people

ˌlong-ˈlasting adj continuing for a long time: *long-lasting damage/harm*

ˈlong-ˌlost adj a long-lost friend or relative is someone who you have not seen for a long time

ˈlong-ˌrange adj **1** continuing or looking far into the future: *a long-range weather forecast* **2** able to travel long distances: *long-range aircraft/missiles*

ˌlong-ˈrunning adj having continued for a long time: *a long-running dispute/conflict*

long·shore·man /ˈlɔŋʃɔrmən/ noun [C] *American* someone whose job is to put goods on ships and take goods off ships

ˌlong-ˈstanding adj having existed for a long time: *a long-standing tradition/arrangement/agreement*

ˌlong-ˈsuffering adj patient despite having problems, or despite being badly treated, over a long period of time

ˌlong-ˈterm adj **1** continuing to exist, be relevant, or have an effect for a long time in the future ≠ SHORT-TERM: *a good long-term investment* **2** having existed for a long time and unlikely to change: *long-term debt*

ˌlong-ˈtime adj having continued or existed as a particular thing for a long time: *his long-time girlfriend*

ˈlongˌwave noun [U] a radio wave of more than 1,000 meters used for broadcasting. The written abbreviation is **LW.** → MEDIUM WAVE, SHORT WAVE

ˌlong weekˈend noun [C] a weekend when you have one or two extra days free in addition to the usual Saturday and Sunday

long·wind·ed /ˌlɔŋˈwɪndəd/ adj using more words and taking more time than necessary to say something

loo /lu/ noun [C] *British informal* a toilet, or a room with a toilet

look¹ /lʊk/ verb ★★★

1 direct eyes at sb/sth	5 for saying how likely
2 search for sb/sth	6 pay attention
3 have an appearance	+ PHRASES
4 seem	+ PHRASAL VERBS

1 [I] to direct your eyes toward someone or something so that you can see them: *Dan* ***looked at*** *his watch.* ♦ *If you* ***look through*** *this window, you can see the cathedral.* → SEE

2 [I] to search for someone or something: *I don't know where the keys are. I've* ***looked everywhere.*** ♦ *I spent most of the morning* ***looking for*** *my passport.*

3 [linking verb] to have a particular appearance: *He looked about twenty.* ♦ *He looked very funny in his hat.* ♦ *It was a first date so Emily wanted to* ***look her best*** (=as attractive as possible).

4 [linking verb] to seem to be something: *That new movie looks good.*

5 [linking verb] used for giving your opinion about how likely it is that something will happen or be true: *It looks pretty certain that Martin will win.*

6 [I] *spoken* used when you want someone to look at something, or when you want them to pay attention to what you are going to say: *Look! There's John!* ♦ *Look, why don't we meet for a drink and talk about it then?*

PHRASES **(I'm) just looking** *spoken* used for telling someone who works in a store that you do not yet know whether you want to buy anything

look good/bad 1 to seem to be going to have a good/bad result: *Things aren't looking too good for him at the moment.* **2** to be considered a good/bad thing to do: *Do you think it will look bad if I don't go and see him?*

looking to do sth planning to do something: *We're looking to expand the business.*

look like 1 to have a particular appearance: *Most people say that Kathleen looks like her dad.* ♦ *I asked him what the house looks like.* **2** to seem likely: *It looks like Bill will be able to come too.*

look out *spoken* used for warning someone to be careful, especially because they are likely to have an accident

PHRASAL VERBS **ˌlook ˈafter 1** to take care of someone or something: *It's hard work looking after three children all day.* **2** to be in charge of something

ˌlook aˈhead to think about what is likely to happen, or to plan what you are going to do in the future: *Looking ahead, I think the company must develop some new services.*

ˌlook aˈround (sth) to walk around a room, building, or place and see what is there: *Do you want to look around the school?*

ˈlook at sb/sth if an expert looks at someone or something, they examine them and decide what to do

ˈlook at sth to think about a situation or subject in a particular way = CONSIDER: *We're looking carefully at all the options before we make our decision.*

ˌlook ˈback to think about a time or event in the past: *Most people* ***look back on*** *their college days with fondness.*

ˌlook ˈdown on sb/sth to think that you are better or more important than someone else

ˈlook for sb/sth 1 to search for someone or something: *I'm looking for Jim. Have you seen him?* **2** to hope to get something that you want or need: *He was looking for work as a builder.*

ˌlook ˈforward to sth to feel happy and excited about something that is going to happen

ˌlook ˈinto sth to try to discover the facts about something such as a problem or crime = INVESTIGATE: *The airline has promised to look into the matter.*

ˌlook ˈon to watch an activity or event without taking part in it: *Phil looked on in disbelief as Maggie got up on the table and started to dance.*

ˌlook ˈout for sb/sth to look carefully at people or things around you in order to try to find a particular person or thing: *We were told to look out for a blue van.*

ˌlook ˈover sth to examine something, usually quickly: *He'd been looking over the leaflets he'd picked up earlier.*

ˌlook ˈthrough sth 1 to read something quickly: *I've just been looking through your cookbooks for inspiration.* **2** to search for something among a lot of other things: *I'll look through these files and see if I can find a copy of my résumé.*

ˌlook ˈup if a situation is looking up, it is getting better: *Finally,* ***things are looking up*** *for me.*

ˌlook sb ˈup to go and see someone who you know when you are visiting the place where they live: *Look me up next time you come to Los Angeles.*

ˌlook sth ˈup to try to find a piece of information by looking in a book or on a list, or by using a computer: *I had to look the word up in a dictionary.*

ˌlook ˈup to sb to admire and respect someone

look² /lʊk/ noun ★★★

1 act of looking at sb/sth	4 appearance of sb's face
2 expression on face	5 act of thinking
3 appearance/style	

1 [C] an act of looking at someone or something: *Come and* ***take a look at*** *this.*

2 [C] an expression that you have on your face or in your eyes: *I could tell by* ***the look on his face*** *that he was not happy.* ♦ *She saw* ***the look of*** *surprise on Nicky's face.* ♦ *She* ***gave me a worried look*** (=looked at me in a worried way) .

3 [C] the appearance that someone or something has: *I don't like the look of him.* ♦ *Let us create a stylish modern look for your home.*

4 **looks** [plural] the attractive appearance of someone, especially their face: *She's got everything – looks, intelligence, and money.*
5 [C] an occasion when you think carefully about a problem or situation: *We need to* ***take a look at*** *the way we deal with orders.*

look·a·like /ˈlʊkəˌlaɪk/ noun [C] someone who is very similar in appearance to a famous person

look·out /ˈlʊkˌaʊt/ noun [C] someone who watches for danger and is ready to warn other people, or the place where they watch from
PHRASE **be on the lookout for** or **keep a lookout for** to be watching carefully for someone or something

loom¹ /lum/ verb [I] **1** if something unpleasant or difficult looms, it seems likely to happen soon: *The administration is denying that a crisis is looming.* **2** to appear as a large shape that is not clear, usually in a threatening way: *Suddenly the mountains loomed up out of the mist.*

loom² /lum/ noun [C] a machine used for making cloth

loop¹ /lup/ noun [C] a shape made by a line that curls back toward itself, or something in this shape
PHRASES **in the loop** *informal* part of the group that has information about something, and therefore knowing the information
out of the loop not part of the group that has information about something, and therefore not knowing the information: *I can't give you an answer – I'm out of the loop on this one.*

loop² /lup/ verb [I/T] to form a loop, or to make something into a loop

loop·hole /ˈlupˌhoʊl/ noun [C] a bad feature of a law or legal document that allows people to avoid obeying it

loose¹ /lus/ adj ★

1 not firmly fixed	4 not tight
2 not grouped together	5 not exact/detailed
3 free to move	6 not official

1 not firmly fixed in position: *a loose tooth* ♦ *One of the screws had* ***come loose****.*
2 not kept together as part of a group or in a container: *Loose oranges are 59 cents each.*
3 free to move around: *A large dog was loose in the yard.* ♦ *The woman managed to* ***break loose*** (=escape) *from her attacker.*
4 loose clothes are large and do not fit your body tightly ≠ TIGHT
5 not exactly accurate in every detail: *This is* ***a loose translation*** *of the letter.*
6 not strictly organized or official: *a system in which political parties form a loose alliance*
→ HELL

loose² /lus/ noun **on the loose** if a dangerous person or animal is on the loose, they have escaped from where they were being kept

ˌloose ˈcannon noun [C] a member of a group who does unexpected things that could cause problems for the other members

ˌloose ˈchange noun [U] coins that you have with you

ˌloose ˈends noun [plural] the final details or parts of something that you have not yet dealt with: *I have to tie up a few loose ends* (=deal with them) *before I go.*

ˌloose-ˈleaf adj containing pages that can be put in or taken out

loose·ly /ˈlusli/ adv **1** not in an exact or detailed way: *loosely translated* **2** not firmly or tightly **3** not according to a strict system or official set of rules: *a loosely organized group of criminal gangs*

loos·en /ˈlus(ə)n/ verb [I/T] to become less firmly attached or fastened, or to make something less firmly fixed or fastened ≠ TIGHTEN: *The screws began to loosen.* ♦ *He loosened his tie.*
PHRASAL VERB **ˌloosen ˈup 1** *informal* to relax or become less serious **2** to exercise your muscles before you do physical activity

loot¹ /lut/ noun [U] things that have been stolen, especially during a war

loot² /lut/ verb [I/T] to steal things from houses or stores during a war, or after a DISASTER such as a fire —**loot·er** noun [C], **loot·ing** noun [U]

lop /lɑp/ PHRASAL VERB **ˌlop sth ˈoff (sth)** to cut something off something else in one smooth movement

lope /loʊp/ verb [I] to run with long slow steps

lop·sid·ed /ˌlɑpˈsaɪdəd/ adj not level because one side is higher than the other

lord /lɔrd/ noun **1 the Lord** a name that Christians use for talking about God or Jesus Christ **2** [C] a man who has a high rank in the British ARISTOCRACY (=highest social class)

lore /lɔr/ noun [U] traditional knowledge about nature and culture that people get from older people, not from books

lose /luz/ (past tense and past participle **lost** /lɔst/) verb ★★★

1 stop having sth	6 waste time/chance
2 be unable to find	7 escape from sb
3 not win	8 confuse sb
4 have less than before	9 when clock is too slow
5 when sb dies	+ PHRASES

1 [T] to not have something anymore: *Mike lost his job last year.* ♦ *The family lost everything when their home burned down.* ♦ *Peter lost a leg in a climbing accident.* ♦ *Jane started to* ***lose interest*** *in her schoolwork.* ♦ *We've* ***lost all hope*** *of finding him alive.*
2 [T] to be unable to find someone or something: *I've lost my purse. Have you seen it?* ♦ *You can easily lose a child in a busy street.*
3 [I/T] to not win a race or competition ≠ WIN: *The Rams* ***lost 24–14 to the Giants.*** ♦ *They* ***lost by*** *only one point.* ♦ **lose sb sth** (=make someone lose something) *Those comments may well have lost them the election.*
4 [T] to have less of something than before because some of it has gone: *He's* ***lost*** *a lot* ***of weight*** *recently.* ♦ *The plane suddenly lost cabin pressure.*
5 [T] if you lose a member of your close family or a close friend, they die: *She lost her son in a car accident.*
6 [T] if you lose time or an opportunity, you waste it
7 [T] to manage to escape from someone who is following you

L

8 [T] to make someone confused when you are explaining something: *I'm sorry, you've **lost me** there. Who's Andrew?*
9 [T] if a clock or watch loses time, it is operating too slowly and shows a time that is earlier than the correct time

PHRASES **have a lot/too much to lose** to be in a position where something bad might happen if you are not successful
have nothing to lose used for saying that someone should try something because their situation will not be any worse if they fail: *You should ask him out! You have nothing to lose.*
lose count 1 to forget a total when you are counting something: *Don't talk to me or I'll lose count.* **2** used for emphasizing that something has happened many times: *I've **lost count of** the times he's asked to borrow money.*
lose ground to go into a position where you are less advanced or successful than someone else
lose it *informal* **1** to start laughing or crying and be unable to stop **2** to suddenly become unable to behave or think in a sensible way **3** to suddenly become very angry
lose your life to die as a result of something such as an accident, war, or illness: *He lost his life in a sailing accident.*
lose your mind *informal* to become crazy or confused
lose touch (with sth) to not know the most recent information about something, so you no longer understand it completely
lose touch/contact (with sb) to not know what someone is doing because you have not talked to or communicated with them for a long time

los•er /ˈluzər/ noun [C] **1** someone who did not win a race or competition ≠ WINNER
2 *informal* someone who has never been successful and is never likely to be
3 someone or something that is affected in a negative way by something ≠ WINNER: *When parents split up the real losers are the children.*

loss /lɔs/ noun ★★★

1 no longer having sth	5 death of sb
2 having less of sth	6 sadness
3 failure to win race	+ PHRASE
4 money lost	

1 [C/U] the state of not having something anymore: *job losses* ♦ *a loss of confidence* ♦ *The **loss of** his sight was a severe blow.*
2 [C/U] the state of having less of something than before: *a new treatment for hair loss* ♦ *Exercise and **weight loss** can help lower your blood pressure.*
3 [C] a failure to win a race or competition =DEFEAT ≠ WIN: *The Mariners have only six losses so far this season.*
4 [C/U] money that a person or company loses when they spend more than they earn ≠ PROFIT: *The company reported **heavy losses** for last year.* ♦ *We **took a loss** on the sale of our house.*
5 [C/U] the death of someone: *Jean never recovered from **the loss of** her husband.* ♦ *There was only minor damage and **no loss of life*** (=no one died).
6 [U] a feeling of sadness that you have when someone leaves or dies, or when you do not have something anymore: *We all felt a tremendous **sense of loss** when Robin left.*

PHRASE **at a loss (to do sth)** not understanding something, or not knowing what to do: *I was at a loss to understand what had happened.*

lost¹ /lɔst/ adj ★

1 not knowing your way	4 not relaxed/confident
2 when sth is missing	5 unable to understand
3 no longer existing	+ PHRASES

1 if you are lost, you do not know where you are: *They decided to drive to New York and ended up **getting lost**.*
2 if something is lost, you cannot find it: *The keys are lost somewhere in the house.*
3 if something is lost, you do not have it anymore: *The strike has cost the airline $3 million in lost profits.* ♦ *lost youth/innocence*
4 someone who feels lost does not feel confident or relaxed because they are in a new situation
5 unable to understand something: *I was completely lost after the first paragraph.*

PHRASES **get lost** *spoken* used for telling someone rudely to go away
lost on sb if something is lost on someone, they do not understand it or are not influenced by it: *The joke was lost on Alex.*

lost² the past tense and past participle of **lose**

lost ˈcause noun [C] someone or something that will never succeed or improve

lot¹ /lɑt/ grammar word ★★★

> **A lot** can be:
> - an **adverb**: *He seems to like her a lot.* ♦ *I feel a lot better.*
> - a **pronoun**: *We didn't get paid a lot, but we had fun.* ♦ *A lot of people don't like the idea much.*
>
> **Lots** can be a **pronoun** like **a lot** but is more informal: *She knows lots about it.*

PHRASE **a lot 1** to a great or greater degree: *I liked her a lot.* ♦ *I can run a lot faster than you.* **2 a lot** or **lots** a large number, amount, or quantity: *We're paying her a lot for her services.* ♦ *There's a lot to see in Paris.* ♦ *Have another piece of cake – there's **lots more** in the kitchen.* ♦ *Barb used to have **a lot of** friends in New York.* ♦ *The idea has attracted **lots of** publicity.* → MANY **3** often: *He's a sensitive child who cries a lot.* ♦ *I think about him a lot.* → MUCH

lot² /lɑt/ noun [C] ★★★
1 *American* a small area of land used for a particular purpose =PLOT: *They bought a small lot behind the church.*
2 a thing or group of things that are to be sold in an AUCTION

lo•tion /ˈloʊʃ(ə)n/ noun [C/U] a thick liquid that you put on your skin to make it feel softer

lot•ter•y /ˈlɑtəri/ noun [C] a game in which people win money if they guess the correct numbers

loud¹ /laʊd/ adj ★★
1 a loud sound is strong and very easy to hear ≠ SOFT: *There was a loud knocking on the door.* ♦ *The music is deafeningly loud.*

2 someone who is loud talks in a loud and confident way that annoys other people ≠ QUIET
3 very bright in a way that does not show good taste = GAUDY: *a loud shirt*
—**loud·ly** adv

loud² /laʊd/ adv loudly
PHRASE **out loud** in a way that other people can hear

loud·speak·er /ˈlaʊdˌspikər/ noun [C] a piece of electrical equipment that allows someone's voice to be heard far away

lounge¹ /laʊndʒ/ noun [C] an area in an airport, hotel, or other public building for sitting and relaxing in

lounge² /laʊndʒ/ verb [I] to lie, sit, or lean in a relaxed or lazy way

lous·y /ˈlaʊzi/ adj *informal* bad, or unpleasant

lov·a·ble /ˈlʌvəb(ə)l/ adj attractive and easy to like

love¹ /lʌv/ verb [T] ★★★
1 to like or enjoy something very much: *She loves all types of music.* ♦ *I would love a glass of wine* (=would like one very much). ♦ **love to do sth** *I would love to see them again.* ♦ **love doing sth** *Bert loves playing the piano.*
2 to be very strongly attracted to someone in an emotional and sexual way: *I love you.* ♦ *We love each other, and we're getting married.*
3 to care very much about someone or something: *She loved her children with all her heart.* ♦ *She went back to the country she loved.*
PHRASE **I'd love to** *spoken* used for saying that you would like to do what someone has suggested: *"Do you want to come?" "I'd love to!"*

love² /lʌv/ noun ★★★

1 romantic feeling	5 used at end of letter
2 feeling of liking/caring	6 no points in tennis
3 sb in relationship	+ PHRASE
4 sth you enjoy	

1 [U] a very strong emotional and sexual feeling for someone: *I think I'm **in love**.* ♦ *They met and **fell in love*** (=started to love each other) *at college.* ♦ *the speech in which Romeo expresses his **love for** Juliet*
2 [U] the feeling of caring about someone or something very much ≠ HATE: *Children need a lot of **love and affection**.* ♦ *his love for his brother* ♦ *a great love of life*
3 [C] someone that you have a sexual or romantic relationship with: *the boy who was her first love*
4 [C] something that you enjoy very much: *Music was his greatest love.*
5 [U] used at the end of a letter to someone you know well: *Hope to see you soon. Love, Ray.* ♦ *Take care. **Lots of love**, Helen.* ♦ *I can't wait to see you. **All my love**, Douglas.*
6 [U] a score of no points in tennis
PHRASE **make love** to have sex with someone

ˈlove afˌfair noun [C] a romantic sexual relationship between people who are not married to each other

loved ones /ˈlʌvd ˌwʌnz/ noun [plural] members of your family

ˈlove ˌlife noun [singular] the romantic or sexual relationships in a person's life

love·ly /ˈlʌvli/ adj **1** enjoyable or nice = WONDERFUL: *What a lovely surprise!* **2** very attractive = BEAUTIFUL: *a city surrounded by lovely countryside*

lov·er /ˈlʌvər/ noun [C] **1** someone that you have a sexual relationship with, often when you are married to someone else **2** someone who likes something very much: *a dog/music lover*

lov·ing /ˈlʌvɪŋ/ adj feeling or showing love

lov·ing·ly /ˈlʌvɪŋli/ adv **1** in a way that expresses love **2** with great care and interest: *The old church has been lovingly restored.*

low¹ /loʊ/ adj ★★★
1 small in height, or not far above the ground: *a low wall/bridge* ♦ *low cloud* ♦ *The water level was very low.*
2 small in amount or level ≠ HIGH: *The bigger stores are able to keep their prices low.* ♦ *low standards/expectations* ♦ *people on **low incomes*** ♦ *Vegetables are **low in fat** and high in nutrition.*
3 someone who is low feels unhappy and does not have much hope or confidence ≠ HIGH: *It was unlike her to be in such **low spirits**.* ♦ *She'd been **feeling low** for a few days.*
4 a low voice or sound is quiet and difficult to hear ≠ HIGH

low² /loʊ/ adv **1** in or to a low position ≠ HIGH **2** quietly, or in a deep voice: *I asked them to turn the volume down low.* ♦ *She can sing high or low.* → LIE[1]

low³ /loʊ/ noun [C] **1** the lowest level, value, or price ≠ HIGH: *Stock prices hit an all-time low.* **2** a bad time in your life ≠ HIGH: *He's experienced all the highs and lows of an actor's life.*

ˌlow-ˈcalorie or **ˌlow-ˈcal** adj low-calorie foods or drinks help people to lose weight because they do not contain many CALORIES

ˌlow-ˈcut adj a low-cut dress or BLOUSE shows a woman's chest and the top part of her breasts because it has a low NECKLINE

low·down, the /ˈloʊˌdaʊn/ noun [singular] *informal* the important or interesting information you need to know about someone or something

low·er¹ /ˈloʊr/ adj **1** below another thing of the same kind ≠ UPPER: *the upper and lower lips* **2** fairly near the bottom of something: *the lower floors of the building* **3** fairly low in status or importance ≠ HIGHER: *the lower ranks of the army*

low·er² /ˈloʊr/ verb [T] ★
1 to move something or someone slowly down from a higher position ≠ RAISE: *He lowered himself into the chair.*
2 to reduce something in number, amount, value, or strength: *The voting age was lowered from 21 to 18 years.* ♦ *Less fat in your diet lowers the risk of heart disease.*

ˌlower ˈcase noun [U] the ordinary small form in which letters are written → UPPER CASE

ˌlower ˈclass noun **the lower class** or **the lower classes** people who have the lowest social status → MIDDLE CLASS, UPPER CLASS, WORKING CLASS

ˌlow-ˈfat adj low-fat food contains only a small amount of fat

ˌlow-ˈkey adj without much activity or excitement: *his usual low-key manner*

low·lands /ˈloʊləndz/ noun [plural] the part of a country that is fairly low and flat ≠ HIGHLANDS

ˌlow-ˈlevel adj **1** without much importance, power, or difficulty: *a low-level sales position* **2** in a low position

low·ly /ˈloʊli/ adj with a low status or position: *a lowly office clerk*

ˌlow-ˈlying adj in a position which is close to the level of the ocean or the ground

ˌlow-ˈpaid adj not receiving or offering much pay

ˈlow ˌpoint noun [C] the worst moment in a situation

ˌlow ˈprofile noun [C] behavior that deliberately does not attract attention: *I've been trying to keep a low profile.* —**low-ˈprofile** adj

ˈlow-ˌrise adj a low-rise building has only a few levels ≠ HIGH-RISE

low-tech /ˌloʊ ˈtek/ adj low-tech equipment is simple and usually old-fashioned

ˌlow ˈtide noun [C/U] the time when the ocean is at its lowest level

loy·al /ˈlɔɪəl/ adj someone who is loyal continues to support a person, organization, or principle in difficult times =FAITHFUL ≠ DISLOYAL: *a loyal friend/customer/employee* ♦ *people who have remained loyal to the company for years* —**loy·al·ly** adv

loy·al·ist /ˈlɔɪəlɪst/ noun [C] someone who supports their government

loy·al·ties /ˈlɔɪəltiz/ noun [plural] feelings of friendship and support

loy·al·ty /ˈlɔɪəlti/ noun [U] support that you always give to someone or something: *I was impressed by his loyalty to his brother.*

loz·enge /ˈlɑzəndʒ/ noun [C] a candy that contains medicine for a sore throat

LSD /ˌel es ˈdi/ noun [U] a powerful illegal drug that makes people see things that are not real =ACID

Ltd. abbrev Limited: used after the name of some companies

lu·bri·cate /ˈlubrɪˌkeɪt/ verb [T] to put oil on the parts of a machine in order to make them move more smoothly —**lu·bri·ca·tion** /ˌlubrɪˈkeɪʃ(ə)n/ noun [U]

lu·cid /ˈlusɪd/ adj **1** describing things in a clear, simple way **2** capable of thinking clearly

luck¹ /lʌk/ noun [U] ★★

1 success that you have by chance: *John never **had much luck** with girls.* ♦ *We'd all like to **wish you luck** in your new job.*

2 an influence that seems to make good things happen to people for no particular reason: *It's a custom that is believed to **bring good luck**.* ♦ *Their luck is bound to **run out** (=end) sometime.* ♦ *He's had nothing but **bad luck** since moving to New York.*

PHRASES **any luck?** *spoken* used for asking someone if they succeeded in doing something they wanted

good luck or **best of luck** used for telling someone that you hope that they will be successful: *Good luck in your exam!*

in luck able to do something that did not seem likely: *You're in luck. We have one pair of shoes left in your size.*

just my luck *spoken* used for saying that something bad happened because you are not a lucky person

out of luck unable to do something that you wanted

with any luck or **with a little luck** used for saying that you hope a particular thing happens: *With any luck, this time next year I'll be living in France.*

luck² /lʌk/ PHRASAL VERB **ˌluck ˈout** *American informal* to be lucky

luck·i·ly /ˈlʌkɪli/ adv used for saying that something good happens in a lucky way =FORTUNATELY: *Luckily he wasn't injured.*

luck·y /ˈlʌki/ adj ★★ if you are lucky, something good happens to you as a result of luck =FORTUNATE ≠ UNLUCKY: *Five **lucky winners** will each receive $1,000.* ♦ *None of his sisters had been **lucky with men**.* ♦ **+(that)** *You're lucky that he was there.* ♦ **it is lucky (that)** *It's lucky that I arrived when I did.* ♦ **be lucky to do sth** *You're really lucky to be alive.* ♦ **be lucky enough to do sth** *I was lucky enough to get a job very easily.*

PHRASE **get lucky** to be successful because of good luck: *Let's buy a lottery ticket – we might get lucky.*

lu·cra·tive /ˈlukrətɪv/ adj bringing a lot of money =PROFITABLE

lu·di·crous /ˈludɪkrəs/ adj extremely silly =ABSURD: *a ludicrous new rule* —**lu·di·crous·ly** adv: *ludicrously expensive*

lug /lʌg/ verb [T] *informal* to carry something with difficulty because it is very heavy

lug·gage /ˈlʌgɪdʒ/ noun [U] bags and suitcases that you take on a trip =BAGGAGE

ˈluggage ˌrack noun [C] *American* a metal frame fixed on the roof of a car, used for carrying large objects, bicycles etc. —*picture* → C6

luke·warm /ˈlukˌwɔrm/ adj **1** not hot or cold enough to be enjoyable **2** not very enthusiastic or interested

lull¹ /lʌl/ verb [T] **1** to make someone relaxed enough to go to sleep **2** to make someone feel so relaxed or confident that they are not prepared when something unpleasant happens

lull² /lʌl/ noun [C] a short period during which noise or activity stops

lum·ber¹ /ˈlʌmbər/ noun [U] *American* rough pieces of wood, or trees cut down for wood

lum·ber² /ˈlʌmbər/ verb [I] to walk with slow heavy steps

lum·ber·jack /ˈlʌmbərˌdʒæk/ noun [C] someone whose job is to cut down trees for wood

lu·mi·nous /ˈlumɪnəs/ adj something that is luminous shines brightly in the dark

lump¹ /lʌmp/ noun [C] **1** a solid piece of something that does not have a regular shape: *a lump of metal/coal/clay* **2** a solid piece in a substance that should be smooth or liquid: *Stir the sauce to get rid of any lumps.* **3** a small hard part on or under your skin, that is caused by illness or injury

lump² /lʌmp/ verb [T] to put people or things into the same group, although they do not really belong together: *Singing and dancing* *tend to be lumped together as "performing arts."*

ˌlump ˈsum noun [C] money in a single large payment rather than separate small payments

lump·y /ˈlʌmpi/ adj full of lumps: *a lumpy sauce/pillow*

lu·na·cy /ˈlunəsi/ noun [U] stupid ideas or behavior = MADNESS

lu·nar /ˈlunər/ adj relating to the moon

lu·na·tic /ˈlunətɪk/ noun [C] someone who behaves in an extreme or dangerous way —**lu·na·tic** adj

lunch /lʌntʃ/ noun [C/U] ★★★ a meal that you eat in the middle of the day: *I'll get a sandwich **for lunch**.* ♦ *Let's **have lunch** at that new restaurant.* ♦ *Did you **eat lunch**?* ♦ *Mr. Miller's already **gone to lunch**.*

lunch·time /ˈlʌntʃˌtaɪm/ noun [U] the time in the middle of the day when people usually eat lunch: *I'm going swimming at lunchtime.* ♦ *the lunchtime news*

lung /lʌŋ/ noun [C] one of the organs in your chest that fill with air when you breathe

lunge /lʌndʒ/ verb [I] to move suddenly and with a lot of force —**lunge** noun [C]

lu·pine /ˈluˌpɪn/ noun [C] a tall plant with several stems and rows of small flowers on each stem —*picture* → C9

lurch¹ /lɜrtʃ/ verb [I] **1** to move suddenly in a way that is not smooth or controlled **2** if your heart or stomach lurches, it seems to jump suddenly because you are excited or upset

lurch² /lɜrtʃ/ noun [C] a sudden uncontrolled movement

PHRASE **leave sb in the lurch** to leave someone in a difficult situation without helping them

lure¹ /lʊr/ verb [T] to persuade someone to do something by making it look very attractive

lure² /lʊr/ noun [C] something that attracts someone into a situation

lu·rid /ˈlʊrɪd/ adj **1** full of shocking or unpleasant details **2** a lurid color is very bright in an ugly way

lurk /lɜrk/ verb [I] **1** to hide somewhere and wait to frighten or attack someone **2** if something is lurking, it is likely to threaten, harm, or upset you

lus·cious /ˈlʌʃəs/ adj **1** very attractive in a sexual way **2** luscious food looks, smells, and tastes especially good = DELICIOUS

lush /lʌʃ/ adj a lush plant or area looks very green and healthy

lust¹ /lʌst/ noun [U] **1** a strong feeling of wanting to have sex = DESIRE **2** great enthusiasm for something = PASSION

lust² /lʌst/

PHRASAL VERBS **ˈlust after sb** to want to have sex with a particular person

ˈlust after sth to want something very much

lux·u·ri·ous /lʌgˈʒʊriəs/ adj very expensive and comfortable

lux·u·ry¹ /ˈlʌgʒ(ə)ri, ˈlʌkʃ(ə)ri/ noun **1** [U] a situation in which you are very comfortable because you have the best and most expensive things: *They live a life of absolute luxury.* **2** [C] something expensive that you enjoy but do not really need **3** [C] something that you enjoy very much but do not have very often: *An evening at home was a real luxury.*

lux·u·ry² /ˈlʌgʒ(ə)ri, ˈlʌkʃ(ə)ri/ adj very expensive and of the highest quality: *a luxury hotel/item/car*

Ly·cra /ˈlaɪkrə/ *trademark* cloth made from artificial fibers that is used for making sports clothes

lynch /lɪntʃ/ verb [T] if a group of angry people lynch someone, they kill that person by hanging them by the neck —**lynch·ing** noun [C/U]

lyr·i·cal /ˈlɪrɪk(ə)l/ adj expressing emotions in a beautiful way

lyr·ics /ˈlɪrɪks/ noun [plural] the words of a song

Mm

m¹ or **M** /em/ noun [C/U] the 13th letter of the English alphabet

m² abbrev minute

M abbrev medium: used on clothes labels

m. abbrev **1** mile **2** meter

ma /mɑ/ noun [C] *informal* your mother

MA abbrev Massachusetts

M.A. /ˌem ˈeɪ/ noun [C] Master of Arts: an advanced degree from a college or university in a subject such as languages or history

ma'am /mæm/ *American* used for talking politely to a woman whose name you do not know

mac /mæk/ noun [C] *British* a RAINCOAT

ma·ca·bre /məˈkɑbrə/ adj something that is macabre is frightening because it involves death or violence

mac·a·ro·ni /ˌmækəˈroʊni/ noun [U] a type of pasta in the form of short curved tubes

PHRASE **macaroni and cheese** *American* a meal consisting of macaroni in a cheese sauce

ma·chet·e /məˈʃeti/ noun [C] a large knife that can be used as a weapon or a tool

ma·chine /məˈʃin/ noun [C] ★★★ a piece of equipment with moving parts that does a particular job: *Sue showed him how to operate the washing machine.* ♦ *These companies do everything by machine these days.*

maˈchine ˌgun noun [C] a gun that fires a lot of bullets very quickly

maˌchine-ˈreadable adj able to be used by a computer

ma·chin·er·y /məˈʃinəri/ noun [U] **1** machines: *agricultural/industrial machinery* **2** an established system for doing something: *the company's decision-making machinery*

ma·cho /ˈmɑtʃoʊ/ adj *showing disapproval* behaving in a way that is considered typical of a man, for example by being strong and not showing your feelings

mack·er·el /ˈmæk(ə)rəl/ noun [C/U] an ocean fish that is eaten as food

mac·ro /ˈmækroʊ/ noun [C] a short computer program that performs a longer series of operations

mad /mæd/ adj ★★
1 *informal* angry: *My boss is **mad at** me for missing the meeting.* ♦ *He makes me so **mad**!*
2 *British* very silly or stupid = CRAZY
3 *British offensive* an offensive way of describing someone who is mentally ill
PHRASES **like mad** *informal* very quickly and with great effort: *We had to work like mad to finish on time.*
mad about sth *British informal* very enthusiastic about something
→ MADLY, MADNESS

mad·am /ˈmædəm/ used for writing politely to a woman whose name you do not know

mad·den·ing /ˈmæd(ə)nɪŋ/ adj making you feel very angry = INFURIATING
—**mad·den·ing·ly** adv

made¹ /meɪd/ adj
PHRASES **be made for each other** *informal* if two people are made for each other, they are perfect partners for each other
have (got) it made *spoken* to be in a very good situation: *She won all that money – she's got it made!*

made² the past tense and past participle of make¹

ˌmade-to-ˈorder adj made according to the specific requests of a particular person

ˌmade-ˈup adj **1** imaginary or false **2** wearing MAKEUP on your face

mad·house /ˈmædˌhaʊs/ noun [C] a place that is very noisy or busy

mad·ly /ˈmædli/ adv very, or very much: *He fell madly in love with her at first sight.*

mad·man /ˈmædmən/ (plural **mad·men** /ˈmædmən/) noun [C] a man who behaves in a crazy way

mad·ness /ˈmædnəs/ noun [U] ideas and actions that show a lack of good judgment and careful thought: *It would be madness to quit your job just now.*

maes·tro /ˈmaɪstroʊ/ noun [C] a musician who people admire and respect a lot

Ma·fi·a, the /ˈmɑfiə, ˈmæfiə/ a secret criminal organization that is involved in illegal activities, especially in the U.S. and Italy

mag·a·zine /ˈmægəˌzin/ noun [C] ★★ a large thin book with a paper cover that is usually published once a month or once a week: *a fashion/gardening/sports magazine* ♦ *a magazine article*

mag·got /ˈmægət/ noun [C] a small soft creature that develops into a fly and is sometimes found in old meat

mag·ic¹ /ˈmædʒɪk/ noun [U] ★
1 a mysterious power that makes impossible things happen if you do special actions or say special words → BLACK MAGIC
2 mysterious tricks that an entertainer performs, for example making things disappear
3 a special attractive quality that something has: ***the magic of** Christmas/Hollywood*
PHRASES **as if by magic** in a surprising or sudden way that is impossible to explain: *I mentioned his name, and he appeared as if by magic.*
like magic *informal* in a very effective or quick way: *This medicine works like magic.*

mag·ic² /ˈmædʒɪk/ adj **1** involving mysterious tricks performed by an entertainer: *a magic show/trick* **2** able to make impossible things happen: *a magic spell/box*

mag·i·cal /ˈmædʒɪk(ə)l/ adj **1** especially enjoyable or attractive: *It was a truly magical evening.* **2** involving magic
—**mag·i·cal·ly** /ˈmædʒɪkli/ adv

ˌmagic ˈbullet noun [C] *informal* a quick and easy solution to a difficult problem

ma·gi·cian /məˈdʒɪʃ(ə)n/ noun [C] someone whose job is to entertain people by performing magic tricks

mag·is·trate /ˈmædʒɪˌstreɪt/ noun [C] a judge in a court for minor crimes

mag·na cum lau·de /ˌmægnə kʌm ˈlaʊdə, ˌmægnə kʌm ˈlaʊdi/ adv a student who receives a degree magna cum laude from a university has achieved the second highest level of degree

mag·nan·i·mous /mægˈnænɪməs/ adj *formal* willing to forgive people, or willing to be kind and fair

mag·nate /ˈmægneɪt/ noun [C] a successful and powerful person in a particular industry = TYCOON: *an oil magnate*

mag·ne·si·um /mægˈniziəm/ noun [U] a light gray metal that burns very brightly

mag·net /ˈmægnət/ noun [C] **1** a piece of iron that can make other iron objects stick to it **2** someone or something that attracts people

mag·net·ic /mægˈnetɪk/ adj **1** able to attract iron objects **2** able to attract and interest people: *his magnetic personality*
—**mag·net·i·cal·ly** /mægˈnetɪkli/ adv

mag·net·ism /ˈmægnəˌtɪzəm/ noun [U] **1** a special ability to attract and interest people **2** the power that a MAGNET has to make iron objects stick to it

mag·ni·fi·ca·tion /ˌmægnəfɪˈkeɪʃ(ə)n/ noun [U] the power of a piece of equipment to make something appear bigger than it really is

mag·nif·i·cent /mægˈnɪfɪsənt/ adj very impressive and beautiful, good, or skillful: *She gave a magnificent performance.*
—**mag·nif·i·cence** noun [U], **mag·nif·i·cent·ly** adv

mag·ni·fy /ˈmægnəˌfaɪ/ verb [T] **1** to make something appear bigger than it really is **2** to make something appear more important or serious than it really is

mag·ni·fy·ing glass /ˈmægnəˌfaɪɪŋ ˌglæs/ noun [C] a small circle of glass with a handle that makes things appear bigger when you look through it

mag·ni·tude /ˈmægnəˌtud/ noun [U] great size or importance

mag·no·lia /mægˈnoʊliə/ noun [C] a small tree with large white or pink flowers, or a flower from this tree —*picture* → C9

mag·pie /ˈmægˌpaɪ/ noun [C] a noisy black and white bird with a long tail

ma·hog·a·ny /məˈhɑgəni/ noun [U] a hard brown-red wood that is used for making furniture

maid /meɪd/ noun [C] a woman whose job is

M

to clean rooms in a hotel or large house

maid•en¹ /ˈmeɪd(ə)n/ noun [C] an old word meaning a girl or young woman who is not married

maid•en² /ˈmeɪd(ə)n/ adj done for the first time: *a maiden flight*

ˈmaiden ˌname noun [C] the original family name of a woman who uses her husband's family name now

mail¹ /meɪl/ noun ★★

1 [U] letters and packages that are delivered by the post office: *The mail came early today.* ♦ *I haven't had a chance to* ***open my mail*** *yet.* ♦ *There was nothing interesting* ***in the mail*** *this morning.*

2 [U] the system for sending and delivering letters and packages: *All our goods can be ordered* ***by mail.*** ♦ *The letter must have gotten lost* ***in the mail.***

3 [C/U] e-mail, or an e-mail message: *Did you read that mail from Cindy?*

mail² /meɪl/ verb [T] ★★

1 to send a letter or package to someone by mail: **mail sth to sb** *Information is mailed regularly to all our members.*

2 *American* to send a message to someone by e-mail

PHRASAL VERB **ˌmail sth ˈout** to send many copies of a letter, advertisement, etc. by mail at one time

mail•box /ˈmeɪlˌbɑks/ noun [C] **1** *American* a container in a public place where you can mail letters **2** *American* a container at your house that the mail carrier puts letters into or takes them out of in order to send them —*picture* → C1 **3** *computing* the part of a computer's memory where e-mail is stored

ˈmail ˌcarrier noun [C] *American* someone whose job is to deliver mail

mail•ing /ˈmeɪlɪŋ/ noun [C] a letter or advertisement sent to many people at the same time

ˈmailing ˌlist noun [C] *business* a list of all the people that letters or e-mail messages are sent to

mail•man /ˈmeɪlˌmæn/ (plural **mail•men** /ˈmeɪlˌmen/) noun [C] *American* a man whose job is to deliver mail

ˌmail ˈorder noun [U] a way of buying goods in which you order them by mail or telephone and they are mailed to you

maim /meɪm/ verb [T] to injure someone severely and permanently

main¹ /meɪn/ adj ★★★ most important, or largest: *We eat our main meal in the evening.* ♦ *The* ***main entrance*** *to the building is on George Street.*

PHRASE **the main thing** *spoken* used for saying what is most important: *The main thing is that you're not injured.*

main² /meɪn/ noun **1** [C] a large pipe or wire that is used for carrying water, gas, or electricity **2 the mains** [plural] *British* the point where the supply of gas, electricity, or water enters a building

ˌmain ˈclause noun [C] *linguistics* a CLAUSE that can be a sentence on its own

ˈmain ˌcourse noun [C] the biggest part of a meal

ˌmain ˈdrag noun [singular] *informal* the main street in a town

main•frame /ˈmeɪnˌfreɪm/ noun [C] *computing* a large powerful computer that has several smaller computers connected to it

main•land, the /ˈmeɪnˌlænd/ noun [singular] a large mass of land that forms the main part of a country but does not include any islands —**main•land** adj

ˌmain ˈline noun [C] an important railroad between two cities

main•ly /ˈmeɪnli/ adv ★★★

1 used for talking about the largest or most important part of something: *This sauce is made mainly of milk and flour.* ♦ *We spent four days there, mainly visiting family.* ♦ *I didn't come mainly because I didn't feel very well.*

2 in most cases: *Our customers are mainly young mothers.*

main•stay /ˈmeɪnˌsteɪ/ noun [C] the person or thing that something depends on in order to continue or be successful

main•stream /ˈmeɪnˌstrim/ adj considered normal, and used or accepted by most people: *mainstream ideas/schools/political parties*

main•stream, the /ˈmeɪnˌstrim/ noun [singular] ideas or methods that most people think are normal

ˈMain ˌStreet noun [U] *American* people who live in small towns and are considered to be traditional and conservative

main•tain /meɪnˈteɪn/ verb [T] ★★

1 to make something stay the same = KEEP: *It's important that you maintain your current weight.* ♦ *Regular inspections ensure that high safety standards are maintained.*

2 to make regular repairs to something, so that it stays in good condition: *The car had been very well maintained.*

3 to continue to say that something is true, even though other people do not believe you = ASSERT: *She maintained her innocence throughout the trial.* ♦ **+(that)** *The company still maintains that the drug is safe.*

4 to provide someone with the money and other things that they need in order to live

main•te•nance /ˈmeɪntənəns/ noun [U] **1** work that is done to keep something in good condition: *aircraft maintenance* **2** the process of continuing something: *the maintenance of international peace and security*

ma•jes•tic /məˈdʒestɪk/ adj very beautiful or impressive —**ma•jes•ti•cal•ly** adv

maj•es•ty /ˈmædʒəsti/ noun [U] the quality of being very beautiful or impressive

ma•jor¹ /ˈmeɪdʒər/ adj ★★★

1 important, large, or great: *one of the major problems facing our planet* ♦ *The major attraction is a huge clock in the entrance hall.* ♦ *Age is a major factor affecting chances of employment.*

2 in the musical SCALE that is used for most tunes in western music → MINOR

Words often used with major

Nouns often used with ***major*** *(adj, sense 1)*

- MAJOR + **drawback, obstacle, problem, setback**: used about problems that are serious

M

- MAJOR + **cause, factor, influence, source**: used about factors that are important
- MAJOR + **change, shake-up, shift, upheaval**: used about changes that have a big effect

ma·jor² /ˈmeɪdʒər/ noun **1** [C] a student's main subject at a college or university, or someone who is studying a particular subject: *I'm a Biology major.* ♦ *Math is her major.* **2** [C] an officer of middle rank in the military **3 the majors** [plural] *American* the MAJOR LEAGUES

ma·jor³ /ˈmeɪdʒər/ PHRASAL VERB ˈ**major in sth** to study something as your main subject at a college or university: *She's majoring in physics.*

ma·jor·i·ty /məˈdʒɔrəti/ noun ★★★
1 [singular] most of the people or things in a group ≠ MINORITY: *His job is to represent the views of the majority.* ♦ ***The majority of** our employees are women.* ♦ ***The vast majority*** (=almost everyone) *had never traveled outside the United States.* ♦ *Young women are **in the majority** in the fashion industry.*
2 [C] the number of votes by which someone wins an election

ˌ**major-ˈleague** adj leading or important

ˌ**Major ˈLeagues, the** noun [plural] the teams that play at the highest level of a professional sport, especially baseball

M

make¹ /meɪk/ (past tense and past participle **made** /meɪd/) verb ★★★

1 create/produce sth	7 give a total
2 do sth	8 cause sth to succeed
3 cause sth to happen	9 have right qualities for
4 force sb to do sth	10 reach place
5 arrange sth	+ PHRASES
6 earn/get money	+ PHRASAL VERBS

1 [T] to create or produce something: *The nail made a hole in my shirt.* ♦ *Jane was **making coffee**.* ♦ *This furniture is **made in** South America.* ♦ *a bowl **made of** metal/plastic/wood* ♦ **make sth from sth** *They make paper from old rags.* ♦ **make sth out of sth** *We made curtains out of some old material we found.* ♦ **make sb sth** *Joan made me a beautiful dress for my wedding.*
2 [T] used with some nouns for showing that someone performs an action: *Have you **made a decision**?* ♦ *Nobody's perfect – we all **make mistakes**.* ♦ *Helen **made an attempt** to stop him.* ♦ *We've **made** some **progress**, but there's still a long way to go.* ♦ *People can eat more healthily without **making** major **changes** to their diet.* ♦ *Stop **making** so much **noise**!* ♦ *Matthew **made a note of** the car's number* (=kept a written record of it) *and informed the police.*
3 [T] to cause someone or something to be in a particular state: *The noise in the school makes learning difficult.* ♦ *Listening to the news just **makes** me **angry** these days.* ♦ *The smell of fish **makes** me **feel** sick.* ♦ *That haircut **makes** you **look** ten years younger.* ♦ *I'd like to **make it clear that** I had nothing to do with this.* ♦ **make sb do sth** *This movie always makes me cry.*
4 [T] to force someone to do something: **make sb do sth** *They made us work for 12 hours a day.*
5 [T] to arrange or organize something: *I've **made an appointment** with the doctor.*
6 [T] to earn or get money: *She makes about $4,000 a month.* ♦ *You can **make** a lot of **money** playing the stock market.* ♦ *Can you **make a living** from painting?* ♦ *The company **made a** small **profit** in its first year.*
7 [linking verb] to give a particular total when added together: *Four multiplied by two makes eight.*
8 [T] to cause something to be successful: *It was the children's singing that really made the performance.*
9 [linking verb] to have the right qualities for a particular job or purpose: *Don't you think the novel would make a great movie?*
10 [T] *informal* to reach a place, or to be present in a place: *At this rate we won't make New York before midnight.* ♦ *I won't be able to make tomorrow's meeting.*

PHRASES **make believe** to pretend that something is real
make do (with/without sth) to succeed in dealing with a situation by using what is available, or despite not having something: *There wasn't much food, but we made do.*
make it 1 to succeed in a particular activity: *She made it in the movies when she was still a teenager.* **2** to manage to arrive on time: *We just made it in time for the wedding.* **3** to be able to be present at a particular event: *I can't make it on Friday.* ♦ *We made it to the meeting.*

PHRASAL VERBS ˈ**make for sth** to help to make something possible: *The new computers make for much greater efficiency.*
ˈ**make sb/sth ˌinto sth** to change someone or something so that they become something else: *The story was made into a movie two years ago.*
ˈ**make sth ˌof sb/sth 1** to understand someone or the meaning of something in a particular way: *I don't know what to make of our new teacher.* ♦ *What do you make of this news?* **2 make the best of sth** to try to get a good result despite a bad situation: *It rained all day, but we made the best of it.* **3 make the most of sth** to use a good situation to get the best possible result: *It's a beautiful day today. Let's make the most of it.*
ˌ**make ˈoff with sth** to leave with something that you have stolen: *They made off with our television.*
ˌ**make ˈout** *American* if two people make out, they kiss and touch in a sexual way
ˌ**make sth ˈout 1** to see, hear, or understand something with difficulty: *I can just make a few words out on this page.* ♦ *I couldn't make out what he was saying.* **2** to write all the necessary information on a check or other document **3 make sb out to be sth** to say that someone is a particular type of person when this is not true: *He made me out to be a liar.*
ˌ**make ˈup** to become friendly with someone again after an argument: *Why don't you two forget your differences and make up?* ♦ *Tom still hasn't **made up with** Alice.*
ˌ**make sth ˈup 1** to invent something such as a story or an explanation: *He made up some excuse about the dog eating his homework.*

♦ *She's good at making up stories for the children.* **2 make it up to sb** to do something good that helps someone to feel better after you did something bad to them

ˌmake ˈup for sth 1 to take the place of something that has been lost or damaged: *Nothing can make up for the loss of a child.* **2** to provide something good, so that something bad seems less important: *He bought her some flowers to make up for being late.*

Words that you can use instead of make

Make is a very general word. Here are some words with more specific meanings that sound more natural and appropriate in particular situations.

things made in factories	assemble, build, manufacture, mass-produce, produce, turn out
buildings/structures	build, erect, put up
power/heat/light	emit, generate, give off, produce
problems/changes/ effects	cause, create, generate, produce
new things	come up with, create, design, develop, invent
things that are made quickly and not very well	churn out, cobble together, throw together

make[2] noun [C] a product that is made by a particular company = BRAND: *a very popular make of car*

ˌmake-beˈlieve noun [U] the activity of pretending that something is real —**make-beˌlieve** adj

make•o•ver /ˈmeɪkˌoʊvər/ noun [C] changes that make a person or thing look much better

mak•er /ˈmeɪkər/ noun [C] a person, company, or machine that produces something

make•shift /ˈmeɪkˌʃɪft/ adj made using whatever is available and therefore not very good

make•up /ˈmeɪkˌʌp/ or **ˈmake-ˌup** noun **1** [U] substances people put on their faces to make them look more attractive = COSMETICS **2** [singular] the people or things that combine to form a single group: *the makeup of society* **3** [C] *American* a special test taken by a student who missed a previous test

mak•ing /ˈmeɪkɪŋ/ noun [U] the activity or process of creating something

PHRASES **have the makings of** to have the qualities that are necessary to become a particular type of thing or person: *I believe you have the makings of a great artist.*

in the making in the process of being created or produced: *We are witnessing a piece of history in the making.*

mal•aise /məˈleɪz/ noun [singular/U] *formal* a situation in which a society or organization is not operating effectively

ma•lar•i•a /məˈleriə/ noun [U] a serious illness that you can get in a hot country if you are bitten by a MOSQUITO

male[1] /meɪl/ adj ★★★

1 belonging to the sex that does not give

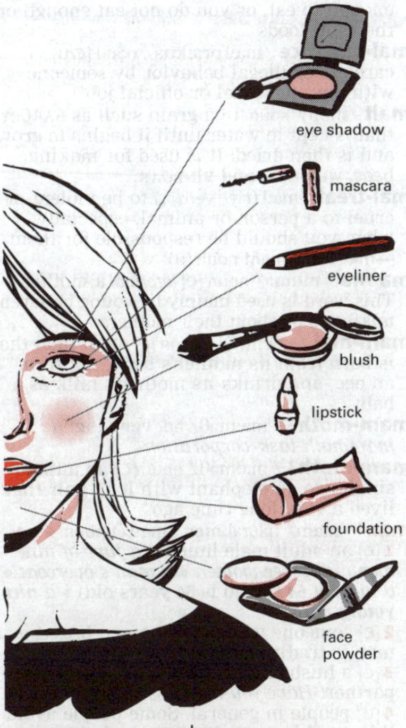

makeup

birth ≠ FEMALE: *male colleagues/workers* ♦ *a male elephant*

2 relating to men ≠ FEMALE: *ideas about female and male sexuality*

male[2] /meɪl/ noun [C] **1** a male animal ≠ FEMALE **2** *formal* a man ≠ FEMALE

ˌmale ˈchauvinist *see* **chauvinist**

ma•lev•o•lent /məˈlevələnt/ adj showing that you want to do something bad to someone

mal•func•tion /mælˈfʌŋkʃ(ə)n/ noun [C/U] an occasion when something does not operate correctly —**mal•func•tion** verb [I]

mal•ice /ˈmælɪs/ noun [U] a strong feeling of wanting to hurt someone or be unkind to them

ma•li•cious /məˈlɪʃəs/ adj intended to hurt or upset someone —**ma•li•cious•ly** adv

ma•lig•nant /məˈlɪgnənt/ adj *medical* a TUMOR that is malignant is dangerous and could cause death ≠ BENIGN —**ma•lig•nan•cy** noun [C/U], **ma•lig•nant•ly** adv

mall /mɔl, mæl/ noun [C] ★ a large building with a lot of stores in it

mal•le•a•ble /ˈmæliəb(ə)l/ adj **1** a malleable metal is easy to press into different shapes **2** a malleable person is easy to persuade or influence

mal•let /ˈmælət/ noun [C] a wooden hammer

mal•nour•ished /mælˈnɜrɪʃt/ adj weak or sick because you do not eat enough, or you do not eat enough of the right foods

mal•nu•tri•tion /ˌmælnuˈtrɪʃ(ə)n/ noun [U] a medical condition in which you are very weak or sick because you do not have

M

enough to eat, or you do not eat enough of the right foods

mal·prac·tice /mælˈpræktɪs/ noun [C/U] careless or illegal behavior by someone with a professional or official job

malt /mɔlt/ noun [U] a grain such as BARLEY that is kept in water until it begins to grow, and is then dried. It is used for making beer, WHISKEY, and VINEGAR.

mal·treat /mælˈtrit/ verb [T] to be violent or cruel to a person or animal, especially when you should be responsible for them —**mal·treat·ment** noun [U]

ma·ma /ˈmɑmə/ noun [C] *informal* a mother. This word is used mainly by young children talking to or about their mothers.

mam·mal /ˈmæm(ə)l/ noun [C] an animal that is born from its mother's body, not from an egg, and drinks its mother's milk as a baby

mam·moth1 /ˈmæməθ/ adj very big: *a mammoth task/corporation*

mam·moth2 /ˈmæməθ/ noun [C] an animal similar to an elephant with long hair that lived a very long time ago

man1 /mæn/ (plural **men** /men/) noun ★★★
1 [C] an adult male human: *a jury of nine men and three women* ♦ *a man's overcoat* ♦ *a man of 64* (=who is 64 years old) ♦ *a nice young man*
2 [C] someone who is strong and brave, as a man is traditionally expected to be
3 [C] a husband, boyfriend, or sexual partner: *Have you met Jessica's new man?*
4 [U] people in general. Some people avoid this word because it suggests that women are not included, or that men are more important than women. They use the word **humans** instead.

M

man2 /mæn/ verb [T] to provide a place, machine, or system with the people who are needed to operate it. Some people avoid using this word because it suggests that women are not included. They use the word **staff** instead.

man3 /mæn/ interjection *informal* used for expressing surprise, admiration, anger, etc.

man·age /ˈmænɪdʒ/ verb ★★★
1 [I/T] to succeed in doing or dealing with something, especially something difficult or something that needs a lot of effort: *I don't think I can manage a long walk today.* ♦ *We couldn't have managed without your help.* ♦ *techniques for managing stress in the workplace* ♦ **manage to do sth** *She managed to escape by diving into the river.*
2 [T] to be in charge of a company, an area, or people that you work with: *He manages the family business.* ♦ *a well-managed restaurant* ♦ *Smith says he wants to manage the team next year.*
3 [T] to be able to provide something such as money or time: *We can only manage $100 a week for rent.*
4 [I] to be able to live with only a limited amount of money: *I don't know how he manages on what he earns.*

man·age·a·ble /ˈmænɪdʒəb(ə)l/ adj able to be dealt with or controlled ≠ UNMANAGEABLE

man·aged care /ˈmænɪdʒd ˌker/ or **ˌmanaged ˈhealth ˌcare** noun [U] a system for managing medical treatment in the U.S. in which insurance companies control what treatment people can have

man·age·ment /ˈmænɪdʒmənt/ noun ★★
1 [U] the control and operation of a business or organization: *In this company we have a new approach to management.* ♦ *a degree in management*
2 [U] the process of controlling or managing something: *stress management* ♦ *an attack on the government's* ***management of*** *the economy*
3 [singular/U] the people who are in charge of a business or organization, or of the people who work there: *the company's senior management* ♦ *Talks between the workers' union and management broke down today.*

man·ag·er /ˈmænɪdʒər/ noun [C] ★★
1 someone whose job is to organize and control the work of a business, a department, or the people who work there: *I'd like to speak to the manager.* ♦ *a marketing/project/sales/office manager* ♦ *For three years I was* ***the manager of*** *a radio station.*
2 someone whose job is to look after the business activities of an entertainer or sports player
3 someone whose job is to organize and train a sports team

man·a·ge·ri·al /ˌmænəˈdʒɪriəl/ adj relating to the job of a manager, especially in a company

ˌmanaging diˈrector noun [C] someone in charge of a company

Man·da·rin /ˈmændərɪn/ noun [U] the official language of China

man·date /ˈmænˌdeɪt/ noun [singular] the authority of an elected government or official to do the things that they promised to do before an election: *He was elected with a clear mandate to reduce taxes.*

man·da·to·ry /ˈmændəˌtɔri/ adj something that is mandatory has to be done because of a law or rule: *a mandatory meeting for all employees*

mane /meɪn/ noun [C] the long hair on the neck of a horse or lion

ma·neu·ver1 /məˈnuvər/ verb [I/T] **1** to use skill to move something or someone, usually when it is difficult to do so **2** to get something you want, often in a way that is not honest

ma·neu·ver2 /məˈnuvər/ noun **1** [C] a movement that you have to make with care or skill **2** [C/U] a clever plan or action that you use to get something you want, especially one that uses illegal or dishonest methods **3** [C] a planned movement by a military group **4 maneuvers** [plural] exercises used for training people in the military

ma·neu·ver·a·ble /məˈnuv(ə)rəb(ə)l/ adj easy to move, especially in situations that need care or skill

ma·neu·ver·ing /məˈnuvərɪŋ/ noun [C/U] clever or skillful behavior that allows someone to get what they want, often in a way that is illegal or dishonest

man·ger /ˈmeɪndʒər/ noun [C] a long low open container that horses or cows eat from

man•gle /ˈmæŋɡ(ə)l/ verb [T] to damage or hurt something seriously by twisting or crushing it —**man•gled** /ˈmæŋɡ(ə)ld/ adj

man•go /ˈmæŋɡoʊ/ noun [C/U] a soft sweet tropical fruit with a red or green skin and yellow flesh —*picture* → C10

man•grove /ˈmæŋˌɡroʊv/ noun [C] a tropical tree that grows beside water and has roots that begin above the ground

man•han•dle /ˈmænˌhænd(ə)l/ verb [T] to touch, push, or pull someone in a rough way

man•hole /ˈmænˌhoʊl/ noun [C] a hole in the surface of a road or street, covered with a metal lid and used for entering an underground passage

man•hood /ˈmænˌhʊd/ noun [U] *formal* the time when a boy becomes a man

man•hunt /ˈmænˌhʌnt/ noun [C] a search that is organized to catch someone that the police think has committed a crime or a prisoner who has escaped

ma•ni•a /ˈmeɪniə/ noun [C/U] an extremely strong enthusiasm for something, especially among a lot of people: *World Cup mania*

ma•ni•ac /ˈmeɪniˌæk/ noun [C] *informal* someone who behaves in a stupid and dangerous way = LUNATIC

man•ic /ˈmænɪk/ adj behaving in an unusually excited way —**man•i•cal•ly** /ˈmænɪkli/ adv

ˌmanic deˈpression noun [U] a serious mental illness in which you experience extreme changes in mood

man•i•cure /ˈmænɪˌkjʊr/ noun [C] a beauty treatment for your hands and nails —**man•i•cure** verb [T]

man•i•fest /ˈmænɪˌfest/ verb [T] *formal* to show something such as a feeling, attitude, or ability

man•i•fes•ta•tion /ˌmænɪfəˈsteɪʃ(ə)n/ noun [C/U] *formal* **a manifestation of sth** evidence that something exists or is present

man•i•fest•ly adv *formal* clearly and without any doubt = OBVIOUSLY

man•i•fes•to /ˌmænɪˈfestoʊ/ (plural **man•i•fes•toes**) noun [C] a formal statement describing the goals and plans of an organization, especially a political party

ma•nip•u•late /məˈnɪpjəˌleɪt/ verb [T] **1** to influence someone, or to control something, in a clever or dishonest way **2** to skillfully handle, control, or use something —**ma•nip•u•la•tion** /məˌnɪpjəˈleɪʃ(ə)n/ noun [U]

ma•nip•u•la•tive /məˈnɪpjələtɪv, məˈnɪpjəˌleɪtɪv/ adj *showing disapproval* someone who is manipulative makes people do what they want by influencing them in a clever or dishonest way

man•kind /ˈmænˌkaɪnd/ noun [U] all humans considered as a single group. Some people avoid using this word because it seems not to include women, and they use **humankind** instead.

man•ly /ˈmænli/ adj typical of traditional good male qualities, for example by being strong and brave —**man•li•ness** noun [U]

ˌman-ˈmade adj something that is man-made has been made by people and does not exist naturally ≠ NATURAL: *Rayon is a man-made fiber.*

manned /mænd/ adj a manned vehicle or place has people working in or on it ≠ UNMANNED: *a manned space flight*

man•ner /ˈmænər/ noun ★★

1 [singular] the way that you do something, or the way that something happens: *The manner of his death aroused a lot of interest in the media.* ♦ *Things had been done in the same manner for centuries.*

2 [singular] the way that you behave towards someone: *The salesman's aggressive manner put us off.*

3 manners [plural] traditionally accepted ways of behaving that show a polite respect for other people: *Children learn manners by observing their parents.* ♦ *It's **bad manners** to interrupt someone.*

PHRASE **all manner of sth** a great variety of people or things

man•ner•ism /ˈmænəˌrɪzəm/ noun [C] a particular way of speaking or moving that someone has

ma•noeu•vre /məˈnuvər/ the British spelling of **maneuver**

man•or /ˈmænər/ or **ˈmanor ˌhouse** noun [C] a large house with a lot of land and small buildings around it

man•pow•er /ˈmænˌpaʊr/ noun [U] all the people who are available to do a particular job or to work in a particular place

man•sion /ˈmænʃ(ə)n/ noun [C] a very large house

man•slaugh•ter /ˈmænˌslɔtər/ noun [U] *legal* the crime of causing someone's death illegally but without intending to → MURDER

man•tel•piece /ˈmænt(ə)lˌpis/ or **man•tel** /ˈmænt(ə)l/ noun [C] a shelf above a FIREPLACE

man•tle /ˈmænt(ə)l/ noun [singular] the authority or responsibility connected with someone's position, duties, or beliefs

man•tra /ˈmæntrə/ noun [C] a sound, word, or phrase that is continuously repeated as a prayer

man•u•al[1] /ˈmænjuəl/ noun [C] a book that contains instructions for doing something, especially for operating a machine

man•u•al[2] /ˈmænjuəl/ adj **1** involving the use of your hands, or doing work with your hands: *The job requires manual skill.* ♦ *manual labor* **2** operated by people instead of automatically or using computers —**man•u•al•ly** adv

man•u•fac•ture[1] /ˌmænjəˈfæktʃər/ verb [T] ★ to make goods in large quantities in a factory: *The firm manufactures women's clothing.*

man•u•fac•ture[2] /ˌmænjəˈfæktʃər/ noun [U] the process of making goods in large quantities in a factory

man•u•fac•tur•er /ˌmænjəˈfæktʃərər/ noun [C] a person or company that makes a particular type of product, especially in a factory

man•u•fac•tur•ing /ˌmænjəˈfæktʃərɪŋ/ noun [U] the business of making goods in large quantities, especially in factories

ma•nure /məˈnʊr/ noun [U] solid waste from

farm animals, often mixed with other substances and used on crops to help them to grow

man•u•script /ˈmænjəˌskrɪpt/ noun [C] **1** a writer's original pages of a book, article, or document before it is published **2** a very old book or document that was written by hand before books began to be printed

man•y /ˈmeni/ (comparative **more** /mɔr/; superlative **most** /moʊst/) grammar word ★★★

> **Many** can be:
> - a **determiner**: *It happened many years ago.*
> - a **pronoun**: *"Did he write any other books?" "Not many."* ♦ *Many of you will be going on to college.*
> - an **adjective**: *He said goodbye to his many friends.*

1 a large number of people, things, places, etc.: *Did you get many replies to your advertisement?* ♦ *I haven't told many people that I am pregnant.* ♦ *I've been to their house many times.* ♦ ***Many of** the world's leading doctors have been trained here.* ♦ *There are **too many** rules and regulations.* ♦ *He has **so many** books, he couldn't possibly read them all.* ♦ ***Not very many** companies can afford the high cost of introducing new technology.* ♦ *We've lived here for **a good many** years.*
2 used for asking or talking about the number of people, things, etc. that there are: ***How many** students are taking the test?* ♦ *It's surprising **how many** different varieties of pasta there are.* ♦ ***How many of** you can remember your first day at school?* ♦ *They try to interview **as many** candidates **as possible**.*
PHRASE **as many as** used before a number for showing how large and surprising it is: *As many as 500,000 people may have become infected with the virus.*
→ WORD[1]

> **Many, a lot**, and **lots** can be used for referring to a large number of things or people.
> - In ordinary spoken English **many** is mainly used in negative sentences and in questions. It is also used in positive sentences after "too," "so," or "as": *We didn't sell many tickets.* ♦ *Were there many children in the audience?* ♦ *You're trying to do too many things at once.*
> - In positive statements **a lot of** is usually used instead of **many**: *A lot of people came.*
> - In written English and in formal spoken English **many** is used in sentences of all types: *Many disabled people use public transportation.*
> - In informal English, **lots** is often used instead of **a lot of**: *Lots of people get divorced these days.*

Mao•ri /ˈmaʊri/ noun [C] someone who belongs to the race of people who were living in New Zealand before Europeans arrived, or the language that they speak —**Mao•ri** adj

map[1] /mæp/ noun [C] ★★
1 a drawing of an area that shows the positions of things such as countries, rivers, cities, and streets: *They never taught us how to **read a map** at school.* ♦ ***a map of** northern Europe/the London Underground/New York City*
2 a drawing that shows the position of things in relation to each other: ***a map of** the human genome*

map[2] /mæp/ verb [T] **1** to make a map of an area **2** to find the position of something, or to find the positions of the parts of something: *Scientists have succeeded in mapping the human genome.*
PHRASAL VERB **ˌmap sth ˈout** to plan or describe in detail how something will happen

ma•ple /ˈmeɪp(ə)l/ noun [C] a tree that grows mainly in northern countries and has wide leaves that turn red and yellow in the fall

mar /mɑr/ verb [T] to spoil something

Mar. abbrev March

mar•a•thon /ˈmerəˌθɑn/ noun [C] **1** a race that is run for 42 kilometers or about 26 miles **2** an activity or event that takes a long time to complete: *marathon talks/negotiations*

ma•raud•ing /məˈrɔdɪŋ/ adj going from place to place in order to attack people or to steal or destroy things —**ma•raud•er** noun [C]

mar•ble /ˈmɑrb(ə)l/ noun **1** [U] a hard smooth stone that is used for building and making STATUES **2** [C] a small colored glass ball, used in children's games

march[1] /mɑrtʃ/ verb [I] **1** when soldiers march, they walk in a group with each person matching the speed and movements of the others **2** to walk somewhere quickly and in a determined, confident, or angry way **3** to walk to a place as part of an organized group protesting about something —**march•er** noun [C]

march[2] /mɑrtʃ/ noun [C] **1** a long walk by an organized group, especially soldiers **2** a walk by a group of people to a place in order to protest about something

March /mɑrtʃ/ noun [C/U] ★★★ the third month of the year, between February and April: *His birthday is in March.* ♦ *The concert is on March 29th.*

mare /mer/ noun [C] an adult female horse

mar•ga•rine /ˈmɑrdʒərɪn/ noun [C/U] a yellow substance made from vegetable oil or animal fat that can be used instead of butter

mar•gin /ˈmɑrdʒɪn/ noun [C] ★

1 space at side of page	4 edge of area
2 amount sth is won by	5 payment in case of loss
3 extra amount	

1 the space at the left or right side of a page that is usually left empty: *I made a couple of notes **in the margin**.*
2 the amount by which a competition or election is won: *The town's citizens voted **by a narrow margin*** (=a small amount) *to reelect the mayor.*
3 an additional amount of time, space, money, etc. that you include to be certain that you will be safe or successful: *There's **no margin for error** – we have to win.* ♦ *It's a business that operates with very small **profit margins*** (=the difference between the cost of providing a product, and the amount that you can charge for providing it).
4 the edge of an area
5 *business* an amount of money you give a

STOCKBROKER to pay for possible losses on money they invest for you

mar•gin•al /ˈmɑrdʒɪn(ə)l/ adj **1** very small **2** *American* not good but not completely bad **3** not important or relevant

mar•gin•al•ize /ˈmɑrdʒɪnəˌlaɪz/ verb [T] to make someone or something seem not important or relevant

mar•gin•al•ly /ˈmɑrdʒɪn(ə)li/ adv by only a very small amount

ma•ri•jua•na /ˌmerəˈhwɑnə, ˌmerəˈwɑnə/ noun [U] an illegal drug in the form of dried leaves that people smoke

ma•ri•na /məˈrinə/ noun [C] an area of water beside the ocean or a lake for keeping small boats in

mar•i•nade /ˌmerəˈneɪd/ noun [C/U] a liquid that you put food into to give it a special flavor before cooking it

mar•i•nate /ˈmerəˌneɪt/ or **mar•i•nade** /ˈmerəˌneɪd/ verb [I/T] to put meat, fish, or vegetables in a marinade

ma•rine¹ /məˈrin/ adj **1** living in, relating to, or happening in the ocean: *marine life/animals/biology* **2** involving ships or the business of moving people and goods in ships

ma•rine² /məˈrin/ noun [C] a soldier whose job is to fight on both land and sea

Maˈrine ˌCorps, the the part of the U.S. military whose members are trained to operate on both land and sea

Ma•rines, the /məˈrinz/ noun [plural] **1** the U.S. MARINE CORPS **2** the British ROYAL MARINES

mar•i•tal /ˈmerət(ə)l/ adj relating to marriage

ˌmarital ˈstatus noun [U] *formal* your marital status is whether you are married, divorced, SINGLE, or WIDOWED

mar•i•time /ˈmerəˌtaɪm/ adj **1** involving ships or the business of moving people and goods in ships **2** close to the ocean

mark¹ /mɑrk/ noun [C] ★★★

1 area of dirt/damage	4 of a quality
2 level/stage/total etc.	5 school score
3 sth printed/written	+ PHRASES

1 a small area of something such as dirt, oil, or damage on the surface of something: *There was a greasy mark on his shirt.* ♦ *There were burn marks all over her hands.*

2 a particular level, stage, total, etc. that something reaches: *Average earnings had not yet **reached** the $40,000 **mark**.* → POINT

3 a printed or written symbol that is not a letter or a number: *Put a mark by the names of the most interesting candidates.*

4 the mark of sth something that shows that a person or thing has a particular quality: *The mark of a good movie is that it leaves you talking about it.*

5 *British* a score or GRADE in school or a competition

PHRASES **leave your/a mark (on)** to have a very strong and noticeable effect on someone or something, usually a bad one: *Years of war have left their mark on these pretty islands.*

on your marks *spoken* used for telling runners in a race to stand in their positions ready to start: *On your marks, get set, go!*

way off the mark incorrect: *Her theory was way off the mark.*

mark² /mɑrk/ verb ★★★

1 make mark on surface	4 show sth is happening
2 write/draw on sth	5 judge student's work
3 show position of sth	+ PHRASAL VERBS

1 [T] to make a mark on the surface of something so that its appearance is spoiled or damaged: **be marked with sth** *Her cheek was marked with scratches.*

2 [I/T] to write or draw words, letters, symbols, etc. on something for a particular purpose: *We entered through a door marked "Private."* ♦ *The teacher **marked** six of the answers **wrong*** (=put a symbol by them to show they were wrong). ♦ **mark sth on sth** *His job is to mark lines on roads.*

3 [T] to show the position of something: *A memorial plaque will **mark the spot** where he died.*

4 [T] to show that something is happening: *This tournament **marks the official start of** the season.*

5 [I/T] *British* to judge the quality of a student's work and write a grade on it

PHRASAL VERBS **ˌmark sth ˈdown** to reduce the price of something: *All shoes are marked down 20 percent.*

ˌmark sth ˈoff to show the limits of an area using a line, fence, rope, etc.: *The crime scene was marked off with official police tape.*

ˌmark sth ˈout to show the shape of something by drawing it on a surface: *The shape of the pond is marked out first with a spade.*

ˌmark sth ˈup to increase the price of something in order to increase your profits: *Foreign cars are often marked up by 40 percent for the American market.*

mark•down /ˈmɑrkˌdaʊn/ noun [C] a reduction in the price of something

marked /mɑrkt/ adj clear and noticeable =DISTINCT —**mark•ed•ly** /ˈmɑrkədli/ adv

mark•er /ˈmɑrkər/ noun [C] **1** an object that is used for showing where something is or where you should go **2** a pen with a thick soft point

mar•ket¹ /ˈmɑrkət/ noun ★★

1 [C] a place, especially outside, where people sell goods: *a flower/fish/antiques market* ♦ *a street market*

2 [singular] trade in goods of a particular type: *Changes in the weather affect **the market in** fruit and vegetables.* ♦ *We're hoping to increase our **share of the market**.*

3 [C] a particular place or group of people that a product is sold to: *overseas markets* ♦ *Europe is the main market for our cars.*

4 [C] a STOCK MARKET: *Trading has been slow on the New York and Tokyo markets this morning.*

PHRASES **be in the market for sth** to want to buy something: *Most people are not in the market for this kind of product.*

on the market available to buy

mar•ket² /ˈmɑrkət/ verb [T] to use advertising and other methods to persuade people to buy something

mar•ket•a•ble /ˈmɑrkətəb(ə)l/ adj **1** a marketable product can be sold because people want to buy it **2** marketable skills

M

are those that employers are likely to want people to have

ˌmarket eˈconomy noun [C] *business* an economic system in which prices, salaries, and the supply of goods are controlled by what and how much people buy, not by the government

ˌmarket ˈforces noun [plural] *business* the economic influences that affect prices, salaries, and the number of jobs available, and that are not controlled by governments

mar•ket•ing /ˈmɑrkətɪŋ/ noun [U] the ways in which a company encourages people to buy its products

mar•ket•place /ˈmɑrkətˌpleɪs/ noun **1** [C] a place where people buy and sell goods in an outdoor market **2 the marketplace** [singular] *business* the part of the economy that involves buying and selling

ˌmarket reˈsearch noun [U] the process of collecting information about what products people like to buy, or what people like or dislike about a particular product

ˌmarket ˈshare noun [C/U] *business* the percentage of the total amount of sales of a particular product that a company has

mark•ing /ˈmɑrkɪŋ/ noun [C] a pattern of marks on the surface of something, for example the skin, fur, or feathers of an animal or bird

M

marks•man /ˈmɑrksmən/ (plural **marks•men** /ˈmɑrksmən/) noun [C] someone who is skillful at shooting with a gun

mar•ma•lade /ˈmɑrməˌleɪd/ noun [C/U] a sweet food that is made from cooked fruit, especially oranges. It is usually spread on TOAST.

ma•roon /məˈrun/ adj dark red-brown in color

ma•rooned /məˈrund/ adj left in a place and unable to leave

mar•quee /mɑrˈki/ noun [C] *American* a sign on the front of a theater with the name of a movie, show, or performer on it

mar•riage /ˈmerɪdʒ/ noun ★★★
1 [C/U] the relationship between two people who are husband and wife: *a long and happy marriage* ♦ *Anne's **marriage to** Daniel lasted ten years.*
2 [C] a WEDDING: *Their marriage is planned for September.*

mar•ried /ˈmerid/ adj ★★★ a married person has a husband or wife ≠ SINGLE: *a married woman/man* ♦ *He's **married to** my older sister.* ♦ *We're **getting married** next year.*

mar•row /ˈmeroʊ/ noun [U] the soft substance inside bones, where blood cells develop =BONE MARROW

mar•ry /ˈmeri/ verb ★★
1 [I/T] to become someone's husband or wife: *Marge married a lawyer.* ♦ *They married in 1996.*
2 [T] to perform the ceremony in which two people become husband and wife

marsh /mɑrʃ/ noun [C] an area of soft wet land

mar•shal¹ /ˈmɑrʃ(ə)l/ noun [C] **1** *American* a government officer whose job is to make certain that the laws of a place or the orders of a court are obeyed: *a federal/district marshal* **2** a police or FIRE DEPARTMENT officer of the highest rank in some parts of the U.S.

mar•shal² /ˈmɑrʃ(ə)l/ verb [T] to organize people or things so that they can be used in an effective way

marsh•mal•low /ˈmɑrʃˌmeloʊ/ noun [C/U] a soft white candy with a thick round shape

mar•su•pi•al /mɑrˈsupiəl/ noun [C] an animal whose babies live in a pocket in their mother's skin until they are completely developed

mart /mɑrt/ noun [C] used in the names of STORES or MARKETS

mar•tial /ˈmɑrʃ(ə)l/ adj *formal* relating to war or fighting

ˌmartial ˈart noun [C] a sport that is a traditional Asian form of fighting such as KARATE or JUDO

ˌmartial ˈlaw noun [U] direct control of a country or area by the military

Mar•tian /ˈmɑrʃ(ə)n/ noun [C] an imaginary creature from Mars

mar•tyr /ˈmɑrtər/ noun [C] **1** someone who suffers or is killed because of their religious or political beliefs **2** *showing disapproval* someone who talks a lot about how much they are suffering, because they want sympathy

mar•tyr•dom /ˈmɑrtərdəm/ noun [U] a martyr's pain or death

mar•vel¹ /ˈmɑrv(ə)l/ verb [I/T] to show or feel surprise or admiration

mar•vel² /ˈmɑrv(ə)l/ noun [C] someone or something that is very surprising or impressive

mar•vel•lous /ˈmɑrvələs/ the British spelling of **marvelous**

mar•vel•ous /ˈmɑrvələs/ adj extremely enjoyable, good, or impressive: *a marvelous performance/trip/party* —**mar•vel•ous•ly** adv

Marx•ism /ˈmɑrksˌɪzəm/ noun [U] the political and economic theories of Karl Marx, from which Communist and SOCIALIST political systems developed

Marx•ist /ˈmɑrksɪst/ adj relating to or based on Marxism —**Marx•ist** noun [C]

mas•car•a /mæˈskerə/ noun [C/U] a substance that is used to make EYELASHES look darker or longer —*picture* → MAKEUP

mas•cot /ˈmæsˌkɑt/ noun [C] an animal, person, or object that is thought to be lucky or that is used as a symbol of a team or organization

mas•cu•line /ˈmæskjəlin/ adj **1** with qualities that are considered typical of men ≠ FEMININE **2** *linguistics* in some languages, masculine nouns, pronouns, and adjectives have different forms from FEMININE or NEUTER words

mas•cu•lin•i•ty /ˌmæskjəˈlɪnəti/ noun [U] the qualities that are considered typical of men ≠ FEMININITY

mash /mæʃ/ verb [T] to crush food so that it is a soft mass: *Mash the potatoes with a little milk.*

mask¹ /mæsk/ noun [C] something that you wear in order to cover part or all of your face

mask² /mæsk/ verb [T] **1** to cover something in order to hide it **2** to hide the smell, taste, or sound of something with a stronger smell or taste or a louder sound

masked /mæskt/ adj wearing a mask

mas•och•ism /ˈmæsəˌkɪzəm/ noun [U] sexual behavior in which someone gets pleasure from being hurt —**mas•och•ist** noun [C], **mas•och•is•tic** /ˌmæsəˈkɪstɪk/ adj

ma•son /ˈmeɪs(ə)n/ noun [C] someone whose job is to cut stones into pieces that can be used in building

ma•son•ry /ˈmeɪsənri/ noun [U] the bricks or stones that make a building, wall, or other structure

mas•quer•ade /ˌmæskəˈreɪd/ verb [I] to pretend to be someone or something that you are not

mass¹ /mæs/ noun ★★

1 [C] a large quantity, number, or amount: *The police had **a mass of** evidence.* ♦ ***a mass** of fallen leaves*

2 [C] a lump or amount of a substance that does not have a clear or definite shape: *The vegetables had turned into a sticky mass at the bottom of the pan.*

3 [U] *science* the amount of MATTER (=physical substance) that something contains → CRITICAL MASS

4 the masses [plural] ordinary people who are not highly educated or rich

mass² /mæs/ adj ★ involving or affecting a large number of people: *the problem of mass unemployment* ♦ *weapons of mass **destruction***

> **Words often used with mass**
>
> *Nouns often used with **mass** (adj)*
>
> ■ MASS + **demonstration, destruction, killings, murder, protest**: used about things that involve a large number of people

mass³ /mæs/ verb [I/T] to come together, or to bring people together, in order to form a large group

Mass /mæs/ noun **1** [C/U] the main religious ceremony of the Roman Catholic Church **2** [C] a piece of music that was written to be played at a Mass

mas•sa•cre /ˈmæsəkər/ noun [C/U] the action of killing a lot of people —**mas•sa•cre** verb [T]

mas•sage /məˈsɑʒ/ noun [C/U] the action of pressing, squeezing, and rubbing someone's body in order to reduce pain in their muscles or to make them relax —**mas•sage** verb [T]

mas•seur /mæˈsɜr, məˈsʊr/ noun [C] someone whose job is to give people massages

mas•seuse /mæˈsuz/ noun [C] a woman whose job is to give people MASSAGES

mas•sive /ˈmæsɪv/ adj **1** very large: *a massive amount of money* **2** very severe: *a massive heart attack* —**mas•sive•ly** adv

ˌmass-ˈmarket adj produced in large quantities in order to be sold to many customers

ˌmass ˈmedia, the noun [plural] the newspapers, television, and radio that communicate news and information to large numbers of people

mass-pro•duced /ˌmæs prəˈdust/ adj made in large quantities using machines —**mass-pro•duce** verb [T]

mast /mæst/ noun [C] a tall pole that the sails hang from on a ship

mas•ter¹ /ˈmæstər/ noun [C] **1** a man who is very good at something: *He's a master of the sarcastic remark.* **2** a man who has control over servants, other people, or an animal **3** a document, photograph, or RECORDING from which copies are made =ORIGINAL

mas•ter² /ˈmæstər/ verb [T] **1** to learn something so that you know it or can do it very well **2** to manage to control a difficult situation or a strong emotion

mas•ter•mind¹ /ˈmæstərˌmaɪnd/ verb [T] to plan and organize a difficult or complicated operation

mas•ter•mind² /ˈmæstərˌmaɪnd/ noun [C] someone who plans a difficult or complicated operation, especially a crime

mas•ter•piece /ˈmæstərˌpis/ noun [C] an excellent work of art, or the best work of art from a particular artist, writer, or musician

ˈmaster's deˌgree noun [C] a university degree that students get if they study for one or two years after their first degree

mas•ter•y /ˈmæstəri/ noun [U] **1** great knowledge or skill **2** power or control over someone or something

mas•tur•bate /ˈmæstərˌbeɪt/ verb [I] to rub your sexual organs in order to get sexual pleasure —**mas•tur•ba•tion** /ˌmæstərˈbeɪʃ(ə)n/ noun [U]

mat¹ /mæt/ noun [C] **1** a piece of thick cloth that is put on a floor to protect it or for decoration **2** a small piece of plastic, cloth, or other material that you put on a table or other surface to protect it **3** a piece of a thick soft material like rubber that you use when doing exercises —*picture* → C16

mat² /mæt/ adj with a surface that is not shiny

match¹ /mætʃ/ noun ★★★

1 [C] a small stick that produces a flame when it is rubbed against a rough surface: *a box of matches* ♦ *He lit a match* (=made it light).

2 [singular] a thing that forms an attractive combination with something else: *The curtains are **a good match for** the sofa.*

3 [C] something that looks the same as something else: *It was difficult to get an **exact match for** the paint.*

4 [C] a game or event in some sports: *a tennis match*

PHRASE **be no match for sb** to be not as good, strong, smart, etc. as someone

match² /mætʃ/ verb ★★

1 [I/T] if one thing matches another, or if they match, they are the same or have similar qualities: *The two signatures match.* ♦ *He matches the description of a man seen in the area.*

2 [I/T] to be equal to something else in amount or level, or to provide something that is equal: *The rise in student numbers has not been matched by an increase in teaching staff.* ♦ *The school promised to match whatever amount we could raise.*

3 [I/T] if one thing matches another, or they match, they form an attractive

combination: *She wore a green dress and a hat to match.*
4 [T] to choose or provide something that is appropriate for a particular situation, person, or purpose: **match sth to sth/sb** *It is important to match the software to the task.* ♦ **match sth with sth/sb** *The children were asked to match words with pictures.*
PHRASAL VERBS **ˌmatch ˈup** if two things match up, they are the same or have similar qualities
ˌmatch ˈup to sb/sth to be as good as someone or something: *The hotel didn't really match up to the description on the website.*

match·book /ˈmætʃˌbʊk/ noun [C] *American* a small piece of thick folded paper that contains paper matches

match·box /ˈmætʃˌbɑks/ noun [C] a small box that contains matches

match·ing /ˈmætʃɪŋ/ adj with the same color, pattern, or design

mate¹ /meɪt/ noun [C] **1** an animal's sexual partner **2** *American* an object that belongs with another and forms a pair with it **3** *British informal* a friend

mate² /meɪt/ verb [I] if one animal mates with another, or if two animals mate, they have sex

ma·te·ri·al¹ /məˈtɪriəl/ noun ★★★
1 [C/U] cloth = FABRIC: *What kind of material is your dress made from?*
2 [C/U] a substance that is used for a particular purpose: *Brick was used as the main building material.*
3 [U] information or ideas that are used as the subject of a book, movie, or song: *Newspaper articles are **a good source of material** for stories.*
4 [C/U] documents, or other things for presenting information, that are used for a particular activity: *publicity material ♦ teaching materials*

ma·te·ri·al² /məˈtɪriəl/ adj **1** relating to things such as money and possessions that affect your physical life rather than your thoughts or emotions **2** *legal* important enough to have an effect: *information material to the decision*

ma·te·ri·al·ism /məˈtɪriəˌlɪzəm/ noun [U] the belief that money and possessions are the most important aspects of human existence —**ma·te·ri·al·is·tic** /məˌtɪriəˈlɪstɪk/ adj

ma·te·ri·al·ize /məˈtɪriəˌlaɪz/ verb [I] **1** to happen, or to become real **2** to appear suddenly and unexpectedly

ma·ter·nal /məˈtɜrn(ə)l/ adj **1** a maternal relative is related to you through your mother **2** typical of a kind and caring mother

ma·ter·ni·ty /məˈtɜrnəti/ adj designed or provided for women who are pregnant or who have just had a baby: *maternity pay/benefits ♦ maternity clothes*

math /mæθ/ noun [U] *American* mathematics

math·e·mat·i·cal /ˌmæθəˈmætɪk(ə)l/ adj relating to or involving mathematics —**math·e·mat·i·cal·ly** /ˌmæθəˈmætɪkli/ adv

math·e·ma·ti·cian /ˌmæθ(ə)məˈtɪʃ(ə)n/ noun [C] someone who studies or teaches mathematics

math·e·mat·ics /ˌmæθəˈmætɪks/ noun [U] *formal* the study or use of numbers and shapes to calculate, represent, or describe things

maths /mæθs/ noun [U] *British* mathematics

mat·i·nee /ˌmæt(ə)nˈeɪ/ noun [C] an afternoon performance of a play or a movie

ma·tri·arch /ˈmeɪtriˌɑrk/ noun [C] a female leader of a family or community

mat·ri·mo·ny /ˈmætrəˌmoʊni/ noun [U] *formal* marriage —**mat·ri·mo·ni·al** /ˌmætrəˈmoʊniəl/ adj

matte /mæt/ another spelling of **mat²**

mat·ted /ˈmætəd/ adj matted hair or fur is twisted or stuck together

mat·ter¹ /ˈmætər/ noun ★★★

1 sth being dealt with	5 substance/thing
2 problem/bad situation	6 all substances
3 situation that sb is in	+ PHRASES
4 when time is short	

1 [C] something that you are discussing, considering, or dealing with: ***an extremely important matter*** ♦ ***Teachers feel this is a matter for discussion with parents.***
2 **the matter** [singular] used for talking about problems or bad situations: *You look sad.* ***What's the matter?*** ♦ ***What's the matter with the car?*** ♦ *I think **there's something the matter with** the printer.* ♦ ***There's nothing the matter*** (=there is no problem) *with you – you're just tired.*
3 **matters** [plural] a situation that someone is involved in: *Her angry attitude didn't improve matters.* ♦ ***To make matters worse,*** *his wife is sick.*
4 [singular] **a matter of sth** used for emphasizing how short a period of time is: *The school could close in a matter of a few weeks.*
5 [U] a particular type of substance or thing: *organic matter* ♦ *Is this appropriate **reading matter** for a young child?*
6 [U] *science* the physical substances that everything in the universe is made of
PHRASES **as a matter of fact 1** used when you are going to give more details about something: *I haven't been here long. As a matter of fact, I just arrived yesterday.* **2** used when you are going to disagree with or correct what has just been said: *"Was he in a bad mood?" "No, as a matter of fact, he seemed fairly cheerful."*
for that matter *spoken* used for emphasizing that something else is also true: *He doesn't like young women, or any women for that matter.*
a matter of life and death a serious or dangerous situation
a matter of opinion/taste something that different people have different opinions about
a matter of time used for saying that something will certainly happen eventually: ***It was only a matter of time*** *before she left the company.*

mat·ter² /ˈmætər/ verb [I] ★★★ to be important: *Education matters.* ♦ *Does it matter if I don't take a present?* ♦ ***It doesn't really matter*** *if we're a little bit late.* ♦ **sth matters to sb** *Winning this award matters a lot to me.*

ˌmatter-of-ˈfact adj calm and showing no emotion when dealing with something —ˌ**matter-of-ˈfactly** adv

mat•ting /ˈmætɪŋ/ noun [U] strong rough material that is used as a floor cover

mat•tress /ˈmætrəs/ noun [C] the thick soft part of a bed that you lie on

ma•ture¹ /məˈtʃʊr/ adj **1** behaving in the sensible way that you would expect an adult to behave ≠ IMMATURE **2** fully developed or fully grown

ma•ture² /məˈtʃʊr/ verb [I] **1** to start behaving like an adult and become more sensible **2** to grow to full adult size

ma•tur•i•ty /məˈtʃʊrəti/ noun [U] **1** the qualities and behavior that you would expect of a sensible adult **2** full growth, or completed development

maud•lin /ˈmɔdlɪn/ adj talking in a sad and emotional way that seems silly

maul /mɔl/ verb [T] if an animal mauls someone, it attacks them, usually causing serious injury

mau•so•le•um /ˌmɔzəˈliəm, ˌmɔsəˈliəm/ noun [C] a large impressive TOMB (=stone structure in which someone is buried)

mauve /moʊv/ adj pale purple in color —**mauve** noun [U]

mav•er•ick /ˈmæv(ə)rɪk/ noun [C] an independent person who has ideas and behavior that are very different from other people's

max¹ /mæks/ PHRASAL VERBS ˌ**max ˈout** *American informal* to do or to have too much of something: *I guess I maxed out on pizza last night!*

ˌ**max sth ˈout** *American informal* to reach the limit of something, or to use all of a supply of something: *I've maxed out all my credit cards.*

max² /mæks/ adv *informal* at the most: *Fixing it should cost about $20 max.*

max³ /mæks/ noun **to the max** *informal* as much or as hard as possible

max. abbrev maximum

max•im /ˈmæksɪm/ noun [C] a phrase or saying that includes a rule or moral about how you should behave

max•i•mize /ˈmæksɪˌmaɪz/ verb [T] to make something as large as possible ≠ MINIMIZE

max•i•mum¹ /ˈmæksɪməm/ noun [C] ★ the largest number, amount, or degree that is allowed or is possible ≠ MINIMUM: *20 kg of luggage is the maximum we allow on the flight.* ♦ *Give yourself **a maximum of** 15 minutes to read the questions.*

max•i•mum² /ˈmæksɪməm/ adj ★★ the largest in amount, size, or number that is allowed or possible ≠ MINIMUM: *The **maximum amount** of cash you can withdraw is $500.*

max•i•mum³ /ˈmæksɪməm/ adv up to a particular amount, size, or number but no more ≠ MINIMUM: *You can invite 25 people maximum.*

may /meɪ/ modal verb ★★★

- **May** is usually followed by an infinitive without "to": *It may rain.*
- Sometimes it is used without a following infinitive: *I'd like to make one or two comments, if I may.*
- **May** has no tenses, no participles, and no infinitive form. It does not change its form, so the third person singular form does not end in "-s": *He may arrive this afternoon.*
- Questions and negatives are formed without "do": *May I make a suggestion?* ♦ *She may not understand.*

1 used for saying that something is possibly true, or that something will possibly happen: *I may not be able to play on Saturday.* ♦ *The injury may have caused brain damage.* ♦ *What you say **may very well be true*** (=it is fairly likely).
2 used for saying or asking whether something is allowed: *May I use your phone?* ♦ *Visitors may use the swimming pool between 5:30 and 7:30 p.m.*
3 *spoken* used when making a polite request or offer: *May I see your ticket, please?* ♦ *May we offer you a glass of wine?* → CAN

May /meɪ/ noun [C/U] ★★★ the fifth month of the year, between April and June: *We're taking an early vacation in May.* ♦ *They were married on May 17th.*

may•be /ˈmeɪbi/ adv ★★★
1 used for showing that you are not sure whether something is true or correct, or whether something will happen: *Maybe it will snow tonight.* ♦ *"Do you think he really loves you?" "Maybe. I'm not sure."* ♦ *The whole process takes maybe ten or fifteen minutes.* ♦ *Maybe things will improve, but then again, **maybe not**.*
2 *spoken* used for making a suggestion when you are not sure what to do: *Maybe we should call a doctor.*

may•hem /ˈmeɪˌhem/ noun [U] a very confused situation = CHAOS

may•on•naise /ˈmeɪəˌneɪz, ˌmeɪəˈneɪz/ noun [U] a thick white sauce made from eggs and oil

may•or /ˈmeɪər/ noun [C] the most important elected official in a town or city —**may•or•al** adj

maze /meɪz/ noun **1** [C] an arrangement of closely connected paths that are separated by tall bushes, walls, or trees, that is designed to be difficult to find your way through **2** [singular] a set of many small streets or paths that is easy to get lost in **3** [singular] a set of closely connected but complicated rules, issues, or ideas: *a maze of new legislation*

MB /ˌem ˈbi/ noun [C] megabyte

M.B.A. /ˌem bi ˈeɪ/ noun [C] Master of Business Administration: a MASTER'S DEGREE in business management

MD abbrev Maryland

M.D. /ˌem ˈdi/ noun [C] Doctor of Medicine: an advanced degree in medicine

me /*weak* mi/ pronoun ★★★ the object form of "I," used for referring to yourself when you are the person who is speaking or writing: *I think Darren really likes me.* ♦ *She wrote me a letter.* ♦ *You can come with me.*

ME abbrev Maine

mead•ow /ˈmedoʊ/ noun [C] a field where grass and wild flowers grow

M

mea·ger /ˈmigər/ adj smaller or less than you want or need: *a meager food supply*

mea·gre /ˈmigər/ the British spelling of meager

meal /mil/ noun [C] ★★★ an occasion when you eat, such as breakfast or lunch, or the food that you eat at that time: *He **cooked** us a delicious **meal**.* → SQUARE MEAL

meal·time /ˈmilˌtaɪm/ noun [C] a time when you eat a meal

mean[1] /min/ (past tense and past participle **meant** /ment/) verb [T] ★★★

1 have a meaning	4 make sth happen
2 intend a meaning	5 be evidence of sth
3 intend sth	+ PHRASES

1 to have a particular meaning: *What does "maudlin" mean?* ♦ *The word means something different in French.*

2 to intend to communicate a particular meaning: *By "partner," I mean your wife, your husband, or someone you live with.* ♦ *Don't be offended, she **meant it as a joke**.* ♦ **+(that)** *She didn't reply to our invitation, which probably means she isn't coming.*

3 to intend something, or to intend to do something: *She had never meant him any real harm.* ♦ **mean to do sth** *I didn't mean to step on your toe.*

4 to make something happen, or to have a particular result: **+(that)** *The company's failure could mean that hundreds of workers lose their jobs.* ♦ **sth means doing sth** *The new contract will mean starting the whole project again.*

5 to be evidence that something exists: *That dark patch means that water is coming in.*

PHRASES **be meant for** to be intended, designed, or appropriate for something or someone: *These books are not meant for grade school students.*

be meant to do sth to have a particular responsibility, duty, or purpose: *You were meant to keep the children out of trouble.*

(do) you mean...? *spoken* used for saying what someone else has said using different words, as a way of asking them if you have understood it correctly: *You mean we do the work and you get the money?*

I know what you mean *spoken* used for telling someone that you understand their situation very well

I mean *spoken* **1** used for adding a comment, or for explaining what you have just said: *We couldn't live on that! I mean, it's ridiculous.* **2** used for correcting a mistake in something you have just said: *Let's ask Mark. I mean Marco.*

I see what you mean *spoken* used for telling someone that you understand what they are saying

mean nothing to have no importance: *He spoke in a relaxed, slow way, as if time meant nothing to him.*

meant to be used for talking about something that seems certain to happen, usually because it has been decided by God or other forces that people cannot control: *Oh well – it was just not meant to be.*

what do you mean? *spoken* **1** used for asking someone to explain what they have said **2** used for showing that you are shocked or annoyed about something that someone has told you: *What do you mean you can't find the keys?*

mean[2] /min/ adj ★★

1 cruel or unkind: *Don't do that – it's mean.* ♦ *The older kids were **mean to** him.*

2 *technical* average: *the mean annual temperature*

3 *informal* very good: *She plays a mean game of tennis.*

PHRASE **no mean feat/achievement** very impressive: *She won her first championship at age 17, which is no mean achievement.*

mean[3] /min/ noun [C] *technical* an average number or amount

me·an·der /miˈændər/ verb [I] **1** if a river or road meanders, it has a lot of turns and curves **2** to move slowly without a particular direction or purpose

mean·ing /ˈminɪŋ/ noun ★★★

1 [C/U] the thing, action, feeling, or idea that a word represents: *The dictionary gives two meanings for this word.* ♦ *The poem's real meaning has always been a puzzle.*

2 [singular/U] the special importance or purpose of something: *Times change and old customs lose their meaning.* ♦ *The book tackles important questions, such as **the meaning of life**.*

mean·ing·ful /ˈminɪŋfəl/ adj **1** serious, useful, or important: *a meaningful debate/discussion* **2** expressing a clear feeling or thought, but without using words: *a meaningful look/glance*
—**mean·ing·ful·ly** adv

mean·ing·less /ˈminɪŋləs/ adj **1** without any clear purpose or importance: *My life seems meaningless since Jim died.* **2** without a clear meaning: *a series of meaningless phrases*

means /minz/ (plural **means**) noun ★★★

1 [C] a method for doing or achieving something = METHOD: *Information is not easily obtained by any other means.* ♦ *The telephone was our only **means of** communication.* ♦ *We had **no means of** warning them.*

2 [plural] *formal* the money that someone has or gets: *She doesn't **have the means to** support herself.*

PHRASES **by all means** *spoken* used for politely giving permission: *"Do you mind if I invite a few friends?" "By all means."*

by no means or **not by any means** not at all: *He was by no means certain that his plan would be successful.*

a means to an end a way of getting or achieving something you want

meant the past tense and past participle of mean[1]

mean·time /ˈminˌtaɪm/ noun **in the meantime** during the time between two events, or between the present time and a future event

mean·while /ˈminˌwaɪl, ˈminˌhwaɪl/ adv ★ between the time that two things happen, or while something is happening: *Put the eggs on to boil and meanwhile slice the onions.*

mea·sles /ˈmiz(ə)lz/ noun [U] an infectious disease in which you have red spots all over your body and a high temperature → GERMAN MEASLES

M

mea•sly /ˈmizli/ adj *informal* too small

meas•ur•a•ble /ˈmeʒ(ə)rəb(ə)l/ adj large enough to be measured, noticed, or important —**meas•ur•a•bly** adv

meas•ure[1] /ˈmeʒər/ noun [C] ★★★
1 an action that is intended to achieve something or deal with something: *This is a temporary measure to stop the problem from getting any worse.* ♦ **take measures to do sth** *Stronger measures will have to be taken to bring down unemployment.*
2 a way of judging something: *The tests are not an accurate **measure of** performance.*
3 an amount of a particular quality that is neither large nor small: ***a measure of** security*
4 a unit used for measuring things
PHRASE **for good measure** as a way of making something complete or better: *Throw in a splash of red wine for good measure.*

Words often used with measure

*Adjectives often used with **measure** (noun, sense 1)*
- **drastic, harsh, severe, strong** + MEASURE: used about measures that are severe

*Verbs often used with **measure** (noun, sense 1)*
- **adopt, implement, introduce, take** + MEASURE: take measures in order to do something

meas•ure[2] /ˈmeʒər/ verb ★★★
1 [I/T] to find the exact size, amount, speed, or rate of something: *We measured from the back of the house to the fence.* ♦ *a device for measuring the flow of water through a pipe*
2 [T] to form an opinion about how good or bad something is: **measure sth by sth** *Success isn't measured by how much money you have.* ♦ *Their rate of economic growth is not very impressive, when you measure it against* (=compare it with) *that of the neighboring countries.*
3 [linking verb] to be a particular size: *The room measures approximately 12 feet by 13 feet.*
PHRASAL VERBS ˌ**measure sth ˈout** to take a particular amount of something from a larger amount: *Measure out half a cup of sugar.*
ˌ**measure ˈup** to be good enough: *The machines that we tested didn't measure up.* ♦ *Will he **measure up to** the challenges that lie ahead of him?*

meas•ure•ment /ˈmeʒərmənt/ noun **1** [C] the exact size, amount, speed, or rate of something, expressed in standard units: *They took measurements of noise levels inside the building.* **2** [U] the process of measuring something

meat /mit/ noun [U] ★★★ the flesh of an animal or bird that is eaten as food

Talking or writing about meat

- **beef** the meat of a cow
- **chicken** the meat of a chicken
- **game** the meat of a wild animal or bird
- **lamb** the meat of a young sheep
- **pork** the meat of a pig
- **poultry** the meat of a chicken, duck, or other farm bird
- **veal** the meat of a young cow
- **red meat** meat that is red in color, such as beef or lamb
- **white meat** meat that is a light color, such as chicken or turkey

meat•ball /ˈmitˌbɔl/ noun [C] meat that is cut into very small pieces, shaped into balls, and cooked

ˈ**meat**ˌ**loaf** noun [C/U] a type of food made from a mixture of small pieces of meat, bread, and eggs, baked in one piece

meat•y /ˈmiti/ adj containing a lot of meat

mec•ca /ˈmekə/ noun [C/U] a place that a lot of people visit

Mec•ca /ˈmekə/ a city in Saudi Arabia that is holy for Muslims

me•chan•ic /məˈkænɪk/ noun **1** [C] someone whose job is to repair vehicles and machines **2 mechanics** [plural] the way in which something works or is done: *the mechanics of newspaper reporting* **3 mechanics** [U] the area of physics that deals with the forces such as GRAVITY that affect all objects

me•chan•i•cal /məˈkænɪk(ə)l/ adj **1** operated by a machine, or relating to machines: *mechanical toys* **2** done without thinking, or without any attempt to be original: *her mechanical responses to my questions* —**me•chan•i•cal•ly** adv

mech•a•nism /ˈmekəˌnɪzəm/ noun [C] **1** a machine, or a part of a machine: *a locking mechanism* **2** a method or process for getting something done: *a mechanism for settling disputes*

mech•a•nize /ˈmekəˌnaɪz/ verb [I/T] to start using machines to do something that was previously done by people

med•al /ˈmed(ə)l/ noun [C] a small flat piece of metal that you are given for winning a competition or for doing something that is very brave

med•al•ist /ˈmed(ə)lɪst/ noun [C] someone who has won a medal in a competition

me•dal•lion /məˈdæljən/ noun [C] a round flat piece of metal that you wear around your neck on a chain as jewelry

med•dle /ˈmed(ə)l/ verb [I] to become involved in a situation that does not affect you, in a way that is annoying = INTERFERE

med•dle•some /ˈmed(ə)lsəm/ adj involving yourself in situations that you have no right to

me•di•a a plural of **medium**

me•di•a, the /ˈmidiə/ noun [plural] ★★★ radio, television, newspapers, the Internet, and magazines, considered as a group: *The story has been widely reported in the media.*
→ MASS MEDIA, MULTIMEDIA

me•di•an /ˈmidiən/ adj *technical* in the middle of a set of numbers when they are arranged in order

me•di•ate /ˈmidiˌeɪt/ verb [I/T] to try to end a disagreement between two people or groups —**me•di•a•tion** /ˌmidiˈeɪʃ(ə)n/ noun [U], **me•di•a•tor** noun [C]

med•ic /ˈmedɪk/ noun [C] *American* someone in the military or in an emergency situation

M

who gives people medical treatment

med•i•cal /ˈmedɪk(ə)l/ adj ★★★ relating to medicine and the treatment of injuries and diseases: *a career in the medical profession* ♦ *a man in need of urgent **medical care*** —**med•i•cal•ly** /ˈmedɪkli/ adv

med•i•ca•tion /ˌmedɪˈkeɪʃ(ə)n/ noun [C/U] drugs that you take to treat or cure an illness

me•dic•i•nal /məˈdɪsən(ə)l/ adj capable of treating an illness: *medicinal herbs*

med•i•cine /ˈmedɪsɪn/ noun ★★
1 [C/U] a substance that you take to treat an illness: *cough medicine* ♦ *You have to **take the medicine** three times a day.*
2 [U] the study and practice of treating or preventing illnesses and injuries: *He went on to study medicine at Johns Hopkins University.*

> **Words often used with medicine**
> *Adjectives often used with **medicine** (sense 2)*
> ■ **alternative, conventional, herbal, traditional** + MEDICINE: used about different types of medicine

me•di•e•val /ˌmidiˈiv(ə)l, ˌmediˈiv(ə)l/ adj relating to the period of European history between about the year 1000 A.D. and the year 1500 A.D.: *a medieval church*

me•di•o•cre /ˌmidiˈoʊkər/ adj not very good: *a mediocre performance* —**me•di•oc•ri•ty** /ˌmidiˈɑkrəti/ noun [U]

med•i•tate /ˈmedɪˌteɪt/ verb [I] to make your mind empty in order to relax, or as a religious exercise —**med•i•ta•tion** /ˌmedɪˈteɪʃ(ə)n/ noun [U]

Med•i•ter•ra•ne•an /ˌmedɪtəˈreɪniən/ adj relating to the countries that surround the Mediterranean, or to the culture of the people in those countries

Med•i•ter•ra•ne•an, the /ˌmedɪtəˈreɪniən/ **1** the sea that has Europe to the north and North Africa to the south **2** the countries that surround the Mediterranean Sea

me•di•um¹ /ˈmidiəm/ adj ★
1 between small and large in size or amount: *Use six medium tomatoes.* ♦ *medium-length blond hair* ♦ *She's slim, **of medium height**, with dark hair.*
2 neither light nor dark in color: *medium-brown hair*

me•di•um² /ˈmidiəm/ noun [C] ★
1 something such as a piece of clothing that is between small and large in size: *Do you have a medium in this style?*
2 (plural **me•di•a** /ˈmidiə/) a way of communicating information and ideas: *Patients can express their emotions through **the medium of** drama.*
3 someone who communicates with the spirits of dead people
→ MEDIA

me•di•um-sized /ˌmidiəm ˈsaɪzd/ adj neither large nor small: *Use a medium-sized saucepan.* ♦ *a medium-sized business*

ˈmedium ˌterm, the noun [singular] the period of time that lasts a few months or years from now —**ˈmedium-ˌterm** adj: *the medium-term effects of the plan*

ˈmedium ˌwave noun [U] a range of radio waves between 100 and 1000 meters in length, used for broadcasting → LONG WAVE, SHORT WAVE

med•ley /ˈmedli/ noun [C] **1** a piece of music that consists of tunes from other pieces of music **2** a mixture of things: *an interesting medley of flavors*

meek /mik/ adj quiet, gentle, and easy to persuade —**meek•ly** adv

meet¹ /mit/ (past tense and past participle **met** /met/) verb ★★★

1 come together with sb	6 do sth necessary
2 for discussions	7 do sth planned
3 meet by accident	8 of roads/lines
4 be introduced to sb	9 look into sb's eyes
5 experience result	+ PHRASAL VERBS

1 [I/T] to come together in order to spend time with someone who you have arranged to see: *I'll meet you in the bar later.* ♦ *We're **meeting for** lunch tomorrow.* ♦ **meet to do sth** *Sally and I met after work to go to the movies.*
2 [I/T] to come together with other people in order to discuss something formally: *The president is meeting world leaders in Brussels.* ♦ **meet to do sth** *The council meets today to decide what action to take.*
3 [T] to see someone and speak to them without planning to: *You'll never guess who I met on the plane.*
4 [I/T] to be introduced to someone that you do not know: *Have you met my wife?* ♦ *I think they met at college.*
5 [T] to get a particular result or reaction: *The plans met strong opposition from local people.*
6 [T] to do what is necessary: *This technology can meet the challenges of the 21st century.* ♦ *The water won't **meet the needs of** the local population.*
7 [T] to do what you planned or promised to do = ACHIEVE: *Will the administration be able to meet its obligations?*
8 [I] if things such as roads or lines meet, they join each other: *The two rivers meet just north of the town.*
9 [I] if two people's eyes meet, they look directly into each other's eyes

PHRASAL VERBS **ˌmeet ˈup** to come together with someone as you have planned to do: *We usually **meet up for** coffee after lunch.*
ˈmeet with sb to have a formal meeting with someone: *Today the President met with Russian leaders in Washington.*
ˈmeet with sth *same as* **meet¹** 5: *Experiments with the new drug have met with some success.*

meet² /mit/ noun [C] a sports event involving a lot of people or teams competing against each other

meet•ing /ˈmitɪŋ/ noun [C] ★★★
1 an occasion when people come together in order to discuss things and make decisions: *We're **holding a meeting** for people who want to join the club.* ♦ *North American leaders **attended a meeting** on air pollution.* ♦ *our **meeting with** the ambassador*
2 an occasion when two people meet

meg•a•byte /ˈmegəˌbaɪt/ noun [C] *computing* a

unit for measuring the size of a computer's memory, equal to just over one million BYTES

meg•a•hertz /ˈmegəˌhɜrts/ (plural **meg•a•hertz**) noun [C] *computing* a unit for measuring the speed of a computer, equal to one million HERTZ

meg•a•lo•ma•ni•ac /ˌmegəloʊˈmeɪniˌæk/ noun [C] someone who loves power over other people and always wants more of it

meg•a•phone /ˈmegəˌfoʊn/ noun [C] a piece of equipment that is used for making your voice louder when you are talking to a crowd

mel•an•chol•y /ˈmelənˌkɑli/ noun [U] *literary* a feeling of being very sad and having no hope —**mel•an•chol•y** adj: *a melancholy tone of voice*

mel•a•nin /ˈmelənɪn/ noun [U] a substance in your skin, eyes, and hair that gives them their color

mel•a•no•ma /ˌmeləˈnoʊmə/ noun [C] *medical* a serious type of skin cancer

meld /meld/ verb [I/T] if things or substances meld, or if you meld them, they combine to form one thing

me•lee /ˈmeɪˌleɪ/ noun [C] *literary* a noisy, confusing, or violent situation

mel•low[1] /ˈmeloʊ/ adj **1** a mellow sound is soft, flowing, and pleasant **2** with a full pleasing taste **3** mellow colors are soft and warm **4** gentle, wise, and easy to talk to

mel•low[2] /ˈmeloʊ/ verb [I] if you mellow, you become gentler and wiser

me•lod•ic /məˈlɑdɪk/ adj pleasant to listen to

mel•o•dra•ma /ˈmeləˌdrɑmə/ noun [C/U] a story, play, or movie in which the characters express extreme emotions

mel•o•dra•mat•ic /ˌmelədrəˈmætɪk/ adj *showing disapproval* behaving in a way that is too emotional or too serious

mel•o•dy /ˈmelədi/ noun **1** [C] a tune or song **2** [C/U] *technical* the main tune in a piece of music

mel•on /ˈmelən/ noun [C/U] a large round fruit with orange, green, or white flesh *—picture* → C10

melt /melt/ verb ★

1 [I/T] to change a solid substance into a liquid, or to be changed from a solid into a liquid: *Melt the butter in a small saucepan.* ♦ *The ice will **melt** quickly in direct sunlight.*

2 [I] to disappear: *My fears melted when I saw his kind expression.*

3 [I/T] to make someone more sympathetic, or to become more sympathetic

melt•down /ˈmeltˌdaʊn/ noun [C/U] **1** a sudden complete failure of a company, organization, or system: *a global financial meltdown* **2** an accident in which nuclear fuel melts through its container

ˈmelting ˌpot noun [C] a situation in which there are many different types of people or ideas existing together

mem•ber /ˈmembər/ noun [C] ★★★

1 someone who belongs to a group or an organization: *a union member* ♦ *She was the only **member of** the family who visited him.*

2 a plant or animal that belongs in a particular group of plants or animals: *members of the cat family*

ˌMember of ˈParliament noun [C] a politician who represents people in a parliament

mem•ber•ship /ˈmembərˌʃɪp/ noun ★

1 [U] the fact of being a member of a club, organization, or group: *Several countries have applied for **membership in** the E.U.*

2 [singular] the members of a club, organization, or group: *They hope to double their membership this year.*

mem•brane /ˈmemˌbreɪn/ noun [C] a thin piece of skin inside your body

me•men•to /məˈmentoʊ/ (plural **me•men•toes**) noun [C] an object that you keep to remind you of someone or something: *a memento of our trip*

mem•o /ˈmemoʊ/ noun [C] a short note about work that you send to someone that you work with

mem•oirs /ˈmemˌwɑrz/ noun [plural] a book that someone famous writes about their own experiences

mem•o•ra•bil•i•a /ˌmem(ə)rəˈbɪliə/ noun [plural] objects that people collect because they are connected with someone famous or something interesting: *Beatles memorabilia*

mem•o•ra•ble /ˈmem(ə)rəb(ə)l/ adj worth remembering, or easy to remember: *a memorable experience*

mem•o•ran•dum /ˌmeməˈrændəm/ noun [C] a short official note from someone in a government or organization

me•mo•ri•al /məˈmɔriəl/ noun [C] a structure that is built to remind people of a famous person or event: *the Vietnam War Memorial* —**me•mo•ri•al** adj: *a memorial service/ceremony*

mem•o•rize /ˈmeməˌraɪz/ verb [T] to learn something so that can you remember it perfectly: *The children had memorized a poem.*

mem•o•ry /ˈmem(ə)ri/ noun ★★★

1 [C] something that you remember: *What are your most **vivid memories*** (=very clear memories) *of that period?* ♦ *I **have many good memories of** my childhood.*

2 [singular] the ability to remember things: *Your memory tends to get worse as you get older.* ♦ *I've never **had a very good memory** for names* (=I can't remember names very well).

3 [C] the part of a computer in which information is stored

PHRASE **in memory of sb** something that is done in memory of someone is done so that people will remember them

> **Words often used with memory**
>
> *Adjectives often used with **memory** (sense 1)*
>
> - **fond, happy, painful** + MEMORY: used about memories that make you feel happy or sad
> - **abiding, clear, distant, vague, vivid** + MEMORY: used about things that you remember well or badly
>
> *Verbs often used with **memory** (sense 1)*
>
> - **arouse, evoke, recall, rekindle, revive, stir, trigger** + MEMORY: make you remember something

men the plural of **man**

men•ace¹ /ˈmenəs/ noun **1** [C] someone or something that is dangerous or very annoying: *the growing menace of global pollution* **2** [U] a threatening quality or feeling

men•ace² /ˈmenəs/ verb [T] to threaten someone or something

men•ac•ing /ˈmenəsɪŋ/ adj intended to threaten someone: *a menacing look* —**men•ac•ing•ly** adv

mend¹ /mend/ verb [T] to repair a hole in a piece of clothing = FIX

mend² /mend/ noun **be on the mend** to be getting better after an illness

me•ni•al /ˈminiəl/ adj menial work does not need much skill

men•in•gi•tis /ˌmenɪnˈdʒaɪtɪs/ noun [U] *medical* a serious illness that affects your brain

men•o•pause /ˈmenəˌpɔz/ noun [singular] the time in a woman's life when her PERIODS stop and she is no longer capable of getting pregnant

ˈmen's ˌroom noun [C] *American* a men's bathroom in a public place

men•stru•al /ˈmenstruəl/ adj relating to the time each month when a woman menstruates

men•stru•ate /ˈmenstruˌeɪt/ verb [I] *formal* when a woman menstruates, blood flows out from her UTERUS each month —**men•stru•a•tion** /ˌmenstruˈeɪʃ(ə)n/ noun [U]

M

men•tal /ˈment(ə)l/ adj ★★ existing in the mind, or relating to the mind: *a child's mental development* ♦ *mental health/illness/problems*

PHRASE **make a mental note** to pay special attention to something so that you will remember it

—**men•tal•ly** adv: *mentally ill*

men•tal•i•ty /menˈtæləti/ noun [C] a particular way of thinking: *a destructive mentality*

men•tion¹ /ˈmenʃ(ə)n/ verb [T] ★★★ to refer to something, but not discuss it much: *He didn't mention her all evening.* ♦ **mention sth to sb** *I'll mention the problem to her.* ♦ **+(that)** *Did I mention that I've got a new job?*

PHRASES **don't mention it** *spoken* used as a polite answer to someone who has just thanked you for something

not to mention used for referring to something else that emphasizes what you have just said: *The fire caused terrible loss of life, not to mention all the damage to the buildings.*

men•tion² /ˈmenʃ(ə)n/ noun [singular/U] the act of referring to someone or something = REFERENCE: *There's no mention of these costs in the contract.*

men•tor /ˈmenˌtɔr, ˈmentər/ noun [C] an experienced person who gives advice to someone with less experience —**men•tor** verb [T], **men•tor•ing** noun [U]

men•u /ˈmenju/ noun [C] ★

1 a list of the food that is available in a restaurant: *Do you see anything you like on the menu?*

2 *computing* a list of choices on a computer screen: *the Edit menu*

me•ow /miˈaʊ/ verb [I] if a cat meows, it makes a short high sound —**me•ow** noun [C]

MEP /ˌem i ˈpi/ noun [C] Member of the European Parliament: a politician who represents one of the regions of a country in the European Union

mer•ce•nar•y¹ /ˈmɜrs(ə)nˌeri/ adj *showing disapproval* interested only in the money or other personal advantages that you can get from something

mer•ce•nar•y² /ˈmɜrs(ə)nˌeri/ noun [C] a soldier who fights for any army that will pay him or her

mer•chan•dise /ˈmɜrtʃənˌdaɪz/ noun [U] goods that people buy and sell

mer•chan•dis•ing /ˈmɜrtʃənˌdaɪzɪŋ/ noun [U] the business of selling products that are related to a popular movie, television show, sports team, etc.

mer•chant /ˈmɜrtʃənt/ noun [C] *formal* a person or business that buys and sells goods

ˌmerchant maˈrine noun [C/U] *American* a country's ships that carry goods rather than soldiers and weapons

mer•ci•ful /ˈmɜrsɪf(ə)l/ adj **1** showing kindness, even when other people are unkind **2** making you feel grateful and lucky by ending something that is bad: *a merciful and painless death*

mer•ci•ful•ly /ˈmɜrsɪfəli/ adv used for saying that you feel grateful and lucky that something bad has ended

mer•ci•less /ˈmɜrsɪləs/ adj very cruel or severe: *a merciless beating* —**mer•ci•less•ly** adv

mer•cu•ry /ˈmɜrkjəri/ noun [U] a silver liquid metal that is used in THERMOMETERS

mer•cy /ˈmɜrsi/ noun [U] the act of treating someone in a kind way when you could have punished them: *the mercy of God*

PHRASE **at the mercy of** in a situation that is controlled by someone or something that can harm you

mere /mɪr/ adj **1** used for emphasizing that something is small or unimportant **2** used for emphasizing the major effect of something that seems unimportant

mere•ly /ˈmɪrli/ adv *formal* **1** used for emphasizing that something is small or unimportant = ONLY **2** used for emphasizing that something is not as bad, severe, or important as someone thinks it is = ONLY

merge /mɜrdʒ/ verb [I] **1** if two organizations merge, they combine to form one bigger organization: *Small publishers were forced to merge with larger companies.* **2** if two things merge, they combine so that you can no longer tell the difference between them: *The hills merged into the dark sky behind them.*

merg•er /ˈmɜrdʒər/ noun [C] *business* an occasion when two companies combine to form a bigger company

me•rid•i•an /məˈrɪdiən/ noun [C] one of the lines on a map that goes around the Earth from the North Pole to the South Pole

me•ringue /məˈræŋ/ noun [C/U] a sweet food made from a mixture of sugar and the white part of eggs

mer•it¹ /ˈmerɪt/ noun [C/U] a good quality that makes you admire something: *Attention to detail is one of the great merits of the book.*

mer•it² /ˈmerɪt/ verb [T] *formal* to deserve

something: *The case merits further investigation.*

mer•maid /ˈmɜrˌmeɪd/ noun [C] an imaginary sea creature that has the body of a woman and the tail of a fish

mer•ri•ly /ˈmerəli/ adv **1** in a happy or lively way **2** without knowing or thinking about any problems = GAILY

mer•ry /ˈmeri/ adj *old-fashioned* happy and lively

PHRASE **Merry Christmas** used for wishing someone a happy time at Christmas

ˈmerry-go-ˌround noun [C] a machine with models of animals that children ride on as it turns around

mesh[1] /meʃ/ noun [C/U] a piece of material that is like a net made of wires or strings

mesh[2] /meʃ/ verb [I] if two things or people mesh, they work well together

mes•mer•ize /ˈmezməˌraɪz/ verb [T] to attract or interest you so much that you do not notice anything else

mess[1] /mes/ noun ★

1 [C/U] a situation in which a place is dirty, not neat, or in bad condition: *Your room is a mess; please pick up your toys.* ♦ *Try not to **make a mess** on the clean carpet.*

2 [singular] a difficult situation with a lot of problems: *an economic mess* ♦ *I don't know how we **got into this mess**.*

3 [singular] *informal* someone who has so many problems that they cannot have a normal life: *I was a complete mess after the divorce.*

mess[2] /mes/ PHRASAL VERBS **ˌmess aˈround** *informal* **1** to behave in a silly way, or to waste time doing things that are not important: *We have to stop messing around, or we won't finish.* **2** to spend time doing things in a relaxed way: *We spent the weekend messing around on John's boat.*

ˌmess (sth) ˈup to make a mistake, or to do something badly: *She thinks she messed up the interview.*

ˌmess sth ˈup 1 to make something dirty or not neat: *The wind had messed his hair up.* **2** to damage or spoil something: *I'm not going to let him mess up my life.*

ˈmess with sb to make someone angry or argue with them: *I wouldn't mess with her if I were you.*

ˈmess with sth or **ˌmess aˈround with sth** *informal* to become involved with something that is dangerous: *A lot of the kids had been messing around with drugs.*

mes•sage /ˈmesɪdʒ/ noun ★★★

1 [C] a piece of written or spoken information that you give or send to someone: *I got your e-mail message, thank you.* ♦ *If I'm not there, just **leave a message** with Chris.* ♦ *She's not here at the moment – can I **take a message**?*

2 [singular] the main idea that is contained in something such as a speech or an advertisement: *The documentary **sends a** clear **message** about the dangers of drug-taking.*

PHRASE **get the message** *informal* to understand what someone is trying to tell you

mes•sag•ing /ˈmesədʒɪŋ/ noun [U] *computing* the process of sending and receiving electronic messages by computer or cellphone

mes•sen•ger /ˈmesəndʒər/ noun [C] someone who delivers messages to people

mes•si•ah /məˈsaɪə/ noun **1** [C] someone who will save people from a difficult situation **2** [C] a religious leader who is sent by God to save the world **3 the Messiah** a name that Christians use for Jesus Christ

mess•y /ˈmesi/ adj ★

1 dirty or not neat: *a messy kitchen/desk/bedroom* ♦ *How did your face get so messy?*

2 complicated, difficult, and unpleasant to deal with: *a messy divorce/relationship*

met the past tense and past participle of **meet**[1]

me•tab•o•lism /məˈtæbəˌlɪzəm/ noun [C/U] the chemical processes in your body that change food and drink into energy —**met•a•bol•ic** /ˌmetəˈbɑlɪk/ adj

met•al /ˈmet(ə)l/ noun [C/U] ★★★ a hard shiny substance such as steel or iron that is used to make things such as tools and machines: *a metal frame/bucket/rod*

me•tal•lic /meˈtælɪk/ adj consisting of metal, or similar to metal

met•a•mor•pho•sis /ˌmetəˈmɔrfəsɪs/ (plural **met•a•mor•pho•ses** /ˌmetəˈmɔrfəˌsiz/) noun [C/U] *formal* a major change that makes someone or something very different

met•a•phor /ˈmetəˌfɔr/ noun [C/U] a way of describing something in which you refer to it as something else with similar qualities: *Writers often use war as a metaphor for business activity and competition.* — **met•a•phor•i•cal** /ˌmetəˈfɔrɪk(ə)l/ adj, **met•a•phor•i•cal•ly** /ˌmetəˈfɔrɪkli/ adv

→ SIMILE

met•a•phys•i•cal /ˌmetəˈfɪzɪk(ə)l/ adj relating to ideas about life, existence, and other things that are not part of the physical world

mete /mit/ PHRASAL VERB **ˌmete sth ˈout** *formal* to give a punishment to someone

me•te•or /ˈmitiər/ noun [C] a large piece of rock from space that appears as a bright light in the sky

me•te•or•ic /ˌmitiˈɔrɪk/ adj becoming very successful very quickly: *his meteoric political career*

me•te•or•ite /ˈmitiəˌraɪt/ noun [C] a piece of rock that has fallen from space and landed on the Earth

me•te•or•ol•o•gy /ˌmitiəˈrɑlədʒi/ noun [U] the scientific study of weather —**me•te•or•o•log•i•cal** /ˌmitiərəˈlɑdʒɪk(ə)l/ adj, **me•te•or•ol•o•gist** noun [C]

me•ter[1] /ˈmitər/ noun ★

1 [C] a piece of equipment for measuring how much gas or electricity you have used

2 [C] a PARKING METER

3 [C/U] a unit for measuring length in the METRIC SYSTEM, equal to 100 CENTIMETERS

me•ter[2] /ˈmitər/ verb [T] to measure something with a meter

meth•a•done /ˈmeθəˌdoʊn/ noun [U] a strong drug that is often taken by people who want to stop using the drug HEROIN

meth•ane /ˈmeˌθeɪn/ noun [U] a gas with no

M

color or smell that is used as a fuel

meth·od /ˈmeθəd/ noun [C] ★★★ a way of doing something, especially a planned or established way: *a rug produced by **traditional methods*** ♦ *We developed new **methods of pollution control.*** ♦ **method of doing sth** *a reliable method of detecting breast cancer*

> Words often used with **method**
>
> *Adjectives often used with **method***
> - **effective, efficient, good, reliable, successful** + METHOD: used about methods that achieve the result you want
>
> *Verbs often used with **method***
> - **adopt, apply, choose, employ, use** + METHOD: use a particular method to do something
> - **develop, devise, pioneer** + METHOD: invent a particular method of doing something

me·thod·i·cal /məˈθɑdɪk(ə)l/ adj always careful to do things in an organized way, or done in an organized way: *a methodical worker* —**me·thod·i·cal·ly** /məˈθɑdɪkli/ adv

Meth·od·ist /ˈmeθədɪst/ noun [C] a member of a Protestant Christian church that was formed by John Wesley in the 18th century —**Meth·od·ist** adj

meth·od·ol·o·gy /ˌmeθəˈdɑlədʒi/ noun [C/U] *formal* the methods and principles that are used for doing research or other work —**meth·od·o·log·i·cal** /ˌmeθədəˈlɑdʒɪk(ə)l/ adj

M

me·tic·u·lous /mɪˈtɪkjələs/ adj done with careful attention to detail: *a meticulous piece of research* —**me·tic·u·lous·ly** adv

me·tre /ˈmitər/ the British spelling of **meter** (=in measurements)

met·ric /ˈmetrɪk/ adj using or relating to the metric system of measurements → IMPERIAL 2

ˈ**metric ˌsystem, the** noun [singular] the system of measurement in which the basic units are meters and kilograms

met·ro /ˈmetroʊ/ noun [C] an underground railroad system in a city

me·trop·o·lis /məˈtrɑpəlɪs/ noun [C] a big city

met·ro·pol·i·tan /ˌmetrəˈpɑlɪt(ə)n/ adj belonging to a big city or typical of big cities: *the metropolitan area*

mg abbrev milligram

mgr. abbrev manager

MHz abbrev megahertz

MI abbrev Michigan

mice the plural of **mouse**

mi·crobe /ˈmaɪˌkroʊb/ noun [C] a MICROORGANISM

mi·cro·chip /ˈmaɪkrəˌtʃɪp/ noun [C] a very small piece of SILICON that contains the electronic connections for making a computer work

mi·cro·cosm /ˈmaɪkrəˌkɑzəm/ noun [C] *formal* something small that contains all the features of something larger: *The village is a microcosm of rural Turkish life.*

mi·cro·fi·ber /ˈmaɪkrəˌfaɪbər/ noun [C/U] a very thin fiber made from chemicals and used for making cloth

mi·cro·man·ag·er /ˈmaɪkroʊˌmænɪdʒər/ noun [C] *American showing disapproval* someone who tries to control every part of a business or system —**mi·cro·man·age** verb [I]

mi·cro·or·gan·ism /ˌmaɪkroʊˈɔrgəˌnɪzəm/ noun [C] a very small living thing that you can see only with a MICROSCOPE

mi·cro·phone /ˈmaɪkrəˌfoʊn/ noun [C] a piece of equipment for making someone's voice louder when they are performing or recording something

mi·cro·proc·es·sor /ˌmaɪkroʊˈprɑˌsesər/ noun [C] *computing* a piece of electronic equipment inside a computer that makes it work

mi·cro·scope /ˈmaɪkrəˌskoʊp/ noun [C] a piece of scientific equipment for looking at things that are too small to see normally

mi·cro·scop·ic /ˌmaɪkrəˈskɑpɪk/ adj very small: *microscopic life*

mi·cro·wave[1] /ˈmaɪkrəˌweɪv/ or ˌ**microwave** ˈ**oven** noun [C] an oven that cooks food very quickly by using ELECTROMAGNETIC waves instead of heat —*picture* → C2

mi·cro·wave[2] /ˈmaɪkrəˌweɪv/ verb [T] to cook food in a microwave —**mi·cro·wav·a·ble** adj

ˌ**mid-air** noun **in mid-air** while someone or something is in the air —ˈ**mid-ˌair** adj: *a mid-air collision*

mid·day /ˌmɪdˈdeɪ/ noun [U] 12 o'clock, when the morning ends and the afternoon begins =NOON

mid·dle[1] /ˈmɪd(ə)l/ noun [singular] ★★★
1 the middle the part of something that is farthest from the sides, edges, or ends =CENTER: *a sheet with a blue stripe down the middle* ♦ *There was a cat sitting **in the middle of** the road.*
2 the middle the part that is between the beginning and the end of a period of time or an event: ***the middle of** the 15th century* ♦ *He fell asleep **in the middle of** the movie.*
PHRASES **in the middle of (doing) sth** busy doing something: *He was in the middle of cooking dinner when I arrived.*
in the middle of nowhere a long way from any town or city

mid·dle[2] /ˈmɪd(ə)l/ adj ★★
1 nearest to the center: *The map's in the middle drawer.* ♦ *middle-income families*
2 between the beginning and end of something: *The middle section of the book deals with training a dog.*

ˌ**middle-ˈaged** adj no longer young but not yet old, usually between 40 and 60 years of age —ˌ**middle ˈage** noun [U]

ˌ**Middle ˈAges, the** the period in European history between about 1000 A.D. and 1500 A.D.

ˌ**middle ˈclass** noun **the middle class** or **the middle classes** the social class that consists mostly of educated people who have professional jobs and are neither very rich nor very poor → LOWER CLASS, UPPER CLASS, WORKING CLASS

ˌ**middle-ˈclass** adj belonging or relating to the middle class: *middle-class families*

ˌ**Middle ˈEast, the** the region of the world that consists of the countries east of the Mediterranean Sea and west of India

ˈ**middle ˌground** noun [singular/U] opinions and attitudes that most people agree with because they are not extreme: *a party that occupies the middle ground of politics*

mid·dle·man /ˈmɪd(ə)lˌmæn/ (plural **mid·dle·men** /ˈmɪd(ə)lˌmen/) noun [C] **1** a person or company that buys things from producers and sells them to customers **2** someone who helps to arrange business deals and discussions between other people

ˌmiddle ˈmanagement noun [U] *business* managers who are in charge of parts of an organization and have less authority than senior managers —**ˌmiddle ˈmanager** noun [C]

ˌmiddle ˈname noun [C] a second name that some people have between their first name and their family name

ˌmiddle-of-the-ˈroad adj not unusual or extreme

ˈmiddle ˌschool noun [C/U] **1** a school in the U.S. for children between the ages of 11 and 14 **2** a school in the U.K. for children between the ages of 8 and 12

Mid•east, the /ˌmɪdˈist/ *American* the MIDDLE EAST

mid•field /ˈmɪdˌfild/ noun [U] the middle part of the field in football, soccer, and other ball games —**mid•field•er** noun [C]

midg•et /ˈmɪdʒɪt/ noun [C] *offensive* an adult who has not grown to a normal size. A more polite expression is **person of restricted growth**.

mid•night /ˈmɪdˌnaɪt/ noun [U] ★ 12 o'clock at night

mid•riff /ˈmɪdrɪf/ noun [C] the front part of your body between your waist and your chest

midst /mɪdst/ noun **in the midst of sth** *formal* while something else is happening or affecting you: *The President went to China in the midst of a crisis at home.*

mid•sum•mer /ˈmɪdˌsʌmər/ noun [U] the middle part of summer, when the weather is usually the hottest: *a midsummer morning*

mid•term /ˈmɪdˌtɜrm/ adj happening in the middle part of a school TERM: *midterm exams*

mid•way /ˈmɪdˌweɪ/ adj, adv **1** in a position that is HALFWAY between two places: *He stopped midway across the room.* **2** at a time in the middle of an event or period: *Our problems started midway through the first year.*

mid•week /ˌmɪdˈwik/ adj, adv in the middle of the week, usually from Tuesday to Thursday: *a midweek game*

Mid•west, the /ˌmɪdˈwest/ the states in the north central region of the U.S. —**Mid•west•ern** adj

mid•wife /ˈmɪdˌwaɪf/ (plural **mid•wives** /ˈmɪdˌwaɪvz/) noun [C] a nurse whose job is to take care of women when they are having a baby

mid•win•ter /ˌmɪdˈwɪntər/ noun [U] the middle part of winter, when the weather is usually the coldest

miffed /mɪft/ adj *informal* slightly annoyed or offended

might¹ /maɪt/ modal verb ★★★

- **Might** is usually followed by an infinitive without "to": *I might change my mind.* Sometimes it is used without a following infinitive: *I don't think we'll need any more help, but we might.*
- **Might** has no tenses, no participles, and no infinitive form. It does not change its form, so the third person singular form does not end in "-s": *She might be late.*
- Questions and negatives are formed without "do": *Might I make a suggestion?* ♦ *Your plan might not work.* The negative short form **mightn't** can also be used, but only in very informal English.

1 used for saying that there is a small possibility that something is true or will happen: *You never know what might happen in the future.* ♦ *I was afraid that someone might recognize me.* ♦ *Did you say anything that might have upset her?*

2 used as the past tense of "may" when you are reporting what someone said: *Roger said they might not be able to come.*

PHRASE **might (just) as well** *informal* **1** used for making a suggestion when you cannot think of anything better to do: *We might as well sit down while we're waiting.* **2** used for saying that it would not make any difference if you did something else: *The meeting was a complete waste of time. I might just as well have stayed at home.*

might² /maɪt/ noun [U] great power or strength

might•y /ˈmaɪti/ adj very large, powerful, or impressive: *a mighty empire*

mi•graine /ˈmaɪˌgreɪn/ noun [C] a very severe HEADACHE

mi•grant /ˈmaɪgrənt/ noun [C] someone who travels to another place in order to work: *migrant workers/laborers*

mi•grate /ˈmaɪˌgreɪt/ verb [I] **1** to go to another place in order to find work **2** if a bird or animal migrates, it travels to another part of the world for warmer weather —**mi•gra•tion** /maɪˈgreɪʃ(ə)n/ noun [U]

mike /maɪk/ noun [C] *informal* a MICROPHONE

mild /maɪld/ adj ★

1 not strong, serious, or severe: *They were both suffering from a mild bout of the flu.* ♦ *There was a note of mild alarm in her voice.* ♦ *a mild recession*

2 mild weather is warm and pleasant: *a mild winter*

3 without a strong taste: *a mild chili*

4 very gentle and not likely to have any bad effects: *a mild soap*

mild•ly /ˈmaɪldli/ adv slightly but not very: *Some of the stories were mildly amusing.*

PHRASE **to put it mildly** *spoken* used for saying that the words you have chosen are not as extreme as they could have been: *The pay cut was unpopular, to put it mildly.*

mile /maɪl/ noun ★★★

1 [C] a unit for measuring distance, equal to 1760 YARDS or 1.609 kilometers: *We drove about 900 miles in two days.* ♦ *The island is **13 miles long**.* ♦ *The car was traveling at 50 **miles an hour**.*

2 miles [plural] a long distance: *They live **miles from** the nearest town.* ♦ *The beach stretched **for miles** in each direction.*

PHRASE **a mile a minute** *informal* very quickly: *The two of them were talking a mile a minute.*

mile•age /ˈmaɪlɪdʒ/ noun **1** [singular/U] the

M

number of miles that a vehicle has traveled: *a car with high mileage* **2 mileage** or **gas mileage** [singular/U] the number of miles that a vehicle can travel using one GALLON of gas **3** [U] *informal* an advantage or opportunity that you get from something: *He has gotten a lot of mileage out of his friendship with the mayor.*

mile•stone /ˈmaɪlˌstoʊn/ noun [C] an event or achievement that marks an important stage in a process

mi•lieu /milˈju/ noun [C] *formal* the type of society that you live in, or the type of people that you spend time with

mil•i•tant¹ /ˈmɪlɪtənt/ adj using violence or extreme methods in order to achieve political change: *The militant group claimed to have killed two soldiers.* —**mil•i•tan•cy** noun [U]

mil•i•tant² /ˈmɪlɪtənt/ noun [C] someone who uses militant methods to achieve something

mil•i•tar•y /ˈmɪlɪˌteri/ adj ★★ relating to ARMED FORCES, or using ARMED FORCES: *military service* ♦ *The government is prepared to take **military action**.* ♦ *a huge **military operation***

mil•i•ta•ry, the /ˈmɪlɪˌteri/ noun [singular] a country's army, navy, air force, etc.: *The military does not have the weapons it needs to defeat the rebels.*

M

mi•li•tia /məˈlɪʃə/ noun [C] a group of ordinary people who are trained as soldiers to fight in an emergency

milk¹ /mɪlk/ noun [U] ★★★

1 a white liquid that women and female animals produce to feed their babies. People drink the milk of cows, goats, and sheep and use it in cooking: *a carton/glass of milk*

2 a white liquid that some plants produce

milk² /mɪlk/ verb [T] **1** to take milk from a cow, goat, or sheep **2** to get a lot of personal advantage from something: *Both parties have milked the political situation for all it's worth.*

milk•shake /ˈmɪlkʃeɪk/ noun [C] a sweet drink made by mixing milk with chocolate or fruit

milk•y /ˈmɪlki/ adj **1** white like milk **2** containing milk or a liquid that looks like milk

mill¹ /mɪl/ noun [C] **1** a building with a machine that is used for crushing grain into flour **2** a factory where a product such as cotton, wool, or steel is made: *a textile mill* **3** a small machine or tool that you use in the kitchen for crushing substances into powder: *a coffee/pepper mill*

mill² /mɪl/ verb [T] to crush grain into flour

PHRASAL VERB ˌ**mill aˈround** *informal* to move around in large numbers in a confused way with no particular purpose

mil•len•ni•um /mɪˈleniəm/ (plural **mil•len•ni•a** /mɪˈleniə/) noun [C] a period of 1000 years —**mil•len•ni•al** adj

mil•li•gram /ˈmɪlɪˌgræm/ noun [C] a unit for measuring weight. There are 1000 milligrams in a **gram**.

mil•li•li•ter /ˈmɪlɪˌlitər/ noun [C] a unit for measuring an amount of liquid. There are 1000 milliliters in a **liter**.

mil•li•me•ter /ˈmɪlɪˌmitər/ noun [C] a unit for measuring length. There are 1000 millimeters in a **meter**.

mil•lion /ˈmɪljən/ number ★★

1 the number 1,000,000

2 millions or **a million** a large number of people or things: *I've got a million things to do before I leave.* ♦ *They received **millions** of letters asking for information.*

—**mil•lionth** /ˈmɪljənθ/ number

mil•lion•aire /ˌmɪljəˈner/ noun [C] someone who has more than a million dollars

mil•li•sec•ond /ˈmɪlɪˌsekənd/ noun [C] a unit for measuring extremely short periods of time. There are 1000 milliseconds in a second.

mime /maɪm/ verb [I/T] to tell a story using only the movements of your body and face, not using words —**mime** noun [U]

mim•ic¹ /ˈmɪmɪk/ (present participle **mim•ick•ing**; past tense and past participle **mim•icked**) verb [T] to copy someone's voice, behavior, or appearance = IMITATE: *She mimicked his accent.* —**mim•ic•ry** noun [U]

mim•ic² /ˈmɪmɪk/ noun [C] someone who is able to copy the voice, behavior, or appearance of someone else

min. abbrev **1** minute **2** minimum

mince /mɪns/ verb **not mince (your) words** *informal* to say exactly what you think and not care about other people's reactions

mind¹ /maɪnd/ noun [C/U] ★★★ your thoughts and attention, or the part of you that thinks, knows, and remembers things: *You never know what's going on **in her mind**.* ♦ *I can't **keep my mind on** work when it's so sunny outside.* ♦ *She's never been able to **get him out of her mind*** (=stop thinking about him). ♦ *She shouldn't drive in her current **state of mind*** (=the way she is thinking and feeling). ♦ *Just try to **put the problem out of your mind**.* ♦ *A good night out will help you **take your mind off** your exams* (=help you to stop thinking about them).

PHRASES **be/go out of your mind** *informal* to be/become crazy or confused: *You must be out of your mind to want to see him again.*

be of two minds (about sth) to not be certain about something, or to have difficulty in making a decision: *I'm of two minds about accepting the job.*

come to mind if something comes to mind, you suddenly remember it or start to think about it

have sb/sth in mind to know the person or thing that you want: *Who do you have in mind for the job?*

have/keep an open mind to be willing to listen to other people's opinions: *I told the committee that I had an open mind on the matter.*

in the back of your mind if something is in the back of your mind, you are not thinking about it now, but you still remember it or know about it: *In the back of her mind, she knew he was lying.*

keep/bear sth in mind to remember or consider something: *Keep that in mind when you come to make your decision.*

keep sb in mind to remember someone because they might be the right person for

something in the future: *Keep me in mind if you need some help.*
make up your mind to make a decision: *I **can't make up my mind** whether to go or not.* ♦ ***My mind's made up.** Nothing will make me change it.*
on your mind if something is on your mind, you are thinking or worrying about it: *She isn't usually so rude; she has **a lot on her mind**.*
put your mind to sth to decide to do something and try very hard to achieve it

mind[2] /maɪnd/ verb ★★★
1 [I/T] to feel annoyed, upset, or unhappy about something: *We had to cancel, but Rosa didn't seem to mind.* ♦ *I don't mind the heat* (=the heat is not a problem to me). ♦ *I **don't mind** going to the store* (=I'm willing to go) *if no one else wants to.* ♦ *He **won't mind** if we're a little late.*
2 [T] *British* to be careful about something: *Mind the step* (=do not fall over it).
3 [T] *British* to take care of someone or something for a short time
PHRASES **do you mind if I do sth?** used for politely asking someone's permission to do something
if you don't mind me/my saying so a polite way of saying that you hope someone is not offended by what you are saying: *You were a little rude, if you don't mind me saying so.*
I wouldn't mind sth used for asking for something politely: *I wouldn't mind a cold drink if you have one.*
mind your own business *spoken* a rude way of telling someone not to ask questions about something that you do not want them to know about: *"Where do you think you're going?" "Mind your own business!"*
never mind 1 *spoken* used for telling someone not to feel upset about something, because you do not think it is important enough to worry about: *"We missed the show!" "Never mind, we can go next week."* **2** used for saying that you do not want to repeat something that you said, or that you want someone to ignore it: *Where's my hat? Oh, never mind, I found it!*
would you mind used for asking politely for something: ***Would you mind** if I brought a friend to the party?* ♦ **would you mind doing sth** *Would you mind closing that window?*

mind-blow·ing /ˈmaɪnd ˌbloʊɪŋ/ adj *informal* extremely impressive, exciting, or shocking

mind·ful /ˈmaɪn(d)fəl/ adj careful about something, or conscious of something: *Travelers ought to be mindful of their surroundings.*

mind·less /ˈmaɪn(d)ləs/ adj **1** done without a reason, or without thinking about the results: *mindless vandalism* **2** not needing any thought or intelligence: *a mindless task*

mind·set /ˈmaɪn(d)ˌset/ noun [C] a way of thinking about things: *The company will have to change its whole mindset if it is to survive.*

mine[1] /maɪn/ pronoun ★★★ used for referring to people or things that belong to you or are connected with you, when you are the person speaking or writing: *Can I borrow your keys? I can't find mine.* ♦ *This must be your T-shirt. Mine has stains on it.* ♦ *I got the idea from a friend **of mine**.*

mine[2] /maɪn/ noun [C] ★
1 a large hole or tunnel in the ground from which people take coal, gold, etc.
2 a bomb that is hidden under the ground or under water and explodes when it is touched

mine[3] /maɪn/ verb **1** [I/T] to dig a large hole or tunnel in the ground in order to get coal, gold, etc.: *People still mine for coal in this area.* **2** [T] to hide bombs under the ground or under water

mine·field /ˈmaɪnˌfild/ noun **1** [singular] a situation with many possible problems or dangers: *The issue of tax cuts is a potential minefield for the government.* **2** [C] an area where bombs have been hidden under the ground or under water

min·er /ˈmaɪnər/ noun [C] someone whose job is to dig coal from a mine

min·er·al /ˈmɪn(ə)rəl/ noun [C] **1** a natural substance in the earth, for example coal, salt, or gold **2** a natural substance in some foods that you need for good health, for example iron and CALCIUM

ˈmineral ˌwater noun [U] water that comes from under the ground and contains minerals

min·gle /ˈmɪŋg(ə)l/ verb [I] **1** if things such as smells or feelings mingle, they become mixed together: *Polly felt hope mingled with fear.* **2** to move around and talk to a lot of people during a social event: *Try to get the guests to mingle.*

mini- /mɪni/ prefix smaller or shorter than other things of the same kind: *a miniskirt*

min·i·a·ture[1] /ˈmɪniətʃər, ˈmɪnɪtʃər/ adj much smaller than things of the same kind: *a miniature railroad*

min·i·a·ture[2] /ˈmɪniətʃər, ˈmɪnɪtʃər/ noun [C] a very small painting or photograph
PHRASE **in miniature** the same in appearance as someone or something else but much smaller

min·i·bar /ˈmɪniˌbɑr/ noun [C] a small cabinet of alcoholic drinks for guests in a hotel room

min·i·bus /ˈmɪniˌbʌs/ noun [C] a small bus for about 10 to 15 people —*picture* → C7

min·i·mal /ˈmɪnɪm(ə)l/ adj extremely small in amount or degree: *a minimal increase* ♦ *minimal damage* —**min·i·mal·ly** adv

min·i·mal·ism /ˈmɪnɪm(ə)lˌɪzəm/ noun [U] a style of art that developed in the 1960s and uses a small number of simple shapes and colors

min·i·mal·ist /ˈmɪnɪm(ə)lɪst/ adj relating to minimalism

min·i·mize /ˈmɪnɪˌmaɪz/ verb [T] **1** to make the amount of something bad as small as possible ≠ MAXIMIZE: *We must minimize the damage to innocent civilians.* **2** to make something seem much less important than it really is ≠ EXAGGERATE: *I don't want to minimize their role in the campaign.* **3** to make a computer program appear as only a small picture on your computer screen when you are not using it

min·i·mum[1] /ˈmɪnɪməm/ adj ★★ as small in

M

amount or degree as possible ≠ MAXIMUM: *the minimum requirements for entry to college* ♦ *the minimum voting age*

min·i·mum² /ˈmɪnɪməm/ noun [singular] ★ the smallest amount or degree of something that is necessary or possible ≠ MAXIMUM: *The project will take **a minimum of six** weeks.* ♦ **keep sth to a minimum** *We need to keep costs to a minimum.*

ˌminimum ˈwage noun [singular/U] the smallest amount of money that an employer is legally allowed to pay a worker

min·ing /ˈmaɪnɪŋ/ noun [U] the process of getting coal, gold, etc. from under the ground

min·i·skirt /ˈmɪniˌskɜrt/ noun [C] a very short skirt

min·is·ter /ˈmɪnɪstər/ noun [C] **1** a priest in some Protestant churches **2** an official who is in charge of a government department in the U.K. and in other countries: *a meeting of trade ministers* —**min·is·te·ri·al** /ˌmɪnɪˈstriəl/ adj

min·is·try /ˈmɪnɪstri/ noun **1 the ministry** [singular] the profession or work of a church MINISTER **2** [C] a government department in the U.K. and in other countries: *the Dutch foreign ministry* ♦ *the Ministry of Education*

min·i·van /ˈmɪniˌvæn/ noun [C] a small van with seats for about eight people

mink /mɪŋk/ noun [C/U] a small animal that is raised for its thick dark fur, or the fur of this animal

min·now /ˈmɪnoʊ/ noun [C] a small fish that lives in rivers and lakes

mi·nor¹ /ˈmaɪnər/ adj ★★

1 not very important in comparison with people or things of the same type: *The damage here was only minor.* ♦ *a minor crime/offence* ♦ *Some **minor changes** may be necessary.*

2 relating to one of the two types of musical KEYS (=set of notes)

→ MAJOR

mi·nor² /ˈmaɪnər/ noun [C] **1** *legal* a young person who is not yet an adult, according to the law **2** *American* a college subject or area of study that is less important and involves less work than a student's main subject

mi·nor³ /ˈmaɪnər/ PHRASAL VERB **ˈminor in sth** *American* to study a particular subject in college in addition to your main subject: *I thought you were going to minor in geography.*

mi·nor·i·ty¹ /maɪˈnɔrəti/ noun [C] ★★

1 a group of people or things that forms less than half of a larger group ≠ MAJORITY: *In a small **minority of** cases, the treatment does not help.* ♦ *Women are **in the minority** in the top ranks of government.*

2 a part of a population that is different in race, religion, or culture from most of the population: *The regulations are intended to prevent discrimination against minorities.* ♦ *Members of ethnic minorities are represented on the committee.* ♦ *a religious minority*

mi·nor·i·ty² /maɪˈnɔrəti/ adj **1** relating to a minority or forming a minority: *They hold a minority interest in the company.* **2** belonging to a RACIAL minority: *kids from minority backgrounds*

mint¹ /mɪnt/ noun **1** [U] a small plant with green leaves that have a strong smell and a cool pleasant taste **2** [C] a piece of candy with a strong fresh taste **3** [C] the place where a country makes its coins

mint² /mɪnt/ verb [T] to make a coin from metal

mi·nus¹ /ˈmaɪnəs/ grammar word ★

> **Minus can be:**
> - a **preposition**: *17 minus 9 is 8.*
> - an **adjective**: *It was minus 12 degrees this morning.*

1 used in mathematics for showing that you are taking one number from another. This word is usually represented by the symbol – ≠ PLUS: *72 minus 5 equals 67.*

2 used before a number to show that a number or temperature is less than zero: *The temperature got down to minus 15 degrees last night.*

3 *informal* without something that you had in the past or usually have: *Anthony returned to work minus his beard.*

PHRASE **A minus/B minus etc.** grades given for students' work that are lower than the grades A, B etc. These grades are usually written "A-," "B-," etc.

mi·nus² /ˈmaɪnəs/ noun [C] *informal* a disadvantage: *Before I decide, I need to weigh up all the pluses and minuses.*

min·us·cule /ˈmɪnəˌskjul/ adj extremely small in size or amount: *The risk to public health is minuscule.*

ˈminus ˌsign noun [C] the symbol –

min·ute /ˈmɪnɪt/ noun [C] ★★★

1 a period of 60 seconds. There are 60 minutes in one hour: *I'll meet you downstairs in ten minutes.* ♦ *A bus leaves at five minutes after the hour.*

2 *informal* a very short period of time: *It will only take a minute.* ♦ ***For a minute** I thought she had left.* ♦ *I'll be ready **in a minute*** (=very soon).

PHRASES **any minute** very soon: *Jack should be here any minute.*

the last minute the latest possible time for doing something: *Jane always waits until the last minute to write her paper.*

hold on a minute *spoken* used for asking someone to wait for a short period of time

the minute you do sth as soon as you do something: *Please call me the minute you hear anything from the hospital.*

wait/just a minute *spoken* **1** used for asking someone to wait or be patient: *Just a minute, sir, and I'll take your order.* **2** used when you are about to disagree with what someone has said: *Wait a minute – that can't be right.*

mi·nute /maɪˈnut/ adj **1** very small: *The soil contained minute quantities of uranium.* **2** very careful and detailed: *a minute examination of the evidence*

min·utes /ˈmɪnɪts/ noun [plural] an official written record of the decisions that people make at a formal meeting: *Carl usually takes the minutes, but he's not here tonight.*

mir·a·cle /ˈmɪrək(ə)l/ noun [C] **1** something

that is extremely lucky and that would not normally be possible: *It's a miracle that no one was killed in the crash.* **2** an event that cannot be explained according to the laws of nature and is considered to be an act of God

PHRASE **perform/work miracles** to achieve extremely impressive results

mi•rac•u•lous /məˈrækjələs/ adj extremely lucky and unexpected —**mi•rac•u•lous•ly** adv

mi•rage /məˈrɑʒ/ noun [C] a strange effect in a desert in which you see something that is not really there

mir•ror[1] /ˈmɪrər/ noun [C] ★★ a piece of special glass in which you can see yourself or what is behind you: *a bathroom mirror* ♦ *Rachel looked at herself in the mirror.*

mir•ror[2] /ˈmɪrər/ verb [T] to match or express the qualities, features, or feelings of someone or something

mirth /mɜrθ/ noun [U] *literary* happy laughter

mis•ap•pre•hen•sion /ˌmɪsæprɪˈhenʃ(ə)n/ noun [C] *formal* a belief that is not correct

mis•be•have /ˌmɪsbɪˈheɪv/ verb [I] to behave badly

mis•be•hav•ior /ˌmɪsbɪˈheɪvjər/ noun [singular/U] bad behavior

misc. abbrev miscellaneous

mis•cal•cu•late /ˌmɪsˈkælkjəˌleɪt/ verb [I/T] **1** to make a mistake in calculating numbers **2** to make a wrong judgment about what will happen or what to do in a situation —**mis•cal•cu•la•tion** /ˌmɪskælkjəˈleɪʃ(ə)n/ noun [C/U]

mis•car•riage /mɪsˈkerɪdʒ/ noun [C/U] the process of giving birth to a baby before it has developed enough to live

PHRASE **miscarriage of justice** a situation in which a court of law punishes someone for a crime that they did not commit

mis•car•ry /mɪsˈkeri/ verb [I/T] to give birth to a baby before it has developed enough to live

mis•cel•la•ne•ous /ˌmɪsəˈleɪniəs/ adj consisting of various kinds of people or things

mis•chief /ˈmɪstʃɪf/ noun [U] behavior or play, especially of children, that causes trouble but not serious harm

mis•chie•vous /ˈmɪstʃɪvəs/ adj a mischievous person, especially a child, enjoys having fun by causing trouble —**mis•chie•vous•ly** adv

mis•con•cep•tion /ˌmɪskənˈsepʃ(ə)n/ noun [C/U] a wrong belief or opinion that is the result of not understanding something

mis•con•duct /mɪsˈkɑnˌdʌkt/ noun [U] *formal* bad or dishonest behavior by someone who has a position of responsibility

mis•de•mean•or /ˌmɪsdɪˈminər/ noun [C] *legal* a crime that is not as serious as a **felony**

mis•er•a•ble /ˈmɪz(ə)rəb(ə)l/ adj **1** extremely unhappy: *He looked cold and miserable.* **2** making you feel very unhappy: *The weather was miserable.* **3** a miserable amount of something is very small and not enough —**mis•er•a•bly** adv

mis•er•y /ˈmɪzəri/ noun [U] the state of being extremely unhappy or uncomfortable

PHRASE **put sth out of its misery** to end the life of an animal that is suffering

put sb out of their misery *humorous* to tell someone something that they are very eager to know, so that they stop worrying about it

mis•fire /mɪsˈfaɪr/ verb [I] **1** if a plan or activity misfires, it does not have the result that you wanted **2** if a gun misfires, the bullet does not come out

mis•fit /ˈmɪsˌfɪt/ noun [C] someone who does not seem to belong to a group, or who is not accepted by a group

mis•for•tune /mɪsˈfɔrtʃ(ə)n/ noun [C/U] bad luck, or a situation in which you have bad luck

mis•giv•ing /mɪsˈgɪvɪŋ/ noun [C/U] a feeling of doubt about whether something is right or will have a good result: *Richard expressed grave misgivings about the deal.*

mis•guid•ed /mɪsˈgaɪdəd/ adj based on judgments or opinions that are wrong

mis•han•dle /mɪsˈhænd(ə)l/ verb [T] to deal with a situation or process badly

mis•hap /ˈmɪsˌhæp/ noun [C/U] a minor mistake or accident

mish•mash /ˈmɪʃˌmæʃ/ noun [singular] *informal* a messy or confused mixture of different things

mis•in•form /ˌmɪsɪnˈfɔrm/ verb [T] to give someone false or incorrect information —**mis•in•for•ma•tion** /ˌmɪsɪnfərˈmeɪʃ(ə)n/ noun [U]

mis•in•ter•pret /ˌmɪsɪnˈtɜrprət/ verb [T] to understand or explain something wrongly —**mis•in•ter•pre•ta•tion** /ˌmɪsɪntɜrprɪˈteɪʃ(ə)n/ noun [C/U]

mis•judge /mɪsˈdʒʌdʒ/ verb [T] **1** to make a wrong judgment about a person or situation **2** to make a mistake in calculating something —**mis•judg•ment** noun [C/U]

mis•lay /mɪsˈleɪ/ (past tense and past participle **mis•laid** /mɪsˈleɪd/) verb [T] to lose something for a short time, because you cannot remember where you put it

mis•lead /mɪsˈlid/ (past tense and past participle **mis•led** /mɪsˈled/) verb [T] to make someone believe something that is incorrect or not true

mis•lead•ing /mɪsˈlidɪŋ/ adj intended or likely to make someone believe something that is incorrect or not true: *He had made misleading statements to the committee.*

mis•man•age•ment /mɪsˈmænɪdʒmənt/ noun [U] the process of managing something badly: *the mismanagement of public funds* —**mis•man•age** verb [T]

mis•match /ˈmɪsˌmætʃ/ noun [C] a difference or disagreement between two facts or two aspects of a situation

mis•no•mer /mɪsˈnoʊmər/ noun [C] a name or description that is incorrect or inappropriate

mi•sog•y•nist /mɪˈsɑdʒənɪst/ noun [U] a man who hates women

mis•placed /ˌmɪsˈpleɪst/ adj a misplaced feeling or opinion is not appropriate for a particular situation, or is directed toward the wrong person: *misplaced fears/loyalty/trust*

mis•print /ˈmɪsˌprɪnt/ noun [C] a mistake such as a wrong spelling in a book, newspaper, etc.

mis·pro·nounce /ˌmɪsprəˈnaʊns/ verb [T] to pronounce a word wrongly

mis·quote /mɪsˈkwoʊt/ verb [T] to report wrongly what someone said or wrote

mis·read /mɪsˈrid/ (past tense and past participle **mis·read** /mɪsˈred/) verb [T] **1** to read something wrongly **2** to understand or judge a person or situation wrongly

mis·rep·re·sent /ˌmɪsreprəˈzent/ verb [T] to deliberately give a false or incorrect description of someone or something —**mis·rep·re·sen·ta·tion** /mɪsˌreprɪzenˈteɪʃ(ə)n/ noun [C/U]

miss[1] /mɪs/ verb ★★★

1 not reach	5 opportunity/chance
2 not be present at	6 avoid sth bad
3 be too late for	7 feel sad about
4 not notice/understand	+ PHRASAL VERB

1 [I/T] to fail to catch, hit, or reach something: *I tried to catch the ball but missed.* ♦ *An official said that the missiles had missed their targets.*
2 [T] to fail to be present for someone or something: *I had to miss a week of school.* ♦ *We must have missed each other by about an hour.* ♦ *I wouldn't miss your party for the world* (=I really want to go to it).
3 [T] to be too late for something such as a train or bus: ***I missed the last bus** home again.*
4 [T] to fail to notice or understand something: *I missed most of what she said.* ♦ *Sue had **missed the point*** (=not understood what someone meant) *completely.* ♦ *The house is next to the store – you can't miss it* (=it is very easy to notice).
5 [T] to fail to take advantage of an opportunity: *She realized she had **missed a chance** to speak to Brian.*
6 [T] to escape something that is unpleasant or uncomfortable: *If I leave at eight, I miss the traffic .*
7 [T] to feel sad because someone is not with you anymore, or because you do not have or cannot do something anymore: *We miss him so much.* ♦ **miss doing sth** *I miss watching her ride her horse.*
PHRASAL VERB ˌ**miss ˈout** to lose an opportunity to do or have something: *We will be repeating the questions later, so you won't miss out.* ♦ *Come with us or you'll **miss out on** all the fun.*

miss[2] /mɪs/ noun **1 Miss** a title used in front of the last name or whole name of a girl or woman who is not married → MRS., MS.
2 *formal* used for talking politely to a girl or young woman whose name you do not know
3 [C] a failure to hit or catch something, or to score in a game

mis·sile /ˈmɪs(ə)l, ˈmisaɪl/ noun [C] **1** a weapon that travels long distances and explodes when it hits something: *a nuclear missile* → BALLISTIC MISSILE, CRUISE MISSILE **2** an object that is thrown or fired at someone or something

miss·ing /ˈmɪsɪŋ/ adj ★★
1 if someone or something is missing, they are not where they should be and you do not know where they are: *We need to look to see if anything is missing.* ♦ *a missing dog* ♦ *The young woman's boyfriend had already **reported her missing**.* ♦ *The key was **missing from** its usual place.*
2 if someone or something is missing, they are not included in something although you would expect them to be there: *Candidates' names were **missing from** the ballots.*
3 not found after a battle or accident, but not known to be dead or taken prisoner: *Five other passengers are **missing, presumed dead**.* ♦ *Over 8,000 American soldiers are listed as **missing in action**.*

mis·sion /ˈmɪʃ(ə)n/ noun

1 important work	4 flight into space
2 group sent to do sth	5 important goal
3 military operation	6 religious work

1 [C] an important piece of work that a person or group of people has to do for a government or large organization, especially one that involves travel: *a fact-finding/rescue mission* **2** [C] a group of people who have been sent to do an important piece of work: *members of the trade mission to Russia* **3** [C] a military operation, especially one by aircraft: *He was shot down during a mission over the Balkans.* **4** [C] a flight into space: *the possibility of a manned mission to Mars* **5** [singular] a goal that is very important to a person or organization: *Helping homeless people was Gina's mission in life.* ♦ *a mission statement* **6** [C/U] the work of religious people who go to other countries in order to make people believe in their religion, or the building where they do this

mis·sion·ar·y /ˈmɪʃ(ə)nˌeri/ noun [C] someone who has been sent to a foreign country by a religious organization to teach people about a particular religion

ˈ**mission ˌstatement** noun [C] a short official statement that an organization makes about the work it does and why it does it

mis·spell /mɪsˈspel/ verb [T] to spell a word wrongly —**mis·spell·ing** noun [C/U]

mis·step /mɪsˈstep/ noun [C] *American formal* a mistake caused by bad judgment

mist[1] /mɪst/ noun [C/U] a mass of small drops of water in the air close to the ground → FOG[1]

mist[2] /mɪst/ or ˌ**mist ˈup** verb [I] to become covered with small drops of water

mis·take[1] /mɪˈsteɪk/ noun [C] ★★
1 something that you have not done correctly, or something you say or think that is not correct: *spelling/grammar mistakes*
2 something that you do that you later wish you had not done, because it causes a lot of problems: *You're **making a big mistake**.* ♦ **it would be a mistake to do sth** *It would be a mistake to think that the trouble is over.* ♦ **make the mistake of doing sth** *I made the mistake of inviting Jennifer to the party.*
PHRASE **by mistake** if you do something by mistake, you do it accidentally = BY ACCIDENT ≠ ON PURPOSE: *Oh no – I sent her the wrong letter by mistake.*

Words often used with mistake

Adjectives often used with **mistake** *(noun, sense 2)*

- **bad, big, costly, dreadful, fatal, serious, terrible** + MISTAKE: used about mistakes that have bad results

mis·take² /mɪˈsteɪk/ (past tense **mis·took** /mɪˈstʊk/; past participle **mis·tak·en** /mɪˈsteɪkən/) verb [T] to not understand something correctly: *I'm afraid I mistook the nature of our relationship.*

PHRASAL VERB **miˈstake sb/sth for sb/sth** to think that a person or thing is someone or something else: *I had mistaken friendship for love.*

mis·tak·en /mɪˈsteɪkən/ adj **1** if someone is mistaken, they are wrong about something: *If you think I'm going to help, you're sadly mistaken.* **2** a mistaken belief, idea, opinion, etc. is not correct —**mis·tak·en·ly** adv: *He mistakenly believed that she was married.*

mis·ter /ˈmɪstər/ *American spoken* used for talking to a man whose name you do not know

mis·tle·toe /ˈmɪs(ə)lˌtoʊ/ noun [U] a plant with small white fruits. It is often used as a Christmas decoration.

mis·took the past tense of **mistake**²

mis·treat /mɪsˈtrit/ verb [T] to treat someone in an unfair or cruel way: *She felt she had been mistreated by the police.* —**mis·treat·ment** noun [U]

mis·tress /ˈmɪstrəs/ noun [C] a woman who is having a sexual relationship with a married man

mis·tri·al /mɪsˈtraɪəl/ noun [C] *legal* a trial that was not done correctly and has to be started again

mis·trust /mɪsˈtrʌst/ noun [singular/U] a feeling that you should not trust someone or something: *Many voters have a deep mistrust of the government.* —**mis·trust** verb [T]

mist·y /ˈmɪsti/ adj it is misty when a mass of small drops of water is in the air close to the ground

mis·un·der·stand /ˌmɪsʌndərˈstænd/ (past tense and past participle **mis·un·der·stood** /ˌmɪsʌndərˈstʊd/) verb [I/T] to not understand someone or something correctly: *I think he has misunderstood the nature of the problem.*

mis·un·der·stand·ing /ˌmɪsʌndərˈstændɪŋ/ noun **1** [C/U] a failure to understand someone or something correctly: *There's been a misunderstanding: Mr. Jones didn't expect you until tomorrow.* **2** [C] an argument that is not very serious

mis·un·der·stood¹ /ˌmɪsʌndərˈstʊd/ adj if someone or something is misunderstood, people do not realize what they are really like

mis·un·der·stood² the past tense and past participle of **misunderstand**

mis·use /mɪsˈjus/ noun [C/U] the use of something in the wrong way or for the wrong purpose: *a misuse of government money* —**mis·use** /mɪsˈjuz/ verb [T]

mite /maɪt/ noun [C] a very small insect that lives in foods, on plants, or on animals

mit·i·gate /ˈmɪtɪˌgeɪt/ verb [T] *formal* to reduce the harmful effects of something —**mit·i·ga·tion** /ˌmɪtɪˈgeɪʃ(ə)n/ noun [U]

mit·i·gat·ing /ˈmɪtɪˌgeɪtɪŋ/ adj **mitigating circumstances** facts that help to explain a crime or mistake and make it seem less bad

mitt /mɪt/ noun [C] a baseball GLOVE, used for catching the ball

mit·ten /ˈmɪt(ə)n/ noun [C] a type of GLOVE with one part for your thumb and another part for your fingers —*picture* → C4

mix¹ /mɪks/ verb ★★

1 [I/T] to combine two or more substances so that they become a single substance: *Add the eggs and mix thoroughly.* ♦ **mix sth with sth** *Mix the flour with the eggs and butter.* ♦ **mix sth together** *Mix the paint and water together.* —*picture* → C2

2 [T] to make something by combining two or more substances: *Phil was mixing a cocktail.*

3 [I/T] to combine things such as activities, ideas, or styles: *In this room, antique and modern furniture have been successfully mixed.* ♦ **mix sth with sth** *Their mood was one of relief mixed with sadness.*

4 [I] to meet other people in social situations and talk to them: *The party gave me a chance to* ***mix with*** *the other students.*

PHRASAL VERBS **ˌmix sb ˈup** to think that someone or something is another person or thing: *I think I'm* ***mixing him up with*** *someone else.*

ˌmix sth ˈup to put things together without any order: *I sorted out all the papers and you've mixed them up again.*

mix² /mɪks/ noun **1** [singular] a combination of different types of people or things: *There was a good mix of people at the party.* **2** [C/U] a powder that you buy and mix with liquid to make a particular type of food: *a cake mix*

mixed /mɪkst/ adj ★

1 consisting of different things: *mixed herbs/vegetables/nuts*

2 partly good and partly bad: *Reactions to the new policy have been mixed.* ♦ *mixed reviews of the new movie*

3 involving people of different ages, abilities, races, etc.: *a mixed population* ♦ *students of mixed abilities* ♦ *a mixed marriage*

PHRASE **mixed feelings/emotions** mixed feelings or emotions make you not certain how you feel about someone or something

ˌmixed ˈblessing noun [C] something that has both advantages and disadvantages

ˌmixed-ˈrace adj involving people of different races: *mixed-raced marriage* ♦ *a mixed-race child* (=with parents who are different races)

ˌmixed ˈup adj **1** confused: *I got mixed up with the dates and went on the wrong day.*

2 *informal* someone who is mixed up has a lot of emotional problems

PHRASES **be/get mixed up in sth** *informal* to be or become involved in something bad or embarrassing

be/get mixed up with sb *informal* to spend time with someone who has a bad influence on you

mix·er /ˈmɪksər/ noun [C] a machine that

M

mixes something: *a cement mixer*

mix·ture /ˈmɪkstʃər/ noun ★★
1 [singular] a combination of two or more different people or things: *Her face showed **a mixture of** fear and excitement.* ♦ *a mixture of volunteers and paid staff*
2 [C/U] a substance such as food that is the result of mixing different things: *Spoon the mixture into the cake pans.*

ˈmix-ˌup noun [C] *informal* a mistake or problem that happens because someone is confused about details

ml abbrev milliliter

mm abbrev millimeter

MN abbrev Minnesota

MO abbrev Missouri

moan /moʊn/ verb [I/T] to make a long low sound because of pain, sadness, or pleasure —**moan** noun [C]

moat /moʊt/ noun [C] a deep wide hole filled with water that surrounds a castle

mob[1] /mɑb/ noun [C] **1** a large crowd of people that is dangerous or difficult to control **2 the Mob** *informal* the MAFIA

mob[2] /mɑb/ verb [T] if a large group of people mob someone or something, they surround them in an angry or excited way

mo·bile[1] /ˈmoʊb(ə)l, ˈmoʊˌbaɪl/ adj ★

1 easily moved	4 owning vehicle
2 contained in vehicle	5 changing job/class
3 able to move	

1 easy to move and use in different places: *a mobile X-ray unit*
2 a mobile library, hospital, etc. is in a vehicle so that it can be moved from one place to another
3 able to move and walk: *He has a broken leg and isn't very mobile.*
4 able to travel from one place to another because you have a vehicle
5 able to move easily from one job, social class, or place to another

mo·bile[2] /ˈmoʊˌbaɪl/ noun [C] **1** a decoration with parts that hang down and move in the air **2** *British* a CELLPHONE

ˌmobile ˈhome noun [C] *American* a house built in a factory and moved to a piece of land on a truck

ˌmobile ˈphone noun [C] *British* a CELLPHONE

mo·bil·i·ty /moʊˈbɪləti/ noun [U] **1** the ability to move a part of your body **2** the ability to travel from one place to another **3** the tendency to move between places, jobs, or social classes

mo·bi·lize /ˈmoʊb(ə)ˌlaɪz/ verb [I/T] **1** to bring together a large group of people, or to be brought together, in order to achieve something **2** to prepare an army to fight a war, or to be prepared to do this —**mo·bi·li·za·tion** /ˌmoʊb(ə)lɪˈzeɪʃ(ə)n/ noun [U]

mob·ster /ˈmɑbstə/ noun [C] a member of the MAFIA

mo·cha /ˈmoʊkə/ noun [C/U] a drink made by mixing coffee and chocolate together, or a cup of this drink

mock[1] /mɑk/ verb [I/T] to make someone or something look stupid by laughing at them or copying them

mock[2] /mɑk/ adj **1** not real but intended to look or seem real = FAKE **2** a mock feeling is one that you pretend to have, usually as a joke **3** a mock test, interview, etc. is one that you do in order to practice for a real one

mock·er·y /ˈmɑkəri/ noun [U] remarks or behavior intended to make someone seem stupid
PHRASE **make a mockery of** to make someone or something seem stupid or useless

mock·ing·bird /ˈmɑkɪŋˌbɜrd/ noun [C] a white and gray North American bird that copies the songs of other birds

mock·up /ˈmɑkʌp/ noun [C] a model of something that is the same size as the real thing

ˌmodal ˈverb or **ˌmodal auxˈiliary** or **mod·al** /ˈmoʊd(ə)l/ noun [C] *linguistics* a verb such as "can," "may," "should," etc. that is used with another verb to express ideas such as possibility, permission, or intention

mode /moʊd/ noun [C] **1** a particular way of doing something **2** one of a series of ways that a machine can be made to work → À LA MODE

mod·el[1] /ˈmɑd(ə)l/ noun [C] ★★★

1 small copy of sth	4 good example
2 sb who shows clothes	5 type of vehicle etc.
3 for artist	

1 a small copy of something such as a building, vehicle, or machine: ***a model of** the Golden Gate Bridge*
2 someone whose job is to appear in magazines or FASHION SHOWS wearing clothes or MAKEUP so that people will want to buy them: *a fashion model*
3 someone whose job is to be drawn or painted by an artist or photographed by a photographer
4 someone or something that is such a good example of a particular quality or method that people should copy them: *The school was **a model of** excellence.* ♦ *The system has been used as **a model for** other organizations.*
5 a particular type of vehicle or machine that a company makes: *I'm going to replace my car with a newer model.*

mod·el[2] /ˈmɑd(ə)l/ (present participle **mod·el·ing** or **mod·el·ling**; past tense and past participle **mod·eled** or **mod·elled**) verb **1** [I/T] to show clothes by wearing them at FASHION SHOWS, in magazine photographs, etc., especially as a job **2** [I] to allow an artist or photographer to draw, paint, or photograph you, especially as your job **3** [T] to copy a method or system: *Their economic structure is closely modeled on the Communist system.*
PHRASE **model yourself on/after sb** to copy the way someone behaves because you admire them

mod·el[3] /ˈmɑd(ə)l/ adj **1** a model aircraft, boat, etc. is a small copy of a real one **2** a model student, husband, etc. behaves in the way a perfect student, husband, etc. would behave

mod·el·ing /ˈmɑd(ə)lɪŋ/ noun [U] the job of working as a fashion model

M

mo•dem /ˈmoʊˌdem/ noun [C] *computing* a piece of equipment that allows you to connect a computer to a telephone line

mod•er•ate¹ /ˈmɑd(ə)rət/ adj **1** neither very big nor very small in amount, size, strength, or degree: *Cook the spinach over a moderate heat.* ♦ *a moderate increase in house prices* **2** reasonable and avoiding extreme opinions or actions: *a moderate political party* ♦ *The tone of his speech was quite moderate.* —**mod•er•ate•ly** /ˈmɑd(ə)rətli/ adv

mod•er•ate² /ˈmɑdəˌr(e)ɪt/ verb [I/T] to make something less extreme, or to become less extreme

mod•er•ate³ /ˈmɑdərət/ noun [C] someone whose opinions and actions are reasonable and not extreme, especially in politics

mod•er•a•tion /ˌmɑdəˈreɪʃ(ə)n/ noun [U] sensible behavior, especially behavior that involves not eating or drinking too much of something: *In moderation, red wine is still thought to be good for health.*

mod•ern /ˈmɑdərn/ adj ★★★
1 relating to or belonging to the present time: *the role of women in modern society*
2 using the most recent methods, ideas, designs, or equipment: *We should replace the equipment with something more modern.*
3 using new styles that are very different from the styles of the past = CONTEMPORARY: *The architecture of the hotel is strikingly modern.*

ˈmodern-ˌday adj existing or happening in the present

mo•der•ni•ty /mɑˈdɜrnəti, moʊˈdɜrnəti/ noun [U] ideas and practices that use modern methods, styles, or equipment

mod•ern•ize /ˈmɑdərˌnaɪz/ verb [I/T] to become less old-fashioned, or to make something become less old-fashioned, as a result of new methods, equipment, or ideas —**mod•ern•i•za•tion** /ˌmɑdərnɪˈzeɪʃ(ə)n/ noun [U]

ˌmodern ˈlanguages noun [plural] languages that are still spoken today

mod•est /ˈmɑdəst/ adj ★
1 a modest person does not like to talk about themselves, their achievements, or their abilities, even if they are successful ≠ BOASTFUL: *Petersen is genuinely modest about his achievements.*
2 fairly small in size, degree, or value: *He earned a modest income.* ♦ *She has had some modest success with her short stories.*
3 feeling shy or embarrassed about other people seeing your body
—**mod•est•ly** adv

mod•es•ty /ˈmɑdəsti/ noun [U] **1** the tendency not to talk about yourself, your achievements, or your abilities even if you are successful **2** a feeling of being shy or embarrassed about other people seeing your body

mod•i•cum /ˈmɑdɪkəm/ noun **a modicum of sth** *formal* a small amount of something good

mod•i•fi•ca•tion /ˌmɑdɪfɪˈkeɪʃ(ə)n/ noun *formal* **1** [C/U] a small change to something = ALTERATION **2** [U] the process of changing something slightly

mod•i•fi•er /ˈmɑdɪˌfaɪər/ noun [C] *linguistics* a word or phrase that slightly changes the meaning of another word or phrase by giving more information about it

mod•i•fy /ˈmɑdɪˌfaɪ/ verb **1** [T] *formal* to change something slightly in order to improve it or in order to make it less extreme = ALTER **2** [I/T] *linguistics* to slightly change the meaning of another word or a phrase by giving more information about it

mod•u•lar /ˈmɑdʒələr/ adj modular buildings, furniture, or other structures are made in separate sections that fit together

mod•ule /ˈmɑdʒul/ noun [C] **1** one of several parts that are made separately and then joined together in order to make a building or other structure **2** a part of a space vehicle that is used separately for doing a particular job

mo•gul /ˈmoʊg(ə)l/ noun [C] an important powerful person in a particular activity or industry

mo•hair /ˈmoʊˌher/ noun [U] soft wool made from the hair of a particular type of goat

moist /mɔɪst/ adj slightly wet

mois•ten /ˈmɔɪs(ə)n/ verb [T] to make something slightly wet

mois•ture /ˈmɔɪstʃər/ noun [U] very small drops of water or another liquid in the air, on the surface of something, or in a substance

mois•tur•ize /ˈmɔɪstʃəˌraɪz/ verb [I/T] to make your skin less dry by using moisturizer

mois•tur•iz•er /ˈmɔɪstʃəˌraɪzər/ noun [C/U] a cream that you put on your skin to make it less dry

mo•lar /ˈmoʊlər/ noun [C] one of the large teeth at the back of your mouth that you use for CHEWING food

mo•las•ses /məˈlæsəz/ noun [U] *American* a sweet brown liquid food, used for making other foods sweeter

mold¹ /moʊld/ noun **1** [U] a green, blue, or white substance that grows on food that is not fresh or on things that are not kept clean and dry **2** [C] a container into which you pour a liquid that then becomes solid in the shape of the container

PHRASE **break the mold** to change a situation by doing something that is very different from what people normally do

mold² /moʊld/ verb [T] **1** to give something a particular shape: *Mold the dough into loaves and bake them in a hot oven.* **2** to influence someone so that they will have particular qualities or behave in a particular way: *The coach must mold a group of individual players into a team.*

mold•ing /ˈmoʊldɪŋ/ noun [C] a small decorated area of stone or wood at the edge of a wall or around a door or picture frame

mold•y /ˈmoʊldi/ adj covered with mold: *moldy bread*

mole /moʊl/ noun [C] **1** a dark-brown lump or spot on your skin that is permanent **2** a small animal with dark fur that digs underground and cannot see well —*picture* → C13 **3** *informal* someone who joins or works for an organization in order to give secret information about it to its enemies

mol•e•cule /ˈmɑləˌkjul/ noun [C] a very small group of atoms that form a particular

M

substance —**mo•lec•u•lar** /məˈlekjələr/ adj

mo•lest /məˈlest/ verb [T] to hurt someone, especially a child, by touching them in a sexual way or forcing them to do sexual acts —**mo•lest•er** noun [C]

mol•li•fy /ˈmɑləˌfaɪ/ verb [T] *formal* to make someone feel less angry or upset

mol•lusk /ˈmɑləsk/ noun [C] a type of animal that has a soft body without bones and is usually covered by a hard shell

mol•ly•cod•dle /ˈmɑliˌkɑd(ə)l/ verb [T] to make someone's life too easy by doing too much for them

molt /moʊlt/ verb [I] to lose an old layer of hair, fur, or feathers so that a new layer can replace it

mol•ten /ˈmoʊlt(ə)n/ adj molten rock, metal, or glass has become liquid because it is very hot

mom /mɑm/ noun [C] *American informal* ★★ your mother: *I talk to my mom on the phone every Saturday.* ♦ *Mom, when will dinner be ready?*

mo•ment /ˈmoʊmənt/ noun [C] ★★★
1 a very short period of time: *A moment later Jane had completely disappeared.* ♦ *He paused **for a moment** before giving his answer.*
2 a particular point in time when something happens: ***At that moment** there was a knock on the door.* ♦ *Ellie had never really given it much thought **until that moment**.* ♦ *This is the proudest **moment of** my career.*
3 a short period of time when you have the opportunity to do something: *I saw he was alone and **seized the moment**.* ♦ *As he stood up, James knew **his big moment** had arrived.*

PHRASES **any moment (now)** *formal* very soon: *They should be here any moment now.*
at the moment now: *They're very upset and don't want to talk at the moment.*
for the moment at the present time, but possibly not in the future: *I thought it was best to say nothing about it for the moment.*
have its/your moments 1 to have some good periods or parts: *Although the movie has its moments, it's not really worth seeing.* **2** to sometimes have problems or cause trouble
in a moment *formal* used for telling someone that you will do something very soon: *"Come and see this." "In a moment."*
just/wait a moment *formal* **1** used for telling someone that you will do something very soon: *"Can you give me a hand?" "Just a moment."* **2** used for asking someone to give you their attention for a short time: *Just a moment, I want to ask you something.*
the moment (that) *formal* as soon as: *The moment he said that, everything became clear to me.*
→ FOR, HEAT[1]

mo•men•tar•i•ly /ˌmoʊmənˈterəli/ adv **1** for a moment **2** *American* very soon

mo•men•tar•y /ˈmoʊmənˌteri/ adj lasting for only a very short time

mo•men•tous /moʊˈmentəs/ adj very important because of having an effect on future events

mo•men•tum /moʊˈmentəm/ noun [U]
1 progress or development that is becoming faster or stronger **2** the speed with which a moving object keeps moving or moves faster

mom•my /ˈmɑmi/ noun [C] *American informal* a word for mother, used especially by young children: *I love my mommy.* ♦ *Mommy, I want to go home.*

Mon. abbrev Monday

mon•arch /ˈmɑnərk/ noun [C] a king or queen

mon•ar•chy /ˈmɑnərki/ noun **1** [C/U] a system of government in which a country is ruled by a king or queen **2** [C] a country that is ruled by a king or queen

mon•as•ter•y /ˈmɑnəˌsteri/ noun [C] a building where a group of MONKS (=religious men) lives and works

mo•nas•tic /məˈnæstɪk/ adj relating to MONKS or MONASTERIES

Mon•day /ˈmʌnˌdeɪ/ noun [C/U] ★★★ the day after Sunday and before Tuesday: *This year's Oscar ceremony will be on a Monday.* ♦ *You can start work next Monday.* ♦ *He goes swimming Mondays* (=every Monday). ♦ *Let's meet for lunch **on Monday**.*

mon•e•tar•y /ˈmʌnəˌteri/ adj relating to money

mon•ey /ˈmʌni/ noun [U] ★★★ the coins and pieces of paper that you earn, save, invest, and use for paying for things: *I don't have any money.* ♦ *We've **spent a lot of money on** this house.* ♦ *It would have **cost us a lot of money** to cancel the event.* ♦ *I have had to **borrow money from** my family.* ♦ *The business has **made** more **money** this year.* ♦ *You can **save money*** (=avoid spending it) *by taking your own lunch.* ♦ *They're trying to **save money*** (=keep it so that they can spend it later) *so that they can go to Florida this winter.* ♦ ***Have you got any money on you*** (=in your pocket/bag)?

PHRASES **get your money's worth** to feel that something that you have is worth the amount that you paid for it: *Get there early to make sure you get your money's worth.*
put money on sth *informal* to BET on something so that you will win money if you are right, but will lose it if you are wrong
throw money at sth to try to solve a problem by spending money on it instead of thinking of more practical ways to deal with it
→ POCKET MONEY, ROLL[1]

ˈmoney ˌmarket noun [C] *business* business activities in which banks and other financial institutions lend money to other organizations in order to make more money

ˈmoney ˌorder noun [C] an official document that you buy in a POST OFFICE as a safe way of sending money to someone

mon•grel /ˈmʌŋgrəl/ noun [C] a dog that is a mixture of different BREEDS (=types with particular features)

mon•i•tor[1] /ˈmɑnɪtər/ verb [T] ★ to regularly check something or watch someone in order to find out what is happening: *a special machine to monitor the baby's breathing* ♦ *Staff will **monitor his progress**.*

mon•i•tor[2] /ˈmɑnɪtər/ noun [C] **1** a screen that shows pictures or information, especially on a computer, or the piece of equipment that contains the screen —*picture* → C3 **2** a piece of equipment that shows and records

M

what is happening in a particular part of someone's body **3** someone who checks to see that something is done fairly or correctly

monk /mʌŋk/ noun [C] a man who lives in a religious community away from other people → NUN

mon•key /ˈmʌŋki/ noun [C] an animal with a long tail that climbs trees and uses its hands in the same way that people do —*picture* → C12

ˈmonkey ˌbusiness noun [U] *informal* dishonest or bad behavior

ˈmonkey ˌwrench noun [C] a WRENCH that you use for turning NUTS of different sizes

mon•o /ˈmɑnoʊ/ noun [U] *American informal* MONONUCLEOSIS

mon•o•chrome /ˈmɑnəˌkroʊm/ adj able to show or produce only black, white, and gray

mo•nog•a•mous /məˈnɑgəməs/ adj having only one husband, wife, or sexual relationship at a time

mo•nog•a•my /məˈnɑgəmi/ noun [U] the practice of having only one husband, wife, or sexual relationship at a time → BIGAMY

mon•o•gram /ˈmɑnəˌgræm/ noun [C] a design using the first letter of each of someone's names —**mon•o•grammed** /ˈmɑnəˌgræmd/ adj

mon•o•lin•gual /ˌmɑnoʊˈlɪŋgwəl/ adj speaking, writing, or using only one language → BILINGUAL

mon•o•lith /ˈmɑnəˌlɪθ/ noun [C] **1** a very large piece of stone standing on one end that was put in position in ancient times **2** a large and extremely powerful organization or system that is not willing to change

mon•o•lith•ic /ˌmɑnəˈlɪθɪk/ adj a monolithic organization or system is large, extremely powerful, and not willing to change

mon•o•logue /ˈmɑnəˌlɑg/ noun [C] **1** a speech made by someone who talks for a long time and does not let anyone else say anything **2** a long speech made by someone in a play or movie

mon•o•nu•cle•o•sis /ˌmɑnoʊˌnukliˈoʊsɪs/ noun [U] *American medical* a disease that makes you feel very tired for several weeks or months

mo•nop•o•lize /məˈnɑpəˌlaɪz/ verb [T] to control something completely and prevent other people or organizations from being involved in it or using it

mo•nop•o•ly /məˈnɑpəli/ noun **1** [C/U] complete control over something by one organization or person **2** [C] a company that has complete control of the product or service it provides because it is the only company that provides it **3** [singular] something that only one person or group of people has

mon•o•rail /ˈmɑnəˌreɪl/ noun [C] a railroad system in which trains travel on a single metal track, or a train on this system

mon•o•syl•lab•ic /ˌmɑnəsɪˈlæbɪk/ adj using very few short words

mon•o•syl•la•ble /ˈmɑnəˌsɪləb(ə)l/ noun [C] *linguistics* a short word with only one SYLLABLE

mon•o•tone /ˈmɑnəˌtoʊn/ noun [singular] a way of talking that is boring because the sound of your voice does not change

mo•not•o•nous /məˈnɑt(ə)nəs/ adj **1** a monotonous sound or voice is boring because it does not change **2** a monotonous job is boring because you have to keep repeating the same activity —**mo•not•o•nous•ly** adv

mo•not•o•ny /məˈnɑt(ə)ni/ noun [U] the fact that something never changes, so that it is boring

mon•soon /mɑnˈsun/ noun [C] a period of heavy rain in India and Southeast Asia

mon•ster[1] /ˈmɑnstər/ noun [C] **1** an imaginary creature that is large, ugly, and frightening **2** something that is very large **3** someone who is very cruel

mon•ster[2] /ˈmɑnstər/ adj *informal* very large

mon•stros•i•ty /mɑnˈstrɑsəti/ noun [C] something that is very large and ugly

mon•strous /ˈmɑnstrəs/ adj **1** cruel, unfair, or morally wrong **2** very large and ugly or frightening —**mon•strous•ly** adv

month /mʌnθ/ noun ★★★

1 [C] one of the 12 periods that a year is divided into, for example January or February: *They hope to finish by **the end of the month**. ♦ A man was arrested **last month** in connection with the robbery. ♦ I give my daughter **$50 a month*** (=each month).

2 [C] a period of about four weeks: *I'll be leaving a month from today. ♦ a three-month-old baby*

3 months [plural] a long time: *It'll take months to finish the work on the house.*

month•ly[1] /ˈmʌnθli/ adj happening or published once a month —**month•ly** adv

month•ly[2] /ˈmʌnθli/ noun [C] a magazine that is published once a month

mon•u•ment /ˈmɑnjəmənt/ noun [C] **1** a structure that is built in a public place in order to celebrate an important person or event **2** a place of historical importance

PHRASE **a monument to sth** something that reminds people of something

mon•u•men•tal /ˌmɑnjəˈment(ə)l/ adj very great in size, degree, or importance

mon•u•men•tal•ly /ˌmɑnjəˈment(ə)li/ adv extremely

moo /mu/ verb [I] to make the long deep sound that a cow makes —**moo** noun [C]

mood /mud/ noun ★★

1 [C/U] the way that someone is feeling, or the way that a group of people is feeling at a particular time: *Politicians have to be in touch with the public mood. ♦ I had never seen Ann **in such a good mood** before. ♦ Jeff's been **in a bad mood** all day. ♦ **a mood of optimism***

2 [C] a period when you feel unhappy or angry: *She refused to put up with her husband's moods. ♦ Just leave her on her own when she's **in a mood**.*

3 [C/U] a quality that something such as a place, movie, or piece of music has that makes you have a particular feeling: *a collection of stories that vary in mood and style ♦ Lighting was particularly important in **setting the mood of** the play.*

4 [C] *linguistics* a group of verb forms that are used to show whether, for example, a sentence is a statement, question, or order

M

PHRASES **be in the mood (for sth)** to want to do something: *I'm in the mood for dancing.* **be in no mood for sth/to do sth** to really not want to do something: *Dad was in no mood for joking.*

mood·y /ˈmudi/ adj likely to become unhappy or angry for no particular reason

moon /mun/ noun ★★
1 the Moon or **the moon** the object similar to a planet that goes around the Earth and that you can see shining in the sky at night: *The moon was shining brightly.*
2 [C] an object similar to a planet that goes around another planet: *How many moons does Jupiter have?*
PHRASE **once in a blue moon** used for emphasizing that something does not happen very often: *We only go out once in a blue moon.*

moon·beam /ˈmunˌbim/ noun [C] a RAY (=thin line) of light from the moon

moon·light /ˈmunˌlaɪt/ noun [U] light from the moon

moon·light·ing /ˈmunˌlaɪtɪŋ/ noun [U] *informal* the activity of working at a second job in the evenings or on weekends

moon·lit /ˈmunˌlɪt/ adj provided with light from the moon

moor /mʊr/ verb [I/T] to stop a ship or boat from moving by fastening it to a place with ropes or chains, or by using an ANCHOR

moor·ing /ˈmʊrɪŋ/ noun **1 moorings** [plural] ropes, chains, or ANCHORS that you use to moor a ship or boat **2** [C] a place where a ship or boat is moored with ropes, chains, or ANCHORS

moose /mus/ (plural **moose**) noun [C] a large DEER that lives in North America, northern Europe, and Asia

moot /mut/ adj a moot point, question, or issue is one that people disagree about

mop¹ /mɑp/ noun [C] an object that has a long handle and is used for washing floors

mop² /mɑp/ verb **1** [I/T] to wash a floor using a mop **2** [T] to wipe SWEAT from your face with a cloth when you are very hot or sick **3** [T] to clean liquid or dirt from a surface using a mop, cloth, or something soft
PHRASAL VERB **ˌmop sth ˈup** *same as* **mop²** 3

mope /moʊp/ verb [I] to feel bored or unhappy and show no interest in doing anything
PHRASAL VERB **ˌmope aˈround** to spend time somewhere with no particular purpose, feeling bored or unhappy

mo·ped /ˈmoʊˌped/ noun [C] a type of MOTORCYCLE with an engine that is not powerful and PEDALS like a bicycle

mor·al¹ /ˈmɔrəl/ adj ★
1 relating to right and wrong and the way that people should behave: *moral standards/principles/values* ♦ *our children's religious and moral education*
2 a moral person always tries to behave in the right way
—**mor·al·ly** adv

mor·al² /ˈmɔrəl/ noun **1 morals** [plural] principles of right or wrong behavior that are generally accepted by a society: *He's shown that he has no morals at all.*
2 [singular] something that you can learn from a story or an experience

mo·rale /məˈrɑl/ noun [U] the amount of enthusiasm that someone feels about the situation that they are in

mor·al·is·tic /ˌmɔrəˈlɪstɪk/ adj *showing disapproval* expressing firm opinions about what is right or wrong

mo·ral·i·ty /məˈræləti/ noun [U] **1** principles of right or wrong behavior: *standards of morality* **2** the degree to which something is thought to be right or wrong: *the continuing debate about the morality of abortion*

mor·al·ize /ˈmɔrəˌlaɪz/ verb [I] *showing disapproval* to tell people how they should behave and what is right and what is wrong

ˌmoral supˈport noun [U] if you give someone moral support, you try to make them more confident

mor·a·to·ri·um /ˌmɔrəˈtɔriəm/ noun [C] an official agreement to stop an activity for a short time

mor·bid /ˈmɔrbɪd/ adj interested in subjects such as death that most people think are unpleasant

more /mɔr/ grammar word ★★★

> **More** is the comparative form of **much** and **many**. It can be:
> - a **determiner**: *He wants to spend more time with his family.*
> - a **pronoun**: *I wish I could do more to help.* ♦ *I'm not going to listen to any more of your lies.*
> - an **adverb**: *The stereos are more expensive in Japan than they are here.* ♦ *I'd like to travel more.*
> - used after numbers or expressions of quantity: *You'll have to wait a few more minutes.*

1 a larger amount or number ≠ LESS: *No matter what her brother gets, she always wants more.* ♦ *Ken already earns* ***more than*** *his father ever did.* ♦ *The merger has created* ***far more*** *problems than it has solved.* ♦ *People in the U.S. are spending* ***more than ever*** *on health and fitness.*
2 to a greater degree ≠ LESS: *The region has become more prosperous in recent years.* ♦ *The storm was* ***more*** *violent* ***than*** *we expected.* ♦ *Beth is obviously* ***a lot more*** *intelligent than the other girls.* ♦ *Could you speak* ***a little more*** *slowly?*

> - **More** is used to form the comparative with adjectives and adverbs with three or more syllables, such as "important," and many adjectives and adverbs with two syllables, such as "often."
> - Adjectives and adverbs with only one syllable form the comparative by adding **-er**, and not with **more**.

3 happening or doing something a greater number of times, for longer periods, or to a greater degree: *You should get out more and meet other people.* ♦ *Rural life has changed* ***more*** *in the last 40 years* ***than*** *at any other time.*
4 an additional amount or number ≠ LESS: *If you need more paper, there's some in the drawer.* ♦ *We'll have to wait for two more days.* ♦ *That's all I know. I can't tell you* ***any more.*** ♦ *I'm not wasting* ***any more of*** *my money on lottery tickets.* ♦ *There are* ***no more*** *eggs.*

PHRASES **more and more** used for saying that something is increasing in number or degree all the time: *More and more people are choosing to spend their vacations abroad.* ♦ *As the situation grew steadily worse, he became more and more depressed.*
the more...the more/less used for saying that when a particular activity, feeling, etc. increases, it causes something else to change at the same time: *The more I thought about Carrie's suggestion, the more doubtful I became.*
more or less almost: *The team is more or less the same as it was last season.*
→ OFTEN, ONCE, WHAT

more•o•ver /mɔrˈoʊvər/ adv *formal* used for introducing an additional important fact that supports or emphasizes what you have just said: *There is growing opposition to capital punishment. Moreover, there is now evidence that many executed prisoners were innocent.*

morgue /mɔrg/ noun [C] a building or room where dead bodies are kept for a short time

morn•ing[1] /ˈmɔrnɪŋ/ noun [C/U] ★★★
1 the part of the day from when the sun rises until noon: *What time did you get up this morning?* ♦ *Call me at my office Monday morning.* ♦ *We spent the morning walking in the park.* ♦ *Let's talk about this **in the morning*** (=during the morning of the next day).
2 the part of the day between midnight and noon: *The phone woke me up at 2 o'clock in the morning.* ♦ *I was working until **the early hours of the morning**.*

morn•ing[2] /ˈmɔrnɪŋ/ interjection *informal* used for saying hello to someone in the morning

mo•ron /ˈmɔˌrɑn/ noun [C] *offensive* an insulting word for someone who behaves in a stupid way

mo•rose /məˈroʊs/ adj unhappy and unfriendly —**mo•rose•ly** adv

mor•phine /ˈmɔrˌfin/ noun [U] a powerful drug that is used for reducing pain

mor•sel /ˈmɔrs(ə)l/ noun [C] **1** *formal* a small piece of food **2** a small amount of something

mor•tal[1] /ˈmɔrt(ə)l/ adj **1** human and not able to live for ever ≠ IMMORTAL **2** serious enough to cause death **3** used for emphasizing that a particular feeling is extremely strong: *people living in mortal fear*

mor•tal[2] /ˈmɔrt(ə)l/ noun [C] a normal person, as opposed to a god or people who are thought to be very important

mor•tal•i•ty /mɔrˈtæləti/ noun [U] **1** the number of deaths in a particular area or group of people **2** the fact that your life will end

mor•tal•ly /ˈmɔrt(ə)li/ adv in a way that is likely to cause death: *mortally wounded/injured*

mor•tar /ˈmɔrtər/ noun **1** [U] a substance that is used in building for joining bricks **2** [C] a large gun that soldiers use for firing bombs over short distances

mort•gage[1] /ˈmɔrgɪdʒ/ noun [C] money that you borrow from a bank and use to buy a house

mort•gage[2] /ˈmɔrgɪdʒ/ verb [T] if you mortgage property, you borrow money from a bank and agree to give the property to the bank if you do not pay back the money

mor•ti•cian /mɔrˈtɪʃ(ə)n/ noun [C] *American formal* someone whose job is to arrange funerals and prepare dead bodies for being buried

mor•ti•fied /ˈmɔrtəˌfaɪd/ adj feeling extremely embarrassed or ashamed —**mor•ti•fy** verb [T]

mor•tu•ar•y /ˈmɔrtʃuˌeri/ noun [C] *American* a place where a dead body is kept and prepared for a funeral

mo•sa•ic /moʊˈzeɪɪk/ noun [C] a pattern made of small pieces of colored stone or glass

mosque /mɑsk/ noun [C] a building in which Muslims worship

mos•qui•to /məˈskitoʊ/ (plural **mos•qui•tos** or **mos•qui•toes**) noun [C] a small flying insect that bites people and can give them diseases —*picture* → C13

moss /mɔs/ noun [U] a soft green or brown plant that grows in a layer on wet ground, rocks, or trees —**mos•sy** adj

most /moʊst/ grammar word ★★★

> **Most** is the superlative form of **much** and **many**. It can be:
> - an **adverb**: *Love is what these children need most.* ♦ *Angie looks the most like her father.*
> - a **determiner**: *Most stores will be closed on Christmas.* ♦ *Which athlete won the most medals?*
> - a **pronoun**: *All the victims were male, and most were between the ages of 15 and 25.* ♦ *Most of my friends live in this area.*

1 the largest part of something, or the majority of people or things ≠ LEAST: *Most people think of robots as machines that look like people.* ♦ *A few of the moths are gray, but most are white.* ♦ *Johnson spent **most of** his life in the South.* ♦ ***Most of the time** we sit around playing cards.*
2 to a greater degree than anyone or anything else ≠ LEAST: *Zurich is Switzerland's most important city.* ♦ *Who do you think is most likely to win the next presidential election?* ♦ The English Patient *was one of **the most** successful movies ever made.*

> - **Most** is used to form the superlative with adjectives and adverbs with three or more syllables, such as "important," and many adjectives and adverbs with two syllables, such as "often."
> - Adjectives and adverbs with only one syllable form the comparative by adding **-est**, and not with **most**.

3 a larger amount or number than any other: *Those who earn most pay most tax.* ♦ *We chose the option that would help **the most** people.*
4 happening or doing something more often or to a greater degree than anyone or anything else ≠ LEAST: *Of the three boys, Eric had changed **the most**.* ♦ *What I want **most of all** is to spend more time with my little girl.*
PHRASES **at (the) most** used for showing that you are mentioning the largest

M

possible amount and that the real amount may be less: *The whole process will take half an hour at the most.*
for the most part used for saying that something is mainly true but not completely true: *For the most part we were happy to live alongside each other.*

most·ly /ˈmoʊs(t)li/ adv ★★
1 most of the time, or in most situations: *We mostly listen to rock music.* ♦ *Mostly, he avoids arguments.*
2 used for saying what the largest part of something consists of: *a group of reporters, mostly American* ♦ *The group is made up mostly of local businesspeople.*
3 used for emphasizing the main reason or purpose of something = MAINLY: *People work mostly because they need the money.* ♦ *This machine was used mostly for agricultural work.*

mo·tel /moʊˈtel/ noun [C] a hotel for people who are traveling by car

moth /mɔθ/ noun [C] a flying insect that flies mainly at night —*picture* → C13

moth·er¹ /ˈmʌðər/ noun [C] ★★★ your female parent: *My mother and father live in New Orleans.* —*picture* → FAMILY TREE

moth·er² /ˈmʌðər/ verb [T] to give someone a lot of care and protection

moth·er·board /ˈmʌðərˌbɔrd/ noun [C] *computing* the main CIRCUIT BOARD in a computer

moth·er·hood /ˈmʌðərˌhʊd/ noun [U] the state of being a mother

ˈmother-in-ˌlaw (plural **ˈmothers-in-ˌlaw**) noun [C] the mother of your husband or wife —*picture* → FAMILY TREE

moth·er·ly /ˈmʌðərli/ adj kind, like a good mother

ˌMother ˈNature nature, or natural forces

ˌmother-of-pearl noun [U] the shiny layer inside some shells that is used for making jewelry

ˈMother's ˌDay noun [C/U] a day when people give cards and presents to their mothers to show their love

ˈmother ˌtongue noun [C] the first language that you learn to speak

mo·tif /moʊˈtif/ noun [C] **1** a shape that is repeated in a design **2** an idea or subject that is frequently repeated in a piece of literature or art

mo·tion¹ /ˈmoʊʃ(ə)n/ noun ★★
1 [U] the process or action of moving: *He studied **the motion of the planets**.* ♦ *photographs of animals **in motion***
2 [C] a movement that someone or something makes: *Rub the horse's coat with a circular motion.*
3 [C] a suggestion that you make at a formal meeting: *propose a motion* (=suggest something for discussion)
PHRASES **go through the motions** to do something without any interest or enthusiasm
in motion if something is in motion, it has already started to happen

mo·tion² /ˈmoʊʃ(ə)n/ verb [I] to move your hand in a particular direction, for example in order to point to something: *He motioned for the waiter to bring the check.*

mo·tion·less /ˈmoʊʃ(ə)nləs/ adj not moving at all = STILL

ˈmotion ˌpicture noun [C] *American* a movie that is made to be shown in theaters

ˈmotion ˌsickness noun [U] *American* a feeling of being sick while traveling in a car, airplane, train, etc.

mo·ti·vate /ˈmoʊtɪˌveɪt/ verb [T] **1** to make someone behave in a particular way: *The crime appears to have been motivated by hatred.* **2** to make someone feel enthusiastic about doing something or determined to do something: *We must motivate students to take charge of their own learning.*
—**mo·ti·va·tor** noun [C]

mo·ti·vat·ed /ˈmoʊtɪˌveɪtəd/ adj
1 enthusiastic about doing something or determined to do something: *highly motivated teachers* **2** caused by a particular belief or emotion: *a racially motivated crime*

mo·ti·va·tion /ˌmoʊtɪˈveɪʃ(ə)n/ noun **1** [U] a feeling of enthusiasm about something, or a feeling of determination to do something: *Some of the students lack motivation.* **2** [C] a reason for doing something: *Our real motivation is to make a profit.*
—**mo·ti·va·tion·al** adj

mo·tive /ˈmoʊtɪv/ noun [C] ★ a reason for doing something: ***The motive for the attack** is still unknown.*

mot·ley /ˈmɑtli/ adj consisting of many different types of people or things that do not seem to belong together

mo·tor¹ /ˈmoʊtər/ noun [C] ★★ the part of a machine or vehicle that makes it work: *The pump is powered by an electric motor.*

mo·tor² /ˈmoʊtər/ adj operated by a motor

mo·tor·boat /ˈmoʊtərˌboʊt/ noun [C] a small boat that has an engine

mo·tor·cade /ˈmoʊtərˌkeɪd/ noun [C] a group of cars that includes a car that an important person is traveling in

mo·tor·cy·cle /ˈmoʊtərˌsaɪk(ə)l/ noun [C] a road vehicle that has two wheels and an engine and looks like a large heavy bicycle

mo·tor·ist /ˈmoʊtərɪst/ noun [C] someone who drives a car

mo·tor·ized /ˈmoʊtəˌraɪzd/ adj something that is motorized has a motor that makes it move

ˌmotor ˈneuron disˌease noun [U] a serious illness in which the part of a person's NERVOUS SYSTEM that controls movement is gradually destroyed

ˈmotor ˌvehicle noun [C] *formal* a road vehicle that has an engine

mo·tor·way /ˈmoʊtərˌweɪ/ noun [C] *British* a large HIGHWAY

mot·tled /ˈmɑt(ə)ld/ adj covered with areas of light and dark colors

mot·to /ˈmɑtoʊ/ (plural **mot·tos** or **mot·toes**) noun [C] a short statement that expresses a principle or goal

mould /moʊld/ the British spelling of **mold**[1]

mould·y /ˈmoʊldi/ the British spelling of **moldy**

mound /maʊnd/ noun [C] **1** a pile of something such as earth or stones **2** a large amount of something in a pile: *a mound of papers* **3** the small hill where the PITCHER stands to throw the ball in baseball —*picture* → C15

mount¹ /maʊnt/ verb ★

1 increase	4 get on horse
2 prepare for and begin	5 climb up
3 put sth in position	+ PHRASAL VERB

1 [I] if a particular feeling mounts, it gets stronger: ***Tension continues to mount** between the two parties.*
2 [T] to prepare and begin an activity: *We are **mounting a campaign** to recruit more volunteers.* ♦ *Government forces have **mounted an attack** on a rebel base.*
3 [T] to put something in a fixed position: *A machine gun was mounted on the roof.* ♦ *Each photograph is mounted on cardboard.*
4 [T] to get on a horse
5 [T] *formal* to go up stairs, or to climb up somewhere

PHRASAL VERB ˌ**mount 'up** to increase a lot: *The costs are beginning to mount up.*

mount² /maʊnt/ noun [C] a base that something is fixed to

Mount /maʊnt/ a word used in the names of mountains: *Mount Everest*

moun·tain /ˈmaʊnt(ə)n/ noun [C] ★★★
1 a very high hill: *They went walking and climbing in the mountains.* ♦ *There was still snow on the mountain tops.*
2 a large pile or amount of something: ***a mountain of** paperwork*

PHRASE **make a mountain out of a molehill** to treat a minor problem as if it were a very serious problem

ˈ**mountain ˌbike** noun [C] a strong bicycle with wide tires, used on rough ground

moun·tain·eer /ˌmaʊnt(ə)nˈɪr/ noun [C] someone who climbs mountains

moun·tain·eer·ing /ˌmaʊnt(ə)nˈɪrɪŋ/ noun [U] the activity of climbing mountains

moun·tain·ous /ˈmaʊnt(ə)nəs/ adj covered with mountains

mount·ed /ˈmaʊntəd/ adj riding on a horse: *mounted police*

mount·ing /ˈmaʊntɪŋ/ adj becoming stronger, greater, or worse: *mounting anger/costs/debts*

mourn /mɔrn/ verb [I/T] **1** to feel extremely sad because someone has died **2** to be sad because something no longer exists

mourn·er /ˈmɔrnər/ noun [C] someone who is at a funeral

mourn·ful /ˈmɔrnfəl/ adj feeling sad, or expressing sadness

mourn·ing /ˈmɔrnɪŋ/ noun [U] **1** expressions of sadness because someone has died **2** *old-fashioned* black clothes that people wear when someone has died

mouse /maʊs/ (plural **mice** /maɪs/) noun [C] ★★
1 a small furry animal with a long tail —*picture* → C13
2 (plural **mouses** or **mice**) a small object connected to a computer that you move in order to do things on the computer screen: *Click on the left mouse button.* —*picture* → C3

ˈ**mouse ˌpad** noun [C] *computing* a piece of soft material that you put under a computer MOUSE so that it can move smoothly —*picture* → C3

mousse /mus/ noun [U] **1** a cold sweet food made with cream, eggs, and fruit or chocolate **2** a white substance that you put in your hair in order to hold it in a particular style

mous·tache /ˈmʌˌstæʃ/ another spelling of **mustache**

mous·y /ˈmaʊsi/ adj **1** mousy hair is a dull pale brown color **2** a mousy person is quiet and prefers not to be noticed

mouth¹ /maʊθ/ (plural **mouths** /maʊðz/) noun [C] ★★★
1 the part of your face that you use when you eat or speak: *She opened her mouth to speak.* ♦ *I have a funny taste in my mouth.* —*picture* → C14
2 the place where a river is widest and joins the ocean
3 the entrance to a tunnel or CAVE

PHRASES **big mouth** used as a criticism of someone when they say things they should not say: *You should have kept your big mouth shut.*
open your mouth to speak: *She didn't open her mouth once during the meeting.*

mouth² /maʊð/ verb [T] **1** to form words with your mouth but not make any sound **2** to say something without really meaning or understanding what you say

PHRASAL VERB ˌ**mouth 'off** *informal* to give your opinions about something in an annoying way

mouth·ful /ˈmaʊθfʊl/ noun [C] **1** an amount of food or drink that you put in your mouth at one time **2** *informal* a word or phrase that is very long or is hard to pronounce

mouth·piece /ˈmaʊθˌpis/ noun [C] the part of something that you put in or near your mouth

mouth·wash /ˈmaʊθˌwɔʃ/ noun [C/U] a liquid that you use for cleaning your mouth

mouth·wa·ter·ing /ˈmaʊθˌwɔtərɪŋ/ adj mouthwatering food smells or looks very good

mov·a·ble /ˈmuvəb(ə)l/ adj able to be moved easily

move¹ /muv/ verb ★★★

1 change position	4 do sth
2 progress/change	5 affect sb emotionally
3 live in a different place	+ PHRASAL VERBS

1 [I/T] to change position, or to make someone or something change position: *Could you help me move the bookcase away from the wall?* ♦ *The traffic was barely moving.* ♦ *She moved quickly toward the door.*
2 [I] to progress or change in a particular way: *Events were moving rapidly.* ♦ *The country has only recently begun **moving toward** democracy.* ♦ *We need to **move to** the next item on the agenda.*
3 [I] to begin to live in a different house or area: *We're moving next week.* ♦ *They moved to Oakland in May.*
4 [I] to do something in order to achieve a goal or solve a problem: *The police moved swiftly to prevent a riot.*
5 [T] to make someone feel sad or sympathetic: *You can't fail to be moved by the plight of these people.* ♦ *Her songs can **move me to tears**.*

M

PHRASAL VERBS ˌ**move ˈin 1** to start living in a different house: *We're moving in next week.* **2** to start living in the same place as someone else: *He's **moving in with** his friends from college.*

ˌ**move ˈinto sth 1** to start living or working in a place: *We're moving into an office in the new building downtown.* **2** to begin a new business or a new type of business: *They're planning to move into publishing.*

ˌ**move ˈon 1** to leave one place and travel to another: *They stay for only a few days before moving on.* **2** to stop doing one thing and begin doing another thing: *Let's **move on to** the next question.* **3** to have a new opinion or way of behaving that is better than the old one: *Public opinion has moved on a great deal since then.*

ˌ**move ˈout** to leave your house and start to live somewhere else

ˌ**move ˈover** to change your position in order to make space for someone or something else: *She moved over to let me pass.*

ˌ**move ˈup** *humorous* **move up in the world** to improve your social status, for example by getting a better job

ˌ**move (sb) ˈup** to go to a better job or position, or to put someone in a better job or position: *He's been moved up to the position of manager.*

M

move² /muv/ noun [C] ★★★

1 something that you do in order to achieve a goal or solve a problem: *Getting rid of the tax would be a welcome move.* ♦ *She's going to have to plan her next move carefully.*

2 a change in an activity or situation: *an upward move in the value of the company* ♦ *The new law is a **move toward** equality.* ♦ *He's considering a **move into** politics.*

3 a change in the place where you live or work: *We're considering a move to the city.*

PHRASES **get a move on** *spoken* used for telling someone to hurry

on the move 1 traveling from one place to other places **2** *informal* developing or progressing quickly: *It's an industry on the move.* **3** *informal* busy or active all the time: *He's always on the move.*

→ FIRST

move·a·ble /ˈmuvəb(ə)l/ another spelling of movable

move·ment /ˈmuvmənt/ noun ★★★

1 group with same goal	4 change of place
2 way of moving	5 sb's activities
3 change in situation	6 part of classical music

1 [C] a group of people who work together in order to achieve a particular goal: *the peace movement* → LABOR MOVEMENT

2 [C/U] a way of moving your body, or the ability to move your body: *rhythmic movements* ♦ *The injury has severely restricted movement in his right arm.*

3 [C/U] change or progress in a situation: *There has been little movement in the peace talks.*

4 [C/U] the process of moving something from one place to another: *The agreement governs the free movement of goods between countries.*

5 movements [plural] someone's activities over a period of time: *Their job is to monitor the movements of suspected terrorists.*

6 [C] one of the main parts of a SYMPHONY

mov·er /ˈmuvər/ noun [C] a person or company whose job is to move people's possessions from one house to another

mov·ie /ˈmuvi/ noun [C] ★★ a story in the form of moving pictures on a screen in a theater or on television

mov·ie·go·er /ˈmuviˌgoʊr/ noun [C] *American* someone who often goes to theaters to see movies

mov·ies, the /ˈmuviz/ noun [plural] **1** movies as a form of entertainment **2** the industry involved in making movies

ˈ**movie ˌstar** noun [C] a famous or popular movie actor

ˈ**movie ˌtheater** noun [C] *American* a building in which movies are shown

mov·ing /ˈmuvɪŋ/ adj **1** making you feel sad or sympathetic **2** a moving object is something that moves: *He was pushed from a moving train.* ♦ *the moving parts of a machine* —**mov·ing·ly** /ˈmuvɪŋli/ adv

mow /moʊ/ (past tense **mowed** /moʊd/; past participle **mown** /moʊn/ or **mowed**) verb [T] to cut grass using a machine with blades

PHRASAL VERB ˌ**mow sb ˈdown** *informal* to kill a person or a crowd of people quickly and violently

mow·er /ˈmoʊr/ noun [C] a machine that is used for cutting grass = LAWN MOWER

MP /ˌem ˈpi/ noun [C] **1** a member of the MILITARY POLICE **2** Member of Parliament: a politician who represents people in a PARLIAMENT

MP3 /ˌem pi ˈθri/ noun [C/U] *computing* a computer program that is used for sending music by e-mail

mpg abbrev miles per gallon: the distance in miles that a vehicle can travel using one GALLON of gas

mph /ˌem pi ˈeɪtʃ/ abbrev miles per hour: a unit for measuring the speed at which a vehicle is traveling

Mr. /ˈmɪstər/ ★★★ a polite or formal title used in front of a man's name: *Mr. Jones* ♦ *Mr. Samuel R. Smith*

MRI /ˌem ɑr ˈaɪ/ noun [C/U] magnetic resonance imaging: a medical test that produces images of the organs inside your body

ˌ**Mr. ˈRight** *informal* a man who would be a perfect partner in a relationship

Mrs. /ˈmɪsɪz/ ★★★ a polite or formal title used in front of the name of a married woman: *Mrs. Grace Talbot* ♦ *Good morning, Mrs. Adams.*

MS¹ /ˌem ˈes/ noun [U] MULTIPLE SCLEROSIS

MS² abbrev Mississippi

Ms. /mɪz/ ★★★ a polite or formal title used in front of the name of a woman, whether she is married or not: *Ms. Gloria Johnson* ♦ *Can I help you, Ms. Jones?*

Words that avoid giving offense: Ms.

Ms. can be used as a title for all women, whether they are married or not. **Mrs.** is usually used only for married women who have the same family name as their husband. **Miss** is used as a title for women who are not married, and **Miss**

is sometimes also used for married women who did not change their name when they got married. However, many women prefer to use **Ms.** as their title.

M.S. /ˌem ˈes/ noun [C] *American* Master of Science: an advanced degree from a college or university in a subject such as physics or biology

M.Sc. noun [C] an M.S.

MT /ˌem ˈti/ abbrev Montana

Mt. abbrev Mount or Mountain: used in the names of mountains

MTV /ˌem ti ˈvi/ *trademark* music television: a U.S. television company that broadcasts music videos

much /mʌtʃ/ (comparative **more** /mɔr/; superlative **most** /moʊst/) grammar word ★★★

Much can be:
- a **determiner**: *There isn't much time left.*
- a **pronoun**: *He didn't say much.* ♦ *Much of the work has already been completed.*
- an **adverb**: *Things haven't changed much.* ♦ *The exam was much easier than I had expected.*

1 a large amount of something: *It's a small car that doesn't use much fuel.* ♦ *I don't know much about art.* ♦ *It wouldn't cost* ***very much*** *to have your old bike repaired.* ♦ ***Much of*** *the evidence was gathered in 1991.* ♦ *We can't talk here. There's* ***too much*** *noise.* ♦ *He spent* ***so much*** *time with Claudia, it seemed as if they were never apart.*

2 used for asking or saying what the amount of something is: ***How much*** *stuff is she taking with her?* ♦ ***How much*** *were the tickets?* ♦ *We didn't spend* ***as much*** *time at the museum* ***as*** *I had hoped.*

3 used for emphasizing that someone or something is a lot bigger, better, worse, etc.: *Richard's much happier now that he's got a permanent job.* ♦ *You will have to try much harder.*

4 a lot, or to a great degree: *People here don't use public transportation much.* ♦ *The trouble with Jean is she talks* ***too much***. ♦ *Aunt Edie laughed* ***so much*** *that her sides ached.* ♦ *We don't go out* ***as much as*** *we used to.* ♦ *It's amazing* ***how much*** *she's changed.* ♦ *It's obvious that they love each other* ***very much***.

PHRASES **as much as** used before an amount for showing how large and surprising it is: *You can pay as much as $500,000 for a one-bedroom condo in San Francisco.*

be too much for sb to be too difficult or tiring for someone to deal with

much less used for saying that something is even less likely or true than something else: *I wouldn't have dinner with him, much less spend the weekend with him.*

not much of a *informal* used for saying that someone or something is not a very good example of something: *We haven't had much of a summer this year.*

not/nothing much *spoken* used for saying that something is not very important, good, or serious: *"What are you doing tomorrow?" "Nothing much."* ♦ *There's not much to get excited about.*

Both **much** and **a lot** can be used for referring to a large amount or a great degree.
- **Much** is mainly used in questions and negative sentences, or in positive statements after "so," "too," and "as": *He drinks too much.*
- **A lot** is usually used instead of **much** in positive statements: *They waste a lot of time.*

muck /mʌk/ noun [U] *informal* a dirty substance that is wet or sticky

mu·cus /mjukəs/ noun [U] a liquid that is produced inside your nose and other parts of your body

mud /mʌd/ noun [U] very soft wet earth

mud·dle¹ /ˈmʌd(ə)l/ noun [singular] a confused situation in which mistakes happen

mud·dle² /ˈmʌd(ə)l/ PHRASAL VERBS
ˌmuddle aˈlong or **ˌmuddle ˈon** to continue living or doing something in a confused way without planning
ˌmuddle ˈthrough to succeed in doing something despite having no clear plan or method

mud·dled /ˈmʌd(ə)ld/ adj not clear or effective

mud·dy¹ /ˈmʌdi/ adj covered with MUD, or full of mud

mud·dy² /ˈmʌdi/ verb [T] to make something muddy
PHRASE **muddy the issue** to make a situation more complicated or difficult than it needs to be

mud·guard /ˈmʌdˌgɑrd/ noun [C] *American* a piece of rubber that hangs behind a wheel of a vehicle and stops dirt from the road from hitting the vehicle —*picture* → C6

mues·li /ˈmjuzli/ noun [U] a food consisting of nuts, seeds, and dried fruit that people eat with milk for breakfast

muf·fin /ˈmʌfɪn/ noun [C] a small sweet cake that often contains fruit

muf·fle /ˈmʌf(ə)l/ verb [T] to make a sound quieter and less easy to hear —**muf·fled** /ˈmʌf(ə)ld/ adj

muf·fler /ˈmʌflər/ noun [C] *American* a piece of equipment that makes the sound of a vehicle's engine quieter

mug¹ /mʌg/ noun [C] a cup with straight sides and no SAUCER —*picture* → CUP

mug² /mʌg/ verb [T] to attack someone in a public place and steal their money or possessions —**mug·ger** noun [C], **mug·ging** noun [C/U]

mug·gy /ˈmʌgi/ adj muggy weather is warm in an unpleasant way because the air feels wet

ˈmug ˌshot noun [C] *informal* a photograph of someone's face that is taken by the police for their records

mule /mjul/ noun [C] an animal that has a horse as its mother and a DONKEY as its father

mul·lah /ˈmʌlə, ˈmʊlə/ noun [C] a Muslim leader or religious teacher

mul·ti·cul·tur·al /ˌmʌltiˈkʌltʃərəl, ˌmʌltaɪˈkʌltʃərəl/ adj consisting of people of different cultures —**mul·ti·cul·tur·al·ism** noun [U]

mul·ti·gym /ˈmʌltiˌdʒɪm, ˈmʌltaɪˌdʒɪm/ noun [C] a piece of exercise equipment that is designed so that you can perform many

M

different exercises on it —*picture* → C16

mul·ti·lat·er·al /ˌmʌltiˈlætərəl, ˌmʌltaɪˈlætərəl/ adj involving several groups or countries: *a multilateral agreement/treaty* → UNILATERAL, BILATERAL

mul·ti·me·di·a /ˌmʌltiˈmidiə, ˌmʌltaɪˈmidiə/ adj multimedia computers and software produce both pictures and sounds —**mul·ti·me·di·a** noun [U]

mul·ti·mil·lion·aire /ˌmʌltiˌmɪljəˈner, ˌmʌltaɪˌmɪljəˈner/ noun [C] someone who has money or property worth many millions of dollars

mul·ti·na·tion·al¹ /ˌmʌltiˈnæʃən(ə)l, ˌmʌltaɪˈnæʃən(ə)l/ adj **1** a multinational company has offices or factories in several countries **2** involving people from many different countries

mul·ti·na·tion·al² /ˌmʌltiˈnæʃən(ə)l, ˌmʌltaɪˈnæʃən(ə)l/ noun [C] a multinational company

mul·ti·ple¹ /ˈmʌltɪp(ə)l/ adj involving many people, things, or parts

mul·ti·ple² /ˈmʌltɪp(ə)l/ noun [C] a number that you can divide by a smaller number an exact number of times: *12 is a multiple of 4.*

ˌmultiple-ˈchoice adj giving you several answers from which you choose the correct answer

M

mul·ti·ple scle·ro·sis /ˌmʌltɪp(ə)l skləˈroʊsɪs/ noun [U] a serious illness that gradually makes you unable to move, speak, or see

mul·ti·plex /ˈmʌltɪˌpleks/ noun [C] a large building that contains several movie theaters

mul·ti·pli·ca·tion /ˌmʌltɪplɪˈkeɪʃ(ə)n/ noun [U] the process of adding a number to itself a particular number of times

mul·ti·plic·i·ty /ˌmʌltɪˈplɪsəti/ noun [singular] *formal* a large quantity or variety of things

mul·ti·ply /ˈmʌltɪˌplaɪ/ verb [I/T] **1** to increase, or to increase something **2** to add a number to itself a particular number of times: *If you multiply 3 by 3, you get 9.*

mul·ti·pur·pose /ˌmʌltiˈpɜrpəs, ˌmʌltaɪˈpɜrpəs/ adj designed to have several different purposes

mul·ti·ra·cial /ˌmʌltiˈreɪʃ(ə)l, ˌmʌltaɪˈreɪʃ(ə)l/ adj involving people of many different races

mul·ti·task·ing /ˈmʌltiˌtæskɪŋ/ noun [U] the activity of doing more than one thing at the same time

mul·ti·tude /ˈmʌltɪˌtud/ noun **a multitude of** *formal* a very large number of people or things

mum /mʌm/ noun [C] *British informal* your mother

mum·ble /ˈmʌmb(ə)l/ verb [I/T] to speak in a way that is not loud enough or clear enough for people to hear

mum·bo-jum·bo /ˌmʌmboʊ ˈdʒʌmboʊ/ noun [U] *informal* ideas, beliefs, or customs that you think are nonsense

mum·my /ˈmʌmi/ noun [C] a dead body that was preserved in special oils and wrapped in cloth in ancient Egypt

mumps /mʌmps/ noun [U] a children's disease that makes the neck swollen and painful

munch /mʌntʃ/ verb [I/T] to eat something in a noisy way

mun·dane /mʌnˈdeɪn/ adj ordinary and not interesting or exciting

mu·nic·i·pal /mjuˈnɪsɪp(ə)l/ adj relating to a town: *municipal elections* ♦ *a municipal swimming pool*

mu·ni·tions /mjuˈnɪʃ(ə)nz/ noun [plural] military weapons and equipment

mu·ral /ˈmjʊrəl/ noun [C] a large painting done on a wall

mur·der¹ /ˈmɜrdər/ noun [C/U] ★★ the crime of deliberately killing someone: *The murder was committed on New Year's Eve.* → MANSLAUGHTER

PHRASE **get away with murder** *informal* to do something bad without being stopped or punished: *They let their children get away with murder.*

mur·der² /ˈmɜrdər/ verb [T] ★ to commit the crime of deliberately killing someone

mur·der·er /ˈmɜrdərər/ noun [C] someone who commits murder

mur·der·ous /ˈmɜrdərəs/ adj likely to kill someone, or intending to kill someone

murk·y /ˈmɜrki/ adj **1** involving activities that are dishonest or morally wrong: *We suspected he had a murky past.* **2** dark and difficult to see through: *murky water*

mur·mur /ˈmɜrmər/ verb [I/T] to say something in a very quiet voice: *Frances murmured an apology as she left.* ♦ *"How strange," she murmured.* —**mur·mur** noun [C]

mus·cle¹ /ˈmʌs(ə)l/ noun ★★
1 [C/U] a piece of flesh that connects bones and moves a particular part of your body: *These exercises are good for your stomach muscles.*
2 [U] power or strength: *financial/political muscle*

muscle

mus·cle² /ˈmʌs(ə)l/ PHRASAL VERB **ˌmuscle ˈin** to use your power or influence to become involved in something

mus·cu·lar /ˈmʌskjələr/ adj **1** having big muscles: *muscular arms/legs* **2** affecting your muscles

muse /mjuz/ verb [I] to think about something in a careful slow way

mu·se·um /mjuˈziəm/ noun [C] ★★★ a building where valuable and important objects are kept for people to see and study

mush /mʌʃ/ noun [singular/U] a solid substance that is much softer than it should be —**mush·y** adj

mush•room[1] /ˈmʌʃˌrum/ noun [C] a small white or brown FUNGUS with a short stem and a round top that is often eaten as a vegetable → TOADSTOOL —*picture* → C11

mush•room[2] /ˈmʌʃˌrum/ verb [I] to increase or develop very quickly

mu•sic /ˈmjuzɪk/ noun [U] ★★★
1 pleasant sounds made by voices or instruments: *She prefers **listening to** classical **music**. ♦ She **writes music** for movies. ♦ We need to play **a new piece of music** for the concert.*
2 the activity of writing, performing, or studying music: *She's planning to major in music. ♦ a music teacher*
3 the printed symbols that represent music: *I'm learning to **read music**.*

mu•si•cal[1] /ˈmjuzɪk(ə)l/ adj ★
1 involving music, or relating to music: *musical instruments ♦ an evening of musical entertainment*
2 a musical sound is pleasant to listen to
3 good at playing or singing music: *They're a very musical family.*
—**mu•si•cal•ly** /ˈmjuzɪk(ə)li/ adv

mu•si•cal[2] /ˈmjuzɪk(ə)l/ noun [C] a play or movie in which there are a lot of songs

mu•si•cian /mjuˈzɪʃ(ə)n/ noun [C] ★ someone who performs or writes music, especially as their job

Mus•lim /ˈmʌzləm, ˈmʊzləm/ noun [C] ★ someone whose religion is Islam —**Mus•lim** adj

mus•lin /ˈmʌzlɪn/ noun [U] a type of thin cotton cloth

mus•sel /ˈmʌs(ə)l/ noun [C] a small SHELLFISH with a black shell and a soft body that can be eaten

must[1] /*weak* məst, *strong* mʌst/ modal verb ★★★

- **Must** is usually followed by an infinitive without "to": *You must stop at the red light.* Sometimes it is used without a following infinitive: *We will act alone if we must.*
- **Must** has no tenses, no participles, and no infinitive form. It does not change its form, so the third person singular form does not end in "-s": *She must be asleep.*
- Questions and negatives are formed without "do": *Must we wear our uniforms?*
- The negative form **must not** is used for saying that something should not be done. This is often shortened in conversation or informal writing to **mustn't**: *You mustn't use the office phone for private calls.* For saying that it is not necessary to do something **not have to**, **not need to**, or **needn't** is used: *Children don't have to pay to go in.*

1 used for saying that you think something is probably true because nothing else seems possible: *You must be tired after your long trip. ♦ There must be some mistake – no one named Shaw lives here. ♦ I must have fallen asleep.*
2 used for saying that something is necessary or important to do: *You must answer all the questions.*
→ SAY[1]

must[2] /mʌst/ noun **a must** something that you definitely need in a particular situation: *Good binoculars are a must for any serious birdwatcher.*

mus•tache /ˈmʌstæʃ/ noun [C] the hair above a man's mouth

mus•tard /ˈmʌstərd/ noun [U] a thick yellow sauce with a hot taste

mus•ter /ˈmʌstər/ verb [T] to try to make yourself feel something as strongly as possible: *The job would need all the energy I could muster.*

must•n't /ˈmʌs(ə)nt/ short form *old-fashioned* a way of saying or writing "must not." This is not often used in formal writing.

must•y /ˈmʌsti/ adj smelling unpleasant and not fresh

mu•tant /ˈmjut(ə)nt/ noun [C] a plant or animal that is different from others of its type because of a change in its genes —**mu•tant** adj

mu•tate /ˈmjuˌteɪt/ verb [I] to become physically different from other plants or animals of the same type because of a genetic change —**mu•ta•tion** /mjuˈteɪʃ(ə)n/ noun [C/U]

mute /mjut/ adj **1** saying nothing, or not willing to speak **2** *old-fashioned* unable to speak. People now think that this word is offensive and prefer to use the expression **speech-impaired**.

mut•ed /ˈmjutəd/ adj not very strong, loud, or bright

mu•ti•late /ˈmjut(ə)lˌeɪt/ verb [T] to damage someone's body permanently by cutting it or cutting off part of it —**mu•ti•la•tion** /ˌmjut(ə)lˈeɪʃ(ə)n/ noun [C/U]

mu•ti•nous /ˈmjut(ə)nəs/ adj refusing to obey someone who is in a position of authority

mu•ti•ny /ˈmjut(ə)ni/ noun [C/U] an occasion when people refuse to obey someone in a position of authority —**mu•ti•ny** verb [I]

mutt /mʌt/ noun [C] *informal* a dog that does not belong to a particular BREED

mut•ter /ˈmʌtər/ verb [I/T] to say something in a quiet voice, especially because you are annoyed

mut•ton /ˈmʌt(ə)n/ noun [U] the meat from an adult sheep → LAMB

mu•tu•al /ˈmjutʃuəl/ adj **1** felt or done in the same way by each person: *mutual respect/support/understanding ♦ His contract was canceled by mutual agreement.* **2** belonging to two or more people: *They were introduced by a mutual friend. ♦ We have a mutual interest in hiking.*

ˈmutual ˌfund noun [C] *American* a company that invests money for you in many different companies

mu•tu•al•ly /ˈmjutʃuəli/ adv to or for each person equally

muz•zle[1] /ˈmʌz(ə)l/ noun [C] **1** the nose and mouth of an animal such as a dog or horse **2** something that you put around the nose and mouth of a dog to prevent it from biting people **3** the end of a gun BARREL where the bullets come out

muz•zle[2] /ˈmʌz(ə)l/ verb [T] **1** to prevent someone from expressing their opinions publicly **2** to put a muzzle on a dog

MVP /ˌem vi ˈpi/ noun [C] *American* Most Valuable Player: the best player in a team in a sport such as baseball and American football

M

my /maɪ/ determiner ★★★ belonging to or connected with you, when you are the person who is speaking or writing: *I shut my eyes.* ♦ *I want you to meet my parents.* ♦ *When my sister went to college I got my own room.*

MYOB abbrev mind your own business: used in e-mails and TEXT MESSAGES

myr•i•ad /ˈmɪriəd/ noun **a myriad of sth** *literary* an extremely large number of people or things —**myr•i•ad** adj

my•self /maɪˈself/ pronoun ★★★
1 the REFLEXIVE form of "I," used for showing that an action that you do affects you: *I fell and hurt myself.* ♦ *I was starting to enjoy myself.* ♦ *I'm going to pour myself another coffee.*
2 used for emphasizing that you are referring to yourself and not to anyone else: *I myself was once a prisoner.*
3 used instead of "I" or "me" when you are trying to be polite. Many people think that this use is incorrect: *Lindsey or myself will be happy to answer any of your questions.*
PHRASES **(all) by myself 1** alone: *I like to spend a little time by myself on weekends.* **2** without help from anyone else: *I made the whole quilt all by myself.*
(all) to myself not sharing something with anyone else: *I had the whole beach to myself.*
be/feel myself to be in your normal mental or physical state: *I'm sorry if I shouted. I'm just not myself today.*

mys•te•ri•ous /mɪˈstɪriəs/ adj **1** not explained, understood, or known: *They are investigating the mysterious disappearance of a young man.* ♦ *He died in mysterious circumstances.* **2** keeping things secret in a way that makes other people want to discover what they are —**mys•te•ri•ous•ly** adv

mys•ter•y¹ /ˈmɪst(ə)ri/ noun ★
1 [C] something that you cannot understand, explain, or get information about: *The exact origin of the universe remains a mystery.* ♦ *Why she left is still **a mystery to him**.*
2 [U] a quality that makes someone or something difficult to explain, understand, or get information about, in a way that makes them seem interesting or exciting: *a woman with an air of mystery about her* ♦ *His past is shrouded in mystery.*
3 [C] a story, movie, or play in which events take place that are not explained until the end: *a murder mystery*

mys•ter•y² /ˈmɪst(ə)ri/ adj a mystery person is someone who you do not know

mys•tic /ˈmɪstɪk/ noun [C] someone who practices MYSTICISM

mys•ti•cal /ˈmɪstɪk(ə)l/ adj **1** relating to MYSTICISM **2** involving mysterious religious or spiritual powers

mys•ti•cism /ˈmɪstɪˌsɪzəm/ noun [U] the belief that you can understand God directly by praying and MEDITATING

mys•ti•fy /ˈmɪstɪˌfaɪ/ verb [T] if something mystifies you, you cannot understand or explain it —**mys•ti•fy•ing** adj

mys•tique /mɪˈstik/ noun [U] an attractive quality that something has because it seems mysterious and special in an exciting way

myth /mɪθ/ noun [C] **1** an ancient traditional story about gods, magic, and HEROES **2** something that people wrongly believe to be true

myth•i•cal /ˈmɪθɪk(ə)l/ adj **1** existing only in MYTHS: *mythical creatures* **2** *formal* imaginary, or not real

my•thol•o•gy /mɪˈθɑlədʒi/ noun [C/U] ancient MYTHS: *Greek/Roman mythology* —**myth•o•log•i•cal** /ˌmɪθəˈlɑdʒɪk(ə)l/ adj

M

LANGUAGE STUDY

These pages have been designed to help you to improve your knowledge and use of the English language. They contain information on how words are formed (Word Formation) and how new meanings develop (Metaphor), how words relate to each other (Collocation, Register, Text Types) and how they are pronounced (Pronunciation).

Increasing your vocabulary is an essential part of learning a foreign language—and remembering new words and phrases is often the hardest part. We have included an eight-page section (Topic Vocabulary) that brings together words and phrases that will help you to talk and write about key topic areas.

Throughout this section there is advice on how to improve your learning strategies, activities to practice these strategies, and exercises to test what you have learned. We hope that you will find these pages informative, useful—and, above all, enjoyable.

Contents

COLLOCATION

What Is Collocation?

Why do we say "to do your homework" and not "to make your homework"? And why do we go somewhere "by car" or "by train" but "on foot"? The reason is "collocation." Collocation means the way that words form predictable relationships with other words. Knowing the "meaning" of a word is not only knowing its dictionary definition but also knowing the kind of words with which it is often associated.

We say, for example, "take a look" and "have a look" but not "make a look." There is no reason or rule that tells us why we use some words with "look" but not others. Looking up the meaning of **take** or **have** in the dictionary won't help us find the answer. Collocations, either fixed or more flexible, are the result of many years of habitual use by fluent speakers of the language.

Why Is Collocation Important?

Collocation is important because:

- it makes speech sound natural and alive
- it provides "chunks" of English that are ready to use
- it saves us a lot of time and effort when we are trying to express ourselves

These pages give you examples of the main kinds of collocation, and some ideas about how to improve your ability to use collocation.

In the case of grammar, once we know the rules we can make new correct sentences all the time, simply by "plugging in" new vocabulary in the right places. But with collocation, there are limits to the changes we can make to a combination of words. In some cases those limits can be very strict, but in others there is more freedom to choose which words can go together.

A collocation may consist of two or more words. Look at this example:

Last year, we spent our summer vacation in Berkeley.

This sentence is made up of nine separate words, but if we look more carefully we can identify four groups of words or "collocations":

- *last + year*—we can also say "last summer/last night/last week," or "next year/this year/every year." But we cannot say "~~last hour~~" or "~~past summer.~~"
- *spend + vacation*—we can also say "spend a week/a month/the winter." But we cannot say "~~pass our vacation.~~"
- *summer + vacation*—we can also say "Christmas vacation/Easter vacation."
- *in + Berkeley*—we often use the preposition **in** with the names of towns, states, and countries. If you say that you spent time "**at** Berkeley" the meaning changes completely. You mean that you studied at the university!

So when we are learning English, it is not enough to know the meaning of words like **spend** and **pass** on their own—the *meanings* of such words may be similar, but the way that they *combine* with other words may be very different.

Fixed Phrases

The relationship between two or more words can be very close. For example, the word **kith** is never seen anywhere but in the company of **kin**, in the phrase "kith and kin" (an old-fashioned way of referring to your relatives). **Kin**, however, also appears with **next** in "next of kin." But both words have very little freedom to combine with other words in English. If you learn these words, it is best to learn them together, as fixed phrases. Other words that form strong partnerships like this are: **ajar** (*she left the* ***door ajar***—which means "she left the door open") and **amends** (*she was sorry for what she had done and decided to* ***make amends***—which means "she decided to try to make the situation better").

Idioms

Many idioms in English are examples of strong collocations. There is very little, if any, room for changing the words that make up expressions such as the following:

- under the weather
- lose face
- spill the beans

Sometimes we can guess the meaning of an idiom if we understand all the individual words that it is formed from. But in many cases, this is not possible. For example, it is difficult to see why "spill the beans" should mean "to give away secret information." The words and grammar that make up these idioms are almost impossible to change, without changing the meaning. We cannot say "on top of the weather" (but we can say "on top of the world"). We cannot say "find face" or "lose faces" (but we can say "save face") and "spill *the peas*" is not an idiomatic expression. A small error in the use of these fixed collocations makes a big difference to their meaning—and will often make them meaningless.

Phrasal Verbs

A special feature of English that is not found in many other languages is the use of combinations of verb + adverb or preposition (particle). These combinations are known as phrasal verbs: **pick up**, **take up**, **bump into**, **set off**, **put up with**.

Phrasal verbs are very common in English and many verbs combine with several different particles. Like other verbs, they also have particular "friends":

- **take up** + an offer/a job/a hobby
- **pick sb up** + from the airport/in your car/at noon
- **run into** + difficulties/an old friend

Thus, there are two layers of collocation to get right if we want to use phrasal verbs correctly. First, we have to choose the correct particle to go with the verb, and then we have to choose the right kind of word or phrase to express the meaning we want. For more information about phrasal verbs, see page 828.

Less Fixed Combinations

"Verb + Noun" Collocations

These are very common in English. In such cases, we have more freedom to make combinations, but there are certain restrictions on what is possible or probable.

Let's take **make**, a verb which has many "friends." We **make**:

- a mistake
- the bed
- (the) dinner
- an effort
- friends

It is difficult to say exactly what **make** means in all these different collocations. We can look up the meaning of **screwdriver** or **digest** in a dictionary and be fairly sure what they refer to, but this strategy does not work very well with **make**. One important part of the meaning of **make** is that it contrasts with the verb **do**. These two verbs tend to have very different friends. For example, we **do**:

- the shopping
- the dishes
- our best
- someone a favor

So we can see that there are many ways of combining **make** and **do** with nouns. There are limits to the number of collocations they have and they don't often share the same collocates.

There are several other very common verbs in English like **make** and **do** (such as **get**, **have**, and **take**) that often do not have much meaning on their own. To really get a feel for the way these very common verbs are used, you need to know the phrases they form with other words and the contexts in which we use them.

Other Common Grammatical Combinations

There are a number of other common grammatical combinations that form collocations in English:

noun + verb:	temperatures **rise**; prices **fall**; dogs **bark**; cats **meow**
adverb + adjective:	**bitterly** cold; **hugely** enjoyable; **deeply** upset
adjective + noun:	**strong** tea; a **powerful** engine; a **heavy** smoker
verb + adverb:	sleep **soundly**; walk **briskly**; rely **heavily** on
adverb + verb:	**distinctly** remember; **flatly** refuse; **categorically** deny

You can find many examples of combinations like these in the 130 "Collocation Boxes" in this dictionary: see for example the boxes at the entries for **cost**, **environment**, **influence**, and **suggestion**.

Functional Expressions

In everyday conversation, there are many collocations that occur with particular grammatical structures. These structures are like frames, into which we can put different words in order to perform a variety of communicative acts. Here are some examples:

- **I'd like** a round-trip ticket to/a ham sandwich... [buying something]
- **I don't suppose you could** tell me the way/open the window... [making requests]
- **Do you have** the time/change for a dollar... [asking for information, asking a favor]
- **Could you** tell me the way to... [asking for directions]
- **By the way**, ... [introducing a new topic of conversation]
- **Well, it's time** we were going/ **Well, that's all** for now... [saying goodbye, ending a conversation]

There are thousands of such sentence frames in English and many are explained in this dictionary. They are one way in which expert users of English manage to sound so fluent.

Learning Collocation

The fact that you are using this dictionary probably means that you would like to be a fluent user of spoken and written English. Here are some techniques to help you to acquire greater "collocational fluency" in English:

- Read widely in English—begin with simplified texts and as quickly as possible go on to authentic, unsimplified texts: newspapers, magazines, stories, etc.

- Use highlighters of different colors to make the new collocations stand out.

- As you read, connect keywords and their collocations by drawing lines between them.

- Copy the examples you come across in your reading into a special notebook.

- Organize your notebook into topics (travel, sports, etc.) and add collocations connected with the topic as you come across them in your reading.

- Organize your notebook into collocational patterns:

Verb + Noun
Noun + Verb
Adverb + Adjective
Verb + Adverb
Adjective + Noun
Functional Expressions
Idioms
Phrasal Verbs

- Organize your notebook into common keywords (**get**, **take**, **come**, **make**, **do**, etc.), and add collocations as you come across them in your reading.

- Make a chart showing common verbs and their collocations:

	a trip	a break	a date	the dishes	a walk	lunch
take	✓	✓			✓	
make			✓			✓
do				✓		
have		✓	✓			✓

- Use your dictionary to enrich your knowledge of collocations. For example, before you use a dull collocation such as "a big storm," look up the word **storm** in your dictionary and try to choose a more interesting adjective (e.g., fierce, raging, terrible, violent).

ACTIVITY

Read the following passage and:

- underline any collocations you find
- organize them into separate groups (for example, verb+noun collocations, adverb+adjective collocations, phrasal verbs, idioms, and functional expressions)

The Dallas Cowboys' decisive victory over the San Francisco 49ers yesterday was overshadowed by news that Phil Harper's knee injury could keep him out of the game for up to a year. By deciding to play in last night's game, the Dallas quarterback had disregarded the advice of his doctor, and it was clear—even during Friday's practice session—that he was hurting. After 30 minutes, he limped off the field in agony, and it is now highly unlikely that he will take any further part in the playoffs.

Harper has made an outstanding contribution to the Cowboys' recent successes, and without him they face a daunting challenge as they gear up for the next game. Coach Don Hansen said, "Of course we're very disappointed that Phil won't make it to the finals with us. But to be honest, we always knew his knee might cause him problems."

ANSWERS

adjective + noun
decisive victory
outstanding contribution
daunting challenge
next round

noun + preposition
victory over
contribution to

preposition + noun
in agony
up to a year

noun + noun
knee injury
practice session

verb + noun
disregard advice
make a contribution
face a challenge
cause problems

adverb + adjective
highly unlikely
bitterly disappointed

phrasal verbs
keep sb out of sth
warm up
gear up for sth

idioms
take part in
make it

functional expressions
to be honest

TOPIC VOCABULARY: ENTERTAINMENT

The following eight pages contain short texts about different topics. Each text is accompanied by a list of vocabulary taken from it along with explanations. There are also some suggestions of other related words and phrases that you might need when talking or writing about one of the topics. Use this dictionary to check their meanings—and add more related words to these lists when you find them in your own reading.

Going to the Movies

I love going to the movies and I'm lucky because there's a big new **multiplex** close to where I live. I always enjoy a good **thriller**—the **nail-biting** type where there's lots of **suspense** and you find yourself gripping the arm of the chair. I don't really like **westerns** or war movies—they usually involve a little too much violence for my taste. But I enjoy **blockbuster sci-fi** movies, especially if the **special effects** are well done. I really like to watch foreign films too, although I hate it if they've been **dubbed**—I prefer the original versions with **subtitles**.

multiplex: a large building with several movie theaters
thriller: an exciting movie about crime, murder, etc.
nail-biting: making you feel nervous and excited
suspense: the nervous, excited feeling that you have when you are waiting to see what will happen next
western: a movie about cowboys and the American West in the 19th century
blockbuster: a very successful film
sci-fi: science fiction—stories about space travel and the future
special effects: exciting images that have been created using computers and other technical methods
dubbed: with the words spoken by actors speaking your own language, not by the film's original actors
subtitles: written words at the bottom of the movie screen, which translate what is being said

Other Useful Vocabulary

You can use the dictionary to check the meanings of these words and expressions.

Types of Movies	People
action movie	director
romantic comedy	producer
horror movie	movie star
sequel	cast

Other Related Vocabulary

script	be set in (Chicago/
scene	the future/ancient
flashback	Rome etc.)

Going Out

I don't **go out** much during the week. Occasionally I go to the movies or meet friends in a bar. But usually I stay in and relax. Sometimes I just read a book or watch television, but now and then I order **takeout** from a local restaurant and rent a **video**. I have a lot more **free time** on the weekend so I do all kinds of things. I try to go to the gym on Saturday mornings, and then in the afternoon I often **go shopping**. I meet up with friends and we go to the **shopping center** together. We usually **go clubbing** on a Saturday night so we go to the clothes stores looking for something new to wear. Every couple of months I try to take a few days off work so that I can have a **long weekend** and go away somewhere nice.

go out: to go somewhere to do something enjoyable, instead of staying at home
takeout: a meal that you buy from a restaurant to eat at home
video: a film on videotape that you watch on your own TV
free time: time when you do not have to work or study
go shopping: to go out to different stores
shopping center: a large place where there are lots of different stores
go clubbing: to go to a place where you can dance and listen to music
long weekend: a weekend when you are also free on the Friday or Monday

PEOPLE AND RELATIONSHIPS

Families

Jake comes from a very **close family**. He spends a lot of time with his **immediate family**—his parents and his brothers and sisters—and he often sees his relatives when they get together for one of their **family reunions**. He has a large **extended family** too with lots of cousins, aunts, and uncles. His friend, Simon, is always telling Jake how lucky he is. Simon is an **only child** and so are both his parents, which means he has very few **close relatives**.

close family: a family in which everyone has a good relationship and talks to each other a lot
immediate family: family members who are most closely related to you
family reunion: a party when family members get together, especially when they have not seen each other for a long time
extended family: family members apart from your immediate family
only child: a child who has no brothers or sisters
close relatives: family members who are closely related to you such as brothers, sisters and cousins

Friends

I've never had trouble **making friends**. I have lots of friends, but there aren't many that I would call **close friends**. Paula's my **best friend**. We **got to know** each other when we were in college. I knew we'd **get along with** each other as soon as we met—we have so much in common. And I was right. We've been friends now for five years, and we've never had a big fight.

make friends: when two people make friends with each other, they become friends
close friend: a friend that you know well and spend a lot of time with
best friend: the friend that you like best
get to know: to become friendly with someone that you have recently met
get along with: to like someone and have a friendly relationship with them

Romantic Relationships

Danuta and Marek first started **going out with** each other when they were 19. Danuta had liked Marek for a long time, and she'd told all her friends how attractive she thought he was. So of course she was really pleased when he **asked her out**. They went to the movies on their first **date**. Their relationship lasted two years and then they **broke up**. A few months later, Danuta met Damien and **fell in love with** him right away. Damien **proposed to** her and now they're **engaged**. They're **living together** and plan to get married some time next year.

go out with: to have a romantic relationship with someone
ask sb out: to invite someone to go with you to a movie, restaurant, etc., because you want to start a relationship with them
date: a romantic meeting with someone
break up: to end a romantic relationship
fall in love with: to feel very strongly attracted to someone
propose to: to ask someone to marry you
engaged: if two people are engaged, they have agreed to get married
live together: to live together in a sexual relationship, but without being married

Other Useful Vocabulary

You can use the dictionary to check the meanings of these words and expressions.

Families

distant (relative/cousin)
single parent
be related to

Friends

old friend
circle of friends
classmate
roommate/housemate

Romantic Relationships

boyfriend/girlfriend
partner
fiancé/fiancée
single
separated
divorced
have an affair (with sb)

TRAVEL AND TOURISM

Choosing a Vacation

If you want to go on a vacation but you're not sure where you want to go or what you want to do, it's a good idea to start by going to a **travel agency**. Take some **brochures** home with you so that you can look at what's available. Think about what sort of **accommodations** you'd like to stay in. Do you enjoy the convenience of a **package tour** or are you the type of person who prefers to travel independently? Do you like staying in hotels or would an apartment or private **villa** be more your type of thing? Most of all though, you should think carefully about your **destination**. Find out what the weather is like there and try to get as much information about the different **resorts**. Are you looking for somewhere quiet, or would you prefer somewhere with plenty of **nightlife**? When you've answered all these questions, you can go ahead and **book** your vacation. And before you set off, if you're going **abroad**, make sure that you have a valid passport and a **visa** if you need one.

travel agency: a business that provides information for travelers and helps them to arrange trips
brochure: a type of magazine with a lot of pictures, giving information about places where you can go on vacation
accommodations: places to stay, such as hotels or rented apartments
package tour: a vacation where everything is organized for you for a single fixed price
villa: a vacation house, especially near the ocean or in the country
destination: the place that you are going to
resort: a town where many people go to spend their vacation
nightlife: evening entertainment in nightclubs, bars, etc.
book (a vacation): to make reservations
abroad: outside your own country
visa: a special stamp in your passport that you must have to visit some countries

My First Vacation

When I was 18 I decided to go traveling with some friends. We really wanted to go to Australia, but we couldn't afford it. So we decided to buy **rail passes** for Europe instead. We spent a long time working out our **itinerary**, deciding which places we'd like to visit in each country. We bought some **guidebooks** to find out more about the countries we were going to and a couple of small **phrase books** so that at least we'd be able to buy food and ask for directions. Since we didn't have much money, we planned to stay mainly in **youth hostels** or cheap **bed and breakfasts**. Although we all wanted to do a lot of **sightseeing**, we also agreed that it would be interesting to get away from the **touristy** areas and try to discover more about the real way of life in our chosen countries.

rail pass: a ticket that allows you to make as many train trips as you want within a particular period
itinerary: a plan of a trip
guidebook: a book for tourists, giving information about a particular place or country
phrase book: a book that gives translations of useful words and phrases
youth hostel: a type of inexpensive hotel for young travelers
bed and breakfast: a small inexpensive hotel that provides rooms and breakfast
sightseeing: the activity of visiting well-known places, museums, etc.
touristy: full of tourists

Other Useful Vocabulary

You can use the dictionary to check the meanings of these words and expressions.

Vacation Activities

go to the beach
go hiking
go skiing

Accommodations

B&B
motel
vacancy

Money

foreign currency
traveler's checks
change money

Other Related Vocabulary

do your packing
go backpacking
travel insurance

WORK

Working for a Big Company

I'm a sales representative. I work for a big **multinational**. I earn about $60,000 a year and get other **benefits** such as a **company car** and a **company pension**. I enjoy what I do even though I often have to **work** very **long hours**. Sometimes I wish I had a **nine-to-five job**, but I enjoy traveling and would hate to be stuck in the office all the time. I'm hoping that I'll **be promoted** to area manager next year—a senior **position** that would be a lot more **challenging**.

multinational: a large company that operates in many different countries
benefits: extra things that you get from your employer, in addition to your salary
company car: a car that your company pays for and provides for you to use
company pension: a system by which you and your company both invest money to provide you with an income when you stop working
work long hours: to work more hours than the usual working day
nine-to-five job: a job in which your working day has fixed hours
be promoted: to be given a more important job, usually with a higher salary
position: a specific job in an organization
challenging: difficult, but also interesting and enjoyable

Applying for a Job

I have just finished college and am now **applying for jobs**. I'd like to work as a recruitment consultant. There have been quite a few **vacancies** advertised in the newspaper recently. Most of them ask you to send your **résumé** and a letter saying why you think you are suitable for the **opening**. Some ask you to send for their **application form** which you then have to **fill out**. Out of the ten companies I've contacted so far, I've already had three **rejections**. I have two interviews next week though, so I hope it won't be long before I'm **offered a job**.

apply for a job: to write to an organization to tell them that you want a job that they have advertised
vacancy: a job that is available for people to apply for
résumé: a document that gives details of your qualifications, skills, and experience
opening: a job that you can apply for
application form: a paper with questions for you to answer when you are applying for a job
fill out: to provide all the necessary information on a form
rejection: when an organization tells you that your application has not been successful
be offered a job: to be told by someone that they want you to work for them

Other Useful Vocabulary

You can use the dictionary to check the meanings of these words and expressions.

Résumés	Working Hours
reference	full-time
qualifications	part-time
communication/ organizational/ interpersonal skills	permanent
	temporary
	flextime
	overtime

Other Related Vocabulary

train as (a nurse/airline pilot/chef etc.)	pay raise
	career
	job offer

ACTIVITY

Rewrite these sentences using words from the reading passage so that the second sentence means the same as the first. You can find the answers on page LS13.

1. I get all sorts of things in addition to my salary—free health insurance, for example.
   I get all sorts of .... in addition to my salary—free health insurance for example.
2. They want me to send them all the details about my qualifications and work experience.
   They want me to send them my ....
3. My job involves a lot of hard work, but it's interesting and I enjoy it.
   I have quite a .... job.
4. Please write all your details on the application form and return it to us.
   Please .... the application form and return it to us.

NEW TECHNOLOGY

Communication

It wasn't such a long time ago that no one had even heard of **cellphones**. These days, they are part of everyday life and one of the main ways we communicate with each other. People use their cellphones to make **personal calls** as well as **business calls**. They are a valuable **form of communication**, enabling people to **be contacted** wherever they are. And you don't always have to speak to someone—you can use a cellphone to send someone a **text message**. **Texting** is a quick and easy way to **get in touch with** someone about something when you don't actually need to talk to them, for example to let them know that you are going to be late. The other option is to leave a message on their **voicemail**—your call gets automatically **diverted to** that if they don't answer the phone.

cellphone: a phone that you carry around with you
personal calls: calls to your friends or family
business calls: calls that you make as part of your job
form of communication: any of the ways that people use to exchange information with each other
be contacted: to be reached by someone who wants to talk to you
text message: a short written message that you send using a mobile phone
texting: the activity of communicating by text messages
get in touch with: to talk to, write to, or send a message to someone
voicemail: a system for recording and storing spoken messages
be diverted to: to be sent to another part of a phone system

ACTIVITY

Complete these sentences using words from the reading passage. You can find the answers on page LS13.

1. I won't be at home all day but you can call me on my ....
2. If I don't answer the phone, just leave a message on my ....
3. You're not supposed to use your phone at work to make ....
4. I often use my cellphone to send someone a ....—it's not always necessary to talk to them directly.

Other Useful Vocabulary

Common Abbreviations Used for Texting

CUL8R: see you later
B4: before
GR8: great
BTW: by the way
2day: today

Emoticons

:) shows that you are pleased
:)) shows that you are very happy
:(shows that you are annoyed or sad
:0 shows that you are surprised
:-D shows that you think that something is funny
;) a wink—shows that you are making a joke

Computers and the Internet

Everyone I know has a home computer so I decided it was time I got one too. I thought it would be best to get a **laptop** since they don't take up so much room. I got a little carried away and bought all the extras—a printer, a **scanner**, a **webcam** and lots of **software** that I didn't really need. Most importantly though, I wanted to have **Internet access** so I arranged for a **broadband connection** as I was told that it would make everything much easier and faster.

laptop or **notebook**: a small computer that you can carry around with you
scanner: a device that converts pictures or documents into computer files
webcam: a small camera attached to a computer. It takes moving pictures that can be seen on a website.
software: computer programs, such as word-processors and web browsers
Internet access: the ability to use the Internet
broadband connection: an Internet connection that allows data to be sent and received at very high speeds

Now I spend a lot of my spare time **going online**. I love **logging on to** some of the **chat rooms**. You can meet some really interesting people. The biggest change for me though has been the **online shopping**. Many of the big stores have great websites and it saves me so much time. The other thing I love is being able to send and receive **e-mails**—it's such an easy way to **keep in touch** with people.

go online: to connect your computer to the Internet
log on to: to enter a particular area of the Internet
chat room: an area on the Internet where several people can have a discussion
online shopping: to buy things using the Internet
e-mail: a written message sent from one computer to another by means of the Internet
keep in touch: to call or write to someone regularly

Computers are really changing the way we live our lives. Some of my friends now work from home. They use their computers to **download** work from their offices and then send it back as an e-mail **attachment** when they've finished. I know they worry a little about getting computer **viruses** but there is plenty of good anti-virus software that you can **install**.

download: to use the Internet to transfer data from another computer system to your own computer
attachment: a computer file that is sent with an e-mail
virus: a computer program that has been deliberately created to cause damage to other people's files
install: to add a new piece of software to your computer system

ACTIVITY

Complete the following paragraph using words from the reading passage. You can find the answers on page LS13.

If you want a computer that you can take anywhere with you, it'd be a good idea to buy a (1)............... . You can use it like an ordinary computer and attach any of the usual things to it, such as a (2).............. if you need to send letters to people. You can use it to connect to an Internet (3) .... if you want to talk to other people about something that you're interested in. I mainly use my computer to send and receive (4) .... because it's such a convenient way of exchanging information.

Other Useful Vocabulary

You can use the dictionary to check the meanings of these words and expressions.

Computers

PC
computer-literate
hardware
hard disk/hard drive
memory
folder
document
program
menu
upgrade

Internet

ISP (Internet Service Provider)
home page
link
search engine
browser

Commands and Actions

edit
delete
save
copy
cut
paste
scroll up/down
click on
right-click/left-click/double-click

MEDIA

Newspapers

Many people don't seem to want **hard news** in their newspapers. In the **tabloids** it's **exclusives** about movie stars, pop stars, and television celebrities that **make the headlines**. And no story is complete without those **intrusive** photographs taken by the **paparazzi**. Tabloids put **sensationalist** stories on their front pages instead of real **investigative journalism** or international news. Most of the Sunday newspapers now come with free **supplements** packed with yet more **trivia**, **gossip columns**, and lifestyle **features** on things like gardening, cooking, and home repair.

hard news: news about important national and international events
tabloids: small newspapers that are full of stories about celebrities, strange events, etc. but not much serious news
exclusive: a story reported in only one newspaper
make the headlines or **hit the headlines**: to get a lot of attention in the newspapers
intrusive: disturbing people's private lives
paparazzi: photographers who follow famous people around to take photos of them
sensationalist: deliberately making facts seem as shocking as possible
investigative journalism: news stories that are based on serious research that tries to find the truth about something
supplement: a type of magazine that is given free with a newspaper
trivia: very unimportant stories
gossip column: an article that is full of stories about famous people
feature: an article that deals with a particular subject, but not with a news story

Other Useful Vocabulary

You can use the dictionary to check the meanings of these words and expressions.

People

journalist	editor
reporter	columnist
correspondent	

Sections of a Newspaper

sports news	letters to the editor
business news	horoscope
editorial	comics

Other Related Vocabulary

the press	the papers
the media	press coverage

ACTIVITY

Rewrite these sentences using words from the reading passage so that the second sentence means the same as the first. You can find the answers on page LS13.

1. I don't like reading serious newspapers.
   I like reading the ....
2. My favorite part of the paper is where you read about all the things famous people have been doing.
   My favorite part of the paper is the ....
3. If it's true that their marriage is breaking up, all the newspapers will have stories about it.
   Their marriage break-up is sure to ....
4. The story about his illness was only in *The Daily News*.
   The Daily News had an .... about his illness.
5. The paper reported his drug problem with a lot of shocking details.
   The paper reported his drug problem in a very .... way.

Television

If we're watching TV together and Miguel has the **remote control**, he spends the whole time **channel surfing**. I'm never allowed to watch the latest **reality show**, listen to a whole interview on a **talk show**, or find out who wins the big prize on a **game show**. When the **commercials** come on, he always **flips channels** to see what else is on. There are so many **channels** to choose from. He usually falls asleep during the news or a **documentary**. So I **turn the volume down**, put the **closed captioning** on, and enjoy an episode of my favorite **soap**.

remote control or **remote**: a device that you hold in your hand and use for changing the channel on your TV
channel surfing: the activity of continually changing from one TV program to another
reality show: a TV program involving ordinary people, not using professional actors
talk show: a show in which a host interviews famous people
game show: a show in which people win prizes by playing games and answering questions
commercials: advertisements that are shown between TV programs or in the middle of programs
flip channels: to change channels continuously
channels: the different television stations and their programs
documentary: a serious program about subjects such as science, history, or politics
turn the volume down: to reduce the level of sound
closed captioning: written words at the bottom of the TV screen, which show what is being said
soap or **soap opera**: a drama series broadcast several times a week, about the lives of a group of imaginary people

Other Useful Vocabulary

You can use the dictionary to check the meanings of these words and expressions.

People

anchor
newscaster
viewer

Types of Television or Program

cable TV
satellite TV
series
sitcom
weather forecast

Actions

turn on/off
turn up/down

ACTIVITY

Rewrite these sentences using words from the reading passage so that the second sentence means the same as the first. You can find the answers at the bottom of this page.

1. On a Friday night I usually watch that program where people try to win prizes.
   On Friday night I usually watch that ....
2. Stop changing channels. I want to watch that.
   Stop .... I was watching that.
3. They are showing a program about the history of Caribbean music.
   They are showing a .... about Caribbean music.
4. Install our new satellite dish, and you can watch shows from over 40 different TV stations.
   Install our new satellite dish, and you can watch over 40 different ....
5. I was working all week, so I missed my favorite daytime drama series.
   I was working all week, so I missed my favorite ....

ANSWERS

Work
1. benefits
2. résumé
3. challenging
4. fill out

New Technology: Communication
1. cellphone
2. voicemail
3. personal calls
4. text message

New Technology: Computers and the Internet
1. laptop/notebook
2. printer
3. chat room
4. emails/email

Newspapers
1. tabloids
2. gossip column
3. make/hit the headlines
4. exclusive
5. sensationalist

Television
1. game show
2. flipping channels
3. documentary
4. channels
5. soap (opera)

PRONUNCIATION

Transcription

The words in this dictionary are followed by a **transcription** to show the pronunciation:

- *come* /kʌm/, *home* /hoʊm/

Often the number of **symbols** in the transcription will be different from the number of **letters** in the written word. This is because symbols in a transcription represent the **sounds** rather than the letters.

Written letters may correspond to a number of different sounds—or to no sound at all! But symbols always represent the same sound. Look at the following groups of words. They all contain the same vowel sound—but the spelling is different:

- *come* /kʌm/, *sum* /sʌm/, *dumb* /dʌm/
- *home* /hoʊm/, *roam* /roʊm/, *comb* /koʊm/

Some symbols are familiar and easy to recognize, for example / p, b, t, d, k, g, f /. Others are less easy. The "ng" sound in words such as *song* /sɔŋ/ and *thing* /θɪŋ/ is represented by the single symbol /ŋ/. And the symbols for "th" show that this pair of letters can cover two different sounds. Compare:

- *thing* /θɪŋ/ and *this* /ðɪs/

If you want to check the sound of a new symbol, look at the list of symbols and words on the inside back cover.

The Schwa Sound /ə/

The **schwa** represents the most common sound in English. It is the first sound in *above* /əˈbʌv/ and the last sound in *pizza* /ˈpitsə/. In fact, almost any written vowel can, when unstressed, be sounded as a schwa:

- *allow* /əˈlaʊ/, *perform* /pərˈfɔrm/, *commit* /kəˈmɪt/, *supply* /səˈplaɪ/.

Stress

Both *above* /əˈbʌv/ and *pizza* /ˈpitsə/ have two **syllables**. But they are different in terms of the relative importance of the syllables. In *above* the first syllable is weak, while the second syllable is strong. In *pizza*, by contrast, it is the first syllable that is strong. In other words, the first syllable in *pizza* is **stressed**, and we indicate this in the dictionary by using the symbol /ˈ/ directly before the stressed syllable. You can imagine these two words written as aBOVE and PIzza.

It is useful to know that:

- most two-syllable nouns and adjectives have **front stress** (the first syllable is stressed): FLOWer, LITTle, VILLage, PREtty, BOdy, FOrest, etc.
- most two-syllable verbs have **end stress** (the second syllable is stressed): forGIVE, aLLOW, coMMIT, etc.

It is worth checking the pronunciation in the dictionary, especially if a two-syllable word can be both a noun and a verb. In such cases one of two things can happen:

- *either* there is no change in the pronunciation or in the stress, for example: *reply* /rɪˈplaɪ/, *damage* /ˈdæmɪdʒ/, and *wonder* /ˈwʌndər/
- *or* the written form stays the same, but the stress changes, often causing a change in the vowel sound: compare *permit* (noun) /ˈpɜrmɪt/ and *permit* (verb) /pərˈmɪt/, *record* (noun) /ˈrekərd/ and *record* (verb) /rɪˈkɔrd/, and *import* (noun) /ˈɪmpɔrt/ and *import* (verb) /ɪmˈpɔrt/.

		weak	secondary	weak	primary	weak
		o	■	o	■	o
station	/ˈsteɪʃ(ə)n/				STA	tion
reaction	/riˈækʃ(ə)n/			re	AC	tion
satisfaction	/ˌsætɪsˈfækʃ(ə)n/		SA	tis	FAC	tion
pronunciation	/prəˌnʌnsiˈeɪʃ(ə)n/	pro	NUN	ci	A	tion

Primary and Secondary Stress

In some words, especially words of three or more syllables, there are sometimes two levels of stress: **primary stress** and **secondary stress**. When this happens, we use the symbol /ˌ/ before the secondary stressed syllable. Look at the examples for *satisfaction* and *pronunciation* in the table above.

Making Sure That People Understand You When You Speak

If you want to be easily understood, then the first thing to do is to make sure that your **consonant sounds** are as clear and accurate as possible.

In the case of **vowel sounds**, you should pay special attention to the group of vowels known as **diphthongs**. These are indicated by double symbols, for example:

- *day* /deɪ/, *nice* /naɪs/, *boy* /bɔɪ/, *go* /goʊ/

In all of these the tongue moves from one position to another as the vowel sound continues.

You should also make sure that your **word stress** is as accurate as possible. You will see that the dictionary shows the stress patterns of compound words and phrasal verbs, for example:

- ˈquestion ˌmark
- ˌput ˈup with sb/sth

Understanding Native Speakers

The dictionary shows the pronunciations of words as they are spoken in their slow, careful form. But in normal rapid speech, this often changes, particularly in the following ways:

1. It is sometimes difficult to hear when one word ends and the next begins. Here are examples of the four main types of **word linking**.

- *an apple* sounds like *a napple*
- *two apples* sounds like *two wapples*
- *three apples* sounds like *three yapples*
- *four apples* sounds like *four rapples*

2. The schwa can disappear between certain consonants. This means that *support* /səˈpɔrt/ may sound like *sport* /spɔrt/ and *parade* /pəˈreɪd/ like *prayed* /preɪd/. The consonants /t/ and /d/ may disappear when found between two other consonants. So *facts* may sound like *fax* and *friendly* like *frienly*.

If you see a symbol in brackets in this dictionary, (as in /ˈsteɪʃ(ə)n/ or /ˈfren(d)li/) it means that the sound may disappear in normal rapid speech.

3. Finally, consonants may change to make it easier to produce the next sound. Sometimes words change permanently, as with *handkerchief* where the /d/ has disappeared completely and it now sounds like *hangkerchief*. Other words change when spoken fast, such as *handbag* which is on its way to sounding permanently like *hambag*.

METAPHOR

You may think that metaphor is only used in poetry and creative writing, but this is not the case. Many words in English have more than one meaning, and these other meanings are often connected to the main meaning in metaphorical ways.

Most of the words that we use for describing familiar objects and familiar experiences also have metaphorical meanings. Groups of metaphors come from many different areas of human life. Here are some examples.

Metaphors about the Body

Some of the first words that you learn in English are for the parts of the body: **hand**, **head**, **eye**, and so on. But these words will sometimes be used in ways that don't fit the meanings that you know:

Could you give Jill a ***hand*** *with these boxes?*
It's very important for us all to put our ***heads*** *together.*
Can you keep an ***eye*** *on things here until I get back?*

If you know only the basic meanings of these words, you will find these sentences strange. Does the first speaker want someone to cut off their hand and give it to Jill, together with the boxes? Does the second speaker want to put their head next to other people's heads? Of course not. The first speaker is asking for help. The second speaker is suggesting that everyone should work together in order to solve a problem. In these sentences, the body parts are being used in ways that are not ***literal*** but ***metaphorical***.

Although the sentences above do not refer literally to body parts, their meanings are influenced by the literal meanings. We use our hands to help people, so to help someone is to **give them a hand**. Our brains are inside our heads, so the head is associated with people thinking. We look at things with our eyes, so if we **keep an eye on something**, we watch it carefully to make sure that it is being done correctly.

Metaphors about the Weather

Most people like sunny weather so, as you might guess, a **sunny** smile or a **sunny** nature or personality are good, positive things.

Storms are powerful and impossible to control, so a **storm** of protest or criticism is difficult to deal with.

Warm weather is pleasant and comfortable, and a **warm** person is kind and friendly in a way that makes other people feel comfortable.

Cold weather, on the other hand, is often less pleasant, and a **cold** person is unfriendly and makes us feel uncomfortable.

ACTIVITY

Have a look in the dictionary at the literal and metaphorical meanings of the following words, and try to find the connections between them:

- cool, icy, heated, hot
- hail, gale, flood, torrent
- to rain, to cloud over

ACTIVITY

Try to think of some more English words connected with temperature and the weather that have metaphorical meanings.

ACTIVITY

There are many metaphors relating to animals in English. Try to find the metaphorical meanings associated with common animals such as **pigs**, **sheep**, **donkeys**, and **rats**.

Are animal metaphors the same in your language as they are in English? Think of some in your own language, and compare them.

Metaphor and the Creation of New Meanings

When new words are needed in order to describe things that did not exist before, they are often created by means of metaphor. With the growth of computer technology, we need words to describe many new objects and activities—and most of these new words have been produced metaphorically:

> When you want to spend some time **surfing** the **Net**, you get connected and start to **browse**. You notice a **website** that looks interesting, and use your **mouse** to click on the **link** that takes you to the website. The **site's home page** may have a **menu** with links to different areas of the site. Having **visited** the site, you like it so much that you will want to return, so you **bookmark** it.

> The first thing I do when I switch on my computer is to check my **mailbox** for any new **emails**. I get about 20 a day but try to keep my **inbox** as neat as possible by **filing** them in a number of different **folders**.

If you look in a dictionary that is over 10 years old, you will find most of the bold words above. But you will not find the meanings that are used here.

Although a website is not a physical place, we can **visit** it as we would visit a friend or a place of interest. Similarly, a **mailbox** can now mean the part of a computer's memory where email is stored. Thinking of it as the physical place where letters written on paper are delivered helps us to understand the technology.

ACTIVITY

The metaphors that are used in computer language come from many different areas of life. Which areas do the following terms come from?

- **virus**, **window**, **exit**, **memory**, **icon**

ACTIVITY

Many computer metaphors come from the language we use to talk about **books**, the **office**, and the traditional **postal system**. Look at the words highlighted in the text above, and try to decide whether they fit into any of these categories.

How Awareness of Metaphor Can Help Your Language Learning

We use metaphors almost every time we write or speak, often without realizing it. Becoming aware of how language works—a process known as "language awareness"—is an essential part of successful language learning.

Here are two ways in which awareness of metaphor can help you to increase your understanding of how English works:

- When you read a piece of English, notice the metaphors, and think about the ways in which *metaphorical* meanings are connected with *literal* meanings.
- Try to relate new words and expressions that you come across in your reading to the words you already know. Thinking about the connections between familiar items of vocabulary and new, unfamiliar ones will help you to remember the new meanings you have learned.

If you develop the habit of thinking about language in this way, you will be able to learn and remember new vocabulary more effectively.

ANSWERS

virus: medicine; *window*: architecture; *exit*: architecture; *memory*: psychology; *icon*: religion

surfing: sports; *browse*: books; *home page*: books; *menu*: restaurants; *bookmark*: books; *mailbox*: postal system; *filing*: office; *folders*: office

WORD FORMATION

Word Families

Look at this group of words and decide what they have in common:

ability	*disability*
disabled	*enable*
inability	*unable*

All of the above words are formed from—and are related to—the adjective **able**. So we can call **able** the "root word" from which all these other words are developed. Can you guess which word is the root word for this next group?

destroyer	*destructive*
destruction	*indestructible*

All these words are formed from the root word **destroy**. We call these groups of related words "word families." Like members of real families, the words that make up a word family share some of the same features: they all share some of the letters of the root word, and their meanings are related too.

ACTIVITY

Look at the following groups of words and try to decide in each case what the root word is. The answers are on page LS19. Then try to guess the meaning of each word. Check in the dictionary to see if you are right.

discomfort	*uncomfortable*
comfortable	*comforting*

decision	*decisive*
undecided	*indecisive*
indecision	

impure	*purify*
purist	*impurity*

How Are Words Formed?

Many English words are formed from combinations of other words, or from combinations of words and prefixes or suffixes. So if you know what each of the parts means, you will often be able to guess the meaning of a new word.

What Are Prefixes and Suffixes?

A *prefix* is added to the *beginning* of a word to make another word. A prefix can be either a short word, or a group of letters that is not a word. An example of the first type is **self**-. **Self**- means "yourself" or "itself," so if you are **self-employed**, you work for yourself, and if something **self-destructs**, it destroys itself. An example of the second type is **non**-, which means "not." So a **nonviolent** protest is a protest that does not involve violence.

A *suffix* is added to the *end* of a word to make another word. A suffix can be either a short word, or a group of letters that is not a word. An example of the first type is **-rich**, which is added to nouns to make adjectives for describing something that "contains a lot" of something. So **oil-rich** rocks are full of oil, and **vitamin-rich** foods contain a lot of vitamins. An example of the second type is **-ish**, which means "slightly" or "rather." So **greenish** water looks slightly green.

ACTIVITY

Look at the words in **bold** in the following sentences and see if you can guess what they mean. After you have guessed, you can check the meanings in the dictionary. All the prefixes and suffixes used in these sentences (and shown here in red) have their own entries in the dictionary.

*The software is **overpriced** and doesn't offer anything more than its rivals.*

*Local residents are calling for the police to crack down on **antisocial** behavior by troublemakers, some of whom are as young as ten.*

***E-commerce** now accounts for 84 percent of the company's sales.*

*The machines are very **user-friendly** and they tell you how hard you are working and how many calories you have used up.*

The new district health boards will be required to act in an efficient and ***businesslike*** *way.*

ACTIVITY
See if you can make some more words using these prefixes and suffixes. Check in the dictionary to see if your words are there.

Compounds

Using prefixes and suffixes is not the only way to form new words. Many English words are *compounds*. Compounds are formed by combining two or three words. Sometimes these combinations remain as two or three separate words and sometimes they combine to form one new word. For example, the word **troublemakers** in the second example above has been formed by combining the two nouns **trouble** and **maker**. This has created a new word meaning "someone who makes (=causes) trouble."

Most compounds are treated as separate entries in this dictionary, so that you can see immediately that they have a meaning of their own that is different from the meanings of the words from which they are formed. Sometimes these meanings are easy to guess. For example, a **bus stop** is a place where buses stop to pick up passengers, and a **bookstore** is a place where you buy books. However, a **soap opera** does not contain any singing and has nothing to do with soap: it is a television or radio show that is broadcast several times a week, and tells the story of the lives of a group of ordinary people.

Other Ways of Forming Words

Some new words are formed by combining part of one word with part of another. For example, **brunch** is a meal you eat in the late morning that combines **breakfast** and **lunch**, and **edutainment** is something such as a video, television program, or software program that combines **education** and **entertainment**.

ACTIVITY
Can you guess which words have combined to form the following computer terms: **emoticon**, **netiquette**, **netizen**, **technophobe**?

And can you guess their meanings from the words that have combined to form them? The answers are at the bottom of this page.

Other new words are formed from the first letters of the words in a compound or phrase. Examples of this are **CD-ROM** (compact disc read-only memory), **FAQs** (frequently-asked questions), and **IT** (information technology). These new words are called *acronyms*.

ACTIVITY
Think about how new words are formed in your own language. Are they formed mainly by using *prefixes* and *suffixes*, by combining words to form *compounds*, by means of *acronyms*, or in other ways?

Spelling Note: Words that are formed from combinations of other words, whether these are compounds or words formed from prefixes or suffixes, are often written in several different ways. You may see them written as separate words, or with hyphens, or as single words. For example: **hard hat**, **hard-hat**, or **hardhat**. Although one form is often more frequent than others, you shouldn't worry too much about which is correct. If you want to be sure, write the word using the form that you find in this dictionary.

ANSWERS

The root words are *comfort, decide, pure*

emoticon: emotion + icon (=a symbol such as :-) or :-(that you type in an e-mail or text message to show how you are feeling)

netiquette: Internet + etiquette (=the rules of polite behavior, used when communicating with people on the Internet)

netizen: Internet + citizen (=someone who spends a lot of time using the Internet)

technophobe: technology + -phobe (=someone who does not like to use new technology, especially computers)

REGISTER

Saying the Right Thing at the Right Time

I recently received an e-mail from a business colleague that began like this:

How are things with you? And your mom? How is she?

She knew that my mother was in the hospital at the time, and wanted to show concern. It was a rather chatty beginning to a letter, which was fine since we are colleagues. What was perhaps less appropriate was her use of the word **mom**. And the reason this sounded a little strange relates to the issue of "register."

Register

The word **mom** has exactly the same *meaning* as **mother**, but it sounds too informal to use in a professional context. Even when trying to sound friendly, you should use the more "neutral" word **mother**, unless you know the person that you are referring to very well. It is a good example of how using the wrong register can make an otherwise successful piece of communication sound strange.

Register in the Dictionary

This dictionary helps learners of English to avoid these (sometimes embarrassing) misuses. At some entries, you will see register "labels," which show that the word is not neutral. Look at the entries for *mother* and *mom*. Notice that *mother* has no register label: this means that it is neutral and safe to use in almost any context. But *mom* is labeled *informal*, which means that you should pay extra attention to when and where you use it.

There are many examples of register labels in the dictionary. These three words express the same idea, for example, but with three different levels of formality:

strike	formal
hit	neutral
bash	informal

Grammatically, they all function in the same way:

He	*struck* *hit* *bashed*	*the nail* *with a* *hammer.*

Which should you use? There is no fixed rule, but when you are not sure which register to use, think of how you want to *sound*.

	Formal	Informal	Neutral
I want to sound friendly.	No	Maybe	OK
I want to sound official.	Yes	No	OK
I want to sound serious.	Yes	No	OK
I want to use the least risky word.	No	No	Yes
I don't want to sound serious.	No	Yes	No

This concept of formality affects expressions as well as individual words. Consider these:

*They found it **most agreeable**.*	formal
*They really **enjoyed themselves**.*	neutral
*They **had a ball**.*	informal

Additional care should be taken before attempting to say a word or expression that is labeled *informal*. Informal words and expressions can sometimes sound strange when spoken by a non-native speaker of English. If you feel that your accent is native-like, a word that is labeled *informal* might be OK to use. Otherwise, be careful.

Domain Labels

Imagine that you are jogging with a friend. She turns to you and says:

*Wait. I'm short of **respiration**.*

Then you pass an ATM and she says:

*I'm just going to take out some **liquid assets**.*

Finally, you invite her to have lunch and she says:

*No, thanks. I'm having lunch in my **abode**.*

If this sounds strange to you, it's because some of the words that your friend is using are not neutral, but belong to specific "domains." The word **respiration** means the same as "breath" or "breathing," but is used mainly by doctors and nurses. In other words, it belongs to the *medical* domain. Similarly, **liquid assets** is a *business* term, and **abode** is *literary*.

When a word belongs to a specific domain, this dictionary shows this by giving "domain labels." These include: *science, journalism, literary,* and *computing*. You can find a list of all the labels on page 829.

Here are some examples that illustrate the contrast between neutral and domain-specific registers:

Domain-Specific Term	Domain	Neutral Term
respiration	*medical*	breath, breathing
liquid assets	*business*	money
abode	*literary*	home, house
minor	*legal*	child, young person
ferrous	*science*	containing iron

So, instead of *short of respiration*, it is more natural to say *short of breath*. Similarly, *take out some money* and *at home* are more natural than *take out some liquid assets* and *in my abode*.

Like formal and informal words, words that belong to specific domains have a more limited use. But they do have a role in the right context. It would sound strange to talk about *minors* if you were talking to a friend, but it would sound completely normal if used in a court of law. The important thing is to know which word to choose to suit the situation.

Conclusion

The register and domain labels given in this dictionary are guides, but there is never a fixed rule as to which register is appropriate to any given situation. Could someone communicate without paying attention to register? Of course. After all, I understood what my colleague was trying to say in her e-mail. However, by using the word **mom**, her message sounded a little strange.

By using the "wrong" register, you may (at best) fail to convey the correct message or (at worst) even cause offense. So when you see a label like *informal* or *literary* next to a word or expression in this dictionary, be careful how you use it. It might help you to avoid uncomfortable situations.

TEXT TYPES

Texts are written for a purpose. The purpose might be to get or give information, to discuss a topic, to present an opinion, or to persuade someone to do something. Writers organize texts in various ways to do these particular jobs. They use different grammar structures and vocabulary depending on the purpose of a text.

Narratives

A narrative tells a story or gives an account (real or imagined) of something that has happened. The events are usually given in the order that they happen.
Past tenses are the most common grammar structures in narratives. The main events are usually told in sentences using the simple past and past progressive tenses. The details or extra information about the story are often in the present or past perfect tenses. Direct speech is used to add variety and interest.

Ordering Events: Useful Vocabulary

after that, afterwards, at first, before, during, in the end, eventually, finally, for, later, meanwhile, next, since, then, till, until, when, while

Sue Miller, who works as an acrobat in a circus, went into a thrift store in St. Louis. She left her bike at the door. While she was in the store, one of the clerks sold her bike for $20. Ms. Miller had paid $1,500 for it. When she came out of the store and discovered what had happened, she was shocked. "At first I thought someone had moved it. Then my knees turned to jelly and I fell down. I felt like I'd been kicked in the stomach," she said.

ACTIVITY

Write a short account of Nelson Mandela's life based on the information below, using some of the useful vocabulary from the Narratives section.

Nelson Mandela Timeline

1918	born in a village in the Transkei
1940	expelled from Fort Hare University for leading a strike
1942	joined the African National Congress, formed the African National Congress Youth League with fellow ANC members
1952	became a lawyer, opened the first black legal firm in the country with Oliver Tambo
1960	Sharpeville Massacre, Mandela detained until 1961
1962	jailed for 5 years
1964	sentenced to life imprisonment while serving the 5-year sentence
1990	released
1990	elected President of the ANC
1993	shared Nobel Peace Prize with President FW de Clerk
1994	became President of South Africa
1999	retired as President of South Africa

Descriptions

A description gives details about what someone or something is like or how something is done.
Descriptions often use present tenses, but they also use past tenses to give background information. Fictional and historical descriptions often use past tenses.

Adjectives

When we are describing people and things, we often use a series of adjectives. The usual order for adjectives before nouns is:

opinion, number	other (size, shape, age, etc.)	color	origin	material	purpose	
a strange	old	red	Moroccan	leather	money	bag
pretty	fluffy	white				clouds
several	tall	gray		concrete	office	buildings

Describing a Person: Useful Vocabulary

Describing a Person's Appearance
he/she is tall/short
he/she has curly/straight/wavy/light/dark hair
he's got a beard/moustache
he/she wears glasses
he/she has wrinkles/freckles/dimples
he/she has a round/oval/long face
he/she looks/seems/appears nervous/relaxed/troubled

My Friend Jane (Part 1)
My friend Jane has short, curly blond hair. She's got an oval face, beautiful green eyes, and a few freckles on her nose. She's about average height for her age—14. Today she's wearing her school uniform—a gray skirt, a long-sleeved white blouse, and black shoes.

Describing a Person's Character
he/she has an outgoing personality/easygoing manner
she/he can be stubborn/difficult/charming

My Friend Jane (Part 2)
Jane is sitting at her desk, staring out the window and seems to be thinking about something else. She is not paying attention to what the teacher is saying. She's often very quiet and doesn't say much in class. Her teachers say that she is a good student—hardworking and intelligent—just not very outgoing.

ACTIVITY

Write a description of a person that you know and/or admire. Write about their appearance and character.

Describing a Scene: Useful Vocabulary

there is/are
in the center/middle
to the right/left, to one side
in the foreground/background
above, behind, between, beyond, in front of, near, over, under

The View from My Bedroom
The clouds look like dark mountains in the distance. There is a small white house to the right with smoke coming out of the chimney. One of the upstairs windows is open and there is a cat asleep on the porch. The trees are beginning to lose their leaves. An old rusty red pickup truck is slowly climbing the rocky road to the house. There is a long wooden table and several cardboard boxes in the back of the truck.

Describing How to Do Something: Useful Vocabulary

first, next, then, before doing something, when/once you have done something

Hot Peanut Sauce
First heat the coconut milk until it boils. Then add the two kinds of curry paste and stir-fry for three minutes. When the mixture has cooked, add peanut butter, sugar, salt, and lemon juice. Mix all the ingredients thoroughly, then return to a low heat, stirring continuously.

Reviews

A review is an article in which someone gives their opinion about a book, play, movie, exhibition, etc. Movie and book reviews often summarize main events in the story or plot.

The movie is set in the early days of the 24th century. Science, technology, and hard work have solved most of the problems humanity faces today but life has become so serious that there is no fun in the world. A team of scientists is sent on a mission to the past to find a sense of humor. This is a delightful, upbeat "feel-good" movie that will leave you laughing.

ACTIVITY

Write a short review of a film or play that you have seen recently.

Discussions and Arguments

A discursive text presents and discusses issues and opinions. The purpose may be to convince or persuade someone that a particular course of action is important or necessary, or simply to present all sides of an argument.

Discursive texts usually:

- compare or contrast two or more things,
- present a problem and suggest a solution, or
- present arguments for or against an action.

The **opening** or **introductory section** may describe the present situation or different sides of an argument. This is followed by a **development section** that describes and illustrates different points. The development section may also consider other points of view or objections. The **closing section** sums up the options or solutions.

Presenting a Discussion: Useful Vocabulary

expressing opinions: in my view/opinion, I think/feel
ordering ideas: first/firstly/in the first place/to begin with, next/secondly, lastly/finally
giving additional information or reasons: additionally, equally, in fact, moreover, what is more, furthermore
giving examples: for example, for instance, such as
showing cause and effect: as a result, consequently, resulting in
contrasting and comparing: compared with/to, however, in contrast, on the one hand ... on the other hand, similarly, whereas, while, yet
summing up: on balance, in conclusion, to sum up

Discuss the following statement:
Ecotourism is responsible for causing many of the problems that it originally set out to solve.

Ecotourism is defined by TIES (The International Ecotourism Society) as "responsible travel to natural areas that conserves the environment and sustains the well-being of local people." This "environmentally friendly" form of tourism aims to help fund environmental protection programs, stimulate the incomes of the local people, especially those on very low incomes, and promote intercultural understanding. These are commendable goals.

Unfortunately, in my view, they are not being achieved. For example, recent reports from a number of developing countries state that locals have been evicted from their houses. These people are being driven from their homes to make way for the development of eco-parks, resorts, and hotels.

While much valuable work has been done and, no doubt, with the best intentions, ecotourism has made many local people homeless.

ACTIVITY

Choose one of the topics below to discuss in writing:

- Smoking should be banned in all public places.
- Parents should control their children's access to the Internet.
- Film censorship is a waste of time.

Nn

n or **N** /en/ noun [C/U] the 14th letter of the English alphabet

n. abbrev noun

N. abbrev **1** north **2** northern

'n' /ən/ conjunction *informal* a way of writing "and" that shows how it sounds in informal conversation

n/a abbrev not applicable: used on forms for showing that a particular question is not relevant to you

NAACP, the /ˌen dʌb(ə)l ˌeɪ si ˈpi/ the National Association for the Advancement of Colored People: an organization that works to improve conditions for African American people

nab /næb/ verb [T] *informal* to catch someone who has done something that is wrong or illegal

na•chos /ˈnɑtʃoʊz/ noun [plural] a Mexican food that consists of pieces of TORTILLA (=thin flat bread) with beans and melted cheese on top

nag /næg/ verb [T] **1** to annoy someone by frequently criticizing them or telling them to do something: *My mom keeps nagging me to clean up my room.* **2** if a doubt, worry, or fear nags you, you cannot stop thinking about it

nag•ging /ˈnægɪŋ/ adj **1** continuously hurting you or making you feel worried: *a nagging doubt/fear/pain* **2** annoying you by frequently criticizing you or telling you to do something

nail¹ /neɪl/ noun [C] ★

1 the smooth hard part that grows over the ends of your fingers and toes

2 a thin pointed piece of metal that you use for attaching one thing to another by hitting it with a hammer

PHRASES **a nail in the coffin** one of a series of events or actions that seriously harm someone or something: *These job losses are the final nail in the region's coffin.*

on the nail *informal* correct: *Her comments were right on the nail.*

→ HIT¹

nail² /neɪl/ verb [T] **1** to attach something with nails **2** *informal* to prove that someone has done something that is wrong or illegal **3** *American informal* to succeed in doing something

nail-bit•ing /ˈneɪl ˌbaɪtɪŋ/ adj a nail-biting situation makes you very excited or worried

ˈnail ˌfile noun [C] a thin piece of metal with a rough side that you use for shaping your nails

ˈnail ˌpolish noun [U] a shiny colored liquid that women put on their nails

na•ive /nɑˈiv/ adj lacking experience of life, and extremely willing to trust and believe people —**na•ive•ly** adv, **na•i•ve•té** /ˌnɑivəˈteɪ, nɑˈivəˌteɪ/ noun [U]

na•ked /ˈneɪkəd/ adj ★

1 not wearing any clothes = BARE: *a drawing of a naked woman*

2 not covered: *a naked flame/bulb*

3 a naked emotion is very strong and can be clearly seen in someone's expression

PHRASE **the naked eye** if you can see something with the naked eye, you can see it without using an instrument such as a TELESCOPE or a MICROSCOPE

name¹ /neɪm/ noun ★★★

1 [C] a word or set of words used for referring to a person or thing: ***My name is** Judith Kramer.* ♦ *What's **the name of** this flower?* ♦ *I think it's a great **name for** a band.*

2 [singular] a reputation: *These people have ruined the school's **good name**.* ♦ *He first **made a name for himself as** a singer.*

3 [C] a famous person or organization: *She's one of the most famous names in country music.* ♦ *This role has turned him into a **household name*** (=known by everyone).

→ BIG NAME

PHRASES **call sb names** to insult someone by using unpleasant words to refer to them

in the name of representing someone or something

the name of the game *informal* something that you must do if you want to be successful at a particular activity: *Personality is the name of the game in sales.*

Talking or writing about names

- **alias** a false name that a criminal uses
- **first name/given name** a personal name that you are given when you are born
- **last name** your family name
- **maiden name** a woman's last name before she was married
- **middle name** the name that comes after your first name but is only used formally
- **nickname** an invented name that other people call you

name² /neɪm/ verb [T] ★★

1 to give someone or something a name: *Have you named the baby yet?* ♦ **name sb/sth sth** *We named our puppy Buddy.*

2 to know and say what the name of someone or something is: *How many state capitals can you name?*

3 to make a decision about a date, time, place, or price, and say what it is: *Name a time, and I'll be there.*

4 to choose someone for a particular job, position, or prize: **name sb sth** *He was named player of the year.*

PHRASE **you name it** *informal* used after a list for saying that many other things of the same type are also available

PHRASAL VERBS **ˈname sb/sth after sb/sth** to give someone or something the same name as someone or something else: *Albert was named after his grandfather.*

ˈname sth for sb/sth *American* to give a place or an object the same name as a person or another thing: *The prize is named for the late Mexican writer, Juan Rulfo.*

ˈname-ˌdropping noun [U] the act of mentioning famous people who you know in order to impress other people

name•less /ˈneɪmləs/ adj not having a name,

or not having a name that you know

name·ly /ˈneɪmli/ adv used for introducing more detailed information about a subject that you are discussing: *Some groups, namely homeowners and landlords, will benefit from the new tax.*

name·sake /ˈneɪmˌseɪk/ noun [C] a person or thing with the same name as someone or something else

nan·ny /ˈnæni/ noun [C] a woman whose job is to take care of someone else's children

nap /næp/ noun [C] a short sleep, usually during the day —**nap** verb [I]

nape /neɪp/ noun [singular] the back of your neck

nap·kin /ˈnæpkɪn/ noun [C] a piece of cloth or paper that you use for protecting your clothes and wiping your mouth and hands when you are eating

nap·py /ˈnæpi/ noun [C] *British* a DIAPER for a baby

narc /nɑrk/ verb [I] *American informal* to tell the police about something that is wrong or illegal that someone has done

nar·cis·sism /ˈnɑrsəˌsɪzəm/ noun [U] the attitude of people who admire themselves a lot —**nar·cis·sist** /ˈnɑrsəˌsɪst/ noun [C], **nar·cis·sis·tic** /ˌnɑrsəˈsɪstɪk/ adj

nar·cot·ic /nɑrˈkɑtɪk/ noun [C] *American* an illegal drug

nar·rate /ˈneˌreɪt/ verb [T] to give information about what is happening in a television program or a movie without appearing on the screen

nar·ra·tion /nəˈreɪʃ(ə)n/ noun [U] spoken information about what is happening in a television program or a movie, given by someone who you do not see

nar·ra·tive /ˈnerətɪv/ noun [C] a story or an account of something that has happened =STORY, TALE

nar·ra·tor /ˌnəˈreɪtər/ noun [C] **1** someone who tells the story in a novel **2** someone whose voice explains what is happening in a television program or a movie, but who you do not see

nar·row¹ /ˈneroʊ/ adj ★★★
1 if something is narrow, there is only a short distance from one side of it to the other ≠ WIDE: *narrow streets*
2 limited ≠ BROAD: *a narrow range of options*
3 used about something that you succeed in doing but nearly failed to do: *a narrow victory/escape*

nar·row² /ˈneroʊ/ verb [I/T] to become narrower, or to make something narrower ≠ WIDEN
PHRASAL VERB **ˌnarrow sth ˈdown** to reduce the number of possibilities or choices

nar·row·ly /ˈneroʊli/ adv by a very small amount: *Three teenagers narrowly escaped death in the accident.*

ˌnarrow-ˈminded adj not interested in ideas or cultures that are different from your own ≠ BROAD-MINDED

na·sal /ˈneɪz(ə)l/ adj **1** relating to your nose **2** someone with a nasal voice sounds as if they are speaking through their nose

nas·ty /ˈnæsti/ adj **1** unkind, offensive, or violent: *She said some very nasty things about him.* **2** very unpleasant =HORRIBLE: *a nasty cold wind* **3** serious or dangerous: *a nasty accident/cough* —**nas·ti·ly** adv

na·tion /ˈneɪʃ(ə)n/ noun [C] ★★★
1 a country: *a meeting of the leaders of the main industrial nations*
2 the people of a particular country: *We want government to serve the whole nation.*

na·tion·al¹ /ˈnæʃən(ə)l/ adj ★★★
1 relating to one particular nation: *the national and international news*
2 relating to the whole of a nation: *House prices in Connecticut are 5% higher than the national average.*
3 owned or controlled by the government: *the Rio Grande National Forest* ♦ *a national park/monument*
—**na·tion·al·ly** adv

> **Word family: national**
> *Words in the same family as **national***
> - **nation** *n*
> - **nationalize** *v*
> - **nationalism** *n*
> - **nationality** *n*
> - **international** *adj*
> - **nationalized** *adj*
> - **nationalistic** *adj*
> - **multinational** *adj, n*

na·tion·al² /ˈnæʃən(ə)l/ noun [C] a citizen of a particular country

ˌnational ˈanthem noun [C] the official national song of a country

na·tion·al·ism /ˈnæʃən(ə)lˌɪzəm/ noun [U] **1** the attitude of people who want political independence from a country that rules them **2** the belief that your country is better than all other countries

na·tion·al·ist /ˈnæʃən(ə)lɪst/ noun [C] **1** a member of a group of people who want political independence from a country that rules them **2** someone who believes that their own country is better than all other countries —**na·tion·al·ist** adj

na·tion·al·is·tic /ˌnæʃ(ə)nəˈlɪstɪk/ adj extremely proud of your own country and believing that it is better than all other countries

na·tion·al·i·ty /ˌnæʃəˈnæləti/ noun ★
1 [U] the legal status of being a citizen of a particular country: *British/American/German nationality*
2 [C] a group of people who have the same race, language, or culture: *There may be as many as 20 different nationalities in a school.*

na·tion·al·ize /ˈnæʃ(ə)nəˌlaɪz/ verb [T] if a government nationalizes a large company or industry, it takes control of it and owns it ≠ PRIVATIZE —**na·tion·al·i·za·tion** /ˌnæʃ(ə)nəlɪˈzeɪʃ(ə)n/ noun [U]

ˌnational ˈpark noun [C] a large area of land that is protected by the government in order to preserve its natural beauty

ˌnational seˈcurity noun [U] the protection or safety of a country

ˌnational ˈservice noun [U] a period of time that young people in some countries must spend in the military

ˌnation ˈstate noun [C] an independent country, especially one in which all the people share the same language and culture

na·tion·wide /ˈneɪʃ(ə)nˌwaɪd/ adj, adv in all parts of a country: *a nationwide strike*

na·tive¹ /ˈneɪtɪv/ adj ★
1 living in a particular country or area since birth: *My wife's a native New Yorker,*

N

but I'm from Atlanta. ♦ *After a long stay in England he's back in his **native land*** (=the country that he was born in).
2 native plants, animals, or people have always existed in a place: *the native population* ♦ *Elephants are **native to** Africa and Asia.*
3 your native language or TONGUE is the first language that you learn

na·tive² /ˈneɪtɪv/ noun [C] **1** someone who was born in a particular place: *He's a native of New Orleans but now lives in Miami.*
2 *offensive* an offensive word for a member of a group of people who lived in a place before Europeans arrived there

ˌNative Aˈmerican noun [C] a member of one of the groups of people who lived in America before Europeans arrived

ˌnative ˈspeaker noun [C] someone who speaks a particular language as their first language

NATO /ˈneɪtoʊ/ North Atlantic Treaty Organization: an organization of North American and European countries that provides military support for its members

nat·u·ral¹ /ˈnætʃ(ə)rəl/ adj ★★★
1 existing in nature, and not produced by people: *This cloth is made from natural fibers.* ♦ *areas of great natural beauty* ♦ *The earthquake is the worst **natural disaster** that Japan has experienced.* ♦ *Mr. Johnson died from **natural causes*** (=not as a result of an accident or crime).
2 reasonable in a particular situation: *His anger was an entirely natural reaction.* ♦ *It's only natural to worry about your child's diet.*
3 existing in someone from an early age: *The best players have **natural talent**.*
4 behaving in a relaxed and sincere way

nat·u·ral² /ˈnætʃ(ə)rəl/ noun [C] someone with a lot of skill that has developed very quickly and easily

ˌnatural ˈgas noun [U] a gas that is found underground and is used for heating and cooking

ˌnatural ˈhistory noun [U] the study of plants and animals

nat·u·ral·ist /ˈnætʃ(ə)rəlɪst/ noun [C] someone who studies plants and animals

nat·u·ral·ize /ˈnætʃ(ə)rəˌlaɪz/ verb [T] to make someone an official citizen of a country that they were not born in
—**nat·u·ra·li·za·tion** /ˌnætʃ(ə)rəlɪˈzeɪʃ(ə)n/ noun [U], **nat·u·ral·ized** /ˈnætʃ(ə)rəˌlaɪzd/ adj

nat·u·ral·ly /ˈnætʃ(ə)rəli/ adv ★
1 as most people would expect or understand = OBVIOUSLY: *Naturally, I was very eager to make a good first impression.* ♦ *His death has naturally come as a shock to us all.*
2 as a basic feature: *Her hair is naturally curly.* ♦ *Many herbs grow naturally in poor dry soils.*
3 in a normal way: *Try to act naturally in front of the camera.*
PHRASE **come naturally (to sb)** to be easy for someone to learn or do: *Being funny comes naturally to him.*

ˌnatural reˈsources noun [plural] useful substances such as coal and oil that exist in a country

na·ture /ˈneɪtʃər/ noun ★★★
1 [U] the physical world and all the living things in it: *the beauty of nature*
2 [C/U] the character, qualities, or features of someone or something: *The pony has a very gentle nature.* ♦ *It isn't **in my nature** to be aggressive.* ♦ *Apes are curious **by nature**.* ♦ ***It's the nature of** plastic to melt at high temperatures.*
3 [singular] a particular type of thing: *His behavior was inappropriate for a meeting **of this nature**.*

ˈnature reˌserve noun [C] an area of land in which the animals and plants are protected

naugh·ty /ˈnɔti/ adj a naughty child behaves badly

nau·se·a /ˈnɔziə, ˈnɔʃə/ noun [U] the feeling that you are going to VOMIT

nau·se·at·ing /ˈnɔziˌeɪtɪŋ, ˈnɔʃiˌeɪtɪŋ/ adj **1** very unpleasant = DISGUSTING **2** making you feel as if you are going to VOMIT
—**nau·se·at·ing·ly** adv

nau·seous /ˈnɔziəs, ˈnɔʃəs/ adj feeling as if you want to VOMIT

nau·ti·cal /ˈnɔtɪk(ə)l/ adj relating to ships, or to sailing them

na·val /ˈneɪv(ə)l/ adj relating to a country's navy

na·vel /ˈneɪv(ə)l/ noun [C] the small round place in the middle of the skin on your stomach

nav·i·ga·ble /ˈnævɪgəb(ə)l/ adj deep and wide enough for ships to travel through

nav·i·gate /ˈnævɪˌgeɪt/ verb **1** [I] to use maps or other equipment in order to decide which way to go in a ship, airplane, or car **2** [T] to follow a path through a difficult place **3** [T] *formal* to deal effectively with a complicated situation

nav·i·ga·tion /ˌnævɪˈgeɪʃ(ə)n/ noun [U] **1** the movement of a ship or an aircraft along a planned path **2** the skill of using maps or other equipment in order to decide which way to go

nav·i·ga·tor /ˈnævɪˌgeɪtər/ noun [C] someone whose job is to plan the direction in which a ship, airplane, or car should travel

na·vy /ˈneɪvi/ noun **1** [C] the part of a country's military that uses ships **2** [U] navy blue

ˌnavy ˈblue adj very dark blue —**ˌnavy ˈblue** noun [U]

Na·zi /ˈnɑtsi/ noun [C] someone who belonged to the political party that governed Germany during World War Two —**Na·zi** adj, **Na·zism** noun [U]

NBC /ˌen bi ˈsi/ National Broadcasting Company: one of the major television broadcasting companies in the U.S.

NC abbrev North Carolina

NCAA, the /ˌen si dʌb(ə)l ˈeɪ/ the National Collegiate Athletic Association: a large U.S. sports organization for college and university teams that decides rules and organizes competitions

ND abbrev North Dakota

NE abbrev **1** Nebraska **2** northeast

near¹ /nɪr/ grammar word ★★★

> **Near** can be:
> - a **preposition**: *I lived near the school.*
> - an **adverb**: *Come nearer, and I'll tell you the whole story.*
> - an **adjective**: *I went into the nearest room.*

1 close to someone or something: *A group*

of students were standing near the entrance. ♦ They live on a ranch 15 miles from the nearest town. ♦ Rosa moved a little **nearer to** the fire.
2 close to a particular time or event: *The incident occurred near the end of the war.* ♦ *The date of the election was* ***drawing near***. ♦ *They plan to start a family sometime* ***in the near future*** (=soon).
3 only a little less than a particular amount or number: *The temperature was near 100 degrees.*
4 getting close to a particular state or situation: *There were rumors that the 66-year-old leader was near death.*
PHRASES **from near and far** from a very wide area
not go near to avoid someone or something: *Dad doesn't go near red meat since his heart attack.*
nowhere/not anywhere near 1 far from a particular point or place: *The photographers were nowhere near the crash when it happened.* **2** not nearly: *She doesn't look anywhere near as old as Rebecca.*

near² /nɪr/ verb [T] to come closer to a place or time: *a man nearing the age of 60*

near•by¹ /ˌnɪrˈbaɪ/ adj a nearby place is not far away

near•by² /ˌnɪrˈbaɪ/ adv not far from where you are: *My cousin lives nearby.*

near•ly /ˈnɪrli/ adv ★★ almost: *It took nearly six hours to do the work.* ♦ *The fall nearly killed him.*
PHRASE **not nearly (as/so)** much less than: *It's not nearly so cold today.* ♦ *There isn't nearly enough food for everyone.*

near•sight•ed /ˌnɪrˈsaɪtəd/ adj *American* not able to see things clearly if they are far away from you ≠ FARSIGHTED

neat /nit/ adj ★★
1 things that are neat look nice because they have been arranged carefully = TIDY: *She arranged the papers into three neat piles on her desk.* ♦ *Her uniform was always neat and clean.*
2 someone who is neat tends to keep things carefully arranged
3 *American informal* good or nice: *She's a really neat person – you'll like her.*
4 producing a result in a simple but intelligent way: *a neat way of solving the problem*
—**neat•ly** adv

nec•es•sar•i•ly /ˌnesəˈserəli/ adv ★ always, or in every situation
PHRASE **not necessarily** not always, or not in every situation: *Our customers will not necessarily understand why we are raising our prices.*

nec•es•sar•y /ˈnesəˌseri/ adj ★★★ if something is necessary, you must have it or must do it: *I don't want to be disturbed unless it's absolutely necessary.* ♦ *I can take your place at the meeting tomorrow* ***if necessary***. ♦ *What type of clothing is* ***necessary for*** *a walk in the mountains?* ♦ **it is necessary for sb to do sth** *It was necessary for all students to attend classes regularly.*
PHRASE **a necessary evil** something that you do not like but cannot avoid: *Paying taxes is a necessary evil.*

Word family: **necessary**

Words in the same family as ***necessary***
- **necessity** *n*
- **necessarily** *adv*
- **necessitate** *v*
- **unnecessary** *adj*
- **unnecessarily** *adv*

ne•ces•si•tate /nəˈsesɪˌteɪt/ verb [T] to make something necessary

ne•ces•si•ty /nəˈsesəti/ noun **1** [U] the fact that something is necessary: *the necessity for a quick solution to the problem* ♦ *doubts about the necessity of the war* **2** [C] something that you must have or must do ≠ LUXURY: *They lacked even the bare necessities* (=the basic things that everyone needs).

neck /nek/ noun [C] ★★★
1 the part of your body that joins your head to the rest of your body —*picture* → C14
2 the part of a piece of clothing that fits around your neck
3 a long narrow part of something such as a bottle or a musical instrument
PHRASES **neck and neck** with each person or group competing as well as the other and equally likely to win
up to your neck in sth *informal* very involved or busy with something
→ BREATHE

neck•lace /ˈnekləs/ noun [C] a piece of jewelry that hangs around your neck —*picture* → JEWELRY

neck•line /ˈnekˌlaɪn/ noun [C] the shape of a piece of clothing around your neck

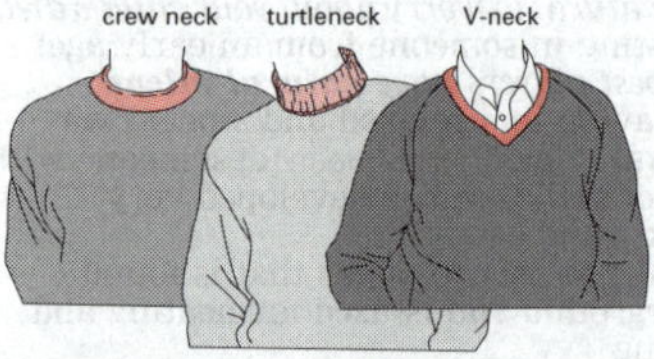

necklines

neck•tie /ˈnekˌtaɪ/ noun [C] *American formal* a TIE that is worn round your neck

nec•tar /ˈnektər/ noun [U] a sweet liquid in flowers that insects and birds drink

nec•tar•ine /ˈnektəˌrin/ noun [C] a fruit with a smooth red and yellow skin. It is yellow inside and has a large seed. —*picture* → C10

need¹ /nid/ verb [T] ★★★
1 if you need something, you must have it because it is necessary: *You'll need some warm clothes for the winter.* ♦ *I don't need any advice from you.* ♦ **need sb to do sth** *I need someone to help me carry these books downstairs.*
2 used for saying whether it is necessary for something to be done or to exist: **need to do sth** *I'll need to know your decision by next week.*

need² /nid/ noun ★★★
1 [singular/U] a situation in which it is necessary for something to be done: *I'll ask someone to help you,* ***if need be*** (=if it becomes necessary). ♦ *He recognizes the* ***need for*** *immediate action.* ♦ **a need to do sth** *We feel there is a need to do more research.*
2 [C] something that you need in order to be healthy, comfortable, successful, etc.:

People with mental health problems ***have*** *special* ***needs****.*

PHRASES **in need** not having enough food, money, clothing, or other things that are necessary: *families in need*

in need of sth needing something: *He was tired and hungry, and badly in need of a bath.*

there is no need (for sb) to do sth or **there is no need for sth** used for saying that something does not have to be done or should not be done: *There's no need for you to stay late – I can finish this.* ♦ *There's no need for all this violence.*

nee·dle¹ /ˈnid(ə)l/ noun [C] ★

1 a thin sharp metal tube that is used for putting medicine or drugs into your body through your skin

2 a thin metal tool that you use for sewing or KNITTING

3 the part of a piece of equipment that points to a number in order to show a measurement: *a compass needle*

4 a very thin sharp leaf that grows on some trees: *pine needles*

nee·dle² /ˈnid(ə)l/ verb [T] *informal* to say things that are intended to make someone angry or embarrassed

need·less /ˈnidləs/ adj unnecessary: *needless waste*

PHRASE **needless to say** used for emphasizing something that people already know

—**need·less·ly** adv

need·y /ˈnidi/ adj **1** without enough money, food, or clothes **2 the needy** people who are poor

ne·gate /nəˈgeɪt/ verb [T] *formal* to make something have no effect —**ne·ga·tion** /nəˈgeɪʃ(ə)n/ noun [U]

neg·a·tive¹ /ˈnegətɪv/ adj ★★

1 saying you disagree	5 expressing "no"
2 harmful/bad	6 less than zero
3 emphasizing bad part	7 about electrical charge
4 of medical test	

1 expressing disagreement or criticism ≠ POSITIVE: *a negative response*

2 harmful, or bad: *I hope the divorce won't have* ***a negative effect*** *on the children.*

3 giving more attention or emphasis to bad aspects than good ones ≠ POSITIVE: *The article presents* ***a rather negative view*** *of professional sports.*

4 showing that someone does not have a particular disease or condition: *Her pregnancy test was negative.* ♦ *He* ***tested negative*** *for drugs.*

5 *linguistics* a negative word expresses "no" or "not," for example "don't" or "never"

6 a negative number or amount is less than zero ≠ POSITIVE

7 *technical* with the same electrical charge as an ELECTRON ≠ POSITIVE

—**neg·a·tive·ly** adv

neg·a·tive² /ˈnegətɪv/ noun [C] **1** *linguistics* a word or expression that means "no" **2** an image on FILM in which dark things appear light, and light things appear dark

ne·glect¹ /nəˈglekt/ verb [T] **1** to not take care of someone or something: *parents who neglect their children* ♦ *The building had been neglected for years.* **2** to not do something that you should do: *He couldn't neglect his duties as an officer.* ♦ *She had neglected to inform me that the company was having financial problems.* **3** to not pay attention to something such as the work of a writer or an artist —**ne·glect·ed** adj

ne·glect² /nəˈglekt/ noun [U] the failure to give someone or something the care that they need: *Our roads have suffered from years of neglect.*

ne·glect·ful /nəˈglektfəl/ adj not doing something that you should do

neg·li·gee /ˌneglɪˈʒeɪ/ noun [C] a long loose thin piece of clothing that women wear over night clothes

neg·li·gence /ˈneglɪdʒəns/ noun [U] the failure to be careful enough, so that something bad happens

neg·li·gent /ˈneglɪdʒənt/ adj failing to be careful enough, so that something bad happens —**neg·li·gent·ly** adv

neg·li·gi·ble /ˈneglɪdʒəb(ə)l/ adj very unimportant or small = INSIGNIFICANT

ne·go·tia·ble /nəˈgoʊʃəb(ə)l, nəˈgoʊʃiəb(ə)l/ adj able to be changed through discussion by the people involved

ne·go·ti·ate /nəˈgoʊʃiˌeɪt/ verb ★

1 [I/T] to try to reach an agreement by discussing something formally: *The two sides have shown their willingness to negotiate.* ♦ ***Negotiating a peace deal*** *will not be an easy task.* ♦ **negotiate sth with sb** *The airline is negotiating a new contract with the union.*

2 [T] to successfully travel on a road or path that is difficult to travel on or travel through: *Only 4-wheel-drive vehicles can negotiate the rough roads around the ranch.*

—**ne·go·ti·a·tor** noun [C]

ne·go·ti·a·tion /nəˌgoʊʃiˈeɪʃ(ə)n/ noun [C/U] formal discussions in which people try to reach an agreement

neigh /neɪ/ verb [I] to make the high loud sound that a horse makes —**neigh** noun [C]

neigh·bor /ˈneɪbər/ noun [C] ★★

1 someone who lives near you: *friends and neighbors*

2 a person or place that is next to another person or place: *She whispered to her neighbor that she thought the play was too long.* ♦ *Turkey and its European neighbors*

neigh·bor·hood /ˈneɪbərˌhʊd/ noun [C] ★ a particular area of a town

neigh·bor·ing /ˈneɪbərɪŋ/ adj next to each other: *neighboring towns/states/countries*

neigh·bor·ly /ˈneɪbərli/ adj showing a helpful and friendly attitude toward people who live near you

neigh·bour /ˈneɪbər/ the British spelling of **neighbor**

neigh·bour·hood /ˈneɪbərˌhʊd/ the British spelling of **neighborhood**

neigh·bour·ing /ˈneɪbərɪŋ/ the British spelling of **neighboring**

neigh·bour·ly /ˈneɪbərli/ the British spelling of **neighborly**

nei·ther /ˈniðər, ˈnaɪðər/ grammar word ★★★

Neither can be:
- an **adverb**: *I can't play tennis, but neither can you.*

N

- a **conjunction** with **nor**: *Neither Simon nor Sally can swim.*
- a **determiner**: *Neither woman seemed sure of what to say.*
- a **pronoun**: *There were two witnesses, but neither would make a statement.* ♦ *Neither of us knew what to do.*

1 used for showing that a negative statement also applies to someone or something else: *Adams was not invited, and neither were any of his friends.* ♦ *"I don't like him." "**Neither do I.**"* ♦ *"I don't feel like going to the party." "**Me neither.**"*
2 used for referring to each of two people or things when saying something negative that applies to both of them: *Neither side trusts the other.* ♦ *Neither company could succeed on its own.* ♦ *It was an experience that **neither of** us will ever forget.*
PHRASE **neither...nor** used for showing that something is not true of two people or things: *Neither his son nor his daughter were at the funeral.* ♦ *Ron's neither as young nor as fast as the other members of the team.*

ne•on /ˈniˌɑn/ noun [U] a gas that is used in lights and signs

neph•ew /ˈnefju/ noun [C] a son of your brother or sister, or a son of your husband's or wife's brother or sister —*picture* → FAMILY TREE

nep•o•tism /ˈnepəˌtɪzəm/ noun [U] the practice of giving jobs to your family and friends

N

nerd /nɜrd/ noun [C] *informal* someone who is boring and not fashionable —**nerd•y** adj

nerve /nɜrv/ noun ★
1 [C] one of the groups of fibers in your body that carry messages to and from your brain
2 [U] the ability to control your fear and stay determined when you are doing something that is difficult = COURAGE: *Suddenly I **lost my nerve** and I couldn't move.* ♦ **the nerve to do sth** *After months of agonizing, she finally found the nerve to tell him he was wrong.*
3 nerves [plural] the worried feeling that you will do something badly: *He asked for a drink to **calm his nerves** before heading out to the plane.*
4 [U] a rude attitude that makes other people angry: **have the nerve to do sth** *She had the nerve to call me a liar after everything I've done for her.*
PHRASE **get on sb's nerves** to annoy someone

nerve-wrack•ing or **nerve-rack•ing** /ˈnɜrvˌrækɪŋ/ adj making you very nervous or worried

nerv•ous /ˈnɜrvəs/ adj ★★
1 feeling excited and worried, or slightly afraid = ANXIOUS: *Driving on icy mountain roads makes me nervous.* ♦ *a nervous laugh* ♦ *I **got** very **nervous** waiting for my turn to be called.* ♦ *She was **nervous about** walking home so late.*
2 a nervous person easily becomes excited or upset because they are not relaxed
3 relating to the nerves in your body: *a nervous condition*
—**nerv•ous•ly** adv

ˌnervous ˈbreakdown noun [C] a mental condition in which you are so upset or unhappy that you cannot take care of yourself

ˈnervous ˌsystem, the noun [singular] the system of nerves that control your body and your mind

nest¹ /nest/ noun [C] **1** a structure that birds make to keep their eggs and babies in **2** a home that insects or small animals make for themselves

nest² /nest/ verb [I] to build or use a nest

nes•tle /ˈnes(ə)l/ verb [I] **1** to put yourself into a comfortable and safe position **2** *literary* to be in a protected position: *a pretty village nestling among rolling hills*

net¹ /net/ noun ★★
1 [C/U] a material made of string or rope that is woven into a loose pattern with spaces in it
2 [C] in some sports, an object made of net that you hit, kick, or throw the ball over or into
3 [C] a bag made of net that you use for catching fish or other animals
4 the Net the INTERNET

net² /net/ adj **1** a net amount of money is the total amount after taxes or costs have been removed → GROSS **2** a net effect or result is the final one, after everything has been considered **3** the net weight of something is its weight without its container

net³ /net/ verb [T] **1** to manage to get or do something **2** to earn a particular amount of money as profit → GROSS

net•tle /ˈnet(ə)l/ noun [C] a wild plant with pointed leaves and small hairs that sting you if you touch them

net•work¹ /ˈnetˌwɜrk/ noun [C] ★★
1 a group of companies that broadcast the same television or radio programs in all parts of a large area: *The president's speech was broadcast on network television.* ♦ *television networks such as NBC and CBS*
2 a group of people or organizations that work together: *We have **a** nationwide **network of** financial advisers.*
3 a number of computers that are connected to each other
4 a system of things such as roads, rivers, or wires that are connected to each other: *a cellular phone network* ♦ ***a network of** canals*

Words often used with network

*Adjectives often used with **network** (noun, sense 2)*
- **extensive, global, international, national, nationwide, wide, worldwide** + NETWORK: used about networks that spread over a large area

*Verbs often used with **network** (noun, sense 2)*
- **build, construct, create, develop, expand, form** + NETWORK: create a network

net•work² /ˈnetˌwɜrk/ verb **1** [I/T] to connect computers together **2** [I] to meet people in order to make friends who will be useful for your business —**net•work•ing** noun [U]

neu•ral /ˈnʊrəl/ adj *technical* relating to your nerves or your NERVOUS SYSTEM

neu•rol•o•gy /nʊˈrɑlədʒi/ noun [U] *medical* the study of your NERVOUS SYSTEM and the diseases that affect it —**neu•ro•log•i•cal** /ˌnʊrəˈlɑdʒɪk(ə)l/ adj

neu•ro•sis /nʊˈroʊsɪs/ (plural **neu•ro•ses** /nʊˈroʊˌsiz/) noun [C/U] *medical* a mental illness that makes you behave or think in an unreasonable way

neu·rot·ic /nʊˈrɑtɪk/ adj extremely worried about something in an unreasonable way

neu·ter¹ /ˈnutər/ verb [T] to perform an operation on an animal's sexual organs so that it cannot have babies

neu·ter² /ˈnutər/ adj *linguistics* a neuter word has a different form and behavior from MASCULINE or FEMININE words in some languages

neu·tral¹ /ˈnutrəl/ adj ★

1 not supporting a particular person, group, or country in an argument, competition, or war: *a neutral country* ♦ *The television coverage was by no means neutral.*

2 not showing strong feelings or opinions in the way you speak or behave: *Her voice remained neutral as she spoke.*

3 neutral colors are not very strong or bright

—**neu·tral·ly** adv

neu·tral² /ˈnutrəl/ noun [U] the position of the GEARS in a car when the car cannot move

neu·tral·i·ty /nuˈtræləti/ noun [U] the attitude of someone who does not support either side in a war or disagreement

neu·tral·ize /ˈnutrəˌlaɪz/ verb [T] to stop something from having any effect

neu·tron /ˈnuˌtrɑn/ noun [C] *science* a part of an atom that does not have an electrical charge

nev·er /ˈnevər/ adv ★★★ at no time, or not at all: *I've never been in love before.* ♦ *You'll never guess who I saw today!* ♦ *He never even said goodbye.* ♦ *I never knew you two were cousins.* ♦ *I went sailing once, but* ***never again.***

PHRASE **you never know** used for saying that something might happen even though it does not seem likely: *You never know – he might offer you a part in his movie.*

nev·er·the·less /ˌnevərðəˈles/ adv ★★ despite a fact or idea that you have just mentioned: *It's a difficult race. Nevertheless, thousands of runners participate every year.*

new /nu/ adj ★★★

1 recently made	4 replacing sb/sth
2 recently bought	5 recently arrived
3 not used	6 not previously known

1 recently made, invented, or developed ≠ OLD: *They are going to build a new office building here.* ♦ *the new Tom Cruise movie* ♦ *I was full of new ideas.*

2 recently bought or obtained ≠ OLD: *Have you seen my new car?* ♦ *When do you start your new job?*

3 never used or owned by anyone before: *I don't need a new printer – a used one is good enough.* → SECONDHAND

4 replacing someone or something else ≠ OLD: *I should get a new passport – my old one's expired.*

5 recently arrived in a new place or situation: *Many companies help new employees with finding accommodations.* ♦ *We are* ***new to*** *the Boston area.*

6 not previously known or discovered: *The police have now been given some new information.*

→ GOOD¹

Words that you can use instead of **new**

New is a very general word. Here are some words with more specific meanings that sound more natural and appropriate in particular situations.

equipment, computers, etc. made using the latest ideas and technology	advanced, cutting-edge, modern, newfangled (*showing disapproval*), state-of-the-art, up-to-date
ideas, methods, etc. that are new and not like anything that has existed before	innovative, fresh, novel, original, revolutionary
movies, books, etc. that have just become available	latest, recent, just out
something you have just bought that has never been used	brand new

ˌNew ˈAge adj not connected with the main religions or with traditional ideas and methods

new·born /ˈnuˌbɔrn/ adj recently born —**new·born** noun [C]

new·com·er /ˈnuˌkʌmər/ noun [C] someone who has recently arrived somewhere

ˌNew ˈEngland the group of states in the NORTHEASTERN part of the U.S.

new·fan·gled /nuˈfæŋg(ə)ld/ adj *showing disapproval* very modern and complicated

new·found /ˈnuˌfaʊnd/ adj recently gained: *a newfound confidence/enthusiasm/optimism*

new·ly /ˈnuli/ adv recently: *the newly appointed chairperson of the company*

new·ly·weds /ˈnuliˌwedz/ noun [plural] two people who have not been married for very long

news /nuz/ noun ★★★

1 [U] information about something that has happened recently: *I'm afraid I have some bad news.* ♦ *She was delighted by this* ***piece of news.*** ♦ *Have you* ***heard the good news?*** *Michael got the job!* ♦ *Friends expressed shock at* ***the news of*** *his death.* ♦ *The leaflet is full of up-to-date* ***news on*** *the environment.*

2 [U] information about recent events that is reported in newspapers or on television or radio: *foreign/sports/financial news* ♦ *a news item* ♦ *Farming methods are back* ***in the news*** *this week.*

3 the news [singular] a television or radio broadcast that gives you information about recent events: *I always listen to the news on my way home.* ♦ *Did you see Bush* ***on the news*** *last night?*

PHRASE **be news to sb** *spoken* to be a piece of information that surprises someone: *"Sally says she's borrowing your car tomorrow." "That's news to me!"*

News looks like a plural, but it is never used with a plural verb and cannot be used with **a**: *I've got a wonderful* ***piece of news*** (NOT a wonderful news) for you. ♦ *Do you have* ***any news*** *about Laura's baby?* ♦ *Here's* ***some news*** *about the World Cup.*

news·cast /ˈnuzˌkæst/ noun [C] *American* a news program —**news·cast·er** noun [C]

news·group /ˈnuzˌgrup/ noun [C] *computing* a

N

place on the Internet where people can leave messages about a subject or activity that interests them

news•let•ter /ˈnuzˌletər/ noun [C] a short simple magazine with information for members of an organization

news•pa•per /ˈnuzˌpeɪpər/ noun ★★★
1 [C] a set of large printed sheets of folded paper containing news, articles, and other information that is published every day or every week: *a local newspaper* ♦ *a newspaper article* ♦ *I saw an interesting article **in the newspaper** this morning.*
2 [U] sheets of paper from a newspaper: *vegetables wrapped in newspaper*

news•print /ˈnuzˌprɪnt/ noun [U] the ink and paper that are used for printing newspapers

news•stand /ˈnuzˌstænd/ noun [C] a place in the street where you can buy newspapers and magazines

news•wor•thy /ˈnuzˌwɜrði/ adj interesting or important enough to be included in a news report

ˌNew ˈTestament, the the part of the Christian Bible that describes Jesus Christ's life

ˌnew ˈwave noun [singular/U] a form of art that uses new styles and ideas —**ˌnew ˈwave** adj

ˌNew ˈWorld, the North, Central, and South America

N

ˌNew Year's ˈDay noun [C] January 1st, the first day of the year

ˌNew Year's ˈEve noun [C] December 31st

next /nekst/ grammar word ★★★

Next can be:
- a **determiner**: *I'll see you next week.*
- an **adjective**: *I'm leaving town on the next train.*
- a **pronoun**: *You're the next in line.*
- an **adverb**: *What happens next?*
- used in the preposition phrase **next to**: *Come sit next to me.*

1 used for referring to the time, event, or person that comes after this one, or that comes after another one: *He said he was leaving for Rome the next day.* ♦ *The next flight to Newark isn't until 1:30.* ♦ *I'll call you the next time I'm in town.* ♦ *Who's next in line?* ♦ *I knew exactly what was going to happen next.* ♦ *I'll see you **next Friday**.* ♦ *A meeting has been arranged for the **weekend after next**.*
2 used for referring to the place that is closest to where you are: *I could hear the sound of laughter in the next room.*
PHRASES **the next best/largest/smallest etc.** one that is almost as good/large/small etc. as another one that you are mentioning: *Britain is Europe's next largest oil producer after Norway.* ♦ *This video game is **the next best thing to** flying a real plane.*
next of kin your closest relative or relatives
next to 1 beside, or very near to, someone or something, with no other person or thing in between: *She sat down next to me.* ♦ *Steve lives next to a lake, so we'll be able to go swimming.* **2** used before negative words to mean "almost, but not completely": *It will be next to impossible to win.* ♦ *She earns **next to nothing**.*

ˌnext ˈdoor adv in the building, room, or position next to yours, or next to another: *The restaurant is next door to the bank.*

ˈnext-ˌdoor adj **1** the next-door apartment, garden, office, etc. is the one next to yours **2** your next-door neighbor lives in the house next to yours

NH abbrev New Hampshire

nib /nɪb/ noun [C] the part of a pen that the ink comes out of

nib•ble /ˈnɪb(ə)l/ verb [I/T] to eat something by taking a lot of small bites —**nib•ble** noun [C]

nice /naɪs/ adj ★★★
1 attractive, enjoyable, or pleasant: *The Garden District is a much nicer place to live nowadays.* ♦ *a nice big smile* ♦ *Your hair **looks nice**.* ♦ *It's **nice and** quiet in here.*
2 friendly, kind, and pleasant: *She's a nice girl.* ♦ *He's always been **nice to me**.* ♦ **it is nice of sb (to do sth)** *It was nice of you to come and see me.*
PHRASES **have a nice day** *spoken* used for saying goodbye to someone, especially to a customer in a store
nice to meet you *spoken* used for saying hello or goodbye to someone when you meet them for the first time

Words that you can use instead of nice

Nice is a very general word. Here are some words with more specific meanings that sound more natural and appropriate in particular situations.

people	easy-going, easy to get along with, friendly, good fun, kind, sweet
behavior	helpful, kind, thoughtful
something that happens or something that you do	good, great, marvelous, wonderful
weather	fantastic, fine, glorious, good, lovely, pleasant
clothes	beautiful, flattering, smart, stylish
food/flowers/gifts/ places	beautiful, delightful, fantastic, great, lovely

nice-look•ing /ˈnaɪsˌlʊkɪŋ/ adj *informal* attractive

nice•ly /ˈnaɪsli/ adv **1** in a satisfactory or appropriate way: *The following story illustrates the point nicely.* **2** in an attractive way: *a nicely furnished apartment* **3** in a polite or friendly way: *If you ask Bob nicely, I'm sure he'll help.*

ni•ce•ty /ˈnaɪsəti/ noun [C] a very small difference or detail

niche /nɪtʃ/ noun [C] **1** a job or activity that is very appropriate for you: *She's never really found her niche in life.* **2** *business* an opportunity to sell a particular product or service that no one else is selling **3** a small space in a wall where you can put small objects

nick[1] /nɪk/ noun [C] a small cut on the surface of something
PHRASE **in the nick of time** just in time to prevent something bad from happening: *The swimmers were rescued in the nick of time.*

nick² /nɪk/ verb [T] to cut the surface of something slightly: *He nicked his finger opening a tin can.*

nick•el /ˈnɪk(ə)l/ noun **1** [C] a coin in the U.S. and Canada that is worth five CENTS **2** [U] a hard silver metal

nick•name¹ /ˈnɪkˌneɪm/ noun [C] an informal name that your friends or family call you that is not your real name

nick•name² /ˈnɪkˌneɪm/ verb [T] to give someone a nickname

nic•o•tine /ˈnɪkəˌtin/ noun [U] the drug in tobacco that makes people ADDICTED to it

niece /nis/ noun [C] a daughter of your brother or sister, or a daughter of your husband's or wife's brother or sister —*picture* → FAMILY TREE

nif•ty /ˈnɪfti/ adj *informal* well designed, effective, or easy to use

nig•gling /ˈnɪg(ə)lɪŋ/ adj causing you slight worries or small problems for a long period of time

nigh /naɪ/ adv *literary* near

PHRASE **nigh on sth** or **well nigh sth** *old-fashioned* almost

night /naɪt/ noun ★★★

1 [C/U] the part of each 24-hour period when it is dark ≠ DAY: *It was a lovely warm night.* ♦ *I woke up **in the middle of the night**.* ♦ *It rained **all night (long)**.* ♦ *The attacks usually take place **at night**.* ♦ *Owls hunt **by night**.*
2 [U] the time between the end of the afternoon and the time when people go to bed = EVENING: *Most nights Jan helps the kids with their homework.* ♦ *What are you doing Friday night?* ♦ *Did you watch the game **last night**?*

PHRASES **an early/late night** an occasion when you go to bed earlier or later than usual

night and day or **day and night** all the time

> **Words often used with night**
>
> *Noun often used with **night** (sense 1)*
>
> ■ **cold, cool, frosty, mild, warm** + NIGHT: used for saying how hot or cold a night is
>
> ■ **dark, moonlit, starlit, starry** + NIGHT: used for saying how much light there is on a particular night

night•club /ˈnaɪtˌklʌb/ noun [C] a place where people go in the evening in order to dance and drink alcohol = CLUB

night•fall /ˈnaɪtˌfɔl/ noun [U] *literary* the time in the evening when it starts to become dark

night•gown /ˈnaɪtˌgaʊn/ or **night•ie** /ˈnaɪti/ *informal* noun [C] a piece of clothing like a dress that women wear for sleeping in

night•in•gale /ˈnaɪtɪŋˌgeɪl/ noun [C] a small bird that is known for the beautiful way that it sings at night

night•life /ˈnaɪtˌlaɪf/ noun [U] evening entertainment that you get in places such as NIGHTCLUBS and bars

night•ly /ˈnaɪtli/ adj, adv happening every night

night•mare /ˈnaɪtˌmer/ noun [C] **1** a very frightening and unpleasant dream: *I still have terrible nightmares about the crash.* **2** a very difficult or frightening situation: *The trip to work was a nightmare.* —**night•mar•ish** /ˈnaɪtˌmerɪʃ/ adj

night•shirt /ˈnaɪtˌʃɜrt/ noun [C] a long loose shirt, used for sleeping in

night•stand /ˈnaɪtˌstænd/ noun [C] a small table beside a bed

night•stick /ˈnaɪtˌstɪk/ noun [C] *American* a short stick that is carried by police officers as a weapon

night•time /ˈnaɪtˌtaɪm/ noun [U] the period of time when it is night

ˌnight ˈwatchman noun [C] someone whose job is to guard a building during the night

nil /nɪl/ noun [U] used for saying that something does not exist: *Their chances of survival are virtually nil.*

nim•ble /ˈnɪmb(ə)l/ adj able to move quickly and easily —**nim•bly** /ˈnɪmbli/ adv

nine /naɪn/ number the number 9

nine•teen /ˌnaɪnˈtin/ number the number 19 —**nine•teenth** number

ˌnine-to-ˈfive adj a nine-to-five job is a normal office job, in which you usually work from nine o'clock until five o'clock

nine•ty /ˈnaɪnti/ number the number 90

PHRASES **be in the nineties** if the temperature is in the nineties, it is in the range of 90 to 99 degrees Fahrenheit

be in your nineties to be an age in the range of 90 to 99

the nineties the years from 1990 to 1999 —**nine•ti•eth** number

ninth /naɪnθ/ number **1** in the place or position counted as number nine: *the ninth of January* **2** one of nine equal parts of something

nip /nɪp/ verb [I/T] to bite someone gently

PHRASE **nip sth in the bud** *informal* to stop a bad situation from becoming worse by taking action at an early stage of its development —**nip** noun [C]

nip•ple /ˈnɪp(ə)l/ noun [C] **1** a small round raised area of flesh on each side of your chest **2** *American* the plastic or rubber part on the end of a baby's bottle that it sucks milk through

nir•va•na /nɪrˈvɑnə, nərˈvɑnə/ noun [U] a state of complete spiritual happiness that Buddhists and Hindus try to achieve

nit•pick /ˈnɪtˌpɪk/ verb [I/T] to criticize unimportant details in an annoying way —**nit•pick•ing** noun [U]

ni•trate /ˈnaɪˌtreɪt/ noun [C/U] a chemical substance that is used for improving the quality of soil

ni•tro•gen /ˈnaɪtrədʒən/ noun [U] a gas with no color or smell that exists in large quantities in the air

nits /nɪts/ noun [plural] the eggs of insects called LICE that people sometimes have in their hair

nit•ty-grit•ty, the /ˌnɪti ˈgrɪti/ noun [singular] *informal* the most basic aspects of a situation or an activity that must be dealt with

nit•wit /ˈnɪtˌwɪt/ noun [C] *informal* a stupid person

NJ abbrev New Jersey

NM abbrev New Mexico

no¹ /noʊ/ grammar word ★★★

> **No** can be:
> - an **adverb**: *"Would you like some tea?" "No, thanks."* ♦ *She's no taller than Jerry.*
> - a **determiner**: *There's no butter in the refrigerator.* ♦ *No smoking.*

1 giving a negative answer used for giving a negative answer to a question or an offer: *"Are you still working at the clinic?" "No, I work at the hospital now."* ♦ *"Do you want another cup of coffee?" **"No, thanks."*** ♦ *I asked Marla to come and help, but she **said no**.*
2 disagreeing with sb used for saying that a statement that someone has made is not true: *"You blame me whenever something goes wrong." "No, I don't."*
3 agreeing with a negative used for agreeing with a negative statement, or agreeing to a negative request: *"Don't forget to make the reservation." "No, I won't."* ♦ *"We're not as young as we used to be." "No, we're certainly not."*
4 not any used for saying that there is not even one person or thing, or not any amount of something: *There was no hospital in the town.* ♦ *I have no living cousins that I know about.* ♦ *There's no time to stop and talk.*
5 telling sb not to do sth used for telling someone not to do something: *No! Don't touch that – it's hot.*
6 not allowed used on signs or in instructions in order to say that something is not allowed: *No smoking.*
7 not at all used for saying that someone or something cannot be described in a particular way: *It is no surprise that the company failed.* ♦ *He's no fool – he can see what you're trying to do.*
PHRASES **in no time** in a very short time: *I'll have it fixed for you in no time.*
no more/less/better etc. not more/less/better etc. than someone or something else: *The painting was no more than a few inches square.* ♦ *In the end, he got no farther than the station.*

no² /noʊ/ (plural **noes**) noun [C] a negative answer or vote: *His answer was a firm no.*

no. abbrev number

no·bil·i·ty /noʊˈbɪləti/ noun **1** [U] an honest and brave way of behaving that people admire **2 the nobility** [singular] the people in the highest social class in some countries

no·ble¹ /ˈnoʊb(ə)l/ adj **1** behaving in an honest and brave way that other people admire **2** belonging to the nobility —**no·bly** /ˈnoʊbli/ adv

no·ble² /ˈnoʊb(ə)l/ noun [C] a member of the nobility

no·ble·man /ˈnoʊb(ə)lmən/ noun [C] a man who is a member of the NOBILITY

no·ble·wom·an /ˈnoʊb(ə)lˌwʊmən/ noun [C] a woman who is a member of the NOBILITY

no·bod·y¹ /ˈnoʊˌbɑdi/ pronoun ★★★ no one: *Nobody understands me.* ♦ ***Nobody else** knows our secret.*

no·bod·y² /ˈnoʊbɑdi/ noun [C] a person who is not at all important: *I'm tired of having everyone treating me like a nobody.*

no-brain·er /ˌnoʊ ˈbreɪnər/ noun [C] *informal* a question or problem that is very easy to deal with

noc·tur·nal /nɑkˈtɜrn(ə)l/ adj **1** nocturnal animals are active at night **2** *formal* happening at night

nod /nɑd/ verb ★
1 [I/T] to move your head up and down in order to answer "yes" or to show that you agree, approve, or understand ≠ SHAKE YOUR HEAD: *I expected an argument, but she just nodded and went out.* ♦ *Alison smiled and nodded in agreement.* ♦ *Luke was nodding his head thoughtfully.*
2 [I] to move your head once in order to make someone look at something, in order to greet someone, or in order to give someone a signal to do something: *"They're having fun," she said, **nodding toward** the kids on the beach.* ♦ ***I nodded to** my friend and she rang the bell.*
—**nod** noun [C]
PHRASAL VERB ˌ**nod ˈoff** *informal* to go to sleep when you do not intend to

nod·ule /ˈnɑˌdʒul/ noun [C] a small round lump

noise /nɔɪz/ noun [C/U] ★★★ a loud or unpleasant sound: *The dog made a deep growling noise in his throat.* ♦ *The neighbors said that we were **making too much noise**.* ♦ *We heard **the noise of** breaking glass.*

noise·less /ˈnɔɪzləs/ adj not making any sound —**noise·less·ly** adv

ˈ**noise pollution** noun [U] dangerous or annoying levels of noise

nois·y /ˈnɔɪzi/ adj ★ making a lot of noise, or full of noise: *noisy neighbors* ♦ *a noisy crowded bar* —**nois·i·ly** adv

no·mad /ˈnoʊˌmæd/ noun [C] someone who belongs to a group of people who do not live in one place but move from place to place —**no·mad·ic** adj

ˈ**no-man's-ˌland** noun [singular/U] an area of land between two countries or armies that is not controlled by either of them

nom·i·nal /ˈnɑmɪn(ə)l/ adj **1** officially described in a particular way, although this is not really true or correct: *He is still the nominal leader of the organization.* **2** a nominal amount of money is very small and is much less than the real cost of something: *Transportation can be provided for a nominal fee.*

nom·i·nal·ly /ˈnɑmɪn(ə)li/ adv officially described as being or doing something, although this is not really true or correct: *John Robbins is nominally in charge of the investigation.*

nom·i·nate /ˈnɑmɪˌneɪt/ verb [T] to officially suggest that someone should be given a job, or that someone or something should receive a prize —**nom·i·na·tion** /ˌnɑmɪˈneɪʃ(ə)n/ noun [C/U]

nom·i·nee /ˌnɑmɪˈni/ noun [C] someone who has been officially suggested for a position or prize

non- /nɑn/ prefix not: *a nonalcoholic drink* ♦ *a nonsmoker*

non·ag·gres·sion /ˌnɑnəˈɡreʃ(ə)n/ noun [U] a policy of not attacking other countries

non·al·co·hol·ic /ˌnɑnælkəˈhɑlɪk/ adj a

N

nonalcoholic drink does not contain alcohol

non•cha•lant /ˌnɑnʃəˈlɑnt, ˈnɑnʃəˌlɑnt/ adj relaxed and not worried about anything —**non•cha•lance** noun [U], **non•cha•lant•ly** adv

non•com•bat•ant /ˌnɑnkəmˈbæt(ə)nt/ noun [C] someone who is not involved in fighting during a war

non•com•mit•tal /ˌnɑnkəˈmɪt(ə)l/ adj avoiding stating clearly what you think or what you plan to do: *He was noncommittal about any future plans.*

non•con•form•ist /ˌnɑnkənˈfɔrmɪst/ noun [C] someone who does not think or behave in the way that most people do —**non•con•form•ist** adj

non•count /nɑnˈkaʊnt/ adj *linguistics* a noncount noun is UNCOUNTABLE

non•de•script /ˌnɑndɪˈskrɪpt/ adj very ordinary, and not interesting or attractive

none /nʌn/ pronoun not any of a group of people or things, or no amount of something: *I thought there was some coffee in the cabinet, but there's none there.* ♦ *The driver was killed, but none of the passengers was hurt.* ♦ *Some people might have only mild symptoms or none at all.* → SECOND[1]

non•en•ti•ty /nɑnˈentəti/ noun [C] someone who is not at all important or interesting

none•the•less /ˌnʌnðəˈles/ adv *formal* despite what has just been said: *Everyone worked very hard. There were still problems, nonetheless.*

non•e•vent /ˌnɑnɪˈvent/ noun [C] an event that is not as exciting as you expected it to be

non•ex•ist•ent /ˌnɑnɪɡˈzɪstənt/ adj not real or present: *Labor is cheap and health and safety regulations virtually nonexistent.*

non•fat /ˌnɑnˈfæt/ adj nonfat food and drinks contain very little fat or no fat

non•fic•tion /nɑnˈfɪkʃ(ə)n/ noun [U] writing that is about real people and events, not imaginary ones —**non•fic•tion** adj

non•flam•ma•ble /nɑnˈflæməb(ə)l/ adj not able to be burned easily

non•gov•ern•men•tal /ˌnɑnɡʌvərnˈment(ə)l/ adj a nongovernmental organization is not part of a government but is usually involved in the type of work that government departments do

non•in•ter•ven•tion /ˌnɑnɪntərˈvenʃ(ə)n/ noun [U] a policy of not getting involved in a disagreement between other people or countries

non•in•va•sive /ˌnɑnɪnˈveɪsɪv/ adj *medical* noninvasive medical tests or treatments do not involve cutting your body or putting things inside it

non•mem•ber /nɑnˈmembər/ noun [C] someone who does not belong to a particular organization

ˈno-ˌno noun [singular] *informal* something that most people do not approve of

ˌno-ˈnonsense adj doing things quickly and effectively without worrying too much about people's feelings: *a no-nonsense approach*

non•pay•ment /nɑnˈpeɪmənt/ noun [U] a failure or a refusal to pay for something

non•plussed /nɑnˈplʌst/ adj so surprised and confused that you do not know what to do or say

non•prof•it /nɑnˈprɑfɪt/ adj a nonprofit organization works in order to help people in some way, rather than in order to make a profit

non•pro•lif•er•a•tion /ˌnɑnprəˌlɪfəˈreɪʃ(ə)n/ noun [U] a policy of not increasing the number of nuclear or chemical weapons in the world

non•re•fund•a•ble /ˌnɑnrɪˈfʌndəb(ə)l/ adj if the money that you pay for something is nonrefundable, you cannot get the money back for any reason: *nonrefundable tickets*

non•re•new•a•ble /ˌnɑnrɪˈnuəb(ə)l/ adj nonrenewable types of energy exist in limited amounts, and when these are all used, there will be none left

non•res•i•dent /nɑnˈrezɪdənt/ noun [C] someone who is in a particular country but does not live there permanently —**non•res•i•dent** adj

non•sense /ˈnɑnˌsens, ˈnɑnsens/ noun [U] ★

1 ideas, behavior, or statements that are not true or sensible: *So you believe the nonsense about ghosts?* ♦ *That's **a lot of nonsense**.* ♦ *These accusations are **absolute nonsense**.*

2 unreasonable or annoying behavior: *I won't **put up with any nonsense** from anybody.*

3 words or sounds that seem like ordinary words but have no meaning: *a nonsense poem*

—**non•sen•si•cal** /nɑnˈsensɪk(ə)l/ adj

non se•qui•tur /nɑnˈsekwɪtər/ noun [C] a statement that has no connection with what was said before

non•smok•er /nɑnˈsmoʊkər/ noun [C] someone who does not smoke

non•smok•ing /ˌnɑnˈsmoʊkɪŋ/ adj a nonsmoking area is one where you are not allowed to smoke

non•stan•dard /ˌnɑnˈstændərd/ adj *linguistics* nonstandard forms of language are different from those that are usually thought to be correct

non•stick /ˌnɑnˈstɪk/ adj nonstick cooking pans have a surface that food will not stick to

non•stop /ˌnɑnˈstɑp/ adj, adv without stopping: *a nonstop flight from New York to Paris* ♦ *We danced nonstop for about an hour.*

non•vi•o•lent /nɑnˈvaɪ(ə)lənt/ adj **1** using peaceful methods to achieve political change: *nonviolent protest/resistance* **2** nonviolent crime does not involve physically hurting people —**non•vi•o•lence** noun [U]

noo•dles /ˈnud(ə)lz/ noun [plural] a type of long thin pasta

nook /nʊk/ noun [C] a small corner, or a quiet place that is protected from bad weather

PHRASE **every nook and cranny** every part of a place

noon /nun/ noun [U] 12 o'clock in the middle of the day = MIDDAY: *We should be there by noon.*

ˈno ˌone pronoun ★★★ not any person = NOBODY: *There was no one around.* ♦ *No one else wanted the job.*

N

noose /nus/ noun [C] a piece of rope that is put around someone's neck and used for killing them by hanging them

nope /noʊp/ adv *informal* used for saying "no" when someone asks you a question

ˌno ˌplace adv *American informal* NOWHERE

nor /nɔr/ conjunction ★★★ used after a negative statement when adding another negative statement: *I have not been asked to resign, nor do I intend to do so.* ♦ *She did not return that night, nor the night after.*

norm /nɔrm/ noun **1 the norm** [singular] something that is average, usual, or expected: *Students who fall below the norm should be encouraged to improve.* ♦ *Fast cars have become the norm.* **2 norms** [plural] standards of behavior that are accepted in a particular society: *Each culture develops its own social norms.*

nor·mal /ˈnɔrm(ə)l/ adj ★★★
1 as expected, and not unusual or surprising in any way: *Temperatures are higher than normal.* ♦ *He didn't like anything to interrupt his normal daily routine.* ♦ *Life is beginning to* ***get back to normal*** *after the fire.* ♦ ***Under normal circumstances,*** *candidates are interviewed by the head of the department.* ♦ **it is normal to do sth** *It's normal to be nervous before an interview.*
2 thinking, behaving, or looking like most people: *He's no hero, just* ***a normal human being.*** ♦ *She's a* ***perfectly normal*** *messy child!*

N

nor·mal·i·ty /nɔrˈmæləti/ or **nor·mal·cy** /ˈnɔrməlsi/ noun [U] a situation in which everything is normal

nor·mal·ize /ˈnɔrm(ə)lˌaɪz/ verb [I/T] to make something normal, or to become normal: *The United States had decided to normalize relations with Vietnam.* —**nor·mal·i·za·tion** /ˌnɔrm(ə)lɪˈzeɪʃ(ə)n/ noun [U]

nor·mal·ly /ˈnɔrm(ə)li/ adv ★★★
1 in most situations or cases = USUALLY: *Normally it takes about six days to arrange a visit.* ♦ *She's not normally late.*
2 in the usual way: *The buses are operating normally.*

north¹ /nɔrθ/ noun ★★★
1 [U] the direction that is on your left when you are facing the rising sun: *We were driving from north to south.*
2 **the north** [singular] the part of a place that is in the north: *How do you like living in the north?* ♦ *She grew up in* ***the north of*** *France.*

north² /nɔrθ/ adv toward the north: *The geese will soon be flying north.* ♦ *It's a lot colder up north.* ♦ *a village 10 miles north of here*

north³ /nɔrθ/ adj **1** in the north, or facing toward the north **2** a north wind blows from the north

north·bound /ˈnɔrθˌbaʊnd/ adj going toward the north

north·east¹ /ˌnɔrθˈist/ noun **1** [U] the direction that is between north and east **2 the northeast** [singular] the part of a place that is in the northeast —**north·east·ern** adj

north·east² /ˌnɔrθˈist/ adj in the northeast, or facing toward the northeast —**north·east** adv

north·east·er·ly /ˌnɔrθˈistərli/ adj **1** a northeasterly wind blows from the northeast **2** toward or in the northeast

north·er·ly /ˈnɔrðərli/ adj **1** a northerly wind blows from the north **2** toward or in the north

north·ern /ˈnɔrðərn/ adj ★★ in or from the north of a country or place: *northern Italy*

north·ern·er /ˈnɔrðərnər/ noun [C] someone who lives in or was born in the northern part of a country

ˌnorthern ˈhemisphere, the noun [singular] the northern half of the Earth, north of the EQUATOR

north·ern·most /ˈnɔrðərnˌmoʊst/ adj farthest toward the north

ˌNorth ˈPole, the the place on the surface of the Earth that is the farthest north

north·ward¹ /ˈnɔrθwərd/ adj toward or in the north

north·ward² /ˈnɔrθwərd/ or **north·wards** /ˈnɔrθwərdz/ adv toward the north

north·west¹ /ˌnɔrθˈwest/ noun **1** [U] the direction that is between north and west **2 the northwest** [singular] the part of a place that is in the northwest **3 the Northwest** [singular] the part of the U.S. that includes the states of Washington, Oregon, and Idaho —**north·west·ern** adj

north·west² /ˌnɔrθˈwest/ adj in the northwest, or facing toward the northwest —**north·west** adv

north·west·er·ly /ˌnɔrθˈwestərli/ adj **1** a northwesterly wind blows from the northwest **2** toward or in the northwest

nose¹ /noʊz/ noun [C] ★★★ the part of your face that is above your mouth that you use for smelling and breathing: *I'd like to punch him in the nose.* ♦ *Can you pass me a tissue – my* ***nose is running*** (=liquid is coming out of it). ♦ *Excuse me, I just need to* ***blow my nose*** (=force liquid from it). —*picture* → C14

PHRASES **look down your nose at** to behave in a way that shows that you think someone or something is not good enough for you: *She looks down her nose at most men.*
poke/stick your nose into sth to become interested or involved in something when you have no right to do this: *You have no right to poke your nose into my business!*
turn your nose up at sth *informal* to refuse to accept something because you do not think that it is good enough
under sb's nose if something happens under someone's nose, it happens in a place or situation where they should notice it, but they do not: *They were dealing drugs right under the noses of the police.*

nose² /noʊz/ verb [I] if a vehicle noses forward, it moves forward slowly and carefully: *The ambulance nosed its way out of the crowd.*

PHRASAL VERB **ˌnose aˈround (sb/sth)** to try to find out information about someone or something: *I found two men nosing around the boat.*

nose·bleed /ˈnoʊzˌblid/ noun [C] an occasion when blood comes out of someone's nose

nose·dive /ˈnoʊzˌdaɪv/ noun [C] **1** a sudden reduction in things such as prices or profits: *The value of the dollar took a nosedive today.* **2** an occasion when an airplane suddenly falls out of the sky with its front end pointing down —**nose•dive** verb [I]

nos•ey /ˈnoʊzi/ another spelling of **nosy**

nos•tal•gi•a /nɑˈstældʒə/ noun [U] thoughts about happy times in your past that make you want to be back in the past

nos•tal•gic /nɑˈstældʒɪk/ adj remembering happy times in the past —**nos•tal•gi•cal•ly** /nɑˈstældʒɪkli/ adv

nos•tril /ˈnɑstrəl/ noun [C] one of the two holes at the end of your nose

nos•y /ˈnoʊzi/ adj *showing disapproval* wanting to know about things that involve other people but not you —**nos•i•ness** noun [U]

not /nɑt/ adv ★★★

1 used for giving a negative or opposite meaning to a sentence, expression, or word: *He would not listen to anything she said.* ♦ *Barbara's not coming to the party.* ♦ *I don't feel sorry for her.* ♦ *Not surprisingly, Greg forgot to bring the key.* ♦ *They told me not to worry.* ♦ *Not all children enjoy sports.* ♦ *The teacher could **not even** remember my name.* ♦ *My parents were **not at all** pleased with my test results.*

2 used instead of repeating something in the negative: *Are you coming with me **or not**?* ♦ *I'll probably see you on Sunday; **if not**, it'll be Monday.* ♦ *"Is it going to be very expensive?" "**I hope not**."*

3 *spoken* used for forming a question when you expect the answer to be "yes": *Isn't it a beautiful day?* ♦ *That was easy, wasn't it?*

PHRASES **not one** or **not a single** used for emphasizing that there are none of the people or things you are talking about: *Not one member voted in favor.*

not that used for adding a negative statement that reduces the effect of what you have just said: *You're using my pen – not that I mind* (=I don't mind).

> In spoken and informal English **not** is often shortened to **n't** on the end of auxiliary verbs ("be," "do," and "have") and modal verbs. For example, **was not** is shortened to **wasn't**.

no•ta•ble /ˈnoʊtəb(ə)l/ adj unusual or interesting enough to be mentioned or noticed

no•ta•bly /ˈnoʊtəbli/ adv *formal* especially

no•ta•tion /noʊˈteɪʃ(ə)n/ noun [U] a set of written signs or shapes that are used in something such as music or mathematics

notch /nɑtʃ/ noun [C] a small cut on the edge or surface of something

note[1] /noʊt/ noun [C] ★★★

1 short message	5 feeling/thought
2 sth that reminds	6 piece of paper money
3 detailed information	+ PHRASES
4 sound/sign in music	

1 a short written message to someone: *I've written him a note asking him to meet me tonight.* ♦ *We left them a note saying dinner was in the refrigerator.*

2 something that you write on a piece of paper in order to remind yourself of something: *I've **made a note of** what needs to be repaired.*

3 notes [plural] details from something such as a lecture or a book that you write on a piece of paper so that you can remember them: *It'll help you later if you **take notes**.*

4 an individual sound in music, or a written sign that represents it: *See if you can **sing** this **note**.* ♦ *He **played** a few **notes** on the piano.*

5 a feeling or mood that is shown in the way that someone speaks or writes: *I'd like to end the discussion on a more cheerful note.* ♦ *There was **a note of** impatience in her voice.*

6 *British* a piece of paper money

PHRASES **of note** *formal* important, or famous: *Several writers of note will be at the conference.*

take note to notice something and try to remember it because you think that it is important: *When the people speak with such passion, politicians should take note.* ♦ *I **took note of** what she said.*

→ COMPARE

note[2] /noʊt/ verb [T] ★★

1 *formal* to notice or realize something: *Liz noted the changes with satisfaction.* ♦ **+that** *Please note that all passengers must have a valid passport.*

2 to write something on a piece of paper so that you will have a record of it: *Isabel noted the details in her diary.*

PHRASAL VERB ˌ**note sth down** *same as* note[2] 2

note•book /ˈnoʊtˌbʊk/ noun [C] **1** a book with empty pages that you use for writing notes **2** a small flat computer that is easy to carry

not•ed /ˈnoʊtəd/ adj well known and admired: *a noted British scientist* ♦ *He is particularly noted for his short stories.*

note•pad /ˈnoʊtˌpæd/ noun [C] several sheets of paper that are joined together along one edge and used for writing notes —*picture* → C3

note•pa•per /ˈnoʊtˌpeɪpər/ noun [U] paper that you use for writing letters

note•wor•thy /ˈnoʊtˌwɜrði/ adj worth giving special attention or praise to: *a noteworthy performance*

noth•ing /ˈnʌθɪŋ/ pronoun ★★★

1 not anything: *There was nothing in the room except for a chair.* ♦ *She waited, but nothing happened.* ♦ *I saw nothing strange in the situation.* ♦ *I knew **nothing at all** about taking care of babies.* ♦ *If there's **nothing else** you want, can we go?* ♦ *The kids complain that there's **nothing to do** there.*

2 not anything that is important or worth thinking about: *You're just making a big fuss about nothing.* ♦ *Do I mean nothing to you?* ♦ *A minor headache is nothing to get too worried about.* ♦ *The beach is **nothing special**, but we like it.*

3 *informal* used in a score to mean "zero": *Our team beat the Eagles, four – nothing.*

PHRASES **be nothing like** to not be similar to someone or something in any way: *Her two daughters are nothing like each other.*

for nothing 1 without any payment: *Some of the men volunteered to work for nothing.* **2** without a reason or purpose: *Why did you call me down here for nothing?*

have nothing to do with 1 to not be connected with a particular fact or situation: *His*

N

resignation has nothing to do with his health. **2** used for saying that someone has no reason to know about something or to be interested in it: *What I do on my own time has nothing to do with you.*
if nothing else used for mentioning what you think may be the only good aspect of something or the only good reason for doing something: *Andrea's work has always been very neat, if nothing else.*
nothing but only: *He has nothing but praise for the managers at his company.*
there's nothing better/worse/more exciting etc. than used for emphasizing how good/bad/exciting etc. something is: *There's nothing worse than not being able to sleep at night.*
there's nothing like sth used for saying that something is very good, enjoyable, or effective: *There's nothing like a cold drink on a hot day.*
there's nothing to it *spoken* used for saying that something is very easy to do
→ STOP[1]

no•tice[1] /ˈnoʊtɪs/ verb [T] ★★★ to become conscious of someone or something by seeing, hearing, or feeling them: *After a few days here you hardly notice the rain!* ♦ *Did you **notice how** pale he looks?* ♦ **+(that)** *I noticed that the door was open.*

no•tice[2] /ˈnoʊtɪs/ noun ★★★
1 [C] a written sign or announcement that gives information or that warns people about something: *They **put up a notice** on the door saying they'd gone out of business.* ♦ *Have you **read the notice** on the board about next week's class?*
2 [U] information or a warning about something that is going to happen: *I need a month's notice if you're planning to move out.* ♦ *If you want to arrive early you must **give advance notice**.* ♦ *Finding a replacement could prove difficult **at short notice**.* ♦ *Lucy was ready to leave **at a moment's notice**.*
PHRASES **give/hand in your notice** to tell your employer that you are leaving your job
take notice to pay attention to something: *Wear what you like – no one seems to take any notice.* ♦ ***Take no notice of** him – he always behaves like that.*
until further notice until someone announces that a situation has changed or no longer exists: *The road is closed to traffic until further notice.*

no•tice•a•ble /ˈnoʊtɪsəb(ə)l/ adj easy to see, hear, or feel: *There was a noticeable chill in the air.* —**no•tice•a•bly** adv

no•ti•fi•ca•tion /ˌnoʊtɪfɪˈkeɪʃ(ə)n/ noun [U] an official announcement about something

no•ti•fy /ˈnoʊtɪˌfaɪ/ verb [T] to tell someone officially about something: *Winners will be notified as soon as possible.*

no•tion /ˈnoʊʃ(ə)n/ noun [C] ★ an idea or belief that is wrong or silly: *Somehow he got the notion that I was interested in dating him.*

no•to•ri•e•ty /ˌnoʊtəˈraɪəti/ noun [U] a situation in which someone or something is famous for something that is bad

no•to•ri•ous /nəˈtɔriəs/ adj famous for something that is bad: *This part of the city is notorious for its high crime rate.* —**no•to•ri•ous•ly** adv

not•with•stand•ing /ˌnɑtwɪðˈstændɪŋ/ adv, preposition *formal* despite something: *Notwithstanding his wealth, his house was simple inside.*

noun /naʊn/ noun [C] *linguistics* ★ a word or group of words used for referring to a person, thing, place, or quality

ˈnoun ˌphrase noun [C] *linguistics* a phrase that is used in a sentence in the same way that a noun is used

nour•ish /ˈnɜrɪʃ/ verb [T] to give a person, animal, or plant the food or the substances in food that they need to live, grow, and be healthy

nour•ish•ing /ˈnɜrɪʃɪŋ/ adj nourishing food provides the substances that you need to live, grow, and be healthy

nour•ish•ment /ˈnɜrɪʃmənt/ noun [U] food or the substances in food that you need to live, grow, and be healthy

nov•el[1] /ˈnɑv(ə)l/ noun [C] ★ a long written story about imaginary characters and events

nov•el[2] /ˈnɑv(ə)l/ adj new, or unusual

nov•el•ist /ˈnɑv(ə)lɪst/ noun [C] someone who writes novels

nov•el•ty /ˈnɑv(ə)lti/ noun **1** [C] something that is new and unusual **2** [U] the excitement or interest that something that is new or unusual creates

No•vem•ber /noʊˈvembər/ noun [C/U] ★★★ the eleventh month of the year, between October and December: *She's arriving in November.* ♦ *The play opens on November 15th.*

nov•ice /ˈnɑvɪs/ noun [C] someone who is just beginning to learn a skill or subject =BEGINNER

now /naʊ/ grammar word ★★★

> **Now** can be:
> - an **adverb**: *We'd better leave now.*
> - a **conjunction** in the phrase **now that**: *Now that I'm married, I don't go out so much.*

1 at the present time: *He is now 48 years old.* ♦ *She's been very sick, but she's much better now.* ♦ *The meeting should have finished **by now**.* ♦ *Nancy will be working full-time **from now on*** (=starting now). ♦ *Prices will remain unchanged **for now*** (=from now until some future time). ♦ ***Right now** I'm not interested in dating.* ♦ *"Can I ask you a question?" "**Not now** – I'm busy."*
2 immediately, or very soon: *If everyone else is finished in the bathroom, I'll take my shower now.* ♦ *"Can you call me back?" "No, I need to talk to you **right now**."*
3 used when you are saying that something happens as a result of something else: *Now I understand why she was so upset.* ♦ ***Now that** the war is over, there is a lot more food in the stores.*
4 *spoken* used when you want to get people's attention, or when you are going to talk about something new: *Now, listen everybody.* ♦ ***Now then**, are there any more questions?*
PHRASES **(every) now and then/again** sometimes, but not regularly or often: *Now*

and then I receive letters from my former students.
just now a very short time ago: *"When did you see him?" "Just now."*

now·a·days /ˈnaʊəˌdeɪz/ adv ★★ at the present time: *Lots of people get divorced nowadays.*

ˌno ˈway adv *spoken* used for saying that you will definitely not do something

no·where /ˈnoʊˌwer, ˈnoʊˌhwer/ adv ★
1 not in any place, or not to any place: *Nowhere does it say that we cannot have guests in our rooms.* ♦ *There is **nowhere else** for me to stay.*
2 in or to no place that is special or important: *The old railroad tracks lead nowhere.*
PHRASES **get/go nowhere** to not be successful in what you are trying to achieve: *Our investigation got nowhere.* ♦ **get sb nowhere** *All this talk is getting us nowhere.*
nowhere near 1 not nearly: *His latest album is nowhere near as good as his last.* **2** a long way away from somewhere
nowhere to be seen/in sight/to be found impossible to see or find: *The children were nowhere in sight.*
out of/from nowhere appearing, arriving, or happening very quickly or unexpectedly: *The car seemed to come out of nowhere.*
→ MIDDLE[1]

ˌno-ˈwin situˌation noun [C] a situation in which there is no chance of success

nox·ious /ˈnɑkʃəs/ adj harmful, or poisonous

noz·zle /ˈnɑz(ə)l/ noun [C] a narrow part at the end of a tube through which a liquid flows

nu·ance /ˈnuˌɑns/ noun [C] a slight difference: *A translator has to be alert to every nuance of meaning.*

nu·cle·ar /ˈnukliər/ adj ★★★
1 relating to energy that is produced by changing the structure of the central part of an atom = ATOMIC: *nuclear power/energy* ♦ *nuclear weapons/arms* ♦ *a nuclear war* ♦ *Are you in favor of **nuclear disarmament*** (=getting rid of nuclear weapons)?
2 relating to the central part of an atom: *nuclear physics*

ˌnuclear ˈfamily noun [C] a family unit that consists of a mother, a father, and their children

ˌnuclear reˈactor noun [C] a machine used for producing nuclear energy, usually in the form of electricity

nu·cle·us /ˈnukliəs/ (plural **nu·cle·i** /ˈnukliˌaɪ/) noun [C] **1** *science* the central part of an atom **2** *science* the central part of a living cell **3** the central or basic part of something: *These groups formed the nucleus of a new political party.*

nude[1] /nud/ adj not wearing clothes = NAKED

nude[2] /nud/ noun [C] a painting or other work of art showing someone who is not wearing clothes
PHRASE **in the nude** not wearing clothes

nudge /nʌdʒ/ verb [T] to use a part of your body, especially your elbow, to give a little push to someone or something —**nudge** noun [C]

nu·dism /ˈnuˌdɪzəm/ noun [U] the practice of wearing no clothes outside, for example on a beach

nud·ist /ˈnudɪst/ noun [C] someone who prefers to wear no clothes —**nud·ist** adj

nu·di·ty /ˈnudəti/ noun [U] the state of not wearing clothes, or of not covering a part of the body that is traditionally covered

nug·get /ˈnʌgət/ noun [C] a rough lump of gold or another metal that is found in the earth

nui·sance /ˈnusəns/ noun [C] someone or something that annoys you or causes problems for you

nuke[1] /nuk/ verb [T] *informal* **1** to attack an enemy with nuclear weapons **2** to heat or cook something in a MICROWAVE oven

nuke[2] /nuk/ noun [C] *informal* a nuclear weapon

nul·li·fy /ˈnʌləˌfaɪ/ verb [T] **1** *legal* to make something lose its legal effect **2** to make something lose its value or effect

numb[1] /nʌm/ adj **1** a part of your body that is numb has no feeling **2** not able to react or to show your emotions, often because of shock —**numb·ly** adv

numb[2] /nʌm/ verb [T] to make a part of your body lose its ability to feel

num·ber[1] /ˈnʌmbər/ noun ★★★

1 sign/word for amount	4 for marking sth
2 for showing position	5 a quantity
3 telephone number	

1 [C] a sign or word that represents an amount or quantity: *Can you read the numbers on the chart?* ♦ *a number between one and ten*
2 [C] used for showing the position of something in a series: *The local trains will be arriving on track number 4.*
3 [C] a telephone number: *Call this number to get a taxi.* ♦ *I must have dialed the **wrong number**.*
4 [C] a number that is given to a particular thing in order to show which one it is out of many others: *Your account number is printed on every check.*
5 [C/U] a quantity of people or things: ***a small number of** stores* → AMOUNT

num·ber[2] /ˈnʌmbər/ verb [T] **1** to give a number to something **2** *formal* to consist of a particular quantity of people or things

ˌnumber ˈone[1] noun [singular] **1** the person or thing that is the first, best, or most important **2** in popular music, the CD or record that has sold the most copies in a particular week

ˌnumber ˈone[2] adj first, best, or most important: *the world's number one female tennis player*

numb·ing /ˈnʌmɪŋ/ adj making you lose feeling in a part of your body

numb·ness /ˈnʌmnəs/ noun [U] the condition of having no feeling in a part of your body

nu·mer·a·cy /ˈnumərəsi/ noun [U] the ability to use numbers in mathematics

nu·mer·al /ˈnumərəl/ noun [C] a symbol that represents a number

nu·mer·ate /ˈnumərət/ adj able to use and calculate numbers

N

nu•mer•i•cal /nuˈmerɪk(ə)l/ adj expressed as numbers, or consisting of numbers —**nu•mer•i•cal•ly** /nuˈmerɪkli/ adv

nu•mer•ous /ˈnumərəs/ adj ★ existing in large numbers=MANY: *She has been seen here on numerous occasions.*

nun /nʌn/ noun [C] a woman who belongs to a religious community of women → MONK

nurse¹ /nɜrs/ noun [C] ★★ someone who is trained to take care of sick or injured people, usually in a hospital

nurse² /nɜrs/ verb **1** [I/T] to take care of someone who is sick or injured **2** [T] to feel a strong emotion for a long time: *He had nursed a grudge* (=had angry feelings) *against them for ages.* **3** [T] to help yourself to get better after an illness or injury, for example by resting or getting medical treatment: *I'm nursing a cold.* ♦ *I took over as captain while she nursed a strained muscle.* **4** [T] if a woman nurses a baby, she feeds it by letting the baby suck milk from her breasts=BREASTFEED

nurs•er•y /ˈnɜrs(ə)ri/ noun [C] **1** a school or a place where very young children are taken care of **2** a place where plants and young trees are grown

ˈnursery ˌrhyme noun [C] a short poem or song for young children

ˈnursery ˌschool noun [C/U] a school for very young children

nurs•ing /ˈnɜrsɪŋ/ noun [U] the job or skills of a nurse

ˈnursing ˌhome noun [C] a place where old people live when they are too old or sick to care for themselves without help

nur•ture /ˈnɜrtʃər/ verb [T] **1** to help someone or something to develop **2** to provide the care and attention that are needed for a young child, animal, or plant to grow and develop

nut /nʌt/ noun [C] ★

1 a dry fruit that grows inside a hard shell on some types of tree. Many kinds of nuts can be eaten: *Do you want some nuts and raisins?*

2 a small metal object with a hole in the middle that you screw a BOLT through in order to fasten things together

3 *informal* someone who is crazy, or who behaves in a crazy way

4 *informal* someone who is extremely enthusiastic about a particular activity, sport, or subject: *a hockey nut*

nut•crack•er /ˈnʌtˌkrækər/ noun [C] a tool for breaking open the shells of nuts

nu•tri•ent /ˈnutriənt/ noun [C] a substance in food that plants, animals, and people need in order to live, grow, and be healthy

nu•tri•tion /nuˈtrɪʃ(ə)n/ noun [U] **1** the food that you eat and its effects on your health and growth **2** the science of food and its effect on health and growth —**nu•tri•tion•al** /nuˈtrɪʃən(ə)l/ adj, **nu•tri•tion•al•ly** /nuˈtrɪʃən(ə)li/ adv

nu•tri•tion•ist /nuˈtrɪʃ(ə)nɪst/ noun [C] someone who is an expert on nutrition

nu•tri•tious /nuˈtrɪʃəs/ adj nutritious food provides the substances that you need in order to live, grow, and be healthy

nuts /nʌts/ adj *informal* crazy: *He'd be nuts to take that job.*

PHRASES **drive sb nuts** to make someone very annoyed

go nuts to suddenly become extremely angry

nuts about/over extremely enthusiastic about something, or very attracted to someone

nut•shell /ˈnʌtʃel/ noun [C] the hard shell around a nut

PHRASE **in a nutshell** *spoken* used for saying that you are going to explain something in a simple direct way

nut•ty /ˈnʌti/ adj **1** *informal* crazy, or very strange: *He had this nutty idea about buying a castle in Scotland.* **2** containing nuts, or having the taste of nuts

nuz•zle /ˈnʌz(ə)l/ verb [I/T] to press your nose or face gently against something

NV abbrev Nevada

NW abbrev northwest

NY abbrev New York

ny•lon /ˈnaɪˌlɑn/ noun **1** [U] a strong artificial substance that is used in making plastic and clothes **2 nylons** [plural] nylon STOCKINGS

nymph /nɪmf/ noun [C] in ancient Greek and Roman stories, one of the female spirits who live in rivers, mountains, or forests

nym•pho•ma•ni•ac /ˌnɪmfəˈmeɪniˌæk/ noun [C] a woman who is always thinking about sex, or is always wanting to have sex —**nym•pho•ma•ni•a** /ˌnɪmfəˈmeɪniə/ noun [U]

O o

o or **O** /oʊ/ noun **1** [C/U] the 15th letter of the English alphabet **2** [C/U] *spoken* a way of saying "zero" **3 O** [U] a common BLOOD TYPE

oak /oʊk/ noun **1** [C] a large tree that can live for a very long time and that produces small hard fruits —*picture* → C9 **2** [U] the wood from an oak tree

oar /ɔr/ noun [C] a long stick with a wide flat blade at one end, used for ROWING a boat

o•a•sis /oʊˈeɪsɪs/ noun [C] a place in a desert where there is water and where plants and trees grow

oath /oʊθ/ (plural **oaths** /oʊðz/) noun [C] a formal promise: *an oath of loyalty*

PHRASE **under oath** if someone is under oath, they have officially promised to tell the truth in a court of law

oat•meal /ˈoʊtˌmil/ noun [U] crushed OATS that are boiled and eaten for breakfast, or used in cooking

oats /oʊts/ noun [plural] a type of grain that people and animals eat

o•be•di•ent /oʊˈbidiənt/ adj doing what a person, law, or rule says that you must do ≠ DISOBEDIENT —**o•be•di•ence** noun [U], **o•be•di•ent•ly** adv

o•bese /oʊˈbis/ adj extremely fat

o•be•si•ty /oʊˈbisəti/ noun [U] a condition in which someone is extremely fat

o•bey /oʊˈbeɪ/ verb [I/T] ★ to do what a person, law, or rule says that you must do: *Officers expect their troops to obey them without question.* ♦ *Drivers are not* ***obeying the*** *new traffic* ***laws.*** ♦ *The commandos were used to* ***obeying orders.***

Word family: obey

Words in the same family as ***obey***

- **obedience** *n*
- **disobedience** *n*
- **obedient** *adj*
- **disobedient** *adj*
- **disobey** *v*

ob/gyn /oʊ bi ˌdʒi waɪ ˈen/ noun [C/U] *American informal* the medical field of OBSTETRICS and GYNECOLOGY, or a doctor whose specialty is in this field

o•bit•u•ar•y /əˈbɪtʃuˌeri/ noun [C] a report in a newspaper that announces someone's death and that gives a short description of their life and achievements

ob•ject[1] /ˈɑbdʒəkt/ noun [C] ★★★ **1** a thing that you can see and touch that is not living: *candles, vases, and other household objects* ♦ *There are thousands of objects in the museum's collection.* **2** something that you plan to achieve: *The decision was made* ***with the object of*** *cutting costs.* ♦ *The* ***main object of*** *the game is to get rid of all your cards.* **3 object of sth** the person or thing that something happens to, or that people have a particular feeling about: *The band is currently* ***the object of*** *a lot of media attention.* **4** *linguistics* a noun, pronoun, or phrase that is affected by the action of a verb, for example "the report" in "I've read the report"

ob•ject[2] /əbˈdʒekt, ɑbˈdʒekt/ verb [I] ★ to be opposed to something, or to say that you oppose it: *I'll take care of it, unless anyone objects.* ♦ *China and India formally* ***objected*** *to the peace plan.* ♦ **object to doing sth** *I object to paying that much for gas.*

ob•jec•tion /əbˈdʒekʃ(ə)n/ noun [C/U] ★ a statement that shows that you disagree with a plan, or a reason for your disagreement: *I think I'll move on to the next point, if you* ***have no objection.*** ♦ *I would like to put forward several* ***objections*** *to this proposal.* ♦ *They* ***raised an objection*** (=expressed an objection) *to the plan.*

ob•jec•tion•a•ble /əbˈdʒekʃənəb(ə)l/ adj unpleasant and offensive

ob•jec•tive[1] /əbˈdʒektɪv/ noun [C] ★ something that you plan to achieve: *I'm not sure I understand* ***the objective of*** *this exercise.* ♦ ***The main objective of*** *our department is to identify market opportunities.*

Words often used with objective

Adjectives often used with ***objective*** *(noun)*

- **key, main, overriding, primary, prime, principal, ultimate** + OBJECTIVE: used for saying that a particular objective is the most important one

Verbs often used with ***objective*** *(noun)*

- **accomplish, achieve, attain, fulfill, meet, reach** + OBJECTIVE: achieve an objective

ob•jec•tive[2] /əbˈdʒektɪv/ adj based only on facts and evidence, and not influenced by personal feelings or beliefs —**ob•jec•tive•ly** adv

ob•jec•tiv•i•ty /ˌɑbdʒekˈtɪvəti/ noun [U] **1** a state or situation in which something is based only on facts and evidence **2** the ability to make decisions that are based on facts rather than on your own personal feelings or beliefs

ob•jec•tor /əbˈdʒektər/ noun [C] someone who disagrees with or opposes something

ob•li•gat•ed /ˈɑblɪˌgeɪtəd/ adj **be/feel obligated to do sth** if you are obligated to do something, you must do it because it is your duty, or because it is morally right

ob•li•ga•tion /ˌɑblɪˈgeɪʃ(ə)n/ noun [C/U] ★ **1** something that you must do for legal or moral reasons: *You are* ***under no obligation*** *to give anyone personal information.* ♦ *The firm* ***has an obligation to*** *its clients.* ♦ *He felt a certain* ***moral obligation*** *to help.* **2** a grateful feeling that you have toward someone who has done something for you: *She felt a certain* ***obligation toward*** *him.*

Words often used with obligation

Adjectives often used with ***obligation*** *(sense 1)*

- **contractual, financial, legal, professional, statutory** + OBLIGATION: used about obligations that are legal or moral

Verbs often used with ***obligation*** *(sense 1)*

- **fulfill, honor, undertake** + OBLIGATION: perform an obligation

o•blig•a•to•ry /əˈblɪgəˌtɔri/ adj *formal* something that is obligatory must be done in order to obey a law or rule

O

o•blige /əˈblaɪdʒ/ verb **1** [T] *formal* to force someone to do something because it is the law, a rule, or a duty: *They felt obliged to offer him hospitality.* ♦ **be/feel obliged to do sth** *You are legally obliged to pay this fine.* **2** [I/T] to help someone by doing something that they have asked you to do: *If you need anything else, I'm always happy to oblige.*

o•blig•ing /əˈblaɪdʒɪŋ/ adj willing to help someone

o•blique /oʊˈblik/ adj not expressing something directly —**o•blique•ly** adv

o•blit•er•ate /əˈblɪtəˌreɪt/ verb [T] to destroy something completely —**o•blit•er•a•tion** /əˌblɪtəˈreɪʃ(ə)n/ noun [U]

o•bliv•i•on /əˈblɪviən/ noun [U] **1** a situation in which someone or something has been completely forgotten **2** a state in which you do not notice what is happening around you

o•bliv•i•ous /əˈblɪviəs/ adj not noticing something, or not knowing about it

ob•long /ˈɑbˌlɔŋ/ noun [C] a shape that is longer than it is wide —**ob•long** adj

ob•nox•ious /ɑbˈnɑkʃəs/ adj very rude, offensive, or unpleasant

o•boe /ˈoʊˌboʊ/ noun [C] a musical instrument that you play by blowing air through a REED —*picture* → WOODWIND

ob•scene /ɑbˈsin/ adj **1** offensive in a sexual way **2** extremely unfair or immoral

ob•scene•ly /ɑbˈsinli/ adv extremely, in a way that makes you angry: *obscenely rich*

ob•scen•i•ty /ɑbˈsenəti/ noun **1** [U] behavior or language that is sexually offensive **2** [C] a word or action that is sexually offensive

ob•scure[1] /əbˈskjʊr/ adj **1** not known about, or not well known **2** not clearly expressed, or not easy to understand —**ob•scure•ly** adv

ob•scure[2] /əbˈskjʊr/ verb [T] **1** to make something difficult to understand **2** to cover something so that it cannot be seen

ob•scu•ri•ty /əbˈskjʊrəti/ noun [U] a state in which a person or thing is not well known, or is not remembered

ob•ser•vance /əbˈzɜrvəns/ noun [U] the practice of obeying a law or rule, or of doing something according to a tradition

ob•ser•vant /əbˈzɜrvənt/ adj noticing the things that happen around you

ob•ser•va•tion /ˌɑbzərˈveɪʃ(ə)n/ noun ★
1 [U] the process of watching someone or something carefully in order to find something out: *She's been admitted to the hospital **for observation**.*
2 [C] a written or spoken comment about something that you have seen, heard, or felt
3 [U] the ability to notice things: *Most children have great **powers of observation**.*
4 [U] the practice of obeying a law, rule, or custom
—**ob•ser•va•tion•al** adj

ob•ser•va•to•ry /əbˈzɜrvəˌtɔri/ noun [C] a building with a TELESCOPE that scientists use to study the stars and planets

ob•serve /əbˈzɜrv/ verb [T] ★
1 to notice or watch someone who is doing something, or something that is happening: *Similar trends may be observed in most modern societies.* ♦ *All evening Jane observed his behavior closely.*
2 to accept and obey something such as a rule or agreement: *The proper procedures must be strictly observed.*
3 *formal* to make a written or spoken comment about someone or something

ob•serv•er /əbˈzɜrvər/ noun [C] someone who watches, sees, or notices something

ob•sess /əbˈses/ verb **1** [T] if someone or something obsesses you, you are unable to stop thinking about them all the time: *The thought of seeing him again completely obsessed her.* **2** [I] to worry about something all the time

ob•sessed /əbˈsest/ adj unable to stop thinking about someone or something all the time

ob•ses•sion /əbˈseʃ(ə)n/ noun **1** [U] an emotional condition in which someone or something is so important to you that you are always thinking about them **2** [C] someone or something that you cannot stop thinking about

ob•ses•sive /əbˈsesɪv/ adj unable to stop thinking about someone or something in a way that is extreme —**ob•ses•sive•ly** adv

ob•so•lete /ˌɑbsəˈlit/ adj something that is obsolete is not used anymore because it has been replaced by something newer

ob•sta•cle /ˈɑbstək(ə)l/ noun [C] **1** a difficulty or problem that prevents you from achieving something = BARRIER **2** an object that you must remove or go around in order to move forward = BARRIER

ob•ste•tri•cian /ˌɑbstəˈtrɪʃ(ə)n/ noun [C] a doctor whose job is to check the health of a woman who is pregnant, and to help with the birth of her child

ob•stet•rics /ɑbˈstetrɪks/ noun [U] the part of medicine that deals with pregnant women and the birth of children —**ob•stet•ric** adj

ob•sti•nate /ˈɑbstɪnət/ adj not willing to be reasonable and change your ideas or behavior = STUBBORN —**ob•sti•na•cy** noun [U], **ob•sti•nate•ly** adv

ob•struct /əbˈstrʌkt/ verb [T] **1** to block a path, passage, door, etc. so that it is difficult or impossible to get past **2** to take action in order to prevent something from happening

ob•struc•tion /əbˈstrʌkʃ(ə)n/ noun **1** [C] something that blocks a path, passage, door, etc. so that it is difficult or impossible to get past **2** [U] the process of taking action in order to prevent something from happening

ob•struc•tive /əbˈstrʌktɪv/ adj trying to prevent something by deliberately causing problems

ob•tain /əbˈteɪn/ verb [T] ★★★ to get something that you want or need: *She has to **obtain** her father's **permission** before she does anything.* ♦ **obtain sth from sb/sth** *Details can be obtained from the Department of Education.*

ob•tain•a•ble /əbˈteɪnəb(ə)l/ adj able to be obtained

ob•tru•sive /ɑbˈtrusɪv/ adj attracting attention in a way that is not pleasant or welcome ≠ UNOBTRUSIVE

ob•tuse /əbˈtus/ adj *technical* an obtuse angle is between 90° and 180° —*picture* → C8

ob•vi•ous /ˈɑbviəs/ adj ★★★ clear to almost anyone: *an obvious mistake* ♦ ***For obvious reasons**, I won't go into details.* ♦ **+(that)** *It's pretty obvious he's crazy about you.*

ob•vi•ous•ly /ˈɑbviəsli/ adv ★★★
1 in a way that is clear for almost anyone to see or understand = CLEARLY: *Richards was obviously disappointed at being left off the team.* ♦ *"Isn't he afraid?" "Obviously not."*
2 as most people would expect or understand = NATURALLY: *Obviously, I'll have to think about your offer carefully.*

oc•ca•sion /əˈkeɪʒ(ə)n/ noun [C] ★★★
1 a special or important time or event: *a great occasion in the nation's history* ♦ *This dress is perfect for **a special occasion**.*
2 a time at which something happens: ***On one occasion** (=once) the defendant was seen trying to get in through a window.* ♦ *He continues to work with us **on occasion*** (=sometimes).

oc•ca•sion•al /əˈkeɪʒən(ə)l/ adj ★ happening sometimes, but not frequently or regularly: *He made occasional visits to Los Angeles.* ♦ *Chocolate is best kept as an occasional treat.*

oc•ca•sion•al•ly /əˈkeɪʒən(ə)li/ adv ★★ sometimes, but not frequently or regularly: *Simmer the sauce for ten minutes, stirring occasionally.*

oc•cult, the /əˈkʌlt/ noun [singular] magic or SUPERNATURAL forces and events —**oc•cult** adj

oc•cu•pan•cy /ˈɑkjəpənsi/ noun [U] *formal* the use of a place, or the period of time for which it is used

oc•cu•pant /ˈɑkjəpənt/ noun [C] someone who is living in or using a place: *the current occupants of the building*

O

oc·cu·pa·tion /ˌɑkjəˈpeɪʃ(ə)n/ noun ★
1 [C/U] a job: *Please give your name, address, and occupation.*
2 [C] something that you do in your free time: *Walking is now Dad's favorite occupation.*
3 [U] the act of living or staying in a building, room, or other place: *The new homes will be **ready for occupation** in August.*
4 [U] the action of using military force to go into a place and take control away from the people or government there: *the Roman occupation of Britain*

oc·cu·pa·tion·al /ˌɑkjəˈpeɪʃən(ə)l/ adj relating to, or caused by, your job

oc·cu·pied /ˈɑkjəˌpaɪd/ adj **1** a seat, room, etc. that is occupied has someone using it **2** an area or country that is occupied has foreign military forces in it that are controlling it **3** busy doing something: *The game kept them occupied for the rest of the afternoon.*

oc·cu·pi·er /ˈɑkjəˌpaɪr/ noun [C] someone who is in control of a place that they have entered in a group using military force

oc·cu·py /ˈɑkjəˌpaɪ/ verb [T] ★★
1 to be using or in a room, building, or other place: *The Smith family has occupied this farm for over a hundred years.*
2 to be in control of a place that you have entered in a group using military force: *The region was quickly occupied by foreign troops.*
3 to keep someone busy at an activity: *I need some way to occupy the kids for an hour.*

oc·cur /əˈkɜr/ verb [I] ★★★
1 to happen: *The police said that the accident occurred at about 4:30 p.m.*
2 *formal* to exist or be found somewhere: *Radon gas occurs naturally in rocks such as granite.*
PHRASAL VERB **ocˈcur to sb** if a thought or idea occurs to you, you suddenly start to think about it: *The thought of giving up never occurred to me.* ♦ **it occurs to sb that** *It suddenly occurred to her that Joe was afraid of being alone.*

oc·cur·rence /əˈkɜrəns/ noun [C/U] something that happens

o·cean /ˈoʊʃ(ə)n/ noun ★★
1 [C] one of the large areas of salt water that cover most of the Earth: *the Atlantic/Pacific/Indian Ocean*
2 **the ocean** [singular] a large area of salt water that lies along the coast of a country: *Our new place is a couple of blocks from the ocean.* → DROP²

- In American English, **the ocean** is the general word for the large area of salt water along the coast of a country: *They live by the ocean.*
- In British English, this is called **the sea**: *He looked out at the sea.*
- In British and American English, an **ocean** is one of the very large areas of salt water that cover most of the Earth: *the Atlantic/Pacific Ocean*

o'clock /əˈklɑk/ adv ★★
PHRASE **one o'clock/four o'clock etc.** used for saying what time it is when a clock shows the exact hour

oc·ta·gon /ˈɑktəˌgɑn/ noun [C] a shape with eight straight sides of equal length —*picture* → C8 —**oc·tag·o·nal** /ɑkˈtægən(ə)l/ adj

oc·tave /ˈɑktəv, ˈɑkˌteɪv/ noun [C] a series of eight musical notes in a musical SCALE

Oc·to·ber /ɑkˈtoʊbər/ noun [C/U] ★★★ the tenth month of the year, between September and November: *We're going to Boston in October.* ♦ *The next meeting will be on October 9th.*

oc·to·pus /ˈɑktəpəs/ noun [C] an ocean animal with a soft round body and eight long arms —*picture* → C13

OD /oʊˈdi/ noun [C] *informal* an OVERDOSE of a dangerous drug —**OD** verb [I]

odd /ɑd/ adj ★
1 unusual, or strange: *Harry's behavior did seem a little odd.* ♦ **it is odd (that)** *It's very odd that he hasn't sent you a birthday present.*
2 an odd number is a WHOLE NUMBER that cannot be divided exactly by two, for example 1, 3, 5, 7, etc. ≠ EVEN
3 without the other thing from a pair of things: *odd socks/shoes/gloves*
→ ODDS

odd·i·ty /ˈɑdəti/ noun [C] someone or something that seems strange or unusual

ˌodd ˈjobs noun [plural] small jobs of various types that you do in your home, such as repairing things

odd·ly /ˈɑdli/ adv in an unusual way that attracts your interest or attention
PHRASE **oddly enough** used for saying that something is not what you would expect in a particular situation

odds /ɑdz/ noun [plural] **1** the chances of something happening: *The odds are* (=it is likely that) *they won't succeed.* **2** the chances that are used for calculating how much money you will get if the person or thing you BET on wins a race or competition
PHRASES **against all (the) odds** if you succeed in doing something against all odds, you succeed in it despite problems and difficulties
at odds (with) 1 disagreeing with someone: *She continued to find herself at odds with the chairman.* **2** if things are at odds with each other, they are different or opposite when they should be the same: *This statement is completely at odds with what was said last week.*
odds and ends small things that are all different and that are not valuable or important

ode /oʊd/ noun [C] a poem that has been written for or about a particular person, thing, or event

o·dom·e·ter /oʊˈdɑmətər/ noun [C] *American* a piece of equipment in a car that shows how many miles it has traveled —*picture* → C6

o·dor /ˈoʊdər/ noun [C] a smell, especially one that is unpleasant

o·dor·less /ˈoʊdərləs/ adj with no smell

o·dour /ˈoʊdər/ the British spelling of **odor**

od·ys·sey /ˈɑdəsi/ noun [C] *literary* a long trip during which many things happen

of /əv, *strong* ɑv/ preposition ★★★
1 **connected with or part of sb/sth** belonging to, connected with, or forming part of someone or something: *the color of the sky* ♦ *I don't remember the name of the street.* ♦ *The roof of the church was damaged.*

O

♦ *the President of Syria* ♦ *Lori is the daughter of my father's sister.* ♦ *a good friend of mine*
2 showing or describing sb/sth concerning or showing someone or something: *She had a photograph of him beside her bed.* ♦ *It was a tale of war and bravery.* ♦ *a history of Russia*
3 containing or consisting of sth containing, including, or formed from a particular type of person or thing: *He handed her a glass of water.* ♦ *a box of chocolates* ♦ *a pound of rice* ♦ *a collection of poems* ♦ *a group of teenage girls* ♦ *a sheet of paper*
4 saying which specific thing used after a general word for giving a specific example: *I had a feeling of duty toward him.* ♦ *She seemed to like the idea of having children.* ♦ *the month of April* ♦ *the city of Rome*
5 from a particular group coming from a particular group: *She's one of my best friends.* ♦ *Three of us went on vacation together.* ♦ *Several of the apartments cannot be lived in.*
6 saying who or what does sth used after nouns that refer to actions for saying who or what does the action, or who or what is affected by the action: *the shouts of excited children* ♦ *the arrival of our train* ♦ *the removal of a tumor*
7 giving a specific number used for giving a specific number or value: *She met Charles at the age of 20.* ♦ *Teachers are asking for a pay raise of 4 percent.*
8 created by sb written or produced by someone: *the paintings of Picasso* ♦ *the plays of Tennessee Williams*
9 giving the cause of sth used for saying what causes something: *He died of lung cancer.* ♦ *As a result of pollution, many species have died out.*
10 in dates used for saying dates: *the 27th of November*
11 saying who has a quality used for saying who shows a particular quality in a situation: *It was nice of you to help me.* ♦ *It was stupid of me to think they would agree.*
12 giving the time before the hour *American* used in saying the time to mean a particular number of minutes before the hour: *It's twenty of two* (=1:40).

of 'course adv ★★★
1 used for saying "yes" very definitely, in answer to a question
2 used for agreeing or disagreeing with someone: *"I'm sure everything's going to be OK." "Of course it is."*
3 used for saying something that someone probably already knows or will not be surprised about: *He finally found out that Doug lied, of course.*
4 used when you have just realized something: *Of course! Now I understand.*
PHRASE **of course not 1** used for saying "no" very definitely, in answer to a question **2** used for agreeing or disagreeing with someone: *"I don't think we should tell anyone." "Of course not."*

off /ɔf, ɑf/ grammar word ★★★

> **Off** can be:
> - an **adverb**: *He waved and drove off.*
> - a **preposition**: *She got off the bus at the next stop.*
> - an **adjective**: *I'm having an off day.*

1 not on sth not on the top or surface of something, especially after being on it: *The wind blew a flowerpot off the balcony.* ♦ *Hold on tight so you don't slip off.* ♦ *She tried to push the dog **off of** her but it kept jumping up.*
2 no longer connected no longer connected to someone or something: *They cut a branch off the tree.* ♦ *One of the doll's legs fell off.* ♦ *The handle came **off of** the coffee pot again.*
3 away from sth leaving a place, or going away from something: *I'd never let an 11-year-old kid go off on his own.*
4 going out of a vehicle leaving a plane, train, bus, etc.: *Let's **get off** at the next bus stop.* ♦ *They didn't see each other till they **got off** the plane.*
5 not working a machine or piece of electrical equipment that is off is not switched on: *The lights were off in the house.*
6 not at work not at work, for example because you are not well or because it is not a normal working day: *I took two weeks off in August.* ♦ *I'm thinking of taking some **time off** work.* ♦ *Today is my **day off**.*
7 when clothes are removed used for saying that clothes or shoes are removed: *Take off your wet clothes.* ♦ *She kicked off her shoes and sat down.*
8 close to sth near an area of land, a room, or a road, or connected to it: *an island five miles off the coast* ♦ *There is a bathroom off the bedroom.* ♦ *We live **just off** the main road.*
9 reduced reduced in price by a particular amount: *There's now 30% off all swimsuits.*
10 no longer planned used for saying that an event is no longer going to take place as planned: *Sorry, but the meeting's off.*
11 a particular time or distance away used for saying how long it will be until something happens, or how far away something is: *Christmas is only three weeks off.* ♦ *We could see a house a few miles off.*
PHRASE **off and on** or **on and off** sometimes but not regularly: *She's been seeing him off and on since she was 16.*

,off-'balance adj **1** surprised by something unexpected **2** in a position in which you feel that you are going to fall down

off•beat /ˈɔfˌbit/ adj *informal* unusual, often in an interesting way

,off-'center adj not exactly in the middle of an area

'off ,chance noun **on the off chance** in the hope that something will happen or succeed, although it seems unlikely: *I called on the off chance he'd be at home.*

,off-'color adj an off-color joke or remark is rude or offensive

,off-'duty adj not working: *an off-duty police officer*

of•fence /əˈfens/ the British spelling of offense

of•fend /əˈfend/ verb **1** [T] to make someone angry and upset by doing or saying something: *They avoided saying anything that might offend their audience.* **2** [I] *formal* to commit a crime —**of•fend•ed** adj: *We feel saddened and offended.*

of•fend•er /əˈfendər/ noun [C] someone who has committed a crime: *juvenile* (=young) *offenders* ♦ *sex offenders*

of·fense /əˈfens/ noun ★★
1 [C] a crime or illegal activity for which there is a punishment: *a traffic/drug/sex offense ♦ The new ruling only applies to suspects who have* ***been charged with an offense.*** *♦ Four people were arrested* ***on minor offenses.*** *♦ Killing these animals is* ***a criminal offense.***
2 [U] something that you do or say that makes someone else angry or upset: *commercials that* ***cause offense***
3 /ˈɑˌfens/ [U] the members of a sports team whose job is to try to score points, or the part of a game that involves trying to score points
4 [C] something that makes you feel angry and upset because it is insulting, unfair, or morally wrong: **+to** *The law is an offense to working people.*
PHRASES **no offense** used for telling someone that you hope that what you are saying will not offend them
take offense (at sth) to feel offended by something that someone has done or said

of·fen·sive¹ /əˈfensɪv/ adj ★
1 unpleasant or insulting, and likely to make people upset or embarrassed ≠ INOFFENSIVE: *offensive language ♦ offensive odors ♦ The advertisement* ***was offensive to*** *many women.*
2 involved in scoring points: *offensive players*
3 used for attacking ≠ DEFENSIVE: *offensive weapons*
—**of·fen·sive·ly** adv

of·fen·sive² /əˈfensɪv/ noun [C] a major military attack
PHRASE **be on the offensive** to be ready to attack or criticize people

of·fer¹ /ˈɔfər, ˈɑfər/ verb [T] ★★★
1 to let someone know that you will give them something or do something for them if they want it: **offer sb sth** *They haven't offered me the job yet.* ♦ **offer sth to sb** *He had offered cocaine to an undercover police officer.* ♦ **offer to do sth** *Thank you for offering to help.*
2 to say that you will pay a particular price for something: **offer sb sth for sth** *I offered Jim $5,000 for his car.* ♦ **offer sth to sb** *Police are offering a reward to anyone with information.*
3 to provide something such as a product or service: *Smaller hotels can offer comfort at lower prices. ♦ The city* ***has a lot to offer*** (=has many attractive features for) *the business traveler.*
4 to express your feelings toward someone: *offer sympathy/regrets/thanks ♦ He called the team manager to offer his congratulations.*

of·fer² /ˈɔfər, ˈɑfər/ noun [C] ★★★
1 a statement in which you offer to give, pay, or do something if someone wants it: *a job offer ♦ I've decided to* ***accept your offer.*** *♦ Did she* ***make you an offer for*** (=tell you how much she would pay for) *the bike? ♦ the government's* ***offer of*** *financial aid*
2 a special price that is lower than the usual price for something: *a half-price offer*
PHRASE **an offer sb can't refuse** *informal* a very good offer

Words often used with offer

Verbs often used with ***offer*** *(noun, sense 1)*
- **make, put in, submit** + OFFER: make someone an offer
- **accept, take, take up, welcome** + OFFER: accept someone's offer
- **decline, refuse, reject, turn down** + OFFER: not accept someone's offer

of·fer·ing /ˈɔfərɪŋ, ˈɑfərɪŋ/ noun [C]
1 something that is offered for sale
2 something that someone gives to a church or to a god

ˌoff-ˈguard adj surprised by something unexpected: *The questions caught her completely off-guard.*

off·hand¹ /ɔfˈhænd, ˈɔfˌhænd/ adj an offhand remark is one that you do not think carefully about

off·hand² /ɔfˈhænd/ adv immediately and without checking the facts: *I can't remember their names offhand.*

of·fice /ˈɔfɪs, ˈɑfɪs/ noun ★★★
1 [C] a room or building where the people in an organization or department work, or the people who work there: *the company's Los Angeles office ♦ Our offices are on the third floor. ♦ office furniture ♦ I share an office with my secretary. ♦ I left* ***the office*** *after 6:00 p.m.*
2 [C/U] a position in a large powerful organization, especially a government: ***the office of*** *President ♦ Bob plans to* ***run for office*** (=try to be elected) *next year. ♦ After one year* ***in office,*** *the President still has the full support of the people.*
3 [C] a room or building where you go for a particular service: *the doctor's office*
4 [C] a government department: *the Mayor's Office ♦ the Office of the Treasury*

ˈoffice ˌbuilding noun [C] *American* a large building that contains many offices

ˌoffice ˈhours noun [plural] the times when a business or other organization is open during the day

of·fi·cer /ˈɔfɪsər, ˈɑfɪsər/ noun [C] ★★★
1 someone with a position of power and authority in the military: *an army officer*
2 a POLICE OFFICER
3 someone with a position of authority in an organization

of·fi·cial¹ /əˈfɪʃ(ə)l/ adj ★★★
1 decided or done by people in authority, especially a government ≠ UNOFFICIAL: *the country's official language ♦ There will be* ***an official investigation*** *into last week's accident.*
2 relating to a job in which you have authority or represent other people: *a list of my official duties*

of·fi·cial² /əˈfɪʃ(ə)l/ noun [C] ★★ someone with an important position in an organization: *a senior government official*

of·fi·cial·ly /əˈfɪʃ(ə)li/ adv ★
1 publicly and formally: *The school won't be officially opened until next month.*
2 according to what governments or people in authority say, although it may not be true: *Officially, the government claims no knowledge of the subject.*

of·fi·cious /əˈfɪʃəs/ adj too serious about your job and duties, in a way that is annoying

O

ˌoff-ˈkey adj, adv music or singing that is off-key does not sound good because the notes are slightly wrong

ˌoff-ˈlimits adj if a place is off-limits, you are not allowed to go there

off•line /ɔfˈlaɪn, ˈɔfˌlaɪn/ adj, adv *computing* **1** not directly connected to a computer **2** working on a computer but not connected to the Internet → ONLINE

ˌoff-ˈpeak adj, adv at times when prices are lower because a service is not usually used by many people: *off-peak hours/prices*

ˈoff-ˌramp noun [C] *American* a road that leads off a big highway

ˈoff-ˌseason noun [singular] **1** the period of the year when there is least business or activity **2** *American* the period of the year when a particular sport is not played

off•set /ˌɔfˈset, ˈɔfˌset/ (past tense and past participle **off•set**) verb [T] to balance the effect of something, with the result that there is no real change or difference: *Falling sales were offset by strong performances in other markets.*

off•shoot /ˈɔfˌʃut/ noun [C] a company, group, or organization that has developed from a larger one

off•shore /ˌɔfˈʃɔr/ adj, adv **1** in the ocean, not on the land ≠ ONSHORE: *an offshore oil rig* ♦ *They're going to be working offshore.* **2** involving money that is invested in another country, or referring to a business that is in another country: *offshore banking* ♦ *offshore investments*

off•spring /ˈɔfˌsprɪŋ/ (plural **off•spring**) noun [C] someone's child, or the baby of an animal

off•stage /ˌɔfˈsteɪdʒ/ adj, adv in or toward the area behind a theater stage where the audience cannot see ≠ ONSTAGE: *He rushed offstage.*

ˌoff-the-ˈcuff adj, adv if you say something off-the-cuff, you do not think about it first: *an off-the-cuff reply*

ˌoff-the-ˈrecord adj, adv said to someone in a private way and not intended as part of an official statement: *an off-the-record remark*

ˌoff-the-ˈwall adj strange, often in a funny or interesting way

ˌoff-ˈwhite adj close to white in color, but with slightly more yellow or gray

of•ten /ˈɔf(ə)n/ adv ★★★
1 on many occasions or in many situations: *Boredom often leads to bad behavior.* ♦ ***Very often** the student can't understand the question.*
2 used for talking about how many times something happens in a particular period of time: ***How often** do you eat meat?*
PHRASES **all too often** used for saying that something happens more often than you think it should: *All too often, parents leave their children at home alone.*
every so often sometimes, but not frequently: *She still calls me every so often.*
more often than not on most occasions, or in most situations: *More often than not, arguments can be avoided.*

o•gle /ˈoʊg(ə)l/ verb [I/T] *showing disapproval* to look at someone in a way that shows you think they are sexually attractive

o•gre /ˈoʊgər/ noun [C] a cruel frightening person

oh¹ /oʊ/ interjection **1** used at the beginning of an answer or reply for showing that you understand or accept new information: *"Joe is her brother, not her boyfriend." "Oh, I see!"* ♦ *"He just resigned." "Oh, did he?"* **2** used for expressing an emotion such as surprise, anger, or happiness: *Oh, what a beautiful view!* ♦ *Oh no! I left my keys in the car.* **3** used when you start telling someone something, for example something that you have just remembered: *Oh honey, did you see that note I left you?*

oh² /oʊ/ number *spoken* a way of saying "zero," for example in saying telephone numbers or a date, such as 1908

OH abbrev Ohio

oil¹ /ɔɪl/ noun ★★★
1 [U] a thick dark smooth liquid used for making gas and other fuels: *The house is heated with oil.* ♦ *oil prices/companies*
2 [C/U] a thick smooth liquid, used in cooking and medicines: *Cook the chicken in oil.* ♦ *vegetable/olive/sunflower oil*
3 [C/U] a thick smooth liquid used in an engine so that it will work smoothly: *Change the oil in your car every 3,000 miles.*
4 [C/U] a thick clear liquid used for protecting your skin or making it soft: *bath/suntan oil* ♦ *baby oil*

oil² /ɔɪl/ verb [T] to put oil on something

oil•field /ˈɔɪlˌfild/ noun [C] an area where there is oil underground

ˈoil ˌpaint noun [C/U] a thick paint used by artists, that contains oil

ˈoil ˌpainting noun [C/U] a picture painted with oil paint, or the art of painting this type of picture

ˈoil ˌrig noun [C] a large structure with equipment on it for getting oil out from underground

ˈoil ˌslick noun [C] a layer of oil on the surface of a large area of water, after an accident

ˈoil ˌtanker noun [C] a large ship that carries oil

ˈoil ˌwell noun [C] a deep narrow hole that is dug in order to obtain oil

oil•y /ˈɔɪli/ adj **1** covered with oil, containing oil, or like oil: *an oily rag* ♦ *oily fish* ♦ *an oily texture* **2** very polite in a way that does not seem sincere

oint•ment /ˈɔɪntmənt/ noun [C/U] a thick smooth substance that you put on sore or injured skin

OJ /ˌoʊ ˈdʒeɪ/ noun [C/U] *American informal* orange juice

OK¹ /oʊˈkeɪ/ interjection ★★★
1 used for showing that you agree, approve, or understand. This is also used to ask if someone agrees, approves, or understands: *"I'd like to buy some new clothes." "OK."* ♦ *So "C" is the best answer. OK?*
2 used when you want to start or continue talking about something: *OK. Is everyone ready?*
3 used for showing that you want to end a conversation or argument: *OK! I'll try to do better next time.*

OK² /oʊˈkeɪ/ adj *spoken* **1** satisfactory, but not usually the best possible: *The food was OK.* **2** allowed, appropriate, or not likely to make you upset: *The teacher said it was OK for me to leave class early.* **3** not injured,

O

damaged, sick, or upset: *Are you OK? You look tired.*

PHRASE **it's/that's OK** *spoken* used for saying that something does not make you angry, upset, or sad: *"I'm sorry I said that." "That's OK."*

—**OK** adv: *I think I did OK on the test.*

OK³ abbrev Oklahoma

o•kay /oʊˈkeɪ/ another spelling of **OK**

old /oʊld/ adj ★★★

1 used for talking about the age of someone or something: *I'm older than my brother.* ♦ *She's the oldest girl in the class.* ♦ *A woman stood watching with her 3-year-old* (=child who is 3). ♦ ***How old** are you? I'm 5 **years old**.* ♦ **old enough to do sth** *He's not old enough to see this movie.*

2 someone who is old has lived a long time ≠ YOUNG: *A lot of **old people** live alone.* ♦ *I hope I'll still be able to play golf when I **get old**.*

3 something that is old has existed or been used for a long time: *an old belief* ♦ *I finally replaced my old sewing machine.* ♦ *Trees are the oldest living things on the planet.* ♦ *I'm meeting **an old friend** for lunch.*

4 used for describing something that existed, happened, or was used in the past: *"Thy" is an old way of saying "your."* ♦ *The old highway only had two lanes.* ♦ *I still get letters from some of my old students* (=people that I taught in the past).

PHRASES **for old times' sake** so that you can remember a happy time in the past

your old self the way you normally were in the past, before something happened: *Now you sound like your old self again!*

> **Words that may cause offense: old**
>
> Avoid saying that someone is **old** or **elderly**, and avoid referring to old or elderly people as **the old** or **the elderly**. Instead, use expressions such as **older people, retired people, seniors**, or **the over 50s/60s** etc.

ˌold ˈage noun [U] the period of time when you are old

old-fash•ioned /oʊldˈfæʃ(ə)nd/ adj ★

1 no longer modern or fashionable: *an old-fashioned leather briefcase*

2 no longer useful or appropriate in the modern world = OUTDATED: *old-fashioned ideas about raising children*

3 used for referring to nice things from the past that still exist: *good old-fashioned home cooking*

ˌold ˈflame noun [C] someone who you had a romantic relationship with in the past

ˌold ˈfolks noun [plural] older people

ˌold ˈguard, the noun [singular] the people in an organization who have been there for a long time and do not like changes

ˌold ˈhand noun [C] someone who has been doing something for a long time and is very good at it

ˌold ˈhat adj *informal* not interesting because people have known or done something for a long time

ˌold ˈpeople's ˌhome noun [C] a place where old people live and are taken care of

ˌold ˌschool, the noun [singular] people who have traditional or old-fashioned ideas

—**ˈold ˌschool** adj

ˌOld ˈTestament, the the first part of the Christian Bible → NEW TESTAMENT

ˌold-ˌtime adj old-fashioned in a way that you admire

ˌold-ˈtimer noun [C] *American* an old person, especially a man

ˌold ˈwives' ˌtale noun [C] a traditional belief that many people think is silly because there is no scientific proof of it

ˈold-ˌworld adj old-fashioned in a pleasant and attractive way: *the town's old-world charm*

ol•ive¹ /ˈɑlɪv/ noun **1** [C] a small black or green fruit that is eaten or used for its oil **2 olive** or **olive green** [U] a dark yellow-green color

ol•ive² /ˈɑlɪv/ adj **1** olive skin is yellowish brown in color **2** dark yellowish green in color

ˈolive ˌbranch noun [singular] something that someone does in order to show that they want to stop arguing

ˌolive ˈoil noun [C/U] a type of cooking oil that is made from OLIVES

O•lym•pi•an¹ /əˈlɪmpiən/ noun [C] **1** someone who competes in the Olympic Games **2** one of the ancient Greek gods

O•lym•pi•an² /əˈlɪmpiən/ adj relating to the ancient Greek gods

O•lym•pic /əˈlɪmpɪk/ adj relating to the Olympic Games

Oˌlympic ˈGames, the or **the O•lym•pics** an international sports event that takes place every four years

ome•let /ˈɑmlət/ noun [C] a flat round food made by mixing eggs together and cooking them —*picture* → EGG

o•men /ˈoʊmən/ noun [C] something that shows whether good or bad things will happen in the future: *He was convinced that seeing the black cat was a bad omen.*

om•i•nous /ˈɑmɪnəs/ adj making you think that something bad will happen: *an ominous silence* —**om•i•nous•ly** adv

o•mis•sion /oʊˈmɪʃ(ə)n/ noun [C/U] someone or something that has not been included, or the fact of not including something: *There are one or two surprising omissions from the list.*

o•mit /oʊˈmɪt/ verb [T] to fail to include someone or something: *Important details had been omitted from the article.*

om•nip•o•tent /ɑmˈnɪpətənt/ adj *formal* powerful enough to do everything —**om•nip•o•tence** noun [U]

on /ɑn, ɔn/ grammar word ★★★

> **On** can be:
>
> - a **preposition**: *She was lying on the floor.*
> - an **adverb**: *When the bus stopped, he got on.*
> - used after the verb "to be": *Is the central heating on?*

1 **supported by a surface** supported by something, or touching the top of it: *Chad was asleep on the floor.* ♦ *He left a note for you on the kitchen table.*

2 **sticking to sth** touching, sticking to, or hanging from something: *There were several posters on the wall.* ♦ *The key is hanging on a hook in the hall.* ♦ *Evelyn kissed him on the cheek.*

3 **at a particular time** used for stating the day or date when something happens: *He's*

O

coming home on Wednesday. ♦ *My birthday is on the 27th of November.*
4 in a particular place at the side of a road, river, or area of water: *Gordie's grandparents live on Crescent Drive.* ♦ *a town on the Mississippi*
5 in an area in a particular area or on a particular type of land: *The house was built on a beautiful piece of land.* ♦ *My father was raised on a farm, but I have lived in the city my whole life.*
6 as part of a page or list included as part of a page of a book, or as part of a list: *Look at the picture on page 94.* ♦ *Why isn't my name on the list?*
7 wearing or carrying sth wearing or carrying a particular thing on a part of your body: *Put your shoes on.* ♦ *She wore a ring on her left hand.* ♦ *You look funny with glasses on.* ♦ *Have you got any cash on you?*
8 being broadcast being broadcast by radio or television: *I usually listen to the news on the radio.* ♦ *What time is the football game on?*
9 saying who or what is affected used for saying who or what is affected by something: *the effect of interest rates on the housing market* ♦ *The attacks on Walters are very unfair.*
10 about sth concerning a particular subject: *a report on the Civil War*
11 continuing continuing to do something or to happen: *Read on to find out the rest of the story.* ♦ *The opera seemed to go* ***on and on*** *for hours.*
12 in or into a vehicle in or into a bus, train, airplane, etc.: *We got on the train in Oakland.* ♦ *I'll get some work done while I'm on the plane.*
13 using particular equipment used for saying what type of machine or equipment is used for doing something: *The work is done on the computer.* ♦ *I recorded our conversation on my tape recorder.*
14 working if a machine or piece of electrical equipment is on, it is working: *Who left the TV on?*
15 using a drug using a particular drug: *She's on antibiotics for an eye infection.* ♦ *He seemed to be on drugs.*
16 taking part in a trip used for saying that someone takes part in an activity in which they travel or see something: *I'll take you on a tour of the factory.* ♦ *I met him when I was on a Mediterranean cruise.*
17 being a member of sth if someone is on a team or committee, they are a member of it: *There are only three directors on the board.*
18 happening immediately *formal* immediately after another event, or at the same time as another event: *Report to the reception desk on arrival.*
19 paid for by sb *spoken* used for saying who will pay for something: *Drink up! The next one is on me.*

PHRASES **from now/then/that moment etc. on** starting at a particular time and continuing to happen: *The new rules will apply to all the members from now on.*
on sb's face used for saying that someone's face has a particular expression: *There was a look of horror on her face.*
on the left/right at or to the left/right side of someone or something: *His office is the last door on the left.*
→ HEAD-ON

ˌon-again, ˈoff-again adj *American* happening, stopping, and then happening again several times

ˈon-ˌair adj broadcast during a radio or television program

once /wʌns/ grammar word ★★★

Once can be:
- an **adverb**: *I only met him once.*
- a **conjunction**: *Once you get there, you'll love it.*
- a **noun**: *For once I wish you'd tell me the truth.* ♦ *Yes, I met him, but just the once.*

1 on one occasion only: *Cathy's only been to visit us once.* ♦ *I'd seen the show once before.* ♦ *We met* ***just the once****, but I remember him well.* ♦ *The class meets* ***once a week.*** ♦ *You should take two pills* ***once every six hours.***
2 used for saying that a particular situation existed in the past, but it does not exist any longer: *Did you know that Dan was once a policeman?* ♦ *Louise bought the house where her grandparents had once lived.*
3 used for saying that as soon as one thing happens, something else happens: *You'll be very happy here once you get to know everyone.*

PHRASES **all at once 1** happening suddenly when you are not expecting it: *All at once thunder shook the whole house.* **2** at the same time: *Everybody started speaking all at once.*
at once 1 immediately: *Bake for 35 minutes and then serve at once.* **2** at the same time: *You're trying to do too many things at once.*
(every) once in a while sometimes, but not very often: *I still see Ken around town once in a while.*
for once *spoken* used for saying that you would like something to happen, and you think it should happen more often: *You can pay the bill for once.*
once again/more 1 used for saying that something happens again: *The fair was once again a tremendous success.* **2** used for saying that a situation becomes as it was before it changed: *We look forward to the day when there will be peace once more.*
once and for all completely and finally: *The Supreme Court's ruling should decide this matter once and for all.*
once or twice a few times, but not very often: *Martin's gone hunting once or twice, but I don't think he really liked it.*
once upon a time used for starting children's stories
→ BLUE[1]

on·com·ing /ˈɑnˌkʌmɪŋ/ adj moving toward you: *oncoming traffic/vehicles*

one /wʌn/ grammar word ★★★

One can be:
- a **number**: *We have one child.*
- a **determiner**: *He grew roses on one side of his garden, and vegetables on the other.*
- a **pronoun**: *They are the ones who suffered.* ♦ *Sydney is one of the world's most exciting cities.*

1 number the number 1: *I've only got one hour free.* ♦ *They have one daughter and five sons.*
2 a single person or thing used for referring to a single person or thing when there are others of the same type: *I bought three T-shirts. Do you want one?* ♦ *One passenger said she had been waiting for 13 hours.* ♦ *I met **one of** her brothers.* ♦ ***one of the best** Japanese restaurants in town*
3 (plural **ones**): **used for referring to things** used for referring to something when that type of thing has already been mentioned: *It was a problem, but not a major one.* ♦ *Your experiences are ones that are shared by many other parents.* ♦ *I'm going to keep those boxes. **The ones** I want to get rid of are in the garage.* ♦ *I'd never seen a game like **that one**.*
4 the one (plural **the ones**): **used for referring to people** used for referring to someone who is part of a group: *David and I are the only ones left who are not married.* ♦ *Who is the one with the beard?*
5 the only the only person or thing of a particular type: *My one concern is that not everyone will be able to attend.* ♦ *We're going to have to play **the one** team we did not want to play.*
6 used for emphasis used for emphasizing a particular fact, person, or thing: *There's one thing you can be sure of – you won't get any help from him.* ♦ *One person who won't be invited is her ex-husband.* ♦ *She's one beautiful lady.*
7 used for comparison used for mentioning the first of two or more similar people or things, especially when you are comparing them: *She had a glass in **one** hand and an empty bottle in **the other**.*

PHRASES **(all) in one** used for saying that someone or something can do many different things at the same time: *The device will give you telephone, television, and Internet all in one.*
one after another or **one after the other** used for saying that actions are done or things happen with very little time between them: *They had four children one after another.*
the one and only used for introducing a famous person, or for saying that someone is very famous
one by one first one, then the next, then the next, separately: *Add the eggs one by one.*
one day/night/year etc. **1** on a particular day/night/year etc. in the past: *One evening Sam didn't come home.* **2** on any day/night/year etc. in the future: *She knew that one day she'd get married.*
one or two a small number of people or things: *Carla said she had one or two ideas of her own.*

ˌone aˈnother pronoun used for saying that each of two or more people does the same thing to the other, or has the same relationship with the other = EACH OTHER: *They all shook hands with one another.* ♦ *We respect one another's privacy.*

ˈone-ˌman adj **1** made for just one person. Many people prefer to use the word ONE-PERSON: *a one-man tent* **2** involving just one person. Many people prefer to use the word ONE-PERSON: *a one-man show*

ˌone-night ˈstand noun [C] a situation in which two people have sex once but do not have a relationship

ˌone-on-ˈone adj, adv happening between only two people: *a one-on-one interview*

ˈone-ˌperson adj involving one person, or made for one person: *a one-person household*

ˈone-ˌshot adj happening or done once and not repeated

one-sid·ed /ˌwʌn ˈsaɪdəd/ adj **1** unfair because of only showing one aspect of something: *a one-sided account of the conflict* **2** in a one-sided activity, one of the people or groups involved has a lot more skill, power, etc. than the other: *a one-sided contest/game/match*

ˈone-ˌstop adj providing a range of products or services in one place: *one-stop shopping*

ˈone-ˌtime adj used for saying what someone or something was in the past = FORMER: *the one-time Communist party leader*

ˌone-track ˈmind noun [C] someone with a one-track mind thinks about one particular thing all the time

one-up·man·ship /wʌn ˈʌpmənʃɪp/ noun [U] attempts to get an advantage by appearing to be more skillful, important, etc. than other people

ˈone-ˌway adj **1** with cars traveling in one direction only: *a one-way street* **2** a one-way ticket allows you to travel from one place to another but not back again

ˈone-ˌwoman adj involving only one woman: *a one-woman comedy act*

on·go·ing /ˈɑnˌɡoʊɪŋ/ adj still happening or being done: *an ongoing discussion*

on·ion /ˈʌnjən/ noun [C] a round vegetable with thin dry skin, many layers inside, and a strong smell —*picture* → C11

on·line /ˈɑnˌlaɪn/ adj, adv *computing* connected to or available through a computer or a computer NETWORK such as the Internet: *an online bookshop* ♦ *online banking* —**on·line** /ˌɑnˈlaɪn/ adv: *Just go online and order it.*

on·look·er /ˈɑnˌlʊkər/ noun [C] someone who watches something happen but does not take part in it

on·ly /ˈoʊnli/ grammar word ★★★

> **Only** can be:
> - an **adverb**: *She's only 18.*
> - an **adjective**: *You're the only person who can help me.*
> - a **conjunction**: *You can come, only make sure you're on time.*

1 showing that an amount is small used for emphasizing that an amount, distance, or time is small: *She was only 18 when she got married.* ♦ *The police station was only 150 yards away.*
2 nothing, no one, nowhere, etc. except used for showing that a statement does not apply to anyone or anything else except the person or thing that you are mentioning: *Everyone promised to come, but only Ted showed up.* ♦ *The flowers grow only on the island of Maui.* ♦ *I only design the dresses, I don't actually make them.*

3 when there are no others used for showing that there are no other things or people of the same kind as the one or ones that you are mentioning: *This is **the only** letter my father ever wrote to me.* ♦ *David's **the only one** of us who has a computer.* ♦ *My only reason for coming here was to see you.*
4 but used for adding a comment to something that you have just said that makes it less true or correct: *Her car is like mine, only it has four doors.* ♦ *I'd love to come. **The only thing is,** I'll have to leave early.*
5 not better, worse, etc. than sth used for saying that something is not better, worse, more important, etc. than you are stating: *"What was that noise?" "Don't worry – it's only the wind."* ♦ *We are only trying to help.*
6 no earlier than sth not before a particular time, or not before a particular thing has happened: *You pay the agent only when you sell the house.*
→ ONE

ˌonly ˈchild noun [C] a child who has no brothers or sisters

ˈon-ˌramp noun [C] *American* a road that leads onto a big highway

ˈon-ˌscreen adj, adv **1** happening or being in a television program or movie: *She plays his on-screen wife, Nancy.* **2** on a computer screen: *The work is edited on-screen.*

on•set /ˈɑnˌset/ noun **the onset of sth** the beginning of something, especially something bad: *the onset of the disease*

on•shore /ˌɑnˈʃɔr/ adj on land rather than on the ocean ≠ OFFSHORE

on•slaught /ˈɑnˌslɔt/ noun [C] **1** large numbers of people or things that come at the same time and are difficult to deal with **2** an attack

on•stage /ˌɑnˈsteɪdʒ/ adj, adv on the stage of a theater ≠ OFFSTAGE

on•to /ˈɑntə/ preposition ★★★
1 into a position on an object or surface: *A tree fell onto a car, trapping the people inside.* ♦ *Marilyn emptied her shopping bag onto the carpet.*
2 into a bus, train, ship, aircraft, etc.: *Slater tried to carry a gun onto the plane.* ♦ *The refugees were put onto buses.*
3 into an area that you consider to be a surface: *A spectator ran onto the field and attacked the referee.*
4 used for saying that something is added to a list, statement, word, etc.: *To form the plural, just add "s" or "es" onto the end.*
PHRASES **be onto sb** to have found out that someone has done something wrong: *He knew the police were onto him.*
be onto sth to have information that will help you to make an important discovery: *I think you could be onto something here.*

o•nus /ˈoʊnəs/ noun [singular] *formal* if the onus is on someone to do something, it is their responsibility or duty to do it

on•ward¹ /ˈɑnwərd/ adj moving forward, or continuing

on•ward² /ˈɑnwərd/ or **on•wards** /ˈɑnwərdz/ adv if something happens or exists from a particular time onward, it starts at that time and continues to happen or exist: *Most nights are very busy from about 7 p.m. onward.*

ooh /u/ interjection used for showing surprise, excitement, or pleasure

oops /ʊps, ups/ interjection used when a small mistake or slight accident has happened

ooze /uz/ verb [I/T] **1** if a thick liquid oozes from something, or if something oozes a liquid, a small amount of it flows out slowly: *Juice oozed from the grapes.* **2** if someone or something oozes a particular quality, or if it oozes from them, they show that quality in a very obvious way: *Her brother oozes charm.*

o•pal /ˈoʊpəl/ noun [U] a smooth white stone used in jewelry

o•paque /oʊˈpeɪk/ adj **1** opaque glass, liquid, etc. is difficult to see through **2** difficult to understand

OPEC /ˈoʊˌpek/ Organization of Petroleum Exporting Countries: an organization that controls the supply and price of oil in the world market

o•pen¹ /ˈoʊpən/ adj ★★★

1 when public can visit	7 anyone can see/join
2 when you can see in	8 considering ideas
3 of a door/window	9 not decided
4 not covered/enclosed	10 when sth can be done
5 not blocked	+ PHRASE
6 not hidden/secret	

1 if a store, restaurant, etc. is open, the public can use it or visit it ≠ CLOSED: *The bar stays open all night.* ♦ *the campaign to keep the hospital open* ♦ *The house is **open to the public** for three weeks each year.*
2 something that is open has no cover, or has its edges separated, so that you can see what is inside: *an open drawer* ♦ *The kids were tearing open presents.* ♦ *A book **lay open** on the table.* ♦ *The baby's **eyes** were **open**.*
3 in a position that allows someone or something to pass through: *The bedroom **door** was **open**.* ♦ *Someone has left the gate **wide open**.*
4 an open space or area is not covered or enclosed, or does not have many buildings, trees, etc.: *The top deck of the bus is open.* ♦ *the **wide open spaces** of the American West*
5 if a road or method of communication is open, it is available for people to use
6 not keeping anything secret: *an open and honest discussion* ♦ *He has always been **open about** his drinking problem.*
7 available for anyone to take part in or see: *The meeting is **open to the public**.*
8 willing to consider many different possibilities: *The police are **keeping an open mind** about the cause of her disappearance.* ♦ *I have some ideas about where to go, but I'm **open to** suggestions.*
9 a situation that is open has at least two possible results: *Should we **leave it open** for now, and decide at the meeting?*
10 if something is open to criticism, doubt, etc., it is possible or reasonable to criticize it, doubt it, etc.: *The system is **open to abuse**.*
PHRASE **welcome sb/sth with open arms** to be very happy to see someone or receive something

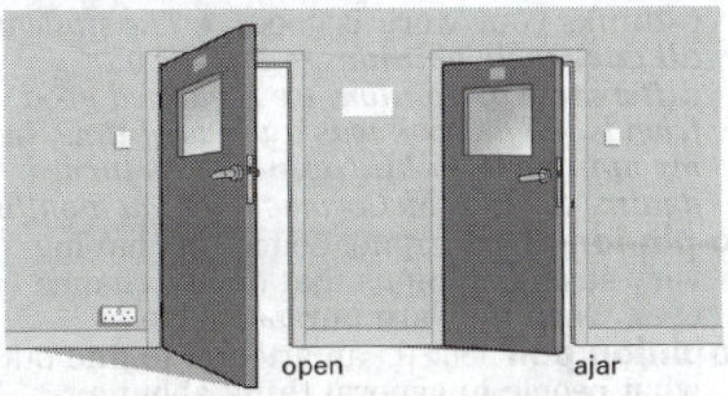

o·pen² /ˈoʊpən/ verb ★★★

1 move sth to see inside	5 first become available
2 of a door/window	6 begin
3 move part of body	+ PHRASES
4 allow people in	+ PHRASAL VERB

1 [T] to separate the edges of something, or take off its cover, so that you can see what is inside: *She opened her purse and took out a lipstick.* ♦ *Can you open this jar?* ♦ ***Open your books** to page 25.*
2 [I/T] if you open a door or window, or if it opens, you move it into a position that allows people or things to pass through: *Do you mind if I **open a window**?*
3 [I/T] if parts of your body open, or if you open them, they move to their widest position: *Open your mouth wide.* ♦ *Her eyes opened slowly.*
4 [I/T] if a store, public building, etc. opens at a particular time, or if someone opens it, it becomes available for people to use or visit at that time: *The library doesn't open until noon today.*
5 [I/T] if a new business, building, etc. opens, or if someone opens it, it becomes available for people to use for the first time: *The college first opened in the 1960s.*
6 [T] to begin something: *I opened an account at the local bank.* ♦ *He opened his talk with a quotation from Shakespeare.* ♦ *The police have **opened an investigation** into his business affairs.*
7 [I] if a movie or play opens, it starts being shown to the public
8 [I] if a flower opens, it moves into its widest position
PHRASES **open the door** to make it possible for something to happen
open doors to give someone opportunities
open sb's eyes to make someone realize the truth about something
open fire to start shooting a gun
PHRASAL VERB ˌ**open (sth) ˈup 1** to open a locked door, container, or building: *He opens up the drugstore every morning.* **2** to talk more about your personal feelings and experiences: *Katy is now starting to **open up to me**.* **3** same as **open²** 5: *Donald wants to open up a bookstore.* **4** to make a situation possible or make something available to people, or to become possible or available in this way: *New markets are opening up every day.* ♦ *The job opened up a lot of opportunities for me.*

o·pen, the /ˈoʊpən/ noun [singular] any place that is outside, not in a building: *It's cold out here in the open.*
PHRASE **(out) in the open** known about and not secret

ˌ**open ˈair, the** noun [singular] any place that is outside

ˌ**open-ˈair** adj happening or existing outside

o·pen-end·ed /ˌoʊpən ˈendəd/ adj **1** an open-ended question is one that asks people for a comment or an opinion rather than a "yes" or "no" answer **2** something that is open-ended has no limits: *an open-ended ticket*

o·pen·er /ˈoʊp(ə)nər/ noun [C] a tool or machine that is used for opening something

ˌ**open ˈhouse** noun [C] **1** a period of time when people are encouraged to visit a place **2** *American* a party to which people can come whenever they want to during a particular time period

o·pen·ing¹ /ˈoʊp(ə)nɪŋ/ noun [C] ★★
1 a hole or place where something opens: *a narrow opening in the fence* ♦ *The doctors had to make an opening in her windpipe.*
2 an opportunity to do something: *His comments created **an opening for** efforts to resolve the crisis.*
3 a job that has become available: *There's an opening in the sales department.*
4 the beginning of a performance or movie: *the opening of the play*

o·pen·ing² /ˈoʊp(ə)nɪŋ/ adj **1** showing that something is open or has begun: *the opening ceremony of the Olympic Games* **2** the first of several similar things: *the opening paragraph*

ˌ**opening ˈnight** noun [C] the first night that a play or other entertainment is performed

ˌ**open ˌinviˈtation** noun [C] an invitation to do something at any time

o·pen·ly /ˈoʊpənli/ adv in a direct or honest way that makes something obvious: *The report openly criticizes the military leadership.*

ˌ**open ˈmarket** noun [C] *business* a situation in which people can buy and sell things without any official rules about prices: *The land will be sold on the open market.*

ˌ**open-ˈminded** adj willing to consider new ideas

o·pen·ness /ˈoʊpənnəs/ noun [U] **1** an honest way of talking or behaving **2** a tendency to accept new ideas, methods, or changes

ˌ**open-ˈplan** adj an open-plan office, house, etc. has few walls and a lot of open space

o·pe·ra /ˈɑp(ə)rə/ noun [C/U] a type of play that is performed by singers and an orchestra, or the art of performing these plays —**op·er·at·ic** /ˌɑpəˈrætɪk/ adj → SOAP OPERA

ˈ**opera ˌhouse** noun [C] a theater where operas are performed

op·er·ate /ˈɑpəˌreɪt/ verb ★★★
1 [I/T] if equipment operates, or if you operate it, you use or control it and it works in the way it should: *The equipment was not operating properly.* ♦ *The motor operates at very high speeds.* ♦ *Do not **operate machinery** after taking this medication.*
2 [I/T] if an organization, company, service, or system operates, or if it is operated, it does its work: *The company has been operating in South America for two years.* ♦

O

Flights operate daily from Miami.
3 [I] to cut into part of someone's body for medical reasons: *Surgeons had to operate to remove the bullet.* ♦ *We may have to* ***operate on*** *your leg.*
4 [I] if something such as a rule, idea, or fact operates, it exists and has an effect in a particular situation: *Racism operates at many levels, conscious and unconscious.*

ˈoperating ˌroom noun [C] *American* a room in a hospital where doctors perform medical operations

ˈoperating ˌsystem noun [C] *computing* the software that tells the parts of a computer how to work together and what to do

op·er·a·tion /ˌɑpəˈreɪʃ(ə)n/ noun ★★★

1 planned activity	4 way sth operates
2 cutting body medically	5 (part of) company
3 actions to achieve sth	+ PHRASES

1 [C] a planned activity involving a lot of people, especially soldiers or police officers: *the biggest* ***military operation*** *in 20 years*
2 [C] the process of cutting into someone's body for medical reasons: *The baby had to* ***have an operation.*** ♦ *She may need an* ***operation on*** *her knee.* ♦ *A very experienced surgeon will* ***perform the operation.***
3 [C] an action or set of actions that is necessary to achieve something: *Connecting the water supply is a very simple operation.*
4 [U] the way that something operates: *We are here to explain* ***the operation of*** *the new exam system.*
5 [C] a company, or a part of a large company: *the company's international operations*
PHRASES **go into operation** to start to work or become effective: *The new production plant went into operation last month.*
in operation 1 working in the normal way: *Only one of our telephone lines is currently in operation.* **2** existing and having an effect in a situation: *Guidelines governing the use of e-mail are now in operation.*

op·er·a·tion·al /ˌɑpəˈreɪʃən(ə)l/ adj **1** working correctly and able to be used: *The new computer system is fully operational.*
2 relating to the way something works, especially a system or business: *operational efficiency*

op·er·a·tive /ˈɑp(ə)rətɪv/ adj working correctly and having the right effect

op·er·a·tor /ˈɑpəˌreɪtər/ noun [C] **1** someone whose job is to operate a machine or piece of equipment: *a crane operator* **2** someone who works for a telephone company and helps people with calls **3** a person or company that runs a business: *bus/ferry operator*

oph·thal·mol·o·gist /ˌɑpθælˈmɑlədʒɪst, ˌɑfθælˈmɑlədʒɪst/ noun [C] a doctor who is an expert in illnesses of the eyes —**oph·thal·mol·o·gy** /ˌɑpθælˈmɑlədʒi/ noun [U]

o·pin·ion /əˈpɪnjən/ noun [C] ★★★ the attitude that someone has toward something, especially about how good it is: *What is your* ***opinion of*** *her latest novel?* ♦ *Professor Wright* ***has a high opinion of*** *your work* (=thinks your work is good). ♦ *The students all* ***gave their opinions.*** ♦ *Despite our* ***differences of opinion,*** *we remained good friends.* ♦ *The book was a waste of time,* ***in my opinion.*** ♦ ***Public opinion*** *has turned against Senator McCormac in recent months.*

o·pin·ion·at·ed /əˈpɪnjəˌneɪtəd/ adj having very strong opinions that do not change even when they are unreasonable

oˈpinion ˌpoll noun [C] an attempt to find out what people in general think about a subject by asking a number of people questions about it

o·pi·um /ˈoʊpiəm/ noun [U] a powerful illegal drug made from the seeds of a type of POPPY (=flower)

o·pos·sum /əˈpɑsəm/ noun [C] an animal found in North America and Australia with thick fur and a long tail

op·po·nent /əˈpoʊnənt/ noun [C] ★★
1 someone who is competing against you: *His Republican opponent received only 36 percent of the vote.*
2 someone who disagrees with something and tries to change or stop it: ***opponents of*** *the legislation*

op·por·tune /ɑpərˈtun/ adj *formal* an opportune moment or time is a good or lucky time for something to happen

op·por·tun·ist /ˈɑpərˌtunɪst, ˌɑpərˈtunɪst/ noun [C] someone who is always trying to gain an advantage and is willing to behave in an unfair way —**op·por·tun·ism** noun [U]

op·por·tun·is·tic /ˌɑpərtuˈnɪstɪk/ adj looking for and taking an opportunity, often in a way that is unfair or harms someone else: *opportunistic crimes*

op·por·tu·ni·ty /ˌɑpərˈtunəti/ noun ★★★
1 [C/U] a chance to do something, or a situation in which it is easy for you to do something: *The trip sounds like a wonderful opportunity.* ♦ *We have given them* ***ample opportunity*** (=a lot of chances) *to voice their complaints.* ♦ *I'd like to* ***take this opportunity to*** *thank all of you for coming.* ♦ *We will inform you of any changes* ***at the earliest opportunity*** (=as soon as possible). ♦ ***an opportunity for*** *career advancement* ♦ **give sb the opportunity to do sth** *The program gives students the opportunity to learn more about global warming.*
2 [C] a job that is available: *There are good opportunities in the marketing division.*

> **Words often used with opportunity**
> *Adjectives often used with* ***opportunity*** *(sense 1)*
> ■ **excellent, golden, good, great, ideal, perfect, rare, unique, wonderful** + OPPORTUNITY: used about opportunities that are good

op·pose /əˈpoʊz/ verb [T] ★ to disagree with a plan or policy, and to try to stop it: *a group that opposes the death penalty* ♦ *There was a campaign to oppose the building of a nuclear reactor.*

op·posed /əˈpoʊzd/ adj ★
1 someone who is opposed to something thinks that it should not happen: *He was bitterly* ***opposed to*** *the war.*
2 completely different: *The two ideas are directly opposed.*

PHRASE **as opposed to** used for referring to something that is very different from the thing that you have just mentioned: *The cost of these airplanes is $3 million, as opposed to the $2 million charged by their competitors.*

op•pos•ing /əˈpoʊzɪŋ/ adj **1** competing against someone else or against each other **2** opposing facts, opinions, or ideas are completely different from each other

op•po•site¹ /ˈɑpəzɪt/ adj ★★
1 completely different: *The car smashed into a truck coming* ***from the opposite direction.***
2 across from, or on the other side of, someone or something: *They sat at* ***opposite ends*** *of the room.* ♦ *On the* ***opposite side*** *of the road from the school was the church.*

op•po•site² /ˈɑpəzɪt/ preposition ★ across from, or facing someone or something: *the bus stop opposite the theater* ♦ *Adam took the seat opposite her.*

op•po•site³ /ˈɑpəzɪt/ noun [C] someone or something that is completely different from someone or something else: *Whatever I suggested, they would go and do the opposite.*

ˌopposite ˈsex, the noun [singular] for men, women are the opposite sex, and for women, men are the opposite sex

op•po•si•tion /ˌɑpəˈzɪʃ(ə)n/ noun ★★
1 [U] strong disagreement with a plan or policy: *Public* ***opposition to*** *the government is growing.*
2 the opposition [singular] a person, organization, etc. that someone is competing against

op•press /əˈpres/ verb [T] to treat people who are less powerful in an unfair and cruel way —**op•pres•sion** /əˈpreʃ(ə)n/ noun [U]

op•pressed /əˈprest/ adj suffering from unfair and cruel treatment

op•pres•sive /əˈpresɪv/ adj **1** unfair and cruel **2** hot in an unpleasant way

op•pres•sor /əˈpresər/ noun [C] a powerful leader or government that treats people in an unfair and cruel way

opt /ɑpt/ verb [I] to choose from a range of possibilities: *We opted for the less expensive car.*

PHRASAL VERB **ˌopt ˈout** to decide not to take part in something, or to stop taking part in it

op•tic /ˈɑptɪk/ adj *medical* relating to the eyes

op•ti•cal /ˈɑptɪk(ə)l/ adj relating to sight, or to light

ˌoptical ˈfiber noun [C/U] a very thin string made from a special type of glass and used in telephone and computer systems for sending information in the form of light

ˌoptical ilˈlusion noun [C] something that looks very different from what it really is, usually because of the way it is drawn or lit

op•ti•cian /ɑpˈtɪʃ(ə)n/ noun [C] *American* someone whose job is to make and sell glasses for people's eyes

op•tics /ˈɑptɪks/ noun [singular] the scientific study of sight and light

op•ti•mal /ˈɑptɪm(ə)l/ adj OPTIMUM

op•ti•mism /ˈɑptɪˌmɪzəm/ noun [U] a tendency to be hopeful and to expect that good things will happen ≠ PESSIMISM

op•ti•mist /ˈɑptɪmɪst/ noun [C] someone who tends to be hopeful and expect that good things will happen ≠ PESSIMIST

op•ti•mis•tic /ˌɑptɪˈmɪstɪk/ adj someone who is optimistic is hopeful about the future and tends to expect that good things will happen ≠ PESSIMISTIC: *She said that she was optimistic about the outcome of the trial.* —**op•ti•mis•ti•cal•ly** /ˌɑptɪˈmɪstɪkli/ adv

op•ti•mize /ˈɑptɪˌmaɪz/ verb [T] to make something as good or as effective as possible

op•ti•mum /ˈɑptɪməm/ adj best, or most appropriate

op•tion /ˈɑpʃ(ə)n/ noun [C] ★★★
1 something that you can choose to do: *We discussed all the marketing options and chose television advertising.* ♦ *She* ***had no option but to*** *admit the truth* (=she had to admit the truth).
2 an extra feature on a new product such as a car, that you can choose when you buy it
3 *business* the right to buy or sell something in the future: *The airline has ordered 16 aircraft and has* ***options on*** *another 29.*

PHRASE **keep/leave your options open** to avoid making a decision now so that you will still have choices later

op•tion•al /ˈɑpʃən(ə)l/ adj something that is optional is available if you want it, but you do not have to have it ≠ COMPULSORY: *The history class is optional.*

op•tom•e•trist /ɑpˈtɑmətrɪst/ noun [C] someone whose job is to test people's sight and to make and sell glasses

op•u•lent /ˈɑpjələnt/ adj *formal* very impressive and expensive —**op•u•lence** noun [U]

or /ɔr/ conjunction ★★★
1 showing possibilities or choices used for connecting possibilities or choices. In a list, "or" is usually used only before the last possibility or choice: *Which color do you want – red, green, yellow, or blue?* ♦ *He's probably at lunch or in a meeting.* ♦ *"When will you get the results?" "****Either*** *tomorrow or the day after."* ♦ *The jury must decide whether the prisoner is guilty* ***or not.***
2 and not used for including someone or something else in a negative statement: *She's had nothing to eat or drink all day.* ♦ *I never had any help or advice from my parents.*
3 when amounts are not exact used between two similar numbers or before "so" for showing that you do not know what the exact number is: *I can photocopy your notes. It'll only take a minute or two.* ♦ *They spent an hour* ***or so*** *searching for the missing file.*
4 in warnings, threats, or advice used for saying what will happen if someone does not do something: *The soldiers told everyone to leave or they would be shot.* ♦ *We must deal with the problem now,* ***or else*** *it will be too late.*
5 correcting or explaining what you have said used for introducing a comment that corrects or adds more information to what you have just said: *He spent time in the Soviet labor camps, or Gulags, as they were called.*

OR abbrev Oregon

o•ral /ˈɔrəl/ adj ★
1 spoken, not written: *an oral agreement*

2 relating to the mouth: *oral health/hygiene* —**o•ral•ly** adv: *The medicine is taken orally.*

or•ange¹ /ˈɔrəndʒ/ noun ★★
1 [C] a round fruit that has a thick orange-colored skin —*picture* → C10
2 [U] a color that is between red and yellow

or•ange² /ˈɔrəndʒ/ adj between red and yellow in color

o•rang•u•tan or **o•rang•u•tang** /əˈræŋəˌtæn/ noun [C] an APE (=a large monkey without a tail) with long orange hair

or•a•tor /ˈɔrətər/ noun [C] someone who is skilled at making speeches in public

or•a•to•ry /ˈɔrəˌtɔri/ noun [U] the skill of making effective and impressive speeches in public

or•bit¹ /ˈɔrbɪt/ noun [C] the path that is taken by an object that is moving around a larger object in space

or•bit² /ˈɔrbɪt/ verb [I/T] to move around a large object in space such as a planet

or•chard /ˈɔrtʃərd/ noun [C] a place where fruit trees are grown

or•ches•tra /ˈɔrkəstrə/ noun [C] ★ a large group of musicians who use many different instruments in order to play mostly classical music —**or•ches•tral** /ɔrˈkestrəl/ adj

or•ches•trate /ˈɔrkəˌstreɪt/ verb [T] to organize a complicated event or course of action so that you achieve the result that you want

or•chid /ˈɔrkɪd/ noun [C] a tropical flower with an unusual shape —*picture* → C9

or•dain /ɔrˈdeɪn/ verb [T] to make someone a priest, MINISTER, or RABBI in an official religious ceremony → ORDINATION

or•deal /ɔrˈdil/ noun [C] an extremely unpleasant experience: *They have suffered a terrible ordeal.*

or•der¹ /ˈɔrdər/ noun ★★★

1 arrangement	5 organized situation
2 request by customer	6 general situation
3 when law is obeyed	7 group of people
4 official instruction	+ PHRASES

1 [C/U] the way in which a set of things is arranged or done so that it is clear which thing is first, second, third, etc.: *Please try to keep the pictures **in order*** (=in the correct order). ♦ *Some of the names on the list are **out of order*** (=in the wrong order).
2 [C] a request for something to be made for you or brought to you: *May I **take your order*** (=write down what you want to eat or drink)? ♦ *A major **order for** six new ships will guarantee the company's future.*
3 [U] a situation in which people obey the law: *The new president's most urgent task will be to **maintain order**.*
4 [C] an instruction that is given by someone in a position of authority: *Try to persuade your employees – don't just **give orders**.* ♦ *Soldiers must **obey orders**.* ♦ *I don't have to **take orders from** you* (=obey you).
5 [U] a situation in which everything is well organized or arranged: *I'm trying to bring some order to the back yard.*
6 [singular] the general situation at a particular time, especially the existing political, economic, or social system: *The old social order was slowly breaking down.*
7 [C] a group of people, especially a religious group, who live according to special rules: *a Buddhist order*

PHRASES **in order** legally or officially correct: *All your papers seem to be in order.*
in order (for sb/sth) to do sth so that someone can do something, or so that something can happen: *What do I have to do in order to convince them?*
out of order a machine or piece of equipment that is out of order is not working correctly

or•der² /ˈɔrdər/ verb ★★★
1 [I/T] to ask for something to be brought to you or be made for you: *Are you ready to order?* ♦ *We sat down and ordered some beers.* ♦ *The airline has ordered 35 new airplanes.*
2 [T] to tell someone to do something, in a way that shows that you have authority: *The government has **ordered an investigation** into the cause of the accident.* ♦ **order sb to do sth** *The judge ordered Hill to serve five years in prison for the robbery.*
3 [T] to put things in a particular order: *The list of books is ordered alphabetically.*

PHRASAL VERB **ˌorder sb aˈround** to keep telling someone what to do, in an annoying way

ˈorder ˌform noun [C] a form that you use to order goods from a company or store, that has spaces where you write your name, address, etc.

or•der•ly¹ /ˈɔrdərli/ adj **1** correctly or neatly organized **2** well-behaved, or well-controlled

or•der•ly² /ˈɔrdərli/ noun [C] someone with no special medical training who works in a hospital, doing jobs such as moving people around

or•di•nance /ˈɔrd(ə)nəns/ noun [C] *American* a law passed by a local government

or•di•nar•i•ly /ˌɔrd(ə)nˌerəli, ˌɔrd(ə)nˈerəli/ adv usually = NORMALLY: *I'm ordinarily gone by this time.*

or•di•nar•y /ˈɔrd(ə)nˌeri/ adj ★★★
1 normal or average, and not unusual or special: *It was just an ordinary Saturday morning.* ♦ *I didn't notice anything **out of the ordinary*** (=unusual).
2 not especially good, interesting, or impressive: *The inside of the house is rather ordinary.*

or•di•na•tion /ˌɔrd(ə)nˈeɪʃ(ə)n/ noun [C/U] the process or religious ceremony by which someone is officially made a priest, MINISTER, or RABBI

ore /ɔr/ noun [C/U] rock or earth from which metal can be obtained

o•reg•a•no /əˈregəˌnoʊ/ noun [U] a plant whose leaves are used in cooking in order to give a special flavor to food

org /ɔrg/ abbrev private organization: used in Internet addresses

or•gan /ˈɔrgən/ noun [C] ★★
1 a part of your body that does a particular job, such as your heart or brain: *organ transplant operations*
2 a large musical instrument with pipes of different lengths, played by pressing KEYS (=narrow bars) on it —*picture* → PIANO
3 an electronic instrument like a piano

or•gan•ic /ɔrˈgænɪk/ adj ★
1 organic food or drink is produced without using artificial chemicals: *organic apples/meat* ♦ *organic farming*

O

2 relating to, or produced by, living things: *organic material/waste/matter*
3 happening or developing as a natural and continuous process: *The business has expanded by 70% through organic growth.*
—**or•gan•i•cal•ly** /ɔrˈgænɪkli/ adv

or•gan•i•sa•tion /ˌɔrgənɪˈzeɪʃ(ə)n/ a British spelling of **organization**

or•gan•ise /ˈɔrgəˌnaɪz/ a British spelling of **organize**

or•gan•ism /ˈɔrgəˌnɪzəm/ noun [C] a living thing

or•gan•ist /ˈɔrgənɪst/ noun [C] someone who plays the organ

or•gan•i•za•tion /ˌɔrgənɪˈzeɪʃ(ə)n/ ★★★
1 [C] an officially organized group of people who work together or have the same goals, for example a company or a political party: *the human rights organization Amnesty International ♦ She belongs to a number of political and charitable organizations.*
2 [U] the way in which the different parts of something are arranged = STRUCTURE: *scientists investigating **the organization of** the human brain ♦ Officials have asked for help with **the organization of** the elections.*
—**or•gan•i•za•tion•al** adj: *her excellent organizational skills*

or•gan•ize /ˈɔrgəˌnaɪz/ verb ★★
1 [T] to prepare or arrange an activity or event: *Who's organizing the conference?*
2 [T] to put things into a sensible order, or to create a system in which all the parts work well together: *Let's organize this agenda a little better.*
3 [I/T] to form a LABOR UNION (=an organization that protects workers' rights): *The National Labor Relations Act gives all employees the right to organize.*

or•gan•ized /ˈɔrgəˌnaɪzd/ adj **1** planned carefully and effectively ≠ DISORGANIZED **2** an organized person arranges and plans activities carefully and effectively ≠ DISORGANIZED

ˌorganized ˈcrime noun [U] criminal activities that are controlled by a large powerful secret organization

or•gan•iz•er /ˈɔrgəˌnaɪzər/ noun [C] someone who makes all the arrangements for an event or activity

or•gasm /ˈɔrˌgæzəm/ noun [C/U] the stage of sexual activity when sexual pleasure is strongest

or•gy /ˈɔrdʒi/ noun [C] **1** a party at which there is a lot of drinking and sexual activity **2 an orgy of sth** an occasion on which someone does something a lot, especially something bad: *an orgy of killing*

O•ri•ent, the /ˈɔriənt/ *old-fashioned* the countries of eastern Asia

o•ri•en•tal /ˌɔriˈent(ə)l/ adj of eastern Asia, or from eastern Asia

o•ri•en•ta•tion /ˌɔriənˈteɪʃ(ə)n/ noun **1** [C/U] someone's basic attitudes or beliefs → SEXUAL ORIENTATION **2** [U] information or training that you are given before you start a new job or activity

o•ri•ent•ed /ˈɔriˌentəd/ adj mainly concerned with, or directed toward a particular group, activity, or situation: *an export-oriented economy*

or•i•gin /ˈɔrədʒɪn/ noun ★★
1 [C] the place or moment at which something begins to exist: *Meteorites may hold clues about **the origin of** life on Earth. ♦ The college **can trace its origins back to** the 18th century.*
2 [C/U] the country, race, or social situation that someone comes from = BACKGROUND
PHRASE **country/place/state of origin** *formal* the place where someone or something comes from

o•rig•i•nal[1] /əˈrɪdʒən(ə)l/ adj ★★★
1 existing at the beginning of a period or process, before any changes have been made = FIRST: *Do you know who the car's original owner was? ♦ The house still has its original doors.*
2 new, interesting, and different from anything else: *a highly original design ♦ a very original songwriter*
3 not copied from something else: *The original painting is in a museum in Vienna.*

o•rig•i•nal[2] /əˈrɪdʒən(ə)l/ noun [C] something such as a document or painting that is not a copy

o•rig•i•nal•i•ty /əˌrɪdʒəˈnæləti/ noun [U] the quality of being new, interesting, and different

o•rig•i•nal•ly /əˈrɪdʒən(ə)li/ adv ★★ at first: *His novels were originally published in magazines. ♦ He's from Germany originally.*

o•rig•i•nate /əˈrɪdʒəˌneɪt/ verb **1** [I] to begin to exist or appear for the first time **2** [T] to create or start something

o•rig•i•na•tor /əˈrɪdʒəˌneɪtər/ noun [C] the first person to create or start something

or•na•ment /ˈɔrnəmənt/ noun [C] a small attractive object that is used for decoration

or•na•men•tal /ˌɔrnəˈment(ə)l/ adj designed to be used as decoration

or•nate /ɔrˈneɪt/ adj decorated with complicated patterns or shapes

or•ner•y /ˈɔrnəri/ adj *American often humorous* quick to argue or become annoyed with people = GRUMPY

or•ni•thol•o•gy /ˌɔrnɪˈθɑlədʒi/ noun [U] the scientific study of birds —**or•ni•thol•o•gist** noun [C]

or•phan[1] /ˈɔrfən/ noun [C] a child whose parents have died

or•phan[2] /ˈɔrfən/ verb **be orphaned** to become an orphan

or•phan•age /ˈɔrfənədʒ/ noun [C] a building where orphans live and are taken care of

or•tho•don•tist /ˌɔrθəˈdɑntɪst/ noun [C] a DENTIST whose job is to make teeth straight

or•tho•dox /ˈɔrθəˌdɑks/ adj **1** accepted by most people as the correct or usual idea or practice ≠ UNORTHODOX **2** accepting and obeying traditional religious beliefs and practices: *orthodox Judaism*

or•tho•dox•y /ˈɔrθəˌdɑksi/ noun [C/U] an idea or practice that is accepted by most people as being correct or usual

or•tho•pe•dic /ˌɔrθəˈpidɪk/ adj *medical*
1 relating to the treatment of injuries and diseases affecting bones and muscles
2 designed to be used by people with injuries or diseases affecting their bones and muscles

or•tho•pe•dics /ˌɔrθəˈpidɪks/ noun [U] the part

O

of medicine that deals with the treatment of injuries or diseases affecting bones and muscles

Os•car /ˈɑskər/ *trademark* a prize that is given to people working in the movie industry

os•cil•late /ˈɑsɪˌleɪt/ verb [I] *science* to move quickly from side to side at a steady speed —**os•cil•la•tion** /ˌɑsɪˈleɪʃ(ə)n/ noun [C/U]

os•mo•sis /ɑzˈmoʊsɪs/ noun [U] *science* the process by which a liquid slowly passes through a thin layer of something

os•ten•si•ble /ɑˈstensəb(ə)l/ adj seeming to be true, or said by someone to be true, but possibly false: *The ostensible reason for the army's presence was to keep the peace.* —**os•ten•si•bly** adv

os•ten•ta•tious /ˌɑstenˈteɪʃəs/ adj *showing disapproval* intended to impress people: *an ostentatious display of wealth* —**os•ten•ta•tion** noun [U], **os•ten•ta•tious•ly** adv

os•te•op•a•thy /ˌɑstiˈɑpəθi/ noun [U] *medical* a treatment for conditions such as back pain or muscle injury —**os•te•o•path** noun [C]

os•te•o•po•ro•sis /ˌɑstioʊpəˈroʊsɪs/ noun [U] *medical* a condition in which your bones become more likely to break

os•tra•cize /ˈɑstrəˌsaɪz/ verb [T] *formal* to no longer accept someone as a member of your social group

os•trich /ˈɑstrɪtʃ/ noun [C] a large African bird that runs very fast but that cannot fly

oth•er /ˈʌðər/ grammar word ★★★

> Other can be:
> - a **determiner**: *He doesn't like other people interfering.*
> - an **adjective**: *She invited all her other friends.*
> - a **pronoun**: *He swerved from one side of the road to the other.* ♦ *Some systems are better than others.*

1 additional used for referring to additional people or things of the type that has already been mentioned: *Apart from the victim's name and age, no other details were given.* ♦ *a book aimed at teachers and others working in education* ♦ ***Among other things**, she enjoys reading and tennis.*

2 different used for referring to a different person or thing from the one that has already been mentioned: *I wanted to go camping, but Carey had other ideas.* ♦ *Not now. We'll talk about it **some other time**.*

3 second of two used for referring to the second of two people or things: *I held onto the rope with my other hand.* ♦ *He sat in front of the fire rubbing one bare foot against **the other**.* ♦ *One of the twins was Reggie. What was **the other one** called?*

4 the rest of a group used for referring to the rest of the people or things in a group: *Beethoven's Ninth is much longer than his other symphonies.* ♦ *We stayed until all **the other** guests had gone home.* ♦ *One boy fell off his chair and **the others** laughed.*

5 people in general used for referring to people in a general way when you are not including yourself as one of them: *I don't care what others think.*

6 opposite opposite, or farthest from you: *Ashley sat at **the other end** of the sofa.* ♦ *A car was coming from **the other direction**.* ♦ *I tried to attract her attention, but she was looking **the other way**.* ♦ *Did the boys do better than the girls, or **the other way around**?*

PHRASES **the other day/night etc.** two or three days/nights etc. ago: *I had a phone call from Mandy the other day.*

other than except for someone or something: *I don't have time to read anything other than the newspaper.*

someone/something/somewhere etc. or other used when you are not saying exactly which person, thing, place etc. that you mean: *He's always complaining about something or other.*

→ ANOTHER, HAND[1], WORD[1]

oth•er•wise /ˈʌðərˌwaɪz/ adv ★★★

1 used for saying that if one thing does not happen or is not true, something else will happen, usually something bad: *I hope the weather improves. Otherwise, we'll have to cancel the picnic.* ♦ *The program has saved thousands of children who would otherwise have died.*

2 in a different or opposite way from what has been mentioned: *I'll plan to wait here unless someone tells me otherwise.*

3 used for saying that something is true except for the fact you have just mentioned: *The show was a little long, but otherwise it was very good.*

ot•ter /ˈɑtər/ noun [C] an animal that has a long body covered in brown fur and that can swim very well

ouch /aʊtʃ/ interjection *spoken* used for expressing a feeling of sudden pain

ought /ɔt/ modal verb ★★★

> - **Ought** is usually followed by "to" and an infinitive: *You ought to tell the truth.* Sometimes it is followed by "to" but no following infinitive: *I don't spend as much time with them as I ought to.*
> - **Ought** has no tenses, no participles, and no infinitive form. It does not change its form, so the third person singular form does not end in " s": *She ought to try a little harder.*
> - Questions and negatives are formed without "do," but these are only used in formal English: *You ought not to be here.* ♦ *Ought I to tell my parents?*

1 ought to (do sth) used for saying what is the right or sensible thing to do, or the right way to behave: *You ought to get up earlier.* ♦ *We don't exercise much, but we really ought to.* ♦ *You **ought to have** listened to the warnings.*

2 ought to (do sth) used when you have strong reasons for believing or expecting something: *Notre Dame ought to win this game.*

> **Should** can be used in the same way as **ought to** and is more common, especially in negatives and questions.

ought•n't /ˈɔt(ə)nt/ short form a way of saying or writing "ought not." This is not often used in formal writing: *You oughtn't to make promises you can't keep.*

ounce /aʊns/ noun [C] a unit for measuring weight, equal to 28.35 grams

our /aʊr/ determiner ★★★ belonging to or connected with you and the group that you are a part of, when you are the person speaking or writing: *When is our next meeting?* ♦ *Most of our friends live on the other side of town.* ♦ *We want to make **our own** decisions.*

ours /aʊrz/ pronoun ★★ used for referring to something that belongs to or is connected with you and the group that you are a part of, when you are the person speaking or writing: *Ours is the third house on the left.* ♦ *If you don't have a grill, you can borrow ours.* ♦ *Friends **of ours** are coming to visit.*

our·selves /aʊr'selvz/ pronoun ★★
1 the REFLEXIVE form of "we," used for showing that both you and the group that you are a part of are affected by what you do together: *We kept ourselves awake by playing card games.* ♦ *Our prayers were for ourselves and our families.*
2 used for emphasizing that you are referring to yourself and your group, and not to anyone else: *If nobody will help us, we will do it ourselves.*

PHRASES **(all) by ourselves 1** alone: *We had dinner by ourselves in our hotel room.*
2 without help from anyone: *We knew that we couldn't organize such a big event all by ourselves.*
(all) to ourselves not sharing something with anyone else: *Freddy's folks were away, so we had the place all to ourselves.*

oust /aʊst/ verb [T] to remove someone from a position of power

oust·er /'aʊstər/ noun [C] *American* an act of removing someone from a position of power

out¹ /aʊt/ grammar word ★★★

> **Out** can be:
> - an **adverb**: *We went out into the yard.*
> - used after the verb "to be": *You were out when I called.*
> - used in the preposition phrase **out of**: *I got out of bed and went downstairs.*
> - a **preposition**: *I looked out the window.*

1 from inside sth from inside a container, building, or place: *I followed him out the door and down the stairs.* ♦ *He opened the drawer and **took out** a large brown envelope.* ♦ *She **went out**, slamming the door behind her.* ♦ *Take that chewing gum **out of** your mouth.*
2 not at home or work away from your home or place of work: *Dr. Hammond is out right now – can I take a message?* ♦ *Try to **get out** more – make new friends.* ♦ *I'm afraid Ms. Davis is **out sick*** (=away from work because of being sick) *today.* ♦ **take sb out** *Why don't you take Dad out for a drink?*
3 outside not inside a building or vehicle: *Is it cold out?* ♦ *The children are out in the back yard.* ♦ *He leaned **out of** his car and called to me.*
4 far away used for saying that someone or something is in another place that is far away, especially toward the west: *Her son's gone out to California.* ♦ *a little town **way out** on the prairie*
5 publicly available available for the public to buy, see, or know about: *Their new album comes out next week.*
6 no longer in a situation used for saying that someone is not in a bad situation anymore: *We are facing a major crisis and there is no easy **way out**.* ♦ *Parents will be relieved that their children are **out of** danger.*
7 no longer in a competition not allowed to continue taking part in a game or competition: *If we don't win today, we'll be **out of** the championships.*
8 unconscious used for saying that someone is unconscious: *Arthur had hit his head on a beam and knocked himself out.* ♦ *I must have been out for five minutes.*
9 not burning no longer burning or shining: *It got so cold when the fire went out.* ♦ *The children were in bed and the **lights** were **out**.*
10 not wanted or not possible *informal* if a particular idea, suggestion, or activity is out, it is not possible, or it cannot be accepted
11 none left with none of something left: *We're **out of** bread.* ♦ *I'm **running out of** ideas – can you suggest anything?*
12 when the sun can be seen if the sun or moon is out, it is not behind clouds
13 when the ocean is low if the TIDE is out, the ocean is at a lower level on the land

PHRASES **be out to do sth** or **be out for sth** to be aiming to do something or get something: *These are dangerous men, and they are out for revenge.*
one out of ten/99 out of 100 etc. used for saying how large a part of a group or number is: *Only one out of ten graduates goes into the teaching profession.*
out of interest/respect/pity etc. because of a particular feeling or attitude: *I went there out of curiosity, really.*
out of it *informal* not conscious of what is happening because you are drunk or have taken drugs

out² /aʊt/ adj a gay person who is out has told other people that he or she is gay

out³ /aʊt/ verb [T] to make it publicly known that someone is gay

out·age /'aʊtɪdʒ/ noun [C] *American* a period of time when the electricity supply in a particular place stops working

out·back, the /'aʊt,bæk/ noun [singular] the large areas of land in Australia that are far away from any city or town

out·bid /aʊt'bɪd/ (past tense and past participle **out·bid**) verb [T] to offer to pay more than someone else for something that you want to buy

'out,box noun [C] *American* a flat open container on your desk where you put letters, documents, etc. that are ready to be sent or put somewhere else *—picture* → C3

out·box /'aʊt,bɑks/ noun [C] *computing* the place on an e-mail program where e-mails are stored before you send them

out·break /'aʊt,breɪk/ noun [C] the sudden start of war, disease, violence, etc.

out·burst /'aʊt,bɜrst/ noun [C] a sudden spoken expression of a strong feeling, especially anger

out·cast /'aʊt,kæst/ noun [C] someone who other people will not accept as a member of society or of a particular group

out•class /aʊt'klæs/ verb [T] to be much better than someone or something else

out•come /'aʊt,kʌm/ noun [C] ★ the final result of a process or activity: *A second game will be played to determine the outcome.* ♦ *He refused to comment on the outcome of the election.*

out•cry /'aʊt,kraɪ/ noun [C/U] an angry expression of protest or shock by a lot of people

out•dat•ed /aʊt'deɪtəd/ adj not modern enough to be useful

out•do /aʊt'du/ (past tense **out•did** /aʊt'dɪd/; past participle **out•done** /aʊt'dʌn/) verb [T] to be better than someone else at doing something

out•door /aʊt'dɔr, 'aʊt,dɔr/ adj done, used, or existing outside ≠ INDOOR

out•doors[1] /aʊt'dɔrz/ adv not in a building = OUTSIDE ≠ INDOORS

out•doors[2] /aʊt'dɔrz/ noun **the (great) outdoors** the countryside, especially considered as somewhere that you visit in order to take part in activities such as walking

out•er /'aʊtər/ adj ★
1 on or around the outside of something ≠ INNER: *The outer walls of the castle were over six feet thick.*
2 farthest away from the center of something ≠ INNER: *the outer limits of the solar system*

out•er•most /'aʊtər,moʊst/ adj farthest away from a particular place or from the center of something ≠ INNERMOST

,outer 'space noun [U] the area outside the Earth's atmosphere that contains the stars and planets

out•fit[1] /'aʊt,fɪt/ noun [C] **1** a set of clothes that are worn together **2** *informal* an organization, especially a small business

out•fit[2] /'aʊt,fɪt/ verb [T] to provide someone or something with the clothes or equipment that they need

out•flank /aʊt'flæŋk/ verb [T] to get an advantage over someone, for example in business or politics

out•go•ing /aʊt'goʊɪŋ/ adj **1** someone who is outgoing is friendly and enjoys meeting and talking to people = SOCIABLE **2** soon to leave a position of authority or power ≠ INCOMING: *the outgoing mayor* **3** going out of or away from a place ≠ INCOMING: *outgoing flights*

out•grow /aʊt'groʊ/ (past tense **out•grew** /aʊt'gru/; past participle **out•grown** /aʊt'groʊn/) verb [T] **1** if you outgrow a piece of clothing, it is too small for you because you have grown **2** if you outgrow an activity or relationship, you have developed and it is now not appropriate for you anymore

out•ing /'aʊtɪŋ/ noun **1** [C] a short trip that you take for enjoyment **2** [C/U] a public announcement saying that someone, especially a famous person, is gay

out•land•ish /aʊt'lændɪʃ/ adj extremely strange and unusual

out•last /aʊt'læst/ verb [T] to last longer than someone or something else: *This system has outlasted many of its rivals.*

out•law[1] /'aʊt,lɔ/ verb [T] to make something illegal: *They signed an agreement outlawing chemical weapons.*

out•law[2] /'aʊt,lɔ/ noun [C] *old-fashioned* a criminal

out•lay /'aʊt,leɪ/ noun [C/U] the amount of money that you must spend in order to buy something or in order to start a new business or project

out•let /'aʊt,let/ noun [C] **1** a place on a wall where you can connect electrical equipment to the power supply **2** a store or place where a particular product is sold **3** a way of expressing strong feelings, or of using extra physical energy

out•line[1] /'aʊt,laɪn/ verb [T] **1** to give the main ideas of a plan or a piece of writing: *The document outlines our company's recycling policy.* **2** to draw a line around the edge of something

out•line[2] /'aʊt,laɪn/ noun [C] ★
1 an explanation that includes the general points about something, but not the details: *The chairman gave them a brief **outline of** the museum's history.*
2 a line that shows the outer edge or shape of something: *Through the mist we could see **the outline of** the island.*

> Words often used with **outline**
>
> *Adjectives often used with **outline** (noun, sense 1)*
>
> ■ **bare, basic, brief, broad, general, rough, vague** + OUTLINE: used for emphasizing that an outline lacks details

out•live /aʊt'lɪv/ verb [T] **1** to live longer than someone else **2** to continue to exist after something else has stopped

out•look /'aʊt,lʊk/ noun [singular] **1** an idea about what a situation will be like in the future: *The outlook for the economy is still uncertain.* **2** your general attitude toward things: *a positive outlook on life*

out•ly•ing /'aʊt,laɪɪŋ/ adj existing away from a particular place: *outlying islands*

out•ma•neu•ver /,aʊtmə'nuvər/ verb [T] to defeat or gain an advantage over someone by being more clever or skillful than they are

out•mod•ed /aʊt'moʊdəd/ adj no longer modern or useful

out•num•ber /aʊt'nʌmbər/ verb [T] if one group outnumbers another, there are more in the first group than in the second

,out-of-'date adj old and no longer useful

,out-of-the-'way adj a long way from other places

,out-of-'town adj coming from another town or area: *out-of-town visitors*

,out-of-'work adj without a job = UNEMPLOYED

out•pa•tient /'aʊt,peɪʃ(ə)nt/ noun [C] someone who receives medical treatment at a hospital, but does not stay there for the night → INPATIENT

out•per•form /,aʊtpər'fɔrm/ verb [T] to do something better than someone or something else

out•post /'aʊt,poʊst/ noun [C] **1** a military camp that is far away from the army **2** a small town that is far away from other towns

out•pour•ing /ˈaʊtˌpɔrɪŋ/ noun [C/U] the act of expressing a strong emotion

out•put¹ /ˈaʊtˌpʊt/ noun [C/U] **1** the amount of something that a person, organization, or system produces ≠ INPUT: *Industrial output increased by four percent last year.* **2** the information that is shown on a screen or printed on paper by a computer: *graphics output*

out•put² /ˈaʊtˌpʊt/ (past tense and past participle **out•put**; present participle **out•put•ting** /ˈaʊtˌpʊtɪŋ/) verb [T] to produce information from a computer, for example by showing it on a screen or printing it ≠ INPUT

out•rage¹ /ˈaʊtˌreɪdʒ/ noun [C/U] a strong feeling of anger and shock, or something that causes this feeling

out•rage² /ˈaʊtˌreɪdʒ/ verb [T] to make someone extremely angry and shocked

out•ra•geous /aʊtˈreɪdʒəs/ adj **1** very shocking or unreasonable **2** extremely unusual and likely to shock people or make them laugh —**out•ra•geous•ly** adv

out•right¹ /aʊtˈraɪt/ adv **1** without hiding your feelings: *I told them outright that they had to leave.* **2** completely in a single process: *They can't afford to buy the house outright.*

out•right² /ˈaʊtˌraɪt/ adj **1** clear and direct: *outright hostility* **2** complete and total: *an outright lie*

out•set /ˈaʊtˌset/ noun [singular] the start of something: *You are going to love this book from the outset.*

out•side /ˌaʊtˈsaɪd, ˈaʊtˌsaɪd/ grammar word ★★★

> **Outside** can be:
> - a **preposition**: *He was sitting at a table outside the café.*
> - an **adverb**: *Why don't you go and play outside?*
> - an **adjective**: *the outside wall of the building*
> - a **noun**: *The house doesn't look very impressive from the outside.*

1 not inside or within a room, building, or area ≠ INSIDE: *Outside the sun was shining.* ♦ *I went to the window and looked outside.* ♦ *Three police cars were parked outside their house.* ♦ *Could you wait outside in the hallway?* ♦ *Her name is almost unknown **outside of** Latin America.*

2 used for referring to the outer part or surface of something ≠ INSIDE: ***The outside** of the house is in urgent need of repair.*

3 not within the limits of a particular time, range, or situation ≠ INSIDE: *classes held outside normal school hours* ♦ *Until then love was something outside my experience.*

4 used for referring to people who do not belong to a particular group or organization: *The company brought in advisers from outside.*

PHRASE **an outside chance** a situation in which something is possible but unlikely: *There's an outside chance that we'll both arrive on the same day.*

out•sid•er /aʊtˈsaɪdər/ noun [C] someone who does not belong to a particular group

out•size /aʊtˈsaɪz/ or **out•sized** /ˈaʊtˌsaɪzd/ adj much larger than usual = OVERSIZED

out•skirts, the /ˈaʊtˌskɜrts/ noun [plural] the areas of a town or city that are farthest away from the center: *a park on the outskirts of Chicago*

out•smart /aʊtˈsmɑrt/ verb [T] to gain an advantage over someone by using a clever or dishonest trick = OUTWIT

out•spo•ken /aʊtˈspoʊkən/ adj an outspoken person states their opinion honestly, even if other people do not like it = FORTHRIGHT

out•stand•ing /aʊtˈstændɪŋ/ adj **1** extremely good or impressive: *an area of outstanding natural beauty* ♦ *an outstanding example of Indian art* **2** not yet completed, dealt with, or paid: *Some tasks are still outstanding.* —**out•stand•ing•ly** adv

out•stay /aʊtˈsteɪ/ *see* **welcome³**

out•stretched /aʊtˈstretʃt/ adj stretched out

out•strip /aʊtˈstrɪp/ verb [T] to go faster, do something better, or become larger than someone or something else: *Demand for the new computers has outstripped supply.*

out•ward¹ /ˈaʊtwərd/ adj relating to something that you can see or notice = EXTERNAL ≠ INWARD: *He had no outward signs of the illness.*

out•ward² /ˈaʊtwərd/ adv away from the center of something, or toward the outside of it ≠ INWARD

out•ward•ly /ˈaʊtwərdli/ adv according to the way that something seems, that is not always the same way that it really is ≠ INWARDLY

out•wards /ˈaʊtwərdz/ adv OUTWARD

out•weigh /aʊtˈweɪ/ verb [T] to be more important, useful, or valuable than something else: *The possible benefits outweigh the risks involved.*

out•wit /aʊtˈwɪt/ verb [T] to gain an advantage over someone by using a clever or dishonest trick = OUTSMART

o•val /ˈoʊv(ə)l/ adj with a shape like a long narrow circle —*picture* → C8 —**o•val** noun [C]

o•va•ry /ˈoʊvəri/ noun [C] one of the two organs in a woman's body that produce eggs

o•va•tion /oʊˈveɪʃ(ə)n/ noun [C] *formal* if an audience gives someone an ovation, they CLAP their hands to express their admiration or enjoyment

ov•en /ˈʌv(ə)n/ noun [C] ★ a large piece of equipment in a kitchen that you cook food in: *Preheat the oven to 400F.* —*picture* → C2

o•ver /ˈoʊvər/ grammar word ★★★

> **Over** can be:
> - a **preposition**: *a bridge over the river* ♦ *It happened over a hundred years ago.*
> - an **adverb**: *He fell over and broke his arm.*
> - used after the verb "to be": *The semester will be over soon.*

1 above sb/sth in a higher position above someone or something, without touching them ≠ UNDER: *Perry glanced at the clock over the door.* ♦ *The Simpsons live in an apartment over the store.* ♦ *Birds circled over their heads.*

2 on sb/sth covering someone or something: *She put her hands over her ears.* ♦ *She spilled coffee **all over** my new dress.*

3 from one side to the other across from one side of something to the other: *Several*

O

bridges over the river were destroyed. ♦ *I crossed over to the other side of the street.* ♦ *Three prisoners had climbed over the fence.*
4 into the opposite position moving into a position so that the side that was facing down now faces up: *He turned the card over.* ♦ *Roll over onto your back.*
5 in or to many parts of sth in, to, or from many different parts of an area: *The drought has spread over much of the southern U.S.* ♦ *The festival attracts music lovers from* ***all over*** *the world.*
6 in or to a place in or to a particular place, for example someone's home: *Why don't you come over and have dinner with us sometime?* ♦ *Lawrence walked over to the window and looked out.*
7 moving downward falling or bending down from an upright position: *Carey fell over and broke his leg.* ♦ *I bent over to tie my shoe.*
8 toward the side toward the side: *The main entrance is farther over on the left.* ♦ *She leaned over and whispered in my ear.*
9 ended used for saying that a particular event, situation, or period of time has ended: *Moore's fourth marriage was over after only 18 months.* ♦ *We're all so relieved that the trial is* ***over and done with.***
10 concerning sth used for talking about the cause of a feeling or argument: *There are worries over the future of the steel industry.* ♦ *We spent a whole hour arguing over the meaning of two words.*
11 no longer affected no longer upset or affected by an illness or a bad experience: *She still isn't over the shock of her brother's death.* ♦ *He'll soon* ***get over*** *his disappointment.*
12 down from an edge falling, hanging, or looking down from the edge of something: *Lava flowed over the rim of the volcano.*
13 controlling or influencing sb/sth used for stating who or what is controlled or influenced by someone or something: *The Church today has little influence over the way people lead their lives.*
14 during during a period of time: *Over the last few years we've become friends.* ♦ *Most hotels are fully booked over the holiday weekend.*
15 more than more than a particular amount or age ≠ UNDER: *Yeltsin was elected with over 45 million votes.* ♦ *The pension will be paid to people aged 65* ***and over.***
PHRASES **all over again** used for saying that you do all of something again starting from the beginning, or that the whole of a long process happens again: *I had to do my essay all over again.*
over and over (again) many times: *They keep asking the same questions over and over again.*
→ ABOVE

o•ver•all¹ /ˌoʊvərˈɔl/ adj ★★
1 considering something as a whole, rather than its details: *My* ***overall impression*** *of the town was not very good.*
2 including everything: *What were the overall costs of the project?*

o•ver•all² /ˌoʊvərˈɔl/ adv when everything is considered: *Overall, our position is stronger than it was last year.*

o•ver•alls /ˈoʊvərˌɔlz/ noun [plural] *American* a piece of clothing consisting of pants and a part covering your chest that is attached to STRAPS that fit over your shoulders —*picture* → C4

o•ver•awed /ˌoʊvərˈɔd/ adj feeling slightly afraid of something that is extremely impressive or powerful

o•ver•bear•ing /ˌoʊvərˈberɪŋ/ adj an overbearing person tries to control other people's behavior and ignores their feelings

o•ver•board /ˈoʊvərˌbɔrd/ adv off a boat or ship and into the water
PHRASE **go overboard** *informal* to do or say more than is reasonable or necessary, for example because you are excited

o•ver•cast /ˈoʊvərˌkæst/ adj an overcast sky is covered in clouds

o•ver•charge /ˌoʊvərˈtʃɑrdʒ/ verb [I/T] to charge someone too much money for something

o•ver•coat /ˈoʊvərˌkoʊt/ noun [C] a long warm coat

o•ver•come /ˌoʊvərˈkʌm/ (past tense **o•ver•came** /ˌoʊvərˈkeɪm/; past participle **o•ver•come**) verb [T] ★
1 to succeed in dealing with a problem: *Jimmy overcame his difficulties to graduate.*
2 to defeat someone or something: *Sampras finally overcame Agassi in the fifth set.*
3 to make someone very emotional, sick, or unconscious: *The entire family was* ***overcome with*** *grief.* ♦ *Two men died when they were* ***overcome by*** *smoke.*

Words often used with overcome
Nouns often used with ***overcome*** *(sense 1)*
■ OVERCOME + **difficulty, disadvantage, fear, obstacle, problem, resistance**: deal successfully with a problem

o•ver•com•pen•sate /ˌoʊvərˈkɑmpənˌseɪt/ verb [I] to do more than you need to do in trying to correct a fault

o•ver•crowd•ed /ˌoʊvərˈkraʊdəd/ adj containing too many people or things: *overcrowded schools*

o•ver•crowd•ing /ˌoʊvərˈkraʊdɪŋ/ noun [U] unpleasant conditions that are caused by too many people or things being in the same place

o•ver•do /ˌoʊvərˈdu/ (past tense **o•ver•did** /ˌoʊvərˈdɪd/; past participle **o•ver•done** /ˌoʊvərˈdʌn/) verb [T] to do or use more of something that you should: *Don't overdo it* (=work too hard) *or you'll make yourself sick.*

o•ver•done /ˌoʊvərˈdʌn/ adj cooked for too long ≠ UNDERDONE

o•ver•dose /ˈoʊvərˌdoʊs/ noun [C] too much of a drug that is taken at one time —**o•ver•dose** verb [I]

o•ver•draft /ˈoʊvərˌdræft/ noun [C] the amount of money that someone owes their bank when they have spent more money than they had in their account

o•ver•drawn /ˌoʊvərˈdrɔn/ adj if you are overdrawn, you have spent more money than the amount that you had in your bank account

o•ver•due /ˌoʊvərˈdu/ adj if something is overdue, it should have been done before now

ˌover-ˈeasy adj *American* eggs that are over-easy have been cooked in oil on one side, then a little on the other side

o•ver•es•ti•mate /ˌoʊvərˈestɪˌmeɪt/ verb [T] to think that something is better or bigger than it really is ≠ UNDERESTIMATE —**o•ver•es•ti•mate** /ˌoʊvərˈestɪmət/ noun [C]

o•ver•flow¹ /ˌoʊvərˈfloʊ/ verb **1** [I/T] to flow over the top of a container because it is too full **2** [I/T] if a river or lake overflows, it floods the land next to it **3** [I] if a place is overflowing with people or things, there are too many of them to fit into it

o•ver•flow² /ˈoʊvərˌfloʊ/ noun [C] **1** an extra number of people or things that do not fit into a particular space **2** a hole or pipe that allows a substance to flow out of a container when it gets too full

o•ver•grown /ˌoʊvərˈgroʊn/ adj covered with plants that have been allowed to grow in an uncontrolled way

o•ver•hand /ˈoʊvərˌhænd/ adj, adv thrown with your arm moving high above your head and then down in front of you

o•ver•hang /ˌoʊvərˈhæŋ/ (past tense and past participle **o•ver•hung** /ˌoʊvərˈhʌŋ/) verb [I/T] to stick out from an edge above something —**o•ver•hang** /ˈoʊvərˌhæŋ/ noun [C]

o•ver•haul /ˌoʊvərˈhɔl/ verb [T] to repair or change a machine or system in order to make it work better —**o•ver•haul** /ˈoʊvərˌhɔl/ noun [C]

o•ver•head¹ /ˌoʊvərˈhed, ˈoʊvərˌhed/ adj, adv above your head

o•ver•head² /ˈoʊvərˌhed/ noun [U] the amount of money that you pay regularly in order to operate a business or organization

o•ver•hear /ˌoʊvərˈhɪr/ (past tense and past participle **o•ver•heard** /ˌoʊvərˈhɜrd/) verb [I/T] to hear what people are saying during a conversation that you are not involved in

o•ver•heat /ˌoʊvərˈhit/ verb [I/T] to become too hot, or to make something too hot

o•ver•joyed /ˌoʊvərˈdʒɔɪd/ adj extremely pleased

o•ver•kill /ˈoʊvərˌkɪl/ noun [U] much more of something than is needed or wanted: *I really did think that four hours of speeches amounted to overkill.*

o•ver•land /ˈoʊvərˌlænd/ adj, adv on land instead of by boat or airplane: *an overland trip*

o•ver•lap /ˌoʊvərˈlæp/ verb [I/T] **1** if two objects overlap, or if one overlaps the other, part of one object covers part of the other **2** if subjects, activities, or ideas overlap, they are partly the same as each other —**o•ver•lap** /ˈoʊvərˌlæp/ noun [C/U], **o•ver•lap•ping** adj

o•ver•load /ˌoʊvərˈloʊd/ verb [T] **1** to put too many people or things in or on something **2** to give someone too much work to do **3** to damage a piece of electrical equipment by putting too much electricity through it —**o•ver•load** /ˈoʊvərˌloʊd/ noun [C/U], **o•ver•load•ed** /ˌoʊvərˈloʊdəd/ adj

o•ver•look /ˌoʊvərˈlʊk/ verb [T] **1** to fail to notice or do something: *Accidents happen when safety checks are overlooked.* **2** to forgive or ignore a mistake or bad behavior: *I'm prepared to overlook what you said.* **3** to have a view of something from above: *Our hotel overlooked the river.* **4** to not consider someone or something: *She claims that she was overlooked for promotion because of her pregnancy.*

o•ver•ly /ˈoʊvərli/ adv *formal* very much, or too much: *It is a problem, but we're not overly worried about it.*

o•ver•night¹ /ˌoʊvərˈnaɪt/ adv **1** during the night, or for one night: *They stayed overnight at the hotel.* **2** in a very short time: *Don't expect to become famous overnight.*

o•ver•night² /ˈoʊvərˌnaɪt/ adj **1** working or happening during the night: *the overnight train/flight/ferry* **2** happening after a very short time: *an overnight success*

o•ver•pass /ˈoʊvərˌpæs/ noun [C] *American* a structure like a bridge that allows one road to pass above another road

o•ver•pow•er /ˌoʊvərˈpaʊr/ verb [T] **1** to control or defeat someone using physical strength: *Two police officers overpowered him and took the gun.* **2** to affect someone so strongly that they cannot think or behave normally

o•ver•pow•er•ing /ˌoʊvərˈpaʊrɪŋ/ adj **1** very strong, so that you do not notice or feel anything else: *an overpowering smell of fish* **2** able to control people because of having a very strong personality

o•ver•priced /ˌoʊvərˈpraɪst/ adj worth less than the price that is being charged

overran the past tense of **overrun**

o•ver•rat•ed /ˌoʊvərˈreɪtəd/ adj not as good or important as some people believe ≠ UNDERRATED

o•ver•re•act /ˌoʊvəriˈækt/ verb [I] to be more worried, annoyed, or offended than you should be

o•ver•ride /ˌoʊvərˈraɪd/ (past tense **o•ver•rode** /ˌoʊvərˈroʊd/; past participle **o•ver•rid•den** /ˌoʊvərˈrɪd(ə)n/) verb [T] **1** to officially change someone else's decision **2** to be much more important than something else: *Passenger safety overrides all other concerns.*

o•ver•rid•ing /ˌoʊvərˈraɪdɪŋ/ adj more important than anything else

overrode the past tense of **override**

o•ver•rule /ˌoʊvərˈrul/ verb [T] to officially change someone else's decision

o•ver•run /ˌoʊvərˈrʌn/ (past tense **o•ver•ran** /ˌoʊvərˈræn/; past participle **o•ver•run**) verb [T] to be present in a place in very large numbers, in a way that is unpleasant: *The mall was overrun with holiday shoppers.*

oversaw the past tense of **oversee**

o•ver•seas¹ /ˌoʊvərˈsiz/ adj ★ existing in, or coming from, a country that is across the ocean from your country: *overseas visitors/students/markets*

o•ver•seas² /ˌoʊvərˈsiz/ adv to or in a country that is across the ocean from your country: *There are plans to move production overseas.*

o•ver•see /ˌoʊvərˈsi/ (past tense **o•ver•saw** /ˌoʊvərˈsɔ/; past participle **o•ver•seen** /ˌoʊvərˈsin/) verb [T] to watch something in order to check that it happens in the way that it should

O

o•ver•shad•ow /ˌoʊvərˈʃædoʊ/ verb [T] **1** to be a negative feature that spoils something: *Violent protests overshadowed the president's visit.* **2** to make someone or something seem less important

o•ver•shoot /ˌoʊvərˈʃut/ (past tense and past participle **o•ver•shot** /ˌoʊvərˈʃɑt/) verb [I/T] to stop or fall at a point that is farther forward than was intended: *The plane seemed in danger of overshooting the runway.*

o•ver•sight /ˈoʊvərˌsaɪt/ noun [C] something that you do not think of that causes problems later

o•ver•sized /ˈoʊvərˌsaɪzd/ or **o•ver•size** /ˈoʊvərˌsaɪz/ adj much larger than usual

o•ver•spend /ˌoʊvərˈspend/ (past tense and past participle **o•ver•spent** /ˌoʊvərˈspent/) verb [I/T] to spend more money than you intended to —**o•ver•spend** /ˈoʊvərˌspend/ noun [C], **o•ver•spend•ing** noun [U]

o•ver•step /ˌoʊvərˈstep/ verb [T] to do something that is not allowed or that is not acceptable: *The committee had overstepped the bounds of its authority.*

o•vert /oʊˈvɜrt, ˈoʊˌvɜrt/ adj not hidden or secret ≠ COVERT: *overt racism/hostility* —**o•vert•ly** adv

o•ver•take /ˌoʊvərˈteɪk/ (past tense **o•ver•took** /ˌoʊvərˈtʊk/; past participle **o•ver•tak•en** /ˌoʊvərˈteɪkən/) verb **1** [T] to become better, bigger, or faster than someone or something else: *The women students seem to be overtaking the men.* **2** [I/T] *British* to pass another vehicle

O

ˌover-the-ˈcounter adj, adv over-the-counter medicine can be bought without a PRESCRIPTION from a doctor

o•ver•throw /ˌoʊvərˈθroʊ/ (past tense **o•ver•threw** /ˌoʊvərˈθru/; past participle **o•ver•thrown** /ˌoʊvərˈθroʊn/) verb [T] to force a leader or government out of their position of power —**o•ver•throw** /ˈoʊvərˌθroʊ/ noun [singular]

o•ver•time /ˈoʊvərˌtaɪm/ noun [U] **1** extra hours that someone works at their job, or money that is paid for working extra hours **2** *American* an extra period of time that is added to a game because neither team won during the normal time

o•ver•tone /ˈoʊvərˌtoʊn/ noun [C] a quality that is noticeable but not obvious

overtook the past tense of **overtake**

o•ver•ture /ˈoʊvərˌtʃʊr/ noun [C] the first part of a long piece of classical music

o•ver•turn /ˌoʊvərˈtɜrn/ verb **1** [I/T] if something overturns, or if you overturn it, it moves so that its bottom or side is upward **2** [T] to officially change a decision or law

o•ver•val•ue /ˌoʊvərˈvælju/ verb [T] to give something a higher price than it should have

o•ver•view /ˈoʊvərˌvju/ noun [C] a description of the main features of something: *The book gives a good overview of the subject.*

o•ver•weight /ˌoʊvərˈweɪt/ adj heavier than you should be ≠ UNDERWEIGHT

o•ver•whelm /ˌoʊvərˈwelm, ˌoʊvərˈhwelm/ verb [T] **1** to affect someone's emotions in a very powerful way: *Her beauty completely overwhelmed him.* **2** to be too much for someone or something to deal with: *In June the town is overwhelmed by tourists.*

o•ver•whelm•ing /ˌoʊvərˈwelmɪŋ, ˌoʊvərˈhwelmɪŋ/ adj ★

1 much larger or more important than anything else in a situation: *An overwhelming majority voted against his proposal.*

2 making you feel a very strong emotion that you cannot control: *I had the overwhelming desire to get up and leave.*

—**o•ver•whelm•ing•ly** adv

Words often used with overwhelming

*Nouns often used with **overwhelming** (sense 2)*

- OVERWHELMING + **desire, emotion, feeling, longing, need, temptation**: used about feelings that are very strong

o•ver•worked /ˌoʊvərˈwɜrkt/ adj forced to work too hard

o•ver•write /ˌoʊvərˈraɪt/ (past tense **o•ver•wrote** /ˌoʊvərˈroʊt/; past participle **o•ver•writ•ten** /ˌoʊvərˈrɪt(ə)n/) verb [T] *computing* to get rid of information in a computer file by replacing it with other information

o•ver•zeal•ous /ˌoʊvərˈzeləs/ adj *showing disapproval* doing something to an unnecessary degree

ow /aʊ/ interjection used for expressing a feeling of sudden pain

owe /oʊ/ verb [T] ★★

1 to have to give someone a particular amount of money because you have bought something from them or have borrowed money from them: **owe sb sth** *Pam still owes me $5.* ♦ **owe sb sth for sth** *How much do we owe you for the tickets?* ♦ **owe sth to sb** *The companies owe as much as $200 billion to foreign lenders.*

2 to have an obligation to do something for someone or to give them something: **owe sb sth** *I think you owe her an apology.* ♦ **owe it to sb to do sth** *They owe it to their children to try to save the marriage.*

3 to feel grateful to someone because of the way that they have helped you: **owe sb sth** *We really owe you a great deal for all your hard work this year.*

4 to have something because someone or something has helped you: **owe sth to sb/sth** *The company owes its success to its excellent training program.*

ow•ing to /ˈoʊɪŋ ˌtu/ preposition because of something: *Owing to the rising cost of fuel, more people are using public transportation.*

owl /aʊl/ noun [C] a large bird with a big head and eyes and a small sharp beak. Owls hunt at night.

own[1] /oʊn/ grammar word ★★★

Own can be:

- an **adjective**: *We grow our own vegetables.*
- a **pronoun**: *Her sister's house is bigger than her own.*

1 belonging to a particular person or thing and not to any other: *You are free to do what you like in your **own home**.* ♦ *She has two small children **of her own**.* ♦ *The club now has its **very own** radio station.*

2 done or caused by a particular person and not by anyone else: *Alan had always done* *his own cooking and cleaning.* ♦ *It's my own fault I didn't get the job.*

PHRASE **(all) on your own 1** alone: *You shouldn't be out on your own at this time of night.* **2** without any help: *Your grandfather did it all on his own.* → YOURSELF

→ HOLD[1]

own² /oʊn/ verb [T] ★★★ to legally have something, especially because you have bought it: *Who owns that house by the lake?* ♦ *Larry doesn't own a car.*

PHRASAL VERB **ˌown ˈup** to admit that you have done something that is bad or embarrassing: *Two local students later owned up to the prank.*

own•er /ˈoʊnər/ noun [C] ★★★ someone who owns something: *a restaurant/supermarket/hotel owner* ♦ *I am* ***the owner of*** *three cars.*

own•er•ship /ˈoʊnərʃɪp/ noun [U] legal possession of something

ox /ɑks/ (plural **ox•en** /ˈɑksən/) noun [C] a large type of male cow that is used for pulling or carrying things

ox•ide /ˈɑkˌsaɪd/ noun [U] *science* a chemical that consists of oxygen mixed with another substance

ox•y•gen /ˈɑksɪdʒən/ noun [U] a gas in the air that has no smell or taste, and that all animals need in order to breathe

oys•ter /ˈɔɪstər/ noun [C] a type of SHELLFISH with a rough shell that is eaten as food, often raw

oz. abbrev ounce

o•zone /ˈoʊˌzoʊn/ noun [U] a type of oxygen that exists high in the Earth's atmosphere

ˈozone ˌlayer noun [singular] a layer of OZONE in the Earth's atmosphere that protects the Earth from the harmful effects of the Sun

Pp

p or **P** /pi/ noun [C/U] the 16th letter of the English alphabet

p. abbrev (plural **pp.**) page

PA¹ /ˌpi ˈeɪ/ noun [C] public address system: a piece of electrical equipment for making announcements or for playing music in a public place

PA² abbrev Pennsylvania

pace¹ /peɪs/ noun ★

1 [singular/U] the speed at which something happens or is done: ***The pace of*** *technological change increased steadily during the 20th century.* ♦ *The course allows students to progress* ***at their own pace.***

2 [singular/U] the speed at which you move: *We wandered along* ***at a leisurely pace.***

3 [C] a step that you take when you walk or run: *I took a few paces toward her.*

PHRASES **keep pace with sth** to develop or progress at the same rate as something else: *The government is not allowing salaries to keep pace with inflation.*

put sb/sth through their/its paces to make a person or machine show how good they are at doing something

set the pace to establish a rate or standard that others have to achieve

pace² /peɪs/ verb **1** [I/T] to walk with regular steps around a small area, because you are worried, nervous, or impatient **2** [T] to make the story in a book, movie, etc. develop in a particular way: *His movies were always well paced and exciting.*

PHRASE **pace yourself** to avoid using all your energy too quickly, so that you have enough left to complete an activity

pace•mak•er /ˈpeɪsˌmeɪkər/ noun [C] a small piece of electronic equipment that is put in someone's heart in order to help the muscles to move regularly

Pa•cif•ic /pəˈsɪfɪk/ adj relating to the Pacific Ocean

Paˌcific ˈRim, the the countries around the Pacific Ocean, considered as a political or economic group

pac•i•fi•er /ˈpæsɪˌfaɪər/ noun [C] *American* a small rubber or plastic object that you put in a baby's mouth to stop it from crying

pac•i•fism /ˈpæsɪˌfɪzəm/ noun [U] the belief that violence is wrong and that people should refuse to fight in wars

pac•i•fist /ˈpæsɪfɪst/ noun [C] someone who believes that violence is wrong and refuses to fight in wars —**pac•i•fist** adj

pac•i•fy /ˈpæsɪˌfaɪ/ verb [T] to make someone who is angry, worried, or upset feel calm

pack¹ /pæk/ verb ★

1 [I/T] to put your possessions into a bag, suitcase, or box so that you can take or send them somewhere ≠ UNPACK: *It didn't take her long to* ***pack a few clothes.*** ♦ *Haven't you packed yet?* ♦ *He was still* ***packing*** *his* ***suitcase*** *when the taxi came.* ♦ **pack sb sth** *I've packed you a few sandwiches in case you get hungry.*

2 [T] to put goods into containers so that they can be sent somewhere and sold: *This is where the fruit is packed.* ♦ **pack sth in sth** *They pack the anchovies in salt.*

3 [T] to fill a place completely: *Eager spectators packed the courtroom.*

4 [T] to press something such as dirt or snow into a solid hard mass

PHRASAL VERBS **ˌpack sth aˈway** to put something back into the place where it is stored: *We packed away the picnic things.*

ˌpack sth ˈin to fill a period of time with a lot of activities: *He packed in an amazing amount in such a short life.*

ˌpack sth ˈinto sth to fit a lot of activities into a period of time: *The festival offers 16 different shows, all packed into one weekend.*

ˌpack ˈup *informal* to finish work for the day by putting work or equipment away: *The workmen have already packed up and left.*

ˌpack (sth) ˈup to put things into a bag, suitcase, or box so that you can take or send them somewhere: *He simply packed up his belongings and moved out.*

pack² /pæk/ noun [C] ★

1 box of cigarettes/cards	4 group of animals
2 set of things	5 group of people/things
3 bag	+ PHRASE

P

1 a paper or cardboard box for something such as cigarettes or PLAYING CARDS
2 a set of things such as products or documents that are wrapped together: *Envelopes are cheaper if you buy them in **packs of 100**.*
3 a bag that you carry on your back
4 a group of animals that live and hunt together: *a pack of wolves*
5 *showing disapproval* a group of people or things: *There was a **pack of reporters** waiting outside.* ♦ *The whole story is **a pack of lies*** (=completely untrue).
PHRASE **lead the pack** or **be ahead of the pack** to be more successful than other people you are competing with: *This kind of innovation will keep the company ahead of the pack.*

pack•age¹ /ˈpækɪdʒ/ noun [C] ★★★
1 an object or set of objects that is wrapped in a box or in paper and sent to someone: *a package full of Christmas presents*
2 *American* a box, bag, or plastic wrapping containing food that is ready to be sold: *The potato chips come in a colorful package.*
3 a plan or offer that is intended to deal with a problem: *a package designed to stabilize the economy*
4 *computing* a set of computer software that is sold as one unit: *the best new graphics package on the market*

pack•age² /ˈpækɪdʒ/ verb [T] **1** to put things into boxes, or to wrap them, so that they can be sold **2** to try to make a product, idea, or person attractive to the public: *Politicians these days are packaged to appeal to a mass market.*

P

ˈpackage ˌtour noun [C] a vacation arranged by a travel company for a fixed price that includes the cost of your hotel and transportation, and sometimes meals and entertainment

pack•ag•ing /ˈpækɪdʒɪŋ/ noun [U] the boxes, plastic, etc. that are used for wrapping products

packed /pækt/ adj **1** extremely crowded: *The movie theater was packed.* **2** *informal* containing a lot of something: *This new series is packed with drama.*

pack•et /ˈpækɪt/ noun [C] **1** a small package or envelope containing a set of similar things: *A packet of brochures arrived in the mail.*
2 *American* a set of documents wrapped together: *a training/information packet*

pack•ing /ˈpækɪŋ/ noun [U] the activity of putting your possessions into bags, suitcases, or boxes so that you can take or send them somewhere: *I haven't done my packing yet.*

pact /pækt/ noun [C] an agreement between two or more people or organizations in which they promise to do something

pad¹ /pæd/ noun [C] **1** a set of sheets of paper that are fastened together along the top or along one side: *a note pad* **2** a thick piece of a soft substance that you use for protecting something, making it more comfortable, or changing its shape: *knee/elbow/shin pads* ♦ *a foam pad* **3** an area of soft flesh on the end of your finger or thumb

pad² /pæd/ verb **1** [T] to cover or fill something with a soft substance in order to protect it, make it more comfortable, or change its shape **2** [I] to walk with quiet light steps —**pad•ded** adj: *a warm padded jacket*

pad•ding /ˈpædɪŋ/ noun [U] a thick soft substance that is used for protecting something, making it more comfortable, or changing its shape

pad•dle¹ /ˈpæd(ə)l/ noun [C] **1** a short pole with a flat end or with two flat ends that is used for moving a small boat such as a CANOE **2** *American* a circular flat object with a handle that is used for hitting the ball in TABLE TENNIS

pad•dle² /ˈpæd(ə)l/ verb [I/T] to move a small boat through the water using a paddle

pad•dock /ˈpædək/ noun [C] a small field where horses are kept

pad•dy /ˈpædi/ noun [C] a RICE PADDY

pad•lock /ˈpædlɑk/ noun [C] a lock that you can attach to something such as a gate or suitcase. It has a curved bar on top that moves when you open the lock. —**pad•lock** verb [T]

pa•gan /ˈpeɪgən/ adj relating to any religion that is not one of the main religions of the world —**pa•gan** noun [C]

page¹ /peɪdʒ/ noun [C] ★★★
1 a sheet of paper in a book, newspaper, or magazine: *the poem **on page** 125* ♦ *For information on hotels in Amsterdam, **see page** 20.* ♦ *Lawrence was eating breakfast while glancing at **the sports page**.* ♦ *She sat on the grass, slowly **turning the pages** of a magazine.*
2 a piece of paper: *Chris wrote her name at the top of the page.*
3 the writing or pictures on a computer screen that you can see at one time, for example as part of a WEBSITE: *Click "Back" to return to the previous page.*
PHRASE **be on the same page** to understand and agree with what is being done

page² /peɪdʒ/ verb [T] **1** to call someone's name in a public place using a PA **2** to communicate with someone by sending a message to their PAGER

pag•eant /ˈpædʒənt/ noun [C] **1** a play, concert, or other performance that is based on a historical or religious story **2** *American* a competition between young women in which judges decide who is the most beautiful

pag•er /ˈpeɪdʒər/ noun [C] a small piece of equipment that makes a noise to tell you to phone someone or go somewhere = BEEPER

pa•go•da /pəˈgoʊdə/ noun [C] a Buddhist religious building with several roofs built on top of each other

paid¹ /peɪd/ adj **1** working or done in exchange for pay: *paid campaign workers* ♦ *paid work* **2** a paid period of time is one when you receive pay although you are not at work ≠ UNPAID: *a paid vacation* **3** earning a particular amount of money: *highly paid managers* ♦ *a new deal for low-paid workers*

paid² the past tense and past participle of **pay¹**

pail /peɪl/ noun [C] an open metal or plastic container with a handle that is used for carrying liquids and soft substances = BUCKET

pain¹ /peɪn/ noun [C/U] ★★★
1 a bad feeling in part of your body when you are hurt or become sick: *An old injury was **causing** him intense **pain**. ♦ He heard Leo scream **in pain**. ♦ I don't think she's **in** any **pain**. ♦ I'm having terrible **pains in** my chest.*
2 a feeling of being very upset or unhappy: *He found it hard to cope with **the pain of** being separated from his children. ♦ The incident must have **caused** my parents great **pain**.*
PHRASES **be a pain (in the neck)** *informal* to be very annoying
go to/take great pains to make a lot of effort to do something well and with care

> **Words often used with pain**
> *Adjectives often used with **pain** (noun, sense 1)*
> ■ **excruciating, intense, searing, severe, sharp, shooting, stabbing, terrible, unbearable** + PAIN: used about pains that are very strong
> *Verbs often used with **pain** (noun, sense 1)*
> ■ **cause, inflict** + PAIN: make someone feel pain
> ■ **alleviate, deaden, dull, ease, lessen, relieve, soothe** + PAIN: make a pain less severe
> ■ **bear, endure, stand, put up with** + PAIN: be able to suffer pain

pain² /peɪn/ verb [T] *formal* to make someone feel very upset, ashamed, or unhappy
pained /peɪnd/ adj showing that you feel very upset or unhappy
pain·ful /ˈpeɪnf(ə)l/ adj ★
1 making you feel upset, ashamed, or unhappy: *painful memories of her unhappy childhood*
2 causing physical pain: *The sting can be excruciatingly painful. ♦ I have a sore throat, and it's really painful when I swallow.*
pain·ful·ly /ˈpeɪnf(ə)li/ adv in a way that makes you feel upset, ashamed, or unhappy: *She was painfully aware of his embarrassment. ♦ She looked painfully thin.*
pain·kill·er /ˈpeɪnˌkɪlər/ noun [C] a medicine that reduces pain
pain·less /ˈpeɪnləs/ adj **1** not causing any physical pain **2** less difficult or unpleasant than you expected: *I was dreading the interview, but in fact it was pretty painless.*
pains·tak·ing /ˈpeɪnzˌteɪkɪŋ/ adj done or doing something very carefully and slowly =METICULOUS —**pains·tak·ing·ly** adv
paint¹ /peɪnt/ noun ★
1 [U] a colored substance that you use for changing the color of a surface or for making a picture: *The paint was peeling off the doors. ♦ You need to apply two **coats of paint**.*
2 paints [plural] a set of small blocks or tubes containing paint that you use for making pictures
paint² /peɪnt/ verb ★★
1 [I/T] to put paint onto something in order to change its color: *Wash the walls before you start to paint. ♦ Will you help me paint the kitchen?*
2 [I/T] to create a picture of something using paints: *I painted a view of the lake.*
3 [T] to describe someone or something in a particular way: *The film **paints a picture** of what life was like during the war.*
paint·brush /ˈpeɪntˌbrʌʃ/ noun [C] a brush used for painting
paint·er /ˈpeɪntər/ noun [C] **1** an artist who paints pictures **2** someone whose job is to paint the inside or outside of buildings
paint·ing /ˈpeɪntɪŋ/ noun ★★
1 [C] a picture made using paint: *a painting by Picasso*
2 [U] the activity of using paint to make a picture or cover a surface: *After retirement he took up painting.*
pair¹ /per/ noun [C] ★★★
1 a set of two things of the same type: *The vases were sold as a pair. ♦ **a pair of** shoes/socks/gloves*
2 a single unit made up of two similar parts joined together: *My glasses are getting old and I probably need a new pair. ♦ **a pair of** pants/tights ♦ **a pair of** scissors/binoculars/pliers*
3 two people who are connected or who do something together: *The pair became good friends. ♦ **a pair of** identical twins ♦ The students worked **in pairs**.*
pair² /per/ PHRASAL VERB **ˌpair (sb) ˈup** to form a pair, or to make two people form a pair
pa·ja·mas /pəˈdʒɑməz/ noun [plural] clothes, usually comfortable pants and a shirt, that you wear when you sleep —*picture* → C5 —**pa·jam·a** adj
pal¹ /pæl/ noun [C] *informal* a friend → PEN PAL
pal² /pæl/ PHRASAL VERB **ˌpal aˈround** *American informal* to spend time with a friend
pal·ace /ˈpæləs/ noun [C] a very large building that is the official home of a royal family, president, or religious leader
pal·at·a·ble /ˈpælətəb(ə)l/ adj **1** tasting good enough to eat or drink **2** acceptable
pal·ate /ˈpælət/ noun [C] **1** the inside upper part of your mouth **2** the ability to taste and judge flavors
pa·la·tial /pəˈleɪʃ(ə)l/ adj a palatial building is very large and impressive
pale¹ /peɪl/ adj ★★
1 light and not bright in color: *pale blue/yellow/green ♦ a pale sky*
2 a pale person has skin that is lighter than usual because they are sick, shocked, or worried: *He **looked pale** and weary.*
pale² /peɪl/ verb [I] to seem less important or serious: *The devastating floods of two years ago pale in comparison with last week's storms.*
pal·ette /ˈpælət/ noun [C] a board that an artist uses for mixing paints on
pall /pɔl/ noun **cast a pall over sth** to create an unpleasant situation or mood: *His comments cast a pall over the meeting.*
pal·lid /ˈpælɪd/ adj very pale in a way that does not look healthy
pal·lor /ˈpælər/ noun [singular] the very pale color that your skin has when you are sick or worried
palm¹ /pɑlm, pɑm/ noun [C] **1** the inside part of your hand, between your fingers and your wrist —*picture* → C14 **2** a PALM TREE
palm² /pɑlm, pɑm/ PHRASAL VERB **ˌpalm sb/sth ˈoff** *informal* to get rid of someone or

P

something that you do not want by persuading someone else to take or buy them from you

'palm ˌtree noun [C] a tropical tree without branches that has large wide leaves growing from the top of its TRUNK —*picture* → C9

pal·pa·ble /ˈpælpəb(ə)l/ adj obvious, or very easily noticed

pal·try /ˈpɔltri/ adj not at all big or important

pam·per /ˈpæmpər/ verb [T] to take care of someone very well, especially by making them feel very comfortable

pam·phlet /ˈpæmflət/ noun [C] a very thin book with a paper cover

pan[1] /pæn/ noun [C] ★

1 a round metal container with a handle that is used for cooking → DUSTPAN

2 *American* a metal container used for baking: *a cake pan*

3 the contents of a pan, or the amount that a pan holds: *a pan of hot water*

→ FLASH[2]

pan[2] /pæn/ verb **1** [T] *informal* to criticize someone or something very strongly **2** [I] if a camera pans, it moves sideways slowly to photograph something

PHRASAL VERB **ˌpan ˈout** *informal* if a situation pans out in a particular way, it develops in that way

pan·a·ce·a /ˌpænəˈsiə/ noun [C] something that people think will solve all their problems

pa·nache /pəˈnæʃ/ noun [U] an impressive way of doing something that shows great skill and confidence

pan·cake /ˈpænˌkeɪk/ noun [C] a small round cake made by cooking a mixture of flour, eggs, and milk

pan·da /ˈpændə/ noun [C] a large Chinese wild animal with black and white fur —*picture* → C12

pan·de·mo·ni·um /ˌpændəˈmoʊniəm/ noun [C/U] a very noisy and confused situation that is caused by a lot of angry or excited people = CHAOS

pan·der /ˈpændər/ PHRASAL VERB **ˈpander to sb/sth** *showing disapproval* to do or say what someone wants in order to please them: *The president was accused of pandering to racial prejudice.*

pane /peɪn/ noun [C] a flat piece of glass in a window or door

pan·el /ˈpæn(ə)l/ noun [C] ★★

1 a flat piece of wood, glass, or other material that forms part of something such as a door or wall: *a door with stained glass panels*

2 a group of well-known people who discuss subjects on television or radio programs

3 a group of people who make decisions or judgments: *an interview panel* ♦ *a panel of judges*

4 the part of a vehicle or machine that contains the switches and other instruments: *a control panel*

pan·el·ing /ˈpæn(ə)lɪŋ/ noun [U] pieces of wood that cover the walls of a room for decoration

pan·el·ist /ˈpæn(ə)lɪst/ noun [C] a member of a PANEL of people who discuss things on television or radio

pan·el·ling /ˈpæn(ə)lɪŋ/ the British spelling of **paneling**

pan·el·list /ˈpæn(ə)lɪst/ the British spelling of **panelist**

pang /pæŋ/ noun [C] a sudden unpleasant physical feeling or emotion: *a pang of guilt*

pan·ic[1] /ˈpænɪk/ noun **1** [singular/U] a sudden strong feeling of fear or worry that makes you unable to think clearly or calmly: *Panic spread quickly through the city.* ♦ *People are fleeing the area in panic.* **2** [C/U] a situation in which a lot of people are hurrying to do something because they are frightened or worried: *News of the incident caused a panic.* —**pan·ick·y** /ˈpænɪki/ adj

pan·ic[2] /ˈpænɪk/ (present participle **pan·ick·ing**; past tense and past participle **pan·icked**) verb [I/T] to have a sudden strong feeling of fear or worry and be unable to think clearly or calmly, or to make someone do this

ˈpanic-ˌstricken adj feeling so afraid or worried that you cannot think clearly or calmly

pan·o·ram·a /ˌpænəˈræmə/ noun [C] a view of a large area of land or water —**pan·o·ram·ic** /ˌpænəˈræmɪk/ adj

pan·sy /ˈpænzi/ noun [C] a small plant with large flowers

pant /pænt/ verb [I] to breathe very loudly with your mouth open, for example when you have been running —**pant** noun [C]

pan·ther /ˈpænθər/ noun [C] a LEOPARD with black fur

pant·ies /ˈpæntiz/ noun [plural] a piece of women's underwear that covers the part of the body from the waist to the top of the legs

pan·to·mime /ˈpæntəˌmaɪm/ noun [C/U] a type of entertainment with only actions and no words

pan·try /ˈpæntri/ noun [C] a small room for storing food

pants /pænts/ noun [plural] *American* ★★ a piece of clothing that covers your body from your waist to your ANKLES and has a separate part for each leg —*picture* → C4

pant·suit /ˈpæntˌsut/ noun [C] *American* a woman's suit that consists of pants and a jacket

pant·y·hose /ˈpæntiˌhoʊz/ noun [U] a piece of women's clothing that covers the body tightly from the toes to the waist and is usually worn under dresses and skirts —*picture* → C5

pa·pa /ˈpɑpɑ/ noun [C] your father

pa·pa·cy, the /ˈpeɪpəsi/ noun [singular] the position of being the POPE

pa·pal /ˈpeɪp(ə)l/ adj relating to the POPE

pa·pa·raz·zi /ˌpɑəˈrɑtsi/ noun [plural] photographers who follow famous people in order to take photographs of them

pa·pa·ya /pəˈpaɪə/ noun [C/U] a fruit with green and yellow skin, orange flesh, and small black seeds inside —*picture* → C10

pa·per[1] /ˈpeɪpər/ noun ★★★

1 for writing/wrapping	4 academic writing/talk
2 newspaper	5 writing by student
3 documents	+ PHRASE

1 [U] the thin flat substance that you use for

writing on or wrapping things in: *a package wrapped in brown paper* ♦ *Stuart handed me **a piece of paper** with an address written on it.*
2 [C] a newspaper: *Is that today's paper?* ♦ *He sat down and **read the paper**.* ♦ *The story was **in all the papers**.*
3 papers [plural] official documents such as your passport, or documents relating to work, study, or personal matters: *We had to show our papers at the security desk.* ♦ *Some important papers are missing from the files.*
4 [C] a piece of writing or talk by an expert on an academic subject: *He has published many **papers on** the subject.*
5 [C] a piece of writing done by a student as part of a course: *I have to write **a paper on** the Cuban Revolution.* → TERM PAPER
PHRASE **on paper 1** in writing: *We need to have something on paper that people can take away with them.* **2** used for saying that something appears to be true but may not in fact be true: *On paper they are the best team in the National League.*

pa·per² /ˈpeɪpər/ adj made of paper

pa·per·back /ˈpeɪpərˌbæk/ noun [C] a book with a cover made of thick paper → HARDBACK

ˈpaper ˌboy noun [C] a boy who earns money by delivering newspapers to people's homes

ˈpaper ˌclip noun [C] a small piece of bent wire used for holding pieces of paper together

ˈpaper ˌgirl noun [C] a girl who earns money by delivering newspapers to people's homes

pa·per·weight /ˈpeɪpərˌweɪt/ noun [C] a small heavy object that you put on top of pieces of paper to keep them in place

pa·per·work /ˈpeɪpərˌwɜrk/ noun [U] **1** the part of a job that involves producing reports, keeping records, and writing letters **2** the documents that you need for a particular activity or occasion

pa·pri·ka /pəˈprikə/ noun [U] a red powder that is used in cooking for adding a slightly hot flavor to food

par /pɑr/ noun [U] **1** the usual or expected standard: *His performance was well below par* (=not as good as usual). **2** in golf, the number of times that a player is expected to hit the ball to get it into the hole, or into all of the holes
PHRASES **on a par with** of the same quality as, or at the same level as someone or something
par for the course *informal* usual or expected in a particular situation: *For a football player, that kind of injury is par for the course.*

par. abbrev paragraph

par·a·ble /ˈperəb(ə)l/ noun [C] a simple story with a moral or religious purpose, especially one told by Jesus Christ in the Bible

par·a·chute¹ /ˈperəˌʃut/ noun [C] a large piece of cloth joined to heavy strings that is used by someone jumping out of an airplane

par·a·chute² /ˈperəˌʃut/ verb [I] to jump from an airplane wearing a parachute

pa·rade¹ /pəˈreɪd/ noun [C] **1** a public celebration in which a large group of people moves through an area, often with decorated vehicles and bands playing music **2** a public ceremony in which a large group of soldiers marches together

pa·rade² /pəˈreɪd/ verb **1** [I] to walk as part of an organized group in order to celebrate or publicly protest something **2** [I] *showing disapproval* to walk around so that people will look at you and admire you **3** [T] to publicly show something that you are proud of

par·a·digm /ˈperəˌdaɪm/ noun [C] *formal* **1** a set of ideas that are used for understanding or explaining something, especially in a particular subject **2** a typical example or model of something

par·a·dise /ˈperəˌdaɪs/ noun **1** [C/U] a perfect place or situation **2 Paradise** Heaven, the place where some people believe that you go when you die if you have lived a good life

par·a·dox /ˈperəˌdɑks/ noun [C] a situation or idea that is strange because it has features or qualities that you would not expect to exist together: *the paradox of people with the best qualifications not being able to get jobs*

par·a·dox·ical /ˌperəˈdɑksɪk(ə)l/ adj strange because of being the opposite of what you expect —**par·a·dox·i·cal·ly** /ˌperəˈdɑksɪkli/ adv

par·af·fin /ˈperəfɪn/ noun [U] a white substance used for making CANDLES

par·a·gon /ˈperəˌgɑn/ noun [C] *formal* someone who is perfect, or who is the best possible example of a particular quality

par·a·graph /ˈperəˌgræf/ noun [C] ★★★ a section of a piece of writing that begins on a new line and contains one or more sentences

par·al·lel¹ /ˈperəˌlel/ adj **1** lines that are parallel are the same distance apart at every point along their length: *He leaned forward so that his body was almost parallel to the ground.* ♦ *The river flows parallel with Main Street.* —*picture* → C8 **2** happening at the same time or in the same way but separately: *Taxes are going up in the U.S., and in a parallel development, Germany is also raising taxes.*

par·al·lel² /ˈperəˌlel/ noun [C] **1** a way in which separate things or people are similar to each other: *There are some interesting parallels between the two wars.* ♦ *Some writers have drawn parallels between computers and the human brain* (=shown how they are similar). **2** someone or something that is similar to another person or thing: *The proposed reforms have parallels in several other countries.* ♦ *Woods is a golfer without parallel* (=no one is better).
PHRASE **in parallel** connected and happening at the same time: *Advertising has developed in parallel with modern industry and the mass media.*

par·al·lel³ /ˈperəˌlel/ verb [T] to be similar or equal to something

par·al·lel·o·gram /ˌperəˈleləˌgræm/ noun [C] a shape with four straight sides in which opposite sides are of equal length and are parallel to each other —*picture* → C8

P

par•a•lyse /ˈperəˌlaɪz/ the British spelling of paralyze

pa•ral•y•sis /pəˈræləsɪs/ noun [U] **1** the loss of the ability to move your body or a part of it **2** the state of being completely unable to operate normally

par•a•lyze /ˈperəˌlaɪz/ verb [T] **1** to make someone lose the ability to move their body or a part of it **2** to make something completely unable to operate normally

par•a•lyzed /ˈperəˌlaɪzd/ adj **1** unable to move your body or part of it because of an illness or injury **2** completely unable to operate normally **3** temporarily unable to move or think clearly

par•a•med•ic /ˌperəˈmedɪk/ noun [C] someone who is not a doctor but is trained to give medical treatment to people at the place where an accident has happened

pa•ram•e•ter /pəˈræmɪtər/ noun [C] a limit that affects how something can be done

par•a•mil•i•tar•y /ˌperəˈmɪˌlɪteri/ adj organized and operating like an army, but not part of an official army —**par•a•mil•i•tar•y** noun [C]

par•a•mount /ˈperəˌmaʊnt/ adj more important than all other things

par•a•noi•a /ˌperəˈnɔɪə/ noun [U] **1** the worried feeling that other people do not like you and are trying to harm you, although you have no proof of this **2** *medical* a mental illness that makes people believe that other people do not like them and want to harm them

par•a•noid /ˈperəˌnɔɪd/ adj **1** worrying that people do not like you and are trying to harm you, although you have no proof of this **2** *medical* suffering from the mental illness PARANOIA

par•a•nor•mal, the /ˌperəˈnɔrm(ə)l/ noun [singular] mysterious events or facts that cannot be explained by science

par•a•pher•na•lia /ˌperəfərˈneɪljə/ noun [U] a set of objects that are used for a particular activity

par•a•phrase /ˈperəˌfreɪz/ verb [T] to express what someone else has said or written using different words in order to make it shorter or clearer —**par•a•phrase** noun [C]

par•a•ple•gic /ˌperəˈplidʒɪk/ noun [C] someone who cannot move the parts of their body below their waist —**par•a•ple•gic** adj

par•a•site /ˈperəˌsaɪt/ noun [C] **1** a plant or animal that lives in or on another type of animal and feeds on it **2** a lazy person who lives by getting things such as money or food from other people —**par•a•sit•ic** /ˌperəˈsɪtɪk/ adj

par•a•sol /ˈpærəˌsɔl/ noun [C] a type of UMBRELLA that provides protection from the sun

par•a•troop•er /ˈperəˌtrupər/ noun [C] a soldier who is trained to jump out of airplanes wearing a PARACHUTE

par•a•troops /ˈperəˌtrups/ noun [plural] soldiers who are paratroopers

par•cel /ˈpɑrs(ə)l/ noun [C] a PACKAGE → PART[1]

parched /pɑrtʃt/ adj **1** *informal* very thirsty **2** extremely dry because of hot weather

par•don[1] /ˈpɑrd(ə)n/ verb [T] to officially forgive someone for committing a crime and free them from prison

PHRASE **pardon me 1** *American* used for politely asking someone to repeat something **2** *American* used when you want to pass someone in a small space **3** used for saying "sorry" when you do something rude, for example when you interrupt someone or make a rude noise with your body

par•don[2] /ˈpɑrd(ə)n/ noun [C] an official decision to forgive someone for committing a crime and to free them from prison → BEG

par•don[3] /ˈpɑrd(ə)n/ interjection used for politely asking someone to repeat something that you did not hear or did not understand

pare /per/ verb [T] to reduce the total number or amount of something

par•ent /ˈperənt/ noun [C] ★★★ your mother or father: *Has Joe met your parents yet?*

par•ent•age /ˈperəntɪdʒ/ noun [U] your parents considered as belonging to a particular country, religion, or social class: *He is of mixed Italian and English parentage.*

pa•ren•tal /pəˈrent(ə)l/ adj involving or provided by parents

ˈparent ˌcompany noun [C] *business* a company that owns or controls a smaller company of the same type → SUBSIDIARY

pa•ren•the•ses /pəˈrenθəˌsiz/ noun [plural] the symbols (and), used in writing for separating a word, phrase, or number from the rest of a sentence: *The students' nationalities are shown in parentheses.*

par•ent•hood /ˈperəntˌhʊd/ noun [U] the fact of being a parent

par•ent•ing /ˈperəntɪŋ/ noun [U] the activities that are involved in being a parent and raising children

par•ish /ˈperɪʃ/ noun **1** [C] in some Christian churches, a district that has its own church building and priest **2** [singular] the people who live in a parish

pa•rish•ion•er /pəˈrɪʃ(ə)nər/ noun [C] someone who lives in a particular parish and regularly goes to church

par•i•ty /ˈperəti/ noun [U] a situation in which different people or things are equal

park[1] /pɑrk/ noun [C] ★★
1 an open public area with grass and trees in a town. Parks often have sports fields or places for children to play: *The tax increase will help pay for the maintenance of city parks.*
2 an area in the countryside that is protected by the government for people to enjoy. Parks often have important natural features such as lakes or mountains: *Yellowstone National Park*

park[2] /pɑrk/ verb [I/T] ★ to move a vehicle into a place where you are going to leave it for a period of time: *Mary **parked the car** in the driveway.*

par•ka /ˈpɑkə/ noun [C] a long warm jacket with a HOOD (=a part to cover your head) —*picture* → C4

park•ing /ˈpɑrkɪŋ/ noun [U] **1** the process of putting a vehicle into a place and leaving it there **2** space where vehicles can be left

ˈparking gaˌrage noun [C] *American* a building where people can park their cars

ˈparking ˌlight noun [C] *American* one of a pair of lights on a vehicle that you use when there is not much light or it is raining —*picture* → C6

ˈparking ˌlot noun [C] *American* an area where people can park their cars

ˈparking ˌmeter noun [C] a machine in the street that you put coins into in order to pay for leaving your car there

ˈparking ˌticket noun [C] an official document that is put on your car telling you that you have broken a rule about parking and must pay a FINE

Par·kin·son's dis·ease /ˈpɑrkɪnsənz dɪˌziz/ noun [U] a serious illness that affects your nerves and makes you shake and move slowly

ˈpark ˌranger noun [C] *American* someone whose job is to take care of a forest, national park, or state park

par·lia·ment /ˈpɑrləmənt/ noun ★
1 [C] an official elected group of people in some countries who meet to make the laws of the country and discuss national issues: *the Russian parliament*
2 Parliament [U] the main law-making institution in some countries such as the U.K.: *The party has a large majority **in Parliament**.* → MEMBER OF PARLIAMENT

par·lia·men·ta·ry /ˌpɑrləˈment(ə)ri/ adj relating to a parliament, or appropriate for a parliament

par·lor /ˈpɑrlər/ noun [C] a name used by some businesses for the store or room where they do their business: *an ice cream parlor* → BEAUTY PARLOR

Par·me·san /ˈpɑrməˌzɑn/ or **Parmesan ˈcheese** noun [U] a hard Italian cheese with a strong flavor, often used on pasta

pa·ro·chi·al /pəˈroʊkiəl/ adj *showing disapproval* not interested in things that do not affect your own local area

par·o·dy¹ /ˈperədi/ noun [C/U] a literary or musical work that copies a serious work in a humorous way

par·o·dy² /ˈperədi/ verb [T] to copy someone or something in a way that makes people laugh

pa·role¹ /pəˈroʊl/ noun [U] permission for a prisoner to leave prison before the official time, if they promise to obey particular rules: *He could be out on parole in two years.*

pa·role² /pəˈroʊl/ verb [T] to give a prisoner parole

par·rot /ˈperət/ noun [C] a brightly colored tropical bird that is often kept as a pet and can be taught to copy what people say

pars·ley /ˈpɑrsli/ noun [U] a small plant that you use for decorating food or giving it a fresh flavor

part¹ /pɑrt/ noun ★★★

1 piece/section/aspect	5 piece for machine
2 person played by actor	6 in hair
3 being involved in sth	7 relative quantity
4 section of book/play	+ PHRASES

1 [C] one of the pieces, sections, or aspects that something consists of: *The top **part of** the shoe is made of leather.* ♦ *We walked part of the way, then took a bus.* ♦ *The hardest **part of** my job is controlling the budgets.* ♦ *This is one of the nicest **parts of** San Francisco.*
2 [C] the person played by an actor in a movie, play, or television program, or the words that the actor speaks: *She'd be really good for that part.* ♦ *He had just two weeks to learn his part.*
3 [singular] the way in which someone is involved in an activity or event, and the effect that they have on what happens: *He was jailed for 10 years for **his part in** the crime.*
4 [C] a section of a book, magazine, play, television series, etc.: *a new 12-part drama starting tonight on HBO*
5 [C] an individual piece of a machine or vehicle: *We're waiting for a part to come from Germany.*
6 [C] *American* a line on your head that you make by brushing or COMBING your hair in two different directions
7 [C] a particular quantity that is used for measuring equal amounts of different substances to form a mixture: *Use a mixture of one part milk to four parts water.*

PHRASES **be part and parcel of sth** to be an aspect of something that has to be accepted: *These little arguments were part and parcel of their relationship.*
the better part of sth almost all of something: *It has taken us the better part of two days to do this job.*
for the most part in most cases, or generally: *There were a few complaints, but for the most part people seemed to enjoy themselves.*
have/play a part (in sth) to be involved in a particular situation or activity and influence its development: *They have worked very hard, but luck has played a part too.*
in part to some degree: *The accidents were due in part to the bad weather.*
look/dress the part to have an appearance or wear clothing that is usual or expected for a particular situation, activity, or job
part of me used for saying that you are not completely sure about what you think or feel about something: *Part of me still wants to believe you.*
part of speech *linguistics* one of the main GRAMMATICAL groups that a particular word belongs to, for example noun, verb, adjective, or adverb
take part (in sth) to be involved in an activity with other people: *They will be taking part in the discussions.*

part² /pɑrt/ verb **1** [I/T] to move apart, or to move two things or two sections of a single unit away from each other: *The crowd parted to let them through.* ♦ *Tony parted the curtains and looked out.* **2** [I] if two people part, they go away from each other: *The marriage failed, but they parted on good terms.* **3** [T] to make a line on your head by brushing or COMBING your hair in two different directions

PHRASES **be parted (from sb)** to be prevented from being with someone who you want to be with
part company (with sb) 1 to go away from each

other: *We parted company in Grand Central Station.* **2** to end a relationship

PHRASAL VERB ˈ**part with sth** to give something to someone although you would prefer to keep it

part³ /pɑrt/ adv **part..., part...** a mixture of two things: *I am part Russian, part English.*

par·tial /ˈpɑrʃ(ə)l/ adj **1** not complete: *a partial withdrawal from enemy territory*
2 supporting one person, group, or opinion more than others, instead of being fair to everyone ≠ IMPARTIAL

PHRASE **be partial to** to like someone or something: *I'm very partial to bacon and eggs.*

par·tial·ly /ˈpɑrʃəli/ adv not completely =PARTLY

par·tic·i·pant /pɑrˈtɪsɪpənt/ noun [C] someone who takes part in something

par·tic·i·pate /pɑrˈtɪsɪˌpeɪt/ verb [I] to take part in something: *The rebels have agreed to participate in the peace talks.*
—**par·tic·i·pa·tion** /pɑrˌtɪsɪˈpeɪʃ(ə)n/ noun [U]

par·ti·ci·ple /ˈpɑrtɪsɪp(ə)l/ noun [C] *linguistics* the form of a verb used in COMPOUND tenses and as an adjective. English uses the **present participle**, which ends in "-ing," and the **past participle**, which usually ends in "-ed."

par·ti·cle /ˈpɑrtɪk(ə)l/ noun [C] **1** an extremely small piece or amount of something
2 *linguistics* an adverb or preposition used with a verb to form a PHRASAL VERB. For example in the sentence "He quickly put on his clothes," "on" is a particle.

P

par·tic·u·lar¹ /pərˈtɪkjələr/ adj ★★★
1 used for emphasizing that you are talking about one specific person or thing and not anyone or anything else=SPECIFIC: *Are there any particular topics that you would like me to explain further?*
2 especially great=SPECIAL: *Two matters need to be given particular attention.*
3 someone who is particular has very clear ideas about what they like and dislike, and is difficult to please: *She's very **particular about** what she eats.*
4 clearly different and belonging to just one person or thing=DISTINCTIVE

par·tic·u·lar² /pərˈtɪkjələr/ noun

PHRASE **in particular 1** especially: *I liked the last candidate in particular.* **2** special, or important: *"What are you doing tonight?" "Nothing in particular."*
→ PARTICULARS

par·tic·u·lar·ly /pərˈtɪkjələrli/ adv ★★★
1 very, or very much: *His remarks were particularly helpful.* ♦ *"Did you have a good time?" "**Not particularly.**"*
2 especially: *The environment has become a major political issue, particularly in the past decade.*
3 in a clear and specific way: *He particularly asked for you to be at the meeting.*

par·tic·u·lars /pərˈtɪkjələrz/ noun [plural] information and details about someone or something

part·ing¹ /ˈpɑrtɪŋ/ adj done or said by someone when they are leaving: *a parting gift/comment*

part·ing² /ˈpɑrtɪŋ/ noun [C/U] the act of leaving someone

PHRASE **a parting of the ways** a point at which two people or groups decide to separate or stop working together

ˌ**parting** ˈ**shot** noun [C] an unpleasant or angry remark made at the end of a conversation by someone when they are leaving

par·ti·san¹ /ˈpɑrtɪzən/ adj showing strong and usually unfair support for one particular person, group, or idea

par·ti·san² /ˈpɑrtɪzən/ noun [C] someone who gives strong support to a particular person, group, or idea

par·ti·tion /pɑrˈtɪʃ(ə)n/ noun **1** [C] a wall, screen, or piece of glass that is used for separating one area from another in a room **2** [U] the process of dividing a country into two or more separate countries —**par·ti·tion** verb [T]

part·ly /ˈpɑrtli/ adv ★★ to some degree, but not completely: *I'll admit I was partly to blame.* ♦ *We get on well together, partly because we share the same sense of humor.*

part·ner¹ /ˈpɑrtnər/ noun [C] ★★★
1 one of two or more people who own a company and share its profits and losses: *He became **a partner in** his father's law firm.*
2 someone who you live with and have a sexual relationship with: *Are partners invited to the office party?*
3 someone who you do a particular activity with: *John is my tennis partner.*
4 a business, organization, or country that has an agreement with another business, organization, or country: *China is one of our major trading partners.*

> **Words that avoid giving offense: partner**
>
> In British English, you can use **partner** to refer to the husband or wife of someone, or to refer to a person who lives with someone and has a sexual relationship with them, but is not married to them. In American English, some people use **partner** only about unmarried people, and many people use **partner** only about gay people.

part·ner² /ˈpɑrtnər/ verb [T] to be someone's partner in an activity

part·ner·ship /ˈpɑrtnəˌʃɪp/ noun **1** [U] the position of being one of two or more people who own a company as partners **2** [C] a company that is owned by two or more partners **3** [C/U] a relationship between two or more people, groups, or countries that are involved in an activity together

ˌ**part-**ˈ**time** adj **1** done for only part of the time that an activity is usually performed: *a part-time job* **2** doing part-time work or study —ˌ**part-**ˈ**time** adv → FULL-TIME

par·ty¹ /ˈpɑrti/ noun [C] ★★★
1 a social event at which people meet in order to celebrate something or have fun: *Did you invite her to your birthday party?* ♦ *We're **having a party** on Saturday night.*
2 an organized group of people who share the same ideas about how a country should be governed, and who try to get elected: *the two main political parties*
3 a group of people who are going somewhere together, or who are involved

in the same activity: *a rescue party* ♦ ***a party of tourists***
4 *formal* a person or group involved in a contract or legal case with another person or group: ***the guilty/innocent party*** (=the person responsible/not responsible for something wrong or illegal)

par·ty² /ˈpɑrti/ verb [I] *informal* to have fun eating and drinking, dancing, etc. with other people

pass¹ /pæs/ verb ★★★

1 go past sth	10 stop happening
2 move somewhere	11 go above amount
3 be successful on test	12 happen
4 let sb have sth	13 give opinion
5 accept on test	14 of body waste
6 be spent	15 change owner
7 spend time	+ PHRASE
8 kick/hit ball to sb	+ PHRASAL VERBS
9 make law, etc. official	

1 [I/T] to go past something: *The procession slowly passed us.* ♦ *They stopped at the crossing, waiting for the train to pass.*
2 [I/T] to move, or to move something, in a particular direction or to a particular place or position: *The railroad line* ***passes through*** *Richmond.* ♦ *Two large birds* ***passed over*** *our heads.* ♦ **pass sth across sth** *He passed his hand across his forehead.*
3 [I/T] to be successful in an examination or test, by achieving a satisfactory standard ≠ FAIL: *Do you think you'll pass?* ♦ *She* ***passed*** *her driver's* ***test***.
4 [T] to put something into someone's hand or into a position where they can take it: *Pass the salt, please.* ♦ **pass sb sth** *Could you pass me that newspaper?* ♦ **pass sth to sb** *He passed the camera to her.*
5 [T] to officially decide that someone has been successful in an examination or test ≠ FAIL: *The examiners passed only 40% of the candidates.*
6 [I] if time passes, it happens and comes to an end: *The summer passed quickly, as usual.*
7 [T] to spend time doing something: *We passed the day swimming and lying in the sun.* ♦ *They watched videos to* ***pass the time*** (=make it seem shorter).
8 [I/T] to kick, hit, or throw the ball to another player in a sports team —*picture* → C15
9 [T] to make a law or proposal become official by voting to accept it
10 [I] to come to an end: *I felt a sharp pain, but it soon passed.*
11 [T] to become more than a particular amount: *The death toll has already passed 200.*
12 [I] to happen, or to be allowed to happen: *Her mistake seemed to have* ***passed unnoticed***. ♦ *Andrew was furious and wasn't going to* ***let this one pass*** (=not react to something annoying).
13 [T] to make a comment or give an opinion: *She was furious that he should have the nerve to* ***pass judgment on*** *her.*
14 [T] *formal* to make something leave your body as a waste product
15 [I] to stop being owned or controlled by one person and start being owned or controlled by another: **pass from sb to sb** *The estate has passed from father to son for generations.*

PHRASE **pass (a) sentence (on sb)** to officially say in a court of law what a criminal's punishment will be
→ BUCK

PHRASAL VERBS ˌ**pass sth aˈround** to give something to one person in a group, who gives it to someone else, who then gives it to someone else, etc.
ˈ**pass as sb/sth** *same as* **pass for sb/sth**
ˌ**pass aˈway** to die. This word is used to avoid saying "die" when you think it might upset someone.
ˌ**pass ˈby (sth)** to go past: *Three buses passed by, but mine never came.* ♦ *I pass by her house every day on my way to school.*
ˌ**pass sb ˈby** if something passes you by, it happens, but you get no advantage from it: *Sometimes I feel that life is just passing me by.*
ˌ**pass sth ˈdown** to give knowledge, or to teach skills, to your children or to younger people
ˈ**pass for sb/sth** to be accepted, wrongly, as being a particular type of person or thing: *He's nearly forty, but he could pass for twenty-five.*
ˌ**pass sb/sth ˈoff as sth** to make people believe that a person or thing is something else: *He put on a suit, intending to pass himself off as a businessman.*
ˌ**pass ˈon** *same as* **pass away**
ˌ**pass sth ˈon 1** to give someone something that someone else has given you: *When you've read this message, please pass it on.* **2** to give someone an infectious illness
ˌ**pass ˈout** to suddenly become unconscious =FAINT
ˌ**pass sth ˈup** *informal* to not take advantage of an opportunity

pass² /pæs/ noun [C] ★
1 an official document that gives you permission to enter a place or to use a particular form of transportation without having to pay each time: *You always have to show your pass before they'll let you in.*
2 a kick, hit, or throw of the ball to another player on your sports team
3 a path or road that goes through an area of mountains
4 a successful result in an examination or test

pass·a·ble /ˈpæːsəb(ə)l/ adj **1** satisfactory, but not of high quality **2** if a road or a river is passable, it is not blocked and can be traveled on ≠ IMPASSABLE

pas·sage /ˈpæsɪdʒ/ noun ★★
1 [C] a long narrow area with walls on each side that leads from one room or place to another: *He left his bike in the passage between the kitchen and the back door.*
2 [C] a short section of a book, article, poem, or piece of music, considered on its own: *He read me a passage from his favorite book.*
3 [U] movement past, over, or through a place: *The passage of heavy guns had left deep ruts in the field.*
4 [C] a tube in your body for air or liquid to pass through: *Her air passages were blocked.*

PHRASE **the passage of time** the process by which time passes: *Her beauty had not faded with the passage of time.*

pas•sage•way /ˈpæsɪdʒˌweɪ/ noun [C] a passage from one room or place to another =PASSAGE

pas•sen•ger /ˈpæsɪndʒər/ noun [C] ★★ someone who travels in a vehicle, aircraft, train, or ship but is not the driver or one of the people who works on it

pas•ser•by /ˌpæsərˈbaɪ/ (plural **pass•ers•by** /ˌpæsərzˈbaɪ/) noun [C] someone who is walking past a place

pass•ing¹ /ˈpæsɪŋ/ adj **1** moving past: *He was found by a passing motorist.* **2** lasting only a short time, and usually not very important or serious

pass•ing² /ˈpæsɪŋ/ noun [U] the process by which time passes: *Even with the passing of time, nothing had happened to change his view.*

PHRASE **in passing** if you say something in passing, you mention it while you are talking about something else

pas•sion /ˈpæʃ(ə)n/ noun ★

1 [C/U] a powerful emotion such as love or anger: *She spoke with great passion about the plight of the refugees.*

2 [C/U] a very strong feeling of sexual love: *I was suddenly seized by **an** overwhelming **passion for** him.*

3 [C] a strong enthusiasm or interest: ***a passion for classical music***

pas•sion•ate /ˈpæʃ(ə)nət/ adj **1** showing or expressing powerful emotions or very strong beliefs **2** involving or affected by very strong feelings of sexual excitement —**pas•sion•ate•ly** adv

pas•sive /ˈpæsɪv/ adj ★★

1 accepting what happens without trying to change events or react to things: *a helpless and passive victim*

2 *linguistics* in a passive sentence, the subject is the person or thing that is affected by the action of the verb. "He was examined by another doctor" is a passive sentence. → ACTIVE 3

—**pas•sive•ly** adv

pas•sive, the /ˈpæsɪv/ or **ˌpassive ˈvoice, the** noun [singular] *linguistics* the passive form of a verb

ˌpassive ˈsmoking noun [U] the act of breathing other people's tobacco smoke into your lungs

Pass•o•ver /ˈpæsˌoʊvər/ noun [C/U] a Jewish religious festival that lasts for seven or eight days in March or April

pass•port /ˈpɑspɔrt/ noun [C] ★

1 an official document that contains your photograph and shows which country you are a citizen of: *Bill has a Canadian passport.*

2 a passport to sth something that makes it possible for you to achieve something good: *In those days a university degree was a passport to a secure job.*

pass•word /ˈpæsˌwɜrd/ noun [C] **1** a secret word or phrase that you need in order to get into a room, building, or area **2** *computing* a set of numbers or letters that you have to type in order to use a computer system

past¹ /pæst/ adv, preposition ★★★

1 passing sb/sth moving near someone or something and then beyond them: *I walked past several hotels on my way to the gas station.* ♦ *She heard music coming from inside the van as it drove past.*

2 after a particular time later than a particular time: *It was **past midnight** by the time we arrived.*

3 farther away than a place farther than a particular place along a road, path, river, etc.: *Turn right a mile past the graveyard and you'll see the church.*

4 after a particular stage used for saying that someone or something has passed a particular stage or point: *I never got past the sixth grade at school.* ♦ *He was past his prime as a player by then.*

5 when time passes used for saying that a period of time passes: *The months went past, and still no word from her.*

6 used for saying the time used for saying what time it is when it is not more than thirty minutes after one, two, etc. o'clock: *It's a quarter past three.* ♦ *It's exactly ten past three* (=3:10).

→ PUT

past² /pæst/ noun ★★★

1 the past [singular] the time before the present, and everything that happened then: *Archaeology helps us to understand the past.* ♦ *He has made similar promises **in the past**.*

2 [C] all the things that someone has done before now: *My past as a player has helped me in my career as a coach.*

3 the past [singular] *linguistics* the form of a verb that is used for describing states that existed or things that happened before the present time

past³ /pæst/ adj ★★★

1 happening or existing in the period immediately before now: *He has spent the past two weeks traveling around the country.*

2 happening or existing at any earlier time: *He is a past president of the union.* ♦ *I know from **past experience** that this work is very time-consuming.*

3 ended, or no longer existing: *My running days are long past.*

pas•ta /ˈpɑstə/ noun [C/U] an Italian food made in many different shapes from flour and water, and sometimes eggs

paste¹ /peɪst/ noun [U] **1** a glue that is used for making something stick to a surface **2** a food that is made by crushing meat, fish, or vegetables. It is spread on bread or added to other food in cooking.

paste² /peɪst/ verb [I/T] **1** to glue paper onto a surface using paste **2** *computing* to copy or move words, pictures, etc. on a computer screen from one place to another

pas•teur•ized /ˈpæstʃəˌraɪzd/ adj a pasteurized liquid such as milk has been heated to a temperature that kills all the harmful bacteria —**pas•teur•i•za•tion** /ˌpæstʃərɪˈzeɪʃ(ə)n/ noun [U]

pas•time /ˈpæsˌtaɪm/ noun [C] something that you do regularly for fun in your free time

pas•tor /ˈpæstər/ noun [C] a priest in some Christian churches

pas•tor•al /ˈpæst(ə)rəl/ adj **1** relating to the

P

work that a priest or other religious leader does to help and advise people **2** *literary* relating to life in the countryside

ˌpast ˈparticiple noun [C] *linguistics* the form of a verb that is used for making perfect tenses and passive forms of verbs. Past participles are also sometimes used as adjectives, for example "cooked" in the phrase "cooked vegetables."

ˌpast ˈperfect, the noun [singular] *linguistics* a verb tense that is formed in English with "had" and a past participle. It is used to express an action that was completed before a particular time in the past, for example "had finished" in the sentence "She offered to help but I had already finished."

pas•tra•mi /pəˈstrɑmi/ noun [U] cooked BEEF with a strong flavor that is usually cut into thin pieces and served cold in sandwiches

pas•try /ˈpeɪstri/ noun **1** [U] a food made by mixing flour, fat, and water. The mixture is rolled flat and used for making PIES and other food. **2** [C] a type of cake made from sweet pastry

ˌpast ˈtense, the noun [singular] *linguistics* the form of a verb that is used for expressing what existed or happened in the past, for example "lived" in the sentence "We lived in France until I was seven."

pas•ture /ˈpærstʃə/ noun [C/U] land covered with grass where sheep or cows are kept

pas•ty /ˈpeɪsti/ adj looking pale and not very healthy

pat¹ /pæt/ verb [T] to touch a person or animal gently several times with a flat hand in a friendly way

pat² /pæt/ noun [C] the action of gently touching a person or animal several times with a flat hand in a friendly way

PHRASE **a pat on the back** *informal* praise for having done something good

pat³ /pæt/ adj pat answers or explanations sound as though they have been used many times before and are not sincere

patch¹ /pætʃ/ noun [C]

1 piece of cloth	4 cover for eye
2 different part of sth	5 piece of software
3 piece of ground	

1 a piece of cloth that you sew over a hole in clothes, or over a part where holes might form **2** an area that is different from what surrounds it: *There were damp patches on the ceiling.* **3** a piece of ground, especially one where you grow fruit or vegetables, or where a particular plant grows: *a patch of grass* **4** a cover that you wear over an injured eye **5** *computing* a piece of software that you add to a computer program in order to improve it or remove a fault

patch² /pætʃ/ verb [T] to cover a hole in clothes by sewing a patch over it

PHRASAL VERB **ˌpatch sth ˈup** to repair something quickly and not very well

patch•work /ˈpætʃˌwɜrk/ noun **1** [singular] something that consists of many different parts **2** [U] the art of sewing pieces of cloth of different colors together to make a pattern or picture

patch•y /ˈpætʃi/ adj **1** happening or existing in some places but not in other places: *patchy rain* **2** not detailed enough or complete enough to be useful: *a patchy knowledge of Spanish history* **3** if someone's performance or work is patchy, it is good sometimes but not always

pâ•té /pɑˈteɪ/ noun [C/U] a soft food made from meat, fish, or vegetables that you spread on bread

pat•ent¹ /ˈpæt(ə)nt/ noun [C] an official document that gives someone who has invented something the legal right to make or sell that thing for a particular period of time, and prevents anyone else from doing so

pat•ent² /ˈpæt(ə)nt/ verb [T] to get a patent for something

pat•ent³ /ˈpæt(ə)nt, ˈpeɪt(ə)nt/ adj extremely obvious —**pat•ent•ly** /ˈpeɪt(ə)ntli/ adv

ˌpatent ˈleather noun [U] very shiny leather, used for making bags and shoes

pa•ter•nal /pəˈtɜrn(ə)l/ adj **1** relating to being a father **2** a paternal relative is related to you through your father **3** typical of a kind and caring father —**pa•ter•nal•ly** adv

pa•ter•ni•ty /pəˈtɜrnəti/ noun [U] *legal* the fact of being the father of a child

paˈternity ˌleave noun [U] a period of time when a father is allowed to be away from work after the birth of his child

path /pæθ/ noun [C] ★★★

1 a way from one place to another that people can walk along: *Amy walked up the path to the house.* → ROAD

2 a way from one place to another passing through a lot of people or objects: *Police tried to* ***clear a path through*** *the rush hour traffic.*

3 the direction that someone or something is moving in: *She ran into the path of an oncoming car.*

4 the way that someone takes to achieve something, or the way that their life develops: *Our lives began to follow separate paths.*

PHRASE **our/your/their paths cross** if two people's paths cross, they meet each other by chance → BEATEN

pa•thet•ic /pəˈθetɪk/ adj **1** useless or not effective in an annoying way **2** if someone or something looks or sounds pathetic, you feel sympathy for them = PITIFUL —**pa•thet•i•cal•ly** /pəˈθetɪkli/ adv

path•o•log•i•cal /ˌpæθəˈlɑdʒɪk(ə)l/ adj **1** pathological behavior or feelings are not based on ordinary practical reasons, and cannot be controlled by the person experiencing them **2** relating to pathology —**path•o•log•i•cal•ly** /ˌpæθəˈlɑdʒɪkli/ adv

pa•thol•o•gist /pəˈθɑlədʒɪst/ noun [C] a scientist who studies the causes of diseases and how they affect people, especially one who studies the causes of a person's death

pa•thol•o•gy /pəˈθɑlədʒi/ noun [U] the study of the causes of diseases and how they affect people

pa•thos /ˈpeɪˌθɑs/ noun [U] a quality in a person or situation that makes you feel sad or sorry for them

path•way /ˈpæθˌweɪ/ noun [C] a PATH that you can walk on

P

pa·tience /ˈpeɪʃəns/ noun [U] ★
1 the ability to remain calm and not get angry, especially when something is annoying or takes too long: *I'm afraid I have no patience with people like them.* ♦ *After waiting for an hour, I was beginning to **run out of patience*** (=stop having any). ♦ *She was quickly **losing patience with** the whole project.*
2 the ability to continue doing something for a long time without losing interest: *Photography **requires** a lot of **patience**.*

pa·tient¹ /ˈpeɪʃənt/ noun [C] ★★★ someone who is receiving medical treatment

pa·tient² /ˈpeɪʃ(ə)nt/ adj ★★ someone who is patient is able to wait for a long time or deal with a difficult situation without becoming angry or upset ≠ IMPATIENT: *Susan's very **patient with** the children.* —**pa·tient·ly** adv

pat·i·o /ˈpætioʊ/ noun [C] a flat area covered with stone or brick at the back of a house, where people can sit outside

pa·tri·ot·ic /ˌpeɪtriˈɑtɪk/ adj feeling a lot of love, respect, and duty toward your country ≠ UNPATRIOTIC —**pa·tri·ot** /ˈpeɪtriət/ noun [C], **pa·tri·ot·ism** /ˈpeɪtriəˌtɪzəm/ noun [U]

pa·trol¹ /pəˈtroʊl/ verb [I/T] to move regularly around a place in order to prevent trouble or crime

pa·trol² /pəˈtroʊl/ noun **1** [C] a group of people or vehicles that move regularly around a place in order to prevent trouble or crime **2** [C/U] the movement of a patrol around a place: *Police officers will be on patrol during the carnival.*

pa·trol·man /pəˈtroʊlmən/ (plural **pa·trol·men** /pəˈtroʊlmən/) noun [C] *American* a police officer walks or drives around a particular area

pa·tron /ˈpeɪtrən/ noun [C] **1** *formal* someone who uses a particular restaurant, bar, or other business **2** someone who supports the work of writers, artists, or musicians by giving them money **3** a famous person who supports an organization and allows it to use their name in its advertising

pa·tron·age /ˈpætrənɪdʒ/ noun [U] help or money that is given by a patron

pa·tron·ize /ˈpeɪtrənaɪz/ verb **1** [I/T] to behave or talk in a way that shows that you think that you are more intelligent or important than someone else **2** [T] *formal* to use a restaurant, bar, or other business

pa·tron·iz·ing /ˈpeɪtrəˌnaɪzɪŋ/ adj behaving or speaking in a way that shows that you think that you are more intelligent or important than someone else

ˌpatron ˈsaint noun [C] a SAINT (=a dead holy person) who is believed to protect a particular place, activity, or group of people

pat·ter /ˈpætər/ noun **1** [singular] a series of short quiet sounds caused by something falling onto or hitting a surface, or by someone walking or running along it
2 [singular/U] very fast continuous talk from someone who is entertaining people or trying to sell something

pat·tern /ˈpætərn/ noun [C] ★★★
1 a series of actions or events that together show how things normally happen or are done: *The study examined **patterns of** behavior in young children.* ♦ *The four murders all seemed to **follow** the same **pattern**.*
2 a set of lines, shapes, or colors that are repeated regularly: *a carpet with a pretty pattern*
3 a drawing or shape that you use when you are making something, so that you get the shape and size correct

pat·terned /ˈpætərnd/ adj decorated with a pattern

paunch /pɔntʃ/ noun [C] a fat stomach that a man has

pause¹ /pɔz/ verb ★
1 [I] to stop moving or doing something for a short time before starting again: *She paused at the door and then left.*
2 [I/T] to make a CD, video, or computer program stop for a short time by pressing a button

pause² /pɔz/ noun **1** [C] a short time when someone stops moving or doing something before starting again **2** [U] a button that stops a CD, video, or computer game for a short time

pave /peɪv/ verb [T] to put a hard flat surface on an area of ground, using bricks, blocks of stone, CONCRETE, etc.
PHRASE **pave the way for sth** to create a situation that makes it possible for something important to happen

pave·ment /ˈpeɪvmənt/ noun **1** [U] *American* the surface of a road **2** [C] *British* a SIDEWALK

pa·vil·ion /pəˈvɪljən/ noun [C] **1** a building in a park or outdoor area for people to sit in **2** a building or tent at an exhibit or show

ˈpaving ˌstone noun [C] a flat square piece of stone or CONCRETE that is used for covering a path or area of ground

paw¹ /pɔ/ noun [C] the foot of some animals such as cats, dogs, and bears

paw² /pɔ/ verb [I/T] to touch something several times with a paw

pawn¹ /pɔn/ noun [C] **1** a person who is used by someone who is more powerful so that they can achieve a goal **2** one of the eight least important pieces that each player has in a game of CHESS —*picture* → C16

pawn² /pɔn/ verb [T] to give something valuable to a pawnbroker, so that you can borrow some money

pawn·bro·ker /ˈpɔnˌbroʊkər/ noun [C] someone whose job is to lend money to people in exchange for a valuable object that they can sell if the person does not return the money

pay¹ /peɪ/ (present participle **pay·ing**; past tense and past participle **paid** /peɪd/) verb ★★★

1 buy goods	5 suffer for sth
2 give money for job	+ PHRASES
3 give money owed	+ PHRASAL VERBS
4 have good result	

1 [I/T] to give money in order to buy something: *Let me **pay for** dinner.* ♦ *Will you be **paying by** cash, check, or credit card?* ♦ *Can I **pay in** dollars?* ♦ *There's a reduction if you **pay cash**.* ♦ **pay sb for sth** *Can I pay you for this?*
2 [I/T] to give money to someone for a job

that they do for you or as their salary: **pay sb sth to do sth** *We had to pay them over $300 to fix it.* ♦ **pay sb for sth** *We still haven't paid them for the repairs to the roof.* ♦ *Some of the workers haven't been paid for weeks.* ♦ **pay to have/get sth done** *Now I'll have to pay to get the car fixed.*

3 [I/T] to give money that you owe for something: *Did you **pay the gas bill**?*

4 [I/T] to have a good result: *The message is simple: **crime doesn't pay**.* ♦ **it pays to do sth** *It pays to cover the pool to keep out falling leaves.*

5 [I] to suffer because of something that you have done: *They had made him look like a fool and now they were going to **pay for it**.*

PHRASES **pay attention (to)** to listen to, watch, or think about someone or something very carefully

pay sb a compliment to say something nice about someone

pay the penalty/price for sth to have to deal with the bad effects of something that you have done

pay tribute to sb to say or do something that shows that you respect and admire someone a lot

pay sb/sth a visit to visit someone or something

pay your way to pay for everything that you need or use, instead of allowing or expecting other people to pay for you

PHRASAL VERBS ˌ**pay sb ˈback 1** to give someone the same amount of money that you borrowed from them **2** to do something bad to someone because they have done something bad to you: *She was determined to **pay them back for** the trouble they had caused.*

ˌ**pay ˈoff** if something that you do pays off, it brings you some benefit

ˌ**pay sth ˈoff** to give back all the money that you borrowed in order to buy something: *In another two years, we will have paid off our mortgage.*

ˌ**pay sth ˈout** to spend or pay a lot of money

ˌ**pay ˈup** to pay money that you owe, especially when you are unwilling to pay

pay[2] /peɪ/ noun [U] ★★ money that you receive for doing your job: *They were demanding higher pay.* ♦ *a pay raise* ♦ *vacation pay*

pay·a·ble /ˈpeɪəb(ə)l/ adj an amount of money that is payable must be paid

PHRASE **payable to sb** a check that is payable to someone has that person's name written on it

pay·check /ˈpeɪˌtʃek/ noun [C] a check from your employer for work that you have done

pay·day /ˈpeɪˌdeɪ/ noun [U] the day when you get your salary

pay·ee /ˌpeɪˈi/ noun [C] the person who you pay a check or money to

pay·ment /ˈpeɪmənt/ noun ★★★

1 [C] an amount of money that you pay or receive: *The first payment is due on January 31.*

2 [U] the process of paying money: *We require prompt **payment of** all bills.*

pay·off /ˈpeɪˌɔf/ noun [C] the benefit that you get from doing something

ˈ**pay ˌphone** noun [C] a telephone in a public place that you pay to use

pay·roll /ˈpeɪˌroʊl/ noun [C] a list of all the people that a company employs and the money that each of them earns

PHRASE **on the payroll** employed by a particular company

PBS /ˌpi bi ˈes/ noun [U] Public Broadcasting Service: a U.S. television company that broadcasts programs without advertisements

PC[1] /ˌpi ˈsi/ noun [C] personal computer: a computer that is designed to be used by one person at home or in an office

PC[2] /ˌpi ˈsi/ adj POLITICALLY CORRECT

P.E. /ˌpi ˈi/ noun [U] physical education: a school subject in which you exercise and play sports

pea /pi/ noun [C] a very small round green vegetable that grows in a long narrow POD —*picture* → C11

peace /pis/ noun [U] ★★★

1 a situation in which there is no war between countries or groups: *For many years the agreement maintained peace in Europe.* ♦ *peace talks/negotiations* ♦ *The U.N. Secretary General urged the two sides to **make peace**.* ♦ *The agreement brought **peace between** the two countries.*

2 a calm quiet situation in which you are not annoyed by noise or other people: *He just wanted to read his newspaper **in peace**.* ♦ *It's not the vacation to choose if you're looking for **peace and quiet**.*

3 a state when you are calm and have no worries: *With this type of insurance, you're buying **peace of mind**.*

PHRASE **make (your) peace (with sb)** to end an argument with someone and stop feeling angry toward them

peace·ful /ˈpisf(ə)l/ adj ★

1 not involving war or violence: *talks aimed at finding a **peaceful solution** to the crisis*

2 calm and quiet: *The hotel is set in peaceful surroundings.*

—**peace·ful·ly** adv

peace·keep·er /ˈpiskipər/ noun [C] a soldier in a military force that has been sent to a place in order to prevent war between groups who have been fighting there

—**peace·keep·ing** /ˈpisˌkipɪŋ/ noun [U]

peace·time /ˈpisˌtaɪm/ noun [U] the time when a country is not involved in a war ≠ WARTIME

peach /pitʃ/ noun **1** [C/U] a fruit with a furry yellow-pink skin that is yellow inside and has a large hard seed —*picture* → C10 **2** [U] a yellow-pink color

pea·cock /ˈpiˌkɑk/ noun [C] a large brightly-colored male bird with long blue-green tail feathers that it can spread out and up

peak[1] /pik/ noun [C] ★

1 the time when something is at its highest or greatest level: *The traffic **reaches its peak** at about 8:30 in the morning.*

2 the top of a mountain: *snow-covered peaks* —*picture* → next page

3 *literary* a mountain

4 the flat curved part of a CAP that continues beyond the main part at the front above your eyes

P

peak

peak² /pik/ verb [I] to reach the highest amount, level, or standard before becoming lower

peak³ /pik/ adj **1** a peak period of time is when the largest number of people are doing or using something **2** a peak level of something is when it is highest

peal /pil/ noun [C] **1** a sound of several bells ringing **2** a loud sound of laughter or THUNDER —**peal** verb [I/T]

pea•nut /ˈpinʌt/ noun [C] a type of nut that you can eat that grows under the ground inside a thin shell

ˌpeanut ˈbutter noun [U] a soft food made by crushing peanuts

pea•nuts /ˈpiˌnʌts/ noun [U] *informal* a very small amount of money

pear /per/ noun [C/U] a fruit that is smaller toward the stem end, is white inside, and has yellow, green, or brown skin *—picture* → C10

pearl /pɜrl/ noun [C] a small round jewel that is white and shiny. Pearls grow inside the shells of OYSTERS.

peas•ant /ˈpezənt/ noun [C] a poor person who works on another person's farm or on their own small farm, especially in the past

peat /pit/ noun [U] a type of soil that consists of decaying plants. It can be used as fuel.

peb•ble /ˈpeb(ə)l/ noun [C] a small stone made smooth by water

pe•can /pɪˈkɑn/ noun [C] a sweet nut with a hard thin smooth shell

peck /pek/ verb **1** [I/T] when a bird pecks, or when it pecks something, it moves its beak quickly forward to hit or bite something **2** [T] to kiss someone in a quick light way: *She pecked him on the cheek.* —**peck** noun [C]

pe•cu•liar /pɪˈkjuljər/ adj **1** strange, often in an unpleasant way: *a peculiar smell* **2** especially true or typical of a particular person, thing, or situation: *features of the environment that are peculiar to the tropics*

pe•cu•li•ar•i•ty /pɪˌkjuliˈerəti/ noun [C] **1** a quality or feature that belongs to a particular person, thing, or situation **2** something strange in the way that a person or animal behaves, or in their appearance

pe•cu•liar•ly /pɪˈkjuljərli/ adv **1** in a strange or unusual way: *He's been behaving very peculiarly lately.* **2** in a way that is true or typical of a particular person, thing, or situation: *a peculiarly American attitude* **3** extremely: *a peculiarly difficult problem*

ped•a•gog•i•cal /ˌpedəˈgɑdʒɪk(ə)l/ adj *formal* relating to educational methods and principles

ped•al /ˈped(ə)l/ noun [C] a part of a bicycle, vehicle, or machine that you push with your foot in order to operate it —**ped•al** verb [I/T]

pe•dan•tic /pəˈdæntɪk/ adj *showing disapproval* giving too much importance to details and formal rules, especially of grammar —**pe•dan•ti•cal•ly** /pəˈdæntɪkli/ adv

ped•dle /ˈped(ə)l/ verb [T] **1** to sell something on the street or by going from place to place in order to find customers **2** to sell illegal drugs —**ped•dler** /ˈpedlər/ noun

ped•es•tal /ˈpedɪst(ə)l/ noun [C] a base on which something such as a STATUE stands PHRASE **put sb on a pedestal** to admire or love someone so much that you believe that they have no faults

pe•des•tri•an¹ /pəˈdestriən/ noun [C] someone who is walking, especially in a town or city, instead of driving or riding

pe•des•tri•an² /pəˈdestriən/ adj **1** used by people who are walking **2** ordinary and boring

pe•di•a•tri•cian /ˌpidiəˈtrɪʃ(ə)n/ noun [C] a doctor who deals with children and their illnesses

pe•di•at•rics /ˌpidiˈætrɪks/ noun [U] the part of medical science that deals with children and their illnesses

ped•i•cure /ˈpedɪkjʊr/ noun [C/U] a treatment for your feet and TOENAILS that makes them look and feel good

ped•i•gree¹ /ˈpedɪˌgri/ noun **1** [C] all the past experiences, achievements, and successes of someone or something: *an investment analyst with a remarkable pedigree* **2** [C/U] the parents, grandparents, etc. of an animal

ped•i•gree² /ˈpedɪˌgri/ adj a pedigree animal comes from a family whose members are all of the same type

ped•o•phile /ˈpedoʊˌfaɪl/ noun [C] an adult who is sexually attracted to children —**ped•o•phi•li•a** /ˌpedoʊˈfɪliə/ noun [U]

pee¹ /pi/ verb [I] *informal* to pass liquid waste from your body

pee² /pi/ noun *informal* **1** [singular] the action of passing liquid waste from your body **2** [U] the liquid waste that you pass from your body

peek¹ /pik/ noun [C] a quick look at something: *Emma took a quick peek inside the box.*

peek² /pik/ verb [I] to look at something quickly

peek•a•boo /ˈpik əˌbu/ noun [U] a game that you play with a baby or small child, in which hide your face, then suddenly show your face, saying "peekaboo"

peel¹ /pil/ verb **1** [T] to remove the skin from a fruit or vegetable *—picture* → C2 **2** [I] if something peels, small pieces of it start to fall off: *Paint was peeling off the walls.* PHRASAL VERB **ˌpeel sth ˈoff** to remove a tight or wet piece of clothing

peel² /pil/ noun [U] the skin of a fruit or vegetable

peep¹ /pip/ verb [I] **1** to look at something quickly and secretly **2** to appear from behind or under something: *His head peeped out from under the blanket.*

peep² /pip/ noun [C] a quick look at something

peep•hole /ˈpipˌhoʊl/ noun [C] a small hole in a door that you can see through

peep•ing Tom /ˌpipɪŋ ˈtɑm/ noun [C] someone who enjoys secretly watching other people when they are doing something private in their homes, such as removing their clothes

peer¹ /pɪr/ verb [I] to look very carefully at something because it is difficult to see

peer² /pɪr/ noun [C] someone who is the same age or who belongs to the same social or professional group as another person

ˈpeer ˌpressure noun [U] the influence that other people of your own age or social class have on the way that you behave or dress

peeve¹ /piv/ noun [C] *American* something that annoys you

peeve² /piv/ verb [T] to make someone feel annoyed

peeved /pivd/ adj annoyed

peg¹ /peg/ noun [C] **1** an object that is attached to a wall or door and used for hanging things on **2** an object that is used for fastening things together: *The furniture is built using wooden pegs instead of nails.* **3 peg** or **tent peg** an object that is pushed or hit into the ground to keep a tent in position

peg² /peg/ verb [T] **1** to keep prices, salaries, or amounts at a particular level **2** *informal* to consider someone as being a particular type of person or having particular qualities: *We had him pegged from the start as a liar and a fraud.* **3** to fasten something, or to keep something in position, with pegs

pel•i•can /ˈpelɪkən/ noun [C] a large bird with a bag of skin that hangs from its beak

pel•let /ˈpelət/ noun [C] a small round piece of a substance

pelt¹ /pelt/ verb [T] to throw a lot of things at someone or something: *Some of the players were pelted with cans and bottles.*

pelt² /pelt/ noun [C] the skin or fur of an animal

pel•vic /ˈpelvɪk/ adj relating to your pelvis

pel•vis /ˈpelvɪs/ noun [C] the large circular bones that support the lower part of your back. They are connected to the bones of your legs.

pen¹ /pen/ noun [C] ★★
1 an object that you use for writing or drawing with ink: *a felt-tip pen*
2 a small area with a fence around it, used for keeping animals in

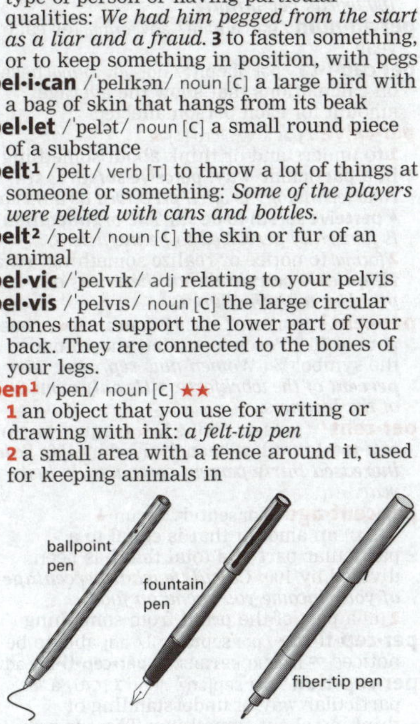

pens

pen² /pen/ verb [T] **1** *mainly journalism* to write something **2** to shut an animal in a small area with a fence around it

pe•nal /ˈpin(ə)l/ adj relating to the punishment of criminals

pe•nal•ize /ˈpin(ə)lˌaɪz/ verb [T] **1** to punish someone for breaking a rule or law **2** to treat someone in an unfair way and make them have a disadvantage: *The tax system seems to penalize people who save for their old age.*

pen•al•ty /ˈpen(ə)lti/ noun [C] ★ a punishment for breaking a rule or law: *the death penalty* ♦ *The maximum* ***penalty for*** *the offense is two years' imprisonment.*

pen•ance /ˈpenəns/ noun [C/U] punishment or suffering that you accept in order to show that you are sorry

pence /pens/ *British* a plural of **penny**

pen•chant /ˈpenʃənt/ noun **a penchant for sth** a feeling of liking something very much or a tendency to do something a lot

pen•cil¹ /ˈpens(ə)l/ noun [C] ★★ a long thin wooden object that you use for writing or drawing: *a colored pencil*

pen•cil² /ˈpens(ə)l/ verb [T] to write or draw something with a pencil
PHRASAL VERB **ˌpencil sb/sth ˈin** to decide or arrange something that may have to be changed later: *The meeting has been penciled in for next Friday.*

ˈpencil ˌsharpener noun [C] an object with a blade inside, used for making a pencil sharper

pen•dant /ˈpendənt/ noun [C] a piece of jewelry that hangs from a chain around your neck

pend•ing¹ /ˈpendɪŋ/ adj **1** waiting to be dealt with **2** likely to happen soon

pend•ing² /ˈpendɪŋ/ preposition *formal* while you are waiting for something to be dealt with

pen•du•lum /ˈpendʒələm/ noun [C] a long thin bar with a weight at the lower end that swings from side to side, usually in order to keep a clock working

pen•e•trate /ˈpenəˌtreɪt/ verb [I/T] to get inside something, get past something, or get through something: *A piece of glass had penetrated the skin.* —**pen•e•tra•tion** /ˌpenəˈtreɪʃ(ə)n/ noun [U]

pen•e•trat•ing /ˈpenəˌtreɪtɪŋ/ adj **1** a person who gives you a penetrating look seems to know what you are thinking=PIERCING **2** intelligent and quick to solve problems or to understand things **3** a penetrating voice or sound is so high or loud that it makes you slightly uncomfortable —**pen•e•trat•ing•ly** adv

pen•guin /ˈpeŋgwɪn/ noun [C] a black and white bird that cannot fly. Penguins live by the ocean, especially around Antarctica. —*picture* → C13

pen•i•cil•lin /ˌpenəˈsɪlɪn/ noun [U] a drug used for treating illnesses that are caused by bacteria

pen•in•su•la /pəˈnɪnsələ/ noun [C] a long piece of land that is mostly surrounded by water but that is joined at one end to a larger area of land —**pen•in•su•lar** adj

pe•nis /ˈpinɪs/ noun [C] the part of a man's

body that he uses for having sex and for getting rid of liquid waste

pen•i•tent /ˈpenɪtənt/ adj sorry for something bad that you have done and willing to change your behavior —**pen•i•tence** noun [U]

pen•i•ten•tia•ry /ˌpenɪˈtenʃəri/ noun [C] a prison

pen•knife /ˈpenˌnaɪf/ (plural **pen•knives** /ˈpenˌnaɪvz/) noun [C] a small knife with one or more blades that fold into the handle

ˈpen ˌname noun [C] a name that a writer uses instead of their real name

pen•nant /ˈpenənt/ noun [C] a long narrow flag with a pointed end, often given as a prize

pen•ni•less /ˈpenɪləs/ adj someone who is penniless has no money

pen•ny /ˈpeni/ noun [C] **1** (plural **pen•nies**) a small coin in the U.S. or Canada that is worth one CENT **2** (plural **pence**) a small unit of money in the U.K. There are 100 pence in one pound.

PHRASES **every penny** all of an amount of money: *The legal case cost them every penny they had.*

not a penny no money at all: *He never gave us a penny.*

ˈpen ˌpal noun [C] someone who you regularly write friendly letters to but have never met

pen•sion /ˈpenʃ(ə)n/ noun [C] ★★ an amount of money that someone receives regularly when they no longer work because of their age or because they are ill

pen•sion•er /ˈpenʃ(ə)nər/ noun [C] someone who receives a pension

pen•sive /ˈpensɪv/ adj someone who is pensive seems to be thinking carefully about something —**pen•sive•ly** adv

pen•ta•gon /ˈpentəˌgɑn/ noun [C] a shape that has five straight sides —*picture* → C8

Pen•ta•gon, the /ˈpentəˌgɑn/ the department of defense in the U.S. government, or the building that belongs to this department

pen•tath•lon /penˈtæθlən/ noun [C] a sports event that consists of five different sports → DECATHLON

pent•house /ˈpentˌhaʊs/ noun [C] an expensive apartment at the top of a tall building

pent-up /ˌpent ˈʌp/ adj pent-up emotions are strong feelings that you have not expressed

pe•nul•ti•mate /pəˈnʌltɪmət/ adj *formal* just before the last in a series

pe•on /ˈpiən/ noun [C] *American humorous* someone who works hard for little money or who feels that they are not respected in their job

peo•ple¹ /ˈpip(ə)l/ noun ★★★

1 [plural] the plural of **person**: *The accident left three people dead and many injured.* ♦ *People were running everywhere.* ♦ *a magazine full of gossip about famous people*

2 the people [plural] ordinary people who are not members of the government or the upper classes: *On this issue, the government has failed to listen to the people.*

3 [C] everyone who belongs to a particular nation, religion, or race: *The Mongols were regarded as a very warlike people.*

PHRASE **of all people** used to express surprise that a particular person did something

peo•ple² /ˈpip(ə)l/ verb **be peopled with** to be filled with a particular type of person

pep¹ /pep/ PHRASAL VERB **ˌpep sb/sth ˈup** *informal* to make someone or something more active and lively

pep² /pep/ noun [U] *informal* lively energy —**pep•py** adj

pep•per¹ /ˈpepər/ noun **1** [U] a black or white powder that adds a strong flavor to food **2** [C] a green, red, or yellow vegetable with small white seeds inside it

pep•per² /ˈpepər/ verb **be peppered with sth** to be full of something: *His conversation was peppered with anti-American comments.*

pep•per•mint /ˈpepərˌmɪnt/ noun **1** [U] a strong fresh flavor that is obtained from a MINT plant and is used in medicines or drinks **2** [C] a piece of candy with a peppermint flavor

pep•per•o•ni /ˌpepəˈroʊni/ noun [U] a type of Italian SAUSAGE

ˈpep ˌrally noun [C] *American* a meeting during which large numbers of people are encouraged to support a school's sports team

ˈpep ˌtalk noun [C] *informal* a talk during which someone encourages you to do something better or to work harder

per /*weak* pə, *strong* pər/ preposition ★ used for stating the rate or cost for each unit of time, quantity, distance, etc.: *I'm charging $20 per hour for the work.* ♦ *Ellen can type 100 words **per minute**.*

per an•num /pər ˈænəm/ adv *formal* for each year

per cap•i•ta /pər ˈkæpɪtə/ adj, adv *formal* based on calculations that show the average amount for each person affected

per•ceive /pərˈsiv/ verb [T] ★

1 to understand or think about something in a particular way: **perceive sb/sth as sth** *New technology is often perceived as a threat.* ♦ **perceive sb/sth to be sth** *The organization is generally perceived to be inefficient.*

2 *formal* to notice or realize something: **+that** *He quickly perceived that there was a problem with the figures.*

per•cent¹ /pərˈsent/ noun [singular] ★★★ one part of 100. Percent is often shown using the symbol %: *Women now represent 50 **percent of** the workforce.* ♦ *He only owns 20% of the business.*

per•cent² /pərˈsent/ adj, adv ★★ equal to part of a total that has been divided by 100: *Sales increased thirty percent compared to last year.*

per•cent•age /pərˈsentɪdʒ/ noun ★

1 [C/U] an amount that is equal to a particular part of a total that has been divided by 100: *Calculate what **percentage of** your income you spend on food.*

2 [C] a part of the profit from something

per•cep•ti•ble /pərˈseptəb(ə)l/ adj able to be noticed ≠ IMPERCEPTIBLE —**per•cep•ti•bly** adv

per•cep•tion /pərˈsepʃən/ noun **1** [C/U] a particular way of understanding or thinking about something: *There is a perception among workers that management only wants to cut costs.* **2** [U] the ability to

P

notice something by seeing, hearing, smelling, etc.

per•cep•tive /pərˈseptɪv/ adj good at noticing or understanding things quickly and easily: *Children are often very perceptive about adults' moods.*

perch¹ /pɜrtʃ/ noun [C] an area or object that a bird uses for resting on

perch² /pɜrtʃ/ verb [I/T] **1** to sit on something that is narrow or small, or to sit on the edge of something **2** to put something high up or on the edge of something, or to be in this position

per•co•late /ˈpɜrkəˌleɪt/ verb [I] if a liquid or gas percolates through a substance, it gradually passes through it —**per•co•la•tion** /ˌpɜrkəˈleɪʃ(ə)n/ noun [U]

per•cus•sion /pərˈkʌʃ(ə)n/ noun [U] musical instruments such as drums that you play by hitting them

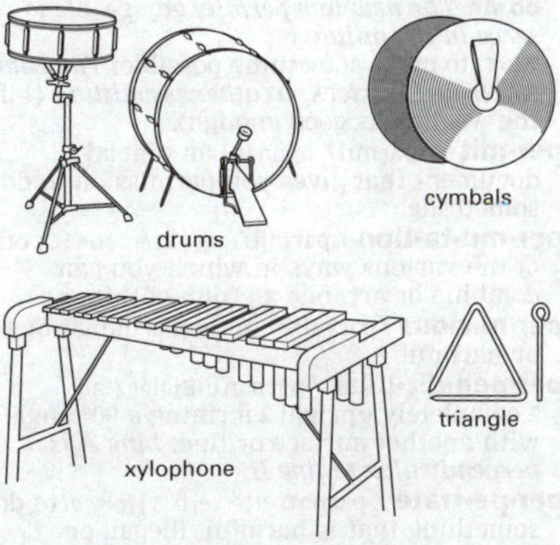

percussion instruments

per•en•ni•al¹ /pəˈreniəl/ adj **1** always existing, or never seeming to change **2** a perennial plant lasts for several years —**per•en•ni•al•ly** adv

per•en•ni•al² /pəˈreniəl/ noun [C] a plant that lasts for several years

per•fect¹ /ˈpɜrfɪkt/ adj ★★
1 as good, accurate, or complete as possible, with no faults = FLAWLESS: *Her English was perfect.* ♦ *These recipes give perfect results every time.*
2 completely appropriate or right = IDEAL: *It seemed like the perfect gift.* ♦ *Their house is absolutely **perfect for** parties.*
3 used for emphasizing what you are saying: *I don't want to share a room with a perfect stranger.*
4 *linguistics* the perfect form of a verb is used for talking about an action that has been completed before the present time
→ PERFECT TENSE

per•fect² /ˈpɜrfɪkt/ verb [T] to make something completely free from faults, or to make it as good as it can be

per•fect, the /ˈpɜrfɪkt/ noun [singular] *linguistics* the PERFECT TENSE

per•fec•tion /pəˈfekʃ(ə)n/ noun [U] a state in which someone or something is perfect

per•fec•tion•ist /pərˈfekʃ(ə)nɪst/ noun [C] someone who always wants things to be done in a perfect way

per•fect•ly /ˈpɜrfɪk(t)li/ adv **1** in a way that could not be better **2** used for emphasizing a particular quality = COMPLETELY

ˈperfect ˌtense, the noun [singular] *linguistics* the form of a verb that is used for talking about an action that has been completed before the present time. It is formed in English with "have" and a past participle. → FUTURE PERFECT, PAST PERFECT, PRESENT PERFECT

per•fo•rat•ed /ˈpɜtfəˌreɪtəd/ adj **1** with a lot of small holes in the surface **2** if an organ or tube inside your body is perforated, it has a small hole or cut in its surface —**per•fo•ra•tion** /ˌpɜrfəˈreɪʃ(ə)n/ noun [C]

per•form /pərˈfɔrm/ verb ★★★
1 [I/T] to do something in front of an audience in order to entertain them: *The opera was first performed in 1992.* ♦ *Akram went on to **perform on stage** in England and India.*
2 [T] to complete an action or activity: *He's a surgeon who has **performed** many heart transplant **operations**.* ♦ *a robot that can **perform** routine **tasks** in the home*
3 [I] to do something with a particular amount of success: *The tires **perform well** in wet or snowy conditions.*

per•form•ance /pəˈfɔrməns/ noun ★★★
1 [C] the act of performing a play, dance, or other form of entertainment: *The first performance of the opera was in 1936.*
2 [C/U] the standard of success that someone or something achieves: *A healthy diet can improve a child's performance in school.* ♦ *We need to test the performance of the equipment.*
3 [C/U] *formal* the process of doing a job or action

per•form•er /pərˈfɔrmər/ noun [C] someone who performs in front of an audience, for example an actor or a musician

per•form•ing arts, the /pərˌfɔrmɪŋ ˈɑrts/ noun [plural] types of art that are performed in front of an audience, such as plays, music, and dance

per•fume /ˈpɜrfjum/ noun **1** [C/U] a liquid with a pleasant smell that you put on your skin **2** [C] *literary* the pleasant smell of something such as a flower or plant —**per•fumed** /pərˈfjumd/ adj

per•haps /pərˈhæps/ adv ★★★
1 *formal* used for saying that you are not certain whether something is true: *I haven't seen them for months – perhaps they've moved away.* ♦ *There were perhaps a dozen women in the audience.*
2 *spoken* used when you are making a suggestion, giving advice, or making a polite request: *You don't look well – perhaps you should go to the doctor.*

per•il /ˈperəl/ noun [U] *literary* serious danger

per•il•ous /ˈperələs/ adj *literary* very dangerous —**per•il•ous•ly** adv

pe•rim•e•ter /pəˈrɪmɪtər/ noun [C] the outer edge of an enclosed area of ground such as a field

pe•ri•od¹ /ˈpɪriəd/ noun [C] ★★★

1 amount of time	4 part of school day
2 symbol in writing	5 for emphasis
3 of woman	

1 an amount of time: *The long dry period ended with heavy rain.* ♦ ***a period of** three months*
2 *American* the symbol . used in writing and printing to show where a sentence ends
3 the time about once a month when a woman who is not pregnant MENSTRUATES (=loses blood)
4 a part of a school day when a particular subject is taught=CLASS
5 *spoken* used for emphasis to show that there is no more to be said about something: *You are not going out tonight, period.*

pe•ri•od² /pɪriəd/ adj typical of a particular historical time: *period costumes/furniture*

pe•ri•od•ic /ˌpɪriˈɑdɪk/ adj happening regularly though not frequently —**pe•ri•od•i•cal•ly** /ˌpɪriˈɑdɪkli/ adv

pe•ri•od•i•cal /ˌpɪriˈɑdɪk(ə)l/ noun [C] a magazine on a particular subject that is published regularly

pe•riph•er•al¹ /pəˈrɪf(ə)rəl/ adj **1** connected with something but not a necessary or important part of it=MARGINAL **2** peripheral areas of a town or country are far from the central area

pe•riph•er•al² /pəˈrɪf(ə)rəl/ noun [C] *computing* a piece of equipment that you can connect to a computer, for example a printer

pe•riph•er•y /pəˈrɪf(ə)ri/ noun [C] the outer part of an area

per•ish /ˈperɪʃ/ verb [I] *literary* to die

per•ish•a•ble /ˈperɪʃəb(ə)l/ adj perishable food decays after a short time

per•ju•ry /ˈpɜrdʒəri/ noun [U] *legal* the crime of lying when you give evidence in a court of law

P

perk¹ /pɜrk/ noun [C] an extra payment or benefit that you get in your job

perk² /pɜrk/
PHRASAL VERBS ˌ**perk (sb) ˈup** if someone perks up, or if something perks them up, they begin to feel happier or more lively
ˌ**perk (sth) ˈup** to become more interesting or exciting, or to make something do this

perk•y /ˈpɜrki/ adj *informal* lively and happy

perm /pɜrm/ noun [C] a chemical treatment for hair that makes straight hair become curly —**perm** verb [T]

per•ma•nent¹ /ˈpɜrmənənt/ adj ★★ happening or existing for a long time, or for all time in the future ≠ TEMPORARY: *The illness can cause permanent blindness.* ♦ *They've offered me a room until I can find something more permanent.* ♦ *I don't have a permanent job.* —**per•ma•nent•ly** adv: *the decision to close down the factory permanently*

per•ma•nent² /ˈpɜrmənənt/ noun [C] *American* a PERM

per•me•ate /ˈpɜrmiˌeɪt/ verb [I/T] to spread gradually through every part of something

per•mis•si•ble /pərˈmɪsəb(ə)l/ adj *formal* if something is permissible, you are allowed to do it

per•mis•sion /pərˈmɪʃ(ə)n/ noun [U] ★★ the right to do something that is given to you by someone in authority: *You are not allowed to camp here without permission.* ♦ *Children should **ask** their parents' **permission** before making long distance phone calls.* ♦ **permission to do sth** *Who gave you permission to come in here?*

> **Words often used with permission**
>
> *Verbs often used with* ***permission***
> - **ask, request, seek** + PERMISSION: ask someone to allow you to do something
> - **gain, get, obtain, receive** + PERMISSION: be allowed to do something
> - **give, grant** + PERMISSION: allow someone to do something
> - **deny, refuse** + PERMISSION: not allow someone to do something

per•mis•sive /pərˈmɪsɪv/ adj allowing people a lot of freedom to behave as they want to

per•mit¹ /pərˈmɪt/ verb ★★
1 [T] *formal* to allow someone to do something, or to allow something to happen: *The use of cellphones is not permitted inside the aircraft.* ♦ **permit sb to do sth** *The new law permits gay people to serve in the military.*
2 [I/T] to make something possible: *The game starts at 11 o'clock, weather permitting* (=if the weather is good enough).

per•mit² /ˈpɜrmɪt/ noun [C] an official document that gives you permission to do something

per•mu•ta•tion /ˌpɜrmjʊˈteɪʃ(ə)n/ noun [C] one of the various ways in which you can combine or arrange a group of things

per•ni•cious /pərˈnɪʃəs/ adj *formal* dangerous or harmful

per•pen•dic•u•lar /ˌpɜrpənˈdɪkjələr/ adj **1** completely upright **2** forming a 90° angle with another surface or line: *Line A is perpendicular to line B.*

per•pe•trate /ˈpɜrpəˌtreɪt/ verb [T] *formal* to do something that is harmful, illegal, or dishonest —**per•pe•tra•tor** noun [C]

per•pet•u•al /pərˈpetʃuəl/ adj happening or continuing all the time —**per•pet•u•al•ly** adv

per•pet•u•ate /pərˈpetʃueɪt/ verb [T] to make a situation or process continue for a long time, especially a bad or dangerous situation

per•plexed /pərˈplekst/ adj confused because you cannot understand something =BEWILDERED

per se /ˌpɜr ˈseɪ/ adv *formal* considered by itself: used for emphasizing that you are not considering something in relation to anything else: *The job, per se, isn't particularly interesting, but it pays well.*

per•se•cute /ˈpɜrsɪˌkjut/ verb [T] to treat someone very badly because of their race, religion, or political beliefs —**per•se•cu•tion** /ˌpɜrsɪˈkjuʃ(ə)n/ noun [U], **per•se•cu•tor** noun [C]

per•se•ver•ance /ˌpɜrsəˈvɪrəns/ noun [U] a determined attitude that makes you continue trying to achieve something that is difficult

per•se•vere /ˌpɜsəˈvɪr/ verb [I] to continue trying to achieve something that is difficult

per•sist /pərˈsɪst/ verb [I] **1** to continue to do or say something in a determined way, especially something bad or annoying **2** *formal* to continue to exist: *Despite* *yesterday's stock market falls, optimism persists among investors.*

per•sist•ent /pər'sɪstənt/ adj **1** continuing to do something in a determined way, especially something bad or annoying **2** continuing to exist —**per•sist•ence** noun [U], **per•sist•ent•ly** adv

per•son /'pɜrs(ə)n/ noun [C] ★★★ an individual human. The plural is **people**, but in formal or official language the form **persons** is used: *Every single person in the room stopped talking.* ♦ *Some people hate camping.* ♦ *Voting is obligatory for all persons between the ages of 18 and 70.*

PHRASES **do sth in person** to do something by going to a place yourself, rather than by writing, telephoning, or sending someone else: *You have to pick up your tickets in person.*

first/second/third person *linguistics* the forms of pronouns and verbs that show who is being referred to. People use the **first person** (I/we) to refer to themselves, the **second person** (you) to refer to the person or people that they are talking to, and the **third person** (he/she/they) to refer to anyone else.

per•so•na /pər'soʊnə/ noun [C] the part of your personality that you deliberately show to most people

per•son•a•ble /'pɜrs(ə)nəb(ə)l/ adj friendly, or nice

per•son•al /'pɜrsən(ə)l/ adj ★★★

1 involving you or belonging to you, not to anyone else: *My own personal view is that boxing should be banned.* ♦ *Most writers use* ***personal experience*** *as the basis for their novels.* ♦ *Many of Tim's* ***personal belongings*** *had been stolen.*

2 private and not known or available to most people: *This is* ***a personal matter*** *and does not concern you.* ♦ *She quit her job for* ***personal reasons.*** ♦ ***My personal life*** *is not your concern.*

3 aimed at one particular person, in an unfriendly or offensive way: *He saw her comments as a personal attack.*

4 done by a person directly, instead of by a representative: *The Dixie Chicks will be making a personal appearance at the awards ceremony.* ♦ *the president's personal involvement in the project*

,personal com'puter noun [C] the usual type of computer, designed to be used by one person on his or her desk

per•son•al•i•ty /,pɜrsə'næləti/ noun ★★

1 [C/U] the part of a person that makes them behave in a particular way in social situations: *He has a very outgoing personality and makes friends very easily.* ♦ *a personality disorder*

2 [U] confidence and lively behavior that make people like you and consider you interesting: *Mary has lots of personality.*

3 [C] a famous or well-known person =CELEBRITY: *a TV personality*

> Words often used with **personality**
>
> *Adjectives often used with* ***personality*** *(sense 1)*
>
> ■ **charismatic, dominant, dynamic, engaging, extroverted, forceful, outgoing, strong +** PERSONALITY: used about personalities that have a strong effect on other people

per•son•al•ized /'pɜrsən(ə)laɪzd/ adj made or changed in order to be especially appropriate for a particular person

per•son•al•ly /'pɜrsənəli/ adv ★

1 *spoken* used for emphasizing that you are giving your own opinion: *Personally, I think we should stick with our original plan.* ♦ *I personally prefer pizza to hamburgers.*

2 used for emphasizing that you are referring to a particular person, not to anyone else: *Were you personally involved in this decision?* ♦ *I have never met the man personally.*

3 in a way that is intended for you only, instead of for a group of people that you belong to: *The invitation was made to me personally, not to the committee.*

PHRASE **take sth personally** to feel that a failure or unpleasant situation is your fault and to be upset about it

,personal 'organizer noun [C] a small book or simple computer that you use for keeping addresses, telephone numbers, and dates

,personal 'pronoun noun [C] *linguistics* a pronoun such as "I," "you," "them," or "it" that refers to a specific person, thing, or group of people or things

,personal 'trainer noun [C] someone whose job is to show you how to exercise effectively —*picture* → C16

per•son•i•fy /pər'sɑnə,faɪ/ verb [T] to be a very clear example of a particular quality: *He personifies Russia's dynamic new business class.* —**per•son•i•fi•ca•tion** /pər,sɑnəfɪ'keɪʃ(ə)n/ noun [C/U]

per•son•nel /,pɜrsə'nel/ noun **1** [plural] the people who work for a company or organization **2** [U] the department in an organization that is responsible for taking care of all the people who work there, and for choosing new workers =HUMAN RESOURCES

per•spec•tive /pər'spektɪv/ noun ★

1 [C] a way of thinking about something: *You can call it brave or foolish, depending on your perspective.*

2 [U] a sensible way of judging something without making it seem too important: *It's important to* ***keep things in perspective*** *and not worry too much.* ♦ *This kind of tragedy* ***puts*** *a mere basketball game* ***into perspective.***

3 [U] a method of showing distance in a picture by making far away objects smaller

per•spi•ra•tion /,pɜrspə'reɪʃ(ə)n/ noun [U] the liquid that your skin produces when you are hot, sick, or nervous =SWEAT

per•spire /pər'spaɪr/ verb [I] to produce liquid on your skin as a result of being hot, sick, or nervous =SWEAT

per•suade /pər'sweɪd/ verb [T] ★★

1 to make someone agree to do something by giving them reasons why they should: *He did finally come with us, although it took a long time to persuade him.* ♦ **persuade sb to do sth** *Nobody could persuade her to change her mind.*

2 to make someone believe that something

P

is true=CONVINCE: **persuade sb (that)** *I managed to persuade him that it was not his fault.* ♦ **persuade sb of sth** *There was no way she could persuade him of her innocence.*

per·sua·sion /pərˈsweɪʒ(ə)n/ noun [U] the process of persuading someone to do or believe something

per·sua·sive /pərˈsweɪsɪv/ adj good at making people agree to do or believe what you want them to —**per·sua·sive·ly** adv

per·tain /pərˈteɪn/ PHRASAL VERB **perˈtain to sth** *formal* to be directly related to something

per·ti·nent /ˈpɜrt(ə)nənt/ adj *formal* relevant

per·turbed /pərˈtɜrbd/ adj worried, or upset ≠ UNPERTURBED —**per·turb** verb [T]

pe·ruse /pəˈruz/ verb [T] *formal* to read something —**pe·rus·al** noun [C/U]

per·vade /pərˈveɪd/ verb [T] *formal* to spread through the whole of something

per·va·sive /pərˈveɪsɪv/ adj spreading through the whole of something: *a pervasive culture of official corruption*

per·verse /pərˈvɜs/ adj behaving in an unreasonable way, by deliberately doing what people do not expect you to do —**per·verse·ly** adv

per·ver·sion /pərˈvɜrʒ(ə)n/ noun [C/U] **1** sexual behavior that is thought to be wrong or not normal **2** the process of changing something that is good or right into something that is bad or wrong

per·vert¹ /pərˈvɜrt/ verb [T] to change something that is good or right into something that is bad or wrong

per·vert² /ˈpɜrˌvɜrt/ noun [C] an insulting word for someone whose sexual behavior is thought to be wrong or not normal

per·vert·ed /pərˈvɜrtəd/ adj relating to sexual behavior that is considered to be wrong or not normal

pes·ky /ˈpeski/ adj *informal* annoying

pe·so /ˈpeɪsoʊ/ noun [C] the unit of money used in the Philippines and several countries in South and Central America

pes·si·mism /ˈpesəˌmɪzəm/ noun [U] the attitude of someone who expects the worst thing to happen in every situation ≠ OPTIMISM

pes·si·mist /ˈpesəmɪst/ noun [C] someone who expects the worst thing to happen in every situation ≠ OPTIMIST

pes·si·mis·tic /ˌpesəˈmɪstɪk/ adj expecting the worst thing to happen in every situation ≠ OPTIMISTIC: *Doctors are pessimistic about his chances of making a full recovery.*

pest /pest/ noun [C] **1** *informal* someone who keeps annoying you=NUISANCE **2** an insect or small animal that damages plants or supplies of food

pes·ter /ˈpestər/ verb [T] to keep annoying someone by asking them for something, or by asking them to do something=NAG

pes·ti·cide /ˈpestɪˌsaɪd/ noun [C] a chemical used for killing insects that damage crops

pet¹ /pet/ noun [C] ★ an animal that you keep in your home and take care of: *a pet dog*

pet² /pet/ verb **1** [T] to touch an animal in a gentle way that shows that you like them **2** [I/T] to hold and touch someone in a sexual way

pet³ /pet/ adj liked more than anything else: *Getting kids to do more sport is one of his pet projects.*

pet·al /ˈpet(ə)l/ noun [C] one of the colored parts around the center of a flower

pe·ter /ˈpitər/ PHRASAL VERB **ˌpeter ˈout** to gradually become smaller or weaker before ending or disappearing completely

pe·tite /pəˈtit/ adj a petite woman is small and thin in an attractive way

pe·ti·tion¹ /pəˈtɪʃ(ə)n/ noun [C] a document that is signed by many people that asks someone in authority to do something

pe·ti·tion² /pəˈtɪʃ(ə)n/ verb [I/T] to ask someone in authority to do something by using a petition

ˌpet ˈpeeve noun [C] *American* something that you dislike very much

pet·ri·fied /ˈpetrɪˌfaɪd/ adj extremely frightened

pet·rol /ˈpetrəl/ noun [U] *British* GASOLINE

pe·tro·le·um /pəˈtroʊliəm/ noun [U] oil that is found under the ground or under the bottom of the ocean. It is used for making gas for cars and chemical products.

pet·ty /ˈpeti/ adj **1** not important and not worth worrying about: *petty arguments* **2** behaving badly toward other people, because you care too much about something that is not really important **3** minor: *a petty criminal/thief/offender*

pet·u·lant /ˈpetʃələnt/ adj behaving in an unreasonable way because you cannot get what you want —**pet·u·lance** noun [U]

pew¹ /pju/ noun [C] a long wooden seat in a church

pew² /pju/ interjection *American spoken* used for saying that you smell something unpleasant

PG /ˌpi ˈdʒi/ adj parental guidance: used for describing a movie that contains scenes, subjects, or language that is considered inappropriate for children unless they have a parent with them

PG-13 /ˌpi dʒi θɜrˈtin/ adj parental guidance 13: used for describing a movie that contains scenes, subjects, or language that is considered inappropriate for children who are younger than 13 unless they have a parent with them

pH /ˌpi ˈeɪtʃ/ noun [singular/U] *science* a number that describes how ACID or ALKALINE a substance is: *Most unpolluted rainwater has a pH of around 5.0.*

phan·tom¹ /ˈfæntəm/ noun [C] the spirit of a dead person that someone sees=GHOST

phan·tom² /ˈfæntəm/ adj imagined, not real: *Sailors often see phantom ships in the fog.*

phar·ma·ceu·ti·cal /ˌfɑrməˈsutɪk(ə)l/ adj relating to medicines and drugs: *the pharmaceutical industry*

phar·ma·cist /ˈfɑrməsɪst/ noun [C] someone whose job is to prepare and sell medicines

phar·ma·col·o·gy /ˌfɑrməˈkɑlədʒi/ noun [U] the scientific study of medicines and drugs —**phar·ma·col·o·gist** noun [C]

phar·ma·cy /ˈfɑrməsi/ noun [C] a place where medicines are prepared and sold

phase¹ /feɪz/ noun [C] ★ a particular period of time during the development of something: *The first **phase** of the project will*

P

be completed by 2010. ♦ *Tim* ***went through a phase*** *of being aggressive at school.* ♦ *a depressing* ***phase in*** *our history*

phase² /feɪz/

PHRASAL VERBS ˌ**phase sth ˈin** to gradually start using something: *The new regulations can be phased in over six months.*

ˌ**phase sth ˈout** to gradually stop using something: *Over the following three years, the use of the drug will be phased out.*

Ph.D. /ˌpi eɪtʃˈdi/ noun [C] Doctor of Philosophy: the highest university degree, or someone who has this degree

pheas•ant /ˈfezənt/ noun [C/U] a large bird with a long tail that is hunted for sport and food, or the meat from this bird

phe•nom•e•nal /fəˈnɑmɪn(ə)l/ adj extremely impressive or surprising: *the phenomenal success of the movie* —**phe•nom•e•nal•ly** adv

phe•nom•e•non /fəˈnɑməˌnɑn/ (plural **phe•nom•e•na** /fəˈnɑmənə/) noun [C] **1** an event or situation: *Some people see "reality TV" shows as a disturbing new phenomenon.* **2** someone or something that is very impressive or surprising: *a publishing phenomenon*

phew /fju/ interjection *spoken* used for showing that you feel hot, tired, or no longer worried about something: *Phew, that's a relief!*

phi•lan•thro•pist /fɪˈlænθrəpɪst/ noun [C] someone who spends a lot of their money on things that benefit society or poor people —**phil•an•throp•ic** /ˌfɪlənˈθrɑpɪk/ adj

phil•is•tine /ˈfɪlɪˌstin/ noun [C] *showing disapproval* someone who does not understand or care about serious art, literature, or music

phi•los•o•pher /fɪˈlɑsəfər/ noun [C] someone who studies and writes about the meaning of things such as life, knowledge, or beliefs

phil•o•soph•i•cal /ˌfɪləˈsɑfɪk(ə)l/ adj **1** able to accept an unpleasant situation calmly because you know that you cannot change it **2** relating to philosophy: *a philosophical argument* —**phil•o•soph•i•cal•ly** /ˌfɪləˈsɑfɪkli/ adv

phi•los•o•phy /fɪˈlɑsəfi/ noun ★
1 [C] a belief that influences someone's decisions and behavior: *the latest philosophies of management* ♦ *My philosophy is "live and let live."*
2 [C/U] the study of theories about the meaning of things such as life, knowledge, and beliefs, or a particular theory that results from this study: *He studied politics and philosophy.* ♦ *a professor of philosophy* ♦ *Eastern philosophies*

phlegm /flem/ noun [U] a thick substance that you get in your nose and throat, especially when you have a cold

phleg•mat•ic /flegˈmætɪk/ adj able to be calm in a dangerous or frightening situation

pho•bi•a /ˈfoʊbiə/ noun [C] a very strong feeling of fear or dislike for something: *a phobia about spiders* —**pho•bic** adj

phone¹ /foʊn/ noun [C] ★★★ a telephone: *The* ***phone rang*** *five times in the next hour.* ♦ *I called his house but his mother* ***answered the phone*** (=picked it up when it rang). ♦ *Our teenagers spend hours* ***on the phone*** (=using the phone) *every day.* ♦ *We take orders* ***by phone*** *or by e-mail.* → CELLPHONE

phone² /foʊn/ verb [I/T] ★ to use a telephone to call someone = CALL

ˈ**phone ˌbook** noun [C] a book that contains lists of names of people, businesses, and organizations with their addresses and phone numbers = TELEPHONE DIRECTORY

ˈ**phone ˌbooth** noun [C] a small structure with a telephone inside that you pay to use

ˈ**phone ˌbox** noun [C] *British* a PHONE BOOTH

ˈ**phone ˌcall** noun [C] an act of telephoning someone: *Excuse me, I have to make a phone call.*

ˈ**phone ˌcard** noun [C] a plastic card that you can use instead of money for paying for a telephone call

ˈ**phone ˌnumber** noun [C] a series of numbers that you press on a telephone in order to call someone

pho•net•ic /fəˈnetɪk/ adj *linguistics* relating to the sounds used in speech, or using special symbols to show speech sounds: *the phonetic alphabet* —**pho•net•i•cal•ly** /fəˈnetɪkli/ adv

pho•net•ics /fəˈnetɪks/ noun [U] *linguistics* the study of the sounds that are used in speech

pho•ny /ˈfoʊni/ adj *informal* **1** not real and intended to trick people **2** pretending to be friendly, smart, kind, etc. in order to impress or trick people = INSINCERE

pho•to /ˈfoʊtoʊ/ noun [C] ★★ a PHOTOGRAPH: ***photos of*** *her grandkids* ♦ *Shall I* ***take a photo*** *of the cathedral?*

pho•to•cop•i•er /ˈfoʊtoʊˌkɑpiər/ noun [C] a COPIER

pho•to•cop•y /ˈfoʊtoʊˌkɑpi/ noun [C] a copy made by a photocopier —**pho•to•cop•y** verb [T]

pho•to•gen•ic /ˌfoʊtoʊˈdʒenɪk/ adj someone who is photogenic looks good in photographs

pho•to•graph¹ /ˈfoʊtəˌgræf/ noun [C] ★★★ a picture of something that you make with a camera: *black and white photographs* ♦ *These are* ***photographs of*** *the Earth, taken from space.* ♦ *We* ***took lots of photographs*** *on vacation.*

pho•to•graph² /ˈfoʊtəˌgræf/ verb [T] to make a photograph of someone or something: *They were photographed shaking hands.*

pho•tog•ra•pher /fəˈtɑgrəfər/ noun [C] someone who takes photographs, especially as their job

pho•to•graph•ic /ˌfoʊtəˈgræfɪk/ adj relating to photographs or photography: *photographic images/equipment*

pho•tog•ra•phy /fəˈtɑgrəfi/ noun [U] **1** the skill, job, or process of taking photographs **2** the photographic images in books, magazines, movies, and television: *fashion/wildlife photography*

ˈ**photo opporˌtunity** noun [C] an occasion when a politician or famous person appears in public and people take photographs of them

phra•sal verb /ˌfreɪz(ə)l ˈvɜrb/ noun [C] *linguistics* a combination of words that is used like a verb. It consists of a verb and an adverb or preposition, for example "give in" or "come up with."

phrase¹ /freɪz/ noun [C] ★★★
1 a group of words that are used together

P

in a fixed expression: *Several of those interviewed used the phrase "being my own boss."*
2 *linguistics* a group of words that form a unit within a CLAUSE (=a group of words containing a subject and verb)

phrase² /freɪz/ verb [T] to express something in a particular way in speech or writing

ˈphrase ˌbook noun [C] a small book that contains useful words and phrases in a particular foreign language

phys·ic·al¹ /ˈfɪzɪk(ə)l/ adj ★★★
1 relating to your body rather than to your mind: *children who have physical disabilities* ♦ *hard **physical work*** → MENTAL
2 real and able to be seen, touched, or felt: *There was no physical evidence to connect Whitman with the crime.*
3 used about activities or relationships that involve people touching or hitting each other a lot: *Football is a very physical game.* ♦ *There was very little **physical contact*** (=touching) *between the mother and her children.*
4 involving sex: *Did they have **a physical relationship**?*

phys·ic·al² /ˈfɪzɪk(ə)l/ noun [C] a PHYSICAL EXAMINATION

ˌphysical eduˈcation noun [U] P.E.

ˌphysical examiˈnation noun [C] a medical examination to find out whether someone is healthy enough to do something such as a particular job

phys·i·cal·ly /ˈfɪzɪkli/ adv **1** in a way that is related to your body or appearance: *physically attractive* ♦ *physically active/fit* **2** used about things in the real world, rather than in your imagination or in stories: *It is physically impossible to be in two places at the same time.*

phys·i·cal·ly chal·lenged /ˌfɪzɪkli ˈtʃælɪndʒd/ adj disabled in a way that prevents you from using part of your body properly =DISABLED

ˌphysical ˈscience noun [C] a science such as geography or physics that deals with things that are not alive

ˌphysical ˈtherapy noun [U] *American* the treatment of injuries using special physical exercises —**physical ˈtherapist** noun [C]

phy·si·cian /fɪˈzɪʃ(ə)n/ noun [C] *formal* a DOCTOR

phys·ics /ˈfɪzɪks/ noun [U] ★ the science that deals with heat, light, and other forms of energy and how they affect objects —**phys·i·cist** /ˈfɪzɪsɪst/ noun [C]

phys·i·o·log·i·cal /ˌfɪziəˈlɑdʒɪk(ə)l/ adj relating to the way that the body of a living thing operates

phys·i·ol·o·gy /ˌfɪziˈɑlədʒi/ noun [U] **1** the science that deals with the way that the bodies of living things operate **2** the way that the body of a particular living thing operates

phy·sique /fɪˈzik/ noun [C] the shape of someone's body: *a boxer with an impressive, muscular physique*

pi·an·ist /piˈænɪst/ noun [C] someone who plays the piano

pi·a·no /piˈænoʊ/ noun [C] ★★ a large musical instrument with a row of black and white KEYS that you press: *Do you **play the piano**?* ♦ *She was accompanied by Helen **on piano**.*

pic·co·lo /ˈpɪkəˌloʊ/ noun [C] a musical instrument like a small FLUTE —*picture* → WOODWIND

pick¹ /pɪk/ verb [T] ★★★
1 to choose someone or something from a group: *Each month we pick a novel, and we all read it and discuss it.* ♦ **pick sb/sth for sth** *She was picked for the school play.*
2 to get flowers or fruit by breaking them off their stems: *They spent the summer picking strawberries.*
3 to keep pulling something with your FINGERNAILS: *If you keep picking that scab, it will never heal.*

PHRASES **pick and choose (sth)** to choose the things you prefer, rather than simply accepting what you are given: *We cannot pick and choose which laws to obey.*
pick sb's brains *informal* to ask someone questions because they have a lot of information or knowledge
pick a fight with sb to start a fight or argument with someone
pick a lock to open a lock without a key, for example with a piece of wire
pick your nose to use your finger to remove MUCUS from inside your nose
pick sb's pocket to steal things from someone's pocket or bag in a crowded place

PHRASAL VERBS **ˈpick at sth 1** to eat only small amounts of a meal when you are not hungry: *Most of the time he just picks at his food.* **2** *same as* **pick¹** 3: *He picked at a loose thread on his coat.*
ˈpick on sb to keep treating someone badly or unfairly, especially by criticizing them: *Why do you always pick on Jill?*
ˌpick sb/sth ˈout to choose one thing or person from a group: *The police organized a lineup, and I had to pick out the man who attacked me.*
ˌpick ˈup to improve: *The economy picked up slightly toward the end of the year.*
ˌpick sb ˈup *informal* to start a relationship with someone because you want to have sex with them: *She picked up some guy at a bar.*
ˌpick sth ˈup 1 to learn a new skill, or to start to have a habit, without intending to: *She picked up a few German phrases while staying in Berlin.* **2** *informal* to get an illness =CATCH: *I must have picked up a bug on vacation.* **3** *informal* to receive an electronic signal on a radio or similar piece of equipment **4 pick up speed** if something picks up speed, it starts to move faster **5 pick up the bill/tab** *informal* to pay for something:

Her father picks up the tab for her expensive lifestyle. =ACCELERATE

ˌpick sb/sth ˈup 1 to lift someone or something up from a surface: *She rushed to pick up the baby.* ♦ *Please pick those toys up and put them away.* —*picture* → CARRY **2** to go to a place in order to get someone or something and take them somewhere, usually in a car: *Will you pick me up at 11:00?* ♦ *Can I pick up my luggage tomorrow?*

ˌpick ˈup on sth to notice something that is not very obvious: *These are mistakes that you would expect an experienced teacher to pick up on.*

pick[2] /pɪk/ noun [C] **1** a tool with a heavy curved blade, used for breaking hard surfaces **2** a piece of plastic used to pull the strings on a guitar when you play it

PHRASES **have your pick of sth** to be able to choose anyone or anything that you want from a group

the pick of sth the best people or things in a particular group

take your pick to choose someone or something

pick•et[1] /ˈpɪkɪt/ or **ˈpicket ˌline** noun [C] a group of people who are protesting outside a building, especially a group of workers who are on STRIKE

pick•et[2] /ˈpɪkɪt/ verb [I/T] to take part in a protest outside a building: *About 100 people picketed the U.S. embassy on Thursday.* —**pick•et•ing** noun [U]

ˈpicket ˌfence noun [C] a fence made of thin flat boards that are pointed at the top

pick•le[1] /ˈpɪk(ə)l/ noun [C] *American* a CUCUMBER or other vegetable preserved in VINEGAR or salt water

pick•le[2] /ˈpɪk(ə)l/ verb [T] to preserve food in VINEGAR or salt water —**pick•led** /ˈpɪk(ə)ld/ adj

pick•pock•et /ˈpɪkˌpɑkɪt/ noun [C] someone who steals things from people's pockets and bags in crowded places

pick•up /ˈpɪkʌp/ noun **1 pickup** or **pickup truck** [C] a truck with an open back and low sides **2** [singular] *informal* an improvement or increase in something =RECOVERY **3** [C] a place or time at which people, goods, or other things are collected =COLLECTION **4** [U] *American informal* the power of a vehicle to ACCELERATE (=go faster) quickly

pick•y /ˈpɪki/ adj *informal* someone who is picky only likes things that are correct or appropriate in every detail =FUSSY

pic•nic[1] /ˈpɪknɪk/ noun [C] a meal that you eat outside

pic•nic[2] /ˈpɪknɪk/ (present participle **pic•nick•ing**; past tense and past participle **pic•nicked**) verb [I] to have a picnic

pic•to•ri•al /pɪkˈtɔriəl/ adj consisting of pictures: *a pictorial history of Williamsburg*

pic•ture[1] /ˈpɪktʃər/ noun ★★★

1 drawing/painting etc.	5 movie
2 situation	6 image on screen
3 description	+ PHRASES
4 mental image	

1 [C] a drawing, painting, or photograph: *I'll stand over here, and you can **take the picture** (=make a photograph with a camera).* ♦ *a **picture of** the house where I was born* ♦ *She asked children to **draw pictures** of their family.*

2 [singular] a situation: *The economic picture has changed a lot recently.*

3 [C] a description or idea of what someone or something is like: *The book **paints a picture of** (=gives a description of) a man with a very lonely life.*

4 [C] an image in your mind: *I have a picture in my head of what he looks like, but I can't quite describe him.*

5 [C] *American* a movie: *It won the award for Best Picture.*

6 [singular] the image on a television or movie screen, or the quality of the image: *The picture isn't very good on this channel.*

PHRASES **the big picture** a whole situation, not just one part of it

get the picture *informal* to understand something

Talking or writing about pictures

- **drawing** a picture that is made using a pen or pencil
- **graphics** the pictures in a magazine or a computer document
- **illustration** a picture that appears in a book or magazine
- **painting** a picture that is made using paints
- **photograph/photo** a picture that is taken with a camera
- **portrait** a picture of a person
- **sketch** a picture that you create quickly, often in preparation for a more detailed drawing or painting

pic•ture[2] /ˈpɪktʃər/ verb [T] **1** to imagine something: *Try to picture what life was like in those days.* ♦ *I pictured myself lying in the sun on a beach.* **2** to show someone in a photograph, painting, etc.: *Pictured above are some of the clothes from the new collection.*

pic•tur•esque /ˌpɪktʃəˈresk/ adj a picturesque place or scene is attractive

pie /paɪ/ noun [C/U] a food that consists of fruit or sometimes meat and vegetables cooked inside a case of PASTRY

PHRASE **a piece/share/slice of the pie** a share of the available money, benefits, etc.

→ PIE CHART

piece[1] /pis/ noun [C] ★★★

1 part of sth	5 writing/art etc.
2 individual object	6 object in board game
3 one of a particular type	+ PHRASES
4 used to make sth	

1 a part that has been cut, broken, or separated from something larger: *Would you like another **piece of** cake?* ♦ *a **piece of** land* ♦ *Jerry **tore** the letter **to pieces*** (=tore it until it was destroyed) *and threw it out.*

2 an individual object of a particular type: *I've used four **pieces of** paper already.* ♦ ***a piece of** equipment/furniture* ♦ *Police found several **pieces of** clothing.*

3 a single instance or amount of something of a particular type: ***a piece of** information/advice/evidence/legislation* ♦ *an impressive **piece of** work* ♦ *I have another **piece of** news for you.*

4 a part that you fit together with other parts to make something: *a jigsaw with 500 pieces* ♦ *I didn't expect the desk to arrive* ***in pieces.***
5 something that a writer, musician, or artist has produced
6 an object that you move in a BOARD GAME: *chess pieces*
PHRASES **give sb a piece of your mind** *informal* to speak angrily to someone about something they have done
in one piece not badly damaged or injured
a piece of the action *informal* the chance to be involved in something exciting
a piece of cake *informal* something that is very easy to do

piece² /pis/ PHRASAL VERB ˌ**piece sth toˈgether 1** to learn the truth about something by considering all the separate pieces of information that you have **2** to make something by combining separate parts

piece•meal /ˈpisˌmil/ adj, adv made or done in separate stages rather than being planned and done as a whole: *a piecemeal approach to the problem*

ˈ**pie ˌchart** noun [C] a circle divided into sections, used in order to show how something is divided into different amounts

pier /pɪr/ noun [C] a structure that is built out from the land over water. It is used for getting on and off boats, fishing, walking, etc.

pierce /pɪrs/ verb [T] **1** to make a hole in something using a sharp object =PENETRATE: *The knife pierced his skin.* **2** if you have a part of your body pierced, you have a small hole made in it so that you can wear jewelry in it: *I had my ears pierced years ago.*

pierc•ing¹ /ˈpɪrsɪŋ/ adj **1** very loud, high, and unpleasant =PENETRATING: *a piercing scream/whistle* **2** piercing wind or cold air is so cold that it hurts you **3** *literary* piercing eyes or looks seem to show that someone understands everything

pierc•ing² /ˈpɪrsɪŋ/ noun [U] the practice of making holes in people's skin for jewelry to fit through

pig¹ /pɪg/ noun [C] ★
1 an animal with no fur and a curly tail that is kept by farmers for its meat —*picture* → C12
2 an insulting word for someone who behaves in an unpleasant way or eats too much
3 *offensive* an insulting word for a police officer

pig² /pɪg/ PHRASAL VERB ˌ**pig ˈout** *informal* to eat an extremely large amount of food at one time

pi•geon /ˈpɪdʒən/ noun [C] a brown or gray bird that often lives in cities

pi•geon•hole¹ /ˈpɪdʒənˌhoʊl/ noun [C] one of the open boxes in a desk or on a wall where you can put papers, letters, messages, etc.

pi•geon•hole² /ˈpɪdʒənˌhoʊl/ verb [T] *showing disapproval* to decide that someone or something belongs to a particular type or group

pi•geon-toed /ˌpɪdʒən ˈtoʊd/ adj having feet that point inward

pig•gy•back /ˈpɪgiˌbæk/ noun [C] if you give someone a piggyback, you carry them on your back with your arms supporting their legs

pig•let /ˈpɪglət/ noun [C] a young pig

pig•ment /ˈpɪgmənt/ noun [C/U] a natural substance that gives color to something such as paint, skin, or hair

pig•men•ta•tion /ˌpɪgmenˈteɪʃ(ə)n/ noun [U] *formal* the natural color of something, for example someone's skin

pig•sty /ˈpɪgˌstaɪ/ noun [C] **1** a small building on a farm where pigs are kept **2** *informal* a place that is very dirty or messy

pig•tails /ˈpɪgteɪlz/ noun [plural] a hairstyle in which the hair is tied at each side of the head and hangs loose —*picture* → HAIRSTYLE

pike /paɪk/ noun [C] a large fish that lives in rivers and lakes

pile¹ /paɪl/ noun ★
1 [C] a number of things that are put on top of each other in a messy way: *Garbage lay* ***in piles*** *in the street.* ♦ ***a pile of*** *books and papers*
2 [C] *informal* a large amount of something: *By the time he was 40, he'd made* ***piles of*** *money.*
3 piles [plural] *old-fashioned* HEMORRHOIDS

pile² /paɪl/ verb [T] to put a large number of things on top of each other: *A group of boys were piling branches next to the tents.* ♦ *a plate piled high with food*
PHRASAL VERBS ˌ**pile ˈin** to enter a place in large numbers, all at the same time: *They opened the doors and all fifteen of us piled in.*
ˌ**pile ˈinto sth** to enter a place in large numbers, all at the same time: *Four huge men piled into the back of the car.*
ˌ**pile ˈup** if something piles up, the amount of it increases a lot: *The bills were piling up.*
ˌ**pile sthˈup** *same as* **pile**²: *Newspapers were piled up on the floor.*

pile-up /ˈpaɪlʌp/ noun [C] an accident in which several vehicles crash into each other

pil•fer /ˈpɪlfər/ verb [I/T] to steal things, especially from the place where you work

pil•grim /ˈpɪlgrɪm/ noun [C] **1** someone who travels to a holy place that is important in their religion **2 Pilgrim** one of the people who left England and went to live in what is now the U.S. in the early 17th century

pil•grim•age /ˈpɪlgrɪmɪdʒ/ noun [C/U] a trip that a religious person makes to a holy place

pill /pɪl/ noun ★
1 [C] a small piece of solid medicine that you swallow with water =TABLET: *vitamin pills* ♦ *Did you remember to* ***take your pills*** *this morning?*
2 the pill [singular] a pill that a woman swallows every day to prevent her from becoming pregnant: *Are you* ***on the pill*** *(=taking it)?*

pil•lage /ˈpɪlɪdʒ/ verb [I/T] to steal things from a place using force during a war

pil•lar /ˈpɪlər/ noun [C] a thick strong upright post that supports part of a building
PHRASE **pillar of the community/nation/church** someone who is important and respected in society or in an organization

P

pil•low /ˈpɪloʊ/ noun [C] a soft object on which you rest your head in bed

pil•low•case /ˈpɪloʊˌkeɪs/ noun [C] a cloth cover for a pillow

pi•lot¹ /ˈpaɪlət/ noun [C] ★
1 someone who flies an aircraft: *an airline pilot*
2 a television program that is broadcast to find out if people would like to watch a whole series
—**pi•lot** verb [T]

pi•lot² adj done with only a few people in order to find out if something will be successful or popular: *a pilot study/project*

pimp /pɪmp/ noun [C] a man who earns money by finding customers for PROSTITUTES —**pimp** verb [I]

pim•ple /ˈpɪmp(ə)l/ noun [C] a small red lump on your skin, especially on your face=SPOT

pin¹ /pɪn/ noun [C] ★
1 a small thin piece of metal with a sharp point, used for holding cloth in place while you are sewing
2 a piece of jewelry that you wear on your clothes
3 a thin piece of metal or wood used for holding things together
4 one of the tall objects that you knock over in the game of BOWLING

pin² /pɪn/ verb [T] to fasten something, or hold it in place, using pins: *She pinned the badge on her jacket.* ♦ *Lucy pinned back her hair.*
PHRASE **pin your hopes on** to hope very much that someone or something will succeed when everyone or everything else has failed
PHRASAL VERBS **ˌpin sb ˈdown 1** to force someone to make a decision about something: *We finally pinned him down and got him to agree to a meeting.* **2** to hold someone firmly on the ground so that they cannot move
ˌpin sth ˈdown to understand or describe something exactly: *Officials are trying to pin down the cause of the power outages.*
ˌpin sth ˈon sb to blame someone for something, often when they are not responsible: *He has managed to pin the blame on the previous government.*
ˌpin sth ˈup to attach a picture or notice to a wall

PIN /pɪn/ noun [C] personal identification number: a set of four numbers that you put into a CASH MACHINE in order to take money out of your bank account

pin•ball /ˈpɪnˌbɔl/ noun [U] a game that you play on a machine with a board that slopes. You use controls to hit a ball into TARGETS on the board.

pinc•er /ˈpɪnsər/ noun [C] a large part like a hand on some insects and SHELLFISH. It is used for attacking and for holding things.

pinch¹ /pɪntʃ/ noun [C] **1** a small amount of something that you can hold between your finger and thumb: *Add a pinch of salt.* **2** the action of squeezing someone's skin between your thumb and finger so that it hurts them
PHRASE **in a pinch** if it becomes necessary and you have no choice

pinch² /pɪntʃ/ verb [T] to squeeze someone's skin between your thumb and finger so that it hurts them: *Roger pinched my arm.*

pine¹ /paɪn/ noun **1** [C] a PINE TREE —*picture* → C9 **2** [U] the wood of a pine tree

pine² /paɪn/ verb [I] to feel very sad because you cannot be with someone who you love

pine•ap•ple /ˈpaɪnˌæp(ə)l/ noun [C/U] a large fruit that is yellow inside and has a thick brown skin with sharp points on it —*picture* → C10

ˈpine ˌcone noun [C] the brown hard fruit of a PINE tree

ˈpine ˌneedle noun [C] the thin sharp leaf of a PINE tree

ˈpine ˌtree noun [C] a tall tree with long thin sharp leaves that do not fall off in winter

ping /pɪŋ/ verb [I] to make a short high sound like the sound of a small bell —**ping** noun [C]

ˈPing-ˌPong *trademark* the game of TABLE TENNIS

pink¹ /pɪŋk/ adj between red and white in color: *His cheeks turned pink with embarrassment.*

pink² /pɪŋk/ noun [U] a color that is between red and white

pink•ish /ˈpɪŋkɪʃ/ adj similar to pink

ˌpink ˈslip noun [C] *American informal* notice that an employer gives to someone telling them they are no longer employed

pin•na•cle /ˈpɪnək(ə)l/ noun [C] *literary* **1** the most successful or exciting part of someone's life: *the pinnacle of her acting career* **2** the top of a very high mountain

pin•point¹ /ˈpɪnˌpɔɪnt/ verb [T] to discover or explain exactly what or where something is: *We couldn't pinpoint the source of the problem.*

pin•point² /ˈpɪnˌpɔɪnt/ adj very accurate and exact: *The missiles can be fired with pinpoint accuracy.*

pin•stripe /ˈpɪnˌstraɪp/ noun [C/U] a thin line in cloth, or cloth with thin lines in it

pint /paɪnt/ noun [C] a unit for measuring liquid, equal to 0.48 liters in the U.S. and 0.57 liters in the U.K.

pin•to bean /ˈpɪntoʊ ˌbin/ noun [C] a small bean with brown spots

pin•up /ˈpɪnʌp/ noun [C] *informal* a sexually attractive person who appears in photographs that people hang on their walls, or a photograph of this person

pi•o•neer¹ /ˌpaɪəˈnɪr/ noun [C] **1** one of the first people to do something important that is later developed by other people: *the pioneers of early color photography* **2** one of the first people to travel to a new place and start living there, especially one of the first Europeans to start living in unknown parts of North America —**pi•o•neer•ing** adj: *pioneering work/research/studies*

pi•o•neer² /ˌpaɪəˈnɪər/ verb [T] to do something that no one else has ever done: *The approach was pioneered by Dr. Bruce Fisher.*

pi•ous /ˈpaɪəs/ adj **1** strict in your religious beliefs and practices **2** *showing disapproval* done or said with the intention of seeming religious and moral —**pi•ous•ly** adv

pipe¹ /paɪp/ noun [C] ★
1 a tube that carries liquid or gas from one

P

place to another: *A pipe runs to the hot water tap in the kitchen.* ♦ *Workers were* ***laying water pipes*** *outside the house.*
2 an object used for smoking tobacco, consisting of a tube with a small bowl at the end
3 a musical instrument with one or more tubes that you blow through
→ PIPING

pipe² /paɪp/ verb [T] to send liquid or gas through a pipe from one place to another
→ PIPING
PHRASAL VERB **ˌpipe ˈup** *informal* to enter a conversation that other people are having

pipe•line /ˈpaɪpˌlaɪn/ noun [C] a long underground pipe that carries water, gas, etc. from one place to another: *a 500-mile oil pipeline*
PHRASE **in the pipeline** something that is in the pipeline is being planned and will happen or be available soon

pip•ing /ˈpaɪpɪŋ/ noun [U] long tubes that are cut to make pipes, or a system of pipes made from these tubes

ˌpiping ˈhot adj food or drink that is piping hot is very hot

piqued /pikt/ adj feeling annoyed and offended because someone has been rude to you

pi•ra•cy /ˈpaɪrəsi/ noun [U] **1** the crime of making and selling illegal copies of computer programs, books, videos, or CDs **2** the crime of stealing things from ships while they are sailing

pi•ra•nha /pəˈrɑnə/ noun [C] a small South American river fish that has sharp teeth and eats meat

pi•rate¹ /ˈpaɪrət/ noun [C] someone who steals things from ships while they are sailing

pirate

pi•rate² /ˈpaɪrət/ verb [T] to illegally make copies of computer programs, books, videos, or CDs —**pi•rat•ed** adj

Pi•sces /ˈpaɪˌsiz/ noun [C/U] one of the 12 signs of the ZODIAC. A **Pisces** is someone who was born between February 20 and March 20.

pis•ta•chi•o /pɪˈstæʃioʊ/ noun [C/U] a small green nut

pis•tol /ˈpɪst(ə)l/ noun [C] a small gun

pis•ton /ˈpɪstən/ noun [C] the part of an engine that moves up and down to create power

pit¹ /pɪt/ noun ★
1 [C] a large hole in the ground: *a gravel pit*
2 [C] *American* a large hard seed inside some types of fruit: *a peach pit*
3 [singular] *informal* an extremely messy place: *Her room was an absolute pit.*
PHRASES **be the pits** *informal* to be very bad: *Having to work on Saturday night is the pits.*
the pit of your stomach the place in your stomach where you experience unpleasant feelings when you are worried, upset, or frightened

pit² /pɪt/ PHRASAL VERB **ˈpit sb/sth aˌgainst sb/sth** to make someone compete or fight against someone or something else → PITTED

pi•ta bread /ˈpitə ˌbred/ or **pi•ta** /ˈpitə/ noun [C/U] a type of flat bread that is hollow inside

ˈpit ˌbull or **ˌpit bull ˈterrier** noun [C] a type of small very strong dog

pitch¹ /pɪtʃ/ noun ★

1 how high/low sound is	4 attempt to persuade
2 a throw of the ball	5 slope of roof etc.
3 strength of emotion	6 sports field

1 [singular/U] the high or low quality of a sound or musical note: *Many actors have been trained to lower* ***the pitch of*** *their voice.*
2 [C] in baseball, a throw of the ball by the PITCHER
3 [singular/U] the level of someone's emotions: *Excitement and enthusiasm* ***rose to fever pitch*** (=reached a high level).
4 [C] the things that you say to persuade someone to buy something or support you: *Most people do not like a very obvious sales* ***pitch.***
5 [singular/U] the slope of something such as a roof
6 [C] *British* a sports field

pitch² /pɪtʃ/ verb

1 aim talk etc. at group	5 fall suddenly
2 throw in baseball	+ PHRASE
3 try to sell/persuade	+ PHRASAL VERB
4 throw with force	

1 [T] to make something such as a speech or explanation appropriate for people who are a particular age or level of ability: *Her book is pitched at a teenage audience.* **2** [I/T] to throw the ball to a BATTER in the game of baseball —*picture* → C15 **3** [T] to try to sell something, or to try to persuade someone to do something: *He tried to pitch the movie to all the major Hollywood studios.* **4** [T] to throw something using a lot of force = FLING: *Jan pitched her books over the fence.* **5** [I] to fall suddenly in a particular direction = PLUNGE: *He tripped and pitched head first into the water.*
PHRASE **pitch a tent** to make a tent ready to use
PHRASAL VERB **ˌpitch ˈin** *informal* to join with other people in doing a job: *If we all pitch in, we can finish today.*

ˌpitch-ˈblack adj completely black or dark

ˌpitch-ˈdark adj completely dark

pitch•er /ˈpɪtʃər/ noun [C] **1** *American* a container for serving drinks, with a handle and a SPOUT **2** the player who throws the ball to the BATTER in baseball —*picture* → C15

pit•fall /ˈpɪtˌfɔl/ noun [C] a problem that is likely to happen in a particular situation: *the pitfalls involved in starting a business*

pith•y /ˈpɪθi/ adj a pithy statement or piece

of writing is short and very effective

pit·i·ful /ˈpɪtɪf(ə)l/ adj **1** someone who is pitiful looks or sounds so unhappy that you feel sympathy for them **2** extremely bad: *a pitiful performance* ♦ *a pitiful excuse* **3** a pitiful amount of something is very small and not enough: *a pitiful salary* —**pit·i·ful·ly** adv

pit·i·less /ˈpɪtɪləs/ adj *literary* cruel and showing no sympathy =MERCILESS

pit·tance /ˈpɪt(ə)ns/ noun [singular] an amount of money that is so small that it seems unfair

pit·ted /ˈpɪtəd/ adj a pitted surface has small marks or holes in it

pit·y¹ /ˈpɪti/ noun [U] a strong feeling of sympathy that you have for someone because they are very unhappy or in a bad situation: *She looked at him with a mixture of pity and disgust.*

PHRASES **(it's a) pity** used for saying that you are disappointed about something: **+(that)** *It's a pity we couldn't stay longer in Boston.*

take pity on sb to feel sorry for someone and try to help them

pit·y² /ˈpɪti/ verb [T] to feel sorry for someone because they are in a bad situation: *I pity the poor person who has to clean this mess up.*

piv·ot¹ /ˈpɪvət/ noun [C] **1** a fixed point or pin that something turns on or balances on **2** the most important thing that something is based on or depends on

piv·ot² /ˈpɪvət/ verb [I/T] to turn or balance on a central point, or to make something do this

piv·ot·al /ˈpɪvət(ə)l/ adj extremely important

pix·el /ˈpɪks(ə)l/ noun [C] *computing* the smallest unit of an image on a computer screen

piz·za /ˈpitsə/ noun [C/U] a food that consists of flat round bread with tomato, cheese, vegetables, meat, etc. on it

ˈpizza ˌparlor noun [C] *American* a PIZZERIA

piz·ze·ri·a /ˌpitsəˈriə/ noun [C] a restaurant that serves PIZZA

pl. abbrev plural

plac·ard /ˈplæˌkɑrd/ noun [C] a large sign that is used for advertising something, or is carried in the street by someone who is protesting against something

pla·cate /ˈpleɪkeɪt/ verb [T] *formal* to stop someone from feeling angry or offended by being nice to them =PACIFY

place¹ /pleɪs/ noun [C] ★★★

1 area/position	5 chance to be in sth
2 town/building etc.	6 importance to people
3 seat/position	7 point in book etc.
4 position in a race etc.	+ PHRASES

1 an area or position: *Carl went back to his place* (=the position where he usually is) *and sat down.* ♦ *Keep your credit cards in **a safe place**.* ♦ *She pushed the couch back **into place*** (=into the correct position). ♦ *The road is very narrow and quite dangerous **in places*** (=in some areas but not all).

2 a particular town, country, building, store, etc.: *They live in a small place called Hunter's Gap.* ♦ *We went back to Jon's place* (=where Jon lives) *after the movie.* ♦ *Cyprus is a great **place for** a vacation.* ♦ **a place to do sth** *Is this a safe place to swim?*

3 a seat on a train, on a bus, in a theater, etc., or a position in a line: *There's no place to sit.* ♦ *Would you mind **saving my place** for a minute?*

4 the position that you achieve in a race or competition: *Brian finished the race in third place.*

5 an opportunity to join an organization, team, etc.: *Jones has **earned a place** on the Olympic team.*

6 the importance that someone or something has in people's lives: *a discussion about **the place of** religion in society*

7 the point that you have reached in a book, speech, etc.

PHRASES **all over the place 1** in or to many different places =EVERYWHERE: *I travel all over the place in my job.* **2** in a messy state: *His papers were all over the place.*

change/trade places (with sb) to take someone's position while they take yours

fall into place 1 if something falls into place, you suddenly understand something that you did not understand before **2** if things fall into place, they start to happen in the way that you want them to

in place 1 existing and capable of being used: *We didn't have the systems in place to deal with so many orders.* **2** *American* without leaving the position you are in: *We had to run in place for five minutes.*

in place of instead of

out of place 1 if someone feels out of place, they are uncomfortable because they feel that they are not like other people around them **2** if something looks out of place, it is in a position where it does not belong or look good

place of work/business/worship *formal* the area where you work/have your business/ practice your religion

take sb's/sth's place or **take the place of sb/sth** to do something instead of someone else, or to be used instead of something else: *Joe resigned as chairperson in 1999 and I took his place.*

Use **room** or **space**, not **place**, to mean an empty area or part of something where people or things can fit: *Is there any room* OR *any space for me in your car?* ♦ *I wanted a big table in here, but there wasn't enough room* OR *enough space.*

place² /pleɪs/ verb [T] ★★★

1 put sth somewhere	4 remember/recognize
2 put sb in situation	5 of advertisement etc.
3 decide importance	+ PHRASE

1 to put something somewhere, usually in a careful way: **place sth on/under/into etc. sth** *Ella placed the dish on the table.*

2 to put someone or something in a particular situation or state: **place sb in/at/under sth** *Her decision places me in an awkward situation.* ♦ *At the end of the war, the island was placed under French control.*

3 to decide how good or important something is in comparison with other things: *The school **places** great **importance** on the safety of its students.* ♦ **place sth above**

P

sth *The company was accused of placing profits above safety.*
4 if you can't place someone, you do not remember them or you cannot remember their name: *He looks familiar, but I can't place him.*
5 if you place an advertisement, an order, or a BET, you give it to someone formally
PHRASE **place first/second/third** *American* to finish a competition in a particular position: *The 23-year-old from Sun Valley, Idaho, placed first in six World Cup downhill races.*

pla•ce•bo /plə'sibou/ noun [C] a substance that a doctor pretends is medicine and gives to a patient, either as part of an experiment or in order to help the patient without drugs

'place ,kick noun [C] a kick of the ball in football while the ball is on the ground or being held by a player —*picture* → C15

place•ment /'pleɪsmənt/ noun **1** [U] the process of finding someone a place where they can live, work, or study: *job placement programs* **2** [C/U] the act of putting something into a position, or the position it is in **3** [C/U] *British* an INTERNSHIP

plac•id /'plæsəd/ adj someone who is placid is not often angry or excited

pla•gia•rism /'pleɪdʒə,rɪzəm/ noun [U] the process of taking another person's work, ideas, or words, and using them as if they were your own

pla•gia•rize /'pleɪdʒə,raɪz/ verb [I/T] to take someone else's work, ideas, or words, and use them as if they were your own

plague¹ /pleɪg/ noun [C] **1** any serious disease that spreads quickly and usually ends in death **2** an uncontrolled increase in the numbers of an animal or insect in a place

plague² /pleɪg/ verb [T] to cause a lot of problems for someone or something for a long period of time: *The east coast has been plagued by blizzards this month.*

plaid /plæd/ noun [U] a type of cloth that has a pattern of squares, especially one that is traditional in Scotland

plain¹ /pleɪn/ adj ★
1 simple, with no decoration or with nothing extra added: *a plain wooden table* ♦ *a plain white T-shirt* ♦ *plain yogurt*
2 expressing what you think honestly, using simple, direct language: *She was admired for her **plain speaking**.*
3 easily seen or understood=OBVIOUS: *Sykes **made it plain** that he had no intention of resigning.* ♦ **it is plain to sb (that)** *It was plain to everyone that Maude was not happy.*
4 not very attractive
PHRASES **plain and simple** used for emphasizing that something is completely true and cannot be described as anything else: *It was cheating plain and simple.*
plain old not at all unusual, interesting, or special: *Just use plain old hamburger.*

plain² /pleɪn/ noun [C] a large flat area of land

plain³ /pleɪn/ adv used for emphasizing that someone or something has a particular negative quality: *It was just plain stupid of him to get involved.*

'plain-,clothes adj plain-clothes police wear ordinary clothes, so that people do not know who they are

P

plain•ly /'pleɪnli/ adv **1** in a way that is easy to see, hear, or notice=CLEARLY: *The climbers were plainly visible on the hillside.* ♦ *Something was plainly wrong with the engine.* **2** without much decoration **3** in a direct and honest way: *Albright told us plainly what the situation was like.*

plain•tiff /'pleɪntɪf/ noun [C] *legal* someone who brings a legal case against someone else in a court of law

plain•tive /'pleɪntɪv/ adj a plaintive sound is high and sad —**plain•tive•ly** adv

plan¹ /plæn/ noun [C] ★★★
1 an idea about what you will do in the future, usually including details about how you will do it: *a five-year **business plan*** ♦ *We need to **make a plan** before we start.* ♦ *We don't have any **plans for** our vacation yet.* ♦ *Everything **went according to plan*** (=there were no problems). ♦ **a plan to do sth** *plans to reduce the use of pesticides in food production*
2 a drawing that shows what something is like or how it will be made=DESIGN: ***plans for** the new public gardens*

plan² /plæn/ verb ★★★
1 [I/T] to think carefully about a series of actions that you need to take in order to achieve something: *They had been planning their trip to Africa for months.* ♦ *We'll need to **plan ahead** if we want to take a year off for traveling.* ♦ *Officials are **planning for** every possibility.* ♦ **plan sth for sth** *The meeting has been planned for next week.*
2 [T] to intend to do something: **plan to do sth** *My boss is planning to retire at 50.*
3 [T] to think about something that you intend to build or make, and draw a picture of how it will look
PHRASAL VERB **'plan on sth** to intend to do something, or to expect something to happen: *We hadn't planned on so many people coming.*

,Plan 'A noun [singular] the first plan that someone tries

,Plan 'B noun [singular] a plan that you intend to use if your first plan fails

plane /pleɪn/ noun [C] ★★★
1 an aircraft with wings and an engine or engines=AIRPLANE: *Most of the passengers got off the plane in Dublin.* ♦ *We traveled **by plane** from Mexico City.*
2 a level in society, or a level of intelligence or ability=LEVEL: *The top players are on a higher plane than the rest.*
3 a tool that is used for making wooden surfaces smooth
4 *technical* a flat surface

plan•et /'plænɪt/ noun ★
1 [C] a very large round object that moves around the sun or around another star: *planet Earth* ♦ *Mars is sometimes known as the red planet.*
2 the planet [singular] the planet Earth and everything on it: *policies to protect the future of the planet*
—**plan•e•tar•y** /'plænə,teri/ adj

plank /plæŋk/ noun [C] **1** a long narrow piece of wood that is used for making structures such as floors **2** an important aspect of something, on which it is based: *the main* *plank of the party's defense policy*

plank·ton /ˈplæŋktən/ noun [U] very small animals and plants that live in water and are eaten by fish

plan·ner /ˈplænər/ noun [C] **1** someone who plans something as their job **2** *American* an APPOINTMENT BOOK

plan·ning /ˈplænɪŋ/ noun [U] ★ the process of deciding how you will do something before you do it: *There was very little planning done for this project.*

plant¹ /plænt/ noun [C] ★★★

1 a living thing that grows in soil and has leaves and roots: *a strawberry plant*

2 a large factory: *a nuclear/chemical plant*

plant² /plænt/ verb [T] ★

1 of seeds etc.	4 hide bomb
2 put firmly in position	5 give sb an idea
3 put sth on sb secretly	

1 to put trees, plants, or seeds in soil so that they will grow there: *I planted a small apple tree in the garden.*

2 to put someone or something firmly in a particular place or position: *Henry planted himself in the seat next to me.*

3 to secretly put something that is illegal or stolen in someone's clothes so that they appear to be guilty when it is found: *Someone must have planted the gun on him.*

4 if someone plants a bomb, they hide it where they want it to explode

5 if you plant an idea in someone's mind, you mention it so that they begin to think about it

plan·ta·tion /plænˈteɪʃ(ə)n/ noun [C] a large farm where crops such as tea, coffee, cotton, and sugar are grown

plaque /plæk/ noun **1** [C] a flat piece of metal or stone that is hung on a wall for decoration, or to give information **2** [U] a substance that forms on your teeth and in which bacteria can grow

plas·ma /ˈplæzmə/ noun [U] *medical* the yellowish liquid that is part of blood

ˈplasma ˌscreen noun [C] a type of television or computer screen made by putting a mixture of gases between two sheets of glass

plas·ter¹ /ˈplæstər/ noun **1** [U] a substance that is spread onto walls and ceilings to form a hard smooth surface **2** [C] *British* a Band-Aid

plas·ter² /ˈplæstər/ verb [T] **1** to cover a surface with labels, advertisements, pictures etc.: *He has posters of rock stars plastered all over the walls of his room.* **2** to cover a wall or ceiling with wet plaster or a similar substance **3** to make something lie flat against something else: *The rain had plastered her hair to her forehead.*

plas·tic¹ /ˈplæstɪk/ noun [C/U] ★★ a very common light, strong substance that is produced by a chemical process and used for making many different things

plas·tic² /ˈplæstɪk/ adj ★★★ made of plastic: *plastic bags*

ˌplastic ˈsurgery noun [U] medical operations to improve the appearance of a part of someone's body → COSMETIC SURGERY —**ˌplastic ˈsurgeon** noun [C]

ˌplastic ˈwrap noun [U] *American* a thin transparent plastic substance that is used for wrapping around food to keep it fresh

plate /pleɪt/ noun ★★★

1 flat round dish	5 thin silver/gold layer
2 amount of food	6 picture in book
3 metal/plastic sign	+ PHRASE
4 sth flat and hard	

1 [C] a flat round dish that you put food on

2 [C] the amount of food that a plate will hold: *a* ***plate of French fries***

3 [C] a small piece of metal or plastic that is attached to something and used for showing information such as someone's name or a number: *He read the name on the brass plate on the door.* → LICENSE PLATE

4 [C] a flat piece of metal or other hard substance: *steel/glass plates*

5 [U] a thin layer of silver or gold that covers a less valuable metal to improve its appearance

6 [C] a picture that is printed on special paper in a book: *The book contains 35 color plates.*

PHRASE **have a lot on your plate** to have a lot of things to worry about or deal with

pla·teau /plæˈtoʊ/ noun [C] **1** a large flat area of land that is higher than the land around it **2** a period of time when something stops increasing or improving: *The recent boom in cellphone sales seems to have reached a plateau.*

plat·ed /ˈpleɪtəd/ adj a metal object that is plated is covered with a thin layer of silver or gold

plate·ful /ˈpleɪtfʊl/ noun [C] the amount of food that a plate will hold

plat·form /ˈplætˌfɔrm/ noun [C] ★

1 raised structure	4 chance to express sth
2 where you get on train	5 in computing
3 policies/goals of party	

1 a raised structure for people to stand on so that they can be seen by an audience: *The two candidates shared the platform for the question and answer session.*

2 an area next to a railroad track where passengers get onto and off trains: *The next train to Brussels will depart from platform 3.*

3 the policies and goals of a political party, especially the ones they state in order to get people to vote for them: *The Democratic platform would provide health insurance for all children.*

4 an opportunity to express your ideas or opinions: *Radio call-ins provide* ***a platform for*** *people with strong opinions.*

5 *computing* the type of computer system you have and the programs you can use with it

plat·i·num /ˈplæt(ə)nəm/ noun [U] a silver-gray metal that is used in industry and for making expensive jewelry

plat·i·tude /ˈplætɪˌtud/ noun [C] something that has been said so often that it is not interesting anymore and shows a lack of imagination

pla·ton·ic /pləˈtɑnɪk/ adj a platonic relationship is friendly but does not involve sex

pla·toon /pləˈtun/ noun [C] a small group of soldiers

P

plat·ter /ˈplætər/ noun [C] a large plate that is used for serving food

plau·si·ble /ˈplɔzəb(ə)l/ adj likely to be true ≠ IMPLAUSIBLE —**plau·si·bil·i·ty** /ˌplɔzəˈbɪləti/ noun [U], **plau·si·bly** adv

play¹ /pleɪ/ verb ★★★

1 take part in game	5 produce sounds
2 compete against sb	6 have part in play etc.
3 make music	+ PHRASES
4 of children	+ PHRASAL VERBS

1 [I/T] to take part in a sport or game: *Do you want to **play cards**? ♦ He used to play for the Yankees.*
2 [I/T] to compete against someone in a sport or game: *She plays the winner of tomorrow's match. ♦ The Bears are **playing against** the Niners tonight.*
3 [I/T] to perform music, or to use an instrument to make music: *He played several organ pieces by Bach. ♦ Gloria **plays the violin** in the London Philharmonic.*
4 [I] if children play, they do things that they enjoy, for example using toys: *The children were playing in the backyard. ♦ Which toys do you want to **play with** today?*
5 [I/T] to produce sounds, or to make something such as a radio or CD produce sounds: *They played the CD at full volume. ♦ I could hear a radio playing in the apartment above.*
6 [T] to have a particular part in a play or movie: *She played Blanche in* A Streetcar Named Desire.

PHRASES **be playing with fire** to be doing something dangerous or risky that could cause lots of problems for you
play ball (with sb) *informal* **1** to agree to do something that someone wants you to do **2** *American* to play a sports game with a ball, especially baseball
play games to behave in a silly way by not saying what you really think or by not being serious enough
play it cool *informal* to behave calmly and not show that you are worried about something
play it safe to avoid taking any risks
→ HARDBALL, HOOKY

PHRASAL VERBS **ˌplay aˈround** to behave in a silly way, especially when you should be doing something else: *The kids were playing around in the pool.*
ˌplay sth ˈback to play a message or video that has been recorded in order to listen to or watch it
ˌplay sth ˈdown to try to make a problem or difficult situation seem less important than it is: *At first the administration played down the threat to public health.*
ˈplay on sth to use a situation or emotions such as fear or worry in order to get what you want: *She plays on the fact that people feel sorry for her.*
ˌplay sth ˈup to try to persuade people to believe that something is more important than it is: *The newspapers have really played up the low voter turnout.*
ˈplay with sth to keep touching something, especially because you are bored

play² /pleɪ/ noun ★★★
1 [C] a piece of writing that is intended to be performed by actors in a theater or on television or the radio: *a Shakespeare/Broadway play ♦ The school's going to **put on a play** this Christmas.*
2 [U] activities that are done because they are enjoyable and fun, especially by children: *She watched the children **at play** in the park.*
3 [U] the action in a sport or game: *Rain stopped play again this afternoon.*

PHRASES **bring sth into play** to make something start to have an effect
come into play to start to happen or have an effect
a play on words a clever or funny use of a word that has two different meanings
→ FOUL PLAY

play·book /ˈpleɪbʊk/ noun [C] *American* a book that contains a team's plans and the PLAYS (=actions) it uses in a sport such as football

play·boy /ˈpleɪˌbɔɪ/ noun [C] a man who is rich and spends his time enjoying himself instead of working

ˌplay-by-ˈplay noun [C/U] *American* a description on television or radio of what happens in a sports competition or game as it happens

play·er /ˈpleɪər/ noun [C] ★★★
1 someone who plays a particular game or sport: *a tennis/baseball player*
2 a person or organization that influences a situation: *Germany is seen as **a key player** within the European Union.*
3 someone who plays a musical instrument: *a piano player*

play·ful /ˈpleɪf(ə)l/ adj **1** lively and full of fun: *playful kittens* **2** intended to be funny or friendly rather than serious: *a playful pat on the back* —**play·ful·ly** adv

play·ground /ˈpleɪˌgraʊnd/ noun [C] an area of land where children can play, especially at a school

play·ing card /ˈpleɪɪŋ ˌkɑrd/ noun [C] a card that is used for playing card games

play·mate /ˈpleɪˌmeɪt/ noun [C] a child who another child plays with

play·off /ˈpleɪˌɔf/ noun **1 playoffs** [plural] a series of games played by the best teams in a sport in order to decide who the final winner will be **2** [C] one of the games in a series of playoffs

play·room /ˈpleɪˌrum/ noun [C] a room for children to play in and keep their toys in

play·thing /ˈpleɪˌθɪŋ/ noun [C] **1** someone or something that you are only interested in when you want pleasure or entertainment and do not care about the rest of the time **2** *formal* a toy

play·time /ˈpleɪˌtaɪm/ noun [C/U] RECESS at school

play·wright /ˈpleɪˌraɪt/ noun [C] someone who writes plays

pla·za /ˈplɑzə/ noun [C] **1** an area in a city where there are several stores and businesses **2** a large open area with a hard surface in a city or town

plea /pli/ noun [C] **1** an urgent or emotional request for something: *The police ignored her pleas for help.* **2** *legal* a statement that someone makes in a court of law to say whether they are guilty or not

ˈplea ˌbargain noun [C] *American* an

arrangement in which someone may be allowed to avoid punishment for a serious crime if they admit that they have committed a less serious crime

plead /plid/ (past tense and past participle **plead•ed** or **pled** /pled/) verb **1** [I] to make an urgent or emotional request: *She pleaded with him to stay, but he would not.* **2** [I/T] *legal* to say in a court of law whether you are guilty of a crime or not: *Both defendants pleaded not guilty.* **3** [T] to mention something as an excuse for doing or not doing something **4** [T] to try to show that something is important or worth trying to achieve: *He pleaded the case for continued cooperation with the Russians.*

pleas•ant /ˈplez(ə)nt/ adj ★
1 enjoyable, or attractive ≠ UNPLEASANT: *They spent a pleasant evening together.*
2 a pleasant person is friendly and behaves correctly in social situations ≠ UNPLEASANT —**pleas•ant•ly** adv

pleas•ant•ries /ˈplezəntriz/ noun [plural] friendly remarks that you make in order to be polite

please¹ /pliz/ interjection ★★★
1 used as a polite way of asking for something, or of asking someone to do something: *Would you help me with these bags, please?* ♦ *Could I please have change for a dollar?*
2 used for emphasizing a request, an order, or a statement: *Please stop making all that noise!*
3 used as a polite way of accepting something that someone has offered you: *"Would you like some more coffee?" "Yes, please."*

please² /pliz/ verb [I/T] ★ to make someone feel happy and satisfied: *He'll do anything to please her.* ♦ *Some of our customers can be very* ***difficult to please.***
PHRASE **whatever/wherever/whenever etc. sb pleases** whatever/wherever/whenever etc. someone wants: *You can go whenever you please.*

pleased /plizd/ adj ★★ happy and satisfied: *I'm really* ***pleased with*** *how you guys performed.* ♦ *I'm really* ***pleased about*** *your new job.* ♦ **+(that)** *We're very pleased that you've accepted our offer.* ♦ **be pleased to do sth** *You'll be pleased to hear that Dave can come tonight!*
PHRASE **pleased to meet you** *spoken* used as a polite way of greeting someone when you meet them for the first time: *"Tony, this is Mr. Wilkins." "Pleased to meet you."*

pleas•ing /ˈplizɪŋ/ adj *formal* **1** making you feel happy and satisfied: *pleasing news*
2 pleasant and enjoyable: *a pleasing aroma*

pleas•ur•a•ble /ˈpleʒ(ə)rəb(ə)l/ adj *formal* giving you a feeling of happiness, enjoyment, or satisfaction = ENJOYABLE

pleas•ure /ˈpleʒər/ noun ★★
1 [U] a feeling of happiness, enjoyment, or satisfaction: *He smiled* ***with pleasure*** *when she walked in.* ♦ **give/bring pleasure to sb** *His books have given enormous pleasure to many people.* ♦ **take pleasure in (doing) sth** *He took great pleasure in pointing out my mistakes.*
2 [C] something that makes you feel happy and satisfied: *Music is one of the greatest pleasures in life.* ♦ **it's a pleasure to do sth** *It's a pleasure to meet you.*
3 [U] the activity of relaxing and enjoying yourself instead of working: *Are you traveling for* ***business or pleasure?***
PHRASE **(it's) my pleasure** *spoken formal* used when someone thanks you as a polite way of saying that you were happy to help them: *"Thanks so much for helping us with our bags." "My pleasure."*

pleat•ed /ˈplitəd/ adj a pleated piece of clothing has regular folds in it

pleb•i•scite /ˈplebɪˌsaɪt, ˈplebɪsɪt/ noun [C] a vote by everyone in a country about a very important issue

pled an American past tense and past participle of **plead**

pledge /pledʒ/ verb [T] to promise seriously and publicly to do something: *Britain, France, and Germany were among the countries pledging their support.* ♦ *He has pledged to fight for a fairer system.* —**pledge** noun [C]

plen•ti•ful /ˈplentɪf(ə)l/ adj present or available in large quantities ≠ SCARCE

plen•ty /ˈplenti/ pronoun ★★★ a lot, or enough: *"How much money will I need?" "Five dollars should be plenty."* ♦ *There's* ***plenty of*** *room for luggage behind the seats.* ♦ *They had* ***plenty of*** *chances to win the game.* ♦ *There's* ***plenty more*** *ice cream in the freezer.* ♦ **plenty to do** *She always has plenty to say.*

pleth•o•ra /ˈpleθərə/ noun [singular] *formal* a greater amount than you need or want

pli•a•ble /ˈplaɪəb(ə)l/ adj able to bend or change shape easily without breaking

pli•ers /ˈplaɪərz/ noun [plural] a metal tool that looks like a strong pair of scissors, used for holding small objects or for bending or cutting wire —*picture* → TOOL

plight /plaɪt/ noun [C] a sad, serious, or difficult situation

plod /plɑd/ verb [I] to walk with slow heavy steps

plop¹ /plɑp/ verb **1** [I] to fall with a short sound like the sound made by a small object falling into a liquid **2** [T] *informal* to drop something carelessly but gently onto a surface

plop² /plɑp/ noun [C] a short sound like the sound made by a small object falling into a liquid

plot¹ /plɑt/ noun ★
1 [C/U] a series of related events that make up the main story in a book, movie, etc.
2 [C] a secret plan to do something bad, made by two or more people: *a kidnapping plot* ♦ ***a plot against*** *the government* ♦ **a plot to do sth** *a plot to kill the president*
3 [C] a piece of land that is used for a particular purpose: *a building/burial plot*

plot² /plɑt/ verb **1** [I/T] to make a secret plan with other people to do something bad = SCHEME **2** [T] to make marks on a map or GRAPH to show the movement or development of something

plough /plaʊ/ the British spelling of **plow²**

plow¹ /plaʊ/ verb [I/T] **1** to turn over the soil

P

with a plow before planting seeds **2** to move snow to the side of a street using a SNOW PLOW

PHRASAL VERBS ˌ**plow ˈinto sb/sth** to crash into someone or something with force, because you are moving or driving too quickly

ˈ**plow through sth** to finish doing something that takes a long time and is difficult or boring

plow² /plaʊ/ noun [C] a piece of equipment that farmers use for turning over the soil before putting seeds into it

ploy /plɔɪ/ noun [C] a way of tricking someone in order to get an advantage, or to make them do what you want them to do

PLS abbrev please: used in e-mails and TEXT MESSAGES

pluck /plʌk/ verb **1** [T] to take someone or something quickly from a particular place: *Rescue crews plucked survivors from the sea.* **2** [T] to pull the feathers off the body of a dead bird so that it can be cooked **3** [I/T] to pull the strings of a musical instrument with your fingers in order to produce a sound **4** [T] *literary* to pull a piece of fruit from a tree, or a flower or leaf from a plant =PICK

PHRASE **pluck your eyebrows** to pull hairs out from around the edges of your EYEBROWS in order to make them look neater

pluck•y /ˈplʌki/ adj brave and determined, especially when success is unlikely =GUTSY

plug¹ /plʌg/ verb **1** [T] to fill a hole so that nothing can get through it: *Plug the hole with newspaper before applying the cement.* **2** [I/T] *American* to block pipes of a SINK, toilet, etc. so that water or waste cannot flow normally down the pipes: *Paper towels will plug the toilet.* **3** [T] to try to make people interested in a book, movie, idea, etc. by talking about it in an enthusiastic way on a radio or television program

PHRASAL VERBS ˌ**plug aˈway (at sth)** to continue doing something in a determined way despite difficulties

ˌ**plug sth ˈin** to connect a piece of equipment to an electricity supply or to another piece of equipment: *I realized I hadn't plugged the TV in.*

ˌ**plug (sth) ˈinto sth** to connect a piece of equipment to an electricity supply or to another piece of equipment, or to be connected in this way: *First plug the keyboard into your computer.*

plug² /plʌg/ noun [C] **1** an object that is used for connecting a piece of equipment to an electricity supply **2** an attempt to make people interested in a book, movie, etc. by talking about it in an enthusiastic way on a radio or television program **3** a small round plastic or rubber object that prevents water from flowing out of the hole in a SINK or BATHTUB

PHRASE **pull the plug (on sth)** to stop an activity, especially by no longer providing money for it

plum /plʌm/ noun [C] a small round fruit with purple, red, or yellow skin and a large hard seed inside —*picture* → C10

plum•age /ˈplumɪdʒ/ noun [U] a bird's feathers

plumb•er /ˈplʌmər/ noun [C] someone whose job is to fit and repair the pipes and equipment that are used for supplying and storing water

plumb•ing /ˈplʌmɪŋ/ noun [U] **1** the job of fitting and repairing the pipes and equipment that are used for supplying and storing water **2** the system of pipes and equipment that are used for supplying and storing water in a building

plume /plum/ noun [C] **1** a long narrow cloud of dust, smoke, etc. that moves upward **2** a large feather or group of feathers, used especially for decorating a hat

plum•met /ˈplʌmɪt/ verb [I] **1** if something such as an amount, rate, or value plummets, it suddenly becomes much lower: *Stock prices plummeted on the New York stock exchange today.* **2** to fall straight down very quickly from a high position =PLUNGE

plump /plʌmp/ adj **1** slightly fat, in a pleasant way **2** large and round in an attractive way: *plump strawberries*

plun•der /ˈplʌndər/ verb [I/T] to take valuable things from a place using force —**plun•der** noun [U]

plunge¹ /plʌndʒ/ verb [I] **1** to fall quickly from a high position =PLUMMET: *The helicopter plunged 500 feet into the ocean.* **2** if an amount or level plunges, it suddenly becomes much lower =PLUMMET: *The temperature is expected to plunge below zero tonight.*

PHRASAL VERBS ˌ**plunge ˈinto sth** to suddenly start doing something with energy and enthusiasm

ˌ**plunge sb/sth ˈinto sth** to suddenly put someone or something in a particular state or situation: *The city was plunged into total darkness when the entire electrical system failed.*

ˌ**plunge sth ˈinto sth** to quickly push something a long way into something else

plunge² /plʌndʒ/ noun [C] **1** a sudden reduction in the amount or level of something: *the plunge in oil prices* **2** a quick fall from a high position: *the plane's plunge into the ocean*

PHRASE **take the plunge** to finally do something that is important, difficult, or dangerous, after thinking about it carefully

plu•per•fect, the /ˌpluˈpɜrfɪkt/ noun [singular] *linguistics* the PAST PERFECT tense of a verb

plu•ral¹ /ˈplʊrəl/ adj *linguistics* ★ a plural word or form is used for referring to more than one person or thing

plu•ral² /ˈplʊrəl/ noun [C] *linguistics* a word or form that is used for referring to more than one person or thing. For example, "students" is the plural of "student," and "mice" is the plural of "mouse."

plu•ral•ism /ˈplʊrəlˌɪzəm/ noun [U] *formal* a situation in which people of different races, religions, cultures, politics, etc. live together in a society —**plu•ral•ist** adj

plus¹ /plʌs/ grammar word ★

Plus can be:
- a **preposition**: *Two plus seven is nine.*
- a **conjunction**: *You can have this bread, plus there's cheese in the fridge.*

■ an **adjective**: *There are 30 plus students in every class.*

1 used for showing that one number or amount is added to another. This word is usually represented in mathematics by +. ≠ MINUS: *36 plus 5 is 41.* ♦ *You have to pay back $100 a month, plus interest.*
2 used when mentioning an additional thing or fact: *He came along with his five children, plus their partners, and his grandchildren.*
3 used after you mention a number or quantity to show that the actual number or quantity may be larger: *Ray Charles' 40-year plus career began in 1954.*
PHRASE **A plus/B plus/C plus/D plus** a grade for a student's work that is higher than a grade of A, B, C, and D. These grades are usually written A+, B+, etc.

plus² /plʌs/ noun [C] an advantage: *For this job, experience in telecommunications is a plus.*

plush /plʌʃ/ adj expensive, comfortable, and attractive

'plus ˌsign noun [C] the symbol +

plu•to•ni•um /pluˈtoʊniəm/ noun [U] a RADIOACTIVE substance that is used in making nuclear power

ply /plaɪ/ verb **ply your trade** *literary* to do your job
PHRASAL VERB **ˈply sb with sth** to keep giving someone a lot of presents, food, or drinks

ply•wood /ˈplaɪˌwʊd/ noun [U] a type of board that is used in building houses, furniture, etc., made by sticking thin layers of wood together with glue

p.m. /ˌpiˈem/ abbrev used after a time for showing that it is between noon and midnight: *3:30 p.m.*

PMS /ˌpi em ˈes/ noun [U] premenstrual syndrome: the pain and unpleasant feelings that some women have just before their PERIOD every month

pneu•mat•ic /nuˈmætɪk/ adj **1** filled with air or gas **2** a pneumatic tool or piece of equipment works by using air

pneu•mo•nia /nuˈmoʊniə/ noun [U] a serious illness that affects your lungs

PO /ˌpi ˈoʊ/ abbrev post office

poach /poʊtʃ/ verb **1** [T] to cook something in liquid that is boiling gently **2** [I/T] to illegally catch or kill an animal, bird, or fish on someone else's property

poach•er /ˈpoʊtʃər/ noun [C] someone who illegally catches or kills animals, birds, or fish on someone else's property

PO Box /ˌpi ˈoʊ ˌbɑks/ noun [C] post office box: used in an address showing the number of a small box at a POST OFFICE where your mail can be sent

pock•et¹ /ˈpɑkɪt/ noun [C] ★★
1 a small bag that forms part of a piece of clothing and is used for holding small objects: *She searched her pockets for the car keys.*
2 a small bag or other container that forms part of an object: *The safety instructions are in the pocket of the seat in front of you.*
3 a supply of money that is available for spending: *Our boss expects us to pay for the trip **out of our own pockets*** (=using our own money)!
4 a small area with a particular quality that makes it different from the areas around it: *She survived thanks to an air pocket.* ♦ ***pockets of resistance to government forces***
→ LINE

pock•et² /ˈpɑkɪt/ verb [T] **1** to put something into your pocket: *He locked the door and pocketed the key.* **2** to take money for yourself that does not belong to you: *He said the officials pocketed some of the taxes they collected.*

pock•et³ /ˈpɑkɪt/ adj small enough to fit into your pocket: *a pocket dictionary*

pock•et•book /ˈpɑkɪtˌbʊk/ noun [C] *American* an amount of money you have to spend

pock•et•ful /ˈpɑkɪtˌfʊl/ noun [C] the amount of something that can be put in a pocket

ˈpocket ˌknife noun [C] a small knife with blades or tools that fold up into the handle

ˈpocket ˌmoney noun [U] a small amount of money that you carry with you for buying inexpensive things

pod /pɑd/ noun [C] the long narrow part that holds the seeds of a bean plant or similar plant

po•di•a•trist /pəˈdaɪətrɪst/ noun [C] someone whose job is to take care of people's feet and to treat foot diseases —**po•di•a•try** noun [U]

po•di•um /ˈpoʊdiəm/ noun [C] **1** a small raised area where someone stands to give a speech or receive a prize **2** *American* a tall box with a top that slopes, used for resting documents on when you are making a speech

po•em /ˈpoʊəm/ noun [C] ★ a piece of writing that uses beautiful or unusual language. It is arranged in lines that have a particular beat and often RHYME.

po•et /ˈpoʊət/ noun [C] someone who writes poetry

po•et•ic /poʊˈetɪk/ adj connected with poetry, or having the qualities of poetry

po•et•ry /ˈpoʊətri/ noun [U] ★ poems: *the poetry of Walt Whitman* ♦ *a poetry book*

poign•ant /ˈpɔɪnjənt/ adj giving you feelings of sadness —**poign•an•cy** noun [U], **poign•ant•ly** adv

point¹ /pɔɪnt/ noun ★★★

1 idea/opinion	7 particular place
2 what you want to say	8 unit for game score
3 reason	9 unit of measurement
4 particular time	10 sharp end of sth
5 stage in process	11 decimal point
6 aspect/feature	+ PHRASES

1 [C] one idea or opinion among a number of others: *I disagree with you on **a couple of points**.*
2 [singular] the thing that you are trying to say: ***My point is** that we're spending too much time on details.* ♦ *She **missed the point*** (=did not understand it) *and thought I was blaming her.*
3 [singular] the reason for something: *I see **no point in** discussing this any more.* ♦ *I'm sorry – I just don't **get the point*** (=understand the reason). ♦ *What is **the point of** your visit?*
4 [C] a particular moment in time: ***At that point** I left the room.* ♦ ***At this point in time***

P

we can't afford to hire any more people.
5 [C] a particular stage in a process: *the freezing/boiling point of water* ♦ *We're just trying to* ***reach a point*** *where both sides will sit down together and talk.*
6 [C] an aspect or feature: *Patience is* ***not one of his strong points.***
7 [C] a particular place: *We'll meet at a point halfway between here and your hotel.*
8 [C] a unit for counting the score in a game or sport: *Our team is two points behind.*
9 [C] a unit of measurement: *Interest rates fell by 2 percentage points.*
10 [C] the sharp end of something: *The potatoes should be soft when pierced with the point of a knife.*
11 [C] the word for a DECIMAL POINT, used when saying a number: 6.3 is said as "six point three"
PHRASES **beside the point** not relevant to what is happening or being said right now
get to the point to stop talking about unimportant details and say what is most important
have (got) a point to have made an important statement
make a point of doing sth to be certain that you do something, usually in an obvious way: *He now made a point of avoiding her.*
more to the point used for saying that something is more relevant and important
the point of no return the moment at which it becomes impossible to change or stop something
point of view a way of judging a situation, based on a particular aspect
up to a point to some degree, but not completely

P

> Words often used with **point**
> *Adjectives often used with* ***point*** *(noun, sense 1)*
> ■ **crucial, fundamental, important, key, main +** POINT: used about points that are important for what you are trying to say

point² /pɔɪnt/ verb ★★★
1 [I/T] to show something by holding out your finger or a long thin object: *Don't point. They'll know we're looking at them.* ♦ *He pointed his stick in the direction of the bird.* ♦ *"What's through there?" he asked,* ***pointing at*** *the door.*
2 [I] to show a particular direction or place, usually using a sign or symbol: *The arrow pointed left toward the exit door.*
3 [I/T] to aim an object at someone or something, or to be aimed at someone or something: *All you have to do is point the camera and shoot.* ♦ **point sth at/toward sb/sth** *He pointed his rifle at the deer.*
4 [I/T] to show someone the direction in which they should go: *Could you point me in the direction of the exit?*
PHRASE **point the/a finger (at sb)** to accuse someone of something
PHRASAL VERBS **ˌpoint sth ˈout** to tell someone something: *Thank you for pointing that out.* ♦ **+that** *He pointed out that we had two hours of free time before dinner.*
ˌpoint sb/sth ˈout to show someone who a person is or where something is: *Which one is Jane's brother? Can you point him out to me?* ♦ *He pointed out the best beaches on the map.*
ˈpoint to sth to show the truth or importance of something: *The evidence clearly points to her guilt.*

ˌpoint-ˈblank adj, adv in a very firm and direct way: *Polly refused point-blank to let me use the car.*
PHRASE **at point-blank range** if you shoot someone at point-blank range, you hold the gun very close to their body

point•ed /ˈpɔɪntəd/ adj **1** with a point on the end **2** done in a way that shows that you are annoyed or do not agree: *a pointed comment/remark* —**point•ed•ly** adv

point•er /ˈpɔɪntər/ noun [C] **1** *informal* a piece of advice or information **2** a long pole for pointing at something such as a map or picture

point•less /ˈpɔɪntləs/ adj lacking any purpose or use —**point•less•ly** adv, **point•less•ness** noun [U]

poise /pɔɪz/ noun [U] **1** a controlled and relaxed way of behaving **2** a graceful calm way of moving, standing, or sitting

poised /pɔɪzd/ adj **1** about to do or achieve something after preparing for it: *Japan was poised to become the biggest foreign investor in Vietnam.* **2** waiting in a position where you can make a movement as soon as you need to: *Two guards stood poised with their hands on their guns.* **3** behaving in a controlled and relaxed way

poi•son¹ /ˈpɔɪz(ə)n/ noun [C/U] a substance that can kill you or make you sick if you eat, drink, or breathe it

poi•son² /ˈpɔɪz(ə)n/ verb [T] **1** to kill someone, or make them very sick, by giving them poison: *He was suspected of poisoning his wife.* **2** to put poison in something: *Waste from the factories is poisoning the water supply.*

poi•son•ing /ˈpɔɪz(ə)nɪŋ/ noun [C/U] an occasion when someone is affected by poison

poi•son•ous /ˈpɔɪz(ə)nəs/ adj **1** containing poison: *poisonous gases/plants* **2** capable of producing poison: *a poisonous snake*

poke¹ /poʊk/ verb **1** [I/T] to push something quickly with your finger or a pointed object: *Jane poked me in the arm to get my attention.* **2** [T] to put something into a space: *The kid was poking a stick down a drain.*
PHRASE **poke fun (at)** to make unkind jokes about someone or something

poke² /poʊk/ noun [C] a quick push with your finger or a pointed object

pok•er /ˈpoʊkər/ noun **1** [U] a card game in which players try to win money **2** [C] a metal stick for moving the coal or wood of a fire around

po•lar /ˈpoʊlər/ adj coming from or relating to an area near the North Pole or the South Pole

ˈpolar ˌbear noun [C] a large white bear that lives in areas near the North Pole

po•lar•ize /ˈpoʊləˌraɪz/ verb [I/T] to form two very different groups, opinions, or situations that are completely opposite to each other, or to cause this to happen —**po•lar•i•za•tion** /ˌpoʊlərɪˈzeɪʃ(ə)n/ noun [U]

Po•lar•oid /ˈpoʊlərɔɪd/ *trademark* a type of camera that produces photographs immediately, or a photograph from this type of camera

pole /poʊl/ noun [C] ★
1 a long thin stick, often used for holding or supporting something: *There were rows of poles supporting young bean plants.*
2 one of the points on the very top or bottom of the Earth, called the North Pole and the South Pole
PHRASE **poles apart** completely different

po•lem•ic /pəˈlemɪk/ noun [C/U] *formal* a strong statement of opinion, especially negative opinion —**po•lem•i•cal** adj

ˈpole ˌvault, the noun [singular] a sport in which you use a long pole to push yourself over a high bar

po•lice¹ /pəˈlis/ noun [plural] ★★★ the official organization that tries to catch criminals and checks that people obey the law, or the people that work for this organization: *traffic/riot police* ♦ *a police car* ♦ *If you don't leave, I'll call* ***the police.***

po•lice² /pəˈlis/ verb [T] to use police officers to control an area or event

poˈlice deˌpartment noun [C] *American* the police organization that is responsible for a particular city

poˈlice ˌforce noun [C] an organized group of police officers in charge of a particular area

po•lice•man /pəˈlismən/ (plural **po•lice•men** /pəˈlismən/) noun [C] a male police officer

poˈlice ˌofficer noun [C] a member of the police

poˈlice ˌstate noun [C] a country where the government controls people and limits their freedom very severely

poˈlice ˌstation noun [C] the building where the police of a particular place work

po•lice•wom•an /pəˈlisˌwʊmən/ (plural **po•lice•wom•en** /pəˈlisˌwɪmɪn/) noun [C] a female police officer

pol•i•cy /ˈpɑləsi/ noun ★★★
1 [C/U] a set of plans or actions that are agreed on by a government, political party, business, or other organization: *the state's economic policy* ♦ *It is not the hospital's policy to disclose the names of patients.* ♦ *What is the party's* ***policy on*** *immigration?*
2 [C] a contract between an insurance company and a person or organization: *Read the wording of your policy very carefully.*

po•li•o /ˈpoʊlioʊ/ noun [U] a serious infectious disease that mostly affects children and destroys muscles

pol•ish¹ /ˈpɑlɪʃ/ verb [T] **1** to rub the surface of something in order to make it shine: *They spend most of their time polishing shoes.* **2** to improve a skill by practicing: *He'd spent the summer polishing his flying skills.*
PHRASAL VERBS **ˌpolish sth ˈoff** *informal* to eat or drink something until it is finished: *Well, it didn't take us long to polish off the ice cream.*
ˌpolish sth ˈup *same as* **polish¹** 2: *I could do the job if I spent some time polishing up my Spanish.*

pol•ish² /ˈpɑlɪʃ/ noun [C/U] a substance that you rub onto an object to make it shine: *furniture/shoe polish*

pol•ished /ˈpɑlɪʃt/ adj **1** clean and shiny because of being rubbed: *a highly polished wooden floor* **2** of very high quality: *a polished performance*

po•lite /pəˈlaɪt/ adj ★ behaving toward other people in a pleasant way that follows all the usual rules of society = COURTEOUS ≠ RUDE: *a polite refusal* ♦ ***It's not polite to*** *talk with your mouth full of food.* ♦ *You must be more* ***polite to*** *the customers.* —**po•lite•ly** adv, **po•lite•ness** noun [U]

po•lit•i•cal /pəˈlɪtɪk(ə)l/ adj ★★★
1 relating to politics: *the importance of political stability* ♦ *the political system in the U.S.* ♦ *political leaders/opponents/parties*
2 interested or involved in politics: *I'm really not very political at all.*
3 relating to relationships of power that exist between people in an organization: *It was a purely political decision to give him the job.*
—**po•lit•i•cal•ly** /pəˈlɪtɪkli/ adv

poˌlitical ˈaction comˌmittee noun [C] an organization in the U.S. created to raise money to help supporters of its ideas to be elected

poˌlitically corˈrect adj using language or behavior that is not offensive to groups of people who have often been affected by DISCRIMINATION (=unfair treatment) —**poˌlitical corˈrectness** noun [U]

poˌlitical ˈprisoner noun [C] someone who is sent to prison for opposing their government

poˌlitical ˈscience noun [U] the study of politics and the way that political power is used in a country

pol•i•ti•cian /ˌpɑləˈtɪʃ(ə)n/ noun [C] ★★ someone who has a job in politics

po•lit•i•cize /pəˈlɪtəˌsaɪz/ verb [T] **1** to cause something to become involved with politics: *The tobacco issue is becoming too politicized.* **2** to make someone more interested and involved in politics

pol•i•tics /ˈpɑlətɪks/ noun ★★★
1 [U] the ideas and activities that are involved in getting power in an area or governing it: *She's heavily involved in* ***local politics.***
2 [plural] your beliefs and attitudes about how government should work: *Her politics became more conservative as she grew older.*
3 [U] the profession of being a politician: *He entered politics at the age of 21.*
4 [U] the ideas and activities that people within a particular group use to try to get power: *Now that I'm self-employed, I don't have to worry about office politics.*

Word family: politics
Words in the same family as politics
- political *adj*
- politically *adv*
- politician *n*
- apolitical *adj*
- politicize *v*

pol•ka /ˈpoʊlkə/ noun [C] a fast lively dance, or the music for this dance

poll¹ /poʊl/ noun ★
1 [C] an occasion when a lot of people are asked their opinions about something, usually as research for a political party,

P

television program, etc.: *A recent poll indicated that most people supported a ban on tobacco advertising.* ♦ *According to a poll conducted last week, 75% of the public support the new law.*
2 the polls [plural] the place where people vote: *The polls close at ten o'clock.* ♦ *Citizens across the country will be* ***going to the polls*** (=voting in an election) *tomorrow.*

poll² /poʊl/ verb [T] **1** to ask a lot of people their opinions about something, especially a political issue: *Over half of those polled said that they were satisfied with the government's performance.* **2** to get a particular number or percentage of votes in an election

pol·len /ˈpalən/ noun [U] a powder that flowers produce. It is carried by the wind or by insects to other flowers so that they can produce seeds.

ˈpollen ˌcount noun [C] a measurement of how much pollen there is in the air

ˈpolling ˌstation or **ˈpolling ˌplace** noun [C] a building where people go to vote in an election

poll·ster /ˈpoʊlstər/ noun [C] *mainly journalism* a person or organization that prepares a POLL

pol·lut·ant /pəˈlut(ə)nt/ noun [C/U] a substance that is harmful to the environment

pol·lute /pəˈlut/ verb [T] to make air, water, or land dirty and dangerous: *The oil spill has polluted the harbor.* —**pol·lut·ed** adj: *heavily/badly polluted rivers* —**pol·lu·ter** noun [C]

P

pol·lu·tion /pəˈluʃ(ə)n/ noun [U] ★★ chemicals and other substances that have a harmful effect on air, water, or land: *new measures to prevent pollution levels from rising* ♦ *The agency is responsible for controlling air pollution.*

Words often used with pollution

Verbs often used with ***pollution***
- **combat, control, prevent, tackle** + POLLUTION: stop pollution from happening
- **cut, limit, reduce** + POLLUTION: make the amount of pollution less

po·lo /ˈpoʊloʊ/ noun [U] a game in which two teams of players ride horses and hit a ball with long wooden hammers

ˈpolo ˌshirt noun [C] a cotton shirt with a collar, a few buttons at the neck, and short sleeves

pol·y·es·ter /ˌpaliˈestər/ noun [U] a light cloth made from artificial fibers

pol·y·graph /ˈpaliˌgræf/ noun [C] *technical* a LIE DETECTOR

pol·yp /ˈpalɪp/ noun [C] a small lump that grows inside your body

pome·gran·ate /ˈpamˌgrænət/ noun [C] a round fruit that has a hard skin and a lot of thick seeds inside

pomp /pamp/ noun [U] formal ceremony, especially involving expensive clothes and special traditions

pom·pom /ˈpampam/ noun [C] **1** a large round ball made of loose plastic strings that is carried by a CHEERLEADER at sports events **2** a ball made of YARN, used as a decoration on clothing

pom·pous /ˈpampəs/ adj *showing disapproval* speaking or behaving in a very serious and formal way that shows that you think you are very important —**pom·pos·i·ty** /pamˈpasəti/ noun [U]

pond /pand/ noun [C] an area of water that is smaller than a lake: *a duck pond*

pon·der /ˈpandər/ verb [I/T] *formal* to think carefully about something for a long time before making a decision: *Mike pondered what he should say to his wife.*

pon·der·ous /ˈpand(ə)rəs/ adj *literary* **1** moving slowly because of being big and heavy **2** ponderous writing or speech is serious and boring

pon·tif·i·cate /panˈtɪfɪˌkeɪt/ verb [I] *formal* to give your opinions in an annoying way that shows that you think you know a lot

po·ny¹ /ˈpoʊni/ noun [C] a small horse

po·ny² /ˈpoʊni/ PHRASAL VERB **ˈpony (sth) up** *American informal* to give money in order to pay for something: *These five energy operators ponied up $4.1 million for the Bush campaign.*

po·ny·tail /ˈpoʊniˌteɪl/ noun [C] long hair that is tied at the back of your head and hangs down —*picture* → HAIRSTYLE

poo /pu/ noun [C/U] *British informal* poop

poo·dle /ˈpud(ə)l/ noun [C] a dog with thick curly fur

pool¹ /pul/ noun ★★

1 water to swim in	4 light shining on area
2 area of liquid	5 group of people
3 name of game	6 competition

1 [C] a large structure filled with water for people to swim in = SWIMMING POOL: *a heated indoor pool*
2 [C] a small area of liquid: *The water collected in a little pool on the floor.* ♦ *a muddy road dotted with* ***pools of*** *rainwater* ♦ ***a pool of blood***
3 [U] a game in which two players hit balls into holes at the edges of a table using a cue (=long stick)
4 [C] a small area of light: *The sun cast* ***a*** *small* ***pool of light*** *on the dirty floor.*
5 [C] a group that shares something, or that someone or something can be chosen from: *a car pool* ♦ *The training program is helping to establish* ***a pool of*** *local qualified craftsmen.*
6 [U] a competition in which people try to guess the result of a game, competition, etc. in order to win money

pool² /pul/ verb [T] to share something such as money, ideas, equipment, etc. with a group of people: *It seemed sensible for us to pool our resources.*

poop /pup/ noun [C/U] *American informal* solid waste that comes out of your body when you use the toilet. This word is used especially by and to children. —**poop** verb [I]

pooped /pupt/ adj *American informal* very tired

poor /pʊr/ adj ★★★

1 lacking money	4 lacking sth important
2 people without money	5 feeling sorry for sb
3 of low quality	6 not skillful

1 having little money and few possessions ≠ RICH: *a poor family/area/country* ♦ *We*

were very poor and could barely afford the necessities of life.
2 the poor people who have little money and few possessions
3 not as good as expected or needed = BAD: *poor health/eyesight/hearing* ♦ *The buildings were all* ***in poor condition.*** ♦ *Wages around here are very poor.*
4 not having enough of something important: *a country poor in natural resources*
5 *spoken* used for showing that you feel sorry for someone: *The poor child had lost both his parents.*
6 *formal* not skillful or clever ≠ GOOD: *I was always put with the poorest students in the class.*

poor·ly /ˈpʊrli/ adv badly: *a poorly written essay*

pop¹ /pɑp/ verb ★

1 burst	5 ears feel pressure
2 make sudden noise	6 when eyes open wide
3 go/move quickly	+ PHRASE
4 put sth somewhere	+ PHRASAL VERB

1 [I/T] if something such as a BALLOON pops, or if you pop it, it bursts
2 [I/T] to make a sudden noise like a small explosion, or to make something do this: *Champagne corks were popping.*
3 [I] *informal* to go somewhere quickly or for a short time: *He kept* ***popping in and out,*** *asking all kinds of questions.*
4 [T] to move something quickly to a particular position: *She picked a berry and popped it into her mouth.*
5 [I] if your ears pop, you feel a sudden change of pressure in them
6 [I] *informal* if your eyes pop, they open very wide in surprise or excitement
PHRASE **pop the question** *informal* to ask someone to marry you
PHRASAL VERB **ˌpop ˈup** to appear very quickly or suddenly: *The daffodils and tulips are popping up everywhere.*

pop² /pɑp/ noun ★
1 [U] POP MUSIC: *Her music combines funk and pop.*
2 [C] a sudden short sound like a small explosion: *The balloon burst with* ***a loud pop.***
3 [U] *informal* a sweet drink containing many BUBBLES: *a can of pop*
4 [C] *American informal old-fashioned* your father

pop³ /pɑp/ adj **1** created for, or popular with, a very large number of people: *pop psychology* **2** relating to POP MUSIC: *a pop singer/record/song*

pop·corn /ˈpɑpˌkɔrn/ noun [U] a food made from dried grains that swell when they are heated

Pope /poʊp/ noun [C] the leader of the Roman Catholic Church

pop·lar /ˈpɑplər/ noun [C] a tall thin tree

ˈpop ˌmusic noun [U] a type of music that is popular with many people, especially young people

pop·py /ˈpɑpi/ noun [C] a red flower with a black center that produces small black seeds —*picture* → C9

ˈpop ˌquiz noun [C] *American* a short test that teachers give to students without any warning

Pop·si·cle /ˈpɑpsɪk(ə)l/ *American trademark* a piece of sweet flavored ice on a stick

pop·u·lace /ˈpɑpjələs/ noun [U] *formal* the people who live in a particular country or area

pop·u·lar /ˈpɑpjələr/ adj ★★★
1 liked by many people ≠ UNPOPULAR: *Jenny is one of the most popular girls in the school.* ♦ *a popular brand of breakfast cereal*
2 intended for, or involving, ordinary people rather than experts or leaders: *popular science/psychology* ♦ *There is little* ***popular support*** *for their economic reform policies.*
3 a popular belief, feeling, attitude, etc. is one that many people have: *It's a popular misconception that all women love shopping.*

pop·u·lar·i·ty /ˌpɑpjəˈlerəti/ noun [U] a situation in which someone or something is popular with many people: *The popularity of professional sports has been increasing steadily.*

pop·u·lar·ize /ˈpɑpjələˌraɪz/ verb [T] to make something popular with many people: *The Beatles popularized British rock in the early 1960s.* —**pop·u·lar·i·za·tion** /ˌpɑpjələrɪˈzeɪʃ(ə)n/ noun [U]

pop·u·lar·ly /ˈpɑpjlərli/ adv by most people, or in most situations: *The duchess is popularly known as "Fergie."*

pop·u·late /ˈpɑpjəˌleɪt/ verb **be populated** if an area is populated by people or animals, they live there: *Burundi is one of the most densely populated countries in the world.*

pop·u·la·tion /ˌpɑpjəˈleɪʃ(ə)n/ noun [singular] ★★★
1 the number of people who live in a particular area: *Los Angeles has* ***a population of*** *over 3 million.* ♦ *Better health care and agriculture have led to rapid* ***population growth.***
2 all the people who live in a particular area: *Less than 40% of the population voted in the last election.* ♦ *the aging* ***population*** *of the U.S.*

pop·u·list /ˈpɑpjəlɪst/ adj representing the interests and opinions of ordinary people —**pop·u·list** noun [C]

pop·u·lous /ˈpɑpjələs/ adj a populous area has many people living in it

por·ce·lain /ˈpɔrs(ə)lɪn/ noun [U] a hard shiny white substance that is used for making things such as dishes, cups, and decorations, or the things that are made from this substance

porch noun [C] **1** *American* an open area with a floor and a roof, attached to the lower level of a house —*picture* → C1 **2** *British* a small area covered by a roof at the entrance to a house or other building

pore¹ /pɔr/ noun [C] one of the very small holes in the surface of your skin

pore² /pɔr/ PHRASAL VERB **ˈpore ˌover sth** to examine or read something very carefully and in a lot of detail: *Ben was poring over computer printouts with an engineer.*

pork /pɔrk/ noun [U] the meat from a pig: *pork chops* → BACON, HAM

porn /pɔrn/ noun [U] *informal* PORNOGRAPHY

por·nog·ra·phy /pɔ'nɑgrəfi/ noun [U] movies, pictures, magazines, etc. that show sexual activities in a very obvious way that is intended to make people sexually excited —**por·no·graph·ic** /ˌpɔrnə'græfɪk/ adj

po·rous /'pɔrəs/ adj with a lot of very small holes that air and water can pass through

por·poise /'pɔrpəs/ noun [C] a large sea animal, similar to a DOLPHIN

por·ridge /'pɔrɪdʒ/ noun [U] *British* OATMEAL

port /pɔrt/ noun ★★
1 [C/U] an area of water on the coast where ships stop, or a city with a port: *New York is the busiest port on the East Coast.* ♦ *We'll have to spend 10 days **in port** for repairs.*
2 [C] *computing* a part of a computer where you can connect another piece of equipment
3 [U] the left side of a ship or airplane
4 [U] a strong sweet wine made in Portugal

port·a·ble /'pɔrtəb(ə)l/ adj easy to carry or move: *a portable television/heater*

por·tal /'pɔrt(ə)l/ noun [C] *computing* a WEBSITE that has LINKS (=connections) to other WEBSITES

por·ter /'pɔrtər/ noun [C] someone in a station, airport, or hotel whose job is helping people with their suitcases and showing them where to go

port·fo·li·o /pɔrt'fouliou/ noun [C] **1** a collection of pictures, photographs, or documents that you use as examples of the work that you have done **2** all of the INVESTMENTS that a person or company has made

port·hole /'pɔrtˌhoul/ noun [C] a small round window in the side of a ship or airplane

P

por·tion /'pɔrʃ(ə)n/ noun [C] **1** a part of something: *Only a small portion of the population could read.* **2** the amount of food that one person eats at a meal: *If you eat smaller portions, you will begin to lose weight.*

port·ly /'pɔrtli/ adj a portly person is fairly fat＝STOUT

por·trait /'pɔrtrət/ noun ★
1 [C] a painting, drawing, or photograph of someone: *A **portrait of** her three children hangs behind her desk.*
2 [C] a description of someone or something, for example in a book: *an interesting **portrait of** life under communism*
3 [U] a way of arranging a page so that its short sides are at the top and bottom → LANDSCAPE

por·tray /pɔr'treɪ/ verb [T] **1** to show or describe someone or something in a particular way: *Opponents portray the president as weak and ineffectual.* **2** to play the part of a particular person in a movie, play, etc. —**por·tray·al** noun [C/U]

pose[1] /pouz/ verb **1** [T] to create a difficult or dangerous situation: *The oil spill poses a threat to marine life in the area.* **2** [I] to sit or stand somewhere so that someone can take a photograph of you or paint a picture of you **3** [I] to dress or behave in a particular way to make people notice you, admire you, or be impressed by you
PHRASE **pose a question** *formal* to ask a question
PHRASAL VERB **'pose as sb/sth** to pretend to be a particular person or type of person in order to trick people: *Police officers posing as customers were sold some of the stolen items.*

pose[2] /pouz/ noun [C] the position that you keep your body in when someone is taking your photograph or painting your picture

posh /pɑʃ/ adj *informal* expensive and attractive: *a posh home/hotel/restaurant*

po·si·tion[1] /pə'zɪʃ(ə)n/ noun [C] ★★★

1 way sth is placed	5 job in company
2 general situation	6 rank/status
3 where sth is	7 place in list etc.
4 opinion about issue	8 where sb plays

1 the way that someone's body or an object is placed: *First, get yourself into a comfortable position.* ♦ *He managed to push the vehicle back to an upright position.*
2 the situation that someone is in: *What would you do if you were in my position?* ♦ *I'm not **in a position to** say who my sources are.*
3 where something is in relation to other things: *Place the plant in a bright sunny position.* ♦ *Here is a chart showing **the positions of** the planets.* ♦ *Put the photographs **into position** on the page.*
4 an opinion about an important issue: *No one was sure of his **position on** any issue.* ♦ *The President will consider the facts carefully before **taking a position** on this case.*
5 a job in a company: *There are 12 women in **management positions** within the company.* ♦ *I'm sorry, **the position has** already **been filled*** (=someone has already been chosen to do the job).
6 someone's rank or status in an organization or in society: *Such behavior was clearly not acceptable for someone in **a position of authority**.*
7 the place that someone or something has in a list or competition: *Following behind in fourth position is Jeff Gordon.*
8 in team sports, the part of the field where a particular player plays

po·si·tion[2] /pə'zɪʃ(ə)n/ verb [T] to put someone or something in a particular place: *Position the microphone as close as possible to the source of the sound.*

pos·i·tive /'pɑzətɪv/ adj ★★★

1 completely certain	4 situation, etc.: good
2 expecting good things	5 showing condition
3 showing agreement	6 number: above zero

1 completely certain: *We'd met before – I was **positive about** that.* ♦ **+(that)** *Are you positive that there's been no mistake?*
2 believing that good things will happen, or that a situation will get better＝OPTIMISTIC ≠ NEGATIVE: *a positive attitude* ♦ *Try to think positive thoughts.*
3 showing agreement or approval ≠ NEGATIVE: *We couldn't be sure if her reaction would be positive.*
4 a positive experience, situation, result, etc. is a good one ≠ NEGATIVE: *The **positive aspects** of parenthood far outweigh the negative ones.* ♦ *School was **a totally positive experience** for me.*

5 a positive result in a medical test means that the person has the disease or condition that was tested for ≠ NEGATIVE
6 *technical* a positive number is higher than zero ≠ NEGATIVE

> **Words often used with positive**
> *Nouns often used with **positive** (sense 2)*
> ■ POSITIVE + **approach, attitude, outlook, view**: used about attitudes that emphasize the good aspects of something
> *Nouns often used with **positive** (sense 3)*
> ■ POSITIVE + **feedback, reaction, response**: used about reactions that show that you approve of someone or something

pos•i•tive•ly /ˈpɑzətɪvli/ adv **1** used for emphasizing that something is true: *His voice changed and became positively angry.* **2** in a way that shows that you approve or agree with something: *Most people reacted positively to the proposal.* **3** in a way that is likely to have good results: *We need to approach this problem positively.*

pos•sess /pəˈzes/ verb [T] *formal* ★★ to own or have something: *Kate is a woman who possesses a rare intelligence.* ♦ *They were all found guilty of illegally possessing firearms.*
PHRASE **what possessed you (to do sth)** *spoken* used for asking someone why they did something when you think that they made a serious mistake: *What possessed you to get involved with such a ridiculous scheme?*
—**pos•ses•sor** noun [C]

pos•sessed /pəˈzest/ adj controlled by an evil spirit

pos•ses•sion /pəˈzeʃ(ə)n/ noun ★★
1 [C] something that you own: *Their family home and possessions were destroyed in the fire.* ♦ *Her most **prized possession** is a locket that she wears constantly.*
2 [U] *formal* a situation in which you have or own something: *The seller is entitled to retain **possession of** the goods until they are paid for.* ♦ *The town of Winterset **took possession of*** (=started owning) *the castle in 1947.*

pos•ses•sive /pəˈʒesɪv/ adj **1** wanting to have all of someone's love and attention: *a jealous and possessive boyfriend* **2** not willing to share things **3** *linguistics* a possessive word or form of a word is a word such as "her," "its," "Jan's," or "dog's" that shows who or what someone or something belongs to or is connected with: *a possessive pronoun* —**pos•ses•sive•ly** adv, **pos•ses•sive•ness** noun [U]

pos•si•bil•i•ty /ˌpɑsəˈbɪləti/ noun ★★★
1 [C/U] something that might happen or be true: *Is everyone **aware of the possibility** of injury when skateboarding?* ♦ **+(that)** *There is a strong possibility that they will win the next election.*
2 [C] a likely or appropriate choice among several possible people or things: *We need to examine other possibilities before we make a final decision.*
3 possibilities [plural] opportunities to develop in a successful, interesting, or exciting way: *This old building has some intriguing possibilities.*

pos•si•ble /ˈpɑsəb(ə)l/ adj ★★★
1 able to be done, or capable of happening or being true ≠ IMPOSSIBLE: *The task will not be possible without access to the Internet.* ♦ *We need to avoid delay **if at all possible**.* ♦ *I relax with a good book **whenever possible**.* ♦ *Get **as much** information **as possible**.* ♦ **it is possible (that)** *I suppose it's possible she didn't know, but I'm fairly sure I told her.* ♦ **it is possible to do sth** *It is possible to see as far as the Golden Gate Bridge on a clear day.*
2 likely or appropriate in a particular situation or for a particular purpose: *a possible explanation* ♦ *a possible site for the new school building*
3 used with a SUPERLATIVE for emphasizing that something has the most or least of a particular quality: *Deb scored the highest score possible on the test.* ♦ *He arrived at **the worst possible** time.*
PHRASE **is it/would it be possible?** *spoken* used for asking politely if you can do something or have something: *Would it be possible to have a look at your newspaper?*

pos•si•bly /ˈpɑsəbli/ adv ★★★ likely to happen or be true, but not certain: *There is a chance of showers today and possibly a thunderstorm.* ♦ *"Do we have enough money to get a hotel room?" "Possibly."* ♦ *He is **quite possibly** the most experienced climber in the world.*
PHRASES **can/could possibly 1** used for emphasizing what is or is not possible: *There was nothing more we could possibly do under the circumstances.* ♦ *You **can't possibly** ask them to risk their lives.* **2** used for emphasizing your surprise or shock at something: *How can anyone possibly spend an hour in the shower?*
can/could sb possibly do sth? *spoken* used for asking someone to do something that you think might not be convenient for them: *Could you possibly give me a ride to work?*

post[1] /poʊst/ noun ★
1 [C] a strong thick pole made of wood or metal that is put upright in the ground
2 [C] a job, especially one with a lot of responsibility: *The President appointed her to **the post of** ambassador.*
3 [C] a place where a soldier or guard must remain in order to do their job
4 [U] *British* the MAIL

post[2] /poʊst/ verb [T] **1** to put information or a message where the public can see it, for example on a wall: *The menu and prices are posted outside the door.* **2** *computing* to put information on the Internet **3** to send someone somewhere to do a job, especially in another country: *Extra guards were posted at the border.* **4** *British* to mail a letter or package to someone
PHRASE **keep sb posted** to regularly give someone information about how something is developing or changing: *We'll keep you posted on the weather situation.*

post- /poʊst/ prefix after or later than: *the post-game show*

post•age /ˈpoʊstɪdʒ/ noun [U] money that you pay in order to send letters and packages in the mail

ˈpostage ˌstamp noun [C] *formal* a stamp that is put on an envelope

P

postures

post·al /ˈpoʊst(ə)l/ adj relating to the system that takes the mail to the people it is addressed to: *a postal clerk*

post·card /ˈpoʊs(t)ˌkɑrd/ noun [C] a small card that you write on one side of and send to someone in the mail

post·er /ˈpoʊstər/ noun [C] a large printed notice or picture that you put on a wall for decoration or to advertise something

pos·ter·i·ty /pɑˈsterəti/ noun [U] the people who will live in the future after you are dead: *We have a duty to preserve great works of art for posterity.*

post·grad·u·ate /ˌpoʊs(t)ˈgrædʒʊət/ adj **1** *American* relating to work or studies that you do after receiving an advanced degree such as an M.A. or a PH.D. **2** *British* relating to study that you do after receiving your first university degree —**post·grad·u·ate** noun [C]

post·hu·mous /ˈpɑstʃəməs/ adj given or happening after someone's death: *posthumous awards for bravery* —**post·hu·mous·ly** adv

post·ing /ˈpoʊstɪŋ/ noun [C] **1** a public notice, especially one advertising a job **2** *computing* a message put on the Internet **3** a job that someone is sent somewhere to do, usually in another country

ˈPost-ˌit *trademark* a small piece of paper with a sticky substance on the back that is used for sticking notes on other papers and surfaces —*picture* → C3

post·mark /ˈpoʊs(t)ˌmɑrk/ noun [C] an official mark that the POST OFFICE puts on a letter or package to show when and where it was mailed —**post·mark** verb [T]

post·na·tal /ˌpoʊs(t)ˈneɪt(ə)l/ adj relating to the period of time after the birth of a baby: *postnatal depression* → PRENATAL

ˈpost ˌoffice noun [C] a place where you can buy stamps, mail letters and packages, and receive mail

ˈpost office ˌbox noun [C] *formal* a PO BOX

post·pone /poʊsˈpoʊn/ verb [T] to decide that something will not be done at the time when it was planned for, but at a later time: *Bad weather forced us to postpone Friday's game.* —**post·pone·ment** noun [C/U]

post·script /ˈpoʊs(t)ˌskrɪpt/ noun [C] information that is added at the end of a letter, e-mail, or other piece of writing

pos·ture /ˈpɑstʃər/ noun [C/U] the position that your body is in when you sit, stand, or walk: *Exercise can improve your posture.*

post·war /ˌpoʊs(t)ˈwɔr/ adj happening or existing in the period of time immediately after a war, especially World War Two

pot¹ /pɑt/ noun [C] ★★
1 a deep round metal container that you cook food in: *a set of* ***pots and pans***
2 a container used for making or serving hot drinks, or the amount of a drink that a pot contains: ***a pot of tea/coffee***
3 a container that you grow plants in: *a plant pot*

pot² /pɑt/ verb [T] to put a plant in a container with soil

po·tas·si·um /pəˈtæsiəm/ noun [U] a soft white metal element that is used for making soap and FERTILIZER

po·ta·to /pəˈteɪtoʊ/ (plural **po·ta·toes**) noun [C/U] ★★ a hard round vegetable that grows under the ground: *baked potatoes* ♦ *potato salad* —*picture* → C11

ˈpotato ˌchips noun [plural] *American* very thin

P

pieces of potato that are cooked in oil and eaten cold

po•tent /ˈpoʊt(ə)nt/ adj powerful or effective: *a potent painkiller* —**po•ten•cy** noun [U]

po•ten•tial¹ /pəˈtenʃ(ə)l/ adj ★ possible or likely in the future: *The disease is a potential killer.* ♦ *a potential disaster* —**po•ten•tial•ly** adv: *a potentially harmful drug*

po•ten•tial² /pəˈtenʃ(ə)l/ noun ★
1 [U] the possibility to develop or achieve something in the future: *As a composer, she still hasn't **realized her potential**.*
2 [singular] a possibility that something will happen: *With this many people involved, there is always **a potential for conflict**.*

pot•hold•er /ˈpɑtˌhoʊldər/ noun [C] a thick piece of cloth used for protecting your hands when you are holding a hot cooking pan

pot•hole /ˈpɑtˌhoʊl/ noun [C] a hole in a road —**pot•holed** /ˈpɑtˌhoʊld/ adj

po•tion /ˈpoʊʃ(ə)n/ noun [C] a drink that is believed to be magic, poisonous, or useful as a medicine

pot•luck /ˌpɑtˈlʌk/ noun [C] *American* an informal meal to which guests bring food

pot•ted /ˈpɑtəd/ adj *American* growing in a pot: *a potted plant*

pot•ter /ˈpɑtər/ noun [C] someone who makes pottery

pot•ter•y /ˈpɑtəri/ noun [U] **1** objects such as plates and cups that are made out of baked clay **2** the activity of making pottery

pot•ty /ˈpɑti/ noun [C] a container that is used as a toilet by young children

pouch /paʊtʃ/ noun [C] **1** a small bag made of cloth or thin leather **2** a fold of skin on the body of an animal, for example the place where a KANGAROO carries its baby

poul•try /ˈpoʊltri/ noun [U] birds such as chickens that are used for meat or eggs, or the meat of these birds

pounce /paʊns/ verb [I] **1** to quickly jump on or hold someone or something: *They pounced on their suspect.* **2** to react in a very sudden way, especially by criticizing someone: *White House aides pounced on the remark.*

pound¹ /paʊnd/ noun [C] ★★★
1 a unit for measuring weight, used in several countries including the U.S. and the U.K., containing 16 OUNCES and equal to 0.454 kilograms: *The baby weighed over 10 pounds.* ♦ *half a pound of cheese*
2 a place where pets that are lost or not wanted are kept
3 **pound** or **pound key** *American* the key with the symbol # on a telephone KEYPAD or computer keyboard
4 a unit of money that is used in the U.K. and several other countries. The symbol for a pound is £.

pound² /paʊnd/ verb **1** [I/T] to hit something many times with a lot of force: *I could hear them pounding on the door.* **2** [I] to walk or run with heavy and regular steps: *She pounded down the hall to see what had happened.* **3** [I] if your heart pounds, it beats strongly and quickly because you are nervous, excited, or afraid

pour /pɔ/ verb ★★
1 [T] to make a liquid or substance flow out of a container that you are holding: **pour sb sth** *Sit down and I'll pour you a drink.* ♦ **pour sth into/over/down sth** *Pour the mixture into a dish and bake for 45 minutes.*
2 [I] to flow continuously and in large amounts: *Tears were **pouring down** her face.* ♦ *The island was evacuated as lava **poured from** the volcano.*
3 [I] to rain very hard: *The thunder and lightning stopped, but it continued to pour.*
4 [I] to arrive or go somewhere quickly in a large group or in large amounts: *Workers **poured out of** the factory train.* ♦ *Election results are beginning to **pour in**.*

PHRASAL VERBS **pour ˌdown** *same as* **pour** 3: *The rain poured down in torrents.*

ˈ**pour sth ˌinto sth** to give a lot of effort, money, or help: *They've already poured a lot of time and money into this project.*

ˌ**pour sth ˈout** to tell someone everything that you are feeling: *She began pouring out her fears about the future.*

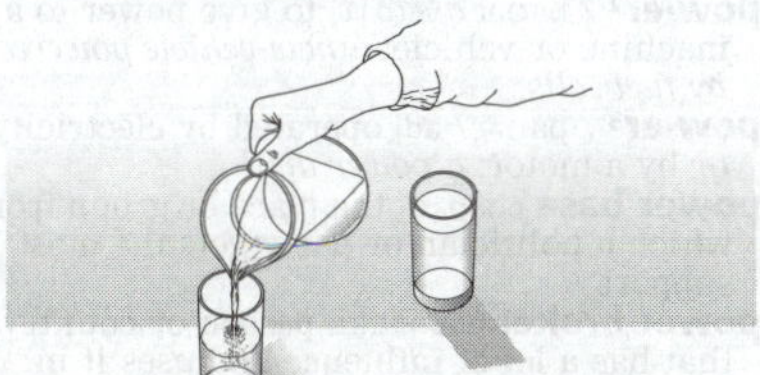

pour

pout /paʊt/ verb [I] to push your lips out in order to show that you are annoyed, or in order to look more sexually attractive —**pout** noun [C]

pov•er•ty /ˈpɑvərti/ noun [U] a situation in which someone does not have enough money to pay for their basic needs ≠ WEALTH: *Half the world's population is living in poverty.*

ˈ**poverty ˌline, the** noun [singular] the amount of money that is considered necessary to live

ˈ**poverty-ˌstricken** adj extremely poor

POW /ˌpi oʊ ˈdʌb(ə)lju/ noun [C] a PRISONER OF WAR

pow•der¹ /ˈpaʊdər/ noun [C/U] ★ a soft dry substance that looks like dust or sand: *chili powder* —**pow•der•y** adj

pow•der² /ˈpaʊdər/ verb [T] to put powder on your face or body

pow•dered /ˈpaʊdərd/ adj in the form of powder: *powdered sugar*

pow•er¹ /ˈpaʊər/ noun ★★★

1 ability to influence	6 physical force
2 ability to achieve	7 strong country
3 political control	8 natural ability
4 legal authority	+ PHRASE
5 energy/electricity	

1 [U] the ability to influence or control people: ***a power struggle** within the party* (=an attempt by each of two people or groups to get control) ♦ *Her parents still have a lot of **power over** her.* ♦ *Don't underestimate **the power of** advertising.*

2 [U] the ability to achieve something or make something happen: *purchasing/bargaining power* ♦ *Willis* ***did everything within his power*** *for his client.*
3 [U] political control of a country or government: *The ruling Social Democratic party has been* ***in power*** *for ten years.* ♦ *Later that year, the generals* ***seized power*** *in a bloody coup.*
4 [C/U] official or legal authority to do something: *An appellate court has* ***power to*** *overturn the lower court's decision.*
5 [U] energy that is used for operating equipment and machines: *solar power*
6 [U] physical force or strength: *The boy was thrown backward by* ***the power of*** *the blast.*
7 [C] a strong country that is able to influence other countries: *China has emerged as a major* ***economic power.***
8 [C/U] a natural or unusual ability for doing something: *He has amazing* ***powers of concentration.***
PHRASE **the powers that be** the people who control a situation

pow•er² /ˈpaʊər/ verb [T] to give power to a machine or vehicle: *a new vehicle powered by fuel cells*

pow•er³ /ˈpaʊər/ adj operated by electricity or by a motor: *a power drill*

ˈpower ˌbase noun [C] the place or group from which a politician or party gets the most support

ˈpower ˌbroker noun [C] a person or country that has a lot of influence and uses it in order to control other people or countries

ˈpower ˌfailure noun [C] a situation in which there is no electricity supply for a period of time = BLACKOUT

pow•er•ful /ˈpaʊrf(ə)l/ adj ★★★
1 able to influence or control what people do or think ≠ WEAK: *We live in a society where the media are extremely powerful.* ♦ *a powerful argument in favor of gun control*
2 with a lot of physical strength or force: *a powerful explosion* ♦ *a powerful athlete* ♦ *The new model has a more powerful engine.*
3 with a strong effect: *powerful drugs*
—**pow•er•ful•ly** adv

pow•er•less /ˈpaʊrləs/ adj not able to control or prevent something: *She was powerless to stop him.* —**pow•er•less•ness** noun [U]

ˈpower ˌplant noun [C] *American* a large building that contains machines that produce power, especially electricity

ˌpower ˈsteering noun [U] a system that makes it easy to turn a car with small movements of the STEERING WHEEL

ˈpower ˌtool noun [C] a tool that uses electricity or a motor

pp. abbrev pages

PR /ˌpi ˈɑr/ abbrev public relations

prac•ti•ca•ble /ˈpræktɪkəb(ə)l/ adj *formal* able to be done or used successfully

prac•ti•cal /ˈpræktɪk(ə)l/ adj ★★★
1 involving, or relating to, real situations rather than theories or ideas alone: *Unfortunately this research has no practical use.* ♦ ***Practical experience*** *can be as valuable as academic qualifications.*
2 making sensible decisions and choices based on what can be successfully achieved ≠ IMPRACTICAL: *Despite their wealth, they were always practical about money.* ♦ *a practical attitude to marriage*
3 intended to be useful or appropriate, not just fashionable or attractive: *a practical car for the family*
4 able to make repairs or do things with your hands in a skillful way

prac•ti•cal•i•ty /ˌpræktɪˈkæləti/ noun **1** [U] the quality of being useful or appropriate for a particular purpose or situation
2 practicalities [plural] the things that need to be dealt with, planned for, or done in order to achieve something

ˌpractical ˈjoke noun [C] a trick that is intended to surprise someone or make them look silly

prac•ti•cal•ly /ˈpræktɪkli/ adv **1** almost: *I was practically begging him to think again.* **2** in a way that is useful, sensible, or practical

prac•tice¹ /ˈpræktɪs/ noun [C/U] ★★★
1 occasions when you do something in order to become better at it, or the time that you spend doing this: *piano/basketball practice* ♦ *Your typing will improve* ***with practice.***
2 a way of doing something, or something that is regularly done: *It is* ***good practice*** *to check your work before handing it in.* ♦ *Bribery is* ***common practice*** *in many countries.*
3 the business or profession of a doctor, lawyer, or other professional person
PHRASES **in practice** used for talking about what really happens rather than what you think will or should happen: *It's a good idea, but I don't think it would work in practice.*
out of practice bad at doing something because you have not been doing it regularly

prac•tice² /ˈpræktɪs/ verb ★★
1 [I/T] to repeat an activity regularly so that you become better at it: *How many hours a day do you practice the piano?* ♦ **practice doing sth** *Practice putting up your tent a few times before going camping.*
2 [T] to do something regularly or in a particular way: *The early settlers seem to have practiced farming.*
3 [T] to perform the activities and duties of your religion: *She practices Catholicism.*
4 [I/T] to work in a particular profession, especially in the medical or legal profession: *She lives in Seattle, where she practices law.* ♦ *He completed his medical training but has never practiced.*

prac•ticed /ˈpræktɪst/ adj **1** skillful in something as a result of experience
2 learned or developed through experience

prac•tic•ing /ˈpræktɪsɪŋ/ adj active in a particular profession, religion, or way of life

prac•tise /ˈpræktɪs/ the British spelling of practice²

prac•ti•tion•er /prækˈtɪʃ(ə)nər/ noun [C] *formal* someone who works in a particular profession, especially medicine

prag•mat•ic /prægˈmætɪk/ adj involving or emphasizing practical results rather than theories and ideas: *a pragmatic approach to problem solving* —**prag•mat•i•cal•ly**

/præg'mætɪkli/ adv, **prag•ma•tism** /'prægmə,tɪzəm/ noun [U], **prag•ma•tist** /'prægmətɪst/ noun [C]

prai•rie /'preri/ noun [C] a large flat area in central North America that is covered with grass and farms but that has no trees

'prairie ,dog noun [C] a small brown animal that lives in holes in the ground on the prairies of North America

praise[1] /preɪz/ verb [T] to express strong approval or admiration for someone or something: *If you never praise your kids, how can they know when they're doing something right?* ♦ *The painting was highly praised.*

praise[2] /preɪz/ noun [U] an expression of strong approval or admiration

praise•wor•thy /'preɪz,wɜrði/ adj *formal* deserving praise or admiration

prance /præns/ verb [I] *showing disapproval* to move around in a lively way that seems silly to other people

prank /præŋk/ noun [C] a silly trick that you play on someone in order to surprise them

prat•tle /'præt(ə)l/ verb [I] to talk in a silly way for a long time about unimportant things —**prat•tle** noun [U]

pray /preɪ/ verb ★
1 [I/T] to speak to God or a SAINT, for example, to give thanks or to ask for help: *They **prayed for** peace.* ♦ **+(that)** *We all prayed that she would soon recover.*
2 [I] to hope or wish very strongly for something: **+(that)** *Everyone prayed that the war wouldn't last long.*

prayer /prer/ noun ★
1 [C] something that you say when you speak to God: *He **said a prayer** for their safe return.* ♦ *a **prayer for** peace*
2 [U] the practice of speaking to God: *the power of prayer*

'prayer ,book noun [C] a book that contains prayers

'prayer ,mat noun [C] a small carpet that Muslims put on the floor under their knees when they pray

pre- /pri/ prefix before: *prewar fashions* ♦ *preschool programs* (=for children who are too young for school)

preach /pritʃ/ verb **1** [I/T] to talk about a religious subject to a group of people, especially in a church **2** [I] *showing disapproval* to tell people how to behave = LECTURE

preach•er /'pritʃər/ noun [C] someone whose job is to give religious speeches or lead religious ceremonies in some Christian churches

pre•ar•ranged /,priə'reɪndʒd/ adj planned or agreed to at an earlier time

pre•car•i•ous /prɪ'keriəs/ adj likely to change or become dangerous without warning: *For the refugees life was always precarious.* —**pre•car•i•ous•ly** adv

pre•cau•tion /prɪ'kɔʃ(ə)n/ noun [C] something that you do in order to protect people or things against possible harm or trouble: *Doctors recommend taking precautions to protect your skin from the sun.*

pre•cau•tion•ar•y /prɪ'kɔʃ(ə)n,eri/ adj done or used for protection against possible harm or trouble: *a precautionary step/measure*

pre•cede /prɪ'sid/ verb [T] *formal* to happen or exist before another person or thing: *These exercises must always be preceded by a warm-up.*

prec•e•dence /'presɪdəns/ noun **take precedence (over)** if something takes precedence over something else, it is more important and should be dealt with first

prec•e•dent /'presɪdənt/ noun [C/U] an action or event in the past that is used as an example when someone wants to do the same thing again: *This decision could set a dangerous precedent.*

pre•ced•ing /prɪ'sidɪŋ/ adj existing or coming immediately before someone or something else

pre•cinct /'pri,sɪŋkt/ noun [C] *American* **1** a district in a town or city, usually organized for voting, police, or government purposes **2** the police station that is in charge of a particular district in a town or city

pre•cious[1] /'preʃəs/ adj ★ very valuable: *a precious jewel* ♦ *Our freedom is the most precious thing we have.*

pre•cious[2] /'preʃəs/ adv **precious little/few** used for emphasizing how little there is of something

,precious 'metal noun [C] a valuable metal such as gold or silver

,precious 'stone noun [C] a valuable stone such as a DIAMOND or RUBY

prec•i•pice /'presəpɪs/ noun [C] a very steep high CLIFF

pre•cip•i•tate /prɪ'sɪpɪtət/ verb [T] *formal* to make something happen or begin to exist: *Such headaches can be precipitated by certain foods as well as stress.*

pre•cip•i•ta•tion /prɪ,sɪpɪ'teɪʃ(ə)n/ noun [U] *technical* rain, snow, HAIL, etc.

pre•cise /prɪ'saɪs/ adj ★ exact and accurate: *The precise date and place of his birth are unknown.* ♦ *Lara was able to tell me everything that had happened **in precise detail**.*
PHRASE **to be precise** used for saying that the information that you are giving about something is more exact than what you have said before = EXACT: *It's her 70th birthday soon, in March to be precise.*

pre•cise•ly /prɪ'saɪsli/ adv **1** clearly **2** used for adding emphasis to a reason or explanation **3** exactly: *He knows precisely what we want.* **4** *spoken* used for showing that you completely agree with what someone says

pre•ci•sion /prɪ'sɪʒ(ə)n/ noun [U] the quality of being accurate and exact

pre•clude /prɪ'klud/ verb [T] *formal* if one thing precludes another, the first thing prevents the second one from happening

pre•co•cious /prɪ'koʊʃəs/ adj a precocious child is more intelligent or behaves in a more developed way than is normal for their age

pre•con•ceived /,prikən'sivd/ adj a preconceived idea or opinion is formed before you have all the facts

pre•con•cep•tion /,prikən'sepʃ(ə)n/ noun [C] an idea or opinion about something that you form before you have all the facts

pre•con•di•tion /,prikən'dɪʃ(ə)n/ noun [C]

P

something that must happen before something else can happen

pre·cur·sor /prɪˈkɜrsər/ noun [C] something that exists before something else

pre·date /ˌpriˈdeɪt/ verb [T] to exist or happen earlier than something else

pred·a·tor /ˈpredətər/ noun [C] **1** an animal that kills and eats other animals **2** *business* a company that tries to take control of other companies —**pred·a·to·ry** /ˈpredəˌtɔri/ adj: *a predatory takeover bid*

pred·e·ces·sor /ˈpredəˌsesər/ noun [C] the person who had a job before someone else

pre·de·ter·mined /ˌpridɪˈtɜrmɪnd/ adj decided in advance

pre·dic·a·ment /ˈpriˈdɪkɑmənt/ noun [C] a difficult or unpleasant situation that is not easy to get out of

pred·i·ca·tive /ˈpredɪkətɪv, ˈpredɪˌkeɪtɪv/ adj *linguistics* predicative adjectives and phrases follow a verb, for example "tired" in the sentence "We were tired"

pre·dict /prɪˈdɪkt/ verb [T] ★ to say what you think will happen in the future: *They're predicting heavy rain for tomorrow.* ♦ **+(that)** *Industry leaders predict that another 8,000 jobs could be lost by the end of the year.*

pre·dict·a·ble /prɪˈdɪktəb(ə)l/ adj **1** something that is predictable happens in the way that you expect it to = FORESEEABLE **2** someone who is predictable always behaves or reacts in the same way ≠ UNPREDICTABLE —**pre·dict·a·bly** adv

pre·dic·tion /prɪˈdɪkʃ(ə)n/ noun [C] a statement about what you think will happen in the future

P

pre·dis·posed /ˌpridɪsˈpoʊzd/ adj **predisposed to/toward sth** likely to think, feel, or behave in a particular way, or to develop a particular medical condition

pre·dis·po·si·tion /ˌpridɪspəˈzɪʃ(ə)n/ noun **have a predisposition to/toward sth** to be likely to think or behave in a particular way, or to develop a particular medical condition

pre·dom·i·nant /prɪˈdɑmɪnənt/ adj **1** most common, or greatest in number or amount **2** most important or powerful —**pre·dom·i·nance** noun [U]

pre·dom·i·nant·ly /prɪˈdɑmɪnəntli/ adv mainly: *a predominantly Catholic country*

pre·dom·i·nate /prɪˈdɑmɪˌneɪt/ verb [I] *formal* to be more important, or greater in number or amount, than other things or people

pre·em·i·nent /priˈemɪnənt/ adj best at a particular activity: *Spain's preeminent guitarist*

pre·empt /priˈempt/ verb [T] **1** to do something in order to try to prevent something from happening **2** to be broadcast instead of another planned program

pre·emp·tive /priˈemptɪv/ adj said or done before someone else has a chance to act or attack so that their plans or actions are prevented from happening

preen /prin/ verb [I/T] if a bird or animal preens, or if it preens itself, it cleans and arranges its feathers or fur

pre·fab·ri·cat·ed /priˈfæbrɪˌkeɪtəd/ or **pre·fab** /ˈprifæb/ adj a prefabricated building is built in sections that can be moved and put together quickly

pref·ace /ˈprefəs/ noun [C] an introduction to a book or a speech

pre·fect /ˈpriˌfekt/ noun [C] a public official in some countries who has authority over a particular district

pre·fer /prɪˈfɜr/ verb [T] ★★★ to like or want someone or something more than someone or something else: *Which do you prefer, the red or the blue one?* ♦ **prefer sb/sth to sb/sth** *Even today, most Americans prefer coffee to tea.* ♦ **prefer to do sth** *Do you prefer to exercise indoors or outdoors?* ♦ **prefer doing sth** *I prefer working alone.*

pref·er·a·ble /ˈpref(ə)rəb(ə)l/ adj more appropriate or useful than something else

pref·er·a·bly /ˈpref(ə)rəbli/ adv used for saying what would be best in a particular situation even if it is not possible: *Applicants should have a degree, preferably in a foreign language.*

pref·er·ence /ˈpref(ə)rəns/ noun [C/U] ★ someone or something that you prefer to something else: *Either tomorrow or Wednesday is fine for me. Do you* ***have a preference?*** ♦ *It's really just a* ***matter of personal preference*** *which you choose.*

PHRASE **in preference to** instead of someone or something else that you like or want less: *They drink beer in preference to wine.*

pref·er·en·tial /ˌprefəˈrenʃ(ə)l/ adj giving one person or group an advantage over all others: *Neither sex should get preferential treatment.*

pre·fix /ˈpriˌfɪks/ noun [C] *linguistics* a group of letters that is added to the beginning of a word in order to change its meaning. For example, the prefix "un-" is added to the word "important" in order to form the word "unimportant."

preg·nan·cy /ˈpregnənsi/ noun [C/U] the condition of being pregnant, or the period of time when a woman is pregnant

preg·nant /ˈpregnənt/ adj ★ if a woman is pregnant, she has a baby developing inside her body: *I was only 19 when I* ***got pregnant.*** ♦ *She was* ***pregnant with*** *twins.*

pre·heat /ˌpriˈhit/ verb [T] to heat an oven so that it is the correct temperature for cooking something

pre·his·tor·ic /ˌprihɪˈstɔrɪk/ adj relating to the period of time before anything was written down by humans: *prehistoric animals*

pre·judge /ˌpriˈdʒʌdʒ/ verb [T] to form an opinion about someone or something before you know everything about them

prej·u·dice¹ /ˈpredʒədɪs/ noun [C/U] an unreasonable opinion or feeling, especially the feeling of not liking a particular group of people: *We've been working hard to overcome prejudice against women in politics.*

prej·u·dice² /ˈpredʒədɪs/ verb [T] to make someone form an opinion about someone or something before they have enough information

prej·u·diced /ˈpredʒədɪst/ adj someone who is prejudiced has an unreasonable opinion or feeling about someone or something, especially about a particular group of people

pre•lim•i•nar•y /prɪˈlɪməˌneri/ adj coming before the main or most important part of something: *a preliminary agreement/discussion*

prel•ude /ˈpreljud/ noun [C] **1** an event that happens before a more important event **2** a short piece of music that introduces a longer piece of music

pre•ma•ture /ˌpriməˈtjʊr/ adj **1** happening too soon or before the usual time **2** a premature baby is born before it should be —**pre•ma•ture•ly** adv

pre•med•i•tat•ed /priˈmedəˌteɪtəd/ adj a premeditated crime is deliberately planned —**pre•med•i•ta•tion** /priˌmedəˈteɪʃ(ə)n/ noun [U]

pre•men•stru•al /priˈmenstruəl/ adj happening in the days before a woman's PERIOD

pre•mier¹ /ˈprɪmɪr, *British* ˈpremiər/ adj best, largest, or most important

pre•mier² /prɪˈmɪr, *British* ˈpremiər/ noun [C] a PRIME MINISTER

pre•miere /prɪˈmɪr, *British* ˈpremieə/ noun [C] the first public performance of a play or a movie—**pre•miere** verb [I/T]

pre•mier•ship /prəˈmɪrˌʃɪp/ noun [U] the position of being Prime Minister, or the period of time that someone is Prime Minister

prem•ise /ˈpremɪs/ noun [C] *formal* a principle or statement that you consider to be true, on which you base other theories and actions

prem•is•es /ˈpremɪsəz/ noun [plural] the buildings and land that a business or organization uses

pre•mi•um¹ /ˈprimiəm/ noun [C] an amount of money that you pay regularly for an insurance policy

PHRASE **at a premium** if something is at a premium, a lot of people want it so that it is difficult to get

pre•mi•um² /ˈprimiəm/ adj more expensive or of higher quality than other similar things

pre•mo•ni•tion /ˌpreməˈnɪʃ(ə)n/ noun [C] a strong feeling that something bad is going to happen

pre•na•tal /ˌpriˈneɪt(ə)l/ adj relating to the period of time when a woman is pregnant

pre•oc•cu•pa•tion /priˌɑkjəˈpeɪʃ(ə)n/ noun **1** [singular/U] a state in which you think about something so much that you do not think about other things: *a preoccupation with death* **2** [C] something that you think about and want to do because it is important = CONCERN

pre•oc•cu•pied /priˈɑkjəˌpaɪd/ adj thinking about something so much that you do not notice other things or cannot think about other things —**pre•oc•cu•py** verb [T]

prep /prep/ verb [T] *American spoken* to prepare someone for something: *They're prepping the patient for surgery now.*

pre•pack•aged /ˌpriˈpækɪdʒd/ adj prepackaged products are already wrapped or in a box when you buy them

pre•paid /ˌpriˈpeɪd/ adj something that is prepaid has already been paid for before you use it: *prepaid postage*

prep•a•ra•tion /ˌprepəˈreɪʃ(ə)n/ noun ★

1 [U] the process of making someone or something ready for something: *The experience was good* ***preparation for*** *a career in journalism.* ♦ *The flowers were ordered* ***in preparation for*** *the wedding.*

2 preparations [plural] things that you do so that you are ready for something: *The U.S. continued its military preparations.* ♦ *Organizers are* ***making*** *the final* ***preparations for*** *next week's Christmas parade.*

pre•par•a•to•ry /prɪˈperəˌtori/ adj done as preparation for something else

pre•pare /prɪˈper/ verb ★★★

1 [I/T] to get ready for something, or to make someone or something ready: **prepare sth for sb/sth** *Wendy helped Karen prepare the room for their guests.* ♦ **prepare to do sth** *Medical teams are preparing to fly to the area tomorrow.*

2 [T] to make food ready to be cooked or eaten: *You can prepare this dish in advance and freeze it.*

PHRASE **prepare the way for** to do things that make it possible or easier for something to happen: *Her research prepared the way for later advances.*

pre•pared /prɪˈperd/ adj **1** ready and able to do something ≠ UNPREPARED: *We have to be prepared for anything.* **2** ready for use: *Make sure the room is prepared before they get there.* **3** done or made earlier: *Bonner read from a prepared statement.*

PHRASE **prepared to do sth** willing and able to do something: *I'm not prepared to listen to excuses.*

pre•pay•ment /priˈpeɪmənt/ noun [C/U] money that you pay before you can use a service

pre•pon•der•ance /prɪˈpɑnd(ə)rəns/ noun [singular] *formal* most of the people or things in a group

prep•o•si•tion /ˌprepəˈzɪʃ(ə)n/ noun [C] *linguistics* a word that usually comes before a noun or a pronoun and that shows its relation to another part of the sentence. In the sentences "I left it on the table" and "She came out of the house," the words "on" and "out of" are prepositions. —**prep•o•si•tion•al** adj

pre•pos•ter•ous /prɪˈpɑst(ə)rəs/ adj *formal* extremely unreasonable or silly = ABSURD

pre•pro•gram /ˌpriˈprouɡræm/ verb [T] to give a computer or other machine a set of instructions so that it will do what you want it to do at a later time

ˈprep ˌschool noun [C/U] **1** in the U.S., a private school for children over the age of 11 that prepares them for college **2** in the U.K., a private school for children between the ages of 7 or 8 and 11 or 13

pre•quel /ˈprikwəl/ noun [C] a book or movie that is about events that happened before the events in another book or movie that was written or made earlier

pre•re•cord•ed /ˌpriɪˈkɔrdəd/ adj prerecorded messages, music, or television or radio programs have been recorded so that they can be used later —**pre•re•cord** verb [T], **pre•re•cord•ing** noun [C]

pre•req•ui•site /priˈrekwəzɪt/ noun [C] *formal* something that must exist or happen before something else is possible

pre•school /ˈpriˌskul/ noun [C/U] *American* a school or class for children between the ages of two or four

pre•school•er /ˈpriskulər/ noun [C] *American* a child who is too young to go to school

pre•scribe /prɪˈskraɪb/ verb [T] if a doctor prescribes a drug or treatment, they say that you should have it

pre•scrip•tion /prɪˈskrɪpʃ(ə)n/ noun [C] a piece of paper that a doctor gives you that says what type of medication you need: *The drug is only available by prescription* (=if you have a prescription).

pre•season /priˈsisən/ adj relating to the time before the SEASON for a particular sport begins: *a preseason game*

pres•ence /ˈprezəns/ noun ★★★

1 [U] the fact of being in a particular place at a particular time: *Mr. Reese didn't even* ***acknowledge*** *my* ***presence.*** ♦ *a device for detecting* ***the presence of*** *submarines*

2 [singular/U] an impressive appearance or way of behaving or speaking

3 [singular] a group of people who are in a place for a particular purpose: *There is still a large* ***military presence*** *in the region.*

PHRASE **presence of mind** the ability to think quickly and clearly in a difficult situation

pres•ent¹ /ˈprezənt/ adj ★★★

1 existing or happening now: *The present situation cannot be allowed to continue.* ♦ *The present owners purchased the farm in 1976.*

2 at an event, or in a place: *Among those* ***present at*** *the ceremony were the ambassador and his wife.*

PHRASE **the present day** now: *It's a tradition that has survived to the present day.*

pres•ent² /prɪˈzent/ verb [T] ★★★

1 give formally/officially	4 describe sb/sth
2 cause situation, etc.	5 produce/organize sth
3 offer to be considered	6 show sth to an official

1 to give something to someone formally or officially: *Who will be* ***presenting the prizes?*** ♦ **present sb with sth** *We are very pleased to have been presented with this award.* ♦ **present sth to sb** *Finally the mayor presented the medals to the winners.*

2 to cause something such as a problem, threat, or opportunity: *The group's activities* ***presented a threat*** *to national security.*

3 to offer something for people to consider: *The commission* ***presented*** *its* ***report*** *in October.*

4 to show someone or something in a particular way: *The movie* ***presents*** *a disturbing* ***image*** *of youth culture.*

5 to produce or organize something such as a play, movie, or exhibit

6 to show something such as a passport to someone in an official position

pres•ent³ /ˈprezənt/ noun ★★★

1 [C] something that you give to someone, for example on their birthday =GIFT: *a wedding/birthday/Christmas present* ♦ *Yuki was wrapping* ***a present for*** *her mother.*

2 the present [singular] the period of time that is happening now: *We must learn to* ***live in the present,*** *not in the past.*

3 the present [singular] *linguistics* the PRESENT TENSE

PHRASE **at present** now: *At present there seems to be no solution to the crisis.*

pre•sent•a•ble /prɪˈzentəb(ə)l/ adj looking good enough for people to see

pres•en•ta•tion /ˌprez(ə)nˈteɪʃ(ə)n/ noun ★

1 [U] the way in which something is shown, arranged, or explained: *Using a computer helped with the spelling and* ***presentation of*** *the report.*

2 [C] a formal talk in which you describe or explain something to a group of people: *I'm going to ask each of you to* ***give a presentation.***

3 [C] a ceremony at which something such as a prize is given to someone: *He will receive the prize at a presentation on Saturday.*

ˌpresent-ˈday adj relating to a situation or place as it exists now: *The novel is set in present-day Russia.*

pre•sent•er /prɪˈzentər/ noun [C] **1** *American* someone who gives a speech or gives someone a prize at a ceremony **2** *British* the HOST or ANNOUNCER on a television or radio program

pres•ent•ly /ˈprezəntli/ adv **1** *old-fashioned* soon **2** *formal* at the present time

ˌpresent ˈparticiple noun [C] *linguistics* in English, the form of a verb that ends in "ing" and that expresses continuing action, for example the word "fishing." It can sometimes be used as an adjective, for example in "the screaming baby."

ˌpresent ˈperfect, the noun [singular] *linguistics* in English, a verb tense that expresses an action that was completed at some time in the past, or that started in the past and continues. The tense is formed by combining the present tense of "have" and the past participle of a verb, as in the sentence "She has paid the bill."

ˌpresent ˈtense, the noun [singular] *linguistics* the form of a verb that expresses what exists now, what is happening now, or what happens regularly

pres•er•va•tion /ˌprezərˈveɪʃ(ə)n/ noun [U] the process of working to protect something so that it is not damaged or destroyed

pres•er•va•tion•ist /ˌprezərˈveɪʃ(ə)nɪst/ noun [C] *American* someone who tries to make certain that things of historical or natural interest such as buildings or trees are not destroyed

pre•ser•va•tive /prɪˈzɜrvətɪv/ noun [C/U] a chemical substance used for preventing food or wood from decaying

pre•serve¹ /prɪˈzɜrv/ verb [T] ★

1 to take care of something in order to prevent it from being harmed or destroyed: *The society works to preserve historic buildings.*

2 to keep food fresh for a long time, for example by adding salt or chemicals to it

pre•serve² /prɪ'zɜrv/ noun **1** [C] *formal* a place or activity that is considered to belong to a particular person or group: *Sailing is no longer the preserve of the rich.* **2** [C] *American* an area where particular animals or plants are kept and protected **3** [C/U] a sweet food made by boiling fruit and sugar together =JAM

pre•side /prɪ'zaɪd/ verb [I] to be in charge of an official meeting, ceremony, or other event

PHRASAL VERB **pre'side ˌover sth** to be in a position of power while important things are happening

pres•i•den•cy /'prezɪdənsi/ noun [C] the job of being president, or the period of time that someone has this job

pres•i•dent /'prezɪdənt/ noun [C] ★★★
1 the political leader of a country that does not have a king or queen: *President Lincoln* ♦ *Clinton was **elected president** in 1992.*
2 the person who has the highest position in an organization or institution: *Lily Chang, our club president*
3 *American* the person in charge of a business or university: ***the president of** Citibank Corporation*

pres•i•den•tial /ˌprezɪ'denʃ(ə)l/ adj **1** relating to a president: *a presidential election/campaign/candidate* **2** behaving like a president or an important leader

press¹ /pres/ noun ★★★

1 newspapers etc.	4 single push on sth
2 machine for printing	5 for crushing fruit etc.
3 publishing business	+ PHRASE

1 the press [singular] newspapers and news magazines, or the reporters who work on them: *the national/local/American press* ♦ *the popular/tabloid press* ♦ *She has been criticized **in the press** for not speaking out on this issue.*
2 [C] a machine that is used for printing newspapers, books, or magazines
→ PRINTING PRESS
3 [C] a business that publishes books: *Harvard University Press*
4 [C] a single push on something such as a button or switch: *Internet shopping brings the store to your home **at the press of a button**.*
5 [C] a piece of equipment that is used for squeezing the juice or oil out of fruit or vegetables: *a garlic press*

PHRASE **give sth a press** to make a piece of clothing smooth using an iron

press² /pres/ verb ★★★
1 [I/T] to push one thing against another: **press sth against sth** *Children were pressing their faces against the window.* ♦ **press sth to sth** *Even with the phone pressed to his ear, he couldn't hear what she was saying.* ♦ **press sth into sth** *The minister pressed a bible into his hand.* ♦ *He felt the enormous weight of the man **pressing down on** his back.*
2 [T] to push something such as a button or switch in order to make a piece of equipment do something: *To read your e-mail, press the return key.*
3 [I] to move as a group by pushing together in a particular direction: *The crowd of fans began to **press** more closely **around** them.* ♦ *A wave of protesters **pressed forward** toward the building.*
4 [T] to make clothes smooth using a hot iron =IRON

PHRASE **press charges (against sb)** to officially accuse someone of committing a crime and make them go to court for a trial

PHRASAL VERBS **ˌpress a'head** to continue doing something in a determined way: *They pressed ahead regardless of objections from local people.*
'press sb for sth to try in a determined way to get something from someone: *The more she pressed him for an explanation, the more he refused to speak.*
ˌpress 'on *same as* **press ahead**

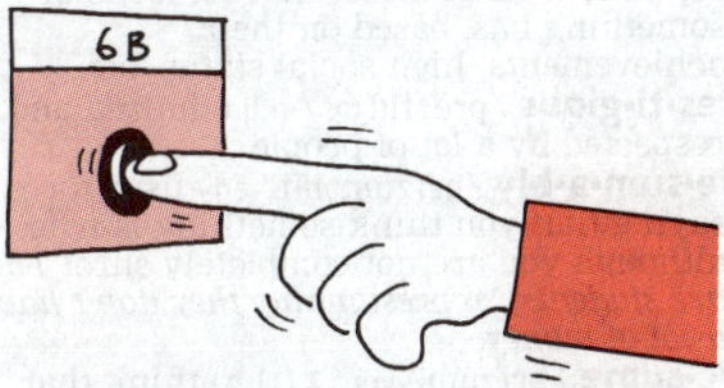

press

'press ˌconference noun [C] an official meeting where someone makes a formal statement about something to reporters and answers questions about it

pressed /prest/ adj in a difficult situation because you do not have enough time, money, or other things that you need

press•ing /'presɪŋ/ adj very important and urgent

'press ˌoffice noun [C] a department of a government or other organization that is responsible for dealing with reporters

'press reˌlease noun [C] an official statement or report that an organization gives to reporters

pres•sure¹ /'preʃər/ noun ★★★
1 [C/U] attempts to persuade or force someone to do something: ***Pressure for** political change increased in the 1990s.* ♦ **be/come under pressure to do sth** *The military is still under pressure to reduce spending.* ♦ *There is now greater **pressure on** the White House to take action.* ♦ *He did not **put** any **pressure on** her to take the job.*
2 [C/U] a worried feeling that you get when you have to deal with a difficult or complicated situation =STRESS: *With greatly increased workloads, everyone is **under pressure** now.* ♦ ***The pressure on** teachers has increased dramatically.*
3 [U] a physical force that is pressing on someone or something: *She became aware of the pressure of his hand on her shoulder.*
4 [U] the force that a liquid, air, or gas produces in an area or a container: *You should check your tire pressure at least once a month.*

pres•sure² /'preʃər/ verb [T] to try to make someone do something that they do not want to do: *Don't be pressured into making any rash decisions.*

pres•sured /'preʃərd/ adj worried because

you have a lot of problems or responsibilities

ˈpressure ˌgroup noun [C] an organized group of people who try to persuade people and influence political decisions about a particular issue

pres•sur•ize /ˈpreʃəˌraɪz/ verb [T] to make the pressure inside something such as a container different from the pressure outside

pres•sur•ized /ˈpreʃəˌraɪzd/ adj **1** with air pressure that is controlled so that it is different from the air pressure outside, for example in an airplane **2** a pressurized container forces a substance out when the container is opened

pres•tige /preˈstiʒ/ noun [U] the good reputation and respect that someone or something has, based on their achievements, high social status, etc.

pres•ti•gious /preˈstidʒəs/ adj admired and respected by a lot of people

pre•sum•a•bly /prɪˈzuməbli/ adv used for saying that you think something is true, although you are not completely sure: *They are students, so presumably they don't have a lot of money.*

pre•sume /prɪˈzum/ verb **1** [T] to think that something is true because it is likely, although you cannot be certain: *I presume you've already ordered lunch.* **2** [I] to behave as though you have the right to behave in a particular way when you do not: *He would never presume to tell me what to do.* **3** [T] *legal* to accept that something is true unless someone proves that it is not true: *Everyone should be presumed innocent until proven guilty.*

P

pre•sump•tion /prɪˈzʌmpʃən/ noun [C] a belief that something is true because it seems reasonable or likely

pre•sump•tu•ous /prɪˈzʌmptʃuəs/ adj *showing disapproval* showing too much confidence and not enough respect

pre•sup•pose /ˌprisəˈpoʊz/ verb [T] *formal* if one thing presupposes another, it cannot exist or happen unless the other thing is also true —**pre•sup•po•si•tion** /ˌprisʌpəˈzɪʃ(ə)n/ noun [C/U]

pre•tax /ˌpriˈtæks/ adj pretax profit or income is the amount of profit or income before tax is paid

pre•teen /ˌpriˈtin/ adj relating to children between the ages of 9 and 12 —**pre•teen** noun [C]

pre•tence /ˈpriˌtens, prɪˈtens/ the British spelling of **pretense**

pre•tend¹ /prɪˈtend/ verb [I/T] ★
1 to behave in a particular way because you want someone to believe that something is true when it is not: *We were never going to make the marriage work, so why pretend?* ♦ **+(that)** *I'm sorry, but I can't just pretend it hasn't happened.* ♦ **pretend to do sth** *She closed her eyes and pretended to be asleep.*
2 to imagine that something is true when you are playing a game: **+(that)** *They're pretending they're astronauts again.* ♦ **pretend to be sb/sth** *The little girl was pretending to be a lion.*

pre•tend² /prɪˈtend/ adj imaginary

pre•tend•ed /prɪˈtendəd/ adj not real or sincere

pre•tense /ˈpriˌtens, prɪˈtens/ noun [C/U] a way of behaving that does not honestly express your real feelings, thoughts, or intentions → FALSE

pre•ten•tious /prɪˈtenʃəs/ adj *showing disapproval* trying to seem more important, intelligent, etc. than you really are ≠ UNPRETENTIOUS

pre•text /ˈpriˌtekst/ noun [C] a reason that you pretend to have for doing something, that is given in order to hide your real reason or intention

pret•ti•ly /ˈprɪt(ə)li/ adv in a pretty way

pret•ty¹ /ˈprɪti/ adv *spoken* ★★
1 fairly: *My TV's getting **pretty old** now.* ♦ *Todd looks **pretty tired**.*
2 very: *The weather is **pretty awful**, isn't it?* ♦ *I can see they've done **a pretty good job** of it.*
PHRASE **pretty much/well/near** almost: *They look **pretty much the same**, don't they?*

pret•ty² /ˈprɪti/ adj ★
1 a pretty child, girl, or woman is attractive: *His girlfriend's **very pretty**.*
2 attractive or nice to look at or listen to: *It's one of the prettiest villages on the south coast.* ♦ *a pretty tune* ♦ *a **pretty little** cottage*
PHRASE **not just a pretty face** or **not just another pretty face** *spoken* used humorously for saying that someone is intelligent or skillful as well as being attractive
—**pret•ti•ness** noun [U]

pret•zel /ˈpretsəl/ noun [C] a type of CRACKER that is baked in the shape of a stick or a knot and is covered with salt

pre•vail /prɪˈveɪl/ verb [I] *formal* **1** to be the strongest influence or element in a situation: *We hope that common sense will prevail in the dispute.* **2** to exist at a particular time or in a particular situation: *A friendly atmosphere prevailed among the crowd.* **3** to defeat someone in a game, competition, argument, etc.

pre•vail•ing /prɪˈveɪlɪŋ/ adj existing or having influence at a particular time or in a particular place: *Our markets were affected by the prevailing economic environment.*

preˌvailing ˈwind noun [C] a wind that blows in a particular area at a particular time of year

prev•a•lent /ˈprevələnt/ adj very common in a particular place or among a particular group —**prev•a•lence** noun [U]

pre•vent /prɪˈvent/ verb [T] ★★★
1 to stop something from happening: **prevent sth (from) happening** *Rubber seals are installed to prevent gas from escaping.*
2 to stop someone from doing something: **prevent sb (from) doing sth** *The owner is prevented by law from making any major changes.*

pre•vent•a•ble /prɪˈventəb(ə)l/ adj capable of being prevented

pre•ven•ta•tive /prɪˈventətɪv/ adj PREVENTIVE

pre•ven•tion /prɪˈvenʃən/ noun [U] the act of preventing something, or things that people do in order to prevent something: *the prevention of cancer* ♦ *crime prevention*

pre•ven•tive /prɪˈventɪv/ adj done so that

something does not become worse or turn into a problem

pre•view /ˈpriˌvju/ noun [C] **1** an opportunity to see something such as a play, movie, or work of art before it is shown to the public **2** a short description of something that will happen or will be available later —**pre•view** verb [T]

pre•vi•ous /ˈpriviəs/ adj ★★★ a previous event, period, or thing happened or existed before the one that you are talking about: *Mark has two children from* ***a previous marriage.*** ♦ *All the other guests had arrived* ***the previous day.*** ♦ *No* ***previous experience*** *is required.*

pre•vi•ous•ly /ˈpriviəsli/ adv ★★★ before the present time, or before the time that you are discussing: *She was previously employed as a nurse.*

pre•war /ˌpriˈwɔr/ adj from a time before a particular war

prey¹ /preɪ/ noun [U] **1** an animal that is caught by another animal and eaten → BIRD **2** someone who is attacked, cheated, or harmed by a criminal or dishonest person =VICTIM

prey² /preɪ/ PHRASAL VERB **ˈprey on sb** or **ˈprey uˌpon sb** to harm someone who is weak or cannot defend themselves

price¹ /praɪs/ noun ★★★
1 [C] the amount of money that you have to pay in order to buy something: *Oil was* ***at its lowest price*** *in 30 years.* ♦ *For a limited period only, all our carpets are being sold* ***at half price.*** ♦ *They'll do the work for you,* ***at a price*** (=for a lot of money).
2 [singular] the bad things that you have to accept in order to achieve something that you want: *For some of these young athletes, success comes* ***at a heavy price.*** ♦ *She has fulfilled her dream, but* ***at what price?***
PHRASE **at any price 1** if you want something at any price, you are determined to get it, even if this brings severe problems **2** if you refuse to do something at any price, you refuse to do it, even for a lot of money or other benefits

Words often used with price

Verb often used with ***price*** *(noun, sense 1)*

- **cut, lower, reduce, slash** + PRICE: make the price of something less
- **increase, raise** + PRICE: make the price of something greater
- PRICE + **come down, fall, plummet, tumble**: become lower in price
- PRICE + **go up, increase, rise, rocket, soar**: become higher in price

price² /praɪs/ verb [T] to set the price of a product or service: *The farmhouse is priced at $300,000.*

price•less /ˈpraɪsləs/ adj **1** very valuable and impossible to replace **2** extremely useful in helping you to achieve something

ˈprice ˌtag noun [C] a label on a product that says how much it costs

pric•ey /ˈpraɪsi/ adj *informal* expensive

prick¹ /prɪk/ verb [T] to make a very small hole in the surface of something with a sharp object

prick² /prɪk/ noun [C] a quick feeling of sharp pain, caused by a sharp object making a hole in your skin

prick•le¹ /ˈprɪk(ə)l/ verb [I/T] if your skin prickles, or if something prickles it, you feel as if something sharp is touching it

prick•le² /ˈprɪk(ə)l/ noun [C] an uncomfortable stinging feeling on your skin

prick•ly /ˈprɪkli/ adj **1** covered with sharp points that cut or sting **2** *informal* a prickly person becomes angry very quickly **3** *informal* a prickly issue makes people disagree

pric•y /ˈpraɪsi/ another spelling of **pricey**

pride¹ /praɪd/ noun ★
1 [U] a feeling of pleasure at your own achievements or those of someone you love: *They* ***take a lot of pride in*** *their daughter's career.*
2 [U] a feeling of respect for yourself =DIGNITY: *Their win has restored national pride.* → SWALLOW¹
3 [U] a feeling that you are better than other people
4 [C] a group of lions
PHRASE **sb's pride and joy** a person or possession that gives someone a lot of happiness and satisfaction

pride² /praɪd/ verb **pride yourself on sth** to feel proud about an achievement, skill, or special quality that you have

priest /prist/ noun [C] ★
1 someone whose job is to perform religious duties and ceremonies in some Christian churches: *a Roman Catholic priest*
2 a man who performs religious duties in some religions that are not Christian —**priest•ly** adv

priest•ess /ˈpristəs/ noun [C] a woman who performs religious duties in some religions that are not Christian

priest•hood /ˈpristˌhʊd/ noun **1 the priesthood** [singular] the work and responsibility of being a priest **2** [C/U] all the priests of a particular religion

prim /prɪm/ adj very careful about your behavior and easily shocked —**prim•ly** adv

pri•ma don•na /ˌprimə ˈdɑnə/ noun [C] someone who thinks that they are very important, and who is very difficult to please

pri•mal /ˈpraɪm(ə)l/ adj relating to something that is very basic, especially very basic needs or emotions =PRIMITIVE

pri•mar•i•ly /ˈpraɪm(ə)rəli, praɪˈmerəli/ adv mainly

pri•mar•y¹ /ˈpraɪm(ə)ri/ adj ★★
1 most important =MAIN: *Dealing with crime is our* ***primary concern.***
2 coming or happening before other things: ***primary sources*** *of information*
3 relating to the education of children between the ages of about five and eleven: *primary education*

pri•mar•y² /ˈpraɪm(ə)ri/ noun [C] an election in which people in a particular state or area in the U.S. choose their CANDIDATE for a political position

ˌprimary ˈcare noun [U] medical treatment and advice that you get in your local community

ˌprimary ˈcolor noun [C] one of the colors red,

P

blue, or yellow that are combined to make other colors

ˌprimary ˈelection noun [C] a PRIMARY

ˈprimary ˌschool noun [C/U] an ELEMENTARY SCHOOL

pri•mate /ˈpraɪˌmeɪt/ noun [C] any animal belonging to the same group as humans, including monkeys and APES

prime[1] /praɪm/ adj **1** most important =PRIMARY: *Our prime concern was the safety of our customers.* **2** of the highest quality: *prime beef* **3** most likely to be chosen or to be appropriate for something: *the prime suspect in a murder case*

prime[2] /praɪm/ verb [T] **1** to prepare someone to behave or react in a particular way **2** to get a weapon or bomb ready to fire or explode **3** to prepare a surface for paint or some other substance

prime[3] /praɪm/ noun [singular] the stage in your life when you are most active or most successful

ˌprime ˈminister noun [C] the political leader in countries such as the U.K. that are governed by a PARLIAMENT

prim•er /ˈpraɪmər/ noun **1** [U] a substance that is used for preparing a surface for paint **2** /ˈprɪmər/ [C] a book that gives very simple instructions or basic information about something

ˈprime ˌrate noun [C] the lowest rate available for borrowing money

ˈprime ˌtime noun [U] the most popular time for watching television, which is in the middle of the evening

P

pri•me•val /praɪˈmiv(ə)l/ adj relating to the period when the universe or the Earth first began to exist

prim•i•tive /ˈprɪmətɪv/ adj **1** relating to a very early stage in the development of people, animals, or plants **2** very simple or old-fashioned: *a primitive computer* **3** natural, and done or experienced without thinking

prim•rose /ˈprɪmˌroʊz/ noun [C] a pale yellow flower that grows wild

prince /prɪns/ noun [C] **1** a male member of a royal family who is not the king **2** the male royal leader of some small countries

prince•ly /ˈprɪnsli/ adj **1** very large, beautiful, or impressive **2** belonging or relating to a prince

prin•cess /ˈprɪnsəs/ noun [C] **1** a female member of a royal family who is not the queen **2** the wife of a prince

prin•ci•pal[1] /ˈprɪnsəp(ə)l/ adj ★ main or most important: *The **principal goal** of the project is to provide an answer to this question.*

prin•ci•pal[2] /ˈprɪnsəp(ə)l/ noun ★★
1 [C] the head of a school: *a high school principal*
2 [singular] the original amount of money that someone borrows

prin•ci•pal•ly /ˈprɪnsəp(ə)li/ adv mainly

prin•ci•ple /ˈprɪnsəp(ə)l/ noun ★★★
1 [C] a basic belief, theory, or rule that has a major influence on the way in which something is done: *It is a basic **principle of** English law that a person is innocent until proven guilty.* ♦ **+that** *the principle that education should be free to everyone*
2 [C/U] a basic rule or belief about what is right, that influences the way you behave: *We are opposed **on principle** to any further building in the valley.* ♦ *It was **against** their **principles** to join the military.*
3 [C] a scientific theory or basic natural law that explains the way something works: *Windmills differ in design, but all operate on exactly the same principle.*
PHRASE **in principle** used for saying that something is possible in theory, although it has not been tried

prin•ci•pled /ˈprɪnsəp(ə)ld/ adj honest and responsible ≠ UNPRINCIPLED

print[1] /prɪnt/ verb ★★
1 [I/T] to produce words, numbers, pictures, etc. on paper, using a printer or PRINTING PRESS: **print sth on sth** *The book is beautifully printed on quality paper.*
2 [T] to publish something in a newspaper or magazine: *They refused to print my letter.*
3 [I/T] to write by hand using individual letters that are not joined together: *Please be sure to **print your name** next to your signature.*
4 [I/T] to produce a photograph on paper
PHRASAL VERB **ˌprint sth ˈout** or **ˌprint sth ˈoff** to produce a copy of a computer document from a printer

print[2] /prɪnt/ noun ★

1 mark	4 picture
2 of fingers	5 photograph
3 letters	+ PHRASES

1 [C] a mark made by pressing something onto a surface: *There were huge paw prints right outside our tent.*
2 [C] a FINGERPRINT
3 [U] letters or other symbols made by pressing ink, paint, etc. on paper or a similar surface: *The print is too small to read.*
4 [C] an image that is created by pressing a raised design onto paper, or by copying an existing image: *a limited edition print*
5 [C] a photograph: *old black and white prints*
PHRASES **in print 1** printed in a book, magazine or newspaper **2** a book that is in print is still available to buy from the company that published it
out of print a book that is out of print is no longer being published

print•er /ˈprɪntər/ noun [C] ★
1 a piece of equipment that you use for printing documents that you have created on a computer —*picture* → C3
2 a person or business that prints books, newspapers, etc.

print•ing /ˈprɪntɪŋ/ noun **1** [U] the process of making books, newspapers, etc., using a printing press **2** [C] the number of copies of something such as a book or newspaper that are printed at one time

ˈprinting ˌpress noun [C] a machine that is used for printing newspapers, books, etc.

ˈprint ˌmedia, the noun [plural] newspapers and magazines

print•out /ˈprɪntˌaʊt/ noun [C/U] paper that is printed with information from a computer file

pri•or /ˈpraɪr/ adj *formal* ★ happening, existing, or done before a particular time =PREVIOUS: *I'm afraid I won't be able to come. I have* ***a prior engagement.*** ♦ *students with no* ***prior knowledge*** *of English*
PHRASE **prior to sth** before something happened or existed: *The plane appeared to catch fire a few seconds prior to taking off.*

pri•or•i•tize /praɪˈɔrəˌtaɪz/ verb **1** [I/T] to decide in what order you should do things, based on how important or urgent they are **2** [T] to treat a particular job or issue as being more important than any others

pri•or•i•ty /praɪˈɔrəti/ noun ★★
1 [C] something important that must be done first, or that needs more attention than anything else: *Health insurance will be our* ***top priority.***
2 [U] the importance that you give to something that must be done: *Their marriage* ***took priority over*** *everything else.* ♦ *Safety must* ***be given*** *the highest* ***priority.***
3 [U] the right to go before someone or something else, or to receive something before they do: *Buses* ***take priority over*** *other vehicles on the road.*

prism /ˈprɪzəm/ noun [C] **1** any solid object that has a regular shape with flat sides and straight edges **2** a glass object in the shape of a prism, used for dividing light into its different colors

pris•on /ˈprɪz(ə)n/ noun [C/U] ★★★ an institution where people are kept as a punishment for committing a crime: *You can* ***go to prison*** *for that, you know.* ♦ *He's currently* ***in prison*** *for tax fraud.* ♦ *She could face a ten-year* ***prison term*** (=period in prison).

ˈprison ˌcamp noun [C] a place where prisoners are kept during a war

pris•on•er /ˈprɪz(ə)nər/ noun [C] ★★ someone who is in prison: *He was* ***taken prisoner*** *during the battle.*
PHRASE **prisoner of war** someone who is held as a prisoner by the enemy during a war =POW

pris•tine /ˈprɪˌstin/ adj something that is pristine looks very clean, neat, or new

pri•va•cy /ˈpraɪvəsi/ noun [U] the freedom to do things without other people watching you or knowing what you are doing

pri•vate¹ /ˈpraɪvət/ adj ★★★

1 not for everyone	5 not government
2 secret	6 not public
3 person	+ PHRASE
4 not work	

1 used only by a particular person or group, or available only to them: *a private bathroom/plane*
2 used about places or situations where other people cannot see or hear you: *They found a private spot where they could talk.*
3 a private person does not talk to other people about their personal life or feelings
4 not connected with someone's work or their public position: *What you do in your* ***private life*** *has nothing to do with your boss.*
5 controlled or owned by individual people or companies, rather than by the government ≠ PUBLIC: *private property*
6 with no position in government or public life: *a private citizen*
PHRASE **in private** in a place or situation where other people cannot watch or listen: *I'd like to talk with you in private, if you don't mind.*

pri•vate² /ˈpraɪvət/ noun [C] the lowest rank of soldier in the army

ˌprivate ˈcompany noun [C] a company that is owned by a person or group of people who do not sell SHARES (=the right to share profits) to the public

ˌprivate deˈtective noun [C] someone who is paid to follow people secretly or to find out information about their lives

ˌprivate ˈenterprise noun [C/U] business or industry that is owned and managed by independent people or businesses, rather than by the government

ˌprivate inˈvestigator noun [C] a PRIVATE DETECTIVE

pri•vate•ly /ˈpraɪvətli/ adv **1** in a place where no other people can see or hear you: *We wanted to speak privately.* **2** used about thoughts or feelings that you do not express: *Privately, he hoped they would refuse.* **3** by people who provide money themselves, rather than by governments: *privately owned businesses*

ˌprivate ˈpractice noun [C] a business that is managed and owned by a professional person such as a doctor or lawyer

ˌprivate ˈschool noun [C] a school that the children's parents pay for directly to the school

ˈprivate ˌsector, the noun [singular] all the businesses, industries, and services that are not owned or managed by the government

pri•va•tize /ˈpraɪvəˌtaɪz/ verb [T] to sell a business or industry that was owned and managed by the government so that it becomes a private business ≠ NATIONALIZE —**pri•va•ti•za•tion** /ˌpraɪvətɪˈzeɪʃ(ə)n/ noun [C/U]

priv•i•lege /ˈprɪvəlɪdʒ/ noun **1** [C] a special benefit that is available only to a particular person or group: *Cheap air travel is one of the privileges of working for the airline.* **2** [C] something nice that you feel lucky to have: *It's been a privilege to be involved in such an interesting project.* **3** [U] a way of life that involves having many advantages and opportunities, without working hard for them: *a life of privilege*

priv•i•leged /ˈprɪvəlɪdʒd/ adj having advantages and opportunities that other people do not have: *a privileged background/upbringing*

prize¹ /praɪz/ noun [C] ★★ a reward that you get for being successful in a competition, or for being good at something: *the Nobel Prize for chemistry* ♦ *Peter Turnbull won* ***first prize*** (=the prize that is given to the person who is first in a competition).

prize² /praɪz/ adj good enough to deserve or win a prize

prize³ /praɪz/ verb [T] to think that something is very important and special

pro /proʊ/ noun [C] *informal* someone who plays a sport or takes part in an activity

P

as a job rather than for enjoyment =PROFESSIONAL

PHRASE **pros and cons** advantages and disadvantages

pro- /proʊ/ prefix supporting or approving of something: *pro-democracy groups*

pro·ac·tive /ˌproʊˈæktɪv/ adj taking action and making changes before they need to be made, instead of waiting until problems develop

prob·a·bil·i·ty /ˌprɑbəˈbɪləti/ noun
1 [singular/U] a measure of how likely something is to happen: *What is the probability of success?* **2** [C] something that is likely to happen or be true: *War is now a probability rather than a possibility.*

prob·a·ble /ˈprɑbəb(ə)l/ adj likely to happen or be true ≠ IMPROBABLE: *It seems probable that the chairman will resign.*

prob·a·bly /ˈprɑbəbli/ adv ★★★ used for saying that you think that something is likely: *You'll probably be gone by the time I get back.* ♦ *"Are you going to accept their offer?" "**Probably not.**"*

pro·ba·tion /prəˈbeɪʃ(ə)n/ noun [U] **1** a system by which someone who has committed a crime is not sent to prison if they promise to behave well for a specific period of time **2** a period of time during which someone who has a new job is watched to see whether they can do the job well

pro·ba·tion·ar·y /prəˈbeɪʃ(ə)nˌeri/ adj relating to someone who has a new job, or to the period during which they are watched to see whether they can do the job well

P

proˈbation ˌofficer noun [C] someone whose job is to give help and advice to people on PROBATION and to check that they are behaving well

probe¹ /proʊb/ verb **1** [I/T] to try to find out the truth about something, especially by asking a lot of questions **2** [T] to examine something by using your fingers or a tool
—**prob·ing** adj

probe² /proʊb/ noun [C] **1** *mainly journalism* an attempt to find out the truth about an issue, problem, or accident =INQUIRY **2** a long thin medical instrument that is used for examining things inside your body **3** a SPACE PROBE

prob·lem /ˈprɑbləm/ noun [C] ★★★
1 something that causes trouble or difficulty: ***the problem of** unemployment* ♦ *We've been **having problems with** our neighbors.* ♦ *They're the best cameras on the market. **The only problem is** they're incredibly expensive.*
2 a question that someone is given to answer as a test of their ability: *mathematical problems*

PHRASES **no problem** *spoken* **1** used for saying that you will be happy to do what someone is asking you to do: *"Can you take care of the children for an hour or so?" "No problem."* **2** used as a polite way of answering someone who has thanked you for something, or said that they are sorry for something: *"You did a good job today – thanks." "No problem."*

not be sb's problem *spoken* used for saying that someone is not responsible for a difficulty and does not have to worry about it

that's your problem *spoken* used for saying in an unkind way that you are not going to help someone

> **Words often used with problem**
>
> *Adjectives often used with **problem** (sense 1)*
> - **big, fundamental, important, major, pressing, serious** + PROBLEM: used about problems that are very difficult to deal with

prob·lem·at·ic /ˌprɑbləˈmætɪk/ or **prob·lem·at·i·cal** /ˌprɑbləˈmætɪk(ə)l/ adj involving or causing problems

pro·ce·dure /prəˈsidʒər/ noun [C] ★ a way of doing something, especially the correct or usual way: *Those ticket holders who **followed the** correct **procedure** will receive a full refund.* ♦ ***The procedure for** doing this is explained fully in the next chapter.*
—**pro·ce·dur·al** /prəˈsidʒ(ə)rəl/ adj

pro·ceed /prəˈsid/ verb [I] ★
1 *formal* to continue doing something: *The team's owner is **proceeding with** his plan to move the stadium.*
2 *formal* to go in a particular direction: *Passengers for flight 406 to New York should **proceed to** Gate 32.*
3 used for telling other people about a surprising or annoying thing that someone has done: **proceed to do sth** *He came into the kitchen and proceeded to eat all of my cake.*

pro·ceed·ings /prəˈsidɪŋz/ noun [plural] **1** the actions that are taken to settle a legal matter, usually in court **2** an event, or series of related events **3** *formal* an official record giving the details of what happened in a meeting

pro·ceeds /ˈproʊˌsidz/ noun [plural] money that a person or organization makes from selling or winning something, or from organizing an event

proc·ess¹ /ˈprɑses/ noun [C] ★★★
1 a series of things that happen naturally and that have a particular result: *Changes occur in the body because of **the process of** aging.*
2 a series of actions that you take that have a particular result: *Learning a language is a slow process.* ♦ *an industrial process*

PHRASE **in the process of doing sth** involved in doing something at the present time

proc·ess² /ˈprɑses/ verb [T] ★
1 to treat food or another substance with chemicals or machines: *processed meat/ cheese*
2 to put information into a computer in order to organize it: ***Data is processed** as it is received.*
3 to deal with a document officially: *28,000 **applications have still to be processed.***
4 to make photographs from FILM by treating it with chemicals
—**pro·cess·ing** noun [U]

pro·ces·sion /prəˈseʃ(ə)n/ noun [C] **1** a line of people or vehicles that are moving in a slow formal way as part of an event **2** a series of people or things

pro·ces·sor /ˈprɑˌsesər/ noun [C] *computing* the part of a computer that controls and performs all its operations

pro•claim /prəˈkleɪm/ verb [T] to announce or state something officially or publicly

proc•la•ma•tion /ˌprɑkləˈmeɪʃ(ə)n/ noun [C/U] an official announcement, or the act of making an official announcement

pro•cras•ti•nate /proʊˈkræst(ə)nˌeɪt/ verb [I] to delay doing something until later because you do not want to do it —**pro•cras•ti•na•tion** /proʊˌkræst(ə)nˈeɪʃ(ə)n/ noun [U]

proc•tor /ˈprɑktər/ noun [C] *American* someone who is in charge of a group of students who are taking an examination —**proc•tor** verb [I/T]

pro•cure /prəˈkjʊr/ verb [T] *formal* to obtain something, especially with effort or difficulty

prod /prɑd/ verb [I/T] **1** to push someone or something quickly with your finger, or with an object that has a long thin end **2** to persuade or encourage someone to do something —**prod** noun [C]

pro•di•gious /prəˈdɪdʒəs/ adj very great, or impressive

prod•i•gy /ˈprɑdədʒi/ noun [C] a young person who has a natural ability to do something extremely well

pro•duce[1] /prəˈdus/ verb ★★★

1 [T] to make or grow something: *We are now producing the same quantity of goods with far fewer workers.* ♦ *The body produces chemicals to control the pain.* ♦ *The region produces some of the best wine in France.*

2 [T] to cause something to happen: *I managed to produce the opposite effect from the one I had intended.*

3 [T] to show or offer something so that it can be examined or used by someone else: *They **produced** very little **evidence** to support their argument.*

4 [I/T] to organize the work and money that are involved in making a movie, play, television or radio program, CD, etc.: *Steve McQueen produced and starred in* The Getaway.

Word family: produce

*Words in the same family as **produce***

- **producer** *n*
- **product** *n*
- **production** *n*
- **productive** *adj*
- **productivity** *n*
- **reproduce** *v*
- **reproduction** *n*
- **reproductive** *adj*
- **unproductive** *adj*

pro•duce[2] /ˈproʊˌdus/ noun [U] fruit, vegetables, and other things that farmers grow

pro•duc•er /prəˈdusər/ noun [C] ★

1 someone whose job is to organize the work and money that are involved in making a movie, play, television or radio program, CD, etc.

2 a person, company, or country that grows food or makes goods to be sold: *an oil/grain/wine producer*

prod•uct /ˈprɑdəkt/ noun ★★★

1 [C/U] something that is made, grown, or obtained in large quantities so that it can be sold: *dairy/pharmaceutical/software products*

2 [C] something or someone that is the result of particular actions, events, or influences: *The system we have now is **the product of** years of research.*

3 [C] *technical* a number that is the result of multiplying two other numbers

pro•duc•tion /prəˈdʌkʃən/ noun ★★★

1 [U] the process of making or growing things in large quantities so that they can be sold: ***the production of** goods for sale in the Far East*

2 [U] the natural process of making a substance: *the body's **production of** hormones*

3 [C/U] a movie, play, television or radio program, CD, etc., or the process of making it: *the Royal Shakespeare Company's **production of*** Macbeth

proˈduction ˌline noun [C] a system for making products in a factory. Each worker or machine does a single job as the product moves past them. = ASSEMBLY LINE

pro•duc•tive /prəˈdʌktɪv/ adj **1** making or growing things in large quantities: *This is highly productive farming country.* **2** producing or achieving a lot ≠ UNPRODUCTIVE: *a very productive meeting* —**pro•duc•tive•ly** adv

pro•duc•tiv•i•ty /ˌprɑdəkˈtɪvəti/ noun [U] the rate at which goods are produced, especially in relation to the time, money, and workers that are needed to produce them

Prof. /prɑf/ abbrev Professor: used in writing before the name of a professor

pro•fess /prəˈfes/ verb [T] *formal* **1** to claim that something is true, especially when it is not **2** to admit publicly that you have a particular feeling or belief

pro•fes•sion /prəˈfeʃ(ə)n/ noun [C] ★

1 a job that you need special skills and qualifications to do: *Her father discouraged her from going into **the legal profession**.* ♦ *He was a teacher **by profession*** (=as his job).

2 all the people who work in a particular profession: ***The medical profession** is always telling us we should exercise more.*

pro•fes•sion•al[1] /prəˈfəʃən(ə)l/ adj ★★★

1 relating to work that needs special skills and qualifications: *Teachers must be free to exercise their **professional judgment**.*

2 playing a sport or taking part in an activity as a job rather than for enjoyment ≠ AMATEUR: *a professional actor/photographer* ♦ *professional football/boxing*

3 showing a high level of skill or training ≠ UNPROFESSIONAL: *They did **a** thoroughly **professional job**.*

pro•fes•sion•al[2] /prəˈfeʃ(ə)nəl/ noun [C] **1** someone who does a job that you need special skills and qualifications to do: *doctors and other professionals* **2** someone who plays a sport or takes part in an activity as a job rather than for enjoyment ≠ AMATEUR **3** someone who has a lot of skill or training ≠ AMATEUR: *You have the makings of a real professional.*

pro•fes•sion•al•ism /prəˈfeʃən(ə)lˌɪzəm/ noun [U] the qualities and skills that someone with a professional job is expected to have

pro•fes•sion•al•ly /prəˈfeʃən(ə)li/ adv **1** with

P

the formal qualifications that are necessary for a particular profession: *professionally qualified staff* **2** showing the type of behavior and skills that someone with a professional job is expected to have: *She hasn't behaved very professionally, has she?* **3** in a way that is connected with your work: *Without Nina's help I wouldn't be where I am today professionally.* **4** as a job rather than for enjoyment: *She has been acting professionally since she was 17.*

pro•fes•sor /prəˈfesər/ noun [C] ★★
1 *American* a teacher in a college or university: *a **professor of** English*
2 *British* a senior teacher in a college or university

prof•fer /ˈprɑfər/ verb [T] *formal* to offer something to someone

pro•fi•cien•cy /prəˈfɪʃənsi/ noun [U] great skill

pro•fi•cient /prəˈfɪʃənt/ adj very good at something —**pro•fi•cient•ly** adv

pro•file¹ /ˈproʊˌfaɪl/ noun [C] **1** the public image of a person or organization, and the attention that they get from the public or reporters: *We have done a lot to change the profile of the company.* ♦ *She's trying to keep a low profile* (=avoid being noticed). **2** a short article or television or radio program about someone: *a profile of the British royal family* **3** the shape of someone's face when you look at them from the side: *She turned his head so she could see his profile.*

pro•file² /ˈproʊˌfaɪl/ verb [T] to give a description of someone in an article or in a television or radio program

prof•it¹ /ˈprɑfɪt/ noun ★★★
1 [C/U] money that you get when you sell something for a price that is higher than the cost of making it or buying it ≠ LOSS: *Investors have **made a** 14% **profit** in just 3 months.* ♦ *the practice of killing whales **for profit*** (=in order to make money) ♦ *They were buying computers and reselling them **at a profit*** (=so that you make a profit). ♦ *The **profit on** that deal was $21 million.* ♦ *All the **profits from** the sales of the CD will go to charity.* ♦ *The company's **profits rose** to $144 million last year.*
2 [U] *formal* the advantage that you get from a situation

prof•it² /ˈprɑfɪt/ PHRASAL VERB ˈ**profit from sth** or ˈ**profit by sth** to get an advantage from a situation

prof•it•a•ble /ˈprɑfɪtəb(ə)l/ adj **1** making a profit ≠ UNPROFITABLE: *a profitable business/company/investment* **2** giving you a benefit or advantage: *The trip should be an enjoyable and profitable experience.* —**prof•it•a•bil•i•ty** /ˌprɑfɪtəˈbɪləti/ noun [U], **prof•it•a•bly** adv

prof•it•eer•ing /ˌprɑfɪˈtɪrɪŋ/ noun [U] the behavior of companies that make large profits by charging people unfairly high prices

ˈ**profit-ˌmaking** adj a profit-making organization exists in order to make a profit

pro•found /prəˈfaʊnd/ adj **1** very great: *My grandfather's death had a profound effect on my father.* **2** showing intelligence and serious thought: *a very profound statement* —**pro•found•ly** adv

pro•fuse /prəˈfjus/ adj existing in large amounts —**pro•fuse•ly** adv

pro•fu•sion /prəˈfjuʒ(ə)n/ noun [singular] *formal* a large quantity of something

prog•no•sis /prɑɡˈnoʊsɪs/ (plural **prog•no•ses** /prɑɡˈnoʊˌsiz/) noun [C] **1** *medical* a doctor's opinion about how a disease is likely to develop **2** *formal* a statement about what is likely to happen in a particular situation → DIAGNOSIS

pro•gram¹ /ˈproʊˌɡræm/ noun [C] ★★★
1 a television or radio broadcast: *More people watch the news than any other program.*
2 a plan of activities for achieving something: *the president's **program for** economic recovery* ♦ *a **program of** political reform*
3 a series of planned events: *a festival with an exciting musical program*
4 *computing* a series of instructions that makes a computer do something: *a word processing/graphics/spreadsheet program*

pro•gram² /ˈproʊˌɡræm/ verb [T] **1** to make a computer or other piece of equipment do something automatically **2** to make a person or animal behave in a particular way —**pro•gram•ma•ble** /ˈproʊˌɡræməb(ə)l/ adj

pro•gramme /ˈproʊˌɡræm/ the British spelling of **program¹**

pro•gram•mer /ˈproʊˌɡræmər/ noun [C] *computing* someone whose job is to create computer programs

pro•gram•ming /ˈproʊˌɡræmɪŋ/ noun [U] *computing* the activity of creating computer programs

pro•gress¹ /ˈprɑɡrəs/ noun [U] ★★★
1 the process of developing or improving: *Keep me informed about **the progress of** the project.* ♦ *I'm worried about my son's lack of **progress in** English.* ♦ *Negotiators have **made** considerable **progress** in the peace talks.*
2 forward movement: *the ship's slow progress across the harbor*
PHRASE **in progress** happening, or being done: *The road will be closed while the maintenance work is in progress.*

> **Words often used with progress**
> *Verbs often used with **progress** (noun, sense 1)*
> - **assess, evaluate, review** + PROGRESS: judge how much progress has been made
> - **chart, check, follow, monitor, track, watch** + PROGRESS: watch how something develops
> - **hamper, hinder, impede, obstruct, slow** + PROGRESS: stop something from developing

pro•gress² /prəˈɡres/ verb [I] ★
1 to continue to develop: *Work on the project is progressing well.*
2 to move forward in space or time: *The situation improved as the century progressed.*

pro•gres•sion /prəˈɡreʃ(ə)n/ noun [U] gradual change or development = PROGRESS: *The drug can slow the progression of the disease.*

pro•gres•sive /prəˈɡresɪv/ adj **1** involving political change that tries to make society fairer: *a progressive tax system* **2** developing gradually: *The disease causes progressive deterioration of the nervous system.* **3** using the most modern ideas or methods:

progressive music **4** *linguistics* the progressive form of a verb is used for showing that an action is continuing =CONTINUOUS —**pro•gres•sive•ly** adv

pro•hib•it /proʊˈhɪbɪt/ verb [T] to officially stop people from doing something =BAN: *Smoking is prohibited inside the building.* —**pro•hi•bi•tion** /ˌproʊəˈbɪʃ(ə)n/ noun [C/U]

pro•hib•i•tive /proʊˈhɪbɪtɪv/ adj a prohibitive price is so high that it prevents people from buying something —**pro•hib•i•tive•ly** adv

proj•ect¹ /ˈprɑdʒekt/ noun [C] ★★★
1 an organized attempt to achieve something: *The first phase of the project is now complete.* ♦ **a project to do sth** *an ambitious project to modernize the road network*
2 a piece of work that involves collecting information: *The university has set up* ***a new research project*** *to study language development in babies.* ♦ *Students must complete* ***a project on*** *a topic of their choice.*
3 *American* a HOUSING PROJECT

> Words often used with **project**
>
> *Adjectives often used with* ***project*** *(noun, sense 1)*
> ■ **ambitious, innovative, major, large-scale** + PROJECT: used about projects that are intended to achieve a lot

proj•ect² /prəˈdʒekt/ verb **1** [T] to calculate how big something will become in the future, using information that is available now =FORECAST, PREDICT: *It is projected that the population will rise by one million by 2008.* **2** [I] to stick out past the edge or surface of something: *The edges of the roof project outward and keep the rain away from the walls.* **3** [T] to make people believe that someone or something has a particular quality: *Ending the talks now would project an image of failure.* **4** [T] to send an image to a screen or other surface

pro•jec•tile /prəˈdʒekt(ə)l/ noun [C] *formal* an object that is shot or thrown as a weapon =MISSILE

pro•jec•tion /prəˈdʒekʃ(ə)n/ noun **1** [C] a calculation of the way that something will develop **2** [U] the action of sending an image to a screen **3** [C] something that sticks out from a surface

pro•jec•tor /prəˈdʒektər/ noun [C] a piece of equipment that is used for showing movies or SLIDES on a screen

pro•lif•er•ate /prəˈlɪfəˌreɪt/ verb [I] *formal* to quickly increase in number or amount

pro•lif•er•a•tion /prəˌlɪfəˈreɪʃ(ə)n/ noun [singular/U] *formal* a sudden increase in number or amount

pro•lif•ic /prəˈlɪfɪk/ adj producing a lot of something: *a prolific writer/artist*

pro•logue /ˈproʊˌlɔg/ noun [C] a short part at the start of a book, play, or movie that introduces the story

pro•long /proʊˈlɔŋ/ verb [T] to make something last longer ≠ CURTAIL

pro•longed /prəˈlɔŋd/ adj continuing for a long time: *a prolonged period of silence*

prom /prɑm/ noun [C] in the U.S., a formal party for students in HIGH SCHOOL

prom•e•nade /ˌprɑməˈneɪd/ noun [C] a wide path that is next to a beach

prom•i•nence /ˈprɑmɪnəns/ noun [U] the state of being important or well known: *a young actor who came to prominence last year*

prom•i•nent /ˈprɑmɪnənt/ adj **1** important and well known: *a prominent member of the government* **2** easy to see or notice: *prominent cheekbones* ♦ *a prominent feature of the landscape* —**prom•i•nent•ly** adv

pro•mis•cu•ous /prəˈmɪskjuəs/ adj someone who is promiscuous has a lot of sexual partners —**prom•is•cu•i•ty** /ˌprɑmɪˈskjuəti/ noun [U]

prom•ise¹ /ˈprɑmɪs/ verb [I/T] ★★★
1 to tell someone that you will definitely do something: *The police chief promised tougher action against young criminals.* ♦ *She phoned at 9 a.m.,* ***as promised.*** ♦ **promise to do sth** *Peter wished he'd never promised to help them.* ♦ **promise sth to sb/promise sb sth** *Relief organizations are promising aid to the country.* ♦ **promise sb (that)** *Promise me you'll be home before dark.*
2 *formal* to make something seem likely: *This evening promises to be a lot of fun.*

prom•ise² /ˈprɑmɪs/ noun ★★
1 [C] a statement in which you say that you will definitely do something: *I'll try to come, but I'm not* ***making any promises!*** ♦ *He swore he would return one day, and he* ***kept his promise.*** ♦ **a promise to do sth** *You made a promise to deal with it immediately.* ♦ *The army* ***broke its promise*** *to bring peace back to the country.*
2 [U] signs that someone or something is likely to be successful in the future =POTENTIAL: *Life was hopeful and* ***full of promise.*** ♦ *He shows great* ***promise*** *as a writer.*

prom•is•ing /ˈprɑmɪsɪŋ/ adj likely to be successful or very good: *a highly promising young artist* —**prom•is•ing•ly** adv

pro•mo /ˈproʊmoʊ/ noun [C] *informal* an advertisement

pro•mote /prəˈmoʊt/ verb [T] ★★
1 to support something, or to help something to develop: *a campaign to promote recycling* ♦ *Young plants are exposed to bright light to* ***promote growth.***
2 to attract people's attention to a product or event, for example by advertising: *They are going on tour to promote their new album.*
3 to move someone to a job at a higher level: **promote sb to sth** *Steve Burrows was recently promoted to senior manager.*

> Words often used with **promote**
>
> *Adverbs often used with* ***promote*** *(sense 1)*
> ■ **actively, heavily, strongly, vigorously** + PROMOTE: promote something in a determined way
>
> *Nouns often used with* ***promote*** *(sense 1)*
> ■ PROMOTE + **awareness, competition, development, efficiency, growth, interest, understanding, use**: increase the level of something

pro•mot•er /prəˈmoʊtər/ noun [C] **1** someone whose job is to arrange and advertise concerts and sports events **2** someone who tries to make people support an idea or issue

P

pro•mo•tion /prəˈmoʊʃ(ə)n/ noun ★
1 [C/U] a move to a job at a higher level: *His main objective is to get a promotion.*
2 [U] the activity of encouraging or supporting something: *The campaign is concerned with the promotion of health.*
3 [U] the process of advertising something: *a ban on the promotion of tobacco products*

pro•mo•tion•al /prəˈmoʊʃən(ə)l/ adj used for advertising something

prompt¹ /prɑmpt/ verb [T] **1** to cause something to happen: *The birth of my first child prompted me to write this article.* **2** to encourage someone to say something **3** to remind an actor which words to say next —**prompt•ing** /ˈprɑmptɪŋ/ noun [U]

prompt² /prɑmpt/ adj **1** immediate or quick: *Prompt action is required.* **2** happening or arriving at exactly a particular time —**prompt•ly** adv, **prompt•ness** noun [U]

prompt³ /prɑmpt/ adv at a particular time exactly

prompt⁴ /prɑmpt/ noun [C] **1** *computing* a sign on a computer screen that shows that the computer is ready for you to TYPE something **2** a word or words that someone says to remind an actor what to say next

prone /proʊn/ adj **1** likely to do something bad, or likely to be affected by something bad **2** *formal* lying flat with the front of your body facing downward

prong /prɔŋ/ noun [C] one of the sharp points on a fork

pro•noun /ˈproʊˌnaʊn/ noun [C] *linguistics* a word used instead of a noun that has been mentioned earlier, for example "she," "this," and "yourself"

P

pro•nounce /prəˈnaʊns/ verb [T] ★
1 to say the sounds of words: *I find some Japanese words very difficult to pronounce.* ♦ *Did I pronounce your name correctly?*
2 *formal* to state an official opinion or decision: *The court pronounced her innocent of all charges.*

pro•nounced /prəˈnaʊnst/ adj very obvious or noticeable: *a pronounced German accent*

pro•nounce•ment /prəˈnaʊnsmənt/ noun [C] *formal* an official public statement

pro•nun•ci•a•tion /prəˌnʌnsiˈeɪʃ(ə)n/ noun [C/U] ★ the way in which a word or language is pronounced: *a guide to French pronunciation* ♦ *What is the correct pronunciation of "rabid?"*

proof /pruf/ noun ★
1 [U] information or evidence that shows that something is definitely true: *We were unable to establish proof of her innocence.* ♦ *Do you have any proof of identity* (=a document that proves who you are)*?*
2 [U] the strength of an alcoholic drink
3 [C] *technical* a copy of a book or article that someone reads and corrects before the final copy is made

> **Words often used with proof**
>
> *Adjectives often used with proof (sense 1)*
> ■ **ample, clear, conclusive, final, irrefutable, tangible** + PROOF: used about proof that is good enough to show that something is true

proof•read /ˈprufˌrid/ (past tense and past participle **proof•read** /ˈprufˌred/) verb [I/T] to correct the mistakes in a piece of writing before the final copy is printed —**proof•read•er** noun [C]

prop¹ /prɑp/ noun [C] **1** something you put under or against an object in order to hold it up **2** an object that is used in a play or movie

prop² /prɑp/ verb [T] to hold something in position by putting an object under or against it, or by leaning it against an object PHRASAL VERB ˌ**prop sth ˈup 1** to stop something from falling by putting an object under it or against it **2** to help something such as a government or an organization to continue to exist

prop•a•gan•da /ˌprɑpəˈgændə/ noun [U] information that a government or an organization spreads in order to influence people's opinions

prop•a•gate /ˈprɑpəˌgeɪt/ verb [T] to spread ideas or beliefs to a lot of people —**prop•a•ga•tion** /ˌprɑpəˈgeɪʃ(ə)n/ noun [U]

pro•pel /prəˈpel/ verb [T] **1** to move something forward: *a car propelled by solar energy* **2** to quickly put someone into a particular situation

pro•pel•ler /prəˈpelər/ noun [C] the part of an airplane or ship that has blades that spin around to make it move

pro•pen•si•ty /prəˈpensəti/ noun [C] a natural tendency to behave in a particular way

prop•er /ˈprɑpər/ adj ★
1 appropriate for a particular purpose or situation: *You have to have the proper tools for the job.* ♦ *That's not the proper way to do it!*
2 behaving in a way that is morally right or polite: *Young people then were all very proper.*
3 understood in its most exact meaning: *Does he live in Chicago proper or in the suburbs?*

prop•er•ly /ˈprɑpərli/ adv ★ in a correct or appropriate way: *You're not properly dressed for this weather.* ♦ *If she doesn't behave properly, send her home.*

ˌ**proper ˈnoun** noun [C] *linguistics* a noun that is the name of a person, place, or thing

prop•er•ty /ˈprɑpərti/ noun ★★★
1 [U] the things that you own: *The books are my personal property.* ♦ *The police found a lot of stolen property in his house.*
2 [C/U] land and the buildings on it: *He owns several properties in London.* ♦ *Property prices are falling.*
3 [C] a quality or feature of something: *The plants are believed to have healing properties.*

proph•e•cy /ˈprɑfəsi/ noun [C] a statement about what will happen in the future

proph•et /ˈprɑfɪt/ noun **1** [C] someone who is believed to have been sent by God to lead people and teach religious beliefs **2 the Prophet** Muhammad, the FOUNDER of Islam

pro•phet•ic /prəˈfetɪk/ adj saying what will happen in the future

pro•po•nent /prəˈpoʊnənt/ noun [C] someone who publicly supports something

pro·por·tion /prəˈpɔrʃ(ə)n/ noun ★★

1 part of whole amount	4 importance
2 relative quantity	5 size or shape
3 of appearance	+ PHRASE

1 [C] a quantity of something that is a part of the whole: *Only a small* ***proportion of*** *graduates fail to get a job.*
2 [U] the relationship between two or more quantities or parts of a whole: **the proportion of sth to sth** *The proportion of trucks to cars on the road has changed dramatically.*
3 [U] the correct or most attractive relationship between things: *Everything about the room* ***is*** *beautifully* ***in proportion.*** ♦ *His head is large* ***in proportion to*** *his body.* ♦ *The figures in the painting* ***are*** *completely* ***out of proportion with*** *their surroundings.*
4 [U] the importance of something in comparison with other things: *We need to keep* ***a sense of proportion*** *about what really matters.*
5 proportions [plural] the size or shape of something: *a chair of graceful proportions* ♦ *The tree can grow to massive proportions.*
PHRASE **blow sth out of proportion** to make a situation seem much worse than it really is

pro·por·tion·al /prəˈpɔrʃən(ə)l/ adj **1** two things that are proportional to each other keep the same relationship to each other when they change in size or amount: *Proportional increases in income maintain the gap between rich and poor.* **2** not too big or too severe in relation to something else =PROPORTIONATE —**pro·por·tion·al·ly** adv

pro·por·tion·ate /prəˈpɔrʃ(ə)nət/ adj **1** not too big or too severe in relation to something else: *a punishment that is proportionate to the crime* **2** keeping the same relationship of size or amount to something else =PROPORTIONAL —**pro·por·tion·ate·ly** adv

pro·pos·al /prəˈpoʊz(ə)l/ noun [C] ★
1 an official plan or suggestion: ***Proposals*** *for a new health service are under discussion.* ♦ **a proposal to do sth** *the latest proposal to impose a tax on fuel*
2 an occasion when you ask someone to marry you

pro·pose /prəˈpoʊz/ verb **1** [T] *formal* to suggest something: *She is proposing that we sell the house.* **2** [T] to make a formal suggestion, especially in a meeting: *I propose Sue Wilson for chairman.* ♦ *It was proposed that we postpone the next meeting.* ♦ *France has proposed creating an international force to deal with the crisis.* **3** [I] to ask someone to marry you **4** [T] *formal* if you propose to do something, you intend to do it

prop·o·si·tion¹ /ˌprɑpəˈzɪʃ(ə)n/ noun [C] **1** an offer or suggestion **2** a statement that people can examine in order to decide whether it is true **3** *American* a suggested law or change in a law that citizens vote for or against

prop·o·si·tion² /ˌprɑpəˈzɪʃ(ə)n/ verb [T] to offer to have sex with someone, especially in an offensive way

pro·pri·e·tor /prəˈpraɪətər/ noun [C] *formal* someone who owns a business

pro·pri·e·ty /prəˈpraɪəti/ noun [U] *formal* behavior that most people think is morally or socially correct ≠ IMPROPRIETY

pro·pul·sion /prəˈpʌlʃən/ noun [U] *technical* the force that makes something move forward

pro ra·ta /ˌproʊ ˈreɪtə/ adj, adv *business* calculated according to how long someone works or how much of an amount is used

pro·rate /proʊˈreɪt/ verb [T] *business* to calculate something in a pro rata way

pro·sa·ic /proʊˈzeɪɪk/ adj not interesting or exciting

prose /proʊz/ noun [U] ordinary written language, not poetry

pros·e·cute /ˈprɑsɪˌkjut/ verb **1** [T] to officially accuse someone of a crime and ask a court of law to judge them **2** [I/T] to try to prove as a lawyer in court that someone is guilty of a crime

pros·e·cu·tion /ˌprɑsɪˈkjuʃ(ə)n/ noun **1** [U] the act of accusing someone of a crime and asking a court of law to judge them **2 the prosecution** [singular] the lawyers in a court who try to prove that someone is guilty ≠ DEFENSE

pros·e·cu·tor /ˈprɑsɪˌkjutər/ noun [C] a lawyer whose job is to prove in court that someone is guilty

pros·pect¹ /ˈprɑsˌpekt/ noun ★
1 [U] the possibility that something good will happen: *Doctors say there is little* ***prospect of*** *any improvement in his condition.*
2 [singular] something that you expect to happen in the future, or the thought of this: *Spending a week at his cousin's ranch was an exciting prospect.* ♦ *We were very excited* ***at the prospect of*** *going home.*
3 prospects [plural] chances of success in a career: *Your employment prospects would be much better if you went to college.*

Words often used with prospect

Adjectives often used with ***prospect*** *(noun, sense 2)*

- **attractive, bright, exciting, inviting** + PROSPECT: used about a prospect that makes you confident or excited about what will happen
- **bleak, daunting, gloomy, grim, terrifying** + PROSPECT: used about a prospect that makes you worried or frightened about what will happen

pros·pect² /prəˈspekt/ verb [I] to search for gold, oil, or another valuable substance

pro·spec·tive /prəˈspektɪv/ adj likely to become a particular thing: *a prospective client/employee*

pro·spec·tus /prəˈspektəs/ noun [C] **1** a small book that describes a school or university and its programs **2** a document that provides details about a business to people who are interested in investing in it

pros·per /ˈprɑspər/ verb [I] to be successful, or to become rich

pros·per·i·ty /prɑˈsperəti/ noun [U] the situation of being successful and having a lot of money

pros·per·ous /ˈprɑsp(ə)rəs/ adj rich and successful

pros·ti·tute /ˈprɑstɪˌtut/ noun [C] someone

P

who has sex with people as their job

pros•ti•tu•tion /ˌprɑstɪˈtuʃ(ə)n/ noun [U] the job of having sex with people

pros•trate /ˈprɑˌstreɪt/ adj *formal* lying completely flat on the ground with your face downward

pro•tag•o•nist /proʊˈtægənɪst/ noun [C] the main character in a play, movie, or book

pro•tect /prəˈtekt/ verb [T] ★★★ to keep someone or something safe: *Are you prepared to protect yourself in case of attack?* ♦ **protect sb/sth from sth** *The hat will protect his face from the sun.* ♦ **protect sb/sth against sth** *The jacket protected him against the cold.* —**pro•tec•tor** noun [C]

pro•tect•ed /prəˈtektəd/ adj used about animals, plants, and other things that the law prevents people from harming

pro•tec•tion /prəˈtekʃ(ə)n/ noun [U] ★★★ the process of keeping someone or something safe: *A healthy diet should provide **protection against** disease.* ♦ *White clothes give your skin good **protection from** the sun.* ♦ *the **protection of** the environment*

pro•tec•tive /prəˈtektɪv/ adj **1** providing protection against something harmful or dangerous: *protective clothing* **2** wanting to protect someone from being harmed or hurt: *He's very protective toward his sister.*

pro•té•gé /ˈproʊtəˌʒeɪ/ noun [C] a young person who receives help or training from an older experienced person

pro•tein /ˈproʊtin/ noun [U] a substance in foods such as meat, eggs, and milk that keeps you healthy

P

pro•test[1] /ˈproʊˌtest/ noun ★★

1 [C/U] a strong complaint or disagreement: *a formal **protest against** the nuclear testing* ♦ *She resigned **in protest** during the scandal.*

2 [C] an occasion when people show strong public opposition to something: *a protest march* ♦ *Students will **stage a protest** this weekend at the federal building.*

> **Words often used with protest**
>
> *Adjectives often used with **protest** (noun, sense 2)*
> - **mass, peaceful, public, violent** + PROTEST: used about a particular type of protest
>
> *Verbs often used with **protest** (noun, sense 2)*
> - **hold, organize, stage** + PROTEST: to arrange for a protest to take place

pro•test[2] /prəˈtest, ˈproʊˌtest/ verb ★

1 [I/T] to show publicly that you oppose something: *The students were marching to protest the war.* ♦ *Workers are **protesting against** high unemployment.*

2 [T] to try to make other people believe that something is true = SWEAR: *She still protests her innocence.*

Prot•es•tant /ˈprɑtɪstənt/ noun [C] a member of a group of Christian churches that separated from the Roman Catholic church in the 16th century —**Prot•es•tant** adj

pro•test•er /prəˈtestər/ noun [C] someone who publicly shows their opposition to something

pro•to•col /ˈproʊtəˌkɔl/ noun [U] rules for correct behavior

pro•to•type /ˈproʊtəˌtaɪp/ noun [C] the first form of something new that is made before it is produced in large quantities

pro•tract•ed /prəˈtræktəd/ adj *formal* continuing for a longer time than normal or necessary = LENGTHY

pro•trude /prəˈtrud/ verb [I] to stick out from a surface

pro•tru•sion /proʊˈtruʒ(ə)n/ noun [C] a part of something that sticks out from a surface

proud /praʊd/ adj ★

1 feeling happy about your achievements, your possessions, or people who you are connected with: *We're so **proud of** her for telling the truth.* ♦ **be proud to do sth** *I'm proud to say we made the right decision.*

2 a proud person does not like other people to help them or to think that they are weak: *a proud and independent nation* ♦ **be too proud to do sth** *I was too proud to admit I didn't understand anything she said.*

3 someone who is proud thinks that they are better than other people = ARROGANT —**proud•ly** adv

prove /pruv/ (past participle **proved** or **prov•en** /ˈpruv(ə)n/) verb ★★★

1 [T] to provide evidence that shows that something is true: *He is still fighting to **prove his innocence**.* ♦ **+(that)** *You have to prove you are sorry for what you've done.* ♦ **prove sb right/wrong** *Recent excellent results have proved the critics wrong.*

2 [linking verb] if something proves to have a particular quality, things happen that show that it has that quality: *My decision proved to be a good one.* ♦ *The movie is proving very profitable.*

PHRASE **prove yourself** to show how good you are at doing something

pro•ven[1] /ˈpruv(ə)n/ adj shown to be true, real, or effective

pro•ven[2] a past participle of **prove**

prov•erb /ˈprɑˌvɜrb/ noun [C] a short well-known statement that gives practical advice about life

pro•vide /prəˈvaɪd/ verb [T] ★★★ to give someone something that they want or need: *A taxi service from the airport will be provided.* ♦ **provide sb with sth** *The book signing provided him with an opportunity to meet one of his heroes.* ♦ **provide sth for sb** *The hotel provides a playroom for children.* ♦ **provide sth to sb** *We provide legal advice to our clients.*

PHRASAL VERBS **proˈvide for sb** to take care of someone by making money in order to buy the things that they need: *She has always provided for her children.*

proˈvide for sth *formal* to make it possible for something to happen in the future: *The budget provides for a salary increase after one year.*

pro•vid•ed /prəˈvaɪdəd/ or **proˈvided that** conjunction ★★ only if a particular thing happens or is done = PROVIDING: *You can go out to play provided that you finish your homework first.*

prov•i•dence /ˈprɑvɪdəns/ noun [U] *literary* a powerful force that some people believe causes everything that happens to us = DESTINY, FATE

pro•vi•der /prəˈvaɪdər/ noun [C] a company that provides a service

pro·vid·ing /prəˈvaɪdɪŋ/ or **proˈviding that** conjunction only if a particular thing happens or is done=PROVIDED: *We'll all be there providing that Al can get time off from work.*

prov·ince /ˈprɑvɪns/ noun [C] one of the large areas that some countries are divided into

pro·vin·cial /prəˈvɪnʃəl/ adj **1** in a province **2** old-fashioned or conservative

pro·vi·sion /prəˈvɪʒ(ə)n/ noun **1** [U] the act of providing something that someone needs **2** [C/U] plans to provide things that you will need in the future: *We've made provisions for our grandchild's education.* **3** [C] a part of a law that deals with a particular problem **4 provisions** [plural] food and other necessary supplies, especially for a trip

pro·vi·sion·al /prəˈvɪʒən(ə)l/ adj intended to be temporary and therefore likely to be changed —**pro·vi·sion·al·ly** adv

pro·vi·so /prəˈvaɪzoʊ/ noun [C] something that someone must agree to do before you will agree to do something else

prov·o·ca·tion /ˌprɑvəˈkeɪʃ(ə)n/ noun [C/U] something that makes you react in an angry or violent way

pro·voc·a·tive /prəˈvɑkətɪv/ adj **1** intended to make you angry or upset **2** intended to make you sexually excited —**pro·voc·a·tive·ly** adv

pro·voke /prəˈvoʊk/ verb [T] **1** to deliberately try to make someone angry: *He's just trying to provoke you.* **2** to cause a particular reaction, especially an angry one: *The Senator's speech has provoked a furious reaction.*

pro·vost /ˈprɑˌvoʊst/ noun [C] an important official in a U.S. university

prow /praʊ/ noun [C] the front of a ship

prow·ess /ˈpraʊəs/ noun [U] great skill, or great ability

prowl[1] /praʊl/ verb [I/T] to move around an area quietly, especially because you are planning to do something bad

prowl[2] /praʊl/ noun **on the prowl** looking for someone or something

prowl·er /ˈpraʊlər/ noun [C] someone who moves around an area quietly, looking for an opportunity to commit a crime

prox·im·i·ty /prɑkˈsɪməti/ noun [U] *formal* the state of being near someone or something

prox·y /ˈprɑksi/ noun **do sth by proxy** if you do something by proxy, someone else does it for you

prude /prud/ noun [C] *showing disapproval* someone who is easily shocked or embarrassed by anything relating to sex —**prud·ish** adj

pru·dent /ˈprud(ə)nt/ adj careful, and using good judgment —**pru·dence** noun [U], **pru·dent·ly** adv

prune[1] /prun/ verb [T] to cut off parts of a tree or plant

prune[2] /prun/ noun [C] a dried PLUM (=type of fruit)

pry /praɪ/ verb **1** [I] to be interested in someone's personal life in a way that is annoying or offensive **2** [T] to force something open, or to force things apart

P.S. /ˌpi ˈes/ abbrev postscript: used for introducing additional information at the end of a letter after you have signed your name

psalm /sɑm/ noun [C] a song or poem from the Bible that praises God

pseu·do·nym /ˈsud(ə)nɪm/ noun [C] a false name that someone uses, especially when they write a book

psych /saɪk/
PHRASAL VERBS ˌ**psych sb ˈout** *informal* to behave very confidently in order to make your opponent feel nervous
ˌ**psych sb ˈup** *informal* to try to make someone feel confident and ready for something

psy·che /ˈsaɪki/ noun [C] the part of your mind that controls your attitudes and behavior

psy·che·del·ic /ˌsaɪkəˈdelɪk/ adj **1** psychedelic drugs make you see things that are not really there **2** psychedelic clothes or designs are very brightly colored and have big unusual patterns

psy·chi·a·trist /sɪˈkaɪətrɪst/ noun [C] a doctor who treats people with mental illnesses

psy·chi·a·try /sɪˈkaɪətri/ noun [U] the study and treatment of mental illness —**psy·chi·at·ric** /ˌsaɪkiˈætrɪk/ adj

psy·chic /ˈsaɪkɪk/ adj **1** someone who is psychic claims to be able to know what other people are thinking or what is going to happen to them **2** connected with mysterious mental powers that cannot be explained by science: *psychic energy* —**psy·chic** noun [C]

psy·cho /ˈsaɪkoʊ/ noun [C] *informal* someone who is crazy and behaves in a frightening and violent way

psy·cho·a·nal·y·sis /ˌsaɪkoʊəˈnæləsɪs/ noun [U] medical treatment in which someone talks to a psychoanalyst about their feelings in order to solve their mental problems —**psy·cho·an·a·lyze** /ˌsaɪkoʊˈæn(ə)lˌaɪz/ verb [T]

psy·cho·an·a·lyst /ˌsaɪkoʊˈæn(ə)lɪst/ noun [C] a doctor whose job is to talk to people about their feelings in order to solve their mental problems

psy·cho·log·i·cal /ˌsaɪkəˈlɑdʒɪk(ə)l/ adj ★
1 involving or affecting your mind: *Harry's problems are more psychological than physical.*
2 connected with the study of how your mind works: *psychological theories* —**psy·cho·log·i·cal·ly** /ˌsaɪkəˈlɑdʒɪkli/ adv

psy·chol·o·gist /saɪˈkɑlədʒɪst/ noun [C] someone who studies how people's minds work and how this affects their behavior

psy·chol·o·gy /saɪˈkɑlədʒi/ noun [U] ★
1 the study of the mind and how it affects behavior
2 the way that the mind affects behavior in a particular person or group of people: *a book on the psychology of murderers*

psy·cho·path /ˈsaɪkəˌpæθ/ noun [C] someone who has a serious mental illness that makes them behave in a very violent way —**psy·cho·path·ic** /ˌsaɪkəˈpæθɪk/ adj

psy·cho·sis /saɪˈkoʊsɪs/ (plural **psy·cho·ses** /saɪˈkoʊˌsiz/) noun [C/U] *medical* a serious mental illness

psy·cho·so·mat·ic /ˌsaɪkoʊsəˈmætɪk/ adj a psychosomatic illness is caused by a problem in your mind

psy•cho•ther•a•py /ˌsaɪkoʊˈθerəpi/ noun [U] a treatment for people with mental illness that involves talking to them instead of giving them drugs —**psy•cho•ther•a•pist** noun [C]

psy•cho•tic /saɪˈkɑtɪk/ adj someone who is psychotic behaves in a dangerous or violent way because they have a serious mental illness —**psy•cho•tic** noun [C]

pt. abbrev **1** pint **2** point

PTA noun [C] Parent-Teacher Association: an organization of parents and teachers who work together in order to improve their school

pub /pʌb/ noun [C] a place where people go to drink alcohol

pu•ber•ty /ˈpjubərti/ noun [U] the period in a person's life when their body changes from a child's body to an adult's body

pu•bic /ˈpjubɪk/ adj relating to the area around the sexual organs

pub•lic[1] /ˈpʌblɪk/ adj ★★★

1 owned by the government, not by a private company ≠ PRIVATE: *public money/institutions*

2 available for people in general to use ≠ PRIVATE: *a public library ♦ the city's public parks*

3 involving a lot of people, or involving people in general: *a public nuisance/hazard ♦ The proposal has a lot of **public support**.*

4 used about places and situations where other people can see you: *Can we go somewhere a little less public? ♦ She keeps her public and private lives very separate.*

PHRASES **in the public eye** well known to people in general: *Her job keeps her in the public eye.*

make sth public to tell everyone about something: *The government has decided to make the results of the inquiry public.*

pub•lic[2] /ˈpʌblɪk/ noun [singular] ★★★ **the public** people in general: *The palace was opened to the public in the 1950s. ♦ The decision was not in the best interests of the traveling public. ♦ The police should be trained to deal politely with **members of the public**.* → GENERAL PUBLIC

PHRASE **in public** if you do something in public, people in general hear about it or see it ≠ IN PRIVATE: *It's unprofessional to criticize your colleagues in public.*

ˌpublic-adˈdress ˌsystem noun [C] a PA system

pub•li•ca•tion /ˌpʌblɪˈkeɪʃ(ə)n/ noun ★

1 [U] the process of producing a book for people to buy: *She became famous after **the publication of** her first novel.*

2 [C] a magazine, newspaper, or book: *a weekly financial publication*

3 [U] the process of making information available to the public: ***Publication of** the report is expected next week.*

ˌpublic deˈfender noun [C] in the U.S., a lawyer who is paid by the government to defend people in court if they cannot pay for themselves

ˌpublic ˈfigure noun [C] a well-known person

pub•li•cist /ˈpʌblɪsɪst/ noun [C] someone whose job is to make a person or thing well known

pub•lic•i•ty /pʌbˈlɪsəti/ noun [U] ★ attention in newspapers and on television: *a publicity campaign* (=an attempt to get publicity) ♦ *Her behavior on the movie set **attracted** a lot of **publicity**.*

> **Words often used with publicity**
>
> *Adjectives often used with **publicity***
> - **adverse, bad, negative, unfavorable, unwelcome** + PUBLICITY: used about bad publicity
> - **considerable, extensive, enormous, massive, maximum, widespread** + PUBLICITY: used about publicity that a large number of people see or hear
>
> *Verbs often used with **publicity***
> - **attract, gain, generate, get, receive** + PUBLICITY: get publicity
> - **avoid, shun** + PUBLICITY: try not to get publicity

pub•li•cize /ˈpʌbləˌsaɪz/ verb [T] to publish or broadcast information about someone or something

pub•lic•ly /ˈpʌblɪkli/ adv **1** in a way that many people notice ≠ PRIVATELY: *Kent publicly disagreed with his fellow doctors on many occasions.* **2** by the government, or by or for people in general: *a publicly funded library system ♦ publicly available information*

ˌpublic reˈlations noun [U] the job of giving people information about something and making it popular = PR

ˌpublic ˈschool noun [C/U] **1** *American* a school that is controlled and paid for by the government **2** *British* an expensive private school

ˈpublic ˈsector noun [singular] the industries and services that are controlled by the government

ˌpublic ˈservice noun **1** [C] a service that the government pays for, such as education **2** [C] a service that helps people without charging them any money **3** [C/U] the business of providing something such as water or electricity that everyone needs **4** [U] the work that is done by people who are employed by the government

ˌpublic ˈtransport noun [U] *British* PUBLIC TRANSPORTATION

ˌpublic transporˈtation noun [U] *American* vehicles such as buses and trains that anyone can use by paying a FARE

pub•lish /ˈpʌblɪʃ/ verb [T] ★★★

1 to produce many copies of a book, magazine, or newspaper for people to buy: *Their company **publishes** a wide selection of **books**.*

2 to make information available for everyone to read: *The department's **report was published** in June.*

3 to have something that you have written printed and sold: *In 1934 he published another successful novel.*

4 to include something such as a letter in a newspaper or magazine: *Our **research is being published** in a well-known medical journal.*

pub•lish•er /ˈpʌblɪʃər/ noun [C] a person or company that produces and sells books

pub•lish•ing /ˈpʌblɪʃɪŋ/ noun [U] the business of producing books

pud•ding /ˈpʊdɪŋ/ noun **1** [C/U] *American* a cold,

soft, sweet food, flavored, for example, with chocolate **2** [C] *British* a soft DESSERT

pud·dle /ˈpʌd(ə)l/ noun [C] a small pool of water that is left on the ground after it has rained

puff¹ /pʌf/ verb **1** [I/T] to smoke a cigarette **2** [I] to breathe noisily after running or doing something else that is physically hard

PHRASAL VERBS **ˌpuff sth ˈout** if you puff out your cheeks or your chest, you fill them with air so that they look bigger

ˌpuff ˈup to swell because of an injury or illness: *The next day his face had really puffed up.*

puff² /pʌf/ noun [C] **1** the action of breathing in smoke from a cigarette **2** a small amount of smoke, wind, or air

puff·y /ˈpʌfi/ adj slightly swollen

pug·na·cious /pʌgˈneɪʃəs/ adj *formal* quick to argue or fight with people

puke /pjuk/ verb [I/T] *informal* to VOMIT food from your stomach out through your mouth = THROW (STH) UP

pull¹ /pʊl/ verb ★★★

1 move sth toward you	6 attract people
2 remove sth attached	7 injure muscle
3 move body with force	8 take gun/knife out
4 take sth behind vehicle	+ PHRASES
5 move window cover	+ PHRASAL VERBS

1 [I/T] to move someone or something toward you using your hands ≠ PUSH: *The little girl pulled gently at my sleeve.* ♦ **pull sb/sth away from/out of/into etc. sth** *I climbed into bed and pulled the comforter over my head.* ♦ *A lifeguard had to pull her out of the water.* ♦ **pull sth open/shut** *Jane pulled the door open.* ♦ **pull sth tight** *Don't pull the string too tight.*

2 [T] to use force to remove something that is attached somewhere: **pull sth up** *She was pulling up the weeds in the garden.* ♦ **pull sth off sth** *Someone pulled the handle off the door.*

3 [T] to move your body or part of your body using effort or force: *He needed all his energy to pull himself up off the ground.*

4 [T] to move something along behind your vehicle by attaching it to the vehicle: *Two horses were pulling the plow.*

5 [T] to open or close something that covers a window: *Alice pulled the curtains shut.*

6 [T] to attract customers, VOTERS, or an audience: *The show is pulling huge audiences all over America.*

7 [T] to injure a muscle by stretching it too much

8 [T] to take a gun or a knife out of your pocket and be ready to use it: **pull sth on sb** *His attacker suddenly pulled a knife on him.*

PHRASES **pull sb's leg** to tell someone a lie as a joke

pull out all the stops to make a big effort so that something happens or is successful: *Her parents pulled out all the stops for her wedding.*

pull strings to use your influence in order to get something: *We might be able to get tickets if I pull a few strings.*

pull up a chair to move a seat near to where someone is sitting, and sit on it

pull your weight to work as hard as the other people who are involved in something

pull the wool over sb's eyes to try to trick someone by giving them wrong information

→ PLUG², PUNCH²

PHRASAL VERBS **ˌpull sb aˈpart** to separate two people or animals that are fighting

ˌpull sth aˈpart to destroy something by violently pulling it into pieces

ˌpull aˈway 1 if a vehicle pulls away, it starts to move away from a place: *The bus pulled away from the station around noon.* **2** to move away from someone who is trying to hold you: *When he tried to kiss her, she pulled away.*

ˌpull ˈback 1 to decide not to do something that you said you would do: *The government has* ***pulled back from*** *sending the navy there.* **2** to move away from someone who is trying to hold you

ˌpull ˈin if a vehicle pulls in, it arrives or stops somewhere

ˌpull ˈinto sth if a vehicle pulls into a place, it stops there: *The train pulled into Grand Central Station.*

ˌpull sth ˈoff to succeed in doing something that is difficult: *Sandy managed to pull off a surprise party for her husband.*

ˌpull ˈoff sth if a vehicle pulls off a road, it stops by the side of it

ˌpull sth ˈon to put clothes on quickly

ˌpull ˈout 1 to leave a place: *The troops are expected to pull out tomorrow.* **2** to decide not take part in something: *The Columbian team pulled out at the last minute.* **3** if a vehicle pulls out, it moves onto a road or onto a part of a road where the traffic is moving faster: *She just pulled out in front of me without signaling!* **4** if a train pulls out, it leaves a station

ˌpull (sth) ˈover to stop at the side of the road, or to make a vehicle stop at the side of the road

ˌpull ˈthrough to manage to stay alive after you have been very sick or badly injured

ˌpull (sb) ˈthrough to succeed in a very difficult situation, or to help someone to do this: *It was a difficult year financially, but we pulled through.*

ˌpull toˈgether if people pull together, they work together to achieve something: *The community pulled together to help the flood victims.*

ˌpull ˈup if a vehicle pulls up, it stops: *Their taxi pulled up outside the church.*

pull² /pʊl/ noun **1** [C] the act of moving someone or something toward you **2** [singular] a strong physical force that causes things to move in a particular direction: *the pull of gravity* **3** [singular] the power that something has to attract people **4** [singular] the power that someone has to get what they want, because they have influence over other people

ˈpull-down ˌmenu noun [C] *computing* a list of choices on a computer screen that you get by CLICKING on something → DROP-DOWN MENU

pul·ley /ˈpʊli/ noun [C] a piece of equipment used for lifting heavy things, consisting of a wheel with a rope around it

P

pull·out /ˈpʊlaʊt/ noun [C] an occasion when an army or business leaves a place

pul·mo·nar·y /ˈpʌlməˌneri/ adj *medical* affecting your lungs

pulp /pʌlp/ noun **1** [U] the inside of a fruit or vegetable = FLESH **2** [singular/U] a thick soft substance made by crushing something

pul·pit /ˈpʊlpɪt/ noun [C] the place where a priest stands to talk to people in a church

pul·sate /ˈpʌlˌseɪt/ verb [I] to make strong regular movements or sounds —**pul·sat·ing** adj

pulse¹ /pʌls/ noun [C] the regular movement of blood as your heart pumps it around your body: *The first thing the doctor does is take your pulse* (=check how fast your heart is beating).

pulse² /pʌls/ verb [I] **1** to move with a strong regular movement **2** to fill a person or place with a quality: *a city pulsing with life*

pul·ver·ize /ˈpʌlvəˌraɪz/ verb [T] to crush something into very small pieces

pum·mel /ˈpʌm(ə)l/ verb [T] to hit someone or something many times

pump¹ /pʌmp/ noun [C] ★ a piece of equipment for sending a liquid or gas into or out of something: *a fuel pump* ♦ *a hand/foot pump* (=operated with your hand or foot)

pump² /pʌmp/ verb ★
1 [T] to send liquid or gas somewhere, especially by using a pump: *Poisonous gases are pumped into the atmosphere every day.*
2 [I/T] to move up and down with a lot of force, or to move something up and down with a lot of force: *Liz pumped the accelerator and tried to start the car.* ♦ *His legs were really pumping.*
3 [T] *informal* to try to get information from someone
PHRASAL VERBS **ˌpump sth ˈinto sth** to invest a lot of money in something
ˌpump sth ˈout 1 to make liquid or gas escape from a place: *Huge generators pump out black smoke.* **2** *informal* to produce a lot of something
ˌpump sth ˈup to fill something with air, using a pump

pump·kin /ˈpʌmpkɪn/ noun [C/U] a large round vegetable with a thick orange skin —*picture* → C11

pumps /pʌmps/ noun [plural] *American* women's plain shoes that have a heel and do not fasten

pun /pʌn/ noun [C] a joke using words that have two meanings

punch¹ /pʌntʃ/ verb [T] **1** to hit someone or something with your FIST (=closed hand) **2** to make a hole in something with a tool or machine

punch² /pʌntʃ/ noun **1** [C] the action of hitting someone or something with your FIST (=closed hand) **2** [U] a sweet drink made with fruit juice and alcohol **3** [C] a tool for making a hole in something
PHRASE **not pull any punches** to criticize someone or something in a very direct honest way

ˈpunch ˌline noun [C] the funny last part of a joke

punch

punc·tu·al /ˈpʌŋktʃuəl/ adj someone who is punctual arrives at the time that they should arrive at —**punc·tu·al·i·ty** /ˌpʌŋktʃuˈæləti/ noun [U], **punc·tu·al·ly** adv

punc·tu·ate /ˈpʌŋktʃuˌeɪt/ verb [I/T] to use PERIODS, COMMAS, and other PUNCTUATION MARKS in your writing
PHRASE **be punctuated by/with sth** to be frequently interrupted by something: *a 15-minute speech punctuated by applause*

punc·tu·a·tion /ˌpʌŋktʃuˈeɪʃ(ə)n/ noun [U] **1** the use of marks such as PERIODS and COMMAS in writing **2** punctuation marks

punctuˈation ˌmark noun [C] a mark such as a PERIOD, COMMA, or QUESTION MARK that you use in order to write in a clear style

punc·ture /ˈpʌŋktʃər/ verb [T] to make a small hole in something —**punc·ture** noun [C]

pun·dit /ˈpʌndɪt/ noun [C] an expert who gives their opinions in newspapers and on television and radio programs

pun·gent /ˈpʌndʒənt/ adj a pungent taste or smell is very strong and sharp

pun·ish /ˈpʌnɪʃ/ verb [T] ★ to do something unpleasant to someone because they have done something bad or illegal: **punish sb for (doing) sth** *He was punished for stealing.*
PHRASE **punish yourself** to do something that makes you suffer: *Why punish yourself by working harder than you need to?*

pun·ish·a·ble /ˈpʌnɪʃəb(ə)l/ adj if someone does something punishable, they can be punished for doing it

pun·ish·ing /ˈpʌnɪʃɪŋ/ adj extremely difficult or tiring

pun·ish·ment /ˈpʌnɪʃmənt/ noun ★
1 [C] a way in which someone is punished: *He had to clean up the mess as a punishment.*
2 [U] the process of punishing someone: *He has cheated people and escaped punishment.*

pu·ni·tive /ˈpjunətɪv/ adj relating to punishment, or intended as a punishment

Pun·ja·bi¹ /pʌnˈdʒɑbi/ noun [U] the language most people speak in the Punjab region of India and Pakistan

Pun·ja·bi² /pʌnˈdʒɑbi/ adj **1** someone who is Punjabi is from Punjab **2** relating to Punjab, or its language or culture

punk /pʌŋk/ noun **1 punk** or **punk rock** [U] a type of loud fast music with angry words **2 punk** or **punk rocker** [C] someone who likes punk music, or who dresses in the style of punk musicians

punt /pʌnt/ verb [I/T] to drop a ball from your hands and kick it in the air in the game of football —*picture* → C15

pu•ny /ˈpjuni/ adj a puny person or animal is small, thin, and weak

pup /pʌp/ noun [C] a PUPPY

pu•pil /ˈpjup(ə)l/ noun [C] **1** the black round part in the middle of your eye **2** someone who is being taught something → STUDENT

pup•pet /ˈpʌpɪt/ noun [C] **1** a toy that looks like a person or animal that you move by pulling wires or strings, or by putting your hand inside it **2** someone who is controlled by someone else

pup•pet•eer /ˌpʌpɪˈtɪr/ noun [C] someone who performs using puppets

pup•py /ˈpʌpi/ noun [C] a very young dog

pur•chase¹ /ˈpɜrtʃəs/ verb [T] *formal* to buy something: *She purchased a number of different stocks.*

pur•chase² /ˈpɜrtʃəs/ noun *formal* **1** [U] the process of buying something: *the purchase of new computers* **2** [C] something that you buy: *Her latest purchase was a long black coat.*

pure /pjʊr/ adj ★★

1 a pure substance has nothing mixed with it that might spoil its quality ≠ IMPURE: *pure gold/alcohol* ♦ *clean, pure drinking water*

2 used for emphasis: *a smile of **pure happiness*** ♦ *Perhaps it was **pure chance** that the other woman happened to be there.*

3 morally good ≠ IMPURE: *He seems to have led a pure life.*

4 a pure science deals only with theory and not with the way the theory is used: *pure mathematics*

Word family: pure

*Words in the same family as **pure***

- **purely** *adv*
- **purify** *v*
- **purity** *n*
- **purist** *n*
- **impure** *adj*
- **impurity** *n*

pu•rée /pjʊˈreɪ/ noun [C/U] food that has been mixed or crushed to form a thick smooth sauce —**pu•rée** verb [T]

pure•ly /ˈpjʊrli/ adv ★ completely, or only: *What I'm saying is purely my own point of view.* ♦ *We meet purely for business reasons.*

pur•ga•to•ry /ˈpɜrgəˌtɔri/ noun [U] **1** the place where Roman Catholics believe that people go to suffer after they die before they are allowed to go to heaven **2** an unpleasant place or experience

purge /pɜrdʒ/ verb [T] **1** to force people to leave an organization **2** to get rid of bad feelings —**purge** noun [C]

pu•ri•fy /ˈpjʊrəfaɪ/ verb [T] to make something clean by removing dirty or harmful substances from it —**pu•ri•fi•ca•tion** /ˌpjʊrɪfəˈkeɪʃ(ə)n/ noun [U]

pur•ist /ˈpjʊrɪst/ noun [C] someone who wants people to follow rules carefully

pu•ri•tan /ˈpjʊrɪt(ə)n/ noun [C] *showing disapproval* someone who does not approve of pleasures such as sex and drinking alcohol —**pu•ri•tan•i•cal** /ˌpjʊrɪˈtænɪk(ə)l/ adj

pu•ri•ty /ˈpjʊrəti/ noun [U] the condition of being pure ≠ IMPURITY

pur•ple¹ /ˈpɜrp(ə)l/ adj between red and blue in color

pur•ple² /ˈpɜrp(ə)l/ noun [U] a color that is between red and blue

pur•port /pərˈpɔrt/ verb [I] *formal* to claim to do something

pur•pose /ˈpɜrpəs/ noun [C] ★★★ a goal or use: ***The purpose of this dictionary is to** help students of English.* ♦ *Another meeting **would serve absolutely no purpose.*** ♦ **for the purpose of doing sth** *He went there for the purpose of making business contacts.*

PHRASE **on purpose** deliberately: *They think the fire was started on purpose.*

→ ALL-PURPOSE

pur•pose•ful /ˈpɜrpəsf(ə)l/ adj showing that you are determined to do something

pur•pose•ly /ˈpɜrpəsli/ adv deliberately

purr /pɜr/ verb [I] **1** if a cat purrs, it makes a continuous low sound because it is happy **2** if a machine purrs, it makes a continuous quiet sound because it is operating correctly —**purr** noun [C]

purse¹ /pɜrs/ noun [C] ★

1 *American* a small bag in which a woman carries money and personal objects = HANDBAG —*picture* → BAG

2 *British* a CHANGE PURSE

purse² /pɜrs/ verb **purse your lips** to press your lips together and outward because you are angry or you are thinking

ˈpurse ˌstrings, the noun [plural] the way in which money is controlled and spent by a group or organization: *Who controls the purse strings?*

pur•sue /pərˈsu/ verb [T] ★

1 to do something, or to try to achieve something: *We're persuading both countries to pursue a peaceful solution.* ♦ *He wants to **pursue a career** in medicine.* ♦ *I intend to **pursue the matter*** (=continue to try to achieve my goal).

2 to chase someone

pur•suit /pərˈsut/ noun **1** [U] the process of trying to achieve something: *the pursuit of happiness* **2** [U] the process of chasing someone: *Several police officers are in pursuit of the stolen car.* **3** [C] *formal* an activity that you enjoy: *his artistic pursuits*

pus /pʌs/ noun [U] a thick yellow liquid that your body produces when you have an infection

push¹ /pʊʃ/ verb ★★★

1 move sb/sth away	5 make sth reach level
2 press button	6 make sb work hard
3 move through group	7 make impatient
4 force sb	+ PHRASAL VERBS

1 [I/T] to move someone or something away from you using your hands ≠ PULL: *Push as hard as you can.* ♦ **push sb/sth away** *She gently pushed him away.* ♦ **push sth open/shut** *I pushed the door open.*

2 [I/T] to press a button on a machine: *To turn on the television, you push this button.*

3 [I/T] to move through a group of people using the force of your body: *Stop pushing and just wait your turn.* ♦ *He just **pushed past** Fred and left.* ♦ *I was **pushing my way through** the crowd.*

4 [T] to force someone to do something: **push sb into (doing) sth** *The police pushed her into giving evidence.*

5 [T] to make something reach a particular level or standard: **push sth into/toward sth**

P

The strong sun pushed temperatures into the nineties. ♦ **push sth up/down** *The Fed had pushed up interest rates sharply to protect the dollar.*
6 [T] to make someone work very hard: *Some parents really push their children.* ♦ *You shouldn't **push yourself** so hard.*
7 [T] to make someone impatient or annoyed by behaving in an unreasonable way: *If you push him too far, he'll resign.*

PHRASAL VERBS **ˌpush aˈhead** to continue trying to achieve something
ˌpush sb aˈround *informal* to keep telling someone what to do in an unfair and unpleasant way
ˌpush sth aˈside to refuse to think about something unpleasant: *She pushed her doubts aside and continued working.*
ˈpush for sth to try hard to get or achieve something: *They continue to push for more pay.*
ˌpush ˈon to continue a trip after stopping for a time
ˌpush sb/sth ˈover to push someone or something hard so that they fall to the ground
ˌpush sth ˈthrough to succeed in making people accept something such as an agreement or a new law
ˌpush sth ˈup to increase the price or level of something

push² /pʊʃ/ noun ★
1 [C] a movement in which you push someone or something: **give sb/sth a push** *Jan helped me give the car a push.*
2 [singular] an occasion when you encourage or force someone to do something: **give sb a push (to do sth)** *I knew I could do it – I just needed someone to give me an extra push.* ♦ **need a push (to do sth)** *Some people need a little push to make new friends.*
3 [C] a determined attempt to do something: **a push to do sth** *The two sides began a final push to reach an agreement before the deadline.*

PHRASE **if/when push comes to shove** if or when you are forced to make a decision or to do something difficult

ˈpush-ˌbutton adj operated by pressing a button or switch

push·er /ˈpʊʃər/ noun [C] *informal* someone who sells illegal drugs

push·o·ver /ˈpʊʃˌoʊvər/ noun [C] **1** someone who is easy to persuade or defeat **2** something that is easy to achieve

push·up /ˈpʊʃʌp/ noun [C] an exercise in which you lie flat on your stomach and use your arms to push yourself up

push·y /ˈpʊʃi/ adj *informal* extremely determined to get what you want, even if it annoys other people

puss·y·cat /ˈpʊsiˌkæt/ noun [C] *informal* a cat. This word is used especially by children.

puss·y·foot /ˈpʊsiˌfʊt/ verb [I] *informal* to avoid saying or doing anything definite because you are afraid

put /pʊt/ (past tense and past participle **put**) verb [T] ★★★

1 move sth to position	6 place somewhere
2 cause to be in situation	7 say in particular way
3 write/print sth	+ PHRASES
4 make sb go to place	+ PHRASAL VERBS
5 give position on list	

1 to move something to a particular position using your hands: *Where did you put the newspaper?* ♦ **put sth in/on/through etc. sth** *Did I put my wallet in your purse?* ♦ *She put her hand on Cliff's arm.*
2 to cause someone or something to be in a particular situation: *She was **put in charge of** the marketing department.* ♦ *The information you've given me **puts** me **in a really difficult position**.* ♦ *I hate being **put under** so much **pressure**.* ♦ *Supermarkets have **put** many smaller stores **out of business**.* ♦ *That argument **put** me **in a bad mood** for the rest of the day.*
3 to write or print something somewhere: *Put a check mark by the correct answer.* ♦ *I'll put a note at the bottom of the card.* ♦ *You've put the comma in the wrong place.*
4 to make someone go to a place: *The government has promised to put more police officers on the street.* ♦ *What time do you **put** the kids **to bed**?*
5 to give something a particular position on a list according to importance, quality, or value: *They're so different, you can't even put them in the same category.* ♦ *I'd put Monet among the best artists of the century.*
6 to build or place something somewhere: *There are plans to put ten new houses on the site.* ♦ *We decided to put the office upstairs.*
7 to say or write something in a particular way: *She **put it very well** when she described him as "brilliant but lazy."*

PHRASES **(let me) put it this way** used when you are going to say something that is honest, but may sound rude: *Let me put it this way, he's rich, but he's certainly not attractive.*
not put it past sb (to do sth) used for saying that you think someone is capable of doing something bad or dishonest: *"Do you think Jake took the money?" "I wouldn't put it past him."*
put sth behind you to stop thinking about something unpleasant that has happened to you: *I was upset at the time, but I've managed to put it behind me.*
put a stop/end to sth to make something stop happening: *He quickly put a stop to the employees' long lunch breaks.*
→ STAY¹

PHRASAL VERBS **ˌput sth aˈside** to not allow yourself to be affected by a problem or argument, so that you can achieve something more important: *Both sides need to **put aside** their **differences** and continue the peace talks.*
ˌput sth aˈway to put something in the place where you usually keep it: *He put the notebook away and stood up.*
ˌput sth ˈback to put something in the place where it was before it was moved: *Can you put the book back when you're finished with it?*
ˌput sb ˈdown to criticize someone in a way that makes them feel stupid
ˌput sth ˈdown **1** to put something onto a surface such as the floor or a table: *Emma put her bag down and went upstairs.* **2** to kill an animal using a drug because it is very old, sick, or dangerous **3** to write

P

something on a piece of paper: *I put my name down on the list.*
ˌ**put sb ˈforward** to officially suggest that someone should be considered for a particular job: *Your name was **put forward** as a possible team leader.*
ˌ**put sth ˈforward** to suggest something so that people can discuss it and make a decision
ˌ**put sth ˈin 1** to spend time or effort doing something: *Wendy has been putting in more hours at the office recently.* **2** to put equipment somewhere and make it ready to use: *We're having a burglar alarm put in.* **3** to make an official request, claim, offer, etc.: *Why don't you put in a claim for the damage?* → APPEARANCE
ˌ**put sth ˈinto sth 1** to invest money in something: *How much are you prepared to put into the business?* **2** to spend time or effort in order to do something: *I put a lot of work into the speech.*
ˌ**put sth ˈoff** to delay doing something that you do not want to do
ˌ**put sb ˈon 1** to pass the telephone to someone so that they can speak to the person that you have been talking to **2 be putting sb on** *informal* to be trying to make someone believe something that is not true: *You're putting me on! Is that true?*
ˌ**put sth ˈon 1** to cover a part of your body with a piece of clothing or jewelry so that you are wearing it ≠ TAKE OFF: *Dorothy put on her coat and went out.* —*picture* → DRESS **2** if you put on weight, you become fatter **3** to organize an event: *We're putting on a concert.* **4** to pretend to have a particular feeling or a particular way of speaking or behaving: *She's not really upset – she's just **putting it on**.*
ˌ**put sb ˈout** to cause problems for someone by making them do something for you: *It would be great to stay with you, but I don't want to put you out.* → PUT OUT
ˌ**put sth ˈout 1** to make something stop burning **2** to put something in a place where someone will see it, so that they can use it or take it: *I put out food for the birds in cold weather.*
ˌ**put sb ˈthrough sth** to make someone do something difficult or unpleasant
ˌ**put sb/sth ˈthrough** if you put a person or a telephone call through, you connect someone to the person that they want to speak to on the telephone
ˈ**put sth to sb** to suggest something so that people can discuss it or consider it
ˌ**put sth toˈgether 1** to make something by joining all its parts: *Will you help me put this desk together?* **2** to produce or organize something using many different things: *The exhibit has been put together by a group of young artists.*
ˌ**put sb ˈup** to let someone stay in your house
ˌ**put sth ˈup 1** to build something such as a wall, fence, or house **2** to attach something to a wall: *The teachers will put a notice up about the new classes.*
ˌ**put sb ˈup to sth** to encourage someone to do something stupid or wrong
ˌ**put ˈup with sb/sth** to accept someone or something unpleasant in a patient way: *How has Jan put up with him for so long?*

put•down /ˈpʊtˌdaʊn/ noun [C] *informal* a comment that is intended to make someone feel stupid
ˌ**put ˈout** adj annoyed, offended, or upset
pu•trid /ˈpjutrɪd/ adj *formal* decaying and smelling very bad
putt /pʌt/ noun [C] in golf, a gentle hit of the ball along the ground toward the hole —**putt** verb [I/T]
put•ter /ˈpʌtər/ verb [I] *American informal* to pass the time in a relaxed way doing unimportant things
put•ty /ˈpʌti/ noun [U] a soft gray substance that is used for putting glass in windows
puz•zle¹ /ˈpʌz(ə)l/ noun [C] **1** a game consisting of many pieces that you have to fit together correctly **2** a game or toy that is designed to test your intelligence
puz•zle² /ˈpʌz(ə)l/ verb [T] if something puzzles you, you cannot understand it
PHRASAL VERB ˈ**puzzle ˌover sb/sth** to think hard about something and try to understand it
puz•zled /ˈpʌz(ə)ld/ adj confused because you cannot understand something
puz•zling /ˈpʌz(ə)lɪŋ/ adj confusing or difficult to understand
py•ja•mas /pəˈdʒɑməz/ the British spelling of **pajamas**
py•lon /ˈpaɪˌlɑn/ noun [C] a tall metal tower that holds electricity wires high above the ground
pyr•a•mid /ˈpɪrəmɪd/ noun [C] **1** a large pointed stone structure with a square base and TRIANGULAR sides **2** an object with the shape of a pyramid —*picture* → C8
pyre /paɪr/ noun [C] a high pile of wood for burning a dead body in a funeral ceremony
py•thon /ˈpaɪˌθɑn/ noun [C] a large snake that kills animals by wrapping itself around them

Q

Qq

q or **Q** /kju/ noun [C/U] the 17th letter of the English alphabet → Q-TIP
Q-tip /ˈkju ˌtɪp/ *American trademark* a short plastic stick with cotton at each end, used for cleaning the inside of your ears, nose, etc.
quack¹ /kwæk/ noun [C] **1** *informal* a bad doctor, or someone who pretends to be a doctor **2** the sound that a DUCK makes
quack² /kwæk/ verb [I] to make the sound that a DUCK makes
quad•ru•ple /kwɑˈdrup(ə)l/ verb [I/T] if a number or an amount quadruples, or if you quadruple it, it becomes four times bigger than it was
quag•mire /ˈkwægˌmaɪr/ noun [C] **1** a situation that is so difficult or complicated that you cannot make much progress **2** an area of

very wet land that is too soft to walk on

quail /kweɪl/ noun [C/U] a small bird that people shoot and eat, or this bird eaten as food

quaint /kweɪnt/ adj interesting or attractive with a slightly strange and old-fashioned quality

quake¹ /kweɪk/ verb [I] **1** to feel so afraid that your body shakes slightly **2** if something such as a building quakes, it shakes violently

quake² /kweɪk/ noun [C] *informal* an EARTHQUAKE

Quak•er /ˈkweɪkər/ noun [C] a member of a Christian religious group whose members avoid violence and hold simple religious services with no priests

qual•i•fi•ca•tion /ˌkwɑləfɪˈkeɪʃ(ə)n/ noun **1** [C] an ability or quality that you need in order to do a particular job or activity **2** [C/U] something that you add to a statement or rule in order to show that it is not true in some situations **3** [U] the action or process of qualifying for something

qual•i•fied /ˈkwɑləˌfaɪd/ adj **1** qualified support or agreement is not completely positive because someone has some doubts or criticisms **2** successfully trained for a particular job: *a qualified doctor/nurse/teacher* **3** able to do something, because you have the knowledge, skill, or experience that is needed: **qualified to do sth** *She is particularly well qualified to give an opinion.*

qual•i•fi•er /ˈkwɑləˌfaɪər/ noun [C] a team or person who competes successfully in an early stage of a competition and is able to go on to the next stage

Q

qual•i•fy /ˈkwɑləˌfaɪ/ verb ★

1 [I/T] to have the right qualities to be or to do something: *Twenty percent of Americans **qualify as** rich.* ♦ *To **qualify for** Olympic status, a sport must be played in 50 countries and on three continents.* ♦ **be qualified to do sth** *Only people over the age of 18 are qualified to vote.* ♦ **qualify sb to do sth** *The fact that his grandparents were Irish qualified him to play in the Irish national team.*

2 [I] to reach a particular stage of a competition by competing successfully in an earlier stage: *It would be incredible if Brazil **failed to qualify**.* ♦ *What are your team's chances of **qualifying for** the finals?*

3 [T] to add something to a statement in order to change it slightly or state the situations in which it is not true: *Let me qualify that last statement by saying that your condition might improve.*

> **Word family: qualify**
>
> *Words in the same family as **qualify***
>
> ■ **qualification** *n* ■ **qualifier** *n*
> ■ **qualified** *adj* ■ **unqualified** *adj*
> ■ **disqualified** *adj* ■ **disqualify** *v*

qual•i•ty¹ /ˈkwɑləti/ noun ★★★

1 [C] a feature of something: *the addictive **qualities of** tobacco*

2 [C] a positive feature of a person's character: *What is the quality you most admire in others?* ♦ *Do you possess the right **personal qualities** to be a teacher?* ♦ *a woman with strong **leadership qualities*** (=the ability to be a good leader)

3 [C/U] the quality of something is how good or how bad it is: *poor-quality workmanship* ♦ *This cut in funding will affect **the quality of** education in our schools.* ♦ *The food is **top quality**.*

4 [U] a high standard: *a company with a reputation for quality and reliability*

qual•i•ty² /ˈkwɑləti/ adj of a high standard

ˈquality ˌtime noun [U] time that you spend with someone, usually your child, doing enjoyable things together so that your relationship remains strong

qualms /kwɑmz/ noun [plural] thoughts that what you are doing might be bad or wrong

quan•da•ry /ˈkwɑndəri/ noun **be in a quandary** to not be certain what decision to make about something

quan•ti•fi•er /ˈkwɑntəˌfaɪər/ noun [C] *linguistics* a word or phrase such as "much" or "a few" that is used with another word in order to show quantity

quan•ti•fy /ˈkwɑntəˌfaɪ/ verb [T] *formal* to measure or describe something as a quantity —**quan•ti•fi•a•ble** /ˈkwɑntəˌfaɪəb(ə)l/ adj, **quan•ti•fi•ca•tion** /ˌkwɑntəfɪˈkeɪʃ(ə)n/ noun [U]

quan•ti•ty /ˈkwɑntəti/ noun **1** [U] the amount of something: *They check both the quantity and the quality of materials used.* **2** [C/U] a particular amount of something: *a small quantity of drugs* ♦ *large quantities of water*

quan•tum leap /ˌkwɑntəm ˈlip/ noun [C] a very big change or improvement

quar•an•tine /ˈkwɔrənˌtin/ noun [U] a situation in which a person or animal that might have a disease is kept separate from other people or animals —**quar•an•tine** verb [T]

quar•rel¹ /ˈkwɔrəl/ noun [C] an argument
PHRASE **have no quarrel with** to have no reason for being unfriendly or for disagreeing with a person, idea, plan, or decision

quar•rel² /ˈkwɔrəl/ (present participle **quar•rel•ing** or **quar•rel•ling**; past tense and past participle **quar•reled** or **quar•relled**) verb [I] to have an argument

quar•rel•some /ˈkwɔrəlsəm/ adj tending to argue with people

quar•ry¹ /ˈkwɔri/ noun **1** [C] a place where stone is dug up out of the ground **2** [singular] *formal* a person or animal that someone is trying to catch

quar•ry² /ˈkwɔri/ verb [T] to dig stone out of the ground

quart /kwɔrt/ noun [C] a unit for measuring an amount of liquid, containing two PINTS

quar•ter /ˈkwɔrtər/ noun [C] ★★★

> 1 one of four equal parts
> 2 coin worth 25 cents
> 3 period of 15 minutes
> 4 period in some sports
> 5 period of 3 months
> 6 part of town
> 7 person/group
> + PHRASES

1 one of four equal parts of something: *Over **a quarter of** our income goes for food.*

2 a coin that is worth one quarter of an American or Canadian dollar, or 25 CENTS

3 one of four periods of 15 minutes that an

hour is divided into when you are telling the time
4 one of four periods that a game is divided into in some sports
5 one of four periods of three months that the year is divided into, especially when you are talking about financial accounts: *The company's profits fell in the third quarter.*
6 a part of a town where you find particular buildings, activities, or people: *the Chinese quarter of the city*
7 *formal* a particular person or group of people: *Concern has been expressed* ***in some quarters*** (=among some people or groups) *about this policy.* ♦ *He has won support* ***from all quarters*** (=from all people or groups).
PHRASES **a quarter after five/six etc.** *American* or **a quarter past five/six etc.** 15 minutes past five o'clock/six o'clock etc.
a quarter of five/six etc. *American* or **a quarter to five/six etc.** 15 minutes before five o'clock/six o'clock etc.
→ QUARTERS

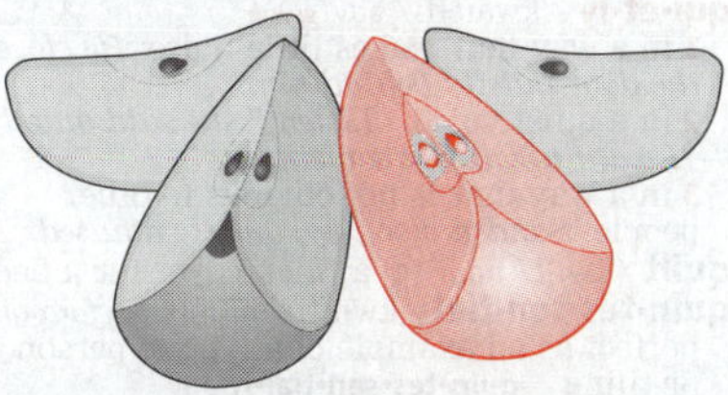

quarter

quar·ter·back /ˈkwɔrtərˌbæk/ noun [C] an important player in the sport of football who gives instructions to the other players and throws the ball —*picture* → C15

quar·ter·fi·nal /ˌkwɔrtərˈfaɪn(ə)l/ noun [C] one of the four games that are played between the eight players or teams that are still left in a competition

quar·ter·ly¹ /ˈkwɔrtərli/ adj, adv done or produced four times a year

quar·ter·ly² /ˈkwɔrtərli/ noun [C] a magazine that is published four times a year

quar·ters /ˈkwɔrtərz/ noun [plural] *formal* rooms or buildings for people to live in

quar·tet /kwɔrˈtet/ noun [C] a group of four musicians or singers, or a piece of music for a quartet to perform

quartz /kwɔrts/ noun [U] a hard shiny stone that is often used inside electronic equipment and watches

quash /kwɑʃ/ verb [T] *formal* **1** to say officially that a decision made by another court was wrong and has no legal force **2** to stop something from continuing

qua·ver /ˈkweɪvər/ verb [I] if your voice quavers, it is not steady because you are feeling nervous or afraid

quay /ki, keɪ/ noun [C] a hard surface next to an ocean or river, where boats can stop

quea·sy /ˈkwizi/ adj feeling that you are going to VOMIT (=get rid of food from your stomach through your mouth)

queen /kwin/ noun [C] ★★★

1 woman who rules	4 in cards
2 king's wife	5 in chess
3 female insect	

1 a woman who belongs to a royal family and who rules a country: *Queen Elizabeth* ♦ *She was* ***crowned queen*** *in 1953.*
2 a woman who is married to a king
3 a large female insect that can lay eggs: *a queen bee*
4 in a game of CARDS, a card with a picture of a queen on it —*picture* → C16
5 a piece that can move in any direction in a game of CHESS —*picture* → C16

queer¹ /kwɪr/ adj **1** *old-fashioned* strange **2** *offensive* an offensive word used for describing gay people

queer² /kwɪr/ noun [C] *offensive* an offensive word for someone who is gay

quell /kwel/ verb [T] *formal* **1** to cause a violent situation to end **2** to get rid of unpleasant thoughts or feelings

quench /kwentʃ/ verb **quench your thirst** to drink something so that you do not feel THIRSTY anymore

que·ry¹ /ˈkwɪri/ noun [C] a question

que·ry² /ˈkwɪri/ verb [T] to ask a question

quest /kwest/ noun [C] *literary* a long difficult search

ques·tion¹ /ˈkwestʃ(ə)n/ noun ★★★
1 [C] something that someone asks you when they want information: *Why won't you* ***answer my question?*** ♦ *I wish I hadn't* ***asked*** *that* ***question.*** ♦ *Does anyone have any* ***questions about*** *the trip?*
2 [C] something that you are asked in a test or competition: *Only one person* ***answered*** *all three* ***questions*** *correctly.*
3 [C] an issue that needs to be discussed and dealt with: *Recent incidents are bound to* ***raise questions*** *about the level of violence in hockey.* ♦ *His report did not* ***address the question*** *of air warfare.*
4 [C/U] a feeling of doubt about something: *This information began to* ***raise questions*** *in her mind about Jack's innocence.* ♦ *New evidence has* ***called into question*** (=made people have doubts about) *the testimony of this witness.* ♦ *There had been some* ***question about*** *whether to interview the boy.*
PHRASES **be out of the question** used for saying that something is definitely not a possibility: *Taking a vacation then is out of the question.*
be a/the question of used for saying what the most important issue is in a situation: *There would definitely be some job losses; it was just a question of how many.* ♦ *We all want to go ahead with the project, but there's the question of finance.*
in question the person, thing, time, etc. in question is the one that you are talking about: *The photograph in question was taken long before I met you.*
(that's a) good question *spoken* used as a way of saying that you do not know something
there is no question of sth if there is no question of something, it definitely will not happen
without question 1 used for saying that

Q

something is definitely true: *He is without question the best player on our team.* **2** if someone does something without question, they do it without asking any questions: *He expected the children to obey without question.*

ques·tion² /ˈkwestʃ(ə)n/ verb [T] ★★
1 to ask someone questions: *A man is being questioned by detectives in connection with a murder.* ♦ *A hundred employers were questioned in the survey.* ♦ **question sb about sth** *Curious friends questioned me about the case.*
2 to have or express doubts about something: *I have never questioned her honesty.*

ques·tion·a·ble /ˈkwestʃənəb(ə)l/ adj
1 possibly not true, accurate, or complete: *The results of the test seem highly questionable.* **2** probably not good, honest, or worth admiring: *questionable behavior/conduct/practices* —**ques·tion·a·bly** adv

ques·tion·ing /ˈkwestʃənɪŋ/ noun [U] a situation in which people ask someone questions

ˈquestion ˌmark noun [C] the symbol ? that is used at the end of a sentence in order to show that it represents a question

ques·tion·naire /ˌkwestʃəˈner/ noun [C] a set of questions that a lot of people are asked as a way of getting information about what people generally think or do

ˈquestion ˌtag noun [C] *linguistics* a word or phrase such as "isn't it?" or "haven't you?" that you can add to a sentence in order to make a question

queue¹ /kju/ noun [C] *British* a line of people that are waiting for something: *We stood in a queue for over an hour.*

Q

queue² /kju/ or **ˌqueue ˈup** verb [I] *British* to LINE UP

quib·ble /ˈkwɪb(ə)l/ verb [I] to argue or complain about things that are not important —**quib·ble** noun [C]

quiche /kiʃ/ noun [C/U] a food with a PASTRY base that is filled with a mixture of eggs and milk and other foods such as cheese and vegetables or meat

quick¹ /kwɪk/ adj ★★★
1 able to move fast or to do something fast: *He's surprisingly quick for such a big man.* ♦ *a quick worker*
2 done or happening in a short time: *He took a quick glance over his shoulder.* ♦ *a quick decision*
3 able to understand things very easily: *a quick learner*
PHRASE **be quick to do sth** to do something very quickly: *Townsend was quick to point out that it has been a team effort.*

quick² /kwɪk/ adv *spoken* quickly

quick·en /ˈkwɪkən/ verb [I/T] if something quickens, or if you quicken it, it happens or moves more quickly

quick·ie /ˈkwɪki/ noun [C] *informal* something that you do quickly —**quick·ie** adj

quick·ly /ˈkwɪkli/ adv ★★★
1 at a fast speed: *We have to work quickly.* ♦ *She walked quickly out of the room.*
2 after only a short time, or lasting only a short time: *Something has to be done about this quickly.* ♦ *Let me explain very quickly what I mean.*

quick·sand /ˈkwɪkˌsænd/ noun [U] soft wet sand that is dangerous to walk on because it pulls your body down into it

qui·et¹ /ˈkwaɪət/ adj ★★★
1 making very little or no noise: *some quiet soothing music* ♦ ***Be quiet**, please. I'm trying to read.*
2 not talking, or not usually talking: *He's a quiet sensitive boy.*
3 not very busy, or with not much activity: *a quiet little coastal town* ♦ *a quiet and relaxing vacation*
PHRASE **keep quiet about sth** or **keep sth quiet** to not tell anyone about something: *Can we trust him to keep quiet about what he's seen?*

qui·et² /ˈkwaɪət/ noun [U] a place or situation in which there is not much noise or activity: *We moved to the countryside for some peace and quiet.*

qui·et³ /ˈkwaɪət/ or **ˌquiet (sb/sth) ˈdown** verb [I/T] *American* to become calmer or less noisy, or to make someone do this

qui·et·ly /ˈkwaɪətli/ adv ★★★
1 in a way that makes little noise: *He closed the door quietly behind him.*
2 in a quiet voice: *"Listen," she said quietly, "I want to tell you something."*
3 in a way that is not obvious to other people: *Sandra stood by, quietly amused.*

quilt /kwɪlt/ noun [C] a thick cover for a bed

quin·tes·sen·tial /ˌkwɪntɪˈsenʃ(ə)l/ adj *formal* perfect as an example of a type of person or thing —**quin·tes·sen·tial·ly** adv

quin·tet /kwɪnˈtet/ noun [C] a group of five musicians or singers, or a piece of music for a quintet to perform

quip /kwɪp/ verb [T] to say something that is funny or clever —**quip** noun [C]

quirk /kwɜrk/ noun [C] **1** a strange or annoying habit **2** something strange that happens

quirk·y /ˈkwɜrki/ adj slightly strange

quit /kwɪt/ (past tense and past participle **quit**) verb *informal* ★★
1 [I/T] to leave a job or school permanently: *She quit after only six months on the job.* ♦ *His decision to quit international soccer has shocked everyone.*
2 [T] to stop doing something: *They encourage younger people to quit smoking.*

quite /kwaɪt/ grammar word ★★

> **Quite** can be:
> - an **adverb**: *I was quite angry with her.*
> - a **determiner**: *I was taking quite a risk when I decided to talk to him.*

1 fairly but not very: *I was feeling quite tired after our walk.* ♦ *They said the dog was quite badly injured.* ♦ *He was **quite a good** musician.*
2 completely, or very: *We haven't quite finished.* ♦ *"Are you ready?" "Not quite."*
PHRASES **quite a lot/a bit/a few** a large number or amount: *My family has moved around quite a bit since then.* ♦ *Quite a few people asked questions.*
quite a or **quite some** used before a noun for emphasizing that something is unusual or

interesting: *The news came as quite a surprise.* ♦ *He's been renting the house for quite some time.*

quits /kwɪts/ adj **call it quits** *informal* **1** to agree that neither person owes the other one anything **2** to leave a job or stop doing something permanently

quiv•er /ˈkwɪvər/ verb [I] to shake with short quick movements —**quiv•er** noun [C]

quiz¹ /kwɪz/ noun [C] a test or competition in which you answer questions

quiz² /kwɪz/ verb [T] to ask someone a lot of questions

quiz•zi•cal /ˈkwɪzɪk(ə)l/ adj showing that you are confused or surprised by something that is rather strange —**quiz•zi•cal•ly** /ˈkwɪzɪkli/ adv

quo•rum /ˈkwɔrəm/ noun [singular] *technical* the smallest number of people who must be present at a meeting in order to allow official decisions to be made

quo•ta /ˈkwoʊtə/ noun [C] an amount of something that someone is allowed or should do

quo•ta•tion /kwoʊˈteɪʃ(ə)n/ noun [C] **1** words from a book, play, movie, etc. that are used by someone else **2** the price that someone says that they will charge you for doing a job

quoˈtation ˌmarks noun [plural] the symbols " and " that are used in writing before and after a quotation or the words that someone speaks

quote¹ /kwoʊt/ verb ★

1 [I/T] to say or write words that someone else has said or written: *He **was quoted as saying** that he was shocked by the judge's decision.* ♦ *Robert **quoted from** one of Churchill's speeches.*

2 [T] to tell someone what price you would charge them to do a particular piece of work: **quote sb sth** *They quoted us $500 to replace the whole window.*

3 [T] to give something as an example to support what you are saying: *He **quoted the example of** a 40-year-old man who has been waiting nearly two years for an operation.*

quote² /kwoʊt/ noun [C] *informal* a QUOTATION

Rr

r or **R** /ɑr/ noun [C/U] the 18th letter of the English alphabet

PHRASE **R and R** rest and relaxation

R¹ adj restricted: used in the U.S. for describing a movie that people under the age of 17 cannot go to unless they go with an adult

R² abbrev **1** Republican **2** are: used in e-mails and TEXT MESSAGES

R & B /ˌɑr ən ˈbi/ noun [U] rhythm and blues: a type of music that combines BLUES and SOUL styles with modern beats

rab•bi /ˈræbaɪ/ noun [C] a Jewish religious leader

rab•bit /ˈræbɪt/ noun [C] a small animal with long ears, soft fur, and a short tail —*picture* → C13

rab•ble /ˈræb(ə)l/ noun [singular] a noisy or violent crowd of people

rab•id /ˈræbɪd/ adj a rabid animal has rabies

ra•bies /ˈreɪbiz/ noun [U] a very serious disease that humans can get if they are bitten by an animal with the disease

rac•coon /rækun/ noun [C] a small animal with a black and white face and a long tail that lives mainly in North and Central America

race¹ /reɪs/ noun ★★★

1 [C] a competition that decides who is the fastest at doing something: *He is training for a big race.* ♦ *Marlene needs to **win the race** to keep her title.*

2 [C] a competition in which a person, organization, business, or country tries to win something or to be the first to do something: *There are three candidates in **the race for** the presidency.* ♦ **a race to do sth** *We are losing the race to find a cure for AIDS.*

3 [C/U] a group of people who are similar because they have the same skin color or other physical features, or because they speak the same language or have the same history or customs: *We do not discriminate on the basis of race or gender.* ♦ *a disaster that could mark the end of **the human race*** (=all of the people of the world, considered as a single group)

4 the races [plural] a series of horse races: *a day at the races*

PHRASE **a race against time** a situation in which someone must do or finish something very quickly because they only have a limited amount of time to do it

race² /reɪs/ verb ★★

1 [I/T] to compete in a race: *The gun sounded and they started to race.* ♦ *I raced my brother down the street.*

2 [I] to move very quickly: *The family **raced** to the basement when they heard Cheryl scream.* ♦ *Thoughts were **racing through** her mind.*

3 [T] to take someone somewhere quickly: *We raced the children to the hospital.*

4 [I] to work or move at a faster speed than usual: *Her heart began to race madly.*

ˈrace ˌcar noun [C] *American* a car that is designed and used for racing

race•horse /ˈreɪsˌhɔrs/ noun [C] a horse that is trained to run in races

ˌrace reˈlations noun [plural] the relationships between people of different races who live in the same community

race•track /ˈreɪsˌtræk/ noun [C] a track that is used for racing in cars, on horses, or on foot

ra•cial /ˈreɪʃ(ə)l/ adj **1** happening between people of different races **2** relating to someone's race —**ra•cial•ly** adv

rac•ing /ˈreɪsɪŋ/ noun [U] a sport in which

R

cars, boats, or horses or other animals race against each other —**rac•ing** adj

ra•cism /ˈreɪˌsɪzəm/ noun [U] a way of behaving or thinking that treats people belonging to some races unfairly

rac•ist /ˈreɪsɪst/ noun [C] someone who thinks that their race is better than others —**rac•ist** adj

rack[1] /ræk/ noun [C] an object with shelves, spaces, or hooks, used for storing things

rack[2] /ræk/ verb [T] if you are racked by pain or unpleasant feelings, you suffer because of them

PHRASE **rack your brains** to try hard to think of something

PHRASAL VERB **ˌrack sth ˈup** *informal* to get a large number or amount of something

rack•et /ˈrækɪt/ noun **1** [singular] *informal* a loud annoying noise **2** [C] an object used for hitting the ball in games such as tennis **3** [C] *informal* an illegal activity that makes money

rack•et•eer•ing /ˌrækəˈtɪrɪŋ/ noun [U] the crime of making money from illegal activities —**rack•et•eer** noun [C]

ra•coon /ræˈkun/ another spelling of **raccoon**

rac•quet•ball /ˈrækɪtˌbɔl/ noun [U] an indoor game in which two players use small RACKETS to hit a ball

rac•y /ˈreɪsi/ adj a racy story, movie, or play is slightly shocking in the way that it describes or shows sex

ra•dar /ˈreɪdɑr/ noun [C/U] a system that uses radio signals in order to find the position of something such as an aircraft or ship

ra•di•ance /ˈreɪdiəns/ noun [singular/U] **1** happiness that you can see in someone's appearance or smile **2** light that shines from something

ra•di•ant /ˈreɪdiənt/ adj **1** someone who is radiant looks extremely happy **2** very bright —**ra•di•ant•ly** adv

R

ra•di•ate /ˈreɪdiˌeɪt/ verb **1** [I/T] to show a particular feeling or attitude: *John radiated charm.* **2** [I/T] to produce heat, light, or energy **3** [I] if lines, paths, or roads radiate from a central point, they spread out from it

ra•di•a•tion /ˌreɪdiˈeɪʃ(ə)n/ noun [U] **1** a form of energy that is produced during a nuclear reaction, used for making electrical power **2** heat or light that is sent out but that you cannot see → RADIOACTIVE

ra•di•a•tor /ˈreɪdiˌeɪtər/ noun [C] **1** a large metal object on a wall, used for heating a room **2** the part of an engine that keeps it from getting too hot

rad•i•cal[1] /ˈrædɪk(ə)l/ adj **1** a radical change or way of doing something is new and very different from the usual way: *a program of radical reforms in schools* ♦ *a radical solution to the problem of juvenile crime* **2** believing that important political and social changes are necessary: *a radical left-wing group* ♦ *He surprised us all with his radical views.*

rad•i•cal[2] /ˈrædɪk(ə)l/ noun [C] someone who believes that important political and social changes are necessary

rad•i•cal•ly /ˈrædɪkli/ adv if something changes radically, it changes completely or in a way that is very noticeable

ra•di•o[1] /ˈreɪdioʊ/ noun ★★★

1 broadcasting system	4 message equipment
2 broadcast equipment	5 programs
3 message system	

1 [U] a system of broadcasting information and programs that people can listen to: *an independent **radio station** ♦ **Radio and television** have had an enormous effect on people's lives.* ♦ *She began her career **in local radio**.*

2 [C] a piece of equipment that you use for listening to radio programs: *a car radio* ♦ *Let's **turn on the radio**.*

3 [U] a system of sending and receiving spoken messages by using electronic signals: *We remained **in constant radio contact**.*

4 [C] the piece of equipment that is used for sending or receiving spoken messages using electronic signals: *a two-way radio*

5 the radio [singular] programs that are broadcast for people to listen to: *Joe's listening to the radio.* ♦ *What's **on the radio**?*

ra•di•o[2] /ˈreɪdioʊ/ verb [I/T] to communicate with someone using a radio

ra•di•o•ac•tive /ˌreɪdioʊˈæktɪv/ adj containing RADIATION (=energy that is produced during nuclear reactions)

ra•di•o•ac•tiv•i•ty /ˌreɪdioʊækˈtɪvəti/ noun [U] the ability that some substances have to produce energy in the form of RADIATION

ra•di•og•ra•phy /ˌreɪdiˈɑgrəfi/ noun [U] the process of taking X-RAY photographs of someone's body as part of a medical treatment —**ra•di•og•raph•er** noun [C]

rad•ish /ˈrædɪʃ/ noun [C] a small white or red vegetable that is eaten raw in salads —*picture* → C11

ra•di•us /ˈreɪdiəs/ (plural **ra•di•i** /ˈreɪdiˌaɪ/ or **ra•di•us•es**) noun [C] **1** the distance from the center of a circle to its edge, or a straight line from the center to the edge —*picture* → C8 **2** a particular distance in all directions from a central point: *Delivery is free within a five mile radius of the city center.*

raf•fle /ˈræf(ə)l/ noun [C] a competition in which you win a prize if the number on your ticket is the same as the number on the prize

raft /ræft/ noun [C] **1** a simple flat boat made by tying long pieces of wood together **2** a small light boat made of rubber or plastic

PHRASE **a raft of** *informal* a very large number of things or people

raft•er /ˈræftər/ noun [C] a large piece of wood that supports a sloping roof

raft•ing /ˈræftɪŋ/ noun [U] the activity of traveling on a river in a small boat

rag /ræg/ noun **1** [C] a piece of old cloth that is used for cleaning or wiping something **2 rags** [plural] clothes that are old, torn, and dirty: *The little girl was dressed in rags.*

rage[1] /reɪdʒ/ noun **1** [C/U] a very strong feeling of anger: *Her eyes filled with tears of rage and frustration.* **2** [U] angry violent behavior in a public situation

rage[2] /reɪdʒ/ verb [I] **1** to continue with a lot of force, violence, or angry arguments:

Fierce fighting raged for several days. **2** to shout angrily at someone

rag•ged /'rægəd/ adj **1** torn and dirty: *a pair of ragged shorts* **2** wearing old dirty clothes: *ragged children playing in the street* **3** not smooth or regular: *a ragged edge*

rag•ing /'reɪdʒɪŋ/ adj **1** happening with a lot of force or violence: *a raging battle* **2** very serious, painful, or strong: *a raging fever/headache/thirst*

ˌrags-to-ˈriches adj used for describing the life of someone who was born into a poor family but later became very rich and successful

raid[1] /reɪd/ noun [C] **1** a sudden short military attack: *Soldiers carried out raids on enemy targets.* **2** an action by police officers in which they suddenly enter a place in order to arrest people or search for something **3** a crime in which someone suddenly enters a place and uses force or threats to steal something

raid[2] /reɪd/ verb [T] **1** to use force to enter a place in order to search for something **2** to suddenly attack a place and cause a lot of damage **3** *informal* to take or steal things from a place: *hungry teenagers raiding the refrigerator*

raid•er /'reɪdər/ noun [C] someone who attacks a place using force

rail /reɪl/ noun ★

1 [C] one of the pair of metal bars that a train travels on

2 [C] a metal or wooden bar that you can hold onto to stop yourself from falling: *a safety rail*

3 [C] a metal bar that is used for hanging clothes and other things on: *a clothes/towel rail*

4 [U] the system of traveling by train: *We ought to transport more heavy goods* ***by rail.*** ♦ *an increase in* ***rail fares***

rail•ing /'reɪlɪŋ/ noun [C] a fence made of narrow posts supporting an upper bar

rail•road[1] /'reɪlˌroʊd/ noun [C] *American* ★★

1 the system of traveling by train, and all the people and things that are connected with it: *the need to invest more money in the railroad* ♦ *a railroad station/bridge*

2 railroad or **railroad track** the metal track that trains travel on: *a railroad that is no longer in use*

3 a train company

rail•road[2] /'reɪlˌroʊd/ verb [T] *informal* to force someone to do something that they do not really want to do

rail•way /'reɪlweɪ/ noun [C] *British* a RAILROAD

rain[1] /reɪn/ noun ★★★

1 [U] water that falls in drops from clouds in the sky: *Visibility was good, with only occasional* ***light rain.*** ♦ *People were standing* ***in the rain.***

2 the rains [plural] the large amounts of rain that fall in tropical regions during a particular season

rain[2] /reɪn/ verb [I] ★

1 if it rains, water falls from clouds in the sky: *Just as we were leaving home* ***it started to rain.*** ♦ *It had been* ***raining heavily*** *all day.*

2 to fall from the air in large amounts

PHRASE **rained out** if a sports game or other outside event is rained out, it does not happen because of rain

PHRASAL VERB **ˌrain ˈdown** *same as* **rain**[2] 2: *Sparks from the fire rained down on the frightened spectators.*

rain•bow /'reɪnˌboʊ/ noun [C] a curved line of colors that appears in the sky when the sun shines while it is raining

ˈrain ˌcheck noun [C] *American* a ticket for a sports game that you can use again if rain stops the game

PHRASE **take a rain check (on sth)** *spoken* used for saying that you are not going to accept an offer or suggestion immediately, but that you may accept it later

rain•coat /'reɪnˌkoʊt/ noun [C] a long coat made of light material that you wear when it is raining —*picture* → C4

rain•drop /'reɪnˌdrɑp/ noun [C] a drop of rain

rain•fall /'reɪnˌfɔl/ noun [C/U] the amount of rain that falls in a particular area during a particular period of time

ˈrain ˌforest noun [C/U] a forest in a tropical region of the world where it rains a lot

rain•storm /'reɪnˌstɔrm/ noun [C] a storm with a lot of rain

rain•wa•ter /'reɪnˌwɔtər/ noun [U] water that falls to the ground in the form of rain

rain•y /'reɪni/ adj a rainy day is one on which it rains a lot

PHRASE **the rainy season** the part of the year in tropical regions when large amounts of rain fall

raise[1] /reɪz/ verb [T] ★★★

1 lift to higher position	6 mention sth
2 lift yourself	7 cause feelings
3 increase	8 of animals/crops
4 take care of children	+ PHRASE
5 collect money	

1 to lift something to a higher place or position: *A number of children raised their hands.* ♦ *He slowly raised the cup to his lips.*

2 to lift yourself from a sitting or lying position: *She could barely raise herself out of the chair.*

3 to increase a number, amount, or level: *They had* ***raised*** *their* ***prices*** *to unreasonable levels.*

4 to take care of children while they are growing up: *For most parents,* ***raising a family*** *is a positive challenge.* ♦ *This seems strange to someone* ***born and raised*** *in the city.*

5 to collect money for a particular purpose: *We need your help to* ***raise money for*** *medical research.*

6 to mention something so that it can be discussed: *Are there any other* ***questions*** *you would like to* ***raise*** *at the meeting?* ♦ **raise sth with sb** *We will raise the issue of working hours with the manager.*

7 to make someone have a particular feeling or reaction: ***Doubts*** *have been* ***raised*** *about the company's right to use this land.*

8 to keep a particular type of animal, or to grow a particular crop: *She's been raising sheep for over 40 years.*

PHRASE **raise your voice** to speak in a loud angry way

→ ALARM[1]

R

raise[2] /reɪz/ noun [C] *American* an increase in the amount of money that your employer pays you

rai•sin /ˈreɪz(ə)n/ noun [C] a dried GRAPE

rake[1] /reɪk/ noun [C] a tool for making soil level and for removing leaves from the ground. It has a long handle with a row of sharp points on one end.

rake[2] /reɪk/ verb **1** [I/T] to use a rake in order to make an area of soil level or to remove leaves from the ground **2** [T] to pull your fingers through or along something
PHRASE **be raking it in** to be earning a lot of money

ral•ly[1] /ˈræli/ noun **1** [C] a public meeting that a lot of people go to in order to support something or protest against something **2** [singular] an increase or improvement in something **3** [C] a car race

ral•ly[2] /ˈræli/ verb **1** [I/T] to join other people in order to support someone or something **2** [I] to increase or improve after being low, weak, or sick

ram[1] /ræm/ verb **1** [I/T] if a vehicle or boat rams something, it hits it very hard **2** [T] to push something into a place with great force: *He rammed his fist through a window.*
PHRASE **ram sth down sb's throat** to force someone to listen to or accept an idea, suggestion, etc. when they do not want to

ram[2] /ræm/ noun [C] a male sheep

RAM /ræm/ noun [U] *computing* random access memory: the part of a computer that programs are loaded into while you are using them

Ram•a•dan /ˌræməˈdɑn/ the ninth month of the Muslim year, when Muslims do not eat or drink anything during the day

ram•ble[1] /ˈræmb(ə)l/ verb [I] **1** to talk for a long time in a confused way **2** to go for a long walk —**ram•bling** adj: *a rambling speech*

ram•ble[2] /ˈræmb(ə)l/ noun [C] a long walk

ram•bunc•tious /ræmˈbʌŋkʃəs/ adj *American* a rambunctious person behaves in a noisy and lively way

ram•i•fi•ca•tions /ˌræməfɪˈkeɪʃ(ə)nz/ noun [plural] *formal* the complicated or unexpected effects of something

ramp /ræmp/ noun [C] **1** a slope connecting two levels of a building or road **2** *American* a road used for driving onto or off of a main highway

ram•page[1] /ˈræmpeɪdʒ/ noun [C] uncontrolled behavior involving damage to property

ram•page[2] /ræmˈpeɪdʒ/ verb [I] to behave in an uncontrolled way, damaging property over a wide area

ram•pant /ˈræmpənt/ adj existing or spreading in an uncontrolled way: *Official corruption here is rampant.*

ram•parts /ˈræmˌpɑrts/ noun [plural] high hills or walls built around a building or town in the past in order to protect it

ram•shack•le /ˈræmˌʃæk(ə)l/ adj in bad condition and likely to fall down

ran the past tense of **run**[1]

ranch /ræntʃ/ noun [C] a very large farm where cows, horses, or sheep are kept

ranch•er /ˈræntʃər/ noun [C] someone who owns or manages a ranch or whose job is to work on a ranch —**ranch•ing** noun [U]

ˈranch ˌhouse noun [C] *American* a house on one level, often with a roof that does not slope much —*picture* → C1

ran•cor /ˈræŋkər/ noun [U] *formal* a feeling of hate or anger that lasts a long time

ran•dom /ˈrændəm/ adj chosen or happening without any particular method or pattern: *a random sample of voters* ♦ *Winning tickets will be chosen at random.* —**ran•dom•ly** adv

ran•dom•ize /ˈrændəmaɪz/ verb [T] *technical* to choose people or things for a test or experiment in a RANDOM way

rang the past tense of **ring**[1]

range[1] /reɪndʒ/ noun ★★★

1 things of same type	5 group of mountains
2 numbers, ages, etc.	6 open area of land
3 of responsibility etc.	7 for cooking
4 distance for sth	

1 [C] a number of different things that are of the same general type: *We discussed **a range of** issues affecting professional women.* ♦ *We stock **a wide range of** office furniture.*
2 [C] all the numbers, ages, measurements, etc. that are included within particular fixed limits: *books for children in the 11-to-14 **age range*** ♦ *Temperatures are expected to be **in the range of** 75 to 85 degrees.*
3 [singular] the limits within which a person or organization is able to deal with something = SCOPE: *Such a decision is not **within the range of** my responsibility.*
4 [singular/U] the distance within which you can see, hear, or reach something: *The children turned their cameras on anyone **in range**.* ♦ *It's best to stay **out of range of** recording equipment.*
5 [C] a number of mountains considered as a group
6 [C] an open area of land where people can practice firing guns
7 [C] *American* a large piece of kitchen equipment that can cook food in different ways

range[2] /reɪndʒ/ verb **1** [I] to be included in a group of numbers, ages, measurements, etc. with particular fixed limits: *Costs range from 50 to several hundred dollars.* ♦ *The team contained ten players whose ages ranged between 10 and 16.* **2** [I] to include a variety of things: *products ranging from televisions to computer software* **3** [I/T] to move with complete freedom around a large area: *There were buffalo ranging the plains of North America.*

rang•er /ˈreɪndʒər/ noun [C] a PARK RANGER

rank[1] /ræŋk/ noun ★★
1 [C/U] someone's position in an organization or in society: *Her rank when she retired was captain.* ♦ *She had reached **the rank of** chief financial officer by the time she was 30.*
2 ranks [plural] all the people within a group or organization: *a dispute within the party ranks* ♦ *Another Republican senator **joined the ranks of** the presidential candidates.*
PHRASES **break ranks** to stop belonging to or supporting a group
close ranks if members of a group close

TREES AND FLOWERS

FRUIT

orange
lemon
lime
grapefruit
peach
apple
pear
apricot
nectarine
plum
grapes
blueberries
cherries
strawberries
raspberries
papaya
watermelon
melon
banana
avocado
kiwi fruit
pineapple
fig
coconut
mango

VEGETABLES

potato
sweet potato
parsnip
beet
carrot
radish
ginger
garlic
shallots
onion
scallions
tomato
zucchini
pumpkin
bell peppers
mushrooms
cucumber
lettuce
celery
fennel
broccoli
Brussels sprouts
eggplant
cabbage
corn on the cob
asparagus
green beans
cauliflower
peas
kidney beans

ANIMALS

cheetah
leopard
koala
lion
elephant
gorilla
tiger
zebra
rhinoceros
monkey
hippopotamus
giraffe
panda
duck
deer
chicken
goose
bull
goat
pig
sheep
cow
donkey

ANIMALS

whale
shark
kangaroo
octopus
penguin
fox
iguana
badger
rat
mole
rabbit
mouse
squirrel
wasp
butterfly
moth
fly
ant
caterpillar
snake
lizard
bee
cockroach
ladybug
crocodile
grasshopper
mosquito
beetle

BODY

head
hand
arm
neck
back
chest
breast
elbow
waist
shoulder
buttocks
hip
stomach
leg
knee
foot

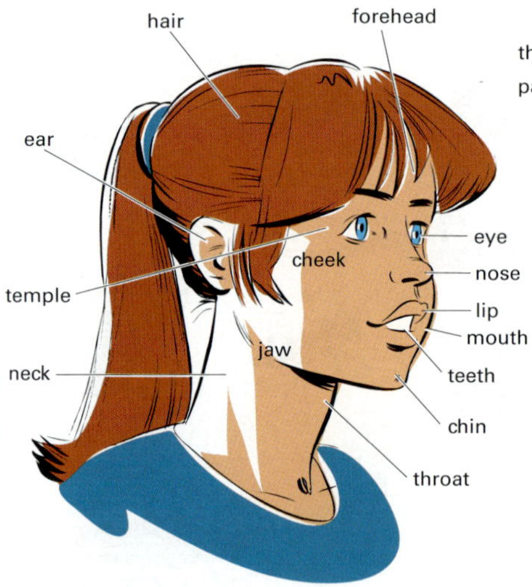
hair
forehead
ear
eye
cheek
temple
nose
lip
mouth
jaw
neck
teeth
chin
throat

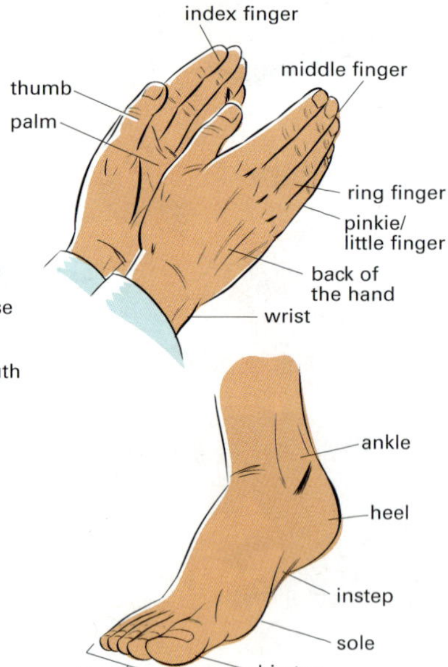
index finger
thumb
middle finger
palm
ring finger
pinkie/
little finger
back of
the hand
wrist
ankle
heel
instep
sole
toes
big toe

SPORTS

Football

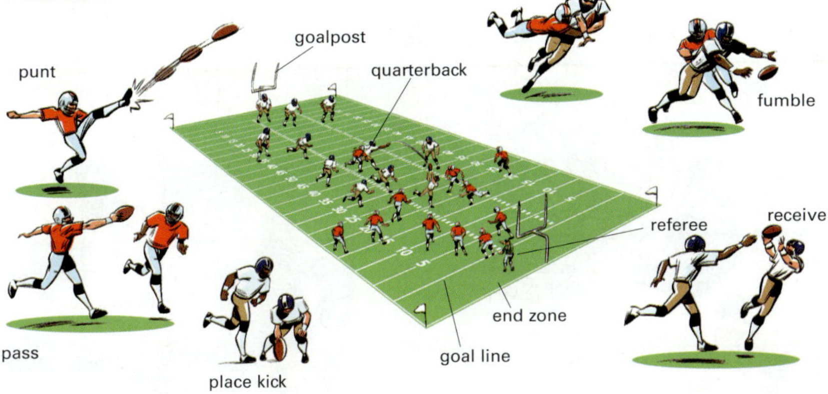

Baseball

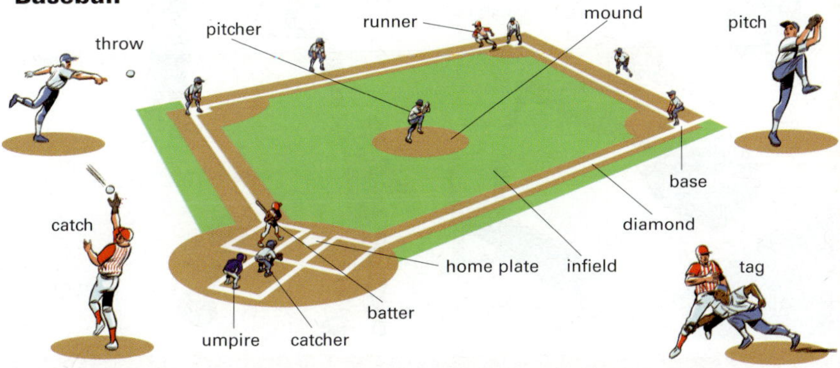

Basketball

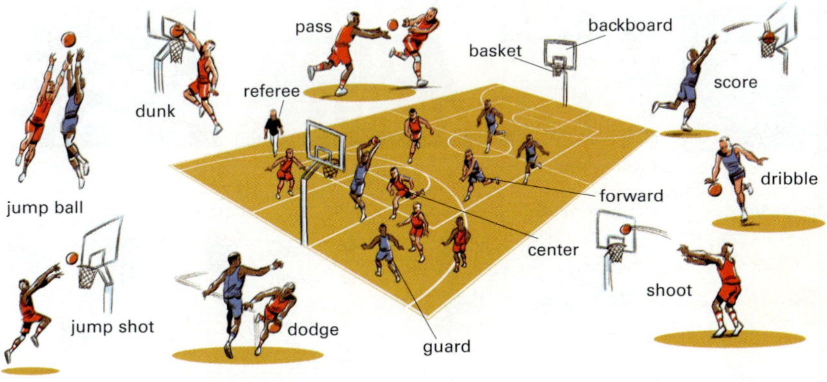

GYM

GAMES

chess

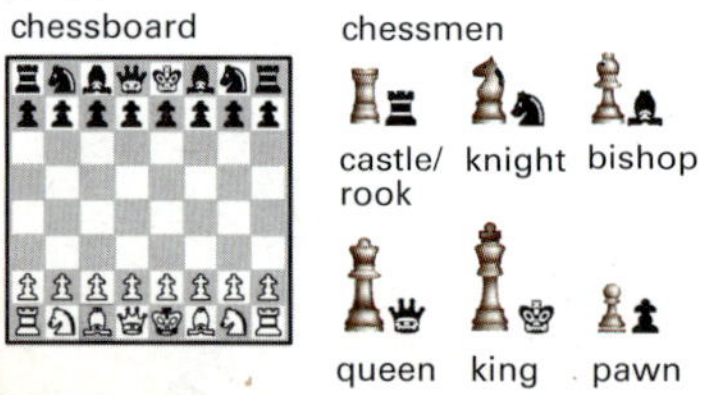

backgammon

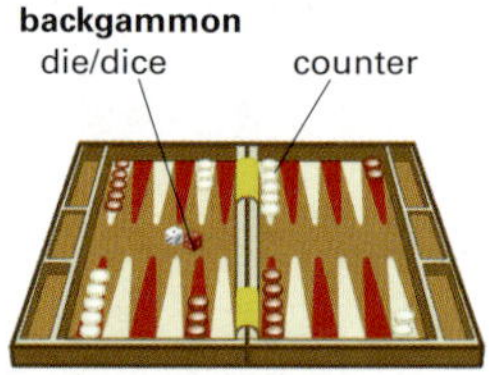

checkers

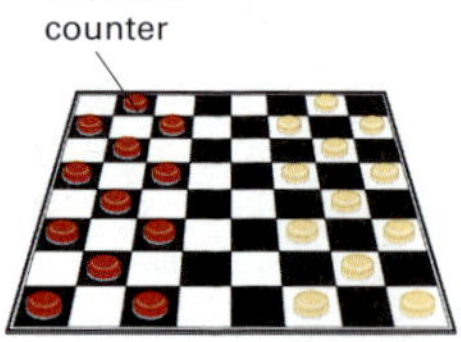

tic-tac-toe

cards

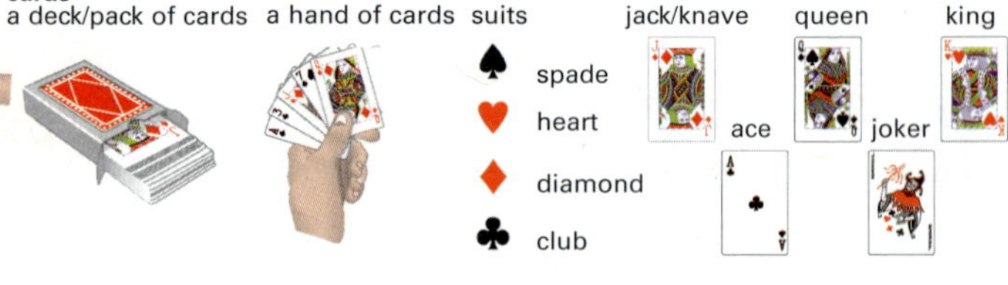

ranks, they support each other against people who are trying to defeat or criticize them
the rank and file all the members of a group or organization except the leaders or officers

rank² /ræŋk/ verb **1** [I] to have a particular quality compared with other similar things: *This must rank as one of the most violent movies ever made.* **2** [T] to put someone or something into a position according to their success, importance, size, etc.: *The survey ranked schools according to their exam results.*

rank•ing /ˈræŋkɪŋ/ noun [C] a position on a list that shows how good someone or something is compared to others

ran•kle /ˈræŋk(ə)l/ verb [I/T] if an action rankles, or if it rankles you, it continues to annoy or upset you for a long time

ran•sack /ˈrænˌsæk/ verb [T] to go through a place stealing or damaging things

ran•som /ˈrænsəm/ noun [C/U] an amount of money that someone asks for, in exchange for a person who they are keeping as a prisoner

rant /rænt/ verb [I] to complain or talk loudly and angrily for a long time: *He was ranting about taxes.*

rap¹ /ræp/ noun **1** [U] a type of music in which words are spoken over a strong beat **2** [C] a quick hard hit, or the sound of this

rap² /ræp/ verb **1** [I/T] to hit something hard and quickly **2** [I] to perform by speaking over a strong musical beat **3** [T] *mainly journalism* to criticize someone

rape /reɪp/ noun [C/U] the crime of forcing someone to have sex by using violence —**rape** verb [T]

rap•id /ˈræpɪd/ adj ★ happening, moving, or acting quickly: *We are seeing a **rapid growth** in the use of the Internet.* ♦ *the **rapid movement** of troops into the area* —**rap•id•i•ty** /rəˈpɪdəti/ noun [U], **rap•id•ly** adv: *a rapidly expanding population*

> **Words often used with rapid**
>
> *Nouns often used with **rapid***
>
> ■ RAPID + **change, decline, deterioration, expansion, growth, increase, progress, rise, succession**: used about things that happen quickly

rap•ids /ˈræpɪdz/ noun [plural] a part of a river where the water moves extremely quickly over rocks

rap•ist /ˈreɪpɪst/ noun [C] someone who forces someone else to have sex with them

rap•pel /ræˈpel/ verb [I] *American technical* to come down the side of a CLIFF or mountain using a rope that is fastened to the top of the cliff or mountain and to your body

rap•per /ˈræpər/ noun [C] someone who performs RAP music

rap•port /ræˈpɔr/ noun [singular/U] a relationship in which people like, understand, and respect each other

rapt /ræpt/ adj *literary* completely interested and involved in something

rap•ture /ˈræptʃər/ noun [U] *literary* a feeling of great happiness or excitement

rare /rer/ adj ★★
1 not happening very often: *I am late only on rare occasions.* ♦ **it is rare (for sb) to do sth** *It's extremely rare for her to lose her temper.*
2 not often seen or found, and therefore valuable: *rare birds* ♦ *He has a rare talent for managing people.*
3 rare meat has been cooked for only a short time and is red inside
→ RARITY

rare•ly /ˈrerli/ adv ★★ not often ≠ FREQUENTLY: *My mother very rarely wears jewelry.*

rar•i•ty /ˈrerəti/ noun [C] something that is unusual or does not happen often

rash¹ /ræʃ/ noun [C] **1** an area of small red spots on your skin that is caused by an illness or a reaction to something **2** a lot of events of the same type taking place in a short period of time

rash² /ræʃ/ adj acting or done too quickly, without thinking —**rash•ly** adv

rasp /ræsp/ verb [I/T] to make an unpleasant sound as if two rough surfaces were rubbing together

rasp•ber•ry /ˈræzˌberi/ noun [C] a small soft red fruit that grows on a bush —*picture* → C10

rat¹ /ræt/ noun [C] **1** an animal like a large mouse with a long tail —*picture* → C13
2 *informal* someone who is not loyal or who tricks you

rat² /ræt/ PHRASAL VERB ˈ**rat on sb** *informal* to tell someone in authority about something that someone you know has done wrong

rate¹ /reɪt/ noun [C] ★★★
1 the number of times that something happens, or the number of examples of something within a particular period of time: *a rising **birth rate*** ♦ *areas where the **rate of unemployment** is high*
2 the speed at which something happens within a particular period of time: *The population was growing at an alarming rate.* ♦ *Doctors monitor the patient's **heart rate**.*
3 an amount of money that is paid or charged: *tax rates* ♦ *They increased the **hourly rate of pay** to $12.*

PHRASES **at any rate** *spoken* used for changing a statement, and telling someone that one part of what has been mentioned is true: *They agree with me – well, at any rate, Maggie does.*
at this rate *spoken* used for saying what will happen if the present situation continues: *At this rate the factory will be closed down by Christmas.*
the going rate the usual amount of money that people pay for something
→ FIRST-RATE, SECOND-RATE, THIRD-RATE

rate² /reɪt/ verb **1** [T] to consider that someone or something has a particular quality or has achieved a particular standard or level: *Many voters rate the environment as the number one issue.* ♦ *She is rated very highly by her colleagues* (=they approve of her).
2 [I] to have a particular quality compared with other similar things: *The exhibit rates as one of the most successful for this museum.*
3 [T] to deserve something: *That should rate a mention in the local newspaper!*

R

rath•er /ˈræðər/ adv ★★

1 to a fairly large degree =QUITE: *He was a rather handsome boy.* ♦ *I realize that I've been rather stupid and selfish.* ♦ *Matt left rather suddenly without any explanation.*

2 used for correcting or explaining what you have just said: *He couldn't help us, or **rather** he didn't want to.*

PHRASES **rather than** instead of: *Doug chose to quit rather than admit that he'd made a mistake.* ♦ *Rather than criticizing your husband, why not find out if there's something wrong?*

would rather used for saying what you would prefer: *He doesn't want to learn – he'd rather stay at home and play video games.* ♦ *They said they **would rather** die **than** abandon their homes.* ♦ *You don't need to come **if you'd rather not**.*

rat•i•fy /ˈrætəˌfaɪ/ verb [T] to make an agreement official by signing it or formally approving it —**rat•i•fi•ca•tion** /ˌrætəfɪˈkeɪʃ(ə)n/ noun [U]

rat•ing /ˈreɪtɪŋ/ noun **1** [C] a measurement of how good or popular someone or something is: *The president's popularity rating fell for the first time.* **2** [C] a letter or letters and sometimes a number that show how old someone needs to be before they are allowed to see a particular movie **3 ratings** [plural] the number that tells how many people watched or listened to a particular television or radio show: *Her new series had high ratings right from the start.*

ra•tio /ˈreɪʃoʊ/ noun [C] ★ a relationship between two things that is expressed by two numbers or amounts: *a teacher-student ratio of 1:20* (=1 teacher for every 20 students) ♦ ***The ratio of men to women** was 4:1.*

R

ra•tion¹ /ˈræʃ(ə)n/ noun [C] a limited amount of something that you are allowed to have when there is not much available

ra•tion² /ˈræʃ(ə)n/ verb [T] to control the supply of something so that people are allowed only a particular amount —**ra•tion•ing** noun [U]

ra•tion•al /ˈræʃ(ə)nəl/ adj a rational person makes decisions based on sensible practical reasons, instead of emotions ≠IRRATIONAL: *There was no rational explanation for his actions.* ♦ *She was perfectly calm and rational.* —**ra•tion•al•ly** adv

ra•tion•ale /ˌræʃəˈnæl/ noun [C] the set of reasons that a plan, decision, or belief is based on

ra•tion•al•ize /ˈræʃ(ə)nəˌlaɪz/ verb [I/T] to try to find a reasonable explanation for your feelings or behavior —**ra•tion•al•i•za•tion** /ˌræʃ(ə)nəlɪˈzeɪʃ(ə)n/ noun [C/U]

rat•tle¹ /ˈræt(ə)l/ verb **1** [I/T] to make short sharp knocking sounds, or to move or shake things so that they make these sounds: *The house shook and the windows rattled.* ♦ *She rattled her keys impatiently.* **2** [T] *informal* to make someone feel nervous or angry

PHRASAL VERB **ˌrattle sth ˈoff** to say something quickly

rat•tle² /ˈræt(ə)l/ noun [C] **1** a baby's toy that rattles when it is shaken **2** the sound that something makes when it rattles

rat•tler /ˈrætlər/ noun [C] *informal* a RATTLESNAKE

rat•tle•snake /ˈræt(ə)lˌsneɪk/ noun [C] a poisonous American snake that makes a noise that sounds like a RATTLE with its tail

rau•cous /ˈrɔkəs/ adj a raucous voice is loud and sounds rough —**rau•cous•ly** adv

rav•age /ˈrævɪdʒ/ verb [T] to destroy something, or to damage it very badly

rav•ag•es /ˈrævɪdʒəz/ noun **the ravages of sth** the damage or destruction caused by something

rave¹ /reɪv/ verb [I] **1** to speak or write in a very enthusiastic way about something or someone: *The critics are raving about her performance.* **2** to talk in an angry and uncontrolled way

rave² /reɪv/ noun [C] **1** a very large party where people dance to loud music **2** *American* a report that praises something or someone in a very enthusiastic way

rav•en /ˈreɪv(ə)n/ noun [C] a large bird with shiny black feathers

rav•en•ous /ˈræv(ə)nəs/ adj very hungry

ra•vine /rəˈvin/ noun [C] a very deep narrow valley with steep sides

rav•ing /ˈreɪvɪŋ/ adj *informal* behaving or talking in a crazy way: *a **raving lunatic***

rav•ish•ing /ˈrævɪʃɪŋ/ adj *literary* very beautiful

raw /rɔ/ adj ★

1 not cooked	5 not trained
2 not processed	6 sore
3 strong/natural	+ PHRASE
4 not examined	

1 raw food has not been cooked: *raw meat* ♦ *The chicken is still raw.*

2 raw substances have not been processed or treated in any way: *raw silk/cotton* ♦ *There was **raw sewage** on the beach.* → RAW MATERIALS

3 a raw quality is strong and natural, without being controlled or made more pleasant: *Her performance was filled with **raw emotion**.*

4 raw DATA consists of information that has not been examined or organized

5 not trained or experienced: *raw recruits*

6 if your skin is raw, it is very sore: *I scrubbed my hands until they were raw.*

PHRASE **a raw deal** unfair treatment

ˌraw maˈterials noun [plural] substances that are in their natural state before being processed or made into something

ray /reɪ/ noun [C] a line of light, heat, or energy

PHRASE **a ray of hope** something that makes you feel slightly more hopeful in a difficult situation

raze /reɪz/ verb [T] to completely destroy a building or town

ra•zor /ˈreɪzər/ noun [C] a small tool or piece of electrical equipment that you use for SHAVING (=removing hair from your skin)

ˈrazor ˌblade noun [C] a thin flat blade with a very sharp edge that you put in a razor

Rd. abbrev Road: used in addresses

re /ri/ preposition used in business letters for

introducing the subject that you are going to write about

re- /ri/ prefix again: *reheated soup* ♦ *She reappeared a few minutes later.* ♦ *the reelection of the Mayor*

reach¹ /ritʃ/ verb ★★★

1 arrive somewhere	6 achieve sth
2 get to point/stage	7 be seen/heard
3 get to level/amount	8 talk by phone
4 move hand toward	+ PHRASAL VERBS
5 manage to touch sth	

1 [T] to arrive somewhere: *We hoped to reach the camp before dark.* ♦ *The money should reach your bank account within three days.* → ARRIVE

2 [T] to get to a particular point in time, or to a particular stage in a process: *You **reach a point** where medicine can't help.* ♦ *The children have **reached the age** when they want more privacy.*

3 [T] to get as high as a particular level or amount: ***Temperatures** here can **reach** 120 degrees Fahrenheit.*

4 [I] to move your hand toward something you are trying to touch or pick up: *He turned around and **reached for** the phone.* ♦ *Travis **reached into** his pocket to get his car keys.*

5 [I/T] to manage to touch something or pick it up by stretching out your arm: *We keep the bottles up here so the children can't reach them.*

6 [T] to achieve something after discussing it or thinking about it for a long time: *The teachers must **reach a decision** before summer.*

7 [T] if something such as a program or message reaches people, they see or hear it

8 [T] to succeed in talking to someone by phone: *I'll leave you a number where I can be reached in an emergency.*

PHRASAL VERBS ˌ**reach (sth)** ˈ**out** to stretch out your arm to try to touch or hold something: *She reached out to touch his face.*
ˌ**reach** ˈ**out to sb** to show someone that you are sympathetic and want to communicate with them

reach

reach² /ritʃ/ noun [U] **1** the distance within which you can touch something by stretching out your arm: *Put the books within reach of your desk.* ♦ *I kicked the knife out of reach.* **2** the distance that you travel to get somewhere: *The hotel is within easy reach of downtown.*

PHRASE **within/beyond sb's reach** used for saying that someone can/cannot have or do something: *Reduced ticket prices put the best seats within everyone's reach.*

re•act /riˈækt/ verb [I] ★

1 to behave in a particular way because of things that are happening around you or things that other people are doing to you: *Workers **reacted** angrily **to** the news of more job cuts.*

2 to become sick when you eat a particular food or medicine: *Some people **react** badly **to** nuts.*

3 if a chemical substance reacts with another substance, it changes as they are mixed together

re•ac•tion /riˈækʃ(ə)n/ noun ★★★

1 [C] the way that you feel or behave as a result of something that happens: *My mother's reaction was quite unexpected.* → KNEE-JERK

2 [C] a bad effect on your body caused by food, medicine, or another substance: ***an allergic reaction to dust***

3 reactions [plural] your ability to think and act quickly in a difficult or dangerous situation: *A tragedy was prevented by the driver's **quick reactions**.*

4 [C] *science* a process in which a chemical change happens → CHAIN REACTION

Words often used with reaction

*Verbs often used with **reaction** (sense 1, 2)*

■ **cause, produce, provoke, trigger** + REACTION: make a reaction happen

re•ac•tion•ar•y /riˈækʃəˌneri/ adj strongly opposed to any political change or social progress —**re•ac•tion•ar•y** noun [C]

re•ac•tor /riˈæktər/ noun [C] a NUCLEAR REACTOR

read /rid/ (past tense and past participle **read** /red/) verb ★★★

1 understand words	7 know what sb thinks
2 speak written words	8 show number etc.
3 get information	9 contain words
4 understand symbols	+ PHRASE
5 examine/copy data	+ PHRASAL VERBS
6 interpret meaning	

1 [I/T] to look at and understand words in a letter, book, newspaper, etc.: *I read a few chapters every night.* ♦ *By the age of five, he could **read and write**.*

2 [I/T] to speak the words that you are looking at: **read (sth) to sb** *Reading to young children helps develop their language skills.* ♦ **read sb sth** *Read me that last sentence again.*

3 [I/T] to get information from books, newspapers, etc.: *He likes **reading about** wildlife.* ♦ **read sth in sth** *We read it in the local paper.*

4 [T] to look at and understand the information, symbols, or numbers on a map or a piece of measuring equipment: *Has the man been here to **read the gas meter**?*

5 [T] if a computer or other piece of electronic equipment reads something, it examines the information on it or copies it to a particular place

6 [T] to understand something in a particular way = INTERPRET: *They had **read the situation** accurately.*

7 [T] to be able to understand what someone is like or what they are thinking: *It was difficult to read his expression.*
8 [T] if a piece of measuring equipment reads something, it shows a particular number or amount: *The thermometer has been reading over 90 degrees all day.*
9 [T] if a short piece of writing reads something, it contains those particular words: *The label read, "Made in Mexico."*
PHRASE **read between the lines** to guess something that is not expressed directly
PHRASAL VERBS **ˌread sth ˈinto sth** to find an extra meaning in someone's words or actions that is not obvious or does not exist: *I think you're reading too much into his remark.*
ˌread sth ˈout to say the words that you are reading so that people can hear them
ˌread sth ˈthrough to read all of a piece of writing in order to check or correct it
ˌread ˈup on sth to get information on a particular subject by reading a lot about it

read•a•ble /ˈridəb(ə)l/ adj **1** easy and pleasant to read **2** clear and able to be read

read•er /ˈridər/ noun [C] ★★★
1 someone who reads
2 someone who reads a particular newspaper, book, or magazine: *The books provide the reader with an introduction to natural history.*
3 someone who reads in a particular way or with a particular level of skill: *a special program for **slow readers***
4 a book containing simple pieces of writing for people who are learning to read or who are learning a language

read•er•ship /ˈridərˌʃɪp/ noun [singular/U] the group or number of people who read a particular newspaper, book, or magazine

read•i•ly /ˈredɪli/ adv **1** easily: *The equipment was cheap and readily available.* **2** in a way that shows that you are willing

read•i•ness /ˈredinəs/ noun **1** [U] a state of being ready and able to deal with what might or will happen **2** [singular/U] the state of being willing to do something

read•ing /ˈridɪŋ/ noun ★★
1 [U] the process of recognizing written or printed words and understanding their meaning: *My little boy is having difficulty with his reading.*
2 [singular/U] the act of reading or studying a book, newspaper, document, etc.: *I haven't done much reading lately.*
3 [C] an event at which someone reads something to a group of people: *a poetry reading*
4 [C] a number or amount shown on a piece of measuring equipment: *compass readings*

re•ad•just /ˌriəˈdʒʌst/ verb **1** [I] to become capable of dealing with a new situation or feeling comfortable in it **2** [T] to make a slight change to something
—**re•ad•just•ment** noun [C/U]

read-out /ˈrid ˌaʊt/ noun [C] a record of information that has been produced by a piece of electronic equipment

read•y /ˈredi/ adj ★★★
1 prepared for what is going to happen: *We'll never be ready in time.* ♦ *She was ready for a new challenge.* ♦ **ready to do sth** *Are you ready to go yet?*
2 in an appropriate condition for use: *Is dinner ready?* ♦ **have sth ready** *We can have your order ready by 5:00.* ♦ **get sth ready** *I'd just gotten the tea ready when they called.*
3 willing or likely to do something: **ready to do sth** *Jack was always ready to work overtime if necessary.*

ˌready-ˈmade adj already made or prepared and ready to be used

re•al¹ /riəl/ adj ★★★

1 in physical world	**5** the most important
2 true, not just claimed	**6** important/serious
3 with true qualities	**7** for emphasis
4 not false/artificial	**+** PHRASES

1 existing in the physical world, not just in someone's imagination or in stories: *Children believe that these characters are real.* ♦ *I had never met a **real live** pop star before.*
2 true, and not just according to what someone claims: *We all know **the** President's **real reason** for refusing to speak.*
3 used for emphasizing that someone or something has the true qualities of a particular type of person or thing: *He had no **real friends**.* ♦ *Few tourists see the real Spain.*
4 not false or artificial **=** GENUINE: *Is that a real diamond?*
5 most important: *Let's deal with **the real issue**.*
6 important or serious enough to be worth thinking or worrying about: *The committee had little real power.* ♦ *The trip was difficult, but we were never in any **real danger**.*
7 *informal* used for emphasizing that a description of someone or something is very accurate: *This walk is a real treat for anyone interested in birds.*
PHRASES **for real** *informal* if something is for real, you are doing it seriously, not just practicing or pretending
get real *spoken* used for telling someone to start thinking about something in a sensible way and stop being silly or unreasonable about it

re•al² /riəl/ adv *American spoken* extremely. Many people think that this use is not correct: *a real nice guy*

ˈreal esˌtate noun [U] *American* **1** land and the buildings on it **2** the business of buying and selling real estate

ˈreal estate ˌagent noun [C] *American* someone whose job is to buy, sell, or rent property for the owner of the property

re•al•ism /ˈriəˌlɪzəm/ noun [U] the ability to accept events and situations as they really exist and to deal with them in a practical way

re•al•ist /ˈriəlɪst/ noun [C] someone who accepts events and situations as they really are and deals with them in a practical way

re•al•is•tic /ˌriəˈlɪstɪk/ adj **1** based on facts and situations as they really are **≠** UNREALISTIC: *He has a realistic chance of winning the election.* ♦ *I don't think it's very realistic to expect her to help us.* **2** able to understand and accept things as they really are: *The*

R

recession has made people more realistic about what they can afford to buy. **3** made to seem natural or real ≠ UNREALISTIC —**re•a•list•i•cal•ly** /ˌriəˈlɪstɪkli/ adv

re•al•i•ty /riˈæləti/ noun ★★
1 [U] the real character or nature of things, not what you imagine or think is possible: *This is a man who has* ***lost touch with reality.*** ♦ *We had to* ***face reality*** *when the business failed.*
2 [C] a fact, event, or situation as it really exists: *After years of hard work, his dream has* ***become a reality.*** ♦ *the grim* ***realities*** *of war*
PHRASE **in reality** used for saying that the true situation is different from what has been said or thought: *Reports put the death toll at 50, when in reality it was closer to 200.*

re•al•i•za•tion /ˌriəlɪˈzeɪʃ(ə)n/ noun [singular/U] **1** the process of understanding something, or the moment when this happens **2** the process of achieving something that you have planned or hoped for, or the moment when this happens

re•al•ize /ˈriəˌlaɪz/ verb ★★★
1 [T] to gradually begin to understand something that you did not know or notice before: *I soon realized my mistake.* ♦ **+why/how etc.** *I now realize how much I miss him.*
2 [I/T] to know and understand something: **+(that)** *It's important to realize that this situation is only temporary.* ♦ **+what/how etc.** *At the time I never even realized how unhappy I was.*
3 [T] *formal* to achieve something that you have planned or hoped for: *He finally* ***realized*** *his* ***dream*** *to become a dancer.*

re•al•ly /ˈriəli/ adv ★★★
1 **very** *spoken* very, or very much: *She really enjoys working with young children.* ♦ *I'm really hungry.* ♦ *We've all been working really hard.*
2 **for saying what is true** used for talking about what is in fact true, when something else seems to be true: *Hamlet isn't really crazy – he's just pretending to be.* ♦ *We'll never know* ***what really happened.***
3 **for emphasis** used for emphasizing what you are saying: *I really must see that film.* ♦ *There's really no need to worry.*
4 **completely** completely: *Rigby had never really recovered from his knee injury.* ♦ *Are you* ***really sure*** *that you want to marry this man?*
5 **for showing surprise or interest** *spoken* used for showing that you are surprised by or interested in what someone has just told you: *"I've decided to move back to Toledo." "Really? But why?"*
PHRASE **not really** used for saying "no" without being very definite: *"Was he sorry for what he'd done?" "Not really."*

realm /relm/ noun [C] *formal* a particular area of knowledge, experience, interest, etc.

ˈreal ˌtime noun [U] if a computer deals with information in real time, it deals with it immediately —**ˈreal-ˌtime** adj

re•al•ty /ˈriəlti/ noun [U] *American* REAL ESTATE

reap /rip/ verb [T] **1** to cut and gather a crop **2** to get something as a result of something else that you do

re•ap•pear /ˌriəˈpɪr/ verb [I] to appear again —**re•ap•pear•ance** noun [C/U]

rear¹ /rɪr/ adj at the back of something

rear² /rɪr/ noun **1 the rear** [singular] the back part of a place or thing: *The main entrance is at the rear.* **2** [C] *informal* the part of your body that you sit on
PHRASE **bring up the rear** to be the last in a line or group

rear³ /rɪr/ verb **1** [T] to take care of a child or young animal until it is fully grown **2** [I] if a horse rears, it lifts its front legs up into the air
PHRASAL VERB **ˌrear ˈup** *same as* **rear³ 2**

ˌrear-ˈend verb [T] *American informal* to drive into the back of another car

re•ar•range /ˌriəˈreɪndʒ/ verb [T] **1** to arrange for an event or meeting to take place at a different time **2** to arrange people or things in a different way

ˌrear-view ˈmirror noun [C] a mirror attached to the front window of a car that lets the driver see what is happening behind the car —*picture* → C6

rea•son¹ /ˈriz(ə)n/ noun ★★★
1 [C] a fact, situation, or intention that explains why something happened, why someone did something, or why something is true: *The council* ***gave no reason*** *for its decision.* ♦ **+why** *The reason why so many people caught the disease is still not clear.* ♦ **reason for doing sth** *Could you explain your reasons for choosing this particular course?*
2 [U] a good or clear cause for doing something or thinking something: *Sometimes the dog would bark* ***for no reason.*** ♦ *With plenty of orders coming in,* ***there is reason for*** *optimism about the company's future.*
3 [U] a way of behaving that most people accept as sensible: *He finally* ***saw reason*** *and gave me the gun.* ♦ *Let your children have their freedom,* ***within reason.***
4 [U] the human ability to think in an intelligent way, make sensible decisions, and form clear arguments
PHRASES **all the more reason** used for emphasizing that what someone has said or done is another reason why they should do a particular thing
for some reason used for saying that you do not know why something happened: *For some reason, they wouldn't let me help them.*

Other words that mean **reason**

- **cause** the reason that something happens, or the reason that you feel a particular emotion
- **excuse** a reason that you give in order to explain why you did something bad
- **explanation** a set of facts that tell you why something happened
- **grounds** a good or fair reason for doing something. This word is used in official or legal situations
- **motivation** someone's personal reason for doing something
- **motive** someone's personal reason for doing something

R

- **pretext** a false reason that you give in order to hide your real reason for doing something
- **purpose** something that you want to achieve

rea•son² /ˈriz(ə)n/ verb [T] *formal* to make a particular judgment after you have thought about the facts of a situation in an intelligent and sensible way
PHRASAL VERB **ˌreason with sb** to try to persuade someone to do something by explaining why you think it is sensible

rea•son•a•ble /ˈriz(ə)nəb(ə)l/ adj ★★
1 sensible and fair: *We have taken all reasonable precautions to avoid an accident.*
2 if something is reasonable, there are good reasons for thinking it is true or correct: *I'm sure there's **a reasonable explanation** for his absence.*
3 fairly good, although not extremely good =ACCEPTABLE: *a reasonable standard of accommodation*
4 not too high or great: *The hotel is situated within a reasonable distance of the beach.* ♦ *reasonable prices*

rea•son•a•bly /ˈriz(ə)nəbli/ adv **1** to a fairly high degree, level, or standard: *He did reasonably well in math.* **2** in a sensible and fair way

rea•soned /ˈriz(ə)nd/ adj thought about and expressed in an intelligent and sensible way

rea•son•ing /ˈriz(ə)nɪŋ/ noun [U] the process of thinking about something in an intelligent and sensible way

re•as•sure /ˌriəˈʃʊər/ verb [T] to make someone feel less worried about something —**re•as•sur•ance** noun [C/U]

re•as•sur•ing /ˌriəˈʃʊrɪŋ/ adj making you feel less worried —**re•as•sur•ing•ly** adv

re•bate /ˈriˌbeɪt/ noun [C] an amount of money that is officially given back to someone

R

re•bel¹ /ˈreb(ə)l/ noun [C] **1** someone who tries to remove a government or leader by using force **2** someone who opposes people in authority or opposes accepted ways of doing things

re•bel² /rɪˈbel/ verb [I] **1** to try to remove a government or leader by using organized force **2** to oppose someone in authority, or to oppose accepted ways of doing things

re•bel•lion /rɪˈbeljən/ noun **1** [C/U] an attempt to remove a government or leader by force **2** [U] opposition to someone in authority or to accepted ways of doing things

re•bel•lious /rɪˈbeljəs/ adj **1** fighting to remove a government or leader by force **2** opposing authority or the accepted rules of society

re•birth /ˌriˈbɜrθ/ noun [singular/U] a situation in which something becomes popular, important, or effective again

re•boot /ˌriˈbut/ verb [I/T] if a computer or system reboots, or if someone reboots it, it starts again after it has been turned off

re•bound¹ /rɪˈbaʊnd/ verb [I] to hit a surface and then move quickly backward again

re•bound² /ˈriˌbaʊnd/ noun **on the rebound** feeling sad after a romantic relationship has ended and impatient to start a new one

re•buff /rɪˈbʌf/ verb [T] *formal* to refuse to talk to someone or do what they suggest —**re•buff** noun [C]

re•build /ˌriˈbɪld/ (past tense and past participle **re•built** /ˌriˈbɪlt/) verb [T] **1** to build something again after it has been damaged or destroyed **2** to improve a situation so that it is as good as it was in the past

re•buke /rɪˈbjuk/ verb [T] *formal* to tell someone angrily that they have behaved badly —**re•buke** noun [C]

re•but /rɪˈbʌt/ verb [T] *formal* to show or say that something is not true =REFUTE

re•call /rɪˈkɔl/ verb ★
1 [I/T] to remember something: **+who/where/why etc.** *He couldn't recall what had happened.* ♦ **recall doing sth** *I don't recall seeing the document.*
2 [T] to ask for a product that people have bought to be returned because there is something wrong with it
3 [T] to order someone to return to their country or the place where they work —**re•call** /rɪˈkɔl, ˈriˌkɔl/ noun [singular/U]

re•cap /ˌriˈkæp/ verb [I/T] to describe what has already been done or decided, without repeating the details —**re•cap** /ˈriˌkæp/ noun [C]

re•cap•ture /ˌriˈkæptʃər/ verb [T] **1** to use force to get an area into your control again **2** to catch an animal or person that has escaped **3** to have a memory or feeling again

re•cede /rɪˈsid/ verb [I] **1** to move farther away **2** to become less strong or likely **3** if a man's hair is receding, less and less of it is growing at the front

re•ceipt /rɪˈsit/ noun ★
1 [C] a document that you get from someone showing that you have given them money or goods: *Keep all your credit card receipts.* ♦ *Make sure you get **a receipt for** the taxi fare.*
2 [U] *formal* the act of receiving something: *Please acknowledge **receipt of** this letter.*
3 **receipts** [plural] *business* the total amount of money that a business or organization receives in a particular period of time

re•ceive /rɪˈsiv/ verb [T] ★★★
1 to get something that someone gives or sends you: *We have not received your letter.* ♦ **receive sth from sb** *The principal has received several calls from angry parents.* —*picture* → C15
2 to have a particular type of treatment or experience: *Several of the victims are **receiving hospital treatment**.*
3 to react to something in a particular way: *Heather's proposals were received without much enthusiasm.*
4 to formally welcome a visitor: *Our group was received by the Brazilian ambassador.*
PHRASE **at/on the receiving end (of sth)** affected by something unpleasant

Word family: receive
Words in the same family as ***receive***
- **receipt** *n*
- **reception** *n*
- **receiver** *n*
- **receptive** *adj*

re•ceiv•er /rɪˈsivər/ noun [C] **1** the part of a phone that you pick up in order to hear and speak **2** the part of a television or radio that receives electronic signals and changes them into pictures and sounds

re·cent /ˈrisənt/ adj ★★★ happening or starting a short time ago: *a recent discovery* ♦ *Business has boomed **in recent years**.*

re·cent·ly /ˈrisəntli/ adv ★★★ not long ago: *She **only recently** discovered the truth.* ♦ *He's been back to America **fairly recently**.*

re·cep·ta·cle /rɪˈseptək(ə)l/ noun [C] *formal* a container

re·cep·tion /rɪˈsepʃən/ noun ★
1 [C] a formal party to welcome someone or to celebrate something: *a wedding reception*
2 [singular] the reaction of people to someone or something: *a friendly reception* ♦ *Crawford's performance had **a mixed reception** from the critics.*
3 [U] the part of a building where there is someone whose job is to welcome visitors, deal with questions, etc.
4 [U] the quality or strength of the picture or sound you receive on a television, radio, or cellphone: *Cellphone users were complaining of **poor reception**.*

re·cep·tion·ist /rɪˈsepʃənɪst/ noun [C] someone who works in reception at a hotel or office and whose job is to welcome visitors, deal with questions, etc.

re·cep·tive /rɪˈseptɪv/ adj willing to listen or consider suggestions

re·cess /ˈriˌses, rɪˈses/ noun **1** [C/U] a short time between periods of work in a court of law or PARLIAMENT **2** [U] *American* a period between classes when students can play or rest **3** [C] a space in a room where part of a wall is farther back than the rest of it

re·ces·sion /rɪˈseʃ(ə)n/ noun [C/U] a period when trade and industry are not successful and there is a lot of unemployment

re·charge /ˌriˈtʃɑrdʒ/ verb [T] to put more power into a BATTERY
PHRASE **recharge your batteries** to rest after being very busy, so that you will be ready to start working again

rec·i·pe /ˈresəpi/ noun [C] ★ a set of instructions for cooking or preparing a particular food: ***a recipe for** apple pie*
PHRASE **be a recipe for sth** to make it extremely likely that something will happen: *Giving your kids too much freedom can be **a recipe for disaster**.*

re·cip·i·ent /rɪˈsɪpiənt/ noun [C] *formal* someone who receives something

re·cip·ro·cal /rɪˈsɪprək(ə)l/ adj done according to an arrangement by which you do something for someone who does the same thing for you

re·cip·ro·cate /rɪˈsɪprəˌkeɪt/ verb [I/T] *formal* to do the same thing for someone that they have done for you

re·cit·al /rɪˈsaɪt(ə)l/ noun [C] a performance of music or poetry

re·cite /rɪˈsaɪt/ verb [I/T] to say a poem or story that you have learned to an audience

reck·less /ˈrekləs/ adj not thinking about the possible bad effects of your actions: *reckless driving* —**reck·less·ly** adv, **reck·less·ness** noun [U]

reck·on /ˈrekən/ verb *spoken* **1** [T] to have a particular opinion about someone or something **2** [I/T] *British* to believe that something is true
PHRASAL VERB ˈ**reckon with sth** to consider something important when you are making plans

reck·on·ing /ˈrekənɪŋ/ noun [C/U] a calculation or measurement

re·claim /rɪˈkleɪm/ verb [T] **1** to get something back that someone has taken from you: *He wants to reclaim the world championship title.* **2** to improve an area of land so that it can be used —**rec·la·ma·tion** /ˌrekləˈmeɪʃ(ə)n/ noun [U]

re·cline /rɪˈklaɪn/ verb [I] **1** to lie or lean in a comfortable position with your back supported by something **2** if a chair reclines, you can make the back of it lean backward to be more comfortable

re·cluse /ˈrekˌlus, *British* ˌrɪˈklus/ noun [C] someone who lives alone and avoids seeing other people —**re·clus·ive** /rɪˈklusɪv/ adj

rec·og·nise /ˈrekəgˌnaɪz/ a British spelling of **recognize**

rec·og·ni·tion /ˌrekəgˈnɪʃ(ə)n/ noun ★
1 [singular/U] agreement that something is true or important: *official **recognition of** the need for affordable childcare*
2 [singular/U] praise, respect, or admiration for something that you have done: *His work has **gained** international **recognition**.* ♦ *She received the award **in recognition of** her work in the community.*
3 [U] the ability to recognize a person or thing: *She looked at me without recognition.*

rec·og·nize /ˈrekəgˌnaɪz/ verb [T] ★★★
1 to know someone or something because you have seen, heard, or met them before: *I recognized the house from your description.* ♦ *I thought I recognized her voice!*
2 to accept that something is true or important: *We **recognize the need for** improvement in our performance.* ♦ **+ (that)** *I recognize that there are some problems with the current system.*
3 to give praise or approval to someone for something they have done: *Her achievement was recognized with a medal.*
4 to accept the authority or status of someone or something: *Many countries refused to recognize the new regime.*
—**rec·og·niz·a·ble** /ˈrekəgˌnaɪzəb(ə)l/ adj, **rec·og·niz·a·bly** adv

re·coil /rɪˈkɔɪl/ verb [I] to move quickly back from someone or something frightening or unpleasant

rec·ol·lect /ˌrekəˈlekt/ verb [I/T] to remember something that has happened

rec·ol·lec·tion /ˌrekəˈlekʃ(ə)n/ noun **1** [U] the ability to remember something that has happened **2** [C] something that you remember

rec·om·mend /ˌrekəˈmend/ verb [T] ★★
1 to advise that something should happen: **+(that)** *I recommend that you buy a more powerful computer.* ♦ **recommend doing sth** *We strongly recommend making reservations early.*
2 to say that someone or something is good and worth using, having, or experiencing: *Can you recommend a good restaurant?* ♦ **recommend sb/sth to sb** *Please recommend our shop to your friends.*

R

Words often used with recommend

Adverbs often used with **recommend** *(sense 2)*

- **heartily, highly, thoroughly, wholeheartedly** + RECOMMEND: say that someone or something is very good

rec•om•men•da•tion /ˌrekəmenˈdeɪʃ(ə)n/ noun **1** [C/U] a suggestion or piece of advice about how to solve a problem, deal with a situation, etc. **2** [C] a written or spoken statement that praises someone's character and ability to do something **3** [C/U] a suggestion that someone or something is especially appropriate or useful for a particular situation

rec•om•pense /ˈrekəmˌpens/ noun [U] *formal* payment that you give to someone who has done something for you or who has suffered injury or loss because of you

rec•on•cile /ˈrekənˌsaɪl/ verb **1** [I/T] if you reconcile two people or groups, or if they reconcile, they become friendly again after a disagreement **2** [T] to make things that are opposed to each other capable of existing together: *We can't reconcile the two versions of what happened.* **3** [T] to force someone to accept a situation that they do not like: *She couldn't reconcile herself to the idea of just giving up.*

rec•on•cil•i•a•tion /ˌrekənsɪliˈeɪʃ(ə)n/ noun [singular/U] **1** a new and friendly relationship with someone who you have argued with or fought with **2** a way of making it possible for things that are opposed to each other to exist together

re•con•nais•sance /rɪˈkɑnɪsəns/ noun [C/U] the use of soldiers or aircraft to go into an area and get information about an enemy

re•con•sid•er /ˌrikənˈsɪdər/ verb [I/T] to think again about a decision in order to decide whether you should change it

R

re•con•sti•tute /ˌriˈkɑnstɪˌtut/ verb [T] **1** to change the form or structure of something **2** to add a liquid to dried food so that you can eat it

re•con•struct /ˌrikənˈstrʌkt/ verb [T] **1** to form an idea of something that happened by connecting pieces of information **2** to build something again

re•con•struc•tion /ˌrikənˈstrʌkʃ(ə)n/ noun **1** [U] the process of building something again **2** [C/U] a situation in which you try to form an idea of something that happened by making something similar happen again

rec•ord[1] /ˈrekərd/ noun ★★★

1 [C] information that is kept about something that has happened: *medical/historical records* ♦ *Try to* ***keep a record of*** *everything you eat this week.* ♦ *This summer has been the hottest* ***on record*** (=hotter than ever before).

2 [singular] the things that someone has done that give an idea of what they are like: *The company has a reasonably good* ***safety record.***

3 [C] the best achievement so far in a particular activity, especially a sport: *She* ***holds the world record*** *in the 800 meters.* → BREAK[1]

4 [C] a large circular black piece of plastic containing music or other sounds: *an original Beatles' record*

PHRASES **(just) for the record** used for giving a piece of information that you want people to know: *It doesn't matter now, but just for the record, you were wrong.*

off the record used for saying that a remark is not official or is not intended to be made public

on (the) record used for stating that you are saying something officially or publicly

set/get the record straight to tell the truth about something after someone else has not told the truth about it

re•cord[2] /rɪˈkɔrd/ verb ★★★

1 [T] to make a record of something that has happened, usually by writing it down: *They were asked to record the time at which the attack happened.*

2 [I/T] to put sounds or images onto a CASSETTE, CD, or video: *Can you record the football game for me at 10 o'clock?*

3 [T] if a piece of equipment records an amount, it measures it and shows it: *Temperatures as low as –70 degrees Celsius have been recorded.*

rec•ord[3] /ˈrekərd/ adj more, better, worse, faster, etc. than ever before: *I made it back to the office in record time.*

rec•ord-break•ing /ˈrekərd ˌbreɪkɪŋ/ adj faster, longer, larger, etc. than anything that has been done before

re•cord•er /rɪˈkɔrdər/ noun [C] a musical instrument that you play by blowing into a hole at the top while putting your fingers over other holes —*picture* → WOODWIND

re•cord•ing /rɪˈkɔrdɪŋ/ noun **1** [C] a piece of music or speech that has been recorded **2** [U] the process of making recordings

re•count[1] /rɪˈkaʊnt/ verb [T] *formal* **1** to say what happened **2** to count something again

re•count[2] /ˈriˌkaʊnt/ noun [C] an occasion when the votes in an election are counted again

re•coup /rɪˈkup/ verb [T] to get back money that you have invested or lost

re•course /ˈriˌkɔrs, rɪˈkɔrs/ noun [U] *formal* the use of something so that you can get what you want or need in a difficult situation

re•cov•er /rɪˈkʌvər/ verb ★★

1 [I] to become fit and healthy again after an illness or injury: *I haven't fully* ***recovered from the flu.***

2 [T] to get back something that has been lost or stolen or is owed: *The thieves were caught, but many of the items were never recovered.*

3 [I] to return to a previous state after a difficult period or unpleasant experience: *The housing market appears to be recovering from the recession.*

4 [T] to get back the ability to do or feel something: *Simon never recovered the use of his arm after the crash.* ♦ *Darren was rushed to hospital, but he never* ***recovered consciousness.***

re•cov•er•y /rɪˈkʌvəri/ noun ★

1 [singular/U] the process of becoming fit and healthy again after an illness or injury: *The doctors expect Josie to* ***make a full recovery.***

2 [singular/U] the process of returning to normal activity after a period of slow activity: *signs of economic recovery*
3 [U] the act of getting something back that has been lost or stolen or is owed: *the **recovery of** stolen property*

re•cre•ate /ˌrikriˈeɪt/ verb [T] to make something exist again

rec•re•a•tion /ˌrekriˈeɪʃ(ə)n/ noun [C/U] *formal* things that you do to enjoy yourself —**rec•re•a•tion•al** adj

re•crim•i•na•tion /rɪˌkrɪmɪˈneɪʃ(ə)n/ noun **1** [U] a situation in which people are accusing or criticizing each other **2** [C] a statement accusing or criticizing someone who has accused or criticized you

re•cruit[1] /rɪˈkrut/ verb [I/T] to get someone to join a company, an organization, or the military —**re•cruit•ment** noun [U]

re•cruit[2] /rɪˈkrut/ noun [C] a new member in a company, an organization, or the military

rec•tan•gle /ˈrekˌtæŋg(ə)l/ noun [C] a shape with four straight sides and four angles of 90° —*picture* → C8 —**rec•tan•gu•lar** /rekˈtæŋgjələr/ adj

rec•ti•fy /ˈrektəˌfaɪ/ verb [T] *formal* to correct a problem or mistake, or to make a bad situation better

rec•tor /ˈrektər/ noun [C] **1** a priest in an Anglican church **2** the person in charge in some schools, colleges, and universities

rec•tum /ˈrektəm/ noun [C] *medical* the lowest part of the tube through which solid waste leaves your body —**rec•tal** adj

re•cu•per•ate /rɪˈkupəˌreɪt/ verb [I] to get better after being sick or injured —**re•cu•per•a•tion** /rɪˌkupəˈreɪʃ(ə)n/ noun [U]

re•cur /rɪˈkɜr/ verb [I] to happen again, once or several times —**re•cur•rence** /rɪˈkʌrəns/ noun [C/U], **re•cur•rent** /rɪˈkʌrənt/ adj

re•cy•cle /riˈsaɪk(ə)l/ verb [T] **1** to treat waste materials so that they can be used again **2** to use something again, often for a different purpose —**re•cy•cla•ble** adj, **re•cy•cling** noun [U]

red[1] /red/ adj ★★★
1 something that is red is the same color as blood: *bright red lipstick*
2 red hair is a red-brown or orange color
3 red wine is dark red or purple in color
PHRASE **turn red** to get red in the face because you are embarrassed

red[2] /red/ noun [C/U] ★ the color of blood: *She was dressed all in red.*
PHRASES **in the red** with more money being spent than there is available: *Their bank account was in the red again.*
see red to become very angry

ˌred-ˈcarpet adj **a red-carpet welcome** special treatment given to a very important visitor when they arrive

red•den /ˈred(ə)n/ verb [I/T] to become red, or to make something become red

red•dish /ˈredɪʃ/ adj similar to red

re•deem /rɪˈdim/ verb [T] **1** to improve something that is not very good by including something that is good: *A difficult year for the company was redeemed by a successful deal.* **2** to make someone free from the power of evil, especially in the Christian religion
PHRASE **redeem yourself** to do something good because you have behaved badly, so that people will realize that you are not a bad person

re•demp•tion /rɪˈdempʃən/ noun [U] the state of being made free from the power of evil, especially in the Christian religion =SALVATION
PHRASE **beyond/past redemption** too bad to be used or made good

re•de•ploy /ˌridɪˈplɔɪ/ verb [T] *formal* to move someone or something to a different place or job —**re•de•ploy•ment** noun [U]

re•de•vel•op /ˌridɪˈveləp/ verb [T] to improve an area in bad condition by destroying or improving old buildings and building new ones —**re•de•vel•op•ment** noun [U]

red-hand•ed /ˌred ˈhændɪd/ adj **be caught red-handed** to be caught doing something wrong

red•head /ˈredˌhed/ noun [C] someone with red hair

ˌred ˈherring noun [C] something that is not relevant that makes you confused or takes your attention away from what you should be concentrating on

ˌred-ˈhot adj extremely hot

re•di•al /ˌriˈdaɪəl/ verb [I/T] to press one or more buttons in order to make a phone call for a second time

redid the past tense of **redo**

re•di•rect /ˌridɪˈrekt, ˌridaɪˈrekt/ verb [T] **1** to send someone or something to a different place **2** to use money or effort for a different purpose: *The money we save will be redirected to other parts of the business.*

re•dis•trib•ute /ˌridɪˈstrɪbjut/ verb [T] to change the way that something is shared between people —**re•dis•tri•bu•tion** /ˌridɪstrɪˈbjuʃ(ə)n/ noun [U]

ˌred ˈmeat noun [U] meat such as BEEF or LAMB that is red before it is cooked

re•do /ˌriˈdu/ (past tense **re•did** /ˌriˈdɪd/; past participle **re•done** /ˌriˈdʌn/) verb [T] to do something again in a different way in order to correct or improve it

re•dress /rɪˈdres/ verb [T] *formal* to improve a bad situation that you are responsible for by doing something for someone or by giving them money —**re•dress** noun [U]

ˌred ˈtape noun [U] documents, rules, or processes that cause delays

re•duce /rɪˈdus/ verb [T] ★★★ to make something smaller or less in size, amount, importance, price, etc. =CUT (STH) DOWN: *Try to reduce the amount of fat in your diet.*
♦ **reduce sth to sth** *All children's shoes are now reduced to $20 a pair.*
PHRASAL VERB **reˈduce sb/sth to sth** to put someone or something into a particular unpleasant state or situation: *Her remarks had **reduced** him **to tears**.*

Words often used with reduce

Adverbs often used with ***reduce***
■ REDUCE + **considerably, dramatically, drastically, greatly, sharply, significantly, substantially**: reduce sth by a large amount

re•duc•tion /rɪˈdʌkʃən/ noun [C/U] ★★ the process or result of making something

R

smaller or less in amount, size, price, importance, etc.: *a $70 reduction for all hotel guests* ♦ *a dramatic **reduction in** the birth rate*

Words often used with reduction

*Adjectives often used with **reduction***

- **considerable, dramatic, drastic, large, marked, sharp, significant, substantial +** REDUCTION: used about reductions that are large

re•dun•dant /rɪˈdʌndənt/ adj **1** not needed because the same thing or a similar thing already exists **2** *British* if someone is made redundant, they have been told that they must leave their job because they are no longer needed —**re•dun•dan•cy** noun [C/U]

red•wood /ˈredˌwʊd/ noun [C/U] a very large tree with red wood that grows in the U.S. —*picture* → C9

reed /rid/ noun **1** [C/U] a tall thin plant that grows near water **2** [C] a thin piece of wood in the top of some musical instruments that makes a sound when you blow over it

reef /rif/ noun [C] a long line of rock or CORAL in the sea, with its top just below or just above the surface

reek /rik/ verb [I] to have a strong unpleasant smell = STINK

reel¹ /ril/ noun [C] an object shaped like a WHEEL that you wind string, THREAD, wire, or FILM around in order to store it

reel² /ril/ verb [I] **1** to move in a way that is not steady **2** to feel very shocked, upset, or confused

PHRASAL VERB **ˌreel sth ˈoff** to say a list of things quickly and without much effort

re•e•lect /ˌriɪˈlekt/ verb [T] to elect someone again —**re•e•lec•tion** /ˌriɪˈlekʃ(ə)n/ noun [U]

re•en•try /reˈentri/ noun [C/U] the moment when a SPACECRAFT enters the Earth's atmosphere again

ref /ref/ noun [C] *informal* a REFEREE

re•fer /rɪˈfɜr/ verb ★★★

PHRASAL VERBS **reˈfer to sb/sth** to mention someone or something when you are speaking or writing: *She referred to the subject several times during her speech.*

reˈfer to sth 1 to describe something, or to be about something: *These notes refer to the case of a teenage murderer.* **2** *formal* to look at a book, map, etc. for information: *Please refer to our catalog for details.*

reˈfer sb to sb/sth to send someone to another person or place in order to get help, information, or advice: *The doctor referred me to a skin specialist.*

ref•e•ree¹ /ˌrefəˈri/ noun [C] someone whose job is to make sure that players in a game obey the rules —*picture* → C15

ref•e•ree² /ˌrefəˈri/ verb [I/T] to be a referee in a game

ref•er•ence /ˈref(ə)rəns/ noun ★★

1 mention of sb/sth	4 a mention in writing
2 statement about you	5 search for information
3 sb who knows you	

1 [C/U] a comment that mentions someone or something: *He **made no reference to** my messy appearance.*

2 [C] a statement giving information about you that you ask someone who knows you or has worked with you to provide when you apply for a new job: *Her former employer **provided a reference for** her.*

3 [C] *American* someone who gives you a reference when you are applying for a job

4 [C] a writer or a piece of work that is mentioned in a piece of writing by someone else: *There was a long list of references at the end of the paper.*

5 [C/U] the process of looking at something in order to get information: *The sentences are numbered **for ease of reference**.*

→ FUTURE²

ˈreference ˌbook noun [C] a book that contains facts and information

ref•er•en•dum /ˌrefəˈrendəm/ noun [C/U] an occasion on which everyone in a country can vote to make a decision about one particular subject

re•fill /ˈriˌfɪl/ noun [C] **1** another amount of something that is put into a container after it has become empty **2** *American* another amount of a medicine that a doctor gives you after you have finished the previous amount —**re•fill** /ˌriˈfɪl/ verb [T]

re•fine /rɪˈfaɪn/ verb [T] **1** to remove things from a natural substance in order to make it pure **2** to make some changes to something in order to improve it: *We've refined the system since it was first launched.*

re•fined /rɪˈfaɪnd/ adj **1** pure, because other things have been removed: *refined sugar/oil* **2** someone who is refined is very polite and enjoys art, music, etc.

re•fine•ment /rɪˈfaɪnmənt/ noun **1** [C/U] a small change that is made to something in order to improve it **2** [U] the quality of being very polite and enjoying art, music, etc.

3 [U] the process of removing things from a natural substance so that it is pure

re•fin•er•y /rɪˈfaɪnəri/ noun [C] a factory where things are removed from a natural substance to make it pure

re•flect /rɪˈflekt/ verb ★★★

1 [T] to show that something is true of a particular situation or person: *He said that the statement did not reflect his own views.*

2 [I] to think about something carefully and seriously

3 [T] if a surface reflects something, you can see the image of that thing on the surface: *I caught a glimpse of them **reflected in** the mirror.*

4 [I/T] if something reflects light, heat, etc., the light, heat, etc. comes back off it

PHRASE **reflect well/badly on sb** to give people a good or bad opinion of someone

re•flec•tion /rɪˈflekʃ(ə)n/ noun ★

1 [C] an image that you see when you look in a mirror or at a shiny surface: *Anna stared at her **reflection in** the hall mirror.*

2 [U] careful thought about something: *At the time I thought I was right, but **on reflection** I'm not so sure.*

3 [C] something that shows that something is true of a particular person or situation: *Your choice of clothes is **a reflection of** your personality.*

4 [U] the process of reflecting light, sound, or images

PHRASE **be a reflection on** to show the faults of someone or something: *These crimes are a sad reflection on modern society.*

re·flec·tive /rɪˈflektɪv/ adj able to reflect light

re·flec·tor /rɪˈflektər/ noun [C] an object that reflects light and shines when light shines onto it

re·flex /ˈriˌfleks/ noun [C] **1** a movement that one of your muscles makes without you thinking about it or being able to control it **2** a quick way of reacting to something, without thinking about it

re·flex·ive /rɪˈfleksɪv/ adj *linguistics* a reflexive verb or pronoun refers back to the subject of the verb. In English, "to enjoy yourself" is a **reflexive verb** and "yourself" is a **reflexive pronoun**.

re·flex·ol·o·gy /ˌriflekˈsɑlədʒi/ noun [U] rubbing and pressing a person's feet in order to make other parts of their body more healthy, or to help the person to relax

re·form¹ /rɪˈfɔrm/ noun [C/U] ★★ a change that is made in order to improve a situation or system: *economic reforms* ♦ ***reform of** the welfare system*

Words often used with **reform**

*Adjectives often used with **reform** (noun)*
- **far-reaching, fundamental, important, major, radical, sweeping** + REFORM: used about reforms that change things a lot

re·form² /rɪˈfɔrm/ verb **1** [T] to change a situation or system in order to improve it **2** [I/T] to improve your own or someone else's behavior

Ref·or·ma·tion, the /ˌrefərˈmeɪʃ(ə)n/ a period of religious change in Europe in the 16th century, in which the Protestant Church was started

re·form·er /rɪˈfɔrmər/ noun [C] someone who tries to change and improve a political or social system

re·frain /rɪˈfreɪn/ verb [I] *formal* to stop yourself from doing something

re·fresh /rɪˈfreʃ/ verb [T] **1** to make you feel that you have more energy again, when you are tired or hot **2** *computing* to make an Internet or other computer document show the most recent changes to it

PHRASE **refresh sb's memory** to make someone remember something

re·fresh·ing /rɪˈfreʃɪŋ/ adj **1** making you feel more lively when you have been feeling tired or hot **2** *showing approval* newer, more interesting, or more exciting than other things that have come before: *a refreshing change* —**re·fresh·ing·ly** adv

re·fresh·ments /rɪˈfreʃmənts/ noun [plural] food and drinks that are provided at an event

re·frig·er·ate /rɪˈfrɪdʒəˌreɪt/ verb [T] to keep food or drinks cold by putting them in a refrigerator —**re·frig·er·a·tion** /rɪˌfrɪdʒəˈreɪʃ(ə)n/ noun [U]

re·frig·er·a·tor /rɪˈfrɪdʒəˌreɪtər/ noun [C] ★ a machine that keeps food and drinks cold —*picture* → C2

re·fu·el /ˌriˈfjuəl/ verb [I/T] if you refuel a vehicle or aircraft, or if it refuels, you put more fuel in it

ref·uge /ˈrefjudʒ/ noun [C/U] a place you go to in order to protect yourself from something dangerous or threatening = SHELTER

ref·u·gee /ˌrefjʊˈdʒi/ noun [C] someone who leaves their country because of a war or other threatening event

re·fund¹ /ˈriˌfʌnd/ noun [C] money that you get back because you have paid too much for something, or because you have decided that you do not want it

re·fund² /rɪˈfʌnd, ˈriˌfʌnd/ verb [T] to give money back to someone because they have paid too much for something or have decided that they do not want it

re·fur·bish /ˌriˈfɜrbɪʃ/ verb [T] to improve a room or a building by cleaning and painting it, by adding new furniture or equipment, etc. —**re·fur·bish·ment** noun [C/U]

re·fus·al /rɪˈfjuz(ə)l/ noun [C/U] ★ the act of refusing to do or accept something, or of not allowing someone to do something: **refusal to do sth** *The rebels' refusal to surrender led to further bloodshed.*

re·fuse¹ /rɪˈfjuz/ verb [I/T] ★★★ to say that you will not do or accept something, or will not let someone do something: *I asked him to apologize, but he refused.* ♦ **refuse to do sth** *He couldn't refuse to help his own son.* ♦ **refuse sb sth** *Judge Mackey refused the defendant the right to appeal.*

ref·use² /ˈrefjus/ noun [U] *formal* garbage

re·fute /rɪˈfjut/ verb [T] *formal* to prove or say that a statement is false

re·gain /rɪˈgeɪn/ verb [T] to get back something that you had lost

re·gal /ˈrig(ə)l/ adj typical of or appropriate for a king or queen —**re·gal·ly** adv

re·gard¹ /rɪˈgɑrd/ verb [T] ★★★
1 to think of someone or something in a particular way: **regard sb/sth as sth** *I regard him as a friend.*
2 *literary* to look at someone or something

PHRASE **as regards** *formal* concerning someone or something

→ REGARDING

re·gard² /rɪˈgɑrd/ noun ★
1 [U] attention or care that you give to someone or something: *The road was built **without regard for** the safety of residents.*
2 [U] respect and admiration for someone or something: *I have very **high regard for** her.*
3 regards [plural] greetings: ***Give my regards** to your parents.*

PHRASES **in this/that regard** relating to this or that

in/with regard to concerning a particular subject

re·gard·ing /rɪˈgɑrdɪŋ/ preposition ★ concerning a particular subject: *Davis had very little to say regarding the accident.*

Regarding is often used to introduce the subject of a business letter or document: *Regarding your inquiry of September 12...*

re·gard·less /rɪˈgɑrdləs/ adv without being affected or influenced by something: *It seemed impossible, but we went on, regardless.* ♦ *There must be equality for all citizens, regardless of nationality.*

re·gen·er·ate /riˈdʒenəreɪt/ verb [T] to develop something again, or to bring it back to its original state —**re•gen•er•a•tion** /rɪˌdʒenəˈreɪʃ(ə)n/ noun [U]

reg•gae /ˈregeɪ/ noun [U] a type of popular music that developed in Jamaica in the 1960s

re•gime /reɪˈʒim/ noun [C] ★ a system of government, especially a strict or unfair one

reg•i•ment /ˈredʒɪmənt/ noun [C] a large group of soldiers made up of several BATTALIONS —**reg•i•men•tal** /ˌredʒɪˈment(ə)l/ adj

reg•i•ment•ed /ˈredʒɪˌmentəd/ adj organized and controlled by strict rules

re•gion /ˈridʒən/ noun [C] ★★★
1 a large area of land: *Peru's eastern jungle region*
2 a particular area of your body: *pain in the abdominal region*

re•gion•al /ˈridʒən(ə)l/ adj ★★★ relating to or typical of a particular region: *a regional council/newspaper/accent*

reg•is•ter¹ /ˈredʒɪstər/ verb ★

1 put information on list	4 show feelings
2 show measurement	5 make opinion known
3 realize/notice sth	6 send by registered mail

1 [I/T] to put a name or other information on an official list: ***Births must be registered*** *within 42 days.* ♦ *Have you* ***registered for*** *classes yet?* ♦ *When you move you need to* ***register with*** *the local draft board.*
2 [T] to show something as a measurement on a piece of equipment: *an earthquake registering 5.1 on the Richter scale*
3 [I/T] to realize or notice something, or to be realized or noticed: *She did tell me she'd be out, but it didn't register.*
4 [T] *formal* to show your feelings about something in your face or voice: *George's look registered his confusion.*
5 [T] *formal* to make your opinion known publicly or officially: *I decided to* ***register a complaint*** *with the manager.*
6 [T] to send a letter or package by REGISTERED mail

reg•is•ter² /ˈredʒɪstər/ noun ★
1 [C] an official list or record of a particular type of thing: *the register of births, deaths, and marriages* ♦ *All guests must sign the hotel register.*
2 [C] a CASH REGISTER
3 [C/U] *linguistics* the type of language that you use in a particular situation or when you are communicating with a particular group of people

reg•is•trar /ˌredʒɪˈstrɑr/ noun [C] someone whose job is to keep official records

reg•is•tra•tion /ˌredʒɪˈstreɪʃ(ə)n/ noun **1** [U] the process of recording names or information on an official list **2** [C] *American* an official document that gives details of a vehicle and its owner

reg•is•try /ˈredʒɪstri/ noun [C] a collection of official records, or the place where it is kept

re•gress /rɪˈgres/ verb [I] to return to a previous and usually less developed state —**re•gres•sion** /rɪˈgreʃ(ə)n/ noun [U]

re•gret¹ /rɪˈgret/ verb [T] ★★ to feel sorry or sad about something that has happened, or about something that you have done: *We regret any inconvenience caused by the delay.* ♦ **regret doing sth** *I don't regret moving to New York.*

PHRASE **I/we regret to inform/tell you that** *formal* used when you are giving someone bad news

re•gret² /rɪˈgret/ noun [C/U] a feeling of sadness about something that has happened or something that you have done

PHRASE **give/send (sb) your regrets** *formal* used as a polite way of refusing an invitation —**re•gret•ful** adj, **re•gret•ful•ly** adv

re•gret•ta•ble /rɪˈgretəb(ə)l/ adj used for talking about something that you wish had not happened —**re•gret•ta•bly** adv

reg•u•lar¹ /ˈregjələr/ adj ★★★

1 arranged evenly	4 with even shape
2 doing sth often	5 with normal grammar
3 ordinary	

1 arranged so that there is the same amount of time or space between things: *regular monthly meetings* ♦ *They come here* ***on a regular basis.***
2 doing something or done frequently: *a regular customer* ♦ *regular exercise*
3 ordinary, or of average size: *regular unleaded gasoline* ♦ *a cheeseburger and regular fries*
4 arranged to form an even shape: *He was a handsome man, with strong* ***regular features.***
5 *linguistics* following the normal patterns of grammar ≠ IRREGULAR: *regular verbs* —**reg•u•lar•i•ty** /ˌregjəˈlerəti/ noun [U]

reg•u•lar² /ˈregjələr/ noun [C] a customer who often goes to the same bar, restaurant, or store

reg•u•lar•ly /ˈregjələrli/ adv ★★
1 after equal amounts of time have passed: *The committee meets regularly.*
2 frequently: *The equipment needs to be checked regularly.*

reg•u•late /ˈregjəˌleɪt/ verb [T] **1** to officially control an activity, process, or industry **2** to control something so that it operates effectively

reg•u•la•tion /ˌregjəˈleɪʃ(ə)n/ noun ★★
1 [C] an official rule that controls the way things are done: *building/safety regulations*
2 [U] official control of an activity, process, or industry: *the government's regulation of the steel industry*

re•hab /ˈriˌhæb/ noun [U] *informal* the process of helping someone to give up drugs or alcohol

re•ha•bil•i•tate /ˌrihəˈbɪlɪˌteɪt/ verb [T] to help someone to return to a normal life after they have been in prison, or after they have been ADDICTED to drugs or alcohol —**re•ha•bil•i•ta•tion** /ˌrihəbɪlɪˈteɪʃ(ə)n/ noun [U]

re•hash /ˌriˈhæʃ/ verb [T] to repeat or use something again without adding anything new

re•hears•al /rɪˈhɜrs(ə)l/ noun [C/U] an occasion when you practice for the performance of a play, concert, etc.

re•hearse /rɪˈhɜrs/ verb [I/T] to practice a play, concert, etc. before giving a performance

reign¹ /reɪn/ noun [C] the period of time when a king or queen rules a country

reign² /reɪn/ verb [I] **1** if a king or queen reigns, they officially rule a country **2** to be the most important feature in a situation: *For weeks, confusion reigned at the office.*

re•im•burse /ˌriːɪmˈbɜrs/ verb [T] to give someone back money that they have spent =PAY SB BACK —**re•im•burse•ment** noun [C/U]

rein /reɪn/ noun [C] a piece of leather fastened to a horse's head that a rider uses to control the horse

re•in•car•nat•ed /ˌriːɪnkɑrˈneɪtəd/ adj born again as a different person, animal, or thing after death, according to some religions

re•in•car•na•tion /ˌriːɪnkɑrˈneɪʃ(ə)n/ noun **1** [U] the belief that after you die you can be born again as a different person, animal, or thing **2** [C] someone who has been born again as a different person, animal, or thing after their death

rein•deer /ˈreɪnˌdɪr/ noun [C] an animal like a DEER with large ANTLERS

re•in•force /ˌriːɪnˈfɔrs/ verb [T] **1** to make an idea, belief, or feeling stronger: *The figures reinforce the view that economic growth is slowing.* **2** to make a building, structure, or object stronger: *Crews started work to reinforce the damaged bridge.* —**re•in•forced** /ˌriːɪnˈfɔrst/ adj

re•in•force•ment /ˌriːɪnˈfɔrsmənt/ noun **1 reinforcements** [plural] extra soldiers or police officers who go to help an existing group of soldiers or police officers **2** [U] the process of REINFORCING something

re•in•state /ˌriːɪnˈsteɪt/ verb [T] **1** to give someone back their previous job or position **2** to bring back something such as a law or benefit that had been stopped —**re•in•state•ment** noun [U]

re•in•vent /ˌriːɪnˈvent/ verb [T] to change something that already exists and give it a different form or purpose

PHRASES **reinvent the wheel** to waste time and effort trying to do something that someone else has already done well
reinvent yourself to change things about yourself, so that people think of you as a different type of person

re•it•er•ate /riˈɪtəˌreɪt/ verb [T] *formal* to repeat something in order to emphasize it —**re•it•er•a•tion** /riˌɪtəˈreɪʃ(ə)n/ noun [C/U]

re•ject¹ /rɪˈdʒekt/ verb [T] ★★
1 to not accept or agree with something such as an offer or an argument: *Our proposal was rejected.*
2 to refuse to accept someone for a job or a course of study
3 to behave in an unkind way to someone who wants kindness or love from you

> **Words often used with reject**
> *Adverbs often used with **reject** (verb, sense 1)*
> ■ REJECT + **categorically, firmly, flatly, outright, totally, vigorously**: reject something in a very clear and definite way

re•ject² /ˈriˌdʒekt/ noun [C] something or someone that is not accepted because they have not reached the necessary standard

re•jec•tion /rɪˈdʒekʃ(ə)n/ noun **1** [C/U] a refusal to accept or agree with something such as an offer or an argument ≠ ACCEPTANCE: *the rejection of the peace plan* **2** [C] a letter that tells you that you did not get a job or were not accepted by a school **3** [C/U] a refusal to show someone the love or kindness that they need or expect: *fear of rejection*

re•joice /rɪˈdʒɔɪs/ verb [I] *literary* to celebrate and express feelings of great happiness —**re•joic•ing** noun [U]

re•join /ˌriˈdʒɔɪn/ verb [T] to return to a person or organization that you were with before

re•ju•ve•nate /rɪˈdʒuvəˌneɪt/ verb [T] to make someone feel or look younger —**re•ju•ve•na•tion** /rɪˌdʒuvəˈneɪʃ(ə)n/ noun [U]

re•kin•dle /ˌriˈkɪnd(ə)l/ verb [T] to make you start feeling or thinking about something again

re•lapse /ˈrilæps/ noun [C/U] **1** a period of illness after you had been getting better **2** a return to a worse state after a period of improvement —**re•lapse** /rɪˈlæps/ verb [I]

re•late /rɪˈleɪt/ verb ★★★
1 [I/T] to show how one thing has a connection with another, or to be connected with another thing: *I can't really see how the two issues relate.* ♦ **relate sth to sth** *We offer courses that relate English literature to other subjects.*
2 [T] *formal* to tell someone about something that has happened

PHRASAL VERB **re'late to sth 1** to be about something, or to be connected with something: *We're only interested in events that relate directly to the murder.* **2** to be able to understand a situation or the way that someone feels and thinks: *The program deals with subjects that ordinary people can relate to.*

re•lat•ed /rɪˈleɪtəd/ adj ★
1 connected ≠ UNRELATED: *We think the two crimes are related in some way.*
2 belonging to the same family: *Annie's **related to** the director.*

re•la•tion /rɪˈleɪʃ(ə)n/ noun ★★★
1 relations [plural] the relationship between countries, people, or organizations: *international relations* ♦ *better **relations between** Japan and China* ♦ *We have very good **relations with** the local police.*
2 [C] a member of your family =RELATIVE: *All our friends and relations came to our wedding.*
3 [C/U] a connection between two or more people or things: *The study found a direct **relation between** smoking and lung cancer.* ♦ *The tax **bears no relation to** people's ability to pay.*

PHRASE **in relation to 1** in comparison to something: *Unemployment here is high in relation to national levels.* **2** concerning something: *I have nothing further to say in relation to this matter.*

> **Word family: relation**
> *Words in the same family as **relation***
>
> | | |
> |---|---|
> | ■ **relate** *v* | ■ **relative** *adj, n* |
> | ■ **related** *adj* | ■ **relatively** *adv* |
> | ■ **relationship** *n* | ■ **unrelated** *adj* |

re•la•tion•ship /rɪˈleɪʃ(ə)nˌʃɪp/ noun [C] ★★★
1 the way in which two or more people or groups behave toward each other: *The **relationships between** players from the two teams were pretty friendly.* ♦ *What was your*

R

relationship with your mother like?
2 the way in which two or more people or things are connected: *There is a close* ***relationship between*** *poverty and crime.*
3 a situation in which two people are sexual or romantic partners: *I was already* ***in a relationship*** *when I met Ben.*

rel•a•tive¹ /ˈrelətɪv/ adj ★★ used for comparing one situation with a more extreme one: *There was relative calm after the violence of the previous night.*
PHRASE **relative to** compared with

rel•a•tive² /ˈrelətɪv/ noun [C] ★ a member of your family, especially one who does not live with you=RELATION

ˌrelative ˈclause noun [C] *linguistics* a CLAUSE that is joined to a previous one by words such as "who," "that," or "which"

rel•a•tive•ly /ˈrelətɪvli/ adv ★★★ in comparison with someone or something similar=COMPARATIVELY: *a relatively small apartment*

ˌrelative ˈpronoun noun [C] *linguistics* a pronoun such as "who," "that," or "which" that introduces a RELATIVE CLAUSE

re•lax /rɪˈlæks/ verb ★★
1 [I] to rest and become calm: *Just sit down and try to relax for half an hour.*
2 [I/T] to make your muscles or a part of your body feel less tight and more comfortable, or to become less tight and more comfortable: *Relax your stomach muscles, then repeat the exercise.*
3 [T] to make rules, controls, conditions, etc. less strict: *Some companies have relaxed their rules about unpaid vacation time.*
—**re•lax•a•tion** /ˌrilækˈseɪʃ(ə)n/ noun [C/U]

re•laxed /rɪˈlækst/ adj ★
1 calm and not worried: *Bill came back from his vacation looking relaxed and tanned.*
2 friendly, informal, and comfortable: *The atmosphere in our office is very relaxed.*

R

re•lax•ing /rɪˈlæksɪŋ/ adj pleasant and making you feel relaxed

re•lay¹ /rɪˈleɪ, ˈriˌleɪ/ verb [T] **1** to communicate information to someone **2** to send out television or radio signals to be broadcast

re•lay² /ˈriˌleɪ/ or **ˈrelay ˌrace** noun [C] a race between two or more teams where each member of the team does part of the race and then another member continues

re•lease¹ /rɪˈlis/ verb [T] ★★★

1 let sb leave	4 offer product
2 stop holding sth	5 move held equipment
3 give information	6 get rid of feeling

1 to let someone leave a place where they have been kept=FREE: *The authorities had recently released two suspects.* ♦ **release sb from sth** *He was released from prison in July.*
2 to stop holding someone or something: *She slowly released her grip on Louisa's hand.*
3 to make information or documents available: *Managers have released few details from yesterday's meeting.*
4 to make a movie, video, or CD available for people to see or buy: *They have just released their second album.*
5 to move a piece of equipment from the position it is held in: *Don't forget to release the brake.*
6 to get rid of a negative feeling, especially by expressing it: *Exercise will release all that tension.*

re•lease² /rɪˈlis/ noun ★★
1 [U] the act of letting someone leave a place such as a prison or hospital: ***The release of*** *Nelson Mandela was watched by millions of people on TV.*
2 [U] a situation in which something such as a chemical spreads into the area around it: *We're doing all we can to prevent* ***the release of*** *toxic waste into the oceans.*
3 [U] the act of making information or documents available: ***the release of*** *secret government information*
4 [C] a new movie, video, or CD that is available for people to see or buy

rel•e•gate /ˈreləˌgeɪt/ verb [T] to move someone or something to a less important position —**rel•e•ga•tion** /ˌreləˈgeɪʃ(ə)n/ noun [U]

re•lent /rɪˈlent/ verb [I] to change your mind about not letting someone do something

re•lent•less /rɪˈlentləs/ adj **1** never seeming to stop or improve **2** determined and never stopping your attempts to achieve something —**re•lent•less•ly** adv

rel•e•vance /ˈreləvəns/ or **rel•e•van•cy** /ˈreləvənsi/ noun [U] the quality of being connected with and important to something else

rel•e•vant /ˈreləvənt/ adj ★★★ important and directly connected with what is being discussed or considered ≠IRRELEVANT: *How is that* ***relevant to*** *this discussion?*

re•li•a•ble /rɪˈlaɪəb(ə)l/ adj ★ able to be trusted =DEPENDABLE ≠UNRELIABLE: *a reliable workman/car* ♦ *reliable information/evidence* —**re•li•a•bil•i•ty** /rɪˌlaɪəˈbɪləti/ noun [U], **re•li•a•bly** adv

re•li•ance /rɪˈlaɪəns/ noun [U] the state of depending on someone or something =DEPENDENCE

re•li•ant /rɪˈlaɪənt/ adj depending on someone or something=DEPENDENT

rel•ic /ˈrelɪk/ noun [C] an object, system, or rule that belongs to the past

re•lief /rɪˈlif/ noun ★★★
1 [singular/U] a relaxed happy feeling that you get because something bad has ended or has not happened: *It's* ***a huge relief*** *to know that everyone is safe.* ♦ ***To her relief,*** *someone had found her keys.*
2 [U] the reduction of pain or the effects of an illness: *The patients experienced no* ***relief from*** *their symptoms.*
3 [U] food, clothes, and money that is given to people who are in need of help: *flood/disaster/earthquake relief*
4 [U] the right to not have to pay the full amount of tax or interest on an amount of money

re•lieve /rɪˈliv/ verb [T] ★
1 to make an unpleasant feeling or situation less severe or unpleasant: *Use a cooling gel to relieve the discomfort of sunburn.* ♦ *Reading helped to* ***relieve the boredom.***
2 to replace someone when they finish work
PHRASE **relieve sb of sth** *formal* to take something from someone: *The new law*

relieves the mayor of responsibility for the police force.

re•lieved /rɪˈlivd/ adj happy and relaxed because something bad has ended or did not happen: *I'm so relieved to know the truth.*

re•li•gion /rɪˈlɪdʒən/ noun [C/U] ★★★ belief in a god or in gods, or a particular system of beliefs in a god or in gods: *the Christian/Hindu/Muslim religion*

re•lig•ious /rəˈlɪdʒəs/ adj ★★★
1 relating to religion: *religious beliefs*
2 believing strongly in your religion =DEVOUT: *a* ***deeply religious*** *man*

re•lig•ious•ly /rəˈlɪdʒəsli/ adv if you do something religiously, you do it regularly and are very serious about it

re•lin•quish /rəˈlɪŋkwɪʃ/ verb [T] *formal* to give up your power, position, or an advantage

rel•ish¹ /ˈrelɪʃ/ verb [T] to get great pleasure or satisfaction from something

rel•ish² /ˈrelɪʃ/ noun **1** [U] great pleasure and satisfaction **2** [C/U] a cold sauce that you put on meat

re•live /ˌriˈlɪv/ verb [T] to remember an experience so clearly that you seem to be in the same situation again

re•load /ˌriˈloʊd/ verb [I/T] to put something into an object such as a gun or camera so that it is ready to use again

re•lo•cate /ˈriloʊˌkeɪt/ verb [I/T] to move to a different place, or to make someone do this —**re•lo•ca•tion** /ˌriloʊˈkeɪʃ(ə)n/ noun [U]

re•luc•tant /rɪˈlʌktənt/ adj ★ not willing to do something: **reluctant to do sth** *She was reluctant to leave.* —**re•luc•tance** noun [U], **re•luc•tant•ly** adv

re•ly /rɪˈlaɪ/ verb ★★
PHRASAL VERBS **reˈly on sth** to need something in order to continue living, existing, or operating: **rely on sth to do sth** *The museum relies on voluntary donations to stay open.*
reˈly on sb/sth to trust someone or something to do something for you: *Sometimes you just have to rely on your own judgment.* ♦ **rely on sb/sth to do sth** *Can we rely on him to support us?*

re•main /rɪˈmeɪn/ verb ★★★
1 [linking verb] to continue to be in a particular situation or condition: *The dictator has remained in power for over 20 years.* ♦ *The economy remains fragile.*
2 [I] to stay in a particular place or position and not leave it: *You must* ***remain in bed*** *for three days after the surgery.*
3 [I] to continue to exist after other things are gone or have been dealt with: *Only a handful of these rare fish remain in North America.*
PHRASE **it remains to be seen (whether/what/how)** used for saying that you do not know yet whether something will happen or will be possible

re•main•der, the /rɪˈmeɪndər/ noun [singular] the part of something that is left after the rest has gone or been finished

re•main•ing /rɪˈmeɪnɪŋ/ adj still left after other people or things have gone or been dealt with

re•mains /rɪˈmeɪnz/ noun [plural] **1** the body of a person or animal that has died **2** the part of something that is left after the rest has been finished, used, or destroyed

re•make /ˈriˌmeɪk/ noun [C] a movie that uses the same story as a previous movie —**re•make** /ˌriˈmeɪk/ verb [T]

re•mand /rɪˈmænd/ verb **be remanded in custody** *legal* to be put in prison until your trial

re•mark¹ /rɪˈmɑrk/ noun [C] ★ a few words that give the facts or give your opinion about something =COMMENT: *Nicholas* ***made a rude remark about*** *her hair.*

re•mark² /rɪˈmɑrk/ verb [T] to make a comment about something
PHRASAL VERB **reˈmark on sth** to make a comment about something that you have noticed

re•mark•a•ble /rɪˈmɑrkəb(ə)l/ adj ★★ unusual in a way that surprises or impresses you: *The play has been a remarkable success.*

re•mark•a•bly /rɪˈmɑrkəbli/ adv in an unusual or surprising way: *All the students did remarkably well.*

re•mar•ry /riˈmeri/ verb [I/T] to get married again —**re•mar•riage** /riˈmerɪdʒ/ noun [C]

re•me•di•al /rɪˈmidiəl/ adj **1** intended to help people who have difficulty learning basic skills such as reading and writing
2 intended to improve or correct something

rem•e•dy¹ /ˈremədi/ noun [C] ★
1 a solution to a particular problem: *There are no easy* ***remedies for*** *learning difficulties.*
2 a cure for pain or for a minor illness: *homeopathic/herbal remedies*

rem•e•dy² /ˈremədi/ verb [T] to correct or improve a situation

re•mem•ber /rɪˈmembər/ verb ★★★
1 [I/T] to have an image in your mind of a person, a place, or something that happened in the past: *I can still remember every word of our conversation.* ♦ **remember doing sth** *She remembers seeing him there.* ♦ **+(that)** *I remember that I was really nervous on my first day at school.* ♦ **+when/where/how etc.** *Try to remember where you put the keys.*
2 [T] to not forget to do something: *I hope she remembers my book* (=brings it with her). ♦ **remember to do sth** *He never remembers to lock the door when he goes out.*

re•mem•brance /rɪˈmembrəns/ noun [U] a way of showing respect for someone who has died or for an important event

re•mind /rɪˈmaɪnd/ verb [T] ★★ to help someone to remember something: **remind sb of/about sth** *Can you remind us about your plans for the building?* ♦ **remind sb to do sth** *Remind Jenny to bring my CD when she comes.* ♦ **remind sb (that)** *She reminded me that we had met before.* ♦ **remind sb what/when/where/how etc.** *I need the notes to remind me what to say.*
PHRASE **remind sb of sb/sth** to be very similar to someone or something else: *She reminded me of my cousin Sarah.*

re•mind•er /rɪˈmaɪndər/ noun [C] something that reminds you of something

rem•i•nisce /ˌremɪˈnɪs/ verb [I] to talk, think,

R

or write about enjoyable experiences in your past —**rem•i•nis•cence** /ˌremɪˈnɪsəns/ noun [C]

rem•i•nis•cent /ˌremɪˈnɪsənt/ adj reminding you of someone or something similar

re•mis•sion /rɪˈmɪʃ(ə)n/ noun [C/U] a period of time when an illness or disease becomes less severe: *Her sister's cancer is in remission.*

re•mit•tance /rɪˈmɪt(ə)ns/ noun [C/U] *formal* payment for goods or services

rem•nant /ˈremnənt/ noun [C] a small remaining part of something

re•mod•el /ˌriˈmɑd(ə)l/ verb [T] to change the structure or appearance of something

re•morse /rɪˈmɔrs/ noun [U] a strong sad and guilty feeling about something bad that you have done —**re•morse•ful** adj, **re•morse•ful•ly** adv

re•morse•less /rɪˈmɔrsləs/ adj not feeling sad or guilty for having done something bad —**re•morse•less•ly** adv

re•mote¹ /rɪˈmoʊt/ adj ★

1 distant in space or time=ISOLATED: *a remote town in Wisconsin ♦ the remote past*

2 slight: *You have only a remote chance of winning.*

3 not showing any friendly interest in other people=ALOOF

—**re•mote•ness** noun [U]

re•mote² /rɪˈmoʊt/ noun [C] a REMOTE CONTROL

reˌmote conˈtrol noun **1** [C] a piece of equipment that you use for controlling something such as a television from a short distance away **2** [U] a system of controlling a machine or a vehicle from a distance —**reˌmote-conˈtrolled** adj

re•mote•ly /rɪˈmoʊtli/ adv in a very small way: *He wasn't even remotely interested in anything we had to say.*

R

re•mov•a•ble /rɪˈmuvəb(ə)l/ adj easily removed

re•mov•al /rɪˈmuv(ə)l/ noun [C/U] the process of removing someone or something

re•move /rɪˈmuv/ verb [T] ★★★

1 to take someone or something away from a place: **remove sb/sth from sth** *Rescue crews removed two people from the collapsed building.*

2 to get rid of a problem, difficulty, or something that annoys you: *We need to remove any obstacles to a peaceful solution.*

3 to take off a piece of clothing: *She removed her coat and sat down.*

4 to take away someone's power or position, especially in politics: *Officials who were involved in the scandal were removed from office.*

re•moved /rɪˈmuvd/ adj **1** different from something: *Paris is far removed from the little town I grew up in.* **2** distant in time or space

re•mov•er /rɪˈmuvər/ noun [C/U] a substance used for removing paint, STAINS, NAIL POLISH, etc.

re•mu•ner•a•tion /rɪˌmjunəˈreɪʃ(ə)n/ noun [U] *formal* payment that you get for your work —**re•mu•ner•ate** /rɪˈmjunəreɪt/ verb [T]

ren•ais•sance /ˌrenəˈsɑns, *British* rɪˈneɪsəns/ noun **1 the Renaissance** the period in Europe between the 14th and 16th centuries when there was increased interest in art, literature, and science **2** [singular] a situation in which something becomes popular again

re•name /riˈneɪm/ verb [T] to change the name of someone or something

ren•der /ˈrendər/ verb [T] *formal* **1** to provide a service, or to help someone **2** to make something be in a particular condition or state: *Failure to supply the information will render the contract invalid.*

ren•dez•vous /ˈrɑndeɪˌvu/ (plural **ren•dez•vous** /ˈrɑndeɪˌvuz/) noun [C] a meeting that is arranged for a particular time and place, or the place where the meeting happens —**ren•dez•vous** verb [I]

ren•di•tion /renˈdɪʃ(ə)n/ noun [C] a particular way of performing a song, poem, piece of music, etc.

re•nege /rɪˈneg, rɪˈnɪg/ verb [I] *formal* to not do something that you promised to do

re•new /rɪˈnu/ verb [T] **1** to arrange for something to continue **2** to do something again after a pause **3** to replace something that is old or damaged —**re•new•al** noun [C/U]

re•new•a•ble /rɪˈnuəb(ə)l/ adj **1** a renewable contract or arrangement can be continued for a longer period of time ≠ NONRENEWABLE **2** renewable energy and natural materials replace themselves by natural processes, so that they are never completely used up ≠ NONRENEWABLE

re•newed /rɪˈnud/ adj happening again after a pause, and with more energy or enthusiasm than before

re•nounce /rɪˈnaʊns/ verb [T] *formal* **1** to say formally that you no longer support or believe in something **2** to say formally that you want to give up a right, title, or position —**re•nun•ci•a•tion** /rɪˌnʌnsiˈeɪʃ(ə)n/ noun [C/U]

ren•o•vate /ˈrenəˌveɪt/ verb [T] to make something old look new again by repairing and improving it —**ren•o•va•tion** /ˌrenəˈveɪʃ(ə)n/ noun [C/U]

re•nowned /rɪˈnaʊnd/ adj famous for a special skill or achievement —**re•nown** noun [U]

rent¹ /rent/ verb ★★

1 [I/T] to pay money regularly to use a house, room, office, etc. that belongs to someone else: *How long have you been renting this place?*

2 [I/T] to pay money to use a vehicle, piece of equipment, etc. for a short time: *You can rent a car at reasonable rates.*

3 [T] to allow a house, room, office, etc. that you own to be used by someone who pays you regularly for using it: *All the rooms are rented out to students.*

PHRASAL VERB ˌ**rent sth ˈout** *same as* **rent¹** 3

rent² /rent/ noun [C/U] ★★ an amount of money that you pay regularly for using a house, room, office, etc. that belongs to someone else: *After she'd* ***paid her rent****, Jan had no money left for food.*

rent•al /ˈrent(ə)l/ noun **1** [C] something you rent, especially a house or car **2** [C/U] the process of renting something, or an amount of money that you pay for renting something —**rent•al** adj

rent•ed /ˈrentəd/ adj used by someone who pays rent to the owner

re•o•pen /ˌriˈoupən/ verb [I/T] if a process reopens, or if someone reopens it, it begins again after stopping for a time

re•or•gan•ize /riˈɔrgəˌnaɪz/ verb [I/T] to organize something in a different way —**re•or•gan•i•za•tion** /riˌɔrgənɪˈzeɪʃ(ə)n/ noun [C/U]

rep /rep/ noun [C] someone who works for a company and whose job it is to deal directly with customers: *a sales/holiday rep*

Rep. 1 Representative 2 Republican

re•pair¹ /rɪˈper/ verb [T] ★
1 to fix something that is broken or damaged: *The cost of repairing the damage was much higher than we thought.*
2 to improve a bad situation: *an attempt to repair the relationship between the two countries*

re•pair² /rɪˈper/ noun ★
1 [C/U] work that is done to fix something that is broken or damaged: *How much will the repairs cost?* ♦ *Unfortunately the engine is **beyond repair*** (=so badly damaged that it cannot be repaired). ♦ *Both of the monuments were **in need of repair**.*
2 [C] a part of something that has been repaired
PHRASE **in good/bad repair** in a good or a bad condition

rep•a•ra•tions /ˌrepəˈreɪʃ(ə)nz/ noun [plural] money paid by the country that loses a war for the damage that it has caused to other countries

re•pa•tri•ate /riˈpeɪtriˌeɪt/ verb [T] to send someone back to the country that is legally their own —**re•pa•tri•a•tion** /riˌpeɪtriˈeɪʃ(ə)n/ noun [U]

re•pay /rɪˈpeɪ/ (past tense and past participle **re•paid** /rɪˈpeɪd/) verb [T] 1 to give someone back the money that you borrowed from them 2 to reward someone who has helped you

re•pay•ment /rɪˈpeɪmənt/ noun [C] an amount of money that you pay back to the person that you borrowed it from

re•peal /rɪˈpil/ verb [T] *legal* to officially end a law —**re•peal** noun [U]

re•peat¹ /rɪˈpit/ verb [T] ★★★
1 to say or do something again: *Can you repeat what you just said, please?*
2 to tell someone something that someone else has told you: **repeat sth to sb** *I'll tell you a secret, but please don't repeat it to anyone.*
3 to say or write something that you have heard or read because you are trying to learn or understand it: **repeat sth after sb** *The students carefully repeated the words after the teacher.*
4 to broadcast a television or radio program again
PHRASE **repeat yourself** to say the same words or idea that you said before, often without realizing you are doing it

> **Word family: repeat**
> *Words in the same family as **repeat***
> - **repetition** *n*
> - **repetitive** *adj*
> - **repeated** *adj*
> - **repeatedly** *adv*
> - **repetitious** *adj*

re•peat² /rɪˈpit/ noun [C] 1 a television or radio program that is broadcast again 2 an event or situation that happens again

re•peat•ed /rɪˈpitəd/ adj done many times —**re•peat•ed•ly** adv

re•pel /rɪˈpel/ verb [T] 1 if something repels you, you think that it is extremely unpleasant 2 to keep someone or something away, or to prevent them from attacking you

re•pel•lent¹ /rɪˈpelənt/ noun [C/U] a substance that keeps insects or animals away

re•pel•lent² /rɪˈpelənt/ adj very unpleasant

re•pent /rɪˈpent/ verb [I/T] *formal* to be very sorry for something bad that you have done —**re•pent•ance** noun [U], **re•pent•ant** adj

re•per•cus•sions /ˌripərˈkʌʃ(ə)nz/ noun [plural] the bad effects that something causes

rep•er•toire /ˈrepərˌtwɑ/ noun [C] all the songs, pieces of music, etc. that a performer knows

rep•e•ti•tion /ˌrepəˈtɪʃ(ə)n/ noun 1 [U] a situation in which someone repeats something 2 [C] something that happens in the same way as an earlier event

re•pet•i•tive /rɪˈpetətɪv/ or **rep•e•ti•tious** /ˌrepəˈtɪʃ(ə)s/ adj repeating the same thing, especially in a way that is boring or annoying

re•phrase /ˌriˈfreɪz/ verb [T] to say or write the same thing, using different words

re•place /rɪˈpleɪs/ verb [T] ★★★
1 to get rid of someone or something and put a new person or thing in their place: *We'll have to replace all the furniture that was damaged in the flood.* ♦ **replace sth with sth** *The plan is to replace state funding with private money.*
2 to do the same job that someone or something did before: *Have they found anyone to replace me yet?* ♦ *E-mail has largely replaced traditional letters.*
3 to put something back in its correct place or position: *She carefully replaced the plate on the shelf.*

re•place•ment /rɪˈpleɪsmənt/ noun [C/U] someone or something that takes the place of another person or thing, or the process of replacing someone or something: *Have you found a replacement for your assistant?*

re•play /ˈriˌpleɪ/ noun [C] part of a sports game that is broadcast again —**re•play** /ˌriˈpleɪ/ verb [T]

re•plen•ish /rɪˈplenɪʃ/ verb [T] *formal* to make something full again, or to bring it back to its previous level by replacing what has been used

rep•li•ca /ˈreplɪkə/ noun [C] an accurate copy of something

rep•li•cate /ˈreplɪˌkeɪt/ verb [T] *formal* to do or make something again in the same way as before —**rep•li•ca•tion** /ˌreplɪˈkeɪʃ(ə)n/ noun [U]

re•ply¹ /rɪˈplaɪ/ verb ★★★
1 [I/T] to say, write, or do something as an answer: *"I know," Corbett replied quietly.* ♦ *It took them a week to **reply to** my letter.* ♦ **+(that)** *When I asked where he was going, he replied that it was none of my business.*
2 [I] to do something as a reaction to what someone else has done = RESPOND

R

re•ply[2] /rɪˈplaɪ/ noun [C] ★★ something that you say or write as an answer: *I wrote to him, but I got no reply.* ♦ *We received **a reply from** the novelist herself.* ♦ *I still haven't had **a reply to** my e-mail.* ♦ *I am writing **in reply to** your letter of August 7.*

re•port[1] /rɪˈpɔrt/ noun [C] ★★★
1 a spoken or written description of a particular subject, situation, or event: *A new report shows violent crime is on the increase.* ♦ *We're **getting reports of** more fighting in the area.* ♦ *the company's annual report* ♦ *We have to write **a short report on** the conference.*
2 an article or broadcast that gives information about something in the news: *Did you see that **report about** poverty in Boston?*

re•port[2] /rɪˈpɔrt/ verb ★★★
1 [T] to provide information about something, especially to people in authority: *Supermarkets report a sharp increase in sales of organic produce.* ♦ **report doing sth** *Witnesses reported hearing a loud noise before the airplane crashed.* ♦ **report sth to sb** *If you see anything suspicious, report it to the police.*
2 [I/T] to give information about something in a news article or broadcast: *Three CNN journalists were sent to **report on** the conflict.* ♦ **+that** *Our sources reported that the president had lost control of the country.*
3 [T] to produce an official statement or a written document about a particular subject: *The committee will report the results of its investigation tomorrow.*
PHRASAL VERB **reˈport to sb** if you report to someone at work, they are responsible for telling you what to do

reˈport ˌcard noun [C] *American* a teacher's written statement about a child's progress in school, sent to the child's parents

re•port•ed•ly /rɪˈpɔrtədli/ adv used for showing that you are not certain that something you are reporting is true

re•port•ed speech /rɪˌpɔrtɪd ˈspitʃ/ noun [U] *linguistics* a way of saying what someone has said that does not repeat their actual words =INDIRECT SPEECH

re•port•er /rɪˈpɔtər/ noun [C] someone whose job is to write articles or make broadcasts about events in the news =JOURNALIST

re•port•ing /rɪˈpɔrtɪŋ/ noun [U] the job of producing written reports or broadcasts about events in the news

re•pose /rɪˈpoʊz/ noun [U] *literary* a calm or relaxed state

re•pos•sess /ˌripəˈzes/ verb [T] to take back something that someone had promised to pay for, because they are unable to pay for it —**re•pos•ses•sion** /ˌripəˈzeʃ(ə)n/ noun [C/U]

rep•re•hen•si•ble /ˌreprɪˈhensəb(ə)l/ adj *formal* very bad

rep•re•sent /ˌreprɪˈzent/ verb [T] ★★★

1 speak/act for sb	4 be example of
2 be sth	5 in sports
3 be sign/symbol of	6 be picture/image of

1 to officially speak or do something for another person or group: *The vice-president will represent the United States at the ceremony.*
2 [linking verb] if something represents another thing, it consists of that thing: *Albanians represent about 90 percent of the population in Kosovo.*
3 to be a sign or symbol of something: *The color red commonly represents danger.*
4 to be an example of a particular quality or type: *His attitude represents everything I dislike about this country.*
5 to take part in a sport as a member of a particular team, country, etc.: *Ben's ambition is to represent Britain at the Olympics.*
6 to be a picture or image of something: *The statue represents Jefferson as a young man.*

rep•re•sen•ta•tion /ˌreprɪzenˈteɪʃ(ə)n/ noun
1 [C] a sign, symbol, or picture of something
2 [U] a person or group that officially speaks or does something for someone else —**rep•re•sen•ta•tion•al** adj

rep•re•sen•ta•tive[1] /ˌreprɪˈzentətɪv/ noun [C] ★★ someone who has been chosen by a person or group to vote, speak, or make decisions for them: *The new government sent a representative to the talks.*

rep•re•sen•ta•tive[2] /ˌreprɪˈzentətɪv/ adj
1 typical of people or things in a particular group ≠ UNREPRESENTATIVE: *His views are not representative of the majority of the population.* **2** a representative form of government is one in which people vote for their politicians

Rep•re•sen•ta•tive /ˌreprɪˈzentətɪv/ noun [C] a politician who is a member of the U.S. House of Representatives

re•press /rɪˈpres/ verb [T] **1** to prevent yourself from showing a feeling **2** to use force to control people —**re•pres•sion** noun [U]

re•pressed /rɪˈprest/ adj having feelings that you do not show or do not admit that you have

re•pres•sive /rɪˈpresɪv/ adj ruling or controlling people with force or violence

re•prieve /rɪˈpriv/ noun [C] an official decision not to kill someone who was going to be killed as a punishment for a crime

rep•ri•mand /ˈreprɪˌmænd/ verb [T] to tell someone officially that something that they have done is wrong —**rep•ri•mand** noun [C]

re•print[1] /ˌriˈprɪnt/ verb [T] to make more copies of a book

re•print[2] /ˈriˌprɪnt/ noun [C] a book that has been reprinted

re•pri•sal /rɪˈpraɪz(ə)l/ noun [C/U] something unpleasant that is done to punish an enemy for something that they have done to you

re•proach[1] /rɪˈproʊtʃ/ noun [C/U] a criticism that you make of someone because of something bad that they have done
PHRASE **beyond reproach** impossible to criticize because of being so good —**re•proach•ful** adj, **re•proach•ful•ly** adv

re•proach[2] /rɪˈproʊtʃ/ verb [T] to criticize someone for something that they have done

re•pro•cess /ˌriˈprɑˌses/ verb [T] to process a waste substance so that it can be used again

re•pro•duce /ˌriprəˈdus/ verb **1** [T] to make a copy of something, or to repeat something **2** [I/T] to have babies, or to produce young animals or plants

re•pro•duc•tion /ˌriprəˈdʌkʃ(ə)n/ noun **1** [U] the

process of having babies or producing young animals or plants **2** [C] a copy of something, especially a work of art

re•pro•duc•tive /ˌriprəˈdʌktɪv/ adj relating to sex, or to the process of having babies or producing young animals or plants

rep•tile /ˈreptɪl/ noun [C] a type of animal such as a snake or LIZARD that lays eggs, and whose body is covered in SCALES (=flat hard pieces of skin) —**rep•til•i•an** /repˈtɪliən/ adj

re•pub•lic /rɪˈpʌblɪk/ noun [C] ★ a country that is not ruled by a king or queen

re•pub•li•can /rɪˈpʌblɪkən/ noun [C] someone who thinks that their country should not have a king or queen —**re•pub•li•can** adj

Re•pub•li•can /rɪˈpʌblɪkən/ noun [C] someone who supports the Republican Party —**Re•pub•li•can** adj

Reˈpublican ˌParty, the one of the two main political parties in the U.S.

re•pu•di•ate /rɪˈpjudiˌeɪt/ verb [T] *formal* to say formally that something is not true, or that you do not accept it —**re•pu•di•a•tion** /rɪˌpjudiˈeɪʃ(ə)n/ noun [U]

re•pug•nant /rɪˈpʌgnənt/ adj *formal* extremely unpleasant or offensive

re•pulse /rɪˈpʌls/ verb [T] *formal* **1** if someone or something repulses you, you think that they are very unpleasant **2** to stop a military attack

re•pul•sion /rɪˈpʌlʃən/ noun [U] a strong feeling of dislike

re•pul•sive /rɪˈpʌlsɪv/ adj extremely unpleasant = DISGUSTING

rep•u•ta•ble /ˈrepjətəb(ə)l/ adj generally considered to be honest and reliable

rep•u•ta•tion /ˌrepjəˈteɪʃ(ə)n/ noun [C/U] ★★ the opinion people have about how good or bad someone or something is: *The town has **a bad reputation**.* ♦ *Our university has an international **reputation as** a center of excellence.*

> **Words often used with reputation**
>
> *Verbs often used with **reputation***
> - **acquire, build, develop, earn, establish, gain, get** + REPUTATION: get a reputation

re•pute /rɪˈpjut/ noun [U] *formal* the reputation that someone or something has

re•put•ed /rɪˈpjutɪd/ adj *formal* said or believed by a lot of people, but not definitely true —**re•put•ed•ly** adv

re•quest¹ /rɪˈkwest/ noun [C] ★★
1 an act of asking for something in a polite or formal way: *Catalogs are available **on request*** (=if you ask). ♦ ***Requests for** visas will be dealt with immediately.* ♦ **at sb's request/at the request of sb** *No photographs of the girl were printed, at her parents' request.*
2 a piece of music that you ask a musician or a DJ to play

re•quest² /rɪˈkwest/ verb [T] to ask for something, or to ask someone to do something, in a polite or formal way

re•quire /rɪˈkwaɪər/ verb [T] ★★★
1 to need someone or something: *Working with these children **requires** a great deal of patience.* ♦ *a medical condition **requiring** treatment*
2 if a rule, law, contract, etc. requires something, you must do that thing: *Car insurance **is required by law**.*

re•quire•ment /rɪˈkwaɪrmənt/ noun [C] ★★★ something that is necessary, or that a rule or law says that you must do: ***a list of safety requirements*** ♦ *Check the car's fuel requirements.*

> **Words often used with requirement**
>
> *Adjectives often used with **requirement***
> - **basic, essential, legal, minimum, statutory** + REQUIREMENT: used about different types of requirement
> - **comply with, fulfill, match, meet, satisfy, suit** + REQUIREMENT: do what is necessary

req•ui•site /ˈrekwɪzɪt/ adj *formal* necessary for a particular purpose

re•re•lease /ˌririˈlis/ verb [T] to make something such as a movie or CD available to the public for a second time —**re•re•lease** noun [C/U]

re•route /ˌriˈrut, ˌriˈraʊt/ verb [T] to send something along a different path than usual

re•run /ˈriˌrʌn/ noun [C] **1** a movie or television program that is being shown again **2** something that happens again in a similar way as before

re•sale /ˈriˌseɪl, ˌriˈseɪl/ noun [U] a situation in which someone sells something that they have bought previously

re•sched•ule /riˈskedʒəl/ verb [T] to change the time when something is planned to happen

res•cue¹ /ˈreskju/ verb [T] ★
1 to save someone from a dangerous or unpleasant situation: *The crew of the ship were rescued just before it sank.*
2 to prevent a business, project, etc. from failing: *an attempt to rescue the peace process*
—**res•cu•er** noun [C]

rescue

res•cue² /ˈreskju/ noun [C/U] ★ an act of saving someone or something from danger or from an unpleasant situation: *Soldiers carried out a dramatic rescue of the hostages last night.*

re•search¹ /rɪˈsɜrtʃ, ˈriˌsɜrtʃ/ noun [U] ★★ the detailed study of something in order to discover new facts: *medical/historical/linguistic research* ♦ *a research project/program* ♦ *He did some **research into** the causes of lung cancer.* → MARKET RESEARCH

Words often used with research

*Verbs often used with **research** (noun)*

- **carry out, conduct, undertake** + RESEARCH: to do research

re·search² /rɪˈsɜrtʃ, ˈriˌsɜrtʃ/ verb [T] to make a detailed study of something in order to discover new facts —**re·search·er** noun [C]

re·sell /ˌriˈsel/ (past tense and past participle **re·sold** /ˌriˈsoʊld/) verb [T] to sell something that you previously bought

re·sem·blance /rɪˈzembləns/ noun [C/U] if there is a resemblance between two people or things, they are similar

re·sem·ble /rɪˈzemb(ə)l/ verb [T] to be similar to someone or something: *The animals make a sound that resembles a cat's meow.*

re·sent /rɪˈzent/ verb [T] to feel angry because you think that you have been treated unfairly

re·sent·ful /rɪˈzentf(ə)l/ adj feeling angry because you think that you have been treated unfairly —**re·sent·ful·ly** adv

re·sent·ment /rɪˈzentmənt/ noun [U] an angry feeling that you have when you think that you have been treated unfairly: *The decision caused a lot of resentment among employees.*

res·er·va·tion /ˌrezərˈveɪʃ(ə)n/ noun ★
1 [C] an arrangement to have something such as a room in a hotel or a seat in a theater kept for you to use = BOOKING: *Do you have a reservation?* ♦ ***I made a reservation for** you on the morning flight.*
2 [C/U] a feeling of doubt about whether something is good or right: *I have some reservations about the plan.*
3 [C] an area of land in the U.S. where NATIVE AMERICANS live as a separate community

re·serve¹ /rɪˈzɜrv/ noun **1** [C] a supply of something that a country, an organization, or a person can use: *Norway's oil reserves* ♦ *We discovered reserves of strength that we didn't realize we had.* **2** [U] the behavior of someone who tends not to talk about or show their feelings
PHRASE **in reserve** available to be used

re·serve² /rɪˈzɜrv/ verb ★
1 [I/T] to make an arrangement so that something such as a room in a hotel or a seat in a theater is kept for you to use: *We've reserved a table for 7:30.*
2 [T] to keep something for a particular person, purpose, or situation: **reserve sth for sb/sth** *This area is reserved for non-smokers.*
PHRASE **reserve judgement** to not form an opinion about someone or something until you have more information

re·served /rɪˈzɜrvd/ adj **1** someone who is reserved tends not to talk about or show their feelings **2** available to be used only by a particular person or group

res·er·voir /ˈrezərˌvwɑ/ noun [C] a lake, often an artificial one, where water is stored so that it can be supplied to houses, factories, etc.

re·set /ˌriˈset/ (past tense and past participle **re·set**) verb [T] **1** to press a special button, or to make changes, so that a machine will work again or will work in a different way **2** to put a broken bone back into its correct position

re·set·tle /ˌriˈset(ə)l/ verb [I/T] to go to live in a different region or country, or to be moved to a different region or country —**re·set·tle·ment** noun [U]

re·shape /ˌriˈʃeɪp/ verb [T] **1** to change the shape of something **2** to change the way that something operates

re·shuf·fle /ˌriˈʃʌf(ə)l, ˈriʃʌf(ə)l/ verb [T] to change the jobs of the people in an organization —**re·shuffle** /ˈriʃʌf(ə)l/ noun [C]

re·side /rɪˈzaɪd/ verb [I] *formal* to live in a particular place

res·i·dence /ˈrezɪdəns/ noun [C] *formal* ★ a house or other place where someone lives: *the President's official residence*
PHRASE **in residence** living or working somewhere

res·i·den·cy /ˈrezɪdənsi/ noun **1** [U] the legal right to live in a country **2** [C/U] *American* a period of time a doctor spends working in a hospital learning more about a particular type of medical treatment

res·i·dent /ˈrezɪdənt/ noun [C] ★★
1 someone who lives in a particular place: *Many **local residents** have objected to the new road.* ♦ *They are both **residents of** the same dormitory.*
2 *American* a junior doctor working in a hospital
—**res·i·dent** adj

res·i·den·tial /ˌrezɪˈdenʃ(ə)l/ adj a residential area is one in which most of the buildings are houses

re·sid·u·al /rɪˈzɪdjuəl/ adj remaining after the rest of something has gone

res·i·due /ˈrezɪdu/ noun [C] the part of something that remains after the rest has gone

re·sign /rɪˈzaɪn/ verb [I/T] ★ to state formally that you are leaving your job: *He was forced **to resign as** mayor.*
PHRASE **resign yourself (to sth)** to accept that something unpleasant must happen and that you cannot change it: *I resigned myself to the fact that I'd never be thin.*

res·ig·na·tion /ˌrezɪgˈneɪʃ(ə)n/ noun **1** [C/U] the act of leaving a job permanently: *The scandal resulted in Allen's resignation from his post.* **2** [U] the attitude of someone who accepts that something unpleasant must happen and that they cannot change it

re·signed /rɪˈzaɪnd/ adj accepting that something unpleasant must happen and that you cannot change it

re·sil·ient /rɪˈzɪljənt/ adj **1** a resilient substance or object can return to its original shape after being bent, stretched, or pressed **2** able to quickly become healthy or strong again after an illness or a problem —**re·sil·ience** noun [U]

res·in /ˈrezɪn/ noun [U] a transparent sticky substance that is used for making paints, glue, and plastic

re·sist /rɪˈzɪst/ verb ★★
1 [T] to oppose someone or something, or to fight against them: *Antibodies help us resist infection.* ♦ *One protester was injured while **resisting arrest**.*
2 [I/T] to stop yourself from doing something that you would like to do: *It's difficult to resist a challenge like that.* ♦ **resist doing sth**

R

She couldn't resist asking him about his date.
3 [T] to not be affected or harmed by something: *The bomb shelters are designed to* ***resist heat.***

re·sis·tance /rɪˈzɪstəns/ noun ★★

1 not being affected	4 force
2 refusal of sth new	5 opposition group
3 opposition to sb/sth	

1 [singular/U] the ability not to be affected or harmed by something: *water resistance* ♦ *Vitamin A helps build* ***resistance to*** *infection.*
2 [singular/U] a refusal to accept something: *political resistance* ♦ *This proposal is* ***meeting*** *some* ***resistance*** (=some people do not accept it) *in the U.N.*
3 [singular/U] military opposition to someone who is attacking you: *There was some resistance in the north.*
4 [U] a force that slows down a moving object: *wind resistance*
5 [singular] a secret organization that fights against the group that controls their country

re·sis·tant /rɪˈzɪstənt/ adj **1** not harmed or affected by something: *a flame-resistant material* **2** opposed to something

resold the past tense and past participle of resell

res·o·lute /ˈrezəlut/ adj extremely determined —**res·o·lute·ly** adv

res·o·lu·tion /ˌrezəˈluʃ(ə)n/ noun ★
1 [C] a formal proposal that is considered by an organization and then voted on: *The U.N.* ***passed a resolution*** (=formally accepted it) *condemning the country's actions.*
2 [U] the act of solving a problem or of dealing with a disagreement: *a peaceful* ***resolution of*** *the conflict*
3 [C] a serious decision to do something: *I made a resolution to lose 15 pounds.*
4 [U] *technical* the amount of detail that you can see on a television or computer screen

re·solve[1] /rɪˈzɑlv/ verb **1** [I] *formal* to make a determined decision to do something **2** [T] to solve a problem, or to find a way of dealing with a disagreement

re·solve[2] /rɪˈzɑlv/ noun [U] *formal* determination

re·sort[1] /rɪˈzɔrt/ noun [C] a place where people go for a vacation: *a ski resort*
PHRASE **(as) a last resort** used for saying that you will do something only after trying everything else to solve a problem: *We would only expel a student as a last resort.*

re·sort[2] /rɪˈzɔrt/ PHRASAL VERB **reˈsort to sth** to do something extreme or unpleasant in order to solve a problem: *protest groups that resort to violence*

re·sound·ing /rɪˈzaʊndɪŋ/ adj **1** a resounding victory, success, defeat etc. is a very definite one **2** very loud

re·source /ˈrizɔrs/ noun ★★★
1 [C] something that you can use to achieve something: *We are increasing resources for our emergency services.* ♦ *The Internet has become* ***a valuable resource*** *in schools.* ♦ ***a lack of educational resources***
2 [C] things that exist in nature and can be used by people: *Many of these countries are rich in mineral resources.*
3 resources [plural] the skills that someone has that they can use for dealing with problems: *He needed all his resources to escape alive.*

re·source·ful /rɪˈzɔrsf(ə)l/ adj good at finding effective ways to deal with problems

re·spect[1] /rɪˈspekt/ noun [U] ★★★
1 the attitude that someone is important and should be admired, and that you should treat them politely: *She has worked hard to* ***gain the respect of*** *her peers.* ♦ *Students* ***show their respect for*** *the teacher by not talking.* ♦ *Children should* ***treat*** *their parents* ***with respect.***
2 respect for sth a feeling that something is important and deserves serious attention: *a healthy respect for the law*
3 an aspect of something: ***In many respects,*** *we are no different from other people.*
PHRASES **with all (due) respect** used for showing that you are going to disagree with someone in a polite way: *With all due respect, I think you're missing the point.*
with respect to *formal* concerning: *The two groups are very similar with respect to age.*

re·spect[2] /rɪˈspekt/ verb [T] ★★
1 to treat someone in a way that shows that you think they are important and should be admired: *He is highly respected in his profession.* ♦ **respect sb for (doing) sth** *People will respect you for telling the truth.*
2 to understand the importance of something: *a promise to respect the rights of minorities*

Word family: respect

Words in the same family as ***respect***

- **respectable** *adj*
- **respectful** *adj*
- **respectability** *n*
- **disrespectful** *adj*
- **respectably** *adv*
- **respectfully** *adv*
- **respected** *adj*
- **disrespect** *n*

re·spect·a·ble /rɪˈspektəb(ə)l/ adj **1** keeping to the accepted moral standards of your society, and not doing anything shocking or illegal **2** if an amount is respectable it is enough: *a respectable salary* —**re·spect·a·bil·i·ty** /rɪˌspektəˈbɪləti/ noun [U], **re·spect·a·bly** adv

re·spect·ed /rɪˈspektəd/ adj admired and approved of by many people

re·spect·ful /rɪˈspektf(ə)l/ adj treating someone with respect —**re·spect·ful·ly** adv

re·spec·tive /rɪˈspektɪv/ adj belonging to each of the people or things that you mentioned previously: *Jane and Patrick talked about their respective childhoods.*

re·spec·tive·ly /rɪˈspektɪvli/ adv in the same order as the people or things you have mentioned: *Walsh and O'Neill were jailed for 12 and 11 years respectively.*

res·pi·ra·tor /ˈrespəˌreɪtər/ noun [C] a machine that is used for helping people to breathe

res·pi·ra·to·ry /ˈresp(ə)rəˌtɔri/ adj *medical* relating to the process of breathing —**res·pi·ra·tion** /ˌrespəˈreɪʃ(ə)n/ noun [U]

res·pite /ˈrespɪt/ noun [singular/U] a short period of time in which a difficult or unpleasant situation stops

R

re·spond /rɪˈspɑnd/ verb [I] ★★
1 to react to something by doing or saying something: *She hugged him, but he didn't respond.*
2 to reply, especially in writing: *Thousands of readers **responded to** our questionnaire.*
3 to react well to medical treatment: *The infection should **respond to** antibiotics.*

re·sponse /rɪˈspɑns/ noun [C] ★★★
1 a reaction: *Her response was to leave the room and slam the door.* ♦ *There was an enthusiastic **response to** the suggestions.* ♦ ***In response to** complaints, the company reviewed its safety procedures.*
2 an answer to a question in a test: *I'm sorry; the correct response was "B."*
3 a reply to a question or letter: *I've left messages, but there's been **no response**.*

re·spon·si·bil·i·ty /rɪˌspɑnsəˈbɪləti/ noun [U] ★★★
1 something that you have to do as a duty or a job: *She has a lot of responsibility as a nurse.* ♦ *Overall **responsibility for** the school lies with the principal.* ♦ *You will **have responsibility for** marketing.*
2 blame for something bad that has happened: *Allan has to **take responsibility for** the failure of the deal.* ♦ *No one has **accepted responsibility for** the attack on the embassy.*

re·spon·si·ble /rɪˈspɑnsəb(ə)l/ adj ★★★
1 if you are responsible for something that has happened, you caused it, or you deserve to be blamed for it: *Parents **feel responsible** when things go wrong.* ♦ *He was **responsible for** the accident.* ♦ *The farmer **was held responsible for** the damage done by his animals.*
2 in charge of someone or something: *The manager is **responsible for** the running of the theater.*
3 sensible, reliable, and able to be trusted ≠ IRRESPONSIBLE: *She may be only 14, but she's very responsible.*

re·spon·si·bly /rɪˈspɑnsəbli/ adv in a sensible way that shows that you can be trusted

re·spon·sive /rɪˈspɑnsɪv/ adj **1** quick to react in the way that is right for a particular situation **2** willing to reply to a question or talk about something

rest¹ /rest/ noun ★★★
1 [singular] the part of something that remains, or the people or things that remain: *I'm not really hungry – do you want **the rest**?* ♦ *Rain will spread to **the rest of** the northeast by evening.*
2 [C/U] a period of time that you spend relaxing or sleeping: *Can we stop for a minute? I need a rest.* ♦ *You should **get some rest**.*
PHRASES **come to rest** to finally stop moving: *The car skidded across the road before coming to rest against a wall.*
set/put sb's mind at rest to stop someone from worrying: *Tell me what happened, just to put my mind at rest.*

rest² /rest/ verb ★★★
1 [I] to spend a period of time relaxing or sleeping: *It would be nice to sit down and rest for a while.*
2 [T] to put something somewhere for support, especially a part of your body: *John was asleep, with his head resting on my shoulder.* ♦ *He rested the bag on the desk.*
3 [T] to not use a part of your body that is tired or injured, so that it can get better: *You'll need to rest your foot for at least two days.*
→ ASSURED
PHRASAL VERB ˈ**rest with sb** if a decision or responsibility rests with someone, they are the person that should decide it or deal with it: *Responsibility for child welfare rests with the government.*

ˈ**rest ˌarea** noun [C] *American* a place beside a highway where drivers can stop and get food, use the bathrooms, etc.

res·tau·rant /ˈrest(ə)rənt/ noun [C] ★★★ a building or room where meals and drinks are sold to customers sitting at tables: *an Italian/Mexican restaurant* → CAFÉ

rest·ed /ˈrestəd/ adj feeling full of energy again because you have had a rest

rest·ful /ˈrestf(ə)l/ adj relaxing and peaceful

rest·less /ˈres(t)ləs/ adj **1** not willing or not able to keep still **2** not satisfied with the way that you are living and wanting to have new experiences —**rest·less·ly** adv, **rest·less·ness** noun [U]

re·store /rɪˈstɔr/ verb [T] ★★
1 to make something exist again: *The government is trying to **restore confidence** in the country's economy.* ♦ *Doctors say there's a possibility that his **sight** can be **restored**.*
2 to clean and repair something that is old and dirty or damaged: *The church has now been beautifully restored.*
3 to give something back to the person that it belongs to after it has been lost, taken, or stolen: *Most of the land has been restored to its original owners.*
—**res·to·ra·tion** /ˌrestəˈreɪʃ(ə)n/ noun [C/U]

re·strain /rɪˈstreɪn/ verb [T] **1** to stop yourself or someone else from doing something **2** to control the movements of a person or animal

re·strained /rɪˈstreɪnd/ adj controlled and not emotional

re·strain·ing or·der /rɪˈstreɪnɪŋ ˌɔrdər/ noun [C] a legal document issued by a judge that stops someone from doing something

re·straint /rɪˈstreɪnt/ noun **1** [U] an attempt to control your emotions, or to not do what you would like to do **2** [C/U] something that limits what you can do

re·strict /rɪˈstrɪkt/ verb [T] ★★
1 to keep something within strict limits: **restrict sth to sth** *Doctors have restricted the number of visits to two per day.*
2 to physically limit or control the movement of something: *The drug restricts blood flow.*

re·strict·ed /rɪˈstrɪktəd/ adj **1** a restricted area is one that only particular people can go into: *This is a restricted area.* **2** not able to develop, to happen, or to do things freely: *Freedom of the press is restricted here.*

re·stric·tion /rɪˈstrɪkʃ(ə)n/ noun [C] something, for example a law, that limits what you can do

re·stric·tive /rɪˈstrɪktɪv/ adj strictly limiting or controlling something

rest•room /ˈrestˌrum/ noun [C] *American* a room with a toilet in it, especially in a public building

re•struc•ture /ˌriˈstrʌktʃər/ verb [T] to change the way that a company is organized —**re•struc•tur•ing** noun [C/U]

re•sult[1] /rɪˈzʌlt/ noun ★★★

1 sth caused by sth else	4 success from actions
2 information obtained	5 financial document
3 votes in election	

1 [C/U] something that is caused directly by something else: *He said the argument was **the result of** a misunderstanding.* ♦ *York Road will be closed and delays are likely **as a result**.* ♦ *Colby died **as the result of** a heart attack.* ♦ *Whichever method you use, **the end result** is the same.*
2 [C] a piece of information that you get by examining, studying, or calculating something: ***The results of** the survey will be published shortly.*
3 results [plural] the number of votes that someone gets in an election: *We'll see who controls Congress when **the results are in*** (=when the winner is announced).
4 results [plural] success that you achieve: *He breaks rules, but he **gets results**.*
5 results [plural] *business* a financial document that shows how well a company has done over a particular period of time

re•sult[2] /rɪˈzʌlt/ verb [I] ★★★ to be caused directly by something that happened previously: *The arrests **resulted from** an anonymous telephone call.*
PHRASAL VERB **reˈsult ˌin sth** to cause or produce something: *The crash resulted in the deaths of 14 passengers.*

re•su•me /rɪˈzum/ verb [I/T] *formal* to start something again after stopping temporarily, or to be started again after stopping temporarily: *Tom resumed his work.* ♦ *Talks will resume today.*

ré•su•mé /ˈrezuˌmeɪ/ noun [C] *American* a document giving details of your educational qualifications and work experience

re•sump•tion /rɪˈzʌmpʃ(ə)n/ noun [singular/U] *formal* the act of starting something again after it had stopped

re•sur•face /ˌriˈsɜrfɪs/ verb **1** [I] to start to be noticed, or to start to be seen again: *Old tensions between the two countries have recently resurfaced.* **2** [I] to come back up to the surface of water **3** [T] to replace the surface of something such as a road

res•ur•rect /ˌrezəˈrekt/ verb [T] **1** to make something exist again or start to be used again **2** to bring someone back to life after they are dead —**res•ur•rec•tion** noun [singular/U]

re•sus•ci•tate /rɪˈsʌsɪˌteɪt/ verb [T] to make an unconscious person start to breathe again —**re•sus•ci•ta•tion** /rɪˌsʌsɪˈteɪʃ(ə)n/ noun [U]

re•tail[1] /ˈriteɪl/ adj relating to the sale of goods directly to the public for their own use: *a retail outlet* (=a store) → WHOLESALE —**re•tail** adv

re•tail[2] /ˈriteɪl/ noun [U] the sale of goods directly to the public for their own use

re•tail•er /ˈriˌteɪlər/ noun [C] a person or company that sells goods directly to the public → WHOLESALER

re•tail•ing /ˈriˌteɪlɪŋ/ noun [U] the business of selling goods directly to the public

re•tain /rɪˈteɪn/ verb [T] *formal* **1** to keep someone or something: *We're trying to recruit and retain skilled staff.* **2** to remember ideas or information

re•take /ˌriˈteɪk/ (past tense **re•took** /ˌriˈtʊk/; past participle **re•tak•en** /ˌriˈteɪkən/) verb [T] **1** to take control of something, or to get something again, after you have lost it: *The army launched an operation to retake land captured by rebels.* **2** to take an examination again because you did not pass it the first time

re•tal•i•ate /rɪˈtæliˌeɪt/ verb [I] to do something unpleasant to someone because they did something unpleasant to you —**re•tal•i•a•tion** /rɪˌtæliˈeɪʃ(ə)n/ noun [U]

re•ten•tion /rɪˈtenʃ(ə)n/ noun [U] *formal* **1** the act of keeping something **2** the ability to remember ideas or facts

re•think /ˌriˈθɪŋk/ (past tense and past participle **re•thought** /ˌriˈθɔt/) verb [I/T] to think about something such as an idea, plan, or system again in order to change it

ret•i•cent /ˈretɪsənt/ adj not willing to talk or provide information about something —**ret•i•cence** noun [U]

ret•i•na /ˈretɪnə/ noun [C] the part at the back of your eye that sends light signals to the brain

ret•i•nue /ˈret(ə)nˌu/ noun [C] a group of people who travel with and take care of an important person

re•tire /rɪˈtaɪr/ verb [I] ★★
1 to stop working permanently, especially when you are old: *He **retired from** the army last month.* ♦ *Mrs. Kenny **retired as** principal in July.*
2 *formal* to leave a place in order to go somewhere quieter: *In the evenings, Lloyd **retired to** his study to write.*

re•tired /rɪˈtaɪrd/ adj no longer working at a job, especially when you are old: *a retired teacher/police officer*

re•tir•ee /rɪˌtaɪˈri/ noun [C] *American* someone who has stopped working, especially because they have reached the age when they can stop

re•tire•ment /rɪˈtaɪrmənt/ noun [C/U] the time after you permanently stop working, or the act of permanently stopping work: *her retirement from politics*

re•tir•ing /rɪˈtaɪrɪŋ/ adj shy and not likely to enjoy social activities

retook the past tense of **retake**

re•tort /rɪˈtɔrt/ verb [T] to reply immediately in an angry or humorous way —**re•tort** noun [C]

re•trace /ˌriˈtreɪs/ verb **retrace your steps** to return along the same path that you have just traveled along

re•tract /rɪˈtrækt/ verb [I/T] to say that something that you previously said is not true —**re•trac•tion** /rɪˈtrækʃən/ noun [C/U]

re•train /ˌriˈtreɪn/ verb [I/T] to learn, or to teach someone, new skills that are needed for a job —**re•train•ing** noun [U]

R

re•treat¹ /rɪ'trit/ verb [I] **1** to move back in order to avoid a dangerous or unpleasant situation: *The army was forced to retreat.* **2** to change your previous opinion or decision about something, especially because of opposition to it

re•treat² /rɪ'trit/ noun **1** [C/U] an act of moving back in order to avoid a dangerous or unpleasant situation **2** [C/U] a change in someone's opinion or decision, especially because there is opposition to it **3** [C] a peaceful and private place where you can go in order to rest

re•tri•al /'ri,traɪəl/ noun [C] a second trial in a court of law because the first one was unfair, or because it did not have a definite result

ret•ri•bu•tion /,retrɪ'bjuʃ(ə)n/ noun [U] severe punishment for something bad, especially one that you think someone deserves

re•trieve /rɪ'triv/ verb [T] **1** *formal* to go and get something back: *Bobby waded out into the lake to retrieve the ball.* **2** *computing* to find information that is stored in a computer —**re•triev•al** noun [U]

ret•ro•ac•tive /,retroʊ'æktɪv/ adj a retroactive law or decision affects things that have happened since a particular date in the past, before the law was introduced or the decision was made —**ret•ro•ac•tive•ly** adv

ret•ro•spect /'retroʊspekt/ noun **in retrospect** used for saying that, when you think about a situation in the past, you would have done something differently if you had known then what you know now: *In retrospect, I should have told her the truth.*

ret•ro•spec•tive¹ /,retroʊ'spektɪv/ adj relating to things that have already happened or that have already been done: *a retrospective study/analysis* —**ret•ro•spec•tive•ly** adv

R

ret•ro•spec•tive² /,retroʊ'spektɪv/ noun [C] an exhibit that includes examples of an artist's work from their whole career

re•try /,ri'traɪ/ verb **1** [T] to judge someone in a court of law again because a previous trial was unfair, or because it ended without a definite result **2** [I] to try to do something again after the first attempt was not successful

re•turn¹ /rɪ'tɜrn/ verb ★★★

1 go/come back	4 go back to activity
2 put/send sth back	5 do/say sth similar back
3 start to happen again	+ PHRASE

1 [I] to go back to a place where you were earlier, or to come back from a place where you have just been: *He **returned home** around midnight.* ♦ *Seven years later we **returned to the village**.* ♦ *And when do you **return from** Paris?*

2 [T] to put, send, or take something back to the place where it came from: *She had to return the dress because it didn't fit.* ♦ **return sth to sb** *Please complete the questionnaire and return it to the personnel department.*

3 [I] to go back to a previous state or situation: *Once the holidays were over, our lives **returned to** normal.*

4 [I] to go back to a previous activity or subject: *She looked up, then **returned to** her reading.* ♦ *I'd like to **return to** what David was saying earlier.*

5 [T] to do or say something to someone that is similar to something that they have done or said to you: *I'm sorry I wasn't able to **return your phone call** earlier.* ♦ *Thanks for helping me. I'll try to **return the favor** some day.*

PHRASE **return a verdict** to say whether someone is guilty or not guilty of a crime in a court of law: *After several hours the jury **returned a verdict** of not guilty.*

re•turn² /rɪ'tɜrn/ noun ★★★

1 going/coming back	5 ticket
2 of activity/condition	6 official (tax) form
3 sending etc. sth back	+ PHRASE
4 profit	

1 [singular/U] a situation in which you go back to a place or come back from a place: *Harry had met Olivia shortly after his **return from** India.* ♦ *John was packing for his **return to** London.*

2 [singular/U] a situation in which a previous activity or condition starts again: *the country's **return to** democratic rule* ♦ *After a long winter, they eagerly awaited the **return of** spring.*

3 [C/U] the action of putting, sending, or taking something back to the place where it came from: *A reward is offered for the safe **return of** the medal.*

4 [C/U] a profit on money that you have invested: *We were able to get **a return of** 10% on our investment.*

5 [C] *British* a ROUND-TRIP

6 [C] an official form on which you say how much your income is, so that the amount of tax that you owe can be calculated

PHRASE **in return** as a payment, exchange, or way of thanking someone: *What can we do **in return** for your kindness?*

re•u•ni•fi•ca•tion /ri,junɪfə'keɪʃ(ə)n/ noun [U] the process of joining together parts of a country that were divided, so that they form one country again

re•un•ion /,ri'junjən/ noun **1** [C] a social event for people who have not seen each other for a long time: *a family reunion* **2** [C/U] a situation in which people meet again after a time when they have been separated

re•u•nite /,riju'naɪt/ verb [I/T] to bring people or groups together again after they have been separated for a time, or to be brought together again after being separated for a time

re•use /,ri'juz/ verb [T] to use something again —**re•us•a•ble** adj

rev /rev/ or **,rev (sth) 'up** verb [I/T] if you rev an engine, or if it revs, you press the GAS PEDAL with your foot when the vehicle is not moving in order to make the engine operate faster

Rev. abbrev Reverend

re•vamp /,ri'væmp/ verb [T] *informal* to improve the way that something looks or operates by making major changes to it —**re•vamp** noun [C]

re•veal /rɪ'vil/ verb [T] ★★★

1 to let something become known that was previously not known: *Cockpit recordings*

may reveal the cause of the crash. ♦ **+how/what etc.** *Neither side revealed what was discussed in the meeting.* ♦ **reveal sth to sb** *Plans for rerouting traffic have been revealed to residents.* ♦ **+(that)** *The survey revealed that many consumers are aware of the risks involved.*
2 to show something that was covered or hidden: *She pulled back the curtain to reveal a table.*

re•veal•ing /rɪˈvilɪŋ/ adj **1** providing new, surprising, or important information **2** showing a part of someone's body that is usually covered

rev•el /ˈrevl/ PHRASAL VERB ˈ**revel ˌin sth** to enjoy something very much

rev•e•la•tion /ˌrevəˈleɪʃ(ə)n/ noun [C] a surprising piece of information: *revelations about his private life*

rev•el•er /ˈrev(ə)lər/ noun [C] someone who enjoys themselves at a lively and noisy party or celebration

re•venge /rɪˈvendʒ/ noun [U] something that you do in order to hurt or punish someone because they have hurt you or someone else: *I wanted to get revenge for the attack.*

rev•e•nue /ˈrevənju/ noun [C/U] income from business activities or taxes

re•ver•ber•ate /rɪˈvɜrbəˌreɪt/ verb [I] if a sound reverberates, it is repeated many times as it hits two opposite surfaces —**re•ver•ber•a•tion** /rɪˌvɜrbəˈreɪʃ(ə)n/ noun [C/U]

re•vere /rɪˈvɪr/ verb [T] *formal* to have a lot of respect and admiration for someone or something

rev•er•ence /ˈrev(ə)rəns/ noun [U] a strong feeling of respect and admiration

Rev•er•end /ˈrev(ə)rənd/ a title that is used for some Christian priests and MINISTERS

rev•er•ie /ˈrevəri/ noun [C/U] *literary* pleasant thoughts that make you forget what is happening around you

re•ver•sal /rɪˈvɜrs(ə)l/ noun [C/U] a change in something, so that it becomes the opposite of what it was: *The decision was a complete reversal of the old policy.*

re•verse¹ /rɪˈvɜrs/ verb ★
1 [T] to change something such as a process, situation, decision, or policy so that it becomes the opposite of what it was: *The judge reversed the court's previous decision.* ♦ *products that claim to reverse the effects of aging*
2 [I/T] to go BACKWARD in a vehicle, or to make a vehicle do this: *She* ***reversed into*** *the parking space.*
3 [T] to trade your status with that of another person: *He's always taught me, but now the* ***roles are reversed*** *and I can teach him.*
4 [T] to turn something so that the part that is usually on the outside is on the inside: *You can reverse the jacket so that the pattern is on the outside.*

re•verse² /rɪˈvɜrs/ adj opposite to what is usual or to what existed previously: *Now arrange the numbers in reverse order.*

re•verse³ /rɪˈvɜrs/ noun **1 the reverse** [singular] the opposite of something: *The situation is the reverse of what it seems.* **2 the reverse** [singular] the back side of a flat object **3** [U] the position in which you put a GEAR in a vehicle in order to make it go BACKWARD: *Put the car in reverse.*

ˈ**reverse ˌlight** noun [C] *American* a light at the back of a car that warns other drivers that it is going backward —*picture* → C6

re•vers•i•ble /rɪˈvɜrsəb(ə)l/ adj **1** able to return or to be changed to a previous state ≠ IRREVERSIBLE: *The effects of the treatment are reversible.* **2** able to be used or worn with either side facing out: *a reversible jacket*

re•vert /rɪˈvɜrt/ PHRASAL VERB reˈ**vert to sth** to return to a previous state or way of behaving: *If you revert to your old eating habits, you'll gain weight again.*

re•view¹ /rɪˈvju/ verb ★★
1 [T] to examine something again in order to check it or make a decision about it: *After reviewing the evidence, the committee decided he had a strong case.* ♦ *The progress of each child must be regularly reviewed.*
2 [T] to write an article giving your opinion of a play, book, exhibit, etc.
3 [I/T] *American* to study your notes and course information again in order to prepare for a test: *We spent most of the class reviewing for the test.*

re•view² /rɪˈvju/ noun ★★
1 [C/U] the process of examining something again in order to check it or make a decision about it: *Several aspects of prison practices are currently* ***under review.*** ♦ *The administration announced* ***a review of all*** *government policies affecting the environment.*
2 [C] an article in which someone gives their opinion of a play, book, exhibit, etc.: *The movie* ***got really good reviews.***
3 [C] *American* a discussion of a particular subject that prepares you for a test

re•view•er /rɪˈvjuər/ noun [C] someone whose job is to write articles giving their opinion about plays, books, exhibits, etc.

re•vile /rɪˈvaɪl/ verb [T] *formal* to hate and criticize someone or something very much

re•vise /rɪˈvaɪz/ verb [T] to change, improve, or make additions to something: *a revised draft of the treaty*

re•vi•sion /rɪˈvɪʒ(ə)n/ noun [C/U] the process of changing, improving, or making additions to something: *He intends to undertake a major revision of the constitution.* ♦ *The article was published with a few revisions.*

re•vi•tal•ize /ˌriˈvaɪt(ə)lˌaɪz/ verb [T] **1** to make something that is failing or weak become strong and successful again **2** to make someone feel or look healthy again

re•viv•al /rɪˈvaɪv(ə)l/ noun **1** [C/U] the process of becoming active, successful, or popular again: *a revival of interest in the subject* **2** [C] a new performance of something that has not been performed for a long time, such as a play

re•vive /rɪˈvaɪv/ verb [I/T] **1** to make someone become conscious or alive again, or to become conscious or alive again: *She had fainted, but soon revived.* **2** to become active, successful, or popular again, or to make something do this: *Jenkins certainly has the ability to revive Australian women's tennis.*

re•voke /rɪˈvoʊk/ verb [T] to officially say that a law or legal right no longer exists

re•volt¹ /rɪˈvoʊlt/ verb **1** [I] to try to remove the government of your country by using force **2** [I] to say that you will not accept someone's authority **3** [T] if someone or something revolts you, they are so unpleasant that you feel slightly sick =DISGUST

re•volt² /rɪˈvoʊlt/ noun [C/U] **1** an attempt to remove the government of a country by using force=REBELLION **2** a refusal to accept someone's authority

re•volt•ing /rɪˈvoʊltɪŋ/ adj extremely unpleasant=DISGUSTING

rev•o•lu•tion /ˌrevəˈluʃ(ə)n/ noun ★
1 [C/U] a situation in which people completely change their government or political system, usually by force: *the French/Russian Revolution ♦ a group committed to promoting revolution*
2 [C] a sudden or major change, especially in ideas or methods: *a sexual/cultural revolution ♦ **the revolution in** information technology*
3 [C/U] the movement of something in a circle around something else

rev•o•lu•tion•ar•y¹ /ˌrevəˈluʃ(ə)nˌeri/ adj **1** relating to or supporting a political revolution: *a revolutionary movement* **2** new and completely changing the way that something is done or thought about: *a revolutionary idea*

rev•o•lu•tion•ar•y² /ˌrevəˈluʃ(ə)nˌeri/ noun [C] someone who supports or takes part in a revolution

rev•o•lu•tion•ize /ˌrevəˈluʃ(ə)nˌaɪz/ verb [T] to completely change the way that something is done or thought about

re•volve /rɪˈvɑlv/ verb [I/T] to turn or spin around a central point, or to make something do this —**re•volv•ing** /rɪˈvɑlvɪŋ/ adj

PHRASAL VERB **reˈvolve aˌround sth** to have something as a very important part or purpose: *Her whole life seems to revolve around her job.*

re•volv•er /rɪˈvɑlvər/ noun [C] a small gun that holds several bullets

re•vul•sion /rɪˈvʌlʃən/ noun [U] a feeling of dislike for someone or something that is enough to make you feel slightly sick =DISGUST

re•ward¹ /rɪˈwɔrd/ noun ★
1 [C/U] something good that happens or that you receive because of something that you have done: *Nursing is a tough job, but it **has its rewards**. ♦ You deserve a day off **as a reward for** working so hard.*
2 [C] money that is offered for help in finding someone or something: *There's **a substantial reward for** information leading to his capture.*

re•ward² /rɪˈwɔrd/ verb [T] to give someone something such as praise or money as a reward

re•ward•ing /rɪˈwɔrdɪŋ/ adj giving you satisfaction, pleasure, or profit ≠UNREWARDING: *rewarding work*

re•wind¹ /ˌriˈwaɪnd/ (past tense and past participle **re•wound** /ˌriˈwaʊnd/) verb [I/T] if you rewind a video or a CASSETTE TAPE, or if it rewinds, it goes BACKWARD to the beginning or to an earlier place

re•wind² /ˌriˈwaɪnd/ noun [singular/U] the button that you use in order to rewind a video or a CASSETTE TAPE

re•work /ˌriˈwɜk/ verb [T] to make changes to something in order to improve it or use it for a new purpose

rewound the past tense and past participle of rewind¹

re•write /ˌriˈraɪt/ (past tense **re•wrote** /ˌriˈroʊt/; past participle **re•writ•ten** /ˌriˈrɪt(ə)n/) verb [T] to make changes to a piece of writing, a computer program, or a law

rhet•o•ric /ˈretərɪk/ noun [U] a style of speaking or writing that is intended to influence people: *anti-American rhetoric* —**rhe•tor•i•cal** /rɪˈtɔrɪk(ə)l/ adj, **rhe•tor•i•cal•ly** /rɪˈtɔrɪk(ə)li/ adv

rheˌtorical ˈquestion noun [C] a question that you ask without expecting or wanting an answer

rheu•ma•tism /ˈruməˌtɪzəm/ noun [U] an illness affecting your JOINTS (=where bones are joined) or muscles so that they swell and become stiff and painful

rhine•stone /ˈraɪnˌstoʊn/ noun [C/U] an artificial jewel made of clear glass

rhi•noc•er•os /raɪˈnɑsərəs/ or **rhino** /ˈraɪnoʊ/ noun [C] a large animal with very thick gray skin and one or two horns on its nose —*picture* → C12

rho•do•den•dron /ˌroʊdəˈdendrən/ noun [C/U] a large bush with big flowers and leaves that stay green all year

rhom•bus /ˈrɑmbəs/ noun [C] *technical* a shape with four straight sides of equal length and angles that are not 90° —*picture* → C8

rhu•barb /ˈruˌbɑrb/ noun [U] a plant with long red or pink stems that is cooked and eaten as a fruit

rhyme¹ /raɪm/ noun **1** [C] a short poem, often for children, that has lines ending in the same sound **2** [C] a word that ends with the same sound as another word **3** [U] the use of words that are rhymes, especially in poetry

rhyme² /raɪm/ verb [I] if two words or lines of poetry rhyme, they end with a similar sound: *"Boy" rhymes with "toy."*

rhythm /ˈrɪðəm/ noun [C] ★ a regular pattern of sounds in music: *He tapped out the rhythm on the table.* —**rhyth•mic** /ˈrɪðmɪk/ adj, **rhyth•mi•cal** /ˈrɪðmɪkl/ adj, **rhyth•mi•cal•ly** /ˈrɪðmɪkli/ adv

RI abbrev Rhode Island

rib /rɪb/ noun [C] one of the long curved bones in your chest

ribbed /rɪbd/ adj ribbed material has raised parallel lines on it

rib•bon /ˈrɪbən/ noun **1** [C/U] a long narrow piece of colored cloth or paper that is used for decorating or tying things **2** [C] *American* a piece of colored cloth that is given to someone who has won a prize in a competition **3** [C] a small piece of colored cloth that is worn on a uniform as a military honor

ˈrib ˌcage noun [C] the bones that curve around

and protect the organs in your chest

rice /raɪs/ noun [U] ★ a food consisting of small white or brown grains that are eaten cooked

ˈrice ˌpaddy noun [C] a field covered in water that is used for growing rice

rich /rɪtʃ/ adj ★★★

1 having a lot of money	**5** of land/soil
2 rich people	**6** interesting
3 having a lot of sth	**7** strong and attractive
4 about food	

1 having a lot of money, property, or valuable possessions = WEALTHY ≠ POOR: *a rich man* ♦ *one of the world's richest countries* ♦ *People wanted to **get rich** by investing in Internet companies.*
2 the rich people who have a lot of money, property, or valuable possessions
3 containing a large quantity of something: *a rich source of protein* ♦ *an area **rich in** natural resources*
4 containing a lot of things such as butter, eggs, or cream that make your stomach feel full very quickly: *a rich chocolate dessert*
5 containing a number of substances that are good for growing plants ≠ POOR: *rich agricultural land*
6 interesting, with a lot of different qualities, experiences, or events: *a town with a rich cultural life*
7 a rich color, sound, or smell is strong in a nice way
—**rich•ness** noun [U]

-rich /rɪtʃ/ suffix full of something: *an oil-rich country*

rich•es /ˈrɪtʃɪz/ noun [plural] *literary* large amounts of money, property, or valuable possessions

rich•ly /ˈrɪtʃli/ adv **1** in a beautiful and expensive way: *a richly decorated palace* **2** with pleasant strong colors, flavors, or smells: *richly colored silks* **3** completely: *He gave them the credit that they very richly deserved.* **4** with a lot of money or benefit: *He was richly rewarded for the help he gave.*

rick•et•y /ˈrɪkəti/ adj a rickety structure or piece of furniture is likely to break if you put any weight on it

rick•shaw /ˈrɪkʃɔ/ noun [C] a small vehicle with two wheels that is used for carrying passengers and is pulled by someone riding a bicycle or walking

ric•o•chet /ˈrɪkəʃeɪ/ verb [I] to hit a surface at an angle and immediately move away from it at a different angle —**ric•o•chet** /ˌrɪkəˈʃeɪ/ noun [C]

rid¹ /rɪd/ adj ★★
PHRASES **be rid of** to be no longer affected by someone or something that is annoying, unpleasant, or not wanted: *Just give him the money and you can be rid of him.*
get rid of 1 to throw away, give away, or sell something that you no longer want or need: *We're moving, so we have to get rid of a lot of our furniture.* **2** to do something so that you stop being affected by someone or something that is annoying or unpleasant: *I wish I could get rid of this cold.* ♦ *I'm sure he knew we were trying to get rid of him!*

rid² /rɪd/ (past tense and past participle **rid**)
PHRASAL VERB **ˈrid sb/sth of sb/sth** to stop a person or thing from being affected by something that is annoying, unpleasant, or harmful, by removing it: *a movement to rid the world of nuclear weapons*

rid•dance /ˈrɪd(ə)ns/ noun **good riddance (to)** used for saying that you are pleased to be free of someone or something that is annoying or unpleasant

ridden the past participle of **ride¹**

rid•dle /ˈrɪd(ə)l/ noun [C] **1** a question that seems impossible or silly but that has a clever or funny answer **2** someone or something that is mysterious or confusing

rid•dled /ˈrɪd(ə)ld/ adj containing a lot of things that are bad or not wanted: *a project riddled with problems*

ride¹ /raɪd/ (past tense **rode** /roʊd/; past participle **rid•den** /ˈrɪd(ə)n/) verb [I/T] ★★
1 to sit on a bicycle, MOTORCYCLE, or an animal such as a horse and control it as it moves: *I learned to **ride a bike** when I was five.* ♦ *Have you ever **ridden on a camel**?*
→ DRIVE
2 to be a passenger in a vehicle, especially a car or bus: *She **rode the bus** all the way across town.* ♦ *You can **ride in** our car.*
3 to take part in a race on a horse, bicycle, MOTORCYCLE, etc.: *Are you **riding in** tomorrow's race?*
4 to float, or to appear to float, on water or in the air: *Surfers rode the huge waves.*
PHRASE **let sth ride** to pay no attention to something, although it upsets you or could cause problems
PHRASAL VERBS **ˈride on sth** to depend on something for success: *I feel as though my whole future is riding on this interview.*
ˌride sth ˈout to get to the end of a difficult or dangerous period or situation without any serious problems

ride² /raɪd/ noun [C] ★
1 a trip on a horse or other animal, on a bicycle or MOTORCYCLE, or in a vehicle: *The **bus ride** from the airport was very pleasant.* ♦ *I **went for a ride** in Jason's new car.* ♦ *Joe let us **take a ride** on his horse.*
2 *American* a free trip that you are given in someone's vehicle: *I'll **get a ride** home with Jeff.* ♦ *Would you like me to **give** you **a ride** to school?*
3 a machine at an AMUSEMENT PARK (=a place outside where there are games and other activities) that people ride in for fun
PHRASES **a rough ride** or **not an easy ride** a period of time when you experience a lot of problems
take sb for a ride to trick, cheat, or lie to someone

rid•er /ˈraɪdər/ noun [C] someone who rides on an animal such as a horse, or on a vehicle such as a bicycle or MOTORCYCLE

ridge /rɪdʒ/ noun [C] **1** the long narrow top of a mountain or group of mountains **2** a long narrow raised line along the surface of something

rid•i•cule¹ /ˈrɪdɪˌkjul/ noun [U] remarks or behavior that are intended to make someone or something seem silly by making fun of them in an unkind way

rid•i•cule² /ˈrɪdɪˌkjul/ verb [T] to try to make

R

someone or something seem silly by making fun of them in an unkind way

ri·dic·u·lous /rɪˈdɪkjələs/ adj silly or unreasonable and deserving to be laughed at = ABSURD: *a ridiculous idea* ♦ *She looks absolutely ridiculous in that hat.* —**ri·dic·u·lous·ly** adv: *The test was ridiculously easy.*

ri·ding /ˈraɪdɪŋ/ noun [U] the activity or sport of riding horses

rife /raɪf/ adj if something that is bad is rife, there is a lot of it

ri·fle¹ /ˈraɪf(ə)l/ noun [C] a large gun with a long BARREL

ri·fle² /ˈraɪf(ə)l/ or ˌ**rifle ˈthrough sth** verb [T] to search quickly through something in order to find something

rift /rɪft/ noun [C] **1** a disagreement between two people or groups **2** a crack or long narrow space that forms in a large mass of something such as rock

rig¹ /rɪg/ verb [T] to influence something such as an election in a dishonest way in order to produce a particular result

PHRASAL VERB ˌ**rig sth ˈup** to make something quickly out of whatever you can find

rig² /rɪg/ noun [C] **1** a tall structure with equipment for getting oil or gas out of the ground **2** *American* a large truck that consists of two parts and is used for carrying goods

rig·ging /ˈrɪgɪŋ/ noun [U] the ropes and chains that are used for supporting a ship's sails and MASTS

right¹ /raɪt/ adv ★★★

1 exactly	4 toward the right
2 immediately	5 all the way
3 correctly/accurately	+ PHRASE

1 exactly: *Their office is **right in the middle** of town.* ♦ *"Am I late?" "No, you're **right on time**."* ♦ *Don't worry – I'm **right behind** you.*

2 immediately: *I liked her right from the start.* ♦ *Paul arrived right after me.* ♦ *She called and asked me to come over **right away**.* ♦ *Just a minute – **I'll be right there**.*

3 correctly, or accurately: *You did it right the first time.*

4 in the direction of your right side: ***Turn right** at the corner.*

5 all the way or completely: *My foot went **right through** the floor.*

PHRASE **right now** *spoken* **1** at the present time: *We're working on it right now.* **2** immediately: *Go to bed right now!*

→ RIGHTLY, SERVE¹

right² /raɪt/ adj ★★★

1 correct	4 with needed qualities
2 morally correct	5 in correct state, etc.
3 on one side of body	+ PHRASE

1 correct according to the facts ≠ WRONG: *"D" is **the right answer**.* ♦ *Is this **the right** way to the station?* ♦ *You were **absolutely right**, my sweater was in the car.* ♦ *I think you were **right about** the color – it doesn't match.*

2 morally correct ≠ WRONG: *You **did the right thing** by telling them you had lied.* ♦ **it is right (of sb) to do sth** *It wasn't right of her to take it without asking.*

3 on or relating to the side of your body that is toward the east when you are facing north ≠ LEFT: *Hold the bat in your **right hand**.*

4 the right person or thing has exactly the qualities that you want or need ≠ WRONG: *I'm not sure this is **the right time** to take a vacation.* ♦ *Harry's definitely **the right person for** the job.*

5 in the position, state, or situation that you would normally expect someone or something to be in ≠ WRONG: *She hadn't been **feeling right** for weeks.* ♦ *I noticed that some of the pictures weren't **in the right place**.*

PHRASE **that's right** *spoken* used instead of "yes" as an answer to a question or statement: *"So you're seeing James again tomorrow?" "That's right."*

→ ALL RIGHT¹, MR. RIGHT

right³ /raɪt/ noun ★★★

1 good behavior	5 a turn to the right
2 sth that is allowed	6 in politics
3 permission to publish	+ PHRASES
4 side of your body	

1 [U] behavior that is considered good or moral ≠ WRONG: *Do children of that age know the difference between **right and wrong**?*

2 [C] something that you are morally or legally allowed to do or have: *We are fighting for workers' rights.* ♦ ***equal rights** for women* ♦ ***the right to** political asylum* ♦ *We **have every right to** complain.* ♦ *You **have no right to** come barging in here like that.*

→ BILL OF RIGHTS, CIVIL RIGHTS

3 rights [plural] the legal authority to publish a book, play, movie, piece of music, etc., or to use it for a performance or production: *the motion-picture **rights to** her book*

4 [singular] the side of your body that is toward the east when you are facing north, or this direction ≠ LEFT: *Could you move a little to the right?* ♦ *It's the second door **on your right**.*

5 [C] a turn toward the right that is made by someone who is walking or driving: ***Take a right** at the art gallery.* ♦ *It's **the first right*** (=the first street where you can turn right) *after the supermarket.*

6 the right [singular] the political party or the group of people within a society who are conservative in their political views

PHRASES **in your own right** as a result of your own ability, achievements, qualifications, etc. and not because of anyone else: *Her father's a well-known author, but she's an excellent writer in her own right.*

right of way the legal right to pass in front of other vehicles when you are entering or crossing a road

right⁴ /raɪt/ interjection ★

1 used for asking whether what you have said is correct: *You told everyone about tomorrow's meeting, right?*

2 used for saying that you agree with a statement or accept a suggestion or an order

3 used for making someone pay attention before you say something

right⁵ /raɪt/ verb [T] to put someone or something back into their usual upright position

PHRASE **right a wrong** to correct something that is bad or wrong that someone has done

ˈright ˌangle noun [C] an angle of 90° —*picture* → C8 —**ˈright-ˌangled** adj

ˈright-ˌclick verb [I] *computing* to press the button on the right side of a computer MOUSE

right·eous /ˈraɪtʃəs/ adj **1** righteous feelings of anger are caused by a belief that you are right to feel angry **2** *literary* morally good or correct

right·ful /ˈraɪtf(ə)l/ adj *formal* officially or legally accepted as right or correct —**right·ful·ly** adv

ˈright-ˌhand adj on the right, or toward the right of someone or something ≠ LEFT-HAND: *the right-hand side of the bed*

right-hand·ed /ˌraɪt ˈhændəd/ adj naturally tending to use your right hand instead of your left to do things such as writing ≠ LEFT-HANDED —**right-handed** adv

ˌright-hand ˈman noun [singular] the person that you regularly depend on to help you

right·ly /ˈraɪtli/ adv **1** for a good reason: *Voters are rightly concerned about what is going to happen.* **2** correctly, or accurately: *As you rightly say, we must work carefully.*

ˌright ˈtriangle noun [C] *American* a flat shape with three straight sides and three angles, one of which is a RIGHT ANGLE

ˌright ˈwing, the noun [singular] the most conservative group within a political party

ˌright-ˈwing adj conservative in your political views ≠ LEFT-WING —**ˌright-ˈwinger** noun [C]

rig·id /ˈrɪdʒɪd/ adj **1** not easily changed: *a rigid class system* **2** done or applied in a strict and unreasonable way: *rigid discipline* **3** stiff, hard, and difficult to bend or move **4** not willing to change your ideas, attitudes, opinions, etc. —**rig·id·i·ty** /rɪˈdʒɪdəti/ noun [U], **rig·id·ly** adv

rig·ma·role /ˈrɪɡməˌroʊl/ noun [singular] a long complicated process that seems unnecessary or silly

rig·or /ˈrɪɡər/ noun [U] **1** the quality of being strict or severe **2** the quality of being thorough and careful

PHRASE **the rigors of sth** the difficult and unpleasant aspects of a situation

rig·or·ous /ˈrɪɡərəs/ adj **1** thorough and careful **2** strict, or severe —**rig·or·ous·ly** adv

rig·our /ˈrɪɡər/ the British spelling of **rigor**

rile /raɪl/ verb [T] to annoy someone

rim /rɪm/ noun [C] the edge of an open container or circular object → PACIFIC RIM

rind /raɪnd/ noun [C/U] **1** the outer skin of a fruit such as a lemon or orange **2** the hard outer edge of BACON or some types of cheese

ring¹ (past tense **rang** /ræŋ/; past participle **rung** /rʌŋ/) verb ★★★

1 of telephone	**5** surround sb/sth
2 of bell	**6** draw circle around sth
3 of ears	+ PHRASES
4 of sound in a place	+ PHRASAL VERBS

1 [I] if a telephone rings, it makes a sound in order to show that someone is calling: *The phone rang again immediately.*

2 [I/T] if a bell rings, or if you ring it, it makes a sound: *He rang the doorbell.* ♦ *The bell rang, and the children stood up.*

3 [I] if your ears are ringing, you continue to hear a loud sound in your head, for example after a loud noise

4 [I] if a sound rings in a place, or if a place rings with sound, the sound is loud and you can hear it clearly: *A great cheer rang through the hall.*

5 [T] to surround someone or something, especially in order to protect them or to prevent them from escaping: *Protesters carrying signs ringed the embassy.* ♦ *Ringed by soldiers for protection, he tried to address the crowd.*

6 [T] to draw a circle around something = CIRCLE: *She ringed the date on the calendar in the kitchen.*

PHRASES **ring a bell** *informal* to sound familiar to you: *The name rings a bell. Isn't he an architect?*

ring true to sound true or sincere: *I didn't think Green's explanation rang true.*

PHRASAL VERBS **ˌring ˈout** *literary* to produce a loud clear sound

ˌring sth ˈup to record an amount of money by pressing the buttons on a CASH REGISTER: *She rang up our purchases quickly and we left.*

ring² /rɪŋ/ noun ★★★

1 jewelry	**4** in boxing/wrestling
2 sth shaped like circle	**5** group doing activity
3 bell sound	**6** quality

1 [C] a piece of jewelry in the form of a circle that you wear on a finger: *She had a ring on every finger.* —*picture* → JEWELRY

2 [C] something that is in the shape of a circle: *onion rings* ♦ *Kia had dark rings under her eyes.* ♦ *The kids sat **in a ring** around the fire.*

3 [C] the sound that a bell or telephone makes: *the ring of the doorbell* ♦ *I answered the phone on the first ring.*

4 [C] a raised area that is surrounded by ropes where people take part in BOXING or WRESTLING

5 [C] a group of people who are involved in an illegal activity: *an international drug ring*

6 [singular] a particular quality that something such as a statement seems to have: *His version of events had a ring of truth.*

ˈring ˌfinger noun [C] the third finger on your left hand, on which a WEDDING RING is traditionally worn —*picture* → C14

ring·lead·er /ˈrɪŋˌlidər/ noun [C] a leader of a group of people who are doing something that is illegal or wrong

ring·let /ˈrɪŋlət/ noun [C] a piece of long hair that hangs down in curls

rink /rɪŋk/ noun [C] a large flat area where people go to SKATE

rinse¹ /rɪns/ verb [T] to wash something quickly in clean water in order to remove soap or dirt

PHRASAL VERB **ˌrinse sth ˈout** to wash the inside of something quickly with clean water

rinse² /rɪns/ noun **1** [C] a quick wash in clean water **2** [C/U] something that you put on your hair to change its color for a short time

ri•ot¹ /ˈraɪət/ noun [C/U] a violent protest by a crowd of people

PHRASE **run riot 1** to behave in a noisy and uncontrolled way **2** if your imagination or emotions run riot, you cannot control them

ri•ot² /ˈraɪət/ verb [I] if people riot, they protest violently about something —**ri•ot•er** noun [C], **ri•ot•ing** noun [U]

ri•ot•ous /ˈraɪətəs/ adj **1** very lively and noisy: *riotous laughter* **2** behaving in a noisy and violent way: *The crowd was becoming riotous.*

rip¹ /rɪp/ verb **1** [I/T] to tear something quickly and with a lot of force, or to be torn in this way: *Stop pulling my shirt – it's going to rip.* ♦ *Jodie ripped the letter open.* ♦ **rip sth on sth** *I ripped my jeans on a sharp nail.* **2** [T] to remove something quickly by pulling hard: *We've ripped out the old fireplace.*

PHRASAL VERBS ˌ**rip sb ˈoff** *informal* to cheat someone by charging them too much money for something

ˌ**rip ˈthrough sth** if something such as a fire, storm, or bomb rips though a place, it damages or destroys the place very quickly

ˌ**rip sth ˈup** to tear something into small pieces

rip² /rɪp/ noun [C] a hole in something that is produced by tearing=TEAR: *My shirt has a big rip.*

ripe /raɪp/ adj ripe fruit or crops have grown to their full size and are ready to eat or use

PHRASES **be ripe for sth** to be ready for something, especially a change: *Some of the smaller firms are ripe for takeover.*

ripe old age an age at which someone is very old: *She lived to the ripe old age of 103.* —**ripe•ness** noun [U]

rip•en /ˈraɪpən/ verb [I/T] to become ripe, or to make something become ripe

ˈ**rip-ˌoff** noun [C] *informal* something that is more expensive than it should be

rip•ple¹ /ˈrɪp(ə)l/ verb [I/T] to move like small waves, or to make something move like small waves

rip•ple² /ˈrɪp(ə)l/ noun [C] **1** a small wave or series of small waves on the surface of a liquid **2** an emotion or reaction that spreads gradually through a person or a group: *a ripple of laughter/applause*

rise¹ /raɪz/ (past tense **rose** /roʊz/; past participle **ris•en** /ˈrɪz(ə)n/) verb [I] ★★★

1 move upward	7 be tall/high
2 increase	8 oppose government
3 achieve success	9 bread/cake grows
4 stand up	+ PHRASE
5 voice gets higher	+ PHRASAL VERBS
6 water increases	

1 to move upward or to a higher position: *The aircraft rose slowly into the air.* ♦ *Thick black* ***smoke rose*** *from the middle of the town.* ♦ *As* ***the sun rose*** *in the sky, the clouds disappeared.*

2 to increase in size, amount, quality, or strength: ***Temperatures will rise*** *steadily toward the end of the week.* ♦ ***Rising unemployment*** *is our biggest problem.* ♦ ***Tensions rose*** *in the city as the day went on.* ♦ *Interest rates* ***rise and fall*** *according to the health of the economy.*

3 to achieve success, power, or a higher status: *I am sure she will* ***rise to the top*** *of her profession.* ♦ *He* ***rose to power*** *as a leader of the miners' union.*

4 *formal* to stand from a sitting, KNEELING, or lying position: *He rose and went to the window.*

5 if your voice rises, it gets higher, often because of a strong feeling

6 if an area of water rises, its level goes up: *The river rose and burst its banks.*

7 if something such as a building or mountain rises somewhere, it is tall or high and can be seen clearly: *Gray mountains rose above the lakes.*

8 to start to protest and fight against a government or leader=REBEL, REVOLT: *Eventually the people rose against the regime.*

9 if something such as bread or a cake rises, it increases in size when it is cooked

PHRASE **rise to the challenge/occasion** to deal successfully with a difficult problem or situation

PHRASAL VERBS ˌ**rise aˈbove sth** to not let something bad affect you, because you have a strong character

ˌ**rise ˈup** *same as* **rise¹** 8: *The peasants rose up in revolt.*

Words often used with rise

Adverbs often used with ***rise*** *(verb, sense 2)*

- RISE + **dramatically, markedly, quickly, rapidly, sharply, significantly, steeply, substantially, suddenly**: rise quickly or by a large amount in a short time

rise² /raɪz/ noun ★★★

1 [C] an increase in size, amount, quality, or strength: *Serious crime is once again* ***on the rise.*** ♦ ***the rise and fall of*** *share prices* ♦ *the threat of a sudden* ***rise in*** *oil prices*

2 [singular] an increase in the power or influence of someone or something: *Fidel Castro's rise to power* ♦ ***the rise of*** *nationalism in Europe* ♦ *The series covers* ***the rise and fall*** *of the Third Reich.*

3 [singular] an upward movement

4 [C] *British* a RAISE in pay

PHRASE **give rise to sth** to make something happen or begin, especially something that is unpleasant or unexpected

Words often used with rise

Adjectives often used with ***rise*** *(noun, sense 1)*

- **dramatic, marked, rapid, sharp, significant, spectacular, steep, substantial, sudden** + RISE: used about rises that are large and happen quickly

ris•er /ˈraɪzər/ noun **an early/late riser** someone who usually gets out of bed early/late

risk¹ /rɪsk/ noun ★★★

1 [C/U] the possibility that something unpleasant or dangerous might happen: *The* ***risks to*** *consumers are being analyzed.* ♦ *There is* ***a*** *serious* ***risk of*** *a major nuclear accident.* ♦ **the risk of doing sth** *the risk of developing lung cancer* ♦ **+(that)** *There is a* *risk that the virus can be transferred from patient to doctor.*

2 [C] someone or something that is likely to be a danger or problem in the future: *a possible fire risk* (=something that could cause fire)

PHRASES **at your own risk** if you do something at your own risk, you are responsible for any harm or damage that you suffer as a result

at risk in a situation in which something that is unpleasant or dangerous could happen to you: *The laws will* ***put*** *many small businesses* ***at risk.***

at the risk of doing sth used for saying that you realize that something bad or unpleasant may happen as a result of what you are going to say: *At the risk of seeming boring, I don't think we should try it.*

a good/bad risk a person or company that is safe/not safe to lend money to or to give CREDIT to

run the risk (of sth) to be in a situation in which something that is bad could happen: *I didn't want to run the risk of seeing Neil again.*

take a risk to do something although you know that something that is unpleasant or dangerous could happen: *Do you think I should take a risk and give her a call?* ♦ **take the risk of doing sth** *I didn't want to take the risk of leaving John alone.*

risk² /rɪsk/ verb [T] ★★ to do something although you know that something that is bad could happen as a result: **risk sth on sth** *He risked a lot of money on the company.* ♦ **risk doing sth** *We don't want to risk becoming involved in a civil war.*

PHRASE **risk your life** to put yourself in a situation in which you could be killed

risk•y /ˈrɪski/ adj involving the possibility of danger, harm, or failure

ris•qué /rɪsˈkeɪ/ adj likely to offend some people, especially by referring to sex

rite /raɪt/ noun [C] a traditional ceremony, especially a religious one

rit•u•al /ˈrɪtʃuəl/ noun [C/U] **1** a formal ceremony **2** something that you do regularly and always in the same way: *Their meetings became a weekly ritual.*

—**rit•u•al** adj

ritz•y /ˈrɪtsi/ adj *informal* expensive and fashionable: *a ritzy hotel/restaurant*

ri•val¹ /ˈraɪv(ə)l/ noun [C] ★

1 a person, team, or business that competes with another: *She scored twice as many points as her rival.*

2 someone or something that is as good as someone or something else: *The band has few rivals in the pop music world.*

—**ri•val** adj: *rival companies*

ri•val² /ˈraɪv(ə)l/ (present participle **ri•val•ing** or **ri•val•ling**; past tense and past participle **ri•valed** or **ri•valled**) verb [T] to be as good as someone or something else: *This small restaurant rivals any that you will find in the city.*

ri•val•ry /ˈraɪv(ə)lri/ noun [C/U] a situation in which people, teams, businesses, etc. compete with one another

riv•er /ˈrɪvər/ noun [C] ★★★ a large area of water that flows toward the ocean: *They were swimming in the river.* ♦ *the Mississippi River*

riv•er•front /ˈrɪvərˌfrʌnt/ noun [C] the part of a town that is next to a river

riv•et¹ /ˈrɪvɪt/ verb **be riveted by/to sth** to be so interested in something that you pay complete attention to it: *I was totally riveted by the pictures.*

riv•et² /ˈrɪvɪt/ noun [C] a metal pin used for joining pieces of metal together

riv•et•ing /ˈrɪvɪtɪŋ/ adj extremely interesting or exciting: *a riveting performance*

roach /roʊtʃ/ noun [C] *American informal* a COCKROACH

road /roʊd/ noun [C] ★★★ a way that leads from one place to another that cars and other vehicles can use: *He was driving on the wrong side of the road.* ♦ *They live on Lockwood Road.* ♦ *The journey is about three hours* ***by road.*** ♦ *There's a supermarket just* ***up the road*** (=not far away on the same road).

PHRASES **down the road** *informal* used for talking about what may happen in the future: *Two years down the road, you might feel very differently.*

on the road traveling in a car, bus, or truck, especially for a long distance or a long period of time

the road to sth a process or series of events that will achieve something or have a particular result: *It's an important step on the road to democracy.*

→ HIT¹

- A **road** is built for vehicles to travel along and can have buildings on each side. It can be wide or narrow, and it can be in a town or can join different towns: *My school is just down the road.* ♦ *the road from the farm into town*
- A **street** is a road in a town, with buildings such as houses and stores along its sides: *They live on a busy street.*
- A **path** is a way from one place to another for people to walk along: *a path leading into the forest*

road•block /ˈroʊdˌblɑk/ noun [C] **1** a part of a road where police or soldiers stop traffic **2** *informal* something that stops someone from making progress: *The issue is still a major roadblock in the negotiations.*

ˈroad ˌmap noun [C] **1** a map that shows all of the roads and highways in a region or country **2** *American* a plan or set of instructions that makes it easier for someone to do something

ˈroad ˌrage noun [U] violent behavior by a driver toward another driver

road•side /ˈroʊdˌsaɪd/ noun [C] the area at the edge of a road

road•way /ˈroʊdˌweɪ/ noun [C] the part of a road that you drive on

road•work /ˈroʊdˌwɜrk/ noun [U] *American* repairs that are done to the surface of a road

road•wor•thy /ˈroʊdˌwɜrði/ adj safe to drive

roam /roʊm/ verb [I/T] to move or travel with no particular purpose: *Young men roamed the streets.*

roar¹ /rɔr/ verb **1** [I/T] to shout, speak, or laugh very loudly: *The crowd roared as the team*

R

ran onto the field. ♦ *Barney roared with laughter.* **2** [I] to make a continuous very loud noise: *Military planes roared overhead.* **3** [I] if a lion roars, it makes a deep loud sound **4** [I] if a vehicle roars somewhere, it travels there very quickly and noisily: *We sat and waited as the traffic roared past.*

roar² /rɔr/ noun [C] **1** a loud continuous sound: *the roar of the waves* ♦ *a roar of anger* **2** the loud deep sound that a lion makes

roar•ing /ˈrɔrɪŋ/ adj **1** a roaring fire burns very brightly and produces a lot of heat **2** making a loud deep noise: *a roaring waterfall*

PHRASE **do a roaring trade (in sth)** to sell large quantities of something in a short period of time

roast¹ /roʊst/ verb [I/T] to cook meat or vegetables in an oven

roast² /roʊst/ noun [C] **1** a large piece of meat that has been cooked in an oven **2** *American* a party that is held outside where meat or vegetables are cooked over a fire

roast³ /roʊst/ adj cooked in an oven: *roast beef*

rob /rɑb/ verb [T] **1** to take money or property from someone illegally: *They were planning to rob the museum.* **2** to take something such as an opportunity, ability, or quality from someone: *The shock had robbed her of the power of speech.*

rob•ber /ˈrɑbər/ noun [C] someone who steals money or property

rob•ber•y /ˈrɑbəri/ noun [C/U] the crime of stealing money or property

robe /roʊb/ noun [C] **1** a BATHROBE **2** a long loose piece of clothing that is worn by a priest or other important person

rob•in /ˈrɑbɪn/ noun [C] **1** a gray North American bird with a red chest **2** a small brown European bird with a red chest

R

ro•bot /ˈroʊˌbɑt/ noun [C] a machine that can do work by itself, often work that humans do —**ro•bot•ic** /roʊˈbɑtɪk/ adj

ro•bust /roʊˈbʌst/ adj **1** a robust person is strong and healthy **2** firm and determined: *a robust approach*

rock¹ /rɑk/ noun ★★★

1 [C/U] the hard solid substance that forms part of the Earth's surface, or a piece of this substance on the ground: *a layer of rock* ♦ *a castle built on a rock* ♦ *The waves crashed against the rocks.*

2 [U] ROCK MUSIC: *a rock star* ♦ *rock concerts*

PHRASE **rock 'n' roll** or **rock and roll** music for dancing that is played on guitars. It was popular in the 1950s.

rock² /rɑk/ verb **1** [I/T] to move gently BACKWARD and forward or from side to side, or to make someone or something do this: *He sat and rocked the baby to sleep.* ♦ *Hold your knees close to your chest and rock from side to side.* **2** [T] *mainly journalism* to shock, surprise, or frighten someone: *Spain has been rocked by another political scandal.* **3** [T] if an explosion or EARTHQUAKE rocks something, it makes it shake violently: *The blast rocked the houses in the street.*

PHRASE **rock the boat** *informal* to cause problems by changing a situation that other people do not want to change

ˌrock ˈbottom noun [U] the lowest possible level: *Confidence in the company is at rock bottom.* —**ˌrock-ˈbottom** adj: *rock-bottom prices*

rock•et¹ /ˈrɑkɪt/ noun [C] **1** a vehicle that is shaped like a tube that travels in space **2** a weapon that is shaped like a tube that flies through the air and explodes when it hits something **3** a FIREWORK that is shaped like a tube that flies up into the air when you light it and then explodes

rock•et² /ˈrɑkɪt/ verb **1** [I/T] *informal* to suddenly become very successful, or to make someone do this **2** [I] to increase suddenly

ˈrocking ˌchair noun [C] a chair on two curved pieces of wood that moves gently BACKWARD and forward when you are sitting in it

ˈrock ˌmusic noun [U] music that has a heavy regular beat and that is played on electric guitars

rock•y /ˈrɑki/ adj covered with rocks, or made of rock

rod /rɑd/ noun [C] a long thin bar or stick made of metal, plastic, or wood

rode the past tense of **ride¹**

ro•dent /ˈroʊd(ə)nt/ noun [C] a type of small animal that has long sharp front teeth, for example a mouse

ro•de•o /roʊˈdeɪoʊ, ˈroʊdioʊ/ (plural **ro•de•os**) noun [C] a sports event in which COWBOYS compete by riding wild horses or catching CATTLE with ropes

roe /roʊ/ noun [U] fish eggs that are eaten as food

rogue /roʊg/ adj a rogue member of a group does not behave in the same way as its other members and is considered dangerous: *a rogue state*

role /roʊl/ noun [C] ★★★

1 the purpose or influence that someone or something has: *It's not my role to tell the politicians what to do.* ♦ *The book examines the role of food and drink in society.* ♦ *We expect parents to have **a key role in** this discussion.* ♦ *Labor unions have **played a** significant **role** in the recent debate.*

2 the character that is played by a particular actor in a movie or play = PART: *Who is playing the role of Hamlet?*

> **Words often used with role**
>
> *Adjectives often used with **role** (sense 1)*
>
> ■ **central, crucial, important, key, leading, major, prominent, significant, vital** + ROLE: used about roles that have an important influence on a situation

ˈrole ˌmodel noun [C] someone whose behavior is a good example for other people to copy

ˈrole-ˌplay noun [C/U] an activity in which you pretend to be someone else, especially in order to learn new skills

roll¹ /roʊl/ verb ★★★

1 move while turning	6 flow
2 move on wheels	7 make substance flat
3 move from side to side	8 machine: work
4 change body position	+ PHRASES
5 wrap sth around itself	+ PHRASAL VERBS

1 [I/T] to move forward while turning over and over, or to make something do this:

The pencil went rolling across the floor. ♦ *Men were rolling tires across the yard.*
2 [I/T] to move on wheels, or to move something that is on wheels: *The car rolled to a stop at the side of the road.* ♦ *We rolled the piano to the front of the stage.*
3 [I] to move from side to side: *The pigs were rolling in the mud.*
4 [I] to change the position of your body when you are lying down: *He* ***rolled onto*** *his back and looked up at me.*
5 [T] to fold something or wrap it around itself so that it forms a tube or a ball: *I always roll my clothes when I pack them.* ♦ **roll sth into sth** *Take a piece of the dough and roll it into a ball.*
6 [I] if a drop of liquid rolls, it moves across a surface without stopping: *Rain drops rolled down the window.*
7 [T] to make a substance flat by pushing something across it: *Roll the pie crust very thinly.*
8 [I] if a machine such as a camera is rolling, it is working: *Although the interview had ended, the cameras were still rolling.*

PHRASES **(all) rolled into one** if someone is several things rolled into one, they are all of those things at the same time
be rolling in money/it *informal* to have a lot of money
roll your eyes to move your eyes upward in order to show that you are annoyed or impatient
→ BALL

PHRASAL VERBS **ˌroll ˈin** to arrive in large numbers or amounts
ˌroll sth ˈup 1 if you roll your sleeves or the legs of your pants up, you fold the cloth several times until they are shorter **2** *same as* **roll**[1] 5: *She rolled her scarf up and put it into her bag.*

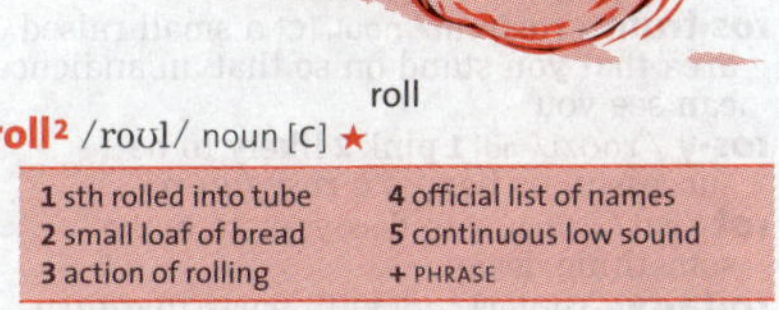
roll

roll[2] /roʊl/ noun [C] ★

1 sth rolled into tube	4 official list of names
2 small loaf of bread	5 continuous low sound
3 action of rolling	+ PHRASE

1 a long piece of something such as paper or carpet that is rolled into the shape of a tube: *We used ten* ***rolls of*** *wallpaper.*
2 bread in the form of a small round or long shape
3 the action of turning over or rolling from side to side: *The constant roll of the ship made her sick.*
4 an official list of names: *The teacher called the roll and checked off the names one by one.* → HONOR ROLL
5 a continuous low sound made by drums or THUNDER

PHRASE **be on a roll** *informal* to be having a lot of success or good luck

ˈroll ˌcall noun [C/U] the process of reading out an official list of people's names in order to see who is present

roll·er /ˈroʊlər/ noun [C] **1** something that is shaped like a tube that goes over a surface in order to make it flat or in order to crush, spread, or print something **2** a small tube that you wind some of your hair around in order to make a curl = CURLER

Rol·ler·blades /ˈroʊlərˌbleɪdz/ *trademark* boots with a single row of small wheels along the bottom

ˈroller ˌcoaster noun [C] **1** a structure like a tall railroad with steep slopes that people ride on for fun at an AMUSEMENT PARK **2** a situation in which there are many big and sudden changes

ˈroller ˌskates noun [plural] boots with four small wheels on the bottom —**ˈroller-ˌskate** verb [I], **ˈroller ˌskating** noun [U]

roll·ing /ˈroʊlɪŋ/ adj rolling land has a lot of gentle slopes

ˈrolling ˌpin noun [C] a piece of kitchen equipment that you roll over PASTRY in order to make it flat and thin

ROM /rɑm/ noun [U] *computing* read-only memory: the part of a computer's memory that is permanent and cannot be changed

Ro·man[1] /ˈroʊmən/ adj of ancient Rome or its EMPIRE, or from ancient Rome or its EMPIRE

Ro·man[2] /ˈroʊmən/ noun [C] someone from ancient Rome or its EMPIRE

ˌRoman ˈCatholic noun [C] a member of the part of the Christian Church that has the POPE as its leader —**ˌRoman ˈCatholic** adj, **ˌRoman Caˈtholicism** noun [U]

ro·mance /roʊˈmæns, ˈroʊˌmæns/ noun **1** [C] a short exciting romantic relationship **2** [U] the behavior that is typical of two people who love each other: *She wasn't in a mood for romance.* **3** [C] a book or movie about a romantic relationship **4** [U] a feeling of excitement that you get from a particular place, activity, or experience: *the romance of traveling through foreign lands*

ˌRoman ˈnumeral noun [C] one of the letters "I," "V," "X," "L," "C," "D," and "M" that are sometimes used for representing numbers

ro·man·tic[1] /roʊˈmæntɪk/ adj **1** involving love, or making you have feelings of love: *We had a romantic dinner in an expensive restaurant.* ♦ *romantic relationships*
2 tending to believe that things are better or more exciting than they really are: *a romantic vision of life on a farm* —**ro·man·ti·cal·ly** /roʊˈmæntɪkli/ adv

ro·man·tic[2] /roʊˈmæntɪk/ noun [C] **1** someone who does things that show their love **2** someone who believes that things are better or more exciting than they really are

ro·man·ti·cize /roʊˈmæntɪˌsaɪz/ verb [T] to think that something is better or more exciting than it really is

Rom·a·ny /ˈrɑməni, ˈroʊməni/ noun [C] a member of a group of people who originally came from India and who sometimes travel

R

around rather than live in one place

romp /rɑmp/ verb [I] to play in a lively way —**romp** noun [singular]

roof /ruf/ noun [C] ★★★
1 the top outer part of a building or vehicle: *The roof is leaking again.* —*picture* → C1
2 the hard top part of the inside of your mouth
PHRASES **go through the roof 1** *informal* to increase quickly to a very high level
2 *informal* to suddenly become extremely angry
a roof over your head a place to live
→ HIT[1]

roof·ing /ˈrufɪŋ/ noun [U] **1** material used for making roofs **2** the process of building or repairing roofs

roof·top /ˈrufˌtɑp/ noun [C] the roof of a building

rook /rʊk/ noun [C] a piece in the shape of a tower used in CHESS —*picture* → C16

rook·ie /ˈrʊki/ noun [C] *American* **1** someone who has been a professional sports player for less than one year **2** *informal* someone who has just started doing a job and does not have much experience

room[1] /rum/ noun ★★★
1 [C] a part of a building with a floor, walls, and a ceiling: *Annie ran out of the room.*
2 [C] a bedroom in a home or a hotel: *My mom told me to clean up my room.* ♦ *I'm staying in Room 52.*
3 [U] the amount of space that you need for a particular purpose: *There isn't much room in here.* ♦ *This table **takes up** too much **room**.* ♦ *Is there **room for** another person in your car?* ♦ **room to do sth** *The band was good, but there was no room to dance.* → PLACE
4 [U] the possibility for something to happen: *There is **room for improvement** in his work* (=it is not very good).
PHRASE **room and board** an arrangement where you have a room to sleep in and meals are also provided for you

room[2] /rum/ verb [I] *American* to share a room or house with other people: *Jean and I roomed together at college.*

room·mate /ˈrumˌmeɪt/ noun [C] someone who you share a room or house with

ˈroom ˌservice noun [U] the service that you use when you ask a hotel to bring food and drinks to your room

room·y /ˈrumi/ adj large and providing you with a lot of space: *a roomy car*

roost /rust/ noun [C] a place where birds rest and sleep
PHRASE **rule the roost** to control a situation
—**roost** verb [I]

roost·er /ˈrustər/ noun [C] a male chicken

root[1] /rut/ noun ★★
1 [C] the part of a plant that grows under the ground: *Olive trees have deep roots.* —*picture* → TREE
2 [C] the part of a hair, tooth, or nail that is under your skin
3 [C] a basic cause or idea: *We need to get to **the root of** the problem.*
4 **roots** [plural] the place, culture, or family that someone comes from originally
PHRASE **take root** if an idea or system takes root, it becomes established

root[2] /rut/ verb [I] to search for something by putting your hand deep into a place and pushing things around: *He rooted around in his coat pocket for some change.*
PHRASAL VERBS **ˈroot for sb** *informal* to support someone in a game or competition
ˌroot sth ˈout to find something that is bad and get rid of it

ˈroot ˌbeer noun [C/U] a sweet CARBONATED drink that is not alcoholic

root·ed /ˈrutəd/ adj **rooted in sth** if one thing is rooted in another, it is based on it or it has developed from it

rope[1] /roʊp/ noun ★★
1 [C/U] a type of very thick string that can be used for tying or pulling things
2 [C] a lot of small objects that are tied together on a string: *a rope of pearls*
3 **the ropes** [plural] the correct way of doing something: *You spend the first few days **learning the ropes**.* ♦ *One of our most experienced workers will **show you the ropes**.*
PHRASES **at the end of your rope** *American spoken* so upset or angry that you cannot deal with a situation calmly
on the ropes *informal* affected by serious problems, and likely to fail

rope[2] /roʊp/ verb [T] to tie people or things together with a piece of rope
PHRASAL VERBS **ˌrope sb ˈin** *informal* to persuade someone to do something that they do not really want to do
ˌrope sth ˈoff to put ropes around an area in order to prevent people from entering it

ro·sa·ry /ˈroʊzəri/ noun [C] a set of BEADS used by Catholics for counting prayers

rose[1] /roʊz/ noun [C] ★ a flower that has a sweet smell and sharp THORNS on its stem, or the bush that it grows on —*picture* → C9

rose[2] the past tense of **rise[1]**

ro·sé /roʊˈzeɪ/ noun [U] a type of wine that is pink

rose·mar·y /ˈroʊzˌmeri/ noun [U] a bush with narrow leaves that are used as an HERB in cooking

ro·sette /roʊˈzet/ noun [C] a decoration or pattern in the shape of a ROSE

ros·ter /ˈrɑstər/ noun [C] a list of the names of the people on a particular sports team

ros·trum /ˈrɑstrəm/ noun [C] a small raised area that you stand on so that an audience can see you

ros·y /ˈroʊzi/ adj **1** pink **2** likely to be successful or happy: *a rosy future*

rot /rɑt/ verb [I/T] to decay, or to make something decay

ro·ta·ry /ˈroʊtəri/ adj with parts that turn around a central point

ro·tate /ˈroʊˌteɪt/ verb [I/T] **1** to move in a circle around a central point, or to move something in this way: *The Earth rotates 360 degrees every 24 hours.* **2** if people or things rotate, or if you rotate them, you change them regularly in a particular order

ro·ta·tion /roʊˈteɪʃ(ə)n/ noun **1** [C/U] movement in a circle around a central point **2** [U] the process of regularly changing people or things in a fixed order

rote /roʊt/ noun **learn sth by rote** to learn

R

something by repeating it many times instead of by understanding it

rot·ten /ˈrɑt(ə)n/ adj **1** decayed: *rotten eggs/fruit/teeth* **2** *informal* unpleasant: *They were really rotten to him!* ♦ *If it rains all the time, we'll have a rotten vacation.* **3** *informal* of a low quality, standard, or ability: *She's a rotten singer.*

rott·wei·ler /ˈrɑtˌwaɪlər/ noun [C] a large strong dog with smooth black and brown hair

rough¹ /rʌf/ adj ★★

1 not smooth	4 not finished/exact
2 difficult	5 with crime/violence
3 not gentle	

1 with a surface that is not smooth: *The walls were built of dark rough stone.* ♦ *a rough dirt road* ♦ *strong winds and **rough waves***
2 *informal* difficult and full of problems: *I've had a really rough day at the office.*
3 not gentle ≠ GENTLE: *Don't be so rough with her, James. She's only a baby.*
4 not completely finished, or not exact: *Can you give me **a rough idea** of the cost?* ♦ *Here is **a rough draft** for you to read.*
5 a rough place is not pleasant because there is a lot of crime or violence there
—**rough·ness** noun [U]
→ ROUGHLY

rough² /rʌf/ verb **rough it** *informal* to live for a short time without things that you usually live with, for example water or electricity
PHRASAL VERB ˌ**rough sb** ˈ**up** *informal* to physically attack someone

ˌ**rough-and-ˈtumble** noun [U] **1** the rough way in which a particular activity is usually done: *the rough-and-tumble of a political campaign* **2** the rough behavior of children who are playing

rough·en /ˈrʌf(ə)n/ verb [T] to make something rough

rough·house /ˈrʌfˌhaʊs/ verb [I] to play in a rough noisy way

rough·ly /ˈrʌfli/ adv ★
1 used for showing that an amount or number is not exact = APPROXIMATELY: *The meeting lasted roughly 45 minutes.*
2 in a way that is not gentle: *He pushed roughly past her.*

rough·shod /ˈrʌfʃɑd/ adv **run/ride roughshod over** to behave in a way that shows that you have no respect for someone or something

rou·lette /ruˈlet/ noun [U] a game in which a small ball is thrown onto a moving wheel. People try to win money by guessing where the ball will stop.

round¹ /raʊnd/ adj ★★★
1 shaped like a circle or a ball: *a round table*
2 not exact, but given as a WHOLE NUMBER or as a number ending in zero: *They quoted a round figure of $100 million.*
—**round·ness** noun [U]

round² /raʊnd/ noun [C] ★★

1 (one of) a series	5 drink for all in group
2 stage in competition	6 part of boxing match
3 bullet/shot	7 series of visits
4 complete game of golf	+ PHRASE

1 one of a series of similar events: *The next **round of** peace talks will be held in Rome.*
2 a stage in a competition or election: *Brazil beat the United States in the second **round of** the World Cup.*
3 a bullet or a shot that is fired from a weapon: *Those guns are capable of firing 1,250 rounds per minute.*
4 a complete game of golf: *He likes to play **a round of golf** on Saturdays.*
5 a drink for each of the people in a group: *Tom bought **a round of drinks**.*
6 one of the periods of fighting in a BOXING or WRESTLING match: *He knocked out his opponent in the fourth round.*
7 a series of visits to different people or places that is made as part of someone's job: *a mailman on his delivery round*
PHRASE **a round of applause** a period of time when an audience reacts by CLAPPING their hands

round³ /raʊnd/ verb [T] **1** to go around something: *The van had just rounded the corner.* **2** to make something round or curved: *You have to round your lips to blow into the flute.*
PHRASAL VERBS ˌ**round sth** ˈ**down** to reduce a number to the nearest WHOLE NUMBER, or to the nearest number ending in zero
ˌ**round sth** ˈ**off** to make an angle or surface curved and smooth: *Use a sharp knife to round off the edges.*
ˌ**round sth** ˈ**up** to increase a number to the nearest WHOLE NUMBER, or to the nearest number ending in zero
ˌ**round sb/sth** ˈ**up** to bring people or animals together in one place for a particular purpose

round⁴ /raʊnd/ *British* AROUND

round·a·bout /ˈraʊndəˌbaʊt/ adj not direct, simple, or short: *a roundabout route*

round·ed /ˈraʊndəd/ adj something that is rounded has a curved shape or surface

round·ly /ˈraʊndli/ adv in a strong clear way: *Their tactics were roundly condemned.*

ˈ**round-the-ˌclock** adj happening all day and all night

ˌ**round** ˈ**trip** noun [C] a trip to a place and back again —**round-ˌtrip** adj

ˈ**round-ˌup** noun [C] **1** a summary of the news **2** an occasion when people or animals are forced together into one place

rouse /raʊz/ verb [T] **1** to make someone have strong feelings, or to make someone want to take strong action **2** *formal* to wake someone up

rous·ing /ˈraʊzɪŋ/ adj making people have strong feelings: *a rousing speech/song*

rout /raʊt/ verb [T] to completely defeat someone in a battle, competition, or election —**rout** noun [C]

route¹ /rut, raʊt/ noun [C] ★★
1 the roads or paths that you use when you go from one place to another: *The tunnel is **the route taken** by most drivers.* ♦ *The most direct **route from** the house **to** the school is through the center of town.*
2 a way of doing something: *I'll need to think carefully before deciding what route to take next.* ♦ ***the route to** success/happiness/disaster*
→ EN ROUTE

R

route² /rut, raʊt/ verb [T] to send someone or something along a particular route

rou·tine¹ /ˌruˈtin/ noun ★

1 [C/U] your usual way of doing things: *It shouldn't take too long to get back to our old routine.*

2 [C] a set of things such as jokes or songs that a performer uses regularly: *a comedy/dance routine*

rou·tine² /ˌruˈtin/ adj **1** usual and not done for any special reason: *a routine check* **2** ordinary and not interesting or special: *routine, repetitive work*

rou·tine·ly /ˌruˈtinli/ adv as part of the normal way of doing something

rov·ing /ˈroʊvɪŋ/ adj traveling around from place to place: *a roving reporter*

row¹ /roʊ/ noun [C] ★★★

1 a series of people or things that are arranged in a straight line: *a row of houses/stores/chairs*

2 a line of seats in a theater

PHRASE **in a row 1** in a straight line: *The children stood in a row against the wall.* **2** one after another, without anything different happening in between: *His job allows him to take several days off in a row.*

row² /roʊ/ verb [I/T] to move a boat through water using poles with flat ends called **oars**

row³ /raʊ/ noun [C] *British* an argument or disagreement between people, organizations, or countries

row·boat /ˈroʊˌboʊt/ noun [C] *American* a small boat that you move by pulling on two poles with flat ends called **oars**

row·dy /ˈraʊdi/ adj noisy and causing trouble

row·ing ma·chine /ˈroʊɪŋ məˌʃin/ noun [C] an exercise machine that you sit on and use as if you were ROWING a boat —*picture* → C16

R

roy·al /ˈrɔɪəl/ adj ★★

1 relating to a king or queen, or to their family: *the royal palace* ♦ *a royal wedding*

2 extremely good or impressive: *a royal welcome*

ˌroyal ˈblue adj deep blue —**ˌroyal ˈblue** noun [U]

roy·al·ist /ˈrɔɪəlɪst/ noun [C] someone who believes that their country should have a king or queen

roy·al·ties /ˈrɔɪəltiz/ noun [plural] money that a writer or performer gets each time their work is sold or performed

roy·al·ty /ˈrɔɪəlti/ noun [U] kings and queens and their families

rpm abbrev revolutions per minute: a unit for measuring the speed at which something goes around in a circle

RSVP /ˌɑr es vi ˈpi/ abbrev used on written invitations for asking for a reply

RTF /ˌɑr ti ˈef/ abbrev *computing* rich text format: a way of storing a computer document so that when you send it to someone, it will look exactly the same on their computer screen

rub /rʌb/ verb ★

1 [I/T] to move your hands or an object over a surface firmly: *Scott gently rubbed her back until the pain went away.* ♦ *Rub your hands together – it will help you to stay warm.*

2 [T] to spread a liquid or substance onto the surface of something: **rub sth on sth** *She rubbed some tanning oil on his back.* ♦ **rub sth with sth** *Rub the chicken with garlic before putting it in the oven.*

PHRASES **rub it in** *spoken* to remind someone of something that is stupid or bad that they have done

rub sb the wrong way *informal* to do or say things that annoy someone

PHRASAL VERBS **ˌrub sb/sth ˈdown** to dry someone or something by rubbing them with a TOWEL

ˌrub (sth) ˈoff if you rub something off, or if it rubs off, you remove it by rubbing it

ˌrub ˈoff on sb if something such as a good quality that you have rubs off on someone, they start to develop it too: *Hopefully her enthusiasm will rub off on the rest of the team.*

rub·ber /ˈrʌbər/ noun **1** [U] a strong substance that bends easily and is used for making things such as tires and boots **2** [C] *American informal* a CONDOM **3** [C] *British* an ERASER

ˌrubber ˈband noun [C] a thin circle of rubber that you use for holding things together

ˌrubber-ˈstamp verb [T] to give official approval for something without thinking about it at all

rub·ber·y /ˈrʌbəri/ adj similar to rubber

rub·bish /ˈrʌbɪʃ/ noun [U] *British* **1** GARBAGE **2** nonsense

rub·ble /ˈrʌb(ə)l/ noun [U] broken pieces of stone and brick from buildings that have been destroyed

ru·bel·la /ruˈbelə/ noun [U] *medical* a minor infectious disease that causes red spots on the skin = GERMAN MEASLES

ru·by /ˈrubi/ noun [C] a valuable red jewel

ruck·sack /ˈrʌkˌsæk/ noun [C] a BACKPACK

ruck·us /ˈrʌkəs/ noun [singular] *informal* a fight or a noisy argument

rud·der /ˈrʌdər/ noun [C] a flat part at the back of a boat or airplane that you move in order to turn the boat or airplane

rud·dy /ˈrʌdi/ adj *literary* a ruddy face is pink and looks healthy

rude /rud/ adj ★

1 not polite: *I don't want to seem rude, but I'd rather be alone.* ♦ **it is rude to do sth** *It's rude to keep people waiting.*

2 offensive because of referring to sex or using the toilet: *a rude word/joke*

—**rude·ly** adv: *What was I saying before I was so rudely interrupted?* —**rude·ness** noun [U]

ru·di·men·ta·ry /ˌrudəˈment(ə)ri/ adj basic: *rudimentary knowledge*

ru·di·ments /ˈrudəmənts/ noun **the rudiments of sth** the basic skills or information that are needed for an activity or subject

rue·ful /ˈruf(ə)l/ adj showing that you are sorry that something has happened —**rue·ful·ly** adv

ruf·fle /ˈrʌf(ə)l/ verb [T] **1** to move or shake something so that it is no longer smooth **2** to make someone feel nervous or upset

rug /rʌg/ noun [C] a small carpet that covers part of a floor

rug·by /ˈrʌgbi/ noun [U] a game like football that is played by two teams of players

rug•ged /ˈrʌgɪd/ adj **1** not smooth or flat: *a rugged landscape* **2** strong and able to deal with difficult conditions: *a rugged piece of equipment* **3** with a strong attractive appearance: *He had a tan rugged face.*

ru•in¹ /ˈruɪn/ verb [T] **1** to spoil or destroy something: *She had ruined her mother's chances of getting a job.* **2** to make someone lose all their money or power: *The scandal that totally ruined him.*

ru•in² /ˈruɪn/ noun **1 ruins** [plural] the parts of a building that remain after it has been severely damaged: *Roman ruins* ♦ *People had built shelters among the ruins of the city.* **2** [U] the loss of all your money or power: *Many of these companies are facing ruin.*

PHRASE **in ruins** destroyed, or severely damaged: *His marriage was over and his career was in ruins.*

ru•in•ous /ˈruɪnəs/ adj **1** causing severe damage **2** something that is ruinous costs so much money that it causes a lot of problems for you

rule¹ /rul/ noun ★★★

1 [C] a statement that explains what you can or cannot do in a particular situation: *grammatical rules* ♦ *Players who* ***break the rules*** *are sent off the field.* ♦ *You should always* ***follow*** *these simple* ***rules*** *when using electrical equipment.* ♦ *You can't do that, it's* ***against the rules!*** ♦ *the basic* ***rules of the game***

2 [U] the person, group, or country that officially controls a place: *In 1999 Hong Kong went back to Chinese rule.*

PHRASES **as a rule** usually: *As a rule, I stay in on Friday nights.*

bend/stretch the rules to allow something that is not normally allowed

rule of thumb a simple method or principle that is not exact, but that is effective

→ GOLDEN RULE, HOME RULE

Words often used with rule

Verbs often used with ***rule*** *(noun, sense 1)*

- **bend, break, flout** + RULES: not accept rules
- **follow, obey, play by, stick to** + RULES: accept rules

rule² /rul/ verb ★★

1 [I/T] to officially control a country or area =GOVERN: *Portugal ruled East Timor for nearly four centuries.*

2 [I/T] to make and announce an official decision: *The judge still has not* ***ruled on*** *the case.* ♦ **+(that)** *The Supreme Court ruled that the law was unconstitutional.*

3 [T] to control someone's thoughts or actions: *Money and music rule Charlie's world.* ♦ *We must not allow ourselves to be ruled by personal feelings.*

PHRASAL VERB ˌ**rule sb/sth** ˈ**out** to stop considering someone or something as a possibility: *The president has ruled out the use of U.S. troops.*

ruled /ruld/ adj ruled paper has straight lines printed on it for writing on

rul•er /ˈrulər/ noun [C] ★

1 a long flat object that you use for measuring or for drawing straight lines

2 someone who controls a country: *Haiti's former military rulers*

rul•ing¹ /ˈrulɪŋ/ adj in control of a country or group: *members of the ruling party*

rul•ing² /ˈrulɪŋ/ noun [C] an official decision

rum /rʌm/ noun [U] a strong alcoholic drink made from SUGAR CANE

rum•ble /ˈrʌmb(ə)l/ verb [I] to make a continuous deep sound —**rum•ble** noun [C]

rum•bling /ˈrʌmblɪŋ/ noun **1** [singular] a continuous deep sound **2 rumblings** [plural] signs that people are becoming unhappy about a situation

ru•mi•nate /ˈrumɪˌneɪt/ verb [I] *formal* to think about something carefully

rum•mage /ˈrʌmɪdʒ/ verb [I] to search for something among a lot of other things

ˈ**rummage** ˌ**sale** noun [C] *American* a sale of old clothes, toys, books, etc.

ru•mor /ˈrumər/ noun [C/U] something that people are saying that may or may not be true: *A student had been spreading rumors about the teachers.* ♦ *Rumor has it that* (=there is a rumor that) *he's seriously ill.* ♦ *Now there are rumors of wedding plans.* ♦ *He denied rumors that a hundred workers would be laid off.*

ru•mored /ˈrumərd/ adj if something is rumored, people are saying it, but it is not definitely true

ru•mour /ˈrumər/ the British spelling of rumor

rump /rʌmp/ noun [C] the part of an animal's body that is above its back legs

rum•pled /ˈrʌmp(ə)ld/ adj something that is rumpled is messy because it is not smooth or flat —**rum•ple** verb [T]

run¹ /rʌn/ (past tense **ran** /ræn/; past participle **run**) verb ★★★

1 move quickly with legs	10 move sth along sth
2 control/organize	11 exist in a place
3 machine: work	12 take sb in car
4 liquid: flow	13 use program
5 make water flow	14 print in newspaper
6 try to be elected	15 liquid/color: spread
7 vehicle: travel	16 do test/check
8 be shown/performed	+ PHRASES
9 reach amount/rate	+ PHRASAL VERBS

1 [I] to move quickly using your legs and feet: *You'll have to run if you want to catch the bus.* ♦ *A cat* ***ran across*** *the road in front of me.* ♦ *I* ***ran to*** *the door and opened it.*

2 [T] to control and organize something such as a business, organization, or event =MANAGE: *He was the man who ran Clinton's election campaign.*

3 [I/T] if a machine or engine runs, or if you run it, it operates: *Don't leave the engine running.* ♦ *I ran the dishwasher even though it wasn't full.*

4 [I] if a liquid runs somewhere, it flows there: *Tears were* ***running down*** *his face.* ♦ *The Mississippi River* ***runs into*** *the Gulf of Mexico.*

5 [T] to make water flow from or into a container: *I'm going to* ***run a bath.***

6 [I] to try to be elected to an official job or position: *How many candidates are running?* ♦ *Jackson announced his intention to* ***run for president.***

7 [I] if a bus or train runs, it travels somewhere at regular times: *The train only runs on the weekend.*

R

8 [I] if a play, movie, or television program runs, it continues to be performed or shown: *a soap opera that has been running for many years*
9 [I] to continue at a particular amount or rate: *Inflation is **running at** 3%.*
10 [T] to move something through or along something else: **run sth through/across/down sth** *Fred ran his fingers gently through her hair.*
11 [I] if something such as a road or wall runs somewhere, it continues from one place to another: *There was a path **running through** the middle of the forest.*
12 [T] to take someone somewhere in your car: *I'll run you there – it's no trouble.* ♦ **run sb to/into sth** *John kindly offered to run me into town.*
13 [I/T] if you run a computer program, or if it runs, you start it or use it: *The software will **run on** any PC.*
14 [T] if newspapers run an article, advertisement, or photograph, they print it
15 [I] if a piece of clothing or a color runs, the color spreads when you wash it
16 [T] to perform something such as a test, or to check on someone or something: *He'd **run a check on** her through his London office.*

PHRASES **run circles around sb** to do something much better than someone else
running late if you are running late, you do something or arrive somewhere later than you planned
run short/low if you run short of something, or if you run low on something, you do not have enough of it left: *We're **running low on** milk.* ♦ *I'm **running short of** ideas.*
sth runs in the family if something such as a quality or disease runs in the family, a lot of people in the family have it
→ COURSE[1]

PHRASAL VERBS **ˌrun aˈcross sb/sth** to meet someone or find something by chance
ˌrun ˈafter sb/sth to chase someone or something: *Velluci ran after the car waving his fists.*
ˌrun aˈround to be very busy doing a lot of different things: *I've been running around all day.*
ˌrun aˈway 1 to secretly leave a place because you are not happy there: *When I was 13, I **ran away from** home.* **2** to try to avoid dealing with a difficult or unpleasant situation: *You can't keep **running away from** the problem.*
ˌrun sth ˈby sb to tell someone your ideas so that they can give you their opinion: *Can I run a few ideas by you?*
ˌrun (sth) ˈdown if something such as a machine runs down, or if you run it down, it gradually stops working because it is losing power: *Switch your headlights off, or you'll run the battery down.*
ˌrun sb/sth ˈdown to hit a person or animal with your car and injure or kill them: *She got run down outside the school.* → RUNDOWN
ˌrun ˈinto sb to meet someone when you did not expect to: ***Guess who I ran into this** morning?*
ˌrun ˈinto sth 1 to start to experience something that is unpleasant: *The project soon **ran into difficulties**.* **2** to reach a particular amount: *The cost of paying for the flood damage could run into millions.*
ˌrun ˈinto sb/sth to hit someone or something by accident while you are driving: *A truck ran into me* (=hit my car) *this morning.*
ˌrun ˈoff to suddenly leave a place or person: *Their dad ran off when they were little.*
ˌrun sth ˈoff to quickly print a copy of something: *Would you mind running off some more copies of the agenda?*
ˌrun ˈoff with sb *informal* to secretly leave a place with someone in order to marry them or have a sexual relationship with them: *They said Phil had run off with his wife's best friend.*
ˌrun ˈoff with sth to steal something, or to take it without permission
ˌrun ˈout 1 to use all of something and not have any left: *Some hospitals are **running out of** blood supplies.* **2** if something such as money or time runs out, there is no more of it left: *They returned home from South Africa when their money ran out.* **3** to stop being legal on a particular date =EXPIRE: *My contract runs out next July.* ♦ *When does your passport run out?*
ˌrun sb/sth ˈover to hit someone or something with a vehicle: *Keeley was run over by a car outside her house.*
ˌrun ˈthrough sth 1 to explain or read something quickly: *Do you want me to run through the details with you?* **2** to practice something so that it is correct for a performance or test: *Let's just run through the piece one more time.*
ˌrun ˈup sth if you run up a bill or a DEBT, you owe someone a lot of money: *My son ran up a huge phone bill.*
ˌrun ˈup aˌgainst sth to have to deal with something that is difficult or unpleasant

run[2] /rʌn/ noun ★★★

1 race	5 a trip
2 period of time	6 hole in stockings
3 amount produced	+ PHRASES
4 baseball point	

1 [C] an act of running, or a race in which you run a long distance: *Lee is doing a six-mile run on Saturday.*
2 [singular] a period of time when something continues: *The play is enjoying a successful run on Broadway.* ♦ *We've had **a run of bad luck** recently.*
3 [C] the amount of something that a company or factory produces at one time: *The plates are a limited edition run of 250.*
4 [C] one point in the game of baseball: *Puckett scored three runs in the game.*
5 [singular] a trip in a vehicle: *We took the new car out for a run in the country.*
6 [C] *American* a long thin hole in STOCKINGS or PANTYHOSE

PHRASES **in the long run** not immediately but at a time in the future: *In the long run, I think you're better off without him.*
in the short run for a short period of time from now: *Most diets produce weight loss only in the short run.*
make a run for sth to suddenly run toward

something and try to reach it: *Mary made a run for the exit.*
a run on sth a situation in which a lot of people want to buy something at the same time
→ RUNS

run·a·way¹ /ˈrʌnəˌweɪ/ noun [C] a child who has secretly left their home

run·a·way² /ˈrʌnəˌweɪ/ adj **1** a runaway vehicle or animal is moving fast without anyone controlling it **2** happening or increasing very quickly: *runaway inflation* **3** a runaway person has left their home or has escaped from somewhere

run·down /ˈrʌnˌdaʊn/ noun [C] a short report

ˌrun-ˈdown adj **1** so tired that you do not feel well **2** in bad condition because no one has spent money on repairs: *a run-down apartment building*

rung¹ /rʌŋ/ noun [C] **1** one of the bars across a LADDER that you put your feet on when you climb up **2** a level of achievement: *You could be on the first rung of a great new career.*

rung² the past participle of **ring¹**

ˈrun-ˌin noun [C] *informal* an argument

run·ner /ˈrʌnər/ noun [C] **1** a person or animal that runs in a race, or someone who runs for pleasure **2** in baseball, a player who is on one of the BASES waiting for the ball to be hit, so that they can try to run and get a point *—picture* → C15 **3** a narrow part on which something such as a drawer or SLED slides **4** someone who carries drugs or weapons illegally from one place to another
→ FRONT-RUNNER

ˈrunner ˌbean noun [C] a long green bean that is cooked and eaten

ˌrunner-ˈup (plural **ˌrunners-ˈup**) noun [C] someone who is second in a competition or race

run·ning¹ /ˈrʌnɪŋ/ noun [U] **1** the activity of running for pleasure or as a sport **2** the activities that are involved in managing or organizing something: *The family is not involved in the day-to-day running of the company.*
PHRASE **be in/out of the running** to have some chance/no chance of success

run·ning² /ˈrʌnɪŋ/ adv **four weeks/five years/six times etc. running** four weeks/five years/six times etc., following one after another

ˌrunning ˈbattle noun [C] an argument that continues over a long period of time

ˌrunning ˈtotal noun [C] a total amount that has new amounts added to it regularly

ˌrunning ˈwater noun [U] water that is supplied by pipes into a building

run·ny /ˈrʌni/ adj **1** a runny nose has liquid coming out of it **2** like a liquid

ˌrun-of-the-ˈmill adj ordinary and not interesting

runs, the /rʌns/ noun [plural] *informal* DIARRHEA

ˈrun-ˌup noun **the run-up to sth** the period of time just before an important event

run·way /ˈrʌnˌweɪ/ noun [C] a long road that is used by airplanes when they land and TAKE OFF

rup·ture /ˈrʌptʃər/ verb [I/T] if something ruptures, or if you rupture it, it bursts or tears suddenly: *The impact ruptured both fuel tanks.* —**rup·ture** noun [C]

ru·ral /ˈrʊrəl/ adj ★★ relating to the parts of a country that are not near cities ≠ URBAN: *rural areas/roads/schools*

ruse /rus, ruz/ noun [C] a way of tricking someone = PLOY

rush¹ /rʌʃ/ verb [I/T] ★★
1 to go somewhere in a hurry, or to take someone or send something somewhere in a hurry: *Suddenly the door burst open and Joe **rushed in**.* ♦ *Ambulance crews **rushed to** the scene of the accident.* ♦ **rush sb to/into sth** *Frank was rushed to the hospital with violent stomach pains.* ♦ **rush sb sth** *Can you rush me a copy of the report?*
2 to do something quickly, or to make someone do something quickly: *There's no need to rush. We have plenty of time.* ♦ *Don't **rush into** a decision.* ♦ **rush sb into (doing) sth** *His parents rushed him into getting married.* ♦ **rush to do sth** *Hayley rushed to answer the phone.*
PHRASAL VERB **ˌrush aˈround** to try to do a lot of things in a short time

rush² /rʌʃ/ noun ★
1 [singular] a sudden strong movement forward: *Everyone **made a rush for** the ice cream stand.* ♦ **a rush to do sth** *Commuters jostled in a rush to get off the subway.*
2 [singular/U] a situation in which you hurry to do something: *Sorry, I can't stop. I'm **in a rush**.*
3 [singular] an occasion when a lot of people suddenly want to do something or have something: *We've had **a rush on** barbecue grills this week.* ♦ **a rush to do sth** *There was a rush to buy tickets for the concert.*
4 the rush [singular] the time of day when a place is very busy and there is a lot of traffic: *Lee left home at six in the morning to avoid the rush.*

rushed /rʌʃt/ adj done in a hurry

rush·es /ˈrʌʃɪz/ noun [plural] tall plants like grass that grow in water

ˈrush ˌhour noun [C/U] the time of day when there is a lot of traffic because people are traveling to or from work

rust¹ /rʌst/ noun [U] the red substance that damages the surface of metal

rust² /rʌst/ verb [I/T] to become damaged by rust, or to make metal develop rust

rus·tic /ˈrʌstɪk/ adj made in the simple style of the countryside

rus·tle /ˈrʌs(ə)l/ verb [I/T] to produce a sound like the sound that leaves or sheets of paper make when they move, or to make something do this —**rus·tle** noun [singular]
PHRASAL VERB **ˌrustle sth ˈup** *informal* to quickly produce something such as a meal using whatever things are available

rust·y /ˈrʌsti/ adj **1** covered in RUST **2** a skill that is rusty has not been used recently

rut /rʌt/ noun [C] **1** a situation that is boring and difficult to change: *If you're in a rut, change jobs.* **2** a deep narrow mark in the ground made by a wheel

ruth·less /ˈruθləs/ adj willing to hurt other people in order to get what you want —**ruth·less·ly** adv

RV /ˌɑr ˈvi/ noun [C] *American* recreational vehicle: a large road vehicle that you can live in

rye /raɪ/ noun [U] **1** plants that produce grain that is used for making bread and WHISKEY **2** bread or WHISKEY made from rye

Ss

s or **S** /es/ noun [C/U] the 19th letter of the English alphabet

S. abbrev **1** small: used on clothes labels **2** South **3** Southern

-'s[1] short form **1** a way of saying or writing "is" and "has." This is not often used in formal writing: *She's in the kitchen.* ♦ *John's gone out.* **2** the usual way of saying or writing "us" when you use it with "let" to make a suggestion: *Let's not tell him now.*

-'s[2] suffix **1** used with nouns for showing who or what something belongs to: *I've never met Andy's wife.* ♦ *The dog's leg was badly cut.* ♦ *the evening's activities* (=activities that happen in the evening) **2** used for talking about the home of a particular person: *We all went back to Alan's for lunch.*

S & L /ˌes ənd ˈel/ noun [C] *American* a savings and loan association

Sab•bath, the /ˈsæbəθ/ noun [singular] a day when the people of some religions rest and pray

sab•bat•i•cal /səˈbætɪk(ə)l/ noun [C/U] a period when a university teacher is away from work because they are doing research

sa•ber /ˈseɪbər/ noun [C] a sword with a curved blade

ˈsaber-ˌrattling noun [U] a threat of violence or military action

sab•o•tage /ˈsæbəˌtɑʒ/ verb [T] **1** to deliberately damage or destroy something that belongs to an enemy **2** to deliberately prevent something from being successful —**sab•o•tage** noun [U]

sab•o•teur /ˌsæbəˈtɜr/ noun [C] someone who deliberately damages or destroys something that belongs to an enemy

sac•cha•rin /ˈsækərɪn/ noun [U] a chemical substance that is used instead of sugar for making food sweet

sack[1] /sæk/ noun [C] a large strong bag for storing and carrying things: *a sack of potatoes/flour* ♦ *The sack was too heavy to lift.*

sack[2] /sæk/ verb [T] **1** if an army sacks a place, they steal property from it and destroy it **2** *British informal* to force someone to leave their job = FIRE

sac•ra•ment /ˈsækrəmənt/ noun [C] an important Christian ceremony such as marriage or BAPTISM

sa•cred /ˈseɪkrəd/ adj **1** connected with religion: *a sacred holiday* **2** holy: *Jerusalem is sacred to Christians, Muslims, and Jews.* **3** something that is sacred is so important that you should not change or criticize it: *the sacred rules of the legal profession*

ˌsacred ˈcow noun [C] something that is too important to change or criticize

sac•ri•fice[1] /ˈsækrɪˌfaɪs/ noun [C/U] **1** a decision not to have or do something that is important to you, so that someone else will have a benefit or so that you will benefit later: *Making sacrifices is part of raising children.* **2** the act of killing a person or animal as part of a ceremony to honor a god or spirit —**sac•ri•fi•cial** /ˌsækrɪˈfɪʃ(ə)l/ adj: *a sacrificial animal*

sac•ri•fice[2] /ˈsækrɪˌfaɪs/ verb [T] **1** to choose not to have something so that other people can have something else: *She sacrificed her career to bring up the children.* **2** to kill a person or animal as part of a ceremony to honor a god or spirit

sac•ri•lege /ˈsækrəlɪdʒ/ noun [U] behavior that shows that someone has no respect for something holy or important —**sac•ri•le•gious** /ˌsækrəˈlɪdʒəs/ adj

sac•ro•sanct /ˈsækroʊˌsæŋkt/ adj too important to change or criticize

sad /sæd/ adj ★★

1 feeling unhappy, making you feel unhappy, or showing that you feel unhappy: *It was a sad day when we sold our home.* ♦ *sad eyes* ♦ *Reading her letter made us all **feel** a little **sad**.* ♦ *I felt **sad about** leaving him, but I had no choice.* ♦ ***I feel sad for** all the children growing up without a father at home.* ♦ **be sad to see/hear sth** *I was very sad to hear that your mother had died.*

2 very bad in a way that makes you feel angry, upset, or shocked: ***The sad truth is** that many people never learn to read.* ♦ *It's **a sad state of affairs** when people can't be bothered to vote anymore.* ♦ **it is sad that/it's a sad fact that** *I think it's sad that children spend so much time watching television.*

3 *very informal* boring or not fashionable

> **Other ways of saying sad**
> - **depressed** feeling very negative about your situation
> - **down** (*informal*) slightly depressed
> - **gloomy** sad and having no hope for the future
> - **low** feeling negative about life, and lacking energy
> - **miserable** very sad because you are uncomfortable, lonely, or sick
> - **unhappy** a general word for "sad"

sad•den /ˈsæd(ə)n/ verb [T] to make someone feel sad

sad•dle[1] /ˈsæd(ə)l/ noun [C] **1** a leather seat that you put on a horse's back **2** the seat on a bicycle or MOTORCYCLE

sad•dle[2] /ˈsæd(ə)l/ verb [T] to put a saddle on a horse

PHRASAL VERB **ˈsaddle sb with sth** to give someone something that is difficult or unpleasant to deal with: *The company was saddled with a huge debt last year.*

sa•dist /ˈseɪdɪst/ noun [C] someone who likes to hurt people —**sa•dism** noun [U]

sa·dis·tic /səˈdɪstɪk/ adj someone who is sadistic likes to hurt people

sad·ly /ˈsædli/ adv **1** used for showing that you think that something is bad or wrong: *Sadly, they chose to ignore our advice.* **2** in a way that shows that you are sad, or that makes you feel sad: *She smiled sadly.*

sad·ness /ˈsædnəs/ noun [U] the feeling of being unhappy: *It is with great sadness that we announce the death of Wilfred White.*

sa·fa·ri /səˈfɑri/ noun [C] a trip, especially to Africa, in order to see wild animals in their natural environment

safe[1] /seɪf/ adj ★★★

1 not likely to be harmed, lost, or stolen: *Will my car be safe if I park it on the street?* ♦ *It's difficult to make airports* ***safe from*** *terrorist attacks.* ♦ **keep sth safe** *Make sure to keep your credit card safe.*

2 not likely to cause damage or harm: *Traveling by airplane is much safer than driving your own car.* ♦ *a safe environment for children*

3 not damaged, hurt, or lost: *Rescuers found the children safe but scared inside the house.* ♦ *Everyone arrived* ***safe and sound.***

4 not involving a lot of risk: *a safe investment*

PHRASE **on the safe side** in a situation that involves very little risk because you have been very careful: *Just to be on the safe side, take an umbrella.*

safe[2] /seɪf/ noun [C] a strong metal box that is used for storing valuable things

ˌsafe-deˈposit ˌbox noun [C] a small box in a bank that a customer uses for storing valuable possessions

safe·guard /ˈseɪfˌgɑrd/ verb [T] to protect something or someone: *a plan to safeguard the environment* —**safe·guard** noun [C]

ˌsafe ˈhaven noun [C] a place where people are safe from danger or attack

safe·keep·ing /seɪfˈkipɪŋ/ noun [U] protection from being damaged or lost: *Sheila gave me the rings for safekeeping.*

safe·ly /ˈseɪfli/ adv **1** in a way that will not cause damage or harm: *Remember to drive safely.* **2** without being damaged, hurt, or lost: *All the children have been returned safely to their parents.*

ˌsafe ˈsex noun [U] sexual activity in which people are careful to avoid getting diseases

safe·ty /ˈseɪfti/ noun [U] ★★★

1 the fact that something is safe to do or use: *Their cars have a reputation for safety and reliability.* ♦ *a safety helmet/harness* ♦ *The airline has a poor* ***safety record*** (=a record of how safe something has been in the past). ♦ *Do we know enough about* ***the safety of*** *these vaccines?*

2 a place or situation in which you are protected from danger: *Refugees walked for several days until they reached safety.* ♦ *We watched the storm from* ***the safety of*** *our home.*

3 a safe way of behaving: *We plan to have frequent training sessions on safety at work.*

ˈsafety ˌbelt noun [C] a SEAT BELT

ˈsafety ˌnet noun [C] **1** a plan or system that is designed to protect people or prevent serious problems **2** a net that you put under something in order to catch people if they fall

ˈsafety ˌpin noun [C] a curved pin with a cover that fits over the sharp point

saf·fron /ˈsæfrən/ noun [U] part of a flower that is used for adding flavor and yellow color to food

sag /sæg/ verb [I] **1** to become soft and start to bend or hang downward **2** to become weaker or less in amount or value

sa·ga /ˈsɑgə/ noun [C] **1** a story about what happens to a group of characters over a long period of time **2** *informal* a long series of events, or a description of them

sage[1] /seɪdʒ/ noun **1** [U] a plant that is used for flavoring food **2** [C] *literary* someone who is wise

sage[2] /seɪdʒ/ adj *literary* wise —**sage·ly** adv

Sag·it·tar·i·us /ˌsædʒɪˈteriəs/ noun [U] one of the twelve signs of the ZODIAC. A **Sagittarius** is someone who was born between November 23 and December 21.

said the past tense and past participle of **say**[1]

sail[1] /seɪl/ verb ★★

1 [I] to travel somewhere by boat or ship: *Sail to Greece aboard the SS Monterey.*

2 [I/T] to control the movement of a boat or ship, especially one that uses the wind to move it: *It's a great opportunity to learn to sail.*

3 [I/T] if a boat sails, it moves across the surface of water: *The yacht sailed into harbor.*

4 [I] to move quickly and easily: *The ball* ***sailed over his head and into the goal.***

PHRASAL VERB **ˈsail ˌthrough sth** to achieve a particular result very easily: *She sailed through the first interview.*

sail[2] /seɪl/ noun [C] a large piece of strong cloth attached to a tall pole on a boat. It uses the wind to move the boat across water.

sail·board /ˈseɪlˌbɔrd/ noun [C] a long board with a MAST and sail, used for moving across water in the sport of WINDSURFING

sail·boat /ˈseɪlˌboʊt/ noun [C] *American* a small boat that is moved by the wind using sails

sail·ing /ˈseɪlɪŋ/ noun [U] the sport or activity of traveling across water in a sailboat

sail·or /ˈseɪlər/ noun [C] someone who works on a boat or ship, or who sails for pleasure

saint /seɪnt/ noun [C] **1** someone who the Christian Church officially honors after their death because they have lived a very holy life **2** someone who is very kind, patient, and helpful —**saint·hood** /ˈseɪntˌhʊd/ noun [U]

saint·ly /ˈseɪntli/ adj very good or holy

sake /seɪk/ noun ★

PHRASES **for God's/goodness'/Heaven's/Pete's sake** *spoken* used for emphasizing what you are saying when you are annoyed or angry. "For God's sake" is offensive to some people: *Oh, for Pete's sake, leave me alone!*

for sb's/sth's sake or **for the sake of sb/sth** for the benefit or good of someone or something: *We hope for her sake that the wedding goes as planned.*

for the sake of sth for the purpose of doing, getting, or achieving something: *I hope you're not doing this just for the sake of the* *money.* ♦ *For clarity's sake, I'd like to reword my statement.*

sal•a•ble /ˈseɪləb(ə)l/ adj able to be sold

sal•ad /ˈsæləd/ noun [C/U] ★
1 a food containing a mixture of raw vegetables such as LETTUCE, tomatoes, and CUCUMBERS, usually served with a salad dressing: *a green salad*
2 food that has been cut into small pieces and mixed together, usually with a sauce, and served cold: *an egg salad sandwich* ♦ *a fruit salad*

ˈ**salad ˌdressing** noun [C/U] a sauce that adds flavor to salads, usually made by mixing oil, VINEGAR, and HERBS or SPICES

sa•la•mi /səˈlɑmi/ noun [C/U] a type of SAUSAGE containing strong SPICES, cut into thin pieces and served cold

sal•a•ried /ˈsælərid/ adj paid a particular amount of money for your job each month or year

sal•a•ry /ˈsæləri/ noun [C] ★ a particular amount of money that you earn each month or year from your job: *an* ***annual salary*** *of $45,000*

sale /seɪl/ noun ★★★

1 when prices are lower	5 selling department
2 event for selling	6 instance of selling
3 process of selling	+ PHRASES
4 total sold	

1 [C] an event or period of time during which a store reduces the prices of some of its goods: *the start of the after-Christmas sales* ♦ *The store is* ***having a sale*** *on appliances next week.*
2 [C] an event at which people meet to buy and sell things: *a second-hand book sale*
3 [C/U] the process of selling goods or services for money: *a ban on* ***the sale of*** *arms*
4 sales [plural] the total number of things that a company sells within a particular period of time, or the money that it earns by selling things: *Sales are up for the month of May.* ♦ *We hope to* ***increase sales*** *this year to $50 million.* ♦ *Do you have* ***the sales figures*** *yet?*
5 sales [plural] the department of a company that sells its goods or services: *Dave works in sales.*
6 [C] a single instance of selling goods or services: *I'm willing to lower the price in order to* ***make a sale.***
PHRASES **for sale** available for people to buy: *That chair is* ***not for sale.***
on sale 1 available for people to buy: *Tickets for the performance are on sale at the box office.* **2** *American* available for people to buy at a price that is less than the usual price: *Furniture usually* ***goes on sale*** *in January.*
up for sale available for people to buy: *We're* ***putting*** *the factory* ***up for sale.***

ˈ**sales ˌclerk** noun [C] *American* someone whose job is to help customers and sell things in a store

sales•man /ˈseɪlzmən/ (plural **sales•men** /ˈseɪlzmən/) noun [C] a man whose job is to sell the products or services of a particular company

sales•per•son /ˈseɪlzˌpɜrs(ə)n/ (plural **sales•peo•ple** /ˈseɪlzˌpip(ə)l/) noun [C] someone whose job is to sell the products or services of a particular company

ˈ**sales repreˌsentative** or ˈ**sales ˌrep** noun [C] someone whose job is to travel to different places and sell the products or services of a particular company

ˈ**sales ˌslip** noun [C] *American* a small piece of paper that a store gives you showing how much money you pay for something you buy=RECEIPT

ˈ**sales ˌtax** noun [C/U] a tax that is added to the basic price of something you buy

sales•wom•an /ˈseɪlzˌwʊmən/ (plural **sales•wom•en** /ˈseɪlzˌwɪmɪn/) noun [C] a woman whose job is to sell the products or services of a particular company

sa•li•ent /ˈseɪliənt/ adj *formal* very noticeable or relevant

sa•line /ˈseɪˌlin/ adj *technical* containing salt

sa•li•va /səˈlaɪvə/ noun [U] the liquid that is produced in your mouth=SPIT

sal•i•vate /ˈsælɪˌveɪt/ verb [I] to produce more than the usual amount of saliva, because you see or smell food

sal•low /ˈsæloʊ/ adj sallow skin is a pale yellow color and does not look healthy

salm•on /ˈsæmən/ (plural **salm•on**) noun [C/U] a large silver fish with pink flesh that is eaten as food

sal•mo•nel•la /ˌsælməˈnelə/ noun [C] a type of bacteria that is found in food and can make you sick

sa•lon /səˈlɑn/ noun [C] a place where you can have your hair cut and STYLED

sa•loon /səˈlun/ noun [C] *British* a SEDAN car

sal•sa /ˈsɑlsə/ noun **1** [U] a sauce usually made from tomatoes, onions, and other herbs or spices. It is served with Mexican or Spanish food. **2** [C/U] a type of Latin-American dance music, or a dance performed to this music

salt¹ /sɔlt/ noun ★
1 [U] a white substance that is often added to food to improve its flavor: *Add* ***a pinch of salt.***
2 [C] *science* a chemical substance formed from an acid
PHRASE **take sth with a grain/pinch of salt** to doubt the truth or value of something: *If I were you, I'd take his advice with a grain of salt.*

salt² /sɔlt/ verb [T] to add salt to food

ˈ**salt ˌshaker** noun [C] *American* a small container with a lid that has holes, used for pouring salt on food

salt•wa•ter /ˈsɔltˌwɔtər/ adj living in the ocean or in water that contains salt ≠FRESHWATER: *saltwater fish*

salt•y /ˈsɔlti/ adj containing salt, or tasting like salt

sa•lute /səˈlut/ verb **1** [I/T] to put your hand to your head as a formal way of showing respect to a senior officer in the military **2** [T] to express praise or respect for a person or an achievement, especially formally and in public —**sa•lute** noun [C]

sal•vage /ˈsælvɪdʒ/ verb [T] **1** to save things from a ship or building that has been damaged or destroyed **2** to succeed in achieving something in a situation that has been a failure —**sal•vage** noun [U]

S

sal·va·tion /sælˈveɪʃ(ə)n/ noun [U] **1** according to the Christian religion, the act of being saved by God from evil =REDEMPTION
2 someone or something that helps you in a bad or dangerous situation

Salˌvation ˈArmy, the an international organization that teaches CHRISTIANITY and helps people who have problems

same /seɪm/ grammar word ★★★

> **Same** can be:
> - an **adjective**: *We both went to the same school.*
> - a **pronoun**: *I'd do the same if I had the chance.*
> - an **adverb**: *The twins always dress the same.*

1 the same used for saying that a particular person or thing is the one that you are referring to, and not a different one: *We were staying at **the same** hotel **as** my parents.* ♦ *Was this **the same** Timothy Evans **that** Carol had gone to school with?* ♦ *I was born on **the very same** day that my father died.*
2 the same exactly like another person, thing, or way of doing something: *She did not want to make the same mistake again.* ♦ *The two pictures **look the same** to me – I can't tell them apart.* ♦ *Her eyes are **the same** color **as** yours.*
3 the same used for saying that someone or something has not changed: *The government policy has **remained the same** since 1991.* ♦ *"How is Frances?" "Oh, she's still **the same as always**."* ♦ *The countryside looks **much the same** as it did 200 years ago.*
4 the same used for saying that one number, amount, price, etc. is equal to another: *The four sides of a square are all the same length.* ♦ *One centimeter **is the same as** ten millimeters.*
PHRASES **at the same time 1** used for saying that two or more things happen together: *The show will make you laugh and cry at the same time.* **2** used for introducing another fact or opinion that needs to be considered as well as the one that has just been stated: *I want to work hard for my family, but at the same time I want to spend time with them.*
same here *spoken* used for saying that you agree or that you have the same feeling: *"I've been looking forward to meeting you." "Same here."*
the same old... familiar and not new or exciting: *Politicians repeat the same old phrases every election.*
→ BOAT, PAGE[1]

> **Other ways of saying same**
> - **alike** almost the same
> - **constant** remaining at the same level
> - **equal/equivalent** at the same level, or the same in quality or quantity
> - **identical** exactly the same, with no differences
> - **similar** almost the same, but with small differences

sam·ple¹ /ˈsæmp(ə)l/ noun [C] ★
1 an example or small amount of something that shows you what all of it is like: *We had to bring some **samples of** our work to the interview.* ♦ *I took home some **samples** of curtain fabrics.*
2 a small amount of a substance that is used for scientific or medical tests: *Tests were performed on hair and blood samples.* ♦ *Researchers are **taking samples of** the air close to the factory.*
3 a group of people that is used for getting information about a larger group, or about the whole population: *The study took **a sample of** 100 students from 3 schools.*

sam·ple² /ˈsæmp(ə)l/ verb [T] **1** to taste a small amount of food or drink in order to see what it is like: *They let us sample some of the wine.* **2** to try doing a new activity for a time: *Here you can relax and sample life in this island paradise.*

sanc·ti·mo·ni·ous /ˌsæŋktəˈmoʊniəs/ adj *showing disapproval* trying to show that you have better moral or religious principles than other people

sanc·tion¹ /ˈsæŋkʃ(ə)n/ noun **1** [C] an official order to stop communication, trade, etc. with a country that has broken international law: *economic/trade/international sanctions* ♦ *The Council wanted to impose sanctions* (=start to use them) *against the countries involved in the dispute.* **2** [U] official permission for taking action: *War was declared without the sanction of parliament.* **3** [C] a punishment for breaking a rule

sanc·tion² /ˈsæŋkʃ(ə)n/ verb [T] *formal* to give approval or permission for something

sanc·ti·ty /ˈsæŋktəti/ noun [U] the special importance that something has

sanc·tu·ar·y /ˈsæŋktʃuˌeri/ noun **1** [C/U] a place that provides official protection for someone: *Refugees sought sanctuary in Thailand.* **2** [C/U] a place where you feel safe or comfortable: *All she wanted now was the sanctuary of her own room.* **3** [C] a special area where animals live in a natural environment protected from people

sand¹ /sænd/ noun ★★
1 [U] a pale brown substance that you find at a beach or in the desert, formed from very small pieces of rock: *The children were playing in the sand.* ♦ *a grain of sand*
2 sands [plural] an area of sand

sand² /sænd/ verb [I/T] to make something such as wood very smooth by rubbing it with SANDPAPER

san·dal /ˈsænd(ə)l/ noun [C] a light shoe that is partly open on top and does not cover your heel or toes *—picture* → SHOE

sand·bag /ˈsæn(d)ˌbæg/ noun [C] a bag that is filled with sand, used for protecting a place from floods or explosions

sand·box /ˈsæn(d)ˌbɑks/ noun [C] *American* a large low container that is filled with sand for children to play in

sand·cas·tle /ˈsæn(d)ˌkæs(ə)l/ noun [C] a pile of sand that is made in the shape of a castle or tower by children on a beach

ˈsand ˌdune noun [C] a hill of sand that is formed by the wind in a desert or near a beach

sand·pa·per /ˈsæn(d)ˌpeɪpər/ noun [U] strong paper with a rough surface that you rub against wood or metal to make it smooth

sand·storm /ˈsæn(d)ˌstɔrm/ noun [C] a strong

S

wind in the desert in which clouds of sand are blown into the air

sand•wich¹ /ˈsæn(d)wɪtʃ/ noun [C] ★ two pieces of bread with a layer of food such as meat, cheese, or egg between them: *a ham/tuna/cheese sandwich* ♦ *I usually just have a sandwich for lunch.*

sand•wich² /ˈsæn(d)wɪtʃ/ verb **be sandwiched between** to be in a small or tight space between two people or things that are larger: *The tiny kingdom was sandwiched between Austria and Czechoslovakia.*

sand•y /ˈsændi/ adj covered with sand, or containing sand

sane /seɪn/ adj **1** able to think, speak, and behave in a reasonable and normal way ≠ INSANE **2** a sane action or decision is a sensible one

sang the past tense of **sing**

san•guine /ˈsæŋgwɪn/ adj *formal* confident and hopeful about what might happen = OPTIMISTIC

san•i•tar•y /ˈsænɪˌteri/ adj **1** relating to people's health, especially to the system of supplying water and dealing with human waste **2** keeping things healthy and clean

ˈsanitary ˌpad or **ˈsanitary ˌnapkin** noun [C] *American* a thick band of soft material that women attach to the inside of their underwear during MENSTRUATION

san•i•ta•tion /ˌsænɪˈteɪʃ(ə)n/ noun [U] conditions and processes relating to people's health, especially the systems that supply water and deal with human waste

san•i•tize /ˈsænɪˌtaɪz/ verb [T] **1** to remove information or details that might be offensive or unpleasant: *books that sanitize history* **2** to make something clean, especially by killing bacteria

san•i•ty /ˈsænəti/ noun [U] the ability to think and speak in a reasonable way and to behave normally: *I was beginning to doubt my own sanity* (=think I was possibly mentally ill).

sank the past tense of **sink**

San•ta Claus /ˈsæntəˌklɔz/ or **San•ta** /ˈsæntə/ an imaginary man with a long white BEARD and a red suit who brings presents for children at Christmas

sap¹ /sæp/ noun [U] a sticky substance that is found in plants and trees

sap² /sæp/ verb [T] to make something become weak: *Years of illness had sapped his strength.*

sap•ling /ˈsæplɪŋ/ noun [C] a young tree

sap•phire /ˈsæˌfaɪr/ noun [C/U] a clear blue jewel

sap•py /ˈsæpi/ adj *American informal* very emotional in a silly way

Sa•ran Wrap /səˈræn ˌræp/ *American trademark* thin plastic used for wrapping food in order to keep it fresh

sar•casm /ˈsɑrˌkæzəm/ noun [U] the activity of saying or writing the opposite of what you mean, in order to make someone feel stupid or to show them that you are angry: *"Fascinating," said Sheila, her voice heavy with sarcasm.*

sar•cas•tic /sɑrˈkæstɪk/ adj using sarcasm —**sar•cas•ti•cal•ly** /sɑrˈkæstɪkli/ adv

sar•dine /sɑrˈdin/ noun [C] a small silver fish that is eaten as food

PHRASE **packed (in) like sardines** placed tightly together in a space so that there is no room to move

sar•don•ic /sɑrˈdɑnɪk/ adj showing a lack of respect for what someone has said or done

sa•ri /ˈsɑri/ noun [C] a very long wide piece of cloth that women in South Asia wrap around their bodies to make a long dress

SASE /ˌes eɪ es ˈi/ noun [C] *American* self-addressed stamped envelope: an envelope with your name, address, and a stamp on it that you send someone so that they can send you something

sash /sæʃ/ noun [C] **1** a long piece of cloth that you put around your waist or over one shoulder and across your chest, for example in an official ceremony **2** *technical* a piece of glass in a wooden frame that forms part of a window

sas•sy /ˈsæsi/ adj *American* **1** showing no respect for someone in authority **2** lively and confident

sat the past tense and past participle of **sit**

SAT /ˌes eɪ ˈti/ *trademark* Scholastic Aptitude Test: in the U.S., an examination that HIGH SCHOOL students must take before they can go to college or university

Sat. abbrev Saturday

Sa•tan /ˈseɪt(ə)n/ the most powerful evil spirit in many religions such as Christianity and Islam = DEVIL

sa•tan•ic /səˈtænɪk/ adj **1** involving the worship of Satan as a god **2** very evil and cruel

sa•tan•ism /ˈseɪt(ə)nˌɪzəm/ noun [U] the worship of Satan as a god —**sa•tan•ist** noun [C]

sat•el•lite /ˈsæt(ə)lˌaɪt/ noun ★

1 [C] an object that is sent into space to travel around the Earth in order to receive and send information: *a spy/weather/communications satellite* ♦ *We have pictures of the disaster live **via satellite*** (=by satellite). ♦ *The new equipment will link vehicles **by satellite** to their office.*

2 [C] a natural object such as a moon that moves around a planet

3 [C] a country, city, or organization that depends on or is controlled by a larger, more powerful one: *She works in a satellite office.*

4 [U] SATELLITE TELEVISION

ˈsatellite ˌdish noun [C] a piece of equipment in the shape of a dish that receives signals from a satellite —*picture* → C1

ˌsatellite ˈtelevision or **ˌsatellite TˈV** noun [U] television programs that are sent to your television by SATELLITE

sat•in /ˈsæt(ə)n/ noun [U] a very smooth shiny cloth that is used for making expensive clothes

sat•ire /ˈsæˌtaɪr/ noun **1** [U] the use of humor to criticize someone or something and make them seem silly **2** [C] a play, book, movie, etc. that uses this humor

sa•tir•i•cal /səˈtɪrɪk(ə)l/ adj using humor to criticize people or things and make them seem silly —**sa•tir•i•cal•ly** /səˈtɪrɪkli/ adv

sat·i·rist /ˈsætərɪst/ noun [C] someone who writes SATIRE

sat·i·rize /ˈsætəˌraɪz/ verb [T] to use SATIRE as a way of criticizing people or things and making them seem silly

sat·is·fac·tion /ˌsætɪsˈfækʃ(ə)n/ noun ★
1 [U] the feeling of pleasure that you get when you achieve or obtain something that you want ≠ DISSATISFACTION: *"My daughter is getting married," she announced with satisfaction.* ♦ *He expressed* ***satisfaction with*** *the results.* ♦ *At least we* ***had the satisfaction of*** *knowing we had done our best.* ♦ ***I get a lot of satisfaction from*** *working in the garden.*
2 [C] something that gives you this feeling: *Being a parent is one of the great satisfactions in life.*
PHRASE **to sb's satisfaction** in the way that a particular person likes or wants: *The problem was resolved to everyone's satisfaction.*

sat·is·fac·to·ry /ˌsætɪsˈfækt(ə)ri/ adj **1** good enough ≠ UNSATISFACTORY: *I have still not received a satisfactory answer to my question.* **2** pleasing —**sat·is·fac·to·ri·ly** adv

sat·is·fied /ˈsætɪsˌfaɪd/ adj **1** pleased with what has happened, or with what you have achieved: *a satisfied customer* ♦ *Honestly, some people are never satisfied!* ♦ *The President declared himself satisfied with the progress of the talks.* **2** if you are satisfied that something is true or correct, you do not need any more proof: *I am satisfied that they are doing all they can.*

sat·is·fy /ˈsætɪsˌfaɪ/ verb ★★
1 [T] to please someone by giving them something that they want or need: *an agreement that is unlikely to satisfy environmental campaigners* ♦ *It's impossible to satisfy everyone.*
2 [I/T] to provide what is needed or wanted: *There's nothing like a cold drink to satisfy your thirst.* ♦ *I just want to satisfy my curiosity – why did he do it?*
3 [T] to have all the qualities or features that are necessary according to a rule, condition, or standard: *Students must* ***satisfy*** *all the* ***requirements*** *to be accepted into the program.*
4 [T] to provide someone with the evidence that they need in order to be certain that something is true = CONVINCE: *The prosecution has to satisfy the jury that the defendant is guilty.*

sat·is·fy·ing /ˈsætɪsˌfaɪɪŋ/ adj making you feel pleased or happy because you have got what you want or need: *a satisfying result/achievement* ♦ *a satisfying meal*

sat·u·rate /ˈsætʃəˌreɪt/ verb [T] **1** to make something completely wet **2** to fill something completely with a large number of things or a large amount of something —**sat·u·ra·tion** /ˌsætʃəˈreɪʃ(ə)n/ noun [U]

ˌsaturated ˈfat noun [C/U] fat from food such as meat or milk products that is difficult for the body to process, and is thought to be bad for your health

Sat·ur·day /ˈsætərˌdeɪ/ noun [C/U] ★★★ the day after Friday and before Sunday: *Christmas is on a Saturday this year.* ♦ *He plays golf Saturdays* (=every Saturday). ♦ *I'm looking forward to the game next Saturday.* ♦ *See you* ***on Saturday.***

sauce /sɔs/ noun [C/U] ★ a liquid food that you put on other foods to give them a particular flavor: *tomato sauce* ♦ *ice cream with chocolate sauce*

sauce·pan /ˈsɔsˌpæn/ noun [C] a round deep metal container with a long handle. It is used for cooking food on a STOVE. —*picture* → C2

sau·cer /ˈsɔsər/ noun [C] a small round flat dish that you put a cup on → FLYING SAUCER

sauc·y /ˈsɔsi/ adj referring to sex in a way that is funny

sau·na /ˈsɔnə/ noun [C] **1** a small hot wooden room where people sit in order to SWEAT (=produce water from their skin) **2** a period of time spent in a sauna

saun·ter /ˈsɔntər/ verb [I] to walk in a slow and relaxed way

sau·sage /ˈsɑsɪdʒ/ noun [C/U] a food that consists of a tube of skin containing meat mixed with SPICES

sau·té /sɔˈteɪ, soʊˈteɪ/ verb [T] to cook something quickly in a small amount of fat or oil

sav·age¹ /ˈsævɪdʒ/ adj **1** extremely violent: *a savage attack/animal* **2** extremely severe: *savage cuts in public services* —**sav·age·ly** adv

sav·age² /ˈsævɪdʒ/ noun [C] *old-fashioned* an insulting word for someone from a culture that is not advanced

sav·age³ /ˈsævɪdʒ/ verb [T] **1** to criticize someone or something severely **2** if an animal savages someone, it attacks them and injures or kills them

sav·age·ry /ˈsævɪdʒ(ə)ri/ noun [U] extremely violent behavior

save¹ /seɪv/ verb ★★★

1 help sb/sth avoid harm	7 in computing
2 avoid using sth	8 collect things
3 put money in bank	9 in sport
4 keep sth for future	+ PHRASE
5 keep sth for sb	+ PHRASAL VERBS
6 help sb avoid doing sth	

1 [T] to make it possible for someone or something to avoid danger, harm, injury, etc.: *campaigns to save the planet* ♦ *A cure for cancer would* ***save*** *thousands of* ***lives*** *each year.* ♦ **save sb/sth from sth** *Nothing can save this company from bankruptcy.*
2 [T] to avoid using something such as money, time, or energy, or to use less of it: *You can save $100 by buying your tickets before Saturday.* ♦ *Traveling by plane is more expensive, but it* ***saves time.*** ♦ **save sb sth** *Democrats argue their plan will save the government money in the future.*
3 [I/T] to regularly put money in a bank, or to invest it so that you can use it later: *Don't wait until you're 40 to start* ***saving for*** *retirement.* ♦ **save sth for sth** *I've managed to save almost $500 for my vacation.* ♦ **save to do sth** *We've been saving to buy a new car.*
4 [T] to keep or store something so that you can use it in the future: *Save some energy for the end of the race.* ♦ *Let's have one piece of cake now and* ***save the rest for later.***

5 [T] to keep something for someone by making sure that other people do not take it: **save sth for sb** *Would you please save a place in line for me?* ♦ **save sb sth** *Save me some dinner and I'll have it when I get in.*
6 [T] to make it possible for someone to avoid doing something: **save sb sth** *If you get some milk on your way home, it'll save me a trip to the store.*
7 [I/T] to make a computer keep information that you have put into it: *Where did you save the file you were working on?* ♦ *It's a good idea to save frequently.*
8 [T] to collect a set of things and keep them for a particular purpose: *Save eight tokens and you can get one of these amazing pens!*
9 [I/T] if a GOALKEEPER saves a ball in a sport such as soccer, they prevent the ball from going into the net
PHRASE **save face** to avoid seeming stupid or feeling embarrassed: *a compromise that allows both sides to save face*
PHRASAL VERBS **'save on sth 1** to spend less money on something than you would normally: *light bulbs that help you save on electricity bills* **2** to avoid using something, or to use less of it: *Keep your showers short to save on water.*
ˌsave (sth) 'up *same as* **save**[1] 3: *I'm saving up for a new car.*
ˌsave sth 'up *same as* **save**[1] 8: *You save up the tokens to get a prize.*

save[2] /seɪv/ noun [C] an action by a GOALKEEPER that prevents a ball from going into the net in a sport such as soccer

sav•er /ˈseɪvər/ noun [C] **1** someone who regularly puts money in a bank so that they can use it later **2** something that makes it possible for you to use or spend less of something: *Our new microwave is great – it's a real time saver.*

ˌsaving 'grace noun [singular] a good quality that makes it possible for you to accept someone or something that is bad in all other ways

S

sav•ing /ˈseɪvɪŋ/ noun **1 savings** [plural] money that you have saved in a bank or invested so that you can use it later: *The money for our trip came out of my savings.* **2** [C] an amount of something that you manage to avoid using or spending: *The TV is 30% off the regular price – that's a saving of $75.*
PHRASE **savings and loan association** a company that gives you interest on the money you have in your account with it and lends you money for a **mortgage** when you want to buy a house

sav•ior /ˈseɪvjər/ noun **1** [C] someone who saves someone or something from trouble or danger **2 the Savior** or **Our Savior** a name that Christians sometimes use for Jesus Christ

sa•vor /ˈseɪvər/ verb [T] to enjoy an experience, activity, or feeling as much as you can and for as long as you can

sa•vor•y /ˈseɪvəri/ adj tasting of salt or SPICES and not sweet

sav•vy[1] /ˈsævi/ adj *informal* knowing a lot about something and able to make good judgments about it

sav•vy[2] /ˈsævi/ noun [U] *informal* the ability to understand and judge people and situations well

saw[1] /sɔ/ noun [C] a tool that is used for cutting wood or metal *—picture* → TOOL

saw[2] /sɔ/ (past participle **sawed** or **sawn** /sɔn/) verb [I/T] to cut something with a saw
PHRASAL VERB **ˌsaw sth 'off** to remove something by cutting through it with a saw or knife

saw[3] the past tense of **see**

saw•dust /ˈsɔˌdʌst/ noun [U] very small pieces of wood like dust that are produced when you cut wood

saw•mill /ˈsɔˌmɪl/ noun [C] a building where wood is cut into boards using machines

sax /sæks/ noun [C] *informal* a SAXOPHONE

sax•o•phone /ˈsæksəfoʊn/ noun [C] a musical instrument consisting of a long curved metal tube that you play by blowing into it as you press its KEYS with your fingers *—picture* → WOODWIND —**sax•o•phon•ist** /ˈsæksəfoʊnɪst/ noun [C]

say[1] /seɪ/ (3rd person singular **says** /sez/; past tense and past participle **said** /sed/) verb ★★★

1 express with words	4 show sth
2 have opinion	5 imagine sth
3 give information	+ PHRASES

1 [I/T] to express something using words: *"Nice to meet you," he said with a smile.* ♦ *"When's he coming back?" "He didn't say."* ♦ *The committee **said yes** (=gave permission), so we can go ahead.* ♦ *What a strange **thing to say**, Carrie thought.* ♦ *I then **said goodbye** and left.* ♦ *I already **said sorry** for hurting his feelings.* ♦ **+(that)** *She said that she liked dancing.* ♦ **+how/what/who etc.** *Did he say who called?* ♦ **say sth to sb** *Tell me what he said to you.* ♦ **say sth on/about** *I want to say something about this subject.*
2 [T] to think something, or to have a particular opinion: *I think we should stop now. What do you say?* ♦ *"Will she meet the deadline?" "I would **say so** (=think it is likely)."* ♦ **+(that)** *He always said you'd be rich and famous one day.* ♦ *I say we go* (=I think we should go) *by car.* ♦ **be said to do sth** *She is said to have great talent as an artist.*
3 [T] to give information or orders in writing, numbers, pictures, etc.: *My watch says quarter of twelve.* ♦ **+(that)** *Her letter says she's coming at noon.* ♦ *The rules say that we need a two-thirds majority to win.* ♦ **+how/when/what etc.** *Does it say on the box how much it costs?*
4 [T] to show indirectly what someone or something is like: *This problem says something about the way the company is run.*
5 [T] to imagine what will happen in a particular situation: *Say you get $2,000 for the car – you'll still need another thousand.*
PHRASES **go without saying (that)** to be completely obvious or true: *It goes without saying that I'm sorry.*
I have to say (that) used for emphasizing a statement: *I'm not very impressed, I have to say.* ♦ *I have to say that the food was awful.*
say it all used for saying that something shows very clearly what someone's feelings

are or what a particular situation is really like: *The look on his face says it all.*
say sth to yourself to think something: *"This is the real thing," he said to himself.* ♦ **+(that)** *I keep saying to myself that I shouldn't do it.*
say when *spoken* used for asking someone to tell you when you have given them enough food or drink
that is to say *formal* used for explaining something that you have just said in a more exact way: *I'll deal with the second point first, that is to say the change to the club's rules.*
that said *spoken* used for adding an opinion that seems to be the opposite of what you have just said, although you think both are true: *The economy is struggling. That said, house prices rose slightly last month.*
to say the least used for saying that you could have expressed something in a much stronger way: *I found the flight uncomfortable, to say the least.*

- You **say** something to someone. **Say** is followed by the words that someone uses, or by reported speech: *She said no to me.* ♦ *"Hello," he said.* ♦ *I said that I was cold.*
- You **tell** someone something when you give them information or an instruction. **Tell** is usually followed by the person who is spoken to: *"It's time to go," he told us.* ♦ *I told Kate to shut up.*
- **Speak** and **talk** mean to say something. They are not usually followed by an object: *Don't interrupt me when I'm speaking.* ♦ *Jade and Adele were talking in the corner.*

say² /seɪ/ noun [singular/U] the right to give your opinion and be involved in a discussion about something: *The junior staff had no say in this decision.*
say·ing /ˈseɪɪŋ/ noun [C] a well-known statement about what often happens in life
SC abbrev South Carolina
scab /skæb/ noun [C] a hard layer of dried blood that forms on a cut on your skin
scaf·fold /ˈskæfəld, ˈskæfoʊld/ noun [C] **1** a structure consisting of poles and boards on the outside of a building. You stand on it when you are working on the building. **2** *American* a structure that can be moved up and down on the outside of a tall building. You stand in it in order to clean the windows. **3** a structure on which criminals were killed in the past by being HANGED or BEHEADED
scaf·fold·ing /ˈskæfəldɪŋ, ˈskæfoʊldɪŋ/ noun [U] poles and boards used for making a scaffold on the outside of a building
scald /skɔld/ verb [T] to burn your skin with very hot liquid or steam
scald·ing /ˈskɔldɪŋ/ adj very hot
scale¹ /skeɪl/ noun ★★★

1 size/rate/level	5 for weighing
2 range	6 series of musical notes
3 set of marks	7 hard piece of skin
4 of map/model	

1 [singular/U] the size, rate, or level of something: *Is the Government aware of the* ***scale of the problem*** (=are they aware of how big it is)?
2 [C] a range of numbers or amounts forming a system for separating things into different groups: *the Celsius scale of temperature* ♦ *The rich are at the top of the social scale.* ♦ *Rate these movies* ***on a scale of 1 to 10.***
3 [C] a set of marks on a piece of equipment or a drawing, used for measuring something: *the vertical scale on the graph*
4 [C/U] the relationship between the actual distance or size of something and how it is shown on a map or in a drawing or model: *This map has* ***a scale of 1:20,000.*** ♦ ***a scale of*** *a half-inch to the mile*
5 [C] a piece of equipment that you use for weighing people or things: *He weighed himself on* ***the bathroom scale.*** → TIP²
6 [C] a series of musical notes in a fixed order: *She was* ***practicing scales*** *on her new piano.*
7 [C] one of the small hard flat pieces of skin on the body of a fish, snake, or similar animal

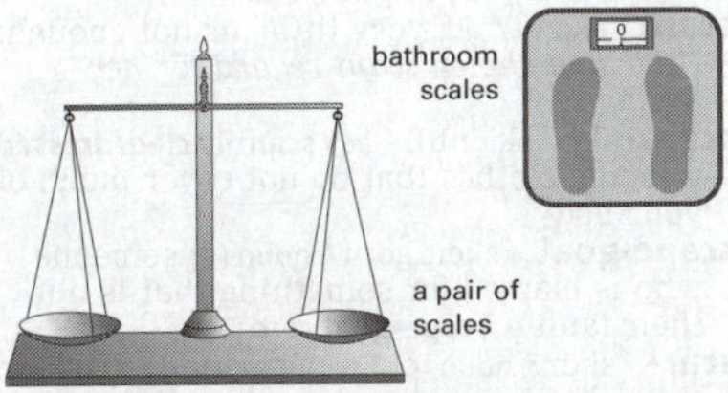

scale² /skeɪl/ verb [T] to climb to or over the top of a mountain, wall, etc.
PHRASAL VERB ˌ**scale sth ˈback** or ˌ**scale sth ˈdown** to make something smaller in size, amount, etc.
scal·lion /ˈskæljən/ noun [C] *American* a small white onion with a long green stem —*picture* → C11
scal·lop /ˈskɑləp, ˈskæləp/ noun [C] a SHELLFISH, eaten as food
scalp¹ /skælp/ noun [C] the skin under the hair on your head
scalp² /skælp/ verb [T] **1** *American* to try to sell a ticket you have bought to someone else at a much higher price **2** to cut the skin and hair off an enemy's head as a sign of victory
scal·pel /ˈskælp(ə)l/ noun [C] a small sharp knife that a doctor uses for doing an operation
scalp·er /ˈskælpər/ noun [C] *American* someone who tries to sell tickets they have bought to other people at a much higher price
scal·y /ˈskeɪli/ adj scaly skin is so dry that small pieces of it fall off
scam /skæm/ noun [C] *informal* a dishonest plan for getting money
scam·per /ˈskæmpər/ verb [I] to move quickly with small light steps
scan¹ /skæn/ verb **1** [T] to look at something very carefully in order to see a particular person or thing: *Ella scanned the crowd for any sign of Geoff.* **2** [I/T] to read something very quickly in order to get a general idea of its meaning or to find particular information: *She scanned the paper for any*

news of them. **3** [I/T] to copy and store information in DIGITAL form using computer equipment **4** [T] to use a piece of equipment to produce a picture of the inside of an object or a part of your body

PHRASAL VERB ˌ**scan ˌthrough (sth)** *same as* scan[1] 2

scan² /skæn/ noun [C] a medical test that uses a piece of equipment to produce a picture of the inside of your body

scan•dal /ˈskænd(ə)l/ noun [C/U] a situation in which people behave in a dishonest or immoral way that shocks people: *a sex scandal*

scan•dal•ize /ˈskænd(ə)lˌaɪz/ verb [T] to do something that shocks someone

scan•dal•ous /ˈskænd(ə)ləs/ adj shocking and immoral or dishonest

scan•ner /ˈskænər/ noun [C] **1** a piece of equipment that you use for copying a picture or document into a computer **2** a piece of equipment that is used for producing a picture of the inside of an object or a part of your body

scant /skænt/ adj very little, or not enough: *Peter had shown scant regard for her feelings.*

scant•i•ly /ˈskæntɪli/ adv **scantily clad/dressed** wearing clothes that do not cover much of your body

scape•goat /ˈskeɪpˌgoʊt/ noun [C] someone who is blamed for something that is not their fault —**scape•goat** verb [T]

scar¹ /skɑr/ noun [C] **1** a permanent mark on your skin where you have been injured: *He has a scar under his left eye.* **2** a permanent effect on someone's mind, caused by an unpleasant experience: *She bore the scars of an unhappy childhood.*

scar² /skɑr/ verb [T] **1** to leave a permanent mark on someone's skin as the result of an injury **2** if an unpleasant experience scars someone, it has a permanent effect on the way that they think and live: *He got involved in drugs at an early age, and it scarred him for life.*

scarce /skers/ adj if something is scarce, there is not very much of it ≠ ABUNDANT: *Fresh water and medicine were scarce in the disaster area.*

scarce•ly /ˈskersli/ adv **1** almost not, or almost none = BARELY, HARDLY **2** only just = BARELY **3** used for showing that something is certainly not true or possible = HARDLY

scar•ci•ty /ˈskersəti/ noun [singular/U] a situation in which there is not enough of something for the people who want or need it = SHORTAGE ≠ ABUNDANCE

scare¹ /sker/ verb **1** [T] to make someone feel frightened: *I'm sorry, I didn't mean to scare you.* **2** [I] to become frightened

PHRASAL VERB ˌ**scare sb aˈway** or ˌ**scare sb ˈoff** **1** to make someone feel so frightened or worried that they do not do something that they had planned to do: *The city's high murder rate has scared away tourists.* **2** to make someone so frightened that they run away

scare² /sker/ noun [C] **1** a situation that makes people suddenly feel frightened or worried about something: *a bomb scare* **2** a sudden feeling of fear: *It gave me a real scare when the cat jumped on me.*

scare•crow /ˈskerˌkroʊ/ noun [C] an object in the shape of a person that farmers put in their fields to frighten birds away

scared /skerd/ adj ★ frightened, or worried: *I'm **scared stiff** (=extremely scared) of having the operation.* ♦ *Louise is **scared of** flying.* ♦ **+(that)** *I'm scared I'll fail all my classes.* ♦ **be scared to do sth** *Mike was too scared to go bungee jumping.*

scarf¹ /skɑrf/ (plural **scarves** /skɑrvz/) noun [C] a piece of cloth that you wear around your neck or head —*picture* → C4

scarf² /skɑrf/ or ˌ**scarf sth ˈdown** verb [T] *American informal* to eat something very quickly

scar•let /ˈskɑrlət/ adj bright red in color —**scar•let** noun [U]

scarves the plural of **scarf¹**

scar•y /ˈskeri/ adj frightening: *a scary story*

scath•ing /ˈskeɪðɪŋ/ adj criticizing someone or something in a very strong way

scat•ter /ˈskætər/ verb **1** [T] to throw or drop things so that they spread over an area **2** [I/T] if a group of people or animals scatter, or if something scatters them, they suddenly move away in different directions

scat•tered /ˈskætərd/ adj **1** spread over a large area: *My relatives are scattered all over the country.* **2** happening in only a few places: *scattered showers*

scat•ter•ing /ˈskætərɪŋ/ noun [C] a small number of people or things that are spread over a large area

scav•enge /ˈskævəndʒ/ verb [I/T] **1** to search through things that other people have thrown away in order to see if there is anything that you want **2** if an animal scavenges, it eats anything that it can find —**scav•en•ger** noun [C]

sce•nar•i•o /səˈneriˌoʊ/ noun [C] a situation that could possibly happen: *The most likely scenario is that Brooks will resign.* ♦ *According to the worst-case scenario, global temperatures could rise by 8 degrees in the next 30 years.*

scene /sin/ noun [C] ★★★

1 part of play/book, etc.	4 activity/interest
2 view	5 argument, etc. in public
3 where sth happens	+ PHRASE

1 a part of a play, book, movie, etc. in which events happen in the same place or period of time: *a love scene* ♦ ***the opening scene of*** *Macbeth*

2 a view that you can see in a picture or from the place where you are: *She stood in the doorway surveying the scene.* ♦ *paintings that depict **scenes of** country life*

3 a place where something happens: ***the scene of the crime/accident/attack*** ♦ *The paramedics will be **at the scene** within a few minutes.*

4 a particular interest or activity, and the people and places that are involved in it: *an important figure on the political scene* ♦ *the music/rave/dance scene*

5 a noisy argument or a strong show of feelings in a public place: *Stop **making** such **a scene**!*

S

PHRASE **behind the scenes** secretly: *These agreements have been drafted by officials behind the scenes.*

scen•er•y /ˈsin(ə)ri/ noun [U] **1** natural things such as trees, hills, and lakes that you can see in a particular place: *Switzerland has some spectacular scenery.* **2** the furniture and painted background on a theater stage

sce•nic /ˈsinɪk/ adj providing beautiful views of nature

scent¹ /sent/ noun **1** [C] a pleasant smell: *an apple with a rich flavor and scent* **2** [C/U] the smell that an animal or person has, that some animals can follow **3** [C/U] PERFUME

PHRASE **the scent of sth** a feeling that a new situation is going to happen: *The scent of victory was in the air.*

scent² /sent/ verb [T] if an animal scents someone or something, it knows that they are there because of their smell

scent•ed /ˈsentəd/ adj having a pleasant smell

scep•tic /ˈskeptɪk/ the British spelling of skeptic

sched•ule¹ /ˈskeˌdʒul, ˈskedʒəl/ noun [C] ★

1 a plan of activities or events and when they will happen: *What's on your schedule today?* ♦ *The president **has a** very busy **schedule**.* ♦ *We're shooting the movie **on a** very **tight schedule*** (=with many things to do in a short time). ♦ *a project completed **ahead of schedule*** (=before the time that was planned)

2 *American* a list that shows when buses, trains, etc. will arrive and leave

sched•ule² /ˈskeˌdʒul, ˈskedʒəl/ verb [T] to plan for something to happen at a particular time: *Let's schedule another meeting for July.* ♦ *The exhibit is scheduled to run from January until March.*

sched•uled /ˈskedʒəld/ adj planned to happen at a particular time, or at the same time each day, week, etc.: *a scheduled flight* ♦ *tonight's scheduled program*

scheme¹ /skim/ noun [C] **1** a plan for achieving something, especially something illegal or dishonest **2** *British* a plan that is developed by a government or large organization in order to provide a particular service for people

scheme² /skim/ verb [I] to make secret plans to achieve something, especially in an illegal or dishonest way = PLOT: *She's convinced that they're scheming against her.* —**schem•er** noun [C], **schem•ing** adj

schiz•o•phre•ni•a /ˌskɪtsəˈfriniə/ noun [U] a serious mental illness in which the way that you think and feel is not connected with what is really happening

schiz•o•phren•ic /ˌskɪtsəˈfrenɪk/ adj relating to schizophrenia, or affected by it —**schiz•o•phren•ic** noun [C]

schol•ar /ˈskɑlər/ noun [C] **1** someone who studies a particular subject and knows a lot about it **2** someone who is given a SCHOLARSHIP to study at a particular school or university

schol•ar•ly /ˈskɑlərli/ adj **1** based on serious academic study: *a scholarly discussion* **2** someone who is scholarly knows a lot about a particular subject or studies something seriously

schol•ar•ship /ˈskɑlərˌʃɪp/ noun **1** [C] an amount of money that an organization gives to someone so that they can study at a particular school or university: *Sophie was awarded a scholarship to attend Boston University.* **2** [U] serious formal study and the knowledge that you get from it: *a work of great scholarship*

scho•las•tic /skəˈlæstɪk/ adj connected with schools, teaching, or studying = ACADEMIC, EDUCATIONAL

school /skul/ noun ★★★

1 where children learn	6 where skill is taught
2 period of education	7 people sharing ideas
3 everyone in school	8 large group of fish, etc.
4 college/university	+ PHRASE
5 department	

1 [C/U] a place where children go to be taught, or the time during the day when they are there: *the biggest school in the city* ♦ *The kids will be **at school** until 3:00 today.* ♦ *It's time to **go to school**.* ♦ *They go swimming **after school**.*

2 [U] the situation or period of years when you receive your education: *Angela's still **in school**, but she graduates in May.* ♦ *I **quit school** when I was fifteen.*

3 [singular] all the students and staff at a school: *The whole school assembled in the auditorium.*

4 [C/U] *American informal* a college or university: *Cornell is a very good school.* ♦ *She's **going to school** at Stanford.*

5 [C/U] a university department or a college that teaches a particular subject: *the School of Management* ♦ *medical/law school*

6 [C/U] a private institution that teaches a particular skill: *the Perkins School of Ballroom Dancing* ♦ *a driving school*

7 [C] a group of writers, artists, etc. whose work or ideas are similar: *the Impressionist school of painting*

8 [C] a large group of fish, DOLPHINS, WHALES, etc.

PHRASE **school of thought** a way of thinking about a particular subject or idea that is shared by a group of people

school•child /ˈskulˌtʃaɪld/ (plural **school•chil•dren** /ˈskulˌtʃɪldrən/) noun [C] a child who goes to school

ˈ**school** ˌ**days** noun [plural] the time in your life when you go to school

ˈ**school** ˌ**district** noun [C] an area within a U.S. state in which all the schools are managed by the same group of people

school•ing /ˈskulɪŋ/ noun [U] the education that you get at school

school•teach•er /ˈskulˌtitʃər/ noun [C] a teacher who works in a school

schwa /ʃwɑ/ noun [C] *linguistics* a vowel sound used in UNSTRESSED SYLLABLES, for example the sound of "a" in "above." Its symbol is /ə/.

sci•ence /ˈsaɪəns/ noun ★★★

1 [U] the study and knowledge of the physical world and its behavior, that is based on experiments and facts and is organized into a system: *recent advances in science* ♦ *a science teacher*

2 [C] a scientific subject such as chemistry, physics, or biology

S

ˌscience ˈfiction noun [U] books and movies about imaginary future events that often include space travel and creatures from other planets

sci·en·tif·ic /ˌsaɪənˈtɪfɪk/ adj ★★
1 relating to science, or based on the methods of science: *scientific research* ♦ *scientific instruments*
2 done in an organized way: *There's nothing scientific about the process they use to select people.*
—**sci·en·tif·i·cal·ly** /ˌsaɪənˈtɪfɪkli/ adv

sci·en·tist /ˈsaɪəntɪst/ noun [C] ★★ someone who is trained in science, especially someone whose job is to do scientific research

sci-fi /ˈsaɪ faɪ/ noun [U] *informal* SCIENCE FICTION

scin·til·lat·ing /ˈsɪnt(ə)ˌleɪtɪŋ/ adj very impressive, interesting, or clever

scis·sors /ˈsɪzərz/ noun [plural] a tool for cutting paper, with two blades that open and shut

scoff /skɑf/ verb [I] to laugh or say things to show that you do not respect someone or something

scold /skoʊld/ verb [T] *old-fashioned* to criticize someone angrily because they have done something that is wrong

scone /skɑn, skoʊn/ noun [C] a small soft cake that sometimes contains dried fruit

scoop[1] /skup/ verb [T] **1** to dig something out, or to pick something up, using an object or your curved hand: *He scooped some water from the stream.* **2** *mainly journalism* to earn or win something: *Advisors will scoop fees of up to one million dollars.*

scoop[2] /skup/ noun [C] **1** a tool like a spoon that is used for measuring or serving something, or the amount that this tool holds **2** *informal* an exciting or important news story that one news organization publishes or broadcasts before anyone else

scoot·er /ˈskutər/ noun [C] **1** a child's vehicle that consists of a board with two small wheels and an upright handle. You stand on the board with one foot and push with the other. **2** a vehicle with an engine and two small wheels that looks like a small MOTORCYCLE —*picture* → C7

scope /skoʊp/ noun [U] ★
1 the things that a particular activity, organization, subject, etc. deals with =RANGE: *The new law is limited **in scope**.* ♦ *These issues are **beyond the scope of** this book.* ♦ *Responsibility for office services is **not within the scope of** the department.*
2 the opportunity or freedom to do something: *There is still much **scope for** improvement.*

scorch /skɔrtʃ/ verb [T] to burn something slightly so that it changes color or is damaged on the surface

scorched /skɔrtʃt/ adj burned on the surface

scorch·ing /ˈskɔrtʃɪŋ/ adj extremely hot

score[1] /skɔr/ verb ★★
1 [I/T] to get a point in a game or sport: *No one scored in the first half.* ♦ *He **scored** the first **touchdown** after five minutes.* —*picture* → C15
2 [T] to achieve a particular amount, level, etc. on a test: *She's hoping to score high on the math test.*
3 [I/T] to be successful in doing something: *She seems to have scored with her latest novel.* ♦ *They scored some big sales successes.*
4 [I/T] *American informal* to obtain something, especially without paying for it or without making much effort: *Maybe I can score some new CDs at the radio station.*

score[2] /skɔr/ noun ★★
1 [C] the number of points that someone gains in a game or test: *The average score for the test was 75.* ♦ *The **final score** was 4–3.*
2 **scores** [plural] a large number of people or things: ***Scores of** volunteers offered to help.*
3 [C] a written copy of a piece of music
PHRASES **know the score** *informal* to know the truth about something, especially when it is unpleasant: *You don't have to lie to me. I know the score.*
on that/this score concerning the thing that has just been mentioned: *We wanted to attract new recruits, and on that score, the campaign has been successful.*

score·board /ˈskɔrˌbɔrd/ noun [C] a large board that shows the score in a game or sports event

score·keep·er /ˈskɔrˌkipər/ noun [C] an official in a game or sports event who keeps a record of the points won

scorn[1] /skɔrn/ noun [U] a feeling that someone or something is not good enough to deserve your approval or respect

scorn[2] /skɔrn/ verb [T] to treat someone or something as if they do not deserve your approval or respect

scorn·ful /ˈskɔrnfəl/ adj feeling or expressing scorn —**scorn·ful·ly** adv

Scor·pi·o /ˈskɔrpiˌoʊ/ noun [C/U] one of the twelve signs of the ZODIAC. A **Scorpio** is someone who was born between October 24 and November 22.

scor·pi·on /ˈskɔrpiən/ noun [C] an animal like a large insect that has a curved tail with a poisonous part on the end

Scot /skɑt/ noun [C] someone from Scotland

Scotch /skɑtʃ/ noun [C/U] WHISKEY that is produced in Scotland, or a glass of this drink

ˌScotch ˈtape *American trademark* a clear plastic material that is sticky on one side and is used for sticking things together

scoun·drel /ˈskaʊndrəl/ noun [C] *old-fashioned* a man who behaves in an unfair or dishonest way

scour /skaʊr/ verb [T] **1** to search a place or document thoroughly for something: *Police officers are scouring the area for the missing child.* **2** to clean something thoroughly by rubbing it hard with something rough

scourge /skɜrdʒ/ noun [C] *formal* something that causes a lot of trouble or harm

scout[1] /skaʊt/ noun [C] **1** a soldier who is sent by an army to get information about the position of the enemy **2** someone whose job is to find and employ people who have special abilities, for example in sports or entertainment: *a talent scout* **3** a BOY SCOUT or GIRL SCOUT

scout² /skaʊt/ verb [I/T] to search for someone or something

scowl /skaʊl/ verb [I] to put an angry expression on your face —**scowl** noun [C]

scram•ble /ˈskræmb(ə)l/ verb [I] **1** to climb somewhere quickly using your feet and hands = CLAMBER: *She managed to scramble over the wall.* **2** to move somewhere quickly and in a way that is not graceful: *He scrambled awkwardly to his feet.* **3** to try very hard to get something that other people are also trying to get: *Companies are scrambling to recruit skilled workers.* —**scram•ble** noun [singular]

scram•bled eggs /ˌskræmb(ə)ld ˈegz/ noun [plural] eggs that are cooked with their white and yellow parts mixed together —*picture* → EGG

scrap¹ /skræp/ noun **1** [C] a small piece of something: *a scrap of paper* ♦ *Every scrap of evidence has to be investigated.* **2** [U] old metal that can be used again after going through a special process: *The car was sold for scrap.*

scrap² /skræp/ verb [T] **1** *informal* to decide not to continue with something such as a plan or event = ABANDON **2** to get rid of something

scrap•book /ˈskræpˌbʊk/ noun [C] a book in which you save pictures, articles, or other material

scrape¹ /skreɪp/ verb **1** [T] to remove something by pulling a hard tool across the surface it is on: *Scrape the mud off your boots before you come inside.* **2** [T] to injure a part of your body or damage something by rubbing it against a rough surface = GRAZE: *I scraped my elbow when I fell.* ♦ *He scraped his van while he was parking it.* **3** [I] to make a rough unpleasant noise by rubbing against a hard surface: *Simon's chair scraped as he pushed it back.* **4** [I/T] if a sharp edge or point scrapes a surface, or if you scrape it across the surface, it moves across a surface: *He felt the knife blade scrape against the back of his neck.*

PHRASAL VERBS **ˌscrape ˈby** to have just enough money to pay for the things that you really need in order to live, but no more: *She just manages to scrape by on her teacher's salary.*

ˌscrape ˈthrough sth to succeed in doing something, but not in a very impressive way: *I think he'll just scrape through the job interview.*

ˌscrape sth toˈgether to succeed in getting enough of something by making a lot of effort: *They have trouble even scraping together their rent.*

scrape² /skreɪp/ noun **1** [C] a slight injury or mark caused by rubbing against a rough surface **2** [singular] the sound caused by something rubbing against a hard surface **3** [C] *informal* a difficult situation that you cause by being careless

scrap•heap /ˈskræpˌhip/ noun [C] a pile of things that are no longer wanted or needed, especially metal objects

scrap•py /ˈskræpi/ adj **1** *American* ready or willing to fight or argue **2** not done in an organized way

scratch¹ /skrætʃ/ verb **1** [I/T] to pull your nails along your skin, especially because you have an ITCH that makes you want to do this: *Scratch my back for me.* **2** [T] to damage a surface by cutting it slightly or marking it with something sharp or rough: *Don't worry, the cat won't scratch you.* ♦ *Someone's scratched my car door.* **3** [I/T] to move something sharp or rough against a hard surface and make a noise: *I could hear the dog scratching at the back door.*

scratch

scratch² /skrætʃ/ noun [C] **1** a narrow mark on your skin or on a surface that is caused by cutting it slightly or marking it with something sharp or rough **2** a sound made by moving something sharp or rough against a hard surface

PHRASE **from scratch** from the beginning, doing everything yourself: *the travel company he built from scratch*

scratch•pad /ˈskrætʃˌpæd/ noun [C] sheets of paper joined together into a book that you use to make notes on

scratch•y /ˈskrætʃi/ adj **1** rough and uncomfortable against your skin **2** a scratchy record, voice, etc. makes an unpleasant sound like two rough surfaces rubbing together

scrawl /skrɔl/ verb [T] to write something carelessly or in a hurry, so that it is difficult to read —**scrawl** noun [C]

scraw•ny /ˈskrɔni/ adj very thin, in a way that is not attractive or healthy

S

scream¹ /skrim/ verb ★

1 [I] to make a loud high cry because you are hurt, frightened, or excited: *She opened her mouth to scream.* ♦ *They were **screaming with delight**.* ♦ *We could hear the passengers **screaming in terror**.* → SHOUT

2 [I/T] to shout something in a very loud voice = YELL: *She heard Anna scream her name.* ♦ *Nobody heard them **screaming for help**.* ♦ *I felt like **screaming at him**.*

3 [I] to make a very loud high noise: *screaming engines*

scream² /skrim/ noun [C] **1** a loud high cry that you make because you are hurt, frightened, or excited = SHRIEK **2** a very loud high noise = SCREECH

PHRASE **be a scream** *informal* to be extremely funny

screech /skritʃ/ verb [I/T] to make a loud, high, and unpleasant cry or noise: *Seagulls were screeching over our heads.* ♦ *The car screeched to a halt.* —**screech** noun [C]

screen¹ /skrin/ noun ★★

1 on television, etc.	4 for keeping insects out
2 for showing movie	5 for separating area
3 movies	

1 [C] the flat surface on a computer, television, or piece of electronic equipment where words and pictures are shown: *Suddenly the screen went blank.*
2 [C] the flat surface in a movie theater where the picture is shown
3 [U] movies in general: *a star of stage and screen*
4 [C] a wire or plastic net in a frame that fits in a door or window and lets air into a building but keeps insects out
5 [C] a flat structure that is used for separating one area of a room from another: *She got undressed behind a folding screen.*

screen² /skrin/ verb [T] **1** to get information about someone in order to decide whether they are appropriate for a job **2** to broadcast a television program, or to show a movie: *The series is currently being screened on PBS on Fridays.* **3** to hide someone or something by being in front of them: *A line of fir trees screened the house from the road.*
—**screen•ing** noun [C/U]
PHRASAL VERB ˌ**screen sth ˈoff** to separate one part of a room from another with a screen

ˈ**screen ˌdoor** noun [C] *American* a door with wire or plastic net in it that lets air into a building but keeps insects out

screen•play /ˈskrinˌpleɪ/ noun [C] a story that someone writes for a movie

ˈ**screen ˌsaver** noun [C] a computer program that makes the screen black or shows a picture when the computer is on but not being used

screen•writ•er /ˈskrinˌraɪtər/ noun [C] someone whose job is to write stories for movies

screw¹ /skru/ verb [T] **1** to fasten one thing to another using screws ≠ UNSCREW: *The rails need to be firmly screwed to the wall.* **2** to put something into its position by turning it ≠ UNSCREW: *Make sure you screw the lid on firmly to keep the contents fresh.* **3** to make something into a smaller shape by squeezing or twisting it: *She was nervously screwing her tissue into a ball.*
PHRASAL VERBS ˌ**screw (sth) ˈup** *very informal* to make a serious mistake or spoil something = MESS (STH) UP
ˌ**screw sth ˈup** if you screw up your eyes, you close them tightly

screw² /skru/ noun [C] a thin pointed piece of metal that you push and turn in order to fasten one thing to another

screw•driv•er /ˈskruˌdraɪvər/ noun [C] a tool used for turning screws —*picture* → TOOL

screwed up /ˌskrud ˈʌp/ adj *informal* upset, unhappy, or confused as a result of bad experiences that you have had

scrib•ble /ˈskrɪb(ə)l/ verb **1** [T] to write something quickly and carelessly **2** [I/T] to make marks or drawings with no meaning —**scrib•ble** noun [C/U]

script¹ /skrɪpt/ noun ★
1 [C] the written words of a play, movie, television program, speech, etc.
2 [C/U] a system of written letters and symbols

script² /skrɪpt/ verb [T] to write the words of something such as a movie, television program, or speech

scrip•ture /ˈskrɪptʃər/ noun [C/U] the holy writings of a religion

script•writ•er /ˈskrɪptˌraɪtər/ noun [C] someone whose job is to write the words for movies or television programs

scroll¹ /skroʊl/ verb [I/T] *computing* to move words or images up or down a computer screen in order to read or look at something: *It shouldn't take long to scroll through the document and check the spelling.*

scroll² /skroʊl/ noun [C] a long roll of paper with ancient writing on it

ˈ**scroll ˌbar** noun [C] *computing* a long narrow area at the edge of a computer screen that is used for moving information up, down, or across the screen

scrounge /skraʊndʒ/ verb [I/T] *informal* to get something that you want by asking someone for it, instead of providing it or paying for it yourself

scrub¹ /skrʌb/ verb [I/T] to wash or clean something by rubbing it hard with a brush or cloth

scrub² /skrʌb/ noun **1** [U] small bushes and trees that grow in areas without much rain **2** [singular] a thorough wash or clean that you give something by rubbing it hard with a brush or cloth

scruff•y /ˈskrʌfi/ adj messy, or dirty

scrunch /skrʌntʃ/ or ˌ**scrunch sth ˈup** verb [T] to press or squeeze something into a smaller shape

scru•ples /ˈskrup(ə)lz/ noun [plural] moral principles that prevent you from doing something that you think is bad

scru•pu•lous /ˈskrupjələs/ adj **1** very careful to be honest and to do what is morally right ≠ UNSCRUPULOUS **2** done very carefully, giving a lot of attention to details
—**scru•pu•lous•ly** adv

scru•ti•nize /ˈskrut(ə)nˌaɪz/ verb [T] to examine someone or something very carefully

scru•ti•ny /ˈskrut(ə)ni/ noun [U] careful examination of someone or something: *The industry comes under scrutiny in tonight's program.*

scu•ba div•ing /ˈskubə ˌdaɪvɪŋ/ noun [U] the activity of swimming under water with a container of air on your back and a tube for breathing through

scuff /skʌf/ verb [T] to make a mark on the surface of something, especially a shoe, by rubbing it against something rough

scuf•fle /ˈskʌf(ə)l/ noun [C] a fight that lasts for a short time and is not very violent
—**scuf•fle** verb [I]

sculp•tor /ˈskʌlptər/ noun [C] an artist who makes sculptures

sculp•ture /ˈskʌlptʃər/ noun **1** [C/U] a solid object that someone makes as a work of art by shaping a substance such as stone, metal, or wood **2** [U] the art of making sculptures

scum /skʌm/ noun [U] **1** a layer of a dirty or unpleasant substance that forms on the surface of a liquid **2** *offensive* an insulting word for a person or people who you think are very unpleasant

scur•ry /ˈskʌri/ verb [I] to hurry to do something or get something

S

scut•tle /ˈskʌt(ə)l/ verb [I] to move quickly with short steps

scythe /saɪð/ noun [C] a tool with a long curved metal blade for cutting long grass or grain

SD abbrev South Dakota

SE abbrev south east

sea /si/ noun ★★★
1 [singular/U] the large area of salt water that covers most of the surface of the Earth: *He died in an accident **at sea**. ♦ Most of his belongings will be transported **by sea**. ♦ She rowed the boat **out to sea**.* → OCEAN
2 [C] a large area of salt water: *The dam will create an enormous inland sea.*
3 [C] the condition of the ocean, especially the way it is affected by the weather: *A fishing boat is missing in **rough seas** off the northern coast.*
PHRASE **a sea of sth** a large amount of something: *She looked out over **a sea of** smiling **faces**.*

sea•bed, the /ˈsiˌbed/ noun [singular] the ground at the bottom of the ocean

sea•board /ˈsiˌbɔrd/ noun [C] the part of a country that is next to the ocean

ˈsea ˌchange noun [singular] a very important change

sea•food /ˈsiˌfud/ noun [U] fish and SHELLFISH that you can eat

sea•gull /ˈsiˌgʌl/ noun [C] a large gray and white bird that lives near the ocean

sea•horse /ˈsiˌhɔrs/ noun [C] a small ocean fish with a head that looks like a horse's head

seal[1] /sil/ verb [T] **1** to close a container or space by covering it with something so that air or other substances cannot get in or out: *Small gaps can be sealed with wax.* **2** to close an envelope by sticking down the top edge
PHRASE **seal a victory/deal/agreement** to make a victory/deal/agreement certain or complete: *We shook hands to seal the deal.*
PHRASAL VERB **ˌseal sth ˈoff** to prevent people from entering an area or building: *Police sealed off the area so that the investigations could begin.*

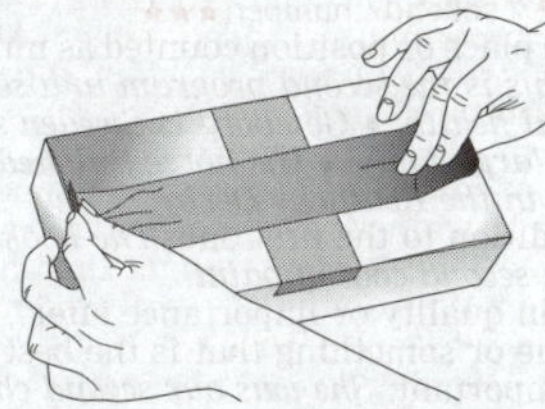
seal

seal[2] /sil/ noun [C] **1** a large sea animal that eats fish and lives mainly in cold parts of the world **2** something that seals a container and that you have to break before you can open the container: *Make sure that the seal on the bottle is intact.* **3** something that stops air or other substances from entering or leaving something: *I replaced the seal, but oil is still leaking out.* **4** a special mark that you put on a document, to show that it is legal or official

ˈsea ˌlevel noun [U] the average level of the ocean. It is used for measuring the height of parts of the land.

ˈsea ˌlion noun [C] a large type of SEAL

seam /sim/ noun [C] **1** a line of stitches that joins two pieces of cloth **2** a long thin layer of coal under the ground

sea•man /ˈsimən/ (plural **sea•men** /ˈsimən/) noun [C] a sailor

seam•less /ˈsimləs/ adj changing or continuing very smoothly and without stopping —**seam•less•ly** adv

se•ance /ˈseɪɑ̃s, ˈseɪɑns/ noun [C] a meeting in which people try to communicate with the spirits of dead people

sea•port /ˈsiˌpɔrt/ noun [C] a town close to the ocean with a large port

search[1] /sɜrtʃ/ noun [C] ★★
1 an attempt to find something: *Despite **a thorough search**, they found no drugs on him. ♦ The authorities carried out several air **searches for** survivors of the crash. ♦ Many people had left their homes to go **in search of** food.*
2 an attempt to find an answer: *The committee is involved in a **search for** solutions to key international problems.*
3 *computing* the process of using a computer to find information, especially on the Internet: *You can probably get the address by doing an Internet search.*

Words often used with search

*Adjectives often used with **search** (noun, sense 1)*
- **careful, painstaking, systematic, thorough** + SEARCH: used about searches that are done with great care
- **desperate, frantic** + SEARCH: used about searches by people who are very eager to find someone or something
- **fruitless, unsuccessful** + SEARCH: used about searches that fail to find someone or something

*Verbs often used with **search** (noun, sense 1)*
- **carry out, conduct, launch, make, mount, undertake** + SEARCH: look for someone or something

search[2] /sɜrtʃ/ verb ★★
1 [I/T] to try to find something or someone by looking carefully: *After three days of searching, I gave up. ♦ Detectives have been brought in to help **search for** clues. ♦ Rescue teams are still **searching through** the wreckage for survivors.*
2 [T] to carefully examine something or someone for something that is hidden: *The police have arrested a man after searching his house.*
3 [T] *computing* to use a computer to look for information, especially on the Internet: *I got most of the answers by **searching the Net**.*

ˈsearch ˌengine noun [C] *computing* a computer program that is used for searching for information on the Internet

search•er /ˈsɜrtʃər/ noun [C] someone who is looking for someone or something that is lost or missing

search•ing /ˈsɜrtʃɪŋ/ adj intending to find out the truth: *searching questions*

ˈsearch ˌparty noun [C] a group of people that

S

is organized to search for someone who is lost or missing

'search ˌwarrant noun [C] an official document that allows the police to search a place

sear•ing /ˈsɪrɪŋ/ adj **1** extreme in degree or strength: *searing pain/heat* **2** severe in your judgment of someone or something

sea•shell /ˈsiˌʃel/ noun [C] the empty shell of a sea animal

sea•shore /ˈsiˌʃɔr/ noun [C] a piece of land next to the ocean

sea•sick /ˈsiˌsɪk/ adj feeling sick from the movement of the boat that you are on

sea•side /ˈsiˌsaɪd/ noun [singular] an area that is near the ocean, especially one where people go for a vacation

sea•son¹ /ˈsiz(ə)n/ noun ★★★

1 one of 4 periods of year	5 period for movies, etc.
2 of weather	6 time for event
3 period sport is played	+ PHRASES
4 time for activity	

1 [C] one of the four periods into which the year is divided according to the weather: *My mood is often affected by the season of the year.* ♦ *She likes to paint the changing seasons in the garden.*

2 [singular] a period of the year when a particular type of weather is expected in some regions of the world: *the dry/rainy season*

3 [C] a period of the year when a particular sport is played: *The baseball season starts next week.*

4 [singular] a particular time or period of the year when something happens: *It's the peak of* ***the vacation season****, so the roads will be crowded.* ♦ *Fruit trees need to be watered regularly during* ***the growing season****.*

5 [singular] a period of time when a series of movies, plays, or television programs are shown: *the season for showing reruns on TV*

6 [singular] a period of time when a particular event takes place: *This topic will be debated throughout the election season.*

PHRASES **in/out of season** grown/not grown at the normal time or under normal conditions: *I don't like to use food that is out of season.*

season's greetings used as a greeting during the Christmas period, especially on cards

sea•son² /ˈsiz(ə)n/ verb [T] to add salt, pepper, or other SPICES to food

sea•son•al /ˈsiz(ə)nəl/ adj available, or happening, at a particular time of year: *seasonal work* ♦ *seasonal changes in temperature* ♦ *seasonal vegetables*

sea•soned /ˈsiz(ə)nd/ adj experienced in a particular activity or job

sea•son•ing /ˈsiz(ə)nɪŋ/ noun [C/U] salt, pepper, or other SPICES that you add to food to improve the taste

'season ˌtickets noun [plural] a set of tickets that you use to see a series of performances or sports games during one year

seat¹ /sit/ noun [C] ★★★

1 something that you can sit on: *Some of the vans have leather seats.* ♦ *The seat next to me was empty.* ♦ *He was in* ***the back seat*** *of the car when the accident happened.* ♦ *She put her purse on* ***the passenger seat*** (=the seat next to the driver) *and started the car.* ♦ *I had* ***a window seat*** *on the plane.*

2 a seat that you pay for as a passenger on a vehicle or as a member of the audience in a theater: *I managed to get us the best seats in the theater.* ♦ *We tried to get on the Friday flight, but there were no seats left.*

3 the part of a chair that you sit on

4 a position as a member of a legislature or committee: *How many* ***seats in*** *Congress did the Democrats win?* ♦ *a* ***seat on*** *the New York Stock Exchange*

PHRASES **take a back seat** to have a less important position than someone or something else

take a seat to sit down: *Hi, come on in and take a seat.*

take your seat to sit down, especially in a place that has been kept for you: *They took their seats in the front row.*

seat² /sit/ verb [T] **1** to have places for a particular number of people to sit: *The new stadium will seat up to 80,000 people.* **2** *formal* to put someone or yourself in a seat somewhere: *He seated himself behind his desk.* ♦ *The general seated them to his right.*

PHRASE **be seated** to be sitting down: *When she entered the room they were already seated.*

'seat ˌbelt noun [C] a strong belt in a car or airplane that you fasten around yourself —*picture* → C6

seat•ing /ˈsitɪŋ/ noun [U] **1** the seats in a public place such as a movie theater, or on a bus or train **2** the way in which seats are arranged

sea•weed /ˈsiˌwid/ noun [U] a green or brown plant that grows in the ocean

sec /sek/ noun [C] *informal* a very short time: *Wait a sec – I just have to brush my teeth.*

SEC, the /ˌes i ˈsi/ the Securities and Exchange Commission: a U.S. government organization that deals with financial markets

se•clud•ed /sɪˈkludəd/ adj private, peaceful, and not near other people or places

se•clu•sion /sɪˈkluʒ(ə)n/ noun [U] a situation in which someone stays apart from other people

sec•ond¹ /ˈsekənd/ number ★★★

1 in the place or position counted as number two: *This is the second program in a series on rural health.* ♦ *Goteborg is Sweden's second largest city.* ♦ *His horse* ***finished second*** *in the Kentucky Derby.*

2 in addition to the first one: *The bookcase needs a second coat of paint.*

3 next in quality or importance after someone or something that is the best or most important: *She was our second choice for the job.* ♦ *In terms of career points, he's* ***second only to*** *Jabbar.*

PHRASES **have second thoughts (about sth)** to begin to doubt a decision that you have made

on second thought used when you want to change something that you have just said, often to say the opposite: *We don't need an umbrella. On second thought, maybe we do.*

second to none the best

sec•ond² /ˈsekənd/ noun ★★★

1 [C] a period of time that is one of the 60

S

parts in a minute: *Each commercial lasts for 30 seconds.*
2 [C] an extremely short period of time: *Just **give me a second** to put my coat on.*
3 seconds [plural] a second amount of the food that you have just eaten

sec•ond³ /ˈsekənd/ adv SECONDLY

sec•ond⁴ /ˈsekənd/ verb [T] to officially support a proposal made by another person in a meeting

sec•ond•ar•y /ˈsekənˌderi/ adj ★
1 less important than something else: *He only played a secondary role.*
2 happening after something else or as a result of it: *a secondary infection*
3 relating to the education of children between the ages of 11 and 16 or 18: *primary and secondary education*

ˈsecondary ˌschool noun [C] a school for children between the ages of 11 and 16 or 18

ˌsecond ˈbest noun [singular/U] **1** someone or something that is not what you wanted, or is not as good as others **2** someone or something that comes directly after the best in order of achievement or quality —**ˌsecond-ˈbest** adj

ˌsecond ˈclass noun [U] the ordinary seats and service on a train or ship

ˌsecond-ˈclass adj **1** low in quality or importance **2** traveling in second class

ˌsecond ˈcousin noun [C] a child of your parent's COUSIN

ˌsecond-deˈgree adj **1** *American legal* second-degree crimes are less serious than FIRST-DEGREE crimes **2** *medical* a second-degree burn is serious

ˌsecond-generˈation adj **1** used for describing someone who was born in the country that they live in but whose parents were not born there **2** developed and improved from an earlier form

ˌsecond-ˈguess verb [T] *American* to criticize a decision after the results of the decision are known

sec•ond•hand /ˌsekəndˈhænd/ adj **1** owned or used by someone else before you: *secondhand books/clothing* **2** heard from someone who was not directly involved in a situation: *secondhand reports/information* —**sec•ond•hand** adv

ˌsecond ˈlanguage noun [C] a language that you can speak but that is not your main language

sec•ond•ly /ˈsekən(d)li/ adv used for introducing the second in a series of two or more things: *Firstly, I didn't know the neighborhood and, secondly, it was night.*

ˌsecond-ˈrate adj not of good quality =MEDIOCRE

se•cre•cy /ˈsikrəsi/ noun [U] a situation in which you keep something secret

se•cret¹ /ˈsikrət/ noun [C] ★★
1 a piece of information that is known by only a small number of people, and is deliberately not told to other people: *I can't tell you what she said – **it's a secret**.* ♦ *Can you promise to **keep a secret** (=not tell anyone)?* ♦ **keep sth a secret (from sb)** *Mandela kept his work a secret from the prison authorities.*
2 something that cannot be explained or is difficult to understand: *What secrets of the universe will the new telescope reveal?*
3 a particular way of achieving something: *She always looks so slim – I wish I knew her secret.* ♦ ***The secret of** our success is having highly skilled workers.*
PHRASE **in secret** without anyone else knowing: *The negotiations were conducted in secret.*

se•cret² /ˈsikrət/ adj ★★
1 deliberately not told to other people, or kept hidden from other people: *The diary records her most secret thoughts and feelings.* ♦ **keep sth secret** *Campaigners have accused the government of keeping the report secret.*
2 not known about by many people: *We love coming here because it's like a secret garden.* —**se•cret•ly** /ˈsikrətli/ adv: *The videotapes were secretly recorded by the FBI.*

ˌsecret ˈagent noun [C] someone whose job involves working for a government and finding out the secrets of other governments =SPY

sec•re•tar•i•al /ˌsekrəˈteriəl/ adj relating to the work or skills of a secretary

sec•re•tar•y /ˈsekrəˌteri/ noun [C] ★★
1 someone in an office who works for someone else and does jobs such as arranging meetings, making phone calls, and preparing letters
2 the member of a committee who writes letters and keeps records of meetings: *secretary of the local golf club*
3 a government official in charge of a department: *the Secretary of Defense*

ˌSecretary of ˈState noun [C] the senior U.S. government official who deals with relations with other countries

se•crete /sɪˈkrit/ verb [T] **1** *science* to produce a liquid **2** *formal* to hide something

se•cre•tion /sɪˈkriʃ(ə)n/ noun [C/U] a liquid that is produced by a plant or animal, or the process of producing this liquid

se•cre•tive /ˈsikrətɪv, sɪˈkritɪv/ adj deliberately not telling people things

ˌsecret ˈservice noun **1** [C] a government department that SECRET AGENTS work for **2 the Secret Service** the U.S. government department responsible for protecting the president

sect /sekt/ noun [C] a religious group whose beliefs are different from the beliefs of an established religion

sec•tar•i•an /sekˈteriən/ adj caused by disagreements among people from different religious groups

sec•tion /ˈsekʃ(ə)n/ noun [C] ★★★
1 a person, group, part, or area that forms part of something larger: *The frozen-foods section is in the back of the store.* ♦ *A large **section of** the population lives in poverty.*
2 a part of a newspaper, book, or other piece of writing that may be considered separately: *The story was reported on the front page of the business section.*
3 *technical* an image that you would see if you cut through something and looked at the flat surface that is created by the cut: *Figure 2 shows a vertical section of the building.*

S

sec·tor /ˈsektər/ noun [C] ★★
1 a part of a country's economic or business activity: *the manufacturing/industrial/financial sector* ♦ *the private/public sector* ♦ *A number of key **sectors of** the economy are in trouble.*
2 a part of an area: *a U.N.-patrolled **sector** of Bosnia*
3 a group that is part of a larger group: *Some **sectors of** the community are opposed to the development plan.*

sec·u·lar /ˈsekjələr/ adj not religious, or not connected with religion

se·cure¹ /sɪˈkjʊr/ adj ★
1 safe from attack, harm, or damage: *Make your home more secure with our burglar alarm system.* ♦ *No store can be completely **secure against** theft.*
2 in a situation where you feel confident and do not need to worry ≠ INSECURE: *The important thing is that children **feel secure** about being loved.* ♦ *You can go home, **secure in the knowledge that** your car is safe.*
3 fastened firmly, in a safe way: *Make sure the pictures are secure.*
4 a secure situation or job is safe and reliable: *She wanted a job with **a more secure future**.*
—**se·cure·ly** adv: *Please make sure that your seat belt is securely fastened.*

se·cure² /sɪˈkjʊr/ verb [T] *formal* ★
1 to get or achieve something important: *The team **secured** their second **victory** of the season.*
2 to make an area or building safe: *We have done our best to secure the embassy against terrorist attacks.*
3 to hold something firmly in place by tying or fastening it: *Screws secure the steel bars to the window frame.*

se·cu·ri·ties /sɪˈkjʊrətiz/ noun [plural] *business* documents showing that you own SHARES in a company

S

se·cu·ri·ty /sɪˈkjʊrəti/ noun [U] ★★★
1 safety from attack, harm, or damage: *The information received is highly confidential and relates to **national security**.* ♦ *The meeting took place amid extremely **tight security**.*
2 a feeling of confidence and safety, or a situation in which you can feel confident and safe: *A predictable routine gives children **a sense of security**.* ♦ *We were lulled into **a false sense of security** and failed to see what was coming.*
3 the department within an organization that protects buildings and workers: *If you won't leave, I'll have to call security.*
4 *business* property or goods that you agree to give to someone who has lent you money if you cannot pay the money back
→ SECURITIES

se·dan /sɪˈdæn/ noun [C] *American* a closed car with a front and back seat for passengers and a TRUNK for carrying things

se·date¹ /sɪˈdeɪt/ adj quiet or slow, and not likely to shock people or attract attention —**se·date·ly** adv

se·date² /sɪˈdeɪt/ verb [T] to give someone a SEDATIVE

se·da·tion /sɪˈdeɪʃ(ə)n/ noun [U] the use of drugs to make someone calmer, or to make them sleep

sed·a·tive /ˈsedətɪv/ noun [C] a drug that makes someone calmer, or makes them sleep

sed·en·tar·y /ˈsed(ə)ntəri/ adj involving a lot of sitting and not much exercise

sed·i·ment /ˈsedəmənt/ noun [C/U] a layer of a substance that forms at the bottom of a liquid

se·duce /sɪˈdus/ verb [T] **1** to persuade someone to have sex with you **2** to persuade someone to do something by making it seem easy or exciting —**se·duc·tion** /sɪˈdʌkʃ(ə)n/ noun [C/U]

se·duc·tive /sɪˈdʌktɪv/ adj **1** sexually attractive **2** attractive and likely to persuade you to do something that may be harmful or wrong —**se·duc·tive·ly** adv

see /si/ (past tense **saw** /sɔ/; past participle **seen** /sin/) verb ★★★

1 notice with eyes	8 find sth out
2 watch movie, etc.	9 experience sth
3 meet/visit sb	10 be in relationship
4 understand sth	11 go with sb
5 consider sb/sth	+ PHRASES
6 imagine sb/sth	+ PHRASAL VERBS
7 make sure	

1 [T] to notice someone or something using your eyes: *She laughed when she saw the expression on his face.* ♦ *She **can't see a thing** without her contact lenses.* ♦ **+what/where/who** *Did you see who it was?* ♦ **+(that)** *I could see she was upset.* ♦ **see sb/sth doing sth** *Didn't you see him talking to her earlier?*
2 [T] to watch something such as a movie or television program: *Have you seen* American Beauty*?*
3 [T] to meet or visit someone: *Are you seeing Jane tomorrow?* ♦ *See you at the station at 6 o'clock.* ♦ *When can Mr. Martin see me?*
4 [I/T] to understand something: *I think I see the problem here.* ♦ *You press this button first, see?* ♦ *"You do it like this." "**I see.**"* ♦ **+why/what/how etc.** *I see why you're angry.* ♦ *"It's not fair to go without him." "Yes, I **see what you mean.**"* ♦ **+(that)** *No one could see he was to blame.*
5 [T] to consider someone or something in a particular way: *A scientist sees things differently from an artist.* ♦ **see sb/sth as sth** *This was seen as an attempt to fool the voters.* ♦ *He seems to see me as a threat.*
6 [T] to imagine someone or something: *Where do you **see yourself** in five years'?* ♦ **see sb as sth** *Can you really see her as the president?* ♦ **see sb/sth doing sth** *I just can't see them winning the game.*
7 [T] to make sure that someone does something or that something happens: **+that** *Could you see that everything's ready in time?*
8 [I/T] to find something out: *As we saw in Chapter 2, the reasons for the war were complex.* ♦ **+if/whether** *He went back to see whether they needed any help.* ♦ **+(that)** *If you read his report, you'll see that he recommends a cautious approach.* ♦ **+who/what/why** *I'll go and see what he wants.*

9 [T] to experience something: *The region has seen some of the fiercest fighting in the war.*
10 [T] to be in a romantic relationship with someone: *Is she seeing anyone at the moment?*
11 [T] to go with someone because you want to make sure that they arrive somewhere: *Can I see you home?*

PHRASES **I don't see why not** *spoken* used for saying yes when someone asks for your permission: *"Can Jason come too, Dad?" "I don't see why not."*
I'll see what I can do *spoken* used for saying that you will try to help: *Bring the car over tomorrow and I'll see what I can do.*
let me see or **let's see** *spoken* used for saying that you are thinking about something or trying to remember something: *It must have been, let me see, 10 years ago.*
see sth coming *spoken* to notice or realize that something is going to happen
see for yourself to check what someone has told you by looking at it: *It's all gone – see for yourself.*
see how it goes/things go *spoken* used for saying that a decision about a situation will be made after allowing it to develop for a period of time
see if you can do sth *spoken* to try to do something: *I'll see if I can find out what he's up to.*
see you *spoken* used for saying goodbye to someone you know when you expect to see them again soon
we'll see *spoken* used for saying that you will decide later: *"Can we go to the park this afternoon, Mom?" "We'll see."*
you'll see *spoken* used for telling someone that they will find out that you are right about something: *It will be wonderful, you'll see.*
you see *spoken* used when you are explaining something: *You see, Harry's coming this afternoon, so I can't come.*
→ DEAD[1], EYE[1], RED[2]

PHRASAL VERBS **ˈsee aˌbout sth** to deal with or organize something: *I should go and see about this job.* ♦ **see about doing sth** *Can you see about getting us a ride home?*
ˌsee sb ˈoff to go somewhere such as a station or airport with someone in order to say goodbye to them: *Anne saw Terry off at the station.*
ˌsee sb ˈout to go with someone to the door when they are leaving in order to say goodbye to them: *My secretary will see you out.*
ˌsee ˈthrough sb/sth to recognize that someone is trying to trick you: *We can all see through your little game, Adam.*
ˌsee sth ˈthrough to continue doing something until it is finished: *Having come this far, she was determined to see things through.*
ˈsee to sb/sth to deal with someone or something: *I'll see to the children's breakfast.*

- If you **see** someone or something, you become aware of them using your eyes: *I saw a flash of light.* ♦ *He saw someone run into the house.*
- If you **look at** someone or something, you deliberately move your eyes toward them so that you can **see** them: *Look at that car!* ♦ *I dropped a glass and everyone turned to look at me.*
- If you **watch** someone or something, you look at them for some time because they are moving or changing and you want to see what happens. You **watch** television or a piece of entertainment: *They were all watching the football game.* ♦ *He sat and watched her clean up.*

seed[1] /sid/ noun ★★★
1 [C/U] a small hard part produced by a plant that can grow into a new plant of the same type: *grass seed* ♦ *a bag of seeds*
2 [C] *American* one of the small hard seeds inside a fruit such as an apple or orange
3 [C] a player who is given a number that shows how likely they are to win a competition: *number one seed, Venus Williams*

seed[2] /sid/ verb **1** [T] to put seeds in the ground so that they can grow **2** [I] if a plant seeds, it produces seeds
PHRASE **be seeded third/tenth etc.** to be in the third/tenth etc. position in an official list of the best players in a competition

seed·less /ˈsidləs/ adj not containing any seeds

seed·ling /ˈsidlɪŋ/ noun [C] a young plant that has grown from a seed

seed·y /ˈsidi/ adj connected with activities that are illegal or morally wrong

see·ing /ˈsiɪŋ/ conjunction **seeing as** or **seeing (that)** *spoken* used for giving the reason why you are saying something: *Maybe we should throw a party, seeing that it's Dan's birthday next week.*

seek /sik/ (past tense and past participle **sought** /sɔt/) verb [T] *formal* ★★
1 to ask for something, or to try to get something: ***Seek medical advice** if symptoms last more than a week.* ♦ *Hundreds of people **sought refuge** in the British Embassy.*
2 to try to find something or someone that you need in your life: *Many single people are seeking that special someone.* ♦ *women who are actively seeking employment*
PHRASE **seek to do sth** *formal* to try to do something: *The law must seek to protect the democratic rights of citizens.*
—**seek·er** /ˈsikər/ noun [C]
PHRASAL VERB **ˌseek sb/sth ˈout** to find someone or something by looking for them in a determined way: *Corbett promised to seek out the truth.*

seem /sim/ linking verb [I] ★★★
1 to appear to be something or appear to have a particular quality: *Going out for lunch **seemed like** a good idea.* ♦ **seem (to be) sb/sth** *Susan seems a very sensible person.* ♦ **seem happy/genuine etc. to sb** *He seems happy enough to me.* ♦ **seem to do sth** *She seemed to take very good care of herself.*
2 used when you want to say something in a more careful and less direct way: **seem to have done sth** *I seem to have forgotten your name.* ♦ **can't seem to do sth** *We can't seem to get this computer to work.*

S

PHRASE **it seems** used for saying that something appears to exist or be true: *It seems like their marriage is over.* ♦ *It seems as if everybody else knew except me.* ♦ **+(that)** *Standing there in the house, it seemed that he had never been away.* ♦ **it seems to sb (that)** *It seems to me this is his most important novel.*

seem·ing·ly /ˈsimɪŋli/ adv in a way that appears to have a particular quality, even though this is probably not true: *Heidi was seemingly calm when she left to take the test.*

seen the past participle of **see**

seep /sip/ verb [I] to flow into or out of something through small holes: *Chemicals from the factory were seeping into the earth.*

see·saw /ˈsiˌsɔ/ noun [C] a long board for children to play on. It is balanced on a support in the middle.

seethe /sið/ verb [I] **1** to be extremely angry **2** to be full of a lot of people or animals that are moving around quickly

seg·ment /ˈsegmənt/ noun [C] a part of something: *certain segments of the population* ♦ *orange/grapefruit segments*

seg·re·gate /ˈsegrəˌgeɪt/ verb [T] to separate groups of people, especially according to race, sex, or religion —**seg·re·ga·tion** /ˌsegrəˈgeɪʃ(ə)n/ noun [U]

seis·mic /ˈsaɪzmɪk/ adj relating to EARTHQUAKES (=sudden shaking of the ground)

seize /siz/ verb [T] **1** to take something using official power or force = CONFISCATE: *Customs officials have seized 100 pounds of cocaine.* **2** to take control of a place or situation: *Their opponents had seized control of the army.* **3** to suddenly and firmly hold someone or something: *"Listen," he said, seizing my wrist.* ♦ *Before he could run away, she seized him by the collar.* **4** if a feeling or emotion seizes someone, it suddenly affects them very strongly: *A wave of panic seized me.*

PHRASE **seize the opportunity/chance to do sth** to act quickly in order to use an opportunity that may not be available later

PHRASAL VERBS **ˈseize on sth** or **ˈseize uˌpon sth** to use something in an enthusiastic way in order to gain an advantage

ˌseize ˈup to suddenly stop moving or working properly

sei·zure /ˈsiʒər/ noun **1** [C/U] the action of taking something, or of taking control of something, using power or force **2** [C] a sudden attack of an illness that makes your body shake

sel·dom /ˈseldəm/ adv not often = RARELY ≠ FREQUENTLY

se·lect¹ /sɪˈlekt/ verb [T] ★

1 to choose someone or something from a group: *You can select one of four colors.* ♦ **select sb to do sth** *We're going to select two students to represent the school.* ♦ **select sb/sth for sth** *The group had been carefully selected for the study because of their lifestyles.*

2 *computing* to mark something on a computer screen before changing it: *You can select a word by double clicking on it.*

se·lect² /sɪˈlekt/ adj **1** carefully chosen from a larger group: *Only a select few companies were allowed to compete for the contract.* **2** very good, or expensive: *a small, very select school*

se·lec·tion /sɪˈlekʃ(ə)n/ noun ★★

1 [C/U] the process of choosing one person or thing from a group: *There are strict rules that govern **the selection of** political candidates.*

2 [C] a set of things for you to choose from: ***a selection of** local cheeses* ♦ *They have **a wide selection of** carpets to suit all tastes.*

3 [C] someone or something that you have chosen: *I'm very happy with my selection.*

se·lec·tive /sɪˈlektɪv/ adj **1** careful about what you choose or accept **2** accepting or using only some things or people: *selective schools* —**se·lec·tive·ly** /sɪˈlektɪvli/ adv

self /self/ (plural **selves** /selvz/) noun [C/U] ★★ who you are and what you think and feel, especially the conscious feeling of being separate and different from other people: *Young babies do not have a fully developed sense of self.*

PHRASES **your old self** the type of person you usually are, especially when you have not been feeling as healthy or happy as usual

your true/real self the type of person you are when you are not trying to impress anyone

self- /self/ prefix relating to yourself or itself: used with many nouns and adjectives: *self-respect* ♦ *a self-cleaning oven*

ˌself-asˈsured adj confident and relaxed because you are sure of your abilities —**ˌself-asˈsurance** noun [U]

ˌself-aˈwareness noun [U] the quality of understanding what your own true thoughts, feelings, and abilities are —**ˌself-aˈware** adj

ˌself-ˈcentered adj too interested in yourself, so that you do not think about what other people feel or need

ˌself-conˈfessed adj admitting to being a particular bad type of person

ˌself-ˈconfidence noun [U] the feeling that you can do things well and that people respect you —**ˌself-ˈconfident** adj

ˌself-ˈconscious adj **1** embarrassed or worried about how you look or what other people think of you **2** not successful in creating a particular effect because of being too obvious —**ˌself-ˈconsciously** adv, **ˌself-ˈconsciousness** noun [U]

self-con·tained /ˌself kənˈteɪnd/ adj not needing the help or friendship of other people

ˌself-conˈtrol noun [U] the ability to control your behavior and not show strong emotions

ˌself-deˈfense noun [U] things that you do in order to protect yourself from being attacked: *Margaret claims she was acting in self-defense when she shot him.*

self-de·scribed /ˌself dɪˈskraɪbd/ adj *American* used for saying what type of person someone says they are

self-de·struct /ˌself dɪˈstrʌkt/ verb [I] if something self-destructs, it destroys itself

ˌself-deˈstructive adj doing things that are

S

likely to harm yourself in some way —ˌ**self-deˈstruction** noun [U]

ˌ**self-deˌterminˈation** noun [U] the freedom of the people in a country to choose their own government and not be controlled by another country

ˌ**self-ˈdiscipline** noun [U] the ability to control your behavior so that you do what you should do —ˌ**self-ˈdisciplined** adj

self-ef•fac•ing /ˌself ɪˈfeɪsɪŋ/ adj someone who is self-effacing does not want to be noticed by other people and tends not to talk about their abilities or achievements

self-em•ployed /ˌself ɪmˈplɔɪd/ adj working for yourself rather than being employed directly by a company or organization —ˌ**self-emˈployment** noun [U]

ˌ**self-esˈteem** noun [U] the feeling that you are as good as other people and that you deserve to be treated well

ˌ**self-ˈevident** adj obvious, and therefore not needing any explanation —ˌ**self-ˈevidently** adv

ˌ**self-exˈplanatory** adj easy to understand without further explanation

ˌ**self-ˈgoverning** adj something such as a country or organization that is self-governing controls itself —ˌ**self-ˈgovernment** noun [U]

ˌ**self-ˈhelp** noun [U] things that you do to solve your own problems instead of depending on other people

ˌ**self-imˈportant** adj behaving in a way that shows you think you are very important

self-im•posed /ˌself ɪmˈpoʊzd/ adj self-imposed rules and conditions are those that you have chosen for yourself, rather than those that someone else has forced you to accept

ˌ**self-inˈdulgent** adj doing things for your own pleasure, rather than for any other purpose: *an idle self-indulgent lifestyle* —ˌ**self-inˈdulgence** noun [U]

self-in•flict•ed /ˌself ɪnˈflɪktəd/ adj a self-inflicted injury, condition, etc. is one that you suffer from and that you have caused: *a self-inflicted gunshot wound*

ˌ**self-ˈinterest** noun [U] the fact of caring only about what will bring advantages for yourself, rather than what will help other people —ˌ**self-ˈinterested** adj

self•ish /ˈselfɪʃ/ adj thinking only about yourself and not caring about other people ≠ UNSELFISH: *a greedy selfish man* —**self•ish•ly** adv, **self•ish•ness** noun [U]

self•less /ˈselfləs/ adj caring about other people's needs and problems more than your own = UNSELFISH —**self•less•ly** adv, **self•less•ness** noun [U]

ˌ**self-ˈmade** adj a self-made person has become successful despite starting with no particular advantages: *a self-made millionaire*

ˌ**self-ˈpity** noun [U] the feeling that your situation is worse than other people's and that they should feel sorry for you —ˌ**self-ˈpitying** adj

ˌ**self-ˈportrait** noun [C] a picture that you draw or paint of yourself

ˌ**self-preserˈvation** noun [U] the wish to stay alive and protect yourself from things that might hurt you

ˌ**self-reˈliant** adj able to do things for yourself without depending on other people —ˌ**self-reˈliance** noun [U]

ˌ**self-reˈspect** noun [U] the feeling that you are as important or as good as other people, and that you should not allow them to treat you badly —ˈ**self-reˌspecting** adj

ˌ**self-ˈrighteous** adj too proud of your own moral behavior or beliefs, especially in a way that annoys other people —ˌ**self-ˈrighteously** adv

ˌ**self-ˈrule** noun [U] government of a country or region by its own people

ˌ**self-ˈsatisfied** adj feeling pleased about your own situation in a way that annoys other people: *a self-satisfied smile* —ˌ**self-satisˈfaction** noun [U]

ˌ**self-ˈservice** or ˌ**self-ˈserve** adj a self-service restaurant or gas station is one where the customers have to serve themselves

ˌ**self-ˈserving** adj showing that you are only willing to do something if it will benefit you

ˌ**self-ˈstudy** noun [U] work that you do without the help of a teacher

ˌ**self-sufˈficient** adj able to provide everything that you need for yourself, without help from other people —ˌ**self-sufˈficiency** noun [U]

self-taught /ˌself ˈtɔt/ adj having learned a particular skill by yourself, instead of being taught by someone

sell[1] /sel/ (past tense and past participle **sold** /soʊld/) verb ★★★

1 [T] to let someone have something in exchange for money: *We've decided to sell our house and move to Florida.* ♦ *My uncle* ***buys and sells*** *secondhand books for a living.* ♦ **sell sb sth** *I sold Chris my old car.* ♦ **sell sth to sb** *Sheila sold her jewelry to an antique dealer.*

2 [T] *informal* to persuade someone to do, have, or use something: **sell sth to sb** *I don't think we could sell the idea to our partners.*

3 [T] if a store or company sells a particular product, people can buy that product from them: *Do you think they sell children's books here?*

4 [I] if a product sells, people buy it: *Her novel sold very well in the first six months.*

PHRASAL VERBS ˌ**sell sth ˈoff** to sell something quickly and for a low price, usually because you need the money

ˌ**sell ˈout 1** if a store sells out of something, it sells all that it has so that there is no more available: *I went to get some bread, but the supermarket had sold out.* ♦ *On a hot day, we can* ***sell out of*** *ice cream in an hour.* **2** if products, tickets, etc. sell out, there are none left for people to buy because they have all been sold **3** *informal* to do something that shows you no longer have the same moral principles you used to have

sell[2] /sel/ noun *see* **hard sell**

sell•er /ˈselər/ noun [C] someone who sells something, especially as their job

ˈ**sell-ˌoff** noun [C] *American business* a situation in which a lot of STOCKS are sold at the same time, making prices go down

S

sell•out /ˈselˌaʊt/ noun [singular] **1** a performance, sports event, etc. for which all the tickets are sold **2** *showing disapproval* a situation in which someone does something that is the opposite of what they had promised, or is against their principles

selves the plural of **self**

se•man•tic /səˈmæntɪk/ adj *linguistics* relating to the meaning of words —**se•man•ti•cal•ly** /səˈmæntɪkli/ adv

sem•blance /ˈsembləns/ noun **a/some semblance of sth** a small amount of a particular quality: *The country was finally returning to some semblance of normality.*

se•men /ˈsimən/ noun [U] the liquid that contains SPERM produced by the male sex organs

se•mes•ter /səˈmestər/ noun [C] one of the two periods of about 18 weeks that the school year is divided into in some countries

sem•i•au•to•mat•ic /ˌsemiɔtəˈmætɪk, ˌsemaɪɔtəˈmætɪk/ adj a semiautomatic weapon keeps moving the next bullet into position and can be fired very quickly

sem•i•cir•cle /ˈsemiˌsɜrk(ə)l/ noun [C] **1** half of a circle **2** a group of people or things arranged in a curved line —**sem•i•cir•cu•lar** /ˌsemiˈsɜrkjələr/ adj

sem•i•co•lon /ˌsemiˈkoʊlən/ noun [C] the symbol ; used in writing for separating words in a list or two parts of a sentence that can be understood separately

sem•i•con•scious /ˌsemiˈkɑnʃəs, ˌsemaɪˈkɑnʃəs/ adj someone who is semiconscious is only partly conscious —**sem•i•con•scious•ness** noun [U]

sem•i•fi•nal /ˌsemiˈfaɪn(ə)l, ˌsemaɪˈfaɪn(ə)l/ noun [C] one of the two games that are played immediately before the last game in a sports competition

sem•i•nar /ˈsemɪˌnɑr/ noun [C] a meeting or class in which a small group of people discuss a subject

S

sem•i•nar•y /ˈsemɪˌneri/ noun [C] a college in which priests are trained

sem•i•pro•fes•sion•al /ˌsemiprəˈfeʃən(ə)l, ˌsemaɪprəˈfeʃən(ə)l/ adj someone who is paid for playing sports, a musical instrument, etc. but who does not do it as their usual job —**sem•i•pro•fes•sion•al•ly** adv

sen•ate /ˈsenət/ noun **1** [C] the more senior part of a legislature that has two parts **2 the Senate** the more senior part of the U.S. Congress

sen•a•tor /ˈsenətər/ noun [C] someone who is a member of a senate

send /send/ (past tense and past participle **sent** /sent/) verb [T] ★★★

1 to arrange for something such as a letter or email to be delivered to someone in another place: *I sent the letters yesterday, so they should arrive today.* ♦ **send sb sth** *Send me an e-mail when you get there!* ♦ **send sth to sb** *I forgot to send a birthday card to Amy.*

2 to arrange for someone or something to go to a place, or to tell someone to go to a place: **send sb/sth somewhere** *Two warships have been sent to the area.* ♦ *My mother sent me back to the store to get the things I'd forgotten.*

3 to make someone move or fall suddenly: *The blow sent him crashing to the floor.*

4 to make a substance such as smoke or a chemical go out into the atmosphere: **send sth out/up** *Forest fires sent up smoke for miles around.*

PHRASAL VERBS ˌ**send sb aˈway** to tell someone to leave a place: *His lawyer was sent away by the security guards.*

send aˈway for sth to write to an organization asking them to send something to you

send sth ˈback to return something to the person who sent it, especially because it is not satisfactory: *If you're not happy with it, you can always send it back.*

send for sb/sth to ask or arrange for someone or something to come to you: *I think we should send for a doctor.*

ˌ**send sb ˈin** to arrange for people to go to a place, especially in order to help with a difficult situation: *Government forces were sent in to fight the rebellion.*

ˌ**send sth ˈin** to send a letter or document to an organization: *Keep sending your letters and suggestions in to NBC News.*

ˌ**send sth ˈoff** to send a letter, e-mail, etc. to someone: *I have to get the package sent off tomorrow.*

ˌ**send sth ˈout** to send a lot of copies of the same document to a large number of people

send•er /ˈsendər/ noun [C] the person who sent a letter, package, e-mail, etc.

se•nile /ˈsiˌnaɪl/ adj someone who is senile is confused, forgets things, or behaves in a strange way, because they are old —**se•nil•i•ty** /səˈnɪləti/ noun [U]

sen•ior¹ /ˈsinjər/ adj ★★

1 with a high position within an organization, or a higher position than someone else ≠ JUNIOR: *a senior officer/manager*

2 belonging to an older age group

sen•ior² /ˈsinjər/ noun [C] **1** *American* a student who is in the last year of HIGH SCHOOL or college **2** a SENIOR CITIZEN

ˌ**senior ˈcitizen** noun [C] someone who is at or past the age when most people stop working

ˌ**senior ˈhigh ˌschool** or ˌ**senior ˈhigh** noun [C] *American* a school in the U.S. for children between the ages of 14 and 18

sen•ior•i•ty /ˌsiniˈɔrəti/ noun [U] greater age or a more important position

sen•sa•tion /senˈseɪʃ(ə)n/ noun **1** [C] a feeling in your mind, especially a strange or uncomfortable one: *He had the eerie sensation that he was being watched.* **2** [C/U] the ability to feel something, or something that you feel: *When she awoke she had lost all sensation in her legs.* ♦ *When applied, the cream may cause a slight burning sensation.* **3** [singular] an event that causes a lot of excitement and interest: *The show caused a sensation when it was first performed.*

sen•sa•tion•al /senˈseɪʃən(ə)l/ adj very exciting and impressive: *a sensational Super Bowl victory* —**sen•sa•tion•al•ly** adv

sen•sa•tion•al•ism /senˈseɪʃən(ə)lˌɪzəm/ noun [U] a way of reporting events, especially in a newspaper, that makes them seem as exciting or shocking as possible —**sen•sa•tion•al•ist** adj

sense¹ /sens/ noun ★★★

1 reasonable behavior	4 natural ability
2 feeling/belief	5 meaning of word
3 way of understanding	+ PHRASES

1 [U] a reasonable way of thinking about something or doing something: **have the sense to do sth** *They must have had the sense to park the car in the shade.* ♦ **there's no sense in doing sth** *There's no sense in going ahead until the costs have been agreed on.*
2 [C] a feeling or belief that you have, especially about yourself: *Beth read Jake's letter with an increasing* ***sense of panic.*** ♦ *All children need to feel* ***a sense of*** *pride in their achievements.*
3 [singular] a way of understanding something, although there may be other ways: *My family's from this area, so* ***in a sense*** *it's like coming home.* ♦ ***In one sense,*** *Robertson is a typical politician.*
4 [C] a natural physical ability that most people have, especially the ability to see, hear, smell, taste, and feel things: *Dogs have* ***a sense of smell*** *that is five times more sensitive than that of humans.*
5 [C] the meaning of a word or phrase: *The word "bank" has a number of senses.*
PHRASES **come to your senses** to start to behave in a reasonable way: *At last she's come to her senses and realizes that we just can't afford it.*
make sense 1 to be practical and sensible: *It makes sense to keep such information on disk.* **2** to be easy to understand: *These instructions don't make any sense to me.*
make sense of sth to understand something that is complicated or unusual
sense of humor the ability to laugh at things and recognize when they are funny

sense² /sens/ verb [T] ★ to know about something through a natural ability or feeling, without being told: **+(that)** *I think she must have sensed there was something wrong.*

Words often used with sense

Nouns often used with sense (verb)
- SENSE + **atmosphere, danger, fear, mood, presence, tension, unease**: know that something exists without being told

sense•less /ˈsensləs/ adj **1** happening or done for no purpose: *the senseless killing of innocent people* **2** unconscious —**sense•less•ly** adv

sen•si•bil•i•ties /ˌsensəˈbɪlətiz/ noun [plural] the ability to be shocked or offended by something: *We have to consider the sensibilities of older people.*

sen•si•ble /ˈsensəb(ə)l/ adj reasonable and practical —**sen•si•bly** adv

sen•si•tive /ˈsensətɪv/ adj

1 reacting quickly	4 easily upset
2 easily damaged	5 secret
3 caring about feelings	6 likely to offend sb

1 reacting quickly or strongly to something: *Bats have very sensitive ears.* ♦ *Coral is very sensitive to changes in water temperature.*
2 needing to be protected because of being easy to harm or destroy: *sensitive skin* **3** caring about someone's feelings and not wanting to offend or upset them ≠ INSENSITIVE: *This is a case that needs sensitive and skillful handling.* **4** likely to become upset very easily: *Paul was always a very sensitive little boy.* **5** sensitive information should be kept secret **6** a sensitive issue needs to be dealt with carefully because it is likely to upset or offend people —**sen•si•tive•ly** adv

sen•si•tiv•i•ty /ˌsensəˈtɪvəti/ noun **1** [U] the quality of understanding how someone feels and being careful not to offend them: *Delivering bad news requires sensitivity on the doctor's part.* **2** [C/U] a tendency to have a strong physical reaction to something: *The drug can cause sensitivity to sunlight.*

sen•sor /ˈsensər/ noun [C] a piece of equipment that reacts to physical changes such as the amount of heat or light that there is in a place

sen•so•ry /ˈsensəri/ adj relating to the physical senses of sight, hearing, smell, taste, and touch

sen•su•al /ˈsenʃuəl/ adj relating to or providing physical pleasure, especially sexual pleasure —**sen•su•al•i•ty** /ˌsenʃuˈæləti/ noun [U]

sen•su•ous /ˈsenʃuəs/ adj relating to physical pleasure

sent the past tense and past participle of **send**

sen•tence¹ /ˈsent(ə)ns/ noun [C] ★★★
1 a group of words, usually including a subject and a verb, that expresses a statement, question, or instruction
2 a punishment that is officially given by a judge: *She received* ***the maximum sentence*** *of ten years.* ♦ *He is* ***serving a*** *three-year* ***sentence*** *for burglary.*

sen•tence² /ˈsent(ə)ns/ verb [T] if a judge sentences someone, they officially say what that person's punishment will be: *He was sentenced to 15 years in prison.*

sen•ti•ment /ˈsentɪmənt/ noun [C/U] *formal* a feeling or attitude

sen•ti•men•tal /ˌsentɪˈment(ə)l/ adj making people experience feelings of sadness, sympathy, love, etc., especially in a deliberate way that many people do not like: *a sentimental song/book/movie*
PHRASE **sentimental value** something that has sentimental value is important because it reminds you of someone or something —**sen•ti•men•tal•i•ty** /ˌsentɪmenˈtæləti/ noun [U], **sen•ti•men•tal•ly** adv

sen•try /ˈsentri/ noun [C] a soldier who stands at the entrance to a place and guards it

Sep. abbrev September

sep•a•ra•ble /ˈsep(ə)rəb(ə)l/ adj capable of being separated ≠ INSEPARABLE

sep•a•rate¹ /ˈsepərət/ adj ★★★
1 not together: *My brother and I always had separate rooms.* ♦ *They're not divorced but they lead completely separate lives* (=do not do things together). ♦ *Clients' funds should be kept* ***separate from*** *the firm's own money.*
2 different or new: *Answer each question on a separate sheet of paper.*
3 not connected with something that is similar: *Police have arrested seven drug*

smugglers in three separate incidents this week.

PHRASE **go your separate ways** to end a relationship with a partner and decide to live or work apart

—**sep•a•rate•ly** adv

sep•a•rate² /ˈsep(ə)ˌreɪt/ verb ★★★

1 [I/T] to keep people or things apart from each other, or to stop being joined to something else: *The army was called in to help separate the warring factions.* ♦ *The newly formed cells will* ***separate from*** *the main organism.* ♦ **separate sb from sb** *The child may be separated from his mother while she receives treatment.*

2 [T] to be between things or people so that they are kept apart: **separate sth from sth** *A large river separates the north of the city from the south.*

3 [I/T] to divide something, or to become divided, into different parts: *The two issues need to be separated to discuss them fairly.* ♦ *The story then* ***separates into*** *several different strands.*

4 [I] to stop living with your husband, wife, or sexual partner

PHRASAL VERB **ˌseparate (sth) ˈout** *same as* **separate²** 3: *The material is processed to separate out any impurities.*

sep•a•rat•ed /ˈsepəˌreɪtəd/ adj no longer living with your husband, wife, or sexual partner → DIVORCED

sep•a•ra•tion /ˌsepəˈreɪʃ(ə)n/ noun **1** [C/U] a period of time that people who are usually together spend apart: *a baby's response to separation from its mother* **2** [U] the act of separating two or more things, or the fact that they are separated: *Quebec wanted some form of separation from the rest of Canada.* **3** [C/U] an arrangement in which a husband and wife live apart even though they are not divorced

sep•a•ra•tist /ˈsep(ə)rətɪst/ noun [C] a member of a group of people who want to be independent of a national, religious, or other group to which they belong

S

Sept. abbrev September

Sep•tem•ber /sepˈtembər/ noun [C/U] ★★★ the ninth month of the year, between August and October: *The last time I saw her was in September.* ♦ *The interview is on September 9th.*

sep•tic /ˈseptɪk/ adj infected with bacteria

ˌseptic ˈtank noun [C] a large container buried under the ground and used for collecting waste from toilets

se•quel /ˈsikwəl/ noun [C] a book, movie, play, etc. that continues the story of an earlier one = FOLLOW-UP

se•quence /ˈsikwəns/ noun [C/U] ★★ a set of related things that happen or are arranged in a particular order: *A computer can store and repeat sequences of instructions.* ♦ *Are the numbers* ***in sequence?*** ♦ *Describe the exact* ***sequence of events*** *that evening.*

se•quin /ˈsikwɪn/ noun [C] a small shiny flat piece of plastic or metal that you sew onto clothes to decorate them

se•rene /səˈrin/ adj calm, or peaceful

—**se•rene•ly** adv, **se•ren•i•ty** /səˈrenəti/ noun [U]

ser•geant /ˈsɑrdʒənt/ noun [C] **1** an officer of middle rank in the army, air force, or MARINES **2** a police officer of middle rank

se•ri•al /ˈsɪriəl/ noun [C] a story that is broadcast or published in a series of separate parts

ˈserial ˌkiller noun [C] someone who murders several people one after the other, often in the same way

ˈserial ˌnumber noun [C] a number that is printed on things such as electrical goods or paper money, so that each one can be recognized

se•ries /ˈsɪriz/ (plural **se•ries**) noun [C] ★★★

1 a set of similar things that come one after another: *We'll need to do* ***a series of*** *tests before we do anything else.*

2 a set of television or radio programs that are all about a particular subject, person, or group of people: *Tonight's episode is the second in a three-part series.*

3 a set of things that are made with the same design, or made in the same way: ***a*** *popular new* ***series of*** *children's books*

se•ri•ous /ˈsɪriəs/ adj ★★★

1 bad or dangerous enough to make you worried: ***a serious*** *head* ***injury*** ♦ *It's not* ***a serious problem.*** ♦ *An accident like this poses* ***a serious threat*** *to the environment.*

2 meaning what you say or do, and not making a joke: *I'm sorry, I didn't realize you were being serious.* ♦ **serious about (doing) sth** *Do you think Mike's serious about going to live in New York?*

3 thinking carefully about things and not laughing much: *Peter seems serious but he actually has a good sense of humor.*

4 if you are in a serious romantic relationship with someone, you intend to stay together for a long time

—**se•ri•ous•ness** noun [U]

se•ri•ous•ly /ˈsɪriəsli/ adv ★★

1 in a way that is bad or dangerous enough to make you worried: *Was anyone in the car* ***seriously hurt?***

2 in a way that shows that you think something is important and should be thought about carefully: *We have to* ***think seriously about*** *what we do next.* ♦ *I'm* ***seriously considering*** *moving to Chicago.*

3 *spoken* really: *Do you* ***seriously think*** *I'm going to lend you the car?*

4 *informal* very: *He must be seriously rich.*

PHRASE **take sb/sth seriously** to behave in a way that shows that you think that someone or something is important

ser•mon /ˈsɜrmən/ noun [C] a religious speech that is made by a priest in church

se•ro•to•nin /ˌsɪrəˈtoʊnɪn/ noun [U] a substance in your body that affects your moods

ser•pent /ˈsɜrpənt/ noun [C] *literary* a snake

ser•vant /ˈsɜrvənt/ noun [C] someone whose job is to cook, clean, or do other work in someone else's home

serve¹ /sɜrv/ verb ★★★

1 provide food/drink	6 spend time in prison
2 do work	7 help customers
3 be used for purpose	8 give document
4 help achieve sth	9 hit ball to start play
5 provide with sth useful	+ PHRASE

1 [I/T] to provide food or a drink for someone, especially at a meal: *A light meal will be served during the flight.* ♦ ***Dinner is served*** *between 7 and 10 p.m.* ♦ **serve sb sth** *Carolyn served them iced tea on the front porch.*
2 [I/T] to do a job, or to perform duties for a person or organization: *He served more than 20 years in the army.* ♦ *Mr. Russell **served as** president of the Association for fifteen years.* ♦ *Henry **served on** numerous committees and commissions.*
3 [I/T] to be used for a particular purpose: *Their spare room also **serves as** an office.* ♦ **serve to do sth** *His death serves to remind us how dangerous drugs can be.*
4 [T] to help to achieve something: **serve sb's interests** *They voted for a chairman who might better serve their interests.* ♦ **serve sb well** *His ability to get along with people served him well in setting up his own business.*
5 [T] to provide a group of people or an area with something useful: *These gas pipes serve the whole area.* ♦ *a new hospital to serve the needs of the local community*
6 [T] to spend time in prison: *He's **serving a life sentence** for murder.*
7 [I/T] to help customers to buy goods in a store
8 [T] to officially give someone a legal document that orders them to do something: **serve sb with sth** *She was served with a summons to appear in court.*
9 [I/T] to hit a ball in order to start playing for a point in a game such as tennis
PHRASE **it serves sb right (for doing sth)** used for saying that you think that someone deserves something unpleasant that happens to them

serve² /sɜrv/ noun [C] a hit of a ball in order to start playing for a point in a game such as tennis = SERVICE

serv·er /ˈsɜrvər/ noun [C] **1** *computing* a computer that stores information for all the computers in a NETWORK **2** *American* someone who brings you your food in a restaurant = WAITER

serv·ice¹ /ˈsɜrvɪs/ noun ★★★

1 system to meet needs	5 sb's work
2 help for customers	6 religious ceremony
3 type of business	7 of machines/vehicles
4 government work	8 the military

1 [C] a system that provides things that the public needs: *transport/education services*
→ HEALTH SERVICE
2 [U] help and advice that is given to customers in a store, hotel, or business: *a store with a reputation for excellent customer service*
3 [C] a business that provides help, information, or advice for the public: *financial/banking services* ♦ *the service sector*
4 [C] an organization that does work for a government: *the prison/diplomatic service*
5 [C/U] work that someone does as a job or in order to help other people: *Jack had given 25 years of **loyal service**.* ♦ *She was praised for her **services to the community**.*
6 [C] a religious ceremony: *a church service*
7 [U] regular examination of a vehicle or machine to check that it works correctly and make repairs: *I need to take my truck in for service.*
8 the service [singular] the military

serv·ice² /ˈsɜrvɪs/ verb [T] to examine and repair a vehicle or machine as part of a regular check

ˈservice ˌcharge noun [C] an amount of money that a company adds to the cost of something in order to be paid for their services

serv·ice·man /ˈsɜrvɪsmən/ (plural **serv·ice·men** /ˈsɜrvɪsmən/) noun [C] a man who is a member of the military

ˈservice proˌvider noun [C] **1** *computing* a company that provides customers with a connection to the Internet = ISP **2** a company that provides a service, for example insurance or medical treatment

ˈservice ˌstation noun [C] a business that sells gas, oil, and other things for vehicles

serv·ice·wom·an /ˈsɜrvɪsˌwʊmən/ (plural **serv·ice·wom·en** /ˈsɜrvɪsˌwɪmɪn/) noun [C] a woman who is a member of the military

serv·ing /ˈsɜrvɪŋ/ noun [C] an amount of food for one person = HELPING

ses·a·me /ˈsesəmi/ noun [U] a plant that produces seeds and oil that are used in cooking

ses·sion /ˈseʃ(ə)n/ noun [C] ★★
1 a period of time that is used for a particular activity: *a question-and-answer session* ♦ *a training/recording session*
2 a formal meeting of an institution such as a legislature or a court of law: *an emergency session of the U.N. Security Council*
PHRASE **in session** meeting to deal with business: *Is the Supreme Court still in session?*

set¹ /set/ (past tense and past participle **set**) verb ★★★

1 put sb/sth somewhere	8 put story in time/place
2 of equipment	9 when sun goes down
3 decide time/place	10 liquid: become solid
4 decide price/value	11 join broken bone
5 establish rule etc.	+ PHRASE
6 give sb sth to do	+ PHRASAL VERBS
7 put sb/sth in state	

1 [T] to put someone or something in a position, or to be in a particular place or position: *Tea's ready, he told them and set down the tray.* ♦ *She set the baby on the floor to play.*
2 [T] to make a piece of equipment ready to operate, or ready to start at a particular time: **set sth to do sth** *The bomb was set to go off at eight o'clock.* ♦ *I'm **setting the alarm** for 6:30.*
3 [T] to decide where or when an event will happen: *Have they **set a date** for the wedding?*
4 [T] to decide the price, value, or level of something: *The central bank is responsible for setting interest rates.*
5 [T] to establish a rule, standard, limit, etc. that people must follow: *Their professor **sets high standards** and expects everyone to meet them.* ♦ *Opposition parties have **set conditions** for cooperating with the*

S

government. ♦ *You should* ***set an example*** *for your younger brothers.*

6 [T] to give something to someone to do or achieve: **set sb sth** *You'll never get anywhere if you don't set yourself any goals.*

7 [T] to put someone or something in a particular state: *The suspect has been accused of* ***setting*** *the restaurant* ***on fire.*** ♦ *Don't* ***set*** *the dog* ***loose.*** ♦ *The hostages have been* ***set free*** *after 34 days in captivity.*

8 [T] if a play, book, movie, etc. is set in a particular time or place, it happens in that time or place: *The film is set in 18th-century New England.*

9 [I] when the sun sets, it goes below the HORIZON at the end of the day ≠ RISE

10 [I] if a liquid sets, it forms a solid substance: *a type of concrete that sets in 15 minutes*

11 [I/T] to put the two ends of a broken bone back together, or to be joined in this way

PHRASE **set the stage for sth** to create the conditions in which something is likely to happen

PHRASAL VERBS **ˌset aˈbout sth** to begin doing something, especially in a determined or enthusiastic way: *She set about the problem with her usual energy.*

ˌset sb aˈgainst sb to cause two people or groups to fight each other

ˌset sb/sth aˈpart to make someone or something different and special: *Graf's natural athleticism* ***set*** *her* ***apart from*** *other tennis players.*

ˌset sth aˈside 1 to keep or save something from a larger amount or supply in order to use it later: *Have you* ***set aside*** *some money for your child's education?* **2** to not let a particular feeling, opinion, or belief influence you, in order to achieve something more important: *They agreed to* ***set aside*** *their* ***differences*** *and work together for peace.*

ˌset sth ˈback to delay the progress of something

ˌset sth ˈdown *formal* to state officially how something should be done

ˌset ˈforth *literary* to leave on a trip

ˌset ˈin if something unpleasant sets in, it starts to happen and is likely to continue: *If the wound is not kept clean, infection could set in.*

ˌset ˈoff to leave on a trip or start going somewhere: *We set off early the next morning.*

ˌset sth ˈoff 1 to cause something to operate or to explode: *Jeff pushed open the front door, which set off the alarm.* **2** to cause a situation or a series of events to happen: *The price increases could set off mass protests.*

ˌset ˈout 1 to leave on a trip: *The group set out from Grand Cayman five days ago.* **2** to start doing something, or trying to achieve something: **set out to do sth** *They set out to build their own house.*

ˌset sth ˈout to explain, describe, or arrange something in a clear and detailed way

ˌset sb ˈup *informal* to arrange for someone to be blamed for doing something illegal

ˌset sth ˈup 1 to start something such as a business, organization, or institution **2** to organize or plan something: *I'll* ***set up a meeting*** *for Thursday.* **3** to make a piece of equipment ready for use: *Will you be able to set up my PC?*

set² /set/ noun [C] ★★★

1 group of things	4 of play/movie
2 piece of equipment	5 songs performed
3 part of tennis match	

1 a group of things that belong together: *Teachers are given* ***a set of*** *guidelines for dealing with violent students.* ♦ ***a set of*** *keys* ♦ *Winners will receive* ***a complete set of*** *REM albums.*

2 a piece of equipment that receives television or radio signals: *a TV set*

3 a part of a tennis match consisting of at least six games

4 a theater stage, or a place where a movie or television program is made: *This photograph was taken on the set of her latest film.*

5 a series of songs that are played or sung in a performance

set³ /set/ adj ★

1 already decided or agreed: *There's no set time limit for the job.* ♦ *He charges* ***a set fee*** *for his services.*

2 ready to do something: *Gillian is* ***getting set*** *to do a world tour.* ♦ *Are you* ***all set for*** *the party tonight?*

3 likely to do something: **be set to do sth** *The costs of many imports are set to rise under the new trade proposals.*

4 not willing to change your opinion or way of doing things: *He's old and stubborn and* ***set in his ways.***

PHRASE **I'm all set** *American spoken* used for saying that you do not need anything, especially food, when someone offers you something

set•back /ˈsetˌbæk/ noun [C] a problem that delays or stops progress

set•ting /ˈsetɪŋ/ noun [C] ★

1 the place where someone or something is, and all the things that are part of that place: *The classroom setting must be calm and safe.* ♦ *a hotel in a charming mountain setting*

2 the time or place in which the events of a play, book, movie, etc. happen: *a love story in a tropical island setting*

3 a position on the controls of a piece of equipment: *To save energy, lower the thermostat setting at night.*

Words often used with setting

Adjectives often used with ***setting*** *(sense 1)*

■ **beautiful, ideal, idyllic, magnificent, perfect, picturesque, tranquil** + SETTING: used about settings that are pleasant

set•tle /ˈset(ə)l/ verb ★★★

1 end disagreement	5 go to live somewhere
2 decide sth	6 pay money owed to sb
3 make sb comfortable	+ PHRASE
4 fall & rest on ground	+ PHRASAL VERBS

1 [T] to end an argument or legal disagreement: *The two sides are holding talks to* ***settle the dispute.*** ♦ *The case was* ***settled out of court*** (=without asking a law court to decide).

2 [T] to decide something definitely: *It was settled that they would leave before dark.*
3 [I/T] to make yourself or someone else comfortable and relaxed in a particular place or position: *I **settled back** into a comfortable chair and waited.*
4 [I] if something settles, it falls downward and stays on the place where it has fallen: *Flakes of snow **settled on** the windshield.*
5 [I] to go to live permanently in a particular place: *Her relatives had come to America and **settled in** Boston.*
6 [T] to pay all the money that you owe to a particular person or company: *He has 30 days to **settle** his **bill**.*
PHRASE **settle a score (with sb)** to do something bad in order to harm someone, because they did something bad to you in the past: *enemies who have an old score to settle*
PHRASAL VERBS ˌ**settle ˈdown** to change your life by choosing to stay in one place or with one partner: *Are you ever going to settle down?*
ˌ**settle (sb) ˈdown** to become calm after being upset, nervous, or excited, or to make someone do this: *The kids will settle down after they've had a nap.*
ˈ**settle for sb/sth** to accept someone or something that is not exactly what you wanted: *Injuries and illness forced the team to settle for third place.*
ˌ**settle ˈin** to become familiar with a new way of life, place, or job: *She seems to have settled in quickly at her new company.*
ˈ**settle on sb/sth** to make a decision between two or more people or things after not being certain which to choose: *The band has yet to settle on a name.*
ˌ**settle ˈup** to pay all of an amount of money that you owe

set•tled /ˈset(ə)ld/ adj **1** happy and relaxed because you are in a familiar or permanent situation **2** if something is settled, people have made a decision about it **3** if you have a settled way of life, you stay permanently in one place or job or with one person **4** not changing or likely to change

set•tle•ment /ˈset(ə)lmənt/ noun ★
1 [C/U] a formal agreement that ends a disagreement: *They are negotiating **a peace settlement**. ♦ **the settlement of** disputes between employers and employees*
2 [C] a place where people have come to live permanently: *They discovered the remains of an early Anglo-Saxon settlement.*

set•tler /ˈsetlər/ noun [C] someone who goes to live in a place where not many people live

set•up /ˈsetʌp/ noun [C] **1** a system by which people or things are organized **2** *informal* a situation in which someone cheats or tricks you, especially by making you look guilty when you are not

sev•en /ˈsev(ə)n/ number the number 7

sev•en•teen /ˌsev(ə)nˈtin/ number the number 17

sev•en•teenth /ˌsev(ə)nˈtinθ/ number **1** in the place or position counted as number 17 **2** one of 17 equal parts of something

sev•enth /ˈsev(ə)nθ/ number **1** in the place or position counted as number 7 **2** one of 7 equal parts of something

sev•en•ti•eth /ˈsev(ə)ntiəθ/ number **1** in the place or position counted as number 70 **2** one of 70 equal parts of something

sev•en•ty /ˈsev(ə)nti/ number the number 70

sev•er /ˈsevər/ verb [T] **1** to cut through a part of something so that it is separated completely from the main part **2** to end something such as a friendship or a connection completely and permanently

sev•er•al /ˈsev(ə)rəl/ grammar word ★★★

> **Several** can be:
> - a **determiner**: *Several buildings were damaged by the explosion.*
> - a **pronoun**: *If you want to see Edward's paintings, there are several in the city art gallery. ♦ I've introduced her to several of my friends.*
> - an **adjective**: *These past several weeks have been difficult for the whole family.*

a number of people or things that is more than two or three, but not many: *He had already been warned several times about speeding. ♦ There are only nine men in the program, but several have drug problems. ♦ **Several of** the passengers were badly injured.*

sev•er•ance /ˈsev(ə)rəns/ noun [U] money that is paid to a worker who is forced to leave a company because they are no longer needed, or a situation in which this happens

se•vere /sɪˈvɪr/ adj ★★
1 very serious and bad, worrying, or unpleasant: *The housing shortage is severe. ♦ a severe thunderstorm ♦ John had suffered **severe bruising** and serious cuts.*
2 very strict or extreme = HARSH: *The most severe penalty he could get is ten years in prison. ♦ The country has come under **severe criticism** for its human rights record.*
3 unfriendly and not smiling: *a severe expression*
—**se•vere•ly** adv, **se•ver•i•ty** /sɪˈverəti/ noun [U]

sew /soʊ/ (past tense **sewed**; past participle **sewn** /soʊn/ or **sewed**) verb [I/T] to make or repair clothes, or to fasten something, using a needle and THREAD
PHRASAL VERB ˌ**sew sth ˈup** **1** *informal* to deal with something successfully, or to make certain that you will win something **2** to repair something such as a hole in a piece of cloth by sewing it

sew•age /ˈsuɪdʒ/ noun [U] waste from people's bodies that is removed from houses and other buildings by a system of large underground pipes

sew•er /ˈsuər/ noun [C] an underground pipe or passage that carries sewage

sew•ing /ˈsoʊɪŋ/ noun [U] **1** work that you do using a needle and THREAD or a sewing machine **2** things such as clothes or curtains that you sew

ˈ**sewing maˌchine** noun [C] a machine that you use for sewing clothes, curtains, etc.

sewn a past participle of sew

sex /seks/ noun ★★★
1 [U] the activity in which people kiss and touch each other's sexual organs, that may

S

also include SEXUAL INTERCOURSE: *the impact of sex and violence in TV programs* ♦ *Parents worry about their teenagers **having sex**.*
2 [C] males or females considered as separate groups: *equal treatment of the sexes* ♦ *The hostel has separate sleeping areas for each sex.*
3 [U] the fact that a person, animal, or plant is either male or female: *We don't want to know the sex of our baby before it is born.*

ˈsex apˌpeal noun [U] the quality of being sexually attractive

sex•ism /ˈsekˌsɪzəm/ noun [U] unfair treatment of someone because they are a woman or a man —**sex•ist** adj

ˈsex ˌlife noun [C] someone's sexual relationships or activities

ˈsex ofˌfender noun [C] someone who has committed a crime involving sex

sex•u•al /ˈsekʃuəl/ adj ★★★
1 involving or relating to sex: *a sexual relationship/partner* ♦ *sexual desire/feelings*
2 concerning relationships between men and women, or the way that people think that men and women should behave: *sexual stereotyping*
—**sex•u•al•ly** adv

ˌsexual ˈharassment noun [U] offensive or threatening behavior that involves regularly making sexual comments or touching someone in a sexual way when they do not want this

ˌsexual ˈintercourse noun [U] *formal* the sexual actions between a man and a woman in which the man puts his PENIS inside the woman's VAGINA

sex•u•al•i•ty /ˌsekʃuˈæləti/ noun [U] sexual feelings, attitudes, and activities

ˌsexual orienˈtation or **ˌsexual ˈpreference** noun [U] the state of preferring sexual relationships with people of one sex rather than the other

ˈsex ˌworker noun [C] a PROSTITUTE

sex•y /ˈseksi/ adj sexually attractive, or causing feelings of sexual excitement

SGML noun [U] *computing* Standard Generalized Markup Language: a computer language that uses normal English words for publishing documents in electronic form

Sgt. abbrev sergeant

sh /ʃ/ interjection used for telling someone to stop talking or to be less noisy

shab•by /ˈʃæbi/ adj **1** old and in bad condition: *shabby clothes/furniture/buildings* **2** not fair or honest: *management's shabby treatment of the workers* —**shab•bi•ly** adv

shack /ʃæk/ noun [C] a small plain building

shack•le /ˈʃæk(ə)l/ verb **be shackled** to be prevented from doing what you want to do

shack•les /ˈʃæk(ə)lz/ noun [plural] a pair of connected metal rings that can be locked onto the wrists or legs of a prisoner

shade¹ /ʃeɪd/ noun ★

1 cool dark area	4 slightly different form
2 screen/cover	5 sunglasses
3 form of a color	

1 [U] a slightly cool dark area where the light and heat from the sun does not reach: *We sat **in the shade** and ate our lunch.* ♦ *I spent the afternoon reading under **the shade of** an umbrella.*
2 [C] a screen or cover that protects something from the sun or from a light
3 [C] a particular form of a color: *a brilliant shade of red*
4 [C] a slightly different form or type of something: *All shades of political opinion were represented.*
5 shades [plural] *informal* a pair of SUNGLASSES

shade² /ʃeɪd/ verb [T] to prevent light from shining directly onto or into something

shad•ow¹ /ˈʃædoʊ/ noun [C/U] ★★ an area of darkness that is created when something blocks light: *The kids jumped out of the shadows, trying to scare us.* ♦ *She stood outside **in the shadow of** an old pine tree.*
PHRASES **beyond/without a shadow of a doubt** used for saying that you are completely certain of something: *I knew beyond a shadow of a doubt that something bad had happened.*
in the shadow of 1 with the influence of someone or something powerful or famous: *aides working in the shadow of senior officials* **2** near in time or space to something: *The farm sits in the shadow of the Rocky Mountains.*
in sb's shadow in a situation where your own qualities are not noticed or recognized because of someone who is more famous or powerful: *For years, she lived in her father's shadow.*

shad•ow² /ˈʃædoʊ/ verb [T] to secretly follow someone wherever they go

shad•ow•y /ˈʃædoʊi/ adj **1** mysterious and secret, or not understood **2** hidden in darkness or shadows

shad•y /ˈʃeɪdi/ adj **1** sheltered from the hot sun **2** probably dishonest or illegal

shaft /ʃæft/ noun [C] **1** a long narrow passage that goes down through a building or down through the ground: *an elevator shaft* **2** *literary* a long thin line of light **3** the handle of a tool

shag•gy /ˈʃægi/ adj shaggy fur or hair is long, thick, and messy

shah /ʃɑ/ noun [C] in the past, a king in Iran and some other countries in the Middle East

shake¹ /ʃeɪk/ (past tense **shook** /ʃʊk/; past participle **shak•en** /ˈʃeɪkən/) verb ★★★
1 [I/T] to make lots of quick small movements up and down, or from side to side, or to make someone or something do this: *Houses shook as a bomb exploded in the neighborhood.* ♦ *An earthquake shook a wide area of southern Italy last year.* ♦ *"You're not listening!" she cried, shaking him.*
2 [T] to frighten someone, or to make them feel very shocked or upset: *The boy's tragic death shook the entire community.* ♦ *He was shaken and upset by the accident.*
3 [T] to make something less strong, powerful, or confident: *Violent conflicts between tribes have shaken the region.* ♦ *You must believe in yourself and not allow anyone to **shake your confidence**.*

4 [I] if your voice shakes, it sounds weak, nervous, or emotional

PHRASES **shake hands (with sb)** or **shake sb's hand** to hold someone's hand and move it up and down, as a way of greeting them or to show that you agree to something: *"Nice to meet you," Larry said, shaking my hand.*

shake your head to say no by turning your head from side to side

PHRASAL VERBS **ˌshake sb ˈoff** to escape from someone who is following you

ˌshake sth ˈoff to get rid of something bad: *I haven't been able to shake this cold off for weeks.*

ˌshake sb ˈup to upset or frighten someone

ˌshake sth ˈout to shake something so that dust and dirt fall off: *Help me shake out this blanket.*

shake

shake2 /ʃeɪk/ noun [C] **1** the action of shaking **2** a MILKSHAKE

ˈshake-up noun [C] an important change in the way that something such as a department or company is organized

shak•y /ˈʃeɪki/ adj **1** feeling weak or unable to walk or move without shaking, for example because you are sick **2** likely to fail or be unsuccessful —**shak•i•ly** adv

shall /*weak* ʃəl, *strong* ʃæl/ modal verb ★★

- **Shall** is usually followed by an infinitive without "to": *I shall explain everything later.* Sometimes it is used without a following infinitive: *I have never visited Africa and probably never shall.*
- **Shall** has no participles and no infinitive form. It does not change its form, so the third person singular form does not end in "-s": *The President shall appoint all ambassadors with the consent of the Senate.*
- Questions and negatives are formed without "do": *Shall I come with you?*
- The negative form **shall not** can be shortened in conversation or informal writing to **shan't**, especially in British English.

1 used for offering help, suggesting something, or asking someone what to do: *Shall we have some lunch?* ♦ *Where shall we meet?* ♦ *Shall I open the champagne?*

2 *British* used after "I" or "we" for saying what you intend to do in the future: *I shall be busy all day tomorrow.*

3 *legal* used in instructions and legal documents for saying that something must be done: *The Court shall have authority to demand the presence of witnesses.*

shal•lot /ʃəˈlɑt/ noun [C] a small vegetable similar to an onion —*picture* → C11

shal•low /ˈʃæloʊ/ adj ★

1 with only a short distance from the top or surface to the bottom ≠ DEEP: *Move to the shallow end of the pool.* ♦ *He dug a shallow trench.* ♦ *The dish needs to be quite shallow.*

2 not interested in serious ideas, strong feelings, or other important things = SUPERFICIAL

sham /ʃæm/ noun [singular] something that people pretend is good, serious, or honest, but is not

sham•bles /ˈʃæmb(ə)lz/ noun [singular] **1** something that is very badly organized **2** an extremely messy place

shame1 /ʃeɪm/ noun ★

1 [U] a guilty and embarrassed feeling that you have when you have behaved badly: *He speaks about his affair without shame.* ♦ *The people who let this happen should* ***hang their heads in shame.***

2 [singular] a reason for feeling sad or disappointed: **it seems a shame to do sth** *It seems a shame to waste all this food.* ♦ **+(that)** *It was a shame that you couldn't come with us.*

shame2 /ʃeɪm/ verb [T] to make someone feel guilty or embarrassed, especially so that they change their behavior

shame•ful /ˈʃeɪmfəl/ adj so bad that you feel ashamed —**shame•ful•ly** adv

shame•less /ˈʃeɪmləs/ adj not feeling ashamed about behaving in a way that other people do not approve of: *a shameless womanizer* —**shame•less•ly** adv

sham•poo /ʃæmˈpu/ noun [C/U] a liquid that you use for washing your hair —**sham•poo** verb [T]

shan't /ʃænt/ short form *British* a way of saying or writing "shall not." This is not often used in formal writing.

shan•ty•town /ˈʃæntiˌtaʊn/ noun [C] an area where very poor people live in houses made from sheets of wood, metal, or other thin material

shape1 /ʃeɪp/ noun ★★★

1 [C/U] the outer form of something: *Trace the shape onto the card and cut it out.* ♦ *There were balloons of* ***all shapes and sizes*** *in the sky.* ♦ *a flowerbed* ***in the shape of*** *a cross* ♦ *My favorite sweater was beginning to* ***lose its shape.***

2 [C] something that you cannot see well because it is far away or there is not enough light: *Ghostly shapes loomed out of the fog.*

3 [U] the features or qualities of something: *It's part of a plan to* ***change the shape of*** *local government.*

4 [U] the condition of something: *The economy is* ***in bad shape.***

PHRASES **in/out of shape** in good/bad physical condition: *I can't believe how out of shape I am.* ♦ *I really want to* ***get in shape*** *before summer.*

take shape to develop into something that can be recognized: *The idea began to take shape about two years ago.*

shape2 /ʃeɪp/ verb [T] ★

1 to influence the way that a person, idea, or situation develops: *We have all been shaped by our past experiences.* ♦ *His generation firmly believed they could* ***shape the future.***

2 to form something into a particular shape:

S

shape sth into sth *Shape the mixture into cubes.*

PHRASAL VERB ˌshape ˈup to develop: *Education is shaping up as the hottest issue on the agenda.*

shaped /ʃeɪpt/ adj with a particular shape

shape•less /ˈʃeɪpləs/ adj without a definite shape

shape•ly /ˈʃeɪpli/ adj attractive in shape

shard /ʃɑrd/ noun [C] a sharp piece of broken glass, metal, or other hard substance

share[1] /ʃer/ verb ★★★

1 use/have with sb	4 have same opinion
2 do sth with sb else	5 tell sb sth
3 let sb use/have sth	6 give part to sb

1 [I/T] to use or to have something at the same time as someone else: *Do you mind sharing a table?* ♦ *There's only one copy left, so we'll have to share.* ♦ **share sth with sb** *I share this apartment with five other people.*
2 [I/T] to do something, or to be responsible for something, with someone else: *We* ***share responsibility*** *for meeting the targets.*
3 [T] to allow someone to use or have something that you own: **share sth with sb** *He would never share his toys with me.*
4 [T] to have the same opinion or feeling as someone else: *Not everyone will share your enthusiasm for this plan.*
5 [I/T] to tell someone something: *Thanks for sharing.* ♦ *Newsgroups enable patients to share information.*
6 [T] to give a part of something to someone else: **share sth between/among sb** *The money will be shared between 30 different environmental organizations.*

share[2] /ʃer/ noun ★★★
1 [C] a part of a total number or amount of something that is divided between two or more people or things: *Britain's* ***share of*** *world trade had steadily declined.*
2 [singular] a part of the total amount of work or responsibility of several people: *He does his* ***share of*** *the cooking.* ♦ *Jane has accepted her* ***share of*** *the blame.*
3 [singular] a reasonable or normal amount of something: *We certainly had our* ***share of*** *good fortune.* ♦ *He has suffered more than his* ***fair share*** *of disappointments.*
4 [C] *business* one of the equal parts of a company that you can buy as a way of investing money: ***Share prices*** *fell on the Tokyo Stock Exchange.*

share•hold•er /ˈʃerˌhoʊldər/ noun [C] someone who owns STOCK in a company

share•ware /ˈʃerˌwer/ noun [U] *computing* computer software that you can use for a period of time before paying for it

sha•ri•a /ʃəˈriə/ noun [U] the traditional system of Islamic law

shark /ʃɑrk/ noun [C] a very large fish with sharp teeth that lives in the ocean *—picture* → C13

sharp[1] /ʃɑrp/ adj ★★★

1 able to cut	6 showing sb is annoyed
2 sudden & big/severe	7 clearly different
3 turning suddenly	8 fashionable
4 clear & with detail	9 wind/frost: very cold
5 quick to notice/react	10 higher in music

1 a sharp object has an edge that can cut or an end that is pointed: *a sharp knife* ♦ *a sharp pencil* ♦ *sharp teeth/claws* ♦ *These scissors aren't very sharp.*
2 sudden and very big or severe: ***a sharp rise*** *in the sale of organic produce* ♦ ***a sharp drop*** *in unemployment* ♦ *I felt* ***a sharp pain*** *in my foot.*
3 changing direction suddenly: *a sharp bend in the road* ♦ *Take a sharp left at the next intersection.*
4 clear and seen in a lot of detail: *The new high-definition TV offers razor-sharp pictures and digital sound.*
5 intelligent and quick to notice something or react to something: *Some of these kids are pretty sharp when it comes to math.* ♦ *a sharp wit*
6 a sharp comment, voice, or expression shows that someone is unfriendly or annoyed: *The deal has come under sharp criticism from the investment community.*
7 clearly recognized as different: *The warm weather was* ***in sharp contrast*** *to last year's cold temperatures.*
8 *informal* fashionable or impressive
9 a sharp wind or FROST is very cold
10 used for showing that a musical note should be played or sung a HALF STEP higher than usual
—**sharp•ly** /ˈʃɑrpli/ adv, **sharp•ness** noun [U]

sharp[2] /ʃɑrp/ adv **1** at a particular time exactly: *We're leaving at 5 o'clock sharp.* **2** at a higher than usual PITCH

sharp[3] /ʃɑrp/ noun [C] a musical note that is played or sung a HALF STEP higher than usual

sharp•en /ˈʃɑrpən/ verb [T] **1** to make something such as a knife, tool, or pencil sharp **2** to make something better, stronger, or more noticeable

shat•ter /ˈʃætər/ verb **1** [I/T] to break suddenly into a lot of small pieces, or to break something into a lot of small pieces: *The blast shattered windows over a wide area.* **2** [T] to destroy or seriously damage something: *His father's constant criticism shattered his confidence.*

shave[1] /ʃeɪv/ verb [I/T] to make a part of your body smooth by cutting off the hair: *I cut myself while I was shaving.*

PHRASAL VERB ˌshave sth ˈoff to remove hair from a part of your body: *You've shaved off your beard.*

shave[2] /ʃeɪv/ noun [singular] an act of making a part of your body smooth by cutting off the hair

shav•en /ˈʃeɪv(ə)n/ adj *formal* with the hair shaved off → CLEAN-SHAVEN

shav•er /ˈʃeɪvər/ noun [C] a small piece of electrical equipment used for cutting hair from a part of your body

shav•ings /ˈʃeɪvɪŋz/ noun [plural] thin pieces that have been cut from the surface of something

shawl /ʃɔl/ noun [C] a large piece of material that is worn by a woman around her shoulders or on her head

she /*weak* ʃɪ, *strong* ʃi/ pronoun ★★★ used for referring to a woman, girl, or female animal, when they have already been mentioned, or when it is obvious which one you are referring to: *I was with Lisa when she bought her wedding dress.*

s/he abbrev she or he

sheaf /ʃif/ (plural **sheaves** /ʃivz/) noun [C] **1** a large number of pieces of paper that are kept together **2** stems of grain that have been cut and tied together

shear /ʃɪr/ (past tense **sheared**; past participle **sheared** or **shorn** /ʃɔrn/) verb [T] to cut the wool from a sheep

shears /ʃɪrz/ noun [plural] a tool like a large pair of scissors

sheath /ʃiθ/ (plural **sheaths** /ʃiðz/) noun [C] a cover that is used for a knife or a sword

sheaves the plural of **sheaf**

she'd /ʃid/ short form **1** the usual way of saying or writing "she had" when "had" is an AUXILIARY VERB. This is not often used in formal writing: *She'd forgotten to lock the door.* **2** the usual way of saying or writing "she would." This is not often used in formal writing: *She'd like to have a vacation.*

shed¹ /ʃed/ (present participle **shed·ding**; past tense and past participle **shed**) verb [T] **1** to let something fall off as part of a natural process: *a snake shedding its skin* **2** to get rid of something that is not wanted: *The company shed another 250 workers this month.*

PHRASES **shed blood** *literary* to cause death or injury

shed light on sth to suggest an explanation for something that is difficult to understand

shed tears to cry, or to feel very sad

shed² /ʃed/ noun [C] a small building that is used for storing things

sheen /ʃin/ noun [singular] a shine on the surface of something

sheep /ʃip/ (plural **sheep**) noun [C] ★★ an animal that is kept by farmers for its wool or meat *—picture* → C12 → BLACK SHEEP

sheep·dog /ˈʃipˌdɔg/ noun [C] a dog that has been trained to guard and control sheep

sheep·ish /ˈʃipɪʃ/ adj embarrassed about something that you have done —**sheep·ish·ly** adv

sheep·skin /ˈʃipˌskɪn/ noun [C/U] the skin of a sheep with the wool still on it

sheer /ʃɪr/ adj **1** used for emphasizing the amount or degree of something: *We were overwhelmed by the sheer volume of work.* ♦ *The trip to work every day was sheer hell.* **2** extremely steep: *a sheer cliff face* **3** sheer cloth is very thin

sheet /ʃit/ noun [C] ★★★

1 a large piece of thin cloth that you put on your bed and use for lying on or for covering your body when you sleep: *I think the maid is waiting to **change the sheets*** (=put clean sheets on the bed).

2 a thin flat piece of paper, metal, plastic, glass, etc.: *The answers are printed on a separate sheet.* ♦ ***a sheet of** cardboard*

3 a wide flat area of something such as water or ice

sheet·ing /ˈʃitɪŋ/ noun [U] large flat pieces of plastic or metal

sheik or **sheikh** /ʃik, ʃeɪk/ noun [C] a male leader in an Arab country

shelf /ʃelf/ (plural **shelves** /ʃelvz/) noun [C] ★★ a flat piece of wood or glass that is attached to a wall or is part of a piece of furniture. It is used for putting things on: *He took a book from the shelf.* ♦ *The plates are on the top shelf.*

ˈshelf ˌlife noun [singular] the amount of time that something can be kept in a store before it is too old to sell

she'll /ʃil/ short form the usual way of saying or writing "she will." This is not often used in formal writing: *She'll be here soon.*

shell¹ /ʃel/ noun ★

1 [C/U] the hard outer part that protects the body of a sea creature or other animal: *a crab/tortoise/snail shell* ♦ *The kids were collecting shells on the beach.*

2 [C/U] the hard outer part of an egg or nut: *pieces of egg shell*

3 [C] a metal container filled with a substance that explodes when it is fired from a large gun: *antiaircraft shells*

shells

shell² /ʃel/ verb [T] **1** to attack or destroy a place by firing shells: *Army bases were shelled overnight by rebel forces.* **2** to remove the outer part that covers nuts or other foods

PHRASAL VERB **ˌshell (sth) ˈout** *informal* to spend a lot of money on something

shell·fish /ˈʃelˌfɪʃ/ (plural **shell·fish**) noun [C/U] sea creatures with a hard shell around them

shel·ter¹ /ˈʃeltər/ noun **1** [C] a place where people are protected from bad weather or from danger: *We built a temporary shelter out of branches.* ♦ *a bomb shelter* **2** [U] protection from bad weather or danger: *We stood and watched from the shelter of our front porch.* ♦ *We took shelter from the rain in a nearby bar.* **3** [C] a temporary place to live for people who do not have their own homes, or for animals who have been treated in a cruel way = REFUGE: *a women's shelter* **4** [U] a place to live, considered as a basic human need: *Everyone has the right to food, clothing, and shelter.*

shel·ter² /ˈʃeltər/ verb **1** [T] to protect someone or something from bad weather: *Hills sheltered the town from the winds.* **2** [T] to protect someone from unpleasant experiences or danger: *You cannot shelter your children from the realities of life.* **3** [I]

S

to stay somewhere where you are protected from danger or bad weather

shel•tered /ˈʃeltərd/ adj **1** not affected by bad weather **2** protected from unpleasant experiences

shelve /ʃelv/ verb [T] to decide not to use something such as a plan or suggestion now, although you may use it later

shelves the plural of **shelf**

shelv•ing /ˈʃelvɪŋ/ noun [U] a set of shelves

she•nan•i•gans /ʃəˈnænɪgənz/ noun [plural] *informal* silly, dishonest, or immoral behavior

shep•herd[1] /ˈʃepərd/ noun [C] someone whose job is to take care of sheep

shep•herd[2] /ˈʃepərd/ verb [T] to take someone to a place in order to make sure that they get there safely: *Carrie was shepherding a party of children toward the museum.*

sher•bet /ˈʃɜrbət/ noun [C/U] *American* a type of food like ICE CREAM

sher•iff /ˈʃerɪf/ noun [C] in the U.S., the most senior police officer in a COUNTY

sher•ry /ˈʃeri/ noun [C/U] a strong wine from southern Spain

she's /ʃiz/ short form **1** the usual way of saying or writing "she has" when "has" is an AUXILIARY VERB. This is not often used in formal writing: *She's gone over to Kerry's house.* **2** the usual way of saying or writing "she is." This is not often used in formal writing: *She's a psychiatrist.*

shh /ʃ/ interjection used for telling someone to stop talking or to be less noisy

shield[1] /ʃild/ noun [C] **1** a large transparent plastic object that police officers carry to protect them when they are controlling crowds: *Riot police with shields had surrounded the building.* **2** someone or something that protects you from harm or bad experiences **3** an object that soldiers carried in the past to protect themselves from being hit **4** an object shaped like a shield that is given to the winner of a competition

S

shield[2] /ʃild/ verb [T] to protect something or someone from something that is dangerous or unpleasant

shift[1] /ʃɪft/ verb ★

1 [I/T] to move, or to move something: *The children are shifting uncomfortably in their seats.* ♦ *She stared at him, then shifted her gaze to the suitcase on the bed.*

2 [I/T] to change, or to change something: *Public opinion had shifted sharply following the war.* ♦ *The government has shifted its attention away from the fight against crime.*

3 [T] to make someone or something else responsible for something: *The lawyers want to **shift the blame** from their client to our company.*

shift[2] /ʃɪft/ noun [C] **1** a period of work time in a place where some people work during the day and some work at night: *a 12-hour shift* ♦ *Rudy works the day shift.* **2** a change in someone's ideas or opinions: *the government's latest policy shift* ♦ *shifts in consumer demand* **3** a SHIFT KEY on a computer keyboard

ˈshift ˌkey noun [C] the BUTTON that you press on a computer keyboard when you want to write a CAPITAL LETTER

shift•y /ˈʃɪfti/ adj *informal* looking dishonest

Shi•ite /ˈʃiˌaɪt/ noun [C] a Muslim who belongs to the Shia group within the religion of Islam

shim•mer /ˈʃɪmər/ verb [I] to reflect a gentle light that seems to shake slightly

shin /ʃɪn/ noun [C] the lower front part of your leg that is between your knee and your foot

shine[1] /ʃaɪn/ (past tense and past participle **shined** or **shone** /ʃoʊn, *British* ʃɑn/) verb ★

1 produce light	4 look happy/excited
2 appear bright	5 show lot of skill
3 point light somewhere	+ PHRASAL VERB

1 [I] to produce a bright light: *Lights were shining from the windows of a few of the houses.* ♦ *The sun was **shining brightly**.*

2 [I/T] to have a bright attractive appearance, or to rub something to make it look bright and attractive: *The wooden tables had been polished until they shone.* ♦ *As a child, he shined shoes and sold newspapers on the streets.*

3 [T] to make a light shine in a particular direction: *Kobe **shone the flashlight** slowly around the room.*

4 [I] if people's eyes or faces shine, they look extremely happy or excited

5 [I] to show that you have a lot of skill when you do something: *It's time we gave some of the younger players a chance to shine.*

PHRASAL VERB **ˌshine ˈthrough** if a good feeling or quality shines through, it is very noticeable

shine[2] /ʃaɪn/ noun [singular] the bright appearance that something such as wood, metal, or leather has when it is in good condition

Shin•to /ˈʃɪntoʊ/ or **Shin•to•ism** /ˈʃɪntoʊˌɪzəm/ noun [U] the traditional religion of Japan

shin•y /ˈʃaɪni/ adj something that is shiny has a bright surface that reflects light: *a shiny red apple*

ship[1] /ʃɪp/ noun [C] ★★★ a very large boat that is used for carrying people or goods long distances: *His ship sailed from Pearl Harbor on Monday.* ♦ *a cargo/cruise ship* ♦ *There were over 350 passengers **aboard the ship**.*

ship[2] /ʃɪp/ verb [T] **1** to send goods to customers, usually by air or land **2** to send people somewhere by ship

ship•build•er /ˈʃɪpˌbɪldər/ noun [C] a company that builds ships —**ship•build•ing** noun [U]

ship•ment /ˈʃɪpmənt/ noun **1** [C] an amount of goods carried on a ship, airplane, train, or truck **2** [U] the process of taking goods from one place to another

ship•ping /ˈʃɪpɪŋ/ noun [U] **1** the business of carrying goods **2** ships and boats that are sailing

ship•wreck[1] /ˈʃɪpˌrek/ noun [C/U] an accident in which a ship is destroyed during a trip

ship•wreck[2] /ˈʃɪpˌrek/ verb **be shipwrecked** to be involved in a shipwreck

ship•yard /ˈʃɪpˌjɑrd/ noun [C] a place where ships are built or repaired

shirk /ʃɜrk/ verb [I/T] to avoid doing something difficult, or to avoid accepting responsibility for something: *A good manager should never shirk difficult decisions.*

shirt /ʃɜrt/ noun [C] ★★★ a piece of clothing that covers the top part of your body. It usually has long sleeves and buttons down the front: *a cotton/silk/denim shirt* ♦ *One of his shirt buttons was missing.* —*picture* → C5

shiv•er /ˈʃɪvər/ verb [I] to shake slightly because you are cold or frightened —**shiv•er** noun [C]

shiver

shoal /ʃoʊl/ noun [C] a group of fish that swim together

shock¹ /ʃɑk/ noun ★★

1 surprise from sth bad	4 electric flow in body
2 sth that surprises you	5 very thick hair
3 being weak and cold	

1 [singular/U] the feeling of being very surprised by something bad that happens unexpectedly: *Jessica's face was blank with shock.* ♦ *My mother* ***got a shock*** *when she saw my new haircut.* ♦ **give sb a shock** *It will give him a shock when he sees how much you've spent.*
2 [C] something that happens unexpectedly and makes you feel very surprised and upset: *The price of the ring was quite a shock for us.* ♦ *The announcement* ***came as a complete shock*** *to me.* ♦ *It was* ***a terrible shock*** *to discover he was already married.*
3 [U] a medical condition in which you suddenly become very weak and cold after a serious accident or injury
4 [C] a sudden flow of electricity that goes through your body
5 [singular] hair that is very thick

shock² /ʃɑk/ verb ★
1 [T] if something bad and unexpected shocks someone, they are very surprised or upset by it: *The news shocked everyone.* ♦ *We were all shocked by the lies he told.*
2 [I/T] to make someone feel embarrassed or offended by saying or doing something that is offensive or immoral: *He only says things like that to shock you.*
—**shocked** /ʃɑkt/ adj: *We were deeply shocked to hear of his sudden death.* ♦ *They listened in shocked silence.*

shock•ing /ˈʃɑkɪŋ/ adj making you feel extremely surprised, upset, or embarrassed —**shock•ing•ly** adv

ˈ**shock** ˌ**wave** noun [C] a severe effect that something has on people

shod•dy /ˈʃɑdi/ adj of a very low standard

shoe /ʃu/ noun [C] ★★★
1 something that you wear on each foot, usually over socks: *She bought several pairs of shoes.* ♦ *walking/running shoes* ♦ *shoe polish*
2 a HORSESHOE
PHRASE **in sb's shoes** in the situation that someone else is in: *What would you do if you were in my shoes?*

shoes

shoe•lace /ˈʃuˌleɪs/ noun [C] a thick string that you use for fastening a shoe tightly on your foot

shoe•string /ˈʃuˌstrɪŋ/ noun [C] *American* a SHOELACE
PHRASE **on a shoestring** using or having a very small amount of money

shone a past tense and past participle of **shine**

shoo /ʃu/ verb [T] to tell an animal or a person to go away, especially by saying "shoo" and waving your hands —**shoo** interjection

shook the past tense of **shake¹**

shoot¹ /ʃut/ (past tense and past participle **shot** /ʃɑt/) verb ★★★

1 fire gun	5 suddenly achieve sth
2 hit with bullet	6 take photographs etc.
3 in sports	+ PHRASES
4 move suddenly	+ PHRASAL VERBS

1 [I/T] to fire a gun: *We were ordered not to shoot until he gave the signal.* ♦ *They were* ***shooting at*** *bottles on a wall.* ♦ *The police officers had instructions to* ***shoot*** *the kidnapper* ***on sight*** (=as soon as they saw him).
2 [T] to hit someone or something with a bullet from a gun: *The man was* ***shot in the head*** *as he left the bar.* ♦ *Two of our officers were* ***shot dead.*** ♦ *The victim had been* ***shot at close range*** (=by someone very close to them).
3 [I/T] in a sport, to throw or kick a ball in an attempt to score points: *She shot the ball from the foul line and scored her first point.* ♦ *He hasn't been shooting very well this season.* —*picture* → C15
4 [I] to move somewhere very suddenly and quickly: *The car* ***shot across*** *the road at high speed.*

5 [I] *informal* to quickly and suddenly become successful or famous: *Clooney shot to stardom after appearing in E.R.*
6 [I/T] to take photographs, or to make a movie or video: *We're going to start shooting early tomorrow morning.* ♦ *All the outdoor scenes were shot on location in Wyoming.*
PHRASES **shoot sb a look/glance** to look at someone quickly: *She shot him an angry look.*
shoot yourself in the foot *informal* to say or do something stupid that causes you trouble
PHRASAL VERBS **ˌshoot sb/sth ˈdown 1** to refuse even to consider something such as an idea or a plan: *Each proposal was quickly shot down.* **2** to shoot someone or something and make them fall to the ground: *Rebels claim to have shot down a military plane.*
ˈshoot ˌfor sth *informal* to try to achieve a particular thing: *She's shooting for her second win at Wimbledon.*
ˌshoot ˈup 1 to increase or grow quickly: *Gasoline prices have shot up in the last six months.* **2** to appear suddenly: *There were fast-food restaurants shooting up all over town.*

shoot

shoot² /ʃut/ noun [C] **1** a very young plant, or a new part growing on a plant **2** an occasion when someone takes a series of photographs or makes a movie
shoot³ /ʃut/ interjection **1** *American* used for expressing anger or disappointment: *Shoot! I forgot to call him back.* **2** used for telling someone to say what they want to say: *"I've got a fantastic idea." "OK, shoot!"*
shoot·ing /ˈʃutɪŋ/ noun **1** [C/U] an occasion when someone is attacked by a person with a gun: *the fatal shooting of two teenagers* **2** [U] any sport or activity in which guns are used: *hunting, shooting, and fishing*
ˌshooting ˈstar noun [C] a piece of rock that makes a line of light as it falls through the sky = METEOR
ˈshoot-ˌout noun [C] a fight using guns
shop¹ /ʃɑp/ noun ★★★
1 [C] a place where you buy things or where you pay for a service = STORE: *We ate lunch at a little coffee shop.*
2 [C] a business where something is made or repaired: *an auto body shop* ♦ *a shoe repair shop* ♦ *Todd works in a machine shop.*
3 [U] *American* a school subject in which students learn to work with tools and machines
PHRASE **set up shop** to start a business or activity
shop² /ʃɑp/ verb [I] **1** to go to stores to look at and buy things: *I like to shop at the mall because there are so many stores to choose from.* **2** *American* to look for something that you want to buy: *Do you know anyone who's shopping for a good used car?*
PHRASAL VERB **ˌshop aˈround 1** to go to several stores before you decide what particular thing to buy: *I'm shopping around for a new coat.* **2** to consider several possibilities before making a choice: *Shop around carefully before investing your money.*
ˌshop ˈfloor noun [C] **1** the area in a factory where products are made **2** the workers in a factory, not the managers
shop·lift·ing /ˈʃɑpˌlɪftɪŋ/ noun [U] the crime of stealing things from a store —**shop·lift** verb [I/T], **shop·lift·er** noun [C]
shop·per /ˈʃɑpər/ noun [C] someone who goes to a store in order to look at or buy the things that are sold there
shop·ping /ˈʃɑpɪŋ/ noun [U] ★★ the activity of going to a store to buy things: *I don't like shopping very much.* ♦ *a shopping list* ♦ *Have you had a chance to **go shopping** yet?* ♦ *Where do you go to **do your shopping**?*
→ WINDOW-SHOPPING
ˈshopping ˌbag noun [C] a bag made of plastic or paper with two handles that a store gives you for carrying home your shopping — *picture* → BAG
ˈshopping ˌcart noun [C] *American* a large basket on wheels that you push. You use it in a supermarket for carrying the things you want to buy.
ˈshopping ˌcenter noun [C] an area where different types of stores and businesses are built next to each other
ˈshopping ˌmall noun [C] a MALL
shore¹ /ʃɔr/ noun [C/U] the land that is on the edge of an ocean or lake: *Three of the sailors managed to swim to the shore.* ♦ *We stayed in a hotel on the shores of Half Moon Bay.*

- The **shore** is the land that is on the edge of a lake, river, or ocean: *They managed to swim to the shore.* ♦ *a cabin on the shores of the lake*
- The **coast** is the land at the edge of a country, near the ocean: *From the deck we could see the coast of Africa.* ♦ *a holiday cottage on the south coast*
- A **beach** is an area of sand or small stones next to the ocean or by a river or lake, where people can sit and enjoy themselves: *Let's have a picnic on the beach.*

shore² PHRASAL VERB **ˌshore sth ˈup 1** to give support or help to something that is having problems or is likely to fail **2** to support something such as a wall, in order to prevent it from falling
shore·line /ˈʃɔrˌlaɪn/ noun [C] the edge of an ocean or lake
shorn a past participle of **shear**
short¹ /ʃɔrt/ adj ★★★

1 small in height etc.	5 not having enough
2 of time	6 about memory
3 with few words	7 rude and unfriendly
4 with fewer letters	+ PHRASES

1 measuring a small height, length, or distance: *She's short and thin, with light brown hair and blue eyes.* ♦ *The theater is a*

S

relatively short distance from here. ♦ *The sleeves are much too short.*
2 a short period of time does not last very long, or seems to pass quickly: *I'm sorry this has been such a short stay.* ♦ *He was here for* ***a short while*** *last week.* ♦ *It will be difficult to reach an agreement in such* ***a short space of time.***
3 expressed in few words, or containing few pages: *Could you give us a short summary of what happened?* ♦ *It was a short book and she read it in one night.*
4 using fewer words or letters than the full form of something: *Memo is* ***short for*** *memorandum.* ♦ *My name is Elizabeth, or Liz* ***for short.***
5 used for saying that you do not have enough of something: *Dad wasn't working and money was short.* ♦ *Skilled workers are* ***in short supply*** *around here.* ♦ *Many of our clients are* ***short of money.*** ♦ *He's very bright but a little* ***short on*** *personality.*
6 if you have a short memory, you are not able or willing to remember things
7 rude and unfriendly when speaking to someone
PHRASES **at/on short notice** without being given much warning before something happens: *I was asked to come on very short notice.*
in the short run/term during the period of time that is not very far into the future: *The policy served him well in the short term, but later backfired.*

short² /ʃɔrt/ adv ★★ without reaching a particular place or position: *The airplane came down just* ***short of*** *the runway.*
PHRASES **cut sth short** to end something before it is completely finished: *We cut our vacation short because Rachel got sick.*
fall short of sth to fail to meet your goal or fail to reach a particular level: *Sales of the CD fell short of expectations.*
run short (of sth) used for saying that there is not much of something left: *Supplies were running short as winter came on.* ♦ *We're running short of time.*
short of (doing) sth except for: *Short of winning the lottery, I don't know how we'll pay for this.* ♦ *Nothing short of a miracle can save us now.*

short³ /ʃɔrt/ noun [C] **1** *informal* a movie that lasts only a few minutes **2** a SHORT CIRCUIT
PHRASE **in short** used for introducing a summary of something that you have just said
→ SHORTS

short·age /ˈʃɔrtɪdʒ/ noun [C/U] ★ a lack of something that you need or want: *Refugees are facing serious* ***food*** *and* ***fuel shortages.***

ˌshort ˈcircuit noun [C] a bad electrical connection that prevents a piece of equipment from working —**ˌshort-ˈcircuit** verb [I/T]

short·com·ing /ˈʃɔrtˌkʌmɪŋ/ noun [C] a fault that makes someone or something less effective

short·cut /ˈʃɔrtˌkʌt/ noun [C] **1** a path or way of going somewhere that is quicker and shorter than the usual way **2** a quicker way than usual to do or achieve something
3 *computing* a combination of keys on a keyboard that helps you to do something more quickly

short·en /ˈʃɔrt(ə)n/ verb [I/T] to become shorter, or to make something shorter

short·en·ing /ˈʃɔrt(ə)nɪŋ/ noun [U] *American* a solid type of fat that is used especially for making PASTRY

short·fall /ˈʃɔrtˌfɔl/ noun [C] a lack of something that you need or want, or the amount that you lack

short·hand /ˈʃɔrtˌhænd/ noun [U] a quick way of writing that uses symbols to represent letters, words, or phrases

ˈshort-ˌhaul adj traveling a short distance, especially by air ≠ LONG-HAUL

ˈshort ˌlist noun [C] a list of people who have been chosen from a larger group by someone who is deciding who should get a job, prize, etc.

short-lived /ʃɔrt ˈlɪvd/ adj lasting for a short period of time

short·ly /ˈʃɔrtli/ adv **1** soon, or happening within a short period of time of something: *We're going to break for lunch very shortly.* ♦ *Police arrived at the scene shortly after midnight.* **2** if you say something shortly, you sound annoyed or rude

shorts /ʃɔrts/ noun [plural] **1** short pants that end at or above the knees —*picture* → C4
2 *American* men's underwear

ˌshort-ˈsighted adj failing to consider what will happen in the future

ˌshort ˈstory noun [C] a short piece of writing about an imaginary situation

ˌshort-ˈterm adj lasting for a short period of time ≠ LONG-TERM: *a short-term solution*

ˈshort ˌwave noun [C] a type of radio wave that is used for broadcasting across large distances → LONG WAVE, MEDIUM WAVE

shot¹ /ʃɑt/ noun [C] ★★★

1 when gun is fired	5 small alcoholic drink
2 throw/hit/kick of ball	6 of drug
3 photograph/view	+ PHRASE
4 attempt to do/get sth	

1 an act of firing a gun, or the sound of a gun being fired: *The man* ***fired two shots*** *from a handgun.* ♦ *The neighbors say they* ***heard four shots.***
2 an act of throwing, hitting, or kicking a ball: *That was another fine shot from Tiger Woods.* ♦ *They didn't manage to get a single* ***shot at*** *our goal.*
3 a photograph, or the view of something that you have because of the position of a camera: *The opening shot is of a man walking across a field.* ♦ *I got* ***a great shot*** *of the dogs playing together.*
4 *informal* a chance or attempt to do or get something: *This is her first* ***shot at*** *an international title.* ♦ *We* ***had a shot at*** *bringing the ship around into the harbor.* ♦ ***Give it your best shot*** (=try as hard as you can) – *that's all you can do.*
5 a small amount of a strong alcoholic drink
6 a medical treatment in which a small amount of a drug is put into your body with a needle
PHRASE **a shot in the arm** *informal* something

S

that quickly makes a bad situation much better

→ BIG SHOT, LONG[1]

shot² the past tense and past participle of **shoot**[1]

shot³ /ʃɑt/ adj *informal* injured, damaged, or destroyed

shot·gun /ˈʃɑtˌgʌn/ noun [C] a long gun that is used especially for hunting birds and animals

ˈshot ˌput, the noun [singular] a sports event in which you throw a heavy metal ball as far as you can

should /ʃʊd/ modal verb ★★★

- **Should** is usually followed by an infinitive without "to": *You should eat more fresh fruit.* Sometimes it is used without a following infinitive: *I don't always do everything I should.*
- **Should** has no tenses, no participles, and no infinitive form. It does not change its form, so the third person singular form does not end in "-s": *She should see a doctor about that cough.*
- Questions and negatives are formed without "do": *Should we come back later?* ♦ *You should not bring up embarrassing topics.*
- The negative form **should not** is often shortened in conversation or informal writing to **shouldn't**: *Those kids shouldn't be in there.*

1 used for saying or asking about the right or sensible thing to do or the right way to behave: *It's an amazing book – you should read it.* ♦ *You shouldn't drive so fast.* ♦ *What should I do? Should I look for another job?* ♦ *You should have taken my advice.*
2 used when you have strong reasons for believing or expecting something: *There should be a knife in the drawer.* ♦ *There'll be lots of games, so it should be fun.* ♦ *That was disappointing – we should have won that game easily.*
3 used for describing a situation that may possibly happen: *Should you need help, do not hesitate to call me.* ♦ *If anything should happen to me, please give this letter to my wife.*

S

shoul·der¹ /ˈʃoʊldər/ noun [C] ★★★
1 one of the two parts of your body between your neck and the top of your arms: *She injured her shoulder in the accident.* ♦ *The man tapped my friend on the shoulder and asked for a cigarette.* ♦ *He just smiled and* ***shrugged his shoulders*** (=moved them quickly up and down). —*picture* → C14
2 the area of ground at the side of a road, where cars can stop if they need to
PHRASE **a shoulder to cry on** someone who listens to you with sympathy when you talk about your problems: *You know where to find me if ever you need a shoulder to cry on.*

→ COLD[1], SHOULDER-LENGTH

shoul·der² /ˈʃoʊldər/ verb [T] **1** to deal with or accept something difficult **2** to push someone with your shoulder

ˈshoulder ˌblade noun [C] one of the two flat bones at the top of your back, near your shoulders

ˈshoulder-ˌlength adj shoulder-length hair reaches down to your shoulders

should·n't /ˈʃʊd(ə)nt/ short form the usual way of saying or writing "should not." This is not often used in formal writing: *We shouldn't assume that everyone will agree.*

shout¹ /ʃaʊt/ verb [I/T] ★★★
1 to say something in a loud voice: *He was one of those speakers who shout into the microphone.* ♦ *Donna* ***shouted at*** *the men furiously.* ♦ *We* ***shouted to*** *the driver to tell him to turn off the engine.*
2 to make a sudden loud noise because you are afraid or you feel pain: *A man in the next bed was shouting wildly in pain.*
PHRASAL VERBS **ˌshout sb ˈdown** to make it difficult to hear what someone says by shouting while they are speaking: *The mayor was shouted down as he tried to justify the government's decision.*
ˌshout (sth) ˈout to say something suddenly in a very loud voice: *I wanted to shout out and stop her, but she was already gone.* ♦ *An officer was shouting out orders.*

shout² /ʃaʊt/ noun [C] the sound of someone shouting, or the words that they shout: *They could hear angry shouts coming from the kitchen.*

shove /ʃʌv/ verb **1** [I/T] to push someone or something with force **2** [T] *informal* to move something, or put it somewhere, quickly and carelessly —**shove** noun [C]

shov·el /ˈʃʌv(ə)l/ noun [C] a tool that is used for digging or moving something such as snow or dirt. It consists of a long handle with a curved metal end. —**shov·el** verb [I/T]

show¹ /ʃoʊ/ (past tense **showed**; past participle **shown** /ʃoʊn/) verb ★★★

1 prove sth is true	7 about movie/program
2 let sb see sth	8 put in exhibit, etc.
3 let sb know sth	9 lead sb somewhere
4 give information	+ PHRASES
5 be/make noticeable	+ PHRASAL VERBS
6 explain sth to sb	

1 [T] to prove that something exists or is true: *The study shows an increase in the disease among the elderly.* ♦ **+what/where/why etc.** *Accidents like this show what can happen when drivers are not alert.* ♦ **+(that)** *The test results show that he could not have committed the murder.*
2 [T] to let someone see something: **show sth to sb** *This is the first time the painting has been shown to the public.* ♦ **show sb sth** *I couldn't wait to show him the letter.*
3 [T] to behave in a way that allows people to know your feelings, opinions, or personal qualities: **+what/how/why etc.** *They have shown what they think of our suggestion.* ♦ **+(that)** *The management has shown that it is not willing to compromise.*
4 [T] if a map, photograph, piece of equipment, etc. shows something, you can see or read that thing on it: *a map showing all the major tourist attractions* ♦ **+(that)** *The dial showed that the pressure had fallen to a dangerously low level.*
5 [I/T] to be easy to see or notice, or to make something easy to see or notice: *A deep sadness showed in his eyes.* ♦ *She had chosen*

*a color that really **showed the dirt**.*
6 [T] to explain something to someone by doing it once and letting them watch: **show sb sth** *Can you show me the right way to do this?* ♦ **show sb how/what/which etc.** *A young girl showed me how to operate the machine.*
7 [I/T] if someone shows a movie or television program, or if it is showing, people can see it: *It was the first time the movie was **shown on television**.*
8 [T] to put something such as a work of art, an animal, or a plant in an exhibit or competition: *Her work was first shown at a gallery in Munich.*
9 [T] to lead someone somewhere: **show sb to sth** *Let me show you to your room.*
PHRASES **have something/nothing to show for sth** to have achieved something/nothing as a result of your efforts: *They had absolutely nothing to show for weeks of hard work.*
show a profit/loss if a company, project, etc. shows a profit/loss, it makes a profit or a loss
PHRASAL VERBS **ˌshow sb aˈround** to lead someone around a place for the first time, so that they can see all parts of it
ˌshow sb ˈin to lead someone into a room where they are going to meet other people
ˌshow ˈoff *showing disapproval* to behave in a way that is intended to attract people's attention and make them admire you: *The children start showing off the minute anyone comes to visit.*
ˌshow sth ˈoff to show people something that you are very proud of so that they will admire it: *Young musicians will get the chance to show off their musical skills.*
ˌshow sb ˈout to lead someone to the door when they are leaving a place
ˌshow ˈup 1 *informal* to arrive in a place where people are expecting you **2** if something shows up, people can see it: *The writing didn't show up very well on yellow paper.*
ˌshow sb ˈup to do something that makes someone look less intelligent or impressive than you

show² /ʃoʊ/ noun ★★★

1 theater performance	4 making sth clear
2 TV/radio program	5 pretending sth
3 exhibit	+ PHRASE

1 [C] a performance in a theater: *the new show at the Winter Garden*
2 [C] a television or radio program: *It's the funniest comedy show on television.*
3 [C] an exhibit: *a fashion/flower show*
4 [singular] something that you do in order to make people realize what your opinions or intentions are: *The attack was clearly intended as **a show of force**.*
5 [singular/U] an occasion when you pretend to have particular feelings: *The friendly behavior was clearly just **for show**.* ♦ *They put on **a show of affection** in front of the reporters.*
PHRASE **get the show on the road** *spoken* to begin an activity

show biz /ˈʃoʊ ˌbɪz/ noun [U] *informal* SHOW BUSINESS

ˈshow ˌbusiness noun [U] the entertainment industry, including movies, television, radio, theater, and music

show•case /ˈʃoʊˌkeɪs/ noun [C] an event that emphasizes the good qualities of someone or something

show•down /ˈʃoʊˌdaʊn/ noun [C] a meeting, argument, or fight that finally settles a disagreement between people, or proves who is the best

show•er¹ /ˈʃaʊər/ noun [C] ★

1 washing equipment	4 group of things
2 act of washing	5 party for a woman
3 period of rain	

1 a piece of equipment that forces small drops of water into the air and is used for washing your body, or a small area with a shower in it: *The shower isn't working.* ♦ *Is Sue still **in the shower**?*
2 the activity of washing yourself by standing under a shower: *I'm going to **take a shower**.*
3 a short period when it rains: *Tonight there's a 50% chance of showers.*
4 a large number of things moving through the air or falling together: ***a shower of** sparks*
5 *American* a party arranged for a woman by her friends, in which they give her presents because she will soon get married or have a baby: *a baby/bridal/wedding shower*

show•er² /ˈʃaʊər/ verb **1** [I] to wash yourself in a shower **2** [T] to give a very large number of things to someone: *He showered her with flowers and jewelry.*

show•er•y /ˈʃaʊri/ adj with frequent short periods of rain

show•ing /ˈʃoʊɪŋ/ noun [C] **1** an occasion when something such as a movie or television program is shown **2** the amount of success that someone or something has in an event or during a particular period: *a strong showing in the last election*

show•man /ˈʃoʊmən/ (plural **show•men** /ˈʃoʊmən/) noun [C] someone such as an entertainer or politician who does things in a lively and enthusiastic way that attracts attention —**show•man•ship** /ˈʃoʊmənʃɪp/ noun [U]

shown the past participle of **show¹**

show•off /ˈʃoʊˌɔf/ noun [C] *informal showing disapproval* someone who tries to show how clever they are in order to get attention and praise from other people

show•piece /ˈʃoʊˌpis/ noun [C] the most impressive feature of something, or the most impressive example of a particular thing: *an architectural showpiece*

show•room /ˈʃoʊˌrum/ noun [C] a large room where you can look at cars or other large objects that are for sale

show•y /ˈʃoʊi/ adj **1** brightly colored and attractive **2** big and expensive in a way that seems ugly = OSTENTATIOUS

shrank a past tense of **shrink¹**

shrap•nel /ˈʃræpnəl/ noun [U] small pieces of metal that fly out of a bomb or bullet when it explodes

shred¹ /ʃred/ noun [C] **1** a long thin piece that has been cut or torn from something **2** a very small amount of something

shred² /ʃred/ verb [T] **1** to destroy a document by putting it into a shredder **2** to cut or tear something into long thin pieces

shred·der /ˈʃredər/ noun [C] a machine that destroys documents by cutting them into long thin pieces

shrewd /ʃrud/ adj **1** able to make good decisions and to judge people and situations very well **2** good at tricking people to get something you want —**shrewd·ly** adv

shriek /ʃrik/ verb [I] to shout in a loud high voice because you are frightened, excited, or surprised = SCREAM —**shriek** noun [C]

shrill /ʃrɪl/ adj a shrill noise or voice is very loud, high, and unpleasant

shrimp /ʃrɪmp/ noun [C] a small SHELLFISH with a lot of legs

shrine /ʃraɪn/ noun [C] a religious place that has been built to remember a particular holy person or event

shrink¹ /ʃrɪŋk/ (past tense **shrank** /ʃræŋk/ or **shrunk** /ʃrʌŋk/; past participle **shrunk** /ʃrʌŋk/) verb **1** [I/T] to become smaller, or to make something become smaller: *Do you think this dress will shrink if I put it in the washing machine?* **2** [I] to move back or away from someone or something because you are frightened or nervous: *He shrank away from her touch.*
PHRASAL VERB **shrink from sth** to not be willing to do something that is difficult or unpleasant

shrink² /ʃrɪŋk/ noun [C] *informal* a PSYCHIATRIST

shrink·age /ˈʃrɪŋkɪdʒ/ noun **1** [U] the process of becoming smaller in size **2** [singular/U] a reduction in something

shrink-wrapped /ˈʃrɪŋk ˌræpt/ adj wrapped very tightly in thin clear plastic

shriv·el /ˈʃrɪv(ə)l/ or **ˌshrivel ˈup** verb [I] if something such as a plant shrivels, it becomes smaller, thinner, and drier, and it does not look fresh and healthy

S

shroud¹ /ʃraʊd/ noun [C] **1** a piece of cloth that is wrapped around a dead body before it is buried **2** *literary* something that covers or hides something

shroud² /ʃraʊd/ verb [T] to cover or hide something
PHRASE **be shrouded in secrecy/mystery** to be very secret or mysterious

shrub /ʃrʌb/ noun [C] a low thick bush

shrub·ber·y /ˈʃrʌb(ə)ri/ noun [U] several shrubs growing together

shrug /ʃrʌg/ verb [I/T] to move your shoulders up and let them drop, in order to show that you do not know something or do not care —**shrug** noun [C]
PHRASAL VERB **ˌshrug sth ˈoff** to not let something worry or upset you

shrug

shrunk the past tense and past participle of **shrink¹**

shrunk·en /ˈʃrʌŋkən/ adj smaller than before, or smaller than is natural

shud·der /ˈʃʌdər/ verb [I] **1** if you shudder, your body shakes several times, for example because you suddenly feel cold or frightened **2** if something shudders, it shakes violently several times —**shud·der** noun [C]

shuf·fle /ˈʃʌf(ə)l/ verb **1** [I] to walk slowly and noisily without lifting your feet **2** [I/T] to keep moving your feet because you are nervous, embarrassed, or bored **3** [T] to change the order of papers or other things in a group **4** [I/T] to put cards into a different order before you DEAL (=give) them to players at the beginning of a game —**shuf·fle** noun [C]

shun /ʃʌn/ verb [T] to deliberately avoid a person, place, or activity

shush /ʃʊʃ/ interjection used for telling someone to be quiet

shut¹ /ʃʌt/ (past tense and past participle **shut**) verb [I/T] ★★★
1 to close something, or to become closed ≠ OPEN: ***Shut the gate or the dog will get out.*** ♦ *I heard the front door shut.*
2 *British* to close a business at the end of the working day or for a short period of time ≠ OPEN
PHRASE **shut your mouth/face/trap** *impolite* an offensive way of telling someone to stop talking
PHRASAL VERBS **ˌshut sb aˈway** to put someone in a place where they are kept apart from other people
ˌshut (sth) ˈdown 1 if a store, school, factory, or business shuts down, or if someone shuts it down, it closes permanently **2** if a machine or computer shuts down, or if someone shuts it down, it stops operating
ˌshut sb/sth ˈin to put a person or animal in a place that they cannot leave
ˌshut sth ˈin sth to crush a part of someone's body by closing a door, window, drawer, etc. on it
ˌshut (sth) ˈoff if a machine shuts off, or if someone shuts it off, it stops working
ˌshut sth ˈoff to stop the flow of something such as water or electricity
ˌshut sb ˈout to not allow someone to enter a particular place
ˌshut sth ˈout if you shut something out, you stop yourself from seeing it, hearing it, or thinking about it: *He closed the door to shut out the noise.*
ˌshut (sb) ˈup *impolite* to stop talking or making a noise, or to make someone stop talking or making a noise: *Why don't you shut up?* ♦ *Can't you shut the kids up for just five minutes?*

shut² /ʃʌt/ adj ★
1 closed: *With the door shut, the room was hot and humid.*
2 *British* not open for business

shut·down /ˈʃʌtˌdaʊn/ noun [C] an occasion when a machine or factory stops working for a short time

shut·ter /ˈʃʌtər/ noun [C] **1** a cover that can be closed over the outside of a window

—*picture* → C1 **2** the part inside a camera that quickly opens and closes to let in light

shut·tle¹ /ˈʃʌt(ə)l/ noun [C] **1** a bus, train, or airplane that makes frequent short trips between two places **2** a SPACE SHUTTLE

shut·tle² /ˈʃʌt(ə)l/ verb [I/T] to travel frequently between two places, or to take people frequently between two places

shy¹ /ʃaɪ/ adj ★

1 nervous and embarrassed in the company of other people, especially people who you do not know: *I'd love to meet her, but I'm too shy to introduce myself.* ♦ *He gave me a shy smile and looked away.*

2 nervous about doing something or being involved in something: *He's **not shy about** saying what he wants.*

—**shy·ly** adv, **shy·ness** noun [U]

shy² /ʃaɪ/ PHRASAL VERB ˌ**shy aˈway** to avoid someone, or to be unwilling to do something, because you are nervous, afraid, or not confident

sib·ling /ˈsɪblɪŋ/ noun [C] *formal* your siblings are your brothers and sisters

sic /sɪk/ adv *formal* written in PARENTHESES after a word that is not spelled or used correctly in order to show that you have written it as someone else spelled or used it

sick /sɪk/ adj ★★

1 if you are sick, you have an illness: *He stayed at home caring for his sick wife.*

2 unpleasant in a way that would upset some people: *sick humor/jokes*

3 if you get sick or you are sick, food that you have eaten suddenly comes out of your stomach through your mouth: *I'm going to be sick!* → SEASICK

4 the sick people who are ill

PHRASES **feel sick (to your stomach)** to feel that food that you have eaten is going to come out of your stomach through your mouth

make sb sick *spoken* to make someone very angry or upset: *The way he treats her makes me sick.*

sick (and tired) of sth *spoken* angry or unhappy about something that keeps happening: *I'm sick of listening to your complaints.*

sick·en /ˈsɪkən/ verb [T] to make you feel shocked and angry

sick·en·ing /ˈsɪkənɪŋ/ adj very unpleasant and shocking

ˈ**sick ˌleave** noun [U] a period of time during which you do not work because you are sick

sick·ly /ˈsɪkli/ adj **1** not healthy and often sick **2** a sickly smell or taste makes you feel sick

sick·ness /ˈsɪknəs/ noun **1** [U] a condition in which you have an illness **2** [C] a particular illness **3** [U] the feeling that you are going to bring up food from your stomach, or the act of doing this

side¹ /saɪd/ noun [C] ★★★

1 one part of area	**7** aspect of situation
2 surface of object	**8** part of family
3 edge of sth flat	**9** additional food
4 surface of sth flat	**10** of opposing groups
5 edge of body	**11** sports team
6 slope of hill	+ PHRASES

1 either of the two parts or areas that something consists of: *Motorists in Japan drive on **the left side** of the road.*

2 a surface of an object or shape, especially one that is not its front, back, bottom, or top: *The ship was found lying on its side.* ♦ *A cube has six sides.* ♦ *The entrance is on **the side of the building**.*

3 any of the edges of a flat shape: *A square has four sides.*

4 either of the flat surfaces of something that is thin such as a piece of paper or a coin: *Use the lined side of the paper.*

5 the general area of your body from your shoulder down to your waist: *I had a sharp pain in **my right side**.* ♦ *His arms hung limply **by his sides**.*

6 the part of a hill that slopes and is between the top and the bottom

7 one aspect of a situation or subject: *I still haven't heard her **side of the story**.* ♦ *Fortunately, my boss **saw the funny side** of the situation.*

8 a part of your family, either your father's set of relatives or your mother's: *Which **side of the family** is his uncle from?* ♦ *Rose is my cousin **on my mother's side**.*

9 *American spoken* an additional food that is served with the main food in a meal: *I'd like a **side of** French fries with that.*

10 one of two or more groups of people who are opposing each other: *The agreement has been signed by both sides.* ♦ *Don't get annoyed with me – I'm **on your side*** (=supporting you)! ♦ *Mary always **takes your side*** (=supports you).

11 a sports team: *Our side lost.*

PHRASES **at/by sb's side 1** beside someone: *She sat by his side.* **2** supporting someone, or remaining loyal to them: *The family will be at her side throughout the trial.*

from all sides from all directions toward one object or person: *Suddenly the crowd came at him from all sides.*

from side to side moving from left to right, then from right to left, then back again

on the side in addition to what is usual: *The band's lead singer has been making solo appearances on the side.*

on the...side slightly, but not very: *It's a nice hotel, but the rooms are on the small side* (=rather small).

put sth to one side to not talk about something, deal with it, or use it now: *Let's put the question of blame to one side for a minute.*

side by side directly next to each other: *The two girls **stood side by side**.*

→ COIN¹

side² /saɪd/ adj **1** not in or on the central part of something: *a side door* **2** less important or less relevant: *a side issue*

side³ /saɪd/ PHRASAL VERB ˈ**side with sb** to agree with and support a particular person in an argument

side·board /ˈsaɪdˌbɔrd/ noun [C] a large piece of furniture with shelves and cupboards that you use for storing dishes, glasses, etc.

ˈ**side efˌfect** noun [C] **1** an effect of a medicine that is not intended and could be unpleasant **2** an additional result that you did not expect or want

S

side•kick /ˈsaɪdˌkɪk/ noun [C] *informal* the friend or ASSISTANT of someone who is more important

side•line¹ /ˈsaɪdˌlaɪn/ noun **1** [C] either of the lines on the sides of a sports field that show where the edges of the field are **2 the sidelines** [plural] the area at the edge of a sports field **3** [C] a job that you do in addition to your main job

PHRASE **be on the sidelines** or **watch from the sidelines** to watch something that is happening without being involved or being able to influence it

side•line² /ˈsaɪdˌlaɪn/ verb [T] to prevent someone from being involved in something that they are normally involved in

side•long /ˈsaɪdˌlɔŋ/ adj a sidelong look is one in which you move your eyes to one side without moving your head much

side•show /ˈsaɪdʃoʊ/ noun [C] **1** something that is less important than something else that is happening at the same time **2** an additional small entertainment at a fair, CIRCUS, etc.

side•step /ˈsaɪdˌstep/ verb [T] to avoid something that is difficult or unpleasant

ˈside ˌstreet noun [C] a small street that is connected to a major street

side•swipe /ˈsaɪdˌswaɪp/ verb [T] *American* to hit the side of another vehicle with your vehicle as you go past it

side•track /ˈsaɪdˌtræk/ verb [T] to delay the progress of something by causing people to waste time on something else that is less important: *It's easy to get sidetracked by talking about unimportant issues like this one.*

side•view mir•ror /ˌsaɪdvju ˈmɪrər/ noun [C] a mirror on the side of a car *—picture* → C6

side•walk /ˈsaɪdˌwɔk/ noun [C] *American* ★ an area along the side of a street that has a hard surface, used by people who are walking

S

side•ways /ˈsaɪdˌweɪz/ adj, adv **1** to, toward, or from one side: *He moved sideways along the bench.* **2** with one side facing forward: *A car was sideways across the road, blocking it.*

si•dle /ˈsaɪd(ə)l/ verb [I] to move slowly in a particular direction, because you are nervous or do not want to be noticed

siege /sidʒ/ noun [C/U] **1** an attack in which an army surrounds a castle or city in order to prevent the people inside from receiving supplies **2** a situation in which a group of soldiers or police surround a building in order to force the people inside to come out

si•es•ta /siˈestə/ noun [C] a short period of sleep in the middle of the day = NAP

sieve /sɪv/ noun [C] an object that you pour a liquid or mixture through in order to remove the large pieces —**sieve** verb [T]

sift /sɪft/ verb [T] **1** to pour a dry substance through a sieve in order to remove the large pieces **2** to examine something carefully in order to find what you are looking for

PHRASAL VERB **ˈsift through sth** *same as* **sift2**

sigh¹ /saɪ/ verb **1** [I] to breathe out slowly making a long soft sound, especially because you are disappointed, tired, annoyed, or relaxed: *Jan sighed heavily and shook her head.* **2** [T] to say something with a sigh: *"I wish you had told me earlier," she sighed.*

sigh² /saɪ/ noun [C] a slow breath out that makes a long soft sound: *She let out a deep sigh.*

sight¹ /saɪt/ noun ★★★

1 ability to see	5 messy person/place
2 act of seeing sb/sth	6 places to visit
3 area you see	7 part of a gun
4 sb/sth that you see	+ PHRASES

1 [U] the ability to see using your eyes = EYESIGHT, VISION: *people with **poor sight***

2 [U] the act of seeing someone or something: *I don't know him personally, but **I know him by sight*** (=I know what he looks like). ♦ *The captain ordered us to shoot any strangers **on sight*** (=as soon as we saw them). ♦ *I can't stand **the sight of** blood.*

3 [U] any place that you can see from where you are = VIEW: *They passed behind the hill and **out of sight**.* ♦ *The rocket **disappeared from sight**.* ♦ *The ship sank **within sight of** the harbor.*

4 [C] a person or thing that you see that has a particular feature: *Windmills are a common sight in this part of the country.*

5 [singular] a person or place that is very unusual, messy, or unpleasant to look at: *The store was quite a sight after the flood.*

6 sights [plural] interesting places that people go to see: *We enjoyed **seeing the sights** of San Francisco.*

7 [C] the part of a gun or other piece of equipment that you look through in order to aim it

PHRASES **catch sight of** to suddenly see someone or something: *As she stood up she caught sight of her reflection in the mirror.*

in/within sight 1 in a place that you can see from where you are: *There was nobody in sight.* **2** going to happen soon: *Political independence seemed to be in sight.*

lose sight of 1 to not be able to see something or someone anymore **2** to forget something that is important, or to forget how important it is: *We shouldn't lose sight of the reasons why we started this campaign.*

set your sights on sth to decide that you want to get or achieve something: *The team has set its sights on the national championship.*

sight² /saɪt/ verb [T] *formal* to see someone or something suddenly or in the distance

sight•ed /ˈsaɪtəd/ adj not blind

sight•ing /ˈsaɪtɪŋ/ noun [C] an occasion when you see someone or something that you do not often see

sight•see•ing /ˈsaɪtˌsiɪŋ/ noun [U] the activity of traveling around a place in order to see the interesting things in it

sign¹ /saɪn/ noun ★★★

1 piece of evidence	4 written symbol
2 sth with information	5 star sign
3 movement/sound	

1 [C/U] a piece of evidence that something exists or is happening = INDICATION: *I couldn't see any **sign of progress**.* ♦ **+that** *He had somehow missed the signs that she was upset.*

2 [C] a flat object with words or pictures on it, put in a public place in order to provide information or to advertise something: *a flashing neon sign* ♦ *Turn right and follow the signs to the zoo.*
3 [C] a movement or sound that you make in order to tell someone something =SIGNAL: *Just give me a sign when you're ready to go.* ♦ **a sign to sb (to do sth)** *He made a sign to me to serve the coffee.*
4 [C] a written symbol that has a particular meaning, for example % meaning "percent" or $ meaning "dollar": *a multiplication/division sign*
5 [C] a STAR SIGN: *I'm a Scorpio. What's your sign?*

sign² /saɪn/ verb ★
1 [I/T] to write your name on something in order to show that you have written it, or that you agree with what is written on it: *You haven't **signed** Rory's birthday **card** yet.* ♦ *Please **sign** and date **the form**.* ♦ *A trade **agreement** was **signed** today by the U.S. and China.*
2 [T] to officially employ someone to work for a particular organization: *The team needs to sign some new players.*
3 [I/T] to communicate using SIGN LANGUAGE → DOTTED LINE

PHRASAL VERBS ˌ**sign sth aˈway** to agree that a property or a right to something does not belong to you anymore, by writing your name on a document
ˈ**sign for sth** to show that you have received something by writing your name on a document
ˌ**sign (sb) ˈin** to write your name, or someone else's name, on an official list when you or they arrive at a place ≠ SIGN (SB) OUT: *All visitors must sign in at the front desk.* ♦ *Mr. Moore signed me in and showed me to his office.*
ˌ**sign (sb) ˈout** to write your name, or someone else's name, on an official list when you or they leave a place ≠ SIGN (SB) IN: *Please sign out when you leave.* ♦ *I'll sign both of us out.*
ˌ**sign sth ˈover** to officially give your property to someone by writing your name on a document: *He's nervous about signing over the whole farm.* ♦ **sign sth over to sb** *Her dad signed the car over to her.*
ˌ**sign ˈup** to agree to do something or to join a program or organization
ˌ**sign sb ˈup** *same as* **sign²** 2: *We have signed up two new players.*

sig•nal¹ /ˈsɪgnəl/ noun [C] ★★★
1 a movement or sound that is made by someone and has a special meaning for another person: *We waited for them to **give us the signal to** move.*
2 a fact, event, or action that shows what someone intends to do, or that shows what is likely to happen =SIGN: **+that** *There were strong signals that she intended to resign.*
3 *technical* pictures, sounds, or other pieces of information that are sent by one piece of electronic equipment and received by another one: *a radio/electrical signal*
4 a piece of equipment with colored lights on it that tells the driver of a vehicle to stop, go, or slow down =TRAFFIC LIGHTS: *The signal was green.*

> **Words often used with signal**
> *Adjectives often used with **signal** (noun, sense 2)*
> ■ **clear, powerful, strong, unmistakable** + SIGNAL: used about signals that show clearly what is likely to happen

sig•nal² /ˈsɪgnəl/ (present participle **sig•nal•ing** or **sig•nal•ling**; past tense and past participle **sig•naled** or **sig•nalled**) verb **1** [I/T] to make a movement or sound that has a special meaning to another person: *The cyclist signaled and turned right.* ♦ *He signaled to his wife, who was on the other side of the room.* ♦ **+that** *He turned on his flashlight to signal that he was ready.* ♦ **signal (to) sb to do sth** *The driver signaled her to cross the road.* **2** [T] to show that something is happening or will happen: *This agreement signaled the end of the war.* **3** [T] to show what you intend to do about something: *The kidnappers have signaled their willingness to negotiate.*

sig•na•to•ry /ˈsɪgnəˌtɔri/ noun [C] a person or organization that has signed an official agreement

sig•na•ture /ˈsɪgnətʃər/ noun [C] ★ a person's name that is written in a special way by that person: *Is this your signature on the letter?* → AUTOGRAPH

sig•nif•i•cance /sɪgˈnɪfɪkəns/ noun [singular/U] ★
1 the importance that something has because it affects other things: *I do not think this case is really **of great significance**.* ♦ *the historical **significance of** these events*
2 the meaning of something, usually a special meaning or a meaning that is not obvious: *I didn't realize **the true significance** of his comment at the time.*

> **Words often used with significance**
> *Adjectives often used with **significance** (sense 1)*
> ■ **considerable, crucial, enormous, great, immense, particular, real, special** + SIGNIFICANCE: used about significance that is great

sig•nif•i•cant /sɪgˈnɪfɪkənt/ adj ★★★
1 very large or noticeable ≠ INSIGNIFICANT: *A significant proportion of the population never actually votes in elections.* ♦ *I think we can save **a significant amount** of time.*
2 very important: *one of the most significant musicians of the last century*
—**sig•nif•i•cant•ly** /sɪgˈnɪfɪkəntli/ adv

sig•ni•fy /ˈsɪgnɪˌfaɪ/ verb [T] to mean something: *What does this symbol signify?*

sign•ing /ˈsaɪnɪŋ/ noun [U] **1** the action of agreeing to a document by writing your name on it **2** the use of sign language to communicate

ˈ**sign ˌlanguage** noun [C/U] a way of communicating with people who cannot hear by making signals with your hands

sign•post¹ /ˈsaɪnˌpoʊst/ noun [C] a sign that is next to a road, that shows where something is

sign•post² /ˈsaɪnˌpoʊst/ verb [T] to mark something with signposts

S

Sikh /sik/ noun [C] a member of an Indian religious group that separated from HINDUISM in the 16th century —**Sikh** adj, **Sikh•ism** /ˈsiˌkɪzəm/ noun [U]

si•lence¹ /ˈsaɪləns/ noun ★★
1 [U] complete quiet: *The **silence was broken** by the soft sound of rain.*
2 [C/U] a period of time when no one speaks: *Long silences make her uncomfortable.* ♦ *They drove home **in silence**.*
3 [singular/U] a refusal to talk about something or provide information: *Her **silence on** the subject has been interpreted as a sign of guilt.*

si•lence² /ˈsaɪləns/ verb [T] **1** to stop someone or something from speaking or making a sound **2** to prevent someone from giving an opinion or criticizing you

si•lent /ˈsaɪlənt/ adj ★★
1 not talking or making any noise: *a crowd of silent onlookers* ♦ *Everyone **fell silent*** (=stopped talking) *as the president walked in.*
2 a silent place is very quiet: *The old house was **completely silent**.*
3 refusing to talk about something: *If you are arrested, you have the right to **remain silent*** (=do not have to give information to the police). ♦ *For now, I prefer to **stay silent** on the matter.*
4 not pronounced: *The "b" in "thumb" is silent.*
—**si•lent•ly** adv

sil•hou•ette /ˌsɪluˈet/ noun [C] the dark shape or shadow of someone or something with the light behind them

sil•hou•et•ted /ˌsɪluˈetəd/ adj seen only as a silhouette

sil•i•con /ˈsɪlɪkən/ noun [U] a chemical element, used especially for making computer CHIPS

ˌsilicon ˈchip noun [C] a small piece of silicon with a set of complicated electronic connections on it, used especially in computers

silk /sɪlk/ noun [U] a thin smooth cloth made from the fibers produced by insects called SILKWORMS: *a silk shirt*

silk•en /ˈsɪlkən/ adj *literary* very soft, smooth, and shiny

silk•y /ˈsɪlki/ adj very soft, smooth, and shiny

sill /sɪl/ noun [C] a narrow shelf at the bottom of a window = LEDGE

sil•ly /ˈsɪli/ adj ★
1 not intelligent or sensible: *a silly mistake* ♦ *You've **been very silly**.*
2 not important: *Don't get upset over silly things that people say.*
3 inappropriate and annoying because it makes you seem stupid or like a child: *a silly hat*

si•lo /ˈsaɪloʊ/ noun [C] **1** a tall round tower on a farm, used for storing things such as grain **2** a large underground structure, used for storing or protecting something

silt /sɪlt/ noun [U] sand, dirt, and very small rocks that are carried from one place to another by moving water

sil•ver¹ /ˈsɪlvər/ noun ★
1 [U] a light gray metal that is used for making jewelry, coins, etc.
2 [U] attractive objects made from silver that people collect: *They had some beautiful silver.*
3 [C/U] a SILVER MEDAL

sil•ver² /ˈsɪlvər/ adj **1** made of silver **2** light gray in color

ˌsilver anniˈversary noun [C] 25 years after a particular event, especially a wedding

ˌsilver ˈmedal noun [C] a round flat silver object that is given as a prize for being second in a competition

sil•ver•ware /ˈsɪlvərˌwer/ noun [U] **1** *American* forks, knives, and spoons for eating or serving food = CUTLERY **2** objects made from silver, especially objects used at meals

sil•ver•y /ˈsɪlvəri/ adj like silver in color or appearance

SIM card /ˈsɪm ˌkɑrd/ noun [C] a small piece of plastic that is inside a cellphone, that contains information about the person who uses the phone

sim•i•lar /ˈsɪmɪlər/ adj ★★★ things that are similar are like each other but are not exactly the same ≠ DIFFERENT: *We have similar interests.* ♦ *A second study produced remarkably similar results.* ♦ *Their situation is very **similar to** ours.* ♦ *The two men are **similar in** appearance.*

sim•i•lar•i•ty /ˌsɪmɪˈlerəti/ noun **1** [C/U] the degree to which one thing is similar to another thing, or the fact that they are similar: *I found some similarities between the two stories.* ♦ *a striking similarity of style* ♦ *His signature bears absolutely no similarity to mine.* **2** [C] something that makes one thing seem like another: *There are many similarities between Ron and his father.*

sim•i•lar•ly /ˈsɪmɪlərli/ adv ★
1 in a similar way: *similarly priced cars*
2 used for showing that two ideas are related or connected: *High inflation usually leads to high interest rates. Similarly, interest rates decline when inflation is low.*

sim•i•le /ˈsɪmɪli/ noun [C] a phrase that describes something by comparing it to something else using the word "like" or "as," for example "His hands were as cold as ice"

sim•mer /ˈsɪmər/ verb [I/T] to cook slowly at a temperature that is near boiling, or to cook something in this way

sim•ple /ˈsɪmp(ə)l/ adj ★★★
1 easy to understand or do: *Students were given **a simple** skills **test**.* ♦ **simple to do** *The machine is fairly simple to operate.*
2 plain, without any complicated features or decoration: *a simple meal* ♦ *simple tools*
3 used for emphasizing one important fact: ***The simple truth** is that I was scared.*
4 *linguistics* a simple sentence has only one subject and one verb

sim•plic•i•ty /sɪmˈplɪsəti/ noun [U] the quality of being simple

sim•pli•fy /ˈsɪmplɪˌfaɪ/ verb [T] to make something less complicated or difficult —**sim•pli•fi•ca•tion** /ˌsɪmplɪfɪˈkeɪʃ(ə)n/ noun [C/U]

sim•plis•tic /sɪmˈplɪstɪk/ adj *showing disapproval* treating a complicated problem or situation in a way that makes it seem much simpler than it really is

sim•ply /ˈsɪmpli/ adv ★★★
1 in a way that is not complicated or confusing: *I've stated my intention as simply as possible.*
2 used for emphasizing one important fact: *He lost simply because he wasn't good enough.*
3 in a very ordinary or plain way: *We live very **simply** and don't spend a lot of money.*

sim•u•late /ˈsɪmjəˌleɪt/ verb [T] to produce the features of something in a way that seems real but is not —**sim•u•lat•ed** adj: *simulated leather/pearls*

sim•u•la•tion /ˌsɪmjəˈleɪʃ(ə)n/ noun [C/U] something that produces the features of something in a way that seems real but is not

sim•u•la•tor /ˈsɪmjəˌleɪtər/ noun [C] a piece of equipment that is used for training people to operate an aircraft or other vehicle, by SIMULATING different situations

si•mul•ta•ne•ous /ˌsaɪm(ə)lˈteɪniəs/ adj happening or done at the same time —**si•mul•ta•ne•ous•ly** adv

sin¹ /sɪn/ noun [C/U] an action, thought, or way of behaving that is wrong according to religious laws: *the sin of pride/greed*

sin² /sɪn/ verb [I] to do something that is wrong according to religious laws

since /sɪns/ grammar word ★★★

> Since can be:
> - a **preposition**: *Everything has changed so much since last spring.*
> - an **adverb**: *She left home in 1993 and hasn't been seen since.*
> - a **conjunction**: *Paul's had several different jobs since he left school.*

1 from a particular point in the past until now, or until another point in the past: *I've known Joanna since she was born.* ♦ *Turkey has been a republic since 1923.* ♦ *I hadn't seen her since she went to live in Hawaii.* ♦ *Since arriving in New York, Thomas has had 15 job interviews.* ♦ *Paul started sailing in 1986 and he's been doing it **ever since**.*
2 used when giving a reason: *Since Barbara is no longer my wife, I'm not responsible for her debts.*
PHRASE **since when?** *spoken* used for showing that you are surprised or annoyed by something: *Since when has it been against the rules to have a coffee break?*

> Both **since** and **for** are used for saying how long something has been happening.
> - Use **since** to introduce a particular time or event when something started: *I've been working here since 1980.*
> - Use **for** to introduce the period of time during which something has continued: *They've been married for over 40 years.*

sin•cere /sɪnˈsɪr/ adj showing that you really mean what you say ≠ INSINCERE: *His apology seemed sincere.*

sin•cere•ly /sɪnˈsɪrli/ adv really, or honestly: *I sincerely hope you will succeed.*
PHRASE **Sincerely yours** or **Yours sincerely** used before your name as a way of ending a formal letter

sin•cer•i•ty /sɪnˈserəti/ noun [U] an honest way of behaving that shows that you really mean what you say or do

sin•ful /ˈsɪnfəl/ adj morally wrong according to religious laws

sing /sɪŋ/ (past tense **sang** /sæŋ/; past participle **sung** /sʌŋ/) verb ★★★
1 [I/T] to make music using your voice: *Grace was singing softly to herself.* ♦ *They **sang** several old familiar **songs**.*
2 [I] if a bird sings, it makes musical sounds
PHRASE **sing sb's/sth's praises** to talk about how good someone or something is
PHRASAL VERB ˌ**sing aˈlong** to sing a song with someone who is already singing

sing. abbrev singular

singe /sɪndʒ/ (present participle **singe•ing**; past tense and past participle **singed**) verb [I/T] to burn something slightly, so that only the edge or surface is affected

sing•er /ˈsɪŋər/ noun [C] someone who sings, especially someone who sings well or as their job

sin•gle¹ /ˈsɪŋg(ə)l/ adj ★★★
1 only one: *a single sheet of paper*
2 not married, or not in a romantic relationship: *Please state whether you are single, married, or divorced.*
3 designed for one person or used by one person: *The room has two **single beds**.*
4 used for emphasizing one thing: *Drugs are the single biggest cause of crime here.* ♦ *Do we have to count **every single** penny we spend?*
PHRASE **not a single** not even one: *You didn't write a single letter the whole time you were away.*

sin•gle² /ˈsɪŋg(ə)l/ noun

1 short musical record	4 one-dollar bill
2 in tennis	5 people not married
3 room/bed	6 one ticket at theater

1 [C] a musical record with only one song or piece of music on each side **2 singles** [plural] in tennis, a match that is played between two people **3** [C] a room or bed for one person **4** [C] *American* a one-dollar bill **5 singles** [plural] people who are not married, or who are not in a romantic relationship **6** [C] one ticket or seat at a theater

sin•gle³ /ˈsɪŋg(ə)l/ PHRASAL VERB ˌ**single sb/sth ˈout** to choose one person or thing from a group for special attention: *In her article, three schools were singled out for particular criticism.*

sin•gle-hand•ed /ˌsɪŋg(ə)l ˈhændəd/ adj, adv done by one person without help from anyone else —**sin•gle-hand•ed•ly** adv

ˌ**single-ˈminded** adj with your attention fixed on only one thing = FOCUSED

ˌ**single ˈparent** noun [C] a parent who raises their children alone, without a partner

ˌ**single-parent ˈfamily** noun [C] a family in which only one parent lives in the home and takes care of the children

sin•gly /ˈsɪŋgli/ adv separately: *You can buy stamps singly or in books of ten.*

sin•gu•lar /ˈsɪŋgjələr/ adj **1** *linguistics* the singular form of a word is used for referring to one person or thing **2** *formal* strange, or unusual

S

sin·gu·lar, the /ˈsɪŋgjələr/ noun [singular] *linguistics* the form of a word that is used for referring to one person or thing

sin·gu·lar·ly /ˈsɪŋgjələrli/ adv in a noticeable way

sin·is·ter /ˈsɪnɪstər/ adj threatening to do something harmful or evil: *a sinister remark*

sink[1] /sɪŋk/ (past tense **sank** /sæŋk/; past participle **sunk** /sʌŋk/) verb ★★

1 go under water	6 invest money
2 go below surface of sth	7 push sth sharp into sth
3 move to lower level	+ PHRASE
4 fall/sit/lie down	+ PHRASAL VERB
5 go down in amount	

1 [I/T] to disappear below the surface of water, or to make something do this: *The ferry sank during a storm.* ♦ *The **ship** was **sunk** by an enemy submarine.*
2 [I] to go below the surface of a soft substance: *Our feet **sank into** the mud as we walked.*
3 [I] to move to a lower level: *The water level in the lake had sunk by several feet.* ♦ *We watched the sun sinking below the horizon.*
4 [I] to fall, sit, or lie down: *All I wanted to do was to **sink into** an armchair and rest.*
5 [I] to go down in value or amount: *Agricultural production had **sunk to** its lowest level in years.*
6 [T] to invest money in something: *We've sunk several thousand dollars into the project so far.*
7 [T] to push something that is sharp into something that is solid: *The cat sank its claws into my leg.*

PHRASE **your spirits/heart sinks** if your spirits sink or your heart sinks, you become sad or lose hope

PHRASAL VERB ˌ**sink ˈin** to become completely understood: *She had to repeat her words several times before they finally sank in.*

sink

sink[2] /sɪŋk/ noun [C] a large open container for water that is attached to a wall and connected to pipes that bring the water and carry it away —*picture* → C2

ˈ**sinking ˌfeeling** noun [singular] a feeling that you get when you realize that something bad has happened or is going to happen

sin·ner /ˈsɪnər/ noun [C] someone who does not obey religious laws

si·nus /ˈsaɪnəs/ noun [C] one of several empty spaces that are in the bones of your face in the area behind your nose

sip[1] /sɪp/ verb [I/T] to drink in small amounts: *She sipped her lemonade.*

sip[2] /sɪp/ noun [C] a small amount of liquid that is taken into your mouth: *He took a sip of coffee.*

si·phon /ˈsaɪf(ə)n/ or ˈ**siphon sth ˌoff** verb [T] **1** to move liquid from one container to another through a tube **2** to move money from one bank account to another illegally or dishonestly

sir /*weak* sər, *strong* sɜr/ **1** *spoken* used as a polite way of speaking to a man **2 Sir** used before the name of a man who is a KNIGHT

PHRASE **Dear Sir** used for beginning a letter to a man whose name you do not know

si·ren /ˈsaɪrən/ noun [C] a piece of equipment that makes a loud sound, used for warning people

sis·ter /ˈsɪstər/ noun [C] ★★★
1 a girl or woman who has the same parents as you: *He has two brothers and two sisters.* → HALF SISTER, STEPSISTER —*picture* → FAMILY TREE
2 a NUN (=a woman who is a member of a religious community): *Sister Mary*
3 used by women for referring to a woman who they feel loyalty and friendship toward: *support for our sisters who are the victims of war*
4 a black woman. This word is mainly used by black people.

PHRASE **sister organization/company etc.** an organization that has close connections with another similar organization

ˈ**sister ˌcity** noun [C] *American* a city that has established a formal connection with another city in a different country in order to encourage visits and exchange information

ˈ**sister-in-ˌlaw** (plural ˈ**sisters-in-ˌlaw**) noun [C] **1** the sister of your husband or wife —*picture* → FAMILY TREE **2** the wife of your brother

sis·ter·ly /ˈsɪstərli/ adj appropriate for a sister, or typical of a sister

sit /sɪt/ (past tense and past participle **sat** /sæt/) verb ★★★

1 rest on seat	6 take care of children
2 lower body into seat	7 be member of sth
3 make someone sit	8 be model
4 be in situation, etc.	9 meet officially
5 be in particular place	+ PHRASAL VERBS

1 [I] to be in a position in which the lower part of your body rests on a seat or the ground, while the upper part of your body is upright: ***Sit still** (=without moving) while I brush your hair.* ♦ *I usually **sit next to** Andrew in history class.* ♦ *They were **sitting in** a café drinking coffee.* ♦ *I was **sitting at** my computer when the phone rang.* ♦ *Matt **sat on** a park bench, eating his lunch.* ♦ *Six of us were **sitting around** the table talking.* —*picture* → POSTURE
2 [I] to lower your body into a sitting position: *He came over and sat on the sofa.*
3 [T] to put someone into a sitting position: *Joanna sat the child on her lap and read him a story.*
4 [I] to be in a particular situation or condition for a period of time: *I was sitting in traffic for over an hour.*
5 [I] to be in a particular place: *The house sits on top of a hill.*

6 [I] *informal* to BABYSIT: ***I'm sitting for the Richardsons tomorrow night.***
7 [I] to be a member of a committee or other official group: *She **sits on** the boards of several large companies.*
8 [I] to be a model for a painter or a PHOTOGRAPHER
9 [I] if a legislature, a court of law, or a committee sits, it has an official meeting
PHRASAL VERBS ˌ**sit aˈround** to spend time doing nothing
ˌ**sit ˈback** to relax and stop making the effort to do something: *We can't just sit back and let them win.*
ˌ**sit ˈby** to take no action while something bad is happening: *Are we just going to sit by and let this happen?*
ˌ**sit ˈdown** *same as* **sit** 2: *Please, sit down and make yourselves comfortable.*
ˌ**sit ˈin on sth** to go to a meeting or a class although you are not directly involved in it: *Do you mind if I sit in on your class this afternoon?*
ˈ**sit through sth** to stay until the end of something, especially if you are not enjoying it: *If I have to sit through one more boring meeting, I think I'll scream.*
ˌ**sit ˈup 1** to sit with your back straight and upright: ***Sit up straight** and pay attention.*
2 to go from a lying position to a sitting position: *Would you like to sit up and read for a while?*
ˌ**sit sb ˈup** to help someone to go from a lying position to a sitting position: *We sat her up in a chair.*

sit•com /ˈsɪtˌkɑm/ noun [C] a humorous television or radio series about a group of characters

site /saɪt/ noun [C] ★★★
1 an area of land where something is being built or could be built: *a construction site*
2 a place where something interesting or important happened: *We visited **the site of** the Battle of Bosworth.*
3 a place used for a particular purpose: *a landing site for helicopters*
4 a WEBSITE

sit•ter /ˈsɪtər/ noun [C] **1** *informal* a BABYSITTER **2** someone who is painted or photographed by an artist

sit•ting /ˈsɪtɪŋ/ noun [C] a period of time when someone is being painted or photographed by an artist
PHRASE **in/at one sitting** during a single period of time while you are sitting: *He read the whole book in one sitting.*

sit•u•at•ed /ˈsɪtʃuˌeɪtɪd/ adj in a particular place

sit•u•a•tion /ˌsɪtʃuˈeɪʃ(ə)n/ noun [C] ★★★ the set of conditions that exist at a particular time in a particular place: *The country is facing a very difficult economic situation.* ♦ *I found myself in **an embarrassing situation**.* ♦ **sb's situation** (=the conditions that affect their life at a particular time) *What prospects are there for a person in his situation?*

six /sɪks/ number the number 6

six•teen /ˌsɪksˈtin/ number the number 16

six•teenth /ˌsɪksˈtinθ/ number **1** in the place or position counted as number 16 **2** one of 16 equal parts of something

sixth /sɪksθ/ number **1** in the place or position counted as number 6 **2** one of 6 equal parts of something

six•ties /ˈsɪkstiz/ noun [plural] **1** the years from 1960 to 1969: *music from the sixties* **2** the numbers 60 to 69, especially as a temperature **3** the period of time from age 60 to age 69: *a woman in her sixties*

six•ti•eth /ˈsɪkstiəθ/ number **1** in the place or position counted as number 60 **2** one of 60 equal parts of something

six•ty /ˈsɪksti/ number the number 60

siz•a•ble /ˈsaɪzəb(ə)l/ adj fairly large =SUBSTANTIAL

size¹ /saɪz/ noun ★★★
1 [C/U] a measurement of how large or small something is: *balloons of **all shapes and sizes*** ♦ *The president has promised to **reduce the size of** the army.*
2 [C] one of a series of standard measurements according to which goods are made or sold: *What size shoe do you wear?* ♦ *He wears a size 12.*
3 [U] the fact that something is very large: ***The size of** the organization makes communication difficult.*

size² /saɪz/ PHRASAL VERB ˌ**size sb/sth ˈup** to think carefully and form an opinion about a person or a situation

size•a•ble /ˈsaɪzəb(ə)l/ another spelling of **sizable**

siz•zle /ˈsɪz(ə)l/ verb [I] to make the sound of food that is cooking in hot oil —**siz•zle** noun [singular]

siz•zling /ˈsɪzlɪŋ/ adj *informal* very hot

skate¹ /skeɪt/ noun [C] **1** a type of shoe with a thin metal blade on the bottom, used for moving quickly on ice=ICE SKATE **2** a type of shoe with four thick wheels on the bottom, used for moving quickly on a smooth surface=ROLLER SKATES

skate² /skeɪt/ verb [I] to move over a surface using skates → THIN —**skat•er** noun [C], **skat•ing** noun [U]

skate•board /ˈskeɪtˌbɔrd/ noun [C] a board with four wheels on the bottom that you stand on and ride —**skate•board•er** noun [C], **skate•board•ing** noun [U]

ˈ**skating** ˌ**rink** noun [C] a place with an area of ice or a smooth floor, used for skating

skel•e•tal /ˈskelɪt(ə)l, skəˈlit(ə)l/ adj **1** relating to a skeleton **2** extremely thin

skel•e•ton /ˈskelɪt(ə)n/ noun [C] the set of bones that supports a human or animal body, or a model of this

ˈ**skeleton** ˌ**crew** noun [C] just enough workers to keep a service or office operating

skep•tic /ˈskeptɪk/ noun [C] someone who has doubts about things that other people think are true or right

skep•ti•cal /ˈskeptɪk(ə)l/ adj having doubts about something that other people think is true or right=DOUBTFUL

skep•ti•cism /ˈskeptɪˌsɪzəm/ noun [U] doubts that someone has about something that other people think is true or right

sketch¹ /sketʃ/ noun [C] **1** a drawing that is made quickly that does not have many details **2** a short funny scene performed within a longer show

sketch² /sketʃ/ verb **1** [I/T] to draw a picture quickly and with few details —*picture* → DRAW **2** [T] to make a general plan of something, with only a few details
PHRASAL VERB ˌ**sketch sth ˈout** *same as* sketch² 2: *I've just sketched out a rough proposal.*

sketch·y /ˈsketʃi/ adj not detailed or complete =VAGUE: *a rather sketchy account*

skewed /skjud/ adj **1** results or judgments that are skewed are not accurate because they have been affected by something **2** not straight

skew·er /ˈskjuər/ noun [C] a long thin piece of metal or wood that you stick through food to hold it while it cooks

ski¹ /ski/ noun [C] a long thin object that you attach to your boot so that you can slide easily over snow

ski² /ski/ verb [I] to slide over snow on skis

skid /skɪd/ verb [I] to slide across the ground in an uncontrolled way —**skid** noun [C]

ski·er /ˈskiər/ noun [C] someone who moves over snow on SKIS

ski·ing /ˈskiɪŋ/ noun [U] the sport or activity of moving over snow on SKIS

skil·ful /ˈskɪlfəl/ the British spelling of **skillful**

skill /skɪl/ noun [C/U] ★★★ the ability to do something well, usually as a result of experience and training: *I admired the skill and dedication of the nursing staff.* ♦ *computer skills*

skilled /skɪld/ adj **1** skillful ≠ UNSKILLED: *a skilled craftsman* **2** a skilled job needs someone who has ability and experience

skil·let /ˈskɪlɪt/ noun [C] a FRYING PAN

skill·ful /ˈskɪlfəl/ adj showing a lot of skill =TALENTED: *a skillful negotiator* ♦ *her skillful use of color* —**skill·ful·ly** adv

skim /skɪm/ verb **1** [I/T] to read something quickly and not very carefully **2** [T] to remove a substance that is floating on the surface of a liquid: *Skim the fat off the soup.* **3** [I/T] to move quickly over the surface of something: *Water skiers skimmed across the lake.* **4** [T] *American* if someone skims money, they take small amounts from somewhere so that people do not notice that it is gone

ˌskim ˈmilk noun [U] milk that has the cream removed from it

skimp·y /ˈskɪmpi/ adj skimpy clothes fit very tightly and do not cover much of someone's body

skin¹ /skɪn/ noun [C/U] ★★★
1 the outer layer of a person's or animal's body: *She has beautiful soft skin.* ♦ *fair/dark skin* ♦ *a skin disease*
2 the outer layer that is cut from an animal's body, used for making clothing and decorations =HIDE
3 the outer layer of a fruit or vegetable =PEEL: *banana skins*
PHRASE **get under sb's skin 1** to make someone very annoyed or upset **2** to make someone feel very attracted to you

skin² /skɪn/ verb [T] to remove the skin from an animal, fruit, or vegetable

skin·head /ˈskɪnˌhed/ noun [C] a young man whose hair has been cut extremely short, especially one who is part of a violent right-wing group

skin·ny /ˈskɪni/ adj *informal* very thin

skip¹ /skɪp/ verb **1** [I] to move forward by jumping first on one foot and then the other: *Julie skipped down the sidewalk.* **2** [I] to jump over a rope that you or two other people swing above your head and then under your feet **3** [T] to not do or have something: *Let's skip that chapter and move on to the next one.* ♦ *It's not a good idea to skip breakfast.* **4** [I] to move quickly from one place or thing to another: *They kept skipping from one topic to another.*

skip

skip² /skɪp/ noun [C] the action of skipping

skip·per /ˈskɪpər/ noun [C] *informal* someone who is in charge of a small ship =CAPTAIN

skir·mish /ˈskɜrmɪʃ/ noun [C] a fight involving a small number of soldiers

skirt¹ /skɜrt/ noun [C] ★★ a piece of clothing for a woman or girl. It hangs from the waist and is not joined between the legs: *She was wearing a long skirt.*

skirt² /skɜrt/ verb **1** [T] to go around the edge of a place or thing: *They skirted the field to avoid the mud.* **2** [I/T] to avoid talking about something that is unpleasant: *He just skirted around the subject.*

ˈski ˌslope noun [C] a part of a hill or mountain that you SKI on

skulk /skʌlk/ verb [I] to move around or wait somewhere in a secret way

skull /skʌl/ noun [C] the bones of the head

skunk /skʌŋk/ noun [C] a small black-and-white North American animal with a long thick tail. It produces a bad smell when it is threatened.

sky /skaɪ/ noun ★★★
1 [C/U] the space above the Earth that you see when you look up into the air: *a clear blue sky* ♦ *Black smoke rose into the sky.* ♦ ***The night sky was filled with stars.***
2 skies [plural] a way of referring to the sky, used especially when talking about the weather: *Tomorrow we expect **clear skies** and sunshine.*
PHRASE **the sky's the limit** used for saying that there is no limit to what someone can do

> **Words often used with sky**
> *Adjectives often used with sky (sense 2)*
> - **cloudy, dark, dull, gloomy, gray, overcast** + SKIES: used about a sky that is not bright or sunny
> - **blue, clear, cloudless, sunny** + SKIES: used about a sky that has no clouds

sky·div·ing /ˈskaɪˌdaɪvɪŋ/ noun [U] the sport of jumping out of an airplane and falling for as long as possible before opening your PARACHUTE —**sky·div·er** noun [C]

sky•light /ˈskaɪˌlaɪt/ noun [C] a window in a roof or ceiling —*picture* → C1

sky•line /ˈskaɪˌlaɪn/ noun [C] the shapes made by buildings or mountains when you see them against the sky

sky•rock•et /ˈskaɪˌrɑkət/ verb [I] if an amount, value, or cost skyrockets, it rises quickly to a very high level

sky•scrap•er /ˈskaɪˌskreɪpər/ noun [C] a very tall building containing offices or apartments

slab /slæb/ noun [C] a large flat piece of something, especially something hard: *a concrete slab* ♦ *a slab of chocolate*

slack[1] /slæk/ adj **1** loose and not pulled tight: *The rope suddenly went slack.* **2** not taking enough care to make sure that something is done well: *slack safety standards* **3** not as busy or successful as usual in business

slack[2] /slæk/ noun [U] **1** the fact that a rope is loose, rather than being pulled tight **2** a period of less activity than usual **3** people, equipment, or money that could be used more effectively in an organization

slack[3] /slæk/ verb [I] to try to avoid working
PHRASAL VERB **ˌslack ˈoff** to slow down or become less

slack•en /ˈslækən/ verb [I/T] **1** to become slower or less active, or to make something become slower or less active **2** to become looser, or to make something looser

slacks /slæks/ noun [plural] *old-fashioned* PANTS that are worn for informal occasions

slain the past participle of **slay**

sla•lom /ˈslɑləm/ noun [C/U] a race, especially on SKIS, in which people move around a series of poles

slam[1] /slæm/ verb **1** [I/T] if a door or lid slams, or if you slam it, it shuts with great force so that it makes a loud noise: *He ran from the room, slamming the door behind him.* ♦ *The heavy gate slammed shut.* **2** [T] to put, move, or hit something somewhere with great force: *He slammed the groceries down on the table.* ♦ *She slammed the brakes on.* **3** [I] to hit against something with great force: *The bicycle slammed into a tree.* **4** [T] *mainly journalism* to criticize someone or something severely: *The movie has been slammed by critics.*

slam[2] /slæm/ noun [C] **1** an instance of something slamming down or slamming shut, or the noise made by this **2** a severe criticism **3** a GRAND SLAM

slan•der /ˈslændər/ noun [C/U] *legal* the crime of saying something about someone that is not true and that is likely to damage their reputation —**slan•der** verb [T]

slang /slæŋ/ noun [U] words or expressions that are very informal and that are not considered appropriate for formal situations

slant[1] /slænt/ verb **1** [I] to be or move at an angle that is not 90 degrees: *Sunlight slanted through the curtains.* **2** [T] to give information or ideas in a way that gives more attention or support to a particular person, group, or opinion: *He was accused of slanting his reports to protect his colleagues.*

slant[2] /slænt/ noun [singular] **1** the angle at which something slopes **2** a particular way of showing or considering information: *Her recipes give us a new slant on Italian cooking.*

slant•ed /ˈslæntəd/ adj **1** at an angle that is not 90 degrees: *a room with a slanted ceiling* **2** done in a way that gives more attention or support to a particular person, group, or opinion: *The book is heavily slanted toward American business methods.*

slap[1] /slæp/ verb **1** [T] to hit someone or something quickly with the palm of the hand **2** [T] to put something down quickly and noisily: *Annie slapped down her cards.* **3** [I] to hit a surface with a sound that is like someone slapping something: *The waves slapped against the stone pier.* **4** [T] to put something on a surface quickly and without much attention: *Just slap some paint on the wall and it will look fine.*

slap[2] /slæp/ noun [C] a sharp hit with the palm of the hand
PHRASE **a slap in the face** an action or criticism that is unkind and that makes you feel sad or disappointed

slap•stick /ˈslæpˌstɪk/ noun [U] humor that is based on physical actions such as people hitting each other or falling down

slash[1] /slæʃ/ verb **1** [T] to cut something in a violent way: *The tires on the car had been slashed.* **2** [T] *mainly journalism* to reduce something by a large amount: *The budget had been slashed by $3 million.* **3** [I/T] to try to cut or hit something by making several swinging movements: *She slashed wildly at the ball.*

slash[2] /slæʃ/ noun [C] **1** a quick swinging movement, especially with something sharp **2** a long deep cut **3** a line (/) that separates numbers, letters, or words in writing

slat /slæt/ noun [C] a thin flat piece of wood, metal, etc., used especially for making furniture or window BLINDS

slate[1] /sleɪt/ noun **1** [U] a type of dark gray stone that breaks easily into flat thin pieces **2** [C] a single flat piece of slate that is that is used with others for covering a roof **3** [C] *American* a list of people who are trying to win an election → CLEAN[1]

slate[2] /sleɪt/ verb [T] to arrange for something to happen: *The meeting is slated for next Tuesday.*
PHRASE **slated to do sth** expected to happen

slaugh•ter[1] /ˈslɔtər/ noun [U] **1** the violent killing of a large number of people **2** the killing of animals, usually for their meat

slaugh•ter[2] /ˈslɔtər/ verb [T] **1** to kill a large number of people in a violent way **2** to kill animals, usually for their meat **3** *informal* to defeat an opponent completely

slaugh•ter•house /ˈslɔtərˌhaʊs/ noun [C] a building where animals are killed for their meat

slave[1] /sleɪv/ noun [C] someone who belongs by law to another person and who has to obey them and work for them

slave[2] /sleɪv/ or **ˌslave aˈway** verb [I] to work very hard

slav•er•y /ˈsleɪv(ə)ri/ noun [U] **1** the system of

S

owning people as slaves **2** the condition of being a slave

slaw /slɔ/ noun [U] *American* COLESLAW

slay /sleɪ/ (past tense **slew** /slu/; past participle **slain** /sleɪn/) verb [T] *mainly journalism* to kill someone in a violent way

sleaze /sliz/ noun [U] behavior that is dishonest or immoral, especially in politics or business

slea•zy /ˈslizi/ adj **1** dishonest or immoral **2** a sleazy place is dirty and unpleasant

sled¹ /sled/ noun [C] *American* a vehicle that rests on long pieces of metal and that you sit on to travel over snow

sled² /sled/ verb [I] *American* to ride on a sled

sledge•ham•mer /ˈsledʒˌhæmər/ noun [C] a long heavy hammer that you swing with both hands

sleek /slik/ adj **1** sleek fur or hair is smooth and shiny **2** with a modern attractive smooth design: *a sleek red sports car*

sleep¹ /slip/ (past tense and past participle **slept** /slept/) verb ★★★

1 [I] to go into a natural state in which your body rests and you are unconscious, especially for several hours at night: *The baby usually sleeps in the afternoon.* ♦ *"Did you **sleep well**?" "Yes, thanks."* ♦ *We both **slept badly** and felt terrible the next day.*

2 [T] to have enough room or beds for a particular number of people to sleep in: *Our house at the beach sleeps six comfortably.*

PHRASAL VERBS **ˌsleep aˈround** *informal* to have sexual relations with a lot of different people

ˌsleep ˈin to continue sleeping after the time that you usually wake up: *The whole family sleeps in on Sundays.*

ˌsleep sth ˈoff to get rid of an unpleasant feeling by sleeping

ˈsleep on sth to wait to make a decision until the next day, after you have rested and had more time to think: *Let me sleep on it and give you an answer tomorrow.*

ˈsleep through sth to continue sleeping although there is a lot of noise around you: *He slept through the whole storm.*

ˈsleep toˌgether if two people sleep together, they have sex, especially when they are not married

ˈsleep with sb to have sex with someone, especially someone who you are not married to

sleep² /slip/ noun ★★

1 [U] a natural state in which your body rests and you are unconscious: *I can't get to sleep if there's any noise.* ♦ *You need to go home and **get some sleep**.* ♦ *The motion of the car **put me to sleep**.* ♦ *You were talking **in your sleep*** (=while you were sleeping) *last night.*

2 [singular] a period of time when you are sleeping: *I haven't had **a good night's sleep** for over a week.* ♦ *She lay down and soon **fell into a deep sleep**.*

PHRASES **can do sth in your sleep** to be able to do something so easily that you do not need to think about it

go to sleep 1 to begin sleeping: *What time do the kids usually go to sleep?* **2** *informal* if a part of your body goes to sleep, you cannot feel it for a short time because it has not been getting enough blood

put sth to sleep to give an animal drugs so that it dies quickly without feeling any pain

sleep•er /ˈslipər/ noun [C] **1** someone who is sleeping: *a light/heavy sleeper* (=someone who wakes/does not wake easily) **2** a train with beds for passengers to sleep in **3** *American* a movie or book that becomes very popular although it was not expected to

ˈsleeping ˌbag noun [C] a warm bag that you sleep in, especially when camping

ˈsleeping ˌpill noun [C] a pill that you take in order to help you to sleep

sleep•less /ˈslipləs/ adj without sleep, or unable to sleep: *a sleepless night*

sleep•o•ver /ˈslipˌoʊvər/ noun [C] a children's party at which the guests stay the night

sleep•walk•ing /ˈslipwɔkɪŋ/ noun [U] the action of walking and sometimes doing things while you are still sleeping

sleep•y /ˈslipi/ adj **1** feeling tired and wanting to sleep **2** a sleepy place is very quiet and does not have much activity —**sleep•i•ly** adv

sleet /slit/ noun [U] a mixture of snow and rain —**sleet** verb [I]

sleeve /sliv/ noun [C] **1** the part of a piece of clothing that covers your arm: *a dress with long sleeves* **2** a paper or plastic cover that protects something such as a record or book

PHRASE **have sth up your sleeve** to have a secret plan that you can surprise people with

sleeve•less /ˈslivləs/ adj a sleeveless dress or shirt does not have sleeves

sleigh /sleɪ/ noun [C] a vehicle that is pulled by animals and used for traveling over snow

sleight of hand /ˌslaɪt əv ˈhænd/ noun [singular/U] clever and slightly dishonest behavior used for achieving something

slen•der /ˈslendər/ adj **1** tall or long and thin in an attractive way: *slender fingers* **2** very small in amount and only just enough: *They won by a slender majority.*

slept the past tense and past participle of **sleep¹**

sleuth /sluθ/ noun [C] *old-fashioned* someone who tries to solve crimes or mysteries =DETECTIVE

slew¹ the past tense of **slay**

slew² /slu/ noun **a slew of sth** *American informal* a lot of something

slice¹ /slaɪs/ noun [C] ★

1 a flat piece of food that has been cut from something larger: *Cut the bread into thick slices.* ♦ ***a slice of** cake/pizza/cheese*

2 *informal* a part or share of something: *We want a bigger **slice of** the tourist trade.*

slice² /slaɪs/ verb **1** [T] to cut something into flat pieces: *I'll slice some bread.* —*picture* → C2 **2** [I] to cut something easily: *The saw quickly sliced through the board.*

slick¹ /slɪk/ adj **1** smooth and shiny or wet: *slick black hair* **2** clever and good at persuading people but probably not honest: *a slick car salesman* **3** done in an impressive

S

way that seems to need little effort: *a slick advertisement*

slick² /slɪk/ noun [C] an OIL SLICK

slick³ /slɪk/ verb [T] if you slick your hair back or down, you put oil or water on it in order to make it stay in place

slide¹ /slaɪd/ noun [C] **1** a structure for children to play on, with steps and a slope to slide down **2** a situation in which an amount gradually becomes less: *a slide in sales* **3** a small piece of FILM in a frame. You shine light through it in order to show the image on a screen. **4** a small thin piece of glass used for looking at things with a MICROSCOPE

slide² /slaɪd/ (past tense and past participle **slid** /slɪd/) verb ★

1 [I/T] to move smoothly and quickly across a surface, or to make something move in this way: *The kids love to **slide down** this hill on their sleds.* ♦ *The doors **slid open**.* ♦ *I **slid** the letter **under** her door.*

2 [I] to gradually get into a worse situation than before: *The company **slid** further **into** debt last year.*

PHRASE **let sth slide 1** *American* to not worry about a small problem, or to forgive someone when they do something wrong: *I'm going to let it slide this time, but don't do it again!* **2** to let a situation become worse and not do anything to stop it

slight /slaɪt/ adj ★★

1 small in size, amount, or degree: *a slight increase in temperature*

2 thin and small: *a slight young woman*

slight·ly /ˈslaɪtli/ adv ★★★ a little: *I feel slightly better today.* ♦ *It looked like Stephen was limping slightly.* ♦ *"Do you know her?" "Only slightly."*

slim¹ /slɪm/ adj ★★

1 thin in an attractive way: *She had a slim youthful figure.*

2 very small: *There is still **a slim chance** that she may be alive.*

slim² /slɪm/

PHRASAL VERBS ˌ**slim ˈdown** to lose weight

ˌ**slim (sth) ˈdown** if you slim down an organization, or if it slims down, you reduce the number of staff in it

slime /slaɪm/ noun [U] a thick, wet, and unpleasant substance

slim·ming /ˈslɪmɪŋ/ adj making you look thinner than you really are

slim·y /ˈslaɪmi/ adj thick, wet, and unpleasant to touch

sling¹ /slɪŋ/ (past tense and past participle **slung** /slʌŋ/) verb [T] to put or throw something somewhere in a careless way: *Just sling all that stuff on the floor.* ♦ *He slung his jacket over one shoulder.*

sling² /slɪŋ/ noun [C] **1** a piece of cloth used for supporting your arm when it is injured **2** a set of belts or ropes used for supporting or lifting something heavy

slink /slɪŋk/ (past tense and past participle **slunk**) verb [I] to go somewhere slowly and quietly so that people will not notice you: *Ray slunk out of the building.*

slip¹ /slɪp/ verb ★★

- 1 (almost) fall
- 2 slide out of position
- 3 go quickly and quietly
- 4 slide sth somewhere
- 5 become less strong
- + PHRASES
- + PHRASAL VERBS

1 [I] if you slip, your feet slide accidentally and you fall or lose your balance: *Margaret slipped and broke her arm.* ♦ *Be careful you don't **slip on** the wet floor.*

2 [I] if something slips, it slides out of the position it should be in: *The knife slipped and cut my finger.* ♦ *The ball **slipped out of** my hands.*

3 [I] to go somewhere quickly and quietly, without anyone noticing you or stopping you: *Several people managed to **slip past** the guards.* ♦ *I **slipped away** before the end of the meeting.*

4 [T] to slide something into a place or position, often so that other people do not notice: *John **slipped** his arm **around** his wife's waist.* ♦ *He **slipped** the money **into** his pocket.*

5 [I] to gradually become less strong or good: *Profits slipped by 13 percent last year.*

PHRASES **let (it) slip** to tell someone something that is secret by mistake: *He let it slip that they intended to move to Canada.*

slip your mind if something slips your mind, you forget to do it

slip through your fingers if something such as an opportunity or a prize slips through your fingers, you fail to get it or to take advantage of it

slip through the net/cracks to fail to be caught or protected by the system that was intended to catch or protect you

PHRASAL VERBS ˌ**slip ˈinto sth** to quickly put on a piece of clothing: *I slipped into my pajamas.*

ˌ**slip sth ˈoff** to take a piece of clothing off quickly: *Slip your shirt off.*

ˌ**slip sth ˈon** to put clothes on: *Ann slipped the jacket on.*

ˌ**slip ˈout** if something slips out, you say it without intending to

ˌ**slip ˈup** *informal* to make a careless mistake

slip

slip² /slɪp/ noun [C] **1** a small piece of paper: *I left the message for you on a slip of paper.* → PINK SLIP **2** a small mistake: *Tom played well, despite a few slips at the beginning.* **3** a small change from a higher level to a lower one: *a slip in the price of technology stocks* **4** a piece of women's underwear consisting of a loose skirt or dress with no sleeves

PHRASE **give sb the slip** *informal* to escape from someone who is following or chasing you

slip·per /ˈslɪpər/ noun [C] a soft comfortable shoe that you wear in your house

slip·per·y /ˈslɪp(ə)ri/ adj **1** a slippery surface or object is difficult to move on or hold because it is smooth or wet **2** *informal* clever but dishonest

slit¹ /slɪt/ noun [C] a long narrow space or cut in something: *a skirt with a slit up the side*

slit² /slɪt/ (past tense and past participle **slit**) verb [T] to make a long thin cut in something: *She grabbed the envelope and slit it open.*

slith·er /ˈslɪðər/ verb [I] to move along the ground like a snake

sliv·er /ˈslɪvər/ noun [C] a small thin piece of something: *slivers of glass*

slob /slɑb/ noun [C] *informal* someone who is lazy or messy

slob·ber /ˈslɑbər/ verb [I] to have SALIVA coming out of your mouth

slog /slɑg/ verb [I] *informal* **1** to work hard and for a long time doing something that is difficult or boring **2** to make a long tiring trip somewhere by walking there

slo·gan /ˈsloʊgən/ noun [C] a short phrase that is used for advertising something, or for supporting someone in politics

slop /slɑp/ verb [I/T] if a liquid slops, or if you slop it, it moves inside its container, or some of it comes out of the container =SLOSH

slope¹ /sloʊp/ noun [C] ★
1 a surface or piece of ground that has one end higher than the other: *At the end of the garden there is* ***a steep slope****.*
2 the angle of a slope: *a 45-degree slope*

slope² /sloʊp/ verb [I] to have one end higher than the other: *The floor slopes a little.*
—**slop·ing** adj

slop·py /ˈslɑpi/ adj **1** done in a very careless way: *a sloppy job* **2** expressing emotions in a way that seems silly or embarrassing

slosh /slɑʃ/ verb **1** [I/T] if a liquid sloshes, or if you slosh it, it moves inside its container, or some of it comes out of the container =SLOP **2** [I] to walk through something wet in a noisy way

S

slot¹ /slɑt/ noun [C] **1** a long narrow hole or space that you can fit something through or into: *He put a coin in the slot.* **2** a time between other events when it is arranged that something will happen: *We circled the airport waiting for a landing slot.*

slot² /slɑt/ PHRASAL VERB ˌ**slot (sth) ˈinto sth** to fit something into a narrow space, or to fit into a narrow space: *She slotted another tape into the cassette player.*

ˈ**slot maˌchine** noun [C] a machine that you put coins into in order to play a game

slouch /slaʊtʃ/ verb [I] to sit, walk, or stand with your shoulders bent forward

slow¹ /sloʊ/ adj ★★★
1 not moving or happening fast: *This bus is really slow.* ♦ *a long slow walk to the top of the hill* ♦ *She's a slow worker, but reliable.* ♦ *Progress has been* ***painfully slow*** (=very slow). ♦ **slow to do sth** *The government has been slow to respond.*
2 not busy, interesting, or exciting: *The first part of the movie is very slow.*
3 a watch or clock that is slow shows a time that is earlier than the correct time: *Your watch is 15 minutes slow.*
4 not intelligent, so that you need a lot of time in order to understand simple things

slow² /sloʊ/ verb [I/T] **1** if you slow something, or if it slows, you reduce the level or amount of it: *Inflation slowed significantly in the 1990s.* **2** if you slow something, or if it slows, you reduce the speed at which it happens or moves: *Drugs can slow the progress of the disease.* ♦ *Traffic on the freeway had slowed to walking pace.*
PHRASAL VERBS ˌ**slow (sb) ˈdown** if someone slows down, or if something slows them down, they become less active or effective: *For me, vacations are a time to slow down and relax.*
ˌ**slow (sb/sth) ˈdown** to move at a slower speed, or to make someone or something move at a slower speed: *Slow down! You're driving too fast.*
ˌ**slow (sth) ˈdown** *same as* **slow² 2**: *The new government is slowing down the pace of reform.*

slow³ /sloʊ/ adv *informal* at a slow speed: *Hurry up! You're driving too slow.*

slow·down /ˈsloʊˌdaʊn/ noun [C] a period when there is less activity: *an economic slowdown*

slow·ly /ˈsloʊli/ adv ★★★ moving or happening at a slow speed: *The city is slowly getting back to normal after a three-day transportation strike.* ♦ *Could you* ***speak*** *a little more* ***slowly****?* ♦ *We're making progress –* ***slowly but surely*** (=slowly but with definite results).

ˌ**slow ˈmotion** noun [U] action in a movie or television program that is shown more slowly than the real speed: *Let's see it again in slow motion.*

slow·poke /ˈsloʊˌpoʊk/ noun [C] *American informal* someone who does things too slowly

sludge /slʌdʒ/ noun [U] **1** a thick soft waste substance from an industrial process **2** an unpleasant thick wet substance

slug¹ /slʌg/ noun [C] a small slow creature with no legs. It looks like a SNAIL without a shell.

slug² /slʌg/ verb [T] *informal* to hit someone or something very hard with your FIST

slug·gish /ˈslʌgɪʃ/ adj not moving, performing, or reacting as well as usual: *a sluggish economy* ♦ *Sasha woke up feeling tired and sluggish.*

slum /slʌm/ noun [C] a poor area of a town where the houses are in very bad condition

slum·ber /ˈslʌmbər/ noun [U] *literary* sleep

slump¹ /slʌmp/ verb [I] **1** to suddenly fall to a much lower level: *Profits slumped to under $250 million.* **2** to suddenly fall or sit down because you are very tired or unconscious: *Sam's body slumped to the floor.*
PHRASE **be slumped in/over etc. sth** to be sitting still in a position that is not upright: *They found him slumped over the wheel of his car.*

slump² /slʌmp/ noun [C] **1** a sudden large reduction in amount: *a slump in prices* **2** a period when someone or something is much less successful than before: *an economic slump*

slung the past tense and past participle of **sling**

slunk the past tense and past participle of **slink**

slur[1] /slɜr/ noun [C] a remark that is intended to insult someone or damage their reputation

slur[2] /slɜr/ verb [I/T] to speak without pronouncing the words clearly or separately —**slurred** /slɜrd/ adj: *slurred speech*

slurp /slɜrp/ verb [I/T] to make loud sucking noises as you drink something

slush /slʌʃ/ noun **1** [U] snow that is starting to MELT (=become water) **2** [C/U] a drink made by mixing a sweet liquid with crushed ice

sly /slaɪ/ adj clever at tricking people or at hurting them without them realizing it: *I noticed his sly smile.*

smack[1] /smæk/ verb [T] to hit someone with your flat hand or with a flat object
PHRASAL VERB ˈ**smack of sth** to be a sign of something bad: *Their decision smacked of discrimination.*

smack[2] /smæk/ noun [C] **1** a hit with your flat hand or with a flat object **2** a loud sound that is made when something hits a surface

smack[3] /smæk/ or ˈ**smack-ˌdab** adv *informal* exactly in a particular place: *The ball hit me smack in the eye.*

small /smɔl/ adj ★★★
1 not large in size, amount, or number: *These shoes are too small for me.* ♦ *I'd rather work for a smaller company.* ♦ ***A small number of** people have complained.*
2 not very important or difficult: *Can you do me a small favor?* ♦ *I noticed a few small mistakes.*
3 not worth a lot of money, or not involving a lot of money: *a new mutual fund that is ideal for small investors*
4 small children are very young
—**small** adv: *Write small so that everything will fit on one page.*
➔ WONDER[2]

Both **small** and **little** can be used to describe something that is not big in size or number.
- **Small** is a more general word: *a woman with a small dog* ♦ *Our house is fairly small.*
- **Little** is usually used when you feel something about the thing that you are describing, for example when you like it, dislike it, or feel surprised that it is so small: *Look at that little baby!* ♦ *She has such little feet.*

ˌ**small inˈtestine** noun [C] the tube in your body that food goes into after it has passed through your stomach

ˌ**small poˈtatoes** noun [plural] *American informal* someone or something that is not important

small·pox /ˈsmɔlˌpɑks/ noun [U] a serious disease in which your skin becomes covered in spots

ˌ**small-ˈscale** adj smaller or less important than other things of the same kind: *a small-scale operation/attack*

ˈ**small ˌtalk** noun [U] informal conversation about things that are not important

smart[1] /smɑrt/ adj ★★★

1 intelligent	4 of appearance
2 clever/funny but rude	5 for rich people
3 about weapons, etc.	

1 intelligent: *Sophie is a smart hard-working student.* ♦ *Wilson made a few smart investments.*
2 behaving in a clever or funny way that shows a lack of respect: ***Don't get smart with me!***
3 smart weapons and machines are very effective because they use computer technology
4 *British* clean and neat in appearance and dressed in nice clothes
5 *British* used by rich fashionable people

smart[2] /smɑrt/ verb [I] **1** to hurt with a sudden sharp pain **2** to be very upset by something that someone has said or done

smart al·eck /ˈsmɑrt ˌælɪk/ noun [C] *showing disapproval* someone who says clever or funny but rude things

ˈ**smart ˌcard** noun [C] a small plastic card that stores information in electronic form

smash[1] /smæʃ/ verb ★
1 [I/T] if something smashes, or if you smash it, it breaks noisily into many pieces when it falls or when you break it: *Someone had smashed a window.* ♦ *The bottle fell and smashed on the floor.*
2 [I/T] to hit against an object or surface with a lot of force, or to hit something against something in this way: *His car smashed into a tree.* ♦ *He fell and smashed his head on the sidewalk.*
3 [T] to completely destroy or defeat an organization, system, etc.
4 [T] in tennis, to hit a ball that is above your head downward and very hard —*picture* ➔ C15
PHRASAL VERB ˌ**smash sth ˈup** *spoken* to destroy something completely by violently breaking it into many pieces: *She got angry and started smashing things up.*

smash[2] /smæʃ/ noun [C] *informal* **1 smash** or **smash hit** something such as a play, movie, or song that is extremely successful **2** a car crash

smear[1] /smɪr/ verb [T] **1** to spread a soft substance on a surface in a messy way: *The kids had smeared glue all over the floor.* ♦ *His face was smeared with mud.* **2** to try to damage someone's reputation by telling lies about them

smear[2] /smɪr/ noun [C] **1** a dirty mark made by rubbing something **2** an attempt to damage someone's reputation by telling lies about them

smell[1] /smel/ noun ★★
1 [C] the quality of something that you notice when you breathe in through your nose: *This paint has **a very strong smell**.* ♦ *the delicious **smell of** fresh bread* ➔ AROMA
2 [U] the ability to notice or recognize smells: *Dogs have an excellent **sense of smell**.*

smell[2] /smel/ (past tense and past participle **smelled**) verb ★
1 [linking verb] to have a particular smell: *That cake **smells so good**!* ♦ *The laboratory **smelled strongly of** chemicals.* ♦ ***It smells like** a bar in here.*
2 [I] to have an unpleasant smell: *It smells in here!* ♦ *His feet really smell.*
3 [T] to notice or recognize the smell of something: *Do you smell gas?*

S

4 [T] to experience the smell of something by putting your nose close to it: *Come and smell these roses.*

→ ROSE

PHRASAL VERB ˌ**smell sth ˈup** to cause a place to have an unpleasant smell: *That fish is smelling up the whole house.*

smell·y /ˈsmeli/ adj with an unpleasant smell

smile¹ /smaɪl/ verb [I] ★★★ to raise the corners of your mouth when you are happy or when you are being friendly: *James looked up and* ***smiled at*** *Karen.*

smile² /smaɪl/ noun [C] ★★★ an expression on your face in which you smile: *Tom had a huge smile on his face.* ♦ *a smile of satisfaction*

> Words often used with **smile**
>
> *Adjectives often used with* ***smile*** *(noun)*
>
> ■ **beaming, dazzling, faint, knowing, radiant, slight, wry** + SMILE: used about different types of smile

smirk /smɜrk/ verb [I] to smile in an unpleasant way because something bad has happened to someone else —**smirk** noun [C]

smock /smɑk/ noun [C] a long loose shirt that is worn over ordinary clothes in order to keep them clean

smog /smɑg/ noun [U] polluted air that forms a cloud close to the ground

smoke¹ /smoʊk/ noun ★★

1 [U] a gray, black, or white cloud that is produced by something that is burning: *A column of black smoke slowly rose above the building.* ♦ *The air was thick with* ***cigarette smoke.*** ♦ *Exploding rockets sent up* ***clouds of smoke.***

2 [C] *informal* a cigarette, or an act of smoking a cigarette: *I'm just going out for a smoke.*

PHRASE **go up in smoke** *informal* to be destroyed

smoke² /smoʊk/ verb ★★

1 [I/T] to suck smoke from a cigarette, pipe, etc. into your mouth and lungs: *Phil was reading the paper and* ***smoking a cigarette.***

2 [I/T] to smoke cigarettes as a regular habit: *I didn't know you smoked!*

3 [I] to produce smoke: *By the time I got home, the engine was smoking badly.*

4 [T] to preserve and give flavor to food by hanging it in smoke

ˈ**smoke aˌlarm** noun [C] a piece of equipment that makes a loud noise when there is smoke in a room, used for warning people that there is a fire

smoked /smoʊkt/ adj smoked food has a special flavor because it has been hung in smoke

ˈ**smoke deˌtector** noun [C] a SMOKE ALARM

smok·er /ˈsmoʊkər/ noun [C] someone who smokes cigarettes, a pipe, etc. ≠ NONSMOKER

ˈ**smoke ˌscreen** noun [C] something that you say or do as a way of hiding your real feelings, intentions, or activities

smoke·stack /ˈsmoʊkˌstæk/ noun [C] a tall structure on a factory or ship through which smoke rises

smok·ing /ˈsmoʊkɪŋ/ noun [U] the activity of breathing smoke from cigarettes, pipes, etc. into your mouth and lungs

smok·y /ˈsmoʊki/ adj **1** with a lot of smoke in the air **2** tasting or smelling of smoke

smol·der /ˈsmoʊldər/ verb [I] **1** to burn slowly, producing smoke but no flames **2** to feel very strong emotions that you do not express in words

smooth¹ /smuð/ adj ★★

1 completely even with no rough areas or lumps ≠ ROUGH: *smooth skin*

2 moving in a way that is steady and well controlled: *With a smooth swing, he hit the ball.*

3 causing no difficulty, problems, or delays: *a smooth process* ♦ *We are changing systems, but we expect a smooth transition.*

4 *showing disapproval* relaxed and confident in a way that usually persuades people to do things: *Steven's a little too smooth if you ask me.* ♦ *a smooth operator* (=someone you cannot trust)

smooth² /smuð/ verb [T] **1** to move your hand across the surface of something until it is flat and even: *Frances smoothed her skirt down over her knees.* **2** to carefully spread a substance over a surface: *Anne gently smoothed cream into the baby's skin.*

PHRASAL VERB ˌ**smooth sth ˈover** to make a problem seem less serious

smooth·ie /ˈsmuði/ noun [C] **1** *showing disapproval* an attractive, relaxed, and confident man who is good at persuading people to do what he wants **2** a drink made from fruit and milk, cream, or ICE CREAM

smooth·ly /ˈsmuðli/ adv **1** without difficulty, problems, or delays **2** with a movement that is steady and well controlled

smoth·er /ˈsmʌðər/ verb [T]

1 cover sth	4 not express sth
2 kill sb	5 love too much
3 cover fire	

1 to cover something completely **2** to kill someone by covering their face until they stop breathing **3** to stop a fire burning by covering it **4** to try not to express a feeling **5** to express your love for someone too much

smoul·der /ˈsmoʊldər/ the British spelling of smolder

smudge¹ /smʌdʒ/ noun [C] a small messy mark made by a substance such as dirt or ink

smudge² /smʌdʒ/ verb [I/T] if you smudge something such as ink, or if it smudges, you make it spread in a messy way by touching it

smug /smʌg/ adj *showing disapproval* too satisfied with your abilities or achievements —**smug·ly** adv, **smug·ness** noun [U]

smug·gle /ˈsmʌg(ə)l/ verb [T] to take someone or something secretly or illegally into or out of a place —**smug·gler** noun [C], **smug·gling** noun [U]

smut /smʌt/ noun [U] *showing disapproval* pictures of sex or stories about sex —**smut·ty** adj

snack /snæk/ noun [C] a small amount of food that you eat between meals: *Coffee, tea, and snacks are available throughout the day.* —**snack** verb [I]

sna·fu /snæˈfu/ noun [singular] *American informal*

a mistake or a problem that prevents you from finishing something

snag¹ /snæg/ noun [C] **1** a problem or disadvantage **2** a small damaged area in a piece of clothing, caused by something that is sharp or rough

snag² /snæg/ verb **1** [I/T] to damage something, especially clothing, with something that is sharp or rough **2** [T] *American informal* to get someone or something that you want: *Did you snag some tickets for us?*

snail /sneɪl/ noun [C] a small animal that has a soft body, no legs, and a hard shell on its back

PHRASE **at a snail's pace** very slowly

ˈsnail ˌmail noun [U] *informal* letters that are sent by mail rather than by e-mail

snake¹ /sneɪk/ noun [C] a long thin animal with no legs and a smooth skin —*picture* → C13

snake² /sneɪk/ verb [I] to move in a series of long curves: *The path snakes through the trees and up the hill.*

snap¹ /snæp/ verb

1 break with loud noise	5 (try to) bite
2 move sth with noise	+ PHRASES
3 become angry/upset	+ PHRASAL VERB
4 speak angrily	

1 [I/T] to suddenly break something with a short loud noise, or to be broken in this way: *When the rope snapped, Davis fell into the water.* ♦ *Ken snapped off the smaller branches.* **2** [I/T] to quickly move something, for example a light switch or something else that makes a short sound, or to be moved quickly in this way: *She quickly snapped her purse shut.* ♦ *It's really simple to build – the pieces just snap together.* **3** [I] to suddenly lose control and become extremely angry or upset: *She was bound to snap under all that pressure.* **4** [I/T] to speak to someone in a sudden angry way: *What do you want now? he snapped angrily.* ♦ *I'm sorry I snapped at you just now.* **5** [I/T] if an animal such as a dog snaps at you, it bites you or tries to bite you: *A terrier was snapping at his heels.*

PHRASES **snap your fingers** to make a short sound by pressing your middle finger against your thumb and moving them suddenly apart

snap out of it to make an effort to stop being unhappy or upset

PHRASAL VERB **ˌsnap sth ˈup 1** to buy something as soon as you see it: *By 10 o'clock most of the best bargains had been snapped up.* **2** to immediately take advantage of an opportunity

snap² /snæp/ noun **1** [singular] a short loud noise, made especially by something breaking or closing **2** [C] *American* a small button on clothes that works by pressing two parts together

PHRASE **cold snap** a short period of time when the weather is very cold

snap³ /snæp/ adj decided or arranged very quickly: *We can't be pushed into making a snap decision.*

snap•per /ˈsnæpər/ noun [C/U] a brightly colored fish with sharp teeth

snap•py /ˈsnæpi/ adj **1** clever and using few words **2** tending to speak to people in an angry way **3** attractive and fashionable

snap•shot /ˈsnæpʃɑt/ noun [C] **1** a photograph that is taken without the use of professional equipment **2** a short explanation or description that tells you what a particular place or situation is like

snare¹ /sner/ noun [C] a piece of equipment that is used for catching an animal

snare² /sner/ verb [T] **1** to catch an animal using a snare **2** to trick someone into an unpleasant situation that they cannot escape from

snarl /snɑrl/ verb **1** [I/T] to speak in an unpleasant angry way **2** [I] if an animal snarls, it makes an angry sound in its throat and shows its teeth **3** [T] to make traffic unable to move —**snarl** noun [C]

snatch¹ /snætʃ/ verb [T] **1** to quickly take something or someone away: *Her brother snatched the letter and tore it open.* **2** to take the opportunity to do something quickly: *They managed to snatch a few hours' sleep.* **3** to manage to get something that you almost did not get: *They snatched victory with a goal in the last minute.*

snatch² /snætʃ/ noun [C] a short piece of something that you hear: *a few snatches of conversation*

snaz•zy /ˈsnæzi/ adj *informal* attractive, bright, and fashionable: *a snazzy tie*

sneak¹ /snik/ (past tense and past participle **sneaked** /snikt/ or **snuck** /snʌk/) verb **1** [I] to move somewhere quietly and secretly so that no one can see you or hear you **2** [T] to take someone or something secretly or illegally

PHRASAL VERB **ˌsneak ˈup** to get very near to someone before they notice you

sneak² /snik/ noun [C] *informal showing disapproval* a person who tells someone in authority about something wrong that you have done

sneak•ers /ˈsnikərz/ noun [plural] *American* shoes made of cloth and rubber. You wear them mainly for playing sports.

sneak•y /ˈsniki/ adj doing or saying things secretly, often in a dishonest or unfair way

sneer /snɪr/ verb [I/T] to smile or speak in an unpleasant way that shows that you do not respect someone or something —**sneer** noun [C]

sneeze /sniz/ verb [I] to loudly blow air out of your nose in a sudden uncontrolled way —**sneeze** noun [C]

snick•er /ˈsnɪkər/ verb [I] *American* to laugh quietly at something that is rude or at something unpleasant that has happened to someone —**snick•er** noun [C]

snide /snaɪd/ adj deliberately unkind in an indirect way

sniff /snɪf/ verb **1** [I] to breathe in noisily through your nose, for example because you have been crying: *Amanda sniffed and wiped her nose.* **2** [T] to breathe in through your nose in order to smell something: *He took off the lid and sniffed the contents of the jar.* —**sniff** noun [C]

snif•fle /ˈsnɪf(ə)l/ verb [I] to keep sniffing

S

because you are crying or because you have a cold

snip /snɪp/ verb [T] to cut something in a short quick movement using scissors —**snip** noun [C]

snip·er /ˈsnaɪpər/ noun [C] someone who shoots at people from a hidden place —**snipe** verb [I]

snip·pet /ˈsnɪpət/ noun [C] a small piece of information or news

snip·py /ˈsnɪpi/ adj *American informal* a snippy person is not patient and speaks to people in an angry way

snit /snɪt/ noun [C/U] *American informal* a feeling of being annoyed

snitch¹ /snɪtʃ/ verb *informal* **1** [I] *showing disapproval* to tell someone about something that is wrong that someone else has done **2** [T] to take something that you are not allowed to have

snitch² /snɪtʃ/ noun [C] *informal showing disapproval* a person who tells someone about something that is wrong that you have done

sniv·el /ˈsnɪv(ə)l/ verb [I] to cry or complain in a way that seems weak or annoying

snob /snɑb/ noun [C] *showing disapproval* someone who thinks that they are better than other people, usually because of their social class

snob·ber·y /ˈsnɑb(ə)ri/ noun [U] the attitudes or behavior of someone who thinks that they are better than other people

snob·bish /ˈsnɑbɪʃ/ or **snob·by** /ˈsnɑbi/ adj behaving in a way that shows that you think you are better than other people

snoop /snup/ verb [I] to secretly try to get information that someone would not want you to have

snooze /snuz/ verb [I] *informal* to sleep for a short period of time, especially during the day —**snooze** noun [C]

snore /snɔr/ verb [I] to breathe noisily while you sleep —**snore** noun [C]

snor·kel /ˈsnɔrk(ə)l/ noun [C] a piece of equipment with a tube that fits in your mouth so that you can breathe when you are looking into the water while swimming

snor·kel·ing /ˈsnɔrk(ə)lɪŋ/ noun [U] the activity of swimming using a snorkel

snort /snɔrt/ verb [I] to make a sudden loud noise through your nose, for example because you are angry or laughing —**snort** noun [C]

snot /snɑt/ noun [U] *impolite* the thick wet substance that is produced in your nose

snot·ty /ˈsnɑti/ adj **1** *impolite* covered in snot **2** *informal* a snotty person thinks that they are better or more important than other people

snout /snaʊt/ noun [C] the long nose of a pig or a similar animal

snow¹ /snoʊ/ noun ★★

1 [U] small soft white pieces of ice that fall from the sky and cover the ground: *The path was hidden under a blanket of snow.* ♦ *Three inches of **snow fell** overnight.*

2 snows [plural] the snow that falls over a period of time: *The first snows of winter are here.*

snow² /snoʊ/ verb [I] if it snows, snow falls from the sky

PHRASES **snowed in** unable to leave a place because a lot of snow has fallen there

snowed under if you are snowed under, you have too much work to deal with

snow·ball¹ /ˈsnoʊˌbɔl/ noun [C] a ball of snow that you can throw

snow·ball² /ˈsnoʊˌbɔl/ verb [I] to develop quickly and become very big or serious

snow·board·ing /ˈsnoʊˌbɔrdɪŋ/ noun [U] a sport in which you stand with both feet on a large curved board and slide down a hill that is covered in snow —**snow·board** noun [C]

snow·drift /ˈsnoʊˌdrɪft/ noun [C] a deep pile of snow that is made by the wind

snow·fall /ˈsnoʊˌfɔl/ noun [C/U] the amount of snow that falls during a particular period

snow·flake /ˈsnoʊˌfleɪk/ noun [C] a single piece of snow that falls from the sky

snow·man /ˈsnoʊˌmæn/ noun [C] a model of a person that children make using snow

snow·plow /ˈsnoʊˌplaʊ/ noun [C] a large vehicle that pushes snow off the road

snow·storm /ˈsnoʊˌstɔrm/ noun [C] a storm with a lot of snow and strong winds

snow·y /ˈsnoʊi/ adj with a lot of snow

snub /snʌb/ verb [T] to insult someone by ignoring them or being rude to them —**snub** noun [C]

snuck a past tense and past participle of **sneak**

snuff¹ /snʌf/ noun [U] tobacco in the form of a powder that you breathe in through your nose

snuff² /snʌf/ PHRASAL VERB ˌ**snuff sth ˈout 1** to make a flame stop burning by squeezing it with your fingers or covering it **2** to make something end quickly

snug /snʌg/ adj **1** warm and comfortable =COZY **2** fitting closely —**snug·ly** adv

snug·gle /ˈsnʌg(ə)l/ verb [I/T] to put yourself into a warm, comfortable, and safe position

so /soʊ/ grammar word ★★★

> So can be:
> - an **adverb**: *Why are you so angry this morning?* ♦ *"I'm hungry." "So am I."*
> - a **conjunction**: *There weren't enough beds, so I had to sleep on the floor.*
> - used in the conjunction phrase **so that**: *He was standing in the shadow so that I could not see his face clearly.*

1 for emphasis used for emphasizing a quality, feeling, or amount: *I'm so glad you could come.* ♦ *The food's wonderful, but it's so expensive!* ♦ *The children couldn't sleep, they were so excited.* ♦ *Like **so many** great artists, he died young.* ♦ *The road surface became **so** hot **that** it melted.*

2 used instead of repeating sth used for referring back to what has just been said instead of repeating it: *You're in love with Rita, aren't you? **I thought so.*** ♦ *If you wanted to leave early, you should have **said so**.* ♦ *Does the President intend to go to Moscow? **And if so**, when?*

3 also used for saying that something that was just said is also true about another person or thing: *Heidi is planning to come, and so is Sylvia.* ♦ *My parents send their love, and so does Rachel.* ♦ *"I'd like to know what's happening out there." "So would I."*

♦ *If I learned how to drive a car, so can you.*
4 because of what has just been mentioned used for saying that something happens because of what you have just mentioned: *A tree had fallen across the road, so they had to turn around and go back.*
5 for stating a purpose used for saying what the purpose of an action is: **+(that)** *He lowered his voice so that no one would hear.*
6 for starting a new subject *spoken* used for starting a new subject or starting to ask a question: *So, let's get down to business.* ♦ *So, what do you suggest we do next?*
7 when showing sth *spoken* used when showing someone what size something is or how something should be done: *She was about so tall.* ♦ *Tie the two ends together, **like so**.*
8 for saying that sth is limited used for saying that a number or amount is limited: *We have only **so much** time before the exams start.* ♦ *There are only **so many** police officers available.*

PHRASES **and so on/forth** used instead of mentioning more of a similar type of thing that has already been mentioned: *Employees were always complaining about their wages, their working conditions, and so forth.*
not so...(as) used for saying that one person or thing has less of a particular quality than another: *The Rosario family managed to flee, but others were not so lucky.*
or so used for showing that a number or amount is not exact: *The job won't take long – about twenty minutes or so.*
so (what)? *informal* used for saying in a slightly rude way that what someone has said is not important: *"Someone might see us." "So what? We're not doing anything illegal."*
→ LONG[2]

soak /soʊk/ verb [I/T] **1** to put something into a liquid and leave it there for a period of time: *Leave the beans to soak overnight.* **2** to make something very wet, or to become very wet: *The rain poured in, soaking the cardboard boxes.*
PHRASAL VERB ˌ**soak sth ˈup** if a dry or soft substance soaks up a liquid, the liquid goes into it

soaked /soʊkt/ adj extremely wet

soak•ing /ˈsoʊkɪŋ/ adj extremely wet

ˈ**so-and-ˌso** noun *informal* **1** [C] an unpleasant person **2** [U] used for referring to someone whose name you do not know

soap /soʊp/ noun ★★
1 [C/U] a substance that you use with water in order to wash your body or an object: *a bar of soap* ♦ *perfumed soaps*
2 [C] *informal* a SOAP OPERA

ˈ**soap ˌopera** noun [C] a television or radio series about the imaginary lives of a group of people

soap•y /ˈsoʊpi/ adj covered in soap, or containing soap

soar /sɔr/ verb [I] **1** to quickly increase to a high level: *Unemployment has soared.* **2** to rise or fly high in the sky —**soar•ing** adj

sob /sɑb/ verb [I/T] to cry noisily while taking short breaths —**sob** noun [C]

so•ber[1] /ˈsoʊbər/ adj **1** not drunk **2** with a serious attitude **3** plain and not brightly colored —**so•ber•ly** adv

so•ber[2] /ˈsoʊbər/ PHRASAL VERB ˌ**sober ˈup** to become sober after being drunk

so•ber•ing /ˈsoʊbərɪŋ/ adj making you think about things in a serious way

so-called /ˈsoʊ ˌkɔld/ adj **1** used for showing that you think a word used for describing something is not appropriate: *His so-called friends betrayed him.* **2** used for saying that a particular word is usually used for referring to something: *They've found the flight recorder, the so-called black box.*

soc•cer /ˈsɑkər/ noun [U] a game in which two teams of 11 players kick a round ball and try to score goals

so•cia•ble /ˈsoʊʃəb(ə)l/ adj a sociable person is friendly and enjoys being with other people = OUTGOING ≠ UNSOCIABLE

so•cial /ˈsoʊʃ(ə)l/ adj ★★★

1 about activities	4 about position
2 about behavior	5 about animals
3 about society	

1 relating to activities that involve being with other people, especially activities that you do for pleasure: *a social activity/engagement* ♦ *The worst thing about working at home is the lack of **social contact**.* ♦ *This is not **a social call**. I'm afraid I have some bad news.*
2 relating to rules about behavior with other people: *We need someone with excellent **social skills**.*
3 relating to society and to people's lives in general: *a period of enormous political and social change* ♦ *the social conditions of rural workers* ♦ ***social problems** such as unemployment*
4 relating to the position that someone has in society in relation to other people: *someone's social background* ♦ *The evidence shows a relationship between crime and **social class**.*
5 used for describing animals that live in groups instead of alone
—**so•cial•ly** adv

so•cial•ism /ˈsoʊʃ(ə)lˌɪzəm/ noun [U] a political system that aims to create a society in which everyone has equal opportunities and in which the most important industries are owned or controlled by the whole community —**so•cial•ist** adj, noun [C]

so•cial•ize /ˈsoʊʃ(ə)lˌaɪz/ verb [I] to spend time with other people socially

so•cial•ized med•i•cine /ˌsoʊʃ(ə)lˌaɪzd ˈmed(ə)sɪn/ noun [U] *American* medical care that is provided by the state

ˌ**social ˈscience** noun [C/U] the study of the way that people live in society, or one of the separate subjects that deal with the way that societies are organized —ˌ**social ˈscientist** noun [C]

ˌ**social seˈcurity** noun [U] **1 Social Security** a U.S. government program that workers must pay money into, that gives money to people who are old or cannot work **2** money that you receive from Social Security

ˌ**Social Seˈcurity ˌnumber** noun [C] an official number that is given to every U.S. citizen

ˌ**social ˈservices** noun [plural] the services that

S

are provided by a government or private organization for people with social problems

ˈsocial ˌworker noun [C] someone who is trained to give help and advice to people who have severe social problems —**ˈsocial ˌwork** noun [U]

so•ci•e•tal /səˈsaɪət(ə)l/ adj *formal* relating to society or the way society is organized

so•ci•e•ty /səˈsaɪəti/ noun ★★★

1 [U] people in general living together in organized communities, with laws and traditions controlling the way that they behave toward each other: *Society has to be prepared to support its elderly people.* ♦ *The program aims to support prisoners who have been released into society.*

2 [C/U] a particular community or type of community, or the people who live in it: *The protesters were drawn from a broad cross section of society.* ♦ *Never forget that we live in a multicultural society.* ♦ *The novels reflect the values of Victorian society.*

3 [U] the group of people in a country who are rich and fashionable or from a high social class: *a big society wedding* ♦ *She moved in **high society** and had many aristocratic friends.*

4 [C] an organization or club for people who have a particular interest or who take part in a particular activity: *She joined the local history society and made some new friends.*

so•ci•o•ec•o•nom•ic /ˌsoʊsioʊˌikəˈnɑmɪk, ˌsoʊʃioʊˌikəˈnɑmɪk/ adj involving a combination of social and economic elements

so•ci•ol•o•gy /ˌsoʊʃiˈɑlədʒi/ noun [U] the study of society, the way that it is organized, and the way that people behave in relation to each other —**so•ci•o•log•i•cal** /ˌsoʊʃiəˈlɑdʒɪk(ə)l/ adj, **so•ci•ol•o•gist** noun [C]

sock¹ /sɑk/ noun [C] **1** a soft piece of clothing that you wear on your foot inside your shoe: *a pair of yellow socks —picture* → C5 **2** *informal* the action of hitting someone or something with a lot of force

sock² /sɑk/ verb [T] *informal* to hit someone or something with a lot of force

sock•et /ˈsɑkət/ noun [C] **1** an electrical OUTLET for connecting a piece of equipment **2** a curved space that something fits into

sod /sɑd/ noun [C/U] a piece of earth that has grass growing on it

so•da /ˈsoʊdə/ noun [C/U] **1** CLUB SODA **2 soda** or **soda pop** *American* a sweet drink with gas in it

sod•den /ˈsɑd(ə)n/ adj completely wet =SOAKING

so•di•um /ˈsoʊdiəm/ noun [U] a chemical element that is a silver-white metal and that is found in salt

so•fa /ˈsoʊfə/ noun [C] a large soft comfortable seat with arms and a back that two or three people can sit on *—picture* → CHAIR

soft /sɔft/ adj ★★★

1 not hard/firm	5 not strict enough
2 not rough/stiff	6 kind/sympathetic
3 quiet/nice	7 about water
4 pale/gentle	

1 a soft substance is easy to press or shape and is not hard or firm: *soft cheese* ♦ *The soil is fairly soft after the rain.*

2 a soft material or surface is nice to touch and not rough or stiff: *I want to get a nice soft carpet for the bedroom.* ♦ *Her skin **felt soft** to his touch.*

3 a soft sound is quiet and nice to listen to: *The engine noise was no more than a soft hum.*

4 a soft light or color is pale, gentle, and nice to look at: *Her bedroom was decorated in soft shades of pink and blue.*

5 not strict enough with other people and allowing them to do things they should not do: *You're **too soft** – I wouldn't let them behave like that.* ♦ *They accused the governor of being **soft on** crime.*

6 kind and sympathetic: *He must have **a soft heart** beneath that stern exterior.*

7 soft water does not contain many MINERALS (=natural substances) and is easy to use with soap

—**soft•ly** adv

soft•ball /ˈsɔftˌbɔl/ noun [U] a game that is similar to baseball but that is played on a smaller field and with a larger softer ball

ˈsoft ˌcopy noun [C/U] *computing* information that is in electronic form, not printed on paper

ˌsoft ˈdrink noun [C/U] a cold drink that does not contain any alcohol

ˌsoft ˈdrug noun [C] a type of illegal drug that is less harmful than other illegal drugs

soft•en /ˈsɔf(ə)n/ verb **1** [I/T] to become softer, or to make something become softer: *Simmer gently until the apple has softened.* **2** [I/T] to become kinder and less severe, or to make someone or something do this: *When Jack spoke to the children his voice softened.* **3** [T] to make something look nicer by making its color or shape less strong: *The warm light softened her features.*

PHRASAL VERB **ˌsoften sb ˈup** to make someone more likely to do what you want by being nice to them: *His strategy was to soften them up with compliments.*

ˌsoft-ˈspoken adj speaking or said in a quiet gentle voice

ˈsoft ˌtouch noun [singular] *informal* someone who is easily persuaded to do something or to give something

soft•ware /ˈsɔf(t)ˌwer/ noun [U] *computing* ★★★ the programs used by computers for doing particular jobs: *word-processing software* ♦ *You log onto our website, then download and install the software.* ♦ *software companies/developers* → HARDWARE

sog•gy /ˈsɑgi/ adj wet and soft

soil¹ /sɔɪl/ noun [C/U] ★★★ the substance on the surface of the Earth in which plants grow: *The dry rocky soil is suitable for planting vines.* ♦ *She scraped away some soil and grasped the top of the root.*

PHRASE **on British/U.S./Japanese etc. soil** in the U.K., the U.S., Japan, etc.: *the presence of foreign troops on Canadian soil*

soil² /sɔɪl/ verb [T] *formal* to make something dirty —**soiled** /sɔɪld/ adj

sol•ace /ˈsɑləs/ noun [singular/U] something that makes you feel better when you are sad or upset

S

so•lar /ˈsoʊlər/ adj relating to the Sun, or coming from the Sun

ˌsolar ˈenergy noun [U] energy that uses the power of the Sun's light and heat

ˌsolar ˈpanel noun [C] a piece of equipment that uses energy from the Sun in order to create power

ˈsolar ˌsystem, the noun [singular] the Sun and the group of planets that move around it

sold the past tense and past participle of **sell**[1]

sol•dier /ˈsoʊldʒər/ noun [C] ★★ someone who is a member of an army

ˌsold ˈout adj if an event is sold out, all the tickets for it have been sold

sole[1] /soʊl/ adj the sole person or thing is the only one of a particular type=ONLY: *She is the sole survivor of the crash.* ♦ *His sole purpose in going there was to see Kelly.*

sole[2] /soʊl/ noun **1** [C] the flat bottom part of your foot —*picture* → C14 **2** [C] the bottom part of your shoe that goes under your foot **3** [C/U] a flat fish that lives in the ocean, or this fish eaten as food

sole•ly /ˈsoʊlli/ adv involving nothing except the person or thing mentioned

sol•emn /ˈsɑləm/ adj involving serious behavior, attitudes, or intentions —**so•lem•ni•ty** /səˈlemnəti/ noun [U], **sol•emn•ly** adv

so•lic•it /səˈlɪsɪt/ verb **1** [T] *formal* to ask people for something such as money or support **2** [I/T] to offer to have sex with someone in exchange for money **3** [I/T] *American* to try to sell something by visiting people and persuading them to buy it

so•lic•i•tor /səˈlɪsɪtər/ noun [C] **1** *American* someone who sells something by visiting people and trying to persuade them to buy it **2** the law officer in some local governments **3** in the U.K., a lawyer who gives legal advice, writes legal contracts, and represents people in the lower courts of law

sol•id[1] /ˈsɑlɪd/ adj ★★

1 not liquid/gas	5 with no pauses
2 with no holes	6 continuous
3 strong	7 of one color
4 with no bad parts	

1 a solid substance is firm and hard and is not a liquid or a gas: *The lake was frozen solid.*

2 a solid object or shape does not have any holes or empty space inside it: *a solid block of ice* → HOLLOW

3 strong enough not to break or become damaged easily: *the solid stone walls of the church* ♦ *The containers have to be solid enough to withstand pressure.*

4 completely good, with no mistakes or bad parts: *Would the evidence be solid enough to convince a jury?* ♦ *She gave another solid performance.*

5 with no pauses or interruptions: *I can't believe I slept for twelve hours solid.* ♦ *It rained for a solid week.*

6 a solid line is continuous, with no breaks in it: ***a solid line of traffic***

7 consisting of one substance or one color only: *a solid oak bookcase* ♦ *solid silver cutlery* ♦ *a solid blue screen*

—**so•lid•i•ty** /səˈlɪdəti/ noun [U], **sol•id•ly** adv

sol•id[2] /ˈsɑlɪd/ noun **1** [C] *technical* a substance that is not a liquid or a gas **2** [C] a shape that is not flat but that can be measured in height, depth, and width **3 solids** [plural] food that is not liquid

sol•i•dar•i•ty /ˌsɑlɪˈderəti/ noun [U] the support that people in a group give each other because they have the same opinions or goals

so•lid•i•fy /səˈlɪdɪˌfaɪ/ verb [I/T] to become solid, or to make something become solid

sol•i•tar•y /ˈsɑləˌteri/ adj **1** tending to spend a lot of time alone **2** done or experienced by someone who is alone **3** in a place or situation where there are no other people or things of the same type

ˌsolitary conˈfinement noun [U] a punishment in which a prisoner is kept alone

sol•i•tude /ˈsɑləˌtud/ noun [U] the state of being completely alone

so•lo[1] /ˈsoʊloʊ/ noun [C] a piece of music that is performed by one person

so•lo[2] /ˈsoʊloʊ/ adj, adv **1** done by one person alone **2** playing or singing alone

so•lo•ist /ˈsoʊloʊɪst/ noun [C] someone who performs a musical solo

so ˈlong interjection *informal* used for saying goodbye to someone who you know well

sol•u•ble /ˈsɑljəb(ə)l/ adj able to mix with a liquid and become part of the liquid ≠ INSOLUBLE

so•lu•tion /səˈluʃ(ə)n/ noun [C] ★★

1 a way to solve a problem or deal with a bad situation: *Putting children in prison is not the solution.* ♦ *The committee has failed to come up with any **solutions for** the crisis.* ♦ *UN leaders are working hard to find **a** peaceful **solution to** the conflict.* ♦ *Solar energy **offers a** low cost **solution** to our fuel problems.*

2 the answer to a question in a game or a problem in mathematics

3 a liquid that is formed by mixing a liquid with another substance

Words often used with solution

*Adjectives often used with **solution** (sense 1)*

- **ideal, peaceful, possible, practical, satisfactory, simple, workable** + SOLUTION: used about different types of solution

solve /sɑlv/ verb [T] ★★

1 to find a solution to something that is causing difficulties: *solve a crisis/dispute/conflict* ♦ *We can help you **solve** your financial **problems**.*

2 to find the reason or explanation for something: *solve a mystery/puzzle/riddle* ♦ *solve a case/crime/murder* (=find out who committed a crime)

3 to find the answer to a question in a game or a problem in mathematics: *solve an equation*

sol•vent[1] /ˈsɑlvənt/ noun [C] a liquid that you add to a substance in order to change it into a liquid

sol•vent[2] /ˈsɑlvənt/ adj able to pay money that you owe ≠ INSOLVENT

som•ber /ˈsɑmbər/ adj **1** serious, or sad **2** dark in color

S

som•bre /ˈsɑmbər/ the British spelling of somber

some /*weak* səm, *strong* sʌm/ grammar word ★★★

> Some can be:
> - a **determiner**: *I brought her some flowers.* ♦ *She married some guy she met on the boat.*
> - a **pronoun**: *The cake's wonderful. Won't you have some?* ♦ *Some of the apples were rotten.*
> - an **adverb**: *The car stopped some twenty-five yards from where we were standing.*

1 an amount or number used for referring to an amount or number, without saying how much or how many: *Let me give you some advice.* ♦ *Tomatoes were only 70 cents a pound, so I bought some.* ♦ *I met some really interesting people at the party.* ♦ *I just wanted **some more** information about language courses.*

> - In negative sentences and questions **any** is usually used: *There aren't any classes today.* ♦ *Do you have any money?*
> - In positive statements and questions expecting the answer "yes" **some** is usually used: *I have some news for you.* ♦ *Would you like some soup?*

2 part of an amount or number used for showing that you are only referring to part of an amount, group, or number and not all of it: ***Some** kids are more adventurous than **others**.* ♦ ***Some** people like cats and **some** don't.* ♦ *I've forgotten **some of** the details.*
3 used for referring to a person or thing without being specific used for referring to a person or thing without saying exactly which one: *There must have been some mistake.* ♦ *Some fool drove into the back of my car.*
4 a fairly large amount or number used for emphasizing that you are talking about a fairly large amount or number: *It took some courage to speak out against her employer.* ♦ *We've been waiting here **for some time** already.*
5 used before a number that is not exact used for showing that you are guessing a number: *Some 130,000 people live in the city.*
6 to a small degree *American very informal* to a small degree but not very much: *They criticized me personally, and that hurt me some.*

some•bod•y /ˈsʌmbədi, ˈsʌmˌbɑdi/ pronoun ★★★ someone: *Somebody called while you were out.* ♦ *When things go wrong, you always say it's **somebody else's** fault.*

some•day /ˈsʌmˌdeɪ/ adv at some time in the future even though you do not know when: *Someday I'll meet the right woman and we'll get married.*

some•how /ˈsʌmhaʊ/ adv ★★
1 in some way, or by some method, that you do not know or understand exactly: *Somehow he managed to pass all his final exams.*
2 for some reason that you do not know or cannot explain: *Somehow, it was easier to deal with him when he was alone.*

some•one /ˈsʌmwʌn/ pronoun ★★★ used for referring to a person when you do not know or do not say who the person is: *I can't find my calculator – someone must have taken it.* ♦ *I've invited someone special that I want you to meet.* ♦ *His wife told him she was in love with **someone else**.*

some•place /ˈsʌmpleɪs/ adv *American* somewhere: *My glasses have to be around here someplace.*

som•er•sault /ˈsʌmərˌsɔlt/ noun [C] a movement in which you form your body into a ball and roll forward or BACKWARD on the ground

some•thing /ˈsʌmθɪŋ/ pronoun ★★★
1 used for referring to a thing, idea, fact, etc. when you do not know or do not say exactly what it is: *I need to buy something for Ted's birthday.* ♦ *Would you like something to drink?* ♦ *Be quiet – I have **something important** to tell you.* ♦ *Jake looks pale – is there **something wrong** with him?* ♦ *I'd love to quit my job and do **something else** with my life.* ♦ *He's always complaining about **something or other**.* ♦ *We should call **or something** and make sure she's all right.* ♦ *Why doesn't the government **do something about** fuel prices?*
2 used for giving a description or amount that is not exact: *The house looks **something like** a castle.* ♦ *A small house in the area costs **something around** $100,000.*

PHRASES **be really/quite something** *spoken* to be very impressive: *What Noreen's done with the business is quite something.*
be something of a 1 used for showing that you are not being very definite in a description: *Woods's performance in the tournament was something of a disappointment.* **2** used for emphasizing that someone is fairly good at something: *My grandmother was something of a poet.*
have something to do with sth used for saying that something is related to something else: *I can't always open my e-mails – it has something to do with the type of attachment they come with.*
that's something *spoken* used for saying that one fact is good, although the general situation is not good: *"I have only enough money for basic necessities." "Well, that's something."*
there is something about used for saying that someone or something has a particular quality but that you are not certain what it is: *There was something about his face that reminded me of my uncle.*
→ UP[1]

some•time /ˈsʌmtaɪm/ adv at a time that you do not know exactly or have not yet decided: *I'd love to visit Norway sometime.* ♦ *Jessica got back from Denver sometime last week.*

some•times /ˈsʌmtaɪmz/ adv ★★★ on some occasions, but not always: *Sometimes it's so cold I don't even want to leave the house.* ♦ *My dad cooks dinner sometimes, but usually my mom does it.*

some•way /ˈsʌmˌweɪ/ adv *American informal* in some way, or by some method that you do not know or understand exactly = SOMEHOW: *We'll get the money someway – don't worry.*

some•what /ˈsʌmwɑt, ˈsʌmhwɑt/ adv to some

S

degree, but not to a large degree: *The situation has improved somewhat during the past year.* ♦ *His behavior has been somewhat unreasonable.*

some•where /ˈsʌmwer/ adv ★★★
1 used for referring to a place when you do not know or do not say exactly where: *I think I've seen you somewhere before.* ♦ *I've lost my watch, but it must be somewhere in the house.* ♦ *Let's go somewhere nice for dinner.* ♦ *If we don't provide a good service, customers will go* ***somewhere else****.*
2 used when giving an amount that is not exact: *You will earn* ***somewhere between*** *$20,000 and $25,000.* ♦ *I'd say there were* ***somewhere around*** *50 people at the meeting.*
PHRASE **be getting somewhere** to be making some progress: *I think at last we're getting somewhere.*

son /sʌn/ noun [C] ★★★ your male child: *My younger son is a doctor.* ♦ *He was* ***the son of*** *an eminent scientist.* —*picture* → FAMILY TREE

so•na•ta /səˈnɑtə/ noun [C] a piece of classical music for the piano, or for one instrument and a piano

song /sɔŋ/ noun ★★★
1 [C] a piece of music with words that you sing: *She knew the words to every song that came on the radio.* ♦ *a popular/patriotic/folk song* ♦ *He* ***sang*** *a beautiful love* ***song****.*
2 [U] the art or activity of singing: *festivals of traditional music and song*
3 [C/U] the musical sound that a bird makes

song•writ•er /ˈsɔŋˌraɪtər/ noun [C] someone who writes songs

son•ic /ˈsɑnɪk/ adj *technical* relating to sound or sound waves

ˈson-in-ˌlaw noun [C] the husband of your daughter —*picture* → FAMILY TREE

son•net /ˈsɑnɪt/ noun [C] a type of poem with 14 lines

soon /sun/ adv ★★★
1 within a short time: *If we don't leave soon, we're going to miss our bus.* ♦ *Mom called and said she'd be home soon.* ♦ *If he doesn't show up pretty soon, I'm leaving.* ♦ *Danny showed up* ***soon after*** *you left.*
2 quickly: ***How soon*** *can this package be delivered to New York?* ♦ *Helen wants you to call her back* ***as soon as possible****.*
PHRASES **as soon as** immediately after something: *I'll call you as soon as I get home from work.*
I would just as soon do sth *spoken* used for saying what you would prefer to do: *I'd just as soon stay at home.*

soon•er /ˈsunər/ adv earlier than expected: *The announcement came sooner than we expected.* ♦ *The investigation may be completed sooner than previously thought.*
PHRASES **the sooner the better** as soon as possible: *You'll have to face her, and the sooner the better.*
sooner or later definitely at some later time, although you do not know exactly when: *The whole thing was going to go wrong sooner or later.*
the sooner...the sooner... used for saying that you want something to happen soon so that something else can also happen: *The sooner you do your homework, the sooner you can go out.*

soot /sʊt/ noun [U] a dirty black powder that is produced when you burn something such as coal —**soot•y** adj

soothe /suð/ verb [T] **1** to make someone more calm when they are feeling worried or upset **2** to make something less sore or painful —**sooth•ing** adj, **sooth•ing•ly** adv

so•phis•ti•cat•ed /səˈfɪstɪˌkeɪtəd/ adj
1 knowing a lot about things such as culture, fashion, and the modern world ≠ UNSOPHISTICATED: *sophisticated dinner-table conversation* **2** knowing and understanding a lot about a subject: *Consumers are getting more sophisticated.*
3 complicated and advanced in design ≠ UNSOPHISTICATED —**so•phis•ti•ca•tion** /səˌfɪstɪˈkeɪʃ(ə)n/ noun [U]

soph•o•more /ˈsɑfəˌmɔr/ noun [C] *American* a student in the second year of college or high school

soph•o•mor•ic /ˌsɑfəˈmɔrɪk/ adj *American* silly in a way that is typical of a child

sop•ping /ˈsɑpɪŋ/ or **ˌsopping ˈwet** adj *informal* completely wet = SOAKING

so•pran•o /səˈprɑnoʊ/ noun [C] a girl, woman, or boy with the highest type of voice for singing

sor•cer•y /ˈsɔrs(ə)ri/ noun [U] magic that is done with the help of evil spirits

sor•did /ˈsɔrdɪd/ adj immoral, dishonest, or unpleasant

sore¹ /sɔr/ adj painful and uncomfortable, usually as a result of an injury, infection, or too much exercise: *a sore throat* ♦ *I always feel stiff and sore after gardening.*
PHRASE **a sore point/spot/subject** something that makes you upset, angry, or embarrassed when someone mentions it

sore² /sɔr/ noun [C] a small painful area of skin that is injured or infected

sore•ly /ˈsɔrli/ adv very much

so•ror•i•ty /səˈrɔrəti/ noun [C] a social club for women students at a U.S. university or college

S

sor•row /ˈsɑroʊ/ noun **1** [U] great sadness **2** [C] an event or problem that makes someone feel very sad —**sor•row•ful** adj

sor•ry /ˈsɑri/ adj ★★★
1 ashamed, embarrassed, or unhappy about something that you have done: *Tell your sister you're sorry!* ♦ *He wasn't* ***sorry for*** *hitting the other boy.* ♦ **+(that)** *I'm sorry I behaved in such a childish way.*
2 feeling sadness or sympathy for someone because something bad has happened to them: *I am* ***sorry to hear*** *that your father died.* ♦ *I'm* ***sorry about*** *your losing your job.*
3 disappointed about a situation, and wishing you could change it: **+(that)** *I'm sorry you have decided to leave the company.*
PHRASES **feel sorry for sb** to feel sympathy for someone because they are in a difficult or unpleasant situation: *I feel sorry for the guys who have to work night shifts.*
feel sorry for yourself to feel sad about your life instead of trying to do things that could make you feel better: *Instead of sitting around feeling sorry for yourself, go out and socialize.*
sorry or **I'm sorry** *spoken* **1** used for telling

someone that you are ashamed or unhappy about something that you have done that has hurt or upset them: *I'm sorry – I shouldn't have blamed you.* ♦ *Sorry, I didn't mean to step on your foot.* **2** used in a social situation as a way of asking someone to forgive you for doing something that is rude or embarrassing: *Sorry, I should have called to let you know I'd be late.* ♦ *I'm **sorry about** the misunderstanding.* **3** used for politely interrupting someone, especially to ask them a question: *Sorry, do you know what time it is?* ♦ *I'm **sorry for** interrupting, but you have a phone call.* **4** used for politely asking someone to repeat something that they have said: *I'm sorry, what was your name again?* **5** used for interrupting yourself in order to correct a mistake that you have made while speaking: *You need to catch the number 3, sorry, the number 23 bus to Market Street.*

sort¹ /sɔrt/ noun [C] ★ a group or type of people or things with the same qualities or features =KIND, TYPE: *What sort are you looking for?* ♦ *Is this a joke **of some sort**?* ♦ *Mistakes **of this sort** happen every day.* ♦ *He was asking us **all sorts of** questions about you.* ♦ *In that **sort of** situation Tom tends to panic.*

PHRASES **of sorts** of a type that is not exactly the same as the actual thing, or not as good as the actual thing: *She's an artist of sorts.*

sort of *spoken* **1** slightly, or in some ways: *"Aren't you hungry?" "Sort of. I'm mostly just tired."* **2** similar, but not exactly the same: *It's sort of a shiny blue-gray color.*

sort² /sɔrt/ verb [T] ★★ to arrange things in groups or in a particular order: **sort sth by sth** *Once the data is collected, the computer will sort it by date.* ♦ **sort sth into sth** *Sort the letters into three piles.*

PHRASAL VERBS **ˌsort sth ˈout 1** to get rid of things that you do not need and arrange things that you do need neatly: *I need to **sort out the mess** on my desk.* **2** to deal with a difficult situation successfully: *This matter could be sorted out if they would just sit down and talk.*

ˈsort through sth to look at a lot of things in order to find something: *Police are now sorting through boxes of documents trying to find evidence.*

ˈso-ˌso adj, adv *informal* not good enough to be described as good

sought the past tense and past participle of seek

sought-af•ter /ˈsɔt ˌæftər/ adj wanted by many people but not easy to get

soul /soʊl/ noun ★

1 [C] the part of a person that is capable of thinking and feeling: *Deep in your **heart and soul** you must know that this is wrong.*

2 [C] a person: *I promise I won't tell a soul.*

3 soul or **soul music** [U] a type of African American music in which the voice of the singer and the words of the songs express deep emotions

4 [C] the spiritual part of a person that most religions believe continues to exist after their body dies

soul•ful /ˈsoʊlfəl/ adj expressing deep emotions, especially sadness

soul•less /ˈsoʊlləs/ adj not at all interesting or attractive

soul-search•ing /ˈsoʊl ˌsɜrtʃɪŋ/ noun [U] careful thought about your beliefs or actions because you want to behave in a moral way

sound¹ /saʊnd/ noun ★★★

1 [C] something that you can hear: *Laura didn't **make a sound** as she left the room.* ♦ *the **sound of** voices/laughter/footsteps*

2 [U] the loudness of a radio, television, etc. =VOLUME: *Turn the sound up a little – I can't hear.*

PHRASES **by the sound of it** used for saying that you are basing your ideas on what you have heard or read: *He's pretty sick by the sound of it.*

like the sound of sth to be pleased by something that you have heard or read: *A vacation in Greece? I like the sound of that!*

> **Types of sound**
> - **bang** a sound like an explosion
> - **clank** a sound like two heavy pieces of metal knocking together
> - **crash** a sound like a large object falling to the ground and breaking
> - **creak** a sound like the sound that is made by an old door when you push it open slowly
> - **rattle** a sound like a loose object hitting another object several times
> - **squeak** a sound like the noise that a mouse makes
> - **thud** a sound like something heavy falling to the ground

sound² /saʊnd/ verb ★★★

1 [linking verb] to seem good, bad, interesting, exciting, etc. based on what you have heard, read, or know: ***It sounds as if** he's never home.* ♦ *You make it **sound as though** he is the most boring man in the world.* ♦ *Costa Rica **sounds like** a great place for a relaxing vacation.*

2 [linking verb] to show a particular emotion or quality in your voice: *He sounded a little bit annoyed.* ♦ ***It sounds as if** you're getting a cold.*

3 [I/T] to produce a sound, or to make something produce a sound: *The sirens sounded, warning of a tornado.* ♦ *Trains are required to sound their whistles as they approach a crossing.*

4 [T] to express a particular attitude or opinion: *Officials sounded a hopeful note about building the new school.*

PHRASE **sounds good/great etc.** *spoken* used for telling someone that their idea or suggestion seems like a good one: *"How about dinner and a movie tonight?" "Sounds great."*

PHRASAL VERB **ˌsound sb ˈout** to try to find out someone's opinions by talking to them: *Candidates will be sounding out voters during the months before the election.*

sound³ /saʊnd/ adj

1 effective/reliable	4 in good condition
2 thorough	5 about sleep
3 healthy	

1 involving the use of good judgment, and therefore likely to be effective or reliable

≠ UNSOUND: *Administrators should make sure the programs are legally sound.* ♦ *He will be able to offer you sound advice and guidance.* **2** thorough: *a sound understanding of basic teaching skills* **3** healthy: *a sound heart* **4** safe, or in good condition: *Investigators found the airplane to be structurally sound.* **5** a sound sleep is one that it is difficult to wake you from

> **Words often used with sound**
>
> *Nouns often used with* ***sound*** *(adj, sense 1)*
>
> ■ SOUND + **advice, approach, decision, judgment, principle**: used about ways of thinking or behaving that are sensible and likely to be effective

sound⁴ /saʊnd/ adv **sound asleep** sleeping very well

ˈsound ˌbite noun [C] a short comment by a politician or other famous person that gets people's attention

ˈsound ˌcard noun [C] *computing* a part inside a computer that changes information into sounds that you can hear

ˈsound efˌfects noun [plural] the special recorded sounds in a movie, television, or radio show

sound•ly /ˈsaʊn(d)li/ adv **1** thoroughly: *soundly beaten/defeated/rejected* **2** if you sleep soundly, you sleep well and it is difficult to wake you

sound•track /ˈsaʊn(d)ˌtræk/ noun [C] the music that is played during a movie or television program, or a CD of this music

soup /sup/ noun [C/U] ★ a liquid food that is made by cooking meat, fish, or vegetables with water: *a bowl of soup* ♦ *chicken/tomato/potato soup*

ˈsoup ˌkitchen noun [C] a place where poor people can go in order to get a free hot meal

sour¹ /saʊr/ adj **1** with a taste like a lemon **2** sour milk has an unpleasant taste or smell because it is not fresh anymore **3** unpleasant, unfriendly, or in a bad mood: *a sour look*

PHRASE **go/turn sour** to be unsuccessful, or to develop in a way that is not satisfactory

sour² /saʊr/ verb [I/T] to stop being successful or satisfactory, or to make something do this

source /sɔrs/ noun [C] ★★

1 a person, place, or thing that provides something that you need or want: *a light/power/energy source* ♦ *A garden was* ***the source of*** *inspiration for the painting.*

2 someone who provides information for a reporter: *The article quoted a senior source at the UN.*

3 the cause of a problem, or the place where it began: *Her son was* ***a constant source of*** *worry to her.*

4 the beginning of a river or stream

south¹ /saʊθ/ noun ★★★

1 [U] the direction that is on your right when you are facing the rising sun: *driving from south to north*

2 the south [singular] the part of a place that is in the south: *Did you like living in the south?*

→ DEEP SOUTH

south² /saʊθ/ adv toward the south: *A room that faces south gets more sunlight.* ♦ *They live 20 minutes south of Dallas.*

south³ /saʊθ/ adj **1** in the south, or facing toward the south **2** a south wind blows from the south

south•bound /ˈsaʊθˌbaʊnd/ adj going toward the south

south•east¹ /ˌsaʊθˈist/ noun **1** [U] the direction that is between south and east **2 the southeast** [singular] the part of a country that is in the southeast: *Another storm has brought snow to the southeast.*

south•east² /ˌsaʊθˈist/ adj in the southeast, or facing toward the southeast —**south•east** adv

south•east•er•ly /ˌsaʊθˈistərli/ adj **1** a southeasterly wind blows from the southeast **2** toward or in the southeast

south•east•ern /ˌsaʊθˈistərn/ adj in or from the SOUTHEAST of a country or place

south•er•ly /ˈsʌðərli/ adj **1** a southerly wind blows from the south **2** toward or in the south

south•ern /ˈsʌðərn/ adj ★★ in or from the south of a place: *southern California* ♦ *the southern shore of the lake*

south•ern•er /ˈsʌðərnər/ noun [C] someone who lives or was born in the southern part of a country

south•ern•most /ˈsʌðərnˌmoʊst/ adj farthest toward the south

ˌSouth ˈPole, the the point on the Earth that is the farthest south

south•ward¹ /ˈsaʊθwərd/ adv toward the south

south•ward² /ˈsaʊθwərd/ adj toward or in the south

south•wards /ˈsaʊθwərdz/ adv SOUTHWARD

south•west¹ /ˌsaʊθˈwest/ noun **1** [U] the direction that is between south and west **2 the southwest** [singular] the part of a country that is in the southwest: *There are reports of heavy fighting in the southwest.*

south•west² /ˌsaʊθˈwest/ adj in the southwest, or facing toward the southwest —**south•west** adv

south•west•er•ly /ˌsaʊθˈwestərli/ adj **1** a southwesterly wind blows from the southwest **2** toward or in the southwest

south•west•ern /ˌsaʊθˈwestərn/ adj in or from the SOUTHWEST of a country or place

sou•ve•nir /ˌsuvəˈnɪr/ noun [C] something that you buy to remind you of a place that you visited on vacation or of a special event

sov•er•eign¹ /ˈsɑvrən/ adj a sovereign nation rules itself

sov•er•eign² /ˈsɑvrən/ noun [C] *formal* a king or queen

sov•er•eign•ty /ˈsɑvrənti/ noun [U] **1** the right of a country to rule itself **2** the right to rule a country

So•vi•et /ˈsoʊviət, ˈsoʊviˌet/ adj from or relating to the former U.S.S.R.

sow¹ /soʊ/ (past participle **sown** /soʊn/ or **sowed** /soʊd/) verb [T] to plant seeds in the ground

sow² /saʊ/ noun [C] an adult female pig

sown a past participle of sow¹

soy•bean /ˈsɔɪˌbin/ noun [C] *American* the seed of a plant, used for making food and oil

soy sauce /ˈsɔɪ ˌsɔs/ noun [U] a dark brown sauce made from soybeans

spa /spɑ/ noun [C] a place with a natural supply of MINERAL water where people go to improve their health

space¹ /speɪs/ noun ★★★

1 empty/available area	4 area everything is in
2 area for purpose	5 period of time
3 beyond atmosphere	+ PHRASE

1 [C/U] an empty or available area: *We replaced the bathtub with a shower to create more space.* ♦ *Their voices sounded loud in the small space.* ♦ *The nursery has* ***space*** *for 48 children.* ♦ *You can grow herbs in the* ***spaces between*** *the plants.* → PLACE
2 [C/U] an area used for a particular purpose: *a parking space* ♦ *Newspapers make money from selling advertising space.*
3 [U] all of the universe outside the Earth's atmosphere: *a space mission* ♦ *The crew have been living* ***in space*** *for over three months.*
4 [U] the area in which everything exists: *different points in space and time*
5 [singular] a period of time: *It was an amazing achievement in such a short* ***space of time.*** ♦ ***In the space of*** *36 hours, I had traveled halfway around the world.*
PHRASE **look/stare into space** to look ahead for a long time but not see anything, because you are thinking about something

space² /speɪs/ verb [T] to arrange objects, events, etc. so that they are a particular time or distance apart

space•craft /ˈspeɪsˌkræft/ (plural **space•craft**) noun [C] a vehicle that can travel in space

ˈspace ˌheater noun [C] *American* a small piece of equipment that you use for heating a particular area

ˈspace ˌprobe noun [C] a vehicle containing cameras and other equipment that is sent into space to collect information and send it back to Earth

S

space•ship /ˈspeɪsˌʃɪp/ noun [C] a SPACECRAFT

ˈspace ˌshuttle noun [C] a vehicle that travels into space and back to Earth and that LANDS like an airplane

ˈspace ˌstation noun [C] a laboratory in space where people can live for long periods

spa•cious /ˈspeɪʃəs/ adj with a lot of space inside

spade /speɪd/ noun **1** [C] a SHOVEL used for digging **2** [C] a playing card with a pattern that is like a pointed black leaf *—picture* → C16 **3 spades** [plural] the SUIT (=group) of playing cards that has a pattern on them that is like a pointed black leaf: *the ace of spades*

spa•ghet•ti /spəˈgeti/ noun [U] a type of pasta that is in the form of long thin pieces like string

spam /spæm/ noun [U] *computing* e-mails that are sent to large numbers of people on the Internet, especially when these are not wanted

span¹ /spæn/ noun [C] **1** the amount of time that something lasts: *Kids these days have a very limited attention span.* → LIFESPAN **2** the width of something

span² /spæn/ verb [T] **1** to last for a particular period of time: *His career spanned half a century.* **2** to cross or cover an area of water or land: *a bridge spanning the Missouri River*

span•iel /ˈspænjəl/ noun [C] a type of small dog with long ears and long shiny hair

spank /spæŋk/ verb [T] to hit a child on their BOTTOM with an open hand

spar /spɑr/ verb [I] to practice fighting with someone

spare¹ /sper/ adj ★
1 kept in addition to other similar things, so that you can use it if you need it: *a spare key/battery* ♦ *Bring a towel and some spare clothes.*
2 available: *Do you have any spare room in your car?*

spare² /sper/ verb [T]

1 give/lend sth	4 use sth
2 have time available	5 not harm sb/sth
3 of bad experience	+ PHRASE

1 if you can spare something, you can give or lend it to someone because you do not need it: *Can you spare a couple of dollars?* ♦ *We can't spare the staff for training sessions.* **2** if you can spare time, effort, or energy, you use it for a particular purpose: *I'm sorry, I can't spare any more energy on this problem right now.* ♦ *We arrived at the airport with just 20 minutes to spare.* **3** to prevent someone from experiencing something that is unpleasant or painful: **spare sb sth** *I want to spare her the embarrassment of asking for money.* **4** if you do not spare something, you use a lot of it in order to make something succeed: *We will spare no effort to find the murderer.* ♦ *No expense was spared in organizing the conference.* **5** *formal* to not harm or kill someone or something: *The commander was so impressed by their bravery that he spared them.*
PHRASE **money/room/time etc. to spare** more than enough money, room, time, etc.: *We have food to spare.*

spare³ /sper/ noun [C] something that you have in addition to other similar things, that you can use if you need it

spar•ing•ly /ˈsperɪŋli/ adv in small quantities

spark¹ /spɑrk/ verb [I/T] **1** to make something start: *The verdict sparked riots all over the city.* **2** to start a fire or explosion, or to make a spark

spark² /spɑrk/ noun **1** [C] a very small fire or electrical flash **2** [C/U] a strong and exciting quality or feeling: *She felt a spark of enthusiasm.*

spar•kle /ˈspɑrk(ə)l/ verb [I] **1** to shine with small points of reflected light **2** to be very lively and interesting —**spar•kle** noun [C/U]

spar•kling /ˈspɑrklɪŋ/ adj **1** shining with small points of reflected light **2** very lively and interesting **3** sparkling drinks are full of BUBBLES

ˈspark ˌplug noun [C] a small part in a car's engine that creates a SPARK that makes the fuel burn

spar•row /ˈsperoʊ/ noun [C] a small brown bird that is common in the U.S. and in northern Europe

sparse /spɑrs/ adj existing in small amounts, or very spread out —**sparse·ly** adv

spar·tan /ˈspɑrt(ə)n/ adj very simple, rather than comfortable or pleasant

spasm /ˈspæzəm/ noun [C/U] a sudden painful movement of a muscle

spat a past tense and past participle of **spit²**

spate /speɪt/ noun **a spate of sth** a large number of similar events that happen in a short period of time: *a spate of bombings*

spa·tial /ˈspeɪʃ(ə)l/ adj *technical* relating to the size, shape, and position of things and their relation to each other in space

spat·ter /ˈspætər/ verb [I/T] to throw small drops of a liquid onto a surface with a lot of force, or to be thrown onto a surface in this way

spawn¹ /spɔn/ noun [U] the eggs of a FROG or fish

spawn² /spɔn/ verb **1** [I/T] to produce spawn **2** [T] to create or produce something

speak /spik/ (past tense **spoke** /spoʊk/; past participle **spo·ken** /ˈspoʊkən/) verb ★★★

1 [I] to talk to someone about something: *We spoke yesterday.* ♦ *I phoned your office and **spoke to** your assistant.* ♦ *Let me **speak with** Jennifer and see what she thinks.* ♦ *He **spoke** movingly **about** his son's struggle with cancer.* ♦ *People **spoke of** their fear as the tornado approached.* ♦ *I know I **speak for** all of us when I say how sorry I am.* → SAY, TALK

2 [I] to use your voice to talk: *There was a long pause before she spoke again.* ♦ *He spoke so softly it was difficult to hear what he said.*

3 [T] to be able to talk in a particular language: *Do you speak Chinese?* ♦ *He speaks three languages.*

4 [I] to give a formal speech: *The governor will be **speaking at** our graduation.* ♦ *Petersen **spoke to** an audience of 2,000.*

PHRASES **broadly/generally speaking** used for showing that what you are saying is usually true, but not in every instance

no... to speak of or **nothing to speak of** used for saying that something is very small or unimportant: *She has no money to speak of.*

so to speak *spoken* used for showing that you have expressed something in an unusual way

speak for itself to be so clear or obvious that no argument is necessary: *His success as a lawyer speaks for itself.*

speaking of *spoken* used for introducing something new that is related to a subject that someone has just mentioned: *Speaking of money, have we paid our credit card bills yet?*

PHRASAL VERBS ˌ**speak ˈout** to state your opinion firmly and publicly about something

ˌ**speak ˈup 1** to talk louder **2** to say what you think instead of saying nothing

Word family: speak

*Words in the same family as **speak***

- **speaker** *n*
- **spoken** *adj*
- **unspoken** *adj*
- **outspoken** *adj*
- **speech** *n*
- **speechless** *adj*
- **unspeakable** *adj*
- **unspeakably** *adv*

speak·er /ˈspikər/ noun [C] ★★

1 someone who talks about a subject to a group: *She's a very interesting speaker.*

2 someone who is able to speak a particular language: *an English speaker*

3 someone who is talking: *expressions that show the speaker is annoyed*

4 a piece of electrical equipment that sends out sound

spear¹ /spɪr/ noun [C] a long weapon that is like a stick with one sharp pointed end

spear² /spɪr/ verb [T] to push something that is sharp and pointed into something else

spear·head /ˈspɪrˌhed/ verb [T] to lead an organized effort or activity

spe·cial¹ /ˈspeʃ(ə)l/ adj ★★★

1 different from and usually better than what is normal or ordinary: *The children can only stay up late on **special occasions**.* ♦ *You're very **special to** me.*

2 more than usual: *Special care must be taken in handling very old books.*

3 relating to one particular person, thing, or purpose: *Many sports have their own special equipment.*

spe·cial² /ˈspeʃ(ə)l/ noun [C] something that is produced for a particular time or day, for example a type of food in a restaurant or a program on television

ˌ**special efˈfects** noun [plural] the artificial images or sounds in a movie that are created with technology

spe·cial·ist /ˈspeʃ(ə)lɪst/ noun [C] ★ someone whose training, education, or experience makes them an expert in a particular subject: *a web design specialist*

spe·ci·al·i·ty /ˌspeʃiˈæləti/ noun [C] *British* a SPECIALTY

spe·cial·ize /ˈspeʃ(ə)lˌaɪz/ verb [I] to be an expert in a particular part of a subject or profession —**spe·cial·i·zation** /ˌspeʃ(ə)lɪˈzeɪʃ(ə)n/ noun [C/U]

spe·cial·ized /ˈspeʃ(ə)lˌaɪzd/ adj designed for a particular purpose, or concentrating on a particular subject

spe·cial·ly /ˈspeʃ(ə)li/ adv in a particular way, or for a particular purpose: *These coats are specially treated to be water repellent.*

ˌ**special ˈneeds** noun [plural] the particular needs of people with disabilities

spe·cial·ty /ˈspeʃ(ə)lti/ noun [C] *American* **1** a food or drink that a region or restaurant is well known for and that you cannot always get in other places **2** a particular part of a wider subject that a person concentrates on or is an expert in

spe·cies /ˈspiʃiz, ˈspisiz/ (plural **spe·cies**) noun [C] ★★ a plant or animal group whose members all have similar general features and are able to produce young plants or animals together: *the human species* ♦ *Over 120 **species of** birds have been recorded in this National Park.*

spe·cif·ic /spəˈsɪfɪk/ adj ★★★

1 involving or limited to only one particular thing or purpose: *You have to enter the information in a specific order.* ♦ *problems that are **specific to** this type of work*

2 exact and detailed: *For specific instructions, please refer to the guide.* ♦ *Can you be more specific?*

S

spe·cif·i·cal·ly /spəˈsɪfɪkli/ adv ★
1 for one particular thing or purpose: *They bought the land specifically for the purpose of building a hotel.*
2 in an exact or detailed way: *She specifically stated that she went to the station because her brother told her to.*

spec·i·fi·ca·tion /ˌspesɪfɪˈkeɪʃ(ə)n/ noun [C] an exact measurement or detailed plan about how something is to be made

spe·cif·ics /spəˈsɪfɪks/ noun [plural] the details of something: *We'll leave the lawyers to deal with the specifics.*

spec·i·fy /ˈspesɪˌfaɪ/ verb [T] to explain something in an exact and detailed way

spec·i·men /ˈspesəmən/ noun [C] **1** a small amount of something such as blood or URINE that is taken from your body so that it can be examined **2** an example of something, especially of a plant or animal

speck /spek/ noun [C] a very small spot or mark

speck·led /ˈspek(ə)ld/ adj covered with a lot of very small spots or marks

spec·ta·cle /ˈspektək(ə)l/ noun [C/U] an unusual, exciting, or impressive event or sight

spec·tac·u·lar /spekˈtækjələr/ adj extremely impressive ≠ UNSPECTACULAR —**spec·tac·u·lar·ly** adv

spec·ta·tor /ˈspekˌteɪtər/ noun [C] someone who watches a public activity or event

spec·ter /ˈspektər/ noun [C] **1** the possibility of something that is unpleasant that might happen in the future **2** *literary* a GHOST

spec·trum /ˈspektrəm/ noun [singular] **1** the whole range of ideas, qualities, situations, etc. that are possible **2** the complete range of colors into which light can be separated

spec·u·late /ˈspekjəˌleɪt/ verb **1** [I/T] to consider or discuss why something has happened **2** [I] to buy things such as STOCK and property, hoping to make a big profit later when you sell them —**spec·u·la·tor** noun [C]

spec·u·la·tion /ˌspekjəˈleɪʃ(ə)n/ noun [C/U] guesses about why something has happened or what might happen

spec·u·la·tive /ˈspekjəˌleɪtɪv, ˈspekjələtɪv/ adj **1** based on guesses or on only a little information **2** done in order to make a big profit, but with a high risk that money will be lost

sped the past tense and past participle of **speed**

speech /spitʃ/ noun ★★★
1 [C] a formal occasion when someone speaks to an audience, or the words that someone speaks to an audience: *He began his speech with a joke.* ♦ *She writes most of the president's speeches.* ♦ *She **made a** wonderful **speech**.*
2 [U] spoken language or the ability to speak: *A stroke can cause difficulties with speech.* ♦ *tapes of recorded speech* ♦ *speech development*

speech·less /ˈspitʃləs/ adj so surprised or angry that you cannot think of anything to say

speed¹ /spid/ noun ★★★
1 [C/U] the rate at which something or someone moves or works: *They were working with incredible speed.* ♦ *The main advantage of this method is its speed.* ♦ *The device measures **the speed and direction of** the wind.*
2 [C] a GEAR: *a car with a 5-speed transmission*
3 [U] an illegal drug that makes people feel as if they have a lot of energy

PHRASE **up to speed 1** *informal* with all the information that you need **2** at the speed or level that is expected

speed² /spid/ (past tense and past participle **sped** /sped/ or **speed·ed**) verb **1** [I] to move somewhere quickly: *an endless stream of traffic speeding toward the city* ♦ *I heard a car speed away.* **2** [I] to drive a car faster than the speed that is allowed **3** [T] to make something happen more quickly: *Regular exercise will help speed your recovery.*

PHRASAL VERB **ˌspeed (sth) ˈup** to move or happen faster, or to make something move or happen faster

speed·boat /ˈspidˌboʊt/ noun [C] a boat with a powerful motor that can go very fast

speed·ing¹ /ˈspidɪŋ/ noun [U] the offense of driving faster than the speed that is allowed in a particular area

speed·ing² /ˈspidɪŋ/ adj moving very fast

ˈspeed ˌlimit noun [singular] the fastest speed that is allowed for vehicles in a particular area

speed·om·e·ter /spɪˈdɑmɪtər/ noun [C] the piece of equipment in a vehicle that shows how fast it is going —*picture* → C6

speed·y /ˈspidi/ adj **1** happening very quickly **2** able to move very fast

spell¹ /spel/ verb ★
1 [I/T] to write or say the letters of a word in the correct order: *Can you spell "beautiful?"* ♦ *You've **spelled** my name **wrong**.* ♦ *Her writing is neat, but she **can't spell**.*
2 [T] to be the letters that make up a word: *L-O-V-E spells "love."*
3 [T] to show that something bad is going to happen: *That look on her face **spells trouble**.*

PHRASAL VERB **ˌspell sth ˈout 1** to say or write the letters of a word in the correct order **2** *informal* to explain something so that it is very clear

spell² /spel/ noun [C] ★
1 words or actions that are believed to make magic things happen: *The witch **cast a spell on** him.*
2 a time when you suddenly feel ill: *He has dizzy spells.*
3 a period of time, usually a short one: *After a short spell in the army, I went to college.* ♦ ***a spell of rain***

spell·bind·ing /ˈspelˌbaɪndɪŋ/ adj something that is spellbinding is so interesting that it holds your attention completely

spell·bound /ˈspelˌbaʊnd/ adj so impressed by something that you do not pay attention to anything else

spell·checker /ˈspelˌtʃekər/ noun [C] *computing* a computer program that checks and corrects the way that you spell words

spell·ing /ˈspelɪŋ/ noun **1** [U] the ability to spell **2** [C] the correct way of writing a word

S

spend /spend/ (past tense and past participle **spent** /spent/) verb ★★★
1 [I/T] to use money to pay for things: *How much money did you spend?* ♦ **spend sth on sth** *You spend too much on clothes.*
2 [T] to stay somewhere, or to do something, for a period of time: *We spent the day at the beach.* ♦ **spend sth on sth** *We have spent too much time on this problem.* ♦ **spend sth with sb** *I'm going to spend Thanksgiving with my family.* ♦ **spend sth doing sth** *He spent hours practicing.*

spend·ing /ˈspendɪŋ/ noun [U] money spent, especially by governments or large organizations

ˈspending ˌmoney noun [U] money for spending on things you want, not on things such as food and bills

spend·thrift /ˈspendˌθrɪft/ noun [C] *showing disapproval* someone who is very careless about money and spends more than they need to

spent¹ the past tense and past participle of spend

spent² /spent/ adj **1** used, and therefore no longer useful: *spent nuclear fuel* **2** *literary* very tired

sperm /spɜrm/ (plural **sperm**) noun **1** [C] a cell from a man that FERTILIZES the egg inside a woman's body **2** [U] the liquid from a man's PENIS that contains sperm = SEMEN

spew /spju/ or **ˌspew (sth) ˈout** verb [I/T] to flow out with a lot of force, or to make something do this

SPF /ˌes pi ˈef/ abbrev sun protection factor: a measurement of how much a product protects your skin from the sun

sphere /sfɪr/ noun [C] **1** an object that is round like a ball —*picture* → C8 **2** a particular area of interest, activity, or responsibility

spher·i·cal /ˈsferɪk(ə)l/ adj *technical* round like a ball

sphinx /sfɪŋks/ noun [C] an animal in ancient Greek and Egyptian MYTHS that has a lion's body and a human head

spice¹ /spaɪs/ noun **1** [U] extra interest or excitement **2** [C/U] a substance made from a plant and added to food to give it flavor

spice² /spaɪs/ PHRASAL VERB **ˌspice sth ˈup 1** to make something more interesting or exciting **2** to add spices to food to give it more flavor

spick and span /ˌspɪk ən ˈspæn/ adj *informal* very clean and neat

spic·y /ˈspaɪsi/ adj with a strong hot flavor

spi·der /ˈspaɪdər/ noun [C] a small creature with eight legs that weaves a WEB in order to catch insects

spi·der·y /ˈspaɪdəri/ adj spidery writing is messy and consists of long thin lines

spiel /ʃpil, spil/ noun [C] *informal* the things that someone says on a particular occasion, especially things that are not interesting or sincere because they sound like a prepared speech

spig·ot /ˈspɪgət/ noun [C] *American* a FAUCET on an OUTDOOR water pipe

spike /spaɪk/ noun [C] a sharp pointed piece of metal or wood —**spik·y** adj

spill¹ /spɪl/ verb ★
1 [I/T] if a liquid spills, or if you spill it, it accidentally flows out of its container: *Oil is still spilling from the ship.* ♦ **spill sth on/over sth** *I spilled coffee all over my desk.*
2 [I] if people spill out of a place, a lot of them leave at the same time

PHRASE **spill the beans** *informal* to tell someone something that should be kept secret

PHRASAL VERB **ˌspill ˈover** to spread to other areas: *The violence has spilled over to other parts of the city.*

spill

spill² /spɪl/ noun [C/U] an amount of liquid that has accidentally flowed out of its container: *an oil spill*

spin¹ /spɪn/ (past tense and past participle **spun** /spʌn/) verb ★
1 [I/T] to turn around and around quickly, or to make something do this: *The dancers were spinning in circles.* ♦ *Spin the wheel with your hand.*
2 [I] when a washing machine spins, it squeezes water out of the clothes by turning them around and around quickly
3 [I/T] to twist fibers into THREAD to make cloth
4 [T] if an insect or SPIDER spins something such as a WEB, it makes it from THREAD that it produces in its body

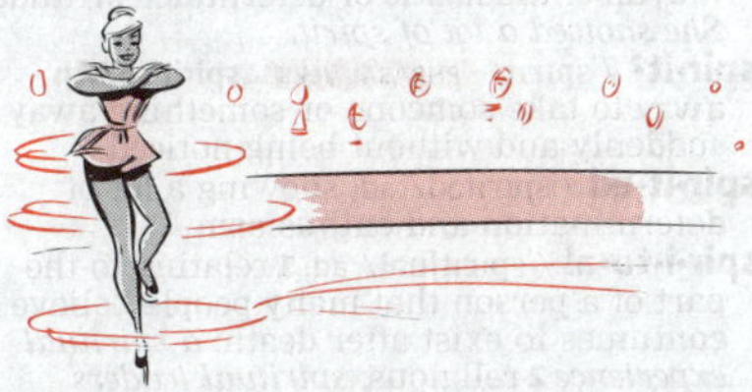
spin

spin² /spɪn/ noun **1** [C/U] a quick turning movement around and around **2** [C] *informal* a short trip for pleasure in a car **3** [singular/U] *informal* a way of giving information that makes something seem less bad

spin·ach /ˈspɪnɪdʒ/ noun [U] a vegetable with dark green leaves

spi·nal /ˈspaɪn(ə)l/ adj relating to your SPINE

ˌspinal ˈcord noun [C] the inner part of your SPINE

ˈspin ˌdoctor noun [C] someone whose job is to give information to reporters in a way that gives people a good opinion of a politician, government, or organization

spine /spaɪn/ noun [C] **1** the row of bones down the middle of your back = BACKBONE **2** the edge of a book where all the pages are attached **3** a sharp point on a plant or animal

spine·less /ˈspaɪnləs/ adj not brave or determined

ˈ**spin-off** noun [C] **1** a new product, service, television program, etc. that is based on another one that already exists **2** something good that happens unexpectedly as a result of something else

spi·ral[1] /ˈspaɪrəl/ noun [C] **1** a shape that looks like a set of circles and is made by one line curving around a central point **2** a situation that gets worse and worse: *the endless spiral of violence and hatred* —**spi·ral** adj

spi·ral[2] /ˈspaɪrəl/ verb **1** [I/T] to move in the shape of a spiral, or to make something do this **2** [I] to become worse and worse: *Crime has begun to spiral out of control.*

spire /ˈspaɪr/ noun [C] the pointed top of a church tower

spir·it[1] /ˈspɪrɪt/ noun ★

1 real meaning	5 sb's attitude
2 non-physical part of sb	6 attitude of group
3 imaginary creature	7 determination
4 mood	

1 [U] the general or real meaning of something: *Their actions go against **the spirit of** the agreement.*

2 [C] the part of a person that many people believe continues to exist after death: *His spirit will always be with us.*

3 [C] an imaginary creature with special powers: *evil spirits*

4 spirits [plural] your mood at a particular time: *She tried singing to **keep her spirits up**.* ♦ *Dad's **in high spirits** today, isn't he?*

5 [C/U] your attitude to life or to other people: *He was always an independent spirit.*

6 [singular/U] the attitude of people in a group: ***a spirit of cooperation*** ♦ *We need more **team spirit**.*

7 [U] an enthusiastic or determined attitude: *She showed a lot of spirit.*

spir·it[2] /ˈspɪrɪt/ PHRASAL VERB ˌ**spirit sb/sth aˈway** to take someone or something away suddenly and without being noticed

spir·it·ed /ˈspɪrɪtəd/ adj showing a lot of determination and enthusiasm

spir·i·tu·al /ˈspɪrɪtʃuəl/ adj **1** relating to the part of a person that many people believe continues to exist after death: *a spiritual experience* **2** religious: *spiritual leaders* —**spir·i·tu·al·ly** adv

spir·i·tu·al·ism /ˈspɪrɪtʃuəˌlɪzəm/ noun [U] the belief that dead people are able to communicate with people who are still alive —**spir·i·tu·al·ist** noun [C]

spit[1] /spɪt/ (past tense and past participle **spit** or **spat** /spæt/) verb [I/T] to force something that is liquid or solid out from your mouth

PHRASE **spit it out** *spoken* used for telling someone to hurry and say something that they are nervous or embarrassed about saying

spit[2] /spɪt/ noun **1** [U] *informal* the clear liquid that is in your mouth =SALIVA **2** [C] a long sharp piece of metal that is used for holding and turning meat as it cooks over a fire

spite[1] /spaɪt/ noun [U] ★ a feeling of wanting to upset someone or to cause problems for them: *She refused to help us **out of spite**.*

PHRASE **in spite of sth** used for referring to a fact that makes something else surprising =DESPITE: *In spite of feeling tired, we decided to go out.* ♦ *The house will certainly sell, **in spite of the fact** that it's overpriced.*

spite[2] /spaɪt/ verb [T] to deliberately upset someone or cause them problems

spite·ful /ˈspaɪtf(ə)l/ adj deliberately trying to upset someone or cause problems for them —**spite·ful·ly** adv

ˌ**spitting ˈimage** noun [C] *informal* someone who looks exactly like someone else

splash[1] /splæʃ/ verb **1** [I/T] if a liquid splashes, or if you splash it, it moves or hits something noisily **2** [I] to move around noisily in water

PHRASE **be splashed across sth** if words, a story, or pictures are splashed across a newspaper, they are large and easy to see

splash[2] /splæʃ/ noun [C] **1** the sound of liquid hitting something, or the sound of something falling into a liquid **2** a mark made by a liquid splashing **3** a small amount of bright color

splat·ter /ˈsplætər/ verb [I/T] if a liquid splatters, or if it splatters something, drops of it hit a surface violently

splay /spleɪ/ or ˌ**splay (sth) ˈout** verb [I/T] to spread part of your body in a way that looks strange

splen·did /ˈsplendɪd/ adj *formal* very good, impressive, or enjoyable =WONDERFUL —**splen·did·ly** adv

splen·dor /ˈsplendər/ noun [U] *formal* the impressive beauty of something

splen·dour /ˈsplendər/ the British spelling of **splendor**

splice /splaɪs/ verb [T] to connect the ends of two pieces of something such as rope, so that they form one piece

splint /splɪnt/ noun [C] a piece of metal, plastic, or wood that is put next to a broken bone in order to hold it in place

splin·ter[1] /ˈsplɪntər/ noun [C] a small sharp piece of wood or glass that has broken off a bigger piece

splin·ter[2] /ˈsplɪntər/ verb [I/T] to break into small sharp pieces, or to make something do this

ˈ**splinter ˌgroup** noun [C] a group of people who have separated from a larger group because of a disagreement

split[1] /splɪt/ (past tense and past participle **split**) verb ★

1 [I/T] to divide something into several parts, or to be divided into several parts: *Let's split into groups and work separately.*

2 [T] to share something by dividing it into separate parts

3 [I/T] if something splits, or if you split it, a long thin cut or break forms in it: *How did you split your pants?* ♦ *One of the boxes fell and split open.*

PHRASES **split the difference** *spoken* to agree on an amount that is the middle point between a larger amount and a smaller one

split hairs to argue or worry about unimportant details

PHRASAL VERB ˌ**split ˈup** to end a sexual or romantic relationship

split² /splɪt/ noun [C] **1** a long thin cut or break in something **2** a disagreement that causes a group to divide into smaller groups

ˌsplit ˈsecond noun [singular] an extremely small amount of time —**ˈsplit-ˌsecond** adj

ˈsplitting ˌheadache noun [C] a very bad pain in your head

splut·ter /ˈsplʌtər/ verb *informal* **1** [I/T] to make noises with your mouth because you suddenly cannot breathe or swallow normally, or to say something while doing this **2** [I] if something such as an engine splutters, it makes a series of short noises because it is not working well —**splut·ter** noun [C]

spoil /spɔɪl/ verb ★
1 [T] to make something worse, less attractive, or less enjoyable: *Radio towers spoiled the view.* ♦ *I really hope it doesn't rain – that would spoil everything.*
2 [T] to allow a child to get everything that they want, so that they behave badly if they do not get something: *His mother **spoils him rotten*** (=spoils him very much).
3 [T] to treat someone with a lot of care and kindness: *It's Mother's Day – let them spoil you a little!*
4 [I] if food spoils, it is not safe to eat because it is too old

spoiled /spɔɪld/ adj a spoiled child behaves badly if they do not get what they want because people have always given them everything that they want

spoils /spɔɪlz/ noun [plural] *literary* the things that someone takes in a war or by stealing

spoil·sport /ˈspɔɪlˌspɔrt/ noun [C] *informal* someone who spoils someone else's enjoyment

spoilt /spɔɪlt/ adj *British* SPOILED

spoke¹ /spoʊk/ noun [C] one of the thin metal bars that connect the center of a wheel to the outside part

spoke² the past tense of **speak**

spo·ken¹ /ˈspoʊkən/ adj said, instead of being written: *examples of spoken and written English*

spo·ken² the past participle of **speak**

spokes·man /ˈspoʊksmən/ (plural **spokes·men** /ˈspoʊksmən/) noun [C] a male spokesperson

spokes·per·son /ˈspoʊksˌpɜrs(ə)n/ (plural **spokes·peo·ple** /ˈspoʊksˌpip(ə)l/) noun [C] someone whose job is to officially represent an organization and to speak to reporters

spokes·wom·an /ˈspoʊksˌwʊmən/ (plural **spokes·wom·en** /ˈspoʊksˌwɪmən/) noun [C] a female spokesperson

sponge¹ /spʌndʒ/ noun [C] a piece of a soft substance that takes in water easily and that is used for cleaning things or for washing yourself

sponge² /spʌndʒ/ verb [T] to wash someone or something with a sponge
PHRASAL VERB **ˈsponge ˌoff sb** *informal* to ask for money and other things from someone and not give anything back or pay for anything yourself

ˈsponge ˌcake noun [C/U] a very light cake made with flour, eggs, and sugar

spong·y /ˈspʌndʒi/ adj light, soft, and full of small holes

spon·sor¹ /ˈspɑnsər/ verb [T] ★
1 to pay for something such as an event or a radio or television program as a way of advertising your company or products
2 to agree to give money to someone who is going to take part in a CHARITY event —**spon·sor·ship** noun [U]

spon·sor² /ˈspɑnsər/ noun [C] **1** a person or business that pays for something such as an event or a radio or television program as a way of advertising their company or products **2** someone who agrees to give money to someone who is taking part in a CHARITY event

spon·sored /ˈspɑnsərd/ adj done in order to make money for a CHARITY: *a sponsored walk*

spon·ta·ne·ous /spɑnˈteɪniəs/ adj happening in a natural way without being planned or thought about: *spontaneous applause/cheers* —**spon·ta·ne·i·ty** /ˌspɑntəˈneɪəti/ noun [U], **spon·ta·ne·ous·ly** adv

spoof /spuf/ noun [C] a piece of entertainment that copies something in a way that is intended to make it seem funny or silly —**spoof** verb [T]

spook /spuk/ verb [T] *informal* to make someone suddenly feel frightened or nervous

spook·y /ˈspuki/ adj *informal* strange and frightening

spool /spul/ noun [C] a round object with a hole in the middle that you wind something such as string around

spoon¹ /spun/ noun [C] ★ an object that you use for eating soup and other liquid foods, and for mixing and preparing food

spoon² /spun/ verb [T] to eat or serve food with a spoon

ˈspoon-feed verb [T] to provide someone with too much help so that they do not learn how to think for themselves

spoon·ful /ˈspunfʊl/ noun [C] the amount that a spoon contains

spo·rad·ic /spəˈrædɪk/ adj not regular or frequent —**spo·rad·i·cal·ly** /spəˈrædɪkli/ adv

sport¹ /spɔrt/ noun [C] ★★★
1 a physical activity in which players or teams compete against each other: *Jess has never liked sports.* ♦ *Bob's favorite sport is tennis.* ♦ *the newspaper's sports section*
2 *informal* someone who always behaves in a reasonable way and is always willing to help: *Thanks, Shelly – you're always **such a good sport**.*

sport² /spɔrt/ verb [T] to wear something in a way that shows that you want people to notice it

sport·ing /ˈspɔrtɪŋ/ adj relating to sports

ˈsports ˌcar noun [C] a small fast car, often with a roof that you can take off

sports·cast /ˈspɔrtsˌkæst/ noun [C] *American* a radio or television program about sports —**sports·cast·er** noun [C]

sports·man /ˈspɔrtsmən/ noun [C] a man who plays sports

sports·man·like /ˈspɔrtsmənˌlaɪk/ adj fair and honest when playing sports

sports·man·ship /ˈspɔrtsmənʃɪp/ noun [U] fair and honest behavior in sports

S

sports·wear /ˈspɔrtsˌwer/ noun [U] *American* comfortable clothes that are appropriate for informal occasions

sports·wom·an /ˈspɔrtsˌwʊmən/ noun [C] a woman who plays sports

ˌsport uˈtility ˌvehicle noun [C] *American* a large vehicle with FOUR-WHEEL DRIVE that is designed to be driven on rough ground

sport·y /ˈspɔrti/ adj **1** sporty clothes are designed to be worn for sports or on informal occasions **2** a sporty car looks fast and expensive

spot¹ /spɑt/ noun [C] ★★

1 particular place	4 on TV/radio
2 small area of color	5 spotlight
3 dirty mark	+ PHRASES

1 a particular place: *We found him sitting in a sunny spot in the yard.* ♦ *one of the region's best-known tourist spots*
2 a small round area of color that is different than the color of the area around it: *The flower is yellow with red spots.*
3 a small unpleasant or dirty mark on something
4 *informal* a period of time in a television or radio program that you get to use for a particular purpose
5 *informal* a SPOTLIGHT

PHRASES **on the spot 1** in the exact place where something is happening
2 immediately

put sb on the spot to ask someone a difficult or embarrassing question

→ BLIND SPOT, HOT SPOT

spot² /spɑt/ verb [T] to notice someone or something: *Maria spotted the book lying under the chair.*

ˌspot ˈcheck noun [C] an occasion when you check someone or something without a warning that you are going to do so

spot·less /ˈspɑtləs/ adj extremely clean —**spot·less·ly** adv

S

spot·light¹ /ˈspɑtˌlaɪt/ noun **1** [C] a powerful light that shines on a small area, for example in a theater = SPOT **2 the spotlight** [singular] a situation in which you get a lot of public attention

spot·light² /ˈspɑtˌlaɪt/ verb [T] **1** to shine a spotlight on someone or something **2** to make people pay a lot of attention to someone or something

spot·ted /ˈspɑtəd/ adj covered with a pattern of spots

spot·ty /ˈspɑti/ adj **1** *American* good, successful, or effective only in some situations **2** covered with a pattern of spots

spouse /spaʊs/ noun [C] *formal* your husband or wife

spout¹ /spaʊt/ noun [C] a part of a container that is shaped like a tube and is used for pouring liquid

spout² /spaʊt/ verb **1** [I/T] if a liquid spouts from somewhere, or if something spouts it, a lot of it comes out fast and continuously **2** [T] *informal* to talk about something for a long time or in a boring way

sprain /spreɪn/ verb [T] to injure a JOINT such as your wrist by suddenly turning it too much —**sprain** noun [C], **sprained** /spreɪnd/ adj: *a sprained ankle*

sprang a past tense of **spring²**

sprawl /sprɔl/ verb [I] **1** to sit or lie with your arms and legs stretched out in a relaxed or careless way **2** to stretch over or across something in an ugly and messy way —**sprawl** noun [singular/U]

spray¹ /spreɪ/ verb [I/T] **1** if you spray a liquid, or if it sprays, very small drops of it are forced out of a container through a small hole: *The chemical is sprayed onto the crops once a week.* **2** if something sprays very small drops or pieces of a substance, or if they spray, they are thrown into the air in different directions

spray² /spreɪ/ noun **1** [C/U] a liquid that is forced out of a container in very small drops when you push a button on it **2** [U] many small drops of water that are forced into the air

spread¹ /spred/ (past tense and past participle **spread**) verb ★★

1 affect larger area	5 of information
2 open sth folded	6 make happen in stages
3 put/be in wide area	7 move arms/legs apart
4 cover with layer	+ PHRASAL VERBS

1 [I/T] to gradually affect a larger area or a large number of people or things, or to make something do this: *Rain will spread from the west this evening.* ♦ *Soldiers returning from the war spread the disease through the region.* ♦ *UN leaders hope to prevent the fighting from spreading.*
2 [T] to open something that is folded so that it covers a surface: *The map was spread on the floor.* ♦ **spread sth on/over sth** *We spread the blanket on the grass and sat down on it.*
3 [I/T] to put things in many parts of an area, or to be present in many parts of a large area: *There are 54 community colleges spread across California.*
4 [T] to cover a surface with a thin layer of a soft food: **spread sth on sth** *Maureen spread jam on her toast.* ♦ **spread sth with sth** *First, spread the bread with mayonnaise.*
5 [I/T] if information spreads, or if you spread it, it becomes known by more people than before: *Someone has been **spreading** nasty **rumors** about Stella's private life.*
6 [T] to make something happen at several times during a long period, instead of all at once: **spread sth over sth** *You can spread your payments over five years.*
7 [T] to move your arms, legs, or hands so that they are far apart = EXTEND

PHRASAL VERBS **ˌspread ˈout** if people in a group spread out, they move away from one another so that they cover a large area
ˌspread sth ˈout *same as* **spread¹** 2: *We spread our papers out on the table.*

spread² /spred/ noun **1** [singular] the growth or development of something, so that it affects a larger area or a larger number of people: *There were concerns about the spread of fighting to other regions.* **2** [C/U] a soft food that you put on bread and similar foods: *a low-fat spread* **3** [C] a long article in a newspaper or magazine: *a two-page spread* **4** [singular] a number of different things = RANGE: *You minimize risk by investing in a spread of companies.*

spread•sheet /ˈspredˌʃit/ noun [C] a CHART that is produced on a computer that shows numbers in a way that makes them easy to compare

spree /spri/ noun [C] a short period that you spend doing a lot of an enjoyable activity

sprig /sprɪg/ noun [C] a stem or very small branch that is cut from a plant

spright•ly /ˈspraɪtli/ adj healthy and full of energy despite being old

spring¹ /sprɪŋ/ noun ★★
1 [C/U] the season between winter and summer: *The garden is so beautiful **in the spring**.*
2 [C] a place where water flows up from under the ground and forms a small stream or pool
3 [C] a long thin piece of metal that is twisted into the shape of a COIL that quickly returns to its original shape after you stop stretching it
4 [C] a quick jump forward or up

spring² /sprɪŋ/ (past tense **sprang** /spræŋ/ or **sprung** /sprʌŋ/; past participle **sprung**) verb [I] **1** to jump or move quickly and with a lot of energy in a particular direction: *The young man turned to hit him, but Corbett sprang back.* ♦ *Robert sprang to his feet* (=stood quickly) *to shout at the referee.* ♦ *The door sprang open, and Jeremy appeared.* **2** to perform an action quickly and with energy or force: *"Let's get going," my father cried, springing into action.* ♦ *"She was just trying to help!" said Eric, springing to her defense.* **3** to happen or appear somewhere suddenly or unexpectedly: *Tears sprang to his eyes as he thought of Helen.*
PHRASES **spring a leak** to crack or break so that water or another liquid can get in or out: *The boat sprang a leak and quickly sank.*
spring to life to begin to be active: *The game finally sprang to life in the second half.*
PHRASAL VERBS ˈ**spring ˌfrom sth** to come from a particular place, family, or situation
ˈ**spring sth on sb** to tell someone something that they do not expect
ˌ**spring ˈup** to appear suddenly and quickly: *New Internet companies were springing up every day.*

spring•board /ˈsprɪŋˌbɔrd/ noun [C] **1** a strong board used for helping you to jump in sports such as DIVING **2** something that helps you to become successful

ˌ**spring ˈbreak** noun [C] *American* a short vacation from school that lasts for a week in March or April

ˌ**spring ˈonion** noun [C] *British* a SCALLION or GREEN ONION

spring•time /ˈsprɪŋˌtaɪm/ noun [U] *literary* the season of spring

spring•y /ˈsprɪŋi/ adj something that is springy quickly returns to its shape after you press it or walk on it

sprin•kle /ˈsprɪŋk(ə)l/ verb **1** [T] to shake small amounts of a liquid or a substance such as sugar over the surface of something: *Sprinkle soy sauce on the chicken.* ♦ *Sprinkle the grated cheese over the pasta, and serve.* **2** [I] *American* to rain slightly —**sprin•kle** noun [singular]

sprin•kler /ˈsprɪŋklər/ noun [C] **1** a piece of equipment that is used for automatically sprinkling water on a garden or yard **2** a piece of equipment on the ceiling that spreads water over the room if a fire starts

sprin•kling /ˈsprɪŋklɪŋ/ noun [C] a small amount of a liquid or a substance such as sugar that is shaken over the surface of something

sprint /sprɪnt/ verb [I] to run at a very fast speed for a short period —**sprint** noun [C]

sprint•er /ˈsprɪntər/ noun [C] a runner who takes part in short fast races

sprout¹ /spraʊt/ verb **1** [I/T] if a plant sprouts, or if it sprouts something, new leaves or SHOOTS begin to grow on it **2** [I] to suddenly appear or increase in number: *A lot of these modern buildings have sprouted suddenly along the shore of the lake.*
PHRASAL VERB ˌ**sprout ˈup** *same as* **sprout¹** 2: *New businesses began to sprout up across the country.*

sprout² /spraʊt/ noun **1** [C] a new SHOOT on a plant **2 sprouts** [plural] *American* seeds or beans that are just beginning to grow and that you eat like vegetables, for example in sandwiches or salads

spruce¹ /sprus/ noun [C] a tall tree with thin sharp leaves that do not fall off in winter

spruce² /sprus/ PHRASAL VERB ˌ**spruce sb/sth ˈup** to improve the appearance of someone or something

sprung the past tense and past participle of **spring²**

spry /spraɪ/ adj healthy and full of energy despite being old

spun the past tense and past participle of **spin¹**

spur¹ /spɜr/ noun [C] **1** a metal object on the heel of a rider's boot that the rider presses into a horse's side in order to make it go faster **2** something that encourages someone to do something
PHRASE **on the spur of the moment** if you do something on the spur of the moment, you do it suddenly and without planning it or thinking carefully about it

spur² /spɜr/ verb [T] **1** to encourage someone to do something **2** to cause something to happen
PHRASAL VERB ˌ**spur sb ˈon** *same as* **spur²** 1

spu•ri•ous /ˈspjʊriəs/ adj *formal* not based on true facts

spurn /spɜrn/ verb [T] *literary* to refuse to accept someone or something

spurt /spɜrt/ verb **1** [I/T] to come out in a sudden strong flow **2** [I] to suddenly increase in speed or energy —**spurt** noun [C]

sput•ter /ˈspʌtər/ verb **1** [I/T] to speak or say something in a confused way, because you are shocked or angry **2** [I] if an engine sputters, it makes noises like small explosions and seems likely to stop

spy¹ /spaɪ/ verb **1** [I] to work as a spy **2** [T] *literary* to notice someone or something
PHRASAL VERB ˈ**spy on sb** to watch someone secretly so that you know everything that they do

spy² /spaɪ/ noun [C] someone whose job is to find out secret information about a country or an organization = SECRET AGENT

sq. abbrev square

S

squab•ble /ˈskwɑb(ə)l/ verb [I] to argue with someone about something that is not important —**squab•ble** noun [C]

squad /skwɑd/ noun [C] **1** a department in a police force that deals with a particular type of crime **2** a small group of soldiers who do a particular job **3** a sports team

ˈsquad ˌcar noun [C] a car used by police officers

squad•ron /ˈskwɑdrən/ noun [C] a section of the military, especially of the air force

squal•id /ˈskwɑlɪd/ adj a place that is squalid is dirty and unpleasant

squall /skwɔl/ noun [C] a storm that happens suddenly

squal•or /ˈskwɑlər/ noun [U] dirty and uncomfortable conditions that people live in or work in

squan•der /ˈskwɑndər/ verb [T] to not use something such as money, time, or an opportunity in a sensible way

square¹ /skwer/ noun [C] ★★★

1 a shape with four straight sides of equal length and four RIGHT ANGLES: *The flower beds form a perfect square.* —*picture* → C8

2 an open area of land in the shape of a square with buildings around it: *The hotel is in the main square.* ♦ *They have an office near Times Square.*

3 the number that is the result of multiplying one number by itself: *The square of 3 is 9.*

PHRASE **back to square one** in the same situation that you were in before you started to do something, so that you have made no progress

square² /skwer/ adj ★★

1 in the shape of a square: *a small square garden*

2 with edges or corners that are not as curved as usual: *He had broad square shoulders.*

3 used for talking about units for measuring the area of something: *an area of over 200 square miles* ♦ *The room is less than four yards square.*

4 *informal* if two people are square, neither person owes the other anything: *You give me back six dollars and then we'll be square.*

PHRASE **a square deal** *informal* fair treatment → FAIR³

square³ /skwer/ verb [T] to multiply a number by itself

PHRASAL VERBS **ˌsquare ˈoff** *American* to prepare to start competing or fighting

ˈsquare with sth if one idea, opinion, explanation, etc. squares with another, they both seem good or reasonable

ˈsquare sth with sb to get permission from someone to do something: *I'll have to square it with the manager first.*

square•ly /ˈskwerli/ adv **1** in a clear and definite way: *Responsibility for it rested squarely on her shoulders.* **2** directly: *She turned and looked him squarely in the eye.*

ˌsquare ˈmeal noun [C] *informal* a large meal that makes you feel satisfied

ˌsquare ˈroot noun [C] a number that you multiply by itself in order to produce a particular number: *The square root of 9 is 3.*

squash¹ /skwɑʃ/ noun **1** [C/U] a large hard vegetable with very thick skin **2** [U] an indoor game in which two players use RACKETS in order to hit a small ball against a wall

squash² /skwɑʃ/ verb **1** [T] to damage something by pressing or crushing it so that it loses its normal shape **2** [I/T] to push someone or something so that they fit into a small space, or to fit into a small space with difficulty **3** [T] to prevent something from happening or being effective

squat¹ /skwɑt/ verb [I] **1** to bend your knees and lower yourself toward the ground so that you balance on your feet = CROUCH **2** to live in a place without permission and without paying the owner

PHRASAL VERB **ˌsquat ˈdown** *same as* squat¹ 1

squat² /skwɑt/ adj wide and not very tall or high

squat•ter /ˈskwɑtər/ noun [C] someone who lives in a place without permission and without paying the owner

squawk /skwɔk/ verb [I] when a bird squawks, it makes a loud unpleasant noise in its throat —**squawk** noun [C]

squeak /skwik/ verb [I] to make a short high noise —**squeak** noun [C]

squeak•y /ˈskwiki/ adj making a short high noise

ˌsqueaky ˈclean adj *informal* **1** extremely clean **2** always behaving in a completely moral and honest way

squeal /skwil/ verb [I] to make a long high sound —**squeal** noun [C]

squea•mish /ˈskwimɪʃ/ adj easily upset by seeing something that is unpleasant

squeeze¹ /skwiz/ verb ★

1 [I/T] to press something firmly: *Ruth smiled, squeezing his hand affectionately.*

2 [T] to press something such as a liquid out of something: *She squeezed some lotion onto her hands.*

3 [I/T] to fit something into a small space, or to get through or into a small space: *We can only squeeze one more thing into the bag.* ♦ *He had **squeezed through** a hole in the fence.* ♦ *Passengers were trying to **squeeze onto** the bus.*

PHRASAL VERB **ˌsqueeze sb/sth ˈin** to be able to do something or meet someone, even though you do not have much time: *I can squeeze a meeting in early tomorrow morning.*

squeeze² /skwiz/ noun **1** [C] an act of squeezing something **2** [C] a small amount of a liquid that is squeezed out of something **3** [singular] a situation in which there are too many people or things in a small space **4** [singular] a situation in which there is strict control over money or goods

squelch /skweltʃ/ verb **1** [T] *American informal* to stop someone or something that is causing you trouble by taking firm action against them = SQUASH **2** [I] to make the sound that your feet make when you walk on wet ground —**squelch** noun [C]

squid /skwɪd/ noun [C] an ocean animal that is like an OCTOPUS but with ten arms instead of eight

S

squig•gle /ˈskwɪɡ(ə)l/ noun [C] a line with a lot of curves in it —**squig•gly** adj

squint /skwɪnt/ verb [I] to close your eyes slightly in order to try to see something more clearly —**squint** noun [C]

squirm /skwɜrm/ verb [I] **1** to move by twisting and turning in a small space **2** to look or feel embarrassed and uncomfortable

squir•rel /ˈskwɪrəl/ noun [C] a gray or red-brown animal with a long thick tail. Squirrels live in trees. —*picture* → C13

squirt /skwɜrt/ verb **1** [I/T] if a liquid squirts somewhere, or if you squirt it, it comes out in a narrow stream with a lot of force **2** [T] to make someone or something wet by squirting a liquid —**squirt** noun [C]

squish /skwɪʃ/ verb [T] *informal* to press hard on something that is soft

squish•y /ˈskwɪʃi/ adj *informal* extremely soft and easy to press or crush

Sr. abbrev Senior: used after the name of someone who has a child with the same name

St. abbrev **1** Saint **2** Street

stab¹ /stæb/ verb [T] to push a knife or other sharp object into someone or something
PHRASE **stab sb in the back** to do something that is not loyal to someone who trusts you

stab² /stæb/ noun [C] **1** *informal* an attempt to do something that is difficult to do or that you have never done: *They decided to take a stab at fixing the car themselves.* **2** an act of stabbing someone **3** a sudden feeling of a negative emotion: *a stab of jealousy*

stab•bing¹ /ˈstæbɪŋ/ adj sudden and very strong: *a stabbing pain*

stab•bing² /ˈstæbɪŋ/ noun [C] an attack in which someone is stabbed

sta•bil•i•ty /stəˈbɪləti/ noun [U] a situation in which things continue without any major changes or problems ≠ INSTABILITY: *The rise of nationalism could threaten the stability of Europe.*

sta•bi•lize /ˈsteɪb(ə)ˌlaɪz/ verb [I/T] to reach a state where there are no longer any major changes or problems, or to make something do this: *Oil prices have stabilized for now.* —**sta•bi•li•za•tion** /ˌsteɪb(ə)lɪˈzeɪʃ(ə)n/ noun [U]

sta•ble¹ /ˈsteɪb(ə)l/ adj ★★
1 not changing frequently, and not likely to suddenly become worse ≠ UNSTABLE: *a stable economic situation* ♦ *Tonight the baby is in a **stable condition** in the hospital.*
2 not likely to fall or move in the wrong way ≠ UNSTABLE: *The suspension keeps the car stable when making a turn.*
3 with a healthy mental and emotional state = BALANCED

sta•ble² /ˈsteɪb(ə)l/ noun [C] a building where horses are kept

stack¹ /stæk/ noun [C] **1** a pile of things that are placed one on top of another: *a stack of unopened mail* **2** *informal* a large amount of something

stack² /stæk/ verb [T] **1** to arrange things by placing one on top of another: *Stack the chairs and put them in the corner when you're finished.* **2** to fill something by arranging things in piles or rows in or on it: *He got a job stacking shelves at the supermarket.*
PHRASAL VERB ˌ**stack sth ˈup** *same as* stack² 1

sta•di•um /ˈsteɪdiəm/ noun [C] a large building, usually without a roof, where people watch sports events such as football games or races

staff¹ /stæf/ noun [singular/U] ★★★ the people who work for a particular company, organization, or institution: *The embassy employs around 50 people on its full-time staff.* ♦ *She **joined the staff** in 1996.* ♦ *Peter became a very valued **member of the staff**.*

staff² /stæf/ verb [T] to provide an organization with workers

staff•er /ˈstafər/ noun [C] *American* a member of the staff of an organization

staff•ing /ˈstæfɪŋ/ noun [U] the activities connected with providing staff for an organization

stag /stæɡ/ noun [C] a male DEER

stage¹ /steɪdʒ/ noun ★★★
1 [C] the part of a theater where the actors or musicians perform: *They had now been **on stage** for over four hours.* ♦ *The band didn't **take the stage*** (=come onto it) *until after ten o'clock.*
2 [C] a particular point in time during a process or series of events: *We were now on **the last stage of** our trip.* ♦ *They had the ball more often **in the early stages of** the game.* ♦ *There's no point arguing about it **at this stage**.*
3 the stage [singular] the theater: *She's written a number of works for the stage.*

> **Words often used with stage**
>
> *Adjectives often used with **stage** (noun, sense 2)*
> ■ **advanced, closing, early, final, formative, initial, last, late, preliminary** + STAGE: used for saying what stage a process has reached

stage² /steɪdʒ/ verb [T] **1** to organize an event: *They staged a protest in front of the embassy.* **2** to organize a performance of a play or opera —**stag•ing** noun [C/U]

stage•coach /ˈsteɪdʒˌkoʊtʃ/ noun [C] a vehicle that is pulled by horses that was used in the past for carrying people, mail, and goods

ˈ**stage ˌfright** noun [U] fear felt by an actor or singer before a performance, or by someone who is going to do something important

ˈ**stage ˌmanager** noun [C] someone who is in charge of the practical arrangements for a play or other show

stag•ger /ˈstæɡər/ verb **1** [I] to walk in an uncontrolled way, as if you are going to fall: *He gave her a slight push, and she staggered backward.* **2** [T] to surprise and shock someone = ASTOUND: *Rory was staggered by his answer.* **3** [T] to arrange for events or activities to start at different times: *We have to stagger meal times because there are so many of us now.*

stag•gered /ˈstæɡərd/ adj extremely surprised

stag•ger•ing /ˈstæɡərɪŋ/ adj extremely surprising —**stag•ger•ing•ly** adv

stag•nant /ˈstæɡnənt/ adj **1** stagnant water does not flow and often smells bad **2** not growing or developing

stag•nate /ˈstæɡˌneɪt/ verb [I] **1** to stay the

same without growing or developing **2** if water stagnates, it does not flow and becomes dirty —**stag•na•tion** /stæg'neɪʃ(ə)n/ noun [U]

staid /steɪd/ adj serious and rather boring

stain¹ /steɪn/ noun **1** [C] a mark that is left accidentally on clothes or surfaces: *oil stains* **2** [C/U] a liquid that is used for coloring wood

stain² /steɪn/ verb **1** [I/T] to leave a mark on something accidentally: *Sweat had stained his shirt.* **2** [T] to color wood with a special liquid

stained glass /ˌsteɪnd 'glæs/ noun [U] colored glass that is traditionally used in church windows —**'stained-ˌglass** adj

stain•less steel /ˌsteɪnləs 'stil/ noun [U] steel that has been treated to stop RUST from forming on its surface. It is used for making knives, tools, etc. —**ˌstainless-'steel** adj

stair /ster/ noun ★★

1 stairs [plural] a set of steps that allow you to go from one level of a building to another: *I **climbed the stairs** to Charles's office.* ♦ *John raced **down the stairs** to answer the door.* ♦ *Someone was waiting **at the top of the stairs**.* —*picture* → C1

2 [C] one of the steps in a set of stairs: *He was standing on the bottom stair.*

stair•case /'sterˌkeɪs/ noun [C] a set of stairs in a building with a BANISTER that you hold onto when you go up or down

Stair•Mas•ter /'sterˌmæstər/ *trademark* a type of exercise equipment that you stand on and move in a way similar to climbing —*picture* → C16

stair•way /'sterˌweɪ/ noun [C] a set of stairs inside or outside a building

stake¹ /steɪk/ noun ★

1 [C] *business* the part of a business that you own because you have invested money in it: *They took a 40% **stake in** the company last year.*

2 [C] an amount of money that you risk losing when you try to guess the result of a race or competition

3 stakes [plural] the things that you can gain or lose by taking a risk: *The Americans have **raised the stakes*** (=risked gaining or losing more) *in a bitter fight over imports.* ♦ *With such **high stakes*** (=a lot that could be won or lost), *the atmosphere was tense.*

4 [C] a wooden or metal post with a pointed end that is used for supporting or marking something

PHRASE **at stake** likely to be lost or damaged if something fails: *People's lives are at stake.*

stake² /steɪk/ verb [T] to risk losing or damaging something that is valuable in order to get or do something = GAMBLE: *The government has staked its reputation on eliminating the deficit.*

PHRASE **stake a claim (to sth)** to say or show clearly that you believe that something is yours

PHRASAL VERB **ˌstake out 'sth** to explain your opinion clearly and defend it in a determined way: *Political leaders are busy staking out their positions on this issue.*

ˌstake sth 'out 1 to stay outside a building and watch it because something that is illegal or exciting is happening there: *The police are staking out his home in case he returns.* **2** to mark an area with fences or posts to show that it belongs to someone: *The settlers would arrive in a place and immediately stake out their territory.*

stale /steɪl/ adj **1** old and no longer fresh: *stale bread* **2** not smelling fresh or nice: *stale air* **3** not new, original, or interesting: *stale news*

stale•mate /'steɪlˌmeɪt/ noun [C/U] **1** a situation in which progress is impossible because the people involved cannot agree: *Management and the unions have reached a stalemate in their negotiations.* **2** the situation in CHESS when the game ends because neither player can win

stalk¹ /stɔk/ noun [C] a long thin part of a plant with a flower, fruit, or leaf at the end

stalk² /stɔk/ verb **1** [T] to follow and watch someone all the time in a threatening way, because of an extremely strong interest in them **2** [T] to hunt a person or animal by following them without being seen **3** [I] to walk in a way that shows that you feel angry or offended: *He shook his head in disgust and stalked off.*

stalk•er /'stɔkər/ noun [C] someone who follows and watches another person all the time in a threatening way, because of an extremely strong interest in them

stall¹ /stɔl/ noun [C] **1** a narrow space for one animal such as a horse or pig **2** *American* a small room for a shower or a toilet **3** a large table or a small building that is open at the front. Stalls are used for selling things or for giving people information.

stall² /stɔl/ verb [I/T] **1** if a process stalls, or if someone stalls it, it stops making progress: *Talks have stalled and both sides are preparing for war.* **2** if a vehicle's engine stalls, or if the driver stalls it, it suddenly stops working **3** to delay, or to delay someone, in order to gain more time: *If he calls again, try to stall him until I get there.*

stal•lion /'stæljən/ noun [C] an adult male horse

stal•wart /'stɔlwərt/ adj very loyal: *a stalwart supporter* —**stal•wart** noun [C]

stam•i•na /'stæmɪnə/ noun [U] the ability to work hard over a long period of time without getting tired

stam•mer /'stæmər/ verb [I/T] to keep repeating a particular sound when trying to speak because you have a speech problem, or because you are nervous or excited —**stam•mer** noun [singular]

stamp¹ /stæmp/ noun ★★

1 [C] a small official piece of paper that you buy and stick on an envelope in order to pay for the cost of mailing a letter or package = POSTAGE STAMP

2 [C] a small tool with a pattern or writing on one side that you press into ink and use for printing a mark on paper

3 [C] a mark that you make with a stamp: *Did you get a stamp in your passport?*

4 [singular] a particular quality that is clearly noticeable in someone or something: *The movie **bears the***

*unmistakable **stamp of** its energetic director.* ♦ *He has a chance to **put his stamp on** government policy.*

PHRASE **stamp of approval** a statement that shows that you approve of someone or something

stamp² /stæmp/ verb ★

1 [T] to put a mark on something using ink and a stamp: *They didn't stamp my passport.*

2 [I/T] to put your foot down hard and noisily on something: *Mary tried to **stamp on** the spider.* ♦ *He **stamped his foot** angrily.*

3 [I] to walk putting your feet down hard and noisily on the ground, usually because you are angry: *Riley **stamped into** the editor's office.*

PHRASAL VERB **ˌstamp sth ˈout** to end something that is bad or unpleasant by taking strong and determined action

stam•pede /ˌstæmˈpid/ noun [C] a situation in which a group of people or animals all start to run in a very fast uncontrolled way because they are frightened or excited —**stam•pede** verb [I/T]

stance /stæns/ noun [C] **1** an attitude or view about an issue that you state publicly =POSITION **2** a particular way of standing

stand¹ /stænd/ (past tense and past participle **stood** /stʊd/) verb ★★★

1 be upright on feet	9 still exist
2 get up	10 be willing to accept
3 be/put sth upright	11 have attitude
4 put foot on/in sth	12 not be affected by sth
5 be in situation/state	13 perform job/service
6 of vehicle	+ PHRASES
7 be particular height	+ PHRASAL VERBS
8 reach level/amount	

1 [I] to have your body in an upright position supported by your feet: *The subway was full and we had to stand all the way to Battery Park.* ♦ ***Stand still*** (=don't move) *and let me brush your hair.* ♦ *Mrs. Carter was **standing by** the open window.* ♦ *The man **standing behind** him spoke.* ♦ **stand doing sth** *He stood looking at them in silence.* ♦ **stand and do sth** *The children stood and watched.* —*picture* → POSTURE

2 [I] to move from lying, sitting, or bending down into an upright position: *Everyone stood as the judge entered the court.*

3 [I/T] to put someone or something in an upright position, or to be in an upright position: *Stand the bookcase against the far wall.* ♦ *His statue stands in the city square.*

4 [I] to put your foot on or in something: *He apologized for **standing on** my foot.*

5 [I] to be in a particular situation or state: *How do negotiations stand at the moment?* ♦ *He might seem rude, but at least you **know where you stand with** him* (=understand your position). ♦ ***As it stands**, the law doesn't allow a local court to take such action.*

6 [I] if a car, train, airplane, etc. stands somewhere, it remains there without moving, waiting to be used: *Luckily, the train was still standing at the platform.*

7 [I] to be a particular height: *The structure stands 40 feet high.*

8 [I] to reach a particular level or amount: *The total amount of money raised so far **stands at** over $100,000.*

9 [I] to remain in existence or use: *Her world record has stood for nearly 20 years.* ♦ *Tell him **my offer still stands**.*

10 [T] to be willing to accept something that is unpleasant: *How can you stand all that noise?* ♦ **stand sb doing sth** *I won't stand them interrupting me all the time.*

11 [I] to have a particular attitude or view about a person or subject: ***Where does** the senator **stand on** this issue?*

12 [T] to be good or strong enough not to be badly affected or damaged by something: *These are plants that do not stand the cold well.* ♦ *I wonder how many of these new businesses will **stand the test of time**.*

13 [T] to perform a particular job or service: *Two men were **standing guard over** the prisoners.*

PHRASES **sb can't stand sb/sth** used for saying that a person dislikes someone or something very much: *James just can't stand his mother-in-law.* ♦ *Sylvia **couldn't stand the sight of** blood.* ♦ **can't stand to do sth** *She couldn't stand to see him leave.* ♦ **can't stand sb('s) doing sth** *He couldn't stand anyone feeling sorry for him.*

sb could stand sth used for saying that you think that someone should do something because it would be a good thing: *Those kids could stand a few lessons in good manners.* ♦ **sb could stand to do sth** *He could stand to lose a bit of weight.*

stand accused of sth to be the person who has been formally accused in a court of law of committing a crime

stand a chance (of doing sth) to be likely to achieve something: *Do they stand any chance of winning the championship?*

stand in line *American* to form or join a row of people waiting one behind the other to do something

stand in sb's way to try to stop someone from doing something

stand in the way of sth to try to prevent something from happening

stand on your own two feet to behave in an independent way, especially by not asking for financial help from anyone

stand to do sth to be in a particular situation or state that makes something likely to happen to you: *Many small companies stand to lose financially if the new law is introduced.*

stand trial (for sth) to be judged for a crime in a court of law

→ LEG

PHRASAL VERBS **ˌstand aˈround** to stand somewhere and do nothing

ˌstand aˈside to move to one side in order to let someone go past you

ˌstand ˈback to move away from something, or to stand at a distance from something

ˌstand ˈby 1 to be ready to do something: *A boat will be standing by in case of an emergency.* **2** to not take action when you should: *We can't just stand by and watch her die.*

ˌstand ˈby sb to be loyal to someone who is in a difficult situation

ˌstand ˈby sth to continue to believe or

S

support something although a situation has changed: *The doctors are standing by their claim that they are not at fault.*

ˈstand for sth 1 if an abbreviation or a symbol stands for something, that is what it means or represents: *The letters ER stand for emergency room.* **2** if someone stands for a particular principle, they believe that principle is important: *I hate them and everything they stand for.* **3** to be willing to accept something that someone does: *No one makes a fool of me. I **won't stand for** it!*

ˌstand ˈin to do someone else's job for a short time while they are not available to do it: *I'll be **standing in for** Peter while he's away.*

ˌstand ˈout 1 to be easy to see or notice because of being different: *His bright yellow tie **stood out against** his black suit.* **2** to be much more impressive or important than others: *It **stands out in my mind** as the most exciting day of my career.*

ˌstand ˈup 1 *same as* **stand**[1] 1: *You can have the chair. I don't mind standing up.* ♦ ***Stand up straight** and take your hands out of your pockets.* **2** *same as* **stand**[1] 2: *A man at the back stood up to ask a question.* **3** to still seem true or correct after being examined carefully: *We all knew her story wouldn't **stand up in court**.*

ˌstand sb ˈup to not meet someone who you have arranged to meet, especially someone who you are having or starting a sexual or romantic relationship with

ˌstand ˈup for sb/sth to defend someone or something that is being criticized or attacked: *You have to stand up for what you believe in.* ♦ *I learned how to **stand up for myself** early on in life.*

ˌstand ˈup to sb to not allow yourself to be treated badly by someone who is more powerful than you

stand[2] /stænd/ noun ★★

1 attitude/opinion	4 for holding sth
2 attempt to oppose	5 in court of law
3 table	

S

1 [C] an attitude or opinion about something that you state publicly: *I couldn't vote for them because of their **stand on** social issues.* ♦ *The president has not **taken a stand** on this.*

2 [C] a determined attempt to oppose someone or something that you think is wrong: *support for their **stand against** racism* ♦ *He must **take a firm stand** against extremists in his party.*

3 [C] a large table or structure that is used for selling things or for providing information or services: *a hot dog stand* ♦ *the Porsche stand at the New York auto show*

4 [C] an object or a piece of furniture that is used for holding, supporting, or storing something: *an umbrella stand* ♦ *a cake stand*

5 [singular] *American* the part of a court of law where people stand in order to answer lawyers' questions: *Would you please **take the stand** (=go into it and give your evidence)?*

→ ONE-NIGHT STAND

stan•dard[1] /ˈstændərd/ noun ★★★

1 [C/U] a level of quality or achievement, especially one that most people think is normal or acceptable: *What can be done to **raise standards** in schools?* ♦ *The food was not **up to standard**.* ♦ *higher **standards of** service in hospitals*

2 [C] a level of quality or achievement that is used for judging someone or something: *The first computers were terribly slow **by today's standards**.* ♦ *The building was still magnificent **by any standards**.*

3 standards [plural] traditional principles of good behavior: *declining **moral standards***

PHRASE **standard of living** the type of life that a person or society has according to the amount of money that they have

stan•dard[2] /ˈstændərd/ adj ★★★

1 generally used or accepted as normal: *It's a standard reply that the company sends out to applicants.* ♦ *It is **standard practice** for the school to inform the parents whenever a child is punished.*

2 generally accepted as correct ≠ NONSTANDARD: *the teaching of **standard English***

3 made or done according to a generally accepted set of rules, measurements, etc.: *The promotional pack was 20 percent bigger than **the standard size**.*

stan•dard•ize /ˈstændərˌdaɪz/ verb [T] to make all the things of a particular type have the same features or level of quality —**stan•dard•i•za•tion** /ˌstændərdɪˈzeɪʃ(ə)n/ noun [U]

stand•by /ˈstændˌbaɪ/ noun [C] someone or something that is always available to be used if they are needed

PHRASE **on standby 1** ready to get on an airplane if there is a seat left when it is about to take off: *The flight is sold out, but we can put you on standby.* **2** available to be used if needed: *The troops are on standby and can return at a moment's notice.*

—**stand•by** adj: *standby passengers*

ˈstand-in noun [C] someone or something that takes the place of another person or thing for a short time, especially in order to do their job

stand•ing[1] /ˈstændɪŋ/ noun **1 standings** [plural] *American* a list of teams or players that are put in order according to how many points they have won in games or competitions against each other **2** [U] the status or reputation that someone or something has

stand•ing[2] /ˈstændɪŋ/ adj always existing: *the members of the standing committee* ♦ *We have a standing invitation to stay with Jen and Mike whenever we want.*

ˌstanding ˈarmy noun [C] a professional army that a country has all the time, not just in a war

ˌstanding ˈjoke noun [C] something that happens regularly that a particular group of people find funny

ˌstanding oˈvation noun [C] an enthusiastic reaction to a performance or speech in which people stand and CLAP their hands

stand•off /ˈstændˌɔf/ noun [C] a situation in a disagreement or fight in which neither opponent can do anything in order to win or to achieve their goal

stand•out /ˈstændˌaʊt/ noun [C] *American*

someone or something that you notice because they are much better than anyone or anything else —**stand•out** adj: *a standout player/performance*

stand•point /ˈstæn(d)ˌpɔɪnt/ noun [C] a way of thinking about something

stand•still /ˈstæn(d)ˌstɪl/ noun [singular] a situation in which something stops moving or happening

ˈstand-up adj consisting of one person standing in front of an audience and entertaining them by telling jokes: *stand-up comedy* —**stand-up** noun [U]

stank the past tense of **stink**[1]

stan•za /ˈstænzə/ noun [C] a group of lines in a poem that form a unit with a pattern that is repeated through the whole poem

sta•ple[1] /ˈsteɪp(ə)l/ noun [C] **1** a small piece of wire that you press through pieces of paper with a STAPLER in order to fasten them together **2** an important food or product that people eat or use regularly

sta•ple[2] /ˈsteɪp(ə)l/ verb [T] to fasten pieces of paper together with a staple

sta•ple[3] /ˈsteɪp(ə)l/ adj a staple food or product is the most basic and important one for a particular place or group of people

ˌstaple ˈdiet noun [singular] the main food or foods that a person or animal eats regularly

sta•pler /ˈsteɪplər/ noun [C] a small object used for fastening pieces of paper with a STAPLE —*picture* → C3

star[1] /stɑr/ noun [C] ★★★

1 small light in night sky	4 pointed object/shape
2 sb famous and popular	5 the best in a group
3 main actor	6 sign of quality

1 a very large hot ball of gas that appears as a small bright light in the sky at night

2 a famous and popular actor, entertainer, or sports player: *a Hollywood/pop star*

3 the main actor or performer in a movie, play, television program, etc.: *Today, he's the star of a hundred-million-dollar movie.*

4 an object, shape, or sign with five or more points that looks like a star: *We always put a star at the top of our Christmas tree.* ♦ *the 50 stars on the US flag* ♦ *I've put stars next to the names I want you to check.* —*picture* → C8

5 someone or something that is clearly better than all the other people or things in a group: *Ewing was most definitely **the star of the team**.* ♦ *Mick was **a star pupil** at his school.*

6 a sign that is shaped like a star that is given to a hotel or restaurant in order to show what level of quality or importance it has: *a five-star hotel*
→ STARS AND STRIPES

star[2] /stɑr/ verb [I/T] ★★ if you star in a movie, play, television program, etc., or if it stars you, you are the main actor or performer in it: The X-Files, *starring David Duchovny and Gillian Anderson* ♦ *He **starred in** the school play.*

star•board /ˈstɑrbərd/ noun [U] the right side of a ship when you are looking toward the front

starch /stɑrtʃ/ noun **1** [U] a substance that is used for making clothes stiff **2** [C/U] a white substance without any taste that is found in rice, potatoes, and other vegetables

starch•y /ˈstɑrtʃi/ adj starchy foods have a lot of STARCH in them

star•dom /ˈstɑrdəm/ noun [U] the state of being very famous and popular as an actor, entertainer, or sports player

stare /ster/ verb [I] ★★ to look at someone or something very directly for a long time: *It's rude to stare.* ♦ *He lifted his head and **stared at** her.* —**stare** noun [C]

star•fish /ˈstɑrˌfɪʃ/ noun [C] a small flat sea animal with five or more arms that is shaped like a star

stark[1] /stɑrk/ adj **1** very clear and plain to look at, in a slightly unpleasant or frightening way: *stark brick walls* **2** very obvious or impossible to avoid: *The stark choice is between moving out or staying here and paying more.* **3** extreme and obvious: *His words were in stark contrast to what he had said earlier.* —**stark•ly** adv

stark[2] /stɑrk/ adv **stark naked** not wearing any clothes

star•light /ˈstɑrˌlaɪt/ noun [U] the light that comes from the stars

star•ling /ˈstɑrlɪŋ/ noun [C] a small bird with dark shiny feathers

star•lit /ˈstɑrˌlɪt/ adj bright with light from the stars

star•ry /ˈstɑri/ adj a starry sky or night is one with a lot of stars

star•ry-eyed /ˌstɑri ˈaɪd/ adj someone who is starry-eyed has a lot of hopes or dreams about success in the future, but does not plan things in a sensible way

ˌStars and ˈStripes, the the flag of the U.S.

ˈstar ˌsign noun [C] one of the 12 signs of the ZODIAC that some people believe influences your character and your future

star-stud•ded /ˈstɑr ˌstʌdəd/ adj including many famous people

start[1] /stɑrt/ verb ★★★

1 begin to happen	7 be the limit of sth
2 begin to do sth	8 be the lowest price
3 begin a trip	9 make sth happen
4 begin job/education	10 make machine work
5 begin a period of time	+ PHRASES
6 of business/project	+ PHRASAL VERBS

1 [I] to begin to happen: *The World Championships start in two weeks.* ♦ **start to do sth** *It's starting to rain.* ♦ **start doing sth** *The leaves have started falling off the trees.*

2 [I/T] to begin doing something: *Please start when you are ready.* ♦ *The class **starts with** some gentle stretching exercises.* ♦ **start to do sth** *I started to unpack my suitcase.* ♦ **start doing sth** *Everyone in the class started laughing.*

3 [I/T] to begin a trip: *We started early enough but got caught in traffic.*

4 [I/T] to begin a new job, career, or period of education: *I **start work** on Monday.* ♦ *Things were very different when I **started in** politics.*

5 [T] to begin a period of time in a particular way: *I always **start the day** with a cup of coffee.*

6 [T] to bring a business or project into

S

existence: *He decided to quit his job and start his own business.*
7 [I] used for talking about the nearest end or edge of something: *The new houses start immediately beyond the bridge.*
8 [I] used for talking about the lowest price or number: *Prices for theater tickets **start from** $15.*
9 [T] to cause something, or to be the first person to do something: *Who wants to start the discussion?* ♦ **start sb doing sth** *What she said started me thinking.*
10 [I/T] if you start a machine, or if it starts, it begins to work: *The car won't start.* ♦ *Scott **started the engine** and drove off.*

PHRASES **back where you started** in the same place or situation where you were before, so that you have not made any progress
get started to begin doing something: *We couldn't wait to **get started on** the next job.*
get sb started 1 to help or cause someone to begin something new: *It was his aunt who got him started in publishing.* **2** *informal* to do or say something that makes someone talk for a long time about something: *It's better not to get him started on that subject.*
to start with 1 as a beginning, or as the first thing: *Let's have a few easy questions to start with.* **2** used for introducing the first or the most important point that supports an opinion: *Well, to start with, you don't have the right qualifications.*

PHRASAL VERBS **ˌstart (sth) ˈoff** to begin, or to cause something to begin: *Let's **start off with** a few questions from the audience.*
ˌstart sb ˈoff to make someone begin doing something: **start sb off on sth** *What started you off on this new career?*
ˈstart on sth to begin working on something or dealing with something: *We could have breakfast before we start on the painting.*
ˌstart ˈout 1 to begin as something before developing into something different: *Some businesses **start out as** hobbies.* **2** to begin a trip: *We started out at five o'clock and got there at eight.*
ˌstart (sth) ˈover *American* to begin doing something again from the beginning: *She counted all the envelopes, put them back in the box, then started over.*
ˌstart (sth) ˈup if you start up a business or project, or if it starts up, you bring it into existence: *The agency helps over 1,000 companies start up each year.* ♦ *She left last year to start up her own business.*

start² /stɑrt/ noun ★★★

1 of period of time	5 in races and games
2 the way sb begins sth	6 new opportunity
3 of trip	7 advantage
4 of movie/story	

1 [C] the beginning of a period of time: *I hated her **right from the start.*** ♦ *The operation takes about 15 minutes **from start to finish.*** ♦ ***At the start of** the final year, students begin to think about going to a university.*
2 [C] the way that someone begins a period of time or activity: *Hakkinen **made a** good **start** and was in second place by the first corner.* ♦ *Her election campaign **got off to a slow start.*** ♦ *There's no better **start to the** day than a healthy breakfast.*
3 [C] the beginning of a trip: *After **an early start**, we were soon out of the city.*
4 [C] the beginning of a movie, story, show, etc.: *Let's take a look at **the start of the** story in more detail.*
5 [singular] the moment when a race begins, or the place where it begins: *The start has been delayed by 30 minutes.* ♦ *The runners were all gathered **at the start.***
6 [C] a big change or new opportunity in your life: *She traveled to Hong Kong, hoping **for a fresh start.***
7 [singular] an advantage that you have, especially in a race or competition = HEAD START: *The women runners are given a 50-meter start.*

start·er /ˈstɑrtər/ noun [C] an official who signals the start of a race

start·ing point /ˈstɑrtɪŋ ˌpɔɪnt/ noun [C] **1** the place where a trip begins **2** something that you use as the first stage in a discussion or other activity

star·tle /ˈstɑrt(ə)l/ verb [T] to make a person or animal suddenly feel frightened or surprised —**star·tled** /ˈstɑrt(ə)ld/ adj, **start·ling** adj

ˈstart-up noun [C/U] **1** the process of starting a business, or a small business that is just being started **2** *computing* the process of switching on a computer, or the action of doing this —**ˈstart-up** adj

star·va·tion /stɑrˈveɪʃ(ə)n/ noun [U] a situation in which people and animals suffer or die because they do not have enough to eat

starve /stɑrv/ verb [I/T] to suffer or die because you do not have enough food, or to make someone do this

starved /stɑrvd/ adj **1** prevented from having enough of what you need **2** *informal* very hungry

starv·ing /ˈstɑrvɪŋ/ adj **1** *informal* very hungry **2** sick or dying because you do not have enough food

stash¹ /stæʃ/ verb [T] *informal* to put something in a safe or secret place

stash² /stæʃ/ noun [C] *informal* an amount of something that you put in a safe or secret place

state¹ /steɪt/ noun ★★★

1 condition of sth	5 government
2 bad condition	6 U.S.A.
3 nation	+ PHRASE
4 region	

1 [C] the condition of something at a particular time: *Experts believe the painting can be restored to its original state.* ♦ *Our city's transportation system is **in a sorry state** (=a very bad condition).* ♦ *We're collecting data on **the state of the** environment.*
2 [C] the physical or mental condition of a person, usually when this is bad: *By the time he got home, he was **in a terrible state.*** ♦ *She was **in a state of** panic.*
3 [C] a nation, or country
4 [C] a region of a country that has its own government: *the state of Michigan*

S

5 [singular/U] the government of a country: *Should the state play a bigger role in industry?*
6 **the States** *informal* the United States of America
PHRASE **state of mind** the way that you are feeling at a particular time
→ STATE-OF-THE-ART

state² /steɪt/ verb [T] ★★★ to express something in speech or writing, especially in a definite or formal way: *"Cheryl is going with me," George stated firmly.* ♦ **+that** *He stated that the project would be completed by April.*

state³ /steɪt/ adj **1** a state occasion or event involves a country's government or leader **2** a state institution is one that is run by the government

ˌstate atˈtorney noun [C] *American* a STATE'S ATTORNEY

state•hood /ˈsteɪtˌhʊd/ noun [U] the status of the states of the U.S.

state•less /ˈsteɪtləs/ adj not officially recognized as a citizen of any country

ˌstate ˈline noun [C] a border between one state and another in a country with states

state•ly /ˈsteɪtli/ adj **1** stately movement is slow and steady **2** a stately person or thing is formal and impressive

state•ment /ˈsteɪtmənt/ noun [C] ★★★
1 something that you say or write, especially officially or in public: *He refused to **make a statement** to the press.*
2 an official document that lists the amounts of money that have been put in or taken out of a bank account

ˌstate-of-the-ˈart adj very new and modern

ˌstate's atˈtorney noun [C] a lawyer who works for the state in the U.S.

states•man /ˈsteɪtsmən/ noun [C] an experienced political leader that many people respect —**states•man•like** adj, **states•man•ship** noun [U]

ˌstate ˈtrooper noun [C] in the U.S., a police officer who is a member of a state police force

state•wide /ˈsteɪtˌwaɪd/ adj, adv *American* affecting or involving the whole state in which it happens

stat•ic¹ /ˈstætɪk/ noun [U] the unpleasant noise that you hear on a radio, television, or telephone that is caused by electricity in the air

stat•ic² /ˈstætɪk/ adj something that is static does not move or change

ˌstatic elecˈtricity noun [U] electricity that is produced when two objects rub together

sta•tion¹ /ˈsteɪʃ(ə)n/ noun [C] ★★★
1 a building or place where trains or buses stop so that passengers can get on or off: *It was dark when we arrived at the station.*
2 a building or place where a particular service or activity is based: *Astronomers at the Salyut Research Station discovered the star.*
3 a company that broadcasts television or radio programs: *Listen to your local radio station for travel information.*

sta•tion² /ˈsteɪʃ(ə)n/ verb [T] to send someone to a particular place in order to do a job, especially for the military

sta•tion•ar•y /ˈsteɪʃ(ə)nˌeri/ adj not moving

sta•tion•er•y /ˈsteɪʃ(ə)nˌeri/ noun [U] **1** paper used for writing letters, often with the name of a company on it and envelopes that match **2** things that you use for writing such as paper and pens

ˈstation ˌwagon noun [C] *American* a long car that has a lot of space behind the seats for carrying things and people

sta•tis•tic /stəˈtɪstɪk/ noun [C] a number that represents a fact or describes a situation

stat•is•ti•cian /ˌstætɪˈstɪʃ(ə)n/ noun [C] someone whose job is to study and work with statistics

sta•tis•tics /stəˈtɪstɪks/ noun **1** [plural] a group of numbers that represent facts or describe a situation **2** [U] the science of using numbers to represent facts and describe situations —**sta•tis•ti•cal** /stəˈtɪstɪk(ə)l/ adj, **sta•tis•ti•cal•ly** /stəˈtɪstɪkli/ adv

stat•ue /ˈstætʃu/ noun [C] an image of a person or animal that is made of stone, wood, metal, etc.

stat•ure /ˈstætʃər/ noun [U] *formal* **1** the degree to which someone or something is respected or admired **2** someone's height

sta•tus /ˈsteɪtəs, ˈstætəs/ noun ★★
1 [C/U] the legal position of someone or something: *Will I be officially self-employed, or will I have employee status?*
2 [U] someone's position in a profession or society, especially in comparison with other people: *Our organization seeks to improve the **social status** of disabled people.*
3 [U] a high social position that makes other people respect and admire you: *a symbol of status and wealth*

sta•tus quo, the /ˌsteɪtəs ˈkwoʊ/ noun [singular] the present situation, or the way that things usually are

ˈstatus ˌsymbol noun [C] a possession that is a symbol of someone's money or power

stat•ute /ˈstætʃut/ noun [C] *formal* a law, or a rule

stat•u•to•ry /ˈstætʃəˌtɔri/ adj *formal* controlled by a statute

ˌstatutory ˈrape noun [C] *American* the crime of having sex with a person who the law says is too young to have sex

staunch /stɔntʃ/ adj loyal and showing strong support

stave /steɪv/ PHRASAL VERB **ˌstave sth ˈoff** to stop something that is unpleasant from happening

stay¹ /steɪ/ verb [I] ★★★
1 to remain in a particular place: *Stay right here, please.* ♦ *I have to **stay late** at work every Thursday.* ♦ *He wanted her to **stay at home** and take care of the children.*
2 to remain in a particular situation or state: *Interest rates should stay low for the next few months.*
3 to live or remain in a place for a while as a guest or visitor: *How long is he planning to **stay with** you?*
PHRASES **sth is here to stay** used for saying that something is generally accepted and is part of all our lives: *Do you think high unemployment is here to stay?*
stay put *spoken* to remain where you are: *Stay put, I'll be back in a minute.*

S

PHRASAL VERBS ˌstay beˈhind to remain somewhere after everyone else has left: *Tony stayed behind and helped us clean the kitchen.*
ˌstay ˈin to remain in your home and not go out: *I think I'd rather stay in tonight.*
ˌstay ˈon to remain at a job, school, or place longer than you had intended to: *James promised to stay on for six more months.*
ˌstay ˈout to remain out of your home for a period of time: *Please don't stay out all night again!*
ˌstay ˈout of sth to refuse to become involved in an argument or a bad situation: *He will go to jail if he doesn't stay out of trouble.*
ˌstay ˈover to sleep in someone's house as a guest for one night: *It's getting late; do you want to stay over?*
ˌstay ˈup to not go to bed: *Josh could stay up all night without getting tired.*

stay² /steɪ/ noun [C] a period of time that you spend somewhere
PHRASE **stay of execution/deportation etc.** *legal* an order that is given by a judge to stop or delay something

STD /ˌes ti ˈdi/ abbrev sexually transmitted disease: a disease that you get from having sex with an infected person

stead•fast /ˈstedˌfæst/ adj not changing your opinions or actions, because you have a strong belief in someone or something

stead•y¹ /ˈstedi/ adj ★
1 firmly held, without moving or shaking: *Hold the flashlight steady so I can see better.* ♦ *You have to have* ***a steady hand*** *to be a surgeon.*
2 slowly and gradually continuing to change, move, or happen: *A steady stream of people passed by.* ♦ ***a steady increase*** *in car sales*
3 staying at the same level, speed, value, etc.: *She listened to the steady rhythm of his breathing as he slept.*
4 likely to continue for a long period of time: *a steady boyfriend/girlfriend* ♦ *a steady relationship* ♦ *It would be nice to have* ***a steady job.***
—**stead•i•ly** adv

stead•y² /ˈstedi/ verb [T] to hold something firmly without moving it
PHRASES **steady your nerves** to stop yourself from feeling nervous
steady yourself to try to get your balance again so that you will not fall

steak /steɪk/ noun [C/U] a large flat piece of meat or fish

steal /stil/ (past tense **stole** /stoʊl/; past participle **sto•len** /ˈstoʊlən/) verb ★★
1 [I/T] to take something that belongs to someone else without permission: **steal sth from sb/sth** *She was caught stealing food from the supermarket.*
2 [I] to move somewhere quietly and secretly: *While Sara wasn't looking, I stole across the hall to make a call.*

> **Other ways of saying steal**
> - **break into sth** to enter a building or vehicle illegally
> - **burglarize** to steal from a house or apartment that you have entered illegally
> - **mug** to attack a person in a public place and steal something from them
> - **rob** to steal things from a place using violence, or threatening to use violence
> - **shoplift** to steal goods from a store

stealth /stelθ/ noun [U] a quiet and secret way of behaving —**stealth•i•ly** adv, **stealth•y** adj

steam¹ /stim/ noun [U] ★
1 the hot wet substance like a cloud that is produced when water is heated: *The steam from the volcano rose into the air.*
2 the power that is created when water is heated: *The equipment was originally powered by steam.* ♦ *a steam engine/locomotive*
PHRASES **let off steam** to express feelings of anger or excitement without harming anyone: *The meeting will be a chance for the protesters to let off steam.*
run out of steam to lose energy, enthusiasm, or importance

steam² /stim/ verb **1** [I/T] to cook food with steam **2** [I] to move using steam power
PHRASAL VERB ˌ**steam (sth) ˈup** to cover something with steam, or to become covered with steam

steam•er /ˈstimər/ noun [C] **1** a STEAMSHIP **2** a container used for cooking food with steam

steam•roll /ˈstimˌroʊl/ verb [T] *informal* **1** to defeat or destroy an opponent completely **2** to make sure that something happens by using all your power

steam•rol•ler /ˈstimˌroʊlər/ noun [C] a heavy vehicle that is used for making a road flat

steam•ship /ˈstimʃɪp/ noun [C] a ship that moves by steam power

steam•y /ˈstimi/ adj **1** *informal* sexually exciting **2** very hot and full of steam

steel¹ /stil/ noun [U] ★ a strong metal made from a mixture of iron and CARBON

steel² /stil/ verb **steel yourself** to prepare yourself for something unpleasant

ˌ**steel ˈwool** noun [U] very thin pieces of wire that are twisted together into a ball, used for cleaning metal

steel•works /ˈstilˌwɜrks/ (plural **steel•works**) noun [C] a factory where steel is made —**steel•work•er** noun [C]

steel•y /ˈstili/ adj showing a calm and firm attitude: *He had a look of steely determination in his eyes.*

steep¹ /stip/ adj ★
1 a steep slope goes up or down very quickly: *a steep hill/path* ♦ *Suddenly the plane went into a steep dive.*
2 steep prices are very high
3 a steep increase or fall in something is sudden and very big: ***a steep rise*** *in oil prices*
—**steep•ly** adv, **steep•ness** noun [U]

steep² /stip/ verb [T] to leave something in a liquid for some time
PHRASE **be steeped in sth** to have a lot of a particular quality or thing

stee•ple /ˈstip(ə)l/ noun [C] a tall pointed tower on a church

steer¹ /stɪr/ verb ★
1 [I/T] to control the direction in which a vehicle moves: *Jack steered while Ken gave*

S

directions. ♦ *We* ***steered*** *the boat* ***into*** *the marina.*

2 [T] to influence the way that something happens or the way that people behave: *Ruth attempted to* ***steer*** *the conversation well* ***away from*** *work.* ♦ *I try to* ***steer*** *my children* ***toward*** *healthier foods.*

3 [T] to control the direction in which someone moves with your hand: *He took her arm to* ***steer*** *her* ***toward*** *the door.*

PHRASE **steer clear (of)** *informal* to avoid someone or something that is dangerous or unpleasant: *Tourists are advised to steer clear of the area.*

steer² /stɪr/ noun [C] a young male cow

steer·ing /ˈstɪrɪŋ/ noun [U] the parts of a vehicle that allow you to control the direction that it travels in

ˈsteering ˌwheel noun [C] the wheel that you hold and turn in order to control the direction that a vehicle travels in —*picture* → C6

stem¹ /stem/ noun [C] **1** the long part of a plant from which the leaves and flowers grow **2** the long thin part of a wine glass that joins the bowl to the base

stem² /stem/ verb [T] to stop something from spreading or increasing

PHRASAL VERB **ˈstem from sth** to be caused by something

stench /stentʃ/ noun [C] a very unpleasant smell

sten·cil¹ /ˈstens(ə)l/ noun [C] a piece of paper or plastic with a shape or letters cut out of it. You place it on a surface and paint over it in order to make a design on something.

sten·cil² /ˈstens(ə)l/ verb [T] to make a design on a surface using a stencil

step¹ /step/ noun [C] ★★★

1 movement or sound	4 stage
2 one of series of actions	5 dance movement
3 for walking up/down	+ PHRASES

1 a movement made by putting one foot in front of the other, or the sound that your feet make while you are walking: *I could hear the steps coming closer.* ♦ *The mini-market is just a few steps from my front door.* ♦ *Tom* ***took a step*** *backward.*

2 one of a series of actions that you take in order to achieve a particular goal: *The government must* ***take steps*** *to control inflation.* ♦ *This agreement is an important* ***step toward*** *our goal.* ♦ *This new law is the first* ***step in*** *making our city safer.* ♦ *It's not the best deal for staff, but it's* ***a step in the right direction.*** ♦ *The new microchip is a major* ***step forward*** (=improvement) *in computer technology.*

3 a flat surface, usually one in a series, that you walk up or down in order to move to a different level: *I met him on the front steps of his house.* ♦ *I climbed* ***a flight of*** *steep* ***steps*** (=a set of steps).

4 one of the stages in a process: *When you finish the exercise, repeat steps five to ten.* ♦ *Her new job is* ***a*** *big* ***step up*** *for her.* ♦ *Don't worry, we'll take things* ***one step at a time*** (=gradually). ♦ *She was congratulating herself on her intelligence, but he was* ***one step ahead of*** *her.*

5 a particular movement or set of movements that you make with your feet while dancing: *Juan was practicing his new* ***dance steps.***

PHRASES **in step 1** if people or things are in step, they agree or move at the same rate: *Prices usually keep* ***in step with*** *inflation.* **2** if people walk in step, each person moves their feet at exactly the same time as the others

out of step if people or things are out of step, they do not agree or move at the same rate

step² /step/ verb [I] ★★

1 to move somewhere by putting one foot down in front of the other: *I* ***stepped on*** *the platform and started to speak.*

2 to move or walk a short distance: *Please* ***step outside*** *and wait a moment.*

PHRASAL VERBS **ˌstep aˈside** to leave an official position or job, especially so that someone else can take your place

ˌstep ˈdown *same as* **step aside**

ˌstep ˈforward to offer help to someone who needs it: *Ron stepped forward and offered to change the tire.*

ˌstep ˈin to become involved in a discussion or argument, especially in order to make it stop: *It is time for the government to step in.*

ˌstep sth ˈup to increase something: *The president has* ***stepped up the pressure*** *on the groups to come to an agreement.*

step·broth·er /ˈstepˌbrʌðər/ noun [C] the son of your STEPFATHER or STEPMOTHER

ˌstep-by-ˈstep adj a step-by-step plan or set of instructions explains each stage of a process in a clear way

step·child /ˈstepˌtʃaɪld/ noun [C] the son or daughter of your husband or wife from a previous relationship

step·daugh·ter /ˈstepˌdɔtər/ noun [C] the daughter of your husband or wife, who is not your child

step·fa·ther /ˈstepˌfɑðər/ noun [C] the man who is married to your mother, but who is not your father

step·lad·der /ˈstepˌlædər/ noun [C] a short LADDER consisting of two sloping parts, that can be folded and carried

step·moth·er /ˈstepˌmʌðər/ noun [C] the woman who is married to your father, but who is not your mother

stepped-up /ˌstept ˈʌp/ adj *mainly journalism* increased in amount or strength

step·ping·stone /ˈstepɪŋˌstoʊn/ noun [C] **1** a step in a process that helps you to move forward to another part of it **2** a flat piece of rock in a river that you stand on in order to cross to the other side

step·sis·ter /ˈstepˌsɪstər/ noun [C] the daughter of your STEPFATHER or STEPMOTHER

step·son /ˈstepˌsʌn/ noun [C] the son of your husband or wife, who is not your child

ster·e·o /ˈsterioʊ/ noun [C] a piece of electronic equipment with two SPEAKERS that you use for listening to the radio, CDs, and CASSETTES

PHRASE **in stereo** recorded or broadcast using a system that sends the sound through two SPEAKERS

—**ster·e·o** adj

S

ster•e•o•type /ˈsteriəˌtaɪp/ noun [C] **1** a firm idea about what a particular type of person or thing is like, especially an idea that is wrong **2** someone who is exactly what many people expect a person of their particular class, NATIONALITY, profession, etc. to be like —**ster•e•o•type** verb [T], **ster•e•o•typ•ic•al** /ˌsteriəˈtɪpɪk(ə)l/ adj

ster•ile /ˈsterəl/ adj **1** completely clean, with no bacteria ≠ DIRTY **2** not able to produce children **3** a sterile argument or discussion does not contain any interesting new ideas —**ste•ril•i•ty** /stəˈrɪləti/ noun [U]

ster•il•ize /ˈsterəˌlaɪz/ verb [T] **1** to kill all the bacteria on or in something and make it completely clean **2** to perform an operation on someone that makes them unable to produce children —**ster•il•i•za•tion** /ˌsterəlɪˈzeɪʃ(ə)n/ noun [C/U]

ster•ling[1] /ˈstɜrlɪŋ/ noun [U] **1 sterling** or **sterling silver** silver that is of a standard quality **2** the standard unit of money in the U.K.

ster•ling[2] /ˈstɜrlɪŋ/ adj *formal* sterling work or a sterling character is good, strong, and reliable

stern[1] /stɜrn/ adj serious and severe —**stern•ly** adv

stern[2] /stɜrn/ noun [C] the back part of a ship

ster•oid /ˈsteˌrɔɪd, stɪˌrɔɪd/ noun [C] a drug that is used by doctors for treating conditions such as swelling, or, illegally, by ATHLETES for improving their performance

steth•o•scope /ˈsteθəˌskoʊp/ noun [C] a piece of equipment that doctors use to listen to your heart or to your breathing

stew[1] /stu/ noun [C/U] a dish made by cooking vegetables, and usually meat or fish, slowly in a liquid

stew[2] /stu/ verb [T] to cook something slowly in a liquid

stew•ard•ess /ˈstuərdəs/ noun [C] *old-fashioned* a female FLIGHT ATTENDANT

S

stick[1] /stɪk/ (past tense and past participle **stuck** /stʌk/) verb ★★★

1 attach sth to sth	5 become attached
2 put quickly	6 of name
3 push sth long into sth	+ PHRASAL VERBS
4 remain in sth	

1 [I/T] to attach one thing to another, or to become attached to something, especially using a sticky substance such as glue: *Can you **stick** the pieces of this vase back **together**?* ♦ *She was **sticking** posters **on** her bedroom wall.* ♦ *The pasta has **stuck to** the bottom of the pan.*

2 [T] *informal* to put something somewhere quickly and without taking much care =SHOVE: *Just **stick** the plates **in** the sink.*

3 [T] to push something that is long and thin into or through something else: *He **stuck** the end of the shovel **in** the ground.* ♦ *a piece of cloth with a pin **stuck through** it*

4 [I] if something sticks in, into, or through something else, its end remains in it or through it: *The knife missed its target and **stuck in** the door.* ♦ *Something sharp was **sticking into** my back.*

5 [I] to become firmly attached in one position, and therefore difficult or impossible to move: *The door is sticking, so give it a good push.* ♦ *The wheels had **stuck in** the mud.*

6 [I] if a new name for someone or something sticks, it becomes accepted and used by everyone: *He'd been called "Tufty" at school, and the name had stuck.*

PHRASAL VERBS **ˌstick aˈround** *informal* to remain in a particular place

ˈstick by sb *informal* to continue to support someone who is in a difficult situation

ˈstick by sth *informal* to do something that you promised or decided that you would do: *The principal is sticking by his decision to retire.*

ˌstick ˈout 1 to continue farther than the end of a surface or the main part of an object: *His ears stick out.* ♦ *A magazine was **sticking out of** his coat pocket.* **2** to be easy to notice or remember because of being unusual or different: *One face in particular stuck out.* ♦ *You **stick out like a sore thumb** in that uniform* (=look very different from everyone else).

ˌstick sth ˈout to push or stretch something forward or away from you, especially a part of your body: *She stuck her arm out of the car window and waved.* ♦ ***Ben stuck out his tongue** at the little girl* (=as an insult).

ˈstick to sth 1 to do something that you promised or decided that you would do, or to do something that you should do: *We said we'd give her the cash, and we must stick to our agreement.* **2** to continue to do or use something, and not change it or stop it: *I think we should stick to our original plan.* ♦ *If everyone **sticks to the rules*** (=obeys the rules), *we shouldn't have any problems.* **3 stick to your guns** *informal* to refuse to change what you are saying or doing

ˌstick toˈgether *informal* if people stick together, they remain close together and support one another

ˌstick ˈup to continue upward farther than the end of a surface or the main part of an object: *You've got some hair sticking up in the back.*

ˌstick ˈup for sb/sth *informal* to speak in support of someone or something, especially when no one else will do this

ˈstick with sb *informal* to stay close to someone and go with them wherever they go

ˈstick with sth *informal* to continue to do or use something, and not change it: *They're going to stick with the same team as last Saturday.*

stick[2] /stɪk/ noun [C] ★★

1 thin piece of wood	4 thin piece of sth
2 for walking	5 for car
3 for a sport	

1 a thin piece of wood, especially one that has been broken or cut from a tree

2 a long strong piece of wood, usually with a handle at the top, that you use for helping you to walk

3 a long thin piece of wood that is used for hitting or carrying something in a sport: *a hockey stick*

4 a long thin piece of something: *a stick of celery/dynamite/butter*

5 *informal* a STICK SHIFT

stick·er /ˈstɪkər/ noun [C] a piece of paper or plastic with a picture or writing on it, that you can stick to something

stick·ler /ˈstɪklər/ noun [C] someone who thinks that a particular thing is very important

sticks, the /stɪks/ noun [plural] *informal* an area far from a town or city

ˈstick ˌshift noun [C] *American* **1** the LEVER in a car that the driver moves in order to change the GEARS —*picture* → C6 **2** a car that uses a stick shift system

ˈstick-up noun [C] *informal* an occasion when someone tries to steal money from a bank, store, etc. by threatening people with a gun

stick·y /ˈstɪki/ adj **1** made of or covered with a substance that sticks to other things: *The dough should be soft but not sticky.* ♦ *sticky fingers* **2** sticky weather is hot and DAMP (=with a lot of water in the air)=HUMID **3** a sticky situation is difficult or dangerous =TRICKY

stiff¹ /stɪf/ adj ★

1 firm & difficult to bend	5 severe/difficult
2 with pain in muscles	6 formal/controlled
3 not moving easily	7 of wind
4 of mixture	8 with much alcohol

1 firm and difficult to bend: *a stiff piece of cardboard* ♦ *a small stiff brush*
2 if a part of your body is stiff, you feel pain in your muscles and cannot move easily: *I have **a really stiff neck**.*
3 not moving or operating as easily as you expect: *The drawer was very stiff, so I pulled on it.*
4 a mixture that is stiff is very thick: *Beat the egg whites until stiff.*
5 more severe or difficult than usual: *Greene is up against some **stiff competition** in this race.* ♦ *Those caught breaking the new law face some pretty **stiff penalties**.*
6 formal in a way that is not friendly or relaxed: *He looked stiff and awkward in his new suit.*
7 a stiff wind or BREEZE is fairly strong
8 a stiff drink contains a lot of alcohol
—**stiff·ly** adv, **stiff·ness** noun [U]

stiff² /stɪf/ adv **bored/scared/worried stiff** extremely bored/frightened/worried

stiff·en /ˈstɪf(ə)n/ verb **1** [I] to suddenly hold your body in a stiff way, often because you are afraid or angry **2** [I/T] to become stiff, or to make something stiff

sti·fle /ˈstaɪf(ə)l/ verb **1** [T] to stop something from happening or developing **2** [I/T] to stop someone from breathing, or to have difficulty in breathing=SUFFOCATE

sti·fling /ˈstaɪf(ə)lɪŋ/ adj so hot that you feel uncomfortable and are unable to breathe easily

stig·ma /ˈstɪgmə/ noun [singular/U] a general attitude in which people treat something as wrong or embarrassing, especially in an unfair way

stig·ma·tize /ˈstɪgməˌtaɪz/ verb [T] to treat something as wrong or embarrassing, especially in an unfair way

sti·let·to /stɪˈletoʊ/ (plural **sti·let·tos** or **sti·let·toes**) noun [C] **1** a small knife with a thin blade **2** a shoe that has a thin high heel, or the heel on this kind of shoe

still¹ /stɪl/ adv ★★★
1 used for saying that a situation continues to exist up to and including a particular time: *Her hair was still damp from her walk in the rain.* ♦ *The car's doors were locked, but the motor was still running.* ♦ *Is Terry still in college?* → YET
2 used for emphasizing that a particular situation has not completely ended or changed: *I still have 50 pages to read before Friday.*
3 used for stating that something remains true despite what you have just said or done: *We knew we wouldn't win the game, but it was still exciting!* ♦ *I hadn't seen him for 25 years. Still, I recognized him immediately.*
4 used for emphasizing that although something is big, good, bad, etc., something else is even bigger, better, worse, etc.: *Greg's medical expenses are enormous and, **worse still**, he may lose his job.*

still² /stɪl/ adj ★
1 not moving: *The water appeared still from a distance.* ♦ *Just **sit still** for a minute and let me tie your shoe.*
2 quiet and calm, with nothing happening: *By 10:00 the streets are pretty still.*

still³ noun [C] **1** a photograph that is taken from one of the scenes in a movie or video **2** a piece of equipment that is used for making strong alcohol

still·born /ˈstɪlˌbɔrn/ adj a stillborn baby is born dead

ˌstill ˈlife (plural **ˌstill ˈlifes**) noun [C/U] a type of art that represents objects instead of people, animals, or the countryside

stilt·ed /ˈstɪltəd/ adj stilted movements or words are not relaxed or natural

stilts /stɪlts/ [plural] **1** a pair of long pieces of wood that you stand on so that you can walk high above the ground **2** a set of posts that a house is built on in order to raise it above the ground or above water

stim·u·lant /ˈstɪmjələnt/ noun [C] a substance that makes you feel more lively or awake

stim·u·late /ˈstɪmjəˌleɪt/ verb [T] **1** to encourage something to happen, develop, or improve: *The government should do more to stimulate investment in the rural areas of the state.* **2** to make someone feel interested in learning new things: *Such questions provide a useful way of stimulating students' interest.* —**stim·u·la·tion** /ˌstɪmjəˈleɪʃ(ə)n/ noun [U]

stim·u·lat·ing /ˈstɪmjəˌleɪtɪŋ/ adj interesting and making you think

stim·u·lus /ˈstɪmjələs/ (plural **stim·u·li** /ˈstɪmjəˌlaɪ/) noun [C/U] **1** something that encourages something else to happen, develop, or improve **2** *science* something that produces a reaction in a person, animal, or plant

sting¹ /stɪŋ/ (past tense and past participle **stung** /stʌŋ/) verb **1** [I/T] if an insect, animal, or plant stings you, it hurts you by putting poison on or into your skin **2** [I/T] to be affected by a sudden pain or uncomfortable feeling, or to make something do this: *My*

S

eyes were stinging because of the salt in the water. **3** [T] to make someone feel angry and upset

sting² /stɪŋ/ noun [C] **1** a sudden pain or uncomfortable feeling **2** the pain that you feel when an insect, animal, or plant stings you

sting•ing /ˈstɪŋɪŋ/ adj strong enough to upset you: *a stinging attack on government policy*

stin•gy /ˈstɪndʒi/ adj *informal* unwilling to spend, give, or use a lot of money = CHEAP ≠ GENEROUS

stink¹ /stɪŋk/ (past tense **stank** /stæŋk/ or **stunk** /stʌŋk/; past participle **stunk**) verb [I] *informal* **1** to smell very unpleasant **2** to be bad or dishonest

stink² /stɪŋk/ noun [singular] *informal* **1** a very strong unpleasant smell **2** a situation in which you complain angrily about something

stint /stɪnt/ noun [C] a period of time that is spent doing something

sti•pend /ˈstaɪˌpend/ noun [C] a small amount of money that is paid regularly to someone for work that they do

stip•u•late /ˈstɪpjəˌleɪt/ verb [T] *formal* to say what is allowed or what is necessary —**stip•u•la•tion** /ˌstɪpjəˈleɪʃ(ə)n/ noun [C]

stir¹ /stɜr/ verb ★

1 [I/T] to move food or a liquid around using a spoon or other object: *Stir the sauce gently over a low heat.*

2 [T] to make someone have a particular feeling or memory: *This crime has stirred a lot of anger in the community.* ♦ *Seeing George again stirred old memories in me.*

3 [I/T] to move slightly, or to make someone or something move slightly: *The curtains stirred gently in the breeze.* ♦ *Mary was asleep and didn't stir.*

PHRASAL VERB ˌ**stir sth ˈup** *same as* **stir¹ 2**: *He was accused of stirring up racial hatred.*

stir² /stɜr/ noun [singular] **1** a situation in which a lot of people feel interested or angry: *His speech caused quite a stir.* **2** the movement that you make with a spoon or other object when you move food or a liquid around

S

ˈ**stir-ˌfry** verb [T] to cook food quickly by moving it around in hot oil —**stir-ˌfry** noun [C]

stir•ring /ˈstɜrɪŋ/ adj causing strong emotions

stir•rup /ˈstɪrəp/ noun [C] a metal object that supports your foot when you ride a horse

stitch¹ /stɪtʃ/ noun **1** [C] one of the short pieces of THREAD that you can see on cloth when it has been sewn **2** [C] a short piece of THREAD that is used for joining someone's skin together after it has been cut **3** [C] a piece of wool that has been put around a needle when you are KNITTING **4** [singular/U] a sharp pain in the side of your body

PHRASE **in stitches** *informal* laughing a lot

stitch² /stɪtʃ/ verb [T] **1** to join pieces of cloth together by sewing them **2** to join someone's skin together with THREAD after it has been cut

PHRASAL VERB ˌ**stitch sth ˈup 1** to repair a piece of cloth that has been torn by sewing it **2** *same as* **stitch² 2**

stock¹ /stɑk/ noun ★★

1 amount kept	4 worth of company
2 goods in store	5 for soups/sauces
3 shares in company	+ PHRASE

1 [C] an amount of something that is kept so that it can be used when it is needed: *Their **stocks of** ammunition were running low.*

2 [U] the goods that are available to buy in a store: *We're having some new stock delivered this afternoon.* ♦ *Do you have any of these batteries **in stock*** (=available to buy) *at the moment?* ♦ *I'm afraid that size is **out of stock*** (=not available to buy).

3 [C/U] *business* a group of SHARES in an individual company: *The value of technology stocks fell sharply today.*

4 [U] *business* the amount of money that a company is worth, represented by the total value of its SHARES

5 [C/U] a liquid made by boiling meat, bones, or vegetables that is used for making soups and sauces: *chicken stock*

PHRASE **take stock (of sth)** to spend some time thinking about the situation that you are in before you decide what to do next: *Millie felt she needed to stop and take stock of her life.*

stock² /stɑk/ verb [T] **1** if a store stocks goods, it has them available for sale **2** to fill a place with things that you will need

PHRASAL VERB ˌ**stock ˈup** to get a lot of something so that it can be used when it is needed: *We like to stock up on firewood before winter sets in.*

stock³ /stɑk/ adj a stock answer, reply, etc. is one that someone always gives when they are asked a particular question

stock•bro•ker /ˈstɑkˌbroʊkər/ noun [C] someone whose job is to buy and sell SHARES in companies for other people —**stock•bro•king** noun [U]

ˈ**stock exˌchange** noun **1** [C] a place where people buy and sell SHARES in companies **2 the stock exchange** [singular] the STOCK MARKET

stock•hold•er /ˈstɑkˌhoʊldər/ noun [C] *American* someone who owns STOCK in a company

stock•ing /ˈstɑkɪŋ/ noun [C] a very thin piece of clothing that is worn on a woman's foot and leg —*picture* → C5

ˈ**stock ˌmarket** noun **1** [C] a STOCK EXCHANGE **2 the stock market** [singular] the activities that are connected with buying and selling SHARES in companies

ˈ**stock ˌoption** noun [C] *American* an opportunity to buy SHARES in the company that you work for

stock•pile /ˈstɑkˌpaɪl/ verb [T] to collect large amounts of things that may be needed —**stock•pile** noun [C]

stock•y /ˈstɑki/ adj a stocky person looks strong but is not tall

sto•i•cal /ˈstoʊɪk(ə)l/ or **stoic** /ˈstoʊɪk/ adj accepting things without complaining —**sto•i•cal•ly** /ˈstoʊɪkli/ adv, **sto•i•cism** /ˈstoʊɪˌsɪzəm/ noun [U]

stoke /stoʊk/ verb [T] **1** to add fuel to a fire **2** to make a feeling stronger

stole the past tense of **steal**

stolen the past participle of **steal**

stom·ach¹ /ˈstʌmək/ noun [C] ★★
1 the soft part at the front of your body that is between your chest and your legs: *A horse had kicked her in the stomach.* —*picture* → C14
2 the organ inside your body where food goes when you have eaten it: *She'll feel better when she has some food in her stomach.*
PHRASES **have the stomach for sth** to have enough determination to do something that is unpleasant or dangerous
on an empty stomach if you do something on an empty stomach, you do not eat anything before you do it: *It's not good to drink alcohol on an empty stomach.*

stom·ach² /ˈstʌmək/ verb [T] if you cannot stomach something, you cannot do it or deal with it because you dislike it very much

ˈstomach ˌache noun [C/U] pain in your stomach

stomp /stɑmp/ verb [I] to walk angrily making a lot of noise with your feet

stone¹ /stoʊn/ noun ★★★
1 [U] the hard substance that rocks are made of: *a cottage built of stone*
2 [C] a small piece of rock: *Children threw stones at him.*
3 [C] a jewel
4 (plural **stones** or **stone**) [C] *British* a unit of weight that is equal to 14 pounds

stone² /stoʊn/ verb [T] to throw stones at someone in order to kill them

ˈStone ˌAge, the the period of history when people made tools and weapons from stone

stoned /stoʊnd/ adj *informal* affected by an illegal drug that makes you feel very relaxed

stone·wall /ˈstoʊnˌwɔl/ verb [I/T] *informal* to refuse to give information

ston·y /ˈstoʊni/ adj **1** covered with stones, or containing stones **2** not friendly and not showing any emotion

ston·y-faced /ˌstoʊni ˈfeɪst/ adj looking unfriendly and not showing any emotion

stood the past tense and past participle of **stand¹**

stool /stul/ noun [C] **1** a seat that has legs but no support for your back or arms —*picture* → CHAIR **2** *technical* a piece of solid waste from your body

stoop¹ /stup/ noun **1** [singular] a way of standing or walking with your head and shoulders bent forward and downward **2** [C] *American* a raised area that is outside the front door of a house, especially a house in the city

stoop² /stup/ verb [I] to bend the top half of your body downward
PHRASAL VERB **ˈstoop to sth** to do something that is bad in order to get what you want

stop¹ /stɑp/ verb ★★★

1 prevent sth	6 ask sb to stop
2 not do sth anymore	7 pause to do sth
3 not move anymore	8 block pipe/hole, etc.
4 bus/train	+ PHRASES
5 not work anymore	+ PHRASAL VERBS

1 [T] to prevent someone from doing something, or to prevent something from happening: *Policies like this aren't going to stop crime.* ♦ **stop sb (from) doing sth** *A broken leg won't stop me from going to the concert.*
2 [I/T] to not do something anymore, or to not happen anymore: *When the rain stops, I'm going out.* ♦ **stop doing sth** *I want to stop smoking.*
3 [I] to not move anymore: *The car stopped at the traffic lights.* ♦ *Lots of people stopped and stared at the accident.*
4 [I] if a bus or train stops somewhere, it stops moving in order to let passengers get on or off: *Does this bus stop in Austin?*
5 [I/T] to not work anymore, or to cause something to not work anymore: *My watch has stopped.*
6 [T] to prevent someone from continuing to walk or drive so that you can talk to them: *I stopped a woman and asked her for directions.*
7 [I] to pause while you are moving or doing something so that you can do something else: *He stopped and listened before opening the door.* ♦ **stop to do sth** *Jeff stopped to get a drink of water.*
8 [T] to block something such as a pipe or hole so that water or another substance cannot go through it
PHRASES **stop at nothing** to do anything in order to get what you want, even if it is very bad
stop it/that used for telling someone not to do something that they are doing: *Stop it! You'll hurt him.*
stop short of (doing) sth to not do something, although you almost do it: *I stopped short of telling him what I really thought.*
PHRASAL VERBS **ˌstop ˈby** to visit someone
ˌstop ˈoff to visit somewhere before continuing to another place
ˈstop up if a sink or BATHTUB stops up, water will not empty out because the pipes are full of something that should not be there

stop² /stɑp/ noun [C] ★
1 a place where you stop on a trip, or the time that you are there: *The president's first stop on his tour will be Honolulu.* ♦ *After a brief stop for coffee, we were on our way.*
2 a place where a bus or train stops in order to let passengers get on or off: *I'm getting off at the next stop.*
PHRASES **come/jerk/skid etc. to a stop** to stop moving
put a stop to sth to prevent or end something
→ PULL¹

stop·gap /ˈstɑpˌgæp/ noun [C] a person or thing that provides a temporary solution

stop·light /ˈstɑpˌlaɪt/ noun [C] *American* a set of lights on a road that tells drivers when to stop and go

stop·o·ver /ˈstɑpˌoʊvər/ noun [C] a stop during a trip, especially during a flight

stop·page /ˈstɑpɪdʒ/ noun [C] a time when people stop working as a protest

stop·per /ˈstɑpər/ noun [C] an object that is put into the top of a bottle in order to prevent the liquid from coming out

stop·watch /ˈstɑpˌwɑtʃ/ noun [C] a small clock that is used for measuring the exact time that it takes to do something

S

stor·age /ˈstɔrɪdʒ/ noun [U] ★ the act of storing something, or the space where something is stored: *The area underneath provides useful storage.* ♦ *Most of our furniture is **in storage**.*

store¹ /stɔr/ noun [C] ★★

1 *American* a place that sells goods: *a grocery store* ♦ *The store manager will be happy to assist you.*

2 a supply of something that is kept so that it can be used later =STOCK: ***a store of** food for the winter*

PHRASES **in store (for sb)** if something is in store for you, it will happen to you in the future

set (great) store by sth to think that something is very important

store² /stɔr/ verb [T] ★★

1 to keep something in a particular place: *Store the cake in an airtight container.*

2 to save information in electronic form, for example in a computer's memory

PHRASAL VERB ˌ**store sth ˈup** to keep a lot of something so that you can use it later: *Many animals store up food for the winter.*

sto·rey /ˈstɔri/ the British spelling of **story** (of a building)

stork /stɔrk/ noun [C] a large bird with long legs and a long beak

storm¹ /stɔrm/ noun ★★

1 [C] an occasion when a lot of rain or snow falls very quickly, often with very strong winds or THUNDER and LIGHTNING: ***A fierce storm** hit the west coast of Florida early this morning.*

2 [singular] a situation in which many people are upset or excited: *His arrest **provoked a storm of protest**.*

PHRASES **take sth by storm** to be very successful in a particular place or among a particular group of people: *Jazz took London and Paris by storm in the 1920s.*

...up a storm *American informal* used for emphasizing that someone does something with all their energy, strength, and ability: *Andy's been cooking up a storm for the party.*

> **Words often used with storm**
>
> *Adjectives often used with **storm** (noun, sense 1)*
>
> ■ **bad, big, fierce, freak, raging, severe, terrible, violent** + STORM: used about storms that are severe
>
> *Verbs often used with **storm** (noun, sense 2)*
>
> ■ **cause, create, provoke, spark, unleash** + STORM: cause a storm by making many people upset or excited

storm² /stɔrm/ verb **1** [T] to use force to enter a place and take control of it **2** [I] to go somewhere very quickly because you are angry or upset: *Rob stormed out of the house and slammed the door.*

storm·y /ˈstɔrmi/ adj **1** with a lot of rain or snow and strong winds **2** involving a lot of anger or arguments

sto·ry /ˈstɔri/ noun [C] ★★★

1 a description of some events. Stories can be imaginary, traditional, or true: *She was **reading a story to** the children.* ♦ ***a story about** a princess and a frog* ♦ ***stories of** his travels in Asia* ♦ *He's written several **children's stories**.*

2 an account of events in a newspaper report or news program: *tonight's **main news stories***

3 an excuse or reason that is not true: *Do you expect me to believe that ridiculous story?*

4 *American* a level of a building: *Our apartment is on the fourth story.* ♦ *A 15-story building is under construction here.*

PHRASES **it's a long story** *spoken* used for saying that you do not want to talk about something because it is complicated

to cut/make a long story short *spoken* used for saying that you are not going to give all the details

sto·ry·tell·er /ˈstɔriˌtelər/ noun [C] someone who tells stories

stout¹ /staʊt/ adj **1** slightly fat **2** strong and thick **3** very determined

stout² /staʊt/ noun [C/U] a type of dark beer

stove¹ /stoʊv/ noun [C] a piece of equipment that provides heat for cooking or for heating a room —*picture* → C2

stove² /stoʊv/ the past tense and past participle of **stave**

stow /stoʊ/ verb [T] to put something somewhere while you are not using it

stow·a·way /ˈstoʊəˌweɪ/ noun [C] someone who hides in a vehicle, ship, or airplane in order to travel without permission

strad·dle /ˈstræd(ə)l/ verb [T] **1** to have one leg on either side of something **2** to be on both sides of something

strag·gle /ˈstræg(ə)l/ verb [I] to move more slowly than other people —**strag·gler** noun [C]

straight¹ /streɪt/ adj ★★

1 not bending/curving	5 attracted to other sex
2 not leaning	6 clean and neat
3 honest and true	7 having highest grades
4 one after the other	+ PHRASES

1 without bends or curves: *a straight line/road* ♦ *She has long straight hair* (=no curls or waves).

2 in the correct position, not leaning to one side or the other: *The picture on that wall isn't straight.* ♦ *Make sure you keep your back straight.*

3 honest and true: *I want **a straight answer**.* ♦ *You have to **be straight with** her.*

4 happening one after the other: *It was the team's sixth straight win.* ♦ *There were five straight days of rain.*

5 *informal* sexually attracted to people of the opposite sex

6 clean and neat: *Is your room straight?*

7 a student who has straight A's has the highest grade in every subject or class: *She got straight A's this term.* ♦ *a straight-A student*

PHRASES **get sth straight** to correctly understand something: ***Let me get this straight** – you didn't know they had your car?*

a straight face if someone has a straight face, they look serious even though they are being funny or they are in a funny situation

straight² /streɪt/ adv ★★★

1 without a bend or curve: *The car was coming **straight at** me.* ♦ *He stared **straight ahead**.*

S

2 directly and immediately: *We decided to go **straight home**.* ♦ *I'll **get straight to the point*** (=say immediately what I want to say).
3 in an upright position, not leaning: *Sit up straight.*
4 without stopping: *We drove for five hours straight.*
PHRASE **straight out** said directly and immediately: *She asked straight out if I liked her.*

ˌstraight aˈway adv *British* immediately

straight·en /ˈstreɪt(ə)n/ verb [I/T] to make something straight, or to become straight: *He straightened his tie.*
PHRASAL VERBS **ˌstraighten sth ˈout** to deal with a problem or a confused situation
ˌstraighten ˈup to stand up straight

straight·for·ward /ˌstreɪtˈfɔrwərd/ adj **1** not complicated or difficult to understand =UNCOMPLICATED: *a straightforward process* **2** clear and honest: *a straightforward answer*

strain¹ /streɪn/ noun **1** [C/U] worries or difficulties that are caused by a difficult situation: *This war will put a strain on the economy.* ♦ *She's been under a lot of strain since the divorce.* **2** [C/U] physical pressure or effort: *All that lifting is putting his back under severe strain.* **3** [C/U] an injury that is caused by twisting or stretching a muscle too much: *a thigh strain* **4** [C] a particular type or aspect of something: *a new strain of the flu virus*

strain² /streɪn/ verb

1 try hard to do sth	4 separate solid & liquid
2 make relationship bad	5 pull/push sth hard
3 injure muscle	

1 [I/T] to try very hard to do something: **strain to do sth** *I strained to hear what they were saying.* **2** [T] to cause problems in a relationship: *Relations between the two countries have been strained by trade disputes.* **3** [T] to injure yourself by twisting or stretching a muscle too much: *Reading in poor light can strain your eyes.* **4** [T] to separate a solid from a liquid by pouring it into a STRAINER **5** [I] to pull or push something very hard: *The elephants strained at their ropes.*

strained /streɪnd/ adj **1** not relaxed or friendly: *a strained atmosphere/silence* **2** done only by trying hard, in a way that is not natural: *a strained smile*

strain·er /ˈstreɪnər/ noun [C] an object like a bowl with holes, used for separating the liquid and solid parts of food

strait /streɪt/ noun [C] a narrow area of water that joins two larger areas of water
PHRASE **in dire straits** in a very difficult situation, especially one that involves a lack of money

strait·jack·et /ˈstreɪtˌdʒækət/ noun [C] a jacket with very long arms that tie behind the back. It is put on someone who is violent in order to stop them from harming anyone.

strand /strænd/ noun [C] **1** a single thin piece of something: *a strand of hair/wire* **2** one of many aspects of something: *the different strands of the story*

strand·ed /ˈstrændəd/ adj left in a place or situation that you cannot get away from: *The passengers were stranded at the airport overnight.*

strange /streɪndʒ/ adj ★★★
1 unusual or unexpected in a way that surprises, worries, or frightens you: *Ian is a very strange person.* ♦ ***It seemed strange** that she would leave so early.* ♦ ***For some strange reason**, I thought she lived in New York.*
2 not familiar or known to you: *When you arrive in a new country, everything **seems strange**.*
—**strange·ly** adv: *Everyone looked at him strangely.*

strang·er /ˈstreɪndʒər/ noun [C] ★
1 someone who you do not know: *I didn't want to share a room with **a complete stranger**.*
2 someone who does not know a place well
PHRASE **be no stranger to sth** to have a lot of experience of something: *Davis is no stranger to tragedy.*

stran·gle /ˈstræŋg(ə)l/ verb [T] **1** to kill a person or an animal by squeezing their throat **2** to stop the development of something

stran·gle·hold /ˈstræŋg(ə)lˌhoʊld/ noun [C] strong power over someone or something that prevents them from having any freedom

strap¹ /stræp/ noun [C] a narrow piece of cloth, plastic, etc. that you use for fastening or carrying something, or for holding something in position: *a bag with leather straps* ♦ *The dress had thin shoulder straps.*

strap² /stræp/ verb [T] to hold or keep something in position by fastening a strap around it: *He strapped down the lid of the basket.*

strata the plural of **stratum**

stra·te·gic /strəˈtidʒɪk/ adj **1** designed to achieve a particular aim in war, business, or politics: *strategic planning* ♦ *a strategic political move* **2** strategic weapons are designed to hit an enemy's home country
—**stra·te·gi·cal·ly** /strəˈtidʒɪkli/ adv: *a strategically located military base*

strat·e·gist /ˈstrætədʒɪst/ noun [C] someone who develops a business, military, or political plan

strat·e·gy /ˈstrætədʒi/ noun ★
1 [C] a plan or method for achieving something: *a strategy to reduce government spending* ♦ *successful **language-learning strategies***
2 [U] the skill of planning how to achieve something: *experts in military strategy*

Words often used with strategy

*Verbs often used with **strategy** (sense 1)*

- **adopt, develop, devise, evolve, formulate, plan, produce** + STRATEGY: invent a strategy for doing something
- **follow, implement, pursue** + STRATEGY: use a strategy in order to do something

stra·tum /ˈstrɑtəm/ (plural **stra·ta** /ˈstrɑtə/) noun [C] **1** a group or class in society **2** a layer of a particular type of rock

straw /strɔ/ noun **1** [U] the yellow stems of

S

dried crops such as wheat. It is given to animals to sleep on. **2** [C] a long thin tube that you use for drinking

PHRASE **the last/final straw** the last of a series of bad events that makes you decide to try to change a situation

straw·ber·ry /ˈstrɔˌberi/ noun [C] a small soft red fruit with a lot of very small seeds on its skin —*picture* → C10

stray¹ /streɪ/ verb [I] **1** to move away from the correct place or path: *The airplane strayed into enemy airspace.* **2** to start talking about a new subject without intending to

stray² /streɪ/ adj **1** lost or without a home: *a stray cat/dog* **2** separated from a group or from the main part of something: *a stray curl of hair*

stray³ /streɪ/ noun [C] a pet that is lost or has left its home

streak¹ /strik/ noun [C] **1** a line or long mark that is different color than the color surrounding it: *The bird has a dark streak on its breast.* ♦ *a streak of lightning* (=a long line of lightning) **2** a part of someone's character that is different from the rest of their character: *The child has a stubborn streak.*

PHRASE **a winning/losing streak** a series of wins/losses in a game or sport

streak² /strik/ verb [I] to move very quickly: *Jet planes streaked overhead.*

PHRASE **be streaked (with sth)** to have lines or marks of a different color: *Jim's face was streaked with paint.*

stream¹ /strim/ noun [C] ★

1 a small narrow river

2 a continuous flow of liquid or gas: *A **stream of** blood was running down his face.*

3 a continuous flow of people or things: ***a stream of** visitors/traffic*

stream² /strim/ verb [I] **1** to flow continuously: *Tears streamed down his face.* **2** to move in large numbers in a continuous flow: *Students streamed into the building.* **3** to shine, or to give off light: *sunlight streaming through the windows*

stream·er /ˈstrimər/ noun [C] a long colored piece of paper or cloth that is used for decoration

stream·ing /ˈstrimɪŋ/ noun [U] *computing* a technology for sending sound or pictures to your computer through the Internet

stream·line /ˈstrimˌlaɪn/ verb [T] **1** to improve something such as an organization or process by making it more modern or simple **2** to design something with a smooth shape so that it will move quickly through air or water

street /strit/ noun [C] ★★★ a road in a town or city with buildings along it: *State Street/Fourth Street* ♦ *I just saw Bill walking down the street.* ♦ *Who lives across the street?* → ROAD

PHRASE **on the street(s)** **1** with no house to live in: *After losing his job, then his family, he ended up on the streets.* **2** in public places in a town: *More police officers are being put on the streets.*

street·light /ˈstritˌlaɪt/ noun [C] a light on top of a long pole on a street or road

ˈstreet-ˌsmart adj *American* able to deal with difficult or dangerous situations in a confident way

strength /streŋθ/ noun ★★★

1 physical power	5 sth sb does very well
2 ability not to break	6 amount of influence
3 of sb's character	+ PHRASE
4 power of sth	

1 [U] the physical energy that someone has to lift or move things: *upper body strength* ♦ *The job requires a lot of **physical strength**.* ♦ *I didn't **have the strength to** get out of bed.*

2 [C/U] the ability of something to pull, push, or support something without breaking: *Test **the strength of** the rope.*

3 [U] the ability to deal with difficult situations: *She has great **strength of character**.*

4 [U] power in a military, political, or economic situation: ***the strength of** the dollar against the euro*

5 [C] something that someone does very well =ABILITY: *Ron's main strength is his ability to motivate his players.* ♦ *The test shows the students' **strengths and weaknesses**.*

6 [U] the amount of influence that a person or group has: ***the strength of** public opinion*

PHRASE **on the strength of** based on what you saw, heard, experienced, etc.

strength·en /ˈstreŋθən/ verb [I/T] ★ to make someone or something stronger, or to become stronger: *Aerobic exercise strengthens the heart.* ♦ *a sense of community that has strengthened over time*

stren·u·ous /ˈstrenjuəs/ adj **1** using a lot of effort, energy, or strength: *strenuous exercise* **2** determined: *strenuous opposition/objections*

stress¹ /stres/ noun ★

1 [C/U] a worried or nervous feeling that makes you unable to relax, or a situation that makes you feel like this: ***the stresses and strains** of everyday living* ♦ *Carol's been **under a lot of stress** lately.*

2 [C/U] physical pressure that can make something break or change its shape: *Judo puts a lot of **stress on** your knee joints.*

3 [U] special importance that is given to something so that you pay more attention to it =EMPHASIS: *The course **puts a lot of stress on** communication.*

4 [C/U] the emphasis that you put on a particular word or part of a word by saying it more loudly → INTONATION

> **Words often used with stress**
>
> *Verbs often used with **stress** (noun, sense 1)*
>
> - **cause, create, generate, produce** + STRESS: cause stress
> - **alleviate, combat, ease, manage, reduce, relieve** + STRESS: reduce stress or deal with it successfully

stress² /stres/ verb [T] ★

1 to emphasize something such as an idea, fact, or detail: *The president **stressed the importance of** controlling spending.* ♦ **+that** *I want to stress that I accept responsibility for these mistakes.*

2 to say a particular word or part of a word more loudly

Words often used with stress

Nouns often used with ***stress*** *(verb, sense 1)*

- STRESS + **desirability, importance, necessity, need, significance, urgency, value:** emphasize that something is important or necessary

stressed /strest/ or ˌ**stressed ˈout** adj worried and unable to relax

stress•ful /ˈstresfəl/ adj making you feel stressed: *My new job is much less stressful.*

ˈ**stress ˌmark** noun [C] a mark that shows you which part of a word is pronounced more loudly

stretch[1] /stretʃ/ verb ★★

1 make longer/wider	5 use money/time etc.
2 make smooth/tight	+ PHRASE
3 of body	+ PHRASAL VERBS
4 continue	

1 [I/T] if you stretch something, or if it stretches, it becomes longer or wider when you pull it: *Can you stretch the material a little?* ♦ *My sweater stretched the first time I washed it.*
2 [T] to pull something so that it becomes smooth, straight, and tight: *The canvas is stretched across a metal frame.*
3 [I/T] to make your arms, legs, or body as long as they can be: *I leaned back in the chair and stretched.* ♦ *Todd stretched his hand toward the rope.*
4 [I] to continue for a particular distance or time: *The beach stretches for miles in each direction.* ♦ *The team has a history that stretches back to 1895.*
5 [T] to use all the money, time, or ability that is available: *I don't think this new job stretches him much.* ♦ *City funds were* ***stretched to the limit.***

PHRASE **stretch your legs** to go for a walk after you have been sitting for a long time

PHRASAL VERBS ˌ**stretch ˈout** to lie down: *I'll just stretch out on the sofa.*

ˌ**stretch sth ˈout** *same as* **stretch**[1] 3: *I stretched out a hand to touch her face.*

stretch[2] /stretʃ/ noun [C] **1** an area of land or water: *a narrow stretch of water* **2** a continuous period of time: *You can't learn it all in such a short stretch of time.* ♦ *He'll surf the Internet for six hours at a stretch* (=continuously). **3** a movement or exercise in which you make a part of your body as long as possible

PHRASE **not by any stretch of the imagination** used for emphasizing that you think that something is not true or possible

stretch[3] /stretʃ/ adj stretch cloth becomes wider or longer when you pull it

stretch•er /ˈstretʃər/ noun [C] a type of bed that is used for carrying someone who is injured or sick

strew /stru/ (past participle **strewn** /strun/) verb **be strewn (with)** to be covered with things that are spread around in a messy way: *One room was strewn with children's toys.*

strick•en /ˈstrɪkən/ adj damaged, destroyed, or affected by serious problems

strict /strɪkt/ adj ★
1 someone who is strict expects people to obey rules completely, or obeys rules completely themselves: *The coach is very strict about our diet.*
2 strict rules or conditions must be obeyed completely: *They operate within* ***strict time limits.*** ♦ *Lynn gave us* ***strict instructions*** *to be good.*
3 exact, or accurate: *He was not depressed* ***in the strict sense of the word.***

strict•ly /ˈstrɪk(t)li/ adv **1** in a strict way: *strictly enforced laws* **2** completely: *It's a strictly neutral organization.* ♦ *I don't think that's strictly true.*

PHRASE **strictly speaking** used for showing that you are trying to be accurate, or trying to follow the rules: *Tomatoes are not, strictly speaking, vegetables.*

stride[1] /straɪd/ (past tense **strode** /stroʊd/; past participle **strid•den** /ˈstrɪd(ə)n/) verb [I] to walk with energy and confidence: *She strode onto the stage.*

stride[2] /straɪd/ noun [C] a long confident step

PHRASES **hit your stride** to begin to do something confidently and well

make strides to make progress toward a goal

take sth in stride to not be upset by something

stri•dent /ˈstraɪd(ə)nt/ adj **1** expressing strong opinions in a way that offends some people: *a strident opponent of the treaty* **2** a strident voice or sound is loud and unpleasant

strife /straɪf/ noun [U] *formal* fighting or disagreement between people

strike[1] /straɪk/ (past tense and past participle **struck** /strʌk/) verb ★★

1 hit against	7 make flame
2 hit with hand, etc.	8 clock: make sound
3 protest by not working	9 make deal/agreement
4 affect sb/sth suddenly	10 find gold/oil etc.
5 when you think sth	+ PHRASES
6 make violent attack	+ PHRASAL VERBS

1 [T] *formal* to hit against someone or something: *The car struck a tree.* ♦ *The ball struck her hard on the left shoulder.* ♦ *About 50 worshippers were inside the church when it was* ***struck by lightning.***
2 [T] *formal* to hit someone or something with your hand, a tool, or a weapon: **strike sb on/in sth** *We watched helplessly as she struck the child in the face.*
3 [I] to refuse to work for a period of time as a protest about your pay or conditions at work: *Automobile workers were threatening to* ***strike over*** *the job losses.*
4 [I/T] if something unpleasant or dangerous strikes, or if it strikes someone or something, it happens to them suddenly and unexpectedly: *Three earthquakes struck Peru on April 5th and 6th.* ♦ *That same year,* ***tragedy struck*** *again.*
5 [T] if a thought or idea strikes you, it enters your mind suddenly: *The first thing that struck me about Alex was her self-confidence.*
6 [I] to make a sudden violent or illegal attack: *Police are worried the man could strike again.*
7 [I/T] to rub a match against a hard surface in order to produce a flame
8 [I/T] if a clock strikes, or if it strikes a particular time, it makes a sound to show

S

what the time is: ***The town hall clock struck** midnight.*

9 [T] to make an agreement: *The two sides had just **struck a deal**.*

10 [T] to find something such as gold or oil by digging or DRILLING

PHRASES **strike sb as sth** to make someone have a particular opinion or feeling: *He didn't strike me as the jealous type.* ♦ ***It struck me as** a little strange that she was always alone.*

strike a balance (between sth and sth) to find a solution that is more reasonable and fair than either of two extreme possibilities

within striking distance (of sth) close to something, or close to achieving something

PHRASAL VERBS **ˌstrike ˈback** to attack, harm, or criticize someone who has attacked, harmed, or criticized you = RETALIATE: *They threatened to **strike back against** the UN forces.*

ˌstrike ˈout 1 to try to hit, attack, or criticize someone or something **2** *informal* to be unsuccessful in trying to do something

ˌstrike (sb) ˈout in baseball, if a BATTER strikes out, or if a pitcher strikes the batter out, the batter misses the ball three times, ending their turn at trying to hit it

ˌstrike ˈup sth to start something such as a relationship or a conversation with someone: *The bartender seemed to have struck up a friendship with Jane.*

strike² /straɪk/ noun ★★

1 [C/U] a period of time during which people refuse to work, as a protest: *A train strike has crippled the city.* ♦ *Workers have been **on strike** since Friday.* → HUNGER STRIKE

2 [C] a failure to hit the ball in baseball

3 [C] a military attack: ***a strike on** the airfield*

PHRASE **two/three strikes against sb/sth** *informal* two or three qualities, facts, or details that are a disadvantage

strik•er /ˈstraɪkər/ noun [C] a worker who is taking part in a strike

S

strik•ing /ˈstraɪkɪŋ/ adj attracting your interest or attention because of an unusual feature: *a striking young woman* ♦ *There are some striking differences in the two theories.* —**strik•ing•ly** adv

string¹ /strɪŋ/ noun ★★

1 [C/U] thin rope that you use for tying things together: *a piece of string* ♦ *The balloon was attached to a long string.*

2 [C] a group of things or events: *He owns **a string of** restaurants in the Midwest.* ♦ *We had **a string of** burglaries in the area last month.*

3 [C] one of several long pieces of NYLON or wire on a musical instrument. You touch them in order to produce sound.

4 the strings [plural] the STRINGED INSTRUMENTS in an orchestra, or the people who play them

PHRASE **no strings (attached)** without any special conditions that limit an offer or agreement

→ PULL¹

string² /strɪŋ/ (past tense and past participle **strung** /strʌŋ/) verb [T] **1** to hang a string or rope somewhere, or to hang something that is like string or rope: *She strung a rope between two trees.* ♦ *Lights were strung all round the garden.* **2** to pass a string through several things in order to make a chain: *The children sat on the floor stringing beads.*

PHRASAL VERB **ˌstring sth toˈgether** to arrange a group of things into a series: *He can hardly string a sentence together.*

stringed in•stru•ment /ˌstrɪŋd ˈɪnstrʊmənt/ noun [C] any musical instrument with strings that you touch to produce sound, for example a VIOLIN

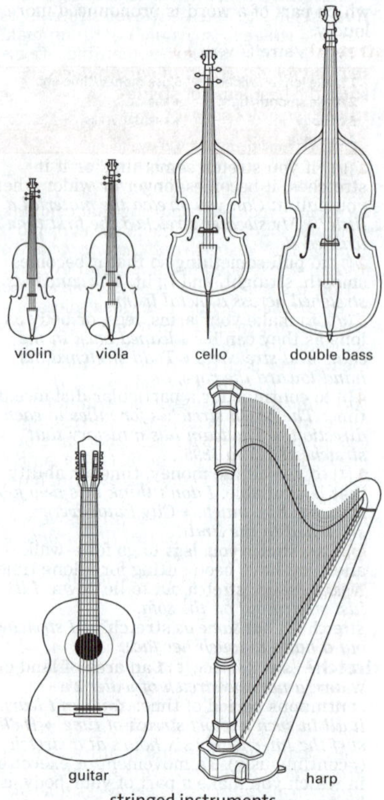

stringed instruments

strin•gent /ˈstrɪndʒənt/ adj stringent rules or conditions are strict —**strin•gent•ly** adv

strip¹ /strɪp/ noun [C] ★ a long narrow piece of something: *a strip of land* ♦ *Cut the paper into strips.*

strip² /strɪp/ verb **1** [I/T] to take off all of your clothes, or to take off all of another person's clothes: *They all stripped and ran into the water.* **2** [T] to remove something that covers something: **strip sth off/from sth** *The wind had stripped the leaves from the trees.* **3** [T] to take something away using force or authority: **strip sb of sth** *They stripped the prisoners of weapons and cash.*

stripe /straɪp/ noun [C] a line of one color on a background of a different color: *a white shirt with red stripes*

striped /straɪpt/ adj with a pattern of stripes: *a blue and white striped tablecloth*

ˈstrip ˌmall noun [C] *American* a row of stores contained in one long building with its own parking lot

ˌstripped-ˈdown adj keeping only the most essential parts and nothing extra

strip·per /ˈstrɪpər/ noun [C] an entertainer who performs stripteases

strip·tease /ˈstrɪpˌtiz/ noun [C/U] an entertainment in which someone takes off their clothes while music is playing

strive /straɪv/ (past tense **strove** /stroʊv/; past participle **striv·en** /ˈstrɪv(ə)n/) verb [I] to make a lot of effort to achieve something: *We are striving for perfection in our products.*

strode the past tense of **stride**[1]

stroke[1] /stroʊk/ noun [C]

1 medical condition	4 in swimming
2 unexpected event	5 single pen/brush mark
3 in sport	6 hand movement

1 a serious medical condition that can make someone suddenly unable to speak or move: *Leni suffered a stroke and died at the age of 89.* **2** an unexpected but important event or action: *a stroke of luck/good fortune* ♦ *It was a real stroke of genius* (=an idea that shows great intelligence). **3** a movement in which someone hits the ball in some sports, or the way in which they make this movement: *He slammed the ball with a powerful backhand stroke.* **4** a style of swimming, or one complete movement of the arms and legs in swimming **5** a single short line or mark made with a pen or brush **6** a gentle movement of your hand across skin, hair, or fur

stroke[2] /stroʊk/ verb [T] to gently move your hand over skin, hair, or fur: *She stroked his hair as he fell asleep.*

stroll /stroʊl/ verb [I] to walk without hurrying —**stroll** noun [C]

strong /strɔŋ/ adj ★★★

1 powerful and healthy	6 firmly believed/felt
2 produced with power	7 of high degree/level
3 not easily damaged	8 with power/influence
4 with confidence, etc.	9 very noticeable
5 good at doing sth	+ PHRASES

1 physically powerful and healthy: *Are you strong enough to carry that?* ♦ *strong hands/arms/muscles* ♦ *Two weeks after her surgery she was **feeling much stronger**.*

2 done with a lot of power or force: *a strong punch/kick*

3 not easily broken, damaged, or destroyed: *a strong fabric/glue/rope* ♦ *a strong friendship/marriage/partnership*

4 someone who is strong has confidence, determination, and emotional strength: *You have to be strong and not let their jokes bother you.*

5 good at doing something: *She's **a strong swimmer**.*

6 firmly believed or felt: *strong views/feelings/opinions*

7 of a high degree or level: *There's **a strong possibility** that they'll get married in the spring.*

8 with a lot of power or influence: *a strong leader/president* ♦ *a strong wind/current* ♦ *Our lawyers say we have **a very strong case**.*

9 very noticeable: *a strong light/color* ♦ *a strong British accent* ♦ *a strong smell/taste*

PHRASES **going strong** successful, or healthy: *The company was founded in 1860 and is still going strong.*

sb's strong point a good quality that makes someone or something effective: *Paula's ability to work quickly is one of her strongest points.* ♦ *Patience is not my strong point* (=I am not a patient person).

strong·hold /ˈstrɔŋˌhoʊld/ noun [C] a place where the majority of people have the same political or religious beliefs: *a Republican stronghold*

strong·ly /ˈstrɔŋli/ adv used for emphasizing that someone is very serious about what they say, feel, or believe: *I would strongly recommend that you don't pay him anything yet.* ♦ *I feel strongly that the trial was unfair.*

strove the past tense of **strive**

struck the past tense and past participle of **strike**[1]

struc·tur·al /ˈstrʌktʃ(ə)rəl/ adj **1** related to the structure of something such as a building: *structural damage* **2** related to the way that something is organized: *structural changes in the industry* —**struc·tur·al·ly** adv

struc·ture[1] /ˈstrʌktʃər/ noun ★★★

1 [C] something large such as a building or a bridge that is built from different parts

2 [C/U] the way in which the parts of something are organized or arranged into a whole: *sentence structure* ♦ ***the structure of** DNA* ♦ *the changing **structure of** agriculture in this country*

3 [C] an organization or system that is made up of many parts: *a social/power/class structure*

struc·ture[2] /ˈstrʌktʃər/ verb [T] to plan or organize something

strug·gle[1] /ˈstrʌg(ə)l/ verb [I] ★

1 to try hard to do something that is very difficult: **struggle to do sth** *She was struggling to cope with her work.* ♦ *a documentary about this species and its **struggle for survival***

2 to try very hard to defeat someone or stop them having power over you: **struggle to do sth** *We have to struggle to win our freedom.* ♦ *women **struggling against** oppression*

3 to use your strength to fight against someone or something: *The man grabbed him, but he struggled free.*

strug·gle[2] /ˈstrʌg(ə)l/ noun ★

1 [C] an attempt to do something that takes a lot of effort over a period of time: ***the struggle for** democracy* ♦ *her **struggle with** the disease* ♦ ***the** community's **struggle against** racism*

2 [C/U] a fight, or a war: *the **armed struggle** against the government*

3 [singular] something that takes a lot of physical or mental effort: *Foreign languages were always a struggle for him.* ♦ **a struggle to do sth** *It was a struggle to get up the hill in the snow.*

strum /strʌm/ verb [T] to play a musical instrument such as a guitar by moving your fingers across its strings

S

strung the past tense and past participle of string[2]

strung out /ˌstrʌŋ ˈaʊt/ adj *informal* very tired and nervous, especially from using illegal drugs

strut /strʌt/ verb [I] to walk in a confident and proud way

PHRASE **strut your stuff** *informal* to show people how good you are at doing something, or how attractive you look

stub¹ /stʌb/ verb [T] to hit your toe against something accidentally so that it hurts

PHRASAL VERB **ˌstub sth ˈout** to press a cigarette hard against a surface to make it stop burning

stub² /stʌb/ noun [C] **1** the part of something that remains after you have used the rest: *a pencil/cigarette stub* **2** the part of a ticket or check that you keep to prove that you paid for something

stub·ble /ˈstʌb(ə)l/ noun [U] **1** the short stiff hairs on a man's face that grow into a BEARD **2** the ends of plants that are left above ground after a farmer cuts a grain crop

stub·born /ˈstʌbərn/ adj **1** not willing to change your ideas or decisions: *Stop being so stubborn!* ♦ *stubborn anger/pride* **2** very difficult to change, defeat, or remove: *stubborn opposition* ♦ *stubborn weeds/stains* —**stub·born·ly** adv, **stub·born·ness** noun [U]

stub·by /ˈstʌbi/ adj short and thick

stuc·co /ˈstʌkoʊ/ noun [U] a substance used for covering walls to give them a rough surface

stuck¹ /stʌk/ adj **1** caught or held in a position so that you cannot move: *Carl's car got stuck in the mud.* **2** unable to solve a problem that prevents you from continuing something: *I'm really stuck on this algebra problem.* **3** *informal* having to deal with someone or something that you do not like but cannot avoid: *I guess I'm stuck with this haircut.*

S

stuck² the past tense and past participle of stick¹

stud¹ /stʌd/ noun [C] **1** a small piece of jewelry on a short metal post that is worn through a part of your body **2** a small piece of metal that sticks up from a surface: *a jacket covered with metal studs*

stud² /stʌd/ verb **be studded with sth** to be covered or decorated with a lot of something: *a sky studded with stars*

stu·dent /ˈstud(ə)nt/ noun [C] ★★★ someone who goes to a university, college, or school: *Jennifer is one of my best students.* ♦ *a physics/art student* ♦ *a student organization/newspaper*

- In American English, a **student** means someone who goes to school, college, or university.
- In British English, a **student** usually means someone who goes to university or college. A child who goes to school is usually called a **pupil**.

ˌstudent ˈcouncil noun [C/U] *American* the elected group of students who make decisions about student activities in a school

ˌstudent ˈgovernment noun *American* **1** [U] the system by which decisions about student life and activities at a high school, college, or university are made by a group of elected students **2** [C] an elected group of student officials

ˌstudent ˈloan noun [C] money that a bank or institution lends to a student so that they can go to a college or university

ˌstudent ˈunion noun [C] a building at a college or university where students can meet and take part in activities

stu·di·o /ˈstudiˌoʊ/ noun [C] ★★
1 a room in which someone such as a painter or photographer works
2 a small apartment that has only one main room
3 a company that produces movies
4 a set of rooms where music or a movie, television show, or radio show is recorded

stu·di·ous /ˈstudiəs/ adj **1** tending to study and read a lot **2** giving a lot of attention and care to what you are doing or learning —**stu·di·ous·ly** adv

stud·y¹ /ˈstʌdi/ noun ★★★
1 [U] the process of learning about a subject or problem: ***the study of*** *criminal behavior* ♦ *a center for* ***the study of*** *Asian languages*
2 [C] a research project that examines a problem or subject: *The study showed a link between the chemicals and cancer.*
3 studies [plural] the work that you do while you are at a college or university: *Sarah wants to continue her studies.*
4 [C] a room in a house where you can read or work quietly

stud·y² /ˈstʌdi/ verb ★★★
1 [I/T] to learn about a subject by going to classes: *She's studying history at the university.* ♦ *Michael was* ***studying to be a*** *lawyer.* → LEARN
2 [I] to do work such as reading and homework: *You need to study hard if you want to pass.*
3 [T] to read or look at something very carefully: *I studied various maps of the area.*
4 [T] to learn about a problem or subject using scientific methods: *They will study the effect of technology on jobs.*

stuff¹ /stʌf/ noun [U] *informal* ★★★
1 objects, or things: *What's all this stuff on my desk?* ♦ *By the time we got to the sale, all the good stuff was gone.* ♦ *I spend most of my time doing really boring stuff.*
2 a material, or a substance: *The costumes were made of thin, gauzy stuff.* ♦ *What's that sticky stuff in your hair?*
3 general information: *I already know all that stuff.*

PHRASES **...and stuff (like that)** *spoken* used for referring to things that are similar or related to the subject that you are discussing: *She wants us to smile more, and stuff like that.*
know your stuff *informal* to know a lot about something

stuff² /stʌf/ verb [T] **1** to push something soft into a space or container: *Alice quickly stuffed her clothes into a suitcase and left.* **2** to fill a container or space with something, especially something soft

stuffed /stʌft/ adj **1** full of things: *The drawer was stuffed with money.* **2** *informal* having eaten until you are full or sick

stuff•ing /ˈstʌfɪŋ/ noun [U] **1** soft material that is used for filling something such as a toy or a seat **2** food that has been cut into small pieces and put inside meat or vegetables

stuff•y /ˈstʌfi/ adj **1** a stuffy room is unpleasant to be in because it is too warm and there is no fresh air in it **2** *informal* if you have a stuffy nose or head, you cannot breathe well because of a cold or similar illness **3** *informal* with strict or old-fashioned attitudes —**stuff•i•ness** noun [U]

stum•ble /ˈstʌmb(ə)l/ verb [I] **1** to fall, or almost fall, while you are walking or running: *Derek stumbled over a fallen tree.* **2** to make a mistake when you are speaking
PHRASAL VERB **ˈstumble aˌcross sb/sth** or **ˈstumble on sb/sth** to find something or meet someone by accident

stum•bling block /ˈstʌmblɪŋ ˌblɑk/ noun [C] a difficulty that causes mistakes or prevents progress

stump[1] /stʌmp/ noun [C] **1** the part of a tree that is left above the ground after it has been cut off at the base **2** the remaining part of someone's arm, leg, or finger after the rest is cut off
PHRASE **on the stump** *American* a politician who is on the stump is traveling around to meet voters and try to get their support

stump[2] /stʌmp/ verb **be stumped by sth** to be unable to explain something mysterious, or to be unable to answer a question

stun /stʌn/ verb [T] **1** to shock and surprise someone so much that they cannot react immediately: *His violent death stunned the nation.* **2** to hit someone so hard on the head that they are unable to move or to react for a short time —**stunned** /stʌnd/ adj

stung the past tense and past participle of sting[1]

stunk the past tense and past participle of stink[1]

stun•ning /ˈstʌnɪŋ/ adj **1** very impressive or beautiful: *The view from the top of the hill is stunning.* ♦ *a stunning man* **2** surprising, powerful, and effective —**stun•ning•ly** adv

stunt[1] /stʌnt/ noun [C] **1** something that is done in order to impress someone or to get their attention: *a publicity stunt* **2** something dangerous that is done to entertain people, often as part of a movie

stunt[2] /stʌnt/ verb **stunt sb's/sth's growth** to stop someone or something from growing

stu•pen•dous /stuˈpendəs/ adj very impressive, large, or surprising

stu•pid /ˈstupɪd/ adj ★★
1 not intelligent, or showing bad judgment: *What a **stupid question**! ♦ I didn't ask because I was afraid of **looking stupid**.*
2 silly or annoying: *He kept singing the same stupid song. ♦ Does this shirt **look stupid**?*
—**stu•pid•i•ty** /stuˈpɪdəti/ noun [U], **stu•pid•ly** adv: *I stupidly loaned him some money.*

stu•por /ˈstupər/ noun [singular/U] the condition of being unable to think or act normally because you are not completely conscious

stur•dy /ˈstɜrdi/ adj strong and thick or solid: *sturdy legs/shoes/plants*

stut•ter /ˈstʌtər/ verb [I/T] to repeat the sounds of words in an uncontrolled way when you speak, because you are nervous or you have a speech problem = STAMMER —**stut•ter** noun [singular]

sty /staɪ/ noun [C] a small building where pigs are kept on a farm

style[1] /staɪl/ noun ★★★
1 [C] the individual way that someone behaves and does things: *I really dislike her teaching style. ♦ Picasso's **style of painting** ♦ Having big parties is **not my style**.*
2 [U] an attractive or impressive way of behaving or doing something: *Greg **has a lot of style**.*
3 [C/U] the way that something is made or done that is typical of a particular group, time, or place: *I don't like **the style of** dresses that are out now. ♦ traditional and modern styles of furniture*
PHRASES **in style 1** fashionable at a particular time **2** in a very comfortable, impressive, or expensive way: *Let's rent a big car and go in style.*
out of style not fashionable

style[2] /staɪl/ verb [T] to give something a particular shape or style

styl•ish /ˈstaɪlɪʃ/ adj attractive and fashionable: *stylish clothes* —**styl•ish•ly** adv

sty•lis•tic /staɪˈlɪstɪk/ adj relating to styles: *stylistic differences between the two books* —**sty•lis•ti•cal•ly** /staɪˈlɪstɪkli/ adv

styl•ized /ˈstaɪˌlaɪzd/ adj in a style that is artificial instead of REALISTIC (=like life)

sty•mie /ˈstaɪmi/ verb [T] *informal* to stop someone or something from continuing or achieving something

Sty•ro•foam /ˈstaɪrəˌfoʊm/ *trademark* a light plastic material, used, for example, for making containers that keep food hot

suave /swɑv/ adj confident and polite in a way that may not be sincere

sub /sʌb/ noun [C] *informal* **1** a SUBMARINE **2** *American* a sandwich made with meat, cheese, vegetables, etc. on a long narrow piece of bread **3** a SUBSTITUTE, especially for a sports player or a teacher

sub- /sʌb/ prefix **1** below a particular level: *sub-zero temperatures* **2** smaller or less important than someone or something: *a subheading* **3** one small part of a larger thing: *a subsection*

sub•com•mit•tee /ˈsʌbkəˌmɪti/ noun [C] a small group of people who are part of a larger committee and who meet to discuss one particular thing

sub•con•scious[1] /sʌbˈkɑnʃəs/ adj relating to thoughts or feelings that you have but do not think about, or that you do not realize that you have —**sub•con•scious•ly** adv

sub•con•scious[2] /sʌbˈkɑnʃəs/ noun [singular] the part of your mind that contains thoughts and feelings that you do not think about, or that you do not realize that you have

sub•con•ti•nent /sʌbˈkɑntɪnənt/ noun [C] a large area of land that forms part of a CONTINENT, especially the part of Asia that contains India, Pakistan, and Bangladesh

S

sub•con•tract /ˌsʌbˈkɑnˌtrækt/ noun [C] a contract in which one person agrees to do some of the work that another person has agreed to do —**sub•con•tract** /ˌsʌbkənˈtrækt/ verb [I/T], **sub•con•tract•or** /ˌsʌbˈkɑnˌtræktər/ noun [C]

sub•cul•ture /ˈsʌbˌkʌltʃər/ noun [C] a group of people whose beliefs and ways of behaving make them different from the rest of society

sub•di•vide /ˌsʌbdɪˈvaɪd/ verb [T] to divide the parts of something that has already been divided

sub•di•vi•sion /ˈsʌbdɪˌvɪʒ(ə)n/ noun [C] **1** *American* an area of land that has been divided into smaller parts for building houses on **2** one small part of something that has already been divided into several larger parts

sub•due /səbˈdu/ verb [T] **1** to make someone stop behaving in an uncontrolled or violent way **2** *formal* to defeat a place or a group of people, and take control of them

sub•dued /səbˈdud/ adj **1** quiet and slightly sad or worried **2** not very loud or bright: *subdued lighting*

sub•group /ˈsʌbˌgrup/ noun [C] a small group of people who form part of a larger group

sub•head•ing /ˈsʌbˌhedɪŋ/ noun [C] the title of one section of a longer piece of writing

sub•ject¹ /ˈsʌbˌdʒekt/ noun [C] ★★★

1 sth you discuss	4 sb in scientific test
2 sth taught at school	5 sth in picture
3 in grammar	6 sb ruled by king/queen

1 something that you discuss or write about =TOPIC: *He's never mentioned **the subject of** money.* ♦ *Someone **raised the subject of*** (=started talking about) *sports facilities.* ♦ *Can we **change the subject*** (=talk about something else), *please?*
2 something that you learn or teach in a school, for example English, mathematics, or biology
3 *linguistics* in English grammar, the person, place, or thing that does what the verb describes. In the sentence "Mary threw the ball," "Mary" is the subject.
4 a person or animal that is used in a medical or scientific test
5 a person or thing that is shown in a picture
6 someone who lives in a country that is controlled by a king or queen: *a British subject*

sub•ject² /ˈsʌbˌdʒekt/ adj
PHRASE **subject to sth 1** likely to be affected by something: *Train times are subject to change during bad weather.* **2** in a situation where you have to obey a rule or law: *All building firms are subject to tight controls.* **3** depending on whether something happens: *Goods will be sent out within 14 days, subject to availability.*

sub•ject³ /səbˈdʒekt/ verb [T] to make someone experience something unpleasant: *Her husband subjected her to years of physical abuse.*

sub•jec•tive /səbˈdʒektɪv/ adj based on your own feelings and ideas, and not on facts ≠OBJECTIVE —**sub•jec•tive•ly** adv, **sub•jec•tiv•i•ty** /ˌsʌbdʒekˈtɪvəti/ noun [U]

ˈ**subject ˌline** noun [C] *computing* the place in an e-mail where you can type what the e-mail is about

ˈ**subject ˌmatter** noun [U] the things that a speech, a piece of writing, an article, etc. is about

sub•junc•tive /səbˈdʒʌŋktɪv/ noun [singular] *linguistics* the form of a verb that is used for expressing doubts and wishes. For example, in the sentence "I wish I were taller," "were" is in the subjunctive. —**sub•junc•tive** adj

sub•lime /səˈblaɪm/ adj **1** extremely good or beautiful **2** *formal* used for describing an extreme feeling or quality

sub•ma•rine /ˈsʌbməˌrin/ noun [C] a ship that can travel both on the surface of the water and under water =SUB

sub•merge /səbˈmɜrdʒ/ verb [I/T] to go completely under water, or to put something completely under water —**sub•merged** /səbˈmɜrdʒd/ adj

sub•mis•sion /səbˈmɪʃ(ə)n/ noun **1** [U] *formal* the action of accepting that someone has defeated you or has power over you **2** [C/U] the process of giving a document to someone for them to consider, or the document that you give them **3** [C] a statement that you make to a judge or official committee

sub•mis•sive /səbˈmɪsɪv/ adj willing to do what other people tell you to do without arguing —**sub•mis•sive•ly** adv, **sub•mis•sive•ness** noun [U]

sub•mit /səbˈmɪt/ verb ★
1 [T] to formally give something to someone so that they can make a decision about it: *The plans will be submitted next week.*
2 [I/T] to accept that someone has power over you, and to do what they want: *The rebels have refused to **submit to** the national government.* ♦ **submit yourself to sb** *Women were supposed to submit themselves totally to their husbands.*

sub•or•din•ate¹ /səˈbɔrdɪnət/ adj **1** having less power or authority than someone else **2** less important than something else —**sub•or•di•na•tion** /səˌbɔrd(ə)nˈeɪʃ(ə)n/ noun [U]

sub•or•din•ate² /səˈbɔrdɪnət/ noun [C] someone who has less power or authority than someone else

subˌordinate ˈclause noun [C] *linguistics* a group of words that gives extra information about a sentence but cannot form a sentence by itself. For example, in the sentence "Marla stayed at home because she was tired," "because she was tired" is a subordinate clause.

sub•poe•na /səˈpinə/ noun [C] an official legal document that says that you must come to a court of law to give evidence —**sub•poe•na** verb [T]

sub•scribe /səbˈskraɪb/ verb [I] **1** to pay money regularly so that you will receive a product such as a magazine, or a service such as an Internet connection **2** *computing* to join an Internet NEWSGROUP ≠UNSUBSCRIBE —**sub•scrib•er** noun [C]
PHRASAL VERB **subˈscribe to sth** to agree with an idea

S

sub•scrip•tion /səbˈskrɪpʃ(ə)n/ noun [C] an agreement to pay an amount of money so that you will receive something such as a magazine or a service, or the amount of money that you pay

sub•sec•tion /ˈsʌbˌsekʃ(ə)n/ noun [C] a section within another section of something

sub•se•quent /ˈsʌbsɪkwənt/ adj *formal* happening or coming after something else: *In subsequent interviews, he contradicted his original story.*

sub•se•quent•ly /ˈsʌbsɪkwəntli/ adv after something else happened: *The disease first appeared in 1890 and subsequently spread to the rest of the country.*

sub•ser•vi•ent /səbˈsɜrviənt/ adj too willing to obey other people —**sub•ser•vi•ence** noun [U]

sub•set /ˈsʌbˌset/ noun [C] a small group of people or things that is a part of a larger group

sub•side /səbˈsaɪd/ verb [I] **1** to become weaker, less violent, or less severe: *Gradually the pain subsided.* **2** if flood water, land, or a building subsides, it sinks to a lower level

sub•sid•i•ar•y¹ /səbˈsɪdiˌeri/ noun [C] a company that is owned by a larger company

sub•sid•i•ar•y² /səbˈsɪdiˌeri/ adj *formal* related to something else, but less important than it

sub•si•dize /ˈsʌbsɪˌdaɪz/ verb [T] to pay some of the cost of goods or services so that they can be sold to people at a lower price

sub•si•dy /ˈsʌbsədi/ noun [C] an amount of money that the government or another organization pays to help to reduce the cost of a product or service

sub•sist /səbˈsɪst/ verb [I] to stay alive when you do not have much food or money —**sub•sis•tence** noun [U]

sub•stance /ˈsʌbstəns/ noun ★★★
1 [C] a particular type of liquid, solid, or gas: *The wood is coated with a special substance that protects it from the sun.*
2 [U] the quality of being important, true, or useful: *The band is all show and no substance.* ♦ *There **is no substance to** his accusations* (=they are not true).
3 [C] a drug that people can become dependent on, especially an illegal drug
4 [U] the most important ideas or basic meaning of a discussion or piece of writing

ˈsubstance aˌbuse noun [U] the practice of drinking too much alcohol or taking illegal drugs

sub•stan•dard /ˌsʌbˈstændərd/ adj not as good as you would normally expect, or not good enough to be accepted

sub•stan•tial /səbˈstænʃ(ə)l/ adj ★★
1 large in amount or degree = CONSIDERABLE: *A **substantial number** of people have called to complain.* ♦ *a **substantial sum** of money*
2 large and strongly built ≠ INSUBSTANTIAL: *a substantial brick building*

sub•stan•tial•ly /səbˈstænʃ(ə)li/ adv by a large amount or degree: *We have substantially increased the number of programs.*

sub•stan•ti•ate /səbˈstænʃiˌeɪt/ verb [T] to provide evidence that proves something

sub•sti•tute¹ /ˈsʌbstɪˌtut/ verb **1** [T] to use something new or different instead of what is normally used: **substitute sth for sth** *You can substitute chicken for beef in this recipe.* **2** [T] to remove one thing and put something else in its place: **substitute sth for sth** *She substituted a picture of herself for the one already attached to the form.* **3** [I] **substitute for sb** to do someone else's job for a short period of time

sub•sti•tute² /ˈsʌbstɪˌtut/ noun [C]
1 something that is used instead of something else **2** someone who does someone else's job for a short time **3** a player who replaces another member of his or her team during a sports game
PHRASE **there is no substitute for sth** used for saying that nothing else is good or useful enough to replace something: *There's no substitute for experience.*

ˌsubstitute ˈteacher noun [C] *American* someone who teaches a class when the regular teacher cannot

sub•sti•tu•tion /ˌsʌbstɪˈtuʃ(ə)n/ noun [C/U] the action of replacing someone or something with someone or something else

sub•sume /səbˈsum/ verb [T] *formal* to include something in a larger group

sub•ter•fuge /ˈsʌbtərˌfjudʒ/ noun [C/U] *formal* the use of lies and tricks = DECEIT

sub•ter•ra•ne•an /ˌsʌbtəˈreɪniən/ adj under the ground

sub•ti•tle /ˈsʌbˌtaɪt(ə)l/ noun **1 subtitles** [plural] a translation of what people are saying in a foreign language movie or television program which appears at the bottom of the screen **2** [C] an additional title that appears after the main title of a piece of writing

sub•tle /ˈsʌt(ə)l/ adj **1** not obvious, and therefore difficult to notice: *subtle changes* ♦ *subtle threats/discrimination* ♦ *subtle advertising* (=that persuades people in a subtle way) ♦ *a subtle hint* **2** showing an ability to notice and understand small things that other people do not: *subtle arguments/humor* **3** delicate and complicated in an attractive way: *a subtle pattern/melody* **4** a subtle color is pleasant because it is not too bright —**sub•tly** adv

sub•tle•ty /ˈsʌt(ə)lti/ noun **1** [U] the quality of being complicated, delicate, or difficult to notice **2** [C] a small detail or feature that is difficult to notice

sub•tract /səbˈtrækt/ verb [I/T] to take a number or amount from another number or amount —**sub•trac•tion** /səbˈtrækʃ(ə)n/ noun [U]

sub•urb /ˈsʌˌbɜrb/ noun [C] an area or town near a large city but away from its center, where there are many houses

sub•ur•ban /səˈbɜrbən/ adj in a suburb, relating to a suburb, or typical of a suburb → URBAN

sub•ur•bi•a /səˈbɜrbiə/ noun [U] SUBURBS in general, the people who live in them, or their way of life

sub•ver•sive /səbˈvɜrsɪv/ adj intended to destroy the power or influence of a government or of an established principle

sub•vert /səbˈvɜrt/ verb [T] to attack or harm a government or established belief —**sub•ver•sion** /səbˈvɜrʒ(ə)n/ noun [U]

S

sub•way /ˈsʌbˌweɪ/ noun [C] **1** *American* a railroad that goes under the ground —*picture* → C7 **2** *British* a tunnel that people can walk through to go under a road =UNDERPASS

sub•ze•ro /ˌsʌbˈzɪroʊ/ adj subzero temperatures are lower than zero degrees

suc•ceed /səkˈsid/ verb ★★★

1 [I] to achieve something that you planned to do or attempted to do ≠ FAIL: *Everyone wants the peace process to succeed.* ♦ **succeed in (doing) sth** *We finally succeeded in getting some extra funding.*

2 [I] to do well in school, in your career, or in some other activity ≠ FAIL: *These days there is a lot of pressure on children to succeed.*

3 [T] to replace someone who was in a powerful job or position: *In 1603, Queen Elizabeth was succeeded by James I.*

Word family: **succeed**

Words in the same family as **succeed**
- **success** *n*
- **successful** *adj*
- **successfully** *adv*
- **unsuccessful** *adj*
- **unsuccessfully** *adv*

suc•ceed•ing /səkˈsidɪŋ/ adj coming after something else

suc•cess /səkˈses/ noun ★★★

1 [U] the achievement of something that you planned to do or attempted to do ≠ FAILURE: *The chairman thanked all those who had contributed to* ***the success of*** *the company.* ♦ **success in (doing) sth** *How do you explain their success in reducing crime?*

2 [C] a plan or attempt that achieves good results: *The party was* ***a great success.*** ♦ *She set up her own business and* ***made a success of it.***

3 [U] the fact that you are successful in your career: *Her success is due mainly to luck and determination.*

suc•cess•ful /səkˈsesfəl/ adj ★★★

1 achieving the result that you want ≠ UNSUCCESSFUL: *The team has had a* ***highly successful*** *season.* ♦ **successful in (doing) sth** *We have been very successful in attracting top quality candidates.*

2 a successful person does well in their career ≠ UNSUCCESSFUL: *a successful businesswoman*

3 a successful business makes a lot of money ≠ UNSUCCESSFUL: *It was another very successful year for the bank.*

—**suc•cess•ful•ly** adv

suc•ces•sion /səkˈseʃ(ə)n/ noun **1** [singular] a series of people or things of the same type: *a succession of low-paying jobs* **2** [U] the process by which one person comes after another as a king, queen, or leader

PHRASE **in succession** in a series: *Hankins has won the tournament five times in succession.*

suc•ces•sive /səkˈsesɪv/ adj coming or happening one after another in a series —**suc•ces•sive•ly** adv

suc•ces•sor /səkˈsesər/ noun [C] **1** someone who has an important position after someone else **2** an organization or machine that replaces something that did the same job before

sucˈcess ˌstory noun [C] someone or something that becomes very successful

suc•cinct /səkˈsɪŋkt/ adj expressed in a very short but clear way —**suc•cinct•ly** adv

suc•cor /ˈsʌkər/ noun [U] *literary* help given to someone who is in serious need

suc•cu•lent /ˈsʌkjələnt/ adj succulent food is full of juice and tastes good

suc•cumb /səˈkʌm/ verb [I] *formal* **1** to lose your ability to fight against someone or something **2** to become very sick, or to die from a disease

such /sʌtʃ/ grammar word ★★★

Such can be:
- a **determiner**: *She's such an intelligent woman.* ♦ *We've had such awful weather lately.*
- a **pronoun**: *I've never really had a career as such.*

1 of the type that is being mentioned: *If this is not genuine champagne, it should not be labeled* ***as such.***

2 used for emphasizing a special or unusual quality in someone or something: *She's such a nice person.* ♦ *If it's such a secret, why did you tell me?*

PHRASES **as such** used after a noun when you are referring to the usual meaning of the word: *She's not really a maid as such. She just helps out in the house sometimes.*

such as used for introducing more examples of the type of person or thing that you have just mentioned: *The money is used to buy basic foods such as flour, rice, and pasta.*

such ... that used for emphasizing the degree of a quality by stating its result: *We had such a good time that we're planning to go again next year.*

there's no such thing/person as used for saying that a particular type of thing or person does not exist: *There's no such thing as luck.*

suck¹ /sʌk/ verb **1** [I/T] to pull liquid, air, or smoke into your mouth: *He sucked in a lungful of air, then jumped into the pool.* **2** [I/T] to put something in your mouth and move your tongue against it: *She sucked on a piece of candy and stared at us.* **3** [T] to pull something somewhere, especially with a lot of force: *The current almost sucked us under the water.* **4** [I] *very informal* to be very bad, very annoying, etc.: *If your job really sucks, leave it.*

PHRASE **be/get sucked into sth** *informal* to be unable to stop yourself from getting involved in something bad

suck² /sʌk/ noun [C] an act of sucking

suck•er¹ /ˈsʌkər/ noun [C] **1** *informal* someone who is easily tricked **2** *American informal* a LOLLIPOP **3** a round structure on the bodies of some animals that allows them to stick to surfaces

suck•er² /ˈsʌkər/ verb [T] *American informal* to trick someone into doing something

suc•tion /ˈsʌkʃ(ə)n/ noun [U] the process of sucking air or a liquid from somewhere by creating a space without air that it can flow into

sud•den¹ /ˈsʌd(ə)n/ adj ★★ happening very quickly and without any sign that it is going to happen: *a sudden rise in violent*

S

crime ♦ *She felt a sudden pain in her hip.*
—**sud•den•ness** noun [U]

sud•den² /ˈsʌd(ə)n/ noun **all of a sudden** if something happens all of a sudden, it happens quickly, and without any sign that it is going to happen: *All of a sudden, the door slammed shut.*

sud•den•ly /ˈsʌd(ə)nli/ adv ★★★ quickly and without any warning: *A strange feeling suddenly came over him.* ♦ *Suddenly, the silence was broken by a loud explosion.*

sue /su/ verb [I/T] to make a legal claim against someone, usually to get money from them because they have done something bad to you

suede /sweɪd/ noun [U] leather with a soft brushed surface

suf•fer /ˈsʌfər/ verb ★★★
1 [I/T] to feel pain in your body or your mind: *When parents argue constantly, it's the children who suffer most.* ♦ *Don't worry, the animal won't* ***suffer any pain.***
2 [T] **suffer from sth** to have a particular illness or physical problem: *patients suffering from heart disease*
3 [I/T] to experience something very unpleasant or painful: *In wars, it's usually innocent civilians that suffer.* ♦ *Our team* ***suffered*** *another humiliating* ***defeat*** *last night.*
4 [I] to become worse or less successful

suf•fer•er /ˈsʌfərər/ noun [C] someone who has a particular problem or disease

suf•fer•ing /ˈsʌfərɪŋ/ noun [C/U] mental or physical pain or problems

suf•fice /səˈfaɪs/ verb [I] *formal* to be enough
PHRASE **suffice (it) to say (that)** *spoken formal* used for saying that the statement you are making contains your main idea, although you could say more about it

suf•fi•cient /səˈfɪʃ(ə)nt/ adj ★★ as much as is needed=ENOUGH ≠ INSUFFICIENT: *The wages were not* ***sufficient for*** *people to live on.* ♦ **sufficient to do sth** *There is now sufficient evidence to prove his claims.* —**suf•fi•cient•ly** adv

suf•fix /ˈsʌfɪks/ noun [C] a letter or group of letters added to the end of a word to make a different word. For example, the suffix "-ness" is added to "great" and "happy" to make "greatness" and "happiness."

suf•fo•cate /ˈsʌfəˌkeɪt/ verb [I/T] to die because you cannot breathe, or to kill someone in this way —**suf•fo•ca•tion** /ˌsʌfəˈkeɪʃ(ə)n/ noun [U]

suf•fo•cat•ing /ˈsʌfəˌkeɪtɪŋ/ adj so hot that you cannot breathe easily

suf•frage /ˈsʌfrɪdʒ/ noun [U] the right to vote

sug•ar /ˈʃʊgər/ noun [U] ★★ a sweet substance that is added to food or drinks to make them taste sweet: *Do you* ***like sugar*** *in your coffee?*

ˈsugar ˌcane noun [C/U] a tall tropical plant with thick stems that is used for producing sugar

sug•ar•y /ˈʃʊgəri/ adj tasting sweet from sugar

sug•gest /səgˈdʒest/ verb [T] ★★★
1 to offer an idea or a plan for someone to consider: **+(that)** *He suggested that we have dinner first, and then watch the movie.* ♦ **suggest doing sth** *If you have computer problems, we suggest calling the manufacturer's helpline.*
2 to tell someone about something that may be appropriate for a particular purpose =RECOMMEND: *Can you suggest a good restaurant?*
3 to make people think that something exists or is true=IMPLY: *Evidence suggests a link between asthma and pollution.* ♦ **+(that)** *I'm not suggesting that giving up smoking will be easy.*

sug•ges•tion /səgˈdʒestʃ(ə)n/ noun ★★★
1 [C] an idea or plan that you offer for someone to consider: *Could I* ***make a suggestion?*** ♦ *People had some helpful* ***suggestions for*** *improving the service.* ♦ **+that** *The suggestion that only rich people go to the opera is inaccurate.*
2 [U] the act of suggesting something: **at sb's suggestion** *It was at Larry's suggestion that I attended the meeting.*
3 [singular] the possibility that something is true, or evidence that shows that something might be true: **+that** *The senator rejected any suggestion that she was to blame.*

Words often used with suggestion

Adjectives often used with ***suggestion*** *(sense 1)*
- **alternative, constructive, helpful, positive, practical, sensible** + SUGGESTION: used about suggestions that are good

Verbs often used with ***suggestion*** *(sense 1)*
- **make, offer, put forward, submit, volunteer** + SUGGESTION: make a suggestion
- **accept, adopt, follow, take up, welcome** + SUGGESTION: accept a suggestion
- **oppose, reject** + SUGGESTION: not accept a suggestion

sug•ges•tive /səgˈdʒestɪv/ adj **1** making you think of sex **2** making you think of, or making you remember, a particular thing

su•i•cid•al /ˌsuɪˈsaɪd(ə)l/ adj **1** someone who is suicidal is likely to try to kill themselves **2** very dangerous, and likely to lead to serious problems or to death

su•i•cide¹ /ˈsuɪˌsaɪd/ noun **1** [C/U] the action of deliberately killing yourself: *Police believe he committed suicide.* **2** [U] something that you do that is likely to have very bad results for you

su•i•cide² /ˈsuɪˌsaɪd/ adj a suicide attack will kill the person who does it: *a suicide bombing*

ˈsuicide ˌnote noun [C] a message left by someone who commits suicide

suit¹ /sut/ noun [C] ★★
1 a set of clothes made from the same cloth, usually a jacket with pants or a skirt: *He was wearing a dark suit and a tie.* —*picture* → C4
2 a type of clothing that you wear for a particular activity: *a diving/jogging suit*
3 a claim or complaint that someone makes in a court of law=LAWSUIT
4 one of four sets of PLAYING CARDS that together make a DECK —*picture* → C16

suit² /sut/ verb [T] ★
1 to be convenient or appropriate for someone: *It's important to find a form of*

S

exercise that suits your lifestyle. ♦ *I work part time, which suits me fine.*
2 if a style or something you wear suits you, it makes you look good: *The new hairstyle really suits her.*

suit•a•bil•i•ty /ˌsutəˈbɪləti/ noun [U] the degree to which someone or something is suitable for a particular job or purpose

suit•a•ble /ˈsutəb(ə)l/ adj ★ right for a particular purpose, person, or situation ≠ UNSUITABLE: *They're trying to find a suitable location for the event.*

suit•a•bly /ˈsutəbli/ adv **1** in a way that is right for a particular purpose or situation: *There is a shortage of suitably qualified and experienced teachers.* **2** used for saying that someone reacts in the way that you expected: *We all looked suitably impressed when she told us her job title.*

suit•case /ˈsutˌkeɪs/ noun [C] a large bag with flat sides and a handle that you use for carrying clothes and other things when you travel

suite /swit/ noun [C] a set of rooms → EN SUITE

suit•ed /ˈsutəd/ adj **1** right for a particular purpose or situation **2** if two people are suited, they are likely to have a successful relationship = COMPATIBLE

suit•or /ˈsutər/ noun [C] *old-fashioned* a man who wants to get married to a particular woman

sul•fur /ˈsʌlfər/ noun [U] a yellow chemical element that has a strong smell

sulk /sʌlk/ verb [I] to show that you are angry about being treated badly by looking unhappy and not talking to anyone —**sulk•y** adj

sul•len /ˈsʌlən/ adj angry, unhappy, and not wanting to talk to anyone —**sul•len•ly** adv

sul•phur /ˈsʌlfər/ another spelling of **sulfur**

sul•tan /ˈsʌlt(ə)n/ noun [C] the leader in some Muslim countries

sul•try /ˈsʌltri/ adj sultry weather is unpleasant because the air is hot and wet

S

sum¹ /sʌm/ noun [C] ★★
1 an amount of money: *We already spend large **sums of money** on advertising.* ♦ *The painting was sold for **the sum of** $1.3 million.*
2 a total amount made by adding several numbers or amounts together: *What's the sum of those three numbers?*

sum² /sʌm/
PHRASAL VERBS ˌ**sum (sth)** ˈ**up** to give a summary of something
ˌ**sum sb/sth** ˈ**up** if something sums someone or something up, it shows exactly what they are like

sum•mar•i•ly /ˈsʌmərɪli/ adv immediately, and without following the usual official methods or processes

sum•ma•rize /ˈsʌməˌraɪz/ verb [I/T] to provide a short account of the most important facts or features of something

sum•ma•ry¹ /ˈsʌməri/ noun [C] ★★ a short account of something that gives only the most important information: *The text provides **summaries** of the plots of Shakespeare's plays.*

sum•ma•ry² /ˈsʌməri/ adj done immediately and without following the usual methods or processes: *summary executions*

sum•mer /ˈsʌmər/ noun [C/U] ★★★ the season between spring and fall, when the weather is hottest: *the summer of 1973* ♦ *a warm summer evening* ♦ *This room is cold even **in summer**.*

ˈ**summer** ˌ**camp** noun [C/U] a place where children can go to stay during the summer and do various activities

ˈ**summer** ˌ**school** noun [C/U] a course of study held at a school, college, or university during the summer vacation

sum•mer•time /ˈsʌmərˌtaɪm/ noun [U] the period of the year when it is summer

ˌ**summer vaˈcation** noun [C] the period of time in the summer when schools, colleges, and universities are closed

sum•mer•y /ˈsʌməri/ adj appropriate for summer, or making you think of summer

sum•mit /ˈsʌmɪt/ noun [C] ★
1 a meeting or series of meetings between leaders of two or more countries: *a summit of EU leaders*
2 the top of a mountain

sum•mon /ˈsʌmən/ verb [T] **1** *formal* to officially order someone to come to a place: *He was urgently summoned to Washington for consultations.* **2** to manage to produce a quality or a reaction that helps you to deal with a difficult situation: *She could barely summon a smile.*
PHRASAL VERB ˌ**summon sth** ˈ**up** *same as* **summon 2**

sum•mons /ˈsʌmənz/ noun [C] an official document that orders someone to appear in a court of law —**sum•mons** verb [T]

su•mo /ˈsumoʊ/ or ˌ**sumo** ˈ**wrestling** noun [U] a Japanese sport in which two very large men WRESTLE —ˌ**sumo** ˈ**wrestler** noun [C]

sump•tu•ous /ˈsʌmptʃuəs/ adj impressive, expensive, and of high quality —**sump•tu•ous•ly** adv

sun¹ /sʌn/ noun ★★★
1 **the Sun** or **the sun** the star in the sky that provides light and warmth to the Earth
2 [singular/U] the light and warmth that you feel from the sun: *Miriam was sitting **in the sun** reading a book.*
3 [C] a very bright star, especially one that a planet travels around

sun² /sʌn/ verb **sun yourself** if a person or animal suns themselves, they sit or lie in the sun

Sun. abbrev Sunday

sun•bathe /ˈsʌnˌbeɪð/ verb [I] to sit or lie in the sun so that your skin becomes darker —**sun•bath•er** noun [C], **sun•bath•ing** noun [U]

sun•bed /ˈsʌnˌbed/ noun [C] a TANNING BED

Sun•belt, the /ˈsʌnˌbelt/ the southern parts of the U.S. from Florida to California that stay warm for most of the year and are often sunny

sun•burn /ˈsʌnˌbɜrn/ noun [U] sore red skin that is caused by staying in the sun for too long

sun•burned /ˈsʌnˌbɜrnd/ or **sun•burnt** /ˈsʌnˌbɜrnt/ adj skin that is sunburned is red and sore from too much sun

Sun•day /ˈsʌnˌdeɪ/ noun [C/U] ★★★ the day after Saturday and before Monday: *Our next meeting is on a Sunday.* ♦ *We usually stay at home Sundays* (=every Sunday). ♦

I'm going to visit my parents next Sunday. ♦ *Are you doing anything nice* ***on Sunday****?*

ˈSunday ˌschool noun [C/U] religious classes for children that are given in a church on Sundays

sun•di•al /ˈsʌnˌdaɪəl/ noun [C] an object that measures time by the position of a shadow made in sunny weather

sun•down /ˈsʌnˌdaʊn/ noun [U] the time when the sun goes below the HORIZON = SUNSET

sun•dry /ˈsʌndri/ adj *formal* sundry things or people are all different from each other and cannot be described as a group

sun•flow•er /ˈsʌnˌflaʊr/ noun [C] a very tall plant that has large yellow flowers with a round brown center *—picture* → C9

sung the past participle of **sing**

sun•glass•es /ˈsʌnˌglæsəz/ noun [plural] dark glasses that you wear to protect your eyes when the sun is bright

sunk the past tense and past participle of **sink**[1]

sunk•en /ˈsʌŋkən/ adj **1** lying at the bottom of the ocean **2** lower than the level of the surrounding land or floor **3** sunken eyes or cheeks curve inward, often showing that someone is sick or old

sun•light /ˈsʌnˌlaɪt/ noun [U] the light from the sun: *bright/strong sunlight*

sun•lit /ˈsʌnˌlɪt/ adj brightly lit by the sun

Sun•ni /ˈsʊni/ noun [C/U] one of the two groups within the religion of Islam, or a Muslim who belongs to this group → SHIITE

sun•ny /ˈsʌni/ adj **1** bright with light from the sun: *It was a beautiful sunny day.* **2** happy: *a sunny smile*

sun•rise /ˈsʌnˌraɪz/ noun [C/U] the time in the early morning when the sun first appears in the sky, or the way the sky looks at this time → SUNSET

sun•roof /ˈsʌnˌruf/ noun [C] a part of a roof of a car that can be opened *—picture* → C6

sun•screen /ˈsʌnˌskrin/ noun [C/U] a cream that you can rub onto your skin to stop it from being burned by the sun

sun•set /ˈsʌnˌset/ noun [C/U] the time in the evening when the sun goes down below the HORIZON and night begins, or the way that the sky looks at this time → SUNRISE

sun•shine /ˈsʌnˌʃaɪn/ noun [U] light from the sun

sun•tan /ˈsʌnˌtæn/ noun [C] the dark color of your skin when you have spent time in the sun **—sun•tanned** /ˈsʌnˌtænd/ adj

ˈsuntan ˌlotion or **ˈsuntan ˌoil** noun [C/U] a substance that you rub onto your skin to stop it from being burned by the sun

su•per[1] /ˈsupər/ adj *informal old-fashioned* very good, nice, or enjoyable

su•per[2] /ˈsupər/ adv *informal* extremely: *a super luxurious hotel*

super- /supər/ prefix more, better, or bigger than usual: *a superhero* ♦ *supersonic*

su•perb /sʊˈpɜrb/ adj of the highest quality = EXCELLENT **—su•perb•ly** adv

su•per•com•put•er /ˌsupərkəmˈpjutər/ noun [C] a very powerful computer

su•per•fi•cial /ˌsupərˈfɪʃ(ə)l/ adj **1** not complete or thorough = CURSORY: *a superficial examination of the damage* **2** affecting or involving only the surface or outside part of something = MINOR: *Her injuries were only superficial.* **3** a superficial person does not think about serious or important things = SHALLOW **—su•per•fi•cial•ly** adv

su•per•flu•ous /sʊˈpɜrfluəs/ adj not needed or wanted = UNNECESSARY

su•per•hu•man /ˌsupərˈhjumən/ adj superhuman qualities are much greater and more impressive than those of an ordinary person

su•per•im•pose /ˌsupərɪmˈpoʊz/ verb [T] **1** to put one image on top of another so that both can be seen **2** to add something such as a feature or idea from one system or situation to another

su•per•in•ten•dent /ˌsupərɪnˈtendənt/ noun [C] **1** *American* someone who takes care of a building, especially an apartment building **2** someone whose job is to be in charge of an area or an activity

su•pe•ri•or[1] /sʊˈpɪriər/ adj **1** of high quality, or better or bigger than something else: *The hotel's service is superior.* ♦ *The sound quality is superior to that on a regular CD.* **2** someone who is superior behaves as if they think that they are better than other people: *I can't stand that superior smile of his.* **3** having a higher status or position than someone or something else: *Rockwood was charged with disobeying a superior officer.*

su•pe•ri•or[2] /sʊˈpɪriər/ noun [C] someone who is senior to you in an organization or job

suˌperior ˈcourt noun [C/U] a court of law in some states of the U.S. that has more authority than many other courts

su•pe•ri•or•i•ty /sʊˌpɪriˈɔrəti/ noun [U] **1** the fact that one person or thing is better than another **2** a way of behaving that shows that you think you are better than other people

su•per•la•tive[1] /sʊˈpɜrlətɪv/ noun [C] *linguistics* the superlative form of an adjective or an adverb

su•per•la•tive[2] /sʊˈpɜrlətɪv/ adj *linguistics* a superlative adjective or adverb is one that expresses the greatest degree of a particular quality. For example the superlative form of "happy" is "happiest." → COMPARATIVE[1]

su•per•mar•ket /ˈsupərˌmɑrkət/ noun [C] ★ a very large store that sells food and other products for the home

su•per•mod•el /ˈsupərˌmɑd(ə)l/ noun [C] a very famous and successful fashion model

su•per•nat•u•ral /ˌsupərˈnætʃ(ə)rəl/ adj used about things that seem to be caused by magic and do not have a natural or scientific explanation

su•per•nat•u•ral, the /ˌsupərˈnætʃ(ə)rəl/ noun [singular] supernatural events, forces, or creatures

su•per•pow•er /ˈsupərˌpaʊər/ noun [C] a country that has great military, economic, and political power

su•per•sede /ˌsupərˈsid/ verb [T] if one thing is superseded by another, it is replaced by it: *Steam trains were gradually superseded by diesel engines.*

su•per•son•ic /ˌsupərˈsɑnɪk/ adj faster than the speed of sound

su•per•star /ˈsupərˌstɑr/ noun [C] someone

such as a movie actor or musician who is extremely famous

su·per·sti·tion /ˌsupərˈstɪʃ(ə)n/ noun [C/U] a belief that things such as magic or luck have the power to affect your life —**su·per·sti·tious** /ˌsupərˈstɪʃəs/ adj

su·per·vise /ˈsupərˌvaɪz/ verb [I/T] to be in charge of people and check that they are behaving or working correctly: *His job was to supervise the loading of the ship.* —**su·per·vis·ion** /ˌsupərˈvɪʒ(ə)n/ noun [U]: *Here children can play safely under supervision.*

su·per·vi·sor /ˈsupərˌvaɪzər/ noun [C] **1** someone who is in charge of an activity, a place, or a group of people **2** someone who is an elected member of the city or COUNTY government in some parts of the U.S. —**su·per·vi·so·ry** /ˌsupərˈvaɪzəri/ adj

sup·plant /səˈplænt/ verb [T] *formal* to replace something or someone

sup·ple /ˈsʌp(ə)l/ adj able to move and bend easily —**sup·ple·ness** noun [U]

sup·ple·ment¹ /ˈsʌpləˌment/ verb [T] **1** to add something extra in order to improve something: *a balanced diet supplemented with vitamin tablets* **2** to add extra money to the amount that you normally earn: *He was able to supplement his income by writing stories.*

sup·ple·ment² /ˈsʌpləmənt/ noun [C] something extra that you add to make something better

sup·ple·men·ta·ry /ˌsʌpləˈment(ə)ri/ or **sup·ple·men·tal** /ˌsʌpləˈment(ə)l/ adj additional

sup·pli·er /səˈplaɪr/ noun [C] a company, organization, or country that supplies or sells a product or service: *Colombia is our main supplier of coffee beans.*

sup·ply¹ /səˈplaɪ/ noun ★★★

1 [C] an amount or quantity of something that is available to use: *The crops need **a** constant **supply of** water.* ♦ *electricity/gas/oil supplies*

2 supplies [plural] things such as food, medicine, and equipment that you need to live or to perform a particular activity: *The trucks carried medicine and other supplies across the border.*

3 [U] the act or process of providing something that is needed: **the supply of sth to sth** *This muscle controls the supply of blood to the heart.*

PHRASE **in short supply** available only in small quantities, so that there is not enough: *Water was in short supply.*

sup·ply² /səˈplaɪ/ verb [T] ★★★ to provide someone or something with something that they need or want: **supply sth to sb/sth** *Two huge generators supply power to farms in the area.* ♦ **supply sb/sth with sth** *They used the money to supply the school with new textbooks.*

sup·port¹ /səˈpɔrt/ verb [T] ★★★

1 approve of and help	4 provide sth necessary
2 help a friend	5 help to prove sth
3 hold/bear weight	

1 to approve of an idea or a person or organization, and help them to be successful: *The United Nations has supported efforts to return the refugees peacefully.* ♦ *Of course we all support the president.*

2 to help someone and be kind to them when they are in a difficult situation: *My friends have supported me through the entire trial.*

3 to hold the weight of someone or something so that they do not move or fall: **support sth with sth** *The plants were supported with wire.* ♦ **be supported by sth** *She was sitting up in bed, supported by pillows.*

4 to provide someone with the money, food, shelter, or other things that they need in order to live: *How can we support our families on such low wages?* ♦ *She's been **supporting herself** since she was 18 years old.*

5 to show that an idea, statement, theory, etc. is true or correct: *Our **conclusions** are **supported** by extensive research.*

Words often used with support

*Nouns often used with **support** (verb, sense 5)*

- SUPPORT + **argument, claim, conclusion, hypothesis, idea, theory, view**: help to show that an idea or argument is true or correct

sup·port² /səˈpɔrt/ noun ★★★

1 help/approval	4 sth that holds sth
2 money	5 proof
3 kindness	

1 [U] help and approval that you give to a particular idea, politician, organization, etc.: *I urge my colleagues to join me **in support of** this plan.*

2 [U] money that is provided to a person or organization in order to help them: *financial **support for** local bus services*

3 [U] help and kindness that you give to someone who is having a difficult time: *I am grateful to my family for their love and support.*

4 [C/U] something that holds the weight of an object, building, or structure so that it does not move or fall

5 [U] proof that something is true or correct: *Do you have any support for your theory?*

Words often used with support

*Adjectives often used with **support** (noun, sense 1)*

- **active, complete, enthusiastic, full, strong, wholehearted** + SUPPORT: used about support that is strong

*Verbs often used with **support** (noun, sense 1)*

- **attract, gain, get, receive, win** + SUPPORT: be thought to be a good idea
- **enlist, mobilize, rally** + SUPPORT: get people to agree to support you
- **give, lend, pledge** + SUPPORT: agree to support someone

sup·port·er /səˈpɔrtər/ noun [C] ★★ someone who supports a particular idea, person, or group: *Jarvis is **a** strong **supporter of** gun control laws.*

supˈport ˌgroup noun [C] a group that is organized by and for people who share a particular problem or medical condition

sup·port·ing /səˈpɔrtɪŋ/ adj **1** used about a part in a play or movie that is important

S

but is not the main part: *a supporting role* **2** helping to prove that a theory or claim is true: *supporting evidence* **3** holding the weight of something, especially in a building

sup·por·tive /səˈpɔrtɪv/ adj helpful and sympathetic

sup·pose /səˈpoʊz/ verb [T] ★★★ to think that something is probably true, right, or possible: **+(that)** *I suppose she must be delighted about getting the job.* ♦ *I suppose I had better get back to work.* ♦ *We have **no reason to suppose that** he's done anything illegal.*

PHRASES **be supposed to do/be sth 1** to be expected to behave in a particular way, especially according to a rule, an agreement, or someone in authority: *You're supposed to make a copy of the contract before you mail it.* **2** to be generally considered to have a particular quality or skill: *Latin America is supposed to be a pretty inexpensive place to travel.* **3** to be expected or intended to happen in a particular way or have a particular result: *The new regulations are supposed to help single parents.*

I suppose (so) *spoken* **1** used when you agree to do something but you are not completely willing to do it: *"Could you loan me $50?" "Yes, I suppose."* **2** used for showing that you mainly agree with something but you have some doubts about it

sup·posed /səˈpoʊzd, səˈpoʊzəd/ adj believed or said by some people to be true, although you may not agree with this: *the supposed economic benefits of lower taxes*

sup·pos·ed·ly /səˈpoʊzədli/ adv as some people believe or say, although you may not agree with this: *The house is supposedly haunted.*

sup·po·si·tion /ˌsʌpəˈzɪʃ(ə)n/ noun [C/U] something that you believe is true although you cannot prove it

sup·press /səˈpres/ verb [T] **1** to stop political opposition, protests, or other forms of disagreement, especially by using force or strict laws: *The revolt was brutally suppressed.* **2** to stop yourself from feeling or showing an emotion: *suppressed anger* **3** to stop a physical process from happening or developing —**sup·pres·sion** /səˈpreʃ(ə)n/ noun [U]

su·prem·a·cy /sʊˈpreməsi/ noun [U] a situation in which one person, group, or thing has more power or influence than any other

su·preme /sʊˈprim/ adj **1** most important or powerful: *the Supreme Commander of the allied forces* **2** very great: *The Church was of supreme importance in medieval Europe.*

suˌpreme ˈcourt noun [C] the most important court in some countries and in most states of the U.S.

SuˌpremeˈCourt, the the most powerful court in the U.S. that has the authority to change the decisions made by other U.S. courts

su·preme·ly /sʊˈprimli/ adv extremely, or to the highest possible degree

sur·charge /ˈsɜrˌtʃɑrdʒ/ noun [C] an extra amount of money that you must pay for something

sure¹ /ʃʊr/ adj ★★★

1 certain that something is real, true, or correct: *I think her name's Monica, but **I'm not sure**.* ♦ *If you're really **sure about** the facts, we'll publish them.* ♦ **+(that)** *I was sure I had left my keys on the counter.* ♦ **+how/why/if etc.** *No one is really sure why he resigned.*

2 certain to happen or succeed: *Everyone thought that the deal was **a sure thing*** (=that it would definitely happen). ♦ **sure to do sth** *If you stay up late, you're sure to feel rotten in the morning.*

3 used about something that is definite and cannot be questioned or doubted: *Bill was chewing his nails, **a sure sign** that he was worried.*

PHRASES **be sure to do sth** *spoken* used for reminding someone to do something: *Be sure to fasten your seat belt.*

for sure definitely or definitely true: *I will call you tomorrow for sure.* ♦ *Ashe was an incredible tennis player, **that's for sure**.*

make sure 1 to check something, so that you can be sure about it: *Always **make sure of** your facts before accusing anyone.* ♦ **+(that)** *I just wanted to make sure you knew where to go.* **2** to take the action that is necessary for something to happen: **+(that)** *Police were there to make sure there was no violence.*

sure of yourself confident

sure² /ʃʊr/ adv ★★★

1 *spoken* used for saying yes or agreeing to something: *"Can I borrow your green sweater?" "Sure, no problem."*

2 used as a reply when someone thanks you: *"I really appreciate all your help." "Sure, anytime."*

PHRASE **sure enough** used for saying that something happened exactly as you thought it would: *I had a feeling we'd get lost, and sure enough, we did.*

sure-foot·ed /ʃʊr ˈfʊtəd/ adj **1** good at walking or climbing and unlikely to fall **2** dealing with a situation confidently and skillfully

sure·ly /ˈʃʊrli/ adv **1** used for showing that you think that something is very likely **2** *spoken* used for showing surprise or doubt

surf¹ /sɜrf/ verb **1** [I] to ride on waves in the ocean on a SURFBOARD **2** [I/T] to look at various places one after another on the Internet or on television: *She spends hours every day just surfing the Net.*

surf

surf² /sɜrf/ noun [U] waves that are falling onto a beach

S

sur·face¹ /ˈsɜrfəs/ noun ★★★
1 [C] the top layer or outside part of something: *a smooth/rough/hard surface* ♦ *Road surfaces are slick from the rain.* ♦ *We saw fish swimming just under **the surface** of the water.*
2 [C] a flat area: *All counter surfaces in the kitchen should be carefully cleaned.* ♦ *Some players complained that the surface was too slippery.*
3 [singular] an appearance that is different from what someone or something is really like: ***On the surface**, they looked like a happily married couple.*

sur·face² /ˈsɜrfəs/ verb **1** [I] if something surfaces, it appears or people start to notice it: *New information about the murder is slowly surfacing.* **2** [I] to come up to the surface of water: *The divers were forced to surface after their equipment was damaged.* **3** [T] to put a smooth surface on a road

sur·face³ /ˈsɜrfəs/ adj **1** on the surface of something: *the surface temperature of the lake* **2** traveling on the surface of land or water, rather than through the air: *surface transportation/mail*

surf·board /ˈsɜrf,bɔrd/ noun [C] a board that you use for riding on waves

surf·ing /ˈsɜrfɪŋ/ noun [U] **1** a sport in which people ride on waves using surfboards **2** the activity of looking at different places on the Internet or on television in order to find something interesting

surge¹ /sɜrdʒ/ verb [I] **1** if a crowd of people surges, they all move forward together very quickly **2** to increase a lot very quickly **3** if a feeling surges, you start to feel it very strongly: *Panic surged inside her.*
PHRASAL VERB ˌ**surge ˈup** *same as* surge¹ 3

surge² /sɜrdʒ/ noun [singular] **1** a sudden increase in something: *a surge in spending* **2** a sudden movement of a large group of people **3** a sudden strong feeling: *a surge of emotion/desire/anxiety*

S

sur·geon /ˈsɜrdʒən/ noun [C] a doctor who does operations

sur·ger·y /ˈsɜrdʒəri/ noun ★
1 [U] medical treatment in which a doctor cuts open someone's body
2 [C] *British* a doctor's or DENTIST's office

sur·gi·cal /ˈsɜrdʒɪk(ə)l/ adj connected with surgery

sur·ly /ˈsɜrli/ adj unfriendly and rude

sur·mise /sərˈmaɪz/ verb [T] *formal* to use information to make a guess about something

sur·mount /sərˈmaʊnt/ verb [T] **1** to deal successfully with a difficult situation **2** to be on top of something

sur·name /ˈsɜr,neɪm/ noun [C] the part of your name that is your family's name = FAMILY NAME, LAST NAME

sur·pass /sərˈpæs/ verb [T] **1** to be better or bigger than something else = EXCEED: *Temperatures surpassed 42 degrees Celsius.* **2** to be even better than what was expected or hoped for: *Winning the gold medal surpassed my wildest dreams.*

sur·plus¹ /ˈsɜrpləs/ noun [C/U] more of something than is necessary: *a surplus of oil*

sur·plus² /ˈsɜrpləs/ adj more than is needed: *They should use the surplus cash to help people who need it.*

sur·prise¹ /sərˈpraɪz/ noun ★★★
1 [C] an unusual event, or an unexpected piece of news: *The news **came as a** big **surprise to** everyone.* ♦ *Given the company's poor performance, the change of management **came as no surprise**.*
2 [U] the feeling that you have when something unusual or unexpected happens: *Many students **expressed surprise** at the news.* ♦ ***Much to my surprise**, the restaurant was actually very nice.*
PHRASE **take/catch sb by surprise** to surprise someone by happening unexpectedly: *The storm caught the fishermen completely by surprise.*

sur·prise² /sərˈpraɪz/ verb [T] ★
1 to give someone a feeling of surprise: *Her angry tone of voice surprised me.* ♦ ***It wouldn't surprise me if** it snowed tonight.* ♦ *She **surprised herself** by finishing the race in less than 45 minutes.*
2 to attack someone when they do not expect it
3 to discover someone doing something bad or embarrassing: *A teacher surprised the boys smoking.*

sur·prised /sərˈpraɪzd/ adj ★★
1 feeling surprise because something unexpected has happened: *We were **surprised by** Ben's reaction to the news.* ♦ ***I wouldn't be surprised** if he got married again soon.* ♦ **be surprised to do sth** *I wasn't surprised to hear that their marriage had ended.*
2 showing surprise: *a surprised look*

sur·pris·ing /sərˈpraɪzɪŋ/ adj ★★ unusual, or unexpected ≠ UNSURPRISING: *It's **hardly surprising** (=not at all surprising) that she's angry, considering what you said.* ♦ **it is surprising how/what/where etc.** *It's surprising what you can do with so little money.* —**sur·pris·ing·ly** adv: *It's a small house, but the garden is surprisingly large.*

sur·re·al /səˈriəl/ adj something surreal is so strange that you cannot believe that it is real

sur·ren·der¹ /səˈrendər/ verb **1** [I] if soldiers surrender, they stop fighting and officially admit that they have been defeated **2** [T] to give something to someone in authority because you have to: *She was ordered to surrender her passport.*

sur·ren·der² /səˈrendər/ noun [U] an occasion when soldiers stop fighting and officially admit that they have been defeated

sur·rep·ti·tious /ˌsʌrəpˈtɪʃəs/ adj done quietly or secretly so that other people will not notice —**sur·rep·ti·tious·ly** adv

sur·ro·gate moth·er /ˌsʌrəgət ˈmʌðər/ noun [C] a woman who gives birth to a baby for another woman who cannot have children

sur·round¹ /səˈraʊnd/ verb [T] ★★
1 to be all around something or someone: *Armed police quickly surrounded the building.* ♦ **surround sth with sth** *People are surrounding their homes with barbed wire fences.*
2 to be closely connected with a situation

or an event: *Uncertainty surrounds the future of the industry.*
3 to be near someone all the time: *She grew up surrounded by older children.* ♦ **surround yourself with sb/sth** *She surrounds herself with talented people.*

sur•round² /sə'raʊnd/ noun [C] a border or edge around something

sur•round•ing /sə'raʊndɪŋ/ adj around a place: *The hotel is ideally located for visiting the surrounding area.*

sur•round•ings /sə'raʊndɪŋz/ noun [plural] a place and all the things in it: *She soon became accustomed to her new surroundings.*

sur•veil•lance /sər'veɪləns/ noun [U] if the police keep someone under surveillance, they watch them closely

sur•vey¹ /'sɜr,veɪ/ noun [C] ★★
1 a set of questions that you ask in order to find out people's opinions: *We **carried out a survey** of local housing needs.*
2 an examination of land by someone who is making a map
3 an examination of the condition of something, especially a house
4 a general book or program about a subject

sur•vey² /sər'veɪ/ verb [T] ★
1 to ask people questions in order to find out their opinions: *19% of those surveyed say they haven't decided who they will vote for.*
2 to look at something or examine something: *He sat quietly, **surveying the scene around him.***

sur•vey•or /sər'veɪər/ noun [C] someone whose job is to measure land in order to make maps

sur•viv•al /sər'vaɪv(ə)l/ noun [U] ★ the fact that someone is still alive, or the fact that something still exists: *survival equipment* ♦ *These animals face a constant **fight for survival.***

sur•vive /sər'vaɪv/ verb [I/T] ★★★
1 to continue to exist or live in a difficult situation: *Only one of the museum's paintings survived the fire.* ♦ *How does the family **survive on** such a small monthly wage?*
2 to stay alive after an injury, illness, or attack: *Doctors don't think the victims will survive.* ♦ *Just eight passengers **survived the plane crash.***
3 to manage to deal with something difficult or unpleasant: *Don't worry about Molly – she'll survive.*

sur•viv•ing /sər'vaɪvɪŋ/ adj still alive, or still existing

sur•vi•vor /sər'vaɪvər/ noun [C] someone who is still alive after an accident, illness, or attack

sus•cep•ti•ble /sə'septəb(ə)l/ adj likely to be influenced or affected by something: *Children are particularly susceptible to the disease.* —**sus•cep•ti•bil•i•ty** /sə,septə'bɪləti/ noun [U]

su•shi /'suʃi/ noun [U] Japanese food that consists of cold rice with fish, egg, or vegetables

sus•pect¹ /sə'spekt/ verb [T] ★★
1 to believe that something is true: **+(that)** *Police suspected that she had some connection with the robbery.*
2 to think that someone might have done something bad: *He wrote a letter naming the people whom he suspected.* ♦ **suspect sb of sth** *men suspected of involvement in the bombing*
3 to think that something might be bad: *Carl seemed very kind, but she suspected his motives.*

> Word family: **suspect**
>
> *Words in the same family as **suspect***
> - **suspected** *adj*
> - **suspicion** *n*
> - **suspicious** *adj*
> - **suspiciously** *adv*
> - **unsuspecting** *adj*

sus•pect² /'sʌ,spekt/ noun [C] **1** someone who might have committed a crime: *a murder suspect* **2** something that might have caused something bad

sus•pect³ /'sʌ,spekt/ adj **1** something that is suspect might not be good, honest, or reliable: *suspect motives* **2** a suspect object might be dangerous or illegal: *a suspect package*

sus•pect•ed /sə'spektəd/ adj if you have a suspected injury or illness, doctors think that you might have that injury or illness

sus•pend /sə'spend/ verb [T] ★
1 to order someone to leave their job or school for a short period of time as a punishment
2 to officially stop something for a short time: *Operations at the plant have been suspended because of safety concerns.*
3 *formal* to hang something from something else

sus•pen•ders /sə'spendərz/ noun [plural]
1 *American* a piece of clothing for keeping trousers up. They fit over your shoulders. —*picture* → C4 **2** *British* a GARTER for holding STOCKINGS up

sus•pense /sə'spens/ noun [U] the excited or worried feeling that you have when you are waiting for something to happen: *Please don't keep me in suspense. I need to know!*

sus•pen•sion /sə'spenʃ(ə)n/ noun **1** [C/U] the act of officially stopping something for a period of time: *the suspension of the peace talks* **2** [C/U] a punishment in which someone is forced to leave their job or school for a short period of time **3** [U] the equipment that makes a vehicle move smoothly when it goes over rough ground

sus'pension ,bridge noun [C] a type of bridge that hangs from strong steel ropes that are attached to towers

sus•pi•cion /sə'spɪʃ(ə)n/ noun **1** [C/U] a feeling that something bad has happened: *She had a suspicion that Mr. Engel was not being completely honest.* ♦ *They were both arrested on suspicion of murder.* **2** [U] a feeling that you do not trust someone: *an atmosphere of suspicion and hostility*
PHRASE **under suspicion** if someone is under suspicion, people think that they might have done something bad: *Several senior party members have come under suspicion.*

sus•pi•cious /sə'spɪʃəs/ adj **1** if you are suspicious, you do not trust someone or you think that something bad might have

S

happened: *Colleagues became suspicious when he started acting strangely.* ♦ *a suspicious glance/look* ♦ *People are often suspicious of strangers.* **2** if something is suspicious, you think that it might be bad or dangerous: *Customers noticed a suspicious package by the door.* —**sus•pi•cious•ly** adv

sus•tain /səˈsteɪn/ verb [T] **1** to provide the conditions that allow something to happen or exist: *Only two of the planets could sustain life.* ♦ *Can the country's economic growth be sustained?* **2** *formal* to give someone strength, energy, or hope: *A cup of coffee isn't enough to sustain you until lunchtime.* **3** *formal* to experience something bad = SUFFER: *One of the officers sustained minor injuries in the fire.*

sus•tain•a•ble /səˈsteɪnəb(ə)l/ adj **1** capable of continuing for a long time at the same level ≠ UNSUSTAINABLE **2** using methods that do not harm the environment

sus•tained /səˈsteɪnd/ adj continuing at the same level for a long time: *sustained economic growth*

sus•te•nance /ˈsʌstənəns/ noun [U] *formal* **1** food and drink **2** a way of earning the money that is necessary to live

SUV /ˌes ju ˈvi/ noun [C] *American* a SPORT UTILITY VEHICLE

SW abbrev **1** southwest **2** southwestern

swab /swɑb/ noun [C] **1** a small piece of a soft substance that is used for cleaning injuries **2** a small amount of a substance from someone's body that a doctor is testing

swag•ger /ˈswæɡər/ verb [I] to walk in a proud confident way —**swag•ger** noun [singular]

Swa•hi•li /swɑˈhili/ noun [U] a major language of eastern Africa

swal•low[1] /ˈswɑloʊ/ verb ★
1 [I/T] to make food or drink go down your throat and into your stomach: *She quickly swallowed the rest of her coffee.* ♦ *I had a sore throat and it hurt to swallow.*
2 [I] to make a movement in your throat as if you are swallowing food: *Tim swallowed nervously before replying.*
3 [T] *informal* to believe something that is unlikely to be true
PHRASE **swallow your pride/disappointment/anger etc.** to not allow your feelings to affect your behavior: *He finally had to swallow his pride and ask for help.*
PHRASAL VERB **ˌswallow sth ˈup 1** if something is swallowed up, it becomes part of something larger: *The company was swallowed up in a corporate merger.* **2** to use a lot of something such as money, time, or effort

swal•low[2] /ˈswɑloʊ/ noun [C] **1** a small bird whose tail has two long points **2** a movement in your throat that makes food or drink go down into your stomach

swam the past tense of **swim**[1]

swamp[1] /swɑmp/ verb **1** [T] if someone is swamped, they have too much to deal with at one time: *Bookstores are always swamped with orders at Christmas.* **2** [T] if a place is swamped, there are very large numbers of people in it: *The hotel lobby was suddenly swamped by reporters and photographers.* **3** [I/T] to fill or cover something with water

swamp[2] /swɑmp/ noun [C/U] an area of land that is covered by water —**swamp•y** adj

swan /swɑn/ noun [C] a large white bird with a long neck that lives near water

ˈswan ˌsong noun [C] the last performance of a performer's career

swap /swɑp/ verb [I/T] to give something to someone in exchange for something else: *If you like this one better, I'll swap with you.* ♦ *Members are encouraged to swap books with each other.* —**swap** noun [singular]

swarm[1] /swɔrm/ verb [I] **1** to go somewhere as a large crowd: *Fans swarmed onto the field to celebrate.* **2** if insects swarm, they fly together in a large group
PHRASAL VERB **ˈswarm with sth** if a place is swarming with people, insects, or animals, it is full of them

swarm[2] /swɔrm/ noun [C] **1** a large group of insects flying together **2** a large number of people moving together as a group

swarth•y /ˈswɔrði/ adj someone who is swarthy has dark skin

swat /swɑt/ verb [T] to hit an insect and try to kill it

swathe /sweɪð/ noun [C] *formal* **1** a large area of land **2** a large number of people, or a large amount of something

swathed /sweɪðd/ adj covered or wrapped in something

sway[1] /sweɪ/ verb **1** [I] to move or swing gently from side to side: *Their bodies swayed to the music.* **2** [T] to change someone's opinion: *Do not allow yourselves to be swayed by these arguments.*

sway[2] /sweɪ/ noun [singular] a slow swinging movement from side to side
PHRASE **hold sway** *formal* **1** to be the main influence on people's opinions or behavior **2** to control an area

swear /swer/ (past tense **swore** /swɔr/; past participle **sworn** /swɔrn/) verb ★
1 [I] to use words that are deliberately offensive, for example because you are angry: *That's the first time I've ever heard him swear.* ♦ *She was shouting and* ***swearing at*** *everyone.*
2 [T] to make a sincere statement or promise: *Members have to* ***swear an oath*** *of secrecy.* ♦ **+(that)** *I swear that's how it happened.* ♦ *She swears that this is the man who attacked her.* ♦ **swear to do sth** *He swore to stay out of politics when he retired.*
PHRASAL VERBS **ˈswear ˌby sth** *informal* to believe that something is very effective: *My father swears by whiskey as a cure for a cold.*
ˌswear sb ˈin to make someone give a formal promise in a law court or at an official ceremony

swear•word /ˈswerˌwɜrd/ noun [C] an offensive word that people use when they swear

sweat[1] /swet/ noun [U] liquid that forms on your skin when you are hot: *She wiped the sweat off her forehead with a towel.*
PHRASES **in a (cold) sweat** very worried or nervous
no sweat *spoken* used for saying that you can easily do something

sweat[2] /swet/ verb [I] **1** to produce liquid on the surface of your skin when you are hot, nervous, or sick: *She could feel the palms of her hands sweating.* **2** *informal* to feel very nervous or worried **3** *informal* to work hard
PHRASE **sweat it out** to wait for something that you are nervous or worried about
sweat·er /ˈswetər/ noun [C] a warm piece of clothing that covers your upper body and arms *—picture* → C5
sweat·pants /ˈswetˌpænts/ noun [plural] *American* loose pants made of thick cotton that you wear for exercising or relaxing *—picture* → C4
sweats /swets/ noun [plural] *American informal* **1** a SWEATSUIT **2** SWEATPANTS
sweat·shirt /ˈswetˌʃɜrt/ noun [C] a shirt made of thick soft cotton that some people wear for exercising *—picture* → C5
sweat·shop /ˈswetˌʃɑp/ noun [C] *informal* a factory where people work very hard in bad conditions and earn very little money
sweat·suit /ˈswetˌsut/ noun [C] *American* a piece of clothing consisting of a SWEATSHIRT and SWEATPANTS that you wear for exercising or relaxing
sweat·y /ˈsweti/ adj covered in SWEAT, or smelling of SWEAT
sweep[1] /swip/ (past tense and past participle **swept** /swept/) verb ★
1 [T] to clean a floor using a long brush: *Her work consisted mainly of making coffee and* ***sweeping the floor.***
2 [I/T] to move quickly or with a lot of force, or to take something somewhere quickly or with a lot of force: *The flood waters swept the car downstream.* ♦ *Disease has* ***swept through*** *this remote city.* ♦ *Fire* ***swept through*** *the building.*
3 [I] to go somewhere quickly and in a confident or angry way: *Several senior officials* ***swept into*** *the room.*
PHRASES **sweep to power** to win an election by a very large number of votes
sweep sth under the rug to try to avoid dealing with a problem
PHRASAL VERBS ˌ**sweep sb/sth aˈside** to ignore someone or something: *He swept aside all her objections.*
ˌ**sweep sth aˈway** to destroy something, or to completely remove something: *Many people died when floods swept their homes away.*
ˌ**sweep ˈup** to clean a floor using a long brush
sweep[2] /swip/ noun [C] **1** a long wide curved area of land or water **2** a long smooth curved movement **3** a SWEEPSTAKES
sweep·ing /ˈswipɪŋ/ adj **1** a sweeping change or development has a major effect **2** a sweeping statement is too general to be true in every case **3** with a wide impressive curved shape
sweep·stakes /ˈswipˌsteɪks/ noun [C] *American* a type of GAMBLING for a group of people. The winner gets all the money that everyone BETS.
sweet[1] /swit/ adj ★★
1 foods and drinks that are sweet taste like sugar ≠ SOUR: *I'd like something sweet, like a piece of cake.* ♦ *This tea is too sweet.*
2 something that is sweet has a nice smell, sound, or appearance: *The room is filled with the sweet fragrance of flowers.* ♦ *a sweet little kitten*
3 kind and gentle: *He's such a sweet man.* ♦ **sweet of sb to do sth** *It was so sweet of you to help me.*
—sweet·ness noun [U]
→ SWEET TOOTH
sweet[2] /swit/ noun *British* **1** [C] a CANDY **2** [C/U] DESSERT
ˈ**sweet ˌcorn** noun [U] the small yellow seeds of a CORN plant that you can cook and eat as a vegetable
sweet·en /ˈswit(ə)n/ verb [T] **1** to make something taste sweeter **2** to make something such as an offer seem more attractive in order to persuade someone to accept it
sweet·en·er /ˈswit(ə)nər/ noun **1** [C/U] a substance that is added to food or drink to make it taste sweeter **2** [C] *informal* something that you offer someone in order to persuade them to do something
sweet·heart /ˈswitˌhɑrt/ noun [C] *spoken* used for talking to someone that you love
sweet·ly /ˈswitli/ adv **1** in a nice, kind, and gentle way **2** in a way that is nice to hear or smell
ˌ**sweet poˈtato** noun [C] a vegetable with a sweet taste that looks like a potato with pink skin *—picture* → C11
ˌ**sweet ˈtooth** noun [singular] someone who has a sweet tooth likes to eat sweet food
swell[1] /swel/ (past tense **swelled** /sweld/; past participle **swelled** or **swol·len** /ˈswoʊlən/) verb [I/T] **1** to become larger than normal, or to make something larger than normal: *My ankles tend to swell when I travel by air.* **2** to increase in amount or number, or to make something increase in amount or number
PHRASAL VERB ˌ**swell (sth) ˈup** *same as* swell[1] 1: *Her injured arm was swelling up.*
swell[2] /swel/ noun [singular] the movement of the waves in the ocean
swell·ing /ˈswelɪŋ/ noun [C] an area of your body that has become bigger because of an injury or illness
swel·ter·ing /ˈsweltərɪŋ/ adj so hot that you feel uncomfortable
swept the past tense and past participle of sweep[1]
swerve /swɜrv/ verb [I] to change direction suddenly in order to avoid something **—swerve** noun [C]
swift /swɪft/ adj **1** happening quickly or immediately **2** moving quickly **—swift·ly** adv
swig /swɪg/ verb [I/T] *informal* to drink something carelessly and in large amounts **—swig** noun [C]
swill /swɪl/ verb [T] **1** to pour water over something in order to clean it **2** to drink a large amount of something
swim[1] /swɪm/ (past tense **swam** /swæm/; past participle **swum** /swʌm/) verb ★★
1 [I/T] to move through water by making movements with your arms and legs: *It's not safe to swim in the lake.* ♦ *Can you swim a length of the pool without stopping?*
2 [I] if your head is swimming, you cannot think or see clearly because you are tired or sick
3 [I] if things are swimming, they appear to

S

be moving when you look at them, because you are tired or sick
—**swim•mer** noun [C], **swim•ming** noun [U]: *I go swimming every evening.*

swim² /swɪm/ noun [singular] an occasion when you swim: *Why don't we go for a swim this afternoon?*

ˈswimming ˌpool noun [C] a large structure filled with water for people to swim in

swim•suit /ˈswɪmˌsut/ noun [C] a BATHING SUIT

swin•dle /ˈswɪnd(ə)l/ verb [T] to cheat someone in order to get their money —**swin•dle** noun [C], **swin•dler** noun [C]

swine /swaɪn/ noun [C] **1** *informal* an extremely unpleasant man **2** (plural **swine**) an old word meaning a "pig"

swing¹ /swɪŋ/ (past tense and past participle **swung** /swʌŋ/) verb [I/T] ★★
1 to move backward and forward from a point, or to make something move in this way: *Swing your arms loosely at your sides.* ♦ *The rope bridge was swinging in the breeze.*
2 to move with a wide curving movement, or to make something move in this way: **swing sth into/around/out etc.** *I swung the car into a side street.* ♦ *The door **swung shut** with a loud bang.* ♦ *She **swung around** and stared angrily at us.*
3 to change from one emotion or condition to another that is very different: *Public opinion has begun to **swing the other way*** (=away from what it was before).
PHRASAL VERB **ˌswing ˈby (sth)** *American informal* to make a short visit to a person or place: *Just swing by on your way home, okay?* ♦ *I'll try and swing by your office later.*

swing² /swɪŋ/ noun [C] **1** a seat that hangs from chains or ropes and moves backward and forward **2** an attempt to hit someone or something: *I clenched my fist and took a swing at him.* **3** a change from one emotion or condition to one that is very different: *He suffers from severe mood swings.* ♦ *a swing away from traditional ideas of family life*
PHRASES **get into the swing of sth** *informal* to become used to a new situation and feel confident that you can deal with it
in full swing at a very busy or active stage: *The party was in full swing when they arrived.*

ˈswing ˌset noun [C] *American* a metal structure with seats hanging from it. Children sit on the seats and move backward and forward.

swipe¹ /swaɪp/ verb [T] **1** *informal* to steal something **2** to pass a plastic card through a piece of electronic equipment that reads the information on it **3** to swing your arm and hit someone or something

swipe² /swaɪp/ noun [C] **1** a movement in which you swing your arm and hit someone or something **2** *informal* an occasion when you criticize someone or something: *Do you think he was taking a swipe at the President?*

ˈswipe ˌcard noun [C] a plastic card that you pass through a piece of electronic equipment that reads the information stored on the card

swirl¹ /swɜrl/ verb [I] to move quickly in circles

swirl² /swɜrl/ noun [C] a fast circular movement, or a circular shape

swish /swɪʃ/ verb [I] to move quickly with a smooth gentle sound —**swish** noun [singular]

switch¹ /swɪtʃ/ verb ★★
1 [I/T] to change from one thing to another, or to make something do this: *He used to vote Republican, but he **switched to** Democrat in 1997.* ♦ *Once you have learned the basics of word processing, **switching between** different programs is quite easy.* ♦ **switch sth (from sth) to sth** *They announced that the tournament would be switched from March to December.*
2 [T] to replace one object with another: *He was accused of switching price labels.* ♦ *Will you switch places with me?*
3 [I/T] to do someone else's work and give them your work: *Will you **switch with** me next week?*
PHRASAL VERBS **ˌswitch ˈoff** *informal* to stop listening to someone, or to stop thinking about something: *He just switches off and ignores me.*
ˌswitch (sth) ˈoff if you switch off something such as a light or a machine, or if it switches off, it stops working: *The heat has switched off.* ♦ *I parked the car and switched off the engine.*
ˌswitch (sth) ˈon if you switch on something such as a light or a machine, or if it switches on, it starts working: *Don't switch on the light.* ♦ *The machine switches on automatically.*
ˌswitch ˈover to stop doing one thing and start doing another: *He played baseball for ten years before switching over to coaching.*

switch² /swɪtʃ/ noun [C] ★★
1 something such as a button or key that makes a piece of equipment work: *a light switch* ♦ *an on-off switch*
2 a change from one thing to another: *a major policy switch by Washington* ♦ *He said **the switch from** electric **to** solar power would be made soon.*

switch•board /ˈswɪtʃˌbɔrd/ noun [C] the electronic equipment that is used to connect telephone calls in a large business or organization

switch•o•ver /ˈswɪtʃˌoʊvər/ noun [C] *American* a complete change from one thing to another

swiv•el /ˈswɪv(ə)l/ verb [I/T] to turn around a fixed point, or to make something turn in this way

swol•len¹ /ˈswoʊlən/ adj **1** bigger than usual because of an injury or illness **2** a swollen river or stream contains more water than normal

swol•len² the past participle of **swell¹**

swoop¹ /swup/ verb [I] **1** to move quickly and suddenly downward through the air in order to attack something **2** to attack a place suddenly and unexpectedly

swoop² /swup/ noun [C] **1** a quick sudden movement downward through the air **2** a sudden unexpected attack on a place
PHRASE **in/at one fell swoop** with one sudden action or on one single occasion

sword /sɔrd/ noun [C] a weapon with a short handle and a long sharp blade
PHRASE **a double-edged/two-edged sword** a

situation that has bad aspects as well as good aspects

sword•fish /ˈsɔrdˌfɪʃ/ (plural **sword•fish**) noun [C] a large sea fish with a long upper jaw

swore the past tense of **swear**

sworn[1] /swɔrn/ adj **1** done by someone who promises to tell the truth: *sworn testimony* **2** sworn enemies hate each other

sworn[2] the past participle of **swear**

swum the past participle of **swim**[1]

swung the past tense and past participle of **swing**[1]

syc•a•more /ˈsɪkəˌmɔr/ noun [C] a tall tree with large leaves —*picture* → C9

syl•la•ble /ˈsɪləb(ə)l/ noun [C] a part of a word that has only one vowel sound. For example, the word "father" has two syllables.

syl•la•bus /ˈsɪləbəs/ noun [C] a list of the main subjects in a course of study → CURRICULUM

sym•bol /ˈsɪmb(ə)l/ noun [C] ★
1 someone or something that represents a particular idea or quality: *Many Catholics saw him as* ***a symbol of*** *hope.*
2 a mark, letter, or number that is used to represent something, for example in chemistry or music
3 a picture or shape that is used to represent something

sym•bol•ic /sɪmˈbɑlɪk/ adj **1** used as a symbol: *The wedding rings are symbolic of their love.* **2** representing something important: *This meeting has great symbolic importance for the people of Ireland.* —**sym•bol•i•cal•ly** /sɪmˈbɑlɪkli/ adv

sym•bol•ism /ˈsɪmbəˌlɪzəm/ noun [U] **1** the use of symbols to represent something **2** the fact that an action or event is a sign of something important

sym•bol•ize /ˈsɪmbəˌlaɪz/ verb [T] **1** to be a symbol of something: *The cross symbolizes Christianity.* **2** to be considered as a perfect example of something: *For many people, cars symbolize personal freedom.*

sym•met•ri•cal /sɪˈmetrɪk(ə)l/ adj a symmetrical shape or object has two halves that are exactly the same —**sym•met•ri•cal•ly** /sɪˈmetrɪkli/ adv

sym•me•try /ˈsɪmətri/ noun [U] the fact that something has two halves that are exactly the same

sym•pa•thet•ic /ˌsɪmpəˈθetɪk/ adj **1** willing to understand someone's problems and help them ≠ UNSYMPATHETIC: *You're not being very sympathetic.* ♦ *Jill was a sympathetic listener.* **2** if you are sympathetic to something such as a plan, you support it ≠ UNSYMPATHETIC **3** a sympathetic character is easy to like ≠ UNSYMPATHETIC —**sym•pa•thet•i•cal•ly** /ˌsɪmpəˈθetɪkli/ adv

> **Sympathetic** and **friendly** have different meanings.
> - **Friendly** is a general word describing someone who is pleasant and wants to make friends with people: *I don't know Tim well, but he always seems friendly.*
> - **Sympathetic** means willing to listen to someone's problems and to try to understand them: *I asked my boss for some time off, but he wasn't very sympathetic.*

sym•pa•thize /ˈsɪmpəˌθaɪz/ verb [I] **1** to show that you understand someone's problems: *We sympathize deeply with the families of the victims.* **2** to support something: *Many people admit they sympathize with the rebels' demands.*

sym•pa•thiz•er /ˈsɪmpəˌθaɪzər/ noun [C] someone who supports something

sym•pa•thy /ˈsɪmpəθi/ noun ★
1 [U] a feeling of kindness and understanding that you have for someone who is experiencing problems: *It's his own fault, so he's not* ***getting any sympathy*** *from me.* ♦ *We all* ***have great sympathy for*** *the victims of the flood.*
2 [C/U] support for something such as a plan or a political party: *journalists with left-wing sympathies* ♦ *Darwin himself had little sympathy for these ideas.*

sym•pho•ny /ˈsɪmfəni/ noun [C] **1** a long piece of classical music played by an orchestra **2** a large orchestra that plays classical music, or the building where they play

symp•tom /ˈsɪmptəm/ noun [C] ★
1 a sign that someone has an illness: *The symptoms include fever and vomiting.* ♦ ***The symptoms of*** *flu may last several days.*
2 a sign of a larger problem: *The fighting is* ***a symptom of*** *growing insecurity in the region.*

symp•to•mat•ic /ˌsɪmptəˈmætɪk/ adj *formal* showing that a bad situation exists

syn•a•gogue /ˈsɪnəˌgɑg/ noun [C] a building that is used by Jewish people for religious services

syn•chro•nize /ˈsɪŋkrəˌnaɪz/ verb [T] to make two or more things happen at the same time or move at the same speed —**syn•chro•ni•za•tion** /ˌsɪŋkrənɪˈzeɪʃ(ə)n/ noun [U]

syn•di•cate /ˈsɪndɪkət/ noun [C] **1** a group of people or organizations that work together to achieve something **2** an organization that sells articles, photographs, or television programs to companies

syn•drome /ˈsɪnˌdroʊm/ noun [C] **1** a medical condition that has a particular set of effects **2** a set of feelings or actions that are typical in a particular situation

syn•o•nym /ˈsɪnənɪm/ noun [C] a word that has the same meaning as another word → ANTONYM

syn•on•y•mous /sɪˈnɑnɪməs/ adj **1** if two words are synonymous, they have the same meaning **2** if one person or thing is synonymous with another, people think of one of them whenever they think of the other one

syn•op•sis /sɪˈnɑpsɪs/ (plural **syn•op•ses** /sɪˈnɑpˌsiz/) noun [C] a short summary of a book, play, or movie

syn•tax /ˈsɪnˌtæks/ noun [U] *linguistics* the rules about how words are arranged to make phrases and sentences

syn•the•sis /ˈsɪnθəsɪs/ (plural **syn•the•ses** /ˈsɪnθəˌsiz/) noun **1** [C] a new combination of ideas or styles **2** [C/U] *technical* the process of producing a substance by a chemical or BIOLOGICAL reaction

syn•the•size /ˈsɪnθəˌsaɪz/ verb [T] **1** *technical* to produce a new substance as a result of a

S

chemical or BIOLOGICAL reaction **2** to combine different ideas or styles

syn·the·siz·er /ˈsɪnθəˌsaɪzər/ noun [C] an electronic machine that produces sounds for music

syn·thet·ic /sɪnˈθetɪk/ adj made from artificial substances

sy·phon /ˈsaɪf(ə)n/ another spelling of **siphon**

sy·ringe /sɪˈrɪndʒ/ noun [C] a plastic tube with a needle that is used for putting medicine into your body through your skin

syr·up /ˈsɪrəp/ noun [U] thick sweet liquid

sys·tem /ˈsɪstəm/ noun ★★★

1 [C] a set of connected things that work together: *a central heating system ♦ the public transportation system ♦ the body's central nervous system ♦ a new computer system*

2 [C] a method of organizing things or doing things: *a legal/educational/political system ♦ the criminal justice system ♦ They are introducing **a new system for** delivering information to the public. ♦ **a democratic system of** government*

3 [C] your body: *The drug stays in your system for hours.*

4 the system [singular] rules that decide how a society should operate: *You can't beat the system.*

PHRASE **get sb/sth out of your system** *informal* to get rid of strong feelings about someone or something

→ IMMUNE SYSTEM

sys·tem·at·ic /ˌsɪstəˈmætɪk/ adj done according to a careful plan —**sys·tem·at·i·cal·ly** /ˌsɪstəˈmætɪkli/ adv

ˌsystems ˈanalyst noun [C] someone whose job is to plan or improve the way that an organization uses computers —**ˌsystems aˈnalysis** noun [U]

T t

t or **T** /ti/ noun [C/U] the 20th letter of the English alphabet

PHRASE **to a T** exactly or completely

→ T-SHIRT

tab¹ /tæb/ noun [C] **1** a part that you pull to open something **2 tab** or **tab key** a button on a computer keyboard that you press in order to move several spaces along the same line **3** a bill for the cost of a meal or drinks: *The company picked up the tab* (=paid) *for lunch.*

PHRASE **keep tabs on** *informal* to watch someone or something carefully

tab² /tæb/ verb [I] to press the tab on a computer keyboard

tab·by /ˈtæbi/ noun [C] a cat with gray or brown and orange bands on its fur

ˈtab ˌkey noun [C] a TAB on a computer keyboard

ta·ble¹ /ˈteɪb(ə)l/ noun [C] ★★★

1 a piece of furniture that consists of a flat surface that is supported by legs: *They sat around a long table in the conference room.*

2 a set of facts or numbers that are arranged in rows and COLUMNS on a page

PHRASES **clear the table** to take away from a table all the knives, forks, plates, etc. after people have finished eating

on the table 1 if a proposal or offer is on the table, someone has suggested it officially and people are considering it **2** *American* if an idea is on the table, people are not discussing it now but they will discuss it in the future

set the table to put knives, forks, plates, etc. on a table at each place where a person will eat

turn the tables (on sb) to succeed in gaining an advantage over someone who had the advantage before

ta·ble² /ˈteɪb(ə)l/ verb [T] *American* to decide not to discuss something until later

ta·ble·cloth /ˈteɪb(ə)lˌklɑθ/ noun [C] a large cloth for covering a table

ta·ble·spoon /ˈteɪb(ə)lˌspun/ noun [C] a unit for measuring an amount of food or liquid, or a spoon that holds this amount

tab·let /ˈtæblət/ noun [C] **1** a small hard round piece of medicine that you swallow = PILL **2** *American* a set of sheets of paper for writing on **3** a flat piece of stone that has writing cut into it

ˈtable ˌtennis noun [U] a game in which players use PADDLES to hit a small light ball across a table with a low net across the middle = PING-PONG

tab·loid /ˈtæbˌlɔɪd/ noun [C] a newspaper that has small pages and not much serious news —**tab·loid** adj: *the tabloid press*

ta·boo /təˈbu/ adj if something is taboo, people do not do it or talk about it because it is offensive or shocking —**ta·boo** noun [C]

tac·it /ˈtæsɪt/ adj expressed or understood without being said directly —**tac·it·ly** adv

tac·i·turn /ˈtæsɪˌtɜrn/ adj someone who is taciturn does not say very much

tack¹ /tæk/ noun **1** [C] a small nail or short pin **2** [singular] a particular way of doing or achieving something: *Let's try a different tack.*

tack² /tæk/ verb [T] to attach something somewhere using small nails or short pins: *There was a note tacked to the door.*

PHRASAL VERB **ˌtack sth ˈon** to add something extra

tack·le¹ /ˈtæk(ə)l/ verb [T] ★

1 to deal with a problem: *Governments have failed to **tackle the question of** homelessness.*

2 to take hold of someone and push them to the ground

3 to try to take the ball from an opponent in a game such as soccer

tack·le² /ˈtæk(ə)l/ noun **1** [C] an attempt to take hold of someone and push them to the ground —*picture* → C15 **2** [C] an attempt to take the ball from an opponent in a game such as soccer **3** [U] special equipment that people use for sports: *fishing tackle*

tack·y /ˈtæki/ adj **1** *informal* looking cheap and

showing bad taste **2** slightly sticky

ta•co /ˈtɑkoʊ/ noun [C] a Mexican food that consists of a flat hard piece of DOUGH that is folded and filled with meat

tact /tækt/ noun [U] a careful way of speaking or behaving that avoids upsetting other people

tact•ful /ˈtæk(t)fəl/ adj careful to avoid upsetting other people —**tact•ful•ly** adv

tac•tic /ˈtæktɪk/ noun [C] a method or plan for achieving something

tac•ti•cal /ˈtæktɪk(ə)l/ adj **1** done as part of a plan for achieving something **2** involving TACTICS —**tac•ti•cal•ly** /ˈtæktɪkli/ adv

tact•less /ˈtæk(t)ləs/ adj not careful about the way that you speak or behave toward other people, so that you often upset them

tad¹ /tæd/ noun **a tad** *informal* a little bit

tad² /tæd/ adv **a tad** *informal* slightly: *I was a tad annoyed.*

tad•pole /ˈtædˌpoʊl/ noun [C] a small animal that develops into a FROG

taf•fe•ta /ˈtæfətə/ noun [U] thick shiny cloth that is used for making women's dresses

tag¹ /tæg/ noun [C] **1** a small label: *a name/price tag* **2** *linguistics* a TAG QUESTION **3** a piece of electronic equipment that is attached to a wild animal. It shows where they are.

tag² /tæg/ verb [T] **1** to attach a label to something **2** to put an electronic tag on a wild animal **3** to touch another player in some children's games **4** to touch a player of the other team with the ball in sports such as baseball —*picture* → C15

PHRASAL VERB ˌ**tag aˈlong** *informal* to go somewhere with someone else although you are not needed

ˈ**tag ˌquestion** noun [C] *linguistics* a word or phrase such as "isn't it?" or "haven't you?" that you can add to a sentence in order to make a question

t'ai chi /ˌtaɪ ˈtʃi/ noun [U] a Chinese activity that involves doing very slow physical exercises to make your mind relax and improve your body's balance

tail¹ /teɪl/ noun ★★

1 [C] a part that sticks out of the back of an animal's body: *When a dog is happy, it **wags its tail**.*

2 [C] the part on the back of an airplane

3 [singular] **the tail of sth** the back or end of something: *at the tail of the line*

4 [C] *informal* someone who secretly follows someone else

→ TAILS

tail² /teɪl/ verb [T] to secretly follow someone

PHRASAL VERB ˌ**tail ˈoff** to become quieter, weaker, or smaller

ˌ**tail ˈend, the** noun [singular] the very last part of something

tail•gate¹ /ˈteɪlˌgeɪt/ noun [C] a door at the back of a van or truck that opens downward

tail•gate² /ˈteɪlˌgeɪt/ verb [T] to drive very close to the vehicle in front of you —**tail•gat•ing** noun [U]

ˈ**tail ˌlight** noun [C] one of the red lights on the back of a vehicle —*picture* → C6

tai•lor¹ /ˈteɪlər/ noun [C] someone whose job is to make and repair clothes

tai•lor² /ˈteɪlər/ verb **tailor sth to/for** to make or change something for a particular person or purpose = CUSTOMIZE

tai•lored /ˈteɪlərd/ adj **1** tailored clothes have the same shape as a person's body **2** made for a particular purpose or situation

ˌ**tailor-ˈmade** adj **1** extremely appropriate **2** designed for a particular person

tail•pipe /ˈteɪlˌpaɪp/ noun [C] *American* the pipe at the back of a motor vehicle that takes waste gases out of the engine

tails /teɪlz/ noun **1** [U] the side of a coin that does not have a picture of a person on it **2** [plural] a man's formal jacket that is long at the back and short at the front

taint•ed /ˈteɪntəd/ adj an event or situation that is tainted is spoiled by an unpleasant feature or quality

take¹ /teɪk/ (past tense **took** /tʊk/; past participle **tak•en** /ˈteɪkən/) verb [T] ★★★

1 move sb/sth	12 use transportation
2 perform action	13 use drugs
3 need sth	14 use milk/sugar
4 accept sth	15 wear a particular size
5 put sb in situation	16 think of
6 reach out and get sth	17 do or have sth
7 study	18 have feeling/opinion
8 remove/steal sth	19 win prize/election
9 get picture/measure	+ PHRASE
10 in calculation	+ PHRASAL VERBS
11 get from opponent	

1 to move or carry someone or something from one place to another: *Remember to take a pen with you.* ♦ **take sb to/into/around sth** *What time do you take Amy to school?* ♦ *The cat had to be taken to the vet.* ♦ *Our guide took us around the cathedral.* ♦ **take sb/sth along** (=with you) *On long trips I always take my dog along.* ♦ **take sb/sth for sth** *We took my mother for a drive in the country.* ♦ **take sb sth** *Take Debbie this cup of coffee, will you?* ♦ **take sth to sb** *Let's take the presents to them tonight.* → BRING

2 to perform an action: ***Take a deep breath.*** ♦ *Let's **take a walk** down to the river.* ♦ *The government must **take action** to stop this trade.*

3 to need something: *Your odd behavior is going to take some explaining.* ♦ *It's going to **take some doing** (=be difficult to do) to persuade them!* ♦ **take sth to do sth** *It takes talent and dedication to become a leading dancer.* ♦ **take sb sth** *The trip will take us about three days.*

4 to accept something: *I've decided not to take the job.* ♦ *Sorry, we don't take credit cards.* ♦ *She won't **take my advice**.* ♦ *In this job you have to be able to **take criticism**.* ♦ *That's my final price, **take it or leave it*** (=the offer will not change). ♦ *You don't have to **take my word for it*** (=believe what I am saying) – *you can ask Tom.*

5 to cause someone or something to be in a new situation: **take sb to/into sth** *Her amazing energy has taken her to the top of her profession.* ♦ *The police took the thief into custody.* ♦ *They'll take us to court if we don't pay up soon.*

6 to reach out and get something with your hand: *Take as many cookies as you want.* ♦ *Let me take your coats.*

T

7 to study a particular subject: *I **took** a **class** in computer programming.*
8 to remove something, or to steal something: *Who's taken my pencil?* ♦ *The thieves didn't take much.* ♦ **take sth away from sb/sth** *Take the knife away from her!*
9 to get a picture or a measurement using a machine: *May I **take a photo** of you?* ♦ *A nurse **took his temperature** every hour.*
10 to remove one number or quantity from another number or quantity: **take sth (away) from sth** *If you take five from ten, you're left with five.*
11 to get control of something from an opponent: *The town was finally taken after a six-week siege.*
12 to use a particular type of transportation or a particular road: *Most drivers take the expressway.* ♦ *I usually **take the bus** to work.*
13 to put drugs or medicine into your body: *People worry that their children will start **taking drugs**.*

> You **eat** food and **drink** drinks, but you **take** liquid or solid medicine: *She took a pill for her headache.* ♦ *You have to keep taking your antibiotics.*

14 to have milk or sugar in your tea or coffee: *Do you take milk in your coffee?*
15 to wear a particular size of clothes or shoes: *What size shoes do you take?*
16 to think about someone or something in a particular way: *He tries hard, but I just can't **take** him **seriously**.* ♦ *She **took** his remarks **as a compliment**.* ♦ *They **took** the rainbow **as** a sign from their god.*
17 to do, or to have something: *Please **take a seat*** (=sit down). ♦ *They're shooting at us! Quick, **take cover**!* ♦ *I did all the work, but Jill **took all the credit**.* ♦ *The rebels are **taking control** of the city.* ♦ *We must encourage fathers to **take** full **responsibility** for their children.*
18 to have a feeling or opinion: *I'm afraid she **took offense** at my remarks.* ♦ *He's never **taken** much **interest** in his kids.* ♦ *Lisa **took pity on** us and invited us to dinner.*
19 to win a prize in a competition or a vote in an election: *Who took the silver medal?* ♦ *The Democratic Party took 45 percent of the votes.*

PHRASE **take place** to happen: *The Olympics take place every four years.*

PHRASAL VERBS **ˈtake ˌafter sb** to look or behave like an older relative

ˌtake sth aˈpart to separate an object into its pieces: *Ben was taking apart an old bicycle.*

ˌtake sth ˈback 1 to take something that you have bought back to a store because it is broken or not appropriate **2** to admit that something that you said was wrong: *I'm sorry – I take it back.*

ˌtake sth ˈdown 1 to separate a large structure into its pieces **2** to write information on a piece of paper: *The police took down our addresses and phone numbers.*

ˌtake sb ˈin 1 to allow someone to stay in your house or your country **2 be taken in** to be tricked so that you believe something that is not true

ˌtake sth ˈin 1 to understand and remember something that you hear or read: *I'm not sure how much of his explanation she took in.* **2** to make a piece of clothing more narrow or more tight, so that it fits you

ˌtake ˈoff 1 if an aircraft takes off, it leaves the ground and starts to fly ≠ LAND **2** to become successful or popular very fast: *Her business has really taken off.* **3** *informal* to leave a place suddenly

ˌtake sth ˈoff 1 to remove a piece of clothing from your body ≠ PUT STH ON **2** to spend a particular amount of time away from work: *I'm taking Monday off to go to the game.*

ˌtake ˈon sth to develop a particular character or appearance: *Our website is taking on a new look.*

ˌtake sb ˈon 1 to start to employ someone **2** to fight or compete against someone

ˌtake sth ˈon to accept some work or responsibility

ˌtake sb ˈout to take someone to a place such as a theater or a restaurant and pay for them: *She's taking her parents out for dinner.*

ˌtake sth ˈout 1 to remove something from a place: *Henry took out his wallet.* **2** to get something officially: *When you take out an insurance policy, read the small print.*

ˌtake sth ˈout on sb to treat someone badly because you are angry, upset, or tired, although it is not their fault

ˌtake (sth) ˈover to begin to do something that someone else was doing: *Jane **took over** as director after Richard retired.*

ˌtake sth ˈover to take control of something, especially another company

ˌtake sb ˈthrough sth to explain something to someone in detail

ˈtake to sth to start doing something as a habit: *Recently he's taken to wearing a hat.*

ˈtake to sb/sth to begin to like someone or something: *I took to John immediately.*

ˌtake ˈup sth to fill a particular amount of space or time: *These files take up a lot of disk space.*

ˌtake sth ˈup to start doing something regularly as a habit, job, or interest: *Chris has taken up jogging.* ♦ *The new teacher will **take up** her **position** in May.*

ˌtake sb ˈup on sth to accept an offer or invitation that someone has made: *I've decided to take you up on that job offer.*

ˌtake sth ˈup with sb to complain to someone about a problem

take² /teɪk/ noun [C] **1** a section of a movie or television program that is recorded without stopping **2** *informal* the amount of money that a business earns in a particular period of time

PHRASE **sb's take on sth** someone's opinion about something: *What's your take on the political crisis?*

taken the past participle of **take¹**

take•off /ˈteɪkˌɔf/ noun [C/U] an occasion when an airplane leaves the ground and starts to fly ≠ LANDING

take•out /ˈteɪkˌaʊt/ noun [C] *American* **1** a meal that you buy in a restaurant and take home to eat **2** a restaurant that sells meals that you take home to eat

take•o•ver /ˈteɪkˌoʊvər/ noun [C] a situation in which one company or country takes control of another company or country → MERGER

tal•cum pow•der /ˈtælkəm ˌpaʊdər/ or **talc** /tælk/ noun [U] a soft white powder that you put on your body after a bath

tale /teɪl/ noun [C] a story about imaginary events or people → OLD WIVES' TALE

tal•ent /ˈtælənt/ noun [C/U] a natural ability for doing a particular activity well: *She had an obvious talent for music.*

tal•ent•ed /ˈtæləntəd/ adj very good at something

tal•is•man /ˈtælɪsmən/ noun [C] an object that some people believe has the power to protect you from bad things

talk¹ /tɔk/ verb ★★★

1 [I] to speak, or to have a conversation: *Can their baby talk yet?* ♦ *Am I talking too much?* ♦ *I saw her **talking to** Matt.* ♦ *Everyone was busily **talking with** their friends.* ♦ *We were **talking about** you last night.* → SAY

2 [I/T] to discuss something: *You and I need to talk.* ♦ *John and Pete spent the evening **talking politics*** (=discussing political issues).

3 [I] to give information that should be secret: *Do you think the prisoners will talk?*

PHRASE **talk sense** *informal* to say something that is sensible

PHRASAL VERBS ˌ**talk ˈback** to reply to someone rudely: *Melanie, don't **talk back** to your mother!*

ˌ**talk ˈdown to sb** to talk to someone in a way that shows that you think that they are less intelligent or important than you are =PATRONIZE

ˈ**talk sb ˌinto sth** to persuade someone to do something: *They talked their mother into taking a rest for a while.*

ˈ**talk sb ˌout of sth** to persuade someone not to do something: *We managed to talk him out of giving up his job.*

ˌ**talk sth ˈover** to discuss a problem or a plan: *You both need to talk over what happened that day.*

Other ways of saying talk

- **chat** to talk informally in a friendly way
- **discuss** to talk about a particular subject in detail
- **gossip** to talk about other people's private lives
- **speak** to talk to someone about something, or to be able to talk in a particular language

talk² /tɔk/ noun ★★★

1 [C/U] a conversation, or conversations in general: *You need time to relax and **have a talk** with your children.* ♦ *There's **a lot of talk** in the school about the new exam system.*

2 [C] an informal lecture about a subject: *Williams **gave a talk on** his travels in Nepal.*

3 talks [plural] discussions between important people that are designed to solve a problem: *peace talks* ♦ *the outcome of **talks between** the government and the rebels* ♦ *preliminary **talks on** the future of the steel industry* ♦ *He visited Egypt in March for **talks with** the president.* ♦ *The management will be **holding** informal **talks** with union officials.*

4 [U] discussions, promises, or threats that are not worth listening to: *She says she's an expert on men, but it's **all talk**!*

talk•a•tive /ˈtɔkətɪv/ adj someone who is talkative talks a lot

talk•er /ˈtɔkər/ noun [C] *informal* someone who talks a lot or who talks in a particular way: *Your brother certainly is a smooth talker* (=good at persuading people by saying nice things).

ˈ**talk ˌshow** noun [C] *American* a television or radio program in which the HOST talks to famous people in an informal way

tall /tɔl/ adj ★★★

1 a tall person or object has greater height than the average person or object: *a tall thin woman* ♦ *tall buildings* → HIGH

2 used for talking about measurements of height: *He must be over six feet tall.*

PHRASE **a tall order** *informal* something very difficult that someone expects you to do

ˌ**tall ˈtale** noun [C] *American informal* something impressive that someone tells you that is probably not true

tal•ly¹ /ˈtæli/ noun [C] a record of the number of things that someone has won or achieved

tal•ly² /ˈtæli/ verb **1** [T] to calculate a total **2** [I] if two things such as statements or calculations tally, they match each other: *Their account doesn't tally with the facts.*

PHRASAL VERB ˌ**tally sth ˈup** *same as* **tally² 1**

Tal•mud, the /ˈtɑlˌmʊd, ˈtælməd/ a collection of Jewish religious writings

tal•on /ˈtælən/ noun [C] one of the sharp nails on the feet of some birds

tam•bou•rine /ˌtæmbəˈrin/ noun [C] a musical instrument that you shake or hit with your hand. It consists of a round frame with small pieces of metal around the edge.

tame¹ /teɪm/ adj **1** a tame animal has been trained not to attack people ≠ WILD **2** not exciting, powerful, or dangerous enough —**tame•ly** adv

tame² /teɪm/ verb [T] to train an animal not to attack people

tam•per /ˈtæmpər/ PHRASAL VERB ˈ**tamper with sth** to touch or change something that you should not touch or change, often because you want to spoil it

tam•pon /ˈtæmˌpɑn/ noun [C] an object that a woman puts inside her VAGINA to collect the blood during her PERIOD (=monthly flow of blood)

tan¹ /tæn/ noun **1** [C] a SUNTAN **2** [U] a light brown color

tan² /tæn/ verb [I/T] if you tan, or if the sun tans your skin, the sun makes your skin darker than it was before

tan³ /tæn/ adj **1** light brown in color **2** *American* someone who is tan has darker skin than before because they have spent time in the sun

tan•dem /ˈtændəm/ noun [C] a bicycle with seats for two people

PHRASE **in tandem** together and at the same time

tan•gent /ˈtændʒənt/ noun [C] *technical* a straight line that touches the edge of a circle but does not pass through it

PHRASE **go off on a tangent** *informal* to

suddenly start doing or discussing something completely different

tan•ger•ine /ˌtændʒəˈrin/ noun [C] a fruit that is like a small orange

tan•gi•ble /ˈtændʒəb(ə)l/ adj able to be seen to exist or be true ≠ INTANGIBLE: *tangible evidence*

tan•gle[1] /ˈtæŋg(ə)l/ noun [C] the messy shape that things make when they are twisted around each other or around something else

tan•gle[2] /ˈtæŋg(ə)l/ verb [I/T] if something tangles, or if you tangle it, its parts become twisted around each other or around something else
PHRASAL VERB **ˈtangle with sb** *informal* to become involved in a fight or argument with someone

tan•gled /ˈtæŋg(ə)ld/ adj **1** if something is tangled, its parts are twisted around each other in a messy way **2** very complicated and difficult to deal with
PHRASE **tangled up in sth** involved in a difficult situation

tan•go /ˈtæŋgoʊ/ noun [C] a dance that is done by two people who hold each other very tightly, or the music for this dance

tang•y /ˈtæŋi/ adj with a taste that is strong and bitter in a pleasant way —**tang** noun [singular]

tank /tæŋk/ noun [C] ★★
1 a large metal container for liquid or gas
2 a very strong military vehicle with a large gun on the top

tank•ard /ˈtæŋkərd/ noun [C] a large metal cup for beer

tank•er /ˈtæŋkər/ noun [C] a large ship or truck that carries gas or oil

ˈtanning ˌbed noun [C] *American* a machine with special lights that you lie under to get a SUNTAN

tan•ta•liz•ing /ˈtænt(ə)lˌaɪzɪŋ/ adj making you feel excited about having something that you want, especially when you cannot have it —**tan•ta•liz•ing•ly** adv

tan•ta•mount /ˈtæntəˌmaʊnt/ adj **be tantamount to sth** *formal* to have the same bad qualities or bad effect as something else

tan•trum /ˈtæntrəm/ noun [C] an occasion when someone, especially a young child, suddenly behaves in a very angry way that is unreasonable or silly

tap[1] /tæp/ verb ★
1 [I/T] to touch someone or something gently: *We could hear someone* ***tapping at the door.*** ♦ **tap sb on sth** *I tapped him on the shoulder and he jumped.*
2 [T] to get something, or to use something: *Several other companies were already tapping this market.*
3 [T] to use electronic equipment to secretly listen to someone's telephone conversations
PHRASAL VERB **ˈtap ˌinto sth** *same as* **tap[1] 2**: *There is a supply of skilled workers that businesses can tap into.*

tap[2] /tæp/ noun [C] **1** the action of touching someone or something gently, or the sound that the touch makes: *I felt a tap on my shoulder.* ♦ *We heard a tap at the window.* **2** an object that is used for controlling how much liquid or gas comes out of a pipe or container **3** a piece of electronic equipment that is used for secretly listening to someone's telephone conversations
PHRASE **on tap 1** if beer is on tap, it can be served from a large container with a tap **2** easily available: *The Internet makes it possible to have all kinds of information on tap at any time.*

ˈtap ˌdancing noun [U] a style of dancing in which you move your feet very quickly and make sounds with the special shoes that you wear

tape[1] /teɪp/ noun ★★
1 [C] a CASSETTE with something recorded on it or for recording something: *This is a great tape – have you heard it?* ♦ *We need a* ***blank tape*** (=one with nothing recorded on it).
2 [U] a very long thin piece of plastic that is used for recording sound, pictures, or information: *We have the concert* ***on tape.***
3 [U] a long thin band of plastic that is sticky on one side and is used for sticking things together
4 [C/U] a long thin band of cloth or plastic that is used for fastening things together or for marking the edges of an area: *Police roped off the area with yellow tape after the incident.*

tape[2] /teɪp/ verb **1** [I/T] to record sounds or pictures onto tape **2** [T] to stick something together using sticky tape **3** [T] to wrap a part of your body tightly with a special band of cloth because it is injured or weak
PHRASAL VERB **ˌtape ˈup** *same as* **tape[2] 3**

ˈtape ˌdeck noun [C] the part of a STEREO system that is used for playing CASSETTES

ˈtape ˌmeasure noun [C] a tool for measuring things that consists of a long narrow piece of cloth, soft plastic, or thin metal with numbers on it

ta•per /ˈteɪpər/ verb [I] to gradually become narrower toward one end
PHRASAL VERB **ˌtaper ˈoff** to gradually become less

ˈtape reˌcorder noun [C] a piece of equipment for playing a TAPE or for recording sound on TAPE

tap•es•try /ˈtæpəstri/ noun [C/U] a thick heavy cloth that has pictures or patterns woven into it

ˈtap ˌwater noun [U] water that comes out of a FAUCET in a building

tar[1] /tɑr/ noun [U] **1** a thick black liquid that is used for making the surfaces of roads **2** a sticky poisonous substance from tobacco

tar[2] /tɑr/ verb [T] to cover the surface of a road with tar

ta•ran•tu•la /təˈræntʃələ/ noun [C] a large poisonous SPIDER

tar•dy /ˈtɑrdi/ adj *formal* arriving late for something

tar•get[1] /ˈtɑrgət/ noun [C] ★★★
1 someone or something that is being attacked: ***military targets*** *such as air bases* ♦ *Foreigners have become* ***targets for attack*** *by terrorists.*
2 a person, organization, or idea that is being criticized or blamed: *The policy has* ***become the target of*** *severe criticism.*

T

3 something that you try to achieve: *The organization is* ***setting a target*** *of 2,000 new members.* ♦ *The government hasn't* ***met its target*** (=achieved it) *for reducing unemployment.* ♦ *The economy was* ***on target*** *to grow by more than 4 percent.* ♦ *The movie's* ***target audience*** *is children in the 11 to 14 age range.*
4 an object that you have to hit in a game: *Few players managed to get their shots* ***on target.***

tar•get² /ˈtɑrgət/ verb [T] **1** to attack or criticize someone or something: *The terrorists were targeting government buildings.* ♦ *The company had been targeted because of its bad record on pollution.* **2** to try to persuade or influence a particular group of people: *television advertising targeted at children*

tar•iff /ˈterɪf/ noun [C] a tax that a government charges on goods that enter or leave their country

tar•mac, the /ˈtɑrˌmæk/ noun [singular] the part of an airport where the planes stop

tar•nish /ˈtɑrnɪʃ/ verb **1** [T] if something tarnishes your reputation or image, it makes people have a bad opinion of you **2** [I] if metal tarnishes, it loses its color and becomes less shiny

tar•ot /ˈteroʊ/ noun [U] a way of telling what will happen in the future by using special cards with pictures on them

tarp /tɑrp/ noun [C] a large piece of thick plastic or other material that you put over something in order to protect it from the rain

tar•pau•lin /tɑrˈpɔlɪn/ noun [C] a TARP

tart¹ /tɑrt/ noun [C] a PIE that has no top and that is filled with fruit

tart² /tɑrt/ adj with a slightly sour taste

tar•tan /ˈtɑrt(ə)n/ noun [U] a pattern of colorful lines and squares on cloth that is typical of Scotland —**tar•tan** adj

task /tæsk/ noun [C] ★★★ something that you have to do, often something that is difficult or unpleasant: *routine/daily tasks* ♦ **the task of doing sth** *Ken began the difficult task of organizing the information.*
PHRASE **take sb to task** to severely criticize someone

> **Words often used with task**
> *Adjectives often used with* ***task***
> ■ **arduous, daunting, difficult, formidable, hopeless, impossible, onerous** + TASK: used about tasks that are difficult to do

task•bar /ˈtæskˌbɑr/ noun [C] *computing* a list that appears along the top or bottom of your computer screen and shows the programs that you are using or the activities that you can perform

ˈtask ˌforce noun [C] a group of people who have been chosen to deal with a particular problem

tas•sel /ˈtæs(ə)l/ noun [C] a decoration on cloth that consists of a group of strings tied together at one end

taste¹ /teɪst/ noun ★★★

1 flavor	4 short experience of sth
2 ability to judge if good	5 sth eaten/drunk
3 types of thing you like	

1 [C/U] the flavor that something creates in your mouth when you eat or drink it: *I love the taste of chocolate.*
2 [U] the ability to judge whether something is good or bad in things such as art, fashion, and social behavior: *She* ***has such good taste in*** *clothes.* ♦ *The joke was* ***in very bad taste.***
3 [C/U] the types of thing that you like: *The meals are designed to suit all tastes.* ♦ *The girls share his* ***taste in*** *music.* ♦ *Even at a young age he* ***had a taste for*** *books.*
4 [singular] a short experience of something that you are not used to: *After 16 years in prison, it was their first* ***taste of*** *freedom.*
5 [singular] a small amount of food or drink that you have in order to find out what flavor it has: ***Have a taste of*** *this wine.*

taste² /teɪst/ verb ★★
1 [linking verb] to have a particular flavor: *Although the meal was cold, it tasted delicious.* ♦ *This lemonade* ***tastes more like*** *water.* ♦ *These cookies don't* ***taste of*** *ginger.*
2 [T] to eat or drink something and experience its flavor: *The dinner was one of the best meals I have ever tasted.* ♦ *Visitors will be able to taste different types of wines.*
3 [T] to experience something: *It's been 13 years since they last tasted victory.*

ˈtaste ˌbuds noun [plural] the areas of your tongue that recognize the flavors of food and drinks

taste•ful /ˈteɪs(t)fəl/ adj showing good judgment about what is attractive or appropriate —**taste•ful•ly** adv

taste•less /ˈteɪs(t)ləs/ adj **1** food or drink that is tasteless has no flavor **2** showing bad judgment about what is attractive or appropriate

tast•y /ˈteɪsti/ adj tasty food has a nice flavor

tat•tered /ˈtætərd/ adj something that is tattered is torn and in very bad condition =RAGGED

tat•ters /ˈtætərz/ noun
PHRASE **in tatters 1** torn and in very bad condition **2** spoiled and likely to fail

tat•tle /ˈtæt(ə)l/ verb [I] *showing disapproval* to tell someone that another person has done something bad

ˈtattle-ˌtale noun [C] *American informal showing disapproval* a child who tells an adult about something bad that another child has done

tat•too /tæˈtu/ noun [C] a permanent picture that is drawn on your body —**tat•too** verb [T]

taught the past tense and past participle of **teach**

taunt /tɔnt/ verb [T] to shout cruel things at someone in order to make them angry or upset —**taunt** noun [C]

Tau•rus /ˈtɔrəs/ noun [U] one of the twelve signs of the ZODIAC. A **Taurus** is someone who was born between April 22 and May 21.

taut /tɔt/ adj stretched tight —**taut•ly** adv

tav•ern /ˈtævərn/ noun [C] a bar that sells beer, wine, and other alcoholic drinks

taw•dry /ˈtɔdri/ adj **1** unpleasant or immoral **2** inexpensive and of bad quality

taw•ny /ˈtɔni/ adj between yellow and brown in color

T

tax¹ /tæks/ noun [C/U] ★★★ an amount of money that you have to pay to the government. It is used for providing public services and for paying for government institutions: *The government has promised to **lower taxes** after the election.* ♦ *I was earning $1,500 a month **after tax*** (=after paying tax). ♦ *an increase in the **tax on** gasoline*

tax² /tæks/ verb [T] **1** to make someone pay a tax **2** to put a tax on something **3** *formal* to cause problems or make things difficult for someone

tax·a·ble /ˈtæksəb(ə)l/ adj something that is taxable is something that you have to pay tax on

tax·a·tion /tækˈseɪʃ(ə)n/ noun [U] **1** the system that a government uses for collecting money in the form of taxes **2** the money that a government collects from taxes

ˈtax eˌvasion noun [U] the use of illegal methods to avoid paying tax

ˌtax-ˈfree adj something that is tax-free is something that you do not pay tax on

tax·i¹ /ˈtæksi/ noun [C] ★★ a car with a driver who you pay to take you somewhere = CAB: *It was late, so I **took a taxi** home.* ♦ *You won't have any problem **getting a taxi**.* ♦ *I tried to **hail a taxi*** (=stop one in the street) *but they all sped past.* —*picture* → C7

tax·i² /ˈtæksi/ verb [I] if an airplane taxies, it moves slowly along the ground

tax·ing /ˈtæksɪŋ/ adj difficult and needing a lot of physical or mental effort

ˈtaxi ˌstand noun [C] *American* a place where taxis wait for customers

tax·pay·er /ˈtæksˌpeɪr/ noun [C] someone who pays tax

ˈtax reˌturn noun [C] an official document for giving details of your income that you use to calculate the amount of tax that you pay. You send the document to the government.

TB /ˌtiˈbi/ noun [U] tuberculosis: a serious infectious disease that affects the lungs

tbs. or **tbsp.** abbrev tablespoon

T

tea /ti/ noun ★

1 [U] a hot brown drink made by pouring boiling water onto the dried leaves of the tea bush: *Do you want some more tea?* ♦ *I'd love **a cup of tea**.*

2 [C/U] a hot drink made by pouring boiling water onto the dried leaves, fruit, or flowers of a particular plant, or a cup of this drink: *a cup of rosehip tea*

3 [U] the dried leaves of the tea bush, used for making tea

ˈtea ˌbag noun [C] a small paper bag with dried leaves inside that you use for making tea

teach /titʃ/ (past tense and past participle **taught** /tɔt/) verb ★★★

1 [I/T] to help students to learn something in a school, college, or university by giving classes: *She teaches children with learning difficulties.* ♦ *I teach English at the high school.* ♦ *How long have you been teaching here?* ♦ *Vivian spent most of her life **teaching school*** (=teaching in a school). ♦ **teach sth to sb/teach sb sth** *John teaches English to adult learners.*

2 [T] to help someone to learn a skill by showing them how to do it: **teach sb sth** *His mother had taught him some words in Spanish.* ♦ **teach sb (how) to do sth** *My uncle is going to teach me to drive this summer.*

3 [T] to change the way that someone behaves or the way that someone thinks or feels about something: **teach sb sth** *The experience taught her the importance of having good friends.* ♦ **teach sb to do sth** *These children have to be taught to share with others.*

PHRASE **teach sb a lesson** *informal* to punish someone for doing something bad so that they do not do it again

teach·er /ˈtitʃər/ noun [C] ★★★ someone whose job is to teach: *a French/math/piano teacher*

teach·ing /ˈtitʃɪŋ/ noun ★★★

1 [U] the job of a teacher: *a career in teaching*

2 [C/U] the religious or political ideas of a particular person or group: *the teachings of Buddha* ♦ *issues that are central to traditional Christian teaching*

tea·cup /ˈtiˌkʌp/ noun [C] a cup for drinking tea —*picture* → CUP

teak /tik/ noun [C/U] a large tree with valuable hard wood that is used for making furniture

tea·ket·tle /ˈtiˌket(ə)l/ noun [C] *American* a container for boiling water that has a lid, a handle, and a part for pouring —*picture* → C2

team¹ /tim/ noun [C] ★★★

1 a group of people who play a sport or game against another group: *a football/basketball team* ♦ *Are you **on the** hockey **team** this year?*

2 a group of people who work together: *a negotiating team* ♦ ***a team of** legal experts*

team² /tim/ PHRASAL VERB **ˌteam ˈup** to work together with someone

team·mate /ˈtimˌmeɪt/ noun [C] someone who is on the same team as you

team·work /ˈtimˌwɜrk/ noun [U] work that you do together with other people

tea·pot /ˈtiˌpɑt/ noun [C] a container with a handle and a SPOUT (=small tube for pouring) that you use for making and pouring tea

tear¹ /ter/ (past tense **tore** /tɔr/; past participle **torn** /tɔrn/) verb ★★

1 [I/T] to pull something so that it separates into pieces or gets a hole in it, or to become damaged in this way = RIP: *He'd torn his raincoat.* ♦ *It's very thin material that tears easily.* ♦ **tear sth to pieces/bits/shreds** *Mary tore the letter to pieces.* ♦ **tear sth open** *He tore the envelope open.*

2 [T] to remove something by pulling it away from something else with force: **tear sth out/off/away from etc.** *You'll need to tear the old wallpaper off the walls.*

3 [I] to move somewhere very quickly, usually in an excited or uncontrolled way: *Those kids are always **tearing around** here on their bicycles.*

PHRASE **torn between** unable to decide which of two people or things you want most: *I was torn between my family and my career.*

PHRASAL VERBS **ˌtear sb aˈpart** to make someone feel very sad, upset, or worried

ˌ**tear sth aˈpart** to damage or destroy something completely by breaking it into pieces
ˌ**tear sb/sth aˈpart** to make the people in a group or organization argue or fight so that the group or organization is destroyed
ˌ**tear sb/sth aˈway** to force someone or yourself to leave, or to stop doing something: *"Sorry," said Douglas, **tearing himself away from the television.***
ˌ**tear sth ˈdown** to destroy or remove a structure or part of a structure
ˌ**tear sth ˈoff** to remove your clothes quickly and carelessly
ˌ**tear sth ˈup** to destroy something such as a piece of paper or cloth by pulling it into pieces

tear² /ter/ noun [C] a hole in something where it has been torn: *There was a tear in her coat.* → WEAR²

tear³ /tɪr/ noun ★★
1 [C] a drop of liquid that comes from your eye when you cry: *Her eyes **filled with tears.***
2 tears [plural] the state of crying: *I was left standing there **in tears*** (=crying). ♦ *She slammed the phone down and **burst into tears*** (=suddenly started crying). ♦ *I was **close to tears*** (=almost crying) *when she said goodbye.*

tear•ful /ˈtɪrf(ə)l/ adj crying, or feeling as if you want to cry —**tear•ful•ly** adv

tear gas /ˈtɪrˌgæs/ noun [U] a gas that makes your eyes sting. It is used by the police for controlling violent crowds.

tease /tiz/ verb [I/T] to say something to someone in order to have fun by embarrassing or annoying them

tea•spoon /ˈtiˌspun/ noun [C] **1** a small spoon that you use for adding sugar to tea or coffee, or for measuring small amounts of liquid or powder **2 teaspoon** or **teaspoonful** the amount of food or liquid that a teaspoon holds

tech•ie /ˈteki/ noun [C] *informal* someone who knows a lot about technology or computers

tech•ni•cal /ˈteknɪk(ə)l/ adj ★★★
1 involving science or industry: *technical experts* ♦ *The job requires someone with technical knowledge.*
2 technical language is difficult to understand for people who do not know a lot about the subject: *The text is interesting and informative, without being too technical.* ♦ ***a technical term** in philosophy*
3 relating to the way that a machine or piece of equipment works: *delays caused by **technical problems***
4 relating to the skills that are needed to perform a particular activity: *The dancers reached extremely high levels of technical skill and ability.*

tech•ni•cal•i•ty /ˌteknɪˈkæləti/ noun
1 technicalities [plural] details about a particular subject that are understood only by an expert **2** [C] a minor detail of the law that can lead to an unfair result

tech•ni•cal•ly /ˈteknɪkli/ adv **1** in a way that involves skill in doing something: *a technically accomplished player* **2** according to a strict way of understanding a rule or set of facts: *Technically the war was over, but there was still some fighting.* **3** in a way that involves the practical use of skills, processes, or equipment in science and industry: *The use of an alternative fuel is not technically feasible.*

tech•ni•cian /tekˈnɪʃ(ə)n/ noun [C] someone with technical training whose job involves working with and taking care of special equipment

tech•nique /tekˈnik/ noun ★★
1 [C] a method of doing something using a special skill that you have developed: *surgical techniques* ♦ ***a useful technique for** dealing with difficult customers* ♦ *modern **techniques of business management***
2 [U] the skills that are needed to perform a particular activity: *Strength, speed, and technique are what you need to be a winner.*

tech•no /ˈteknoʊ/ noun [U] a type of popular music with a fast strong beat and electronic sounds

tech•no•log•i•cal /ˌteknəˈlɑdʒɪk(ə)l/ adj relating to or involving technology —**tech•no•log•i•cal•ly** /ˌteknəˈlɑdʒɪkli/ adv

tech•nol•o•gy /tekˈnɑlədʒi/ noun ★★★
1 [C/U] advanced scientific knowledge that is used for practical purposes, especially in industry: *computer/military technology* ♦ *the development of new technologies*
→ INFORMATION TECHNOLOGY
2 [U] advanced machines and equipment that are developed using technology

ˈ**teddy ˌbear** noun [C] a soft toy bear

te•di•ous /ˈtidiəs/ adj boring and continuing for too long

tee /ti/ noun [C] in golf, a small object that you place the ball on so that you can hit it

teem /tim/ PHRASAL VERB ˈ**teem with sb/sth** to contain an extremely large number of people, animals, or objects that are all moving around

teem•ing /ˈtimɪŋ/ adj containing an extremely large number of people, animals, or objects that are all moving around: *the teeming streets of the old city*

teen¹ /tin/ adj *informal* teenage

teen² /tin/ noun [C] *informal* a TEENAGER

teen•age /ˈtinˌeɪdʒ/ adj **1** between the ages of 13 and 19: *a teenage girl/boy* **2** relating to, or intended for, young people between the ages of 13 and 19: *teenage magazines* ♦ *teenage pregnancies*

teen•aged /ˈtinˌeɪdʒd/ adj between the ages of 13 and 19

teen•ag•er /ˈtinˌeɪdʒər/ noun [C] ★ a young person between the ages of 13 and 19 —*picture* → CHILD

teens /tinz/ noun [plural] the years of your life between the ages of 13 and 19: *She became a tennis champion while she was still in her teens.*

tee•ny /ˈtini/ or **tee•ny wee•ny** /ˌtini ˈwini/ adj *informal* very small

ˈ**tee ˌshirt** another spelling of **T-shirt**

tee•ter /ˈtitər/ verb [I] to stand or move in a way that is not steady, so that you seem about to fall
PHRASE **teetering on the brink/edge (of sth)** in a situation in which something bad is very likely to happen

T

teeth the plural of **tooth**

teethe /tið/ verb **be teething** if a baby is teething, it is getting its first teeth

ˈteething ˌproblems or **ˈteething ˌtroubles** noun [plural] minor problems that a new company, project, or product has in the beginning

tee•to•tal•er /tiˈtoʊtlər/ noun [C] someone who never drinks alcohol

TEFL /ˈtef(ə)l/ noun [U] the Teaching of English as a Foreign Language

tel. abbrev telephone number

tel•e•com•mu•ni•ca•tions /ˌtelɪkəˌmjunɪˈkeɪʃ(ə)nz/ noun [U] the science and technology of sending information by telephone, radio, or television

tel•e•com•mut•ing /ˌtelɪkəˈmjutɪŋ/ noun [U] the activity of working from home and sending your work to your office by e-mail —**tel•e•com•mute** verb [I], **tel•e•com•mut•er** noun [C]

tel•e•con•fer•ence /ˌteləˈkɑnf(ə)rəns/ noun [C] a meeting that is held among people in different places using an electronic communications system

tel•e•gram /ˈteləˌɡræm/ noun [C] a message that you send by telegraph

tel•e•graph /ˈteləˌɡræf/ noun [U] an old-fashioned method of communicating, by sending signals through wires or by radio waves

tel•e•mar•ket•ing /ˈteləˌmɑrkətɪŋ/ noun [U] the activity or job of using the telephone to sell goods or services —**tel•e•mar•ket•er** noun [C]

te•lep•a•thy /təˈlepəθi/ noun [U] the ability of people to communicate directly with each other's minds, without using words —**tel•e•path•ic** /ˌteləˈpæθɪk/ adj

tel•e•phone¹ /ˈteləˌfoʊn/ noun ★★★

1 [C] a piece of electronic equipment that you use for speaking to someone in a different place = PHONE: *Suddenly, the* ***telephone rang.*** ♦ *Pascoe* ***answered the telephone*** *and said "Hello."* ♦ *He's been* ***on the telephone*** *for the past two hours.* —*picture* → C3

2 [U] the system of communicating using telephones: *a telephone line/conversation* ♦ *People are interviewed* ***over the telephone.*** ♦ *I placed my order* ***by telephone*** *two weeks ago.*

tel•e•phone² /ˈteləˌfoʊn/ verb [I/T] *formal* to speak to someone using the telephone = PHONE

ˈtelephone diˌrectory noun [C] a book that contains the names, telephone numbers, and addresses of people and businesses in a particular area = PHONE BOOK

ˈtelephone ˌnumber noun [C] a series of single numbers that you use for phoning a particular person

ˈtelephone ˌpole noun [C] a tall pole that supports telephone or electric wires

tel•e•scope /ˈteləˌskoʊp/ noun [C] a piece of equipment shaped like a tube that you use to make distant objects look closer and larger

tel•e•vise /ˈteləˌvaɪz/ verb [T] to broadcast something on television

tel•e•vi•sion /ˈteləˌvɪʒ(ə)n/ noun ★★★

1 [C] a piece of electrical equipment with a screen that is used for watching programs = TV: *Kelly* ***turned on the television*** *and stared blankly at the screen.*

2 [U] the system of broadcasting pictures and sounds by electronic signals: *a television show/program/channel*

3 [U] the programs that are shown on television: *I spent Saturday evening* ***watching television.*** ♦ *I'm sure I've seen him* ***on television.***

4 [U] the business of creating and broadcasting television programs: *She* ***works in television.***

Types of television program

- **current affairs program** a program about politics or other subjects that are being discussed in the news
- **documentary** a program that deals with facts or historical events
- **drama** any serious program that tells a story
- **episode** a single program of a series
- **game show** a program in which people compete to win prizes
- **the news** a program that provides the latest information about the day's events
- **series** a group of related programs that are broadcast over a period of time
- **sitcom** a type of humorous program in which the same characters regularly appear in funny situations
- **soap (opera)** a type of program in which the same characters regularly appear in situations that are like ordinary life
- **talk show** a program in which a well-known person interviews famous people

ˈtelevision ˌset noun [C] a TELEVISION

tel•e•work•er /ˈteləˌwɜrkər/ noun [C] someone who works at home on a computer and communicates with their office or customers by telephone or e-mail —**tel•e•work•ing** noun [U]

tell /tel/ (past tense and past participle **told** /toʊld/) verb ★★★

1 sb gives information	6 see difference
2 sth gives information	7 have clear effect
3 talk about story	8 fail to keep secret
4 order/advise to do sth	+ PHRASES
5 know sth	+ PHRASAL VERBS

1 [T] to give information to someone: *If you see anything suspicious, tell the police.* ♦ **tell sb (that)** *Didn't he tell you that I wanted to see you?* ♦ **tell sb who/what/why/how etc.** *Just tell me what she said.* ♦ **tell sb sth** *He finally told me the reason he was so upset.* ♦ **tell sb (sth) about sth** *"Tell me about your day," she said.* → SAY

2 [T] if something such as a fact, event, or piece of equipment tells you something, it gives you or shows you some information: *The flashing light tells you when the battery needs recharging.* ♦ *What does this room tell you about the person who lived here?*

3 [T] if you tell a story or a joke, you give someone a spoken account of it: *Grandpa* ***tells*** *wonderful* ***stories*** *about the old days.* ♦ **tell sb sth** *I have to tell you this joke.*

4 [T] to order or strongly advise someone to

do something: *I'm not asking you – I'm telling you!* ♦ **tell sb to do sth** *I told you to be here on time this morning.* ♦ **tell sb what/how/when etc.** *I told him what to do, but he wouldn't listen.*

5 [I/T] to recognize something as a result of experience or evidence: *He's lying. I can always tell.* ♦ **+whether/if** *It's never easy to tell whether he's being serious or not.* ♦ **+(that)** *Peter could tell that she was bored.*

6 [I/T] to recognize the difference between one person or thing and another: *Which is which? I can't tell.* ♦ *These days it's hard to* ***tell the difference*** *between the good guys and the bad guys.* ♦ **tell sb/sth from sb/sth** *Can you tell butter from margarine?*

7 [I] to have an effect that can be clearly seen, especially a bad effect: *The strain of the last few days was* ***beginning to tell.***

8 [I] *informal* to not keep a secret: *You promised you wouldn't tell.*

PHRASES **(I'll) tell you what** used when you are going to make a suggestion, proposal, or offer: *I'll tell you what – let's have the party here.*

I told you (so) used for saying that you warned someone that something bad would happen and that you have now been proven to be right

tell time to know what time it is when you look at a clock or watch

there's no telling who/what/when/how etc. used for saying that it is impossible to be certain about something: *There was no telling how he would react.*

to tell (you) the truth used for saying what you really think or feel: *To tell you the truth, the whole thing bored me.*

you never can tell used for saying that it is impossible to be certain about something → TELLING

PHRASAL VERBS **ˌtell sb/sth aˈpart** to recognize the difference between two people or things that are very similar: *I couldn't tell the two pictures apart.*

ˌtell sb ˈoff *informal* to criticize someone angrily for doing something wrong

tel·ler /ˈtelər/ noun [C] someone whose job is to take your money from you or give your money to you in a bank → FORTUNE-TELLER, STORYTELLER

tell·ing /ˈtelɪŋ/ adj **1** very important or effective **2** showing or suggesting the truth about a situation

tell·tale /ˈtelˌteɪl/ adj showing that something exists or has happened

temp¹ /temp/ noun [C] someone who works in an office for a limited period of time

temp² /temp/ verb [I] *informal* to work as a temp

tem·per¹ /ˈtempər/ noun **1** [C/U] a tendency to get angry very quickly: *That temper of yours is going to get you into trouble.*

2 [singular/U] a particular emotional state or mood: *Mark was in a foul temper.*

PHRASES **keep your temper (with)** to stay calm and not get angry

lose your temper (with) to become very angry

tem·per² /ˈtempər/ verb [T] *formal* to make something less strong or extreme

tem·per·a·ment /ˈtemp(ə)rəmənt/ noun [C/U] someone's temperament is their basic character, for example their tendency to be happy or angry, or calm or worried

tem·per·a·men·tal /ˌtemp(ə)rəˈment(ə)l/ adj **1** someone who is temperamental gets angry easily or changes from one mood to another very quickly **2** a machine that is temperamental often does not work correctly

tem·per·ate /ˈtemp(ə)rət/ adj never having extremely hot or extremely cold weather

tem·per·a·ture /ˈtemp(ə)rəˌtʃʊr/ noun [C/U] ★★★

1 a measurement of how hot or cold a place or object is: *The plants need* ***a temperature of*** *at least 65°F to grow well.* ♦ ***Temperatures dropped*** *below freezing last night.* ♦ *The* ***temperature rose*** *steadily throughout the day.*

2 the measurement of how hot your body is: *She had a very high temperature.* ♦ **take sb's temperature** (=measure it) *She took his temperature and sent him to bed.*

tem·pest /ˈtempəst/ noun [C] *literary* a severe storm with strong winds and heavy rain or snow

tem·pes·tu·ous /temˈpestʃuəs/ adj full of strong emotion

tem·plate /ˈtemplət/ noun [C] something that is used as a pattern or example for something else

tem·ple /ˈtemp(ə)l/ noun [C] **1** a building that is used for worship in some religions **2** the flat area that is on either side of your forehead next to your eyes —*picture* → C14

tem·po /ˈtempoʊ/ noun **1** [C/U] the speed at which music is played or sung **2** [singular] the speed at which something happens

tem·po·rar·y /ˈtempəˌreri/ adj ★★★

1 existing, done, or used for only a limited period of time ≠ PERMANENT: *These measures are only temporary.* ♦ *a temporary job*

2 temporary workers do a job for a limited period of time: *a temporary lecturer* —**tem·po·rar·i·ly** /ˌtempəˈrerəli/ adv

tempt /tempt/ verb [T] to make you want to do or have something, especially something that is wrong or bad for you

temp·ta·tion /tempˈteɪʃ(ə)n/ noun **1** [C/U] a strong feeling of wanting to do or have something, especially something that is wrong or bad for you: *I resisted the temptation to have another piece of cake* (=stopped myself from having another piece). **2** [C] something that tempts you

tempt·ing /ˈtemptɪŋ/ adj something that is tempting makes you feel that you would like to do or have it

ten /ten/ number the number 10

te·na·cious /təˈneɪʃəs/ adj very determined and not willing to stop trying to do something = DOGGED —**te·na·cious·ly** adv, **te·nac·i·ty** /təˈnæsəti/ noun [U]

ten·an·cy /ˈtenənsi/ noun [C/U] the right to use an apartment, office, building, or piece of land that you rent from the person who owns it

ten·ant /ˈtenənt/ noun [C] someone who rents an apartment, office, building, or piece of land from the person who owns it

T

tend /tend/ verb ★★★
1 [I] to usually do a particular thing: **tend to do sth** *He tends to exaggerate.* ♦ **tend not to do sth** *I tend not to go out so much in the winter.*
2 [I/T] to take care of someone or something: *Eddie kept himself busy tending the garden.* ♦ *Doctors were tending the wounded.* ♦ *I have to* ***tend to*** *the children before I go out.*
3 [I] **tend toward sth** to usually have a particular quality: *Her study found that sociologists tended toward liberalism and radicalism.*

ten•den•cy /ˈtendənsi/ noun [C] ★
1 an aspect of your character that you show by behaving in a particular way: *artistic/criminal/suicidal tendencies* ♦ **have a tendency to do sth** *You have a tendency to avoid arguments.*
2 a situation that is starting to develop in a particular way = TREND: *We continue to see* ***a tendency toward*** *globalization of brands.* ♦ **a tendency (for sb/sth) to do sth** *There is a growing tendency for students to use the Internet to do their research.*

ten•der¹ /ˈtendər/ adj **1** soft, and easy to cut and eat **2** gentle in a way that shows that you care about someone or something: *Her voice was low and tender.* **3** if a part of your body is tender, it is painful when you touch it —**ten•der•ly** adv, **ten•der•ness** noun [U]

ten•der² /ˈtendər/ verb [T] *formal* to formally offer something: *The Deputy Prime Minister tendered his resignation Thursday.*

ten•don /ˈtendən/ noun [C] a part of your body that connects a muscle to a bone

ten•e•ment /ˈtenəmənt/ noun [C] a large building containing apartments

ten•et /ˈtenət/ noun [C] a principle or belief

ten•nis /ˈtenɪs/ noun [U] a game in which two or four people hit a ball across a net using a RACKET

ten•or /ˈtenər/ noun **1** [C/U] the middle and higher range of musical notes written for men to sing, or a man who sings this range **2** [singular] **the tenor of sth** the feeling, mood, or main message that you get from something

T

tense¹ /tens/ adj **1** making you feel nervous and not relaxed: *a tense situation* **2** feeling nervous and not relaxed: *He was too tense to sleep.* **3** stretched tight: *tense muscles*

tense² /tens/ noun [C/U] *linguistics* a form of a verb that is used for showing when something happens. For example "I go" is the present tense and "I went" is the past tense of the verb "to go."

tense³ /tens/ or ˌ**tense (sth)** ˈ**up** verb [I/T] if your muscles tense, or if you tense them, they become tight

ten•sion /ˈtenʃ(ə)n/ noun ★
1 [U] the feeling of being so nervous, worried, or excited that you cannot relax: *I tried to* ***ease the tension*** (=make it less strong) *with a joke.* ♦ *Symptoms include* ***nervous tension****, depression, and insomnia.*
2 [C/U] a situation in which there is a lack of trust between people, groups, or countries and they may attack each other: *racial tensions* ♦ *Measures are needed to* ***reduce tension*** *between the two states.*
3 [C/U] a situation in which opposing aims, ideas, or influences cause problems: *There is* ***a certain tension between*** *the freedom of individuals and the need for public safety.*
4 [U] the degree to which something such as a rope or muscle is pulled tight: *Can you feel the tension in your neck and shoulders?*

tent /tent/ noun [C] a structure made of cloth and supported with poles and ropes. You sleep in it when you are camping.

ten•ta•cle /ˈtentək(ə)l/ noun [C] one of the long thin arms that some sea creatures have

ten•ta•tive /ˈtentətɪv/ adj **1** not definite, or not certain **2** not confident —**ten•ta•tive•ly** adv

tenth /tenθ/ number **1** in the place or position that is counted as number ten **2** one of ten equal parts of something

ten•u•ous /ˈtenjuəs/ adj weak, or not certain: *a tenuous connection*

ten•ure /ˈtenjər/ noun [U] **1** the right of a teacher to stay in their job permanently **2** the period of time during which someone has an important job **3** *legal* someone's right to live on land and own it

ten•ured /ˈtenjərd/ adj having a job that you can stay in until you retire

tep•id /ˈtepɪd/ adj a tepid liquid is slightly warm

te•qui•la /təˈkilə/ noun [C/U] a strong, clear or yellow alcoholic drink from Mexico

term¹ /tɜrm/ noun ★★★

1 word/phrase	5 part of year
2 aspects	6 of agreement
3 time sth lasts	+ PHRASES
4 when court etc. meets	

1 [C] a word or phrase that is used for referring to or describing someone or something: *a technical/medical term*
2 **terms** [plural] used for saying which aspects of something you are considering or including: ***In practical terms****, this change is unlikely to affect many people.* ♦ *The savings, both* ***in terms of*** *time and money, could be considerable.*
3 [C] a period of time that something lasts: *In 1988 he was reelected for a five-year term.* ♦ *He received* ***a prison term*** *of six months.*
4 [C] a period of time during which a government, court, or other official organization regularly meets: *The Supreme Court's term always begins in October.*
5 [C] one of the periods of time that the year is divided into for students: *What classes are you taking this term?* ♦ *You will be required to take an exam at the end of the term.*
6 **terms** [plural] the conditions of a legal, business, or financial agreement that the people making it accept: *We have agreed the terms of the lease.* ♦ *the terms for their release from prison* ♦ *Do you accept these* ***terms and conditions****?*

PHRASES **be on good/bad/friendly etc. terms** to have a good/bad/friendly etc. relationship with someone: *We ended the meeting on good terms.*
come to terms with sth to learn to accept and deal with an unpleasant situation or event
in the long/short term for or after a long/short period of time: *In the long term,*

you'll be happier if you quit smoking. **on speaking terms** feeling friendly toward someone, and not angry with them

term² /tɜrm/ verb [T] to use a particular word or phrase for describing or referring to someone or something

ter•mi•nal¹ /ˈtɜrmɪn(ə)l/ noun [C] **1** a part of an airport where passengers arrive and leave **2** a large building where train, boat, or bus services start and finish **3** a computer screen and a keyboard connected to a computer NETWORK

ter•mi•nal² /ˈtɜrmɪn(ə)l/ adj a terminal illness cannot be cured and will cause someone to die —**ter•mi•nal•ly** adv

ter•mi•nate /ˈtɜrmɪˌneɪt/ verb *formal* **1** [I/T] to end, or to make something end **2** [T] to remove someone from a job —**ter•mi•na•tion** /ˌtɜrmɪˈneɪʃ(ə)n/ noun [C/U]

ter•mi•nol•o•gy /ˌtɜrmɪˈnɑlədʒi/ noun [U] the words and phrases that are used in a particular subject or profession

ter•mi•nus /ˈtɜrmɪnəs/ noun [C] the place where a bus or train service ends

ter•mite /ˈtɜrˌmaɪt/ noun [C] a small insect that eats wood and can damage buildings

ˈterm ˌpaper noun [C] *American* a long piece of writing on a particular subject that you do as part of a course in high school or college

ter•race /ˈterəs/ noun [C] **1** a flat area outside a building where you can sit and eat meals **2** one of a series of areas on a slope that look like wide steps, used for growing crops

ter•ra cot•ta /ˌterəˈkɑtə/ noun [U] a brown-red clay

ter•rain /təˈreɪn/ noun [U] an area of land with a particular physical feature

ter•res•tri•al /təˈrestriəl/ adj existing on the Earth, or happening on the Earth instead of in the sky or the ocean

ter•ri•ble /ˈterəb(ə)l/ adj ★★

1 making you feel very upset or afraid: *A few minutes later there was a terrible scream.* ♦ *Her mother's sudden death came as a terrible shock.*

2 causing or involving serious harm or damage: *She suffered terrible injuries in the attack.* ♦ *A terrible storm hit the island last night.*

3 sick, unhappy, or feeling guilty: ***I feel terrible** about what I said.* ♦ *What's wrong? You **look terrible**.*

4 very bad: *The food was terrible.* ♦ *I've always been really **terrible at** math.*

ter•ri•bly /ˈterəbli/ adv **1** very or extremely: *Something is terribly wrong.* **2** in a very bad way: *What's wrong? You're playing terribly today.*

ter•ri•er /ˈteriər/ noun [C] a type of small dog

ter•rif•ic /təˈrɪfɪk/ adj **1** very good or interesting **2** very big or great: *We suddenly heard a terrific bang.* —**ter•rif•i•cal•ly** /təˈrɪfɪkli/ adv

ter•ri•fied /ˈterəˌfaɪd/ adj extremely frightened

ter•ri•fy /ˈterəˌfaɪ/ verb [T] to make someone very frightened —**ter•ri•fy•ing** adj

ter•ri•to•ri•al /ˌterəˈtɔriəl/ adj relating to the land or the part of the ocean that is controlled by a particular country

ter•ri•to•ry /ˈterəˌtɔri/ noun ★★

1 [C/U] an area of land that is controlled by a particular country, leader, or army: *Russian troops crossed into Austrian territory in February 1849.*

2 [C/U] an area that an animal considers to be its own, and tries to prevent others from entering: *A lion will fearlessly **defend its territory**.*

3 [U] an area of knowledge, study, or experience: *Social work is familiar territory to her.*

PHRASE **come/go with the territory** to be a necessary or accepted part of a situation or activity: *In professional football, serious injuries come with the territory.*

ter•ror /ˈterər/ noun ★

1 [singular/U] a strong feeling of fear: *I remember **the sheer terror** of those bombing raids.* ♦ *Thousands of people fled **in terror** as the volcano erupted.*

2 [U] violence that is used for achieving political aims: *the war against terror* ♦ *a deliberate **campaign of terror***

3 [C] something or someone that makes you very frightened: *the terrors of the night*

ter•ror•ism /ˈterəˌrɪzəm/ noun [U] ★ the use of violence in order to achieve political aims: *They were charged with conspiring to commit **acts of terrorism**.*

ter•ror•ist /ˈterərɪst/ noun [C] ★ someone who uses violence in order to achieve political aims: *a terrorist bombing* ♦ *a suspected/convicted terrorist*

ter•ror•ize /ˈterəˌraɪz/ verb [T] to frighten someone by threatening them or by using violence

ter•ry•cloth /ˈteriˌklɑθ/ or **ter•ry** /ˈteri/ noun [U] a thick cotton cloth

terse /tɜrs/ adj a terse statement or remark is very short and shows that you are annoyed: *a terse reply* —**terse•ly** adv

TESOL /ˈtiˌsɑl/ noun [U] **1** Teaching English to Speakers of Other Languages **2** *American* Teachers of English to Speakers of Other Languages: an organization of teachers

test¹ /test/ noun [C] ★★★

1 check of knowledge	4 check of object
2 check of ability	5 difficult situation
3 check of body	+ PHRASE

1 a set of written or spoken questions that is used for finding out how much someone knows about a subject: *Did you get a good grade on your physics test?* ♦ *You're going to have to **take the test** again.* ♦ *I **passed** my English **test** today.* ♦ *I know I'm going to **fail** this **test**.*

2 a series of actions that someone must perform in order to show how well they can do a particular activity: *I'm still too young to **take** my driver's **test**.*

3 an examination of a part of your body or of a substance that is taken from your body: *an eye test* ♦ ***a test for** HIV* ♦ *Your **test results** are fine.*

4 a process that is designed to find out whether something is satisfactory, whether something works correctly, or whether something exists somewhere: *nuclear tests in the Pacific* ♦ *Researchers **conducted tests***

on more than 220 electric blankets.
5 a difficult situation that shows what qualities someone or something has: ***a test of** strength/character*
PHRASE **put sb/sth to the test** to find out how good or effective someone or something is

test² /test/ verb [T] ★★★
1 to find out how much someone knows or how well they can do something, by giving them a set of questions to answer or an activity to perform: *The aim of the examination is to test your writing skills.* ♦ **test sb on sth** *You won't be tested on anything that you haven't already studied.*
2 to try using something such as a machine or product to find out whether it works correctly or is satisfactory: *The theory will be tested by computer simulation.* ♦ **test sth on sth** *a skin-care product that isn't tested on animals* → TRIED²
3 to examine someone's body in order to check that it is in good condition, or in order to find out whether they have a particular illness: *Debbie has to have her eyes tested.* ♦ **test sb for sth** *She was tested for hepatitis.*
4 to show how good or effective someone or something is by putting pressure on them: *They were never seriously tested by their opponents in the first half of the game.*

tes·ta·ment /ˈtestəmənt/ noun **(a) testament to sth** *formal* evidence that something exists or is true
→ NEW TESTAMENT, OLD TESTAMENT

ˈtest ˌcase noun [C] a legal case whose result will be used as a model for similar cases in the future

tes·ti·cles /ˈtestɪk(ə)lz/ noun [plural] the two round male sex organs that hang in a bag of skin behind the PENIS

tes·ti·fy /ˈtestɪˌfaɪ/ verb [I/T] to make a formal statement in a court of law about something that you saw, know, or experienced

tes·ti·mo·ny /ˈtestəˌmoʊni/ noun [C/U] a formal statement that you make in a court of law about something that you saw, know, or experienced
PHRASE **(a) testimony to sth** evidence that something exists or is true

T

ˈtest ˌtube noun [C] a long thin glass container that is open at one end and is used in laboratories

tet·a·nus /ˈtet(ə)nəs/ noun [U] an illness in which your jaw and neck become stiff

teth·er /ˈteðər/ verb [T] to tie an animal to something so that it will stay in a particular area —**teth·er** noun [C]

text¹ /tekst/ noun ★★★

1 writing not pictures	4 textbook
2 words of speech	5 message
3 book you study	

1 [U] the part of a book, magazine, or computer document that consists of writing and not pictures: *There are 200 pages of text and illustrations.*
2 [C/U] a written record of the words of a speech, lecture, program, or play: *The text of the lecture is available from the departmental office.*
3 [C] a piece of writing such as a book or play that you study: *We'll be analyzing the language of literary texts.*
4 [C] *American* a TEXTBOOK: *history texts*
5 [C] a TEXT MESSAGE

text² /tekst/ verb [T] to send a written message to someone using a cellphone: *Karen didn't call or text me all day.* —**text·ing** noun [U]

text·book /ˈteks(t)ˌbʊk/ noun [C] a book that contains information about a particular subject

tex·tile /ˈtekˌstaɪl/ noun [C] any type of woven cloth = FABRIC

ˈtext ˌmessage noun [C] a written message that you send or receive using a cellphone

text mes·sag·ing /ˈteks(t) ˌmesɪdʒɪŋ/ noun [U] the process of sending and receiving written messages using a cellphone

tex·ture /ˈtekstʃər/ noun [C/U] the way that something feels when you touch it: *a soft/rough/firm texture*

than /*weak* ðən, *strong* ðæn/ preposition, conjunction ★★★
1 used when making comparisons: *Nylon is considerably stronger than cotton.* ♦ *Is the world a safer place than it was a year ago?* ♦ *We don't want to do more than is necessary.*
2 used when you are saying that a number or amount is above or below a particular level: *a city of **more than** 5 million people* ♦ *I'll be back in **less than** a week.*
→ RATHER

thank /θæŋk/ verb [T] ★★★ to tell someone that you are grateful for something that they have done or given to you: *She didn't even thank me.* ♦ **thank sb for (doing) sth** *I just wanted to thank you for the flowers – they're beautiful.* ♦ *I'd like to thank everybody for coming today.*
PHRASE **thank God/goodness/heaven(s)** used for saying that you are happy that something unpleasant has ended or has not happened: *Thank heaven nobody was injured in the crash.*

thank·ful /ˈθæŋkf(ə)l/ adj grateful for something, or pleased that something unpleasant is no longer happening or did not happen

thank·ful·ly /ˈθæŋkf(ə)li/ adv used for saying you are pleased that something unpleasant is no longer happening or did not happen: *Thankfully the boys are safe.*

thank·less /ˈθæŋkləs/ adj a thankless activity is unpleasant, and other people are not grateful to you for doing it

thanks¹ /θæŋks/ interjection *informal* ★★★
1 used for telling someone that you are grateful for something that they have said or done: *"You're looking well." "Thanks."* ♦ ***Thanks for** dinner – it was great.* ♦ ***Thanks for** reminding me.*
2 used for politely accepting something that is offered to you: *"Do you want a piece of candy?" "Thanks, I'd love one."*
PHRASE **no, thanks** used for politely refusing something that is offered to you: *"Can I get you a drink?" "No, thanks."*

thanks² /θæŋks/ noun [plural] ★★★ things that you say or do in order to tell someone that you are grateful to them: *Please accept* *my heartfelt **thanks for** your concern and generosity.*

Thanks·giv·ing /ˈθæŋks,gɪvɪŋ/ or **ˈThanksgiving ˌDay** noun [C/U] in the U.S., the fourth Thursday in November, and in Canada, the second Monday in October, when families have a special meal

ˈthank ˌyou interjection ★★★
1 used for telling someone that you are grateful for something that they have said or done: *"That's a nice jacket." "Thank you."* ♦ ***Thank you for** coming here today.*
2 used for politely accepting something that is offered to you: *"Would you like a cup of coffee?" "Oh, thank you, that would be great."*
PHRASE **no, thank you** used for politely refusing something that is offered to you

thank·you /ˈθæŋk,ju/ noun [C] something that you say or do to tell someone that you are grateful to them

that /ðæt/ grammar word ★★★

> That can be:
> - a **determiner**: *Give me that hammer.*
> - a **pronoun**: *Who gave you that?*
> - a **conjunction**: *I didn't know that she was married.*
> - a **relative pronoun**: *It's a song that my mother taught me.*
> - an **adverb**: *Three years? I can't wait that long.*

1 (plural **those** /ðoʊz/) **the one that is known about** used for referring to someone or something that has already been mentioned or is already known about: *I know there's a problem, but I haven't got time to worry about that now.* ♦ *Why don't you ask Carmen? That's who I'd choose.* ♦ *The engine's started making that noise again.*
2 (plural **those** /ðoʊz/) **the one that you are looking at** *spoken* used for referring to someone or something that you can see or point at, although they are not very near to you: *That's Jerry's car, over there.* ♦ *Where did that stain on the carpet come from?* ♦ *Do you know who that woman in the blue dress is?* ♦ *I need these books, but you can borrow any of those.*
3 (plural **those** /ðoʊz/) **a past time or event** used for referring to a period, event, or experience in the past: *Remember that time we all went to the lake?* ♦ *There were no telephones in those days.* ♦ *That was fun. We'll have to do it again some time.*
4 /*strong* ðæt, *weak* ðət/ **introducing a statement** used after some verbs, adjectives, and nouns in order to state an idea, fact, or reason: *Dawkins believes that his sister was murdered.* ♦ *We cannot ignore the fact that there is a shortage of qualified nurses.* ♦ *It is surprising that no one warned them of the danger.* ♦ *I'm sorry that I missed the first meeting.*

> The conjunction **that** is often left out, especially in spoken English: *I told them I was busy.*

5 /*strong* ðæt, *weak* ðət/ **used instead of "which" or "who"** used instead of "which" or "who" in order to give more information about a noun or pronoun: *We haven't met the people that live next door.* ♦ *It was the worst winter that anyone could remember.* ♦ *Is there anything else that you want to ask?*

> The relative pronoun **that** is often left out when it is the object of a relative clause: *Did you find the book you were looking for?* In formal written English **that** is not generally left out.

6 /*strong* ðæt, *weak* ðət/ **introducing a result** used after "so" or "such" for showing the result of something: *It was so cold that the lake froze in some places.*

> The conjunction **that** is often left out of expressions with "so" and "such," especially in spoken English: *I was so excited I couldn't sleep.*

7 showing how big *spoken* used when you use your hands for showing the size or level of something: *There was only that much left in the bottle.*
8 very *spoken* to a very great degree: *There's no need to get upset – it isn't that important.*
PHRASES **that is** used when explaining or correcting what you have just said: *I've always enjoyed my work – that is, I did until this new manager arrived.*
that's it or **that does it** *spoken* used when a series of situations has made you angry, so that you decide to leave or stop what you are doing
that's that *spoken* used for saying that something has been finished or finally decided
→ THIS

thatched /θætʃt/ adj with a roof made from dried plants such as STRAW

thaw¹ /θɔ/ verb **1** [I/T] if ice or snow thaws, or if something thaws it, it becomes warmer and changes into liquid **2** [I/T] if frozen food thaws, or if you thaw it, it becomes softer and ready to cook **3** [I] to become more friendly
PHRASAL VERB ˈ**thaw (sth) out 1** *same as* **thaw¹** 1 **2** *same as* **thaw¹** 2

thaw² /θɔ/ noun [singular] **1** a period of warmer weather that causes ice and snow to turn into water **2** an improvement in the relationship between people, countries, etc.

the /*weak* ðə, ði, *strong* ði/ determiner ★★★

> The is used as the **definite article** before a noun.

1 talking about sb/sth when you know who or which used before a noun when that person or thing has already been mentioned or is known about, or when there is only one: *Have you locked the door?* ♦ *I have to take care of the children.* ♦ *She brought me some cake and coffee, but the cake was stale.* ♦ *The sun was hidden behind a cloud.* ♦ *the best hotel in Paris*
2 talking in general about one type of thing or person used before a singular noun when making a general statement about things or people of a particular type: *People have come to depend on the automobile as their only means of transportation.*

> DO NOT use **the** when you are referring to things or people in a general way: *Children need love and attention.*

3 with a part of an object or body used before a part of a particular thing, or a part

T

of the body: *the sharp end of a pencil* ♦ *He had a gunshot wound in the neck.*
4 used when explaining which person or thing you are referring to: *Who was the actor who played Romeo?* ♦ *We live in the house with green shutters.*
5 in dates and times used before dates or periods of time: *the 4th of July* ♦ *popular music of the 1960s*
6 with nouns referring to actions used before a noun that refers to an action, especially when it is followed by "of": *the destruction of a whole city* ♦ *the death of Queen Victoria*
7 with names of oceans, rivers, etc. used before the names of oceans, rivers, deserts, or groups of mountains: *the Pacific Ocean* ♦ *the Sahara* ♦ *the Alps*

> **The** is not usually used before the names of streets, cities, countries, states, or continents: *My parents live in Florida.*

8 used before an adjective in order to form a plural noun that refers to people of a particular type or people from a particular country: *a policy of taxing the rich to help the poor* ♦ *The Japanese eat a lot of seafood.*

> You should avoid using "the" with adjectives that refer to disabilities, for example **the blind** and **the handicapped**. Many people now think that this use is offensive and prefer expressions such as **the visually impaired** and **people with disabilities**.

9 used when you are saying what type of musical instrument someone plays: *Lorna plays the violin.*
PHRASE **the...the...** used with "more," "less," and other COMPARATIVES for showing that when one thing increases or is reduced, it causes something else to increase or be reduced at the same time: *The more people who help, the better.*

the·a·ter /ˈθiətər/ noun **1** [C] a building or room that is used for performing plays: *We're going to the theater on Saturday.* **2** [C] *American* a building or room that is used for showing movies = MOVIE THEATER **3** [U] the activity of writing, performing, or organizing performances of plays: *a career in the theater*

the·a·tre /ˈθiətər/ another spelling of **theater**

the·at·ri·cal /θiˈætrɪk(ə)l/ adj **1** relating to the theater **2** theatrical behavior is very emotional and aims to attract attention

theft /θeft/ noun [C/U] the crime of stealing something

their /ðer/ determiner ★★★
1 belonging to, or relating to, a particular group of people or things that have already been mentioned or when it is obvious which ones you are referring to: *chemical fertilizers and their effect on the environment* ♦ *They have children of **their own**.*
2 used instead of "his or her," especially when you are referring back to a word such as "everyone," "someone," or "anyone": *Everyone has their own way of doing things.*

theirs /ðerz/ pronoun ★
1 used for referring to someone or something that belongs to or is connected with a particular group of people or animals that have already been mentioned: *Your yard is big, but I think theirs is bigger.* ♦ *They introduced us to some friends **of theirs**.*
2 used instead of "his or hers," especially when you are referring back to a word such as "everyone," "someone," or "anyone": *I haven't gotten my grades yet, but everyone else has gotten theirs.*

them /*strong* ðem, *weak* ðəm/ pronoun ★★★
1 the object form of "they," used for referring to a particular group of people or things that have already been mentioned, or when it is obvious which group you are referring to: *They've taken their families with them.* ♦ *Sykes stole the paintings and then tried to sell them.*
2 used instead of "him or her," especially when you are referring back to a word such as "everyone," "someone," or "anyone": *Someone called, but I told them to call back later.*

theme /θim/ noun [C] ★
1 the main subject of something such as a book, speech, or art exhibit: *Love and honor are the main **themes of** the book.*
2 theme or **theme tune** a short piece of music that is played at the beginning and end of a radio or television program or a movie: *the theme from the movie* Rocky

ˈtheme ˌpark noun [C] a large park where people pay to play games and have fun and where all the entertainment is designed according to one theme

them·selves /ðəmˈselvz/ pronoun ★★★
1 the REFLEXIVE form of "they" that is used for showing that the people or things that do something are also affected by what they do: *They have no weapons to defend themselves.* ♦ *The couple had been saving up to buy themselves a house.*
2 used for emphasizing that a particular group of people are the ones that you are referring to, and not any others: *The two youths died in a fire that they themselves had started.*
PHRASES **(all) by themselves 1** alone: *Why were these two small children wandering around all by themselves?* **2** without any help: *It's a brilliant idea, and they thought it up all by themselves!*
(all) to themselves not sharing something with anyone else: *Helen and Philip were able to get a table to themselves.*

then /ðen/ grammar word ★★★

> **Then** can be:
> - an **adverb**: *I was still at school then.*
> - an **adjective**: *the then prime minister, Harold Wilson*

1 at a particular time in the past or in the future: *"Did you hear him when he left the house?" "Yes, I heard him then and when he came back."* ♦ *I can see you next weekend. Can you wait until then?*
2 used for introducing the next thing that happens: *He glanced quickly at Sally and then looked away again.* ♦ *First Lewis will give a TV interview. Then comes the main news conference.*

3 used for saying what you think the result must be if something is true: *"Sue and I grew up together." "You must know her fairly well then."* ♦ ***If no one else is willing, then** I'll have to do the job myself.*
4 used for referring to someone who had a particular job or position at a particular time in the past: *the then Secretary of State, Warren Christopher*
PHRASE **okay then** or **all right then** used for getting someone's attention when you are starting to talk about something new: *Okay then, are we ready to start?*
→ THERE

thence /ðens/ adv *literary* from a particular place or point

the•ol•o•gy /θiˈɑlədʒi/ noun [U] the study of God and religion —**the•o•log•i•cal** /ˌθiəˈlɑdʒɪk(ə)l/ adj

the•o•rem /ˈθiərəm/ noun [C] *technical* a statement that can be proved to be true

the•o•ret•i•cal /ˌθiəˈretɪk(ə)l/ adj **1** based on theories instead of practical experience **2** possible but not definite

the•o•ret•i•cal•ly /ˌθiəˈretɪkli/ adv used for saying that something could be true or could exist: *Transmission of the virus is theoretically possible, but very unlikely.*

the•o•rist /ˈθiərɪst/ noun [C] someone who develops or studies theories about a particular subject

the•o•rize /ˈθiəˌraɪz/ verb [I/T] to develop ideas in order to explain something

the•o•ry /ˈθiəri/ noun ★★
1 [C] an idea that explains how or why something happens: *Einstein's theory of relativity* ♦ **+that** *He had a theory that the germs caused disease.*
2 [U] the set of general principles that a particular subject is based on: *Marxist/literary theory*
3 [C] an idea that you believe is true, although you have no proof: *I have my own **theory about** why he resigned.*
PHRASE **in theory** used for saying that something is believed to be true, although it may not be true: *In theory the country is a democracy, but in practice the military holds most of the power.*

ther•a•peu•tic /ˌθerəˈpjutɪk/ adj **1** helping to treat or cure illness **2** helping you to feel better or calmer

ther•a•pist /ˈθerəpɪst/ noun [C] someone whose job is to help people with physical, mental, or emotional problems

ther•a•py /ˈθerəpi/ noun **1** [C/U] a form of treatment for an illness or medical condition **2** [U] treatment for someone with mental illness or emotional problems that involves talking to them

there /ðer/ grammar word ★★★

> There can be:
> - a **pronoun**: *There's a spider in the bathtub.*
> - an **adverb**: *Wait there until I get back.*
> - an **interjection**: *There, that didn't hurt so much, did it?*

1 /*weak* ðər, *strong* ðer/ **used for saying what exists** used for introducing a statement about someone or something that exists or happens: ***There is** plenty of time left.* ♦ *There are 24 teams competing in the tournament.* ♦ ***Are there** any other suggestions?*
2 in or to that place in or to a place that has already been mentioned, or that you are looking at or pointing to: *They're going to Hawaii, and they plan to stay there until the end of March.* ♦ *It's only a hundred miles to Westport. You could drive **there and back** in a day.* ♦ *Would you like to sit **over there** by the window?* ♦ ***There's** Angela now, coming up the street.*
3 at a point in a process at a particular point in a series of events, in a speech, or in a story: *I'll stop there, and answer questions.*
4 available available, and ready to help or to be used: *The opportunity was there, so I took it.* ♦ *If you need me, I'll **be there for** you.*
5 referring to what has just happened *spoken* used when something has just happened, for showing that you feel satisfied, sorry, annoyed, etc. about it: *There, everything's clean now.*
PHRASES **there and then** or **then and there** immediately at that moment and in that place: *They wanted me to make a decision there and then.*
there goes sth *spoken* used for expressing disappointment that something has failed, has been lost, or has been destroyed
there you go *spoken* a polite expression used when you are giving someone something
→ AGAIN

there•a•bouts /ˌðerəˈbaʊts/ adv near a particular place, amount, or time that has just been mentioned

there•af•ter /ðerˈæftər/ adv *formal* after a particular time that has just been mentioned

there•by /ðerˈbaɪ/ adv *formal* because of or by means of what has just been mentioned

there•fore /ˈðerfɔr/ adv *formal* ★★ as a result of what has just been mentioned: *The new boots are lighter and softer, and therefore more comfortable to wear.* ♦ *This is a binding contract. Therefore, we recommend that you review it with a lawyer.*

there•in /ðerˈɪn/ adv *formal* in a particular place or piece of writing that has just been mentioned
PHRASE **therein lies sth** used for explaining the cause of a situation that you have just described

ther•mal /ˈθɜrm(ə)l/ adj **1** *science* relating to or caused by heat **2** thermal clothing is made of special material that keeps you warm

ther•mom•e•ter /θərˈmɑmətər/ noun [C] a piece of equipment that measures temperature

Ther•mos /ˈθɜrməs/ *trademark* a container that keeps liquids hot or cold

ther•mo•stat /ˈθɜrməˌstæt/ noun [C] a piece of equipment that controls the temperature in a building, machine, or engine

the•sau•rus /θəˈsɔrəs/ (plural **the•sau•rus•es** or **the•sau•ri** /θəˈsɔˌraɪ/) noun [C] a book that contains lists of words that have similar meanings

these /ðiz/ grammar word ★★★ the plural of **this**

T

the•sis /ˈθisɪs/ (plural **the•ses** /ˈθiˌsiz/) noun [C] **1** a long piece of writing that is the final part of an advanced university degree **2** *formal* a theory that is used for explaining something

they /ðeɪ/ pronoun ★★★
1 used for referring to a group of people or things that have already been mentioned, or that are already known about: *I called her parents because I knew they were worried.* ♦ *It's hard to choose. They're all very nice.*
2 used instead of "he or she": *We should give everyone a chance to say what they think.*

- In spoken English and in informal written English, **they, them, their,** and **themselves** are used by many people for referring to a person without mentioning whether the person is male or female, especially when referring back to a pronoun such as "everyone" or "someone": *What happens if someone changes their mind?*
- In more formal English, "he or she," "him or her," or "himself or herself" are used instead.

3 used for referring to people in general: *They say there's going to be a war.*
4 used for referring to a government, an organization, or a group of people in authority: *They're going to ban logging in the region.*
→ HE

they'd /ðeɪd/ short form **1** the usual way of saying or writing "they would." This is not often used in formal writing: *They said they'd be happy to help.* **2** the usual way of saying or writing "they had" when "had" is an AUXILIARY VERB. This is not often used in formal writing: *He knew they'd met somewhere before.*

they'll /ðeɪl/ short form the usual way of saying or writing "they will." This is not often used in formal writing: *Hurry up! They'll be here any minute.*

they're /ðer/ short form the usual way of saying or writing "they are." This is not often used in formal writing: *They believe that what they're doing is right.*

they've /ðeɪv/ short form the usual way of saying or writing "they have" when "have" is an AUXILIARY VERB. This is not often used in formal writing: *They've been talking about buying a new house for years.*

thick¹ /θɪk/ adj ★★★

1 long between edges	5 filling air completely
2 of measurement	6 of accent
3 of plants/hair	+ PHRASES
4 not flowing easily	

1 a thick object or material has a long distance between two opposite sides, edges, or surfaces: *a thick wool sweater* ♦ *a thick layer of snow*
2 used for stating the distance between the opposite surfaces or edges of a solid object: *The walls are only a few inches thick.*
3 growing very close together: *her thick dark hair* ♦ *a thick cluster of trees*
4 a thick liquid is more stiff or solid than normal and does not flow easily: *a thick cream sauce*
5 thick smoke or cloud fills the air completely, so that it is difficult to see or difficult to breathe
6 a thick ACCENT shows very clearly that the speaker comes from a particular place
PHRASES **have thick skin** to not be easily upset or offended by what other people say about you
thick with sth full of something: *The air was thick with smoke.*
—**thick•ly** adv

thick² /θɪk/ noun
PHRASES **in the thick of sth** in the most busy, active, or dangerous part of a situation, event, or activity
through thick and thin in all situations, especially the most difficult ones

thick•en /ˈθɪkən/ verb [I/T] to become thick, or to make something become thick

thick•et /ˈθɪkɪt/ noun [C] an area with a lot of bushes and small trees growing very close together

thick•ness /ˈθɪknəs/ noun **1** [C/U] the measurement of how thick something is **2** [C] a layer of something

thick-skinned /ˌθɪk ˈskɪnd/ adj not easily upset or offended by what other people say about you

thief /θif/ (plural **thieves** /θivz/) noun [C] someone who steals something

thigh /θaɪ/ noun [C] the top part of your leg, above your knee

thim•ble /ˈθɪmb(ə)l/ noun [C] a small metal or plastic object that you wear on your finger in order to protect it when you are sewing

thin¹ /θɪn/ adj ★★★

1 short between edges	5 without much detail
2 with little fat on body	6 with little oxygen
3 flowing easily	7 small in amount
4 of hair/fur	+ PHRASE

1 a thin object or material has only a short distance between two opposite sides, edges, or surfaces: *a thin layer of dust* ♦ *Cut the tomatoes into **thin slices**.*
2 someone who is thin has very little fat on their body: *Charles was thin and very tall.*
3 a thin liquid contains mostly water, so that it flows easily: *a plate of meat covered with thin gravy*
4 thin hair or fur grows with spaces between the individual hairs: *a thin mustache*
5 without much detail or many facts: *The evidence for his theory is pretty thin.*
6 thin air has less oxygen in it than usual
7 small in number or amount: *It was a day of thin trading on the stock market.*
PHRASE **thin air** if something appears out of thin air or disappears into thin air, it appears or disappears in a sudden mysterious way
→ THINLY

Other ways of saying thin

- **emaciated** extremely thin because you have been sick, or because you do not have enough food to eat
- **lean/wiry** thin and strong
- **skinny** (*informal*) thin in a way that is not attractive
- **slender** thin in a graceful way

T

- **slim** thin in an attractive way
- **trim** thin because you exercise regularly

thin² /θɪn/ verb **1** [I] to become less in number, amount, or thickness: *As it grew dark, the crowd started to thin.* ♦ *Did you notice that his hair is thinning on top?* **2** [T] to make a thick liquid become less thick by adding water or another liquid to it

thin³ /θɪn/ adv in a way that produces a thin layer or piece of something: *Cut the cheese thin, so that it melts.*

thing /θɪŋ/ noun ★★★

1 object	5 general situation
2 action/activity	6 idea/information
3 situation/event	7 possessions
4 aspect/quality	+ PHRASES

1 [C] used for referring to an object that you cannot or do not want to refer to in a more specific way: *What's that thing over there on the table?* ♦ *It's one of those gadget things, isn't it?* ♦ *It's a thing used for looking inside people's ears.*
2 [C] an action or activity: *I have a lot of things to do today.* ♦ *I gave back the money. Did I **do the right thing**?*
3 [C] a situation or event: *A funny thing happened to me today.* ♦ *I think we should just forget the whole thing.* ♦ *She doesn't find that **kind of thing** funny.*
4 [C] an aspect of a situation, or a quality that someone has: *If you could change three things about your job, what would they be?* ♦ *The thing I really like about Theresa is her sense of humor.* ♦ *The funny thing is, I miss him now.* ♦ ***It's a good thing that** you don't need to work late.*
5 things [plural] used for talking about a situation in a general way: *Things have been getting better lately.* ♦ *The police soon got things under control.*
6 [C] an idea, comment, fact, or subject: *There are some interesting things in your report.* ♦ *I have a few things to say to you.* ♦ *If anyone asks you what I said, don't say a thing.*
7 things [plural] the objects that belong to a particular person or are used for a particular purpose

PHRASES **among other things** used for saying that there are other details, examples, etc. in addition to the ones that you are mentioning: *He's a liar and a thief, among other things.*
be seeing/hearing things to think that you see or hear something that is not really there
first thing (in the morning) early in the morning
for one thing used for saying that the reason or example that you are giving is not the only one: *Well, for one thing, I'm not tall enough to play basketball.*
the thing is *spoken* used for introducing an answer, comment, or explanation that is related to something that was just mentioned: *"Why didn't you invite me?" "Well, the thing is, I didn't think you would want to come."*

thing·y /ˈθɪŋi/ or **thing·a·ma·jig** /ˈθɪŋəməˌdʒɪɡ/ noun [C] *spoken* used for referring to something when you do not know or cannot remember the name of it

think /θɪŋk/ (past tense and past participle **thought** /θɔt/) verb ★★★

1 believe sth is true	6 remember sb/sth
2 have opinion	7 consider sb
3 consider facts carefully	+ PHRASES
4 have sth in your mind	+ PHRASAL VERBS
5 imagine sth	

1 [T] to believe something based on facts or ideas: *"Is Dan coming tonight?" "**I think so**, but I'm not sure."* ♦ **+(that)** *I don't think there's a computer store in town.* ♦ **be thought to do sth** *Faulty wiring is thought to have caused the fire.*
2 [I/T] to have a particular opinion about someone or something: *His colleagues **think a lot of** him* (=have a very good opinion of him). ♦ ***I don't think much of** Sam's new girlfriend* (=I don't like her very much). ♦ **think of sb/sth as sth** *Nobody seriously thought of him as a candidate for the job.* ♦ *I've always thought of that as a love song.*
3 [I] to carefully consider facts in order to understand something, make a decision, or solve a problem: *Let's **stop and think** before we do anything else.* ♦ *I need to **think** seriously **about** their offer.* ♦ *I've got to **think of** a way to earn more money.*
4 [I/T] to have something in your mind: *I wasn't worried – I just thought, "Why is she doing that?"* ♦ *I guess we were all thinking the same thing.*
5 [I/T] to imagine something: *Just **think of** what she's suffered!* ♦ **+(that)** *I never thought that I'd end up working here.*
6 [I] to remember someone or something: *He could never **think of** the woman's name.* ♦ *I often **think about** the time we spent in Rome.*
7 [I] to consider someone and their needs or situation: *It was kind of you to **think of** our daughter.*

PHRASES **come to think of it** *spoken* used for adding something to what you have said because you have just remembered something: *Come to think of it, he did mention going to the house.*
I thought (that) *spoken* used as a polite way of suggesting something: *I thought we'd have a drink before dinner.*
think twice/again to carefully consider whether what you are planning to do is a good idea

PHRASAL VERBS ˌ**think ˈback** to think about something that happened in the past: *I've been trying to think back to that last evening.*
ˌ**think sth ˈover** to consider a problem or decision carefully: *Let's think his proposal over before we see him again.*
ˌ**think sth ˈthrough** to consider the facts about something in an organized and thorough way: *Have you had time to **think things through**?*
ˌ**think sth ˈup** to invent or imagine something, especially an excuse: *She'd have to think up a good reason for being late.*

think·er /ˈθɪŋkər/ noun [C] someone who thinks about important subjects and develops new ideas

think·ing /ˈθɪŋkɪŋ/ noun [U] **1** an opinion, or a

set of ideas: *Can you explain the thinking behind your proposal?* **2** the way that you consider things or react to them: *What's needed here is some positive thinking.* **3** the process of considering something or reacting to something: *He had some serious thinking to do.*

ˈthink ˌtank noun [C] a group of people who work together to produce new ideas on a particular subject

thin•ly /ˈθɪnli/ adv **1** in a thin layer or piece: *thinly sliced tomatoes* **2** with only a few people or things that are far apart from each other: *a thinly populated area* **3** in a way that makes it easy to recognize what the true situation really is: *a thinly disguised/veiled/concealed threat*

third /θɜrd/ number **1** in the place or position counted as number 3 **2** one of 3 equal parts of something

third•ly /ˈθɜrdli/ adv used for introducing the third idea in a list

ˌthird ˈparty noun [C] *formal* a person or organization that is not one of the two main people or organizations involved in something

ˌthird ˈperson, the noun [singular] *linguistics* the set of pronouns and verb forms that are used for referring to someone or something that is not the speaker or the person who is being spoken to

ˌthird-ˈrate adj of very low quality

ˌThird ˈWorld, the noun [singular] countries that are poor and do not have much industrial development. People now prefer to use the expression **developing countries**.

thirst /θɜrst/ noun **1** [singular/U] the feeling or state of being thirsty **2** [singular] a strong feeling of wanting to have or do something

thirst•y /ˈθɜrsti/ adj ★ feeling that you want or need to drink something: *I'm really thirsty – could I have a glass of water?* —**thirst•i•ly** adv

thir•teen /ˌθɜrˈtin/ number the number 13

thir•teenth /ˌθɜrˈtinθ/ number **1** in the place or position counted as number 13 **2** one of 13 equal parts of something

T

thir•ti•eth /ˈθɜrtiəθ/ number **1** in the place or position counted as number 30 **2** one of 30 equal parts of something

thir•ty /ˈθɜrti/ number the number 30

this /ðɪs/ grammar word ★★★

> This can be:
> - a **determiner**: *He gave me this diamond ring.*
> - a **pronoun**: *This is the photograph you asked for.*
> - an **adverb**: *It's a long time since I felt this good.*

1 (plural **these** /ðiz/) **the one that is here** used for referring to a person, thing, or place that is near you: *I bought these shoes in Italy.* ♦ *This is where I catch the bus.* ♦ *This is my towel and that's yours.* ♦ *This is our new secretary, Veronica Taylor.*

2 (plural **these** /ðiz/) **the present one** used for referring to the present time or a present action, or to a time or action that will happen soon: *I'm going to be away all this week.* ♦ *Is this your first visit to Wyoming?* ♦ *Are we going to have enough fuel this winter?* ♦ *Benson was late again **this morning*** (=the morning of today). ♦ *I don't get much spare time **these days**.*

3 (plural **these** /ðiz/) **the one that is known** used for referring to a particular fact, thing, person, etc. that has just been mentioned, or when it is obvious which one you are referring to: *Sometimes there's flooding, and this is why no one wants to live here.*

4 so *spoken* so, or to such a degree: *I haven't had this much fun since I was a kid.* ♦ *It was cold in Toronto, but it wasn't as cold **as this**.*

5 saying who you are used when you are saying who you are in a telephone conversation, or when asking who you are speaking to on the telephone: *Hello, this is Kim Riley speaking.* ♦ *Hello, is this Mrs. Baker?*

PHRASE **this and that** or **this, that, and the other** *spoken* various things

> - **This** refers to something that you are holding or wearing, or that is nearest to you, and **that** refers to something that someone else is holding or wearing, or that is farther away from you: *Do you like this shirt?* ♦ *Where did you get that hat?*
> - **This** refers to things that are happening now or are just about to happen, but **that** refers to things that happened in the past, that have just ended, or that will happen in the future: *I'm enjoying this party.* ♦ *What happened at that meeting?*

this•tle /ˈθɪs(ə)l/ noun [C] a wild plant with a thick round purple or white flower and leaves with sharp points

THNQ abbrev thank you: used in TEXT MESSAGES

thong /θɔŋ/ noun [C] **1** a piece of underwear with a very narrow piece of cloth in the back **2** *American* a FLIP-FLOP

thorn /θɔrn/ noun [C] a sharp point that sticks out from the stem of a plant

PHRASE **a thorn in sb's side** a person or thing that causes a lot of problems for someone

thorn•y /ˈθɔrni/ adj **1** difficult to deal with: *a thorny issue/question* **2** covered with thorns

thor•ough /ˈθʌrə/ adj ★

1 including everything that is possible or necessary: *a thorough investigation/examination/search* ♦ *She has **a thorough understanding** of the business.*

2 someone who is thorough does everything that they should and leaves nothing out: *The doctor was very thorough and asked lots of questions.*

—**thor•ough•ness** noun [U]

thor•ough•bred /ˈθʌrəˌbred/ noun [C] a horse that belongs to a BREED (=type) that is considered of very high quality

thor•ough•fare /ˈθʌrəˌfer/ noun [C] *formal* a main road through a place

thor•ough•ly /ˈθʌrəli/ adv **1** very carefully, so that nothing is missed: *The case will be thoroughly studied before any decision is made.* **2** very much or completely: *The children thoroughly enjoyed the show.*

those /ðoʊz/ grammar word ★★★ the plural of that

though /ðoʊ/ adv, conjunction ★★★

1 used for introducing a statement that

makes your main statement seem surprising=ALTHOUGH: *Though the U.K. is only a small country, it has played an important role in history.* ♦ *He went on fighting* ***even though*** *he was wounded.*
2 but=ALTHOUGH: *I really enjoyed your lecture, though there were some parts I didn't quite understand.*
3 used when adding a statement or question that seems surprising after the previous statement: *"The Savoy's a very nice hotel." "Isn't it expensive, though?"* ♦ *The movie has some interesting parts. I wouldn't rush out to see it, though.*
→ AS

thought¹ /θɔt/ noun ★★★
1 [C] a word, idea, or image that comes into your mind: *a comforting/sobering/chilling thought* ♦ *His mind was filled with* ***thoughts of*** *revenge.* ♦ *She couldn't stand* ***the thought of*** *seeing him again.* ♦ ***The thought had crossed my mind*** *that we were taking a big risk.*
2 [U] the mental effort that you make to understand something, make decisions, or solve problems: ***Deep in thought,*** *he did not hear the doorbell ring.* ♦ *I hope you'll* ***give*** *our conversation* ***some thought*** (=think about it).
3 [C] an idea or opinion about something: *Does anyone want to express their* ***thoughts on*** *this question?*
4 [C/U] an intention or wish to do something: *He insists he has no thought of running for office.*
PHRASE **with no thought for sth** without any feeling of being worried about what might happen as a result of an action
→ FOOD

thought² the past tense and past participle of think

thought•ful /ˈθɔtf(ə)l/ adj **1** kind and showing that you think that what other people want or need is important: *Thank you – the flowers were a very thoughtful gift.* **2** thinking seriously about something: *Beth stood there, silent and thoughtful.*
—**thought•ful•ly** adv

thought•less /ˈθɔtləs/ adj not thinking about what other people want or need
—**thought•less•ly** adv, **thought•less•ness** noun [U]

thou•sand /ˈθaʊz(ə)nd/ number ★★
1 the number 1,000
2 thousands or **a thousand** a large number or amount of people or things: *The floods have left thousands homeless.* ♦ *I still have a thousand things to do.*

thou•sandth /ˈθaʊz(ə)ndθ/ number **1** in the place or position counted as number 1,000 **2** one of 1,000 equal parts of something

thrash /θræʃ/ verb **1** [T] to defeat an opponent very easily in a game or competition **2** [T] to hit someone hard several times as a punishment **3** [I] to move in a violent uncontrolled way
PHRASAL VERB ˌ**thrash sth ˈout** to discuss something until you find a solution or reach an agreement

thrash•ing /ˈθræʃɪŋ/ noun [C] **1** *informal* an easy victory in a game or competition **2** an act of hitting someone hard several times as a punishment

thread¹ /θred/ noun **1** [C/U] a long thin fiber used for sewing: *cotton/silk/nylon thread* ♦ *You need a longer piece of thread.* **2** [C] an idea or quality that forms a connection between things: *There is a common thread running through all the problems.* **3** [C] the raised line that curves around a screw **4** [C] *computing* a series of e-mail messages about a particular subject

thread² /θred/ verb **1** [T] to put something long and thin through a hole or space: *Can you thread this needle for me?* **2** [I/T] to move carefully through a place, avoiding people or things that are in your way

thread•bare /ˈθredˌber/ adj very thin because of being worn or used a lot: *a threadbare carpet/shirt*

threat /θret/ noun ★★
1 [C] an occasion when someone says that they will cause you harm or problems, especially if you do not do what they tell you to do: *He would not* ***make threats*** *he wasn't prepared to carry out.* ♦ *After* ***threats*** *of legal action they stopped the construction.* ♦ *He had received several* ***death threats.*** ♦ *This isn't just an* ***idle threat*** (=a threat that is not serious).
2 [C] someone or something that could cause harm or danger: *She is not viewed as a threat by her former employer.* ♦ *a* ***threat to*** *freedom* ♦ *The dispute* ***poses a threat*** (=is a threat) ***to*** *peace.*
3 [C/U] the possibility that something bad is going to happen: *Constant* ***threat of*** *attack makes everyday life dangerous here.* ♦ *They* ***face the threat*** *of terrorism every day.* ♦ *With the closure of the hospital, local jobs are* ***under threat.***

threat•en /ˈθret(ə)n/ verb ★★
1 [T] to tell someone that you will cause them harm or problems, especially in order to make them do something: *He's been threatening me for months.* ♦ **threaten to do sth** *The terrorists are threatening to kill the hostages.* ♦ **threaten sb with sth** *One man has been threatened with legal action.*
2 [T] to be likely to harm or destroy something: *Many workers feel that their jobs are threatened.* ♦ *Nearly 1,000 of the world's bird species are* ***threatened with*** *extinction.* ♦ **threaten to do sth** *Nuclear testing threatens to destroy our environment.*
3 [I] if something bad or unpleasant threatens, it is likely to happen or to affect you: *The animals return to the herd when danger threatens.*
—**threat•en•ing** adj, **threat•en•ing•ly** adv

three /θri/ number the number 3

three-di•men•sion•al /ˌθri dɪˈmenʃən(ə)l/ adj not flat, but able to be measured in height, depth, and width

ˌ**three-ˈquarters** noun [plural] three of four equal parts of something: *It took an hour and three-quarters to get home.*

thresh•old /ˈθreʃˌhoʊld/ noun [C] the point at which a limit is reached or a rule starts to apply
PHRASE **on the threshold of sth** starting a new stage in your life, or soon to discover something

threw the past tense of **throw**[1]

thrift shop /ˈθrɪft ʃɑp/ or ˈ**thrift ˌstore** noun [C] *American* a store that sells used things at low prices

thrift·y /ˈθrɪfti/ adj careful about how you spend money so that you do not waste any

thrill[1] /θrɪl/ noun [C] **1** a sudden feeling of being very pleased and excited **2** something that makes you feel excited

thrill[2] /θrɪl/ verb [T] to make someone feel very pleased and excited

thrilled /θrɪld/ adj very pleased and excited: *We are thrilled that Kevin is going to join the team.*

thrill·er /ˈθrɪlər/ noun [C] a book, play, or movie that tells an exciting story

thrill·ing /ˈθrɪlɪŋ/ adj extremely exciting

thrive /θraɪv/ verb [I] to become very successful, happy, or healthy —**thriv·ing** adj: *a thriving economy*

PHRASAL VERB ˈ**thrive on sth** to become successful or happy in a particular situation, especially a situation that other people would not enjoy: *Some couples thrive on conflict.*

throat /θroʊt/ noun [C] ★★

1 the area at the back of your mouth and inside your neck: *She's in bed with a throat infection.* ♦ *Have we got any medicine for **a sore throat**?*

2 the front part of your neck: *The bigger man grabbed him by the throat.* —*picture* → C14

throb /θrɑb/ verb [I] **1** if a painful part of your body throbs, the pain comes and goes in a fast regular pattern **2** to make a repeated low sound: *Loud dance music throbbed in the air.* —**throb** noun [C]

throes /θroʊz/ noun **in the throes of sth** involved in a difficult or unpleasant situation or activity

throm·bo·sis /θrɑmˈboʊsɪs/ noun [C/U] a serious medical condition in which your blood gets thicker and forms a CLOT that stops the blood from flowing normally

throne /θroʊn/ noun **1** [C] a special chair that a king or queen sits on **2 the throne** [singular] the position of being a king or queen

throng[1] /θrɔŋ/ noun [C] *literary* a large crowd of people

throng[2] /θrɔŋ/ verb [I/T] if people throng somewhere, a lot of them go there

throt·tle[1] /ˈθrɑt(ə)l/ verb [T] to hurt or kill someone by squeezing their throat so that they cannot breathe

throt·tle[2] /ˈθrɑt(ə)l/ noun [C] a piece of equipment that controls how fast a vehicle is moving by controlling the amount of fuel going into the engine

through /θru/ grammar word ★★★

> **Through** can be:
> - a **preposition**: *They were riding through a forest.*
> - an **adverb**: *There's a hole in the roof where the rain comes through.*
> - an **adjective**: *Are you through with that?*

1 from one end or side to the other from one side of a hole, object, or area to the other: *The train runs through a tunnel.* ♦ *The man at the gate would not let us through.* ♦ *Workers had cut through an electrical cable while they were digging.* ♦ *The path climbs steeply through the trees.*

2 during a period of time during all of a period of time until the end of it: *the period from February 1 through June 30* ♦ *He lay awake **all through** the night.* ♦ *The training program will continue **through to** mid-April.*

3 by means of sth by means of something, or because of something: *Most accidents occur through human error.* ♦ *skills that we can only learn through experience* ♦ *Concert tickets are being sold through the Internet.*

4 finished finished doing or using something: *Only one more letter to write. I'm nearly through.* ♦ *I'm not sure what time he'll be **through with** his meeting.* ♦ *Let me know when you're **through with** the hairdryer.*

5 communicating by phone used for saying that you are connected to someone by phone: *I tried to call the mayor's office, but I couldn't **get through**.* ♦ *Can you **put** me **through** to Mr. Hearst, please?*

6 affecting every part affecting every part of someone or something: *A rumor spread through the camp.* ♦ *Problems extend through the entire system.* ♦ *When she heard Bruno's voice, it sent a chill of terror through her.*

7 reading or looking at every part reading or looking at every part of something, from the beginning to the end of it: *You'd better read through the instructions carefully.* ♦ *I've been searching through all the files, but I can't find Hamilton's letter.*

through·out /θruˈaʊt/ adv, preposition ★

1 in every part of a place: *The hotel has recently been redecorated throughout.* ♦ *Pollution is a serious problem in major cities **throughout the world**.*

2 during all of a period of time or an event: *House prices continued to rise throughout the 1980s.*

through·way /ˈθruˌweɪ/ noun [C] *American* a wide divided highway on which traffic can travel fast. You have to pay to use many throughways.

throw[1] /θroʊ/ (past tense **threw** /θru/; past participle **thrown** /θroʊn/) verb ★★★

1 send through air	5 put sb/sth in bad state
2 put sth somewhere	6 confuse sb
3 move your body	+ PHRASES
4 look etc. in direction	+ PHRASAL VERBS

1 [I/T] to make something leave your hand and move through the air, by moving your arm quickly: **throw sth at sb/sth** *Kids were throwing stones at the windows.* ♦ **throw sth to sb** *She threw the ball to the little boy.* ♦ **throw sb sth** *Can you throw me that rope?* —*picture* → C15

2 [T] to put something somewhere carelessly: *She hastily threw her books into a bag.*

3 [T] to suddenly move your body or a part of your body: *Throwing back his head, he started laughing.*

4 [T] to suddenly look, smile, etc. in a particular direction: *Marco threw an angry glance at her.*

5 [T] to cause someone or something to be in a particular state or situation, especially a bad one: *A single computer problem can throw the whole office* ***into chaos.***
6 [T] if something throws you, it makes you confused because you were not expecting it and do not know how to deal with it
PHRASES **throw a party** to organize a party, especially in your own home
throw a punch to hit someone with your FIST (=closed hand)
throw yourself into sth to start giving all of your attention and energy to something: *After my girlfriend left me, I threw myself into my work.*
PHRASAL VERBS ˌ**throw sth aˈway 1** to get rid of something that you no longer want: *Have you thrown the papers away?* **2** to waste something such as an opportunity or advantage: *They lost the game after throwing away a fourteen-point lead.*
ˌ**throw sth ˈin** to include something extra with something that you are selling, without asking for more money
ˌ**throw sb ˈout** to force someone to leave a place or group: *Several people were* ***thrown out of*** *the party.*
ˌ**throw sth ˈout** *same as* **throw sth away** 1: *I've thrown out my old boots.*
ˌ**throw (sth) ˈup** *informal* if you throw up, or if you throw something up, food and drink comes back up from your stomach and out of your mouth = VOMIT

throw² /θroʊ/ noun [C] **1** an action of throwing something such as a ball **2** a large piece of cloth that you put over a chair, bed, etc.

throw·back /ˈθroʊˌbæk/ noun [singular] someone or something that seems to belong to an earlier period of time

thrown the past participle of **throw**¹

ˈ**throw ˌpillow** noun [C] *American* a small PILLOW that you keep on a seat for decoration

thru /θru/ adv, preposition an informal way of writing "through"

thrush /θrʌʃ/ noun [C] a brown bird with light spots on its breast

thrust¹ /θrʌst/ (past tense and past participle **thrust**) verb [T] to put something somewhere with a quick hard push: *A reporter thrust a microphone under her nose.*

thrust² /θrʌst/ noun **1** [singular] **the thrust of sth** the main idea or intention of something such as a document, speech, or policy **2** [C] a quick hard push **3** [U] *technical* the force that an engine produces to push something forward

thru·way /ˈθruweɪ/ another spelling of **throughway**

thud /θʌd/ noun [C] a low sound that is made by something heavy falling or hitting something —**thud** verb [I]

thug /θʌg/ noun [C] someone who behaves in an unpleasant and violent way, especially in a public place

thumb¹ /θʌm/ noun [C] ★ the part like a wide finger at the side of your hand: *She held the jewel carefully between her finger and thumb.* —*picture* → C14

thumb² /θʌm/ PHRASAL VERB ˈ**thumb through sth** to quickly turn the pages of a book, magazine, or newspaper

thumb·nail /ˈθʌmˌneɪl/ noun [C] **1** the nail on your thumb **2** a small picture of something shown on a computer screen, especially on a WEB PAGE

ˌ**thumbs ˈdown, the** noun [singular] if a plan, idea, or suggestion gets or is given the thumbs down, people do not like or accept it

ˌ**thumbs ˈup, the** noun [singular] if a plan, idea, or suggestion gets or is given the thumbs up, people like or accept it

thumb·tack /ˈθʌmˌtæk/ noun [C] *American* a short pin with a flat round top, used especially for fastening papers to walls

thump¹ /θʌmp/ verb **1** [I] if your heart is thumping, you can feel it beating very fast, for example because you are frightened or excited **2** [T] to hit someone or something with your FIST (=closed hand) = PUNCH

thump² /θʌmp/ noun [C] **1** a low loud sound that is made when something heavy hits something else: *He brought his hand down on the table with a thump.* **2** an action of hitting someone or something with your FIST (=closed hand) = PUNCH

thun·der¹ /ˈθʌndər/ noun [U] the loud noise that you sometimes hear in the sky during a storm

thun·der² /ˈθʌndər/ verb [I] **1** if it thunders, you hear thunder in the sky **2** to make a lot of noise while moving somewhere fast: *An express train thundered through the station.*

thun·der·ous /ˈθʌnd(ə)rəs/ adj very loud —**thun·der·ous·ly** adv

thun·der·storm /ˈθʌndərˌstɔrm/ noun [C] a storm with THUNDER (=loud noise) and LIGHTNING (=flashes of light) in the sky

Thurs. abbrev Thursday

Thurs·day /ˈθɜrzˌdeɪ/ noun [C/U] ★★★ the day after Wednesday and before Friday: *The election is being held on a Thursday.* ♦ *We often go swimming Thursdays* (=every Thursday). ♦ *Could I make an appointment for next Thursday?* ♦ *Adam has his piano lesson* ***on Thursdays*** (=every Thursday).

thus /ðʌs/ adv *formal* ★
1 as a result of the fact that you have just mentioned = HENCE, THEREFORE: *Fewer pupils will attend the schools, and they will thus need fewer teachers.*
2 by the method that has been mentioned: *The oil producers will raise prices, thus increasing their profits.*

thwart /θwɔrt/ verb [T] *formal* to prevent someone from doing something that they were planning to do

thyme /taɪm/ noun [U] a small plant with very small leaves, used for adding flavor to food

ti·ar·a /tiˈɑrə, tiˈerə/ noun [C] a piece of jewelry that a woman wears on her head on formal occasions

tic /tɪk/ noun [C] a sudden movement of a muscle that you cannot control

tick¹ /tɪk/ verb [I] if a clock or watch ticks, it makes a quiet sound every second
PHRASE **what makes sb tick** *informal* the basic aspects of someone's personality that make them behave the way they do
PHRASAL VERB ˌ**tick sb ˈoff** *informal* **1** *American* to annoy someone **2** *British* to speak angrily

T

to someone who has done something wrong

tick² /tɪk/ noun [C] **1** an insect that sucks blood **2** the quiet sound that some clocks and watches make every second **3** *British* a CHECK that you write next to a correct answer

tick·et /ˈtɪkɪt/ noun [C] ★★★
1 a piece of paper that shows that you have paid to do something such as go to a concert, visit a museum, or travel on a train, bus, airplane, etc.: *a movie/theater ticket* ♦ *We'll send your tickets a week before your flight.*
2 a piece of paper that says you must pay an amount of money as a punishment for breaking a traffic law: *a speeding ticket*
3 the politicians or policies that a political party is supporting: *Bush ran for president on the Republican ticket.*

tick·le¹ /ˈtɪk(ə)l/ verb **1** [T] to move your fingers gently on someone's skin in order to make them laugh **2** [I/T] if a part of your body tickles, or if something that touches your skin tickles it, you have an uncomfortable feeling on your skin

tick·le² /ˈtɪk(ə)l/ noun [singular] a slightly sore feeling in your throat that makes you want to cough

tic-tac-toe /ˌtɪk tæk ˈtoʊ/ noun [U] *American* a game in which two players take turns to draw an X or an O on a paper marked with squares. The player who draws a line of three X's or three O's wins. *—picture* → C16

tid·al /ˈtaɪd(ə)l/ adj connected with the regular movement of the ocean toward and away from the land

ˈtidal ˌwave noun [C] a very large wave that causes a lot of damage when it hits the land

tid·bit /ˈtɪdˌbɪt/ noun [C] *American* a small piece of food or information

tide¹ /taɪd/ noun [C] the regular movement of the ocean toward and away from the land

tide² /taɪd/ PHRASAL VERB **ˌtide sb ˈover** to help someone to get to the end of a difficult period of time, especially by giving them money

ti·dy¹ /ˈtaɪdi/ adj ★
1 a tidy room, desk, etc. has everything in the correct place or arranged properly =NEAT
2 a tidy person always puts their things away in the correct place
—**ti·di·ly** adv, **ti·di·ness** noun [U]

ti·dy² /ˈtaɪdi/ verb [I/T] to make a place look better by putting things in the correct place

tie¹ /taɪ/ (present participle **ty·ing**) verb ★★
1 [T] to fasten two ends of a piece of string, rope, etc. together with a knot, or to fasten things together with string, rope, etc.: *Sally bent down to tie her shoelaces.* ♦ **tie sth to sth** *They tied one end of the rope to a tree.* ♦ **tie sth together** *Tie the newspapers together before you throw them away.*
2 [T] to form a close connection between people or things: *This series **ties together** events from the past and present.* ♦ *Portugal's economy **is closely tied** to Spain's.*
3 [I/T] if two players or teams tie, they both have the same number of points at the end of a game or competition
4 [T] if something ties you to a particular place or situation, you cannot leave it: *Many young mothers feel **tied to** the home and children.*

PHRASAL VERBS **ˌtie sb ˈdown** to stop someone from being free to do what they want: *I don't want a relationship that ties me down.*
ˌtie ˈin with sth if one statement, fact, etc. ties in with another, they both contain the same information and are therefore likely to be true
ˌtie sb ˈup to tie a rope, etc. tightly around someone so that they cannot move or escape
ˌtie sth ˈup 1 to tie the ends of something together **2** to tie an animal to something such as a post so that it cannot get away

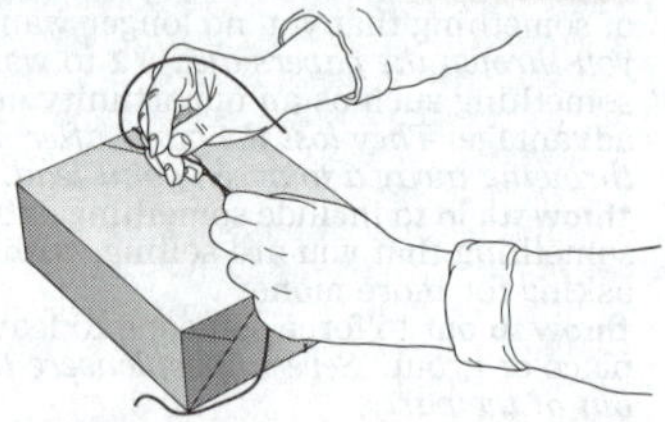
tie

tie² /taɪ/ noun [C] ★

1 narrow cloth for neck	4 equal points/votes
2 connection	5 sth limiting freedom
3 for fastening	

1 a long narrow piece of colored cloth that a man wears around his neck with a shirt: *a silk tie* ♦ *Do you have to wear a tie to work? —picture* → C4
2 a relationship or connection between people or things: *the ties of marriage* ♦ *The treaty should **strengthen ties** between the two countries.*
3 a short piece of string or wire that is used for fastening something
4 a result of a game or competition in which each person or team has the same number of points, votes, etc.: *The game finished in a tie.*
5 something that limits your freedom: *He still feels a tie to the land where he grew up.*

tie·break·er /ˈtaɪˌbreɪkər/ or **tie·break** /ˈtaɪˌbreɪk/ noun [C] an extra part of a game or competition to decide who will win when the players have the same number of points

tied up /ˌtaɪd ˈʌp/ adj **1** very busy **2** *American* if traffic is tied up, it is not moving very quickly **3** if your money is tied up in something, it is being used for that thing and you cannot use it for anything else

ˈtie-ˌin noun [C] *business* a product such as a toy or book that is connected with a successful movie or television program

tier /tɪr/ noun [C] **1** one of several rows or layers of something that are all at different heights: *a wedding cake with three tiers* **2** one of several levels in an organization or system: *the lower tiers of management*

tiff /tɪf/ noun [C] *informal* a minor argument

ti·ger /ˈtaɪgər/ noun [C] a large Asian wild animal that has yellowish fur with black lines. It is a member of the cat family. *—picture* → C12

tight¹ /taɪt/ adj ★★

1 close against body	5 stretched straight/flat
2 holding sth firmly	6 of bend on a road
3 controlled carefully	+ PHRASE
4 only just enough	

1 fitting closely around your body or part of your body ≠ LOOSE: *a tight shirt/dress*
2 holding someone or fastening something very firmly ≠ LOOSE: *a tight knot* ♦ *Baxter kept **a tight grip** on the prisoner's arm.*
3 controlled very carefully and strictly ≠ LAX: ***Security** has been very **tight** throughout the Prince's visit.*
4 if something such as time or money is tight, you have only just enough of it: *vacations for people on **a tight budget***
5 if something such as cloth or rope is tight, it is stretched so that it is completely straight or flat
6 a tight bend on a road is difficult to drive around because it curves a lot
PHRASE **keep a tight grip/hold on sth** to control something in a very strict way
—**tight•ly** adv: *Keep the windows tightly closed.* —**tight•ness** noun [U]

tight² /taɪt/ adv very firmly: *She held on tight to the handrail.*

tight•en /ˈtaɪt(ə)n/ verb **1** [T] to turn something such as a screw or cover until it is tight and you cannot turn it any more ≠ LOOSEN **2** [I/T] to become tighter, or to make something become tighter ≠ LOOSEN: *He tightened his hold on the steering wheel.* **3** [T] to make a set of rules stricter or harder to avoid: *Airport security has been tightened up since September 11.*
PHRASE **tighten your belt** to spend less money

tight•knit /ˌtaɪtˈnɪt/ adj **1** a tightknit group of people have a very close relationship to each other **2** *American* a tightknit plan has been thought about and prepared carefully so that it is unlikely to fail

tight-lipped /ˌtaɪt ˈlɪpt/ adj *mainly journalism* refusing to comment on something

tight•rope /ˈtaɪtˌroʊp/ noun [C] a piece of rope or wire high above the ground that a CIRCUS performer walks along
PHRASE **walk a tightrope** to be in a difficult situation that you have to deal with very carefully, because even a small mistake could have very bad results

tights /taɪts/ noun [plural] a piece of women's clothing that tightly covers the feet and legs up to the waist

tile¹ /taɪl/ noun [C] a flat piece of baked clay or stone that is used for covering a roof, floor, or wall —*picture* → C1

tile² /taɪl/ verb [T] **1** to cover a roof, floor, or wall with tiles **2** *computing* to arrange different WINDOWS on a computer screen so that you can see all of them next to each other

tiled /taɪld/ adj covered with tiles

till¹ /tɪl/ preposition, conjunction ★ until: *You'll have to wait till tomorrow.* ♦ *Just sit here till I come back.*

till² /tɪl/ noun [C] *old-fashioned* a CASH REGISTER

tilt /tɪlt/ verb [I/T] to move, or to move something, so that one side is lower than the other: *The tray was tilted at an angle.* —**tilt** noun [singular]

tim•ber /ˈtɪmbər/ noun [U] **1** trees that are used for producing wood **2** wood that is used for building houses or making furniture

time¹ /taɪm/ noun ★★★

1 hours, years, etc.	6 when sth happens
2 measurement on clock	7 time available/needed
3 period	8 part of history/sb's life
4 occasion/experience	9 in a race
5 moment/situation	+ PHRASES

1 [U] the quantity that is measured in minutes, hours, days, years, etc.: *Einstein tried to define the relationship between space and time.* ♦ ***Time** seemed to **pass** more quickly than before.*
2 [singular/U] the hours, minutes, etc. as shown on a clock: *Do you know what time it is?* ♦ ***What time** does the show start?* ♦ *Can your daughter **tell the time** yet* (=is she able to say what time is shown on a clock)*?*
3 [C/U] a particular period of minutes, hours, days, years, etc.: *She thought about it for **a long time**.* ♦ *She left **a short time** ago.* ♦ *How much **time** did it **take** to get here?* ♦ *I've been thinking of changing my job **for some time*** (=for a fairly long time). ♦ *There have been improvements in **the length of time** patients have to wait for treatment.*
4 [C] an occasion on which you do something or on which something happens: ***The next time** you need financial advice, come and see me.* ♦ *It was **the first time** we'd met.* ♦ *Did you **have a good time** at camp?*
5 [singular/U] the moment or situation when something happens: *I was still living with my parents **at that time**.* ♦ ***By the time** we arrived, the other guests were already there.* ♦ *When would be **a good time** to discuss the proposal?* ♦ *It seemed like **the right time** to make the change.*
6 [U] the particular point when something should happen: *Is it closing time already?* ♦ *Come on, everyone. **It's time for** dinner.* ♦ *Did your plane arrive **on time**?*
7 [U] time that you have available for doing something in: *She will **have less time** to spend with family and friends now.* ♦ *Come and see me next week, if you **get the time**.* ♦ *I should be able to **find time** to call him tomorrow.*
8 [C] a period in history or in someone's life: *The fort was built in Roman times.* ♦ ***a time** of political instability* ♦ *I thoroughly enjoyed my **time as** a teacher.*
9 [C] the amount of time that someone takes to finish a race: *She's cut two seconds off her previous best time.*
PHRASES **about time 1** *spoken* used for showing that you are annoyed because something has happened later than it should: *Here they are, and about time too.* **2** used for saying that someone should do something soon: *Isn't it about time we got a new car?*
ahead of time at an earlier time than people expected
ahead of your/its etc. time much more modern or advanced than most other

people or things: *As an artist, he was years ahead of his time.*
all the time 1 often: *It's a very good restaurant. We go there all the time.* **2** continuously: *It rained all the time they were there.*
at a time used for saying how many things there are in each group or on each occasion: *Deal with each question separately, one at a time.*
at all times *formal* always: *Please keep your bags with you at all times.*
at one time in the past, but not now: *At one time, that kind of thing would have made me really mad.*
at times sometimes but not often: *She was fun to be with at times.*
before your time used for saying that you are too young to remember something: *These styles were a bit before my time.*
for days/weeks etc. at a time continuously for a period of several days/weeks etc.
for the time being at the present time, but not permanently
from time to time sometimes, but not often
in no time (at all) or **in next to no time** very soon or very quickly
in time 1 early enough to do something: *I want to be home **in time for** dinner.* ♦ *We got to the hospital **just in time**.* ♦ **in time to do sth** *Luckily, they got there in time to warn him about what had happened.* **2** after a fairly long period of time: *He'll forget about it in time.*
most of the time usually, or very often
of all time used for talking about people or things that are better than all others that have existed: *the greatest boxer of all time*
out of time with no more time available to finish something
time after time or **time and again** happening so often that you become annoyed
take your time 1 to spend too much time doing something: *They're taking their time over that report, aren't they?* **2** *spoken* used for telling someone that they do not need to hurry: *You don't have to do everything at once. Just take your time.*
→ FOR, HARD[1]

time² /taɪm/ verb [T] **1** to use a clock to measure how long something takes or how often something happens: *a simple device for timing the human heartbeat* **2** to arrange something so that it happens at a particular time: *The exhibit has been timed to coincide with the publication of her new book.*

ˈtime ˌbomb noun [C] something that is likely to have a sudden and bad effect on a situation in the future

time-con·sum·ing /ˈtaɪm kənˌsumɪŋ/ adj something that is time-consuming takes a long time to do

ˈtime ˌframe noun [C] the period of time in which something happens or should be done = TIMESCALE

time·less /ˈtaɪmləs/ adj not affected by time or changes in fashion

ˈtime ˌlimit noun [C] an amount of time in which you must do something

time·line /ˈtaɪmˌlaɪn/ noun [C] **1** *American* a plan of when something should happen or how much time something should take **2** a line showing particular dates, for example dates of historical events

time·ly /ˈtaɪmli/ adj happening at the most appropriate time ≠ UNTIMELY: *a timely reminder*

ˌtime ˈoff noun [U] time when you are not at work or in school

ˌtime ˈout noun **1** [C] a short period of time in a game of basketball or ICE HOCKEY when players rest and plan their game **2** [U] a period of time when you stop working or stop doing what you usually do: *It's very beneficial to take time out to relax each day.*

tim·er /ˈtaɪmər/ noun [C] a piece of equipment used for measuring time, or for turning a machine on or off at a particular time

times /taɪmz/ preposition *informal* multiplied by: *Two times four is eight.*

time·scale /ˈtaɪmˌskeɪl/ noun [C] the period of time in which something happens or should be done = TIME FRAME

time·ta·ble /ˈtaɪmˌteɪb(ə)l/ noun [C] **1** a plan that shows the dates and times when something will take place = SCHEDULE **2** *British* a list of the times when buses, trains, etc. arrive and leave

ˈtime ˌzone noun [C] one of the areas that the world is divided into for measuring time

tim·id /ˈtɪmɪd/ adj shy and nervous —**ti·mid·i·ty** /tɪˈmɪdəti/ noun [U], **tim·id·ly** adv

tim·ing /ˈtaɪmɪŋ/ noun **1** [C/U] the date or time when something happens or is planned to happen: *They objected to the timing of the election.* **2** [U] the ability to do or say things at the right moment

tin /tɪn/ noun **1** [U] a soft light silver metal: *There used to be tin mines all around this area.* **2** [C] a metal container with a lid, used for storing things: *a cookie tin*

tin·foil /ˈtɪnˌfɔɪl/ noun [U] a substance that looks like shiny silver paper, used for wrapping and covering food

tinge /tɪndʒ/ noun [C] a very small amount of a color, feeling, or quality: *a tinge of sadness/nostalgia*

tinged /tɪndʒd/ adj containing a very small amount of something: *white flowers tinged with blue*

tin·gle /ˈtɪŋg(ə)l/ verb [I] if a part of your body tingles, it stings slightly, for example because it is very cold or hot —**tin·gle** noun [C]

tin·ker /ˈtɪŋkər/ or **tinker aˈround** verb [I] to make small changes to something in order to improve or repair it

tin·kle /ˈtɪŋk(ə)l/ verb [I] to make a high ringing sound: *Silver bells tinkled.* —**tin·kle** noun [singular]

tin·sel /ˈtɪns(ə)l/ noun [U] long thin pieces of shiny paper that you use especially as a Christmas decoration

tint¹ /tɪnt/ noun [C] a small amount of a particular color

tint² /tɪnt/ verb [T] to change the color of your hair

tint·ed /ˈtɪntəd/ adj slightly colored: *a car with tinted windows*

ti·ny /ˈtaɪni/ adj ★★ extremely small: *She is one of a tiny minority of female sports* writers. ♦ *The floor was covered in* ***tiny pieces*** *of paper.* ♦ *a* ***tiny little*** *baby*

tip¹ /tɪp/ noun [C] ★
1 a narrow or pointed end, especially of something long or thin: ***the tip of your*** *nose/finger* ♦ *The village is* ***on the southern tip*** *of the island.*
2 an amount of money that you give to someone in addition to the price of a service: *Did you* ***leave a tip*** *for the waiter?*
3 a useful suggestion or piece of information that someone gives you: *The booklet gives some good* ***tips on*** *getting the most out of your software.*
PHRASES **on the tip of your tongue** if a word, name, etc. is on the tip of your tongue, you know it but cannot remember it at the time you are speaking
the tip of the iceberg a bad situation that shows that a much more serious problem exists: *The recent riots are just the tip of the iceberg.*

tip² /tɪp/ verb **1** [I/T] to give someone an amount of money in addition to what you owe for a service: *Don't forget to tip the driver.* **2** [I/T] to move into a position that is at an angle instead of upright, or to put something into a position like this: *He tipped his chair back and looked at me.* **3** [T] to pour something from a container: *She tipped the sand out of her pail.* **4** [T] to hit something very gently: *His bat just tipped the ball.*
PHRASE **tip the balance/scales** to give someone or something an advantage, so that they get or achieve something
PHRASAL VERBS **ˌtip sb ˈoff** to give someone a warning, or to give them secret information about something
ˌtip (sth) ˈover if something tips over, or if someone tips it over, it falls onto its side: *Be careful that the vase doesn't tip over.* ♦ *He tipped his drink over.*

ˈtip-ˌoff noun [C] *informal* a warning or secret information that you give to someone

tip·sy /ˈtɪpsi/ adj *informal* slightly drunk

tip·toe¹ /ˈtɪpˌtoʊ/ noun **on tiptoe(s)** if you stand or walk on tiptoe, you stand or walk with only the front part of your foot touching the ground

tip·toe² /ˈtɪpˌtoʊ/ verb [I] to walk very quietly with only the front part of your foot touching the ground

ti·rade /ˈtaɪˌreɪd, taɪˈreɪd/ noun [C] a long angry speech criticizing someone or something

tire¹ /ˈtaɪr/ noun [C] ★ the rubber cover of a wheel, that is filled with air: *Oh no! Not another* ***flat tire*** (=a tire without air in it)! —*picture* → C6

tire² /ˈtaɪr/ verb [I/T] to become tired, or to make someone feel tired
PHRASE **tire of sb/sth** to become bored with someone or something
PHRASAL VERB **ˌtire sb ˈout** to make someone feel very tired

tired /ˈtaɪrd/ adj ★★★ needing to rest or sleep: *Your mother* ***looked tired.*** ♦ *Kids can suddenly* ***get very tired*** *after playing for a time.*
PHRASE **tired of (doing) sth** not wanting something, or not wanting to do something, because you are bored or annoyed with it: *I'm tired of hearing about politics.*

tire·less /ˈtaɪrləs/ adj *showing approval* working very hard to achieve something, with a lot of energy and determination —**tire·less·ly** adv

tire·some /ˈtaɪrsəm/ adj making you feel bored or annoyed

tir·ing /ˈtaɪrɪŋ/ adj making you feel tired

tis·sue /ˈtɪʃu/ noun **1** [C] a piece of soft thin paper that you use for wiping your nose: *a* ***box of tissues*** **2** [U] the substance that animal and plant cells are made of: ***brain/muscle tissue***

tit /tɪt/ noun [C] *impolite* a woman's breast
PHRASE **tit for tat** *informal* something that you do to harm someone because they have harmed you

ti·tle /ˈtaɪt(ə)l/ noun ★★★

1 name of book/movie	4 claim to property
2 before sb's name	5 in competition
3 name for job	

1 [C] the name of a book, movie, or other work of art: *What's* ***the title of*** *her new book?*
2 [C] a word or abbreviation that is used before someone's name, for example "Doctor," "General," or "Mrs."
3 [C] a name for someone's job within a company or organization: *His new title is senior vice president.*
4 [singular/U] *legal* a right or claim to something, especially property
5 [C] the position of a winner in a sports competition: *She's won several important singles titles this year.*

ˈtitle ˌrole noun [C] the main part for someone in a movie, play, or opera, that has the same name as its title

tit·ter /ˈtɪtər/ verb [I] to laugh quietly because you are nervous or embarrassed —**tit·ter** noun [C]

TN abbrev Tennessee

TNT /ˌti en ˈti/ noun [U] a chemical used for making powerful explosions

to /*weak* tə, *strong* tu/ grammar word ★★★

To can be:
- used before the basic form of a verb to form the infinitive: *I want to go home.*
- a **preposition**: *We drove to Newport.*

1 part of an infinitive used before a verb for forming an infinitive, often when you are stating the purpose of an action, or used without the following verb instead of an infinitive: *I hope to see you next week.* ♦ *The system is very easy to understand.* ♦ *Nobody came to help me.* ♦ *You don't need to come if you don't want to.*
2 going somewhere used for saying the place or event where someone or something goes: *She rushed to the phone.* ♦ *There are daily flights to Boston.* ♦ *the road to the farm* ♦ *Robert hates going to parties.*
3 for showing who is affected by an action used for saying who or what is told, given, or shown something, or is treated or affected in a particular way: *Prizes were presented to the winners.* ♦ *I have already explained to everyone what the problem is.*

♦ *They were very kind to my mother when she was ill.* ♦ *Look what you've done to my new carpet!* ♦ *cruelty to animals*
4 in a particular direction used for saying in which direction someone or something is, is pointing, or is looking: *She pointed to a sign on the wall.* ♦ *Henry was standing with his back to me.* ♦ *There was a large bookcase to the left of the fireplace.* ♦ *a large township just to the south of Johannesburg*
5 in a particular relationship with sb/sth used for explaining a relationship between people or things: *a political party with ties to a terrorist group* ♦ *She is personal assistant to the CEO.*
6 when sth is connected or fastened used for stating where something is fastened or where a connection is: *The carpet had been nailed to the floor.* ♦ *Your computer is connected to the main network.*
7 when sth changes or develops used for saying what stage of development or change is reached: *an event that brought matters to crisis point* ♦ *When will all this suffering come to an end?*
8 as far as as far as a particular point or limit: *The cancer had spread to his lungs.* ♦ *How far is it from here to Salem?*
9 until until a particular time or event: *Only another 18 days to the final exam!* ♦ *The store stays open **from** 7 a.m. **to** 9 p.m.*
10 before the hour used when telling the time, for saying how many minutes it is before the hour: *I'll meet you at quarter to six* (=5:45).
11 for stating sb's opinion used for saying whose opinion, attitude, or knowledge is being referred to: *To most of us, work is an unpleasant necessity.* ♦ ***It seems to me** that there has been a lack of discipline.*
12 for showing how numbers are related used for showing the relationship between two numbers or amounts: *You get about five of these apples to the pound.*
13 for giving a score used for saying what the score is in a game: *Our team won by five goals to three.*
14 for showing a possible range used for showing one of the ends of a possible range: *Only about 20 to 25 percent of the population voted for the government.* ♦ *the numbers **from** one **to** ten*
15 needed for sth used for showing that something is an important or necessary part of something else: *the answer to an important question* ♦ *the keys to my desk*
16 causing a particular reaction used for saying what your reaction is when something happens: *To her surprise, she saw that he was crying.*
PHRASES **(all) to yourself** not sharing something with anyone else: *My parents were away, so I had the house to myself.*
to and fro *literary* in one direction and then back again = BACKWARD AND FORWARD

toad /toʊd/ noun [C] a small animal that is similar to a FROG but has brown skin and lives mainly on land

toad·stool /ˈtoʊdˌstul/ noun [C] a wild plant that is similar to a MUSHROOM and is often poisonous

toast¹ /toʊst/ noun **1** [U] bread that has been heated until its outside is brown and hard **2** [C] an occasion when people all drink together and say someone's name in order to express their admiration or good wishes

toast² /toʊst/ verb [T] **1** to make bread into toast **2** to drink a toast to someone

toast·er /ˈtoʊstər/ noun [C] a piece of electrical equipment that you use for making toast —*picture* → C2

toast·y /ˈtoʊsti/ adj *informal* warm and comfortable

to·bac·co /təˈbækoʊ/ noun [U] a substance that people smoke in cigarettes

to·bog·gan /təˈbɑgən/ noun [C] a small vehicle without wheels that is used for moving over snow

to·day¹ /təˈdeɪ/ adv ★★★
1 on this day: *I'm working today.* ♦ *Did you get any mail today?*
2 at the period of time that is happening now: *Teenagers today are so sophisticated.*

to·day² /təˈdeɪ/ noun [U] **1** this day: *Today is Wednesday.* **2** the present period of time: *Think about today, not yesterday!* ♦ *Today's computers are so much more powerful than those of five years ago.*

tod·dler /ˈtɑdlər/ noun [C] a very young child who is learning how to walk —*picture* → CHILD

toe¹ /toʊ/ noun [C] ★
1 one of the five individual parts at the end of your foot: *Vera slipped off her shoes and **wriggled her toes**.* —*picture* → C14
2 the part of a shoe or sock that covers your toes: *shoes with **pointed toes***
PHRASE **keep sb on their toes** to make someone concentrate so that they are ready to deal with any problem

toe² /toʊ/ verb **toe the line** to accept rules and obey people in authority

TOEFL /ˈtoʊf(ə)l/ *trademark* Test of English as a Foreign Language: an English language test for speakers of other languages that shows how well they speak English

toe·hold /ˈtoʊˌhoʊld/ noun [singular] a small or unimportant position in a place, organization, or activity that you hope will help you to get a better one

TOEIC /ˈtoʊɪk/ *trademark* Test of English for International Communication: an English language test for speakers of other languages that shows how well they speak English

toe·nail /ˈtoʊˌneɪl/ noun [C] the hard part over the top of a toe

tof·fee /ˈtɑfi/ noun [C/U] a sticky brown candy made by cooking together sugar, butter, and water

to·fu /ˈtoʊˌfu/ noun [U] a soft white food made from SOYBEANS

to·geth·er¹ /təˈgeðər/ adv ★★★
1 if you put or join two or more things together, you combine or connect them: *Mix together the flour, eggs, and water.* ♦ *small patches of cloth sewn together* ♦ *Now add the numbers together.*
2 with each other: *Kevin, Jack, and Dave share a house together.* ♦ *Bob and I worked together many years ago.* ♦ *Are Tanya and*

T

Pete still together (=still in a romantic relationship)?
3 near each other, or in one place: *Get all your things together.* ♦ *The book brings together essays by several different authors.*
4 at the same time: *Everyone arrived together at around four o'clock.*

to•geth•er² /təˈgeðər/ adj *spoken* confident, sensible, and clear about what you are doing

to•geth•er•ness /təˈgeðərnəs/ noun [U] a feeling of friendship and happiness in a close relationship

tog•gle /ˈtɑg(ə)l/ verb [I/T] *computing* to move from one computer operation or program to another and back again by using one key or COMMAND (=instruction)

toil /tɔɪl/ verb [I] *literary* to work very hard —**toil** noun [U]

toi•let /ˈtɔɪlət/ noun [C] ★
1 a structure like a seat over a hole where you get rid of waste from your body
2 *British* a bathroom

ˈtoilet ˌpaper noun [U] soft thin paper that you use to clean yourself after using the toilet

toi•let•ries /ˈtɔɪlətriz/ noun [plural] things such as soap and SHAMPOO that you use for keeping yourself clean

to•ken¹ /ˈtoʊkən/ noun [C] **1** a small flat round piece of metal or plastic that you use instead of money in some machines **2** *formal* something that you do or give as a way of showing your feelings toward someone: *a token of your appreciation/gratitude/respect*

to•ken² /ˈtoʊkən/ adj done in order to pretend to people that you are trying to achieve something: *a token gesture*
PHRASE **a token woman/black/gay etc.** *showing disapproval* someone who is included in a group in order to make people believe that the group is trying to include all types of people

told the past tense and past participle of **tell**

tol•er•a•ble /ˈtɑlərəb(ə)l/ adj *formal* acceptable but not very good ≠ INTOLERABLE —**tol•er•a•bly** adv

tol•er•ance /ˈtɑlərəns/ noun [U] the attitude of someone who is willing to accept other people's beliefs, way of life, etc. without criticizing them, even if they disagree with them ≠ INTOLERANCE: *We need to show greater tolerance toward each other.*

tol•er•ant /ˈtɑlərənt/ adj willing to accept other people's beliefs, way of life, etc. without criticizing them, even if you disagree with them ≠ INTOLERANT

tol•er•ate /ˈtɑləˌreɪt/ verb [T] **1** to allow someone to do something that you do not like or approve of: *He won't tolerate anyone questioning his decisions.* **2** to accept something that is unpleasant without becoming impatient or angry: *They have tolerated poor working conditions for too long.* **3** if plants or animals tolerate particular conditions, they are able to exist in those conditions —**tol•er•a•tion** /ˌtɑləˈreɪʃ(ə)n/ noun [U]

toll¹ /toʊl/ noun **1** [singular] the total number of people who have been killed or hurt: *The death toll from the earthquake is not yet known.* **2** [C] an amount of money that you pay to use a bridge or road
PHRASE **take its toll** or **take a heavy toll** to gradually harm or damage someone or something

toll² /toʊl/ verb [I/T] if you toll a bell, or if it tolls, it makes a slow repeated sound

ˈtoll-ˌfree adj *American* a toll-free telephone number is one that you can call without having to pay —**ˌtoll-ˈfree** adv

to•ma•to /təˈmeɪtoʊ/ (plural **to•ma•toes**) noun [C] a round red fruit that you eat raw in salads or cooked as a vegetable —*picture* → C11

tomb /tum/ noun [C] a place or large stone structure where a dead person is buried

tom•boy /ˈtɑmˌbɔɪ/ noun [C] a girl who behaves and dresses in a way that people think is more appropriate for a boy

tomb•stone /ˈtumˌstoʊn/ noun [C] a large stone that is put over the place where a dead person is buried

tom•cat /ˈtɑmˌkæt/ noun [C] a male cat

tome /toʊm/ noun [C] *literary* a large heavy book, usually about a serious subject

to•mor•row¹ /təˈmɔroʊ/ adv ★★★
1 on the day after today: *Are you going back home tomorrow?* ♦ *They're arriving tomorrow morning.*
2 in the future: *Who can say what will happen tomorrow?*

to•mor•row² /təˈmɔroʊ/ noun [U] **1** the day after today: *Tomorrow is Tuesday.* **2** the future: *These students are the leaders of tomorrow.*

ton /tʌn/ noun [C] **1** *American* a unit for measuring weight, containing 2,000 POUNDS and equal to 907 kilograms **2** *informal* a very large number or amount: *I have tons of* (=a lot of) *things to do.* ♦ *That bag of yours weighs a ton* (=is extremely heavy)*!* **3** *British* a unit for measuring weight, containing 2,240 POUNDS and equal to 1,016 kilograms

tone¹ /toʊn/ noun ★

1 sound of voice	4 phone sound
2 character of sth	5 color
3 quality of sound	6 firmness of muscles

1 [C/U] the sound of someone's voice that shows what they are feeling: *His tone was angry.* ♦ *"Really?" Simone said in a disbelieving **tone of voice**.*
2 [singular/U] the general character of something: ***The positive tone of the evening** had changed completely.* ♦ *The opening remarks **set the tone** for the rest of the interview.*
3 [C/U] the quality of a sound: *a flute with a clear bright tone*
4 [C] a sound made by a piece of equipment such as a telephone: *I picked up the phone and just got a beeping tone.*
5 [C] a color, or a particular SHADE (=type) of a color: *The room is decorated in cool blue tones.*
6 [U] the firmness or healthy quality of your body, muscles, or skin: *The patient's general muscle tone is good.*

tone² /toʊn/
PHRASAL VERBS **ˌtone sth ˈdown** to make

T

something less severe, shocking, or offensive

ˌ**tone sth ˈup** to make your body, muscles, or skin more firm and healthy

ˌ**tone ˈdeaf** adj unable to sing a tune correctly because you cannot hear the difference between musical notes

ton·er /ˈtoʊnər/ noun [U] ink in the form of a powder that you put into a printer or a PHOTOCOPIER

tongs /tɔŋz/ noun [plural] a metal or plastic object that consists of two connected arms that you push together in order to pick something up

tongue /tʌŋ/ noun [C] ★★

1 the long soft piece of flesh that is attached to the bottom of your mouth that you use for tasting, speaking, etc.

2 a language: *English was clearly not his **mother tongue*** (=the one he first learned as a child).

→ BITE, SLIP, TIP[1]

ˌ**tongue-in-ˈcheek** adj intended to be humorous and not meant seriously: *a tongue-in-cheek answer* —ˌ**tongue-in-ˈcheek** adv

ˈ**tongue-ˌtied** adj unable to speak because you are nervous or embarrassed

ˈ**tongue ˌtwister** noun [C] a word or phrase that is difficult to say because it contains many similar sounds

ton·ic /ˈtɑnɪk/ noun **1 tonic** or **tonic water** [C/U] a type of CARBONATED water that has a bitter taste and is often mixed with a strong alcoholic drink **2** [singular] something that makes you feel happier or healthier

to·night[1] /təˈnaɪt/ adv ★★★ in the evening or during the night of today: *Call me tonight when you get home.*

to·night[2] /təˈnaɪt/ noun [U] the evening or night of today: *tonight's performance*

tonne /tʌn/ noun [C] a unit for measuring weight, equal to 1,000 kilograms

ton·sil /ˈtɑns(ə)l/ noun [C] one of the two small pieces of flesh on each side of your throat at the back of your mouth

T

ton·sil·li·tis /ˌtɑns(ə)lˈaɪtɪs/ noun [U] an illness in which your tonsils become infected, swollen, and painful

too /tu/ adv ★★★

1 more than is necessary or acceptable: *You're driving too fast.* ♦ *It's too cold to sit outside.* ♦ *This film is **too** scary **for** seven-year-old kids.* ♦ *You've put **too much** sugar in my coffee.*

2 used after mentioning an additional person, thing, or fact to show that they are also included in what you are saying=ALSO: *Helen's got a beautiful voice, and she's a good dancer too.* ♦ *"I'm starting to feel hungry." "**Me too.**"*

> Do not use **too** for making additions to negative sentences. Use **not...either**: *I didn't tell my friends, and I didn't tell my wife either.*

3 *spoken* used for emphasizing that something is true when someone does not believe it: *"You don't know how to change a tire." "I do too."*

PHRASES **all/only too** used for emphasizing that you wish that something did not happen so much, or that something was not true: ***All too often** it is the victim who gets blamed.* ♦ *I knew **only too well** how dangerous the operation might be.*

not too *spoken* not very: *Barbara won't be too pleased if we get there late.* ♦ *"How are you feeling?" "Oh, **not too bad.**"*

took the past tense of **take[1]**

tool /tul/ noun [C] ★★

1 a piece of equipment that you hold to do a particular type of work: *kitchen/garden tools* ♦ *a set of tools*

2 something that you use in order to perform a job or achieve a goal: *The Internet has become an important research **tool for** students.*

tool·bar /ˈtulˌbɑr/ noun [C] *computing* a row of ICONS (=small pictures) on a computer screen that perform particular actions when you CLICK on them

ˈ**tool ˌshed** noun [C] a small building, often made of wood and usually in a yard, used for storing tools —*picture* → C1

toot /tut/ verb [I/T] if you toot a horn, or if it toots, it makes a loud high sound —**toot** noun [C]

tooth /tuθ/ (plural **teeth** /tiθ/) noun [C] ★★★

1 any of the hard white objects inside your mouth that you use for biting: *a loose/missing/broken tooth* ♦ *It's important to **brush your teeth** at least twice a day.* —*picture* → C14

2 one of a row of narrow pointed parts that form the edge of a tool or machine: *the teeth on a saw/comb*

→ GRIT[2]

tooth·ache /ˈtuθˌeɪk/ noun [singular/U] a pain in one or more of your teeth

tooth·brush /ˈtuθˌbrʌʃ/ noun [C] a small brush that you use for cleaning your teeth

tooth·paste /ˈtuθˌpeɪst/ noun [C/U] a soft thick substance that you put on a toothbrush to clean your teeth

tooth·pick /ˈtuθˌpɪk/ noun [C] a thin pointed piece of wood that you use for removing bits of food from between your teeth

top[1] /tɑp/ noun ★★★

1 highest place/part	4 container lid/cover
2 upper surface	5 piece of clothing
3 highest/best position	+ PHRASES

1 [C] the highest place, point, part, or surface of something: *We could see mountain tops in the distance.* ♦ *I left my purse **at the top of** the stairs.* ♦ *He sprinkled sugar **on top of** the cake.*

2 [C] a flat upper surface of something: *a table top*

3 the top [singular] the highest status or most important position: *Scott has reached **the top of** his profession.*

4 [C] a lid or cover for a container or pen: *the top of the shampoo bottle*

5 [C] a piece of clothing that covers the upper part of your body: *She was wearing a red skirt and a black top.*

PHRASES **off the top of your head** immediately and without thinking very much: *Off the top of my head, I'd say we have about 200 members.*

on top in a situation where you are in

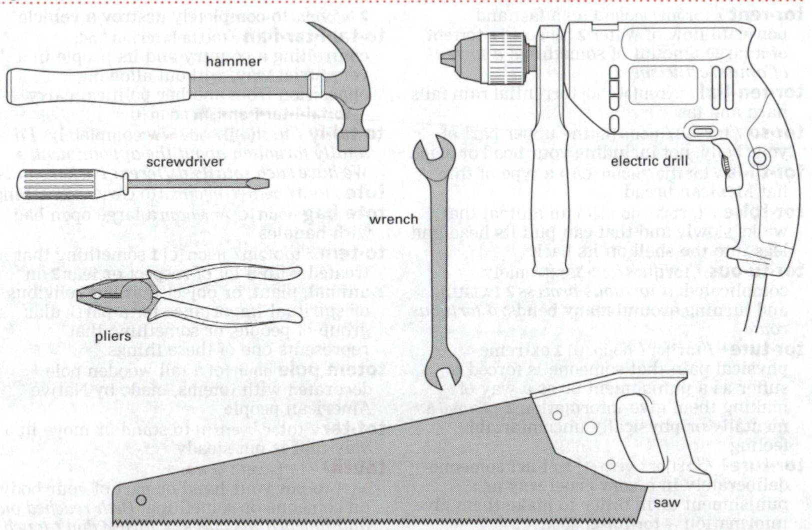

tools

control or winning: *The Bears stayed on top throughout most of the game.*
on top of 1 in addition to something else: *On top of all his financial problems, his wife left him.* **2** in control of what is happening: *I try to stay on top of things.* **3** very close to someone or something: *The truck was almost on top of me.*
on top of the world in a very good mood because things are going well for you

top[2] /tɑp/ adj ★★★
1 at or on the highest part of something: *Our room is on the top floor.*
2 highest in status, degree, or importance: *He's one of the top players in the league.* ♦ *Our top priority now is finding shelter for the flood victims.*

top[3] /tɑp/ verb [T] **1** to be larger than a particular amount: *The costs for the project may top $50 million.* **2** to cover something with a layer of something else: *pizza topped with pepperoni* **3** to be in the most important or popular position in a list of things **4** to be better or more impressive than something else: *I don't think I can top your fishing story.*
PHRASAL VERBS **ˌtop sth ˈoff** to finish something with a final activity or detail
ˌtop ˈout if a rate or an amount tops out, it reaches its highest level: *Mortgage rates topped out at 10% before falling last spring.*

ˌtop-ˈdown adj starting at a general level and then moving to more specific things

ˌtop ˈhat noun [C] a man's tall hat that is worn on formal occasions —*picture* → HAT

ˌtop-ˈheavy adj **1** something that is top-heavy lacks balance because it is heavier at the top than at the bottom **2** a company or organization that is top-heavy has too many workers at higher levels and not enough at lower levels

top•ic /ˈtɑpɪk/ noun [C] ★★ a subject that you write or speak about: *There has been little research on this particular topic.* ♦ *She tried to think of another topic of conversation.*

top•i•cal /ˈtɑpɪk(ə)l/ adj relating to a subject that is of particular interest at the present time

top•less /ˈtɑpləs/ adj not wearing any clothes on the upper part of your body

top•most /ˈtɑpˌmoʊst/ adj highest

to•pog•ra•phy /təˈpɑgrəfi/ noun [C/U] the features of a particular area of land, such as hills, rivers, and roads —**top•o•graph•i•cal** /ˌtɑpəˈgræfɪk(ə)l/ adj

top•ping /ˈtɑpɪŋ/ noun [C] a layer of food that you put on top of other food, for example on ice cream or a PIZZA

top•ple /ˈtɑp(ə)l/ verb **1** [I/T] to fall, or to make someone or something fall **2** [T] to make someone in authority lose their power

ˌtop ˈsecret adj containing or involving very important and secret information

top•sy-tur•vy /ˌtɑpsi ˈtɜrvi/ adj *informal* confused and in the wrong order

To•rah, the /ˈtɔrə/ the first five books of the Jewish Bible

torch[1] /tɔrtʃ/ noun [C] a piece of wood with a flame at one end that is used as a light

torch[2] /tɔrtʃ/ verb [T] to set fire to something

tore the past tense of **tear**[1]

tor•ment[1] /ˈtɔrˌment/ noun [C/U] severe physical or mental pain, or something that causes this

tor•ment[2] /tɔrˈment/ verb [T] to make someone suffer severe physical or mental pain —**tor•men•tor** noun [C]

torn the past participle of **tear**[1]

tor•na•do /tɔrˈneɪdoʊ/ (plural **tor•na•does** or **tor•na•dos**) noun [C] a very strong wind that goes quickly around in a circle or FUNNEL

tor•pe•do[1] /tɔrˈpidoʊ/ (plural **tor•pe•does**) noun [C] a weapon that is shot under water in order to hit a ship or a SUBMARINE

tor•pe•do[2] /tɔrˈpidoʊ/ verb [T] to hit a ship or a SUBMARINE with a torpedo

tor•rent /ˈtɔrənt/ noun **1** [C] a fast and powerful flow of water **2** [singular] **a torrent of** a large amount of something: *a torrent of abuse/criticism*

tor•ren•tial /tɔˈrenʃəl/ adj torrential rain falls hard and fast

tor•so /ˈtɔrsoʊ/ noun [C] the upper part of your body, not including your head or arms

tor•til•la /tɔrˈtijə/ noun [C/U] a type of thin flat Mexican bread

tor•toise /ˈtɔrtəs/ noun [C] an animal that walks slowly and that can pull its head and legs into the shell on its back

tor•tu•ous /ˈtɔrtʃuəs/ adj **1** extremely complicated: *a tortuous process* **2** twisting and turning around many bends: *a tortuous route*

tor•ture¹ /ˈtɔrtʃər/ noun [U] **1** extreme physical pain that someone is forced to suffer as a punishment or as a way of making them give information **2** *informal* a mentally or physically uncomfortable feeling

tor•ture² /ˈtɔrtʃər/ verb [T] to hurt someone deliberately in a very cruel way as a punishment or in order to make them give information —**tor•tur•er** noun [C]

toss¹ /tɔs/ verb **1** [T] to throw something somewhere gently or in a careless way: *Brendon tossed the ball into the air.* **2** [T] *informal* to get rid of something because you do not want or need it **3** [I/T] to throw a coin into the air in order to make a decision based on which side the coin falls on **4** [T] to mix food with a liquid so that it becomes covered in the liquid: *Can you toss the salad for me?*

PHRASES **toss and turn** to be unable to sleep, or to sleep badly

toss your head/hair to move your head quickly upward

PHRASAL VERB ˌ**toss sth** ˈ**out** *informal same as* toss¹ 2

toss² /tɔs/ noun [C] **1** the act of throwing something somewhere gently or in a careless way **2** the act of throwing a coin into the air in order to make a decision based on which side the coin falls on **3** the act of moving your head quickly upward

tot /tɑt/ noun [C] *informal* a small child

to•tal¹ /ˈtoʊt(ə)l/ adj ★★★

1 with all the numbers or things added together: ***The total cost** of the project came to about $700,000.* ♦ ***The total number** of votes was over one million.*

2 complete = ABSOLUTE: *Why would you let **a total stranger** into the house?* ♦ *They sat in almost **total silence** the whole evening.*

to•tal² /ˈtoʊt(ə)l/ noun [C] ★★★ the amount that you get when you add several numbers or things together: *The total for your books comes to $63.61.* ♦ ***A total of** 17 students signed up for the course.* ♦ ***In total*** (=counting everyone) *over 100 people attended.*

to•tal³ /ˈtoʊt(ə)l/ (present participle **to•tal•ing** or **to•tal•ling**; past tense and past participle **to•taled** or **to•talled**) verb [T] **1** to be a particular total as a result of everything being added together: *The company went bankrupt, with debts totaling $60 million.* **2** *informal* to completely destroy a vehicle

to•tal•i•tar•i•an /toʊˌtæləˈteriən/ adj controlling a country and its people in a very strict way, without allowing opposition from another political party —**to•tal•i•tar•i•an•ism** noun [U]

to•tal•ly /ˈtoʊt(ə)li/ adv ★★ completely: *I'd totally forgotten about the appointment.* ♦ *We have such **totally different** backgrounds.*

tote /toʊt/ verb [T] *informal* to carry something

ˈ**tote** ˌ**bag** noun [C] *American* a large open bag with handles

to•tem /ˈtoʊtəm/ noun [C] **1** something that is treated with a lot of respect or fear **2** an animal, plant, or object that has religious or spiritual importance for a particular group of people, or something that represents one of these things

ˈ**totem** ˌ**pole** noun [C] a tall wooden pole decorated with totems, made by Native American people

tot•ter /ˈtɑtər/ verb [I] to stand or move in a way that is not steady

touch¹ /tʌtʃ/ verb ★★★

1 [T] to put your hand or part of your body on someone or something: *Beth reached out and touched his cheek.* ♦ *Please don't touch the paintings.* ♦ *He fell asleep as soon as his head touched the pillow.*

2 [I/T] if two things touch, or if something touches something else, there is no space between them: *The chair was so high that his feet couldn't touch the ground.* ♦ *They stood next to each other, barely touching.*

3 [T] to affect your emotions, so that you feel sad, sympathetic, pleased, or grateful: *His comments really touched me.* ♦ *Everyone was touched by the tragedy.*

4 [T] to eat or drink a particular thing: *I never touch alcohol.*

PHRASAL VERBS ˌ**touch** ˈ**down** if an aircraft or space vehicle touches down, it lands

ˈ**touch** ˌ**on sth** to mention something when you are talking or writing

ˌ**touch sth** ˈ**up** to make a surface look better with small improvements

touch² /tʌtʃ/ noun ★★★

1 putting hand on sth	4 small feature
2 very small amount	5 ability to do sth well
3 ability to feel things	+ PHRASES

1 [singular] the action of putting your hand or part of your body on someone or something: *Bill was wakened by her touch on his shoulder.* ♦ *He shook her hand and his touch was warm and firm.*

2 [singular] a very small amount of something: *Add **a touch of** olive oil.*

3 [U] the SENSE that tells you what something feels like, through your skin, or when you put your fingers on it: *Children's imaginations can be stimulated through sight, touch, and smell.*

4 [C] a small feature that improves something: *The flowers in the room were **a nice touch**.* ♦ *The band is **putting the finishing touches on** their third album.*

5 [singular] your ability to do something well

PHRASES **in touch (with sb)** to see, speak to, or write to someone: *I'll be in touch next week about our trip to Paris.* ♦ *Why don't*

*you **get in touch** with Jerry and tell him the news?* ♦ *They moved away five years ago, but we still **keep in touch**.*
lose touch (with sb) to not see, speak to, or write to someone any longer: *She moved to France and we lost touch with each other.*
out of touch (with sb) no longer seeing, speaking to, or writing to someone
out of touch (with sth) no longer having recent knowledge or information about something: *I haven't taught for a while so I'm a little out of touch.*

ˌtouch-and-ˈgo adj not certain and with a risk of death or serious failure

touch•down /ˈtʌtʃˌdaʊn/ noun [C] the moment when an aircraft or space vehicle lands on the ground

touched /tʌtʃt/ adj feeling sad, sympathetic, pleased, or grateful

touch•ing /ˈtʌtʃɪŋ/ adj making you feel sad, sympathetic, pleased, or grateful

touch•line /ˈtʌtʃˌlaɪn/ noun [C] one of the two lines marking the sides of a playing area in a sport, especially soccer

ˈtouch ˌscreen noun [C] a computer screen that you touch in order to choose what you want to see next

touch•stone /ˈtʌtʃˌstoʊn/ noun [C] a standard that is used for testing or judging other things

touch•y /ˈtʌtʃi/ adj **1** tending to become angry or upset very easily **2** likely to make people angry or upset

tough /tʌf/ adj ★★

1 difficult	5 with crime/violence
2 strong	6 of meat
3 confident/determined	7 hard to break/damage
4 very strict/severe	

1 difficult: *He's having **a really tough time** at the moment.* ♦ *It was **a tough decision** to move overseas.* ♦ *Many companies are facing **tough competition**.*
2 strong and able to deal with difficult situations or pain: *The divorce was difficult, but she's always been tough.*
3 confident and determined to get what you want: *a tough businessman*
4 very strict and severe: *tough criticism* ♦ *We must take tough action against terrorism.* ♦ *The new mayor promises to be **tough on** crime.*
5 a tough place is one in which there is a lot of crime and violence: *a tough neighborhood*
6 tough meat is very difficult to cut and CHEW
7 difficult to break or damage
—**tough•ness** noun [U]

Words often used with tough

Nouns often used with ***tough*** *(sense 1)*

- TOUGH + **battle, fight, challenge, competition**: used about situations in which you face strong opposition
- TOUGH + **call, choice, decision**: used about situations in which it is difficult to decide what to do

tough•en /ˈtʌf(ə)n/ verb [I/T] to become mentally or physically stronger, or to make someone become mentally or physically stronger

tou•pee /tuˈpeɪ/ noun [C] artificial hair that a man wears on top of his head where he has no hair

tour¹ /tʊr/ noun ★★
1 [C] a trip in which you visit several different places: *The president plans a European tour next month.* ♦ *We went on a 10-day **tour of** central Africa.*
2 [C] a short trip around a building or place in order to see what is there: *Every weekend there are free **guided tours** of the museum.*
3 [C/U] a trip in which a person or group visits several different places in order to perform: *The group is currently **on tour** in Europe.*

tour² /tʊr/ verb [I/T] to visit different several places for pleasure or to perform

ˈtour ˌguide noun [C] **1** someone whose job is to show tourists around a place and explain its history, ARCHITECTURE, etc. **2** *American* someone whose job is to help and take care of tourists on an organized vacation

tour•ism /ˈtʊˌrɪzəm/ noun [U] the business of providing services for people who are traveling for their vacation

tour•ist /ˈtʊrɪst/ noun [C] ★★ someone who is visiting a place on vacation: *The islands attract more than 17,000 tourists a year.* ♦ *a tourist hotel/destination*

tour•na•ment /ˈtɜrnəmənt/ noun [C] a series of games in which the winner of each game plays in the next game until there is only one player or team left

tour•ni•quet /ˈtɜrnɪkət/ noun [C] a piece of cloth that you tie very tight around someone's leg or arm in order to stop blood from flowing from a cut

tou•sled /ˈtaʊz(ə)ld/ adj tousled hair looks messy

tout /taʊt/ verb **1** [T] to praise someone or something because you want other people to think that they are good or important: *The club is being touted as the best place to hear live music.* **2** [I/T] to try to persuade people to buy something by telling them about it

tow¹ /toʊ/ verb [T] to pull a vehicle or boat by attaching it to another vehicle or boat

tow² /toʊ/ noun [singular] the activity of pulling one vehicle behind another
PHRASE **in tow** *informal* if you have someone in tow, you are taking them somewhere

to•ward /tɔrd, təˈwɔrd/ or **to•wards** /tɔrdz, təˈwɔrdz/ preposition ★★★
1 going, facing, or looking in a particular direction: *I saw Joanna hurrying toward me along the sidewalk.* ♦ *Victor was standing with his back toward me.* ♦ *a path leading towards the river*
2 used for saying how you feel about someone or something or how you treat them: *He's not feeling very friendly toward you at the moment.* ♦ *the Church's attitude toward divorce*
3 in a way that brings a process closer to a particular result: *progress toward European unity* ♦ *Not much has been done toward improving safety.*
4 near or nearer a time or place: *I'll call*

T

you some time toward the end of the week. ♦ *Caroline's name appeared toward the bottom of the list.*

tow•el /ˈtaʊəl/ noun [C] ★ a piece of material that you use for drying your hands or body, or for drying dishes

tow•er¹ /ˈtaʊr/ noun [C] ★★ a tall narrow structure, building, or part of a building: *a water tower* ♦ *the Leaning Tower of Pisa* ♦ *a church tower*

tow•er² /ˈtaʊr/ verb [I] to be much taller than the people or things that are near you

ˈtower ˌblock noun [C] *British* a HIGH-RISE building

town /taʊn/ noun ★★★

1 [C] a place where people live and work that is smaller than a city: *a small town* ♦ *a town on the Mississippi River* ♦ *the northern Wisconsin town of Rhinelander*
→ CITY

2 [U] the town or city that you live in or that you are talking about: *He moved to another part of town.* ♦ *The crew was **in town** last week filming a new television series.* ♦ *His girlfriend flew in from **out of town**.*

3 [singular] the people who live in a town: *Most of the town was involved with the carnival.*

4 [U] the center of a town where all the stores are: *We're going **into town** this afternoon.*

PHRASE **go to town (on sth)** *informal* to do something very well, or to make something look very good by spending a lot of time or money on it
→ HOME TOWN

ˌtown ˈhall noun [C] a building that has all the offices of a town's local government

town•house /ˈtaʊnˌhaʊs/ or **town•home** /ˈtaʊnˌhoʊm/ noun [C] *American* a house that shares walls with houses on either side of it —*picture* → C1

ˌtown ˈmeeting noun [C] *American* **1** a meeting where people discuss problems affecting the town where they live **2** a meeting at which people can meet a national politician to ask questions and talk about issues

towns•peo•ple /ˈtaʊnzˌpip(ə)l/ noun [plural] the people who live in a town or city

ˈtow ˌtruck noun [C] *American* a truck used for moving vehicles that cannot be driven

tox•ic /ˈtɑksɪk/ adj poisonous, and harmful to humans, animals, or the environment

tox•in /ˈtɑksɪn/ noun [C] a poisonous substance

toy¹ /tɔɪ/ noun [C] ★★ an object that is designed for a child to play with: *boxes full of books, toys, and games* ♦ *a toy soldier/gun/car*

toy² /tɔɪ/ PHRASAL VERB **ˈtoy with sth 1** to think about an idea in a way that is not serious: *I've been toying with the idea of starting my own business.* **2** to keep touching or moving something

trace¹ /treɪs/ verb [T] ★

1 to find someone or something that you are looking for by asking questions and getting information: *Detectives have failed to trace the missing woman.*

2 to discover the origin or cause of something: *The source of the infection was traced to a farm in Wisconsin.*

3 to describe what happened in a long process or series of events: *The book traces the history of the regiment.*

4 to copy an image by putting transparent paper on top and following the lines with your pencil —*picture* → DRAW

trace² /treɪs/ noun **1** [C/U] a slight sign that someone has been present or that something has happened **2** [C] a very small amount of something

track¹ /træk/ noun ★★★

1 train line	5 course of study
2 running/racing course	6 recorded music
3 athletic events	7 rough path/road
4 marks on ground	+ PHRASES

1 [C/U] a railroad line: *a long stretch of track*

2 [C] a piece of ground that is used for running or racing

3 [U] *American* athletic events in which the runners run around a circular course: *Are you going to run track in the spring?*

4 **tracks** [plural] marks that a person, animal, or vehicle leaves on the ground: *He followed the tracks of a car to the edge of the lake.*

5 [C] *American* a course of study that students of one level or ability all take together: *a vocational/academic track*

6 [C] a song or piece of music that is recorded on a CD: *Which is your favorite track?*

7 [C] *British* a path or road with a rough surface: *I walked along a track to the mountain village.*

PHRASES **keep track of sth** to have information about how something is developing: *We need to keep track of how we are spending our money.*

lose track (of sth) to forget something, or to not know exactly what is happening: *I've lost track of how many times he called last week.*

off track unlikely to be successful or correct

on the right/wrong track doing or thinking the right or wrong things

on track doing things that are likely to be successful or correct: *a desperate attempt to keep the peace talks on track* ♦ **on track to do sth** *We're right on track to create two million new jobs.*

stop (dead) in your tracks to suddenly stop, for example because you are surprised

track and field sports that involve running, jumping, and throwing objects
→ BEATEN, FAST TRACK

track² /træk/ verb [T] **1** to follow someone or something by looking for evidence that shows where they have gone, or by using special equipment: *The radar system tracks planes up to 50 miles from the airport.* **2** to follow the development of something: *Live television coverage allows you to track the progress of the competitors.* **3** *American* to leave a line of dirt on the floor when you walk

PHRASAL VERB **ˌtrack sb/sth ˈdown** to find someone or something after a long search: *I finally managed to track him down in Manchester.*

track•ball /ˈtrækˌbɔl/ noun [C] *computing* a ball

that is used instead of a computer MOUSE

'track ˌrecord noun [C] your reputation, based on the things that you have done or not done

tract /trækt/ noun [C] **1** a large area of land **2** *medical* a group of organs and tubes that work together in your body

trac•tion /ˈtrækʃ(ə)n/ noun [U] *technical* the ability of something to move over a surface without slipping

trac•tor /ˈtræktər/ noun [C] a vehicle that is used on farms for pulling machines

'tractor-ˌtrailer noun [C] *American* a large truck that pulls one or two TRAILERS (=long containers with wheels)

trade¹ /treɪd/ noun ★★★

1 [U] the activity of buying and selling goods or services: *Spain wants to develop its **trade with** the Philippines.* ♦ *the illegal **trade in** drugs*

2 [C] the exchange of one thing for another of the same value: *a fair trade*

3 [C] a particular area of business or industry: *the book/drug/jewelry trade*

4 [C] a job or type of work that someone is trained to do: *He **learned his trade** in the 1960s.*

trade² /treɪd/ verb ★★

1 [I/T] to buy and sell goods or services: *Investors can now **trade stocks online**.* ♦ *Cuba continues to **trade with** other countries around the world.*

2 [T] to exchange something that you have for something else: **trade sth for sth** *Tony traded his computer for a bike.*

3 [I] to operate as a business: *The company will continue to trade under its original name.*

PHRASE **trade places** to move into someone else's place or position: *I wouldn't want to trade places with anyone in politics.*

PHRASAL VERB **ˌtrade sth 'in** to give something old as part of the payment for something new: *She **traded in** her old car for a new one.*

'trade ˌdeficit noun [C] a situation in which a country is buying more things from other countries than it is selling to other countries

trade•mark /ˈtreɪdˌmɑrk/ noun [C] a name or design that belongs to a particular company and is used on its products

'trade ˌname noun [C] a BRAND NAME

'trade-ˌoff noun [C] a situation in which you accept a disadvantage so that you can have a benefit

trad•er /ˈtreɪdər/ noun [C] someone who buys and sells things: *market/street traders*

'trade ˌshow noun [C] an event at which companies show their new products

trades•man /ˈtreɪdzmən/ noun [C] *American* a man who is trained to do a skilled job using his hands

ˌtrade 'union noun [C] *British* a LABOR UNION

tra•di•tion /trəˈdɪʃ(ə)n/ noun [C/U] ★★★ a very old custom, belief, or story: *Native American culture and traditions* ♦ *His son **followed** the family **tradition** and entered politics.*

tra•di•tion•al /trəˈdɪʃən(ə)l/ adj ★★★

1 relating to very old customs, beliefs, or stories: *traditional Mediterranean cooking* ♦ *All the dancers and musicians wore **traditional costumes**.*

2 typical of the things people have usually done: *Our house was built in a traditional style.* ♦ *Many women have abandoned their **traditional role** as wife and mother.*

—tra•di•tion•al•ly adv

tra•di•tion•al•ist /trəˈdɪʃən(ə)lɪst/ noun [C] someone who supports traditional ideas or methods

traf•fic /ˈtræfɪk/ noun [U] ★★★

1 the vehicles that are traveling in an area at a particular time: *At that time of night, there was no traffic on the roads.* ♦ *the huge volume of traffic on the highway* ♦ *rush-hour traffic* ♦ *traffic noise/fumes/congestion*

2 aircraft, ships, and trains that travel from one place to another: *an increase in **air traffic***

3 the information that passes through a communications system: *Internet traffic*

4 the process of buying and selling things such as drugs and weapons illegally: *measures to reduce the illegal **traffic in** heroin*

'traffic ˌcircle noun [C] *American* a circular area where three or more roads meet

'traffic ˌjam noun [C] a line of vehicles waiting behind something that is blocking the street

traf•fick•ing /ˈtræfɪkɪŋ/ noun [U] the business of illegally buying and selling things such as drugs and weapons **—traf•fick•er** noun [C]

'traffic ˌlights noun [plural] a set of red, yellow, and green lights that control traffic

trag•e•dy /ˈtrædʒədi/ noun **1** [C/U] a very sad event that involves death or human suffering: *The trip ended in tragedy.* ♦ *We need new safety laws to prevent tragedies like this from happening again.* **2** [C] a bad situation that makes people very upset or angry: *It's a tragedy that so many young people are out of work.* **3** [C] a play in which people suffer or die, especially one in which the main character dies: *Shakespeare's tragedies*

trag•ic /ˈtrædʒɪk/ adj **1** causing or involving great sadness, because someone suffers or dies **2** relating to tragedy in plays or literature **—trag•i•cal•ly** /ˈtrædʒɪkli/ adv

trail¹ /treɪl/ noun [C] ★

1 a path through the countryside, especially one designed for walking for pleasure: *The trail led down to the lake.* ♦ *We followed a winding trail into the mountains.*

2 a series of marks that shows where someone or something has been: ***a trail of** blood* ♦ *He **left a trail** of muddy footprints.*

3 damage or harm caused by something bad: *Hurricane Andrew left **a trail of** destruction along the coast.*

4 many pieces of connected evidence that prove someone did something wrong or illegal: *Detectives are **on the trail of** a serial killer.*

trail² /treɪl/ verb

1 in competition	4 follow sb
2 pull sth behind you	5 leave marks
3 move slowly	+ PHRASAL VERB

1 [I/T] to be losing in a competition or election: *A recent poll shows the Democrats*

T

trailing the Republicans. ♦ *At the end of the round, Garcia trailed by two strokes.* **2** [I/T] to pull something behind you, or to be pulled behind someone or something **3** [I] to move slowly behind someone in a tired or unhappy way: *My husband usually trails behind me when I'm shopping.* **4** [T] to follow someone secretly in order to learn something about them: *Detectives trailed Evans for weeks.* **5** [T] to leave marks on a surface as you go through a place: *The dogs came in, trailing mud everywhere.*
PHRASAL VERB **ˌtrail aˈway** or **ˌtrail ˈoff** if someone's voice trails away, they gradually become silent

trail·er /ˈtreɪlər/ noun [C] **1** *American* a home on wheels that can be pulled by a car **2** a long container that can be attached to a vehicle and used for moving heavy objects or large animals **3** an advertisement for a movie or television program that shows short parts of that movie or program

ˈtrailer ˌpark noun [C] *American* a place where people park trailers and live in them

train¹ /treɪn/ noun [C] ★★★
1 a group of railroad cars that are connected and pulled by an engine: *a freight/passenger train* ♦ *We traveled across China* ***by train.*** ♦ *I met her* ***on a train*** *to New York.* ♦ *More and more people* ***got on the crowded train.*** ♦ *We'll be waiting for you when you* ***get off the train.*** ♦ *If we don't leave now we'll* ***miss the train.*** ♦ *I'll meet you at the* ***train station.*** *—picture* → C7
2 a series of events or thoughts: *I'm sorry,* ***I lost my train of thought*** (=forgot what I was thinking).
3 a long part at the back of a formal dress that spreads out over the ground

train² /treɪn/ verb ★★★
1 [T] to teach someone to do a particular job or activity: *We need to recruit and train more police officers.* ♦ **train sb to do sth** *They were training him to use the new security system.*
2 [I] to learn how to do a particular job or activity: *He* ***trained as*** *a chef in Paris.* ♦ **train to do sth** *I have an uncle who trained to be a pilot.*
3 [I] to practice a sport regularly before a game or competition: *The players train five days a week.*
4 [T] to teach an animal to obey you or to do something: **train sth to do sth** *He had trained the dogs to attack.*

train·ee /ˌtreɪˈni/ noun [C] someone who is learning how to do a particular job or activity

train·er /ˈtreɪnər/ noun [C] **1** someone whose job is to teach people skills, or to help people to practice a sport **2** someone whose job is to train animals

train·ing /ˈtreɪnɪŋ/ noun [U] ★★★
1 the process of teaching or learning a particular job or activity: *Counseling is a difficult job requiring skill and training.* ♦ *Employees are given* ***training in*** *the use of safety equipment.* ♦ *The college* ***provides*** *vocational* ***training*** *for actors.*
2 physical exercise that someone does regularly in order to practice for a sport or to stay healthy: *McColgan is currently* ***in training*** *for the New York marathon.*

trait /treɪt/ noun [C] a particular quality in someone's character

trai·tor /ˈtreɪtər/ noun [C] someone who is not loyal to their country, friends, or family

tra·jec·to·ry /trəˈdʒektəri/ noun [C] *technical* the high curving line that is formed by the movement of an object through the air

tram /træm/ noun [C] *British* a TROLLEY for carrying passengers

tramp¹ /træmp/ noun [C] **1** someone without a home or a job who moves from one place to another **2** a long tiring walk

tramp² /træmp/ verb [I/T] to walk with slow heavy steps, or to walk a long way

tram·ple /ˈtræmp(ə)l/ verb [I/T] to put your feet down on someone or something in a heavy way that causes injury or damage

tram·po·line /ˈtræmpəˌlin/ noun [C] a piece of equipment that you jump up and down on, consisting of a metal frame with a strong material stretched across it

trance /træns/ noun [C] a state in which you are awake but not really conscious of where you are

tran·quil /ˈtræŋkwɪl/ adj calm, still, and quiet —**tran·quil·i·ty** /træŋˈkwɪləti/ noun [U]

tran·quil·iz·er /ˈtræŋkwəˌlaɪzər/ noun [C] a drug that makes people calmer when they are very worried or nervous

trans·ac·tion /trænˈzækʃ(ə)n/ noun [C] *formal* an occasion when someone buys or sells something

trans·at·lan·tic /ˌtrænsətˈlæntɪk/ adj **1** crossing the Atlantic Ocean **2** involving countries on both sides of the Atlantic Ocean

tran·scend /trænˈsend/ verb [T] *formal* to become free of things that limit what you can achieve

tran·scribe /trænˈskraɪb/ verb [T] to write something exactly as it was spoken

tran·script /ˈtrænˌskrɪpt/ noun [C] **1** a written copy of the exact words that someone said **2** *American* an official record of the classes a student has taken and the grades they have received

trans·fer¹ /trænsˈfɜr, ˈtrænsfər/ verb ★★
1 [I/T] to move, or to move someone, from one job or department to another in the same company or organization: *I'm* ***transferring to*** *our Tokyo office next year.* ♦ **transfer sb from sth to sth** *Helen was transferred from marketing to sales.*
2 [T] to move something or someone from one place to another: **transfer sb/sth to sth** *Wait until the cookies cool before transferring them to a plate.* ♦ *The prisoner will be transferred to a maximum security unit.* ♦ *I need to transfer $1,000 to my daughter's account.*
3 [T] to let someone speak to another person by changing telephone lines for them: *Please hold while I transfer you.*
4 [T] to officially arrange for someone else to become the owner of something

trans·fer² /ˈtrænsfər/ noun ★★
1 [C/U] the process of moving, or being moved, from one job or place to another: *We're currently dealing with the paperwork for your transfer.* ♦ *the transfer of supplies*

T

2 [C] *American* a ticket that allows you to move from one bus or train to another without paying again

trans·fixed /trænsˈfɪkst/ adj so surprised, shocked, or interested that you continue to look at something without moving

trans·form /trænsˈfɔrm/ verb [T] ★ to make someone or something completely different, especially in a positive way: *E-mail has transformed the way people communicate.* ♦ **transform sb/sth into sth** *They've transformed the old train station into a science museum.* —**trans·for·ma·tion** /ˌtrænsfərˈmeɪʃ(ə)n/ noun [C/U]

trans·form·er /trænsˈfɔrmər/ noun [C] *technical* an object that changes the VOLTAGE of a flow of electricity

trans·fu·sion /trænsˈfjuʒ(ə)n/ noun [C/U] a medical treatment in which blood from one person is put into another person's body

trans·gen·ic /ˌtrænzˈdʒenɪk/ adj *science* a transgenic plant or animal contains genes from a different plant or animal

trans·gress /trænzˈgres/ verb [I/T] *formal* to do something that is not allowed by a law, custom, or religion —**trans·gres·sion** /trænzˈgreʃ(ə)n/ noun [C/U]

tran·sient[1] /ˈtrænʃənt, ˈtrænziənt/ adj existing, happening, or staying somewhere for a short period of time only

tran·sient[2] /ˈtrænʃənt, ˈtrænziənt/ noun [C] someone without a permanent home or job who moves from one place to another

tran·sis·tor /trænˈzɪstər/ noun [C] *technical* an object that controls the flow of electricity inside electronic equipment

tran·sit /ˈtrænsɪt/ noun [U] **1** the movement of people or things from one place to another: *Our suitcases were damaged in transit.* **2** *American* a system of buses, trains, etc. that people use to travel around a particular city or area

tran·si·tion /trænˈzɪʃ(ə)n/ noun [C/U] the process of changing from one situation, form, or state to another: *It's not always a smooth transition from high school to college.* —**tran·si·tion·al** adj

tran·si·tive /ˈtrænzɪtɪv/ adj *linguistics* a transitive verb is always used with a DIRECT OBJECT. Transitive verbs are marked [T] in this dictionary.

tran·si·to·ry /ˈtrænzɪˌtɔri/ adj temporary

trans·late /trænsˈleɪt/ verb ★

1 [I/T] to change spoken or written words into a different language: *I don't speak Russian, so someone will have to translate.* ♦ **translate sth into sth** *The Bible has been translated into more than 100 languages.*

2 [I] to cause a particular situation or result: *Will the sales increase **translate into** more jobs?*

trans·la·tion /trænsˈleɪʃ(ə)n/ noun ★

1 [C] a piece of work in which spoken or written words have been changed into a different language: *an English **translation of*** Candide

2 [U] the activity of changing spoken or written words into a different language: *Most legal translation is done by lawyers with foreign language training.* ♦ *Try to read Baudelaire **in the original** and not **in translation**.*

trans·la·tor /trænsˈleɪtər/ noun [C] someone whose job is to translate spoken or written words into a different language

trans·lu·cent /trænsˈlus(ə)nt/ adj clear enough for light to pass through, but not completely clear

trans·mis·sion /trænzˈmɪʃ(ə)n/ noun **1** [C/U] the process of sending electronic signals such as radio or television signals, or a signal that is sent in this way: *New telephone lines allow faster data transmission by fax or modem.* **2** [U] *formal* the process by which something spreads from one person to another: *the transmission of disease* **3** [C] the part of a vehicle that takes power from the engine to the wheels

trans·mit /trænzˈmɪt/ verb [T] **1** to send an electronic signal such as a radio or television signal **2** *formal* to pass information, beliefs, or attitudes to other people **3** *formal* to spread a disease from one person to another

trans·mit·ter /trænzˈmɪtər/ noun [C] a piece of electronic equipment that is used for sending radio, television, or telephone signals through the air

trans·par·en·cy /trænsˈperənsi/ noun [C] a photograph, drawing, or piece of writing on plastic that you shine light through in order to look at it on a screen

trans·par·ent /trænsˈperənt/ adj **1** clear or thin enough for you to see things through **2** not trying to keep anything secret

tran·spire /trænˈspaɪr/ verb [I] *formal* **1** to become known: *It later transpired that the driver of her car was drunk.* **2** to happen

trans·plant[1] /ˈtrænsˌplænt/ noun [C/U] a medical operation in which a new organ is put into someone's body

trans·plant[2] /ˌtrænsˈplænt/ verb [T] **1** to take a plant out of the ground and put it in a different place **2** to take an organ from one person's body and put it into another person's body

trans·port[1] /trænsˈpɔrt/ verb [T] ★ to move people or things from one place to another, usually in a vehicle: *We will need a big truck to transport all the boxes.* ♦ *Volunteers will be transported to the island by boat.*

trans·port[2] /ˈtrænsˌpɔrt/ noun [U] ★

1 the action of moving goods from one place to another

2 *British* TRANSPORTATION

trans·por·ta·tion /ˌtrænspərˈteɪʃ(ə)n/ noun [U] ★★★

1 the system used for traveling or for moving goods from one place to another: *rising transportation costs* ♦ *In New York, most people rely on public transportation to get to work.*

2 a method of traveling or moving things from one place to another: *What will we do for transportation to the airport?*

3 the action of moving goods from one place to another: *the possession and transportation of illegal drugs*

trans·pose /trænsˈpoʊz/ verb [T] *formal* to change the order or position of something

T

trans•ves•tite /trænzˈvesˌtaɪt/ noun [C] someone who wears clothing typical of the opposite sex, especially for sexual pleasure

trap¹ /træp/ verb [T] ★

1 prevent from escaping	4 catch an animal
2 of bad situation	5 trick sb
3 catch a criminal	

1 to prevent someone from leaving a place: *Both men were trapped inside the burning car.* ♦ *The bomb exploded, trapping victims in the building.*
2 to make someone unable to change a bad situation or way of thinking: *The two communities are trapped in a cycle of violence.* ♦ *I felt* ***trapped*** *by my marriage.*
3 to catch someone such as a criminal, especially by forcing them into a place that they cannot escape from: *Police officers trapped both suspects before they left the bank.*
4 to catch an animal using a trap
5 to trick someone in order to make them do or say something that they did not mean to do: **trap sb into (doing) sth** *I was trapped into admitting I had lied.*

trap² /træp/ noun [C] **1** a piece of equipment that is used for catching animals: *We set traps for the mice.* **2** a bad situation that is difficult to change or escape from: *He was caught in a trap of poverty.* **3** a trick that is designed to catch someone or make them do something that they did not mean to do: *We didn't know that we were walking straight into a trap.* **4** a mistake or problem that you should try to avoid: *I fell into the trap of putting work before family.* → DEATH TRAP

trap•door /ˈtræpˌdɔr/ noun [C] a small door that covers an opening in a floor, ceiling, or wall

tra•peze /trəˈpiz/ noun [C] a short bar that hangs on two ropes from a high ceiling and is used by performers in a CIRCUS

tra•pe•zi•um /trəˈpiziəm/ noun [C] *American technical* a shape with four straight sides that are not parallel to each other —*picture* → C8

trap•e•zoid /ˈtræpəˌzɔɪd/ noun [C] *American* a shape with four straight sides, two of which are parallel —*picture* → C8

trap•pings /ˈtræpɪŋz/ noun [plural] possessions that show that someone is rich, powerful, or important

trash¹ /træʃ/ noun [U] ★
1 *American* garbage such as paper, plastic bags, used containers, etc. that you get rid of = GARBAGE: *There was trash all over the fairgrounds for weeks afterward.*
2 the trash *American* the container where you keep garbage: *Did you put the newspaper in the trash?*
3 *informal* something that is of very bad quality: *I can't watch this trash any longer. Let's go.*
4 *offensive* an extremely insulting word for people you think are dishonest, immoral, or badly educated

trash² /træʃ/ verb [T] *informal* **1** to damage or destroy something **2** to criticize someone or something in a very strong way

ˈtrash ˌcan noun [C] *American* a metal or plastic container for things you want to get rid of —*picture* → C2

trash•y /ˈtræʃi/ adj *informal* very badly made, or of very bad quality

trau•ma /ˈtrɔmə/ noun [U] a feeling of being very upset, afraid, or shocked because of a bad experience, or the experience that causes this feeling

trau•mat•ic /trɔˈmætɪk/ adj causing you to feel very upset, afraid, or shocked

trau•ma•tized /ˈtrɔməˌtaɪzd/ adj very upset, afraid, or shocked because of a bad experience —**trau•ma•tize** verb [T]

trav•el¹ /ˈtræv(ə)l/ (present participle **trav•el•ing** or **trav•el•ling**; past tense and past participle **trav•eled** or **trav•elled**) verb ★★★
1 [I] to go on a trip, or visit different places: *Matt spends much of his time traveling abroad.* ♦ *We traveled around Spain for two weeks.* ♦ *I usually* ***travel by bus.*** ♦ *Joe recently* ***traveled to*** *Australia on business.*
2 [I/T] to move a particular distance, or at a particular speed: *We traveled 300 miles on Saturday.* ♦ *The car was* ***traveling at*** *about 50 miles per hour.*
3 [I] to spread from one place to another in a way that affects or influences a lot of people: *The news traveled quickly.*

trav•el² /ˈtræv(ə)l/ noun [U] ★★★ the activity of traveling: *Foreign travel never really appealed to him until he retired.* ♦ *Our agency deals mostly with business travel.* ♦ *travel arrangements/insurance*
PHRASE **sb's travels** trips that someone makes to different places: *We met a lot of interesting people* ***on our travels.***

ˈtravel ˌagency or **ˈtravel ˌagent's** noun [C] a business that helps people to plan trips and to make travel arrangements

ˈtravel ˌagent noun [C] someone whose job is to help people to plan trips and to make travel arrangements

trav•el•er /ˈtræv(ə)lər/ noun [C] someone who is traveling, or who travels often

ˈtraveler's ˌcheck noun [C] a printed piece of paper that you sign and use as money when you are traveling

trav•el•ler /ˈtræv(ə)lər/ the British spelling of traveler

tra•verse /trəˈvɜrs/ verb [T] *formal* to move over or across an area

trav•es•ty /ˈtrævəsti/ noun [singular] something that is shocking because it is unfair or very different from what you expect

trawl /trɔl/ verb [I/T] to look for someone or something by searching through a large number of things

trawl•er /ˈtrɔlər/ noun [C] a boat used for fishing that pulls a large net through the water

tray /treɪ/ noun [C] **1** a flat piece of plastic, metal, or wood with raised edges, used for carrying food or drinks **2** a flat open container with raised edges, used for holding paper

treach•er•ous /ˈtretʃərəs/ adj **1** very dangerous: *treacherous driving conditions* **2** someone who is treacherous cannot be trusted

T

treach•er•y /ˈtretʃəri/ noun [U] the act of harming people who trusted you

tread¹ /tred/ verb **tread water 1** to not make progress **2** to stay upright in deep water by moving your legs and arms and keeping your head out of the water

tread² /tred/ noun [C] the pattern of lines on a tire

tread•mill /ˈtredˌmɪl/ noun [C] **1** a piece of exercise equipment with a moving surface that you walk or run on —*picture* → C16 **2** a situation that is very tiring or boring because you always do the same things

trea•son /ˈtriz(ə)n/ noun [U] the crime of trying to harm or destroy your country's government

treas•ure¹ /ˈtreʒər/ noun **1** [C] a valuable piece of art, or a valuable historical object: *the treasures of the Vatican Museum* **2** [U] a collection of valuable things, for example jewels, gold, etc.: *There are rumors of buried treasure in the old house.*

treasure

treas•ure² /ˈtreʒər/ verb [T] to think that something is very important because it gives you a lot of pleasure —**treas•ured** /ˈtreʒərd/ adj

treas•ur•er /ˈtreʒərər/ noun [C] someone who is in charge of an organization's money

Treas•ur•y, the /ˈtreʒəri/ the government department that is responsible for a country's financial matters

treat¹ /trit/ verb [T] ★★★

1 behave toward sb	4 protect sth
2 cure illness	5 buy sb sth special
3 deal with sth	

1 to behave toward someone in a particular way: *Rachel felt she had been unfairly treated.* ♦ *They treat their guests very well.* ♦ **treat sb like/as sth** *I wish you would stop treating me like a child!* ♦ **treat sb with sth** *Dean always treated my grandfather with the greatest respect.*

2 to use medicine or medical methods to cure an illness: *Patients are treated using both medication and exercise.* ♦ **treat sb for sth** *She was treated for minor injuries.*

3 to deal with something in a particular way: **treat sth with sth** *You should treat this new evidence with caution.* ♦ **treat sth as sth** *These payments will be treated as income.*

4 to put a substance on something in order to protect it or to make it stronger: **treat sth with sth** *The wood is treated with chemicals.*

5 to pay for something special for someone: **treat sb to sth** *Bob treated us to dinner at a nice restaurant.*

Words often used with treat

*Adverbs often used with **treat** (verb, sense 1)*

- TREAT + **badly, cruelly, harshly, unfairly, unjustly**: treat someone in an unkind or unfair way
- TREAT + **equally, fairly, kindly, leniently, well**: treat someone in a kind or fair way

treat² /trit/ noun **1** [C] a very enjoyable event or occasion: *It's a real treat to see you again.* ♦ *The band is great – you're in for a treat* (=you will enjoy it). **2** [singular] an occasion when you pay for something special for someone else: *I'd like this lunch to be my treat.* → TRICK¹

trea•tise /ˈtritɪs/ noun [C] *formal* a serious book or piece of writing about a particular subject

treat•ment /ˈtritmənt/ noun ★★★

1 [C/U] the process of providing medical care, or a particular type of medical care: *medical/dental/psychiatric treatment* ♦ *She was receiving treatment for breast cancer.* ♦ *a new treatment for heroin addiction* ♦ *the treatment of tropical diseases*

2 [U] the particular way in which you deal with someone: *the treatment of prisoners*

trea•ty /ˈtriti/ noun [C] an official written agreement between countries: *a treaty on arms reduction*

treb•le /ˈtreb(ə)l/ noun [C/U] the highest range of musical sounds, or the part of a radio or STEREO that controls the higher sounds —**treb•le** adj

tree /tri/ noun [C] ★★★ a very tall plant that has branches and a thick stem made of wood: *a maple/pine/olive tree* → BARK¹, FAMILY TREE

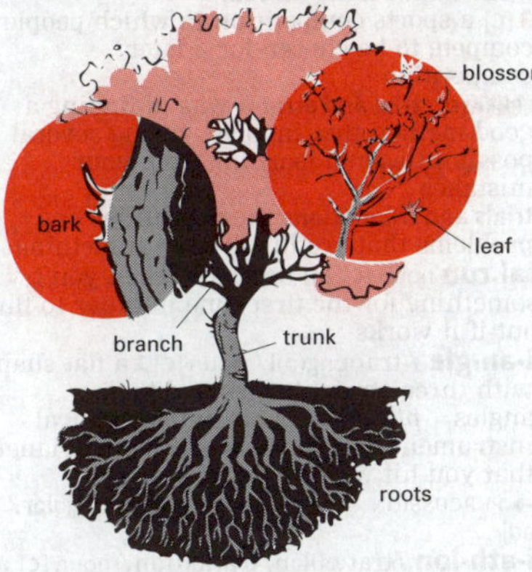

tree

trek /trek/ noun [C] a long tiring walk —**trek** verb [I]

trel•lis /ˈtrelɪs/ noun [C] an upright frame for plants to grow on

trem•ble /ˈtremb(ə)l/ verb [I] if you are trembling, your body is shaking, for example because you are nervous or weak: *She was trembling with anger.*

tre•men•dous /trəˈmendəs/ adj **1** extremely great, important, or strong: *I have tremendous respect for my parents.* ♦ *We have*

T

a tremendous amount of work to do. **2** extremely good: *We had a tremendous time on vacation.* —**tre•men•dous•ly** adv

trem•or /ˈtremər/ noun [C] **1** a small EARTHQUAKE **2** a slight shaking movement in your body or your voice that you cannot control

trench /trentʃ/ noun [C] a long narrow hole in the ground

trend /trend/ noun [C] ★ a gradual change or development that produces a particular result: *His designs often **set the trend*** (=start something that becomes popular) *for the new season.* ♦ *We've seen **a trend toward** more violent movies this year.* ♦ *the latest **trends in** popular music*

Words often used with trend

Adjectives often used with ***trend***

- **current, general, growing, increasing, present, recent, rising, underlying** + TREND: used about different types of trend

trend•y /ˈtrendi/ adj fashionable, but sometimes in a way that is silly or annoying

trep•i•da•tion /ˌtrepɪˈdeɪʃ(ə)n/ noun [U] *formal* fear, or nervousness

tres•pass /ˈtresˌpæs, ˈtrespəs/ verb [I] to go into a place without the owner's permission —**tres•pass•er** noun [C]

tri•al /ˈtraɪəl/ noun ★★

1 [C/U] the process of examining a case in a court of law and deciding whether someone is guilty of a crime: *a murder/rape/fraud trial* ♦ *They're **on trial for** armed robbery.*

2 [C/U] the process of testing something over a period of time: *The system will operate for a six-month **trial period**.*

3 [C] a sports competition in which people compete to be chosen for a later competition

PHRASES **trial and error** a way of finding a good method that involves trying several possibilities and learning from your mistakes

trials and tribulations the difficulties and problems that are involved in something

ˌtrial ˈrun noun [C] an occasion when you try something for the first time in order to find out if it works

tri•an•gle /ˈtraɪˌæŋg(ə)l/ noun [C] **1** a flat shape with three straight sides and three angles *—picture* → C8 **2** a simple musical instrument that consists of a metal triangle that you hit with a bar *—picture* → PERCUSSION —**tri•an•gu•lar** /traɪˈæŋgjələr/ adj

tri•ath•lon /traɪˈæθlən, traɪˈæθˌlɑn/ noun [C] a type of race in which each person swims, rides a bicycle, and runs

tribe /traɪb/ noun [C] a large group of related families who live in the same area and share a common language, religion, and customs: *Native American tribes* —**trib•al** adj

trib•u•la•tion /ˌtrɪbjəˈleɪʃn/ noun [C] *see* **trial**

tri•bu•nal /traɪˈbjun(ə)l, trɪˈbjun(ə)l/ noun [C] a special law court that is organized in order to judge a particular case: *a war crimes tribunal*

trib•u•tar•y /ˈtrɪbjəˌteri/ noun [C] a small river that flows into a larger river

trib•ute /ˈtrɪbjut/ noun [C/U] something that you do, say, or make in order to show that you respect and admire someone: *They showed the program as a tribute to Nelson Mandela.*

PHRASES **be a tribute to** to show how good someone or something is: *This year's success is a tribute to all your hard work.*

pay tribute to to praise someone or something publicly

trick[1] /trɪk/ noun [C] ★★

1 a deliberate attempt to make someone believe something that is not true, either as a joke or as a serious attempt to harm them: *At first I thought Joe was **playing a trick on** me.*

2 a way of entertaining people by doing something that looks like magic: *a street performer **doing tricks** for the crowd*

3 an effective and skillful way of doing something: *There's **a trick to** folding up this umbrella.* ♦ *If you want to see her, **the trick is to** go early.*

PHRASES **do the trick** to do what is needed in order to achieve something

trick or treat a custom in which children visit your home at HALLOWEEN and say "Trick or treat?" as a way of asking for candy

trick[2] /trɪk/ verb [T] to make someone believe something that is not true: *I suddenly realized that I'd been tricked.* ♦ **trick sb into doing sth** *He tricked me into believing that he was somebody famous.*

trick•er•y /ˈtrɪk(ə)ri/ noun [U] the use of tricks to get what you want

trick•le /ˈtrɪk(ə)l/ verb [I] **1** if a liquid trickles somewhere, a small amount of it flows there slowly: *A tear trickled down his cheek.* **2** if people or things trickle into or out of a place, a few of them arrive or leave —**trick•le** noun [C]

ˌtrick ˈquestion noun [C] a question that seems to have an easy answer but is really designed to trick you

trick•y /ˈtrɪki/ adj difficult to do, or difficult to deal with: *a tricky problem/situation*

tried[1] the past tense and past participle of **try**[1]

tried[2] /traɪd/ adj **tried and true** known to be good or effective

tri•fle /ˈtraɪf(ə)l/ noun **a trifle** *formal* slightly

trig•ger[1] /ˈtrɪgər/ verb [T] **1** to cause something to happen: *The news of his death triggered more violence.* **2** to make a machine or piece of equipment start to work: *Someone broke a window, and this triggered the alarm.*

trig•ger[2] /ˈtrɪgər/ noun [C] **1** the part of a gun that you pull with your finger to make the gun fire **2** something that causes something bad to happen

tril•lion /ˈtrɪljən/ number the number 1,000,000,000,000

tril•o•gy /ˈtrɪlədʒi/ noun [C] a series of three books, movies, or plays

trim[1] /trɪm/ verb [T] **1** to cut a small amount off something so that it looks neat: *I just wanted her to trim my hair.* **2** to reduce the amount or number of something: *The company has trimmed $46,000 from its*

T

advertising budget. **3** to decorate something

trim² /trɪm/ adj healthy and thin in an attractive way

trim³ /trɪm/ noun **1** [singular] the act of trimming something, especially hair **2** [singular/U] decoration on the edges of something: *cream leather seats with brown trim*

tri•mes•ter /traɪˈmestər/ noun [C] **1** a period of three months, especially during the time when a woman is pregnant **2** one of three periods that a year is divided into in some U.S. schools and colleges

trim•mings /ˈtrɪmɪŋz/ noun [plural] small objects or pieces of cloth that are used for decorating things such as clothes

trin•ket /ˈtrɪŋkɪt/ noun [C] a small object or decoration that is not very valuable

tri•o /ˈtrioʊ/ noun [C] a group of three people or things that do something together

trip¹ /trɪp/ noun ★★

1 [C] an occasion when you go somewhere and come back again: *a fishing/camping/sightseeing trip* ♦ *a bus/train/boat trip* ♦ *We* ***took a trip*** *across the country.* ♦ ***a trip to*** *Brazil* ♦ *The whole family* ***went on a trip*** *to Hawaii.* → FIELD TRIP, ROUND TRIP

2 [singular] *American spoken* an unusual but interesting or exciting experience

Other words that mean trip

- **crossing** a trip across water from one piece of land to another
- **drive** a trip in a car
- **excursion** an organized trip for a group of people
- **expedition** a long and difficult trip to a place that is very far away, often made by people who are doing scientific research
- **flight** a trip in an airplane
- **journey** a long trip from one place to another
- **outing** a short trip made by a group of people who are visiting a place
- **ride** a short trip in a car or bus, or on a bicycle or motorcycle
- **tour** a trip to a place where there are interesting things to see

trip

trip² /trɪp/ verb **1** [I/T] to hit your foot on something and fall down, or to make someone hit their foot on something and fall down: *I'm sure she tripped me!* ♦ *I tripped over a rock.* **2** [T] to make a switch go on or off, especially by accident

PHRASAL VERB ˌ**trip (sb)** ˈ**up 1** to make a mistake, or to cause someone to make a mistake: *The tests are designed to trip you up.* **2** *same as* **trip²** 1

tri•ple¹ /ˈtrɪp(ə)l/ adj **1** involving three things of the same kind: *a triple killing* **2** three times bigger than the usual size or amount: *a triple vodka*

tri•ple² /ˈtrɪp(ə)l/ determiner three times as much or as many: *The price they wanted was triple the amount we expected.*

tri•ple³ /ˈtrɪp(ə)l/ verb [I/T] if something triples, or if you triple it, it increases so that it is three times bigger than before: *We had tripled our money by the end of the year.*

trip•let /ˈtrɪplət/ noun [C] one of three children who were born at the same time to the same mother

tri•pod /ˈtraɪˌpɑd/ noun [C] an object with three legs, used for supporting something such as a camera

tri•state /ˈtraɪˌsteɪt/ adj *American* relating to three states near each other

trite /traɪt/ adj a trite remark is not interesting or original because people have used it too much

tri•umph¹ /ˈtraɪəmf/ noun **1** [C/U] an exciting victory or success **2** [U] the proud or excited feeling that you get when you have been successful

tri•umph² /ˈtraɪəmf/ verb [I] to win a great victory, or to have a great success

tri•um•phant /traɪˈʌmfənt/ adj showing that you are very pleased about a victory or success: *a triumphant smile/laugh/yell* —**tri•um•phant•ly** adv

triv•i•a /ˈtrɪviə/ noun [U] **1** facts about subjects such as sports, history, movies, or television programs that people use to answer questions in a game **2** unimportant facts or details: *The papers are just full of trivia about celebrities.*

triv•i•al /ˈtrɪviəl/ adj not very interesting, serious, or valuable: *Why are they so upset over such a trivial matter?*

triv•i•al•ize /ˈtrɪviəˌlaɪz/ verb [T] to make something seem less important or serious than it really is

trol•ley /ˈtrɑli/ noun [C] **1 trolley** or **trolley car** *American* an electric vehicle for carrying passengers that moves along RAILS in the road —*picture* → C7 **2** *British* a SHOPPING CART or a CART for suitcases, etc.

trom•bone /trɑmˈboʊn/ noun [C] a musical instrument consisting of two metal tubes. You play it by blowing into it and sliding one tube forward and backward. —*picture* → BRASS

troop /trup/ verb [I] to walk somewhere in a group

troop•er /ˈtrupər/ noun [C] **1** *American* a STATE TROOPER **2** someone of low rank in the army

troops /trups/ noun [plural] soldiers

tro•phy /ˈtroʊfi/ noun [C] a large silver cup or similar object that is given as a prize to the winner of a sports competition

trop•i•cal /ˈtrɑpɪk(ə)l/ adj in or from the hottest parts of the world

tro•pics, the /ˈtrɑpɪk/ the hottest parts of the world, that are near the EQUATOR (=imaginary line around the middle of the Earth)

trot¹ /trɑt/ verb [I] to walk quickly with short steps, but without running

PHRASAL VERB ˌ**trot sth** ˈ**out** *showing*

T

disapproval to provide an explanation, excuse, or piece of information that has been used many times before

trot² /trɑt/ noun [singular] the speed of a horse or other animal when it trots

trou•ble¹ /ˈtrʌb(ə)l/ noun ★★★

1 problems/worries	4 when blame is likely
2 additional effort	5 violence
3 unpleasant situation	+ PHRASES

1 [C/U] problems, worries, or difficulties: *The company has had serious financial troubles recently.* ♦ *The plane had engine trouble and had to land in Miami.* ♦ *This old car has **caused a lot of trouble** for us.* ♦ *I'm **having** some **trouble with** my knee.* ♦ *He was **having trouble** hearing her* (=finding it difficult to hear her).

2 [U] additional or special effort that causes you problems: *I don't mind waiting – **it's no trouble**.* ♦ *Thank you for **taking the trouble to** reply.* ♦ *Growing roses **is more trouble than it is worth**.* ♦ *He'd **gone to a lot of trouble to** make the evening go perfectly.*

3 [U] an unpleasant, difficult, or dangerous situation: *I knew we were **in trouble** when the elevator stopped.* ♦ *The airplane **ran into** serious **trouble** soon after takeoff.*

4 [U] a situation for which you are likely to be blamed, criticized, or punished: *I hear she's **in trouble with** the police again.* ♦ *If he hears about this, you'll be **in big trouble**.* ♦ *I **got into trouble** for being late.*

5 [C/U] fighting, violence, or bad behavior: *There's been **a lot of trouble** in the neighborhood recently.* ♦ ***The trouble started** after a youth was arrested.*

PHRASES **asking for trouble** doing something that is very likely to cause you problems or difficulties: *Delaying surgery is just asking for trouble.*

the trouble with sb/sth used for talking about something that causes problems, worries, or difficulties: *The trouble with my parents is they think I'm still a child.*

trou•ble² /ˈtrʌb(ə)l/ verb [T] to make someone worried: *I could tell that something was troubling her.*

T

trou•bled /ˈtrʌb(ə)ld/ adj **1** worried about the problems that you have **2** a troubled place, time, or situation is affected by many problems

trou•ble•mak•er /ˈtrʌb(ə)lˌmeɪkər/ noun [C] someone who deliberately causes a lot of problems

trou•ble•shoot•ing /ˈtrʌb(ə)lˌʃutɪŋ/ noun [U] the activity of finding out the cause of a problem and then solving it
—**trou•ble•shoot•er** noun [C]

trou•ble•some /ˈtrʌb(ə)lsəm/ adj causing annoying problems or difficulties

ˈtrouble ˌspot noun [C] a place where there is often fighting between groups

trough /trɔf/ noun [C] **1** a long open container that is used for holding food or water for animals **2** a period when something that rises and falls regularly is at a low level: *the peaks and troughs in demand*

trounce /traʊns/ verb [T] to easily defeat an opponent in a game, competition, election, etc.

troupe /trup/ noun [C] a group of performers

trou•sers /ˈtraʊzərz/ noun [plural] PANTS

trout /traʊt/ (plural **trout**) noun [C/U] a fish that lives in rivers and lakes, or this fish eaten as food

trow•el /ˈtraʊəl/ noun [C] **1** a small tool with a curved blade that is used in gardens for digging **2** a small tool with a flat blade that is used for spreading substances such as CEMENT

tru•an•cy /ˈtruənsi/ noun [U] the act or habit of staying away from school without permission

tru•ant /ˈtruənt/ noun [C] a child who stays away from school without permission

truce /trus/ noun [C] a temporary agreement between two opponents to stop fighting

truck¹ /trʌk/ noun [C] ★★

1 a large road vehicle that is used for carrying goods: *a truck driver*

2 a vehicle like a car in the front, but with a flat open space in the back = PICKUP

truck² /trʌk/ verb [T] to take goods somewhere in a truck

truck•er /ˈtrʌkər/ noun [C] someone whose job is to drive a truck

truck•ing /ˈtrʌkɪŋ/ noun [U] the job or business of carrying goods in trucks

ˈtruck ˌstop noun [C] *American* an area beside a major road where trucks can stop and the drivers can get a meal and gas

trudge /trʌdʒ/ verb [I] to walk somewhere with slow heavy steps

true /tru/ adj ★★★

1 based on facts or on things that really happened ≠ FALSE: *The film is based on **a true story**.* ♦ *It rains a lot in the northwest, and that is especially **true of** Vancouver.* ♦ **+that** *Is it true that you're looking for a new job?*

2 real or actual, especially when compared with how something seems to be: *Lara never shows her **true feelings**.* ♦ *The study shows that **the true cost** of the system is much higher than people think.*

3 having all the qualities that you expect in a particular type of person, thing, or feeling = GENUINE: *Curry was a true champion in every way.* ♦ *The country is not yet a true democracy.* ♦ *true love*

4 if you are true to someone or something, you continue to be loyal to them: *Through the years, Doug **stayed true to** his wife.*

PHRASES **come true** if a wish, dream, fear, etc. comes true, it really happens: *Meeting Joe was like **a dream come true*** (=exactly what you have always wanted).

true to life similar to what really happens in people's lives: *The characters in this novel are so true to life.*

truf•fle /ˈtrʌf(ə)l/ noun [C] **1** a plant that you eat that grows under the ground and is very expensive to buy **2** a soft chocolate candy

tru•ly /ˈtruli/ adv **1** completely: *a truly wonderful job* ♦ *She was someone who truly understood children.* **2** used for emphasizing that you really mean what you are saying: *I truly believe you are the right person for the job.*

trump card /ˈtrʌmp ˌkɑrd/ noun [C] an

advantage that you have that your opponent does not have

trum•pet /ˈtrʌmpət/ noun [C] a metal musical instrument that you play by blowing into it as you press buttons on the top *—picture* → BRASS

trun•dle /ˈtrʌnd(ə)l/ verb [I/T] to roll slowly on wheels, or to make something roll slowly on wheels

trunk /trʌŋk/ noun [C]

1 main part of tree	4 elephant's nose
2 covered space in car	5 main part of body
3 large strong box	

1 the main part of a tree that the branches grow out of *—picture* → TREE **2** *American* the covered space in the back of a car, used for carrying things in *—picture* → C6 **3** a large strong box with a lid, used for storing things **4** an elephant's long nose **5** the part of your body between your waist and your head, not including your arms or head

trunks /trʌŋks/ noun [plural] a piece of clothing that men wear for swimming *—picture* → C5

trust¹ /trʌst/ verb [T] ★★ to believe that someone or something is good, honest, or reliable: *Both communities have to trust each other.* ♦ *Never trust cheap locks like these.* ♦ **trust sb to do sth** *Can we trust you to give John the message?* ♦ **trust sb with sth** *I trust Dana with all my secrets.*

Word family: trust

Words in the same family as ***trust***

- **trusting** *adj*
- **trusty** *adj*
- **trustworthy** *adj*
- **untrustworthy** *adj*
- **distrust** *n, v*
- **mistrust** *n, v*

trust² /trʌst/ noun ★★
1 [U] a feeling that you trust someone or something: *The doctor-patient relationship has to be based on trust.* ♦ *We have to* ***put our trust in*** *the democratic system.*
2 [C/U] *legal* an arrangement in which a person or an organization manages someone else's money or property, or the money or property that they manage: *The land will* ***be held in trust*** *by the Church.*

trus•tee /trʌˈsti/ noun [C] someone who is responsible for taking care of money or property that belongs to someone else

ˈtrust ˌfund noun [C] an amount of money that is invested and managed for someone, usually a child

trust•ing /ˈtrʌstɪŋ/ adj willing to trust people, especially when it is not a sensible thing to do

trust•wor•thy /ˈtrʌs(t)ˌwɜrði/ adj someone who is trustworthy can be trusted ≠ UNTRUSTWORTHY

trust•y /ˈtrʌsti/ adj *humorous* a trusty person or possession is one that you know that you can depend on

truth /truθ/ noun ★★★
1 [U] the actual facts about something, rather than what people think or say is true: *We finally learned* ***the truth about*** *Gina's past.* ♦ ***Tell me the truth:*** *did you take the money?* ♦ ***The truth is that*** *they haven't solved the problem.*
2 [U] the quality of being true: ***There is some truth to*** *his story* (=it is partly true). ♦ *Are you questioning* ***the truth of*** *his accusations?*
3 [C] an idea that is accepted by most people as being true: *Is it* ***a universal truth*** (=something that is true in all situations) *that exercise is good for you?*

PHRASE **to tell (you) the truth** used for admitting something, or for saying what you really think about something: *To tell you the truth, I don't care.*

Words often used with truth

Verbs often used with ***truth*** *(sense 1)*

- **discover, establish, find out, get at, learn, uncover** + THE + TRUTH: find out the truth
- **admit, reveal, tell** + THE + TRUTH: say what the truth is

truth•ful /ˈtruθf(ə)l/ adj **1** a truthful person says what is true, and does not lie: *He was sure she wasn't being completely truthful.* **2** a truthful statement only contains things that are true —**truth•ful•ly** adv

try¹ /traɪ/ (past tense and past participle **tried** /traɪd/) verb ★★★
1 [I/T] to attempt to do something: *Don't try any of your tricks with me!* ♦ *We'll just have to* ***try harder*** *next time.* ♦ **try to do sth** *Just try to stay calm.* ♦ **try and do sth** *I will try and get the report to you today.*
2 [T] to do something in order to find out whether it is enjoyable, appropriate, or effective: *Have you tried these cookies? They're great!* ♦ *Let's try something different with your hair this time.* ♦ *You should try yoga if you're feeling stressed – you might like it.* ♦ **try doing sth** *She tried talking about it to Steve, but couldn't make him change his mind.*
3 [I/T] to go to a particular place in order to find something, or to go to a particular person in order to get information: *There's a hardware store down the street – you could try there.* ♦ *Try Dina – she knows a lot about the law.*
4 [T] to judge a person or case in a court of law: *Franklin's case will be tried on August 25th.* ♦ **try sb for sth** *He was tried for murder and found guilty.*

PHRASE **try your hand at sth** to do an activity for the first time in order to find out whether you like it, or whether you are good at it

PHRASAL VERBS **ˌtry sth ˈon** to put on a piece of clothing in order to see how it looks and whether it fits

ˌtry sth ˈout to test something in order to see what it is like or whether it is appropriate or effective

ˌtry ˈout for sth *American* to try to become a member of a team, or to try to get a part in a play or movie, by showing someone how well you can play or perform

try² /traɪ/ noun [C] an attempt to do something: *Charlie passed the test on his first try.* ♦ *There are no guarantees that it will work, but it's worth a try.* ♦ *"I can't lift it." "Here, let me give it a try."*

try•ing /ˈtraɪɪŋ/ adj difficult to deal with in a way that makes you annoyed or tired: *We've all had a very trying day.*

ˈtry-ˌout noun [C] *American* a test for someone

T

who wants to become a member of a team or wants to get a part in a play or movie

T-shirt /ˈtiˌʃɜrt/ noun [C] a soft shirt that has short sleeves and no collar or buttons *—picture* → C5

tsp. abbrev teaspoon

tub /tʌb/ noun [C] **1** a BATHTUB **2** a small container with a lid, used for holding or storing food: *ice cream tubs* **3** a large round container with a flat bottom: *tubs of flowers and shrubs* → HOT TUB

tu•ba /ˈtubə/ noun [C] a large metal musical instrument that is a curved tube with a wide open end. You play it by blowing into it as you press buttons on the top. *—picture* → BRASS

tube /tub/ noun [C] ★
1 a long narrow object similar to a pipe that liquid or gas can move through: *Nurses had to feed Dan through a tube.*
2 a long narrow plastic or metal container that you squeeze in order to push out the soft substance inside: ***a tube of toothpaste***

tu•ber•cu•lo•sis /tʊˌbɜrkjəˈloʊsɪs/ noun [U] a serious infectious disease that affects your lungs

tub•ing /ˈtubɪŋ/ noun [U] a piece of tube, or a system of tubes

tuck /tʌk/ verb [T] to put something in a place where it looks neat or is hidden: *She tucked her glasses into her pocket.*
PHRASAL VERB **ˌtuck sb ˈin** to make sure that a child is warm and comfortable in bed, by covering them well: *I'll be right upstairs to tuck you in.*

Tues. or **Tue.** abbrev Tuesday

Tues•day /ˈtuzˌdeɪ/ noun [C/U] ★★★ the day after Monday and before Wednesday: *New Year's Day will be on a Tuesday this year.* ♦ *Do you work Tuesdays* (=every Tuesday)*?* ♦ *Last Tuesday they went to the zoo.* ♦ *We are leaving **on Tuesday**.*

tuft /tʌft/ noun [C] several pieces of grass, hair, feathers, or fibers that are all growing together

tug¹ /tʌg/ verb [I/T] to pull someone or something by making a short strong movement: *The little boy tugged on his mother's skirt.* → HEARTSTRINGS

tug² /tʌg/ noun [C] **1** a short strong pull **2** a TUG BOAT

ˈtug ˌboat noun [C] a small powerful boat that is used for pulling ships in ports

ˌtug-of-ˈwar noun [C] a situation in which two people or groups try very hard to get something that they both want

tu•i•tion /tuˈɪʃ(ə)n/ noun [U] money that you pay to take classes at a college, university, or private school

tu•lip /ˈtulɪp/ noun [C] a colorful flower that is shaped like a cup *—picture* → C9

tum•ble /ˈtʌmb(ə)l/ verb [I] **1** if a price or value tumbles, it suddenly becomes much lower **2** to suddenly fall to the ground —**tum•ble** noun [C]

tum•bler /ˈtʌmblər/ noun [C] a drinking glass without a handle or STEM (=long thin part connected to the base)

tum•my /ˈtʌmi/ noun [C] *informal* your stomach

tu•mor /ˈtumər/ noun [C] a mass of cells in your body that grow in a way that is not normal and that can cause serious illness

tu•mul•tu•ous /tuˈmʌltʃuəs/ adj noisy and excited: *tumultuous applause*

tu•na /ˈtunə/ noun [C/U] a large fish that lives in the Pacific and Atlantic Oceans, or this fish eaten as food

tune¹ /tun/ noun [C] *informal* ★ a song or simple piece of music: *the station that plays all your favorite tunes* ♦ *a Russian folk tune*
PHRASES **change your tune** to change your opinion or attitude
in tune producing the right note when you sing or play music: *He can sing any song perfectly in tune.*
in tune with understanding the feelings, opinions, or needs of a group of people: *Voters felt she was in tune with their needs and problems.*
out of tune producing the wrong note when you sing or play music: *One of the guitars sounded a little out of tune.*
to the tune of used for emphasizing how large an amount of money is: *The company is in debt to the tune of $2.1 billion.*

tune² /tun/ verb [T] **1** to make small changes to a musical instrument so that it will produce the correct notes **2** to make small changes to an engine or machine so that it works better
PHRASAL VERBS **ˌtune ˈin 1** to listen to or watch a particular broadcast on the radio or television: *Millions of people tuned in to watch the election results.* **2 be tuned in (to sth)** to understand something such as a situation or other people's feelings
ˌtune (sb/sth) ˈout *very informal* to stop paying attention
ˌtune ˈup if a group of musicians tune up, they make small changes to their instruments so that they can play well together

tu•nic /ˈtunɪk/ noun [C] **1** a long loose shirt **2** a short jacket that is part of a uniform

tun•nel¹ /ˈtʌn(ə)l/ noun [C] ★ a passage through a hill or under the ground: *We watched the train enter a tunnel.*

tun•nel² /ˈtʌn(ə)l/ verb [T] to dig a tunnel

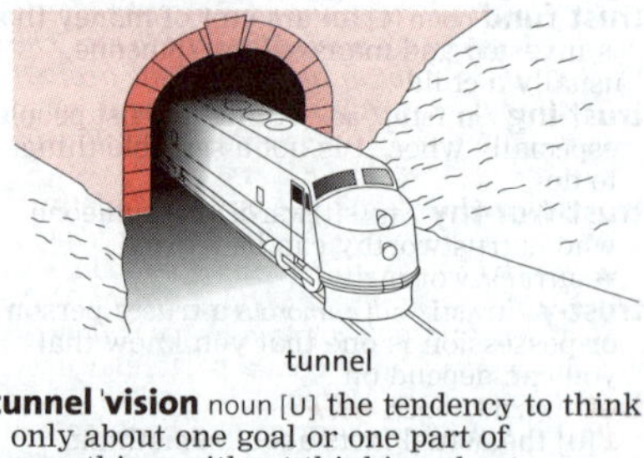
tunnel

ˌtunnel ˈvision noun [U] the tendency to think only about one goal or one part of something, without thinking about anything else

tur•ban /ˈtɜrbən/ noun [C] a long piece of cloth that is wrapped around the head like a hat. It is worn by some men in the Sikh, Hindu, and Muslim religions.

T

tur•bine /ˈtɜrˌbaɪn/ noun [C] a machine that produces power by using the pressure of liquid or gas on a wheel

tur•bu•lence /ˈtɜrbjələns/ noun [U] **1** sudden violent movements of air or water **2** a confusing situation in which everything is changing in an uncontrolled way: *a period of turbulence after the death of the dictator*

tur•bu•lent /ˈtɜrbjələnt/ adj **1** turbulent air or water moves suddenly and violently in different directions **2** a turbulent situation, place, or time is one in which there is a lot of uncontrolled change: *the country's turbulent history*

turf /tɜrf/ noun [U] **1** *informal* an area that one person or group considers to be their own, and that they may fight to keep **2** artificial grass used for covering a sports field **3** short grass and the earth that is under it

tur•key /ˈtɜrki/ noun [C/U] a large bird that is similar to a chicken, or the meat from this bird

tur•moil /ˈtɜrˌmɔɪl/ noun [U] a situation in which there is a lot of excitement or uncontrolled activity: *economic/political turmoil* ♦ *Her life seemed to be in turmoil.*

turn[1] /tɜrn/ verb ★★★

1 change your position	6 become particular age
2 change sth's position	7 move page
3 change direction	+ PHRASES
4 move in circle	+ PHRASAL VERBS
5 do/become sth else	

1 [I/T] to change the position of your body or your head so that you are facing in a different direction: *She turned and smiled at me.* ♦ *He **turned his head** and looked around the room.* ♦ *Lopez just glared at the other man and then **turned away**.* ♦ *The girls in front **turned around** and smiled.* ♦ *Maria **turned to** the reporters and said: "I'm innocent."*

2 [T] to change the position of something so that it is pointing in a different direction: **turn sth around** *Turn your chairs around so you're facing me.*

3 [I/T] to change the direction in which you are moving or traveling, or to make something change direction: *We **turned into** our driveway, glad to get home.* ♦ *The truck **turned around** and came back down the hill.* ♦ *Follow this road, then **turn right** after the school.* ♦ **turn sth around/back/into etc.** *They ordered the pilot to turn the plane around.*

4 [I/T] to make a circular movement, or to make something move in a circle: *I heard the key turn in the lock.*

5 [linking verb] to change and do something else, or to become something else: *The weather turned chilly in the afternoon.* ♦ *The crowd was beginning to turn violent.* ♦ *The lizard's skin turned green as we watched.*

6 [linking verb] to become a particular age: *He turned 40 in March.*

7 [T] if you turn the page of a book or magazine, you move it in order to read a different page

PHRASES **turn your back on sb/sth** to refuse to accept someone or something that you have previously accepted

turn a corner to reach a stage in which a situation improves, after a difficult period

PHRASAL VERBS **ˌturn (sb) aˈgainst sb/sth** to stop liking or supporting someone or something and start opposing them, or to make someone do this: *She's turned your whole family against you.*

ˌturn sth aˈround to make something such as a company or team successful again after a period of being unsuccessful: *The $400 million loan will help turn the country's economy around.*

ˌturn sb aˈway to refuse to let someone come into a place: *Reporters who visited the training camp were turned away.*

ˌturn ˈback to return the same way that you came instead of continuing on your journey: *Bad weather forced them to turn back.*

ˌturn sth ˈdown 1 to refuse to accept an offer or request: *How could you turn down such a fantastic job?* **2** to reduce the amount of sound, heat, or light that is produced by a piece of equipment, by pressing a button or by moving a switch ≠ TURN STH UP: *Could you **turn the music down** a little?*

ˌturn sb ˈin to tell the police about someone who has committed a crime: *His own brother turned him in.* ♦ *She turned herself in to local police.*

ˌturn sth ˈin 1 to give something to someone in authority: *You're the only person who hasn't turned in their report.* **2** to return something that you have been using to the organization or company that owns it: *I think Mr. Watkins has already turned in his pass and his pager.*

ˌturn (sth) ˈinto sth to change or develop into something different, or to make something change or develop into something different: *Our vacation turned into a nightmare.* ♦ *They turned her first book into a movie.*

ˌturn ˈoff to leave the road that you are traveling along in order to go along another one: *Drive east along I-95, and **turn off at** exit 35.*

ˌturn sb ˈoff 1 to make someone feel bored or no longer interested in something: *This sort of talk could turn a lot of voters off.* **2** to stop someone from feeling sexually attracted or sexually excited ≠ TURN SB ON

ˌturn sth ˈoff to stop using a piece of equipment or a supply of gas, electricity, or water by pressing, turning, or moving something ≠ TURN STH ON: *Will you turn the television off, please?* ♦ *The emergency crew turned off the power and gas supplies.*

ˌturn sb ˈon to make someone feel sexually attracted or sexually excited ≠ TURN SB OFF

ˌturn sth ˈon to start using a piece of equipment or a supply of gas, electricity, or water by pressing, turning, or moving something ≠ TURN STH OFF: *Is your computer turned on?* ♦ *Let's turn the radio on and see if it works.*

ˈturn on sb to make a sudden and unexpected attack on someone using violence or very angry words: *The dog suddenly turned on me.*

ˌturn ˈout 1 to develop in a particular way, or to have a particular result: *I'm sure it will **turn out all right** in the end.* ♦ ***As it turned out**, the storm missed Puerto Rico.* ♦

T

It all ***turned out to be*** *a mistake.* **2** to go somewhere in order to be present at an event or in order to take part in an activity: *Only 47 percent of the electorate* ***turned out*** *to vote.*

ˌturn sth ˈout 1 to stop using a light by pressing a button or moving a switch ≠ TURN STH ON **2** to produce something in large numbers: *The company turns out 2,000 small planes a year.*

ˌturn (sth) ˈover to turn a page in a book or a sheet of paper so that the other side is towards you: *You may turn your exam papers over now.*

ˌturn sb/sth ˈover to give someone or something to someone who is in a position of authority: *The local police* ***turned him over to*** *the FBI.*

ˈturn to sb to go to someone for help: *There are plenty of people you can turn to for advice.*

ˈturn (sth) to sth *same as* **turn (sth) into sth**: *Shock at the killings quickly turned to anger.* ♦ *Roads were turned to mud by days of rain.*

ˈturn to sth to look for a particular page in a book: *Turn to page 17 for our prices.*

ˌturn ˈup 1 to arrive somewhere: *She failed to turn up for work on Monday.* **2** to be found by accident after being lost or not known about: *The documents finally turned up in an office down the hall.* **3** to happen unexpectedly: *You'll get another job:* ***something is bound to turn up*** *soon.*

ˌturn sth ˈup to increase the amount of sound, heat, or light that is produced by a piece of equipment, by pressing a button or by moving a switch ≠ TURN STH DOWN: *Can you turn the volume up a little?*

turn² /tɜrn/ noun [C] ★★★

1 time to do sth	4 change in situation
2 in a road	5 movement in circle
3 change of direction	+ PHRASES

1 the time when you can or must do something, because you are part of a group of people who are each doing the same activity, one after the other: *You've already moved your piece – it's my turn now.* ♦ *You'll just have to* ***wait your turn*** (=be patient until it is your turn). ♦ **sb's turn to do sth** *I think it's your turn to wash the dishes.*

2 a place where a road bends to the right or left, or where one road leads away from another: *There's* ***a very sharp turn*** *at the end of the road.* ♦ *We* ***took a wrong turn*** (=turned onto the wrong road) *about two miles back.*

3 a change of direction made by a person or vehicle: *He* ***made a left turn*** *onto a quiet street.*

4 a change in a situation: *The weather suddenly* ***took a turn for the worse*** (=became worse). ♦ *We wanted to express our shock at today's tragic* ***turn of events*** (=unexpected change in the situation).

5 a circular movement, when something is turned around

PHRASES **in turn 1** one after the other in a particular order: *We will deal with each of these problems in turn.* **2** as a result of something that is part of a connected series of events: *Bad farming methods caused soil erosion, and this in turn made the land less productive.*

take turns if people take turns to do something, each of them does their share of it, one after the other: *We took turns steering the boat.*

the turn of the century the time around the end of one century and the beginning of the next one: *a mansion built at the turn of the century*

turn·a·round /ˈtɜrnəˌraʊnd/ noun [C] a situation in which something changes completely from a bad situation to a good one: *an economic turnaround*

ˈturning ˌpoint noun [C] a time when an important change takes place =CROSSROADS: *1956 marked a turning point in Franco's political and personal life.*

tur·nip /ˈtɜrnɪp/ noun [C] a large round vegetable that grows under the ground

ˈturn-ˌoff noun [C] **1** a road that leads off a main road or highway **2** *informal* something that stops you from feeling sexually attracted or excited

turn·out /ˈtɜrnˌaʊt/ noun [singular] the number of people who come to an event: *We're expecting a good turnout at tonight's meeting.*

turn·o·ver /ˈtɜrnˌoʊvər/ noun **1** [C/U] the rate at which people leave a business, school, etc. and new people arrive: *a high turnover of staff* **2** [C/U] the value of the goods and services that a company sells in a particular period of time **3** [C] a sweet food like a small PIE, filled with fruit

turn·pike /ˈtɜrnˌpaɪk/ noun [C] *American* a highway that drivers must pay to use

ˈturn ˌsignal noun [C] *American* a light on a vehicle that flashes to show in which direction it is going to turn —*picture* → C6

turn·stile /ˈtɜrnˌstaɪl/ noun [C] a gate with metal bars that move in a circle so that only one person can go through at a time

turn·ta·ble /ˈtɜrnˌteɪb(ə)l/ noun [C] a RECORD PLAYER, especially of the type used by DJS

tur·quoise /ˈtɜrˌkwɔɪz/ adj bright green-blue in color —**tur·quoise** noun [U]

tur·ret /ˈtʌrət/ noun [C] a small tower on the top of a building such as a castle

tur·tle /ˈtɜrt(ə)l/ noun [C] *American* an animal with a shell and four short legs that lives on the land or in water

tur·tle·neck /ˈtɜrt(ə)lˌnek/ noun [C] *American* a sweater with a high neck that folds over —*picture* → NECKLINE

tusk /tʌsk/ noun [C] one of the two very long pointed teeth on an animal such as an elephant

tus·sle /ˈtʌs(ə)l/ noun [C] *informal* a short fight —**tus·sle** verb [I]

tu·tor¹ /ˈtutər/ noun [C] **1** someone who gives private lessons in a particular subject **2** someone who teaches and advises a group of students at a university

tu·tor² /ˈtutər/ verb [T] *formal* to teach one person or a small group of people

tu·to·ri·al /tuˈtɔriəl/ noun [C] **1** a book or a computer program that gives instructions on how to do something **2** a class in which a small group of students discusses a subject with a tutor at a university or college

tux•e•do /tʌkˈsidoʊ/ or **tux** /tʌks/ noun [C] a type of suit that men wear on very formal occasions

TV /ˌtiˈvi/ noun [C/U] ★★★ television: *a TV show* ♦ *What's on TV tonight?*

twang /twæŋ/ noun [singular] **1** the way that someone's voice sounds when it comes through their nose as well as through their mouth **2** the sound that a tight string makes when you pull it —**twang** verb [I/T]

tweak /twik/ verb [T] **1** *informal* to make small changes to something in order to improve it **2** to pull or twist a part of someone's body —**tweak** noun [C]

tweed /twid/ noun [U] a type of thick rough cloth made from wool of different colors

tweez•ers /ˈtwizərz/ noun [plural] a tool that you use for picking up very small objects or for pulling out hairs. It consists of two narrow pieces of metal joined at one end.

twelfth /twelfθ/ number in the place or position counted as number 12

twelve /twelv/ number the number 12

twen•ti•eth /ˈtwentiəθ/ number in the place or position counted as number 20

twen•ty /ˈtwenti/ number the number 20

twice[1] /twaɪs/ adv ★★★

1 two times: *He's called twice already this morning.* ♦ *I go to the gym twice a week.*

2 two times the amount or rate of something: *The United States has **twice as many** people as Japan.*

twice[2] /twaɪs/ determiner ★ two times the amount or rate of something: *Wages are rising at twice the rate of inflation.*

twig /twɪg/ noun [C] a very small thin branch on a tree or bush

twi•light /ˈtwaɪˌlaɪt/ noun [U] the time in the evening when the sky is beginning to get dark = DUSK

twin[1] /twɪn/ noun [C] ★ one of two children who were born at the same time to the same mother: *my twin brother/sister*

twin[2] /twɪn/ adj forming a pair of two similar things: *a plane with twin engines*

ˌtwin ˈbed noun [C] the smallest size of bed, made for one adult

twinge /twɪndʒ/ noun [C] **1** a sudden short pain **2** a sudden unpleasant feeling: *a twinge of sadness/regret/guilt*

twin•kle /ˈtwɪŋk(ə)l/ verb [I] **1** if lights or stars twinkle, the light from them seems to get brighter then weaker **2** if someone's eyes twinkle, they seem to shine because the person is happy —**twin•kle** noun [singular]

twirl /twɜrl/ verb [I/T] to move in circles, or to make something move in circles —**twirl** noun [C]

twist[1] /twɪst/ verb ★

1 bend out of shape	4 change meaning
2 turn sth in circle	5 have many bends
3 injure part of body	+ PHRASE

1 [I/T] to bend or turn into a different shape, or to force something out of its original shape by bending it or turning it: *The force of the explosion had twisted the metal.*

2 [T] to turn something in a circle with your hands or fingers: *Kathryn sat anxiously twisting a handkerchief in her hands.*

3 [T] to injure a part of your body by suddenly bending it too much: ***I twisted my ankle**, so I won't be able to play.*

4 [T] to change the intended meaning of something slightly, so that it means what you want it to mean: *You're twisting my words.*

5 [I] if a road or river twists, it has a lot of bends in it: *The path twists and turns up the mountainside.*

PHRASE **twist sb's arm** *informal* to persuade someone to do something that they do not want to do

twist[2] /twɪst/ noun [C] **1** a sudden unexpected change in a situation: *This is the final tragic twist in a long story.* **2** a bend in a road or river: *The island roads are full of twists and turns.* **3** a movement in which you turn something: *With a twist of his wrist, he untied the ropes.*

twist•ed /ˈtwɪstəd/ adj **1** bent into a shape that is not normal: *All that was left of the car was a tangle of twisted metal.* **2** *informal* someone who is twisted behaves in a strange and cruel way

twist•er /ˈtwɪstər/ noun [C] *informal* a TORNADO

twitch /twɪtʃ/ verb [I] if part of your body twitches, it makes an uncontrolled movement —**twitch** noun [C]

two /tu/ number ★★★ the number 2

PHRASES **in two** into two pieces: *The explosion had broken the plane in two.*

put two and two together to guess what is happening based on what you have seen or heard

two-di•men•sion•al /ˌtu dɪˈmenʃən(ə)l/ adj **1** a two-dimensional shape is flat **2** a two-dimensional character in a book, play, or movie does not have the complicated personality of a real person

ˈtwo-ˌtime verb [T] *informal* to be dishonest with your sexual partner by secretly having a relationship with another person

ˌtwo-way ˈstreet noun [singular] *American* a situation in which two people or two groups of people need to work together

TX abbrev Texas

ty•coon /ˌtaɪˈkun/ noun [C] someone rich and powerful who is involved in business or industry

tying the present participle of **tie**[1]

type[1] /taɪp/ noun ★★★

1 [C] a group of people or things with similar qualities that make them different from other groups = KIND, SORT: *What **type of** dog do you have?* ♦ *It's a good price for a bike of **this type**.* ♦ *We provide advice to **all types of** businesses.*

2 [U] letters that are printed in a book, magazine, or newspaper, or typed using a keyboard: *The book is produced **in large type**.*

3 [C] someone with particular interests or qualities: *The bar is popular with arty types.* ♦ *Sam isn't the romantic type.*

PHRASE **be sb's type** to have the particular qualities that someone finds attractive: *Joe's nice, but he's not really my type.*

T

type² /taɪp/ verb [I/T] to write something using a keyboard

type·face /ˈtaɪpˌfeɪs/ noun [C] a set of letters and numbers of the same design, used in printing or computing

type·writ·er /ˈtaɪpˌraɪtər/ noun [C] a machine with a keyboard that you use for typing words directly onto a sheet of paper

type·writ·ten /ˈtaɪpˌrɪt(ə)n/ adj produced using a typewriter, not written by hand

ty·phoid /ˈtaɪˌfɔɪd/ noun [U] a serious disease that you can get from food or dirty water

ty·phoon /ˌtaɪˈfun/ noun [C] a tropical storm with strong winds

ty·phus /ˈtaɪfəs/ noun [U] a serious disease spread by some small insects

typ·i·cal /ˈtɪpɪk(ə)l/ adj ★★★
1 like most things of the same type: *It's a typical working-class community.* ♦ *a typical reaction/response/comment* ♦ *His opinions are fairly **typical of** people of his generation.*
2 behaving in a way that is usual for a particular person: *She responded with typical enthusiasm.* ♦ *It was **typical of** him to want to help.*
3 *spoken* used for saying that you are not surprised that something bad has happened: *The show's been canceled? Typical!* ♦ ***It's typical**, just when we might win, two of our players got injured.*

typ·i·cal·ly /ˈtɪpɪkli/ adv **1** usually: *The courses typically last for three days.* **2** with the typical qualities of a particular person or group of people

typ·i·fy /ˈtɪpɪˌfaɪ/ verb [T] to be a typical example or feature of something

typ·ing /ˈtaɪpɪŋ/ noun [U] the skill of using a TYPEWRITER or computer keyboard to write documents

typ·ist /ˈtaɪpɪst/ noun [C] someone who types using a TYPEWRITER or a computer keyboard, especially as their job

tyr·an·ny /ˈtɪrəni/ noun [C/U] cruel and unfair treatment by someone in a position of power, especially a government —**ty·ran·ni·cal** /tɪˈrænɪk(ə)l/ adj

ty·rant /ˈtaɪrənt/ noun [C] someone in a position of power who behaves in a cruel and unfair way

tyre /ˈtaɪr/ the British spelling of **tire¹**

U

Uu

u or **U** /ju/ noun [C/U] the 21st letter of the English alphabet → U-TURN

U /ju/ pronoun *informal* a written form of "you," used in e-mails and TEXT MESSAGES

u·biq·ui·tous /juˈbɪkwɪtəs/ adj *formal* seeming to be everywhere

ud·der /ˈʌdər/ noun [C] the part under the body of a cow and some other female animals that produces milk

UFO /ˌju ef ˈoʊ/ noun [C] unidentified flying object: a mysterious object that flies through the sky, that some people think is a sign of life from other planets

ugh /ʌg/ interjection used for writing the sound that people make when they think that something is extremely unpleasant

ug·ly /ˈʌgli/ adj ★
1 unpleasant to look at ≠ BEAUTIFUL
2 an ugly situation involves violent or angry behavior: *an ugly confrontation*

uh huh /ʌ ˈhʌ/ interjection used for writing the sound that people make when they agree with something

uh-oh /ˈʌ ˌoʊ/ interjection used for writing the sound that people make when they realize that something has gone wrong

uh-uh /ə ˈhʌ/ interjection used for writing the sound that people make when they disagree with something

U.K., the /ˌju ˈkeɪ/ the United Kingdom

ul·cer /ˈʌlsər/ noun [C] a sore area in your body or on your skin that sometimes BLEEDS or produces a poisonous substance: *a mouth/stomach ulcer* —**ul·cer·at·ed** /ˈʌlsəˌreɪtəd/ adj

ul·te·ri·or mo·tive /ʌlˌtɪriər ˈmoʊtɪv/ noun [C] a secret reason for doing something

ul·ti·mate¹ /ˈʌltɪmət/ adj **1** happening at the end of a process or activity = EVENTUAL: *Independence remains their ultimate political goal.* **2** as good or as bad as possible: *The Nobel Prize is the ultimate award for any scientist.* **3** if you have something such as ultimate power or responsibility, you have more power or responsibility than anyone else: *Parents must have ultimate responsibility for their children's safety.*

ul·ti·mate² /ˈʌltɪmət/ noun **the ultimate in sth** the best or most perfect example of something

ul·ti·mate·ly /ˈʌltɪmətli/ adv **1** after a process or activity has ended: *Computerization could ultimately lead to more job losses.* **2** used for emphasizing the main point that you are talking about: *What worries me, ultimately, is the cost of the program.*

ul·ti·ma·tum /ˌʌltɪˈmeɪtəm/ noun [C] a statement that orders someone to do something and threatens to punish or attack them if they do not do it

ultra- /ʌltrə/ prefix extremely: *an ultra-modern kitchen*

ul·tra·son·ic /ˌʌltrəˈsɑnɪk/ adj used for describing sounds that are higher than the range of sounds that humans can hear

ul·tra·sound /ˈʌltrəˌsaʊnd/ noun [U] a way of producing an image of an organ or of a baby inside someone's body, using sound waves

ul·tra·vi·o·let /ˌʌltrəˈvaɪ(ə)lət/ adj ultraviolet light is beyond the normal range of colors that humans can see —**ul·tra·vi·o·let** noun [U]

um /ʌm/ interjection used for writing the sound that people make when they are thinking about what to say next

um·bil·i·cal cord /ʌmˌbɪlɪk(ə)l ˈkɔrd/ noun [C] a tube that connects a baby to its mother before it is born

um·brage /ˈʌmbrɪdʒ/ noun **take umbrage (at sth)** to be offended by something

um·brel·la¹ /ʌmˈbrelə/ noun [C] an object that you hold over your head when it is raining

umbrella

um•brel•la[2] /ʌmˈbrelə/ adj an umbrella organization consists of a lot of small groups

um•pire /ˈʌmˌpaɪr/ noun [C] someone whose job is to make sure that players obey the rules in some sports, for example tennis and baseball —*picture* → C15 —**um•pire** verb [I/T]

ump•teen /ˌʌmpˈtin/ determiner *informal* many —**ump•teenth** adj

UN, the /ˌjuˈen/ the United Nations: an international organization that encourages countries to work together in order to solve world problems

un- /ʌn/ prefix used with many adjectives, adverbs, and verbs to give the opposite meaning: *unhappy* ♦ *unhurriedly* ♦ *unzip*

un•a•bashed /ˌʌnəˈbæʃt/ adj not ashamed or embarrassed

un•a•bat•ed /ˌʌnəˈbeɪtəd/ adj *formal* without stopping

un•a•ble /ʌnˈeɪb(ə)l/ adj ★★★
unable to do sth *formal* not able to do something: *Some of the children were unable to read.* ♦ *Many teenagers feel unable to talk to their parents about their problems.*

un•a•bridged /ˌʌnəˈbrɪdʒd/ adj an unabridged book or article has not had any parts removed from it

un•ac•cept•a•ble /ˌʌnəkˈseptəb(ə)l/ adj too bad to be allowed to continue —**un•ac•cept•a•bly** adv

un•ac•com•pa•nied /ˌʌnəˈkʌmpənid/ adj **1** someone who is unaccompanied goes somewhere alone **2** an unaccompanied singer or musician sings or plays alone

un•ac•count•a•ble /ˌʌnəˈkaʊntəb(ə)l/ adj **1** people or organizations that are unaccountable do not have to explain their actions or decisions to anyone else **2** *formal* difficult or impossible to explain or understand —**un•ac•count•a•bly** adv

un•ac•count•ed /ˌʌnəˈkaʊntəd/ adj
unaccounted for if something is unaccounted for, you are unable to explain what happened to it or where it is

un•ac•cus•tomed /ˌʌnəˈkʌstəmd/ adj unusual
PHRASE **unaccustomed to sth** not used to something

un•ac•knowl•edged /ˌʌnəkˈnɑlɪdʒd/ adj not given the praise or admiration that you deserve

un•a•dul•ter•at•ed /ˌʌnəˈdʌltəˌreɪtəd/ adj **1** complete: used for emphasizing how good or bad a quality or feeling is **2** in a pure form with nothing added

un•ad•ven•tur•ous /ˌʌnədˈventʃərəs/ adj not interested in trying anything new or exciting

un•af•fect•ed /ˌʌnəˈfektəd/ adj **1** not changed or influenced by something **2** sincere and natural in your behavior

un•aid•ed /ʌnˈeɪdəd/ adv *formal* without help

un•al•tered /ʌnˈɔltərd/ adj not changed

un•am•big•u•ous /ˌʌnæmˈbɪgjʊəs/ adj clear and with only one possible meaning

u•nan•i•mous /jʊˈnænɪməs/ adj **1** a unanimous decision, vote, agreement, etc. is one that everyone agrees with **2** a group of people who are unanimous about something all agree about it —**u•na•nim•i•ty** /ˌjunəˈnɪməti/ noun [U], **u•nan•i•mous•ly** adv

un•an•nounced /ˌʌnəˈnaʊnst/ adv unexpectedly

un•an•swered /ʌnˈænsərd/ adj **1** an unanswered question or problem has not been answered or solved **2** an unanswered letter, message, or phone call has not had a reply

un•ap•peal•ing /ˌʌnəˈpilɪŋ/ adj not attractive or enjoyable

un•ap•pe•tiz•ing /ʌnˈæpəˌtaɪzɪŋ/ adj food that is unappetizing does not look or smell good

un•ap•proach•a•ble /ˌʌnəˈproʊtʃəb(ə)l/ adj not friendly and not easy to talk to

un•armed /ʌnˈɑrmd/ adj not carrying a weapon

un•a•shamed•ly /ˌʌnəˈʃeɪmədli/ adv in a way that shows that you are not embarrassed or worried about what other people think of you —**un•a•shamed** /ˌʌnəˈʃeɪmd/ adj

un•asked /ʌnˈæskt/ adj **1** an unasked question is a question that people have not asked **2** if you do something unasked, you do it without being asked or told to

un•as•sail•a•ble /ˌʌnəˈseɪləb(ə)l/ adj *formal* impossible to defeat, criticize, or argue with

un•as•sist•ed /ˌʌnəˈsɪstəd/ adj without help

un•as•sum•ing /ˌʌnəˈsumɪŋ/ adj behaving in a quiet pleasant way, without wanting to attract attention = MODEST

un•at•tached /ˌʌnəˈtætʃt/ adj not married, or not having a boyfriend or girlfriend

un•at•tain•a•ble /ˌʌnəˈteɪnəb(ə)l/ adj impossible to achieve or obtain

un•at•tend•ed /ˌʌnəˈtendəd/ adj left without being taken care of or dealt with

un•at•trac•tive /ˌʌnəˈtræktɪv/ adj **1** ugly **2** unpleasant or not enjoyable

un•au•thor•ized /ʌnˈɔθəˌraɪzd/ adj done without official permission

un•a•vail•a•ble /ˌʌnəˈveɪləb(ə)l/ adj **1** not able to go somewhere, meet someone, or do something **2** impossible to obtain

un•a•void•a•ble /ˌʌnəˈvɔɪdəb(ə)l/ adj impossible to stop from happening = INEVITABLE —**un•a•void•a•bly** adv

un•a•ware /ˌʌnəˈwer/ adj not realizing that something exists or is happening

un•a•wares /ˌʌnəˈwerz/ adv **catch/take sb unawares** to surprise someone, often making them feel confused or embarrassed

un•bal•anced /ʌnˈbælənst/ adj **1** giving only one view or opinion of a situation or subject = BIASED **2** mentally ill **3** not containing all the necessary parts in the correct amount: *an unbalanced diet*

un•bear•a•ble /ʌnˈberəb(ə)l/ adj too

unpleasant or painful to deal with —**un•bear•a•bly** adv

un•beat•a•ble /ʌnˈbitəb(ə)l/ adj **1** impossible to defeat **2** better than anything else of the same type

un•beat•en /ʌnˈbit(ə)n/ adj if a team, player, etc. is unbeaten, they have not been defeated

un•be•com•ing /ˌʌnbɪˈkʌmɪŋ/ adj *formal* behavior that is unbecoming is inappropriate for a particular type of person

un•be•liev•a•ble /ˌʌnbɪˈlivəb(ə)l/ adj **1** *informal* used for emphasizing how good, bad, impressive, etc. something is **2** too unlikely to be true or to be believed —**un•be•liev•a•bly** adv

un•bend•ing /ʌnˈbendɪŋ/ adj unwilling to change your opinions or beliefs

un•bi•ased /ʌnˈbaɪəst/ adj fair in the way that you describe or deal with a situation

un•blem•ished /ʌnˈblemɪʃt/ adj **1** without any faults or mistakes **2** without any marks that harm the appearance of something

un•block /ʌnˈblɑk/ verb [T] to remove something that is blocking a pipe or tube

un•born /ʌnˈbɔrn/ adj an unborn child is still inside its mother's body

un•break•a•ble /ʌnˈbreɪkəb(ə)l/ adj impossible to break

un•bro•ken /ʌnˈbroʊkən/ adj **1** continuing for a long time without stopping = CONTINUOUS **2** not broken or damaged

un•but•ton /ʌnˈbʌt(ə)n/ verb [T] to UNDO (=open) the buttons on a piece of clothing

un•called for /ʌnˈkɔld fɔr/ adj insulting or offensive

un•can•ny /ʌnˈkæni/ adj strange and mysterious —**un•can•ni•ly** adv

un•car•ing /ʌnˈkerɪŋ/ adj without any sympathy for other people

un•cer•e•mo•ni•ous•ly /ˌʌnserəˈmoʊniəsli/ adv done suddenly, with no attempt to be polite

un•cer•tain /ʌnˈsɜrt(ə)n/ adj **1** not clearly known or understood: *It is uncertain how they entered the property.* ♦ *The whole industry faces a very uncertain future.* **2** not feeling sure about something: *I left the meeting feeling uncertain about what to do.*
PHRASE **in no uncertain terms** in a way that is clear and definite: *She was told in no uncertain terms that she would have to accept the deal.*
—**un•cer•tain•ty** noun [C/U]

un•chal•lenged /ʌnˈtʃæləndʒd/ adj **1** accepted as right or correct **2** not stopped from going somewhere **3** a leader or CANDIDATE who is unchallenged is not opposed by anyone

un•chal•leng•ing /ʌnˈtʃæləndʒɪŋ/ adj too easy, and therefore not very interesting

un•changed /ʌnˈtʃeɪndʒd/ adj remaining the same

un•chang•ing /ʌnˈtʃeɪndʒɪŋ/ adj always remaining the same

un•char•ac•ter•is•tic /ʌnˌkerəktəˈrɪstɪk/ adj not typical of someone or something, and therefore surprising —**un•char•ac•ter•is•ti•cal•ly** /ʌnˌkerəktəˈrɪstɪkli/ adv

un•char•i•ta•ble /ʌnˈtʃerɪtəb(ə)l/ adj unkind in what you say or think about someone

un•chart•ed /ʌnˈtʃɑrtəd/ adj not shown on any map = UNEXPLORED
PHRASE **uncharted territory/waters** an activity or subject that people do not know anything about, or one that they have not experienced before

un•checked /ʌnˈtʃekt/ adj *formal* not controlled or prevented from happening

un•civ•i•lized /ʌnˈsɪv(ə)lˌaɪzd/ adj behaving in a rude or offensive way

un•claimed /ʌnˈkleɪmd/ adj without a known owner

un•clas•si•fied /ʌnˈklæsɪˌfaɪd/ adj unclassified information is available to everyone and is not secret

un•cle /ˈʌŋk(ə)l/ noun [C] ★ the brother of one of your parents, or the husband of your AUNT: *The business was owned by my uncle.* ♦ *a letter from Uncle Richard* —*picture* → FAMILY TREE

un•clear /ʌnˈklɪr/ adj not obvious, definite, or easy to understand
PHRASE **be unclear about/as to sth** to not understand something, or to not be certain about something

Un•cle Sam /ˌʌŋk(ə)l ˈsæm/ *informal* a way of referring to the U.S. or the U.S. government

un•clut•tered /ʌnˈklʌtərd/ adj simple, neat, and not containing any unnecessary things

un•com•fort•a•ble /ʌnˈkʌmfərtəb(ə)l/ adj ★
1 if you are uncomfortable, you have an unpleasant or slightly painful feeling in part of your body: *You'll be uncomfortable for a few days after the surgery.* ♦ *They were sitting in a very uncomfortable position.*
2 used for describing something that makes you have an unpleasant or slightly painful feeling in part of your body: *uncomfortable clothes/shoes*
3 feeling embarrassed or nervous, or making you feel embarrassed or nervous = UNEASY: *A long **uncomfortable silence** followed.*
—**un•com•fort•a•bly** adv

un•com•mon /ʌnˈkɑmən/ adj unusual or rare

un•com•mu•ni•ca•tive /ˌʌnkəˈmjunɪˌkeɪtɪv/ adj not willing to talk or give information

un•com•pli•cat•ed /ʌnˈkɑmplɪˌkeɪtəd/ adj simple

un•com•pro•mis•ing /ʌnˈkɑmprəˌmaɪzɪŋ/ adj very determined, and not willing to change your opinions, plans, or actions

un•con•cerned /ˌʌnkənˈsɜrnd/ adj not worried about a situation or about what might happen

un•con•di•tion•al /ˌʌnkənˈdɪʃən(ə)l/ adj without limits or conditions —**un•con•di•tion•al•ly** adv

un•con•firmed /ˌʌnkənˈfɜrmd/ adj with no definite proof to show that something is true: *unconfirmed reports of fighting*

un•con•nect•ed /ˌʌnkəˈnektəd/ adj not related or linked

un•con•scious[1] /ʌnˈkɑnʃəs/ adj **1** in a condition similar to sleep in which you do not see, feel, or think, usually because you are injured **2** an unconscious feeling or thought is one that you do not realize you have —**un•con•scious•ly** adv, **un•con•scious•ness** noun [U]

un•con•scious² /ʌnˈkɑnʃəs/ noun [singular] the part of your mind that contains unconscious feelings and thoughts that influence your behavior

un•con•sti•tu•tion•al /ˌʌnkɑnstɪˈtuʃən(ə)l/ adj not allowed or not legal according to the rules of a particular country or organization

un•con•trol•la•ble /ˌʌnkənˈtroʊləb(ə)l/ adj **1** impossible to control or stop **2** someone who is uncontrollable behaves badly and refuses to do what other people tell them —**un•con•trol•la•bly** adv

un•con•trolled /ˌʌnkənˈtroʊld/ adj continuing without being controlled or stopped

un•con•tro•ver•sial /ˌʌnkɑntrəˈvɜrʃ(ə)l/ adj if an idea, statement, or situation is uncontroversial, the majority of people accept that it is right

un•con•ven•tion•al /ˌʌnkənˈvenʃən(ə)l/ adj different from what most people consider to be usual or normal —**un•con•ven•tion•al•ly** adv

un•con•vinced /ˌʌnkənˈvɪnst/ adj not certain that something is true or right

un•con•vinc•ing /ˌʌnkənˈvɪnsɪŋ/ adj not likely to persuade you that something is true or right

un•cooked /ʌnˈkʊkt/ adj raw, or not yet cooked

un•cool /ʌnˈkul/ adj *informal* not considered popular, attractive, or fashionable

un•co•op•er•a•tive /ˌʌnkoʊˈɑp(ə)rətɪv/ adj not willing to work with or to help another person or group

un•co•or•di•nat•ed /ˌʌnkoʊˈɔrdɪˌneɪtəd/ adj **1** not graceful, or not able to fully control your movements **2** badly planned or organized

un•cork /ʌnˈkɔrk/ verb [T] to open a bottle by taking the CORK out of it

un•count•a•ble /ʌnˈkaʊntəb(ə)l/ adj *linguistics* an uncountable noun has no plural form and cannot be counted in individual units. Uncountable nouns are marked [U] in this dictionary.

un•couth /ʌnˈkuθ/ adj behaving in a way that polite people think is rude or offensive

un•cov•er /ʌnˈkʌvər/ verb [T] **1** to find out about something that has been hidden or kept secret **2** to take the lid or cover off something

un•crit•i•cal /ʌnˈkrɪtɪk(ə)l/ adj not criticizing someone or something, even when they should be criticized

un•cul•ti•vat•ed /ʌnˈkʌltɪˌveɪtəd/ adj uncultivated land has not been used for growing crops

un•cut /ʌnˈkʌt/ adj **1** allowed to grow longer without being cut: *uncut hair* **2** an uncut movie or book is complete and has not had parts removed

un•dam•aged /ʌnˈdæmɪdʒd/ adj not damaged

un•daunt•ed /ʌnˈdɔntəd/ adj not afraid to continue doing something, even though it might be difficult

un•de•cid•ed /ˌʌndɪˈsaɪdəd/ adj if someone is undecided, they have not yet made a decision about something

un•de•clared /ˌʌndɪˈklerd/ adj undeclared goods or profits have been illegally kept secret from the authorities, by someone who wants to avoid paying tax on them

un•de•feat•ed /ˌʌndɪˈfitəd/ adj not having been defeated in a particular period of time

un•de•fend•ed /ˌʌndɪˈfendəd/ adj not effectively guarded or protected

un•de•fined /ˌʌndɪˈfaɪnd/ adj **1** not clearly explained, or without clear rules or limits **2** without a clear shape or form

un•de•mand•ing /ˌʌndɪˈmændɪŋ/ adj **1** not expecting other people to do things for you or to pay attention to you **2** not needing much mental or physical effort

un•dem•o•crat•ic /ˌʌndeməˈkrætɪk/ adj **1** controlled by officials or politicians who have not been elected by the people **2** not representing the wishes of the majority of people, and therefore unfair

un•de•ni•a•ble /ˌʌndɪˈnaɪəb(ə)l/ adj certainly correct or true = INDISPUTABLE —**un•de•ni•a•bly** adv

un•der /ˈʌndər/ adv, preposition ★★★

1 below or covered by sth in or to a position directly below or covered by something: *What are you kids doing under the table?* ♦ *We drove under the bridge and came out on Elm Street.* ♦ *I found the letter under a pile of books.* ♦ *Charlotte saw a light coming* ***from under*** *the door.*

2 below the surface below the surface of water: *The ducks kept diving* ***under the water*** *to catch fish.* ♦ *Jump into the water and see how long you can* ***stay under****.*

3 less than less than a particular amount, or younger than a particular age ≠ OVER: *A visa is not required for a stay of under three months.* ♦ *The day care center is open to children aged four and under.* → UNDERAGE

4 affected by sth in the process of being affected by a particular action, situation, or state: *A number of proposals are* ***under consideration****.* ♦ *I've been* ***under a lot of stress*** *at work lately.*

5 according to a rule according to a particular law, agreement, or system: ***Under the terms of the agreement****, our company will receive 40% of the profits.*

6 controlled or taught by sb with a particular person or group in control of you as your leader, manager, or teacher: *He studied under Chomsky in the 1960s.*

7 using a particular name using a particular name in some situations, often a name that is not your own: *Carson had been traveling under a false name.*

8 where sth can be found if something is under a particular title, letter, etc., that is where it can be found: *Look under Section Q and you'll find all the details.*

→ UNDERWAY

un•der•age /ˌʌndərˈeɪdʒ/ adj not old enough to do something legally, for example drink alcohol or drive a car

un•der•arm /ˈʌndərˌɑrm/ noun [C] the area of your body under your arm = ARMPIT

un•der•car•riage /ˈʌndərˌkerɪdʒ/ noun [C] the wheels of an airplane and the whole structure that supports it

un•der•class /ˈʌndərˌklæs/ noun [C] the lowest social class in a society, consisting of people who are the poorest and have the least power

U

un•der•cov•er /ˌʌndərˈkʌvər/ adj working or done secretly in order to catch criminals or get secret information —**un•der•cov•er** adv

un•der•cur•rent /ˈʌndərˌkʌrənt/ noun [C] **1** a current that moves below the surface in an ocean or a river **2** a feeling that exists and affects the way people behave, but is not obvious or stated directly

un•der•cut /ˌʌndərˈkʌt/ (past tense and past participle **un•der•cut**) verb [T] **1** to sell something for less money than another company or store **2** *American* to make someone or something become gradually less effective, confident, or successful

un•der•de•vel•oped /ˌʌndərdɪˈveləpt/ adj **1** an underdeveloped country or region is poor. Many people think that this word is offensive, and prefer to use the word **developing**. **2** an underdeveloped person or body has not grown as much as it should have

un•der•dog /ˈʌndərˌdɔg/ noun [C] a person or team that seems least likely to win something

un•der•done /ˌʌndərˈdʌn/ adj underdone food has not been cooked for long enough ≠ OVERDONE

un•der•es•ti•mate /ˌʌndərˈestɪˌmeɪt/ verb [T] **1** to think that someone has less power or ability than they really do **2** to think or guess that something is smaller, less important, etc. than it really is ≠ OVERESTIMATE —**un•der•es•ti•mate** /ˌʌndərˈestɪmət/ noun [C]

un•der•foot /ˌʌndərˈfʊt/ adv **1** under your feet in the place where you are walking **2** *American* in your way and preventing you from moving easily: *I can't get dinner ready with all you kids underfoot.*

un•der•fund /ˌʌndərˈfʌnd/ verb [T] to not provide an organization, project, etc. with enough money to operate effectively —**un•der•fund•ed** adj, **un•der•fund•ing** noun [U]

un•der•go /ˌʌndərˈgoʊ/ (past tense **un•der•went** /ˌʌndərˈwent/; past participle **un•der•gone** /ˌʌndərˈgɔn/) verb [T] to experience something, especially a change or medical treatment: *Sue underwent knee surgery in April.* ♦ *The bridge has undergone repairs.*

U

un•der•grad•u•ate /ˌʌndərˈgrædʒuət/ noun [C] a student who is studying for a first degree at a college or university

un•der•ground /ˈʌndərˌgraʊnd/ adj **1** below the surface of the ground **2** secret and usually illegal —**un•der•ground** /ˌʌndərˈgraʊnd/ adv

Un•der•ground, the /ˈʌndərˌgraʊnd/ noun [singular] *British* the SUBWAY

un•der•growth /ˈʌndərˌgroʊθ/ noun [U] small thick bushes that cover the ground

un•der•hand /ˌʌndərˈhænd/ adj *American* thrown with your arm low, so that it does not go above your shoulder

un•der•hand•ed /ˌʌndərˈhændəd/ adj secret and dishonest —**un•der•hand•ed•ly** adv, **un•der•hand•ed•ness** noun [U]

un•der•lie /ˌʌndərˈlaɪ/ (present participle **un•der•ly•ing** /ˌʌndərˈlaɪɪŋ/; past tense **un•der•lay** /ˌʌndərˈleɪ/; past participle **un•der•lain** /ˌʌndərˈleɪn/) verb [T] to be the real or basic cause of or reason for something

un•der•line /ˌʌndərˈlaɪn/ verb [T] **1** to draw a line under something **2** to show or emphasize that something is important or true: *The recent violence underlines the need for continuing peace talks.*

un•der•ly•ing /ˌʌndərˈlaɪɪŋ/ adj underlying causes, facts, ideas, etc. are the real or basic ones, although they are not obvious: *The underlying causes of the riots have been ignored.*

un•der•mine /ˌʌndərˈmaɪn/ verb [T] to make something or someone become gradually less effective, confident, or successful =UNDERCUT

un•der•neath /ˌʌndərˈniθ/ adv, preposition ★★
1 in, to, or through a place directly below something, or below something that covers it: *I'll leave the key underneath the mat.* ♦ *He hid underneath the bed.* ♦ *The artist's name was printed underneath.*
2 on the lower surface of something: *The pancakes should be golden underneath.*
3 used for describing what someone or something is really like, despite how they may seem: *Gary acts tough, but underneath he's really very kind.*

un•der•paid /ˌʌndərˈpeɪd/ adj not earning enough money for the work that you do —**un•der•pay** verb [I/T]

un•der•pants /ˈʌndərˌpænts/ noun [plural] underwear for men and women worn on the lower half of the body

un•der•pass /ˈʌndərˌpæs/ noun [C] part of a road or path that goes under another road or a railroad

un•der•pin /ˌʌndərˈpɪn/ verb [T] to be an important basic part of something, allowing it to succeed or continue to exist

un•der•priv•i•leged /ˌʌndərˈprɪv(ə)lɪdʒd/ adj not having as many advantages or opportunities as most other people

un•der•rat•ed /ˌʌndərˈreɪtəd/ adj if a person or thing is underrated, most people do not recognize how good that person or thing really is —**un•der•rate** verb [T]

un•der•score /ˌʌndərˈskɔr/ verb [T] to emphasize something, or to show that it is important =UNDERLINE

un•der•sea /ˈʌndərˌsi/ adj existing or happening under the surface of the ocean

un•der•served /ˌʌndərˈsɜrvd/ adj *American* not getting enough help or services

un•der•shirt /ˈʌndərˌʃɜrt/ noun [C] *American* underwear that you wear on the top half of your body —*picture* → C5

un•der•side /ˈʌndərˌsaɪd/ noun [C] the bottom side or surface of something

un•der•staffed /ˌʌndərˈstæft/ adj not having enough workers

un•der•stand /ˌʌndərˈstænd/ (past tense and past participle **un•der•stood** /ˌʌndərˈstʊd/) verb ★★★
1 [I/T] to know what someone or something means: *I didn't understand a word he was saying.* ♦ *The instructions were easy to understand.* ♦ *I'm sorry, I don't understand French.*
2 [I/T] to know how or why something happens, or what effect or influence something has: *Do they fully understand the implications of their decision?* ♦ **+how/why/what etc.** *We are only beginning to*

understand how the brain functions.
3 [I/T] to know how someone feels, or why someone does something: *I understand your concern, but the operation is completely safe.*
4 [T] *formal* to believe that something is true because you have heard or read it somewhere: **+(that)** *We understand that a major announcement is to be made tomorrow.*
PHRASE **make yourself understood** to know enough of another language to be able to deal with ordinary situations

Word family: understand
*Words in the same family as **understand***
- **understandable** *adj*
- **understandably** *adv*
- **understanding** *n*
- **misunderstand** *v*
- **misunderstood** *adj*
- **misunderstanding** *n*

un•der•stand•a•ble /ˌʌndərˈstændəb(ə)l/ adj **1** normal and reasonable in a particular situation **2** clear and easy to understand —**un•der•stand•a•bly** adv
un•der•stand•ing[1] /ˌʌndərˈstændɪŋ/ noun ★★
1 [singular/U] knowledge about a particular subject, process, or situation: *The course will help you develop a deeper **understanding of** yourself.*
2 [U] sympathy that comes from knowing how other people feel and why they do things: *Suzy just needs **a little understanding**.*
3 [C] an agreement that is made in an informal way, or that is not expressed in words: *We **have an understanding with** them that we won't compete.* ♦ *We gave them the details **with the understanding that** they would not be made public.*
4 [C/U] the particular way in which you understand the meaning of something =INTERPRETATION: *My understanding was that the meeting would end at 5 o'clock.*
un•der•stand•ing[2] /ˌʌndərˈstændɪŋ/ adj willing to forgive other people or to be sympathetic, because you understand how they feel
un•der•stat•ed /ˌʌndərˈsteɪtəd/ adj not trying to impress people or attract their attention, and therefore attractive or effective
un•der•state•ment /ˈʌndərˌsteɪtmənt/ noun [C/U] something that you say that makes something seem less important or serious than it really is
understood the past tense and past participle of **understand**
un•der•stud•y /ˈʌndərˌstʌdi/ noun [C] an actor whose job is to learn someone else's part in a play, so that they can perform it if that person is sick
un•der•take /ˌʌndərˈteɪk/ (past tense **un•der•took** /ˌʌndərˈtʊk/; past participle **un•der•tak•en** /ˌʌndərˈteɪkn/) verb [T] to agree to be responsible for a job or project, and to do it: *It is one of the largest dam projects ever undertaken.*
un•der•tak•er /ˈʌndərˌteɪkər/ noun [C] someone whose job is to make arrangements for funerals
un•der•tak•ing /ˈʌndərˌteɪkɪŋ/ noun [C] something that you do that is difficult or complicated
un•der•tone /ˈʌndərˌtoʊn/ noun [C] an idea or feeling that exists, but is not obvious
undertook the past tense of **undertake**
un•der•used /ˌʌndərˈjuzd/ adj not used enough
un•der•val•ue /ˌʌndərˈvælju/ verb [T] **1** to not recognize how important or valuable someone or something is **2** to think that something is worth less money than it really is —**un•der•val•ued** /ˌʌndərˈvæljud/ adj
un•der•wa•ter /ˌʌndərˈwɔtər/ adj, adv existing, happening, or used under the surface of the water
un•der•way /ˌʌndərˈweɪ/ adj **1** already started or happening: *Rescue efforts are underway.* **2** already moving
un•der•wear /ˈʌndərˌwer/ noun [U] clothes that you wear next to your skin under your regular clothes
un•der•weight /ˌʌndərˈweɪt/ adj below the normal weight ≠ OVERWEIGHT
un•der•went the past tense of **undergo**
un•der•world /ˈʌndərˌwɜrld/ noun **1** [singular] the criminals in a particular community, considered as a group **2 the Underworld** in old stories, a place below the Earth's surface where people go when they die
un•de•served /ˌʌndɪˈzɜrvd/ adj if something is undeserved, you get it even though you have not done anything to deserve it
un•de•sir•a•ble /ˌʌndɪˈzaɪrəb(ə)l/ adj bad or harmful
un•de•tect•ed /ˌʌndɪˈtektəd/ adj not noticed
un•de•terred /ˌʌndɪˈtɜrd/ adj continuing to do something, even though you are not successful or people do not support you
un•de•vel•oped /ˌʌndɪˈveləpt/ adj **1** not fully grown **2** undeveloped land has not been used for building or industry
undid the past tense of **undo**
un•dig•ni•fied /ʌnˈdɪgnɪˌfaɪd/ adj embarrassing or silly
un•di•lut•ed /ˌʌndɪˈlutəd, ˌʌndaɪˈlutəd/ adj **1** strong, with no water mixed in **2** without any attempt to make something less offensive or easier to accept
un•dip•lo•mat•ic /ˌʌndɪpləˈmætɪk/ adj very direct, in a way that is likely to cause offense =TACTLESS —**un•dip•lo•mat•i•cal•ly** /ˌʌndɪpləˈmætɪkli/ adv
un•dis•ci•plined /ʌnˈdɪsəˌplɪnd/ adj not well controlled
un•dis•closed /ˌʌndɪsˈkloʊzd/ adj not reported publicly
un•dis•cov•ered /ˌʌndɪˈskʌvərd/ adj not noticed or known about
un•dis•crim•i•nat•ing /ˌʌndɪˈskrɪmɪˌneɪtɪŋ/ adj deciding what you like without thinking carefully about the value or qualities of different things
un•dis•guised /ˌʌndɪsˈgaɪzd/ adj without any attempt to make your feelings less obvious
un•dis•put•ed /ˌʌndɪˈspjutəd/ adj agreed or accepted by everyone
un•dis•turbed /ˌʌndɪˈstɜrbd/ adj **1** not touched or moved **2** not interrupted by anyone
un•di•vid•ed /ˌʌndɪˈvaɪdəd/ adj complete and total: *You should give this matter your undivided attention.*
un•do /ʌnˈdu/ (past tense **un•did** /ʌnˈdɪd/; past participle **un•done** /ʌnˈdʌn/) verb **1** [T] to open or untie something so that it is no longer closed or fastened: *He undid the screws that held the lid on.* ♦ *I can't undo my belt.* **2** [T]

U

to have the effect of changing something back into its original, usually worse, state: *One mistake could undo all our achievements.* **3** [I/T] *computing* to give a computer an instruction to ignore the last change that you made

un·done /ʌnˈdʌn/ adj **1** not finished **2** not closed or fastened

un·doubt·ed·ly /ʌnˈdaʊtədli/ adv used for saying something is certainly true or accepted by everyone —**un·doubt·ed** adj

un·dress /ʌnˈdres/ verb [I/T] to remove your clothes, or to remove someone else's clothes

un·dressed /ʌnˈdrest/ adj not wearing any clothes

un·due /ˌʌnˈdu/ adj *formal* not necessary or reasonable

un·du·lat·ing /ˈʌndʒəˌleɪtɪŋ/ adj having slopes and curves, or moving gently up and down in the shape of waves —**un·du·late** verb [I]

un·du·ly /ʌnˈduli/ adv *formal* too much

un·dy·ing /ʌnˈdaɪɪŋ/ adj never-ending

un·earth /ʌnˈɜrθ/ verb [T] **1** to discover someone or something that was not known before **2** to find something that is buried in the ground

un·eas·y /ʌnˈizi/ adj slightly nervous or worried about something —**un·ease** noun [U], **un·eas·i·ly** adv

un·ed·u·cat·ed /ʌnˈedʒəˌkeɪtəd/ adj not having had much education

un·e·mo·tion·al /ˌʌnɪˈmoʊʃən(ə)l/ adj not showing any feelings

un·em·ployed /ˌʌnɪmˈplɔɪd/ adj ★ without a job: *About 8.4 million people are unemployed in the United States today.* ♦ *an unemployed actor/engineer/teacher*

un·em·ploy·ment /ˌʌnɪmˈplɔɪmənt/ noun [U] ★★

1 a situation in which people do not have jobs, or the fact that someone does not have a job: *Unemployment rose last month to its highest level in five years.*

2 **unemployment** or **unemployment compensation** *American informal* money provided by the government to someone who loses their job until they find another job

un·end·ing /ʌnˈendɪŋ/ adj continuing without stopping, or seeming to last for ever

U

un·en·thu·si·as·tic /ˌʌnɪnˌθuziˈæstɪk/ adj not excited or enthusiastic about something

un·en·vi·a·ble /ʌnˈenviəb(ə)l/ adj difficult and not enjoyable

un·e·qual /ʌnˈikwəl/ adj **1** not giving the same treatment or opportunities to everyone, and therefore unfair **2** not the same in amount, number, or size **3** involving one person, team, army, etc. that is much stronger than another **4** not good enough or skillful enough to do something

un·e·quiv·o·cal /ˌʌnɪˈkwɪvək(ə)l/ adj *formal* clear and definite —**un·e·quiv·o·cal·ly** adv

un·err·ing /ʌnˈɜrɪŋ/ adj always right or accurate

un·eth·i·cal /ʌnˈeθɪk(ə)l/ adj morally wrong

un·e·ven /ʌnˈiv(ə)n/ adj **1** not smooth or level **2** not the same in size or length **3** not fairly balanced or equally shared **4** not of the same quality in all its parts —**un·e·ven·ly** adv

un·e·vent·ful /ˌʌnɪˈventfəl/ adj without anything unusual or exciting happening

un·ex·cep·tion·al /ˌʌnɪkˈsepʃən(ə)l/ adj not especially good or unusual

un·ex·cit·ing /ˌʌnɪkˈsaɪtɪŋ/ adj not interesting or exciting

un·ex·pect·ed /ˌʌnɪkˈspektəd/ adj ★ surprising: *Her divorce was totally unexpected.* ♦ *Belgium's unexpected victory over France* —**un·ex·pect·ed·ly** adv

un·ex·plained /ˌʌnɪkˈspleɪnd/ adj an unexplained event seems to have no explanation or reason

un·ex·plored /ˌʌnɪkˈsplɔrd/ adj **1** never visited by people **2** not thought about or considered before

un·fail·ing /ʌnˈfeɪlɪŋ/ adj never changing or ending —**un·fail·ing·ly** adv

un·fair /ʌnˈfer/ adj ★

1 not fair or reasonable = UNJUST: *The students complained that the test was unfair.* ♦ *an unfair trial* ♦ *He claims the tax laws are unfair to single people.*

2 not treating people equally: *It is unfair that not everyone got the chance to vote.*

—**un·fair·ly** adv

un·faith·ful /ʌnˈfeɪθf(ə)l/ adj having a sexual relationship with someone who is not your husband, wife, or usual partner —**un·faith·ful·ly** adj

un·fa·mil·iar /ˌʌnfəˈmɪljər/ adj if you are unfamiliar with something, you have no knowledge or experience of it —**un·fa·mil·iar·i·ty** /ˌʌnfəˌmɪliˈerəti/ noun [U]

un·fash·ion·a·ble /ʌnˈfæʃ(ə)nəb(ə)l/ adj not popular or fashionable

un·fas·ten /ʌnˈfæs(ə)n/ verb [T] to open or untie something, especially a piece of clothing or a belt = UNDO

un·fath·om·a·ble /ʌnˈfæðəməb(ə)l/ adj *formal* impossible to explain, or impossible to understand

un·fa·vor·a·ble /ʌnˈfeɪv(ə)rəb(ə)l/ adj **1** not positive or not showing approval = CRITICAL: *The report makes unfavorable comparisons with the system used in France.* **2** an unfavorable situation or set of conditions is one that involves difficult problems and makes success harder to achieve —**un·fa·vor·a·bly** adv

un·fazed /ˌʌnˈfeɪzd/ adj not worried or upset by something bad that happens

un·fea·si·ble /ʌnˈfizəb(ə)l/ adj not possible or practical to do or believe

un·feel·ing /ʌnˈfilɪŋ/ adj not showing sympathy for other people

un·fin·ished /ʌnˈfɪnɪʃt/ adj not finished, or not dealt with completely

un·fit /ʌnˈfɪt/ adj **1** below the accepted quality or standard for a particular use or purpose: *an unfit mother* **2** not feeling healthy or strong because you do not do enough exercise

un·flat·ter·ing /ʌnˈflæt(ə)rɪŋ/ adj making someone seem unpleasant or not attractive

un·fold /ʌnˈfoʊld/ verb **1** [T] to open something that was folded **2** [I] to happen or develop

un·fore·see·a·ble /ˌʌnfɔrˈsiəb(ə)l/ adj impossible to know about or expect

un·fore·seen /ˌʌnfɔrˈsin/ adj an unforeseen situation is one that you did not expect = UNEXPECTED

un·for·get·ta·ble /ˌʌnfərˈgetəb(ə)l/ adj something that is unforgettable will be remembered for a very long time =MEMORABLE —**un·for·get·ta·bly** adv

un·for·giv·a·ble /ˌʌnfərˈgɪvəb(ə)l/ adj extremely bad and impossible to forgive =INEXCUSABLE

un·for·giv·ing /ˌʌnfərˈgɪvɪŋ/ adj not willing to forgive people

un·forth·com·ing /ˌʌnforθˈkʌmɪŋ/ adj not willing to talk or provide information

un·for·tu·nate /ʌnˈfortʃənət/ adj **1** experiencing bad luck, or caused by bad luck=UNLUCKY: *The unfortunate woman had had her purse stolen.* **2** *formal* if something is unfortunate, you do not approve of it, or you wish that it had not happened: *an unfortunate accident*

un·for·tu·nate·ly /ʌnˈfortʃənətli/ adv ★ used for saying that you wish that something had not happened, or that it was not true: *Unfortunately, Jack is leaving the company.* ♦ *Effective treatments do exist, but unfortunately they are very expensive.*

un·found·ed /ʌnˈfaʊndəd/ adj not supported with facts or evidence

un·friend·ly /ʌnˈfren(d)li/ adj not friendly

un·ful·filled /ˌʌnfʊlˈfɪld/ adj unhappy because you have not achieved what you want

un·furl /ʌnˈfɜrl/ verb [I/T] to untie or open something that was rolled up, or to spread out after being untied

un·furn·ished /ʌnˈfɜrnɪʃt/ adj without any furniture

un·gain·ly /ʌnˈgeɪnli/ adj not moving in an attractive or graceful way

un·gra·cious /ʌnˈgreɪʃəs/ adj not polite or friendly —**un·gra·cious·ly** adv

un·gram·mat·i·cal /ˌʌngrəˈmætɪk(ə)l/ adj not correct according to the rules of grammar

un·grate·ful /ʌnˈgreɪtfəl/ adj not grateful to someone who has helped you or been kind to you —**un·grate·ful·ly** adv

un·hap·py /ʌnˈhæpi/ adj ★★ **1** feeling sad or upset, or making someone feel sad or upset: *Why are you so unhappy?* ♦ *an unhappy childhood/memory* **2** not satisfied: *People are very **unhappy about** the high ticket prices.* —**un·hap·pi·ly** adv, **un·hap·pi·ness** noun [U]

un·harmed /ʌnˈhɑrmd/ adj not hurt or damaged

un·health·y /ʌnˈhelθi/ adj **1** sick, or not physically fit **2** not good for you

un·heard /ʌnˈhɜrd/ adj not heard by anyone, or ignored

unˈheard-ˌof adj something that is unheard-of is very unusual or has never happened before

un·help·ful /ʌnˈhelpfəl/ adj **1** not willing or able to help **2** not useful —**un·help·ful·ly** adv

un·hur·ried /ʌnˈhʌrid/ adj slow, without any worry about taking a long time —**un·hur·ried·ly** adv

un·hurt /ʌnˈhɜrt/ adj not injured

u·ni·corn /ˈjunɪˌkorn/ noun [C] an imaginary creature like a horse with a single long horn on its head

un·i·den·ti·fied /ˌʌnaɪˈdentɪfaɪd/ adj not recognized or known

u·ni·fi·ca·tion /ˌjunɪfɪˈkeɪʃ(ə)n/ noun [U] the process of uniting groups or countries, or the fact that they have been united

u·ni·form¹ /ˈjunɪˌform/ noun [C] ★★ a set of clothes that you wear to show that you are part of a particular organization or school: *He was still wearing his school uniform.* ♦ *a police uniform*

PHRASE **in uniform** wearing a uniform: *soldiers in uniform*

u·ni·form² /ˈjunɪˌform/ adj the same everywhere: *a uniform standard of health care* —**u·ni·form·ly** adv

u·ni·formed /ˈjunɪˌformd/ adj wearing a uniform

u·ni·fy /ˈjunɪˌfaɪ/ verb [T] to unite people or countries so that they will work together —**u·ni·fied** /ˈjunɪˌfaɪd/ adj

u·ni·lat·er·al /ˌjunɪˈlætrəl/ adj done or decided by one country, group, or person without the agreement of others —**u·ni·lat·er·al·ly** adv

un·i·mag·i·na·ble /ˌʌnɪˈmædʒɪnəb(ə)l/ adj very difficult to imagine —**un·i·mag·i·na·bly** adv

un·i·mag·i·na·tive /ˌʌnɪˈmædʒɪnətɪv/ adj unable to think of new and interesting things

un·im·por·tant /ˌʌnɪmˈportənt/ adj not important or relevant

un·im·pres·sive /ˌʌnɪmˈpresɪv/ adj not very good

un·in·form·a·tive /ˌʌnɪnˈformətɪv/ adj not giving enough information and therefore unhelpful

un·in·formed /ˌʌnɪnˈformd/ adj not based on knowledge or correct information, and therefore wrong or inappropriate

un·in·hab·it·a·ble /ˌʌnɪnˈhæbɪtəb(ə)l/ adj not appropriate for living in

un·in·hab·it·ed /ˌʌnɪnˈhæbɪtəd/ adj an uninhabited place has no people living there

un·in·hib·it·ed /ˌʌnɪnˈhɪbɪtəd/ adj not embarrassed about doing or saying something that other people might be unwilling to do or say

un·in·spired /ˌʌnɪnˈspaɪrd/ adj not interesting or exciting

un·in·tel·li·gent /ˌʌnɪnˈtelɪdʒənt/ adj not intelligent

un·in·tel·li·gi·ble /ˌʌnɪnˈtelɪdʒəb(ə)l/ adj impossible to understand

un·in·tend·ed /ˌʌnɪnˈtendəd/ adj not deliberate or planned

un·in·ten·tion·al /ˌʌnɪnˈtenʃənəl/ adj not deliberate or planned

un·in·ter·est·ed /ʌnˈɪntrəstəd/ adj not interested

un·in·ter·rupt·ed /ˌʌnɪntəˈrʌptəd/ adj continuous and not interrupted by anything

un·in·vit·ing /ˌʌnɪnˈvaɪtɪŋ/ adj not attractive or pleasant

un·ion /ˈjunjən/ noun ★★ **1** [C] an organization that represents the workers in a particular industry: *the International Ladies' Garment Workers' Union* ♦ *We encourage all employees to join a union.* → LABOR UNION **2** **Union** [C] a group of states or countries that have joined together: *the European Union*

U

3 [singular/U] the process of joining things together, or the state of being joined together
4 [C/U] *formal* the process of getting married, or the state of being married

ˌUnion ˈJack the national flag of the U.K.

u•nique /juˈnik/ adj ★
1 very special, unusual, or good: *It is her use of color that makes her work unique.* ♦ *Mark had a* ***unique opportunity*** *to travel with the President.*
2 not the same as anything or anyone else: *Each individual is unique.*
3 only existing or happening in one place or situation: *The problem is not* ***unique to*** *British students.*
—**u•nique•ly** adv

u•ni•sex /ˈjuniˌseks/ adj for both men and women

u•ni•son /ˈjunɪsən/ noun **in unison** together, or at the same time

u•nit /ˈjunɪt/ noun [C] ★★★

1 individual thing	5 small machine
2 part of institution	6 part of a book
3 for measuring	7 piece of furniture
4 apartment	8 team of people

1 an individual thing that is part of a larger group: *low-cost housing units* ♦ *The sen is the smallest* ***unit of currency*** *in Malaysia.*
2 a department of an institution that has a particular purpose: *an intensive care unit*
3 a standard quantity that is used for measuring something: *The gram is a unit for measuring weight.*
4 one of the apartments that a building or group of buildings is divided into: *thirty units of affordable housing*
5 a small machine that does a particular job: *an air-conditioning unit*
6 one of the parts that an educational book or a school course is divided into
7 a piece of furniture that fits together with other pieces of the same type: *kitchen units*
8 a group of people who work as a team within a larger group or organization: *an army unit*

u•nite /juˈnaɪt/ verb [I/T] to join together, or to join people or groups together: *They all united to demand a safer neighborhood.*

u•nit•ed /juˈnaɪtəd/ adj ★
1 if people are united, they agree with each other: *Local people are* ***united in*** *their opposition to the site.*
2 joined together: *a united Germany*

ˌUnited ˈKingdom, the England, Scotland, Wales, and Northern Ireland, considered as a political unit

UˌnitedˈNations, the the UN

u•ni•ty /ˈjunəti/ noun [U] a situation in which people, groups, or countries join together or agree about something

u•ni•ver•sal /ˌjunɪˈvɜrs(ə)l/ adj ★ involving or affecting everyone in the world, or all the members of a group or society: *universal human rights* ♦ *universal health care*
—**u•ni•ver•sal•ly** adv

u•ni•verse, the /ˈjunɪvɜrs/ noun [singular] space and everything that exists in it, including the Earth and all the other planets

u•ni•ver•si•ty /ˌjunɪˈvɜrsəti/ noun [C] ★★★ an educational institution where students study for degrees and where academic research is done: *He was at the University of Wisconsin* (=studied there). ♦ *Which university do you want to go to?*

un•just /ʌnˈdʒʌst/ adj not fair or reasonable =UNFAIR —**un•just•ly** adv

un•jus•ti•fied /ʌnˈdʒʌstɪˌfaɪd/ adj not fair, or not based on any good reason

un•kempt /ʌnˈkempt/ adj dirty and messy

un•kind /ʌnˈkaɪnd/ adj ★ unfriendly, insulting, or cruel: *an unkind remark* ♦ *You're being very* ***unkind to*** *your sister.*
—**un•kind•ly** adv, **un•kind•ness** noun [U]

un•know•ing•ly /ʌnˈnoʊɪŋli/ adv without realizing what type of situation you are involved in

un•known¹ /ʌnˈnoʊn/ adj ★
1 if something is unknown, people do not know about it or do not know what it is: ***For some unknown reason****, the plane landed at the wrong airport.*
2 not famous: *an unknown poet*

un•known² /ʌnˈnoʊn/ noun **1** [C] someone who is not famous **2 the unknown** [singular] things that you do not know about or have not experienced

un•law•ful /ʌnˈlɔf(ə)l/ adj *legal* illegal
—**un•law•ful•ly** adv

un•lead•ed /ʌnˈledəd/ adj unleaded gas does not contain LEAD

un•leash /ʌnˈliʃ/ verb [T] to do or cause something that has a very powerful or harmful effect

un•less /ənˈles/ conjunction ★★★ used for saying that if something does not happen, something else will happen or will be true as a result: *I can't help you unless you tell me what's wrong.* ♦ *Unless you come now, I'm going to leave without you.* ♦ *"Are you going to stay overnight?" "****Not unless*** (=only if) *it's absolutely necessary."*

un•li•censed /ʌnˈlaɪs(ə)nst/ adj without an official LICENSE to do something

un•like /ʌnˈlaɪk/ preposition ★★
1 different from someone or something else: *The show was unlike anything we'd ever seen before.*
2 not typical of a particular person or thing: *It's so unlike Mary to go off on her own.*

un•like•ly /ʌnˈlaɪkli/ adj ★★
1 not likely to happen: *It's* ***highly unlikely*** *that we'll be invited.* ♦ **unlikely to do sth** *He's unlikely ever to find a job again.* ♦ **+(that)** *It seems unlikely that she will make the same mistake next time.*
2 not typical: *He's a very unlikely romantic hero.*

un•lim•it•ed /ʌnˈlɪmɪtəd/ adj with no limits

un•lit /ʌnˈlɪt/ adj dark because there are no lights

un•load /ʌnˈloʊd/ verb **1** [I/T] to take goods off a vehicle **2** [T] to take the bullets out of a gun, or the film out of a camera

un•lock /ʌnˈlɑk/ verb [T] to open the lock on something, usually with a key

un•luck•y /ʌnˈlʌki/ adj **1** having bad luck **2** believed to bring bad luck **3** happening because of bad luck —**un•luck•i•ly** adv

un•man•age•a•ble /ʌnˈmænɪdʒəb(ə)l/ adj extremely difficult to control or organize

un•manned /ˌʌnˈmænd/ adj an unmanned building, vehicle, or machine does not have anyone working in it or on it

un•marked /ˌʌnˈmɑrkt/ adj something that is unmarked has no words or symbols on it to show what or where it is

un•mar•ried /ʌnˈmerid/ adj not married =SINGLE

un•mis•tak•a•ble /ˌʌnmɪˈsteɪkəb(ə)l/ adj very easy to recognize

un•mit•i•gat•ed /ʌnˈmɪtɪˌgeɪtəd/ adj used for emphasizing how bad or unpleasant something is: *The whole project was an unmitigated disaster.*

un•moved /ʌnˈmuvd/ adj feeling no sympathy or sadness

un•named /ˌʌnˈneɪmd/ adj used for describing a person or thing whose name is not mentioned

un•nat•u•ral /ʌnˈnætʃ(ə)rəl/ adj different from what you would normally expect or experience, especially in a way that makes you feel uncomfortable: *an unnatural silence* —**un•nat•u•ral•ly** adv

un•nec•es•sar•y /ʌnˈnesəˌseri/ adj ★
1 used for describing something that should not have happened because it could have been avoided: *The policy had caused thousands of families unnecessary suffering.* ♦ *The delay was totally unnecessary.*
2 not needed: *Remove all unnecessary files from your computer.*
—**un•nec•es•sar•i•ly** /ˌʌnnesəˈserəli/ adv

un•no•ticed /ʌnˈnoʊtɪst/ adj, adv not seen or noticed by anyone

un•ob•served /ˌʌnəbˈzɜrvd/ adj, adv not seen by anyone

un•ob•tru•sive /ˌʌnəbˈtrusɪv/ adj not attracting much attention —**un•ob•tru•sive•ly** adv

un•oc•cu•pied /ʌnˈɑkjəˌpaɪd/ adj an unoccupied room, building, or seat is not being used by anyone

un•of•fi•cial /ˌʌnəˈfɪʃ(ə)l/ adj **1** not organized or formally approved by anyone in authority **2** not having an official position or status —**un•of•fi•cial•ly** adv

un•op•posed /ˌʌnəˈpoʊzd/ adj, adv if someone does something unopposed, no one competes against them or tries to stop them

un•or•tho•dox /ʌnˈɔrθəˌdɑks/ adj not following the usual rules or beliefs of your religion or society

un•pack /ʌnˈpæk/ verb [I/T] to take things out of a suitcase, bag, etc.

un•paid /ˌʌnˈpeɪd/ adj **1** unpaid work is work that you are not paid for **2** not yet paid: *unpaid debts/bills/rent*

un•par•al•leled /ʌnˈperəˌleld/ adj *formal* much greater than anything else or anyone else

un•pa•tri•ot•ic /ˌʌnpeɪtriˈɑtɪk/ adj not proud of your country, or involved in something that harms your country

un•per•turbed /ˌʌnpərˈtɜrbd/ adj not worried or upset by something that has happened

un•planned /ˌʌnˈplænd/ adj not intended or expected

un•pleas•ant /ʌnˈplez(ə)nt/ adj ★★
1 if something is unpleasant, you do not like or enjoy it: *The smell was very unpleasant.* ♦ *an unpleasant experience*
2 not friendly or kind: *She was really unpleasant on the phone.*
—**un•pleas•ant•ly** adv

un•plug /ʌnˈplʌg/ verb [T] to separate a piece of equipment from a power supply by taking its PLUG out of an electric SOCKET

un•pop•u•lar /ʌnˈpɑpjələr/ adj disliked by many people —**un•pop•u•lar•i•ty** /ˌʌnpɑpjəˈlerəti/ noun [U]

un•prec•e•dent•ed /ʌnˈpresɪdentəd/ adj never having happened or existed before

un•pre•dict•a•ble /ˌʌnprɪˈdɪktəb(ə)l/ adj changing often, in a way that is impossible to prepare for =ERRATIC —**un•pre•dict•a•bly** adv

un•pre•pared /ˌʌnprɪˈperd/ adj not ready for a particular situation, event, or process

un•pre•ten•tious /ˌʌnprɪˈtenʃəs/ adj not trying to impress people with money, style, intelligence, importance, etc. This word shows that you approve of this quality.

un•prin•ci•pled /ˌʌnˈprɪnsəp(ə)ld/ adj willing to use dishonest or unfair methods in order to get what you want

un•pro•duc•tive /ˌʌnprəˈdʌktɪv/ adj not achieving any benefits or positive results

un•pro•fes•sion•al /ˌʌnprəˈfeʃən(ə)l/ adj not behaving according to the normal standards of work or behavior of your profession: *The rude way she treats clients is very unprofessional.* —**un•pro•fes•sion•al•ly** adv

un•prof•it•a•ble /ʌnˈprɑfɪtəb(ə)l/ adj an unprofitable business does not make enough money —**un•prof•it•a•bly** adv

un•pro•voked /ˌʌnprəˈvoʊkt/ adj an unprovoked attack is made on someone who has done nothing to deserve it

un•qual•i•fied /ʌnˈkwɑlɪˌfaɪd/ adj not having the education, experience, or right qualifications to do a particular job

un•ques•tion•a•ble /ʌnˈkwestʃənəb(ə)l/ adj used for emphasizing how true something is, or for saying that most people believe it: *His commitment to the job is unquestionable.* —**un•ques•tion•a•bly** adv

un•re•al /ʌnˈriəl/ adj extremely unusual and not normal —**un•re•al•i•ty** /ˌʌnriˈæləti/ noun [U]

un•re•al•is•tic /ˌʌnriəˈlɪstɪk/ adj based on hopes or wishes, and not on what is likely or possible —**un•re•al•is•ti•cal•ly** /ˌʌnriəˈlɪstɪkli/ adv

un•rea•son•a•ble /ʌnˈriz(ə)nəb(ə)l/ adj **1** not fair **2** not sensible —**un•rea•son•a•bly** adv

un•rec•og•niz•a•ble /ʌnˈrekəgˌnaɪzəb(ə)l/ adj very different from the person or place that you remember

un•re•lat•ed /ˌʌnrɪˈleɪtəd/ adj **1** not connected with another event, situation, subject, etc.: *His decision to quit was unrelated to the company's performance.* **2** not part of the same family

un•re•lent•ing /ˌʌnrɪˈlentɪŋ/ adj done or happening in a severe or determined way

un•re•li•a•ble /ˌʌnrɪˈlaɪəb(ə)l/ adj someone or something that is unreliable cannot be depended on

un•re•mark•a•ble /ˌʌnrɪˈmɑrkəb(ə)l/ adj very ordinary and not interesting or impressive

un•re•mit•ting /ˌʌnrɪˈmɪtɪŋ/ adj continuing

U

for a long time without getting better

un·re·pent·ant /ˌʌnrɪˈpentənt/ adj *formal* not sorry for something bad that you have done

un·rep·re·sen·ta·tive /ˌʌnreprɪˈzentətɪv/ adj not typical of other people or things in the same group

un·re·quit·ed /ˌʌnrɪˈkwaɪtəd/ adj unrequited love is love that you feel for someone who does not love you

un·re·served /ˌʌnrɪˈzɜrvd/ adj complete and sincere —**un·re·serv·ed·ly** /ˌʌnrɪˈzɜrvədli/ adv

un·re·solved /ˌʌnrɪˈzɑlvd/ adj not dealt with or agreed on

un·re·spon·sive /ˌʌnrɪˈspɑnsɪv/ adj not reacting in the way that you want or expect

un·rest /ʌnˈrest/ noun [U] angry or violent behavior by people who are protesting against something

un·re·ward·ing /ˌʌnrɪˈwɔrdɪŋ/ adj giving you no pleasure or satisfaction

un·ri·valed /ʌnˈraɪv(ə)ld/ adj used for emphasizing that something is much better or greater than other similar things

un·roll /ʌnˈroʊl/ verb [T] to open out something that has been rolled up

un·ruf·fled /ʌnˈrʌf(ə)ld/ adj not nervous or upset in a difficult situation

un·ru·ly /ʌnˈruli/ adj very difficult to control

un·safe /ˌʌnˈseɪf/ adj **1** dangerous **2** involving a lot of risk

un·said /ʌnˈsed/ adj something that is unsaid is something that you think but do not say

un·sat·is·fac·to·ry /ˌʌnsætɪsˈfæktəri/ adj not good enough

un·sa·vor·y /ʌnˈseɪv(ə)ri/ adj involving unpleasant, dishonest, or immoral things

un·scathed /ʌnˈskeɪðd/ adj not harmed or damaged

un·screw /ʌnˈskru/ verb [T] to open something by twisting its lid or top

un·scru·pu·lous /ʌnˈskrupjələs/ adj willing to do things that are unfair, dishonest, or illegal

un·seem·ly /ʌnˈsimli/ adj *formal* unseemly behavior is not appropriate and is embarrassing or upsetting

un·seen¹ /ˌʌnˈsin/ adj not seen or known about by anyone

U

un·seen² /ˌʌnˈsin/ adv without being seen by anyone

un·sel·fish /ʌnˈselfɪʃ/ adj thinking about what other people want or need rather than what you want or need yourself —**un·sel·fish·ly** adv

un·set·tled /ʌnˈset(ə)ld/ adj **1** something such as a problem or argument that is unsettled has not been dealt with successfully **2** nervous, confused, or upset **3** an unsettled place, situation, or period of time is one in which people feel nervous because things are changing **4** unsettled weather changes a lot and has a lot of wind and rain

un·set·tling /ʌnˈsetlɪŋ/ adj making you feel nervous, confused, or upset

un·shak·a·ble or **un·shake·a·ble** /ʌnˈʃeɪkəb(ə)l/ adj impossible to change or destroy

un·shav·en /ʌnˈʃeɪv(ə)n/ adj a man who is unshaven has hair growing on his face because he has not SHAVED recently

un·sight·ly /ʌnˈsaɪtli/ adj not pleasant to look at: *an unsightly scar*

un·skilled /ˌʌnˈskɪld/ adj **1** not needing much education, training, or experience **2** not having enough education, training, or experience to do a job that needs skill

un·so·cia·ble /ʌnˈsoʊʃəb(ə)l/ adj not interested in meeting people or in doing things with other people

un·so·lic·it·ed /ˌʌnsəˈlɪsɪtəd/ adj unsolicited offers, advice, gifts, etc. are those that you get but did not ask for

un·solved /ʌnˈsɑlvd/ adj an unsolved problem or mystery is one that has not been dealt with or explained

un·so·phis·ti·cat·ed /ˌʌnsəˈfɪstɪˌkeɪtəd/ adj **1** simple and not advanced in design **2** not knowing much about things such as culture, fashion, and the modern world

un·sound /ˌʌnˈsaʊnd/ adj **1** not based on sensible ideas **2** not safe

un·speak·a·ble /ʌnˈspikəb(ə)l/ adj used for emphasizing how bad something is —**un·speak·a·bly** adv

un·spec·i·fied /ʌnˈspesɪˌfaɪd/ adj not mentioned or known

un·spec·tac·u·lar /ˌʌnspekˈtækjələr/ adj not especially good

un·spoiled /ˌʌnˈspɔɪld/ adj an unspoiled place has not been changed in ways that make it less beautiful or enjoyable

un·spo·ken /ʌnˈspoʊkn/ adj not expressed in words but understood

un·sta·ble /ʌnˈsteɪb(ə)l/ adj **1** an unstable person often becomes suddenly angry or upset **2** often affected by serious problems **3** likely to move or change and become dangerous

un·stead·y /ʌnˈstedi/ adj **1** not regular, calm, or normal **2** too weak or sick to walk well

un·sub·scribe /ˌʌnsəbˈskraɪb/ verb [I/T] *computing* to take your name off an Internet MAILING LIST (=list of people who receive e-mails)

un·sub·stan·ti·at·ed /ʌnsəbˈstænʃiˌeɪtəd/ adj not proved to be true

un·suc·cess·ful /ˌʌnsəkˈsesfəl/ adj **1** something that is unsuccessful does not achieve what you want: *another unsuccessful attempt to reach agreement* **2** someone who is unsuccessful does not get what they want: *Letters are sent to all unsuccessful candidates.* —**un·suc·cess·ful·ly** adv

un·suit·a·ble /ʌnˈsutəb(ə)l/ adj not appropriate for a particular situation, purpose, or person: *Some of the material may be unsuitable for children.*

un·sung /ˌʌnˈsʌŋ/ adj not famous, praised, or admired, although deserving to be

un·sure /ʌnˈʃʊr/ adj not certain about something

PHRASE **unsure of yourself** not having much confidence

un·sur·pris·ing /ˌʌnsərˈpraɪzɪŋ/ adj something unsurprising is what you expected

un·sus·pect·ing /ˌʌnsəˈspektɪŋ/ adj not knowing that something bad is happening or will happen

un·sus·tain·a·ble /ˌʌnsəˈsteɪnəb(ə)l/ adj not capable of continuing at the same rate or level

un·sym·pa·thet·ic /ˌʌnsɪmpəˈθetɪk/ adj **1** not

kind enough to want to know about other people's problems **2** not willing to support something

un·tan·gle /ʌnˈtæŋg(ə)l/ verb [T] **1** to understand a complicated situation, or to solve a difficult problem **2** to separate things that are twisted around each other

un·tapped /ˌʌnˈtæpt/ adj not being used, but existing in large amounts that could bring profits or benefits

un·ten·a·ble /ʌnˈtenəb(ə)l/ adj impossible to defend as fair, appropriate, or true

un·think·a·ble /ʌnˈθɪŋkəb(ə)l/ adj impossible to imagine

un·ti·dy /ʌnˈtaɪdi/ adj not arranged in a way that is neat

un·tie /ʌnˈtaɪ/ verb [T] to take the knot out of a piece of rope or string that fastens something

un·til /ənˈtɪl/ preposition, conjunction ★★★

1 happening or done up to a particular point in time, and then stopping: *Baker is expected to be here until the end of the week.* ♦ *You'll just have to wait until they call your name.* ♦ ***Up until** now, Katherine has had no major problems in her life.*

2 continuing as far as a particular place: *Keep on the bus until the big supermarket, then get off.*

PHRASE **not (...) until** used for stating the point at which something finally happens, becomes possible, or becomes true: *They didn't see each other again until the fall.* ♦ *It was not until six o'clock that we got the first reports of trouble.*

un·time·ly /ʌnˈtaɪmli/ adj **1** happening earlier than you expected **2** happening at a time that is not appropriate, for example because it causes additional problems

un·told /ˌʌnˈtoʊld/ adj too great to be measured

un·touched /ˌʌnˈtʌtʃt/ adj **1** not harmed or spoiled: *Few families were untouched by the war.* **2** food or drink that is untouched has not been eaten or drunk

un·trained /ˌʌnˈtreɪnd/ adj not trained to do a particular job

PHRASE **to the untrained eye** to someone with little knowledge or experience of something

un·treat·ed /ʌnˈtritəd/ adj **1** receiving no medical treatment **2** in a natural state, and perhaps harmful

un·tried /ˌʌnˈtraɪd/ adj never done or used before and therefore not certain to succeed

un·true /ˌʌnˈtru/ adj not based on fact

un·trust·wor·thy /ʌnˈtrʌstˌwɜrði/ adj not capable of being trusted or depended on

un·truth /ʌnˈtruθ/ noun [C] *formal* a lie

un·used[1] /ʌnˈjuzd/ adj not used

un·used[2] /ʌnˈjust/ adj **be unused to (doing) sth** to not have much experience of something

un·u·su·al /ʌnˈjuʒuəl/ adj ★★

1 different from other people or things in a way that is interesting, attractive, or impressive: *The designers have chosen unusual color combinations.* ♦ *Ewing is a player with unusual talent.*

2 not normal, common, or ordinary: *You're in a very unusual situation.* ♦ *Residents should contact the police if they notice anything unusual.* ♦ *There's **nothing unusual** about this man's appearance.* ♦ **it is unusual for sb to do sth** *It's unusual for Sue to get so angry.* ♦ **it is unusual to do sth** *It's unusual to find so many different plants in one garden.*

un·u·su·al·ly /ʌnˈjuʒuəli/ adv **1** in a way that is not usual or typical: *Boris seemed unusually quiet.* **2** extremely: *Cambridge has several unusually good restaurants.*

un·veil /ʌnˈveɪl/ verb [T] **1** to announce something officially **2** to remove the cover from something as part of an official ceremony

un·want·ed /ʌnˈwɑntəd/ adj not wanted

un·war·rant·ed /ʌnˈwɔrəntəd/ adj not fair or necessary

un·war·y /ʌnˈweri/ adj not paying attention to the dangers around you

un·wa·ver·ing /ʌnˈweɪv(ə)rɪŋ/ adj strong and steady

un·wel·come /ʌnˈwelkəm/ adj **1** unpleasant or annoying **2** an unwelcome guest or visitor is someone who you do not want to spend time with

un·well /ʌnˈwel/ adj *formal* sick

un·wield·y /ʌnˈwildi/ adj *formal* **1** too big or complicated to work well **2** large or heavy and difficult to carry

un·will·ing /ʌnˈwɪlɪŋ/ adj **1** if you are unwilling to do something, you do not want to do it or you refuse to do it: *Jane was unwilling to admit she was wrong.*

2 involved in doing something that you do not want to do: *an unwilling participant* —**un·will·ing·ly** adv, **un·will·ing·ness** noun [U]

un·wind /ʌnˈwaɪnd/ (past tense and past participle **un·wound** /ʌnˈwaʊnd/) verb **1** [I] *informal* to begin to relax after you have been working hard or feeling nervous **2** [I/T] to become straighter or looser after being wrapped around something else, or to make something do this

un·wise /ˌʌnˈwaɪz/ adj not sensible —**un·wise·ly** adv

un·wit·ting·ly /ʌnˈwɪtɪŋli/ adv in a way that is not conscious or deliberate —**un·wit·ting** adj

un·work·a·ble /ʌnˈwɜrkəb(ə)l/ adj not practical, and therefore unlikely to be successful

unwound the past tense and past participle of **unwind**

un·wrap /ʌnˈræp/ verb [T] to remove the paper or plastic that is covering something

un·writ·ten /ʌnˈrɪt(ə)n/ adj known or understood by everyone but not official

un·zip /ʌnˈzɪp/ verb [T] **1** to open a piece of clothing or a bag by pulling a ZIPPER (=an object with two pieces of metal that fit together to fasten something) **2** *computing* to increase the size of a file to its original size after it has been reduced

up[1] /ʌp/ grammar word ★★★

> Up can be:
> - an **adverb**: *Their voices could be heard up in our room.*
> - a **preposition**: *He climbed up the steps.*
> - an **adjective**: *the up escalator*
> - used after the verb "to be": *He was up early the next morning.*

1 higher in or toward a higher position:

U

She's up in the bathroom. ♦ *I got off my bike and walked up the hill.* ♦ *Pick your clothes up off the floor and put them away.* ♦ *The hotel is 1,500 feet up in the Black Mountains.* ♦ *We rolled on our backs and looked up at the sky.* ♦ *The kids were jumping* ***up and down*** *on the bed.*
2 upright upright, or moving toward an upright position: *He stood up and pulled a chair out for me to sit on.* ♦ *I found Hattie sitting up in bed.*
3 north in or toward the north of a region or country: *We're going up to Seattle soon.*
4 moving near to sb/sth moving near to someone or something and then stopping: *A salesperson came up and asked if she could help.* ♦ *Just go* ***up to*** *him and say hello.*
5 farther along a road, etc. farther along a road, path, etc., in a direction away from you: *He lives up the street from me.*
6 increased in amount/level at or toward an increased amount or level: *Total car sales were up $3 million over last year.* ♦ *Turn the volume up – I can't hear anything.* ♦ *Fuel prices* ***went up*** *by 3 percent.*
7 not in bed awake and out of bed: *Get up! It's almost 10:00.* ♦ *I was up till midnight preparing the presentation.*
8 in or into smaller parts divided or broken into smaller pieces or equal parts: *The prize money will be divided up among the team members.*
9 completely completely done or used so that there is nothing left: *He ate up all his dinner.* ♦ *The stream dries up in summer.*
10 at an end used for stating that a period of time has ended: *Put your pencils down! Time's up!*
11 fastened fastened or closed completely: *She kept Albert's letters in a bundle tied up with ribbon.* ♦ *Did you lock the house up before you left?*
12 collected collected, added, or brought together in one place: *She was busy gathering up her papers.* ♦ *Our profits are quite large when you add them all up.*
13 working a system that is up is working properly: *By ten o'clock we had the computers up again.* ♦ *The new records system should be* ***up and running*** *soon.*
14 happening *spoken* used for saying or asking if something is wrong or if something is happening: *When Sara didn't come, I knew* ***something was up.*** ♦ *You seem rather quiet today.* ***What's up?***
PHRASES **up against sb/sth** competing with someone, or having a serious problem to deal with
up and down 1 backward and forward: *He kept walking up and down the hallway all night long.* **2** sometimes happy and well and sometimes not: *"How are things going?" "Kind of up and down."*
up for sth 1 being considered for a particular status or job: *The senator is up for re-election in 2006.* ♦ *The contract is up for renewal soon.* **2** available for a particular purpose: *Most of the houses are up for sale.* **3** *spoken* willing to do a particular activity: *"What do you feel like doing?" "I'd be up for just about anything."*
up to/until/till sth used for stating the latest time that something can happen, or the end of a period of time: *Laura was here up until about 5 minutes ago.* ♦ *We can make the delivery any time today up till about 10 p.m.*
up to sb if something is up to you, you are responsible for deciding about it or doing it: *Do you want to stay or go? It's up to you.* ♦ *It's up to all of us to make our streets safe for children.*
up to sth 1 used for stating the most that an amount can be, or what level it can reach: *Some dinosaurs were up to twenty-seven meters long.* **2** used for stating a particular standard that something can reach: *I'm afraid the play wasn't up to our expectations.* **3** doing something wrong or secret: *When the children are quiet like this, I know they're up to something.* **4** well enough, strong enough, or good enough to do something: *She's supposed to leave the hospital now, but I don't think she's up to it.*

up² /ʌp/ verb [T] *informal* to increase an amount, or raise something to a higher level

up³ /ʌp/ noun **ups and downs** *informal* a mixture of good and bad situations or experiences: *Like all couples, we've had our ups and downs.*

ˌup-and-ˈcoming adj likely to become successful or popular soon

up·beat /ˈʌpˌbit/ adj *informal* happy and positive

up·bring·ing /ˈʌpˌbrɪŋɪŋ/ noun [singular] the way that parents take care of their children and teach them to behave

up·com·ing /ˈʌpˌkʌmɪŋ/ adj **1** happening soon **2** an upcoming book, CD, or movie will soon be available to buy or see

up·date¹ /ʌpˈdeɪt/ verb **1** [I/T] to add the most recent information to something such as a book, document, or list: *The latest edition has been completely updated.* **2** [T] to tell someone the most recent news or information about something: **update sb on sth** *Dr. Cooper can update us on the latest developments.* **3** [T] to make something more modern: *Our software is continually updated and improved.* → UP-TO-DATE

up·date² /ˈʌpˌdeɪt/ noun [C] **1** a report or broadcast that contains the most recent information **2** *computing* a piece of software that contains recent improvements to a computer program

up·end /ʌpˈend/ verb [T] to turn something upside down

ˌup ˈfront adv **1** if you pay for something up front, you pay for it before you receive it **2** if you tell someone something up front, you are very honest from the beginning about something that might affect them —**up·front** /ʌpˈfrʌnt/ adj

up·grade¹ /ˈʌpˌgreɪd/ verb **1** [I/T] to make a computer or machine more powerful or effective **2** [T] to officially give someone or something a higher status

up·grade² /ˈʌpˌgreɪd/ noun [C] a piece of equipment or software that is designed to make a computer more powerful or effective

up·heav·al /ʌpˈhiv(ə)l/ noun [C/U] a sudden or violent change

up·hill /ˈʌphɪl/ adj **1** toward the top of a slope or hill **2** difficult to do or achieve —**up·hill** /ˌʌpˈhɪl/ adv

up·hold /ʌpˈhoʊld/ (past tense and past

participle **up•held** /ʌp'held/) verb [T] if a court of law upholds something, it says that it is correct: *The Appeals Court upheld the decision of the lower court.*

up•hol•ster•y /ʌp'hoʊlst(ə)ri/ noun [U] soft material that is used for covering chairs and other seats

up•keep /'ʌpˌkip/ noun [singular/U] the process or cost of keeping property in good condition

up•lift•ing /ʌp'lɪftɪŋ/ adj making you feel happier or more hopeful

up•load /'ʌpˌloʊd/ verb [T] *computing* to send information from your computer to a larger system using the Internet

up•on /ə'pɑn/ preposition ★
1 *literary* on or onto something: *He believes we were put upon this earth for a purpose.*
2 *formal* used after some verbs with the same meaning as "on": *My whole future depended upon the decision of one manager.*
3 *formal* immediately after doing something, or immediately after something happens: *Upon his release, Davis went to his mother's.*

up•per /'ʌpər/ adj ★
1 higher than something else, especially higher than one of two things that are a pair ≠ LOWER: *He had a scar on his upper lip.* ♦ *You'll be able to see more if you sit on the upper bunk.*
2 near the top, or at the top of something ≠ LOWER: *There is already some snow on the upper slopes.* ♦ *upper-body strength*
3 higher in status or rank ≠ LOWER: *the upper ranks of the army*
4 to the north: *New York's Upper East Side*

ˌupper 'case adj upper case letters of the alphabet are CAPITAL LETTERS, for example "A," "F," and "T"

ˌupper 'class noun **the upper class** or **the upper classes** people who have the highest social status → LOWER CLASS, MIDDLE CLASS, WORKING CLASS

ˌupper 'hand, the noun [singular] control or an advantage over a person or situation: *Agassi got the upper hand in the last set.*

up•per•most /'ʌpərˌmoʊst/ adj **1** more important than anything else **2** at or near the top

up•right¹ /'ʌpˌraɪt/ adv **1** sitting or standing with a straight back: *Sara was wide awake, sitting upright in her bed.* **2** in or into a straight or standing position: *Pictures were propped upright against all the walls.*

up•right² /'ʌpˌraɪt/ adj **1** straight and tall: *Make sure your seat is in an upright position for landing.* **2** *formal* honest: *an upright citizen*

up•ris•ing /'ʌpˌraɪzɪŋ/ noun [C] a political situation in which a large group of people opposes and tries to defeat the government or the person who rules their country = REBELLION

up•riv•er /ʌp'rɪvər/ adv in the opposite direction to the way that a river flows

up•roar /'ʌpˌrɔr/ noun [singular/U] **1** angry public criticism of something **2** a lot of noise made by people who are shouting

up•root /ʌp'rut/ verb [T] **1** to force someone to leave the place where they live **2** to pull a whole tree or plant from the ground

up•scale /'ʌpˌskeɪl/ adj *American* very expensive, fashionable, and intended for people who have a lot of money

up•set¹ /ˌʌp'set/ adj ★
1 sad, worried, or angry about something: *Why are you so upset?* ♦ *They're all still very **upset about** losing the case.* ♦ **+(that)** *She feels upset that we didn't tell her the truth.*
2 if your stomach is upset, you have an illness affecting your stomach, usually caused by something that you have eaten or drunk: *Call and tell them you've got an upset stomach.*

up•set² /ʌp'set, 'ʌpˌset/ (present participle **up•set•ting**; past tense and past participle **up•set**) verb [T] ★
1 to make someone feel sad, worried, or angry: *I'm sorry, I didn't mean to upset you.* ♦ *Tim was upset by Hansen's rude remarks.*
2 to spoil something: *I'm sorry if I've upset your plans for this evening.*
3 to knock something over accidentally = SPILL

up•set³ /'ʌpˌset/ noun [C] an occasion when someone defeats an opponent who is considered better than them

up•set•ting /ʌp'setɪŋ/ adj making you feel sad, worried, or angry

up•shot /'ʌpˌʃɑt/ noun **the upshot (of sth)** the result of a process or event

up•side /'ʌpˌsaɪd/ noun [singular] the positive aspect of a bad situation

ˌupside 'down adv ★ with the top part at the bottom or lower than the bottom part: *The car landed upside down in a ditch.*
PHRASES **turn sb's life/world upside down** to change someone's life completely
turn sth upside down to make a place very messy while you are searching for something
—**ˌupside-'down** adj

up•stage /ʌp'steɪdʒ/ verb [T] to do something so that you get more attention and admiration than someone else

up•stairs /ʌp'sterz/ adv ★
1 on an upper level of a building with stairs ≠ DOWNSTAIRS: *The children are upstairs in bed.* ♦ *Do you know who lives in the apartment upstairs?*
2 to an upper level of a building ≠ DOWNSTAIRS: *I'm going upstairs for a nap.*
—**up•stairs** /'ʌpˌsterz/ adj: *an upstairs room*

up•start /'ʌpˌstɑrt/ noun [C] a new person in a group who behaves as if they are more important than the people who are already there

up•state /ʌp'steɪt/ adj in the northern part of a state in the U.S. —**up•state** adv

up•stream /ʌp'strim/ adv in the opposite direction to the way that a river or stream flows

up•surge /'ʌpˌsɜrdʒ/ noun [singular] a sudden increase in something

up•swing /'ʌpˌswɪŋ/ noun **on the upswing** increasing or improving

up•take /'ʌpˌteɪk/ noun **be quick/slow on the uptake** *informal* to take a short/long time to understand or realize something

up•tight /'ʌpˌtaɪt/ adj nervous and easily annoyed

ˌup-to-'date adj **1** giving the most recent news and information: *Visit our website for the most up-to-date sports news.* **2** modern and

U

using the latest ideas or knowledge: *up-to-date technology*

ˌup-to-the-ˈminute adj containing all the most recent news and information

up•town /ˌʌpˈtaʊn/ adv *American* in or toward the areas of a city that are farthest away from the center —**up•town** adj → DOWNTOWN

up•turn /ˈʌpˌtɜrn/ noun [singular] an increase in something

up•turned /ˌʌpˈtɜrnd/ adj **1** curving, pointing, or facing upward **2** an upturned object has been moved so that its top part is at the bottom

up•ward¹ /ˈʌpwərd/ or **up•wards** /ˈʌpwərdz/ adv **1** toward a higher position ≠ DOWNWARD: *The road climbed upward.* **2** toward a higher or more important level ≠ DOWNWARD: *Share prices have moved sharply upward.* **3** more than a number or amount: *They spent upward of a million dollars on that project.*

up•ward² /ˈʌpwərd/ adj **1** moving or turned toward a higher position **2** moving toward a higher level or amount

u•ra•ni•um /jʊˈreɪniəm/ noun [U] a metal used for producing nuclear energy

ur•ban /ˈɜrbən/ adj ★ relating to towns and cities ≠ RURAL: *People moved to the urban areas for jobs.* ♦ *urban poverty*

ur•bane /ɜrˈbeɪn/ adj behaving in a pleasant, relaxed, and correct way in social situations

urge¹ /ɜrdʒ/ verb [T] ★
1 to advise someone very strongly about what action or attitude they should take: *He urged restraint in dealing with the protesters.* ♦ **urge sb to do sth** *The United Nations has urged them to honor the treaty.*
2 to make a person or animal move in a particular direction: *He urged the horse forward.*
PHRASAL VERB **ˌurge sb ˈon** to encourage someone to keep trying to do something

urge² /ɜrdʒ/ noun [C] a strong feeling of wanting or needing to do something: *I had an overwhelming urge to kiss him.*

ur•gen•cy /ˈɜrdʒənsi/ noun [U] the need to deal with something immediately

ur•gent /ˈɜrdʒənt/ adj ★
1 urgent things are things that you need to deal with immediately: *The problem is becoming increasingly urgent.* ♦ *The refugees are* ***in urgent need of*** *food.*
2 expressing the feeling of wanting something very much or wanting it immediately: *an urgent whisper*
—**ur•gent•ly** adv

u•ri•nate /ˈjʊrɪˌneɪt/ verb [I] *formal* to get rid of urine from your body

u•rine /ˈjʊrɪn/ noun [U] liquid waste from a person's or animal's body

URL /ˌju ɑr ˈel/ noun [C] *computing* Uniform Resource Locator: an Internet address

us /*weak* əs, *strong* ʌs/ pronoun ★★★ the object form of "we," used for referring to yourself and other people with you or in your group when you are the person speaking or writing: *It wasn't our idea, so don't blame us.* ♦ *Angela came with us in our rented car.* ♦ *No one told us when we should be there.*

U.S., the /ˌjuˈes/ the United States

U.S.A., the /ˌju es ˈeɪ/ the United States of America

us•a•ble /ˈjuzəb(ə)l/ adj available or appropriate to be used for a particular purpose

us•age /ˈjusɪdʒ/ noun **1** [C/U] the way that words are used by people when they speak and write their language: *differences between British and American usage* **2** [U] the process of using something **3** [U] the amount of something that you use

use¹ /juz/ verb ★★★

1 do sth with tool, etc.	5 take illegal drugs
2 get benefit from sth	6 say particular words
3 take from supply	+ PHRASE
4 treat sb in unfair way	+ PHRASAL VERB

1 [T] to do something using a machine, tool, skill, method, etc. to do a job or to achieve a result: *Using a computer is so much quicker.* ♦ *What type of soap do you use?* ♦ **use sth for sth** *Psychological tests are used for selection purposes.* ♦ **use sth for doing sth** *We use methane gas for heating.* ♦ **use sth as sth** *The land is being used as a parking lot.*
2 [T] to get a benefit for yourself from something available to you: *Only about 30 people regularly use the bus service.*
3 [T] to take an amount from a supply of something: *You've used all the hot water.*
4 [T] to treat someone in an unfair way, for example by pretending to care about them so that they do what you want: *You know he's just using you.*
5 [I/T] to take illegal drugs regularly: *In jail, he continued to use drugs.*
6 [T] to say or write particular words: *Don't use language like that in front of your mom.*
PHRASE **could use sth** *spoken* used for saying someone or something needs a particular thing very much: *You both look as if you could use a drink.*
PHRASAL VERB **ˌuse sth ˈup** to use all of a supply of something: *I've used up all my vacation days, and it's only August.*

Word family: use

Words in the same family as ***use***

- **usage** *n*
- **used** *adj*
- **useful** *adj*
- **useless** *adj*
- **reusable** *adj*
- **user** *n*
- **unused** *adj*
- **misuse** *n, v*
- **reuse** *v*

use² /jus/ noun ★★★
1 [singular/U] the act of using something: *an unnecessary use of force* ♦ ***the use of*** *resources/technology/computers*
2 [C/U] a way of using something: *This material has a variety of manufacturing uses.* ♦ *This is not the best* ***use of*** *your talents.*
3 [U] the right, an opportunity, or permission to use something: *We can* ***have the use of*** *the hall every Thursday.* ♦ *The pool was built* ***for the use of*** *residents* (=only for them to use).
4 [U] the ability to use a part of your body: *He* ***lost the use of*** *his legs in a car accident.*
PHRASES **be of use (to sb)** to be helpful or useful: *This leaflet may be of use to him.*
be (of) no use (to sb) to not be helpful or useful
come into/go out of use to start or stop being used by people: *Computers first came into use in the early 1950s.*
in/out of use being used regularly, or not

being used any longer: *I'll be glad to see the building in use again.*
make use of to use someone or something for a particular purpose, especially one that brings a benefit to you: *Why doesn't she make use of her singing talent?*
put sth to good use to use something you have for a sensible purpose that brings a benefit to you

used /juzd/ adj ★★
1 owned by someone else before you =SECONDHAND: *a used car*
2 no longer completely clean because of having been used: *a used towel*

used to¹ /ˈjust tu/ modal verb ★★★

> ■ **Used to** is usually followed by an infinitive: *We used to swim in the river.* But sometimes the following infinitive is left out: *I don't play golf now, but I used to.*
> ■ **Used to** only exists as a past tense.
> ■ Questions and negatives are usually formed with "did" + **use to** (with no "d"): *Did you use to work here?* ♦ *We didn't use to earn much.*

used for saying what was true or what happened regularly in the past, especially when this is not true or does not happen now: *I used to enjoy gardening, but I don't have time for it now.* ♦ *Where did you use to live before you moved here?* ♦ *I didn't use to like him, but now we're good friends.*

used to² /ˈjust tu/ adj ★★ familiar with something because you have often experienced it before, so that it no longer seems difficult or strange: **used to (doing) sth** *Deborah was used to working on difficult assignments.* ♦ *I'm tired – I'm not used to these late nights.* ♦ *I haven't **gotten used to** the new system yet.*

use•ful /ˈjusf(ə)l/ adj ★★★ helpful for doing or achieving something: *a useful tool/ technique/gadget* ♦ *Here's some **useful information** about travel in Canada.* ♦ **useful for (doing) sth** *Old pictures are useful for seeing how people used to dress.* —**use•ful•ly** adv, **use•ful•ness** noun [U]

use•less /ˈjusləs/ adj **1** useless objects have no purpose or cannot do what they were designed to do: *This technology is useless if you can't operate it.* ♦ *Why do you keep this completely useless umbrella?* **2** useless activities are not effective in achieving the purpose they were intended to achieve: *All of my efforts to persuade him were useless.* ♦ **it's useless trying to do sth** *It's useless trying to talk to her because she never listens.* **3** *impolite* if someone is useless, they are not capable of achieving anything: *Don't ask Jeff – he's useless!* —**use•less•ly** adv

us•er /ˈjuzər/ noun [C] ★
1 someone who uses something such as a service or a piece of equipment: *Software should meet the needs of users.* ♦ *Bicyclists, like all **road users**, must obey traffic signs.*
2 someone who regularly takes illegal drugs

ˌuser-ˈfriendly adj easy to use or understand

us•er•name /ˈjuzərˌneɪm/ noun [C] *computing* the name that is used by someone for operating a computer program

ush•er¹ /ˈʌʃər/ verb [T] to lead someone politely somewhere
PHRASAL VERB **ˌusher sth ˈin** to make an activity or process begin

ush•er² /ˈʌʃər/ noun [C] someone whose job is to show people where to sit

USS /ˌju es ˈes/ United States Ship: used before the name of a ship belonging to the U.S. Navy

u•su•al /ˈjuʒuəl/ adj ★★★ typical of what happens in most situations, or of what people do in most situations: *She gave us her usual polite smile.* ♦ *The trip to work took longer than usual.*
PHRASE **as usual** used for saying what usually happens: *We went to bed that evening around 10:30 as usual.*

u•su•al•ly /ˈjuʒuəli/ adv ★★★ used for saying what happens in most situations, or what people do in most situations =NORMALLY: *What time do you usually go to bed?* ♦ *She's usually home by this time.*

u•surp /juˈzɜrp/ verb [T] *formal* to take a job or position that belongs to someone else

UT abbrev Utah

u•ten•sil /juˈtens(ə)l/ noun [C] something that you use to cook or eat with

u•ter•us /ˈjutərəs/ noun [C] the organ in a woman's body where babies grow

u•til•i•ties /juˈtɪlətiz/ noun [plural] services such as gas, water, or electricity that are used by everyone

u•til•i•ty pole /juˈtɪləti ˌpoʊl/ noun [C] *American* one of a series of tall poles that hold telephone or electricity wires high above the ground

u•til•ize /ˈjut(ə)lˌaɪz/ verb [T] *formal* to use something —**u•til•i•za•tion** /ˌjut(ə)lɪˈzeɪʃ(ə)n/ noun [U]

ut•most¹ /ˈʌtˌmoʊst/ adj as much as possible: *We attach the utmost importance to safety.*

ut•most² /ˈʌtˌmoʊst/ noun [singular] the greatest amount or degree possible
PHRASE **do/try your utmost (to do sth)** to try as hard as possible

u•to•pi•a /juˈtoʊpiə/ noun [C/U] an imaginary place or situation in which everything is perfect —**u•to•pi•an** adj

ut•ter¹ /ˈʌtər/ adj complete: *It's been an utter waste of time.*

ut•ter² /ˈʌtər/ verb [T] *literary* **1** to say something **2** to make a sound

ut•ter•ance /ˈʌt(ə)rəns/ noun [C] *formal* something that someone says

ut•ter•ly /ˈʌtərli/ adv completely: *You're being utterly unreasonable.*

U-turn /ˈju ˌtɜrn/ noun [C] **1** a sudden and complete change of policy **2** a movement in which you turn a vehicle in order to travel in the opposite direction

V v

v or **V** /vi/ noun [C/U] the 22nd letter of the alphabet → V-CHIP, V-NECK

V abbrev volt

v. abbrev **1** verb **2** versus **3** very

VA abbrev Virginia

va•can•cy /ˈveɪkənsi/ noun [C] **1** a job that is

available: *We have several vacancies to fill in the Sales Department.* **2** a room in a hotel that is available: *We have no vacancies at all in July.*

va•cant /ˈveɪkənt/ adj **1** a place that is vacant is available because no one else is using it **2** if a job is vacant, someone is needed to do it **3** looking as if you do not understand or are not paying attention —**va•cant•ly** adv

va•cate /ˈveɪˌkeɪt/ verb [T] *formal* to leave a place or a job so that it is available for someone else

va•ca•tion /veɪˈkeɪʃ(ə)n/ noun ★★
1 [C/U] *American* a period of time when you do not work and you do things for pleasure, often when you travel somewhere: *a vacation home* ♦ *I only get one week of vacation per year in this job.* ♦ *She's **on vacation** this week.* ♦ *We're **taking a vacation** in Europe this summer.*
2 [C] a period of time when a school is closed: *I'm planning on visiting my parents during Christmas vacation.*
—**va•ca•tion** verb [I]

va•ca•tion•er /veɪˈkeɪʃ(ə)nər/ noun [C] *American* someone who is on vacation

vac•ci•nate /ˈvæksɪˌneɪt/ verb [T] to treat a person or animal with a vaccine to protect them against a disease —**vac•ci•na•tion** /ˌvæksɪˈneɪʃ(ə)n/ noun [C/U]

vac•cine /ˈvækˌsin/ noun [C/U] a substance that is put into your body in order to provide protection against a disease

vac•u•um[1] /ˈvækjuəm, ˈvækjum/ noun **1** [C] a VACUUM CLEANER **2** [C] an enclosed space with all the air and other gases removed from it **3** [singular] a situation in which something is missing: *the political vacuum left by his death*
PHRASE **in a vacuum** existing or happening separately from other people or things, and not influenced by them: *Learning cannot occur in a vacuum.*

vac•u•um[2] /ˈvækjuəm, ˈvækjum/ verb [I/T] to clean a room using a vacuum cleaner

ˈvacuum ˌcleaner noun [C] a piece of electrical equipment that cleans floors by sucking up dirt

va•ga•ries /ˈveɪgəriz/ noun [plural] *formal* unexpected changes that you cannot control

va•gi•na /vəˈdʒaɪnə/ noun [C] a woman's sex organ, consisting of a tube that connects the outer sex organs to the UTERUS (=place where babies grow) —**vag•i•nal** /ˈvædʒən(ə)l/ adj

V

vague /veɪg/ adj **1** not clearly or fully explained: *Witnesses gave only a vague description of the driver.* ♦ *the vague promises of politicians* **2** a vague feeling or memory is not complete or definite: *I have a vague memory of the hotel.* ♦ *a vague idea/feeling* **3** someone who is vague does not clearly or fully explain something: *He was always vague when I asked about deadlines.* **4** a vague shape is not clear or not easy to see

vague•ly /ˈveɪgli/ adv **1** in a way that is not clear: *He vaguely remembered his mother talking about it.* **2** slightly: *The interview made him look vaguely ridiculous.* **3** in a way that shows that you are not paying attention

vain /veɪn/ adj **1** unsuccessful or useless: *a vain attempt* **2** *showing disapproval* someone who is vain is very proud and thinks that they are attractive or special
PHRASE **in vain** without success
—**vain•ly** adv

val•en•tine /ˈvælənˌtaɪn/ noun [C] **1** a card or present that you give to someone on Valentine's Day **2** someone who you give a valentine to

ˈValentine's ˌDay noun [C/U] February 14th, the day on which people give cards and small presents to the person who they love

val•et /ˈvælət, ˈvæleɪ/ noun [C] **1** *American* someone who works at a hotel or restaurant whose job is to park your car **2** a man whose job is to take care of another man's clothes and cook his meals

val•iant /ˈvæliənt/ adj *formal* very brave and determined —**val•i•ant•ly** adv

val•id /ˈvælɪd/ adj ★
1 legally or officially acceptable ≠ INVALID: *a valid claim* ♦ *You will need **a valid passport**.*
2 reasonable and generally accepted ≠ INVALID: *a valid argument* ♦ *These are valid reasons why we should ban tobacco advertising.*
3 accepted by a computer system ≠ INVALID: *a valid password*
—**va•lid•i•ty** /vəˈlɪdəti/ noun [U]

val•i•date /ˈvælɪˌdeɪt/ verb [T] *formal* **1** to officially prove that something is true or correct **2** to officially state that something is of an appropriate standard —**val•i•da•tion** /ˌvælɪˈdeɪʃ(ə)n/ noun [C/U]

val•ley /ˈvæli/ noun [C] ★ a low area of land between two mountains or hills, often with a river flowing through it: *the Ohio River Valley*

val•u•a•ble /ˈvæljəb(ə)l/ adj ★★
1 worth a lot of money: *a valuable antique* ♦ *The necklace is not very valuable.*
2 very useful and important: *an opportunity to gain **valuable experience***
3 valuable time is important because there is not much of it available

val•u•a•bles /ˈvæljəb(ə)lz/ noun [plural] small possessions that are worth a lot of money

val•u•a•tion /ˌvæljuˈeɪʃ(ə)n/ noun [C/U] a decision about how much money something is worth, or the process of making this decision

val•ue[1] /ˈvælju/ noun ★★★
1 [C/U] the amount that something is worth, measured especially in money: *The value of the painting is not known.* ♦ *a drop/rise/fall in value* ♦ *You can't put a value on a human life.* ♦ *The ring was **of little value**.*
2 [U] the degree to which someone or something is useful or important: *educational/nutritional value* ♦ *documents that will be **of great value to** future historians*
3 [U] the amount that something is worth compared to the money that it costs: *This wine is an excellent value at $5.98 a bottle.*

val•ue[2] /ˈvælju/ verb [T] ★
1 to consider someone or something important: *a valued friend/colleague* ♦ *a community in which people value the knowledge of their elders*

2 to state how much something is worth: *I had the necklace valued.* ♦ **value sth at sth** *a contract valued at approximately $3 billion*

val•ues /ˈvæljuz/ noun [plural] the principles and beliefs that influence the behavior and way of life of a particular group or community: *Western/Islamic values*

valve /vælv/ noun [C] something that opens and closes in order to control the flow of air or liquid

vam•pire /ˈvæmˌpaɪr/ noun [C] a character in stories who appears at night to bite people's necks and suck their blood

van /væn/ noun [C] ★ a vehicle that is used for carrying goods or several people: *We'll have to **rent a van** to move all this stuff.*

van•dal /ˈvænd(ə)l/ noun [C] someone who deliberately damages or destroys things, especially public property

van•dal•ism /ˈvænd(ə)lˌɪzəm/ noun [U] the act of deliberately damaging or destroying things, especially public property

van•dal•ize /ˈvænd(ə)lˌaɪz/ verb [T] to deliberately damage or destroy things, especially public property

van•guard, the /ˈvænˌgɑrd/ noun [singular] the people who introduce and develop new ways of thinking, new technologies, etc.

va•nil•la /vəˈnɪlə/ noun [U] a flavor from the bean of a tropical plant, used in some sweet foods

van•ish /ˈvænɪʃ/ verb [I] ★
1 to disappear in a sudden or mysterious way: *The plane circled the airport once, then vanished.* ♦ *He **vanished into** the darkness.*
2 to stop existing completely: *a rapidly vanishing way of life*

van•i•ty /ˈvænəti/ noun [U] the quality of being too proud of your abilities, or too interested in your appearance

van•tage point /ˈvæntɪdʒ ˌpɔɪnt/ noun [C] **1** a position from which you can see things well **2** the particular ideas or beliefs that influence the way you think about things

va•por /ˈveɪpər/ noun [C] very small drops of water or another liquid in the air

va•pour /ˈveɪpər/ the British spelling of **vapor**

var•i•a•ble[1] /ˈveriəb(ə)l/ adj capable of being changed, or changing often

var•i•a•ble[2] /ˈveriəb(ə)l/ noun [C] something that can change and affect a situation

var•i•ance /ˈveriəns/ noun **at variance (with)** *formal* if one thing is at variance with another, they are completely different and seem to oppose each other

var•i•ant /ˈveriənt/ noun [C] **1** something that is related to another thing but is not exactly the same **2** *linguistics* a different form, spelling, or pronunciation of a word

var•i•a•tion /ˌveriˈeɪʃ(ə)n/ noun ★
1 [C/U] differences in amount, level, etc.: *There was **wide variation in** the test scores.* ♦ ***variations in** temperature*
2 [C] something that is slightly different from similar things: *The dessert is a **variation of** a classic recipe.*

var•ied /ˈverid/ adj including a wide range of things or people

va•ri•e•ty /vəˈraɪəti/ noun ★★★
1 [singular] a number of different people or things: *Adults study for **a variety of** reasons.* ♦ *We've interviewed **a wide variety of** people.*
2 [C] a particular type of thing: *a new variety of tomato*
3 [U] the fact that something consists of different things: *Consumers are demanding more variety.*

> **Words often used with variety**
>
> *Adjectives often used with **variety** (sense 1)*
>
> ■ **astonishing, bewildering, enormous, great, huge, immense, infinite, large, rich, wide +** VARIETY: used about a very large number of different people or things

var•i•ous /ˈveriəs/ adj ★★★ several different: *There are **various ways** of solving the problem.* ♦ *vehicles of **various shapes and sizes***

var•i•ous•ly /ˈveriəsli/ adv in different ways, by different people, or at different times

var•nish[1] /ˈvɑrnɪʃ/ noun [C/U] **1** a clear sticky liquid that is put onto wood to protect it and make it shiny **2** the surface formed when varnish dries

var•nish[2] /ˈvɑrnɪʃ/ verb [T] to put varnish on something

var•si•ty /ˈvɑrsəti/ adj *American* a varsity team, sport, etc. at a school, college, or university is involved in the highest level of competition

var•y /ˈveri/ verb ★★
1 [I] to change according to the situation: *People's reactions to the drug can **vary widely**.* ♦ *Prices **vary according to** the size of the job.*
2 [I] if things vary, they are different from each other: *Rooms **vary in size** but all have a television and a telephone.*
3 [T] to change something: *The software allows you to vary the size of the print.*

vase /veɪs, veɪs/ noun [C] a container for cut flowers

va•sec•to•my /vəˈsektəmi/ noun [C] a medical operation that makes a man unable to have children

vast /væst/ adj ★ extremely large = HUGE: *I believe **the vast majority** of people* (=almost everyone) *will support us.*

vast•ly /ˈvæs(t)li/ adv to a great degree: *The hotel has been vastly improved.*

vat /væt/ noun [C] a large container for holding or storing liquids

VAT /ˌvi eɪ ˈti, væt/ noun [U] value added tax: a tax on goods and services

vault[1] /vɔlt/ noun [C] **1** a strongly protected room in a bank where money, gold, etc. is kept **2** a curved structure that supports or forms a roof, especially in a church

vault[2] /vɔlt/ or **ˌvault ˈover sth** verb [T] to jump over something, especially using your hands or a pole to support you

V-chip /ˈvi ˌtʃɪp/ noun [C] an electronic CHIP that is put in a television so that parents can control what their children watch

VCR /ˌvi si ˈɑr/ noun [C] video cassette recorder: a machine for recording and watching videos

've /əv/ short form the usual way of saying or writing "have," added to the end of "I," "you," "we," or "they" to form the present perfect tense. This is not often used in formal writing: *We've been trying to call you.*

veal /vil/ noun [U] meat from a young cow

veer /vɪr/ verb [I] to suddenly move in a different direction

veg /vedʒ/ or ˌ**veg ˈout** verb [I] *informal* to sit and relax without thinking about anything

veg·an /ˈvigən, ˈvedʒən/ noun [C] someone who chooses not to eat anything made from animals or fish, including eggs, milk, and cheese

veg·e·ta·ble /ˈvedʒ(ə)təb(ə)l/ noun [C] ★★★ a part of a plant used as food, for example a potato, bean, or CABBAGE: *We grow all our own vegetables.* ♦ *a vegetable garden*

veg·e·tar·i·an /ˌvedʒəˈteriən/ noun [C] someone who chooses not to eat meat or fish —**veg·e·tar·i·an** adj

veg·e·ta·tion /ˌvedʒəˈteɪʃ(ə)n/ noun [U] *formal* plants and trees

veg·gie /ˈvedʒi/ noun [C] *spoken* a vegetable —**veg·gie** adj

ve·he·ment /ˈviəmənt/ adj involving extremely strong feelings or beliefs —**ve·he·mence** noun [U], **ve·he·ment·ly** adv

ve·hi·cle /ˈviɪk(ə)l/ noun [C] ★★★
1 a machine that you travel in or on, especially one with an engine that travels on roads, for example a car, bus, van, truck, or MOTORCYCLE: *Don't forget to lock your vehicle while it is parked.*
2 a way of expressing ideas or of making something happen: *He launched the newspaper as **a vehicle for** his campaign.*
3 a movie, television show, etc. that is created for one actor: *The movie was a vehicle for Tom Hanks.*

veil /veɪl/ noun [C] **1** a thin piece of cloth worn over a woman's head or face **2** a layer of something such as rain that prevents you from seeing very far **3** a lack of knowledge or information that prevents you from discovering the truth: *a veil of secrecy*

veiled /veɪld/ adj **1** a veiled threat, attack, or warning is not direct but is easily understood **2** covered with a veil

vein /veɪn/ noun ★
1 [C] one of the tubes in your body that carry blood to your heart
2 [C] one of the tubes that carry liquids through plants or insects
3 [singular] a supply or amount of a particular thing: *a rich vein of talent*
4 [C] a thin layer of a metal or other substance inside the Earth
PHRASE **in the same/a similar etc. vein** in the same/a similar etc. style or subject: *The second CD continues in the same vein as the first.*

Vel·cro /ˈvelˌkroʊ/ *trademark* two narrow bands of cloth with special surfaces that stick together, used for fastening clothes, shoes, etc.

ve·loc·i·ty /vəˈlɑsəti/ noun [U] *technical* the speed that something moves at in one direction

vel·vet /ˈvelvət/ noun [U] cloth that is very soft on one side and smooth on the other

vel·vet·y /ˈvelvəti/ adj very soft or smooth

ven·det·ta /venˈdetə/ noun [C] a situation in which one person or group keeps trying to harm another, especially because of something that happened in the past

vend·ing ma·chine /ˈvendɪŋ məˌʃin/ noun [C] a machine that you can buy things from, for example cigarettes, candy, or drinks

ven·dor /ˈvendər/ noun [C] someone who sells something, but not in a store

ve·neer /vəˈnɪr/ noun **1** [C/U] a thin layer of wood or plastic that covers something and improves its appearance **2** [singular] a pleasant appearance or polite way of behaving that is not sincere

ven·er·a·ble /ˈvenərəb(ə)l/ adj very old, and wise or respected

ve·ne·re·al dis·ease /vəˈnɪriəl dɪˌziz/ noun [C/U] *old-fashioned* a disease that is spread when people have sex

ve·ne·tian blind /vəˌniʃ(ə)n ˈblaɪnd/ noun [C] a BLIND across a window, made of flat narrow pieces joined with string

ven·geance /ˈvendʒəns/ noun [U] the act of harming or killing someone because they have done something bad to you = REVENGE
PHRASE **with a vengeance** used for emphasizing that something happens in an extreme way or with a lot of force

venge·ful /ˈvendʒfəl/ adj *literary* wanting or trying to harm someone because they have done something bad to you

ven·i·son /ˈvenɪs(ə)n/ noun [U] meat from a DEER

ven·om /ˈvenəm/ noun [U] **1** poison produced by some animals, especially snakes and insects **2** very strong anger or hate

ven·om·ous /ˈvenəməs/ adj **1** capable of producing poison **2** extremely unpleasant and full of very strong anger or hate

vent[1] /vent/ noun [C] a hole that allows air, gas, or smoke to escape or fresh air to enter

vent[2] /vent/ verb [I/T] to express your feelings of anger very strongly

ven·ti·late /ˈvent(ə)lˌeɪt/ verb [T] to allow fresh air to enter a room or building

ven·ti·la·tion /ˌvent(ə)lˈeɪʃ(ə)n/ noun [U] the movement of fresh air around a room or building

ven·ture[1] /ˈventʃər/ noun [C] a new business or activity

ven·ture[2] /ˈventʃər/ verb **1** [I] to go somewhere unpleasant, dangerous, or exciting **2** [T] to be brave enough to say something

ˈ**venture** ˌ**capital** noun [U] money invested in a new business that may or may not be successful

ven·ue /ˈvenˌju/ noun [C] the place where an activity or event happens

ve·ran·da or **ve·ran·dah** /vəˈrændə/ noun [C] a covered area along the outside of a house = PORCH

verb /vɜrb/ noun [C] *linguistics* ★ a word that shows an action or a state, for example "run" or "remain"

ver·bal /ˈvɜrb(ə)l/ adj **1** using words, or relating to words: *verbal communication* **2** using spoken communication rather than writing: *a verbal agreement* **3** *linguistics* acting as a verb or relating to a verb **4** using words, not physical force: *verbal abuse* —**ver·bal·ly** adv

ˌ**verbal** ˈ**noun** noun [C] *linguistics* a noun that is formed from a verb and ends in "ing," for example "swimming" in the sentence "Swimming is my favorite sport" = GERUND

V

ver•ba•tim /vɜrˈbeɪtɪm/ adj, adv repeating the exact words that were used

ver•dict /ˈvɜrdɪkt/ noun [C] ★
1 an official judgment made in a court about whether someone is guilty of a crime: *The jury took 16 hours to **reach a verdict**.*
2 an opinion that you have or a decision that you make: *What's your **verdict on** the movie?*

verge¹ /vɜrdʒ/ PHRASAL VERB **ˈverge on sth** to almost be in a particular state: *The test was so difficult it was verging on the ridiculous.*

verge² /vɜrdʒ/ noun **on the verge of sth** about to do something or experience something: *The two countries were on the verge of war.*

ver•i•fy /ˈverɪˌfaɪ/ verb [T] *formal* to check or prove that something is true or correct —**ver•i•fi•ca•tion** /ˌverɪfɪˈkeɪʃ(ə)n/ noun [U]

ver•i•ta•ble /ˈverɪtəb(ə)l/ adj *formal* real: used for emphasizing what you saying

ver•min /ˈvɜrmɪn/ noun [plural] small animals or insects that cause damage or disease

versa *see* **vice versa**

ver•sa•tile /ˈvɜrsət(ə)l/ adj **1** able to be used in many different ways: *a versatile summer jacket* **2** having a wide range of different skills and abilities: *a versatile actor* —**ver•sa•til•i•ty** /ˌvɜrsəˈtɪləti/ noun [U]

verse /vɜrs/ noun **1** [C] a group of words or sentences that form one section of a poem or song **2** [U] *formal* poetry **3** [C] a small group of sentences in the Bible that has a number next to it

ver•sion /ˈvɜrʒ(ə)n/ noun [C] ★
1 a form of something that is different from other forms or from the original: *The software comes in several different versions.* ♦ *The latest **version of** the movie is more like the book.*
2 a description of something that happened, according to one person: *I want to hear his **version of** the story now.*

ver•sus /ˈvɜrsəs/ preposition **1** used for saying that two things are being compared, usually to show how they are different: *the grades of male versus female students at the university* **2** used for showing that two people, groups, or teams are competing against each other: *the South Africa versus New Zealand Davis Cup*

ver•te•bra /ˈvɜrtəbrə/ (plural **ver•te•brae** /ˈvɜrtəˌbreɪ/) noun [C] one of the small bones that form a row down the center of your back

ver•ti•cal /ˈvɜrtɪk(ə)l/ adj ★ standing, pointing, or moving straight up: *vertical lines* ♦ *The cliff face is almost vertical.* —*picture* → C8 —**ver•ti•cal•ly** /ˈvɜrtɪkli/ adv

ver•ti•go /ˈvɜrtɪˌgoʊ/ noun [U] a loss of balance or a feeling that things around you are spinning, when you are in a very high place

verve /vɜrv/ noun [U] energy and enthusiasm

ver•y /ˈveri/ grammar word ★★★

> **Very** can be:
> - an **adverb**: *She writes very well.*
> - an **adjective**: *They went down to the very bottom of the ocean.*

1 used for emphasizing that a quality exists or is true to a great degree: *The building looks very old.* ♦ *I took my music lessons very seriously.* ♦ *It was a **very good** movie.* ♦ *Thank you **very much**.*
2 used for emphasizing a noun, especially a place or time that is at the top, bottom, or end of something: *Can you see that little bird right up at **the very top** of the tree?*
PHRASE **not very** used before adjectives and adverbs for saying that something is only slightly true, or that it is not true at all: *Victor's suggestions were not very helpful.* ♦ *She said "hello," but not very politely.*

ves•sel /ˈves(ə)l/ noun [C] **1** *formal* a large boat or ship **2** a tube in people, animals, or plants through which liquid flows: *blood vessels*

vest /vest/ noun [C] **1** *American* a piece of clothing with no sleeves or collar and with buttons down the front, usually worn over a shirt —*picture* → C4 **2** *British* an undershirt —*picture* → C5

vest•ed in•ter•est /ˌvestəd ˈɪntrəst/ noun [singular] a special reason for wanting things to happen in a particular way, because you will benefit from this

ves•tige /ˈvestɪdʒ/ noun [C] *formal* a very small sign that remains when something has almost disappeared = TRACE

vet¹ /vet/ noun [C] *informal* **1** a VETERINARIAN **2** *American* a VETERAN of the military

vet² /vet/ verb [T] to check someone's character or reputation to find out if they are appropriate for a particular job = SCREEN

vet•er•an¹ /ˈvet(ə)rən/ noun [C] **1** someone who was in the military, especially during a war **2** someone who has a lot of experience of doing a particular activity: *jazz veteran Dave Brubeck*

vet•er•an² /ˈvet(ə)rən/ adj very experienced and skilled in a particular activity: *veteran politicians*

ˈVeteran's ˌDay noun [C/U] November 11th, a holiday in the U.S. and Canada for honoring the people who have fought in a war

vet•er•i•nar•i•an /ˌvet(ə)rɪˈneriən/ noun [C] *American* a doctor for animals

vet•er•i•nar•y /ˈvet(ə)rɪˌneri/ adj relating to the care of sick or injured animals

ve•to¹ /ˈvitoʊ/ verb [T] to officially refuse to approve or allow something

ve•to² /ˈvitoʊ/ (plural **ve•toes**) noun [C/U] an official refusal to approve or allow something

VHF /ˌvi eɪtʃ ˈef/ noun [U] very high frequency: a range of radio waves that produces good sound quality

VHS /ˌvi eɪtʃ ˈes/ noun [U] video home system: a system for recording television programs at home

vi•a /ˈvaɪə, ˈviə/ preposition ★
1 going through one place on the way to another place: *They flew from New York to New Delhi via Frankfurt.*
2 using a particular method or person to send or deliver something: *Blake spoke to the audience **via satellite** from San Diego.*

vi•a•ble /ˈvaɪəb(ə)l/ adj **1** able to be done, or worth doing **2** *science* able to live and grow in an independent way —**vi•a•bil•i•ty** /ˌvaɪəˈbɪləti/ noun [U]

vi•a•duct /ˈvaɪəˌdʌkt/ noun [C] a long bridge on high posts, usually across a valley

vibe /vaɪb/ noun [C] *informal* a general feeling

V

that you get from a person or place: *good/bad vibes*

vi•brant /ˈvaɪbrənt/ adj **1** lively and exciting **2** bright and colorful —**vi•bran•cy** noun [U], **vi•brant•ly** adv

vi•brate /ˈvaɪˌbreɪt/ verb [I] to shake very quickly with small movements —**vi•bra•tion** /vaɪˈbreɪʃ(ə)n/ noun [C/U]

vic•ar /ˈvɪkər/ noun [C] a priest in the U.S. EPISCOPAL Church or the Church of England

vi•car•i•ous /vaɪˈkeriəs, vɪˈkeriəs/ adj experienced through the actions of other people —**vi•car•i•ous•ly** adv

vice /vaɪs/ noun **1** [C] a bad habit, or a bad personal quality ≠ VIRTUE **2** [U] crimes relating to sex **3** the British spelling of **vise**

ˌvice ˈpresident noun [C] **1** a politician who is next in rank after the president **2** a senior manager in a business, especially the person in charge of a department

vi•ce ver•sa /ˌvaɪs ˈvɜrsə, ˌvaɪsi ˈvɜrsə/ adv the opposite of what has been said: *Should I come to your house or vice versa?*

vi•cin•i•ty /vɪˈsɪnəti/ noun [singular] the area near a particular place: *a university in the vicinity of Boston*

vi•cious /ˈvɪʃəs/ adj **1** extremely violent: *a vicious attack* **2** extremely unkind or unpleasant: *He had a vicious temper.* —**vi•cious•ly** adv

ˌvicious ˈcircle or **ˌvicious ˈcycle** noun [singular] a process in which the existence of a problem causes other problems, and this makes the original problem worse

vic•tim /ˈvɪktɪm/ noun [C] ★★★

1 someone who has been harmed or killed as the result of a crime: *a murder victim* ♦ ***victims of violence***

2 someone who has been affected by something such as an accident or illness: *flood/earthquake victims* ♦ *She **fell victim to** a rare disease.*

3 someone who has suffered as a result of the actions or attitudes of other people: ***victims of racism/discrimination***

vic•tim•ize /ˈvɪktɪˌmaɪz/ verb [T] to treat someone in a deliberately unfair way —**vic•tim•i•za•tion** /ˌvɪktɪmɪˈzeɪʃ(ə)n/ noun [U]

vic•tor /ˈvɪktər/ noun [C] *formal* the winner of a competition or battle

V

Vic•to•ri•an[1] /vɪkˈtɔriən/ adj relating to the period from 1837 to 1901, when Queen Victoria was queen in the U.K.

Vic•to•ri•an[2] /vɪkˈtɔriən/ noun [C] **1** a house built during or in the style of the Victorian period **2** someone who lived during the Victorian period

vic•to•ri•ous /vɪkˈtɔriəs/ adj having won a competition or battle

vic•to•ry /ˈvɪkt(ə)ri/ noun [C/U] ★★ the fact of winning a competition or battle, or an occasion when someone wins ≠ DEFEAT: *a decisive election **victory for** the Democrats* ♦ *Spain's 3–2 **victory over** Russia in last night's game*

vid•e•o /ˈvɪdiˌoʊ/ noun ★★★

1 [C/U] a movie or television program recorded onto VIDEOTAPE: *The movie will soon be available **on video**.* ♦ *We stayed in and **watched a video**.* ♦ *They **made a video** of the wedding.*

2 [U] the activity of making movies using VIDEOTAPE

ˈvideo arˌcade noun [C] *American* a place where you can play games on machines by putting money in them

ˈvideo ˌcamera noun [C] a piece of equipment that you use for recording something onto VIDEOTAPE

ˈvideo ˌgame noun [C] a game in which players use electronic controls to move images on a television or computer screen

vid•e•o•phone /ˈvɪdioʊˌfoʊn/ noun [C] a telephone with a screen, on which you can see the person who you are talking to

ˈvideo reˌcorder noun [C] a VCR

vid•e•o•tape /ˈvɪdioʊˌteɪp/ noun [C/U] a thin band of film in a plastic case, used for recording television programs, etc.

vie /vaɪ/ (present participle **vy•ing**; past tense and past participle **vied**) verb [I] *formal* to compete with other people for something that is difficult to get

Vi•et•nam War, the /viˌetnæm ˈwɔr/ a war between North and South Vietnam from 1954 to 1975, in which the U.S. supported South Vietnam

view[1] /vju/ noun ★★★

1 [C/U] the things that you can see from a particular place: *We had **a spectacular view** of the mountains from our room.* ♦ *The showers were **in full view of*** (=easily seen by) *everyone in the pool.* ♦ *The castle **came into view*** (=became able to be seen) *as we turned the corner.*

2 [C] your personal opinion about something = POINT OF VIEW: *What are your **views on** the election?* ♦ *He has strong **views about** global warming.* ♦ **+that** *It's our view that women should get paid the same as men.*

3 [C] a picture or photograph of a place, especially an attractive place

PHRASES **in view of sth** because of something: *In view of the shortage of time, each person may only speak for five minutes.*

with a view to (doing) sth with the hope of doing something in the future

> **Words often used with view**
>
> *Adjectives often used with **view** (noun, sense 1)*
>
> ■ **breathtaking, magnificent, panoramic, spectacular, splendid, superb** + VIEW: used about views that are attractive and impressive

view[2] /vju/ verb [T] ★★

1 to have a particular opinion or attitude toward something: **view sb/sth as** *The Internet is viewed by many as a revolutionary educational tool.* ♦ **view sth with sth** *These results must be viewed with caution.*

2 to look at or watch something: **view sth from sth** *Viewed from the road, the wall looked too high to climb.*

3 to look at information on a computer screen: *To view the next page, press "tab."*

view•er /ˈvjuər/ noun [C] someone who watches television programs

view•find•er /ˈvjuˌfaɪndər/ noun [C] a small window in a camera, used for seeing exactly what you are photographing or RECORDING

view•ing /ˈvjuɪŋ/ noun [C/U] **1** the activity of

watching a television program or movie, or an occasion when someone does this **2** the activity of looking at something, or an occasion when someone does this

view•point /ˈvjuˌpɔɪnt/ noun [C] an opinion that you have about something

vig•il /ˈvɪdʒɪl/ noun [C] a period of time when you stay quietly in a place, for example as a protest or when you are looking after someone who is sick

vig•i•lant /ˈvɪdʒɪlənt/ adj *formal* watching a person or situation very carefully so that you will notice any problems immediately —**vig•i•lance** noun [U]

vig•i•lan•te /ˌvɪdʒɪˈlænti/ noun [C] someone who tries to catch and punish criminals by themselves, without waiting for the police

vig•or /ˈvɪgər/ noun [U] energy, enthusiasm, and determination

vig•or•ous /ˈvɪgərəs/ adj **1** full of energy, enthusiasm, and determination: *a vigorous debate/campaign* **2** strong and healthy: *a vigorous young man* —**vig•or•ous•ly** adv

vig•our /ˈvɪgər/ the British spelling of **vigor**

vile /vaɪl/ adj extremely unpleasant

vil•i•fy /ˈvɪlɪˌfaɪ/ verb [T] *formal* to criticize someone very strongly, especially in a way that is not fair —**vil•i•fi•ca•tion** /ˌvɪlɪfɪˈkeɪʃ(ə)n/ noun [U]

vil•la /ˈvɪlə/ noun [C] a large house, especially one used for vacation

vil•lage /ˈvɪlɪdʒ/ noun [C] ★★★ a very small old town in the countryside, usually in a country outside the U.S. and Canada: *a fishing village* ♦ *the village shop* → CITY

vil•lag•er /ˈvɪlɪdʒər/ noun [C] someone who lives in a village

vil•lain /ˈvɪlən/ noun [C] **1** a bad character in a story, play, movie, etc. ≠ HERO **2** an evil person or criminal

vin•di•cate /ˈvɪndɪˌkeɪt/ verb [T] to prove that someone is right, especially when most people believed that they were wrong —**vin•di•ca•tion** /ˌvɪndɪˈkeɪʃ(ə)n/ noun [C/U]

vin•dic•tive /vɪnˈdɪktɪv/ adj someone who is vindictive will not forgive a person who has hurt them, and tries to hurt them back —**vin•dic•tive•ness** noun [U]

vine /vaɪn/ noun [C] the plant on which GRAPES grow = GRAPEVINE

vin•e•gar /ˈvɪnɪgər/ noun [U] a sour liquid that is used for adding flavor to food

vine•yard /ˈvɪnˌjərd/ noun [C] a piece of land where GRAPES are grown and wine is produced

vin•tage[1] /ˈvɪntɪdʒ/ adj **1** vintage wine is excellent in quality and was made several years ago **2** a vintage object or vehicle is old, but is kept in good condition **3** showing the best or most typical qualities of someone: *The record is vintage early Elvis.*

vin•tage[2] /ˈvɪntɪdʒ/ noun [C] all of the wine that is produced in a particular year, or the year that it was produced

vi•nyl /ˈvaɪn(ə)l/ noun [U] a light strong plastic

vi•o•la /viˈoʊlə/ noun [C] a musical instrument that is like a large VIOLIN —*picture* → STRINGED INSTRUMENT

vi•o•late /ˈvaɪəˌleɪt/ verb [T] to break a law, agreement, etc. —**vi•o•la•tor** noun [C]

vi•o•la•tion /ˌvaɪəˈleɪʃ(ə)n/ noun [C/U] an action that breaks a law, agreement, etc.

vi•o•lence /ˈvaɪələns/ noun [U] ★★
1 violent behavior: *acts of violence* ♦ ***Violence against** women must stop.*
2 a strong force that something has, often one that causes a lot of damage: ***the violence of the storm***

vi•o•lent /ˈvaɪələnt/ adj ★★★

1 using physical force **4** movies, etc.
2 causing damage **5** emotions/opinions
3 difficult to control

1 using physical force to hurt people or damage property: *There were several violent incidents on the streets.* ♦ *a fall in **violent crime*** ♦ *He **gets violent** when he's been drinking.*
2 a violent wind, storm, or explosion happens with a lot of force and causes serious damage
3 painful and difficult to control: *a violent coughing fit*
4 containing a lot of violent action: *a violent movie*
5 involving very strong and angry emotions or opinions: *a violent argument*
—**vi•o•lent•ly** adv

vi•o•let[1] /ˈvaɪələt/ noun **1** [C] a small plant with purple flowers and a sweet smell **2** [U] a blue-purple color

vi•o•let[2] /ˈvaɪələt/ adj blue-purple in color

vi•o•lin /ˌvaɪəˈlɪn/ noun [C] a musical instrument that you hold under your chin and play by pulling a long object called a **bow** across its strings —*picture* → STRINGED INSTRUMENT —**vi•o•lin•ist** noun [C]

VIP /ˌvi aɪ ˈpi/ noun [C] very important person: used for referring to someone who receives special treatment because they are powerful or famous

vi•per /ˈvaɪpər/ noun [C] a type of poisonous snake

vi•ral /ˈvaɪrəl/ adj caused by or relating to a VIRUS

vir•gin[1] /ˈvɜrdʒɪn/ noun [C] someone who has never had sex

vir•gin[2] /ˈvɜrdʒɪn/ adj in a natural or original state

vir•gin•i•ty /vərˈdʒɪnəti/ noun [singular] the state of being a virgin

Vir•go /ˈvɜrgoʊ/ noun [C/U] one of the 12 signs of the ZODIAC. A **Virgo** is someone who was born between August 22 and September 22.

vir•ile /ˈvɪrəl, ˈvɪˌraɪl/ adj a man who is virile is strong, active, and full of sexual energy

vi•ril•i•ty /vɪˈrɪləti/ noun [U] the strength and power that are considered typical qualities of a man

vir•tu•al /ˈvɜrtʃuəl/ adj **1** very close to a particular condition, quality, etc.: *Over the years they had become virtual strangers.* ♦ *It's a virtual impossibility.* **2** *computing* created or shown by computers, or existing on computers or on the Internet: *a virtual community*

vir•tu•al•ly /ˈvɜrtʃuəli/ adv ★ used for emphasizing that a statement is almost completely true = ALMOST: *It's **virtually impossible** to get him to eat vegetables.*

ˌvirtual reˈality noun [U] *computing* images and sounds that are produced by a computer in

V

a way that makes the user feel as if they are real

vir·tue /ˈvɜrtʃu/ noun ★
1 [C] a good quality that someone has, especially a moral one ≠ VICE: *Patience is not one of my virtues.*
2 [U] *formal* a way of behaving in which you do what is morally good and right, and avoid doing things that are morally wrong
3 [C] an advantage or good feature that something has: *The plan had the virtue of simplicity.*
PHRASE **by virtue of sth** because of something, or as a result of something: *By virtue of its natural beauty, Hawaii attracts millions of visitors each year.*

vir·tu·o·so /ˌvɜrtʃuˈoʊsoʊ/ noun [C] someone who is very good at a particular activity, especially playing a musical instrument

vir·tu·ous /ˈvɜrtʃuəs/ adj behaving in a way that is morally good and right —**vir·tu·ous·ly** adv

vir·u·lent /ˈvɪrələnt/ adj **1** a virulent illness is very dangerous and affects people very quickly **2** virulent feelings or actions are extremely strong and angry —**vir·u·lence** noun [U], **vir·u·lent·ly** adv

vi·rus /ˈvaɪrəs/ noun [C] ★
1 a very small living thing that can enter your body and make you sick, or a disease or illness caused by this: *Malaria is caused by a virus.* ♦ *the AIDS virus* ♦ *I've been in bed all week with a virus.* → BACTERIA
2 *computing* a program that enters your computer and damages or destroys information that you have stored: *Most viruses are spread over the Internet.*

vi·sa /ˈvizə/ noun [C] an official document or mark in your passport that allows you to enter or leave a country

vis-à-vis /ˌvizəˈvi/ preposition *formal* compared to or relating to someone or something

vis·cous /ˈvɪskəs/ adj *technical* a viscous liquid is thick and sticky —**vis·cos·i·ty** /vɪˈskɑsəti/ noun [U]

vise /vaɪs/ noun [C] a tool used for holding an object firmly while you are working with it

vis·i·bil·i·ty /ˌvɪzəˈbɪləti/ noun [U] the distance that you can see, depending on conditions such as the weather

V

vis·i·ble /ˈvɪzəb(ə)l/ adj **1** able to be seen: *The house is visible from the road.* **2** clear or obvious = NOTICEABLE: *There has been a visible improvement in your work.*

vis·i·bly /ˈvɪzəbli/ adv in a way that is easy to see or notice

vi·sion /ˈvɪʒ(ə)n/ noun ★★
1 [U] the ability to think about and plan for the future, using your intelligence and imagination: *Tackling these challenges will require real vision.*
2 [C] someone's idea of how something should be done, or of how it will be in the future: *The speech gives her vision of the country's economic future.*
3 [U] the ability to see = SIGHT: *He suffers from blurred vision and headaches.*
4 [C] something that someone sees in a dream or as a religious experience

vi·sion·ar·y /ˈvɪʒ(ə)nˌeri/ adj with imagination and clear, often new ideas of how things should be done: *his visionary leadership* —**vi·sion·ar·y** noun [C]

vis·it¹ /ˈvɪzɪt/ verb ★★★
1 [I/T] to go to see someone and spend some time with them: *I visit my family every year at Christmas.* ♦ *We only use this room when friends come to visit.*
2 [T] to go to a place for a short period of time: *Have you visited Venezuela before?*
3 [T] to use a WEBSITE: *For more information, visit our website.*
4 [I] *American informal* to have a conversation with someone: *I didn't get a chance to visit with Mabel.*

vis·it² /ˈvɪzɪt/ noun [C] ★★★
1 an occasion when you visit a person or place: *What did you see on your visit to India?* ♦ *It's been a long time since I've* ***paid*** *my grandmother* ***a visit.***
2 an occasion when an important person such as a political leader visits a place: *The president arrived in Taiwan today for a three-day visit.*
3 *American informal* an occasion when you spend time talking to someone

vis·i·ta·tion /ˌvɪzɪˈteɪʃ(ə)n/ noun [U] the right of a divorced parent to visit children who live with the other parent

ˌvisiting proˈfessor noun [C] a professor from one university who is teaching in another university for a short period

vis·i·tor /ˈvɪzɪtər/ noun [C] ★★★
1 someone who visits a person or place: *Did you* ***have any visitors*** *today?* ♦ ***Visitors to*** *the museum will notice many improvements.*
2 *computing* someone who looks at a particular page on the Internet: *Visitors to our website can purchase books online.*

vi·sor /ˈvaɪzər/ noun [C] **1** a piece of clear plastic on the front of a HELMET (=hard hat) that protects your face **2** a curved piece of plastic or other material on a band that you wear on your head to protect your eyes from the sun **3** *American* the front part of a CAP (=type of hat) that sticks out over your eyes **4** a flat object at the top of the front window of a car that you pull down to protect your eyes from the sun

vis·ta /ˈvɪstə/ noun [C] the view that you can see from a particular place, especially a beautiful view

vi·su·al¹ /ˈvɪʒuəl/ adj **1** relating to things that you can see: *the visual arts* **2** relating to sight: *a visual impairment/acuity* —**vi·su·al·ly** adv

vi·su·al² /ˈvɪʒuəl/ noun [C] something such as a drawing or photograph, especially one that helps to explain something

ˌvisual ˈaid noun [C] a drawing, map, movie, etc. that people can look at when they are learning about a particular subject

vi·su·al·ize /ˈvɪʒuəˌlaɪz/ verb [T] to form a picture of someone or something in your mind —**vi·su·al·i·za·tion** /ˌvɪʒuəlɪˈzeɪʃ(ə)n/ noun [U]

vi·tal /ˈvaɪt(ə)l/ adj ★
1 very important or necessary = ESSENTIAL: *He* ***played a vital role in*** *setting up the organization.* ♦ *Skillful employees are* ***vital to*** *the success of any company.*
2 full of energy and life: *He was young, vital, and handsome.*

3 necessary to keep you alive: *vital organs*

vi•tal•i•ty /vaɪˈtæləti/ noun [U] **1** energy or enthusiasm **2** the quality of being exciting or successful

vi•tal•ly /ˈvaɪt(ə)li/ adv used for emphasizing that something is very important or necessary: *It is vitally important that we find him.*

vi•ta•min /ˈvaɪtəmɪn/ noun [C] a natural substance in food that is necessary to keep your body healthy

vit•ri•ol•ic /ˌvɪtriˈɑlɪk/ adj vitriolic language or behavior is cruel and full of hate

vi•va•cious /vɪˈveɪʃəs/ adj lively and attractive

viv•id /ˈvɪvɪd/ adj **1** very clear and detailed: *a vivid description/image/memory* **2** a vivid example of something shows very clearly that something exists or is true **3** a vivid color is strong and bright —**viv•id•ly** adv, **viv•id•ness** noun [U]

viv•i•sec•tion /ˌvɪvɪˈsekʃ(ə)n/ verb [U] the practice of performing operations on living animals for scientific experiments

V-neck /ˈvi ˌnek/ noun [C] an opening for the neck in a piece of clothing, in the shape of a "V" —**ˈV-ˌnecked** adj —*picture* → NECKLINE

vo•cab /ˈvoʊˌkæb/ noun [U] *informal* vocabulary

vo•cab•u•lar•y /voʊˈkæbjəˌleri/ noun [C/U] ★ all the words that someone knows, or all the words in a particular language, a particular book, etc.: *exercises designed to increase your vocabulary*

vo•cal /ˈvoʊk(ə)l/ adj **1** relating to the voice, or done with the voice **2** a vocal group of people express their opinions strongly with the result that people in authority notice them

ˈvocal ˌcords or **ˈvocal ˌchords** noun [plural] the very thin muscles inside your throat that you use for making sounds

vo•cal•ist /ˈvoʊk(ə)lɪst/ noun [C] a singer, especially one who sings popular music

vo•ca•tion /voʊˈkeɪʃ(ə)n/ noun [C] a job that you do because you feel that it is your purpose in life and you have special skills for doing it

vo•ca•tion•al /voʊˈkeɪʃən(ə)l/ adj relating to the skills that you need for a particular job: *a vocational course*

vo•cif•er•ous /voʊˈsɪfərəs/ adj *formal* expressing opinions loudly and with force —**vo•cif•er•ous•ly** adv

vod•ka /ˈvɑdkə/ noun [C/U] a strong clear alcoholic drink, or a glass of this drink

vogue /voʊg/ noun [singular] a fashion, or something that is fashionable

voice[1] /vɔɪs/ noun ★★★

1 [C/U] the sounds that someone makes when they speak, or the way that someone speaks: *We could **hear voices** in the next apartment.* ♦ *The woman at the desk greeted him **in a** bored **voice**.* ♦ *The children were very well-behaved, and I never had to **raise my voice*** (=speak louder or shout).

2 [singular] the right or opportunity to express your opinions or feelings and influence what happens: **give voice to sth** (=express something publicly) *Her article gave voice to the anger felt by many local people.*

3 [singular] a person, organization, etc. that represents a particular type of opinion or group of people: *Carter is the voice of the black minority in this area.* ♦ *the voice of reason/authority/experience*

> **Words often used with voice**
>
> *Adjectives often used with **voice** (noun, sense 1)*
> - **big, booming, loud** + VOICE: used about voices that are loud
> - **gentle, low, quiet, small, soft** + VOICE: used about voices that are quiet
> - **high-pitched, piercing, shrill** + VOICE: used about voices that are high
> - **deep, gruff, hoarse, husky, low** + VOICE: used about voices that are low

voice[2] /vɔɪs/ verb [T] *formal* to express your opinions or feelings about something: *Human rights groups have voiced their concern over the treatment of refugees.*

voice-ac•ti•vat•ed /ˌvɔɪsˈæktɪˌveɪtəd/ adj a machine or piece of equipment that is voice-activated can recognize and obey spoken instructions

ˈvoice ˌbox noun [C] the part of your throat from which you produce sounds

voice•mail /ˈvɔɪsmeɪl/ noun [U] an electronic system that records and stores phone messages

void /vɔɪd/ noun [singular] *formal* **1** a situation in which someone or something that is important to you is not there anymore **2** an extremely large empty space

vol•a•tile /ˈvɑlət(ə)l/ adj **1** a volatile situation can suddenly change or become more dangerous **2** someone who is volatile can quickly become angry or violent

vol•can•ic /vɑlˈkænɪk/ adj coming from, or relating to, a volcano: *a layer of volcanic ash* ♦ *volcanic activity*

vol•ca•no /vɑlˈkeɪnoʊ/ noun [C] a mountain that forces hot gas, rocks, ASH, and LAVA (=melted rock) into the air through a hole at the top

vole /voʊl/ noun [C] a small animal similar to a mouse but with a short tail

vol•ley[1] /ˈvɑli/ noun [C] **1** a lot of questions, insults, etc. that are all spoken or made at the same time **2** the action of hitting or kicking a ball back to an opponent before it touches the ground

vol•ley[2] /ˈvɑli/ verb [I/T] to hit or kick a ball back to an opponent before it touches the ground

vol•ley•ball /ˈvɑliˌbɔl/ noun [U] a sport in which two teams use their hands and arms to hit a ball to each other over a high net

volt /voʊlt/ noun [C] a unit for measuring the power of an electric current

volt•age /ˈvoʊltɪdʒ/ noun [C/U] the amount of power in an electric current, measured in volts

vol•ume /ˈvɑljəm, ˈvɑlˌjum/ noun ★★★

1 [U] the loudness of a sound, especially from something such as a television, CD player, etc.

2 [C/U] an amount of something: *an increase in the volume of traffic* ♦ *Some students cannot cope with **the huge volume of work**.*

3 [C] *formal* a book

4 [U] the amount of space that is contained in something or that is filled by something:

V

How do you calculate the volume of a cube?

vol·un·tar·y /ˈvɑlənˌteri/ adj ★★
1 something that is voluntary is done because you choose to do it, and not because you have to ≠ COMPULSORY, MANDATORY: *voluntary participation in the research study*
2 voluntary work is done for no pay: *All the teachers work on a voluntary basis.*
—**vol·un·tar·i·ly** /ˌvɑlənˈterəli/ adv

vol·un·teer¹ /ˌvɑlənˈtɪr/ noun [C] **1** someone who offers to do something and does not have to be made to do it **2** someone who works without expecting to be paid for what they do **3** someone who joins the military without being forced to —**vol·un·teer** adj: *volunteer work*

vol·un·teer² /ˌvɑlənˈtɪr/ verb **1** [I] to offer or choose to do something for someone else **2** [I/T] to work without expecting to be paid for what you do **3** [I/T] to say something or give information without being asked **4** [I] to join the military without being forced to

vo·lup·tu·ous /vəˈlʌptʃuəs/ adj a voluptuous woman has a large curved body and is sexually attractive

vom·it¹ /ˈvɑmɪt/ verb [I/T] if you vomit, food comes up from your stomach and out through your mouth because you are sick

vom·it² /ˈvɑmɪt/ noun [U] food or other substances that come up from your stomach when you vomit

voo·doo /ˈvuˌdu/ noun [U] a religion whose followers believe in magic and WITCHCRAFT

vo·ra·cious /vəˈreɪʃəs/ adj *formal* **1** a voracious person or animal eats a lot **2** enjoying something very much and wanting to do it a lot: *a voracious reader* —**vo·ra·cious·ly** adv

vote¹ /voʊt/ verb [I/T] ★★★ to decide something, or to choose a representative or winner, by officially stating your choice, for example in an election: *68 percent of the union **voted against** striking.* ♦ *I'm going to **vote for** Jackson.* ♦ *The Council will **vote on** the proposal next Friday.* ♦ **vote to do sth** *The committee voted unanimously to ban alcohol from the concert.*

vote² /voʊt/ noun ★★★
1 [C] an official choice you make between two or more issues, people, etc., for example in an election: *My vote will go to the candidate who promises tax reform.* ♦ *I **cast my vote for*** (=gave my vote to) *the candidate who seemed the most honest.*
2 the vote [singular] the right to vote in an election

vot·er /ˈvoʊtər/ noun [C] someone who votes in an election

vouch /vaʊtʃ/
PHRASAL VERBS ˈ**vouch for sb** to say that you believe that someone is good and will behave well in future
ˈ**vouch for sth** to say that something is true, correct, or good

vouch·er /ˈvaʊtʃər/ noun [C] a piece of paper that you buy something with instead of using money

vow¹ /vaʊ/ noun **1** [C] a serious promise
2 vows [plural] a set of formal promises that people make to each other, for example during a wedding ceremony

vow² /vaʊ/ verb [I/T] *formal* to promise that you will do something

vow·el /ˈvaʊəl/ noun [C] *linguistics* one of the letters a, e, i, o, or u, or the sounds that they represent

voy·age /ˈvɔɪɪdʒ/ noun [C] a long trip, especially on a ship

VP /ˌviˈpi/ abbrev vice president

vs. abbrev versus

VT abbrev Vermont

vul·gar /ˈvʌlgər/ adj **1** a vulgar joke, comment, action, etc. has a sexual meaning that is rude or offensive **2** someone who is vulgar is rude, unpleasant, and offensive
3 showing a lack of ability to judge what is attractive, appropriate, etc. —**vul·gar·ly** adv

vul·ner·a·ble /ˈvʌln(ə)rəb(ə)l/ adj weak and therefore easy to hurt, harm, or attack: *The government must help the most vulnerable groups in our society.* —**vul·ner·a·bil·i·ty** /ˌvʌln(ə)rəˈbɪləti/ noun [U]

vul·ture /ˈvʌltʃər/ noun [C] a large bird that eats the bodies of dead animals

Ww

w or **W** /ˈdʌb(ə)lˌju/ noun [C/U] the 23rd letter of the English alphabet

W. abbrev **1** watt **2** West **3** Western

WA /ˌdʌb(ə)lju ˈeɪ/ abbrev Washington

wack·y /ˈwæki/ adj *informal* funny, or silly

wad¹ /wɑd/ noun [C] **1** a thick pile of papers, documents, or paper money **2** a round mass of something soft

wad² /wɑd/ or ˌ**wad sth** ˈ**up** verb [T] to form something such as paper into the shape of a ball

wad·dle /ˈwɑd(ə)l/ verb [I] to walk with short steps that make your body move from side to side —**wad·dle** noun [C]

wade /weɪd/ verb [I] to walk in water that is not very deep
PHRASAL VERB ˈ**wade** ˌ**through sth** to read a lot of boring information

wa·fer /ˈweɪfər/ noun [C] a very thin COOKIE

waf·fle¹ /ˈwɑf(ə)l/ noun [C] a flat cake that has deep square marks on both sides

waf·fle² /ˈwɑf(ə)l/ verb [I] *American* to avoid making a decision or stating a clear opinion

waft /wɑft/ verb [I] if a smell or a noise wafts, it floats through the air

wag /wæg/ verb [I/T] **1** if a dog wags its tail, it moves its tail from one side to the other several times **2** if a person wags a finger, they move it up and down, especially in order to show that they disapprove of something

wage¹ /weɪdʒ/ noun [C] ★★ a regular amount of money that you earn for working: *a daily/hourly/weekly wage* ♦ *What is the **minimum wage** here?* → PAYCHECK

wage² /weɪdʒ/ verb [T] to start and continue a war or fight: *The administration has pledged to wage war on drugs.*

wa•ger /ˈweɪdʒər/ noun [C] an agreement to win or lose an amount of money depending on the result of a competition or other event = BET

wag•on /ˈwægən/ noun [C] **1** a covered vehicle with four wheels that is usually pulled by horses **2** *American* a small open CART with four wheels and a long handle, used by children as a toy **3** *American informal* a STATION WAGON
PHRASE **on the wagon** *informal* not drinking alcohol any more

waif /weɪf/ noun [C] a child who is very thin and pale

wail /weɪl/ verb **1** [I/T] to shout or cry with a long high sound because you are in pain or are very sad **2** [I] to make a long high sound: *wailing sirens* —**wail** noun [C]

waist /weɪst/ noun [C] **1** the middle part of the human body that is usually narrower than the parts above and below —*picture* → C14 **2** the part of a piece of clothing that covers your waist

waist•band /ˈweɪs(t)ˌbænd/ noun [C] a piece of cloth on a pair of pants or a skirt that goes around your waist

waist•coat /ˈwes(t)kɪt, ˈweɪs(t)ˌkoʊt/ noun [C] *British* a VEST

waist•line /ˈweɪs(t)ˌlaɪn/ noun [C] the measurement around your waist, used especially as a way of judging how fat or thin someone is

wait¹ /weɪt/ verb [I] ★★★
1 to stay in one place until a particular thing happens or until someone arrives: *Sheryl said she'd be waiting in the lobby.* ♦ *He was attacked while he was **waiting for** a bus.* ♦ *They **waited** anxiously **for** news of survivors.* ♦ *Let's sit down and **wait until** Bob gets here.* ♦ **wait to do sth** *The TV showed thousands of people waiting to board buses.*
2 to delay doing something until something happens or until someone arrives: *I'm busy so you'll just have to wait.* ♦ *Should we start eating or should we **wait for** the others?*
3 to be hoping or expecting that something will happen: *I've been **waiting for** a refund check for several months.* ♦ **wait for sb/sth to do sth** *There's no point waiting for her to change her mind.*
4 to be ready for someone to take or use: *There's a package **waiting for** you at home.*
PHRASES **sb can't wait/can hardly wait** used for saying that someone is very excited about something that is going to happen: *I can't wait for the holidays.*
keep sb waiting to make someone stay in one place or do nothing until you are ready to see them or talk to them: *We were kept waiting outside his office for over an hour.*
wait a minute/second *spoken* **1** used for telling someone to stop and wait for you **2** used for saying that you have just remembered or noticed something: *Wait a second, wasn't Jackie supposed to be here?* **3** used when you are slightly annoyed by something that someone has just said: *Wait a minute, that's not what I said!*
wait tables to serve food to people in a restaurant
PHRASAL VERBS ˌ**wait aˈround** to do nothing because you are expecting something to happen, and you cannot do anything until it does: *I don't feel like **waiting around for** him to make up his mind.*
ˈ**wait ˌon sb** to serve people in a store or restaurant
ˌ**wait ˈup 1** to not go to sleep until someone comes home **2** *American spoken* used for asking someone to stop so that you can walk with them

Words often used with wait

*Adverbs often used with **wait** (verb, sense 1)*

- WAIT + **anxiously, eagerly, expectantly, impatiently, nervously, patiently, quietly**: wait in a particular mental state

Wait for and **expect** have different meanings.

- If you **wait for** something to happen, you do not leave a place or do something else until it happens: *We waited for Alex to finish his lunch.* ♦ *I'm waiting for a bus.*
- If you **expect** something to happen, you believe that it will happen: *We expected Lee to be upset.* ♦ *I'm expecting a phone call later.*

wait² /weɪt/ noun [singular] a period of time during which you wait for something: *Expect a long wait if you intend to buy tickets.* → LIE¹

wait•er /ˈweɪtər/ noun [C] a man who brings food and drink to your table in a restaurant

wait•ing list /ˈweɪtɪŋ ˌlɪst/ noun [C] a list of people who are waiting for something to become available

wait•ing room /ˈweɪtɪŋ ˌrum/ noun [C] a room where you wait for something such as a train, or for someone such as a doctor to be ready to see you

wait•ress /ˈweɪtrəs/ noun [C] a woman who brings food and drink to your table in a restaurant

waive /weɪv/ verb [T] to choose to officially ignore a rule, right, or claim

waiv•er /ˈweɪvər/ noun [C] an official statement or document that says that a right, claim, or law can be ignored

wake¹ /weɪk/ (past tense **woke** /woʊk/; past participle **wok•en** /ˈwoʊkən/) verb [I/T] ★ to stop sleeping, or to make someone stop sleeping: *I woke at 5 o'clock this morning.* ♦ *Be quiet or you'll wake the baby.*
PHRASAL VERB ˌ**wake (sb) ˈup** *same as* **wake¹**: *Wake up! It's almost ten o'clock!* ♦ *Don't wake me up when you come in.*

wake² /weɪk/ noun [C] **1** the track that appears in the water behind a moving boat **2** a meeting of friends and relations before or after a funeral in order to remember the person who has died
PHRASE **in the wake of sth** or **in sth's wake** happening after an event or as a result of it: *An inquiry has been set up in the wake of the crash.*

wak•en /ˈweɪkən/ verb [I/T] *formal* to wake up, or to wake someone up

ˈ**wake-up ˌcall** noun [C] **1** a telephone call that you receive in order to wake you up **2** a bad experience that makes you take action in order to improve a situation: *The low test scores should serve as a loud wake-up call to teachers.*

wak•ing /ˈweɪkɪŋ/ adj relating to the time that you are awake: *I spent every waking hour working on the report.*

walk[1] /wɔk/ verb ★★★
1 [I] to move forward by putting one foot in front of the other: *Has your little boy learned to walk yet?* ♦ *It takes me 25 minutes to **walk to work**.* ♦ *Greg **walked** slowly **toward** her, smiling.* ♦ *Howard **walked in** with two men I'd never seen before.* ♦ *As we **walked along** she talked about her plans.*
2 [T] to go a particular distance by walking: *She walked three miles each day.*
3 [T] to walk somewhere with someone in order to be sure that they reach the place safely: *When Valerie worked late, Carl always **walked** her **home**.*
PHRASES **walk all over sb** to treat someone very badly
walk the dog to walk somewhere with a dog so that it gets exercise
→ TIGHTROPE
PHRASAL VERBS ˌ**walk aˈway** to leave a place, situation, or person: *Spencer turned to walk away, then stopped.*
ˌ**walk aˈway with sth** to win something easily: *The Bears could walk away with the championship.*
ˌ**walk ˈin on sb** to walk into a room where someone is doing something that is private or secret
ˌ**walk ˈoff with sth 1** to steal something: *You can't just walk off with his jacket.* **2** to win something easily
ˌ**walk ˈon** to continue walking in the direction that you were going in
ˌ**walk ˈout 1** to suddenly leave a job or relationship: *Her husband had **walked out on** her a year before.* **2** to stop working as a way to protest something: *All of the workers walked out on Friday night.*

Other ways of saying walk
- **march** to walk in a military way or with a lot of energy
- **shuffle** to walk slowly without lifting your feet off the ground
- **stagger** to walk with uneven steps, almost falling over
- **step** to move one foot forward
- **stride** to walk fast, taking big steps
- **stroll** to walk for pleasure in a relaxed way
- **tiptoe** to walk very quietly, standing on your toes
- **trudge** to walk slowly because you are very tired

W

walk[2] /wɔk/ noun [C] ★★
1 a short trip that you make by walking, or the distance of this trip: *It's a five-minute walk from our house to the post office.* ♦ *It's a beautiful walk down to the beach.* ♦ *Does anyone want to **go for a walk**?* ♦ *Let's **take a walk** after we eat.*
2 the way that someone walks
PHRASE **from all walks of life** used for saying that a group consists of all types of people with different backgrounds, jobs, etc.

walk•er /ˈwɔkər/ noun [C] **1** someone who walks for pleasure or for exercise **2** *American* a special frame that some people use to help them to walk

walk•ie-talk•ie /ˌwɔki ˈtɔki/ noun [C] a small radio that you can carry and use for communicating with someone else who also has one

walk•ing /ˈwɔkɪŋ/ noun [U] the activity of going for walks: *We went walking in the Marin Headlands.* ♦ *a pair of strong walking boots*

Walk•man /ˈwɔkmən/ (plural **Walk•mans**) *trademark* a type of small CASSETTE or CD player with HEADPHONES that you can carry with you

walk•out /ˈwɔkˌaʊt/ noun [C] a form of protest in which people stop what they are doing, and leave the place where they work or study

walk•way /ˈwɔkˌweɪ/ noun [C] a path built for people to walk along, especially one that is above ground level and that connects two buildings

wall[1] /wɔl/ noun [C] ★★★
1 an upright side of a room or building: *The walls of the factory were covered in graffiti.* ♦ *Several paintings hung **on the wall**.*
2 an upright structure made of stone or brick that surrounds or divides an area of land: *The children got into the yard by climbing over the wall.*
3 a large amount of something that forms a tall mass: ***A wall of** dark water approached their small boat.*
PHRASES **like talking to a (brick) wall** used for saying that someone does not listen or react to you when you talk
run into/hit a (brick) wall to reach a point in a process where there are problems that seem impossible to solve

wall[2] /wɔl/
PHRASAL VERBS ˌ**wall sth ˈin** to surround something with a wall
ˌ**wall sth ˈoff** to separate a small space from a larger one by building a wall

wal•la•by /ˈwɑləbi/ noun [C] an animal like a small KANGAROO

walled /wɔld/ adj surrounded by a wall

wal•let /ˈwɑlət/ noun [C] a small flat case that you keep money, CREDIT CARDS, etc. in

wal•lop /ˈwɑləp/ verb [T] *informal* to hit someone or something very hard

wal•low /ˈwɑloʊ/ verb [I] **1** *showing disapproval* to spend a lot of time feeling sad or upset: *George still seems determined to wallow in self-pity.* **2** to lie down and roll around in water, dirt, or MUD

wall•pa•per[1] /ˈwɔlˌpeɪpər/ noun [C/U] **1** thick paper that you can stick on the walls inside a house in order to decorate them **2** the background color or pattern that you can put on your computer screen

wall•pa•per[2] /ˈwɔlˌpeɪpər/ verb [I/T] to put wallpaper onto walls

ˈ**Wall ˌStreet 1** the U.S. STOCK MARKET **2** the area in New York City where the U.S. STOCK EXCHANGE and other major financial institutions are based

ˌ**wall-to-ˈwall** adj **1** covering the whole floor of a room: *wall-to-wall carpet* **2** *informal* filling a space or time completely: *wall-to-wall TV coverage*

wal•nut /ˈwɔlˌnʌt/ noun **1** [C] a nut you can eat that has a hard round shell **2** [C/U] the tree that this nut grows on, or the wood of a walnut tree

wal•rus /ˈwɔlrəs/ noun [C] a large sea animal that has two very long TUSKS (=teeth)

waltz[1] /wɔlts/ noun [C] a dance in which a

pair of dancers turns continuously while moving around the dance floor, or the music for this dance

waltz² /wɔlts/ verb [I] **1** to dance a waltz **2** *informal* to walk somewhere in a relaxed and confident way

wan /wɑn/ adj **1** someone who is wan looks very pale and weak because they are sick **2** a wan light is not bright

wand /wɑnd/ noun [C] a thin stick that is used for doing magic tricks

wan•der /ˈwɑndər/ verb **1** [I/T] to go from place to place without a particular direction or purpose: *Jim wandered into the kitchen and made some tea.* ♦ *We spent the afternoon in the old city, just wandering the streets.* **2** [I] if your mind or thoughts wander, you stop concentrating and start thinking about other things **3** [I] if your eyes or your GAZE wanders, you stop looking at one thing and start looking at another **4** [I] *same as* **wander off** —**wan•der•er** noun [C]

PHRASAL VERB ˌ**wander ˈoff** to move away from a place where you are usually, or where people expect you to be: *It's a safe place where kids can wander off on their own.*

wane /weɪn/ verb [I] **1** to become weaker or less important **2** when the moon is waning, it looks smaller each night ≠ WAX

wan•gle /ˈwæŋg(ə)l/ verb [T] *informal* to get something that is difficult to get, especially by persuading someone in an indirect way: *I'll see if I can wangle some tickets for you.*

wan•na /ˈwɑnə/ short form *informal* a way of writing "want to" that shows how it sounds in informal conversation

wan•na•be /ˈwɑnəbi/ noun [C] *informal* someone who wants to be famous or successful —**wan•na•be** adj

want¹ /wɑnt/ verb [T] ★★★

1 to feel that you would like to have, keep, or do something: *Do you still want these old letters?* ♦ **want to do sth** *Liz wants to go to the circus.* ♦ **want sth for sth** *She wants a ticket to the concert for her birthday.*

2 to feel that you would like someone to do something, or would like something to happen: **want sb to do sth** *I want you to come with me.* ♦ **want sth from sb/sth** *I'm not sure what he wants from me.*

3 to ask for someone because you would like to see or speak to them: *Mom wants you – she's in the kitchen.* ♦ *You're wanted on the phone.*

PHRASES **all sb wants** *spoken* used for saying that someone's needs or requests are reasonable: *All I want is the truth.*

do you want sth? *spoken* used for offering something to someone, or for asking them if they would like to do something: *Do you want a cup of coffee?*

if you want *spoken* **1** used for offering to do something: *I'll make some coffee if you want.* **2** used for giving permission, or for agreeing with a suggestion that someone has made: *"Can I come with you?" "If you want."*

who wants (to do) sth? used for offering something to a group of people, or for asking if they would like to do something: *Who wants another glass of wine?*

want² /wɑnt/ noun **1** [C/U] *formal* a situation in which people do not have basic things such as food or money **2 wants** [plural] things that you want or need

ˈ**want** ˌ**ad** noun [C] *American* a small advertisement that you put in a newspaper if you want to give someone a job, buy something, etc. = CLASSIFIED AD

want•ed /ˈwɑntəd/ adj **1** being looked for by the police in connection with a crime **2** loved by other people

want•ing /ˈwɑntɪŋ/ adj not as good as something should be: *UN peacekeeping forces were found wanting.*

wan•ton /ˈwɑntən/ adj *formal* causing harm or damage for no reason: *wanton destruction*

war /wɔr/ noun ★★★

1 [C/U] fighting between two or more countries or groups, that involves the use of the military and usually continues for a long time: *the Vietnam War* ♦ *They have **been at war** for five years.* ♦ *I joined the Navy when **war broke out**.* ♦ *The Allies **declared war*** (=officially said they were at war) *in 1939.*

2 [C/U] a determined effort to control or stop something, for example a disease or crime: *This is a major victory in **the war against** drugs.* ♦ ***the war on** poverty*

3 [C] a situation in which countries, organizations, or businesses compete with each other in order to gain economic advantages: *a trade war*

→ WARRING

ˈ**war** ˌ**crime** noun [C] the crime of killing or harming people during a war for reasons that are not allowed by international law —ˈ**war** ˌ**criminal** noun [C]

ward¹ /wɔrd/ noun [C] **1** a large room in a hospital with beds for people to stay in **2** *legal* a child who is officially being taken care of by a court of law or by someone who is not their parents

ward² /wɔrd/ PHRASAL VERB ˌ**ward sb/sth** ˈ**off** to do something in order to prevent someone or something from harming you

war•den /ˈwɔrd(ə)n/ noun [C] *American* someone whose job is to be responsible for everything that happens in a prison

ward•robe /ˈwɔrdˌroʊb/ noun [C] **1** all the clothes that someone has **2** a large piece of furniture where you can hang your clothes

ware•house /ˈwerˌhaʊs/ noun [C] a big building where large amounts of goods are stored

war•fare /ˈwɔrˌfer/ noun [U] the activity of fighting a war, or the methods that are used for fighting wars: *the rules of warfare* ♦ *germ/biological warfare*

ˈ**war** ˌ**game** noun [C] a military training exercise in which soldiers practice for a real war

war•head /ˈwɔrˌhed/ noun [C] the front part of a missile that explodes

war•like /ˈwɔrˌlaɪk/ adj likely to start wars, or always ready to go to war

war•lord /ˈwɔrˌlɔrd/ noun [C] a military leader who controls part of a country but does not belong to the country's official armed forces

warm¹ /wɔrm/ adj ★★★

1 fairly hot in a comfortable, pleasant way ≠ COOL: *It was warm enough for us to sit*

outside. ♦ *I walked fast to **keep warm**.*
2 warm clothes and buildings prevent you from feeling cold: *The kitchen was the warmest room in the house.* ♦ *a thick warm coat*
3 kind and friendly in a way that makes other people feel comfortable: *a warm smile* ♦ *Please give **a warm welcome** to tonight's special guests.*
4 warm colors have red, orange, or yellow in them
—**warm•ly** adv

warm² /wɔrm/ verb [T] to make someone or something warm: *The morning sun warms the kitchen nicely.*
PHRASAL VERBS **ˈwarm to sb/sth** to begin to like someone or something
ˌwarm (sb/sth) ˈup 1 to become warm, or to make someone or something become warm: *I'll warm up some soup for lunch.* ♦ *Drink this – it'll warm you up.* **2** to prepare for a sport or activity by doing gentle exercises or practicing just before it starts: *The players are already on the field warming up.*

warmed-o•ver /ˌwɔrmd ˈoʊvər/ adj *American* **1** warmed-over ideas or arguments are not new or original **2** warmed-over food had gotten cold but has been heated again, so that you can eat it

ˈwar meˌmorial noun [C] a structure that is built to remind people of the soldiers and other people who were killed in a war

warm-heart•ed /ˌwɔrm ˈhɑrtəd/ adj friendly, kind, and generous ≠ COLD-HEARTED

warmth /wɔrmθ/ noun [U] **1** heat: *We sat near the warmth of the fire.* **2** a kind, friendly quality in someone or something

ˈwarm-ˌup noun **1** [C] a set of exercises that you do just before you start to play a sport, in order to prepare your body **2 warm-ups** [plural] *American* a loose jacket and pants that you wear for exercising or playing sports

warn /wɔrn/ verb [I/T] ★★★
1 to tell someone about a possible problem or danger, so that they can avoid it or deal with it: *Recent studies **warn against** drinking too much caffeine.* ♦ *Scientists **warned of** the threat to beaches and rivers from pollution.* ♦ **warn sb to do sth** *Police are warning all women in the area to take extra care when going out alone.* ♦ **+that** *The report warns that consumers could end up paying higher prices.* ♦ **warn sb about sth** *Travel agents are not warning tourists about the dangers of crime in ski resorts.*
2 to tell someone that they will be punished or that something bad will happen if they do something: *I warned you not to go out with him.*

W

warn•ing /ˈwɔrnɪŋ/ noun ★★
1 [C/U] an action or statement telling someone of a possible problem or danger: *By law, cigarette packs must carry **a health warning**.* ♦ ***a warning against** driving on the icy roads*
2 [C] a statement telling someone that they will be punished or that something bad will happen if they do something: *This is your last warning – if you're late again, you'll lose your job.*

warp /wɔrp/ verb [I/T] to become bent or curved because of damage by heat or water, or to make something do this

war•path /ˈwɔrˌpɑθ/ noun **on the warpath** *informal* angry about something and looking for someone to punish for it

warped /wɔrpt/ adj **1** bent or curved because of damage by heat or water **2** *informal* someone who is warped has opinions or thoughts that most people think are strange or shocking

war•rant¹ /ˈwɔrənt/ noun [C] a document written by a judge that gives the police permission to do something, for example to arrest someone or to search a house

war•rant² /ˈwɔrənt/ verb [T] *formal* to make an action seem reasonable or necessary = JUSTIFY

war•ran•ty /ˈwɔrənti/ noun [C] a company's written promise to repair or replace a product that you buy from them if it breaks or does not work = GUARANTEE

war•ren /ˈwɔrən/ noun [C] a place that is very difficult to find your way around because there are so many ways that you could go

war•ring /ˈwɔrɪŋ/ adj arguing or fighting with each other

war•ri•or /ˈwɔriər/ noun [C] *literary* a soldier

war•ship /ˈwɔrˌʃɪp/ noun [C] a large ship with a lot of weapons, used for fighting in wars

wart /wɔrt/ noun [C] a small hard lump that grows on your skin

war•time /ˈwɔrˌtaɪm/ noun [U] the period when a war is taking place ≠ PEACETIME
—**war•time** adj

war-torn /ˈwɔr ˌtɔrn/ adj a war-torn country or place has been badly damaged by a war

war•y /ˈweri/ adj careful or nervous about someone or something, because you think that they might cause a problem —**war•i•ly** adv

was /*weak* wəz, *strong* wɑz/ *see* **be**

wash¹ /wɑʃ/ verb ★★★
1 [T] to clean something with water or with soap and water: *I have to wash the dishes.* ♦ *a freshly washed shirt* ♦ *You should always wash fruit before eating it.*
2 [I/T] to clean yourself or a part of your body with water or with soap and water: *He washed and dressed quickly.* ♦ ***Wash your hands** before you touch the food.*
3 [T] if water washes a person or object somewhere, it carries them there: *Some very strange things get washed ashore here.*
4 [I/T] to flow, or to flow to a place: *Waves were washing against the side of the boat.*
PHRASE **wash your hands of** to say or show that you do not want to be involved with something, and that you are not responsible for it: *The government had washed its hands of the affair.*
PHRASAL VERBS **ˌwash sth aˈway** if water washes something away, it carries it away: *Heavy rains have washed away the bridge.*
ˌwash sth ˈdown to drink a liquid in order to help you to swallow food or medicine more easily: *He had a large slice of pizza **washed down with** beer.*
ˌwash (sth) ˈoff if you wash dirt off, or if dirt washes off, you remove it by washing: *Wash all the dirt off before you cook the potatoes.* ♦ *Don't worry – that'll wash off.*
ˌwash ˈout to be able to be removed by washing: *Permanent dyes won't wash out.*
ˌwash sth ˈout to wash something quickly,

especially the inside of a container

ˌwash ˈup *American* to wash yourself, especially your hands and face: *Why don't you go wash up before we eat.*

ˌwash sth ˈup if water washes something up, it carries it somewhere and leaves it there: *A whale has been washed up on the beach.*

wash

wash² /wɑʃ/ noun **1** [C] the process of washing someone or something: *These pants need a wash.* ♦ *After a few washes the color faded.* **2 the wash** [singular] clothes that will be washed or that have just been washed =LAUNDRY: *Did you put my blue shirt in the wash?*

wash·a·ble /ˈwɑʃəb(ə)l/ adj able to be washed without being damaged

wash·cloth /ˈwɑʃˌklɑθ/ noun [C] *American* a small square towel used for washing your face or body

washed-out /ˌwɑʃt ˈaʊt/ adj *informal* very pale and sick or tired

washed-up /ˌwɑʃt ˈʌp/ adj *informal* someone who is washed-up will never be popular or successful again =FINISHED

wash·er /ˈwɑʃər/ noun [C] **1** *informal* a WASHING MACHINE **2** a small flat ring that is used for filling the space between two metal parts, for example between a surface and the top of a screw

ˈwashing maˌchine noun [C] a machine for washing clothes

wash·out /ˈwɑʃˌaʊt/ noun [C] *informal* a failure: *The party was a total washout.*

was·n't /ˈwʌz(ə)nt/ short form the usual way of saying or writing "was not." This is not often used in formal writing: *The food looked good, but I wasn't hungry.*

wasp /wɑsp/ noun [C] a black and yellow flying insect that can sting you —*picture* → C13

wast·age /ˈweɪstɪdʒ/ noun [U] the amount of something that is wasted, or a situation in which something is wasted

waste¹ /weɪst/ noun ★★

1 [singular/U] the failure to use something that is valuable or useful in an effective way: *All this uneaten food – what a waste!* ♦ *It's **a waste of time** trying to get her to change her mind.* ♦ *The cherries will just **go to waste** (=be spoiled or thrown away) if we don't pick them soon.*

2 [C/U] the useless materials, substances, or parts that are left after you have used something: *nuclear waste*

waste² /weɪst/ verb [T] ★★ to use more of something than is necessary, or to use it in a way that does not produce the best results: *There were accusations that the government was wasting public money.* ♦ *A great deal of time was wasted arguing over the details of the contract.* ♦ **waste sth on sth** *Why do you waste your money on the lottery?*

PHRASES **be wasted on sb** if something is wasted on someone, they do not understand it or realize how good it is

waste no time (in) doing sth to do something immediately

PHRASAL VERB **ˌwaste aˈway** to gradually become thinner and weaker over a period of time, usually because of an illness

waste³ /weɪst/ adj **1** waste substances are what is left of something after the valuable parts of it have been used **2** waste land or waste ground is land that is not being used or has not been built on

ˈwaste ˌbasket noun [C] *American* a small open container for garbage such as used paper —*picture* → C3

wast·ed /ˈweɪstəd/ adj **1** not used effectively: *a wasted day* **2** *informal* very drunk or strongly affected by illegal drugs **3** extremely thin and weak

waste·ful /ˈweɪs(t)fəl/ adj using something carelessly, so that some of it is wasted

waste·land /ˈweɪs(t)ˌlænd/ noun [C/U] an area of land that is empty or that cannot be used

waste·pa·per bas·ket /ˈweɪs(t)ˌpeɪpər ˌbæskət/ noun [C] a WASTE BASKET

watch¹ /wɑtʃ/ verb ★★★

1 [I/T] to look at someone or something for a period of time: *Did you watch the news last night?* ♦ *We watched helplessly as the car rolled into the river.* ♦ **watch sb/sth do sth** *Jill watched the children build sandcastles.* ♦ **watch sb/sth doing sth** *We arrived early to watch the players warming up.* → LOOK

2 [T] to be careful of something: *Watch the knife! It's sharp!* ♦ **+(that)** *Watch that the ball doesn't go into the street.* ♦ **+how/who/what etc.** *They need to watch what they spend very carefully.*

3 [T] to take care of someone or something for a short time and make sure that nothing bad happens to them: *Dennis is going to watch the kids tonight while I'm out.*

PHRASES **watch it** *spoken* **1** used for telling someone to be careful **2** used for threatening someone

watch your step *spoken* **1** used for telling someone to be careful where they walk **2** used for telling someone to be careful about what they say or do, because they could get into trouble

PHRASAL VERBS **ˌwatch ˈout** used for telling someone to be careful: *Watch out – you're going to hit that car!*

ˌwatch ˈout for sb/sth to be careful so that you can avoid someone or something

ˌwatch ˈover sb/sth to guard, protect, or be in charge of someone or something

> Words often used with **watch**
>
> *Adverbs often used with **watch** (verb, sense 1)*
>
> ■ WATCH + **anxiously, carefully, closely, helplessly, idly, incredulously, intently, nervously, quietly, silently**: watch in a particular way

watch² /wɑtʃ/ noun [C] ★★ a small clock that you wear on your wrist

PHRASE **keep (a) watch** to pay attention to a situation carefully so that you can deal with any changes or problems: *Scientists are **keeping** a close **watch on** pollution levels.*

watch•dog /ˈwɑtʃˌdɔg/ noun [C] **1** a person or organization whose job is to make sure that companies that provide a particular type of service or product do not break the law or do anything harmful: *the water industry watchdog* **2** a dog that is used for guarding a building

watch•ful /ˈwɑtʃfəl/ adj looking at something carefully, or noticing everything that is happening = VIGILANT

watch•man /ˈwɑtʃmən/ noun [C] a NIGHT WATCHMAN

watch•word /ˈwɑtʃˌwɜrd/ noun [C] a word or phrase that expresses the quality that someone believes is most important in a particular situation

wa•ter[1] /ˈwɔtər/ noun ★★★

1 [U] the clear liquid that falls as rain and is used for drinking, washing, and cooking: *Wash your hands with soap and water.*

2 [U] an area of water such as a lake or ocean: *From the hotel there's a beautiful view of the water.*

3 [C/U] the surface of a lake or the ocean: *I swam under the water near the beach.*

4 **waters** [plural] an area of water that belongs to a particular place, state, country, etc.: *Cuban waters*

→ HEAD[1]

wa•ter[2] /ˈwɔtər/ verb **1** [T] to pour water on plants in order to keep them healthy **2** [I] if your eyes water, tears form in them because something is hurting them **3** [I] if your mouth waters when you see or smell good food, SALIVA begins to form in your mouth

PHRASAL VERB ˌ**water sth ˈdown 1** to make something such as a statement or newspaper article less offensive, powerful, or detailed **2** to add water to a drink or liquid in order to make it less strong = DILUTE

wa•ter•col•or /ˈwɑtərˌkʌlər/ noun **1** [C/U] a type of paint that is mixed with water for painting pictures **2** [C] a painting that is done with watercolor paints

ˈ**water ˌcooler** noun **1** [C] a machine that makes cool water available for people to drink, especially in an office or other place where people work —*picture* → C16 **2** [singular] *journalism* used for referring to the situation or place in an office where people talk in an informal way: *jokes around the water cooler*

wa•ter•cress /ˈwɔtərˌkres/ noun [U] a plant with leaves that are eaten in salads

wa•ter•fall /ˈwɔtərˌfɔl/ noun [C] a place where water flows over the edge of a steep place onto another level below

wa•ter•front /ˈwɔtərˌfrʌnt/ noun [C] an area that is next to a river, lake, or ocean

wa•ter•hole /ˈwɔtərˌhoʊl/ noun [C] a small area of water in a hot country where wild animals go to drink

wa•ter•ing can /ˈwɔt(ə)rɪŋ ˌkæn/ noun [C] a container used for pouring water on plants. It has a handle and a long SPOUT.

wa•ter•logged /ˈwɔtərˌlɔgd/ adj waterlogged ground is too wet to walk on or play sports on

wa•ter•mark /ˈwɔtərˌmɑrk/ noun [C] a hidden design on a piece of paper that you can only see when you hold the paper in front of a light

wa•ter•mel•on /ˈwɔtərˌmelən/ noun [C/U] a large round fruit that has a hard green skin and is red with small black seeds inside —*picture* → C10

ˈ**water ˌpolo** noun [U] a game that is played in water by two teams of seven players who get points by throwing a ball into the other team's goal

wa•ter•proof /ˈwɔtərˌpruf/ adj waterproof clothes or materials do not let water pass through them

wa•ter•shed /ˈwɔtərˌʃed/ noun [C] a time or event when a major change takes place = TURNING POINT

ˈ**water-ˌskiing** noun [U] a sport in which you stand on SKIS and ride on the surface of water while being pulled behind a boat —ˈ**water-ˌski** verb [I], ˈ**water-ˌskier** noun [C]

ˈ**water ˌtable** noun [C] the level below the Earth's surface where water is found

wa•ter•tight /ˈwɔtərˌtaɪt/ adj **1** a watertight container or room is made so that water cannot enter it **2** a watertight excuse, argument, or case is so good that no one can find anything wrong with it

wa•ter•way /ˈwɔtərˌweɪ/ noun [C] *formal* a river or CANAL that boats use for traveling from one place to another

wa•ter•y /ˈwɔt(ə)ri/ adj **1** containing or filled with water: *watery eyes* **2** watery food or drink contains a lot of water and has a weak taste **3** weak or pale: *watery sunlight*

watt /wɑt/ noun [C] a unit for measuring electrical power

wave[1] /weɪv/ noun [C] ★★

1 of water	4 sudden emotion
2 movement	5 lots of people
3 increase	6 of sound/radio, etc.

1 a line of water that rises up on the surface of an ocean, lake, or river: *The boat was smashed by a huge wave.* ♦ *Children swam and played in the waves.*

2 a movement that you make with your hand or with an object as a way of saying hello or goodbye to someone or as a signal to them

3 a sudden increase of a particular type of behavior or activity: ***a frightening wave of*** *drug-related killings* ♦ ***a new wave of*** *company bankruptcies*

4 a sudden strong emotion that affects a person or group: *The invasion caused a* ***wave of*** *anti-American feeling.*

5 a large number of people moving or arriving somewhere at the same time: ***Waves of*** *protesters began arriving at the stadium.*

6 the way in which sound, light, a radio signal, etc. travels → LONG WAVE, MEDIUM WAVE, SHORT WAVE

→ NEW WAVE

wave[2] /weɪv/ verb ★★

1 [I/T] to move your hand in order to say hello or goodbye: *He smiled and waved when he saw me.* ♦ *Mrs. Clinton* ***waved to*** *the crowd.* ♦ *We* ***waved goodbye*** *to them as the car drove off.*

2 [T] to move your hand in order to tell someone to move, to leave, or to stop annoying you: **wave sb away/off/on** *He waved me away when I offered to help.*

3 [T] to move something around in the air: *People clapped and children waved flags.*
4 [I] to move smoothly and gently from side to side: *The trees were waving in the wind.*
PHRASAL VERB **ˌwave sth aˈside** to ignore someone's ideas, feelings, or opinions because you do not think that they are important

wave·band /ˈweɪvˌbænd/ noun [C] a range of radio waves that have lengths that come between particular limits

wave·length /ˈweɪvˌleŋθ/ noun [C] **1** the length of the radio wave that a radio station uses for broadcasting **2** the distance between two waves of sound or light that are next to each other
PHRASE **be on the same wavelength** to understand the way that another person thinks because you have the same ideas and opinions

wa·ver /ˈweɪvər/ verb [I] **1** to not be certain about what to do = HESITATE **2** to shake and not be steady: *Her voice wavered as she said goodbye.*

wav·y /ˈweɪvi/ adj a wavy line or wavy hair has a lot of waves or curls in it

wax¹ /wæks/ noun [U] **1** a solid substance that becomes liquid when it is heated. Wax is used, for example, to make CANDLES. **2** a dark yellow substance in your ears —**wax·y** adj

wax² /wæks/ verb [T] **1** to make wood shiny by rubbing wax onto it **2** to remove hair by putting wax on your skin

way¹ /weɪ/ noun [C] ★★★

1 method	5 distance in space
2 manner/style	6 distance in time
3 road/path	7 aspect
4 direction/position	+ PHRASES

1 a method for doing something: **+(that)** *There are so many delicious ways you can prepare chicken.* ♦ **way of doing sth** *Is there any way of contacting you while you're in Africa?* ♦ **way to do sth** *The students are learning new ways to communicate in writing.* → EASY¹, HARD¹
2 the manner or style in which something happens or is done: **+(that)** *I love to watch the way she plays with the children.* ♦ **no way to do sth** (=not the right thing to do) *That's no way to talk to your mother.*
3 the particular road, path, or track that you use in order to go from one place to another: *I don't think this is* ***the right way.*** ♦ *The tourists* ***lost their way*** (=became lost) *and had to ask for directions.* ♦ *Is this* ***the way to*** *the Eiffel Tower?* ♦ *Does Tim* ***know the way*** *to your house from here?* ♦ *Could you please* ***show me the way*** *to the bus station?* ♦ *Don't bother picking me up. It's really* ***out of your way*** (=far from the road you use). → LEAD¹
4 the direction or position where something is, or the direction in which something is standing or moving: *The bathroom is this way.* ♦ *The car was going* ***the wrong way.***
5 the distance from one place to another: *The nearest store is quite* ***a long way*** *from here.* ♦ *The children were arguing* ***all the way*** *home.*
6 a distance in time from one event to another: *The Christmas holidays were still* ***a long way off.***
7 a particular aspect of something: *The evening was a great success,* ***in more ways than one.*** ♦ ***In a way,*** *I agree with you.*

PHRASES **be/get in the/sb's way** to be in the area where someone is, so that it is difficult for them to do something: *Can I move your bags? They're in my way.*
be/get/keep out of the/sb's way to be away from, or to stay away from, the area where someone is, so that you do not make it difficult for them to do something: *Keep the kids out of the way while I'm working.*
be on the/its way to be about to arrive or happen: *We fear a recession is on the way.*
by the way used for introducing a new or extra fact or comment into a conversation: *By the way, I'll be late home tonight.*
get/have your (own) way to be allowed to do what you want, although other people want something different
get in the way of sth to prevent something from happening: *The new rules are just getting in the way of progress.*
get sth out of the way to finish doing something that is difficult or unpleasant: *I want to get this out of the way before lunch.*
give way 1 if something gives way, it breaks because there is too much weight or pressure on it **2** to agree to something that someone else wants instead of what you want: *We will not* ***give way to*** *terrorism.*
go out of your way to do sth to make an extra effort to do something, even though it is not convenient or easy to do
have come a long way to have made a lot of progress or improvement
have a long way to go to need a lot more progress or improvement
in a big way *informal* a lot: *Investors were buying Internet stocks in a big way.*
know your way around (sth) to be very familiar with a particular place or activity
make way to move in order to allow someone to go forward or get past: *The crowd made way as police officers entered the building.*
make way for sth to provide space for something new by removing what was there before: *They plan to demolish the houses to make way for a gas station.*
no way *spoken* **1** used for saying that something will definitely not happen: *"Are you inviting Phil to your party?" "No way!"* **2** used for expressing surprise, or for telling someone that you do not believe them: *She said that to you? No way!*
one way or another used for saying that something will definitely happen, even though you do not know how it will happen: *One way or another, I'm going to go to Europe.*
way of life the way people normally live in a place, or the things that they normally do or experience: *Fishing has been a way of life here for centuries.* ♦ *People see this as a threat to their way of life.*
way to go *spoken* used for telling someone that they have done something well
you can't have it both ways used for saying that someone cannot have all the benefits from two possible situations: *What's more important, your family or your job? You can't have it both ways.*
→ FIND¹

Other words meaning way

- **means** a way that makes it possible to do something
- **method** a way of doing something that involves following a detailed plan
- **procedure** a way of doing something that involves doing specific activities in a particular order
- **strategy** a way of achieving a goal that involves detailed planning
- **system** a way of doing something that involves following an organized set of rules
- **technique** a way of doing something that involves using particular skills

way² /weɪ/ adv *informal* by a large amount or distance: *Michael was way ahead of the other runners.*
PHRASE **way back** *informal* a long time ago in the past: *I graduated from high school way back in 1982.*

way·lay /ˈweɪˌleɪ/ (past tense and past participle **way·laid** /ˈweɪˌleɪd/) verb [T] to stop someone who is going somewhere, in order to talk to them or to harm them

ˌway ˈout noun [C] a way of dealing with a problem

way·side /ˈweɪˌsaɪd/ noun **fall by the wayside** to not be successful or effective anymore

way·ward /ˈweɪwərd/ adj difficult to control and tending to do unexpected things

we /wi/ pronoun ★★★
1 used for referring to yourself and one or more other people when you are the person speaking or writing: *We moved here soon after we were married.* ♦ *We were all glad to get back home.*
2 used for referring to people in general: *We live in a competitive world.*

weak /wik/ adj ★★

1 not physically strong	6 easily criticized
2 not strongly built	7 with a lot of water
3 not effective	8 hard to see/hear
4 easily persuaded	+ PHRASE
5 bad in quality	

1 lacking physical strength or good health ≠ STRONG: *The illness had left him too weak to speak.* ♦ *He has always had a weak heart.*
2 not strongly built and easily damaged or destroyed: *The floorboards are weak in some places.*
3 not powerful or effective, and unlikely to be successful ≠ STRONG: *We are in a weak negotiating position.* ♦ *a weak economy/ currency*
4 lacking determination and easily persuaded to do something that you should not do: *weak, indecisive leadership*
5 bad in quality or ability ≠ STRONG: *Her written work is good, but her oral skills are weak.*
6 a weak argument or idea is one that you can easily criticize or prove to be wrong ≠ STRONG: *The government's case is weak.*
7 a weak liquid contains a lot of water and does not have much taste ≠ STRONG: *a cup of weak coffee*
8 a weak light, sound, or heat is one that you cannot easily see, hear, or feel ≠ STRONG
PHRASE **weak point** a fault or problem that makes something or someone less effective or attractive
—**weak·ly** adv

weak·en /ˈwikən/ verb [I/T] **1** to become less strong or healthy, or to make someone or something do this **2** to become less powerful, effective, or determined, or to make someone or something do this

weak·ling /ˈwiklɪŋ/ noun [C] *showing disapproval* a person or animal that is physically weak

weak·ness /ˈwiknəs/ noun ★
1 [U] the state or condition of being weak: *the increasing* ***weakness of*** *the government*
2 [C] a fault or problem that makes someone or something less effective or attractive: *They listed* ***the strengths and weaknesses of*** *their product.*
3 [C] a strong liking or enjoyment of something: *You know my* ***weakness for*** *chocolate.*

wealth /welθ/ noun [U] ★★
1 a large amount of money and other valuable things: *a man of immense wealth*
2 the state of being rich ≠ POVERTY: *He had an obsession with power and wealth.*
3 a large amount of something that is useful or interesting: ***a wealth of*** *exciting opportunities*

wealth·y /ˈwelθi/ adj rich: *a wealthy businessman*

wean /win/ verb [T] to make a baby stop taking its mother's milk and start to eat solid food
PHRASAL VERB **ˈwean sb off sth** to make someone gradually stop depending on something that they like and have become used to

weap·on /ˈwepən/ noun [C] ★★★ an object that can be used for hurting people or damaging property, for example a gun, knife, or bomb

weap·on·ry /ˈwepənri/ noun [U] weapons

wear¹ /wer/ (past tense **wore** /wɔr/; past participle **worn** /wɔrn/) verb ★★★

1 have sth on body	5 have expression
2 form hole in sth	+ PHRASES
3 become thin/weak	+ PHRASAL VERBS
4 have hairstyle	

1 [T] to have something on your body as clothing, decoration, or protection: *He was wearing jeans and a T-shirt.* ♦ *She wasn't* ***wearing any makeup.*** ♦ *He wears glasses now.* —*picture* → DRESS
2 [T] if you wear a hole in something, you form a hole in it by using it or rubbing it a lot
3 [I] to become thinner or weaker because of being used a lot: *The carpet has* ***worn thin*** *in places.*
4 [T] to have a particular hairstyle: *It was fashionable for men to wear their hair long then.*
5 [T] to have a particular expression on your face: *They all wore puzzled frowns.*
PHRASES **wear thin** if something such as a feeling or explanation wears thin, it becomes gradually weaker or harder to accept
wear well to stay in good condition even after a lot of use

W

PHRASAL VERBS ˌ**wear (sth) aˈway** to disappear, or to make something disappear, because it has been used or rubbed a lot: *The inscription on the ring had almost worn away.*
ˌ**wear sb ˈdown** to make someone gradually lose their energy or confidence
ˌ**wear sth ˈdown** to make something gradually disappear or become thinner by using or rubbing it: *The old stone steps had been worn down by years of use.*
ˌ**wear ˈoff** if a feeling wears off, it gradually disappears
ˌ**wear ˈon** if time wears on, it passes
ˌ**wear sb ˈout** to make someone feel very tired: *Those kids wore me out today.*
ˌ**wear (sth) ˈout** to become extremely thin or damaged because of being used a lot, or to make something do this

wear² /wer/ noun [U] **1** the continuous use that something has over a period of time **2** a type of clothes for a particular activity or a particular group of people: *a menswear store* ♦ *I didn't bring any evening wear.* **3** changes or damage that affect something when it has been used a lot
PHRASE **wear and tear** the changes or damage that normally happen to something that has been used a lot

wear•ing /ˈwerɪŋ/ adj making you physically or mentally tired

wea•ry /ˈwɪri/ adj **1** very tired **2** bored or annoyed with something that you feel has continued for too long —**wea•ri•ly** adv, **wea•ri•ness** noun [U]

wea•sel /ˈwiz(ə)l/ noun [C] **1** a small thin animal with brown fur, short legs, and a long tail **2** *informal* an insulting word for a dishonest person

weath•er¹ /ˈweðər/ noun [U] ★★★ the conditions that exist in the atmosphere, for example, whether it is hot, cold, sunny, or wet: *The hot weather will continue through the weekend.* ♦ *We couldn't paint the outside because of the weather.*
PHRASE **under the weather** *informal* not feeling well

Words often used with weather

*Adjectives often used with **weather** (noun)*

- **beautiful, bright, fine, glorious, good, perfect, sunny** + WEATHER: used about weather that is pleasant
- **appalling, awful, bad, foul, terrible** + WEATHER: used about weather that is unpleasant
- **cold, freezing, frosty, wintry** + WEATHER: used about weather that is cold
- **hot, muggy, warm** + WEATHER: used about weather that is hot
- **changeable, uncertain, unsettled** + WEATHER: used about weather that changes often

weath•er² /ˈweðər/ verb **1** [I/T] if something weathers, or if it is weathered, its appearance changes because of the effects of wind, rain, etc. **2** [T] to manage a difficult experience without being seriously harmed

ˈ**weather-ˌbeaten** adj a weather-beaten face has rough skin as a result of being outside for long periods

ˈ**weather ˌforecast** noun [C] a report on what the weather will be like for a period of time in the future —ˈ**weather ˌforecaster** noun [C]

weave /wiv/ (past tense **wove** /woʊv/; past participle **wo•ven** /ˈwoʊv(ə)n/) verb **1** [I/T] to make cloth by crossing long THREADS over and under each other on a special machine **2** [T] to create an object by weaving or by twisting pieces of things together: *She was weaving a basket.* **3** (past tense and past participle **weaved**) [I/T] to move somewhere by going around and between things —**weav•er** noun [C]

web /web/ noun [C] **1** a net of thin THREADS that a SPIDER makes in order to catch insects **2** a complicated set of related things: *a web of lies*

Web, the /web/ *computing* all the WEBSITES that organizations have created on their computers for people to look at using the Internet = WORLD WIDE WEB, THE

webbed /webd/ adj if a bird or animal has webbed feet, it has skin between its toes to help it to swim

ˈ**web ˌbrowser** noun [C] *computing* a software program that you use for finding and looking at pages on the Internet

web•cam /ˈwebˌkæm/ noun [C] *computing* a camera that is connected to a computer and produces images on a WEBSITE

web•cast /ˈwebˌkæst/ noun [C] *computing* a broadcast on the Internet —**web•cast** verb [I/T]

web•mas•ter /ˈwebˌmæstər/ noun [C] *computing* someone whose job is to manage a WEBSITE

ˈ**web ˌpage** noun [C] *computing* a page or document that you can read on a WEBSITE

web•site noun [C] *computing* a place on the Internet where information is available about a particular subject, company, university, etc.

we'd /wid/ short form the usual way of saying or writing "we had" or "we would." This is not often used in formal writing: *We'd like to hear from you.*

wed /wed/ (past tense and past participle **wed** or **wed•ded**) verb [I/T] *mainly journalism* to marry, or to marry someone

Wed. abbrev Wednesday

wed•ding /ˈwedɪŋ/ noun [C] ★★ a ceremony in which two people get married: *We wanted a quiet wedding.* ♦ *a wedding present/cake*

ˈ**wedding anniˌversary** noun [C] a celebration of the number of years that two people have been married

ˈ**wedding ˌring** noun [C] a ring that you wear on your left hand in order to show that you are married

wedge¹ /wedʒ/ noun [C] **1** a piece of wood, plastic, or other material that is thin at one end and wider at the other. You press it into a space to hold something in place or to force things apart. **2** a piece of something that is shaped like a wedge

wedge² /wedʒ/ verb [T] **1** to push something tightly into a small space: *I wedged a piece of paper into the crack.* **2** to hold something in position with a wedge

Wednes•day /ˈwenzˌdeɪ/ noun [C/U] ★★★ the day after Tuesday and before Thursday: *I was born on a Wednesday.* ♦ *I go swimming*

Wednesdays (=every Wednesday). ♦ *I saw Sharon last Wednesday.* ♦ *They are arriving* ***on Wednesday.***

weed¹ /wid/ noun [C] a wild plant that grows in places where you do not want it

weed² /wid/ verb [I/T] to remove weeds from the ground

PHRASAL VERB ˌ**weed sb/sth ˈout** to remove people or things from a group because they are not appropriate or not good enough

week /wik/ noun [C] ★★★

1 a period of seven days, usually counted from a Sunday: *They spent two weeks in Florida.* ♦ *He works from home two days* ***a week.*** ♦ *He will meet his uncle in Boston* ***next week.*** ♦ *We're seeing Jim* ***a week from*** *Tuesday* (=seven days from next Tuesday).

2 the five days from Monday to Friday, when most people work: *They work a 35-hour week.* ♦ *She stays in the city during the week.*

week·day /ˈwikˌdeɪ/ noun [C] a day that is not Saturday or Sunday

week·end /ˈwikˌend/ noun [C] ★★★ Saturday and Sunday: *Let's go away for the weekend.* ♦ *The bus service is free* ***on weekends.***

week·ly¹ /ˈwikli/ adj happening or published once every week

week·ly² /ˈwikli/ noun [C] a newspaper or magazine that is published once a week

week·ly³ /ˈwikli/ adv every week

weep /wip/ (past tense and past participle **wept** /wept/) verb [I/T] to cry

weigh /weɪ/ verb ★★

1 [linking verb] to have a particular weight: *How much do you weigh?* ♦ *The baby weighed 7 pounds at birth.* ♦ *Your suitcase* ***weighs a ton*** (=is very heavy).

2 [T] to measure how heavy someone or something is: *I weigh myself once a week.*

3 [T] to consider all the aspects of a situation carefully before making a decision: *The judge weighed all the facts before reaching a verdict.* ♦ **weigh sth against sth** *Those costs must be weighed against the environmental benefits.*

PHRASAL VERBS ˌ**weigh sb ˈdown 1** to be very heavy and prevent someone from moving easily **2** to cause problems for someone or something

ˈ**weigh ˌon sb** to make someone worried

weight¹ /weɪt/ noun ★★★

1 measurement	4 sth difficult to move
2 being heavy	5 influence
3 for exercise/sport	6 sth causing trouble

1 [U] a measurement of how heavy a person or thing is: *Have you* ***lost weight*** (=become thinner)? ♦ *Susan* ***put on weight*** (=became fatter) *after her accident.* ♦ *I am trying to* ***watch my weight*** (=control how much I eat).

2 [U] the fact or effect of being heavy: ***The weight of*** *the backpack made her fall over.*

3 [C] a piece of heavy metal that is designed for lifting for exercise or as a sport —*picture* → C16

4 [C] a heavy object that is difficult to lift or move

5 [U] the influence or importance that someone or something has: *Simpson's opinions* ***carry a lot of weight with*** (=have a lot of influence on) *the President.* ♦ *The Chief Executive is* ***throwing his full weight behind*** *the proposal.*

6 [singular] something that causes you trouble or difficulty: *Obviously the verdict* ***is a huge weight off my mind*** (=something I do not have to worry about anymore).

weight² /weɪt/ or ˈ**weight sth ˌdown** verb [T] to make something heavier by putting a weight on it in order to stop it from moving

weight·ed /ˈweɪtəd/ adj designed to produce a particular effect or result by giving more importance to one thing than to another: *The tax laws are heavily weighted in favor of the wealthy.*

weight·less /ˈweɪtləs/ adj having no weight, because of being outside the Earth's atmosphere —**weight·less·ness** noun [U]

weight·lift·ing /ˈweɪtˌlɪftɪŋ/ noun [U] the sport of lifting heavy weights —**weight·lift·er** noun [C]

ˈ**weight ˌtraining** noun [U] exercise that involves lifting weights

weight·y /ˈweɪti/ adj serious and important

weird /wɪrd/ adj strange and unusual —**weird·ly** adv

weird·o /ˈwɪrdoʊ/ noun [C] *informal* someone who behaves in a way that seems strange

wel·come¹ /ˈwelkəm/ verb [T] ★★

1 to greet someone in a polite and friendly way when they arrive: *My aunt and uncle were waiting at the door to welcome us.*

2 to say that you approve of something that has happened, or that you are pleased about it: *They welcomed the new proposals.*

wel·come² /ˈwelkəm/ adj ★

1 if you are welcome somewhere, people are pleased that you are there ≠ UNWELCOME: *Your friends are always welcome here.* ♦ *The neighbors* ***made us feel very welcome.***

2 if something is welcome, people are happy about it because it is pleasant or because they need it ≠ UNWELCOME: *A cold drink would be very welcome.*

3 if someone tells you that you are welcome to do something, they mean that you are allowed to do it if you want to: *Members of the public are welcome to attend the meeting.* ♦ *You're* ***more than welcome*** *to stay overnight.*

4 if someone tells you that you are welcome to something, they mean that you can have it or use it, because they do not want it themselves

PHRASE **you're welcome** used as a reply to someone who has thanked you

wel·come³ /ˈwelkəm/ noun [C/U] an act of welcoming someone to a place: *He gave us a warm welcome and invited us to lunch.*

PHRASE **outstay/overstay your welcome** to stay at a place for longer than people want you to be there

wel·come⁴ /ˈwelkəm/ interjection used for welcoming someone to a place: *Welcome to Springfield.*

weld /weld/ verb [T] to join two pieces of metal by heating them and pressing them together —**weld·er** noun [C]

wel·fare /ˈwelˌfer/ noun [U] ★

1 care that is provided by the government or another organization for people in need: *the welfare system*

2 *American* money given to people who do not have work or who are in need: *A*

quarter of the town's population ***is on welfare*** (=is receiving it).
3 the health, happiness, and safety of a person or group=WELL-BEING: *Police are concerned for the welfare of the child.*

ˌwelfare ˈstate noun **1** [C] a country that takes care of its citizens by providing social and financial support **2 the welfare state** [singular] the system by which a country takes care of its citizens by providing them with education, medical care, or money if they are unable to work

we'll /wil/ short form the usual way of saying or writing "we shall" or "we will." This is not often used in formal writing: *We'll come to meet you at the airport.*

well[1] /wel/ (comparative **bet·ter** /ˈbetər/; superlative **best** /best/) adv ★★★

1 skillfully/effectively	4 very/very much
2 in satisfactory way	5 by large amount
3 completely	+ PHRASES

1 skillfully, or effectively: *She speaks Japanese really well.*
2 in a satisfactory way: *The boys were not behaving very well.*
3 completely, or thoroughly: *Shake the can well before opening.* ♦ *I don't know these people very well.*
4 very, or very much: *Rostov was* ***well aware*** *of the scandal he was creating.* ♦ *A trip to the new museum is* ***well worth*** *the effort.*
5 by a large amount of time, or by a large distance: *We left the party* ***well before*** *you.*

PHRASES **as well (as)** in addition to someone or something else: *I need to go to the bookstore as well as the bank.* ♦ *I'd like a cup of coffee, and a glass of water as well.*
→ ALSO
be doing well to be getting better after an illness
be doing well for yourself to be successful in life
could/may/might well used for saying that something is likely: *The two murder cases may well be connected.*
may/might (just) as well do sth *informal* used for saying that it might be a good idea to do something, although it is not essential: *We might as well go home.*
well done used for giving someone praise when they do something well

well[2] /wel/ interjection ★★★

1 when replying	4 expressing emotion
2 when asking sth	5 for ending talk
3 after a pause	+ PHRASES

1 used for introducing a statement, especially one that you make as a reply: *Well, I agree with you about that.* ♦ *"So you told him what you thought of his idea, then?" "Well, not exactly."*
2 used for asking a question or for asking for an explanation: *Well, what did they say?* ♦ *Well, who's responsible for this mess?*
3 used after a pause, for continuing with what you were saying: *Well, as I was saying...*
4 used for expressing surprise or anger: *Well, they have a lot of nerve!*
5 used for ending a discussion or talk: *Well thanks for calling. I'll get back to you again tomorrow.*

PHRASES **oh well** used for accepting a bad situation or disappointment: *Oh well, I suppose I can borrow the money from someone else.*
well, well used for expressing surprise

well[3] /wel/ (comparative **bet·ter** /ˈbetər/; superlative **best** /best/) adj ★ healthy: *"How are you?"* ***"Very well, thank you."*** ♦ *I'm* ***not feeling very well*** *today.* ♦ *You don't* ***look*** *too* ***well.*** ♦ *Take care and* ***get well soon!***

PHRASES **all is well** used for saying that a situation or arrangement is satisfactory: *I hope all is well back home.*
just as well helpful or convenient in the situation that exists: **+(that)** *It's just as well we have neighbors who don't mind noise.*

well[4] /wel/ noun [C] a deep hole that is dug in the ground where there is a supply of water, oil, or gas

well[5] /wel/ or **ˌwell ˈup** verb [I] **1** if a feeling wells inside you, it becomes very strong **2** if a liquid wells, it comes to the surface and begins to flow

well-ad·vised /ˌwel ədˈvaɪzd/ adj sensible and following good advice

ˌwell-ˈbalanced adj **1** made up of various things that form a satisfactory or healthy combination: *a well-balanced meal/diet* **2** sensible and mentally strong

well-be·haved /ˌwel bɪˈheɪvd/ adj behaving in a way that is polite and quiet and does not upset people

ˌwell-ˈbeing noun [U] a satisfactory state in which you are happy, healthy, and safe, and have enough money=WELFARE

well-brought-up /ˌwel brɔt ˈʌp/ adj knowing how to behave politely because you have been taught well by your parents

well-built /ˌwel ˈbɪlt/ adj a well-built person has an attractive, strong body

ˌwell-conˈnected adj knowing a lot of people who are important or who have influence

ˌwell-ˈdone adj well-done meat has been cooked thoroughly until all of it is brown
→ RARE 3

ˌwell-ˈdressed adj wearing good, fashionable clothes

well-earned /ˌwel ˈɜrnd/ adj earned or deserved because of hard work or a difficult experience

ˌwell-esˈtablished adj having existed for a long time, and having been successful or accepted for a long time

well-fed /ˌwel ˈfed/ adj getting a lot of good food to eat

well-heeled /ˌwel ˈhild/ adj *informal* rich

ˌwell-inˈformed adj knowing a lot about a subject or a situation

well-in·ten·tioned /ˌwel ɪnˈtenʃənd/ adj trying to help, but often making a situation worse=WELL-MEANING

ˌwell-ˈkept adj a well-kept place looks good because someone takes good care of it
PHRASE **well-kept secret** a fact that some people know but do not share with everyone

ˌwell-ˈknown adj known by many people, or by the people involved in a particular situation

ˌwell-ˈmannered adj polite ≠ IMPOLITE

ˌwell-ˈmeaning adj trying to help, but often making a situation worse=WELL-INTENTIONED

ˌwell-ˈoff adj *informal* rich
ˌwell-ˈpaid adj receiving a satisfactory amount of money for the work that you do
well-pre·served /ˌwel prɪˈzɜrvd/ adj *informal* looking younger than you really are
well-read /ˌwel ˈred/ adj having read many books so that you know about a lot of things
well-timed /ˌwel ˈtaɪmd/ adj effective because of happening at the right time = TIMELY
ˌwell-to-ˈdo adj rich
well-wish·er /ˈwel ˌwɪʃər/ noun [C] someone who expresses their good wishes or sympathy to a person who they do not know
went the past tense of go[1]
wept the past tense and past participle of weep
we're /wɪr/ short form the usual way of saying or writing "we are." This is not often used in formal writing: *We're having a party on Saturday.*
were /*weak* wər, *strong* wɜr/ *see* **be**
were·n't /wɜrnt/ short form the usual way of saying or writing "were not." This is not often used in formal writing: *You weren't listening.*
were·wolf /ˈwerˌwʊlf/ (plural **were·wolves** /ˈwerˌwʊlvz/) noun [C] an imaginary creature who is human during the day but becomes a WOLF at night when there is a FULL MOON
west[1] /west/ noun ★★★
1 [U] the direction that is behind you when you are facing the rising sun: *We've been driving from east to west.* → EAST
2 **the west** [singular] the part of a place that is in the west: *The country's major cities are all **in the west**. ♦ I work in the west of the city.*
3 **the West** [singular] the western part of the world, especially Europe and North America
west[2] /west/ adv toward the west: *You drive west to get to the lake. ♦ We'll camp ten miles west of town.*
west[3] /west/ adj **1** in the west, or facing toward the west **2** a west wind blows from the west
west·bound /ˈwes(t)ˌbaʊnd/ adj going toward the west
ˈWest ˌCoast, the the western part of the U.S., along the Pacific Ocean
ˌWest ˈEnd, the the part of London where there are many theaters
west·er·ly /ˈwestərli/ adj **1** toward or in the west **2** a westerly wind blows from the west
west·ern[1] /ˈwestərn/ adj ★★
1 in the west of a place: *a western accent ♦ the western United States*
2 relating to or typical of the western part of the world, especially Europe and North America: *western attitudes ♦ Wages there are much lower than western levels.*
west·ern[2] /ˈwestərn/ noun [C] a movie about COWBOYS in the western United States in the 19th century
west·ern·er /ˈwestərnər/ noun [C] **1** someone who lives in or was born in the western part of a country **2** someone who is from Europe or North America
west·ern·ized /ˈwestərnaɪzd/ adj influenced by American or Western European culture, technology, or values —**west·ern·i·za·tion** /ˌwestərnɪˈzeɪʃ(ə)n/ noun [U]
west·ern·most /ˈwestərnˌmoʊst/ adj farthest toward the west
West·min·ster /ˈwes(t)mɪnstər/ the U.K. government, based in Westminster, London
west·ward[1] /ˈwestwərd/ adj toward or in the west
west·ward[2] /ˈwestwərd/ adv *American* toward the west
wet[1] /wet/ adj ★★★
1 covered with water or another liquid: *You'd better come in or you'll get wet. ♦ My socks and shoes were **soaking wet*** (=very wet). *♦ Her forehead was **wet with** sweat.*
2 not yet dry or solid: *wet paint*
3 if the weather is wet, it is raining
wet[2] /wet/ (past tense and past participle **wet** or **wet·ted**) verb [T] **1** to make something wet with water or another liquid **2** to make something such as a bed or clothes wet with URINE (=liquid waste from your body)
ˌwet ˈblanket noun [C] *informal* someone who spoils other people's fun by criticizing what they are doing, or by refusing to take part in it
wet·suit /ˈwetˌsut/ noun [C] a suit made of rubber that you wear for water sports such as DIVING and SURFING
we've /wiv/ short form the usual way of saying or writing "we have." This is not often used in formal writing: *We've been waiting for a long time.*
whack /wæk, hwæk/ verb [T] *informal* to hit someone or something with a lot of force —**whack** noun [C]
whale /weɪl, hweɪl/ noun [C] a very large sea animal that looks like a fish but breathes air through a hole on the top of its head —*picture* → C13
PHRASE **have a whale of a time** *informal* to have a lot of fun
whal·ing /ˈweɪlɪŋ, ˈhweɪlɪŋ/ noun [U] the activity of hunting WHALES
wham /wæm, hwæm/ interjection used for representing the loud sound of something being hit hard
wharf /wɔrf, hwɔrf/ (plural **wharves** /wɔrvz, hwɔrvz/) noun [C] a structure built at the edge of the land where boats can stop = DOCK
what /wɑt, hwɑt/ grammar word ★★★

> What can be:
> - a **question pronoun**: *What do you want?*
> - a **relative pronoun**: *She showed me what she had bought.*
> - a **determiner**: *What subjects are you studying? ♦ What a nuisance!*
> - an **interjection**: *What! You mean I've been wasting my time?*

1 **which thing** used for asking which thing or which type of thing something is: *What's your name? ♦ What time is it? ♦ I asked her what kind of music she liked.*
2 **which thing sth is** used when someone knows or says which thing something is: *I told him what the problem was. ♦ We suddenly realized what was happening.*
3 **a particular thing** used for referring to a particular thing that is being described or explained: *You haven't given me what I asked for. ♦ What annoys me is the way he boasts about what he's done.*

4 asking sb to repeat sth *spoken* used for asking someone to repeat what they have just said because you did not hear it clearly: *"Turn the radio down!" "What?"*

It is more polite to say "excuse me," "pardon me," or "I beg your pardon."

5 when sb calls your name *spoken* used for replying to someone when they have just called your name: *"Hey, Julie!" "What?" "I have something to show you."*
6 emphasizing a quality *spoken* used for introducing a remark in which you emphasize how big, good, bad, etc. someone or something is: *What awful weather we've been having!* ♦ *What a kind man!*
7 showing surprise *spoken* used for showing that you are surprised by something that you have just heard: *What! You mean he can't read or write?*
PHRASES **so what?** *spoken* used for showing someone that you think that a particular fact that they have mentioned is not important: *"But they're living together and they aren't married." "So what?"*
what about...? *spoken* **1** used for making a suggestion: *"When do you want to meet?" "What about Tuesday?"* **2** used for reminding someone that a particular person or thing needs to be considered: *What about Sue? Shouldn't we invite her?*
what for *spoken* used for asking the reason for something: *"I need to have your name and address." "What for?"* ♦ *What did you hit him for?*
what if...? 1 used for asking what would happen in a particular situation, especially an unpleasant situation: *It sounds like a good offer, but what if it's a trick?* **2** used when you are making a helpful suggestion: *What if I lend you the money?*
what's more *spoken* used for introducing an additional statement that supports what you have already said
what with *spoken* used when you are giving a number of reasons for a particular situation or problem: *The police are having a difficult time, what with all the drugs and violence on our streets.*

what·ev·er /wɑtˈevər, hwɑtˈevər/ grammar word ★★★

Whatever can be:
- a **relative pronoun**: *You can choose whatever you like.*
- a **determiner**: *We'll be ready at whatever time you get here.*
- a **conjunction**: *We must stay together whatever happens.*
- an **adverb**: *There is nothing whatever to worry about.*

1 anything or everything used for referring to anything or everything that happens or is available, needed, wanted, etc.: *Now you are free to do whatever you want.* ♦ *We will be grateful for whatever help you can give.*
2 when sth does not matter used for saying that what happens or what is true is not important, because it makes no difference to the situation: *You know that you have our full support whatever you decide.*
3 sth you do not know used for referring to something when you do not know what it is: *He said there were "technical difficulties," **whatever that means**.*
4 at all used with a noun for emphasis in a negative statement: *I have no intention whatever of leaving.*
5 used as an annoyed reply *spoken* used for showing that you are annoyed about something, or that you do not care about it, but that you will accept it: *"They say we all have to attend the meeting." "Whatever."*

what·not /ˈwɑtˌnɑt, ˈhwɑtˌnɑt/ noun [U] *informal* other similar things: *brochures, leaflets, and whatnot*

what's /wɑts, hwɑts/ short form the usual way of saying or writing "what is" or "what has." This is not often used in formal writing: *What's the time?* ♦ *What's happened?*

what·so·ev·er /ˌwɑtsoʊˈevər, ˌhwɑtsoʊˈevər/ adv used for emphasizing a negative statement = WHATEVER: *It had no effect whatsoever.*

wheat /wit, hwit/ noun [U] **1** tall plants that produce grain for making bread and other foods **2** wheat grains, or food made from them

whee·dle /ˈwid(ə)l, ˈhwid(ə)l/ verb [I/T] to persuade someone using tricks, lies, or praise that is not sincere

wheel¹ /wil, hwil/ noun ★★★
1 [C] a circular object that turns around in order to make a car, bicycle, or other vehicle move —*picture* → C6
2 the wheel [singular] the STEERING WHEEL that is used for controlling a car or other vehicle: *He had a heart attack **at the wheel** of his car* (=while driving).
→ REINVENT

wheel² /wil, hwil/ verb **1** [T] to move something that has wheels by pushing it **2** [T] to move someone in or on an object that has wheels **3** [I/T] to move in a circle in the air, or to make something do this
PHRASE **wheel and deal** *informal* to use clever or slightly dishonest methods in order to get advantages in business or politics
PHRASAL VERB **ˌwheel aˈround** to turn around quickly where you are standing

wheel·bar·row /ˈwilˌberoʊ, ˈhwilˌberoʊ/ noun [C] a large open container with a wheel in the front and handles in the back. You use it outside for moving things such as dirt, wood, or supplies.

wheel·chair /ˈwilˌtʃer, ˈhwilˌtʃer/ noun [C] a chair with large wheels that someone who cannot walk uses for moving around —*picture* → CHAIR

wheel·er-deal·er /ˌwilər ˈdilər, ˌhwilər ˈdilər/ noun [C] *informal* someone who uses clever or slightly dishonest methods in order to get advantages in business or politics

wheeze /wiz, hwiz/ verb [I] to breathe in a noisy way that is uncomfortable, because you are sick —**wheez·y** adj

when /wen, hwen/ grammar word ★★★

When can be:
- a **conjunction**: *When he saw me, he waved.*
- a **question adverb**: *When should we meet?*
- a **relative adverb**: *I remember the day when the war began.*

1 at what time or in what situation used

W

for asking at what time or in what situation something happens: *When will we know our test results?* ♦ *I asked him when he was going to start work.*
2 what time sth happens used when someone knows or says at what time something happens, or in what situation it happens: *He didn't say when they would leave.*
3 at the time that sth else happens at the same time as something, or just after it has finished: *I always wear a hat when I work in the garden.* ♦ *She claims she was at a friend's house when the shooting took place.* ♦ *When it stops raining, we'll go outside.*
4 at a particular time or in a particular situation used for referring to a particular occasion or situation: *Do you remember **the time when** we took your mother camping?*
5 introducing surprising information used for introducing a situation that makes someone's action or behavior seem surprising: *Why does she always drive to work when she could easily take the subway?*

when·ev·er /wen'evər, hwen'evər/ adv, conjunction ★
1 every time that something happens: *Whenever I hear that song, I think of you.*
2 at any time, or in any situation: *You can come and stay with us whenever you want.*
3 used for showing that you do not know when something happened or will happen: *We'll have to wait until the next committee meeting, **whenever that is**.*

where /wer, hwer/ grammar word ★★★

> **Where** can be:
> - a **question adverb**: *Where are you going?*
> - a **relative adverb**: *I know a place where you can hide.*
> - a **conjunction**: *I've hidden the money where no one will find it.*

1 used for asking what place someone or something is in, or what place they go to: *Where would you like to sit?* ♦ *I wonder where Jack went.* ♦ *Where did the package come from?*
2 used when someone knows or says what place someone or something is in or what place they go to: *She didn't say where she works.* ♦ *We can't decide where to go on vacation.*
3 used for referring to a particular place that someone or something is in or that they go to: *We were led to the dining room, where lunch was being served.*
4 used for asking about or referring to a situation or a point in a process, discussion, story, etc.: *Where shall I start?* ♦ *Eventually I reached the point where I was beginning to enjoy my work.*
PHRASE **where does sb/sth go from here?** used for asking what will happen or what will be done next in a particular situation: *The big question everyone is asking is, where does the economy go from here?*

where·a·bouts¹ /'werə,baʊts, 'hwerə,baʊts/ noun [plural] the place where someone or something is

where·a·bouts² /'werə,baʊts, 'hwerə,baʊts/ adv used for asking in general where someone or something is: *Whereabouts in America was he born?*

where·as /wer'æz, hwer'æz/ conjunction used for showing that there is an important difference between two things, people, situations, etc.: *Doctors' salaries have risen substantially, whereas nurses' pay has actually fallen.*

where·by /wer'baɪ, hwer'baɪ/ adv *formal* done according to the method, arrangement, rule, etc. that has been referred to

where·up·on /'werə,pɑn, 'hwerə,pɑn/ conjunction *formal* happening just after or because of something that has been mentioned

wher·ev·er /wer'evər, hwer'evər/ adv, conjunction ★
1 everywhere, or anywhere: *Wherever he went, he took his dog with him.* ♦ *Garlic grows wherever there is a warm climate.*
2 used for showing that you do not know where something is: *He said he was calling from Landsford Park, **wherever that is**.*

where·with·al, the /'werwɪ,ðɔl, 'hwerwɪ,ðɔl/ noun [singular] the money or other things that you need in order to be able to do a particular thing

whet /wet, hwet/ verb **whet your appetite (for sth)** to make you feel that you want more of something

wheth·er /'weðər, 'hweðər/ conjunction ★★★
1 used when someone does not know which of two possibilities is true: *They asked us whether we were married.* ♦ *She doesn't even know whether her daughter is dead or alive.*
2 used when someone can choose between two possibilities: *Employees are deciding whether to accept the offer.* ♦ *There was a debate over **whether or not** to send troops.*
3 used for saying that it does not matter which of two possibilities is true, because the situation will be the same: *Whether you like it or not, you'll have to change your lifestyle.*

> - Both **whether** and **if** can be used to introduce indirect questions: *She asked if/whether I liked jazz.*
> - Use **whether**, not **if**, before an infinitive or after a preposition: *She can't decide whether to marry him.* ♦ *I was worried about whether he would come.*
> - Use **whether**, not **if**, before "or not": *I don't know whether or not we can afford it.*

whew /fju, hju/ interjection a way of writing the sound that you make when you are tired, hot, or surprised, or when you feel happy that something difficult or frightening has finished

which /wɪtʃ, hwɪtʃ/ grammar word ★★★

> **Which** can be:
> - a **determiner**: *Which color do you like best?*
> - a **question pronoun**: *Which is the hottest month of the year?*
> - a **relative pronoun**: *My car, which I have owned for five years, is a Ford.*

1 used for asking for a specific choice from a limited number of possibilities: *Which would you like, tea or coffee?* ♦ *Which way did they go?* ♦ ***Which of** the secretaries did you talk to?*
2 used when someone knows or says who or what is chosen from a group of

possibilities: *They're all so pretty – I don't know which one to choose.* ♦ *It was either whiskey or vodka – I forget which.* ♦ *Did he say which hotel he was staying at?*

3 used for adding information or a comment about a thing or fact: *Bogart starred in the film* Casablanca, *which was made in 1942.* ♦ *It's a story which every child will enjoy.* ♦ *A skilled workforce is essential, which is why our training program is so important.*

which•ev•er /wɪtʃˈevər, hwɪtʃˈevər/ determiner, pronoun **1** used for saying that it does not matter which person or thing is involved: *I'm sure you'll have a good time whichever cruise you decide to take.* **2** used for referring to any person or thing from a group: *Whichever of us gets home first will turn the heating on.*

whiff /wɪf, hwɪf/ noun [singular] a slight smell of something that lasts for a very short time

while¹ /waɪl, hwaɪl/ conjunction ★★★

1 during the time that something is happening: *Someone called while you were out.*

2 used when comparing things, situations, or people and showing how they are different: *While most children learn to read easily, some need extra help.*

3 *formal* despite a particular fact: *While I support you, I do not believe that you will succeed.*

while² /waɪl, hwaɪl/ noun [singular] ★★ a period of time: *We haven't seen Barry **for a while**.* ♦ *I've been waiting here **quite a while**.* ♦ *Couldn't you stay just **a little while** longer?* ♦ *Her mother died **a while ago**.* → ONCE

while³ /waɪl, hwaɪl/ PHRASAL VERB **ˌwhile sth aˈway** to spend time in a relaxed way when you have nothing else to do

whim /wɪm, hwɪm/ noun [C] a sudden feeling that you must have or must do something that other people think is unnecessary or silly

whim•per /ˈwɪmpər, ˈhwɪmpər/ verb [I] to make small sounds of pain, fear, or sadness —**whim•per** noun [C]

whim•si•cal /ˈwɪmzɪk(ə)l, ˈhwɪmzɪk(ə)l/ adj slightly strange and funny

whine /waɪn, hwaɪn/ verb [I] **1** to complain in a way that annoys other people **2** if a dog whines, it makes a high noise, usually because it wants something —**whine** noun [C]

whip¹ /wɪp, hwɪp/ noun [C] **1** a long thin piece of leather with a handle on one end that is used for making horses move faster

2 someone in a political party whose job is to make certain that other members are present and vote in the correct way when they are needed

whip² /wɪp, hwɪp/ verb [T] **1** to hit a person or animal with a whip **2** *informal* to defeat someone thoroughly **3** to remove something or move something somewhere very fast: *Sykes whipped out a gun and demanded the money.* **4** to mix a food such as cream very quickly in order to make it thicker = BEAT

PHRASE **whip sb/sth into shape** to quickly make someone or something improve or work more effectively

PHRASAL VERB **ˌwhip sth ˈup 1** to encourage strong emotions in people **2** *informal* to quickly prepare something to eat

whir /wɜr, hwɜr/ verb [I] to make a fast repeated quiet sound —**whir** noun [singular]

whirl¹ /wɜrl, hwɜrl/ verb **1** [I/T] to move quickly in circles, or to make something move in this way **2** [I] if your mind, thoughts, or feelings whirl, you feel very confused or upset

whirl² /wɜrl, hwɜrl/ noun [C] **1** a lot of confused activity and movement **2** a quick movement around in circles

PHRASE **give sth a whirl** *informal* to try a new activity

whirl•pool /ˈwɜrlˌpul, ˈhwɜrlˌpul/ noun [C] an area in a river or stream where the water moves around in circles very quickly and pulls things under the surface

whirl•wind /ˈwɜrlˌwɪnd, ˈhwɜrlˌwɪnd/ noun [C] a situation that changes very quickly, in a way that is confusing or out of control: *a whirlwind of emotions*

whirr /wɜr, hwɜr/ another spelling of **whir**

whisk¹ /wɪsk, hwɪsk/ noun [C] a kitchen tool, used for mixing, that consists of several curves of wire joined to a handle

whisk² /wɪsk, hwɪsk/ verb [T] **1** to mix something such as eggs or cream using a whisk or a fork = BEAT —*picture* → C2 **2** to move someone or something very quickly: *The police whisked her away in a van.*

whisk•er /ˈwɪskər, ˈhwɪskər/ noun **1** [C] one of several long stiff hairs that grow near the mouth of an animal such as a cat **2 whiskers** [plural] *old-fashioned* hair on a man's face

whis•key /ˈwɪski, ˈhwɪski/ noun [C/U] a strong alcoholic drink from the U.S., Ireland, or Scotland that is made from grain such as BARLEY or RYE, or a glass of this drink

whis•per¹ /ˈwɪspər, ˈhwɪspər/ verb ★

1 [I/T] to speak very quietly to someone, so that other people cannot hear you: *Please stop whispering and pay attention!* ♦ **whisper (sth) to sb** *Pop whispered a warning to us to keep quiet.*

2 [I] *literary* to make a quiet gentle sound

whis•per² /ˈwɪspər, ˈhwɪspər/ noun [C] **1** a very quiet way of saying something to someone so that other people cannot hear you **2** *literary* a quiet gentle sound

whis•tle¹ /ˈwɪs(ə)l, ˈhwɪs(ə)l/ noun [C] **1** a small metal or plastic object that you put in your mouth and blow in order to make a high sound **2** a sound that you make by blowing through a whistle or by forcing air through your lips

whis•tle² /ˈwɪs(ə)l, ˈhwɪs(ə)l/ verb **1** [I/T] to make a high sound with a whistle or by forcing air through your lips **2** [I] to produce a high sound as a result of air passing quickly through or over something **3** [I] to move very quickly through the air

white¹ /waɪt, hwaɪt/ adj ★★★

1 of same color as milk	4 sick/upset
2 of race with pale skin	5 of wine
3 of white people	

1 something that is white is the same color as milk or snow: *a white tablecloth* ♦ *The hills **were white with** snow.* → BLACK

2 a white person belongs to a race of people

W

with pale skin: *The attacker was described as white, with short hair.* → BLACK
3 relating to white people, or consisting of white people: *a white neighborhood*
4 with a very pale face because you are frightened, angry, or sick: *She suddenly **turned** very **white** and fainted.* ♦ *Luke's face was **white with** anger.*
5 white wine is a pale yellow color
—**white•ness** noun [U]

white² /waɪt, hwaɪt/ noun ★
1 [C/U] the color of milk or snow: *The sign was written in white on a black background.* ♦ *We painted the walls a creamy white.* ♦ *The bride **wore white*** (=white clothes).
2 [C] someone who belongs to a race of people with pale skin
3 [C/U] the clear part inside an egg that surrounds the YOLK (=yellow part)
PHRASE **the whites of sb's eyes** the white parts of your eyes

white•board /ˈwaɪtˌbɔrd, ˈhwaɪtˌbɔrd/ noun [C] a white plastic board in a classroom that a teacher writes on with large thick pens

ˈwhite-ˌcollar adj white-collar workers work in offices

ˈWhite ˌHouse, the **1** the official home of the President of the U.S., in Washington, D.C. **2** the people who work at the White House, including the President

ˌwhite ˈlie noun [C] a lie about something that is not important that you tell in order to avoid making someone upset

ˌwhite ˈmeat noun [U] meat such as chicken or PORK that is pale after you have cooked it

whit•en /ˈwaɪt(ə)n, ˈhwaɪt(ə)n/ verb [I/T] to become pale or white, or to make something pale or white

ˌWhite ˈPages, the a book containing a list of the names, telephone numbers, and addresses of the people who live in a particular city or area in the U.S. → YELLOW PAGES

ˌwhite ˈpaper noun [C] in some countries, a government report that gives details of policy on a particular issue

white•wash /ˈwaɪtˌwɑʃ, ˈhwaɪtˌwɑʃ/ noun
1 [singular] an attempt to stop people from discovering the true facts about something
2 [U] a substance that is used for painting walls or buildings white —**white•wash** verb [T]

white•wa•ter raft•ing /ˌwaɪtwɔtər ˈræftɪŋ, ˌhwaɪtwɔtər ˈræftɪŋ/ noun [U] the activity of floating in a rubber boat along rivers where the current is very fast and rough

whit•ish /ˈwaɪtɪʃ, ˈhwaɪtɪʃ/ adj almost white in color

whit•tle /ˈwɪt(ə)l, ˈhwɪt(ə)l/
PHRASAL VERBS **ˌwhittle (sth) aˈway** to gradually reduce the amount or importance of something
ˌwhittle sth ˈdown to reduce the number of people or things, or the size of something

whiz /wɪz, hwɪz/ verb [I] *informal* to move very quickly

ˈwhiz ˌkid noun [C] *informal* a young person who is very intelligent or successful

whizz /wɪz, hwɪz/ another spelling of **whiz**

who /hu/ pronoun ★★★
1 used for asking which person is involved in something, or what someone's name is: *Who works in that office?* ♦ *Who did you hire for the sales position?* ♦ *"Who is that?" "It's Karen – don't you recognize her?"* ♦ ***Who else** did you tell the secret to?*
2 used when someone knows or says which person is involved in something or what their name is: *Curry refused to say who had organized the meeting.*
3 used for adding more information about a person: *I recently talked to Michael Hall, who teaches music at the university.* ♦ *We only employ people who already have computer skills.*
PHRASE **who knows/cares etc.** *spoken* used for saying that you do not know/care etc., and you think that no one else does: *"Won't Terry be upset?" "Who cares? He never thinks about anyone but himself."*

who'd /hud/ short form the usual way of saying or writing "who had" or "who would." This is not often used in formal writing: *He was the one who'd complained the loudest.*

who•ev•er /huˈevər/ pronoun ★
1 someone, or anyone: *Whoever finishes first will get a prize.* ♦ *You may choose whoever you would like to represent you.*
2 used for saying that it does not matter who is involved: *Whoever you ask, the answer is always the same.*
3 *spoken* used when you do not know who someone is or what their name is: *The movie is about Celia Carr, **whoever that is.***

whole¹ /hoʊl/ adj ★★★
1 all of something=ENTIRE: *My whole family came to watch me playing in the concert.* ♦ *Come on, let's just forget **the whole thing**.* ♦ *She told Tilly **the whole story**.*
2 not divided or broken: *Add three whole eggs plus two additional yolks.* ♦ *Some of the statues were broken, but others were still whole.*
3 used for emphasizing what you are saying: *A whole bunch of kids were waiting to get his autograph.* ♦ ***The whole point** of this meeting was to discuss finances.* ♦ *They're the best pizzas **in the whole world**.*

whole² /hoʊl/ noun [C] ★★★ a complete thing made of several parts: *Two halves make a whole.*
PHRASES **as a whole** considering all the parts of something as one unit: *His views are not popular with the community as a whole.*
on the whole used for talking about the general situation: *It was a pretty good conference on the whole.*
the whole of all of something: *The problem will affect the whole of Europe.*

whole³ /hoʊl/ adv **1** as a single piece: *The bird swallowed the fish whole.* **2** completely: *E-commerce is a whole new way of doing business.*

whole•heart•ed /ˌhoʊlˈhɑrtəd/ adj enthusiastic and complete
—**whole•heart•ed•ly** adv

ˌwhole ˈnumber noun [C] *technical* a number such as 1, 32, 144, etc., rather than a number such as 0.1, 0.32, $\frac{1}{2}$, $\frac{3}{4}$, etc.

whole•sale /ˈhoʊlˌseɪl/ adj **1** relating to the business of selling large quantities of

W

goods, especially to people who are going to sell them in a store **2** affecting every part of something, or affecting every person: *the wholesale destruction of entire communities* —**whole•sale** adv

whole•sal•er /ˈhoʊlˌseɪlər/ noun [C] a person or company that sells large quantities of goods to stores or small businesses

whole•some /ˈhoʊlsəm/ adj **1** wholesome food is good for you **2** thought to have a good influence on people

ˈwhole ˌwheat adj made from flour that contains all the wheat grain, including the outer part

who'll /hul/ short form the usual way of saying or writing "who will." This is not often used in formal writing: *You're the one who'll have to decide.*

whol•ly /ˈhoʊli/ adv *formal* completely: *His behavior is wholly unacceptable.*

whom /hum/ pronoun *formal* ★

1 used for asking or stating which person is affected by an action or is involved in something: *To whom did you speak?*

2 used for adding more information about a person: *This is the gentleman whom I mentioned a moment ago.*

whoop /wup, hwup, hup/ verb [I] to shout in a happy or excited way —**whoop** noun [C]

whoop•ing cough /ˈhupɪŋ ˌkɔf/ noun [U] an infectious disease of children that causes them to cough and make a loud noise when they breathe

whoops /wʊps, hwʊps/ interjection used when a small accident happens, or when you make a small mistake

whop•ping /ˈwɑpɪŋ, ˈhwɑpɪŋ/ adj *informal* extremely large

who's /huz/ short form the usual way of saying or writing "who is" or "who has." This is not often used in formal writing: *Who's that talking to Michael?* ♦ *Do you know anyone who's been to New Zealand?*

whose /huz/ determiner, pronoun ★★★

> Whose can be:
> - a **determiner**: *Whose idea was it to come here?*
> - a **question pronoun**: *Whose is this jacket?*
> - a **relative pronoun**: *I asked whose it was.*

1 used for asking who someone or something belongs to or who they are connected with: *What about these glasses? Whose are they?* ♦ *Whose little girl is she?*

2 used when someone knows or says who someone or something belongs to or who they are connected with: *He wouldn't say whose names were on the list.*

3 used for showing that someone or something belongs to or is connected with the person or thing that you have just mentioned: *Help is needed for families whose homes were destroyed in the bombing.* ♦ *a school whose reputation is excellent*

who've /huv/ short form the usual way of saying or writing "who have." This is not often used in formal writing: *Talk to people who've been doing the job for a while.*

why /waɪ, hwaɪ/ adv ★★★

1 used for asking the reason for something: *Why are you so angry?* ♦ *He asked me why I was leaving early.*

2 used when someone knows or says the reason for something: *I don't know why she's always so rude.* ♦ *There are a lot of things we need to discuss, and that's why I'm here.* ♦ *I can only think of one **reason why** Frank should be jealous.*

PHRASE **why not...?** *spoken* **1** used for making a suggestion: *Why not stay for lunch?* **2** used for agreeing to a suggestion or request: *"Maybe we could all meet up at your house?" "Yes, of course, why not?"*

WI abbrev Wisconsin

wick•ed /ˈwɪkəd/ adj **1** morally wrong and deliberately intending to hurt people **2** slightly cruel, but in a way that is intended to be funny: *a wicked sense of humor* **3** *informal* very good —**wick•ed•ly** adv, **wick•ed•ness** noun [U]

wick•er /ˈwɪkər/ noun [U] long thin pieces of wood that are woven together to make furniture or baskets

wide¹ /waɪd/ adj ★★★

1 far from side to side	4 large
2 with measurement	5 about general aspects
3 including a lot	

1 measuring a large distance from one side to the other: *Beijing's wide avenues and boulevards* ♦ *An earthquake shook a wide area of southern Italy on Saturday.*

2 measuring a particular distance from one side to the other: *The stream is about 4 feet wide.* ♦ *The roads are barely wide enough for cars.*

3 including or involving many different things or people: *Her proposal has gained **wide support**.* ♦ *Workers must carry out **a wide range of** tasks.*

4 large: *There can be wide differences in temperature between the north and the south.* ♦ *a wide smile*

5 concerning the basic aspects of something rather than the details: *The report looks at women's employment in its **wider** social context.*

→ WIDTH

wide² /waɪd/ adv **1** as much as possible: *The door opened wide and people came streaming out.* ♦ *He was now wide awake and sitting up in bed.* **2** over a large area: *The news spread far and wide.*

wide-eyed /ˌwaɪd ˈaɪd/ adj with an expression that shows that you are very surprised, frightened, or impressed

wide•ly /ˈwaɪdli/ adv ★★

1 by a lot of people, or in a lot of places: *He has traveled widely in South America.* ♦ *The drug is **widely used** to treat cancer.*

2 by a large amount, or to a large degree: *widely different views* ♦ *Prices vary widely from one store to the next.*

wid•en /ˈwaɪd(ə)n/ verb [I/T] **1** to increase, or to make something increase ≠ NARROW **2** to become wider, or to make something wider ≠ NARROW

wide-rang•ing /ˌwaɪd ˈreɪndʒɪŋ/ adj dealing with a large variety of subjects

wide•screen /ˈwaɪdˌskrin/ adj with a screen that gives a wider view than a normal screen

wide•spread /ˈwaɪdˌspred/ adj happening or existing in many places, or affecting many people: *The project has received widespread* *support.* ♦ *Foxes are becoming more widespread in urban areas.*

wid·ow /ˈwɪdoʊ/ noun [C] a woman whose husband has died

wid·owed /ˈwɪdoʊd/ adj if someone is widowed, their husband or wife has died

wid·ow·er /ˈwɪdoʊr/ noun [C] a man whose wife has died

width /wɪdθ, wɪtθ/ noun **1** [C/U] the distance from one side of something to the other: *The path is about two yards in width.* **2** [U] the quality of being wide: *the width of his shoulders*

wield /wild/ verb [T] **1** to hold a weapon or tool and use it **2** to have, and be able to use, power or influence

wife /waɪf/ (plural **wives** /waɪvz/) noun [C] ★★★ the woman that a man is married to: *I'd better phone my wife and tell her I'll be late.* ♦ *a reception for* ***the wives of the*** *ambassadors* —*picture* → FAMILY TREE

wig /wɪg/ noun [C] a cover of artificial hair that you wear on your head

wig·gle /ˈwɪg(ə)l/ verb [I/T] to make short quick movements from side to side, or to move something in this way —**wig·gle** noun [C]

wild¹ /waɪld/ adj ★★

1 not raised by humans	4 not accurate
2 of weather/ocean	5 exciting
3 with strong emotions	6 with no people

1 a wild animal or plant lives or grows on its own in natural conditions and is not raised by humans: *a wild rose* ♦ *This trait is common to both domestic and wild dogs.*
2 if the weather or the ocean is wild, there is a storm with strong winds: *a wet and wild night*
3 expressing or feeling strong emotions: *Ali entered the boxing ring to wild cheers.* ♦ *The noise drove him* ***wild with*** *terror.* ♦ *When Iverson scored, the fans* ***went wild.***
4 not accurate, or not thought about carefully: *wild accusations/claims* ♦ *They make all sorts of wild promises.*
5 exciting and enjoyable: *They have some pretty wild parties.*
6 a wild area is one where people do not live or cannot live: *wild mountainous regions*
—**wild·ness** noun [U]

wild² /waɪld/ adv in a natural or uncontrolled way: *Daisies grew wild in the meadow.*

W

wild, the /waɪld/ noun [singular] an environment that is natural

ˈwild ˌcard noun [C] *computing* a sign or symbol used for representing any letter or number

wil·der·ness /ˈwɪldərnəs/ noun **1** [C] an area of land where people do not live or grow crops and where there are no buildings
2 [singular] a period when someone is not as successful or powerful as they were previously

ˈwilderness ˌarea noun [C] *American* an area where the government has decided that no roads or buildings can be built so that it can be enjoyed for its natural beauty

wild·fire /ˈwaɪldˌfaɪr/ noun [C] a fire that starts in an area of countryside and spreads very quickly

wild·life /ˈwaɪldˌlaɪf/ noun [U] animals, birds, and plants that live in natural conditions

wild·ly /ˈwaɪldli/ adv **1** in an uncontrolled way: *Italian fans cheered wildly.*
2 extremely: used for emphasizing what you are saying: *The figures are wildly inaccurate.*

wiles /waɪlz/ noun [plural] ways of persuading or tricking someone so that they do what you want

will¹ /wɪl/ modal verb ★★★

- **Will** is usually followed by an infinitive without "to": *She will be angry.* Sometimes it is used without a following infinitive: *I have never borrowed money, and I never will.*
- In conversation or informal writing **will** is often shortened to **'ll**: *Do you think it'll rain?*
- **Will** has no participles and no infinitive form. **Will** does not change its form, so the third person singular form does not end in "-s": *Robert will be there.*
- Questions and negatives are formed without "do": *Will you help me?* ♦ *They will not accept our offer.*
- The negative form **will not** is often shortened to **won't** in conversation or informal writing: *Don't worry – the dog won't bite you.*

1 talking about future actions or events used for saying what is planned or expected for the future: *The President will attend a lunch hosted by the Queen.* ♦ *Let's finish the job now – it won't take long.*
2 to be willing used for saying that you are willing to do something or that you intend to do it: *If you won't tell him, I will.*
3 polite requests and offers used for asking or inviting someone to do something or for offering them something: *Will you please listen to what I'm saying!* ♦ *Won't you stay for lunch?*
4 showing possibility used for saying whether something is possible: *Will these gloves fit you?* ♦ *Forty dollars will buy enough food for a family for a week.*
5 when sth always happens used for saying what always happens in certain situations: *Natural rubber will stretch easily when pulled.*
PHRASE **sth will not work/start/open etc.** used for saying that you cannot make something do what it should do, although you have tried: *The engine won't start.*

will² /wɪl/ noun ★★
1 [C/U] someone's determination to do what is necessary in order to achieve what they want: *a child with* ***a very strong will*** ♦ **the will to do sth** *Without the will to win, the team won't go far.*
2 [singular] what someone wants to happen: ***the will of the people*** ♦ *He claims he was kept in the apartment* ***against his will.*** → GOODWILL
3 [C] a legal document that explains what you want to happen to your money and possessions after you die: *Ed's father didn't leave him anything in his will.*
PHRASE **at will** at any time that you want or choose: *Children were allowed to enter and leave at will.*

will³ /wɪl/ verb [T] to make something happen by wishing for it very strongly

will·ful /ˈwɪlfəl/ adj **1** done deliberately in

order to cause damage or harm
2 determined to do what you want and not caring if you upset other people —**will•ful•ly** adv

will•ing /ˈwɪlɪŋ/ adj ★★
1 if you are willing to do something, you do it when someone asks you ≠ UNWILLING: *They are very willing to give her the job.* ♦ *I wasn't willing to accept his gifts.*
2 enthusiastic about doing something ≠ UNWILLING: *a willing helper/partner/volunteer*
—**will•ing•ly** adv: *I'll willingly help you.*
—**will•ing•ness** noun [U]

wil•low /ˈwɪloʊ/ noun [C] a tree with long thin branches and narrow leaves that grows near water —*picture* → C9

will•pow•er /ˈwɪlˌpaʊr/ noun [U] the ability to control your thoughts and behavior in order to achieve something

wilt /wɪlt/ verb [I] if a plant wilts, it gradually bends toward the ground because it needs water or is dying

wi•ly /ˈwaɪli/ adj clever and willing to trick people in order to get what you want =CUNNING

wimp /wɪmp/ noun [C] *informal* someone who is not brave, strong, or confident

win¹ /wɪn/ (past tense and past participle **won** /wʌn/) verb ★★★
1 [I/T] to defeat everyone else by being the best, or by finishing first in a competition ≠ LOSE: *Every time we play tennis, she wins.* ♦ *Who **won the race**?* ♦ *The Liberals **won the election**.* ♦ *I never **win at cards**.*
2 [I/T] to achieve victory in a war, battle, or argument ≠ LOSE: *In an argument like that, nobody wins.* ♦ *No one knows who will **win the war**.*
3 [T] to get something as a prize for defeating other people or because you are lucky: *He won $4,000 in the lottery.* ♦ *Our ski team **won a gold medal** at the Olympics.* ♦ *Raoul **won first prize** in a spelling contest.*
4 [T] to succeed in getting something that you want because of hard work or ability: *We've won a $3 million contract to build the new bridge.* ♦ *The bill is **winning** a lot of **support** from farmers.*
—**win•ning** adj: *the winning team/goal/ticket*
PHRASAL VERBS ˌ**win sth ˈback** to get back something that you have lost: *She tried hard to win back his trust.*
ˌ**win ˈout** to succeed after great difficulty: *Truth won out in the end.*
ˌ**win sb ˈover** to persuade someone to agree with you: *We've finally won him over to our point of view.*

win² /wɪn/ noun [C] an occasion when someone wins something: *This is their fourth win of the season.*

wince /wɪns/ verb [I] to make a sudden expression or movement that shows that you are embarrassed or feel pain

winch /wɪntʃ/ noun [C] a piece of equipment that uses a rope or chain for lifting or pulling things or people —**winch** verb [T]

wind¹ /wɪnd/ noun ★★★
1 [C/U] a natural current of air that moves fast enough for you to feel it: *A cold wind blew.* ♦ *During the night the wind picked up* (=got stronger). ♦ *The helicopter can't reach them until the wind drops* (=becomes less strong). ♦ ***A large gust of wind swept** his hat into the sea.* → HEADWIND
2 [singular] the air in your lungs: *The heavy blow knocked the wind out of him.*

wind² /waɪnd/ (past tense and past participle **wound** /waʊnd/) verb ★
1 [T] to wrap or twist something around something else: *I put on my coat and wound a scarf around my neck.*
2 [I/T] to follow a course or path that curves or twists a lot: *The River Nile winds through Sudan and Egypt.* ♦ *The bus wound its way up the mountain.*
3 [T] to make a video or a CASSETTE TAPE move forward or backward in a machine: *I've wound it back to the beginning.* → REWIND
4 [T] if you wind a watch or clock, you make it operate by turning a part of it around and around
PHRASAL VERBS ˌ**wind ˈdown** to relax after a period of excitement or worry =UNWIND
ˌ**wind (sth) ˈdown** to end gradually, or to finish something gradually: *The party started to wind down around 2:00 a.m.*
ˌ**wind ˈup** to be in a particular place or situation that you did not plan to be in: *There were no hotels available in San Francisco, so we wound up in Oakland.*
ˌ**wind sth ˈup 1** to end something: *I'd like to wind up the meeting soon.* **2** *informal* to make someone angry or upset

wind•fall /ˈwɪn(d)ˌfɔl/ noun [C] an amount of money that you get unexpectedly

wind•ing /ˈwaɪndɪŋ/ adj with a lot of bends: *a winding lane*

wind in•stru•ment /ˈwɪnd ˌɪnstrʊmənt/ noun [C] a musical instrument that you play by blowing through it, such as a FLUTE or CLARINET —*picture* → WOODWIND

wind•mill /ˈwɪn(d)ˌmɪl/ noun [C] a tall building with long pieces of wood or metal that turn in the wind, used for producing power or crushing grain

win•dow /ˈwɪndoʊ/ noun [C] ★★★
1 a hole with a frame in a wall or vehicle that lets in light and air and lets you see outside, or the glass that covers this hole: *She just stood there staring out of the window.* ♦ *She was watching him from an upstairs window.* ♦ *Do you mind if I **open a window**?* ♦ *Rioters set fire to cars and **smashed store windows**.*
2 one of the different work areas on a computer screen: *Click on the X to close the window.*
3 a short period of time when you can do something: *I've got a window on Friday when I could see you.*

ˈ**window ˌpane** noun [C] a piece of glass used in a window —*picture* → C1

ˈ**window-ˌshopping** noun [U] the activity of looking at things in store windows but not buying anything

win•dow•sill /ˈwɪndoʊˌsɪl/ noun [C] a shelf under a window —*picture* → C1

wind•pipe /ˈwɪn(d)ˌpaɪp/ noun [C] the tube that carries air into your lungs from your nose or mouth

wind pow•er /ˈwɪnd ˌpaʊər/ noun [U] electricity that is created using the power of wind

W

wind·screen /ˈwɪn(d)ˌskrin/ noun [C] *British* a WINDSHIELD

wind·shield /ˈwɪn(d)ʃild/ noun [C] *American* the large window at the front of a vehicle —*picture* → C6

ˈ**windshield** ˌ**wiper** noun [C] *American* a long thin piece of equipment that moves across a vehicle's windshield in order to wipe and clean it —*picture* → C6

wind·surf·ing /ˈwɪn(d)ˌsɜrfɪŋ/ noun [U] a sport in which you move across the water standing on a flat board with a sail that you can move —**wind·surf·er** noun [C]

wind·swept /ˈwɪn(d)ˌswept/ adj **1** a windswept place has a lot of wind and not many buildings or trees to protect it **2** looking messy because your clothes and hair have been blown around by the wind

wind·y /ˈwɪndi/ adj with a lot of wind: *a windy day*

wine¹ /waɪn/ noun [C/U] ★★★ an alcoholic drink made from grapes: *a bottle/glass of wine* ♦ *Spanish wines* ♦ *I'll have a red wine, please* (=a glass of red wine).

wine² /waɪn/ verb **wine and dine sb** to entertain someone by taking them out for a meal

win·er·y /ˈwaɪn(ə)ri/ noun [C] a place where wine is made

wing /wɪŋ/ noun [C] ★★

1 part of bird/insect	4 part of organization
2 part of airplane	5 in sports
3 part of building	+ PHRASES

1 one of the parts on a bird or insect that move up and down and allow it to fly: *a moth's delicate wings* ♦ *a blackbird flapping its wings*

2 one of the long flat parts on both sides of an airplane that allow it to fly

3 a part of a building that sticks out from the main part, especially one with a particular purpose: *the east/main wing* ♦ *He works in the psychiatric wing of the hospital.*

4 a part of an organization or political party that has particular responsibilities or opinions: *the Libertarian Party's youth wing*

5 the left or right side of a sports field, or a player who plays on the side of a sports field

PHRASES **under sb's wing** being taken care of by someone who is older or more experienced

waiting in the wings ready to do something, or ready to be used when needed

W

winged /wɪŋd, ˈwɪŋɪd/ adj with wings

wink /wɪŋk/ verb [I] to quickly close and open one eye as a sign to someone: *Marcus winked at me.* —**wink** noun [C]

win·ner /ˈwɪnər/ noun [C] ★★

1 someone who wins a competition, race, or prize: *The winner of the tournament gets $50,000.* ♦ *She was a gold medal winner at the last Olympics.*

2 *informal* something that is very popular or successful: *Her latest book looks like another winner.*

win·nings /ˈwɪnɪŋz/ noun [plural] money that you win

ˌ**winning** ˈ**streak** noun [C] a period of time when you win a series of things

win·ter¹ /ˈwɪntər/ noun [C/U] ★★★ the season after fall and before spring, when it is usually cold: *a cold/severe/hard winter* ♦ *a cold winter's night* ♦ *We usually go skiing **in winter**.* ♦ *This town is deserted **in the winter**.* ♦ *She wore **a heavy winter coat**.*

win·ter² /ˈwɪntər/ verb [I] to spend the winter in a particular place

ˌ**winter** ˈ**solstice** noun [C/U] the day of the year when the sun is above the HORIZON for the shortest amount of time

ˌ**winter** ˈ**sports** noun [plural] sports that are done on snow or ice

win·try /ˈwɪntri/ adj cold and typical of winter

ˈ**win-**ˌ**win** adj a win-win situation is one in which everyone benefits

wipe¹ /waɪp/ verb [T] ★

1 to clean or dry something by moving something such as a cloth over it: *Let me just wipe the table before you sit down.* ♦ *She wiped away her tears.* ♦ **wipe sth with sth** *He wiped his mouth with his napkin.*

2 to clean or dry something by moving it over a surface: ***Wipe your feet** before you come inside.* ♦ **wipe sth on sth** *I wish you wouldn't wipe your hands on your clothes.*

3 to remove something, or to make something disappear: *Nearly $20 billion was wiped off share prices yesterday.* ♦ *She wanted to wipe the image from her mind.*

PHRASAL VERBS ˌ**wipe** ˈ**out** *informal* to fall and have a big crash when you are riding something such as a bicycle or SURFBOARD

ˌ**wipe sth** ˈ**out** to destroy or get rid of something completely = ERADICATE: *We want to wipe out world hunger by the year 2010.*

ˌ**wipe sth** ˈ**up** to remove a liquid from a surface using a cloth

wipe² /waɪp/ noun [C] **1** the action of wiping something to make it clean **2** a small wet cloth for cleaning something that you use only once

wiped out /ˌwaɪpt ˈaʊt/ adj *informal* extremely tired

wipe·out /ˈwaɪpˌaʊt/ noun [C/U] *informal* **1** total destruction or failure **2** a crash or fall when you are riding something such as a SNOWBOARD

wip·er /ˈwaɪpər/ noun [C] a WINDSHIELD WIPER

wire¹ /waɪr/ noun [C/U] ★

1 a long piece of metal like a very thin piece of string: *The sticks were tied in bundles with wire.* ♦ *a wire fence/cage*

2 a long thin piece of metal that carries electricity or telephone signals: *telephone wires*

PHRASE **(right) down to the wire** *informal* at the latest possible time

wire² /waɪr/ verb [T] **1** to connect a piece of electrical equipment to something, or to connect the wires inside a piece of equipment **2** to send money using an electronic system **3** *American* to send a message to someone by TELEGRAM

wire·less /ˈwaɪrləs/ adj not using wires: *wireless phones* ♦ *wireless data transfer*

ˈ**wire** ˌ**service** noun [C] an organization that sends news of recent events to newspapers and to television and radio companies

wire·tap /ˈwaɪrˌtæp/ noun [C] a piece of equipment used for secretly listening to and recording telephone conversations —**wire•tap** verb [I/T], **wire•tap•ping** noun [U]

wir•ing /ˈwaɪrɪŋ/ noun [U] the electric wires in a building, vehicle, or machine

wir•y /ˈwaɪri/ adj **1** a wiry person is thin but looks strong **2** wiry hair is stiff and rough

wis•dom /ˈwɪzdəm/ noun [U] the ability to make good decisions based on knowledge and experience: *The Egyptian leader was praised for his courage and wisdom.*

PHRASES **in his/her/their wisdom** *humorous* used for emphasizing that you do not understand why someone has done something that you think is silly

question/doubt the wisdom of (doing) sth to feel that something is probably not a sensible thing do to

ˈwisdom ˌtooth noun [C] one of the four large teeth that grow at the back of your mouth when you are an adult

wise /waɪz/ adj ★

1 a wise action or decision is sensible and shows that you have good judgment: *You made **a wise decision** when you chose to study Spanish.* ♦ *Buying those shares was **a wise move**.* ♦ **wise to do sth** *I don't think it's wise to teach your children at home.*

2 a wise person is able to make good choices and decisions because they have a lot of experience

PHRASE **none the wiser** *spoken* used for saying that you still do not know or understand something, or that someone has not found out about what you have done

—**wise•ly** adv: *They spent the money wisely.*

wish[1] /wɪʃ/ verb ★★★

1 [T] to want something to happen although it is unlikely: **+(that)** *I wish I was rich!* ♦ *Andy wished that he could think of a way to help.* ♦ *I wish Beth would stop interfering.*

2 [T] used for saying that you feel sorry or disappointed about something that you did or did not do: **+(that)** *I wish I'd never come!* ♦ *Now he wished that he had listened more carefully.*

3 [I/T] *formal* to want something, or to want to do something: *You may attend the meeting **if you wish**.* ♦ **wish to do sth** *Please do not hesitate to contact me if you wish to discuss the matter.*

4 [T] **wish sb sth** used for saying that you hope someone enjoys something or that something good happens to them: *May I **wish you all a very Merry Christmas**.* ♦ *I **wish you every success**.* ♦ *The crowd **wished them well** as they left for their honeymoon.*

PHRASES **I wish** used for saying that something is not true, although you would be pleased if it were true: *"Did she give you some money?" "I wish!"*

you wish *spoken* used for telling someone that the thing that they want to happen is completely impossible: *"I told Ben that Sally was my girlfriend." "You wish!"*

PHRASAL VERB **ˈwish for sth** *formal* to want something

wish[2] /wɪʃ/ noun [C] ★

1 a feeling that you want something or want to do something: *He'd **expressed a wish** to go there.* ♦ *I have to **respect the wishes** of my client.* ♦ *She married him **against** her parents' **wishes**.* → DEATH WISH

2 the thing that you want to have or to do: *His last wish was to see his grandson once more.* ♦ *Our one wish is to find a cure for this disease.*

3 something that you hope will happen by magic or by the power of your mind: ***Make a wish** and then blow out the candles.*

PHRASE **best wishes** used for saying that you hope that something good will happen to someone: *Please give them our best wishes for their anniversary.*

wish•ful think•ing /ˌwɪʃfəl ˈθɪŋkɪŋ/ noun [U] a belief that something is true, based only on the fact that you want it to be true, not on the real situation

wisp /wɪsp/ noun [C] something that has a long, thin, delicate shape: *a wisp of smoke/hair* —**wisp•y** adj

wist•ful /ˈwɪstfəl/ adj slightly sad because you want to have or to do something —**wist•ful•ly** adv

wit /wɪt/ noun **1** [singular/U] the ability to use words in a clever way that makes people laugh: *a novel of great inventiveness and wit* **2 wits** [plural] the ability to think quickly and make sensible decisions: *You've got to keep your wits about you in this job.*

PHRASE **at your wits' end** so worried and tired because of your problems that you cannot think of any more ways of solving them

witch /wɪtʃ/ noun [C] a woman with magic powers

witch•craft /ˈwɪtʃˌkræft/ noun [U] the practice of magic, especially for evil purposes

ˈwitch-ˌhunt noun [U] *showing disapproval* an attempt to find all the people in a particular group in order to punish them unfairly

Wite-Out /ˈwaɪt ˌaʊt/ *American trademark* a white liquid used for covering mistakes in writing, typing, etc.

with /wɪð, wɪθ/ preposition ★★★

1 together if one person or thing is with another or does something with them, they are together or they do it together: *Hannah lives with her parents.* ♦ *chicken served with vegetables and mushrooms* ♦ *a problem you should discuss with your teacher*

2 sharing or exchanging used for saying that people share or exchange things: *She shares her food with all the family.* ♦ *Most countries had stopped trading with South Africa.*

3 having or holding sth used for saying what someone or something has or is holding: *a girl with red hair* ♦ *a room with a high ceiling* ♦ *Servants arrived with trays of tea.*

4 by means of sth used for saying what is used for doing something: *Stir the mixture with a spoon.* ♦ *Stan wiped his eyes with his hand.*

5 toward or concerning sb/sth used for saying what person or thing you have a particular feeling toward: *Why are you angry with me?* ♦ *We were disappointed with the court's decision.*

6 caused by sth used for saying what feeling causes someone or something to have a particular reaction or to be in a particular state: *She was trembling with rage.* ♦ *His face was **red with embarrassment**.* ♦ *The air was **thick with smoke**.*

7 against sb used for showing who you compete, fight, or argue against: *The war with France lasted for nearly 20 years.* ♦ *Don't argue with me.*
8 in a particular way used for describing the qualities that someone shows or the feelings that they have when they do something: *He spoke with great confidence.*
9 while doing sth used for describing the sound or expression that someone or something makes when they do something: *The bomb exploded with a loud bang.* ♦ *"Are you enjoying yourself?" he asked with a friendly smile.*
10 holding your body in a position used for describing the position of someone's body when they do something: *Gordon was standing with his back to the window.*
11 covered or filled by sth used for saying what is in or on something: *Fill the pitcher with boiling water.* ♦ *The hills were **covered with** snow.*
12 relating to sth used for saying what a particular action or problem is related to: *There's nothing wrong with my eyesight.* ♦ *We're making good progress with our investigations.*
PHRASE **be with sb** *spoken* to understand what someone is telling you

with·draw /wɪðˈdrɔ/ (past tense **with·drew** /wɪðˈdru/; past participle **with·drawn** /wɪðˈdrɔn/) verb ★

1 stop providing sth	4 leave a place
2 stop taking part	5 say sth is not true
3 get money from bank	

1 [T] to take something back, or to stop providing something: *The bus service in many rural areas has been withdrawn.* ♦ *Some parents have **withdrawn** their **support** from the school.*
2 [I] to no longer take part in something: *Two of the competitors threatened to withdraw.* ♦ *The injury has forced him to **withdraw from** the competition.*
3 [T] to take money from a bank account: *You can **withdraw cash** at any of our branches.*
4 [I/T] to leave a place, or to make someone leave a place: *The troops began to **withdraw from** the northern region.*
5 [T] to say that something that you said earlier is not in fact true: *He **withdrew** his **remarks** and apologized.*

W

with·draw·al /wɪðˈdrɔəl/ noun **1** [C/U] the act of stopping something or removing something: *Their withdrawal of support forced the official to resign.* ♦ *Illness led to her withdrawal from the contest.* **2** [C/U] the process of taking an amount of money out of your bank account, or the amount of money that you take out: *You can make a withdrawal from most ATMs.* **3** [U] a period during which someone feels sick because they have stopped taking a drug that they have been taking regularly: *You may experience withdrawal symptoms.*
with·drawn¹ /wɪðˈdrɔn/ adj very quiet and preferring not to talk to other people
with·drawn² the past participle of **withdraw**
with·drew the past tense of **withdraw**
with·er /ˈwɪðər/ verb [I] **1** if a plant withers, it becomes dry and starts to die **2** to become weaker and then disappear
PHRASAL VERB ˌ**wither aˈway** *same as* **wither** 2
with·er·ing /ˈwɪðərɪŋ/ adj intended to make someone feel silly or embarrassed: *a withering look/remark*
with·hold /wɪðˈhoʊld/ (past tense and past participle **with·held** /wɪðˈheld/) verb [T] *formal* to deliberately not give something to someone
with·in /wɪˈðɪn/ adv, preposition ★★★
1 during a period of time, or before a period of time ends: *Within the past few weeks, 215 people have been arrested.* ♦ *We expect an announcement within the next 24 hours.*
2 inside a place, organization, group, or person: *There were four churches within the walls of the ancient city.* ♦ *Mr. Potter complained about the lack of leadership within the department.* ♦ *She has a kind of spiritual strength that comes **from within**.*
3 not more than a particular distance or amount: *A bomb exploded within 150 feet of the Allied headquarters.*
4 included in the range of things that are possible, reasonable, or allowed: *Private security firms must still operate **within the limits of the law**.*
with·out /wɪðˈaʊt/ adv, preposition ★★★
1 used for saying what someone or something does not have: *I can't find the answer without a calculator.* ♦ *a dress without sleeves* ♦ *I can't afford new tennis shoes, so I'll have to **do without*** (=manage despite not having them).
2 used for saying that you do not have someone with you: *If the others don't want to come, we'll go without them.*
3 used for saying what does not happen when something else happens: *Liz closed the door without making a sound.* ♦ *an attack that came without any warning*
with·stand /wɪðˈstænd/ (past tense and past participle **with·stood** /wɪðˈstʊd/) verb [T] to be strong enough not to be harmed or destroyed by something
wit·ness¹ /ˈwɪtnəs/ noun [C] ★
1 someone who sees a crime, accident, or other event happen: *Witnesses reported hearing two gunshots.* ♦ *Any **witnesses to** the incident are asked to contact the police.*
2 someone who tells a court what they know about a crime: *More than 20 witnesses will be called.* ♦ *a witness for the defense/prosecution*
3 someone who watches you sign an official document and then signs it to state that they have watched you
wit·ness² /ˈwɪtnəs/ verb [T] ★
1 to see something happen, for example a crime or an accident: *Several journalists **witnessed** the **incident**.*
2 to be present when something important happens: *We are witnessing the third change of government in three years.*
3 used for saying that something happened at a particular time or in a particular place: *The 1980s witnessed enormous growth in the financial sector.*
4 to watch someone sign an official document, and then sign it yourself to state that you have watched them: *Could you*

witness my signature on this visa application?

ˈwitness ˌstand noun [C] *American* the place in a court of law where the witness stands or sits when they are answering questions

wit•ty /ˈwɪti/ adj clever and funny

wives the plural of **wife**

wiz•ard /ˈwɪzərd/ noun [C] **1** a man in stories who has magic powers **2** someone who is very good at something: *a financial wizard*

wiz•ard•ry /ˈwɪzərdri/ noun [U] a very high level of skill at something

wiz•ened /ˈwɪz(ə)nd/ adj old and with a lot of WRINKLES (=lines on the skin)

wob•ble /ˈwɑb(ə)l/ verb [I/T] to rock slightly from side to side, or to make something do this —**wob•bly** adj

woe /woʊ/ noun **1 woes** [plural] *formal* problems and worries **2** [U] *literary* a strong feeling of sadness

woe•ful•ly /ˈwoʊf(ə)li/ adv used for emphasizing that something is very bad: *Medical supplies are woefully inadequate.*

wok /wɑk/ noun [C] a metal pan that is shaped like a large bowl, and is used for cooking Chinese food —*picture* → C2

woke the past tense of **wake**[1]

woken the past participle of **wake**[1]

wolf[1] /wʊlf/ (plural **wolves** /wʊlvz/) noun [C] a wild animal that looks like a large dog

wolf[2] /wʊlf/ or **ˌwolf sth ˈdown** verb [T] *informal* to eat something very quickly

wom•an /ˈwʊmən/ (plural **wom•en** /ˈwɪmɪn/) noun [C] ★★★ an adult female person: *We need more women in government.* ♦ *a study of women writers* → WOMEN'S

wom•an•hood /ˈwʊmənˌhʊd/ noun [U] the state of being a woman

wom•an•iz•er /ˈwʊməˌnaɪzər/ noun [C] *showing disapproval* a man who has sexual relationships with many women —**wom•an•iz•ing** noun [U]

wom•an•kind /ˈwʊmənˌkaɪnd/ noun [U] *formal* all women when they are thought of as a group

wom•an•ly /ˈwʊmənli/ adj typical of a woman, or appropriate for a woman

womb /wum/ noun [C] the organ in a woman's body where a baby grows before it is born

women the plural of **woman**

wom•en's /ˈwɪmɪnz/ adj relating to women: *women's magazines*

won the past tense and past participle of **win**[1]

won•der[1] /ˈwʌndər/ verb ★★★

1 [I/T] to think about something because you want to know more facts, or because you are worried: *"How did they find out?" she wondered.* ♦ *I was* ***wondering about*** *the best way to tell her the news.* ♦ **+how/what/when etc.** *I wonder what we can do to help Sylvia.* ♦ *I wonder if they'll get married.* ♦ *I wonder whether it was wise to let her travel alone.*

2 [I] to be very impressed or surprised by something: *It's hard not to* ***wonder at*** *the miracle of a newborn baby.*

PHRASE **I wonder if/whether** a polite way of asking something: *I wonder if you would do me a favor?* ♦ *I was wondering whether you would like to come to the theater with me?*

won•der[2] /ˈwʌndər/ noun ★

1 [U] a strong feeling of surprise or admiration: *She gazed at the ocean* ***in wonder***. ♦ *Where is the* ***sense of wonder*** *we felt when we were younger?*

2 [C] something that is very impressive or surprising: ***the wonders of*** *modern technology* ♦ *Coral reefs are among* ***the natural wonders of the world***.

PHRASES **it's a wonder (that)** used for saying that something is so bad that it is surprising that a good result can come from it: *Your writing is so small, it's a wonder anyone can read it.*

no wonder (that) used for showing that you are not surprised by something: *No wonder they were bored – it was such a long speech.*

won•der[3] /ˈwʌndər/ adj extremely good or effective: *The treatment was first regarded as a wonder cure.*

won•der•ful /ˈwʌndərfəl/ adj ★★ extremely good: *There was a wonderful view from the window.* ♦ *Thank you so much – I had a wonderful time!* —**won•der•ful•ly** adv

won't /woʊnt/ short form the usual way of saying or writing "will not." This is not often used in formal writing: *I'm sorry I won't be able to come to your party.*

wont /woʊnt/ adj **be wont to do sth** *literary* to have a habit of doing something

woo /wu/ verb [T] **1** to try to persuade people to support you or buy something from you **2** *old-fashioned* if a man woos a woman, he tries to start a sexual or romantic relationship with her

wood /wʊd/ noun ★★★

1 [U] the substance that trees are made of, used for making furniture and other objects: *a piece of wood* ♦ *a wood floor* ♦ *tables* ***made of wood***

2 the woods [plural] an area where there are many trees and wild plants: *We walk the dog in the woods behind our house.*

PHRASE **knock on wood** *American* used for saying that you hope for good luck, especially while you hit something wooden with your hand

→ DEAD WOOD

wood•ed /ˈwʊdəd/ adj covered with trees

wood•en /ˈwʊd(ə)n/ adj ★★ made of wood: *a wooden box*

wood•land /ˈwʊdlənd/ noun [C/U] an area of land that is filled with trees

wood•peck•er /ˈwʊdˌpekər/ noun [C] a bird that makes holes in trees using its long beak

wood•wind /ˈwʊdˌwɪnd/ noun [U] musical instruments made of wood that you play by blowing into them → BRASS, —*picture* → next page

wood•work /ˈwʊdˌwɜrk/ noun [U] **1** the doors, window frames, and other wooden parts of a room **2** the activity or skill of making objects from wood

wood•worm /ˈwʊdˌwɜrm/ noun [U] damage to wood that is caused by woodworms

wood•y /ˈwʊdi/ adj a woody plant has a strong hard stem

woof /wʊf/ noun [C] the sound that a dog makes when it BARKS

wool /wʊl/ noun [U] ★★

1 thick hair that grows on sheep and some other animals

2 fiber or cloth made from wool: *a ball of wool* ♦ *a wool jacket*

W

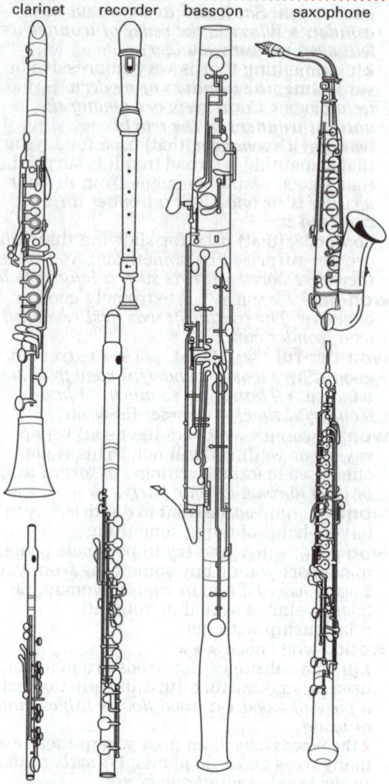

woodwind instruments

wool·en /ˈwʊlən/ adj made from wool

wool·len /ˈwʊlən/ the British spelling of woolen

wool·ly /ˈwʊli/ the British spelling of wooly

wool·y /ˈwʊli/ adj made of wool, or feeling like wool: *wooly hair*

wooz·y /ˈwuzi/ adj *informal* feeling slightly sick and unable to see or think clearly

word[1] /wɜrd/ noun ★★★

1 unit of language	4 of advice/praise etc.
2 short conversation	5 things sb says
3 news/information	+ PHRASES

1 [C] a single unit of language that expresses a particular meaning by itself: *The Latin word for a table is "mensa." ♦ The first word that many babies can say is "Mama." ♦ Can you read the words on this page?*

2 [singular] a short conversation or discussion, usually without other people listening: *David **wants a word with** you. ♦ Can I **have a word with** you?*

3 [singular/U] news or information: *We haven't received any **word from** Brian yet. ♦ He **sent word** that they had arrived safely.*

4 [C] if someone gives you a word of something such as advice, praise, or warning, they advise, praise, or warn you: *a few **words of** encouragement*

5 words [plural] someone's words are the things that they say: *The nation was facing – **in the words of** the President – a choice between two evils.*

PHRASES **give/say the word** to give someone an order to do something

give (sb) your word to promise to do something: *You gave me your word that you would take care of them.*

in other words used for introducing a simpler way of saying something

keep your word to do what you promised to do

not hear/understand etc. a (single) word used for emphasizing that someone does not hear/understand etc. anything that you say to them: *Jane could hardly understand a word Mervyn said. ♦ I don't believe a single word he told me.*

not in so many words used for saying that someone says something in a very indirect way: *"Did he say he was unhappy?" "Not in so many words."*

put in a (good) word for sb to praise someone so that someone else will like them, choose them, or employ them

put words into sb's mouth to claim that someone said or meant a particular thing that they did not really say or mean

take my word for it used for emphasizing that what you are saying is completely true

word for word if you repeat something word for word, you repeat it exactly as someone said it or wrote it

word of mouth informal conversations between people: *Most of our customers hear about us by word of mouth.*

→ LAST WORD

word[2] /wɜrd/ verb [T] to use words to express something in a particular way: *You could have worded your message a little more clearly.*

word·ing /ˈwɜrdɪŋ/ noun [U] the words that are used in a particular piece of writing

word·play /ˈwɜrdˌpleɪ/ noun [U] clever or funny use of words

ˈword ˌprocessing noun [U] the work or skill of producing written documents on a computer or word processor

ˈword ˌprocessor noun [C] a computer program that you use for creating documents

word·y /ˈwɜrdi/ adj using too many words

wore the past tense of wear[1]

work[1] /wɜrk/ verb ★★★

1 have job	6 do calculation
2 spend time doing sth	7 move gradually
3 operate well	8 grow crops on land
4 succeed/have effect	+ PHRASAL VERBS
5 operate equipment	

1 [I] to have a job: *Dominic works part-time. ♦ She **works for** a big law firm in the city. ♦ She **worked as** a journalist. ♦ I hope to **work in** marketing when I'm older.*

2 [I] to spend time and use effort trying to achieve something: *I've been working in the garden all day. ♦ Our thanks go to everybody who has **worked on** this project.* ♦ **work to do sth** *He worked tirelessly to improve safety conditions in the mines.*

3 [I] to operate in a satisfactory way: *The new telephone system seems to be working*

W

perfectly. ♦ *This pen doesn't work.*
4 [I] to succeed, or to have a particular effect: *If this plan doesn't work, we'll have to think of something else.* ♦ *The drug works by blocking the spread of the virus.* ♦ *Criticizing your former employer usually* ***works against*** *you in an interview.* ♦ *The new tax system is* ***working in*** *the company's* ***favor****.*
5 [T] to operate a piece of equipment: *I don't know how to work this thing.*
6 [T] *American* to solve a problem in mathematics by doing a calculation: *Some students may be able to work the problems if they are given more time.*
7 [I/T] to move gradually, or to move something gradually: *He managed to work one hand free of the rope.*
8 [T] to prepare land and grow crops on it
PHRASAL VERBS **ˈwork at sth** to try hard to develop or improve something: *Successful relationships don't just happen – you have to work at them.*
ˈwork on sth to spend time producing or improving something: *He'll have to work on getting in shape before the game.*
ˌwork ˈout 1 to be successful, or to end in a particular way: *If your new arrangement doesn't work out, you can always come back here.* **2** to do physical exercise as a way of staying in shape
ˌwork sth ˈout 1 to find a way of dealing with a problem: *We can't work out how to get the Internet connection going.* **2** to find an answer to something by calculating it
ˌwork sb/sth ˈout to understand someone or something: *I can't work him out.*
ˌwork ˈup to sth to prepare yourself for doing something difficult: *Are you working up to telling me that you can't pay?*

work² /wɜrk/ noun ★★★

1 job	4 sth made/done in job
2 activity needing effort	5 repairs
3 place sb does their job	+ PHRASES

1 [U] a job that you are paid to do: *Many people are having difficulty* ***finding work*** (=getting a job) *in this town.* ♦ *I* ***started work*** (=got my first job) *when I was 16.* ♦ *She's been* ***out of work*** (=unemployed) *for over a year.*
2 [U] activity that involves physical or mental effort: *I know you've got a lot of work to do.* ♦ *Thank you for all your* ***hard work****.*
3 [U] a place where someone goes to do their job: *I walk to work and take the bus home.*
4 [C/U] something that someone makes or does: *As a writer, she did some of her best work in her late twenties.* ♦ *It's not the best* ***piece of work*** *you've ever done.* ♦ ***works of*** *literature*
5 [C/U] the activity of repairing or building something: *There will be no disruption of traffic while the construction work is carried out.*
PHRASES **at work 1** at the place where you work: *If he's not at home, he must still be at work.* **2** in the process of doing or making something: *She's currently* ***at work on*** *a new book.*
get/go/set to work (on sth) to start doing something: *Let's get to work on finding a solution to the problem.*
have your work cut out to have something difficult that you have to do
make quick/short work of sth to deal with something quickly and easily
work of art 1 something such as a painting or SCULPTURE that an artist produces **2** something that is done in a very skillful or impressive way
→ DIRTY¹

- You can refer to what someone does in order to get paid as their **work** or their **job**: *Do you find your work* OR *your job interesting?* ♦ *What kind of work* OR *job does he do?*
- **Work** is uncountable with this meaning, so it never has **a** in front of it and is never plural: *He's looking for work.* ♦ *It's fascinating work.* ♦ *Has he found a job?* ♦ *She has had many different jobs.*

work·a·ble /ˈwɜrkəb(ə)l/ adj practical and likely to be effective
work·a·hol·ic /ˌwɜrkəˈhɔlɪk/ noun [C] someone who spends most of their time working and is not interested in other things
work·book /ˈwɜrkˌbʊk/ noun [C] a book for students that contains exercises
work·day /ˈwɜrkˌdeɪ/ noun [C] *American* **1** the period of time that you work in one day **2** a day of the week when people have to work
worked up /ˌwɜrkt ˈʌp/ adj upset, angry, or excited
work·er /ˈwɜrkər/ noun [C] ★★★
1 someone who works in a company or industry and is below the level of a manager = EMPLOYEE: *About 1,000 workers at the factory lost their jobs.* ♦ *farm/ factory/shipyard workers*
2 used for describing how well or how quickly someone works: *He's a nice man, but quite a slow worker.* ♦ *Jan has always been* ***a hard worker****.*
ˌworker's compenˈsation or **ˌworker's ˈcomp** *informal* noun [C] in the U.S., money that a company must pay to a worker who becomes sick or injured because of their job
work·force /ˈwɜrkˌfɔrs/ noun [singular] the total number of people who work in a particular company, industry, or country
work·ing /ˈwɜrkɪŋ/ adj ★★★
1 a working person has a job: *working parents*
2 relating to or involving work: *After the meeting there will be* ***a working lunch****.* ♦ *The strikers are demanding better* ***working conditions****.*
3 something that is working can be operated or used: *The dining room has an attractive working fireplace.*
4 satisfactory, but not perfect or completely developed: *Applicants should have* ***a working knowledge of*** *Greek.*
PHRASE **in working order** working correctly, without any problems
ˌworking ˈclass noun **the working class** or **the working classes** the social class consisting of people who have little money, education, or power, and who work mainly in jobs that require physical skills → LOWER CLASS, MIDDLE CLASS, UPPER CLASS
work·ings /ˈwɜrkɪŋz/ noun [plural] the parts

W

of something such as a system, organization, or piece of equipment that control it or make it work

work•load /ˈwɜrk,loʊd/ noun [C] the amount of work that a person or organization has to do

work•man /ˈwɜrkmən/ (plural **work•men** /ˈwɜrkmən/) noun [C] a man whose job is building or repairing things

work•man•like /ˈwɜrkmən,laɪk/ adj done or made in a professional way

work•man•ship /ˈwɜrkmənʃɪp/ noun [U] the standard of someone's work, or the skill that they use in making something

work•out /ˈwɜrk,aʊt/ noun [C] an occasion when you do physical exercise

work•place /ˈwɜrk,pleɪs/ noun [C] the place where you work, or all the places where people work

work•sheet /ˈwɜrkʃit/ noun [C] a piece of paper with exercises on it that help you to learn something

work•shop /ˈwɜrkʃɑp/ noun [C] **1** an occasion when a group of people meet in order to learn about a particular subject **2** a room or building where things are made using tools and machines

work•sta•tion /ˈwɜrk,steɪʃ(ə)n/ noun [C] **1** a desk with a computer for one person to work at **2** a powerful computer used in an office

world¹ /wɜrld/ noun ★★★

1 all countries	4 being alive
2 our planet	5 sb's situation
3 group of countries	+ PHRASES

1 [singular] people and society in all countries: *We want to create a safer world for our children.* ♦ *They control about a quarter of the world's oil supply.* ♦ *The terrorists pose a threat to* ***the whole world.*** ♦ *The same problems are faced by workers* ***throughout the world.***

2 the world [singular] the planet that we live on: *changes in the world's climate*

3 [C] a particular group of countries: *the economies of* ***the western world*** (=the countries of western Europe and North America) ♦ *It is the oldest institution in* ***the English-speaking world.***

4 [singular] the state of being alive: *Thousands of babies* ***come into the world*** (=are born) *every day.*

5 [C] the particular type of place or situation in which someone lives or works: *the entertainment world*

PHRASES **do sb a/the world of good** to make someone feel very happy or healthy

in the world 1 used for emphasizing a particular quality that something has: *They produce some of the finest wines in the world.* **2** used for adding emphasis to a question in order to show that you are surprised or annoyed: *How in the world did they make a mistake like that?*

mean the world to sb *informal* to be very important to someone

out of this world *informal* extremely good or impressive

think the world of *informal* to like someone or something very much

→ BEST, TOP¹

world² /wɜrld/ adj involving all the countries of the world: *the world championships* ♦ *a world war*

,world-ˈclass adj at a level where you are one of the best in the world

,world-ˈfamous adj known by people in all parts of the world

world•ly /ˈwɜrldli/ adj a worldly person has a lot of experience and knowledge of life

PHRASE **sb's worldly goods/possessions** all the things someone owns

,world ˈmusic noun [U] in western Europe and North America, music from other cultures

World War I /,wɜrld wɔr ˈwʌn/ *American* a war that was fought mainly in Europe from 1914 to 1918

World War II /,wɜrld wɔr ˈtu/ *American* a war that was fought in Europe, Africa and Asia between 1939 and 1945

world•wide /ˈwɜrld,waɪd/ adj, adv happening or existing all over the world: *a worldwide network of over 100 organizations* ♦ *Our company has 1,500 employees worldwide.*

,World Wide ˈWeb, the all the WEBSITES that organizations have created on their computers for people to look at using the Internet = WEB, THE

worm¹ /wɜrm/ noun [C] **1** a small creature with a long soft body and no bones or legs **2** *computing* a program that deliberately damages computer systems by making copies of itself

worm² /wɜrm/ verb **worm your way into/out of sth** to use clever methods in order to do something or in order to avoid doing something

PHRASAL VERB **,worm sth ˈout of sb** to gradually get information from someone who does not want to give it to you

worn¹ /wɔrn/ adj **1** something that is worn looks old and damaged because it has been used a lot **2** looking tired and old

worn² the past participle of **wear¹**

,worn ˈout adj **1** too old or damaged to be used anymore **2** extremely tired = EXHAUSTED

wor•ried /ˈwʌrid/ adj ★ nervous and upset because you are thinking about your problems or about bad things that could happen: *Everyone was very worried when John didn't show up.* ♦ *a worried look/glance/frown* ♦ *We are very* ***worried about*** *our future.* ♦ *Your parents are* ***worried sick*** *about you* (=extremely worried). ♦ **+that** *I'm worried that he might have gotten lost.*

wor•ry¹ /ˈwʌri/ verb ★★★

1 [I/T] to feel nervous and upset because you keep thinking about your problems or about bad things that could happen: *People* ***worry*** *more* ***about*** *their health than they used to.* ♦ *If companies are following the rules, they've got* ***nothing to worry about.*** ♦ **+that** *She worried that she might have taken on too much work.*

2 [T] to make someone feel nervous and upset: *What worries me most is the possibility of complete failure.*

PHRASE **don't worry** used for telling someone that they do not need to do something: ***Don't worry about*** *dinner; I'll make it when I get back.*

wor•ry² /ˈwʌri/ noun **1** [C] a problem or possibility that makes you feel worried: *financial worries* ♦ *My biggest worry now is* *how we are going to pay for it.* **2** [U] the feeling of being worried: *She was making herself sick with worry.*

wor•ry•ing /ˈwʌriɪŋ/ adj making you feel worried

worse¹ /wɜrs/ adj ★★★

1 more unpleasant or bad than something else, or than before ≠ BETTER: *Our performance **got worse** as the game went on.* ♦ *The company's financial problems are getting **worse and worse**.* ♦ *The injury looked a lot **worse than** it really was.*

2 sicker than before ≠ BETTER: *She's **feeling** much **worse** today.*

PHRASE **make matters/things worse** to make a bad situation even worse

worse² /wɜrs/ adv **1** more badly ≠ BETTER: *They played even worse in the second half.* **2** more severely: *His leg seemed to be hurting worse than ever.*

worse³ /wɜrs/ noun [U] something that is more unpleasant or bad: *Things were looking bad, but worse was to follow.*

PHRASE **for the worse** in a way that makes a situation worse

wors•en /ˈwɜrs(ə)n/ verb [I/T] to become worse, or to make something worse ≠ IMPROVE —**wors•en•ing** adj

ˌworse ˈoff adj **1** in a worse situation than someone else, or than before ≠ BETTER OFF **2** having less money than someone else, or than before ≠ BETTER OFF

wor•ship¹ /ˈwɜrʃɪp/ noun [U] the activity of showing respect and love for God or a god

wor•ship² /ˈwɜrʃɪp/ verb **1** [I/T] to show respect and love for God or a god **2** [T] to love and admire someone or something very much —**wor•ship•er** noun [C]

worst¹ /wɜrst/ adj ★★★ worse than all others, or worse than at all other times: *It was the worst accident in the company's history.* ♦ *The noise from the airport is worst at night.*

worst² /wɜrst/ noun [singular] **the worst** someone or something that is worse than all others: *Even if the worst happens, you shouldn't give up hope.*

PHRASES **at worst** used for talking about the worst possibility in a situation: *At worst, we'll lose $100.*

if worse/worst comes to worst *informal* used for saying what you will do if a bad situation happens

worst³ /wɜrst/ adv more badly than all others: *the areas that were worst hit by Monday's heavy rains*

worth¹ /wɜrθ/ adj ★★★

1 if you say how much something is worth, you state its value in money: *How much do you think the house is worth?* ♦ *a Gucci watch worth $1,500*

2 used for saying that there is a good enough reason for doing something, because it is important, enjoyable, useful, etc.: *The book is definitely worth reading.* ♦ *It's worth talking to your financial adviser before making your final decision.* ♦ *It was hard work, but **it was worth it** in the end.* ♦ ***It's not worth my while** to do the job for less than $150.*

3 used for saying how rich someone is: *She is now worth 20 million dollars.*

PHRASE **for what it's worth** *mainly spoken* used when you are telling someone something and you are not sure how useful it is

worth² /wɜrθ/ noun [U] **1** the financial value of something: *Houses are being sold at prices far below their true worth.* ♦ *millions of dollars' worth of equipment* **2** the degree to which someone or something is good, useful, or important: *The NATO alliance has proved its worth over the years.* **3** an amount measured by the time it lasts: *a week's worth of work*

worth•less /ˈwɜrθləs/ adj **1** with no value, or not useful **2** a worthless person has no good qualities

worth•while /ˌwɜrθˈwaɪl, ˌwɜrθˈhwaɪl/ adj if something is worthwhile, it is worth the time, money, or effort that you spend on it: *We felt the meeting had been very worthwhile.* ♦ *It might be worthwhile to remember a few important facts.*

wor•thy /ˈwɜrði/ adj **1** *formal* deserving something: *He had shown himself to be worthy of their respect.* **2** a worthy person or thing has qualities that make people respect them: *a worthy opponent* ♦ *The money will go to a worthy cause* (=an activity or organization that helps people).

would /wʊd/ modal verb ★★★

- **Would** is usually followed by an infinitive without "to": *A picnic would be nice.* Sometimes it is used without a following infinitive: *They didn't do as much as they said they would.*
- In conversation and informal writing, **would** is often shortened to **'d**: *I thought you'd like a drink before dinner.*
- **Would** has no tenses, no participles, and no infinitive form. **Would** does not change its form, so the third person singular form does not end in "-s": *As a child, she would often run away from home.*
- Questions and negatives are formed without "do": *Would you like a cup of coffee?* ♦ *He would not tell us his secret.*
- The negative form **would not** is often shortened in conversation or informal writing to **wouldn't**: *I wouldn't want to have your job.*

1 for talking about what was going to happen in the past used for showing what someone expected, intended, promised, etc. when they were thinking or talking about the future: *James said he would never forgive her.*

2 for talking about results of an unlikely situation used for talking about the possible results of a situation that is unlikely to happen, or that did not happen: *I'd travel first class if I could afford it.* ♦ *If I'd known you were coming, I **would have** gotten your room ready.*

3 for giving opinions about possible situations used for saying or asking what someone thinks about a possible situation: *You wouldn't recognize the place now – it's changed so much.* ♦ *Why would anyone want to kill Jerry?*

4 for talking about past habits used for saying what someone used to do in the past: *The Campbells would sometimes invite us over for the weekend.*

5 in requests and offers used for politely

asking someone for something, or for offering them something: ***Would you like** a cup of coffee or something?* ♦ ***Would it be** all right if I used your phone?* ♦ ***Would you mind** waiting outside?*
6 **to be willing** used when you think that someone is willing to do something: *Bruce would lend you the money, I'm sure.*
7 **for saying what sb wants** used for saying what someone wants to do, or wishes that they could do: *I wish it would stop raining.* ♦ *I think David **would like** to see you alone.*
PHRASE **sth would not work/start/open etc.** used for saying that you could not make something do what it was meant to do, although you tried: *I turned the key, but the motor wouldn't start.*

ˈwould-ˌbe adj hoping to do something: *a would-be author*

would·n't /ˈwʊd(ə)nt/ short form the usual way of saying or writing "would not." This is not often used in formal writing: *I told you he wouldn't come.*

would've /ˈwʊdəv/ short form *spoken* the usual way of saying "would have." This is not often used in formal writing: *It would've been nice to see him again.*

wound[1] /wund/ noun [C] ★ an injury in which your skin or flesh is seriously damaged: *a head wound* ♦ *a stab wound* ♦ *He **had** serious **wounds to** his stomach.*

wound[2] /wund/ verb [T] **1** to injure someone so that their skin or flesh is seriously damaged: *Two soldiers died and three others were wounded in the attack.* **2** to hurt someone's feelings by doing or saying something unpleasant: *Her remark had deeply wounded him.*

wound[3] the past tense and past participle of wind[2]

wound·ed /ˈwundəd/ adj **1** seriously injured: *wounded soldiers* ♦ *his wounded arm* **2** feeling emotional pain: *wounded pride*

wound up /ˌwaʊnd ˈʌp/ adj *informal* nervous, worried, or angry

wove the past tense of **weave**

woven the past participle of **weave**

wow /waʊ/ interjection *informal* used for showing that you are very surprised or impressed by something

wran·gle /ˈræŋg(ə)l/ verb [I] to argue for a long time about something complicated —**wran·gle** noun [C]

W

wrap /ræp/ verb [T] ★ to cover someone or something by putting paper, cloth, etc. around them: *Keep the cheeses fresh by wrapping each one individually.* ♦ **wrap sth in sth** *We wrapped the baby in a blanket to keep it warm.*
PHRASE **be wrapped up in sth** to spend so much time doing something that you do not notice anything else
PHRASAL VERBS **ˌwrap sth aˈround sth** to put something around something else: *He grabbed a towel to wrap around his waist.* ♦ *couples with their arms wrapped around each other*
ˌwrap ˈup to wear enough clothes to keep you warm
ˌwrap sth ˈup 1 *same as* **wrap**: *We've just finished wrapping up Susie's birthday present.* **2** *informal* to finish something

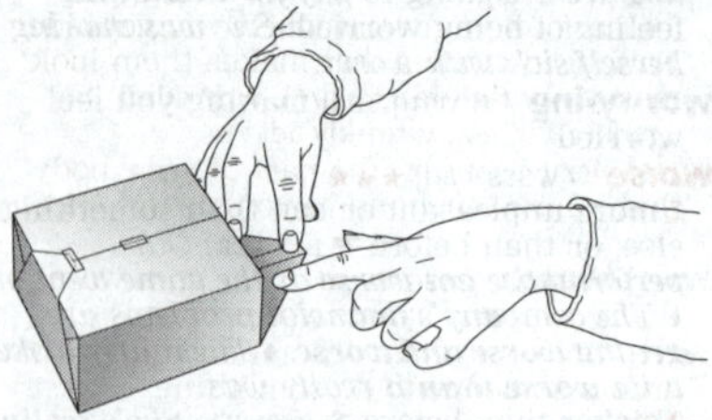

wrap

wrap·per /ˈræpər/ noun [C] a piece of paper or plastic that is wrapped around something that you buy: *candy wrappers*

wrap·ping /ˈræpɪŋ/ noun [U] the paper or plastic that is wrapped around something

ˈwrapping ˌpaper noun [U] paper that you use for wrapping presents

ˈwrap-ˌup noun [C] *American* a short summary at the end of a news program

wrath /rɑθ/ noun [U] *formal* extreme anger

wreak /rik/ verb **wreak havoc (on)** to cause a lot of harm or damage to someone or something

wreath /riθ/ noun [C] a circle of flowers that you put on a dead person's GRAVE

wreck[1] /rek/ verb [T] to destroy or damage something badly

wreck[2] /rek/ noun [C] **1** *American* an accident that involves a vehicle = CRASH **2** *informal* someone who looks or feels very sick or tired **3** something that has been badly damaged or is in very bad condition

wreck·age /ˈrekɪdʒ/ noun [singular/U] the parts of a vehicle or building that remain after it has been severely damaged

wrench[1] /rentʃ/ noun [C] *American* a tool with a round end that fits around a NUT of a particular size *—picture* → TOOL

wrench[2] /rentʃ/ verb [T] **1** to injure a part of your body by twisting it suddenly **2** to pull and twist something strongly: *The door had been wrenched off its hinges.*

wrest /rest/ verb [T] *mainly journalism* to use force to get land, power, or possessions from someone

wres·tle /ˈres(ə)l/ verb [I/T] to fight by holding someone and trying to push or throw them to the ground, especially as a sport
PHRASAL VERB **ˈwrestle with sth** to try to deal with a difficult problem

wres·tling /ˈres(ə)lɪŋ/ noun [U] a sport in which two people fight by holding each other and trying to push or throw each other to the ground —**wres·tler** noun [C]

wretch·ed /ˈretʃəd/ adj **1** *formal* very unhappy or sick **2** *informal* used for emphasizing how much someone or something annoys you: *I eventually found the wretched letter.*

wrig·gle /ˈrɪg(ə)l/ verb [I/T] to move by twisting or turning quickly, or to make something move in this way
PHRASAL VERB **ˈwriggle ˌout of sth** to try to avoid something

wring /rɪŋ/ (past tense and past participle **wrung** /rʌŋ/) or **ˌwring sth ˈout** verb [T] to twist and squeeze something in order to remove liquid from it

wrin•kle /ˈrɪŋk(ə)l/ noun [C] **1** a line that appears on your skin when you get older **2** a fold in clothes that makes them look messy —**wrink•le** verb [I/T], **wrin•kled** /ˈrɪŋk(ə)ld/ adj, **wrin•kly** adj

wrist /rɪst/ noun [C] the part of your body that joins your hand to your arm —*picture* → C14

wrist•watch /ˈrɪs(t)ˌwɑtʃ/ noun [C] a watch that you wear around your wrist

writ /rɪt/ noun [C] an official document that orders someone to do something

write /raɪt/ (past tense **wrote** /roʊt/; past participle **writ•ten** /ˈrɪt(ə)n/) verb ★★★
1 [I/T] to use something such as a pen or pencil to make words, numbers, or symbols: *Emily is just learning to write.* ♦ *Write your full name in Box A.*
2 [I/T] to create something such as a book, a piece of music, or a computer program, by putting together words or symbols: *I have to write a review of my favorite movie.* ♦ *Matt writes software for computer games.* ♦ *He traveled around Mexico and **wrote about** his experiences.* ♦ *She **writes for** several fashion magazines.*
3 [I/T] to create a letter or other message and send it: **write sb** *Don't forget to write me.* ♦ **write sth to sb** *She'd written a letter to the newspaper to complain.*
4 [T] to create a formal document by writing: **write sb sth** *I'll write you a check for the full amount.*
PHRASAL VERBS ˌ**write ˈback** to send a reply to someone who has sent you a letter
ˌ**write sth ˈdown** to write something on a piece of paper
ˌ**write ˈin** to send a letter to an organization
ˌ**write sth ˈoff** to accept that you will not receive money that someone owes you: *The U.S. government agreed to write off debts of $170 billion.*
ˌ**write sb/sth ˈoff** to decide that someone or something will not succeed, so that you stop giving them your attention and energy: *He thought the teachers had written him off.*
ˌ**write sth ˈup** to write something such as a report or research paper, using notes

write-pro•tect•ed /ˌraɪt prəˈtektəd/ adj *computing* containing information that cannot be changed or removed

writ•er /ˈraɪtər/ noun [C] ★★★ someone who writes books, stories, or articles as their job

ˈ**write-up** noun [C] an article in a newspaper that gives the writer's opinion about something such as a new book or movie =REVIEW

writhe /raɪð/ verb [I] to twist your body because you are feeling a lot of pain

writ•ing /ˈraɪtɪŋ/ noun ★★★

1 act of writing	4 things that are written
2 job of creating stories	5 everything sb has written
3 written words	+ PHRASE

1 [U] the skill of producing written material by putting words together: *In the first two years, the children focus on reading and writing.*
2 [U] the job or activity of creating things such as books, poems, or newspaper articles
3 [U] words that are written or printed on something: *The label was torn and I couldn't read the writing.*
4 [U] books, poems, articles, etc. that have been written by a particular person or about a particular subject: *Her writing on environmental issues has been very influential.* ♦ *a course on women's writing*
5 writings [plural] all the books, poems, or articles that someone has written
PHRASE **in writing** in the form of a document that you can keep as proof of something: *Customers are expected to **put** their complaints **in writing**.*

writ•ten[1] /ˈrɪt(ə)n/ adj in the form of a letter or other document

writ•ten[2] the past participle of **write**

wrong[1] /rɔŋ/ adj ★★★
1 not accurate, correct, or sensible =INCORRECT: *We must have gone the wrong way.* ♦ *the wrong answer* ♦ *If you think carefully, you won't make the wrong decision.*
2 not morally right: *Do you think it's wrong to use animals for testing new medicines?* ♦ *There's **nothing wrong with** living with your boyfriend in my opinion.*
3 if there is something wrong, there is a problem: *You don't look well. Is anything wrong?* ♦ *I checked the engine, but I couldn't find anything wrong.* ♦ *There was **something wrong with** one of the tires.* ♦ *She had some blood tests, but they still don't know **what's wrong with** her.* ♦ ***What's wrong with** the washing machine?*
4 not appropriate: *It's **the wrong place** to build a factory.* ♦ *The colors just look **wrong for** a room this size.*
PHRASE **get off on the wrong foot** to start something badly, especially a relationship
→ CORRECT[2]

Words often used with wrong

*Adverbs often used with **wrong** (adj, sense 1)*
- **completely, entirely, hopelessly, plainly, totally** + WRONG: used for saying that something is not at all correct

*Adverbs often used with **wrong** (adj, sense 3)*
- **badly, disastrously, horribly, seriously, terribly** + WRONG: used for saying that there is a serious problem with something

wrong[2] /rɔŋ/ adv ★ in a way that is not correct: *Someone had tied the rope on wrong.*
PHRASES **don't get me wrong** used for explaining your comments when you think that someone has not understood them
get sth wrong to make a mistake about something: *The police got the name wrong and arrested an innocent man.*
go wrong 1 to stop working: *Then something went wrong with the engine.* **2** used when a problem happens and causes something to fail: *It's difficult to say when the relationship started to go wrong.*

wrong[3] /rɔŋ/ noun [U] behavior that is morally wrong or breaks a rule: *Small children do not know the difference between right and wrong.*
PHRASE **in the wrong** someone who is in the wrong has made a mistake and deserves the blame for it

W

wrong⁴ /rɔŋ/ verb [T] *formal* to treat or judge someone unfairly

wrong·do·ing /ˈrɔŋˌduɪŋ/ noun [C/U] *formal* behavior that is illegal or immoral

wrong·ful /ˈrɔŋfəl/ adj unfair or illegal: *a wrongful arrest*

wrong·ly /ˈrɔŋli/ adv not correctly, or by mistake

wrote the past tense of **write**

wrought /rɔt/ a past tense and past participle of **wreak**

ˌwrought ˈiron noun [U] iron that is used for making things such as fences and gates, especially for decoration

wrung the past tense and past participle of **wring**

wry /raɪ/ adj showing that you think that something is funny but not very pleasant: *a wry smile* —**wry·ly** adv

wt. abbrev weight

WV abbrev West Virginia

www /ˌdʌb(ə)lju dʌb(ə)lju ˈdʌb(ə)lju/ abbrev the World Wide Web: used in some website addresses

WY abbrev Wyoming

X x

x or **X** /eks/ noun [C/U] **1** the 24th letter of the English alphabet **2** a symbol that you use for showing that an answer is wrong **3** X used instead of saying the name of a person or place when you do not know it, or when you want to keep it secret: *Mr. X* **4** *informal* a symbol that you use for writing a kiss at the end of a letter

xen·o·pho·bi·a /ˌzinəˈfoʊbiə, ˌzenəˈfoʊbiə/ noun [U] hate of people from other countries and cultures —**xen·o·pho·bic** adj

XL abbrev extra large: used on labels showing clothes sizes

X·mas /ˈkrɪsməs, ˈeksməs/ noun [C/U] *informal* CHRISTMAS

XML /ˌeks em ˈel/ noun [U] *computing* a computer language that is used for creating WEBSITES

X-rat·ed /ˈeks ˌreɪtəd/ adj an X-rated movie contains so much sex or violence that it is only appropriate for adults to watch

X-ray¹ /ˈeks ˌreɪ/ noun [C] **1** a type of RADIATION that is used for looking inside things such as your body **2** a picture of the inside of someone's body that is taken using X-rays

X-ray² /ˈeks ˌreɪ/ verb [T] to take a picture of the inside of something using X-rays

xy·lo·phone /ˈzaɪləˌfoʊn/ noun [C] a musical instrument with a row of narrow wooden pieces that you hit with a wooden hammer —*picture* → PERCUSSION

Y y

y or **Y** /waɪ/ noun [C/U] the 25th letter of the English alphabet

yacht /jɑt/ noun [C] a boat that is used for racing or sailing

y'all /jɔl/ pronoun *American spoken* a way of saying "you all": used for talking to or getting the attention of a group of people, especially in the southern U.S.

yam /jæm/ noun [C/U] *American* a SWEET POTATO

yank /jæŋk/ verb [I/T] to pull something suddenly using force = JERK

Yan·kee /ˈjæŋki/ noun [C] **1** someone from the northern part of the U.S., especially from New England **2** someone from the U.S. This word is often used as an insulting word for referring to an American by people who are not from the U.S.

yap /jæp/ verb [I] if a dog yaps, it makes short high sounds

yard /jɑrd/ noun [C] ★★

1 *American* the area around a house usually with grass, plants, trees, etc., used for relaxing and playing in —*picture* → C1

2 a unit for measuring length that is equal to 0.91 meters

3 an enclosed area around a large building where people can do activities outside: *a school/prison yard*

4 a large open area that is used for a particular purpose: *a lumber yard*

PHRASE **the whole nine yards** *American informal* everything

ˈyard ˌsale noun [C] *American* a sale where someone sells things in their yard

yard·stick /ˈjɑrdˌstɪk/ noun [C] something that you compare similar things to, as a way of judging their quality or value

yarn /jɑrn/ noun **1** [U] cotton, wool, or other fibers in the form of thick THREAD (=a substance like string) **2** [C] *informal* a long story with a lot of exciting details

yawn /jɔn/ verb [I] to open your mouth wide and take a big breath, because you are tired or bored —**yawn** noun [C]

yawn

yd. abbrev yard

yeah /jeə/ adv *informal* YES

year /jɪr/ noun ★★★
1 [C] a period of 365 or 366 days divided into 12 months: *He lived in Paris for **a few years**. ♦ I started my job two **years ago**. ♦ He returned to China **year after year*** (=continuously for many years).
2 years [plural] a very long time: *It wasn't until **years later** that I realized how foolish I'd been. ♦ He hasn't been back to his country **for years**.*
3 [C] a year beginning on January 1 and ending on December 31: *We're hoping to sell the house by the end of the year. ♦ one of this year's best movies*
4 [C] the period during which an institution operates, or the system it uses for dividing time: *the school year ♦ the tax year*
PHRASE **five/ten etc. years old** the number of years that someone has lived or that something has existed

year·book /ˈjɪrˌbʊk/ noun [C] *American* a book containing pictures of people and the activities they did at a school or college during one particular year

year·ly /ˈjɪrli/ adj, adv happening every year, or once every year = ANNUAL

yearn /jɜrn/ verb [I] *literary* to want something very much —**yearn·ing** noun [C/U]

yeast /jist/ noun [U] a white substance that is used in making bread and beer

yell /jel/ verb [I/T] to shout loudly —**yell** noun [C]

yel·low¹ /ˈjeloʊ/ adj ★★★ something that is yellow is the same color as the sun or the middle of an egg: *yellow flowers*

yel·low² /ˈjeloʊ/ noun [C/U] the color of the sun or the middle of an egg

yel·low·ish /ˈjeloʊɪʃ/ adj similar to yellow

ˌYellow ˈPages *trademark* a large book that contains the telephone numbers and addresses of businesses and organizations in a particular area

yelp /jelp/ verb [I/T] to make a short loud high noise, because you are excited, angry, or in pain —**yelp** noun [C]

yep /jep/ adv *informal* YES

yes¹ /jes/ adv ★★★
1 used for saying that something is true or correct, for giving permission, or for agreeing to do something: *"Is that your car?" "Yes, it is." ♦ "Can I borrow your pen?" "Yes, of course." ♦ "Would you like me to open a window?" "**Yes, please.**"*
2 used for answering someone who calls you in order to show that you have heard them: *"Erica!" "Yes?"*
3 used for correcting someone when they make a wrong negative statement: *"She won't go." "Yes, she will. She just told me she would."*
PHRASE **yes and no** *spoken* used for saying that something is only partly true: *"Were you angry?" "Well, yes and no."*

yes² /jes/ noun [C] an answer or a vote that expresses agreement or gives permission

yes·ter·day¹ /ˈjestərˌdeɪ/ adv ★★★ on the day before today: *Yesterday, we went to the zoo. ♦ I saw her **yesterday afternoon**.*

yes·ter·day² /ˈjestərˌdeɪ/ noun [C/U] **1** the day before today **2** *formal* a time in the past

yet /jet/ adv, conjunction ★★★
1 not before a particular time used for talking or asking about something that has not happened at a particular time, but will probably happen in the future: *She hasn't decided yet if she wants to come. ♦ "Are you feeling hungry?" "**Not yet.**"*
2 not now, but later used for saying that something cannot or should not be done now, but will be done at a time in the future: *I can't leave the hospital yet – the doctor says maybe tomorrow.*
3 possibly now or in the future used for saying that something could still happen in the future: *The team may yet make it to the finals.*
4 ever used for saying that someone or something is the best, worst, biggest, etc. of their kind up to now: *This will be the president's most important speech yet.*
5 despite sth used for introducing a statement that is surprising after what has just been mentioned: *The new computer is much more powerful; yet it costs the same.*
6 used for emphasizing a greater amount, degree, or number of times used for emphasizing that someone or something is even bigger, better, worse, more, etc.: *We woke to **yet another** gray rainy day. ♦ Seth knew that he had failed **yet again**.*
PHRASE **as (of) yet** *formal* used for talking about something that has not happened or been done up to now

Both **already** and **yet** are used for talking about something that happened before a particular time or before now.

- Use **already** in positive sentences or in questions when you think it is likely that something has happened, or when you know it has happened and are surprised: *Thanks, but I've already eaten. ♦ Did I already give you my e-mail address? ♦ Is John married already? He hardly looks old enough.*
- Use **yet** in negative sentences and in questions, especially when you think that something should happen soon: *Kim hasn't seen the movie yet, so don't tell her how it ends. ♦ Have you told her yet that you're leaving?*
- Use **still** for talking about things that continue happening without changing: *Are you still working downtown? ♦ I still love him.*
- You can also use **still** for expressing surprise that a situation has not changed: *Why are you still here?*

yew /ju/ noun [C] a tree with dark green leaves

yield¹ /jild/ verb **1** [T] to produce something: *We're hoping the farm will yield a big harvest in the fall. ♦ The search for truth is beginning to yield results.* **2** [I] to finally agree to do what someone wants you to do: *The sport should not yield to every demand from the television companies.* **3** [I] *American* to allow another vehicle to go before you when you are driving **4** [T] to give something to someone else: *After the war, Mexico yielded a large amount of its territory to the United States.*

yield² /jild/ noun [C] the amount of something that is produced

YMCA, the /ˌwaɪ em si ˈeɪ/ the Young Men's Christian Association: an organization that

Y

provides places for people to exercise, take classes, and sometimes rent a room for the night while traveling

yo /joʊ/ interjection *American informal* used for getting someone's attention or for greeting someone

yo•ga /ˈjoʊgə/ noun [U] an activity that involves exercises that are intended to make you stronger and more relaxed

yo•gurt or **yoghurt** /ˈjoʊgərt/ noun [C/U] a food made from milk that has become thick and slightly sour

yoke /joʊk/ noun [C] a wooden object used for connecting animals that are pulling a vehicle
PHRASE **the yoke of sth** *formal* a situation or experience that limits your freedom

yolk /joʊk/ noun [C/U] the yellow part of an egg

you /*weak* jə, *weak* jʊ, *strong* ju/ pronoun ★★★
1 used for referring to the person or people that you are talking to or writing to: *Do you like oranges?* ♦ *I can't really trust you, can I?* ♦ *I'll give it to you if you want it.*
2 used for referring to people in general: ♦ *You don't have to be a great cook to make pasta.*

you'd /jud/ short form **1** the usual way of saying or writing "you had" when "had" is an AUXILIARY VERB. This is not often used in formal writing: *You look very tired – you'd better take a break.* **2** the usual way of saying or writing "you would." This is not often used in formal writing: *The doctor can see you at 3 p.m. if you'd like to come then.*

you'll /jul/ short form the usual way of saying or writing "you will." This is not often used in formal writing: *You'll get cold if you don't wear a coat.*

young[1] /jʌŋ/ adj ★★★
1 someone who is young has lived for only a short time: *a young man/woman* ♦ *She has two **young children**.*
2 something that is young has existed for only a short time: *It's still quite a young organization.*
3 appropriate for young people: *That dress is a little young for you.*
4 the young children and young adults in general
PHRASE **young at heart** behaving or thinking in a way that is considered typical of a young person, although you are old

young[2] /jʌŋ/ noun [plural] a group of young animals that belong to the same family

young•er /ˈjʌŋgər/ adj not as old as you are, or not as old as someone else who you are discussing: *My younger sister, Karen, is moving to Japan.*

young•ster /ˈjʌŋstər/ noun [C] a child, or a young person

your /*weak* jə, *strong* jʊr, jɔr/ determiner ★★★
1 used for showing that something belongs to or is connected with the person or people who you are talking to or writing to: *You never really talk to your parents, do you?* ♦ *What's your address?*
2 used for showing that something belongs to or is connected with people in general: *You never forget your first kiss.*

you're /jʊr, jɔr/ short form the usual way of saying or writing "you are." This is not often used in formal writing: *You're looking well, Peter.*

yours /jʊrz, jɔrz/ pronoun ★★★ used for referring to something that belongs to or is connected with the person or people who you are talking to or writing to: *My pen isn't working – can I borrow yours?* ♦ *A friend **of yours** called while you were out.*
PHRASE **Yours** or **Sincerely yours** used at the end of a formal letter before your name

your•self /jʊrˈself, jɔrˈself/ (plural **your•selves** /jʊrˈselvz, jɔrˈselvz/) pronoun ★★★
1 the REFLEXIVE form of "you," used for showing that the person or people who you are talking to or writing to are affected by something that they do: *Did you hurt yourself?* ♦ *Go get yourselves a drink.*
2 used with "you" for emphasizing that you mean the person or people who you are talking to or writing to, and no one else: *Think about how you yourself would like to be treated in a similar situation.*
3 *formal* used instead of "you" in order to be formal or polite. Many people think that this use is incorrect: *Someone like yourself would be a suitable buyer for the property.*
PHRASES **(all) by yourself 1** without help from anyone else: *Did you paint the room all by yourself?* **2** alone: *I'm sure you like to be by yourself sometimes.*
(all) to yourself not shared with anyone else: *You have the house to yourself until five o'clock.*
be/feel/look etc. yourself to be, or appear to be, in your normal mental or physical state: *Take a rest – you're not quite yourself today.*

youth /juθ/ noun ★★
1 [U] the time in your life when you are young: *In his youth, he traveled around the world.* ♦ *the energy of youth*
2 [C] a male teenager: *a gang of youths*
3 [U] young people in general: *the youth of the nation*

youth•ful /ˈjuθf(ə)l/ adj **1** typical of young people **2** looking or behaving like a young person, although you are not young anymore

ˈyouth ˌhostel noun [C] an inexpensive place where travelers can stay for a short period of time

you've /juv/ short form the usual way of saying or writing "you have" when "have" is an AUXILIARY VERB. This is not often used in formal writing: *You've got mail.*

ˈyo-yo noun [C] a toy that consists of a round plastic or wooden object on the end of a string. You make it rise and fall by tying the string to your finger and moving your hand up and down.

yr. (plural **yrs.**) abbrev **1** year **2** your

yuck /jʌk/ interjection *informal* used for saying that you think that someone or something is dirty, ugly, or unpleasant

yuck•y /ˈjʌki/ adj *informal* dirty, ugly, or unpleasant

yum /jʌm/ interjection *informal* used for saying that you like the taste or smell of something

yum•my /ˈjʌmi/ adj *informal* food that is yummy tastes good

yup•pie /ˈjʌpi/ noun [C] *showing disapproval* someone who is young, earns a lot of money, and lives in a city in a style that is too expensive for most people

Y

YWCA, the /ˌwaɪ dʌb(ə)lju si ˈeɪ/ the Young Women's Christian Association: an organization that helps women by providing them with a place to live, giving them information, etc.

Zz

z or **Z** /zi, *British* zed/ noun [C/U] the 26th and last letter of the English alphabet

za•ny /ˈzeɪni/ adj *informal* strange or unusual in a funny way

zap /zæp/ verb *informal* **1** [T] to hit, harm, or destroy someone or something **2** [I/T] to quickly change the program that you are watching on television using a REMOTE CONTROL

zeal /zil/ noun [U] a lot of energy, effort, and enthusiasm

zeal•ous /ˈzeləs/ adj full of energy, effort, and enthusiasm —**zeal•ous•ly** adv

ze•bra /ˈzibrə/ noun [C] an African animal that is similar to a horse but has black and white STRIPES on its body —*picture* → C12

ˌzebra ˈcrossing noun [C] *British* a CROSSWALK with black and white lines

ze•nith /ˈzenɪθ/ noun [C] *literary* the time when someone or something is most successful or effective

ze•ro¹ /ˈzɪroʊ/ (plural **ze•roes**) noun ★
1 [C/U] the number 0: *Add a zero to 3 and you get 30.*
2 [U] a temperature below freezing on the Fahrenheit SCALE, used for talking about very cold temperatures. It is also the temperature on the Celsius SCALE at which water freezes: *The temperature was 40 degrees below zero.*

ze•ro² /ˈzɪroʊ/ PHRASAL VERB **ˌzero ˈin on sb/sth 1** to start to give all your attention to someone or something **2** to aim at someone or something

zest /zest/ noun [U] **1** a feeling of a lot of enthusiasm or interest **2** the skin of an orange or lemon when it is used in cooking

zig•zag¹ /ˈzɪgˌzæg/ noun [C] a line or movement that makes very sharp angles, because it suddenly changes from one direction to another

zig•zag² /ˈzɪgˌzæg/ verb [I] to move forward in a line that makes very sharp angles, by suddenly changing from one direction to another

zilch /zɪltʃ/ noun [U] *informal* nothing

zil•lion /ˈzɪljən/ number *informal* a very large number

zinc /zɪŋk/ noun [U] a chemical element that is a blue-white metal

zip¹ /zɪp/ noun **1** [C] *American* a ZIP CODE **2** [U] *informal* nothing **3** [C] *British* a ZIPPER

zip² /zɪp/ verb **1** [T] to close or fasten something with a ZIPPER ≠ UNZIP **2** [I] *informal* to move very quickly **3** [T] *computing* to make a computer document fill less space ≠ UNZIP

ˈzip ˌcode noun [C] *American* a series of numbers that are added to your address in order to make it easier to deliver letters to you

ˈzip ˌdrive noun [C] *computing* part of a computer, or a small machine that you connect to your computer, used for copying large documents onto a special DISK

zip•per /ˈzɪpər/ noun [C] *American* a long narrow metal or plastic object with two rows of teeth. It is used for opening or closing something such as a piece of clothing.

zit /zɪt/ noun [C] *informal* a small raised infected mark on your face = PIMPLE

zo•di•ac, the /ˈzoʊdiˌæk/ noun [singular] 12 groups of stars that some people believe affect your character according to the positions that they are in when you are born

zom•bie /ˈzɑmbi/ noun [C] **1** *informal* someone who does not seem to know or care about what is happening around them and moves very slowly **2** a dead person who is believed to behave as though they are alive as a result of magic

zone¹ /zoʊn/ noun [C] ★ an area where a particular thing happens: *an earthquake zone* ♦ *a traffic-free zone*

zone² /zoʊn/ verb [T] to officially make land available for a particular use —**zon•ing** noun [U]: *zoning laws*

zoo /zu/ noun [C] a place where many types of wild animals are kept so that people can see them

zoo•keep•er /ˈzuˌkipər/ noun [C] someone whose job is to take care of the animals in a zoo

zo•ol•o•gist /zoʊˈɑlədʒɪst, zuˈɑlədʒɪst/ noun [C] a scientist who studies animals

zo•ol•o•gy /zoʊˈɑlədʒi, zuˈɑlədʒi/ noun [U] the scientific study of animals

zoom /zum/ verb [I] **1** to move with a lot of speed and energy **2** if a camera zooms in or out, it makes something seem much closer or farther away: *The camera zoomed in on the action.*

ˈzoom ˌlens noun [C] a piece of equipment that you attach to a camera so that you can take photographs of things that are very close or very far away

zuc•chi•ni /zuˈkini/ (plural **zuc•chi•ni**) noun [C] *American* a long vegetable with dark green skin —*picture* → C11

zzz a way of writing the sound that someone makes when they are sleeping

GEOGRAPHICAL NAMES AND NATIONALITIES

The following lists show you the names and pronunciations of countries and the adjectives that are related to them. Most adjectives can be used as nouns to describe a person from a particular country (e.g., a **Mexican** is a person from **Mexico**). When the adjective cannot be used as a noun, it is followed by an asterisk (*) and the correct term is given in the Nationalities table at the end.

Countries

NOTE: Inclusion in the following list does not imply status as a sovereign state.

Name	**Adjective**
Afghanistan /æfˈgænəˌstæn/	Afghan /ˈæfˌgæn/
Albania /ælˈbeɪniə/	Albanian /ælˈbeɪniən/
Algeria /ælˈdʒɪriə/	Algerian /ælˈdʒɪriən/
Andorra /ænˈdɔrə/	Andorran /ænˈdɔrən/
Angola /æŋˈgoʊlə/	Angolan /æŋˈgoʊlən/
Antigua and Barbuda /ænˌtigə ənd bɑrˈbudə/	Antiguan /ænˈtigən/
Argentina /ˌɑrdʒənˈtinə/	Argentine* /ˈɑrdʒəntin/
Armenia /ɑrˈminiə/	Armenian /ɑrˈminiən/
Australia /ɔˈstreɪliə/	Australian /ɔˈstreɪliən/
Austria /ˈɔstriə/	Austrian /ˈɔstriən/
Azerbaijan /ˌæzərbaɪˈdʒɑn/	Azerbaijani* /ˌæzərbaɪˈdʒɑni/
Bahamas, the /bəˈhɑməz/	Bahamian /bəˈheɪmiən/
Bahrain /bɑˈreɪn/	Bahraini /bɑˈreɪni/
Bangladesh /ˌbɑŋgləˈdeʃ/	Bangladeshi /ˌbɑŋgləˈdeʃi/
Barbados /bɑrˈbeɪdoʊs/	Barbadian /bɑrˈbeɪdiən/
Belarus /ˌbeləˈrus/	Belorussian /ˌbeləˈrʌʃ(ə)n/
Belgium /ˈbeldʒəm/	Belgian /ˈbeldʒən/
Belize /bəˈliz/	Belizian /bəˈliziən/
Benin /bəˈnin/	Beninese /ˌbenɪˈniz/
Bermuda /bərˈmjudə/	Bermudan /bərˈmjud(ə)n/
Bhutan /buˈtɑn/	Bhutanese /ˌbut(ə)ˈniz/
Bolivia /bəˈlɪviə/	Bolivian /bəˈlɪviən/
Bosnia-Herzegovina /ˌbɑzniə ˌhɜrtsəgəˈvinə/	Bosnian /ˈbɑzniən/
Botswana /bɑtˈswɑnə/	Botswanan /bɑtˈswɑnən/
Brazil /brəˈzɪl/	Brazilian /brəˈzɪliən/
Brunei /bruˈnaɪ/	Bruneian /bruˈnaɪən/
Bulgaria /bʌlˈgeriə/	Bulgarian /bʌlˈgeriən/
Burkina Faso /bərˌkinə ˈfɑsoʊ/	Burkinan /bərˈkinən/
Burundi /bʊˈrundi/	Burundian /bʊˈrundiən/
Cambodia /kæmˈboʊdiə/	Cambodian /kæmˈboʊdiən/
Cameroon /ˌkæməˈrun/	Cameroonian /ˌkæməˈruniən/
Canada /ˈkænədə/	Canadian /kəˈneɪdiən/
Cape Verde /ˌkeɪp ˈvɜrd/	Cape Verdean /ˌkeɪp ˈvɜrdiən/
Caribbean, the /ˌkærɪˈbiən, kəˌrɪˈbiən/	Caribbean /ˌkærɪˈbiən, kəˌrɪˈbiən/
Cayman Islands, the /ˈkeɪmən ˌaɪləndz/	Cayman Island* /ˈkeɪmən ˌaɪlənd/
Central African Republic, the /ˌsentrəl ˌæfrɪkən rɪˈpʌblɪk/	Central African /ˌsentrəl ˈæfrɪkən/
Chad /tʃæd/	Chadian /ˈtʃædiən/
Chile /ˈtʃɪli/	Chilean /ˈtʃɪliən/
China /ˈtʃaɪnə/	Chinese /ˌtʃaɪˈniz/
Colombia /kəˈlʌmbiə/	Colombian /kəˈlʌmbiən/
Comoros /ˈkɑməˌroʊz/	Comoran /ˈkɑmərən/
Democratic Republic of Congo, the /ˌdeməkrætɪk rɪˌpʌblɪk əv ˈkɑŋgoʊ/	Congolese /ˌkɑŋgəˈliz/
Republic of Congo, the /ˌrɪpʌblɪk əv ˈkɑŋgoʊ/	Congolese /ˌkɑŋgəˈliz/
Costa Rica /ˌkɑstə ˈrikə/	Costa Rican /ˌkɑstə ˈrikən/
Côte d'Ivoire /ˌkoʊt diˈvwɑr/	Ivorian /aɪˈvɔriən/
Croatia /kroʊˈeɪʃə/	Croatian* /kroʊˈeɪʃ(ə)n/
Cuba /ˈkjubə/	Cuban /ˈkjubən/
Cyprus /ˈsaɪprəs/	Cypriot /ˈsɪpriət/
Czech Republic, the /ˌtʃek rɪˈpʌblɪk/	Czech /tʃek/
Denmark /ˈdenmɑrk/	Danish* /ˈdeɪnɪʃ/
Djibouti /dʒɪˈbuti/	Djiboutian /dʒɪˈbutiən/

Dominica /ˌdɑməˈnikə/	Dominican /ˌdɑməˈnikən/
Dominican Republic, the /dəˌmɪnɪkən rɪˈpʌblɪk/	Dominican /dəˈmɪnɪkən/
East Timor /ˌist ˈtimɔr/	East Timorese /ˌist timɔˈriz/
Ecuador /ˈekwəˌdɔr/	Ecuadorian /ˌekwəˈdɔriən/
Egypt /ˈidʒɪpt/	Egyptian /ɪˈdʒɪpʃ(ə)n/
El Salvador /el ˈsælvəˌdɔr/	Salvadorian /ˌsælvəˈdɔriən/
England /ˈɪŋglənd/	English* /ˈɪŋglɪʃ/
Equatorial Guinea /ˌekwətɔriəl ˈgɪni/	Equatorial Guinean /ˌekwətɔriəl ˈgɪniən/
Eritrea /ˌerɪˈtriə/	Eritrean /ˌerɪˈtriən/
Estonia /eˈstoʊniə/	Estonian /eˈstoʊniən/
Ethiopia /ˌiθiˈoʊpiə/	Ethiopian /ˌiθiˈoʊpiən/
Fiji /ˈfidʒi/	Fijian /ˈfidʒiən/
Finland /ˈfɪnlənd/	Finnish* /ˈfɪnɪʃ/
France /fræns/	French* /frentʃ/
Gabon /gæˈboʊn/	Gabonese /ˌgæbəˈniz/
Gambia, the /ˈgæmbiə/	Gambian /ˈgæmbiən/
Georgia /ˈdʒɔrdʒə/	Georgian /ˈdʒɔrdʒən/
Germany /ˈdʒɜrməni/	German /ˈdʒɜrmən/
Ghana /ˈgɑnə/	Ghanaian /gɑˈneɪən/
Gibraltar /dʒɪˈbrɔltər/	Gibraltarian /ˌdʒɪbrɔlˈteriən/
Great Britain /ˌgreɪt ˈbrɪt(ə)n/	British* /ˈbrɪtɪʃ/
Greece /gris/	Greek /grik/
Greenland /ˈgrinlənd/	Greenlandic* /grinˈlændɪk/
Grenada /grəˈneɪdə/	Grenadian /grəˈneɪdiən/
Guatemala /ˌgwɑtəˈmɑlə/	Guatamalan /ˌgwɑtəˈmɑlən/
Guinea /ˈgɪni/	Guinean /ˈgɪniən/
Guinea-Bissau /ˌgɪni bɪˈsaʊ/	Guinea-Bissauan /ˌgɪni bɪˈsaʊən/
Guyana /gaɪˈɑnə/	Guyanese /ˌgaɪəˈniz/
Haiti /ˈheɪti/	Haitian /ˈheɪʃ(ə)n/
Honduras /hɑnˈdʊrəs/	Honduran /hɑnˈdʊrən/
Hungary /ˈhʌŋgəri/	Hungarian /hʌŋˈgeriən/
Iceland /ˈaɪslənd/	Icelandic* /aɪsˈlændɪk/
India /ˈɪndiə/	Indian /ˈɪndiən/
Indonesia /ˌɪndəˈniʒə/	Indonesian /ˌɪndəˈniʒ(ə)n/
Iran /ɪˈræn/	Iranian /ɪˈreɪniən/
Iraq /ɪˈræk/	Iraqi /ɪˈræki/
Northern Ireland /ˌnɔrð(ə)n ˈaɪ(ə)rlənd/	
Republic of Ireland, the /rɪˌpʌblɪk əv ˈaɪ(ə)rlənd/	Irish* /ˈaɪ(ə)rɪʃ/
Israel /ˈɪzriəl/	Israeli /ɪzˈreɪli/
Italy /ˈɪt(ə)li/	Italian /ɪˈtæliən/
Ivory Coast, the /ˌaɪv(ə)ri ˈkoʊst/	Ivorian /aɪˈvɔriən/
Jamaica /dʒəˈmeɪkə/	Jamaican /dʒəˈmeɪkən/
Japan /dʒəˈpæn/	Japanese /ˌdʒæpəˈniz/
Jordan /ˈdʒɔrd(ə)n/	Jordanian /dʒɔrˈdeɪniən/
Kazakhstan /ˈkæzækˌstæn/	Kazakh /ˈkæzæk/
Kenya /ˈkenjə/	Kenyan /ˈkenjən/
Kiribati /ˈkɪrəˌbæs, kɪrɪˈbɑti/	Kiribati /ˈkɪrəˌbæs, ˌkɪrɪˈbɑti/
North Korea /ˌnɔrθ kəˈriə/	North Korean /ˌnɔrθ kəˈriən/
South Korea /ˌsaʊθ kəˈriə/	South Korean /ˌsaʊθ ˈkəˈriən/
Kuwait /kʊˈweɪt/	Kuwaiti /kʊˈweɪti/
Kyrgyzstan /ˈkɪrgɪˌstæn/	Kyrgyz /kɪrˈgiz/
Laos /laʊs/	Laotian /leɪˈoʊʃ(ə)n/
Latvia /ˈlætviə/	Latvian /ˈlætviən/
Lebanon /ˈlebəˌnɑn/	Lebanese /ˌlebəˈniz/
Lesotho /ləˈsoʊtoʊ/	Sotho* /ˈsoʊtoʊ/
Liberia /laɪˈbɪriə/	Liberian /laɪˈbɪriən/
Libya /ˈlɪbiə/	Libyan /ˈlɪbiən/
Liechtenstein /ˈlɪktənˌstaɪn/	Liechtenstein* /ˈlɪktənˌstaɪn/
Lithuania /ˌlɪθuˈeɪniə/	Lithuanian /ˌlɪθuˈeɪniən/
Luxembourg /ˈlʌksəmˌbɜrg/	Luxembourg* /ˈlʌksəmˌbɜrg/
Madagascar /ˌmædəˈgæskər/	Malagasy /ˌmæləˈgæsi/
Malawi /məˈlɑwi/	Malawian /məˈlɑwiən/
Malaysia /məˈleɪʒə/	Malaysian /məˈleɪʒ(ə)n/
Maldives, the /ˈmɔldaɪvz/	Maldivian /mɔlˈdɪviən/
Mali /ˈmɑli/	Malian /ˈmɑliən/
Malta /ˈmɔltə/	Maltese /ˌmɔlˈtiz/
Marshall Islands, the /ˈmɑrʃ(ə)l ˌaɪləndz/	Marshallese* /ˌmɑrʃəˈliz/
Mauritania /ˌmɔrəˈteɪniə/	Mauritanian /ˌmɔrəˈteɪniən/

Mauritius /mɔˈrɪʃəs/	Mauritian /mɔˈrɪʃ(ə)n/
Melanesia /ˌmeləˈniʒə/	Melanesian /ˌmeləˈniʒ(ə)n/
Mexico /ˈmeksɪˌkoʊ/	Mexican /ˈmeksɪkən/
Micronesia /ˌmaɪkrəˈniʒə/	Micronesian /ˌmaɪkrəˈniʒ(ə)n/
Moldova /mɑlˈdoʊvə/	Moldovan /mɑlˈdoʊvən/
Monaco /ˈmɑnəˌkoʊ/	Monegasque /ˌmɑneɪˈgæsk/
Mongolia /mɑŋˈgoʊliə/	Mongolian /mɑŋˈgoʊliən/
Montserrat /ˌmɑntsəˈræt/	Montserratian /ˌmɑntsəˈreɪʃ(ə)n/
Morocco /məˈrɑkoʊ/	Moroccan /məˈrɑkən/
Mozambique /ˌmoʊzəmˈbik/	Mozambican /ˌmoʊzəmˈbikən/
Myanmar /ˈmjɑnmɑr/	Burmese /bərˈmiz/
Namibia /nəˈmɪbiə/	Namibian /nəˈmɪbiən/
Nauru /nɑˈuru/	Nauruan /nɑˈuruən/
Nepal /nəˈpɔl/	Nepalese /ˌnepəˈliz/
Netherlands, the /ˈneðərləndz/	Dutch* /dʌtʃ/
New Zealand /ˌnu ˈzilənd/	New Zealand* /ˌnu ˈzilənd/
Nicaragua /ˌnɪkəˈrɑgwə/	Nicaraguan /ˌnɪkəˈrɑgwən/
Niger /ˈnaɪdʒər/	Nigerien /naɪˈdʒɪriən/
Nigeria /naɪˈdʒɪriə/	Nigerian /naɪˈdʒɪriən/
Norway /ˈnɔrweɪ/	Norwegian /nɔrˈwidʒən/
Oman /oʊˈmɑn/	Omani /oʊˈmɑni/
Pakistan /ˈpækɪˌstæn/	Pakistani /ˌpækɪˈstæni/
Panama /ˈpænəˌmɑ/	Panamanian /ˌpænəˈmeɪniən/
Papua New Guinea /ˌpæpjuə nu ˈgɪni/	Papua New Guinean /ˌpæpjuə nuˈgɪniən/
Paraguay /ˈpærəˌgwaɪ/	Paraguayan /ˌpærəˈgwaɪən/
Peru /pəˈru/	Peruvian /pəˈruviən/
Philippines, the /ˈfɪləˌpinz/	Philippine* /ˈfɪləˌpin/
Poland /ˈpoʊlənd/	Polish* /ˈpoʊlɪʃ/
Polynesia /ˌpɑləˈniʒə/	Polynesian /ˌpɑləˈniʒ(ə)n/
Portugal /ˈpɔrtʃəg(ə)l/	Portuguese /ˌpɔrtʃəˈgiz/
Puerto Rico /ˌpɔrtə ˈrikoʊ/	Puerto Rican /ˌpɔrtə ˈrikən/
Qatar /ˈkɑtɑr/	Qatari /kɑˈtɑri/
Romania /roʊˈmeɪniə/	Romanian /roʊˈmeɪniən/
Russia /ˈrʌʃə/	Russian /ˈrʌʃ(ə)n/
Russian Federation, the /ˌrʌʃ(ə)n fedəˈreɪʃ(ə)n/	
Rwanda /ruˈɑndə/	Rwandese /ruˈɑndiz/
Saint Kitts and Nevis /seɪnt ˌkɪts ən ˈnivɪs/	Kittitian /kɪˈtɪʃ(ə)n/ Nevisian /nəˈviʃ(ə)n/
Saint Lucia /seɪnt ˈluʃə/	Saint Lucian /seɪnt ˈluʃ(ə)n/
Saint Vincent and the Grenadines /seɪnt ˌvɪns(ə)nt ən ðə ˌgrenəˈdinz/	Vincentian /vɪnˈsenʃ(ə)n/
Samoa /səˈmoʊə/	Samoan /səˈmoʊən/
San Marino /ˌsæn məˈrinoʊ/	Sanmarinese /ˌsænmærəˈniz/
São Tomé and Príncipe /ˌsaʊn təˌmeɪ ən ˈprɪnsəpə/	Sao Tomean /ˌsaʊn təˈmeɪən/
Saudi Arabia /ˌsaʊdi əˈreɪbiə/	Saudi Arabian /ˌsaudi əˈreɪbiən/ Saudi /ˈsaʊdi/
Scandinavia /ˌskændɪˈneɪviə/	Scandinavian /ˌskændɪˈneɪviən/
Scotland /ˈskɑtlənd/	Scottish* /ˈskɑtɪʃ/
Senegal /ˈsenɪˌgɔl/	Senegalese /ˌsenɪgɔˈliz/
Seychelles, the /seɪˈʃelz/	Seychellois /ˌseɪʃelˈwɑ/
Sierra Leone /siˌerə liˈoʊn/	Sierra Leonean /siˌerə liˈoʊniən/
Singapore /ˈsɪŋgəˌpɔr/	Singaporean /ˌsɪŋgəˈpɔriən/
Slovakia /sloʊˈvɑkiə/	Slovak /ˈsloʊvɑk/ Slovakian /sloʊˈvɑkiən/
Slovenia /sloʊˈviniə/	Slovene /ˈsloʊvin/ Slovenian /sloʊˈviniən/
Solomon Islands, the /ˈsɑləmən ˌaɪləndz/	Solomon Island* /ˌsɑləmən ˈaɪlənd/
Somalia /səˈmɑliə/	Somali /səˈmɑli/
South Africa /ˌsaʊθ ˈæfrɪkə/	South African /ˌsaʊθ ˈæfrɪkən/
Spain /speɪn/	Spanish* /ˈspænɪʃ/
Sri Lanka /sri ˈlɑŋkə/	Sri Lankan /sri ˈlɑŋkən/
Sudan /suˈdæn/	Sudanese /ˌsud(ə)ˈniz/
Suriname /ˌsʊrɪˈnɑm/	Surinamese* /ˌsurənɑˈmiz/
Swaziland /ˈswɑziˌlænd/	Swazi /ˈswɑzi/
Sweden /ˈswid(ə)n/	Swedish* /ˈswidɪʃ/
Switzerland /ˈswɪtsərlənd/	Swiss /swɪs/
Syria /ˈsɪriə/	Syrian /ˈsɪriən/
Tajikistan /tɑˈdʒikɪˌstæn/	Tajik /tɑˈdʒik/

Tanzania /ˌtænzəˈniə/	Tanzanian /ˌtænzəˈniən/
Thailand /ˈtaɪlænd/	Thai /taɪ/
Togo /ˈtoʊgoʊ/	Togolese /ˌtoʊgəˈliz/
Tonga /ˈtɑŋgə/	Tongan /ˈtɑŋgən/
Trinidad and Tobago /ˌtrɪnɪdæd ən təˈbeɪgoʊ/	Trinidadian /ˌtrɪnɪˈdædiən/
	Tobagan /təˈbeɪgən/
Tunisia /tuˈniʒə/	Tunisian /tuˈniʒ(ə)n/
Turkey /ˈtɜrki/	Turkish* /ˈtɜrkɪʃ/
Turkmenistan /ˌtɜrkmenɪˈstæn/	Turkmen /ˈtɜrkmən/
Tuvalu /tuˈvɑlu/	Tuvaluan /tuˈvɑluən/
Uganda /juˈgændə/	Ugandan /juˈgændən/
Ukraine /juˈkreɪn/	Ukrainian /juˈkreɪniən/
United Arab Emirates, the /juˌnaɪtəd ˌærəb ɪˈmɪrɪts/	Emirati /ɪmɪˈrɑti/
United Kingdom, the /juˌnaɪtəd ˈkɪŋdəm/	British* /ˈbrɪtɪʃ/
United States of America, the /juˌnaɪtəd steɪts ev əˈmerɪkə/	American /əˈmerɪkən/
Uruguay /ˈjʊrəˌgwaɪ/	Uruguayan /jʊrəˈgwaɪən/
Uzbekistan /ʊzˈbekɪˌstæn/	Uzbek /ˈʊzbek/
Vanuatu /ˌvænuˈɑtu/	Vanuatuan /ˌvænuˈɑtuən/
Vatican City /ˌvætɪkən ˈsɪti/	Vatican /ˈvætɪkən/
Venezuela /ˌvenəˈzweɪlə/	Venezuelan /ˌvenəˈzweɪlən/
Vietnam /ˌvjetˈnɑm/	Vietnamese /ˌvjetnəˈmiz/
Wales /weɪlz/	Welsh* /welʃ/
Western Sahara /ˌwestərn səˈhɑrə/	Sahrawian /səˈrɑwiən/
Yemen /ˈjemən/	Yemeni /ˈjeməni/
Yugoslavia /jugoʊˈslɑviə/	Yugoslav /ˈjugoʊˌslɑv/
	Yugoslavian /ˌjugoʊˈslɑviən/
Zambia /ˈzæmbiə/	Zambian /ˈzæmbiən/
Zimbabwe /zɪmˈbɑbweɪ/	Zimbabwean /zɪmˈbɑbweɪən/

Nationalities

Country	**Person**
Argentina /ˌɑrdʒənˈtinə/	Argentinian /ˌɑrdʒənˈtɪniən/
Azerbaijan /ˌæzərbaɪˈdʒɑn/	Azeri /ɑˈzeri/
	Azerbaijani /ˌæzərbaɪˈdʒɑni/
Cayman Islands, the /ˈkeɪmən ˌaɪləndz/	Cayman Islander /ˌkeɪmən ˈaɪləndər/
Croatia /kroʊˈeɪʃə/	Croat /ˈkroʊæt/
Denmark /ˈdenmɑrk/	Dane /deɪn/
England /ɪŋglənd/	Englishman /ˈɪŋglɪʃmən/
Finland /ˈfɪnlənd/	Finn /fɪn/
France /fræns/	Frenchman /ˈfrentʃmən/
Great Britain /ˌgreɪt ˈbrɪt(ə)n/	Briton (*mainly journalism*) /ˈbrɪt(ə)n/
Greenland /ˈgrinlənd/	Greenlander /ˈgrinləndər/
Iceland /ˈaɪslənd/	Icelander /ˈaɪsləndər/
Republic of Ireland, the /rɪpʌblɪk əv ˈaɪ(ə)rlənd/	Irishman /ˈaɪ(ə)rɪʃmən/
Lesotho /ləˈsoʊtoʊ/	Mosotho /məˈsoʊtoʊ/
	plural Basotho /bəˈsoʊtoʊ/
Liechtenstein /ˈlɪktənˌstaɪn/	Liechtensteiner /ˈlɪktənˌstaɪnər/
Luxembourg /ˈlʌksəmˌbɜrg/	Luxembourger /ˈlʌksəmˌbɜrgər/
Marshall Islands, the /ˈmɑrʃ(ə)l ˌaɪləndz/	Marshall Islander /ˌmarʃ(ə)l ˈaɪləndər/
Netherlands, the /ˈneðərləndz/	Dutchman /ˈdʌtʃmən/
New Zealand /ˌnu ˈzilənd/	New Zealander /ˌnu ˈziləndər/
Philippines, the /ˈfɪləˌpinz/	Filipino /ˌfɪlɪˈpinoʊ/
Poland /ˈpoʊlənd/	Pole /poʊl/
Scotland /ˈskɑtlənd/	Scot /skɑt/
Solomon Islands, the /ˈsɑləmən ˌaɪləndz/	Solomon Islander /ˌsɑləmən ˈaɪləndər/
Spain /speɪn/	Spaniard /ˈspænjərd/
Suriname /ˌsʊrɪˈnɑm/	Surinamer /ˌsʊrɪˈnɑmər/
Sweden /ˈswid(ə)n/	Swede /swid/
Turkey /ˈtɜrki/	Turk /tɜrk/
United Kingdom, the /juˌnaɪtəd ˈkɪŋdəm/	Briton (*mainly journalism*) /ˈbrɪt(ə)n/
Wales /weɪlz/	Welshman /ˈwelʃmən/

CAPITAL LETTERS AND PUNCTUATION

Capital Letters

Capital letters (or upper case letters) are used:

- to begin a sentence
  You've done a fantastic job.
- for the names of people
  ***J**im, **H**elen, **A**ndrew **W**alker*
- for calling people by their title
  ***M**rs. **J**ones, **U**ncle **P**eter, **M**om*
- for the personal pronoun "I"
  *Can **I** help?*
- for the titles of films, books, etc.
  Notting **H**ill *is a funny movie.*

  NOTE: Small words like *and, a, the,* and prepositions do not usually have capitals, unless they are the first word of the title: *The film was based on* The End of the Affair *by Graham Greene.*
- for names of organizations
  ***F**riends of the **E**arth, the **E**uropean **U**nion*
- for the names of places (towns, countries, etc.)
  ***P**aris, **H**ungary*
- for nationalities and languages
  ***E**nglish, **S**outh **A**frican*
- for days, months etc
  ***W**ednesday, **M**arch, **N**ew **Y**ear's **D**ay*

Some words can be written with capitals or in lower case, depending on the meaning:

- jobs
  *Sanderson was a good **p**resident.* (general use)
  *Paul met **P**resident Brunswick.* (job title)
- compass points
  *I live in the **n**orth of Scotland.* (description)
  *Sally works in the **F**ar **E**ast.* (place name)

Period (.)

Periods are used:

- at the end of a sentence
  His sister's name is Kate.
- in abbreviations *Sat.* (Saturday), *pl.* (plural), *approx.* (approximately), *Mr.* (Mister), *Dr.* (Doctor), *Rd.* (Road), *Ave.* (Avenue)

  NOTE: In modern British English, periods are not usually added when the abbreviation contains the last letter of the full word:
  Mr, Dr, Rd, Ave

Comma (,)

Commas are used:

- in writing to represent a brief pause in a long sentence
  Everyone agrees that Anna is a very intelligent girl, but she is kind of lazy.
- in lists of two or more items
  I bought some bananas, some oranges, and some potatoes.

  NOTE: This is the style used in this dictionary, but the final comma (before "and") can be left out.
- in lists of adjectives that appear before a noun
  a large, green, wooden table

  NOTE: In the above example, commas can be left out. Commas are not used to separate adjectives in this dictionary.
- after linking words at the beginning of a sentence
  First of all, this can be dangerous.
- before and after linking words in the middle of a sentence
  Ann, on the other hand, did not agree.
- when giving additional information that can be left out
  Tony, who is usually late, showed up at 10:30.
- to introduce direct speech
  Jim said, "I'll be late."

  NOTE: Commas are not used after reporting verbs in reported speech:
  Jim said he would be late.
- before tag questions
  You're from India, aren't you?

- in large numbers to separate digits
  6,550 17,500 387,100 2,000,000

  NOTE: In some languages a period (.) is used here. In English, a period represents a decimal point (e.g., 3.5 million = "three and a half million" or "three point five million").

Semicolon (;)

Semicolons are used:

- to join together two sentences with related meanings
  We need better technology; better technology costs money.
- to separate long items in a list
  Students are asked not to leave bicycles by the entrance; not to leave bags in the sitting room; and not to leave coats in the dining room.

Colon (:)

Colons are used:

- to introduce items in a list
  You will need to provide one of the following pieces of identification: a passport, a students ID, or a driver's license.

- to introduce an explanation of the previous part of the sentence
  Finally, we had to stop: we were tired and it was dark.

Quotation Marks (" ")

Quotation marks are used:

- around direct speech
  "Why are we leaving so early?" Helen asked.

- around words you want to emphasize or treat in a special way:
  What does "plethora" mean?

Question mark (?)

Question marks are used:

- after a question
  What time is it?

  NOTE: In modern British English, single quotation marks (' ') are used.

Exclamation Point (!)

Exclamation points are used:

- to show a strong emotion such as surprise or anger
  You'll never guess what! I just got engaged!

  NOTE: Exclamation points are used in informal writing, but are not considered appropriate in formal writing.

Apostrophe (')

Apostrophes are used:

- with "s" to show who or what someone or something belongs to or is connected with
  Mike is having dinner with Nicky's sister.

  Did you go to yesterday's meeting?

  NOTE: -'s is used when referring to a single person or thing, -s' is used when referring to more than one person or thing:

  The boy's father (=the father of one boy) *demanded an explanation.*

  The boys' father (=the father of more than one boy) *demanded an explanation.*

- in contractions (short forms) to show that some letters are missing
  The talk wasn't (=was not) *any good.*

  I'm (=I am) *only here for a week.*

  That can't (cannot) *be right.*

  NOTE: Do not confuse **its** (=belonging to or connected with "it") and **it's** (=it is).

  The dog was chasing ***its*** *tail.*

  It's *too late to do anything now.*

PHRASAL VERBS

What is a Phrasal Verb?

A phrasal verb is a verb with two parts: a verb (such as *go, put,* or *set*), and a "particle" (an adverb or preposition, such as *away, out,* or *on*). The meanings of phrasal verbs are often very different from the meaning of the verb that they are based on: for example, *hold up* can mean "to cause a delay" or "to try to rob someone," and these meanings have no obvious connection with the idea of holding something in your hands.

How Do I Find Phrasal Verbs in the *Macmillan Essential Dictionary*?

Phrasal verbs appear at the end of the entry for the verb that they are formed from. A box saying PHRASAL VERBS makes them easy to find. Look in your dictionary at the entry for the verb *count*. You will see that *count* has five main meanings, and these are followed by some phrases that include the word *count*. After the phrases, you will see the PHRASAL VERBS box, and this is followed by several phrasal verbs, such as **count against sb** and **count on sth**.

How Do Phrasal Verbs Combine with Other Words?

There are several types of phrasal verb. The main ones are:

- intransitive phrasal verbs (with no object): *What time can we **check in**?*

  These are shown like this:

  ˌ**check ˈin 1** to arrive at a hotel and give your personal details to the person at the RECEPTION desk

- transitive phrasal verbs where the object can come in two positions – after the verb, or after the particle: *I think I'll **put** my jacket **on**.* OR *I think I'll **put on** my jacket.*

  These are shown like this:

  ˌ**put sth ˈon 1** to cover a part of your body with a piece of clothing or jewelry so that you are wearing it

  ˌ**beat sb ˈup** *informal* to hurt someone by hitting or kicking them many times

  The word **sb** (=someone) means that the object is a person, and the word **sth** (= something) means that the object is a thing.

- transitive phrasal verbs where the object must come after the particle: *The baby **takes after** his mother*.

  These are shown like this:

  ˈ**take ˌafter sb** to look or behave like an older relative

- phrasal verbs that sometimes have an object and sometimes have no object: *It took a while for the house to warm up.* ♦ *The drink soon warmed her up.*

  These are shown like this:

  ˌ**warm (sb/sth) ˈup 1** to become warm, or to make someone or something become warm

- phrasal verbs with *two* objects – one after the verb, the other after the particle: He didn't want to ***put** his wife **through** the pain of divorce.*

  These are shown like this:

  ˈ**put sb ˈthrough sth** to make someone do something difficult or unpleasant

How Are Phrasal Verbs Pronounced?

You will notice that all these phrasal verbs include symbols that show which part is "stressed" (=spoken with more force). The symbols at ˌ**check ˈin** show that you stress the word "in."

LABELS

Style and Attitude Labels

formal in current use but not used in ordinary conversation or in normal everyday writing: *augur, permissible, remuneration*

humorous used in an ironic and often friendly way: *ill-gotten gains* (=money obtained dishonestly)

impolite not taboo but will certainly offend some people

informal more common in speech than in writing and not used on a formal occasion: *comfy, guy, yeah*

literary old but still used in some kinds of creative writing: *bountiful, forsake, spurn*

offensive extremely rude and likely to cause offense

old-fashioned no longer in current use but still used by some older people: *slacks*

showing approval used when it is not obvious from a definition that a word says something good about someone or something: *fearless, tireless*

showing disapproval used when it is not obvious from a definition that a word says something bad about someone or something: *babyish, smooth* (=relaxed and confident)

spoken used in speech rather than writing: *after you, would you believe it?*

Subject Labels

These labels show that a word is used as part of the language of a particular subject and is not used in normal everyday English:

business ***legal*** ***science***
computing ***linguistics*** ***technical***
journalism ***medical***

Regional Labels

American used in American English but not in British English

British used in British English but not in American English

Software licence for the Macmillan Essential Dictionary CD-ROM

This is an agreement between you (the **'User'**) and Macmillan Publishers Limited (the **'Supplier'**).

1 Licence
The Supplier grants the User a personal, non-exclusive, non-transferable licence to use the Supplier's software product, the Macmillan Essential Dictionary, as acquired with this licence (the **'Program'**). Macmillan grants the User the licence to use one copy of the Program **either** (i) on a single stand-alone computer for use by the User and one or more people provided that only one person uses it at any one time, **or** (ii) by the User on more than one computer (provided the Program is only used on one stand-alone computer at a time). The User shall not: (i) loan, rent, lease or license the Program; (ii) copy or authorize copying of the Program, reverse-engineer, disassemble or decompile the Program (other than to the extent permitted under applicable law); (iii) operate the Program from a network or mainframe system.

2 Copyright and other intellectual property rights
The intellectual property rights in the Program and any documentation or materials supplied with the Program are owned by and remain with the Supplier or its third party licensors.

3 Statutory rights
If the User is a consumer and has in that capacity purchased the Program, the exclusions and limitations contained in this agreement do not affect any statutory rights to which the User is entitled as a consumer and which may not under applicable law be excluded or limited.

4 Warranty
Subject to clause 3, the Supplier warrants that the Program and any disk or other medium on which the Program is supplied will be free from defects which have a materially adverse effect on its use in accordance with this agreement. The Supplier does not warrant that the Program will be entirely free from errors or that the information accessible via use of the Program is entirely accurate or error free. The User's sole remedy for breach of this warranty is to return the Program and all documentation to the Supplier, together with proof of purchase, and the Supplier will, at the User's option, either replace the Program or provide the User with a full refund.

5 No other warranties
SUBJECT TO CLAUSE 3, EXCEPT AS EXPRESSLY PROVIDED OTHERWISE BY THIS AGREEMENT, NO CONDITIONS, WARRANTIES, REPRESENTATIONS OR OTHER TERMS APPLY WITH RESPECT TO THE PROGRAM OR USER DOCUMENTATION (INCLUDING ANY SUCH TERMS AS TO QUALITY, PERFORMANCE, SUITABILITY OR FITNESS FOR A PARTICULAR PURPOSE).

6 Limitation of liability
SUBJECT TO CLAUSE 3 AND SAVE AS EXPRESSLY PROVIDED OTHERWISE BY THIS AGREEMENT:

(A) THE SUPPLIER SHALL NOT BE LIABLE TO THE USER OR TO ANY THIRD PARTY FOR: LOSS OF PROFITS; LOSS OF SALES OR BUSINESS; LOSS OF USE OF COMPUTER EQUIPMENT, SOFTWARE OF DATA OR ANY INDIRECT OR CONSEQUENTIAL LOSS HOWSOEVER SUCH LOSS ARISES; AND

(B) THE SUPPLIER'S TOTAL AGGREGATE LIABILITY UNDER THIS AGREEMENT SHALL BE LIMITED IN ALL CASES TO THE PRICE OF THE PROGRAM;

PROVIDED THAT NOTHING IN THIS AGREEMENT LIMITS THE SUPPLIER'S LIABILITY TO THE USER IN THE EVENT OF DEATH OR PERSONAL INJURY RESULTING FROM THE SUPPLIER'S NEGLIGENCE OR FOR ANY OTHER LIABILITY THAT MAY NOT BE EXCLUDED OR LIMITED UNDER APPLICABLE LAW.

7 Termination
The User's licence to use the Program automatically terminates if the User fails to comply with any provisions of this agreement.

8 Title
The Supplier shall at all times retain ownership of the Program but the User shall retain title in the media on which the Program is supplied.

9 Entire agreement, applicable law and jurisdiction
This agreement is the complete and exclusive statement of the agreement between the User and the Supplier with respect to the Program. This agreement is governed by English law and both parties submit to the exclusive jurisdiction of the English Court.

Minimum system requirements for the CD-ROM

- IBM-compatible PC running Windows® 98 or later
- Microsoft Windows® 98 operating on a Pentium® 133 processor with 32 MB RAM
or Microsoft Windows® NT 4.0 Workstation with Service Pack 3 operating on a Pentium® 133 processor with 64 MB RAM
or Microsoft Windows® ME operating on a Pentium® 200 processor with 64 MB RAM
or Microsoft Windows® 2000 Professional Workstation operating on a Pentium® 200 processor with 64 MB RAM
or Microsoft Windows® XP operating on a Pentium® 400 processor with 128 MB RAM
- 120 MB of free hard-disk space
- CD-ROM or DVD-ROM drive
- DirectX-compatible screen card and monitor supporting 800 x 600 resolution with 16-bit colour resolution
- Microsoft-compatible mouse or pointing device
- For playback and practice of pronunciations: 16-bit Windows® and DirectX-compatible sound card with speakers or headphones, and microphone